Presented to

you are Precious. I love you!

Sabrina

By

Aunt Kathleen

Date

12 - 12 - 10

You are
precious.
I love
you!

Sabrina

Aunt Kathleen

12 - 12 - 10

N/rv Kids' Quest

study Bible

**New International
Reader's Version**

N/rv Kids' Quest

study Bible

**New International
Reader's Version**

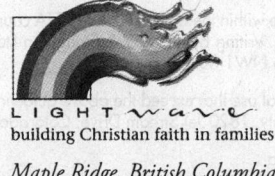

LIGHT*ware*

building Christian faith in families

Maple Ridge, British Columbia

Table of Contents

Contents

BOOKS OF THE BIBLE ALPHABETICALLY

Introduction to This Bible

NIrV Kids' Quest Study Bible

What's a quest anyway?

Have you ever spent a whole afternoon looking for something that was lost? Maybe your dad couldn't find the car keys. Maybe your little sister lost her favorite stuffed animal. Or maybe you lost your homework. When you go looking for something, you're on a quest.

How can this Bible be a quest?

If you read the Bible, you probably have lots of questions. Most people do. You wonder things like:

Why did God make mosquitoes?
Were there dinosaurs on the ark?
What's a parable?

So you go on a quest to find the answers. You look for answers in the Bible. *Kids' Quest Study Bible* will answer almost all of the questions you could possible ask! Over 500 of them!

Who asked these questions?

You did! Or at least kids just like you. They asked the questions, and then we looked in the Bible for answers. You'll find all the questions and all the answers right next to the passage that fits them best. For example, if you ask, "Why did Solomon want to cut the baby in half?" you'll find the answer right next to the story in 1 Kings 3. Your quest will be fun, but it won't be too hard. You'll find all the answers you're looking for very easily.

What is the NIrV?

The NIrV is the New International Reader's Version. This is a Bible version that is easy to read and understand. You won't find really hard words or really long sentences in this Bible version. So you'll be able to read and understand what you read when you're on your quest.

Introduction to This Bible continued

What else can I find in my *Kids' Quest Study Bible*?

In the back of your Bible, you'll find a dictionary (see page 1668). Maybe there are some words in this Bible that you're not sure you understand. Look those words up in this dictionary to find out what they mean. You'll also find a topical index (see page 1676) in the back of this Bible. This index will help you find the questions and answers you have on certain topics. Are you looking for information about money or angels? Look it up in your topical index.

Quest Challenge is a new feature found at the end of many books of the Bible. It will challenge you to apply God's word to your life. Read the question. Check out the Quest Clue. Then find and read the listed chapter or chapters in the Bible. When you see the ??? in the text you will know that you are close to finding the answer.

Do you have anything you want to say?

We would sure like to hear it! You can write to us with any comments about your Kids' Quest Study Bible to:

> Kids' Quest Editors
> Zondervan
> 5300 Patterson Ave., S.E.
> Grand Rapids, MI 49530

Now what?

Now you can start your quest! God's Word, the Bible, has so much power and has so much to say about God's love for you. Go on your quest and you'll find all the great treasures God has stored for you in your *Kids' Quest Study Bible*.

A Word About the New International Reader's Version

Have you ever heard of the New International Version?

We call it the NIV. A lot of people read the NIV. In fact, more people read the NIV than any other English Bible. They like it because it's easy to read.

And now we are happy to give you another Bible that's easy to read and understand. It's the New international Reader's Version. We call it the NIrV.

Who will enjoy reading the New International Reader's Version?

We made sure that people who are just starting to read could understand and enjoy the NIrV. Children will be able to read it and understand it. So will older people who are learning how to read or those who are reading the Bible for the first time. So will people who have a hard time understanding what they read. And so will people who use English as their second language. We hope this Bible will be just right for you.

How is the NIrV different from the NIV?

The NIrV is based on the NIV. The NIV Committee on Bible Translation (CBT) didn't produce the NIrV. But several members of CBT worked hard to make the NIrV possible. We used the words of the NIV when we could. When the NIV words were long, we used words that were shorter. We wanted to use words that are easy to understand. We explained words that might be hard to understand in a dictionary at the back of the Bible. We also made the NIV sentences much shorter.

Why did we do all of those things? Because we wanted to make the NIrV really easy to read and understand.

What other helps does the NIrV have?

We decided to give you a lot of other help too. For example, sometimes a verse is quoted from another place in the Bible. When it is, we put the Bible book's name, chapter and verse right after the verse that quotes another place.

We separated each chapter into shorter sections. We gave a title to almost every chapter. Sometimes we even gave a title to a section. We did it to help you understand what the chapter or section is all about.

Sometimes the writers of the Bible used more than one name for the same person or place. For example, in the New Testament the Sea of Galilee is also called the Sea of Gennesaret and the Sea of Tiberias. But in the NIrV we decided to call it the Sea of Galilee everywhere it appears in the New Testament. We did it because that is its most familiar name.

New International Reader's Version

We also wanted to help our readers learn the names of people and places even in verses where those names don't actually appear. For example, when we knew that "the River" meant "the Euphrates River," we used those words even in verses where only the words "the River" are found. When we knew that the name of "Pharaoh" in a certain verse was "Hophra," we wrote his name in that verse. We did all of these things because we wanted to make the NIrV as clear as possible.

Does the NIrV say what the first writers of the Bible said?

We wanted the NIrV to say just what the first writers of the Bible said. So we kept checking the Hebrew Old Testament and the Greek New Testament as we did our work. That's because the Bible's first writers used the Hebrew and Greek languages.

We used the best and oldest copies of the Hebrew and Greek. Earlier English Bibles couldn't use those copies because they had not yet been found. The oldest copies are best because they are closer in time to the ones the first Bible writers wrote. That's why we kept checking the older copies instead of newer ones.

Newer copies of the Greek New Testament added several verses that the older ones don't have. Sometimes it's just a single verse. When that's the case, we put the verse itself in the list below. But sometimes it's several verses in a row. When that's the case, we included them in the NIrV. But we set those verses off with a long line. That tells you that the first writers didn't write them. The verses were added later on. You will find the long lines at Mark 16:9-20 and John 7:53—8:11.

What is our prayer for you?

The Lord has blessed the New International Version in a wonderful way. He has used it to help millions of Bible readers. Many people have put their faith in Jesus after reading it. Many others have become stronger believers because they have read it.

We hope and pray that the New International Reader's Version will help you in the same way. If that happens, we will give God all of the glory.

Verses that were not found in earliest Greek New Testaments

Later copies of the Greek New Testament added several verses that the earlier ones don't have. An example is Mark 9:44. That verse is not in the oldest Greek New Testaments. So we put the number 43/44 right before Mark 9:43. The verse for Mark 9:44 is listed below.

Matthew 17:21   But that kind does not go out except by prayer and fasting.
Matthew 18:11   The Son of Man came to save what was lost.
Matthew 23:14   How terrible for you, teachers of the law and Pharisees! You pretenders! You take over the houses of widows. You say long prayers to show off. So God will punish you much more.
Mark 7:16   Everyone who has ears to hear should listen.

Mark 9:44	In hell, "the worms don't die,/ and the fire doesn't go out."
Mark 9:46	In hell, "the worms don't die,/ and the fire doesn't go out."
Mark 11:26	But if you do not forgive, your Father who is in heaven will not forgive your sins either.
Mark 15:28	Scripture came true. It says, "And he was counted among those who disobey the law."
Luke 17:36	Two men will be in the field. One will be taken and the other left.
Luke 23:17	It was Pilate's duty to let one prisoner go free for them at the Feast.
John 5:4	From time to time an angel of the Lord would come down. The angel would stir up the waters. The first disabled person to go into the pool after it was stirred would be healed.
Acts 8:37	Philip said, "If you believe with all your heart, you can." The official answered, "I believe that Jesus Christ is the Son of God."
Acts 15:34	But Silas decided to remain there.
Acts 24:7	But Lysias, the commander, came. By using a lot of force, he took Paul from our hands.
Acts 28:29	After he said that, the Jews left. They were arguing strongly among themselves.
Romans16:24	May the grace of our Lord Jesus Christ be with all of you. Amen.

Acknowledgments

Questions Children Ask About God series

Project Manager
Betsy Schmitt

General Editors
Jennifer Karrer
Daryl J. Lucas

Project Staff
Phoebe Blaustein
Andy Culbertson

Contributors
Bruce B. Barton
Jonathan Farrar
James C. Galvin
Jennifer Karrer
Richard Osborne
James C. Wilhoit
David R. Veerman

Illustrations
Lillian Crump
Sharon VanLoozenoord

Production Staff
Ashley Taylor
Kathleen Ristow
Thomas Ristow

NIrV Kids' Quest Study Bible: Revised Edition
Project Management and Editorial: Catherine DeVries, Doris Rikkers
Editorial Assistance: Kristen Tuinstra
Editorial Services: The Livingstone Corporation, Carol Stream, IL
Interior Design: Sarah Jongsma, Amy Peterman
Interior Typesetting: The Livingstone Corporation, Carol Stream, IL
Cover Design: Merit Alderink
Cover Illustration: Craig Phillips
Printing: R.R. Donnelley & Sons Company, Crawfordsville, IN

NIrV Kids' Quest Study Bible: First Edition
Project Management and Editorial: Jean E. Syswerda, Donna Huisjen
Editorial Services: The Livingstone Corporation, Carol Stream, IL
Interior Design: Gary Gnidovic
Interior Typesetting: The Livingstone Corporation, Carol Stream, IL
Interior Proofreading: Peachtree Editorial and Proofreading Service, Peachtree City, GA
Cover Design: Jody Langley, Cindy Tobey
Printing: R. R. Donnelley & Sons Company, Crawfordsville, IN

Old
Testament

Genesis

Who wrote this book?
Moses.

Why was this book written?
Genesis tells how God created the universe and human beings. It also covers the special promises God made to Abraham.

What happens in this book?
God creates the universe and people. People sin, and God punishes them with a great flood. God speaks to Abraham and gives his family special promises.

What do we learn about God in this book?
God created all things. God loves people but will punish sin. God promises to save people who trust him.

Who is important in this book?
The important people in this book are Adam and Eve, Noah, Abraham, Isaac, Jacob and Joseph.

When did this happen?
No one knows when the creation or the flood happened. Abraham was born about 2150 B.C. His great-grandson Joseph died about 1800 B.C.

THE BEGINNING

1 In the beginning, God created the heavens and the earth. ²The earth didn't have any shape. And it was empty. Darkness was over the surface of the ocean. At that time, the ocean covered the earth. The Spirit of God was hovering over the waters.

³God said, "Let there be light." And there was light. ⁴God saw that the light was good. He separated the light from the darkness. ⁵God called the light "day." He called

the darkness "night." There was evening, and there was morning. It was day one.

⁶God said, "Let there be a huge space between the waters. Let it separate water from water." ⁷And that's exactly what happened. God made the huge space between the waters. He separated the water that was under the space from the water that was above it. ⁸God called the huge space "sky." There was evening, and there was morning. It was day two.

⁹God said, "Let the water under the sky be gathered into one place. Let dry ground appear." And that's exactly what happened. ¹⁰God called the dry ground "land." He called the waters that were gathered together "oceans." And God saw that it was good.

¹¹Then God said, "Let the land produce plants. Let them bear their own seeds. And let there be trees on the land that bear fruit with seeds in it. Let each kind of plant or tree have its own kind of seeds." And that's exactly what happened.

¹²The land produced plants. Each kind of plant had its own kind of seeds. The land produced trees that bore fruit with seeds in it. Each kind of tree had its own kind of seeds.

God saw that it was good. ¹³And there was evening, and there was morning. It was day three.

¹⁴God said, "Let there be lights in the huge space of the sky. Let them separate the day from the night. Let them serve as signs to mark off the seasons and the days and the years. ¹⁵Let them serve as lights in the huge space of the sky to give light on the earth." And that's exactly what happened.

¹⁶God made two great lights. He made the larger light to rule over the day. He made the smaller light to rule over the night. He also made the stars.

¹⁷God put the lights in the huge space of the sky to give light on the earth. ¹⁸He put them there to rule over the day and the night. He put them there to separate light from darkness.

God saw that it was good. ¹⁹And there was evening, and there was morning. It was day four.

²⁰God said, "Let the waters be filled with living things. Let birds fly above the earth across the huge space of the sky." ²¹So God created the great creatures of the ocean. He created every living and moving thing that fills the waters. He created all kinds of them. He created every kind of bird that flies. And God saw that it was good.

²²God blessed them. He said,

KIDS' QUESTion — Why did God make people?

People are special creations, not just smart animals. God created people to be his friends and to take care of the world. Human beings can talk to each other and to God. Animals can't. People are the only part of God's wonderful creation that can be special friends with God. And he created them perfect. That's why Adam and Eve did not feel any shame for their nakedness. But people are also the only ones who can sin.

checkout
Genesis 1:26,27

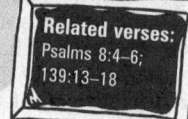

Related verses:
Psalms 8:4–6;
139:13–18

"Have little ones and increase your numbers. Fill the water in the oceans. Let there be more and more birds on the earth."

²³There was evening, and there was morning. It was day five.

²⁴God said, "Let the land produce all kinds of living creatures. Let there be livestock, and creatures that move along the ground, and wild animals. Let there be all kinds of them." And that's exactly what happened.

²⁵God made all kinds of wild animals. He made all kinds of live-stock. He made all kinds of creatures that move along the ground. And God saw that it was good.

²⁶Then God said, "Let us make man in our likeness. Let them rule over the fish in the waters and the birds of the air. Let them rule over the livestock and over the whole earth. Let them rule over all of the creatures that move along the ground."

²⁷So God created man in his own likeness.

He created him in the likeness of God.

He created them as male and female.

²⁸God blessed them. He said to them, "Have children and increase your numbers. Fill the earth and bring it under your control. Rule over the fish in the waters and the birds of the air. Rule over every living creature that moves on the ground."

²⁹Then God said, "I am giving you every plant on the face of the whole earth that bears its own seeds. I am giving you every tree that has fruit with seeds in it. All of them will be given to you for food.

³⁰"I am giving every green plant to all of the land animals and the birds of the air for food. I am also giving the plants to all of the creatures that move on the ground. I am giving them to every living thing that breathes." And that's exactly what happened.

³¹God saw everything he had made. And it was very good. There was evening, and there was morning. It was day six.

2 So the heavens and the earth and everything in them were completed.

²By the seventh day God had finished the work he had been doing. So

KIDS' QUESTION

Why did God make people red and yellow, black and white?

Can you imagine a world in which everyone looked the same? All people would have the same height, weight, color of hair, length of nose, color of eyes, size of ears and color of skin. That would be very boring. And how would we tell people apart? Instead, God created all kinds and colors of people. Some are tall. Some are short. Some are brown. Some are pink. Some have straight black hair. Some have curly red hair. They are all special to God. Don't you just love the differences and the things that make you special? God does!

JASON'S IMAGINATION

BABIES: singles, twins, triplets
COLORS: red, yellow, black, white
TODAY'S SPECIAL: 7lbs. 9ozs.

Related verses: Jeremiah 13:23; Acts 17:26

checkout
Genesis 1:31

on the seventh day he rested from all of his work. ³God blessed the seventh day and made it holy. He rested on it. After he had created everything, he rested from all of the work he had done.

ADAM AND EVE

⁴Here is the story of the heavens and the earth when they were created.

The LORD God made the earth and the heavens. ⁵At that time, bushes had not appeared on the earth. Plants had not come up in the fields. The LORD God had not sent rain on the earth. And there wasn't any man to work the ground. ⁶But streams came up from the earth. They watered the whole surface of the ground.

⁷Then the LORD God formed a man. He made him out of the dust of the ground. He breathed the breath of life into him. And the man became a living person.

⁸The LORD God had planted a garden in the east. It was in Eden. There he put the man he had formed. ⁹The LORD God made all kinds of trees grow out of the ground. Their fruit was pleasing to look at and good to eat.

The tree that gives life forever was in the middle of the garden. The tree that gives the ability to tell the difference between good and evil was also there.

¹⁰A river watered the garden. It flowed from Eden. From there it separated into four other rivers.

¹¹The name of the first river is the Pishon. It winds through the whole land of Havilah. Gold is found there. ¹²The gold of that land is good. Onyx and sweet-smelling resin are also found there.

¹³The name of the second river is the Gihon. It winds through the whole land of Cush. ¹⁴The name of the third river is the Tigris. It runs along the east side of Asshur. And the fourth river is the Euphrates.

¹⁵The LORD God put the man in the Garden of Eden. He put him there to work its ground and to take care of it. ¹⁶The LORD God gave the man a command. He said, "You can eat the fruit of any tree that is in the garden. ¹⁷But you must not eat the fruit of the tree of the knowledge of good and evil. If you do, you can be sure that you will die."

¹⁸The LORD God said, "It is not good for the man to be alone. I will make a helper who is just right for him." ¹⁹The LORD God had formed all of the wild animals. He had also formed all of the birds of the air. He had made all of them out of the ground. He brought them to the man to see what names he would give them. And the name the man gave each living creature became its name.

²⁰So the man gave names to all of the livestock. He gave names to all of the birds of the air. And he gave names to all of the wild animals.

But Adam didn't find a helper that was right for him. ²¹So the LORD God

---

What can children do to help take better care of the world?

Children can and should help to take care of our world. Here are a few ideas to get you started. (1) Do not litter. Throw your trash away. (2) Recycle. Paper, plastic, glass, oil and even batteries can be recycled. (3) Take good care of your pets. They are part of God's world too. (4) Don't waste food. Take only as much as you can eat. (5) Don't waste water. Turn off the faucet when you're done using it. (6) Don't waste electricity. Turn off the lights when you don't need them.

Related verses:
Genesis 1:28–31;
Psalm 8:6;
Proverbs 12:10;
24:30–34;
John 6:12

checkout Genesis 2:15

caused him to fall into a deep sleep. While the man was sleeping, the LORD God took out one of his ribs. He closed up the opening that was in his side. ²²Then the LORD God made a woman. He made her from the rib he had taken out of the man. And he brought her to him. ²³The man said,

"Her bones have come from my
   bones.
Her body has come from my
   body.
She will be named 'woman,'
   because she was taken out of a
   man."

²⁴That's why a man will leave his father and mother and be joined to his wife. The two of them will become one. ²⁵The man and his wife were both naked. They didn't feel any shame.

ADAM AND EVE FALL INTO SIN

3 The serpent was more clever than any of the wild animals the LORD God had made. The serpent said to the woman, "Did God really say, 'You must not eat the fruit of any tree that is in the garden'?" ²The woman said to the serpent, "We can eat the fruit of the trees that are in the garden. ³But God did say, 'You must not eat the fruit of the tree

that is in the middle of the garden. Do not even touch it. If you do, you will die.' " ⁴"You can be sure that you won't die," the serpent said to the woman. ⁵"God knows that when you eat the fruit of that tree, you will know things you have never known before. You will be able to tell the difference between good and evil. You will be like God." ⁶The woman saw that the fruit of the tree was good to eat. It was also pleasing to look at. And it would make a person wise. So she took some of the fruit and ate it. She also gave some to her husband, who was with her. And he ate it. ⁷Then both of them knew things they had never known before. They realized they were naked. So they sewed fig leaves together and made clothes for themselves.

⁸Then the man and his wife heard the LORD God walking in the garden. It was the coolest time of the day. They hid from the LORD God among the trees of the garden. ⁹But the LORD God called out to the man. "Where are you?" he asked. ¹⁰"I heard you in the garden," the man answered. "I was afraid. I was naked, so I hid." ¹¹The LORD God said, "Who told you that you were naked? Have you eaten the fruit of the tree I commanded you not to eat?"

KIDS' QUESTION

Why did Adam and Eve eat the fruit if God said not to?

They chose to do it because they thought the devil was right and God was wrong. Adam and Eve were perfect when God created them. But they were still able to choose to do wrong. The devil knew this and tempted them to disobey God. He told them it would be all right for them to disobey God. Pretty soon they wanted to eat the fruit more than they wanted to obey God's rule. They thought it would be OK and that it would not hurt them. They soon found out that they were wrong. People often say that Adam and Eve ate an apple, but we don't know what the fruit was. We only know that it was the one fruit they were not supposed to eat.

Related verses:
Matthew 6:13;
26:41

checkout Genesis 3:1–6

¹²The man said, "It was the woman you put here with me. She gave me some fruit from the tree. And I ate it."

¹³Then the LORD God said to the woman, "What have you done?"

The woman said, "The serpent tricked me. That's why I ate the fruit."

¹⁴So the LORD God spoke to the serpent. He said, "Because you have done this,

"I am putting a curse on you.
    You are cursed more than all of
        the livestock
    and all of the wild animals.
You will crawl on the ground.
    You will eat dust
    all of the days of your life.
¹⁵I will put hatred
    between you and the woman.
    Your children and her children
        will be enemies.
Her son will crush your head.
    And you will crush his heel."

¹⁶The LORD God said to the woman,

"I will greatly increase your pain
    when you give birth.
You will be in pain when you
    have children.
You will long for your husband.
    And he will rule over you."

¹⁷The LORD God said to Adam, "You listened to your wife. You ate the fruit of the tree that I commanded you about. I said, 'You must not eat its fruit.'

"So I am putting a curse on the
    ground because of what you
    did.
All the days of your life you will
    have to work hard
    to get food from the ground.
¹⁸You will eat the plants of the field,
    even though the ground
        produces thorns and thistles.
¹⁹You will have to work hard and
    sweat a lot
    to produce the food you eat.
You were made out of the ground.
    And you will return to it.
You are dust.
    So you will return to it."

²⁰Adam named his wife Eve. She would become the mother of every living person.

²¹The LORD God made clothes out of animal skins for Adam and his wife to wear. ²²The LORD God said, "The man has become like one of us. He can now tell the difference between good and evil. He must not be allowed to reach out his hand and pick fruit from the tree of life and eat it. If he does, he will live forever."

²³So the LORD God drove the man out of the Garden of Eden to work the ground he had been made out of. ²⁴The LORD God drove him out and then placed cherubim on the east side of the Garden of Eden. He also placed a flaming sword there. It flashed back and forth. The cherubim and the

Why were there angels and a flaming sword guarding the entrance to the Garden of Eden?

Angels stood at the entrance to the Garden of Eden to keep Adam and Eve from going back in. God had sent them out of the garden because they had sinned. They would never be allowed to live in Eden again.

Related verse: Numbers 22:31

checkout
Genesis 3:24

JASON'S IMAGINATION

sword guarded the way to the tree of life.

CAIN AND ABEL

4 Adam made love to his wife Eve. She became pregnant and gave birth to Cain. She said, "With the LORD's help I have had a baby boy." ²Later she gave birth to his brother Abel.

Abel took care of sheep. Cain worked the ground. ³After some time, Cain gathered some of the things he had grown. He brought them as an offering to the LORD.

⁴But Abel brought the fattest parts of some of the lambs from his flock. They were the male animals that were born first to their mothers.

The LORD was pleased with Abel and his offering. ⁵But he wasn't pleased with Cain and his offering. So Cain became very angry. His face was sad.

⁶Then the LORD said to Cain, "Why are you angry? Why are you looking so sad? ⁷Do what is right. Then you will be accepted. If you don't do what is right, sin is waiting at your door to grab you. It longs to have you. But you must rule over it."

⁸Cain said to his brother Abel, "Let's go out to the field." So they went out. There Cain attacked his brother Abel and killed him.

⁹Then the LORD said to Cain, "Where is your brother Abel?"

"I don't know," he replied. "Am I supposed to look after my brother?"

¹⁰The LORD said, "What have you done? Listen! Your brother's blood is crying out to me from the ground. ¹¹So I am putting a curse on you. I am driving you away from the ground. It has opened its mouth to receive your brother's blood from your hand. ¹²When you work the ground, it will not produce its crops for you anymore. You will be a restless person who wanders around on the earth."

¹³Cain said to the LORD, "You are punishing me more than I can take. ¹⁴Today you are driving me away from the land. I will be hidden from you. I'll be a restless person who wanders around on the earth. Anyone who finds me will kill me."

¹⁵But the LORD said to him, "No. Anyone who kills you will be paid back seven times." The LORD put a mark on Cain. Then anyone who found him wouldn't kill him.

¹⁶So Cain went away from the LORD. He lived in the land of Nod. It was east of Eden.

¹⁷Cain made love to his wife. She became pregnant and gave birth to Enoch. At that time Cain was building a city. He named it after his son Enoch.

KIDS' QUESTION

How did God make everyone else after Adam and Eve?

God created animals and plants with the ability to make more animals and plants. The same is true of Adam and Eve. God created them with the ability to make babies. Adam and Eve had babies. When Adam and Eve's babies grew up, they had babies. Those babies grew up and had babies. Soon there were a lot of people on the earth. God does not make people today the same way he made Adam and Eve. But he still creates each one. He puts together every person just the way he wants. He put *you* together just the way he wanted, too, without making any mistakes.

Related verses:
Psalm 139:13–16;
Jeremiah 1:5

checkout
Genesis 4:1,2

¹⁸Enoch had a son named Irad. Irad was the father of Mehujael. Mehujael was the father of Methushael. And Methushael was the father of Lamech.

¹⁹Lamech married two women. One was named Adah, and the other was named Zillah. ²⁰Adah gave birth to Jabal. He was the father of those who live in tents and raise livestock. ²¹His brother's name was Jubal. He was the father of everyone who plays the harp and flute.

²²Zillah also had a son. His name was Tubal-Cain. He made all kinds of tools out of bronze and iron. Tubal-Cain's sister was Naamah.

²³Lamech said to his wives,

"Adah and Zillah, listen to me.
    You wives of Lamech, hear my
        words.
I have killed a man because he
    wounded me.
I have killed a young man
    because he hurt me.
²⁴Anyone who would have killed
    Cain would have been paid
        back seven times.
But anyone who hurts me will be
    paid back 77 times."

²⁵Adam made love to his wife again. She gave birth to a son and named him Seth. She said, "God has given me another child. The child will take the place of Abel, because Cain killed him."

²⁶Seth also had a son. He named him Enosh.

At that time people began to worship the LORD.

THE FAMILY LINE OF ADAM

5 Here is the written story of Adam's family line.

When God created man, he made him in his own likeness. ²He created them as male and female. He blessed them. And he called them "man" when they were created.

³When Adam was 130 years old, he had a son in his own likeness. He named him Seth. ⁴Adam lived 800 years after Seth was born. He also had other sons and daughters. ⁵Adam lived a total of 930 years. Then he died.

⁶Seth lived 105 years. Then he became the father of Enosh. ⁷Seth lived 807 years after Enosh was born. He also had other sons and daughters. ⁸Seth lived a total of 912 years. Then he died.

⁹Enosh lived 90 years. Then he became the father of Kenan. ¹⁰Enosh lived 815 years after Kenan was born. He also had other sons and daughters. ¹¹Enosh lived a total of 905 years. Then he died.

¹²Kenan lived 70 years. Then he became the father of Mahalalel. ¹³Kenan lived 840 years after Mahalalel was born. He also had other sons and daughters. ¹⁴Kenan lived a total of 910 years. Then he died.

¹⁵Mahalalel lived 65 years. Then he

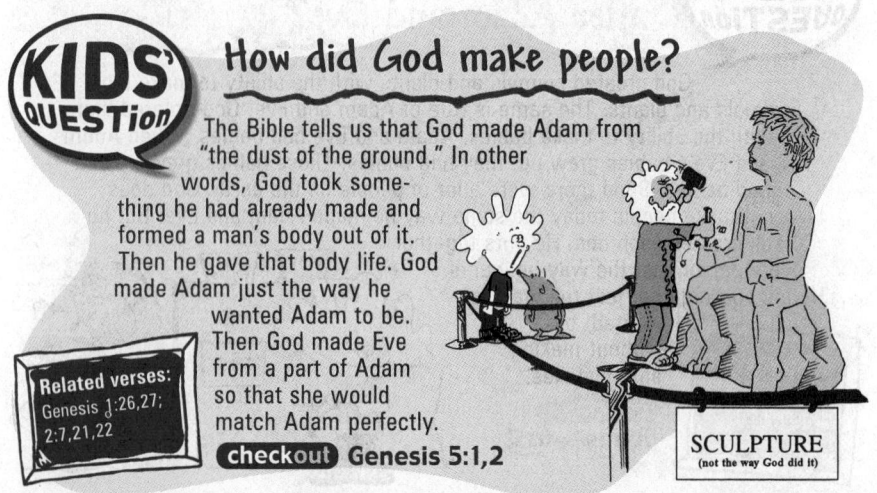

KIDS' QUESTION — How did God make people?

The Bible tells us that God made Adam from "the dust of the ground." In other words, God took something he had already made and formed a man's body out of it. Then he gave that body life. God made Adam just the way he wanted Adam to be. Then God made Eve from a part of Adam so that she would match Adam perfectly.

Related verses: Genesis 1:26,27; 2:7,21,22

checkout Genesis 5:1,2

SCULPTURE
(not the way God did it)

became the father of Jared. [16]Mahala-lel lived 830 years after Jared was born. He also had other sons and daughters. [17]Mahalalel lived a total of 895 years. Then he died.

[18]Jared lived 162 years. Then he became the father of Enoch. [19]Jared lived 800 years after Enoch was born. He also had other sons and daughters. [20]Jared lived a total of 962 years. Then he died.

[21]Enoch lived 65 years. Then he became the father of Methuselah. [22]Enoch walked with God 300 years after Methuselah was born. He also had other sons and daughters. [23]Enoch lived a total of 365 years.

[24]Enoch walked with God. Then he couldn't be found, because God took him from this life.

[25]Methuselah lived 187 years. Then he became the father of Lamech. [26]Methuselah lived 782 years after Lamech was born. He also had other sons and daughters. [27]Methuselah lived a total of 969 years. Then he died.

[28]Lamech lived 182 years. Then he had a son. [29]He named him Noah. Lamech said, "He will comfort us when we are working. He'll comfort us when our hands work so hard they hurt. We have to work hard. That's because the LORD has put a curse on the ground."

[30]Lamech lived 595 years after Noah was born. He also had other sons and daughters. [31]Lamech lived a total of 777 years. Then he died.

[32]After Noah was 500 years old, he became the father of Shem, Ham and Japheth.

THE FLOOD

6 Men began to increase their numbers on the earth, and daughters were born to them. [2]The sons of God saw that the daughters of men were beautiful. So they married any of them they chose.

[3]Then the LORD said, "My Spirit will not struggle with man forever. He will die. He will have only 120 years to live until I judge him."

[4]The Nephilim were on the earth in those days. That was when the sons of God went to the daughters of men and had children by them. The Nephilim were the heroes of long ago. They were famous men. Nephilim were also on the earth later on.

[5]The LORD saw how bad the sins of man had become on the earth. All of the thoughts in his heart were always directed only toward what was evil. [6]The LORD was very sad that he had made man on the earth. His heart was filled with pain. [7]So the LORD said, "I created man on the earth. But I will

Can God take a person who is still alive to heaven?

God can do anything. He can take a person to heaven any time he likes. He does not have to wait for the person to die. The Bible tells about two people who got to go to heaven without dying. God took both Enoch and Elijah directly to heaven this way. The Bible also tells us that someday Jesus will come back and take all his people to heaven. Those who have died will rise first. Then those still alive will go with Jesus.

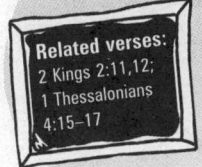

Related verses:
2 Kings 2:11,12;
1 Thessalonians
4:15–17

checkout Genesis 5:24

wipe them out. I will destroy people and animals alike. I will also destroy the creatures that move along the ground and the birds of the air. I am very sad that I have made man."

⁸But the LORD was pleased with Noah.

⁹Here is the story of Noah.

Noah was a godly man. He was without blame among the people of his time. He walked with God. ¹⁰Noah had three sons. Their names were Shem, Ham and Japheth.

¹¹The earth was very sinful in God's eyes. It was full of mean and harmful acts. ¹²God saw how sinful the earth had become. All of the people on earth were leading very sinful lives.

¹³So God said to Noah, "I am going to put an end to all people. They have filled the earth with their harmful acts. You can be sure that I am going to destroy both them and the earth.

¹⁴"So make yourself an ark out of cypress wood. Make rooms in it. Cover it with tar inside and out. ¹⁵Here is how I want you to build it. The ark has to be 450 feet long. It has to be 75 feet wide and 45 feet high. ¹⁶Make a roof for it. Leave the sides of the ark open a foot and a half from the top. Put a door in one side of the ark. Make lower, middle and upper decks.

¹⁷"I am going to bring a flood on the earth. It will destroy all life under the sky. It will destroy every living creature that breathes. Everything on earth will die.

¹⁸"But I will make my covenant with you. You will enter the ark. Your sons and your wife and your sons' wives will enter it with you.

¹⁹"Bring two of every living thing into the ark. Bring male and female of them into it. They will be kept alive with you. ²⁰Two of every kind of bird will come to you. Two of every kind of animal will come to you. And two of every kind of creature that moves along the ground will come to you. All of them will be kept alive with you.

²¹"Take every kind of food that you will need. Store it away. It will be food for you and for them."

²²Noah did everything exactly as God commanded him.

7 Then the LORD said to Noah, "Go into the ark with your whole family. I know that you are a godly man among the people of today.

²"Take seven of every kind of 'clean' animal with you. Take male and female of them. Take two of every kind

KIDS' QUESTion

Why did God flood the whole earth?

God flooded the earth because of sin. People had gotten worse and worse since Adam and Eve first sinned. They were evil and mean to each other all the time. It was so bad that God was sorry he had made people at all. God gave them 120 years to do better. They had many chances to obey God. But they only got worse. There was only one man in the whole world who was trying to live God's way. That was Noah. So God decided to destroy everyone on earth except Noah and his family.

checkout Genesis 6:11

Related verses:
Hebrews 11:7;
2 Peter 2:5

of animal that is not 'clean.' Take male and female of them. ³Also take seven of every kind of bird. Take male and female of them. That will keep every kind alive. Then they can spread out again over the whole earth.

⁴"Seven days from now I will send rain on the earth. It will rain for 40 days and 40 nights. I will destroy from the face of the earth every living thing I have made."

⁵Noah did everything the LORD commanded him to do.

⁶Noah was 600 years old when the flood came on the earth. ⁷He and his sons entered the ark. His wife and his sons' wives went with them. They entered the ark to escape the waters of the flood.

⁸Pairs of "clean" animals and pairs of animals that were not "clean" came to Noah. So did pairs of birds and pairs of all of the creatures that move along the ground. ⁹Male and female of all of them came to Noah and entered the ark.

Everything happened exactly as God had commanded Noah. ¹⁰After seven days the flood came on the earth.

¹¹Noah was 600 years old. It was the 17th day of the second month of the year. On that day all of the springs at the bottom of the oceans burst open. God opened the windows of the skies. ¹²Rain fell on the earth for 40 days and 40 nights.

¹³On that same day Noah entered the ark together with Shem, Ham and Japheth. Noah's wife and the wives of his three sons also entered it. ¹⁴They had every kind of wild animal with them. They had every kind of livestock. They had every kind of creature that moves along the ground. And they had every kind of bird that flies. ¹⁵Pairs of all living creatures that breathe came to Noah and entered the ark. ¹⁶The animals going in were male and female of every living thing.

Everything happened exactly as God had commanded Noah. Then the LORD shut him in.

¹⁷For 40 days the flood kept coming on the earth. As the waters rose higher, they lifted the ark high above the earth. ¹⁸The waters rose higher and higher on the earth. And the ark floated on the water.

¹⁹The waters rose on the earth until all of the high mountains under the entire sky were covered. ²⁰The waters continued to rise until they covered the mountains by more than 20 feet.

²¹Every living thing that moved on the earth died. The birds, the livestock

How did Noah build a boat that was so big?

We do not know exactly *how* Noah built the big boat we call an ark. We know that God told him what size to make it and what kind of wood to use. Noah did just what God had told him. The boat had to be very large because it would have to hold so many people and animals. Noah, his children, their families and hundreds of animals would have to go on the ark. It had to be a boat because God was going to flood the whole earth. It took a long time for Noah to build the boat. His family probably helped him.

Related verse:
Hebrews 11:7

checkout
Genesis 6:22

and the wild animals died. All of the creatures that fill the earth also died. And so did every human being. ²²Everything on dry land that had the breath of life in it died. ²³Every living thing on the earth was wiped out. People and animals were destroyed. The creatures that move along the ground and the birds of the air were wiped out.

Everything was destroyed from the earth. Only Noah and those who were with him in the ark were left. ²⁴The waters flooded the earth for 150 days.

8 But God showed concern for Noah. He also showed concern for all of the wild animals and livestock that were with Noah in the ark.

So God sent a wind over the earth. And the waters began to go down. ²The springs at the bottom of the oceans had been closed. The windows of the skies had been closed. And the rain had stopped falling from the sky. ³The water continued to go down from the earth. At the end of the 150 days the water had gone down. ⁴On the 17th day of the seventh month, the ark came to rest on the mountains of Ararat. ⁵The waters continued to go down until the tenth month. On the first day of the month, the tops of the mountains could be seen.

⁶After 40 days Noah opened the window he had made in the ark. ⁷He sent a raven out. It kept flying back and forth until the water had dried up from the earth.

⁸Then Noah sent a dove out. He wanted to see if the water had gone down from the surface of the ground. ⁹But the dove couldn't find any place to put its feet down. There was still water over the whole surface of the earth. So the dove returned to Noah in the ark. Noah reached out his hand and took the dove in. He brought it back to himself in the ark.

¹⁰He waited seven more days. Then he sent the dove out from the ark again. ¹¹In the evening the dove returned to him. There in its beak was a freshly picked olive leaf! So Noah knew that the water on the earth had gone down.

¹²He waited seven more days. Then he sent the dove out again. But that time it didn't return to him.

¹³It was the first day of the first month of Noah's 601st year. The water had dried up from the earth. Then Noah removed the covering from the ark. He saw that the surface of the ground was dry. ¹⁴By the 27th day of the second month the earth was completely dry.

¹⁵Then God said to Noah, ¹⁶"Come out of the ark. Bring your wife and your sons and their wives with you.

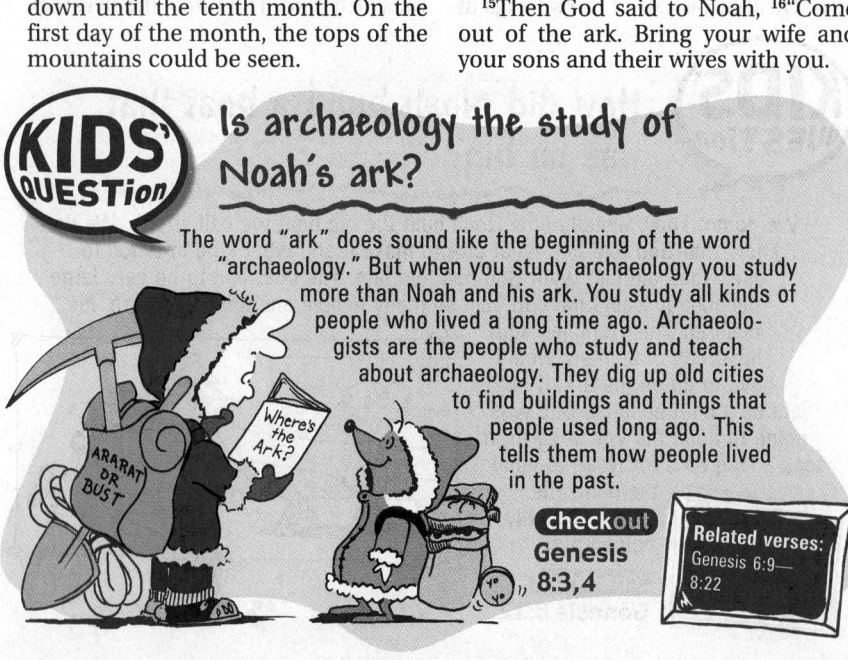

KIDS' QUESTION

Is archaeology the study of Noah's ark?

The word "ark" does sound like the beginning of the word "archaeology." But when you study archaeology you study more than Noah and his ark. You study all kinds of people who lived a long time ago. Archaeologists are the people who study and teach about archaeology. They dig up old cities to find buildings and things that people used long ago. This tells them how people lived in the past.

checkout
Genesis 8:3,4

Related verses:
Genesis 6:9—
8:22

¹⁷"Bring out every kind of living thing that is with you. Bring the birds, the animals, and all of the creatures that move along the ground. Then they can multiply on the earth. They can have little ones and increase their numbers."

¹⁸So Noah came out of the ark. His sons and his wife and his sons' wives were with him. ¹⁹All of the animals came out of the ark. The creatures that move along the ground also came out. So did all of the birds. Everything that moves on the earth came out of the ark. One kind after another came out.

²⁰Then Noah built an altar to honor the LORD. He took some of all of the "clean" animals and birds. He sacrificed burnt offerings to the LORD on the altar.

²¹Their smell was pleasant to the LORD. He said to himself, "I will never put a curse on the ground again because of man. I will not do it even though his heart is always directed toward what is evil. His thoughts are evil from the time he is young. I will never destroy all living things again, as I have just done.

²²"As long as the earth lasts,
there will always be a time to plant
and a time to gather the crops.
As long as the earth lasts,
there will always be cold and heat.
There will always be summer and winter,
day and night."

GOD MAKES A COVENANT WITH NOAH

9 Then God gave his blessing to Noah and his sons. He said to them, "Have children and increase your numbers. Fill the earth.

²"All of the land animals will be afraid of you. All of the birds of the air will fear you. Every creature that moves along the ground will fear you. Every fish in the oceans will also be afraid of you. Every living thing is put under your control.

³"Everything that lives and moves will be food for you. I have already given you the green plants for food. Now I am giving you everything.

⁴"But you must not eat meat that still has blood in it. ⁵You can be sure that I will hold someone accountable if you are murdered. I will even hold animals accountable if they kill you. I will also hold anyone accountable who murders another person.

⁶"Anyone who murders man
will be killed by man.
That is because I have made man
in my own likeness.

⁷"Have children and increase your numbers. Multiply on the earth and increase your numbers on it."

⁸Then God spoke to Noah and to his sons who were with him. He said, ⁹"I am now making my covenant with you and with all of your children who will be born after you. ¹⁰I am making it also with every living thing that was with you in the ark. I am making my covenant with the birds, the livestock and all of the wild animals. I am making it with all of the creatures that came out of the ark with you. I am making it with every living thing on earth.

¹¹"Here is my covenant that I am making with you. The waters of a flood will never destroy all life again. A flood will never destroy the earth again."

¹²God continued, "My covenant is between me and you and every living thing with you. It is a covenant for all time to come.

"Here is the sign of the covenant I am making. ¹³I have put my rainbow in the clouds. It will be the sign of the covenant between me and the earth. ¹⁴Sometimes when I bring clouds over the earth, a rainbow will appear in them. ¹⁵Then I will remember my covenant between me and you and every kind of living thing. The waters will never become a flood to destroy all life again.

¹⁶"When the rainbow appears in the clouds, I will see it. I will remember that my covenant will last forever. It is a covenant between me and every kind of living thing on earth."

¹⁷So God said to Noah, "The rainbow is the sign of my covenant. I have made my covenant between me and all life on earth."

THE SONS OF NOAH

¹⁸The sons of Noah who came out of the ark were Shem, Ham and Japheth. Ham was the father of Canaan. ¹⁹The people who were scattered over the earth came from Noah's three sons.

²⁰Noah was a man who worked the ground. He decided to plant a vineyard. ²¹He drank some of its wine. It made him drunk. Then he lay down inside his tent without any clothes on. ²²Ham saw his father's naked body. Ham was the father of Canaan. Ham went outside and told his two brothers. ²³But Shem and Japheth took a piece of clothing. They laid it across their shoulders. Then they walked backward into the tent. They covered their father's body. They turned their faces away. They didn't want to see their father's naked body. ²⁴Then Noah woke up from his sleep that was caused by the wine. He found out what his youngest son had done to him. ²⁵He said,

"May a curse be put on Canaan.
  He will be the lowest of slaves to
    his brothers."

²⁶Noah also said,

"May the LORD, the God of Shem,
  be blessed.
May Canaan be the slave of
  Shem.
²⁷May God add land to Japheth's
  territory.
May Japheth live in the tents of
  Shem.
And may Canaan be their slave."

²⁸After the flood Noah lived 350 years. ²⁹Noah lived a total of 950 years. Then he died.

A LIST OF NATIONS

10 Here is the story of Shem, Ham and Japheth. They were Noah's sons. After the flood, they too had sons.

THE SONS OF JAPHETH

²The sons of Japheth were
  Gomer, Magog, Madai, Javan,
  Tubal, Meshech and Tiras.
³The sons of Gomer were
  Ashkenaz, Riphath and Togarmah.
⁴The sons of Javan were
  Elishah, Tarshish, the Kittim
  and the Rodanites. ⁵The people
  who lived by the sea came from
  all of them. Their tribes and

KIDS' QUESTION

Why did God put a rainbow in the sky?

It was a sign of his promise to Noah. It rained for forty days while Noah and his family and the animals were on the ark. Then the flood waters went down bit by bit. It took many months for the ark to come to rest on dry land once again. Then Noah and his family and the animals left the ark. They offered a sacrifice to God. And God promised that he would never again send a flood to destroy the earth. The rainbow in the clouds reminds us of this promise. Whenever we see a rainbow we can remember God's promise never to flood the earth again.

checkout
Genesis 9:11–15

Related verse:
Hebrews 11:7

nations spread out into their own territories. Each tribe and nation had its own language.

THE SONS OF HAM

[6] The sons of Ham were
Cush, Egypt, Put and Canaan.
[7] The sons of Cush were
Seba, Havilah, Sabtah, Raamah and Sabteca.
The sons of Raamah were
Sheba and Dedan.

[8] Cush was the father of Nimrod. Nimrod grew up to be a mighty hero on the earth. [9] He was a mighty hunter in the LORD's eyes. That's why people sometimes compare others with Nimrod. They say, "They are like Nimrod, who is a mighty hunter in the LORD's eyes."

[10] At first Nimrod's kingdom was made up of Babylon, Erech, Akkad and Calneh. Those cities were in the land of Babylonia. [11] From that land he went to Assyria. There he built Nineveh, Rehoboth Ir and Calah. [12] He also built Resen. It is between Nineveh and Calah. Nineveh is the great city.

[13] Egypt was the father of
the Ludites, Anamites, Lehabites and Naphtuhites. [14] He was also the father of the Pathrusites, Casluhites and Caphtorites. The Philistines came from the Casluhites.
[15] Canaan was the father of
Sidon. Sidon was his oldest son. Canaan was also the father of the Hittites, [16] Jebusites, Amorites and Girgashites. [17] And he was the father of the Hivites, Arkites, Sinites, [18] Arvadites, Zemarites and Hamathites.

Later the Canaanite tribes scattered. [19] The borders of Canaan went from Sidon toward Gerar all the way to Gaza. Then they went toward Sodom, Gomorrah, Admah and Zeboiim all the way to Lasha.
[20] Those are the sons of Ham. They are listed by their tribes and languages in their territories and nations.

THE SONS OF SHEM

[21] Sons were also born to Shem. Shem was Japheth's younger brother. All of the sons of Eber came from Shem.

[22] The sons of Shem were
Elam, Asshur, Arphaxad, Lud and Aram.
[23] The sons of Aram were
Uz, Hul, Gether and Meshech.
[24] Arphaxad was the father of Shelah.
Shelah was the father of Eber.
[25] Eber was the father of two sons. One was named Peleg. That's because the earth was divided up in his time. His brother was named Joktan.
[26] Joktan was the father of
Almodad, Sheleph, Hazarmaveth and Jerah. [27] He was also the father of Hadoram, Uzal, Diklah, [28] Obal, Abimael, Sheba, [29] Ophir, Havilah and Jobab. All of them were sons of Joktan.

[30] The area where they lived stretched from Mesha toward Sephar. It was in the eastern hill country.
[31] Those are the sons of Shem. They are listed by their tribes and languages in their territories and nations.

[32] Those are the tribes of Noah's sons. They are listed by their family lines within their nations. From them the nations spread out over the earth after the flood.

THE TOWER OF BABEL

11 The whole world had only one language. All people spoke it. [2] They moved to the east and found a broad valley in Babylonia. There they settled down.

[3] They said to each other, "Come. Let's make bricks and bake them well." They used bricks instead of stones. They used tar to hold the bricks together.
[4] Then they said, "Come. Let's build a city for ourselves. Let's build a tower that reaches to the sky. We'll make a name for ourselves. Then we won't be scattered over the face of the whole earth."
[5] But the LORD came down to see the city and the tower the people were

building. **6**The LORD said, "They are one people. And all of them speak the same language. That is why they can do this. Now they will be able to do anything they plan to. **7**Come. Let us go down and mix up their language. Then they will not understand each other."

8So the LORD scattered them from there over the whole earth. And they stopped building the city. **9**The LORD mixed up the language of the whole world there. That's why the city was named Babel. From there the LORD scattered them over the face of the whole earth.

THE FAMILY LINE OF SHEM

10Here is the story of Shem.

It was two years after the flood. When Shem was 100 years old, he became the father of Arphaxad. **11**After Arphaxad was born, Shem lived 500 years. And he had other sons and daughters.

12When Arphaxad had lived 35 years, he became the father of Shelah. **13**After Shelah was born, Arphaxad lived 403 years. And he had other sons and daughters.

14When Shelah had lived 30 years, he became the father of Eber. **15**After Eber was born, Shelah lived 403 years. And he had other sons and daughters.

16When Eber had lived 34 years, he became the father of Peleg. **17**After Peleg was born, Eber lived 430 years. And he had other sons and daughters.

18When Peleg had lived 30 years, he became the father of Reu. **19**After Reu was born, Peleg lived 209 years. And he had other sons and daughters.

20When Reu had lived 32 years, he became the father of Serug. **21**After Serug was born, Reu lived 207 years. And he had other sons and daughters.

22When Serug had lived 30 years, he became the father of Nahor. **23**After Nahor was born, Serug lived 200 years. And he had other sons and daughters.

24When Nahor had lived 29 years, he became the father of Terah. **25**After Terah was born, Nahor lived 119 years. And he had other sons and daughters.

26Terah lived for 70 years. Then he became the father of Abram, Nahor and Haran.

27Here is the story of Terah.

Terah became the father of Abram, Nahor and Haran. And Haran became the father of Lot. **28**Haran died in Ur in Babylonia. That was the land where he had been born. Haran died while his father Terah was still alive.

29Abram and Nahor both got married. The name of Abram's wife was Sarai. The name of Nahor's wife was Milcah. She was the daughter of Haran. Haran was the father of Milcah and Iscah. **30**But Sarai wasn't able to have children.

31Terah started out from Ur in Babylonia. He took his son Abram with him. He also took his grandson Lot. Lot was the son of Haran. And Terah took his daughter-in-law Sarai. She was the wife of his son Abram.

All of them left together to go to Canaan. But when they came to Haran, they settled down.

32Terah lived for 205 years. He died in Haran.

GOD CHOOSES ABRAM

12 The LORD had said to Abram, "Leave your country and your people. Leave your father's family. Go to the land I will show you.

2 "I will make you into a great
　　nation.
I will bless you.
I will make your name great.
　You will be a blessing to others.
3 I will bless those who bless you.
　I will put a curse on anyone who
　　calls down a curse on you.
All nations on earth
　will be blessed because of you."

4So Abram left, just as the LORD had told him. Lot went with him. Abram was 75 years old when he left Haran.
5He took his wife Sarai and his nephew Lot. They took all of the things they had gotten in Haran. They also took the workers they had gotten there.

They set out for the land of Canaan. And they arrived there.
6Abram traveled through the land. He went as far as the large tree of Moreh at Shechem. At that time the

people of Canaan were living in the land.

[7]The LORD appeared to Abram at Shechem. He said, "I will give this land to your children after you." So Abram built an altar there to honor the LORD, who had appeared to him.

[8]From there, Abram went on toward the hills east of Bethel. He set up his tent there. Bethel was to the west, and Ai was to the east.

Abram built an altar there and worshiped the LORD. [9]Then Abram left and continued toward the Negev Desert.

ABRAM GOES TO EGYPT

[10]At that time there wasn't enough food in the land. So Abram went down to Egypt to live there for a while.

[11]As he was about to enter Egypt, he spoke to his wife Sarai. He said, "I know what a beautiful woman you are. [12]The people of Egypt will see you. They will say, 'This is his wife.' And they will kill me. But they will let you live. [13]Say you are my sister. Then I'll be treated well because of you. My life will be spared because of you."

[14]Abram arrived in Egypt. The people of Egypt saw that Sarai was a very beautiful woman. [15]When Pharaoh's officials saw her, they bragged to Pharaoh about her. Sarai was taken into his palace.

[16]Pharaoh treated Abram well because of her. So Abram gained more sheep and cattle. He also got more male and female donkeys. And he gained more male and female servants and some camels.

[17]But the LORD sent terrible sicknesses on Pharaoh and everyone in his palace. He did it because of Abram's wife Sarai.

[18]So Pharaoh sent for Abram. "What have you done to me?" he said. "Why didn't you tell me she was your wife? [19]Why did you say, 'She's my sister'? That's why I took her to be my wife. Now then, here's your wife. Take her and go!"

[20]Then Pharaoh gave orders about Abram to his men. They sent him on his way. He left with his wife and everything he had.

ABRAM AND LOT SEPARATE

13 Abram went up from Egypt to the Negev Desert. He took his wife and everything he had. Lot went with him. [2]Abram had become very rich. He had a lot of livestock and silver and gold.

[3]From the Negev Desert, he went from place to place until he came to Bethel. He came to a place between Bethel and Ai. That's where his tent had been earlier. [4]He had also built an

Why did God choose Abram to go to the promised land instead of someone else?

The Bible does not give us God's reasons for choosing Abram. It was not that Abram was better than everyone else. God chose Abram because he was the right person for the job. But only God knows exactly why. That is true of many of God's actions. He does not always tell us why he does what he does. But he knows everything and does only what is good. That much we know for sure.

checkout
Genesis 12:1,2

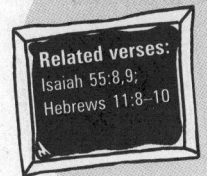

Related verses:
Isaiah 55:8,9;
Hebrews 11:8–10

DEAR GOD please choose me

altar there. He worshiped the LORD there.

⁵Lot was moving around with Abram. Lot also had flocks and herds and tents.

⁶But the land didn't have enough food for both of them. They had large herds and many servants. So they weren't able to stay together. ⁷The people who took care of Abram's herds and those who took care of Lot's herds began to argue.

The Canaanites and Perizzites were also living in the land at that time.

⁸So Abram said to Lot, "Let's not argue with each other. The people who take care of your herds and those who take care of mine shouldn't argue with one another. After all, we're part of the same family.

⁹"Isn't the whole land in front of you? Let's separate. If you go to the left, I'll go to the right. If you go to the right, I'll go to the left."

¹⁰Lot looked up. He saw that the whole Jordan River valley had plenty of water. It was like the garden of the LORD. It was like the land of Egypt near Zoar. That was before the LORD destroyed Sodom and Gomorrah.

¹¹So Lot chose the whole Jordan River valley for himself. Then he started out toward the east.

The two men separated. ¹²Abram lived in the land of Canaan. Lot lived among the cities of the Jordan River valley. He set up his tents near Sodom. ¹³The men of Sodom were evil. They were sinning greatly against the LORD.

¹⁴The LORD spoke to Abram after Lot had left him. He said, "Look up from where you are. Look north and south. Look east and west. ¹⁵I will give you all of the land that you see. I will give it to you and your children after you forever.

¹⁶"I will make your children like the dust of the earth. Can dust be counted? If it can, then your children can be counted. ¹⁷Go. Walk through the land. See how long and wide it is. I am giving it to you."

¹⁸So Abram moved his tents. He went to live near the large trees of Mamre at Hebron. There he built an altar to honor the LORD.

ABRAM SAVES LOT

14 At that time Amraphel was the king of Babylonia. Arioch was the king of Ellasar. Kedorlaomer was the king of Elam. And Tidal was the king of Goiim. ²They went to war against five kings. The kings were Bera king of Sodom,

KIDS' QUESTION

When was money invented?

Money was invented many thousands of years ago, during Bible times. For example, we know that early Egyptians used valuable minerals as money. In Old Testament times, people traded gold and silver by its weight. People measured Abram's wealth by the gold, silver and animals he owned. They did not use coins. Later, governments started making coins. People throughout the Roman empire used coins to buy and sell in New Testament times. Jesus paid taxes with money and told other people to pay their taxes too. Jesus and the apostle Paul also warned people about the dangers of loving money.

JASON'S IMAGINATION

Related verses:
Matthew 6:19,24

checkout
Genesis 13:1,2

Birsha king of Gomorrah, Shinab king of Admah, Shemeber king of Zeboiim, and the king of Bela. Bela was also called Zoar.

³Those five kings all gathered their armies together in the Valley of Siddim. It was the valley of the Dead Sea. ⁴For 12 years they had been under the rule of Kedorlaomer. But in the 13th year they opposed him.

⁵In the 14th year, Kedorlaomer and the kings who helped him went to war. They won the battle against the Rephaites in Ashteroth Karnaim. They also won the battle against the Zuzites in Ham and the Emites in Shaveh Kiriathaim. ⁶They did the same thing to the Horites in the hill country of Seir. They marched all the way to El Paran near the desert.

⁷Then they turned back. They went to En Mishpat. En Mishpat was also called Kadesh. They took over the whole territory of the Amalekites. They also won the battle against the Amorites who were living in Hazazon Tamar.

⁸Then the king of Sodom and the king of Gomorrah marched out. The kings of Admah, Zeboiim and Bela went with them. Bela was also called Zoar.

They lined up their armies for battle in the Valley of Siddim. ⁹They got ready to fight against Kedorlaomer king of Elam, Tidal king of Goiim, Amraphel king of Babylonia, and Arioch king of Ellasar. There were four kings against five.

¹⁰The Valley of Siddim was full of tar pits. The kings of Sodom and Gomorrah ran away from the battle. Some of their men fell into the pits. The rest escaped to the hills. ¹¹The four kings took all of the things that belonged to Sodom and Gomorrah. They also took all of their food. Then they went away.

¹²They carried away Lot, Abram's nephew, and the things he owned. Lot was living in Sodom at that time.

¹³One man escaped. He came and reported everything to Abram. Abram was a Hebrew. He was living near the large trees of Mamre the Amorite. Mamre was a brother of Eshcol and Aner. All of them helped Abram.

¹⁴Abram heard that Lot had been captured. So he called out his 318 trained men. All of them were sons of his servants. They chased the enemy as far as Dan. ¹⁵During the night Abram separated his men into groups. They attacked the enemy and drove them away. They chased them north of Damascus as far as Hobah.

¹⁶Abram took back all of the things the kings had taken. He brought back his nephew Lot and the things Lot owned. He also brought back the women and the other people.

¹⁷After Abram won the battle over Kedorlaomer and the kings who helped him, he returned. The king of Sodom came out to meet him in the Valley of Shaveh. The Valley of Shaveh was also called the King's Valley.

¹⁸Melchizedek was the king of Jerusalem. He brought out bread and wine. He was the priest of God Most High. ¹⁹He gave a blessing to Abram. He said,

"May God Most High bless Abram.
    May the Creator of heaven and
        earth bless him.
²⁰Give praise to God Most High.
    He gave your enemies into your
        hand."

Then Abram gave Melchizedek a tenth of everything.

²¹The king of Sodom said to Abram, "Give me the people. Keep everything else for yourself."

²²But Abram said to the king of Sodom, "I have raised my hand to the LORD. He is God Most High. He is the Creator of heaven and earth. I have taken an oath. ²³I have said that I won't accept anything that belongs to you. I won't take even a thread or the strap of a sandal. You will never be able to say, 'I made Abram rich.'

²⁴"I'll accept only what my men have eaten and what belongs to Aner, Eshcol and Mamre. Those three men went with me. Let them have their share."

GOD MAKES A COVENANT WITH ABRAM

15 Some time later, Abram had a vision. The LORD said to him,

"Abram, do not be afraid.
I am like a shield to you.
I am your very great reward."

²But Abram said, "LORD and King, what can you give me? I still don't have any children. My servant Eliezer comes from Damascus. When I die, he will get everything I own." ³Abram continued, "You haven't given me any children. So a servant in my house will get everything I own."

⁴Then a message came to Abram from the LORD. He said, "This man will not get what belongs to you. A son will come from your own body. He will get everything you own."

⁵The LORD took Abram outside and said, "Look up at the sky. Count the stars, if you can." Then he said to him, "That is how many children you will have."

⁶Abram believed the LORD. The LORD accepted Abram because he believed. So his faith made him right with the LORD.

⁷He also said to Abram, "I am the LORD. I brought you out of Ur in Babylonia. I wanted to give you this land to take as your very own."

⁸But Abram said, "LORD and King, how can I know I will take this land as my own?"

⁹So the LORD said to him, "Bring me a young cow. Also bring a goat and a ram. All of them must be three years old. Bring a dove and a young pigeon along with them."

¹⁰Abram brought all of them to the LORD. Abram cut them in two. He placed the halves opposite each other. But he didn't cut the birds in half. ¹¹Then large birds came down to eat the dead bodies of the animals and birds. But Abram chased the large birds away.

¹²As the sun was going down, Abram fell into a deep sleep. A thick and terrible darkness covered him. ¹³Then the LORD said to him, "You can be sure of what I am about to tell you. Your children who live after you will be strangers in a country that does not belong to them. They will become slaves. They will be treated badly for 400 years. ¹⁴But I will punish the nation that makes them slaves. After

that, they will leave with all kinds of valuable things.

¹⁵"But you will die in peace. You will join the members of your family who have already died. You will be buried when you are very old.

¹⁶"Your children's grandchildren will come back here. That is because the sin of the Amorites has not yet reached the point where I must judge them."

¹⁷The sun set and darkness fell. Then a burning torch and a fire pot filled with smoke appeared. They passed between the pieces of the animals.

¹⁸On that day the LORD made a covenant with Abram. He said, "I am giving this land to your children after you. It reaches from the river of Egypt to the great river Euphrates. ¹⁹It includes the land of the Kenites, Kenizzites, Kadmonites, ²⁰Hittites, Perizzites and Rephaites. ²¹The Amorites, Canaanites, Girgashites and Jebusites also live there."

HAGAR AND ISHMAEL

16 Abram's wife Sarai had never had any children by him. But she had a female servant from Egypt named Hagar. ²So she said to Abram, "The LORD has kept me from having children. Go and make love to my servant. Maybe I can have a family through her."

Abram agreed to what Sarai had said. ³After he had been living in Canaan for ten years, his wife Sarai gave him her servant Hagar to be his wife. ⁴He made love to Hagar. And she became pregnant.

When Hagar knew she was pregnant, she began to look down on the woman who owned her.

⁵Then Sarai said to Abram, "It's your fault that I'm suffering like this. I put my servant in your arms. Now that she knows she's pregnant, she looks down on me. May the LORD judge between you and me. May he decide which of us is right."

⁶"Your servant belongs to you," Abram said. "Do with her what you think is best." Then Sarai treated Hagar badly. So Hagar ran away from her.

⁷The angel of the LORD found Hagar near a spring of water in the desert.

The spring was beside the road to Shur. [8]He said, "Hagar, you are the servant of Sarai. Where have you come from? Where are you going?"

"I'm running away from my owner Sarai," she answered.

[9]Then the angel of the LORD told her, "Go back to the woman who owns you. Obey her." [10]The angel continued, "I will greatly increase the number of your children after you. You will have more of them than anyone can count."

[11]The angel of the LORD also said to her,

"You are now pregnant.
You will have a son.
You will name him Ishmael.
That is because the LORD has
　heard about your suffering.
[12]He will be like a wild donkey.
He will use his power against
　everyone.
And everyone will be against
　him.
He will not be friendly
　toward any of his relatives."

[13]She gave a name to the LORD who spoke to her. She called him "You are the God who sees me." That's because she said, "I have now seen the One who sees me."

[14]That's why the well was named Beer Lahai Roi. It's still there, between Kadesh and Bered.

[15]So Hagar had a son by Abram. And Abram gave the name Ishmael to the son she had by him. [16]Abram was 86 years old when Hagar had Ishmael by him.

THE COVENANT OF CIRCUMCISION

17 When Abram was 99 years old, the LORD appeared to him. He said, "I am the Mighty God. Walk with me and live without any blame. [2]I will now put into practice my covenant between me and you. I will greatly increase your numbers."

[3]Abram fell with his face to the ground. God said to him, [4]"As for me, this is my covenant with you. You will be the father of many nations. [5]"You will not be called Abram any-more. Your name will be Abraham, because I have made you a father of many nations. [6]I will give you many children. Nations will come from you. And kings will come from you.

[7]"I will make my covenant with you. It will last forever. It will be between me and you and your children after you for all time to come. I will be your God. And I will be the God of all of your family after you.

[8]"You are now living in Canaan as an outsider. But I will give you the whole land of Canaan. You will own it forever. So will your children after you. And I will be their God."

[9]Then God said to Abraham, "As for you, you must keep my covenant. You and your children after you for all time to come must keep it.

[10]"Here is my covenant that you and your children after you must keep. Every male among you must be circumcised. [11]You must be circumcised. That will be the sign of the covenant between me and you. [12]It must be done for all time to come.

"Every male among you who is eight days old must be circumcised. That includes those who are born in your house. It also includes those who are bought with money from a stranger. Even those who are not your own children must be included. [13]Any male who is born in your house or bought with your money must be circumcised.

"My covenant will last forever. Your body will have the mark of my covenant on it.

[14]"Any male who has not been circumcised will be cut off from his people. He has broken my covenant."

[15]God also said to Abraham, "As for Sarai your wife, do not call her Sarai anymore. Her name will be Sarah. [16]I will give her my blessing. You can be sure that I will give you a son by her. I will bless her so that she will be the mother of nations. Kings of nations will come from her."

[17]Abraham fell with his face to the ground. He laughed and said to himself, "Will a son be born to a man who is 100 years old? Will Sarah have a child at the age of 90?"

[18]Abraham said to God, "I wish Ishmael could receive your blessing!"

¹⁹Then God said, "I will bless Ishmael. But your wife Sarah will have a son by you. And you will name him Isaac. I will establish my covenant with him. It will be a covenant that lasts forever. It will be for Isaac and for his family after him.

²⁰"As for Ishmael, I have heard you. You can be sure that I will bless him. I will give him children. I will greatly increase his numbers. He will be the father of 12 rulers. And I will make him into a great nation.

²¹"But I will establish my covenant with Isaac. By this time next year, Sarah will have a son by you."

²²When he had finished speaking with Abraham, God left him.

²³On that very day Abraham circumcised his son Ishmael. He also circumcised every male who was born in his house or bought with his money. He did exactly as God had told him. ²⁴Abraham was 99 years old when he was circumcised. ²⁵His son Ishmael was 13.

²⁶Abraham and his son Ishmael were both circumcised on that same day. ²⁷And every male in Abraham's house was circumcised along with him. That included those who were born in his house or bought from a stranger.

THREE MEN VISIT ABRAHAM

18 The LORD appeared to Abraham near the large trees of Mamre. Abraham was sitting at the entrance to his tent. It was the hottest time of the day.

²Abraham looked up and saw three men standing nearby. He quickly left the entrance to his tent to meet them. He bowed low to the ground.

³He said, "My lord, if you are pleased with me, don't pass me by. ⁴Let a little water be brought. All of you can wash your feet and rest under this tree.

⁵"Let me get you something to eat to give you strength. Then you can go on your way. I want to do this for you now that you have come to me."

"All right," they answered. "Go ahead and do it."

⁶So Abraham hurried into the tent to Sarah. "Quick!" he said. "Get about half a bushel of fine flour. Mix it and bake some bread."

⁷Then he ran to the herd. He picked out a choice, tender calf. He gave it to a servant, who hurried to prepare it. ⁸Then he brought some butter and milk and the calf that had been prepared. He served them to the three men.

Can an angel be a person to us like a real person?

Sometimes angels have taken on human form and appeared to people. That is how they appeared to Abraham one day. Abraham was sitting outside his tent when three men walked up and greeted him. Abraham thought they were travelers looking for a place to stay. But in fact they were angels. One was the Lord God himself! That is why the Bible tells you to be kind and neighborly to visitors. You never know when a visitor might be an angel. It is possible that you have met an angel and did not know it. But do not go looking for angels. Angels almost always stay invisible.

checkout
Genesis 18:1,2

Related verse: Hebrews 13:2

HERE YOU GO, ANGEL

While they ate, he stood near them under a tree.

⁹"Where is your wife Sarah?" they asked him.

"Over there, in the tent," he said.

¹⁰Then the LORD said, "You can be sure that I will return to you about this time next year. Your wife Sarah will have a son."

Sarah was listening at the entrance to the tent behind him. ¹¹Abraham and Sarah were already very old. Sarah was too old to have a baby. ¹²So she laughed to herself. She thought, "I'm worn out, and my husband is old. Can I really know the joy of having a baby?"

¹³Then the LORD said to Abraham, "Why did Sarah laugh? Why did she say, 'Will I really have a baby, now that I am old?' ¹⁴Is anything too hard for me? I will return to you at the appointed time next year. Sarah will have a son."

¹⁵Sarah was afraid. So she lied and said, "I didn't laugh."

But the LORD said, "Yes, you did."

ABRAHAM MAKES AN APPEAL FOR SODOM

¹⁶The men got up to leave. They looked down toward Sodom. Abraham walked along with them to see them on their way.

¹⁷Then the LORD said, "Should I hide from Abraham what I am about to do? ¹⁸He will certainly become a great and powerful nation. All nations on earth will be blessed because of him. ¹⁹"I have chosen him. He must direct his children. He must see that the members of his family after him live the way I want them to. So he must direct them to do what is right and fair. Then I, the LORD, will do for Abraham what I have promised him."

²⁰The LORD said, "The cries against Sodom and Gomorrah are very great. Their sin is so bad ²¹that I will go down and see for myself. I want to see if what they have done is as bad as the cries that have reached me. If it is not, then I will know."

²²The men turned away. They went toward Sodom. But Abraham remained standing in front of the LORD. ²³Then Abraham came up to him. He said, "Will you sweep away godly

people along with those who are evil? ²⁴What if there are 50 godly people in the city? Will you really sweep it away? Won't you spare the place because of the 50 godly people in it?

²⁵"You would never kill godly people along with those who are evil, would you? You wouldn't treat godly and evil people alike. You would never do anything like that! Won't the Judge of the whole earth do what is right?"

²⁶The LORD said, "If I find 50 godly people in the city of Sodom, I will save it. I will spare the whole place because of them."

²⁷Then Abraham spoke up again. He said, "I have been very bold to speak to the Lord. After all, I'm only dust and ashes. ²⁸What if the number of godly people is five less than 50? Will you destroy the whole city because of five people?"

"If I find 45 there," he said, "I will not destroy it."

²⁹Once again Abraham spoke to him. He asked, "What if only 40 are found there?"

He said, "If there are 40, I will not do it."

³⁰Then Abraham said, "Lord, don't let your anger burn against me. Let me speak. What if only 30 can be found there?"

He answered, "If there are 30, I will not do it."

³¹Abraham said, "I have been very bold to speak to the Lord. What if only 20 are found there?"

He said, "If there are 20, I will not destroy it."

³²Then he said, "Lord, don't let your anger burn against me. Let me speak just one more time. What if only ten are found there?"

He answered, "If there are ten, I will not destroy it."

³³When the LORD had finished speaking with Abraham, he left. And Abraham returned home.

THE LORD DESTROYS SODOM AND GOMORRAH

19 The two angels arrived at Sodom in the evening. Lot was sitting near the gate of the city.

When Lot saw them, he got up to

meet them. He bowed down with his face to the ground. ²"My lords," he said, "please come to my house. You can wash your feet and spend the night here. Then you can go on your way early in the morning."

"No," they answered. "We'll spend the night in the street."

³But Lot wouldn't give up. So they went with him and entered his house. He prepared a meal for them. He baked bread without using yeast. And they ate.

⁴Before Lot and his guests had gone to bed, all of the men came from every part of the city of Sodom. Young and old men alike surrounded the house. ⁵They called out to Lot. They said, "Where are the men who came to you tonight? Bring them out to us. We want to have sex with them."

⁶Lot went outside to meet them. He shut the door behind him. ⁷He said, "No, my friends. Don't do such an evil thing. ⁸Look, I have two daughters. No man has ever made love to them. I'll bring them out to you now. Then do to them what you want to. But don't do anything to these men. I've brought them inside so they can be safe."

⁹"Get out of our way!" the men of Sodom replied. They said, "This fellow came here as an outsider. Now he wants to act like a judge! We'll treat you worse than them." They kept trying to force Lot to open the door. Then they moved forward to break it down.

¹⁰But the men inside reached out and pulled Lot back into the house. They shut the door. ¹¹Then they made the men who were at the door of the house blind. They blinded young and old men alike. So the men couldn't find the door.

¹²The two men said to Lot, "Do you have anyone else here? Do you have sons-in-law, sons or daughters? Does anyone else in the city belong to you? Get them out of here. ¹³We are going to destroy this place. There has been a great cry to the LORD against the people of this city. So he has sent us to destroy it."

¹⁴Then Lot went out and spoke to his sons-in-law. They had promised to get married to his daughters. He said, "Hurry up! Get out of this place! The LORD is about to destroy the city!" But his sons-in-law thought he was joking.

¹⁵The sun was coming up. So the angels tried to get Lot to leave. They

Why do some angels look like real people?

JASON'S IMAGINATION

ANGEL COSTUME DEPARTMENT

The word *angel* means "messenger." God sometimes sends angels to take messages to people. The Bible describes them as taking the form of human beings when they bring these messages. God can send angels to cheer up a person, to comfort someone or to deliver news. Angels would scare people away if they always appeared as blazing towers of fire. Sometimes God does want angels to frighten people. At other times he wants his messengers to hide their true selves as angels for a while. Then they appear as people.

Related verses:
Judges 6:11–22

checkout
Genesis 19:1

said, "Hurry up! Take your wife and your two daughters who are here. Get out! If you don't, you will be swept away when the city is punished."

¹⁶Lot didn't move right away. So the men grabbed him by the hand. They also took hold of the hands of his wife and two daughters. They led all of them safely out of the city. The LORD had mercy on them.

¹⁷As soon as the angels had brought them out, one of them spoke. He said, "Run for your lives! Don't look back! Don't stop anywhere in the valley! Run to the mountains! If you don't, you will be swept away!"

¹⁸But Lot said to them, "No, my lords! Please! ¹⁹You have done me a big favor. You have been very kind to me by sparing my life. But I can't run to the mountains. This horrible thing that's going to happen will catch up with me. And then I'll die.

²⁰"Look, here's a town near enough to run to. It's small. Let me run to it. It's very small, isn't it? Then my life will be spared."

²¹The LORD said to Lot, "All right. I will also give you what you are asking for. I will not destroy the town you are talking about. ²²But run there quickly. I can't do anything until you reach it."

The town was named Zoar. Zoar means "small."

²³By the time Lot reached Zoar, the sun had risen over the land. ²⁴Then the LORD sent down burning sulfur. It came down like rain on Sodom and Gomorrah. It came from the LORD out of the sky. ²⁵He destroyed those cities and the whole valley. All of the people who were living in the cities were wiped out. So were the plants in the land.

²⁶But Lot's wife looked back. When she did, she became a pillar made out of salt.

²⁷Early the next morning Abraham got up. He returned to the place where he had stood in front of the LORD. ²⁸He looked down toward Sodom and Gomorrah and the whole valley. He saw thick smoke rising from the land. It looked like smoke from a furnace.

²⁹So when God destroyed the cities of the valley, he showed concern for Abraham. He brought Lot out safely when he destroyed the cities where Lot had lived.

LOT AND HIS DAUGHTERS

³⁰Lot and his two daughters left Zoar. They went to settle down in the mountains. Lot was afraid to stay in Zoar. So he and his daughters lived in a cave.

³¹One day the older daughter spoke to the younger one. She said, "Our father is old. There aren't any other men around here to make love to, as people all over the earth do. ³²So let's get our father to drink wine. Then we can make love to him. We can use our father to continue our family line."

³³That night they got their father to drink wine. Then the older daughter went in and made love to him. He didn't know when she lay down or when she got up.

³⁴The next day the older daughter spoke to the younger one again. She said, "Last night I made love to my father. Let's get him to drink wine again tonight. Then you go in and make love to him. In that way, we can use our father to continue our family line."

³⁵So they got their father to drink wine that night also. Then the younger daughter went and made love to him. Again he didn't know when she lay down or when she got up.

³⁶So both of Lot's daughters became pregnant by their father. ³⁷The older daughter had a son. She named him Moab. He's the father of the Moabites of today. ³⁸The younger daughter also had a son. She named him Ben-Ammi. He's the father of the Ammonites of today.

ABRAHAM AND ABIMELECH

20 Abraham moved away from there into the Negev Desert. He lived between Kadesh and Shur. For a while he stayed in Gerar.

²There Abraham said about his wife Sarah, "She's my sister." Then Abimelech sent for Sarah and took her. He was the king of Gerar.

³God came to Abimelech in a dream one night. He said to him, "You are as

good as dead because of the woman you have taken. She is already married."

⁴But Abimelech hadn't gone near her. So he said, "Lord, will you destroy a nation that hasn't done anything wrong? ⁵Didn't Abraham say to me, 'She's my sister'? And didn't she also say, 'He's my brother'? I had no idea I was doing anything wrong. I'm not guilty."

⁶Then God spoke to him in the dream. He said, "Yes, I know you had no idea you were doing anything wrong. So I have kept you from sinning against me. That is why I did not let you touch her.

⁷"Now return the man's wife to him. He is a prophet. He will pray for you, and you will live. But what if you do not return her? Then you can be sure that you and all of your people will die."

⁸Early the next morning Abimelech sent for all of his officials. He told them everything that had happened. They were really afraid.

⁹Then Abimelech called Abraham in. He said, "What have you done to us? Have I done something wrong to you? Why have you brought so much guilt on me and my kingdom? You have done things to me that shouldn't be done."

¹⁰Abimelech also asked Abraham, "Why did you do this?"

¹¹Abraham replied, "I thought, 'There isn't any respect for God in this place at all. They will kill me because of my wife.' ¹²Besides, she really is my sister. She's the daughter of my father, but not the daughter of my mother. And she became my wife.

¹³"God had me wander away from my father's house. So I said to her, 'Here is how you can show your love to me. Everywhere we go, say about me, "He's my brother." ' "

¹⁴Then Abimelech gave Abraham sheep and cattle and male and female slaves. He also returned his wife Sarah to him. ¹⁵Abimelech said, "Here is my land. Live anywhere you want to."

¹⁶He said to Sarah, "I'm giving your brother 25 pounds of silver. It will take care of the problem we caused you. And all those who are with you will know that you aren't guilty of doing anything wrong."

¹⁷Then Abraham prayed to God. And God healed Abimelech. He also healed his wife and his female slaves so they could have children again. ¹⁸The LORD had kept the women in Abimelech's house from having children. He had done it because of Abraham's wife Sarah.

ISAAC IS BORN

21 The LORD was gracious to Sarah, just as he had said he would be. He did for Sarah what he had promised to do. ²Sarah became pregnant. She had a son by Abraham when he was old. He was born at the exact time God had promised him.

³Abraham gave the name Isaac to the son Sarah had by him. ⁴When his son Isaac was eight days old, Abraham circumcised him. He did it exactly as God had commanded him. ⁵Abraham was 100 years old when his son Isaac was born to him.

⁶Sarah said, "God has given laughter to me. Everyone who hears about this will laugh with me."

⁷She continued, "Who would have said to Abraham that Sarah would nurse children? But I've had a son by him when he is old."

ABRAHAM SENDS HAGAR AND ISHMAEL AWAY

⁸Isaac grew. The time came for his mother to stop nursing him. On that day Abraham had a big dinner prepared.

⁹But Sarah saw Ishmael making fun of Isaac. Ishmael was the son Hagar had by Abraham. Hagar was Sarah's servant from Egypt.

¹⁰Sarah said to Abraham, "Get rid of that slave woman. Get rid of her son. The slave woman's son will never have a share of the family's property with my son Isaac."

¹¹What Sarah said upset Abraham very much. After all, Ishmael was his son.

¹²But God said to him, "Do not be so upset about the boy and your servant Hagar. Listen to what Sarah tells you, because your family line will continue

through Isaac. [13]I will make the son of your servant into a nation also. I will do it because he is your child."

[14]Early the next morning Abraham got some food and a bottle of water. The bottle was made out of animal skin. He gave the food and water to Hagar. He placed them on her shoulders. Then he sent her away with the boy. She went on her way and wandered in the desert of Beersheba.

[15]When the water in the bottle was gone, she put the boy under a bush. [16]Then she went off and sat down nearby. She was about as far away as a person can shoot an arrow. She thought, "I can't stand to watch the boy die." As she sat nearby, she began to sob.

[17]God heard the boy crying. Then the angel of God called out to Hagar from heaven. He said to her, "What is the matter, Hagar? Do not be afraid. God has heard the boy crying as he lies there. [18]Lift the boy up. Take him by the hand. I will make him into a great nation."

[19]Then God opened Hagar's eyes. She saw a well of water. So she went and filled the bottle with water. And she gave the boy a drink.

[20]God was with the boy as he grew up. He lived in the desert and learned to shoot with a bow. [21]While he was living in the Desert of Paran, his mother got him a wife from Egypt.

THE PEACE TREATY AT BEERSHEBA

[22]At that time Abimelech and Phicol spoke to Abraham. Phicol was the commander of Abimelech's army. They said, "God is with you in everything you do. [23]Now make a promise to me here while God is watching. Take an oath that you will treat me fairly. Promise that you will treat my children and their children the same way. "I've been kind to you. Now you be kind to me. And be kind to the country where you are living as an outsider."

[24]Abraham said, "I promise with an oath that I'll do it."

[25]Then Abraham objected to Abimelech about what Abimelech's servants had done. They had taken over a well of water.

[26]But Abimelech said, "I don't know who has done this. You didn't tell me. Today is the first time I heard about it."

[27]So Abraham gave Abimelech sheep and cattle. The two men made a peace treaty. [28]Then Abraham took out seven female lambs from his flock.

[29]Abimelech asked Abraham, "What's the meaning of these seven female lambs? Why have you taken them out and put them by themselves?"

[30]Abraham replied, "Accept the seven lambs from me. They will be a witness that I dug this well."

[31]That place was named Beersheba. That's because there the two men made a promise with an oath.

[32]After the peace treaty had been made at Beersheba, Abimelech went back to the land of the Philistines. His army commander Phicol went with him.

[33]Abraham planted a tamarisk tree in Beersheba. There he worshiped the LORD, the God who lives forever. [34]Abraham stayed in the land of the Philistines for a long time.

GOD PUTS ABRAHAM TO THE TEST

22 Some time later God put Abraham to the test. He said to him, "Abraham!"

"Here I am," Abraham replied.

[2]Then God said, "Take your son, your only son. He is the one you love. Take Isaac. Go to Moriah. Give him to me there as a burnt offering. Sacrifice him on one of the mountains I will tell you about."

[3]Early the next morning Abraham got up. He put a saddle on his donkey. He took two of his servants and his son Isaac with him. He cut enough wood for the burnt offering. Then he started out for the place God had told him about.

[4]On the third day Abraham looked up. He saw the place a long way off. [5]He said to his servants, "Stay here with the donkey. The boy and I will go over there and worship. Then we'll come back to you."

[6]Abraham put the wood for the burnt offering on his son Isaac. He himself carried the fire and the knife.

The two of them walked on together.

[7]Then Isaac spoke up. He said to his father Abraham, "Father?"

"Yes, my son?" Abraham replied.

"The fire and wood are here," Isaac said. "But where is the lamb for the burnt offering?"

[8]Abraham answered, "God himself will provide the lamb for the burnt offering, my son." The two of them walked on together.

[9]They reached the place God had told Abraham about. There Abraham built an altar. He arranged the wood on it. He tied up his son Isaac. He placed him on the altar, on top of the wood. [10]Then he reached out his hand. He took the knife to kill his son.

[11]But the angel of the LORD called out to him from heaven. He said, "Abraham! Abraham!"

"Here I am," Abraham replied.

[12]"Do not lay a hand on the boy," he said. "Do not do anything to him. Now I know that you have respect for God. You have not held back from me your son, your only son."

[13]Abraham looked up. There in a bush he saw a ram. It was caught by its horns. He went over and took the ram. He sacrificed it as a burnt offering instead of his son.

[14]So Abraham named that place The LORD Will Provide. To this day people say, "It will be provided on the mountain of the LORD."

[15]The angel of the LORD called out to Abraham from heaven a second time. [16]He said, "I am taking an oath in my own name. I will bless you because of what you have done," announces the LORD. "You have not held back your son, your only son. [17]So I will certainly bless you. I will make your children after you as many as the stars in the sky. I will make them as many as the grains of sand on the seashore. Your children will take over the cities of their enemies. [18]All nations on earth will be blessed because of your children. All of that will happen because you have obeyed me."

[19]Then Abraham returned to his servants. They started out together for Beersheba. And Abraham stayed in Beersheba.

NAHOR'S SONS

[20]Some time later Abraham was told, "Milcah has become a mother. She has had sons by your brother Nahor. [21]Uz was born first. Then came his brother Buz. Next came Kemuel, the father of Aram. [22]The other sons are Kesed, Hazo, Pildash, Jidlaph and Bethuel." [23]Bethuel became the father of Rebekah. Milcah had the eight sons by Abraham's brother Nahor. [24]Nahor had a concubine named Reumah. She also had sons. They were Tebah, Gaham, Tahash and Maacah.

SARAH DIES

23 Sarah lived to be 127 years old. [2]She died at Kiriath Arba. Kiriath Arba is also called Hebron. It's in the land of Canaan.

Sarah's death filled Abraham with sorrow. He went to the place where her body was lying. There he sobbed over her.

[3]Then Abraham got up from beside his dead wife. He spoke to the Hittites. He said, [4]"I'm an outsider. I'm a stranger among you. Sell me some property here as a place for a family tomb. Then I can bury my wife's body."

[5]The Hittites replied to Abraham, [6]"Sir, listen to us. You are a mighty prince among us. Bury your dead wife in the best of our tombs. None of us will refuse to sell you his tomb for burying her."

[7]Then Abraham bowed down in front of the Hittites, the people of the land. [8]He said to them, "If you are willing to let me bury my dead wife, then listen to me. Speak to Zohar's son Ephron for me. [9]Ask him to sell me the cave of Machpelah. It belongs to him and is at the end of his field. Ask him to sell it to me for the full price. I want it as a place to bury my dead wife among you."

[10]Ephron the Hittite was sitting there among his people. He replied to Abraham. All of the Hittites who had come to the gate of his city heard him. [11]"No, sir," Ephron said. "Listen to me. I will sell you the field. I'll also sell you the cave that's in the field. I will sell it

to you in front of my people. Bury your wife."

¹²Again Abraham bowed down in front of the people of the land. ¹³He spoke to Ephron so they could hear him. He said, "Please listen to me. I'll pay the price of the field. Accept it from me. Then I can bury my dead wife there."

¹⁴Ephron answered Abraham, ¹⁵"Sir, listen to me. The land is worth ten pounds of silver. But what is that between you and me? Bury your wife."

¹⁶Abraham agreed to Ephron's offer. He weighed out for him the price he had named. The Hittites there had heard it. The price was ten pounds of silver. Abraham measured it by the weights that were used by those who bought and sold.

¹⁷So Ephron sold his field in Machpelah near Mamre to Abraham. He bought the field and the cave that was in it. He also bought all of the trees that were inside the borders of the field. Everything was sold ¹⁸to Abraham as his property. He bought it in front of all of the Hittites who had come to the gate of the city.

¹⁹Then Abraham buried the body of his wife Sarah. He buried her in the cave in the field of Machpelah near Mamre in the land of Canaan. Mamre is at Hebron. ²⁰So the field and the cave that was in it were sold to Abraham by the Hittites. The property became a place for his family tomb.

ABRAHAM'S SERVANT FINDS A WIFE FOR ISAAC

24 By that time Abraham was very old. The LORD had blessed him in every way. ²The best servant in his house was in charge of everything he had.

Abraham said to him, "Put your hand under my thigh. ³The LORD is the God of heaven and the God of earth. I want you to make a promise with an oath in his name.

"I'm living among the people of Canaan. But I want you to promise me that you won't get a wife for my son from their daughters. ⁴Instead, promise me that you will go to my country and to my own relatives. Get a wife for my son Isaac from there."

⁵The servant asked him, "What if the woman doesn't want to come back with me to this land? Then should I take your son back to the country you came from?"

⁶"Make sure you don't take my son back there," Abraham said. ⁷"The LORD, the God of heaven, took me away from my father's family. He brought me out of my own land. And he made me a promise with an oath. He said, 'I will give this land to your family after you.' The LORD will send his angel ahead of you. So you will be able to get a wife for my son from there.

⁸"The woman may not want to come back with you. If she doesn't, you will be free from your oath. But don't take my son back there."

⁹So the servant put his hand under Abraham's thigh. He promised with an oath to do what his master wanted.

¹⁰The servant took ten of his master's camels and left. He took with him all kinds of good things from his master. He started out for Aram Naharaim. He made his way to the town of Nahor.

¹¹He stopped near the well outside the town. There he made the camels get down on their knees. It was almost evening. It was the time when women go out to get water.

¹²Then he prayed, "LORD, you are the God of my master Abraham. Give me success today. Be kind to my master Abraham. ¹³I'm standing beside this spring. The daughters of the people who live in the town are coming out here to get water. ¹⁴"I will speak to a young woman. I'll say, 'Please lower your jar so I can have a drink.' Suppose she says, 'Have a drink of water. And I'll get some for your camels too.' Then let her be the one you have chosen for your servant Isaac. That's how I'll know you have been kind to my master."

¹⁵Before he had finished praying, Rebekah came out. She had a jar on her shoulder. She was the daughter of Bethuel, the son of Milcah. Milcah was the wife of Abraham's brother Nahor. ¹⁶The young woman was very beautiful. She was a virgin. No man had made love to her. She went down to

the spring. She filled her jar and came up again.

[17]The servant hurried to meet her. He said, "Please give me a little water from your jar."

[18]"Have a drink, sir," she said. She quickly lowered the jar to her hands. And she gave him a drink.

[19]After she had given him a drink, she said, "I'll get water for your camels too. I'll keep doing it until they finish drinking." [20]So she quickly emptied her jar into the stone tub. Then she ran back to the well to get more water. She got enough for all of his camels.

[21]The man didn't say a word. He watched her closely. He wanted to learn whether the LORD had given him success on the journey he had made.

[22]The camels finished drinking. Then the man took out a gold nose ring. It weighed a fifth of an ounce. He also took out two gold bracelets. They weighed four ounces.

[23]Then he asked, "Whose daughter are you? And please tell me something else. Is there room in your father's house for us? Can we spend the night there?"

[24]She answered, "I'm the daughter of Bethuel. He's the son Milcah had by Nahor." [25]She continued, "We have plenty of straw and feed for your camels. We also have room for you to spend the night."

[26]Then the man bowed down and worshiped the LORD. [27]He said, "I praise the LORD, the God of my master Abraham. He hasn't stopped being kind and faithful to my master. The LORD has led me on this journey. He has brought me to the house of my master's relatives."

[28]The young woman ran home. She told her mother's family what had happened.

[29]Rebekah had a brother named Laban. He hurried out to the spring to meet the man. [30]Laban had seen the nose ring. He had seen the bracelets on his sister's arms. And he had heard Rebekah tell what the man had said to her. So he went out to the man. He found him standing by the camels near the spring. [31]"The LORD has given you his blessing," he said. "So come. Why are you standing out here? I've

prepared my house for you. I also have a place for the camels."

[32]So the man went to the house. The camels were unloaded. Straw and feed were brought for the camels. And water was brought for him and his men to wash their feet.

[33]Then food was placed in front of him. But he said, "I won't eat until I've told you what I have to say."

"Then tell us," Laban said.

[34]So he said, "I am Abraham's servant. [35]The LORD has blessed my master greatly. He has become wealthy. The LORD has given him sheep and cattle. He has given him silver and gold. He has also given him male and female servants, and camels and donkeys.

[36]"My master's wife Sarah had a son by him when she was old. He has given that son everything he owns. [37]My master made me take an oath. He said, 'I'm living in the land of the people of Canaan. But promise me that you won't get a wife for my son from their daughters. [38]Instead, go to my father's family and to my own relatives. Get a wife for my son there.'

[39]"Then I asked my master, 'What if the woman won't come back with me?'

[40]"He replied, 'I have walked with the LORD. He will send his angel with you. He will give you success on your journey. So you will be able to get a wife for my son. You will get her from my own relatives and from my father's family.

[41]" 'When you go to my relatives, suppose they refuse to give her to you. Then you will be free from your oath.'

[42]"Today I came to the spring. I said, 'LORD, you are the God of my master Abraham. Please give me success on this journey I've made.

[43]" 'I'm standing beside this spring. A young woman will come out to get water. I will speak to her. I'll say, "Please let me drink a little water from your jar." [44]Suppose she says, "Have a drink of water. And I'll get some for your camels too." Then let her be the one the LORD has chosen for my master's son.'

[45]"Before I finished praying in my heart, Rebekah came out. She had a jar

on her shoulder. She went down to the spring and got water. I said to her, 'Please give me a drink.'

⁴⁶"She quickly lowered her jar from her shoulder. She said, 'Have a drink. And I'll get water for your camels too.' So I drank. She also got water for the camels.

⁴⁷"I asked her, 'Whose daughter are you?'

"She said, 'The daughter of Bethuel. He's the son Milcah had by Nahor.'

"Then I put the ring in her nose. I put the bracelets on her arms. ⁴⁸And I bowed down and worshiped the LORD. I praised the LORD, the God of my master Abraham. He had led me on the right road. He had led me to get for my master's son the granddaughter of my master's brother.

⁴⁹"Now will you be kind and faithful to my master? If you will, tell me. And if you won't, tell me. Then I'll know which way to turn."

⁵⁰Laban and Bethuel answered, "The LORD has done all of this. We can't say anything to you one way or the other. ⁵¹Here is Rebekah. Take her and go. Let her become the wife of your master's son, just as the LORD has said."

⁵²Abraham's servant heard what they said. So he bowed down to the LORD with his face to the ground. ⁵³He brought out gold and silver jewelry. He brought out articles of clothing. He gave all of it to Rebekah. He also gave expensive gifts to her brother and her mother.

⁵⁴Then Abraham's servant and the men who were with him ate and drank. They spent the night there.

They got up the next morning. Abraham's servant said, "Send me back to my master."

⁵⁵But her brother and her mother replied, "Let the young woman stay with us ten days or so. Then you can go."

⁵⁶But he said to them, "Don't make me wait. The LORD has given me success on my journey. Send me on my way so I can go to my master."

⁵⁷Then they said, "Let's get Rebekah. We'll ask her about it." ⁵⁸So they sent for her. They asked her, "Will you go with this man?"

"Yes," she said.

⁵⁹So they sent their sister Rebekah on her way with Abraham's servant and his men. They also sent Rebekah's attendant with her. ⁶⁰And they gave Rebekah their blessing. They said to her,

"Dear sister, may your family grow
    by thousands and thousands.
May your children after you take
    over
    the cities of their enemies."

⁶¹Then Rebekah and her female servants got ready. They got on their camels to go with the man. So the servant took Rebekah and left.

⁶²By that time Isaac had come from Beer Lahai Roi. He was living in the Negev Desert.

⁶³One evening he went out to the field. He wanted to spend some time thinking. When he looked up, he saw camels approaching.

⁶⁴Rebekah also looked up and saw Isaac. She got down from her camel. ⁶⁵She asked the servant, "Who is that man in the field coming to meet us?"

"He's my master," the servant answered. So she took her veil and covered her face.

⁶⁶Then the servant told Isaac everything he had done.

⁶⁷Isaac brought Rebekah into the tent that had belonged to his mother Sarah. And he married Rebekah. She became his wife, and he loved her. So Isaac was comforted after his mother died.

ABRAHAM DIES

25 Abraham married another woman. Her name was Keturah. ²She had Zimran, Jokshan, Medan, Midian, Ishbak and Shuah by Abraham. ³Jokshan was the father of Sheba and Dedan. The children of Dedan were the Asshurites, the Letushites and the Leummites. ⁴The sons of Midian were Ephah, Epher, Hanoch, Abida and Eldaah. All of them came from Keturah.

⁵Abraham left everything he owned to Isaac. ⁶But while he was still living, he gave gifts to the sons of his concubines. Then he sent them away from his son Isaac. He sent them to the land of the east.

[7]Abraham lived a total of 175 years. [8]He took his last breath and died when he was very old. He had lived a very long time. Then he joined the members of his family who had already died.

[9]Abraham's sons Isaac and Ishmael buried his body. They put it in the cave of Machpelah near Mamre. It was in the field of Ephron, the son of Zohar the Hittite. [10]Abraham had bought it from the Hittites. He was buried there with his wife Sarah.

[11]After Abraham died, God blessed his son Isaac. At that time Isaac lived near Beer Lahai Roi.

THE SONS OF ISHMAEL

[12]Here is the story of Abraham's son Ishmael. Hagar had Ishmael by Abraham. She was Sarah's servant from Egypt.

[13]Here are the names of the sons of Ishmael. They are listed in the order they were born. Nebaioth was Ishmael's oldest son. Then came Kedar, Adbeel, Mibsam, [14]Mishma, Dumah, Massa, [15]Hadad, Tema, Jetur, Naphish and Kedemah. [16]All of them were Ishmael's sons. They were rulers of 12 tribes. They all lived in their own settlements and camps.

[17]Ishmael lived a total of 137 years. Then he took his last breath and died. He joined the members of his family who had already died. [18]His children settled in the area between Havilah and Shur. It was near the eastern border of Egypt, as you go toward Asshur. Ishmael's children weren't friendly toward any of the tribes that were related to them.

JACOB AND ESAU

[19]Here is the story of Abraham's son Isaac.

Abraham was the father of Isaac. [20]Isaac was 40 years old when he married Rebekah. She was the daughter of Bethuel the Aramean from Paddan Aram. She was also the sister of Laban the Aramean.

[21]Rebekah couldn't have children. So Isaac prayed to the LORD for her. And the LORD answered his prayer. His wife Rebekah became pregnant. [22]The babies struggled with each other inside her. She said, "Why is this happening to me?" So she went to ask the LORD what she should do.

[23]The LORD said to her,

"Two nations are in your body.
Two tribes that are now inside
    you will be separated.
One nation will be stronger than
    the other.
The older son will serve the
    younger one."

[24]The time came for Rebekah to have her babies. There were twin boys in her body. [25]The first one to come out was red. His whole body was covered with hair. So they named him Esau. [26]Then his brother came out. His hand was holding onto Esau's heel. So he was named Jacob. Isaac was 60 years old when Rebekah had them.

[27]The boys grew up. Esau became a skillful hunter. He was a man who liked the open country. But Jacob was a quiet man. He stayed at home among the tents. [28]Isaac liked the meat of wild animals. So Esau was his favorite son. But Rebekah's favorite was Jacob.

[29]One day Jacob was cooking some stew. Esau came in from the open country. He was very hungry. [30]He said to Jacob, "Quick! Let me have some of that red stew! I'm very hungry!" That's why he was also named Edom.

[31]Jacob replied, "First sell me the rights that belong to you as the oldest son in the family."

[32]"Look, I'm dying of hunger," Esau said. "What good are those rights to me?"

[33]But Jacob said, "First promise me with an oath that you are selling me your rights." So Esau promised to do it. He sold Jacob all of the rights that belonged to him as the oldest son.

[34]Jacob gave Esau some bread and some lentil stew. Esau ate and drank. Then he got up and left.

So Esau didn't care anything at all about the rights that belonged to him as the oldest son.

ISAAC AND ABIMELECH

26 There was very little food in the land. The same thing had been true earlier, in Abraham's time. Isaac went to Abimelech in Gerar. Abimelech was the king of the Philistines.

²The LORD appeared to Isaac. He said, "Do not go down to Egypt. Live in the land where I tell you to live. ³Stay here for a while. I will be with you and give you my blessing. I will give all of these lands to you and your children after you. And I will keep the promise I made with an oath to your father Abraham. ⁴I will make your children after you as many as the stars in the sky. And I will give them all these lands. All nations on earth will be blessed because of your children.

⁵"I will do all of those things because Abraham obeyed me. He did what I required. He kept my commands, my rules and my laws." ⁶So Isaac stayed in Gerar.

⁷The men of that place asked him about his wife. He said, "She's my sister." He was afraid to say, "She's my wife." He thought, "The men of this place might kill me because of Rebekah. She's a beautiful woman."

⁸Isaac had been there a long time. One day Abimelech, the king of the Philistines, looked down from a window. He saw Isaac hugging and kissing his wife Rebekah.

⁹So Abimelech sent for Isaac. He said, "She's really your wife, isn't she? Why did you say, 'She's my sister'?"

Isaac answered him, "I thought I might lose my life because of her."

¹⁰Then Abimelech said, "What have you done to us? What if one of the men had sex with your wife? Then you would have made us guilty."

¹¹So Abimelech gave orders to all of the people. He said, "You can be sure that anyone who harms this man or his wife will be put to death."

¹²Isaac planted crops in that land. That same year he gathered 100 times more than he planted. That was because the LORD blessed him.

¹³Isaac became rich. His wealth continued to grow until he became very rich. ¹⁴He had many flocks and herds and servants.

Isaac had so much that the Philistines became jealous of him. ¹⁵So they stopped up all of the wells the servants of his father Abraham had dug. They filled them with dirt.

¹⁶Then Abimelech said to Isaac, "Move away from us. You have become too powerful for us."

¹⁷So Isaac moved away from there. He camped in the Valley of Gerar and settled there. ¹⁸Isaac opened up the wells again. They had been dug in the time of his father Abraham. The Philistines had stopped them up after Abraham died. Isaac gave the wells the same names his father had given them.

¹⁹Isaac's servants dug for wells in the valley. There they discovered a well of fresh water. ²⁰But the people of Gerar who took care of their herds argued with the people who took care of Isaac's herds. "The water is ours!" the people of Gerar said. So Isaac named the well Esek. That's because they argued with him.

²¹Then Isaac's servants dug another well. They argued about that one too. So he named it Sitnah.

²²He moved on from there and dug another well. But no one argued about that one. So he named it Rehoboth. He said, "Now the LORD has given us room. Now we will do well in the land."

²³From there Isaac went up to Beersheba. ²⁴That night the LORD appeared to him. He said, "I am the God of your father Abraham. Do not be afraid. I am with you. I will bless you. I will increase the number of your children because of my servant Abraham."

²⁵Isaac built an altar there and worshiped the LORD. There he set up his tent. And there his servants dug a well.

²⁶During that time, Abimelech had come to him from Gerar. Ahuzzath had come with him. So had Phicol, Abimelech's army commander. Ahuzzath was Abimelech's personal adviser.

²⁷Isaac asked them, "Why have you come to me? You were angry with me and sent me away."

²⁸They answered, "We saw clearly that the LORD was with you. So we said, 'We should make an agreement by taking an oath.' The agreement should be between us and you. We want to make a peace treaty with you. ²⁹Promise that you won't harm us. We didn't harm you. We always treated you well. We

sent you away in peace. Now the LORD has blessed you."

³⁰Then Isaac had a big dinner prepared for them. They ate and drank. ³¹Early the next morning the men made an agreement with an oath. Then Isaac sent the men of Gerar on their way. And they left in peace.

³²That day Isaac's servants came to him. They told him about the well they had dug. They said, "We've found water!" ³³So he named it Shibah. To this day the name of the town has been Beersheba.

³⁴When Esau was 40 years old, he got married to Judith. She was the daughter of Beeri the Hittite. He also married Basemath. She was the daughter of Elon the Hittite. ³⁵Isaac and Rebekah became very upset because Esau had married Hittite women.

ISAAC GIVES JACOB HIS BLESSING

27 Isaac had become old. His eyes were so weak he couldn't see anymore. One day he called for his older son Esau. He said to him, "My son."

"Here I am," he answered.

²Isaac said, "I'm an old man now. And I don't know when I'll die. ³Now then, get your weapons. Get your bow and arrows. Go out to the open coun-try. Hunt some wild animals for me. ⁴Prepare for me the kind of tasty food I like. Bring it to me to eat. Then I'll give you my blessing before I die."

⁵Rebekah was listening when Isaac spoke to his son Esau. Esau left for the open country. He went to hunt for a wild animal and bring it back.

⁶Then Rebekah said to her son Jacob, "Look, I heard your father speaking to your brother Esau. ⁷He said, 'Bring me a wild animal. Prepare some tasty food for me to eat. Then I'll give you my blessing before I die. The LORD will be my witness.' "

⁸Rebekah continued, "My son, listen carefully. Do what I tell you. ⁹Go out to the flock. Bring me two of the finest young goats. I will prepare tasty food for your father. I'll make it just the way he likes it. ¹⁰I want you to take it to your father to eat. Then he'll give you his blessing before he dies."

¹¹Jacob said to his mother Rebekah, "My brother Esau's body is covered with hair. But my skin is smooth. ¹²What if my father touches me? He would know I was trying to trick him. That would bring a curse down on me instead of a blessing."

¹³His mother said to him, "My son, let the curse fall on me. Just do what I say. Go and get the goats for me."

¹⁴So he went and got the goats. He

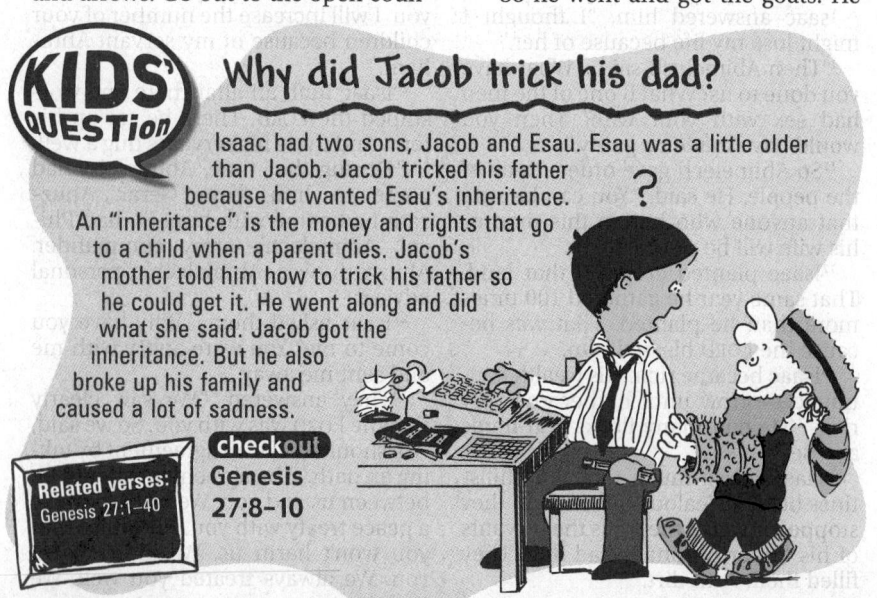

KIDS' QUESTION

Why did Jacob trick his dad?

Isaac had two sons, Jacob and Esau. Esau was a little older than Jacob. Jacob tricked his father because he wanted Esau's inheritance. An "inheritance" is the money and rights that go to a child when a parent dies. Jacob's mother told him how to trick his father so he could get it. He went along and did what she said. Jacob got the inheritance. But he also broke up his family and caused a lot of sadness.

checkout
Genesis 27:8-10

Related verses:
Genesis 27:1–40

brought them to his mother. And she prepared some tasty food. She made it just the way his father liked it.

¹⁵The clothes of her older son Esau were in her house. She took the best of them and put them on her younger son Jacob. ¹⁶She covered his hands with the skins of the goats. She also covered the smooth part of his neck with them.

¹⁷Then she handed to her son Jacob the tasty food and the bread she had made.

¹⁸He went to his father and said, "My father."

"Yes, my son," Isaac answered. "Who is it?"

¹⁹Jacob said to his father, "I'm your oldest son Esau. I've done as you told me. Please sit up. Eat some of my wild meat. Then give me your blessing."

²⁰Isaac asked his son, "How did you find it so quickly, my son?"

"The LORD your God gave me success," he replied.

²¹Then Isaac said to Jacob, "Come near so I can touch you, my son. I want to know whether you really are my son Esau."

²²Jacob went close to his father. Isaac touched him and said, "The voice is the voice of Jacob. But the hands are the hands of Esau."

²³Isaac didn't recognize him. His hands were covered with hair like those of his brother Esau. So Isaac blessed him. ²⁴"Are you really my son Esau?" he asked.

"I am," Jacob replied.

²⁵Isaac said, "My son, bring me some of your wild meat to eat. Then I'll give you my blessing."

Jacob brought it to him. So Isaac ate. Jacob also brought some wine. And Isaac drank. ²⁶Then Jacob's father Isaac said to him, "Come here, my son. Kiss me."

²⁷So Jacob went to him and kissed him. When Isaac smelled the clothes, he gave Jacob his blessing. He said,

"It really is the smell of my son.
    It's like the smell of a field
    that the LORD has blessed.
²⁸May God give you dew from heaven.
    May he give you the richness of
        the earth.

May he give you plenty of grain
    and fresh wine.
²⁹May nations serve you.
    May they bow down to you.
Rule over your brothers.
    May the sons of your mother
        bow down to you.
May those who call down curses
    on you be cursed.
    And may those who bless you be
        blessed."

³⁰When Isaac finished blessing him, Jacob left his father. Just then his brother Esau came in from hunting. ³¹He too prepared some tasty food. He brought it to his father. Then Esau said to him, "My father, sit up. Eat some of my wild meat. Then give me your blessing."

³²His father Isaac asked him, "Who are you?"

"I'm your son," he answered. "I'm your oldest son. I'm Esau."

³³Isaac was shaking all over. He said, "Then who was it that hunted a wild animal and brought it to me? I ate it just before you came. I gave him my blessing. And he will certainly be blessed!"

³⁴Esau heard his father's words. Then he began crying loudly and bitterly. He said to his father, "Bless me! Bless me too, my father!"

³⁵But Isaac said, "Your brother came and tricked me. He took your blessing."

³⁶Esau said, "Isn't Jacob just the right name for him? He has cheated me two times. First, he took my rights as the oldest son. And now he's taken my blessing!" Then Esau asked, "Haven't you saved any blessing for me?"

³⁷Isaac answered Esau, "I've made him ruler over you. I've made all of his relatives serve him. And I've provided him with grain and fresh wine. So what can I possibly do for you, my son?"

³⁸Esau said to his father, "Do you have only one blessing, my father? Bless me too, my father!" Then Esau sobbed loudly.

³⁹His father Isaac answered him,

"You will live far away from the
    richness of the earth.
You will live far away from the
    dew of heaven above.

⁴⁰You will live by the sword.
And you will serve your brother.
But you will grow restless.
Then you will throw off the heavy
load
he put on your shoulders."

JACOB RUNS AWAY TO LABAN

⁴¹Esau was angry with Jacob. He was angry because of the blessing his father had given to Jacob. He said to himself, "My father will soon die. The days of sorrow over him are near. Then I'll kill my brother Jacob."

⁴²Rebekah was told what her older son Esau had said. So she sent for her younger son Jacob. She said to him, "Your brother Esau is comforting himself with the thought of killing you.

⁴³"Now then, my son, do what I say. Go at once to my brother Laban in Haran. ⁴⁴Stay with him until your brother's anger calms down. ⁴⁵Stay until your brother isn't angry with you anymore. When he forgets what you did to him, I'll let you know. Then you can come back from there. Why should I lose both of you in one day?"

⁴⁶Then Rebekah spoke to Isaac. She said, "I'm sick of living because of Esau's Hittite wives. Suppose Jacob also marries a Hittite woman. If he does, my life won't be worth living."

28 So Isaac called for Jacob and blessed him. He commanded him, "Don't get married to a woman from Canaan. ²Go at once to Paddan Aram. Go to the house of your mother's father Bethuel. Find a wife for yourself there. Take her from among the daughters of your mother's brother Laban.

³"May the Mighty God bless you. May he give you children. May he increase your numbers until you become a community of nations. ⁴May he give you and your children after you the blessing he gave to Abraham. Then you can take over the land where you now live as an outsider. It's the land God gave to Abraham."

⁵Isaac sent Jacob on his way. Jacob went to Paddan Aram. He went to Laban, the son of Bethuel the Aramean. Laban was the brother of Rebekah. And Rebekah was the mother of Jacob and Esau.

⁶Esau found out that Isaac had blessed Jacob and had sent him to Paddan Aram. Isaac wanted him to get a wife from there. Esau heard that when Isaac blessed Jacob, he commanded him, "Don't get married to a woman from Canaan." ⁷Esau also learned that Jacob had obeyed his father and mother and had gone to Paddan Aram.

⁸Then Esau realized how much his father Isaac disliked the women of Canaan. ⁹So he went to Ishmael and married Mahalath. She was the sister of Nebaioth and the daughter of Abraham's son Ishmael. Esau added her to the wives he already had.

JACOB HAS A DREAM AT BETHEL

¹⁰Jacob left Beersheba and started out for Haran. ¹¹He reached a certain place and stopped for the night. The sun had already set. He took one of the stones there and placed it under his head. Then he lay down to sleep.

¹²In a dream he saw a stairway standing on the earth. Its top reached to heaven. The angels of God were going up and coming down on it. ¹³The LORD stood above the stairway. He said, "I am the LORD. I am the God of your grandfather Abraham and the God of Isaac. I will give you and your children after you the land on which you are lying. ¹⁴They will be like the dust of the earth that can't be counted. They will spread out to the west and to the east. They will spread out to the north and to the south. All nations on earth will be blessed because of you and your children after you.

¹⁵"I am with you. I will watch over you everywhere you go. And I will bring you back to this land. I will not leave you until I have done what I have promised you."

¹⁶Jacob woke up from his sleep. Then he thought, "The LORD is certainly in this place. And I didn't even know it."

¹⁷Jacob was afraid. He said, "How holy this place is! This must be the house of God. This is the gate of heaven."

¹⁸Early the next morning Jacob took

the stone he had placed under his head. He set it up as a pillar. And he poured oil on top of it. ¹⁹He named that place Bethel. But the city used to be called Luz.

²⁰Then Jacob made a promise. He said, "May God be with me. May he watch over me on this journey I'm taking. May he give me food to eat and clothes to wear. ²¹May he do as he has promised so that I can return safely to my father's home. Then you, LORD, will be my God. ²²This stone I've set up as a pillar will be God's house. And I'll give you a tenth of everything you give me."

JACOB ARRIVES IN PADDAN ARAM

29 Then Jacob continued on his journey. He came to the land where the eastern tribes lived. ²There he saw a well in the field. Three flocks of sheep were lying near it. The flocks were given water from the well. The stone over the opening of the well was large. ³All of the flocks would gather there. The shepherds would roll the stone away from the well's opening. They would give water to the sheep. Then they would put the stone back in its place over the opening of the well.

⁴Jacob asked the shepherds, "My friends, where are you from?"

"We're from Haran," they replied.

⁵He said to them, "Do you know Nahor's grandson Laban?"

"Yes, we know him," they answered.

⁶Then Jacob asked them, "How is he?"

"He's fine," they said. "Here comes his daughter Rachel with the sheep now."

⁷"Look," he said, "the sun is still high in the sky. It's not time for the flocks to be brought together. Give water to the sheep and take them back to the grasslands."

⁸"We can't," they replied. "We have to wait until all of the flocks are brought together. The stone has to be rolled away from the opening of the well. Then we'll give water to the sheep."

⁹He was still talking with them when Rachel came with her father's sheep. It was her job to take care of the flock. ¹⁰Rachel was the daughter of Laban. He was the brother of Jacob's mother.

When Jacob saw Rachel with Laban's sheep, he went over to the well. He rolled the stone away from the opening. He gave water to his uncle's sheep.

¹¹Jacob kissed Rachel. Then he began to sob loudly. ¹²He had told Rachel he was a relative of her father. He had also said he was Rebekah's son. Rachel ran and told her father what Jacob had said.

¹³As soon as Laban heard the news about his sister's son Jacob, he hurried to meet him. Laban hugged Jacob and kissed him. Then he brought him to his home. There Jacob told him everything. ¹⁴Then Laban said to him, "You are my own flesh and blood."

JACOB GETS MARRIED TO LEAH AND RACHEL

Jacob stayed with Laban for a whole month. ¹⁵Then Laban said to him, "You are one of my relatives. But is that any reason for you to work for me for nothing? Tell me what your pay should be."

¹⁶Laban had two daughters. The name of the older one was Leah. And the name of the younger one was Rachel. ¹⁷Leah had weak eyes. But Rachel was beautiful. She had a nice figure. ¹⁸Jacob was in love with Rachel. He said to Laban, "I'll work for you for seven years to get your younger daughter Rachel."

¹⁹Laban said, "It's better for me to give her to you than to some other man. Stay here with me." ²⁰So Jacob worked for seven years to get Rachel. But they seemed like only a few days to him because he loved her so much.

²¹Then Jacob said to Laban, "Give me my wife. I've completed my time. I want to make love to her."

²²So Laban brought all of the people of the place together and had a big dinner prepared. ²³But when evening came, he gave his daughter Leah to Jacob. And Jacob made love to her. ²⁴Laban gave his female servant Zilpah to his daughter as her servant.

²⁵When Jacob woke up the next

morning, there was Leah next to him! So he said to Laban, "What have you done to me? I worked for you to get Rachel, didn't I? Why did you trick me?" ²⁶Laban replied, "It isn't our practice here to give the younger daughter to be married before the older one. ²⁷Complete this daughter's wedding week. Then we'll give you the younger one also. But you will have to work for another seven years."

²⁸So Jacob did it. He completed the week with Leah. Then Laban gave him his daughter Rachel to be his wife. ²⁹Laban gave his female servant Bilhah to his daughter Rachel as her servant. ³⁰Jacob made love to Rachel also. He loved Rachel more than he loved Leah. And he worked for Laban for another seven years.

JACOB BECOMES THE FATHER OF MANY CHILDREN

³¹The LORD saw that Jacob didn't love Leah as much as he loved Rachel. So he let Leah have children. But Rachel wasn't able to have children. ³²Leah became pregnant. She had a son. She named him Reuben. She said, "The LORD has seen me suffer. Certainly my husband will love me now." ³³She became pregnant again. She had a son. Then she said, "The LORD heard that Jacob doesn't love me very much. That's why the LORD gave me this one too." So she named him Simeon. ³⁴She became pregnant again. She had a son. Then she said, "Now at last my husband will want me. I have had three sons by him." So the boy was named Levi. ³⁵She became pregnant again. She had a son. Then she said, "This time I'll praise the LORD." So she named him Judah. Then she stopped having children.

30 Rachel saw that she couldn't have any children by Jacob. So she became jealous of her sister. She said to Jacob, "Give me children, or I'll die!"

²Jacob became angry with her. He said, "Do you think I'm God? He's the one who has kept you from having children."

³Then she said, "Here's my servant Bilhah. Make love to her so that she can have children for me. Then I too can have a family through her."

⁴So she gave him her servant Bilhah as a wife. Jacob made love to her. ⁵And Bilhah became pregnant. She had a son by him. ⁶Then Rachel said, "God has stood up for my rights. He has listened to my prayer and given me a son." So she named him Dan.

⁷Rachel's servant Bilhah became pregnant again. She had a second son by Jacob. ⁸Then Rachel said, "I've had a great struggle with my sister. Now I've won." So she named him Naphtali.

⁹Leah saw that she had stopped having children. So she gave her servant Zilpah to Jacob as a wife. ¹⁰Leah's servant Zilpah had a son by Jacob. ¹¹Then Leah said, "What good fortune!" So she named him Gad.

¹²Leah's servant Zilpah had a second son by Jacob. ¹³Then Leah said, "I'm so happy! The women will call me happy." So she named him Asher.

¹⁴While the wheat harvest was being gathered, Reuben went out into the fields. He found some mandrake plants. He brought them to his mother Leah. Rachel said to Leah, "Please give me some of your son's mandrakes."

¹⁵But Leah said to her, "Isn't it enough that you took my husband away? Are you going to take my son's mandrakes too?"

Rachel said, "All right. Jacob can make love to you tonight if you give me your son's mandrakes."

¹⁶Jacob came in from the fields that evening. Leah went out to meet him. "You have to sleep with me tonight," she said. "I've bought you with my son's mandrakes." So he made love to her that night.

¹⁷God listened to Leah. She became pregnant and had a fifth son by Jacob. ¹⁸Then Leah said, "God has rewarded me because I gave my female servant to my husband." So she named the boy Issachar.

¹⁹Leah became pregnant again. She had a sixth son by Jacob. ²⁰Then Leah said, "God has given me a priceless gift. This time my husband will treat me with honor. I've had six sons by him." So she named the boy Zebulun.

²¹Some time later she had a daughter. She named her Dinah. ²²Then God listened to Rachel. He showed concern for her. He made it possible for her to have children. ²³She became pregnant. She had a son. She said, "God has taken my shame away." ²⁴She continued, "May the LORD give me another son." So she named him Joseph.

JACOB'S FLOCKS INCREASE THEIR NUMBERS

²⁵After Rachel had Joseph, Jacob spoke to Laban. He said, "Send me on my way. I want to go back to my own home and country. ²⁶Give me my wives and children. I worked for you to get them. So I'll be on my way. You know how much work I've done for you."

²⁷But Laban said to him, "If you are pleased with me, stay here. I've discovered that the LORD has blessed me because of you." ²⁸He continued, "Name your pay. I'll give it to you."

²⁹Jacob said to him, "You know how hard I've worked for you. You know that your livestock has done better under my care. ³⁰You had only a little before I came. But that little has become a lot. The LORD has blessed you everywhere I've been. But when can I do something for my own family?"

³¹"What should I give you?" Laban asked.

"Don't give me anything," Jacob replied. "Just do one thing for me. Then I'll go on taking care of your flocks and watching over them. ³²"Let me go through all of your flocks today. Let me remove every sheep that has speckles or spots on it. Let me remove every dark-colored lamb. Let me remove every goat that has spots or speckles on it. They will be my pay. ³³"My honesty will give witness about me in days to come. It will give witness every time you check on what you have paid me. Suppose I have a goat that doesn't have speckles or spots. Or suppose I have a lamb that isn't dark-colored. Then it will be considered stolen."

³⁴"I agree," said Laban. "Let's do what you have said."

³⁵That same day Laban removed all of the male goats that had stripes or spots. He removed all of the female goats that had speckles or spots. They were the ones that had white on them. He also removed all of the dark-colored lambs. He had his sons take care of them.

³⁶Then he put a journey of three days between himself and Jacob. But Jacob continued to take care of the rest of Laban's flocks.

³⁷Jacob took branches that were freshly cut from poplar, almond and plane trees. He made white stripes on them by peeling off the bark. He uncovered the white wood inside the branches. ³⁸Then he placed the peeled branches in all of the stone tubs where the animals drank water. He placed them so they would be right in front of the flocks when they came to drink. The flocks were ready to mate when they came to drink. ³⁹So they mated in front of the branches. And they had little ones that were striped or speckled or spotted. ⁴⁰Jacob put the little ones of the flock to one side by themselves. But he made the older ones face the striped and dark-colored animals that belonged to Laban. In that way, he made separate flocks for himself. He didn't put them with Laban's animals.

⁴¹Every time the stronger females were ready to mate, Jacob would place the branches in the stone tubs. He would place them in front of the animals so they would mate near the branches. ⁴²But if the animals were weak, he wouldn't place the branches there. So the weak animals went to Laban. And the strong ones went to Jacob.

⁴³In this way, Jacob became very rich. He became the owner of large flocks. He also had many male and female servants. And he had many camels and donkeys.

JACOB RUNS AWAY FROM LABAN

31 Jacob heard what Laban's sons were saying. "Jacob has taken everything our father owned," they said. "He has gained all of this wealth from what belonged to our father."

²Jacob noticed that Laban's feelings toward him had changed.

³Then the LORD spoke to Jacob. He said, "Go back to your father's land and to your relatives. I will be with you."

⁴So Jacob sent word to Rachel and Leah. He told them to come out to the fields where his flocks were.

⁵He said to them, "I see that your father's feelings toward me have changed. But the God of my father has been with me. ⁶You know that I've worked for your father with all of my strength.

⁷"But your father has cheated me. He has changed my pay ten times. In spite of everything that's happened, God hasn't let him harm me. ⁸Sometimes Laban would say, 'The speckled ones will be your pay.' Then all the flocks had little ones with speckles. At other times he would say, 'The striped ones will be your pay.' Then all the flocks had little ones with stripes. ⁹So God has taken away your father's livestock and given it to me.

¹⁰"Once during the mating season I had a dream. In my dream I looked up and saw male goats mating with the flock. The goats had stripes, speckles or spots. ¹¹"The angel of God said to me in the dream, 'Jacob.' I answered, 'Here I am.' ¹²He said, 'Look up. See the male goats mating with the flock. All of them have stripes, speckles or spots. That is because I have seen everything that Laban has been doing to you.

¹³" 'I am the God of Bethel. That is where you poured oil on a pillar. There you made a promise to me. Now leave this land. Go back to your own land.' "

¹⁴Rachel and Leah replied, "Do we still have any share in our father's property? ¹⁵Doesn't our father think of us as strangers? First he sold us. Now he has used up what he was paid for us. ¹⁶All of the wealth God took away from our father really belongs to us and our children. So do what God has told you to do."

¹⁷Then Jacob put his children and wives on camels. ¹⁸He drove all of his livestock ahead of him. He also took with him everything he had gotten in Paddan Aram. He left to go to his father Isaac in the land of Canaan.

¹⁹Laban had gone to clip the wool from his sheep. While he was gone, Rachel stole the statues of family gods that belonged to her father. ²⁰And that's not all. Jacob tricked Laban the Aramean. He didn't tell him he was running away.

²¹So Jacob ran off with everything he had. He crossed the Euphrates River. And he headed for the hill country of Gilead.

LABAN CHASES JACOB

²²On the third day Laban was told that Jacob had run away. ²³He took his relatives with him and went after Jacob. Seven days later he caught up with him in the hill country of Gilead.

²⁴Then God came to Laban the Aramean in a dream at night. He said to him, "Be careful. Do not say anything to Jacob, whether it is good or bad."

²⁵Jacob had set up his tent in the hill country of Gilead. That's where Laban caught up with him. Laban and his relatives camped there too.

²⁶Laban said to Jacob, "What have you done? You have tricked me. You have taken my daughters away like prisoners of war. ²⁷Why did you run away in secret and trick me? Why didn't you tell me? Then I could have sent you away happily. We could have sung to the music of tambourines and harps. ²⁸You didn't even let me kiss my grandchildren and my daughters good-by. You have done a foolish thing.

²⁹"I have the power to harm you. But last night the God of your father spoke to me. He said, 'Be careful. Do not say anything to Jacob, whether it is good or bad.'

³⁰"Now you have run away. You longed to go back to your father's home. But why did you have to steal my gods?"

³¹Jacob answered Laban, "I was afraid. I thought you would take your daughters away from me by force. ³²"But if you find anyone who has your gods, he will not remain alive. While our relatives are watching, look for yourself. See if there's anything of yours here with me. If you find any-

thing belonging to you, take it." But Jacob didn't know that Rachel had stolen the gods.

³³So Laban went into Jacob's tent and Leah's tent. He went into the tent of their two female servants. But he didn't find anything.

After he came out of Leah's tent, he entered Rachel's tent. ³⁴Rachel was the one who had taken his family gods. She had put them inside her camel's saddle. She was sitting on them. Laban searched the whole tent. But he didn't find anything.

³⁵Rachel said to her father, "I'm sorry, sir. I can't get up for you right now. But don't be angry with me. I'm having my monthly period." So he searched everywhere but couldn't find his family gods.

³⁶Jacob was very angry with Laban. "What have I done wrong?" he asked. "What sin have I committed to make you hunt me down like this? ³⁷You have searched through all of my things. What have you found that belongs to your family? Put it here in front of your relatives and mine. Let them decide between the two of us.

³⁸"I've been with you for 20 years now. The little ones of your sheep and goats were not dead when they were born. I haven't eaten rams from your flocks. ³⁹I didn't bring you animals that were torn apart by wild beasts. I made up for the loss myself. Also, you made me pay for anything that was stolen by day or night.

⁴⁰"And what was my life like? The heat burned me in the daytime. And it was so cold at night that I froze. I couldn't sleep. ⁴¹That's what it was like for the 20 years I was living with you.

"I worked for 14 years to get your two daughters. I worked for six years to get my share of your flocks. You changed my pay ten times.

⁴²"But the God of my father was with me. He is the God of Abraham and the God Isaac worshiped. If he hadn't been with me, you would certainly have sent me away without anything to show for all of my work. But God has seen my hard times. He has seen all of the work my hands have done. So last night he warned you."

⁴³Laban answered Jacob, "The women are my daughters. The children are my children. The flocks are my flocks. Everything you see is mine. But what can I do today about these daughters of mine? What can I do about the children they've had?

⁴⁴"Come now. Let's make a covenant, you and I. Let it be a witness between us."

⁴⁵So Jacob took a stone. He set it up as a pillar. ⁴⁶He said to his relatives, "Get some stones." So they took stones and put them in a pile. And they ate there by it.

⁴⁷Laban named the pile of stones Jegar Sahadutha. Jacob named it Galeed.

⁴⁸Laban said, "This pile of stones is a witness between you and me today." That's why it was named Galeed. ⁴⁹It was also called Mizpah. That's because Laban said, "May the LORD keep watch between you and me when we are away from each other. ⁵⁰Don't treat my daughters badly. Don't get married to any women besides my daughters. There isn't anyone here to see what we're doing. But remember that God is a witness between you and me."

⁵¹Laban also said to Jacob, "Here is this pile of stones. And here is this pillar. I've set them up between you and me. ⁵²This pile is a witness. And this pillar is a witness. They give witness that I won't go past this pile to harm you. And they give witness that you won't go past this pile and pillar to harm me.

⁵³"The God of Abraham and Nahor is also the God of their father. May their God decide which of us is right."

So Jacob took an oath in the name of the God his father Isaac worshiped. ⁵⁴He offered a sacrifice there in the hill country. And he invited his relatives to a meal. After they had eaten, they spent the night there.

⁵⁵Early the next morning Laban kissed his grandchildren and his daughters. He gave them his blessing. Then he left and returned home.

JACOB GETS READY TO MEET ESAU

32 Jacob also went on his way. The angels of God met him. ²Jacob saw them. He said, "This is the army of God!" So he named that place Mahanaim.

³Jacob sent messengers ahead of him to his brother Esau. Esau lived in the land of Seir. It was also called the country of Edom. ⁴Jacob told the messengers what to do. He said, "Here's what you must tell my master Esau. 'Your servant Jacob says, "I've been staying with Laban. I've remained there until now. ⁵I have cattle and donkeys and sheep and goats. I also have male and female servants. Now I'm sending this message to you. I hope I can please you."'"

⁶The messengers came back to Jacob. They said, "We went to your brother Esau. He's coming now to meet you. He has 400 men with him."

⁷Jacob was very worried and afraid. So he separated the people who were with him into two groups. He also separated the flocks and herds and camels. ⁸He thought, "Esau may come and attack one group. If he does, the group that's left can escape."

⁹Then Jacob prayed, "You are the God of my grandfather Abraham. You are the God of my father Isaac.

"LORD, you are the one who said to me, 'Go back to your country and your relatives. Then I will give you success.' ¹⁰You have been very kind and faithful to me. But I'm not worthy of any of this. When I crossed this Jordan River, all I had was my walking stick. But now I've become two groups.

¹¹"Please save me from the hand of my brother Esau. I'm afraid he'll come and attack me and the mothers with their children. ¹²But you have said, 'I will certainly give you success. I will make your children as many as the grains of sand on the seashore. People will not be able to count them.'"

¹³Jacob spent the night there. He chose a gift for his brother Esau from what he had with him. ¹⁴He chose 200 female goats and 20 male goats. He chose 200 female sheep and 20 male sheep. ¹⁵He chose 30 female camels with their little ones. He chose 40 cows and ten bulls. And he chose 20 female donkeys and ten male donkeys. ¹⁶He put each herd by itself.

Then he put his servants in charge of them. He said to his servants, "Go

on ahead of me. Keep some space between the herds."

¹⁷Jacob spoke to his servant who was leading the way. He said, "My brother Esau will meet you. He'll ask, 'Who is your master? Where are you going? And who owns all of these animals in front of you?'

¹⁸"Then say to Esau, 'They belong to your servant Jacob. They are a gift to you from him. And he is coming behind us.'"

¹⁹He also spoke to the second and third servants. He told them and all of the others who followed the herds what to do. He said, "Say the same thing to Esau when you meet him. ²⁰Make sure you say, 'Your servant Jacob is coming behind us.'" Jacob was thinking, "I'll make peace with him with these gifts I'm sending on ahead. When I see him later, maybe he'll welcome me."

²¹So Jacob's gifts went on ahead of him. But he himself spent the night in the camp.

JACOB STRUGGLES WITH GOD

²²That night Jacob got up. He took his two wives, his two female servants and his 11 sons and sent them across the Jabbok River. ²³After they had crossed the stream, he sent over everything he owned.

²⁴So Jacob was left alone. A man struggled with him until morning. ²⁵The man saw that he couldn't win. So he touched the inside of Jacob's hip. As Jacob struggled with the man, Jacob's hip was twisted. ²⁶Then the man said, "Let me go. It is morning."

But Jacob replied, "I won't let you go unless you bless me."

²⁷The man asked him, "What is your name?"

"Jacob," he answered.

²⁸Then the man said, "Your name will not be Jacob anymore. Instead, it will be Israel. You have struggled with God and with men. And you have won."

²⁹Jacob said, "Please tell me your name."

But he replied, "Why do you want to know my name?" Then he blessed Jacob there.

³⁰So Jacob named the place Peniel. He said, "I saw God face to face. But I'm still alive!"

³¹The sun rose above Jacob as he passed by Peniel. He was limping because of his hip. ³²That's why the people of Israel don't eat the meat attached to the inside of the hip. They don't eat it to this very day. It's because the inside of Jacob's hip was touched.

JACOB MEETS ESAU

33 Jacob looked up. And there was Esau, coming with his 400 men! So Jacob separated the children. He put them with Leah, Rachel and the two female servants. ²He put the servants and their children in front. He put Leah and her children next. And he put Rachel and Joseph last.

³He himself went on ahead. As he came near his brother, he bowed down to the ground seven times.

⁴But Esau ran to meet Jacob. He hugged him and threw his arms around his neck. He kissed him, and they cried. ⁵Then Esau looked up and saw the women and children. "Who are these people with you?" he asked.

Jacob answered, "They are the children God has so kindly given to me."

⁶Then the female servants and their children came near and bowed down. ⁷Next, Leah and her children came and bowed down. Last of all came Joseph and Rachel. They bowed down too.

⁸Esau asked, "Why did you send all of those herds I saw?"

"I hoped I could do something to please you," Jacob replied.

⁹But Esau said, "I already have plenty, my brother. Keep what you have for yourself."

¹⁰"No, please!" said Jacob. "If I've pleased you, accept this gift from me. Seeing your face is like seeing the face of God. You have welcomed me so kindly. ¹¹Please accept the present that was brought to you. God has been gracious to me. I have everything I need." Jacob wouldn't give in. So Esau accepted it.

¹²Then Esau said, "Let's be on our way. I'll go with you."

¹³But Jacob said to him, "You know that the children are young. You also know that I have to take care of the cows and female sheep that are nursing their little ones. If the animals are driven hard for just one day, all of them will die.

¹⁴"So you go on ahead of me. I'll move along only as fast as the herds and the children can go. I'll go slowly until I come to you in Seir."

¹⁵Esau said, "Then let me leave some of my men with you."

"Why do that?" Jacob asked. "I just hope I've pleased you."

¹⁶So that day Esau started on his way back to Seir. ¹⁷But Jacob went to Succoth. There he built a place for himself. He also made shelters for his livestock. That's why the place is named Succoth.

¹⁸After Jacob came from Paddan Aram, he arrived safely at the city of Shechem in Canaan. He camped where he could see the city. ¹⁹For 100 pieces of silver he bought a piece of land. He got it from the sons of Hamor. Hamor was the father of Shechem. Jacob set up his tent on that piece of land. ²⁰He also set up an altar there. He named it El Elohe Israel.

SIMEON AND LEVI KILL THE MEN OF SHECHEM

34 Dinah was the daughter Leah had by Jacob. Dinah went out to visit the women of the land.

²Hamor the Hivite was the ruler of that area. When his son Shechem saw Dinah, he took her and raped her. ³Then his heart longed for Jacob's daughter Dinah. He fell in love with her and spoke tenderly to her.

⁴Shechem said to his father Hamor, "Get me that woman. I want her to be my wife."

⁵Jacob heard that his daughter Dinah had been made "unclean." His sons were in the fields with his livestock. So he kept quiet about it until they came home.

⁶Then Shechem's father Hamor went out to talk with Jacob. ⁷Jacob's sons had come in from the fields. They came as soon as they heard what had happened. They were filled with sadness and anger.

Shechem had done a very terrible thing. He had forced Jacob's daughter to have sex with him. He had done something that should never be done in Israel.

⁸But Hamor said to them, "My son Shechem wants your daughter. Please give her to him to be his wife.

⁹"Let your people and ours get married to each other. Give us your daughters as our wives. You can have our daughters as your wives. ¹⁰You can settle among us. Here is the land. Live in it. Trade in it. Buy property in it."

¹¹Then Shechem spoke to Dinah's father and brothers. He said, "I want to please you. I'll give you anything you ask. ¹²Make the price for the bride as high as you want to. I'll pay anything you ask me. Just give me the woman. I want to get married to her."

¹³Their sister Dinah had been made "unclean." So Jacob's sons lied to Shechem and his father Hamor. ¹⁴They said to them, "We can't do it. We can't give our sister to a man who isn't circumcised. That would bring shame on us. ¹⁵We'll agree, but only on one condition. You will have to become like us. You will have to circumcise all of your males.

¹⁶"Then we'll give you our daughters as your wives. And we'll take your daughters as our wives. We'll settle among you and become one people with you. ¹⁷But if you won't agree to it, then we'll take our sister and go."

¹⁸Their offer seemed good to Hamor and his son Shechem. ¹⁹The young man was the most honored of all of the men in his father's family. He didn't lose any time in doing what they said, because he was delighted with Jacob's daughter.

²⁰Hamor and his son Shechem went to the city gate. They spoke to the other men in town. ²¹"These men are friendly toward us," they said. "Let them live in our land. Let them trade in it. The land has plenty of room for them. We can get married to their daughters. And they can marry ours. ²²But they will agree to live with us as one people only on one condition. All of our males must be circumcised, just as they are. ²³Won't their livestock and their property belong to us? Won't all of their animals become ours? So let's say yes to them. Then they'll settle among us."

²⁴All of the men who went out through the city gate agreed with Hamor and his son Shechem. So every male in the city was circumcised.

²⁵Three days later, all of them were still in pain. Then Simeon and Levi took their swords. They were Jacob's sons and Dinah's brothers. They attacked the city when the people didn't expect it. They killed every male. ²⁶They also killed Hamor and his son Shechem with their swords. Then they took Dinah from Shechem's house and left.

²⁷Jacob's other sons found the dead bodies. They robbed the city where their sister had been made "unclean." ²⁸They took the flocks and herds and donkeys. They took everything that was in the city and out in the fields. ²⁹They carried everything away. And they took all of the women and children. They took away everything that was in the houses.

³⁰Then Jacob said to Simeon and Levi, "You have brought trouble on me. Now I'm like a very bad smell to the Canaanites and Perizzites who live in this land. There aren't many of us. They may join together against me and attack me. Then I and my family will be destroyed."

³¹But they replied, "Should he have treated our sister like a prostitute?"

JACOB RETURNS TO BETHEL

35 Then God said to Jacob, "Go up to Bethel and settle there. Build an altar there to honor me. That's where I appeared to you when you were running away from your brother Esau."

²So Jacob spoke to his family and to everyone who was with him. He said, "Get rid of the strange gods you have with you. Make yourselves pure, and change your clothes. ³Come, let's go up to Bethel. There I'll build an altar to honor God. He answered me when I was in trouble. He's been with me everywhere I've gone."

⁴So they gave Jacob all of the strange gods they had. They also gave him

their earrings. Jacob buried them under the oak tree at Shechem.

⁵Then Jacob and everyone who was with him started out. The terror of God fell on the towns all around them. So no one chased them.

⁶Jacob and all of the people who were with him came to Luz. Luz is also called Bethel. It's in the land of Canaan. ⁷Jacob built an altar at Luz. He named the place El Bethel. There God made himself known to Jacob when he was running away from his brother.

⁸Rebekah's attendant Deborah died. They buried her body under the oak tree below Bethel. So it was called Allon Bacuth.

⁹After Jacob returned from Paddan Aram, God appeared to him again. And God blessed him. ¹⁰God said to him, "Your name is Jacob. But you will not be called Jacob anymore. Your name will be Israel." So he named him Israel.

¹¹God said to him, "I am the Mighty God. Have children and increase your numbers. A nation and a community of nations will come from you. Kings will come from your body. ¹²I am giving you the land I gave to Abraham and Isaac. I will also give it to your children after you."

¹³Then God left him at the place where he had talked with him.

¹⁴Jacob set up a stone pillar at the place where God had talked with him. He poured out a drink offering on it. He also poured oil on it. ¹⁵Jacob named the place Bethel. That's where God had talked with him.

RACHEL AND ISAAC DIE

¹⁶They moved on from Bethel. Ephrath wasn't very far away when Rachel began to have a baby. She was having a very hard time of it.

¹⁷The woman who helped her saw that she was having problems. So she said to her, "Don't be afraid. You have another son."

¹⁸But Rachel was dying. As she took her last breath, she named her son Ben-Oni. But his father named him Benjamin.

¹⁹So Rachel died. Her body was buried beside the road to Ephrath. Ephrath was also called Bethlehem. ²⁰Jacob set up a pillar over her tomb. The pillar marks the place of Rachel's tomb to this very day.

²¹Israel moved on again. He set up his tent beyond Migdal Eder.

²²While Israel was living in that area, Reuben went in and made love to Bilhah. She was the concubine of Reuben's father. And Israel heard about it.

Here are the 12 sons Jacob had.
²³Leah was the mother of
   Reuben, Jacob's oldest son.
  Her other sons were
   Simeon, Levi, Judah, Issachar
   and Zebulun.
²⁴The sons of Rachel were
   Joseph and Benjamin.
²⁵The sons of Rachel's female servant Bilhah were
   Dan and Naphtali.
²⁶The sons of Leah's female servant Zilpah were
   Gad and Asher.
Those were Jacob's sons. They were born in Paddan Aram.

²⁷Jacob came home to his father Isaac in Mamre. Mamre is near Kiriath Arba, where Abraham and Isaac had stayed. The place is also called Hebron.

²⁸Isaac lived 180 years. ²⁹Then he took his last breath and died. He was very old when he joined the members of his family who had already died. His sons Esau and Jacob buried his body.

THE FAMILY LINE OF ESAU

36 Here is the story of Esau. Esau was also called Edom.

²Esau got his wives from among the women of Canaan. He married Adah, the daughter of Elon the Hittite. He also married Oholibamah, the daughter of Anah and the granddaughter of Zibeon the Hivite. ³And he married Basemath, the daughter of Ishmael and the sister of Nebaioth.

⁴Adah had Eliphaz by Esau. Basemath had Reuel. ⁵Oholibamah had Jeush, Jalam and Korah. All of

them were Esau's sons. They were born in Canaan.

[6]Esau moved to a land far away from his brother Jacob. He took with him his wives, his sons and daughters, and all of the people who lived with him. He also took his livestock and all of his other animals. He took everything he had gotten in Canaan.

[7]Jacob and Esau owned so much that they couldn't remain together. There wasn't enough land for both of them. They had too much livestock. [8]So Esau settled in the hill country of Seir. Esau was also called Edom.

[9]Here is the story of Esau. He's the father of the people of Edom. They live in the hill country of Seir.

[10]Here are the names of Esau's sons.
They are Eliphaz, the son of Esau's wife Adah, and Reuel, the son of Esau's wife Basemath.
[11]The sons of Eliphaz were
Teman, Omar, Zepho, Gatam and Kenaz.
[12]Esau's son Eliphaz also had a concubine named Timna. She had Amalek by Eliphaz. They were grandsons of Esau's wife Adah.
[13]The sons of Reuel were
Nahath, Zerah, Shammah and Mizzah. They were grandsons of Esau's wife Basemath.
[14]Esau's wife Oholibamah was the daughter of Anah and the granddaughter of Zibeon. She had Jeush, Jalam and Korah by Esau.

[15]Here are the chiefs who were among Esau's sons.
Eliphaz was Esau's oldest son. The sons of Eliphaz were
Chiefs Teman, Omar, Zepho, Kenaz, [16]Korah, Gatam and Amalek. They were the chiefs in Edom who were sons of Eliphaz. They were Adah's grandsons.
[17]The sons of Esau's son Reuel were
Chiefs Nahath, Zerah, Sham-mah and Mizzah. They were the chiefs in Edom who were sons of Reuel. They were grandsons of Esau's wife Basemath.
[18]The sons of Esau's wife Oholibamah were
Chiefs Jeush, Jalam and Korah. They were the chiefs who were sons of Esau's wife Oholibamah. She was Anah's daughter.

[19]That was the family line of Esau. And those were the chiefs. Esau was also called Edom.

[20]Seir the Horite had sons living in the same area.
They were Lotan, Shobal, Zibeon, Anah, [21]Dishon, Ezer and Dishan. The sons of Seir in Edom were Horite chiefs.
[22]The sons of Lotan were
Hori and Homam. Timna was Lotan's sister.
[23]The sons of Shobal were
Alvan, Manahath, Ebal, Shepho and Onam.
[24]The sons of Zibeon were
Aiah and Anah. He was the Anah who discovered the hot springs of water in the desert. He found them while he was taking care of the donkeys that belonged to his father Zibeon.
[25]The children of Anah were
Dishon and Oholibamah. Oholibamah was the daughter of Anah.
[26]The sons of Dishon were
Hemdan, Eshban, Ithran and Keran.
[27]The sons of Ezer were
Bilhan, Zaavan and Akan.
[28]The sons of Dishan were
Uz and Aran.
[29]The Horite chiefs were
Lotan, Shobal, Zibeon, Anah, [30]Dishon, Ezer and Dishan. They were the Horite chiefs in the land of Seir. They are listed tribe by tribe.

THE RULERS OF EDOM

[31]Before Israel had a king, there were kings who ruled in Edom.

³²Bela became the king of Edom. Bela was the son of Beor. Bela's city was called Dinhabah.

³³When Bela died, Jobab became the next king. Jobab was the son of Zerah from Bozrah.

³⁴When Jobab died, Husham became the next king. Husham was from the land of the Temanites.

³⁵When Husham died, Hadad became the next king. Hadad was the son of Bedad. Hadad had won the battle over Midian in the country of Moab. Hadad's city was called Avith.

³⁶When Hadad died, Samlah became the next king. Samlah was from Masrekah.

³⁷When Samlah died, Shaul became the next king. Shaul was from Rehoboth on the river.

³⁸When Shaul died, Baal-Hanan became the next king. Baal-Hanan was the son of Acbor.

³⁹When Baal-Hanan died, Hadad became the next king. Hadad's city was called Pau. His wife's name was Mehetabel. She was the daughter of Matred. Matred was the daughter of Me-Zahab.

⁴⁰Here are the chiefs who were in the family line of Esau. They are listed by name as chiefs in charge of their tribes and territories. They are Timna, Alvah, Jetheth, ⁴¹Oholibamah, Elah, Pinon, ⁴²Kenaz, Teman, Mibzar, ⁴³Magdiel and Iram. They were the chiefs of Edom. They ruled over their settlements in the land where they lived.

That's the end of the story of Esau. He was the father of the people of Edom.

JOSEPH HAS TWO DREAMS

37 Jacob lived in the land of Canaan. It's the land where his father had stayed.

²Here is the story of Jacob.

Joseph was a young man. He was 17 years old. He was taking care of the flocks with some of his brothers. They were the sons of Bilhah and the sons of Zilpah, his father's wives. Joseph brought their father a bad report about them.

³Israel loved Joseph more than any of his other sons. Joseph had been born to him when he was old. Israel made him a beautiful robe.

⁴Joseph's brothers saw that their father loved him more than any of them. So they hated Joseph. They couldn't even speak one kind word to him.

⁵Joseph had a dream. When he told it to his brothers, they hated him even more. ⁶He said to them, "Listen to the dream I had. ⁷We were tying up bundles of grain out in the field. Suddenly my bundle rose and stood up straight. Your bundles gathered around my bundle and bowed down to it."

⁸His brothers said to him, "Do you plan to be king over us? Will you really rule over us?" So they hated him even more because of his dream. They didn't like what he had said.

⁹Then Joseph had another dream. He told it to his brothers. "Listen," he said. "I had another dream. This time the sun and moon and 11 stars were bowing down to me."

¹⁰He told his father as well as his brothers. Then his father objected. He said, "What about this dream you had? Will your mother and I and your brothers really do that? Will we really come and bow down to the ground in front of you?"

¹¹His brothers were jealous of him. But his father kept the matter in mind.

JOSEPH IS SOLD BY HIS BROTHERS

¹²Joseph's brothers had gone to take care of their father's flocks near Shechem. ¹³Israel said to Joseph, "As you know, your brothers are taking care of the flocks near Shechem. Come. I'm going to send you to them."

"All right," Joseph replied.

¹⁴So Israel said to him, "Go to your brothers. See how they are doing. Also see how the flocks are doing. Then come back and tell me." So he sent him away from the Hebron Valley.

Joseph arrived at Shechem. ¹⁵A man found him wandering around in the fields. He asked Joseph, "What are you looking for?"

¹⁶He replied, "I'm looking for my brothers. Can you tell me where they are taking care of their flocks?"

¹⁷"They've moved on from here," the man answered. "I heard them say, 'Let's go to Dothan.' "

So Joseph went to look for his brothers. He found them near Dothan. ¹⁸But they saw him a long way off. Before he reached them, they made plans to kill him.

¹⁹"Here comes that dreamer!" they said to one another. ²⁰"Come. Let's kill him. Let's throw him into one of these empty wells. Let's say that a wild animal ate him up. Then we'll see whether his dreams will come true."

²¹Reuben heard them. He tried to save Joseph from them. "Let's not take his life," he said. ²²"Let's not spill any blood. Throw him into this empty well here in the desert. But don't harm him yourselves."

Reuben said that to save Joseph from them. He was hoping he could take him back to his father.

²³When Joseph came to his brothers, he was wearing his beautiful robe.

They took it away from him. ²⁴And they threw him into the well. The well was empty. There wasn't any water in it.

²⁵Then they sat down to eat their meal. As they did, they saw some Ishmaelite traders coming from Gilead. Their camels were loaded with spices, lotion and myrrh. They were on their way to take them down to Egypt.

²⁶Judah said to his brothers, "What will we gain if we kill our brother and try to cover up what we've done? ²⁷Come. Let's sell him to these traders. Let's not harm him ourselves. After all, he's our brother. He's our own flesh and blood." Judah's brothers agreed with him.

²⁸The traders from Midian came by. Joseph's brothers pulled him up out of the well. They sold him to the Ishmaelite traders for eight ounces of silver. Then the traders took him to Egypt.

²⁹Later, Reuben came back to the empty well. He saw that Joseph wasn't there. He was so upset that he tore his clothes. ³⁰He went back to his brothers and said, "The boy isn't there! Now what should I do?"

KIDS' QUESTION

Why did Joseph's brothers sell him?

Joseph had ten older brothers and one younger brother. Joseph's older brothers were angry with him for three reasons. First, Joseph was their dad's favorite. Second, Joseph told on his brothers for the bad things they did. Third, Joseph's brothers were mad because Joseph told them that he was going to be their boss someday. The brothers became so angry at Joseph that they decided to kill him. But then they changed their minds and just threw him in a well. Some traders came by and the brothers sold Joseph to them. At last they had Joseph out of the way.

checkout
Genesis 37:19,20

Related verses:
Genesis 37:1–36

4 SALE
1 SISTER
20 pieces of silver
or reptile of any sort

³¹Then they got Joseph's beautiful robe. They killed a goat and dipped the robe in the blood. ³²They took it back to their father. They said, "We found this. Take a look at it. See if it's your son's robe."

³³Jacob recognized it. He said, "It's my son's robe! A wild animal has eaten him up. Joseph must have been torn to pieces."

³⁴Jacob tore his clothes. He put on black clothes. Then he sobbed over his son for many days.

³⁵All of Jacob's other sons and daughters came to comfort him. But they weren't able to. He said, "I'll be full of sorrow when I go down into the grave to be with my son." So Joseph's father sobbed over him.

³⁶But the traders from Midian sold Joseph to Potiphar in Egypt. Potiphar was one of Pharaoh's officials. He was the captain of the palace guard.

JUDAH AND TAMAR

38 At that time, Judah left his brothers. He went down to stay with a man named Hirah. Hirah was from the town of Adullam.

²There Judah met the daughter of a man from Canaan. His name was Shua. Judah married her and made love to her. ³She became pregnant. She had a son. They named him Er. ⁴She became pregnant again and had another son. She named him Onan. ⁵She had still another son. She named him Shelah. He was born at Kezib.

⁶Judah got a wife for his oldest son Er. Her name was Tamar. ⁷But Judah's oldest son Er was evil in the LORD's eyes. So the LORD put him to death.

⁸Then Judah said to Onan, "Make love to your brother's wife. After all, you are her brother-in-law. So carry out your duty to her. Produce children for your brother."

⁹But Onan knew that the children wouldn't belong to him. So every time he made love to his brother's wife, he spilled his semen on the ground. He did it so he wouldn't produce children for his brother.

¹⁰What he did was evil in the LORD's eyes. So the LORD put him to death also.

¹¹Then Judah spoke to his daughter-in-law Tamar. He said, "Live as a widow in your father's home. Wait there until my son Shelah grows up."

Judah was thinking, "Shelah might die too, just like his brothers." So Tamar went to live in her father's home.

¹²After a long time Judah's wife died. She was the daughter of Shua. When Judah got over his sadness, he went up to Timnah. His friend Hirah from Adullam went with him. Men were clipping the wool from Judah's sheep at Timnah.

¹³Tamar was told, "Your father-in-law is on his way to Timnah to clip the wool from his sheep." ¹⁴So she took off her widow's clothes. She covered her face with a veil so people wouldn't know who she was. Then she sat down at the entrance to Enaim. Enaim is on the road to Timnah. Tamar knew that Shelah had grown up. But she hadn't been given to him as his wife.

¹⁵Judah saw her. He thought she was a prostitute because she had covered her face with a veil. ¹⁶He didn't realize that she was his daughter-in-law. He went over to her by the side of the road. He said, "Come. Let me make love to you."

"What will you give me to make love to you?" she asked.

¹⁷"I'll send you a young goat from my flock," he said.

"Will you give me something that belongs to you?" she asked. "I'll keep it until you send the goat."

¹⁸He said, "What should I give you?"

"Give me your seal and its string," she answered. "And give me your walking stick."

So he gave them to her. Then he had sex with her. And she became pregnant by him. ¹⁹After she left, she took off her veil. She put on her widow's clothes again.

²⁰Judah sent his friend Hirah with the young goat he had promised. He wanted to get back what he had given to the woman.

But his friend Hirah couldn't find her. ²¹He asked the men who lived at Enaim, "Where's the temple prostitute? She used to sit beside the road here."

"There hasn't been any temple prostitute here," they said.

²²So Hirah went back to Judah. He said, "I couldn't find her. Besides, the men who lived there didn't know anything about her. They said, 'There hasn't been any temple prostitute here.' "

²³Then Judah said, "Let her keep what she has. I don't want people making fun of us. After all, I did send her this young goat. We can't help it if you couldn't find her."

²⁴About three months later people brought word to Judah. They said, "Your daughter-in-law Tamar is guilty of being a prostitute. Now she's pregnant."

Judah said, "Bring her out! Have her burned to death!"

²⁵As Tamar was being brought out, she sent a message to her father-in-law. She said, "I am pregnant by the man who owns these." She continued, "Do you recognize this seal and string and walking stick? Do you know who they belong to?"

²⁶Judah recognized them. He said, "She's a better person than I am. I should have given her to my son Shelah, but I didn't." Judah never had sex with Tamar again.

²⁷The time came for Tamar to have her baby. There were twin boys inside her.

²⁸As the babies were being born, one of them stuck out his hand. So the woman who was helping Tamar took a bright red thread. The woman tied it on the baby's wrist. She said, "This one came out first."

²⁹But he pulled his hand back, and his brother came out first instead. She said, "Just look at how you have broken out!" So he was called Perez.

³⁰Then his brother, who had the red thread on his wrist, came out. So he was named Zerah.

JOSEPH AND POTIPHAR'S WIFE

39 Joseph had been taken down to Egypt. An Egyptian named Potiphar had bought him from the Ishmaelite traders who had taken him there. Potiphar was one of Pharaoh's officials. He was the captain of the palace guard.

²The LORD was with Joseph. He gave him great success. Joseph lived in Potiphar's house.

³Joseph's master saw that the LORD was with him. He saw that the LORD gave Joseph success in everything he did. ⁴So Potiphar was pleased with Joseph. He made him his attendant. He put Joseph in charge of his house. He told Joseph to take good care of everything he owned.

⁵From that time on, the LORD blessed Potiphar's family and servants because of Joseph. He blessed everything Potiphar had in his house and field.

⁶So Potiphar told Joseph to take good care of everything he owned. With Joseph in charge, he didn't have to worry about anything except the food he ate.

Joseph was strong and handsome. ⁷After a while, his master's wife noticed Joseph. She said to him, "Make love to me!"

⁸But he said no. "My master has put me in charge," he told her. "Now he doesn't have to worry about anything in the house. He trusts me to take care of everything he owns.

⁹"No one in this house is in a higher position than I am. My master hasn't held anything back from me, except you. You are his wife. So how could I do an evil thing like that? How could I sin against God?"

¹⁰She spoke to Joseph day after day. But he told her he wouldn't make love to her. He didn't even want to be with her.

¹¹One day Joseph went into the house to take care of his duties. None of the family servants was inside.

¹²Potiphar's wife grabbed hold of him by his coat. "Make love to me!" she said. But he left his coat in her hand. And he ran out of the house.

¹³She saw that he had left his coat in her hand and had run out of the house. ¹⁴So she called her servants.

"Look," she said to them, "this Hebrew slave has been brought here to make fun of us! He came in here to sleep with me. But I screamed for help. ¹⁵He heard my scream. So he left his coat beside me and ran out of the house."

[16]She kept Joseph's coat with her until Potiphar came home. [17]Then she told him her story. She said, "That Hebrew slave you brought us came to me to make sport of me. [18]But I screamed for help. So he left his coat beside me and ran out of the house."

[19]Potiphar's wife told him, "That's how your slave treated me." When Joseph's master heard her story, he became very angry. [20]So he put Joseph in prison. It was the place where the king's prisoners were kept.

While Joseph was there in the prison, [21]the LORD was with him. He was kind to him.

So the man who was running the prison was pleased with Joseph. [22]He put Joseph in charge of all of the prisoners. He made him accountable for everything that was done there. [23]The man who ran the prison didn't pay attention to anything that was in Joseph's care.

The LORD was with Joseph. He gave Joseph success in everything he did.

THE WINE TASTER AND THE BAKER

40 Some time later, the Egyptian king's baker and wine taster did something their master didn't like.

[2]So Pharaoh became angry with his two officials, the chief wine taster and the chief baker. [3]He put them in prison in the house of the captain of the palace guard. It was the same prison where Joseph was kept.

[4]The captain put Joseph in charge of those men. So Joseph took care of them.

Some time passed while they were in prison. [5]Then each of the two men had a dream. The men were the Egyptian king's baker and wine taster. They were being held in prison. Both of them had dreams the same night. Each of their dreams had its own meaning.

[6]Joseph came to them the next morning. He saw that they were sad. [7]They were Pharaoh's officials, and they were in prison with Joseph in his master's house. So he asked them, "Why do you look so sad today?"

[8]"We both had dreams," they answered. "But no one can tell us what they mean."

Then Joseph said to them, "Only God knows what dreams mean. Tell me your dreams."

[9]So the chief wine taster told Joseph his dream. He said to him, "In my dream I saw a vine in front of me. [10]There were three branches on the vine. As soon as it budded, it flowered. And bunches of ripe grapes grew on it. [11]"Pharaoh's cup was in my hand. I took the grapes. I squeezed them into Pharaoh's cup. Then I put the cup in his hand."

[12]"Here's what your dream means," Joseph said to him. "The three branches are three days. [13]In three days Pharaoh will let you out of prison. He'll give your position back to you. And you will put Pharaoh's cup in his hand. That's what you used to do when you were his wine taster.

[14]"But when everything is going well with you, remember me. Do me a favor. Speak to Pharaoh about me. Get me out of this prison. [15]I was taken away from the land of the Hebrews by force. Even here I haven't done anything to be put in prison for."

[16]The chief baker saw that Joseph had given a positive meaning to the wine taster's dream. So he said to Joseph, "I had a dream too. There were three baskets of bread on my head. [17]All kinds of baked goods for Pharaoh were in the top basket. But the birds were eating them out of the basket that was on my head."

[18]"Here's what your dream means," Joseph said. "The three baskets are three days. [19]In three days Pharaoh will cut your head off. Then he will stick a pole through your body and set the pole up. The birds will eat up your body."

[20]The third day was Pharaoh's birthday. He had a big dinner prepared for all of his officials. He brought the chief wine taster and the chief baker out of prison. He did it in front of his officials. [21]He gave the chief wine taster's position back to him. Once again the wine taster put the cup into Pharaoh's hand.

[22]But Pharaoh had a pole stuck through the chief baker's body. Then he had the pole set up.

Everything happened exactly as Joseph had told them when he explained their dreams. [23]But the chief wine taster didn't remember Joseph. In fact, he forgot all about him.

PHARAOH HAS TWO DREAMS

41

When two full years had passed, Pharaoh had a dream. In his dream, he was standing by the Nile River. [2]Seven cows came up out of the river. They looked healthy and fat. They were eating some of the tall grass that was growing along the river.

[3]After them, seven other cows came up out of the Nile. They looked ugly and skinny. They were standing beside the other cows on the riverbank.

[4]The ugly, skinny cows ate up the seven cows that looked healthy and fat. Then Pharaoh woke up.

[5]He fell asleep again and had a second dream. In that dream, seven heads of grain were growing on one stem. They were healthy and good.

[6]After them, seven other heads of grain came up. They were thin and dried up by the east wind.

[7]The thin heads of grain swallowed up the seven healthy, full heads. Then Pharaoh woke up. It had been a dream.

[8]In the morning he was worried. So he sent for all of the magicians and wise men of Egypt. Pharaoh told them his dreams. But no one could tell him what they meant.

[9]Then the chief wine taster spoke up. He said to Pharaoh, "Now I remember that I've done something wrong. [10]Pharaoh was once angry with his servants. He put me and the chief baker in prison. We were in the house of the captain of the palace guard. [11]Each of us had a dream the same night. Each dream had its own meaning.

[12]"A young Hebrew servant was there with us. He was a servant of the captain of the guard. We told him our dreams. And he explained them to us. He told each of us the meaning of our dreams. [13]Things turned out exactly as he said they would. I was given back my position. The other man had a pole stuck through his body."

[14]So Pharaoh sent for Joseph. He was quickly brought out of the prison. Joseph shaved himself and changed his clothes. Then he came to Pharaoh.

[15]Pharaoh said to Joseph, "I had a dream. No one can tell me what it means. But I've heard that when you hear a dream you can explain it."

[16]"I can't do it," Joseph replied to Pharaoh. "But God will give Pharaoh the answer he wants."

[17]Then Pharaoh told Joseph what he had dreamed. He said, "I was standing on the bank of the Nile River. [18]Seven cows came up out of the river. They were fat and good-looking. They were eating the tall grass that was growing along the river.

[19]"After them, seven other cows came up. They were bony and very ugly and thin. I had never seen such ugly cows in the whole land of Egypt. [20]"The thin, ugly cows ate up the seven fat cows that came up first. [21]But even after the thin cows ate up the fat ones, no one could tell that they had eaten them. They looked just as ugly as before. Then I woke up.

[22]"In my dreams I also saw seven heads of grain. They were full and good. They were all growing on one stem. [23]"After them, seven other heads of grain came up. They were weak and thin and dried up by the east wind. [24]"The thin heads of grain swallowed up the seven good heads. I told my dreams to the magicians. But none of them could explain them to me."

[25]Then Joseph said to Pharaoh, "Both of Pharaoh's dreams have the same meaning. God has shown Pharaoh what he is about to do. [26]The seven good cows are seven years. And the seven good heads of grain are seven years. Both dreams mean the same thing.

[27]"The seven thin, ugly cows that came up later are seven years. So are the seven worthless heads of grain that were dried up by the east wind. They are seven years when there won't be enough food.

[28]"It's exactly as I said to Pharaoh. God has shown Pharaoh what he's about to do. [29]Seven years with plenty of food are coming to the whole land of Egypt.

³⁰"But seven years when there won't be enough food will follow them. Then everyone will forget about all of the food Egypt had. Terrible hunger will destroy the land. ³¹There won't be anything left to remind people of the years when there was plenty of food in the land. That's how bad the hunger that follows will be.

³²"God gave the dream to Pharaoh in two forms. That's because the matter has been firmly decided by God. And it's because God will do it soon.

³³"So Pharaoh should look for a wise and understanding man. He should put him in charge of the land of Egypt.

³⁴"Pharaoh should appoint officials to be in charge of the land. They should take a fifth of the harvest in Egypt during the seven years when there's plenty of food. ³⁵They should collect all of the extra food of the good years that are coming. Pharaoh should give them authority to store up the grain. They should keep it in the cities for food.

³⁶"The grain should be stored up for the country to use later. It will be needed during the seven years when there isn't enough food in Egypt. Then the country won't be destroyed just because it doesn't have enough food."

³⁷The plan seemed good to Pharaoh and all of his officials. ³⁸So Pharaoh said to them, "The spirit of God is in this man. We can't find anyone else like him, can we?"

³⁹Then Pharaoh said to Joseph, "God has made all of this known to you. No one is as wise and understanding as you are. ⁴⁰You will be in charge of my palace. All of my people must obey your orders. I will be greater than you only because I'm the one who sits on the throne."

JOSEPH IS PUT IN CHARGE OF EGYPT

⁴¹So Pharaoh said to Joseph, "I'm putting you in charge of the whole land of Egypt."

⁴²Then Pharaoh took his ring off his finger. It was the ring he used to stamp all of the official papers. He put it on Joseph's finger. He dressed him in robes that were made out of fine linen. He put a gold chain around his neck.

⁴³He also had him ride in a chariot. Joseph was now next in command after Pharaoh. People went in front of him and shouted, "Get down on your knees!"

By doing all of those things, Pharaoh put Joseph in charge of the whole land of Egypt.

⁴⁴Then Pharaoh said to Joseph, "I am Pharaoh. But without your word, no one will do anything in the whole land of Egypt."

⁴⁵Pharaoh gave Joseph the name Zaphenath-Paneah. He gave him a wife. She was Asenath, the daughter of Potiphera. Potiphera was the priest of On.

Joseph traveled all over the land of Egypt.

⁴⁶Joseph was 30 years old when he began serving Pharaoh, the king of Egypt. He left Pharaoh's palace and traveled all over Egypt.

⁴⁷During the seven years when there was plenty of food, the land produced more than the people needed.

⁴⁸Joseph collected all of the extra food produced in those seven years in Egypt. He stored it in the cities. In each city he stored up the food that was grown in the fields around it. ⁴⁹Joseph stored up huge amounts of grain. It was like the sand of the sea. There was so much grain it couldn't be measured. So Joseph stopped keeping records of it.

⁵⁰Before the years when there wasn't enough food, two sons were born to Joseph. He had them by Asenath, the daughter of Potiphera. Potiphera was the priest of On.

⁵¹Joseph named his first son Manasseh. That's because he said, "God has made me forget all of my trouble and my father's whole family."

⁵²He named the second son Ephraim. That's because he said, "God has given me children in the land where I've suffered so much."

⁵³The seven years when there was plenty of food in Egypt came to an end. ⁵⁴Then the seven years when there wasn't enough food began. It happened exactly as Joseph had said it would. There wasn't enough food in any of the other lands. But in the whole land of Egypt there was food.

⁵⁵When all of the people of Egypt

began to get hungry, they cried out to Pharaoh for food. He told all of the Egyptians, "Go to Joseph. Do what he tells you."

⁵⁶There wasn't enough food anywhere in the country. So Joseph opened the storerooms. He sold grain to the Egyptians because people were very hungry all over Egypt.

⁵⁷People from all of the other countries came to Egypt. They came to buy grain from Joseph. That's because people were very hungry all over the world.

JOSEPH'S BROTHERS GO DOWN TO EGYPT

42 Jacob found out that there was grain in Egypt. So he said to his sons, "Why do you just keep looking at each other?" ²He continued, "I've heard there's grain in Egypt. Go down there. Buy some for us. Then we'll live and not die."

³So ten of Joseph's brothers went down to Egypt to buy grain there. ⁴But Jacob didn't send Joseph's brother Benjamin with them. He was afraid Benjamin might be harmed.

⁵Israel's sons were among the people who went to buy grain. There wasn't enough food in the land of Canaan.

⁶Joseph was the governor of the land. He was the one who sold grain to all of its people. When Joseph's brothers arrived, they bowed down to him with their faces to the ground.

⁷As soon as Joseph saw his brothers, he recognized them. But he pretended to be a stranger. He spoke to them in a mean way. "Where do you come from?" he asked.

"From the land of Canaan," they replied. "We've come to buy food."

⁸Joseph recognized his brothers, but they didn't recognize him. ⁹Then Joseph remembered his dreams about them. So he said to them, "You are spies! You have come to see the places where our land isn't guarded very well."

¹⁰"No, sir," they answered. "We've come to buy food. ¹¹All of us are the sons of one man. We're honest men. We aren't spies."

¹²"No!" he said to them. "You have come to see the places where our land isn't guarded very well."

¹³But they replied, "We were 12 brothers. All of us were the sons of one man. He lives in the land of Canaan. Our youngest brother is now with our father. And one brother is gone."

¹⁴Joseph said to them, "I still say you are spies! ¹⁵So I'm going to put you to the test. You can be sure that Pharaoh lives. And you can be just as sure that you won't leave this place unless your youngest brother comes here. I promise with an oath that you won't leave here. ¹⁶Send one of you back to get your brother. The rest of you will be kept in prison.

"I'll put your words to the test. Then we'll find out whether you are telling the truth. You can be sure that Pharaoh lives. And you can be just as sure that if you aren't telling the truth, we'll know that you are spies!"

¹⁷So Joseph kept all of them under guard for three days.

¹⁸On the third day, Joseph spoke to them again. He said, "Do what I say. Then you will live, because I have respect for God. ¹⁹If you are honest men, let one of your brothers stay here in prison. The rest of you may go and take grain back to your hungry families. ²⁰But you must bring your youngest brother to me. That will prove that your words are true. Then you won't die." So they did what he said.

²¹They said to one another, "God is certainly punishing us because of our brother. We saw how troubled he was when he begged us to let him live. But we wouldn't listen. That's why all of this trouble has come to us."

²²Reuben replied, "Didn't I tell you not to sin against the boy? But you wouldn't listen! Now we're being held accountable for killing him."

²³They didn't realize that Joseph could understand what they were saying. He was using someone else to explain their words to him in the Egyptian language.

²⁴Joseph turned away from them and began to sob. Then he turned around and spoke to them again. He had Simeon taken and tied up right there in front of them.

²⁵Joseph gave orders to have their

bags filled with grain. He had each man's money put back into his sack. He also made sure they were given food for their journey.

²⁶Then the brothers loaded their grain on their donkeys and left.

²⁷When night came, they stopped. One of them opened his sack to get feed for his donkey. He saw his money in the top of his sack. ²⁸"My money has been given back," he said to his brothers. "Here it is in my sack."

They had a sinking feeling in their hearts. They began to tremble. They turned to each other and said, "What has God done to us?"

²⁹They came to their father Jacob in the land of Canaan. They told him everything that had happened to them.

They said, ³⁰"The man who is the governor of the land spoke to us in a mean way. He treated us as if we were spying on the land. ³¹But we said to him, 'We're honest men. We aren't spies. ³²We were 12 brothers. All of us were the sons of one father. But now one brother is gone. And our youngest brother is with our father in Canaan.'

³³"Then the man who is the governor of the land spoke to us. He said, 'Here's how I will know whether you are honest men. Leave one of your brothers here with me. Take food for your hungry families and go.

³⁴" 'But bring your youngest brother to me. Then I'll know that you are honest men and not spies. I'll give your brother back to you. And you will be free to trade in the land.' "

³⁵They began emptying their sacks. There in each man's sack was his bag of money! When they and their father saw the money bags, they were afraid. ³⁶Their father Jacob said to them, "You have taken my children away from me. Joseph is gone. Simeon is gone. Now you want to take Benjamin. Everything is going against me!"

³⁷Then Reuben spoke to his father. He said, "You can put both of my sons to death if I don't bring Benjamin back to you. Place him in my care. I'll bring him back."

³⁸But Jacob said, "My son will not go down there with you. His brother is dead. He's the only one left here with me. Suppose he's harmed on the jour-

ney you are taking. Then I would die as a sad old man. I would go down into the grave full of sorrow."

JOSEPH'S BROTHERS GO DOWN TO EGYPT AGAIN

43 There still wasn't enough food anywhere in the land. ²After a while Jacob's family had eaten all of the grain the brothers had brought from Egypt.

So their father said to them, "Go back. Buy us a little more food."

³But Judah said to him, "The man gave us a strong warning. He said, 'You won't see my face again unless your brother comes with you.' ⁴So send our brother along with us. Then we'll go down and buy food for you.

⁵"If you won't send him, we won't go down. The man said to us, 'You won't see my face again unless your brother comes with you.' "

⁶Israel asked, "Why did you bring this trouble to me? Why did you tell the man you had another brother?"

⁷They replied, "The man questioned us closely about ourselves and our family. 'Is your father still living?' he asked us. 'Do you have another brother?'

"We just answered his questions. How could we possibly know he would say, 'Bring your brother down here'?"

⁸Judah spoke to Israel his father. "Send the boy along with me," he said. "We'll go at once. Then we and you and our children will live and not die.

⁹"I myself promise to keep him safe. You can hold me accountable for him. I'll bring him back to you. I'll set him right here in front of you. If I don't, you can put the blame on me for the rest of my life.

¹⁰"As it is, we've already waited too long. We could have gone to Egypt and back twice by now."

¹¹Then their father Israel spoke to them. He said, "If that's the way it has to be, then do what I tell you. Put some of the best things from our land in your bags. Take them down to the man as a gift. Take some lotion and a little honey. Take some spices and myrrh. Take some pistachio nuts and almonds. ¹²Take twice the amount of money with you. You have to give back

the money that was put in your sacks. Maybe it was a mistake.

¹³"Also take your brother. Go back to the man at once. ¹⁴May the Mighty God cause him to show you mercy. May the man let your other brother and Benjamin come back with you. And if I lose my sons, I lose them."

¹⁵So the men took the gifts. They took twice the amount of money. They also took Benjamin. They hurried down to Egypt and went to Joseph.

¹⁶When Joseph saw Benjamin with them, he spoke to the manager of his house. "Take these men to my house," he said. "Kill an animal and prepare dinner. I want them to eat with me at noon."

¹⁷The manager did what Joseph told him to do. He took the men to Joseph's house.

¹⁸They were afraid when they were taken to Joseph's house. They thought, "We were brought here because of the money that was put back in our sacks the first time. He wants to attack us and overpower us. Then he can hold us as slaves and take our donkeys."

¹⁹So they went up to Joseph's manager. They spoke to him at the entrance to the house. ²⁰"Please, sir," they said. "We came down here the first time to buy food. ²¹We opened our sacks at the place where we stopped for the night. Each of us found in our sacks the money we had paid. So we've brought it back with us. ²²We've also brought more money with us to buy food. We don't know who put our money in our sacks."

²³"It's all right," the manager said. "Don't be afraid. Your God, the God of your father, has given you riches in your sacks. I received your money." Then he brought Simeon out to them.

²⁴The manager took the men into Joseph's house. He gave them water to wash their feet. He provided feed for their donkeys. ²⁵They prepared their gifts for Joseph. He was planning to arrive at noon. They had heard that they were going to eat there.

²⁶When Joseph came home, they gave him the gifts they had brought into the house. They bowed down to the ground in front of him.

²⁷He asked them how they were.

Then he said, "How is your old father you told me about? Is he still living?"

²⁸They replied, "Your servant our father is still alive and well." And they bowed low to show him honor.

²⁹Joseph looked around. Then he saw his brother Benjamin, his own mother's son. He asked, "Is this your youngest brother? Is he the one you told me about?" He continued, "May God be gracious to you, my son."

³⁰It moved him deeply to see his brother. So Joseph hurried out and looked for a place to cry. He went into his own room and cried there.

³¹Then he washed his face and came out. He calmed down and said, "Serve the food."

³²They served Joseph by himself. They served the brothers by themselves. They also served the Egyptians who ate with him by themselves. Because of their beliefs, Egyptians couldn't eat with Hebrews.

³³The brothers had been given places in front of Joseph. They had been seated in the order of their ages, from the oldest to the youngest. That made them look at each other in great surprise.

³⁴While they were eating, some food was brought to them from Joseph's table. Benjamin was given five times as much as anyone else. So all of Joseph's brothers ate and drank a lot with him.

A SILVER CUP IN A SACK

44 Joseph told the manager of his house what to do. "Fill the men's sacks with as much food as they can carry," he said. "Put each man's money in his sack.

²"Then put my silver cup in the youngest one's sack. Put it there along with the money he paid for his grain." So the manager did what Joseph told him to do.

³When morning came, the men were sent on their way with their donkeys.

⁴They hadn't gone very far from the city when Joseph spoke to his manager. "Go after those men at once," he said. "Catch up with them. Say to them, 'My master was good to you. Why have you paid him back by doing

evil? [5]Isn't this the cup my master drinks from? Doesn't he also use it to figure things out? You have done an evil thing.' "

[6]When the manager caught up with them, he told them what Joseph had said.

[7]But they said to him, "Why do you say these things? We would never do anything like that! [8]We even brought back to you from Canaan the money we found in our sacks. So why would we steal silver or gold from your master's house?

[9]If you find out that any of us has the cup, he will die. And the rest of us will become your slaves."

[10]"All right, then," he said. "As you wish. The one who is found to have the cup will become my slave. But the rest of you will be free from blame."

[11]Each of them quickly put his sack down on the ground and opened it.

[12]Then the manager started to search. He began with the oldest and ended with the youngest. The cup was found in Benjamin's sack.

[13]When that happened, they were so upset they tore their clothes. Then all of them loaded their donkeys and went back to the city.

[14]Joseph was still in the house when Judah and his brothers came in. They threw themselves down on the ground in front of him.

[15]Joseph said to them, "What have you done? Don't you know that a man like me has ways to figure things out?"

[16]"What can we say to you?" Judah replied. "What can we say? How can we prove we haven't done anything wrong? God has shown you that we are guilty. We are now your slaves. All of us are, including the one who was found to have the cup."

[17]But Joseph said, "I would never do anything like that! Only the man who was found to have the cup will become my slave. The rest of you may go back to your father in peace."

[18]Then Judah went up to him. He said, "Please, sir. Let me speak a word to you. Don't be angry with me, even though you are equal to Pharaoh himself. [19]You asked us, 'Do you have a father or a brother?' [20]We answered, 'We have an old father. A young son was born to him when he was old. His brother is dead. He's the only one of his mother's sons left. And his father loves him.'

[21]"Then you said to us, 'Bring him down to me. I want to see him for myself.'

[22]"We said to you, 'The boy can't leave his father. If he does, his father will die.'

[23]"But you told us, 'Your youngest brother must come down here with you. If he doesn't, you won't see my face again.' [24]So we went back to my father. We told him what you had said.

[25]"Then our father said, 'Go back. Buy a little more food.'

[26]"But we said, 'We can't go down. We'll only go if our youngest brother goes there with us. We can't even see the man's face unless our youngest brother goes with us.'

[27]"Your servant my father said to us, 'You know that my wife had two sons by me. [28]One of them went away from me. And I said, "He must have been torn to pieces." I haven't seen him since. [29]What if you take this one from me too and he is harmed? Then you would cause me to die as a sad old man. I would go down into the grave full of pain and suffering.'

[30]"So now, what will happen if the boy isn't with us when I go back to my father? His life is closely tied up with the boy's life. [31]When he sees that the boy isn't with us, he'll die as a sad old man. Because of us, he'll go down into the grave full of sorrow.

[32]"I promised my father I would keep the boy safe. I said, 'Father, I'll bring him back to you. If I don't, you can put the blame on me for the rest of my life.'

[33]"Now then, please let me stay here. Let me be your slave in place of the boy. Let the boy return with his brothers. [34]How can I go back to my father if the boy isn't with me? Don't let me see the pain and suffering that would come to my father."

JOSEPH TELLS HIS BROTHERS WHO HE IS

45 Joseph couldn't control himself anymore in front of all of his attendants.

He cried out, "Have everyone leave me!"

So there wasn't anyone with Joseph when he told his brothers who he was. [2]He sobbed so loudly that the Egyptians heard him. Everyone in Pharaoh's house heard about it.

[3]Joseph said to his brothers, "I am Joseph! Is my father still alive?"

But his brothers weren't able to answer him. They were too afraid of him.

[4]Joseph said to his brothers, "Come close to me." So they did.

Then he said, "I am your brother Joseph. I'm the one you sold into Egypt. [5]But don't be upset. And don't be angry with yourselves because you sold me here. God sent me ahead of you to save many lives.

[6]"For two years now, there hasn't been enough food in the land. And for the next five years, people won't be plowing or gathering crops. [7]But God sent me ahead of you to keep some of you alive on earth. He sent me here to save your lives by an act of mighty power.

[8]"So then, it wasn't you who sent me here. It was God. He made me like a father to Pharaoh. He made me master of Pharaoh's whole house. He made me ruler of the whole land of Egypt.

[9]"Now hurry back to my father. Say to him, 'Your son Joseph says, "God has made me master of the whole land of Egypt. Come down to me. Don't waste any time. [10]You will live in the area of Goshen. You, your children and grandchildren, your flocks and herds, and everything you have will be near me. [11]There I will provide everything you need.

" ' "Five years without enough food are still coming. If you don't come down here, you and your family and everyone who belongs to you will lose everything." ' '

[12]"Brothers, you can see for yourselves that it's really I, Joseph, speaking to you. My brother Benjamin can see it too.

[13]"Tell my father about all of the honor that has been given to me in Egypt. Tell him about everything you

Why didn't Joseph go back home?

He was not able to. Joseph probably wanted to go back home. But he was a slave when he first got to Egypt. Then he was in prison for a while. Even after he got out of prison he was a long way from home, and it was much harder to travel back then than it is now. Also, Joseph may have been afraid to face his brothers again. Remember that they had wanted to kill him at one point and sold him to slave traders. But Joseph also stayed in Egypt because he knew that God had put him there. He knew that God had a plan for his life in Egypt. He got to save his family and many others when there was no food. Joseph knew this was God's plan and that made him feel that it was OK to stay in Egypt.

checkout
Genesis 45:8

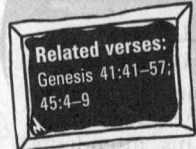

Related verses:
Genesis 41:41–57;
45:4–9

have seen. And bring my father down here quickly."

¹⁴Then Joseph threw his arms around his brother Benjamin and sobbed. Benjamin also hugged him and sobbed. ¹⁵Joseph kissed all of his brothers and sobbed over them. After that, his brothers talked with him.

¹⁶The news reached Pharaoh's palace that Joseph's brothers had come. Pharaoh and all of his officials were pleased.

¹⁷Pharaoh said to Joseph, "Here's what I want you to tell your brothers. Say to them, 'Load your animals. Return to the land of Canaan. ¹⁸Bring your father and your families back to me. I'll give you the best land in Egypt. You can enjoy all of the good things in the land.'

¹⁹"And here's something else I want you to tell them. Say to them, 'Take some carts from Egypt. Your children and your wives can use them. Get your father and come back. ²⁰Don't worry about the things you have back there. The best of everything in Egypt will belong to you.' "

²¹So the sons of Israel did it. Joseph gave them carts, as Pharaoh had commanded. He also gave them supplies for their journey. ²²He gave new clothes to each of them.

But he gave more than seven pounds of silver to Benjamin. He also gave him five sets of clothes.

²³He sent his father ten donkeys loaded with the best things from Egypt. He also sent ten female donkeys loaded with grain and bread and other supplies for his journey.

²⁴Then Joseph sent his brothers away. As they were leaving he said to them, "Don't argue on the way!"

²⁵So they went up out of Egypt. They came to their father Jacob in the land of Canaan. ²⁶They told him, "Joseph is still alive! In fact, he is ruler of the whole land of Egypt."

Jacob was shocked. He didn't believe them. ²⁷So they told him everything Joseph had said to them.

Jacob saw the carts Joseph had sent to carry him back. That gave new life to their father Jacob. ²⁸Israel said, "I believe it now! My son Joseph is still alive. I'll go and see him before I die."

JACOB GOES DOWN TO EGYPT

46 So Israel started out with everything that belonged to him. When he reached Beersheba, he offered sacrifices to the God of his father Isaac.

²God spoke to Israel in a vision at night. "Jacob! Jacob!" he said.

"Here I am," Jacob replied.

³"I am God. I am the God of your father," he said. "Do not be afraid to go down to Egypt. There I will make you into a great nation. ⁴I will go down to Egypt with you. You can be sure that I will bring you back again. And when you die, Joseph will close your eyes with his own hand."

⁵Then Jacob left Beersheba. Israel's sons put their father Jacob and their families in the carts that Pharaoh had sent to carry them.

⁶So Jacob and his whole family went to Egypt. They took their livestock with them. And they took everything they had gotten in Canaan. ⁷Jacob took his sons and grandsons with him to Egypt. He also took his daughters and granddaughters. He took all of his children and grandchildren with him.

⁸Here are the names of Israel's children and grandchildren who went to Egypt. Jacob and all of his children and grandchildren are included.

Reuben was Jacob's oldest son.

⁹The sons of Reuben were
Hanoch, Pallu, Hezron and Carmi.
¹⁰The sons of Simeon were
Jemuel, Jamin, Ohad, Jakin, Zohar and Shaul. Shaul was the son of a woman from Canaan.
¹¹The sons of Levi were
Gershon, Kohath and Merari.
¹²The sons of Judah were
Er, Onan, Shelah, Perez and Zerah. But Er and Onan had died in the land of Canaan. The sons of Perez were Hezron and Hamul.
¹³The sons of Issachar were
Tola, Puah, Jashub and Shimron.

¹⁴The sons of Zebulun were
   Sered, Elon and Jahleel.

¹⁵Those were the sons and grandsons who were born to Jacob and Leah in Paddan Aram. Leah also had a daughter by Jacob. Her name was Dinah. The total number of people in the family line of Jacob and Leah was 33.

¹⁶The sons of Gad were
   Zephon, Haggi, Shuni, Ezbon,
   Eri, Arodi and Areli.
¹⁷The sons of Asher were
   Imnah, Ishvah, Ishvi and Beriah. Their sister was Serah.
   The sons of Beriah were Heber and Malkiel.

¹⁸Those were the children and grandchildren who were born to Jacob and Zilpah. Laban had given Zilpah to his daughter Leah. The total number of people in the family line of Jacob and Zilpah was 16.

¹⁹The sons of Jacob's wife Rachel were
   Joseph and Benjamin. ²⁰In Egypt, Asenath had Manasseh and Ephraim by Joseph. Asenath was the daughter of Potiphera. Potiphera was the priest of On.
²¹The sons of Benjamin were
   Bela, Beker, Ashbel, Gera, Naaman, Ehi, Rosh, Muppim, Huppim and Ard.

²²Those were the sons and grandsons who were born to Jacob and Rachel. The total number of people in the family line of Jacob and Rachel was 14.

²³The son of Dan was
   Hushim.
²⁴The sons of Naphtali were
   Jahziel, Guni, Jezer and Shillem.

²⁵Those were the sons and grandsons who were born to Jacob and Bilhah. Laban had given Bilhah to his daughter Rachel. The total number of people in the family line of Jacob and Bilhah was seven.

²⁶The total number of those who went to Egypt with Jacob was 66. That number includes only his own children and grandchildren. It doesn't include his sons' wives or his grandsons' wives.

²⁷The total number of the members of Jacob's family who went to Egypt was 70. That includes the two sons who had been born to Joseph in Egypt.

²⁸Jacob sent Judah ahead of him to Joseph. He sent him to get directions to Goshen. And so they arrived in the area of Goshen.

²⁹Then Joseph had his servants get his chariot ready. He went to Goshen to meet his father Israel. As soon as he came to his father, Joseph threw his arms around him. Then Joseph sobbed for a long time.

³⁰Israel said to Joseph, "I have seen for myself that you are still alive. Now I'm ready to die."

³¹Then Joseph spoke to his brothers and to the rest of his father's family. He said, "I will go up and speak to Pharaoh. I'll say to him, 'My brothers and the rest of my father's family have come to me. They were living in the land of Canaan. ³²The men are shepherds. They take care of livestock. They've brought along their flocks and herds and everything they own.'

³³"Pharaoh will send for you. He'll ask, 'What do you do for a living?' ³⁴You should answer, 'We've taken care of livestock from the time we were boys. We've done just as our fathers did.' It's the practice of the people of Egypt not to mix with shepherds.

"So Pharaoh will let you settle in the area of Goshen."

47 Joseph went to Pharaoh. He told him, "My father and brothers have come from the land of Canaan. They've brought along their flocks and herds and everything they own. They are now in Goshen."

²Joseph had chosen five of his brothers to meet with Pharaoh.

³Pharaoh asked the brothers, "What do you do for a living?"

"We're shepherds," they replied to Pharaoh. "And that's what our fathers were." ⁴They also said to him, "We've come to live in Egypt for a while. There isn't enough food anywhere in Canaan. There isn't any grass for our flocks. So please let us settle in Goshen."

⁵Pharaoh said to Joseph, "Your father and your brothers have come to you. ⁶The land of Egypt is open to you. Settle your father and brothers in the best part of the land. Let them live in Goshen. Do any of them have special skills? If they do, put them in charge of my own livestock."

⁷Then Joseph brought his father Jacob in. He brought him in to meet Pharaoh. Jacob gave Pharaoh his blessing. ⁸Then Pharaoh asked him, "How old are you?"

⁹Jacob said to Pharaoh, "The years of my journey through life are 130. My years have been few and hard. They aren't as many as the years of my fathers before me."

¹⁰Jacob gave Pharaoh his blessing. Then he left him.

¹¹So Joseph settled his father and his brothers in Egypt. He gave them property in the best part of the land, just as Pharaoh had directed him to do. That part was known as the territory of Rameses.

¹²Joseph also provided food for his father and brothers. He provided for them and the rest of his father's family. He gave them enough for all of their children.

JOSEPH SAVES MANY LIVES

¹³But there wasn't any food in the whole area. In fact, there wasn't enough food anywhere. Both Egypt and Canaan lost their strength because there wasn't enough food to go around.

¹⁴Joseph collected all of the money that was in Egypt and Canaan. People paid it to him for the grain they were buying. And Joseph brought it to Pharaoh's palace.

¹⁵When the money of the people of Egypt and Canaan was gone, all of the Egyptians came to Joseph. They said, "Give us food. Why should we die right in front of your eyes? Our money is all gone."

¹⁶"Then bring your livestock," said Joseph. "You say your money is gone. So I'll trade you food for your livestock."

¹⁷They brought their livestock to Joseph. He traded them food for their animals. They gave him their horses,

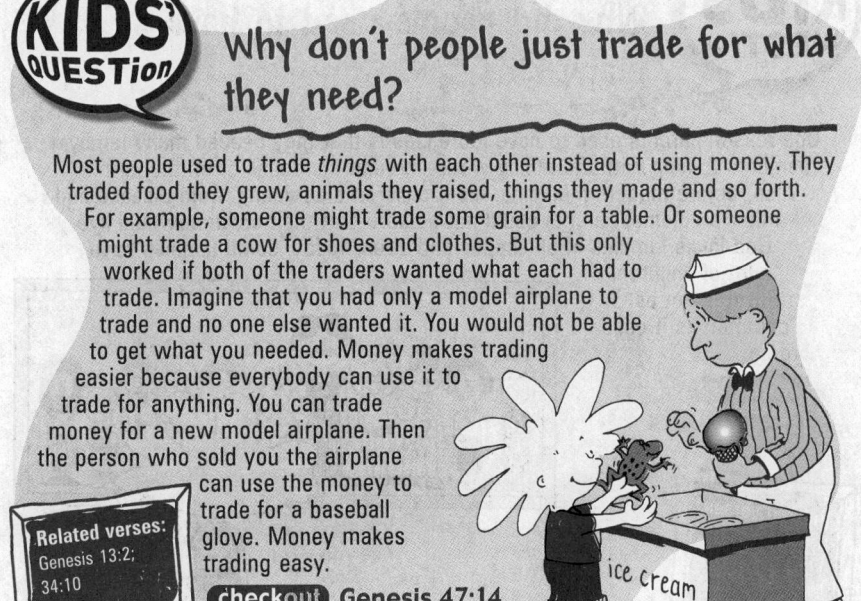

KIDS' QUESTION

Why don't people just trade for what they need?

Most people used to trade *things* with each other instead of using money. They traded food they grew, animals they raised, things they made and so forth. For example, someone might trade some grain for a table. Or someone might trade a cow for shoes and clothes. But this only worked if both of the traders wanted what each had to trade. Imagine that you had only a model airplane to trade and no one else wanted it. You would not be able to get what you needed. Money makes trading easier because everybody can use it to trade for anything. You can trade money for a new model airplane. Then the person who sold you the airplane can use the money to trade for a baseball glove. Money makes trading easy.

Related verses: Genesis 13:2; 34:10

checkout Genesis 47:14

sheep, goats, cattle and donkeys. He brought the people through that year by trading them food for all of their livestock.

¹⁸When that year was over, they came to him the next year. They said, "We can't hide the truth from you. Our money is gone. Our livestock belongs to you. We don't have anything left to give you except our bodies and our land.

¹⁹"Why should we die right in front of your eyes? Why should our land be destroyed as well? Trade us food for ourselves and our land. Then we and our land will belong to Pharaoh. Give us some seeds so we can live and not die. We don't want the land to become a desert."

²⁰So Joseph bought all of the land in Egypt for Pharaoh. All of the people of Egypt sold their fields. They did that because there wasn't enough food anywhere. In that way, the land became Pharaoh's. ²¹Joseph made the people slaves from one end of Egypt to the other.

²²But he didn't buy the land that belonged to the priests. They received a regular share of food from Pharaoh. They had enough food from what Pharaoh gave them. That's why they didn't have to sell their land.

²³Joseph said to the people, "I've bought you and your land today for Pharaoh. So here are some seeds for you to plant in the ground. ²⁴But when the crop comes in, give a fifth of it to Pharaoh. Keep the other four-fifths for yourselves. They will be seeds for the fields. And they will be food for yourselves, your children, and the other people who live with you."

²⁵"You have saved our lives," they said. "If you are pleased with us, we will be slaves to Pharaoh."

²⁶So Joseph made a law about land in Egypt. It's still the law today. A fifth of the produce belongs to Pharaoh. Only the land belonging to the priests didn't become Pharaoh's.

²⁷The people of Israel settled in Egypt in the area of Goshen. They received property there. They had children and greatly increased their numbers.

²⁸Jacob lived 17 years in Egypt. He lived a total of 147 years.

Why did people used to have so many kids?

One reason parents used to have more kids is that they needed many family members to help with the family work—around the house or on the farm. Also, before modern medicine, more children died young, from disease and other problems. Parents could not be sure that their children would live. God loves families of all shapes and sizes. Today, some families have a lot of children. But it is not as common as it used to be.

checkout
Genesis 48:3,4

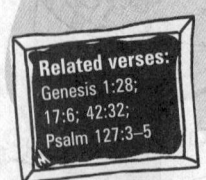

Related verses:
Genesis 1:28;
17:6; 42:32;
Psalm 127:3–5

²⁹The time came near for Israel to die. So he sent for his son Joseph. He said to him, "If you are pleased with me, put your hand under my thigh. Promise me that you will be kind and faithful to me. Don't bury me in Egypt. ³⁰When I join the members of my family who have already died, carry me out of Egypt. Bury me where they are buried."

"I'll do exactly as you say," Joseph said.

³¹"Promise me with an oath that you will do it," Jacob said. So Joseph promised him. And Israel worshiped God as he leaned on the top of his wooden staff.

EPHRAIM AND MANASSEH

48 Some time later Joseph was told, "Your father is sick." So he took his two sons Manasseh and Ephraim along with him. ²Jacob was told, "Your son Joseph has come to you." So Israel became stronger and sat up in bed.

³Jacob said to Joseph, "The Mighty God appeared to me at Luz in the land of Canaan. He blessed me there. ⁴He said to me, 'I am going to give you children. I will increase your numbers. I will make you a community of nations. And I will give this land to your children after you. It will belong to them forever.'

⁵"Now then, two sons were born to you in Egypt. It happened before I came to you here. They will be counted as my own sons. Ephraim and Manasseh will belong to me, in the same way that Reuben and Simeon belong to me.

⁶"Any children who are born to you after them will belong to you. Any territory they receive will come from the land that is given to Ephraim and Manasseh.

⁷"As I was returning from Paddan, Rachel died. It made me very sad. She died in the land of Canaan while we were still on the way. We weren't very far away from Ephrath. So I buried her body there beside the road to Ephrath." Ephrath was also called Bethlehem.

⁸Israel saw Joseph's sons. He asked, "Who are they?"

⁹"They are the sons God has given me here," Joseph said to his father.

Then Israel said, "Bring them to me. I want to give them my blessing."

¹⁰Israel's eyes were weak because he was old. He couldn't see very well. So Joseph brought his sons close to him. His father kissed them and hugged them.

¹¹Israel said to Joseph, "I never thought I'd see your face again. But now God has let me see your children too."

¹²Then Joseph took his sons away from Israel's knees. He bowed down with his face to the ground. ¹³Joseph placed Ephraim on his right, toward Israel's left hand. He placed Manasseh on his left, toward Israel's right hand. Then he brought them close to Jacob.

¹⁴But Israel reached out his right hand and put it on Ephraim's head. He did it even though Ephraim was the younger son. He crossed his arms and put his left hand on Manasseh's head. He did it even though Manasseh was the older son.

¹⁵Then Israel gave Joseph his blessing. He said,

"May God bless these boys.
  He is the God of my grandfather
    Abraham and my father Isaac.
  They walked with him.
He is the God who has been my
    shepherd
  all of my life to this very day.
¹⁶He is the Angel who has saved me
    from all harm.
  May he bless these boys.
  May they be called by my name.
  May they also be called by the
    names of my grandfather
    Abraham and my father Isaac.
  And may they greatly increase
    their numbers
    on the earth."

¹⁷Joseph saw his father putting his right hand on Ephraim's head. And Joseph didn't like it. So he took hold of his father's hand to move it over to Manasseh's head. ¹⁸Joseph said to him, "No, my father. Here's my older son. Put your right hand on his head."

¹⁹But his father wouldn't do it. He said, "I know, my son. I know. He too

will become a nation. He too will become great. But his younger brother will be greater than he is. His children after him will become a group of nations."

²⁰On that day, Jacob gave them his blessing. He said,

> "In the land of Israel, people will bless others in your names.
> They will say, 'May God make you like Ephraim and Manasseh.' "

So he put Ephraim ahead of Manasseh.

²¹Then Israel said to Joseph, "I'm about to die. But God will be with all of you. He'll take you back to the land of your fathers. ²²But you, Joseph, are over your brothers. So I'm giving you the range of hills I took from the Amorites. I took it with my sword and bow."

JACOB GIVES BLESSINGS TO HIS SONS

49 Then Jacob sent for his sons. He said, "Gather around me so I can tell you what will happen to you in days to come.

² "Sons of Jacob, come together and listen.
> Listen to your father Israel.

³ "Reuben, you are my oldest son.
> You were my first child. You were the first sign of my strength.
> You were first in honor. You were first in power.
⁴ But you are as unsteady as water.
> So you won't be first anymore.
> You had sex with your father's concubine in his bed.
> You lay on his couch and made it 'unclean.'

⁵ "Simeon and Levi are brothers.
> Their swords have killed a lot of people.
⁶ I won't share in their plans.
> I won't have anything to do with them.
> They became angry and killed people.
> They cut the legs of oxen just for the fun of it.
⁷ May the LORD put a curse on them because of their terrible anger.

I will scatter them in Jacob's land.
> I will spread them around in Israel.

⁸ "Judah, your brothers will praise you.
> Your enemies will be brought under your control.
> Your father's sons will bow down to you.
⁹ Judah, you are like a lion's cub.
> You return from hunting, my son.
> Like a lion, you lie down and sleep.
> You are like a mother lion. Who dares to wake you up?
¹⁰ The right to rule will not leave Judah.
> The ruler's rod will not be taken from between his feet.
> It will be his until the king it belongs to comes.
> It will be his until the nations obey him.
¹¹ He will tie his donkey to a vine.
> He will tie his colt to the very best branch.
> He will wash his clothes in wine.
> He will wash his robes in the red juice of grapes.
¹² His eyes will be darker than wine.
> His teeth will be whiter than milk.

¹³ "Zebulun will live by the seashore.
> He will become a safe harbor for ships.
> His border will go out toward Sidon.

¹⁴ "Issachar is like a donkey lying down between two saddlebags.
¹⁵ He sees how good his resting place is.
> He sees that his land is pleasant.
> So he'll carry a heavy load on his back.
> He will obey when he's forced to work.

¹⁶ "Dan will do what is fair for his people.
> He will do it as one of the tribes of Israel.
¹⁷ Dan will be a serpent by the side of the road.
> He will be a poisonous snake along the path.
> It bites the horse's heels

so that the rider falls off
backward.

[18] "LORD, I look to you to save me.

[19] "Gad will be attacked by a group of
robbers.
But he'll attack them as they run
away.

[20] "Asher's food will be rich and sweet.
He will provide food that even a
king would enjoy.

[21] "Naphtali is a female deer that is
set free
and gives birth to beautiful fawns.

[22] "Joseph is a vine that grows a lot of
fruit.
It grows close by a spring.
Its branches climb over a wall.

[23] Mean people shot arrows at him.
They shot at him because they
were angry.

[24] But his bow remained steady.
His strong arms moved freely.
The hand of the Mighty One of
Jacob was with him.
The Shepherd, the Rock of Israel,
stood by him.

[25] Your father's God helps you.
The Mighty One blesses you.
He gives you blessings from the
highest heavens.
He gives you blessings from the
deepest oceans.
He blesses you with children and
with a mother's milk.

[26] Your father's blessings are great.
They are greater than the
blessings from the age-old
mountains.
They are greater than the gifts
from the ancient hills.
Let all of those blessings rest on
the head of Joseph.
Let them rest on the head of the
one who is prince among his
brothers.

[27] "Benjamin is a hungry wolf.
In the morning he eats what he
has killed.
In the evening he shares what he
has stolen."

[28] All of those are the 12 tribes of Israel. That's what their father said to
them when he blessed them. He gave
each one the blessing that was just
right for him.

JACOB DIES

[29] Then Jacob gave directions to his
sons. He said, "I'm about to join the
members of my family who have
already died. Bury me with them in
the cave in the field of Ephron the
Hittite.
[30] "The cave is in the field of Machpelah near Mamre in Canaan. Abraham had bought it as a place where he
could bury his wife's body. He had
bought the cave from Ephron the
Hittite, along with the field.
[31] "The bodies of Abraham and his
wife Sarah were buried there. So were
the bodies of Isaac and his wife
Rebekah. I also buried Leah's body
there. [32] Abraham bought the field and
the cave from the Hittites."
[33] When Jacob had finished telling
his sons what to do, he pulled his feet
up into his bed. Then he took his last
breath and joined the members of his
family who had already died.

50

Joseph threw himself on his
father's body. He sobbed
over him and kissed him.
[2] Then Joseph talked to the doctors
who served him. He told them to prepare the body of his father Israel to be
buried. So the doctors prepared it.
[3] They took 40 days to do it. They
needed that much time to prepare a
body in the right way. The Egyptians
sobbed over Jacob for 70 days.
[4] After the days of sorrow had
passed, Joseph went to Pharaoh's
officials. He said to them, "If you are
pleased with me, speak to Pharaoh for
me. Tell him, [5] 'My father made me take
an oath and make a promise to him.
He said, "I'm about to die. Bury me in
the tomb I dug for myself in the land of
Canaan." So let me go up and bury my
father. Then I'll come back.' "
[6] Pharaoh said, "Go up and bury your
father. Do what he made you promise
to do."
[7] So Joseph went up to bury his father. All of Pharaoh's officials went
with him. They were the important
people of his court and all of the leaders of Egypt.

⁸All of Joseph's family also went. His brothers and all of the rest of his father's family went too. Only their children and their flocks and herds were left in Goshen.

⁹Chariots and horsemen also went up with him. It was a very large group.

¹⁰They came to the threshing floor of Atad. It was near the Jordan River. There they sobbed loudly and bitterly. Joseph set apart seven days of sadness to honor his father's memory.

¹¹The people of Canaan who were living there saw how sad all of them were at the threshing floor of Atad. They said, "The Egyptians are having a very special service for the dead." That's why that place near the Jordan River is called Abel of the Egyptians.

¹²So Jacob's sons did exactly as he had commanded them. ¹³They carried his body to the land of Canaan. They buried it in the cave in the field of Machpelah near Mamre. Abraham had bought the cave as a place where he could bury his wife's body. He had bought it from Ephron the Hittite, along with the field.

¹⁴After Joseph buried his father, he went back to Egypt. His brothers and all of the others who had gone to help him bury his father went back with him.

JOSEPH SETS HIS BROTHERS FREE FROM THEIR FEARS

¹⁵Now that their father was dead, Joseph's brothers were worried. They said, "Remember all of the bad things we did to Joseph? What if he decides to hold those things against us? What if he pays us back for them?"

¹⁶So they sent a message to Joseph. They said, "Your father gave us directions before he died. ¹⁷He said, 'Here's what you must say to Joseph. Tell him, "I'm asking you to forgive your brothers. Forgive the terrible things they did to you. Forgive them for treating you so badly." ' Now then, please forgive our sins. We serve the God of your father."

When their message came to Joseph, he sobbed.

¹⁸Then his brothers came and threw themselves down in front of him. "We are your slaves," they said.

¹⁹But Joseph said to them, "Don't be afraid. Do you think I'm God? ²⁰You planned to harm me. But God planned it for good. He planned to do what is now being done. He wanted to save many lives.

²¹"So then, don't be afraid. I'll provide for you and your children." He set them free from their fears. And he spoke in a kind way to them.

JOSEPH DIES

²²Joseph stayed in Egypt, along with all of his father's family. He lived 110 years. ²³He lived long enough to see Ephraim's children and grandchildren. When the children of Makir were born, they were placed on Joseph's knees and counted as his own children. Makir was the son of Manasseh.

²⁴Joseph said to his brothers, "I'm about to die. But I'm sure that God will come to help you. He'll take you up out of this land. He'll bring you to the land he promised with an oath to give to Abraham, Isaac and Jacob."

²⁵Joseph made the sons of Israel take an oath and make a promise to him. He said, "I'm sure that God will come to help you. Then you must carry my bones up from this place."

²⁶So Joseph died at the age of 110. They prepared his body to be buried. Then he was placed in a casket in Egypt.

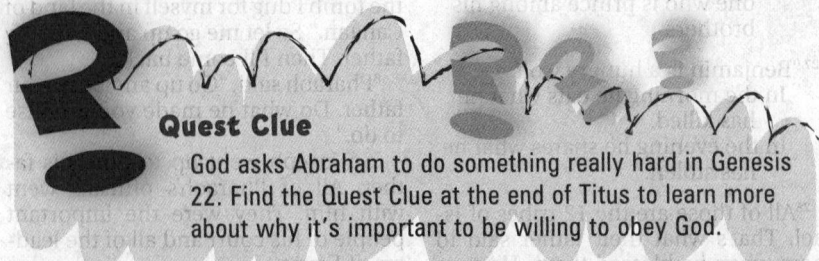

Quest Clue

God asks Abraham to do something really hard in Genesis 22. Find the Quest Clue at the end of Titus to learn more about why it's important to be willing to obey God.

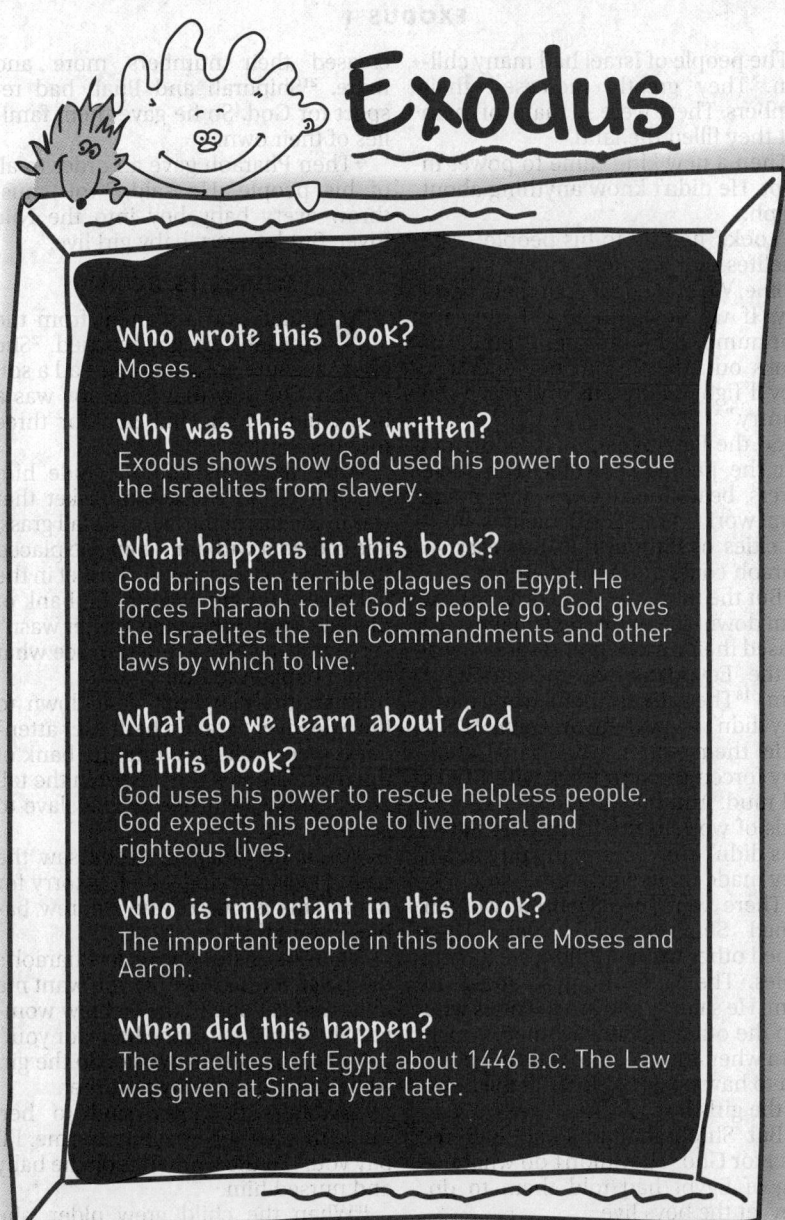

Exodus

Who wrote this book?
Moses.

Why was this book written?
Exodus shows how God used his power to rescue the Israelites from slavery.

What happens in this book?
God brings ten terrible plagues on Egypt. He forces Pharaoh to let God's people go. God gives the Israelites the Ten Commandments and other laws by which to live.

What do we learn about God in this book?
God uses his power to rescue helpless people. God expects his people to live moral and righteous lives.

Who is important in this book?
The important people in this book are Moses and Aaron.

When did this happen?
The Israelites left Egypt about 1446 B.C. The Law was given at Sinai a year later.

THE PEOPLE OF ISRAEL ARE SLAVES IN EGYPT

1 Here are the names of Israel's children who went to Egypt with Jacob. Each one went with his family. ²Jacob's sons were Reuben, Simeon, Levi, Judah, ³Issachar, Zebulun, Benjamin, ⁴Dan, Naphtali, Gad and Asher. ⁵The total number of Jacob's children and grandchildren was 70. Joseph was already in Egypt.

⁶Joseph and all of his brothers died. So did all of their children.

[7]The people of Israel had many children. They greatly increased their numbers. There were so many of them that they filled the land.

[8]Then a new king came to power in Egypt. He didn't know anything about Joseph.

[9]"Look," he said to his people. "The Israelites are far too many for us. [10]Come. We must deal with them carefully. If we don't, they will increase their numbers even more. Then if war breaks out, they'll join our enemies. They'll fight against us and leave the country."

[11]So the Egyptians put slave drivers over the people of Israel. The slave drivers beat them down and made them work hard. The Israelites built the cities of Pithom and Rameses so Pharaoh could store things there.

[12]But the more the slave drivers beat them down, the more the Israelites increased their numbers and spread out. So the Egyptians became afraid of them. [13]They made them work hard. They didn't show them any pity. [14]They made them suffer with hard labor. They forced them to work with bricks and mud. And they made them do all kinds of work in the fields. The Egyptians didn't show them any pity at all. They made them work very hard.

[15]There were two Hebrew women named Shiphrah and Puah. They helped other women who were having babies. The king of Egypt spoke to them. He said, [16]"You are the ones who help the other Hebrew women. Watch them when they get into a sitting position to have their babies. Kill the boys. Let the girls live."

[17]But Shiphrah and Puah had respect for God. They didn't do what the king of Egypt had told them to do. They let the boys live.

[18]Then the king of Egypt sent for the women. He asked them, "Why have you done this? Why have you let the boys live?"

[19]The women answered Pharaoh, "Hebrew women are not like the women of Egypt. They are strong. They have their babies before we get there."

[20]So God was kind to Shiphrah and Puah. And the people of Israel increased their numbers more and more. [21]Shiphrah and Puah had respect for God. So he gave them families of their own.

[22]Then Pharaoh gave an order to all of his people. He said, "You must throw every baby boy into the Nile River. But let every baby girl live."

MOSES IS BORN

2 A man and a woman from the tribe of Levi got married. [2]She became pregnant and had a son by him. She saw that her baby was a fine child. So she hid him for three months.

[3]After that, she couldn't hide him any longer. So she got a basket that was made out of the stems of tall grass. She coated it with tar. Then she placed the child in it. She put the basket in the tall grass that grew along the bank of the Nile River. [4]The child's sister wasn't very far away. She wanted to see what would happen to him.

[5]Pharaoh's daughter went down to the Nile River to take a bath. Her attendants were walking along the bank of the river. She saw the basket in the tall grass. So she sent her female slave to get it.

[6]When she opened it, she saw the baby. He was crying. She felt sorry for him. "This is one of the Hebrew babies," she said.

[7]Then his sister spoke to Pharaoh's daughter. She asked, "Do you want me to go and get one of the Hebrew women? She could nurse the baby for you."

[8]"Yes. Go," she answered. So the girl went and got the baby's mother.

[9]Pharaoh's daughter said to her, "Take this baby. Nurse him for me. I'll pay you." So the woman took the baby and nursed him.

[10]When the child grew older, she took him to Pharaoh's daughter. And he became her son. She named him Moses. She said, "I pulled him out of the water."

MOSES ESCAPES TO MIDIAN

[11]Moses grew up. One day, he went out to where his own people were. He watched them while they were hard at work. He saw an Egyptian hitting a Hebrew man. The man was one of

Moses' own people. ¹²Moses looked around and didn't see anyone. So he killed the Egyptian. Then he hid his body in the sand.

¹³The next day Moses went out again. He saw two Hebrew men fighting. He asked the one who had started the fight a question. He said, "Why are you hitting another Hebrew man?"

¹⁴The man said, "Who made you ruler and judge over us? Are you thinking about killing me as you killed the Egyptian?"

Then Moses became afraid. He thought, "People must have heard about what I did."

¹⁵When Pharaoh heard about what had happened, he tried to kill Moses. But Moses escaped from Pharaoh and went to live in Midian. There he sat down by a well.

¹⁶A priest of Midian had seven daughters. They came to fill the stone tubs with water. They wanted to give water to their father's flock. ¹⁷Some shepherds came along and drove the women away. But Moses got up and helped them. Then he gave water to their flock.

¹⁸The young women returned to their father Reuel. He asked them, "Why have you returned so early today?"

¹⁹They answered, "An Egyptian saved us from the shepherds. He even got water for us and gave it to the flock."

²⁰"Where is he?" he asked his daughters. "Why did you leave him? Invite him to have something to eat."

²¹Moses agreed to stay with the man. And the man gave his daughter Zipporah to Moses to be his wife. ²²Zipporah had a son by him. Moses named him Gershom. Moses said, "I'm an outsider in a strange land."

²³After a long time, the king of Egypt died. The people of Israel groaned because they were slaves. They also cried out to God. Their cry for help went up to him. ²⁴God heard their groans. He remembered his covenant with Abraham, Isaac and Jacob. ²⁵So God looked on the Israelites with favor. He was concerned about them.

THE LORD SENDS MOSES TO SAVE HIS PEOPLE

3 Moses was taking care of the flock of his father-in-law Jethro. Jethro was the priest of Midian. Moses led the flock to the western side of the desert. He came to Horeb. It was the mountain of God.

²There the angel of the LORD appeared to him from inside a burning

Why didn't the bush burn up?

KIDS' QUESTION

God was keeping the bush from burning up because he wanted to get Moses' attention. God knew that a bush that kept on burning without turning to ashes would catch Moses' eye. Moses would wonder what was going on. It worked, too. As soon as Moses saw the bush, he went over to look at it. And as soon as he heard God's voice, he was ready to listen because he knew he had seen a miracle. God used the burning bush to help Moses see that God could do anything. Moses needed to know that before he went to rescue the people of Israel from slavery in Egypt.

checkout
Exodus 3:2-4

Related verses:
Exodus 3:1—4:18

bush. Moses saw that the bush was on fire. But it didn't burn up. ³So Moses thought, "I'll go over and see this strange sight. Why doesn't the bush burn up?"

⁴The LORD saw that Moses had gone over to look. So God spoke to him from inside the bush. He called out, "Moses! Moses!"

"Here I am," Moses said.

⁵"Do not come any closer," God said. "Take off your sandals. The place you are standing on is holy ground." ⁶He continued, "I am the God of your father. I am the God of Abraham. I am the God of Isaac. And I am the God of Jacob."

When Moses heard that, he turned his face away. He was afraid to look at God.

⁷The LORD said, "I have seen my people suffer in Egypt. I have heard them cry out because of their slave drivers. I am concerned about their suffering.

⁸"So I have come down to save them from the Egyptians. I will bring them up out of that land. I will bring them into a good land. It has a lot of room. It is a land that has plenty of milk and honey. It is the home of the Canaanites, Hittites, Amorites, Perizzites, Hivites and Jebusites.

⁹"And now Israel's cry for help has reached me. I have seen the way the Egyptians are beating them down. ¹⁰So now, go. I am sending you to Pharaoh. I want you to bring the Israelites out of Egypt. They are my people."

¹¹But Moses spoke to God. "Who am I that I should go to Pharaoh?" he said. "Who am I that I should bring the Israelites out of Egypt?"

¹²God said, "I will be with you. I will give you a miraculous sign. It will prove that I have sent you. When you have brought the people out of Egypt, all of you will worship me on this mountain."

¹³Moses said to God, "Suppose I go to the people of Israel. Suppose I say to them, 'The God of your fathers has sent me to you.' Suppose they ask me, 'What is his name?' Then what should I tell them?"

¹⁴God said to Moses, "I AM WHO I AM.

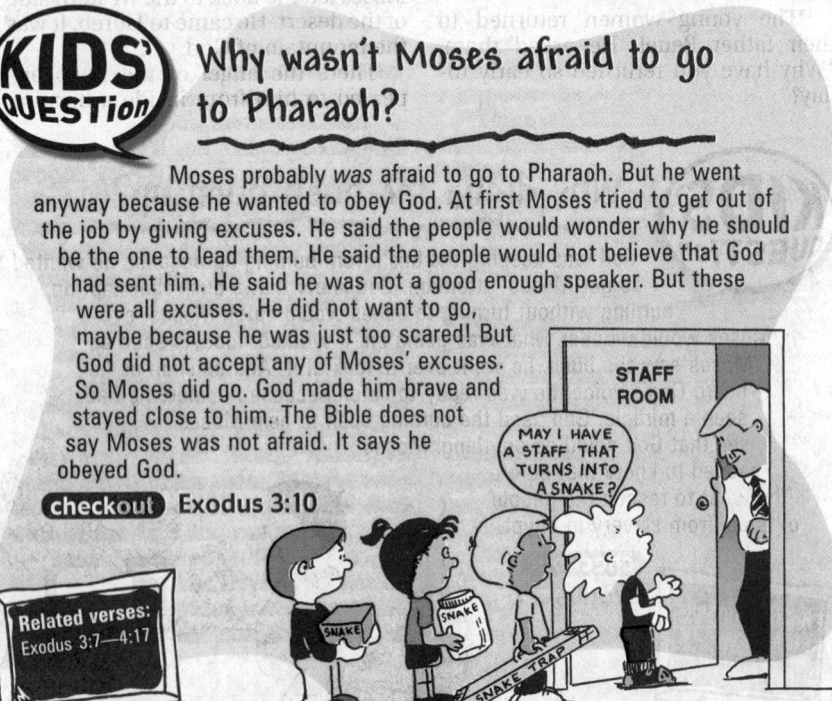

KIDS' QUESTION

Why wasn't Moses afraid to go to Pharaoh?

Moses probably *was* afraid to go to Pharaoh. But he went anyway because he wanted to obey God. At first Moses tried to get out of the job by giving excuses. He said the people would wonder why he should be the one to lead them. He said the people would not believe that God had sent him. He said he was not a good enough speaker. But these were all excuses. He did not want to go, maybe because he was just too scared! But God did not accept any of Moses' excuses. So Moses did go. God made him brave and stayed close to him. The Bible does not say Moses was not afraid. It says he obeyed God.

checkout   Exodus 3:10

Related verses:
Exodus 3:7—4:17

STAFF ROOM

MAY I HAVE A STAFF THAT TURNS INTO A SNAKE?

SNAKE

SNAKE

SNAKE TRAP

Here is what you must say to the Isra-elites. Tell them, 'I AM has sent me to you.' "

¹⁵God also said to Moses, "Say to the Israelites, 'The LORD is the God of your fathers. He has sent me to you. He is the God of Abraham. He is the God of Isaac. And he is the God of Jacob.' My name will always be The LORD. Re-member me by that name for all time to come.

¹⁶"Go. Gather the elders of Israel to-gether. Say to them, 'The LORD, the God of your fathers, appeared to me. He is the God of Abraham, Isaac and Jacob.

" 'He said, "I have watched over you. I have seen what the Egyptians have done to you. ¹⁷I have promised to bring you up out of Egypt where you are suffering. I will bring you into the land of the Canaanites, Hittites, Amor-ites, Perizzites, Hivites and Jebusites. It is a land that has plenty of milk and honey." '

¹⁸"The elders of Israel will listen to you. Then you and the elders must go to the king of Egypt. You must say to him, 'The LORD has met with us. He is the God of the Hebrews. Let us take a journey that lasts about three days. We want to go into the desert to offer sac-rifices to the LORD our God.'

¹⁹"But I know that the king of Egypt will not let you and your people go. Only a mighty hand could make him do that. ²⁰So I will reach my hand out. I will strike the Egyptians with all kinds of miracles. After that, he will let you go.

²¹"I will cause the Egyptians to treat you in a kind way. Then when you leave, you will not go out with your hands empty. ²²Every woman should ask her neighbor and any woman liv-ing in her house for articles made out of silver and gold. Ask them for clothes too. Put them on your children. In that way, you will take the wealth of Egypt along with you."

MIRACULOUS SIGNS FOR MOSES TO DO

4 Moses answered, "What if the elders of Israel won't believe me? What if they won't listen to me? Suppose they say, 'The LORD

didn't appear to you.' Then what should I do?"

²The LORD said to him, "What do you have in your hand?"

"A wooden staff," he said.

³The LORD said, "Throw it on the ground."

So Moses threw it on the ground. It turned into a snake. He ran away from it. ⁴Then the LORD said to Moses, "Reach your hand out. Take the snake by the tail." So he reached out and grabbed hold of the snake. It turned back into a staff in his hand.

⁵The LORD said, "When they see this miraculous sign, they will believe that I appeared to you. I am the God of their fathers. I am the God of Abra-ham. I am the God of Isaac. And I am the God of Jacob."

⁶Then the LORD said, "Put your hand inside your coat." So Moses put his hand inside his coat. When he took it out, it was as white as snow. It was cov-ered with a skin disease.

⁷"Now put it back into your coat," the LORD said. So Moses put his hand back into his coat. When he took it out, the skin was healthy again. His hand was like the rest of his skin.

⁸Then the LORD said, "Suppose they do not believe you or pay attention to the first miracle. Then maybe they will believe the second one.

⁹"But suppose they do not believe either miracle. Suppose they will not listen to you. Then get some water from the Nile River. Pour it on the dry ground. The water you take from the river will turn to blood on the ground."

¹⁰Moses spoke to the LORD. He said, "Lord, I've never been a good speaker. And I haven't gotten any better since you spoke to me. I don't speak very well at all."

¹¹The LORD said to him, "Who makes a man able to talk? Who makes him unable to hear or speak? Who makes him able to see? Who makes him blind? It is I, the LORD. ¹²Now go. I will help you speak. I will teach you what to say."

¹³But Moses said, "Lord, please send someone else to do it."

¹⁴Then the LORD's anger burned against Moses. He said, "What about your brother, Aaron the Levite? I know

he can speak well. He is already on his way to meet you. He will be glad to see you. ¹⁵Speak to him. Put your words in his mouth. Tell him what to say. I will help both of you speak. I will teach you what to do. ¹⁶He will speak to the people for you. He will be like your mouth. And you will be like God to him.

¹⁷"But take this wooden staff in your hand. You will be able to do miraculous signs with it."

MOSES RETURNS TO EGYPT

¹⁸Then Moses went back to his father-in-law Jethro. He said to him, "Let me go back to my own people in Egypt. I want to see if any of them are still alive."

Jethro said, "Go. I hope everything goes well with you."

¹⁹The LORD had said to Moses in Midian, "Go back to Egypt. All of the men who wanted to kill you are dead."

²⁰So Moses got his wife and sons. He put them on a donkey. Together they started back to Egypt. And he took the wooden staff in his hand. It was the staff God would use in a powerful way.

²¹The LORD spoke to Moses. He said, "When you return to Egypt, do all of the miracles I have given you the power to do. Do them in the sight of Pharaoh. But I will make his heart stubborn. He will not let the people go.

²²"Then say to Pharaoh, 'The LORD says, "Israel is like an oldest son to me. ²³I told you, 'Let my son go. Then he will be able to worship me.' But you refused to let him go. So I will kill your oldest son." ' "

²⁴On the way to Egypt, Moses stopped for the night. There the LORD met him and was about to kill him. ²⁵But Zipporah got a knife that was made out of hard stone. She circumcised her son with it. Then she touched Moses' feet with the skin she had cut off. "You are a husband who has forced me to spill my son's blood," she said. ²⁶So the LORD didn't kill Moses. When she said "husband who has forced me to spill my son's blood," she was talking about circumcision.

²⁷The LORD said to Aaron, "Go into the desert to see Moses." So he greeted Moses at the mountain of God and kissed him.

²⁸Then Moses told Aaron everything the LORD had sent him to say. He also told him about all of the miraculous signs he had commanded him to do.

²⁹Moses and Aaron gathered all of the elders of Israel together. ³⁰Aaron told them everything the LORD had said to Moses. He also did the miracles in the sight of the people.

³¹And they believed. They heard that the LORD was concerned about them. He had seen their suffering. So they bowed down and worshiped him.

PHARAOH MAKES THE ISRAELITES WORK EVEN HARDER

5 Later on, Moses and Aaron went to Pharaoh. They said, "The LORD is the God of Israel. He says, 'Let my people go. Then they will be able to hold a feast in my honor in the desert.' "

²Pharaoh said, "Who is the LORD? Why should I obey him? Why should I let Israel go? I don't even know the LORD. And I won't let Israel go."

³Then Moses and Aaron said, "The God of the Hebrews has met with us. Now let us take a journey that lasts about three days. We want to go into the desert to offer sacrifices to the LORD our God. If we don't, he might strike us with plagues. Or he might let us be killed with swords."

⁴But the king of Egypt said, "Moses and Aaron, why are you taking the people away from their work? Get back to work!" ⁵Pharaoh continued, "There are large numbers of your people in the land. But you are stopping them from working."

⁶That same day Pharaoh gave orders to the slave drivers and the others who were in charge of the people. ⁷He said, "Don't give the people any more straw to make bricks. Let them go and get their own straw. ⁸But require them to make the same number of bricks as before. Don't lower the number they have to make. They don't want to work. That's why they are crying out, 'Let us go. We want to offer sacrifices to our God.' ⁹Make them work harder. Then they will be too busy to pay attention to lies."

¹⁰The slave drivers and the others

who were in charge left. They said to the people, "Pharaoh says, 'I won't give you any more straw. ¹¹Go and get your own straw anywhere you can find it. But you still have to make the same number of bricks.' "

¹²So the people scattered all over Egypt. They went to gather any pieces of straw that were left in the fields.

¹³The slave drivers kept making the people work hard. They said, "Finish the work you are required to do each day. Make the same number of bricks you made when you had straw." ¹⁴They whipped the Israelites who were in charge of the people. Those Israelites had been appointed by Pharaoh's slave drivers. The slave drivers asked, "Why didn't you make the same number of bricks yesterday or today, just as before?"

¹⁵Then the Israelites who were in charge of the people made their appeal to Pharaoh. They asked, "Why have you treated us like this? ¹⁶You didn't give us any straw. But you told us, 'Make bricks!' We are being whipped. But it's the fault of your own people."

¹⁷Pharaoh said, "You just don't want to work! That's why you keep saying, 'Let us go. We want to offer sacrifices to the LORD.' ¹⁸Now get to work. We won't give you any straw. But you still have to make the same number of bricks."

¹⁹The Israelites who were in charge of the people realized they were in trouble. They knew it when they were told, "Don't lower the number of bricks you are required to make each day."

²⁰When they left Pharaoh, they found Moses and Aaron waiting to meet them. ²¹They said to Moses and Aaron, "We want the LORD to look at what you have done! We want him to judge you for it! We are like a very bad smell to Pharaoh and his officials. You have given them an excuse to kill us with their swords."

THE LORD PROMISES TO SAVE THE ISRAELITES

²²Moses returned to the LORD. He said to him, "Lord, why have you brought trouble on these people? Is this why you sent me? ²³I went to Pharaoh to speak to him in your name. Ever

since then, he has brought nothing but trouble on these people. And you haven't saved your people at all."

6 Then the LORD spoke to Moses. He said, "Now you will see what I will do to Pharaoh. Because of my powerful hand, he will let the people of Israel go. Because of my mighty hand, he will drive them out of his country."

²God continued, "I am the LORD. ³I appeared to Abraham, Isaac and Jacob as the Mighty God. But I did not show them the full meaning of my name, The LORD.

⁴"I also made my covenant with them. I promised to give them the land of Canaan. That is where they lived as outsiders. ⁵Also, I have heard the groans of the Israelites. The Egyptians are keeping them as slaves. But I have remembered my covenant.

⁶"So tell the people of Israel, 'I am the LORD. I will throw off the heavy load the Egyptians have put on your shoulders. I will set you free from being slaves to them. I will reach out my arm and save you with mighty acts when I judge Egypt.

⁷" 'I will take you to be my own people. I will be your God. You will know that I am the LORD your God when I throw off the load the Egyptians have put on your shoulders.

⁸" 'I will bring you to the land I promised with an oath to give to Abraham, Isaac and Jacob. I lifted up my hand and promised it to them. The land will belong to you. I am the LORD.' "

⁹Moses reported those things to the Israelites. But they didn't listen to him. That's because they had lost all hope and had to work very hard.

¹⁰Then the LORD said to Moses, ¹¹"Go. Tell Pharaoh, the king of Egypt, to let the people of Israel leave his country."

¹²But Moses spoke to the LORD. "The people won't listen to me," he said. "So why would Pharaoh listen to me? After all, I don't speak very well."

THE FAMILY LINE OF MOSES AND AARON

¹³The LORD had spoken to Moses and Aaron. He had talked with them

about the Israelites and about Pharaoh, the king of Egypt. He had commanded Moses and Aaron to bring the people of Israel out of Egypt.

¹⁴Here were the leaders of the family groups of Reuben, Simeon and Levi.

Reuben was the oldest son of Israel. His sons were Hanoch, Pallu, Hezron and Carmi. Those were the family groups of Reuben.

¹⁵The sons of Simeon were Jemuel, Jamin, Ohad, Jakin, Zohar and Shaul. Shaul was the son of a woman from Canaan. Those were the family groups of Simeon.

¹⁶Here were the names of the sons of Levi that were recorded in their family history. They were Gershon, Kohath and Merari. Levi lived for 137 years.

¹⁷The sons of Gershon, by their family groups, were Libni and Shimei.

¹⁸The sons of Kohath were Amram, Izhar, Hebron and Uzziel. Kohath lived for 133 years.

¹⁹The sons of Merari were Mahli and Mushi.

Those were the family groups of Levi that were recorded in their family history.

²⁰Amram got married to his father's sister Jochebed. Aaron and Moses were born in Amram's family line. Amram lived for 137 years.

²¹The sons of Izhar were Korah, Nepheg and Zicri.

²²The sons of Uzziel were Mishael, Elzaphan and Sithri.

²³Aaron married Elisheba. She was the daughter of Amminadab and the sister of Nahshon. She had Nadab, Abihu, Eleazar and Ithamar by Aaron.

²⁴The sons of Korah were Assir, Elkanah and Abiasaph. Those were the family groups of Korah.

²⁵Eleazar, the son of Aaron, married one of the daughters of Putiel. She had Phinehas by Eleazar.

Those were the leaders of the families of Levi that were recorded by their groups.

²⁶The LORD had spoken to that same Aaron and Moses. He had told them, "Bring the Israelites out of Egypt like an army on the march." ²⁷They spoke to Pharaoh, the king of Egypt, about bringing the people of Israel out of Egypt. They were that same Moses and Aaron.

AARON SPEAKS FOR MOSES

²⁸The LORD had spoken to Moses in Egypt. ²⁹He had told him, "I am the LORD. Tell Pharaoh, the king of Egypt, everything I tell you."

³⁰But Moses said to the LORD, "I don't speak very well. So why would Pharaoh listen to me?"

7 Then the LORD said to Moses, "I have made you like God to Pharaoh. And your brother Aaron will be like a prophet to you. ²You must say everything I command you to say. Then your brother Aaron must tell Pharaoh to let the people of Israel leave his country.

³"But I will make Pharaoh's heart stubborn. I will multiply my miraculous signs and wonders in Egypt. ⁴In spite of that, he will not listen to you. So I will use my powerful hand against Egypt. When I judge them with mighty acts, I will bring my people Israel out like an army on the march.

⁵"Then the Egyptians will know that I am the LORD. I will reach out my powerful hand against Egypt. I will bring the people of Israel out of it."

⁶Moses and Aaron did exactly as the LORD had commanded them. ⁷Moses was 80 years old and Aaron was 83 when they spoke to Pharaoh.

AARON'S WOODEN STAFF BECOMES A SNAKE

⁸The LORD spoke to Moses and Aaron. ⁹He said, "Pharaoh will say to you, 'Do a miracle.' When he does, speak to Aaron. Tell him, 'Take your wooden staff and throw it down in front of Pharaoh.' It will turn into a snake."

¹⁰So Moses and Aaron went to Pharaoh. They did exactly as the LORD had commanded them. Aaron threw his staff down in front of Pharaoh and his officials. It turned into a snake.

¹¹Then Pharaoh sent for wise men and those who do evil magic. By doing

their magic tricks, the Egyptian magicians did the same things Aaron had done. [12]Each one threw his staff down. Each staff turned into a snake. But Aaron's staff swallowed theirs up.

[13]In spite of that, Pharaoh's heart became stubborn. He wouldn't listen to them, just as the LORD had said.

THE NILE RIVER TURNS INTO BLOOD

[14]Then the LORD said to Moses, "Pharaoh's heart is very stubborn. He refuses to let the people go. [15]In the morning Pharaoh will go down to the water. Go and wait on the bank of the Nile River to meet him. Take in your hand the wooden staff that turned into a snake.

[16]"Say to Pharaoh, 'The LORD, the God of the Hebrews, has sent me to you. He says, "Let my people go. Then they will be able to worship me in the desert. But up to now you have not listened."

[17]" 'The LORD says, "Here is how you will know that I am the LORD. I will strike the water of the Nile River with the staff that is in my hand. The river will turn into blood. [18]The fish in the river will die. The river will stink. The Egyptians will not be able to drink its water." ' "

[19]The LORD said to Moses, "Tell Aaron, 'Get your staff. Reach your hand out over the waters of Egypt. The streams, waterways, ponds and all of the lakes will turn into blood. There will be blood everywhere in Egypt. It will even be in the wooden buckets and stone jars.' "

[20]Moses and Aaron did exactly as the LORD had commanded them. Aaron held out his staff in front of Pharaoh and his officials. He struck the water of the Nile River. And all of the water turned into blood. [21]The fish in the Nile died. The river smelled so bad the Egyptians couldn't drink its water. There was blood everywhere in Egypt.

[22]But the Egyptian magicians did the same things by doing their magic tricks. So Pharaoh's heart became stubborn. He wouldn't listen to Moses and Aaron, just as the LORD had said. [23]Even that miracle didn't change Pharaoh's mind. In fact, he turned around and went into his palace.

[24]All of the Egyptians dug holes near the Nile River to get drinking water. They couldn't drink water from the river.

THE PLAGUE OF FROGS

8 [25]Seven days passed after the LORD struck the Nile River. [1]Then the LORD said to Moses, "Go to Pharaoh. Tell him, 'The LORD says, "Let my people go. Then they will be able to worship me.

[2]" ' "If you refuse to let them go, I will plague your whole country with frogs. [3]The Nile River will be full of frogs. They will come up into your palace. You will have frogs in your bedroom and on your bed. They will be in the homes of your officials and your people. They will be in your ovens and in your bread pans. [4]The frogs will be on you, your people and all of your officials." ' "

[5]Then the LORD spoke to Moses. He said, "Tell Aaron, 'Reach your hand out. Hold your staff over the streams, waterways and ponds. Make frogs come up on the land of Egypt.' "

[6]So Aaron reached his hand out over the waters of Egypt. The frogs came up and covered the land. [7]But the magicians did the same things by doing their magic tricks. They also made frogs come up on the land of Egypt.

[8]Pharaoh sent for Moses and Aaron. He said to them, "Pray to the LORD to take the frogs away from me and my people. Then I'll let your people go to offer sacrifices to the LORD."

[9]Moses said to Pharaoh, "You can have the honor of setting the time for me to pray. I will pray for you, your officials and your people. I'll pray that the frogs will leave you and your homes. The only frogs left will be the ones in the Nile River."

[10]"Tomorrow," Pharaoh said.

Moses replied, "It will happen just as you say. Then you will know that there is no one like the LORD our God. [11]The frogs will leave you and your houses. They will leave your officials and your people. They will remain only in the Nile River."

[12]Moses and Aaron left Pharaoh.

Then Moses cried out to the LORD about the frogs he had brought on Pharaoh. [13]And the LORD did what Moses asked. The frogs died in the houses, courtyards and fields. [14]The Egyptians piled them up. The land smelled very bad because of them.

[15]But when Pharaoh saw that the frogs were dead, his heart became stubborn. He wouldn't listen to Moses and Aaron, just as the LORD had said.

THE PLAGUE OF GNATS

[16]Then the LORD spoke to Moses. He said, "Tell Aaron, 'Reach your wooden staff out. Strike the dust on the ground with it.' Then all over the land of Egypt the dust will turn into gnats."

[17]So they did it. Aaron reached out the staff that was in his hand. He struck the dust on the ground with it. The dust all over the land of Egypt turned into gnats. They landed on people and animals alike.

[18]The magicians tried to produce gnats by doing their magic tricks. But they couldn't. The gnats stayed on people and animals alike.

[19]The magicians said to Pharaoh, "God's powerful finger has done this." But Pharaoh's heart was stubborn. He wouldn't listen, just as the LORD had said.

THE PLAGUE OF FLIES

[20]Then the LORD spoke to Moses. He said, "Get up early in the morning. Talk to Pharaoh as he goes down to the river. Say to him, 'The LORD says, "Let my people go. Then they will be able to worship me. [21]If you do not let my people go, I will send large numbers of flies. I will send them on you and your officials. I will send them on your people and into your homes. The houses of the Egyptians will be full of flies. Even the area where they live will be full of flies.

[22]" ' "But on that day I will treat the area of Goshen differently from yours. That is where my people live. There will not be large numbers of flies in Goshen. Then you will know that I, the LORD, am in this land. [23]I will treat my people differently from yours. The miraculous sign will take place tomorrow." ' "

[24]So the LORD did it. Huge numbers

Why wouldn't Pharaoh let the people go?

A pharaoh was like a king. The pharaoh in Egypt made the Israelites into slaves. He was angry when Moses asked him to let the Israelites leave Egypt. Pharaoh wanted to keep his slaves because they did a lot of work for free. That made his life easier. He was also too proud to let them go. It would look like Moses was pushing him around. And he also would not let the people go because he did not believe in God. Pharaoh was in charge of Egypt and he liked it that way. He did not want God, Moses or anyone else telling him what to do.

checkout
Exodus 8:19

Related verses:
Exodus 5:1,2

of flies poured into Pharaoh's palace. They came into the homes of his officials. All over Egypt the flies destroyed the land.

²⁵Then Pharaoh sent for Moses and Aaron. He said to them, "Go. Offer sacrifices to your God here in the land."

²⁶But Moses said, "That wouldn't be right. The sacrifices we offer to the LORD our God wouldn't be accepted by the Egyptians because of their beliefs. Suppose we offered sacrifices they couldn't accept. Then they would throw stones at us and try to kill us. ²⁷We have to take a journey that lasts about three days. We want to go into the desert to offer sacrifices to the LORD our God, exactly as he commands us."

²⁸Pharaoh said, "I will let you and your people go to offer sacrifices. You can offer them to the LORD your God in the desert. But you must not go very far. And pray for me."

²⁹Moses replied, "As soon as I leave you, I will pray to the LORD. Tomorrow the flies will leave you. They will also leave your officials and your people.

Just be sure you don't try to trick us again. Let the people go to offer sacrifices to the LORD."

³⁰Then Moses left Pharaoh and prayed to the LORD. ³¹And the LORD did what Moses asked. The flies left Pharaoh, his officials and his people. Not one fly remained. ³²But Pharaoh's heart became stubborn that time also. He wouldn't let the people go.

THE PLAGUE ON LIVESTOCK

9 Then the LORD spoke to Moses. He said, "Go to Pharaoh. Tell him, 'The LORD, the God of the Hebrews, says, "Let my people go. Then they will be able to worship me. ²Do not refuse to let them go. Do not keep holding them back.

³" ' "If you refuse, my powerful hand will bring a terrible plague on you. I will strike your livestock in the fields. I will strike your horses, donkeys, camels, cattle, sheep and goats. ⁴But I will treat Israel's livestock differently from yours. No animal that belongs to the people of Israel will die." ' "

⁵The LORD set a time for the plague.

KIDS' QUESTION

Why did God send plagues on Egypt?

A "plague" is a bad thing that happens to a lot of people at the same time. God sent the plagues on Egypt to show Pharaoh who was in charge. God also sent them to show his power. God kept telling Pharaoh to let the Israelite slaves go free. But Pharaoh kept saying no. Whenever Pharaoh would say no, God would send a plague. After some of the plagues Pharaoh did decide to let the Israelites go. But then he would change his mind and say no again. It took ten plagues to get Pharaoh to let the Israelite slaves go free!

checkout
Exodus 9:1–3

Related verse:
Exodus 7:14

He said, "Tomorrow I will send it on the land." ⁶So the next day the LORD sent it. All of the livestock of the Egyptians died. But not one animal that belonged to the Israelites died.

⁷Pharaoh sent people to find out what had happened. They discovered that not even one animal that belonged to the Israelites had died. But his heart was still very stubborn. He wouldn't let the people go.

THE PLAGUE OF BOILS

⁸Then the LORD spoke to Moses and Aaron. He said, "Take handfuls of ashes from a furnace. Have Moses toss them into the air in front of Pharaoh. ⁹The ashes will turn into fine dust all over the whole land of Egypt. Then boils will break out on people and animals all over the land. Their bodies will be covered with them."

¹⁰So Moses and Aaron took ashes from a furnace and stood in front of Pharaoh. Moses tossed them into the air. Then boils broke out on people and animals alike. ¹¹The bodies of all of the Egyptians were covered with boils. The magicians couldn't stand in front of Moses because of the boils that were all over them.

¹²But the LORD made Pharaoh's heart stubborn. Pharaoh wouldn't listen to Moses and Aaron, just as the LORD had said to Moses.

THE PLAGUE OF HAIL

¹³Then the LORD spoke to Moses. He said, "Get up early in the morning. Go to Pharaoh and say to him, 'The LORD, the God of the Hebrews, says, "Let my people go. Then they will be able to worship me.

¹⁴" ' "If you do not let them go, I will send the full force of my plagues against you this time. They will strike your officials and your people. Then you will know that there is no one like me in the whole earth.

¹⁵" ' "By now I could have reached out my hand. I could have struck you and your people with a plague that would have wiped you off the earth. ¹⁶But I had a special reason for making you king. I decided to show you my power. I wanted my name to become known everywhere on earth.

¹⁷" ' "But you are still against my people. You will not let them go. ¹⁸So at this time tomorrow I will send the worst hailstorm ever to fall on Egypt in its entire history.

¹⁹" ' "Give an order now to bring your livestock inside to a safe place. Bring in everything that is outside. The hail will fall on all of the people and animals that are left outside. They will die." ' "

²⁰The officials of Pharaoh who had respect for what the LORD had said obeyed him. They hurried to bring their slaves and their livestock inside.

²¹But others didn't pay attention to what the LORD had said. They left their slaves and livestock outside.

²²Then the LORD spoke to Moses. He said, "Reach your hand out toward the sky. Then hail will fall all over Egypt. It will beat down on people and animals alike. It will strike everything that is growing in the fields of Egypt."

²³Moses reached his wooden staff out toward the sky. Then the LORD sent thunder and hail. Lightning flashed down to the ground. The LORD rained hail on the land of Egypt. ²⁴Hail fell and lightning flashed back and forth. It was the worst storm in Egypt's entire history.

²⁵All over Egypt hail struck everything in the fields. It fell on people and animals alike. It beat down everything that was growing in the fields. It tore all of the leaves off the trees.

²⁶The only place it didn't hail was in the area of Goshen. That's where the people of Israel were.

²⁷Then Pharaoh sent for Moses and Aaron. "This time I've sinned," he said to them. "The LORD has done what is right. I and my people have done what is wrong. ²⁸Pray to the LORD, because we've had enough thunder and hail. I'll let you and your people go. You don't have to stay here any longer."

²⁹Moses replied, "When I've left the city, I'll lift up my hands and pray to the LORD. The thunder will stop. There won't be any more hail. Then you will know that the earth belongs to the LORD. ³⁰But I know that you and your officials still don't have any respect for the LORD God."

³¹The barley was ripe. The flax was

blooming. So they were both destroyed. ³²But the wheat and spelt weren't destroyed. That's because they ripen later.

³³Then Moses left Pharaoh and went out of the city. He lifted up his hands and prayed to the LORD. The thunder and hail stopped. The rain didn't pour down on the land any longer.

³⁴Pharaoh saw that the rain, hail and thunder had stopped. So he sinned again. He and his officials made their hearts stubborn. ³⁵So Pharaoh's heart was stubborn. He wouldn't let the people of Israel go, just as the LORD had said through Moses.

THE PLAGUE OF LOCUSTS

10 Then the LORD said to Moses, "Go to Pharaoh. I have made his heart stubborn. I have also made the hearts of his officials stubborn so I can do my miraculous signs among them. ²Then you will be able to tell your children and grandchildren how hard I was on the Egyptians. You can tell them I did great miracles among the people of Egypt. And all of you will know that I am the LORD."

³So Moses and Aaron went to Pharaoh. They said to him, "The LORD, the God of the Hebrews, says, 'How long will you refuse to obey me? Let my people go. Then they will be able to worship me.

⁴" 'If you refuse to let them go, I will bring locusts into your country tomorrow. ⁵They will cover the ground so that it can't be seen. They will eat what little you have left after the hail. That includes every tree that is growing in your fields. ⁶They will fill your houses. They will be in the homes of all of your officials and your people. Your parents and your people before them have never seen anything like it as long as they have lived here.' " Then Moses turned around and left Pharaoh.

⁷Pharaoh's officials said to him, "How long will this man be a trap for us? Let the people go. Then they'll be able to worship the LORD their God. After everything that's happened, don't you realize that Egypt is destroyed?"

⁸Moses and Aaron were brought back to Pharaoh. "Go. Worship the LORD your God," he said. "But just who will be going?"

⁹Moses answered, "We'll go with our young people and old people. We'll go with our sons and daughters. We'll take our flocks and herds. We are supposed to hold a feast in the LORD's honor."

¹⁰Pharaoh said, "The LORD will really be with all of you if I ever let you go, along with your women and children! Clearly you are planning to do something bad. ¹¹No! I'll only allow the men to go. Then all of you can worship the LORD. After all, that's what you have been asking for."

Then Pharaoh drove Moses and Aaron out of his sight.

¹²The LORD said to Moses, "Reach out your hand over Egypt. Locusts will cover the land. They will eat up everything that is growing in the fields. They will eat up everything that was left by the hail."

¹³So Moses reached his wooden staff out over Egypt. Then the LORD made an east wind blow across the land. It blew all that day and all that night. By morning the wind had brought the locusts. ¹⁴They came into every part of Egypt. They settled down in every area of the country in large numbers. There had never been a plague of locusts like it before. And there will never be one like it again.

¹⁵The locusts covered the ground until it was black. They ate up everything that was left after the hail. They ate up everything that was growing in the fields. They ate up the fruit on the trees. There was nothing green left on any tree or plant in the whole land of Egypt.

¹⁶Pharaoh quickly sent for Moses and Aaron. He said, "I have sinned against the LORD your God. I've also sinned against you. ¹⁷Now forgive my sin one more time. Pray to the LORD your God to take this deadly plague away from me."

¹⁸After Moses left Pharaoh, he prayed to the LORD. ¹⁹The LORD changed the wind to a very strong west wind. The wind picked up the locusts. It blew them into the Red Sea. Not even one locust was left anywhere in Egypt.

20But the LORD made Pharaoh's heart stubborn. And Pharaoh wouldn't let the people of Israel go.

THE PLAGUE OF DARKNESS

21The LORD spoke to Moses. He said, "Reach out your hand toward the sky. Darkness will spread over Egypt. It will be so dark that people can feel it."

22So Moses reached out his hand toward the sky. Then complete darkness covered Egypt for three days. **23**No one could see anyone else or go anywhere for three days. But all of the people of Israel had light where they lived.

24Then Pharaoh sent for Moses. He said to him, "Go. Worship the LORD. Even your women and children can go with you. Just leave your flocks and herds behind."

25But Moses said, "You must allow us to take animals to offer as sacrifices and burnt offerings to the LORD our God. **26**Our livestock must also go with us. We have to use some of them to worship the LORD our God. We can't leave even one animal behind. Until we get there, we won't know what we are supposed to use to worship the LORD."

27But the LORD made Pharaoh's heart stubborn. So he wouldn't let the people go. **28**Pharaoh said to Moses, "Get out of my sight! Make sure you don't come to see me again! If you do, you will die."

29"I'll do just as you say," Moses replied. "I will never come to see you again."

THE LORD ANNOUNCES THE TENTH PLAGUE

11 The LORD had spoken to Moses. He had said, "I will bring one more plague on Pharaoh and on Egypt. After that, he will let you and your people go. When he does, he will drive you completely away. **2**Tell the men and women alike to ask their neighbors for articles made out of silver and gold."

3The LORD caused the Egyptians to treat the Israelites in a kind way. Pharaoh's officials and the people had great respect for Moses.

4Moses said, "The LORD says, 'About midnight I will go through every part of Egypt. **5**Every oldest son in Egypt will die. The oldest son of Pharaoh, who sits on the throne, will die. The oldest son of the female slave, who works at her hand mill, will die. All of the male animals that were born first to their mothers among the cattle will also die. **6**There will be loud crying all over Egypt. It will be worse than it's ever been before. And nothing like it will ever be heard again.

7" 'But among the people of Israel not even one dog will bark at any man or animal.' Then you will know that the LORD treats Egypt differently from us.

8"All of your officials will come and bow down to me. They will say, 'Go, you and all of the people who follow you!' After that, I will leave."

Moses burned with anger when he left Pharaoh.

9The LORD had spoken to Moses. He had said, "Pharaoh will refuse to listen to you. So I will multiply my miracles in Egypt."

10Moses and Aaron did all of those miracles in the sight of Pharaoh. But the LORD made Pharaoh's heart stubborn. He wouldn't let the people of Israel go out of his country.

THE FIRST PASSOVER SACRIFICE

12 The LORD spoke to Moses and Aaron in Egypt. **2**He said, "From now on, this month will be your first month. Each of your years will begin with it.

3"Speak to the whole community of Israel. Tell them that on the tenth day of this month each man must get a lamb from his flock. A lamb should be chosen for each family and home.

4"Suppose there are not enough people in your family to eat a whole lamb. Then you must share some of it with your nearest neighbor. You must add up the total number of people there are. You must decide how much lamb is needed for each person.

5"The animals you choose must be males that are a year old. They must not have any flaws. You may choose either sheep or goats. **6**Take care of them until the 14th day of the month. Then the whole community of Israel must kill them when the sun goes down. ⁷Take some of the blood. Put it on the sides and tops of the doorframes of the houses where you eat the lambs.

⁸"That same night eat the meat cooked over the fire. Also eat bitter plants. And eat bread that is made without yeast. ⁹Do not eat the meat raw or boiled in water. Instead, cook it over the fire. Cook the head, legs and inside parts. ¹⁰Do not leave any of it until morning. If some is left over until morning, burn it.

¹¹"Eat the meat while your coat is tucked into your belt. Put your sandals on your feet. Take your walking stick in your hand. Eat the food quickly. It is the LORD's Passover.

¹²"That same night I will pass through Egypt. I will strike down every oldest son. I will also kill all of the male animals that were born first to their mothers. And I will judge all of the gods of Egypt. I am the LORD.

¹³"The blood on your houses will be a sign for you. When I see the blood, I will pass over you. No deadly plague will touch you when I strike Egypt.

¹⁴"Always remember this day. For all time to come, you and your children after you must celebrate this day as a feast in honor of the LORD. It is a law that will last forever.

¹⁵"Eat bread made without yeast for seven days. On the first day remove the yeast from your homes. For the next seven days, anyone who eats anything that has yeast in it must be cut off from Israel.

¹⁶"On the first and seventh days, come together for a special service. Do not work at all on those days. All you are allowed to do is prepare food for everyone to eat.

¹⁷"Celebrate the Feast of Unleavened Bread. I brought you out of Egypt on this very day like an army on the march. It is a law that will last for all time to come. ¹⁸In the first month eat bread that is made without yeast. Eat it

KIDS' QUESTION

What does Passover mean?

Passover is a special feast that many Jews observe every year during the Feast of Unleavened Bread. It reminds them of when the Israelite slaves left Egypt and started their trip to the promised land. It reminds them of when God told the Israelites to put the blood of a lamb over their doors. Each family did this so the angel of death would see the blood and *pass over* the house. Nobody in that house died that night. So the Passover is a celebration of God's love and care for his people. Have you ever heard of the Last Supper? That was when Jesus celebrated the Passover with his disciples for the last time.

checkout
Exodus 12:17

Related verses:
Exodus 12:1–30;
Matthew 26:17–19

WAX MUSEUM

from the evening of the 14th day until the evening of the 21st day.

¹⁹"For seven days do not let any yeast be found in your homes. Anyone who eats anything that has yeast in it must be cut off from the community of Israel. That applies to outsiders and Israelites alike. ²⁰Do not eat anything that is made with yeast. No matter where you live, eat bread that is made without yeast."

²¹Then Moses sent for all of the elders of Israel. He said to them, "Go at once. Choose the animals for your families. Each family must kill a Passover lamb. ²²Get a branch of a hyssop plant. Dip it into the blood in the bowl. Put some of the blood on the top and on both sides of the doorframe. None of you can go out the door of your house until morning.

²³"The LORD will go through the land to strike the Egyptians down. He'll see the blood on the top and sides of the doorframe. He will pass over that house. He won't let the destroying angel enter your homes to kill you.

²⁴"Obey all of these directions. It's a law for you and your children after you for all time to come. ²⁵The LORD will give you the land, just as he promised. When you enter it, keep this holy day.

²⁶"Your children will ask you, 'What does this holy day mean to you?' ²⁷Tell them, 'It's the Passover sacrifice in honor of the LORD. He passed over the houses of the people of Israel in Egypt. He spared our homes when he struck the Egyptians down.' "

Then the people of Israel bowed down and worshiped. ²⁸They did just what the LORD commanded Moses and Aaron.

²⁹At midnight the LORD struck down every oldest son in Egypt. He killed the oldest son of Pharaoh, who sat on the throne. He killed all of the oldest sons of prisoners, who were in prison. He also killed all of the male animals that were born first to their mothers among the livestock.

³⁰Pharaoh and all of his officials got up during the night. So did all of the Egyptians. There was loud crying in Egypt because someone had died in every home.

Why did the Israelites smear blood on their doors?

The last plague that God sent on Egypt was the plague that killed the oldest son in each Egyptian family. God told the Israelites to mark their doors with blood. This blood came from a perfect lamb that they killed for food that night. The angel of death would see the blood on the doorframe and know that the family was a family of Israelites. The oldest son of that family would not die. This was God's plan for protecting the Israelites and getting them ready to leave Egypt.

checkout Exodus 12:23

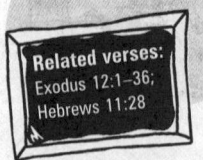

Related verses:
Exodus 12:1–36;
Hebrews 11:28

THE PEOPLE OF ISRAEL LEAVE EGYPT

³¹During the night, Pharaoh sent for Moses and Aaron. He said to them, "Get out of here! You and the Israelites, leave my people! Go. Worship the LORD, just as you have asked. ³²Go. Take your flocks and herds, just as you have said. And also give me your blessing."

³³The Egyptians begged the people of Israel to hurry up and leave the country. "If you don't," they said, "we'll all die!"

³⁴So the people took their dough before the yeast was added to it. They carried it on their shoulders in bread pans that were wrapped in clothes. ³⁵They did just as Moses had directed them. They asked the Egyptians for articles that were made out of silver and gold. They also asked them for clothes. ³⁶The LORD had caused the Egyptians to treat the people of Israel in a kind way. So they gave them what they asked for. The people of Israel took many expensive things that belonged to the Egyptians.

³⁷The Israelites traveled from Rameses to Succoth. There were about 600,000 men who were old enough to go into battle. The women and children went with them. ³⁸So did many other people. The Israelites also took large flocks and herds with them.

³⁹They brought dough from Egypt. With it they baked bread without yeast. The dough didn't have any yeast in it. That's because the people had been driven out of Egypt before they had time to prepare their food.

⁴⁰The people of Israel lived in Egypt for 430 years. ⁴¹At the end of the 430 years, to the very day, all of the LORD's people marched out of Egypt like an army.

⁴²The LORD kept watch that night to bring them out of Egypt. So on that same night every year all of the Israelites must keep watch. They must do it to honor the LORD for all time to come.

RULES FOR THE PASSOVER

⁴³The LORD spoke to Moses and Aaron. He said, "Here are the rules for the Passover.

"No one from another country is allowed to eat the Passover meal. ⁴⁴Any slave you have bought is allowed to eat it after you have circumcised him. ⁴⁵But a hired worker or someone who lives with you for a while is not allowed to eat it.

⁴⁶"It must be eaten inside a house. Do not take any of the meat outside. Do not break any of the bones. ⁴⁷The whole community of Israel must celebrate the Passover.

⁴⁸"Suppose an outsider who is living among you wants to celebrate the LORD's Passover. Then all of the males in that home must be circumcised. After that, the person can take part, just like an Israelite. Only males who are circumcised can eat it.

⁴⁹"The same law applies to Israelites and to outsiders who are living among you."

⁵⁰All of the people of Israel did just what the LORD had commanded Moses and Aaron. ⁵¹On that very day the LORD brought the Israelites out of Egypt like an army on the march.

SETTING APART THE OLDEST SONS

13 The LORD said to Moses, ²"Set apart for me the first boy born in every family. The oldest son of every Israelite mother belongs to me. Every male animal that is born first to its mother also belongs to me."

³Then Moses said to the people, "Remember this day. It's the day you came out of Egypt. That's the land where you were slaves. The LORD used his mighty hand to bring you out of Egypt. Don't eat anything that has yeast in it. ⁴You are leaving today. It's the month of Abib.

⁵"The LORD will bring you into the land of the Canaanites, Hittites, Amorites, Hivites and Jebusites. He took an oath and promised your people of long ago that he would give that land to you. It's a land that has plenty of milk and honey. When you get there, keep this holy day in this month.

⁶"For seven days eat bread that is made without yeast. On the seventh day hold a feast in the LORD's honor.

[7]Eat bread that is made without yeast during those seven days. Nothing that has yeast in it should be found among you. No yeast should be seen anywhere inside your borders.

[8]"On that day talk to your son. Tell him, 'I'm doing this because of what the LORD did for me when I came out of Egypt.'

[9]"When you celebrate this day, it will be like a mark on your hand. It will be like a reminder on your forehead. The law of the LORD must be on your lips. The LORD used his mighty hand to bring you out of Egypt. [10]Obey this law at the appointed time year after year.

[11]"The LORD will bring you into the land of Canaan. He will give it to you, just as he promised he would. He even took an oath when he made the promise to you and your people of long ago. [12]"After you arrive there, give to the LORD the oldest son of every mother. Every male animal that is born first to its mother among your livestock belongs to the LORD. [13]By sacrificing a lamb, buy back every male donkey that is born first to its mother. But if you don't buy the donkey back, break its neck. Buy back every oldest son.

[14]"In days to come, your son will ask you, 'What does this mean?'

"When he does, say to him, 'The LORD used his mighty hand to bring us out of Egypt. That's the land where we were slaves. [15]Pharaoh was stubborn. He refused to let us go. So the LORD killed every oldest son in Egypt. He also killed every male animal that was born first to its mother. That's why I sacrifice to the LORD every male animal that was born first. And that's why I buy back each oldest son for him.'

[16]"This day will be like a mark on your hand. It will be like a sign on your forehead. It will remind you that the LORD used his mighty hand to bring us out of Egypt."

ISRAEL GOES THROUGH
THE RED SEA

[17]Pharaoh let the people go. The shortest road from Goshen to Canaan went through the Philistine country. But God didn't lead them that way. God said, "If they have to go into battle, they might change their minds. They might return to Egypt."

[18]So God led the people toward the Red Sea by taking them on a road through the desert. The Israelites were prepared for battle when they went up out of Egypt.

[19]Moses took the bones of Joseph along with him. Joseph had made the sons of Israel take an oath and make a promise. He had said, "I'm sure that God will come to help you. When he does, you must carry my bones up from this place with you." *(Genesis 50:25)*

[20]The people left Succoth. They camped at Etham on the edge of the desert.

[21]By day the LORD went ahead of them in a pillar of cloud. It guided them on their way. At night he led them with a pillar of fire. It gave them light. So they could travel by day or at night. [22]The pillar of cloud didn't leave its place in front of the people during the day. And the pillar of fire didn't leave its place at night.

14 Then the LORD spoke to Moses. [2]He said, "Tell the people of Israel to turn back. Have them camp near Pi Hahiroth between Migdol and the Red Sea. They must camp by the sea, right across from Baal Zephon. [3]Pharaoh will think, 'The people of Israel are wandering around the land. They don't know which way to go. The desert is all around them.'

[4]"I will make Pharaoh's heart stubborn. He will chase them. But I will gain glory for myself because of what will happen to Pharaoh and his whole army. And the Egyptians will know that I am the LORD." So the Israelites camped by the Red Sea.

[5]The king of Egypt was told that the people had gotten away. Then Pharaoh and his officials changed their minds about them. They said, "What have we done? We've let the people of Israel go! We've lost our slaves and all of the work they used to do for us!"

[6]So he had his chariot made ready. He took his army with him. [7]He took 600 of the best chariots in Egypt. He also took along all of the other chariots. Officers were in charge of all of them.

⁸The LORD made the heart of Pharaoh, the king of Egypt, stubborn. So he chased the Israelites, who were marching out boldly. ⁹The Egyptians went after the Israelites. All of Pharaoh's horses and chariots and horsemen and troops went after them. They caught up with them as they camped by the sea. The Israelites were near Pi Hahiroth, across from Baal Zephon.

¹⁰As Pharaoh approached, the people of Israel looked up. There were the Egyptians marching after them! The Israelites were terrified. They cried out to the LORD.

¹¹They said to Moses, "Why did you bring us to the desert to die? Weren't there any graves in Egypt? What have you done to us by bringing us out of Egypt? ¹²We told you in Egypt, 'Leave us alone. Let us serve the Egyptians.' It would have been better for us to serve the Egyptians than to die here in the desert!"

¹³Moses answered the people. He said, "Don't be afraid. Stand firm. You will see how the LORD will save you today. Do you see those Egyptians? You will never see them again. ¹⁴The LORD will fight for you. Just be still."

¹⁵Then the LORD spoke to Moses. He said, "Why are you crying out to me? Tell the people of Israel to move on. ¹⁶Hold your wooden staff out. Reach your hand out over the Red Sea to part the water. Then the people can go through the sea on dry ground.

¹⁷"I will make the hearts of the Egyptians stubborn. They will go in after the Israelites. I will gain glory for myself because of what will happen to Pharaoh, his whole army, his chariots and his horsemen.

¹⁸"The Egyptians will know that I am the LORD. I will gain glory because of what will happen to all of them."

¹⁹The angel of God had been traveling in front of Israel's army. Now he moved back and went behind them. The pillar of cloud also moved away from in front of them. Now it stood behind them. ²⁰It came between the armies of Egypt and Israel. All through the night the cloud brought darkness to one side and light to the other. Neither army went near the other all night long.

²¹Then Moses reached his hand out over the Red Sea. All that night the LORD pushed the sea back with a strong east wind. He turned the sea

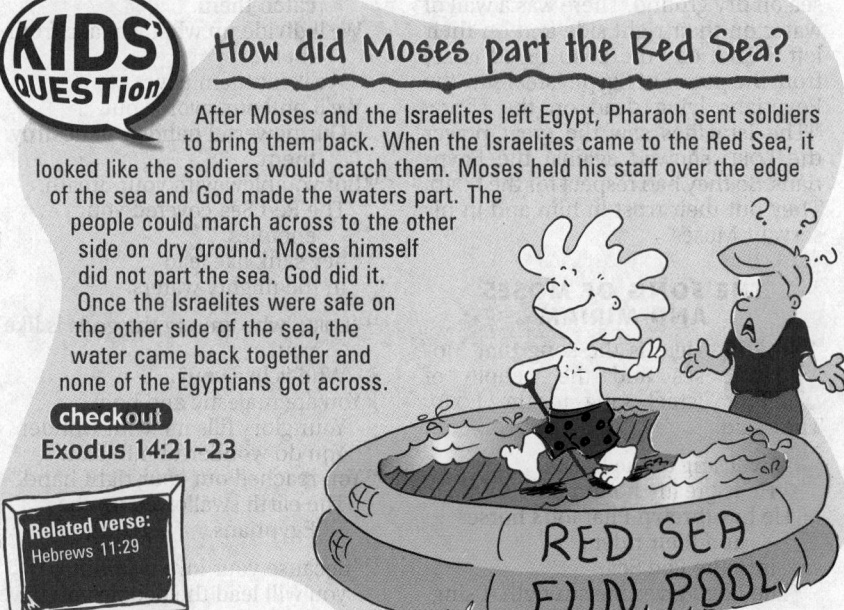

KIDS' QUESTION

How did Moses part the Red Sea?

After Moses and the Israelites left Egypt, Pharaoh sent soldiers to bring them back. When the Israelites came to the Red Sea, it looked like the soldiers would catch them. Moses held his staff over the edge of the sea and God made the waters part. The people could march across to the other side on dry ground. Moses himself did not part the sea. God did it. Once the Israelites were safe on the other side of the sea, the water came back together and none of the Egyptians got across.

checkout
Exodus 14:21–23

Related verse:
Hebrews 11:29

RED SEA FUN POOL

into dry land. The waters were parted. ²²The people of Israel went through the sea on dry ground. There was a wall of water on their right side and on their left.

²³The Egyptians chased them. All of Pharaoh's horses and chariots and horsemen followed them into the sea. ²⁴Near the end of the night the LORD looked down from the pillar of fire and cloud. He saw the Egyptian army and threw it into a panic. ²⁵He kept their chariot wheels from turning freely. That made the chariots hard to drive.

The Egyptians said, "Let's get away from the Israelites! The LORD is fighting for Israel against Egypt."

²⁶Then the LORD spoke to Moses. He said, "Reach your hand out over the sea. The waters will flow back over the Egyptians and their chariots and horsemen." ²⁷So Moses reached his hand out over the sea. At sunrise the sea went back to its place. The Egyptians tried to run away from the sea. But the LORD swept them into it. ²⁸The water flowed back and covered the chariots and horsemen. It covered the entire army of Pharaoh that had followed the people of Israel into the sea. Not one of the Egyptians was left.

²⁹But the Israelites went through the sea on dry ground. There was a wall of water on their right side and on their left. ³⁰That day the LORD saved Israel from the power of Egypt. Israel saw the Egyptians lying dead on the shore. ³¹The Israelites saw the great power the LORD showed against the Egyptians. So they had respect for the LORD. They put their trust in him and in his servant Moses.

THE SONG OF MOSES AND MIRIAM

15 Here is the song that Moses and the people of Israel sang to the LORD. They said,

"I will sing to the LORD.
  He is greatly honored.
He has thrown Pharaoh's horses
    and their riders
  into the Red Sea.
²The LORD gives me strength. I sing
    about him.

He has saved me.
He is my God. I will praise him.
  He is my father's God. I will
    honor him.
³The LORD goes into battle.
  The LORD is his name.
⁴He has thrown Pharaoh's chariots
    and army
  into the Red Sea.
Pharaoh's best officers
  drowned in the sea.
⁵The deep waters covered them.
  They sank to the bottom like a
    stone.

⁶"LORD, your right hand
  was majestic and powerful.
LORD, your right hand
  destroyed your enemies.
⁷Because of your great majesty,
  you threw down those who
    opposed you.
Your burning anger blazed out.
  It burned them up like straw.
⁸The powerful blast from your nose
  piled up the waters.
The rushing waters stood firm like
    a wall.
The deep waters stood up in the
    middle of the sea.

⁹"Your enemies bragged,
  'We will chase Israel. We will
    catch them.
We'll divide up what we take from
    them.
  We'll eat them alive.
We'll pull our swords out.
  Our powerful hands will destroy
    them.'
¹⁰But you blew with your breath.
  The Red Sea covered your
    enemies.
They sank like lead
  in the mighty waters.

¹¹"LORD, who among the gods is like
    you?
  Who is like you?
You are majestic and holy.
  Your glory fills me with wonder.
  You do wonderful miracles.
¹²You reached out your right hand.
  The earth swallowed up the
    Egyptians.

¹³"Because your love is faithful,
  you will lead the people you have
    set free.

Because you are so strong,
you will guide them to the holy
place where you live.
[14] The nations will hear about it and
tremble.
Pain and suffering will take hold
of the Philistines.
[15] The chiefs of Edom will be
terrified.
The leaders of Moab will tremble
with fear.
The people of Canaan will melt
away.
[16] Fear and terror will fall on them.
Your powerful arm
will make them as still as a stone.
Then your people will pass by,
LORD.
Then the people you created will
pass by.
[17] You will bring them in.
You will plant them on the
mountain you gave them.
LORD, you have made that place
your home.
Lord, your hands have made
your holy place secure.
[18] "The LORD will rule
for ever and ever."

[19] Pharaoh's horses, chariots and horsemen went into the Red Sea. The LORD brought the waters of the sea back over them. But the people of Israel walked through the sea on dry ground. [20] Aaron's sister Miriam was a prophet. She took a tambourine in her hand. All the women followed her. They played tambourines and danced. [21] Miriam sang to them,

"Sing to the LORD.
He is greatly honored.
He has thrown Pharaoh's horses
and their riders
into the Red Sea."

AT THE WATERS OF MARAH AND ELIM

[22] Then Moses led Israel away from the Red Sea. They went into the Desert of Shur. For three days they traveled in the desert. They didn't find any water there. [23] When they came to Marah, they couldn't drink its water. It was bitter. That's why the place is named

Marah. [24] The people told Moses they weren't happy with him. They said, "What are we supposed to drink?"

[25] Then Moses cried out to the LORD. The LORD showed him a stick. Moses threw it into the water. The water became sweet.

There the LORD made a rule and a law for the people. And there he put them to the test. [26] He said, "I am the LORD your God. Listen carefully to my voice. Do what is right in my eyes. Pay attention to my commands. Obey all of my rules. If you do, I will not send on you any of the sicknesses I sent on the Egyptians. I am the LORD who heals you."

[27] The people came to Elim. It had 12 springs and 70 palm trees. They camped there near the water.

THE LORD GIVES ISRAEL FOOD EVERY DAY

16 The whole community of Israel started out from Elim. They came to the Desert of Sin. It was between Elim and Sinai. They arrived there on the 15th day of the second month after they had come out of Egypt.

[2] In the desert the whole community told Moses and Aaron they weren't happy with them. [3] The Israelites said to them, "We wish the LORD had put us to death in Egypt. There we sat around pots of meat. We ate all of the food we wanted. But you have brought us out into this desert. You must want this entire community to die of hunger."

[4] Then the LORD spoke to Moses. He said, "I will rain down bread from heaven for you. The people must go out each day. Have them gather enough bread for that day. Here is how I will put them to the test. I will see if they will follow my directions.

[5] "On the sixth day they must prepare what they bring in. On that day they must gather twice as much as on the other days."

[6] So Moses and Aaron spoke to all of the people of Israel. They said, "In the evening you will know that the LORD brought you out of Egypt. [7] And in the morning you will see the glory of the LORD. He has heard you say you aren't happy with him. Who are we? Why are

you telling us you aren't happy with us?"

[8]Moses also said, "You will know that the LORD has heard you speak against him. He will give you meat to eat in the evening. He'll give you all of the bread you want in the morning. But who are we? You aren't speaking against us. You are speaking against the LORD."

[9]Then Moses told Aaron, "Talk to the whole community of Israel. Say to them, 'Come to the LORD. He has heard you speak against him.' "

[10]While Aaron was talking to the whole community of Israel, they looked toward the desert. There was the glory of the LORD appearing in the cloud!

[11]The LORD said to Moses, [12]"I have heard the people of Israel talking about how unhappy they are. Tell them, 'When the sun goes down, you will eat meat. In the morning you will be filled with bread. Then you will know that I am the LORD your God.' "

[13]That evening quail came and covered the camp. In the morning the ground around the camp was covered with dew. [14]When the dew was gone, thin flakes appeared on the desert floor. They looked like frost on the ground. [15]The people of Israel saw the flakes. They asked each other, "What's that?" They didn't know what it was.

Moses said to them, "It's the bread the LORD has given you to eat. [16]Here is what the LORD has commanded. He has said, 'Each one of you should gather as much as you need. Take two quarts for each person who lives in your tent.' "

[17]The people of Israel did as they were told. Some gathered a lot, and some gathered a little. [18]When they measured it out, those who gathered a lot didn't have too much. And those who gathered a little had enough. All of them gathered only what they needed.

[19]Then Moses said to them, "Don't keep any of it until morning."

[20]Some of them didn't pay any attention to Moses. They kept part of it until morning. But it was full of maggots and began to stink. So Moses became angry with them.

[21]Each morning all of them gathered as much as they needed. But by the hottest time of the day, the thin flakes had melted away.

[22]On the sixth day, the people gathered twice as much. It amounted to four quarts for each person. The leaders of the community came and reported that to Moses. [23]He said to them, "Here is what the LORD commanded. He said, 'Tomorrow will be a day of rest. It will be a holy Sabbath day. It will be set apart for the LORD. So bake what you want to bake. Boil what you want to boil. Save what is left. Keep it until morning.' "

[24]So they saved it until morning, just as Moses commanded. It didn't stink or get maggots in it.

[25]"Eat it today," Moses said. "Today is a Sabbath day in the LORD's honor. You won't find any flakes on the ground today. [26]Gather them for six days. But on the seventh day there won't be any. It's the Sabbath."

[27]In spite of what Moses said, some of the people went out on the seventh day to gather the flakes. But they didn't find any.

[28]Then the LORD spoke to Moses. He said, "How long will all of you refuse to obey my commands and my teachings? [29]Keep in mind that I have given you the Sabbath day. That is why on the sixth day I give you bread for two days. All of you must stay where you are on the seventh day. No one can go out." [30]So the people rested on the seventh day.

[31]The people of Israel called the bread manna. It was white like coriander seeds. It tasted like wafers that were made with honey.

[32]Moses said, "Here is what the LORD has commanded. He has said, 'Get two quarts of manna. Keep it for all time to come. Then those who live after you will see the bread I gave you to eat in the desert. I gave it to you when I brought you out of Egypt.' "

[33]So Moses said to Aaron, "Get a jar. Put two quarts of manna in it. Then place it in front of the LORD. Keep it there for all time to come."

[34]Aaron did exactly as the LORD had commanded Moses. He put the manna in front of the tablets of the covenant. He put it there so it would be kept for all time to come.

³⁵The people of Israel ate manna for 40 years. They ate it until they came to a land that was settled. They ate it until they reached the border of Canaan. ³⁶The jar had an omer of manna in it. An omer was two quarts.

THE LORD GIVES ISRAEL WATER OUT OF THE ROCK

17 The whole community of Israel started out from the Desert of Sin. They traveled from place to place, just as the LORD commanded.

They camped at Rephidim. But there wasn't any water for the people to drink. ²So they argued with Moses. They said, "Give us water to drink."

Moses replied, "Why are you arguing with me? Why are you putting the LORD to the test?"

³But the people were thirsty for water there. So they told Moses they weren't happy with him. They said, "Why did you bring us up out of Egypt? Did you want us, our children and our livestock to die of thirst?"

⁴Then Moses cried out to the LORD. He said, "What am I going to do with these people? They are almost ready to kill me by throwing stones at me."

⁵The LORD answered Moses. He said, "Walk on ahead of the people. Take some of the elders of Israel along with you. Take in your hand the wooden staff you used when you struck the Nile River. Go. ⁶I will stand there in front of you by the rock at Mount Horeb. Hit the rock. Then water will come out of it for the people to drink." So Moses hit the rock in the sight of the elders of Israel.

⁷Moses called the place Massah and Meribah. That's because the people of Israel argued with him there. They also put the LORD to the test. They asked, "Is the LORD among us or not?"

JOSHUA WINS THE BATTLE OVER THE AMALEKITES

⁸The Amalekites came and attacked the Israelites at Rephidim. ⁹Moses said to Joshua, "Choose some of our men. Then go out and fight against the Amalekites. Tomorrow I will stand on top of the hill. I'll stand there with the staff of God in my hands."

¹⁰So Joshua fought against the Amalekites, just as Moses had ordered. Moses, Aaron and Hur went to the top of the hill. ¹¹As long as Moses held his hands up, the Israelites were winning. But every time he lowered his hands, the Amalekites began to win.

¹²When Moses' arms got tired, Aaron and Hur got a stone and put it under him. Then he sat on it. Aaron and Hur held his hands up. Aaron was on one side, and Hur was on the other. Moses' hands remained steady until sunset.

¹³So Joshua destroyed the Amalekite army with swords.

¹⁴Then the LORD said to Moses, "That is something to be remembered. So write it on a scroll. Make sure Joshua knows you have done it. I will completely erase the memory of the Amalekites from the earth."

¹⁵Then Moses built an altar. He called it The LORD Is My Banner. ¹⁶He said, "I raised my hands toward the throne of the LORD. The LORD will fight against the Amalekites for all time to come."

JETHRO VISITS MOSES

18 Moses' father-in-law Jethro was the priest of Midian. He heard about everything God had done for Moses and for his people Israel. He heard how the LORD had brought Israel out of Egypt.

²Moses had sent his wife Zipporah to his father-in-law. So Jethro welcomed her ³and her two sons. One son was named Gershom. That's because Moses had said, "I'm an outsider in a strange land." ⁴The other was named Eliezer. That's because Moses had said, "My father's God helped me. He saved me from Pharaoh's sword."

⁵Moses' father-in-law Jethro came to Moses in the desert. Moses' sons and wife came with Jethro. Moses was camped near the mountain of God. ⁶Jethro had sent a message to him. It said, "I, your father-in-law Jethro, am coming to you. I'm bringing your wife and her two sons."

⁷So Moses went out to meet his father-in-law. Moses bowed down and kissed him. They greeted each other. Then they went into the tent.

⁸Moses told his father-in-law about

everything the LORD had done to Pharaoh and the Egyptians because of how much he loved Israel. He told him about all of their hard times along the way. He told him about how the LORD had saved them.

⁹Jethro was delighted to hear about all of the good things the LORD had done for Israel. He heard about how God had saved them from the power of Egypt. ¹⁰He said, "I praise the LORD. He saved you and your people from the power of Pharaoh and Egypt. ¹¹Now I know that the LORD is greater than all other gods. See what he did to those who looked down on Israel."

¹²Then Moses' father-in-law Jethro brought a burnt offering and other sacrifices to God. Aaron came with all of the elders of Israel. They ate with Moses' father-in-law in the sight of God.

¹³The next day Moses took his seat to serve the people as their judge. They stood around him from morning until evening. ¹⁴His father-in-law saw everything Moses was doing for the people. So he said, "Aren't you trying to do too much for the people? You are the only judge. And all of these people are standing around you from morning until evening."

¹⁵Moses answered him. He said, "The people come to me to find out what God wants them to do. ¹⁶Anytime they don't agree, they come to me. I decide between them. I tell them about God's rules and laws."

¹⁷Moses' father-in-law replied, "What you are doing isn't good. ¹⁸You will just get worn out. And so will these people who come to you. There's too much work for you. You can't possibly handle it by yourself.

¹⁹"Listen to me. I'll give you some advice, and may God be with you. You must speak to God for the people. Take their problems to him. ²⁰Teach them the rules and laws. Show them how to live and what to do.

²¹"But choose men of ability from all of the people. They must have respect for God. You must be able to trust them. They must not try to get money by cheating others. Appoint them as officials over thousands, hundreds, fifties and tens. ²²Let them serve the people as judges. But have them bring every hard case to you. They can decide the easy ones themselves. That will make your load lighter. They will share it with you.

²³"If this is what God wants and if you do it, then you will be able to carry the load. And all of these people will go home satisfied."

²⁴Moses listened to his father-in-law. He did everything Jethro said. ²⁵He chose men of ability from the whole community of Israel. He made them leaders of the people. They became officials over thousands, hundreds, fifties and tens. ²⁶They judged the people at all times. They brought the hard cases to Moses. But they decided the easy ones themselves.

²⁷Moses sent his father-in-law on his way. So Jethro returned to his own country.

ISRAEL COMES TO MOUNT SINAI

19 Exactly three months after the people of Israel left Egypt, they came to the Desert of Sinai. ²After they started out from Rephidim, they entered the Desert of Sinai. They camped there in the desert in front of the mountain.

³Then Moses went up to God. The LORD called out to him from the mountain. He said, "Here is what I want you to say to my people, who came from Jacob's family. Tell the Israelites, ⁴'You have seen for yourselves what I did to Egypt. You saw how I carried you on the wings of eagles and brought you to myself.

⁵"'Now obey me completely. Keep my covenant. If you do, then out of all of the nations you will be my special treasure. The whole earth is mine. ⁶But you will be a kingdom of priests to serve me. You will be my holy nation.' That is what you must tell the Israelites."

⁷So Moses went back. He sent for the elders of the people. He explained to them everything the LORD had commanded him to say. ⁸All of the people answered together. They said, "We will do everything the LORD has said."

So Moses brought their answer back to the LORD.

⁹The Lord spoke to Moses. He said, "I am going to come to you in a thick cloud. The people will hear me speaking with you. They will always put their trust in you." Then Moses told the Lord what the people had said.

¹⁰The Lord said to Moses, "Go to the people. Today and tomorrow set them apart for me. Have them wash their clothes. ¹¹Have the people ready by the third day. On that day I will come down on Mount Sinai. Everyone will see it.

¹²"Put limits for the people around the mountain. Tell them, 'Be careful that you do not go up the mountain. Do not even touch the foot of it. You can be sure that all who touch the mountain will be put to death. ¹³Do not lay a hand on any of them. Kill them with stones or shoot them with arrows. Whether they are people or animals, do not let them live.' They may go up to the mountain only when the ram's horn gives out a long blast."

¹⁴Moses went down the mountain to the people. After he set them apart for the Lord, they washed their clothes. ¹⁵Then he spoke to the people. He said, "Get ready for the third day. Don't make love."

¹⁶On the morning of the third day there was thunder and lightning. A thick cloud covered the mountain. A trumpet gave out a very loud blast. Everyone in the camp trembled with fear.

¹⁷Then Moses led the people out of the camp to meet with God. They stood at the foot of the mountain.

¹⁸Smoke covered Mount Sinai, because the Lord came down on it in fire. The smoke rose up from it like smoke from a furnace. The whole mountain trembled and shook. ¹⁹The sound of the trumpet got louder and louder. Then Moses spoke. And the voice of God answered him.

²⁰The Lord came down to the top of Mount Sinai. He told Moses to come to the top of the mountain. So Moses went up.

²¹The Lord said to him, "Go down and warn the people. They must not force their way through to see me. If they do, many of them will die. ²²The priests approach me when they serve

me. But even they must set themselves apart for me. If they do not, my anger will break out against them."

²³Moses said to the Lord, "The people can't come up Mount Sinai. You yourself warned us. You said, 'Put limits around the mountain. Set it apart as holy.' "

²⁴The Lord replied, "Go down. Bring Aaron up with you. But the priests and the people must not force their way through. They must not come up to me. If they do, my anger will break out against them."

²⁵So Moses went down to the people and told them.

GOD GIVES HIS PEOPLE THE TEN COMMANDMENTS

20 Here are all of the words God spoke. He said,

²"I am the Lord your God. I brought you out of Egypt. That is the land where you were slaves.

³"Do not put any other gods in place of me.

⁴"Do not make statues of gods that look like anything in the sky or on the earth or in the waters. ⁵Do not bow down to them or worship them. I, the Lord your God, am a jealous God. I punish the children for the sin of their parents. I punish the grandchildren and great-grandchildren of those who hate me. ⁶But for all time to come I show love to all those who love me and keep my commandments.

⁷"Do not misuse the name of the Lord your God. The Lord will find guilty anyone who misuses his name.

⁸"Remember to keep the Sabbath day holy. ⁹Do all of your work in six days. ¹⁰But the seventh day is a Sabbath in honor of the Lord your God. Do not do any work on that day. The same command applies to your sons and daughters, your male and female servants, and

your animals. It also applies to any outsiders who live in your cities. ¹¹In six days I made the heavens and the earth. I made the oceans and everything in them. But I rested on the seventh day. So I blessed the Sabbath day and made it holy.

¹² "Honor your father and mother. Then you will live a long time in the land the LORD your God is giving you.

¹³ "Do not commit murder.

¹⁴ "Do not commit adultery.

¹⁵ "Do not steal.

¹⁶ "Do not give false witness against your neighbor.

¹⁷ "Do not long for anything that belongs to your neighbor. Do not long for your neighbor's house, wife, male or female servant, ox or donkey."

¹⁸The people saw the thunder and lightning. They heard the trumpet. They saw the mountain covered with smoke. They trembled with fear and stayed a long way off.

¹⁹They said to Moses, "Speak to us yourself. Then we'll listen. But don't let God speak to us. If he does, we'll die."

²⁰Moses said to the people, "Don't be afraid. God has come to put you to the test. He wants you to have respect for him. That will keep you from sinning."

²¹Moses approached the thick darkness where God was. But the people remained a long way off.

WORSHIPING THE LORD

²²Then the LORD said to Moses, "Here is what you must tell the people of Israel. Say to them, 'You have seen for yourselves what I said to you from heaven. ²³Do not put any other gods in place of me. Do not make silver or gold statues of them for yourselves.

²⁴ " 'Make an altar out of dirt for me. Sacrifice your burnt offerings and friendship offerings on it. Sacrifice your sheep, goats and cattle on it. I will come to you and bless you everywhere I cause my name to be honored.

²⁵ " 'If you make an altar out of stones in honor of me, do not build it with blocks of stone. You will make it "unclean" if you use a tool on it.

 **Is it wrong to put my fingers in my ears so I can't hear my parents?**

Some children think that they do not have to do what their parents tell them if they cannot hear them. But God tells us to *honor* our parents, not just obey them. That means treating them with respect. It means we look at them when they talk to us and we listen carefully to what they say. It means we do *not* plug our ears or ignore them. And it means having a good attitude and not talking back. God gives us parents to protect us and give us what we need. It will be hard for them to do that if we do not listen to them.

checkout
Exodus 20:12

Related verses: Deuteronomy 5:16; Luke 6:31

26" 'Do not walk up steps to my altar. If you do, someone might see your naked body under your robes.'

21

"Here are the laws you must explain to the people of Israel.

SET YOUR HEBREW SERVANTS FREE

2"Suppose you buy a Hebrew servant. He must serve you for six years. But in the seventh year, you must set him free. He does not have to pay anything.

3"If he does not have a wife when he comes, he must go free alone. But if he has a wife when he comes, she must go with him. 4Suppose his master gives him a wife. And suppose she has sons or daughters by him. Then only the man will go free. The woman and her children will belong to her master.

5"But suppose the servant says, 'I love my master and my wife and children. I don't want to go free.' 6Then his master must take him to the judges. He must be taken to the door or doorpost of his master's house. His master must poke a hole through his ear lobe into the doorpost. Then he will become his servant for life.

7"Suppose a man sells his daughter as a servant. Then she can't go free as male servants do.

8"But what if the master who has chosen her does not like her? Then he must let the man buy her back. He has no right to sell her to strangers. He has broken his promise to her.

9"What if he chooses her to get married to his son? Then he must grant her the rights of a daughter.

10"What if he marries another woman? He must still give the first one her food and clothes and make love to her. 11If he does not provide her with those three things, she can go free. She does not have to pay anything.

LAWS ABOUT HARMING OTHERS

12"You can be sure that if anyone hits and kills someone else, he will be put to death. 13Suppose he did not do it on purpose. Suppose I let it happen. Then he can escape to a place I will choose. 14But suppose he kills someone on

KIDS' QUESTiON

Why is it wrong to steal things?

Stealing is wrong because it goes against God's nature. God is honest, true and loving toward others. That is why he tells us to be honest, true and loving toward others. God also wants us to trust him to give us what we need. People who steal show that they do not trust God. He will provide what we need. When we steal, we miss out on God's care, get a bad reputation and make other people feel like stealing from us. God really has our best interests in mind when he tells us not to steal.

checkout

Exodus 20:15

Related verses:
Ephesians 4:28;
James 4:2

purpose. Then take him away from my altar and put him to death.

¹⁵"If anyone attacks his father or mother, he will be put to death.

¹⁶"If anyone kidnaps and sells another person, he will be put to death. If he still has the person with him when he is caught, he will be put to death.

¹⁷"If anyone calls down a curse on his father or mother, he will be put to death.

¹⁸"Suppose two men get into a fight and argue with each other. One hits the other with a stone or his fist. He does not die but has to stay in bed. ¹⁹And later he gets up and walks around outside with his walking stick. Then the man who hit him will not be held accountable. But he must pay the one who was hurt for the time he spent in bed. He must be sure that the person is completely healed.

²⁰"Suppose a man beats his male or female slave to death with a club. Then he must be punished. ²¹But he will not be punished if the slave gets up after a day or two. After all, the slave is his property.

²²"Suppose some men are fighting and one of them hits a pregnant woman. And suppose she has her baby early but is not badly hurt. Then the man who hurt her must pay a fine. He must pay what the woman's husband asks for and the court allows.

²³"But if someone is badly hurt, a life must be taken for a life. ²⁴An eye must be put out for an eye. A tooth must be knocked out for a tooth. A hand must be cut off for a hand and a foot for a foot. ²⁵A burn must be given for a burn, a wound for a wound, and a bruise for a bruise.

²⁶"Suppose a man hits his male or female servant in the eye and destroys it. Then he must let the servant go free to pay for the eye.

²⁷"Suppose he knocks out the tooth of a male or female servant. Then he must let the servant go free to pay for the tooth.

²⁸"Suppose a bull kills a man or woman with its horns. Then you must kill the bull by throwing stones at it. Its meat must not be eaten. The owner of the bull will not be held accountable. ²⁹But suppose the bull has had the

habit of attacking people. And suppose the owner has been warned but has not kept it fenced in. Then if it kills a man or woman, you must kill it with stones. The owner must also be put to death.

³⁰"But suppose payment is required of him instead. Then he can save his life by paying what is required.

³¹"The same law applies if the bull wounds a son or daughter with its horns.

³²"Suppose the bull wounds a male or female slave. Then the owner must pay the slave's master 12 ounces of silver. You must kill the bull with stones.

³³"Suppose a man uncovers a pit or digs one and does not cover it. And suppose an ox or donkey falls into it. ³⁴Then the owner of the pit must pay the animal's owner for the loss. The dead animal will belong to the owner of the pit.

³⁵"Suppose a man's bull wounds a neighbor's bull and it dies. Then they must sell the live one. And they must share the money and the dead animal equally.

³⁶"But suppose people knew that the bull had the habit of attacking. And suppose the owner did not keep it fenced in. Then he must give another animal to pay for the dead animal. The dead animal will belong to him.

LAWS ABOUT KEEPING PROPERTY SAFE

22 "Suppose a man steals an ox or a sheep. And suppose he kills it or sells it. Then he must pay back five head of cattle for the ox. Or he must pay back four sheep or goats for the sheep.

²"Suppose you catch a thief breaking into your house. And suppose you hit the thief and kill him. Then you are not guilty of murder. ³But suppose it happens after the sun has come up. Then you are guilty of murder.

"A thief must pay for what he has stolen. But suppose he does not have anything. Then he must be sold to pay for what he has stolen.

⁴"What if the stolen ox, donkey or sheep is found alive with him? Then

the thief must pay back twice as much as he stole.

⁵"Suppose a man lets his livestock eat grass in someone else's field or vineyard. Then he must pay that person back from the best crops of his own field or vineyard.

⁶"Suppose a fire breaks out and spreads into bushes. It burns grain that has been cut and stacked. Or it burns grain that is still growing. Or it burns the whole field. Then the one who started the fire must pay for the loss.

⁷"Suppose a man gives his neighbor silver or other things to keep safe. And suppose they are stolen from the neighbor's house. If the thief is caught, he must pay back twice as much as he stole.

⁸"But suppose the thief is not found. Then the neighbor must go to the judges. They will decide whether the neighbor has stolen the other person's property.

⁹"Suppose you have an ox, donkey, sheep or clothing that does not belong to you. Or you have other property that was lost by someone else. And suppose someone says, 'That belongs to me.' Then both people must bring their case to the judges. The one the judges decide is guilty must pay back twice as much to the other person.

¹⁰"Suppose a man asks his neighbor to take care of a donkey, ox, sheep or any other animal. And suppose the animal dies or gets hurt. Or suppose it is stolen while no one is looking. ¹¹Then the problem will be settled by taking an oath and promising the LORD to tell the truth.

"Suppose the neighbor takes an oath and says, 'I didn't steal your property.' Then the owner must accept what the neighbor says. No payment is required.

¹²"But suppose the animal really was stolen. Then the neighbor must pay the owner back.

¹³"Or suppose it was torn to pieces by a wild animal. Then the neighbor must bring in what is left as proof. No payment is required.

¹⁴"Suppose a man borrows an animal from his neighbor. And it gets hurt or dies while the owner is not there. Then the man must pay for it.

¹⁵"But suppose the owner is with the animal. Then the man will not have to pay. If he hired the animal, the money he paid to hire it covers the loss.

LAWS ABOUT SOCIAL PROBLEMS

¹⁶"Suppose a man meets a virgin who is not engaged. And he talks her into having sex with him. Then he must pay her father the price for a bride. And he must get married to her.

¹⁷"But suppose her father absolutely refuses to give her to him. Then he must still pay the price for getting married to a virgin.

¹⁸"Do not let a woman who does evil magic stay alive. Put her to death.

¹⁹"Anyone who has sex with an animal must be put to death.

²⁰"Anyone who sacrifices to any god other than me must be destroyed.

²¹"Do not treat outsiders badly. Do not beat them down. Remember, you were outsiders in Egypt.

²²"Do not take advantage of widows. Do not take advantage of children whose fathers have died.

²³"If you do, they might cry out to me. Then I will certainly hear them. ²⁴And I will get angry. I will kill you with a sword. Your wives will become widows. Your children's fathers will die.

²⁵"Suppose you lend money to one of my people among you who is in need. Then do not be like those who lend money and charge interest. Do not charge any interest.

²⁶"Suppose your neighbor owes you money and gives you a coat as a promise to pay it back. Then return it to him by sunset. ²⁷That coat is the only thing he owns to wear or sleep in. When he cries out to me, I will listen, because I am loving and kind.

²⁸"Do not speak evil things against me. Do not call down a curse on the ruler of your people.

²⁹"Do not hold back your grain offerings or wine offerings.

"You must give me the oldest of your sons. ³⁰Do the same with your cattle and sheep. Let them stay with their mothers for seven days. But give them to me on the eighth day.

³¹"I want you to be my holy people. So do not eat the meat of any animal that has been torn by wild animals. Throw it to the dogs.

LAWS ABOUT MERCY AND FAIRNESS

23 "Do not spread reports that are false. Do not help an evil person by telling lies in court.

²"Do not follow the crowd when they do what is wrong. When you are a witness in court, do not turn what is right into wrong. Do not go along with the crowd. ³Do not show favor to a poor person in court.

⁴"Suppose you come across your enemy's ox or donkey wandering away. Then be sure to take it back to him.

⁵"Suppose you see that the donkey of someone who hates you has fallen down under its load. Then do not leave it there. Be sure you help him with it.

⁶"Be fair to your poor people in their court cases. ⁷Do not have anything to do with a charge that is false. Do not put to death those who are not guilty of doing anything wrong. I will not let those who are guilty go free.

⁸"Do not take money from people who want special favors. It makes you blind to the truth. It twists the words of godly people.

⁹"Do not beat an outsider down. You yourselves know how it feels to be outsiders. Remember, you were outsiders in Egypt.

LAWS ABOUT SABBATHS

¹⁰"For six years plant your fields and gather your crops. ¹¹But during the seventh year do not plow your land or use it. Then the poor people who are among you can get food from it. The wild animals can eat what is left over. Do the same thing with your vineyards and your groves of olive trees.

¹²"Do all of your work in six days. But do not do any work on the seventh day. Then your oxen and donkeys can rest. The slaves who are born in your house can be renewed. And so can the outsiders.

¹³"Be careful to do everything I have

KIDS' QUESTion
Why is it wrong to do something if all the other kids do it?

If something is wrong, it is wrong no matter how many people do it. Suppose a group of your friends started throwing stones at windows in the neighborhood. Would it be OK just because everyone did it? Of course not! It would be wrong whether *one* person did it or *everyone in school* did it. You can be sure that the police and the homeowners would say it was wrong. You should do what is right even if you are the only one doing it. That is what God wants. If you are hanging around with kids who want to do bad things, find some other kids to hang around with. Get away from kids who are always wanting you to do wrong.

checkout
Exodus 23:2

PRIVATE PROPERTY
NO
SKATE BOARDING

Related verses:
Psalm 1:1–3;
Proverbs 13:20

said to you. Do not use the names of other gods. Do not even let them be heard on your lips.

LAWS ABOUT CELEBRATING THE MAIN FEASTS

[14]"Three times a year you must celebrate a feast in my honor.

[15]"Celebrate the Feast of Unleavened Bread. Eat bread that is made without yeast for seven days, just as I commanded you. Do it at the appointed time in the month of Abib. You came out of Egypt in that month.

"You must not come to worship me with your hands empty.

[16]"Celebrate the Feast of Weeks. Bring the first share of your crops from your field.

"Celebrate the Feast of Booths. Hold it in the fall when you gather in your crops from the field.

[17]"Three times a year all of your men must come to worship me. I am your LORD and King.

[18]"Do not include anything that is made with yeast when you offer me the blood of a sacrifice.

"Suppose the fat from sacrifices is left over from my feasts. Then do not keep it until morning.

[19]"Bring the best of the first share of your crops to my house. I am the LORD your God.

"Do not cook a young goat in its mother's milk.

GOD'S ANGEL WILL PREPARE THE WAY

[20]"I am sending an angel ahead of you. He will guard you along the way. He will bring you to the place I have prepared. [21]Pay attention to him. Listen to what he says. Do not refuse to obey him. He will not forgive you if you turn against him. My very Name is in him. [22]Listen carefully to what he says. Do everything I say. Then I will be an enemy to your enemies. I will fight against those who fight against you.

[23]"My angel will go ahead of you. He will bring you into the land of the Amorites, Hittites, Perizzites, Canaanites, Hivites and Jebusites. I will wipe them out.

[24]"Do not do what they do. Do not bow down to their gods or worship them. You must destroy the statues of

Is it wrong to keep money that you find on the street?

An honest person always tries to return things to their rightful owners, even when no one is watching. An honest person who found a wallet or a large amount of money on the sidewalk would try to get it back to the owner. Sometimes it is impossible to find the owner. For example, you would probably never find the rightful owner of a nickel in the street or a dollar blowing across a field. Just remember that a *person* lost that money. You should do for them what you would want them to do for you. Do not make excuses for keeping what does not belong to you. Try to find the owner if you can.

Related verses:
Matthew 22:37–40

checkout
Exodus 23:4,5

their gods. You must break their sacred stones to pieces.

²⁵"I am the LORD your God. Worship me. Then I will bless your food and water. I will take away sickness from among you. ²⁶In your land no woman will give birth to a dead baby. Every woman will be able to have children. I will give you a long life.

²⁷"I will send my terror ahead of you. I will throw every nation you meet into a panic. I will make all of your enemies turn their backs and run away. ²⁸I will send hornets ahead of you. They will drive the Hivites, Canaanites and Hittites out of your way.

²⁹"But I will not drive them out in just one year. If I did, the land would be deserted. There would be too many wild animals for you. ³⁰I will drive them out ahead of you little by little. I will do it until your numbers have increased enough for you to take control of the land.

³¹"I will make your borders secure from the Red Sea to the Mediterranean Sea. They will go from the desert to the Euphrates River.

"I will hand over to you the people who live in the land. You will drive them out to make room for you. ³²Do not make a covenant with them or with their gods. ³³Do not let them live in your land. If you do, they will cause you to sin against me. If you worship their gods, that will certainly be a trap for you."

THE BLOOD OF THE COVENANT

24 The LORD said to Moses, "You and Aaron, Nadab and Abihu, and 70 of the elders of Israel must come up to me. Do not come close when you worship. ²Only Moses can come close to me. The others must not come near. And the people may not go up with him."

³Moses went and told the people all of the LORD's words and laws. They answered with one voice. They said, "We will do everything the LORD has told us to do." ⁴Then Moses wrote down everything the LORD had said.

Moses got up early the next morning. He built an altar at the foot of the mountain. He set up 12 stone pillars. They stood for the 12 tribes of Israel.

⁵Then he sent young Israelite men to offer burnt offerings. They also sacrificed young bulls as friendship offerings to the LORD. ⁶Moses took half of the blood and put it in bowls. He sprinkled the other half on the altar. ⁷Then he took the Scroll of the Covenant and read it to the people.

They answered, "We will do everything the LORD has told us to do. We will obey him."

⁸Then Moses took the blood and sprinkled it on the people. He said, "This is the blood that puts the covenant into effect. The LORD has made this covenant with you in keeping with all of these words."

⁹Moses and Aaron, Nadab and Abihu, and the 70 elders of Israel went up. ¹⁰They saw the God of Israel. Under his feet was something like a street made out of sapphire. It was as clear as the sky itself. ¹¹But God didn't raise his hand against those leaders of the people of Israel. They saw God. And they ate and drank.

¹²The LORD said to Moses, "Come up to me on the mountain. Stay here. I will give you the stone tablets. They contain the law and commands I have written to teach the people."

¹³Then Moses and Joshua, his helper, started out. Moses went up on the mountain of God. ¹⁴He said to the elders, "Wait for us here until we come back to you. Aaron and Hur are with you. Anyone who has a problem can go to them."

¹⁵Moses went up on the mountain. Then the cloud covered it. ¹⁶The glory of the LORD settled on Mount Sinai. The cloud covered the mountain for six days.

On the seventh day the LORD called out to Moses from inside the cloud. ¹⁷The people of Israel saw the glory of the LORD. It looked like a fire burning on top of the mountain. ¹⁸Moses entered the cloud as he went on up the mountain. He stayed on the mountain for 40 days and 40 nights.

OFFERINGS FOR THE HOLY TENT

25 The LORD said to Moses, ²"Tell the people of Israel to bring me an offering.

You must receive the offering for me from all whose hearts move them to give.

³"Here are the offerings you must receive from them.

"gold, silver and bronze
⁴blue, purple and bright red yarn and fine linen
goat hair
⁵ram skins that are dyed red
the hides of sea cows
acacia wood
⁶olive oil for the lights
spices for the anointing oil and for the sweet-smelling incense
⁷onyx stones and other jewels for the linen apron and chest cloth

⁸"Have them make a sacred tent for me. I will live among them. ⁹Make the holy tent and everything that belongs to it. Make them exactly like the pattern I will show you.

THE ARK OF THE COVENANT

¹⁰"Have them make a chest out of acacia wood. Make it three feet nine inches long and two feet three inches wide and high. ¹¹Cover it inside and outside with pure gold. Put a strip of gold around it.

¹²"Make four gold rings for it. Join them to its four bottom corners. Put two rings on one side and two rings on the other.

¹³"Then make poles out of acacia wood. Cover them with gold. ¹⁴Put the poles through the rings on the sides of the chest to carry it. ¹⁵The poles must remain in the rings of the chest. Do not remove them. ¹⁶I will give you the tablets of the covenant. When I do, put them into the chest.

¹⁷"Make its cover out of pure gold. The cover is the place where sin will be paid for. Make it three feet nine inches long and two feet three inches wide.

¹⁸"Make two cherubim out of hammered gold at the ends of the cover. ¹⁹Put one cherub on each end of it. Make the cherubim as part of the cover itself. ²⁰The cherubim must have their wings spread up over the cover. The cherubim must face each other and look toward the cover.

²¹"Place the cover on top of the chest. I will give you the tablets of the covenant. Put them into the chest. ²²"The chest is the ark where the tablets of the covenant are kept. I will meet with you above the cover between the two cherubim that are over the ark. There I will give you all of my commands for the people of Israel.

THE TABLE FOR THE HOLY BREAD

²³"Make a table out of acacia wood. Make it three feet long, one foot six inches wide and two feet three inches high. ²⁴Cover it with pure gold. Put a strip of gold around it. ²⁵Also make a rim around it that is three inches wide. Put a strip of gold around the rim.

²⁶"Make four gold rings for the table. Join them to the four corners, where the four legs are. ²⁷The rings must be close to the rim. They must hold the poles that will be used to carry the table.

²⁸"Make the poles out of acacia wood. Cover them with gold. Use them to carry the table.

²⁹"Make its plates and dishes out of pure gold. Also make its pitchers and bowls out of pure gold. Use the pitchers and bowls to pour out drink offerings.

³⁰"Put the holy bread on the table. It must be near my holy throne on the ark of the covenant at all times.

THE GOLD LAMPSTAND

³¹"Make a lampstand out of pure gold. Hammer out its base and stem. Its buds, blooms and cups must branch out from it.

³²"Six branches must come out from the sides of the lampstand. Make three on one side and three on the other. ³³On one branch make three cups that are shaped like almond flowers with buds and blooms. Then put three on the next branch. Do the same with all six branches that come out from the lampstand.

³⁴"On the lampstand there must be four cups that are shaped like almond flowers with buds and blooms. ³⁵One bud must be under the first pair of branches that come out from the lampstand. Put a second bud under

the second pair. And put a third bud under the third pair. Make a total of six branches. [36]The buds and branches must come out from the lampstand.

"The whole lampstand must be one piece that is hammered out of pure gold. [37]Then make its seven lamps. Set them up on it so that they light the space in front of it. [38]The trays and wick cutters must be made out of pure gold. [39]Use 75 pounds of pure gold to make the lampstand and everything that is used with it.

[40]"Be sure to make everything just like the pattern I showed you on the mountain.

THE HOLY TENT

26 "Make ten curtains out of finely twisted linen for the holy tent. Make them with blue, purple and bright red yarn. Have a skilled worker sew cherubim into the pattern. [2]Make all of the curtains the same size. They must be 42 feet long and six feet wide.

[3]"Join five of the curtains together. Do the same thing with the other five. [4]Make loops out of blue strips of cloth along the edge of the end curtain in one set. Do the same thing with the end curtain in the other set. [5]Make 50 loops on the end curtain of the one set. Do the same thing on the end curtain of the other set. Put the loops across from each other. [6]Make 50 gold hooks. Use them to join the curtains together so that the holy tent is all one piece.

[7]"Make a total of 11 curtains out of goat hair to put over the holy tent. [8]Make all 11 curtains the same size. They must be 45 feet long and six feet wide.

[9]"Join five of the curtains together into one set. Do the same thing with the other six. Fold the sixth curtain in half at the front of the tent. [10]Make 50 loops along the edge of the end curtain in the one set. Do the same thing with the other set. [11]Then make 50 bronze hooks. Put them in the loops to join the tent together all in one piece.

[12]"Let the extra half curtain hang down at the rear of the holy tent. [13]The tent curtains will be one foot six inches longer on both sides. What is left over will hang over the sides of the holy tent and cover it.

[14]"Make a covering for the tent. Make it out of ram skins that are dyed red. Put a covering of the hides of sea cows over that.

[15]"Make frames out of acacia wood for the holy tent. [16]Make each frame 15 feet long and two feet three inches wide. [17]Add two small wooden pins to each frame. Make the pins stick out so that they are even with each other. Make all of the frames for the holy tent in the same way.

[18]"Make 20 frames for the south side of the holy tent. [19]And make 40 silver bases to go under them. Make two bases for each frame. Put one under each pin that sticks out.

[20]"For the north side of the holy tent make 20 frames [21]and 40 silver bases. Put two bases under each frame.

[22]"Make six frames for the west end of the holy tent. [23]Make two frames for the corners at the far end. [24]At those two corners the frames must be double from top to bottom. They must be fitted into a single ring. Make both of them the same. [25]There will be eight frames and 16 silver bases. There will be two bases under each frame.

[26]"Also make crossbars out of acacia wood. Make five for the frames on one side of the holy tent. [27]Make five for the frames on the other side. And make five for the frames on the west, at the far end of the holy tent. [28]The center crossbar must reach from end to end at the middle of the frames.

[29]"Cover the frames with gold. Make gold rings to hold the crossbars. Also cover the crossbars with gold.

[30]"Set up the holy tent in keeping with the plan I showed you on the mountain.

[31]"Make a curtain out of blue, purple and bright red yarn and finely twisted linen. Have a skilled worker sew cherubim into the pattern. [32]Hang the curtain with gold hooks on four posts that are made out of acacia wood. Cover the posts with gold. Stand them on four silver bases. [33]Hang the curtain from the hooks.

"Place the ark of the covenant behind the curtain. The curtain will separate the Holy Room from the Most

Holy Room. ³⁴Put the cover on the ark of the covenant in the Most Holy Room. The cover will be the place where sin is paid for.

³⁵"Place the table outside the curtain on the north side of the holy tent. And put the lampstand across from it on the south side.

³⁶"For the entrance to the tent make a curtain out of blue, purple and bright red yarn and finely twisted linen. Have a person who sews skillfully make it. ³⁷Make gold hooks for the curtain. Make five posts out of acacia wood. Cover them with gold. And make five bronze bases for them.

THE ALTAR FOR BURNT OFFERINGS

27 "Build an altar out of acacia wood. It must be four feet six inches high and seven feet six inches square. ²Make a horn stick out from each of its upper four corners. Cover the altar with bronze.

³"Make all of its tools out of bronze. Make its pots to remove the ashes. Make its shovels, sprinkling bowls, meat forks, and pans for carrying ashes.

⁴"Make a bronze grate for the altar. Make a bronze ring for each of the four corners of the grate. ⁵Put the grate halfway up the altar on the inside.

⁶"Make poles out of acacia wood for the altar. Cover them with bronze. ⁷Put the poles through the rings. They will be on two sides of the altar for carrying it.

⁸"Make the altar out of boards. Make it hollow. You must make it just as I showed you on the mountain.

THE COURTYARD

⁹"Make a courtyard for the holy tent. The south side must be 150 feet long. It must have curtains that are made out of finely twisted linen. ¹⁰The curtains must be hung on 20 posts and 20 bronze bases. The posts must have silver hooks and bands on them.

¹¹"The north side must also be 150 feet long. It must have curtains with 20 posts and 20 bronze bases. The posts must have silver hooks and bands on them.

¹²"The west end of the courtyard must be 75 feet wide. It must have curtains with ten posts and ten bases.

¹³"The east end of the courtyard, toward the sunrise, must also be 75 feet wide. ¹⁴On one side of the entrance you must put curtains that are 22 feet six inches long. Hang them on three posts. Each post must have a base. ¹⁵On the other side you must also put curtains that are 22 feet six inches long. Hang them on three posts. Each post must have a base.

¹⁶"For the entrance to the courtyard, provide a curtain that is 30 feet long. Make it out of blue, purple and bright red yarn and finely twisted linen. Have someone who sews skillfully make it. Hang it on four posts. Each post must have a base.

¹⁷"All of the posts that are around the courtyard must have silver bands and hooks. They must also have bronze bases. ¹⁸The courtyard must be 150 feet long and 75 feet wide. It must have curtains that are made out of finely twisted linen. They must be seven feet six inches high. The posts must have bronze bases.

¹⁹"Make all of the other articles used for any purpose in the holy tent out of bronze. That includes all of the tent stakes for the tent and the courtyard.

OIL FOR THE LAMPSTAND

²⁰"Command the people of Israel to bring you clear oil that is made from pressed olives. Use it to keep the lamps burning and giving light. ²¹"Aaron and his sons must keep the lamps burning in the Tent of Meeting. The lamps will be outside the curtain that is in front of the tablets of the covenant. The lamps must be kept burning in my sight from evening until morning. That is a law for the people of Israel that will last for all time to come.

CLOTHES FOR THE PRIESTS

28 "Have your brother Aaron brought to you from among the people of Israel. His sons Nadab, Abihu, Eleazar and Ithamar must also be brought. They will serve me as priests.

²"Make sacred clothes for your

brother Aaron. When he is wearing them, people will honor him. They will have respect for him.

³"Speak to all of the skilled workers. I have given them the skill to do this kind of work. Tell them to make clothes for Aaron. He will wear them when he is set apart to serve me as priest. ⁴They must make a chest cloth, a linen apron, an outer robe, an inner robe, a turban and a belt. They must make sacred clothes for your brother Aaron and his sons. Then they will serve me as priests. ⁵Have them use fine gold wire, and blue, purple and bright red yarn, and fine linen.

THE LINEN APRON

⁶"Make the linen apron out of fine gold wire, and out of blue, purple and bright red yarn, and out of finely twisted linen. Have a skilled worker make it. ⁷It must have two shoulder straps joined to two of its corners.

⁸"Its skillfully made waistband must be like it. The waistband must be part of the apron itself. Make the waistband out of fine gold wire, and out of blue, purple and bright red yarn, and out of finely twisted linen.

⁹"Get two onyx stones. Carve the names of the sons of Israel on them. ¹⁰Arrange them in the order of their birth. Carve six names on one stone and six on the other. ¹¹Carve the names of the sons of Israel on the two stones the way a jewel cutter carves a seal.

"Then put the stones in fancy gold settings. ¹²Connect them to the shoulder straps of the linen apron. The stones will stand for the sons of Israel. Aaron must carry the names on his shoulders as a reminder while he is serving me. ¹³Make fancy gold settings. ¹⁴Make two braided chains out of pure gold. Make them like ropes. Join the chains to the settings.

THE CHEST CLOTH

¹⁵"Make a chest cloth that will be used for making decisions. Have a skilled worker make it. Make it like the linen apron. Use fine gold wire, and blue, purple and bright red yarn, and finely twisted linen. ¹⁶Make it nine inches square. Fold it in half.

¹⁷"Put four rows of valuable jewels on it. Put a ruby, a topaz and a beryl in the first row. ¹⁸Put a turquoise, a sapphire and an emerald in the second row. ¹⁹Put a jacinth, an agate and an amethyst in the third row. ²⁰And put a chrysolite, an onyx and a jasper in the fourth row. Put them in fancy gold settings.

²¹"Use a total of 12 stones. Use one for each of the names of the sons of Israel. Each stone must be carved like a seal with the name of one of the 12 tribes.

²²"Make braided chains out of pure gold for the chest cloth. Make them like ropes. ²³Make two gold rings for the chest cloth. Connect them to two corners of it. ²⁴Join the two gold chains to the rings at the corners of the chest cloth. ²⁵Join the other ends of the chains to the two settings. Join them to the shoulder straps on the front of the linen apron.

²⁶"Make two gold rings. Connect them to the other two corners of the chest cloth. Put them on the inside edge next to the apron. ²⁷Make two more gold rings. Connect them to the bottom of the shoulder straps on the front of the apron. Put them close to the seam. Put them right above the waistband of the apron. ²⁸The rings of the chest cloth must be tied to the rings of the apron. Tie them to the waistband with blue cord. Then the chest cloth will not swing out from the linen apron.

²⁹"When Aaron enters the Holy Room, he will carry the names of the sons of Israel over his heart. Their names will be on the chest cloth of decision. They will be a continuing reminder while he is serving me.

³⁰"Also put the Urim and Thummim into the chest cloth. Then they will be over Aaron's heart when he comes to serve me. In that way, Aaron will always have what he needs to make decisions for the people of Israel. He will carry the Urim and Thummim over his heart while he is serving me.

MORE CLOTHES FOR THE PRIESTS

³¹"Make the outer robe of the linen apron completely from blue cloth. ³²In

the center of the robe, make an opening for the head of the priest. Make an edge like a collar around the opening. Then it will not tear.

³³"Make pomegranates out of blue, purple and bright red yarn. Sew them around the hem of the robe. Sew gold bells between them. ³⁴Sew a gold bell between every two pomegranates all around the hem of the robe.

³⁵"Aaron must wear the robe when he serves. The bells will jingle when he enters the Holy Room while he is serving me. And they will jingle when he goes out. Then he will not die.

³⁶"Make a plate out of pure gold. Carve words on it as if it were a seal. Carve the words SET APART FOR THE LORD. ³⁷Tie the plate to the front of the turban with a blue cord.

³⁸"Aaron must wear it on his forehead all the time. He will be held accountable for all of the sacred gifts the Israelites set apart. Then I will accept the gifts.

³⁹"Make the inner robe out of fine linen. And make the turban out of fine linen. Have the belt made by a person who sews skillfully.

⁴⁰"Make inner robes, belts and headbands for Aaron's sons. When they are wearing them, people will honor them. They will also have respect for them.

⁴¹"Put all of the clothes on your brother Aaron and his sons. Then pour olive oil on them and prepare them to serve me. Set them apart to serve me as priests.

⁴²"Make linen underwear that reaches from the waist to the thigh. ⁴³Aaron and the priests who are in his family line must wear it when they enter the Tent of Meeting. They must wear it when they approach the altar to serve in the Holy Room. Then they will not be found guilty and die.

"For all time to come, that will be a law for Aaron and the priests who are in his family line.

DIRECTIONS FOR SETTING THE PRIESTS APART

29 "Here is what you must do to set Aaron and his sons apart to serve me as priests.

"Get a young bull and two rams. They must not have any flaws. ²Get fine wheat flour that does not have yeast in it. Use the flour to make bread, flat cakes that are mixed with olive oil, and wafers that are spread with oil. ³Put everything in a basket. Offer them along with the bull and the two rams.

⁴"Then bring Aaron and his sons to the entrance to the Tent of Meeting. Wash them with water.

⁵"Take the inner robe, the outer robe of the linen apron, the apron itself and the chest cloth. Dress Aaron in them. Take the skillfully made waistband and tie the apron on him with it. ⁶Put the turban on his head. Connect the sacred crown to the turban. ⁷Take the anointing oil and pour it on his head.

⁸"Bring his sons and dress them in their inner robes. ⁹Put headbands on them. Tie belts on Aaron and his sons. The work of the priests belongs to them. This is my law that will last for all time to come.

"And that is how you must prepare Aaron and his sons to serve me.

¹⁰"Bring the bull to the front of the Tent of Meeting. Have Aaron and his sons place their hands on its head. ¹¹Kill it in my sight at the entrance to the Tent of Meeting.

¹²"Dip your finger into some of the bull's blood. Put it on the horns that stick out from the upper four corners of the altar. Pour the rest of it out at the base of the altar.

¹³"Then take all of the fat around the inside parts. Take the covering of the liver. Take both kidneys with the fat on them. And burn all of it on the altar.

¹⁴"But burn the bull's meat, hide and guts outside the camp. It is a sin offering.

¹⁵"Get one of the rams. Have Aaron and his sons place their hands on its head. ¹⁶Kill it. Take the blood and sprinkle it against every side of the altar.

¹⁷"Cut the ram into pieces. Wash the inside parts and the legs. Put them with the head and the other pieces. ¹⁸Then burn the whole ram on the altar. It is a burnt offering to me. It has a pleasant smell. It is an offering that is made to me with fire.

¹⁹"Get the other ram. Have Aaron

and his sons place their hands on its head. ²⁰Kill it. Put some of its blood on the right ear lobes of Aaron and his sons. Put some on the thumbs of their right hands. Also put some on the big toes of their right feet. Then sprinkle blood against every side of the altar.

²¹"Get some of the blood from the altar. Also get some of the anointing oil. Sprinkle both of them on Aaron and his clothes and his sons and their clothes. Then he and his sons and their clothes will be set apart to serve me.

²²"Here is what you must take from the second ram. Take the fat, the fat tail, the fat around the inside parts, the covering of the liver, both kidneys with the fat on them, and the right thigh. It is the ram you must use when you prepare the priests to serve me. ²³Get a loaf, a flat cake that is made with oil, and a wafer. Take them from the basket of bread that was made without yeast. It is the one that is in front of me.

²⁴"Put everything in the hands of Aaron and his sons. Tell them to lift it up and wave it in front of me as a wave offering. ²⁵Then take it from their hands. Burn it on the altar along with the burnt offering. It gives a smell that is pleasant to me. It is an offering that is made to me with fire.

²⁶"Get the breast of the ram that is used when you prepare Aaron to serve me. Wave it in front of me as a wave offering. It will be your share of the meat.

²⁷"Here are the parts of the second ram that belong to Aaron and his sons. You must set apart the breast that was waved and the thigh that was offered. ²⁸It will always be the regular share from the people of Israel for Aaron and his sons. The people must give it to me from their friendship offerings.

²⁹"Aaron's sacred clothes will belong to his sons who will come after him. Then they can wear them when you anoint them and prepare them to serve me. ³⁰The son who comes after him as priest must wear them seven days. He will come and serve in the Holy Room in the Tent of Meeting.

³¹"Get the ram that is sacrificed when you prepare Aaron and his sons to serve me. Cook the meat in a sacred place.

³²"Aaron and his sons must eat the ram's meat. And they must eat the bread that is in the basket. They must eat all of it at the entrance to the Tent of Meeting. ³³Those are the offerings to pay for their sins. They must eat them. The offerings must be made when Aaron and his sons are set apart and prepared to serve me. No one else can eat them. They are sacred.

³⁴"And if any parts of the ram or bread that are sacrificed when you prepare Aaron and his sons to serve me are left until morning, burn them up. They must not be eaten. They are sacred.

³⁵"Do everything I have commanded you to do for Aaron and his sons. Take seven days when you prepare them to serve me. ³⁶Sacrifice a bull each day. It is a sin offering to pay for their sins.

"Make the altar pure. Pour olive oil on it to set it apart. ³⁷Take seven days to make the altar pure. Set it apart. Then the altar will be a very holy place. Anything that touches it will be holy.

³⁸"Every day offer on the altar two lambs that are a year old. ³⁹Offer one in the morning. Offer the other one when the sun goes down. ⁴⁰Along with the first lamb, offer eight cups of fine flour. Mix it with a quart of oil that is made from pressed olives. Along with that, offer a quart of wine as a drink offering.

⁴¹"Sacrifice the other lamb when the sun goes down. Sacrifice it along with the same grain offering and its drink offering as you do in the morning. It has a pleasant smell. It is an offering that is made to me with fire.

⁴²"For all time to come, the burnt offering must be sacrificed regularly. Sacrifice it at the entrance to the Tent of Meeting in my sight. There I will meet you and speak to you. ⁴³There I will also meet with the people of Israel. My glory will make the place holy.

⁴⁴"So I will set the Tent of Meeting and the altar apart. And I will set Aaron and his sons apart to serve me as priests.

⁴⁵"Then I will live among the people of Israel. And I will be their God. ⁴⁶They will know that I am the LORD their God. They will know that I

brought them out of Egypt so I could live among them. I am the LORD their God.

THE ALTAR FOR
BURNING INCENSE

30 "Make an altar for burning incense. Make it out of acacia wood. ²It must be one foot six inches square and three feet high. Make a horn stick out from each of its upper four corners. ³Cover the top, sides and horns with pure gold. Put a strip of gold around it.

⁴"Make two gold rings for the altar below the strip. Put the rings across from each other. They will hold the poles that are used to carry it. ⁵Make the poles out of acacia wood. Cover them with gold.

⁶"Put the altar in front of the curtain that hangs in front of the ark where the tablets of the covenant are kept. The ark will have a cover. It will be the place where sin is paid for. There I will meet with you.

⁷"Aaron must burn sweet-smelling incense on the altar. He must do it every morning when he takes care of the lamps. ⁸He must burn incense again when he lights the lamps at sunset. Incense must be burned regularly to me. Do it for all time to come.

⁹"Do not burn any other incense on the altar. Do not use the altar for burnt offerings or grain offerings. Do not pour drink offerings on it.

¹⁰"Once a year Aaron must put the blood of a sin offering on its horns to make it pure. He must do it on the day Israel's sin is paid for. Do it for all time to come. The altar is a very holy place to me."

MONEY TO PAY FOR THE
PEOPLE'S LIVES

¹¹Then the LORD spoke to Moses. He said, ¹²"When you make a list of the people of Israel and count them, they must pay me for their lives at the time they are counted. Then a plague will not come on them when you count them.

¹³"Each one who is counted must pay a fifth of an ounce of silver. It must be weighed out in keeping with the standard weights that are used in the sacred tent. The payment is an offering to me. ¹⁴Each one who is counted must be 20 years old or more. He must give an offering to me.

¹⁵"When you make the offering, rich people must not give more than a fifth of an ounce of silver. And poor people must not give less. The offering you give to me will pay for your lives.

¹⁶"Receive the money from the people of Israel. Use it for any purpose in the Tent of Meeting. It will remind the people that they are paying me for their lives."

THE LARGE BOWL
FOR WASHING

¹⁷Then the LORD spoke to Moses. He said, ¹⁸"Make a large bronze bowl for washing. Make a bronze stand to put it on. Place the bowl between the Tent of Meeting and the altar. Put water in it.

¹⁹"Aaron and his sons must wash their hands and feet with water from it. ²⁰When they enter the Tent of Meeting, they must wash with water so that they will not die. They will come to the altar to serve me. They will bring an offering that is made to me with fire. ²¹When they do, they must wash their hands and feet so that they will not die. For all time to come, that will be a law for Aaron and the priests who are in his family line."

ANOINTING OIL

²²Then the LORD spoke to Moses. ²³He said, "Get some fine spices. Get 12 pounds eight ounces of liquid myrrh. Get six pounds four ounces of sweet-smelling cinnamon and the same amount of sweet-smelling cane. ²⁴Also get 12 pounds eight ounces of cassia. All of the spices must be weighed out in keeping with the standard weights that are used in the sacred tent. Get four quarts of olive oil.

²⁵"Have a person who makes perfume mix everything into a sacred anointing oil. It will smell sweet.

²⁶"Then anoint the Tent of Meeting and the ark where the tablets of the covenant are kept. ²⁷Anoint the table for the holy bread and all of its articles. Anoint the lampstand and the things that are used with it. Anoint the altar for burning incense. ²⁸Anoint the altar

for burnt offerings and all of its tools. And anoint the large bowl together with its stand. [29]You must set them apart so that they will be very holy. Anything that touches them will be holy.

[30]"Anoint Aaron and his sons. Set them apart so that they can serve me as priests.

[31]"Say to the people of Israel, 'This will be my sacred anointing oil for all time to come. [32]Do not pour it on the bodies of any other men. Do not make any other oil in the same way. It is sacred. So you must think of it as sacred. [33]Anyone who makes perfume in the same way and puts it on someone who is not a priest must be cut off from his people.' "

INCENSE

[34]Then the LORD spoke to Moses. He said, "Get some sweet-smelling spices. Get some gum resin, onycha and galbanum. Also get some pure frankincense. Make sure everything is in equal amounts.

[35]"Have a person who makes perfume mix it all up into a sweet-smelling incense. It must have salt in it. It will be pure and sacred. [36]Grind some of it into powder. Place it in front of the tablets of the covenant in the Tent of Meeting. There I will meet with you. The incense will be very holy to you.

[37]"Do not make any incense for yourselves in the same way. Think of it as holy to me. [38]Anyone who makes incense in the same way to enjoy its sweet smell must be cut off from his people."

BEZALEL AND OHOLIAB

31 Then the LORD spoke to Moses. [2]He said, "I have chosen Bezalel, the son of Uri. Uri is the son of Hur. Bezalel is from the tribe of Judah. [3]I have filled him with the Spirit of God. I have filled him with skill, ability and knowledge in all kinds of crafts. [4]He can make beautiful patterns in gold, silver and bronze. [5]He can cut and set stones. He can work with wood. In fact, he can work in all kinds of crafts.

[6]"I have also appointed Oholiab, the son of Ahisamach, to help him. Oholiab is from the tribe of Dan.

"I have given ability to all of the skilled workers. They can make everything I have commanded you to make. Here is the complete list.

[7]"the Tent of Meeting
    the ark where the tablets of the covenant are kept
    the cover for the ark
[8]the table for the holy bread and its articles
    the pure gold lampstand and everything that is used with it
    the altar for burning incense
[9]the altar for burnt offerings and all of its tools
    the large bowl with its stand
[10]the sacred clothes for Aaron the priest
    the clothes for his sons when they serve as priests
[11]the anointing oil
    the sweet-smelling incense for the Holy Room

"The skilled workers must make them just as I commanded you."

THE SABBATH DAY

[12]Then the LORD spoke to Moses. [13]He said, "Tell the people of Israel, 'You must always keep my Sabbath days. That will be the sign of the covenant I have made between me and you for all time to come. Then you will know that I am the LORD. I make you holy.

[14]" 'Keep the Sabbath day. It is holy to you. Those who misuse it must be put to death. Those who do any work on that day must be cut off from their people. [15]Do your work in six days. But the seventh day is a Sabbath. You must rest on it. It is set apart for me. Those who work on the Sabbath day must be put to death.

[16]" 'The people of Israel must keep the Sabbath. They must celebrate it for all time to come. It will be a covenant that lasts forever. [17]It will be the sign of the covenant I have made between me and the people of Israel forever.

" 'I made the heavens and the earth in six days. But on the seventh day I did not work. I rested.' "

[18]The LORD finished speaking to Moses on Mount Sinai. Then he gave him the two tablets of the covenant.

They were made out of stone. The words on them were written by the finger of God.

ISRAEL WORSHIPS A GOLDEN CALF

32 The people saw that Moses took a long time to come down from the mountain. So they gathered around Aaron. They said to him, "Come. Make us a god that will lead us. This fellow Moses brought us up out of Egypt. But we don't know what has happened to him."

²Aaron answered them, "Take the gold earrings off your wives, your sons and your daughters. Bring the earrings to me."

³So all of the people took off their earrings. They brought them to Aaron. ⁴He took what they gave him and made it into a metal statue of a god. It looked like a calf. He shaped it with a tool.

Then the people said, "Israel, here is your god who brought you up out of Egypt."

⁵When Aaron saw it, he built an altar in front of the calf. He said, "Tomorrow will be a feast day in the LORD's honor."

⁶So the next day the people got up early. They sacrificed burnt offerings and brought friendship offerings. They sat down to eat and drink. Then they got up to dance wildly in front of their god.

⁷The LORD spoke to Moses. He said, "Go down. Your people you brought up out of Egypt have become very sinful. ⁸They have quickly turned away from what I commanded them. They have made themselves a statue of a god that looks like a calf. They have bowed down and sacrificed to it. And they have said, 'Israel, here is your god who brought you up out of Egypt.'

⁹"I have seen those people," the LORD said to Moses. "They are stubborn. ¹⁰Now leave me alone. My anger will burn against them. I will destroy them. Then I will make you into a great nation."

¹¹But Moses asked the LORD his God to show favor to the people. "LORD," he said, "why should your anger burn against your people? You used your great power and mighty hand to bring them out of Egypt. ¹²Why should the Egyptians say, 'He brought them out to hurt them. He wanted to kill them in the mountains. He wanted to wipe them off the face of the earth'? Turn away from your burning anger. Please take pity on your people. Don't destroy them!

¹³"Remember your servants Abraham, Isaac and Israel. You made a promise. You took an oath in your name. You said, 'I will make your children after you as many as the stars in the sky. I will give them all of this land I promised them. It will belong to them forever.' "

¹⁴Then the LORD took pity on his people. He didn't destroy them as he had said he would.

¹⁵Moses turned and went down the mountain. He had the two tablets of the covenant in his hands. Words were written on both sides of the tablets, front and back. ¹⁶The tablets were the work of God. The words had been written by God. They had been carved on the tablets.

¹⁷Joshua heard the noise of the people shouting. So he said to Moses, "It sounds like war in the camp."

¹⁸Moses replied,

"It's not the sound of winning.
    It's not the sound of losing.
    It's the sound of singing that I
        hear."

¹⁹As Moses approached the camp, he saw the calf. He also saw the people dancing. So he burned with anger. He threw the tablets out of his hands. They broke into pieces at the foot of the mountain.

²⁰He took the calf the people had made. He burned it in the fire. Then he ground it into powder. He scattered it on the water. And he made the people of Israel drink it.

²¹He said to Aaron, "What did these people do to you? How did they make you lead them into such terrible sin?"

²²"Please don't be angry," Aaron answered. "You know how these people like to do what is evil. ²³They said to me, 'Make us a god that will lead us. This fellow Moses brought us up out of Egypt. But we don't know what has happened to him.'

²⁴"So I told them, 'Anyone who has any gold jewelry, take it off.' They gave me the gold. I threw it into the fire. And out came this calf!"

²⁵Moses saw that the people were running wild. Aaron had let them get out of control. The people had become a joke to their enemies.

²⁶Moses stood at the entrance to the camp. He said, "Anyone who is on the LORD's side, come to me." All of the Levites joined him.

²⁷Then he spoke to them. He said, "The LORD, the God of Israel, says, 'Each man must put on his sword. Then he must go back and forth through the camp from one end to the other. Each man must kill his brother, friend and neighbor.' " ²⁸The Levites did as Moses commanded. About 3,000 of the people died that day. ²⁹Then Moses said to the Levites, "You have been set apart for the LORD today. You stood against your own sons and brothers. And he has blessed you this day."

³⁰The next day Moses said to the people, "You have committed a terrible sin. But now I will go up to the LORD. Maybe if I pray to him, he will forgive your sin."

³¹So Moses went back to the LORD. He said, "These people have committed a terrible sin. They have made a god out of gold for themselves. ³²Now please forgive their sin. But if you won't, then erase my name from the scroll you have written."

³³The LORD replied to Moses, "I will erase from my scroll only the names of those who have sinned against me. ³⁴Now go. Lead the people to the place I spoke about. My angel will go ahead of you. But when the time comes for me to punish, I will punish them for their sin."

³⁵The LORD struck the people with a plague. That's because of what they did with the calf Aaron had made.

33 Then the LORD spoke to Moses. He said, "Leave this place. You and the people you brought up out of Egypt must leave it. Go up to the land I promised with an oath to give to Abraham, Isaac and Jacob. I said to them, 'I will give it to your children after you.' ²I will send an angel ahead of you. I will drive out the Canaanites, Amorites, Hittites, Perizzites, Hivites and Jebusites. ³"Go up to the land that has plenty of milk and honey. But I will not go with you. You are stubborn. I might destroy you on the way."

⁴When the people heard those painful words, they became sad and began to sob. No one put on any jewelry. ⁵The LORD had said to Moses, "Tell the people of Israel, 'You are stubborn. If I went with you even for a moment, I might destroy you. Now take off your jewelry. Then I will decide what to do with you.' " ⁶So the people took off their jewelry at Mount Horeb.

THE TENT OF MEETING

⁷Moses used to take a tent and set it up far outside the camp. He called it the "tent of meeting." Anyone who wanted to ask the LORD a question would go to the tent of meeting that was outside the camp. ⁸When Moses would go out to the tent, all of the people would get up and stand at the entrances to their tents. They would watch Moses until he entered the tent.

⁹As Moses would go into the tent, the pillar of cloud would come down. It would stay at the entrance while the LORD spoke with Moses. ¹⁰The people would see the pillar of cloud standing at the entrance to the tent. Then all of them would stand and worship at the entrances to their tents.

¹¹The LORD would speak to Moses face to face. It was like a man speaking to his friend. Then Moses would return to the camp.

But Joshua, his young helper, didn't leave the tent. Joshua was the son of Nun.

THE LORD SHOWS MOSES HIS GLORY

¹²Moses said to the LORD, "You have been telling me, 'Lead these people.' But you haven't let me know whom you will send with me. You have said, 'I know your name. I know all about you. And I am pleased with you.' ¹³If you are pleased with me, teach me more about yourself. Then I can know you. And I can continue to please you. Remember that this nation is your people."

[14]The LORD replied, "I will go with you. And I will give you rest."

[15]Then Moses said to him, "If you don't go with us, don't send us up from here. [16]How will anyone know that you are pleased with me and your people? You must go with us. How else will we be different from all of the other people on the face of the earth?"

[17]The LORD said to Moses, "I will do exactly what you have asked. I am pleased with you. And I know your name. I know all about you."

[18]Then Moses said, "Now show me your glory."

[19]The LORD said, "I will make all of my goodness pass in front of you. And I will announce my name, The LORD, in front of you. I will have mercy on whom I have mercy. And I will show love to those I love. [20]But you can't see my face," he said. "No one can see me and stay alive."

[21]The LORD continued, "There is a place near me where you can stand on a rock. [22]When my glory passes by, I will put you in an opening in the rock. I will cover you with my hand until I have passed by. [23]Then I will remove my hand. You will see my back. But my face must not be seen."

THE NEW STONE TABLETS

34 The LORD said to Moses, "Cut out two stone tablets that are just like the first ones. I will write on them the words that were on the first tablets, which you broke.

[2]"Be ready in the morning. Then come up on Mount Sinai. Meet with me there on top of the mountain. [3]No one must come with you. No one must be seen anywhere on the mountain. Not even the flocks and herds must be allowed to eat grass in front of the mountain."

[4]So Moses carved out two stone tablets that were just like the first ones. Early in the morning he went up Mount Sinai. He carried the two tablets in his hands. He did as the LORD had commanded him to do.

[5]Then the LORD came down in the cloud. He stood there with Moses and announced his name, The LORD.

[6]As he passed in front of Moses, he called out. He said, "I am the LORD, the LORD. I am a God who is tender and kind. I am gracious. I am slow to get angry. I am faithful and full of love. [7]I continue to show my love to thousands of people. I forgive those who do

KIDS' QUESTION

What does God look like?

No one knows what God looks like because God is invisible and does not have a body. But we can learn about God and see what God acts like by learning about his Son, Jesus. The Bible tells us a lot about him. We can read about how Jesus lived, how he treated people and what he taught. That's what God is like.

checkout
Exodus 33:20

Related verses:
John 1:18; 6:46

evil. I forgive those who refuse to obey. And I forgive those who sin. But I do not let guilty people go without punishing them. I punish the children, grandchildren and great-grandchildren for the sin of their parents."

8Moses bowed down to the ground at once and worshiped. 9"Lord," he said, "if you are pleased with me, then go with us. Even though these people are stubborn, forgive the evil things we have done. Forgive our sin. And accept us as your people."

10Then the LORD said, "I am making a covenant with you. I will do wonderful things in front of all of your people. I will do miracles that have never been done before in any nation in the whole world. The people you live among will see the things that I, the LORD, will do for you. And they will see how wonderful those things really are.

11"Obey what I command you today. I will drive out the Amorites, Canaanites, Hittites, Perizzites, Hivites and Jebusites to make room for you.

12"Be careful. Do not make a peace treaty with those who live in the land where you are going. They will be a trap to you. 13Tear down their altars. Smash their sacred stones. Cut down the poles they use to worship the goddess Asherah. 14Do not worship any other god. I am a jealous God. In fact, my name is Jealous.

15"Be careful not to make a peace treaty with those who live in the land. They commit sin by offering sacrifices to their gods. They will invite you to eat their sacrifices. 16You will choose some of their daughters as wives for your sons. And those daughters will commit sin by worshiping their gods. Then they will lead your sons to do the same thing.

17"Do not make statues of gods.

18"Celebrate the Feast of Unleavened Bread. For seven days eat bread that is made without yeast, just as I commanded you. Do it at the appointed time in the month of Abib. You came out of Egypt in that month.

19"Every male animal that is born first to its mother belongs to me. That includes your livestock. It includes herds and flocks alike. 20Sacrifice a lamb to buy back every male donkey that is born first to its mother. But if you do not buy the donkey back, break its neck. Buy back every oldest son.

"You must not come to worship me with your hands empty.

21"Do your work in six days. But you must rest on the seventh day. Even when you are plowing your land or gathering your crops, you must rest on the seventh day.

22"Celebrate the Feast of Weeks. Bring the first share of your wheat crop.

"Celebrate the Feast of Booths. Hold it in the fall.

23"Three times a year all of your men must come to worship me. I am your LORD and King, the God of Israel. 24I will drive out nations ahead of you. I will increase your territory. Go up three times a year to worship me. While you are doing that, I will keep others from wanting to take any of your land for themselves. I am the LORD your God.

25"Do not include anything that is made with yeast when you offer me the blood of a sacrifice. You must not keep any of the meat from the sacrifice of the Passover Feast until morning.

26"Bring the best of the first share of your crops to my house. I am the LORD your God.

"Do not cook a young goat in its mother's milk."

27Then the LORD said to Moses, "Write down the words I have spoken. I have made a covenant with you and with Israel in keeping with those words."

28Moses was there with the LORD for 40 days and 40 nights. He didn't eat any food or drink any water. The LORD wrote on the tablets the words of the covenant. Those words are the Ten Commandments.

THE FACE OF MOSES SHINES

29Moses came down from Mount Sinai. He had the two tablets of the covenant in his hands. His face was shining because he had spoken with the LORD. But he didn't realize it. 30Aaron and all of the people of Israel saw Moses. His face was shining. So they were afraid to come near him.

31But Moses called out to them. So

Aaron and all of the leaders of the community came to him. And Moses spoke to them. ³²After that, all of the people came near him. And he gave them all of the commands the LORD had given him on Mount Sinai.

³³Moses finished speaking to them. Then he put a veil over his face. ³⁴But when he would go to speak with the LORD, he would remove the veil. He would keep it off until he came out. Then he would tell the people what the LORD had commanded. ³⁵They would see that his face was shining. So Moses would put the veil back over his face. He would keep it on until he went in again to speak with the LORD.

RULES FOR THE SABBATH DAY

35 Moses gathered the whole community of Israel together. He said to them, "Here are the things the LORD has commanded you to do. ²You must do your work in six days. But the seventh day will be your holy day. It will be a Sabbath in the LORD's honor. You must rest on it. Anyone who does any work on it must be put to death. ³Do not even light a fire in any of your homes on the Sabbath day."

SUPPLIES FOR THE HOLY TENT

⁴Moses spoke to the whole community of Israel. He said, "Here is what the LORD has commanded. ⁵Take an offering for the LORD from what you have. Those who want to can bring an offering to the LORD. Here is what they can bring.

"gold, silver and bronze
⁶blue, purple and bright red yarn and fine linen
goat hair
⁷ram skins that are dyed red
the hides of sea cows
acacia wood
⁸olive oil for the lights
spices for the anointing oil and for the sweet-smelling incense
⁹onyx stones and other jewels for the linen apron and the chest cloth
¹⁰"All of the skilled workers among

you must come. They must make everything the LORD has commanded ¹¹for the holy tent and its covering. Here is what they must make.

"hooks
frames
crossbars
posts
bases
¹²the ark of the covenant
the poles and cover for the ark
the curtain that screens the ark
¹³the table for the holy bread
the poles and all of the articles for the table
the holy bread
¹⁴the lampstand for light and everything that is used with it
the lamps and the olive oil that gives light
¹⁵the altar for burning incense
the poles for the altar
the anointing oil
the sweet-smelling incense
the curtain for the entrance to the holy tent
¹⁶the altar for burnt offerings with its bronze grate
its poles and all of its tools
the large bronze bowl with its stand
¹⁷the curtains of the courtyard with their posts and bases
the curtain for the entrance to the courtyard
¹⁸the ropes and tent stakes for the holy tent and for the courtyard
¹⁹the sacred clothes for Aaron the priest
the clothes for his sons when they serve as priests"

²⁰Then the whole community of Israel left Moses. ²¹Everyone who wanted to give offerings to the LORD brought them to him. The offerings were for the work on the Tent of Meeting, for the sacred clothes, and for any other purpose there.

²²Every man and woman who wanted to give came. They brought gold jewelry of all kinds. They brought pins, earrings, rings and other jewelry. All of them gave their gold as a wave offering to the LORD.

²³People brought what they had.

They brought blue, purple or bright red yarn or fine linen. They brought goat hair, ram skins that were dyed red, or the hides of sea cows. ²⁴Some brought silver or bronze as an offering to the LORD. Others brought acacia wood for any part of the work.

²⁵All of the skilled women spun yarn with their hands. They brought blue, purple or bright red yarn or fine linen. ²⁶All of the skilled women who wanted to spin the goat hair did so.

²⁷The leaders brought onyx stones and other jewels for the linen apron and the chest cloth. ²⁸They also brought spices and olive oil. They brought them for the light, for the anointing oil, and for the sweet-smelling incense.

²⁹All of the men and women of Israel who wanted to bring offerings to the LORD brought them to him. The offerings were for all of the work the LORD had commanded Moses to tell them to do.

BEZALEL AND OHOLIAB

³⁰Then Moses spoke to the people of Israel. He said, "The LORD has chosen Bezalel, the son of Uri. Uri is the son of Hur. Bezalel is from the tribe of Judah. ³¹The LORD has filled him with the Spirit of God. He has filled him with skill, ability and knowledge in all kinds of crafts. ³²He can make beautiful patterns in gold, silver and bronze. ³³He can cut and set stones. He can work with wood. In fact, he can work in all kinds of arts and crafts.

³⁴"And the LORD has given both him and Oholiab the ability to teach others. Oholiab, the son of Ahisamach, is from the tribe of Dan.

³⁵"The LORD has filled them with skill to do all kinds of work. They carve things and make patterns. They sew skillfully with blue, purple and bright red yarn and on fine linen. They use thread to make beautiful cloth. They have the skill to work in all kinds of

36 crafts. ¹Bezalel and Oholiab must do the work just as the LORD has commanded. So must every skilled worker to whom the LORD has given skill and ability. They must know how to do all of the work for every purpose con-

nected with the sacred tent. And that includes setting it up."

²Then Moses sent for Bezalel and Oholiab. He sent for every skilled worker to whom the LORD had given ability and who wanted to come and do the work.

³They received from Moses all of the offerings the people of Israel had brought. They had brought the offerings for all of the work for every purpose connected with the holy tent. That included setting it up. The people kept bringing the offerings they chose to give. They brought them morning after morning.

⁴So all of the skilled workers who were working on the holy tent stopped what they were doing. ⁵They said to Moses, "The people are bringing more than enough for doing the work the LORD commanded us to do."

⁶Then Moses gave an order. A message was sent through the whole camp. It said, "No man or woman should make anything else and offer it for the holy tent." And so the people were kept from bringing more offerings. ⁷There was already more than enough to do all of the work.

THE HOLY TENT

⁸All of the skilled workers made the holy tent. They made ten curtains out of finely twisted linen. They made them with blue, purple and bright red yarn. A skilled worker sewed cherubim into the pattern. ⁹All of the curtains were the same size. They were 42 feet long and six feet wide.

¹⁰The workers joined five of the curtains together. They did the same thing with the other five. ¹¹Then they made loops out of blue strips of cloth along the edge of the end curtain in one set. They did the same thing with the end curtain in the other set. ¹²They also made 50 loops on the end curtain of the one set. They did the same thing on the end curtain of the other set. They put the loops across from each other. ¹³Then they made 50 gold hooks. They used them to join curtains together so that the holy tent was all one piece.

¹⁴The workers made a total of 11 curtains out of goat hair to put over the

holy tent. ¹⁵All 11 curtains were the same size. They were 45 feet long and six feet wide.

¹⁶The workers joined five of the curtains together into one set. They did the same thing with the other six. ¹⁷Then they made 50 loops along the edge of the end curtain in the one set. They did the same thing with the other set. ¹⁸They made 50 bronze hooks. They used them to join the tent together all in one piece. ¹⁹They made a covering for the tent. They made it out of ram skins that were dyed red. They put a covering of the hides of sea cows over that.

²⁰The workers made frames out of acacia wood for the holy tent. ²¹Each frame was 15 feet long and two feet three inches wide. ²²The workers added two small wooden pins to each frame. The pins stuck out so that they were even with each other. The workers made all of the frames of the holy tent in the same way.

²³They made 20 frames for the south side of the holy tent. ²⁴And they made 40 silver bases to go under them. They made two bases for each frame. They put one under each pin that stuck out.

²⁵For the north side of the holy tent they made 20 frames ²⁶and 40 silver bases. They put two bases under each frame.

²⁷The workers made six frames for the west end of the holy tent. ²⁸They made two frames for the corners of the holy tent at the far end. ²⁹At those two corners the frames were double from top to bottom. They were fitted into a single ring. The workers made both of them the same. ³⁰So there were eight frames and 16 silver bases. There were two bases under each frame.

³¹The workers also made crossbars out of acacia wood. They made five for the frames on one side of the holy tent. ³²They made five for the frames on the other side. And they made five for the frames on the west, at the far end of the holy tent. ³³The center crossbar reached from end to end at the middle of the frames.

³⁴They covered the frames with gold. They made gold rings to hold the crossbars. They also covered the crossbars with gold.

³⁵They made the curtain out of blue, purple and bright red yarn and finely twisted linen. A skilled worker sewed cherubim into the pattern. ³⁶The workers made four posts out of acacia wood for the curtain. They covered the posts with gold. They made gold hooks and four silver bases for the posts.

³⁷For the entrance to the tent the workers made a curtain out of blue, purple and bright red yarn and finely twisted linen. A person who sewed skillfully made it. ³⁸The workers made five posts with hooks for the curtains. They covered the tops of the posts and their bands with gold. And they made five bronze bases for them.

THE ARK OF THE COVENANT

37 Bezalel made the ark of the covenant out of acacia wood. It was three feet nine inches long and two feet three inches wide and high. ²He covered it inside and outside with pure gold. He put a strip of gold around it.

³He made four gold rings for it. He joined them to its four bottom corners. He put two rings on one side and two rings on the other.

⁴Then he made poles out of acacia wood. He covered them with gold. ⁵He put the poles through the rings on the sides of the ark to carry it.

⁶He made its cover out of pure gold. It was three feet nine inches long and two feet three inches wide. The cover is the place where sin is paid for.

⁷He made two cherubim out of hammered gold at the ends of the cover. ⁸He put one cherub on each end of it. ⁹He made the cherubim as part of the cover itself. The cherubim's wings spread up over the cover. The cherubim faced each other and looked toward the cover.

THE TABLE FOR THE HOLY BREAD

¹⁰The workers made the table out of acacia wood. It was three feet long, one foot six inches wide and two feet three inches high. ¹¹They covered it with pure gold. They put a strip of gold around it. ¹²They also made a rim three

inches wide around it. They put a strip of gold around the rim.

¹³They made four gold rings for the table. They joined them to the four corners, where the four legs were. ¹⁴The rings were close to the rim. They held the poles that were used to carry the table.

¹⁵The workers made the poles out of acacia wood. They covered them with gold.

¹⁶They made plates, dishes and bowls out of pure gold for the table. They also made pure gold pitchers to pour out drink offerings.

THE GOLD LAMPSTAND

¹⁷The workers made the lampstand out of pure gold. They hammered out its base and stem. Its buds, blooms and cups branched out from it.

¹⁸Six branches came out from the sides of the lampstand. There were three on one side and three on the other. ¹⁹On one branch there were three cups that were shaped like almond flowers with buds and blooms. There were three on the next branch. There were three on all six branches that came out from the lampstand.

²⁰On the lampstand there were four cups that were shaped like almond flowers with buds and blooms. ²¹One bud was under the first pair of branches that came out from the lampstand. A second bud was under the second pair. And a third bud was under the third pair. There was a total of six branches. ²²The buds and branches came out from the lampstand.

The whole lampstand was one piece that was hammered out of pure gold. ²³The workers made its seven lamps out of pure gold. They also made its trays and wick cutters out of pure gold. ²⁴They used 75 pounds of pure gold to make the lampstand and everything that was used with it.

THE ALTAR FOR BURNING INCENSE

²⁵The workers made an altar for burning incense. They made it out of acacia wood. It was one foot six inches square and three feet high. A horn stuck out from each of its upper four corners. ²⁶The workers covered the top, sides and horns with pure gold. They put a strip of gold around it.

²⁷They made two gold rings below the strip. They put the rings across from each other. The rings held the poles that were used to carry it. ²⁸The workers made the poles out of acacia wood. They covered them with gold.

²⁹They also made the sacred anointing oil and the pure, sweet-smelling incense. A person who makes perfume made them.

THE ALTAR FOR BURNT OFFERINGS

38 The workers made the altar for burnt offerings out of acacia wood. It was four feet six inches high and seven feet six inches square. ²They made a horn stick out from each of its four upper corners. They covered the altar with bronze.

³They made all of its tools out of bronze. They made its pots, shovels, sprinkling bowls, meat forks, and pans for carrying ashes.

⁴They made a bronze grate for the altar. They put the grate halfway up the altar on the inside. ⁵They made a bronze ring for each of the four corners of the grate.

⁶They made poles out of acacia wood. They covered them with bronze. ⁷They put the poles through the rings. The poles were on two sides of the altar for carrying it.

The workers made the altar out of boards. They made it hollow.

THE LARGE BOWL FOR WASHING

⁸The workers made the large bronze bowl and its bronze stand. They made them out of the bronze mirrors that belonged to the women who served at the entrance to the Tent of Meeting.

THE COURTYARD

⁹Next, the workers made the courtyard. The south side was 150 feet long. It had curtains that were made out of finely twisted linen. ¹⁰The curtains had 20 posts and 20 bronze bases. The posts had silver hooks and bands on them.

¹¹The north side was also 150 feet long. Its curtains had 20 posts and 20 bronze bases. The posts had silver hooks and bands on them.

¹²The west end was 75 feet wide. It had curtains with ten posts and ten bases. The posts had silver hooks and bands on them.

¹³The east end, toward the sunrise, was also 75 feet wide. ¹⁴Curtains that were 22 feet six inches long were on one side of the entrance. They were hung on three posts. Each post had a base. ¹⁵Curtains that were 22 feet six inches long were also on the other side of the entrance to the courtyard. They were hung on three posts. Each post had a base.

¹⁶All of the curtains that were around the courtyard were made out of finely twisted linen. ¹⁷The bases for the posts were made out of bronze. The hooks and bands that were on the posts were made out of silver. Their tops were covered with silver. So all of the posts of the courtyard had silver bands.

¹⁸The curtain for the entrance to the courtyard was made out of blue, purple and bright red yarn and finely twisted linen. A person who sewed skillfully made it. It was 30 feet long. Like the curtains of the courtyard, it was seven feet six inches high. ¹⁹It had four posts and four bronze bases. Their hooks and bands were made out of silver. Their tops were covered with silver.

²⁰All of the tent stakes of the holy tent were made out of bronze. So were all of the stakes of the courtyard that was around it.

THE AMOUNTS OF THE METALS USED

²¹Here are the amounts of the metals that were used for the holy tent, where the tablets of the covenant were kept. Moses commanded the Levites to record the amounts. The Levites did the work under the direction of Ithamar. Ithamar was the son of the priest Aaron.

²²Bezalel, the son of Uri, made everything the LORD had commanded Moses. Uri was the son of Hur. Bezalel was from the tribe of Judah. ²³Oholiab,

the son of Ahisamach, helped Bezalel. Oholiab was from the tribe of Dan. He could carve things and make patterns. And he could sew skillfully with blue, purple and bright red yarn and on fine linen.

²⁴The total weight of the gold from the wave offering was more than a ton. It was weighed out in keeping with the standard weights that are used in the sacred tent. The gold was used for all of the work that was done in connection with the sacred tent.

²⁵The silver that was received from the men in the community who were listed and counted weighed four tons. It was weighed out in keeping with the weights used in the sacred tent. ²⁶It amounted to a fifth of an ounce for each person. It was weighed out in keeping with the weights used in the sacred tent. The silver was received from the men who had been listed and counted. All of them were 20 years old or more. Their total number was 603,550.

²⁷The four tons of silver were used to make the bases for the holy tent and for the curtain. The 100 bases were made from the four tons. Each base used more than 75 pounds of silver. ²⁸The workers used 45 pounds to make the hooks for the posts, to cover the tops of the posts, and to make their bands.

²⁹The bronze from the wave offering weighed two and a half tons. ³⁰The workers used some of it to make the bases for the entrance to the Tent of Meeting. They used some for the bronze altar for burnt offerings and its bronze grate and all of its tools. ³¹They used some for the bases for the courtyard that was around the holy tent. They used some for the bases for the courtyard entrance. And they used the rest to make all of the tent stakes for the holy tent and the courtyard that was around it.

THE CLOTHES FOR THE PRIESTS

39 The workers made clothes from the blue, purple and bright red yarn. The clothes were worn by those who served in the holy tent. The workers also made sacred clothes for Aaron. They made them just as the LORD had commanded Moses.

THE LINEN APRON

[2]The workers made the linen apron out of fine gold wire, and out of blue, purple and bright red yarn, and out of finely twisted linen. [3]They hammered out thin sheets of gold. They cut it into fine wire. They sewed it into the blue, purple and bright red yarn and fine linen. A skilled worker made it. [4]The workers made shoulder straps for the apron. The straps were joined to two of its corners.

[5]Its skillfully made waistband was made like it. The waistband was part of the apron itself. It was made out of fine gold wire, and out of blue, purple and bright red yarn, and out of finely twisted linen. The workers made it just as the LORD had commanded Moses.

[6]They put the onyx stones in fancy gold settings. They carved the names of the sons of Israel on them. They did it the way a person carves a seal. [7]Then they connected them to the shoulder straps of the linen apron. The stones stood for the sons of Israel and were a reminder for them. The workers did those things just as the LORD had commanded Moses.

THE CHEST CLOTH

[8]Skilled workers made the chest cloth. They made it like the linen apron. They used fine gold wire, and blue, purple and bright red yarn, and finely twisted linen. [9]The chest cloth was nine inches square. It was folded in half.

[10]They put four rows of valuable jewels on it. A ruby, a topaz and a beryl were in the first row. [11]A turquoise, a sapphire and an emerald were in the second row. [12]A jacinth, an agate and an amethyst were in the third row. [13]And a chrysolite, an onyx and a jasper were in the fourth row. The workers put them in fancy gold settings.

[14]They used a total of 12 stones. There was one stone for each of the names of the sons of Israel. Each stone was carved like a seal with the name of one of the 12 tribes.

[15]The workers made braided chains out of pure gold for the chest cloth. They made them like ropes. [16]They made two fancy gold settings and two gold rings. They connected them to two corners of the chest cloth. [17]They joined the two gold chains to the rings at the corners of the chest cloth. [18]They joined the other ends of the chains to the two settings. They joined them to the shoulder straps on the front of the linen apron.

[19]The workers made two gold rings. They connected them to the other two corners of the chest cloth. They put them on the inside edge next to the apron. [20]They made two more gold rings. They connected them to the bottom of the shoulder straps on the front of the apron. They put them close to the seam right above the waistband of the apron. [21]They tied the rings of the chest cloth to the rings of the apron with blue cord. That connected it to the waistband. Then the chest cloth would not swing out from the linen apron. The workers did those things just as the LORD had commanded Moses.

MORE CLOTHES FOR THE PRIESTS

[22]The workers made the outer robe of the linen apron completely from blue cloth. The cloth was made by a skillful person. [23]The workers made an opening like a collar in the center of the robe. They made an edge around the opening. Then it couldn't tear.

[24]They made pomegranates out of blue, purple and bright red yarn and finely twisted linen. They sewed them around the hem of the robe.

[25]They made bells out of pure gold. They sewed them around the hem between the pomegranates. [26]They sewed a bell between every two pomegranates all around the hem of the robe. Aaron had to wear the robe when he served as priest. That's what the LORD commanded Moses.

[27]The workers made inner robes out of fine linen for Aaron and his sons. The linen cloth was made by a skillful person. [28]The workers also made the turban out of fine linen. And they made the headbands and the underwear out of finely twisted linen. [29]The

belt was made out of finely twisted linen and blue, purple and bright red yarn. A person who sewed skillfully made it. The workers did those things just as the LORD had commanded Moses.

³⁰They made the plate out of pure gold. It was a sacred crown. They carved words on it as if it were a seal. They carved the words SET APART FOR THE LORD. ³¹Then they tied the plate to the turban with a blue cord. They did those things just as the LORD had commanded Moses.

THE HOLY TENT IS COMPLETED

³²So all of the work on the holy tent, the Tent of Meeting, was completed. The people of Israel did everything just as the LORD had commanded Moses.

³³Then they brought the holy tent to Moses along with everything that belonged to it. Here are the things they brought.

hooks
frames
crossbars
posts
bases
³⁴the covering of ram skins that were dyed red
the covering of the hides of sea cows
the curtain that screens the ark
³⁵the ark where the tablets of the covenant are kept
the poles and cover for the ark
³⁶the table for the holy bread with all of its articles
the holy bread
³⁷the pure gold lampstand with its row of lamps and everything that is used with it
the olive oil that gives light
³⁸the gold altar for burning incense
the anointing oil
the sweet-smelling incense
the curtain for the entrance to the tent
³⁹the bronze altar for burnt offerings with its bronze grate
its poles and all of its tools
the large bowl with its stand

⁴⁰the curtains of the courtyard with their posts and bases
the curtain for the entrance to the courtyard
the ropes and tent stakes for the courtyard
⁴¹the sacred clothes for the priest Aaron
the clothes for his sons when they serve as priests

⁴²The people of Israel had done all of the work just as the LORD had commanded Moses. ⁴³Moses looked over the work carefully. He saw that the workers had done it just as the LORD had commanded. So Moses gave them his blessing.

MOSES SETS UP THE HOLY TENT

40 Then the LORD said to Moses, ²"Set up the holy tent, the Tent of Meeting. Set it up on the first day of the first month.

³"Place in it the ark where the tablets of the covenant are kept. Screen the ark with the curtain. ⁴Bring in the table for the holy bread. Arrange the loaves of bread on it. Then bring in the lampstand. Set up its lamps. ⁵Place the gold altar for burning incense in front of the ark where the tablets of the covenant are kept. Put up the curtain at the entrance to the holy tent.

⁶"Place the altar for burnt offerings in front of the entrance to the holy tent, the Tent of Meeting. ⁷Place the large bowl between the Tent of Meeting and the altar. Put water in the bowl.

⁸"Set up the courtyard around the holy tent. Put the curtain at the entrance to the courtyard.

⁹"Get the anointing oil. Anoint the holy tent and everything that is in it. Set apart the holy tent and everything that belongs to it. Then it will be holy. ¹⁰Anoint the altar for burnt offerings and all of its tools. Set the altar apart. Then it will be a very holy place. ¹¹Anoint the large bowl and its stand. Set them apart.

¹²"Bring Aaron and his sons to the entrance to the Tent of Meeting. Wash them with water. ¹³Dress Aaron in the

sacred clothes. Anoint him and set him apart. Then he will be able to serve me as priest. [14]"Bring his sons and dress them in their inner robes. [15]Anoint them just as you anointed their father. Then they will be able to serve me as priests. They will be anointed to do the work of priests. That work will last for all time to come."

[16]Moses did everything just as the LORD had commanded him.

[17]So the holy tent was set up. It was the first day of the first month in the second year. [18]Moses set up the holy tent. He put the bases in place. He put the frames in them. He put in the crossbars. He set up the posts. [19]He spread the holy tent over the frames. Then he put the coverings over the tent. Moses did it as the LORD had commanded him.

[20]He got the tablets of the covenant. He placed them in the ark. He put the poles through its rings. And he put the cover on it. The cover was the place where sin is paid for. [21]Moses brought the ark into the holy tent. He hung the curtain to screen the ark where the tablets of the covenant are kept. Moses did it as the LORD had commanded him.

[22]He placed the table for the holy bread in the Tent of Meeting. It was on the north side of the holy tent outside the curtain. [23]He arranged the loaves of bread on it in the sight of the LORD. Moses did it as the LORD had commanded him.

[24]He placed the lampstand in the Tent of Meeting. It stood across from the table on the south side of the holy tent. [25]He set up the lamps in the sight of the LORD. Moses did it as the LORD had commanded him.

[26]He placed the gold altar for burning incense in the Tent of Meeting. He placed it in front of the curtain. [27]He burned sweet-smelling incense on it. Moses did it as the LORD had commanded him.

[28]Then he put up the curtain at the entrance to the holy tent.

[29]He set the altar for burnt offerings near the entrance to the holy tent, the Tent of Meeting. He sacrificed burnt offerings and grain offerings on it. Moses did it as the LORD had commanded him.

[30]He placed the large bowl between the Tent of Meeting and the altar. He put water in the bowl for washing. [31]Moses and Aaron and his sons used it to wash their hands and feet. [32]They washed when they entered the Tent of Meeting or approached the altar. They did it as the LORD had commanded Moses.

[33]Then Moses set up the courtyard around the holy tent and altar. He put up the curtain at the entrance to the courtyard. And so Moses completed the work.

THE GLORY OF THE LORD

[34]Then the cloud covered the Tent of Meeting. The glory of the LORD filled the holy tent. [35]Moses couldn't enter the Tent of Meeting because the cloud had settled on it. The glory of the LORD filled the holy tent.

[36]The people of Israel continued their travels. When the cloud lifted from above the holy tent, they started out. [37]But if the cloud didn't lift, they did not start out. They stayed until the day it lifted.

[38]So the cloud of the LORD was above the holy tent during the day. Fire was in the cloud at night. The whole community of Israel could see the cloud during all of their travels.

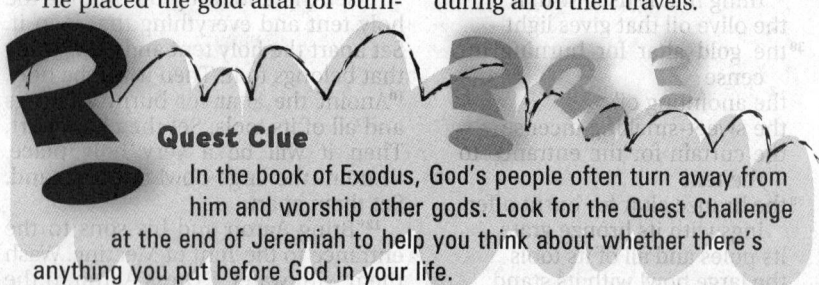

Quest Clue

In the book of Exodus, God's people often turn away from him and worship other gods. Look for the Quest Challenge at the end of Jeremiah to help you think about whether there's anything you put before God in your life.

Leviticus

Who wrote this book?
Moses.

Why was this book written?
Leviticus shows the Israelites how to worship God and live a holy life.

What happens in this book?
Moses gives the people and the priests of Israel God's instructions.

What do we learn about God in this book?
God is holy and expects his people to be holy. God accepts sacrifice and forgives people who sin.

Who is important in this book?
The important people in this book are Moses and Aaron.

When did this happen?
God's instructions were given about 1445 B.C.

Where did this happen?
The Israelites were camped at Mount Sinai when these instructions were given.

RULES FOR BURNT OFFERINGS

1 The LORD called out to Moses. He spoke to him from the Tent of Meeting. He said, ²"Speak to the people of Israel. Tell them, 'Sup-pose any one of you brings an offering to the LORD. You must bring an animal from your herd or flock.

³" 'If a man brings a burnt offering from the herd, he must offer a male animal. It must not have any flaws. He

must bring it to the entrance to the Tent of Meeting. Then the LORD will accept it.

⁴" 'The man must place his hand on the head of the burnt offering. Then the LORD will accept it in place of him. It will pay for his sin. ⁵The young bull must be killed there in the sight of the LORD.

" 'Then the priests who are in Aaron's family line must bring its blood to the altar. They must sprinkle it against every side of the altar. The altar stands at the entrance to the Tent of Meeting.

⁶" 'The skin must be removed from the animal that is brought for the burnt offering. Then the animal must be cut into pieces.

⁷" 'The priests who are in Aaron's family line must build a fire on the altar. They must place wood on the fire. ⁸Then they must place the pieces of the animal on the burning wood on the altar. The pieces include the head and the fat.

⁹" 'The inside parts of the animal must be washed with water. The legs must also be washed. The priest must burn all of it on the altar.

" 'It is a burnt offering. It is an offering that is made with fire. It gives a smell that is pleasant to the LORD.

¹⁰" 'If the offering is a burnt offering from the flock, it must be a male animal. It can be a sheep or a goat. It must not have any flaws.

¹¹" 'It must be killed at the north side of the altar in the sight of the LORD. The priests who are in Aaron's family line must sprinkle its blood against every side of the altar.

¹²" 'The animal must be cut into pieces. The priest must place them on the burning wood on the altar. The pieces include the head and the fat.

¹³" 'The inside parts must be washed with water. The legs must also be washed. The priest must bring all of it to the altar. He must burn it there.

" 'It is a burnt offering. It is an offering that is made with fire. It gives a smell that is pleasant to the LORD.

¹⁴" 'If the offering to the LORD is a burnt offering of birds, it must be a dove or a young pigeon.

¹⁵" 'The priest must bring it to the altar. He must twist its head off. Then he must burn the rest of the bird on the altar. Its blood must be emptied out on the side of the altar.

¹⁶" 'The priest must remove the small bag inside the bird's throat. He must also remove what is in the bag. Then he must throw all of it to the east side of the altar. That is where the ashes are. ¹⁷He must take hold of the wings of the bird and tear it open. But he must not tear it in two. Then the priest will burn it on the wood that is on the fire on the altar.

" 'It is a burnt offering. It is an offering that is made with fire. It gives a smell that is pleasant to the LORD.

RULES FOR GRAIN OFFERINGS

2 " 'Suppose someone brings a grain offering to the LORD. Then his offering must be made out of fine flour. He must pour olive oil on it. He must also put incense on it.

²" 'He must take it to the priests who are in Aaron's family line. A priest must take a handful of the fine flour and oil. He must mix it with all of the incense. Then he must burn that part on the altar. It will be a reminder that all good things come from the LORD. It is an offering that is made with fire. It gives a smell that is pleasant to the LORD.

³" 'The rest of the grain offering belongs to Aaron and to the priests who are in his family line. It is a very holy part of the offerings that are made to the LORD with fire.

⁴" 'If you bring a grain offering that is baked in an oven, make it out of fine flour. It can be flat cakes that are made without yeast. Mix them with olive oil. Or it can be wafers that are made without yeast. Spread oil on them. ⁵If your grain offering is grilled on a metal plate, make it out of fine flour. Mix it with oil. Make it without yeast. ⁶Break it into pieces. Pour oil on it. It is a grain offering. ⁷If your grain offering is cooked in a pan, make it out of fine flour and oil.

⁸" 'Bring to the LORD your grain offering that is made out of all of those things. Give it to the priest. He must take it to the altar. ⁹He must take out the part of the grain offering that re-

minds you that all good things come from the LORD. He must burn it on the altar. It is an offering that is made with fire. It gives a smell that is pleasant to the LORD.

¹⁰" 'The rest of the grain offering belongs to Aaron and the priests who are in his family line. It is a very holy part of the offerings that are made to the LORD with fire.

¹¹" 'Every grain offering you bring to the LORD must be made without yeast. You must not burn any yeast or honey in an offering that is made to the LORD with fire.

¹²" 'You can bring them to the LORD as an offering of the first share of the food you gather or produce. But they must not be offered on the altar as a pleasant smell.

¹³" 'Put salt on all of your grain offerings. Salt stands for the lasting covenant between you and your God. So do not leave it out of your grain offerings. Add it to all of your offerings.

¹⁴" 'Suppose you bring to the LORD a grain offering of the first share of your food. Then offer crushed heads of your first grain that have been cooked in fire. ¹⁵Put olive oil and incense on it. It is a grain offering.

¹⁶" 'The priest must burn part of the crushed grain and the oil. It will remind you that all good things come from the LORD. The priest must burn it together with all of the incense. It is an offering that is made to the LORD with fire.

RULES FOR FRIENDSHIP OFFERINGS

3 " 'Suppose someone brings a friendship offering. If he offers an animal from the herd, it can be either male or female. It must not have any flaws. He must offer it in the sight of the LORD.

²" 'The man must place his hand on the animal's head. It must be killed at the entrance to the Tent of Meeting. Then the priests who are in Aaron's family line must sprinkle the blood against every side of the altar.

³" 'Part of the friendship offering must be given to the LORD as an offering that is made with fire. It must include all of the fat that covers the

inside parts or is connected to them. ⁴It must include both kidneys with the fat on them next to the lower back muscles. It must also include the covering of the liver. All of it must be removed together with the kidneys.

⁵" 'Then the priests who are in Aaron's family line must burn it on the altar. They must burn it on top of the burnt offering on the burning wood.

" 'It is an offering that is made with fire. It gives a smell that is pleasant to the LORD.

⁶" 'If a man brings an animal from the flock as a friendship offering to the LORD, it can be either male or female. It must not have any flaws. ⁷If he brings a lamb, he must offer it in the sight of the LORD. ⁸The man must place his hand on the lamb's head. It must be killed there in front of the Tent of Meeting. Then the priests who are in Aaron's family line must sprinkle its blood against every side of the altar. ⁹Part of the offering must be brought as a sacrifice that is made to the LORD with fire. It must include the lamb's fat and the entire fat tail cut off close to the backbone. It must include all of the fat that covers the inside parts or is connected to them. ¹⁰It must include both kidneys with the fat on them next to the lower back muscles. It must also include the covering of the liver. All of it must be removed together with the kidneys.

¹¹" 'Then the priest must burn it on the altar as food. It is an offering that is made to the LORD with fire.

¹²" 'If a man brings a goat, he must offer it in the sight of the LORD. ¹³The man must place his hand on its head. It must be killed there in front of the Tent of Meeting. Then the priests who are in Aaron's family line must sprinkle its blood against every side of the altar.

¹⁴" 'Part of the offering must be brought as an offering that is made to the LORD with fire. It must include all of the fat that covers the inside parts or is connected to them. ¹⁵It must include both kidneys with the fat on them next to the lower back muscles. It must also include the covering of the liver. All of it must be removed together with the kidneys.

¹⁶" 'Then the priest must burn it on

the altar as food. It is an offering that is made with fire. It has a pleasant smell. All of the fat belongs to the LORD.

[17] " 'You must not eat any fat or any blood. That is a law that will last for all time to come. It applies no matter where you live.' "

RULES FOR SIN OFFERINGS

4 The LORD spoke to Moses. He said, [2] "Speak to the people of Israel. Tell them, 'Suppose someone sins without meaning to. And that person does something the LORD commands us not to do.

[3] " 'Suppose it is the anointed priest who sins. And suppose he brings guilt on the people. Then he must bring a young bull to the LORD. It must not have any flaws. He must bring it as a sin offering for the sin he has committed. [4] He must bring the bull to the entrance to the Tent of Meeting in the sight of the LORD. He must place his hand on its head. He must kill it there in the sight of the LORD.

[5] " 'Then the priest must take some of the bull's blood. He must carry it into the Tent of Meeting. [6] He must dip his finger into the blood. He must sprinkle some of it seven times in the sight of the LORD. He must do it in front of the curtain of the Most Holy Room.

[7] " 'Then the priest must put some of the blood on the horns that stick out from the upper four corners of the altar for burning incense. The incense has a sweet smell. The altar stands in front of the LORD in the Tent of Meeting. The priest must pour out the rest of the bull's blood at the bottom of the altar for burnt offerings. That altar stands at the entrance to the tent.

[8] " 'He must remove all of the fat from the bull for the sin offering. It includes the fat that covers the inside parts or is connected to them. [9] It includes both kidneys with the fat on them next to the lower back muscles. It also includes the covering of the liver. He must remove all of it together with the kidneys. [10] He must remove it in the same way the fat is removed from an ox that is sacrificed as a friendship offering. Then the priest

must burn all of it on the altar for burnt offerings.

[11] " 'But the bull's hide must be taken away. So must all of its meat. So must its head and legs. And so must its inside parts and guts. [12] In other words, all of the rest of the bull must be taken away. The priest must take it outside the camp. He must take it to a place that is "clean." He must take it to the place where the ashes are thrown. There he must burn it in a wood fire on a pile of ashes.

[13] " 'Or suppose the whole community of Israel sins without meaning to. They do something the LORD commands us not to do. Even if they are not aware of what they have done, they are guilty.

[14] " 'But suppose they become aware of the sin they have committed. Then they must bring a young bull as a sin offering. They must offer it in front of the Tent of Meeting. [15] The elders of the community must place their hands on the bull's head in the sight of the LORD. The bull must be killed in the sight of the LORD.

[16] " 'Then the anointed priest must take some of the bull's blood into the Tent of Meeting. [17] He must dip his finger into the blood. He must sprinkle it seven times in the sight of the LORD. He must do it in front of the curtain. [18] He must put some of the blood on the horns that stick out from the upper four corners of the altar. The altar stands in front of the LORD in the Tent of Meeting. The priest must pour out the rest of the blood at the bottom of the altar for burnt offerings. That altar stands at the entrance to the tent.

[19] " 'He must remove all of the fat from the bull. He must burn it on the altar. [20] He must do the same thing with that bull as he did with the bull for the sin offering. When he does, he will pay for the sin of the people. And they will be forgiven.

[21] " 'Then he must take the bull outside the camp. He must burn it just as he burned the first bull. It is the sin offering for the whole community.

[22] " 'Or suppose a leader sins without meaning to. If he disobeys any of the

commands of the LORD his God, he is guilty.

23" 'But suppose he is made aware of the sin he has committed. Then he must bring an offering. It must be a male goat. It must not have any flaws. 24He must place his hand on the goat's head. He must kill it. He must do it at the place where the animals for burnt offerings are killed in the sight of the LORD. His offering is a sin offering.

25" 'Then the priest must dip his finger into some of the blood of the sin offering. He must put it on the horns that stick out from the upper four corners of the altar for burnt offerings. He must pour out the rest of the blood at the bottom of the altar.

26" 'He must burn all of the fat on the altar. He must burn it in the same way he burned the fat of the friendship offering. When he does, he will pay for the sin of the leader. And the leader will be forgiven.

27" 'Or suppose someone in the community sins without meaning to. If he disobeys any of the LORD's commands, he is guilty.

28" 'But suppose he is made aware of the sin he has committed. Then he must bring an offering for the sin he has committed. It must be a female goat. It must not have any flaws. 29He must place his hand on the head of the animal for the sin offering. It must be killed at the place where the animals for burnt offerings are killed.

30" 'Then the priest must dip his finger into some of the blood. He must put it on the horns that stick out from the upper four corners of the altar for burnt offerings. He must pour out the rest of the blood at the bottom of the altar.

31" 'He must remove all of the fat in the same way the fat is removed from the friendship offering. He must burn it on the altar. It gives a smell that is pleasant to the LORD. When the priest burns the offering, he will pay for the sin of that person. And he will be forgiven.

32" 'Suppose he brings a lamb as his sin offering. Then he must bring a female animal. It must not have any flaws. 33He must place his hand on its head. He must kill it as a sin offering.

He must do it at the place where the animals for burnt offerings are killed.

34" 'Then the priest must dip his finger into some of the blood of the sin offering. He must put it on the horns that stick out from the upper four corners of the altar for burnt offerings. He must pour out the rest of the blood at the bottom of the altar.

35" 'He must remove all of the fat in the same way the fat is removed from the lamb for the friendship offering. He must burn it on the altar on top of the offerings that are made to the LORD with fire. When he does, he will pay for the sin that person has committed. And he will be forgiven.

5 " 'Suppose a person has been called as a witness to something he has seen or learned about. Then if he does not tell what he knows, he has sinned. And he will be held accountable for it.

2" 'Or suppose a person touches something that is not "clean." It could be the dead bodies of wild animals or of livestock. Or it could be the dead bodies of creatures that move along the ground. Even though he is not aware that he touched them, he has become "unclean." And he is guilty.

3" 'Or suppose he touches something "unclean" that comes from a human being. It could be anything that would make him "unclean." Suppose he is not aware that he touched it. When he finds out about it, he will be guilty.

4" 'Or suppose a person takes an oath and makes a promise to do something without thinking it through. It does not matter what he promised. It does not matter whether he took the oath without thinking about it carefully. And suppose he is not aware that he did not think it through. When he finds out about it, he will be guilty.

5" 'When someone is guilty in any of those ways, he must admit he has sinned. 6He must bring a sin offering to pay for the sin he has committed. He must bring to the LORD a female lamb or goat from the flock. The priest will sacrifice the animal. That will pay for the person's sin.

7" 'Suppose he can't afford a lamb.

Then he must get two doves or two young pigeons. He must bring them to the LORD to pay for his sin. One of them is for a sin offering. The other is for a burnt offering.

⁸" 'He must bring them to the priest. The priest will offer the one for the sin offering first. He must twist its head. But he must not twist it off completely.

⁹" 'Then he must sprinkle some of the blood of the sin offering against the side of the altar. He must empty out the rest of the blood at the bottom of the altar. It is a sin offering.

¹⁰" 'Then the priest will offer the other bird as a burnt offering. He must do it in the way the law requires. That will pay for the sin the person has committed. And he will be forgiven.

¹¹" 'But suppose he can't afford two doves or two young pigeons. Then he must bring eight cups of fine flour as an offering for his sin. It is a sin offering. He must not put olive oil or incense on it. That is because it is a sin offering.

¹²" 'He must bring it to the priest. The priest must take a handful of it. He must burn that part on the altar. It will be a reminder that all good things come from the LORD. The priest must burn it on top of the offerings that are made to the LORD with fire. It is a sin offering.

¹³" 'In that way the priest will pay for any of the sins the person has committed. And he will be forgiven. The rest of the offering will belong to the priest. It is the same as in the case of the grain offering.' "

RULES FOR GUILT OFFERINGS

¹⁴The LORD spoke to Moses. He said, ¹⁵"Suppose a person sins by breaking the law. And he does it without meaning to. He sins against me or my priests by refusing to give them one of the holy things that are set apart for them.

"Then he must bring me a ram from the flock. It must not have any flaws. It must be worth the required amount of silver. It must be weighed out in keeping with the standard weights that are used in the sacred tent. It is a guilt offering. It will pay for his sin.

¹⁶"He must also pay for the holy thing he refused to give. He must add a fifth of its value to it. He must give all of it to the priest. The priest will pay for the person's sin with the ram. It is a guilt offering. And he will be forgiven.

¹⁷"Suppose a person sins by doing something I command him not to do. Even though he does not know it, he is guilty. He will be held accountable for it.

¹⁸"He must bring to the priest a ram from the flock as a guilt offering. It must not have any flaws. And it must be worth the required amount of money.

"The priest will sacrifice the animal. That will pay for what the person has done wrong without meaning to. And he will be forgiven. ¹⁹It is a guilt offering. He has been guilty of doing wrong against me."

6 The LORD spoke to Moses. He said, ²"Suppose a person sins by not being faithful to me. He does it by tricking his neighbors. He tricks them in connection with something they have placed in his care. He steals from them. Or he cheats them. ³Or he finds something they have lost and then tells a lie about it. Or he goes to court. He takes an oath and tells a lie when he witnesses about it. Or he commits any other sin like those sins.

⁴"When he sins in any of those ways, he becomes guilty. He must return what he stole. He must give back what he took by cheating his neighbors. He must return what they placed in his care. He must return the lost property he found. ⁵He must return anything he told a lie about when he witnessed in court. He must pay back everything in full. He must add a fifth of its value to it. He must give all of it to the owner on the day he brings his guilt offering.

⁶"He must bring his guilt offering to the priest to pay for his sin. It is an offering to me. He must bring a ram from the flock. It must not have any flaws. It must be worth the required amount of money.

⁷"The priest will sacrifice the ram to pay for the person's sin. He will do it in my sight. And the person will be forgiven for any of the things he did that made him guilty."

MORE RULES FOR BURNT OFFERINGS

[8]The LORD spoke to Moses. He said, [9]"Give Aaron and the priests who are in his family line a command. Tell them, 'Here are some more rules for burnt offerings. The burnt offering must remain on the altar through the whole night. The fire on the altar must be kept burning until morning.

[10]" 'The priest must put on his linen clothes. He must put on linen underwear next to his body. He must remove the ashes of the burnt offering that the fire has burned up on the altar. He must place them beside the altar. [11]Then he must take his clothes off and put others on. He must carry the ashes outside the camp to a place that is "clean."

[12]" 'The fire on the altar must be kept burning. It must not go out. Every morning the priest must add more wood to the fire. He must place the burnt offering on the fire. He must burn the fat of the friendship offerings on it. [13]The fire must be kept burning on the altar all the time. It must not go out.

MORE RULES FOR GRAIN OFFERINGS

[14]" 'Here are some more rules for grain offerings. The priests who are in Aaron's family line must bring the grain offering to the LORD in front of the altar.

[15]" 'The priest must take a handful of fine flour and olive oil. He must add to it all of the incense that is on the grain offering. He must burn that part on the altar. It will remind him that all good things come from the LORD. It gives a smell that is pleasant to the LORD.

[16]" 'Aaron and the priests who are in his family line will eat the rest of it. But they must eat it without yeast in a holy place. They must eat it in the courtyard of the Tent of Meeting. [17]It must not be baked with yeast. The LORD has given it to the priests as their share of the offerings that are made to him with fire. It is very holy, just like the sin offering and the guilt offering.

[18]" 'Any priests who are in Aaron's family line can eat it. It is their regular share of the offerings that are made to

Why do people cheat?

People cheat mostly because they're lazy. They don't want to work hard to finish an assignment or do well on a test. Cheating is wrong because it's lying, and God tells us not to lie. People cheat in many areas, not just school. Some cheat in games—trying to win without following the rules. Some cheat with money, and others cheat by not being honest with their friends. People who fall into a pattern of cheating find it hard to stop. Kids who cheat in school keep themselves from learning. Then they have to cheat again. After a while, people who cheat stop believing that they can learn on their own. Don't be a cheater—you will cheat yourself.

checkout
Leviticus 6:1–3

Related verses:
Proverbs 11:1;
20:23;
Luke 16:10

I WOULDN'T RECOMMEND IT. I DIDN'T STUDY EITHER.

the LORD with fire. It is their share for all time to come. Anyone who touches those offerings will become holy.' "

¹⁹The LORD spoke to Moses. He said, ²⁰"On the day each high priest who is in Aaron's family line is anointed, he must bring an offering to me. He must bring eight cups of fine flour as a regular grain offering. He must bring half of it in the morning. He must bring the other half in the evening. ²¹Mix it with olive oil. Grill it on a metal plate. Break it in pieces. Bring it as a grain offering. It gives a smell that is pleasant to me. ²²"The son of Aaron who will become the next high priest after him will prepare the grain offering. It is my regular share. It must be completely burned up. ²³Every grain offering a high priest offers must be completely burned up. It must not be eaten."

MORE RULES FOR SIN OFFERINGS

²⁴The LORD spoke to Moses. He said, ²⁵"Speak to Aaron and the priests who are in his family line. Tell them, 'Here are some more rules for sin offerings. You must kill the animal for the sin offering in the sight of the LORD. Kill it in the place where the burnt offering is killed. It is very holy. ²⁶The priest who offers it will eat it. He must eat it in a holy place. He must eat it in the courtyard of the Tent of Meeting. ²⁷'Anyone who touches any of its meat will become holy. Suppose some of the blood is spilled on someone's clothes. Then you must wash them in a holy place. ²⁸Break the clay pot the meat is cooked in. But suppose you cook it in a bronze pot. Then you must scrub the pot and rinse it with water. ²⁹'Any male in a priest's family can eat the meat. It is very holy. ³⁰'But suppose some of the blood of a sin offering is brought into the Tent of Meeting. And that blood is brought into the Holy Room to pay for sin. Then that sin offering must not be eaten. It must be burned.

MORE RULES FOR GUILT OFFERINGS

7 " 'Here are some more rules for guilt offerings. The guilt offering is very holy. ²You must kill the animal for the guilt offering in the same place where you kill the animal for the burnt offering. Sprinkle its blood against every side of the altar. ³" 'Offer all of its fat. It must include the fat tail and the fat that covers the inside parts. ⁴It must include both kidneys with the fat on them next to the lower back muscles. It must also include the covering of the liver. Remove all of it together with the kidneys. ⁵The priest must burn all of it on the altar. It is an offering that is made to the LORD with fire. It is a guilt offering. ⁶" 'Any male in a priest's family can eat it. But he must eat it in a holy place. It is very holy.

⁷" 'The same law applies to the sin offering and the guilt offering. Both of them belong to the priest who offers them to pay for sin. ⁸The priest who offers a burnt offering for anyone can keep its hide for himself. ⁹" 'Every grain offering that is baked in an oven belongs to the priest who offers it. So does every grain offering that is cooked in a pan or grilled on a metal plate. ¹⁰Every grain offering belongs equally to all of the priests who are in Aaron's family line. That is true whether it is mixed with olive oil or it is dry.

MORE RULES FOR FRIENDSHIP OFFERINGS

¹¹" 'Here are some more rules for friendship offerings a person may bring to the LORD. ¹²" 'Suppose he offers a friendship offering to show he is thankful. Then together with the thank offering he must offer flat cakes of bread. He must make them without yeast. He must mix them with olive oil. Or he must offer wafers that are made without yeast. He must spread oil on them. Or he must offer flat cakes that are made out of fine flour. He must add oil to it. He must work the flour and mix it well. ¹³" 'He must bring another friendship offering along with his thank offering. It should be flat cakes of bread that are made with yeast. ¹⁴He must bring one of each kind of bread as an offering. One kind is made with yeast. The other is not. Both of them are a gift to the LORD. They belong to the priest

who sprinkles the blood of the friendship offerings.

¹⁵" 'The person must eat the meat from his thank offering on the day he offers it. He must not leave any of it until morning.

¹⁶" 'But suppose he brings a friendship offering to keep a promise he has made. Or suppose he brings an offering he chooses to give. Then he must eat the sacrifice on the day he offers it. But if anything is left over, he may eat it the next day.

¹⁷" 'He must burn up any meat from the sacrifice that is left over until the third day. ¹⁸Suppose he eats any meat from the friendship offering on the third day. Then the LORD will not accept the offering. He will not accept it as a gift from that person. It is not pure. If the person eats any of it, he will be held accountable for it.

¹⁹" 'He must not eat meat that touches anything that is "unclean." He must burn it up. Anyone who is "clean" may eat any other meat.

²⁰" 'But suppose a person is not "clean" and eats any meat from the friendship offering that belongs to the LORD. Then that person will be cut off from his people.

²¹" 'Suppose a person touches something that is not "clean." It does not matter whether it comes from a human being who is not "clean." It does not matter whether it comes from an animal that is not "clean." It does not matter whether it comes from something that is hated and is not "clean." And suppose the person eats any of the meat from the friendship offering that belongs to the LORD. Then that person will be cut off from his people.' "

ISRAEL MUST NOT EAT FAT OR BLOOD

²²The LORD spoke to Moses. He said, ²³"Speak to the people of Israel. Tell them, 'Do not eat any of the fat of cattle, sheep or goats. ²⁴Do not eat the fat of any animal that is found dead. Do not eat the fat of an animal that wild animals have torn apart. But you can use the fat for any other purpose.

²⁵" 'Suppose an animal has been sacrificed as an offering that is made to the LORD with fire. No one may eat its fat. If he does, he will be cut off from his people.

²⁶" 'No matter where you live, do not eat the blood of any bird or animal. ²⁷If anyone does, he will be cut off from his people.' "

THE SHARE THAT BELONGS TO THE PRIESTS

²⁸The LORD spoke to Moses. He said, ²⁹"Speak to the people of Israel. Tell them, 'Suppose a person brings a friendship offering to the LORD. Then he must bring part of it as his special gift to the LORD. ³⁰He must bring it with his own hands. It is an offering that is made to the LORD with fire. He must bring the fat together with the breast. He must lift the breast up and wave it in front of the LORD as a wave offering. ³¹The priest will burn the fat on the altar.

" 'But the breast belongs to Aaron and the priests who are in his family line. ³²Give the right thigh from your friendship offerings to the priest as a gift. ³³The priest who offers the blood and fat from the friendship offering must be given the right thigh. It is his share.

³⁴" 'I, the LORD, have taken the breast that is waved and the thigh that is given. I have taken them from the friendship offerings of the people of Israel. And I have given them to the priest Aaron and the priests who are in his family line. The offerings are their regular share from the people of Israel.' "

³⁵That is the part of the offerings that are made to the LORD with fire and given to Aaron and the priests who are in his family line. It was given to Aaron and his sons on the day they were set apart to serve the LORD as priests. ³⁶On the day they were anointed, the LORD commanded the people of Israel to give that part to them. For all time to come, it will be the regular share of Aaron and the priests who are in his family line.

³⁷Those are the rules for burnt offerings, grain offerings, sin offerings, guilt offerings and friendship offerings. They are also the rules for the of-

ferings that are given when priests are being prepared to serve the LORD. ³⁸They are the rules the LORD gave Moses on Mount Sinai. He gave them on the day he commanded the people of Israel to bring their offerings to the LORD. That took place in the Sinai Desert.

PREPARING THE PRIESTS TO SERVE THE LORD

8 The LORD spoke to Moses. He said, ²"Bring Aaron and his sons to the entrance to the Tent of Meeting. Bring their clothes and the anointing oil. Bring the bull for the sin offering. Also bring two rams. And bring the basket with the bread that is made without yeast. ³Then gather the whole community at the entrance to the Tent of Meeting."

⁴Moses did just as the LORD had commanded him. All of the people gathered together at the entrance to the Tent of Meeting.

⁵Moses said to the people, "Here is what the LORD has commanded us to do."

⁶Then Moses brought Aaron and his sons to the people. He washed Aaron and his sons with water. ⁷He put the inner robe on Aaron. He tied the belt around him. He dressed him in the outer robe. He put the linen apron on him. He took the skillfully made waistband and tied the apron on him with it. He wanted to make sure it was securely tied to him.

⁸Moses placed the chest cloth on Aaron. He put the Urim and Thummim in the chest cloth. ⁹Then he placed the turban on Aaron's head. On the front of the turban he put the gold plate. It was a sacred crown. Moses did everything just as the LORD had commanded him.

¹⁰Then Moses took the anointing oil and poured it on the holy tent. He also poured it on everything that was in it. That's how he set those things apart for the LORD. ¹¹He sprinkled some of the oil on the altar seven times. He poured oil on the altar and all of its tools. He poured it on the large bowl and its stand. He did it to set them apart.

¹²He poured some of the anointing oil on Aaron's head. He anointed him to set him apart to serve the LORD. ¹³Then Moses brought Aaron's sons to the people. He put the inner robes on them. He tied belts around them. He put headbands on them. He did everything just as the LORD had commanded him.

¹⁴Then he brought the bull for the sin offering. Aaron and his sons placed their hands on its head. ¹⁵Moses killed the bull. He dipped his finger into some of the blood. He put it on all of the horns that stick out from the upper four corners of the altar. He did it to make the altar pure. He poured out the rest of the blood at the bottom of the altar. So he set it apart to make it pure.

¹⁶Moses also removed all of the fat that was around the inside parts of the bull. He removed the covering of the liver. He took both kidneys and their fat. Then he burned all of it on the altar.

¹⁷But he burned the rest of the bull outside the camp. He burned up its hide, its meat and its guts. He did it just as the LORD had commanded him.

¹⁸Then Moses brought the ram for the burnt offering. Aaron and his sons placed their hands on its head. ¹⁹Moses killed the ram. He sprinkled the blood against every side of the altar.

²⁰He cut the ram into pieces. He burned the head, the other pieces and the fat. ²¹He washed the inside parts and the legs with water. He burned the whole ram on the altar as a burnt offering. It had a pleasant smell. It was an offering that was made to the LORD with fire. Moses did everything just as the LORD had commanded him.

²²Then he brought the other ram. It was sacrificed to prepare the priests for serving the LORD. Aaron and his sons placed their hands on its head.

²³Moses killed the ram. He put some of its blood on Aaron's right ear lobe. He put some on the thumb of Aaron's right hand. He also put some on the big toe of Aaron's right foot. ²⁴Then Moses brought Aaron's sons to the people. He put some of the blood on their right ear lobes. He put some on the thumbs of their right hands. He also put some on the big toes of their right feet. Then he sprinkled the rest of

the blood against every side of the altar.

²⁵He removed the fat, the fat tail and all of the fat around the inside parts. He removed the covering of the liver. He removed both kidneys and their fat. And he removed the right thigh. ²⁶Then he took a flat cake of bread from the basket of bread that was made without yeast. The basket was in front of the LORD. Moses took a cake of bread that was made with olive oil. He also took a wafer. He put all of it on the fat parts of the ram and on its right thigh.

²⁷He put everything in the hands of Aaron and his sons. He told them to lift it up and wave it in front of the LORD as a wave offering.

²⁸Then Moses took it from their hands. He burned it on the altar on top of the burnt offering. It was the offering that was sacrificed to prepare the priests for serving the LORD. It had a pleasant smell. It was an offering that was made to the LORD with fire.

²⁹Moses also lifted the ram's breast up and waved it in front of the LORD as a wave offering. The breast was Moses' share of the ram that was sacrificed to prepare the priests for serving the LORD. Moses did everything just as the LORD had commanded him.

³⁰Then Moses took some of the anointing oil. He also took some of the blood from the altar. He sprinkled some of the oil and blood on Aaron and his clothes. He also sprinkled some on Aaron's sons and their clothes. That's how he set apart Aaron and his clothes. And that's how he set apart Aaron's sons and their clothes.

³¹Then Moses spoke to Aaron and his sons. He said, "Cook the meat at the entrance to the Tent of Meeting. Eat it there along with the bread from the basket of the offerings that are brought to prepare the priests for serving the LORD. Do it just as I commanded you. I said, 'Aaron and his sons must eat it.' ³²Then burn up the rest of the meat and the bread.

³³"Don't leave the entrance to the Tent of Meeting for seven days. Don't leave until the days that are required to prepare you for serving the LORD have been completed. Stay here for the full seven days. ³⁴The LORD commanded what has been done here today. It was done to pay for your sin. ³⁵Stay at the entrance to the Tent of Meeting for seven days. Stay here day and night. Do what the LORD requires. Then you won't die. That's the command the LORD gave me."

³⁶So Aaron and his sons did everything just as the LORD had commanded through Moses.

THE PRIESTS OFFER SACRIFICES

9 On the eighth day Moses sent for Aaron, his sons and the elders of Israel. ²He said to Aaron, "Bring a bull calf for your sin offering. Bring a ram for your burnt offering. They must not have any flaws. Offer them to the LORD.

³"Then speak to the people of Israel. Tell them, 'Bring a male goat for a sin offering. Bring a calf and a lamb for a burnt offering. Both of them must be a year old. They must not have any flaws. ⁴Bring an ox and a ram for a friendship offering. Sacrifice all of them to the LORD. Also bring a grain offering. Mix it with olive oil. Today the LORD will appear to you.' "

⁵The people got the things Moses commanded them to get. They took them to the front of the Tent of Meeting. The whole community came up close to the tent. They stood there in front of the LORD.

⁶Then Moses said, "You have done what the LORD has commanded. So the glory of the LORD will appear to you."

⁷Moses said to Aaron, "Come to the altar. Sacrifice your sin offering and your burnt offering. Pay for your sin and the sin of the people. Sacrifice the people's offering. Pay for their sin. Do just as the LORD has commanded."

⁸So Aaron came to the altar. He killed the calf as a sin offering for himself. ⁹His sons brought its blood to him. He dipped his finger into the blood. He put some on the horns that stick out from the upper four corners of the altar. He poured out the rest at the bottom of the altar.

¹⁰He burned the fat and the kidneys on the altar. He also burned the covering

of the liver. All of those parts were from the sin offering. Aaron did just as the LORD had commanded Moses. [11]He burned up the meat and the hide outside the camp.

[12]Then he killed the animal for the burnt offering. His sons handed him its blood. He sprinkled it against every side of the altar. [13]They handed him the burnt offering piece by piece. It included the animal's head. Aaron burned everything on the altar. [14]He washed the inside parts and the legs. He burned them on top of the burnt offering on the altar.

[15]Then Aaron brought the people's offering. He took the goat for their sin offering and killed it. He offered it for a sin offering. He did just as he had done with his own sin offering.

[16]He brought the animal for the burnt offering. He offered it in the way the law requires. [17]He also brought the grain offering. He took a handful of it and burned it on the altar. It was in addition to that morning's burnt offering.

[18]Aaron killed the ox and the ram as the friendship offering for the people. His sons handed him the blood. He sprinkled it against every side of the altar.

[19]His sons also brought the fat parts of the ox and the ram. They included the fat tail and the layer of fat. They also included the kidneys and the covering of the liver. [20]Aaron's sons placed everything on the breasts of the animals.

Aaron burned the fat on the altar. [21]He lifted up the breasts and the right thigh and waved them in front of the LORD as a wave offering. He did it just as Moses had commanded.

[22]Then Aaron lifted up his hands toward the people. He gave them a blessing. He had already sacrificed the sin offering, the burnt offering and the friendship offering. So he stepped down from the altar.

[23]Moses and Aaron went into the Tent of Meeting. When they came out, they gave the people a blessing. The glory of the LORD appeared to all of the people. [24]The LORD sent fire on the altar. It burned up the burnt offering and the fat parts that were on it. All of the people saw it. Then they shouted for joy. They fell with their faces to the ground.

THE LORD KILLS NADAB AND ABIHU

10 Nadab and Abihu were two of Aaron's sons. They got their shallow cups for burning incense. They put fire in them. They added incense to it. They made an offering to the LORD by using fire that wasn't allowed. They did it against his command. [2]So the LORD sent fire on them. It burned them up. They died in front of the LORD.

[3]Then Moses spoke to Aaron. He said, "That's what the LORD was talking about when he said,

" 'Among those who approach me
    I will show that I am holy.
In the sight of all of the people
    I will be honored.' "

So Aaron remained silent.

[4]Moses sent for Mishael and Elzaphan. They were sons of Aaron's uncle Uzziel. Moses said to them, "Come here. Carry the bodies of your cousins outside the camp. Take them away from in front of the Holy Room." [5]So they came and carried them outside the camp. It was just as Moses had ordered. The bodies of Nadab and Abihu still had their inner robes on them.

[6]Moses spoke to Aaron and to Eleazar and Ithamar. They were Aaron's sons. Moses said, "Don't let your hair hang loose. Don't tear your clothes. If you do, you will die. And the LORD will be angry with the whole community.

"But all of the people of Israel are allowed to show they are sad. They are your relatives. They can sob over those the LORD has destroyed with fire.

[7]"Don't leave the entrance to the Tent of Meeting. If you do, you will die. That's because the LORD's anointing oil has made you holy." So they did what Moses told them to do.

[8]Then the LORD spoke to Aaron. He said, [9]"You and your sons must not drink any kind of wine when you go into the Tent of Meeting. If you do, you will die. That is a law that will last for all time to come.

[10]"You must be able to tell the difference between what is holy and what is not. You must be able to tell the difference between what is 'clean' and what is not. [11]You must teach the people of Israel all of the rules I have given them through Moses."

[12]Moses spoke to Aaron and to Eleazar and Ithamar. They were Aaron's two remaining sons. Moses said, "Take the grain offering that is left over from the offerings that are made to the LORD with fire. It is very holy. Make bread without yeast from it. Eat it beside the altar. [13]Eat it in a holy place. It's your share and your sons' share of the offerings that are made to the LORD with fire. Those rules are in keeping with the command the LORD gave me.

[14]"But you and your sons and your daughters can eat the breast that was waved. You can also eat the thigh that was offered. Eat them in a place that is 'clean.' They have been given to you and your children. They are your share of the friendship offerings the people of Israel bring.

[15]"The thigh that was offered must be brought together with the fat parts of the offerings that are made with fire. The breast that was waved must be brought in the same way. All of it must be lifted up and waved in front of the LORD as a wave offering. It will be the regular share for you and your children. That's what the LORD has commanded."

[16]Moses asked about the goat that was brought as the sin offering. He found out that it had been burned up. So he became angry with Eleazar and Ithamar. They were Aaron's two remaining sons.

Moses asked them, [17]"Why didn't you eat the sin offering in a place that is near the Holy Room? The offering is very holy. It was given to you to take the people's guilt away. It paid for their sin in the sight of the LORD. [18]The blood of the offering wasn't taken into the Holy Room. So you should have eaten the goat in a place that is near the Holy Room. That's what I commanded."

[19]Aaron replied to Moses, "Today the people sacrificed their sin offering to the LORD. They also sacrificed their burnt offerings to him. But a terrible thing has happened to me. Two of my sons have died. Would the LORD have been pleased if I had eaten the sin offering today?" [20]When Moses heard that, he was satisfied.

FOOD THAT IS "CLEAN" AND FOOD THAT IS NOT

11 The LORD spoke to Moses and Aaron. He said to them, [2]"Speak to the people of Israel. Tell them, 'Many animals live on land. Here are the only ones you can eat. [3]You can eat any animal that has hoofs that are separated completely in two. But it must also chew the cud.

[4]" 'Some animals only chew the cud. Some only have hoofs that are separated in two. You must not eat those animals.

" 'Camels chew the cud. But their hoofs are not separated in two. So they are not "clean" for you.

[5]" 'Rock badgers chew the cud. But their hoofs are not separated in two. So they are not "clean" for you.

[6]" 'Rabbits chew the cud. But their hoofs are not separated in two. So they are not "clean" for you.

[7]" 'Pigs have hoofs that are separated completely in two. But they do not chew the cud. So they are not "clean" for you.

[8]" 'You must not eat the meat of those animals. You must not even touch their dead bodies. They are not "clean" for you.

[9]" 'Many creatures live in the water of the oceans and streams. You can eat all of those that have fins and scales.

[10]" 'But be sure to avoid all of the creatures in the oceans or streams that do not have fins and scales. That includes all of those that move together in groups and all of those that do not. [11]Be sure to avoid them. Do not eat their meat. Do not even touch their dead bodies. [12]Be sure to avoid everything that lives in the water that does not have fins and scales.

[13]" 'Here are the birds you must be sure to avoid. Do not eat them. Be sure to avoid them.

" 'They include eagles, vultures and black vultures. [14]They include red kites and all kinds of black kites. [15]They include all kinds of ravens. [16]They include horned owls, screech owls, gulls and all kinds of hawks.

[17]" 'They include little owls, cormorants and great owls. [18]They include white owls, desert owls and ospreys. [19]They also include storks, hoopoes, bats and all kinds of herons.

[20]" 'Be sure to avoid every flying insect that walks on all fours. [21]But you can eat some creatures that have wings and walk on all fours. Their legs have joints so they can hop on the ground.

[22]" 'Here are the insects you can eat. You can eat all kinds of locusts, katydids, crickets and grasshoppers. [23]But be sure to avoid every other creature that has wings and four legs.

[24]" 'You will make yourselves "unclean" if you eat those things. If you touch their dead bodies, you will be "unclean" until evening. [25]If a person picks up one of their dead bodies, he must wash his clothes. He will be "unclean" until evening.

[26]" 'Suppose an animal has hoofs that are not separated completely in two. Or suppose an animal does not chew the cud. Then those animals are not "clean" for you. If you touch the dead body of any of them, you will not be "clean."

[27]" 'Many animals walk on all fours. But those that walk on their paws are not "clean" for you. Anyone who touches their dead bodies will be "unclean" until evening. [28]If he picks up their dead bodies, he must wash his clothes. He will be "unclean" until evening. They are not "clean" for him.

[29]" 'Many animals move around on the ground. Here are the ones that are not "clean" for you. They include weasels, rats and all kinds of large lizards. [30]They also include geckos, monitor lizards, wall lizards, skinks and chameleons. [31]Those are the animals that move around on the ground that are not "clean" for you. If you touch their dead bodies, you will be "unclean" until evening.

[32]" 'Suppose one of them dies and falls on something. Then that article will not be "clean." It does not matter what it is used for. It does not matter

whether it is made out of wood, cloth, hide or black cloth. Put it in water. It will be "unclean" until evening. After that, it will be "clean."

[33]" 'Suppose one of those animals falls into a clay pot. Then everything that is in the pot will be "unclean." You must break the pot. [34]Any food that could be eaten but has water on it that came from that pot is not "clean." And any liquid that could be drunk from it is not "clean."

[35]" 'Anything that the dead body of one of those animals falls on becomes "unclean." If it is an oven or cooking pot, break it. It is "unclean." And you must consider it "unclean."

[36]" 'But a spring or a well for collecting water remains "clean." That is true even if the dead body of one of those animals falls into it. But anyone who touches the dead body is not "clean."

[37]" 'If the dead body falls on any seeds that have not been planted yet, the seeds remain "clean." [38]But suppose water has already been put on the seeds. And suppose the dead body falls on them. Then they are not "clean" for you.

[39]" 'Suppose an animal you are allowed to eat dies. If anyone touches its dead body, he will be "unclean" until evening. [40]If he eats part of the dead body, he must wash his clothes. He will be "unclean" until evening. If he picks up the dead body, he must wash his clothes. He will be "unclean" until evening.

[41]" 'Be sure to avoid every creature that moves around on the ground. Do not eat it. [42]Do not eat any of those creatures. It does not matter whether they move on their bellies. It does not matter whether they walk on all fours or on many feet. Be sure to avoid them. [43]Do not make yourselves "unclean" by eating any of those animals. Do not make yourselves "unclean" because of them. Do not let them make you "unclean."

[44]" 'I am the LORD your God. Set yourselves apart. Be holy, because I am holy. Do not make yourselves "unclean" by eating any creatures that move around on the ground. [45]I am the LORD. I brought you up out of Egypt to

be your God. So be holy, because I am holy.

⁴⁶" 'Those are the rules about animals and birds. Those are the rules about every living thing that moves in the water. And those are the rules about every creature that moves around on the ground. ⁴⁷You must be able to tell the difference between what is "clean" and what is not. You must also be able to tell the difference between the living creatures that can be eaten and those that can't.' "

BECOMING "CLEAN" AFTER HAVING A BABY

12 The LORD spoke to Moses. He said, ²"Speak to the people of Israel. Tell them, 'Suppose a woman becomes pregnant and has a baby boy. Then she will be "unclean" for seven days. It is the same as when she is "unclean" during her monthly period. ³On the eighth day the boy must be circumcised.

⁴" 'After that, the woman must wait for 33 days to be made pure from her bleeding. She must not touch anything that is sacred until the 33 days are over. During that time she must not go to the sacred tent.

⁵" 'But suppose she has a baby girl. Then she will be "unclean" for two weeks. It is the same as during her period. After the two weeks, she must wait for 66 days to be made pure from her bleeding.

⁶" 'After she has waited the required number of days to be made pure, she must bring two offerings. She must take them to the priest at the entrance to the Tent of Meeting. She must bring a lamb that is a year old for a burnt offering. She must also bring a young pigeon or a dove for a sin offering. ⁷The priest must offer them to the LORD. They will pay for her sin. Then she will be "clean" from her bleeding.

" 'Those are the rules for a woman who has a baby boy or girl.

⁸" 'But suppose she can't afford a lamb. Then she must bring two doves or two young pigeons. One is for a burnt offering. The other is for a sin offering. The priest will sacrifice those offerings. That will pay for her sin. And she will be "clean." ' "

RULES ABOUT SKIN DISEASES

13 The LORD spoke to Moses and Aaron. He told them to say to the people, ²"Suppose someone's skin has a swelling or a rash or a bright spot. And suppose it could become a skin disease. Then he must be brought to the priest Aaron. Or he must be brought to a priest who is in Aaron's family line.

³"The priest must look carefully at the sore on the person's skin. He must see whether the hair in the sore has turned white. He must also see whether the sore seems to be under the skin. If the sore is white and is under the skin, it is a skin disease. When the priest looks that person over carefully, he must announce that the person is 'unclean.'

⁴"Suppose the spot on the skin is white but does not seem to be under the skin. And suppose the hair in the spot has not turned white. Then the priest must make the person stay away from everyone else for seven days. ⁵On the seventh day the priest must look carefully at the sore again. Suppose it has not changed and has not spread in the skin. Then the priest must make the person stay away from everyone else for another seven days. ⁶On the seventh day the priest must look carefully at the sore again. If it has faded and has not spread, he must announce that the person is 'clean.' It is only a rash. He must wash his clothes. He will be 'clean.'

⁷"But suppose the rash spreads in the skin after he has shown himself to the priest a second time. Then he must appear in front of the priest again. ⁸The priest must look carefully at the sore. If the rash has spread, he must announce that the person is 'unclean.' He has a skin disease.

⁹"When anyone has a skin disease, he must be brought to the priest. ¹⁰The priest must look him over carefully. Suppose there is a white swelling in the skin. Suppose it has turned the hair white. And suppose there are open sores in the swelling. ¹¹Then the person has a skin disease that will never go away. The priest must announce that he is 'unclean.' The priest must

not make the person stay away from everyone else. He is already 'unclean.'

¹²"Suppose the disease breaks out all over his skin. And suppose it covers him from head to foot, as far as the priest can tell. ¹³Then the priest must look him over carefully. If the disease has covered his whole body, the priest must announce that he is 'clean.' All of his skin has turned white. So he is 'clean.'

¹⁴"But when open sores appear on his skin, he will not be 'clean.' ¹⁵When the priest sees the open sores, he must announce that he is 'unclean.' The open sores are not 'clean.' He has a skin disease.

¹⁶"But if the open sores change and turn white, he must go to the priest. ¹⁷The priest must look him over carefully. If the sores have turned white, the priest must announce that the person is 'clean.' Then he will be 'clean.'

¹⁸"Suppose someone has a boil on his skin and it heals. ¹⁹And suppose a white swelling or shiny pink spot appears where the boil was. Then he must show himself to the priest.

²⁰"The priest must look at the boil carefully. Suppose it seems to be under the skin. And suppose the hair in it has turned white. Then the priest must announce that the person is 'unclean.' A skin disease has broken out where the boil was.

²¹"But suppose that when the priest looks at the boil carefully, there is no white hair in it. The boil is not under the skin. And it has faded. Then the priest must make the person stay away from everyone else for seven days. ²²If the boil is spreading in the skin, the priest must announce that the person is 'unclean.' He has a skin disease.

²³"But suppose the spot has not changed. And suppose it has not spread. Then it is only a scar from the boil. And the priest must announce that the person is 'clean.'

²⁴"Suppose someone has a burn on his skin. And suppose a white or shiny pink spot shows up in the open sores of the burn. ²⁵Then the priest must look at the spot carefully. Suppose the hair in it has turned white. And suppose the spot seems to be under the skin. Then the person has a skin dis-

ease. It has broken out where he was burned. The priest must announce that the person is 'unclean.' He has a skin disease.

²⁶"But suppose the priest looks at the spot carefully. Suppose there is no white hair in it. Suppose the spot is not under the skin. And suppose it has faded. Then the priest must make the person stay away from everyone else for seven days. ²⁷On the seventh day the priest must look him over carefully. If the spot is spreading in the skin, the priest must announce that the person is 'unclean.' He has a skin disease.

²⁸"But suppose the spot has not changed. It has not spread in the skin. And it has faded. Then the burn has caused it to swell. The priest must announce that the person is 'clean.' It is only a scar from the burn.

²⁹"Suppose a man or woman has a sore on the head or chin. ³⁰Then the priest must look at the sore carefully. Suppose it seems to be under the skin. And suppose the hair in the sore is yellow and thin. Then the priest must announce that the person is 'unclean.' The sore is an itch. It is a skin disease on the head or chin.

³¹"But suppose the priest looks carefully at that kind of sore. It does not seem to be under the skin. And there is no black hair in it. Then the priest must make the person stay away from everyone else for seven days.

³²"On the seventh day the priest must look at the sore carefully. Suppose the itch has not spread in the skin. It does not have any yellow hair in it. And it does not seem to be under the skin. ³³Then the person must shave his head. But he must not shave the area where the disease is. And the priest must make him stay away from everyone else for another seven days.

³⁴"On the seventh day the priest must look at the itch carefully. Suppose it has not spread in the skin. And suppose it does not seem to be under the skin. Then the priest must announce that the person is 'clean.' He must wash his clothes. He will be 'clean.'

³⁵"But suppose the itch spreads in the skin after the priest announces that the person is 'clean.' ³⁶Then the

priest must look him over carefully. Suppose the itch has spread. Then the priest does not have to look for yellow hair. The person is not 'clean.'

[37]"But suppose the itch has been stopped and black hair has grown in it, as far as the priest can tell. Then the itch is healed. The person is 'clean.' The priest must announce that he is 'clean.'

[38]"Suppose a man or woman has white spots on the skin. [39]Then the priest must look at them carefully. Suppose he sees that the spots are dull white. Then a harmless rash has broken out on the skin. That person is 'clean.'

[40]"Suppose a man loses all of the hair on his head. Then he is 'clean.' [41]Suppose he loses only the hair on the front of his head. Then he is 'clean.'

[42]"But suppose he has a shiny pink sore on his head where his hair was. Then he has a skin disease. It is breaking out on his whole head or on the front of his head.

[43]"The priest must look him over carefully. Suppose the swollen sore on his head or on the front of it is pink and shiny. And suppose it looks like a skin disease. [44]Then he has a skin disease. He is not 'clean.' The priest must announce that the man is 'unclean.' That is because he has a sore on his head.

[45]"Suppose someone has a skin disease that makes him 'unclean.' Then he must wear torn clothes. He must let his hair hang loose. He must cover the lower part of his face. He must cry out, 'Unclean! Unclean!' [46]As long as he has the disease, he remains 'unclean.' He must live alone. He must live outside the camp.

RULES ABOUT MOLD

[47]"Suppose some clothes have mold on them. The clothes could be made out of wool or linen. [48]Or there could be cloth that is woven or knitted out of linen or wool. There could be pieces of leather. Or there could be articles that are made out of leather. [49]And suppose the mold that is on the clothes or on the woven or knitted cloth looks green or red. Or suppose the green or red mold is on the pieces of leather or the

leather articles. Then it is mold that spreads. It must be shown to the priest.

[50]"The priest must look at it carefully. He must keep the article with the mold on it away from everything else for seven days. [51]On the seventh day he must look at it carefully. Suppose the mold has spread in the clothes or in the woven or knitted cloth. Or suppose it has spread on the pieces of leather or on the leather articles. Then it is mold that destroys. The article is not 'clean.'

[52]"The priest must burn up everything that has the mold in it. He must burn up the clothes or the woven or knitted cloth that is made out of wool or linen. He must burn up the leather articles. The mold destroys. So everything must be burned up.

[53]"But suppose the priest looks at the article carefully. The mold has not spread in the clothes. And it has not spread in the woven or knitted cloth or in the leather articles. [54]Then he will order someone to wash the article that has the mold on it. After that, the priest must keep the articles away from everything else for another seven days.

[55]"After the article that has the mold on it has been washed, the priest must look at it carefully. Suppose the way the mold looks has not changed. Then even though the mold has not spread, it is not 'clean.' Burn it up. It does not matter which side of the article the mold is on.

[56]"But suppose the priest looks at it carefully. And suppose the mold has faded after the article has been washed. Then the priest must tear out the part that has mold on it. He must tear it out of the clothes or leather. He must tear it out of the woven or knitted cloth.

[57]"But suppose it shows up again in the clothes. Or suppose it shows up again in the woven or knitted cloth or in the leather articles. Then it is spreading. Everything that has the mold on it must be burned up.

[58]"The clothes that have been washed and do not have any more mold on them must be washed again. So must the woven or knitted cloth or

the leather articles. Then they will be 'clean.' "

⁵⁹Those are the rules about what to do with anything that has mold on it. They apply to clothes that are made out of wool or linen. They apply to woven and knitted cloth and to leather articles. They give a priest directions about when to announce whether something is "clean" or not.

MAKING PEOPLE "CLEAN" FROM SKIN DISEASES

14 The LORD spoke to Moses. He told him to say to the people, ²"Here are the rules for making someone 'clean' if he has had a skin disease. They apply when he is brought to the priest.

³"The priest must go outside the camp. He must look the person over carefully. Suppose he has been healed of his skin disease. ⁴Then the priest will order someone to bring him two live 'clean' birds. He will also order someone to bring him some cedar wood, bright red yarn and branches of a hyssop plant. All of those things will be used to make the person 'clean.'

⁵"The priest will order someone to kill one of the birds. It must be killed over fresh water in a clay pot. ⁶Then the priest must take the live bird. He must dip it into the blood of the bird that was killed over the fresh water. He must dip it into the blood together with the cedar wood, the bright red yarn and the hyssop plant.

⁷"The priest will sprinkle the blood on the person who had the skin disease. That will make him 'clean.' The priest must sprinkle him seven times. Then the priest must announce that he is 'clean.' After that, the priest must let the live bird go free in the open fields.

⁸"The person must also wash his clothes to be made 'clean.' He must shave off all of his hair. He must take a bath. Then he will be 'clean.' After that, he may come into the camp. But he must stay outside his tent for seven days.

⁹"On the seventh day he must shave off all of his hair. He must shave his head. He must shave off his beard. He must also shave off his eyebrows and the rest of his hair. He must wash his clothes. He must take a bath. Then he will be 'clean.'

¹⁰"On the eighth day he must bring two male lambs and one female lamb as an offering. The female must be a year old. The lambs must not have any flaws. He must also bring 24 cups of fine flour as a grain offering. He must mix it with olive oil. He must also bring five ounces of oil. ¹¹The priest who announces that the person is 'clean' must bring him and his offerings to me. He must do it at the entrance to the Tent of Meeting.

¹²"Then the priest must take one of the male lambs. He must offer it as a guilt offering. He must offer it along with five ounces of oil. He must lift all of it up and wave it in front of me as a wave offering.

¹³"He must kill the lamb in the holy place where sin offerings and burnt offerings are killed. The guilt offering belongs to the priest, just as the sin offering does. The guilt offering is very holy.

¹⁴"The priest must take some of the blood from the guilt offering and put it on the person's right ear lobe. He must put some on the thumb of his right hand. He must also put some on the big toe of his right foot.

¹⁵"Then the priest must take some of the oil and pour it into his own left hand. ¹⁶He must dip his right forefinger into the oil that is in his hand. He must use his finger to sprinkle some of the oil in front of me seven times.

¹⁷"The priest must put some of the oil that is in his hand on the same places he put the blood of the guilt offering. He must put some on the person's right ear lobe. He must put some on the thumb of his right hand. He must put some on the big toe of his right foot. ¹⁸He must put on his head the rest of the oil that is in his hand. It will pay for the person's sin in my sight.

¹⁹"Then the priest must sacrifice the sin offering. It will pay for the person's sin. He will be made 'clean' after being 'unclean.' After that, the priest will kill the burnt offering. ²⁰He will offer it on the altar. He will offer it together with the grain offering. It will pay for the person's sin. Then he will be 'clean.'

²¹"But suppose he is poor. Suppose he can't afford all of those offerings. Then he must bring one male lamb as a guilt offering. It must be lifted up and waved in front of me to pay for his sin. He must also bring eight cups of fine flour along with the lamb. He must mix the flour with olive oil. It is a grain offering. He must offer it along with five ounces of oil. ²²He must also bring two doves or two young pigeons that he can afford. One is for a sin offering. The other is for a burnt offering.

²³"On the eighth day he must bring them to the priest so he can be made 'clean.' He must bring them to the entrance to the Tent of Meeting. He must do it in my sight.

²⁴"The priest must take the lamb for the guilt offering. He must take it together with the five ounces of oil. He must lift all of it up and wave it in front of me as a wave offering. ²⁵He must kill the lamb for the guilt offering. He must take some of its blood and put it on the person's right ear lobe. He must put some on the thumb of his right hand. He must also put some on the big toe of his right foot.

²⁶"The priest must pour some of the oil into his own left hand. ²⁷He must dip his right forefinger into the oil that is in his hand. He must use his finger to sprinkle some of it seven times in front of me.

²⁸"He must put some of the oil that is in his hand on the same places he put the blood of the guilt offering. He must put some on the person's right ear lobe. He must put some on the thumb of his right hand. He must also put some on the big toe of his right foot. ²⁹He must put on his head the rest of the oil that is in his hand. It will pay for the person's sin in my sight.

³⁰"The priest will sacrifice the doves or the young pigeons that the person can afford. ³¹One is for a sin offering. The other is for a burnt offering. The priest must offer them together with the grain offering. In that way he will pay for the person's sin in my sight. He will do it to make him 'clean.' "

³²Those are the rules for anyone who has a skin disease. They are for people who can't afford the regular offerings that are required to make them "clean."

MAKING THINGS "CLEAN" FROM MOLD

³³The LORD spoke to Moses and Aaron. He told them to say to the people, ³⁴"You will enter the land of Canaan. I am giving it to you as your own. When you enter it, suppose I put mold in one of your houses. And suppose the mold spreads. ³⁵Then the owner of that house must go and speak to the priest. He must say, 'I've seen something that looks like mold in my house.'

³⁶"The priest must order everything to be taken out of the house. It must be done before he goes in to look carefully at the mold. If it is not done, the priest must announce that everything in the house is 'unclean.'

"After the house is empty the priest must go in and check it. ³⁷He must look carefully at the mold that is on the walls. Suppose it looks as if it has green or red dents in it. And suppose the dents look as if they are behind the surface of the wall. ³⁸Then the priest must go out the door. He must close the house up for seven days.

³⁹"On the seventh day the priest will return to check the house. Suppose the mold that is on the walls has spread. ⁴⁰Then he must order someone to tear out the stones that have mold on them. He must have them thrown into an 'unclean' place outside the town. ⁴¹He must have all of the inside walls of the house scraped. Everything that is scraped off must be dumped into an 'unclean' place outside the town.

⁴²"Then other stones must be put in the place of the stones that had mold on them. The inside walls of the house must be coated with new clay.

⁴³"Suppose the stones have been torn out. The house has been scraped. And the walls have been coated with new clay. But the mold appears again. ⁴⁴"Then the priest must go and look things over carefully. Suppose the mold has spread in the house. Then it is the kind of mold that destroys things. The house is not 'clean.'

⁴⁵"It must be torn down. The stones, the wood and all of the clay coating

must be torn out. All of it must be taken out of the town to an 'unclean' place.

⁴⁶"Suppose someone goes into the house while it is closed up. Then he will be 'unclean' until evening. ⁴⁷If he sleeps or eats in the house, he must wash his clothes.

⁴⁸"But suppose the priest comes to look things over carefully. And suppose the mold has not spread after the walls had been coated with new clay. Then he will announce that the house is 'clean.' The mold is gone.

⁴⁹"To make the house pure, the priest must get two birds. He must also get some cedar wood, bright red yarn and branches of a hyssop plant. ⁵⁰He must kill one of the birds over fresh water in a clay pot.

⁵¹"Then he must take the cedar wood, the hyssop plant, the bright red yarn and the live bird. He must dip all of them into the blood of the dead bird. He must also dip them into the fresh water. He must sprinkle the house seven times.

⁵²"The priest will use the blood and the water to make the house pure. He will use the live bird to make it pure. He will also use the cedar wood, the hyssop plant and the bright red yarn to make it pure.

⁵³"Then he must let the live bird go free in the open fields outside the town. In that way he will make the house pure. It will be 'clean.' "

⁵⁴Those are the rules for skin diseases. They apply to itches. ⁵⁵They apply to mold in clothes or in houses. ⁵⁶They also apply to swellings, rashes or bright red spots on the skin. ⁵⁷Use those rules to decide whether something is "clean" or not.

Those are the rules for skin diseases and for mold.

RULES ABOUT LIQUID BODY WASTES

15 The LORD spoke to Moses and Aaron. He said, ²"Speak to the people of Israel. Tell them, 'Suppose liquid waste is flowing out of a man's body. That liquid is not "clean." ³It does not matter whether it continues to flow out of his body or is blocked. It will make him "unclean."

Here is how his liquid body waste will make him "unclean."

⁴" 'Any bed the man who has the flow of liquid body waste lies on will not be "clean." Anything he sits on will not be "clean."

⁵" 'If any of you touches the man's bed, you must wash your clothes. You must take a bath. You will be "unclean" until evening. ⁶Suppose you sit on anything the man sat on. Then you must wash your clothes. You must take a bath. You will be "unclean" until evening.

⁷" 'Suppose you touch the man who has the flow of liquid body waste. Then you must wash your clothes. You must take a bath. You will be "unclean" until evening.

⁸" 'Suppose you are "clean." And suppose the man who has the flow of liquid waste spits on you. Then you must wash your clothes. You must take a bath. You will be "unclean" until evening.

⁹" 'Everything the man sits on when he is riding will be "unclean." ¹⁰Suppose you touch any of the things that were under him. Then you will be "unclean" until evening. Even if you pick up those things, you must wash your clothes. You must take a bath. You will be "unclean" until evening.

¹¹" 'Suppose the man who has the liquid flow touches you. And suppose he does it without rinsing his hands with water. Then you must wash your clothes. You must take a bath. You will be "unclean" until evening.

¹²" 'Suppose the man touches a clay pot. Then that pot must be broken. Any wooden article he touches must be rinsed with water.

¹³" 'Suppose the man has been healed from his liquid flow. Then he must wait seven days. He must wash his clothes. He must take a bath in fresh water. After that, he will be "clean."

¹⁴" 'On the eighth day he must get two doves or two young pigeons. He must come to the LORD at the entrance to the Tent of Meeting. There he must give the birds to the priest. ¹⁵The priest must sacrifice them. One is for a sin offering. The other is for a burnt offering. In that way the priest will pay for

the man's sin in the sight of the LORD. He will do it because the man had a liquid flow.

¹⁶" 'Suppose semen flows from a man's body. Then he must wash his whole body with water. He will be "unclean" until evening.

¹⁷" 'Suppose clothes or leather have semen on them. Then they must be washed with water. They will be "unclean" until evening.

¹⁸" 'Suppose a man makes love to a woman. And suppose semen flows from his body and touches both of them. Then they must take a bath. They will be "unclean" until evening.

¹⁹" 'Suppose a woman is having her regular period. Then for seven days she will not be pure. Anyone who touches her will be "unclean" until evening.

²⁰" 'Anything she lies on during her period will be "unclean." Anything she sits on will be "unclean."

²¹" 'If anyone touches her bed, he must wash his clothes. He must take a bath. He will be "unclean" until evening. ²²If anyone touches anything she sits on, he must wash his clothes. He must take a bath. He will be "unclean" until evening.

²³" 'It does not matter whether it was her bed or anything she was sitting on. If anyone touches it, he will be "unclean" until evening.

²⁴" 'Suppose a man makes love to that woman. And suppose blood from her monthly period touches him. Then he will be "unclean" for seven days. Any bed he lies on will be "unclean."

²⁵" 'Suppose blood flows from a woman's body for many days. And it happens at a time other than her monthly period. Or blood keeps flowing after her period is over. Then she will be "unclean" as long as the blood continues to flow. She will be "unclean," just as she is during the days of her period.

²⁶" 'Any bed she lies on while her blood continues to flow will be "unclean." It is the same as it is when she is having her period. Anything she sits on will be "unclean." It is the same as it is when she is having her period.

²⁷" 'If anyone touches those things, he will not be "clean." He must wash his clothes. He must take a bath. He will be "unclean" until evening.

²⁸" 'Suppose the woman has been healed from her flow of blood. Then she must wait seven days. After that, she will be "clean." ²⁹On the eighth day she must get two doves or two young pigeons. She must bring them to the priest at the entrance to the Tent of Meeting.

³⁰" 'The priest must sacrifice them. One is for a sin offering. The other is for a burnt offering. In that way he will pay for her sin in the sight of the LORD. He will do it because her flow of blood made her "unclean."

³¹" 'You must keep the people of Israel away from things that make them "unclean." Then they will not die for being "unclean." And they will not die for making the place where the LORD lives "unclean." It is in the middle of the camp.' "

³²Those are the rules for a man who has liquid waste flowing out of his body. They apply to a man who is made "unclean" by semen that flows from his body. ³³They apply to a woman who is having her monthly period. They apply to a man or woman who has a liquid flow. And they apply to a man who makes love to a woman who is not "clean."

THE DAY WHEN SIN IS PAID FOR

16 The LORD spoke to Moses after two of Aaron's sons had died. They were the sons who died when they came near the LORD. ²The LORD said to Moses, "Speak to your brother Aaron. Tell him not to come into the Most Holy Room just anytime he wants to. Tell him not to come behind the curtain that is in front of the cover of the ark. The cover is the place where sin is paid for. If he comes behind the curtain, he will die. That is because I appear in the cloud over the cover.

³"Aaron must not enter the area of the sacred tent without bringing a sacrifice. He must bring a young bull for a sin offering. He must also bring a ram for a burnt offering.

⁴"He must put on the sacred inner

robe that is made out of linen. He must wear linen underwear next to his body. He must tie the linen belt around him. And he must put on the linen turban. Those are sacred clothes. So he must take a bath before he puts them on.

⁵"The community of Israel must give him two male goats and a ram. The goats are for a sin offering. The ram is for a burnt offering.

⁶"Aaron must offer the bull for his own sin offering. It will pay for his own sin and the sin of his whole family.

⁷"Then he must take the two goats and bring them to me at the entrance to the Tent of Meeting. ⁸He must cast lots for the two goats. One lot is for me. The other is for the goat that carries the people's sins away. ⁹Aaron must bring the goat that is chosen for me by lot. He must sacrifice it for a sin offering.

¹⁰"But the goat that is chosen by the other lot must remain alive. First it must be brought in to me to pay for the people's sin. Then it must be sent into the desert as a goat that carries the people's sins away.

¹¹"Aaron must bring the bull for his own sin offering. It will pay for his own sin and the sin of his whole family. He must kill the bull for his own sin offering.

¹²"He must take a shallow cup full of burning coals from the altar in my sight. He must get two handfuls of incense that is completely ground up. The incense must smell sweet. He must take the cup and the incense behind the curtain. ¹³He must put the incense on the fire in my sight. The smoke from the incense will hide the cover of the ark where the tablets of the covenant are kept. The cover is the place where sin is paid for. Aaron must burn the incense so that he will not die.

¹⁴"He must dip his finger in the bull's blood. He must sprinkle it on the front of the cover of the ark. He must sprinkle some in front of the cover. He must do it seven times.

¹⁵"Then Aaron must kill the goat for the sin offering for the people. He must take its blood behind the curtain. There he must do the same thing with it as he did with the bull's blood.

He must sprinkle it on the cover of the ark. He must also sprinkle some in front of it.

¹⁶"That is how he will make the Most Holy Room pure. He must do it because the people of Israel are not 'clean.' They have not obeyed me. They have also committed other sins. Aaron must do the same for the Tent of Meeting because it stands in the middle of the camp. And the camp is not 'clean.'

¹⁷"No one can be in the Tent of Meeting when Aaron goes into the Most Holy Room to pay for the people's sin. No one can enter the tent until Aaron comes out. He will not come out until he has paid for his own sin and the sin of his whole family. He will not come out until he has also paid for the sin of the whole community of Israel.

¹⁸"Then he will come out to the altar for burnt offerings. It is in front of the tent where the ark of the LORD is. He will make the altar pure and clean. He will take some of the bull's blood and some of the goat's blood. Then he will put the blood on all of the horns that stick out from the upper four corners of the altar. ¹⁹He will sprinkle some of the blood on it with his finger seven times. He will do it to make the altar pure. He will do it to set it apart from the people of Israel. They are not 'clean.'

²⁰"Aaron will finish making the Most Holy Room pure and clean. He will finish making the Tent of Meeting and the altar pure.

"Then he will bring the live goat out. ²¹He must place both of his hands on its head. While he does that, he must tell me about all of the sins the people of Israel have committed. He must tell me about all of their evil acts and the times they did not obey me. In that way he puts their sins on the goat's head.

"Then he will send the goat away into the desert. The goat will be led away by a man who was appointed to do it. ²²The goat will carry all of their sins on itself to a place where there are no people. And the man will set the goat free in the desert.

²³"Then Aaron must go into the Tent of Meeting. He must take off the linen

clothes he put on before he entered the Most Holy Room. He must leave them there. ²⁴He must take a bath in a holy place. And he must put on his regular clothes.

"Then he will come out and sacrifice the burnt offering for himself. He will also sacrifice the burnt offering for the people. That will pay for his own sin and the people's sin. ²⁵He will also burn the fat of the sin offering on the altar.

²⁶"The man who sets free the goat that carries the people's sins away must wash his clothes. He must take a bath. After that, he can come back into the camp.

²⁷"The bull and the goat for the sin offerings must be taken outside the camp. Their blood was brought into the Most Holy Room. It paid for sin. The hides, meat and guts must be burned up.

²⁸"The man who burns them must wash his clothes. He must take a bath. After that, he can come back into the camp.

²⁹"Here is a law for you that will last for all time to come. On the tenth day of the seventh month you must not eat anything. You must not do any work. It does not matter whether you are Israelites or outsiders.

³⁰"On that day your sin will be paid for. You will be made pure and clean. You will be clean from all of your sins in my sight. ³¹That day is a sabbath for you. You must rest on it. You must not eat anything on that day. That is a law that will last for all time to come.

³²"The high priest must pay for sin. He must make everything pure and clean. He has been anointed and prepared to become the next high priest after his father. He must put on the sacred clothes that are made out of linen. ³³He must make the Most Holy Room, the Tent of Meeting and the altar pure. And he must pay for the sin of the priests and all of the people in the whole community.

³⁴"Here is a law for you that will last for all time to come. Once a year you must pay for all of the sin of the people of Israel."

So it was done, just as the LORD commanded Moses.

DO NOT EAT MEAT THAT HAS BLOOD IN IT

17 The LORD spoke to Moses. He said, ²"Speak to Aaron and his sons. Speak to all of the people of Israel. Tell them, 'Here is what the LORD has commanded. He has said, ³"Suppose someone sacrifices an ox, a lamb or a goat. He sacrifices it in the camp or outside of it. ⁴He does it instead of bringing the animal to the entrance to the Tent of Meeting. He sacrifices it instead of giving it as an offering to me in front of my holy tent. Then he will be thought of as guilty of spilling blood. Because he has done that, he must be cut off from his people.

⁵" ' "The people of Israel are now making sacrifices in the open fields. But they must bring their sacrifices to the priest. They must bring them to me at the entrance to the Tent of Meeting. There they must sacrifice them as friendship offerings. ⁶The priest must sprinkle the blood against my altar. It is the altar at the entrance to the Tent of Meeting. He must burn the fat. It will give a pleasant smell to me.

⁷" ' "Israel must stop offering any of their sacrifices to statues of gods that look like goats. When they offer sacrifices to those statues, they are not faithful to me. That is a law for them that will last for all time to come." '

⁸"Tell them, 'Suppose someone offers a burnt offering or sacrifice. It does not matter whether he is an Israelite or an outsider. ⁹And suppose he does not bring it to the entrance to the Tent of Meeting to sacrifice it to me. Then he must be cut off from his people.

¹⁰" 'Suppose someone eats meat that still has blood in it. It does not matter whether he is an Israelite or an outsider. I will turn against him if he eats it. I will cut him off from his people.

¹¹" 'The life of each creature is in its blood. So I have given you the blood of animals to pay for your sin on the altar. Blood is life. That is why blood pays for your sin.

¹²" 'So I say to the people of Israel, "You must not eat meat that still has blood in it. And an outsider who lives among you must not eat it either."

¹³" 'Suppose any of you hunts any animal or bird that can be eaten. It does not matter whether you are an Israelite or an outsider. You must let the blood flow out of the animal or bird. You must cover the blood with dirt.

¹⁴" 'That is because every creature's life is its blood. And that is why I have said to the people of Israel, "You must not eat any creature's meat that still has blood in it. Every creature's life is its blood. Anyone who eats that kind of meat must be cut off."

¹⁵" 'Suppose someone eats anything that is found dead or is torn apart by wild animals. It does not matter whether he is an Israelite or an outsider. He must wash his clothes. He must take a bath. He will be "unclean" until evening. After that, he will be "clean."

¹⁶" 'But suppose he does not wash his clothes. And suppose he does not take a bath. Then he will be held accountable for what he has done.' "

DO NOT COMMIT SEXUAL SINS

18 The LORD spoke to Moses. He said, ²"Speak to the people of Israel. Tell them, 'I am the LORD your God. ³You must not do what the people of Egypt do. You used to live there. And you must not do what the people of Canaan do. I am bringing you into their land. Do not follow their practices.

⁴" 'You must obey my laws. You must be careful to follow my rules. I am the LORD your God. ⁵Keep my rules and laws. The one who obeys them will live by them. I am the LORD.

⁶" 'Do not have sex with any of your close relatives. I am the LORD.

⁷" 'Do not bring shame on your father by having sex with your mother. Do not have sex with her. She is your mother.

⁸" 'Do not have sex with any other wife of your father. That would bring shame on your father.

⁹" 'Do not have sex with your sister.

KIDS' QUESTION

Why did people kill animals for church?

Every person sins against God and that sin must be paid for. Before Jesus died for our sins, God's people brought animals to pay for their sins. The animal took the person's place. When Jesus did come, he died for every person's sin for all time. That is why John the Baptist called him the *Lamb* of God. Jesus was a lot like the lambs that were offered for sins. But he was the *perfect* Son of God. His death paid for all sins once and for all. No more animals ever have to die for our sins again.

checkout Leviticus 17:11

Related verses:
John 1:29;
Hebrews 9:22;
10:1–18

It does not matter whether she is your father's daughter or your mother's daughter. It does not matter whether she was born in the same home as you were or somewhere else.

[10] " 'Do not have sex with your son's daughter or your daughter's daughter. That would bring shame on you.

[11] " 'Do not have sex with the daughter of your father's wife. She was born to your father. She is your sister.

[12] " 'Do not have sex with your father's sister. She is a close relative on your father's side.

[13] " 'Do not have sex with your mother's sister. She is a close relative on your mother's side.

[14] " 'Do not bring shame on your father's brother by having sex with his wife. She is your aunt.

[15] " 'Do not have sex with your daughter-in-law. She is your son's wife. Do not have sex with her.

[16] " 'Do not have sex with your brother's wife. That would bring shame on your brother.

[17] " 'Do not have sex with both a woman and her daughter. Do not have sex with either her son's daughter or her daughter's daughter. They are close relatives on her side. Having sex with them is an evil thing.

[18] " 'Do not take your wife's sister as another wife and have sex with her. Do not do it while your wife is still living.

[19] " 'Do not make love to a woman during her monthly period. She is not "clean" at that time.

[20] " 'Do not have sex with your neighbor's wife. That would make you "unclean."

[21] " 'Do not hand over any of your children to be sacrificed to the god Molech. That would be treating my name as if it were not holy. I am the LORD your God.

[22] " 'Do not have sex with a man as you would have sex with a woman. I hate that.

[23] " 'Do not have sex with an animal. Do not make yourself "unclean" by doing that. A woman must not offer herself to an animal to have sex with it. That is a twisted use of sex.

[24] " 'Do not make yourselves "unclean" in any of those ways. That is how other nations became "unclean."

So I am going to drive those nations out of the land to make room for you. [25] Even their land was not "clean." So I punished it because of its sin. The land itself threw out the people who lived there.

[26] " 'But you must keep my rules and my laws. You must not do any of the things I hate. It does not matter whether you are Israelites or outsiders.

[27] " 'All of those things were done by the people who lived in the land before you. That is how the land became "unclean." [28] If you make the land "unclean," it will throw you out. It will get rid of you just as it got rid of the nations that were there before you.

[29] " 'Suppose you do any of the things I hate. Then you must be cut off from your people.

[30] " 'Do exactly what I require. When you arrive in Canaan, do not follow any of the practices of its people. I hate the things they do. Do not make yourselves "unclean" by doing them. I am the LORD your God.' "

OTHER LAWS

19 The LORD spoke to Moses. He said, [2] "Speak to the whole community of Israel. Tell them, 'Be holy, because I am holy. I am the LORD your God.

[3] " 'All of you must have respect for your mother and father. You must always keep my Sabbath days. I am the LORD your God.

[4] " 'Do not turn away from me to worship statues of gods. Do not make gods out of metal for yourselves. I am the LORD your God.

[5] " 'Suppose you sacrifice a friendship offering to me. Then do it in the right way. And I will accept it from you. [6] You must eat it on the same day you sacrifice it or on the next day. Anything that is left over until the third day must be burned up.

[7] " 'If you eat any of it on the third day, it is not pure. I will not accept it. [8] If you eat it, you will be held accountable. You have misused what is holy to me. You will be cut off from your people.

[9] " 'Suppose you are harvesting your crops. Then do not harvest all the way to the edges of your field. And do not

pick up the grain you missed. ¹⁰Do not go over your vineyard a second time. Do not pick up the grapes that have fallen to the ground. Leave them for poor people and outsiders. I am the LORD your God.

¹¹" 'Do not steal.

" 'Do not tell lies.

" 'Do not cheat one another.

¹²" 'Do not take an oath and give false witness in my name. That would be treating it as if it were not holy. I am the LORD your God.

¹³" 'Do not cheat your neighbor. Do not rob him.

" 'Do not hold back the pay of a hired worker until morning.

¹⁴" 'Do not call a curse down on deaf people. Do not put anything in front of blind people that will make them trip. Instead, have respect for me. I am the LORD your God.

¹⁵" 'Do not make something that is wrong appear to be right. Treat poor people and rich people in the same way. Do not favor one person over another. Instead, judge everyone fairly.

¹⁶" 'Do not go around spreading lies among your people.

" 'Do not do anything that puts your neighbor's life in danger. I am the LORD.

¹⁷" 'Do not hate your brother in your heart. Correct your neighbor boldly when he does something wrong. Then you will not share his guilt.

¹⁸" 'Do not try to get even. Do not hold anything against one of your people. Instead, love your neighbor as you love yourself. I am the LORD.

¹⁹" 'Obey my rules.

" 'Do not let different kinds of animals mate with each other.

" 'Do not mix two kinds of seeds and then plant them in your field.

" 'Do not wear clothes that are made out of two kinds of cloth.

²⁰" 'Suppose a man has sex with a female slave. But she and another man have promised to get married to each other. And her freedom has not yet been paid for or given to her. Then she and the man who had sex with her must be punished. But they must not be put to death, because she had not been set free.

²¹" 'The man must bring a ram to the entrance to the Tent of Meeting. It is for a guilt offering to me. ²²The priest must take the ram for the guilt offer-

KIDS' QUESTION

Why would your friends expect you to lie for them?

Some people think that friends should do anything for them—even lie. But that's not part of friendship. More important than doing what your friends want is doing what God wants. That's what you need to consider first. Your relationship with God should be your most important friendship, and God says that lying is wrong.

checkout
Leviticus 19:11

IF MY MOM ASKS WHERE WE WERE, SAY WE WERE AT THE LIBRARY, OK?

THAT WAS A LIBRARY?

Related verse:
Ephesians 4:25

ing. He must sacrifice it to pay for the man's sin in my sight. Then his sin will be forgiven.

²³" 'When you enter the land, suppose you plant a fruit tree. Then do not eat its fruit for the first three years. The fruit is not "clean." ²⁴In the fourth year all of the fruit will be holy. Offer it as a way of showing praise to me. ²⁵But in the fifth year you can eat the fruit. Then you will gather more and more fruit. I am the LORD your God.

²⁶" 'Do not eat any meat that still has blood in it.

" 'Do not practice any kind of evil magic at all.

²⁷" 'Do not cut the hair on the sides of your head. Do not clip off the edges of your beard.

²⁸" 'Do not make cuts on your bodies when someone dies. Do not put marks on your skin. I am the LORD.

²⁹" 'Do not dishonor your daughter's body by making a prostitute out of her. If you do, the people of Israel will start using prostitutes. The land will be filled with evil.

³⁰" 'You must always keep my Sabbath days. Have respect for my sacred tent. I am the LORD.

³¹" 'Do not look for advice from people who get messages from those who have died. Do not go to people who talk to the spirits of the dead. If you do, they will make you "unclean." I am the LORD your God.

³²" 'Stand up in order to show your respect for old people. Also have respect for me. I am the LORD your God.

³³" 'Suppose an outsider lives with you in your land. Then do not treat him badly. ³⁴Treat him as if he were one of your own people. Love him as you love yourself. Remember that all of you were outsiders in Egypt. I am the LORD your God.

³⁵" 'Be honest when you measure lengths, weights or amounts. ³⁶Use honest scales and honest weights. Use honest dry measures. And use honest liquid measures. I am the LORD your God. I brought you out of Egypt.

³⁷" 'Obey all of my rules and laws. Follow them. I am the LORD.' "

ISRAEL WILL BE PUNISHED FOR THEIR SINS

20 The LORD spoke to Moses. He said, ²"Say to the people of Israel, 'Suppose a person

How should I treat kids who are different?

Kids are different in many ways. They may be different races, come from different cultures, or be different sizes. Some children may have trouble learning, or may have trouble using their hands and feet. People in a school or neighborhood may even speak different languages. It's never right to make fun of people or ignore them because of those differences. Just because kids are different doesn't mean that they are wrong or that you should be afraid of them. Think about this: God made the different races and gave people the ability to do things differently. Even if people have different ideas about God, he still wants us to be kind and to respect others. No matter how different kids are, God wants us to treat them in the way we would like to be treated.

Related verses:
Matthew 25:37–40;
Luke 19:1–5;
John 4:9

checkout
Leviticus 19:33

sacrifices one of his children to the god Molech. It does not matter whether that person is an Israelite or an outsider who lives in Israel. He must be put to death. The people of the community must kill him by throwing stones at him. ³I will turn against that man. I will cut him off from his people. That is because he sacrificed his child to Molech. He has made my sacred tent "unclean." He has treated my name as if it were not holy.

⁴" 'Suppose the people of the community close their eyes to the fact that the man sacrificed his child to Molech. And suppose they fail to put him to death. ⁵Then I will turn against that man and his family. I will cut him off from his people. I will also cut off all those who follow him by joining themselves to Molech. They are not faithful to me.

⁶" 'Suppose someone looks for advice from people who get messages from those who have died. Or he goes to people who talk to the spirits of the dead. And he follows their advice. Then he has not been faithful to me. So I will turn against him. I will cut him off from his people.

⁷" 'Set yourselves apart for me. Be holy, because I am the LORD your God. ⁸Obey my rules. Follow them. I am the LORD. I make you holy.

⁹" 'If anyone calls down a curse on his father or mother, he will be put to death. He has cursed his father or mother. Anything that happens to him will be his own fault.

¹⁰" 'Suppose a man commits adultery with his neighbor's wife. Then the man and the woman must be put to death.

¹¹" 'Suppose a man has sex with his father's wife. Then he has brought shame on his father. The man and the woman must be put to death. Anything that happens to them will be their own fault.

¹²" 'Suppose a man has sex with his daughter-in-law. Then they must be put to death. They have used sex in a twisted way. Anything that happens to them will be their own fault.

¹³" 'Suppose a man has sex with another man as he would have sex with a woman. I hate what they have done. They must be put to death. Anything that happens to them will be their own fault.

¹⁴" 'Suppose a man gets married to both a woman and her mother. That is evil. All of them must be burned to death. Then there will not be any evil among you.

¹⁵" 'Suppose a man has sex with an animal. Then he must be put to death. You must also kill the animal.

Is it OK to hit my brother back if he hit me first?

No. That is called revenge. God says in the Bible that revenge is his job. He has given you people like police, teachers and parents to settle fights. It is not your place to hit back. So if your brother or sister hits you, be nice back. If he or she continues to be mean, tell your father and mother and let them take care of it. God wants you to learn how to get along with people. Sometimes that can be difficult at home. But if you can learn to love and to be kind to your family members, you probably will be able to get along with almost anyone else.

Related verses:
Matthew 5:9;
Romans 12:14,
17–20

checkout
Leviticus 19:18

¹⁶" 'Suppose a woman has sex with an animal. Then kill the woman and the animal. They must be put to death. Anything that happens to them will be their own fault.

¹⁷" 'Suppose a man gets married to his sister and has sex with her. That is a shameful thing to do. It does not matter whether she is the daughter of his father or of his mother. They must be cut off right in front of their own people. That man has brought shame on his sister. He will be held accountable for what he has done.

¹⁸" 'Suppose a man makes love to a woman during her monthly period. He has uncovered the place where her bleeding was coming from. And she has let him do it. So they must be cut off from their people.

¹⁹" 'Do not have sex with the sister of either your mother or your father. That would bring shame on a close relative. Both of you would be held accountable for what you have done.

²⁰" 'Suppose a man has sex with his aunt. Then he has brought shame on his uncle. Both of them will be held accountable for what they have done. They will die without having any children.

²¹" 'Suppose a man gets married to his brother's wife. That is something that should never be done. He has brought shame on his brother. Neither of them will have any children.

²²" 'Obey all of my rules and laws. Follow them. Then the land where I am bringing you to live will not throw you out. ²³To make room for you, I am going to drive out the nations that are in the land. You must not follow the practices of those nations. I hated those nations because they did all of those things.

²⁴" 'But I said to you, "You will take over their land as your own. I will give it to you. It will belong to you. It is a land that has plenty of milk and honey." I am the LORD your God. I have set you apart from the other nations.

²⁵" 'So you must be able to tell the

Why do they put horoscopes in the newspaper?

Newspapers print horoscopes because many people read them. They believe that big parts of life are controlled by forces beyond their control. They think the horoscopes will guide them.

Believers do not need horoscopes. Only God controls what happens and only God knows the future. If you need advice, you can do three things. (1) You can read the Bible. (2) You can talk to wise people. (3) You can ask God for wisdom (James 1:5). Pray to God if you are worried about the future. Tell him about your worries and ask him to take care of you. That is the best thing to do. He is more powerful than any other force in the universe.

I DON'T HAVE ENOUGH NEWS FOR THE NEWSPAPER. WHAT WILL I DO?

checkout Leviticus 20:6

Related verses:
Proverbs 13:20;
Philippians 4:6

difference between animals that are "clean" and those that are not. You must know which birds are "clean" and which are not. Do not make yourselves "unclean" by eating any animal or bird that is not "clean." Do not make yourselves "unclean" by eating anything that moves along the ground. I have set all of them apart. They are "unclean" for you.

²⁶" 'You must be holy. You must be set apart to me. I am the LORD. I am holy. I have set you apart from the other nations to be my own people.

²⁷" 'Suppose a man or woman gets messages from those who have died. Or suppose a man or woman talks to the spirits of the dead. Then you must put that man or woman to death. You must kill them by throwing stones at them. Anything that happens to them will be their own fault.' "

RULES FOR PRIESTS

21 The LORD said to Moses, "Speak to the priests, the sons of Aaron. Tell them, 'A priest must not make himself "unclean" by going near the dead body of any of his people. ²But he can go near the body of a close relative. It could be his mother, father, son, daughter or brother. ³He can also go near a sister who is not married. She would have depended on him because she did not have a husband. The priest can make himself "unclean" by going near her body. ⁴But he must not make himself "unclean" by going near the bodies of people who were only related to him by marriage. Going near them would make him "unclean."

⁵" 'Priests must not shave any part of their heads. They must not shave off the edges of their beards. They must not make cuts on their bodies when someone dies.

⁶" 'Priests must be holy. They must be set apart for me. I am their God. They must not treat my name as if it were not holy. They must be holy because they bring offerings that are made to me with fire. That is my food.

⁷" 'They must not get married to women who are "unclean" because they are prostitutes. They must not marry women who are divorced from

their husbands. That is because priests are holy. They are set apart for me. I am their God. ⁸Consider them as holy, because they offer up food to me. Consider them as holy, because I am holy. I am the LORD. I make you holy.

⁹" 'Suppose a priest's daughter makes herself "unclean" by becoming a prostitute. Then she brings shame on her father. She must be burned to death.

¹⁰" 'The high priest is the one among his brothers whose head has been anointed with olive oil. He has been appointed to wear the priest's clothes. " 'When someone dies, the high priest must not let his hair hang loose. He must not tear his clothes to show how sad he is. ¹¹He must not enter a place where there is a dead body. He must not make himself "unclean," even if his father or mother dies. ¹²He must not leave my sacred tent to take part in burying a body. That would bring shame on the tent. My anointing oil has set the high priest apart. I am the LORD.

¹³" 'The woman the high priest gets married to must be a virgin. ¹⁴He must not marry a widow or a woman who is divorced. He must not marry a woman who is "unclean" because she is a prostitute. He must only get married to a virgin. She must come from his own people. ¹⁵If he marries a virgin, he makes the children he has by her "clean." I am the LORD. I make him holy.' "

¹⁶The LORD spoke to Moses. He said, ¹⁷"Speak to Aaron. Tell him, 'For all time to come, no man in your family line who has any flaws can come near to offer food to me.

¹⁸" 'No man who has any flaws can come near. No man who is blind or disabled can come. No man whose body is scarred or twisted can come. ¹⁹No man whose foot or hand is disabled can come. ²⁰No man whose back is bent can come. No man who is too short can come. No man who has anything wrong with his eyes can come. No man who has boils or running sores can come. No man whose sex glands are crushed can come.

²¹" 'No man in the family line of the priest Aaron who has any flaws can

come near me. He can't come to bring the offerings that are made to me with fire. If he has any flaws, he must not come near to offer food to me. ²²He can eat the holy food. He can also eat my very holy food. ²³But because he has a flaw, he must not go near the curtain or approach the altar. If he does, he will make my sacred tent "unclean." I am the LORD. I make everything holy.' "

²⁴So Moses told all of those things to Aaron and his sons. He also told them to all of the people of Israel.

22 The LORD spoke to Moses. He said, ²"Here is what I want you to tell Aaron and his sons. Tell them to treat the sacred offerings with respect. They are the offerings the people of Israel set apart to honor me. So Aaron and his sons must never treat my name as if it were not holy. I am the LORD.

³"Say to them, 'Suppose a man in your family line is "unclean." And suppose he comes near the sacred offerings. They are the offerings the people of Israel set apart to honor me. That man must be cut off from serving me as a priest. That applies for all time to come. I am the LORD.

⁴" 'Suppose a man in Aaron's family line has a skin disease. Or suppose liquid waste is flowing out of his body. Then he can't eat the sacred offerings until he is made pure and clean.

" 'Suppose he touches something that has been made "unclean" by coming near a dead body. Or suppose he touches someone who has semen flowing from his body. Then he will not be "clean." ⁵Or suppose he touches any crawling thing that makes him "unclean." Or suppose he touches any person who makes him "unclean." It does not matter what he touches that is "unclean." It will make him "unclean."

⁶" 'The one who touches anything of that kind will be "unclean" until evening. He must not eat any of the sacred offerings unless he has taken a bath. ⁷When the sun goes down, he will be "clean." After that, he can eat the sacred offerings. They are his food.

⁸" 'He must not eat anything that is found dead or torn apart by wild animals. If he does, it will make him "unclean." I am the LORD.

⁹" 'The priests must do what I require. But suppose they make fun of what I require. Then they will become guilty and die. I am the LORD. I make them holy.

¹⁰" 'Only a member of a priest's family can eat the sacred offering. The guest of a priest can't eat it. A priest's hired worker can't eat it either.

¹¹" 'But suppose a priest buys a slave with money. Or suppose a slave is born in his house. Then that slave can eat the sacred food.

¹²" 'Suppose a priest's daughter gets married to someone who is not a priest. Then she can't eat any of the food that is brought as a sacred gift. ¹³But suppose the priest's daughter becomes a widow or is divorced. She does not have any children. And she returns to live in her father's house, where she lived when she was young. Then she can eat her father's food. But a person who does not belong to a priest's family can't eat any of it.

¹⁴" 'Suppose someone eats a sacred offering by mistake. Then he must pay back the priest for the offering. He must also add a fifth of its value to it.

¹⁵" 'The priests must not allow the sacred offerings to become "unclean." They are the offerings the people of Israel bring to me. ¹⁶The priests must not allow the offerings to become "unclean" by letting the people eat them. If they do, they will bring guilt on the people. They will have to pay for what they have done. I am the LORD. I make them holy.' "

SACRIFICES THE LORD DOES NOT ACCEPT

¹⁷The LORD spoke to Moses. He said, ¹⁸"Speak to Aaron and his sons. Speak to all of the people of Israel. Tell them, 'Suppose any of you brings a gift for a burnt offering to the LORD. It does not matter whether you are an Israelite or an outsider who lives in Israel. It does not matter whether you bring the offering to keep a promise or because you choose to give it. ¹⁹You must bring a male animal that does not have any flaws if you want the LORD to accept it from you. It does not matter whether it

is from your cattle, sheep or goats. [20]Do not bring an animal that has any flaws. If you do, the LORD will not accept it from you.

[21]" 'Suppose any of you brings an animal for a friendship offering to the LORD. Then it must not have any flaws at all. If it does, the LORD will not accept it. It does not matter whether the animal is from your herd or flock. It does not matter whether you bring it to keep a promise or because you choose to give it. [22]Do not offer a blind animal to the LORD. Do not bring an animal that is hurt or wounded. And do not offer one that has warts or boils or running sores. Do not place any of them on the altar as an offering that is made to the LORD with fire.

[23]" 'But suppose you bring an offering you choose to give. Then you can bring an ox or a sheep whose body is twisted or too small. But the LORD will not accept it if you offer it to keep a promise.

[24]" 'You must not offer the LORD a male animal whose sex glands have been hurt. The glands also must not be crushed, torn or cut. You must not offer that kind of animal in your own land. [25]And you must not accept that kind of animal from someone who comes from another land. You must not offer it as food for your God. He will not accept it from you. Its body is twisted and has flaws.' "

[26]The LORD spoke to Moses. He said, [27]"When a calf, lamb or goat is born, it must remain with its mother for seven days. From the eighth day on, I will accept it as an offering that is made to me with fire. [28]Do not kill a cow and its calf on the same day. Do not kill a female sheep and its lamb on the same day. [29]"Sacrifice a thank offering to me in the right way. Then I will accept it from you. [30]You must eat it that same day. Do not leave any of it until morning. I am the LORD.

[31]"Obey my commands. Follow them. I am the LORD. [32]Do not treat my name as if it were not holy. The people of Israel must recognize me as the holy God. I am the LORD. I make you holy. [33]I brought you out of Egypt to be your God. I am the LORD."

23

The LORD spoke to Moses. He said, [2]"Speak to the people of Israel. Tell them, 'Here are my appointed feast days. They are the appointed feast days of the LORD. Tell the people that they must come together for these sacred feasts.

THE SABBATH DAY

[3]" 'There are six days when you can work. But the seventh day is a Sabbath. You must rest on it. Come together on that sacred day. You must not do any work on it. No matter where you live, it is a Sabbath day in my honor.

PASSOVER AND UNLEAVENED BREAD

[4]" 'Here are my appointed feasts. Tell the people that they must come together for these sacred feasts at their appointed times. [5]My Passover begins when the sun goes down on the 14th day of the first month.

[6]" 'My Feast of Unleavened Bread begins on the 15th day of that month. For seven days you must eat bread that is made without yeast. [7]On the first day you must come together for a special service. Do not do any regular work on that day. [8]On each of the seven days bring an offering that is made to me with fire. On the seventh day come together for a special service. Do not do any regular work on that day.' "

THE FIRST SHARE OF ISRAEL'S CROPS BELONGS TO THE LORD

[9]The LORD spoke to Moses. He said, [10]"Speak to the people of Israel. Tell them, 'When you enter the land I am going to give you, bring an offering to me. Gather your crops. Bring the first bundle of grain to the priest. [11]He must lift the grain up and wave it in front of me. Then I will accept it from you. The priest must wave it on the day after the Sabbath.

[12]" 'On the day he waves the grain for you, you must sacrifice a burnt offering to me. It must be a lamb that does not have any flaws. It must be a year old. [13]You must bring it together with its grain offering. The grain offer-

ing must be 16 cups of fine flour. Mix it with olive oil. It is an offering that is made to me with fire. It has a pleasant smell. You must offer a drink offering along with the burnt offering. It must be a quart of wine.

¹⁴" 'You must not eat any bread until the very day you bring your offering to me. You must not eat any grain that has been cooked or any of your first grain until that time. That is a law that will last for all time to come. It applies no matter where you live.

THE FEAST OF WEEKS

¹⁵" 'The day you brought the grain for the wave offering was the day after the Sabbath. Count off seven full weeks from that day. ¹⁶Count off 50 days up to the day after the seventh Sabbath. On that day bring me an offering of your first grain. ¹⁷Bring two loaves of bread that are made with 16 cups of fine flour. They must be baked with yeast. Bring them to me as a wave offering from the first share of your crops. That applies no matter where you live.

¹⁸" 'Together with the bread, bring seven male lambs. Each lamb must be a year old. It must not have any flaws. Also bring one young bull and two rams. They will be a burnt offering to me. They will be offered together with their grain offerings and drink offerings. They are an offering that is made with fire. They give a pleasant smell to me.

¹⁹" 'Then sacrifice one male goat for a sin offering. Also sacrifice two lambs for a friendship offering. Each of the lambs must be a year old. ²⁰The priest must lift the two lambs up and wave them in front of me as a wave offering. He must offer them together with the bread that is made out of the first share of your crops. They are a sacred offering to me. They will be given to the priest.

²¹" 'On that same day tell the people that they must come together for a special service. They must not do any regular work. That is a law that will last for all time to come. It applies no matter where you live.

²²" 'Suppose you are gathering your crops. Then do not harvest all the way to the edges of your field. And do not pick up the grain you missed. Leave some for poor people and outsiders. I am the LORD your God.' "

THE FEAST OF TRUMPETS

²³The LORD spoke to Moses. He said, ²⁴"Say to the people of Israel, 'On the first day of the seventh month you must have a day of rest. It must be a special service that is announced with trumpet blasts. ²⁵Do not do any regular work on that day. Instead, bring an offering that is made to me with fire.' "

THE DAY WHEN SIN IS PAID FOR

²⁶The LORD spoke to Moses. He said, ²⁷"The tenth day of the seventh month is the day when sin is paid for. Come together for a special service. Do not eat any food. Bring an offering that is made to me with fire. ²⁸Do not do any work on that day. It is the day when sin is paid for. On that day your sin will be paid for in my sight. I am the LORD your God.

²⁹"Suppose you do eat food on that day. Then you will be cut off from your people. ³⁰I will destroy anyone among your people who does any work on that day. ³¹You must not do any work at all. That is a law that will last for all time to come. It applies no matter where you live.

³²"That day is a sabbath for you. You must rest on it. You must not eat anything on that day. You must keep your sabbath from the evening of the ninth day of the month until the following evening."

THE FEAST OF BOOTHS

³³The LORD spoke to Moses. He said, ³⁴"Say to the people of Israel, 'On the 15th day of the seventh month my Feast of Booths begins. It lasts for seven days.

³⁵" 'On the first day you must come together for a special service. Do not do any regular work on that day. ³⁶On each of the seven days bring an offering that is made to me with fire. On the eighth day come together for a special service. Bring an offering that is made to me with fire. That special service is

the closing service. Do not do any regular work on that day.

³⁷" 'Those are my appointed feasts. Tell the people that they must come together for those sacred feasts. During those times, the people must bring offerings that are made to me with fire. They are burnt offerings and grain offerings. They are sacrifices and drink offerings. Each offering must be brought at its required time.

³⁸" 'The feasts are in addition to my Sabbath days. The offerings are in addition to your gifts and anything you have promised. They are also in addition to all of the offerings you choose to give me.

³⁹" 'Begin with the 15th day of the seventh month. That is after you have gathered your crops. On that day celebrate my Feast of Booths for seven days. The first day is a day of rest. The eighth day is also a day of rest. ⁴⁰On the first day you must get the best fruit from the trees. You must also get palm leaves, leafy branches and poplar branches. You must be filled with joy in my sight for seven days. I am the LORD your God.

⁴¹" 'Celebrate my Feast of Booths for seven days each year. That is a law that will last for all time to come. Celebrate the feast in the seventh month. ⁴²Live in booths for seven days. All of the people of Israel must live in booths. ⁴³Then your children after you will know that I made the people of Israel live in booths. I made them do it after I brought them out of Egypt. I am the LORD your God.' "

⁴⁴So Moses announced to the people of Israel the appointed feasts of the LORD.

OLIVE OIL, BREAD AND INCENSE

24 The LORD spoke to Moses. He said, ²"Command the people of Israel to bring you clear oil that is made from pressed olives. Use it to keep the lamps burning and giving light all the time.

³"Aaron must take care of the lamps in my sight from evening until morning all the time. That is a law that will last for all time to come. The lamps are outside the curtain that is in front of the tablets of the covenant in the Tent of Meeting. ⁴The lamps are on the pure gold lampstand in front of me. They must be taken care of all the time.

⁵"Get fine flour and bake 12 loaves of bread. Use 16 cups of flour for each loaf. ⁶Place them in two rows. Put six loaves in each row on the table that is made out of pure gold. The table stands in front of me.

⁷"Along each row put some pure incense. It will remind you that all good things come from me. Burn the incense in place of the bread. The incense is an offering that is made to me with fire.

⁸"The bread must be set out in front of me regularly. Do it every Sabbath day. It will be Israel's duty to provide it for all time to come.

⁹"The bread belongs to Aaron and his sons. They must eat it in a holy place. It is a very holy part of their regular share of the offerings that are made to me with fire."

A PERSON WHO SPEAKS EVIL IS PUT TO DEATH

¹⁰There was a man who had an Israelite mother. His father was born in Egypt. The man went out among the people of Israel. A fight broke out in the camp between him and an Israelite. ¹¹The son of the Israelite woman spoke evil things against the LORD by using a curse. So the people brought him to Moses. The name of the man's mother was Shelomith. She was the daughter of Dibri. Dibri was from the tribe of Dan. ¹²The people kept her son under guard until they could find out what the LORD wanted them to do.

¹³Then the LORD spoke to Moses. He said, ¹⁴"Get the man who spoke evil things against me. Take him outside the camp. All those who heard him say those things must place their hands on his head. Then the whole community must kill him by throwing stones at him.

¹⁵"Say to the people of Israel, 'If anyone calls down a curse on me, he will be held accountable. ¹⁶If anyone speaks evil things against my Name, he must be put to death. The whole community must kill him by throwing stones at him. It does not matter

whether he is an outsider or an Israelite. When he speaks evil things against my Name, he must be put to death.

17" 'If anyone kills another human being, he must be put to death. 18If anyone kills someone's animal, he must pay its owner. A life must be taken for a life.

19" 'Suppose someone hurts his neighbor. Then what he has done must be done to him. 20A bone must be broken for a bone. An eye must be put out for an eye. A tooth must be knocked out for a tooth. He must be hurt in the same way he hurt someone else.

21" 'If anyone kills an animal, he must pay its owner. But if he kills a human being, he must be put to death. 22The same law applies whether he is an outsider or an Israelite. I am the LORD your God.' "

23Then Moses spoke to the people of Israel. They got the man who had spoken evil things against the LORD. They took him outside the camp. There they killed him by throwing stones at him. The people of Israel did just as the LORD had commanded Moses.

THE SABBATH YEAR

25 The LORD spoke to Moses on Mount Sinai. He said, 2"Speak to the people of Israel. Tell them, 'You will enter the land I am going to give you. When you do, you must honor me every seventh year by not farming the land that year.

3" 'For six years plant your fields. Trim the branches in your vineyards and gather your crops.

4" 'But the seventh year must be a sabbath for the land. The land must rest during it. It is a sabbath year in my honor. Do not plant your fields. Do not trim the branches in your vineyards. 5Do not gather what grows without being planted. And do not gather the grapes from the vines you have not taken care of. The land must have a year of rest.

6" 'Anything the land produces during the sabbath year will be food for you. It will be for you and your male and female servants. Your hired workers will eat it. So will people who live with you for a while. 7And so will your

livestock and the wild animals that are in your land. Anything the land produces can be eaten.

THE YEAR OF JUBILEE

8" 'Count off seven sabbaths of years. Count off seven times seven years. The seven sabbaths of years add up to a total of 49 years. 9The tenth day of the seventh month is the day when sin is paid for. On that day blow the trumpet all through your land.

10" 'Set the 50th year apart. Announce freedom all over the land to everyone who lives there. The 50th year will be a Year of Jubilee for you. Each of you must return to your own family property. And each of you must return to your own tribe.

11" 'The 50th year will be a Year of Jubilee for you. Do not plant anything. Do not gather what grows without being planted. And do not gather the grapes from the vines you have not taken care of. 12It is a Year of Jubilee. It will be holy for you. Eat only what the fields produce.

13" 'In the Year of Jubilee all of you must return to your own property.

14" 'Suppose you sell land to one of your own people. Or you buy land from him. Then do not take advantage of each other. 15The price you pay must be based on the number of years since the last Year of Jubilee. And the price you charge must be based on the number of years left for gathering crops before the next Year of Jubilee.

16" 'When there are many years left, you must raise the price. When there are only a few years left, you must lower the price. That is because what the man is really selling you is the number of crops the land will produce. 17Do not take advantage of each other. Instead, have respect for me. I am the LORD your God.

18" 'Follow my rules. Be careful to obey my laws. Then you will live safely in the land. 19The land will produce its fruit. You will eat as much as you want. And you will live there in safety.

20" 'Suppose you say, "In the seventh year we will not plant anything or gather our crops. So what will we eat?" 21I will send you a great blessing in the sixth year. The land will produce enough for three years. ²²While you plant during the eighth year, you will eat food from the old crop. You will continue to eat food from it until the crops from the ninth year are gathered.

²³" 'The land must not be sold without a way of getting it back. That is because it belongs to me. You are only outsiders who rent my land. ²⁴You must make sure that you can buy the land back. That applies to all of the land that belongs to you.

²⁵" 'Suppose one of your own people becomes poor. And suppose he has to sell some of his land. Then his nearest relative must come and buy back what he has sold.

²⁶" 'But suppose he does not have anyone to buy it back for him. And suppose things go well for him and he earns enough money to buy it back himself. ²⁷Then he must decide how much the crops have become worth since the time he sold the land. He must take that amount off the price the land was sold for. He must give the man who is selling it back to him the money that is left. Then he can go back to his own property.

²⁸" 'But suppose he has not earned enough money to pay the man back. Then the buyer he sold the land to will keep it until the Year of Jubilee. At that time it will be returned to him. Then he can go back to his property.

²⁹" 'Suppose a man sells a house in a city that has a wall around it. Then for a full year after he sells it he has the right to buy it back.

³⁰" 'But suppose he does not buy it back before the full year has passed. Then the house in the walled city will continue to belong to the buyer and his children after him. It will not be returned to the seller in the Year of Jubilee.

³¹" 'But houses in villages that do not have walls around them must be treated like property outside walled cities. Those houses can be bought back at any time. And they must be returned in the Year of Jubilee.

³²" 'The Levites always have the right to buy back their houses in the towns that belong to them. ³³So their property among the people of Israel can be bought back. That applies to a house that is sold in any of their towns. Any house that is sold must be returned to its original owner in the Year of Jubilee. That is because the houses

KIDS' QUESTION

Why are some countries rich and others poor?

Wealthy countries sometimes have many natural resources (such as gold mines or tourist attractions) that make them rich. They also have business systems that reward people for making and selling goods and services. Poor countries don't usually have a lot of natural resources. Sometimes they have the resources, but the business system makes it hard for people to sell them. Also, some countries have been hurt by war, hurricanes, or not having enough food. Whether you live in a rich country or a poor country, everyone has to work together and support good business systems. Everyone has to make rules and keep them. When we follow God's rules, life works better.

checkout
Leviticus 25:18

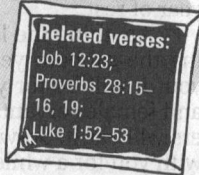

Related verses:
Job 12:23;
Proverbs 28:15–16, 19;
Luke 1:52–53

of the Levites will always belong to them.

³⁴" 'But the grasslands around their towns must never be sold. They will belong to them for all time to come.

³⁵" 'Suppose one of your own people becomes poor. And suppose he can't take care of himself. Then help him just as you would help an outsider or someone who is living among you for a while. In that way, the man who is poor can continue to live among you.

³⁶" 'Do not charge him interest of any kind. Instead, have respect for me. Then the man who has become poor can continue to live among you. ³⁷If you lend him money, you must not charge him interest. And you must not sell him food for more than it cost you.

³⁸" 'I am the LORD your God. I brought you out of Egypt. I did it to give you the land of Canaan. I wanted to be your God.

³⁹" 'Suppose one of your own people becomes poor. And suppose he sells himself to you. Then do not make him work as a slave. ⁴⁰You must treat him like a hired worker. Or you must treat him like someone who is living among you for a while.

" 'He must work for you until the Year of Jubilee. ⁴¹Then he and his children must be set free. He will go back to his own tribe. He will go back to the property his people have always owned.

⁴²" 'The people of Israel are my servants. I brought them out of Egypt. So they must not be sold as slaves. ⁴³Show them pity when you rule over them. Have respect for me.

⁴⁴" 'You must get your male and female slaves from the nations that are around you. You can buy slaves from them. ⁴⁵You can buy as slaves some of the people who are living among you for a while. You can also buy members of their families who were born among you. They will become your property. ⁴⁶You can leave them to your children as their share of your property. You can make them slaves for life. But when you rule over your own people, you must be kind to them.

⁴⁷" 'Suppose an outsider or someone who is living among you for a

Do we have to give money to poor people?

Christians have the responsibility to help people who have needs, including poor people. One reason for this is that God cares about people in need, and we should all try to be like God. God is kind to his people, so we should be kind to others. Another reason we should give is that God shows his love to others through us.

You can help the poor in many ways. For example, you can give food to a community food pantry or soup kitchen. You can serve meals at a rescue mission. You can give money to programs that help poor children. You can give money to groups that help the poor.

Everything you have comes from God's goodness and kindness to you. He wants you to treat others the way he treats you.

checkout Leviticus 25:35

Related verses: Deuteronomy 15:7–11; Luke 12:33,34

while becomes rich. Then suppose one of your own people becomes poor. He sells himself to the outsider who is living among you. Or he sells himself to a member of the outsider's family. ⁴⁸Then he keeps the right to buy himself back after he has sold himself. One of his relatives can buy him back. ⁴⁹An uncle or a cousin can buy himself back after he has sold himself. In fact, any relative in his tribe can do it. Or suppose things go well for him. Then he can buy himself back.

⁵⁰ 'He and his buyer must count the number of years from the time of the sale up to the Year of Jubilee. The price for his freedom must be based on the amount that is paid to a hired man for that number of years.

⁵¹ 'Suppose there are many years until the Year of Jubilee. Then for his freedom he must pay a larger share of the price that was paid for him. ⁵²But suppose there are only a few years left until the Year of Jubilee. Then he must count the number of years that are

left. The payment for his freedom must be based on that number.

⁵³ 'He must be treated as if he had been hired from year to year. You must make sure that his owner is kind to him when he rules over him.

⁵⁴ 'Suppose he is not bought back in any of those ways. Then he and his children must still be set free in the Year of Jubilee. ⁵⁵That is because the people of Israel belong to me. They are my servants. I brought them out of Egypt. I am the LORD their God.

REWARDS FOR OBEYING THE LORD

26 " 'Do not make statues of gods for yourselves. Do not set up a likeness of a god or a sacred stone for yourselves. Do not place a carved stone in your land and bow down in front of it. I am the LORD your God.

²" 'You must always keep my Sabbath days. Have respect for my sacred tent. I am the LORD.

Why do people have to pay interest on money they borrow?

People have to pay interest only if they agree to do so when they borrow the money. Credit cards come with a contract that tells how much the user of the card has to pay. People who borrow money from a bank agree to pay a certain amount of interest. Banks charge interest on loans and credit cards because that is how they make money. It is like paying rent on the money. You want to use the money for a while, so you pay the bank a fee as long as you have it.

God told the Israelites not to charge each other interest for loans. Many people today will loan money to relatives and close friends without charging interest to help them in an emergency.

checkout Leviticus 25:36,37

Related verse:
Exodus 22:25

³" 'Follow my rules. Be careful to obey my commands. ⁴Then I will send you rain at the right time. The ground will produce its crops. The trees of the field will bear their fruit. ⁵You will continue to thresh your grain until you gather your grapes. You will continue to gather your grapes until you plant your crops. You will have all you want to eat. And you will live in safety in your land.

⁶" 'I will give you peace in the land. You will sleep, and no one will make you afraid. I will remove wild animals from the land. There will not be any war in your country. ⁷You will hunt down your enemies. You will kill them with your swords. ⁸Five of you will chase 100. And 100 of you will chase 10,000. You will kill your enemies with your swords.

⁹" 'I will look with favor on you. I will give you many children and increase your numbers. And I will keep my covenant with you. ¹⁰You will still be eating last year's crops when you have to move them out to make room for new crops.

¹¹" 'I will live among you. I will not turn away from you. ¹²I will walk among you. I will be your God. And you will be my people. ¹³I am the LORD your God. I brought you out of Egypt. I did not want you to be slaves in Egypt anymore. I threw off your heavy load. I helped you walk with your heads held high.

PUNISHMENT FOR NOT OBEYING THE LORD

¹⁴" 'But suppose you will not listen to me. You will not carry out all of my commands. ¹⁵You will say no to my rules and turn away from my laws. And you will break my covenant by failing to carry out all of my commands. ¹⁶Then here is what I will do to you. All at once I will bring terror on you. I will send sicknesses that will make you weak. I will send fever that will destroy your sight. It will slowly take your life away. When you plant seeds, it will not do you any good. Instead, your enemies will eat what you have planted. ¹⁷I will turn against you. Then your enemies will win the battle over you. Those who hate you will rule

over you. You will run away even when no one is chasing you.

¹⁸" 'After all of that, suppose you still will not listen to me. Then I will punish you for your sins seven times. ¹⁹I will break down your stubborn pride. I will make the sky above you like iron, and it will not rain. I will make the ground under you like bronze, and you will not be able to farm it. ²⁰You will work with all of your strength, but it will not do you any good. That is because your soil will not produce any crops. The trees of the land will not bear any fruit.

²¹" 'Suppose you continue to be my enemy. And suppose you still refuse to listen to me. Then I will multiply your troubles many times because of your sins. ²²I will send wild animals against you. They will kill your children. They will destroy your cattle. There will be so few of you left that your roads will be deserted.

²³" 'After all of those things, suppose you still do not accept my warnings. And suppose you continue to be my enemy. ²⁴Then I myself will be your enemy. I will make you suffer for your sins again and again. ²⁵I will send war against you to punish you for breaking my covenant. When you go back into your cities, I will send a plague among you. You will be handed over to your enemies. ²⁶I will cut off your supply of bread. Ten women will need only one oven to bake your bread. They will weigh out the bread piece by piece. Even when you eat all of it, it will not be enough to satisfy you.

²⁷" 'After all of that, suppose you still do not listen to me. And suppose you continue to be my enemy. ²⁸Then I will be angry with you. I will be your enemy. I myself will again punish you for your sins over and over. ²⁹You will eat the dead bodies of your sons. You will also eat the dead bodies of your daughters.

³⁰" 'I will destroy the high places where you worship other gods. I will pull down your incense altars. I will pile up your dead bodies on the lifeless statues of your gods. And I will turn away from you. ³¹I will completely destroy your cities. I will destroy your places of worship. The pleasant smell

of your offerings will not give me any delight.

³²" 'I will destroy your land so completely that your enemies who live there will be shocked. ³³I will scatter you among the nations. I will pull out my sword and hunt you down. Your land and your cities will be completely destroyed.

³⁴" 'Then the deserted land will enjoy its sabbath years. It will rest. It will not be farmed. It will enjoy its sabbaths. But you will become prisoners in the country of your enemies. ³⁵The land will rest the whole time it is deserted. It was not able to rest during the sabbaths you lived in it.

³⁶" 'Some of you will be left in the lands of your enemies. I will fill your hearts with fear. The sound of a leaf that is blown by the wind will scare you away. You will run as if you were escaping from swords. You will fall down, even though no one is chasing you. ³⁷You will trip over one another as if you were running away from the battle. You will run away, even though no one is chasing you. You will not be able to stand and fight against your enemies.

³⁸" 'While you are still scattered among the nations, you will die. The lands of your enemies will destroy you. ³⁹You who are left in those lands will become weaker and weaker. You will die because of your sins and the sins of your parents.

⁴⁰" 'But suppose you admit that you and your parents have sinned. You admit the evil and dishonest things you have done against me. And you admit you have become my enemy. ⁴¹What you did made me become your enemy. I let your enemies take you into their land. But suppose you stop being stubborn. You stop being proud. And you pay for your sin. ⁴²Then I will remember my covenant with Jacob. I will remember my covenant with Isaac. I will remember my covenant with Abraham. I will remember what I said to them about the land.

⁴³" 'You will leave the land. It will enjoy its sabbaths while it lies deserted because you are not there. You will pay for your sins because you said no to my laws. You turned away from my rules.

⁴⁴" 'But even after all of that, I will not say no to you or turn away from you. I will not destroy you completely in the land of your enemies. I will not break my covenant with you. I am the LORD your God. ⁴⁵Because of you, I will remember the covenant I made with the people of Israel who lived before you. I brought them out of Egypt to be their God. The nations saw me do it. I am the LORD.' "

⁴⁶Those are the orders, the laws and the rules of the covenant the LORD made on Mount Sinai. He made it between himself and the people of Israel through Moses.

KEEP YOUR PROMISES TO THE LORD

27 The LORD spoke to Moses. He said, ²"Speak to the people of Israel. Tell them, 'Suppose someone makes a special promise to set a person apart to serve me. Here is how much it will cost to set that person free from the promise to serve.

³" 'The cost for a male between the ages of 20 and 60 is 20 ounces of silver. It must be weighed out in keeping with the standard weights that are used in the sacred tent. ⁴The cost for a female of the same age is 12 ounces of silver.

⁵" 'The cost for a male between the ages of five and 20 is eight ounces of silver. The cost for a female of the same age is four ounces of silver.

⁶" 'The cost for a male between the ages of one month and five years is two ounces of silver. The cost for a female of the same age is one and a fourth ounces of silver.

⁷" 'The cost for a male who is 60 years old or more is six ounces of silver. The cost for a female of the same age is four ounces of silver.

⁸" 'But suppose the one who makes the special promise is too poor to pay the required amount. Then he must bring to the priest the person who will be set free. The priest will decide the right value for that person. It will be based on how much the one who makes the promise can afford.

⁹" 'Suppose what he promised is an animal that I will accept as an offering.

Then the animal that is given to me becomes holy. [10]The one who makes the promise must not trade it. He must not trade a good animal for a bad one. And he must not trade a bad animal for a good one. Suppose he chooses one animal instead of another. Then both animals become holy.

[11]" 'Suppose the animal he promised is not "clean." Suppose I will not accept it as an offering. Then the animal must be brought to the priest. [12]He will decide whether it is good or bad. Its value will be what he decides it will be. [13]Suppose the owner wants to buy the animal back. Then he must add a fifth to its cost.

[14]" 'Suppose a man sets his house apart as something that is holy to me. Then the priest will decide whether it is good or bad. Its value will remain what he decides it will be. [15]Suppose the man sets his house apart. And suppose later he wants to buy it back. Then he must add a fifth to its value. The house will belong to him again.

[16]" 'Suppose a man sets apart a piece of his family's land to me. Then its value must be decided based on the number of seeds that are required to grow a full crop on it. That value will be 20 ounces of silver for every six bushels of barley seeds.

[17]" 'Suppose he sets his field apart during the Year of Jubilee. Then the value that has been decided will not be changed. [18]But suppose he sets his field apart after the Year of Jubilee. Then the priest will decide its value based on the number of years that are left until the next Year of Jubilee. The value that was decided will be reduced.

[19]" 'Suppose the man who sets his field apart wants to buy it back. Then he must add a fifth to its value. The field will belong to him again. [20]But suppose he does not buy the field back. Instead, suppose he sells it to someone else. Then he can never buy it back.

[21]" 'When the field is set free in the Year of Jubilee, it will become holy. It will be like a field that is set apart to me. It will become the property of the priests.

[22]" 'Suppose a man sets apart to me a field he has bought. And suppose it is not part of his family's land. [23]Then the priest will decide its value based on the number of years that are left until the Year of Jubilee. The man must pay that value on the day it is decided. The money is holy. It is set apart for me.

[24]" 'In the Year of Jubilee the field will go back to the person the man bought it from. That person is the one who had owned the land before.

[25]" 'Every amount of money must be weighed out in keeping with the standard weights that are used in the sacred tent.

[26]" 'But no one can set apart the first male animal that is born to its mother. That animal already belongs to me. It does not matter whether it is an ox or a sheep. It belongs to me.

[27]" 'Suppose it is an animal that is not "clean." Then the owner may buy it back at the value that has been decided. And he must add a fifth to its value. But suppose he does not buy it back. Then it must be sold at the value that has been decided.

[28]" 'But nothing a man owns and sets apart to me can be sold or bought back. It does not matter whether it is a person or an animal or a family's land. Everything that is set apart to me is very holy to me.

[29]" 'No one who is set apart in a special way to be destroyed can be bought back. He must be put to death.

[30]" 'A tenth of everything the land produces belongs to me. That includes grain from the soil and fruit from the trees. It is holy. It is set apart for me. [31]Suppose a man buys back some of his tenth. Then he must add a fifth of the cost to it.

[32]" 'The whole tenth of his herds and flocks will be holy. They will be set apart for me. That includes every tenth animal that its shepherd marks with his wooden staff. [33]The owner must not pick out the good animals from the bad. He must not choose one animal instead of another. But if he does, both animals become holy. They can't be bought back.' "

[34]The LORD gave Moses all of those commands on Mount Sinai for the people of Israel.

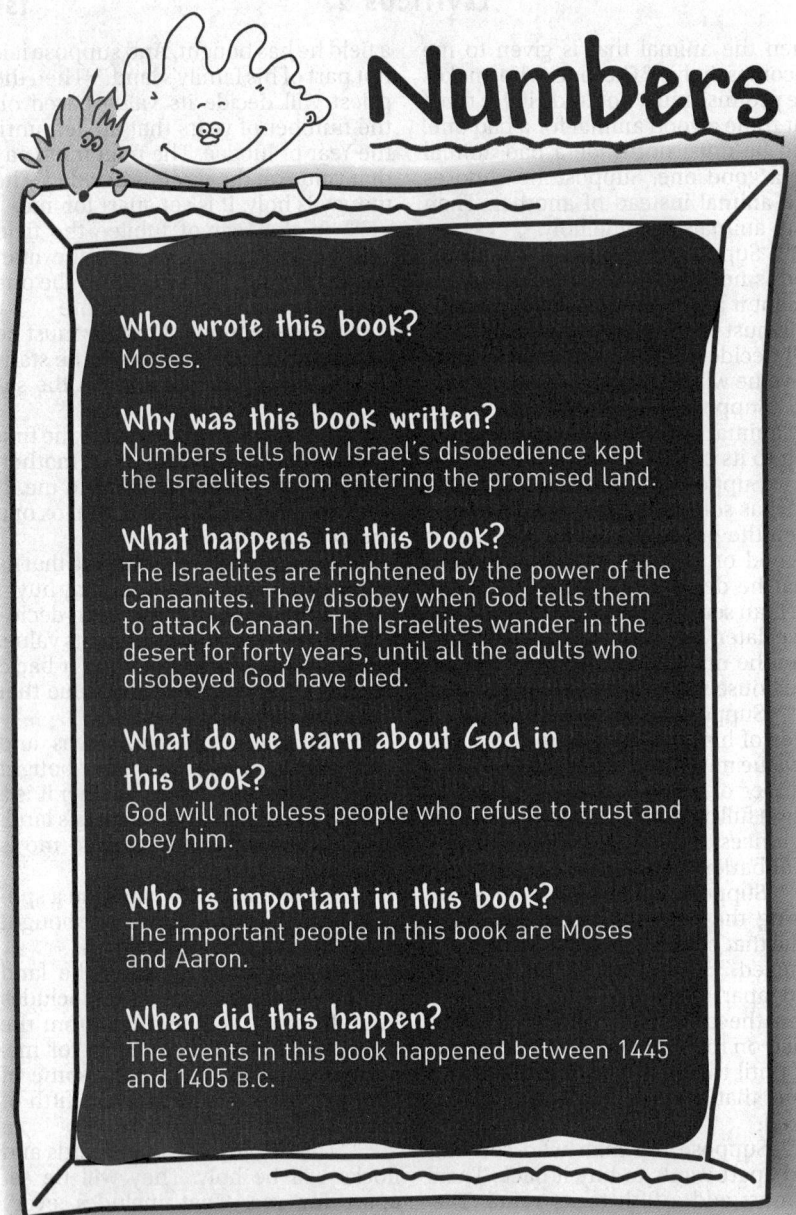

Numbers

Who wrote this book?
Moses.

Why was this book written?
Numbers tells how Israel's disobedience kept the Israelites from entering the promised land.

What happens in this book?
The Israelites are frightened by the power of the Canaanites. They disobey when God tells them to attack Canaan. The Israelites wander in the desert for forty years, until all the adults who disobeyed God have died.

What do we learn about God in this book?
God will not bless people who refuse to trust and obey him.

Who is important in this book?
The important people in this book are Moses and Aaron.

When did this happen?
The events in this book happened between 1445 and 1405 B.C.

THE MEN OF ISRAEL ARE COUNTED

1 The LORD spoke to Moses in the Tent of Meeting. It happened in the Desert of Sinai. The LORD spoke to him on the first day of the second month. It was the second year after the people of Israel came out of Egypt.

The LORD said, ²"Count all of the men of Israel. Make a list of them by their tribes and families. List every man by name. List them one by one. ³Count all of the men who are able to serve in the army. They must be 20 years old or more. I want you and Aaron to make a list of them company by company. ⁴One man from each tribe must help you. Those who help must be the heads of their families.

⁵"Here are the names of the men who must help you.

"From the tribe of Reuben will come Elizur, the son of Shedeur.
⁶From the tribe of Simeon will come Shelumiel, the son of Zurishaddai.
⁷From the tribe of Judah will come Nahshon, the son of Amminadab.
⁸From the tribe of Issachar will come Nethanel, the son of Zuar.
⁹From the tribe of Zebulun will come Eliab, the son of Helon.
¹⁰From the tribe of Ephraim will come Elishama, the son of Ammihud.
From the tribe of Manasseh will come Gamaliel, the son of Pedahzur.
Ephraim and Manasseh were Joseph's two sons.
¹¹From the tribe of Benjamin will come Abidan, the son of Gideoni.
¹²From the tribe of Dan will come Ahiezer, the son of Ammishaddai.
¹³From the tribe of Asher will come Pagiel, the son of Ocran.
¹⁴From the tribe of Gad will come Eliasaph, the son of Deuel.
¹⁵From the tribe of Naphtali will come Ahira, the son of Enan."

¹⁶Those were the men who were appointed from the community. They were the leaders of the tribes of their people. They were the heads of the major families in Israel.

¹⁷Moses and Aaron went and got the men whose names had been given to them. ¹⁸Then Moses and Aaron gathered all of the men of Israel together. It was the first day of the second month. The men announced the tribe and family they belonged to. Those who were 20 years old or more were listed by name. They were listed one by one.

¹⁹Everything was done just as the LORD had commanded Moses. So Moses counted them in the Desert of Sinai.

²⁰Here is the number of men from the tribe of Reuben, Israel's oldest son.

All of the men who were able to serve in the army were counted. They were 20 years old or more. They were listed by name. They were listed one by one. They were listed in keeping with the records of their tribes and families. ²¹The number from the tribe of Reuben was 46,500.

²²Here is the number of men from the tribe of Simeon.

All of the men who were able to serve in the army were counted. They were 20 years old or more. They were listed by name. They were listed one by one. They were listed in keeping with the records of their tribes and families. ²³The number from the tribe of Simeon was 59,300.

²⁴Here is the number of men from the tribe of Gad.

All of the men who were able to serve in the army were counted. They were 20 years old or more. They were listed by name. They were listed in keeping with the records of their tribes and families. ²⁵The number from the tribe of Gad was 45,650.

²⁶Here is the number of men from the tribe of Judah.

All of the men who were able to serve in the army were counted. They were 20 years old or more. They were listed by name. They were listed in keeping with the records of their tribes and families. ²⁷The number from the tribe of Judah was 74,600.

²⁸Here is the number of men from the tribe of Issachar.

All of the men who were able to serve in the army were counted. They were 20 years old or more. They were listed by name. They were listed in keeping with the records of their tribes and families. [29]The number from the tribe of Issachar was 54,400.

[30]Here is the number of men from the tribe of Zebulun.

All of the men who were able to serve in the army were counted. They were 20 years old or more. They were listed by name. They were listed in keeping with the records of their tribes and families. [31]The number from the tribe of Zebulun was 57,400.

[32]Here is the number of men from the tribe of Ephraim, the son of Joseph.

All of the men who were able to serve in the army were counted. They were 20 years old or more. They were listed by name. They were listed in keeping with the records of their tribes and families. [33]The number from the tribe of Ephraim was 40,500.

[34]Here is the number of men from the tribe of Manasseh, the son of Joseph.

All of the men who were able to serve in the army were counted. They were 20 years old or more. They were listed by name. They were listed in keeping with the records of their tribes and families. [35]The number from the tribe of Manasseh was 32,200.

[36]Here is the number of men from the tribe of Benjamin.

All of the men who were able to serve in the army were counted. They were 20 years old or more. They were listed by name. They were listed in keeping with the records of their tribes and families. [37]The number from the tribe of Benjamin was 35,400.

[38]Here is the number of men from the tribe of Dan.

All of the men who were able to serve in the army were counted. They were 20 years old or more. They were listed by name. They were listed in keeping with the records of their tribes and families. [39]The number from the tribe of Dan was 62,700.

[40]Here is the number of men from the tribe of Asher.

All of the men who were able to serve in the army were counted. They were 20 years old or more. They were listed by name. They were listed in keeping with the records of their tribes and families. [41]The number from the tribe of Asher was 41,500.

[42]Here is the number of men from the tribe of Naphtali.

All of the men who were able to serve in the army were counted. They were 20 years old or more. They were listed by name. They were listed in keeping with the records of their tribes and families. [43]The number from the tribe of Naphtali was 53,400.

[44]Those were the men Moses and Aaron counted. The 12 leaders of Israel helped them. There was one leader from each tribe. [45]The men who were counted were able to serve in Israel's army. All of them were 20 years old or more. They were counted family by family. [46]The total number was 603,550.

[47]But the families of the tribe of Levi were not counted along with the others. [48]The LORD had spoken to Moses. He had said, [49]"You must not count the men from the tribe of Levi. Do not include them when you list the other men of Israel.

[50]"Instead, put the Levites in charge of the holy tent. That is where the tablets of the covenant are kept. The Levites will be in charge of everything that belongs to the holy tent. They must carry the tent and everything

that belongs to it. They must take care of it. They must set up camp around it. ⁵¹"When the holy tent must be moved, the Levites must take it down. And when the tent must be set up, the Levites must do it. Anyone else who goes near it will be put to death. ⁵²"The people of Israel must set up their tents by companies. All of them must be in their own camps under their own flags. ⁵³"But the Levites must set up their tents around the holy tent where the tablets of the covenant are kept. Then my anger will not fall on the community of Israel. The Levites will be held accountable for taking care of the tent."

⁵⁴The people of Israel did everything just as the LORD had commanded Moses.

THE TRIBES CAMP AROUND THE TENT OF MEETING

2 The LORD spoke to Moses and Aaron. He said, ²"The people of Israel must camp around the Tent of Meeting. But they must not camp too close to it. All of them must camp under their flags and under the banners of their families."

³The companies of the camp of Judah must be on the east side. They must set up camp toward the sunrise. They must camp under their flag. The leader of the tribe of Judah is Nahshon, the son of Amminadab. ⁴There are 74,600 men in his company.

⁵The tribe of Issachar will camp next to them. The leader of the tribe of Issachar is Nethanel, the son of Zuar. ⁶There are 54,400 men in his company.

⁷The tribe of Zebulun will be next. The leader of the tribe of Zebulun is Eliab, the son of Helon. ⁸There are 57,400 men in his company.

⁹So a total of 186,400 men will be set apart for the camp of Judah. They will be arranged company by company. They will start out first.

¹⁰The companies of the camp of Reuben will be on the south side. They will be under their flag. The leader of the tribe of Reuben is Elizur, the son of Shedeur. ¹¹There are 46,500 men in his company.

¹²The tribe of Simeon will camp next to them. The leader of the tribe of Simeon is Shelumiel, the son of Zurishaddai. ¹³There are 59,300 men in his company.

¹⁴The tribe of Gad will be next. The leader of the tribe of Gad is Eliasaph, the son of Deuel. ¹⁵There are 45,650 men in his company.

¹⁶So a total of 151,450 men will be set apart for the camp of Reuben. They will be arranged company by company. They will start out second.

¹⁷Then the camp of the Levites will start out. The Tent of Meeting will go with them. They will march in the middle of the other camps. They will start out in the same order as they do when they set up camp. Each one will be in his own place under his flag.

¹⁸The companies of the camp of Ephraim will be on the west side. They will be under their flag. The leader of the tribe of Ephraim is Elishama, the son of Ammihud. ¹⁹There are 40,500 men in his company.

²⁰The tribe of Manasseh will be next to them. The leader of the tribe of Manasseh is Gamaliel, the son of Pedahzur. ²¹There are 32,200 men in his company.

²²The tribe of Benjamin will be next. The leader of the tribe of Benjamin is Abidan, the son of Gideoni. ²³There are 35,400 men in his company.

²⁴So a total of 108,100 men will be set apart for the camp of Ephraim. They will be arranged company by company. They will start out third.

²⁵The companies of the camp of Dan will be on the north side. They will be under their flag. The leader of the tribe of Dan is Ahiezer, the son of Ammishaddai. ²⁶There are 62,700 men in his company.

[27]The tribe of Asher will camp next to them. The leader of the tribe of Asher is Pagiel, the son of Ocran. [28]There are 41,500 men in his company.

[29]The tribe of Naphtali will be next. The leader of the tribe of Naphtali is Ahira, the son of Enan. [30]There are 53,400 men in his company.

[31]So a total of 157,600 men will be set apart for the camp of Dan. They will start out last. They will march under their flags.

[32]Those are the men of Israel. They were counted in keeping with their families. The total number of all of the men who were in the camps is 603,550, company by company. [33]But the Levites weren't counted along with the other men of Israel. That's what the LORD had commanded Moses.

[34]So the people of Israel did everything the LORD had commanded Moses. That's the way they set up camp under their flags. And that's the way they started out. Each man marched out with his own tribe and family.

THE LEVITES

3 Here is the story of the family of Aaron and Moses. It belongs to the time when the LORD talked with Moses on Mount Sinai.

[2]Aaron's oldest son was Nadab. His other sons were Abihu, Eleazar and Ithamar. [3]Those were the names of Aaron's sons. They were the anointed priests. They were prepared to serve the LORD as priests. [4]But Nadab and Abihu made an offering to the LORD by using fire that wasn't allowed. So they fell dead in front of him. That happened in the Desert of Sinai. They didn't have any sons. Only Eleazar and Ithamar served as priests while their father Aaron was living.

[5]The LORD spoke to Moses. He said, [6]"Bring the men of the tribe of Levi to the priest Aaron. They will help him. [7]They must work at the Tent of Meeting for Aaron and for the whole community. They must do what needs to be done at the holy tent. [8]They must take care of everything that is connected with the Tent of Meeting. When they do, they are acting for all of the people of Israel. [9]Give the Levites to Aaron and his sons. They are the men of Israel who must be given completely to him.

[10]"Appoint Aaron and his sons to serve as priests. Anyone else who approaches the sacred tent must be put to death."

[11]The LORD also said to Moses, [12]"I have taken the Levites from among the people of Israel. I have taken them in place of the oldest son who is born to each woman in Israel. The Levites belong to me. [13]That is because every male that is born first to a mother is mine. In Egypt I struck down all of the males that were born first. I did it when I set apart for myself every male that is born first to a mother in Israel. That is true for men and animals alike. They belong to me. I am the LORD."

[14]The LORD spoke to Moses in the Desert of Sinai. He said, [15]"Count the Levites by their family groups. Count every male who is a month old or more." [16]So Moses counted them. He did just as the word of the LORD had commanded him.

[17]The sons of Levi were
  Gershon, Kohath and Merari.
[18]The major families from Gershon were
  Libni and Shimei.
[19]The major families from Kohath were
  Amram, Izhar, Hebron and Uzziel.
[20]The major families from Merari were
  Mahli and Mushi.
Those were the major families of the Levites.

[21]The families of Libni and Shimei belonged to the family of Gershon. [22]All of the males who were a month old or more were counted. There were 7,500 of them. [23]The families of Gershon had to camp on the west side. They had to camp behind the holy tent. [24]The leader of the families of Gershon was Eliasaph, the son of Lael. [25]Here are the duties of the families

of Gershon at the Tent of Meeting. They were held accountable for taking care of the holy tent and its coverings. They took care of the curtain at the entrance to the Tent of Meeting. ²⁶They took care of the curtains of the courtyard. They took care of the curtain at the entrance to the courtyard. The courtyard was all around the holy tent and altar. They also took care of the ropes. In fact, they had to take care of everything that was connected with the use of all of those things.

²⁷The families of Amram, Izhar, Hebron and Uzziel belonged to the family of Kohath. ²⁸All of the males who were a month old or more were counted. There were 8,600 of them. The families of Kohath were held accountable for taking care of the sacred tent. ²⁹They had to camp on the south side of the holy tent. ³⁰The leader of the families of Kohath was Elizaphan, the son of Uzziel.

³¹They were held accountable for taking care of the ark of the covenant. They took care of the table for the holy bread. They took care of the lampstand and the two altars. They took care of the articles that were used for serving in the sacred tent. They also took care of the inner curtain. In fact, they had to take care of everything that was connected with the use of all of those things.

³²The chief leader of the Levites was Eleazar. He was the son of the priest Aaron. Eleazar was appointed over those who were held accountable for taking care of the sacred tent.

³³The families of Mahli and Mushi belonged to the family of Merari. ³⁴All of the males who were a month old or more were counted. There were 6,200 of them. ³⁵The leader of the families of Merari was Zuriel, the son of Abihail. They had to camp on the north side of the holy tent.

³⁶They were appointed to take care of the frames of the tent. They took care of its crossbars, posts and bases. They took care of all of its supplies. In fact, they had to take care of everything that was connected with the use of all of those things. ³⁷They also took care of the posts of the courtyard that was around the holy tent. And they took care of the bases, tent stakes and ropes.

³⁸Moses, Aaron and Aaron's sons had to camp to the east of the holy tent. They had to camp toward the sunrise in front of the Tent of Meeting. They were held accountable for taking care of the sacred tent. They had to do it for the people of Israel. Anyone else who approached the tent would be put to death.

³⁹The total number of the Levites was 22,000. They were counted family by family. Every male who was a month old or more was counted. Moses and Aaron counted them, just as the LORD had commanded.

⁴⁰The LORD said to Moses, "Count the males among the people of Israel who were the oldest sons born in their families. Count all those who are a month old or more. Make a list of their names. ⁴¹Take the Levites for me in their place. And take the livestock of the Levites in place of all of the male animals in Israel that were born first to their mothers. I am the LORD."

⁴²So Moses counted all of the oldest sons in Israel. He did just as the LORD had commanded him. ⁴³There were 22,273 of those sons who were a month old or more. They were listed by name.

⁴⁴The LORD also said to Moses, ⁴⁵"Take the Levites in place of all the males who were born first in Israel. Also take the livestock of the Levites in place of the livestock of Israel. The Levites belong to me. I am the LORD.

⁴⁶"But there are 273 more males who were born first in Israel than there are male Levites. ⁴⁷Collect two ounces of silver for each of them. Weigh it out in keeping with the standard weights that are used in the sacred tent. ⁴⁸Give the silver to Aaron and his sons. It will buy the freedom of the additional sons in Israel."

⁴⁹So Moses collected the silver from the additional sons in Israel to buy their freedom. The Levites took the place of all of the others. ⁵⁰Moses col-

lected 35 pounds of silver. It was weighed out in keeping with the weights that are used in the sacred tent. Moses collected it from the oldest sons in Israel. [51]He gave the silver to Aaron and his sons. He did just as the LORD had commanded him.

THE KOHATH FAMILIES

4 The LORD spoke to Moses and Aaron. He said, [2]"Count the Kohath families of the Levites. Make a list of them family by family. [3]Count all of the men who are from 30 to 50 years old. Those are the men who must come and serve at the Tent of Meeting.

[4]"Here is the work the men of Kohath must do at the Tent of Meeting. They must take care of the things that are very holy.

[5]"When the camp is ready to move, Aaron and his sons must go into the tent. They must take down the curtain that screens the ark where the tablets of the covenant are kept. They must cover the ark with the curtain. [6]Then they must cover that with the hides of sea cows. They must spread a solid blue cloth over the hides. And they must put the poles in place.

[7]"They must spread a blue cloth over the table for the holy bread. They must put the plates, dishes and bowls on the cloth. They must also put the jars for drink offerings on it. The bread that is always kept there must remain on it. [8]They must spread a bright red cloth over everything. Then they must cover that with the hides of sea cows. And they must put the poles of the table in place.

[9]"They must get a blue cloth. With it they must cover the lampstand that gives light. They must also cover its lamps, trays and wick cutters. And they must cover all of its jars. The jars are for the olive oil that is used in the lampstand. [10]Then Aaron and his sons must wrap the lampstand and all of the things that are used with it. They must cover it with the hides of sea cows. And they must put it on a frame to carry it.

[11]"They must spread a blue cloth over the gold altar for burning incense. They must cover that with the hides of sea cows. And they must put the poles of the altar in place.

[12]"They must get all of the articles that are used for serving in the sacred tent. They must wrap them in a blue cloth. They must cover that with the hides of sea cows. Then they must put the articles on a frame to carry them.

[13]"They must remove the ashes from the bronze altar for burnt offerings. They must spread a purple cloth over it. [14]Then they must place all of the tools on it. The tools are used for serving at the altar. They include the pans for carrying ashes. They also include the meat forks, shovels and sprinkling bowls. Aaron and his sons must cover the altar with the hides of sea cows. And they must put its poles in place.

[15]"Aaron and his sons must cover all of the holy articles that belong to the holy tent. Then the men of Kohath must get ready to carry everything. They must do it when the camp is ready to move. But they must not touch the holy things. If they do, they will die. The men of Kohath must carry everything that is in the Tent of Meeting.

[16]"The priest Eleazar will be in charge of the olive oil for the light. He is the son of Aaron. Eleazar will be in charge of the sweet-smelling incense. He will be in charge of the regular grain offering and the anointing oil. He will be in charge of the entire holy tent. He will also be in charge of everything that is in it. That includes all of the articles that belong to the tent."

[17]The LORD spoke to Moses and Aaron. He said, [18]"Make sure that the Kohath families are not cut off from the Levites. [19]I want them to live and not die when they come near the very holy things. So here is what you must do for them. Aaron and his sons must go into the sacred tent and tell each man what to do. They must tell each man what to carry. [20]But the men of Kohath must not go in and look at the holy things. They must not look at them even for a moment. If they do, they will die."

THE GERSHON FAMILIES

[21]The LORD said to Moses, [22]"Count the Gershon families. Make a list of them family by family. [23]Count all of the men who are from 30 to 50 years

old. Those are the men who must come and serve at the Tent of Meeting.

²⁴"Here is how the Gershon families must serve. They must carry things. ²⁵They must carry the curtains of the holy Tent of Meeting. They must carry its covering and the outside covering of the hides of sea cows. They must carry the curtains that cover the entrance to the Tent of Meeting. ²⁶They must carry the curtains of the courtyard. The courtyard is all around the holy tent and altar. They must carry the curtain for the entrance. They must carry the ropes. They must also carry all of the supplies that are used for any purpose in the tent. The men of Gershon must do everything that needs to be done with those things.

²⁷"All of their work must be done under the direction of Aaron and his sons. That includes carrying and everything else they do. Aaron and his sons must tell them what to carry. And that will be their work. ²⁸It is what the Gershon families must do at the Tent of Meeting. They must work under the direction of the priest Ithamar. He is the son of Aaron.

THE MERARI FAMILIES

²⁹"Count the Merari families. Count them family by family. ³⁰Count all of the men who are from 30 to 50 years old. Those are the men who must come and serve at the Tent of Meeting. ³¹"Here is the work they must do at the Tent of Meeting. They must carry the frames of the holy tent. They must carry its crossbars, posts and bases. ³²They must also carry the posts of the courtyard. The courtyard is all around the holy tent. And they must carry the bases for the posts as well as their tent stakes and ropes. They must also carry all of the supplies and everything that is connected with their use. Tell each man exactly what to carry. ³³That is the work the Merari families must do at the Tent of Meeting. They must work under the direction of the priest Ithamar. He is the son of Aaron."

COUNTING THE FAMILIES OF THE LEVITES

³⁴Moses, Aaron and the leaders of the community counted the men of Kohath. They counted them family by family. ³⁵They counted all of the men who were from 30 to 50 years old. Those were the men who came and served at the Tent of Meeting. ³⁶There were 2,750 men. They were counted family by family. ³⁷That was the total of all of the men in the Kohath families who served at the Tent of Meeting. Moses and Aaron counted them. They did just as the LORD had commanded through Moses.

³⁸The men of Gershon were counted family by family. ³⁹All of the men who were from 30 to 50 years old were counted. They were the men who came and served at the Tent of Meeting. ⁴⁰There were 2,630 men. They were counted family by family. ⁴¹That was the total of the men in the Gershon families who served at the Tent of Meeting. Moses and Aaron counted them. They did just as the LORD had commanded.

⁴²The men of Merari were counted family by family. ⁴³All of the men who were from 30 to 50 years old were counted. They were the men who came and served at the Tent of Meeting. ⁴⁴There were 3,200 men. They were counted family by family. ⁴⁵That was the total of the men in the Merari families. Moses and Aaron counted them. They did just as the LORD had commanded through Moses.

⁴⁶So Moses and Aaron counted all of the Levites. The leaders of Israel helped them. They counted the Levites family by family. ⁴⁷All of the men who were from 30 to 50 years old were counted. They were the men who came and served at the Tent of Meeting. They were also supposed to carry it. ⁴⁸The total number of men was 8,580. ⁴⁹Everything was done as the LORD had commanded through Moses. Each man was given his work. And each one was told what to carry.

So they were counted, just as the LORD had commanded Moses.

MAKING THE CAMP PURE

5 The LORD spoke to Moses. He said, ²"Tell the Israelites that certain people must be sent away from the camp. Command them to send away anyone who has a skin

disease. They must send away all those who have a liquid waste coming from their bodies. And they must send away those who are not 'clean' because they have touched a dead body. ³That applies to men and women alike. Send them out of the camp. They must not make their camp 'unclean.' That is where I live among them."

⁴So the people of Israel did what the LORD commanded. They sent those who were not "clean" out of the camp. They did just as the LORD had directed Moses.

SINS AGAINST OTHERS MUST BE PAID FOR

⁵The LORD said to Moses, ⁶"Speak to the people of Israel. Say to them, 'Suppose a man or woman does something wrong to someone else. Then that person is not being faithful to the LORD. People like that are guilty.

⁷" 'They must admit they have committed a sin. They must pay in full for what they did wrong. And they must add a fifth to it. Then they must give all of it to the person they have sinned against.

⁸" 'But suppose the person has died. And suppose there is not a close relative who can be paid for the sin that was committed. Then what is paid belongs to the LORD. It must be given to the priest. A ram must be given along with it. The ram must be sacrificed to the LORD to pay for the sin.

⁹" 'All of the sacred gifts the people of Israel bring to a priest will belong to him. ¹⁰Sacred gifts belong to the man who gives them. But what he gives to a priest will belong to the priest.' "

THE TEST FOR A WIFE WHO IS NOT FAITHFUL

¹¹Then the LORD spoke to Moses again. He said, ¹²"Speak to the people of Israel. Say to them, 'Suppose a man's wife goes down the wrong path. And suppose she is not faithful to him. ¹³She has sex with another man. And suppose what she has done is hidden from her husband. No one knows she is not "clean." So there is no witness against her. And she has not been caught in the act.

¹⁴" 'Suppose her husband becomes jealous. He does not trust his wife, and she is really not "clean." Or suppose he does not trust her even though she is "clean." ¹⁵Then he must take his wife to the priest.

" 'He must also bring an offering. It must be eight cups of barley flour. The offering is for his wife. He must not pour olive oil on it. And he must not put incense on it. It is a grain offering for being jealous. It calls attention to a person's guilt.

¹⁶" 'The priest must have her stand in front of the LORD. ¹⁷He must pour some holy water into a clay jar. He must get some dust from the floor of the holy tent. And he must put it into the water. ¹⁸The priest must have the woman stand in front of the LORD. Then he must untie her hair. He must place in her hands the offering that calls attention to a person's guilt. It is the grain offering for being jealous. The priest must keep the bitter water with him. It is the water that brings a curse.

¹⁹" 'Then the priest must have the woman take an oath. He must say to her, "Suppose no other man has had sex with you. And suppose you haven't gone down the wrong path. You have kept yourself pure while you are married to your husband. Then may the bitter water that brings a curse not harm you. ²⁰But suppose you have gone down the wrong path while you are married to your husband. You have made yourself 'unclean.' You have had sex with a man who isn't your husband."

²¹" 'At that point the priest must put the woman under the curse of the oath. He must say, "May the LORD cause your people to call a curse down on you. May he cause them to speak against you. May they do it when the LORD makes your body unable to have children. ²²May this water that brings a curse enter your body. May it make your body unable to have children."

" 'Then the woman must say, "Amen. Let it happen."

²³" 'The priest must write the curses on a scroll. He must wash them off in the bitter water. ²⁴It is the water he will have the woman drink. It is bitter wa-

ter that brings a curse. It will enter her body. And it will cause her to suffer bitterly.

25" 'The priest must take from her hands the grain offering for being jealous. He must lift it up and wave it in front of the LORD. He must bring it to the altar. 26Then the priest must take a handful of the grain offering. It is the offering that calls attention to a person's guilt. He must burn it on the altar. After that, he must have the woman drink the water.

27" 'Suppose she has made herself "unclean." She has not been faithful to her husband. And she has drunk the water that brings a curse. Then it will go into her body. It will cause her to suffer bitterly. It will make her body unable to have children. Her people will call a curse down on her.

28" 'But suppose the woman has not made herself "unclean." And suppose she is free from anything that is not "clean." Then she will be free of guilt. And she will be able to have children.

29" 'That is the law about being jealous. It applies to a woman who has gone down the wrong path. She has made herself "unclean" while she is married to her husband. 30And it applies to a man who becomes jealous. He has doubts about his wife. The priest must have her stand in front of the LORD. He must apply the entire law to her. 31The husband will not be guilty of doing anything wrong. But the woman will be punished for her sin.' "

BECOMING A NAZIRITE

6 The LORD said to Moses, 2"Speak to the people of Israel. Say to them, 'Suppose a man or woman wants to make a special promise. They want to set themselves apart to the LORD for a certain period of time. They want to be Nazirites.

3" 'Then they must not drink any kind of wine. They must not drink vinegar that is made out of wine of any kind. They must not drink grape juice. They must not eat grapes or raisins. 4As long as they are Nazirites, they must not eat anything grapevines produce. They must not even eat the seeds or skins of grapes.

5" 'They must not use razors on their heads. They must not cut their hair during the whole time they have set themselves apart to the LORD. They must be holy until that time is over. They must let the hair on their heads grow long. 6And they must not go near a dead body during that whole time.

7" 'But what if their father or mother dies? Or what if their brother or sister dies? Then they must not make themselves "unclean" because of them. The hair on their heads shows they are set apart for God. 8During the whole time they are set apart they are holy to the LORD.

9" 'Suppose someone dies suddenly in front of them. That makes the hair they have set apart to the LORD "unclean." So they must shave their heads on the day they will be made "clean." That is the seventh day.

10" 'Then on the eighth day they must bring two doves. Or they can bring two young pigeons. They must bring them to the priest. He will be at the entrance to the Tent of Meeting. 11The priest must offer one of the birds as a sin offering. And he must offer the other as a burnt offering. The sacrifices will pay for the sin of the Nazirite man or woman. They sinned by being near a dead body. That same day they must set their heads apart as holy.

12" 'They must set themselves apart to the LORD again. They must do it for the same period of time they had agreed to at first. And they must bring a male lamb that is a year old as a guilt offering. The days before that day do not count. That is because they became "unclean" during the time they were set apart.

13" 'The time when the Nazirites are set apart will come to an end. Here is the law that applies to them at that time. They must be brought to the entrance to the Tent of Meeting.

14" 'There they must sacrifice their offerings to the LORD. They must bring a male lamb that is a year old. It must not have any flaws. It is for a burnt offering. Then they must bring a female lamb that is a year old. It must not have any flaws. It is for a sin offering. And they must bring a ram that does not have any flaws. It is for a friendship offering.

¹⁵" 'They must sacrifice the offerings together with their grain offerings and drink offerings. And they must also bring a basket of bread that is made without yeast. The offering must include flat cakes that are made out of fine flour mixed with olive oil. And it must include wafers that are spread with oil.

¹⁶" 'The priest must bring all of those things to the LORD. He must sacrifice the sin offering and the burnt offering. ¹⁷He must bring the basket of bread that is made without yeast. And he must sacrifice the ram. It will be a friendship offering to the LORD. The priest must bring it together with its grain offering and drink offering.

¹⁸" 'Then the Nazirites must shave off the hair they had set apart to the Lord. They must do it at the entrance to the Tent of Meeting. And they must put the hair in the fire that burns the sacrifice of the friendship offering.

¹⁹" 'After the Nazirites have shaved off their hair, the priest must take a boiled shoulder of the ram. He must remove a cake and a wafer from the basket. They must be made without yeast. And he must place the shoulder and the bread in the hands of the Nazirites.

²⁰" 'Then he must lift up the shoulder and bread and wave them in front of the LORD. They are a wave offering. They are holy. They belong to the priest. The breast that was waved belongs to him. The thigh that was offered belongs to him too. After the offering is waved, the Nazirites can drink wine.

²¹" 'That is the law of the Nazirites. They promise to sacrifice offerings to the LORD. They do it when they set themselves apart. And they should bring anything else they can afford. They must carry out the promises they have made. They must do it in keeping with the law of the Nazirites.' "

HOW THE PRIESTS BLESS THE PEOPLE

²²The LORD spoke to Moses. He said, ²³"Tell Aaron and his sons, 'Here is how I want you to bless the people of Israel. Say to them,

²⁴" ' "May the LORD bless you
    and take good care of you.
²⁵May the LORD smile on you
    and be gracious to you.
²⁶May the LORD look on you with favor
    and give you his peace." ' '

²⁷"In that way they will put the blessing of my name on the people of Israel. And I will bless them."

ISRAEL'S LEADERS BRING OFFERINGS FOR THE HOLY TENT

7 Moses finished setting up the holy tent. Then he anointed it with olive oil. He set it apart to the LORD. He did the same thing with everything that belonged to it. He also anointed the altar. And he set apart to the LORD the altar and all of its tools.

²Then the leaders of Israel brought their offerings. The leaders were the heads of the families. They were the leaders of the tribes. They were in charge of the men who had been counted. ³They brought gifts to the LORD. They brought six covered carts and 12 oxen. Each leader gave an ox. And every two leaders gave a cart. They put their gifts in front of the holy tent.

⁴The LORD spoke to Moses. He said, ⁵"Accept the gifts from the leaders. I want their gifts to be used in the work at the Tent of Meeting. Give them to the Levites. They need them to do their work."

⁶So Moses gave the carts and the oxen to the Levites. ⁷He gave two carts and four oxen to the men from the family of Gershon. They needed them to do their work. ⁸He gave four carts and eight oxen to the men from the family of Merari. They needed them to do their work. All of those men were under the direction of the priest Ithamar, the son of Aaron.

⁹But Moses didn't give any carts or oxen to the men from the family of Kohath. They had to carry the holy things on their shoulders. They were accountable for the holy things.

¹⁰When the altar was anointed, the leaders brought their offerings. They placed them in front of the altar. They

brought their offerings to set the altar apart. [11]The LORD had spoken to Moses. He had said, "Each day one leader must bring his offering. He must bring it to set the altar apart."

[12]On the first day Nahshon, the son of Amminadab, brought his offering. Nahshon was from the tribe of Judah. [13]He brought one silver plate and one silver sprinkling bowl. The plate weighed three pounds four ounces. The sprinkling bowl weighed one pound 12 ounces. They were weighed in keeping with the standard weights that are used in the sacred tent. Each plate and bowl was filled with fine flour that was mixed with olive oil. It was a grain offering. [14]He brought one gold dish. It weighed four ounces. It was filled with incense. [15]Nahshon brought one young bull, one ram, and one male lamb that was a year old. They would be sacrificed as a burnt offering. [16]He brought one male goat to be sacrificed as a sin offering. [17]He brought two oxen, five rams and five male goats. He also brought five male lambs that were a year old. All of them would be sacrificed as a friendship offering.

That was everything that Nahshon, the son of Amminadab, brought as his offering.

[18]On the second day Nethanel, the son of Zuar, brought his offering. Nethanel was the leader of the tribe of Issachar. [19]He brought one silver plate and one silver sprinkling bowl. The silver plate weighed three pounds four ounces. The sprinkling bowl weighed one pound 12 ounces. Both were weighed in keeping with the standard weights that are used in the sacred tent. Each plate and bowl was filled with fine flour that was mixed with olive oil. It was a grain offering. [20]He brought one gold dish. It weighed four ounces. It was filled with incense. [21]Nethanel brought one young bull, one ram, and one male lamb that was a year old. They would be sacrificed as a burnt offering. [22]He brought one male goat to be sacrificed as a sin offering. [23]He brought two oxen, five rams and five male goats. He also brought five male lambs that were a year old. All of them would be sacrificed as a friendship offering.

That was everything that Nethanel, the son of Zuar, brought as his offering.

[24]On the third day Eliab, the son of Helon, brought his offering. Eliab was the leader of the people of Zebulun. [25]He brought one silver plate and one silver sprinkling bowl. The plate weighed three pounds four ounces. The sprinkling bowl weighed one pound 12 ounces. They were weighed in keeping with the standard weights that are used in the sacred tent. Each plate and bowl was filled with fine flour that was mixed with olive oil. It was a grain offering. [26]He brought one gold dish. It weighed four ounces. It was filled with incense. [27]Eliab brought one young bull, one ram, and one male lamb that was a year old. They would be sacrificed as a burnt offering. [28]He brought one male goat to be sacrificed as a sin offering. [29]He brought two oxen, five rams and five male goats. He also brought five male lambs that were a year old. All of them would be sacrificed as a friendship offering.

That was everything that Eliab, the son of Helon, brought as his offering.

[30]On the fourth day Elizur, the son of Shedeur, brought his offering. Elizur was the leader of the people of Reuben. [31]He brought one silver plate and one silver sprinkling bowl. The plate weighed three pounds four ounces. The sprinkling bowl weighed one pound 12 ounces. They were weighed in keeping with the standard weights that are used in the sacred tent. Each plate and bowl was filled with fine flour that was mixed with olive oil. It was a grain offering. [32]He brought one gold dish. It weighed four

ounces. It was filled with incense.
³³Elizur brought one young bull, one ram, and one male lamb that was a year old. They would be sacrificed as a burnt offering. ³⁴He brought one male goat to be sacrificed as a sin offering. ³⁵He brought two oxen, five rams and five male goats. He also brought five male lambs that were a year old. All of them would be sacrificed as a friendship offering.

That was everything that Elizur, the son of Shedeur, brought as his offering.

³⁶On the fifth day Shelumiel, the son of Zurishaddai, brought his offering. Shelumiel was the leader of the people of Simeon.

³⁷He brought one silver plate and one silver sprinkling bowl. The plate weighed three pounds four ounces. The sprinkling bowl weighed one pound 12 ounces. They were weighed in keeping with the standard weights that are used in the sacred tent. Each plate and bowl were filled with fine flour that was mixed with olive oil. It was a grain offering. ³⁸He brought one gold dish. It weighed four ounces. It was filled with incense.

³⁹Shelumiel brought one young bull, one ram, and one male lamb that was a year old. They would be sacrificed as a burnt offering. ⁴⁰He brought one male goat to be sacrificed as a sin offering. ⁴¹He brought two oxen, five rams and five male goats. He also brought five male lambs that were a year old. All of them would be sacrificed as a friendship offering.

That was everything that Shelumiel, the son of Zurishaddai, brought as his offering.

⁴²On the sixth day Eliasaph, the son of Deuel, brought his offering. Eliasaph was the leader of the people of Gad.

⁴³He brought one silver plate and one silver sprinkling bowl. The plate weighed three pounds four ounces. The sprinkling bowl weighed one pound 12 ounces. They were weighed in keeping

with the standard weights that are used in the sacred tent. Each plate and bowl was filled with fine flour that was mixed with olive oil. It was a grain offering. ⁴⁴He brought one gold dish. It weighed four ounces. It was filled with incense.

⁴⁵Eliasaph brought one young bull, one ram, and one male lamb that was a year old. They would be sacrificed as a burnt offering. ⁴⁶He brought one male goat to be sacrificed as a sin offering. ⁴⁷He brought two oxen, five rams and five male goats. He also brought five male lambs that were a year old. All of them would be sacrificed as a friendship offering.

That was everything that Eliasaph, the son of Deuel, brought as his offering.

⁴⁸On the seventh day Elishama, the son of Ammihud, brought his offering. Elishama was the leader of the people of Ephraim.

⁴⁹He brought one silver plate and one silver sprinkling bowl. The plate weighed three pounds four ounces. The sprinkling bowl weighed one pound 12 ounces. They were weighed in keeping with the standard weights that are used in the sacred tent. Each plate and bowl was filled with fine flour that was mixed with olive oil. It was a grain offering. ⁵⁰He brought one gold dish. It weighed four ounces. It was filled with incense.

⁵¹Elishama brought one young bull, one ram, and one male lamb that was a year old. They would be sacrificed as a burnt offering. ⁵²He brought one male goat to be sacrificed as a sin offering. ⁵³He brought two oxen, five rams and five male goats. He also brought five male lambs that were a year old. All of them would be sacrificed as a friendship offering.

That was everything that Elishama, the son of Ammihud, brought as his offering.

⁵⁴On the eighth day Gamaliel, the son of Pedahzur, brought his offering. Gamaliel was the leader of the people of Manasseh.

⁵⁵He brought one silver plate and one silver sprinkling bowl. The plate weighed three pounds four ounces. The sprinkling bowl weighed one pound 12 ounces. They were weighed in keeping with the standard weights that are used in the sacred tent. Each plate and bowl was filled with fine flour that was mixed with olive oil. It was a grain offering. ⁵⁶He also brought one gold dish. It weighed four ounces. It was filled with incense.

⁵⁷Gamaliel brought one young bull, one ram, and one male lamb that was a year old. They would be sacrificed as a burnt offering. ⁵⁸He brought one male goat to be sacrificed as a sin offering. ⁵⁹He brought two oxen, five rams and five male goats. He also brought five male lambs that were a year old. All of them would be sacrificed as a friendship offering.

That was everything that Gamaliel, the son of Pedahzur, brought as his offering.

⁶⁰On the ninth day Abidan, the son of Gideoni, brought his offering. Abidan was the leader of the people of Benjamin.

⁶¹He brought one silver plate and one silver sprinkling bowl. The plate weighed three pounds four ounces. The sprinkling bowl weighed one pound 12 ounces. They were weighed in keeping with the standard weights that are used in the sacred tent. Each plate and bowl was filled with fine flour that was mixed with olive oil. It was a grain offering. ⁶²He brought one gold dish. It weighed four ounces. It was filled with incense.

⁶³Abidan brought one young bull, one ram, and one male lamb that was a year old. They would be sacrificed as a burnt offering. ⁶⁴He brought one male goat to be sacrificed as a sin offering. ⁶⁵He brought two oxen, five rams and five male goats. He also brought five male lambs that were a year old. All of them would be sacrificed as a friendship offering.

That was everything that Abidan, the son of Gideoni, brought as his offering.

⁶⁶On the tenth day Ahiezer, the son of Ammishaddai, brought his offering. Ahiezer was the leader of the people of Dan.

⁶⁷He brought one silver plate and one silver sprinkling bowl. The plate weighed three pounds four ounces. The sprinkling bowl weighed one pound 12 ounces. They were weighed in keeping with the standard weights that are used in the sacred tent. Each plate and bowl was filled with fine flour that was mixed with olive oil. It was a grain offering. ⁶⁸He brought one gold dish. It weighed four ounces. It was filled with incense.

⁶⁹Ahiezer brought one young bull, one ram, and one male lamb that was a year old. They would be sacrificed as a burnt offering. ⁷⁰He brought one male goat to be sacrificed as a sin offering. ⁷¹He brought two oxen, five rams and five male goats. He also brought five male lambs that were a year old. All of them would be sacrificed as a friendship offering.

That was everything that Ahiezer, the son of Ammishaddai, brought as his offering.

⁷²On the eleventh day Pagiel, the son of Ocran, brought his offering. Pagiel was the leader of the people of Asher.

⁷³He brought one silver plate and one silver sprinkling bowl. The plate weighed three pounds four ounces. The sprinkling bowl weighed one pound 12 ounces. They were weighed in keeping with the standard weights that are used in the sacred tent. Each plate and bowl was filled with fine flour that was mixed with olive oil. It was a grain offering. ⁷⁴He brought one gold dish. It weighed four ounces. It was filled with incense.

⁷⁵Pagiel brought one young bull, one ram, and one male lamb that was a year old. They would be sacrificed as a burnt offering. ⁷⁶He brought one male goat to be sacrificed as a sin offering. ⁷⁷He

brought two oxen, five rams and five male goats. He also brought five male lambs that were a year old. All of them would be sacrificed as a friendship offering.

That was everything that Pagiel, the son of Ocran, brought as his offering.

78On the twelfth day Ahira, the son of Enan, brought his offering. Ahira was the leader of the people of Naphtali.

79He brought one silver plate and one silver sprinkling bowl. The plate weighed three pounds four ounces. The sprinkling bowl weighed one pound 12 ounces. They were weighed in keeping with the standard weights that are used in the sacred tent. Each plate and bowl was filled with fine flour that was mixed with olive oil. It was a grain offering. 80He brought one gold dish. It weighed four ounces. It was filled with incense.

81Ahira brought one young bull, one ram, and one male lamb that was a year old. They would be sacrificed as a burnt offering. 82He brought one male goat to be sacrificed as a sin offering. 83He brought two oxen, five rams and five male goats. He also brought five male lambs that were a year old. All of them would be sacrificed as a friendship offering.

That was everything that Ahira, the son of Enan, brought as his offering.

84Those were the offerings the leaders of the people of Israel brought. They gave them to set the altar apart when it was anointed with olive oil. They gave 12 silver plates, 12 silver sprinkling bowls and 12 gold dishes. 85Each silver plate weighed three pounds four ounces. Each sprinkling bowl weighed one pound 12 ounces. The total weight of the silver dishes was 60 pounds. Everything was weighed in keeping with the standard weights that are used in the sacred tent. 86Each of the 12 gold dishes weighed four ounces. They were filled with incense. They were weighed in keeping with the weights used in the sacred

tent. The total weight of the gold dishes was three pounds.

87The leaders brought 12 young bulls, 12 rams and 12 male lambs that were a year old. That was the total number of animals they gave for the burnt offering. They gave them together with the grain offering. They brought 12 male goats for the sin offering.

88The leaders brought 24 oxen, 60 rams, 60 male goats and 60 male lambs that were a year old. That was the total number of animals that were sacrificed as the friendship offering.

Those were the offerings they brought to set the altar apart. The leaders brought them after the altar was anointed with oil.

89Moses entered the Tent of Meeting. He wanted to speak with the LORD. There Moses heard the LORD talking to him. The LORD's voice was speaking to him from between the two cherubim. The cherubim were over the place where sin is paid for. It was the cover on the ark where the tablets of the covenant were kept. The LORD spoke with Moses there.

AARON SETS UP THE LAMPS

8 The LORD said to Moses, 2"Speak to Aaron. Say to him, 'Set up the seven lamps. They will give light to the area that is in front of the lampstand.' "

3So Aaron did it. He set up the lamps so that they faced forward on the lampstand. He did just as the LORD had commanded Moses. 4The lampstand was made out of hammered gold. From its base to its blooms it was made out of hammered gold. The lampstand was made exactly like the pattern the LORD had shown Moses.

MOSES SETS THE LEVITES APART

5The LORD spoke to Moses. He said, 6"Take the Levites from among the other men of Israel. Make them 'clean' in the usual way. 7Here is how to make them pure. Sprinkle the special water on them. Then have them shave their whole bodies. Also have them wash their clothes. That is how they will make themselves pure.

⁸"Have them get a young bull along with its grain offering. The offering must be made out of fine flour mixed with olive oil. Then you must get a second young bull. You must sacrifice it as a sin offering.

⁹"Bring the Levites to the front of the Tent of Meeting. Gather the whole community of Israel together. ¹⁰You must bring the Levites to me. The men of Israel must place their hands on them. ¹¹Aaron must bring the Levites to me. They are a wave offering from the people of Israel. That is how they will be set apart to do my work.

¹²"I want the Levites to place their hands on the heads of the bulls. Then they must sacrifice one bull as a sin offering to me. And they must sacrifice the other as a burnt offering. The blood of the bulls will pay for the sin of the Levites.

¹³"Have the Levites stand in front of Aaron and his sons. Then give them as a wave offering to me. ¹⁴That is how I want you to set the Levites apart from the other men of Israel. The Levites will belong to me.

¹⁵"Make the Levites pure. Give them to me as a wave offering. Then they must come to do their work at the Tent of Meeting. ¹⁶They are the men of Israel who will be given to me completely. I have taken them to be my own. I have taken them in place of every son who is born first in his family in Israel.

¹⁷"Every male that is born first in Israel belongs to me. That is true whether it is a man or an animal. I struck down all of the males that were born first to a mother in Egypt. Then I set apart for myself all of the males that were born first in Israel. ¹⁸And I have taken the Levites in place of all of the sons who are born first in Israel.

¹⁹"I have given the Levites as gifts to Aaron and his sons. I have taken them from all of the men of Israel. I have appointed them to do the work at the Tent of Meeting. They will do it in place of the men of Israel.

"That is how they will keep the men of Israel from being guilty when they go near the sacred tent. Then no plague will strike the people of Israel when they go near the tent."

²⁰So Moses and Aaron and the whole community of Israel did with the Levites just as the LORD had commanded Moses. ²¹The Levites made themselves pure. They washed their clothes. Then Aaron gave them to the LORD as a wave offering. That's how he paid for their sin to make them pure.

²²After that, the Levites came to do their work at the Tent of Meeting. They worked under the direction of Aaron and his sons. And so Moses and Aaron and the whole community of Israel did with the Levites just as the LORD had commanded Moses.

²³The LORD spoke to Moses. He said, ²⁴"Here is what the Levites must do. Men who are 25 years old or more must come and take part in the work at the Tent of Meeting. ²⁵"But when they reach the age of 50, they must not work any longer. They must stop doing their regular work. ²⁶They can help their brothers with their duties at the Tent of Meeting. But they themselves should not do the work. That is how you must direct the Levites to do their work."

ISRAEL CELEBRATES THE PASSOVER FEAST

9 The LORD spoke to Moses in the Desert of Sinai. It was the first month of the second year after the people came out of Egypt. He said, ²"Tell the people of Israel to celebrate the Passover Feast. Have them do it at the appointed time. ³Celebrate it when the sun goes down on the 14th day of this month. Obey all of its rules and laws."

⁴So Moses told the people of Israel to celebrate the Passover Feast. ⁵They did it in the Desert of Sinai. They celebrated it when the sun went down on the 14th day of the first month. The people of Israel did everything just as the LORD had commanded Moses.

⁶But some of them couldn't celebrate the Passover Feast on that day. That's because they weren't "clean." They had gone near a dead body. So they came to Moses and Aaron that same day. ⁷They said to Moses, "We went near a dead body. So we aren't 'clean.' But why should we be kept from bringing the LORD's offering at

the appointed time? Why shouldn't we bring it along with the other people of Israel?"

[8] Moses answered them, "Wait until I find out what the LORD wants you to do."

[9] Then the LORD spoke to Moses. He said, [10] "Tell the people of Israel, 'Suppose any of you or your children are not "clean" because you have gone near a dead body. Or suppose you are away on a journey. You can still celebrate the LORD's Passover.

[11] " 'I want you to celebrate it on the 14th day of the second month. You have to do it when the sun goes down. You have to eat the lamb together with bread that is made without yeast. Eat it with bitter plants. [12] Do not leave any of it until morning. Do not break any of its bones. When you celebrate the Passover Feast, follow all of the rules.

[13] " 'But suppose a man is "clean." He is not on a journey. And he fails to celebrate the Passover Feast. Then he must be cut off from the community of Israel. He did not bring the LORD's offering at the appointed time. He will be punished for his sin.

[14] " 'What if there is an outsider living among you? And what if he wants to celebrate the LORD's Passover? Then he must obey its rules and laws. You must have the same laws for outsiders as you do for the people of Israel.' "

THE CLOUD COVERS THE HOLY TENT

[15] The holy tent was set up. It was the tent where the tablets of the covenant were kept. On the day it was set up, the cloud covered it. From evening until morning the cloud that was above the tent looked like fire. [16] That's what continued to happen. The cloud covered the tent. At night the cloud looked like fire.

[17] When the cloud lifted from its place above the tent, the people of Israel started out. Where the cloud settled, the people of Israel camped. [18] When the LORD gave the command, the people of Israel started out. And when he gave the command, they camped. As long as the cloud stayed above the holy tent, they remained in camp.

[19] Sometimes the cloud remained above the tent for a long time. Then the people of Israel obeyed the LORD's order. They didn't start out. [20] Sometimes the cloud was above the tent for only a few days. When the LORD would give the command, they would camp. Then when he would give the command, they would start out.

[21] Sometimes the cloud stayed only from evening until morning. When it lifted in the morning, they started out. It didn't matter whether it was day or night. When the cloud lifted, the people started out. [22] It didn't matter whether the cloud stayed above the holy tent for two days or a month or a year. The people of Israel would remain in camp. They wouldn't start out. But when the cloud lifted, they would start out.

[23] When the LORD gave the command, they camped. And when he gave the command, they started out. They obeyed the LORD's order. They obeyed him, just as he had commanded them through Moses.

THE SILVER TRUMPETS

10 The LORD spoke to Moses. He said, [2] "Make two trumpets out of hammered silver. Blow them when you want the community to gather together. And blow them when you want the camps to start out. [3] When both trumpets are blown, the whole community must gather in front of you. They must come to the entrance to the Tent of Meeting. [4] Suppose only one trumpet is blown. Then the leaders must gather in front of you. They are the heads of the tribes of Israel. [5] When a trumpet blast is blown, the tribes that are camped on the east side must start out. [6] When the second blast is blown, the camps on the south side must start out. The blast will tell them when to start. [7] Blow the trumpets to gather the people together. But do not use the same kind of blast.

[8] "The sons of Aaron, the priests, must blow the trumpets. That is a law for you and your children after you for all time to come. [9] Suppose you go into battle in your own land. And suppose it is against an enemy who is beating

you down. Then blow a blast on the trumpets. If you do, I will remember you. I will save you from your enemies. I am the LORD your God. ¹⁰You must also blow the trumpets when you are happy. Blow them at your appointed feasts. Blow them at your New Moon Feasts. Blow them when you sacrifice your burnt offerings. Blow them when you sacrifice your friendship offerings. They will remind me of you. I am the LORD your God."

THE PEOPLE OF ISRAEL LEAVE THE SINAI DESERT

¹¹It was the 20th day of the second month of the second year. On that day the cloud began to move. It went up from above the holy tent where the tablets of the covenant were kept.

¹²Then the people of Israel started out from the Desert of Sinai. They traveled from place to place. They kept going until the cloud came to rest in the Desert of Paran. ¹³The first time they started out, the LORD commanded Moses to tell them to do it. And they did it.

¹⁴The companies of the camp of Judah went first. They went out under their flag. Nahshon was their commander. He was the son of Amminadab. ¹⁵Nethanel was over the company of the tribe of Issachar. Nethanel was the son of Zuar. ¹⁶Eliab was over the company of the tribe of Zebulun. Eliab was the son of Helon.

¹⁷The holy tent was taken down. The men of Gershon and Merari started out. They carried the tent.

¹⁸The companies of the camp of Reuben went next. They went out under their flag. Elizur was their commander. He was the son of Shedeur. ¹⁹Shelumiel was over the company of the tribe of Simeon. Shelumiel was the son of Zurishaddai. ²⁰Eliasaph was over the company of the tribe of Gad. Eliasaph was the son of Deuel.

²¹The men of Kohath started out. They carried the holy things. The holy tent had to be set up before they arrived.

²²The companies of the camp of Ephraim went next. They went out under their flag. Elishama was their commander. He was the son of Ammihud. ²³Gamaliel was over the company of the tribe of Manasseh. Gamaliel was the son of Pedahzur. ²⁴Abidan was over the company of the tribe of Benjamin. Abidan was the son of Gideoni.

²⁵Finally, the companies of the camp of Dan started out. They marched out under their flag. They followed behind all of the other companies and guarded them. Ahiezer was their commander. He was the son of Ammishaddai. ²⁶Pagiel was over the company of the tribe of Asher. Pagiel was the son of Ocran. ²⁷Ahira was over the company of the tribe of Naphtali. Ahira was the son of Enan.

²⁸As the companies of Israel started out, that was the order they marched in.

²⁹Moses spoke to Hobab, the son of Reuel. Reuel was Moses' father-in-law. Reuel was from Midian. Moses said to Hobab, "We're starting out for the place the LORD promised to us. He said to us, 'I will give it to you.' So come with us. We'll treat you well. The LORD has promised to give good things to Israel."

³⁰Hobab answered, "No. I can't go. I'm going back to my own land. I'm returning to my own people."

³¹But Moses said, "Please don't leave us. You know where we should camp in the desert. You can be our guide. ³²So come with us. The LORD will give us good things. We'll share them with you."

³³So they started out from the mountain of the LORD. They traveled for three days. The ark of the covenant of the LORD went in front of them during those three days. It went ahead of them to find a place for them to rest. ³⁴They started out from the camp by day. And the cloud of the LORD was above them.

³⁵When the ark started out, Moses said,

"LORD, rise up!
Let your enemies be scattered.
Let them run away from you."

³⁶When the ark came to rest, Moses said,

"LORD, return.

Return to the many thousands of people in Israel."

THE LORD SENDS FIRE AMONG THE PEOPLE

11 The people weren't happy about the hard times they were having. The LORD heard what they were saying. It made him burn with anger. Then the LORD sent fire on them. It blazed out among the people. It burned up some of the outer edges of the camp.

²The people cried out to Moses. Then he prayed to the LORD. And the fire died down.

³So that place was named Taberah. That's because fire from the LORD had blazed out among them there.

THE LORD SENDS MEAT FOR THE PEOPLE

⁴Some people who were with them began to long for other food. Again the people of Israel began to cry out. They said, "We wish we had meat to eat. ⁵We remember the fish we ate in Egypt. It didn't cost us anything. We also remember the cucumbers, melons, leeks, onions and garlic. ⁶But now we've lost all interest in eating. We never see anything but this manna!"

⁷The manna was like coriander seeds. It looked like sap from a tree. ⁸The people went around gathering it. Then they ground it in a small mill they held in their hands. Or they crushed it in a stone bowl. They cooked it in a pot. Or they made cakes out of it. It tasted like something made with olive oil. ⁹When the dew came down on the camp at night, the manna also came down.

¹⁰Moses heard people from every family crying. They were sobbing at the entrances to their tents.

The LORD burned with hot anger. So Moses became troubled. ¹¹He asked the LORD, "Why have you brought this trouble on me? Why aren't you pleased with me? Why have you loaded me down with the troubles of all of these people?

¹²"Am I like a mother to them? Are they my children? Why do you tell me to carry them in my arms? Do I have to carry them the way a nurse carries a baby? Do I have to carry them to the land you promised? You took an oath and promised the land to their people of long ago.

¹³"Where can I get meat for all of these people? They keep crying out to me. They say, 'Give us meat to eat!' ¹⁴I can't carry all of these people by myself. The load is too heavy for me.

¹⁵"Is this how you are going to treat me? If you are pleased with me, just put me to death right now. Don't let me live if I have to see myself destroyed anyway."

¹⁶The LORD said to Moses, "Bring me 70 of Israel's elders. Bring men that you know are leaders and officials among the people. Have them come to the Tent of Meeting. I want them to stand there with you. ¹⁷I will come down. I will speak with you there. I will take some of my Spirit that is on you. And I will put the Spirit on them. They will help you carry the people's load. Then you will not have to carry it alone.

¹⁸"Tell the people, 'Set yourselves apart for tomorrow. At that time you will eat meat. The LORD heard you when you cried out. You said, "We wish we had meat to eat. We were better off in Egypt."

" 'Now the LORD will give you meat. And you will eat it. ¹⁹You will not eat it for just one or two days. You will not eat it for just five, ten or 20 days. ²⁰Instead, you will eat it for a whole month. You will eat it until it comes out of your nose. You will eat it until you hate it.

" 'The LORD is among you. But you have turned your back on him. You have cried out while he was listening. You have said, "Why did we ever leave Egypt?" ' "

²¹But Moses said, "Here I am among 600,000 men on the march. And you say, 'I will give them meat to eat for a whole month'! ²²Would they have enough if flocks and herds were killed for them? Would they have enough even if all of the fish in the ocean were caught for them?"

²³The LORD answered Moses, "Am I not strong enough? Now you will see whether what I say will come true for you."

²⁴So Moses went out. He told the people what the LORD had said. He gathered 70 of their elders together. He had them stand around the Tent of Meeting.

²⁵Then the LORD came down in the cloud. He spoke with Moses. He took some of his Spirit that was on Moses. And he put the Spirit on the 70 elders. When the Spirit came on them, they prophesied. But they didn't do it again.

²⁶Two men had remained in the camp. Their names were Eldad and Medad. They were listed among the elders. But they didn't go out to the Tent of Meeting. In spite of that, the Spirit came on them too. So they prophesied in the camp.

²⁷A young man ran up to Moses. He said, "Eldad and Medad are prophesying in the camp."

²⁸Joshua spoke up. He was the son of Nun. Joshua had been Moses' helper from the time he was young. He said, "Moses! Please stop them!"

²⁹But Moses replied, "Are you jealous for me? I wish that all of the LORD's people were prophets. And I wish that the LORD would put his Spirit on them." ³⁰Then Moses and the elders of Israel returned to the camp.

³¹The LORD sent out a wind. It drove quail in from the Red Sea. It brought them down all around the camp. They were about three feet above the ground. They could be seen in every direction as far as a person could walk in a day. ³²The people went out all day and gathered quail. They gathered them all night and all the next day. No one gathered less than 60 bushels. Then they spread the quail out all around the camp. ³³But while the meat was still in their mouths, the LORD acted. Before the people could swallow it, his anger burned against them. He struck them with a terrible plague. ³⁴So the place was named Kibroth Hattaavah. That's where the bodies of the people who had longed for other food were buried.

³⁵From Kibroth Hattaavah the people traveled to Hazeroth. And they stayed there.

MIRIAM AND AARON SPEAK AGAINST MOSES

12 Miriam and Aaron began to say bad things about Moses. That's because Moses had married a woman from Cush. ²"Has the LORD spoken only through Moses?" they asked. "Hasn't he also spoken through us?" The LORD heard what they said.

³Moses wasn't very proud at all. In fact, he had less pride than anyone else on the face of the earth.

⁴The LORD spoke to Moses, Aaron and Miriam. He said, "All three of you, come out to the Tent of Meeting." So they did. ⁵Then the LORD came down in a pillar of cloud. He stood at the entrance to the tent. And he told Aaron and Miriam to come to him. Both of them stepped forward.

⁶Then the LORD said, "Listen to my words.

"Suppose one of my prophets is
    among you.
I make myself known to him in
    visions.
I speak to him in dreams.
⁷But that is not true of my servant
    Moses.
He is faithful in everything he
    does in my house.
⁸With Moses I speak face
    to face.
I speak with him clearly. I do not
    speak in riddles.
I let him see something of what I
    look like.
So why were you not afraid
    to speak against my servant
    Moses?"

⁹The anger of the LORD burned against them. And he left them. ¹⁰When the cloud went up from above the tent, there stood Miriam. She had a disease that made her skin as white as snow.

Aaron turned toward her. He saw that she had a skin disease. ¹¹So he said to Moses, "We have committed a very foolish sin. Please don't hold it against us. ¹²Don't let Miriam be like a baby that was born dead. Don't let her look like a dead baby whose body is half eaten away."

¹³So Moses cried out to the LORD. He said, "God, please heal her!"

¹⁴The LORD answered Moses. He said, "Suppose her father had spit in her face. Then she would have been put to shame for seven days. So keep her outside the camp for seven days. After that, you can bring her back."

¹⁵So Miriam was kept outside the camp for seven days. The people didn't move on until she was brought back.

¹⁶After that, the people left Hazeroth. They camped in the Desert of Paran.

SOME MEN CHECK OUT THE LAND OF CANAAN

13 The LORD spoke to Moses. He said, ²"Send some men to check out the land of Canaan. I am giving it to the people of Israel. Send one leader from each of Israel's tribes."

³So Moses sent them out from the Desert of Paran. He sent them as the LORD had commanded. All of them were leaders of the people of Israel.

⁴Here are their names.

There was Shammua from the tribe of Reuben. Shammua was the son of Zaccur.
⁵There was Shaphat from the tribe of Simeon. Shaphat was the son of Hori.
⁶There was Caleb from the tribe of Judah. Caleb was the son of Jephunneh.
⁷There was Igal from the tribe of Issachar. Igal was the son of Joseph.
⁸There was Hoshea from the tribe of Ephraim. Hoshea was the son of Nun.
⁹There was Palti from the tribe of Benjamin. Palti was the son of Raphu.
¹⁰There was Gaddiel from the tribe of Zebulun. Gaddiel was the son of Sodi.
¹¹There was Gaddi from the tribe of Manasseh. Gaddi was the son of Susi. Manasseh was a tribe of Joseph.
¹²There was Ammiel from the tribe of Dan. Ammiel was the son of Gemalli.
¹³There was Sethur from the tribe of Asher. Sethur was the son of Michael.
¹⁴There was Nahbi from the tribe of Naphtali. Nahbi was the son of Vophsi.
¹⁵There was Geuel from the tribe of Gad. Geuel was the son of Maki.

¹⁶Those are the men Moses sent to check out the land. He gave the name Joshua to Hoshea, the son of Nun.

¹⁷Moses sent them to check out Canaan. He said, "Go up through the Negev Desert. Go on into the central hill country. ¹⁸See what the land is like. See whether the people who live there are strong or weak. See whether they are few or many.

¹⁹"What kind of land do they live in? Is it good or bad? What kind of towns do they live in? Do the towns have high walls around them or not? ²⁰How is the soil? Is it rich land or poor land? Are there trees on it or not? Do your best to bring back some of the fruit of the land." It was the season for the first ripe grapes.

²¹So the men went up and checked out the land. They went from the Desert of Zin as far as Rehob. It was in the direction of Lebo Hamath. ²²They went up through the Negev Desert and came to Hebron. That's where Ahiman, Sheshai and Talmai lived. They belonged to the family line of Anak. Hebron had been built seven years before Zoan. Zoan was a city in Egypt.

²³The men came to the Valley of Eshcol. There they cut off a branch that had a single bunch of grapes on it. Two of them carried it on a pole between them. They carried some pomegranates and figs along with it. ²⁴That place was called the Valley of Eshcol. That's because the men of Israel cut off a bunch of grapes there.

²⁵At the end of 40 days, the men returned from checking out the land.

THE MEN REPORT ON WHAT THEY FOUND

²⁶The men came back to Moses, Aaron and the whole community of

Israel. The people were at Kadesh in the Desert of Paran. There the men reported to Moses and Aaron and all of the people. They showed them the fruit of the land.

²⁷They gave Moses their report. They said, "We went into the land you sent us to. It really does have plenty of milk and honey! Here's some fruit from the land.

²⁸"But the people who live there are powerful. Their cities have high walls around them and are very large. We even saw members of the family line of Anak there. ²⁹The Amalekites live in the Negev Desert. The Hittites, Jebusites and Amorites live in the central hill country. The Canaanites live near the Mediterranean Sea. They also live along the Jordan River."

³⁰Then Caleb interrupted the men who were speaking to Moses. He said, "We should go up and take the land. We can certainly do it."

³¹But the men who had gone up with him spoke. They said, "We can't attack those people. They are stronger than we are." ³²The men spread a bad report about the land among the people of Israel. They said, "The land we checked out destroys those who live in it. All of the people we saw there are very big and tall. ³³We saw the Nephilim there. We seemed like grasshoppers in our own eyes. And that's also how we seemed to them." The children of Anak came from the Nephilim.

THE PEOPLE REFUSE TO OBEY THE LORD

14 That night all of the people in the community raised their voices. They sobbed out loud.

²The people of Israel spoke against Moses and Aaron. The whole community said to them, "We wish we had died in Egypt or even in this desert.

Did people have ice cream in Bible times?

No. Ice cream was invented only about 200 years ago. Bible times were a lot longer ago than that. They did not have refrigerators to keep anything as cold as ice cream. But the people of Israel did have lots of good food to eat. Their land had good soil for growing food and raising animals. They had all kinds of foods. They had figs, dates, honey, grapes, raisins, bread, rice, milk, cheese, all kinds of vegetables and many kinds of meat. They made flat cakes out of barley, raisins and figs. Often they would flavor their food with salt and spices just as we do today. They had plenty of good food.

checkout
Numbers 13:27

Related verses:
Genesis 9:3;
1 Samuel 25:18

JASON'S IMAGINATION

³Why is the LORD bringing us to this land? We're going to be killed with swords. Our enemies will capture our wives and children. Wouldn't it be better for us to go back to Egypt?"

⁴They said to one another, "We should choose another leader. We should go back to Egypt."

⁵Then Moses and Aaron fell with their faces to the ground. They did it in front of the whole community of Israel that was gathered there.

⁶Joshua, the son of Nun, tore his clothes. So did Caleb, the son of Jephunneh. Joshua and Caleb were two of the men who had checked out the land. ⁷They spoke to the whole community of Israel. They said, "We passed through the land and checked it out. It's very good. ⁸If the LORD is pleased with us, he'll lead us into that land. It's a land that has plenty of milk and honey. He'll give it to us.

⁹"But don't refuse to obey him. And don't be afraid of the people of the land. We will swallow them up. The LORD is with us. So nothing can save them. Don't be afraid of them."

¹⁰But all of the people talked about killing Joshua and Caleb by throwing stones at them.

Then the glory of the LORD appeared at the Tent of Meeting. All of the people of Israel saw it. ¹¹The LORD spoke to Moses. He said, "How long will these people make fun of me? How long will they refuse to believe in me? They refuse even though I have done many miraculous signs among them. ¹²So I will strike them down with a plague. I will destroy them. But I will make you into a greater and stronger nation than they are."

¹³Moses said to the LORD, "Then the Egyptians will hear about it. You used your power to bring these people up from among them.

¹⁴"And the Egyptians will tell the people who live in Canaan about it. LORD, they have already heard a lot about you. They've heard that you are with these people. They've heard that you have been seen face to face. They've been told that your cloud stays over them. They've heard that you go in front of them in a pillar of cloud by day. They've been told that

you go in front of them in a pillar of fire at night.

¹⁵"Suppose you put these people to death all at one time. Then the nations who have heard those things about you will talk. They'll say, ¹⁶'The LORD took an oath. He promised to give these people the land of Canaan. But he wasn't able to bring them into it. So he killed them in the desert.'

¹⁷"Now, Lord, show your strength. You have said, ¹⁸'I am the LORD. I am slow to get angry. I am full of love. I forgive those who sin. I forgive those who refuse to obey. But I do not let guilty people go without punishing them. I punish the children, grandchildren and great-grandchildren for the sin of their parents.'

¹⁹"LORD, your love is great. So forgive the sin of these people. Forgive them just as you have done from the time they left Egypt until now."

²⁰The LORD replied, "I have forgiven them, just as you asked. ²¹You can be sure that I live. You can be sure that my glory fills the whole earth.

²²"And you can be just as sure that these men will not see the land I promised to give them. They have seen my glory. They have seen the miraculous signs I did in Egypt. And they have seen what I did in the desert. But they did not obey me. And they have put me to the test ten times. ²³So not even one of them will ever see the land I promised with an oath to give to their people of long ago. No one who has made fun of me will ever see it.

²⁴"But my servant Caleb has a different spirit. He follows me with his whole heart. So I will bring him into the land he went to. And his children after him will receive land there.

²⁵"The Amalekites and Canaanites are living in the valleys. So turn back tomorrow. Start out toward the desert. Go along the way that leads to the Red Sea."

²⁶The LORD spoke to Moses and Aaron. He said, ²⁷"How long will this evil community speak against me? I have heard these Israelites talk about how unhappy they are. ²⁸So tell them, 'Here is what I, the LORD, am announcing. You can be sure that I live. And you can be just as sure that I will do to you the very things that I heard you say.

²⁹" 'You will die in this desert. Every one of you who is 20 years old or more will die. Every one of you who was counted in the list of the people will die. Every one of you who has spoken out against me will be wiped out. ³⁰I lifted up my hand and promised with an oath to make this land your home. But now not all of you will enter the land. Caleb, the son of Jephunneh, will enter it. So will Joshua, the son of Nun. They are the only ones who will enter the land.

³¹" 'You have said that your enemies would capture your children. But I will bring your children in to enjoy the land you have turned your backs on. ³²As for you, you will die in the desert. ³³Your children will be shepherds here for 40 years. They will suffer because you were not faithful. They will suffer until the last of your bodies lies here in the desert. ³⁴For 40 years you will suffer for your sins. That is one year for each of the 40 days you checked out

the land. You will know what it is like to have me against you.'

³⁵"I, the LORD, have spoken. You can be sure that I will do those things to this whole evil community. They have joined together against me. They will meet their end in this desert. They will die here."

³⁶So the LORD struck down the men Moses had sent to check out the land. They had returned and had spread a bad report about the land. And that had made the whole community speak out against Moses. ³⁷Those men were to blame for spreading the bad report. So the LORD struck them down. They died of a plague. ³⁸Only two of the men who went to check out the land remained alive. One of them was Joshua, the son of Nun. The other was Caleb, the son of Jephunneh.

³⁹Moses reported to all of the people of Israel what the LORD had said. And they became very sad. ⁴⁰Early the next

Why did the Israelites who left Egypt have to wander in the desert until they died?

God led the Israelites to the land he had promised to Abraham. Before they went in, Moses sent 12 spies into the land to see what it was like. Ten spies came back scared. They said that the giant people in the land would get them. But two of the spies knew God would help them beat the giants. They were Joshua and Caleb. They said to trust God and go on into the land. The people listened to the ten scared spies instead of to Joshua and Caleb. The people who did not trust God never saw the promised land. They wandered in the desert for 40 years. They did not have faith to do what God wanted them to do.

checkout
Numbers 14:34,35

Related verses:
Numbers 13:1—14:45

WILDERNESS TRAIL

morning they went up toward the high hill country. "We have sinned," they said. "We will go up to the place the LORD promised to give us."

⁴¹But Moses said, "Why aren't you obeying the LORD's command? You won't succeed. ⁴²So don't go up. The LORD isn't with you. Your enemies will win the battle over you. ⁴³The Amalekites and Canaanites will meet you on the field of battle. You have turned away from the LORD. So he won't be with you. And you will be killed with swords."

⁴⁴But they wouldn't listen. They still went up toward the high hill country. They went up even though Moses didn't move from the camp. They went even though the ark of the LORD's covenant didn't move from the camp.

⁴⁵Then the Amalekites and Canaanites who lived in that hill country came down. They attacked the people of Israel. They won the battle over them. They chased them all the way to Hormah.

OTHER OFFERINGS

15 The LORD said to Moses, ²"Speak to the people of Israel. Say to them, 'You are going to enter the land I am giving you as a home. ³When you do, you will give offerings that are made to the LORD with fire. The animals must come from your herd or flock. The offerings will give a smell that is pleasant to the LORD. They can be either burnt offerings or sacrifices. They can be either for special promises or for feast offerings. Or they can be for offerings you choose to give.

⁴" 'With each of the offerings, the one who brings it must give the LORD a grain offering. It must be eight cups of fine flour. It must be mixed with a quart of olive oil. ⁵Also prepare a quart of wine as a drink offering. You must give it with each lamb that you bring for the burnt offering or the sacrifice.

⁶" 'With a ram prepare a grain offering. It must be 16 cups of fine flour. It must be mixed with two and a half pints of olive oil. ⁷You must bring two and a half pints of wine as a drink offering. Offer everything as a smell that is pleasant to the LORD.

⁸" 'Suppose you prepare a young bull as a burnt offering or sacrifice. You prepare it to keep a special promise to the LORD. Or you prepare it to give as a friendship offering. ⁹Then bring a grain offering with the bull. The grain offering must be 24 cups of fine flour. It must be mixed with two quarts of olive oil. ¹⁰Also bring two quarts of wine as a drink offering. It will be an offering that is made with fire. It will give a smell that is pleasant to the LORD.

¹¹" 'Each bull or ram must be prepared in the same way. Each lamb or young goat must also be prepared in that way. ¹²Do it for each animal. Do it for as many animals as you prepare.

¹³" 'Everyone in Israel must do those things in that way. He must do them when he brings an offering that is made with fire. Offerings like that give a smell that is pleasant to the LORD.

¹⁴" 'Everyone must always do what the law requires. It does not matter whether he is an outsider or someone else who is living among you. He must do exactly as you do when he brings an offering that is made with fire. Offerings like that give a smell that is pleasant to the LORD.

¹⁵" 'The community must have the same rules for you and for the outsider who is living among you. That law will last for all time to come. In the sight of the LORD, the law applies to you and the outsider alike. ¹⁶The same laws and rules will apply to you and to the outsider who is living among you.' "

¹⁷The LORD said to Moses, ¹⁸"Speak to the people of Israel. Say to them, 'You are going to enter the land I am taking you to. ¹⁹You will eat its food. When you do, bring part of it as an offering to the LORD. ²⁰Bring a loaf that is made from the first flour you grind. Give it as an offering from the threshing floor. ²¹You must bring the offering to the LORD. You must give it from the first grain you grind. You must do it for all time to come.

OFFERINGS FOR SINS THAT AREN'T COMMITTED ON PURPOSE

²²" 'Suppose you fail to keep any of the commands the LORD gave Moses.

And suppose you do it without meaning to. ²³That applies to any of the commands the LORD told Moses to give you. And they are in effect from the day the LORD gave them and for all time to come. ²⁴Suppose the community sins without meaning to. And suppose they do not know they have sinned. Then the whole community must offer a young bull. They must offer it for a burnt offering. It will give a smell that is pleasant to the LORD. Along with it, they must offer its required grain offering and drink offering. They must also offer a male goat for a sin offering.

²⁵" 'With it the priest will pay for the sin of the whole community of Israel. Then they will be forgiven. They did not mean to commit that sin. And they have brought to the LORD an offering that is made with fire for the wrong thing they did. They have brought a sin offering with it.

²⁶" 'The LORD will forgive the whole community of Israel and the outsiders living among them. All of the people had a part in the sin, even though they did not mean to do it.

²⁷" 'But suppose just one person sins without meaning to. Then he must bring a female goat for a sin offering. It must be a year old. ²⁸With it the priest will pay for the person's sin in the sight of the LORD. He will do it for the one who did wrong by sinning without meaning to. When the sin is paid for, that person will be forgiven.

²⁹" 'The same law applies to everyone who sins without meaning to. It does not matter whether he is an Israelite or an outsider.

³⁰" 'But suppose someone sins on purpose. It does not matter whether he is an Israelite or an outsider. He speaks evil things against the LORD. He must be cut off from his people. ³¹He has made fun of what the LORD has said. He has broken the LORD's commands. He must certainly be cut off. He is still guilty.' "

A MAN BREAKS THE SABBATH DAY

³²The people of Israel were in the desert. One Sabbath day, people saw a man gathering wood. ³³They brought him to Moses and Aaron and the whole community. ³⁴They kept him under guard. It wasn't clear what should be done to him.

³⁵Then the LORD said to Moses, "The man must die. The whole community must kill him by throwing stones at him. They must do it outside the camp."

³⁶So the people took the man outside the camp. There they killed him by throwing stones at him. They did just as the LORD had commanded Moses.

TASSELS ON CLOTHES

³⁷The LORD said to Moses, ³⁸"Speak to the people of Israel. Say to them, 'You must make tassels on the corners of your clothes. A blue cord must be on each tassel. You must do it for all time to come. ³⁹You will have the tassels to look at. They will remind you to obey all of the LORD's commands. Then you will be faithful to him. You will not go after what your own hearts and eyes long for.

⁴⁰" 'You will remember to obey all of my commands. And you will be set apart for your God. ⁴¹I am the LORD your God. I brought you out of Egypt to be your God. I am the LORD your God.' "

KORAH, DATHAN AND ABIRAM

16 Korah was the son of Izhar, the son of Kohath. Kohath was the son of Levi. Korah and certain men from the tribe of Reuben turned against Moses. The men from Reuben were Dathan, Abiram and On. Dathan and Abiram were the sons of Eliab. On was the son of Peleth. ²All of those men rose up against Moses. And 250 men of Israel joined them. All of them were known as leaders in the community. They had been appointed as members of the ruling body.

³They came as a group to oppose Moses and Aaron. They said to Moses and Aaron, "You have gone too far! The whole community is holy. Every one in it is holy. And the LORD is with them. So why do you put yourselves above the LORD's people?"

⁴When Moses heard what they said, he fell with his face to the ground. ⁵Then he spoke to Korah and all of his followers. He said, "In the morning the LORD will show who belongs to him. He will show who is holy. He'll bring that person near him. He'll bring the man he chooses near him.

⁶"Korah, here's what you and all of your followers must do. Get some shallow cups for burning incense. ⁷Tomorrow put fire and incense in them. Offer it to the LORD. The man the LORD chooses will be the one who is holy. You Levites have gone too far!"

⁸Moses also said to Korah, "Listen, you Levites! ⁹The God of Israel has separated you from the rest of the community of Israel. He has brought you near him to work at the LORD's holy tent. He has given you to the people so that you can serve them. Isn't all of that enough for you? ¹⁰He has already brought you and all of the other Levites near him. But now you want to be priests too. ¹¹You and all of your followers have joined together against the LORD. Why are you telling Aaron you aren't happy with him?"

¹²Then Moses sent for Dathan and Abiram, the sons of Eliab. But they said, "We won't come! ¹³You have brought us up out of a land that has plenty of milk and honey. You have brought us here to kill us in this desert. Isn't that enough? Now do you also want to act as if you were ruling over us?

¹⁴"Besides, you haven't brought us into a land that has plenty of milk and honey. You haven't given us fields and vineyards of our own. Are you going to poke out the eyes of these men? No! We won't come!"

¹⁵Then Moses became very angry. He said to the LORD, "Don't accept their offering. I haven't taken even a donkey from them. In fact, I haven't done anything wrong to any of them."

¹⁶Moses said to Korah, "You and all of your followers must stand in front of the LORD tomorrow. You must appear there along with Aaron. ¹⁷Each man must get his shallow cup. He must put incense in it. There will be a total of 250 incense cups. Each man must bring his cup to the LORD. You and Aaron must also bring your cups."

¹⁸So each man got his cup. He put fire and incense in it. All of the men came with Moses and Aaron. They stood at the entrance to the Tent of Meeting. ¹⁹Korah gathered all of his followers together at the entrance to the tent. They opposed Moses and Aaron.

Then the glory of the LORD appeared to the whole community. ²⁰The LORD spoke to Moses and Aaron. He said, ²¹"Separate yourselves from these people. Then I can put an end to all of them at once."

²²But Moses and Aaron fell with their faces to the ground. They cried out, "God, you are the God who creates the spirits of all people. Will you be angry with the whole community when only one man sins?"

²³Then the LORD spoke to Moses. He said, ²⁴"Tell the community, 'Move away from the tents of Korah, Dathan and Abiram.' "

²⁵Moses got up. He went to Dathan and Abiram. The elders of Israel followed him. ²⁶Moses warned the community. He said, "Move away from the tents of those evil men! Don't touch anything that belongs to them. If you do, the LORD will sweep you away because of all of their sins."

²⁷So they moved away from the tents of Korah, Dathan and Abiram. Dathan and Abiram had already come out. They were standing at the entrances to their tents. Their wives, children and little ones were standing there with them.

²⁸Then Moses said, "What is about to happen wasn't my idea. The LORD has sent me to do everything I'm doing. Here is how you will know I'm telling you the truth. ²⁹Those men won't die a natural death. Something will happen to them that doesn't usually happen to people. If what I'm telling you isn't true, then you will know that the LORD hasn't sent me. ³⁰But the LORD will make something totally new happen. The ground will open its mouth and swallow them up. It will swallow up everything that belongs to them. They will go down into the grave alive. When that happens, you will know that those men have made fun of the LORD."

³¹As soon as Moses finished speaking all of those words, what he had said came true. The ground under them broke open. ³²It opened its mouth. It swallowed up those men. In fact, it swallowed up everyone who lived in their houses. It swallowed all of Korah's men. And it swallowed up everything they owned. ³³They went down into the grave alive. Everything they owned went down with them. The ground closed over them. They died. And so they disappeared from the community.

³⁴All of the people of Israel who were around them heard their cries. They ran away from them. They shouted, "The ground is going to swallow us up too!"

³⁵Then the LORD sent down fire. It burned up the 250 men who were offering the incense.

³⁶The LORD spoke to Moses. He said, ³⁷"Speak to the priest Eleazar. He is the son of Aaron. Remind him that the shallow cups are holy. He must take them out of the fire. He must scatter the burning coals away from there. ³⁸The men who sinned used those cups. And it cost them their lives. Hammer the cups into bronze sheets that will cover the altar. The cups were offered to the LORD. They have become holy. Let them serve as a warning to the people of Israel."

³⁹So the priest Eleazar collected the bronze incense cups. They had been brought by the men who had been burned up. He had them hammered out to cover the altar. ⁴⁰He did just as the LORD had directed Moses to tell him to do. The covering would be a reminder to the people of Israel. It would remind them that no one except a son of Aaron should come and burn incense to the LORD. If people other than priests did that, they would become like Korah and his followers.

⁴¹The next day the whole community of Israel told Moses and Aaron they weren't happy with them. "You have killed the LORD's people," they said.

⁴²The community gathered together to oppose Moses and Aaron. The people walked toward the Tent of Meeting. Suddenly the cloud covered it. The glory of the LORD appeared. ⁴³Then Moses and Aaron went to the front of the Tent of Meeting. ⁴⁴The LORD spoke to Moses. He said, ⁴⁵"Get away from these people. Then I can put an end to all of them at once." And Moses and Aaron fell with their faces to the ground.

⁴⁶Moses said to Aaron, "Take your incense cup. Put incense in it. And put fire from the altar in it. Then hurry to the people and pay for their sin. The LORD has sent his anger. The plague has started."

⁴⁷So Aaron did as Moses said. He ran in among the people. The plague had already started among them. But Aaron offered the incense and paid for their sin. ⁴⁸He stood between those who were alive and those who were dead. And the plague stopped. ⁴⁹But 14,700 people died from the plague. That doesn't include those who had died because of what Korah did. ⁵⁰Then Aaron returned to Moses at the entrance to the Tent of Meeting. The plague had stopped.

AARON'S WOODEN STAFF PRODUCES BUDS

17 The LORD spoke to Moses. He said, ²"Speak to the people of Israel. Get 12 wooden staffs from them. Get one from the leader of each of Israel's tribes. Write the name of each man on his staff. ³Write Aaron's name on the staff of Levi. There must be one staff for the head of each of Israel's tribes. ⁴"Put the staffs in the Tent of Meeting. Place them in front of the ark where the tablets of the covenant are kept. That is where I meet with you. ⁵The staff that belongs to the man I choose will begin to grow new shoots. The people of Israel are never happy with what you do. I will put an end to what they are saying."

⁶So Moses spoke to the people of Israel. Their leaders gave him 12 wooden staffs. They gave one for the leader of each of Israel's tribes. Aaron's staff was among them. ⁷Moses put the staffs in front of the LORD in the tent where the tablets of the covenant were kept.

⁸The next day Moses entered the

tent. He looked at Aaron's staff. It stood for the tribe of Levi. Moses saw that it had not only begun to grow new shoots. It had also produced buds and flowers and almonds.

[9]Then Moses brought out all of the staffs from in front of the LORD. He brought them to all of the people of Israel. They looked at them. And each man took his own staff.

[10]The LORD said to Moses, "Put Aaron's staff back in front of the ark where the tablets of the covenant are kept. The staff will be kept there as a warning to those who refuse to obey. They are never happy with what I do. Aaron's staff will put an end to what they are saying. Then they will not die." [11]Moses did just as the LORD commanded him.

[12]The people of Israel said to Moses, "We'll die! We are lost! All of us are lost! [13]Anyone who even comes near the LORD's holy tent will die. Are all of us going to die?"

DUTIES OF PRIESTS AND LEVITES

18 The LORD spoke to Aaron. He said, "You, your sons and your father's family are in charge of the sacred tent. You will be held accountable for sins that are committed against it. And you and your sons will be held accountable for sins that are committed against the office of priest.

[2]"Bring the Levites from your tribe to join you. They will help you when you and your sons serve at the tent where the tablets of the covenant are kept. [3]They will work for you. They must do everything that needs to be done at the tent. But they must not go near anything that belongs to the sacred tent. And they must not go near the altar. If they do, they and you will die. [4]They will help you take care of the Tent of Meeting. They will join you in all of the work at the tent. No one else can come near you there.

[5]"You will be held accountable for taking care of the sacred tent and the altar. Then my anger will not fall on the people of Israel again. [6]I myself have chosen the Levites. I have chosen them from among the people of Israel.

They are a gift to you. I have set them apart to do the work at the Tent of Meeting.

[7]"But only you and your sons can serve as priests. Only you and your sons can work with everything at the altar and inside the curtain. I am letting you serve as priests. It is a gift from me. Anyone else who comes near the sacred tent must be put to death."

OFFERINGS FOR PRIESTS AND LEVITES

[8]Then the LORD spoke to Aaron. He said, "I have put you in charge of the offerings that are brought to me. The people of Israel will give me holy offerings. I will give all of their offerings to you and your sons. They are the part that belongs to you. They are your regular share.

[9]"You will have a part of the very holy offerings. It is the part that is not burned in the fire. That part belongs to you and your sons. You will have a part of all of the gifts the people bring me as very holy offerings. It does not matter whether they are grain offerings or sin offerings or guilt offerings. [10]Eat your part as something that is very holy. Every male will eat it. You must consider it holy.

[11]"Part of the gifts the people of Israel bring as wave offerings will be set to one side. That part will also belong to you. I will give it to you and your sons and daughters. It is your regular share. Everyone in your home who is 'clean' can eat it.

[12]"I will give you all of the finest olive oil and grain the people give me. And I will give you all of the finest fresh wine they give me. They give all of those things as the first share of their harvest. [13]All of the first shares of the harvest they bring me will belong to you. Everyone in your home who is 'clean' can eat it.

[14]"Everything in Israel that is set apart to me belongs to you. [15]Offer to me every male that is born first to its mother. It belongs to you. That is true for men and animals alike. But you must buy back every oldest son. Suppose certain animals are not 'clean.' Then you must buy back every male that is born first to its mother. [16]When

they are a month old, you must buy them back. You must pay the price to buy them back. The price is set at two ounces of silver. It must be weighed out in keeping with the standard weights that are used in the sacred tent.

¹⁷"But you must not buy back any male calf that is born first. And you must not buy back any male sheep or goat that is born first. They are holy. Sprinkle their blood on the altar. And burn their fat as an offering that is made with fire. It gives a smell that is pleasant to me.

¹⁸"The meat will belong to you. It is just like the breast and the right thigh of the wave offering. Those parts belong to you. ¹⁹Part of the holy offerings the people of Israel bring to me will be set to one side. No matter what it is, I will give it to you and your sons and daughters. It is your regular share. It is a covenant of salt from me. The salt means that the covenant will last for all time to come for you and your children."

²⁰The LORD spoke to Aaron. He said, "You will not receive any part of the land I am giving to Israel. You will not have any share among them. I am your share. I am what you will receive among the people of Israel.

²¹"The people of Israel will give me a tenth of everything they produce. And I will give it to the Levites. They serve at the Tent of Meeting. I will give them the tenth for the work they do there. ²²From now on the people of Israel must not go near the Tent of Meeting. If they do, they will be punished for their sin. They will die.

²³"The Levites will do the work at the Tent of Meeting. They will be held accountable for sins that are committed against it. That is a law that will last for all time to come. The Levites will not receive any share among the people of Israel. ²⁴Instead, I will give the Levites the tenth as their share. It is the tenth that the people of Israel bring me as an offering. That is why I said the Levites would not have any share of land among the people of Israel."

²⁵The LORD said to Moses, ²⁶"Speak to the Levites. Say to them, 'You will receive the tenth from the people of

Israel. I will give it to you as your share. When I do, you must give a tenth of that tenth as an offering to the LORD. ²⁷Your offering will be considered as if you gave grain from a threshing floor. It will be considered as juice from a winepress.

²⁸" 'In that way, you also will bring an offering to the LORD. You will bring it from the tenth you receive from the people of Israel. You must give the LORD's part to the priest Aaron. You must bring it from the tenth you receive. ²⁹You must bring to the LORD a part of everything that is given to you. It must be the best and holiest part.'

³⁰"Say to the Levites, 'You must bring the best part. Then it will be considered as if you gave grain from a threshing floor. It will be considered as juice from a winepress. ³¹You and your families can eat the rest of it anywhere. It is your pay for your work at the Tent of Meeting. ³²Bring the best part of what you receive. Then you will not be guilty of holding anything back. You will not make the holy offerings of the people of Israel "unclean." You will not die.' "

THE SPECIAL WATER THAT MAKES PEOPLE "CLEAN"

19 The LORD spoke to Moses and Aaron. He said, ²"Here is what the law I have commanded requires. Tell the people of Israel to bring you a young red cow. It must not have any flaws at all. It must never have pulled a load.

³"Give it to the priest Eleazar. It must be taken outside the camp and killed in front of him. ⁴Then the priest Eleazar must put some of its blood on his finger. He must sprinkle the blood toward the front of the Tent of Meeting. He must do it seven times.

⁵"While he watches, the young cow must be burned. Its hide, meat, blood and guts must be burned. ⁶The priest must get some cedar wood, branches of a hyssop plant, and bright red wool. He must throw them on the young cow as it burns.

⁷"After that, the priest must wash his clothes. He must also take a bath. Then he can come into the camp. But he will be 'unclean' until evening.

⁸"The man who burns the young

cow must wash his clothes. He must also take a bath. He too will be 'unclean' until evening.

⁹"A man who is 'clean' will gather up the ashes of the young cow. He must put them in a place that is 'clean.' The place must be outside the camp. The ashes will be kept by the community of Israel. They will be added to the special water. The water will be used to make people pure from their sin.

¹⁰"The man who gathers up the ashes of the young cow must wash his clothes. He too will be 'unclean' until evening. That law is for the people of Israel. It is also for the outsiders who are living among them. The law will last for all time to come.

¹¹"Anyone who touches a dead person's body will be 'unclean' for seven days. ¹²He must make himself pure and clean with the special water. He must do it on the third day. He must also do it on the seventh day. Then he will be 'clean.'

"But suppose he does not make himself pure and clean on the third and seventh days. Then he will not be 'clean.' ¹³Anyone who touches a dead person's body and does not make himself pure and clean makes my holy tent 'unclean.' He must be cut off from Israel. The special water has not been sprinkled on him. So he is 'unclean.' And he remains 'unclean.'

¹⁴"Here is the law that applies when a person dies in a tent. Anyone who enters the tent will be 'unclean' for seven days. Anyone who is in the tent will also be 'unclean' for seven days. ¹⁵And anything in it that is open and has no lid will be 'unclean.'

¹⁶"Suppose someone is out in the country. And suppose he touches someone who has been killed with a sword. Or he touches someone who has died a natural death. Or he touches a human bone or a grave. Then anyone who touches any of those things will be 'unclean' for seven days.

¹⁷"Here is what I want you to do for someone who is not 'clean.' Put some ashes from the burned young cow into a jar. Pour fresh water on the ashes. ¹⁸Then a man who is 'clean' must dip branches of a hyssop plant in the wa-

ter. He must sprinkle the tent with it. Everything that belongs to the tent must be sprinkled with it. The people who were in the tent must also be sprinkled. Anyone who has touched a human bone or a grave must be sprinkled. So must anyone who has touched someone who has been killed. So must anyone who has touched someone who has died a natural death.

¹⁹"The man who is 'clean' must sprinkle the person who is not. That must be done on the third and seventh days. On the seventh day the person who is not 'clean' must be made pure and clean. The one who is being made 'clean' must wash his clothes. He must take a bath. Then that evening he will be 'clean.'

²⁰"But what if a person who is 'unclean' does not make himself pure and clean? Then he must be cut off from the community. He has made my holy tent 'unclean.' The special water has not been sprinkled on him. He is not 'clean.' ²¹That law will apply to all of those people for all time to come.

"The man who sprinkles the special water must also wash his clothes. Anyone who touches the water will be 'unclean' until evening. ²²Anything that an 'unclean' person touches becomes 'unclean.' And anyone who touches it becomes 'unclean' until evening."

THE LORD GIVES ISRAEL WATER OUT OF THE ROCK

20 In the first month the whole community of Israel arrived at the Desert of Zin. They stayed at Kadesh. Miriam died there. Her body was also buried there.

²The people didn't have any water. So they gathered together to oppose Moses and Aaron. ³They argued with Moses. They said, "We wish we had died when our people fell dead in front of the LORD.

⁴"Why did you bring the LORD's people into this desert? We and our livestock will die here. ⁵Why did you bring us up out of Egypt? Why did you bring us to this terrible place? It doesn't have any grain or figs. It doesn't have any grapes or pomegran-

ates. There isn't even any water for us to drink!"

⁶Moses and Aaron left the people. They went to the entrance to the Tent of Meeting. There they fell with their faces to the ground.

Then the glory of the LORD appeared to them. ⁷The LORD spoke to Moses. He said, ⁸"Get your wooden staff. You and your brother Aaron gather the people together. Then speak to that rock while everyone is watching. It will pour out its water. You will bring water out of the rock for the community. Then they and their livestock can drink it."

⁹So Moses took the wooden staff from the tent. He did just as the LORD had commanded him. ¹⁰He and Aaron gathered the people together in front of the rock. Moses said to them, "Listen, you who refuse to obey! Do we have to bring water out of this rock for you?"

¹¹Then Moses raised his arm. He hit the rock twice with his staff. Water poured out. And the people and their livestock drank it.

¹²But the LORD spoke to Moses and Aaron. He said, "You did not trust in me enough to honor me. You did not honor me as the holy God in front of the people of Israel. So you will not bring this community into the land I am giving them."

¹³Those were the waters of Meribah. That's where the people of Israel argued with the LORD. And that's where he showed them he is holy.

EDOM DOESN'T LET ISRAEL PASS THROUGH ITS TERRITORY

¹⁴Moses sent messengers from Kadesh to the king of Edom. The messengers said,

"The nation of Israel is your brother. They say, 'You know about all of the hard times we've had. ¹⁵Long ago our people went down into Egypt. We lived there for many years. The Egyptians treated us and our people badly. ¹⁶But we cried out to the LORD. He heard our cry. He sent an angel and brought us out of Egypt.

" 'Now here we are at the town of Kadesh. It's on the edge of your territory. ¹⁷Please let us pass through your country. We won't go through any field or vineyard. We won't drink water from any well. We'll travel along the king's highway. We won't turn to the right or the left. We'll just go straight through your territory.' "

¹⁸But the people of Edom answered,

"You can't pass through here. If you try to, we'll march out against you. We'll attack you with our swords."

¹⁹The people of Israel replied,

"We'll go along the main road. We and our livestock won't drink any of your water. If we do, we'll pay for it. We only want to walk through your country. That's all we ask."

²⁰Again the people of Edom answered,

"You can't pass through here."

Then the people of Edom came out against them. They came with a large and powerful army. ²¹Edom refused to let Israel go through their territory. So Israel turned away from them.

AARON DIES

²²The whole community of Israel started out from Kadesh. They arrived at Mount Hor. ²³It was near the border of Edom. There the LORD spoke to Moses and Aaron. He said, ²⁴"Aaron will join the members of his family who have already died. He will not enter the land I am giving to the people of Israel. Both of you refused to obey my command. You did it at the waters of Meribah.

²⁵"So get Aaron and his son Eleazar. Take them up Mount Hor. ²⁶Take Aaron's official robes off him. Put them on his son Eleazar. Aaron will die on Mount Hor. He will join the members of his family who have already died."

²⁷Moses did just as the LORD had commanded. The three men went up Mount Hor while the whole commu-

nity was watching. [28]Moses took Aaron's official robes off him. He put them on Aaron's son Eleazar. And Aaron died there on top of the mountain. Then Moses and Eleazar came down from the mountain.

[29]The whole community found out that Aaron had died. So the entire nation of Israel sobbed over him for 30 days.

ISRAEL DESTROYS ARAD

21 The Canaanite king of the city of Arad lived in the Negev Desert. He heard that Israel was coming along the road to Atharim. So he attacked the people of Israel. He captured some of them.

[2]Then Israel made a promise to the LORD. They said, "Hand these people over to us. If you do, we will set their cities apart to you in a special way to be destroyed."

[3]The LORD gave Israel what they asked for. He handed the Canaanites over to them. Israel completely destroyed them. They also destroyed their towns. So that place was named Hormah.

MOSES MAKES A BRONZE SNAKE

[4]The people of Israel traveled from Mount Hor along the way to the Red Sea. They wanted to go around Edom. But they grew tired on the way. [5]So they spoke against God. They also spoke against Moses. They said to them, "Why have you brought us up out of Egypt? Do you want us to die here in the desert? We don't have any bread! We don't have any water! And we hate this awful food!"

[6]Then the LORD sent poisonous snakes among the people of Israel. The snakes bit them. Many of the people died. [7]The others came to Moses. They said, "We sinned when we spoke against the LORD and against you. Pray that the LORD will take the snakes away from us." So Moses prayed for the people.

How did the people travel?

People in Bible times did not have cars, trains, buses or airplanes. They usually walked from town to town. If you have ever taken a hike, you probably walked until you were tired. Then you rested. You may have even put up a tent and camped out for the night. That is what people did back then whenever they went a long way. Some who had enough money to pay for it rode on donkeys, camels or horses. Sometimes kings, soldiers or rich people rode in chariots that were pulled by horses. And when they had to travel over water, they went in boats or ships.

checkout
Numbers 20:19

Related verses:
Exodus 12:11,34, 37,38

JASON'S IMAGINATION

SCHOOL BUS

[8]The LORD said to Moses, "Make a snake. Put it up on a pole. Then anyone who is bitten can look at it and remain alive." [9]So Moses made a bronze snake. He put it up on a pole. Then anyone who was bitten by a snake and looked at the bronze snake remained alive.

THE PEOPLE CONTINUE ON TO MOAB

[10]The people of Israel moved on. They camped at Oboth. [11]Then they started out from Oboth. They camped in Iye Abarim. It's in the desert on the eastern border of Moab. [12]From there they moved on. They camped in the Zered Valley. [13]They started out from there and camped by the Arnon River. It's in the desert that spreads out into the territory of the Amorites. The Arnon is the border of Moab. It's between Moab and the Amorites.

[14]Here is what the Book of the Wars of the LORD says about it. It says,

"Sing about Waheb in Suphah and
   the valleys.
Sing about the Arnon [15]and the
   slopes of the valleys.
They lead to the place called Ar.
They lie along the border of
   Moab."

[16]From there the people of Israel continued on to Beer. That was the well where the LORD spoke to Moses. He said, "Gather the people together. I will give them water to drink."

[17]Then Israel sang a song. They said,

"Spring up, you well!
Sing about it.
[18]Sing about the well the princes
   dug.
Sing about the well the nobles of
   the people dug.
All of their rulers were holding
   their rods and staffs."

Then the people of Israel went from the desert to Mattanah. [19]They went from Mattanah to Nahaliel. They went from Nahaliel to Bamoth. [20]And they went from Bamoth to a valley in Moab. It's the valley where the highest slopes of Pisgah look out over a dry and empty land.

ISRAEL WINS THE BATTLE OVER SIHON AND OG

[21]The people of Israel sent messengers to speak to Sihon. He was the king of the Amorites. The messengers said to him,

[22]"Let us pass through your country. We won't go off the road into any field or vineyard. We won't drink water from any well. We'll travel along the king's highway. We'll just go straight through your territory."

[23]But Sihon wouldn't let Israel pass through his territory. He gathered his whole army together. Then he marched out into the desert against Israel. When he reached Jahaz, he fought against Israel. [24]But Israel put him to death with their swords. They took over his land. They took everything from the Arnon River to the Jabbok River. But they didn't take over any of the land of the Ammonites. That's because the Ammonites had built strong forts along their border. [25]The people of Israel captured all of the cities of the Amorites. Then they settled down in them. They captured the city of Heshbon. They also captured all of the settlements that were around it.

[26]Sihon, the king of the Amorites, ruled in Heshbon. He had fought against an earlier king of Moab. Sihon had taken from him all of his land all the way to the Arnon River.

[27]That's why the poets say,

"Come to Heshbon. Let it be built
   again.
Let Sihon's city be made as good
   as new.
[28]"Fire went out from Heshbon.
A blaze went out from the city of
   Sihon.
It burned up Ar in Moab.
It burned up the citizens who
   lived on Arnon's hills.
[29]Moab, how terrible it is for you!
People of Chemosh, you are
   destroyed!
Chemosh has deserted his sons
   and daughters.

His sons have run away from the
battle.
His daughters have become
prisoners.
He has handed all of them over
to Sihon,
the king of the Amorites.

30 "But we have taken them over.
Heshbon is destroyed all the way
to Dibon.
We have destroyed them as far as
Nophah.
Nophah goes all the way to
Medeba."

31 So Israel settled in the land of the Amorites.

32 Moses sent spies to the city of Jazer. The people of Israel captured the settlements that were around it. They drove out the Amorites who were there. 33 Then they turned and went up along the road toward Bashan. Og was the king of Bashan. He and his whole army marched out. They went to fight against Israel at Edrei.

34 The LORD said to Moses, "Do not be afraid of Og. I have handed him over to you. I have given you his whole army. I have also given you his land. Do to him what you did to Sihon, the king of the Amorites. He ruled in Heshbon."

35 So the people of Israel struck Og down. They struck his sons down. And they wiped out his whole army. They didn't leave anyone alive. They took over his land for themselves.

BALAK SENDS FOR BALAAM

22 Then the people of Israel traveled to the flatlands of Moab. They camped along the Jordan River across from Jericho.

2 Balak saw everything that Israel had done to the Amorites. Balak was the son of Zippor. 3 The people of Moab were terrified because there were so many Israelites. In fact, Moab was filled with panic because of the people of Israel.

4 The Moabites spoke to the elders of Midian. They said, "This huge mob is going to lick up everything around us. They'll lick it up as an ox licks up all of the grass in the fields."

Balak, the son of Zippor, was the king of Moab at that time. 5 He sent messengers to get Balaam. Balaam was the son of Beor. Balaam was at the city of Pethor near the Euphrates River. Pethor was in the land where Balaam had been born. Balak told the messengers to say to Balaam,

"A nation has come out of Egypt. They are covering the face of the land. They've settled down next to me. 6 So come and put a curse on those people. They are too powerful for me. Maybe I'll be able to win the battle over them. Maybe I'll be able to drive them out of the country. I know that those you bless will be blessed. And I know that those you put a curse on will be cursed."

7 The elders of Moab and Midian left. They took with them the money they knew Balaam would ask for. They wanted him to use magic and figure things out for them. They came to where Balaam was. And they told him what Balak had said.

8 "Spend the night here," Balaam said to them. "I'll bring you back the answer the LORD gives me." So the princes of Moab stayed with him.

9 God came to Balaam. He asked, "Who are these men who are with you?"

10 Balaam said to God, "Balak king of Moab, the son of Zippor, sent me a message. 11 He said, 'A nation has come out of Egypt. They are covering the whole surface of the land. So come. Put a curse on them for me. Maybe I'll be able to fight them. Maybe I'll be able to drive them away.' "

12 But God said to Balaam, "Do not go with them. You must not put a curse on those people. I have blessed them."

13 The next morning Balaam got up. He said to Balak's princes, "Go back to your own country. The LORD won't let me go with you."

14 So the princes of Moab returned to Balak. They said, "Balaam wouldn't come with us."

15 Then Balak sent other princes. They were more important than the first ones. And there were more of them. 16 They came to Balaam. They said,

"Balak, the son of Zippor, says, 'Don't let anything keep you from coming to me. [17]I'll make you very rich. I'll do anything you say. Come. Put a curse on those people for me.' "

[18]But Balaam gave them his answer. He said, "Balak could give me his palace filled with silver and gold. Even then, I still couldn't do anything at all that goes beyond what the LORD my God commands. [19]Stay here tonight, just as the others did. I'll find out what else the LORD will tell me."

[20]That night God came to Balaam. He said, "These men have come to get you. So go with them. But do only what I tell you to do."

BALAAM'S DONKEY

[21]Balaam got up in the morning. He put a saddle on his donkey. Then he went with the princes of Moab.

[22]But God was very angry when Balaam went. So the angel of the LORD stood in the road to oppose him. Balaam was riding on his donkey. His two servants were with him. [23]The donkey saw the angel of the LORD standing in the road. The angel was holding a sword. He was ready for battle. So the donkey left the road and went into a field. Balaam hit the donkey. He wanted to get it back on the road.

[24]Then the angel of the LORD stood in a narrow path. The path went between two vineyards. There were walls on both sides. [25]The donkey saw the angel of the LORD. So it moved close to the wall. It crushed Balaam's foot against the wall. He hit the donkey again.

[26]Then the angel of the LORD moved on ahead. He stood in a narrow place. There was no room to turn, either right or left. [27]The donkey saw the angel of the LORD. So it lay down under Balaam. That made him angry. He hit the donkey with his walking stick.

[28]Then the LORD opened the donkey's mouth. It said to Balaam, "What have I done to you? Why did you hit me those three times?"

[29]Balaam answered the donkey. He said, "You have made me look foolish! I wish I had a sword in my hand. If I did, I'd kill you right now."

[30]The donkey said to Balaam, "I'm your own donkey. I'm the one you have always ridden. Haven't you been riding me to this very day? Have I ever made you look foolish before?"

"No," he said.

[31]Then the LORD opened Balaam's

KIDS' QUESTION

Are there angels in this room with us?

There may be. We should not expect them to be with us at every moment the way God is. Angels are not *everywhere*. But angels can be with us without our knowing about it. And they may be in the room with us right now. That is what happened to Balaam (Numbers 22:21–41). He did not know there was an angel with him until God allowed him to see it.

checkout
Numbers 22:31

Related verses:
2 Kings 6:16,17;
Hebrews 13:2

eyes. He saw the angel of the LORD standing in the road. He saw that the angel was holding a sword. The angel was ready for battle. So Balaam bowed down. He fell with his face to the ground. ³²The angel of the LORD spoke to him. He asked him, "Why have you hit your donkey three times? I have come here to oppose you. What you are doing is foolish. ³³The donkey saw me. It turned away from me three times. Suppose it had not turned away. Then I would certainly have killed you by now. But I would have spared the donkey."

³⁴Balaam spoke to the angel of the LORD. He said, "I have sinned. I didn't realize you were standing in the road to oppose me. Tell me whether you are pleased with me. If you aren't, I'll go back."

³⁵The angel of the LORD spoke to Balaam. He said, "Go with the men. But say only what I tell you to say." So Balaam went with the princes of Balak.

³⁶Balak heard that Balaam was coming. So he went out to meet him. They met at a Moabite town near the Arnon River. The town was on the border of Balak's territory. ³⁷Balak spoke to Balaam. He said, "Didn't I send messengers to you? I wanted you to come quickly. So why didn't you come? I can make you very rich."

³⁸"Well, I've come to you now," Balaam replied. "But I can't say just anything. I can only speak the words God puts in my mouth."

³⁹Then Balaam went with Balak to Kiriath Huzoth. ⁴⁰Balak sacrificed cattle and sheep. He gave some to Balaam. He also gave some to the princes who were with him.

⁴¹The next morning Balak took Balaam up to Bamoth Baal. From there he saw part of the people of Israel.

BALAAM'S FIRST MESSAGE FROM GOD

23 Balaam said to Balak, "Build me seven altars here. Prepare seven bulls and seven rams for me to sacrifice."

²Balak did just as Balaam said. The two of them offered a bull and a ram on each altar.

³Then Balaam said to Balak, "Stay here beside your offering. I'll go and try to find out what the LORD wants me to do. Maybe he'll come and meet with me. Then I'll tell you what he says to me." So Balaam went off to a bare hilltop.

⁴God met with him there. Balaam said, "I've prepared seven altars. On each altar I've offered a bull and a ram."

⁵The LORD put a message in Balaam's mouth. The LORD said, "Go back to Balak. Give him my message."

⁶So Balaam went back to him. He found Balak standing beside his offering. All of the princes of Moab were with him.

⁷Then Balaam spoke the message he had received from God. He said,

"Balak brought me from the land of Aram.
    The king of Moab sent for me from the mountains in the east.
'Come,' he said. 'Put a curse on Jacob's people for me.
    Come. Speak against Israel.'
⁸But how can I put a curse on people God hasn't cursed?
How can I speak against people the LORD hasn't spoken against?
⁹I see them from the rocky peaks.
    I view them from the hills.
I see a group of people who live by themselves.
    They don't consider themselves to be one of the nations.
¹⁰Jacob's people are like the dust of the earth.
    Can dust be counted?
Who can count even a fourth of the people of Israel?
Let me die as godly people die.
    Let my death be like theirs!"

¹¹Balak said to Balaam, "What have you done to me? I brought you here to put a curse on my enemies! But all you have done is give them a blessing!"

¹²He answered, "I have to speak only the words the LORD puts in my mouth."

BALAAM'S SECOND MESSAGE FROM GOD

¹³Then Balak said to Balaam, "Come with me to another place. You can see the people of Israel from there. You will see only some of them. You won't see all of them. From there, put a curse on them for me."

¹⁴So Balak took Balaam to the field of Zophim. It was on the highest slopes of Pisgah. There he built seven altars. He offered a bull and a ram on each altar.

¹⁵Balaam said to Balak, "Stay here beside your offering. I'll meet with the LORD over there."

¹⁶The LORD met with Balaam. He put a message in Balaam's mouth. The LORD said, "Go back to Balak. Give him my message."

¹⁷So he went to him. He found him standing beside his offering. The princes of Moab were with him. Balak asked him, "What did the LORD say?"

¹⁸Then Balaam spoke the message he had received from God. He said,

"Balak, rise up and listen.
 Son of Zippor, hear me.
¹⁹God isn't a mere man. He can't lie.
 He isn't a human being. He
 doesn't change his mind.
He speaks, and then he acts.
 He makes a promise, and then he
 keeps it.
²⁰He has commanded me to bless
 Israel.
 He has given them his blessing.
 And I can't change it.

²¹ "I don't see any trouble coming on
 the people of Jacob.
 I don't see any suffering in
 Israel.
The LORD their God is with them.
 The shout of the King is among
 them.
²²God brought them out of Egypt.
 They are as strong as a wild ox.
²³There isn't any magic that can hurt
 the people of Jacob.
 No one can use magic words to
 harm Israel.
Here is what will be said about the
 people of Jacob.
Here is what will be said about
 Israel.

People will say, 'See what God
 has done!'
²⁴The people of Israel are going to
 wake up like a female lion.
 They are going to get up like a
 male lion.
They are like a lion that won't rest
 until it eats what it has caught.
They are like a lion that won't rest
 until it drinks the blood of what
 it has killed."

²⁵Then Balak said to Balaam, "Don't put a curse on them at all! And don't give them a blessing at all!"

²⁶Balaam answered, "Didn't I tell you that I have to do only what the LORD says?"

BALAAM'S THIRD MESSAGE FROM GOD

²⁷Then Balak said to Balaam, "Come. Let me take you to another place. Perhaps God will be pleased to let you put a curse on them for me from there."

²⁸Balak took Balaam to the top of Mount Peor. It looks out over a dry and empty land.

²⁹Balaam said, "Build me seven altars here. Prepare seven bulls and seven rams for me to sacrifice." ³⁰Balak did just as Balaam said. He offered a bull and a ram on each altar.

24 Balaam saw that the LORD was pleased to give Israel his blessing to Israel. So he didn't try to use evil magic as he had done at other times. Instead, he turned and looked toward the desert. ²He looked out and saw Israel. They had set up their camps tribe by tribe. The Spirit of God came on him.

³Balaam spoke the message he had received from God. He said,

"Here is the message God gave
 Balaam, the son of Beor.
 It's the message God gave to the
 one who sees clearly.
⁴It's the message God gave to the
 one who hears the words of
 God.
He sees a vision from the Mighty
 One.
He falls down flat with his face
 toward the ground.
 His eyes have been opened by
 the LORD.

⁵"People of Jacob, your tents are
    very beautiful.
  Israel, the places where you live
    are very beautiful.

⁶"They spread out like valleys.
  They are like gardens beside a
    river.
  They are like aloes the LORD has
    planted.
  They are like cedar trees beside a
    stream.
⁷Their water buckets will run over.
  Their seeds will have plenty of
    water.

  "Their king will be greater than
    King Agag.
  Their kingdom will be honored.

⁸"God brought them out of Egypt.
  They are as strong as a wild ox.
  They eat up nations that are at war
    with them.
  They break their bones in pieces.
  They wound them with their
    arrows.
⁹Like a male lion they lie down and
    sleep.
  They are like a female lion.
  Who dares to wake them up?

  May those who bless you be
    blessed!
  May those who call down a curse
    on you be cursed!"

¹⁰Then Balak's anger burned against
Balaam. He slapped his hands together. He said to Balaam, "I sent for
you to put a curse on my enemies. But
you have given them a blessing three
times. ¹¹Get out of here right away! Go
home! I said I'd make you very rich.
But the LORD has kept you from getting rich."

¹²Balaam answered Balak, "Here is
what I told the messengers you sent
me. ¹³I said, 'Balak could give me his
palace filled with silver and gold. Even
if I wanted to, I still couldn't do anything at all that goes beyond what the
LORD commands. I have to say only
what the LORD tells me to say.'

¹⁴"Now I'm going back to my people.
But come. Let me warn you about
what these people will do to your
people in days to come."

BALAAM'S FOURTH MESSAGE FROM GOD

¹⁵Then Balaam spoke the message
he had received from God. He said,

  "Here is the message God gave
    Balaam, the son of Beor.
  It's the message God gave to the
    one who sees clearly.
¹⁶It's the message God gave to the one
    who hears the words of God.
  The Most High God has given
    him knowledge.
  He sees a vision from the Mighty
    One.
  He falls down flat with his face
    toward the ground.
  His eyes have been opened by
    the LORD.
¹⁷"I see him, but I don't see him
    now.
  I view him, but he isn't near.
  A star will come from among the
    people of Jacob.
  A king will rise up out of Israel.
  He'll crush the foreheads of the
    people of Moab.
  He'll crush the skulls of all of the
    sons of Sheth.
¹⁸He'll win the battle over Edom.
  He'll win the battle over his
    enemy Seir.
  But Israel will grow strong.
¹⁹A ruler will come from among the
    people of Jacob.
  He'll destroy those from the city
    who are still alive."

BALAAM'S FIFTH MESSAGE FROM GOD

²⁰Then Balaam saw the people of
Amalek. He spoke the message he had
received from God. He said,

  "Amalek was the first nation to
    attack Israel.
  But they will finally be
    destroyed."

BALAAM'S SIXTH MESSAGE FROM GOD

²¹Then he saw the Kenites. He spoke
the message he had received from
God. He said,

  "The place where you live is safe.
  Your nest is on a high cliff.

²²But you Kenites will be destroyed.
Assyria will take you as
prisoners."

BALAAM'S SEVENTH MESSAGE FROM GOD

²³Then he spoke the message he had received from God. He said,

"Who can live when God does
this?
²⁴ Ships will come from the shores
of Kittim.
They will bring Assyria and Eber
under their control.
But they themselves will also be
destroyed."

²⁵Then Balaam got up and returned home. And Balak went on his way.

MOAB LEADS ISRAEL DOWN THE WRONG PATH

25 Israel was staying in Shittim. The men of Israel began to commit sexual sins with the women of Moab. ²The women invited the men to feasts and sacrifices in honor of their gods. The people ate and bowed down in front of the statues of those gods.

³So Israel joined in worshiping the god Baal that was worshiped at Peor. The LORD's anger burned against Israel.

⁴The LORD said to Moses, "Take all of the leaders of these people. Kill them. Put their dead bodies out in the open. I want to see you do it in the middle of the day. Then my anger will not burn against Israel."

⁵So Moses spoke to Israel's judges. He said, "Some of your men have joined in worshiping the god Baal that is worshiped at Peor. Each of you must kill the men in your tribe who have done that."

⁶Then a man of Israel brought a woman of Midian to his family. He did it right in front of the eyes of Moses and the whole community of Israel. They were sobbing at the entrance to the Tent of Meeting.

⁷Phinehas was a priest. He was the son of Eleazar, the son of Aaron. When Phinehas saw what had happened, he left the people. He took a spear in his hand. ⁸He followed the man into a tent. Phinehas stuck the spear through both the man and the woman.

Then the LORD stopped the plague against the people of Israel. ⁹But the plague had already killed 24,000 of them.

¹⁰The LORD spoke to Moses. He said, ¹¹"Phinehas is a priest. He is the son of Eleazar, the son of Aaron. Phinehas has turned my anger away from the people of Israel. I am committed to making sure I am honored among them. And he is as committed as I am. Even though I was angry with them, I did not put an end to them.

¹²"So tell Phinehas I am making my covenant with him. It promises to give him peace. ¹³He and his sons after him will have a covenant to be priests forever. That is because he was committed to making sure that I, his God, was honored. In that way he paid for the sin of the people of Israel."

¹⁴The name of the man of Israel who was killed was Zimri. He was the son of Salu. Zimri was killed along with the woman of Midian. Salu was a family leader in the tribe of Simeon. ¹⁵The name of the woman of Midian who was killed was Cozbi. She was the daughter of Zur. Zur was the chief of a family in Midian.

¹⁶The LORD spoke to Moses. He said, ¹⁷"Treat the people of Midian just as you would treat enemies. Kill them. ¹⁸After all, they treated you like enemies. They tricked you into worshiping the god Baal that is worshiped at Peor. They also tricked you because of what Cozbi did. She was the woman who was killed when the plague that was connected with Peor came. Cozbi was the daughter of a leader of Midian."

THE MEN OF ISRAEL ARE COUNTED A SECOND TIME

26 After the plague the LORD spoke to Moses and the priest Eleazar. Eleazar was the son of Aaron. The LORD said, ²"Count all of the men of Israel. Make a list of them by their families. Count all of the men who are able to serve in Israel's army. They must be 20 years old or more."

³At that time the people of Israel

were on the flatlands of Moab. They were by the Jordan River across from Jericho. Moses and the priest Eleazar spoke with them. They said, [4]"Count all of the men who are 20 years old or more. Do it just as the LORD commanded Moses."

Here are the men of Israel who came out of Egypt.

[5]Reuben was Israel's oldest son. Here are the names of his sons.

The Hanochite family came from Hanoch.

The Palluite family came from Pallu.

[6]The Hezronite family came from Hezron.

The Carmite family came from Carmi.

[7]Those were the families of Reuben. The number of men was 43,730.

[8]Eliab was the son of Pallu. [9]Eliab's sons were Nemuel, Dathan and Abiram. Dathan and Abiram were the same community officials who refused to obey Moses and Aaron. They were among the followers of Korah who refused to obey the LORD. [10]The ground opened its mouth. It swallowed them up along with Korah. The followers of Korah died when fire burned up 250 men. Their deaths were a warning to the rest of Israel. [11]But the family line of Korah didn't die out completely.

[12]Here are the names of Simeon's sons. They are listed by their families.

The Nemuelite family came from Nemuel.

The Jaminite family came from Jamin.

The Jakinite family came from Jakin.

[13]The Zerahite family came from Zerah.

The Shaulite family came from Shaul.

[14]Those were the families of Simeon. The number of men was 22,200.

[15]Here are the names of Gad's sons. They are listed by their families.

The Zephonite family came from Zephon.

The Haggite family came from Haggi.

The Shunite family came from Shuni.

[16]The Oznite family came from Ozni.

The Erite family came from Eri.

[17]The Arodite family came from Arodi.

The Arelite family came from Areli.

[18]Those were the families of Gad. The number of the men was 40,500.

[19]Er and Onan were sons of Judah. But they died in Canaan. [20]Here are the names of Judah's sons. They are listed by their families.

The Shelanite family came from Shelah.

The Perezite family came from Perez.

The Zerahite family came from Zerah.

[21]Here are the names of the sons of Perez.

The Hezronite family came from Hezron.

The Hamulite family came from Hamul.

[22]Those were the families of Judah. The number of the men was 76,500.

[23]Here are the names of Issachar's sons. They are listed by their families.

The Tolaite family came from Tola.

The Puite family came from Puah.

[24]The Jashubite family came from Jashub.

The Shimronite family came from Shimron.

[25]Those were the families of Issachar. The number of the men was 64,300.

[26]Here are the names of Zebulun's sons. They are listed by their families.

The Seredite family came from Sered.

The Elonite family came from Elon.

The Jahleelite family came from Jahleel.

[27]Those were the families of Zebulun. The number of the men was 60,500.

[28]Here are the names of Joseph's sons. They are listed by their families. The families came from Manasseh and Ephraim, the sons of Joseph.

²⁹Here are the names of Manasseh's sons.

The Makirite family came from Makir. Makir was the father of Gilead.

The Gileadite family came from Gilead.

³⁰Here are the names of Gilead's sons.

The Iezerite family came from Iezer.

The Helekite family came from Helek.

³¹The Asrielite family came from Asriel.

The Shechemite family came from Shechem.

³²The Shemidaite family came from Shemida.

The Hepherite family came from Hepher.

³³Zelophehad was the son of Hepher. Zelophehad didn't have any sons. All he had was daughters. Their names were Mahlah, Noah, Hoglah, Milcah and Tirzah.

³⁴Those were the families of Manasseh. The number of the men was 52,700.

³⁵Here are the names of Ephraim's sons. They are listed by their families.

The Shuthelahite family came from Shuthelah.

The Bekerite family came from Beker.

The Tahanite family came from Tahan.

³⁶The sons of Shuthelah were the Eranite family.

They came from Eran.

³⁷Those were the families of Ephraim. The number of the men was 32,500.

Those were the sons of Joseph. They are listed by their families.

³⁸Here are the names of Benjamin's sons. They are listed by their families.

The Belaite family came from Bela.

The Ashbelite family came from Ashbel.

The Ahiramite family came from Ahiram.

³⁹The Shuphamite family came from Shupham.

The Huphamite family came from Hupham.

⁴⁰Bela's sons came from Ard and Naaman.

The Ardite family came from Ard.

The Naamite family came from Naaman.

⁴¹Those were the families of Benjamin. The number of the men was 45,600.

⁴²Here is the name of Dan's son. He is listed by his family.

The Shuhamite family came from Shuham.

That was the family of Dan. ⁴³All of the men in Dan's family were Shuhamites. The number of the men was 64,400.

⁴⁴Here are the names of Asher's sons. They are listed by their families.

The Imnite family came from Imnah.

The Ishvite family came from Ishvi.

The Beriite family came from Beriah.

⁴⁵Here are the names of the families that came from Beriah's sons.

The Heberite family came from Heber.

The Malkielite family came from Malkiel.

⁴⁶Asher also had a daughter named Serah.

⁴⁷Those were the families of Asher. The number of the men was 53,400.

⁴⁸Here are the names of Naphtali's sons. They are listed by their families.

The Jahzeelite family came from Jahzeel.

The Gunite family came from Guni.

⁴⁹The Jezerite family came from Jezer.

The Shillemite family came from Shillem.

⁵⁰Those were the families of Naphtali. The number of the men was 45,400.

⁵¹The total number of the men of Israel was 601,730.

⁵²The LORD spoke to Moses. He said, ⁵³"I will give the land to them. The amount of land each family receives

will be based on the number of its men. ⁵⁴Give a larger share to a larger family. Give a smaller share to a smaller family. Each family will receive its share based on the number of men who are listed in it.

⁵⁵"Be sure that you use lots when you give out the land. What each family receives will be based on the number of men listed in its tribe. ⁵⁶Use lots when you give out each share. Use lots for the larger and smaller families alike."

⁵⁷Here are the names of the Levites. They are listed by their families.

The Gershonite family came from Gershon.
The Kohathite family came from Kohath.
The Merarite family came from Merari.

⁵⁸Here are the names of the other Levite families. They are

the Libnite family,
the Hebronite family,
the Mahlite family,
the Mushite family,
the Korahite family.

Amram came from the Kohathite family.

⁵⁹The name of Amram's wife was Jochebed. She was from the family line of Levi. She was born to the Levites in Egypt. Aaron, Moses and their sister Miriam were born in the family line of Amram and Jochebed.

⁶⁰Aaron was the father of Nadab and Abihu. He was also the father of Eleazar and Ithamar. ⁶¹But Nadab and Abihu made an offering to the LORD by using fire that wasn't allowed. So they died.

⁶²The number of male Levites who were a month old or more was 23,000. They weren't listed along with the other men of Israel. That's because they didn't receive a share among them.

⁶³Those are the men who were counted by Moses and the priest Eleazar. At that time the people of Israel were on the flatlands of Moab. They were by the Jordan River across from Jericho. ⁶⁴The men of Israel had been counted before in the Sinai Desert by Moses and the priest Aaron. But not one of them was among the men who were counted this time. ⁶⁵The LORD had told the people of Israel at Kadesh Barnea that they would certainly die in the desert. Not one of them was left alive except Caleb, the son of Jephunneh, and Joshua, the son of Nun.

ZELOPHEHAD'S DAUGHTERS

27 The daughters of Zelophehad belonged to the family groups of Manasseh. Zelophehad was the son of Hepher. Hepher was the son of Gilead. Gilead was the son of Makir. Makir was the son of Manasseh. And Manasseh was the son of Joseph. The names of Zelophehad's daughters were Mahlah, Noah, Hoglah, Milcah and Tirzah. They approached ²the entrance to the Tent of Meeting. There they stood in front of Moses and the priest Eleazar. The leaders and the whole community were there too.

Zelophehad's daughters said, ³"Our father died in the Sinai Desert. But he wasn't one of the men who followed Korah. He wasn't one of those who joined together against the LORD. Our father died because of his own sin. He didn't leave any sons. ⁴"Why should our father's name disappear from his family just because he didn't have a son? Give us property among our father's relatives."

⁵So Moses brought their case to the LORD. ⁶The LORD spoke to him. He said, ⁷"What Zelophehad's daughters are saying is right. You must certainly give them property. Give them a share among their father's relatives. Turn their father's property over to them.

⁸"Say to the people of Israel, 'Suppose a man dies who doesn't have a son. Then turn his property over to his daughter. ⁹Suppose the man doesn't have a daughter. Then give his property to his brothers. ¹⁰Suppose the man doesn't have any brothers. Then give his property to his father's brothers. ¹¹Suppose his father doesn't have any brothers. Then give his property to the nearest male relative in his family group. It will belong to him. That is what the law will require of the people

of Israel. It is just as the LORD commanded me.' "

JOSHUA BECOMES ISRAEL'S NEW LEADER

[12]Then the LORD spoke to Moses. He said, "Go up this mountain in the Abarim range. See the land I have given the people of Israel. [13]After you have seen it, you too will join the members of your family who have already died. You will die, just as your brother Aaron did.

[14]"The community refused to obey me at the waters of Meribah Kadesh. At that time, you and Aaron did not obey my command. You did not honor me in front of them as the holy God." Meribah Kadesh is in the Desert of Zin.

[15]Moses spoke to the LORD. He said, [16]"LORD, you are the God who creates the spirits of all people. Please appoint a man to lead this community. [17]Put him in charge of them. Tell him to take care of them. Then your people won't be like sheep that don't have a shepherd."

[18]So the LORD said to Moses, "Joshua, the son of Nun, has the ability to be a wise leader. Get him and place your hand on him. [19]Have him stand in front of the priest Eleazar and the whole community. Put him in charge while everyone is watching. [20]Give him some of your authority. Then the whole community of Israel will obey him.

[21]"Joshua will stand in front of the priest Eleazar. Eleazar will help him make decisions. Eleazar will get help from me by using the Urim. Joshua and the whole community of Israel must not make any move at all unless I command them to."

[22]Moses did just as the LORD commanded him. He got Joshua and had him stand in front of the priest Eleazar and the whole community. [23]Then Moses placed his hands on Joshua. And he put him in charge of the people. He did just as the LORD had directed through Moses.

OFFERINGS THAT ISRAEL MUST BRING EACH DAY

28 The LORD spoke to Moses. He said, [2]"Here is a command I want you to give the people of Israel. Tell them, 'Be sure to bring to the LORD the food for the offerings that are made to him with fire. Do it at the appointed time. It will give a smell that is pleasant to him.'

[3]"Tell them, 'Here is the offering you must bring to the LORD. It should be made with fire. Bring him two lambs that are a year old. They must not have any flaws. Bring them as a regular burnt offering each day.

[4]" 'Prepare one lamb in the morning. Prepare the other when the sun goes down. [5]Bring a grain offering along with them. It must have eight cups of fine flour. Mix it with a quart of oil that is made from pressed olives. [6]It is the regular burnt offering. The LORD established it at Mount Sinai. It has a pleasant smell. It is an offering that is made to him with fire. [7]Along with that, offer a quart of wine as a drink offering. It must be given along with each lamb. Pour out the drink offering to the LORD at the sacred tent.

[8]" 'Prepare the second lamb when the sun goes down. Sacrifice it along with the same kind of grain offering and drink offering that you prepare in the morning. It is an offering that is made with fire. It gives a smell that is pleasant to the LORD.

OFFERINGS THAT ISRAEL MUST BRING ON THE SABBATH DAY

[9]" 'On the Sabbath day, bring an offering of two lambs. They must be a year old. They must not have any flaws. Offer them along with their drink offering. Offer them along with a grain offering of 16 cups of fine flour. Mix it with olive oil. [10]It is the burnt offering for every Sabbath day. It is in addition to the regular burnt offering and its drink offering.

OFFERINGS THAT ISRAEL MUST BRING EVERY MONTH

[11]" 'On the first day of every month, bring to the LORD a burnt offering. Bring two young bulls and one ram. Also bring seven male lambs that are a year old. They must not have any flaws.

[12]" 'Bring a grain offering along with each bull. It must have 24 cups of fine

flour. Mix it with olive oil. Bring a grain offering along with the ram. It must have 16 cups of fine flour. Mix it with oil. [13]Bring a grain offering along with each lamb. It must have eight cups of fine flour. Mix it with oil. It is for a burnt offering. It has a pleasant smell. It is an offering that is made to the LORD with fire.

[14]" 'Bring a drink offering along with each bull. It must have two quarts of wine. Offer two and a half pints along with the ram. And offer one quart along with each lamb.

" 'It is the burnt offering for each month. It must be made on the day of each New Moon Feast during the year.

[15]" 'One male goat must be brought to the LORD as a sin offering. It is in addition to the regular burnt offering and its drink offering.

THE PASSOVER FEAST

[16]" 'The LORD's Passover Feast must be held on the 14th day of the first month. [17]On the 15th day of the month there must be a feast. For seven days eat bread that is made without yeast. [18]On the first day come together for a special service. Do not do any regular work.

[19]" 'Bring to the LORD an offering that is made with fire. Bring a burnt offering of two young bulls and one ram. Also bring seven male lambs that are a year old. They must not have any flaws.

[20]" 'Prepare a grain offering along with each bull. The offering must have 24 cups of fine flour. Mix it with olive oil. Offer 16 cups along with the ram. [21]Offer eight cups along with each of the seven lambs.

[22]" 'Include a male goat as a sin offering. It will pay for your sin.

[23]"Prepare everything in addition to the regular morning burnt offering. [24]Prepare the food in that way for the offering that is made with fire. Do it every day for seven days. The offering will give a smell that is pleasant to the LORD. You must prepare the offering in addition to the regular burnt offering and its drink offering.

[25]" 'On the seventh day come together for a special service. Do not do any regular work.

THE FEAST OF WEEKS

[26]" 'On the day you gather the first share of your crops, bring to the LORD an offering of your first grain. Do it during the Feast of Weeks. Come together for a special service. Do not do any regular work.

[27]" 'Bring a burnt offering of two young bulls and one ram. Also bring seven male lambs that are a year old. The offering will give a smell that is pleasant to the LORD.

[28]" 'Bring a grain offering along with each bull. It must have 24 cups of fine flour. Mix it with olive oil. Offer 16 cups along with the ram. [29]Offer eight cups along with each of the seven lambs.

[30]" 'Include a male goat to pay for your sin.

[31]" 'Prepare everything along with the drink offerings. Do it in addition to the regular burnt offering and its grain offering. Be sure the animals do not have any flaws.

THE FEAST OF TRUMPETS

29 " 'On the first day of the seventh month, come together for a special service. Do not do any regular work. Blow the trumpets on that day.

[2]" 'Prepare a burnt offering. It will give a smell that is pleasant to the LORD. Prepare one young bull and one ram. Also prepare seven male lambs that are a year old. They must not have any flaws.

[3]" 'Prepare a grain offering along with the bull. It must have 24 cups of fine flour. Mix it with olive oil. Offer 16 cups along with the ram. [4]Offer eight cups along with each of the seven lambs.

[5]" 'Include a male goat as a sin offering. It will pay for your sin.

[6]" 'Each month and each day you must bring burnt offerings. Bring them along with their grain offerings and drink offerings as they are required.

" 'The offerings for the Feast of Trumpets are in addition to them. They are offerings that are made to the LORD with fire. They have a pleasant smell.

THE DAY WHEN SIN IS PAID FOR

7" 'On the tenth day of the seventh month, come together for a special service. You must not eat anything on that day. You must not do any work on it.

8" 'Bring a burnt offering. It will give a smell that is pleasant to the LORD. Bring one young bull and one ram. Also bring seven male lambs that are a year old. They must not have any flaws.

9" 'Prepare a grain offering along with the bull. It must have 24 cups of fine flour. Mix it with olive oil. Offer 16 cups along with the ram. 10Offer eight cups along with each of the seven lambs.

11" 'Include a male goat as a sin offering. It is in addition to the offering that pays for sin. It is in addition to the regular burnt offering along with its grain offering. It is also in addition to their drink offerings.

THE FEAST OF BOOTHS

12" 'On the 15th day of the seventh month, come together for a special service. Do not do any regular work. Celebrate the Feast of Booths in honor of the LORD for seven days.

13" 'Bring an offering that is made with fire. It will give a smell that is pleasant to the LORD. Bring a burnt offering of 13 young bulls and two rams. Also bring 14 male lambs that are a year old. They must not have any flaws.

14" 'Prepare a grain offering along with each of the 13 bulls. It must have 24 cups of fine flour. Mix it with olive oil. Offer 16 cups along with each of the two rams. 15Offer eight cups along with each of the 14 lambs.

16" 'Include a male goat as a sin offering. It is in addition to the regular burnt offering. It is also in addition to its grain offering and drink offering.

17" 'On the second day prepare 12 young bulls and two rams. Also prepare 14 male lambs that are a year old. They must not have any flaws.

18" 'Prepare their grain offerings and drink offerings. Prepare them along with the bulls, rams and lambs. Pre-pare them in keeping with the required number.

19" 'Include a male goat as a sin offering. It is in addition to the regular burnt offering along with its grain offering. It is also in addition to their drink offerings.

20" 'On the third day prepare 11 bulls and two rams. Also prepare 14 male lambs that are a year old. They must not have any flaws.

21" 'Prepare their grain offerings and drink offerings. Prepare them along with the bulls, rams and lambs. Prepare them in keeping with the required number.

22" 'Include a male goat as a sin offering. It is in addition to the regular burnt offering. It is also in addition to its grain offering and drink offering.

23" 'On the fourth day prepare ten bulls and two rams. Also prepare 14 male lambs that are a year old. They must not have any flaws.

24" 'Prepare their grain offerings and drink offerings. Prepare them along with the bulls, rams and lambs. Prepare them in keeping with the required number.

25" 'Include a male goat as a sin offering. It is in addition to the regular burnt offering. It is also in addition to its grain offering and drink offering.

26" 'On the fifth day prepare nine bulls and two rams. Also prepare 14 male lambs that are a year old. They must not have any flaws.

27" 'Prepare their grain offerings and drink offerings. Prepare them along with the bulls, rams and lambs. Prepare them in keeping with the required number.

28" 'Include a male goat as a sin offering. It is in addition to the regular burnt offering. It is also in addition to its grain offering and drink offering.

29" 'On the sixth day prepare eight bulls and two rams. Also prepare 14 male lambs that are a year old. They must not have any flaws.

30" 'Prepare their grain offerings and drink offerings. Prepare them along with the bulls, rams and lambs. Prepare them in keeping with the required number.

31" 'Include a male goat as a sin offering. It is in addition to the regular burnt offering. It is also in addition to its grain offering and drink offering.

³²" 'On the seventh day prepare seven bulls and two rams. Also prepare 14 male lambs that are a year old. They must not have any flaws.

³³" 'Prepare their grain offerings and drink offerings. Prepare them along with the bulls, rams and lambs. Prepare them in keeping with the required number.

³⁴" 'Include a male goat as a sin offering. It is in addition to the regular burnt offering. It is also in addition to its grain offering and drink offering.

³⁵" 'On the eighth day come together for a sacred service. Do not do any regular work.

³⁶" 'Bring an offering that is made with fire. It will give a smell that is pleasant to the LORD. Bring a burnt offering of one bull and one ram. Also bring seven male lambs that are a year old. They must not have any flaws.

³⁷" 'Prepare their grain offerings and drink offerings. Prepare them along with the bull, the ram and the lambs. Prepare them in keeping with the required number.

³⁸" 'Include a male goat as a sin offering. It is in addition to the regular burnt offering. It is also in addition to the grain offering and drink offering.

³⁹" 'Here are the offerings you must prepare for the LORD at your appointed feasts. They are burnt offerings, grain offerings, drink offerings and friendship offerings. They are in addition to the offerings you bring to keep a special promise you make to the LORD. They are also in addition to the offerings you choose to give.' "

⁴⁰Moses told the people of Israel everything the LORD had commanded him.

OATHS AND SPECIAL PROMISES

30 Moses spoke to the heads of the tribes of Israel. He said, "Here is what the LORD commands. ²Suppose a man makes a special promise to the LORD. Or suppose he takes an oath and agrees to do something. Then he must keep his promise. He must do everything he said he would do.

³"Suppose a young woman is still living in her father's house. She makes a special promise to the LORD. Or she takes an oath and agrees to do something.

⁴"Suppose her father hears about her promise or oath. And he doesn't say anything to her about it. Then she must keep her promise. She must do what she agreed to do.

⁵"But suppose her father doesn't allow her to keep her promises when he hears about them. Then she doesn't have to do what she promised or agreed to do. The LORD will set her free. He'll do it because her father hasn't allowed her to keep her promises.

⁶"Suppose she gets married after she makes a special promise. Or she gets married after agreeing to do something without thinking it through. ⁷Suppose her husband hears about what she did. And he doesn't say anything to her about it. Then she must keep her promise. She must do what she agreed to do.

⁸"But suppose her husband doesn't allow her to keep her promises when he hears about them. Then she doesn't have to do what she promised. She doesn't have to do what she agreed to do without thinking it through. The LORD will set her free.

⁹"Suppose a widow makes a special promise. Or suppose she takes an oath and agrees to do something. Then she must keep her promise. She must do what she agreed to do. The same rules apply to a woman who has been divorced.

¹⁰"Suppose a woman who is living with her husband makes a special promise. Or she takes an oath and agrees to do something. ¹¹Suppose her husband hears about what she did. He doesn't say anything to her about it. And he doesn't try to stop her from keeping her promises. Then she must keep her promise. She must do what she agreed to do.

¹²"But suppose her husband doesn't allow her to keep her promises when he hears about them. Then she doesn't have to do what she promised. She doesn't have to do what she agreed to do. Her husband has kept her from doing what she said she would do. The LORD will set her free.

¹³"Her husband can let her keep any special promise she makes. Or he can refuse to let her keep it.

"Suppose she takes an oath and agrees not to eat anything. Then her husband can let her keep her promise. Or he can refuse to let her keep it.

¹⁴"But suppose day after day her husband doesn't say anything to her about what she did. Then he lets her keep all of her promises. He lets her do everything she agreed to do. That's because he didn't say anything to her when he heard about what she had done.

¹⁵"But suppose some time after he hears about her promises he doesn't let her keep them. Then she will be guilty. But he will be held accountable for it."

¹⁶Those are the rules the LORD gave Moses about a man and his wife. And those are the rules the LORD gave about a father and his young daughter who is still living in his house.

THE LORD PUNISHES THE PEOPLE OF MIDIAN

31 The LORD spoke to Moses. He said, ²"Pay the people of Midian back for what they did to the Israelites. After that, you will join the members of your family who have already died."

³So Moses said to the people, "Prepare some of your men for battle. They must go to war against Midian. They will carry out the LORD's plan to punish Midian. ⁴Send 1,000 men from each of the tribes of Israel into battle." ⁵So Moses prepared 12,000 men for battle. There were 1,000 from each tribe. They came from the families of Israel.

⁶Moses sent them into battle. He sent 1,000 from each tribe. The priest Phinehas went along with them. Phinehas was the son of Eleazar. Phinehas took some articles from the sacred tent with him. He also took the trumpets. The trumpet blasts would tell the people what to do and when to do it.

⁷They fought against Midian, just as the LORD had commanded Moses. They killed every man. ⁸Evi, Rekem, Zur, Hur and Reba were among the men they killed. Those men were the five kings of Midian. The people of Is-

rael also killed Balaam, the son of Beor, with a sword.

⁹They captured the women and children of Midian. They took for themselves all of the herds, flocks and goods.

¹⁰They burned up all of the towns where the people of Midian had settled. They also burned up all of their camps.

¹¹They carried off everything they had taken. That included the people and the animals. ¹²They brought back to Israel's camp the prisoners and everything else they had taken. They took them to Moses and to the priest Eleazar. They brought them to the whole community. Israel was camped on the flatlands of Moab. They were by the Jordan River across from Jericho.

¹³Moses and the priest Eleazar went to meet them outside the camp. So did all of the leaders of the community. ¹⁴Moses was angry with the officers of the army who had returned from the battle. Some of them were the commanders of thousands of men. Others were the commanders of hundreds.

¹⁵"Have you let all of the women remain alive?" Moses asked them. ¹⁶"The women followed Balaam's advice. They caused the people of Israel to turn away from the LORD. The people worshiped the god Baal that was worshiped at Peor. So a plague struck them. ¹⁷Kill all of the boys. And kill every woman who has made love to a man. ¹⁸But save for yourselves every woman who has never made love to a man.

¹⁹"All of you who have killed anyone must stay outside the camp for seven days. And all of you who have touched anyone who was killed must do the same thing. On the third and seventh days you must make yourselves pure. You must also make your prisoners pure. ²⁰Make all of your clothes pure and clean. Everything that is made out of leather, goat hair or wood must be made pure."

²¹Then the priest Eleazar spoke to the soldiers who had gone into battle. He said, "Here is what the law the LORD gave Moses requires. ²²All of your gold, silver, bronze, iron, tin and lead ²³must be put through fire. So must every-

thing else that doesn't burn up. Then those things will be 'clean.' But they must also be made pure with the special water. In fact, everything that won't burn up must be put through that water. ²⁴On the seventh day wash your clothes. And you will be 'clean.' Then you can come into the camp."

THE PEOPLE DIVIDE UP WHAT THEY HAD TAKEN

²⁵The LORD spoke to Moses. He said, ²⁶"Here is what you and the priest Eleazar and the family heads of the community must do. You must count all of the people and animals you took. ²⁷Divide up some of what you took with the soldiers who fought in the battle. Divide up the rest with the others in the community.

²⁸"Set apart a gift for me. Take something from the soldiers who fought in the battle. Set apart one out of every 500 people, cattle, donkeys, sheep and goats. ²⁹Take my gift from the soldiers' half. Give it to the priest Eleazar. It is my share.

³⁰"Also take something from the half that belongs to the people of Israel. Choose one out of every 50 people, cattle, donkeys, sheep, goats or other animals. Give them to the Levites. They are accountable for taking care of my holy tent."

³¹So Moses and the priest Eleazar did just as the LORD had commanded Moses.

³²What the soldiers took included 675,000 sheep. ³³There were also 72,000 cattle ³⁴and 61,000 donkeys. ³⁵And there were 32,000 women who had never made love to a man.

³⁶Here is the half that belonged to those who had fought in the battle.

There were 337,500 sheep. ³⁷From among them, the LORD's gift was 675.

³⁸There were 36,000 cattle. From among them, the LORD's gift was 72.

³⁹There were 30,500 donkeys. From among them, the LORD's gift was 61.

⁴⁰There were 16,000 women. From among them, the LORD's gift was 32.

⁴¹Moses gave the gift to the priest Eleazar. It was the LORD's share. Moses did just as the LORD had commanded him.

⁴²The other half belonged to the people of Israel. Moses set it apart from what belonged to the fighting men. ⁴³The community's half was 337,500 sheep, ⁴⁴36,000 cattle, ⁴⁵30,500 donkeys ⁴⁶and 16,000 women. ⁴⁷Moses chose one out of every 50 people and animals. He gave them to the Levites. They were accountable for taking care of the LORD's holy tent. Moses did just as the LORD had commanded him.

⁴⁸Then the army officers went to Moses. Some of them were the commanders of thousands of men. Others were the commanders of hundreds. ⁴⁹All of them said to Moses, "We have counted the soldiers under our command. Not a single one is missing. ⁵⁰So we've brought an offering to the LORD. We've brought the gold articles each of us took in the battle. We've also brought armbands, bracelets, rings, earrings and necklaces. We've brought them to pay for our sin in the sight of the LORD."

⁵¹Moses and the priest Eleazar accepted the beautiful gold articles from the army officers. ⁵²The gold that was received from the commanders of thousands and commanders of hundreds weighed 420 pounds. Moses and Eleazar offered all of it as a gift to the LORD. ⁵³Each soldier had taken things from the battle for himself. ⁵⁴Moses and the priest Eleazar accepted the gold from all of the commanders. They brought it into the Tent of Meeting. It reminded the LORD of the people of Israel.

THE TRIBES ON THE EAST SIDE OF THE JORDAN RIVER

32 The tribes of Reuben and Gad had very large herds and flocks. They looked at the lands of Jazer and Gilead. They saw that those lands were just right for livestock.

²So they came to Moses and the priest Eleazar. They also came to the leaders of the community. They said, ³"We have seen the cities of Ataroth, Dibon, Jazer, Nimrah and Heshbon.

We've seen Elealeh, Sebam, Nebo and Beon. ⁴All of them are in the land the LORD has brought under Israel's control. This land is just right for livestock. And we have livestock.

⁵"We hope you are pleased with us," they continued. "If you are, please give us this land. Then it will belong to us. But don't make us go across the Jordan River."

⁶Moses spoke to the people of Gad and Reuben. He said, "Should the rest of us go to war while you stay here? ⁷The LORD has given the land of Canaan to the people of Israel. So why would you want to keep them from going over into it?

⁸"That's what your fathers did. I sent them from Kadesh Barnea to check out the land. ⁹They went up to the Valley of Eshcol and looked at the land. Then they talked the people of Israel out of entering the land the LORD had given them.

¹⁰"The LORD's anger was stirred up that day. So he took an oath and made a promise. He said, ¹¹'Not one of the men who is 20 years old or more who came up out of Egypt will see the land. They have not followed me with their whole heart. I took an oath and promised to give the land to Abraham, Isaac and Jacob.

¹²" 'But not one of these men will see it except Caleb and Joshua. Caleb is the son of Jephunneh, the Kenizzite. And Joshua is the son of Nun. They will see the land. They followed me with their whole heart.'

¹³"The LORD's anger burned against Israel. He made them wander around in the desert for 40 years. They wandered until all of the people who had done evil in his sight had died.

¹⁴"Now here you are, you bunch of sinners! You have taken the place of your fathers. And you are making the LORD even more angry with Israel. ¹⁵What if you turn away from following him? Then he'll leave all of these people in the desert again. And it will be your fault when they are destroyed."

¹⁶Then they came up to Moses. They said, "We would like to build pens here for our livestock. We would also like to build cities for our women and children.

¹⁷"But we're ready to prepare ourselves for battle. We're even ready to go ahead of the people of Israel. We'll go with them until we've brought them to their place. While we're gone, our women and children will live in cities that have high walls around them. That will keep them safe from the people who are living in this land.

¹⁸"We won't return to our homes until all of the people of Israel have received their share of the land.

¹⁹"We won't receive any share with them on the west side of the Jordan River. We've already received our share here on the east side."

²⁰Then Moses said to them, "Do what you have promised to do. Prepare yourselves to fight for the LORD. ²¹Prepare yourselves and go across the Jordan River. Fight for the LORD until he has driven out his enemies in front of him.

²²"When the land is under the LORD's control, you can come back here. Your duty to the LORD and Israel will be over. Then the LORD will give you this land as your own.

²³"But what if you fail to do your duty? Then you will be sinning against the LORD. And you can be sure that your sin will be discovered. It will be brought out into the open.

²⁴"So build up cities for your women and children. Make sheep pens for your flocks. But do what you have promised to do."

²⁵The people of Gad and Reuben spoke to Moses. They said, "We will do just as you command. ²⁶Our children and wives will remain here in the cities of Gilead. So will our flocks and herds. ²⁷But we will prepare ourselves for battle. We'll go across the Jordan River and fight for the LORD. We will do just as you have said."

²⁸Then Moses gave orders about them to the priest Eleazar. He gave the same orders to Joshua, the son of Nun. He also spoke to the family heads of the tribes of Israel.

²⁹He said, "The men of Gad and Reuben must prepare themselves for battle. They must go across the Jordan River with you. They must help you fight for the LORD. They must stay with you until the land has been brought

under your control. If they do, give them the land of Gilead as their own.

³⁰"But what if they don't get ready for battle? What if they don't go across the Jordan with you? Then they must accept a share with you in Canaan."

³¹The people of Gad and Reuben gave their answer. They said, "We will do what the LORD has said. ³²We'll get ready for battle. We'll go across the Jordan into Canaan. We'll fight for the LORD there. But the property we receive will be on this side of the Jordan River."

³³Then Moses gave their land to them. He gave it to the tribes of Gad and Reuben and half of the tribe of Manasseh. Manasseh was Joseph's son. One part of that land had belonged to the kingdom of Sihon, the king of the Amorites. The other part had belonged to the kingdom of Og, the king of Bashan. Moses gave that whole land to those two and a half tribes. It included its cities and the territory around them.

³⁴The people of Gad built up the cities of Dibon, Ataroth and Aroer. ³⁵They built up Atroth Shophan, Jazer, Jogbehah, ³⁶Beth Nimrah and Beth Haran. They built a high wall around each of those cities. They also built sheep pens for their flocks.

³⁷The people of Reuben built up Heshbon, Elealeh and Kiriathaim. ³⁸They also built up Nebo, Baal Meon and Sibmah. They gave new names to the cities they had built up.

³⁹The people of Makir, the son of Manasseh, went to the land of Gilead. They captured it. They drove out the Amorites who were living there. ⁴⁰So Moses gave Gilead to the people of Makir, the son of Manasseh. And they settled there. ⁴¹Jair was a man in the family line of Manasseh. Jair captured Gilead's settlements. He called them Havvoth Jair. ⁴²Nobah captured Kenath and the settlements that were around it. He named it after himself.

THE PLACES WHERE ISRAEL STOPPED DURING THEIR JOURNEY

33 Here are the places where the people of Israel stopped during their journey. When they came out of Egypt, they marched in companies like an army. Moses and Aaron led them. ²The LORD commanded Moses to record their journey. Here are the places where they stopped.

³The people of Israel started out from Rameses. It was the 15th day of the first month. It was the day after the Passover Feast. They marched out boldly in plain sight of all of the Egyptians. ⁴The Egyptians were burying all of their oldest sons. The LORD had struck them down. He had done it when he punished their gods.

⁵The people of Israel left Rameses and camped at Succoth.

⁶They left Succoth and camped at Etham. Etham was on the edge of the desert.

⁷They left Etham and turned back to Pi Hahiroth. It was east of Baal Zephon. They camped near Migdol.

⁸They left Pi Hahiroth. Then they passed through the Red Sea into the desert. They traveled for three days in the Desert of Etham. Then they camped at Marah.

⁹They left Marah and went to Elim. Twelve springs and 70 palm trees were there. So they camped at Elim.

¹⁰They left Elim and camped by the Red Sea.

¹¹They left the Red Sea and camped in the Desert of Sin.

¹²They left the Desert of Sin and camped at Dophkah.

¹³They left Dophkah and camped at Alush.

¹⁴They left Alush and camped at Rephidim. But there was no water there for the people to drink.

¹⁵They left Rephidim and camped in the Desert of Sinai.

¹⁶They left the Desert of Sinai and camped at Kibroth Hattaavah.

¹⁷They left Kibroth Hattaavah and camped at Hazeroth.

¹⁸They left Hazeroth and camped at Rithmah.

¹⁹They left Rithmah and camped at Rimmon Perez.

²⁰They left Rimmon Perez and camped at Libnah.

²¹They left Libnah and camped at Rissah.

²²They left Rissah and camped at Kehelathah.

²³They left Kehelathah and camped at Mount Shepher.

²⁴They left Mount Shepher and camped at Haradah.

²⁵They left Haradah and camped at Makheloth.

²⁶They left Makheloth and camped at Tahath.

²⁷They left Tahath and camped at Terah.

²⁸They left Terah and camped at Mithcah.

²⁹They left Mithcah and camped at Hashmonah.

³⁰They left Hashmonah and camped at Moseroth.

³¹They left Moseroth and camped at Bene Jaakan.

³²They left Bene Jaakan and camped at Hor Haggidgad.

³³They left Hor Haggidgad and camped at Jotbathah.

³⁴They left Jotbathah and camped at Abronah.

³⁵They left Abronah and camped at Ezion Geber.

³⁶They left Ezion Geber and camped at Kadesh. Kadesh was in the Desert of Zin.

³⁷They left Kadesh and camped at Mount Hor. It was on the border of Edom.

³⁸The priest Aaron went up Mount Hor when the LORD commanded him to. That's where he died. It happened on the first day of the fifth month. It was the 40th year after the people of Israel came out of Egypt. ³⁹Aaron was 123 years old when he died on Mount Hor.

⁴⁰The Canaanite king of Arad lived in the Negev Desert in Canaan. He heard that the people of Israel were coming.

⁴¹They left Mount Hor and camped at Zalmonah.

⁴²They left Zalmonah and camped at Punon.

⁴³They left Punon and camped at Oboth.

⁴⁴They left Oboth and camped at Iye Abarim. It was on the border of Moab.

⁴⁵They left Iyim and camped at Dibon Gad.

⁴⁶They left Dibon Gad and camped at Almon Diblathaim.

⁴⁷They left Almon Diblathaim and camped in the mountain range of Abarim near Nebo.

⁴⁸They left the mountain range of Abarim and camped on the flatlands of Moab. They were by the Jordan River across from Jericho. ⁴⁹They camped there along the Jordan River from Beth Jeshimoth to Abel Shittim.

⁵⁰On the flatlands of Moab the LORD spoke to Moses. He spoke to him by the Jordan River across from Jericho. The LORD said, ⁵¹"Speak to the people of Israel. Tell them, 'Go across the Jordan River into Canaan. ⁵²Drive out all those who are living in the land. The statues of their gods are made out of stone and metal. Destroy all of those statues. And destroy all of the high places where they are worshiped.

⁵³" 'Take the land as your own. Settle down in it. I have given it to you. ⁵⁴Use lots when you give out the land. Do it based on the number of men who are in each tribe and family. Give a larger share to a larger group. And give a smaller group a smaller share. The share they receive by using lots will belong to them. Give out the shares based on the number of men in Israel's tribes.

⁵⁵" 'But suppose you do not drive out the people who are living in the land. Then those you allow to remain there will become like needles in your eyes. They will become like thorns in your sides. They will give you trouble in the land where you will live. ⁵⁶Then I will do to you what I plan to do to them.' "

ISRAEL ARRIVES AT THE BORDERS OF CANAAN

34 The LORD spoke to Moses. He said, ²"Give the people of Israel a command. Tell them, 'You are going to enter Canaan.

The land will be given to you as your own. Here are the borders it will have.

³" 'Your southern border will include some of the Desert of Zin. It will be along the border of Edom. On the east, your southern border will start from the end of the Dead Sea. ⁴It will cross south of Scorpion Pass. It will continue on to Zin. From there it will go south of Kadesh Barnea. Then it will go to Hazar Addar and over to Azmon. ⁵There it will turn and join the Wadi of Egypt. It will come to an end at the Mediterranean Sea.

⁶" 'Your western border will be the coast of the Mediterranean Sea. That will be your border on the west.

⁷" 'For your northern border, run a line from the Mediterranean Sea to Mount Hor. ⁸Continue it from Mount Hor to Lebo Hamath. Then the border will go to Zedad. ⁹It will continue to Ziphron. It will come to an end at Hazar Enan. That will be your border on the north.

¹⁰" 'For your eastern border, run a line from Hazar Enan to Shepham. ¹¹The border will go down from Shepham to Riblah. Riblah is on the east side of Ain. From there the border will continue along the slopes east of the Sea of Galilee. ¹²Then the border will go down along the Jordan River. It will come to an end at the Dead Sea.

" 'That will be your land. And those will be its borders on every side.' "

¹³Moses gave the people of Israel a command. He said, "Use lots when you give out the land. Each tribe will have its own share. The LORD has ordered it to be given to the nine and a half tribes.

¹⁴"The families of the tribes of Reuben and Gad have already received their shares. The families of half of the tribe of Manasseh have also received their share. ¹⁵Those two and a half tribes have received their shares east of the Jordan River. It flows near Jericho. Their land is toward the sunrise."

¹⁶The LORD spoke to Moses. He said, ¹⁷"Here are the names of the men who will give out the shares of the land to your people. They are the priest Eleazar and Joshua, the son of Nun. ¹⁸Also

appoint one leader from each tribe to help give out the land. ¹⁹Here are their names.

"Caleb, the son of Jephunneh,
    is from the tribe of Judah.
²⁰Shemuel, the son of Ammihud,
    is from the tribe of Simeon.
²¹Elidad, the son of Kislon,
    is from the tribe of Benjamin.
²²Bukki, the son of Jogli,
    is the leader from the tribe of Dan.
²³Hanniel, the son of Ephod,
    is the leader from the tribe of Manasseh. Manasseh was the son of Joseph.
²⁴Kemuel, the son of Shiphtan,
    is the leader from the tribe of Ephraim. Ephraim was the son of Joseph.
²⁵Elizaphan, the son of Parnach,
    is the leader from the tribe of Zebulun.
²⁶Paltiel, the son of Azzan,
    is the leader from the tribe of Issachar.
²⁷Ahihud, the son of Shelomi,
    is the leader from the tribe of Asher.
²⁸Pedahel, the son of Ammihud,
    is the leader from the tribe of Naphtali."

²⁹Those are the men the LORD commanded to give out the shares of the land. They were commanded to give them to Israel in the land of Canaan.

THE LEVITES RECEIVE THEIR TOWNS

35 On the flatlands of Moab, the LORD spoke to Moses. It was by the Jordan River across from Jericho. The LORD said, ²"Command the people of Israel to give the Levites towns to live in. The towns must come from the shares of land the people will have as their own. Also give the Levites the grasslands that are around the towns. ³Then the Levites will have towns to live in. They will also have grasslands that are for their cattle, flocks and all of their other livestock.

⁴"The grasslands that are around each town you give them will go out to 1,500 feet from the town wall. ⁵Outside

each town, the east side will measure 3,000 feet. The south side will measure 3,000 feet. The west side will measure 3,000 feet. And the north side will measure 3,000 feet. The town must be in the center. The Levites will have the area around it as grasslands.

CITIES TO GO TO FOR SAFETY

⁶"Six of the towns you give the Levites will be cities to go to for safety. A person who has killed someone can run to one of them. Also give the Levites 42 other towns. ⁷You must give the Levites a total of 48 towns. Also give them the grasslands that are around the towns.

⁸"The towns you give the Levites must come from the land the people of Israel have as their own. So the number you give from each tribe will depend on the size of that tribe's share. Take many towns from a tribe that has many. But take only a few towns from a tribe that has only a few."

⁹Then the LORD spoke to Moses. He said, ¹⁰"Speak to the people of Israel. Tell them, 'You will soon go across the Jordan River. You will enter Canaan. ¹¹When you do, choose the cities to go to for safety. People who have killed someone by accident can run to one of those cities. ¹²They will be places of safety for them. People will be safe there from those who want to kill them. Then those who are charged with murder will not die before their case has been brought to the community court.

¹³" 'Six towns will be the cities you can go to for safety. ¹⁴Three will be east of the Jordan River. The other three will be in Canaan.

¹⁵" 'Those six towns will be places where the people of Israel can go for safety. Outsiders and any other people living in Israel can also go to them for safety. So anyone who has killed another person by accident can run there.

¹⁶" 'Suppose a person uses an iron object to hit and kill someone. Then he is a murderer. He must be put to death. ¹⁷Or suppose a person is holding a stone that could kill. And he uses it to hit and kill someone. Then he is a murderer. He must be put to death. ¹⁸Or

suppose a person is holding a wooden object that could kill. And he uses it to hit and kill someone. Then he is a murderer. He must be put to death.

¹⁹" 'The dead person's nearest male relative should kill the murderer. When he meets him, he should kill him.

²⁰" 'What if a person makes evil plans against someone else? And what if that person pushes him so that he dies? Or what if that person throws something at him so that he dies? ²¹Or what if that person hits the other person with a fist so that the other dies? Then the person who does any of those things must be put to death. He is a murderer.

" 'The dead person's nearest male relative should kill the murderer. When he meets him, he should kill him.

²²" 'But what if a person suddenly pushes someone else without being angry? Or what if that person throws something at him without meaning to? ²³Or what if that person does not see him and drops a stone on him that kills him? He was not the dead person's enemy. He did not mean to harm him.

²⁴" 'Then the court must decide between the person who did the act and the nearest male relative of the one who was killed. Here are the rules the court must follow.

²⁵" 'The court must provide a safe place for the person who is charged with murder. It must keep him safe from those who want to kill him. The court must send him back to the city he ran to for safety. He must stay there until the high priest dies. The priest is the one who has been anointed with the holy oil.

²⁶" 'But suppose the one who has been charged with murder goes outside that city. ²⁷And suppose the dead person's nearest male relative finds that one outside the city. Then the relative can kill the one who has been charged. The relative will not be guilty of murder.

²⁸" 'The one who has been charged must stay in that city until the high priest dies. Only then can the one who has been charged return home.

²⁹" 'That is what the law requires of you for all time to come. It will apply to you no matter where you live.

³⁰" 'Suppose a person kills someone. That person must be put to death as a murderer. But do it only when there are witnesses who can tell what happened. Do not put anyone to death if only one witness tells what happened.

³¹" 'Do not accept payment for a murderer's life. He should die. He must certainly be put to death.

³²" 'Do not accept payment for anyone who has run to a city for safety. Do not let him buy his freedom to return home. He must not go back and live on his own land before the high priest dies.

³³" 'Do not pollute the land where you are. Murder pollutes the land. Only one thing can pay to remove the pollution in the land where murder has been committed. The blood of the one who spilled another's blood must be spilled. ³⁴So do not make the land where you live "unclean." I live there too. I live among the people of Israel. I am the LORD.' "

THE PROPERTY ZELOPHEHAD'S DAUGHTERS WILL RECEIVE

36 The heads of the families of Gilead came to Moses. Gilead was the son of Makir. The family heads were from the tribe of Manasseh. So they were in the family line of Joseph. They spoke to Moses in front of the leaders of the families of Israel.

²They said, "The LORD commanded you to give shares of the land to the people of Israel. He told you to use lots when you do it. At that time the LORD ordered you to give our brother Zelophehad's share to his daughters.

³"Suppose they get married to men who are from other tribes in Israel. Then their share will be taken away from our family's land. It will be added to the land of the tribe they marry into. So a part of the share that was given to us will be taken away. ⁴The Year of Jubilee for the people of Israel will come. Then their share will be added to the land of the tribe they marry into. Their land will be taken away from the share that was given to our tribe."

⁵Then the LORD gave a command to Moses. He told Moses to give an order to the people of Israel. Moses said, "What the tribe in the family line of Joseph is saying is right.

⁶"Here is what the LORD commands for Zelophehad's daughters. They can get married to anyone they want to. But they have to get married to someone in their own family's tribe.

⁷"Property in Israel must not pass from one tribe to another. Everyone in Israel must keep his family's share of his tribe's land.

⁸"Suppose a daughter in any tribe of Israel receives land from her parents. Then she must get married to someone in her father's family and tribe. In that way, every family's share will remain in its family line in Israel.

⁹"Property can't pass from one tribe to another. Each tribe of Israel must keep the land it receives."

¹⁰So Zelophehad's daughters did just as the LORD commanded Moses. ¹¹The names of the daughters were Mahlah, Tirzah, Hoglah, Milcah and Noah. All of them got married to their cousins on their father's side. ¹²They married men who were in the family line of Manasseh, the son of Joseph. So the land they received remained in their father's family and tribe.

¹³Those are the commands and rules the LORD gave through Moses. He gave them to the people of Israel on the flatlands of Moab. They were by the Jordan River across from Jericho.

Deuteronomy

Who wrote this book?
Moses.

Why was this book written?
Deuteronomy tells a new generation of Israelites how to please God, so that God could bless them.

What happens in this book?
Moses speaks to the Israelites. He tells what God has done for them and reviews God's rules for holy living. The Israelites promise to obey God.

What do we learn about God in this book?
God helps people because he loves them. God's rules for living are given in love, and he blesses people who keep his rules.

Who is important in this book?
The important person in this book is Moses.

When did this happen?
These events happened about 1405 B.C.

Where did this happen?
During this time the Israelites were camped across the Jordan River from Canaan, the promised land.

THE LORD COMMANDS ISRAEL TO LEAVE MOUNT HOREB

1 These are the words Moses spoke to all of the people of Israel. At that time, they were in the desert east of the Jordan River. It's in the Arabah Valley across from Suph. They were between Paran and Tophel, Laban, Hazeroth and Dizahab. ²It takes 11 days to go from Mount Horeb to Kadesh Barnea if you travel on the Mount Seir road.

³It was now the 40th year since the people of Israel had left Egypt. On the

first day of the 11th month, Moses spoke to them. He told them everything the LORD had commanded him to tell them. ⁴They had already won the battle over Sihon. Sihon was the king of the Amorites. He had ruled in Heshbon. Israel had also won the battle over Og at Edrei. Og was the king of Bashan. He had ruled in Ashtaroth.

⁵The people were east of the Jordan River in the territory of Moab. There Moses began to explain the law. Here is what he said.

⁶The LORD our God spoke to us at Mount Horeb. He said, "You have stayed long enough at this mountain. ⁷Take your tents down. Go into the hill country of the Amorites. Go to all of the people who are their neighbors. Go to the people who live in the Arabah Valley. Travel to the mountains and the western hills. Go to the people in the Negev Desert and along the coast. Travel to the land of Canaan and to Lebanon. Go as far as the great Euphrates River.

⁸"I have given you all of that land. Go in and take it as your own. I took an oath. I promised I would give the land to your fathers. I promised it to Abraham, Isaac and Jacob. I also said I would give it to their children after them."

SOME OFFICIALS HELP MOSES

⁹At that time I spoke to you. I said, "You are too heavy a load for me to carry alone. ¹⁰The LORD your God has increased your numbers. Today you are as many as the stars in the sky. ¹¹The LORD is the God of your people. May he increase your numbers a thousand times. May he bless you, just as he promised he would. ¹²But I can't handle your problems and troubles all by myself. I can't settle your arguments.

¹³"So choose some wise men from each of your tribes. They must understand how to give good advice. The people must have respect for them. I will appoint those men to have authority over you."

¹⁴You answered me, "Your suggestion is good."

¹⁵So I took the leading men of your tribes who were wise and respected. I appointed them to have authority over you. I made them commanders of thousands, hundreds, fifties and tens. I appointed them to be officials over the tribes.

¹⁶Here is what I commanded your judges at that time. I said, "Listen to your people's cases when they argue with one another. Judge them fairly. It doesn't matter whether the case is between fellow Israelites or between an Israelite and an outsider. ¹⁷When you judge them, treat everyone the same. Listen to those who are important and those who are not. Don't be afraid of any man. God is the highest judge. Bring me any case that is too hard for you. I'll listen to it." ¹⁸At that time I told you everything you should do.

TWELVE MEN CHECK OUT THE LAND OF CANAAN

¹⁹The LORD our God commanded us to start out from Mount Horeb. So we did. We went toward the hill country of the Amorites. We traveled all through the huge and terrible desert you saw. Finally, we reached Kadesh Barnea.

²⁰Then I said to you, "You have reached the hill country of the Amorites. The LORD our God is giving it to us. ²¹The LORD your God has given you the land. Go up and take it. Do what the LORD says. He's the God of your people. Don't be afraid. Don't lose hope."

²²Then all of you came to me. You said, "Let's send some men ahead of us. They can check out the land for us and bring back a report. They can suggest to us which way to go. They can tell us about the towns we'll come to."

²³That seemed like a good idea to me. So I chose 12 of you. I picked one man from each tribe. ²⁴They left and went up into the hill country. There they came to the Valley of Eshcol. They checked it out. ²⁵They got some of the fruit of that land. They brought it down to us and gave us their report. They said, "The LORD our God is giving us a good land."

ISRAEL REFUSES TO OBEY THE LORD

²⁶But you wouldn't go up. You refused to obey the command of the

LORD your God. ²⁷You spoke against him in your tents. You said, "The LORD hates us. That's why he brought us out of Egypt to hand us over to the Amorites. He wanted to destroy us. ²⁸Where can we go? The men who checked out the land have made us lose hope. They say, 'The people are stronger and taller than we are. The cities are large. They have walls that reach up to the sky. We even saw the Anakites there.' "

²⁹Then I said to you, "Don't be terrified. Don't be afraid of them. ³⁰The LORD your God will go ahead of you. He will fight for you. With your own eyes you saw how he fought for you in Egypt. ³¹"You also saw how the LORD your God brought you through the desert. He carried you everywhere you went, just as a father carries his son. And now you have arrived here."

³²In spite of that, you didn't trust in the LORD your God. ³³He went ahead of you on your journey. He was in the fire at night and in the cloud during the day. He found places for you to camp. He showed you the way you should go.

³⁴The LORD heard what you said. So he became angry. He took an oath and made a promise. He said, ³⁵"I promised to give this good land to your people long ago. But not one of you evil men who are alive today will see it.

³⁶"Only Caleb will see the land. He is the son of Jephunneh. I will give him and his children after him the land he walked on. He followed me with his whole heart."

³⁷Because of you, the LORD became angry with me also. He said, "You will not enter the land either. ³⁸But Joshua, the son of Nun, is your helper. Joshua will enter the land. Help him to be brave. Give him hope. He will lead Israel to take the land as their own.

³⁹"You said your little ones would be taken prisoner. But they will enter the land. They do not know right from wrong yet. But I will give them the land. They will take it as their own. ⁴⁰As for you, turn around. Start out toward the desert. Go along the road that leads to the Red Sea."

⁴¹Then you replied, "We have sinned against the LORD. We will go up and fight. We'll do just as the LORD our God has commanded us." So all of you got your swords and put them on. You thought it would be easy to go up into the hill country.

⁴²But the LORD spoke to me. He said, "Tell them, 'Do not go up and fight. I will not be with you. Your enemies will win the battle over you.' "

⁴³So I told you what the LORD said. But you wouldn't listen. You refused to obey his command. You were so filled with pride that you marched up into the hill country. ⁴⁴The Amorites who lived in those hills came out and attacked you. Like large numbers of bees they chased you. They beat you down from Seir all the way to Hormah.

⁴⁵You came back and sobbed in front of the LORD. But he didn't pay any attention to your sobs. He wouldn't listen to you. ⁴⁶So you stayed in Kadesh for many years. You spent a long time in that area.

ISRAEL WANDERS IN THE DESERT

2 We turned back and started out toward the desert. We went along the road that leads to the Red Sea. That's how the LORD had directed me. For a long time we made our way around the hill country of Seir.

²Then the LORD spoke to me. He said, ³"You have made your way around this hill country long enough. So now turn north.

⁴"Here are the orders I want you to give the people. Tell them, 'You are about to pass through the territory of your relatives. They are from the family line of Esau. They live in Seir. They will be afraid of you. But be very careful. ⁵Do not make them angry. If you do, they will go to war against you. I will not give you any of their land. You will not have even enough to put your foot on. I have given Esau the hill country of Seir as his own. ⁶Pay them with silver for the food you eat and the water you drink.' "

⁷The LORD your God has blessed you in everything your hands have done. He watched over you when you traveled through that huge desert. For these 40 years the LORD your God has

been with you. So you have had everything you need.

⁸We went on past our relatives. They are from the family line of Esau. They live in Seir. We turned away from the Arabah Valley road. It comes up from Elath and Ezion Geber. We traveled along the desert road of Moab.

⁹Then the LORD said to me, "Do not attack the Moabites. Do not even make them angry. If you do, they will go to war against you. I will not give you any part of their land. I have given Moab to the people in the family line of Lot. I have given it to them as their own."

¹⁰The Emites used to live there. They were strong people. There were large numbers of them. They were as tall as the Anakites. ¹¹Like the Anakites, they too were thought of as Rephaites. But the Moabites called them Emites.

¹²The Horites used to live in Seir. But the people of Esau drove them out. They destroyed the Horites to make room for themselves. Then they settled in their territory. They did just as Israel has done in the land the LORD gave them as their own.

¹³The LORD said, "Now get up. Go across the Zered Valley." So we went across it.

¹⁴Between the time we left Kadesh Barnea and the time we went across the Zered Valley, 38 years passed. By then, all of the fighting men who had been in our camp from the beginning had died. The LORD had warned them with an oath that it would happen. ¹⁵He used his power against them until he had gotten rid of all of them. Not one was left in the camp.

¹⁶Finally, the last of the fighting men among the people died.

¹⁷Then the LORD spoke to me. He said, ¹⁸"Today you must pass near the border of Moab. Moab is also called Ar. ¹⁹"When you come to the Ammonites, do not attack them. Do not make them angry. If you do, they will go to war against you. I will not give you any of their land as your own. I have given it to the people in the family line of Lot. I have given it to them as their own."

²⁰That land was also thought of as a land of the Rephaites. They used to live there. But the Ammonites called them Zamzummites. ²¹The Rephaites were strong people. There were large numbers of them. They were as tall as the Anakites. The LORD destroyed the Rephaites to make room for the Ammonites. So the Ammonites drove them out. Then they settled in the territory of the Rephaites.

²²The LORD had done the same thing for the people of Esau. They lived in Seir. He destroyed the Horites to make room for them. They drove the Horites out. So the people of Esau have lived in Seir in the territory of the Horites to this very day.

²³The Avvites lived in villages as far away as Gaza. But people came from Crete. They destroyed the Avvites. Then they settled in the territory of the Avvites.

ISRAEL WINS THE BATTLE OVER SIHON

²⁴The LORD said, "Start out and go across the valley of the Arnon River. I have handed Sihon over to you. He is the Amorite king of Heshbon. I have also given you his country. Begin to take it as your own. Go to war against him. ²⁵"This very day I will bring fear and terror on all of the nations because of you. They will hear about you. They will tremble with fear. Pain and suffering will take hold of them because of you."

²⁶I sent messengers from the Desert of Kedemoth. I told them to go to Sihon, the king of Heshbon. They offered him peace. They said, ²⁷"Let us pass through your country. We'll stay on the main road. We won't turn off it to one side or the other. ²⁸We'll pay you the right amount of silver for food to eat and water to drink. Just let us walk through your country. ²⁹The people of Esau, who live in Seir, allowed us to do that. The people of Moab, who live in Ar, also allowed us to do it. So let us walk through until we go across the Jordan River. Then we'll be able to go into the land the LORD our God is giving us."

³⁰But Sihon, the king of Heshbon, refused to let us walk through. The LORD your God had made his heart and spirit stubborn. The LORD wanted

to hand him over to you. And that's exactly what he has done.

[31]The LORD said to me, "I have begun to hand Sihon and his country over to you. So begin the battle to take his land as your own."

[32]Sihon and his whole army came out to fight against us at Jahaz. [33]But the LORD our God handed him over to us. We struck him down together with his sons and his whole army. [34]At that time we took all of his towns. We completely destroyed them. We killed all of the men, women and children. We didn't leave any of them alive. [35]But we took for ourselves the livestock and everything else from the towns we had captured.

[36]Not a single town was too strong for us. That includes all of the towns from Aroer on the rim of the Arnon River valley all the way to Gilead. It also includes the town in the valley. The LORD our God gave us all of them. [37]And you obeyed the LORD's command. You didn't go near any part of the land of the Ammonites. That includes the land along the Jabbok River. It also includes the land around the towns that are in the hills.

ISRAEL WINS THE BATTLE OVER OG

3 Next, we turned and went up along the road toward Bashan. Og, the king of Bashan, marched out with his whole army. They fought against us at Edrei. [2]The LORD said to me, "Do not be afraid of Og. I have handed him over to you. I have also handed over his whole army and his land. Do to him what you did to Sihon. Sihon was the Amorite king who ruled in Heshbon."

[3]So the LORD our God also handed Og, the king of Bashan, and his whole army over to us. We struck them down. We didn't leave any of them alive. [4]At that time we took all of his cities. There were 60 of them. We took the whole area of Argob. That was Og's kingdom in Bashan.

[5]All of those cities had high walls around them. The city gates were made secure with heavy metal bars. There were also large numbers of villages that didn't have walls. [6]We completely destroyed them. We did to them just as we had done to Sihon, the king of Heshbon. We destroyed all of their cities. We destroyed the men, women and children. [7]But we kept for ourselves the livestock and everything else we took from their cities.

[8]So at that time we took the territory east of the Jordan River. We captured it from those two Amorite kings. The territory goes all the way from the Arnon River valley to Mount Hermon. [9]Hermon is called Sirion by the people of Sidon. The Amorites call it Senir.

[10]We captured all of the towns on the high flatlands. We took the whole land of Gilead. And we captured the whole land of Bashan as far away as Salecah and Edrei. Those were towns that belonged to Og's kingdom in Bashan. [11]Og, the king of Bashan, was the only Rephaite left. His bed was made out of iron. It was more than 13 feet long and six feet wide. It is still in the Ammonite city of Rabbah.

MOSES DIVIDES UP THE LAND

[12]I divided up the land we took over at that time. I gave the tribes of Reuben and Gad the territory north of Aroer by the Arnon River valley. It includes half of the hill country of Gilead together with its towns.

[13]I gave the rest of Gilead to half of the tribe of Manasseh. I also gave them the whole land of Bashan, the kingdom of Og. The whole area of Argob in Bashan used to be known as a land of the Rephaites.

[14]Jair took the whole area of Argob. He was from the family line of Manasseh. Argob goes all the way to the border of the people of Geshur and Maacah. It was named after Jair. So Bashan is called Havvoth Jair to this very day. [15]I gave Gilead to Makir.

[16]But I gave to the tribes of Reuben and Gad the territory that reaches from Gilead down to the Arnon River valley. It reaches all the way to the Jabbok River. The Jabbok is the northern border of Ammon. The middle of the Arnon River valley is its southern border.

[17]The western border of Reuben and Gad is the Jordan River in the Arabah Valley. It reaches from the Sea of Gali-

lee to the Dead Sea. It runs below the slopes of Pisgah.

[18]Here is the command I gave at that time to the tribes of Reuben and Gad and half of the tribe of Manasseh. I said, "The LORD your God has given you this land as your very own. But all of your strong men must be prepared for battle. They must cross over ahead of the rest of your fellow Israelites.

[19]"But your wives and children can stay in the towns I've given you. You can keep your livestock there too. I know you have a lot of livestock. [20]Let your families and livestock stay in those towns until the LORD gives peace and rest to the other tribes, just as he has given you peace and rest. And let them stay until the other tribes have taken over the land the LORD your God is giving them. That land is across the Jordan River. After that, each of you may go back to the land I've given you as your very own."

THE LORD WILL NOT ALLOW MOSES TO CROSS THE JORDAN RIVER

[21]At that time I gave Joshua a command. I said, "Your own eyes have seen everything the LORD your God has done to Sihon and Og. He will do the same thing to all of the kingdoms in the land where you are going. [22]Don't be afraid of them. The LORD your God himself will fight for you."

[23]At that time I made my appeal to the LORD. I said, [24]"LORD and King, you have begun to show me how great you are. You have shown me how strong your hand is. You do great works and mighty acts. There isn't any god in heaven or on earth that can do what you do. [25]Let me go across the Jordan River. Let me see the good land that is beyond it. I want to see that fine hill country and Lebanon."

[26]But the LORD was angry with me because of what you did. He wouldn't listen to me. "That is enough!" the LORD said. "Do not speak to me anymore about this matter. [27]Go up to the highest slopes of Pisgah. Look west and north and south and east. Look at the land with your own eyes. But you are not going to go across that Jordan River.

[28]"So appoint Joshua as the new leader. Help him to be brave. Give him hope and strength. He will take these people across the Jordan. You will see the land. But he will lead them into it to take it as their own." [29]So we stayed in the valley near Beth Peor.

OBEY THE LORD

4 Israel, listen to the rules and laws I'm going to teach you. Follow them. Then you will live. You will go in and take over the land. The LORD was the God of your people long ago. He's giving you the land. [2]Don't add to what I'm commanding you. Don't subtract from it either. Instead, obey the commands of the LORD your God that I'm giving you.

[3]Your own eyes saw what the LORD your God did at Baal Peor. He destroyed every one of your people who followed the Baal that was worshiped at Peor. [4]But all of you who remained true to the LORD your God are still alive today.

[5]I have taught you rules and laws, just as the LORD my God commanded me. Follow them in the land you are entering to take as your very own. [6]Be careful to keep them. That will show the nations how wise and understanding you are. They will hear about all of those rules. They'll say, "That great nation certainly has wise and understanding people."

[7]The LORD our God is near us every time we pray to him. What other nation is great enough to have its gods that close to them? [8]I'm giving you the laws of the LORD today. What other nation is great enough to have rules and laws that are as fair as these?

[9]Don't be careless. Instead, be very careful. Don't forget the things your eyes have seen. As long as you live, don't let them slip from your mind. Teach them to your children and their children after them. [10]Remember the day you stood at Mount Horeb. The LORD your God was there. He said to me, "Bring the people to me to hear my words. I want them to learn to have respect for me as long as they live in the land. I want them to teach my words to their children."

[11]You came near and stood at the

foot of the mountain. It blazed with fire that reached as high as the very heavens. There were black clouds and deep darkness.

¹²Then the LORD spoke to you out of the fire. You heard the sound of his words. But you didn't see any shape or form. You only heard a voice. ¹³He announced his covenant to you. That covenant is the Ten Commandments. He commanded you to follow them. Then he wrote them down on two stone tablets.

¹⁴At that time the LORD directed me to teach you his rules and laws. You must follow them in the land you are crossing the Jordan River to take as your own.

DON'T MAKE OR WORSHIP STATUES OF GODS

¹⁵The LORD spoke to you at Mount Horeb out of the fire. But you didn't see any shape or form that day. So be very careful.

¹⁶Make sure you don't commit a horrible sin. Don't make for yourselves a statue of a god. Don't make a god that looks like a man or woman or anything else. ¹⁷Don't make one that looks like any animal on earth or any bird that flies in the sky. ¹⁸Don't make a statue that looks like any creature that moves along the ground or any fish that swims in the water.

¹⁹When you look up at the heavens, you will see the sun and moon. And you will see huge numbers of stars. Don't let anyone tempt you to bow down to the sun, moon or stars. Don't worship things the LORD your God has provided for all of the nations on earth.

²⁰Egypt was like a furnace that melts iron down and makes it pure. But the LORD took you and brought you out of Egypt. He wanted you to be his very own people. And that's exactly what you are.

²¹The LORD was angry with me because of what you did. He took an oath that he would never let me go across the Jordan River. He promised that I would never enter that good land. It's the land the LORD your God is giving you as your own. ²²I'll die here in this land. I won't go across the Jordan. But you are about to cross over it. And you

are about to take that good land as your own.

²³Be careful. Don't forget the covenant the LORD your God made with you. Don't make for yourselves a statue of any god at all. He has told you not to. So don't do it. ²⁴The LORD your God is like a fire that burns everything up. He's a jealous God.

²⁵You will have children and grandchildren. And you will live in the land a long time.

But don't commit a horrible sin. Don't make a statue of a god. If you do, that will be an evil thing in the sight of the LORD your God. You will make him angry. ²⁶I'm calling out to heaven and earth to be witnesses against you this very day. If you do those things, you will quickly die in the land you are going across the Jordan River to take over. You won't live there very long. You will certainly be destroyed. ²⁷The LORD will drive you out of your land. He will scatter you among the nations. Only a few of you will remain alive there. ²⁸There you will worship gods that men have made out of wood and stone. Those gods can't see, hear, eat or smell.

²⁹Perhaps while you are there, you will look to the LORD your God. You will find him if you look for him with all your heart and with all your soul.

³⁰All of the things I've told you about might happen to you. And you will be in trouble. But later you will return to the LORD your God. You will obey him. ³¹The LORD your God is tender and loving. He won't leave you or destroy you. He won't forget the covenant he made with your people long ago. He took an oath when he made it.

THE LORD IS GOD

³²Ask now about the days of long ago. Learn what happened long before your time. Ask about what has happened since the time God created man on the earth. Ask from one end of the world to the other. Has anything as great as this ever happened? Has anything like it ever been heard of? ³³You heard the voice of God speaking out of fire. And you lived! Has that happened to any other people?

³⁴Has any god ever tried to take one nation out of another to be his own? Has any god done it by putting his people to the test? Has any god done it with miraculous signs and wonders or with a war? Has any god reached out his mighty hand and powerful arm? Or has any god shown his people his great and wonderful acts?

The LORD your God did all of those things for you in Egypt. With your very own eyes you saw him do them.

³⁵The LORD showed you those things so that you might know he is God. There is no other God except him. ³⁶From heaven he made you hear his voice. He wanted to teach you. On earth he showed you his great fire. You heard his words coming out of the fire.

³⁷He loved your people long ago. He chose their children after them. So he brought you out of Egypt. He used his great strength to do it. ³⁸He drove out nations to make room for you. They were greater and stronger than you are. He will bring you into their land.

He wants to give it to you as your very own. The whole land is as good as yours right now.

³⁹The LORD is God in heaven above and on the earth below. Today you must agree with that and take it to heart. There is no other God.

⁴⁰I'm giving you his rules and commands today. Obey them. Then things will go well with you and your children after you. You will live a long time in the land. The LORD your God is giving you the land for all time to come.

CITIES TO GO TO FOR SAFETY

⁴¹I set apart three cities east of the Jordan River. ⁴²Anyone who killed a person he didn't hate and without meaning to do it could run to one of those cities. He could go there and stay alive.

⁴³Here are the names of the cities. Bezer was for the people of Reuben. It was in the high flatlands in the desert. Ramoth was for the people of Gad. It was in Gilead. Golan was for the people of Manasseh. It was in Bashan.

Did the Bible stories really happen or are they like fairy tales?

The stories in the Bible really happened. Some of the stories may seem impossible to us because they tell about things only God can do. But they still happened. We know that the stories are true because the Bible says that every word in it is true. Some people do not believe the Bible. Some have not even read it. And some do not believe that God can do things that we think are impossible. But we know that God can do anything, and he is the best one to tell us how to live.

checkout Deuteronomy 4:35

Related verses:
Luke 1:1–4;
John 21:24,25

MOSES GIVES THE LAW TO ISRAEL

⁴⁴Here is the law I gave the people of Israel. ⁴⁵Here are its terms, rules and laws. I gave them to the people when they came out of Egypt.

⁴⁶They were now east of the Jordan River in the valley near Beth Peor. They were in the land of Sihon, the king of the Amorites. He ruled in Heshbon. But the people of Israel and I won the battle over him after we came out of Egypt. ⁴⁷We captured his land and made it our own. We also took the land of Og, the king of Bashan. Sihon and Og were the two Amorite kings east of the Jordan River.

⁴⁸Their land reached from Aroer on the rim of the Arnon River valley to Mount Hermon. ⁴⁹It included the whole Arabah Valley east of the Jordan. It included land all the way to the Dead Sea below the slopes of Pisgah.

THE TEN COMMANDMENTS

5 I sent for all of the people of Israel. Here is what I said to them.

Israel, listen to me. Here are the rules and laws I'm announcing to you today. Learn them well. Be sure to follow them.

²The LORD our God made a covenant with us at Mount Horeb. ³He didn't make it only with our parents. He also made it with us. In fact, he made it with all of us who are alive here today. ⁴The LORD spoke to you face to face. His voice came out of the fire on the mountain.

⁵At that time I stood between the LORD and you. I announced to you the LORD's message. I did it because you were afraid of the fire. You didn't go up the mountain.

The LORD said,

⁶ "I am the LORD your God. I brought you out of Egypt. That is the land where you were slaves.

⁷ "Do not put any other gods in place of me.

⁸ "Do not make statues of gods that look like anything in the sky or on the earth or in the waters. ⁹Do not bow down to them or worship them. I am the LORD your God. I am a jealous God. I punish the children for

Why did God give Moses so many laws for the Israelites to obey?

Bible books like Leviticus and Deuteronomy do have a lot of laws in them. It may seem as if God gave the Israelites a very long list of laws to obey. But each law had a purpose. The basic laws are the Ten Commandments. Many of the other laws explained one of the Ten Commandments. Some of the laws helped the Israelites become a nation. Some helped keep the people healthy. Others told the people how to live together peacefully. God knew what was best for the people and that was why he gave all those laws. We have a lot of laws today, too. We just do not see them written down in one book.

(checkout)
Deuteronomy 5:1

Related verses:
Exodus 20:1–17;
Galatians 3:24

the sin of their parents. I judge the grandchildren and great-grandchildren of those who hate me. ¹⁰But for all time to come I show love to all those who love me and keep my commandments.

¹¹ "Do not misuse the name of the LORD your God. The LORD will find guilty anyone who misuses his name.

¹² "Observe the Sabbath day. Keep it holy, just as the LORD your God commanded you. ¹³Do all of your work in six days. ¹⁴But the seventh day is a Sabbath in honor of the LORD your God. Do not do any work on that day. The same command applies to your sons and daughters, your male and female servants, your oxen, your donkeys and your other animals. It also applies to any outsiders who live in your cities. I want your male and female servants to rest, just as you do. ¹⁵Remember that you were slaves in Egypt. The LORD your God reached out his mighty hand and powerful arm and brought you out of there. So he has commanded you to observe the Sabbath day.

¹⁶ "Honor your father and mother, just as the LORD your God commanded you. Then you will live a long time in the land he is giving you. And things will go well with you there.

¹⁷ "Do not commit murder.

¹⁸ "Do not commit adultery.

¹⁹ "Do not steal.

²⁰ "Do not give false witness against your neighbor.

²¹ "Do not long for your neighbor's wife. Do not long to have anything that belongs to your neighbor. Do not long to have your neighbor's house or land, male or female servant, ox or donkey."

²²Those are the commandments the LORD announced in a loud voice to your whole community. He gave them

KIDS' QUESTION

Why is it wrong to complain when my mom asks me to do something?

The Bible tells us to honor our parents. We should be polite to them, have a good attitude toward them and show them respect. That includes the times when we disagree with them. We can tell our parents how we feel if we do not agree with them. But we do not need to complain or say cruel things to them. If we try to think about how much our parents do for us, we will be thankful instead of complaining.

COMPLAINT FREE ZONE!
CHECK ATTITUDES AT THE DOOR MOM

ATTITUDE CHECKER

checkout
Deuteronomy 5:16

Related verses:
1 Corinthians 10:10,11;
Philippians 2:14

to you there on the mountain. He spoke out of the fire, cloud and deep darkness. He didn't add anything else. Then he wrote the commandments on two stone tablets. And he gave them to me.

²³The mountain was blazing with fire. You heard the voice coming out of the darkness. So your elders and all of the leaders of your tribes came to me.

²⁴You said, "The LORD our God has shown us his glory and majesty. We have heard his voice coming out of the fire. Today we have seen that a man can still stay alive even if God speaks with him. ²⁵But why should we die? This great fire will burn us up. We'll die if we hear the voice of the LORD our God again.

²⁶"We have heard the voice of the living God. We've heard him speaking out of the fire. Has any other human being ever heard him speak like that and stayed alive? ²⁷Go near and listen to everything the LORD our God says. Then tell us what he tells you. We will listen and obey."

²⁸The LORD heard you when you spoke to me. He said to me, "I have heard what these people said to you. Everything they said was good. ²⁹But I wish they would always have respect for me in their hearts. I wish they would always obey all of my commands. Then things would go well with them and their children forever.

³⁰"Go and tell them to return to their tents. ³¹But you stay here with me. Then I will give you all of my commands, rules and laws. You must teach the people to follow them in the land I am giving them as their very own."

³²So be careful to do what the LORD your God has commanded you. Don't turn away from his commands to the right or the left. ³³Live exactly as the LORD your God has commanded you to live. Then you will enjoy life in the land you will soon own. Things will go well with you there. You will live there for a long time.

LOVE THE LORD YOUR GOD

6 The LORD your God has directed me to teach you his commands, rules and laws. Obey them in the land you will take over when you go across the Jordan River. ²Then you, your children and their children after them will have respect for the LORD your God as long as you live. Keep all of his rules and commands I'm giving you. If you do, you will enjoy long life.

³Israel, listen to me. Make sure you obey me. Then things will go well with you. Your numbers will increase greatly in a land that has plenty of milk and honey. That's what the LORD, the God of your parents, promised you.

⁴Israel, listen to me. The LORD is our God. The LORD is the one and only God. ⁵Love the LORD your God with all your heart and with all your soul. Love him with all your strength.

⁶The commandments I give you today must be in your hearts. ⁷Make sure your children learn them. Talk about them when you are at home. Talk about them when you walk along the road. Speak about them when you go to bed. And speak about them when you get up. ⁸Write them down and tie them on your hands as a reminder. Also tie them on your foreheads. ⁹Write them on the doorframes of your houses. Also write them on your gates.

¹⁰The LORD your God will bring you into the land of Canaan. He took an oath. He promised he would give the land to your fathers. He promised it to Abraham, Isaac and Jacob.

The land has large, wealthy cities you didn't build. ¹¹It has houses that are filled with all kinds of good things you didn't provide. It has wells you didn't dig. And it has vineyards and groves of olive trees you didn't plant. You will have plenty to eat.

¹²But be careful that you don't forget the LORD. Remember that he brought you out of Egypt. That's the land where you were slaves.

¹³Worship the LORD your God. He is the only one you should serve. When you make promises, take your oaths in his name. ¹⁴Don't follow other gods. Don't worship the gods of the nations that are around you.

¹⁵The LORD your God is among you. He is a jealous God. If you worship other gods, his anger will burn against you. And he will destroy you from the face of the land. ¹⁶Don't put the LORD

your God to the test as you did at Massah.

¹⁷Be sure to obey the LORD's commands. Follow the terms and rules he has given you. ¹⁸Do what is right and good in the LORD's eyes. Then things will go well with you. You will go in and take over the land. It's the good land the LORD promised with an oath to your people long ago. ¹⁹You will drive out all of your enemies to make room for you. That's what the LORD said would happen.

²⁰Later on, your son might ask you, "What is the meaning of the terms, rules and laws the LORD our God has commanded you to obey?"

²¹If he does, tell him, "We were Pharaoh's slaves in Egypt. But the LORD used his mighty hand to bring us out of Egypt. ²²With our own eyes we saw the LORD send miraculous signs and wonders. They were great and terrible. He sent them on Egypt and Pharaoh and everyone in his house.

²³"But the LORD brought us out of Egypt. He planned to bring us into the land of Canaan and give it to us. It's the land he promised with an oath to our people long ago.

²⁴"The LORD our God commanded us to obey all of his rules. He commanded us to have respect for him. If we do, we will always succeed and be kept alive. That's what is happening today. ²⁵We must make sure we obey the whole law in the sight of the LORD our God. That's what he has commanded us to do. If we obey his law, we'll be doing what he requires of us."

THE LORD WILL DRIVE MANY NATIONS OUT

7 The LORD your God will bring you into the land. You are going to enter it and take it as your own. He'll drive many nations out to make room for you. He'll drive out the Hittites, Girgashites, Amorites, Canaanites, Perizzites, Hivites and Jebusites. Those seven nations are larger and stronger than you are.
²The LORD your God will hand them over to you. You will win the battle over them. You must completely destroy them. Don't make a peace treaty with them. Don't show them any

mercy. ³Don't get married to any of them. Don't give your daughters to their sons. And don't take their daughters for your sons. ⁴If you do, those people will turn your children away from following the LORD. Then your children will serve other gods. The LORD's anger will burn against you. It will quickly destroy you.

⁵So here is what you must do to those people. Break down their altars. Smash their sacred stones. Cut down the poles they use to worship the goddess Asherah. Burn the statues of their gods in the fire.

⁶You are a holy nation. The LORD your God has set you apart for himself. He has chosen you to be his special treasure. He chose you out of all of the nations on the face of the earth to be his people.

⁷The LORD chose you because he loved you very much. He didn't choose you because you had more people than other nations. In fact, you had the smallest number of all.

⁸The LORD chose you because he loved you. He wanted to keep the promise he had made with an oath to your people long ago. That's why he brought you out of Egypt with a mighty hand. He bought you back from the land where you were slaves. He set you free from the power of Pharaoh, the king of Egypt.

⁹So I want you to realize that the LORD your God is God. He is the faithful God. He keeps his covenant for all time to come. He keeps it with those who love him and obey his commands. He shows them his love. ¹⁰But he will pay back those who hate him. He'll destroy them. He'll quickly pay back those who hate him. ¹¹So be careful to follow the commands, rules and laws I'm giving you today.

¹²Pay attention to the laws of the LORD your God. Be careful to obey them. Then he will keep his covenant of love with you. That's what he promised with an oath to your people long ago. ¹³The LORD will love you and bless you. He'll increase your numbers. He'll give you many children. He'll bless the crops of your land. He'll give you plenty of grain, olive oil and fresh wine. He'll bless your herds with many

calves. He'll give your flocks many lambs. He'll do all of those things for you in the land of Canaan. It's the land he promised your people long ago that he would give you. ¹⁴He will bless you more than any other nation. All of your men and women will have children. All of your livestock will have little ones.

¹⁵The LORD will keep you from getting sick. He won't send on you any of the horrible sicknesses you saw all around you in Egypt. But he'll send them on everyone who hates you.

¹⁶You must destroy all of the nations the LORD your God hands over to you. Don't feel sorry for them. Don't serve their gods. If you do, they will be a trap for you.

¹⁷You might say to yourselves, "These nations are stronger than we are. How can we drive them out?" ¹⁸But don't be afraid of them.

Be sure to remember what the LORD your God did to Pharaoh and all of the Egyptians. ¹⁹With your own eyes you saw what the LORD did to them. You saw his miraculous signs and wonders. He reached out his mighty hand and powerful arm. The LORD your God used all of those things to bring you out. He will do the same things to all of the nations you are now afraid of.

²⁰The LORD your God will also send hornets among them. Some of the people who are left alive will hide from you. But even they will die. ²¹So don't be terrified by them. The LORD your God is with you. He is a great and wonderful God.

²²The LORD your God will drive out those nations to make room for you. But he will do it little by little. You won't be allowed to get rid of them all at once. If you did, wild animals would multiply all around you.

²³But the LORD your God will hand those nations over to you. He will throw them into a panic until they are destroyed. ²⁴He will hand their kings over to you. You will wipe out their names from the earth. No one will be able to stand up against you. You will destroy them.

²⁵Burn the statues of their gods in the fire. Don't long for the silver and gold that is on those statues. Don't

take it for yourselves. If you do, it will be a trap for you. The LORD your God hates it. ²⁶Don't bring anything he hates into your house. If you do, you will be completely destroyed along with it. So hate it with all your heart. It is set apart to be destroyed.

REMEMBER WHAT THE LORD HAS DONE

8 Make sure you follow every command I'm giving you today. Then you will live. You will increase your numbers. You will enter the land and take it as your own. It's the land the LORD promised with an oath to your people long ago.

²Remember how the LORD your God led you all the way. He guided you in the desert for these 40 years. He wanted to take your pride away. He wanted to put you to the test and know what was in your hearts. He wanted to see whether you would obey his commands.

³He took your pride away. He let you go hungry. Then he gave you manna to eat. You and your parents had never even known anything about manna before. He tested you to teach you that man doesn't live only on bread. He also lives on every word that comes from the mouth of the LORD. ⁴Your clothes didn't wear out during these 40 years. Your feet didn't swell.

⁵Here is what I want you to know in your hearts. The LORD your God trains you, just as parents train their children.

⁶Obey the commands of the LORD your God. Live as he wants you to live. Have respect for him.

⁷The LORD your God is bringing you into a good land. It has streams and pools of water. Springs flow in its valleys and hills. ⁸It has wheat, barley, vines, fig trees, pomegranates, olive oil and honey. ⁹There is plenty of food in that land. You will have everything you need. Its rocks have iron in them. And you can dig copper out of its hills.

¹⁰When you have eaten and are satisfied, praise the LORD your God. Praise him for the good land he has given you. ¹¹Make sure you don't forget the LORD your God. Don't fail to obey his commands, laws and rules. I'm giving them to you today.

¹²But suppose you don't obey his commands. And suppose you have plenty to eat. You build fine houses and settle down in them. ¹³Your herds and flocks increase their numbers. You also get more and more silver and gold. And everything you have multiplies. ¹⁴Then your hearts will become proud. And you will forget the LORD your God.

The LORD brought you out of Egypt. That's the land where you were slaves. ¹⁵He led you through that huge and terrible desert. It was a dry land. It didn't have any water. It had poisonous snakes and scorpions. The LORD gave you water out of solid rock. ¹⁶He gave you manna to eat in the desert. Your parents had never even known anything about manna before.

The LORD took your pride away. He put you to the test. He did it so that things would go well with you in the end. ¹⁷You might say to yourselves, "Our power and our strong hands have made us rich."

¹⁸But remember the LORD your God.

He gives you the ability to produce wealth. That shows he stands by the terms of his covenant. He promised it with an oath to your people long ago. And he's still faithful to his covenant today.

¹⁹Don't forget the LORD your God. Don't follow other gods. Don't worship them and bow down to them. I give witness against you today that if you do, you will certainly be destroyed. ²⁰You will be destroyed just like the nations the LORD your God is destroying to make room for you. That's what will happen if you don't obey him.

WHY THE LORD GAVE CANAAN TO ISRAEL

9 Israel, listen to me. You are now about to go across the Jordan. You will take over the land of the nations that live there.

Those nations are greater and stronger than you are. Their large cities have walls that reach up to the sky. ²The people who live there are Anakites. They are strong and tall. You

What should we know about saving money?

Here are six important facts about saving money.
1. It is important because it is part of God's plan for meeting our needs.
2. It is hard now but it will reward us later.
3. It takes planning and work, but it is less effort than getting out of debt.
4. Responsible people do it because they know they will need the money someday.
5. We should save with a purpose in mind so we know when to use the money we have saved.
6. God gives us the ability to earn money, but he wants us to use it wisely. This includes saving.

checkout

Deuteronomy 8:17,18

Related verses:
Genesis 41:35,36;
Proverbs 13:11

Advanced Seminar on Savings and Investment

know all about them. You have heard people say, "Who can stand up against the Anakites?"

³But today you can be sure the LORD your God will go over there ahead of you. He is like a fire that will burn them up. He'll destroy them. He'll bring them under your control. You will drive them out. You will put an end to them quickly, just as the LORD has promised you.

⁴The LORD your God will drive them out to make room for you. When he does, don't say to yourselves, "The LORD has done it because we are godly. That's why he brought us here to take over this land." That isn't true. The LORD is going to drive out those nations to make room for you because they are very evil.

⁵You are not going in to take over their land because you have done what is right or honest. It's because those nations are so evil. That's why the LORD your God will drive them out ahead of you. He will do what he said he would do. He took an oath and made a promise to your fathers. He made it to Abraham, Isaac and Jacob.

⁶The LORD your God is giving you this good land to take as your own. But you must understand that it isn't because you are a godly nation. In fact, you are stubborn.

ISRAEL WORSHIPED THE GOLDEN CALF

⁷Here is something you must remember. Never forget it. You made the LORD your God angry in the desert. You refused to obey him from the day you left Egypt until you arrived here.

⁸At Mount Horeb you made the LORD angry enough to destroy you. ⁹I went up the mountain. I went there to receive the tablets of the covenant. They were made out of stone. It was the covenant the LORD had made with you. I stayed on the mountain for 40 days and 40 nights. I didn't eat any food or drink any water.

¹⁰The LORD gave me two stone tablets. The words on them were written by the finger of God. All of the commandments the LORD gave you were written on the tablets. He announced them to you out of the fire on the

mountain. He wrote them on the day you gathered together there.

¹¹The 40 days and 40 nights came to an end. Then the LORD gave me the two stone tablets. They were the tablets of the covenant. ¹²The LORD told me, "Go down from here right away. The people you brought out of Egypt have become very sinful. They have quickly turned away from what I commanded them. They have made a metal statue of a god for themselves."

¹³The LORD said to me, "I have seen these people. They are so stubborn! ¹⁴Do not try to stop me. I am going to destroy them. I will wipe them out from the earth. Then I will make you into a great nation. Your people will be stronger than they were. There will be more of you than there were of them."

¹⁵So I turned and went down the mountain. It was blazing with fire. I was carrying the two tablets of the covenant.

¹⁶When I looked, I saw that you had sinned against the LORD your God. You had made for yourselves a metal statue of a god. It looked like a calf. You had quickly turned away from the path the LORD had commanded you to follow.

¹⁷So I threw the two tablets out of my hands. You watched them break into pieces.

¹⁸Then once again I fell down flat in front of the LORD with my face toward the ground. I lay there for 40 days and 40 nights. I didn't eat any food or drink any water. You had committed a terrible sin. You had done an evil thing in the LORD's sight. You had made him angry.

¹⁹I was afraid of the LORD's burning anger. He was so angry with you he wanted to destroy you. But the LORD listened to me again. ²⁰And he was so angry with Aaron he wanted to destroy him too. But at that time I prayed for Aaron.

²¹I also got that sinful calf you had made. I burned it in the fire. I crushed it and ground it into fine powder. Then I threw the powder into a stream that was flowing down the mountain.

²²You also made the LORD angry at Taberah, Massah and Kibroth Hattaavah.

²³The LORD sent you out from Kadesh Barnea. He said, "Go up and take over the land I have given you." But you refused to do what the LORD your God had commanded you to do. You didn't trust him or obey him. ²⁴You have been refusing to obey the LORD as long as I've known you.

²⁵I lay down in front of the LORD with my face toward the ground for 40 days and 40 nights. I did it because the LORD had said he would destroy you.

²⁶I prayed to him. "LORD and King," I said, "don't destroy your people. They belong to you. You set them free by your great power. You used your mighty hand to bring them out of Egypt. ²⁷Remember your servants Abraham, Isaac and Jacob. Forgive the people of Israel for being so stubborn. Don't judge them for the evil and sinful things they've done.

²⁸"If you do, the Egyptians will say, 'The LORD wasn't able to take them into the land he had promised to give them. He hated them. So he brought them out of Egypt to put them to death in the desert.' ²⁹But they are your people. They belong to you. You used your great power to bring them out of Egypt. You reached out your mighty arm and saved them."

THE NEW STONE TABLETS

10

At that time the LORD spoke to me. He said, "Carve out two stone tablets, just like the first ones. Then come up to me on the mountain. Also make a wooden chest. ²I will write on the tablets the words that were on the first tablets, which you broke. Then you must put the tablets in the chest."

³So I made the ark out of acacia wood. I carved out two stone tablets that were just like the first ones. I went up the mountain. I carried the two tablets in my hands. ⁴The LORD wrote on the tablets what he had written before. It was the Ten Commandments. He had announced them to you out of the fire on the mountain. It was on the day you had gathered together there. So the LORD gave the tablets to me. ⁵Then I came back down the mountain. I put the tablets in the ark I had

made, just as the LORD had commanded me. And that's where they are now.

⁶Remember how the people of Israel traveled from the wells of Bene Jaakan to Moserah. That's where Aaron died. And his body was buried there. His son Eleazar became the next priest after him. ⁷From Moserah the people traveled to Gudgodah. Then they went on to Jotbathah. That land has streams of water.

⁸At that time the LORD set the tribe of Levi apart. He appointed them to carry the ark of the covenant of the LORD. He wanted them to serve him. He told them to bless the people in his name. And they still do it today. ⁹That's why the Levites don't have any part of the land the LORD gave the other tribes in Israel. They don't have any share among them. The LORD himself is their share. That's what the LORD your God told them.

¹⁰I had stayed on the mountain for 40 days and nights, just as I did the first time. The LORD listened to me that time also. He didn't want to destroy you.

¹¹"Go," the LORD said to me. "Lead the people on their way. Then they can enter the land and take it over. I have taken an oath. I promised I would give the land to their fathers. I promised it to Abraham, Isaac and Jacob."

HAVE RESPECT FOR THE LORD

¹²And now, Israel, what is the LORD your God asking you to do? Have respect for him. Live exactly as he wants you to live. Love him. Serve him with all your heart and with all your soul. ¹³Obey the LORD's commands and rules. I'm giving them to you today for your own good.

¹⁴The heavens belong to the LORD your God. Even the highest heavens belong to him. He owns the earth and everything in it. ¹⁵But the LORD loved your people very much long ago. You are their children. And he chose you above all of the other nations. His love and his promise remain with you to this very day. ¹⁶So don't let your hearts be stubborn anymore. Obey the LORD. ¹⁷The LORD your God is the greatest

God of all. He is the greatest Lord of all. He is the great God. He is mighty and wonderful. He treats everyone the same. He doesn't accept any money from those who want special favors. [18]He stands up for widows and for children whose fathers have died. He loves outsiders. He gives them food and clothes. [19]So you also must love outsiders. Remember that you yourselves were outsiders in Egypt.

[20]Have respect for the LORD your God. Serve him. Remain true to him. When you make promises, take your oaths in his name. [21]He is the one you should praise. He's your God. With your own eyes you saw the great and wonderful miracles he did for you. [22]Long ago, your people went down into Egypt. The total number of them was 70. And now the LORD your God has made you as many as the stars in the sky.

LOVE AND OBEY THE LORD

11 Love the LORD your God. Do what he requires. Always obey his rules, laws and commands.

[2]Remember today that your children weren't the ones the LORD your God taught and trained. They didn't see his majesty. They weren't in Egypt when he reached out his mighty hand and powerful arm. [3]They didn't see the miraculous signs and the other things he did in Egypt. They didn't see what he did to Pharaoh, the king of Egypt, and to his whole country. [4]They weren't there when he destroyed the army of Egypt and its horses and chariots. The LORD swept the waters of the Red Sea over the Egyptians while they were chasing you. He wiped them out forever.

[5]Your children didn't see what he did for you in the desert before you arrived here. [6]They didn't see what he did to Dathan and Abiram, who were the sons of Eliab. Eliab was from the tribe of Reuben. The earth opened its mouth right in the middle of the Israelite camp. It swallowed up Dathan and Abiram. It swallowed them up together with their families, tents and every living thing that belonged to them.

[7]But with your own eyes you saw all of the great things the LORD has done. [8]So obey all of the commands I'm giving you today. Then you will be strong enough to go in and take over the land. You will go across the Jordan River and take it as your own.

[9]You will live in the land for a long time. It's the land the LORD promised to give to Abraham, Isaac and Jacob and their children after them. He took an oath when he made that promise. It's a land that has plenty of milk and honey. [10]You will enter it and take it over.

It isn't like the land of Egypt. That's where you came from. You planted your seeds there. You had to water them, just as you have to water a vegetable garden.

[11]But you will soon go across the Jordan River. The land you are going to take over has mountains and valleys in it. It drinks rain from heaven. [12]It's a land the LORD your God takes care of. His eyes always look on it with favor. He watches over it from the beginning of the year to its end. [13]So be faithful. Obey the commands the LORD your God is giving you today. Love him. Serve him with all your heart and with all your soul. [14]Then the LORD will send rain on your land at the right time. He'll send rain in the fall and in the spring. You will be able to gather your grain. You will also be able to make olive oil and fresh wine. [15]He'll provide grass in the fields for your cattle. You will have plenty to eat.

[16]But be careful. Don't let anyone tempt you to do something wrong. Don't turn away and worship other gods. Don't bow down to them. [17]If you do, the LORD's anger will burn against you. He'll close up the sky. It won't rain. The ground won't produce its crops. Soon you will die. You won't live to enjoy the good land the LORD is giving you.

[18]So keep my words in your hearts and minds. Write them down and tie them on your hands as a reminder. Also tie them on your foreheads. [19]Teach them to your children. Talk about them when you are at home. Talk about them when you walk along

the road. Speak about them when you go to bed. And speak about them when you get up. ²⁰Write them on the doorframes of your houses. Also write them on your gates.

²¹Then you and your children will live for a long time in the land. The LORD took an oath and promised to give the land to Abraham, Isaac and Jacob. Your family line will continue as long as the heavens remain above the earth.

²²So be careful. Obey all of the commands I'm giving you to follow. Love the LORD your God. Live exactly as he wants you to live. Remain true to him. ²³Then the LORD will drive out all of the nations to make room for you. They are larger and stronger than you are. But you will take their land.

²⁴Every place you walk on will belong to you. Your territory will go all the way from the desert to Lebanon. It will go from the Euphrates River to the Mediterranean Sea.

²⁵No man will be able to stand up against you. The LORD your God will throw the whole land into a panic because of you. He'll do it everywhere you go, just as he promised you.

²⁶Listen to me. I'm setting a blessing and a curse in front of you today. ²⁷I'm giving you the commands of the LORD your God today. You will be blessed if you obey them. ²⁸But you will be cursed if you don't obey them. So don't turn away from the path I'm now commanding you to take. Don't worship other gods. You haven't known anything about them before.

²⁹The LORD your God will bring you into the land to take it over. When he does, you must announce the blessings from Mount Gerizim. You must announce the curses from Mount Ebal. ³⁰As you know, those mountains are across the Jordan River. They are beyond the road that runs along the west side of the Jordan. They are near the large trees of Moreh. The mountains are in the territory of the Canaanites, who live in the Arabah Valley near Gilgal.

³¹You are about to go across the Jordan River. You will enter the land and take it over. The LORD your God is giving it to you. You will take it over and

live there. ³²When you do, make sure you obey all of the rules and laws I'm giving you today.

WORSHIP ONLY WHERE THE LORD WANTS YOU TO

12 Here are the rules and laws you must obey. Be careful to follow them in the land the LORD has given you to take as your own. He's the God of your people who lived long ago. Obey these rules and laws as long as you live in the land.

²You will soon drive the nations out of it. Completely destroy all of the places where they worship their gods. Destroy them on the high mountains, on the hills, and under every green tree. ³Break down their altars. Smash their sacred stones. Burn up the poles they use to worship the goddess Asherah. Cut down the statues of their gods. Wipe out the names of their gods from those places.

⁴You must not worship the LORD your God the way those nations worship their gods. ⁵Instead, go to the special place he will choose from among all of your tribes. He will put his Name there. That's where you must go.

⁶Take your burnt offerings and sacrifices to that place. Bring your special gifts and a tenth of everything you produce. Take with you what you have promised to give. Bring any other offerings you choose to give. And bring the male animals among your livestock that were born first to their mothers.

⁷You and your families will eat at the place the LORD your God will choose. He will be with you there. You will find joy in everything you have done. That's because he has blessed you.

⁸You must not do as we're doing here today. All of us are doing only what we think is right. ⁹That's because you haven't yet reached the place the LORD is giving you. Your God will give you peace and rest there.

¹⁰But first you will go across the Jordan River. You will settle in the land he's giving you. It will belong to you as your share. He will give you peace and rest from all of your enemies around you. You will live in safety.

¹¹The LORD your God will choose a

special place. He will put his Name there. That's where you must bring everything I command you to bring. That includes your burnt offerings and sacrifices. It includes your special gifts and a tenth of everything you produce. It also includes all of the things of value that you promised to give to the LORD.

¹²Be filled with joy there in the sight of the LORD your God. Your children should also be joyful. So should your male and female servants. And so should the Levites from your towns. The Levites won't receive any part of the land as their share.

¹³Be careful not to sacrifice your burnt offerings anywhere you want to. ¹⁴Offer them only at the place the LORD will choose in one of your tribes. There obey everything I command you.

¹⁵But you can kill your animals in any of your towns. You can eat as much of the meat as you want to. You can eat it as if it were antelope or deer meat. That's in keeping with the blessing the LORD your God is giving you. Those who are "clean" and those who are not can eat it.

¹⁶But you must not eat meat that still has blood in it. Pour the blood out on the ground like water.

¹⁷Here are the things you must not eat in your own towns. You must not eat the tenth part of your grain, olive oil and fresh wine. It belongs to the LORD. You must not eat the male animals among your livestock that were born first to their mothers. Don't eat anything you have promised to give. Don't eat any offerings you have chosen to give. And you must not eat any of your special gifts.

¹⁸Instead, you must eat all of those things in the sight of the LORD your God. Do it at the place he will choose. You, your children, your male and female servants and the Levites from your towns can eat them.

Be filled with joy in the sight of the LORD your God. Be joyful in everything you do.

¹⁹Don't forget to take care of the Levites as long as you live in your land.

²⁰The LORD your God will increase your territory, just as he has promised you. When he does, you might get hungry for meat. You might say, "I'd really like some meat." Then you can eat as much of it as you want to.

²¹The LORD your God will choose a special place. He will put his Name there. But suppose it's too far away for you to go to it. Then you can kill animals from the herds and flocks the LORD has given you. Do it just as I have commanded you. In your own towns you can eat as much of the meat as you want to. ²²Eat it as you would eat antelope or deer meat. Those who are "clean" and those who are not can eat it.

²³But be sure you don't eat meat that still has blood in it. The blood is the animal's life. So you must not eat the life along with the meat. ²⁴You must not eat the blood. Pour it out on the ground like water. ²⁵Don't eat it. Then things will go well with you and your children after you. You will be doing what is right in the eyes of the LORD.

²⁶But go to the place the LORD will choose. Take with you the things you have set apart for him. Bring what you have promised to give him. ²⁷Sacrifice your burnt offerings on the altar of the LORD your God. Offer the meat and the blood there. The blood of your sacrifices must be poured out beside his altar. But you can eat the meat.

²⁸Make sure you obey all of the rules I'm giving you. Then things will always go well with you and your children after you. That's because you will be doing what is good and right in the eyes of the LORD your God.

²⁹You are about to attack the land and take it over as your own. When you do, the LORD your God will cut off the nations who live there. He will do it to make room for you. You will drive them out. You will settle in their land. ³⁰They will be destroyed to make room for you. But when they are, be careful.

Don't be trapped. Don't ask questions about their gods. Don't say, "How do these nations serve their gods? We'll do it in the same way." ³¹You must not worship the LORD your God the way they worship their gods. When they worship, they do all kinds of evil things the LORD hates. They even burn up their children in the fire as sacrifices to their gods.

³²Be sure you do everything I'm commanding you to do. Don't add anything to my commands. And don't take anything away from them.

DON'T WORSHIP OTHER GODS

13

Suppose a prophet appears among you. Or someone comes who uses dreams to tell what's going to happen. He tells you that a miraculous sign or wonder is going to take place. ²The sign or wonder he has spoken about might really take place. And he might say, "Let's follow other gods. Let's worship them." But you haven't known anything about those gods before. ³So you must not listen to what that prophet or dreamer has said.

The LORD your God is putting you to the test. He wants to know whether you love him with all your heart and with all your soul. ⁴You must follow him. You must have respect for him. Keep his commands. Obey him. Serve him. Remain true to him.

⁵That prophet or dreamer must be put to death. He told you not to obey the LORD your God. The LORD brought you out of Egypt. He set you free from the land where you were slaves. He

commanded you to live the way he wants you to. But that prophet or dreamer has tried to make you turn away from it. Get rid of that evil person.

⁶Suppose your very own brother or sister secretly tempts you to do something wrong. Or your child or the wife you love tempts you. Or your closest friend does it. Suppose one of them says, "Let's go and worship other gods." But you and your people long ago hadn't known anything about those gods before. ⁷They are the gods of the nations that are around you. Those nations might be near or far away. In fact, they might reach from one end of the land to the other. ⁸Don't give in to those who are tempting you. Don't listen to them. Don't feel sorry for them. Don't spare them or save them.

⁹You must certainly put them to death. You must be the first to throw stones at them. Then all of the people must do the same thing. ¹⁰Put them to death by throwing stones at them. They tried to turn you away from the LORD your God. He brought you out of Egypt. That's the land where you were slaves.

¹¹After you kill those who tempted

How can people find out what is right and wrong?

We can know what is right by knowing God. For example, we know it is right to be loving because God is love. Everything that is wrong goes against what God is like. We can learn what God is like by reading the Bible. The Bible helps us know how to be like God and act like him. God has given us rules and guidance for how to live. Those are also in the Bible. When we read rules such as the Ten Commandments, we know how God wants us to act.

checkout
Deuteronomy 12:28

Related verses: 2 Timothy 3:16,17

you, all of the people of Israel will hear about it. And they will be too scared to do an evil thing like that again.

¹²The LORD your God is giving you towns to live in. But suppose you hear something bad about one of those towns. ¹³You hear that evil men have appeared among you. They've tried to get the people of their town to do something wrong. They've said, "Let's go and worship other gods." But you haven't known anything about those gods before. ¹⁴So you must question people. You must check the matter out carefully.

If it's true, an evil thing has really happened among you. It's something the LORD hates. ¹⁵Then you must certainly kill with your swords everyone who lives in that town. Destroy it completely. Wipe out its people and livestock. ¹⁶Gather all of the goods of that town into the middle of the main street. Burn the town completely. Burn up everything in it.

It's a whole burnt offering to the LORD your God. The town must remain a pile of stones forever. It must never be built again.

¹⁷Don't keep anything that should be destroyed. Then the LORD will turn away from his burning anger. He will show you mercy. He'll have deep concern for you. He'll increase your numbers. That's what he promised your people long ago. He took an oath when he made the promise.

¹⁸The LORD your God will do those things if you obey him. I'm giving you his commands today. And you must obey all of them. You must do what is right in his eyes.

FOOD THAT IS "CLEAN" AND FOOD THAT IS NOT

14 You are the children of the LORD your God. Don't cut yourselves to honor the dead. Don't shave the front of your heads to honor them.

²You are a holy nation. The LORD your God has set you apart for himself. He has chosen you to be his special treasure. He chose you out of all of the nations on the face of the earth.

³Don't eat anything the LORD hates. ⁴Here are the only animals you can eat.

You can eat oxen, sheep, goats, ⁵deer, gazelles, roe deer, wild goats, ibexes, antelope and mountain sheep.

⁶You can eat any animal that has hoofs that are separated completely in two. But it must also chew the cud. ⁷Some animals only chew the cud. Others only have hoofs that are completely separated in two. The camel, rabbit and rock badger chew the cud, but they don't have hoofs that are completely separated. So you can't eat them. They are not "clean" for you. ⁸Pigs aren't "clean" for you either. They have hoofs that are completely separated, but they don't chew the cud. So don't eat their meat. And don't touch their dead bodies.

⁹Many creatures live in water. You can eat all of the ones that have fins and scales. ¹⁰But don't eat anything that doesn't have fins and scales. It isn't "clean" for you.

¹¹You can eat any "clean" bird. ¹²But there are many birds you can't eat. They include eagles, vultures, and black vultures. ¹³They include red kites, black kites and all kinds of falcons. ¹⁴They include all kinds of ravens. ¹⁵They include horned owls, screech owls, gulls and all kinds of hawks. ¹⁶They include little owls, great owls, white owls ¹⁷and desert owls. They include ospreys and cormorants. ¹⁸They include storks and all kinds of herons. They also include hoopoes and bats.

¹⁹All insects that fly together in groups are "unclean" for you. So don't eat them. ²⁰But you can eat any creature that has wings and is "clean."

²¹If you find something that's already dead, don't eat it. You can give it to an outsider who is living in any of your towns. He can eat it. Or you can sell it to someone who is from another country. But you are a holy nation. The LORD your God has set you apart for himself.

Don't cook a young goat in its mother's milk.

GIVE A TENTH OF WHAT YOU PRODUCE

²²Be sure to set apart a tenth of everything your fields produce each year. ²³Here are the things you should

eat in the sight of the LORD your God. You should eat a tenth part of your grain, olive oil and fresh wine. You should also eat the male animals among your livestock that were born first to their mothers. Eat all of those things at the special place the LORD your God will choose. He will put his Name there. You will learn to have respect for him always.

²⁴But suppose the place the LORD will choose for his Name is too far away from you. And suppose your God has blessed you. And your tenth part is too heavy for you to carry. ²⁵Then sell it for silver. Take the silver with you. Go to the place the LORD your God will choose. ²⁶Use the silver to buy anything you like. It can be cattle or sheep. It can be any kind of wine. In fact, it can be anything else you wish. Then you and your family can eat there in the sight of the LORD your God. You can be filled with joy.

²⁷Don't forget to take care of the Levites who will live in your towns. They won't receive any part of the land as their share.

²⁸At the end of every three years, bring a tenth of everything you produce that year. Store it in your towns. ²⁹Then the Levites can come and eat. That's because they won't receive any part of the land as their share. The outsiders and widows who live in your towns can come. So can the children whose fathers have died. Everyone can have plenty to eat. Then the LORD your God will bless you in everything you do.

THE YEAR FOR FORGIVING PEOPLE WHAT THEY OWE

15 At the end of every seven years you must forgive people what they owe you. ²Have you made a loan to one of your own people? Then forgive what is owed to you. You can't require that person to pay you back. The LORD's

KIDS' QUESTiON
Why do people fight over money?

One of the biggest reasons is greed. Greedy people want more money than they need, and they want it so much that they may do nasty things to hold on to it. They may fight about it and do other hurtful things. They may be stingy and not share with the poor. God wants us to share freely and not fight over how much we have.

Always remember that people are more important than money. Talk over your money problems rather than fighting about them. If you cannot agree, let the other person win. It is better to let someone else have his or her way than to lose a friend to a fight over money.

checkout
Deuteronomy 15:7,8

Related verses:
Luke 12:15;
Colossians 3:5

time to forgive what is owed has been announced. ³You can require someone from another nation to pay you back. But you must forgive your own people what they owe you.

⁴There shouldn't be any poor people among you. The LORD will greatly bless you in the land he is giving you. You will take it over as your own. ⁵The LORD your God will bless you if you obey him completely. Be careful to follow all of the commands I'm giving you today.

⁶The LORD your God will bless you, just as he has promised. You will lend money to many nations. But you won't have to borrow from any of them. You will rule over many nations. But none of them will rule over you.

⁷Suppose there are poor people among you. And suppose they live in one of the towns in the land the LORD your God is giving you. Then don't be mean to them. They are poor. So don't hold back money from them. ⁸Instead, open your hands and lend them what they need. Do it freely.

⁹Be careful not to have an evil thought in your mind. Don't say to yourself, "The seventh year will soon be here. It's the year for forgiving people what they owe." If you think like that, you might treat your needy people badly. You might not give them anything. Then they might make their appeal to the LORD against you. And he will find you guilty of sin.

¹⁰So give freely to those who are needy. Open your hearts to them. Then the LORD your God will bless you in all of your work. He will bless you in everything you do. ¹¹There will always be poor people in the land. So I'm commanding you to give freely to those who are poor and needy in your land. Open your hands to them.

SET YOUR HEBREW SERVANTS FREE

¹²Suppose Hebrew men or women sell themselves to you. If they do, they will serve you for six years. Then in the seventh year you must let them go free.

¹³But when you set them free, don't send them away without anything to show for all of their work. ¹⁴Freely give them some animals from your flock. Also give them some of your grain and

How can we help someone who is poor if we don't have much money?

There are a lot of poor people in the world. It makes us sad to see poor people, and we wish we could help everybody. But what if we don't have very much money ourselves? What can we do then? There are lots of things we can do! We can help people in the neighborhood by working around their homes and giving them food. We can give our time to a local mission. We can give food to food pantries. We can give our used clothes and toys and furniture to groups that help the poor people in our cities.

checkout
Deuteronomy 15:11

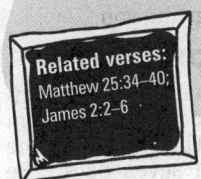

Related verses:
Matthew 25:34–40;
James 2:2–6

wine. The LORD your God has blessed you richly. Give to them as he has given to you. [15]Remember that you were slaves in Egypt. The LORD your God set you free. That's why I'm giving you this command today.

[16]But suppose your servant says to you, "I don't want to leave you." He loves you and your family. And you are taking good care of him. [17]Then take him to the door of your house. Poke a hole through his ear lobe into the doorpost. And he will become your servant for life. Do the same with your female servant.

[18]Don't think you are being cheated when you set your servants free. After all, they have served you for six years. The service of each of them has been worth twice as much as the service of a hired worker. And the LORD your God will bless you in everything you do.

MALE ANIMALS THAT ARE BORN FIRST TO THEIR MOTHERS

[19]Set apart to the LORD your God every male animal among your livestock that was born first to its mother. Don't put that kind of ox to work. Don't clip the wool from that kind of sheep. [20]Each year you and your family must eat them. Do it in the sight of the LORD your God at the place he will choose.

[21]Suppose an animal has something wrong with it. It might not be able to see or walk. Or it might have a bad flaw. Then you must not sacrifice it to the LORD your God. [22]You must eat it in your own towns. Those who are "clean" and those who are not can eat it. Eat it as if it were antelope or deer meat. [23]But you must not eat meat that still has blood in it. Pour the blood out on the ground like water.

THE PASSOVER FEAST

16 Celebrate the Passover Feast of the LORD your God in the month of Abib. In that month he brought you out of Egypt at night. [2]Sacrifice an animal from your flock or herd. It is the Passover sacrifice in honor of the LORD your God. Sacrifice

it at the special place the LORD will choose. He will put his Name there. [3]Don't eat the animal along with bread that is made with yeast. Instead, for seven days eat bread that is made without yeast. It's the bread that reminds you of how much you suffered. Remember that you left Egypt in a hurry. Remember it all the days of your life. Don't forget the day you left Egypt. [4]Don't keep any yeast anywhere in your land for seven days.

Don't let any of the meat you sacrifice on the evening of the first day be left over until the next morning. [5]You must not sacrifice the Passover animal in any town the LORD your God is giving you. [6]Sacrifice it only in the special place he will choose for his Name. Sacrifice it there in the evening when the sun goes down. Do it on the same day every year. Be sure it's the day you left Egypt. [7]Cook it and eat it. Do it at the place the LORD your God will choose. Then in the morning return to your tents.

[8]For six days eat bread that is made without yeast. On the seventh day come together for a service in honor of the LORD your God. Don't do any work.

THE FEAST OF WEEKS

[9]Count off seven weeks from the time you begin to cut your grain in the field. [10]Then celebrate the Feast of Weeks in honor of the LORD your God. Give anything you choose to give as an offering. Do it in keeping with the blessings the LORD has given you.

[11]Be filled with joy in the sight of the LORD your God. Be joyful at the special place he will choose for his Name. You, your children, and your male and female servants should be joyful. So should the Levites who are living in your towns. So should the outsiders and widows who are living among you. And so should the children whose fathers have died. [12]Remember that you were slaves in Egypt. Be careful to obey the rules I'm giving you.

THE FEAST OF BOOTHS

[13]Gather the grain from your threshing floors. Take the fresh wine from your winepresses. Then celebrate the Feast of Booths for seven days. [14]Be

filled with joy at your Feast. You, your children, and your male and female servants should be joyful. So should the Levites, the outsiders, and the widows who are living in your towns. And so should the children whose fathers have died.

¹⁵For seven days celebrate the Feast in honor of the LORD your God. Do it at the place he will choose. The LORD will bless you when you gather all of your crops. He'll bless you in everything you do. And you will be full of joy.

¹⁶All of your men must appear in front of the LORD your God at the holy tent. They must go to the place he will choose. They must do it three times a year. They must go there to celebrate the Feast of Unleavened Bread, the Feast of Weeks and the Feast of Booths.

No man should appear in front of the LORD without bringing something with him. ¹⁷Each of you must bring a gift. Do it in keeping with the way the LORD your God has blessed you.

APPOINT JUDGES AND OFFICIALS

¹⁸Appoint judges and officials for each of your tribes. Do it in every town the LORD your God is giving you. They must judge the people fairly. ¹⁹Do what is right. Treat everyone the same. Don't take money from people who want special favors. It makes those who are wise close their eyes to the truth. It twists the words of those who do what is right. ²⁰Follow only what is right. If you do, you will live. You will take over the land the LORD your God is giving you.

DON'T WORSHIP OTHER GODS

²¹Don't set up a wooden pole that is used to worship the goddess Asherah. Don't set it up beside the altar you build to worship the LORD your God. ²²Don't set up a sacred stone to honor another god. The LORD your God hates Asherah poles and sacred stones.

17 Suppose an ox or sheep has anything at all wrong with it. Then don't sacrifice it to the LORD your God. He hates it.

²Someone who is living among you might do what is evil in the sight of the LORD your God. It might happen in one of the towns the LORD is giving you. That person is breaking the LORD's covenant. ³The person might have worshiped or bowed down to other gods. That person might have bowed down to the sun or moon or stars in the sky. I have commanded you not to do those things. ⁴When you hear that people have done something like that, check the matter out carefully. If it's true, an evil thing has been done in Israel. It's something the LORD hates.

⁵So take the person who has done that evil thing to your city gate. Put that person to death with stones. ⁶The witness of two or three people is required to put someone to death. No one can be put to death because of what only one witness says. It needs the witness of two or three people. ⁷The witnesses must throw the first stones. Then the rest of the people must also throw stones. Get rid of that evil person.

LAW COURTS

⁸People will bring their cases to your courts. But some cases will be too hard for you to judge. They might be about murders, attacks or other crimes. Then take those hard cases to the place the LORD your God will choose. ⁹Go to a priest, who is a Levite. And go to the judge who is in office at that time. Ask them for their decision. They will give it to you.

¹⁰They'll hand down their decisions at the place the LORD will choose. You must do what they decide. Be careful to do everything they direct you to do. ¹¹Act in keeping with the laws they teach you. Accept the decisions they give you. Don't turn away from what they tell you. Don't turn to the right or the left.

¹²Someone might make fun of the judge. Or he might make fun of the priest who serves the LORD your God at the place he will choose. If the man does that, he must be put to death. Remove that evil person from Israel. ¹³All of the people of Israel will hear about it. And they will be afraid to make fun of a judge or priest again.

APPOINT THE KING THE LORD CHOOSES

¹⁴You will enter the land the LORD your God is giving you. You will take it as your own. You will settle down in it. When you do, you will say, "Let's appoint a king over us, just like all of the nations around us." ¹⁵When that happens, make sure you appoint over you the king the LORD your God chooses. He must be from among your own people. Don't appoint over you someone from another country. Don't choose anyone who isn't from one of the tribes of Israel.

¹⁶The king must not get large numbers of horses for himself. He must not make the people return to Egypt to get more horses. The LORD has told you, "You must not go back there again."

¹⁷The king must not have a lot of wives. If he does, he will be led down the wrong path. He must not store up large amounts of silver and gold.

¹⁸When he sits on the throne of his kingdom, he must make himself a copy of the law I'm teaching you. He must write it on a scroll. He must copy it from the scroll of a priest, who is a Levite.

¹⁹The king must keep the scroll close to him at all times. He must read it all the days of his life. Then he can learn to have respect for the LORD his God. He can carefully follow all of the words of that law and those rules. ²⁰He won't think of himself as being better than his people are. He won't turn away from the law. He won't turn to the right or the left. Then he and his sons after him will rule over his kingdom in Israel for a long time.

OFFERINGS FOR PRIESTS AND LEVITES

18 The priests, who are Levites, won't receive any part of the land of Israel. That also applies to the whole tribe of Levi. They will eat the offerings that are made to the LORD with fire. That will be their share. ²They won't have any part of the land the LORD gave the other tribes in Israel. The LORD himself is their share, just as he promised them.

³Anyone who sacrifices a bull or a sheep owes a share of it to the priests. Their share is the shoulder, jaws and inside parts. ⁴You must give the priests the first share of the harvest of your grain, olive oil and fresh wine. You must also give them the first wool you clip from your sheep. ⁵The LORD your God has chosen the Levites and their sons after them to serve him in his name always. He hasn't chosen priests from any of your other tribes.

⁶Sometimes a Levite will move from the town in Israel where he's living. And he will come to the place the LORD will choose. He'll do it because he really wants to. ⁷Then he can serve in the name of the LORD his God. He'll be like all of the other Levites who serve the LORD there. ⁸He must have an equal share of the good things they have. That applies even if he has already received money by selling things his family owned.

PRACTICES THE LORD HATES

⁹You will enter the land the LORD your God is giving you. When you do, don't copy the practices of the nations that are there. The LORD hates those practices.

¹⁰Here are things you must not do. Don't sacrifice your children in the fire to other gods. Don't practice any kind of evil magic at all. Don't use magic to try to explain the meaning of warnings in the sky or of any other signs. Don't take part in worshiping evil powers. ¹¹Don't put a spell on anyone. Don't get messages from those who have died. Don't talk to the spirits of the dead. Don't get advice from the dead.

¹²The LORD your God hates it when anyone does those things. The nations that are in the land he's giving you practice the things he hates. So he will drive out those nations to make room for you. ¹³You must be without blame in the sight of the LORD your God.

THE PROPHET OF THE LORD

¹⁴You will take over the nations that are in the land the LORD is giving you. They listen to those who practice all kinds of evil magic. But you belong to the LORD your God. He says you must not do those things.

¹⁵The LORD your God will raise up for you a prophet like me. He will be one of your own people. You must listen to him. ¹⁶At Mount Horeb you asked the LORD your God for a prophet. You asked him on the day you gathered together. You said, "We don't want to hear the voice of the LORD our God. We don't want to see this great fire anymore. If we do, we'll die."

¹⁷The LORD said to me, "What they are saying is good. ¹⁸I will raise up for them a prophet like you. He will be one of their own people. I will put my words in his mouth. He will tell them everything I command him to say.

¹⁹"The prophet will speak in my name. But someone might not listen to what I say through the prophet. Then that person will be accountable to me.

²⁰"But suppose a prophet dares to speak in my name something I have not commanded him to say. Or he speaks in the name of other gods. Then that prophet must be put to death."

²¹You will say to yourselves, "How can we know when a message hasn't been spoken by the LORD?" ²²Sometimes a prophet will announce something in the name of the LORD. And it won't take place or come true. Then that's a message the LORD hasn't told him to speak. That prophet has dared to speak on his own authority. So don't be afraid of him or what he says.

CITIES TO GO TO FOR SAFETY

19 The LORD your God will destroy the nations whose land he is giving you. You will drive them out. And you will settle down in their towns and houses.

²When you do, set apart for yourselves three cities in the land. It's the land the LORD your God is giving you to take as your own. ³Build roads to those cities and separate the land into three parts. Then anyone who kills another person can run to one of the cities for safety. They are in the land the LORD your God is giving you as your own.

Were prophets the people in Bible days who made lots of money?

Many words sound alike but have different meanings. The word *profit* means the money you make when you sell something. But the word *prophet* means a person who talked for God in Bible times. A prophet spoke God's messages and told the people to obey God. People did not become prophets to get rich or famous. Most of the time prophets were not popular. Some were put in prison. Some were even killed. Moses, Elijah, Isaiah, Jeremiah and Daniel were all prophets of God. And there were many others.

checkout Deuteronomy 18:18

Related verses:
Deuteronomy
18:15–22;
Hebrews 1:1

⁴Here is the rule about a person who kills someone. That person can run to one of those cities for safety. The rule applies to all those who kill a neighbor they didn't hate and didn't mean to kill.

⁵For example, suppose a man goes into a forest with his neighbor to cut wood. When he swings his ax to chop down a tree, the head of the ax flies off. And it hits his neighbor and kills him. Then that man can run to one of those cities and save his life.

⁶If he doesn't go to one of those cities, the dead man's nearest male relative might become very angry. He might chase the man. If the city is too far away, he might catch him and kill him. But he isn't worthy of death, because he didn't hate his neighbor. ⁷That's why I command you to set apart for yourselves three cities.

⁸The LORD your God will increase the size of your territory. He took an oath and promised your fathers he would do it. He will give you the whole land he promised them. ⁹But he'll do it only if you are careful to obey all of the laws I'm commanding you today. I'm commanding you to love the LORD your God. I want you to live always as he wants you to live.

When he gives you additional land, you must set apart three more cities. ¹⁰Do it so the blood of those who aren't guilty of murder won't be spilled in your land. It's the land the LORD your God is giving you as your own.

¹¹But suppose a man hates his neighbor. So he hides and waits for him. Then he attacks him and kills him. And he runs to one of those cities for safety. ¹²If he does, the elders of his own town must send for him. He must be brought back from the city and handed over to the dead man's nearest male relative. The relative will kill him.

¹³Don't feel sorry for him. He has killed someone who hadn't done anything wrong. Crimes like that must be punished in Israel. Then things will go well with you.

¹⁴Don't move your neighbor's boundary stone. It was set up by people who lived there before you. It marks the border of a field in the land

you will receive as your own. The LORD your God is giving you that land. You will take it over.

WITNESSES

¹⁵Suppose someone is charged with committing a crime of any kind. Then one witness won't be enough to prove he is guilty. Every matter must be proved by the words of two or three witnesses.

¹⁶Suppose a witness who tells lies goes to court and brings charges against someone. The witness says that person committed a crime. ¹⁷Then the two people in the case must stand in front of the LORD. They must stand in front of the priests and the judges who are in office at that time. ¹⁸The judges must check out the matter carefully. And suppose the witness is proved to be lying. Then he has given false witness against another Israelite.

¹⁹So do to the lying witness what he tried to do to the other person. Get rid of that evil person. ²⁰The rest of the people will hear about it. And they will be afraid. They won't allow such an evil thing to be done among them again.

²¹Don't feel sorry for that evil person. A life must be taken for a life. An eye must be put out for an eye. A tooth must be knocked out for a tooth. A hand must be cut off for a hand and a foot for a foot.

GOING TO WAR

20 When you go to war against your enemies, you might see that they have horses and chariots. They might even have an army that is stronger than yours. But don't be afraid of them. The LORD your God will be with you. After all, he brought you up out of Egypt.

²Just before you go into battle, the priest will come forward. He'll speak to the army. ³He'll say, "Men of Israel, listen to me. Today you are going into battle against your enemies. Don't be scared. Don't be afraid. Don't panic. Don't be terrified by them. ⁴The LORD your God is going with you. He'll fight for you. He'll help you win the battle over your enemies."

⁵The officers will speak to the army.

They will say, "Has anyone built a new house and not started to live in it? Let him go home. If he doesn't, he might die in battle. Then someone else will live in his house. ⁶Has anyone planted a vineyard and not started to enjoy it? Let him go home. If he doesn't, he might die in battle. Then someone else will enjoy his vineyard. ⁷Has anyone promised to get married to a woman but hasn't done it yet? Let him go home. If he doesn't, he might die in battle. Then someone else will marry her." ⁸The officers will continue, "Is any man afraid? Is anyone scared? Let him go home. Then the other men won't lose hope too."

⁹The officers will finish speaking to the army. When they do, they'll appoint commanders over it.

¹⁰Suppose you march up to attack a city. Before you attack it, offer peace to its people. ¹¹Suppose they accept your offer and open their gates. Then force all of the people in the city to be your slaves. They will have to work for you.

¹²But suppose they refuse your offer of peace and prepare for battle. Then surround that city. Get ready to attack it. ¹³The LORD your God will hand it over to you. When he does, kill all of the men with your swords.

¹⁴But you can take the women and children for yourselves. You can also take the livestock and everything else in the city. What you have captured from your enemies you can use for yourselves. The LORD your God has given it to you.

¹⁵That's how you must treat all of the cities that are far away from you. Those cities don't belong to the nations that are nearby.

¹⁶But what about the cities the LORD your God is giving you as your own? Kill everything in those cities that breathes. ¹⁷Completely destroy them. Wipe out the Hittites, Amorites, Canaanites, Perizzites, Hivites and Jebusites. That's what the LORD your God commanded you to do.

¹⁸If you don't destroy them, they'll teach you to follow all of the things the LORD hates. He hates the way they worship their gods. If you do those things, you will sin against the LORD your God.

¹⁹Suppose you surround a city and get ready to attack it. And suppose you fight against it for a long time in order to capture it. Then don't chop its trees down and destroy them. You can eat their fruit. So don't cut them down. The trees of the field aren't people. So why should you attack them?

²⁰But you can cut down trees that you know aren't fruit trees. You can build war machines out of their wood. You can use them until you capture the city you are fighting against.

WHAT TO DO WHEN YOU DON'T KNOW WHO KILLED SOMEONE

21 Suppose you find someone who has been killed. The body is lying in a field in the land the LORD your God is giving you to take as your own. But no one knows who the killer was. ²Then your elders and judges will go out and measure how far it is from the body to the nearby towns.

³The elders from the town that is nearest to the body will get a young cow. It must never have been used for work. It must never have pulled a load. ⁴The elders must lead it down into a valley. The valley must not have been farmed. There must be a stream flowing through it. There in the valley the elders must break the cow's neck.

⁵The priests, who are sons of Levi, will step forward. The LORD your God has chosen them to serve him. He wants them to bless the people in his name. He wants them to decide all cases that have to do with people arguing and attacking others.

⁶Then all of the elders from the town that is nearest to the body will wash their hands. They will wash them over the young cow whose neck they broke in the valley. ⁷They'll say to the LORD, "We didn't kill that person. We didn't see it happen. ⁸Accept this payment for the sin of your people Israel. LORD, you have set your people free. Don't hold them guilty for spilling the blood of someone who hasn't done anything wrong." That will pay for the death of that person.

⁹So you will get rid of the guilt of kill-

ing someone who didn't do anything wrong. That's because you have done what is right in the LORD's eyes.

GETTING MARRIED TO A WOMAN WHO IS YOUR PRISONER

¹⁰Suppose you go to war against your enemies. And the LORD your God hands them over to you and you take them as prisoners. ¹¹Then you notice a beautiful woman among them. If you like her, you can get married to her.

¹²Bring her home. Have her shave her head. Have her cut her nails. ¹³Have her throw away the clothes she was wearing when she was captured. Let her live in your house and sob over her parents for a full month. Then you can go to her and be her husband. And she will be your wife.

¹⁴But suppose you aren't pleased with her. Then let her go where she wants to. You must not sell her. You must not treat her as a slave. You have already brought shame on her.

THE RIGHTS OF THE OLDEST SON

¹⁵Suppose a man has two wives. He loves one but not the other. And both of them have sons by him. But the oldest son is the son of the wife the man doesn't love. ¹⁶Someday he'll leave his property to his sons. When he does, he must not give the rights of the oldest son to the son of the wife he loves. He must give those rights to his oldest son. He must do it even though his oldest son is the son of the wife he doesn't love.

¹⁷He must recognize the full rights of the oldest son, even though that son is the son of the wife he doesn't love. He must give that son a double share of everything he has. That son is the first sign of his father's strength. So the rights of the oldest son belong to him.

If we are running out of trees, why doesn't God just make more?

God *is* making more trees. But it is up to us not to use them faster than he replaces them. Some trees are cut down and used for wood and paper. Other trees are cut down to make room for houses, shopping centers, roads and other construction projects. Some people say that we are running out of trees. God created trees with the ability to make new trees. But it takes many years for a tree to grow to be big and tall. We should be careful not to cut down more trees than can be replaced by the seeds. God has given us the job of taking care of the earth. That includes using the trees well and planting new ones.

checkout

Deuteronomy 20:19

Related verse:
Genesis 1:29

A STUBBORN SON

¹⁸Suppose someone has a very stubborn son. He doesn't obey his father and mother. And he won't listen to them when they try to correct him. ¹⁹Then his parents will take hold of him and bring him to the elders at the gate of his town. ²⁰They will say to the elders, "This son of ours is very stubborn. He won't obey us. He wastes his money. He's always getting drunk." ²¹Then all of the people in his town will put him to death by throwing stones at him. Get rid of that evil person. All of the people of Israel will hear about it. And they will be afraid to disobey their parents.

SEVERAL OTHER LAWS

²²Suppose a man is put to death for a crime that is worthy of death. And a pole is stuck through his body and set up where people can see it. ²³Then you must not leave the body on the pole all night. Make sure you bury it that same day.

Everyone who is hung on a pole is under God's curse. You must not make the land "unclean." The LORD your God is giving it to you as your own.

22 Suppose you see your neighbor's ox or sheep wandering away. Then don't act as if you didn't see it. Instead, make sure you take it back to him.

²Your neighbor might not live near you. Or you might not know who he is. Then take the animal home with you. Keep it until he comes looking for it. Then give it back.

³Do the same thing if you find his donkey, coat or anything he loses. Don't act as if you didn't see it.

⁴Suppose you see your neighbor's donkey or ox that has fallen down on the road. Then don't act as if you didn't see it. Help him get it up on its feet again.

⁵A woman must not wear men's clothes. And a man must not wear women's clothes. The LORD your God hates it when anyone does that.

⁶Suppose you happen to find a bird's nest beside the road. It might be in a tree or on the ground. And suppose the mother bird is sitting on her little birds or on the eggs. Then don't take the mother along with the little ones. ⁷You can take the little ones. But make sure you let the mother go. Then things will go well with you. You will live for a long time.

⁸If you build a new house, put a low wall around the edge of your roof. Then you won't be held accountable if someone falls off your roof and dies.

KIDS' QUESTion

What if you find something that doesn't belong to you and you can't find who it belongs to. Is that stealing?

Try hard to find the owner if the thing you found is valuable. You do not need to put an ad in the paper to find the person who lost a penny or nickel. But an album of wedding pictures, a box of diamonds or a wallet is worth a great deal. You should try to find the owner of such valuable items. Often your mom or dad will know how to look for the owner. If you find something at school, you can take it to the "lost and found." Never use "I just found it and can't see anybody around" as an excuse to call something yours.

Related verse:
Philippians 2:4

checkout Deuteronomy 22:1-3

⁹Don't plant two kinds of seeds in your vineyard. If you do, the crops you grow there will be polluted. Your grapes will also be polluted.

¹⁰Don't let an ox and a donkey pull the same plow together.

¹¹Don't wear clothes made of wool and linen that are woven together.

¹²Make tassels on the four corners of the coat you wear.

BREAKING MARRIAGE LAWS

¹³Suppose a man gets married to a woman and makes love to her. But then he doesn't like her. ¹⁴So he tells lies about her and says she's a bad woman. He says, "I got married to this woman. But then I made love to her, I discovered she wasn't a virgin." ¹⁵Then the woman's parents must bring proof that she was a virgin. They must give the proof to the elders at the gate of the town.

¹⁶The woman's father will speak to the elders. He'll say, "I gave my daughter to this man to be his wife. But he doesn't like her. ¹⁷So now he has told lies about her. He has said, 'I discovered that your daughter wasn't a virgin.' But here's the proof that my daughter was a virgin." Then her parents will show the elders of the town the cloth that has her blood on it.

¹⁸The elders will punish the man. ¹⁹They'll make him weigh out two and a half pounds of silver. They'll give it to the woman's father. That's because the man has said an Israelite virgin is a bad woman. She will continue to be his wife. He must not divorce her as long as he lives.

²⁰But suppose the charge is true. And there isn't any proof that the woman was a virgin. ²¹Then she must be brought to the door of her father's house. There the people of her town will put her to death by throwing stones at her. She has done a very terrible thing in Israel. She has had sex before she got married. Get rid of that evil person.

²²Suppose a man is seen having sex with another man's wife. Then the man and the woman must both die. Get rid of those evil people.

²³Suppose a man happens to see a virgin in a town. And she has promised to get married to another man. But the man who happens to see her has sex with her. ²⁴Then you must take both of them to the gate of that town. You must put them to death by throwing stones at them. You must kill the woman because she was in a town and didn't scream for help. And you must kill the man because he had sex with another man's wife. Get rid of those evil people.

²⁵But suppose a man happens to see a woman out in the country. And she has promised to marry another man. But the man who happens to see her rapes her. Then only the man who has done that will die. ²⁶Don't do anything to the woman. She hasn't committed a sin that is worthy of death. That case is like the case of someone who attacks and murders his neighbor. ²⁷The man found the woman out in the country. And she screamed. But there wasn't anyone around who could save her.

²⁸Suppose a man happens to see a virgin who hasn't promised to marry another man. And the man who happens to see her rapes her. But someone discovers them. ²⁹Then the man must weigh out 20 ounces of silver. He must give it to the woman's father. The man must marry the woman, because he raped her. And he can never divorce her as long as he lives.

³⁰A man must not get married to his stepmother. He must not bring shame on his father by having sex with her.

WHO CAN WORSHIP WITH THE LORD'S PEOPLE?

23 No man whose sex organs have been crushed or cut can join in worship with the LORD's people.

²No one who was born to a woman who wasn't married can join in worship with the LORD's people. That also applies to the person's children for all time to come.

³The people of Ammon and Moab can't join in worship with the LORD's people. That also applies to their children after them for all time to come. ⁴The Ammonites and Moabites didn't come to meet you with food and water on your way out of Egypt. They even hired Balaam from Pethor in Aram

Naharaim to call down a curse on you. Balaam was the son of Beor. [5]The LORD your God wouldn't listen to Balaam. Instead, he turned the curse into a blessing for you. He did it because he loves you. [6]So don't make a peace treaty with the Ammonites and Moabites as long as you live.

[7]Don't hate the people of Edom. They are your relatives. Don't hate the people of Egypt. After all, you lived as outsiders in their country. [8]The great-grandchildren of the Edomites and Egyptians can join in worship with the LORD's people.

KEEP THE CAMP OF THE SOLDIERS PURE AND CLEAN

[9]There will be times when you are at war with your enemies. And your soldiers will be in camp. Then keep away from anything that isn't pure and clean. [10]Suppose semen flows from the body of one of your soldiers during the night. Then that will make him "unclean." He must go outside the camp and stay there. [11]But as evening approaches, he must wash himself. When the sun goes down, he can return to the camp.

[12]Choose a place outside the camp where you can go to the toilet. [13]Keep a shovel among your tools. When you go to the toilet, dig a hole. Then cover up your waste.

[14]The LORD your God walks around in your camp. He's there to keep you safe. He's also there to hand your enemies over to you. So your camp must be holy. Then he won't see anything among you that is shameful. He won't turn away from you.

SEVERAL OTHER LAWS

[15]If a slave comes to you for safety, don't hand him over to his master. [16]Let him live among you anywhere he wants to. Let him live in any town he chooses. Don't crush him.

[17]A man or woman in Israel must not become a temple prostitute. [18]The LORD your God hates the money that men and women get for being prostitutes. So don't take that money into the house of the LORD to pay what you promised to give.

[19]Don't charge your own people any interest. Don't charge them when they borrow money, food or anything else. [20]You can charge interest to people from another country. But don't charge your own people. Then the LORD your God will bless you in everything you do. He will bless you in the land you are entering to take as your own.

[21]Don't put off giving to the LORD your God everything you promise him. He will certainly require it from you. And you will be guilty of committing a sin. [22]But if you don't make a promise, you won't be guilty. [23]Make sure you do what you promised to do. With your own mouth you made the promise to the LORD your God. No one forced you to do it.

[24]When you enter your neighbor's vineyard, you can eat all of the grapes you want. But don't put any of them in your basket. [25]When you enter your neighbor's field, you can pick heads of grain. But don't cut down his standing grain.

24 Suppose a man gets married to a woman. But later he decides he doesn't like her. He finds something shameful about her. So he gives her a letter of divorce and sends her away from his house. [2]Then after she leaves his house she becomes another man's wife. [3]But her second husband doesn't like her either. So he gives her a letter of divorce and sends her away from his house. Or perhaps he dies. [4]Then her first husband isn't allowed to marry her again. The LORD would hate that. When her first husband divorced her, she became "unclean." Don't bring sin on the land the LORD your God is giving you as your own.

[5]Suppose a man has just gotten married. Then don't send him into battle. Don't give him any other duty either. He's free to stay home for one year. He needs time to make his new wife happy.

[6]Someone might borrow money from you and give you two millstones to keep until you are paid back. Don't keep them. Don't even keep the upper one. That person depends on the millstones to make a living.

[7]Suppose a man is caught kidnapping another Israelite. And he sells or treats that person as a slave. Then the kidnapper must die. Get rid of that evil person.

[8]What about skin diseases? Be very careful to do exactly what the priests, who are Levites, tell you to do. You must be careful to follow the commands I've given them. [9]Remember what the LORD your God did to Miriam on your way out of Egypt.

[10]Suppose your neighbor borrows something from you. And he offers you something to keep until you get paid back. Then don't go into his house to get it. [11]Stay outside. Let the man bring it out to you.

[12]He might be poor. You might be given his coat to keep until you get paid back. Don't go to sleep while you still have it. [13]Return it before the sun goes down. He needs it to sleep in and will thank you for returning it. The LORD your God will see it and know that you have done the right thing.

[14]Don't take advantage of any hired worker who is poor and needy. That applies to your own people. It also applies to outsiders who are living in one of your towns. [15]Give them their pay every day. They are poor and are counting on it. If you don't pay them, they might cry out to the LORD against you. Then you will be guilty of committing a sin.

[16]Parents must not be put to death because of what their children do. And children must not be put to death because of what their parents do. People must die because of their own sins.

[17]Do what is right and fair for outsiders and for children whose fathers have died. Suppose a widow borrows something from you. And she offers to give you her coat until she pays you back. Don't take it.

[18]Remember that you were slaves in Egypt. Remember that the LORD your God set you free from there. That's why I'm commanding you to do those things.

[19]When you are gathering crops in your field, you might leave some grain behind by mistake. Don't go back to get it. Leave it for outsiders and widows. Leave it for children whose fa-

thers have died. Then the LORD your God will bless you in everything you do.

[20]When you knock olives off your trees, don't go back over the branches a second time. Leave what remains for outsiders and widows. Leave it for children whose fathers have died. [21]When you pick grapes in your vineyard, don't go back over the vines a second time. Leave what remains for outsiders and widows. Leave it for children whose fathers have died.

[22]Remember that you were slaves in Egypt. That's why I'm commanding you to do those things.

25 Suppose two men don't agree about something. Then they must take their case to court. The judges will decide the case. They will let the one who isn't guilty go free. And they will punish the one who is guilty.

[2]The guilty one might have done something that's worthy of a beating. Then the judge will make him lie down and be beaten with a whip right there in court. The number of strokes should fit the crime. [3]But the judge must not give the guilty man more than 40 strokes. If more than that are used, you will look down on your Israelite neighbor.

[4]Don't stop an ox from eating while you use it to separate grain from straw.

[5]Suppose two brothers are living near each other. And one of them dies without having a son. Then his widow must not get married to anyone outside the family. Her husband's brother should marry her. That's what a brother-in-law is supposed to do. [6]Her first baby boy will be named after her first husband. Then the dead man's name will not be wiped out in Israel.

[7]But suppose the man doesn't want to get married to his brother's wife. Then she will go to the elders at the gate of the town. She will say, "My husband's brother refuses to keep his brother's name alive in Israel. He won't do for me what a brother-in-law is supposed to do."

[8]Then the elders in his town will send for him. They will talk to him. But he still might say, "I don't want to marry her." [9]Then his brother's widow

will go up to him in front of the elders. She'll pull one of his sandals off his foot. She'll spit in his face. And she'll say, "That's what we do to a man who won't build up his brother's family line." [10]That man's family line will be known in Israel as The Family of the Man Whose Sandal Was Pulled Off.

[11]Suppose two men are fighting. And the wife of one of them comes to save her husband from his attacker. So she reaches out and grabs hold of his sex organs. [12]Then you must cut off her hand. Don't feel sorry for her.

[13]Don't have two different scales. You must not have one that weighs things heavier than they really are and another that weighs them lighter than they are. [14]And don't have two different sets of measures. You must not have one set that measures things larger than they really are and another that measures them smaller than they are. [15]You must use weights and measures that are honest and exact. Then you will live a long time in the land the LORD your God is giving you. [16]He hates anyone who cheats.

[17]Remember what the Amalekites did to you on your way out of Egypt.

[18]You were tired and worn out. They met you on your journey. They attacked everyone who was lagging behind. They didn't have any respect for God. [19]The LORD your God will give you peace and rest from all of the enemies who are around you. He'll do it in the land he's giving you to take over as your very own. Then you will wipe out the memory of the Amalekites from the earth. Don't forget to do it!

GIVE THE LORD HIS SHARE

26 You will enter the land the LORD your God is giving you as your own. You will take it over. You will settle down in it. [2]When you do, get some of the first share of everything your soil produces. Put it in a basket. It's from the land the LORD your God is giving you. Take your gifts and go to the special place he will choose. He will put his Name there.

[3]Speak to the priest who is in office at that time. Tell him, "I announce today to the LORD your God that I have come to this land. It's the land he promised with an oath to our fathers to give us." [4]The priest will take the

What's so bad about cheating in sports?

Sometimes it seems as though winning a game is the most important thing in the world. We forget that it is only a game. We let winning become so important that we will cheat to win. But nothing is so important that it should make us cheat. God wants us to be honest, truthful and fair in *all* that we do. Remember that we play sports to improve our skills and health. Sports help us learn about teamwork and how to win and lose with grace. We should do our best, play fair, play clean and enjoy the game whenever we play any sport. That is much more important than winning or losing.

checkout
Deuteronomy 25:16

Related verse:
Mark 10:19

basket from you. He'll set it down in front of the altar of the LORD your God.

⁵Then you will speak while the LORD is listening. You will say, "My father Jacob was a wanderer from the land of Aram. He went down into Egypt with a few people. He lived there and became the father of a great nation. It had huge numbers of people.

⁶"But the people of Egypt treated us badly. They made us suffer. They made us work very hard. ⁷Then we cried out to the LORD. He is the God of our people who lived long ago. He heard our voice. He saw how much we were suffering. The Egyptians were crushing us. They were making us work very hard.

⁸"So the LORD reached out his mighty hand and powerful arm and brought us out of Egypt. He did great and wonderful things. He did miraculous signs and wonders. ⁹He brought us to this place. He gave us this land. It's a land that has plenty of milk and honey.

¹⁰"Now, LORD, I'm bringing you the first share of crops from the soil. After all, you have given them to me." Place the basket in front of the LORD your God. Bow down to him.

¹¹You and the Levites and the outsiders among you will be full of joy. You will enjoy all of the good things the LORD your God has given to you and your family.

¹²You will set apart a tenth of everything you produce in the third year. That's the year for giving the tenth to people who have special needs. You will give it to the Levites, outsiders and widows. You will also give it to children whose fathers have died. Then all of them will have plenty to eat in your towns.

¹³Speak to the LORD your God. Say to him, "I have taken your sacred share from my house. I have given it to the Levites, outsiders and widows. I have also given it to children whose fathers have died. I've done everything you commanded me to do. I haven't turned away from your commands. I haven't forgotten any of them. ¹⁴I haven't eaten any part of your sacred share while I was sobbing over someone who had died. I haven't taken any

of it from my house while I was 'unclean.' And I haven't offered any of it to the dead. LORD my God, I've obeyed you. I've done everything you commanded me to do.

¹⁵"Look down from the holy place where you live in heaven. Bless your people Israel. Bless the land you have given us. It's the land you promised with an oath to give to our fathers. It's a land that has plenty of milk and honey."

FOLLOW THE LORD'S COMMANDS

¹⁶This very day the LORD your God commands you to follow all of those rules and laws. Be careful to obey them with all your heart and with all your soul.

¹⁷Today you have announced that the LORD is your God. You have said you would live exactly as he wants you to live. You have agreed to keep his rules, commands and laws. And you have said you would obey him.

¹⁸Today the LORD has announced that you are his people. He has said that you are his special treasure. He promised that you would be. He has told you to keep all of his commands. ¹⁹He has announced that he will make you famous. He'll give you more praise and honor than all of the other nations he has made. And he has said that you will be a holy nation. The LORD your God has set you apart for himself. That's exactly what he promised to do.

THE ALTAR ON MOUNT EBAL

27 The elders of Israel and I gave commands to the people. We said, "Obey all of the commands we're giving you today.

²"You will go across the Jordan River. You will enter the land the LORD your God is giving you. When you do, set up some large stones. Put a coat of plaster on them. ³Write all of the words of this law on them. Do it when you have crossed over into the land the LORD your God is giving you. It's a land that has plenty of milk and honey. The LORD is the God of your fathers. He promised you that you would enter

the land. ⁴After you have gone across the Jordan, set up those stones on Mount Ebal. Put a coat of plaster on them. We're commanding you today to do that.

⁵"Build an altar there to honor the LORD your God. Make it out of stones. Don't use any iron tool on them. ⁶Use stones you find in the fields to build his altar. Then offer burnt offerings on it to the LORD your God. ⁷Sacrifice friendship offerings there. Eat them and be filled with joy in the sight of the LORD your God.

⁸"You must write all of the words of this law on the stones you have set up. Write the words very clearly."

CURSES FOR NOT OBEYING THE LORD

⁹Then the priests, who are Levites, and I spoke to all of the people of Israel. We said, "Israel, be quiet! Listen! You have now become the people of the LORD your God. ¹⁰Obey him. Follow his commands and rules that we're giving you today."

¹¹Here are the commands I gave the people that very day.

¹²You will go across the Jordan River. When you do, I want six tribes to stand on Mount Gerizim to bless the people. Those tribes are Simeon, Levi, Judah, Issachar, Joseph and Benjamin. ¹³I want the other six tribes to stand on Mount Ebal to announce some curses. Those tribes are Reuben, Gad, Asher, Zebulun, Dan and Naphtali.

¹⁴The Levites will speak to all of the people of Israel in a loud voice. They will say,

¹⁵"May any man who makes a wooden or metal statue of a god and sets it up in secret be under the LORD's curse. That statue is made by a skilled worker. And the LORD hates it."

Then all of the people will say, "Amen!"

¹⁶"May anyone who brings shame on his father or mother be under the LORD's curse."

Then all of the people will say, "Amen!"

¹⁷"May anyone who moves his neighbor's boundary stone be under the LORD's curse."

Then all of the people will say, "Amen!"

¹⁸"May anyone who leads blind people down the wrong road be under the LORD's curse."

Then all of the people will say, "Amen!"

¹⁹"May anyone who isn't fair in the way he treats outsiders, widows, and children whose fathers have died be under the LORD's curse."

Then all of the people will say, "Amen!"

²⁰"May any man who has sex with his stepmother be under the LORD's curse. That man brings shame on his father by doing that."

Then all of the people will say, "Amen!"

²¹"May anyone who has sex with animals be under the LORD's curse."

Then all of the people will say, "Amen!"

²²"May any man who has sex with his sister be under the LORD's curse. It doesn't matter whether she is his full sister or his half sister."

Then all of the people will say, "Amen!"

²³"May any man who has sex with his mother-in-law be under the LORD's curse."

Then all of the people will say, "Amen!"

²⁴"May anyone who kills his neighbor secretly be under the LORD's curse."

Then all of the people will say, "Amen!"

²⁵"May anyone who accepts money to kill someone who isn't guilty of doing anything wrong be under the LORD's curse."

Then all of the people will say, "Amen!"

²⁶"May anyone who doesn't honor the words of this law by obeying them be under the LORD's curse."

Then all of the people will say, "Amen!"

BLESSINGS FOR OBEYING THE LORD

28 Make sure you obey the LORD your God completely. Be careful to follow all of his commands. I'm giving them to you today. If you do those things, the LORD will honor you more than all of the other nations on earth. ²If you obey the LORD your God, here are the blessings that will come to you and remain with you.

³You will be blessed in the cities. You will be blessed out in the country.

⁴Your children will be blessed. Your crops will be blessed. The young animals among your livestock will be blessed. That includes your calves and lambs.

⁵Your baskets and bread pans will be blessed.

⁶You will be blessed no matter where you go.

⁷Enemies will rise up against you. But the LORD will help you win the battle over them. They will come at you from one direction. But they'll run away from you in seven directions.

⁸The LORD your God will bless your barns with plenty of grain and other food. He will bless everything you do. He'll bless you in the land he's giving you.

⁹The LORD your God will make you his holy people. He will set you apart for himself. He took an oath and promised to do that. He promised to do it if you would keep his commands and live exactly as he wants you to live. ¹⁰All of the nations on earth will see that you belong to the LORD. And they will be afraid of you.

¹¹The LORD will give you more than you need. You will have many children. Your livestock will have many little ones. Your crops will do very well. All of that will happen in the land he promised with an oath to your fathers to give you.

¹²The LORD will open up the heavens. That's where he stores his riches. He will send rain on your land at just the right time. He'll bless everything you do. You will lend money to many nations. But you won't have to borrow from any of them. ¹³The LORD your God will make you leaders, not followers.

Pay attention to his commands that I'm giving you today. Be careful to follow them. Then you will always be on top. You will never be on the bottom. ¹⁴Don't turn away from any of the commands I'm giving you today. Don't turn to the right or the left. Don't follow other gods. Don't worship them.

MORE CURSES FOR NOT OBEYING THE LORD

¹⁵But suppose you don't obey the LORD your God. And you aren't careful to follow all of his commands and rules I'm giving you today. Then he will send curses on you. They'll catch up with you. Here are those curses.

¹⁶You will be cursed in the cities. You will be cursed out in the country.

¹⁷Your baskets and bread pans will be cursed.

¹⁸Your children will be cursed. Your crops will be cursed. Your calves and lambs will be cursed.

¹⁹You will be cursed no matter where you go.

²⁰The LORD will send curses on you. You won't know what's going on. In everything you do, he will be angry with you. You will be destroyed suddenly and completely. That will happen because you did an evil thing when you deserted the LORD.

²¹He will send all kinds of sicknesses on you. He'll send them until he has destroyed you. He'll remove you from the land you are entering to take as your own. ²²The LORD will make you sick and very weak. He will strike you with fever and swelling. He'll send burning heat. There won't be any rain. The hot winds will completely dry up your crops. All of those things will happen until you die.

²³The sky above you will be like bronze. The ground beneath you will be like iron. ²⁴The LORD will turn the rain of your country into dust and powder. It will come down from the skies until you are destroyed.

²⁵The LORD will help your enemies win the battle over you. You will come at them from one direction. But you will run away from them in seven directions. You will look so bad that all of the kingdoms on earth will be completely shocked when they see you. ²⁶Birds and wild animals will eat up

your dead bodies. There won't be anyone left to scare them away.

²⁷The LORD will send boils on you, just like the ones he sent on the Egyptians. You will have growths in your bodies and boils on your skin. You will itch all over. No one will be able to heal you.

²⁸The LORD will make you lose your mind. He will make you blind. You won't know what's going on. ²⁹Even at noon you will have to feel your way around like a blind person in the dark. You won't have success in anything you do. Day after day you will be robbed and beaten down. No one will be able to save you.

³⁰You and a woman will promise to get married to each other. But another man will take her and rape her. You will build a house. But you won't live in it. You will plant a vineyard. But you won't eat a single grape from it. ³¹Your ox will be killed right in front of your eyes. But you won't eat any of it. Your donkey will be taken away from you by force. And you will never get it back. Your sheep will be given to your enemies. No one will be able to save them.

³²Your children will be given to another nation. Day after day you will watch for them to come back. But you will only wear out your eyes. You won't be able to help your children.

³³A nation you don't know anything about will eat what you work to produce on your land. You will be completely beaten down as long as you live. ³⁴The things you see will make you lose your mind. ³⁵The LORD will send painful boils on your knees and legs. No one will be able to heal them. They will cover you from head to toe.

³⁶The LORD will drive you out of the land. And he will drive out the king you place over you. All of you will go to a nation you and your people long ago didn't know anything about. There you will worship other gods. They will be made out of wood and stone. ³⁷You will look very bad to all of the nations where the LORD sends you. They will be completely shocked when they see you. They will laugh at you and make fun of you.

³⁸You will plant many seeds in your field. But you will gather very little food. Locusts will eat it up. ³⁹You will plant vineyards and take care of them. But you won't drink the wine. You won't gather the grapes. Worms will eat them up. ⁴⁰You will have olive trees through your whole country. But you won't use the oil. The olives will drop off the trees. ⁴¹You will have children. But you won't be able to keep them. They'll be taken away as prisoners. ⁴²Large numbers of locusts will eat up the leaves on all of your trees. They will also eat up the crops on your land.

⁴³Outsiders who live among you will become your leaders. They will rise higher and higher. But you will sink lower and lower. ⁴⁴They will lend money to you. But you won't be able to lend money to them. They will be the leaders. But you will be the followers.

⁴⁵The LORD your God will send all of those curses on you. They will follow you everywhere. They'll catch up with you. You will be under the LORD's curse until you are destroyed. That's because you didn't obey him. You didn't keep the commands and rules he gave you. ⁴⁶Those curses will remain as miraculous signs and wonders against you and your children after you forever.

⁴⁷You didn't serve the LORD your God with joy and gladness when times were good. ⁴⁸So he will send enemies against you. You will have to serve them. You will be hungry and thirsty. You will be naked and poor. The LORD will put the iron chains of slavery around your necks until he has destroyed you.

⁴⁹The LORD will bring a nation against you from far away. It will come from the ends of the earth. It will dive down on you like an eagle. You won't understand that nation's language. ⁵⁰Its people will look mean. They won't have any respect for old people. They won't show any kindness to young people.

⁵¹They will eat up the young animals among your livestock. They'll eat up the crops on your land. They'll destroy you. They won't leave you any grain, olive oil or fresh wine. They won't leave you any calves or lambs. They'll destroy you. ⁵²They'll surround all of the cities through your whole land.

They'll get ready to attack them. They'll do those things until the high, strong walls you trust in fall down. That's what will happen to the cities in the land the LORD your God is giving you. ⁵³Your enemies will surround you and get ready to attack you. They will make you suffer greatly. So you will eat your own children. You will eat the dead bodies of the sons and daughters the LORD your God has given you.

⁵⁴There may be a gentle and caring man among you. But he will treat his own brother badly. He'll be just as mean to the wife he loves and to any of his children who are still alive. ⁵⁵He won't give to a single one of them any part of the dead bodies of his children that he's eating. It will be all he has left to eat. That's how much your enemies will make you suffer when they surround all of your cities to attack them.

⁵⁶There may be a gentle and caring woman among you. She wouldn't even touch the ground with her feet without first putting her sandals on. But she will not share anything with the husband she loves. She won't share with her own children either. ⁵⁷She will eat what comes out of her body after she has a baby. Then she'll even eat her baby. She won't share it with anyone in her family. She'll plan to eat it in secret. There won't be anything else for her to eat because the city she lives in will be surrounded. That's an example of how much your enemies will make you suffer when they are getting ready to attack your cities.

⁵⁸Be careful to follow all of the words of this law. They are written in this scroll. Have respect for the glorious and wonderful name of the LORD your God. If you don't, ⁵⁹he will send terrible plagues on you and your children after you. He'll send horrible and lasting troubles. He'll make you very sick for a long time. ⁶⁰He'll bring on you all of the sicknesses you were afraid of getting when you were in Egypt. You won't be able to get rid of them. ⁶¹The LORD will also bring on you all of the other kinds of sickness and trouble I haven't written down in this Scroll of the Law. You will be destroyed.

⁶²At one time you were as many as the stars in the sky. But there will only be a few of you left. That's because you didn't obey the LORD your God. ⁶³It pleased the LORD to give you success and to increase your numbers. But it will please him just as much to wipe you out and destroy you. You will be removed from the land you are entering to take as your own.

⁶⁴Then the LORD will scatter you among all of the nations. He'll spread you around from one end of the earth to the other. There you will worship statues of gods that are made out of wood and stone. You and your people long ago hadn't known anything about those gods.

⁶⁵Among those nations you won't find any peace. There won't be any place where you can settle down and rest your feet. There the LORD will give you minds that are filled with worry. He'll give you eyes that are worn out from sobbing. Your hearts won't have any hope. ⁶⁶Your lives will always be in danger. You will be filled with fear night and day. You will never be sure you are safe. ⁶⁷In the morning you will say, "We wish it were evening!" In the evening you will say, "We wish it were morning!" Your hearts will be filled with fear. The things you see will terrify you. ⁶⁸The LORD will send you back to Egypt in ships. He'll send you on a journey I said you should never have to make again. You will offer to sell yourselves to your enemies as slaves in Egypt. But no one will buy you.

FOLLOW THE TERMS OF THE COVENANT

29 These are the terms of the covenant the LORD commanded me to make with the people of Israel in Moab. The terms were added to the covenant he had made with them at Mount Horeb.

²I sent for all of the Israelites. Here is what I said to them.

With your own eyes you have seen everything the LORD did in Egypt to Pharaoh. You have seen what he did to all of Pharaoh's officials and to his whole land. ³With your own eyes you saw how the LORD really made them suffer. You saw his miraculous signs and great wonders.

⁴But to this very day the LORD hasn't given you a mind that understands. He hasn't given you eyes that see. He hasn't given you ears that hear.

⁵He led you through the desert for 40 years. During that time your clothes didn't wear out. The sandals on your feet didn't wear out either. ⁶You didn't eat any bread. You didn't drink any kind of wine. The LORD did all of those things because he wanted you to know that he is the LORD your God.

⁷When we got here, Sihon and Og came out to fight against us. Sihon was the king of Heshbon. And Og was the king of Bashan. But we won the battle over them. ⁸We took their land. We gave it to the tribes of Reuben and Gad and half of the tribe of Manasseh as their share.

⁹Be careful to obey the terms of this covenant. Then you will have success in everything you do.

¹⁰Today all of you are standing here in the sight of the LORD your God. Your leaders and chief men are here. Your elders and officials are here. So are all of the other men of Israel. ¹¹Your children and wives are here with you too. So are the outsiders who are living in your camps. They chop your wood and carry your water.

¹²All of you are standing here in order to enter into a covenant with the LORD your God. He is making the covenant with you today. He's sealing it with an oath. ¹³Today he wants to show you that you are his people and that he is your God. That's what he promised with an oath to your fathers. He promised it to Abraham, Isaac and Jacob.

¹⁴I'm making this covenant. I'm sealing it with an oath. I'm not making it only with you ¹⁵who are standing here

Why does God sometimes wait until the last minute to supply our needs?

Wandering in the desert was hard for the Israelites. But God gave them everything they needed. It may seem as though God waits until the last minute to supply your needs, but remember that God has a timetable that you cannot see. He has a plan for you. Nothing can stop that plan, not even a shortage of money. God may wait because he wants you to trust him more. God always remembers you and hears your prayers. And he never runs out of anything.

Sometimes people wait until the last minute to pray. Instead, we should pray to God about every need. We can trust him to take care of us just like he took care of the Israelites in the desert.

checkout
Deuteronomy 29:5,6

Related verses:
Psalm 138:7,8

JASON'S IMAGINATION

HEAVEN'S PAYROLL

with us today in the sight of the LORD our God. I'm also making it with those who aren't here today.

¹⁶You yourselves know how we lived in Egypt. You also know how we passed through other countries on the way here. ¹⁷You saw the statues of their gods that were made out of wood, stone, silver and gold. The LORD hates those statues.

¹⁸Make sure there isn't a man or woman among your families or tribes who turns away from the LORD our God. No one must worship the gods of those nations. Make sure that kind of worship doesn't spread like bitter poison through your whole community.

¹⁹Some people who worship those gods will hear the oath that seals the covenant I'm making. They think they can escape trouble by saying to themselves, "We'll be safe, even though we're stubborn and go our own way." But trouble will come on them everywhere in the land.

²⁰The LORD will never be willing to forgive these people. His burning anger will blaze out against them. All of the curses I've written down in this scroll will fall on them. And the LORD will wipe out their names from the earth. ²¹He will find those people in all of the tribes of Israel and give them nothing but trouble. That will be in keeping with all of the curses of the covenant. They are written down in this Scroll of the Law.

²²Even your children's children will see the troubles that have fallen on the land. They'll see the sicknesses the LORD has brought on it. People who come from countries far away will also see those things. ²³The whole land will be burned up. Nothing but salt and sulfur will be left. Nothing will be planted there. Nothing will grow there. In fact, nothing will even start to grow there. The land will be like Sodom, Gomorrah, Admah and Zeboiim after they were destroyed. The LORD wiped out those cities because he was very angry.

²⁴All of the nations will ask, "Why has the LORD done this to the land? What could have made him so very angry?"

²⁵And they will hear the answer, "It's because the people who are living there have broken the covenant of the LORD. He's the God of their parents. He made that covenant with them when he brought them out of Egypt. ²⁶They went off and worshiped other gods. They bowed down to them. They hadn't known anything about those gods before. The LORD hadn't given those gods to them.

²⁷"So the LORD's anger burned against the land. He brought on it all of the curses that are written down in this scroll. ²⁸The LORD's anger blazed out against his people. So he pulled them up out of their land. He threw them into another land. And that's where they are now."

²⁹The LORD our God keeps certain things hidden. But he makes other things known to us and our children forever. He does it so we can obey all of the words of this law.

THE LORD WILL BLESS HIS PEOPLE

30 I have told you about all of those blessings and curses. The LORD will bring them on you. Then you will think carefully about them everywhere the LORD your God scatters you among the nations. ²You and your children will return to the LORD your God. You will obey him with all your heart and with all your soul. That will be in keeping with everything I'm commanding you today.

³When all of that happens, the LORD your God will bless you with great success again. He will be very kind to you. He'll bring you back from all of the nations where he scattered you. ⁴Suppose you have been forced to go away to the farthest land on earth. The LORD your God will bring you back even from there.

⁵He will bring you to the land that belonged to your people long ago. You will take it over. He'll make you better off than your people were. He'll increase your numbers more than he increased theirs. ⁶The LORD your God will keep your hearts from being stubborn. He'll do the same thing for your children and their children. Then you will love him with all your heart and with all your soul. And you will live.

[7]The LORD your God will put all of those curses on your enemies. They hated you and hunted you down.

[8]You will obey the LORD again. You will follow all of his commands that I'm giving you today. [9]Then the LORD your God will give you great success in everything you do. You will have many children. Your livestock will have many little ones. Your crops will do very well. The LORD will take delight in you again. He'll give you success. That's what he did for your people long ago.

[10]But you must obey the LORD your God. You must keep his commands and rules. They are written in this Scroll of the Law. You must turn to the LORD your God with all your heart and with all your soul.

CHOOSE LIFE

[11]What I'm commanding you today is not too hard for you. It isn't beyond your reach. [12]It isn't up in heaven. So you don't have to ask, "Who will go up into heaven to get it? Who will announce it to us so we can obey it?" [13]And it isn't beyond the ocean. So you don't have to ask, "Who will go across the ocean to get it? Who will announce it to us so we can obey it?"

[14]No, the message isn't far away at all. In fact, it's really near you. It's in your mouth and in your heart so that you can obey it.

[15]Today I'm giving you a choice. You can have life and success. Or you can have death and harm. [16]I'm commanding you today to love the LORD your God. I'm commanding you to live exactly as he wants you to live. You must obey his commands, rules and laws. Then you will live. Your numbers will increase. The LORD your God will bless you in the land you are entering to take as your own.

[17]Don't let your hearts turn away from the LORD. Instead, obey him. Don't let yourselves be drawn away to other gods. And don't bow down to them and worship them. [18]If you do, I announce to you this very day that you will certainly be destroyed. You are about to go across the Jordan River and take over the land. But you won't live there very long.

[19]I'm calling for heaven and earth to give witness against you this very day. I'm offering you the choice of life or death. You can choose either blessings or curses. But I want you to choose life. Then you and your children will live. [20]And you will love the LORD your God. You will obey him. You will remain true to him. The LORD is your very life. He will give you many years in the land. He took an oath. He promised to give that land to your fathers. He promised it to Abraham, Isaac and Jacob.

JOSHUA BECOMES THE NEW LEADER

31

Here are the words I spoke to all of the people of Israel. [2]I said, "I am now 120 years old. I'm not able to lead you anymore. The LORD has said to me, 'You will not go across the Jordan River.'

[3]"The LORD your God himself will go across ahead of you. He'll destroy the nations that are there in order to make room for you. You will take over their land. Joshua will also go across ahead of you, just as the LORD said he would.

[4]"The LORD will do to those nations what he did to Sihon and Og. He destroyed those Amorite kings along with their land. [5]The LORD will hand those nations over to you. Then you must do to them everything I've commanded you to do.

[6]"Be strong and brave. Don't be afraid of them. Don't be terrified because of them. The LORD your God will go with you. He will never leave you. He'll never desert you."

[7]Then I sent for Joshua. I spoke to him in front of all of the people of Israel. I said, "Be strong and brave. You must go with these people. They are going into the land the LORD promised with an oath to give to their fathers. You must divide it up among them. They will each receive their share. [8]The LORD himself will go ahead of you. He will be with you. He will never leave you. He'll never desert you. So don't be afraid. Don't lose hope."

THE LAW MUST BE READ

[9]I wrote down that law. I gave it to the priests, who are sons of Levi. They carried the ark of the covenant of the

LORD. I also gave the law to all of the elders of Israel.

[10]Then I commanded them, "You must read this law at the end of every seven years. Do it in the year when you forgive people what they owe. Read it during the Feast of Booths. [11]That's when all of the people of Israel come to appear in front of the LORD your God at the holy tent. It will be at the place he will choose. You must read this law to them.

[12]"Gather the people together. Gather the men, women and children. Also bring together the outsiders who are living in your towns. Then they can listen and learn to have respect for the LORD your God. And they'll be careful to obey all of the words of this law. [13]Their children must hear it read too. They don't know this law yet. They too must learn to have respect for the LORD your God. They must respect him as long as you live in the land. You are about to go across the Jordan River and take that land as your very own."

ISRAEL WILL REFUSE TO OBEY THE LORD

[14]The LORD spoke to me. He said, "The day when you will die is near. Have Joshua go to the Tent of Meeting. Join him there. That is where I will appoint him as the new leader." So Joshua and I went to the Tent of Meeting.

[15]Then the LORD appeared at the tent in a pillar of cloud. It stood over the entrance to the tent. [16]The LORD spoke to me. He said, "You are going to join the members of your family who have already died. The people will not be faithful to me. They will soon join themselves to the strange gods that are worshiped in the land they are entering. The people will desert me. They will break the covenant I made with them.

[17]"On that day I will become angry with them. I will desert them. I will turn my face away from them. And they will be destroyed. Many horrible troubles and hard times will come on them. On that day they will say, 'Trouble has come on us. Our God isn't with us!'

[18]"I will certainly turn away from them on that day. I will do it because they did a very evil thing when they turned to other gods.

[19]"I want you to write down a song for yourselves. Teach it to the people of Israel. Have them sing it. It will be my witness against them.

[20]"I will bring them into a land that has plenty of milk and honey. I prom-

Why are there spooky things like skeletons and monsters?

Some people like to be frightened by funny skeletons and make-believe monsters. They like to scare others too. They like spooky times like Halloween. But you do not have to be afraid of ghosts and goblins. They are not real. Besides, God is with you and will take care of you. Keep trusting in him to protect you.

checkout Deuteronomy 31:6

Related verses:
Matthew 28:20;
Romans 8:38,39

ised the land to their fathers. I took an oath when I promised it. In that land they will eat until they have had enough. They will get fat. When they do, they will turn to other gods and worship them. They will turn their backs on me. They will break my covenant.

²¹"Many horrible troubles and hard times will come on them. Then the song I am giving you will be a witness against them. That is because the song will not be forgotten by their children and their children's children. I know what they are likely to do. I know it even before I bring them into the land I promised them with an oath."

²²So that day I wrote the song down. And I taught it to the people of Israel.

²³The LORD gave a command to Joshua, the son of Nun. He said, "Be strong and brave. You will bring the Israelites into the land I promised them with an oath. I myself will be with you."

²⁴I finished writing the words of that law in a scroll. I wrote them down from beginning to end. ²⁵Then I gave a command to the Levites who carried the ark of the covenant of the LORD. I said, ²⁶"Take this Scroll of the Law. Place it beside the ark of the covenant of the LORD your God. It will remain there as a witness against you. ²⁷I know how you refuse to obey the LORD. I know how stubborn you are. You have refused to obey him while I've been living among you. So you will certainly refuse to obey him after I'm dead!

²⁸Gather together all of the elders of your tribes and all of your officials. Bring them to me. Then I can speak these words to them. I can call for heaven and earth to give witness against them. ²⁹I know that after I'm dead you will certainly become very sinful. You will turn away from the path I've commanded you to take. In days to come, trouble will fall on you. That's because you will do what is evil in the sight of the LORD. You will make him very angry because of the statues of gods your hands have made."

THE SONG OF MOSES

³⁰I spoke the words of this song from beginning to end. The whole commu-

nity of Israel heard them. Here is what I said.

32 Heavens, listen to me.
 Then I will speak.
 Earth, hear the words of my mouth.
² Let my teaching fall like rain.
 Let my words come down like dew.
 Let them be like raindrops on new grass.
 Let them be like rain on tender plants.

³ I will make known the name of the LORD.
 Praise God! How great he is!
⁴ He is the Rock. His works are perfect.
 All of his ways are right.
 He is faithful. He doesn't do anything wrong.
 He is honest and fair.

⁵ Israel, you have sinned against him very much.
 It's too bad for you that you aren't his children anymore.
 You have become a twisted and evil nation.
⁶ Is that how you thank the LORD?
 You aren't wise. You are foolish.
 Remember, he's your Father. He's your Creator.
 He made you. He formed you.

⁷ Remember the days of old.
 Think about what the LORD did through those many years.
 Ask your father. He will tell you.
 Ask your elders. They'll explain it to you.
⁸ The Most High God gave the nations their lands.
 He divided up the human race.
 He set up borders for the nations.
 He did it based on the number of the sons of Israel.
⁹ The LORD's people are his share.
 Jacob is the nation he has received.
¹⁰ The LORD found Israel in a desert land.
 He found them in an empty and windy wasteland.
 He took care of them and kept them safe.

He guarded them as he would
guard his own eyes.
¹¹He was like an eagle that stirs up
its nest.
It hovers over its little ones.
It spreads out its wings to catch
them.
It carries them on its feathers.
¹²The LORD was the only one who
led Israel.
No other god was with them.

¹³The LORD made them ride on the
highest places in the land.
He fed them what grew in the
fields.
He gave them the sweetest honey.
He fed them olive oil from a
rocky hillside.
¹⁴He gave them butter and milk
from the herds and flocks.
He fed them the fattest lambs
and goats.
He gave them the best of Bashan's
rams.
He fed them the finest wheat.
They drank the bubbling red
juice of grapes.

¹⁵When Israel grew fat, they became
stubborn.
When they were filled with food,
they became fat and heavy.
They left the God who made them.
They turned away from the Rock
who saved them.
¹⁶They made him jealous by serving
strange gods.
They made him angry by
worshiping statues of gods.
He hated those gods.
¹⁷The people sacrificed to demons,
not to God.
The demons were gods they
hadn't known anything about.
Those gods were new to them.
Their people long ago didn't
worship them.
¹⁸But then they deserted the Rock.
He was their Father.
They forgot the God who created
them.

¹⁹When the LORD saw that, he
turned away from them.
His sons and daughters made
him angry.

²⁰"I will turn my face away from
them," he said.
"I will see what will happen to
them in the end.
They are sinful people.
They are unfaithful children.
²¹They made me jealous by serving
what is not even a god.
They made me angry by
worshiping worthless statues
of gods.
I will use people who are not a
nation to make them jealous.
I will use a nation that has no
understanding to make them
angry.
²²My anger has started a fire.
It burns down to the kingdom of
the dead.
It will eat up the earth and its crops.
It will set the base of the
mountains on fire.

²³"I will pile troubles on my people.
I will shoot all of my arrows at
them.
²⁴I will send them hunger. It will
make them weak.
I will send terrible sickness. I will
send deadly plagues.
I will send wild animals that will
tear them apart.
Snakes that glide through the
dust will bite them.
²⁵In the streets their children will be
killed with swords.
Their homes will be filled with
terror.
Young men and women will die.
Babies and old people will die.
²⁶I said I would scatter them.
I said I would wipe them from
human memory.
²⁷But I was afraid their enemies
would make fun of that.
I was afraid their attackers would
not understand.
I was sure they would say, 'We're
the ones who've beaten them!
The LORD isn't the one who did
it.' "

²⁸Israel is a nation that doesn't have
any sense.
They can't understand anything.
²⁹I wish they were wise. Then they
would understand what's
coming.

They'd realize what would happen to them in the end.

³⁰ How could one person chase a thousand?

How could two make ten thousand run away?

It couldn't happen unless their Rock had deserted them.

It couldn't take place unless the LORD had given them up.

³¹ Their rock is not like our Rock. Even our enemies know that.

³² Their vine comes from the vines of Sodom.

It comes from the vineyards of Gomorrah.

Their grapes are filled with poison. Their bunches of grapes taste bitter.

³³ Their wine is like the poison of snakes.

It's like the deadly poison of cobras.

³⁴ The LORD says, "I have kept all of those terrible things stored away.

I have kept them sealed up in my strongbox.

³⁵ I punish people. I will pay them back.

The time will come when their feet will slip.

Their day of trouble is near.

Very soon they will be destroyed."

³⁶ The LORD will judge his people.

He'll show tender love to those who serve him.

He will know when their strength is gone.

He'll see that no one at all is left.

³⁷ He'll say, "Where are their gods now?

Where is the rock they went to for safety?

³⁸ Where are the gods who ate the fat of their sacrifices?

Where are the gods who drank the wine of their drink offerings?

Let them rise up to help you!

Let them keep you safe!

³⁹ "Look! I am the One!

There is no other God except me.

I put some people to death. I bring others to life.

I have wounded, and I will heal.

No one can save you from my powerful hand.

⁴⁰ I raise my hand to heaven. Here is the oath I take.

You can be sure that I live forever.

⁴¹ And you can be just as sure that I will sharpen my flashing sword.

My hand will hold it when I judge.

I will get even with my enemies.

I will pay back those who hate me.

⁴² I will make my arrows drip with blood.

My sword will destroy people.

It will kill some. It will even kill prisoners.

It will cut off the heads of enemy leaders."

⁴³ You nations, be full of joy. Be joyful together with God's people.

The LORD will get even with his enemies.

He will pay them back for killing those who serve him.

He will wipe away the sin of his land and people.

⁴⁴ I spoke all of the words of that song to the people. Joshua, the son of Nun, was with me. ⁴⁵ I finished speaking all of those words to all of the people of Israel. ⁴⁶ Then I said to the people, "Think carefully about all of the words I have announced to you today. I want you to command your children to be careful to obey all of the words of this law. ⁴⁷ They aren't just useless words for you. They are your very life. If you obey them, you will live in the land for a long time. It's the land you are going across the Jordan River to take as your own."

MOSES WILL DIE ON MOUNT NEBO

⁴⁸ On that same day the LORD spoke to me. He said, ⁴⁹ "Go up into the Abarim Mountains. Go to Mount Nebo in Moab. It is across from Jericho. From there look out over Canaan. It is the land I am giving the people of Israel to take as their own.

⁵⁰"You will die there on the mountain you have climbed. You will join the members of your family who have already died. In the same way, your brother Aaron died on Mount Hor. He joined the members of his family who had already died. ⁵¹"You and Aaron disobeyed me in front of the Israelites. It happened at the waters of Meribah Kadesh in the Desert of Zin. You did not honor me among the Israelites as the holy God. ⁵²So you will see the land. But you will see it only from far away. You will not enter the land I am giving to the people of Israel."

MOSES BLESSES THE TRIBES

33 Here is the blessing that Moses, the man of God, gave to the people of Israel before he died. ²He said,

"The LORD came from Mount
    Sinai.
Like the rising sun, he shone on
    his people from Mount Seir.
He shone on them from Mount
    Paran.
He came with large numbers of
    angels.
He came from his mountain
    slopes in the south.
³LORD, I'm sure you love your
    people.
All of the Israelites are in your
    hands.
At your feet all of them bow down.
And you teach them.
⁴They learn the law I gave them.
It belongs to the community of
    the people of Jacob.
⁵The LORD was king over Israel
    when the leaders of the people
    came together.
The tribes of Israel were also
    there."

⁶Here's what Moses said about Reuben.

"Let Reuben live. Don't let him die.
    But let his people be few."

⁷Here's what Moses said about Judah.

"LORD, listen to Judah cry out.
    Bring him to his people.

By his own power he stands up for
    himself.
LORD, help him fight against his
    enemies!"

⁸Here's what Moses said about Levi.

"Your Thummim and Urim belong
    to the man you favored.
You put him to the test at
    Massah.
You argued with him at the
    waters of Meribah.
⁹Levi didn't show special favor to
    anyone.
He did not spare his father and
    mother.
He didn't excuse his relatives or
    his children.
But he watched over your word.
He guarded your covenant.
¹⁰He teaches your rules to the
    people of Jacob.
He teaches your law to Israel.
He offers incense to you.
He sacrifices whole burnt
    offerings on your altar.
¹¹LORD, bless all of his skills.
Be pleased with everything he
    does.
Destroy those who rise up against
    him.
Strike down his enemies until
    they can't get up."

¹²Here's what Moses said about Benjamin.

"Let the one the LORD loves rest
    safely in him.
The LORD guards him all day
    long.
The one the LORD loves rests in
    his arms."

¹³Here's what Moses said about Joseph.

"May the LORD bless Joseph's land.
May he bless it with dew from
    the highest heavens.
May he bless it with water from
    the deepest oceans.
¹⁴May he bless it with the best crops
    the sun can produce.
May he bless it with the finest
    crops the moon can give.
¹⁵May he bless it with the best
    products of the age-old
    mountains.

May he bless it with the many
crops of the ancient hills.
[16] May he bless it with the best gifts
that fill the earth.
May he bless it with the favor of
the One who spoke out of the
burning bush.
Let all of those blessings rest on
the head of Joseph.
Let them rest on the head of the
one who is prince among his
brothers.
[17] His glory is like the glory of a bull
that was born first to its
mother.
His horns are like the horns of a
wild ox.
He will destroy the nations with
them.
He'll wipe out the nations that
are very far away.
The ten thousands of men in
Ephraim's army are like the
bull and the ox.
So are the thousands in the army
of Manasseh."

[18] Here's what Moses said about
Zebulun and Issachar.

"Zebulun, be filled with joy when
you go out.
Issachar, be joyful in your tents.
[19] You will call for all of the other
Israelites to go to the
mountain.
There you will offer proper
sacrifices.
You will enjoy the many good
things your ships bring you.
You will enjoy treasures that are
hidden in the sand."

[20] Here's what Moses said about Gad.

"May the One who gives Gad more
land be praised!
Gad lives there like a lion
that tears off arms and heads.
[21] He chose the best land for his
livestock.
The leader's share was kept for
him.
The leaders of the people came
together.
Then Gad carried out the LORD's
holy plan.
He carried out the LORD's
decisions for Israel."

[22] Here's what Moses said about Dan.

"Dan is like a lion's cub
that charges out of the land of
Bashan."

[23] Here's what Moses said about
Naphtali.

"The LORD greatly favors Naphtali.
The LORD fills him with his
blessing.
Naphtali's land will reach south
to the Sea of Galilee."

[24] Here's what Moses said about
Asher.

"Asher is the most blessed of sons.
Let his brothers show favor to
him.
Let him wash his feet with olive
oil.
[25] The bars of his gates will be made
out of iron and bronze.
His strength will last as long as
he lives.
[26] "There is no one like the God of
Israel.
He rides in the heavens to help
you.
He rides on the clouds in his
glory.
[27] God lives forever! You can run to
him for safety.
His powerful arms are always
there to carry you.
He will drive out your enemies to
make room for you.
He'll say to you, 'Destroy them!'
[28] So Israel will live alone in safety.
Jacob's spring of water is safe
in a land that has grain and fresh
wine.
There the heavens drop their dew.
[29] Israel, how blessed you are!
Who is like you?
The LORD has saved you.
He keeps you safe. He helps you.
He's like a glorious sword to you.
Your enemies will bow down to
you in fear.
You will bring them under your
control."

MOSES DIES

34 Moses climbed Mount
Nebo. He went up from the
flatlands of Moab to the

highest slopes of Pisgah. It's across from Jericho.

At Pisgah the LORD showed him the whole land from Gilead all the way to Dan. ²Moses saw the whole land of Naphtali. He saw the territory of Ephraim and Manasseh. The LORD showed him the whole land of Judah all the way to the Mediterranean Sea. ³Moses saw the Negev Desert. He saw the whole area from the Valley of Jericho all the way to Zoar. Jericho was also known as The City of Palm Trees.

⁴Then the LORD spoke to Moses. He said, "This is the land I promised with an oath to Abraham, Isaac and Jacob. I told them, 'I will give this land to your children and their children.' Moses, I have let you see it with your own eyes. But you will not go across the Jordan River to enter it."

⁵Moses, the servant of the LORD, died there in Moab, just as the LORD had said. ⁶The LORD buried the body of Moses in Moab. His grave is in the valley across from Beth Peor. But to this day no one knows where it is. ⁷Moses was 120 years old when he died. But his eyes were not weak. He was still very strong.

⁸The people of Israel sobbed over Moses on the flatlands of Moab for 30 days. They did it until their time for sobbing and crying was over.

⁹Joshua, the son of Nun, was filled with wisdom. That's because Moses had placed his hands on him. So the Israelites listened to Joshua. They did what the LORD had commanded Moses.

¹⁰Since then, Israel has never had a prophet like Moses. The LORD knew him face to face. ¹¹Moses did many miraculous signs and wonders. The LORD had sent him to do them in Egypt. Moses did them against Pharaoh, against all of his officials and against his whole land. ¹²No one has ever had the mighty power Moses had. No one has ever done the wonderful acts he did in the sight of all of the people of Israel.

Why do people put stones on people's graves?

A gravestone or metal plate on a grave marks the place where the person's body is buried. Friends and family will sometimes go to the cemetery after a person has died. They will put flowers on the grave and think about the person. The stone helps them find the grave. They can go there and remember the person instead of forgetting. Just think what it would be like if a family member was buried and no one marked where it was. That is what happened to Moses. No one knew where he was buried.

checkout
Deuteronomy 34:6

Related verse:
Acts 13:36

Joshua

Who wrote this book?
The author of Joshua is not named, but probably was someone who witnessed the events described.

Why was this book written?
Joshua tells how God helped the Israelites defeat the Canaanites.

What happens in this book?
Joshua becomes Israel's leader. Joshua leads Israel's armies to victory. Joshua assigns land to Israel's twelve tribes.

What do we learn about God in this book?
God will give victory to his people when they obey him.

Who is important in this book?
The important person in this book is Joshua.

When did this happen?
The Israelite conquest of Canaan probably happened between 1405 and 1390 B.C.

THE LORD GIVES COMMANDS TO JOSHUA

1 Moses, the servant of the LORD, died. After that, the LORD spoke to Joshua, the son of Nun. Joshua was Moses' helper. The LORD said to Joshua, ²"My servant Moses is dead. Now then, I want you and all of these people to get ready to go across the Jordan River. I want all of you to go into the land I am about to give to the people of Israel.

³"I will give all of you every place you walk on, just as I promised Moses. ⁴Your territory will reach from the Negev Desert all the way to Lebanon. The great Euphrates River will be to the east. The Mediterranean Sea will

be to the west. Your territory will include all of the Hittite country.

⁵"Joshua, no one will be able to stand up against you as long as you live. I will be with you, just as I was with Moses. I will never leave you. I will never desert you.

⁶"Be strong and brave. You will lead these people, and they will take the land as their very own. It is the land I promised with an oath to give their people long ago.

⁷"Be strong and very brave. Make sure you obey the whole law my servant Moses gave you. Do not turn away from it to the right or the left. Then you will have success everywhere you go. ⁸Never stop reading this Scroll of the Law. Day and night you must think about what it says. Make sure you do everything that is written in it. Then things will go well with you. And you will have great success.

⁹"Here is what I am commanding you to do. Be strong and brave. Do not be terrified. Do not lose hope. I am the LORD your God. I will be with you everywhere you go."

JOSHUA GIVES COMMANDS TO THE PEOPLE

¹⁰So Joshua gave orders to the officers of the people. He said, ¹¹"Go through the camp. Tell the people, 'Get your supplies ready. Three days from now you will go across the Jordan River right here. You will go in and take over the land. The LORD your God is giving it to you as your very own.' "

¹²Joshua also spoke to the tribes of Reuben and Gad and half of the tribe of Manasseh. He said to them, ¹³"Remember what Moses, the servant of the LORD, commanded you. He said, 'The LORD your God is giving you this land. It's a place where you can settle down and live in peace and rest.'

¹⁴"Your wives, children and livestock can stay here east of the Jordan River. Moses gave you this land. But all of your fighting men must get ready for battle. They must go across ahead of the other tribes. You must help them ¹⁵until the LORD gives them rest. In the same way, he has already given you rest. You must help them until they also have taken over their land. It's the

KIDS' QUESTION — How can Kids study the Bible?

First, start out by reading it. Get a Bible you can understand and read a few verses in it. Second, get someone to explain any words that you do not understand. Find someone like a parent, teacher or pastor to answer your questions. Third, memorize verses that tell you what God wants you to do. Fourth, look through some books that tell you more about the Bible. A Bible dictionary tells you what Bible words mean. A Bible atlas shows you where Bible places are. And a concordance tells you where certain words are found.

checkout Joshua 1:8

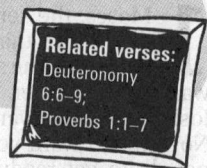

Related verses:
Deuteronomy
6:6–9;
Proverbs 1:1–7

land the LORD your God is giving them. After that, you can come back here. Then you can live in your own land. It's the land that Moses, the servant of the LORD, gave you east of the Jordan River. It's toward the sunrise."

¹⁶Then the tribes of Reuben and Gad and half of the tribe of Manasseh answered Joshua. They said, "We'll do what you have commanded us to do. We'll go where you send us. ¹⁷We obeyed Moses completely. And we'll obey you just as completely. But may the LORD your God be with you, just as he was with Moses.

¹⁸"Suppose people question your authority. And suppose they refuse to obey anything you command them to do. Then they will be put to death. Just be strong and brave!"

RAHAB HELPS THE SPIES

2 Joshua, the son of Nun, sent two spies from Shittim. He sent them in secret. He said to them, "Go. Look the land over. Most of all, check out Jericho."

So they went to Jericho. They stayed at the house of a prostitute. Her name was Rahab.

²The king of Jericho was told, "Look! Some of the people of Israel have come here tonight. They've come to check out the land."

³So the king sent a message to Rahab. It said, "Bring out the men who came into your house. They've come to check out the whole land."

⁴But the woman had hidden the two men. She said, "It's true that the men came here. But I didn't know where they had come from. ⁵They left at sunset, when it was time to close the city gate. I don't know which way they went. Go after them quickly. You might catch up with them."

⁶But in fact she had taken them up on the roof. There she had hidden them under some flax she had piled up.

⁷The king's men left to hunt down the spies. They took the road that leads to where the Jordan River can be crossed. As soon as they had gone out of the city, the gate was shut.

⁸Rahab went up on the roof before the spies settled down for the night. ⁹She said to them, "I know that the LORD has given this land to you. We are very much afraid of you. Everyone

KIDS' QUESTion

If lying is a sin, why did some people in the Bible tell lies?

It is true that the Bible has stories about people who told lies. But God never says in the Bible that lying is right. And he never said that people who told lies were right for doing it. Most Bible people who loved God told the truth. God is truth, and he wants us to tell the truth. Honesty is very important for families, neighborhoods, cities, schools, companies and friendships. Honesty protects us from danger and helps us to be happier people. Be a person who always tells the truth.

checkout
Joshua 2:4-6

Related verses:
Proverbs 6:17;
Ephesians 4:25

SAMSON

who lives in this country is weak with fear because of you.

¹⁰"We've heard how the LORD dried up the Red Sea for you when you came out of Egypt. We've heard what you did to Sihon and Og, the two Amorite kings. They ruled east of the Jordan River. You completely destroyed them. ¹¹"When we heard about it, our hearts melted away in fear. Because of you, we aren't brave anymore. The LORD your God is the God who rules over heaven above and earth below.

¹²"Now then, please take an oath. Promise me in the name of the LORD that you will be kind to my family. I've been kind to you. Promise me ¹³that you will spare the lives of my father and mother. Spare my brothers and sisters. Also spare everyone in their families. Promise that you won't put any of us to death."

¹⁴So the men made a promise to her. "We'll give up our lives to save yours," they said. "But don't tell anyone what we're doing. Then we'll be kind and faithful to you when the LORD gives us the land."

¹⁵The house Rahab lived in was part of the city wall. So she let the spies down by a rope through the window. ¹⁶She had said to them, "Go up into the hills. The men who are chasing you won't be able to find you. Hide yourselves there for three days until they return. Then you can go on your way."

¹⁷The men said to her, "You made us take an oath and make a promise. But we won't keep it ¹⁸unless you do what we say. When we enter the land, you must tie this bright red rope in the window. Tie it in the window you let us down through.

"Bring your father and mother into your house. Also bring your brothers and everyone else in your family into your house. ¹⁹None of you must go out into the street. If you do, anything that happens to you will be your own fault. Don't hold us accountable.

"But if anyone hurts someone who is inside the house with you, it will be our fault. And you can hold us accountable.

²⁰"Don't tell anyone what we're doing. If you do, we won't have to keep the promise you asked us to make."

²¹"I agree," Rahab replied. "I'll do as you say." So she sent them away, and they left. Then she tied the bright red rope in the window.

²²When the spies left, they went up into the hills. They stayed there for three days. By that time the men who were chasing them had searched all along the road. They couldn't find them. So they returned.

²³Then the two spies started back. They went down out of the hills. They went across the Jordan River. They came to Joshua, the son of Nun. They told him everything that had happened to them. ²⁴They said, "We're sure the LORD has given the whole land over to us. All of the people there are weak with fear because of us."

ISRAEL GOES ACROSS THE JORDAN RIVER

3 Early one morning Joshua and all of the people of Israel started out from Shittim. They went down to the Jordan River. They camped there before they went across it.

²After three days the officers went all through the camp. ³They gave orders to the people. They said, "Watch for the ark of the covenant of the LORD your God. The priests, who are Levites, will be carrying it. When you see it, you must move out from where you are and follow it. ⁴Then you will know which way to go. You have never gone this way before. But don't go near the ark. Stay about 1,000 yards away from it."

⁵Joshua spoke to the people. He said, "Set yourselves apart to the LORD. Tomorrow he'll do amazing things among you."

⁶Joshua said to the priests, "Go and get the ark of the covenant. Walk on ahead of the people." So they went and got it. Then they walked on ahead of them.

⁷The LORD said to Joshua, "Today I will begin to honor you in the eyes of all of the people of Israel. Then they will know that I am with you, just as I was with Moses. ⁸Speak to the priests who carry the ark of the covenant. Tell them, 'When you reach the edge of the

Jordan River, go into the water and stand there.' "

⁹Joshua spoke to the people of Israel. He said, "Come here. Listen to what the LORD your God is saying. ¹⁰You will soon know that the living God is among you. You can be sure that he'll drive out the people who are now living in the land. He'll do it to make room for you. He'll drive out the Canaanites, Hittites, Hivites, Perizzites, Girgashites, Amorites and Jebusites.

¹¹"The ark will go into the Jordan River ahead of you. It's the ark of the covenant of the Lord of the whole earth.

¹²"Choose 12 men from the tribes of Israel. Choose one from each tribe.

¹³"The priests will carry the ark of the LORD. He's the Lord of the whole earth. As soon as the priests step into the Jordan, it will stop flowing. The water that's coming down the river will pile up in one place. That's how you will know that the living God is among you."

¹⁴So the people took their tents down. They prepared to go across the Jordan River. The priests who were carrying the ark of the covenant went ahead of them.

¹⁵The water of the Jordan was going over its banks. It always does that at the time the crops are being gathered. The priests came to the river. Their feet touched the water's edge. ¹⁶Right away the water that was coming down the river stopped flowing. It piled up far away at a town called Adam near Zarethan. The water that was flowing down to the Dead Sea was completely cut off. So the people went across the Jordan River opposite Jericho.

¹⁷The priests carried the ark of the covenant of the LORD. They stood firm on dry ground in the middle of the river. They stayed there until the whole nation of Israel had gone across on dry ground.

4 After the whole nation had gone across the Jordan River, the LORD spoke to Joshua. He said, ²"Choose 12 men from among the people. Choose one from each tribe. ³Tell them to get 12 stones from the middle of the river. They must pick

them up from right where the priests stood. They must carry the stones over with all of you. And they must put them down at the place where you will stay tonight."

⁴So Joshua called together the 12 men he had appointed from among the people of Israel. There was one man from each tribe. ⁵He said to them, "Go back to the middle of the Jordan River. Go to where the ark of the LORD your God is. Each one of you must pick up a stone. You must carry it on your shoulder. There will be as many stones as there are tribes in Israel.

⁶"The stones will serve as a reminder to you. In days to come, your children will ask you, 'What do these stones mean?' ⁷Tell them that the LORD cut off the flow of water in the Jordan River. Tell them its water stopped flowing when the ark of the covenant of the LORD went across. The stones will always remind the Israelites of what happened there."

⁸So the people of Israel did as Joshua commanded them. They took 12 stones from the middle of the Jordan River. There was one stone for each of the tribes of Israel. It was just as the LORD had told Joshua. The people carried the stones with them to their camp. There they put them down.

⁹Joshua piled up the 12 stones that had been in the middle of the river. They had been right where the priests who carried the ark of the covenant had stood. And they are still there to this very day.

¹⁰The priests who carried the ark remained standing in the middle of the Jordan River. They stayed there until the people had done everything the LORD had commanded Joshua. It was just as Moses had directed Joshua. All of the people went across quickly. ¹¹As soon as they did, the ark of the LORD and the priests also went across to the other side. The people were watching them.

¹²Among the people who went across the river were men from the tribes of Reuben and Gad and half of the tribe of Manasseh. The men were armed. They went across ahead of the rest of the people of Israel. It was just as Moses had directed them. ¹³There

were about 40,000 of them. All of them were ready for battle. They went across in front of the ark of the LORD. They went to the flatlands around Jericho. They were prepared to go to war.

¹⁴That day the LORD honored Joshua in the eyes of all of the people of Israel. They had respect for Joshua as long as he lived. They respected him just as much as they had respected Moses.

¹⁵Then the LORD spoke to Joshua. He said, ¹⁶"Command the priests to come up out of the Jordan River. They are carrying the ark where the tablets of the covenant are kept."

¹⁷So Joshua gave a command to the priests. He said, "Come up out of the Jordan River."

¹⁸Then the priests came up out of the river. They were carrying the ark of the covenant of the LORD. As soon as they stepped out on dry ground, the water of the Jordan began to flow again. It went over its banks, just as it had done before.

¹⁹On the tenth day of the first month the people went up out of the Jordan River. They camped at Gilgal on the eastern border of Jericho.

²⁰Joshua set up the 12 stones at Gilgal. They were the ones the people had taken out of the Jordan.

²¹Then he spoke to the people of Israel. He said, "In days to come, your children after you will ask their parents, 'What do these stones mean?' ²²Their parents must tell them, 'Israel went across the Jordan River on dry ground.' ²³The LORD your God dried up the Jordan for you until you had gone across it. He did to the Jordan River the same thing he had done to the Red Sea. He dried up the Red Sea ahead of us until we had gone across it. ²⁴He did it so that all of the nations on earth would know that he is powerful. He did it so that you would always have respect for the LORD your God."

JOSHUA CIRCUMCISES THE MEN OF ISRAEL

5 All of the Amorite and Canaanite kings heard how the LORD had dried up the Jordan River. They heard how he had dried it up for the people of Israel until they had gone across it. The Amorite kings lived west of the Jordan. The kings of Canaan lived along the Mediterranean Sea.

When all of those kings heard what the LORD had done, their hearts melted away in fear. They weren't brave enough to face the people of Israel anymore.

²At that time the LORD spoke to Joshua. He said, "Make knives out of hard stone. Circumcise the men of Israel."

³So Joshua made knives out of hard stone. Then he circumcised the men of Israel at Gibeath Haaraloth.

⁴Here is why Joshua circumcised them. All of the men who came out of Egypt had died. They died while they were going through the Sinai Desert after they had left Egypt. They were the men who were old enough to serve in the army. ⁵All of the men who came out had been circumcised. But all of the men who were born in the desert during the journey from Egypt hadn't been circumcised.

⁶The people of Israel had moved around in the desert for 40 years. By the end of that time all of the men who were old enough to serve in the army when they left Egypt had died. That's because they hadn't obeyed the LORD. The LORD had taken an oath. He had told them they wouldn't see the land. It's the land he had promised with an oath to their people to give us. It's a land that has plenty of milk and honey. ⁷Because they hadn't obeyed him, he raised up their sons to take their place. They were the ones Joshua circumcised. They hadn't been circumcised yet. That's because no one had circumcised them during the journey. ⁸So Joshua circumcised all of those men. The whole nation remained in the camp until the men were healed.

⁹Then the LORD spoke to Joshua. He said, "Today I have taken away from you the shame of being laughed at by Egypt." That's why the place where the men were circumcised has been called Gilgal to this very day.

¹⁰The people of Israel celebrated the Passover Feast. They observed it on the evening of the 14th day of the month. They did it while they were camped at Gilgal on the flatlands

around Jericho. ¹¹The day after the Passover, they ate some of the food that was grown in the land. On that very day they ate grain that had been cooked. They also ate bread that was made without yeast. ¹²The manna stopped coming down the day after they ate the food that was grown in the land. The people of Israel didn't have manna anymore. Instead, that year they ate food that was grown in Canaan.

ISRAEL CAPTURES JERICHO

¹³When Joshua was near Jericho, he looked up and saw a man standing in front of him. The man was holding a sword. He was ready for battle. Joshua went up to him. He asked, "Are you on our side? Or are you on the side of our enemies?"

¹⁴"I am not on either side," he replied. "I have come as the commander of the LORD's army." Then Joshua fell with his face to the ground. He asked the man, "What message does my Lord have for me?"

¹⁵The commander of the LORD's army replied, "Take off your sandals. The place you are standing on is holy ground." So Joshua took them off.

6 The gates of Jericho were shut tight and guarded closely because of the people of Israel. No one went out. No one came in.

²Then the LORD spoke to Joshua. He said, "I have handed Jericho over to you. I have also handed its king and its fighting men over to you.

³"March around the city once with all of your fighting men. In fact, do it for six days. ⁴Have seven priests get trumpets that are made out of rams' horns. They must carry them in front of the ark. On the seventh day, march around the city seven times. Have the priests blow the trumpets as you march.

⁵"You will hear them blow a long blast on the trumpets. When you do, have all of the men give a loud shout. The wall of the city will fall down. Then the whole army will go up to the city. Every man will go straight in."

⁶So Joshua, the son of Nun, called for the priests. He said to them, "Go and get the ark of the covenant of the LORD.

I want seven of you to carry trumpets in front of it." ⁷He gave an order to the men. He said, "Move out! March around the city. Some of the fighting men must march in front of the ark of the LORD."

⁸When Joshua had spoken to the men, the seven priests went forward. They were carrying the seven trumpets as they marched in front of the ark of the LORD. They were blowing the trumpets. The ark of the LORD's covenant was carried behind the priests. ⁹Some of the fighting men marched ahead of the priests who were blowing the trumpets. The others followed behind the ark and guarded all of them. That whole time the priests were blowing the trumpets.

¹⁰But Joshua had given an order to the fighting men. He had said, "Don't give a war cry. Don't raise your voices. Don't say a word until the day I tell you to shout. Then shout!"

¹¹So he had the ark of the LORD carried around the city once. Then the men returned to camp. They spent the night there.

¹²Joshua got up early the next morning. The priests went and got the ark of the LORD. ¹³The seven priests who were carrying the seven trumpets started out. They marched in front of the ark of the LORD. They blew the trumpets. Some of the fighting men marched ahead of them. The others followed behind the ark and guarded all of them. The priests kept blowing the trumpets.

¹⁴On the second day they marched around the city once. Then the men returned to camp. They did all of those things for six days.

¹⁵On the seventh day, they got up at sunrise. They marched around the city, just as they had done before. But on that day they went around it seven times.

¹⁶On the seventh time around, the priests blew a long blast on the trumpets. Then Joshua gave a command to the men. He said, "Shout! The LORD has given you the city! ¹⁷The city and everything that is in it must be set apart to the LORD in a special way to be destroyed. But the prostitute Rahab and

all those who are with her in her house must be spared. That's because she hid the spies we sent.

¹⁸"But keep away from the things that have been set apart to the LORD. If you take any of them, you will be destroyed. And you will bring trouble on the camp of Israel. You will cause it to be destroyed. ¹⁹All of the silver and gold is holy. It is set apart to the LORD. So are all of the articles that are made out of bronze and iron. All of those things must be added to the treasures that are kept in the LORD's house."

²⁰The priests blew the trumpets. As soon as the fighting men heard the sound, they gave a loud shout. Then the wall fell down. Every man charged straight in. So they took the city. ²¹They set it apart to the LORD in a special way to be destroyed. They destroyed every living thing in it with their swords. They killed men and women. They wiped out young people and old people. They destroyed cattle, sheep and donkeys.

²²Then Joshua spoke to the two men who had gone in to check out the land. He said, "Go into the prostitute's house. Bring her out. Also bring out everyone who is with her. That's what you promised her you would do when you took an oath."

²³So the young men who had checked out the land went into Rahab's house. They brought her out along with her parents and brothers. They brought out everyone else who was there with her. They put them in a place that was outside the camp of Israel.

²⁴Then they burned the whole city and everything that was in it. But they added the silver and gold to the treasures that were kept in the LORD's house. They also put there the articles that were made out of bronze and iron.

²⁵But Joshua spared the prostitute Rahab. He spared her family. He also spared everyone else who was in the house with her. He did it because she hid the spies he had sent to Jericho. Rahab lives among the people of Israel to this very day.

²⁶At that time Joshua took an oath and called down a curse. He said, "May the man who tries to rebuild this city of Jericho be under the LORD's curse.

"If he lays its foundations,
    it will cost the life of his oldest
        son.
If he sets up its gates,
    it will cost the life of his youngest
        son."

²⁷So the LORD was with Joshua. And Joshua became famous everywhere in the land.

ACHAN SINS AGAINST THE LORD

7 But the people of Israel weren't faithful to the LORD. They didn't do what they were told to do with the things that had been set apart to him in a special way to be destroyed.

Achan had taken some of those things. So the LORD's anger burned against Israel. Achan was the son of Carmi. Carmi was the son of Zimri. And Zimri was the son of Zerah. They were from the tribe of Judah.

²Joshua sent men from Jericho to Ai. Ai is near Beth Aven east of Bethel. Joshua told the men, "Go up and check out the area around Ai." So the men went up and checked it out.

³Then they returned to Joshua. They said, "The whole army doesn't have to go up and attack Ai. Send only two or three thousand men. They can take the city. Don't make the whole army go up there. Ai only has a few men."

⁴So only about 3,000 men went up. But the men of Ai drove them away. ⁵They chased the men of Israel from the city gate all the way to Shebarim. They killed about 36 of them on the way down.

So the hearts of the people of Israel melted away in fear.

⁶Joshua and the elders of Israel became sad. Joshua tore his clothes. He fell in front of the ark of the LORD with his face to the ground. He remained there until evening. The elders did the same thing. They also sprinkled dust on their heads.

⁷Joshua said, "LORD and King, why did you ever bring these people across the Jordan River? Did you want to

hand us over to the Amorites? Did you want them to destroy us? I wish we had been content to stay on the other side of the Jordan!

[8]"Lord, our enemies have driven us away. What can I say? [9]The people of Canaan will hear about it. So will everyone else in the country. They will surround us. They'll wipe our name from the face of the earth. Then what will you do when people don't honor your great name anymore?"

[10]The LORD said to Joshua, "Get up! What are you doing down there on your face?

[11]"Israel has sinned. I made a covenant with them. I commanded them to keep it. But they have broken it. They have taken some of the things that had been set apart to me in a special way to be destroyed. They have stolen. They have lied. They have taken the things they stole and have put them with their own things.

[12]"That is why the men of Israel can't stand up against their enemies. They turn their backs and run. It is because I have decided to let them be destroyed. You must destroy the things you took that had been set apart to me. If you do not, I will not be with you anymore.

[13]"Go. Set the people apart. Tell them, 'Make yourselves pure. Get ready for tomorrow. Here is what the LORD, the God of Israel, wants you to do. He says, "People of Israel, you have kept some of the things that had been set apart to me in a special way to be destroyed. You can't stand up against your enemies until you get rid of those things."

[14]" 'In the morning, come forward tribe by tribe. The tribe the LORD chooses will come forward group by group. The group the LORD chooses will come forward family by family. And the men in the family the LORD chooses will come forward one by one.

[15]" 'Anyone who is caught with the things that had been set apart to the LORD will be destroyed by fire. Everything that belongs to that person will also be destroyed. He has broken the LORD's covenant. He has done a very terrible thing in Israel!' "

[16]Early the next morning Joshua had Israel come forward by tribes.

The tribe of Judah was picked. [17]The groups of Judah came forward. Joshua picked the group of Zerah. He had the group of Zerah come forward by families. The family of Zimri was picked. [18]He had their men come forward one by one. Achan was picked. Achan was the son of Carmi. Carmi was the son of Zimri. And Zimri was the son of Zerah. Zerah was from the tribe of Judah.

[19]Joshua spoke to Achan. He said, "My son, the LORD is the God of Israel. So give him glory by telling the truth! Give him praise by admitting you have sinned! Tell me what you have done. Don't hide it from me."

[20]Achan replied, "It's true! I've sinned against the LORD, the God of Israel. Here is what I've done. [21]I saw a beautiful robe from Babylonia among the things we had taken. I saw five pounds of silver. And I saw a gold bar that weighed 20 ounces. I wanted them, so I took them. I hid them in the ground inside my tent. The silver is on the bottom."

[22]So Joshua sent some messengers. They ran to Achan's tent. And there was everything, hidden in his tent! The silver was on the bottom. [23]They brought the things out of the tent. They took them to Joshua and all of the people of Israel. And they spread them out in the sight of the LORD.

[24]Then Joshua and all of the people grabbed hold of Achan, the son of Zerah. They took the silver, the robe and the gold bar. They took Achan's sons and daughters. They took his cattle, donkeys and sheep. They also took his tent and everything he had. They took all of it to the Valley of Achor.

[25]Joshua said to Achan, "Why have you brought this trouble on us? The LORD will bring trouble on you today."

Then all of the people killed Achan by throwing stones at him. They also killed the rest of his family with stones. They burned all of them up. [26]They placed a large pile of rocks on top of Achan's body. The place has been called the Valley of Achor ever since. That pile is still there to this very day.

After the people killed Achan, the LORD turned his burning anger away from them.

ISRAEL DESTROYS AI

8 Then the LORD spoke to Joshua. He said, "Do not be afraid. Do not lose hope. Go up and attack Ai. Take the whole army with you. I have handed the king of Ai over to you. I have given you his people, his city and his land.

[2] "Remember what you did to Jericho and its king. You will do the same thing to Ai and its king. But this time you can keep for yourselves the livestock and everything else you take from them. Have some of your fighting men hide behind the city and take them by surprise."

[3] So Joshua and the whole army moved out to attack Ai. He chose 30,000 of his best fighting men. He sent them out at night. [4] He gave them orders. He said, "Listen carefully to what I'm saying. You must hide behind the city. Don't go very far away from it. All of you must be ready to attack it.

[5] "I and all of the men who are with me will go up to the city. The men of Ai will come out to fight against us, just as they did before. Then we'll run away from them. [6] They'll chase us until we've drawn them away from the city. They'll say, 'They are running away from us, just as they did before.'

"When we run away from them, [7] come out of your hiding place. Take over the city. The LORD your God will hand it over to you. [8] When you have taken it, set it on fire. Do what the LORD has commanded. Make sure you obey my orders."

[9] Then Joshua sent them away. They went to the place where they had planned to hide. They hid in a place west of Ai. It was between Bethel and Ai. But Joshua spent that night with his men.

[10] Early the next morning Joshua brought his men together. He and the leaders of Israel marched in front of them to Ai. [11] The whole army that was with him marched up to the city. They stopped in front of it. They set up camp north of Ai. There was a valley between them and the city.

[12] Joshua had chosen about 5,000 soldiers. He had ordered them to hide in a place west of Ai. It was between Bethel and Ai. [13] The men took up their battle positions. All of the men who were in the camp that was north of the city took up their positions. So did those who were supposed to hide west of the city. That night Joshua went into the valley.

[14] The king of Ai saw what the army of Israel was doing. So he and all of his men hurried out of the city early in the morning. They marched out to meet Israel in battle. They went to a place that looked out over the Arabah Valley. The king didn't know that some of Israel's fighting men were hiding behind the city.

[15] Joshua and all of his men let the men of Ai drive them back. The men of Israel ran away toward the desert.

[16] All of the men of Ai were called out to chase them. They chased Joshua. So they were drawn away from the city. [17] Not even one man remained in Ai or Bethel. All of them went out to chase Israel. When they did, they left the city wide open.

[18] Then the LORD spoke to Joshua. He said, "Point the javelin that is in your hand at Ai. I will hand the city over to you." So Joshua pointed his javelin at Ai.

[19] As soon as he did, the men who were hiding behind the city got up quickly. They came out of their hiding places and rushed forward. They entered the city and captured it. They quickly set it on fire.

[20] The men of Ai looked back. They saw smoke rising up from the city into the sky. But they couldn't escape in any direction.

The men of Israel had been running away toward the desert. But now they turned around to face those who were chasing them. [21] Joshua and all of his men saw that the men who had been hiding behind the city had captured it. They also saw the smoke that was going up from it. So they turned around and attacked the men of Ai. [22] The men who had set Ai on fire came out of the city. They also fought against the men of Ai.

So the men of Ai were caught in the middle. The army of Israel was on both sides of them. Israel struck them down. They didn't let anyone remain alive or get away. ²³But they took the king of Ai alive. They brought him to Joshua.

²⁴Israel finished killing all of the men of Ai. They destroyed them in the fields and in the desert where they had chased them. They struck every one of them down with their swords. Then all of the men of Israel returned to Ai. And they killed those who were left in it.

²⁵The total number of men and women they killed that day was 12,000. They put to death all of the people of Ai.

²⁶Joshua kept the javelin that was in his hand pointed at Ai. He didn't lower his hand until he and his men had totally destroyed everyone who lived there.

²⁷But this time Israel kept for themselves the livestock and everything else they had taken from the city. The LORD had directed Joshua to let them do it.

²⁸So Joshua burned Ai down. He tore it down so it could never be built again. It has been deserted to this very day.

²⁹Joshua killed the king of Ai. He stuck a pole through the body. Then he set it up where people could see it. He left it there until evening. At sunset, Joshua ordered his men to remove the body from the pole. He told them to throw the body down at the entrance of the city gate. They put a large pile of rocks over the body. That pile is still there to this very day.

JOSHUA READS THE SCROLL OF THE LAW TO THE PEOPLE

³⁰Joshua built an altar to honor the LORD, the God of Israel. He built it on Mount Ebal. ³¹Moses, the servant of the LORD, had commanded the people of Israel to do that. Joshua built the altar in keeping with what is written in the Scroll of the Law of Moses. He built an altar out of stones that iron tools had never touched. Then the people offered on the altar burnt offerings to the LORD. They also sacrificed friendship offerings on it.

³²Joshua copied the written law of Moses on stones. He did it while all of

the people of Israel were watching. ³³They were standing on both sides of the ark of the covenant of the LORD. All of the people of Israel, including outsiders and citizens, were there. Israel's elders, officials and judges were also there. All of them faced the priests, who were Levites. They were carrying the ark. Half of the people stood in front of Mount Gerizim. The other half stood in front of Mount Ebal. Moses, the servant of the LORD, had earlier told them to do it. It was when he had given directions to bless the people of Israel.

³⁴Then Joshua read all of the words of the law out loud. He read the blessings and the curses. He read them in keeping with what is written in the Scroll of the Law. ³⁵Joshua read every word Moses had commanded. He read them to the whole community of Israel. That included the women and children. It also included the outsiders who were living among them.

THE PEOPLE OF GIBEON TRICK ISRAEL

9 All of the kings who ruled west of the Jordan River heard about the battles Israel had won. That included the kings who ruled in the central hill country and the western hills. It also included those who ruled along the entire coast of the Mediterranean Sea all the way to Lebanon. They were the kings of the Hittites, Amorites, Canaanites, Perizzites, Hivites and Jebusites. ²They brought their armies together to fight against Joshua and Israel.

³The people of Gibeon heard about what Joshua had done to Jericho and Ai. ⁴So they decided to trick the people of Israel. They packed supplies as if they were going on a long trip. They loaded their donkeys with old sacks and old wineskins. The wineskins were cracked but had been mended. ⁵The men put worn-out sandals on their feet. The sandals had been patched. The men also wore old clothes. All of the bread they took along was dry and moldy.

⁶They went to Joshua in the camp at Gilgal. They spoke to him and the men of Israel. They said, "We've come from

a country that's far away. Make a peace treaty with us."

⁷The men of Israel spoke to the Hivites. They said, "But suppose you live close to us. If you do, we can't make a peace treaty with you."

⁸"We'll serve you," they said to Joshua.

But Joshua asked, "Who are you? Where do you come from?"

⁹They answered, "We've come from a country that's very far away. We've come because the LORD your God is famous. We've heard reports about him. We've heard about everything he did in Egypt.

¹⁰"We've heard about everything he did to Sihon and Og. They were the two kings of the Amorites. They ruled east of the Jordan River. Sihon was the king of Heshbon. Og was the king of Bashan. He ruled in Ashtaroth.

¹¹"Our elders and all of the people who are living in our country spoke to us. They said, 'Take supplies for your trip. Go and meet the people of Israel. Say to them, "We'll serve you. Make a peace treaty with us." '

¹²"Look at our bread. It was warm when we packed it. We packed it at home on the day we left to come and see you. But look at how dry and moldy it is now. ¹³When we filled these wineskins, they were new. But look at how cracked they are now. And our clothes and sandals are worn out because we've traveled so far."

¹⁴The men of Israel looked over the supplies those men had brought. But they didn't ask the LORD what they should do.

¹⁵Joshua made a peace treaty with the men who had come. He agreed to let them live. The leaders of the community took an oath to show that they agreed with the treaty.

¹⁶The people of Israel made a peace treaty with the people of Gibeon. But three days later they heard that the people of Gibeon lived close to them. ¹⁷So the people of Israel started out to go to the cities of those men. On the third day they came to Gibeon, Kephirah, Beeroth and Kiriath Jearim. ¹⁸But they didn't attack those cities. That's because the leaders of the community had taken an oath and made a peace treaty with them. They had taken the oath in the name of the LORD, the God of Israel.

The whole community told the leaders they weren't happy with them. ¹⁹But all of the leaders answered, "We've made a peace treaty with them. We've taken an oath in the name of the LORD, the God of Israel. So we can't touch them now. ²⁰"But here is what we'll do to them. We'll let them live. Then the LORD's anger won't fall on us because we didn't keep the oath we took." ²¹They continued, "Let them live. But let them cut wood and carry water for the whole community." So the leaders kept their promise to them.

²²Joshua sent for the people of Gibeon. He said, "Why did you trick us? You said, 'We live far away from you.' But in fact you live close to us. ²³So now you are under a curse. You will always serve us. You will always cut wood and carry water for the house of my God."

²⁴They answered Joshua, "We were clearly told what the LORD your God had commanded his servant Moses to do. He commanded him to give you the whole land. He also ordered him to wipe out all of its people to make room for you. So we were afraid you would kill us. That's why we tricked you. ²⁵We are now in your hands. Do to us what you think is good and right."

²⁶So Joshua saved the people of Gibeon. He didn't let the people of Israel kill them. ²⁷That day he made them cut wood and carry water. They had to serve the community of Israel. They also had to serve at the altar of the LORD at the place where he would choose to put it. And they still serve the people of Israel to this very day.

THE SUN STANDS STILL

10 Adoni-Zedek was the king of Jerusalem. He heard that Joshua had taken Ai. He found out that the city had been set apart to the LORD in a special way to be destroyed. He heard that Joshua had done to Ai and its king the same thing he had done to Jericho and its king.

Adoni-Zedek heard that the people of Gibeon had made a peace treaty with Israel. He also found out that they were living among the people of Israel. [2]The things he heard alarmed him and his people very much. That's because Gibeon was an important city. It was like one of the royal cities. It was larger than Ai. All of its men were good soldiers.

[3]So Adoni-Zedek, the king of Jerusalem, made an appeal to Hoham, the king of Hebron. He appealed to Piram, the king of Jarmuth. He appealed to Japhia, the king of Lachish. He also made an appeal to Debir, the king of Eglon. [4]"Come up and help me attack Gibeon," he said. "Its people have made peace with Joshua and the people of Israel."

[5]The kings of Jerusalem, Hebron, Jarmuth, Lachish and Eglon gathered their armies together. Those five Amorite kings moved all of their troops into position to fight against Gibeon. Then they attacked it.

[6]Joshua was in the camp at Gilgal. The people of Gibeon sent a message to him there. It said, "Don't desert us. We serve you. Come up to us quickly! Save us! Help us! All of the Amorite kings from the central hill country have gathered their armies together to fight against us."

[7]So Joshua marched up from Gilgal with his whole army. The army included all of his best fighting men.

[8]The LORD said to Joshua, "Do not be afraid of them. I have handed them over to you. Not one of them will be able to fight against you and win."

[9]Joshua marched all night from Gilgal. He took the Amorite armies by surprise. [10]The LORD threw them into a panic as Israel marched toward them. Then Israel won a great battle over them at Gibeon. They chased them along the road that goes up to Beth Horon. They struck them down all the way to Azekah and Makkedah.

[11]The Amorites ran away as Israel marched toward them. They ran down the road from Beth Horon to Azekah. As they ran, the LORD threw large hailstones down on them from the sky. The hailstones killed more of them than the swords of the men of Israel did.

[12]So the LORD gave the Amorites over to Israel. On that day Joshua spoke to the LORD while the people of Israel were listening. He said,

"Sun, stand still over Gibeon.
  Moon, stand still over the Valley of Aijalon."
[13]So the sun stood still.
  The moon stopped.
  They didn't move again until the nation won the battle over its enemies.

You can read about it in the Book of Jashar.

The sun stopped in the middle of the sky. It didn't go down for about a full day. [14]There has never been a day like it before or since. It was a day when the LORD listened to a mere man. You can be sure that the LORD was fighting for Israel!

[15]Joshua and his whole army returned to the camp at Gilgal.

JOSHUA KILLS THE FIVE AMORITE KINGS

[16]The five Amorite kings had run away. They had hidden in the cave at Makkedah. [17]Joshua was told that the five kings had been found. He was also told that they were hiding in the cave at Makkedah. [18]He said, "Roll some large rocks up to the opening of the cave. Put some men there to guard it. [19]But keep on going! Chase your enemies. Attack them from behind. Don't let them get back to their cities. The LORD your God has handed them over to you."

[20]So Joshua and the men of Israel completely destroyed them. They killed almost every one of them. But a few escaped. They went back to their cities that had high walls around them.

[21]Then Israel's whole army returned safely to Joshua. He was in the camp at Makkedah. No one in the land dared to say anything against the people of Israel.

[22]Joshua said, "Open up the cave. Bring those five kings out to me." [23]So Joshua's men brought the five kings out of the cave. They were the kings of Jerusalem, Hebron, Jarmuth, Lachish and Eglon.

[24]The men brought them to Joshua. Then he sent for all of the men of Israel. He spoke to the army command-

ers who had come with him. He said, "Come here. Put your feet on the necks of these kings." So they came forward and placed their feet on the necks of the kings.

²⁵Joshua said to them, "Don't be afraid. Don't lose hope. Be strong and brave. This is what the LORD will do to all of the enemies you are going to fight."

²⁶Joshua struck the five kings down and killed them. He stuck a pole through each of their bodies. Then he set the poles up where people could see the bodies. He left them there until evening.

²⁷At sunset Joshua ordered his men to take the bodies down. So they took them down and threw them into the cave where the kings had been hiding. They placed large rocks at the opening of the cave. And the rocks are still there to this very day.

²⁸That day Joshua took Makkedah. He killed its people and their king with the sword. He totally destroyed everyone in it. He didn't leave anyone alive. He did to the king of Makkedah the same thing he had done to the king of Jericho.

THE CAMPAIGN AGAINST THE CITIES IN THE SOUTH

²⁹Joshua moved on from Makkedah to Libnah. Israel's whole army went with him. They attacked Libnah. ³⁰The LORD also handed that city and its king over to Israel. Joshua destroyed the city. He and his men killed everyone in it with their swords. He didn't leave anyone alive there. He did to its king the same thing he had done to the king of Jericho.

³¹Joshua moved on from Libnah to Lachish. Israel's whole army went with him. The men took up their battle positions. Then Joshua attacked Lachish. ³²The LORD handed it over to Israel. Joshua took the city on the second day of the battle. He destroyed the city. He and his men killed everyone in it with their swords. He had done the same thing to Libnah.

³³While all of that was happening, Horam had come up to help Lachish. He was the king of Gezer. But Joshua won the battle over him and his army. No one was left alive.

³⁴Joshua moved on from Lachish to Eglon. Israel's whole army went with him. They took up their battle positions. Then they attacked Eglon. ³⁵They captured it that same day. They totally destroyed everyone in it with their swords. They had done the same thing to Lachish.

³⁶Joshua went up from Eglon to Hebron. Israel's whole army went with him. Then they attacked Hebron. ³⁷They took the city. They destroyed it and its villages. They killed all of its people and their king with their swords. They didn't leave anyone alive. They totally destroyed the city and everyone in it. They had done the same thing at Eglon.

³⁸Joshua turned back and attacked Debir. Israel's whole army went with him. ³⁹They took the city, its king and its villages. They totally destroyed everyone in Debir with their swords. They didn't leave anyone alive. They did to Debir and its king the same thing they had done to Libnah and its king. They had also done the same thing to Hebron.

⁴⁰So Joshua brought the whole area under his control. That included the central hill country and the Negev Desert. It included the western hills and the mountain slopes. It also included all of the kings in that whole area. Joshua didn't leave anyone alive. He totally destroyed everyone who breathed. He did just as the LORD, the God of Israel, had commanded.

⁴¹Joshua brought everyone from Kadesh Barnea to Gaza under his control. He also brought everyone from the whole area of Goshen to Gibeon under his control. ⁴²He won the battle over all of those kings and their lands. He did it in one campaign. That's because the LORD, the God of Israel, fought for Israel.

⁴³Then Joshua returned to the camp at Gilgal. Israel's whole army went with him.

THE CAMPAIGN AGAINST THE CITIES IN THE NORTH

11 Jabin was the king of Hazor. He heard about the battles Israel had won. So he sent a message to Jobab. Jobab was the king of Madon. Jabin sent the same message to the kings of Shimron and Acshaph. ²He also sent it to a lot of other kings. Some ruled in the mountains in the north. Some ruled in the Arabah Valley south of Kinnereth. Others ruled in the western hills. Still others ruled in Naphoth Dor in the west. ³Jabin sent the same message to the people of east Canaan and west Canaan. He sent it to the Amorites, Hittites, Perizzites and Jebusites. They lived in the central hill country. He also sent it to the Hivites who lived below Mount Hermon in the area of Mizpah.

⁴Those kings marched out with all of their troops. They had a large number of horses and chariots. It was a huge army. The fighting men were as many as the grains of sand on the seashore. ⁵All of those kings gathered their armies together to fight against Israel. They set up camp together at the Waters of Merom.

⁶The Lord spoke to Joshua. He said, "Do not be afraid of them. By this time tomorrow I will hand all of them over to Israel. All of them will be killed. You must cut the legs of their horses. You must burn up their chariots."

⁷So Joshua and his whole army attacked them suddenly. They fought against them at the Waters of Merom. ⁸The Lord handed them over to Israel. Israel won the battle over them. They hunted them down all the way to Greater Sidon. They chased them to Misrephoth Maim. They chased them to the Valley of Mizpah in the east. Not one of them was left alive.

⁹Joshua did to them what the Lord had directed him to do. He cut the legs of their horses. He burned up their chariots.

¹⁰At that time Joshua turned back. He captured Hazor. He killed its king with his sword. Hazor was the most important city in all of those kingdoms. ¹¹The army of Israel killed everyone in Hazor with their swords. Its people had been set apart to the Lord in a special way to be destroyed. Israel's army didn't spare anything that breathed. Then Joshua burned up the city.

¹²Joshua took all of those royal cities and their kings. He and his men killed everyone in those cities with their swords. He totally destroyed them. He did just as Moses, the servant of the Lord, had commanded. ¹³Many cities were built on top of earlier cities that had been destroyed. Israel didn't burn up any of those except Hazor. Joshua burned it up.

¹⁴The army of Israel kept for themselves the livestock and everything else they took from those cities. But they killed all of the people with their swords. They completely destroyed them. They didn't spare anyone who breathed.

¹⁵The Lord had commanded his servant Moses to do all of those things. Moses had passed that command on to Joshua. And Joshua carried it out. He did everything the Lord had commanded Moses.

¹⁶So Joshua took the whole land. He took the central hill country and the whole Negev Desert. He took the whole area of Goshen. He took the western hills. He took the Arabah Valley. He took the mountains of Israel and the hills around them. ¹⁷He took the area that begins at Mount Halak, which rises toward Seir. The area ends at Baal Gad in the Valley of Lebanon below Mount Hermon.

Joshua captured the kings who ruled over that whole land. He struck them down and killed them. ¹⁸He fought battles against all of those kings for a long time.

¹⁹Only the Hivites who lived in Gibeon made a peace treaty with the people of Israel. No other city made a treaty with them. So Israel captured all of those cities in battle. ²⁰The Lord himself made the hearts of their people stubborn. He made them go to war against Israel so he could totally destroy them. He wanted to wipe them out. He didn't show them any mercy. The Lord had commanded Moses to destroy the people of Canaan.

²¹At that time Joshua went and destroyed the Anakites. They lived all through the hill country of Judah and Israel. They lived in Hebron, Debir and Anab. Joshua totally destroyed the Anakites and their towns. ²²There weren't any Anakites left alive in

Israel's territory. But a few were left alive in Gaza, Gath and Ashdod.

²³So Joshua took the whole land, just as the LORD had directed Moses. Joshua gave the land to Israel as their very own. He divided it up and gave each tribe its share.

Then the land had peace and rest.

ISRAEL WINS THE BATTLE OVER THE KINGS IN THE LAND

12 The people of Israel took over the territory east of the Jordan River. The land they took reached from the Arnon River valley to Mount Hermon. It included the whole east side of the Arabah Valley. Israel won the battle over the kings of that whole territory. Here are the lands Israel took from the kings they won the battle over.

²They took the land of Sihon. He was the king of the Amorites.

He ruled in Heshbon. The land he ruled over begins at Aroer. Aroer is on the rim of the Arnon River valley. He ruled from the middle of the valley to the Jabbok River. The Jabbok is the border of Ammon. Sihon's territory included half of Gilead. ³He also ruled over the east side of the Arabah Valley. That land begins at the Sea of Galilee. It goes to the Dead Sea and over to Beth Jeshimoth. Then it goes south, below the slopes of Pisgah.

⁴Israel also took the territory of Og. He was the king of Bashan.

He was one of the last of the Rephaites. He ruled in Ashtaroth and Edrei. ⁵He ruled over Mount Hermon, Salecah and the whole land of Bashan. He ruled all the way to the border of Geshur and Maacah. He ruled over half of Gilead. His land reached the border of Sihon. Sihon was the king of Heshbon.

⁶Moses was the servant of the LORD. Moses and the people of Israel won the battle over those two kings. He gave their land to the tribes of Reuben and Gad and half of the tribe of Manasseh. He gave it to them as their share.

⁷Joshua and the people of Israel won the battle over the kings who ruled west of the Jordan River. The lands of the kings reached from Baal Gad in the Valley of Lebanon to Mount Halak, which rises toward Seir.

Joshua gave their lands to the tribes of Israel as their very own. He divided them up and gave each tribe its share. ⁸Those lands included the central hill country, the western hills and the Arabah Valley. They also included the mountain slopes, the Desert of Judah and the Negev Desert. Those lands belonged to the Hittites, Amorites, Canaanites, Perizzites, Hivites and Jebusites. Here are the kings Israel won the battle over.

⁹the king of Jericho	one
the king of Ai, which is near Bethel	one
¹⁰the king of Jerusalem	one
the king of Hebron	one
¹¹the king of Jarmuth	one
the king of Lachish	one
¹²the king of Eglon	one
the king of Gezer	one
¹³the king of Debir	one
the king of Geder	one
¹⁴the king of Hormah	one
the king of Arad	one
¹⁵the king of Libnah	one
the king of Adullam	one
¹⁶the king of Makkedah	one
the king of Bethel	one
¹⁷the king of Tappuah	one
the king of Hepher	one
¹⁸the king of Aphek	one
the king of Lasharon	one
¹⁹the king of Madon	one
the king of Hazor	one
²⁰the king of Shimron Meron	one
the king of Acshaph	one
²¹the king of Taanach	one
the king of Megiddo	one
²²the king of Kedesh	one
the king of Jokneam in Carmel	one
²³the king of Dor in Naphoth Dor	one
the king of Goyim in Gilgal	one
²⁴the king of Tirzah	one

The total number of kings was 31.

THE LAND THAT REMAINED TO BE TAKEN OVER

13 Joshua was now very old. The LORD said to him, "You are very old. And there are still very large areas of land that have not been taken over yet.

2"Here is the land that remains to be taken over. It includes all of the areas of Philistia and Geshur. 3Those areas begin at the Shihor River in the eastern part of Egypt. They go to the territory of Ekron in the north. All of that land is considered as belonging to the people of Canaan. The land that remains to be taken over includes the territory of the five rulers of Philistia. They rule over Gaza, Ashdod, Ashkelon, Gath and Ekron. The Avvites 4live south of them. The rest of the land of Canaan that remains to be taken over reaches from Arah all the way to Aphek. Arah belongs to the people of Sidon. The land that remains to be taken over includes the area where the Amorites live. 5It includes the area where the people of Byblos live. It also includes all of Lebanon to the east. It reaches from Baal Gad below Mount Hermon to Lebo Hamath.

6"I myself will drive out all of the people who live in the mountain areas. Those areas reach from Lebanon to Misrephoth Maim. They include the area where all of the people of Sidon live. I myself will drive those people out to make room for the people of Israel.

"Make sure you set that land apart for Israel. Give it to them as their share, just as I have directed you. 7Divide it up among the nine tribes and half of the tribe of Manasseh. Give each tribe its share."

MOSES HAD GIVEN THE EASTERN TRIBES THEIR LAND

8The other half of Manasseh's tribe had already received the share of land Moses had given them. Their share was east of the Jordan River. The tribes of Reuben and Gad had already received their share too. Moses, the servant of the LORD, had given it to them.

9That land starts at Aroer on the rim of the Arnon River valley. It includes the town in the middle of the valley. It includes the high flatlands of Medeba all the way to Dibon. 10It also includes all of the towns of Sihon, the king of the Amorites. He had ruled in Heshbon. That area reaches to the border of Ammon. 11It also includes Gilead. It includes the territory of Geshur and Maacah. It includes Mount Hermon and the whole land of Bashan all the way to Salecah.

12So it includes the entire kingdom of Og in Bashan. Og had ruled in Ashtaroth and Edrei. He was one of the last of the Rephaites. Moses had won the battle over Sihon and Og. He had taken over their land.

13But the people of Israel didn't drive out the people of Geshur and Maacah. So they continue to live among the people of Israel to this very day.

14Moses hadn't given any share of the land to the tribe of Levi. That's because the offerings that are made with fire are their share. Those offerings are made to the LORD, the God of Israel. Moses gave the Levites what he had promised them.

15Here is what Moses had given to the tribe of Reuben, family group by family group.

16Their territory starts at Aroer on the rim of the Arnon River valley. It includes the town in the middle of the valley. It includes all of the high flatlands that are near Medeba. 17It includes Heshbon and all of its towns on those flatlands. Those towns include Dibon, Bamoth Baal, Beth Baal Meon, 18Jahaz, Kedemoth and Mephaath. 19They include Kiriathaim, Sibmah and Zereth Shahar on the hill in the valley. 20They also include Beth Peor, Beth Jeshimoth and the slopes of Pisgah. 21All of those towns are on the high flatlands.

The territory includes the whole kingdom of Sihon, the king of the Amorites. He had ruled in Heshbon. Moses had won the battle over him and over the chiefs of Midian. Those chiefs were Evi, Rekem, Zur, Hur and Reba. They were princes who helped Sihon fight against Israel. They lived in that country. ²²The people of Israel killed many of them in battle. They also killed Balaam with a sword. He was the son of Beor. Balaam used magic to find out what was going to happen.

²³The border of the tribe of Reuben was the bank of the Jordan River. All of those towns and their villages were given to the tribe of Reuben as their very own. Each family group received its share.

²⁴Here is what Moses had given to the tribe of Gad, family group by family group.

²⁵Their territory includes Jazer and all of the towns of Gilead. It includes half of the country of Ammon all the way to Aroer, which was near Rabbah. ²⁶Their territory reaches from Heshbon to Ramath Mizpah and Betonim. It reaches from Mahanaim to the territory of Debir. ²⁷In the valley their land includes Beth Haram, Beth Nimrah, Succoth and Zaphon. It also includes the rest of the kingdom of Sihon. He was the king of Heshbon. His kingdom included the east side of the Jordan River. It reached up to the south end of the Sea of Galilee. ²⁸All of those towns and their villages were given to the tribe of Gad as their very own. Each family group received its share.

²⁹Here is what Moses had given to half of the tribe of Manasseh, family group by family group. It's what Moses had given to half of Manasseh's family line.

³⁰Their territory starts at Mahanaim. It includes the whole land of Bashan. That was the entire kingdom of Og, the king of Bashan. Manasseh's territory includes all of the 60 towns of Jair in Bashan. ³¹It includes half of the land of Gilead. It also includes Ashtaroth and Edrei. They were the royal cities of Og in Bashan. That land was given to half of the family line of Makir. He was the son of Manasseh. Each family group received its share.

³²Those were the shares of land Moses had given the eastern tribes when he was in the flatlands of Moab. The flatlands are across the Jordan River east of Jericho. ³³But Moses hadn't given any share to the tribe of Levi. The LORD, the God of Israel, is their share. Moses gave the Levites what he had promised them.

THE WESTERN TRIBES ARE GIVEN THEIR LAND

14 The rest of the tribes of Israel received their shares of land in Canaan. The priest Eleazar and Joshua, the son of Nun, decided what each of the tribes should receive. The leaders of the tribes helped them make those decisions. ²The shares of nine tribes and half of the tribe of Manasseh were decided by using lots. That's what the LORD had commanded through Moses. ³Moses had given two tribes and the other half of the tribe of Manasseh their shares east of the Jordan River. But Moses had not given the Levites a share among the other tribes. ⁴Manasseh and Ephraim were the sons of Joseph. They had become two tribes. The Levites didn't receive any share of the land. They only received towns to live in and grasslands for their flocks and herds. ⁵So the people of Israel divided up the land, just as the LORD had commanded Moses.

JOSHUA GIVES HEBRON TO CALEB

⁶The men of Judah approached Joshua at Gilgal. Caleb, the son of Jephunneh the Kenizzite, spoke to Joshua. He said, "You know what the LORD said to Moses, the man of God.

He spoke to him at Kadesh Barnea about you and me. [7]Moses, the servant of the LORD, sent me from Kadesh Barnea to check out the land. I was 40 years old at that time. I brought back an honest report to him. I told him exactly what I had seen. [8]Several other men of Israel went up with me. What they reported made the hearts of the people melt away in fear. But I followed the LORD my God with my whole heart.

[9]"So on that day Moses took an oath and made a promise to me. He said, 'The land your feet have walked on will be your share. It will be the share of your children forever. That's because you have followed the LORD my God with your whole heart.'
(Deuteronomy 1:36)

[10]"The LORD has done just as he promised. He made the promise while Israel was wandering around in the desert. That was 45 years ago. He has kept me alive all of this time. So here I am today, 85 years old! [11]I'm still as strong today as I was the day Moses sent me out. I'm just as able to go out to battle now as I was then.

[12]"So give me this hill country. The LORD promised it to me that day. At that time you yourself heard that the Anakites were living there. You also heard that their cities were large and had high walls. But I'll drive them out, just as the LORD said I would. He will help me do it."

[13]Then Joshua blessed Caleb, the son of Jephunneh. He gave him Hebron as his share. [14]So ever since that time Hebron has belonged to Caleb, the son of Jephunneh the Kenizzite. That's because he followed the LORD, the God of Israel, with his whole heart.

[15]Hebron used to be called Kiriath Arba. It was named after Arba. He was the greatest man among the Anakites. So the land had peace and rest.

LAND IS GIVEN TO JUDAH

15 Land was given to the tribe of Judah, family group by family group. It reached down to the territory of Edom. It went as far south as the Desert of Zin. [2]Judah's border on the south started from the bay at the south end of the Dead Sea. [3]It went across to the south of Scorpion Pass. It continued on to Zin. It went over to the south of Kadesh Barnea. Then it ran past Hezron up to Addar. It curved around to Karka. [4]It then went along to Azmon. There it joined the Wadi of Egypt and ended at the Mediterranean Sea. That was the southern border of Judah.

[5]The border on the east was the Dead Sea. It went north all the way to where the Jordan River enters the sea.

The border on the north started at the bay of the Dead Sea. That's where the Jordan River enters the sea. [6]From there it went up to Beth Hoglah. It continued north of Beth Arabah to the Stone of Bohan, the son of Reuben. [7]Then it went from the Valley of Achor up to Debir. It turned north to Gilgal. Gilgal faces the Pass of Adummim south of the valley. The border continued along to the springs of En Shemesh. It came to an end at En Rogel. [8]Then it ran up the Valley of Ben Hinnom. It went along the south slope of Jerusalem. From there it climbed to the top of the hill that is west of the Hinnom Valley. The hill is also at the north end of the Valley of Rephaim. [9]From the top of the hill the border headed toward the springs of Nephtoah. It went to the towns near Mount Ephron. It went down toward Kiriath Jearim. [10]Then it curved west from Kiriath Jearim to Mount Seir. It ran along the north slope of Mount Kesalon. It continued down to Beth Shemesh and crossed over to Timnah. [11]It went to the north slope of Ekron. Then it turned toward Shikkeron. It passed along to Mount Baalah and reached Jabneel. The border came to an end at the Mediterranean Sea. [12]The border on the west was the coastline of the Mediterranean Sea.

Those were the borders of the family groups of the tribe of Judah.

[13]Joshua gave a part of Judah's share of land to Caleb, the son of Jephunneh. That was in keeping with the LORD's command to Joshua. The share Caleb received was the city of Hebron. It was also called Kiriath Arba. Anak came from the family line of Arba. [14]Caleb drove three Anakites out of Hebron. Their names were Sheshai, Ahiman and Talmai. They were from the family line of Anak.

[15]From Hebron, Caleb marched out against the people who were living in Debir. It used to be called Kiriath Sepher. [16]Caleb said, "I will give my daughter Acsah to be married. I'll give her to the man who attacks and captures Kiriath Sepher."

[17]Othniel captured it. So Caleb gave his daughter Acsah to him to be his wife. Othniel was the son of Kenaz. He was Caleb's brother.

[18]One day Acsah came to Othniel. She begged him to ask her father for a field. When she got off her donkey, Caleb spoke to her. He asked, "What can I do for you?"

[19]She replied, "Do me a special favor. You have given me some land in the Negev Desert. Give me springs of water also." So Caleb gave her the upper and lower springs.

[20]Here is the share of land that was given to the tribe of Judah, family group by family group.

[21]The towns farthest south that were given to Judah were in the Negev Desert. They were near the border of Edom. Here is a list of those towns.

Kabzeel, Eder, Jagur, [22]Kinah, Dimonah, Adadah, [23]Kedesh, Hazor, Ithnan, [24]Ziph, Telem, Bealoth, [25]Hazor Hadattah, Hazor, [26]Amam, Shema, Moladah, [27]Hazar Gaddah, Heshmon, Beth Pelet, [28]Hazar Shual, Beersheba, Biziothiah, [29]Baalah, Iim, Ezem, [30]Eltolad, Kesil, Hormah, [31]Ziklag, Madmannah, Sansannah, [32]Lebaoth, Shilhim, Ain and Rimmon. The total number of towns was 29. Some of them had villages near them.

[33]Towns were also given to Judah in the western hills. Here is a list of those towns.

Eshtaol, Zorah, Ashnah, [34]Zanoah, En Gannim, Tappuah, Enam, [35]Jarmuth, Adullam, Socoh, Azekah, [36]Shaaraim, Adithaim and Gederah. Gederah is also called Gederothaim. The total number of towns was 14. Some of them had villages near them.

[37]Here's another list of towns that were given to Judah in the western hills.

Zenan, Hadashah, Migdal Gad, [38]Dilean, Mizpah, Joktheel, [39]Lachish, Bozkath, Eglon, [40]Cabbon, Lahmas, Kitlish, [41]Gederoth, Beth Dagon, Naamah and Makkedah. The total number of towns was 16. Some of them had villages near them.

[42]Here's another list of towns that were given to Judah in the western hills.

Libnah, Ether, Ashan, [43]Iphtah, Ashnah, Nezib, [44]Keilah, Aczib and Mareshah. The total number of towns was nine. Some of them had villages near them.

[45]Judah was also given Ekron and the settlements and villages that were around it. [46]West of Ekron, Judah was given all of the settlements and villages that were near Ashdod. [47]Judah was given Ashdod and the settlements and villages that were around it. And Judah was given Gaza and its settlements and villages. Judah's territory went all the way to the Wadi of Egypt and the coast of the Mediterranean Sea.

[48]Towns were also given to Judah in the central hill country. Here is a list of those towns.

Shamir, Jattir, Socoh, [49]Dannah, Debir, [50]Anab, Eshtemoh, Anim, [51]Goshen, Holon and Giloh. The total number of towns was 11. Some of them had villages near them.

[52]Here's another list of towns that were given to Judah in the central hill country.

Arab, Dumah, Eshan, [53]Janim, Beth Tappuah, Aphekah, [54]Humtah, Hebron and Zior. The total number of towns was nine. Some of them had villages near them.

[55]Here's another list of towns that

were given to Judah in the central hill country.

Maon, Carmel, Ziph, Juttah, [56]Jezreel, Jokdeam, Zanoah, [57]Kain, Gibeah and Timnah. The total number of towns was ten. Some of them had villages near them.

[58]Here's another list of towns that were given to Judah in the central hill country.

Halhul, Beth Zur, Gedor, [59]Maarath, Beth Anoth and Eltekon. The total number of towns was six. Some of them had villages near them.

[60]Here's another list of towns that were given to Judah in the central hill country.

Kiriath Jearim and Rabbah. The total number of towns was two. They had villages near them.

[61]Towns were also given to Judah in the desert. Here is a list of those towns.

Beth Arabah, Middin, Secacah, [62]Nibshan, the City of Salt and En Gedi. The total number of towns was six. Some of them had villages near them.

[63]Judah couldn't drive out the Jebusites who were living in Jerusalem. So they live there with the people of Judah to this very day.

LAND IS GIVEN TO EPHRAIM AND MANASSEH

16 The land that was given to the two tribes in the family line of Joseph began at the Jordan River near Jericho. Their border started east of the springs of Jericho. It went up from there through the desert into the hill country of Bethel. [2]Bethel is also called Luz. From Bethel it crossed over to Ataroth. That's where the Arkites live. [3]Then it went west down to the territory of the Japhletites. It went all the way to the area of Lower Beth Horon. It went on to Gezer. It came to an end at the Mediterranean Sea.

[4]The tribes of Manasseh and Ephraim were from the family line of Joseph. So they received that land as their share.

[5]Here is the territory that was given to the tribe of Ephraim, family group by family group.

The border of their share of land started at Ataroth Addar in the east. It went to Upper Beth Horon. [6]It continued toward the Mediterranean Sea. From Micmethath on the north, it curved toward the east. It went to Taanath Shiloh. It passed by Taanath Shiloh to Janoah on the east. [7]Then it went down from Janoah to Ataroth and Naarah. It touched Jericho and came to an end at the Jordan River. [8]From Tappuah the border went west to the Kanah Valley. It came to an end at the Mediterranean Sea. That was the land that was given to the tribe of Ephraim. Each family group received its share.

[9]The tribe of Ephraim was also given other towns and villages that were set apart for them. Those towns and villages were in the share of land that was given to the tribe of Manasseh.

[10]The people of Ephraim didn't drive out the people of Canaan who were living in Gezer. The people of Canaan live among the people of Ephraim to this very day. But they are forced to work hard for the people of Ephraim.

17 Land was given to the tribe of Manasseh. It was given to Makir. Manasseh was Joseph's oldest son. Makir was Manasseh's oldest son. The people of Gilead came from the family line of Makir. The people of Gilead had received the lands of Gilead and Bashan. That's because the people of Makir were great soldiers. [2]So land was given to the rest of the people of Manasseh. It was given to the family groups of Abiezer, Helek, Asriel, Shechem, Hepher and Shemida. They were the other men in the family line of Manasseh, the son of Joseph. Those were their names by their family groups.

[3]Makir was the son of Manasseh. Gilead was the son of Makir. Hepher was the son of Gilead. And Zelophehad was the son of Hepher. Zelophehad didn't have any sons. He only

had daughters. Their names were Mahlah, Noah, Hoglah, Milcah and Tirzah.

⁴The daughters of Zelophehad went to the priest Eleazar and to Joshua, the son of Nun. They also went to the other leaders. They said, "The LORD commanded Moses to give us our share of land among our male relatives." So Joshua gave them land along with their male relatives. That was in keeping with what the LORD had commanded.

⁵Manasseh's share was made up of ten pieces of land. That land was in addition to Gilead and Bashan east of the Jordan River. ⁶So the five granddaughters of Hepher in the family line of Manasseh received land, just as the other five sons of Manasseh did. The land of Gilead belonged to the rest of the family line of Manasseh.

⁷The territory of Manasseh reached from Asher to Micmethath. Micmethath was east of Shechem. The border ran south from Micmethath. The people who were living at En Tappuah were inside the border. ⁸Manasseh had the land around Tappuah. But the town of Tappuah itself was on the border of Manasseh's land. It belonged to the people of Ephraim. ⁹The border continued south to the Kanah Valley. Some of the towns that belonged to Ephraim were located among the towns of Manasseh. But the border of Manasseh was the north side of the valley. The border came to an end at the Mediterranean Sea.

¹⁰The land on the south belonged to Ephraim. The land on the north belonged to Manasseh. The territory of Manasseh reached the Mediterranean Sea. The tribe of Asher was the border on the north. The tribe of Issachar was the border on the east. ¹¹Inside the land that was given to Issachar and Asher, the towns of Beth Shan and Ibleam belonged to Manasseh. The towns of Dor, Endor, Taanach and Megiddo and their people also belonged to Manasseh. Manasseh was given

all of those towns and the settlements that were around them. The third town in the list was also called Naphoth Dor.

¹²But the people of Manasseh weren't able to take over those towns. That's because the people of Canaan had made up their minds to live in that area. ¹³The people of Israel grew stronger. Then they forced the people of Canaan to work hard for them. But they didn't drive them out completely.

¹⁴The people in the family line of Joseph spoke to Joshua. They said, "Why have you given us only one share of the land to have as our own? There are large numbers of us. The LORD has blessed us greatly."

¹⁵"That's true," Joshua said. "There are large numbers of you. And the hill country of Ephraim is too small for you. So go up into the forest. Clear out some land for yourselves in the territory of the Perizzites and Rephaites."

¹⁶The people in Joseph's family line replied. They said, "The hill country isn't big enough for us. And all of the people of Canaan who live in the flatlands use chariots that have iron parts. They include the people of Beth Shan and its settlements. They also include the people who live in the Valley of Jezreel."

¹⁷Joshua spoke again to the people in Joseph's family line. He said to the people of Ephraim and Manasseh, "There are large numbers of you. And you are very powerful. You will have more than one piece of land. ¹⁸You will also have the central hill country. It's covered with trees. Cut them down and clear the land. That whole land from one end to the other will belong to you. The people of Canaan use chariots that have iron parts. And those people are strong. But you can drive them out."

THE REST OF THE LAND IS DIVIDED UP

18 The whole community of Israel gathered together at Shiloh. They set up the Tent of Meeting there. The country was brought under their control. ²But there were still seven tribes in Israel who had not yet received their shares of land.

[3]So Joshua spoke to the people of Israel. He said, "The LORD, the God of your people, has given you this land. How long will you wait before you begin to take it over? [4]Appoint three men from each tribe. I'll send them to map out the land. Then they'll write a report about its features. The report will point out the share of land each tribe will receive. Then the men will return to me.

[5]"You must divide the land up into seven shares. Judah must remain in its territory in the south. The people in Joseph's family line must remain in their territory in the north. [6]Write reports about the features of those seven shares of land. Bring them here to me. Then I'll cast lots for you in the sight of the LORD our God.

[7]"But the Levites don't get any share of your land. That's because their share is to serve the LORD as priests.

"The tribes of Gad and Reuben and half of the tribe of Manasseh have already received their shares. They are on the east side of the Jordan River. Moses, the servant of the LORD, gave their shares to them."

[8]The men started out on their way to map out the land. Joshua directed them, "Go and map out the land. Write a report about its features. Then return to me. I'll cast lots for you here at Shiloh in the sight of the LORD."

[9]So the men left and went through the land. They wrote a report about its features on a scroll. It showed how they divided up the land into seven shares. It listed the towns that were in each share. The men returned to Joshua in the camp at Shiloh.

[10]Then Joshua cast lots for them in Shiloh in the sight of the LORD. There he gave out a share of land to each of the remaining tribes in Israel.

LAND IS GIVEN TO BENJAMIN

[11]The first lot that was drawn out was for the tribe of Benjamin, family group by family group. The territory they were given was located between the tribes of the people of Judah and the people of Joseph. Here are the borders of Benjamin's territory.

[12]On the north side their border started at the Jordan River. It went past the north slope of Jericho. Then it headed west into the central hill country. It came to an end at the Desert of Beth Aven. [13]From there it crossed to the south slope of Bethel. Then it went down to Ataroth Addar on the hill south of Lower Beth Horon.

[14]From the hill that faces Beth Horon on the south the border turned south along the west side of the hill. It came to an end at Kiriath Jearim. That town belongs to the people of Judah. That was the border on the west.

[15]The border on the south side started at the west edge of Kiriath Jearim. It came to an end at the springs of Nephtoah. [16]It went down to the foot of the hill that faces the Valley of Ben Hinnom. The hill is north of the Valley of Rephaim. The border continued down the Hinnom Valley. It went along the south slope of Jerusalem, where the people of Jebus live. It continued on to En Rogel. [17]Then it curved north. It went to En Shemesh. It continued on to Geliloth. Geliloth faces the Pass of Adummim. The border ran down to the Stone of Bohan, the son of Reuben. [18]It continued to the north slope of Beth Arabah. It went on down into the Arabah Valley. [19]From there it went to the north slope of Beth Hoglah. It came to an end at the north bay of the Dead Sea. That's where the Jordan River flows into the Dead Sea. That was the border on the south.

[20]The Jordan River formed the border on the east side. Those were the borders that marked out on all sides the land the family groups of Benjamin received as their share.

[21]Here is a list of towns that were given to the tribe of Benjamin, family group by family group.

Jericho, Beth Hoglah, Emek Keziz, [22]Beth Arabah, Zemaraim, Bethel, [23]Avvim, Parah, Ophrah,

[24]Kephar Ammoni, Ophni and Geba. The total number of towns and their villages was 12. [25]Here is another list of towns that were given to Benjamin.

Gibeon, Ramah, Beeroth, [26]Mizpah, Kephirah, Mozah, [27]Rekem, Irpeel, Taralah, [28]Zelah, Haeleph, Jerusalem, Gibeah and Kiriath. The total number of towns and their villages was 14.

That was the share of land the family groups of Benjamin received.

LAND IS GIVEN TO SIMEON

19 The second lot that was drawn out was for the tribe of Simeon, family group by family group. The share of land they were given was in the territory of Judah. [2]Here is what Simeon's share included.

Beersheba, Moladah, [3]Hazar Shual, Balah, Ezem, [4]Eltolad, Bethul, Hormah, [5]Ziklag, Beth Marcaboth, Hazar Susah, [6]Beth Lebaoth and Sharuhen. The total number of towns was 13. Some of them had villages near them. [7]Here's another list of towns that were given to Simeon.

Ain, Rimmon, Ether and Ashan. The total number of towns was four. Some of them had villages near them. [8]The towns and all of the villages that were around them reached all the way to Ramah in the Negev Desert.

That was the share of land the tribe of Simeon received, family group by family group. [9]Simeon's share of land was taken from Judah's share. That's because Judah had more land than they needed. So the people of Simeon received their share of land inside the territory of Judah.

LAND IS GIVEN TO ZEBULUN

[10]The third lot that was drawn out was for the tribe of Zebulun, family group by family group. Here are the borders of Zebulun's territory.

The border of their share of land went as far as Sarid. [11]It ran west to Maralah and touched Dabbesheth. It reached to the valley near Jokneam. [12]It turned east

from Sarid toward the sunrise. It went to the territory of Kisloth Tabor. It went on to Daberath and up to Japhia. [13]Then it continued east to Gath Hepher and Eth Kazin. It came to an end at Rimmon and turned toward Neah. [14]There the border went around on the north to Hannathon. It came to an end at the Valley of Iphtah El. [15]Zebulun's territory included Kattath, Nahalal, Shimron, Idalah and Bethlehem. The total number of towns was 12. Some of them had villages near them. [16]Those towns and their villages were Zebulun's share, family group by family group.

LAND IS GIVEN TO ISSACHAR

[17]The fourth lot that was drawn out was for the tribe of Issachar, family group by family group. [18]Here is what Issachar's share included.

Jezreel, Kesulloth, Shunem, [19]Hapharaim, Shion, Anaharath, [20]Rabbith, Kishion, Ebez, [21]Remeth, En Gannim, En Haddah and Beth Pazzez. [22]The border touched Tabor, Shahazumah and Beth Shemesh. It came to an end at the Jordan River. The total number of towns was 16. Some of them had villages near them. [23]Those towns and their villages were the share the tribe of Issachar received, family group by family group.

LAND IS GIVEN TO ASHER

[24]The fifth lot that was drawn out was for the tribe of Asher, family group by family group. [25]Here is what Asher's share included.

Helkath, Hali, Beten, Acshaph, [26]Allammelech, Amad and Mishal. On the west the border touched Carmel and Shihor Libnath. [27]Then it turned east toward Beth Dagon. It touched Zebulun and the Valley of Iphtah El. It went north to Beth Emek and Neiel. It went past Cabul on the left. [28]It went to Abdon, Rehob, Hammon and Kanah. It reached all the way to Greater Sidon. [29]The border then turned back toward Ramah.

It went to Tyre, a city that had high walls around it. It turned toward Hosah. It came to an end at the Mediterranean Sea in the area of Aczib, ³⁰Ummah, Aphek and Rehob. The total number of towns was 22. Some of them had villages near them.

³¹Those towns and their villages were the share the tribe of Asher received, family group by family group.

LAND IS GIVEN TO NAPHTALI

³²The sixth lot that was drawn out was for Naphtali, family group by family group.

³³Their border started at Heleph and the large tree in Zaanannim. It went past Adami Nekeb and Jabneel. It went to Lakkum and came to an end at the Jordan River. ³⁴The border ran west through Aznoth Tabor. It came to an end at Hukkok. It touched Zebulun on the south. It touched Asher on the west. It touched the Jordan on the east.

³⁵The cities that had high walls around them were Ziddim, Zer, Hammath, Rakkath, Kinnereth, ³⁶Adamah, Ramah, Hazor, ³⁷Kedesh, Edrei, En Hazor, ³⁸Iron, Migdal El, Horem, Beth Anath and Beth Shemesh. The total number of towns was 19. Some of them had villages near them.

³⁹Those towns and their villages were the share the tribe of Naphtali received, family group by family group.

LAND IS GIVEN TO DAN

⁴⁰The seventh lot that was drawn out was for the tribe of Dan, family group by family group. ⁴¹Here is what Dan's share of land included.

Zorah, Eshtaol, Ir Shemesh, ⁴²Shaalabbin, Aijalon, Ithlah, ⁴³Elon, Timnah, Ekron, ⁴⁴Eltekeh, Gibbethon, Baalath, ⁴⁵Jehud, Bene Berak, Gath Rimmon, ⁴⁶Me Jarkon and Rakkon. Dan's share included the area that faces Joppa.

⁴⁷The people of Dan had trouble taking over their territory. So they went up and attacked Leshem. They took it. They killed its people with their swords. Then they moved into Leshem

and settled down there. They named it Dan. That's because they traced their family line back to him.

⁴⁸All of those towns and their villages were the share the tribe of Dan received, family group by family group.

LAND IS GIVEN TO JOSHUA

⁴⁹The people of Israel finished dividing up the shares of land the tribes received. Then they gave a share to Joshua, the son of Nun. ⁵⁰They did what the LORD had commanded them to do. They gave Joshua the town he asked for. It was Timnath Serah in the hill country of Ephraim. He built up the town and settled down there.

⁵¹All of those territories were given out by using lots at Shiloh. The lots were drawn out by the priest Eleazar and by Joshua, the son of Nun. The leaders of the tribes of Israel helped them. The lots were drawn out in front of the LORD at the entrance to the Tent of Meeting. So the work of dividing up the land was finished.

CITIES TO GO TO FOR SAFETY

20 Then the LORD spoke to Joshua. He said, ²"Tell the people of Israel to choose the cities to go to for safety, just as I directed you through Moses. ³Anyone who kills a person by accident can run there for safety. So can anyone who kills a person without meaning to. The one who is charged with murder will be kept safe from the nearest male relative of the person who was killed.

⁴"Suppose the one who is charged runs for safety to one of those cities. Then he must stand in the entrance of the city gate. He must state his case in front of the elders of that city. They must let him come into their city. They must give him a place to live there.

⁵"Suppose the nearest male relative of the person who was killed comes after him. Then the elders must not hand him over to that relative. That's because he didn't mean to kill his neighbor. He didn't make evil plans to do it.

⁶"He must stay in that city until his case has been brought to the community court. He must stay there until the

high priest who is serving at that time dies. Then he can go back to his own home. He can return to the town he ran away from."

[7]So the people of Israel set apart Kedesh in Galilee. It's in the hill country of Naphtali. They set apart Shechem. It's in the hill country of Ephraim. They set apart Kiriath Arba. It's in the hill country of Judah. Kiriath Arba is also called Hebron.

[8]On the east side of the Jordan River near Jericho they chose Bezer. It's in the desert on the high flatlands. It's in the territory of the tribe of Reuben. They chose Ramoth in Gilead. It's in the territory of the tribe of Gad. They chose Golan in the land of Bashan. It's in the territory of the tribe of Manasseh.

[9]Suppose you kill someone by accident. Or another Israelite does it. Or an outsider who lives among you does it. Then any of you can run for safety to one of those cities that have been chosen. There you won't be killed by the nearest male relative of the person who was killed. First your case must be brought to the community court.

TOWNS ARE GIVEN TO THE LEVITES

21 The leaders of the Levite family groups approached the priest Eleazar and Joshua, the son of Nun. They also approached the leaders of the family groups of Israel's other tribes. [2]They went to all of them at Shiloh in Canaan. They said to them, "Give us towns to live in. Also give us grasslands for our livestock. That's what the LORD commanded through Moses."

[3]So the people of Israel gave the Levites towns and grasslands out of their own shares of land. They did what the LORD had commanded. Here are the towns the Levites were given.

[4]The first lot that was drawn out was for the people of Kohath, family group by family group. Some of the Levites came from the family line of the priest Aaron. They were given 13 towns from the tribes of Judah, Simeon and Benjamin. [5]The rest of Kohath's family groups were given ten towns from the family groups of the tribes of Ephraim and Dan and half of the tribe of Manasseh.

[6]The family groups of Gershon were given 13 towns from the family groups of the tribes of Issachar, Asher and Naphtali and half of the tribe of Manasseh. That part of Manasseh was in the land of Bashan.

[7]The family groups of Merari received 12 towns from the tribes of Reuben, Gad and Zebulun. Each family group received its share.

[8]So the people of Israel gave those towns and their grasslands to the Levites. They did what the LORD had commanded through Moses.

[9]They gave some towns from the territories of the tribes of Judah and Simeon [10]to the members of the family line of Aaron. The towns were given to the family groups of Kohath. They were Levites. The first lot that was drawn out was for them. Here are the towns the family groups of Kohath were given.

[11]The people of Israel gave them Kiriath Arba and the grasslands that were around it. Kiriath Arba is also called Hebron. It's in the hill country of Judah. Anak came from the family line of Arba. [12]But Israel had already given away the fields and villages around the city. They had given them to Caleb as his share. Caleb was the son of Jephunneh.

[13]So they gave Hebron to the members of the family line of the priest Aaron. Hebron was a city where anyone who was charged with murder could go for safety. They also gave them Libnah, [14]Jattir, Eshtemoa, [15]Holon, Debir, [16]Ain, Juttah and Beth Shemesh. They gave those towns and their grasslands to the family groups of Kohath. The total number of towns from the tribes of Judah and Simeon was nine.

[17]The people of Israel gave some towns from the tribe of Benjamin to the family groups of Kohath. The towns were Gibeon, Geba, [18]Anathoth and Almon. The

total number of those towns and their grasslands was four.

¹⁹So the total number of towns and their grasslands that were given to the priests in the family line of Aaron was 13.

²⁰There were other family groups of Kohath among the Levites. They were given towns from the tribe of Ephraim. Here are the towns those other family groups of Kohath were given.

²¹In the hill country of Ephraim they were given Shechem. It was a city where anyone who was charged with murder could go for safety. They were also given Gezer, ²²Kibzaim and Beth Horon. The total number of those towns and their grasslands was four.

²³From the tribe of Dan they received Eltekeh, Gibbethon, ²⁴Aijalon and Gath Rimmon. The total number of those towns and their grasslands was four.

²⁵From half of the tribe of Manasseh they received Taanach and Gath Rimmon. The total number of those towns and their grasslands was two.

²⁶So all of those ten towns and their grasslands were given to the other family groups of Kohath.

²⁷Here are the towns the family groups of Gershon among the Levites were given.

From half of the tribe of Manasseh they received Golan in the land of Bashan. Golan was a city where anyone who was charged with murder could go for safety. They also received Be Eshtarah. The total number of those towns and their grasslands was two.

²⁸From the tribe of Issachar they received Kishion, Daberath, ²⁹Jarmuth and En Gannim. The total number of those towns and their grasslands was four.

³⁰From the tribe of Asher they received Mishal, Abdon, ³¹Helkath and Rehob. The total number of those towns and their grasslands was four.

³²From the tribe of Naphtali they received Kedesh in Galilee.

Kedesh was a city where anyone who was charged with murder could go for safety. They also received Hammoth Dor and Kartan. The total number of those towns and their grasslands was three.

³³So the total number of towns and their grasslands that were given to the family groups of Gershon was 13.

³⁴The rest of the Levites were from the family groups of Merari. Here are the towns they were given.

From the tribe of Zebulun they received Jokneam, Kartah, ³⁵Dimnah and Nahalal. The total number of those towns and their grasslands was four.

³⁶From the tribe of Reuben they received Bezer, Jahaz, ³⁷Kedemoth and Mephaath. The total number of those towns and their grasslands was four.

³⁸From the tribe of Gad they received Ramoth in Gilead. Ramoth was a city where anyone who was charged with murder could go for safety. They also received Mahanaim, ³⁹Heshbon and Jazer. The total number of those towns and their grasslands was four.

⁴⁰So the total number of towns that were given to the family groups of Merari was 12. That concludes the list of towns the rest of the Levites received.

⁴¹The total number of Levite towns and their grasslands in the territory that was given to Israel was 48. ⁴²Each of those towns had grasslands around it. That was true of all of them.

⁴³So the LORD gave Israel all of the land he had promised with an oath to give to Abraham, Isaac and Jacob. And Israel took it over. Then they settled down there. ⁴⁴The LORD gave them peace and rest on every side. That's what he had promised their fathers he would do. Not one of their enemies was able to fight against Israel and win. The LORD handed all of their enemies over to them.

⁴⁵The LORD kept all of the good promises he had made to the people of Israel. Every one of them came true.

THE EASTERN TRIBES RETURN HOME

22 Joshua sent for the tribes of Reuben and Gad and half of the tribe of Manasseh. ²He said to them, "You have done everything that Moses, the servant of the LORD, commanded. You have also obeyed everything I commanded. ³For a long time now you haven't deserted the other Israelites. Instead, you have done what the LORD your God sent you to do. You have obeyed him to this very day.

⁴"Now the LORD your God has given the other tribes peace and rest. That's what he promised to do. So return to your homes. They are in the land that Moses, the servant of the LORD, gave you. It's on the east side of the Jordan River.

⁵"Be very careful to obey the law that Moses, the servant of the LORD, gave you. He commanded you to love the LORD your God. He told you to live exactly as the LORD wants you to. He told you to obey the LORD's commands. He told you to remain true to the LORD. And he told you to serve the LORD with all your heart and with all your soul."

⁶Joshua gave the eastern tribes his blessing. Then he sent them home. So they went.

⁷Moses had given land in Bashan to half of the tribe of Manasseh. Joshua had given land to the other half of the tribe along with the other tribes on the west side of the Jordan River.

When Joshua sent them home, he blessed them. ⁸He said, "Return to your homes. Take your great wealth with you. Return with your large herds of livestock. Take your silver, gold, bronze and iron with you. Return with all of your clothes. Divide up the things you have taken from your enemies. Share them with your people."

⁹So the tribes of Reuben and Gad and half of the tribe of Manasseh went home. They left the other people of Israel at Shiloh in Canaan. They returned to Gilead. That was their own land. They had gotten it in keeping with the LORD's command through Moses.

¹⁰The tribes of Reuben and Gad and half of the tribe of Manasseh came to Geliloth. It was near the Jordan River in the land of Canaan. They built a large altar there by the Jordan.

¹¹The rest of the people of Israel heard that they had built the altar. They heard that they had built it on the border of Canaan at Geliloth. It was near the Jordan River on the west side.

¹²So the whole community of Israel gathered together at Shiloh. They decided to go to war against the eastern tribes.

¹³The people of Israel sent the priest Phinehas to the land of Gilead. Phinehas was the son of Eleazar. They sent him to the tribes of Reuben and Gad and half of the tribe of Manasseh.

¹⁴They sent ten of their leaders with him. There was one for each of the tribes of Israel. Each man was the leader of a family group among the larger family groups of Israel.

¹⁵They went to the tribes of Reuben and Gad and half of the tribe of Manasseh in the land of Gilead. They said to them, ¹⁶"We're speaking for the LORD's whole community. How could you disobey the God of Israel like this? How could you turn away from the LORD? How could you disobey him by building an altar for yourselves?

¹⁷"Don't you remember how we sinned at Peor? The LORD struck us with a plague because of what we did. Up to this very day we're still suffering because of that sin. ¹⁸Are you turning away from the LORD now?

"Suppose you disobey the LORD today. If you do, he'll be angry with the whole community of Israel tomorrow.

¹⁹"If your own land isn't 'clean,' come over to the LORD's land. It's where his holy tent stands. Share our land with us. But don't disobey the LORD. Don't turn against us by building an altar for yourselves. Don't build any altar other than the altar of the LORD our God.

²⁰"Remember Achan, the son of Zerah. Achan wasn't faithful to the LORD. He took the things that had been set apart to the LORD in a special way to be destroyed. Didn't the LORD's anger come on the whole community of

Israel? And Achan wasn't the only one who died because of his sin."

²¹Then the tribes of Reuben and Gad and half of the tribe of Manasseh replied. They answered the leaders of the family groups of Israel. ²²They said, "The Mighty One, God, the LORD! The Mighty One, God, the LORD! He knows! And we want Israel to know! Have we opposed the LORD? Have we refused to obey him? If we have, don't spare us today.

²³"Have we built our own altar so we can turn away from the LORD? Have we built it to offer burnt offerings and grain offerings on it? Have we built it to sacrifice friendship offerings on it? If we have, may the LORD himself hold us accountable.

²⁴"No! We built it because we were afraid. Someday your children might speak to our children. We were afraid they might say, 'What do you have to do with the LORD? What do you have to do with the God of Israel?' ²⁵The LORD has made the Jordan River a border between us and you. You people of Reuben! You people of Gad! You don't have anything to do with the LORD.' If your children say that, they might cause our children to stop worshiping the LORD.

²⁶"That's why we said to ourselves, 'Let's get ready and build an altar. But let's not build it to offer burnt offerings or sacrifices on it.'

²⁷"So just the opposite is true. The altar will be a witness between us and you. It will be a witness between our children and yours after us. It will also be a witness that we will worship the LORD at his sacred tent. We'll worship him there with our burnt offerings, sacrifices and friendship offerings. Then in days to come your children won't be able to say to ours, 'You don't have anything to do with the LORD.'

²⁸"So we said to ourselves, 'Suppose they say that to us sometime. Or suppose they say it to our children after us. Then we'll answer, "Look at this altar. It's exactly like the LORD's altar. Our people built it. They didn't build it to offer burnt offerings and sacrifices on it. Instead, they built it to be a witness between us and you." '

²⁹"We would never refuse to obey the LORD. We would never turn away from him now. We wouldn't build an altar to offer burnt offerings, grain offerings and sacrifices on it. We wouldn't use any altar other than the altar of the LORD our God. That altar stands in front of his holy tent."

³⁰The priest Phinehas heard what the tribes of Reuben, Gad and Manasseh had to say. The leaders of the family groups of the community of Israel heard it too. All of them were pleased with what they heard.

³¹The priest Phinehas spoke to the tribes of Reuben, Gad and Manasseh. Phinehas was the son of Eleazar. He said, "Today we know that the LORD is with us. That's because you have been faithful to him in this matter. Now you have saved the people of Israel from the LORD's anger against them."

³²Then the priest Phinehas, the son of Eleazar, returned to Canaan. So did the leaders. All of them went back from their meeting with the tribes of Reuben and Gad in Gilead. They brought a report back to the people of Israel. ³³The people were glad to hear the report. They praised God. They didn't talk anymore about going to war against the eastern tribes. And they didn't talk anymore about destroying the country where the tribes of Reuben and Gad lived.

³⁴The tribes of Reuben and Gad gave the altar a name. They called it A Witness Between Us That the LORD Is God.

JOSHUA SAYS GOOD-BY TO THE LEADERS

23 A long time had passed. The LORD had given Israel peace and rest from all of their enemies who were around them. By that time Joshua was very old. ²So he sent for all of the elders, leaders, judges and officials of Israel. He said to them, "I'm very old. ³You yourselves have seen everything the LORD your God has done. You have seen what he's done to all of those nations because of you. The LORD your God fought for you.

⁴"Remember how I've given you all of the land of the nations that remain here. I've given each of your tribes a share of it. It's the land of the nations I

won the battle over. It's between the Jordan River and the Mediterranean Sea in the west. ⁵The LORD your God himself will drive those nations out of your way. He will push them out to make room for you. You will take over their land, just as the LORD your God promised you.

⁶"Be very strong. Be careful to obey everything that is written in the Scroll of the Law of Moses. Don't turn away from it to the right or the left.

⁷"Don't have anything to do with the nations that remain among you. Don't use the names of their gods for any reason at all. Don't take oaths and make promises in their names. You must not serve them. You must not bow down to them. ⁸You must remain true to the LORD your God, just as you have done until now.

⁹"The LORD has driven out great and powerful nations to make room for you. To this very day no one has been able to fight against you and win. ¹⁰One of you can chase a thousand away. That's because the LORD your God fights for you, just as he promised

he would. ¹¹So be very careful to love the LORD your God.

¹²"But suppose you turn away from him. You mix with the people who are left alive in the nations that remain among you. Later, you and they get married to each other. And you do other kinds of things with them. ¹³Then you can be sure of what the LORD your God will do. He won't drive out those nations to make room for you anymore. Instead, they will become traps and snares for you. They will be like whips on your backs. They will be like thorns in your eyes. All of that will continue until you are destroyed. It will continue until you are removed from this good land. It's the land the LORD your God has given you.

¹⁴"Now I'm about to die, just as everyone else on earth does. The LORD your God has kept all of the good promises he gave you. Every one of them has come true. Not one has failed to come true. And you know that with all your heart and soul.

¹⁵"Every good promise of the LORD your God has come true. So you know

What should I do if my friend turns on a show that I'm not allowed to watch?

You can explain that you're not allowed to watch that show and ask your friend to change the channel. If that doesn't work, you can excuse yourself and go to another room or even go home, telling your friend, in a nice way, how you feel. You can explain that your parents don't want you to watch that show. This may help your friend make wiser choices when it comes to watching television. You may also want to explain that your parents will get very upset if they find out—it's just not worth the risk. Then you can suggest something else to do.

checkout

Joshua 23:6

Related verses:
Proverbs 1:10;
1 Corinthians 10:13;
2 Timothy 2:22

that the LORD will bring on you all of the evil things he has warned you about. He'll do it until he has destroyed you. He'll do it until he has removed you from this good land. It's the land he has given you.

¹⁶"Suppose you break the covenant the LORD your God made with you. He commanded you to obey it. But suppose you go and serve other gods. And you bow down to them. Then the LORD's anger will burn against you. You will quickly be destroyed. You will be removed from the good land he has given you."

JOSHUA TELLS ISRAEL TO SERVE THE LORD

24 Joshua gathered all of Israel's tribes together at Shechem. He sent for the elders, leaders, judges and officials of Israel. They came and stood there in the sight of God.

²Joshua spoke to all of the people. He said, "The LORD is the God of Israel. He says, 'Long ago your people lived east of the Euphrates River. They worshiped other gods there. Your people included Terah. He was the father of Abraham and Nahor.

³" 'I took your father Abraham from the land that is east of the Euphrates. I led him all through Canaan. I gave him many children and grandchildren. I gave him Isaac. ⁴To Isaac I gave Jacob and Esau. I gave the hill country of Seir to Esau. But Jacob and his children went down to Egypt.

⁵" 'Then I sent Moses and Aaron. I made the people of Egypt suffer because of the plagues I sent on them. But I brought you out of Egypt.

⁶" 'When I brought your parents out, they came to the Red Sea. The people of Egypt chased them with chariots and with men on horses. They chased them all the way to the sea. ⁷But your people cried out to me for help. So I put darkness between you and the people of Egypt. I swept them into the sea. It completely covered them. Your own eyes saw what I did to them. After that, you lived in the desert for a long time.

⁸" 'I brought you to the land of the Amorites. They lived east of the Jordan River. They fought against you. But I handed them over to you. I destroyed them to make room for you. Then you took over their land.

⁹" 'Balak, the son of Zippor, prepared to fight against Israel. Balak was king of Moab. He sent for Balaam. He wanted him to put a curse on you. Balaam was the son of Beor. ¹⁰But I would not listen to Balaam's curses. So he blessed you again and again. And I saved you from his power.

¹¹" 'Then you went across the Jordan River. You came to Jericho. Its people fought against you. So did the Amorites, Perizzites, Canaanites, Hittites, Girgashites, Hivites and Jebusites. But I handed them over to you.

¹²" 'I sent hornets ahead of you. They drove your enemies out to make room for you. That included the two Amorite kings. You did not do that with your own swords and bows. ¹³So I gave you a land you had never farmed. I gave you cities you had not built. You are now living in them. And you are eating the fruit of vineyards and olive trees you did not plant.'

¹⁴"So have respect for the LORD. Serve him. Be completely faithful to him. Throw away the gods your people worshiped east of the Euphrates River and in Egypt. Serve the LORD.

¹⁵"But suppose you don't want to serve him. Then choose for yourselves right now whom you will serve. You can choose the gods your people served east of the Euphrates River. Or you can choose the gods the Amorites serve. After all, you are living in their land. But as for me and my family, we will serve the LORD."

¹⁶Then the people answered Joshua. They said, "We would never desert the LORD! We would never serve other gods! ¹⁷The LORD our God himself brought us and our parents up out of Egypt. He brought us out of that land where we were slaves. With our own eyes, we saw those great and miraculous signs he did. He kept us safe on our entire journey. He kept us safe as we traveled through all of the nations. ¹⁸He drove them out to make room for us. That included the Amorites. They also lived in the land. We too will serve

the LORD. That's because he is our God."

¹⁹Joshua spoke to the people. He said, "You aren't able to serve the LORD. He is a holy God. He is a jealous God. He won't forgive you when you disobey him. He won't forgive you when you sin against him.

²⁰"Suppose you desert the LORD. Suppose you serve the gods that people in other lands serve. If you do, he will turn against you. He will bring trouble on you. He will destroy you, even though he has been good to you."

²¹But the people spoke to Joshua. They said, "No! We will serve the LORD."

²²Then Joshua said, "You are witnesses against yourselves. You have said that you have chosen to serve the LORD."

"Yes. We are witnesses," they replied.

²³"Now then," said Joshua, "throw away the gods that are among you. People from other lands serve those gods. Give yourselves completely to the LORD, the God of Israel."

²⁴Then the people spoke to Joshua. They said, "We will serve the LORD our God. We will obey him."

²⁵On that day Joshua made a covenant for the people. There at Shechem he wrote down rules and laws for them. ²⁶He recorded those things in the Scroll of the Law of God. Then he got a large stone. He set it up in Shechem under the oak tree. It was near the place that had been set apart for the LORD.

²⁷"Look!" he said to all of the people. "This stone will be a witness against us. It has heard all of the words the LORD has spoken to us. Suppose you aren't true to your God. Then the stone will be a witness against you."

JOSHUA DIES

²⁸Joshua sent the people away. He sent all of them to their own shares of land.

²⁹Then Joshua, the servant of the LORD, died. He was the son of Nun. He was 110 years old when he died. ³⁰His people buried his body at Timnath Serah on his own property. It's north of Mount Gaash in the hill country of Ephraim.

³¹Israel served the LORD as long as Joshua lived. They also served him as long as the elders lived. Those were the elders who lived longer than Joshua did. They had seen for themselves everything the LORD had done for Israel.

³²The people of Israel had brought Joseph's bones up from Egypt. They buried his bones at Shechem in the piece of land Jacob had bought. He had bought it from the sons of Hamor. He had paid 100 pieces of silver for it. Hamor was the father of Shechem. That piece of land became the share that belonged to Joseph's children after him.

³³Aaron's son Eleazar died. His body was buried at Gibeah in the hill country of Ephraim. Gibeah had been given to Eleazar's son Phinehas.

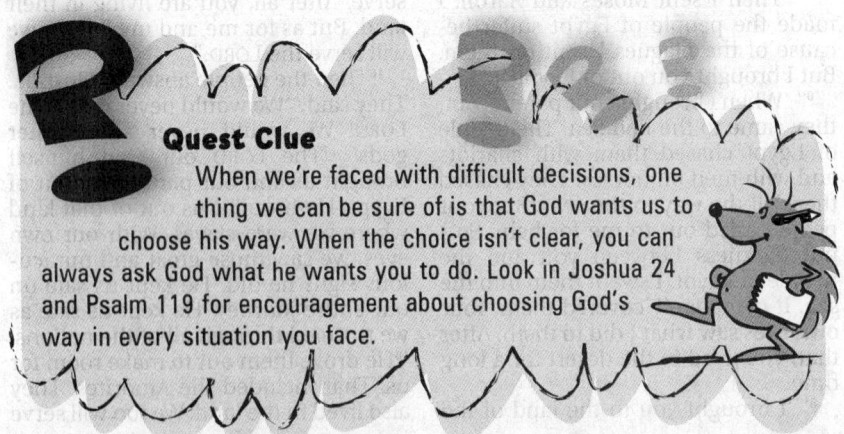

Quest Clue
When we're faced with difficult decisions, one thing we can be sure of is that God wants us to choose his way. When the choice isn't clear, you can always ask God what he wants you to do. Look in Joshua 24 and Psalm 119 for encouragement about choosing God's way in every situation you face.

Judges

Who wrote this book?
No one knows for sure. Many people think Samuel is the author.

Why was this book written?
Judges shows what happened when the Israelites turned away from God to worship idols.

What happens in this book?
God's people sin again and again. God lets Israel's enemies win. When the Israelites suffer, they turn to God. Then God sends a "judge" to defeat the enemy and lead Israel.

What do we learn about God in this book?
God is eager to forgive and help people who have sinned if only they will turn to him.

Who is important in this book?
The most important people in this book are Deborah, Gideon, Jephthah and Samson.

When did this happen?
The events in this book happened between 1390 and 1050 B.C.

ISRAEL FIGHTS AGAINST THE CANAANITES WHO ARE STILL LEFT

1 Joshua died. After that, the people of Israel spoke to the LORD. They asked him, "Who will go up first and fight for us against the people of Canaan?"

²The LORD answered, "The tribe of Judah will go. I have handed the land over to them."

³Then the men of Judah spoke to their fellow Israelites, the men of Simeon. They said, "Come up with us. Come into the territory Joshua gave us. Help us fight against the people of

Canaan. Then we'll go with you into your territory." So the men of Simeon went with them.

⁴When the men of Judah attacked, the LORD helped them. He handed the Canaanites and Perizzites over to them. They struck down 10,000 men at Bezek.

⁵Judah found Adoni-Bezek there. They fought against him. They struck down the Canaanites and Perizzites. ⁶But Adoni-Bezek ran away. Judah chased him and caught him. Then they cut off his thumbs and big toes.

⁷Adoni-Bezek said, "I cut off the thumbs and big toes of 70 kings. I made them pick up scraps under my table. Now God has paid me back for what I did to them." The men of Judah brought Adoni-Bezek to Jerusalem. That's where he died.

⁸The men of Judah attacked Jerusalem and took it. They set the city on fire. They killed its people with their swords.

⁹After that, the men of Judah went down to fight against the people of Canaan who were living in the central hill country. They also fought against those who were living in the Negev Desert and the western hills.

¹⁰Then the men of Judah marched out against the Canaanites who were living in Hebron. The men of Judah won the battle over Sheshai, Ahiman and Talmai. Hebron used to be called Kiriath Arba.

¹¹From Hebron they marched out against the people who were living in Debir. It used to be called Kiriath Sepher.

¹²Caleb said, "I will give my daughter Acsah to be married. I'll give her to the man who attacks and captures Kiriath Sepher."

¹³Othniel captured it. So Caleb gave his daughter Acsah to him to be his wife. Othniel was the son of Kenaz. He was Caleb's younger brother.

¹⁴One day Acsah came to Othniel. She begged him to ask her father for a field. When she got off her donkey, Caleb spoke to her. He said, "What can I do for you?"

¹⁵She replied, "Do me a special favor. You have given me some land in the Negev Desert. Give me springs of wa-ter also." So Caleb gave her the upper and lower springs.

¹⁶Moses' father-in-law was a Kenite. His family went up from Jericho. They went up with the people of Judah to the Desert of Judah. They went there to live among its people. Those people were living in the Negev Desert near Arad. Jericho was also known as The City of Palm Trees.

¹⁷The men of Judah went with their fellow Israelites, the men of Simeon. They attacked the people of Canaan who were living in Zephath. They set the city apart to the LORD in a special way to be destroyed. That's why the city was called Hormah.

¹⁸The men of Judah took Gaza, Ashkelon and Ekron. They also took the territory that was around each of those cities.

¹⁹The LORD was with the men of Judah. They took over the central hill country. But they weren't able to drive the people out of the flatlands. That's because those people used chariots that had some iron parts.

²⁰Moses had promised to give Hebron to Caleb. So Hebron was given to Caleb. He drove the three sons of Anak out of it.

²¹But the people of Benjamin failed to drive out the Jebusites who were living in Jerusalem. So they live there with the people of Benjamin to this very day.

²²The men of Joseph attacked Bethel. The LORD was with them. ²³They sent men to Bethel to check it out. It used to be called Luz.

²⁴Those who were sent saw a man coming out of the city. They said to him, "Show us how to get into the city. If you do, we'll see that you are treated well." ²⁵So he showed them how to get in.

The men of Joseph killed the people in the city with their swords. But they spared the man from Bethel. They also spared his whole family. ²⁶Then he went to the land of the Hittites. He built a city there. He called it Luz. That's still its name to this very day.

²⁷But the tribe of Manasseh didn't drive out the people of Beth Shan. They didn't drive out the people of Taanach, Dor, Ibleam and Megiddo.

And they didn't drive out the people of the settlements that are around those cities either. That's because the people of Canaan had made up their minds to continue living in that land.

²⁸Later, Israel became stronger. Then they forced the people of Canaan to work hard for them. But Israel never drove them out completely.

²⁹The tribe of Ephraim didn't drive out the Canaanites who were living in Gezer. So they continued to live there among them.

³⁰The tribe of Zebulun didn't drive out the Canaanites who were living in Kitron and Nahalol. So they remained among them. But Zebulun forced the Canaanites to work hard for them.

³¹The tribe of Asher didn't drive out the people who were living in Acco and Sidon. They didn't drive out the people of Ahlab, Aczib, Helbah, Aphek and Rehob. ³²So the people of Asher lived among the Canaanites who were in the land.

³³The tribe of Naphtali didn't drive out the people who were living in Beth Shemesh and Beth Anath. So the people of Naphtali lived among the Canaanites who were in the land. The people of Beth Shemesh and Beth Anath were forced to work hard for them.

³⁴The Amorites made the people of Dan stay in the central hill country. They didn't let them come down into the flatlands. ³⁵The Amorites made up their minds to stay in Mount Heres. They also stayed in Aijalon and Shaalbim.

But the power of the tribes of Joseph grew. Then the Amorites were forced to work hard for them.

³⁶The border of the Amorites started at Scorpion Pass. It went to Sela and even past it.

THE ANGEL OF THE LORD WARNS ISRAEL

2 The angel of the LORD went up from Gilgal to Bokim. There he spoke to the people of Israel. "I brought you up out of Egypt," he said. "I led you into this land. It is the land I promised with an oath to give to Abraham, Isaac and Jacob. I said, 'I will never break the covenant I made with you. ²So you must not make a covenant with the people of this land. Instead, you must tear down their altars.'

"But you have disobeyed me. Why did you do it? ³I have something to tell you. I will not drive those people out to make room for you. They will be like thorns in your sides. Their gods will be a trap to you."

⁴The angel of the LORD spoke those things to all of the people of Israel. Then the people began to sob out loud. ⁵So that place was called Bokim. The people offered sacrifices to the LORD there.

THE PEOPLE TURN AWAY FROM THE LORD

⁶Joshua sent the people of Israel away. Then they went to take over the land. All of them went to their own shares of land.

⁷The people served the LORD as long as Joshua lived. They also served him as long as the elders lived. Those were the elders who lived longer than Joshua did. They had seen all of the great things the LORD had done for Israel.

⁸Joshua, the servant of the LORD, died. He was the son of Nun. He was 110 years old when he died. ⁹His people buried his body on his own property at Timnath Heres. It's north of Mount Gaash in the hill country of Ephraim.

¹⁰All of the people of Joshua's time joined the members of their families who had already died. Then those who were born after them grew up. They didn't know the LORD. They didn't know what he had done for Israel.

¹¹The people of Israel did what was evil in the sight of the LORD. They served the gods that were named after Baal. ¹²They deserted the LORD, the God of their people. He had brought them out of Egypt. But now the people of Israel followed other gods and worshiped them. They served the gods of the nations that were around them. They made the LORD angry ¹³because they deserted him. They served Baal. They also served the goddesses that were named after Ashtoreth.

¹⁴The LORD became angry with Israel. So he handed them over to rob-

bers. The robbers stole everything from them. He gave them over to their enemies who were all around them. Israel wasn't able to fight against them anymore and win. ¹⁵When Israel went out to fight, the LORD's power was against them. He let their enemies win the battle over them. The LORD had warned them with an oath that it would happen. And now they were suffering terribly.

¹⁶Then the LORD gave them leaders. The leaders saved them from the power of those robbers. ¹⁷But the people wouldn't listen to their leaders. They weren't faithful to the LORD. They joined themselves to other gods and worshiped them. They didn't obey the LORD's commands as their people before them had done. They quickly turned away from the path their people had taken.

¹⁸When the LORD gave them a leader, he was with that leader. He saved the people from the power of their enemies. He did it as long as the leader lived. He was very sorry for the people. They groaned because of what their enemies did to them. The enemies beat them down. They treated them badly.

¹⁹But when the leader died, the people returned to their evil ways. The things they did were even more sinful than the things their people before them had done. They followed other gods. They served them. They worshiped them. They refused to give up their evil practices. They wouldn't change their stubborn ways.

²⁰So the LORD's anger burned against the people of Israel. He said, "This nation has broken my covenant. I made it with their people of long ago. But this nation has not listened to me. ²¹Joshua left some nations in the land when he died. I will not drive those nations out to make room for you anymore. ²²I will use them to put Israel to the test. I will see whether Israel will live the way I want them to. I will see whether they will follow my path, just as their people did long ago."

²³The LORD had let those nations remain in the land. He didn't drive them out right away. He didn't hand them over to Joshua.

3 The LORD left some nations in the land. He left them there in order to put the people of Israel to the test. He did it for all those who hadn't lived through any of the wars in Canaan. ²He wanted to teach the men in Israel who had never been in battle before. He wanted them to learn how to fight. ³So he left the five rulers of the Philistines. He left the people of Canaan and the people of Sidon. He left the Hivites who were living in the Lebanon mountains. They lived in the area that was between Mount Baal Hermon and Lebo Hamath.

⁴The LORD left those nations where they were in order to put Israel to the test. He wanted to see whether they would obey his commands. He had given those commands through Moses to their people of long ago.

⁵So the people of Israel lived among the Canaanites, Hittites, Amorites, Perizzites, Hivites and Jebusites. ⁶They got married to the daughters of those people. They gave their own daughters to the sons of those people. And they served the gods of those people.

OTHNIEL

⁷The people of Israel did what was evil in the sight of the LORD. They forgot the LORD their God. They served the gods that were named after Baal. They also served the goddesses that were named after Asherah.

⁸So the LORD's anger burned against Israel. He gave them over to the power of Cushan-Rishathaim. He was the king of Aram Naharaim. For eight years Israel was under his rule.

⁹They cried out to the LORD. Then he gave them a man to save them. His name was Othniel, the son of Kenaz. He was Caleb's younger brother. ¹⁰The Spirit of the LORD came on Othniel. So he became Israel's leader. He went to war. The LORD handed Cushan-Rishathaim, the king of Aram, over to him. Othniel overpowered him.

¹¹So the land was at peace for 40 years. Then Othniel, the son of Kenaz, died.

EHUD

¹²Once again the people of Israel did what was evil in the sight of the LORD.

Because they did that, the LORD gave Eglon power over Israel. Eglon was the king of Moab. ¹³He got the Ammonites and Amalekites to join him. All of them came and attacked Israel. They took over Jericho. Jericho was also known as The City of Palm Trees. ¹⁴For 18 years the people of Israel were under the rule of Eglon, the king of Moab.

¹⁵Again the people of Israel cried out to the LORD. Then he gave them a man to save them. His name was Ehud, the son of Gera. Ehud was left-handed. He was from the tribe of Benjamin.

The people of Israel sent Ehud to Eglon, the king of Moab. They sent him to give the king what he required them to bring him. ¹⁶Ehud had made a sword that had two edges. It was about a foot and a half long. He tied it to his right leg under his clothes. ¹⁷Eglon, the king of Moab, was a very fat man. Ehud gave him the gift he had brought. ¹⁸After that, he sent away those who had carried it.

¹⁹At the place where some statues of gods stood near Gilgal, Ehud turned back. He said, "King Eglon, I have a secret message for you."

The king said, "I want everyone to be quiet." And all of his attendants left him.

²⁰Then Ehud approached him. King Eglon was sitting alone in the upstairs room of his summer palace. Ehud said, "I have a message from God for you." So the king got up from his seat.

²¹Then Ehud reached out his left hand. He pulled out the sword that was tied to his right leg. He stuck it into the king's stomach. ²²Even the handle sank in after the blade. The blade came right out the king's back. Ehud didn't pull the sword out. And the fat closed over it.

²³Ehud went out to the porch. He shut the doors of the upstairs room behind him. Then he locked them.

²⁴After he had gone, the servants came. They found the doors of the upstairs room locked. They said, "Eglon must be going to the toilet in the inside room of the house."

²⁵They waited for a long time. They waited so long they became worried. But the king still didn't open the doors of the room. So they took a key and

unlocked them. There they saw their king. He had fallen to the floor. He was dead.

²⁶While Eglon's servants had been waiting, Ehud had gotten away. He passed by the statues of gods and escaped to Seirah. ²⁷There in the hill country of Ephraim he blew a trumpet. Then he led the people of Israel down from the hills.

²⁸"Follow me," Ehud ordered. "The LORD has handed your enemy Moab over to you."

So they followed him down. They took over the only places where people could go across the Jordan River to get to Moab. They didn't let anyone go across. ²⁹At that time they struck down about 10,000 men of Moab. All of those men were strong and powerful. But not even one escaped. ³⁰That day Moab was brought under the rule of Israel.

So the land was at peace for 80 years.

SHAMGAR

³¹After Ehud, Shamgar became the next leader. He was the son of Anath. He struck down 600 Philistines with a large, pointed stick that was used to drive oxen. He saved Israel too.

DEBORAH

4 After Ehud died, the people of Israel once again did what was evil in the sight of the LORD. ²So the LORD gave them over to the power of Jabin. He was a king in Canaan. He ruled in Hazor. The commander of his army was Sisera. Sisera lived in Harosheth Haggoyim. ³Jabin used 900 chariots that had some iron parts. He treated the people of Israel very badly for 20 years. So they cried out to the LORD for help.

⁴Deborah was a prophet. She was the wife of Lappidoth. She was leading Israel at that time. ⁵Under The Palm Tree of Deborah she served the people as their judge. That place was between Ramah and Bethel in the hill country of Ephraim. The people of Israel came to her there. They came to have her decide cases for them. She settled matters between them.

⁶Deborah sent for Barak. He was the son of Abinoam. Barak was from

Kedesh in the land of Naphtali. Deborah said to Barak, "The LORD, the God of Israel, is giving you a command. He says, 'Go! Take 10,000 men from the tribes of Naphtali and Zebulun with you. Then lead the way to Mount Tabor. [7]I will draw Sisera into a trap. He is the commander of Jabin's army. I will bring him, his chariots and his troops to the Kishon River. There I will hand him over to you.' "

[8]Barak said to her, "If you go with me, I'll go. But if you don't go with me, I won't go."

[9]"All right," Deborah said. "I'll go with you. But because of the way you are doing this, you won't receive any honor. The LORD will hand Sisera over to a woman."

So Deborah went to Kedesh with Barak. [10]There he sent for Zebulun and Naphtali. And 10,000 men followed him. Deborah also went with him.

[11]Heber, the Kenite, had left the other Kenites. They came from the family line of Hobab. He was the brother-in-law of Moses. Heber set up his tent by the large tree in Zaanannim near Kedesh.

[12]Sisera was told that Barak, the son of Abinoam, had gone up to Mount Tabor. [13]So Sisera gathered together his 900 chariots that had some iron parts. He also gathered all of his men together. He brought them from Harosheth Haggoyim to the Kishon River.

[14]Then Deborah said to Barak, "Go! Today the LORD will hand Sisera over to you. Hasn't the LORD gone ahead of you?" So Barak went down Mount Tabor. His 10,000 men followed him.

[15]As Barak's men marched out, the LORD drove Sisera away from the field of battle. He scattered all of Sisera's chariots. Barak's men struck down Sisera's army with their swords. Sisera left his chariot behind. He ran away on foot.

[16]But Barak chased Sisera's chariots and army. He chased them all the way to Harosheth Haggoyim. All of Sisera's men were killed with swords. Not even one was left.

[17]But Sisera ran away on foot. He ran to the tent of Jael. She was the wife of Heber, the Kenite. Sisera ran there because Heber's family was friendly toward Jabin, the king of Hazor.

KIDS' QUESTION

Did the Israelites have lawyers and courts for their judges?

Joshua was the Israelites' leader when they first got to the promised land. After Joshua died, God used judges to lead his people. We can read about these judges in the book called Judges. These were not like judges that we have today. They did not have courts or listen to lawyers. Their job was to help the people live together, to rescue them from enemies and to lead them to God.

checkout Judges 4:4,5

Related verses:
Judges 2:16–23;
1 Samuel 8:1–22

¹⁸Jael went out to meet Sisera. "Come in, sir," she said. "Come right in. Don't be afraid." So he entered her tent. Then she covered him up.

¹⁹"I'm thirsty," he said. "Please give me some water." So Jael opened a bottle of milk. The bottle was made out of animal skin. She gave him a drink of milk. Then she covered him up again.

²⁰"Stand in the doorway of the tent," he told her. "Someone might come by and ask you, 'Is anyone here?' If that happens, say 'No.'"

²¹But Heber's wife Jael picked up a tent stake and a hammer. She went quietly over to Sisera. He was lying there, fast asleep. He was very tired. She drove the stake through his head right into the ground. So he died.

²²Barak came by because he was chasing Sisera. Jael went out to meet him. "Come right in," she said. "I'll show you the man you are looking for." So he went in with her. Sisera was lying there with the stake through his head. He was dead.

²³On that day God brought Jabin under Israel's control. He was a king in Canaan. ²⁴Israel's power grew stronger and stronger against Jabin, a king in Canaan. They became so strong that they destroyed him.

THE SONG OF DEBORAH

5 On that day Deborah and Barak sang a song. Barak was the son of Abinoam. Here is what Deborah and Barak sang.

² "The princes in Israel lead the way.
The people follow them just
  because they want to.
Praise the LORD!

³ "Kings, hear this! Rulers, listen!
I will sing to the LORD. I will sing.
I will make music to the LORD. He
  is the God of Israel.

⁴ "LORD, you went out from Mount
  Seir.
You marched out from the land
  of Edom.
The earth shook. The heavens
  poured.
The clouds poured down their
  water.

⁵ The mountains shook because of
  the LORD. He was at Mount
  Sinai.
They shook because of the LORD.
  He is the God of Israel.

⁶ "The roads were deserted. So
  travelers used the winding
  paths.
That happened in the days of
  Shamgar, the son of Anath.
It happened in the days of Jael.
⁷ Life in the villages of Israel
  stopped.
It stopped until I, Deborah,
  came.
I came as a mother in Israel.
⁸ The people chose new gods.
Then war came to the city gates.
But no shields or spears were seen
  anywhere.
There weren't any among 40,000
  men in Israel.
⁹ My heart is with the princes in
  Israel.
It's with the people who follow
  them just because they want
  to.
Praise the LORD!

¹⁰ "Some of you ride on white
  donkeys.
Some of you sit on your saddle
  blankets.
Some of you walk along the road.
Think about ¹¹the voices of the
  singers at the watering places.
They sing about the right things
  the LORD does.
They sing about the right things
  his warriors in Israel do.

"The people of the LORD
  went down to the city gates.
¹² 'Wake up, Deborah! Wake up!' they
  said.
'Wake up! Wake up! Begin to sing!
Barak, get up!
Son of Abinoam, capture your
  prisoners!'

¹³ "Then the people who were left
  came down to the nobles.
The people of the LORD
  came to me against the powerful
  enemy.
¹⁴ Some came from the part of
  Ephraim where some
  Amalekites lived.

Benjamin was with the people
who followed Ephraim.
Captains came down from Makir.
Those who rule like commanders
came down from Zebulun.
¹⁵ The princes of Issachar were with
Deborah.
The men of Issachar were with
Barak.
They rushed behind him into the
valley.
In the territories of Reuben,
men looked deeply into their
hearts.
¹⁶ Why did they stay among the
campfires?
Why did they stay to hear
shepherds whistling for the
flocks?
In the territories of Reuben,
men looked deeply into their
hearts.
¹⁷ Gilead stayed east of the Jordan
River.
Why did Dan stay near the ships?
The men of Asher remained on the
coast of the Mediterranean
Sea.
They stayed in their safe harbors.
¹⁸ The people of Zebulun put their
very lives in danger.
So did Naphtali on the hills in
the open country.
¹⁹ "Kings came and fought.
The kings of Canaan fought
at Taanach by the streams of
Megiddo.
But they didn't carry any silver
away.
They didn't take anything at all.
²⁰ From the heavens the stars fought.
From the sky they fought against
Sisera.
²¹ The Kishon River swept them away.
The Kishon is a very old river.
My spirit, march on! Be strong!
²² The hoofs of the horses pounded
like thunder.
The powerful horses of our
enemies galloped away.
²³ 'Let Meroz be cursed,' said the
angel of the LORD.
'Let bitter curses fall on its
people.
They did not come to help the
LORD.

They did not come to help him
against our powerful
enemies.'
²⁴ "May Jael be the most blessed
woman of all.
May the wife of the Kenite Heber
be blessed.
May she be the most blessed
woman of all those who live in
tents.
²⁵ Sisera asked for water. She gave
him milk.
In a bowl that was fit for nobles
she brought him buttermilk.
²⁶ Her hand reached out for a tent
stake.
Her right hand reached for a
hammer.
She hit Sisera. She crushed his
head.
She drove the stake right through
his head.
²⁷ He sank down. He fell at her feet.
He was lying there.
At her feet he sank down. He fell.
He fell where he sank down.
That's where he died.
²⁸ "Sisera's mother looked out
through the window.
From behind the wooden screen
she cried out.
'Why is his chariot taking so long
to get here?' she said.
'Why can't I hear the noise of his
chariots yet?'
²⁹ Her wisest ladies answer her.
And here's what she keeps saying
to herself.
³⁰ She says, 'They must be finding
riches to bring back.
They must be dividing them up.
Each man is getting a woman or
two.
They are giving colorful clothes
to Sisera.
The clothes are very beautiful.
He will bring some for me to
wear.
The men must be finding many
things to bring home.'
³¹ "LORD, may all of your enemies be
destroyed.
But may those who love you be
like the morning sun.

May they be like the sun when it
shines the brightest."

So the land was at peace for 40 years.

GIDEON

6 Once again the people of Israel
did what was evil in the sight of
the LORD. So for seven years he
handed them over to the people of
Midian.

²The Midianites treated the people
of Israel very badly. That's why they
made hiding places for themselves.
They hid in holes in the mountains.
They also hid in caves and in other
safe places.

³Each year the people planted their
crops. When they did, the Midianites
came into the country and attacked it.
So did the Amalekites and other tribes
from the east. ⁴They camped on the
land. They destroyed the crops all the
way to Gaza. They didn't spare any living thing for Israel. They didn't spare
sheep or cattle or donkeys.

⁵The Midianites came up with their
livestock and tents. They came like
huge numbers of locusts. It was impossible to count all of those men and
their camels. They came into the land
to destroy it.

⁶Midian made the people of Israel
very poor. So they cried out to the
LORD for help.

⁷They cried out to the LORD because
of what Midian had done. ⁸So he sent a
prophet to them. The prophet said,
"The LORD is the God of Israel. He says,
'I brought you up out of Egypt. That is
the land where you were slaves. ⁹I
saved you from the power of Egypt. I
saved you from all those who were
beating you down. I drove the people
of Canaan out to make room for you. I
gave you their land.

¹⁰' I said to you, "I am the LORD your
God. You are now living in the land of
the Amorites. Do not worship their
gods." But you have not listened
to me.' "

¹¹The angel of the LORD came. He sat
down under an oak tree in Ophrah.
The tree belonged to Joash. He was
from the family line of Abiezer.

Gideon was threshing wheat in a
winepress at Ophrah. He was the son
of Joash. Gideon was threshing in a
winepress to hide the wheat from the
Midianites.

¹²The angel of the LORD appeared to
Gideon. He said, "Mighty warrior, the
LORD is with you."

¹³"But sir," Gideon replied, "you say
the LORD is with us. Then why has all of
this happened to us? Where are all of
the wonderful things he has done? Our
parents told us about them. They said,
'Didn't the LORD bring us up out of
Egypt?' But now the LORD has deserted

KIDS' QUESTION

Who was the angel of the Lord?

The Bible mentions the angel of
the Lord many times. In the desert,
Moses saw a bush that was burning but was
not burning up. Then the angel of the Lord
spoke to him out of it. Some people think
that was a special appearance of God
and not actually an angel. The angel of
the Lord appeared here to Gideon, too.
Sometimes the phrase "angel of the
Lord" is just a good way
to describe an angel.

... AND THE ANGEL OF THE LORD
SHONE AROUND THEM ...

Related verses:
2 Samuel 24:16;
1 Chronicles 21:16

checkout
Judges 6:12

us. He has handed us over to Midian."

¹⁴The LORD turned to Gideon. He said to him, "You are strong. Go and save Israel from the power of Midian. I am sending you."

¹⁵"But Lord," Gideon asked, "how can I possibly save Israel? My family group is the weakest in the tribe of Manasseh. And I'm the least important member of my family."

¹⁶The LORD answered, "I will be with you. So you will strike down the men of Midian all at one time."

¹⁷Gideon replied, "If you are pleased with me, give me a special sign. Then I'll know that it's really you talking to me. ¹⁸Please don't go away until I come back. I'll bring my offering and set it down in front of you."

The LORD said, "I will wait until you return."

¹⁹Gideon went and prepared a young goat. From more than half a bushel of flour he made bread without using yeast. He put the meat in a basket. In a pot he put soup that was made from the meat. Then he brought all of it and offered it to the LORD under the oak tree.

²⁰The angel of God spoke to Gideon.

He said, "Take the meat and the bread. Place them on this rock. Then pour out the soup." So Gideon did it.

²¹The angel of the LORD had a wooden staff in his hand. With the tip of his staff he touched the meat and the bread. Fire blazed out of the rock. It burned up the meat and the bread. Then the angel of the LORD disappeared.

²²Gideon realized it was the angel of the LORD. He cried out, "LORD and King, I have seen the angel of the LORD face to face!"

²³But the LORD said to him, "May peace be with you! Do not be afraid. You are not going to die."

²⁴So Gideon built an altar to honor the LORD there. He called it The LORD Is Peace. It still stands in Ophrah to this very day. Ophrah is in the territory that belongs to the family line of Abiezer.

²⁵That same night the LORD spoke to Gideon. He said, "Get the second bull from your father's herd. Get the one that is seven years old. Tear down the altar your father built in honor of Baal. Cut down the pole that is beside it. The pole is used to worship the goddess Asherah.

Why do people worship idols instead of God?

Idols in the Bible were often pictures or statues of fake gods. People wanted to worship something they could see and touch, so they made their own gods out of metal or wood. Today, most people who have idols don't worship the idols but the fake gods they represent.

Today we still have idols, but they usually aren't statues. Money, rock stars or wanting to be famous can become an idol. When we make anything in our lives more important than loving, serving and obeying God, it may become an idol to us. Nothing in our lives should take the place of God.

checkout
Judges 6:25, 30–31

TEEN IDOL

IZZY A. BUZZARD

IZZY

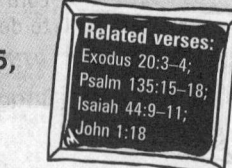

Related verses:
Exodus 20:3–4;
Psalm 135:15–18;
Isaiah 44:9–11;
John 1:18

²⁶"Then build the right kind of altar. Build it in honor of the LORD your God. Build it on top of this hill. Then use the wood from the Asherah pole you cut down. Sacrifice the second bull as a burnt offering."

²⁷So Gideon went and got ten of his servants. He did just as the LORD had told him. But he was afraid of his family. He was also afraid of the men in the town. So he did everything at night instead of during the day.

²⁸In the morning the men in the town got up. They saw that Baal's altar had been torn down. The Asherah pole that was beside it had been cut down. And the second bull had been sacrificed on the new altar that had been built.

²⁹They asked each other, "Who did this?"

They looked into the matter carefully. Someone told them, "Gideon, the son of Joash, did it."

³⁰The men in the town spoke to Joash. They ordered him, "Bring your son out here. He must die. He has torn down Baal's altar. He has cut down the Asherah pole that was beside it."

³¹But Joash replied to the angry crowd that was around him. He said, "Are you going to stand up for Baal? Are you trying to save him? Those who stand up for him will be put to death by morning! Is Baal really a god? If he is, he can stand up for himself when someone tears down his altar."

³²That's why Gideon was called Jerub-Baal that day. He said, "Let Baal take his stand against him." Gideon had torn down Baal's altar.

³³All of the Midianites and Amalekites gathered their armies together. Other tribes from the east joined them. All of them went across the Jordan River. They camped in the Valley of Jezreel.

³⁴Then the Spirit of the LORD came on Gideon. So Gideon blew the trumpet to send for the men of Abiezer. He told them to follow him. ³⁵He sent messengers all through Manasseh. He called for the men of Manasseh to fight. He also sent messengers to the men of Asher, Zebulun and Naphtali. So all of those men went up to join the others.

³⁶Gideon said to God, "You promised you would use me to save Israel. ³⁷Please do something for me. I'll put a piece of wool on the threshing floor. Suppose dew is only on the wool tomorrow morning. And suppose the ground all around it is dry. Then I will know that you will use me to save Israel. I'll know that your promise will come true."

³⁸And that's what happened. Gideon got up early the next day. He squeezed the dew out of the wool. The water filled a bowl.

³⁹Then Gideon said to God, "Don't let your anger burn against me. Let me ask you for just one more thing. Let me use the wool for one more test. This time make the wool dry. And cover the ground with dew."

⁴⁰So that night God did it. Only the wool was dry. The ground all around it was covered with dew.

GIDEON WINS THE BATTLE OVER THE MIDIANITES

7 Early in the morning Jerub-Baal and all of his men camped at the spring of Harod. Jerub-Baal was another name for Gideon. The camp of Midian was north of Gideon's camp. It was in the valley near the hill of Moreh.

²The LORD spoke to Gideon. He said, "I want to hand Midian over to you. But you have too many men for me to do that. I do not want Israel to brag that their own strength has saved them. ³So here is what I want you to announce to your men. Tell them, 'Those who tremble with fear can turn back. They can leave Mount Gilead.'" So 22,000 men left. But 10,000 remained.

⁴The LORD spoke to Gideon again. He said, "There are still too many men. So take them down to the water. I will sort them out for you there. If I say, 'This one will go with you,' he will go. But if I say, 'That one will not go with you,' he will not go."

⁵So Gideon took the men down to the water. There the LORD spoke to him. He said, "Some men will drink the way dogs do. They will lap up the water with their tongues. Separate

them from those who get down on their knees to drink."

⁶Three hundred men lapped up the water. They brought it up to their mouths with their hands. All of the rest got down on their knees to drink.

⁷The LORD spoke to Gideon. He said, "With the help of the 300 men who lapped up the water I will save you. I will hand the Midianites over to you. Let all of the other men go home."

⁸So Gideon sent the rest of the men of Israel to their tents. But he kept the 300 men. They took over the supplies and trumpets the others had left.

The Midianites had set up their camp in the valley below where Gideon was.

⁹During that night the LORD spoke to Gideon. He said, "Get up. Go down against the camp. I am going to hand it over to you. ¹⁰But what if you are afraid to attack? Then go down to the camp with your servant Purah. ¹¹Listen to what they are saying. After that, you will not be afraid to attack the camp."

So Gideon and his servant Purah went down to the edge of the camp. ¹²The Midianites had settled in the valley. So had the Amalekites and all of the other tribes from the east. There were so many of them that they looked like huge numbers of locusts. Like the grains of sand on the seashore, their camels couldn't be counted.

¹³Gideon arrived just as a man was telling a friend about his dream. "I had a dream," he was saying. "A round loaf of barley bread came rolling into the camp of Midian. It hit a tent with great force. The tent turned over and fell down flat."

¹⁴His friend replied, "That can only be the sword of Gideon, the son of Joash. Gideon is from Israel. God has handed the Midianites over to him. He has given him the whole camp."

¹⁵Gideon heard the man explain what the dream meant. Then Gideon worshiped God. He returned to the camp of Israel. He called out, "Get up! The LORD has handed the Midianites over to you."

¹⁶Gideon separated the 300 men into three companies. He put a trumpet and an empty jar into the hands of each man. And he put a torch inside each jar.

¹⁷"Watch me," he told them. "Do what I do. I'll go to the edge of the enemy camp. Then do exactly as I do. ¹⁸I and everyone who is with me will blow our trumpets. Then blow your trumpets from your positions all around the camp. And shout the battle cry, 'For the LORD and for Gideon!' "

¹⁹Gideon and the 100 men who were with him reached the edge of the enemy camp. It was about ten o'clock at night. It was just after the guard had been changed. Gideon and his men blew their trumpets. They broke the jars that were in their hands.

²⁰The three companies blew their trumpets. They smashed their jars. They held their torches in their left hands. They held in their right hands the trumpets they were going to blow. Then they shouted the battle cry, "A sword for the LORD and for Gideon!"

²¹Each man stayed in his position around the camp. But all of the Midianites ran away in fear. They were crying out as they ran.

²²When the 300 trumpets were blown, the LORD caused all of the men in the enemy camp to start fighting each other. They attacked each other with their swords. The army ran away to Beth Shittah toward Zererah. They ran all the way to the border of Abel Meholah near Tabbath.

²³The men of Israel from the tribes of Naphtali, Asher and all of Manasseh were called out. They chased the Midianites.

²⁴Gideon sent messengers through the entire hill country of Ephraim. They said, "Come on down against the Midianites. Take control of the waters of the Jordan River before they get there. Do it all the way to Beth Barah."

So all of the men of Ephraim were called out. They took control of the waters of the Jordan all the way to Beth Barah.

²⁵They also captured Oreb and Zeeb. Those men were two of the Midianite leaders. The men of Ephraim killed Oreb at the rock of Oreb. They killed Zeeb at the winepress of Zeeb. They chased the Midianites. And they

brought the heads of Oreb and Zeeb to Gideon. He was by the Jordan River.

GIDEON DESTROYS MIDIAN'S WHOLE ARMY

8 The men of Ephraim spoke to Gideon. They asked, "Why have you treated us like this? Why didn't you ask us to help you when you went out to fight against Midian?" They spoke very sharply against Gideon.

²But he answered them, "What I've done isn't anything compared to what you have done. After Ephraim's grapes have been gathered, isn't what is left over better than all of the grapes that have been gathered from Abiezer's vines? ³God handed Oreb and Zeeb over to you. They were Midianite leaders. So what was I able to do compared to what you did?"

After Gideon had said that, they didn't feel angry with him anymore.

⁴Gideon and his 300 men were very tired. But they kept on chasing their enemies. They came to the Jordan River and went across it. ⁵Gideon spoke to the men of Succoth. He said, "Give my troops some bread. They are worn out. And I'm still chasing Zebah and Zalmunna. They are the kings of Midian."

⁶But the officials of Succoth objected. They said, "Have you already killed Zebah and Zalmunna? Have you cut their hands off and brought them back to prove it? If you haven't, why should we give bread to your troops?"

⁷Gideon replied, "The LORD will hand Zebah and Zalmunna over to me. When he does, I'll tear your skin with thorns from desert bushes."

⁸From there Gideon went up to Peniel. He asked its men for the same thing. But they answered as the men of Succoth had. ⁹So he said to the men of Peniel, "I'll be back after I've won the battle. Then I'll tear down this tower."

¹⁰Zebah and Zalmunna were in Karkor. They had an army of about 15,000 men. That's all that was left of the armies of the tribes from the east. About 120,000 men who carried swords had died in battle.

¹¹Gideon went up the trail the people of the desert had made. It ran east of Nobah and Jogbehah. He attacked the army by surprise. ¹²Zebah and Zalmunna ran away. They were the two kings of Midian. Gideon chased them and captured them. He destroyed their whole army.

¹³Then Gideon, the son of Joash, returned from the battle. He came back through the Pass of Heres. ¹⁴He caught a young man from Succoth. He asked him about the elders of the town. The young man wrote down for him the names of Succoth's 77 officials. ¹⁵Then Gideon came and spoke to the men of Succoth. He said, "Here are Zebah and Zalmunna. You made fun of me because of them. You said, 'Have you already killed Zebah and Zalmunna? Have you cut their hands off and brought them back to prove it? If you haven't, why should we give bread to your tired men?' "

¹⁶Gideon went and got the elders of the town. Then he taught the men of Succoth a lesson. He tore their skin with thorns from desert bushes. ¹⁷He also pulled down the tower at Peniel. He killed the men in the town.

¹⁸Then he spoke to Zebah and Zalmunna. He asked, "What were the men like that you killed at Tabor?"

"Men like you," they answered. "Each one walked as if he were a prince."

¹⁹Gideon replied, "Those were my brothers. They were the sons of my own mother. You can be sure that the LORD lives. And you can be just as sure that if you had spared their lives, I wouldn't kill you."

²⁰Then Gideon turned to his oldest son Jether. He said, "Kill them!" But Jether didn't pull out his sword. He was only a boy. So he was afraid.

²¹Zebah and Zalmunna said, "Come on. Do it yourself. 'The older the man, the stronger he is.' "

So Gideon stepped forward and killed them. Then he took the moon-shaped necklaces off the necks of their camels.

GIDEON REFUSES TO BE ISRAEL'S RULER

²²The people of Israel spoke to Gideon. They said, "Rule over us. We

want you, your son and your grandson to be our rulers. You have saved us from the power of Midian."

²³But Gideon told them, "I will not rule over you. My son won't rule over you either. The LORD will rule over you."

²⁴He continued, "I do ask one thing. I want each of you to give me an earring. I'm talking about the earrings you took from your enemies." It was the practice of the people in the family line of Ishmael to wear gold earrings.

²⁵The people of Israel said, "We'll be glad to give them to you." So they spread out a piece of clothing. Each man threw a ring on it from what he had taken. ²⁶The weight of the gold rings Gideon asked for was 43 pounds. That didn't include the moon-shaped necklaces the kings of Midian had worn. It didn't include their other necklaces or their purple clothes. And it didn't include the gold chains that had been on the necks of their camels.

²⁷Gideon made an object out of all of the gold. It looked like the linen apron the high priest of Israel wore. He placed it in Ophrah. That was his hometown. All of the people of Israel worshiped it there. They weren't faithful to the LORD. So the gold object became a trap to Gideon and his family.

GIDEON DIES

²⁸Israel brought Midian under their control. Midian wasn't able to attack Israel anymore. So the land was at peace for 40 years. The peace lasted as long as Gideon was living.

²⁹Jerub-Baal, the son of Joash, went back home to live. Jerub-Baal was another name for Gideon. ³⁰He had 70 sons of his own. That's because he had a lot of wives. ³¹And he had a concubine who lived in Shechem. She also had a son by him. Gideon named that son Abimelech.

³²Gideon, the son of Joash, died when he was very old. His body was buried in the tomb of his father Joash in Ophrah. Ophrah was in the territory that belonged to the family line of Abiezer.

³³As soon as Gideon had died, the people of Israel joined themselves to the gods that were named after Baal.

Israel wasn't faithful to the LORD. They worshiped Baal-Berith as their god. ³⁴They forgot what the LORD their God had done for them. He had saved them from the power of their enemies who were all around them.

³⁵Jerub-Baal had done many good things for the people of Israel. But they weren't kind to his family. Jerub-Baal was another name for Gideon.

ABIMELECH BECOMES KING OF SHECHEM

9 Abimelech was the son of Jerub-Baal. He went to his mother's brothers in Shechem. He spoke to them and to all of the members of his mother's family group. He said, ²"Speak to all of the citizens of Shechem. Tell them, 'You can have all 70 of Jerub-Baal's sons rule over you. Or you can have just one man rule over you. Which would you rather have?' Remember, I'm your own flesh and blood."

³The brothers told all of that to the citizens of Shechem. Then the people decided to follow Abimelech. They said, "He's related to us."

⁴They gave him 28 ounces of silver. They had taken it from the temple of the god Baal-Berith. Abimelech used it to hire some men. They were wild. They weren't good for anything. They became his followers.

⁵Abimelech went to his father's home in Ophrah. There on a big rock he murdered his 70 brothers. All of them were the sons of Jerub-Baal. But Jotham escaped by hiding. He was Jerub-Baal's youngest son.

⁶All of the citizens of Shechem and Beth Millo came together. They gathered at the stone pillar that was beside the large tree in Shechem. They wanted to crown Abimelech as their king.

⁷Jotham was told about it. So he climbed up on top of Mount Gerizim. He shouted down to them, "Citizens of Shechem! Listen to me! Then God will listen to you. ⁸One day the trees went out to anoint a king for themselves. They said to an olive tree, 'Be our king.' ⁹"But the olive tree answered, 'Should I give up my olive oil? It's used to honor gods and people alike.

Should I give that up just to rule over the trees?'

¹⁰"Next, the trees spoke to a fig tree. They said, 'Come and be our king.'

¹¹"But the fig tree replied, 'Should I give up my fruit? It's so good and sweet. Should I give that up just to rule over the trees?'

¹²"Then the trees spoke to a vine. They said, 'Come and be our king.'

¹³"But the vine answered, 'Should I give up my wine? It cheers up gods and people alike. Should I give that up just to rule over the trees?'

¹⁴"Finally, all of the trees spoke to a bush that had thorns. They said, 'Come and be our king.'

¹⁵"The bush spoke to the trees. It said, 'Do you really want to anoint me as king over you? If you do, come and rest in my shade. But if you don't, I will destroy you! Fire will come out of me and burn up the cedar trees of Lebanon!'

¹⁶"Did you act in an honest way when you made Abimelech your king? Did you really do the right thing? Have you been fair to Jerub-Baal and his family? Have you given him the honor he's worthy of?

¹⁷"Remember that my father fought for you. He put his life in danger for you. He saved you from the power of Midian. ¹⁸But today you have turned against my father's family. You have murdered his 70 sons on a big rock. Abimelech is only the son of my father's female slave. But you have made him king over the citizens of Shechem. You have done that because he's related to you.

¹⁹"Have you citizens of Shechem and Beth Millo acted in an honest way toward Jerub-Baal? Have you done the right thing to his family today? If you have, may you be happy with Abimelech! And may he be happy with you! ²⁰But if you haven't, let fire come out from Abimelech and burn you up! And let fire come out from you and burn Abimelech up!"

²¹Then Jotham ran away. He escaped to Beer. He lived there because he was afraid of his brother Abimelech.

²²Abimelech ruled over Israel for three years. ²³Then God sent an evil spirit to cause trouble between Abim-elech and the citizens of Shechem. They turned against Abimelech. They decided not to follow him anymore.

²⁴God made that happen because of what Abimelech had done to Jerub-Baal's 70 sons. He had spilled their blood. God wanted to pay back their brother Abimelech for doing that. He also wanted to pay back the citizens of Shechem. They had helped Abimelech murder his brothers.

²⁵The citizens of Shechem opposed Abimelech. So they hid some men on top of the hills. They wanted them to attack and rob everyone who passed by. Abimelech was told about it.

²⁶Gaal and his relatives moved into Shechem. He was the son of Ebed. The citizens of Shechem put their trust in Gaal.

²⁷The people of Shechem went out into the fields. They gathered the grapes. They pressed the juice out of them by stomping on them. Then they held a feast in the temple of their god. While they were eating and drinking, they called down curses on Abimelech.

²⁸Then Gaal, the son of Ebed, spoke up. "Who is Abimelech?" he said. "And who is Shechem? Why should we be under Abimelech's rule? Isn't he Jerub-Baal's son? Isn't Zebul his helper? It would be better to serve the men of Hamor. He was the father of Shechem. So why should we serve Abimelech? ²⁹I wish these people were under my command. Then I would get rid of him. I would say to him, 'Call out your whole army!' "

³⁰Zebul was the governor of Shechem. He heard about what Gaal, the son of Ebed, had said. So he burned with anger. ³¹Zebul sent messengers to Abimelech secretly. They said, "Gaal, the son of Ebed, has come to Shechem. His relatives have come with him. They are stirring up the city against you. ³²So come with your men during the night. Hide in the fields and wait. ³³In the morning at sunrise, attack the city. Gaal and his men will come out against you. Then do what you can."

³⁴So Abimelech and all of his troops started out at night. They went into their hiding places near Shechem.

Abimelech had separated them into four companies.

³⁵Gaal, the son of Ebed, had already gone out. He was standing at the entrance of the city gate. He had arrived there just as Abimelech and his troops came out of their hiding places.

³⁶Gaal saw them. He said to Zebul, "Look! People are coming down from the tops of the mountains!"

Zebul replied, "You are wrong. Those aren't people. They are just the shadows of the mountains."

³⁷But Gaal spoke up again. He said, "Look! People are coming down from the center of the land. Another company is coming from the direction of the fortune tellers' tree."

³⁸Then Zebul said to Gaal, "Where is your big talk now? You said, 'Who is Abimelech? Why should we be under his rule?' Aren't these the people you looked down on? Go out and fight against them!"

³⁹So Gaal led the citizens out of Shechem. They fought against Abimelech. ⁴⁰He chased Gaal from the field of battle. Many men were wounded as they ran away. Abimelech chased them all the way to the entrance of the city gate. ⁴¹He stayed in Arumah. Zebul drove Gaal and his relatives out of Shechem.

⁴²The next day the people of Shechem went out to work in the fields. Abimelech was told about it. ⁴³So he gathered his men together. He separated them into three companies. Then he hid them in the fields and told them to wait. When he saw the people coming out of the city, he got up to attack them.

⁴⁴Abimelech and the men who were with him ran forward. They placed themselves at the entrance of the city gate. Then the other two companies rushed over to the people who were in the fields. There they struck them down. ⁴⁵Abimelech kept up his attack against the city all day long. He didn't stop until he had captured it. Then he killed its people. He destroyed the city. He scattered salt on it to make sure that nothing would be able to grow there.

⁴⁶The citizens who were in the tower of Shechem heard about what was happening. So they went to the safest place in the temple of the god El-Berith.

⁴⁷Abimelech heard that they had gathered together there. ⁴⁸He and all of his men went up Mount Zalmon. He got an ax and cut off some branches. He carried them on his shoulders. He ordered the men who were with him to do the same thing. "Quick!" he said. "Do what you have seen me do!"

⁴⁹So all of the men cut branches and followed Abimelech. They piled them against the place where the people had gone for safety. Then they set the place on fire with the people inside. There were about 1,000 men and women in the tower of Shechem. All of them died.

⁵⁰Next, Abimelech went to Thebez. He surrounded it. Then he attacked it and captured it.

⁵¹But inside the city there was a strong tower. All of the people in the city ran to it for safety. All of the men and women went into it. They locked themselves in. They climbed up on the roof of the tower. ⁵²Abimelech went to the tower and attacked it. He approached the entrance to the tower to set it on fire. ⁵³But a woman dropped a large millstone on him. It broke his head open.

⁵⁴He quickly called out to the man who was carrying his armor. He said, "Pull out your sword and kill me. Then people can't say, 'A woman killed him.'" So his servant stuck his sword through him. And Abimelech died. ⁵⁵When the people of Israel saw he was dead, they went home.

⁵⁶That's how God paid Abimelech back for the evil thing he had done to his father. He had murdered his 70 brothers. ⁵⁷God also made the men of Shechem pay for all of the evil things they had done. The curse of Jotham came down on them. He was the son of Jerub-Baal.

TOLA

10 Tola rose up to save Israel. That happened after the time of Abimelech. Tola was from the tribe of Issachar. He was the son of Puah, who was the son of Dodo. Tola lived in Shamir. It's in the hill country of Ephraim. ²Tola led Israel for 23 years. After he died, his body was buried in Shamir.

JAIR

³Jair became the leader after Tola. Jair was from the land of Gilead. He led Israel for 22 years. ⁴He had 30 sons. They rode on 30 donkeys. They controlled 30 towns in Gilead. Those towns are called Havvoth Jair to this very day. ⁵After Jair died, his body was buried in Kamon.

JEPHTHAH

⁶Once again the people of Israel did what was evil in the sight of the LORD. They served the gods that were named after Baal. They served the goddesses that were named after Ashtoreth. They worshiped the gods of Aram and Sidon. They served the gods of Moab and Ammon. They also worshiped the gods of the Philistines. The people of Israel deserted the LORD. They didn't serve him anymore.

⁷So the LORD's anger burned against them. He handed them over to the Philistines and the Ammonites. ⁸That year they broke Israel's power completely. They treated the people of Israel badly for 18 years. Those people lived east of the Jordan River. They lived in Gilead. That was the land of the Amorites.

⁹The Ammonites also went across the Jordan. They crossed over to fight against Judah, Benjamin and the people of Ephraim. Israel was suffering terribly.

¹⁰Then the people of Israel cried out to the LORD. They said, "We have sinned against you. We have deserted our God. We have served the gods that are named after Baal."

¹¹The LORD replied, "The Egyptians and Amorites beat you down. So did the Ammonites and Philistines. ¹²And so did the Amalekites and the people of Sidon and Maon. Each time you cried out to me for help. And I saved you from their power.

¹³"But you have deserted me. You have served other gods. So I will not save you anymore. ¹⁴Go and cry out to the gods you have chosen. Let them save you when you get into trouble!"

¹⁵But the people of Israel replied to the LORD. They said, "We have sinned. Do to us what you think is best. But please save us now." ¹⁶Then they got rid of the strange gods that were among them. They served the LORD. And he couldn't stand to see Israel suffer anymore.

¹⁷The Ammonites were called together to fight. They camped in the land of Gilead. Then the men of Israel gathered together. They camped at the city of Mizpah.

¹⁸The leaders of Gilead spoke to each other. They said, "Who will lead the attack against the Ammonites? That man will be the ruler of all of the people who live in Gilead."

11 Jephthah was a mighty warrior. He was from the land of Gilead. His father's name was Gilead. Jephthah's mother was a prostitute.

²Gilead's wife also had sons by him. When they had grown up, they drove Jephthah away. "You aren't going to get any share of our family's property," they said. "You are the son of another woman."

³So Jephthah ran away from his brothers. He settled in the land of Tob. A group of men who weren't good for anything gathered around him there. And they followed him.

⁴Some time later, the Ammonites went to war against Israel. ⁵So the elders of Gilead went to get Jephthah from the land of Tob. ⁶"Come with us," they said. "Be our commander. Then we can fight against the Ammonites."

⁷Jephthah said to them, "Didn't you hate me? Didn't you drive me away from my father's house? Why are you coming to me only when you are in trouble?"

⁸The elders of Gilead replied to him. "You are right," they said. "That's why we're turning to you now. Come with us and fight against the Ammonites. Then you will be our leader. You will rule over everyone who lives in Gilead."

⁹Jephthah said, "Suppose you take me back to fight against the Ammonites. And suppose the LORD gives them over to me. Then will I really be your leader?"

¹⁰The elders of Gilead replied, "The LORD is our witness. We'll certainly do as you say." ¹¹So Jephthah went with the elders of Gilead. And the people made him their leader and commander. He went to Mizpah. There he repeated to the LORD everything he had said.

¹²Then Jephthah sent messengers to the king of Ammon. They asked, "What do you have against us? Why have you attacked our country?"

¹³The king of Ammon answered Jephthah's messengers. He said, "Israel came up out of Egypt. At that time they took my land away. They took all of the land that was between the Arnon River and the Jabbok River. It reached all the way to the Jordan River. Now give it back. Then there will be peace."

¹⁴Jephthah sent messengers back to the king of Ammon. ¹⁵They said,

"Here is what Jephthah says to you. Israel didn't take the land of Moab. They didn't take the land of Ammon. ¹⁶When Israel came up out of Egypt, they went through the desert to the Red Sea. From there they went on to Kadesh.

¹⁷"Then Israel sent messengers to the king of Edom. They said, 'Please let us go through your country.' But the king of Edom wouldn't listen to them.

"They sent the same message to the king of Moab. But he refused too. So Israel stayed at Kadesh.

¹⁸"Next, they traveled through the desert. They traveled along the borders of the lands of Edom and Moab. They passed along the east side of the country of Moab. They camped on the other side of the Arnon River. They didn't enter the territory of Moab. The Arnon River was Moab's border.

¹⁹"Then Israel sent messengers to Sihon. He was the king of the Amorites. He ruled in Heshbon. They said to him, 'Let us pass through your country to our own land.'

²⁰"But Sihon didn't trust Israel to pass through his territory. Instead, he gathered all of his men together. They camped at Jahaz. And they fought against Israel.

²¹"Then the LORD, the God of Israel, handed Sihon and all of his men over to Israel. Israel won the battle over them. Amorites were living in the country at that time. And Israel took over all of their land. ²²They captured all of the land that was between the Arnon River and the Jabbok River. It reached from the desert all the way to the Jordan River.

²³"The LORD, the God of Israel, has driven the Amorites out to make room for his people. So what right do you have to take it over? ²⁴You will take what your god Chemosh gives you, won't you? In the same way, we will take over what the LORD our God has given us. ²⁵Are you better than Balak, the son of Zippor? Balak was the king of Moab. Did he ever argue with Israel? Did he ever fight against them?

²⁶"For 300 years Israel has been living in Heshbon and Aroer. They have been living in the settlements that are around those cities. They have also been living in all of the towns that are along the Arnon River. Why didn't you take those places back during that time?

²⁷"I haven't done anything wrong to you. But you are doing something wrong to me. You have gone to war against me. The LORD is the Judge. So let him decide our case today. Let him settle matters between the people of Israel and the people of Ammon."

²⁸But the king of Ammon didn't pay any attention to the message Jephthah sent him.

²⁹Then the Spirit of the LORD came on Jephthah. He went across the territories of Gilead and Manasseh. He passed through Mizpah in the land of Gilead. From there he attacked the people of Ammon.

³⁰Jephthah made a promise to the LORD. He said, "Hand the Ammonites over to me. ³¹If you do, here's what I'll do when I come back from winning

the battle. Anything that comes out the door of my house to meet me will belong to you. I will sacrifice it as a burnt offering."

³²Then Jephthah went over to fight against the Ammonites. The LORD handed them over to him. ³³Jephthah destroyed 20 towns between Aroer and the area of Minnith. He destroyed them all the way to Abel Keramim. So Israel brought Ammon under their control.

³⁴Jephthah returned to his home in Mizpah. And guess who came out to meet him. It was his daughter! She was dancing to the music of tambourines. She was his only child. He didn't have any other sons or daughters.

³⁵When Jephthah saw her, he was so upset that he tore his clothes. He cried out, "My daughter! You have filled me with trouble and sorrow. I've made a promise to the LORD. And I can't break it."

³⁶"My father," she replied, "you have given your word to the LORD. So do to me just what you promised to do. The Ammonites were your enemies. And the LORD has paid them back for what they did to you.

³⁷"But please do one thing for me," she continued. "Give me two months to wander around in the hills. Let me sob there with my friends. I want to do that because I'll never get married."

³⁸"You can go," he said. He let her go for two months. She and her friends went into the hills. They were filled with sadness because she would never get married.

³⁹After the two months were over, she returned to her father. He did to her just what he had promised to do. And she was a virgin.

So that became a practice in Israel. ⁴⁰Each year the young women of Israel go away for four days. They do it in honor of the daughter of Jephthah. He was from the land of Gilead.

JEPHTHAH WINS THE BATTLE OVER EPHRAIM

12 The men of Ephraim called out their troops. The troops went across the Jordan River to Zaphon. When they arrived, they said to Jephthah, "You went

to fight against the Ammonites. Why didn't you ask us to go with you? We're going to burn down your house over your head."

²Jephthah answered, "I and my people were taking part in a great struggle. We were at war with the Ammonites. I asked you for help. But you didn't come to save me from their power. ³I saw that you wouldn't help. So I put my own life in danger. I went across the Jordan to fight against the Ammonites. The LORD helped me win the battle over them. So why have you come up today to fight against me?"

⁴Then Jephthah called the men of Gilead together. They fought against Ephraim. The men of Gilead struck them down. The people of Ephraim had said, "You people of Gilead are nothing but deserters from Ephraim and Manasseh."

⁵The men of Gilead captured the places where people go across the Jordan River to get to Ephraim. Some men of Ephraim weren't killed in the battle. When they arrived at the river, they would say, "Let us go across."

Then the men of Gilead would ask each one, "Are you from Ephraim?" Suppose he replied, "No." ⁶Then they would say, "All right. Say 'Shibboleth.' " If he said "Sibboleth," the way he said the word would give him away. He couldn't say it correctly. So they would grab hold of him. Then they would kill him at one of the places where people go across the Jordan. At that time, 42,000 men of Ephraim were killed.

⁷Jephthah led Israel for six years. Then he died. His body was buried in a town in Gilead. Jephthah was from the land of Gilead.

IBZAN, ELON AND ABDON

⁸After Jephthah, Ibzan from Bethlehem led Israel. ⁹He had 30 sons and 30 daughters. He gave his daughters to be married to men who were outside his family group. He brought in 30 young women to be married to his sons. Those women also came from outside his family group. Ibzan led Israel for seven years. ¹⁰Then he died. His body was buried in Bethlehem.

¹¹After Ibzan, Elon led Israel. He was

from the tribe of Zebulun. Elon led Israel for ten years. ¹²Then he died. His body was buried in Aijalon. It was in the land of Zebulun.

¹³After Elon, Abdon led Israel. Abdon was the son of Hillel. Abdon was from Pirathon. ¹⁴He had 40 sons and 30 grandsons. They rode on 70 donkeys. He led Israel for eight years. ¹⁵Then he died. His body was buried at Pirathon in Ephraim. Pirathon was in the hill country of the Amalekites. Abdon was the son of Hillel.

SAMSON IS BORN

13 Once again the people of Israel did what was evil in the sight of the LORD. So the LORD handed them over to the Philistines for 40 years.

²A certain man from Zorah was named Manoah. He was from the tribe of Dan. Manoah had a wife who wasn't able to have children.

³The angel of the LORD appeared to Manoah's wife. He said, "You are not able to have children. But you are going to become pregnant. You will have a baby boy. ⁴Make sure you do not drink any kind of wine. Also make sure you do not eat anything that is 'unclean.'

⁵"You will become pregnant. You will have a son. He must not use a razor on his head. He must not cut his hair. That is because the boy will be a Nazirite. He will be set apart to God from the day he is born. He will begin to save Israel from the power of the Philistines."

⁶Then the woman went to her husband. She told him, "A man of God came to me. He looked like an angel of God. His appearance was so amazing that it filled me with great wonder. I didn't ask him where he came from. And he didn't tell me his name.

⁷"But he said to me, 'You will become pregnant. You will have a son. So do not drink any kind of wine. Do not eat anything that is "unclean." That is because the boy will be a Nazirite. He will belong to God in a special way from the day he is born until the day he dies.' "

⁸Then Manoah prayed to the LORD. He said, "Lord, I beg you to let the man of God you sent to us come again. He

KIDS' QUESTION

Was Samson a good guy or a bad guy?

He was a little bit of both. Samson was one of Israel's judges. He served God and wanted to please him. But Samson was not perfect. God chose him to rescue his people from their enemies. Samson did that job well. But he also did some foolish things. Samson could use his abilities for good or bad. Sometimes he chose to go his own way instead of God's.

checkout
Judges 13:3,5

Related verses:
Judges
13:1—16:31

Samson the HULK

LIL'S FAVORITE DOLLS

told us we would have a son. We want the man of God to teach us how to bring up the boy."

⁹God heard Manoah. And the angel of God came again to the woman. He came while she was out in the field. But her husband Manoah wasn't with her. ¹⁰The woman hurried to her husband. She told him, "He's here! The man who appeared to me the other day is here!"

¹¹Manoah got up and followed his wife. When he came to the man, he spoke to him. He said, "Are you the one who talked to my wife?"

"I am," he replied.

¹²So Manoah asked him, "What will happen when your words come true? What rules should we follow for the boy's life and work?"

¹³The angel of the LORD answered him. He said, "Your wife must do everything I have told her to do. ¹⁴She must not eat anything that comes from grapevines. She must not drink any kind of wine. She must not eat anything that is 'unclean.' She must do everything I have commanded her to do."

¹⁵Manoah spoke to the angel of the LORD. He said, "We would like you to stay and eat. We want to prepare a young goat for you."

¹⁶The angel of the LORD replied, "Even if I stay, I will not eat any of your food. But if you still want to prepare a burnt offering, you must offer it to the LORD." Manoah didn't realize it was the angel of the LORD.

¹⁷Then Manoah asked the angel of the LORD a question. "What is your name?" he said. "We want to honor you when your word comes true."

¹⁸The angel replied, "Why are you asking me what my name is? You would not be able to understand it."

¹⁹Manoah got a young goat. He brought it together with the grain of-

KIDS' QUESTION

Why do some kids get their own way when they cry and get angry?

Some adults give in when children cry, complain or throw tantrums. The adults let those children get what they want. Kids who have been treated that way think they can always get what they want by acting like that. But someday those actions won't work. Can you imagine adults lying on the floor in a store, crying loudly and rolling this way and that way just because the store didn't have what they wanted? It's much better to learn to talk things through, be cooperative and not try to get our way all the time.

checkout
Judges
14:16, 17

Related verses:
Psalm 37:8
James 1:19–20

WAAAA I WANT CANDY!

CANDY

fering. He sacrificed it on a rock to the LORD.

Then the LORD did an amazing thing. It happened while Manoah and his wife were watching. ²⁰A flame blazed up from the altar toward heaven. The angel of the LORD rose up in the flame. When Manoah and his wife saw it, they fell with their faces to the ground.

²¹The angel of the LORD didn't show himself again to Manoah and his wife. Then Manoah realized it was the angel of the LORD.

²²"We're going to die!" he said to his wife. "We've seen God!"

²³But his wife answered, "The LORD doesn't want to kill us. If he did, he wouldn't have accepted a burnt offering and a grain offering from us. He wouldn't have shown us all of those things. He wouldn't have told us we're going to have a son."

²⁴Later, the woman had a baby boy. She named him Samson. As he grew up, the LORD blessed him. ²⁵The Spirit of the LORD began to work in his life. It happened while he was in Mahaneh Dan. It's between Zorah and Eshtaol.

SAMSON GETS MARRIED

14 Samson went down to Timnah. There he saw a young Philistine woman. ²When he returned, he spoke to his father and mother. He said, "I've seen a Philistine woman in Timnah. Get her for me. I want her to be my wife."

³His father and mother replied, "Can't we find a wife for you among your relatives? Isn't there one among any of our people? Do you have to go to the Philistines to get a wife? They aren't God's people. They haven't even been circumcised."

But Samson said to his father, "Get her for me. She's the right one for me."

⁴Samson's parents didn't know that the LORD wanted things to happen that way. He was working out his plans against the Philistines. That's because the Philistines were ruling over Israel at that time.

⁵Samson went down to Timnah. His father and mother went with him. They approached the vineyards of Timnah. Suddenly a young lion came roaring toward Samson.

⁶Then the Spirit of the LORD came on Samson with power. He tore the lion apart with his bare hands. He did it as easily as he might have torn a young goat apart. But he didn't tell his father or mother what he had done.

⁷Then he went down and talked with the woman. He liked her.

⁸Some time later, he was going back to get married to her. But he turned off the road to look at the lion's dead body. Large numbers of bees and some honey were in it. ⁹He dug the honey out with his hands. He ate it as he walked along. Then he joined his parents again. He gave them some honey. They ate it too. But he didn't tell them he had taken it from the lion's dead body.

¹⁰Samson's father went down to see the woman. Samson had a big dinner prepared there. He was following the practice of men when they got married. ¹¹When the people saw Samson, they gave him 30 companions.

¹²"Let me tell you a riddle," Samson said to the companions. "The dinner will last for seven days. Give me the answer to the riddle before the dinner ends. If you do, I'll give you 30 linen shirts. I'll also give you 30 sets of clothes. ¹³But suppose you can't give me the answer. Then you must give me 30 linen shirts. You must also give me 30 sets of clothes."

"Tell us your riddle," they said. "Let's hear it."

¹⁴Samson replied,

"Out of the eater came something
    to eat.
Out of the strong came
    something sweet."

For three days they couldn't give him the answer.

¹⁵On the fourth day they spoke to Samson's wife. "Get your husband to explain the riddle for us," they said. "If you don't, we'll burn you to death. We'll burn up everyone in your family. Did you invite us here to rob us?"

¹⁶Then Samson's wife threw herself on him. She sobbed, "You hate me! You don't really love me. You have given my

people a riddle. But you haven't told me the answer."

"I haven't even explained it to my father or mother," he replied. "So why should I explain it to you?"

¹⁷She cried during the whole seven days the dinner was going on. So on the seventh day he finally told her the answer to the riddle. That's because she kept on asking him to tell her. Then she explained the riddle to her people.

¹⁸Before sunset on the seventh day the men of the town spoke to Samson. They said,

"What is sweeter than honey?
What is stronger than a lion?"

Samson said to them,

"You have plowed with my young cow.
If you hadn't, you wouldn't have known the answer to my riddle."

¹⁹Then the Spirit of the LORD came on Samson with power. He went down to Ashkelon. He struck down 30 of their men. He took everything they had with them. And he gave their clothes to those who had explained the riddle. Samson was burning with anger as he went up to his father's house.

²⁰Samson's wife was given to someone else. She was given to a friend of Samson. The friend had helped him at his wedding.

SAMSON GETS EVEN WITH THE PHILISTINES

15 Later on, Samson went to visit his wife. He took a young goat with him. He went at the time the wheat was being gathered. He said, "I'm going to my wife's room." But her father wouldn't let him go in.

²Her father said, "I was sure you really hated her. So I gave her to your friend. Isn't her younger sister more beautiful? Take her instead."

³Samson said to them, "This time I have a right to get even with the Philistines. I'm going to hurt them badly."

⁴So he went out and caught 300 foxes. He tied them in pairs by their tails. Then he tied a torch to each pair of tails. ⁵He lit the torches. He let the foxes loose in the fields of grain that belonged to the Philistines. He burned up the grain that had been cut and stacked. He burned up the grain that was still growing. He also burned up the vineyards and olive trees.

⁶The Philistines asked, "Who did this?" They were told, "Samson did. He's the son-in-law of the man from Timnah. Samson did it because his wife was given to his friend."

So the Philistines went up and burned the woman and her father to death.

⁷Samson said to them, "Is that how you act? Then I won't stop until I pay you back." ⁸He struck them down with heavy blows. He killed many of them. Then he went down and stayed in a cave. It was in the rock of Etam.

⁹The Philistines went up and camped in Judah. They spread out near Lehi. ¹⁰The men of Judah asked, "Why have you come to fight against us?"

"We've come to take Samson as our prisoner," they answered. "We want to do to him what he did to us."

¹¹Then 3,000 men from Judah went to get Samson. They went down to the cave that was in the rock of Etam. They said to Samson, "Don't you realize the Philistines are ruling over us? What have you done to us?"

Samson answered, "I only did to them what they did to me."

¹²The men of Judah said to him, "We've come to tie you up. We're going to hand you over to the Philistines."

Samson said, "Take an oath and promise me you won't kill me yourselves."

¹³"We agree," they answered. "We'll only tie you up and hand you over to them. We won't kill you." So they tied him up with two new ropes. They led him up from the rock.

¹⁴Samson approached Lehi. The Philistines came toward him shouting. Then the Spirit of the LORD came on Samson with power. The ropes on his arms became like burned thread. They dropped off his hands. ¹⁵He found a fresh jawbone of a donkey. He grabbed hold of it and struck down 1,000 men.

[16]Then Samson said,

"By using a donkey's jawbone
    I've made them look like
        donkeys.
By using a donkey's jawbone
    I've struck down 1,000 men."

[17]Samson finished speaking. Then he threw the jawbone away. That's why the place was called Ramath Lehi. [18]Samson was very thirsty. So he cried out to the LORD. He said, "You have helped me win this great battle. Do I have to die of thirst now? Must I fall into the power of people who haven't even been circumcised? They aren't your people."

[19]Then God opened up the hollow place in Lehi. Water came out of it. When Samson drank the water, his strength returned. He felt as good as new. So the spring was called En Hakkore. It's still there in Lehi.

[20]Samson led Israel for 20 years. In those days the Philistines were in the land.

SAMSON AND DELILAH

16 One day Samson went to Gaza. There he saw a prostitute. He went in to spend the night with her. [2]The people of Gaza were told, "Samson is here!" So they surrounded the place. They hid and waited for him at the city gate all night long. They didn't make any move against him during the night. They said, "Let's wait until the sun comes up. Then we'll kill him."

[3]But Samson stayed there only until the middle of the night. Then he got up. He took hold of the doors of the city gate. He also took hold of the two doorposts. He tore them loose, together with their metal bar. He picked them up and put them on his shoulders. Then he carried them to the top of the hill that faces Hebron.

[4]Some time later, Samson fell in love again. The woman lived in the Valley of Sorek. Her name was Delilah. [5]The rulers of the Philistines went to her. They said, "See if you can get him to tell you the secret of why he's so strong. Find out how we can overpower him. Then we can tie him up.

We can bring him under our control. Each of us will give you 28 pounds of silver."

[6]So Delilah spoke to Samson. She said, "Tell me the secret of why you are so strong. Tell me how you can be tied up and controlled."

[7]Samson answered her, "Let someone tie me up with seven new leather straps. They must be straps that aren't completely dry. Then I'll become as weak as any other man."

[8]So the Philistine rulers brought seven new leather straps to her. They weren't completely dry. Delilah tied Samson up with them. [9]Men were hiding in the room. She called out to him. She said, "Samson! The Philistines are attacking you!" But he snapped the leather straps easily. They were like pieces of string that had come too close to a flame. So the secret of why he was so strong wasn't discovered.

[10]Delilah spoke to Samson again. "You have made me look foolish," she said. "You told me a lie. Come on. Tell me how you can be tied up."

[11]Samson said, "Let someone tie me tightly with new ropes. They must be ropes that have never been used. Then I'll become as weak as any other man."

[12]So Delilah got some new ropes. She tied him up with them. Men were hiding in the room. She called out to him. She said, "Samson! The Philistines are attacking you!" But he snapped the ropes off his arms. They fell off just as if they were threads.

[13]Delilah spoke to Samson again. "Until now, you have been making me look foolish," she said. "You have been telling me lies. This time really tell me how you can be tied up."

He replied, "Weave the seven braids of my hair into the cloth on a loom. Then pin my hair to the loom. If you do, I'll become as weak as any other man."

So while Samson was sleeping, Delilah took hold of the seven braids of his hair. She wove them into the cloth on a loom. [14]Then she pinned his hair to the loom.

Again she called out to him. She said, "Samson! The Philistines are attacking you!" He woke up from his sleep. He pulled up the pin and the loom, together with the cloth.

¹⁵Then she said to him, "How can you say, 'I love you'? You won't even share your secret with me. This is the third time you have made me look foolish. And you still haven't told me the secret of why you are so strong."

¹⁶She continued to pester him day after day. She nagged him until he was sick and tired of it.

¹⁷So he told her everything. "I've never used a razor on my head," he said. "I've never cut my hair. That's because I've been a Nazirite since the day I was born. A Nazirite is set apart to God. If you shave my head, I won't be strong anymore. I'll become as weak as any other man."

¹⁸Delilah realized he had told her everything. So she sent a message to the Philistine rulers. She said, "Come back one more time. He has told me everything." So the rulers returned. They brought the silver with them.

¹⁹Delilah got Samson to go to sleep on her lap. Then she called for a man to shave off the seven braids of his hair. That's how she began to bring him under her control. And he wasn't strong anymore.

²⁰She called out, "Samson! The Philistines are attacking you!"

He woke up from his sleep. He thought, "I'll go out just as I did before. I'll shake myself free." But he didn't know that the LORD had left him.

²¹Then the Philistines grabbed hold of him. They poked his eyes out. They took him down to Gaza. They put bronze chains around him. Then they made him grind grain in the prison. ²²His head had been shaved. But the hair on it began to grow again.

SAMSON DIES

²³The rulers of the Philistines gathered together. They were going to offer a great sacrifice to their god Dagon. They were going to celebrate. They said, "Our god has handed our enemy Samson over to us."

²⁴When the people saw Samson, they praised their god. They said,

"Our god has handed our enemy
over to us.

KIDS' QUESTion

Why did Samson tell Delilah his secret?

Samson was in love with a woman named Delilah. Delilah did not really love Samson. She was a friend of his enemies. When his enemies offered her money to help them capture Samson, Delilah agreed to help. Delilah asked Samson for the secret of his strength. At first he gave her the wrong answers. But she nagged him until he told her the truth. He told her that God's strength would leave him if his hair was cut. Samson let himself be tricked because he loved Delilah so much.

checkout
Judges 16:16, 17

Related verses:
Judges 16:1–22

Our enemy has destroyed our
    land.
He has killed large numbers of
    our people."

[25]After they had drunk a lot of wine, they shouted, "Bring Samson out. Let him put on a show for us." So they called Samson out of the prison. He put on a show for them.

They had him stand near the temple pillars. [26]Then he spoke to the servant who was holding his hand. He said, "Put me where I can feel the pillars. I'm talking about the ones that hold the temple up. I want to lean against them."

[27]The temple was crowded with men and women. All of the Philistine rulers were there. About 3,000 men and women were on the roof. They were watching Samson put on a show.

[28]Then he prayed to the LORD. He said, "LORD and King, show me that you still have concern for me. God, please make me strong just one more time. Let me pay the Philistines back for what they did to my two eyes. Let me do it with only one blow."

[29]Then Samson reached toward the two pillars that were in the middle of the temple. They held the temple up. He put his right hand on one of them. He put his left hand on the other. He leaned hard against them.

[30]Samson said, "Let me die together with the Philistines!" Then he pushed with all his might. The temple came down on the rulers. It fell on all of the people who were in it. So Samson killed many more Philistines when he died than he did while he lived.

[31]Then his brothers went down to get him. So did his father's whole family. All of them brought Samson's body back home. They buried his body in the tomb of his father Manoah. It's between Zorah and Eshtaol. Samson had led Israel for 20 years.

MICAH MAKES SOME STATUES OF GODS

17 A man named Micah lived in the hill country of Ephraim. [2]He said to his mother, "Someone took 28 pounds of silver from you. I heard you call down a curse because of it. I have the silver with me. I'm the one who took it."

Then his mother said, "My son, may the LORD bless you!"

[3]He gave the 28 pounds of silver back to his mother. She said to him, "I'm taking an oath and setting my silver apart to the LORD. My son, I want you to use part of it for a statue of a god that is made out of wood or stone and covered with silver. Use the rest of it to have another statue made out of silver. That's why I'll give the silver back to you."

[4]He gave the silver back to his mother. She gave five pounds of it to a skilled worker who made things out of silver. He used the silver for the two statues. They were put in Micah's house.

[5]That same Micah had a small temple. He made a sacred linen apron and some statues of gods. He prepared one of his sons to serve as his priest.

[6]In those days Israel didn't have a king. The people did anything they thought was right.

[7]A young Levite had been living in land that belonged to the tribe of Judah. He was from Bethlehem in Judah. [8]He left that town to look for some other place to stay. On his way he came to Micah's house. It was in the hill country of Ephraim.

[9]Micah asked him, "Where are you from?"

"I'm a Levite," he said. "I'm from Bethlehem in Judah. I'm looking for a place to stay."

[10]Then Micah said to him, "Live with me. Be my father and priest. I'll give you four ounces of silver a year. I'll also give you clothes and food."

[11]So the Levite agreed to live with him. The young man was just like a son to Micah.

[12]Then Micah prepared the Levite to serve as his priest. He lived in Micah's house. [13]Micah said, "Now I know that the LORD will be good to me. This Levite has become my priest."

THE PEOPLE OF DAN SETTLE DOWN IN LAISH

18 In those days Israel didn't have a king.

And in those days the tribe of Dan was looking for a place

where they could settle down. They hadn't been able to take over their own share of land among the tribes of Israel.

²So the people of Dan sent out five warriors from Zorah and Eshtaol. They told them to look the land over and check it out. Those men did it for all of their family groups. The people of Dan told the men, "Go. Check out the land."

So they entered the hill country of Ephraim. They went to the house of Micah. That's where they spent the night.

³When they came near Micah's house, they recognized a voice. It was the voice of the young Levite. So they turned off the road and stopped there. They asked him, "Who brought you here? What are you doing in this place? Why are you here?"

⁴The Levite told them what Micah had done for him. He said, "He has hired me. I'm his priest."

⁵Then they said to him, "Please ask God for advice. Try to find out whether we'll have success on our journey."

⁶The priest answered them, "Go in peace. The LORD is pleased with your journey."

⁷So the five men left. They came to Laish. There they saw that the people felt secure. They were living in safety. Like the people in Sidon, they weren't expecting anything bad to happen to them. Their land had everything they needed. Things were going very well for them. They lived a long way from the people of Sidon. And they didn't think they would ever need help from anyone else.

⁸The men returned to Zorah and Eshtaol. Their people asked them, "What did you find out?"

⁹They answered, "Come on! Let's attack them! We've seen that the land is very good. Aren't you going to do something? Don't wait any longer. Go there and take it over. ¹⁰When you get there, you will find people who aren't expecting anything bad to happen to them. Their land has plenty of room. God has handed it over to you. It's a land that has everything you will ever need."

¹¹So 600 men from the tribe of Dan started out from Zorah and Eshtaol.

They were prepared for battle. ¹²On their way they set up camp. Their camp was near Kiriath Jearim in Judah. That's why the place is called Mahaneh Dan to this very day. It's west of Kiriath Jearim. ¹³From there they went to the hill country of Ephraim. They came to Micah's house.

¹⁴Then the five men who had looked over the land of Laish spoke to the other members of their tribe. They said, "Don't you know that one of these houses has a sacred linen apron in it? Some statues of family gods are there. It also has two statues of other gods in it. One of them is made out of wood or stone. The other is made out of silver. Now you know what to do."

¹⁵So they turned off the road and stopped there. They went to the house of the young Levite. He was at Micah's place. They greeted the young man. ¹⁶The 600 men from Dan stood at the entrance of the gate. They were prepared for battle.

¹⁷The five men who had looked over the land went inside. They took the two statues. They also took the family gods and the linen apron.

During that time, the priest stood at the entrance of the gate. The 600 men stood there with him. They were prepared for battle.

¹⁸When those men went into Micah's house and took all of those things, the priest spoke to them. He asked, "What are you doing?"

¹⁹They answered him, "Be quiet! Don't say a word. Come with us. Be our father and priest. You can serve a whole tribe and family group in Israel as our priest. Isn't that better than serving just one man's family?"

²⁰The priest was glad. He took the linen apron and the family gods. He also took the statue of a god that was made out of wood or stone. Then he left with the people.

²¹They put their little children and their livestock in front of them. They also put everything else they owned in front of them. And they turned and went on their way.

²²The men who lived near Micah were called together. Then they left and caught up with the people of Dan. That's because Dan's people hadn't

gone very far from Micah's house.
²³Those who lived near Micah shouted at them. The people of Dan turned around and spoke to Micah. "What's the matter with you?" they asked. "Why did you call your men out to fight against us?"

²⁴He replied, "You took away the gods I made. And you took my priest away. What do I have left? So how can you ask, 'What's the matter with you?' "

²⁵The people of Dan answered, "Don't argue with us. Some men get angry quickly. They might attack you. Then you and your family will lose your lives."

²⁶So the people of Dan went on their way. Micah saw that they were too strong for him. So he turned around and went back home.

²⁷The people of Dan took what Micah had made. They also took his priest. They continued on their way to Laish. They went there to fight against peaceful people who weren't expecting to be attacked. They struck them down with their swords. They burned their city down. ²⁸No one could save them. They lived a long way from Sidon. And they didn't think they would ever need help from anyone else. Their city was located in a valley near Beth Rehob.

The people of Dan rebuilt the city. Then they settled down there. ²⁹They named it Dan. That's because they traced their family line back to Dan. He was a son of Israel. The city used to be called Laish.

³⁰There the people of Dan set up the statues of gods for themselves. Jonathan and his sons were priests for the tribe of Dan. Jonathan was the son of Gershom, the son of Moses. Jonathan and his sons were priests until the time when the land was captured. ³¹They continued to use the statues Micah had made. They used them during the whole time the house of God was in Shiloh.

A LEVITE AND HIS CONCUBINE

19 In those days Israel didn't have a king.

There was a Levite who lived deep in the hill country of Ephraim. He got a concubine from Bethlehem in Judah. ²But she wasn't faithful to him. She left him. She went back to her father's house in Bethlehem in Judah. She stayed there for four months.

³Then her husband went to see her. He tried to talk her into coming back with him. He had his servant and two donkeys with him. She took her husband into her father's house. When her father saw him, he gladly welcomed him.

⁴His father-in-law, the woman's father, begged him to stay. So he remained with him for three days. He ate, drank and slept there.

⁵On the fourth day they got up early. The Levite prepared to leave. But the woman's father spoke to his son-in-law. He said, "Have something to eat. It will give you strength. Then you can go on your way."

⁶So the two of them sat down. They ate and drank together. After that, the woman's father said, "Please stay tonight. Enjoy yourself."

⁷The man got up to go. But his father-in-law talked him into staying. So he stayed there that night.

⁸On the morning of the fifth day, he got up to go. But the woman's father said, "Have something to eat. It will give you strength. Wait until this afternoon!" So the two of them ate together.

⁹Then the man got up to leave. His concubine and his servant got up when he did. But his father-in-law, the woman's father, spoke to him again. "Look," he said. "It's almost evening. The day is nearly over. So spend another night here. Please stay. Enjoy yourself. Early tomorrow morning you can get up and go back home."

¹⁰But the man didn't want to stay another night. So he left. He went toward Jebus. He had his two donkeys and his concubine with him. The donkeys had saddles on them. Jebus is also called Jerusalem.

¹¹By the time the travelers came near Jebus, the day was almost over. So the servant said to his master, "Come. Let's stop at this Jebusite city. Let's spend the night here."

¹²His master replied, "No. We won't go into a city where strangers live. The people there aren't from Israel. We'll continue on to Gibeah." ¹³He added, "Come. Let's try to reach Gibeah or Ramah. We can spend the night in one of those places."

¹⁴So they continued on. As they came near Gibeah in Benjamin, the sun went down. ¹⁵They stopped there to spend the night. They went to the city's main street and sat down. But no one took them home for the night.

¹⁶That evening an old man came into the city. He had been working in the fields. He was from the hill country of Ephraim. But he was living in Gibeah. The people who lived there were from the tribe of Benjamin. ¹⁷The old man saw the traveler in the main street. He asked, "Where are you going? Where did you come from?"

¹⁸The Levite answered, "We've come from Bethlehem in Judah. We're on our way to Ephraim. I live deep in the hill country there. I've been to Bethlehem. Now I'm going to the house of the LORD. But no one has taken me home for the night. ¹⁹We have straw and feed for our donkeys. We have food and wine for ourselves. We have enough for me, my female servant and the young man who is with us. We don't need anything."

²⁰"You are welcome at my house," the old man said. "I'd be happy to supply anything you might need. But don't spend the night in the street."

²¹So the old man took him into his house and fed his donkeys. After the travelers had washed their feet, they had something to eat and drink.

²²They were inside enjoying themselves. But some of the evil men who lived in the city surrounded the house. They pounded on the door. They shouted to the old man who owned the house. They said, "Bring out the man who came to your house. We want to have sex with him."

²³The owner of the house went outside. He said to them, "No, my friends. Don't do such an evil thing. This man is my guest. So don't do this terrible thing.

²⁴"Look, here is my virgin daughter. And here's the Levite's concubine. I'll bring them out to you now. You can have them. Do to them what you want to. But don't do such a terrible thing to this man."

²⁵The men wouldn't listen to him. So the Levite sent his concubine out to them. They forced her to have sex with them. They raped her all night long. As the night was ending, they let her go.

²⁶At sunrise she went back to the house where her master was staying. She fell down at the door. She stayed there until daylight.

²⁷Later that morning her master got up. He opened the door of the house. He stepped out to continue on his way. But his concubine was lying there. She had fallen at the doorway of the house. Her hands were reaching out toward the door. ²⁸He said to her, "Get up. Let's go." But there wasn't any answer. Then he put her dead body on his donkey. And he started out for home.

²⁹When he reached home, he got a knife. He cut up his concubine. He cut her into 12 pieces. He sent them into all of the territories of Israel.

³⁰Everyone who saw it said, "Nothing like this has ever been seen or done before. Nothing like this has happened since the day the people of Israel came up out of Egypt. Think about it! Consider it! Tell us what to do!"

THE TRIBE OF BENJAMIN IS ATTACKED BY THE OTHER TRIBES

20 Then all of the people of Israel came out. They came from the whole land between Dan and Beersheba. They also came from the land of Gilead. All of them gathered together in the sight of the LORD at Mizpah. ²The leaders of all of the tribes of Israel came. They took their places among the people of God who were gathered together. There were 400,000 fighting men who were carrying swords. ³The tribe of Benjamin heard that the people of Israel had gone up to Mizpah. The people of Israel said, "Tell us how that awful thing happened."

⁴So the Levite spoke. He was the husband of the woman who had been murdered. He said, "I and my concu-

bine went to Gibeah in Benjamin. We spent the night there. ⁵During the night the men of Gibeah came after me. They surrounded the house. They were planning to kill me. They raped my concubine, and she died.

⁶"I took my concubine and cut her into pieces. I sent one piece to each part of Israel's territory. I did it because they had done a very terrible thing in Israel. ⁷All of you men of Israel, speak up now. Give your decision."

⁸All of the men got up together. They said, "None of us will go home. Not one of us will return to his house. ⁹Here is what we'll do to Gibeah. We'll use lots to tell us how to attack the city. ¹⁰We'll take ten men out of every 100 from all of the tribes of Israel. We'll take 100 from every 1,000. We'll take 1,000 from every 10,000. The men we take will get supplies for the army. Then the army will go to Gibeah in Benjamin. They'll give Gibeah exactly what they should get because of the evil thing they did in Israel."

¹¹So all of the men of Israel came together to fight against the city.

¹²The tribes of Israel sent men through the whole tribe of Benjamin. They said, "What about this awful crime that was committed among you? ¹³Hand over those evil men of Gibeah. We'll put them to death. In that way we'll get rid of those evil people."

But the people of Benjamin wouldn't listen to the other people of Israel. ¹⁴They came together at Gibeah from their towns. They came to fight against the other people of Israel.

¹⁵Right away the people of Benjamin gathered together 26,000 men from their towns. They were carrying swords. The men were added to the 700 who had been chosen from those who were living in Gibeah. ¹⁶Among all of those men there were 700 who were left-handed. Each of them could sling a stone at a hair and not miss.

¹⁷Israel gathered 400,000 men together. They were carrying swords. All of them were fighting men. That number didn't include the tribe of Benjamin.

¹⁸The people of Israel went up to Bethel. There they spoke to God. They asked him, "Who will go up first and fight for us against the people of Benjamin?"

The LORD answered, "The tribe of Judah will go first."

¹⁹The next morning the people of Israel got up. They set up camp near Gibeah. ²⁰The men of Israel went out to fight against the men of Benjamin. They took up their battle positions against them at Gibeah. ²¹The men of Benjamin came out of Gibeah. They killed 22,000 men of Israel on the field of battle that day. ²²But the men of Israel cheered each other on. They again took up their positions in the places where they had been the first day.

²³The men of Israel went and sobbed in the sight of the LORD until evening. They spoke to the LORD. They asked, "Should we go up again to fight against the men of Benjamin? They are our fellow Israelites."

The LORD answered, "Go up and fight against them."

²⁴The men of Israel came near the men of Benjamin on the second day. ²⁵The men of Benjamin came out from Gibeah to oppose them. That time they killed 18,000 more men of Israel. All of the men who died had been carrying swords.

²⁶Then all of the people of Israel went up to Bethel. They sat there and sobbed in the sight of the LORD. They didn't eat anything that day until evening. Then they brought burnt offerings and friendship offerings to the LORD.

²⁷Again the people of Israel spoke to the LORD. In those days the ark of the covenant of God was there. ²⁸Phinehas was serving as priest at the ark. He was the son of Eleazar. Eleazar was the son of Aaron. The people of Israel asked, "Should we go up again to fight against the men of Benjamin? They are our fellow Israelites."

The LORD answered, "Go. Tomorrow I will hand them over to you."

²⁹Then Israel hid some men and had them wait all around Gibeah. ³⁰They went up to fight against the men of Benjamin on the third day. They took up their positions against Gibeah, just as they had done before.

³¹The men of Benjamin came out to fight against them. They were drawn away from the city. They began to wound and kill the men of Israel just as they had done before. About 30 men fell in battle. They fell in the open fields and on the roads. One of the roads led to Bethel. The other led to Gibeah.

³²The men of Benjamin said, "We're winning the battle over them, just as we did before."

But the men of Israel said, "Let's pull back. Let's draw them away from the city to the roads."

³³All of the men of Israel moved away from their places. They took up new battle positions at Baal Tamar. The men who had been hiding charged out. They came from west of Gibeah.

³⁴Then 10,000 of Israel's finest men attacked Gibeah. The men of Benjamin didn't realize they were about to be destroyed. The fighting was very heavy.

³⁵The LORD helped Israel win the battle over Benjamin. On that day the men of Israel struck down 25,100 men of Benjamin. All of the men who died had been carrying swords. ³⁶Then the men of Benjamin saw that they had lost the battle.

The men of Israel had moved away from their positions in front of Benjamin. They had depended on the men they had hidden near Gibeah. ³⁷Suddenly the men who had been hiding rushed into Gibeah. They spread out. Then they killed everyone in the city with their swords.

³⁸The men of Israel had made a plan with those who had been hiding. They had told them to send up a large cloud of smoke from the city. ³⁹Then the men of Israel would turn around and attack.

The men of Benjamin had begun to wound and kill the men of Israel. They had struck down about 30 of them. They had said, "We're winning the battle over them, just as we did the first time."

⁴⁰But a column of smoke began to go up from the city. The men of Benjamin turned around. They saw the smoke of the whole city going up into the sky.

⁴¹Then the men of Israel turned around and attacked them.

The men of Benjamin were terrified. They realized they were going to be destroyed. ⁴²So they ran away from the men of Israel. They ran toward the desert. But they couldn't escape the battle. Other men of Israel came out of the towns. There they struck the men of Benjamin down. ⁴³They surrounded them. They chased them and easily caught up with them. That happened east of Gibeah.

⁴⁴So 18,000 men of Benjamin fell in battle. All of them were brave fighters. ⁴⁵Some men of Benjamin turned back. They ran toward the desert to the rock of Rimmon. As they did, the men of Israel struck down 5,000 of them along the roads. They kept chasing the men of Benjamin all the way to Gidom. Along the way they struck down 2,000 more.

⁴⁶On that day 25,000 men of Benjamin fell in battle. They had been carrying swords. All of them were brave fighters. ⁴⁷But 600 men turned back. They ran into the desert to the rock of Rimmon. They stayed there for four months.

⁴⁸The men of Israel went back to Benjamin. They killed the people in all of the towns with their swords. They even killed the animals. So they killed everything they found. They set on fire all of the towns they came to.

THE MEN OF BENJAMIN RECEIVE WIVES

21 The men of Israel had taken an oath and made a promise at Mizpah. They had said, "Not one of us will give his daughter to be married to a man from Benjamin."

²The people went to Bethel. They sat there until evening in the sight of God. They sobbed loudly and bitterly. ³"LORD, you are the God of Israel," they cried. "Why has this happened to Israel? Why is one tribe missing from Israel today?"

⁴Early the next day the people built an altar. They brought burnt offerings and friendship offerings.

⁵Then the people of Israel asked, "Has anyone failed to come here in the

sight of the LORD? Is anyone missing from all of the tribes of Israel?"

The people had made a promise with an oath. They had said that anyone who failed to come to Mizpah in the sight of the LORD should certainly be put to death.

⁶The people of Israel were very sad because of what had happened to the tribe of Benjamin. After all, they were their fellow Israelites. "Today one tribe has been cut off from Israel," they said. ⁷"How can we provide wives for the men who are left? We've made a promise with an oath in the sight of the LORD. We've promised not to give any of our daughters to be married to them."

⁸Then they asked, "Has any tribe of Israel failed to come here to Mizpah in the sight of the LORD?"

They discovered that no one from Jabesh Gilead had come. No one from there had gathered together with the others in the camp. ⁹They counted the people. They found that none of the people of Jabesh Gilead had come to Mizpah.

¹⁰So the community sent 12,000 fighting men to Jabesh Gilead. They directed them to take their swords and kill those who were living there. That included the women and children. ¹¹"Here is what you must do," they said. "Kill every male. Also kill every woman who is not a virgin."

¹²They found 400 young women in Jabesh Gilead who had never made love to a man. So they took them to the camp at Shiloh in Canaan.

¹³Then the whole community sent an offer of peace to the men of Benjamin. The men were at the rock of Rimmon. ¹⁴So the men of Benjamin returned at that time. They were given the women of Jabesh Gilead who had been spared. But there weren't enough women for all of them.

¹⁵The people were very sad because of what had happened to the tribe of Benjamin. The LORD had left a gap in the tribes of Israel. They weren't complete without Benjamin.

¹⁶The elders of the community spoke up. They said, "All of the women of Benjamin have been wiped out. So how will we find wives for the men who are left? ¹⁷The men of Benjamin who are still alive need to have children," they said. "If they don't, a tribe of Israel will be wiped out.

¹⁸"But we can't give them our daughters to be their wives. We Israelites have taken an oath and made a promise. We've said, 'May anyone who gives a wife to a man from Benjamin be under the LORD's curse.'

¹⁹"Look, a feast is celebrated every year in Shiloh in honor of the LORD. Shiloh is north of Bethel. It's east of the road that goes from Bethel to Shechem. It's south of Lebonah."

²⁰So they told the men of Benjamin what to do. They said, "Go. Hide in the vineyards ²¹and watch. The young women of Shiloh will come out. They'll join in the dancing. When they do, run out of the vineyards. Each of you grab hold of a young woman from Shiloh to be your wife. Then go to the land of Benjamin.

²²"Their fathers or brothers might not be happy with what we're doing. If they aren't, we'll say to them, 'Do us a favor. Help the men of Benjamin. We didn't get wives for them during the battle. You aren't guilty of doing anything wrong. After all, you didn't give your daughters to them. They were stolen from you.' "

²³So that's what the men of Benjamin did. While the young women were dancing, each man caught one. He carried her away to be his wife. Then the men returned to their own share of land. They built the towns again. They settled down in them.

²⁴At that time the men of Israel also left. They went home to their tribes and family groups. Each one went to his own share of land.

²⁵In those days Israel didn't have a king. The people did anything they thought was right.

Ruth

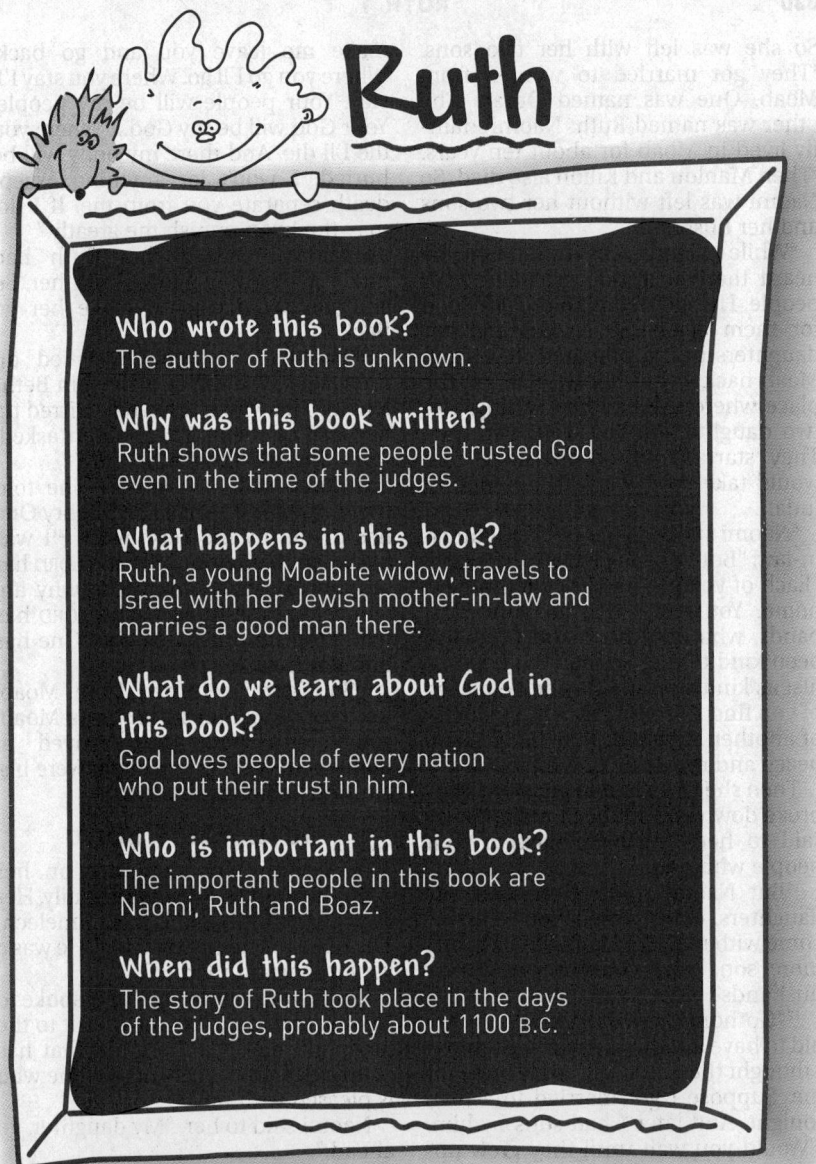

Who wrote this book?
The author of Ruth is unknown.

Why was this book written?
Ruth shows that some people trusted God even in the time of the judges.

What happens in this book?
Ruth, a young Moabite widow, travels to Israel with her Jewish mother-in-law and marries a good man there.

What do we learn about God in this book?
God loves people of every nation who put their trust in him.

Who is important in this book?
The important people in this book are Naomi, Ruth and Boaz.

When did this happen?
The story of Ruth took place in the days of the judges, probably about 1100 B.C.

RUTH GOES TO BETHLEHEM WITH NAOMI

1 There was a time when Israel didn't have kings to rule over them. But they had leaders to help them. This is a story about some things that happened during that time.

There wasn't enough food in the land of Judah. So a man went to live in the country of Moab for a while. He was from Bethlehem in Judah. His wife and two sons went with him.

²The man's name was Elimelech. His wife's name was Naomi. The names of his two sons were Mahlon and Kilion. They were Ephrathites from Bethlehem in Judah. They went to Moab and lived there.

³Naomi's husband Elimelech died.

So she was left with her two sons. [4]They got married to women from Moab. One was named Orpah. The other was named Ruth. Naomi's family lived in Moab for about ten years. [5]Then Mahlon and Kilion also died. So Naomi was left without her two sons and her husband.

[6]While Naomi was in Moab, she heard that the LORD had helped his people. He had begun to provide food for them again. So Naomi and her daughters-in-law prepared to go from Moab back to her home. [7]She left the place where she had been living. Her two daughters-in-law went with her. They started out on the road that would take them back to the land of Judah.

[8]Naomi spoke to her two daughters-in-law. "Both of you go back," she said. "Each of you go to your own mother's home. You were kind to your husbands, who have died. You have also been kind to me. So may the LORD be just as kind to you. [9]May he help each of you find a secure place in the home of another husband. May he give you peace and rest."

Then she kissed them good-by. They broke down and sobbed loudly. [10]They said to her, "We'll go back to your people with you."

[11]But Naomi said, "Go home, my daughters. Why would you want to come with me? Am I going to have any more sons who could become your husbands?

[12]"Go home, my daughters. I'm too old to have another husband. Suppose I thought there was still some hope for me. Suppose I got married to a man tonight. And later I had sons by him. [13]Would you wait until they grew up? Would you stay single until you could get married to them? No, my daughters. My life is more bitter than yours. The LORD's powerful hand has been against me!"

[14]When they heard that, they broke down and sobbed again. Then Orpah kissed her mother-in-law good-by. But Ruth held on to her.

[15]"Look," said Naomi. "Your sister-in-law is going back to her people and her gods. Go back with her."

[16]But Ruth replied, "Don't try to make me leave you and go back. Where you go I'll go. Where you stay I'll stay. Your people will be my people. Your God will be my God. [17]Where you die I'll die. And there my body will be buried. I won't let anything except death separate you from me. If I do, may the LORD punish me greatly."

[18]Naomi realized that Ruth had made up her mind to go with her. So she stopped trying to make her go back.

[19]The two women continued on their way. At last they arrived in Bethlehem. The whole town was stirred up because of them. The women asked, "Can this possibly be Naomi?"

[20]"Don't call me Naomi," she told them. "Call me Mara. The Mighty One has made my life very bitter. [21]I was full when I went away. But the LORD has brought me back empty. So why are you calling me Naomi? The LORD has made me suffer. The Mighty One has brought trouble on me."

[22]So Naomi returned from Moab. Ruth, her daughter-in-law from Moab, came with her. They arrived in Bethlehem just when people were beginning to harvest the barley.

RUTH MEETS BOAZ

2 Naomi had a relative on her husband's side of the family. Her husband's name was Elimelech. The relative's name was Boaz. He was a very important man.

[2]Ruth, who was from Moab, spoke to Naomi. She said, "Let me go out to the fields. I'll pick up the grain that has been left. I'll do it behind anyone who is pleased with me."

Naomi said to her, "My daughter, go ahead."

[3]So Ruth went out and began to pick up grain. She worked in the fields behind those who were cutting and gathering the grain. As it turned out, she was working in a field that belonged to Boaz. He was from the family of Elimelech.

[4]Just then Boaz arrived from Bethlehem. He greeted those who were cutting and gathering the grain. He said, "May the LORD be with you!"

"And may the LORD bless you!" they replied.

⁵Boaz spoke to the man who was in charge of his workers. He asked, "Who is that young woman?"

⁶The man replied, "She's from Moab. She came back from there with Naomi. ⁷She said, 'Please let me walk behind the workers. Let me pick up the grain that is left.' Then she went into the field. She has kept on working there from morning until now. She took only one short rest in the shade."

⁸So Boaz said to Ruth, "Dear woman, listen to me. Don't pick up grain in any other field. Don't go anywhere else. Stay here with my female servants. ⁹Keep your eye on the field where the men are cutting grain. Walk behind the women who are gathering it. Pick up the grain that is left. I've told the men not to touch you. When you are thirsty, go and get a drink. Take water from the jars the men have filled."

¹⁰When Ruth heard that, she bowed down with her face to the ground. She asked, "Why are you being so kind to me? In fact, why are you even noticing me? I'm from another country."

¹¹Boaz replied, "I've been told all about you. I've heard about everything you have done for your mother-in-law since your husband died. I know that you left your father and mother. I know that you left your country. You came to live with people you didn't know before. ¹²"May the LORD reward you for what you have done. May the God of Israel bless you richly. You have come to him to find safety under his care."

¹³"Sir, I hope you will continue to be kind to me," Ruth said. "You have comforted me. You have spoken kindly to me. And I'm not even as important as one of your female servants!"

¹⁴When it was time to eat, Boaz spoke to Ruth again. "Come over here," he said. "Have some bread. Dip it in the wine vinegar."

She sat down with the workers. Then Boaz offered her some grain that had been cooked. She ate all she wanted. She even had some left over.

¹⁵Ruth got up to pick up more grain. Then Boaz gave orders to his men. He said, "Suppose she takes some stalks from what the women have tied up. If she does, don't make her look bad. ¹⁶Instead, pull some stalks out for her. Leave them for her to pick up. Don't tell her she shouldn't do it."

¹⁷So Ruth picked up grain in the field until evening. Then she separated the barley from the straw. It amounted to more than half a bushel. ¹⁸She carried it back to town. Her mother-in-law saw how much she had gathered. Ruth also brought out the food that was left over from the lunch Boaz had given her. She gave it to Naomi.

¹⁹Her mother-in-law asked her, "Where did you pick up grain today? Where did you work? May the man who noticed you be blessed!"

Then Ruth told her about the man whose field she had worked in. "The name of the man I worked with today is Boaz," she said.

²⁰"May the LORD bless him!" Naomi said to her daughter-in-law. "The LORD is still being kind to those who are living and those who are dead."

She continued, "That man is a close relative of ours. He's one of our family protectors."

²¹Then Ruth, who was from Moab, said, "He told me more. He even said, 'Stay with my workers until they have finished bringing in all of my grain.' "

²²Naomi replied to her daughter-in-law Ruth. She said, "That will be good for you, my daughter. Go with his female servants. You might be harmed if you go to someone else's field."

²³So Ruth stayed close to the female servants of Boaz as she picked up grain. She worked until the time when all of the barley and wheat had been harvested. And she lived with her mother-in-law.

RUTH GOES TO BOAZ AT THE THRESHING FLOOR

3 One day Ruth's mother-in-law Naomi spoke to her. She said, "My daughter, shouldn't I try to find a secure place for you? Shouldn't you have peace and rest? Shouldn't I find a home where things will go well with you? ²You have been with the female servants of Boaz. He's a relative of ours. Tonight he'll be separating the straw from his barley on the threshing floor.

³"So wash yourself. Put on some perfume. And put on your best clothes. Then go down to the threshing floor. But don't let Boaz know you are there. Wait until he has finished eating and drinking. ⁴Notice where he lies down. Then go over and uncover his feet. Lie down there. He'll tell you what to do."

⁵"I'll do everything you say," Ruth answered. ⁶So she went down to the threshing floor. She did everything her mother-in-law had told her to do.

⁷When Boaz had finished eating and drinking, he was in a good mood. He went over to lie down at the far end of the grain pile. Then Ruth approached quietly. She uncovered his feet and lay down there.

⁸In the middle of the night, something surprised Boaz and woke him up. He turned and found a woman lying there at his feet.

⁹"Who are you?" he asked.

"I'm Ruth," she said. "You are my family protector. So take good care of me by making me your wife."

¹⁰"Dear woman, may the LORD bless you," he replied. "You are showing even more kindness now than you did earlier. You didn't run after the younger men, whether they were rich or poor. ¹¹Dear woman, don't be afraid. I'll do for you everything you ask. All of the people of my town know that you are a noble woman.

¹²"It's true that I'm a relative of yours. But there's a family protector who is more closely related to you than I am. ¹³So stay here for the night. In the morning if he wants to help you, good. Let him help you. But if he doesn't want to, then I'll do it. You can be sure that the LORD lives. And you can be just as sure that I'll help you. Lie down here until morning."

¹⁴So she stayed at his feet until morning. But she got up before anyone could be recognized. Boaz thought, "No one must know that a woman came to the threshing floor."

¹⁵He said to Ruth, "Bring me the coat you have around you. Hold it out." So she did. He poured more than fifty pounds of barley into it and helped her pick it up. Then he went back to town.

¹⁶Ruth came to her mother-in-law. Naomi asked, "How did it go, my daughter?"

Then Ruth told her everything Boaz had done for her. ¹⁷She said, "He gave me all of this barley. He said, 'Don't go back to your mother-in-law with your hands empty.'"

¹⁸Naomi said, "My daughter, sit down until you find out what happens. The man won't rest until he settles the whole matter today."

BOAZ GETS MARRIED TO RUTH

4 Boaz went up to the town gate and sat down there. The family protector he had talked about came by. Then Boaz said, "Come over here, my friend. Sit down." So the man went over and sat down.

²Boaz brought ten of the elders of the town together. He said, "Sit down here." So they did.

³Then he spoke to the family protector. He said, "Naomi has come back from Moab. She's selling the piece of land that belonged to our relative Elimelech. ⁴I thought I should bring the matter to your attention. I suggest that you buy the land while those who are sitting here and the elders of my people are looking on as witnesses.

"If you are willing to buy it back, do it. But if you aren't, tell me. Then I'll know. No one has the right to buy it back except you. And I'm next in line."

"I'll buy it," he said.

⁵Then Boaz said, "When you buy the land from Naomi and Ruth, who is from Moab, you must get married to Ruth. She's the dead man's widow. So you must take her as your wife. His name must stay with his property."

⁶When the family protector heard that, he said, "Then I can't buy the land. If I did, I might put my own property in danger. So you buy it. I can't do it."

⁷In earlier times in Israel, there was a certain practice. It was used when family land was bought back and changed owners. The practice made the sale final. One person would take

his sandal off and give it to the other. That was how people in Israel showed that a business matter had been settled.

⁸So the family protector said to Boaz, "Buy it yourself." And he took his sandal off.

⁹Then Boaz spoke to the elders and all of the people. He said, "Today you are witnesses. You have seen that I have bought land from Naomi. I have bought all of the property that had belonged to Elimelech, Kilion and Mahlon.

¹⁰"I've also taken Ruth, who is from Moab, to become my wife. She is Mahlon's widow. I've decided to get married to her so the dead man's name will stay with his property. Now his name won't disappear from his family line. It won't disappear from the town records. Today you are witnesses!"

¹¹Then the elders and all who were at the gate spoke. They said, "We are witnesses. The woman is coming into your home. May the LORD make her to be like Rachel and Leah. Together they built up the nation of Israel. May you be an important person in Ephrathah. May you be famous in Bethlehem. ¹²The LORD will give you children through this young woman. May your family be like the family of Perez. He was the son Tamar had by Judah."

THE FAMILY LINE OF DAVID

¹³So Boaz got married to Ruth. She became his wife. Then he made love to her. The LORD blessed her so that she became pregnant. And she had a son. ¹⁴The women said to Naomi, "We praise the LORD. Today he has provided a family protector for you. May this child become famous all over Israel! ¹⁵He will make your life new again. He'll take care of you when you are old. He's the son of your very own daughter-in-law. She loves you. She is better to you than seven sons." ¹⁶Then Naomi put the child on her lap and took care of him. ¹⁷The women who were living there said, "Naomi has a son." They named him Obed. He was the father of Jesse. Jesse was the father of David.

¹⁸Here is the family line of Perez.

Perez was the father of Hezron.
¹⁹Hezron was the father of Ram.
Ram was the father of Amminadab.
²⁰Amminadab was the father of Nahshon.
Nahshon was the father of Salmon.
²¹Salmon was the father of Boaz.
Boaz was the father of Obed.
²²Obed was the father of Jesse.
And Jesse was the father of David.

KIDS' QUESTION

Did people have shoes in Bible days?

People usually wore sandals instead of shoes because it was very sunny, hot and dry where they lived. They made their sandals of leather and fastened them to their feet with strips of leather. The leather was attached to the bottom of the sandal and wrapped up around the ankle. Sandals protected their feet without making them hot. This also meant that their feet got dirty. Whenever people entered a home, they had to clean off the dust and dirt that had stuck to their sweaty feet. That is why Jesus talked about washing people's feet when they came to visit.

BIBLE COSTUME PARTY

checkout Ruth 4:7,8

Related verses:
John 13:5–15.

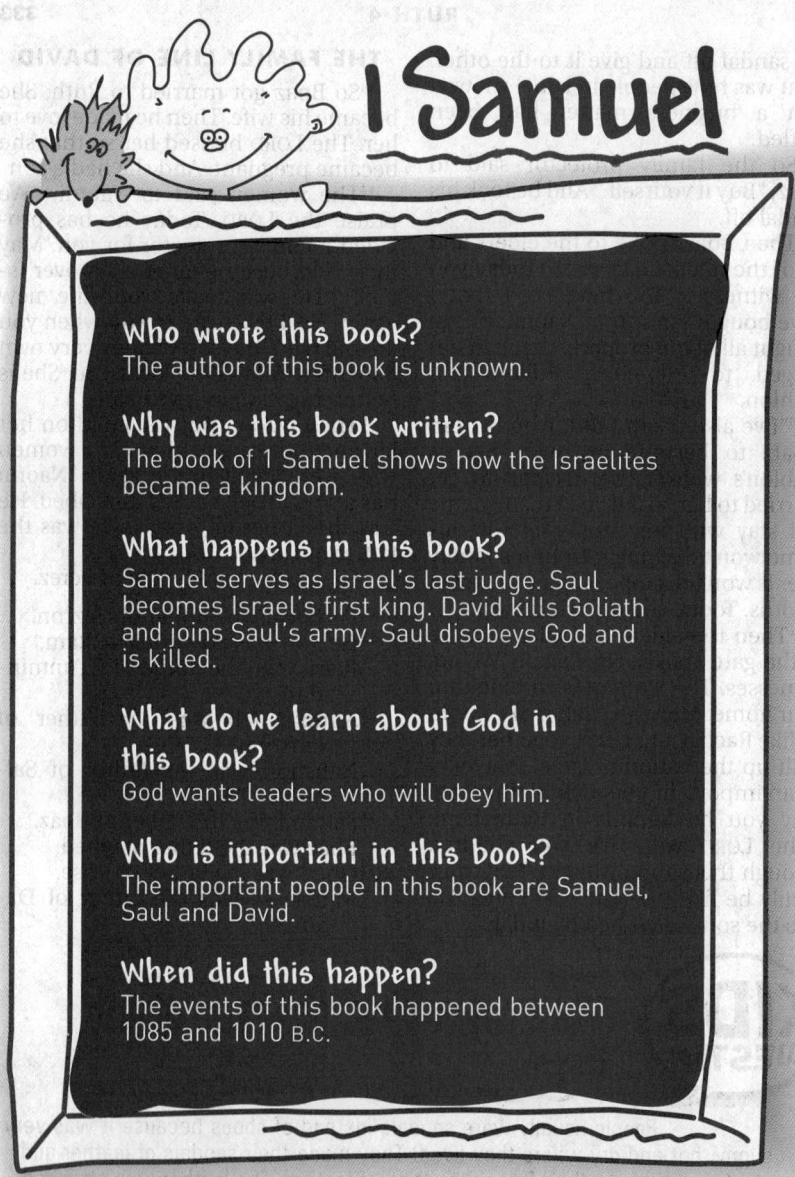

1 Samuel

Who wrote this book?

The author of this book is unknown.

Why was this book written?

The book of 1 Samuel shows how the Israelites became a kingdom.

What happens in this book?

Samuel serves as Israel's last judge. Saul becomes Israel's first king. David kills Goliath and joins Saul's army. Saul disobeys God and is killed.

What do we learn about God in this book?

God wants leaders who will obey him.

Who is important in this book?

The important people in this book are Samuel, Saul and David.

When did this happen?

The events of this book happened between 1085 and 1010 B.C.

SAMUEL IS BORN

1 A certain man from Ramathaim in the hill country of Ephraim was named Elkanah. He was the son of Jeroham. Jeroham was the son of Elihu. Elihu was the son of Tohu. Tohu was the son of Zuph. Elkanah belonged to the family line of Zuph. Elkanah lived in the territory of Ephraim.

²Elkanah had two wives. One was named Hannah. The other was named Peninnah. Peninnah had children, but Hannah didn't.

³Year after year Elkanah went up from his town to Shiloh. He went there to worship and sacrifice to the LORD who rules over all. Hophni and Phinehas served as priests of the LORD at Shiloh. They were the two sons of Eli.

⁴Every time the day came for Elka-

nah to offer a sacrifice, he would give a share of the meat to his wife Peninnah. He would also give a share to each of her sons and daughters. ⁵But he would give two shares of meat to Hannah. That's because he loved her. He also gave her two shares because the LORD had kept her from having children.

⁶Peninnah teased Hannah to make her angry. She did it because the LORD had kept Hannah from having children. ⁷Peninnah teased Hannah year after year. Every time Hannah would go up to the house of the LORD, Elkanah's other wife would tease her. She would keep doing it until Hannah cried and wouldn't eat.

⁸Her husband Elkanah would speak to her. He would say, "Hannah, why are you crying? Why don't you eat? Why are you so angry and unhappy? Don't I mean more to you than ten sons?"

⁹One time when they had finished eating and drinking in Shiloh, Hannah stood up. The priest Eli was sitting on a chair by the doorpost of the LORD's house. ¹⁰Hannah was very bitter. She sobbed and sobbed. She prayed to the LORD. ¹¹She made a promise to him. She said, "LORD, you rule over all. Please see how I'm suffering! Show concern for me! Don't forget about me! Please give me a son! If you do, I'll give him back to you. Then he will serve you all the days of his life. He'll never use a razor on his head. He'll never cut his hair."

¹²As Hannah kept on praying to the LORD, Eli watched her lips. ¹³She was praying in her heart. Her lips were moving. But she wasn't making a sound.

Eli thought Hannah was drunk. ¹⁴He said to her, "How long will you keep on getting drunk? Get rid of your wine."

¹⁵"That's not true, sir," Hannah replied. "I'm a woman who is deeply troubled. I haven't been drinking wine or beer. I was telling the LORD all of my troubles. ¹⁶Don't think of me as an evil woman. I've been praying here because I'm very sad. My pain is so great."

¹⁷Eli answered, "Go in peace. May the God of Israel give you what you have asked him for."

¹⁸She said, "May you be pleased with me." Then she left and had something to eat. Her face wasn't sad anymore.

¹⁹Early the next morning Elkanah and his family got up. They worshiped the LORD. Then they went back to their home in Ramah.

Elkanah made love to his wife Hannah. And the LORD showed concern for her. ²⁰After some time, Hannah became pregnant. She had a baby boy. She said, "I asked the LORD for him." So she named him Samuel.

HANNAH GIVES SAMUEL TO THE LORD

²¹Elkanah went up to Shiloh to offer the yearly sacrifice to the LORD. He also went there to keep a promise he had made. His whole family went with him.

²²But Hannah didn't go. She said to her husband, "When the boy doesn't need me to nurse him anymore, I'll take him to the LORD's house. I'll give him to the LORD there. He'll stay there for the rest of his life."

²³Her husband Elkanah told her, "Do what you think is best. Stay here at home until Samuel doesn't need you to nurse him anymore. May the LORD make his promise to you come true."

So Hannah stayed home. She nursed her son until he didn't need her milk anymore.

²⁴When the boy didn't need her to nurse him anymore, she took him with her to Shiloh. She took him there even though he was still very young. She brought him to the LORD's house. She brought along a bull that was three years old. She brought more than half a bushel of flour. She also brought a bottle of wine. The bottle was made out of animal skin.

²⁵After the bull was killed, Elkanah and Hannah brought the boy to Eli. ²⁶Hannah said to Eli, "Sir, I'm the woman who stood here beside you praying to the LORD. And that's just as sure as you are alive. ²⁷I prayed for this child. The LORD has given me what I asked him for. ²⁸So now I'm giving him to the LORD. As long as he lives he'll be given to the LORD." And all of them worshiped the LORD there.

HANNAH GIVES THANKS TO THE LORD

2 Then Hannah prayed. She said,
"The LORD has filled my heart
  with joy.
He has made me strong.
I can laugh at my enemies.
I'm so glad he saved me.

2 "There isn't anyone holy like the
  LORD.
There isn't anyone except him.
There isn't any Rock like our God.

3 "Don't keep talking so proudly.
Don't let your mouth say such
  proud things.
The LORD is a God who knows
  everything.
He judges everything people do.

4 "The bows of great heroes are
  broken.
But those who trip and fall are
  made strong.

5 Those who used to be full have to
  work for food.
But those who used to be hungry
  aren't hungry anymore.

The woman who couldn't have
  children has seven of them
  now.
But the woman who has had
  many children is sad now
  because hers has died.

6 "The LORD causes people to die.
He also gives people life.
He brings people down to the
  grave. He also brings people
  up.

7 The LORD makes people poor. He
  also makes people rich.
He brings people down. He also
  lifts people up.

8 He raises poor people up from the
  trash pile.
He lifts needy people out of the
  ashes.
He lets them sit with princes.
He gives them places of honor.

"The foundations of the earth
  belong to the LORD.
On them he has set the world.

9 He guards the paths of those who
  are faithful to him.
But evil people will lie silent in
  their dark graves.

Why did Hannah leave her son at the church?

Hannah was unable to have children for a long time. That bothered her very much. One day she prayed about it. She promised that if God would give her a son, she would give him back to God. God answered her prayer and gave her Samuel. When Samuel was born, Hannah remembered her promise to God. When Samuel was a little older she brought him to the temple. There was a school there. Leaving Samuel there was like leaving him at a school where the kids stay all the time. He was with people who would love and care for him. Hannah's son was in good hands and she got to visit him.

Related verses:
1 Samuel 1:1–28;
2:20–21

checkout
1 Samuel 1:27,28

"People don't win just because they are strong.

[10] Those who oppose the LORD will be totally destroyed.
He will thunder against them from heaven.
He will judge the earth from one end to the other.

"He will give power to his king.
He will give honor to his anointed one."

[11]Then Elkanah went home to Ramah. But the boy Samuel served the LORD under the direction of the priest Eli.

ELI'S EVIL SONS

[12]Eli's sons were evil men. They didn't know the LORD. [13]When anyone came to offer a sacrifice, here is what the priests would do. While the meat was being boiled, the servant of the priest would come with a large fork in his hand. [14]He would stick it into the pan or pot or small or large kettle. Then the priest would take for himself everything the fork brought up. That's how Eli's sons treated all of the people of Israel who came to Shiloh.

[15]Even before the fat was burned, the servant of the priest would come over. He would speak to the man who was offering the sacrifice. He would say, "Give the priest some meat to cook. He won't accept boiled meat from you. All he'll accept is raw meat."

[16]Sometimes the man would say to him, "Let the fat be burned up first. Then take what you want."

But the servant would answer, "No. Hand it over right now. If you don't, I'll take it away from you by force."

[17]That sin of Eli's sons was very great in the LORD's sight. That's because they were making fun of his offering.

[18]But the boy Samuel served the LORD. He wore a sacred linen apron. [19]Each year his mother made him a little robe. She took it to him when she went up to Shiloh with her husband. She did it when her husband went to offer the yearly sacrifice.

[20]Eli would bless Elkanah and his wife. He would say, "May the LORD give you children by this woman. May they take the place of the boy she prayed for and gave to him." Then they would go home.

[21]The LORD was gracious to Hannah. She became pregnant. Over a period of years she had three more sons and two daughters. During that whole time the boy Samuel grew up serving the LORD.

[22]Eli was very old. He kept hearing about everything his sons were doing to all of the people of Israel. He also heard how they were sleeping with the women who served at the entrance to the Tent of Meeting.

[23]So Eli said to his sons, "Why are you doing those things? All of the people are telling me about the evil things you are doing. [24]No, my sons. The report I hear isn't good. And it's spreading among the LORD's people. [25]If a man sins against someone else, God can help that sinner. But if a man sins against the LORD, who can help him?"

In spite of what their father Eli said, his sons didn't pay any attention to his warning. That's because the LORD had already decided to put them to death.

[26]The boy Samuel continued to grow stronger. He also became more and more pleasing to the LORD and to people.

A MAN OF GOD PROPHESIES AGAINST ELI'S FAMILY

[27]A man of God came to Eli. He told him, "The LORD says, 'I made myself clearly known to your relatives who lived long ago. I did it when they were in Egypt under Pharaoh. [28]I chose your father Aaron to be my priest. I chose him out of all of the tribes of Israel. I told him to go up to my altar. I told him to burn incense. I chose him to wear a linen apron when he served me. I also gave his family all of the offerings that are made with fire by the people of Israel.

[29]" 'Why do all of you laugh at my sacrifices and offerings? I require them to be brought to the house where I live. Why do you honor your sons more than me? Why do you fatten yourselves on the best parts of every offering that is made by my people Israel?'

[30]"The LORD is the God of Israel. He

announced, 'I promised that your family and the family of Aaron would serve me as priests forever.'

"But now the LORD announces, 'I will not let that happen! I will honor those who honor me. But I will turn away from those who look down on me. [31]The time is coming when I will cut your life short. I will also cut short the lives of those in your family. No man in your family line will grow old.

[32]"'You will see nothing but trouble in the house where I live. Good things will still happen to Israel. But no man in your family line will ever grow old. [33]A member of your family will serve me at my altar. But what he does will bring tears to your eyes. Your heart will be sad. And the rest of the men in your family line will die while they are still young.

[34]"'Something is going to happen to your two sons Hophni and Phinehas. When it does, it will show you that what I am saying is true. They will both die on the same day.

[35]"'I will raise up for myself a faithful priest. He will do what my heart and mind want him to do. I will make his family line very secure. They will always serve as priests to my anointed king. [36]Everyone who is left in your family line will come and bow down to him. They will beg him for a piece of silver and a crust of bread. They will say, "Please give me a place to serve among the priests. Then I can have food to eat."' "

THE LORD CALLS OUT TO SAMUEL

3 The boy Samuel served the LORD under the direction of Eli. In those days the LORD didn't give many messages to his people. He didn't give them many visions.

[2]One night Eli was lying down in his usual place. His eyes were becoming so weak he couldn't see very well. [3]Samuel was lying down in the LORD's house. That's where the ark of God was kept. The lamp of God was still burning. [4]The LORD called out to Samuel.

Samuel answered, "Here I am." [5]He ran over to Eli. He said, "Here I am. You called out to me."

But Eli said, "I didn't call you. Go

back and lie down." So he went and lay down.

[6]Again the LORD called out, "Samuel!" Samuel got up and went to Eli. He said, "Here I am. You called out to me."

"My son," Eli said, "I didn't call you. Go back and lie down."

[7]Samuel didn't know the LORD yet. That's because the LORD still hadn't given him a message.

[8]The LORD called out to Samuel for the third time. Samuel got up and went to Eli. He said, "Here I am. You called out to me."

Then Eli realized that the LORD was calling the boy. [9]So Eli told Samuel, "Go and lie down. If someone calls out to you again, say, 'Speak, LORD. I'm listening.' " So Samuel went and lay down in his place.

[10]The LORD came and stood there. He called out, just as he had done the other times. He said, "Samuel! Samuel!"

Then Samuel replied, "Speak. I'm listening."

[11]The LORD said to Samuel, "Pay attention! I am about to do something terrible in Israel. It will make the ears of everyone who hears about it ring.

[12]"At that time I will do everything to Eli and his family that I said I would. I will finish what I have started. [13]I told Eli I would punish his family forever. He knew his sons were sinning. He knew they were making fun of me. In spite of that, he failed to stop them.

[14]"So I took an oath and made a promise to the family of Eli. I said, 'The sins of Eli's family will never be paid for by bringing sacrifices or offerings.' "

[15]Samuel lay down until morning. Then he opened the doors of the LORD's house. He was afraid to tell Eli about the vision he had received. [16]But Eli called out to him. He said, "Samuel, my son."

Samuel answered, "Here I am."

[17]"What did the LORD say to you?" Eli asked. "Don't hide from me anything he told you. If you do, may God punish you greatly."

[18]So Samuel told him everything. He didn't hide anything from him.

Then Eli said, "He is the LORD. Let him do what he thinks is best."

¹⁹As Samuel grew up, the LORD was with him. He made everything Samuel said come true. ²⁰So all of the people of Israel recognized that Samuel really was a prophet of the LORD. Everyone from Dan all the way to Beersheba knew it.

²¹The LORD continued to appear at Shiloh. There he made himself known to Samuel through the messages he gave him.

4 And Samuel gave those messages to all of the people of Israel.

THE PHILISTINES CAPTURE THE ARK

The people of Israel went out to fight against the Philistines. The Israelites camped at Ebenezer. The Philistines camped at Aphek. ²The Philistines brought their forces together to fight against Israel. As the fighting spread, the men of Israel lost the battle to the Philistines. The Philistines killed about 4,000 of them on the field of battle.

³The rest of the Israelite soldiers returned to camp. Then the elders asked them, "Why did the LORD let the Philistines win the battle over us today? Let's bring the ark of the LORD's covenant from Shiloh. Let's take it with us. It will save us from the power of our enemies."

⁴So the people sent men to Shiloh. They brought back the ark of the covenant of the LORD. He sits there on his throne between the cherubim. He is the One who rules over all. Eli's two sons Hophni and Phinehas were with the ark of the covenant of God in Shiloh.

⁵The ark of the LORD's covenant was brought into the camp. Then all of the people of Israel shouted so loudly that the ground shook.

⁶The Philistines heard the noise. They asked, "What's all that shouting about in the Hebrew camp?"

Then the Philistines found out that the ark of the LORD had come into the camp. ⁷So they were afraid. "A god has come into their camp," they said. "We're in trouble! Nothing like this has ever happened before. ⁸How terrible it will be for us! Who will save us from

the power of those mighty gods? They struck down the people of Egypt in the desert. They sent all kinds of plagues on them.

⁹"Philistines, be strong! Fight like men! If you don't, you will come under the control of the Hebrews. You will become their slaves, just as they have been your slaves. Fight like men!"

¹⁰So the Philistines fought. The people of Israel lost the battle. Every man ran back to his tent. A large number of them were killed. Israel lost 30,000 soldiers who were on foot.

¹¹The ark of God was captured. And Eli's two sons Hophni and Phinehas died.

ELI DIES

¹²That same day a man from the tribe of Benjamin ran from the front lines of the battle. He went to Shiloh. His clothes were torn. He had dust on his head. ¹³When he arrived, there was Eli sitting on his chair. He was by the side of the road. He was watching because his heart was really concerned about the ark of God. The man entered the town and told everyone what had happened. Then the whole town cried out.

¹⁴Eli heard the people crying out. He asked, "What's the meaning of all of this noise?"

The man hurried over to Eli. ¹⁵Eli was 98 years old. His eyes were so bad he couldn't see. ¹⁶The man told Eli, "I've just come from the front lines of the battle. I ran away from there this very day."

Eli asked, "What happened, son?"

¹⁷The man who brought the news replied, "Israel ran away from the Philistines. Large numbers of men in the army were wounded or killed. Your two sons Hophni and Phinehas are also dead. And the ark of God has been captured."

¹⁸When the man spoke about the ark of God, Eli fell backward off his chair. He had been sitting by the side of the gate. When he fell, he broke his neck and died. He was old and fat. He had led Israel for 40 years.

¹⁹The wife of Phinehas was pregnant. She was Eli's daughter-in-law. It was near the time for her baby to be

born. She heard the news that the ark of God had been captured. She heard that her father-in-law and her husband were dead. So she went into labor and had her baby. Her pain was so great that her life was slipping away.

²⁰As she was dying, the women who were helping her spoke up. They said, "Don't be afraid. You have had a son." But she didn't reply. She didn't pay any attention.

²¹She named the boy Ichabod. She said, "The God of glory has left Israel." She said it because the ark of God had been captured. She also said it because her father-in-law and her husband had died. ²²She said, "The God of glory has left Israel." She said it because the ark of God had been captured.

THE ARK IS TAKEN TO ASHDOD AND EKRON

5 The Philistines had captured the ark of God. They took it from Ebenezer to Ashdod. ²They carried the ark into the temple of their god Dagon. They set it down beside the statue of Dagon.

³The people of Ashdod got up early the next day. They saw the statue of Dagon. There it was, lying on the ground! It had fallen on its face in front of the ark of the LORD. So they picked the statue of Dagon up. They put it back in its place.

⁴But the following morning when they got up, they saw the statue of Dagon. There it was, lying on the ground again! It had fallen on its face in front of the ark of the LORD. Its head and hands had been broken off. Only the body of the statue was left. Its head and hands were lying in the doorway of the temple. ⁵That's why to this very day no one steps on the bottom part of the doorway of Dagon's temple at Ashdod. Not even the priests of Dagon step there.

⁶The LORD's powerful hand punished the people of Ashdod and the settlements that were near it. He destroyed them. He made them suffer with growths in their bodies.

⁷The people of Ashdod saw what was happening. They said, "The ark of the god of Israel must not stay here with us. His powerful hand is punishing us and our god Dagon."

⁸So they called all of the rulers of the Philistines together. They asked them, "What should we do with the ark of the god of Israel?"

The rulers answered, "Have the ark moved to Gath." So they moved it.

⁹But after the people of Ashdod had moved the ark, the LORD's hand punished Gath. That threw its people into a great panic. The LORD made them break out with growths in their bodies. It happened to young people and old people alike. ¹⁰So the ark of God was sent to Ekron.

As the ark was entering Ekron, the people of the city cried out. They shouted, "They've brought the ark of the god of Israel to us. They want to kill us and our people."

¹¹So they called all of the rulers of the Philistines together. They said, "Send the ark of the god of Israel away. Let it go back to its own place. If you don't, it will kill us and our people." The death of so many people had filled the city with panic. God's powerful hand was punishing the city. ¹²Those who didn't die suffered with growths in their bodies. The people of Ekron cried out to heaven for help.

THE PHILISTINES RETURN THE ARK TO ISRAEL

6 The ark of the LORD had been in Philistine territory for seven months. ²The Philistines called for the priests and for those who practice evil magic. They wanted their advice. They said to them, "What should we do with the ark of the LORD? Tell us how we should send it back to its place."

³They answered, "If you return the ark of the god of Israel, don't send it away empty. Be sure you send a guilt offering to their god along with it. Then you will be healed. You will find out why his hand hasn't stopped punishing you."

⁴The Philistines asked, "What guilt offering should we send to him?"

Their advisers replied, "There are five Philistine rulers. So send five gold models of the growths that are in your bodies. Also send five gold models of rats. Do it because the same plague has struck you and your rulers alike. ⁵Make models of the growths and of the rats that are destroying the country. Pay honor to Israel's god. Perhaps his hand will stop punishing you. Maybe it will stop punishing your gods and your land.

⁶"Why are you stubborn, as Pharaoh and the people of Egypt were? God was very hard on them. Only then did they send the people of Israel out. Only then did they let them go on their way.

⁷"Now then, get a new cart ready. Get two cows that have just had calves. Be sure the cows have never pulled a cart before. Tie the cart to them. But take their calves away and put them in a pen.

⁸"Then put the ark of the LORD on the cart. Put the gold models in a chest beside the ark. Send them back to the LORD as a guilt offering. Send the cart on its way.

⁹"But keep an eye on the cart. See if it goes up toward Beth Shemesh to its own territory. If it does, then it's the LORD who has brought this horrible trouble on us. But if it doesn't, then we'll know it wasn't his hand that struck us. We'll know it happened to us by chance."

¹⁰So that's what they did. They took the two cows and tied the cart to them. They put the calves in a pen. ¹¹They placed the ark of the LORD on the cart. They put the chest there along with it. The chest held the gold models of the rats and of the growths.

¹²Then the cows went straight up toward Beth Shemesh. They stayed on the road. They were mooing all the way. They didn't turn to the right or the left. The Philistine rulers followed them all the way to the border of Beth Shemesh.

¹³The people of Beth Shemesh were working in the valley. They were gathering their wheat crop. They looked up and saw the ark. When they saw it, they were filled with joy.

¹⁴The cart came to the field of Joshua of Beth Shemesh. It stopped there beside a large rock. The people chopped up the wood the cart was made out of.

They sacrificed the cows as a burnt offering to the LORD.

¹⁵Some Levites had taken the ark of the LORD off the cart. They had also taken off the chest that held the gold models. They placed them on the large rock. On that day the people of Beth Shemesh offered burnt offerings to the LORD. They also made sacrifices to him.

¹⁶The five Philistine rulers saw everything that happened. On that same day they returned to Ekron.

¹⁷The Philistines sent gold models of growths as a guilt offering to the LORD. There was one each for Ashdod, Gaza, Ashkelon, Gath and Ekron. ¹⁸They also sent five gold models of rats. There was one for each of the Philistine towns that belonged to the five rulers. Each of those towns had high walls around it. The towns also had country villages around them.

The Levites set the ark of the LORD on a large rock. To this very day the rock gives witness to what happened there. It's in the field of Joshua of Beth Shemesh.

¹⁹But some of the people of Beth Shemesh looked into the ark of the LORD. So he struck them down. He put 70 of them to death. The rest of the people were filled with sorrow. That's because the LORD had killed so many of them.

²⁰The people of Beth Shemesh said, "The LORD is a holy God. Who can stand in front of him? Where can the ark go up to from here?"

²¹Then messengers were sent to the people of Kiriath Jearim. They said, "The Philistines have returned the ark of the LORD. Come down and take it up

7 to your place." ¹So the men of Kiriath Jearim came and got the ark of the LORD. They took it up to Abinadab's house on the hill. They set his son Eleazar apart to guard the ark.

SAMUEL BRINGS THE PHILISTINES UNDER ISRAEL'S CONTROL

²The ark remained at Kiriath Jearim for a long time. It was there for a full 20 years. All of the people of Israel were filled with sorrow. They looked to the LORD for help.

³Samuel spoke to the whole community of Israel. He said, "Do you really want to return to the LORD with all your hearts? If you do, get rid of your strange gods. Get rid of your statues of goddesses that are named after Ashtoreth. Commit yourselves to the LORD. Serve him only. Then he will save you from the powerful hand of the Philistines."

⁴So the people of Israel put away their statues of gods that were named after Baal. They put away their statues of goddesses named after Ashtoreth. They served the LORD only. ⁵Then Samuel said, "Gather all of the people of Israel together at Mizpah. I will pray to the LORD for you."

⁶When the people had come together at Mizpah, they went to the well and got water. They poured it out in the sight of the LORD. On that day they didn't eat any food. They admitted they had sinned. They said, "We've sinned against the LORD." Samuel was the leader of Israel at Mizpah.

⁷The Philistines heard that Israel had gathered together at Mizpah. So the Philistine rulers came up to attack them.

When the people of Israel heard about it, they were afraid. ⁸They said to Samuel, "Don't stop crying out to the LORD our God to help us. Keep praying that he'll save us from the powerful hand of the Philistines."

⁹Then Samuel got a very young lamb. He sacrificed it as a whole burnt offering to the LORD. He cried out to the LORD to help Israel. And the LORD answered his prayer.

¹⁰The Philistines came near to attack Israel. At that time Samuel was sacrificing the burnt offering. But that day the LORD thundered loudly against the Philistines. He threw them into such a panic that the Israelites were able to chase them away. ¹¹The men of Israel rushed out of Mizpah. They chased the Philistines all the way to a point below Beth Car. They killed them all along the way.

¹²Then Samuel got a big stone. He set it up between Mizpah and Shen. He named it Ebenezer. He said, "The LORD has helped us every step of the way."

¹³So Samuel brought the Philistines under Israel's control. The Philistines didn't attack their territory again.

The LORD used his powerful hand against the Philistines as long as Samuel lived. ¹⁴The Philistines had captured many towns between Ekron and Gath. But they had to give all of them back. Israel took back the territories near those towns from the powerful hand of the Philistines.

During that time Israel and the Amorites were friendly toward each other.

¹⁵Samuel continued to lead Israel all the days of his life. ¹⁶From year to year he traveled from Bethel to Gilgal to Mizpah. He served Israel as judge in all of those places. ¹⁷But he always went back to Ramah. That's where his home was. He served Israel as judge there too. And he built an altar there to honor the LORD.

ISRAEL ASKS SAMUEL FOR A KING

8 When Samuel became old, he appointed his sons to serve as judges for Israel. ²The name of his oldest son was Joel. The name of his second son was Abijah. They served as judges at Beersheba. ³But his sons didn't live as he did. They were only interested in making money. They accepted money from people who wanted special favors. They made things that were wrong appear to be right.

⁴So all of the elders of Israel gathered together. They came to Samuel at Ramah. ⁵They said to him, "You are old. Your sons don't live as you do. So appoint a king to lead us. We want a king just like the kings all of the other nations have."

⁶Samuel wasn't pleased when they said, "Give us a king to lead us." So he prayed to the LORD. ⁷The LORD told him, "Listen to everything the people are saying to you. You are not the one they have turned their backs on. I am the one they do not want as their king. ⁸They are doing just as they have always done. They have deserted me and served other gods. They have done that from the time I brought them up out of Egypt

until this very day. Now they are deserting you too.

⁹"Let them have what they want. But give them a strong warning. Let them know what the king who rules over them will do."

¹⁰Samuel told the people who were asking him for a king everything the LORD had said. ¹¹Samuel told them, "Here's what the king who rules over you will do. He will take your sons. He'll make them serve with his chariots and horses. They will run in front of his chariots. ¹²He'll choose some of your sons to be commanders of thousands of men. Some will be commanders of fifties. Others will have to plow his fields and gather his crops. Still others will have to make weapons of war and parts for his chariots.

¹³"He'll also take your daughters. Some will have to make perfume. Others will be forced to cook and bake.

¹⁴"He will take away your best fields and vineyards and olive groves. He'll give them to his attendants. ¹⁵He will take a tenth of your grain and a tenth of your grapes. He'll give it to his officials and attendants. ¹⁶He will also take your male and female servants. He'll take your best cattle and donkeys. He'll use all of them any way he wants to.

¹⁷"He will take a tenth of your sheep and goats. You yourselves will become his slaves.

¹⁸"When that time comes, you will cry out for help because of the king you have chosen. But the LORD won't answer you at that time."

¹⁹In spite of what Samuel said, the people refused to listen to him. "No!" they said. "We want a king to rule over us. ²⁰Then we'll be like all of the other nations. We'll have a king to lead us. He'll go out at the head of our armies and fight our battles."

²¹Samuel heard everything the peo-

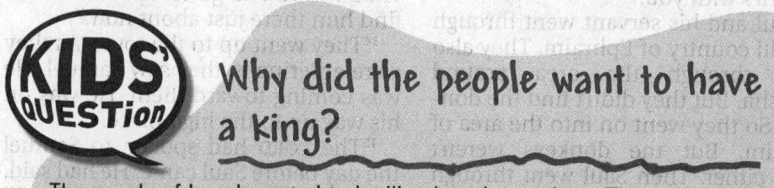

Why did the people want to have a king?

The people of Israel wanted to be like the other nations. They did not want God for a king. They wanted a man for a king. They wanted a king they could see. They wanted a king who would lead them in battle. Samuel knew that God wanted the people to trust in him and not in a king. And God warned them that a king could make life harder instead of easier. But they said they wanted a king anyway. So God told Samuel to give them a king. The first king of Israel was Saul. It turned out just the way God had said. At first Saul did well. But after a while he disobeyed God and led the people the wrong way.

checkout 1 Samuel 8:7

...and I'll focus on your kids' education–more instruction time, more discipline, more homework...

POLITICAL CAMPAIGN

Related verses: 1 Samuel 8:1–22

ple said. He told the LORD about it. [22]The LORD answered, "Listen to them. Give them a king."

Then Samuel said to the men of Israel, "Each of you go back to your own town."

SAMUEL ANOINTS SAUL TO BE ISRAEL'S LEADER

9 There was a man named Kish from the tribe of Benjamin. Kish was a very important person. He was the son of Abiel, the son of Zeror. Zeror was the son of Becorath, the son of Aphiah from the tribe of Benjamin. [2]Kish had a son named Saul. Saul was a handsome young man. There wasn't anyone like him among the people of Israel. He was a head taller than any of them.

[3]The donkeys that belonged to Saul's father Kish were lost. So Kish spoke to his son Saul. He said, "Go and look for the donkeys. Take one of the servants with you."

[4]Saul and his servant went through the hill country of Ephraim. They also went through the area around Shalisha. But they didn't find the donkeys. So they went on into the area of Shaalim. But the donkeys weren't there either. Then Saul went through the territory of Benjamin. But they still didn't find the donkeys.

[5]When Saul and the servant who was with him reached the area of Zuph, Saul spoke to him. He said, "Come on. Let's go back. If we don't, my father will stop thinking about the donkeys and start worrying about us."

[6]But the servant replied, "There's a man of God here in Ramah. People have a lot of respect for him. Everything he says comes true. So let's go and see him now. Perhaps he'll tell us which way to go."

[7]Saul said to his servant, "If we go to see the man, what can we give him? There isn't any food in our sacks. We don't have a gift for the man of God. So what can we give him?"

[8]The servant answered Saul again. "Look," he said. "I've got a tenth of an ounce of silver. I'll give it to the man of God. Then maybe he'll tell us which way to go."

[9]In Israel, prophets used to be called seers. So if a man wanted to ask God for advice, he would say, "Come on. Let's go to the seer."

[10]Saul said to his servant, "That's a good idea. Come on. Let's go and ask the seer." So they started out for the town where the man of God lived.

[11]They were going up the hill toward the town. Along the way they met some young women who were coming out to get water from the well. Saul and his servant asked them, "Is the seer here?"

[12]"Yes, he is," they answered. "In fact, he's just up ahead of you. So hurry along. He has just come to our town today. The people are going to offer a sacrifice at the high place where they worship. [13]As soon as you enter the town, you will find him. He'll be there until he goes up to the high place to eat. The people won't start eating until he gets there. He must bless the sacrifice first. After that, those who are invited will eat. So go on up. You should find him there just about now."

[14]They went up to the town. As they were entering it, they saw Samuel. He was coming toward them. He was on his way up to the high place.

[15]The LORD had spoken to Samuel the day before Saul came. He had said, [16]"About this time tomorrow I will send you a man. He is from the land of Benjamin. Anoint him to be the leader of my people Israel. He will save them from the powerful hand of the Philistines. I have seen how much my people are suffering. Their cry for help has reached me."

[17]When Samuel saw a man coming toward him, the LORD spoke to Samuel again. He said, "He is the man I told you about. His name is Saul. He will govern my people."

[18]Saul approached Samuel at the gate of the town. He asked Samuel, "Can you please show me the house where the seer is staying?"

[19]"I'm the seer," Samuel replied. "Go on up to the high place ahead of me. I want you and your servant to eat with me today. Tomorrow morning I'll tell you what's on your mind. Then I'll let you go. [20]Don't worry about the donkeys you lost three days ago. They've already been found. But who are all of

the people of Israel longing for? You and your father's whole family!"

²¹Saul answered, "But I'm from the tribe of Benjamin. It's the smallest tribe in Israel. And my family group is the least important in the whole tribe of Benjamin. So why are you saying that to me?"

²²Then Samuel brought Saul and his servant into the room where they would be eating. He seated them at the head table. About 30 people had been invited. ²³Samuel said to the cook, "Bring the piece of meat I gave you. It's the one I told you to put to one side."

²⁴So the cook went and got a choice piece of thigh. He set it in front of Saul. Samuel said, "Here is what has been kept for you. Eat it. It was put to one side for you for this special occasion. We've saved it for you ever since I invited the guests." And Saul ate with Samuel that day.

²⁵They came down from the high place to the town. After that, Samuel talked with Saul on the roof of Samuel's house.

²⁶The next day they got up at about the time the sun was rising. Samuel called out to Saul on the roof. He said, "Get ready. Then I'll send you on your way." So Saul got ready. And he and Samuel went outside together.

²⁷As they were on their way down to the edge of town, Samuel spoke to Saul. He said, "Tell the servant to go ahead of us." So the servant went on ahead. Then Samuel continued, "Stay here awhile. I'll give you a message from God."

10 Then Samuel took a bottle of olive oil. He poured it on Saul's head and kissed him. He said, "The LORD has anointed you to be the leader of his people. ²When you leave me today, you will meet two men. They will be near Rachel's tomb at Zelzah on the border of Benjamin. They'll say to you, 'The donkeys you have been looking for have been found. Now your father has stopped thinking about them. Instead, he's worried about you. He's asking, "What can I do to find my son?" '

³"You will go on from Zelzah until you come to the large tree at Tabor.

Three men will meet you there. They'll be on their way up to Bethel to worship God. One of them will be carrying three young goats. Another will be carrying three loaves of bread. A third will be carrying a bottle of wine. It will be a bottle that is made out of animal skin. ⁴The men will greet you. They'll offer you two loaves of bread. You will accept the loaves from them.

⁵"After that, you will go to Gibeah of God. Some Philistine soldiers are stationed there. As you approach the town, you will meet a group of prophets. They'll be coming down from the high place where they worship. People will be playing lyres, tambourines, flutes and harps at the head of the group. The prophets will be prophesying. ⁶The Spirit of the LORD will come on you with power. Then you will prophesy along with them. You will become a different person.

⁷"All of those things will happen. Then do what you want to do. God is with you.

⁸"Go down ahead of me to Gilgal. You can be sure that I'll come down to you there. I'll come and sacrifice burnt offerings and friendship offerings. But you must wait there for seven days until I come to you. Then I'll tell you what to do."

SAUL IS MADE KING OF ISRAEL

⁹As Saul turned to leave Samuel, God changed Saul's heart. All of those things happened that day. ¹⁰When Saul and his servant arrived at Gibeah, a group of prophets met Saul. Then the Spirit of God came on him with power. He prophesied along with them. ¹¹Those who had known Saul before saw him prophesying with the prophets. They asked one another, "What has happened to the son of Kish? Is Saul also one of the prophets?"

¹²A man who lived in Gibeah answered, "Yes, he is. In fact, he's their leader." That's why people say, "Is Saul also one of the prophets?"

¹³After Saul stopped prophesying, he went to the high place to worship.

¹⁴Later, Saul's uncle spoke to him and his servant. He asked, "Where have you been?"

"Looking for the donkeys," he said. "But we couldn't find them. So we went to Samuel."

¹⁵Saul's uncle said, "Tell me what Samuel said to you."

¹⁶Saul replied, "He told us the donkeys had been found." But Saul didn't tell his uncle that Samuel had said he would become king.

¹⁷Samuel sent a message to the people of Israel. He told them to meet with the LORD at Mizpah. ¹⁸He said to them, "The LORD is the God of Israel. He says, 'Israel, I brought you up out of Egypt. I saved you from their powerful hand. I also saved you from the powerful hand of all of the kingdoms that had beaten you down.'

¹⁹"But now you have turned your backs on your God. He saves you out of all of your trouble and suffering. In spite of that, you have said, 'We refuse to listen. Place a king over us.'

"So now gather together to meet with the LORD. Do it tribe by tribe and family group by family group."

²⁰Then Samuel had each tribe of Israel come forward. The tribe of Benjamin was chosen. ²¹Next he had the tribe of Benjamin come forward, family group by family group. Matri's group was chosen. Finally Saul, the son of Kish, was chosen. But when people looked for him, they realized he wasn't there. ²²They needed more help from the LORD. So they asked him, "Has the man come here yet?"

The LORD said, "Yes. He has hidden himself among the supplies."

²³So they ran over there and brought him out. When he stood up, the people saw that he was a head taller than any of them.

²⁴Samuel spoke to all of the people. He said, "Look at the man the LORD has chosen! There isn't anyone like him among all of the people."

Then the people shouted, "May the king live a long time!"

²⁵Samuel explained to the people what the king who ruled over them should do. He wrote it down on a scroll. He placed it in front of the LORD in the holy tent. Then he sent the people away. He sent each of them to their own homes.

²⁶Saul also went to his home in Gibeah. Some brave men whose hearts God had touched went with Saul.

²⁷But some evil people who wanted to stir up trouble said, "How can this fellow save us?" They looked down on him. They didn't bring him any gifts. But Saul kept quiet about it.

SAUL SAVES THE CITY OF JABESH GILEAD

11 Nahash was the king of Ammon. He and his army went up to Jabesh Gilead. They surrounded it and got ready to attack it. All of the men of Jabesh spoke to Nahash. They said, "Make a peace treaty with us. Then we'll be under your control."

²Nahash, the king of Ammon, replied, "I will make a peace treaty with you. But I'll do it only on one condition. You must let me put out the right eye of every one of you. I want to bring shame on the whole nation of Israel."

³The elders of Jabesh said to him, "Give us seven days to report back to you. We'll send messengers all through Israel. If no one comes to save us, we'll hand ourselves over to you."

⁴The messengers came to Gibeah of Saul. They reported to the people the terms Nahash had required. Then all of the people sobbed out loud.

⁵Just then Saul was coming in from the fields. He was walking behind his oxen. He asked, "What's wrong with the people? Why are they sobbing?" He was told what the men of Jabesh had said.

⁶When Saul heard their words, the Spirit of God came on him with power. He burned with anger. ⁷He got a pair of oxen and cut them into pieces. He sent the pieces by messengers all through Israel. They announced, "You must follow Saul and Samuel. If you don't, this is what will happen to your oxen."

The terror of the LORD fell on the people. So all of them came together with one purpose in mind.

⁸Saul brought his army together at Bezek. There were 300,000 men from Israel and 30,000 from Judah.

⁹The messengers who had come were told, "Go back and report to the men of Jabesh Gilead. Tell them, 'By

the hottest time of the day tomorrow, you will be saved.' "

The messengers went and reported it to the men of Jabesh. It made those men very happy. [10]They said to the people of Ammon, "Tomorrow we'll hand ourselves over to you. Then you can do to us what seems best to you."

[11]The next day Saul separated his men into three groups. While it was still dark, they broke into the camp of the Ammonite army. They kept killing the men of Ammon until the hottest time of the day. Those who got away alive were scattered. There weren't two of them left together anywhere.

THE PEOPLE AGREE TO HAVE SAUL AS KING

[12]The people said to Samuel, "Who asked, 'Is Saul going to rule over us?' Bring those people to us. We'll put them to death."

[13]But Saul said, "We won't put anyone to death today! After all, this is the day the LORD has saved Israel."

[14]Then Samuel said to the people, "Come on. Let's go to Gilgal. There we'll agree to have Saul as our king."

[15]So all of the people went to Gilgal. There, with the LORD as witness, they agreed to have Saul as their king. There they sacrificed friendship offerings to the LORD. And there Saul and all of the people of Israel celebrated with great joy.

SAMUEL TELLS ISRAEL TO SERVE THE LORD

12 Samuel spoke to all of the people of Israel. He said, "I've done everything you asked me to do. I've placed a king over you. [2]Now you have a king as your leader. But I'm old. My hair is gray. My sons are here with you. I've been your leader from the time I was young until this very day.

[3]"Here I stand. Bring charges against me if you can. The LORD is a witness. And so is his anointed king. Whose ox have I taken? Whose donkey have I taken? Have I cheated anyone? Have I beaten anyone down? Have I accepted money from anyone who wanted special favors? If I've done any of those things, I'll make it right."

[4]"You haven't cheated us," they replied. "You haven't beaten us down. You haven't taken anything from anyone."

[5]Samuel said to them, "The LORD is a witness against you this very day. And so is his anointed king. They are witnesses that I haven't taken anything from any of you."

"The LORD is a witness," they said.

[6]Then Samuel said to the people, "The LORD appointed Moses and Aaron. He brought up out of Egypt your people who lived long ago. [7]Now then, stand here. I'm going to remind you of all of the good things the LORD has done for you and your people. He is a witness.

[8]"After Jacob's family entered Egypt, they cried out to the LORD for help. The LORD sent Moses and Aaron. They brought your people out of Egypt. They settled them in this land.

[9]"But the people forgot the LORD their God. So he gave them over to the powerful hand of Sisera. Sisera was the commander of the army of Hazor. The LORD also gave the people of Israel over to the powerful hand of the Philistines and the king of Moab. All of those nations fought against Israel.

[10]"So the people cried out to the LORD. They said, 'We have sinned. We've deserted the LORD. We've served the gods that are named after Baal. We've served the goddesses that are named after Ashtoreth. But save us now from the powerful hands of our enemies. Then we will serve you.'

[11]"The LORD sent Gideon, Barak, Jephthah and me. He saved you from the hands of your enemies, who were all around you. So you lived in safety.

[12]"But then you saw that Nahash, the king of Ammon, was about to attack you. So you said to me, 'No! We want a king to rule over us.' You said it even though the LORD your God was your king. [13]Now here is the king you have chosen. He's the one you asked for. The LORD has placed a king over you.

[14]"But you must have respect for the LORD. You must serve him and obey him. You must not say no to his commands. Both you and the king who rules over you must follow the LORD

your God. If you do, that's good. ¹⁵But you must not disobey him. You must not say no to his commands. If you do, his powerful hand will punish you. That's what happened to your people who lived before you.

¹⁶"So stand still. Watch the great thing the LORD is about to do right here in front of you! ¹⁷It's time to gather in the wheat, isn't it? I'll call out to the LORD to send thunder and rain. Then you will realize what an evil thing you did in the sight of the LORD. You shouldn't have asked for a king."

¹⁸Samuel called out to the LORD. That same day the LORD sent thunder and rain. So all of the people had great respect for the LORD and for Samuel.

¹⁹They said to Samuel, "Pray to the LORD your God for us. Pray that we won't die because we asked for a king. That was an evil thing to do. We added it to all of our other sins."

²⁰"Don't be afraid," Samuel replied. "It's true that you have done all of those evil things. But don't turn away from the LORD. Serve him with all your heart.

²¹"Don't turn away and worship statues of gods. They are useless. They can't do you any good. They can't save you either. They are completely useless.

²²"But the LORD will be true to his great name. He won't turn his back on his people. That's because he was pleased to make you his own people.

²³"I would never sin against the LORD by failing to pray for you. I'll teach you to live in a way that is good and right.

²⁴"But be sure to have respect for the LORD. Serve him faithfully. Do it with all your heart. Think about the great things he has done for you. ²⁵But don't be stubborn. Don't continue to do what is evil. If you do, both you and your king will be swept away."

SAUL REFUSES TO OBEY THE LORD'S COMMAND

13 Saul was 30 years old when he became king. He ruled over Israel for 42 years. ²He chose 3,000 of Israel's men. Two thousand of them were with him at Micmash and in the hill country of

Bethel. One thousand were with Jonathan at Gibeah in the land of Benjamin. Saul sent the rest back to their homes.

³Some Philistine soldiers were stationed at Geba. Jonathan attacked them. The other Philistines heard about it.

Saul announced, "Let the Hebrew people hear about what has happened!" He had trumpets blown all through the land. ⁴So all of the people of Israel heard the news. They were told, "Saul has attacked the Philistine army camp at Geba. He has made Israel smell very bad to the Philistines." The people of Israel were called out to join Saul at Gilgal.

⁵The Philistines gathered together to fight against Israel. They had 3,000 chariots and 6,000 chariot drivers. Their soldiers were as many as the grains of sand on the seashore. They went up and camped at Micmash. It was east of Beth Aven.

⁶The men of Israel saw that their army was in deep trouble. So they hid in caves and bushes. They hid among the rocks. They hid in pits and empty wells. ⁷Some of them even went across the Jordan River. They went to the lands of Gad and Gilead.

Saul remained at Gilgal. All of the troops who were with him were shaking with fear. ⁸He waited seven days, just as Samuel had told him to. But Samuel didn't come to Gilgal. And Saul's men began to scatter. ⁹So he said, "Bring me the burnt offering and the friendship offerings." Then he offered up the burnt offering.

¹⁰Just as Saul finished offering the sacrifice, Samuel arrived. Saul went out to greet him.

¹¹"What have you done?" asked Samuel.

Saul replied, "I saw that the men were scattering. I saw that the Philistines were gathering together at Micmash. You didn't come when you said you would. ¹²So I thought, 'Now the Philistines will come down to attack me at Gilgal. And I haven't asked the LORD to show us his favor.' So I felt I had to sacrifice the burnt offering."

¹³"You did a foolish thing," Samuel

said. "You haven't obeyed the command the LORD your God gave you. If you had, he would have made your kingdom secure over Israel for all time to come. ¹⁴But now your kingdom won't last. The LORD has already looked for a man who is dear to his heart. He has appointed him leader of his people. That's because you haven't obeyed the LORD's command."

¹⁵Then Samuel left Gilgal and went up to Gibeah in the land of Benjamin. Saul counted the men who stayed with him. The total number was about 600.

ISRAEL DOESN'T HAVE SWORDS OR SPEARS

¹⁶Saul and his son Jonathan were staying in Gibeah in the land of Benjamin. What was left of the army was there with them. At the same time, the Philistines camped at Micmash.

¹⁷Three groups of soldiers went out from the Philistine camp to attack Israel. One group turned and went toward Ophrah in the area of Shual. ¹⁸Another went toward Beth Horon. The third went toward the border that looked out over the Valley of Zeboim. That valley faces the desert.

¹⁹There weren't any blacksmiths in the whole land of Israel. That's because the Philistines had said, "The Hebrews might hire them to make swords or spears!"

²⁰So all of the people of Israel had to go down to the Philistines. They had to go to them to get their plows, hoes, axes and sickles sharpened. ²¹It cost a fourth of an ounce of silver to sharpen a plow or a hoe. It cost an eighth of an ounce to sharpen a pitchfork or an axe. That's also what it cost to put new tips on large sticks that were used to drive oxen.

²²So not one of Saul's or Jonathan's soldiers had a sword or spear in his hand when he went out to battle. Only Saul and his son Jonathan had those weapons.

JONATHAN ATTACKS THE PHILISTINES

²³A group of Philistine soldiers had gone out to the pass at Micmash. ¹One day Jonathan, the son of Saul, spoke to the young man who was carrying his armor. "Come on," he said. "Let's go over to the Philistine army camp on the other side of the pass." But he didn't tell his father about it.

²Saul was staying just outside Gibeah. He was under a pomegranate tree in Migron. He had about 600 men with him. ³Ahijah was one of them. He was wearing a sacred linen apron. He was a son of Ichabod's brother Ahitub. Ahitub was the son of Eli's son Phinehas. Eli had been the LORD's priest in Shiloh. No one was aware that Jonathan had left.

⁴Jonathan planned to go across the pass to reach the Philistine camp. But there was a cliff on each side of the pass. One cliff was called Bozez. The other was called Seneh. ⁵One cliff stood on the north side of the pass toward Micmash. The other stood on the south side toward Geba.

⁶Jonathan spoke to the young man who was carrying his armor. He said, "Come on. Let's go over to the camp of those fellows who aren't circumcised. Perhaps the LORD will help us. If he does, it won't matter how many or how few of us there are. That won't keep the LORD from saving us."

⁷"Go ahead," the young man said. "Do everything you have in mind. I'm with you all the way."

⁸Jonathan said, "Come on, then. We'll go across the pass toward the Philistines and let them see us. ⁹Suppose they say to us, 'Wait there until we come to you.' Then we'll stay where we are. We won't go up to them. ¹⁰But suppose they say, 'Come up to us.' Then we'll climb up. That will show us that the LORD has handed them over to us."

¹¹So Jonathan and the young man let the soldiers in the Philistine camp see them. "Look!" said the Philistines. "Some of the Hebrews are crawling out of the holes they were hiding in."

¹²The men in the Philistine camp shouted to Jonathan and the young man who was carrying his armor. They said, "Come on up here. We'll teach you a thing or two."

So Jonathan said to the young man, "Climb up after me. The LORD has handed them over to Israel."

[13]Using his hands and feet, Jonathan climbed up. The young man was right behind him. Jonathan struck the Philistines down. The young man followed him and killed those who were still alive. [14]In that first attack, Jonathan and the young man killed about 20 men. They did it in an area of about half an acre.

ISRAEL CHASES THE PHILISTINES AWAY

[15]Then panic struck the whole Philistine army. It struck those who were in the camp and the field. It struck those who were at the edge of the camp. It also struck those who were in the groups that had been sent out to attack Israel. The ground shook. It was a panic that God had sent.

[16]Saul's lookouts at Gibeah in the land of Benjamin saw what was happening. They saw the Philistine army melting away in all directions.

[17]Then Saul spoke to the men who were with him. He said, "Bring the troops together. See who has left our camp." When they did, they discovered that Jonathan and the young man who was carrying his armor weren't there.

[18]Saul said to the priest Ahijah, "Bring the ark of God." At that time it was with the people of Israel.

[19]While Saul was talking to the priest, the noise in the Philistine camp increased more and more. So Saul said to him, "Stop what you are doing."

[20]Then Saul and all of his men gathered together. They went to the battle. They saw that the Philistines were in total disorder. They were striking each other with their swords.

[21]At an earlier time some of the Hebrews had been on the side of the Philistines. They had gone up with them to their camp. But now they changed sides. They joined the people of Israel who were with Saul and Jonathan.

[22]Some of the people had hidden in the hill country of Ephraim. They heard that the Philistines were running away. They quickly joined the battle and chased after them.

[23]So the LORD saved Israel that day. And the fighting continued on past Beth Aven.

JONATHAN EATS HONEY

[24]The men of Israel became very hungry that day. That's because Saul had put the army under an oath. He had said, "None of you must eat any food before evening comes. You must not eat until I've paid my enemies back for what they did. If you do, may you be under a curse!" So none of the troops ate any food at all.

[25]The whole army entered the woods. There was honey on the ground. [26]When they went into the woods, they saw the honey dripping out of a honeycomb. No one put any of the honey in his mouth. That's because they were afraid of the oath.

[27]But Jonathan hadn't heard that his father had put the army under an oath. Jonathan had a long stick in his hand. He reached out and dipped the end of it into the honeycomb. He put some honey in his mouth. It gave him new life.

[28]Then one of the soldiers told him, "Your father put the army under a strong oath. He said, 'None of you must eat any food today. If you do, may you be under a curse!' That's why the men are weak and ready to faint."

[29]Jonathan said, "My father has made trouble for the country. See how I gained new life after I tasted a little of this honey. [30]Our soldiers took food from their enemies today. Suppose they had eaten some of it. How much better off they would have been! Even more Philistines would have been killed."

[31]That day the men of Israel struck the Philistines down. They killed them from Micmash to Aijalon. By that time they were tired and worn out. [32]They grabbed what they had taken from their enemies. They killed some of the sheep, cattle and calves right there on the ground. They ate the meat while the blood was still in it.

[33]Then someone said to Saul, "Look! The men are sinning against the LORD. They're eating meat that still has blood in it."

Saul said to them, "You have broken your promise. Roll a large stone over here at once." [34]He continued, "Go out among the men. Tell them, 'Each of you bring me your cattle and sheep. Kill them here and eat them. Don't sin against the LORD by eating meat that still has blood in it.' "

So that night everyone brought the ox he had taken and killed it there.

35Then Saul built an altar to honor the LORD. It was the first time he had done that.

36Saul said, "Let's go down after the Philistines tonight. Let's not leave even one of them alive. Let's take everything they have before it gets light."

"Do what you think is best," they replied.

But the priest said, "Let's ask God for advice first."

37So Saul asked God, "Should I go down after the Philistines? Will you hand them over to Israel?" But God didn't answer him that day.

38Saul said to the leaders of the army, "Come here. Let's find out what sin has been committed today. 39You can be sure that the LORD who saves Israel lives. And you can be just as sure that the sinner must die. He must die even if he's my son Jonathan." But no one said anything.

40Then Saul spoke to all of Israel's men. He said, "You stand over there. I and my son Jonathan will stand over here."

"Do what you think is best," the men replied.

41Then Saul prayed to the LORD, the God of Israel. He said, "Give me an answer." Jonathan and Saul were chosen by using lots. The other men were cleared of blame.

42Saul said, "Cast the lot to find out whether I or my son Jonathan is to blame." And Jonathan was chosen.

43Then Saul said to Jonathan, "Tell me what you have done."

So Jonathan told him, "I only used the end of my stick to get a little honey and taste it. And now do I have to die?"

44Saul said, "Jonathan, I must certainly put you to death. If I don't, may God punish me greatly."

45But the men said to Saul, "Should Jonathan be put to death? Never! He has saved Israel in a wonderful way. He did it today with God's help. You can be sure that the LORD lives. And you can be just as sure that not even one hair on Jonathan's head will fall to the ground." So the men saved Jonathan. He wasn't put to death.

46Then Saul stopped chasing the Philistines. They went back to their own land.

47After Saul's kingdom was set firmly in place in Israel, he fought against their enemies who were all around them. He went to war against Moab, Ammon and Edom. He fought against the kings of Zobah and the Philistines. No matter where he went, he punished his enemies. 48He fought bravely. He won the battle over the Amalekites. He saved Israel from the power of those who had carried off what belonged to Israel.

SAUL'S FAMILY

49Saul's sons were Jonathan, Ishvi and Malki-Shua. His older daughter was named Merab. His younger daughter was named Michal. 50Saul's wife was named Ahinoam. She was the daughter of Ahimaaz.

The commander of Saul's army was named Abner. He was the son of Ner. Ner was Saul's uncle. 51Saul's father Kish and Abner's father Ner were sons of Abiel.

52As long as Saul was king, he had to fight hard against the Philistines. So every time Saul saw a strong or brave man, he took him into his army.

THE LORD IS SORRY HE HAS MADE SAUL KING

15 Samuel said to Saul, "The LORD sent me to anoint you as king over his people Israel. So listen now to a message from him. 2The LORD who rules over all says, 'I will punish the Amalekites because of what they did to Israel. As the people of Israel came up from Egypt, the Amalekites attacked them.

3" 'Now go. Attack the Amalekites. Set everything apart that belongs to them. Set it apart to me in a special way to be destroyed. Do not spare the Amalekites. Put the men and women to death. Put the children and babies to death. Also kill the cattle, sheep, camels and donkeys.' "

4So Saul brought his men together at Telaim. The total number was 200,000 soldiers on foot from Israel and 10,000 men from Judah. ⁵He went to the city of Amalek. He had some of his men hide and wait in the valley.

⁶Then Saul said to the Kenites, "You were kind to all of the people of Israel when they came up out of Egypt. Get away from the Amalekites. Then I won't have to destroy you along with them." So the Kenites moved away from the Amalekites.

⁷Saul attacked the Amalekites. He struck them down all the way from Havilah to Shur. Shur was near the eastern border of Egypt. ⁸He took Agag, the king of the Amalekites, alive. He and his men totally destroyed all of Agag's people with swords.

⁹But Saul and the army spared Agag. They spared the best of the sheep and cattle. They spared the fat calves and lambs. They spared everything that was valuable. They weren't willing to completely destroy any of those things. But they totally destroyed everything that was worthless and weak.

¹⁰Then the LORD gave Samuel a message. He said, ¹¹"I am very sorry I have made Saul king. He has turned away from me. He has not done what I directed him to do."

When Samuel heard that, he was troubled. He cried out to the LORD during that whole night.

¹²Early the next morning Samuel got up. He went to see Saul. But Samuel was told, "Saul went to Carmel. There he set up a monument in his own honor. Now he has gone on down to Gilgal."

¹³When Samuel got there, Saul said, "May the LORD bless you. I've done what he directed me to do."

¹⁴But Samuel said, "Then why do I hear the baaing of sheep? Why do I hear the mooing of cattle?"

¹⁵Saul answered, "The soldiers brought them from the Amalekites. They spared the best of the sheep and cattle. They did it to sacrifice them to the LORD your God. But we totally destroyed everything else."

¹⁶"Stop!" Samuel said to Saul. "Let me tell you what the LORD said to me last night."

"Tell me," Saul replied.

¹⁷Samuel said, "There was a time when you didn't think you were important. But you became the leader of the tribes of Israel. The LORD anointed you to be king over Israel. ¹⁸He sent you to do something for him. He said, 'Go and set the Amalekites apart. Set those sinful people apart to me in a special way to be destroyed. Fight against them until you have wiped them out.'

¹⁹"Why didn't you obey the LORD? Why did you grab what you had taken from your enemies? Why did you do what is evil in the sight of the LORD?"

²⁰"But I did obey the LORD," Saul said. "I went to do what he sent me to do. I totally destroyed the Amalekites. I brought back Agag, their king. ²¹"The soldiers took sheep and cattle from what had been taken from our enemies. They took the best of what had been set apart to God. They wanted to sacrifice them to the LORD your God at Gilgal."

²²But Samuel replied,

"What pleases the LORD more?
　Burnt offerings and sacrifices, or
　　obeying him?
It is better to obey than to offer a
　sacrifice.
It is better to do what he says
　than to offer the fat of rams.
²³Refusing to obey him is as sinful as
　using evil magic.
Being proud is as evil as
　worshiping statues of gods.
You have refused to do what the
　LORD told you to do.
So he has refused to have you as
　king."

²⁴Then Saul said to Samuel, "I have sinned. I've broken the LORD's command. I haven't done what you directed me to do. I was afraid of the people. So I did what they said I should do. ²⁵Now I beg you, forgive my sin. Come back into town with me so I can worship the LORD."

²⁶But Samuel said to him, "I won't go back with you. You have refused to do what the LORD told you to do. So he has refused to have you as king over Israel!"

²⁷Samuel turned to leave. But Saul grabbed hold of the hem of his robe, and it tore.

²⁸Samuel said to Saul, "The LORD has torn the kingdom of Israel away from you today. He has given it to one of your neighbors. He has given it to someone who is better than you. ²⁹The One who is the Glory of Israel does not lie. He doesn't change his mind. That's because he isn't a mere man. If he were, he might change his mind."

³⁰Saul replied, "I have sinned. But please honor me in front of the elders of my people and in front of Israel. Come back with me so I can worship the LORD your God."

³¹So Samuel went back with Saul. And Saul worshiped the LORD.

³²Then Samuel said, "Bring me Agag, the king of the Amalekites."

Agag wasn't afraid when he came to Samuel. He thought, "The time for me to be put to death must have passed by now."

³³But Samuel said,

"Your sword has killed the
  children of other women.
So the child of your mother will
  be killed."

Samuel put Agag to death at Gilgal in the sight of the LORD.

³⁴Then Samuel left to go to Ramah. But Saul went up to his home in Gibeah of Saul. ³⁵Until the day Samuel died, he didn't go to see Saul again. Samuel was filled with sorrow because of Saul. And the LORD was very sorry he had made Saul king over Israel.

SAMUEL ANOINTS DAVID TO BE ISRAEL'S KING

16 The LORD said to Samuel, "How long will you be filled with sorrow because of Saul? I have refused to have him as king over Israel. Fill your animal horn with olive oil and go on your way. I am sending you to Jesse in Bethlehem. I have chosen one of his sons to be king."

²But Samuel said, "How can I go? Saul will hear about it. Then he'll kill me."

The LORD said, "Take a young cow with you. Tell the elders of Bethlehem, 'I've come to offer a sacrifice to the LORD.' ³Invite Jesse to the sacrifice. Then I will show you what to do. You must anoint for me the one I point out to you."

⁴Samuel did what the LORD said. He arrived at Bethlehem. The elders of the town met him. They were trembling with fear. They asked, "Have you come in peace?"

⁵Samuel replied, "Yes, I've come in peace. I've come to offer a sacrifice to the LORD. Set yourselves apart to him and come to the sacrifice with me."

Then he set Jesse and his sons apart to the LORD. He invited them to the sacrifice.

⁶When they arrived, Samuel saw Eliab. He thought, "This has to be the one the LORD wants to anoint for him."

⁷But the LORD said to Samuel, "Do not consider how handsome or tall he is. I have not chosen him. I do not look at the things people look at. Man looks at how someone appears on the outside. But I look at what is in the heart."

⁸Then Jesse called for Abinadab. He had him walk in front of Samuel. But Samuel said, "The LORD hasn't chosen him either."

⁹Then Jesse had Shammah walk by. But Samuel said, "The LORD hasn't chosen him either."

¹⁰Jesse had seven of his sons walk in front of Samuel. But Samuel said to him, "The LORD hasn't chosen any of them." ¹¹So he asked Jesse, "Are these the only sons you have?"

"No," Jesse answered. "My youngest son is taking care of the sheep."

Samuel said, "Send for him. We won't sit down to eat until he arrives."

¹²So Jesse sent for his son and had him brought in. His skin was tanned. He had a fine appearance and handsome features.

Then the LORD said, "Get up and anoint him. He is the one."

¹³So Samuel got the animal horn that was filled with olive oil. He anointed David in front of his brothers. From that day on, the Spirit of the LORD came on David with power. Samuel went back to Ramah.

DAVID SERVES SAUL

¹⁴The Spirit of the LORD had left Saul. And an evil spirit that was sent by the LORD terrified him.

¹⁵Saul's attendants said to him, "An evil spirit that was sent by God is terrifying you. ¹⁶Give us an order to look for someone who can play the harp. He will play it when the evil spirit that was sent by God comes on you. Then you will feel better."

¹⁷So Saul said to his attendants, "Find someone who plays the harp well. Bring him to me."

¹⁸One of the servants said, "I've seen someone who knows how to play the harp. He is a son of Jesse from Bethlehem. He's a brave man. He would make a good soldier. He's a good speaker. He's very handsome. And the LORD is with him."

¹⁹Then Saul sent messengers to Jesse. He said, "Send me your son David, the one who takes care of your sheep."

²⁰So Jesse got some bread and a bottle of wine. The bottle was made out of animal skin. He also got a young goat. He loaded everything on the back of a donkey. He sent all of it to Saul with his son David.

²¹David went to Saul and began to serve him. Saul liked him very much. David became one of the men who carried Saul's armor.

²²Saul sent a message to Jesse. It said, "Let David stay here. I want him to serve me. I'm pleased with him."

²³When the evil spirit that was sent by God would come on Saul, David would get his harp and play it. That would help Saul. He would feel better, and the evil spirit would leave him.

DAVID KILLS GOLIATH

17 The Philistines gathered their army together for war. They came to Socoh in Judah. They set up camp at Ephes Dammim. It was between Socoh and Azekah. ²Saul and the army of Israel gathered together. They camped in the Valley of Elah. They lined up their men to fight against the Philistines. ³The Philistine army was camped on one hill. Israel's army was on another. The valley was between them.

⁴A mighty hero named Goliath came

What did Goliath eat that made him so big?

Goliath was a very big man. He was more than nine feet tall. If he were alive today, he would be able to dunk a basketball without jumping. His head would touch the net. We do not know how Goliath got to be so big. It was not something he ate. It was just the way God made him. David was a lot smaller. But that did not really matter. What mattered was that David believed in God and Goliath did not.

checkout
1 Samuel 17:4

Related verses:
1 Samuel 17:1–51

out of the Philistine camp. He was from Gath. He was more than nine feet tall. ⁵He had a bronze helmet on his head. He wore a coat of bronze armor. It weighed 125 pounds. ⁶On his legs he wore bronze guards. He carried a bronze javelin on his back. ⁷His spear was as big as a weaver's rod. Its iron point weighed 15 pounds. The man who carried his shield walked along in front of him.

⁸Goliath stood and shouted to the soldiers of Israel. He said, "Why do you come out and line up for battle? I'm a Philistine. You are servants of Saul. Choose one of your men. Have him come down and face me. ⁹If he's able to fight and kill me, we'll become your slaves. But if I win and kill him, you will become our slaves and serve us." ¹⁰Goliath continued, "This very day I dare the soldiers of Israel to send a man down to fight against me."

¹¹Saul and the whole army of Israel heard what the Philistine said. They were terrified.

¹²David was the son of an Ephrathite. His name was Jesse. He was from Bethlehem in Judah. Jesse had eight sons. When Saul was king, Jesse was already very old. ¹³Jesse's three oldest sons had followed Saul into battle. The oldest son was Eliab. The second was Abinadab. The third was Shammah. ¹⁴David was the youngest. The three oldest sons followed Saul. ¹⁵But David went back and forth from Saul's camp to Bethlehem. He went to Bethlehem to take care of his father's sheep.

¹⁶Every morning and evening Goliath came forward and stood there. He did it for 40 days.

¹⁷Jesse said to his son David, "Get at least half a bushel of grain that has been cooked. Also get ten loaves of bread. Take all of it to your brothers. Hurry to their camp. ¹⁸Take along these ten chunks of cheese to the commander of their company. Find out how your brothers are doing. Bring me back some word about them. ¹⁹They are with Saul and all of the men of Israel. They are in the Valley of Elah. They are fighting against the Philistines."

²⁰Early in the morning David left his father's flock in the care of a shepherd.

David loaded up the food and started out, just as Jesse had directed.

David reached the camp as the army was going out to its battle positions. The soldiers were shouting the war cry. ²¹Israel and the Philistines were lining up their armies for battle. The armies were facing each other.

²²David left what he had brought with the man who took care of the supplies. He ran to the battle lines and greeted his brothers. ²³As David was talking with them, Goliath stepped forward from his line. Goliath was a mighty Philistine hero from Gath. He again dared someone to fight him, and David heard it.

²⁴When Israel's army saw Goliath, all of them ran away from him. That's because they were filled with fear.

²⁵The men of Israel had been saying, "Just look at how this man keeps stepping forward! Again and again he dares Israel to fight him. The king will make the man who kills him very wealthy. He will also give him his daughter to be his wife. He won't require anyone in his family to pay any taxes in Israel."

²⁶David spoke to the men who were standing near him. He asked them, "What will be done for the man who kills this Philistine? Goliath is bringing shame on Israel. What will be done for the one who removes it? This Philistine isn't even circumcised. He dares the armies of the living God to fight him. Who does he think he is?"

²⁷The men told David what Israel's soldiers had been saying. The men told him what would be done for the man who killed Goliath.

²⁸David's oldest brother Eliab heard him speaking with the men. So he burned with anger at him. He asked him, "Why have you come down here? Who did you leave those few sheep in the desert with? I know how proud you are. I know how evil your heart is. The only reason you came down here was to watch the battle."

²⁹"What have I done now?" said David. "Can't I even speak?"

³⁰Then he turned away to speak to some other men. He asked them the same question he had asked before. And they gave him the same answer.

³¹Someone heard what David said and reported it to Saul. So Saul sent for him.

³²David said to Saul, "Don't let anyone lose hope because of that Philistine. I'll go out and fight him."

³³Saul replied, "You aren't able to go out there and fight that Philistine. You are too young. He's been a fighting man ever since he was a boy."

³⁴But David said to Saul, "I've been taking care of my father's sheep. Sometimes a lion or a bear would come and carry off a sheep from the flock. ³⁵Then I would go after it and hit it. I would save the sheep it was carrying in its mouth. If it turned around to attack me, I would grab hold of its hair. I would strike it down and kill it. ³⁶In fact, I've killed both a lion and a bear. I'll do the same thing to this Philistine. He isn't even circumcised. He has dared the armies of the living God to fight him.

³⁷"The Lord saved me from the paw of the lion. He saved me from the paw of the bear. And he'll save me from the powerful hand of this Philistine too."

Saul said to David, "Go. And may the Lord be with you."

³⁸Then Saul dressed David in his own military clothes. He put a coat of armor on him. He put a bronze helmet on his head. ³⁹David put on Saul's sword over his clothes. He walked around for a while in all of that armor because he wasn't used to it.

"I can't go out there in all of this armor," he said to Saul. "I'm not used to it." So he took it off.

⁴⁰Then David picked up his wooden staff. He went down to a stream and chose five smooth stones. He put them in the pocket of his shepherd's bag. Then he took his sling in his hand and approached Goliath.

⁴¹At that same time, the Philistine kept coming closer to David. The man who was carrying Goliath's shield walked along in front of him.

⁴²Goliath looked David over. He saw how young he was. He also saw how tanned and handsome he was. And he hated him. ⁴³He said to David, "Why are you coming at me with sticks? Do you think I'm only a dog?" The Philistine called down curses on David in the name of his god. ⁴⁴"Come over here," he said. "I'll feed your body to the birds of the air! I'll feed it to the wild animals!"

⁴⁵David said to Goliath, "You are coming to fight against me with a sword, a spear and a javelin. But I'm coming against you in the name of the Lord who rules over all. He is the God of the armies of Israel. He's the one you have dared to fight against.

⁴⁶"This very day the Lord will hand you over to me. I'll strike you down. I'll cut your head off. This very day I'll feed the bodies of the Philistine army to the birds of the air. I'll feed them to the wild animals. Then the whole world will know there is a God in Israel.

⁴⁷"The Lord doesn't save by using a sword or a spear. And everyone who is here will know it. The battle belongs to the Lord. He will hand all of you over to us."

⁴⁸As the Philistine moved closer to attack him, David ran quickly to the battle line to meet him. ⁴⁹He reached into his bag. He took out a stone. He put it in his sling. He slung it at Goliath. The stone hit him on the forehead and sank into it. He fell to the ground on his face.

⁵⁰So David won the fight against Goliath with a sling and a stone. He struck the Philistine down and killed him. He did it without even using a sword.

⁵¹David ran and stood over him. He took hold of Goliath's sword and pulled it out. After he killed him, he cut off his head with the sword.

The Philistines saw that their hero was dead. So they turned around and ran away.

⁵²Then the men of Israel and Judah shouted and rushed forward. They chased the Philistines to the entrance of Gath. They chased them to the gates of Ekron. The dead bodies of the Philistines were scattered all along the road to Gath and Ekron. That's the road that leads to Shaaraim.

⁵³Israel's army returned from chasing the Philistines. They had taken everything from the Philistine camp.

⁵⁴David picked up Goliath's head. He brought it to Jerusalem. He put Goliath's weapons in his own tent.

⁵⁵Saul had been watching David as he went out to meet the Philistine. He spoke to Abner, the commander of the army. He said to him, "Abner, whose son is that young man?"

Abner replied, "King Saul, I don't know. And that's just as sure as you are alive."

⁵⁶The king said, "Find out whose son that young man is."

⁵⁷After David killed Goliath, he returned to the camp. Then Abner brought him to Saul. David was still carrying Goliath's head.

⁵⁸"Young man, whose son are you?" Saul asked him.

David said, "I'm the son of Jesse from Bethlehem."

SAUL BECOMES JEALOUS OF DAVID

18 David finished talking with Saul. After that, Jonathan and David became close friends. Jonathan loved David just as he loved himself.

²From that time on, Saul kept David with him. He didn't let him return to his father's home.

³Jonathan made a covenant with David because he loved him just as he loved himself. ⁴Jonathan took off the robe he was wearing and gave it to David. He also gave him his military clothes. He even gave him his sword, his bow and his belt.

⁵David did everything Saul sent him to do. He did it so well that Saul gave him a high rank in the army. That pleased Saul's whole army, including his officers.

⁶After David had killed Goliath, the men of Israel returned home. The women came out of all of the towns of Israel to meet King Saul. They danced and sang joyful songs. They played lutes and tambourines. ⁷As they danced, they sang,

"Saul has killed thousands of men.
David has killed tens of
      thousands."

⁸That song made Saul very angry. It really upset him. He said to himself, "They are saying David has killed tens of thousands of men. But they are saying I've killed only thousands. The only thing left for him to get is the

How did David fight Goliath if he was so small?

David was only about 16 years old when he fought the bragging bully Goliath. He was not a big man or a soldier. But he trusted in God. He knew that God was on his side and would help him. He remembered that God had helped him fight lions and bears. So he used the weapon that he knew best. It was not a sharp sword or a big spear. It was not strong armor. It was his shepherd's sling. With his sling he could attack Goliath. David was a lot smaller than Goliath. But he was a lot smarter, too. He trusted in God instead of his weapons.

checkout

1 Samuel 17:45

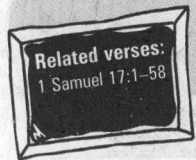

Related verses:
1 Samuel 17:1–58

kingdom itself."⁹From that time on, Saul became very jealous of David. So he watched him closely.

¹⁰The next day an evil spirit that was sent by God came on Saul with power. Saul began to prophesy in his house. At that same time David began to play the harp, just as he usually did. Saul was holding a spear. ¹¹He threw it at David. As he did, he said to himself, "I'll pin David to the wall." But David got away from him twice.

¹²The LORD had left Saul and was with David. So Saul was afraid of David. ¹³He sent David away. He put him in command of 1,000 men. David led the troops in battle. ¹⁴In everything he did, he was very successful. That's because the LORD was with him.

¹⁵When Saul saw how successful David was, he became afraid of him. ¹⁶But all of the troops of Israel and Judah loved David. That's because he led them in battle.

¹⁷Saul said to David, "Here is my older daughter Merab. I'll give her to you to be your wife. Just serve me bravely and fight the LORD's battles."

Saul said to himself, "I won't have to lift my hand to strike him down. The Philistines will do that!"

¹⁸But David said to Saul, "Who am I? Is anyone in my whole family that important in Israel? Am I worthy to become the king's son-in-law?"

¹⁹The time came for Saul to give his daughter Merab to David. Instead, Saul gave her to Adriel from Meholah to be his wife.

²⁰Saul's daughter Michal was in love with David. When they told Saul about it, he was pleased. ²¹"I'll give her to him to be his wife," he said to himself. "Then maybe she'll trap him. And maybe the powerful hand of the Philistines will strike him down." So Saul said to David, "Now you have a second chance to become my son-in-law."

²²Then Saul gave an order to his attendants. He said, "Speak to David in private. Tell him, 'The king is pleased with you. All of his attendants like you. So become his son-in-law.' "

²³Saul's attendants spoke those very words to David. But David said, "Do you think it's a small thing to become the king's son-in-law? I'm only a poor man. I'm not very well known."

²⁴Saul's attendants told him what David had said. ²⁵Saul said, "Tell David, 'Here's the price the king wants for the bride. He wants you to kill 100 Philistines. Then bring back the skins you cut off when you circumcise them.

KIDS' QUESTION

Why was Saul jealous of David?

After David killed Goliath, people compared Saul to David. Saul began to feel like everyone liked David better than him. This made Saul angry. Saul knew that David was a better man, a better soldier and a better person. Saul tried to kill David for a long time. Finally God told Saul he could not be king anymore. Saul died a little bit later. Then David became king.

checkout
1 Samuel 18:8,9

Related verses:
1 Samuel 18:6–9

That's how Saul will get even with his enemies.' " Saul hoped that the powerful hand of the Philistines would strike David down.

²⁶Saul's attendants also told David those things. Then David was pleased to become the king's son-in-law. So before the day that was set for the wedding, ²⁷David and his men went out and killed 200 Philistines. They circumcised them. Then David brought all of the skins and gave them to the king. By doing that, he could become the king's son-in-law. So Saul gave David his daughter Michal to be his wife.

²⁸Saul realized that the LORD was with David. He also realized that his daughter Michal loved David. ²⁹So Saul became even more afraid of him. He remained David's enemy as long as he was king.

³⁰The Philistine commanders kept on going out to battle. Every time they did, David had more success against them than the rest of Saul's officers. So his name became well known.

MICHAL HELPS DAVID GET AWAY

19 Saul told his son Jonathan and all of the attendants to kill David. But Jonathan liked David very much. ²So Jonathan warned him, "My father Saul is looking for a chance to kill you. Be very careful tomorrow morning. Find a place to hide and stay there. ³My father and I will come and stand in the field where you are hiding. I'll speak to him about you. Then I'll tell you what I find out."

⁴Jonathan told his father Saul some good things about David. He said to him, "Please don't do anything to harm David. He hasn't done anything to harm you. And what he's done has helped you a lot. ⁵He put his own life in danger when he killed Goliath. The LORD used him to win a great battle for the whole nation of Israel. When you saw it, you were glad. So why would you do anything to harm a man like David? He isn't guilty of doing anything to harm you. Why would you want to kill him without any reason?"

⁶Saul paid attention to Jonathan. He took an oath and made a promise. He said, "You can be sure that the LORD lives. And you can be just as sure that David will not be put to death."

⁷So Jonathan sent for David and told him everything he and Saul had said. Then he brought David to Saul. David served Saul as he had done before.

⁸Once more war broke out. So David went out and fought against the Philistines. He struck them down with so much force that they ran away from him.

⁹But an evil spirit that was sent by the LORD came on Saul. It happened as he was sitting in his house and holding his spear. While David was playing the harp, ¹⁰Saul tried to pin him to the wall with his spear. But David got away from him just as Saul drove the spear into the wall. That night David escaped.

¹¹Saul sent some men to watch David's house. He told them to kill David the next morning.

But David's wife Michal warned him. She said, "You must run for your life tonight. If you don't, tomorrow you will be killed." ¹²So Michal helped David escape through a window. He ran and got away.

¹³Then Michal got a statue of a god. She laid it on David's bed. She covered it with clothes. And she put some goat hair at the place where David's head would have been.

¹⁴Saul sent the men to capture David. But Michal told them, "He's sick."

¹⁵Then Saul sent the men back to see David. He told them, "Bring him up here to me in his bed. Then I'll kill him."

¹⁶But when the men entered, they found nothing but the statue in the bed. Some goat hair was at the place where David's head would have been.

¹⁷Saul said to Michal, "Why did you trick me like this? Why did you help my enemy escape?"

Michal told him, "He said to me, 'Help me get away. If you don't, I'll kill you.' "

¹⁸After David had run away and escaped, he went to Samuel at Ramah. He told him everything Saul had done to him. Then David and Samuel went to Naioth and stayed there.

[19]Saul was told, "David is in Naioth at Ramah." [20]So Saul sent some men to capture him. When they got there, they saw a group of prophets who were prophesying. Samuel was standing there as their leader. Then the Spirit of God came on Saul's men. So they also began to prophesy. [21]Saul was told about it. So he sent some more men. They began to prophesy too. Saul sent some men a third time. And they also began to prophesy.

[22]Finally, Saul decided to go to Ramah himself. He went to the large well at Secu. He asked some people, "Where are Samuel and David?"

"Over in Naioth at Ramah," they said.

[23]So Saul went to Naioth at Ramah. But the Spirit of God even came on him. He walked along and prophesied until he came to Naioth. [24]There he took off his royal robes. Then he prophesied in front of Samuel. He lay there without his robes on all that day and night. That's why people say, "Is Saul also one of the prophets?"

JONATHAN HELPS DAVID GET AWAY

20 David was in Naioth at Ramah. He ran away from there to where Jonathan was. He asked him, "What have I done? What crime have I committed? I haven't done anything to harm your father. So why is he trying to kill me?"

[2]"That will never happen!" Jonathan replied. "You aren't going to die! My father doesn't do anything at all without telling me. So why would he hide that from me? He isn't going to kill you!"

[3]But David took an oath. Then he said, "Your father knows very well that you are pleased with me. He has said to himself, 'I don't want Jonathan to know I'm planning to kill David. If he finds out, he'll be very sad.' But I'm very close to being killed. And that's just as sure as the LORD and you are alive."

[4]Jonathan said to David, "I'll do anything you want me to do for you."

[5]So David said, "Tomorrow is the time for the New Moon Feast. I'm supposed to eat with the king. But let me go and hide in the field. I'll stay there until the evening of the day after tomorrow. [6]Your father might miss me. If he does, then tell him, 'David begged me to let him hurry home to Bethlehem. A yearly sacrifice is being offered there for his whole family group.' [7]Your father might say, 'That's all right.' If he does, it will mean I'm safe. But he might become very angry. If he does, you can be sure he's made up his mind to harm me.

[8]"Please be kind to me. You have made a covenant with me in the sight of the LORD. If I'm guilty, kill me yourself! Don't hand me over to your father!"

[9]"I would never do that!" Jonathan said. "Suppose I had even the smallest clue that my father had made up his mind to harm you. Then I would tell you."

[10]David asked, "Who will tell me if your father answers you in a mean way?"

[11]"Come on," Jonathan said. "Let's go out to the field." So they went there together.

[12]Then Jonathan spoke to David. He said, "I promise you that I'll find out what my father is planning to do. I'll find out by this time the day after tomorrow. The LORD, the God of Israel, is my witness. Suppose my father feels kind toward you. Then I'll send you a message and let you know. [13]But suppose he wants to harm you. And I don't let you know about it. I don't help you get away safely. Then may the LORD punish me greatly. May he be with you, just as he has been with my father.

[14]"But always be kind to me, just as the LORD is. Be kind to me as long as I live. Then I won't be killed. [15]And never stop being kind to my family. Don't stop even when the LORD has cut off every one of your enemies from the face of the earth."

[16]So Jonathan made a covenant with David and his family. He said, "May the LORD make David's enemies accountable for what they've done." [17]Jonathan had David take an oath again because he loved him. In fact, Jonathan loved David just as he loved himself.

[18]Then Jonathan said to David, "To-

morrow is the time for the New Moon Feast. You will be missed, because your seat at the table will be empty. [19]Go to the place where you hid when all of this trouble began. Go there the day after tomorrow, when evening is approaching. There's a stone out there called Ezel. [20]Wait by it.

"I'll shoot three arrows to one side of the stone. I'll pretend I'm practicing my shooting. [21]Then I'll send a boy out there. I'll tell him, 'Go and find the arrows.' Suppose I say to him, 'The arrows are on this side of you. Bring them here.' Then come. That will mean you are safe. You won't be in any danger. And that's just as sure as the LORD is alive. [22]But suppose I tell the boy, 'The arrows are far beyond you.' Then go. That will mean the LORD is sending you away.

[23]"And remember what we talked about. Remember that the LORD is a witness between you and me forever."

[24]So David hid in the field. When the time for the New Moon Feast came, the king sat down to eat. [25]He sat in his usual place by the wall. Jonathan sat across from him. Abner sat next to Saul. But David's place was empty.

[26]Saul didn't say anything that day. He said to himself, "Something must have happened to David to make him 'unclean.' That must be why he isn't here."

[27]But the next day, David's place was empty again. It was the second day of the month.

Finally, Saul spoke to his son Jonathan. He said, "Why hasn't the son of Jesse come to the meal? He hasn't been here yesterday or today."

[28]Jonathan replied, "David begged me to let him go to Bethlehem. [29]He said, 'Let me go. Our family is offering a sacrifice in the town. My brother has ordered me to be there. Are you pleased with me? If you are, let me go and see my brothers.' That's why he hasn't come to eat at your table."

[30]Saul burned with anger against Jonathan. He said to him, "You are an evil son. You have refused to obey me. I know that you are on the side of Jesse's son. You should be ashamed of that. And your mother should be ashamed of having a son like you. [31]You will

never be king as long as Jesse's son lives on this earth. And you will never have a kingdom either. So send for the son of Jesse. Bring him to me. He must die!"

[32]"Why do you want to put him to death?" Jonathan asked his father. "What has he done?"

[33]But Saul threw his spear at Jonathan to kill him. Then Jonathan knew that his father wanted to kill David.

[34]So Jonathan got up from the table. He was burning with anger. On that second day of the month, he refused to eat. He was very sad that his father was treating David so badly.

[35]The next morning Jonathan went out to the field to meet David. He took a young boy with him. [36]He said to the boy, "Run and find the arrows I shoot." As the boy ran, Jonathan shot an arrow far beyond him. [37]The boy came to the place where Jonathan's arrow had fallen.

Then Jonathan shouted to him, "The arrow went far beyond you, didn't it?" [38]He continued, "Hurry up! Run fast! Don't stop!"

The boy picked up the arrow and returned to his master. [39]The boy didn't know what was going on. Only Jonathan and David knew. [40]Jonathan gave his weapons to the boy. He told him, "Go back to town. Take the weapons with you."

[41]After the boy had gone, David got up from the south side of the stone. He bowed down in front of Jonathan with his face to the ground. He did it three times. Then they kissed each other and cried. But David cried more than Jonathan did.

[42]Jonathan said to David, "Go in peace. In the name of the LORD we have taken an oath. We've promised to be friends. We've said, 'The LORD is a witness between you and me. He's a witness between your children and my children forever.'"

Then David left, and Jonathan went back to the town.

AHIMELECH HELPS DAVID

21 David went to the priest Ahimelech at Nob. Ahimelech trembled with fear when he met him. He asked David,

"Why are you alone? Why isn't anyone with you?"

²David answered the priest Ahimelech, "The king gave me a special job to do. He said to me, 'I don't want anyone to know what I'm sending you to do. So don't say anything about it.' I've told my men to meet me at a certain place. ³Do you have anything for us to eat? Give me five loaves of bread, or anything else you can find."

⁴But the priest answered David, "I don't have any bread that isn't holy. I only have some holy bread here. But it's for men who haven't made love to women recently."

⁵David replied, "Well, we haven't made love to women recently. That's the way it is every time I lead my men out to battle. We keep ourselves holy even when we do jobs that aren't holy. And that's even more true today."

⁶So the priest gave him the holy bread. It was the only bread he had. It had been removed from the table that was in front of the LORD. On the same day, hot bread had been put in its place.

⁷One of Saul's servants was there that day. He had been made to stay at the holy tent for a while. He was Doeg from Edom. He was Saul's chief shepherd.

⁸David asked Ahimelech, "Don't you have a spear or sword here? I haven't brought my sword or any other weapon. That's because the king's business had to be done right away."

⁹The priest replied, "The sword of Goliath, the Philistine, is here. You killed him in the Valley of Elah. His sword is wrapped in a cloth. It's behind the sacred linen apron. If you want it, take it. It's the only sword here."

David said, "There isn't any sword like it. Give it to me."

DAVID MEETS A PHILISTINE KING

¹⁰That day David ran away from Saul. He went to Achish, the king of Gath. ¹¹But the servants of Achish spoke to him. They said, "Isn't this David, the king of the land? Isn't he the one the Israelites sing about when they dance? They sing,

" 'Saul has killed thousands of men.

David has killed tens of thousands.' "

¹²David paid close attention to what the servants were saying. He became very much afraid of what Achish, the king of Gath, might do. ¹³So he pretended to be out of his mind when he was with them. As long as he was in Gath, he acted like someone who was crazy. He made marks on the doors of the city gate. He let spit run down his beard.

¹⁴Achish said to his servants, "Just look at the man! He's out of his mind! Why are you bringing him to me? ¹⁵Don't I have enough crazy people around me already? So why do you have to bring this fellow here? Just look at how he's carrying on in front of me! Why do you have to bring this man into my house?"

DAVID GOES TO ADULLAM AND MIZPAH

22 David left Gath and escaped to the cave of Adullam. His brothers and the other members of his family heard about it. So they went down to join him there. ²Everyone who was in trouble or owed money or was unhappy gathered around him. He became their leader. About 400 men were with him.

³From there David went to Mizpah in Moab. He spoke to the king of Moab. He said, "Please let my father and mother come and stay with you. Let them stay until I learn what God will do for me." ⁴So David left his parents with the king of Moab. They stayed with him as long as David was in his usual place of safety.

⁵But the prophet Gad spoke to David. He said, "Don't stay in your usual place of safety. Go into the land of Judah." So David left and went to the forest of Hereth.

SAUL KILLS THE PRIESTS OF NOB

⁶Saul heard that the place where David and his men were hiding had been discovered. Saul was sitting un-

der a tamarisk tree on the hill at Gibeah. He was holding his spear. All of his officials were standing around him.

⁷Saul said to them, "Men of Benjamin, listen to me! Do you think Jesse's son will give all of you fields and vineyards? Do you think he'll make some of you commanders of thousands of men? Do you think he'll make the rest of you commanders of hundreds? ⁸Is that why all of you have joined together against me? No one tells me when my son makes a covenant with Jesse's son. None of you is concerned about me. No one tells me that my son has stirred up Jesse's son to hide and wait to attack me. But that's exactly what's happening now."

⁹Doeg was standing with Saul's officials. He was from Edom. He said, "I saw Jesse's son David come to Ahimelech at Nob. Ahimelech is the son of Ahitub. ¹⁰Ahimelech asked the LORD a question for David. He also gave him food and the sword of Goliath, the Philistine."

¹¹Then the king sent for the priest Ahimelech, the son of Ahitub. He sent for all of the men in his family. They were the priests at Nob. All of them came to the king.

¹²Saul said, "Son of Ahitub, listen to me."

"Yes, master," he answered.

¹³Saul said to him, "Why have you and Jesse's son joined together against me? Why did you give him bread and a sword? Why did you ask God a question for him? Now he has turned against me. He is hiding and waiting to attack me right now."

¹⁴Ahimelech answered the king, "David is true to you. In fact, he's more true to you than anyone else who serves you. He's your own son-in-law. He's the captain of your own personal guards. He's highly respected by everyone in your palace. ¹⁵Was that day the first time I asked God a question for him? Of course not!

"Please don't bring charges against me. Please don't bring charges against anyone in my family. I don't know anything at all about this whole matter."

¹⁶But the king said, "Ahimelech, you will certainly be put to death. You and your whole family will be put to death."

¹⁷Then the king gave an order to the guards who were at his side. He said, "Go and kill the priests of the LORD. They are on David's side too. They knew he was running away from me. And they didn't even tell me."

But the king's officials wouldn't raise a hand to strike down the priests of the LORD.

¹⁸Then the king ordered Doeg, "You go and strike the priests down."

So Doeg, the Edomite, went and struck them down. That day he killed 85 men who wore linen aprons. ¹⁹He also killed the people of Nob with his sword. Nob was a town where priests lived. Doeg killed its men and women. He killed its children and babies. He also destroyed its cattle, donkeys and sheep.

²⁰But Abiathar, a son of Ahimelech, escaped. Ahimelech was the son of Ahitub. Abiathar ran away and joined David. ²¹He told David that Saul had killed the priests of the LORD.

²²Then David said to Abiathar, "One day I was at Nob. I saw Doeg, the Edomite, there. I knew he would be sure to tell Saul. Your whole family has been killed. And I'm accountable for it. ²³So stay with me. Don't be afraid. The man who wants to kill you wants to kill me too. You will be safe with me."

DAVID SAVES THE PEOPLE OF KEILAH

23 David was told, "The Philistines are fighting against the town of Keilah. They are stealing grain from the threshing floors." ²So he asked the LORD for advice. He said, "Should I go and attack those Philistines?"

The LORD answered him, "Go and attack them. Save Keilah."

³But David's men said to him, "We're afraid here in Judah. Suppose we go to Keilah and fight against the Philistine army. Then we'll be even more afraid."

⁴Once again David asked the LORD what he should do.

The LORD answered him, "Go down to Keilah. I am going to hand the Philistines over to you."

⁵So David and his men went to Keilah. They fought against the Philis-

tines and carried off their livestock. David wounded and killed large numbers of Philistines. And he saved the people of Keilah.

⁶Abiathar, the son of Ahimelech, had brought the linen apron down with him from Nob. He did it when he ran away to David at Keilah.

SAUL CHASES DAVID

⁷Saul was told that David had gone to Keilah. He said, "God has handed him over to me. David has trapped himself by entering a town that has gates and heavy metal bars." ⁸So Saul brought together all of his soldiers to go to battle. He ordered them to go down to Keilah. He told them to surround David and his men. He told them to get ready to attack them.

⁹David learned that Saul was planning to attack him. So he said to the priest Abiathar, "Bring the linen apron." ¹⁰Then David said, "LORD, you are the God of Israel. I know for sure that Saul plans to come to Keilah. He plans to destroy the town because of me. ¹¹Will the citizens of Keilah hand me over to him? Will Saul come down here, as I've heard he would? LORD, you are the God of Israel. Please answer me."

The LORD said, "He will come down."

¹²Again David asked, "Will the citizens of Keilah hand me and my men over to Saul?"

And the LORD said, "They will."

¹³So David and his men left Keilah. The total number of them was about 600. They kept moving from place to place. Saul was told that David had escaped from Keilah. So he didn't go there.

¹⁴Sometimes David stayed in places of safety in the desert. At other times he stayed in the hills of the Desert of Ziph. Day after day Saul looked for him. But God didn't hand David over to him.

¹⁵David was at Horesh in the Desert of Ziph. There he learned that Saul had come out to kill him.

¹⁶Saul's son Jonathan went to David at Horesh. He told David that God would make him strong. ¹⁷"Don't be afraid," he said. "My father Saul won't lay a hand on you. You will be king over Israel. And I will be next in command. Even my father Saul knows this."

¹⁸The two of them made a covenant in the sight of the LORD. Then Jonathan went home. But David remained at Horesh.

¹⁹The people of Ziph went up to Saul at Gibeah. They said, "David is hiding among us. He's hiding in places of safety at Horesh. Horesh is south of Jeshimon on the hill of Hakilah. ²⁰King Saul, come down when it pleases you to come. It will be our duty to hand David over to you."

²¹Saul replied, "May the LORD bless you because you were concerned about me. ²²Make sure you are right. Go and check things out again. Find out where David usually goes. Find out who has seen him there. People tell me he's very tricky. ²³Find out about all of the hiding places he uses. Come back to me with all of the facts. I'll go with you. Suppose he's in the area. Then I'll track him down among all of the family groups of Judah."

²⁴So they started out. They went to Ziph ahead of Saul. David and his men were in the Desert of Maon. Maon is south of Jeshimon in the Arabah Valley. ²⁵Saul and his men started out to look for David. David was told about it. So he went down to a rock in the Desert of Maon to hide. Saul heard he was there. So he went into the Desert of Maon to chase David.

²⁶Saul was going along one side of the mountain. David and his men were on the other side. They were hurrying to get away from Saul. Saul and his army were closing in on David and his men. They were about to capture them. ²⁷Just then a messenger came to Saul. He said, "Come quickly! The Philistines are attacking the land."

²⁸So Saul stopped chasing David. He went to fight against the Philistines. That's why they call that place Sela Hammahlekoth.

²⁹David left that place. He went and lived in places of safety near En Gedi.

DAVID SPARES SAUL'S LIFE

24 Saul returned from chasing the Philistines. Then he was told, "David is in the

Desert of En Gedi." ²So Saul took 3,000 of the best soldiers from the whole nation of Israel. He started out to look for David and his men. He planned to look near the Rocky Cliffs of the Wild Goats.

³He came to some sheep pens along the way. A cave was there. Saul went in to go to the toilet. David and his men were far back in the cave.

⁴David's men said, "This is the day the LORD told you about. He said to you, 'I will hand your enemy over to you. Then you can deal with him as you want to.' "

So David came up close to Saul without being seen. He cut off a corner of Saul's robe.

⁵Later, David felt sorry that he had cut off a corner of Saul's robe. ⁶He said to his men, "May the LORD keep me from doing a thing like that to my master again. He is the LORD's anointed king. So I promise that I will never lift my hand to strike him down. The LORD has anointed him."

⁷David said that to warn his men. He didn't allow them to attack Saul. So Saul left the cave and went on his way.

⁸Then David went out of the cave. He called out to Saul, "King Saul! My master!" When Saul looked behind him, David bowed down. He lay down flat with his face toward the ground.

⁹He said to Saul, "Why do you listen when men say, 'David is trying to harm you'? ¹⁰This very day you have seen with your own eyes how the LORD handed you over to me in the cave. Some of my men begged me to kill you. But I spared you. I said, 'I will never lift my hand to strike my master down. He is the LORD's anointed king.'

¹¹"Look, my father! Look at this piece of your robe in my hand! I cut off the corner of your robe. But I didn't kill you. I want you to know and understand that I'm not guilty of doing anything wrong. I haven't turned against you. I haven't done anything to harm you. But you are hunting me down. You want to kill me.

¹²"May the LORD judge between you and me. And may the LORD pay you back because of the wrong things you have done to me. But I won't lay a hand on you. ¹³People say, 'Evil acts come from those who do evil.' So I won't lay a hand on you.

¹⁴"King Saul, who are you trying to catch? Who do you think you are chasing? I'm nothing but a dead dog or a flea! ¹⁵May the LORD be our judge. May he decide between us. May he consider my case and stand up for me. May he show that I'm not guilty of doing anything wrong. May he save me from your powerful hand."

¹⁶When David finished speaking, Saul asked him a question. He said, "My son David, is that your voice?" And Saul sobbed out loud. ¹⁷"You are a better person than I am," he said. "You have treated me well. But I've treated you badly. ¹⁸You have just now told me about the good things you did to me. The LORD handed me over to you. But you didn't kill me. ¹⁹Suppose a man finds his enemy. He doesn't let him get away without harming him. May the LORD reward you with many good things. May he do it because of the way you treated me today. ²⁰I know for sure that you will be king. I know that the kingdom of Israel will be made secure under your control. ²¹Now take an oath in the name of the LORD. Promise me that you won't cut off my children from my family. Also promise me that you won't wipe out my name from my family line."

²²So David took an oath and made that promise to Saul. Then Saul returned home. But David and his men went up to his usual place of safety.

DAVID GETS MARRIED TO ABIGAIL

25 Samuel died. The whole nation of Israel gathered together. They were filled with sorrow because he was dead. They buried his body at his home in Ramah.

Then David went down into the Desert of Maon. ²A certain man in Maon was very wealthy. He owned property there at Carmel. He had 1,000 goats and 3,000 sheep. He was clipping the wool off the sheep in Carmel. ³His name was Nabal. His wife's name was Abigail. She was a wise and beautiful woman. But her husband was rude and mean in the way he treated others. He was from the family of Caleb.

[4]David was staying in the Desert of Maon. While he was there, he heard that Nabal was clipping the wool off his sheep. [5]So he sent for ten young men. He said to them, "Go up to Nabal at Carmel. Greet him for me. [6]Say to him, 'May you live a long time! May everything go well with you and your family! And may things go well with everything that belongs to you!

[7]" 'I hear that you are clipping the wool off your sheep. When your shepherds were with us, we treated them well. The whole time they were at Carmel nothing that belonged to them was stolen. [8]Ask your own servants. They'll tell you. We've come to you now at a happy time of the year. Please show favor to my young men. Please give me and my men anything you can find for us.' "

[9]When David's men arrived, they gave Nabal the message from David. Then they waited.

[10]Nabal answered David's servants, "Who is this David? Who is this son of Jesse? Many servants are running away from their masters these days. [11]Why should I give away my bread and water? Why should I give away the meat I've prepared for those who clip the wool off my sheep? Why should I give food to men who come from who knows where?"

[12]So David's men turned around and went back. When they arrived, they reported to David every word Nabal had spoken. [13]David said to his men, "Put on your swords!" So they put their swords on. David put his on too. About 400 men went up with David. Two hundred men stayed behind with the supplies.

[14]One of the servants warned Nabal's wife Abigail. He said, "David sent some messengers from the desert to give his greetings to our master. But Nabal shouted at them and made fun of them. [15]"David's men had been very good to us. They treated us well. The whole time we were near them out in the fields, nothing was stolen. [16]We were taking care of our sheep near them. During that time, they were like a wall around us night and day. They kept us safe.

[17]"Now think it over. See what you can do. Horrible trouble will soon come to our master and his whole family. He's such an evil man that no one can even talk to him."

[18]Abigail didn't waste any time. She got 200 loaves of bread and two bottles of wine. The bottles were made out of animal skins. She got five sheep that were ready to be cooked. She got a bushel of grain that had been cooked. She got 100 raisin cakes. And she got 200 cakes of pressed figs. She loaded all of it on the backs of donkeys. [19]Then she told her servants, "Go on ahead. I'll follow you." But she didn't tell her husband Nabal about it.

[20]Abigail rode her donkey into a mountain valley. There she saw David and his men. They were coming down toward her. [21]David had just said, "Everything we've done hasn't been worth a thing! I watched over that fellow's property in the desert. I made sure none of it was stolen. But he has paid me back evil for good. [22]I won't leave even one of his men alive until morning. If I do, may God punish me greatly!"

[23]When Abigail saw David, she quickly got off her donkey. She bowed down in front of David with her face toward the ground. [24]She fell at his feet. She said, "Please let me speak to you, sir. Listen to what I'm saying. Let me take the blame myself. [25]Don't pay any attention to that evil man Nabal. His name means Foolish Person. And that's exactly what he is. He's always doing foolish things. I'm sorry I didn't get a chance to see the men you sent.

[26]"Sir, the LORD has kept you from killing Nabal and his men. He has kept you from using your own hands to get even. May what's about to happen to Nabal happen to all of your enemies. May it also happen to everyone who wants to harm you. And may it happen just as surely as the LORD and you are alive.

[27]"I've brought a gift for you. Give it to the men who follow you. [28]Please forgive me for what I've done wrong.

"The LORD will certainly give you and your family line a kingdom that will last. That's because you fight the LORD's battles. Don't do anything wrong as long as you live.

29"Someone may chase you and try to kill you. But the LORD your God will keep your life safe like a treasure that is hidden in a bag. And he'll destroy your enemies. Their lives will be thrown away, just as a stone is thrown from a sling.

30"The LORD will do for you every good thing he promised to do. He'll appoint you leader over Israel. 31When that happens, you won't have this heavy load on your mind. You won't have to worry about how you killed people without any reason. You won't have to worry about how you got even. The LORD will give you success. When that happens, please remember me."

32David said to Abigail, "Give praise to the LORD. He is the God of Israel. He has sent you today to find me. 33May the LORD bless you for what you have done. You have shown a lot of good sense. You have kept me from killing Nabal and his men this very day. You

have kept me from using my own hands to get even.

34"It's a good thing you came quickly to meet me. If you hadn't come, not one of Nabal's men would have been left alive by sunrise. And that's just as sure as the LORD, the God of Israel, is alive. He has kept me from harming you."

35Then David accepted from her what she had brought him. He said, "Go home in peace. I've heard your words. I'll do what you have asked."

36Abigail went back to Nabal. He was having a dinner party in the house. It was the kind of dinner a king would have. He had been drinking too much wine. He was very drunk. So she didn't tell him anything at all until sunrise.

37The next morning Nabal wasn't drunk anymore. Then his wife told him everything. When she did, his heart grew weak. He became like a stone. 38About ten days later, the LORD struck Nabal down. And he died.

39David heard that Nabal was dead. So he said, "Give praise to the LORD.

Why did people in Bible times sometimes bow down to each other?

People in Bible times usually greeted each other with a hug or a kiss on the cheek. That was like a handshake today. They almost never bowed down unless they wanted to show a lot of respect. They always bowed before a king or other important leaders. Sometimes they bowed down when they wanted to make peace with an angry person. A bow meant, "You are more important than I am. I am at your service." Friends who were just meeting on the street or visiting somebody's home would usually just give each other a hug.

checkout
1 Samuel 25:23

Related verses:
Isaiah 60:14;
1 Thessalonians
5:26

Nabal made fun of me. But the LORD stood up for me. He has kept me from doing something wrong. He has paid Nabal back for the wrong things he did."

Then David sent a message to Abigail. He asked her to become his wife. [40]His servants went to Carmel. They said to Abigail, "David has sent us to you. He wants you to come back with us and become his wife."

[41]Abigail bowed down with her face toward the ground. She said, "Here I am. I'm ready to serve him. I'm ready to wash the feet of his servants."

[42]Abigail quickly got on a donkey and went with David's messengers. Her five female servants went with her. She became David's wife.

[43]David had also gotten married to Ahinoam from Jezreel. Both of them became his wives.

[44]But Saul had given his daughter Michal, David's first wife, to Paltiel. Paltiel was from Gallim. He was the son of Laish.

DAVID SPARES SAUL'S LIFE AGAIN

26 Some people from Ziph went to Saul at Gibeah. They said, "David is hiding on the hill of Hakilah. It faces Jeshimon."

[2]So Saul went down to the Desert of Ziph. He took 3,000 of the best soldiers in Israel with him. They went to the desert to look for David. [3]Saul set up his camp beside the road. It was on the hill of Hakilah facing Jeshimon.

But David stayed in the desert. He saw that Saul had followed him there. [4]So he sent out scouts. From them he learned that Saul had arrived.

[5]Then David started out. He went to the place where Saul had camped. He saw where Saul and Abner were lying down. Saul was lying inside the camp. The army was camped all around him. Abner was commander of the army. He was the son of Ner.

[6]Then David spoke to Ahimelech, the Hittite. He also spoke to Joab's brother Abishai, the son of Zeruiah. He asked them, "Who will go down with me into the camp to Saul?"

"I'll go with you," said Abishai.

[7]So that night David and Abishai went into the camp. They found Saul lying asleep inside the camp. His spear was stuck in the ground near his head. Abner and the soldiers were lying asleep around him.

[8]Abishai said to David, "Today God has handed your enemy over to you. So let me pin him to the ground. I can do it with one jab of my spear. I won't even have to strike him twice."

[9]But David said to Abishai, "Don't destroy him! No one can lay a hand on the LORD's anointed king and not be guilty. [10]You can be sure that the LORD lives," he said. "And you can be just as sure that the LORD himself will strike Saul down. Perhaps he'll die a natural death. Or perhaps he'll go into battle and be killed. [11]May the LORD keep me from laying a hand on his anointed king. Now get the spear and water jug that are near his head. Then let's leave."

[12]So David took the spear and water jug that were near Saul's head. Then he and Abishai left. No one saw them. No one knew about what they had done. In fact, no one even woke up. Everyone was sleeping. That's because the LORD had put them into a deep sleep.

[13]David went across to the other side of the valley. He stood on top of a hill far away from Saul's camp. There was a wide space between them. [14]He called out to the army and to Abner, the son of Ner. He said, "Abner! Aren't you going to answer me?"

Abner replied, "Who is calling out to the king?"

[15]David said, "You are a great soldier, aren't you? There isn't anyone else like you in Israel. So why didn't you guard the king? He's your master, isn't he? Someone came into the camp to destroy him. [16]You didn't guard him. And that isn't good. You can be sure that the LORD lives. And you can be just as sure that you and your men are worthy of death. That's because you didn't guard your master. He's the LORD's anointed king. Look around you. Where are the king's spear and water jug that were near his head?"

[17]Saul recognized David's voice. He said, "My son David, is that your voice?"

David replied, "Yes it is, King Saul, my master." ¹⁸He continued, "Why are you chasing me? What evil thing have I done? What am I guilty of?

¹⁹"King Saul, please listen to what I'm saying. Was it the LORD who made you angry with me? If it was, may he accept my offering. Was it people who made you angry at me? If it was, may the LORD send down a curse on them. They have now driven me from my share of the LORD's land. By doing that, they might as well have said, 'Go and serve other gods.'

²⁰"Don't spill my blood on the ground far away from where the LORD lives. King Saul, you have come out to look for nothing but a flea. It's as if you were hunting a partridge in the mountains."

²¹Then Saul said, "I have sinned. My son David, come back. Today you thought my life was very special. So I won't try to harm you again. I've really acted like a foolish person. I've made a huge mistake."

²²"Here's your spear," David answered. "Send one of your young men over to get it.

²³"The LORD rewards everyone for doing what is right and being faithful. He handed you over to me today. But I wouldn't lay a hand on you. You are the LORD's anointed king. ²⁴Today I thought your life had great value. In the same way, may the LORD think of my life as having great value. May he save me from all trouble."

²⁵Then Saul said to David, "My son David, may the LORD bless you. You will do great things. You will also have great success."

So David went on his way. And Saul returned home.

DAVID LIVES IN PHILISTINE TERRITORY

27 David thought, "Some day the powerful hand of Saul will destroy me. So the best thing I can do is escape. I'll go to the land of the Philistines. Then Saul will stop looking for me everywhere in Israel. His hand won't be able to reach me."

²So David and his 600 men left Israel. They went to Achish, the king of Gath. He was the son of Maoch. ³David and his men settled down in Gath near Achish. Each of David's men had his family with him. David had his two wives with him. They were Ahinoam from Jezreel and Abigail from Carmel. Abigail was Nabal's widow.

⁴Saul was told that David had run away to Gath. So he didn't look for David anymore.

⁵David said to Achish, "If you are pleased with me, give me a place in one of your country towns. I can live there. I don't really need to live near you in the royal city."

⁶So on that day Achish gave David the town of Ziklag. It has belonged to the kings of Judah ever since that time. ⁷David lived in Philistine territory for a year and four months.

⁸Sometimes David and his men would go up and attack the Geshurites. At other times they would attack the Girzites or the Amalekites. All of those people had lived in the land that reached all the way to Shur and Egypt. They had been there for a long time.

⁹When David would attack an area, he wouldn't leave a man or woman alive. But he would take their sheep, cattle, donkeys, camels and clothes. Then he would return to Achish.

¹⁰Achish would ask, "Who did you attack today?" David would answer, "The people who live in the Negev Desert of Judah." Or he would answer, "The people in the Negev Desert of Jerahmeel." Or he would answer, "The people in the Negev Desert of the Kenites."

¹¹David wouldn't leave a man or woman alive to be brought back to Gath. He thought, "They might tell on us. They might tell Achish who we really attacked." That's what David did as long as he lived in Philistine territory.

¹²Achish trusted David. He thought, "David has made himself smell very bad to his people, the Israelites. So he'll serve me forever."

SAUL DISOBEYS THE LORD AT ENDOR

28 While David was living in Ziklag, the Philistines gathered their army together. They planned to fight against Israel.

Achish said to David, "I want you to understand that you and your men must march out with me and my army."

²David said, "I understand. You will see for yourself what I can do."

Achish replied, "All right. I'll make you my own personal guard for life."

³Samuel had died. The whole nation of Israel was filled with sorrow because he was dead. They had buried his body in his own town of Ramah.

Saul had gotten rid of people who get messages from those who have died. He had also gotten rid of people who talk to the spirits of the dead. He had thrown all of them out of the land.

⁴The Philistines gathered together and set up camp at Shunem. At the same time, Saul gathered all of the fighting men of Israel together. They set up camp at Gilboa.

⁵When Saul saw the Philistine army, he was afraid. Terror filled his heart. ⁶He asked the LORD for advice. But the LORD didn't answer him through

dreams or prophets. He didn't answer him when Saul had the priest use the Urim.

⁷Saul spoke to his attendants. He said, "Find me a woman who gets messages from those who have died. Then I can go and ask her some questions."

"There's a woman like that in Endor," they said.

⁸Saul put on different clothes so people wouldn't know who he was. At night he and two of his men went to see the woman. "I want you to talk to a spirit for me," he said. "Bring up the spirit of the dead person I choose."

⁹But the woman said to him, "By now you must know what Saul has done. He has cut off everyone who gets messages from those who have died. He has also cut off everyone who talks to the spirits of the dead. He has thrown all of them out of the land. Why are you trying to trap me? Why do you want to have me put to death?"

¹⁰Saul took an oath in the name of the LORD. He promised the woman, "You can be sure that the LORD lives.

KIDS' QUESTion

Why did Saul go to a fortune-teller?

King Saul went to see a fortune-teller because he did not know what else to do. He did not trust God to lead him. Saul wanted to find out things that he did not have a right to know. God had told his people that they should never get involved with witchcraft and fortune-tellers. Saul disobeyed God and did it anyway.

(checkout) 1 Samuel 28:7

Related verses:
Deuteronomy
18:10,11

And you can be just as sure that you won't be punished for helping me."

¹¹Then the woman asked, "Whose spirit should I bring up for you?"

"Bring Samuel up," he said.

¹²When the woman saw Samuel, she let out a loud scream. She said to Saul, "Why have you tricked me? You are King Saul!"

¹³He said to her, "Don't be afraid. Tell me what you see."

The woman said, "I see a spirit. He's coming up out of the ground."

¹⁴"What does he look like?" Saul asked.

"An old man wearing a robe is coming up," she said.

Then Saul knew it was Samuel. He bowed down. He lay down flat with his face toward the ground.

¹⁵Samuel said to Saul, "Why have you troubled me by bringing me up from the dead?"

"I'm having big problems," Saul said. "The Philistines are fighting against me. God has turned away from me. He doesn't answer me anymore. He doesn't speak to me through prophets or dreams. So I've called on you to tell me what to do."

¹⁶Samuel said, "The Lord has turned away from you. He has become your enemy. So why are you asking me what you should do? ¹⁷The Lord has spoken through me and has done what he said he would do. He has torn the kingdom out of your hands. He has given it to one of your neighbors. He has given it to David. ¹⁸You didn't obey the Lord. You didn't carry out his burning anger against the Amalekites. So he's punishing you today.

¹⁹"He will hand both Israel and you over to the Philistines. Tomorrow you and your sons will be down here with me. The Lord will also hand Israel's army over to the Philistines."

²⁰Immediately Saul fell flat on the ground. What Samuel had said filled Saul with fear. His strength was gone. He hadn't eaten anything all that day and night.

²¹The woman went over to Saul because she saw that he was very upset. She said, "Look, I've obeyed you. I put my own life in danger by doing what you told me to do. ²²So please listen to me. Let me give you some food. Eat it. Then you will have the strength to go on your way."

²³But he refused. He said, "I don't want anything to eat."

Then his men joined the woman in begging him to eat. Finally, he paid attention to them. He got up from the ground and sat on a couch.

²⁴The woman had a fat calf at her house. She killed it at once. She got some flour. She mixed it and baked some bread that didn't have any yeast in it. ²⁵Then she set the food in front of Saul and his men. They ate it. That same night they got up and left.

ACHISH SENDS DAVID BACK TO ZIKLAG

29 The Philistines gathered their whole army together at Aphek. Israel's army camped by the spring of water at Jezreel. ²The Philistine rulers marched out in companies of hundreds and thousands. David and his men were marching with Achish behind the others.

³The commanders of the Philistines asked, "Why are these Hebrews here?"

Achish replied, "That's David, isn't it? Wasn't he an officer of Saul, the king of Israel? He has already been with me for more than a year. I haven't found any fault in him. That's been true from the day he left Saul until now."

⁴But the Philistine commanders were angry with Achish. They said, "Send David back. Let him return to the town you gave him. He must not go with us into battle. If he does, he'll turn against us during the fighting. In fact, he might even cut off the heads of our own men. What better way could he choose to win back his master's favor? ⁵Isn't David the one the Israelites sang about when they danced? They sang,

" 'Saul has killed thousands of
   men.
David has killed tens of
   thousands.' "

⁶So Achish called David over to him. He said, "You have been faithful to me. And that's just as sure as the Lord is alive. I would be pleased to have you

serve with me in the army. I haven't found any fault in you. That's been true from the day you came to me until now. But the Philistine rulers aren't pleased to have you come along. ⁷So go back home in peace. Don't do anything that wouldn't please the Philistine rulers."

⁸"But what have I done?" asked David. "What have you found against me from the day I came to you until now? Why can't I go and fight against your enemies? After all, you are my king and master."

⁹Achish answered, "You have been as pleasing to me as an angel of God. But the Philistine commanders have said, 'We don't want David to go up with us into battle.' ¹⁰So get up early in the morning. Take with you the men who used to serve Saul. Leave as soon as the sun begins to come up."

¹¹So David and his men got up early in the morning. They went back to the land of the Philistines. And the Philistines went up to Jezreel.

DAVID DESTROYS THE AMALEKITES

30 On the third day David and his men arrived in Ziklag. The Amalekites had attacked the people of the Negev Desert. They had also attacked Ziklag and burned it. ²They had captured the women and everyone else who was in Ziklag. They had taken as prisoners young people and old people alike. But they didn't kill any of them. Instead, they carried them off as they went on their way.

³David and his men came to Ziklag. They saw that it had been destroyed by fire. They found out that their wives and sons and daughters had been captured. ⁴So David and his men began to sob out loud. They sobbed until they couldn't sob anymore. ⁵David's two wives had been captured. Their names were Ahinoam from Jezreel and Abigail from Carmel. Abigail was Nabal's widow.

⁶David was greatly troubled. His men were even talking about killing him by throwing stones at him. All of them were very bitter because their sons and daughters had been taken away. But David was made strong by the LORD his God.

⁷Then David spoke to the priest Abiathar, the son of Ahimelech. He said, "Bring me the linen apron." Abiathar brought it to him. ⁸David asked the LORD for advice. He said, "Should I chase after the men who attacked Ziklag? If I do, will I catch up with them?"

"Chase after them," the LORD answered. "You will certainly catch up with them. You will succeed in saving those who were captured."

⁹David and his 600 men came to the Besor Valley. Some of them stayed behind there. ¹⁰That's because 200 of them were too tired to go across the valley. But David and the other 400 continued the chase.

¹¹David's men found an Egyptian in a field. They brought him to David. They gave him water to drink and food to eat. ¹²They gave him part of a cake of pressed figs. They also gave him two raisin cakes. After he ate them, he felt as good as new. That's because he hadn't eaten any food for three days and three nights. He hadn't drunk any water during that time either.

¹³David asked him, "Who do you belong to? Where do you come from?"

The man said, "I'm from Egypt. I'm the slave of an Amalekite. My master deserted me when I became ill three days ago. ¹⁴We attacked the people in the Negev Desert of the Kerethites. We attacked the territory that belongs to Judah. We attacked the people in the Negev Desert of Caleb. And we burned Ziklag."

¹⁵David asked him, "Can you lead me down to the men who attacked Ziklag?"

He answered, "Take an oath in the name of God. Promise me that you won't kill me. Promise that you won't hand me over to my master. Then I'll take you down to them."

¹⁶He led David down to where the men were. They were scattered all over the countryside. They were eating and drinking and dancing wildly. That's because they had taken a large amount of goods from those they had attacked. They had taken it from the land of the Philistines and from the people of Judah.

¹⁷David fought against them from sunset until the evening of the next day. None of them escaped except 400 young men. They rode off on camels and got away.

¹⁸David got everything back that the Amalekites had taken. That included his two wives. ¹⁹Nothing was missing. Not one young person or old person or boy or girl was missing. None of the goods or anything else the Amalekites had taken was missing. David brought everything back. ²⁰He brought back all of the flocks and herds. His men drove them on ahead of the other livestock. They said, "Here's what David has captured."

²¹Then David came to the 200 men who had been too tired to follow him. They had been left behind in the Besor Valley. They came out to welcome David and the people who were with him. As David and his men approached, he greeted them. ²²But some of the men who had gone out with David were evil. They wanted to stir up trouble. They said, "The 200 men didn't go out into battle with us. So we won't share with them the goods we brought back. But each man can take his wife and children and go home."

²³David replied, "No, my friends. You must not hold back their share of what the LORD has given us. He has kept us safe. He has handed over to us the men who attacked Ziklag. ²⁴So no one will pay any attention to what you are saying. Each man who stayed with the supplies will receive the same share as each man who went down to the battle. Everyone's share will be the same." ²⁵David made that a law and a rule for Israel. It has been followed from that day until now.

²⁶David arrived in Ziklag. He sent some of the goods to the elders of Judah. They were his friends. He said, "Here's a present for you. It's part of the things we took from the LORD's enemies."

²⁷He sent some goods to the elders who were in Bethel, Ramoth Negev and Jattir. ²⁸He sent some to those who were in Aroer, Siphmoth, Eshtemoa ²⁹and Racal. He sent some to those who were in the towns of the Jerahmeelites and Kenites. ³⁰He sent some to those who were in Hormah, Bor Ashan, Athach ³¹and Hebron. He also sent some to those who were in all of the other places where he and his men had wandered around.

SAUL TAKES HIS OWN LIFE

31 The Philistines fought against Israel. The men of Israel ran away from them. But many Israelites were killed on Mount Gilboa.

²The Philistines kept chasing Saul and his sons. They killed his sons Jonathan, Abinadab and Malki-Shua. ³The fighting was heavy around Saul. Men who were armed with bows and arrows caught up with him. They shot their arrows at him and wounded him badly.

⁴Saul spoke to the man who was carrying his armor. He said, "Pull out your sword. Stick it through me. If you don't, those fellows who aren't circumcised will come. They'll stick their swords through me and hurt me badly."

But the man was terrified. He wouldn't do it. So Saul took his own sword and fell on it. ⁵The man saw that Saul was dead. So he fell on his own sword and died with him.

⁶Saul and his three sons died together that same day. The man who carried his armor also died with them that day. So did all of Saul's men.

⁷The Israelites who lived along the valley saw that their army had run away. So did those who lived across the Jordan River. They saw that Saul and his sons were dead. So they left their towns and ran away. Then the Philistines came and settled down in them.

⁸The day after the Philistines had won the battle, they came to take what they wanted from the dead bodies. They found Saul and his three sons dead on Mount Gilboa. ⁹So they cut off Saul's head. They took his armor from his body. Then they sent messengers through the whole land of the Philistines. They announced the news in the temple where they had set up statues of their gods. They also announced it among their people.

¹⁰They put Saul's armor in the

temple where they had set up statues of goddesses that were named after Ashtoreth. They hung his body up on the wall of Beth Shan.

¹¹The people of Jabesh Gilead heard about what the Philistines had done to Saul. ¹²So all of their brave men traveled through the night to Beth Shan.

They took down the bodies of Saul and his sons from the wall of Beth Shan. They brought them to Jabesh. There they burned them.

¹³Then they got the bones of Saul and his sons and buried them under a tamarisk tree at Jabesh. They didn't eat anything for seven days.

quest challenge

I Wonder . . .

How can I pray for my friends?

Real Life Challenge

Maybe one of your friends is having trouble in school or with his or her parents' divorce. You want to do something to help, but you feel powerless. Yet God's Word tells us that each one of us can do something very powerful to help our friends—pray! God gives us several examples from Paul's letters to show us how to pray for others in a way that will really help them.

Quest Clue

Look in 1 Samuel 12 to see what God thinks about praying for your friends. Then find chapter 1 in Ephesians, Philippians, and Colossians for some specific ideas on how to pray for them.

2 Samuel

Who wrote this book?
The writer is unknown.

Why was this book written?
The book of 2 Samuel tells the story of David's forty-year reign as Israel's king.

What happens in this book?
David becomes king of Israel. During his reign foreign enemies are defeated and Israel becomes a great nation.

What do we learn about God in this book?
God uses people who love and want to please him, as King David did.

Who is important in this book?
The important person in this book is King David.

When did this happen?
Events in this book happened between 1010 and 970 B.C.

Where did this happen?
These events took place in Israel.

DAVID HEARS THAT SAUL HAS DIED

1 After Saul died, David returned to Ziklag. He had won the battle over the Amalekites. He stayed in Ziklag for two days.

²On the third day a man arrived from Saul's camp. His clothes were torn. He had dust on his head. When he came to David, he fell to the ground to show him respect.

³"Where have you come from?" David asked him.

He answered, "I've escaped from Israel's camp."

⁴"What happened?" David asked. "Tell me."

He said, "Israel's men ran away from

the battle. Many of them were killed. Saul and his son Jonathan are dead."

⁵David spoke to the young man who brought him the report. He asked him, "How do you know that Saul and his son Jonathan are dead?"

⁶"I just happened to be there on Mount Gilboa," the young man said. "Saul was there too. He was leaning on his spear. The enemy chariots and chariot drivers had almost caught up with him. ⁷Then he turned around and saw me. He called out to me. I said, 'What do you want me to do?'

⁸"He asked me, 'Who are you?'

" 'An Amalekite,' I answered.

⁹"Then he said to me, 'Stand over me and kill me! I'm close to death, but I'm still alive.'

¹⁰"So I stood over him and killed him. I did it because I knew that after he had lost the battle he would be killed anyway. So I took the crown that was on his head. I also took his armband. I've brought them here to you. You are my master."

¹¹Then David took hold of his clothes and tore them. All of his men did the same thing. ¹²All of them were filled with sadness. They sobbed over the whole nation of Israel. They didn't eat anything until evening. That's because Saul and Jonathan and the LORD's army had been killed with swords.

¹³David spoke to the young man who had brought him the report. He asked, "Where are you from?"

"I'm the son of an outsider, an Amalekite," he answered.

¹⁴David asked him, "Why weren't you afraid to lift your hand to kill the LORD's anointed king?"

¹⁵Then David called for one of his men. He said, "Go! Strike him down!" So he struck the man down, and the man died. ¹⁶That's because David had said to him, "Anything that happens to you will be your own fault. What your own mouth has spoken is a witness against you. You said, 'I killed the LORD's anointed king.' "

DAVID'S SONG OF SADNESS ABOUT SAUL AND JONATHAN

¹⁷David sang a song of sadness about Saul and his son Jonathan. ¹⁸He ordered that it be taught to the people of Judah. It is called The Song of the Bow. It is written down in the Book of Jashar.

David sang,

¹⁹"Israel, your glorious leaders lie
　　dead on your hills.
　Your mighty men have fallen.

²⁰"Don't announce it in Gath.
　Don't tell it in the streets of
　　Ashkelon.
　If you do, the daughters of the
　　Philistines will be glad.
　The daughters of men who
　　haven't been circumcised will
　　be joyful.

²¹"Mountains of Gilboa,
　may no dew or rain fall on you.
　May your fields not produce any
　　offerings of grain.
　The shield of the mighty king lies
　　polluted there.
　The shield of Saul lies there. It
　　isn't rubbed with oil anymore.

²²The bow of Jonathan didn't turn
　　back.
　The sword of Saul didn't return
　　without being satisfied.
　They spilled the blood of their
　　enemies.
　They killed mighty men.

²³"In life Saul and Jonathan were
　　loved and gracious.
　In death they were not parted.
　They were faster than eagles.
　They were stronger than lions.

²⁴"Daughters of Israel, sob over Saul.
　He dressed you in the finest
　　clothes.
　He decorated your clothes with
　　ornaments of gold.

²⁵"Your mighty men have fallen in
　　battle.
　Jonathan lies dead on your hills.
²⁶My brother Jonathan, I'm filled
　　with sadness because of you.
　You were very special to me.
　Your love for me was wonderful.
　It was more wonderful than the
　　love of women.

²⁷"Israel's mighty men have fallen.
　Their weapons of war are
　　broken."

DAVID IS ANOINTED TO BE KING OVER JUDAH

2 After Saul and Jonathan died, David asked the LORD for advice. "Should I go up to one of the towns of Judah?" he asked.

The LORD said, "Go up."

David asked, "Where should I go?"

"To Hebron," the LORD answered.

²So David went up there with his two wives. Their names were Ahinoam from Jezreel and Abigail from Carmel. Abigail was Nabal's widow. ³David also took his men and their families with him. They settled down in Hebron and its towns.

⁴Then the men of Judah came to Hebron. There they anointed David to be king over the people of Judah.

David was told that the men of Jabesh Gilead had buried Saul's body. ⁵So he sent messengers to them to speak for him.

The messengers said, "You were kind to bury the body of your master Saul. May the LORD bless you for that. ⁶And may he now be kind and faithful to you. David will treat you well for being kind to Saul's body. ⁷Now then, be strong and brave. Your master Saul is dead. And the people of Judah have anointed David to be king over them."

THE ARMIES OF DAVID AND SAUL FIGHT EACH OTHER

⁸Abner, the son of Ner, was commander of Saul's army. He had brought Saul's son Ish-Bosheth to Mahanaim. ⁹There he made him king over Gilead, Ashuri and Jezreel. He also made him king over Ephraim, Benjamin and other areas of Israel.

¹⁰Ish-Bosheth was 40 years old when he became king over Israel. He ruled for two years. But the people of Judah followed David. ¹¹David was king in Hebron over the people of Judah for seven and a half years.

¹²Abner, the son of Ner, left Mahanaim and went to Gibeon. The men of

How come the husbands could have so many wives?

Very few husbands had more than one wife. Most of them had only one wife and lived with their families just like husbands do today. Some kings and rich men were married to several women at once. A king might marry a princess from a neighboring country just to keep peace with that country. Other men married more than one wife because their first wives could not have children. But God's plan is for a man to have one wife and for a woman to have one husband. God never said that men could have lots of wives.

checkout 2 Samuel 2:2

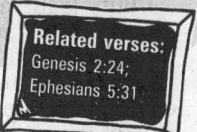

Related verses:
Genesis 2:24;
Ephesians 5:31

Ish-Bosheth, the son of Saul, went with him. [13]Joab, the son of Zeruiah, and David's men also went out. All of them met at the pool in Gibeon. One group sat down on one side of the pool. The other group sat on the other side.

[14]Then Abner said to Joab, "Let's have some of the young men get up and fight. Let's tell them to fight hand to hand in front of us."

"All right. Let them do it," Joab said.

[15]So the young men stood up and were counted off. There were 12 on the side of Benjamin and Saul's son Ish-Bosheth. And there were 12 on David's side. [16]Each man grabbed one of his enemies by the head. Each one stuck his dagger into the other man's side. And all of them fell down together and died. So that place in Gibeon was named Helkath Hazzurim.

[17]The fighting that day was very heavy. Abner and the men of Israel lost the battle to David's men.

[18]The three sons of Zeruiah were there. Their names were Joab, Abishai and Asahel. Asahel was as quick on his feet as a wild antelope. [19]He chased Abner. He didn't turn to the right or the left as he chased him. [20]Abner looked behind him. He asked, "Asahel, is that you?"

"It is," he answered.

[21]Then Abner said to him, "Turn to the right or the left. Fight one of the young men. Take his weapons away from him." But Asahel wouldn't stop chasing him.

[22]Again Abner warned Asahel, "Stop chasing me! If you don't, I'll strike you down. Then how could I look your brother Joab in the face?"

[23]But Asahel refused to give up the chase. So Abner drove the dull end of his spear into Asahel's stomach. The spear came out of his back. He fell and died right there on the spot. Every man stopped when he came to the place where Asahel had fallen and died.

[24]But Joab and Abishai chased Abner. As the sun was going down, they came to the hill of Ammah. It was near Giah on the way to the dry and empty land close to Gibeon. [25]The men of Benjamin gathered in a group around Abner. They took their stand on top of a hill.

[26]Abner called out to Joab, "Do you want our swords to keep on killing us off? Don't you know that all of this fighting will end in bitter feelings? How long will it be before you order your men to stop chasing their fellow Israelites?"

[27]Joab answered, "It's a good thing you spoke up. If you hadn't, the men would have kept on chasing their fellow Israelites until morning. And that's just as sure as God is alive."

[28]So Joab blew a trumpet. All of the men stopped. They didn't chase Israel anymore. They didn't fight anymore either.

[29]All that night Abner and his men marched through the Arabah Valley. They went across the Jordan River. They kept on going through the whole Bithron. Finally, they came to Mahanaim.

[30]Then Joab returned from chasing Abner. He gathered all of his men together. Besides Asahel, only 19 of David's men were missing. [31]But David's men had killed 360 men from Benjamin who were with Abner. [32]They got Asahel's body and buried it in his father's tomb at Bethlehem. Then Joab and his men marched all night. They arrived at Hebron at sunrise.

3 The war between Saul's royal house and David's royal house lasted a long time. David grew stronger and stronger. But the royal house of Saul grew weaker and weaker.

[2]Sons were born to David in Hebron. His first son was Amnon. Amnon's mother was Ahinoam from Jezreel.

[3]His second son was Kileab. Kileab's mother was Abigail. She was Nabal's widow from Carmel.

The third son was Absalom. His mother was Maacah. She was the daughter of Talmai, the king of Geshur.

[4]The fourth son was Adonijah. His mother was Haggith.

The fifth son was Shephatiah. His mother was Abital.

[5] The sixth son was Ithream. His mother was David's wife Eglah. Those sons were born to David in Hebron.

ABNER GOES OVER TO DAVID'S SIDE

[6] The fighting continued between David's royal house and Saul's royal house. Abner gained more and more power in the royal house of Saul.

[7] While Saul was still alive, he had a concubine named Rizpah. She was the daughter of Aiah. Ish-Bosheth said to Abner, "Why did you have sex with my father's concubine?"

[8] Abner burned with anger because of what Ish-Bosheth said. He answered, "Do you think I'm only a dog's head? Am I on Judah's side? To this very day I've been true to the royal house of your father Saul. I've been true to his family and friends. I haven't handed you over to David. But now you claim that I've sinned with this woman!

[9] "I will do for David what the LORD promised him with an oath. If I don't, may God punish me greatly. [10] I'll take the kingdom away from Saul's royal house. I'll set up the throne of David's kingdom over Israel and Judah. He will rule from Dan all the way to Beersheba."

[11] Ish-Bosheth didn't dare to say another word to Abner. He was much too afraid of him.

[12] Then Abner sent messengers to David to speak for him. They said, "Who will rule over this land? Make a covenant with me. Then I'll help you bring all of the people of Israel over to your side."

[13] "Good," said David. "I will make a covenant with you. But there's one thing I want you to do. Bring Saul's daughter Michal to me. Don't come to see me unless she's with you."

[14] Then David sent messengers to Saul's son Ish-Bosheth. He ordered them to say, "Give me my wife Michal. She was promised to me. I paid for her with the skins I cut off when I circumcised 100 Philistines."

[15] So Ish-Bosheth gave the order. He sent men who took Michal away from her husband Paltiel. Paltiel was the son of Laish. [16] But her husband followed her to Bahurim. He was crying all the way. Then Abner said to him, "Go back home!" So he did.

[17] Abner talked with the elders of Israel. He said, "For some time you have wanted to make David your king. [18] Now do it! The LORD made a promise to David. He said, 'I will save my people Israel from the powerful hand of the Philistines. I will also save them from all of their enemies. I will save them through my servant David.' "

[19] Abner also spoke to the people of Benjamin in person. Then he went to Hebron to tell David everything. He told him what Israel and all of the people of Benjamin wanted to do. [20] Abner had 20 men with him. They came to David at Hebron. So David prepared a big dinner for Abner and his men.

[21] Then Abner said to David, "Let me go right now. I'll gather together all of the people of Israel for you. After all, you are now my king and master. The people can make a covenant with you. Then you can rule over everyone you want to." So David sent Abner away. And he went in peace.

JOAB MURDERS ABNER

[22] Just then David's men and Joab came back from attacking their enemies. They brought with them the large amount of goods they had taken. But Abner wasn't with David in Hebron anymore. That's because David had sent him away, and he had gone in peace.

[23] Joab and all of the soldiers who were with him arrived. Then he was told that Abner, the son of Ner, had come to see the king. He was told that the king had sent Abner away. He was also told that Abner had gone in peace.

[24] So Joab went to the king. He said, "What have you done? Abner came to you. Why did you let him get away? Now he's gone! [25] You know what Abner, the son of Ner, is like. He came to trick you. He wanted to watch your every move. He came to find out everything you are doing."

[26] Then Joab left David. He sent messengers to get Abner. They brought Abner back from the well of Sirah. But David didn't know about it.

²⁷When Abner returned to Hebron, Joab took him to one side. He brought him to the entrance of the city gate. Joab acted as if he wanted to speak to him in private. But he really wanted to get even with him. That's because Abner had spilled the blood of Joab's brother Asahel. So Joab stabbed him in the stomach. And Abner died.

²⁸Later on, David heard about it. He said, "I and the people of my kingdom aren't guilty of spilling the blood of Abner, the son of Ner. We are free of blame forever in the sight of the LORD. ²⁹"May Joab and his whole family line be held accountable for spilling Abner's blood! May someone in Joab's family always have an open sore or skin disease. May someone in his family always have to use a crutch to walk. May someone in his family be killed with a sword. And may someone in his family never have enough food to eat."

³⁰Joab and his brother Abishai murdered Abner. They did it because he had killed their brother Asahel in the battle at Gibeon.

³¹David spoke to Joab and all of the people who were with him. He said, "Tear your clothes. Put on black clothes. Sob when you walk in front of Abner's body." King David himself walked behind it.

³²Abner's body was buried in Hebron. The king sobbed out loud at Abner's tomb. So did the rest of the people.

³³King David sang a song of sadness over Abner. He said,

"Should Abner have died as sinful
    people do?
³⁴ His hands were not tied.
    His feet were not chained.
He died as if he had been killed by
    evil people."

All of the people sobbed over Abner again.

³⁵Then all of them came and begged David to eat something. They wanted him to eat while it was still day. But David took an oath. He said, "I won't taste bread or anything else before the sun goes down. If I do, may God punish me greatly!"

³⁶All of the people heard it and were pleased. In fact, everything the king did pleased them. ³⁷So on that day all of the people of Judah and Israel understood. They knew that the king didn't have anything to do with the murder of Abner, the son of Ner.

³⁸The king spoke to his men. He said, "Don't you realize that a great commander has died in Israel today? ³⁹I'm the anointed king. But today I'm weak. These sons of Zeruiah are too powerful for me. May the LORD pay back the one who killed Abner! May he pay him back for the evil thing he has done!"

ISH-BOSHETH IS MURDERED

4 Ish-Bosheth, the son of Saul, heard that Abner had died in Hebron. Then he wasn't so brave anymore. And all of the people of Israel became alarmed.

²Two men in Ish-Bosheth's army led small companies that attacked their enemies. The names of the men were Baanah and Recab. They were sons of Rimmon from the town of Beeroth. Rimmon was from the tribe of Benjamin. Beeroth is considered to be part of Benjamin. ³That's because the people who used to live in Beeroth had run away to Gittaim. They have lived there as outsiders to this very day.

⁴Jonathan, the son of Saul, had a son named Mephibosheth. Both of Mephibosheth's feet were hurt. He was five years old when the news that Saul and Jonathan had died came from Jezreel. His nurse picked him up and ran. But as she hurried to get away, he fell down. That's how his feet were hurt.

⁵Recab and Baanah started out for the house of Ish-Bosheth. They were the sons of Rimmon from Beeroth. They arrived there during the hottest time of the day. Ish-Bosheth was taking his early afternoon nap. ⁶Recab and his brother Baanah went into the inside part of the house. They acted as if they were going to get some wheat. Instead, they stabbed Ish-Bosheth in the stomach. Then they slipped away.

⁷They had gone into the house while Ish-Bosheth was lying on his bed in his bedroom. They stabbed him and killed him. Then they cut off his head and took it with them. They traveled all night through the Arabah Valley.

⁸They brought the head of Ish-Bosheth to King David at Hebron. They said to him, "Here's the head of Ish-Bosheth, the son of Saul. Saul was your enemy. He often tried to kill you. Today the LORD has paid Saul and his family back. He has let you get even with them. You are our king and master."

⁹David gave an answer to Recab and his brother Baanah. They were the sons of Rimmon of Beeroth. David said, "The LORD has saved me from all of my troubles. ¹⁰A man once told me, 'Saul is dead.' He thought he was bringing me good news. But I grabbed hold of him. I had him put to death in Ziklag. That's the reward I gave him for his news! And that's just as sure as the LORD is alive.

¹¹"Now you evil men have killed a man in his own house. He hadn't done anything wrong. You killed him while he was lying on his own bed. You spilled his blood. So shouldn't I spill your blood? Shouldn't I wipe you off the face of the earth?"

¹²Then David gave an order to his men. They killed Recab and Baanah. They cut off their hands and feet. They hung their bodies by the pool in Hebron. But they buried the head of Ish-Bosheth in Abner's tomb at Hebron.

DAVID BECOMES KING OVER ISRAEL

5 All of the tribes of Israel came to see David at Hebron. They said, "We are your own flesh and blood. ²In the past, Saul was our king. But you led the men of Israel on their military campaigns. And the LORD said to you, 'You will be the shepherd over my people Israel. You will become their ruler.' "

³All of the elders of Israel came to see King David at Hebron. There the king made a covenant with them in the sight of the LORD. They anointed David as king over Israel.

⁴David was 30 years old when he became king. He ruled for 40 years. ⁵In Hebron he ruled over Judah for seven and a half years. In Jerusalem he ruled over all of Israel and Judah for 33 years.

DAVID CAPTURES JERUSALEM

⁶The king and his men marched to Jerusalem. They went to attack the Jebusites who lived there.

The Jebusites said to David, "You won't get in here. Even blind people and those who are disabled can keep you from coming in." They thought, "David can't get in here."

⁷But David captured the fort of Zion. It became known as the City of David.

⁸On that day David said, "Anyone who wins the battle over the Jebusites will have to crawl through the water tunnel to get into the city. That's the only way he can reach those 'disabled and blind' enemies of mine." That's why people say, "Those who are 'blind and disabled' won't enter David's palace."

⁹David moved into the fort. He called it the City of David. He built up the area around the fort. He filled in the low places. He started at the bottom and worked his way up. ¹⁰David became more and more powerful. That's because the LORD God who rules over all was with him.

¹¹Hiram was king of Tyre. He sent messengers to David. He sent cedar logs along with them. He also sent skilled workers. They worked with wood and stone. They built a palace for David.

¹²David knew that the LORD had made his position as king secure. He knew that he had made him king over the whole nation of Israel. He knew that the LORD had greatly honored his kingdom. The LORD had done it because the Israelites were his people.

¹³After David left Hebron, he got more concubines and wives in Jerusalem. More sons and daughters were born to him there. ¹⁴Here is a list of the children who were born to him in Jerusalem. Their names were Shammua, Shobab, Nathan, Solomon, ¹⁵Ibhar, Elishua, Nepheg, Japhia, ¹⁶Elishama, Eliada and Eliphelet.

DAVID WINS THE BATTLE OVER THE PHILISTINES

¹⁷The Philistines heard that David had been anointed king over Israel. So their whole army went to look for him.

But David heard about it. He went down to his usual place of safety. [18]The Philistines had come and spread out in the Valley of Rephaim.

[19]So David asked the LORD for advice. He said, "Should I go and attack the Philistines? Will you hand them over to me?"

The LORD answered him, "Go. You can be sure that I will hand the Philistines over to you."

[20]So David went to Baal Perazim. There he won the battle over the Philistines. He said, "The LORD has broken through against my enemies when I've attacked them, just as water breaks through a dam." That's why the place was called Baal Perazim. [21]The Philistines left the statues of their gods there. So David and his men carried the statues off.

[22]Once more the Philistines came up. They spread out in the Valley of Rephaim. [23]So David asked the LORD for advice. The LORD answered, "Do not go straight up. Instead, circle around behind them. Attack them in front of the balsam trees. [24]Listen for the sound of marching in the tops of the trees. Then move quickly. The sound will mean that I have gone out in front of you. I will strike down the Philistine army." [25]So David did just as the LORD had commanded him. He struck down the Philistines. He struck them down from Gibeon all the way to Gezer.

DAVID BRINGS THE ARK TO JERUSALEM

6 Again David brought together the best soldiers in Israel. The total number was 30,000. [2]He and all of his men started out from Baalah in Judah. They wanted to bring the ark of God up to Jerusalem from there. The ark is named after the LORD. He is the LORD who rules over all. He sits on his throne between the cherubim that are on the ark.

[3]The ark of God was placed on a new cart. Then it was brought from Abinadab's house, which was on a hill. Uzzah and Ahio were guiding the cart. They were the sons of Abinadab. [4]The ark of God was on the cart. Ahio was walking in front of it.

[5]David was celebrating with all his might in the sight of the LORD. So was the whole community of Israel. All of them were singing songs. They were also playing harps, lyres, tambourines, rattles and cymbals.

[6]They came to the threshing floor of Nacon. The oxen nearly fell there. So Uzzah reached out and took hold of the ark of God. [7]Then the LORD's anger burned against Uzzah. That's because what Uzzah did showed that he didn't have any respect for the LORD. So God struck him down. He died there beside the ark of God.

[8]David was angry because the LORD's burning anger had broken out against Uzzah. That's why the place is still called Perez Uzzah to this very day.

[9]David was afraid of the LORD that day. He asked, "How can the ark of the LORD ever be brought to me?" [10]He didn't want to take the ark of the LORD to be with him in the City of David. Instead, he took it to the house of Obed-Edom. Obed-Edom was from Gath. [11]The ark of the LORD remained in Obed-Edom's house for three months. And the LORD blessed him and his whole family.

[12]King David was told, "The LORD has blessed the family of Obed-Edom. He has also blessed everything that belongs to him. That's because the ark of God is in Obed-Edom's house."

So David went down there and brought up the ark. With great joy he brought it up from the house of Obed-Edom. He took it to the City of David. [13]Those who were carrying the ark of the LORD took six steps forward. Then David sacrificed a bull and a fat calf. [14]David was wearing a sacred linen apron. He danced in the sight of the LORD with all his might. [15]He did it while he was bringing up the ark of the LORD. The whole community of Israel helped him bring it up. They shouted. They blew trumpets.

[16]The ark of the LORD was brought into the City of David. Saul's daughter Michal was watching from a window. She saw King David leaping and dancing in the sight of the LORD. That made her hate him in her heart.

¹⁷The ark of the LORD was brought into Jerusalem. It was put in its place in the tent David had set up for it. David sacrificed burnt offerings and friendship offerings to the LORD.

¹⁸After he finished sacrificing those offerings, he blessed the people in the name of the LORD who rules over all. ¹⁹He gave to each Israelite man and woman a loaf of bread. He also gave each one a date cake and a raisin cake. Then all of the people went home.

²⁰David returned home to bless his family. Saul's daughter Michal came out to meet him. She said, "You are the king of Israel. You have really brought honor to yourself today, haven't you? You have taken off your royal robe right in front of the female slaves of your officials. You acted like someone who is very foolish!"

²¹David said to Michal, "I did it to honor the LORD. He chose me instead of your father or anyone else in Saul's family. He appointed me ruler over his people Israel. I will celebrate in honor of the LORD. ²²And that's not all. I will bring even less honor to myself. I will bring even more shame on myself. But those female slaves you spoke about will honor me."

²³Saul's daughter Michal didn't have any children as long as she lived.

GOD MAKES A PROMISE TO DAVID

7 The king settled down in his palace. The LORD had given him peace and rest from all of his enemies who were around him.

²Then the king spoke to the prophet Nathan. He said, "Here I am, living in a palace that has beautiful cedar walls. But the ark of God remains in a tent."

³Nathan replied to the king, "Go ahead and do what you want to. The LORD is with you."

⁴That night the word of the LORD came to Nathan. The LORD said,

⁵"Go and speak to my servant David. Tell him, 'The LORD says, "Are you the one to build me a house to live in? ⁶I have not lived in a house from the day I brought the people of Israel up out of Egypt until now. I have been moving from place to place. I have been living in a tent. ⁷I have moved from place to place with all of the people of Israel. I commanded their rulers to be shepherds over them. I never asked any of those rulers, 'Why haven't you built me a house that has beautiful cedar walls?' " '

⁸"So tell my servant David, 'The LORD who rules over all says, "I took you away from the grasslands. That's where you were taking care of your father's sheep and goats. I made you ruler over my people Israel. ⁹I have been with you everywhere you have gone. I cut off all of your enemies when you were attacking them.

" ' "Now I will make you famous. Your name will be just as respected as the names of the most important people on earth. ¹⁰I will provide a place where my people Israel can live. I will plant them in the land. Then they will have a home of their own. They will not be bothered anymore. Evil people will no longer crush them, as they did at first. ¹¹That is what your enemies have done ever since I appointed leaders over my people Israel. But I will give you peace and rest from all of them.

" ' "I tell you that I myself will set up a royal house for you. ¹²Some day your life will come to an end. You will join the members of your family who have already died. Then I will make one of your own sons the next king after you. And I will make his kingdom secure. ¹³He is the one who will build a house where I will put my Name.

" ' "I will set up the throne of his kingdom. It will last forever. ¹⁴I will be his father. And he will be my son. When he does what is wrong, I will use other men to beat him with rods and whips. ¹⁵I took my love away from Saul. I removed him from being king. You were there when I did it. But I will never take my love away from your son.

16" ' "Your royal house and your kingdom will last forever in my sight. Your throne will last forever." ' "

17Nathan reported to David all of the words that the LORD had spoken to him.

DAVID PRAYS TO THE LORD

18Then King David went into the holy tent. He sat down in front of the LORD. He said,

"LORD and King, who am I? My family isn't important. So why have you brought me this far? 19I would have thought that you had already done more than enough for me. But now, LORD and King, you have also spoken about what is going to happen to my royal house in days to come. LORD and King, is this your usual way of dealing with people? 20"What more can I say to you? LORD and King, you know all about me. 21You have done a wonderful thing. You have made it known to me. You have done it because that's what you said you would do. It's exactly what you wanted to do for me. 22"LORD and King, how great you are! There isn't anyone like you. There isn't any God but you. We have heard about it with our own ears. 23"Who is like your people Israel? God, we are the one nation on earth you have saved. You have set us free for yourself. Your name has become famous. You have done great and wonderful things. You have driven out nations and their gods to make room for your people. You saved us when you set us free from Egypt. 24You made Israel your very own people forever. LORD, you have become our God. 25"And now, LORD God, keep forever the promise you have made to me and my royal house. Do exactly as you promised. 26Then your name will be honored forever. People will say, 'The LORD rules over all. He is God over Is-

rael.' My royal house will be made secure in your sight.

27"LORD who rules over all, you are the God of Israel. Here's what you have shown me. You told me, 'I will build you a royal house.' So I can boldly offer this prayer to you. 28LORD and King, you are God! Your words can be trusted. You have promised many good things to me.

29"Now please bless my royal house. Then it will continue forever in your sight. LORD and King, you have spoken. Because you have given my royal house your blessing, it will be blessed forever."

DAVID WINS MANY BATTLES

8 While David was king of Israel, he won many battles over the Philistines. He brought them under his control. He took Metheg Ammah away from them.

2David also won the battle over the people of Moab. He made them lie down on the ground. Then he measured them off with a piece of rope. He put two-thirds of them to death. He let the other third remain alive. So the Moabites were brought under David's rule. They gave him the gifts he required them to bring him.

3David fought against Hadadezer, the son of Rehob. Hadadezer was king of Zobah. He had gone to take back control of the land along the Euphrates River. 4David captured 1,000 of Hadadezer's chariots, 7,000 chariot riders and 20,000 soldiers on foot. He cut the legs of all but 100 of the chariot horses.

5The Arameans of Damascus came to help Hadadezer, the king of Zobah. But David struck down 22,000 of them. 6He stationed some soldiers in the Aramean kingdom of Damascus. The people of Aram were brought under his rule. They gave him the gifts he required them to bring him. The LORD helped David win his battles everywhere he went.

7David took the gold shields that belonged to the officers of Hadadezer. He brought the shields to Jerusalem. 8He took a huge amount of bronze from Tebah and Berothai. Those towns belonged to Hadadezer.

⁹Tou was king of Hamath. He heard that David had won the battle over the entire army of Hadadezer. ¹⁰So Tou sent his son Joram to King David. Joram greeted David. He praised him because he had won the battle over Hadadezer. Hadadezer had been at war with Tou. So Joram brought with him articles that were made out of silver, gold and bronze.

¹¹King David set those articles apart for the LORD. He had done the same thing with the silver and gold he had taken from the other nations he had brought under his control. ¹²Those nations were Edom, Moab, Ammon, Philistia and Amalek. He also set apart for the LORD what he had taken from Hadadezer, the son of Rehob. Hadadezer was king of Zobah.

¹³David returned after he had struck down 18,000 men of Edom in the Valley of Salt. He became famous for doing it.

¹⁴He stationed some soldiers all through Edom. The whole nation of Edom was brought under his rule. The LORD helped David win his battles everywhere he went.

DAVID'S OFFICIALS

¹⁵David ruled over the whole nation of Israel. He did what was fair and right for all of his people. ¹⁶Joab, the son of Zeruiah, was commander over the army. Jehoshaphat, the son of Ahilud, kept the records. ¹⁷Zadok, the son of Ahitub, was a priest. Ahimelech, the son of Abiathar, was also a priest. Seraiah was the secretary. ¹⁸Benaiah, the son of Jehoiada, was commander over the Kerethites and Pelethites. And David's sons were royal advisers.

DAVID IS KIND TO MEPHIBOSHETH

9 David asked, "Is anyone left from the royal house of Saul? If there is, I want to be kind to him because of Jonathan."

²Ziba was a servant in Saul's family. David sent for him to come and see him. The king said to him, "Are you Ziba?"

"I'm ready to serve you," he replied.

³The king asked, "Isn't anyone left from the royal house of Saul? God has been very kind to me. I would like to be kind to someone in the same way."

Ziba answered the king, "A son of Jonathan is still living. Both of his feet were hurt."

⁴"Where is he?" the king asked.

Ziba answered, "He's in the town of Lo Debar. He's staying at the house of Makir, the son of Ammiel."

⁵So King David had Mephibosheth brought from Makir's house in Lo Debar.

⁶Mephibosheth came to David. He was the son of Jonathan, the son of Saul. Mephibosheth bowed down to David to show him respect.

David said, "Mephibosheth!"

"I'm ready to serve you," he replied.

⁷"Don't be afraid," David told him. "You can be sure that I will be kind to you because of your father Jonathan. I'll give back to you all of the land that belonged to your grandfather Saul. And I'll always provide what you need."

⁸Mephibosheth bowed down to David. He said, "Who am I? Why should you pay attention to me? I'm nothing but a dead dog."

⁹Then the king sent for Saul's servant Ziba. He said to him, "I'm giving your master's grandson everything that belonged to Saul and his family. ¹⁰You and your sons and your servants must farm the land for him. You must bring in the crops. Then he'll be taken care of. I'll always provide what he needs." Ziba had 15 sons and 20 servants.

¹¹Then Ziba said to the king, "I'll do anything you command me to do. You are my king and master." So David provided what Mephibosheth needed. He treated him like one of the king's sons.

¹²Mephibosheth had a young son named Mica. All of the members of Ziba's family became servants of Mephibosheth. ¹³Mephibosheth lived in Jerusalem. The king always provided what he needed. Both of his feet were hurt.

DAVID GOES TO WAR AGAINST THE PEOPLE OF AMMON

10 The king of Ammon died. His son Hanun became the next king after him. ²David thought, "I'm going to be kind to Hanun. His father Nahash was kind to me." So David sent messengers to Hanun. He wanted them to tell Hanun how sad he was that Hanun's father had died.

David's messengers went to the land of Ammon. ³The Ammonite nobles spoke to their master Hanun. They said, "David has sent messengers to tell you he is sad. They say he wants to honor your father. But the real reason they've come is to look the city over. They want to destroy it."

⁴So Hanun grabbed hold of David's men. He shaved off half of each man's beard. He cut their clothes off just below the waist and left them half naked. Then he sent them away.

⁵David was told about it. So he sent messengers to his men because they were filled with shame. King David said to them, "Stay at Jericho until your beards grow out again. Then come back here."

⁶The Ammonites realized that what they had done had made David very angry with them. So they hired 20,000 Aramean soldiers who were on foot. The soldiers came from Beth Rehob and Zobah. The Ammonites also hired the king of Maacah and 1,000 men. And they hired 12,000 men from Tob.

⁷David heard about it. So he sent Joab out with the entire army of Israel's fighting men.

⁸The Ammonites marched out. They took up their battle positions at the entrance of their city gate. The Arameans of Zobah and Rehob gathered their troops together in the open country. So did the men of Tob and Maacah.

⁹Joab saw that there were lines of soldiers in front of him and behind him. So he chose some of the best troops in Israel. He sent them to march out against the Arameans.

¹⁰He put the rest of the men under the command of his brother Abishai. Joab sent them to march out against the Ammonites. ¹¹He said, "Suppose the Arameans are too strong for me. Then you must come and help me. But suppose the Ammonites are too strong for you. Then I'll come and help you.

¹²"Be strong. Let's be brave as we fight for our people and the cities of our God. The LORD will do what he thinks is best."

¹³Then Joab and the troops who were with him marched out to attack the Arameans. They ran away from him. ¹⁴The Ammonites saw that the Arameans were running away. So they ran away from Abishai. They went inside the city. After Joab had fought against the Ammonites, he went back to Jerusalem.

¹⁵The Arameans saw that they had been driven away by Israel. So they brought their troops together. ¹⁶Hadadezer had some Arameans brought from east of the Euphrates River. They went to Helam under the command of Shobach. He was the commander of Hadadezer's army.

¹⁷David was told about it. So he gathered the whole army of Israel together. They went across the Jordan River to Helam. The Arameans lined up their soldiers to go to war against David. They began to fight against him. ¹⁸But then they ran away from Israel. David killed 700 of their chariot riders. He killed 40,000 of their soldiers who were on foot. He also struck down Shobach, the commander of their army. Shobach died there.

¹⁹All of the kings who were under the rule of Hadadezer saw that Israel had won the battle over them. So they made a peace treaty with the Israelites. They were brought under Israel's rule. After that, the Arameans were afraid to help the Ammonites anymore.

DAVID AND BATHSHEBA

11 It was spring. It was the time when kings go off to war. So David sent Joab out with the king's special troops and the whole army of Israel. They destroyed the Ammonites. They went to the city of Rabbah. They surrounded it and got ready to attack it. But David remained in Jerusalem.

²One evening David got up from his bed. He walked around on the roof of his palace. From the roof he saw a woman taking a bath. She was very beautiful.

³David sent a messenger to find out

who she was. The messenger returned and said, "She is Bathsheba. She's the daughter of Eliam. She's the wife of Uriah. He's a Hittite."

[4] Then David sent messengers to get her. She came to him. And he slept with her. Then she went back home. All of that took place after she had already made herself "clean" from her monthly period.

[5] Later, Bathsheba found out she was pregnant. She sent a message to David. It said, "I'm pregnant."

[6] So David sent a message to Joab. It said, "Send me Uriah, the Hittite." Joab sent him to David.

[7] Uriah came to David. David asked him how Joab and the soldiers were doing. He also asked him how the war was going.

[8] David said to Uriah, "Go home and enjoy some time with your wife." So Uriah left the palace. Then the king sent him a gift.

[9] But Uriah didn't go home. Instead, he slept at the entrance to the palace. He stayed there with all of his master's servants.

[10] David was told, "Uriah didn't go home." So he sent for Uriah. He said to him, "You have been away for a long time. Why didn't you go home?"

[11] Uriah said to David, "The ark and the army of Israel and Judah are out there in tents. My master Joab and your special troops are camped in the open fields. How could I go to my house to eat and drink? How could I go there and make love to my wife? I could never do a thing like that. And that's just as sure as you are alive!"

[12] Then David said to him, "Stay here one more day. Tomorrow I'll send you back to the battle." So Uriah remained in Jerusalem that day and the next.

[13] David invited Uriah to eat and drink with him. David got him drunk. But Uriah still didn't go home. In the evening he went out and slept on his mat. He stayed there among his master's servants.

[14] The next morning David wrote a letter to Joab. He sent it along with Uriah. [15] In it he wrote, "Put Uriah on the front lines. That's where the fighting is the heaviest. Then pull your men back from him. When you do, the Am-

monites will strike him down and kill him."

[16] So Joab attacked the city. He put Uriah at a place where he knew the strongest enemy fighters were. [17] The troops came out of the city. They fought against Joab. Some of the men in David's army were killed. Uriah, the Hittite, also died.

[18] Joab sent David a full report of the battle. [19] He told the messenger, "Tell the king everything that happened in the battle. When you are finished, [20] his anger might explode. He might ask you, 'Why did you go so close to the city to fight against it? Didn't you know that the enemy soldiers would shoot arrows down from the wall? [21] Don't you remember how Abimelech, the son of Jerub-Besheth, was killed? A woman dropped a large millstone on him from the wall. That's how he died in Thebez. So why did you go so close to the wall?' If the king asks you that, tell him, 'Your servant Uriah, the Hittite, is also dead.' "

[22] The messenger started out for Jerusalem. When he arrived there, he told David everything Joab had sent him to say. [23] The messenger said to David, "The men who were in the city were more powerful than we were. They came out to fight against us in the open. But we drove them back to the entrance of the city gate. [24] Then those who were armed with bows shot arrows at us from the wall. Some of your special troops were killed. Your servant Uriah, the Hittite, is also dead."

[25] David told the messenger, "Tell Joab, 'Don't get upset over what happened. Swords kill one person as well as another. So keep on attacking the city. Destroy it.' Tell that to Joab. It will cheer him up."

[26] Uriah's wife heard that her husband was dead. She sobbed over him. [27] When her time of sadness was over, David had her brought to his house. She became his wife. And she had a son by him. But the LORD wasn't pleased with what David had done.

DAVID'S SON DIES

12 The LORD sent the prophet Nathan to David. When Nathan came to him, he said, "Two men lived in the same town. One was rich. The other was poor. ²The rich man had a very large number of sheep and cattle. ³But all the poor man had was one little female lamb. He had bought it. He raised it. It grew up with him and his children. It shared his food. It drank from his cup. It even slept in his arms. It was just like a daughter to him.

⁴"One day a traveler came to the rich man. The rich man wanted to prepare a meal for him. But he didn't want to kill one of his own sheep or cattle. Instead, he took the little female lamb that belonged to the poor man. Then he cooked it for the traveler who had come to him."

⁵David burned with anger against the rich man. He said to Nathan, "The man who did that is worthy of death. And that's just as sure as the LORD is alive. ⁶The man must pay back four times as much as that lamb was worth. How could he do such a thing? And he wasn't even sorry he had done it."

⁷Then Nathan said to David, "You are the man! The LORD, the God of Israel, says, 'I anointed you king over Israel. I saved you from Saul's powerful hand. ⁸I gave you everything that belonged to your master Saul. I even put his wives into your arms. I made you king over the people of Israel and Judah. And if all of that had not been enough for you, I would have given you even more.

⁹" 'Why did you turn your back on what I told you to do? You did what is evil in my sight. You made sure that Uriah, the Hittite, would be killed in battle. You took his wife to be your own. You let the men of Ammon kill him with their swords.

¹⁰" 'So time after time members of your own royal house will be killed with swords. That's because you turned your back on me. You took the wife of Uriah, the Hittite, to be your own.'

¹¹"The LORD also says, 'I am going to bring trouble on you. It will come from your own family. I will take your wives away. Your own eyes will see it. I will give your wives to a man who is close to you. He will lie with them in the middle of the day. ¹²You committed your sins in secret. But I will make

sure that the sin the man commits with your wives will take place in the middle of the day. Everyone in Israel will see it.' "

¹³Then David said to Nathan, "I have sinned against the LORD."

Nathan replied, "The LORD has taken away your sin. You aren't going to die. ¹⁴But you have dared to make fun of the LORD. So the son who has been born to you will die."

¹⁵Nathan went home. Then the LORD made the child that had been born to Uriah's wife by David very sick.

¹⁶David begged God to heal the child. David didn't eat anything. He spent his nights lying on the ground. ¹⁷His most trusted servants stood beside him. They wanted him to get up from the ground. But he refused to do it. And he wouldn't eat any food with them.

¹⁸On the seventh day the child died. David's servants were afraid to tell him the child was dead. They thought, "While the child was still alive, we spoke to David. But he wouldn't listen to us. So how can we tell him the child is dead? He might do something terrible to himself."

¹⁹David saw that his servants were whispering to each other. Then he realized the child was dead. "Has the child died?" he asked.

"Yes," they replied. "He's dead."

²⁰Then David got up from the ground. After he washed himself, he put on lotions. He changed his clothes. He went into the house of the LORD and worshiped him. Then he went to his own house. He asked for some food. They served it to him. And he ate it.

²¹His servants asked him, "Why are you acting like this? While the child was still alive, you wouldn't eat anything. You cried a lot. But now that the child is dead, you get up and eat!"

²²He answered, "While the child was still alive, I didn't eat anything. And I cried a lot. I thought, 'Who knows? The LORD might show favor to me. He might let the child live.' ²³But now he's dead. So why should I go without eating? Can I bring him back to life again? Someday I'll go to him. But he won't return to me."

²⁴Then David comforted his wife Bathsheba. He went to her and made love to her. Some time later she had a son. He was given the name Solomon. The LORD loved him. ²⁵So the LORD sent a message through the prophet Nathan. It said, "Name the boy Jedidiah."

DAVID CAPTURES THE CITY OF RABBAH

²⁶During that time, Joab fought against Rabbah. It was the royal city of the Ammonites. It had high walls around it. Joab was about to capture it. ²⁷He sent messengers to David. He told them to say, "I have fought against Rabbah. I've taken control of its water supply. ²⁸So bring the rest of the troops together. Surround the city and get ready to attack. Then capture it. If you don't, I'll capture it myself. Then it will be named after me."

²⁹So David brought the whole army together and went to Rabbah. He attacked it and captured it. ³⁰He took the gold crown off the head of the king of Ammon. The crown weighed 75 pounds. It had jewels in it. It was placed on David's head. He took a huge amount of goods from the city. ³¹He brought out the people who were there. He made them work with saws and iron picks and axes. He forced them to make bricks. He did that to all of the towns in Ammon. Then he and his entire army returned to Jerusalem.

AMNON RAPES TAMAR

13 Some time later, David's son Amnon fell in love with Tamar. She was the beautiful sister of Absalom. He was another one of David's sons.

²Amnon's sister Tamar was a virgin. It seemed impossible for him to do what he wanted to do with her. But he wanted her so much it almost made him sick.

³Amnon had a friend named Jonadab. He was the son of David's brother Shimeah. Jonadab was a very clever man. ⁴He asked Amnon, "You are the king's son, aren't you? So why do you look so worn out every morning? Won't you tell me?"

Amnon answered, "I'm in love with Tamar. She's the sister of my brother Absalom."

⁵"Go to bed," Jonadab said. "Pretend to be sick. Your father will come to see you. When he does, tell him, 'I would like my sister Tamar to come and give me something to eat. Let her prepare the food right here in front of me where I can watch her. Then she can feed it to me.' "

⁶So Amnon went to bed. He pretended to be sick. The king came to see him. Amnon said to him, "I would like my sister Tamar to come here. I want to watch her make some special bread. Then she can feed it to me."

⁷David sent a message to Tamar at the palace. It said, "Go to your brother Amnon's house. Prepare some food for him."

⁸So Tamar went to the house of her brother Amnon. He was lying in bed. She got some dough and mixed it. She shaped the bread right there in front of him. And she baked it. ⁹Then she took the bread out of the pan and served it to him. But he refused to eat it.

"Send everyone out of here," Amnon said. So everyone left him.

¹⁰Then he said to Tamar, "Bring the food here into my bedroom. Please feed it to me."

So Tamar picked up the bread she had prepared. She brought it to her brother Amnon in his bedroom. ¹¹She took it to him so he could eat it.

But he grabbed hold of her. He said, "My sister, come and have sex with me."

¹²"Don't do this, my brother!" she said to him. "Don't force me to have sex with you. An evil thing like that should never be done in Israel! Don't do it! ¹³What about me? How could I ever get rid of my shame? And what about you? You would be as foolish as any evil person in Israel. Please speak to the king. He won't keep me from getting married to you."

¹⁴But Amnon refused to listen to her. He was stronger than she was. So he raped her.

¹⁵Then Amnon was filled with deep hatred for Tamar. In fact, he hated her now more than he had loved her before. He said to her, "Get up! Get out!"

¹⁶"No!" she said to him. "Don't send me away. That would be worse than what you have already done to me."

But he refused to listen to her. ¹⁷He sent for his personal servant. He said, "Get this woman out of here. Lock the door behind her."

¹⁸So his servant threw her out. Then he locked the door behind her.

Tamar was wearing a beautiful robe. It was the kind of robe the virgin daughters of the king wore. ¹⁹She put ashes on her head. She tore the beautiful robe she was wearing. She put her hands on her head and went away. She was sobbing out loud as she went.

²⁰When her brother Absalom saw her, he spoke to her. He said, "Has Amnon, that brother of yours, forced you to have sex with him? My sister, don't let it upset you. Don't let it bother you. He's your brother."

After that, Tamar lived in her brother Absalom's house. She was very lonely.

²¹King David heard about everything that had happened. So he became very angry.

²²Absalom never said a word of any kind to Amnon. He hated Amnon because he had brought shame on his sister Tamar.

ABSALOM KILLS AMNON

²³Two years later, Absalom invited all of the king's sons to come to Baal Hazor. It was near the border of Ephraim. The workers who clipped the wool off Absalom's sheep were there.

²⁴Absalom went to the king. He said, "I've had my workers come to clip the wool. Will you and your officials please join me?"

²⁵"No, my son," the king replied. "All of us shouldn't go. It would be too much trouble for you." Although Absalom begged him, the king still refused to go. But he gave Absalom his blessing.

²⁶Then Absalom said, "If you won't come, please let my brother Amnon come with us."

The king asked him, "Why should he go with you?" ²⁷But Absalom begged him. So the king sent Amnon with him. He also sent the rest of his sons.

²⁸Absalom ordered his men, "Listen! When Amnon has had too much wine to drink, I'll say to you, 'Strike Amnon down.' When I do, kill him. Don't be afraid. I've given you an order, haven't I? Be strong and brave."

²⁹So Absalom's men killed Amnon, just as Absalom had ordered. Then all of the king's sons got on their mules and rode away.

³⁰While they were on their way, a report came to David. It said, "Absalom has struck down all of your sons. Not one of them is left alive."

³¹The king stood up and tore his clothes. Then he lay down on the ground. All of his servants stood near him. They had also torn their clothes.

³²Jonadab, the son of David's brother Shimeah, spoke up. He said, "You shouldn't think that all of the princes have been killed. The only one who is dead is Amnon. Absalom had planned to kill him ever since the day Amnon raped his sister Tamar. ³³You are my king and master. You shouldn't be concerned about this report. It's not true that all of your sons are dead. The only one who is dead is Amnon."

³⁴While all of that was taking place, Absalom ran away.

The man on guard duty at Jerusalem looked up. He saw many people coming on the road west of him. They were coming down the side of the hill. He went and spoke to the king. He said, "I see men coming down the road from Horonaim. They are coming down the side of the hill."

³⁵Jonadab said to the king, "See, your sons are coming. It has happened just as I said it would."

³⁶As he finished speaking, the king's sons came in. They were sobbing out loud. The king and all of his servants were also sobbing very bitterly.

³⁷When Absalom ran away, he went to Talmai, the son of Ammihud. Talmai was king of Geshur. King David sobbed over his son every day.

³⁸So Absalom ran away and went to Geshur. He stayed there for three years.

³⁹After some time the king got over his sorrow because of Amnon's death. Then he longed to go to Absalom.

ABSALOM RETURNS TO JERUSALEM

14 Joab, the son of Zeruiah, knew that the king longed to see Absalom. ²So Joab sent someone to Tekoa to have a wise woman brought back from there. Joab said to her, "Pretend you are filled with sadness. Put on black clothes. Don't use any makeup. Act like a woman who has spent many days sobbing over someone who has died. ³Then go to the king. Give him the message I'm about to give you." And Joab told her what to say.

⁴The woman from Tekoa went to the king. She bowed down with her face toward the ground. She did it to show him respect. She said, "King David, please help me!"

⁵The king asked her, "What's bothering you?"

She said, "I'm a widow. My husband is dead. ⁶I had two sons. They got into a fight with each other in the field. No one was there to separate them. One of my sons struck the other one down and killed him.

⁷"Now my whole family group has risen up against me. They say, 'Hand over the one who struck his brother down. Then we can put him to death for killing his brother. That will also get rid of the one who will receive the family property.' They want to kill the only living son I have left, just as someone would put out a burning coal. That would leave my husband without any son on the face of the earth to carry on his name."

⁸The king said to the woman, "Go home. I'll give an order to make sure you are taken care of."

⁹But the woman from Tekoa said to him, "You are my king and master. No matter what you do, I and my family will take the blame for it. You and your royal family won't be guilty of doing anything wrong."

¹⁰The king replied, "If people give you any trouble, bring them to me. They won't bother you again."

¹¹She said, "Please pray to the LORD your God. Pray that he will keep our nearest male relative from killing my other son. Then my son won't be destroyed."

"You can be sure that the LORD lives," the king said. "And you can be just as sure that not one hair of your son's head will fall to the ground."

¹²Then the woman said, "King David, please let me say something else to you."

"Go ahead," he replied.

¹³The woman said, "You are the king. So why have you done something that brings so much harm on God's people? When you do that, you hand down a sentence against yourself. You won't let the son you drove away come back. ¹⁴All of us must die. We are like water that is spilled on the ground. It can't be put back into the jar. But God doesn't take life away. Instead, he finds a way to bring back anyone who was driven away from him.

¹⁵"King David, I've come here to say this to you now. I've done it because people have made me afraid. I thought, 'I'll go and speak to the king. Perhaps he'll do what I'm asking. ¹⁶Perhaps he'll agree to save me from the man who is trying to cut off me and my son from the property God gave us.'

¹⁷"So now I'm saying, 'May what you have told me bring me peace and rest. You are like an angel of God. You know what is good and what is evil. May the LORD your God be with you.' "

¹⁸Then the king said to the woman, "I'm going to ask you a question. I want you to tell me the truth."

"Please ask me anything you want to," the woman said.

¹⁹The king asked, "Joab told you to say all of this, didn't he?"

The woman answered, "What you have told me is exactly right. And that's just as sure as you are alive. It's true that Joab directed me to do this. He told me everything he wanted me to say. ²⁰He did it to change the way things now are. You are as wise as an angel of God. You know everything that happens in the land."

²¹Later the king said to Joab, "All right. I'll do what you want. Go. Bring the young man Absalom back."

²²Joab bowed down with his face toward the ground. He did it to honor the king. And he asked God to bless

the king. He said, "You are my king and master. Today I know that you are pleased with me. You have given me what I asked for."

²³Then Joab went to Geshur. He brought Absalom back to Jerusalem. ²⁴But the king said, "He must go to his own house. I don't want him to come and see me."

So Absalom went to his own house. He didn't go to see the king.

²⁵In the whole land of Israel there wasn't any man as handsome as Absalom was. That's why everyone praised him. From the top of his head to the bottom of his feet he didn't have any flaws. ²⁶He used to cut his hair when it became too heavy for him. Then he would weigh it. It weighed five pounds in keeping with the standard weights that were used in the palace.

²⁷Three sons and a daughter were born to Absalom. The daughter's name was Tamar. She became a beautiful woman.

²⁸Absalom lived in Jerusalem for two years without going to see the king. ²⁹Then Absalom sent for Joab. He wanted to send him to the king. But Joab refused to come to Absalom. So Absalom sent for him a second time. But Joab still refused to come.

³⁰Then Absalom said to his servants, "Joab's field is next to mine. He has barley growing there. Go and set it on fire." So Absalom's servants set the field on fire.

³¹Joab finally went to Absalom's house. He said to Absalom, "Why did your servants set my field on fire?"

³²Absalom said to Joab, "I sent a message to you. It said, 'Come here. I want to send you to the king. I want you to ask him for me, "Why did you bring me back from Geshur? I would be better off if I were still there!" ' Now then, I want to go and see the king. If I'm guilty of doing anything wrong, let him put me to death."

³³So Joab went to the king and told him that. Then the king sent for Absalom. He came in and bowed down to the king with his face toward the ground. And the king kissed Absalom.

ABSALOM MAKES SECRET PLANS AGAINST DAVID

15 Some time later, Absalom got a chariot and horses for himself. He also got 50 men to run in front of him. ²He would get up early. He would stand by the side of the road that led to the city gate. Sometimes a person would come with a case for the king to decide. Then Absalom would call out to him, "What town are you from?"

He would answer, "I'm from one of the tribes of Israel."

³Absalom would say, "Look, your claims are based on the law. So you have every right to make them. But the king doesn't have anyone here who can listen to your case." ⁴Absalom would continue, "I wish I were appointed judge in the land! Then anyone who has a case or a claim could come to me. I would make sure he is treated fairly."

⁵Sometimes people would approach Absalom and bow down to him. Then he would reach out his hand. He would take hold of them and kiss them.

⁶Absalom did that to all of the people of Israel who came to the king with their cases or claims. That's why the hearts of the people were turned toward him.

⁷After Absalom had lived in Jerusalem for four years, he went and spoke to the king. He said, "Let me go to Hebron. I want to keep a promise I made to the LORD. ⁸When I was living at Geshur in Aram, I made a promise. I said, 'If the LORD takes me back to Jerusalem, I'll go to Hebron and worship him there.' "

⁹The king said to him, "Go in peace." So he went to Hebron.

¹⁰Then Absalom sent messengers secretly to all of the tribes of Israel. They said, "Listen for the sound of trumpets. As soon as you hear them, say, 'Absalom has become king in Hebron.' "

¹¹Absalom had taken 200 men from Jerusalem with him to Hebron. He had invited them to be his guests. They went without having any idea what was going to happen. ¹²While Absalom

was offering sacrifices, he sent for Ahithophel. Ahithophel was David's adviser. He came to Absalom from Giloh, his hometown. The number of people who followed Absalom kept growing. So he became more and more able to carry out his plans against David.

DAVID RUNS AWAY FROM ABSALOM

¹³A messenger came and spoke to David. He told him, "The hearts of the people are turned toward Absalom."

¹⁴Then David spoke to all of his officials who were with him in Jerusalem. He said, "Come on! We have to leave right away! If we don't, none of us will escape from Absalom. He'll move quickly to catch up with us. He'll destroy us. His men will kill everyone in the city with their swords."

¹⁵The king's officials answered him, "You are our king and master. We're ready to do anything you want."

¹⁶The king started out. Everyone in his whole family went with him. But he left ten concubines behind to take care of the palace. ¹⁷So the king and all those who were with him left. They stopped at a place that wasn't very far away.

¹⁸All of David's officials marched past him. All of the Kerethites and Pelethites marched along with them. And all of the 600 men who had come with him from Gath marched in front of him.

¹⁹The king spoke to Ittai. He was from Gath. The king said to him, "Why do you want to come along with us? Go back. Stay with King Absalom. You are a stranger. You left your own country. ²⁰You came to join me only a short time ago. So why should I make you wander around with us now? I don't even know where I'm going. So go on back. Take with you the others who are from your country. And may the LORD be kind and faithful to you."

²¹But Ittai replied to the king, "You are my king and master. I want to be where you are. It doesn't matter whether I live or die. And that's just as sure as the LORD and you are alive."

²²David said to Ittai, "Go ahead then. Keep marching with my men."

So Ittai, the Gittite, kept marching. All of his men and their families marched with him.

²³All of the people in the countryside sobbed out loud as David and all of his followers passed by. The king went across the Kidron Valley. He and all of the people who were with him moved on toward the desert.

²⁴Zadok also went with them. Some of the Levites went with him. They were carrying the ark of the covenant of God. They set the ark down. Abiathar offered sacrifices until all of the people had left the city.

²⁵Then the king said to Zadok, "Take the ark of God back into the city. If the LORD is pleased with me, he'll bring me back. He'll let me see the ark again. He'll also let me see Jerusalem again. That's the place where he lives. ²⁶But suppose he says, 'I am not pleased with you.' Then I accept that. Let him do to me what he thinks is best."

²⁷The king spoke again to the priest Zadok. He said, "You are a prophet, aren't you? Go back to the city in peace. Take your son Ahimaaz with you. Also take Abiathar and his son Jonathan with you. ²⁸I'll wait at the place in the desert where we can go across the Jordan River. I'll wait there until you send word to let me know what's happening."

²⁹So Zadok and Abiathar took the ark of God back to Jerusalem. They stayed there.

³⁰But David went on up the Mount of Olives. He was sobbing as he went. His head was covered, and he was barefoot. All of the people who were with him covered their heads too. And they were sobbing as they went up.

³¹David had been told, "Ahithophel is one of those who are making secret plans with Absalom against you." So David prayed, "LORD, make Ahithophel's advice look foolish."

³²David arrived at the top of the Mount of Olives. That's where people used to worship God. Hushai, the Arkite, was there to meet him. His robe was torn. There was dust on his head.

³³David said to him, "If you go with me, you will be too much trouble for me. ³⁴So return to the city. Say to Absalom, 'King Absalom, I'll be your ser-

vant. In the past, I was your father's servant. But now I'll be your servant.' If you do that, you can help me by making sure Ahithophel's advice fails. ³⁵The priests Zadok and Abiathar will be there with you. Tell them everything you hear in the king's palace. ³⁶They have their sons Ahimaaz and Jonathan there with them. Send them to tell me everything you hear."

³⁷So David's friend Hushai went to Jerusalem. He arrived just as Absalom was entering the city.

ZIBA LIES TO DAVID

16 David went just beyond the top of the Mount of Olives. Ziba was waiting there to meet him. He was Mephibosheth's manager. He had several donkeys with saddles on them. They were carrying 200 loaves of bread and 100 raisin cakes. They were also carrying 100 fig cakes and a bottle of wine. The bottle was made out of animal skin.

²The king asked Ziba, "Why have you brought all of these things?"

Ziba answered, "The donkeys are for the king's family to ride on. The bread and fruit are for the people to eat. The wine will make those who get tired in the desert feel like new again."

³Then the king asked, "Where is your master's grandson Mephibosheth?"

Ziba said to him, "He's staying in Jerusalem. He thinks, 'Today the people of Israel will give me back my grandfather Saul's kingdom.' "

⁴Then the king said to Ziba, "Everything that belonged to Mephibosheth belongs to you now."

"You are my king and master," Ziba said. "I make myself low in front of you. I bow down to you. May you be pleased with me."

SHIMEI CALLS DOWN CURSES ON DAVID

⁵King David approached Bahurim. As he did, a man came out toward him. The man was from the same family group that Saul was from. His name was Shimei. He was the son of Gera. As he came out of the town, he called down curses on David. ⁶He threw stones at David and all of his officials.

He did it even though all of the troops and the special guard were there. They were to the right and left of David.

⁷As Shimei called down curses, he said, "Get out! Get out, you murderer! You are a worthless and evil man! ⁸You spilled the blood of a lot of people in Saul's family. You took over his kingdom. Now the LORD is paying you back. He has handed the kingdom over to your son Absalom. You have been destroyed because you are a murderer!"

⁹Then Abishai, the son of Zeruiah, spoke to the king. He said, "King David, why should we let this dead dog call down curses on you? Let me go over there. I'll cut off his head."

¹⁰But the king said, "You and Joab are sons of Zeruiah. What do you and I have in common? Maybe the LORD said to him, 'Call down curses on David.' If he did, who can ask him, 'Why are you doing this?' "

¹¹Then David spoke to Abishai and all of his officials. He said, "My very own son Absalom is trying to kill me. How much more should this man from Benjamin want to kill me! Leave him alone. Let him call down curses. The LORD has told him to do it. ¹²Maybe the LORD will see how much I'm suffering. Maybe he'll reward me with good things in place of the curses that are being called down on me today."

¹³So David and his men kept going along the road. At the same time, Shimei was going along the hillside across from him. He was calling down curses as he went. He was throwing stones at David. He was showering him with dirt.

¹⁴The king and all of the people who were with him came to the place they had planned to go to. They were very tired. So David rested there.

HUSHAI AND AHITHOPHEL GIVE ADVICE TO ABSALOM

¹⁵During that time, Absalom and all of the men of Israel came to Jerusalem. Ahithophel was with him. ¹⁶Then Hushai, the Arkite, went to Absalom. He said to him, "May the king live a long time! May the king live a long time!" Hushai was David's friend.

[17]Absalom asked Hushai, "Is this the way you show love to your friend? Why didn't you go with him?"

[18]Hushai said to Absalom, "Why should I? You are the one the LORD has chosen. These people and all of the men of Israel have also chosen you. I want to be on your side. I want to stay with you. [19]After all, who else should I serve? Shouldn't I serve the king's son? I will serve you, just as I served your father."

[20]Absalom said to Ahithophel, "Give us your advice. What should we do?"

[21]Ahithophel answered, "Your father left some concubines behind to take care of the palace. Go and have sex with them. Then all of the people of Israel will hear about it. They will hear that you have made yourself smell very bad to your father. Everyone who is with you will become braver."

[22]So they set up a tent for Absalom on the roof of the palace. He went in and had sex with his father's concubines. Everyone in Israel saw it.

[23]In those days the advice Ahithophel gave was as good as advice from someone who asks God for guidance. That's what David and Absalom thought about all of Ahithopel's advice.

17 One day Ahithophel said to Absalom, "Here's what I suggest. Choose 12,000 men. Start out tonight and go after David. [2]Attack him while he's tired and weak. Fill him with terror. Then all of the people who are with him will run away. Don't strike down anyone except the king. [3]Bring all of the other people back. After the man you want to kill is dead, everyone else will return to you. And none of the people will be harmed."

[4]Ahithophel's plan seemed good to Absalom. It also seemed good to all of the elders of Israel.

[5]But Absalom said, "Send for Hushai, the Arkite. Then we can find out what he suggests."

[6]Hushai came to him. Absalom said, "Ahithophel has given us his advice. Should we do what he says? If we shouldn't, tell us what you would do."

[7]Hushai replied to Absalom, "The advice Ahithophel has given you isn't good this time. [8]You know your father and his men. They are fighters. They are as strong as a wild bear whose cubs have been stolen from her. Besides, your father really knows how to fight. He won't spend the night with his troops. [9]In fact, he's probably hiding in a cave or some other place right now.

"Suppose he attacks your troops first. When people hear about it, they'll say, 'Many of the troops who followed Absalom have been killed.' [10]Then the hearts of your soldiers will melt away in fear. Even those who are as brave as a lion will be terrified. That's because everyone in Israel knows that your father is a fighter. They know that those who are with him are brave.

[11]"So here's what I suggest. Bring together all of the men of Israel from the town of Dan all the way to Beersheba. They are as many as the grains of sand on the seashore. You yourself should lead them into battle.

[12]"Then we'll attack David no matter where we find him. As dew completely covers the ground, we'll completely overpower his entire army. We won't leave him or any of his men alive. [13]He might try to get away by going into a city. If he does, all of us will bring ropes to that city. We'll drag the whole city down into the valley. No one will be able to find even a piece of that city."

[14]Absalom and all of the men of Israel agreed. They said, "The advice of Hushai, the Arkite, is better than the advice of Ahithophel." The LORD had decided that Ahithophel's good advice would fail. The LORD wanted to bring horrible trouble on Absalom.

[15]Hushai spoke to the priests Zadok and Abiathar. He said, "Ahithophel has given advice to Absalom and the elders of Israel. He suggested that they should do one thing. But I suggested something else.

[16]"Send a message right away. Tell David, 'Don't spend the night at the place in the desert where people can go across the Jordan River. Make sure you go on across. If you don't, you and all of the people who are with you will be swallowed up.' "

[17]Jonathan and Ahimaaz were staying at En Rogel just outside Jerusalem.

They knew they would be in danger if anyone saw them entering the city. A female servant was supposed to go and tell them what had happened. Then they were supposed to go and tell King David. [18]But a young man saw Jonathan and Ahimaaz and told Absalom about it. So the two men left quickly. They went to the house of a man in Bahurim. He had a well in his courtyard. They climbed down into it. [19]The man's wife got a covering and spread it out over the opening of the well. Then she scattered grain on the covering. So no one knew that the men were hiding in the well.

[20]Absalom's men came to the house. They asked the woman, "Where are Ahimaaz and Jonathan?"

She answered, "They went across the brook." When the men looked around, they didn't find anyone. So they returned to Jerusalem.

[21]After the men had gone, Jonathan and Ahimaaz climbed out of the well. They went to tell King David what they had found out. They said to him, "Go across the river right away. Ahithophel has told Absalom how to come after you and strike you down."

[22]So David and all of the people who were with him started out. They went across the Jordan River. By sunrise, everyone had crossed over.

[23]Ahithophel saw that his advice wasn't being followed. So he put a saddle on his donkey. He started out for his house in his hometown. When he got there, he put everything in order. He made out his will. Then he killed himself. So he died, and his body was buried in his father's tomb.

[24]David went to Mahanaim. Absalom went across the Jordan River with all of the men of Israel. [25]Absalom had made Amasa commander of the army in place of Joab. Amasa was the son of a man named Jether. Jether belonged to the family line of Ishmael. He had gotten married to Abigail. She was the daughter of Nahash and the sister of Zeruiah. Zeruiah was the mother of Joab. [26]Absalom and the people of Israel camped in the land of Gilead.

[27]David came to Mahanaim. Shobi, the son of Nahash, met him there.

Shobi was from Rabbah in the land of Ammon. Makir, the son of Ammiel from Lo Debar, met him there too. So did Barzillai from Rogelim in the land of Gilead. [28]They brought beds, bowls and clay pots. They brought wheat, barley, flour, and grain that had been cooked. They brought beans and lentils. [29]They brought honey, butter, sheep and cheese that was made from cows' milk. They brought all of that food for David and his people to eat. They said, "These people have become hungry. They've become tired and thirsty in the desert."

ABSALOM DIES

18 David brought together the men who were with him. He appointed commanders of thousands over some of them. He appointed commanders of hundreds over the others.

[2]Then David sent the troops out in three companies. One company was under the command of Joab. Another was under Joab's brother Abishai, the son of Zeruiah. The last was under Ittai, the Gittite. The king told the troops, "You can be sure that I myself will march out with you."

[3]But the men said, "You must not march out. If we are forced to run away, our enemies won't care about us. Even if half of us die, they won't care. But you are worth 10,000 of us. So it would be better for you to stay here in the city. Then you can send us help if we need it."

[4]The king said, "I'll do what you think is best."

So the king stood beside the city gate. The whole army marched out in companies of hundreds and companies of thousands.

[5]The king gave an order to Joab, Abishai and Ittai. He commanded them, "Be gentle with the young man Absalom. Do it for me." All of the troops heard the king give the commanders that order about Absalom.

[6]David's army marched into the field to fight against Israel. The battle took place in the forest of Ephraim. [7]There David's men won the battle over Israel's army. A huge number of men

were wounded or killed that day. The total number was 20,000. ⁸The fighting spread out over the whole countryside. But more men were killed in the forest that day than out in the open.

⁹Absalom happened to come across some of David's men. He was riding his mule. The mule went under the thick branches of a large oak tree. Absalom's head got caught in the tree. He was left hanging in the air. The mule he was riding kept on going.

¹⁰One of David's men saw what had happened. He told Joab, "I just saw Absalom hanging in an oak tree."

¹¹Joab said to the man, "What! You saw him? Why didn't you strike him down right there? Then I would have had to give you four ounces of silver and a soldier's belt."

¹²But the man replied, "I wouldn't lift my hand to harm the king's son. I wouldn't do it even for 25 pounds of silver. We heard the king's command to you and Abishai and Ittai. He said, 'Be careful not to hurt the young man Absalom. Do it for me.' ¹³Suppose I had put my life in danger by killing him. The king would have found out about it. Nothing is hidden from him. And you wouldn't have stood up for me."

¹⁴Joab said, "I'm not going to waste any more time on you." So he got three javelins. Then he went over and drove them into Absalom's heart. He did it while Absalom was still hanging there alive in the oak tree.

¹⁵Ten of the men who were carrying Joab's armor surrounded Absalom. They struck him down and killed him.

¹⁶Then Joab blew his trumpet. He ordered his troops to stop chasing Israel's army. ¹⁷Joab's men threw Absalom's body into a big pit in the forest. They covered his body with a large pile of rocks. While all of that was going on, all of the Israelites ran back to their homes.

¹⁸Earlier in his life Absalom had set up a pillar in the King's Valley. He had put it up as a monument to himself. He thought, "I don't have a son to carry on the memory of my name." So he named the pillar after himself. It is still called Absalom's Monument to this very day.

DAVID SOBS OVER ABSALOM

¹⁹Ahimaaz said to Joab, "Let me run and take the news to the king. Let me tell him that the LORD has saved him from the power of his enemies." Ahimaaz was the son of Zadok.

²⁰"I don't want you to take the news to the king today," Joab told him. "You can do it some other time. But you must not do it today, because the king's son is dead."

²¹Then Joab said to a man from Cush, "Go. Tell the king what you have seen." The man bowed down in front of Joab. Then he ran off.

²²Ahimaaz, the son of Zadok, spoke again to Joab. He said, "I don't care what happens to me. Please let me run behind the man from Cush."

But Joab replied, "My son, why do you want to go? You don't have any news that will bring you a reward."

²³He said, "I don't care what happens. I want to run."

So Joab said, "Run!" Then Ahimaaz ran across the flatlands of the Jordan River. As he ran, he passed the man from Cush.

²⁴David was sitting in the area between the inner and outer gates of the city. The man on guard duty went up to the roof over the entrance of the gate by the wall. As he looked out, he saw someone running alone. ²⁵He called out to the king and reported it.

The king said, "If the runner is alone, he must be bringing good news." The man came closer and closer.

²⁶Then the man on guard duty saw another man running. He called out to the man who was guarding the gate. He said, "Look! There's another man running alone!"

The king said, "He must be bringing good news too."

²⁷The man on guard duty said, "I can see that the first one runs like Ahimaaz, the son of Zadok."

"He's a good man," the king said. "He's bringing good news."

²⁸Then Ahimaaz called out to the king, "Everything's all right!" He bowed down in front of the king with his face toward the ground. He said, "You are my king and master. Give

praise to the LORD your God! He has handed over to you the men who lifted their hands to kill you."

²⁹The king asked, "Is the young man Absalom safe?"

Ahimaaz answered, "I saw total disorder. I saw it just as Joab was about to send the king's servant and me to you. But I don't know what it was all about."

³⁰The king said, "Stand over there and wait." So he stepped over to one side and stood there.

³¹Then the man from Cush arrived. He said, "You are my king and master. I'm bringing you some good news. The LORD has saved you today from all those who were trying to kill you."

³²The king asked the man from Cush, "Is the young man Absalom safe?"

The man replied, "King David, may your enemies be like that young man. May all those who rise up to harm you be like him."

³³The king was very upset. He went up to the room over the entrance of the gate and sobbed. As he went, he said, "My son Absalom! My son, my son Absalom! I wish I had died instead of you. Absalom! My son, my son!"

19 Someone told Joab, "The king is sobbing over Absalom. He's filled with sadness because his son has died."

²The army had won a great battle that day. But their joy turned into sadness. That's because someone had told the troops, "The king is filled with sorrow because his son is dead." ³The men came quietly into the city that day. They were like fighting men who are ashamed because they've run away from a battle.

⁴The king covered his face. He sobbed out loud, "My son Absalom! Absalom, my son, my son!"

⁵Then Joab went into the king's house. He said to him, "Today you have made all of your men feel ashamed. They have just saved your life. They have saved the lives of your sons and daughters. And they have saved the lives of your wives and concubines.

⁶"You love those who hate you. You hate those who love you. The commanders and their troops don't mean

anything to you. You made that very clear today. I can see that you would be pleased if Absalom were alive today and all of us were dead.

⁷"Now go out there and cheer up your men. If you don't, you won't have any of them left with you by sunset. That will be worse for you than all of the troubles you have ever had in your whole life. That's what I promise you with an oath in the LORD's name."

⁸So the king got up and took his seat in the entrance of the city gate. His men were told, "The king is sitting in the entrance of the gate." Then all of them came and stood in front of him.

DAVID RETURNS TO JERUSALEM

While all of that was going on, the Israelites had run back to their homes. ⁹People from all of the tribes of Israel began to argue with one another. They were saying, "The king saved us from the power of our enemies. He saved us from the power of the Philistines. But now he has left the country because of Absalom. ¹⁰We anointed Absalom to rule over us. But he has died in battle. So why aren't any of you talking about bringing the king back?"

¹¹King David sent a message to the priests Zadok and Abiathar. It said, "Speak to the elders of Judah. Tell them I said, 'News has reached me where I'm staying. People all over Israel are talking about bringing me back to my palace. Why should you be the last to do something about it? ¹²You are my relatives. You are my own flesh and blood. So why should you be the last to bring me back?'

¹³"Say to Amasa, 'Aren't you my own flesh and blood? From now on you will be the commander of my army in place of Joab. If that isn't true, may God punish me greatly.' "

¹⁴So the hearts of all of the men of Judah were turned toward David. All of them had the same purpose in mind. They sent a message to the king. It said, "We want you to come back. We want all of your men to come back too." ¹⁵Then the king returned. He went as far as the Jordan River.

The men of Judah had come to Gilgal to welcome the king back. They had come to bring him across the Jordan. ¹⁶Shimei, the son of Gera, was among them. Shimei was from Bahurim in the territory of Benjamin. He hurried down to welcome King David back. ¹⁷There were 1,000 people from Benjamin with him. Ziba, the manager of Saul's house, was with him too. And so were Ziba's 15 sons and 20 servants. All of them rushed down to the Jordan River. That's where the king was. ¹⁸They went across at the place where people usually cross it. Then they brought the king's family back over with them. They were ready to do anything he wanted them to do.

Shimei, the son of Gera, had also gone across the Jordan. When he did, he fell down flat with his face toward the ground in front of the king. ¹⁹He said to him, "You are my king and master. Please don't hold me guilty. Please forgive me for the wrong things I did on the day you left Jerusalem. Please forget all about them. ²⁰I know I've sinned. But today I've come down here to welcome you. I'm the first member of Joseph's whole family to do it."

²¹Then Abishai, the son of Zeruiah, said, "Shouldn't Shimei be put to death for what he did? He called down curses on you. And you are the LORD's anointed king."

²²But David replied, "You and Joab are sons of Zeruiah. What do you and I have in common? Abishai, you have now become my enemy! Should anyone be put to death in Israel today? Don't I know that today I am king over Israel again?"

²³So the king took an oath and made a promise to Shimei. He said to him, "You aren't going to be put to death."

²⁴Mephibosheth was Saul's grandson. He had also gone down to welcome the king back. He had not taken care of his feet. He hadn't trimmed his mustache or washed his clothes. He hadn't done any of those things from the day the king left Jerusalem until the day he returned safely. ²⁵He came from Jerusalem to welcome the king. The king asked him, "Mephibosheth, why didn't you go with me?"

²⁶He said, "You are my king and master. I'm disabled. So I thought, 'I'll have a saddle put on my donkey. I'll ride on

it. Then I can go with the king.' But my servant Ziba turned against me. ²⁷He has told you lies about me. King David, you are like an angel of God. So do what pleases you. ²⁸You should have put all of the members of my grandfather's family to death, including me. Instead, you always provided what I needed. So what right do I have to make any more appeals to you?"

²⁹The king said to him, "You don't have to say anything else. I order you and Ziba to divide up Saul's fields between you."

³⁰Mephibosheth said to the king, "I'm happy that you have arrived home safely. So just let Ziba have everything."

³¹Barzillai had also come down to go across the Jordan River with the king. He wanted to send the king on his way from there. Barzillai was from Rogelim in the land of Gilead. ³²He was a very old man. He was 80 years old. He had given the king everything he needed while the king was staying in Mahanaim. That's because Barzillai was very wealthy.

³³The king said to Barzillai, "Come across the river with me. Stay with me in Jerusalem. I'll take good care of you."

³⁴But Barzillai said to the king, "I won't live for many more years. So why should I go up to Jerusalem with you? ³⁵I'm already 80 years old. I can hardly tell the difference between what is good and what isn't. I can hardly taste what I eat and drink. I can't even hear the voices of male and female singers anymore. So why should I add my problems to yours?

³⁶"I'll go across the Jordan River with you for a little way. Why should you reward me by taking care of me? ³⁷Let me go back home. Then I can die in my own town. I can be buried there in the tomb of my father and mother. But let Kimham take my place. Let him go across the river with you. Do for him what pleases you."

³⁸The king said, "Kimham will go across with me. I'll do for him what pleases you. And I'll do for you anything you want me to do."

³⁹So all of the people went across the Jordan River. Then the king crossed over. The king kissed Barzillai and

gave him his blessing. And Barzillai went back home.

⁴⁰After the king had gone across the river, he went to Gilgal. Kimham had gone across with him. All of the troops of Judah and half of the troops of Israel had taken the king across.

⁴¹Soon all of the men of Israel were coming to the king. They were saying to him, "Why did the men of Judah take you away from us? They are our relatives. What right did they have to bring you and your family across the Jordan River? What right did they have to bring all of your men over with you?"

⁴²All of the men of Judah answered the men of Israel. They said, "We did that because the king is our close relative. So why should you be angry about what happened? Have we eaten any of the king's food? Have we taken anything for ourselves?"

⁴³Then the men of Israel answered the men of Judah. They said, "We have ten of the 12 tribes in the kingdom. So we have a stronger claim on David than you have. Why then are you acting as if you hate us? Weren't we the first ones to talk about bringing back our king?"

But the men of Judah answered in an even meaner way than the men of Israel.

SHEBA TELLS ISRAEL NOT TO FOLLOW DAVID

20 An evil man who always stirred up trouble happened to be in Gilgal. His name was Sheba, the son of Bicri. Sheba was from the tribe of Benjamin. He blew his trumpet. Then he shouted,

"We don't have any share in
    David's kingdom!
Jesse's son is not our king!
Men of Israel, every one of you
    go back home!"

²So all of the men of Israel deserted David. They followed Sheba, the son of Bicri. But the men of Judah stayed with their king. They remained with him from the Jordan River all the way to Jerusalem.

³David returned to his palace in Jerusalem. He had left ten concubines there to take care of the palace. He put them in a house and kept them under guard. He gave them what they needed. But he didn't make love to them. They were kept under guard until the day they died. They lived as if they were widows.

⁴The king said to Amasa, "Send for the men of Judah. Tell them to come to me within three days. And be here yourself." ⁵So Amasa went to get the men of Judah. But he took longer than the time the king had set for him.

⁶David said to Abishai, "Sheba, the son of Bicri, will do more harm to us than Absalom ever did. Take my men and go after him. If you don't, he'll find cities that have high walls around them. He'll go into one of them and escape from us."

⁷So Joab's men marched out with the Kerethites and Pelethites. They went out with all of the mighty soldiers. All of them were under Abishai's command. They marched out from Jerusalem and went after Sheba, the son of Bicri.

⁸They arrived at the great rock in Gibeon. Amasa went there to welcome them. Joab was wearing his military clothes. Over them at his waist he strapped on a belt that held a dagger. As he stepped forward, the dagger fell out.

⁹Joab said to Amasa, "How are you, my friend?" Then Joab reached out his right hand. He took hold of Amasa's beard to kiss him.

¹⁰Amasa didn't pay any attention to the dagger that was in Joab's left hand. Joab stuck it into his stomach. His insides spilled out on the ground. Joab didn't have to stab him again. Amasa was already dead. Then Joab and his brother Abishai went after Sheba, the son of Bicri.

¹¹One of Joab's men stood beside Amasa's body. He said to the other men, "Are you pleased with Joab? Are you on David's side? Then follow Joab!"

¹²Amasa's body lay covered with his blood in the middle of the road. The man saw that all of the troops stopped there. He realized that everyone was

stopping to look at Amasa's body. So he dragged it from the road into a field. Then he threw some clothes on top of it. ¹³After that happened, all of the men continued on with Joab. They went after Sheba, the son of Bicri.

¹⁴Sheba passed through all of the territory of the tribes of Israel. He arrived at the city of Abel Beth Maacah. He had gone through the entire area of the Berites. They had gathered together and followed him.

¹⁵Joab and all of his troops came to Abel Beth Maacah. They surrounded it because Sheba was there. They built a ramp up to the city. It stood against the outer wall. They pounded the wall with huge logs to bring it down.

¹⁶While that was going on, a wise woman called out from the city. She shouted, "Listen! Listen! Tell Joab to come here. I want to speak to him." ¹⁷So Joab went toward her. She asked, "Are you Joab?"

"I am," he answered.

She said, "Listen to what I have to say."

"I'm listening," he said.

¹⁸She continued, "Long ago people used to say, 'Get your answer at Abel.' And that would settle the matter. ¹⁹We are the most peaceful and faithful people in Israel. You are trying to destroy a city that is like a mother in Israel. Why do you want to swallow up what belongs to the LORD?"

²⁰"I would never do anything like that!" Joab said. "I would never swallow up or destroy what belongs to the LORD! ²¹That isn't what I have in mind at all. There's a man named Sheba, the son of Bicri, in your city. He's from the hill country of Ephraim. He's trying to kill King David. Hand that man over to me. Then I'll pull my men back from your city."

The woman said to Joab, "We'll throw his head down to you from the wall."

²²Then the woman gave her wise advice to all of the people in the city. They cut off the head of Sheba, the son of Bicri. They threw it down to Joab. So he blew his trumpet. Then his men pulled back from the city. Each of them returned to his home. And Joab went back to the king in Jerusalem.

²³Joab was commander over Israel's entire army. Benaiah, the son of Jehoiada, was commander over the Kerethites and Pelethites. ²⁴Adoniram was in charge of those who were forced to work hard. Jehoshaphat, the son of Ahilud, kept the records. ²⁵Sheva was the secretary. Zadok and Abiathar were priests. ²⁶Ira, the Jairite, was David's priest.

DAVID MAKES THINGS RIGHT FOR THE PEOPLE OF GIBEON

21 For three years in a row there wasn't enough food in the land. That was while David was king. So David asked the LORD why he wasn't showing his favor to his people. The LORD said, "It is because Saul and his family committed murder. He put the people of Gibeon to death."

²The people of Gibeon weren't a part of Israel. Instead, they were some of the Amorites who were still left alive. The people of Israel had promised with an oath to spare them. But Saul had tried to put an end to them. That's because he wanted to make Israel and Judah strong.

So now King David sent for the people of Gibeon and spoke to them. ³He asked them, "What would you like me to do for you? How can I make up for the wrong things that were done to you? I want you to be able to pray that the LORD will once again bless his land."

⁴The people of Gibeon answered him. They said, "No amount of silver or gold can make up for what Saul and his family did to us. And we can't put anyone in Israel to death."

"What do you want me to do for you?" David asked.

⁵They answered the king, "Saul nearly destroyed us. He made plans to wipe us out. We don't have anywhere to live in Israel. ⁶So let seven of the males in his family line be given to us. We'll kill them. We'll put their dead bodies out in the open in the sight of the LORD. We'll do it at Gibeah of Saul. Saul was the LORD's chosen king."

So King David said, "I'll give seven males to you."

⁷The king spared Mephibosheth. He was the son of Jonathan and the

grandson of Saul. David had taken an oath in the sight of the LORD. He had promised to be kind to Jonathan and the family line of his father Saul.

⁸But the king chose Armoni and another Mephibosheth. They were the two sons of Aiah's daughter Rizpah. Saul was their father. The king also chose the five sons of Saul's daughter Merab. Adriel, the son of Barzillai, was their father. Adriel was from Meholah.

⁹King David handed them over to the people of Gibeon. They killed them. They put their dead bodies out in the open on a hill in the sight of the LORD. All seven of them died together. They were put to death during the first days of the harvest. It happened just when people were beginning to harvest the barley.

¹⁰Aiah's daughter Rizpah got some black cloth. She spread it out for herself on a rock. She stayed there from the beginning of the harvest until it rained. The rain poured down from the sky on the dead bodies of the seven males. She didn't let the birds of the air touch them by day. She didn't let the wild animals touch them at night.

¹¹Someone told David what Rizpah had done. She was Aiah's daughter and Saul's concubine.

¹²David got the bones of Saul and his son Jonathan. He got them from the citizens of Jabesh Gilead. They had taken them in secret from the main street in Beth Shan. That's where the Philistines had hung their bodies up on the city wall. They had done it after they struck Saul down on Mount Gilboa.

¹³David brought the bones of Saul and his son Jonathan from Jabesh Gilead. The bones of the seven males who had been killed and put out in the open were also gathered up.

¹⁴The bones of Saul and his son Jonathan were buried in the tomb of Saul's father Kish. The tomb was at Zela in the territory of Benjamin. Everything the king commanded was done. After that, God answered prayer and blessed the land.

ISRAEL GOES TO WAR AGAINST THE PHILISTINES

¹⁵Once again there was a battle between the Philistines and Israel. David went down with his men to fight against the Philistines. He became very tired.

¹⁶Ishbi-Benob belonged to the family line of Rapha. The tip of his bronze spear weighed seven and a half pounds. He was also armed with a new sword. He said he would kill David.

¹⁷But Abishai, the son of Zeruiah, came to save David. He struck the Philistine down and killed him.

Then David's men took an oath and made a promise. They said to David, "We never want you to go out with us to battle again. You are the lamp of Israel's kingdom. We want that lamp to keep on burning brightly."

¹⁸There was another battle against the Philistines. It took place at Gob. At that time Sibbecai killed Saph. Sibbecai was a Hushathite. Saph was from the family line of Rapha.

¹⁹In another battle against the Philistines at Gob, Elhanan killed Goliath's brother. Elhanan was the son of Jaare-Oregim from Bethlehem. Goliath was from the city of Gath. His spear was as big as a weaver's rod.

²⁰There was still another battle. It took place at Gath. A huge man lived there. He had six fingers on each hand and six toes on each foot. So the total number of his toes and fingers was 24. He was also from the family of Rapha. ²¹He made fun of Israel. So Jonathan killed him. Jonathan was the son of David's brother Shimeah.

²²Those four Philistine men lived in Gath. They were from the family line of Rapha. David and his men killed them.

DAVID SINGS PRAISES TO THE LORD

22 David sang the words of this song to the LORD. He sang them when the LORD saved him from the powerful hand of all of his enemies and of Saul. ²He said,

"The LORD is my rock and my fort. He is the One who saves me.
³ My God is my rock. I go to him for safety.
He is like a shield to me. He's the power that saves me.

He's my place of safety. I go to him
for help. He's my Savior.
He saves me from those who
want to hurt me.
⁴I call out to the LORD. He is worthy
of praise.
He saves me from my enemies.

⁵"The waves of death were all
around me.
A destroying flood swept over
me.
⁶The ropes of the grave were tight
around me.
Death set its trap in front of me.
⁷When I was in trouble I called out
to the LORD.
I called out to my God.
From his temple he heard my
voice.
My cry for help reached his ears.

⁸"The earth trembled and shook.
The pillars of the heavens rocked
back and forth.
They trembled because the LORD
was angry.
⁹Smoke came out of his nose.
Flames of fire came out of his
mouth.
Burning coals blazed out of it.
¹⁰He opened the heavens and came
down.
Dark clouds were under his feet.
¹¹He got on the cherubim and flew.
The wings of the wind lifted him
up.
¹²He covered himself with darkness.
The dark rain clouds of the sky
were like a tent around him.
¹³From the brightness that was all
around him
flashes of lightning blazed out.
¹⁴The LORD thundered from heaven.
The voice of the Most High God
was heard.
¹⁵He shot his arrows and scattered
our enemies.
He sent flashes of lightning and
chased the enemies away.
¹⁶The bottom of the sea could be
seen.
The foundations of the earth
were uncovered.
It happened when the LORD's
anger blazed out.
It came like a blast of breath
from his nose.

¹⁷"He reached down from heaven.
He took hold of me.
He lifted me out of deep waters.
¹⁸He saved me from my powerful
enemies.
He set me free from those who
were too strong for me.
¹⁹They stood up to me when I was in
trouble.
But the LORD helped me.
²⁰He brought me out into a wide
and safe place.
He saved me because he was
pleased with me.

²¹"The LORD has been good to me
because I do what is right.
He has rewarded me because I
lead a pure life.
²²I have lived the way the LORD
wanted me to.
I haven't done evil by turning
away from my God.
²³I keep all of his laws in mind.
I haven't turned away from his
commands.
²⁴He knows that I am without
blame.
He knows I've kept myself from
sinning.
²⁵The LORD has rewarded me for
doing what is right.
He has rewarded me because I
haven't done anything wrong.

²⁶"LORD, to those who are faithful
you show that you are faithful.
To those who are without blame
you show that you are without
blame.
²⁷To those who are pure you show
that you are pure.
But to those whose paths are
crooked you show that you are
clever.
²⁸You save those who aren't proud.
But you watch the proud to bring
them down.
²⁹LORD, you are my lamp.
You bring light into my darkness.
³⁰With your help I can attack a troop
of soldiers.
With the help of my God I can
climb over a wall.

³¹"God's way is perfect.
The word of the LORD doesn't
have any flaws.

He is like a shield
to all who go to him for safety.
³² Who is God except the LORD?
Who is the Rock except our God?
³³ God gives me strength for the
battle.
He makes my way perfect.
³⁴ He makes my feet like the feet of a
deer.
He helps me stand on the highest
places.
³⁵ He trains my hands to fight every
battle.
My arms can bend a bow of
bronze.
³⁶ LORD, you are like a shield that
keeps me safe.
You help me win the battle.
You bend down to make me
great.
³⁷ You give me a wide path to walk in
so that I don't twist my ankles.

³⁸ "I chased my enemies and
crushed them.
I didn't turn back until they were
destroyed.
³⁹ I crushed them completely so that
they couldn't get up.
They fell under my feet.
⁴⁰ LORD, you gave me strength to
fight the battle.
You made my enemies bow down
at my feet.
⁴¹ You made them turn their backs
and run away.
So I destroyed my enemies.
⁴² They cried out for help. But there
was no one to save them.
They called out to you. But you
didn't answer them.
⁴³ I beat them as fine as the dust of
the earth.
I pounded them and walked on
them like mud in the streets.

⁴⁴ "You saved me when my own
people attacked me.
You have kept me as the ruler
over nations.
People I didn't know serve me now.
⁴⁵ People from other lands bow
down to me in fear.
As soon as they hear me, they
obey me.
⁴⁶ All of them give up hope.
They come trembling out of their
hiding places.

⁴⁷ "The LORD lives! Give praise to my
Rock!
Give honor to God, the Rock! He
is my Savior!
⁴⁸ He is the God who pays my
enemies back.
He brings the nations under my
control.
⁴⁹ He sets me free from my
enemies.
You have honored me more than
them.
You have saved me from men
who want to hurt me.
⁵⁰ LORD, I will praise you among the
nations.
I will sing praises to you.
⁵¹ You help me win great battles.
You show your faithful love to
your anointed king.
You show it to me and my family
forever."

DAVID'S LAST WORDS

23 Here are David's last
words. He said,

"I am David, the son of Jesse. God
has given me a message.
The Most High God has greatly
honored me.
The God of Jacob anointed me as
king.
I am Israel's singer of songs.

² "The Spirit of the LORD spoke
through me.
I spoke his word with my tongue.
³ The God of Israel spoke.
The Rock of Israel said to me,
'A king must rule over people in a
way that is right.
He must have respect for me
when he rules.
⁴ Then he will be like the light of
morning at sunrise
when there aren't any clouds.
He will be like the bright sun after
rain
that makes the grass grow on the
earth.'

⁵ "Isn't my royal family right with
God?
Hasn't he made a covenant with
me that will last forever?
Every part of it was well prepared
and made secure.

Won't he save me completely?
Won't he give me everything I
long for?
⁶But evil people are like thorns that
are thrown away.
You can't pick them up with your
hands.
⁷Even if you touch them,
you must use an iron tool or a
spear.
Thorns are burned up right
where they are."

DAVID'S MIGHTY MEN

⁸Here are the names of David's
mighty men.

Josheb-Basshebeth was chief of the
Three. He was a Tahkemonite. He used
his spear against 800 men. He killed all
of them at one time.

⁹Next to him was Eleazar. He was
one of the three mighty men. He was
the son of Dodai, the Ahohite. Eleazar
was with David at Pas Dammim. That's
where Israel's army made fun of the
Philistines who were gathered there
for battle. Then the men of Israel
pulled back.

¹⁰But Eleazar stayed right where he
was. He struck the Philistines down
until his hand grew tired. But he still
held on to his sword. The LORD helped
him win a great battle that day. The
troops returned to Eleazar. They came
back to him only to take what they
wanted from the dead bodies.

¹¹Next to him was Shammah, the
son of Agee. Shammah was a Hararite.
The Philistines gathered together at a
place where there was a field full of
lentils. Israel's troops ran away from
them.

¹²But Shammah took his stand in the
middle of the field. He didn't let the
Philistines capture it. He struck them
down. The LORD helped him win a
great battle.

¹³David was at the cave of Adullam.
During harvest time, three of the 30
chief men came down to him there. A
group of Philistines was camped in the
Valley of Rephaim. ¹⁴At that time
David was in his usual place of safety.
Some Philistine troops were stationed
at Bethlehem.

¹⁵David longed for water. He said, "I
wish someone would get me a drink of
water from the well that is near the
gate of Bethlehem."

¹⁶So the three mighty men fought
their way past the Philistine guards.
They got some water from the well
that was near the gate of Bethlehem.
They took the water back to David.

But David refused to drink it. Instead, he poured it out as a drink offering to the LORD. ¹⁷"LORD, I would
never drink that water!" David said.
"It stands for the blood of these men.
They put their lives in danger by going
to Bethlehem to get it." So David
wouldn't drink it.

Those were some of the brave things
the three mighty men did.

¹⁸Abishai was chief over the Three.
He was the brother of Joab, the son of
Zeruiah. He used his spear against 300
men. He killed all of them. So he became as famous as the Three were. ¹⁹In
fact, he was even more honored than
the Three. He became their commander. But he wasn't included
among them.

²⁰Benaiah was a great hero from
Kabzeel. He was the son of Jehoiada.
Benaiah did many brave things. He
struck down two of Moab's best fighting men. He also went down into a pit
on a snowy day. He killed a lion there.

²¹And he struck down a huge Egyptian. The Egyptian was holding a
spear. Benaiah went out to fight
against him with a club. He grabbed
the spear out of the Egyptian's hand.
Then he killed him with it.

²²Those were some of the brave
things Benaiah, the son of Jehoiada,
did. He too was as famous as the three
mighty men were. ²³He was honored
more than any of the Thirty. But he
wasn't included among the Three.
David put him in charge of his own
personal guards.

²⁴Here is a list of David's men who
were among the Thirty.

Asahel, the brother of Joab
Elhanan, the son of Dodo,
from Bethlehem
²⁵Shammah, the Harodite
Elika, the Harodite
²⁶Helez, the Paltite
Ira, the son of Ikkesh, from
Tekoa

²⁷Abiezer from Anathoth
Mebunnai, the Hushathite
²⁸Zalmon, the Ahohite
Maharai from Netophah
²⁹Heled, the son of Baanah,
from Netophah
Ithai, the son of Ribai, from
Gibeah in Benjamin
³⁰Benaiah from Pirathon
Hiddai from the valleys of
Gaash
³¹Abi-Albon, the Arbathite
Azmaveth, the Barhumite
³²Eliahba, the Shaalbonite
the sons of Jashen
Jonathan, ³³the son of Shammah, the Hararite
Ahiam, the son of Sharar, the
Hararite
³⁴Eliphelet, the son of Ahasbai,
the Maacathite
Eliam, the son of Ahithophel,
from Giloh
³⁵Hezro from Carmel
Paarai, the Arbite
³⁶Igal, the son of Nathan, from
Zobah
the son of Hagri
³⁷Zelek from Ammon
Naharai from Beeroth, who
carried the armor of Joab,
the son of Zeruiah
³⁸Ira, the Ithrite
Gareb, the Ithrite
³⁹Uriah, the Hittite

The total number of men
was 37.

DAVID COUNTS HIS FIGHTING MEN

24 The LORD's anger burned
against Israel. He stirred
up David against them. He
said, "Go! Count the men of Israel and
Judah."

²So the king spoke to Joab and the
army commanders who were with
him. He said, "Go all through the territories of the tribes of Israel. Go from
Dan all the way to Beersheba. Count
the fighting men. Then I'll know how
many there are."

³Joab replied to the king. He said,
"King David, you are my master. May
the LORD your God multiply the troops
100 times. And may you live to see it.

But why would you want me to count
the fighting men?"

⁴In spite of what Joab said, the king's
word had more authority than the
word of Joab and the army commanders did. So they left the king and went
out to count the fighting men of Israel.

⁵They went across the Jordan River.
They camped south of the town in the
middle of the Arnon River valley near
Aroer. Then they went through Gad
and continued on to Jazer. ⁶They went
to Gilead and the area of Tahtim Hod-
shi. They continued to Dan Jaan and
on around toward Sidon. ⁷Then they
went toward the fort of Tyre. They
went to all of the towns of the Hivites
and Canaanites. Finally, they went on
to Beersheba. It was in the Negev
Desert of Judah.

⁸They finished going through the
entire land. Then they came back to
Jerusalem. They had been gone for
nine months and 20 days.

⁹Joab reported to the king how many
fighting men he had counted. In Israel
there were 800,000 men who were able
to handle a sword. In Judah there were
500,000.

¹⁰David felt sorry that he had
counted the fighting men. So he said
to the LORD, "I committed a great sin
when I counted Judah and Israel's
men. LORD, I beg you to take away my
guilt. I've done a very foolish thing."

¹¹Before David got up the next
morning, a message from the LORD
came to the prophet Gad. He was
David's seer. The message said, ¹²"Go
and tell David, 'The LORD says, "I could
punish you in three different ways.
Choose one of them for me to use
against you." ' "

¹³So Gad went to David. He said to
him, "Take your choice. Do you want
three years when there won't be
enough food in your land? Or do you
want three months when you will run
away from your enemies while they
chase you? Or do you want three days
when there will be a plague in your
land? Think it over. Then take your
pick. Tell me how to answer the One
who sent me."

¹⁴David said to Gad, "I'm suffering
terribly. Let us fall into the hands
of the LORD. His mercy is great. But

don't let me fall into the hands of men."

¹⁵So the LORD sent a plague on Israel. It lasted from that morning until he decided to end it. From Dan all the way to Beersheba 70,000 people died.

¹⁶The angel reached his hand out to destroy Jerusalem. But the LORD was very sad because of the plague. So he spoke to the angel who was making the people suffer. He said, "That is enough! Do not kill any more people." The angel of the LORD was at Araunah's threshing floor. Araunah was from the city of Jebus.

¹⁷David saw the angel who was striking the people down. David said to the LORD, "I'm the one who has sinned. I'm the one who has done what is wrong. These people are like sheep. What have they done? Let your powerful hand punish me and my family."

DAVID BUILDS AN ALTAR

¹⁸On that day Gad went to David. Gad said to him, "Go up to the threshing floor of Araunah, the Jebusite. Build an altar there to honor the LORD."

¹⁹So David went up and did it. He did what the LORD had commanded through Gad.

²⁰Araunah looked and saw the king and his officials coming toward him.

So he went out to welcome them. He bowed down to the king with his face toward the ground.

²¹Araunah said, "King David, you are my master. Why have you come to see me?"

"To buy your threshing floor," David answered. "I want to build an altar there to honor the LORD. When I do, the plague on the people will be stopped."

²²Araunah said to David, "Take anything that pleases you. Offer it up. Here are oxen for the burnt offering. Here are threshing sleds. And here are wooden collars from the necks of the oxen. Use all of the wood to burn the offering. ²³King David, I'll give all of it to you." Araunah continued, "And may the LORD your God accept you."

²⁴But the king replied to Araunah, "No. I want to pay you for it. I won't sacrifice to the LORD my God burnt offerings that haven't cost me anything."

So David bought the threshing floor and the oxen. He paid 20 ounces of silver for them. ²⁵David built an altar there to honor the LORD. He sacrificed burnt offerings and friendship offerings.

Then the LORD answered prayer and blessed the land. The plague on Israel was stopped.

KIDS' QUESTion

Why is there such a thing as money?

David gave Araunah money for a valuable piece of land. By giving him silver, David was showing how much the land was worth. People use money to trade one thing for another. Think of the times you go to the store. How would you buy something without money? You would have to trade something you have for what you want. The store would have to want what you have to trade. But what if the store didn't want what you were offering? That is why there is money. It is something that everyone is willing to trade for anything.

Related verse: Ecclesiastes 5:19

checkout
2 Samuel 24:24

$999.⁹⁹

FULLY OPERATIONAL MINI·4×4

1 Kings

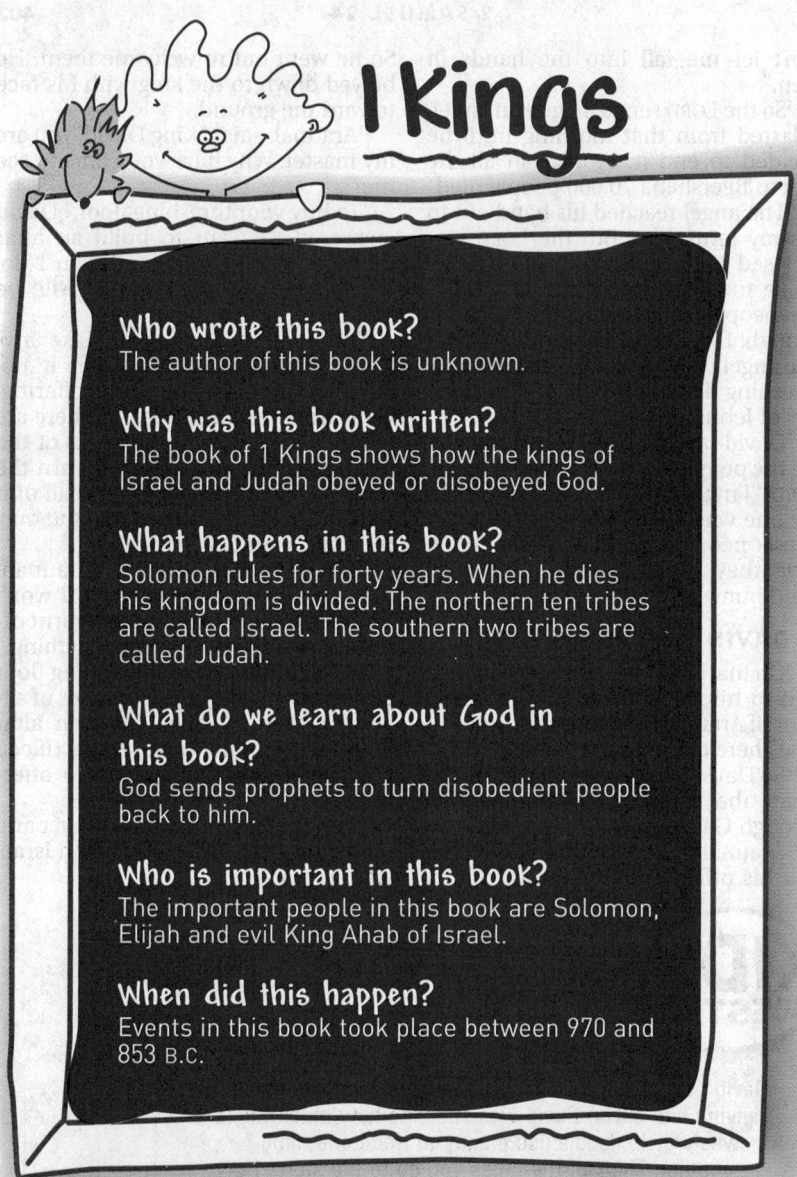

Who wrote this book?
The author of this book is unknown.

Why was this book written?
The book of 1 Kings shows how the kings of Israel and Judah obeyed or disobeyed God.

What happens in this book?
Solomon rules for forty years. When he dies his kingdom is divided. The northern ten tribes are called Israel. The southern two tribes are called Judah.

What do we learn about God in this book?
God sends prophets to turn disobedient people back to him.

Who is important in this book?
The important people in this book are Solomon, Elijah and evil King Ahab of Israel.

When did this happen?
Events in this book took place between 970 and 853 B.C.

ADONIJAH MAKES HIMSELF KING

1 King David was now very old. He couldn't keep warm even when blankets were spread over him. ²So his servants spoke to him. They said, "You are our king and master. Please let us try to find a young virgin to help you. She can take care of you. She can lie down beside you. Then you can keep warm."

³So David's servants looked all over Israel for a beautiful young woman. They found Abishag. She was from the town of Shunem. They brought her to the king. ⁴The woman was very beautiful. She took care of the king and served him. But the king didn't have sex with her.

⁵Adonijah was the son of David and his wife Haggith. He came forward and announced, "I'm going to be the

next king." So he got chariots and horses ready. He also got 50 men to run in front of him.

⁶His father had never tried to stop him from doing what he wanted to. His father had never asked him, "Why are you acting the way you do?"

Adonijah was also very handsome. Now that Absalom was dead, Adonijah was David's oldest son.

⁷Adonijah talked things over with Joab, the son of Zeruiah. He also talked with the priest Abiathar. They agreed to help him.

⁸But the priest Zadok and Benaiah, the son of Jehoiada, didn't join Adonijah. The prophet Nathan didn't join him. Shimei and Rei didn't join him. And neither did David's special guard.

⁹Adonijah sacrificed sheep, cattle and fat calves. He sacrificed them at the Stone of Zoheleth near En Rogel. He invited all of his brothers, the king's sons, and all of the men of Judah who were royal officials.

¹⁰But he didn't invite Benaiah or the prophet Nathan. He didn't invite the special guard or his brother Solomon either.

¹¹Nathan spoke to Solomon's mother Bathsheba. He asked, "Haven't you heard? Adonijah, the son of Haggith, has made himself king. And King David doesn't even know about it.

¹²"So let me tell you what to do to save your life. It will also save the life of your son Solomon. ¹³Go in and see King David. Say to him, 'You are my king and master. You took an oath. You promised me, "You can be sure that your son Solomon will be king after me. He will sit on my throne." If that's really true, why has Adonijah become king?'

¹⁴"While you are still talking to the king, I'll come in. I'll tell him that what you have said is true."

¹⁵So Bathsheba went to see the old king in his room. Abishag, the Shunammite, was taking care of him there. ¹⁶Bathsheba bowed low. She got down on her knees in front of the king.

"What do you want?" the king asked.

¹⁷She said to him, "My master, you took an oath in the name of the LORD your God. You promised me, 'Your son Solomon will be king after me. He will sit on my throne.'

¹⁸"But now Adonijah has made himself king. And you don't even know about it. ¹⁹He has sacrificed large numbers of cattle, fat calves and sheep. He has invited all of the king's sons. He has also invited the priest Abiathar and Joab, the commander of the army. But he hasn't invited your son Solomon.

²⁰"You are my king and master. All of the people of Israel are watching to see what you will do. They want to find out from you who will sit on the throne after you. ²¹If you don't do something, I and my son Solomon will be treated like people who have committed crimes. That will happen as soon as you join the members of your family who have already died."

²²While she was still speaking with the king, the prophet Nathan arrived. ²³The king was told, "The prophet Nathan is here." So Nathan went to the king. He bowed down with his face toward the ground.

²⁴Nathan said, "You are my king and master. Have you announced that Adonijah will be king after you? Have you said he will sit on your throne? ²⁵Today he has gone down outside the city. He has sacrificed large numbers of cattle, fat calves and sheep. He has invited all of the king's sons. He has also invited the commanders of the army and the priest Abiathar. Even now they are eating and drinking with him. They are saying, 'May King Adonijah live a long time!'

²⁶"But he didn't invite me. He didn't invite the priest Zadok or Benaiah, the son of Jehoiada. He didn't invite your son Solomon either.

²⁷"King David, have you allowed all of that to happen? Did you do it without letting us know about it? Why didn't you tell us who is going to sit on your throne after you?"

DAVID MAKES SOLOMON KING

²⁸King David said, "Tell Bathsheba to come in." So she came and stood in front of the king.

²⁹Then the king took an oath and made a promise. He said, "The LORD

has saved me from all of my troubles. You can be sure that he lives. ³⁰And you can be just as sure that I will do today what I promised in the name of the LORD. He is the God of Israel. I promised you that your son Solomon would be king after me. He will sit on my throne in my place."

³¹Then Bathsheba bowed low with her face toward the ground. She got down on her knees in front of the king. She said, "King David, you are my master. May you live forever!"

³²King David said, "Tell the priest Zadok and the prophet Nathan to come in. Also tell Benaiah, the son of Jehoiada, to come." So they came to the king.

³³He said to them, "Take my officials with you. Put my son Solomon on my own mule. Take him down to the Gihon spring. ³⁴Have the priest Zadok and the prophet Nathan anoint him as king over Israel there. Blow a trumpet. Shout, 'May King Solomon live a long time!' ³⁵Then come back up to the city with him. Have him sit on my throne. He will rule in my place. I've appointed him ruler over Israel and Judah."

³⁶Benaiah, the son of Jehoiada, answered the king. "Amen!" he said. "May the LORD your God make it come true. ³⁷You are my king and master. The LORD has been with you. May he also be with Solomon. King David, may the LORD make Solomon's kingdom even greater than yours!"

³⁸So the priest Zadok and the prophet Nathan left the palace. Benaiah, the son of Jehoiada, went with them. So did the Kerethites and Pelethites. They put Solomon on King David's mule. And they brought him down to the Gihon spring.

³⁹The priest Zadok had gotten an animal horn that was filled with olive oil. He had taken it from the sacred tent. He anointed Solomon with the oil. The trumpet was blown. All of the people shouted, "May King Solomon live a long time!"

⁴⁰Then they went up toward the city. Solomon was leading the way. The people were playing flutes. They were filled with great joy. The ground shook because of all of the noise.

⁴¹Adonijah and all of his guests heard it. They were just finishing their meal. Joab heard the sound of the trumpet. So he asked, "What does all of that noise in the city mean?"

⁴²While Joab was still speaking, Jonathan arrived. Jonathan was the son of the priest Abiathar. Adonijah said, "Come in. I have respect for you. You must be bringing good news."

⁴³"No! I'm not!" Jonathan answered. "Our master King David has made Solomon king. ⁴⁴David sent the priest Zadok and the prophet Nathan along with Solomon. He also sent Benaiah, the son of Jehoiada, with him. He sent the Kerethites and Pelethites with him too. They put him on the king's mule. ⁴⁵They took him down to the Gihon spring. There the priest Zadok and the prophet Nathan anointed him as king. Now they've gone back up to the city. They were cheering all the way. The city is filled with the sound of it. That's the noise you hear.

⁴⁶"And that's not all. Solomon has taken his seat on the royal throne. ⁴⁷The royal officials came to give their blessing to our master King David. They said, 'May your God make Solomon's name more famous than yours! May he make Solomon's kingdom greater than yours!'

"While King David was sitting on his bed, he bowed in worship. ⁴⁸He said, 'I praise the LORD. He is the God of Israel. He has let me live to see my son sitting on my throne today as the next king.' "

⁴⁹When all of Adonijah's guests heard that, they were terrified. So they got up and scattered.

⁵⁰Adonijah was afraid of what Solomon might do to him. So he went and grabbed hold of the horns that stuck out from the upper corners of the altar for burnt offerings.

⁵¹Then Solomon was told, "King Solomon, Adonijah is afraid of you. He's holding onto the horns of the altar. He says, 'I want King Solomon to take an oath today. I want him to promise that he won't kill me with his sword.' "

⁵²Solomon replied, "Let him show that he's a man people can respect. Then not even one hair on his head will fall to the ground. But if I find

out he's done something evil, he will die."

⁵³King Solomon got some men to bring Adonijah down from the altar. He came and bowed down to King Solomon. Solomon said, "Go on home."

DAVID GIVES ORDERS TO SOLOMON

2 The time came near for David to die. So he gave orders to his son Solomon. He said,

²"I'm about to die, just as everyone else on earth does. So be strong. Show how brave you are. ³Do everything the LORD your God requires. Live the way he wants you to. Obey his orders and commands. Keep his laws and rules. Do everything that is written in the Law of Moses. Then you will have success in everything you do. You will succeed everywhere you go.

⁴"The LORD will keep the promise he made to me. He said, 'Your sons must be careful about how they live. They must be faithful to me with all their heart and soul. Then you will always have a man sitting on the throne of Israel.'

⁵"You yourself know what Joab, the son of Zeruiah, did to me. You know that he killed Abner, the son of Ner, and Amasa, the son of Jether. They were the two commanders of Israel's armies. He killed them in a time of peace. It wasn't a time of war. Joab spilled the blood of Abner and Amasa. It stained the belt that was around his waist. It also stained the sandals on his feet. ⁶You are wise. So I leave him in your hands. Just don't let him live to become an old man. Don't let him die peacefully.

⁷"But be kind to the sons of Barzillai from Gilead. Provide what they need. They were faithful to me when I had to run away from your brother Absalom.

⁸"Don't forget Shimei, the son of Gera. He's still around. He's from Bahurim in the territory of Benjamin. He called down bitter curses on me. He did it on the day I went to Mahanaim. Later, he came down to welcome me at the Jordan River. At that time I took an oath in the name of the LORD. I promised Shimei, 'I won't put you to death with my sword.' ⁹But now

I want you to think of him as guilty. You are wise. You will know what to do to him. Don't let him live to become an old man. Put him to death."

¹⁰David joined the members of his family who had already died. His body was buried in the City of David. ¹¹He had ruled over Israel for 40 years. He ruled for seven years in Hebron. Then he ruled for 33 years in Jerusalem.

¹²So Solomon sat on the throne of his father David. His position as king was made secure.

SOLOMON'S KINGDOM IS MADE SECURE

¹³Adonijah was the son of David's wife Haggith. He went to Bathsheba. She was Solomon's mother. She asked Adonijah, "Have you come in peace?"

He answered, "Yes. I've come in peace." ¹⁴He continued, "I want to ask you something."

"Go ahead," she replied.

¹⁵He said, "As you know, the kingdom belonged to me. The whole nation of Israel thought of me as their king. But now things have changed. The kingdom belongs to my brother. The LORD has given it to him. ¹⁶But I have a favor to ask of you. Don't say no to me."

"Go ahead," she said.

¹⁷So he continued, "Please ask King Solomon for a favor. He won't say no to you. Ask him to give me Abishag from Shunem to be my wife."

¹⁸"All right," Bathsheba replied. "I'll speak to the king for you."

¹⁹So Bathsheba went to King Solomon. She went to him to speak for Adonijah. The king stood up to greet her. He bowed down to her. Then he sat down on his throne. He had a throne brought for his mother. She sat down at his right side.

²⁰"I have one small favor to ask of you," she said. "Don't say no to me."

The king replied, "Mother, go ahead and ask. I won't say no to you."

²¹She said, "Let your brother Adonijah get married to Abishag, the Shunammite."

²²King Solomon answered his mother, "Why are you asking for Abishag, the Shunammite, for Adonijah? You might as well ask me to give him the

whole kingdom! After all, he's my older brother. And he doesn't want the kingdom only for himself. He also wants it for the priest Abiathar and for Joab, the son of Zeruiah."

²³Then King Solomon took an oath and made a promise in the name of the LORD. He said, "Adonijah will pay with his life because of what he has asked for. If he doesn't, may God punish me greatly. ²⁴The LORD has made my position as king secure. I'm sitting on the throne of my father David. The LORD has built a royal house for me, just as he promised. You can be sure that the LORD lives. And you can be just as sure that Adonijah will be put to death today."

²⁵So King Solomon gave the order to Benaiah, the son of Jehoiada. Benaiah struck Adonijah down. And Adonijah died.

²⁶The king spoke to the priest Abiathar. He said, "Go back to your fields in Anathoth. You should really be put to death. But I won't have it done now. That's because you carried the ark of the LORD and King. You did it for my father David. You shared all of his hard times."

²⁷So Solomon wouldn't let Abiathar serve as a priest of the LORD anymore. That's how the message the LORD had spoken at Shiloh came true. He had spoken it about the family of Eli.

²⁸News of what Solomon had done reached Joab. Joab had never made evil plans along with Absalom. But he had joined Adonijah. So he ran to the tent of the LORD. He took hold of the horns that stuck out from the upper corners of the altar for burnt offerings.

²⁹King Solomon was told that Joab had run to the tent. He was also told that Joab was by the altar.

Then Solomon gave the order to Benaiah, the son of Jehoiada. He told him, "Go! Strike him down!"

³⁰So Benaiah entered the tent of the LORD. He said to Joab, "The king says, 'Come on out!' "

But Joab answered, "No. I'd rather die here."

Benaiah told the king what Joab had said to him.

³¹Then the king commanded Benaiah, "Do what he says. Strike him down. Bury his body. Then I and my family won't be held accountable for the blood Joab spilled. He killed people who weren't guilty of doing anything wrong. ³²The LORD will pay him back for the blood he spilled. Joab attacked two men. He killed them with his sword. And my father David didn't even know anything about it.

"Joab killed Abner, the son of Ner. Abner was the commander of Israel's army. Joab also killed Amasa, the son of Jether. Amasa was the commander of Judah's army. Abner and Amasa were better men than Joab is. They were more honest than he is. ³³May Joab and his children after him be held forever accountable for spilling the blood of Abner and Amasa.

"But may David and his children after him enjoy the LORD's peace and rest forever. May the LORD also give his peace to David's royal house and kingdom forever."

³⁴So Benaiah, the son of Jehoiada, went up to the LORD's tent. There he struck Joab down. And he killed him. Joab's body was buried on his own land in the desert.

³⁵The king put Benaiah in charge of the army. Benaiah took Joab's place. The king also put the priest Zadok in Abiathar's place.

³⁶Then the king sent for Shimei. He said to him, "Build yourself a house in Jerusalem. Live there. Don't go anywhere else. ³⁷You must not leave the city and go across the Kidron Valley. If you do, you can be sure you will die. And it will be your own fault."

³⁸Shimei replied to the king, "You are my king and master. What you say is good. I'll do it." Shimei stayed in Jerusalem for a long time.

³⁹Three years after Solomon had talked with Shimei, two of Shimei's slaves ran off. They went to Achish, the king of Gath. He was the son of Maacah. Shimei was told, "Your slaves are in Gath." ⁴⁰When Shimei heard that, he put a saddle on his donkey. Then he went to Achish at Gath to look for his slaves. Shimei found them and brought them back from Gath.

⁴¹Solomon was told that Shimei had left Jerusalem. He was told he had gone to Gath and had returned.

⁴²So the king sent for Shimei. He said to him, "Didn't I make you take an oath in the name of the LORD? Didn't I warn you? I said, 'You must not leave the city and go somewhere else. If you do, you can be sure you will die.' At that time you said to me, 'What you say is good. I'll obey your command.' ⁴³So why didn't you keep your oath to the LORD? Why didn't you obey the command I gave you?"

⁴⁴The king continued, "You know all of the wrong things you did to my father David. In your heart you know them. Now the LORD will pay you back for what you did. ⁴⁵But I will be blessed. The LORD will make David's kingdom secure forever."

⁴⁶Then the king gave the order to Benaiah, the son of Jehoiada. Benaiah left the palace and struck Shimei down. And he killed him.

So the kingdom was now made secure in Solomon's hands.

SOLOMON ASKS GOD FOR WISDOM

3 Solomon and Pharaoh, the king of Egypt, agreed to help each other. So Solomon got married to Pharaoh's daughter. He brought her to the City of David. She stayed there until he finished building his palace, the LORD's temple, and the wall that was around Jerusalem. ²But the people continued to offer sacrifices at the high places where they worshiped. That's because a temple hadn't been built yet where the LORD would put his Name. ³Solomon showed his love for the LORD. He did it by obeying the laws his father David had taught him. But Solomon offered sacrifices at the high places. He also burned incense there.

⁴King Solomon went to the city of Gibeon to offer sacrifices. That's where the most important high place was. He offered 1,000 burnt offerings on the altar that was there.

⁵The LORD appeared to Solomon at Gibeon. He spoke to him in a dream during the night. God said, "Ask for anything you want me to give you."

⁶Solomon answered, "You have been very kind to my father David, your servant. That's because he was faithful to you. He did what was right. His heart was honest. And you have continued to be very kind to him. You have given him a son to sit on his throne this very day.

⁷"LORD my God, you have now made me king. You have put me in the place of my father David. But I'm only a little child. I don't know how to carry out my duties. ⁸I'm here among the people you have chosen. They are a great nation. They are more than anyone can count. ⁹So give me a heart that understands. Then I can rule over your people. I can tell the difference between what is right and what is wrong. Who can possibly rule over this great nation of yours?"

¹⁰The Lord was pleased that Solomon had asked for that. ¹¹So God said to him, "You have not asked to live for a long time. You have not asked to be wealthy. You have not even asked to have your enemies killed. Instead, you have asked for understanding. You want to do what is right and fair when you judge people. Because that is what you have asked for, ¹²I will give it to you. I will give you a wise and understanding heart. So here is what will be true of you. There has never been anyone like you. And there never will be.

¹³"And that is not all. I will give you what you have not asked for. I will give you riches and honor. As long as you live, no other king will be as great as you are. ¹⁴Live the way I want you to. Obey my laws and commands, just as your father David did. Then I will let you live for a long time."

¹⁵Solomon woke up. He realized he had been dreaming.

He returned to Jerusalem. He stood in front of the ark of the LORD's covenant. He sacrificed burnt offerings and friendship offerings. Then he gave a big dinner for all of his officials.

SOLOMON JUDGES WISELY

¹⁶Two prostitutes came to the king. They stood in front of him. ¹⁷One of them said, "My master, this woman and I live in the same house. I had a baby while she was there with me. ¹⁸Three days after my child was born, this woman also had a baby. We were

alone. There wasn't anyone in the house but the two of us.

19"During the night this woman's baby died. It happened because she was lying on top of him. 20So she got up in the middle of the night. She took my son from my side while I was asleep. She put him by her breast. Then she put her dead son by my breast. 21The next morning, I got up to nurse my son. But he was dead! I looked at him closely in the morning light. And I saw that it wasn't my baby."

22The other woman said, "No! The living baby is my son. The dead one belongs to you."

But the first woman said, "No! The dead baby is yours. The living one belongs to me." So they argued in front of the king.

23The king said, "One of you says, 'My son is alive. Your son is dead.' The other one says, 'No! Your son is dead. Mine is alive.' "

24He continued, "Bring me a sword." So a sword was brought to him. 25Then he gave an order. He said, "Cut the living child in two. Give half to one woman and half to the other."

26The woman whose son was alive

was filled with deep concern for her son. She said to the king, "My master, please give her the living baby! Don't kill him!"

But the other woman said, "Neither one of us will have him. Cut him in two!"

27Then the king made his decision. He said, "Give the living baby to the first woman. Don't kill him. She's his mother."

28All of the people of Israel heard about the decision the king had given. That gave them great respect for him. They saw that God had given him wisdom. They knew that Solomon would do what was right and fair when he judged people.

SOLOMON'S OFFICIALS AND GOVERNORS

4 So King Solomon ruled over the whole nation of Israel. 2Here are the names of his chief officials.

Azariah was the priest. He was the son of Zadok.

3Elihoreph and Ahijah were secretaries. They were the sons of Shisha.

Why did Solomon want to cut the baby in half?

God gave King Solomon a lot of wisdom. When two women were fighting over a baby, Solomon needed a way to know who the real mother was. He was not really going to cut the baby in half. He suggested that they cut the baby in half so he could see which woman cared more for the baby. Solomon knew that the real mother would never let such a thing happen to her baby. Solomon's plan worked. The baby was given to his real mother.

checkout 1 Kings 3:25

Related verses:
1 Kings 3:5–28

Jehoshaphat kept the records. He was the son of Ahilud.

⁴Benaiah was the commander in chief. He was the son of Jehoiada.

Zadok and Abiathar were priests.

⁵Azariah was in charge of the local officials. He was the son of Nathan.

Zabud was a priest. He was the king's personal adviser. He was the son of Nathan.

⁶Ahishar was in charge of the palace.

Adoniram was in charge of those who were forced to work for the king. He was the son of Abda.

⁷Solomon also had 12 local governors over the whole land of Israel. They provided supplies for the king and the royal family. Each governor had to provide supplies for one month out of each year. ⁸Here are their names and areas.

Ben-Hur's area was the hill country of Ephraim.

⁹Ben-Deker's area was Makaz, Shaalbim, Beth Shemesh and Elon Bethhanan.

¹⁰Ben-Hesed's area was Arubboth. Socoh and the whole land of Hepher were included in his area.

¹¹Ben-Abinadab's area was Naphoth Dor. He got married to Solomon's daughter Taphath.

¹²Baana's area was Taanach, Megiddo and the whole territory of Beth Shan. Beth Shan was next to Zarethan below Jezreel. Baana's area reached from Beth Shan all the way to Abel Meholah. It also went across to Jokmeam. Baana was the son of Ahilud.

¹³Ben-Geber's area was Ramoth Gilead. The settlements of Jair, the son of Manasseh, were included in his area in Gilead. The area of Argob in Bashan was also included. That area had 60 large cities that had high walls around them. The city gates were made secure with heavy bronze bars.

¹⁴Ahinadab's area was Mahanaim. He was the son of Iddo.

¹⁵Ahimaaz's area was Naphtali. He had gotten married to Basemath. She was Solomon's daughter.

¹⁶Baana's area was Asher and Aloth. He was the son of Hushai.

¹⁷Jehoshaphat's area was Issachar. He was the son of Paruah.

¹⁸Shimei's area was Benjamin. He was the son of Ela.

¹⁹Geber's area was Gilead. He was the only governor over the area. He was the son of Uri. Gilead had been the country of Sihon and Og. Sihon had been king of the Amorites. Og had been king of Bashan.

SOLOMON'S DAILY SUPPLIES

²⁰There were many people in Judah and Israel. In fact, they were as many as the grains of sand on the seashore. They ate, drank and were happy.

²¹Solomon ruled over all of the kingdoms from the Euphrates River to the land of the Philistines. He ruled as far as the border of Egypt. All of those countries brought the gifts he required them to bring him. And Solomon ruled over those countries for his whole life.

²²Here are the supplies Solomon required every day.

185 bushels of fine flour
375 bushels of meal
²³ten head of cattle that had been fed by hand
20 head of cattle that had been fed on grasslands
100 sheep and goats
deer, antelopes and roebucks
the finest birds

²⁴Solomon ruled over all of the kingdoms that were west of the Euphrates River. He ruled from Tiphsah all the way to Gaza. And he had peace and rest on every side. ²⁵While Solomon was king, Judah and Israel lived in safety. They were secure from Dan all the way to Beersheba. Each man had his own vine and fig tree. ²⁶Solomon had 4,000 spaces where

he kept his chariot horses. He had a total of 12,000 horses.

²⁷The local officials provided supplies for King Solomon. They provided them for all who ate at the king's table. Each official provided supplies for one month every year. The officials made sure the king had everything he needed. ²⁸They also brought barley and straw for the chariot horses and the other horses. Each of them brought the amounts that were required of them. They brought them to the proper places.

GOD MAKES SOLOMON VERY WISE

²⁹God made Solomon very wise. His understanding couldn't even be measured. It was like the sand on the seashore. People can't measure that either.

³⁰Solomon's wisdom was greater than the wisdom of all of the people of the east. It was greater than all of the wisdom of Egypt. ³¹Solomon was wiser than any other man. He was wiser than Ethan, the Ezrahite. He was wiser than Heman, Calcol and Darda. They were the sons of Mahol. Solomon became famous in all of the nations that were around him.

³²He spoke 3,000 proverbs. He wrote 1,005 songs. ³³He explained all about plants. He knew everything about them, from the cedar trees in Lebanon to the hyssop plants that grow out of walls. He taught about animals and birds. He also taught about reptiles and fish.

³⁴The kings of all of the world's nations heard about how wise Solomon was. So they sent their people to listen to him.

SOLOMON ASKS HIRAM TO HELP BUILD THE TEMPLE

5 Hiram was the king of Tyre. He heard that Solomon had been anointed as king. He heard that Solomon had become the next king after his father David. Hiram had always been David's friend. So Hiram sent his messengers to Solomon.

²Then Solomon sent a message back to Hiram. It said,

³"As you know, my father David had to fight many battles. His enemies attacked him from every side. So he couldn't build a temple where the LORD his God would put his Name. That wouldn't be possible until the LORD had put his enemies under his control.

⁴"But now the LORD my God has given me peace and rest on every side. We don't have any enemies. And we don't have any other major problems either. ⁵So I'm planning to build a temple. I want to build it for the Name of the LORD my God. That's what he told my father David he wanted me to do. He said, 'I will put your son on the throne in your place. He will build a temple. I will put my Name there.'

⁶"So give your men orders to cut down cedar trees in Lebanon for me. My men will work with yours. I'll pay you for your men's work. I'll pay any amount you decide on. As you know, we don't have anyone who is as skilled in cutting down trees as the men of Sidon are."

⁷When Hiram heard Solomon's message, he was very pleased. He said, "May the LORD be praised today. He has given David a wise son to rule over that great nation."

⁸So Hiram sent a message to Solomon. It said,

"I have received the message you sent me. I'll do everything you want me to. I'll provide the cedar and pine logs. ⁹My men will bring them from Lebanon down to the Mediterranean Sea. I'll make them into rafts. I'll float them to the place you want me to. When the rafts arrive, I'll separate the logs from each other. Then you can take them away.

"And here's what I want in return. Provide food for all of the people in my palace."

¹⁰So Hiram supplied Solomon with all of the cedar and pine logs he wanted. ¹¹Solomon gave Hiram 125,000 bushels of wheat as food for the peo-

ple in his palace. He also gave him 115,000 gallons of oil that was made from pressed olives. He did that for Hiram year after year.

¹²The LORD made Solomon wise, just as he had promised him. There was peace between Hiram and Solomon. The two of them made a peace treaty.

¹³King Solomon forced men from all over Israel to work hard for him. There were 30,000 of them. ¹⁴He sent them off to Lebanon in groups of 10,000 each month. They spent one month in Lebanon. Then they spent two months at home. Adoniram was in charge of the people who were forced to work. ¹⁵Solomon had 70,000 people who carried things. He had 80,000 who cut stones in the hills. ¹⁶He had 3,300 men who were in charge of the project. They also directed the workers.

¹⁷The people did what the king commanded. They removed large blocks of fine stone from a rock pit. They used them to provide a foundation for the temple. ¹⁸The skilled workers of Solomon and Hiram cut and prepared the logs and stones. They would later be used in building the temple. The people of Byblos helped the workers.

SOLOMON BUILDS THE TEMPLE

6 Solomon began to build the temple of the LORD. It was 480 years after the people of Israel had come out of Egypt. It was in the fourth year of Solomon's rule over Israel. He started in the second month. That was the month of Ziv.

²The temple King Solomon built for the LORD was 90 feet long. It was 30 feet wide. And it was 45 feet high. ³The temple had a porch in front of the main hall. The porch was as wide as the temple itself. It was 30 feet wide. It came out 15 feet from the front of the temple. ⁴Solomon made narrow windows high up in the temple walls.

⁵He built side rooms around the temple. They were built against the walls of the main hall and the Most Holy Room. ⁶On the first floor the side rooms were seven and a half feet wide. On the second floor they were nine feet wide. And on the third floor they

were ten and a half feet wide. Solomon made the walls of the temple thinner as they went up floor by floor. The result was ledges along the walls. So the floor beams of the side rooms rested on the ledges. The beams didn't go into the temple walls.

⁷All of the stones that were used for building the temple were shaped where they were cut. So hammers, chisels and other iron tools couldn't be heard where the temple was being built.

⁸The entrance to the first floor was on the south side of the temple. A stairway led up to the second floor. From there it went on up to the third floor.

⁹So Solomon built the temple and finished it. He made its roof out of beams and cedar boards. ¹⁰He built side rooms all along the temple. Each room was seven and a half feet high. They were joined to the temple by cedar beams.

¹¹A message came to Solomon from the LORD. The LORD said, ¹²"You are now building this temple. Follow my orders. Keep my rules. Obey all of my commands. Then I will make the promise I gave your father David come true. I will do it through you. ¹³I will live among my people Israel. I will not desert them."

¹⁴So Solomon built the temple and finished it. ¹⁵He put cedar boards on its inside walls. He covered them from floor to ceiling. He covered the temple floor with pine boards. ¹⁶He put up a wall 30 feet from the back of the temple. He made it with cedar boards from floor to ceiling. That formed a room inside the temple. It was the Most Holy Room. ¹⁷The main hall in front of the room was 60 feet long. ¹⁸The inside of the temple was covered with cedar wood. Gourds and open flowers were carved on the wood. Everything was cedar. There wasn't any stone showing anywhere.

¹⁹Solomon prepared the Most Holy Room inside the temple. That's where the ark of the covenant of the LORD would be placed. ²⁰The Most Holy Room was 30 feet long. It was 30 feet wide. And it was 30 feet high. Solomon covered the inside of it with pure gold.

He prepared the cedar altar for burning incense. He covered it with gold. ²¹Solomon covered the inside of the main hall with pure gold. He placed gold chains across the front of the Most Holy Room. That room was covered with gold. ²²So Solomon covered the inside of the whole temple with gold. He also covered the altar for burning incense with gold. It was right in front of the Most Holy Room.

²³For the Most Holy Room Solomon made a pair of cherubim. He made them out of olive wood. Each cherub was 15 feet high. ²⁴One wing of the first cherub was seven and a half feet long. The other wing was also seven and a half feet long. So the wings measured 15 feet from tip to tip. ²⁵The second cherub's wings also measured 15 feet from tip to tip. The two cherubim had the same size and shape. ²⁶Each cherub was 15 feet high.

²⁷Solomon placed the cherubim inside the Most Holy Room in the temple. Their wings were spread out. The wing tip of one cherub touched one wall. The wing tip of the other touched the other wall. The tips of their wings touched each other in the middle of the room. ²⁸Solomon covered the cherubim with gold.

²⁹On the walls that were all around the temple he carved cherubim, palm trees and open flowers. He carved them on the walls of the Most Holy Room and the main hall. ³⁰He also covered the floors of those two rooms with gold.

³¹For the entrance to the Most Holy Room he made two doors out of olive wood. Each doorpost had five sides. ³²On the two olive wood doors he carved cherubim, palm trees and open flowers. He covered the cherubim and palm trees with hammered gold.

³³In the same way he made olive wood doorposts for the entrance to the main hall. Each doorpost had four sides. ³⁴He also made two pine doors. Each door had two parts. They turned in bases that were shaped like cups. ³⁵He carved cherubim, palm trees and open flowers on the doors. He covered the doors with gold. He hammered the gold evenly over the carvings.

³⁶He used blocks of stone to build a wall around the inside courtyard. The first three layers of the wall were made out of stone. The top layer was made out of beautiful cedar wood.

³⁷The foundation of the LORD's temple was laid in Solomon's fourth year. It was in the month of Ziv. ³⁸The temple was finished in his 11th year. It was in the month of Bul. That was the eighth month. Everything was finished just as the plans required. Solomon had spent seven years building the temple.

SOLOMON BUILDS HIS PALACE

7 But it took Solomon 13 years to finish constructing his palace and the other buildings that were related to it.

²He built the Palace of the Forest of Lebanon. It was 150 feet long. It was 75 feet wide. And it was 45 feet high. It had four rows of cedar columns. They held up beautiful cedar beams. ³Above the beams was a roof that was made out of cedar boards. It rested on the columns. There were three rows of beams with 15 in each row. The total number of beams was 45. ⁴The windows of the palace were placed high up in the walls. They were in groups of three. And they faced each other. ⁵All of the doorways had frames that were shaped like rectangles. They were in front. They were in groups of three. And they faced each other.

⁶Solomon made a covered area. It was 75 feet long. And it was 45 feet wide. Its roof was held up by columns. In front of it was a porch. In front of that were pillars and a roof that went out beyond them.

⁷Solomon built the throne hall. It was called the Hall of Justice. That's where he would serve as judge. He covered the hall with cedar boards from floor to ceiling.

⁸The palace where he would live was set farther back. Its plan was something like the plan for the hall. Solomon had gotten married to Pharaoh's daughter. He made a palace for her. It was like the hall.

⁹All of those buildings were made out of blocks of very fine stone. They

were cut to the right size. They were shaped with a saw on the back and front sides. Those stones were used for the outside of each building and for the large courtyard. They were also used from the foundations up to the roofs. ¹⁰Large blocks of very fine stone were used for the foundations. Some were 15 feet long. Others were 12 feet long. ¹¹The walls that were above them were made out of very fine stones. The stones were cut to the right size. On top of them was a layer of cedar beams.

¹²The large courtyard had a wall around it. The first three layers of the wall were made out of blocks of stone. The top layer was made out of beautiful cedar wood. The same thing was done with the inside courtyard of the LORD's temple and its porch.

MORE FACTS ABOUT THE TEMPLE

¹³King Solomon sent messengers to Tyre. He wanted them to bring Huram back with them. ¹⁴Huram's mother was a widow. She was from the tribe of Naphtali. Huram's father was from Tyre. He was skilled in working with bronze. Huram also was very skilled. He had done all kinds of work with bronze. He came to King Solomon and did all of the work he was asked to do.

¹⁵Huram made two bronze pillars. Each of them was 27 feet high. And each was 18 feet around. ¹⁶Each pillar had a decorated top that was made out of bronze. Each top was seven and a half feet high.

¹⁷Chains that were linked together hung down from the tops of the pillars. There were seven chains for each top. ¹⁸Huram made two rows of pomegranates. They circled the chains. The pomegranates decorated the tops of the pillars. Huram did the same thing for each pillar. ¹⁹The tops on the pillars of the porch were shaped like lilies. The lilies were 6 feet high. ²⁰On the tops of both pillars were 200 pomegranates. They were in rows all around the tops. They were above the part that was shaped like a bowl. And they were next to the chains.

²¹Huram set the pillars up at the temple porch. The pillar on the south he named Jakin. The one on the north he named Boaz. ²²The tops of the pillars were shaped like lilies. So the work on the pillars was finished.

²³Huram made a huge metal bowl for washing. Its shape was round. It measured 15 feet from rim to rim. It was seven and a half feet high. And it was 45 feet around. ²⁴Below the rim there was a circle of gourds around the bowl. In every 18 inches around the bowl there were ten gourds. The gourds were arranged in two rows. They were made as part of the bowl itself.

²⁵The huge bowl stood on 12 bulls. Three of them faced north. Three faced west. Three faced south. And three faced east. The bowl rested on top of them. Their rear ends were toward the center. ²⁶The bowl was three inches thick. Its rim was like the rim of a cup. The rim was shaped like the bloom of a lily. The bowl held 11,500 gallons of water.

²⁷Huram also made ten stands out of bronze. They could be moved around. Each stand was six feet long. It was six feet wide. And it was four and a half feet high. ²⁸Here is how the stands were made. They had sides that were joined to posts. ²⁹On the sides between the posts were lions, bulls and cherubim. They were also on all of the posts. Above and below the lions and bulls were wreaths that were made out of hammered metal.

³⁰Each stand had four bronze wheels with bronze axles. Each one had a bowl that rested on four supports. They had wreaths on each side. ³¹There was a round opening on the inside of each stand. The opening had a frame that was 18 inches deep. The sides were 27 inches high from the top of the opening to the bottom of the base. There was carving around the opening. The sides of the stands were square, not round. ³²The four wheels were under the sides. The axles of the wheels were connected to the stand. Each wheel was 27 inches across. ³³The wheels were made like chariot wheels. All of the axles, rims, spokes and hubs were made out of metal. ³⁴Each stand had four handles on it.

There was one on each corner. They came out from the stand. ³⁵At the top of the stand there was a round band. It was nine inches deep. The sides and supports were connected to the top of the stand.

³⁶Huram carved cherubim, lions and palm trees on the sides of the stands. He also carved them on the surfaces of the supports. His carving covered every open space. He had also carved wreaths all around.

³⁷That's how he made the ten stands. All of them were made in the same molds. And they had the same size and shape.

³⁸Then Huram made ten bronze bowls. Each one held 230 gallons. The bowls measured six feet across. There was one bowl for each of the ten stands. ³⁹He placed five of the stands on the south side of the temple. He placed the other five on the north side. He put the huge bowl on the south side. It was at the southeast corner of the temple. ⁴⁰He also made the bowls, shovels and sprinkling bowls.

So Huram finished all of the work he had started for King Solomon. Here's what he made for the LORD's temple.

⁴¹ He made the two pillars.

He made the two tops for the pillars. The tops were shaped like bowls.

He made the two sets of chains that were linked together. They decorated the two bowl-shaped tops of the pillars.

⁴² He made the 400 pomegranates for the two sets of chains. There were two rows of pomegranates for each chain. They decorated the bowl-shaped tops of the pillars.

⁴³ He made the ten stands with their ten bowls.

⁴⁴ He made the huge bowl. He made the 12 bulls that were under it.

⁴⁵ He made the pots, shovels and sprinkling bowls.

Huram made all of those objects for King Solomon for the LORD's temple. He made them out of bronze. Then he shined them up. ⁴⁶The king had made them in clay molds. It was done on the flatlands of the Jordan River between Succoth and Zarethan.

⁴⁷Solomon didn't weigh any of those things. There were too many of them to weigh. No one even tried to weigh the bronze they were made out of.

⁴⁸Solomon also made all of the articles that were in the LORD's temple.

He made the golden altar.

He made the golden table for the holy bread.

⁴⁹ He made the pure gold lampstands. There were five on the right and five on the left. They were in front of the Most Holy Room.

He made the gold flowers. He made the gold lamps and tongs.

⁵⁰ He made the bowls, wick cutters, sprinkling bowls, dishes, and shallow cups for burning incense. All of them were made out of pure gold.

He made the gold bases for the doors of the inside room. That's the Most Holy Room. He also made gold bases for the doors of the main hall of the temple.

⁵¹King Solomon finished all of the work for the LORD's temple. Then he brought in the things his father David had set apart for the LORD. They included the silver and gold and all of the articles for the LORD's temple. Solomon placed them with the other treasures that were there.

SOLOMON BRINGS THE ARK TO THE TEMPLE

8 Then King Solomon sent for the elders of Israel. He told them to come to him in Jerusalem. They included all of the leaders of the tribes. They also included the chiefs of the families of Israel. Solomon wanted them to bring up the ark of the LORD's covenant from Zion. Zion was the City of David. ²All of the men of Israel came together to where King Solomon was. It was at the time of the Feast of Booths. The feast was held in the month of Ethanim. That's the seventh month.

³All of the elders of Israel arrived.

Then the priests picked up the ark and carried it. [4]They brought up the ark of the LORD. They also brought up the Tent of Meeting and all of the sacred articles that were in the tent. The priests and Levites carried everything up.

[5]The entire community of Israel had gathered around King Solomon. All of them were in front of the ark. They sacrificed huge numbers of sheep and cattle. There were so many that they couldn't be recorded. In fact, they couldn't even be counted.

[6]The priests brought the ark of the LORD's covenant to its place in the Most Holy Room of the temple. They put it under the wings of the cherubim. [7]The cherubim's wings were spread out over the place where the ark was. They covered the ark. They also covered the poles that were used to carry it. [8]The poles were so long that their ends could be seen from the Holy Room in front of the Most Holy Room. But they couldn't be seen from outside the Holy Room. They are still there to this very day.

[9]There wasn't anything in the ark except the two stone tablets. Moses had placed them in it at Mount Horeb. That's where the LORD had made a covenant with the Israelites. He made it after they came out of Egypt.

[10]The priests left the Holy Room. Then the cloud filled the temple of the LORD. [11]The priests couldn't do their work because of it. That's because the glory of the LORD filled his temple.

[12]Then Solomon said, "LORD, you have said you would live in a dark cloud. [13]As you can see, I've built a beautiful temple for you. You can live in it forever."

[14]The whole community of Israel was standing there. The king turned around and gave them his blessing. [15]Then he said,

"I praise the LORD. He is the God of Israel. With his own mouth he made a promise to my father David. With his own powerful hand he made it come true. He said, [16]'I brought my people Israel out of Egypt. Ever since I did that, I have not chosen a city in any tribe of Israel where a temple could be built for my Name. But I have chosen David to rule over my people Israel.'

[17]"With all his heart my father David wanted to build a temple. He wanted to do it so the LORD could put his Name there. The LORD is the God of Israel.

[18]"But the LORD spoke to my father David. He said, 'With all your heart you wanted to build a temple for my Name. It is good that you wanted to do that. [19]But you will not build the temple. Instead, your son will build the temple for my Name. He is your own flesh and blood.'

[20]"The LORD has kept the promise he made. I've become the next king after my father David. Now I'm sitting on the throne of Israel. That's exactly what the LORD promised would happen. I've built the temple where the LORD will put his Name. He is the God of Israel. [21]I've provided a place for the ark there. The tablets of the LORD's covenant are inside it. He made that covenant with our people of long ago. He made it when he brought them out of Egypt."

SOLOMON PRAYS TO SET THE TEMPLE APART TO THE LORD

[22]Then Solomon stood in front of the LORD's altar. He stood in front of the whole community of Israel. He spread out his hands toward heaven. [23]He said,

"LORD, you are the God of Israel. There is no God like you in heaven above or on earth below. You keep the covenant you made with us. You show us your love. You do that when we follow you with all our hearts. [24]You have kept your promise to my father David. He was your servant. With your mouth you made a promise. With your powerful hand you have made it come true. And today we can see it.

[25]"LORD, you are the God of Israel. Keep the promises you made to my father David. Do it for him.

He was your servant. You said to him, 'You will always have a man to sit on the throne of Israel in my sight. That will be true only if your sons are careful in everything they do. They must live in my sight the way you have lived.' ²⁶God of Israel, let your promise to my father David come true.

²⁷"But will you really live on earth? After all, the heavens can't hold you. In fact, even the highest heavens can't hold you. So this temple I've built certainly can't hold you!

²⁸"But please pay attention to my prayer. LORD my God, show me your favor as I make my appeal to you. Listen to my cry for help. Hear the prayer I'm praying to you today. ²⁹Let your eyes look toward this temple night and day. You said, 'I will put my Name there.' So please listen to the prayer I'm praying toward this place.

³⁰"Hear me when I ask you to show us your favor. Listen to your people Israel when they pray toward this place. Listen to us from heaven. It's the place where you live. When you hear us, forgive us.

³¹"Suppose a man does something wrong to his neighbor. And he is required to take an oath and make a promise. He must come and do it in front of your altar in this temple. ³²When he does, listen to him from heaven. Take action. Judge between those people. Punish the one who is guilty. Do to him what he has done to his neighbor. Tell everyone that the one who hasn't done anything wrong is free from blame. That will prove he isn't guilty.

³³"Suppose your people Israel have lost the battle against their enemies. And suppose they've sinned against you. But they turn back to you and praise your name. They pray to you in this temple.

KIDS' QUESTION

Where does God live?

He lives everywhere all at once. Sometimes we think that God must live in only one place at a time because that's the way we do it. We need a place to live so we think that God does, too. But God isn't limited by a body or a place. We call church "God's house" because that's where people who love God get together to worship him. And God loves being with his people. But no matter where we are, God is with us. We can never be lost to his love. God also lives in heaven. Someday we will live there, too.

checkout

1 Kings 8:27,30

Related verses:
Psalm 139:7–12;
Isaiah 66:1,2

And they ask you to show them your favor. [34]Then listen to them from heaven. Forgive the sin of your people Israel. Bring them back to the land you gave to their people who lived long ago.

[35]"Suppose your people have sinned against you. And because of that, the sky is closed up and there isn't any rain. But your people pray toward this place. They praise you by admitting they've sinned. And they turn away from their sin because you have made them suffer. [36]Then listen to them from heaven. Forgive the sin of your people Israel. Teach them the right way to live. Send rain on the land you gave them as their share.

[37]"Suppose there isn't enough food in the land. And a plague strikes the land. The hot winds completely dry up our crops. Or locusts or grasshoppers come and eat them up. Or an enemy surrounds one of our cities and gets ready to attack it. Or trouble or sickness comes. [38]But suppose one of your people prays to you. He asks you to show him your favor. He is aware of how much his own heart is suffering. And he spreads out his hands toward this temple to pray. [39]Then listen to him from heaven. It's the place where you live. Forgive him. Take action. Deal with him in keeping with everything he does. You know his heart. In fact, you are the only one who knows every human heart. [40]Your people will have respect for you. They will respect you as long as they are in the land you gave our people long ago.

[41]"Suppose there are strangers who don't belong to your people Israel. And they have come from a land far away. They've come because they've heard about your name. [42]When they get here, they will find out even more about your great name. They'll hear about how you reached out your mighty hand and powerful arm. So they'll come and pray toward this temple.

[43]"Then listen to them from heaven. It's the place where you live. Do what those strangers ask you to do. Then all of the nations on earth will know you. They will have respect for you. They'll respect you just as your own people Israel do. They'll know that your Name is in this house I've built.

[44]"Suppose your people go to war against their enemies. It doesn't matter where you send them. And suppose they pray to you toward the city you have chosen. They pray toward the temple I've built for your Name. [45]Then listen to them from heaven. Listen to their prayer. Listen to them when they ask you to show them your favor. Stand up for them.

[46]"Suppose your people sin against you. After all, there isn't anyone who doesn't sin. And suppose you get angry with them. You hand them over to their enemies. They take them as prisoners to their own land. It doesn't matter whether it's near or far away.

[47]"But suppose your people change their ways in the land where they are held as prisoners. They turn away from their sins. They beg you to help them in the land of those who won the battle over them. They say, 'We have sinned. We've done what is wrong. We've done what is evil.' [48]And they turn back to you with all their heart and soul. Suppose it happens in the land of their enemies who took them away as prisoners. There they pray to you toward the land you gave their people long ago. They pray toward the city you have chosen. And they pray toward the temple I've built for your Name.

[49]"Then listen to them from heaven. It's the place where you live. Listen to their prayer. Listen to them when they ask you to show them your favor. Stand up for them.

[50]"Your people have sinned against you. Please forgive them. Forgive them for all of the wrong things they've done against you.

And make those who won the battle over them show mercy to them. ⁵¹After all, they are your people. They belong to you. You brought them out of Egypt. You brought them out of that furnace that melts iron down and makes it pure.

⁵²"Let your eyes be open to me when I ask you to show us your favor. Let them be open to your people Israel when they ask you to show them your favor. Pay attention to them every time they cry out to you.

⁵³"After all, you chose them out of all of the nations in the world. You made them your very own people. You did it just as you had announced through your servant Moses. That's when you brought our people out of Egypt. You are our LORD and King."

⁵⁴Solomon finished all of those prayers. He finished asking the LORD to show his favor to his people. Then he got up from in front of the LORD's altar. He had been down on his knees with his hands spread out toward heaven. ⁵⁵He stood in front of the whole community of Israel. He blessed them with a loud voice. He said,

⁵⁶"I praise the LORD. He has given peace and rest to his people Israel. That's exactly what he promised to do. He gave his people good promises through his servant Moses. Every single word of those promises has come true.

⁵⁷"May the LORD our God be with us, just as he was with our people who lived long ago. May he never leave us. May he never desert us. ⁵⁸May he turn our hearts to him. Then we will live the way he wants us to. We'll obey the commands, rules and directions he gave our people.

⁵⁹"I've prayed these words to the LORD our God. May he keep them close to him day and night. May he stand up for me. May he also stand up for his people Israel. May he give us what we need every day. ⁶⁰Then all of the nations on earth will know that the LORD is

God. They'll know that there isn't any other god.

⁶¹"But you must commit your lives completely to the LORD our God. You must live by his rules. You must obey his commands. You must always do as you are doing now."

SOLOMON SETS THE TEMPLE APART TO THE LORD

⁶²Then the king and the whole community of Israel offered sacrifices to the LORD. ⁶³Solomon sacrificed friendship offerings to the LORD. He sacrificed 22,000 head of cattle. He also sacrificed 120,000 sheep and goats. So the king and the whole community set the temple of the LORD apart to him.

⁶⁴On that same day the king set the middle area of the courtyard apart to the LORD. It was in front of the LORD's temple. There Solomon sacrificed burnt offerings and grain offerings. He also sacrificed the fat of the friendship offerings there. He did it there because the bronze altar in front of the LORD was too small. It wasn't big enough to hold all of the burnt offerings, the grain offerings and the fat of the friendship offerings.

⁶⁵At that time Solomon celebrated the Feast of Booths. The whole community of Israel was with him. It was a huge crowd. People came from as far away as Lebo Hamath and the Wadi of Egypt. For seven days they celebrated in front of the LORD our God. The feast continued for seven more days. That made a total of 14 days.

⁶⁶On the following day Solomon sent the people away. They asked the LORD to bless the king. Then they went home. The people were glad. Their hearts were full of joy. That's because the LORD had done so many good things for his servant David and his people Israel.

THE LORD APPEARS TO SOLOMON

9 Solomon finished building the LORD's temple and the royal palace. He had accomplished everything he had planned to do. ²The

LORD appeared to him a second time. He had already appeared to him at Gibeon. ³The LORD said to him,

"I have heard you pray to me. I have heard you ask me to show you my favor. You have built this temple. I have set it apart for myself. My Name will be there forever. My eyes and my heart will always be there.

⁴"But you must walk with me, just as your father David did. Your heart must be honest. It must be without blame. Do everything I command you to do. Obey my rules and laws. ⁵Then I will set up your royal throne over Israel forever. I promised your father David I would do that. I said to him, 'You will always have a man on the throne of Israel.'

⁶"But suppose all of you turn away from me. Or your sons turn away from me. You refuse to obey the commands and rules I have given you. And you go off to serve other gods and worship them. ⁷Then I will cut Israel off from the land. It is the land I gave them. I will turn my back on this temple. I will do it even though I have set it apart for my Name to be there. Then Israel will be hated by all of the nations. They will laugh and joke about Israel.

⁸"This temple is now grand and beautiful. But the time is coming when all those who pass by it will be shocked. They will make fun of it. And they will say, 'Why has the LORD done a thing like this to this land and temple?'

⁹"People will answer, 'Because they have deserted the LORD their God. He brought their people out of Egypt. But they have been holding on to other gods. They've been worshiping them. They've been serving them. That's why the LORD has brought all of this horrible trouble on them.' "

OTHER THINGS SOLOMON DID

¹⁰Solomon built the LORD's temple and the royal palace. It took him 20 years to construct those two buildings.

¹¹King Solomon gave 20 towns in Galilee to Hiram. That's because Hiram had provided him with all of the cedar and pine logs he wanted. He had also provided him with all of the gold he wanted. Hiram was king of Tyre. ¹²Hiram went from Tyre to see the towns Solomon had given him. But he wasn't pleased with them. ¹³"My friend," he asked, "what have you given me? What kind of towns are these?" So he called them the Land of Cabul. And that's what they are still called to this very day. ¹⁴Hiram had sent four and a half tons of gold to Solomon.

¹⁵King Solomon forced people to work hard for him. Here is a record of what they did. They built the LORD's temple and Solomon's palace. They filled in the low places. They rebuilt the wall of Jerusalem. They built up Hazor, Megiddo and Gezer. ¹⁶Pharaoh, the king of Egypt, had attacked Gezer and captured it. He had set it on fire. He had killed the Canaanites who lived there. Then he had given Gezer as a wedding gift to his daughter. She was Solomon's wife. ¹⁷Solomon rebuilt Gezer. He built up Lower Beth Horon ¹⁸and Baalath. He built up Tadmor in the desert. All of those towns were in his land. ¹⁹He built up all of the cities where he could store things. He also built up the towns for his chariots and horses. He built anything he wanted to build in Jerusalem, Lebanon and all of the territory he ruled over.

²⁰There were still many people left in the land who weren't Israelites. They included Amorites, Hittites, Perizzites, Hivites and Jebusites. ²¹They were children of the people who had lived in the land before the Israelites came. Those people had been set apart to the LORD in a special way to be destroyed. But the Israelites hadn't been able to kill all of them. Solomon had forced them to work very hard as his slaves. And they still work for Israel to this very day.

²²But Solomon didn't force any of the men of Israel to work as his slaves. Instead, some were his fighting men. Others were his government officials, his officers and his captains. Others

were commanders of his chariots and chariot drivers. ²³Still others were the chief officials who were in charge of his projects. There were 550 officials in charge of those who did the work.

²⁴Pharaoh's daughter moved from the City of David up to the palace Solomon had built for her. After that, he filled in the low places near the palace.

²⁵Three times a year Solomon sacrificed burnt offerings and friendship offerings. He sacrificed them on the altar he had built to honor the LORD. Along with the offerings, he burned incense to the LORD. So he carried out his duties for the temple.

²⁶King Solomon also built ships at Ezion Geber. It's near Elath in Edom. It's on the shore of the Red Sea. ²⁷Hiram sent his men to serve on the ships together with Solomon's men. Hiram's sailors knew the sea. ²⁸All of them sailed to Ophir. They brought back 16 tons of gold. They gave it to King Solomon.

THE QUEEN OF SHEBA VISITS SOLOMON

10 The queen of Sheba heard about how famous Solomon was. She also heard about how he served and worshiped the LORD. So she came to test him with hard questions. ²She arrived in Jerusalem with a very large group of attendants. Her camels were carrying spices, huge amounts of gold, and valuable jewels. She came to Solomon and asked him about everything she wanted to know. ³Solomon answered all of her questions. There wasn't anything that was too hard for the king to explain to her. ⁴So the queen of Sheba saw how very wise Solomon was. She saw the palace he had built. ⁵She saw the food that was on his table. She saw his officials sitting there. She saw the robes of the servants who waited on everyone. She saw his wine tasters. And she saw the burnt offerings Solomon sacrificed at the LORD's temple. She could hardly believe everything she had seen.

⁶She said to the king, "Back in my own country I heard a report about

you. I heard about how much you had accomplished. I also heard about how wise you are. Everything I heard is true. ⁷But I didn't believe those things. So I came to see for myself. And now I believe it! You are twice as wise and wealthy as people say you are. The report I heard doesn't even begin to tell the whole story about you.

⁸"How happy your men must be! How happy your officials must be! They always get to serve you and hear the wise things you say. ⁹May the LORD your God be praised. He must take great delight in you. He placed you on the throne of Israel. The LORD will love Israel for all time to come. That's why he has made you king. He knows that you will do what is fair and right."

¹⁰She gave the king four and a half tons of gold. She also gave him huge amounts of spices and valuable jewels. No one would ever bring to King Solomon as many spices as the queen of Sheba gave him.

¹¹Hiram's ships brought gold from Ophir. From there they also brought huge amounts of almugwood and valuable jewels. ¹²The king used the almugwood to make supports for the LORD's temple and the royal palace. He also used it to make harps and lyres for those who played the music. That much almugwood has never been brought into Judah or seen there since that day.

¹³King Solomon gave the queen of Sheba everything she wanted and asked for. That was in addition to what he had given her out of his royal riches. Then she left. She returned to her own country with her attendants.

SOLOMON IN ALL OF HIS GLORY

¹⁴Each year Solomon received 25 tons of gold. ¹⁵That didn't include the money that was brought in by business and trade. It also didn't include the money from all of the kings of Arabia and the governors of Israel.

¹⁶King Solomon made 200 large shields out of hammered gold. Each one weighed seven and a half pounds. ¹⁷He also made 300 small shields out of

hammered gold. Each one weighed almost four pounds. The king put all of the shields in the Palace of the Forest of Lebanon.

[18]Then he made a large throne. It was decorated with ivory. It was covered with fine gold. [19]The throne had six steps. Its back had a rounded top. The throne had armrests on both sides of the seat. A statue of a lion stood on each side of the throne. [20]Twelve lions stood on the six steps. There was one at each end of each step. Nothing like that throne had ever been made for any other kingdom.

[21]All of King Solomon's cups were made out of gold. All of the articles that were used in the Palace of the Forest of Lebanon were made out of pure gold. Nothing was made out of silver. When Solomon was king, silver wasn't considered to be worth very much.

[22]He had many ships that carried goods to be traded. His ships went to sea along with Hiram's ships. Once every three years the ships returned. They brought gold, silver, ivory, apes and baboons.

[23]King Solomon was richer than all of the other kings on earth. He was also wiser than they were. [24]People from the whole world wanted to meet Solomon in person. They wanted to see for themselves how wise God had made him. [25]Year after year, everyone who came to him brought a gift. They brought articles that were made out of silver and gold. They brought robes, weapons and spices. They also brought horses and mules.

[26]Solomon had 1,400 chariots and 12,000 horses. He kept some of his horses and chariots in the chariot cities. He kept the others with him in Jerusalem.

[27]The king made silver as common in Jerusalem as stones. He made cedar wood as common there as sycamore-fig trees in the western hills.

[28]Solomon got horses from Egypt and from Kue. The royal traders bought them from Kue. [29]They weighed out 15 pounds of silver for a chariot from Egypt. And they weighed out almost four pounds of silver for a horse. They also sold horses and chariots to all of the kings of the Hittites and the kings of the Arameans.

KIDS' QUESTion

Is it OK to be popular?

Nothing is wrong with being popular if it's for the right reasons. Some kids are popular because they are kind and caring. King Solomon was popular because he used the wisdom that he got from God. Sometimes Christians are very unpopular, however, because they stand up for what is right. They have to say things that people don't want to hear and do what is right even though other people are doing what is wrong. (The prophets in the Bible sure weren't very popular!) It's much more important to have God's approval than to be popular with people.

checkout
1 Kings 10:6-9

Related verses:
John 5:44;
12:42-43;
Acts 5:29;
Romans 2:13;
Galatians 1:10

SOLOMON'S WIVES TURN HIM AWAY FROM THE LORD

11 King Solomon loved many women besides Pharaoh's daughter. They were from other lands. They were Moabites, Ammonites, Edomites, Sidonians and Hittites.

²The LORD had warned Israel about women from other nations. He had said, "You must not get married to them. If you do, you can be sure they will turn your hearts toward their gods." But Solomon continued to love them anyway. He wouldn't give them up. ³He had 700 wives who came from royal families. And he had 300 concubines. His wives led him down the wrong path.

⁴As Solomon grew older, his wives turned his heart toward other gods. He didn't follow the LORD his God with all his heart. So he wasn't like his father David. ⁵Solomon worshiped Ashtoreth. Ashtoreth was the goddess of the people of Sidon. He also worshiped Molech. Molech was the god of the people of Ammon. The LORD hated that god.

⁶Solomon did what was evil in the sight of the LORD. He didn't follow the LORD completely. He didn't do what his father David had done.

⁷There is a hill east of Jerusalem. Solomon built a high place for worshiping Chemosh there. He built a high place for worshiping Molech there too. Chemosh was the god of Moab. Molech was the god of Ammon. The LORD hated both of those gods.

⁸Solomon also built high places so that all of his wives from other nations could worship their gods. Those women burned incense and offered sacrifices to their gods.

⁹The LORD became angry with Solomon. That's because his heart had turned away from the LORD. He is the

Why does everybody want to do things that other people do?

Because they feel pressured. They want to be liked, fit in and not be too different. They may be afraid that kids will make fun of them if they don't do what everyone else is doing. Sometimes we assume that a movie, TV show or product is good because it's popular. We may think, *If so many people do that, it must be fun.* Or, *If so many people have seen that movie, it must be good.* That's OK as long as what's popular is pleasing to God. But no one has to give into pressure to do things that are wrong.

checkout
1 Kings 11:4–5

Related verses:
Matthew 5:19;
1 Corinthians 9:20;
Philemon 1:14

God of Israel. He had appeared to Solomon twice. ¹⁰He had commanded Solomon not to follow other gods. But Solomon didn't obey him.

¹¹So the LORD said to Solomon, "You have chosen not to keep my covenant. You have decided not to obey my rules. I commanded you to do what I told you. But you did not do it. So you can be absolutely sure I will tear the kingdom away from you. I will give it to one of your officials.

¹²"But I will not do that while you are still living. Because of your father David I will wait. I will tear the kingdom out of your son's hand. ¹³But I will not tear the whole kingdom away from him. I will give him one of the tribes because of my servant David. I will also do it because of Jerusalem. That is the city I have chosen."

THE LORD BRINGS ENEMIES AGAINST SOLOMON

¹⁴Then the LORD brought an enemy against Solomon. The enemy's name was Hadad. He was from Edom. In fact, he belonged to the royal family of Edom.

¹⁵David had fought against Edom. Joab had been the commander of the army. He had gone up to bury the dead bodies of the Israelites who had been killed in battle. At that time he had struck down all of the men in Edom. ¹⁶In fact, Joab and all of the men of Israel stayed there for six months. During that time they destroyed all of the men in Edom.

¹⁷But when Hadad was only a boy, he ran away to Egypt. Some officials from Edom went with him. They had served Hadad's father. ¹⁸They started out from Midian and went to Paran. They took some men from Paran with them. Then they went to Egypt. They went to Pharaoh, the king of Egypt. He gave Hadad a house and some land. He also supplied him with food.

¹⁹Pharaoh was very pleased with Hadad. Pharaoh's wife was Queen Tahpenes. He gave Hadad her sister to be his wife. ²⁰The sister of Tahpenes had a son by Hadad. The baby was named Genubath. Tahpenes brought him up in the royal palace. Genubath lived there with Pharaoh's own children.

²¹Hadad heard that David had joined the members of his family who had already died. He also heard that Joab, the commander of the army, was dead. Hadad heard those things while he was in Egypt. He said to Pharaoh, "Let me go. I want to return to my own country."

²²"Why do you want to go back to your own country?" Pharaoh asked. "Don't you have everything you need right here?"

"Yes," Hadad replied. "But I want you to let me go anyway!"

²³God brought another enemy against Solomon. The enemy's name was Rezon. He was the son of Eliada. Rezon had run away from his master Hadadezer, the king of Zobah. ²⁴He gathered some men together to follow him. He became the leader of a group of men who had refused to follow David. It happened when David destroyed the troops of Zobah. Then the group that was against David went to Damascus. They settled down there and took control of it. ²⁵Rezon was Israel's enemy as long as Solomon was living. Rezon added to the trouble Hadad had caused. So Rezon ruled in Aram. He was Israel's enemy.

JEROBOAM REFUSES TO FOLLOW SOLOMON

²⁶Jeroboam refused to follow King Solomon. He was one of Solomon's officials. He was from Zeredah in the territory of Ephraim. His father was Nebat. His mother was a widow named Zeruah.

²⁷Here is the story of how Jeroboam refused to follow the king. Solomon had filled in the low places near the palace. He had also repaired the wall of the city of his father David. ²⁸Jeroboam was a very important young man. Solomon saw how well he did his work. So he put him in charge of all of the workers in northern Israel.

²⁹About that time Jeroboam was going out of Jerusalem. The prophet Ahijah met him on the road. Ahijah was from Shiloh. He was wearing a new coat. The two of them were all alone out in the country.

³⁰Ahijah grabbed hold of the new coat he had on. He tore it up into 12

pieces. ³¹Then he said to Jeroboam, "Take ten pieces for yourself. The LORD is the God of Israel. He says, 'I am going to tear the kingdom out of Solomon's hand. I will give you ten of its tribes. ³²Solomon will have one of its tribes. I will let him keep it because of my servant David and because of Jerusalem. I have chosen that city out of all of the cities in the tribes of Israel.

³³" 'I will do those things because the tribes have deserted me. They have worshiped Ashtoreth, the goddess of the people of Sidon. They have worshiped Chemosh, the god of the people of Moab. And they have worshiped Molech, the god of the people of Ammon. They have not lived the way I wanted them to. They have not done what is right in my eyes. They have not obeyed my rules and laws as Solomon's father David did.

³⁴" 'But I will not take the whole kingdom out of Solomon's hand. I have made him ruler all the days of his life. I have done it because of my servant David. I chose him. He obeyed my commands and rules.

³⁵" 'I will take the kingdom out of his son's hands. And I will give you ten of the tribes.

³⁶" 'I will give one of the tribes to David's son. Then my servant David will always have a son on his throne in Jerusalem. The lamp of David's kingdom will always burn brightly in my sight. Jerusalem is the city I chose for my Name.

³⁷" 'But I will make you king over Israel. You will rule over everything your heart longs for. So you will be the king of Israel. ³⁸Do everything I command you to do. Live the way I want you to. Do what is right in my eyes. Obey my rules and commands. That is what my servant David did. If you do those things, I will be with you. I will build you a kingdom. It will last as long as the one I built for David. I will give Israel to you.

³⁹" 'I will punish David's family because of what Solomon has done. But I will not punish them forever.' "

⁴⁰Solomon tried to kill Jeroboam. But Jeroboam ran away to Egypt. He went to Shishak, the king of Egypt. He stayed there until Solomon died.

SOLOMON DIES

⁴¹The other events of Solomon's rule are written down. Everything he did and the wisdom he showed are written down. They are written in the official records of Solomon.

⁴²Solomon ruled in Jerusalem over the whole nation of Israel for 40 years. ⁴³Then he joined the members of his family who had already died. His body was buried in the city of his father David. Solomon's son Rehoboam became the next king after him.

ISRAEL REFUSES TO FOLLOW REHOBOAM

12 Rehoboam went to Shechem. All of the people of Israel had gone there to make him king. ²Jeroboam heard about it. He was the son of Nebat. Jeroboam was still in Egypt at that time. He had gone there for safety. He wanted to get away from King Solomon. But now he returned from Egypt.

³So the people sent for Jeroboam. He and the whole community of Israel went to Rehoboam. They said to him, ⁴"Your father put a heavy load on our shoulders. But now make our hard work easier. Make the heavy load on us lighter. Then we'll serve you."

⁵Rehoboam answered, "Go away for three days. Then come back to me." So the people went away.

⁶King Rehoboam asked the elders for advice. They had served his father Solomon while he was still living. Rehoboam asked them, "What advice can you give me? How should I answer these people?"

⁷They replied, "Serve them today. Give them what they are asking for. Then they'll always serve you."

⁸But Rehoboam didn't accept the advice the elders gave him. Instead, he asked for advice from the young men who had grown up with him and were now serving him. ⁹He asked them, "What's your advice? How should I answer these people? They say to me, 'Make the load your father put on our shoulders lighter.' "

¹⁰The young men who had grown up with him gave their answer. They replied, "These people say to you, 'Your

father put a heavy load on our shoulders. Make it lighter.' Tell them, 'My little finger is stronger than my father's legs. ¹¹My father put a heavy load on your shoulders. But I'll make it even heavier. My father beat you with whips. But I'll beat you with bigger whips.' "

¹²Three days later Jeroboam and all of the people returned to Rehoboam. That's because the king had said, "Come back to me in three days."

¹³The king answered the people in a mean way. He didn't accept the advice the elders had given him. ¹⁴Instead, he followed the advice of the young men. He said, "My father put a heavy load on your shoulders. But I'll make it even heavier. My father beat you with whips. But I'll beat you with bigger whips."

¹⁵So the king didn't listen to the people. That's because the LORD had planned it that way. What he had said through Ahijah came true. Ahijah had spoken the LORD's message to Jeroboam, the son of Nebat. Ahijah was from Shiloh.

¹⁶All of the people of Israel saw that the king refused to listen to them. So they answered the king. They said,

"We don't have any share in
    David's royal family.
We don't have any share in Jesse's
    son.
People of Israel, let's go back to
    our homes.
David's royal family, take care of
    your own kingdom!"

So the people of Israel went home. ¹⁷But Rehoboam still ruled over the Israelites who were living in the towns of Judah.

¹⁸Adoniram was in charge of those who were forced to work hard for King Rehoboam. The king sent him out among all of the Israelites. But they killed him by throwing stones at him. King Rehoboam was able to get away in his chariot. He escaped to Jerusalem. ¹⁹Israel has refused to follow the royal family of David to this very day.

²⁰All of the people of Israel heard that Jeroboam had returned. They sent for him. They wanted him to meet with the whole community. Then they made him king over the entire nation of Israel. Only the tribe of Judah remained true to David's royal family.

²¹Rehoboam arrived in Jerusalem. He brought together 180,000 fighting men from the royal house of Judah and the tribe of Benjamin. He had decided to make war against the royal house of Israel. Solomon's son Rehoboam wanted his fighting men to get the kingdom of Israel back for him.

²²But a message from God came to Shemaiah. He was a man of God. God said to him, ²³"Speak to Solomon's son Rehoboam, the king of Judah. Speak to the royal house of Judah and Benjamin. Also speak to the rest of the people. Tell all of them, ²⁴'The LORD says, "Do not go up to fight against the Israelites. They are your relatives. I want every one of you to go back home. Things have happened exactly the way I planned them." ' " So the fighting men obeyed the LORD's message. They went home again, just as he had ordered.

JEROBOAM SETS UP GOLDEN CALVES AT BETHEL AND DAN

²⁵Jeroboam built up the walls of Shechem. It was in the hill country of Ephraim. Jeroboam made Shechem his home. From there he went out and built up Peniel.

²⁶Jeroboam thought, "My kingdom still isn't secure. It could very easily go back to the royal family of David. ²⁷Suppose the people of Israel go up to Jerusalem to offer sacrifices at the LORD's temple. If they do, they will again decide to follow Rehoboam as their master. Then they'll kill me. They'll return to King Rehoboam. He is king of Judah."

²⁸So King Jeroboam asked for advice. Then he made two golden statues that looked like calves. He said to the people, "It's too hard for you to go up to Jerusalem. Israel, here are your gods who brought you up out of Egypt." ²⁹He set up one statue in Bethel. He set up the other one in Dan.

³⁰What Jeroboam did was sinful. And it caused Israel to sin. The people even went all the way to Dan to worship the statue that was there.

³¹Jeroboam built temples for worshiping gods on high places. He appointed all kinds of people as priests. They didn't even have to be Levites. ³²He established a feast. It was on the 15th day of the eighth month. He wanted to make it like the Feast of Booths that was held in Judah.

Jeroboam built an altar at Bethel. He offered sacrifices on it. He sacrificed to the calves he had made. He also put priests in Bethel. He did it at the high places he had made. ³³He offered sacrifices on the altar he had built at Bethel. It was on the 15th day of the eighth month. That's the month he had chosen for it. So he established the feast for the people of Israel. And he went up to the altar to sacrifice offerings.

A MAN OF GOD GOES TO BETHEL

13 A man of God went from Judah to Bethel. He had received a message from the LORD. He arrived in Bethel just as Jeroboam was standing by the altar to offer a sacrifice. ²The man cried out. He shouted a message from the LORD against the altar. He said, "Altar! Altar! The LORD says, 'A son named Josiah will be born into the royal family of David. Altar, listen to me! Josiah will sacrifice the priests of the high places on you. They will be the children of the priests who are offering sacrifices here now. So human bones will be burned on you.' "

³That same day the man of God spoke about a miraculous sign. He said, "Here is the sign the LORD has announced. This altar will be broken to pieces. The ashes on it will be spilled out."

⁴The man of God announced that message against the altar at Bethel. When King Jeroboam heard it, he reached out his hand from the altar. He said, "Grab him!" But as he reached out his hand toward the man, it dried up. He couldn't even pull it back.

⁵Also, the altar broke into pieces. Its ashes spilled out. That happened in keeping with the miraculous sign the man of God had announced. He had received a message from the LORD.

⁶King Jeroboam spoke to the man of God. He said, "Pray to the LORD your God for me. Pray that my hand will be as good as new again."

So the man of God prayed to the LORD for the king. And the king's hand became as good as new. It was just as healthy as it had been before.

⁷The king said to the man of God, "Come home with me. Have something to eat. I'll give you a gift."

⁸But the man of God replied to the king. He said, "What if you were to give me half of what you own? Even then I wouldn't go with you. I wouldn't eat bread or drink water here. ⁹The LORD gave me a command. He said, 'Do not eat bread or drink water there. Do not return the same way you came.' " ¹⁰So he took another road. He didn't go back on the same road he had taken when he came to Bethel.

¹¹An old prophet was living in Bethel. His sons came and spoke to him. They told him everything the man of God had done there that day. They also told their father what the man had said to the king.

¹²Their father asked them, "Which way did he go?"

His sons showed him the road the man of God from Judah had taken.

¹³So he said to his sons, "Put a saddle on the donkey for me."

When they had done it, he got on the donkey. ¹⁴He traveled on the same road the man of God had taken. He found the man sitting under an oak tree. He asked him, "Are you the man of God who came from Judah?"

"I am," he replied.

¹⁵So the prophet said to him, "Come home with me. I'll give you something to eat."

¹⁶The man of God said, "I can't go back to Bethel with you. I can't eat bread or drink water with you there. ¹⁷I've received a message from the LORD. He told me, 'Do not eat bread or drink water there. Do not return the same way you came.' "

¹⁸The old prophet answered, "I'm also a prophet, just like you. An angel gave me a message from the LORD. The message said, 'Bring the man of God back with you to your house. Then he can eat bread and drink water with

you.' " But the old prophet was telling him a lie.

¹⁹The man of God returned with him. He ate and drank in his house. ²⁰They were sitting at the table. The LORD gave a message to the old prophet who had brought the man of God back. ²¹He cried out to the man who had come from Judah. He told him, "The LORD says, 'You have not done what I told you to do. You have not obeyed the command I gave you. I am the LORD your God. ²²You came back here and ate bread and drank water. You did it in the place where I told you not to. So your body will not be buried in your family tomb.' "

²³The man of God finished eating and drinking. Then the old prophet who had brought him back put a saddle on the man's donkey for him. ²⁴And the man went on his way. A lion attacked him on the road and killed him. His body was left lying on the road. The donkey and the lion were standing beside it.

²⁵Some people passed by. They saw the body lying on the road. They saw the lion standing beside the body. Then they went and reported it in the city where the old prophet lived.

²⁶The prophet who had brought the man back from his journey heard about what had happened. He said, "It's the man of God. He didn't do what the LORD told him to do. So the LORD has given him over to the lion. The lion has attacked him and killed him. Everything has happened just as the LORD's message had warned him it would."

²⁷The old prophet said to his sons, "Put a saddle on the donkey for me." So they did. ²⁸Then he went out. He found the body of the man of God lying on the road. The donkey and the lion were standing beside it. The lion hadn't eaten the body. It hadn't attacked the donkey either.

²⁹So the prophet picked up the man's body. He put it on the donkey. He brought it back to his own city. He wanted to sob over him and bury him. ³⁰Then he placed the body in his own tomb. People sobbed over him. They said, "My friend! My dear friend!"

³¹After the old prophet had buried the body of the man of God, he spoke to his sons. He said, "When I die, bury my body in the grave where the man of God is buried. Put my bones next to his bones. ³²I want you to do that because he announced a message from the LORD. He spoke against the altar in Bethel. He also spoke against all of the temples that were on the high places. They are in the towns of Samaria. What the man of God said will certainly come true."

³³Even after all of that happened, Jeroboam still didn't change his evil ways. Once more he appointed priests for the high places. He made priests out of all kinds of people. In fact, he let anyone become a priest who wanted to. He set them apart to serve at the high places. ³⁴All of that was the great sin the royal family of Jeroboam committed. It led to their fall from power. Because of it, they were destroyed from the face of the earth.

AHIJAH PROPHESIES AGAINST JEROBOAM

14 At that time Abijah became sick. He was the son of Jeroboam. ²Jeroboam said to his wife, "Go. Put on some different clothes. Then no one will recognize you as my wife. Go to Shiloh. That's where the prophet Ahijah is. He told me I would be king over the people of Israel. ³Take ten loaves of bread with you. Take some cakes and a jar of honey. Go to him. He'll tell you what will happen to our son."

⁴So Jeroboam's wife did what he said. She went to Ahijah's house in Shiloh.

Ahijah couldn't see. He was blind because he was so old. ⁵But the LORD had told Ahijah, "Jeroboam's wife is coming. Her son is sick. She'll ask you about him. Give her the answer I give you. When she arrives, she'll pretend to be someone else."

⁶Ahijah heard the sound of her footsteps at the door. He said, "Come in. I know that you are Jeroboam's wife. Why are you pretending to be someone else? I have some bad news for you.

⁷"Go. Tell Jeroboam that the LORD has a message for him. The LORD is the

God of Israel. He says, 'I chose you from among the people. I made you the leader of my people Israel. [8]I tore the kingdom away from the royal house of David. I gave it to you. But you have not been like my servant David. He obeyed my commands. He followed me with all his heart. He did only what was right in my eyes. [9]You have done more evil things than all those who lived before you. You have made other gods for yourself. You have made statues of gods out of metal. You have made me very angry. You have turned your back on me.

[10]" 'Because of that, I am going to bring horrible trouble on your royal house. I will cut off from you every male in Israel. It does not matter whether they are slaves or free. I will burn up your royal house, just as someone burns up trash. I will burn it until it is all gone. [11]Some of the people who belong to you will die in the city. Dogs will eat them up. Others will die in the country. The birds of the air will eat them. I have spoken!'

[12]"Now go back home. When you enter your city, your son will die. [13]All of the people of Israel will sob over him. Then his body will be buried. He is the only one who belongs to Jeroboam who will be buried. That is because he is the only one in Jeroboam's royal house in whom I have found anything good. I am the LORD, the God of Israel.

[14]"I will choose for myself a king over Israel. He will cut off the family of Jeroboam. This very day your son will die. Can that really be true? Yes. Even now, that is what I am telling you.

[15]"I will strike Israel down. Israel will be like tall grass swaying in the water. I will pull Israel up from this good land by the roots. I gave it to their people who lived long ago. I will scatter Israel to the east side of the Euphrates River. That is because they made me very angry. They made poles that were used to worship the goddess Asherah.

[16]"I will give Israel up because of the sins Jeroboam has committed. He has also caused Israel to commit those same sins."

[17]Then Jeroboam's wife got up and left. She went to the city of Tirzah. As soon as she stepped through the door-way of the house, her son died. [18]His body was buried. All of the people of Israel sobbed over him. That's what the LORD had said would happen. He had said it through his servant, the prophet Ahijah.

[19]The other events of Jeroboam's rule are written down. His wars and how he ruled are written down. They are written in the official records of the kings of Israel. [20]Jeroboam ruled for 22 years. Then he joined the members of his family who had already died. Jeroboam's son Nadab became the next king after him.

REHOBOAM, THE KING OF JUDAH

[21]Rehoboam was king in Judah. He was the son of Solomon. Rehoboam was 41 years old when he became king. He ruled for 17 years in Jerusalem. It was the city the LORD had chosen out of all of the cities in the tribes of Israel. He wanted to put his Name there. Rehoboam's mother was Naamah from Ammon.

[22]The people of Judah did what was evil in the sight of the LORD. The sins they had committed stirred up his jealous anger. They did more to make him angry than their people who lived before them had done.

[23]Judah also set up for themselves high places for worship. They set up sacred stones. They set up poles that were used to worship the goddess Asherah. They did it on every high hill and under every green tree.

[24]There were even male prostitutes at the temples in the land. The people took part in all of the practices of other nations. The LORD hated those practices. He had driven those nations out to make room for the people of Israel.

[25]Shishak attacked Jerusalem. It was in the fifth year that Rehoboam was king. Shishak was king of Egypt. [26]He carried away the treasures of the LORD's temple. He also carried the treasures of the royal palace away. He took everything. That included all of the gold shields Solomon had made.

[27]So King Rehoboam made bronze shields to take their place. He gave them to the commanders of the guards who were on duty at the en-

trance to the royal palace. ²⁸Every time the king went to the LORD's temple, the guards carried the shields. Later, they took them back to the room where they were kept.

²⁹The other events of Rehoboam's rule are written down. Everything he did is written down. All of those things are written in the official records of the kings of Judah. ³⁰Rehoboam and Jeroboam were always at war with each other. ³¹Rehoboam joined the members of his family who had already died. His body was buried in his family tomb in the City of David. His mother was Naamah from Ammon. His son Abijah became the next king after him.

ABIJAH BECOMES KING OF JUDAH

15 Abijah became king of Judah. It was in the 18th year of Jeroboam's rule over Israel. Jeroboam was the son of Nebat. ²Abijah ruled in Jerusalem for three years. His mother's name was Maacah. She was Abishalom's daughter.

³Abijah committed all of the sins his father had committed before him. Abijah didn't follow the LORD his God with all his heart. He didn't do what King David had done.

⁴But the LORD still kept the lamp of Abijah's kingdom burning brightly in Jerusalem. He did it by giving him a son to be the next king after him. He also did it by making Jerusalem strong. The LORD did those things because of David. ⁵David had done what was right in the eyes of the LORD. He had kept all of the LORD's commands. He had obeyed them all the days of his life. But he hadn't obeyed the LORD in the case of Uriah, the Hittite.

⁶There was war between Jeroboam and Abijah's father Rehoboam. The war continued all through Abijah's life. ⁷The other events of Abijah's rule are written down. Everything he did is written down. All of those things are written in the official records of the kings of Judah. There was war between Abijah and Jeroboam.

⁸Abijah joined the members of his family who had already died. His body was buried in the City of David. His son Asa became the next king after him.

ASA BECOMES KING OF JUDAH

⁹Asa became king of Judah. It was in the 20th year that Jeroboam was king of Israel. ¹⁰Asa ruled in Jerusalem for 41 years. His grandmother's name was Maacah. She was Abishalom's daughter.

¹¹Asa did what was right in the eyes of the LORD. That's what King David had done.

¹²Asa threw out of the land the male prostitutes who were at the temples. He got rid of all of the statues of gods his people before him had made. ¹³He even removed his grandmother Maacah from her position as queen mother. That's because she had made a pole that was used to worship the goddess Asherah. The LORD hated it. So Asa cut it down. He burned it in the Kidron Valley.

¹⁴Asa didn't remove the high places from Israel. But he committed his whole life completely to the LORD. ¹⁵He and his father had set apart silver, gold and other articles to the LORD. He brought them into the LORD's temple.

¹⁶There was war between Asa and Baasha, the king of Israel. It lasted the whole time they were kings. ¹⁷Baasha was king of Israel. He marched out against Judah. He built up the walls of Ramah. He did it to keep people from leaving or entering the territory of Asa, the king of Judah.

¹⁸Asa took all of the silver and gold that was left among the treasures of the LORD's temple and his own palace. He put his officials in charge of it. He sent the officials to Ben-Hadad. Ben-Hadad was king of Aram. He was ruling in Damascus. He was the son of Tabrimmon and the grandson of Hezion.

¹⁹"Let's make a peace treaty between us," Asa said. "My father and your father had made a peace treaty between them. Now I'm sending you a gift of silver and gold. So break your treaty with Baasha, the king of Israel. Then he'll go back home."

²⁰Ben-Hadad agreed with King Asa. He sent his army commanders against

the towns of Israel. He attacked Ijon, Dan, Abel Beth Maacah and the whole area of Kinnereth in addition to Naphtali. ²¹Baasha heard about it. So he stopped building up Ramah. He went back home to Tirzah.

²²Then King Asa gave an order to all of the men of Judah. Everyone was required to help. They carried away from Ramah the stones and wood Baasha had been using there. King Asa used them to build up Geba in the territory of Benjamin. He also used them to build up Mizpah.

²³All of the other events of Asa's rule are written down. Everything he accomplished is written down. Everything he did and the cities he built are written down. They are written in the official records of the kings of Judah. But when Asa became old, his feet began to give him trouble. ²⁴He joined the members of his family who had already died. His body was buried in his family tomb. It was in the city of King David. Asa's son Jehoshaphat became the next king after him.

NADAB BECOMES KING OF ISRAEL

²⁵Nadab became king of Israel. It was in the second year that Asa was king of Judah. Nadab ruled over Israel for two years. He was the son of Jeroboam. ²⁶Nadab did what was evil in the sight of the LORD. He lived the way his father had lived. He sinned as his father had sinned. Jeroboam had also caused Israel to commit the same sins.

²⁷Baasha was from the tribe of Issachar. He was the son of Ahijah. Baasha made plans against Nadab and struck him down at Gibbethon. It was a Philistine town. Baasha struck him down while Nadab and all of the men of Israel were getting ready to attack Gibbethon. ²⁸He killed Nadab in the third year that Asa was king of Judah. Baasha became the next king after Nadab.

²⁹As soon as Baasha became king, he killed Jeroboam's whole family. He didn't leave any of them alive. He destroyed every one of them. He did what the LORD had said would happen. The LORD had spoken that message through his servant Ahijah from Shiloh.

³⁰The LORD judged Jeroboam's family because of the sins Jeroboam had committed. He had also caused Israel to commit those same sins. He had made the LORD very angry. The LORD is the God of Israel.

³¹The other events of Nadab's rule are written down. Everything he did is written down. All of those things are written in the official records of the kings of Israel.

³²There was war between Asa and Baasha, the king of Israel. It lasted the whole time they were kings.

BAASHA BECOMES KING OF ISRAEL

³³Baasha became king of Israel in Tirzah. It was in the third year that Asa was king of Judah. Baasha ruled for 24 years. He was the son of Ahijah. ³⁴Baasha did what was evil in the sight of the LORD. He lived the way Jeroboam had lived. He sinned as Jeroboam had sinned. Jeroboam had also caused Israel to commit the same sins.

16 The LORD's message against Baasha came to Jehu. Jehu was the son of Hanani. The LORD said, ²"I lifted you up from the dust. I made you leader of my people Israel. But you lived the way Jeroboam had lived. You also caused my people Israel to sin. And their sins made me very angry.

³"So I am about to destroy you and your royal house. I will make your house like the royal house of Jeroboam, the son of Nebat. ⁴Some of the people who belong to you will die in the city. Dogs will eat them up. Others will die in the country. The birds of the air will eat them."

⁵The other events of Baasha's rule are written down. What he did and what he accomplished are written down. All of those things are written in the official records of the kings of Israel. ⁶Baasha joined the members of his family who had already died. His body was buried in Tirzah. His son Elah became the next king after him.

⁷The LORD's message came through the prophet Jehu, the son of Hanani. It was against Baasha and his royal

house. Baasha had done all kinds of evil things in the sight of the LORD. What he did had made the LORD very angry. So Baasha had become as sinful as the royal house of Jeroboam had been. He had also destroyed it.

ELAH BECOMES KING OF ISRAEL

⁸Elah became king of Israel. It was in the 26th year that Asa was king of Judah. Elah ruled in Tirzah for two years. He was the son of Baasha. ⁹Zimri was one of Elah's officials. He commanded half of Elah's chariot drivers. He made plans against Elah. Elah was in Tirzah at the time. He was getting drunk in the home of Arza. Arza was in charge of the palace at Tirzah. ¹⁰Zimri came in. He struck Elah down and killed him. It was in the 27th year of Asa, the king of Judah. Zimri became the next king after Elah.

¹¹As soon as Zimri was seated on the throne as king, he killed off Baasha's whole family. He didn't even spare one male. It didn't matter whether it was a relative or a friend. ¹²So Zimri destroyed the whole family of Baasha. That's what the LORD had said would happen. He had spoken against Baasha through the prophet Jehu. ¹³Baasha and his son Elah had committed all kinds of sin. They had also caused Israel to commit the same sins. So Israel made the LORD very angry. They did it by worshiping worthless statues of gods. The LORD is the God of Israel.

¹⁴The other events of Elah's rule are written down. Everything he did is written down. All of those things are written in the official records of the kings of Israel.

ZIMRI BECOMES KING OF ISRAEL

¹⁵Zimri ruled in Tirzah for seven days. It was in the 27th year that Asa was king of Judah. The army of Israel had set up camp near Gibbethon. It was a Philistine town. ¹⁶The people of Israel who were in the camp heard that Zimri had made plans against King Elah. They also heard that Zimri had murdered him. So they announced that Omri was king over Israel. He was the commander of the army. They made him king that very day in the camp.

¹⁷Then Omri and all of his men pulled back from Gibbethon. They marched to Tirzah and surrounded it. They attacked it and captured it. ¹⁸Zimri saw that they had taken over the city. So he went into the safest place in the royal palace. He set the palace on fire all around him. He died there ¹⁹because of the sins he had committed. He had done what was evil in the sight of the LORD. He had lived the way Jeroboam had lived. He had sinned as Jeroboam had sinned. Jeroboam had also caused Israel to commit the same sins.

²⁰The other events of Zimri's rule are written down. The way he turned against King Elah and killed him is written down. All of those things are written in the official records of the kings of Israel.

OMRI BECOMES KING OF ISRAEL

²¹The people of Israel divided up into two groups. Half of them wanted Tibni to be king. He was the son of Ginath. The other half wanted Omri. ²²But Omri's followers were stronger than those of Tibni, the son of Ginath. So Tibni died. And Omri began to rule.

²³Omri became king of Israel. It was in the 31st year that Asa was king of Judah. Omri ruled for 12 years. He ruled in Tirzah for six of those years. ²⁴He bought the hill of Samaria from Shemer. He weighed out 150 pounds of silver for it. Then he built a city on the hill. He called it Samaria. He named it after Shemer. Shemer had owned the hill before him.

²⁵But Omri did what was evil in the sight of the LORD. He sinned more than all of the kings who had ruled before him. ²⁶He lived the way Jeroboam, the son of Nebat, had lived. He sinned as Jeroboam had sinned. Jeroboam had also caused Israel to commit the same sins. Israel made the LORD very angry. They did it by worshiping worthless statues of gods. The LORD is the God of Israel.

²⁷The other events of Omri's rule are

written down. Everything he did and the things he accomplished are written down. All of those things are written in the official records of the kings of Israel. ²⁸Omri joined the members of his family who had already died. His body was buried in Samaria. His son Ahab became the next king after him.

AHAB BECOMES KING OF ISRAEL

²⁹Ahab became king of Israel. It was in the 38th year that Asa was king of Judah. Ahab ruled over Israel in Samaria for 22 years. He was the son of Omri. ³⁰Ahab, the son of Omri, did what was evil in the sight of the LORD. He did more evil things than any of the kings who had ruled before him. ³¹He thought it was only a small thing to commit the sins Jeroboam, the son of Nebat, had committed.

Ahab also got married to Jezebel. She was Ethbaal's daughter. Ethbaal was king of the people of Sidon. Ahab began to serve the god Baal and worship him. ³²He set up an altar to honor Baal. He set it up in the temple of Baal that he built in Samaria. ³³Ahab also made a pole that was used to worship the goddess Asherah.

He made the LORD very angry. He did more to make him angry than all of the kings of Israel had done before him. The LORD is the God of Israel.

³⁴In Ahab's time, Hiel from Bethel rebuilt Jericho. When he laid its foundations, it cost him the life of his oldest son Abiram. When he set up its gates, it cost him the life of his youngest son Segub. That's what the LORD had said would happen. He had spoken it through Joshua, the son of Nun.

ELIJAH IS FED BY RAVENS

17 Elijah was from Tishbe in the land of Gilead. He said to Ahab, "I serve the LORD. He is the God of Israel. You can be sure that he lives. And you can be just as sure that there won't be any dew or rain on the whole land. There won't be any during the next few years. It won't come until I say so."

²Then a message from the LORD came to Elijah. It said, ³"Leave this place. Go east and hide in the Kerith Valley. It is east of the Jordan River. ⁴You will drink water from the brook. I have ordered some ravens to feed you there."

⁵So Elijah did what the LORD had told him to do. He went to the Kerith Valley. It was east of the Jordan River. He stayed there. ⁶The ravens brought him bread and meat in the morning. They also brought him bread and meat in the evening. He drank water from the brook.

ELIJAH VISITS A WIDOW AT ZAREPHATH

⁷Some time later the brook dried up. It hadn't rained in the land for quite a while. ⁸A message came to Elijah from the LORD. He said, ⁹"Go right away to Zarephath in the territory of Sidon. Stay there. I have commanded a widow in that place to supply you with food."

¹⁰So Elijah went to Zarephath. He came to the town gate. A widow was there gathering sticks. He called out to her. He asked, "Would you bring me a little water in a jar? I need a drink." ¹¹She went to get the water.

Then he called out to her, "Please bring me a piece of bread too."

¹²"I don't have any bread," she replied. "And that's just as sure as the LORD your God is alive. All I have is a small amount of flour in a jar and a little olive oil in a jug. I'm gathering a few sticks to take home. I'll make one last meal for myself and my son. We'll eat it. After that, we'll die."

¹³Elijah said to her, "Don't be afraid. Go home. Do what you have said. But first make a little bread for me. Make it out of what you have. Bring it to me. Then make some for yourself and your son.

¹⁴"The LORD is the God of Israel. He says, 'The jar of flour will not be used up. The jug will always have oil in it. You will have flour and oil until the day the LORD sends rain on the land.' "

¹⁵She went away and did what Elijah had told her to do. So Elijah had food every day. There was also food for the woman and her family. ¹⁶The jar of flour wasn't used up. The jug always had oil in it. That's what the LORD had

said would happen. He had spoken that message through Elijah.

¹⁷Some time later the son of the woman who owned the house became sick. He got worse and worse. Finally he stopped breathing.

¹⁸The woman said to Elijah, "You are a man of God. What do you have against me? Did you come to bring my sin out into the open? Did you come to kill my son?"

¹⁹"Give me your son," Elijah replied. He took him from her arms. He carried him to the upstairs room where he was staying. He put him down on his bed.

²⁰Then Elijah cried out to the LORD. He said, "LORD my God, I'm staying with this widow. Have you brought pain and sorrow to her? Have you caused her son to die?"

²¹Then he lay down on the boy three times. He cried out to the LORD. He said, "LORD my God, give this boy's life back to him!"

²²The LORD answered Elijah's prayer. He gave the boy's life back to him. So the boy lived. ²³Elijah picked up the boy. He carried him down from the upstairs room into the house. He gave him to his mother. He said, "Look! Your son is alive!"

²⁴Then the woman said to Elijah, "Now I know that you are a man of God. I know that the message you have brought from the LORD is true."

ELIJAH GIVES OBADIAH A MESSAGE FOR AHAB

18 It was now three years since it had rained. A message came to Elijah from the LORD. He said, "Go. Speak to Ahab. Then I will send rain on the land."

²So Elijah went to speak to Ahab. There wasn't enough food in Samaria. The people there were very hungry. ³Ahab had sent for Obadiah. He was in charge of Ahab's palace. Obadiah had great respect for the LORD.

⁴Ahab's wife Jezebel had been killing off the LORD's prophets. So Obadiah had hidden 100 prophets in two caves. He had put 50 in each cave. He had supplied them with food and water.

⁵Ahab had said to Obadiah, "Go through the land. Go to all of the springs of water and to the valleys. Maybe we can find some grass there. It will keep the horses and mules alive. Then we won't have to kill any of our animals." ⁶So they decided where each of them would look. Ahab went in one direction. Obadiah went in another.

⁷As Obadiah was walking along, Elijah met him. Obadiah recognized him. He bowed down to the ground. He said, "My master Elijah! Is it really you?"

⁸"Yes," he replied. "Go and tell your master Ahab, 'Elijah is here.' "

⁹"What have I done wrong?" asked Obadiah. "Why are you handing me over to Ahab to be put to death? ¹⁰My master has sent people to look for you everywhere. There isn't a nation or kingdom where he hasn't sent someone to look for you. Suppose a nation or kingdom would claim you weren't there. Then Ahab would make them take an oath and say they couldn't find you. And that's just as sure as the LORD your God is alive. ¹¹But now you are telling me to go to my master. You want me to say, 'Elijah is here.' ¹²But the Spirit of the LORD might carry you away when I leave you. Then I won't know where you are. If I go and tell Ahab and he doesn't find you, he'll kill me.

"But I've worshiped the LORD ever since I was young. ¹³My master, haven't you heard what I did? Jezebel was killing the LORD's prophets. But I hid 100 of them in two caves. I put 50 in each cave. I supplied them with food and water. ¹⁴And now you are telling me to go to my master Ahab. You want me to say to him, 'Elijah is here.' He'll kill me!"

¹⁵Elijah said, "I serve the LORD who rules over all. You can be sure that he lives. And you can be just as sure that I will speak to Ahab today."

THE LORD ANSWERS ELIJAH'S PRAYER ON MOUNT CARMEL

¹⁶Obadiah went back to Ahab. He told Ahab that Elijah wanted to see him. So Ahab went to where Elijah was. ¹⁷When he saw Elijah, he said to him, "Is that you? You are always stirring up trouble in Israel."

¹⁸"I haven't made trouble for Israel,"

Elijah replied. "But you and your father's family have. You have turned away from the LORD's commands. You have followed the gods that are named after Baal.

¹⁹"Now send for people from all over Israel. Tell them to meet me on Mount Carmel. And bring the 450 prophets of the god Baal. Also bring the 400 prophets of the goddess Asherah. All of them eat at Jezebel's table."

²⁰So Ahab sent that message all through Israel. He gathered the prophets together on Mount Carmel. ²¹Elijah went there and stood in front of the people. He said, "How long will it take you to make up your minds? If the LORD is the one and only God, follow him. But if Baal is the one and only God, follow him."

The people didn't say anything.

²²Then Elijah said to them, "I'm the only one of the LORD's prophets left. But Baal has 450 prophets. ²³Get two bulls for us. Let Baal's prophets choose one for themselves. Let them cut it into pieces. Then let them put it on the wood. But don't let them set fire to it. I'll prepare the other bull. I'll put it on the wood. But I won't set fire to it. ²⁴Then you pray to your god. And I'll pray to the LORD. The god who answers by sending fire down is the one and only God."

Then all of the people said, "What you are saying is good."

²⁵Elijah spoke to the prophets of Baal. He said, "Choose one of the bulls. There are many of you. So prepare your bull first. Pray to your god. But don't light the fire."

²⁶So they prepared the bull they had been given.

They prayed to Baal from morning until noon. "Baal! Answer us!" they shouted. But there wasn't any reply. No one answered. Then they danced around the altar they had made.

²⁷At noon Elijah began to tease them. "Shout louder!" he said. "I'm sure Baal is a god! Perhaps he has too much to think about. Or maybe he has gone to the toilet. Or perhaps he's away on a trip. Maybe he's sleeping. You might have to wake him up."

²⁸So they shouted louder. They cut themselves with swords and spears until their blood flowed. That's what they usually did when things really looked hopeless. ²⁹It was now past noon. The prophets of Baal continued to prophesy with all their might. They did it until the time came to offer the evening sacrifice. But there wasn't any reply. No one answered. No one paid any attention.

³⁰Then Elijah said to all of the people, "Come here to me." So they went to him. He rebuilt the altar of the LORD. It had been destroyed. ³¹Elijah got 12 stones. There was one for each tribe in the family line of Jacob. The LORD's message had come to Jacob. It had said, "Your name will be Israel." ³²Elijah used the stones to build an altar in honor of the LORD. He dug a ditch around it. The ditch was large enough to hold 13 quarts of seeds. ³³He arranged the wood for the fire. He cut the bull into pieces. He placed the pieces on the wood.

Then he said to some of the people, "Fill four large jars with water. Pour it on the offering and the wood." So they did.

³⁴"Do it again," he said. So they did it again.

"Do it a third time," he ordered. And they did it the third time. ³⁵The water ran down around the altar. It even filled the ditch.

³⁶When it was time to offer the evening sacrifice, the prophet Elijah stepped forward. He prayed, "LORD, you are the God of Abraham, Isaac and Israel. Today let everyone know that you are God in Israel. Let them know I'm your servant. Let them know I've done all of these things because you commanded me to. ³⁷Answer me. LORD, answer me. Then these people will know that you are the one and only God. They'll know that you are turning their hearts back to you again."

³⁸The fire of the LORD came down. It burned up the sacrifice. It burned up the wood and the stones and the soil. It even licked up the water in the ditch. ³⁹All of the people saw it. Then they fell down flat with their faces toward the ground. They cried out, "The LORD is the one and only God! The LORD is the one and only God!"

⁴⁰Then Elijah commanded them, "Grab hold of the prophets of Baal. Don't let a single one of them get away!"

So they grabbed them. Elijah had them brought down to the Kishon Valley. There he had them put to death.

⁴¹Elijah said to Ahab, "Go. Eat and drink. I can hear the sound of a heavy rain."

⁴²So Ahab went off to eat and drink. But Elijah climbed to the top of Mount Carmel. He bent down toward the ground. Then he put his face between his knees.

⁴³"Go and look toward the sea," he told his servant. So he went up and looked.

"I don't see anything there," he said.

Seven times Elijah said, "Go back."

⁴⁴The seventh time the servant said, "I see a cloud. It's as small as a man's hand. It's coming up over the sea."

Elijah said, "Go to Ahab. Tell him, 'Tie your chariot to your horse. Go down to Jezreel before the rain stops you.' "

⁴⁵Black clouds filled the sky. The wind came up, and a heavy rain began to fall. Ahab rode off to Jezreel.

⁴⁶The power of the LORD came on Elijah. He tucked his coat into his belt. And he ran ahead of Ahab all the way to Jezreel.

ELIJAH RUNS AWAY TO MOUNT HOREB

19 Ahab told Jezebel everything Elijah had done. He told her how Elijah had killed all of the prophets with his sword.

²So Jezebel sent a message to Elijah. She said, "You can be sure that I will kill you, just as I killed the other prophets. I'll do it by this time tomorrow. If I don't, may the gods punish me greatly."

³Elijah was afraid. So he ran for his life. He came to Beersheba in Judah. He left his servant there.

⁴Then he traveled for one day into the desert. He came to a small tree. He sat down under it. He prayed that he would die. "LORD, I've had enough," he said. "Take my life. I'm no better than my people of long ago." ⁵Then he lay down under the tree. And he fell asleep.

Suddenly an angel touched him. The angel said, "Get up and eat." ⁶Elijah looked around. Near his head he saw a flat cake of bread. It had been baked over hot coals. A jar of water was also there. So Elijah ate and drank. Then he lay down again.

⁷The angel of the LORD came to him a second time. He touched him and said, "Get up and eat. Your journey will be long and hard."

⁸So he got up. He ate and drank. The food gave him new strength. He traveled for 40 days and 40 nights. He kept going until he arrived at Horeb. It was the mountain of God. ⁹There he went into a cave and spent the night.

THE LORD APPEARS TO ELIJAH

A message came to Elijah from the LORD. He said, "Elijah, what are you doing here?"

¹⁰He replied, "LORD God who rules over all, I've been very committed to you. The people of Israel have turned their backs on your covenant. They have torn down your altars. They've put your prophets to death with their swords. I'm the only one left. And they are trying to kill me."

¹¹The LORD said, "Go out. Stand on the mountain in front of me. I am going to pass by."

As the LORD approached, a very powerful wind tore the mountains apart. It broke up the rocks. But the LORD wasn't in the wind.

After the wind there was an earthquake. But the LORD wasn't in the earthquake.

¹²After the earthquake a fire came. But the LORD wasn't in the fire.

And after the fire there was only a gentle whisper. ¹³When Elijah heard it, he pulled his coat over his face. He went out and stood at the entrance to the cave.

Then a voice said to him, "Elijah, what are you doing here?"

¹⁴He replied, "LORD God who rules over all, I've been very committed to you. The people of Israel have turned their backs on your covenant. They have torn down your altars. They've

put your prophets to death with their swords. I'm the only one left. And they are trying to kill me."

¹⁵The LORD said to him, "Go back the way you came. Go to the Desert of Damascus. When you get there, anoint Hazael as king over Aram. ¹⁶Also anoint Jehu as king over Israel. He is the son of Nimshi. And anoint Elisha from Abel Meholah as the next prophet after you. He is the son of Shaphat. ¹⁷Jehu will put to death anyone who escapes Hazael's sword. And Elisha will put to death anyone who escapes Jehu's sword.

¹⁸"But I will keep 7,000 people in Israel for myself. They have not bowed down to Baal. And they have not kissed him."

THE LORD CHOOSES ELISHA

¹⁹Elijah left Mount Horeb. He saw Elisha, the son of Shaphat. Elisha was plowing in a field. He was driving the last of 12 pairs of oxen. Elijah went up to him. He threw his coat around him. ²⁰Then Elisha left his oxen. He ran after Elijah. "Let me kiss my father and mother good-by," he said. "Then I'll come with you."

"Go back," Elijah replied. "What have I done to you?"

²¹So Elisha left him and went back. He got his two oxen and killed them. He burned the plow to cook the meat. He gave it to the people, and they ate it. Then he started to follow Elijah. He became Elijah's assistant.

BEN-HADAD ATTACKS SAMARIA

20 Ben-Hadad brought his whole army together. He was king of Aram. He went up to Samaria. He took 32 kings and their horses and chariots with him. All of them surrounded Samaria and attacked it.

²Ben-Hadad sent messengers into the city. They spoke to Ahab, the king of Israel. They told him, "Ben-Hadad says, ³'Your silver and gold belong to me. The best of your wives and children also belong to me.' "

⁴The king of Israel replied, "What you say is true. You are my king and master. I belong to you. And everything I have belongs to you."

⁵The messengers came again. They told Ahab, "Ben-Hadad says, 'I commanded you to give me your silver and gold. I also commanded you to give me your wives and children. ⁶But now I'm going to send my officials to you. They will come about this time tomorrow. They'll search your palace. They'll search the houses of your officials. They'll take everything you value. And they'll carry all of it away.' "

⁷The king of Israel sent for all of the elders of the land. He said to them, "This man is really looking for trouble! He sent for my wives and children. He sent for my silver and gold. And I agreed to give them to him."

⁸All of the elders and people answered, "Don't listen to him. Don't agree to give him what he wants."

⁹So Ahab replied to Ben-Hadad's messengers. He said, "Tell my king and master, 'I will do everything you commanded me to do the first time. But this time, I can't do what you want me to do.' "

They took Ahab's answer back to Ben-Hadad.

¹⁰Then Ben-Hadad sent another message to Ahab. It said, "There won't be enough dust left in Samaria to give each of my followers even a handful. If there is, may the gods punish me greatly."

¹¹The king of Israel replied. He said, "Tell him, 'Someone who puts his armor on shouldn't brag like someone who takes it off.' "

¹²Ben-Hadad and the kings were in their tents drinking. That's when he heard the message. He ordered his men, "Get ready to attack." So they prepared to attack the city.

AHAB WINS THE BATTLE OVER BEN-HADAD

¹³During that time a prophet came to Ahab, the king of Israel. He announced, "The LORD says, 'Do you see this huge army? I will hand it over to you today. Then you will know that I am the LORD.' "

¹⁴"But who will do it?" Ahab asked. The prophet answered, "The LORD

says, 'The young officers who are under the area commanders will do it.' "

"And who will start the battle?" he asked.

The prophet answered, "You will."

¹⁵So Ahab sent for the young officers who were under the area commanders. The total number of officers was 232. Ahab gathered together the rest of the men of Israel. The total number of them was 7,000. ¹⁶They started out at noon. At that time Ben-Hadad and the 32 kings who were helping him were in their tents. They were getting drunk. ¹⁷The young officers who were under Ahab's area commanders marched out first.

Ben-Hadad had sent out scouts. They came back and reported, "Men are marching against us from Samaria."

¹⁸Ben-Hadad said, "They might be coming to make peace. If they are, take them alive. Or they might be coming to make war. If they are, take them alive."

¹⁹The young officers marched out of the city. The army was right behind them. ²⁰Each man struck down the one who was fighting against him. When that happened, the army of Aram ran away. The men of Israel chased them. But Ben-Hadad, the king of Aram, escaped on a horse. Some of his horsemen escaped with him.

²¹The king of Israel attacked them. He overpowered the horses and chariots. Large numbers of the men of Aram were wounded or killed.

²²After that, the prophet came to the king of Israel again. He said, "Make your position stronger. Do what needs to be done. Next spring the king of Aram will attack you again."

²³During that time, the officials of the king of Aram gave him advice. They said, "The gods of Israel are gods of the hills. That's why they were too strong for us. But suppose we fight them on the flatlands. Then we'll certainly be stronger than they are.

²⁴"Here's what you should do. Don't let any of the kings continue as military leaders. Have other officers take their places. ²⁵You must also put another army together. It should be just like the one you lost. It should have the same number of horses and chariots.

Then we'll be able to fight against Israel on the flatlands. And we'll certainly be stronger than they are."

Ben-Hadad agreed with their advice. He did what they suggested.

²⁶The next spring Ben-Hadad brought together the men of Aram. They went up to the city of Aphek to fight against Israel.

²⁷The men of Israel were also brought together. They were given supplies. They marched out to fight against their enemies. Israel's army camped across from Aram's army. The men of Israel looked like two small flocks of goats that had become separated from the others. But the men of Aram covered the countryside.

²⁸The man of God came up to the king of Israel again. He told him, "The LORD says, 'The men of Aram think I am a god of the hills. They do not think I am a god of the valleys. So I will hand their huge army over to you. Then you will know that I am the LORD.' "

²⁹For seven days the two armies camped across from each other. On the seventh day the battle began. The men of Israel wounded or killed 100,000 Aramean soldiers on foot. That happened in a single day. ³⁰The rest of the men of Aram escaped to the city of Aphek. Its wall fell down on 27,000 of them. Ben-Hadad ran to the city. He hid in a secret room.

³¹His officials said to him, "Look, we've heard that the kings of Israel's royal house often show mercy. So let's go to the king of Israel. Let's wear black clothes. Let's tie ropes around our heads. Perhaps Ahab will spare your life."

³²So they wore black clothes. They tied ropes around their heads. Then they went to the king of Israel. They told him, "Your servant Ben-Hadad says, 'Please let me live.' "

The king answered, "Is he still alive? He used to be my friend."

³³The men thought that was good news. So they quickly used the word Ahab had used. "Yes! Your friend Ben-Hadad!" they said.

"Go and get him," the king said.

Ben-Hadad came out of the secret room. Then Ahab had him get into his chariot.

³⁴"I'll return the cities my father took from your father," Ben-Hadad offered. "You can set up your own market areas in Damascus. That's what my father did in Samaria."

Ahab said, "If we sign a peace treaty, I'll set you free."

So he made a treaty with him. Then Ahab let him go.

A PROPHET BRINGS CHARGES AGAINST AHAB

³⁵There was a group that was called the company of the prophets. A message from the LORD came to one of their members. He said to his companion, "Strike me down with your weapon." But the man wouldn't do it. ³⁶The prophet said, "You haven't obeyed the LORD. So as soon as you leave me, a lion will kill you."

The companion went away. And a lion found him and killed him.

³⁷The prophet found another man. He said, "Please strike me down."

So the man struck him down and wounded him. ³⁸Then the prophet went and stood by the road. He waited for the king to come by. He pulled his headband down over his eyes so no one would recognize him. ³⁹The king passed by. Then the prophet called out to him. He said, "I went into the middle of the battle. Someone came to me with a prisoner. He said, 'Guard this man. Don't let him get away. If he does, you will pay for his life with yours. Or you can pay 75 pounds of silver.' ⁴⁰While I was busy here and there, the man disappeared."

"That's your sentence," the king of Israel told him. "You have said so yourself."

⁴¹Then the prophet quickly removed the headband from his eyes. The king of Israel recognized him as one of the prophets. ⁴²He told the king, "The LORD says, 'You have set a man free. But I had said he should be set apart to the LORD in a special way to be destroyed. So you must pay for his life with yours. You must pay for his people's lives with the lives of your people.' "

⁴³The king of Israel was angry. He was in a bad mood. He went back to his palace in Samaria.

AHAB TAKES OVER NABOTH'S VINEYARD

21 Some time later King Ahab wanted a certain vineyard. It belonged to Naboth from Jezreel. The vineyard was in Jezreel. It was close to the palace of Ahab, the king of Samaria.

²Ahab said to Naboth, "Let me have your vineyard. It's close to my palace. I want to use it for a vegetable garden. I'll trade you a better vineyard for it. Or, if you prefer, I'll pay you what it's worth."

³But Naboth replied, "May the LORD keep me from giving you the land my family handed down to me."

⁴So Ahab went home. He was angry. He was in a bad mood because of what Naboth from Jezreel had said. He had told him, "I won't give you the land my family handed down to me."

So Ahab lay on his bed. He was in a very bad mood. He wouldn't even eat anything.

⁵His wife Jezebel came in. She asked him, "Why are you in such a bad mood? Why won't you eat anything?"

⁶He answered her, "Because I spoke to Naboth from Jezreel. I said, 'Sell me your vineyard. Or, if you prefer, I'll give you another vineyard in its place.' But he said, 'I won't sell you my vineyard.' "

⁷His wife Jezebel said, "Is this how the king of Israel acts? Get up! Eat something! Cheer up. I'll get you the vineyard of Naboth from Jezreel."

⁸So she wrote some letters in Ahab's name. She stamped them with his seal. Then she sent them to the elders and nobles who lived in the city where Naboth lived. ⁹In those letters she wrote,

"Announce a day when people are supposed to go without eating. Have Naboth sit in an important place among the people. ¹⁰But put two worthless and evil men in seats across from him. Have them witness to the fact that he has called down curses on God and the king. Then take him out of the city. Kill him by throwing stones at him.”

¹¹So the elders and nobles who lived in that city did what Jezebel wanted. They did everything she directed in the letters she had written to them. ¹²They announced a day of fasting. They had Naboth sit in an important place among the people.

¹³Then two worthless and evil men came and sat across from him. They brought charges against Naboth in front of the people. The two men said, “Naboth has called down curses on God and the king.” So they took him outside the city. They killed him by throwing stones at him.

¹⁴Then they sent a message to Jezebel. They said, “Naboth is dead. We killed him by throwing stones at him.”

¹⁵Jezebel heard that Naboth had been killed. As soon as she heard it, she said to Ahab, “Get up. Take over the vineyard of Naboth from Jezreel. It’s the one he wouldn’t sell to you. He isn’t alive anymore. He’s dead.”

¹⁶Ahab heard that Naboth was dead. So he got up. He went down to take over Naboth’s vineyard.

¹⁷Then a message from the LORD came to Elijah, who was from Tishbe. It said, ¹⁸“Go down to see Ahab, the king of Israel. He rules in Samaria. You will find him in Naboth’s vineyard. He has gone there to take it over. ¹⁹Tell him, ‘The LORD says, “Haven’t you murdered a man? Haven’t you taken over his property?” ’ Then tell him, ‘The LORD says, “Dogs licked up Naboth’s blood. In that same place dogs will lick up your blood. Yes, I said your blood!” ’ ”

²⁰Ahab said to Elijah, “My enemy! You have found me!”

“I have found you,” he answered. “That’s because you gave yourself over to do evil things. You did what was evil in the sight of the LORD. ²¹So the LORD says, ‘I am going to bring horrible trouble on you. I will destroy your children after you. I will cut off every male in Israel who is related to you. It does not matter whether they are slaves or free. ²²I will make your royal house like the house of Jeroboam, the son of Nebat. I will make it like the house of Baasha, the son of Ahijah. You have made me very angry. You have caused Israel to commit sin.’

²³“The LORD also says, ‘Dogs will eat up Jezebel near the wall of Jezreel.’

²⁴“Some of the people who belong to Ahab will die in the city. Dogs will eat them up. Others will die in the country. The birds of the air will eat them.”

²⁵There was never anyone like Ahab. He gave himself over to do what was evil in the sight of the LORD. His wife Jezebel talked him into it. ²⁶He acted in the most evil way. He worshiped statues of gods. He was like the Amorites. The LORD drove them out to make room for Israel.

²⁷When Ahab heard what Elijah had said, he tore his clothes. He put on black clothes. He went without eating. He even slept in his clothes. He went around looking sad.

²⁸Then a message from the LORD came to Elijah, who was from Tishbe. It said, ²⁹“Have you seen how Ahab has made himself low in my sight? Because he has done that, I will not bring trouble on him while he lives. But I will bring it on his royal house when his son is king.”

MICAIAH PROPHESIES AGAINST AHAB

22 For three years there wasn’t any war between Aram and Israel. ²In the third year Jehoshaphat went down to see Ahab, the king of Israel. Jehoshaphat was king of Judah.

³The king of Israel had spoken to his officials. He had said, “Don’t you know that Ramoth Gilead belongs to us? And we aren’t even doing anything to take it back from the king of Aram.”

⁴So Ahab asked Jehoshaphat, “Will you go with me to fight against Ramoth Gilead?”

Jehoshaphat replied to the king of Israel, “Yes. I’ll go with you. My men will go with you. My horses will also go with you.” ⁵Jehoshaphat continued, “First ask the LORD for advice.”

⁶So the king of Israel brought about 400 prophets together. He asked them, “Should I go to war against Ramoth Gilead? Or should I stay here?”

"Go," they answered. "The Lord will hand it over to you."

⁷But Jehoshaphat asked, "Isn't there a prophet of the LORD here? If there is, ask him what we should do."

⁸The king of Israel answered Jehoshaphat. He said, "There is still one other man we can go to. We can ask the LORD for advice through him. But I hate him. He never prophesies anything good about me. He only prophesies bad things. His name is Micaiah. He's the son of Imlah."

"You shouldn't say bad things about him," Jehoshaphat replied.

⁹So the king of Israel called for one of his officials. He told him, "Bring Micaiah, the son of Imlah, at once."

¹⁰The king of Israel and Jehoshaphat, the king of Judah, were wearing their royal robes. They were sitting on their thrones at the threshing floor. It was near the entrance of the gate of Samaria. All of the prophets were prophesying in front of them.

¹¹Zedekiah was the son of Kenaanah. Zedekiah had made horns out of iron. They looked like animal horns. He announced, "The LORD says, 'With these horns you will drive back the men of Aram until they are destroyed.' "

¹²All of the other prophets were prophesying the same thing. "Attack Ramoth Gilead," they said. "Win the battle over it. The LORD will hand it over to you."

¹³A messenger went to get Micaiah. He said to him, "Look. The other prophets agree. All of them are saying the king will have success. So agree with them. Say the same thing they do."

¹⁴But Micaiah said, "You can be sure that the LORD lives. And you can be just as sure that I can only tell the king what the LORD tells me to say."

¹⁵When Micaiah arrived, the king spoke to him. He asked, "Should we go to war against Ramoth Gilead? Or should I stay here?"

"Attack," he answered. "You will win. The LORD will hand Ramoth Gilead over to you."

¹⁶The king said to him, "I've made you promise to tell the truth many times before. So don't tell me anything but the truth in the name of the LORD."

¹⁷Then Micaiah answered, "I saw all of the people of Israel scattered on the hills. They were like sheep that didn't have a shepherd. The LORD said, 'These people do not have a master. Let each of them go home in peace.' "

¹⁸The king of Israel spoke to Jehoshaphat. He said, "Didn't I tell you he never prophesies anything good about me? He only prophesies bad things."

¹⁹Micaiah continued, "Listen to the LORD's message. I saw the LORD sitting on his throne. Some of the angels of heaven were standing at his right side. The others were standing at his left side. So all of them were standing around him. ²⁰The LORD said, 'Who will try to get Ahab to attack Ramoth Gilead? I want him to die there.'

"One angel suggested one thing. Another suggested something else. ²¹Finally, a spirit came forward and stood in front of the LORD. The spirit said, 'I'll try to get Ahab to do it.'

²²" 'How?' the LORD asked.

"The spirit said, 'I'll go out and put lies in the mouths of all of his prophets.'

" 'You will have success in getting Ahab to attack Ramoth Gilead,' said the LORD. 'Go and do it.'

²³"So the LORD has put lies in the mouths of all of your prophets. He has said that great harm will come to you."

²⁴Then Zedekiah, the son of Kenaanah, went up and slapped Micaiah in the face. "So you think the spirit that was sent by the LORD went away from me to speak to you, do you?" he asked. "Which way did he go?"

²⁵Micaiah replied, "You will find out on the day you go to hide in an inside room to save your life."

²⁶Then the king of Israel gave an order. He said, "Take Micaiah away. Send him back to Amon. Amon is the ruler of the city of Samaria. And send him back to Joash. Joash is a member of the royal court. ²⁷Tell him, 'The king says, "Put this fellow in prison. Don't give him anything but bread and water until I return safely." ' "

²⁸Micaiah announced, "Do you really think you will return safely? If

you do, the LORD hasn't spoken through me." He continued, "All of you people, remember what I've said!"

AHAB IS KILLED AT RAMOTH GILEAD

²⁹So the king of Israel went up to Ramoth Gilead. Jehoshaphat, the king of Judah, went there too.

³⁰The king of Israel spoke to Jehoshaphat. He said, "I'll go into battle wearing different clothes. Then people won't recognize me. But you wear your royal robes."

So the king of Israel put on different clothes. Then he went into battle.

³¹The king of Aram had given an order to his 32 chariot commanders. He had said, "Fight only against the king of Israel. Don't fight against anyone else."

³²The chariot commanders saw Jehoshaphat. They thought, "That has to be the king of Israel." So they turned to attack him. But Jehoshaphat cried out. ³³Then the commanders saw he wasn't the king of Israel after all. So they stopped chasing him.

³⁴But someone shot an arrow without taking aim. The arrow hit the king of Israel between the parts of his armor. The king told his chariot driver, "Turn the chariot around. Get me out of this battle. I've been wounded." ³⁵All day long the battle continued. The king kept himself standing up by leaning against the inside of his chariot. He kept his face toward the men of Aram. The blood from his wound ran down onto the floor of the chariot. That evening he died.

³⁶As the sun was setting, a cry spread through the army. "Every man must go to his own town!" they said. "Everyone must go to his own land!"

³⁷So the king died. He was brought to Samaria. They buried his body there. ³⁸They washed the chariot at a pool in Samaria. It was where the prostitutes took baths. The dogs licked up Ahab's blood. It happened exactly as the LORD had said it would.

³⁹The other events of Ahab's rule are written down. Everything he did is written down. That includes the palace he built and decorated with ivory. It also includes the cities he built up

and put high walls around. All of those things are written in the official records of the kings of Israel. ⁴⁰Ahab joined the members of his family who had already died. His son Ahaziah became the next king after him.

JEHOSHAPHAT'S RULE COMES TO AN END

⁴¹Jehoshaphat began to rule over Judah. It was in the fourth year that Ahab was king of Israel. Jehoshaphat was the son of Asa. ⁴²Jehoshaphat was 35 years old when he became king. He ruled in Jerusalem for 25 years. His mother's name was Azubah. She was the daughter of Shilhi.

⁴³Jehoshaphat followed all of the ways of his father Asa. He didn't wander away from them. He did what was right in the eyes of the LORD. But the high places weren't removed. The people continued to offer sacrifices and burn incense at them.

⁴⁴Jehoshaphat was also at peace with the king of Israel.

⁴⁵The other events of Jehoshaphat's rule are written down. The brave things he did in battle and everything else he accomplished are written down. All of those things are written in the official records of the kings of Judah.

⁴⁶Jehoshaphat got rid of the rest of the male prostitutes who were at the temples. They had remained in the land even after the rule of his father Asa.

⁴⁷At that time Edom didn't have a king. An appointed official was in charge.

⁴⁸Jehoshaphat built many ships that he used to carry goods to be traded. The ships were supposed to go to Ophir for gold. But they never had a chance to sail. They were wrecked at Ezion Geber. ⁴⁹At that time Ahaziah, the son of Ahab, spoke to Jehoshaphat. He said, "Let my men sail with yours." But Jehoshaphat refused.

⁵⁰Jehoshaphat joined the members of his family who had already died. His body was buried in the family tomb in the city of King David. His son Jehoram became the next king after him.

AHAZIAH BECOMES KING OF ISRAEL

⁵¹Ahaziah became king of Israel in Samaria. It was in the 17th year that Jehoshaphat was king of Judah. Ahaziah ruled over Israel for two years. He was the son of Ahab.

⁵²Ahaziah did what was evil in the sight of the LORD. He lived the way his father and mother had lived. He lived the way Jeroboam, the son of Nebat, had lived. Jeroboam had caused Israel to commit sin. ⁵³Ahaziah served and worshiped the god Baal. He made the LORD, the God of Israel, very angry. That's exactly what his father had done.

quest challenge

I Wonder . . .

What is the most important thing I can do in my life?

Real Life Challenge

Take a minute to think about how you spend your free time: sports, piano lessons, dance, video games, TV, movies, the Internet and much more. While all of these things can be a really important part of your life, keep the *most* important thing in mind: knowing the God who loves you.

Quest Clue

Take a look at 1 Kings 2 (at the very beginning of the chapter) to see the advice one father gave his son about what was important in life. Then find Philippians 3 to see what Paul has to say.

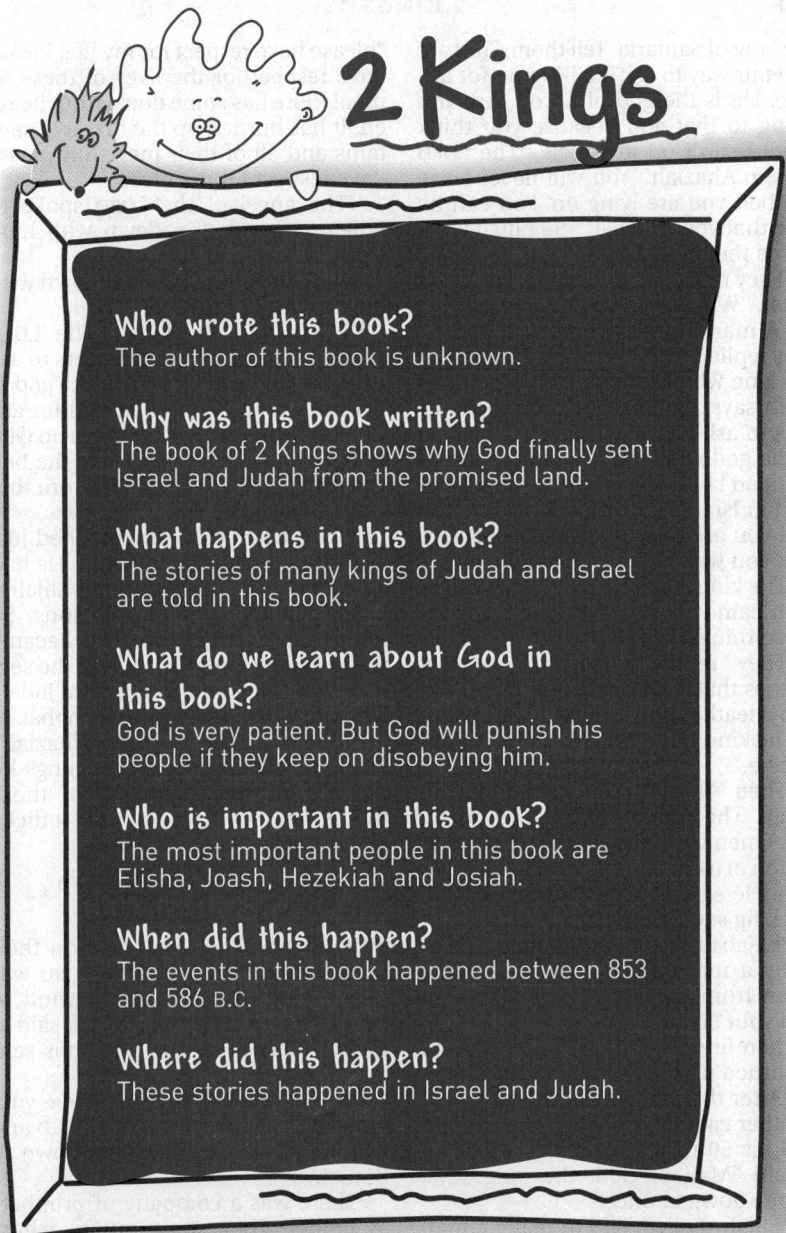

2 Kings

Who wrote this book?
The author of this book is unknown.

Why was this book written?
The book of 2 Kings shows why God finally sent Israel and Judah from the promised land.

What happens in this book?
The stories of many kings of Judah and Israel are told in this book.

What do we learn about God in this book?
God is very patient. But God will punish his people if they keep on disobeying him.

Who is important in this book?
The most important people in this book are Elisha, Joash, Hezekiah and Josiah.

When did this happen?
The events in this book happened between 853 and 586 B.C.

Where did this happen?
These stories happened in Israel and Judah.

THE LORD JUDGES AHAZIAH

1 After Ahab died, Moab refused to remain under Israel's control. ²Ahaziah had fallen through the window of his upstairs room in Samaria. He had hurt himself. So he sent messengers to ask the god Baal-Zebub for advice. Baal-Zebub was the god of the city of Ekron. Ahaziah said to the messengers, "Go and ask Baal-Zebub whether I will get well again."

³But the angel of the LORD spoke to Elijah, who was from Tishbe. He said, "Go up to see the messengers of Ahaziah,

the king of Samaria. Tell them, 'You are on your way to ask Baal-Zebub for advice. He is the god of Ekron. Are you going to that god because you think there is no God in Israel?' ⁴The LORD says to Ahaziah, 'You will never leave the bed you are lying on. You can be sure that you will die!' " So Elijah went to see the messengers.

⁵They returned to the king. He asked them, "Why have you come back?"

⁶"A man met us on our way there," they replied. "He said to us, 'Go back to the king who sent you. Tell him, "The LORD says, 'You are sending messengers to ask Baal-Zebub for advice. He is the god of Ekron. Are you going to that god because you think there is no God in Israel? You will never leave the bed you are lying on. You can be sure that you will die!' " ' "

⁷The king asked them, "What kind of man came to see you? Who told you those things?"

⁸They replied, "He was wearing clothes that were made out of hair. He had a leather belt around his waist."

The king said, "That was Elijah from Tishbe."

⁹Then Ahaziah sent a captain to Elijah. The captain had his company of 50 men with him. Elijah was sitting on top of a hill. The captain went up to him. He said to Elijah, "Man of God, the king says, 'Come down!' "

¹⁰Elijah answered the captain, "If I'm really a man of God, may fire come down from heaven! May it burn you and your 50 men up!"

Then fire came down from heaven. It burned up the captain and his men.

¹¹After that happened, the king sent another captain to Elijah. The captain had his 50 men with him. He said to Elijah, "Man of God, the king says, 'Come down at once!' "

¹²Elijah replied, "If I'm really a man of God, may fire come down from heaven! May it burn you and your 50 men up!"

Then the fire of God came down from heaven. It burned up the captain and his 50 men.

¹³So the king sent a third captain with his 50 men. The captain went up to Elijah. He fell on his knees in front of him. "Man of God," he begged,

"please have respect for my life! Please have respect for the lives of these 50 men! ¹⁴Fire has come down from heaven. It has burned up the first two captains and all of their men. But please have respect for my life!"

¹⁵The angel of the LORD spoke to Elijah. He said, "Go down with him. Don't be afraid of him."

So Elijah got up. He went down with the captain to the king.

¹⁶Elijah told the king, "The LORD says, 'You have sent messengers to ask Baal-Zebub for advice. He is the god of Ekron. Did you go to that god for advice because you think there is no God in Israel? You will never leave the bed you are lying on. You can be sure that you will die!' "

¹⁷So Ahaziah died. It happened just as the LORD had said it would. He had spoken that message through Elijah.

Ahaziah didn't have any sons. So Joram, his younger brother, became the next king after him. It was the second year of Jehoram, the king of Judah. Jehoram was the son of Jehoshaphat.

¹⁸All of the other events of Ahaziah's rule are written down. The things he did are written down. All of those things are written in the official records of the kings of Israel.

ELIJAH IS TAKEN UP TO HEAVEN

2 Elijah and Elisha were on their way from Gilgal. The LORD was going to use a strong wind to take Elijah up to heaven. ²Elijah said to Elisha, "Stay here. The LORD has sent me to Bethel."

But Elisha said, "I won't leave you. And that's just as sure as the LORD and you are alive." So they went down to Bethel.

³There was a company of prophets at Bethel. They came out to where Elisha was. They asked him, "Do you know what the LORD is going to do? He's going to take your master away from you today."

"Yes, I know," Elisha replied. "But don't talk about it."

⁴Then Elijah said to him, "Stay here, Elisha. The LORD has sent me to Jericho."

Elisha replied, "I won't leave you.

And that's just as sure as the LORD and you are alive." So they went to Jericho.

⁵There was a company of prophets at Jericho. They went up to where Elisha was. They asked him, "Do you know what the LORD is going to do? He's going to take your master away from you today."

"Yes, I know," Elisha replied. "But don't talk about it."

⁶Then Elijah said to him, "Stay here. The LORD has sent me to the Jordan River."

Elisha replied, "I won't leave you. And that's just as sure as the LORD and you are alive." So the two of them walked on.

⁷Fifty men from the company of the prophets followed them. The men stopped and stood not far away from them. They faced the place where Elijah and Elisha had stopped at the Jordan River. ⁸Elijah rolled his coat up. Then he struck the water with it. The water parted to the right and to the left. The two of them went across the river on dry ground.

⁹After they had gone across, Elijah spoke to Elisha. He said, "Tell me. What can I do for you before I'm taken away from you?"

"Please give me a double share of your spirit," Elisha replied.

¹⁰"You have asked me for something I can't give you," Elijah said. "Only the LORD can give it. But suppose you see me when I'm taken away from you. Then you will receive what you have asked for. If you don't see me, you won't receive it."

¹¹They kept walking along and talking together. Suddenly a chariot and horses appeared. Fire was all around them. The chariot and horses came between the two men. Then Elijah went up to heaven in a strong wind.

¹²Elisha saw it. He cried out to Elijah, "My father! You are like a father to me! You are the true chariots and horsemen of Israel!"

Elisha didn't see Elijah anymore. Then Elisha took hold of his own clothes and tore them apart.

¹³He picked up the coat that had fall-

Why did Elijah go up to heaven without dying?

Elijah was a prophet. He spent most of his life telling others about God and telling others what God said. He is one of the two people mentioned in the Bible who did not die before going to heaven. When God took Elijah, he used a chariot of fire and a whirlwind. The whirlwind and fire did not kill Elijah or burn him. The chariot separated him from his good friend Elisha. The whirlwind carried him to heaven. God took Elijah to heaven at just the right time. We do not know how old Elijah was when God took him. He may have been a very old man.

2 Kings 2:11

Related verses:
Genesis 5:24;
2 Kings 2:1–12

en from Elijah. He went back and stood on the bank of the Jordan River. ¹⁴Then he struck the water with Elijah's coat. "Where is the power of the LORD?" he asked. "Where is the power of the God of Elijah?" When Elisha struck the water, it parted to the right and to the left. He went across the river.

¹⁵The company of the prophets from Jericho were watching. They said, "The spirit of Elijah has been given to Elisha." They went over to him. They bowed down to him with their faces toward the ground. ¹⁶"Look," they said. "We have 50 able men. Let them go and look for your master. Perhaps the Spirit of the LORD has lifted him up. Maybe he has put him down on a mountain or in a valley."

"No," Elisha replied. "Don't send them."

¹⁷But they kept asking until he felt he couldn't say no. So he said, "Send them." And they sent 50 men. They looked for Elijah for three days. But they didn't find him.

¹⁸So they returned to Elisha. He was staying in Jericho. Elisha said to them, "Didn't I tell you not to go?"

ELISHA MAKES JERICHO'S WATER PURE

¹⁹The men of Jericho spoke to Elisha. "Look," they said. "This town has a good location. You can see that for yourself. But the spring of water here is bad. So the land doesn't produce anything."

²⁰"Bring me a new bowl," Elisha said. "Put some salt in it." So they brought it to him.

²¹Then he went out to the spring. He threw the salt into it. He told them, "The LORD says, 'I have made this water pure. It will never cause death again. It will never keep the land from producing crops again.'" ²²The water has stayed pure to this very day. That's what Elisha had said would happen.

SOME YOUNG FELLOWS MAKE FUN OF ELISHA

²³Elisha left Jericho and went up to Bethel. He was walking along the road. Some young fellows came out of the town. They made fun of him. "Go on

up! You don't even have any hair on your head!" they said. "Go on up! You don't even have any hair on your head!"

²⁴He turned around and looked at them. And he called down a curse on them. He did it in the name of the LORD. Then two bears came out of the woods. They attacked 42 of the young fellows.

²⁵Elisha went on to Mount Carmel. From there he returned to Samaria.

MOAB'S KING REFUSES TO OBEY ISRAEL'S KING

3 Joram became king of Israel in Samaria. It was in the 18th year that Jehoshaphat was king of Judah. Joram ruled for 12 years. He was the son of Ahab.

²Joram did what was evil in the sight of the LORD. But he wasn't as bad as his father and mother had been. His father had made a sacred stone that was used to worship the god Baal. Joram got rid of it. ³But he kept on committing the sins of Jeroboam, the son of Nebat. Jeroboam had also caused Israel to commit those same sins. Joram didn't turn away from them.

⁴Mesha raised sheep. He was king of Moab. He had to supply the king of Israel with 100,000 lambs a year. He also had to supply him with the wool of 100,000 rams a year.

⁵Ahab died. Moab's king refused to obey the next king of Israel. ⁶So at that time King Joram started out from Samaria. He gathered all of Israel's troops together.

⁷He also sent a message to Jehoshaphat, the king of Judah. It said, "The king of Moab is refusing to obey me. Will you go with me to fight against Moab?"

"Yes. I'll go with you," he replied. "My men will go with you. My horses will also go with you."

⁸"What road should we take to attack Moab?" Joram asked.

"The one that goes through the Desert of Edom," Jehoshaphat answered.

⁹So the king of Israel started out. The king of Judah and the king of Edom went with him. Their armies marched around the southern end of the Dead

Sea. After seven days they ran out of water. There wasn't any water for the men or their animals.

¹⁰"What should we do now?" exclaimed the king of Israel. "The LORD has called us three kings together. Did he do it only to hand us over to Moab?"

¹¹But Jehoshaphat asked, "Isn't there a prophet of the LORD here? Can't we ask the LORD for advice through him?"

An officer of the king of Israel spoke up. He answered, "Elisha is here. He's the son of Shaphat. Elisha used to serve Elijah."

¹²Jehoshaphat said, "The LORD speaks through him." So the king of Israel went down to see Elisha. Jehoshaphat and the king of Edom also went there.

¹³Elisha spoke to the king of Israel. He said, "What do you and I have in common? Go to your father's prophets. Go to your mother's prophets."

"No," the king of Israel answered. "The LORD called us three kings together. He did it to hand us over to Moab."

¹⁴Elisha said, "I serve the LORD who rules over all. You can be sure that he lives. And you can be just as sure that I have respect for Jehoshaphat, the king of Judah. If I didn't, I wouldn't look at you or even notice you. ¹⁵But now bring me someone who plays the harp."

While that person was playing the harp, the LORD's powerful hand came on Elisha. ¹⁶Elisha announced, "The LORD says, 'Dig a lot of ditches in this valley.' ¹⁷Do it because the LORD says, 'You will not see wind or rain. But this valley will be filled with water. Then you, your cattle and your other animals will have water to drink.'

¹⁸"That's an easy thing for the LORD to do. He will also hand Moab over to you. ¹⁹You will destroy every city that has high walls around it. You will destroy every major town. You will cut down every good tree. You will stop up all of the springs of water. And you will cover every good field with stones."

²⁰The next day, the time came to offer the morning sacrifice. And then it happened! Water was flowing from the direction of Edom! In fact, the land was filled with water!

²¹Now all of the people of Moab had heard that the kings had come to fight against them. So Moab sent for all of its fighting men. It didn't matter whether they were young or old. They sent for everyone who could carry a weapon. All of them were stationed at the border.

²²They got up early in the morning. The sun was already shining on the water. Across the way, the water looked red to the men of Moab. It looked like blood. ²³"That's blood!" they said. "Those kings must have fought and killed each other. Let's go, Moab! Let's take everything that has any value."

²⁴So the men of Moab went to the camp of Israel. Just as they arrived there, the men of Israel got ready to fight. They fought against the men of Moab until they ran away. The men of Israel marched into the land and attacked it. They killed the people of Moab. ²⁵They destroyed the towns. Each man threw a large stone on every good field. They did that until the fields were covered. They stopped up all of the springs of water. And they cut down every good tree. The only town that was left with any stones in place was Kir Hareseth. But men who were armed with slings surrounded it. Then they attacked it.

²⁶The king of Moab saw that the battle had gone against him. So he took with him 700 men who had swords. They tried to break through the battle lines to the king of Edom. But they couldn't do it.

²⁷Then the king of Moab got his oldest son. He was the son who would become the next king after him. He offered his son as a sacrifice on the city wall. That shocked and terrified the men of Israel. So they pulled back. And they returned to their own land.

ELISHA PROVIDES OLIVE OIL FOR A WIDOW

4 The wife of a man from the company of the prophets cried out to Elisha. She said, "My husband is dead. You know how much respect he had for the LORD. But he owed money to someone. And now that person is coming to take my two boys away. They will become his slaves."

²Elisha replied to her, "How can I help you? Tell me. What do you have in your house?"

"I don't have anything there at all," she said. "All I have is a little olive oil."

³Elisha said, "Go around to all of your neighbors. Ask them for empty jars. Get as many as you can. ⁴Then go inside your house. Shut the door behind you and your sons. Pour oil into all of the jars. As each jar is filled, put it over to one side."

⁵The woman left him. After that, she shut the door behind her and her sons. They brought the jars to her. And she kept pouring. ⁶When all of the jars were full, she spoke to one of her sons. She said, "Bring me another jar."

But he replied, "There aren't any more left." Then the oil stopped flowing.

⁷She went and told the man of God about it. He said, "Go and sell the oil.

Pay what you owe. You and your sons can live on what is left."

THE SON OF A WOMAN FROM SHUNEM IS BROUGHT BACK TO LIFE

⁸One day Elisha went to the town of Shunem. A rich woman lived there. She begged him to stay and have a meal. So every time he came by, he stopped there to eat.

⁹The woman said to her husband, "That man often comes by here. I know that he is a holy man of God. ¹⁰Let's make a small room for him on the roof. We'll put a bed and a table in it. We'll also put a chair and a lamp in it. Then he can stay there when he comes to visit us."

¹¹One day Elisha came. He went up to his room. He lay down there. ¹²He said to his servant Gehazi, "Go and get the Shunammite woman." So he did. She stood in front of Elisha.

¹³He said to Gehazi, "Tell her, 'You

 **Does it matter how much faith we have?**

Jesus said that even if we have a very tiny amount of faith, we can accomplish great things. Having faith just means that we believe that God is faithful. In other words, we decide to trust that he loves us and will do what he said he would do. Great faith in God comes from deciding that God is faithful and that we are going to trust him no matter what.

We should put all our trust in God and depend on him, not on our own words, strength or clever plans. If we trust even a little in our mighty God, it will make a huge difference.

checkout
2 Kings 4:22–25, 30

Related verses:
Psalm 22:4–5;
Matthew 17:20;
Mark 9:22–24;
Luke 17:6;
James 1:6–7

FAITH CHRISTIAN BOOKSTORE

BIBLES

YES, I'D LIKE TO BUY A MUSTARD SEED'S WORTH OF FAITH PLEASE.

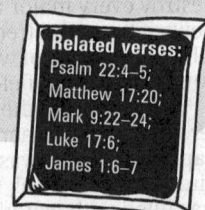

have gone to a lot of trouble for us. Now what can we do for you? Can we speak to the king for you? Or can we speak to the commander of the army for you?' "

She replied, "I live among my own people. I have everything I need here."

¹⁴After she left, Elisha asked Gehazi, "What can we do for her?"

Gehazi said, "Well, she doesn't have a son. And her husband is old."

¹⁵Then Elisha said, "Bring her here again." So he did. She stood in the doorway. ¹⁶"You will hold a son in your arms," Elisha said. "It will be about this time next year."

"No, my master!" she objected. "You are a man of God. So don't lie to me!"

¹⁷But the woman became pregnant. She had a baby boy. It happened the next year about that same time. That's exactly what Elisha had told her would happen.

¹⁸The child grew. One day he went out to get his father. His father was with those who were gathering the crops.

¹⁹The boy said to his father, "My head hurts! It really hurts!"

His father told a servant, "Carry him to his mother." ²⁰The servant lifted the boy up. He carried him to his mother.

The boy sat on her lap until noon. Then he died. ²¹She went up to the room on the roof. There she laid him on the bed of the man of God. Then she shut the door and went out.

²²She sent for her husband. She said, "Please send me one of the servants and a donkey. Then I can go quickly to the man of God and return."

²³"Why do you want to go to him today?" he asked. "It isn't the time for the New Moon Feast. It isn't the Sabbath day."

"Don't let that bother you," she said.

²⁴She put a saddle on her donkey. She said to her servant, "Let's go. Don't slow down for me unless I tell you to."

²⁵So she started out. She came to Mount Carmel. That's where the man of God was.

When she was still a long way off, he saw her coming. He said to his servant Gehazi, "Look! There's the woman from Shunem! ²⁶Run out there to meet her. Ask her, 'Are you all right? Is your husband all right? Is your child all right?' "

"Everything is all right," she said.

²⁷She came to the man of God at the mountain. Then she took hold of his feet. Gehazi came over to push her away. But the man of God said, "Leave her alone! She is suffering terribly. But the LORD hasn't told me the reason for it. He has hidden it from me."

²⁸"My master, did I ask you for a son?" she said. "Didn't I tell you, 'Don't get my hopes up'?"

²⁹Elisha said to Gehazi, "Tuck your coat into your belt. Take my wooden staff and run to Shunem. Don't say hello to anyone you see. If anyone says hello to you, don't answer. Lay my staff on the boy's face."

³⁰But the child's mother said, "I won't leave you. And that's just as sure as the LORD and you are alive." So Elisha got up and followed her.

³¹Gehazi went on ahead. He laid Elisha's wooden staff on the boy's face. But there wasn't any sound. The boy didn't move at all.

So Gehazi went back to Elisha. He told him, "The boy hasn't awakened."

³²Elisha arrived at the house. The boy was dead. He was lying on Elisha's bed.

³³Elisha went into the room. He shut the door. He was alone with the boy. He prayed to the LORD.

³⁴Then he got on the bed. He lay down on the boy. His mouth touched the boy's mouth. His eyes touched the boy's eyes. And his hands touched the boy's hands. As Elisha lay on the boy, the boy's body grew warm.

³⁵Elisha turned away. He walked back and forth in the room. Then he got on the bed again. He lay down on the boy once more. The boy sneezed seven times. After that, he opened his eyes.

³⁶Elisha sent for Gehazi. He said to him, "Go and get the Shunammite woman." So he did. When she came, Elisha said, "Take your son."

³⁷She came in. She fell at Elisha's feet. She bowed down with her face toward the ground. Then she took her son and went out.

DEADLY FOOD IN A POT

[38]Elisha returned to Gilgal. There wasn't enough food to eat in that area. The company of the prophets was meeting with Elisha. So he said to his servant, "Put the large pot over the fire. Cook some stew for these men."

[39]One of them went out into the fields to gather herbs. He found a wild vine. He gathered up some of its gourds. He brought them back with him in his coat. Then he cut them up into the pot of stew. But no one knew what they were.

[40]The stew was poured out for the men. They began to eat it. But then they cried out, "Man of God, the food in that pot will kill us!" They couldn't eat it.

[41]Elisha said, "Get some flour." He put it in the pot. He said, "Serve it to the men to eat." Then there wasn't anything in the pot that could harm them.

ELISHA FEEDS 100 PEOPLE

[42]A man came from Baal Shalishah. He brought the man of God 20 loaves of barley bread. They had been baked from the first grain that had ripened. He also brought some heads of new grain. "Give this food to the people to eat," Elisha said.

[43]"How can I put this in front of 100 men?" his servant asked.

But Elisha answered, "Give it to the people to eat. Do it because the LORD says, 'They will eat and have some left over.'"

[44]Then the servant put the food in front of them. They ate it and had some left over. It happened just as the LORD had said it would.

NAAMAN IS HEALED OF A SKIN DISEASE

5 Naaman was commander of the army of the king of Aram. He was a very important man in the eyes of his master. And he was highly respected. That's because the LORD had helped him win the battle over Aram's enemies. He was a brave soldier. But he had a skin disease.

[2]Companies of soldiers from Aram had marched out. They had captured a young girl from Israel. She became a servant of Naaman's wife. [3]She spoke to the woman she was serving. She said, "I wish my master would go and see the prophet who is in Samaria. He would heal my master of his skin disease."

[4]Naaman went to see his own master. He told him what the girl from Israel had said.

[5]"I think you should go," the king of Aram replied. "I'll give you a letter to take to the king of Israel."

So Naaman left. He took 750 pounds of silver with him. He also took 150 pounds of gold. And he took ten sets of clothes. [6]He carried the letter to the king of Israel. It said, "I'm sending my servant Naaman to you with this letter. I want you to heal him of his skin disease."

[7]The king of Israel read the letter. As soon as he did, he tore his royal robes. He said, "Am I God? Can I kill people and bring them back to life? Why does this fellow send someone to me to be healed of his skin disease? He must be trying to pick a fight with me!"

[8]Elisha, the man of God, heard that the king of Israel had torn his robes. So he sent the king a message. It said, "Why have you torn your robes? Tell the man to come to me. Then he will know there is a prophet in Israel."

[9]So Naaman went to see Elisha. He took his horses and chariots with him. He stopped at the door of Elisha's house.

[10]Elisha sent a messenger out to him. The messenger said, "Go. Wash yourself in the Jordan River seven times. Then your skin will be healed. You will be pure and clean again."

[11]But Naaman went away angry. He said, "I was sure he would come out to me. I thought he would stand there and pray to the LORD his God. I thought he would wave his hand over my skin. Then I would be healed. [12]And what about the Abana and Pharpar rivers of Damascus? Aren't they better than any of the rivers of Israel? Couldn't I wash in them and be made pure and clean?" So he turned and went away. He was burning with anger.

[13]Naaman's servants went over to

him. They said, "You are like a father to us. What if the prophet Elisha had told you to do some great thing? Wouldn't you have done it? But he only said, 'Wash yourself. Then you will be pure and clean.' You should be even more willing to do that!"

¹⁴So Naaman went down to the Jordan River. He dipped himself in it seven times. He did exactly what the man of God had told him to do. Then his skin was made pure again. It became clean like the skin of a young boy.

¹⁵Naaman and all of his attendants went back to the man of God. Naaman stood in front of Elisha. He said, "Now I know that there is no God anywhere in the whole world except in Israel. Please accept a gift from me."

¹⁶The prophet answered, "I serve the LORD. You can be sure that he lives. And you can be just as sure that I won't accept a gift from you." Even though Naaman begged him to take it, Elisha wouldn't.

¹⁷"I can see that you won't accept a gift from me," said Naaman. "But please let me have some soil from your land. Give me as much as a pair of mules can carry. Here's why I want it. I won't ever bring burnt offerings and sacrifices to any other god again. I'll bring them only to the LORD. I'll worship him on his own soil.

¹⁸"But there is one thing I hope the LORD will forgive me for. From time to time my master will enter the temple to bow down to his god Rimmon. When he does, he'll lean on my arm. Then I'll have to bow down there also. I hope the LORD will forgive me for that."

¹⁹"Go in peace," Elisha said.

Naaman started out on his way.

²⁰Gehazi was the servant of Elisha, the man of God. Gehazi said to himself, "My master was too easy on Naaman from Aram. He should have accepted the gift he brought. I'm going to run after Naaman. I'm going to get something from him. And that's just as sure as the LORD is alive."

²¹Gehazi hurried after Naaman. Naaman saw him running toward him. So he got down from the chariot to greet him. "Is everything all right?" he asked.

²²"Everything is all right," Gehazi answered. "My master sent me to say, 'Two young men from the company of the prophets have just come to me. They've come from the hill country of Ephraim. Please give them 75 pounds of silver and two sets of clothes.' "

²³"I wish you would take twice as much silver," said Naaman. He begged Gehazi to accept it. Then Naaman tied up 150 pounds of silver in two bags. He also gave Gehazi two sets of clothes. He gave all of it to two of his own servants. They carried it ahead of Gehazi.

²⁴Gehazi came to the hill where Elisha lived. Then the servants handed the things over to Gehazi. He put them away in Elisha's house. He sent the men away, and they left. ²⁵Then he went back inside the house. He stood in front of his master Elisha.

"Gehazi, where have you been?" Elisha asked.

"I didn't go anywhere," Gehazi answered.

²⁶But Elisha said to him, "Didn't my spirit go with you? I know that the man got down from his chariot to greet you. Is this the time for you to accept money or clothes? Is it the time to take olive groves, vineyards, flocks or herds? Is it the time to accept male and female servants? ²⁷You and your children after you will have Naaman's skin disease forever."

Then Gehazi left Elisha. And he had Naaman's skin disease. His skin was as white as snow.

AN AX BLADE FLOATS

6 The company of the prophets spoke to Elisha. They said, "Look. The place where we meet with you is too small for us. ²We would like to go to the Jordan River. Each of us can get some wood there. We want to build a place there for us to live in."

Elisha said, "Go."

³Then one of them said, "Won't you please come with us?"

"I will," Elisha replied. ⁴And he went with them.

They went to the Jordan. There they began to cut down trees. ⁵One of them was cutting a tree down. The iron blade of his ax fell into the water.

"Master!" he cried out. "This ax was borrowed!"

⁶The man of God asked, "Where did the blade fall?" He showed him the place. Then Elisha cut a stick and threw it there. That made the iron blade float. ⁷"Take it out of the water," he said. So the man reached out and took it.

ELISHA MAKES THE SOLDIERS OF ARAM BLIND

⁸The king of Aram was at war with Israel. He talked things over with his officers. Then he said, "I'm going to set up my camp in a certain place."

⁹The man of God sent a message to the king of Israel. It said, "Try to stay away from that place. Aram's army is going to be down there." ¹⁰The king of Israel checked on the place the man of God had told him about. Time after time Elisha warned the king. So the king was on guard in those places.

¹¹All of that made the king of Aram very angry. He sent for his officers. He said to them, "Tell me. Which of us is on the side of the king of Israel?"

¹²"You are my king and master," said one of his officers. "None of us is on Israel's side. But Elisha is a prophet in Israel. He tells the king of Israel the very words you speak in your own bedroom."

¹³"Go and find out where he is," the king ordered. "Then I can send my men and capture him." The report came back. It said, "He's in Dothan."

¹⁴Then the king sent horses and chariots and a strong army there. They went at night and surrounded the city.

¹⁵The servant of the man of God got up the next morning. He went out early. He saw that an army with horses and chariots had surrounded the city. "My master!" the servant said. "What can we do?"

¹⁶"Don't be afraid," the prophet answered. "Those who are with us are more than those who are with them."

¹⁷Elisha prayed, "LORD, open my servant's eyes so he can see." Then the LORD opened his eyes. He looked up and saw the hills. He saw that Elisha was surrounded by horses and chariots. Fire was all around them.

¹⁸Aram's army came down toward Elisha. Then he prayed to the LORD. He said, "Make these soldiers blind." So the LORD made them blind, just as Elisha had prayed.

¹⁹Elisha told them, "This isn't the right road. This isn't the right city. Follow me. I'll lead you to the man you are looking for." He led them to Samaria.

²⁰They entered the city. Then Elisha said, "LORD, open the eyes of these men. Help them see again." Then the LORD opened their eyes. They looked around. And there they were, inside Samaria!

²¹The king of Israel saw them. So he asked Elisha, "Should I kill them? I need your advice. You are like a father to me. Should I kill them?"

²²"Don't kill them," he answered. "Would you kill men you have captured with your own sword or bow? Put some food and water in front of them. Then they can eat and drink. They can go back to their master."

²³So he prepared a big dinner for them. After they had finished eating and drinking, he sent them away. They returned to their master. So the companies of soldiers from Aram stopped attacking Israel's territory.

ARAM'S ARMY ATTACKS SAMARIA

²⁴Some time later, Ben-Hadad gathered his entire army together. Ben-Hadad was the king of Aram. His army marched up and surrounded Samaria. Then they attacked it.

²⁵There wasn't enough food anywhere in the city. It was surrounded for so long that people had to weigh out two pounds of silver for a donkey's head. They had to weigh out two ounces of silver for half a pint of seed pods.

²⁶One day the king of Israel was walking on top of the wall. A woman cried out to him, "You are my king and master. Please help me!"

²⁷The king replied, "If the LORD doesn't help you, where can I get help for you? From the threshing floor? From the winepress?" ²⁸He continued, "What's wrong?"

She answered, "A woman said to me, 'Give up your son. Then we can eat him today. Tomorrow we'll eat my son.' ²⁹So we cooked my son. Then we ate him. The next day I said to her, 'Give up your son. Then we can eat him.' But she had hidden him."

³⁰When the king heard the woman's words, he tore his royal robes. As he walked along the wall, the people looked up at him. They saw that he was wearing black clothes under his robes. ³¹He said, "I'll cut the head of Shaphat's son Elisha off his shoulders today. If I don't, may God punish me greatly!"

³²Elisha was sitting in his house. The elders were sitting there with him. The king went to see Elisha. He sent a messenger on ahead of him. Before the messenger arrived, Elisha spoke to the elders. He said, "That murderer is sending someone here to cut my head off. Can't you see that? When the messenger comes, close the door. Hold it shut against him. Can't you hear his master's footsteps right behind him?"

³³Elisha was still talking to the elders when the messenger came down to him. The king also arrived. He said, "The LORD has sent this horrible trouble on us. Why should I wait any longer for him to help us?"

7 Elisha said, "Listen to a message from the LORD. He says, 'About this time tomorrow, you will be able to buy seven quarts of flour for less than half of an ounce of silver. You will also be able to buy 13 quarts of barley for the same price. That's all you will have to pay for those things at the gate of Samaria.' "

²The king was leaning on an officer's arm. The officer spoke to the man of God. He said, "Suppose the LORD opens the windows of the skies. Suppose he pours food down on us. Even if he does, could what you are saying really happen?"

"You will see it with your own eyes," answered Elisha. "But you won't eat any of it!"

THE ATTACK ON SAMARIA ENDS

³There were four men who had a skin disease. They were at the entrance of the gate of Samaria. They said to one another, "Why should we stay here until we die? ⁴Suppose we say, 'We'll go into the city.' There isn't any food there, and we'll die. But if we stay here, we'll die anyway. So let's go over to Aram's army camp. Let's give ourselves up. If they spare us, we'll live. If they kill us, we'll die."

⁵At sunset they got up. They went to Aram's army camp. They arrived at the edge of it. But no one was there. ⁶The Lord had caused the soldiers of Aram to hear a noise. It sounded like chariots and horses and a huge army. So the soldiers spoke to one another. They said, "Listen! The king of Israel has hired the Hittite and Egyptian kings. He has paid them to attack us!" ⁷So they had gotten up and had run away at sunset. They had left their tents and horses and donkeys behind. They had left the camp as it was. And they had run for their lives.

⁸The men who had a skin disease arrived at the edge of the camp. They entered one of the tents. They ate and drank. Then they carried away silver, gold and clothes. They went off and hid them. They returned and entered another tent. They took some things from it and hid them also.

⁹But then they said to one another, "What we're doing isn't right. This is a day of good news. And we're keeping it to ourselves. If we wait until sunrise, we'll be punished. Let's go at once. Let's report this to the royal palace."

¹⁰So they went. They called out to the people who were guarding the city gates. They told them, "We went into Aram's army camp. No one was there. We didn't hear anyone. The horses and donkeys were still tied up. The tents were left just as they were."

¹¹The people who guarded the gates shouted the news. It was reported inside the palace.

¹²The king of Israel got up in the night. He spoke to his officers. He said, "I'll tell you what the men of Aram have done to us. They know we are very hungry. So they have left the camp to hide in the countryside. They are thinking, 'We are sure they'll come out. Then we'll take them alive. And we'll get into the city.' "

¹³One of the king's officers spoke up. He said, "A few horses are still left in the city. Have some men get five of

them. They won't be any worse off than all of the other Israelites who are left here. In fact, all of us will soon be dead. So let's send the men to find out what happened."

[14]The men chose two chariots and their horses. The king sent them out to look for Aram's army. He commanded the drivers, "Go and find out what has happened."

[15]They followed the trail of Aram's soldiers all the way to the Jordan River. They found clothes and supplies all along the road. The soldiers had thrown them down when they ran away. So the men returned. They reported to the king what they had seen.

[16]Then the people went out of the city. They took everything of value from Aram's army camp. So seven quarts of flour sold for less than half of an ounce of silver. And 13 quarts of barley sold for the same price. That's exactly what the LORD had said would happen.

[17]The king had put an officer in charge of the city gate. He was the officer on whose arm the king leaned. On their way out of the city, the people knocked the officer down. In the entrance of the gate they walked all over him. And he died. That's exactly what the man of God had said would happen. He had said it when the king came down to his house.

[18]What the man of God had told the king came true. He had said, "About this time tomorrow, you will be able to buy seven quarts of flour for less than half of an ounce of silver. You will also be able to buy 13 quarts of barley for the same price. That's all you will have to pay for those things at the gate of Samaria."

[19]The officer had spoken to the man of God. He had said, "Suppose the LORD opens the windows of the skies. Suppose he pours food down on us. Even if he does, could what you are saying really happen?" The man of God had replied, "You will see it with your own eyes. But you won't eat any of it!"

[20]And that's exactly what happened to the officer. On their way out of the city, the people knocked him down. In the entrance of the gate they walked all over him. And he died.

THE WOMAN FROM SHUNEM GETS HER LAND BACK

8 Elisha had brought a woman's son back to life. He had said to her, "Go away with your family. Stay for a while anywhere you can. The LORD has decided that there won't be enough food in the land. That will be true for seven years."

[2]The woman did just as the man of God told her to. She and her family went away. They stayed in the land of the Philistines for seven years.

[3]The seven years passed. Then she came back from the land of the Philistines. She went to the king of Israel. She wanted to beg him to get her house and land back.

[4]The king was talking to Gehazi. Gehazi was the servant of the man of God. The king had said, "Tell me about all of the great things Elisha has done."
[5]Gehazi was telling the king how Elisha had brought a dead boy back to life. Just then the woman came to beg the king to get her house and land back. She was the woman whose son Elisha had brought back to life.

Gehazi said, "King Joram, this is the woman I've been telling you about. And this is her son. He's the one Elisha brought back to life." [6]The king asked the woman about her house and land. And she told him.

Then he appointed an official to look into her case. The king told him, "Give her back everything that belonged to her. That includes all of the money that was earned from her land. It was earned from the day she left the country until now."

HAZAEL MURDERS BEN-HADAD

[7]Elisha went to Damascus. Ben-Hadad was sick. He was king of Aram. The king was told, "The man of God has come all the way up here."
[8]Then the king said to Hazael, "Take a gift with you. Go and see the man of God. Ask him for the LORD's advice. Ask him whether I will get well again."
[9]Hazael went to see Elisha. He took 40 camels with him as a gift. The cam-

els were loaded with all of the finest goods of Damascus. Hazael went into Elisha's house and stood in front of him. He said, "Ben-Hadad has sent me. He is the king of Aram. He asks, 'Will I get well again?' "

¹⁰Elisha answered, "Go and speak to him. Tell him, 'Yes. You will get well again.' But the LORD has shown me that he will in fact die."

¹¹Elisha stared at him without looking away. He did it until Hazael felt ashamed. Then the man of God began to sob.

¹²"Why are you sobbing?" asked Hazael.

"Because I know how much harm you will do to the people of Israel," he answered. "You will set fire to their cities that have high walls around them. You will kill their young men with your sword. You will smash their little children on the ground. You will rip open their pregnant women."

¹³Hazael said, "How could I possibly do a thing like that? I'm nothing but a dog. I don't have that kind of power."

"You will become king of Aram," Elisha answered. "That's what the LORD has shown me."

¹⁴Then Hazael left Elisha. He returned to his master. Ben-Hadad asked, "What did Elisha say to you?"

Hazael replied, "He told me you would get well again."

¹⁵But the next day Hazael got a thick cloth. He soaked it in water. He spread it over the king's face. He held it there until the king died. Then Hazael became the next king after him.

JEHORAM BECOMES KING OF JUDAH

¹⁶Jehoram began to rule as king over Judah. It was in the fifth year that Joram was king of Israel. Joram was the son of Ahab. Jehoram was the son of Jehoshaphat. ¹⁷Jehoram was 32 years old when he became king. He ruled in Jerusalem for eight years.

¹⁸He followed the ways of the kings of Israel, just as the royal family of Ahab had done. In fact, he got married to a daughter of Ahab. Jehoram did what was evil in the sight of the LORD.

¹⁹But the LORD didn't want to destroy Judah. That's because the LORD had

made a covenant with his servant David. He had promised to keep the lamp of David's kingdom burning brightly for him and his children after him forever.

²⁰When Jehoram was king over Judah, Edom refused to remain under Judah's control. They set up their own king. ²¹So Jehoram went to Zair. He took all of his chariots with him. The men of Edom surrounded him and his chariot commanders. He got up at night and fought his way out. But his army ran back home.

²²To this very day Edom has refused to remain under Judah's control. At that same time, Libnah also refused to remain under the control of Judah.

²³The other events of Jehoram's rule are written down. Everything he did is written down. All of those things are written in the official records of the kings of Judah.

²⁴Jehoram joined the members of his family who had already died. His body was buried in the family tomb in the City of David. His son Ahaziah became the next king after him.

AHAZIAH BECOMES KING OF JUDAH

²⁵Ahaziah began to rule as king over Judah. It was in the 12th year that Joram was king of Israel. Joram was the son of Ahab. Ahaziah was the son of Jehoram. ²⁶Ahaziah was 22 years old when he became king. He ruled in Jerusalem for one year. His mother's name was Athaliah. She was a granddaughter of Omri. Omri had been the king of Israel.

²⁷Ahaziah followed the ways of the royal family of Ahab. Ahaziah did what was evil in the sight of the LORD, just as the family of Ahab had done. That's because he had married into Ahab's family.

²⁸Ahaziah joined forces with Joram. They went to war against Hazael at Ramoth Gilead. Joram was the son of Ahab. Hazael was king of Aram. The soldiers of Aram wounded King Joram. ²⁹So he returned to Jezreel to give his wounds time to heal. The soldiers of Aram had wounded him at Ramoth in his battle against Hazael, the king of Aram.

Ahaziah, the son of Jehoram, went down to Jezreel. He went there to see Joram. That's because Joram had been wounded. Ahaziah was king of Judah. Joram was the son of Ahab.

JEHU IS ANOINTED AS KING OF ISRAEL

9 The prophet Elisha sent for a man from the company of the prophets. Elisha said to him, "Tuck your coat into your belt. Take this bottle of olive oil with you. Go to Ramoth Gilead.

2"When you get there, look for Jehu. He's the son of Jehoshaphat, the son of Nimshi. Go to him. Get him away from his companions. Take him into an inside room. 3Then get the bottle. Pour the oil on his head. Announce to him, 'The LORD says, "I anoint you as king over Israel."' After that, open the door and run away. Do it quickly!"

4So the young prophet went to Ramoth Gilead. 5When he arrived, he found the army officers sitting together. "Commander, I have a message for you," he said.

"For which one of us?" asked Jehu.

"For you, commander," he replied.

6Jehu got up and went into the house. Then the prophet poured the oil on Jehu's head. He announced, "The LORD is the God of Israel. He says, 'I am anointing you as king over my people Israel. 7You must destroy the royal house of your master Ahab. I will pay them back for spilling the blood of my servants the prophets. I will also pay them back for the blood of all of my servants that Jezebel spilled. 8The whole house of Ahab will die out. I will cut off every male in Israel who is related to Ahab. It does not matter whether they are slaves or free.

9"'I will make Ahab's royal house like the house of Jeroboam, the son of Nebat. I will make it like the house of Baasha, the son of Ahijah. 10Dogs will eat up Jezebel on a piece of land at Jezreel. No one will bury her.'" Then the prophet opened the door and ran away.

11Jehu went out to where the other officers were. One of them asked him, "Is everything all right? Why did that crazy man come to you?"

"You know the man. You know the kinds of things he says," Jehu replied. 12"That's not true!" they said. "Tell us."

Jehu said, "Here is what he told me. He announced, 'The LORD says, "I am anointing you as king over Israel."'"

13The officers quickly grabbed their coats. They spread them out under Jehu on the bare steps of the house. Then they blew a trumpet. They shouted, "Jehu is king!"

JEHU KILLS JORAM AND AHAZIAH

14Jehu was the son of Jehoshaphat, the son of Nimshi. Jehu made plans against Joram. During that time Joram and Israel's whole army had been guarding Ramoth Gilead. They had been guarding it against Hazael, the king of Aram. 15But King Joram had returned to Jezreel. He had gone there to give his wounds time to heal. The soldiers of Aram had wounded him in his battle against Hazael, the king of Aram.

Jehu said to his men, "Are you really on my side? If you are, don't let anyone sneak out of the city. Don't let them go and tell the news in Jezreel." 16Then Jehu got into his chariot. He rode off to Jezreel. Joram was resting there. And Ahaziah, the king of Judah, had gone down to see him.

17A lookout was standing on the roof of the tower in Jezreel. He saw Jehu's troops approaching. So he called out, "I see some troops coming."

"Get a horseman," Joram ordered. "Send him to ride out to them. Have him ask, 'Are you coming in peace?'"

18The horseman rode out to where Jehu was. He said, "The king asks, 'Are you coming in peace?'"

"What do you know about peace?" Jehu answered. "Get in line behind me."

The lookout reported, "The messenger has reached them. But he isn't coming back."

19So the king sent out a second horseman. When he came to them, he told them, "The king asks, 'Are you coming in peace?'"

Jehu replied, "What do you know about peace? Get in line behind me."

²⁰The lookout reported, "The second messenger has reached them. But he isn't coming back either. The one driving the chariot drives like Jehu, the son of Nimshi. He's driving like a crazy man."

²¹"Get my chariot ready," King Joram ordered. When it was ready, he rode out. Ahaziah, the king of Judah, rode out with him. Each of them was in his own chariot. They both went to meet Jehu. They met him at the piece of land that had belonged to Naboth from Jezreel.

²²When Joram saw Jehu he asked, "Have you come here in peace, Jehu?"

"Your mother Jezebel worships statues of gods," Jehu replied. "She also worships evil powers. The evil things she does have spread everywhere. As long as all of that goes on, how can there be peace?"

²³Joram turned around and tried to get away. He called out to Ahaziah. He said, "It's treason, Ahaziah!"

²⁴Then Jehu shot an arrow at Joram. It hit him between the shoulders. It went through his heart. He sank down slowly in his chariot.

²⁵Jehu spoke to Bidkar, his chariot officer. He said, "Pick him up. Throw him on the field that belonged to Naboth from Jezreel. Remember how you and I were riding together in chariots behind Joram's father Ahab? It was when the LORD made a prophecy about him. He announced, ²⁶'Yesterday I saw the blood of Naboth and the blood of his sons. You can be sure that I will make you pay for it on this piece of land.' So pick him up. Throw him on that piece of land. That's what the LORD said would happen."

²⁷Ahaziah, the king of Judah, saw what had happened. So he tried to get away. He went up the road toward Beth Haggan.

Jehu chased him. He shouted, "Kill him too!" Jehu's men wounded Ahaziah in his chariot. It happened on the way up to Gur near Ibleam. But he escaped to Megiddo. And that's where he died.

²⁸Ahaziah's servants took him to Jerusalem in his chariot. They buried his body in his family tomb in the City of David. ²⁹Ahaziah had become king of

Judah. It was in the 11th year of Joram, the son of Ahab.

JEHU KILLS JEZEBEL

³⁰Jehu went to Jezreel. Jezebel heard about it. So she put makeup on her eyes and fixed her hair. She looked out of a window. ³¹Jehu entered the gate below. Then Jezebel said, "You are just like Zimri. You murdered your master. Have you come here in peace?"

³²He looked up at the window. "Who is on my side?" he called out. "Who?" Two or three officials looked down at him. ³³"Throw her down!" Jehu said. So they threw her down. Some of her blood splashed on the wall. Some of it splashed on Jehu's chariot horses as they ran over her.

³⁴Jehu went inside. He ate and drank. "The LORD put a curse on that woman," he said. "Take proper care of her body. Bury it. After all, she was a king's daughter."

³⁵So they went out to bury her body. But all they found was her skull, feet and hands.

³⁶They went back and reported it to Jehu. He told them, "That's what the LORD said would happen. He announced it through his servant Elijah, who was from Tishbe. He said, 'On a piece of land at Jezreel, dogs will eat up Jezebel's body. ³⁷Her body will be left to rot on that piece of land. So no one will be able to say, "Here's where Jezebel is buried." ' "

JEHU WIPES OUT AHAB'S ROYAL HOUSE

10 Ahab's royal family in the city of Samaria had a total of 70 sons. Jehu wrote some letters to the officials of the city. He also sent them to the elders there. And he sent them to those who took care of Ahab's children. He said, ²"Your master's sons are with you. You also have chariots and horses and weapons. And you are living in a city that has high walls around it. As soon as you read this letter, here's what I want you to do. ³Choose the best and most respected son of your master. Place him on his father Joram's throne. Then fight for your master's royal house."

⁴The leaders of Samaria were terri-

fied. They said, "King Joram and King Ahaziah couldn't stand up against Jehu. So how can we?"

⁵The city governor and the person who was in charge of the palace sent a message to Jehu. The message was also from the elders and those who took care of Ahab's children. It said, "We will serve you. We'll do anything you say. We won't appoint anyone to be king. Do what you think is best."

⁶Then Jehu wrote them a second letter. It said, "You say you are on my side. You say you will obey me. If you really mean it, bring me the heads of your master's sons. Meet me in Jezreel by this time tomorrow."

There were 70 royal princes. They were with the most important men of the city. Those men were in charge of raising them. ⁷When Jehu's letter arrived, the men went and got the princes. They killed all 70 of them. They put their heads in baskets. Then they sent them to Jehu in Jezreel.

⁸When the messenger arrived, he spoke to Jehu. He told him, "The heads of the princes have been brought here."

Then Jehu ordered his men, "Put them in two piles. Stack them up at the entrance of the city gate until morning."

⁹The next morning Jehu went out. He stood in front of all of the people. He said, "You aren't guilty of doing anything wrong. I'm the one who made plans against my master Joram. I killed him. But who killed all of these? ¹⁰I want you to know that the LORD has spoken against Ahab's royal house. Not a word of what he has said will fail. The LORD has done exactly what he promised through his servant Elijah."

¹¹So Jehu killed everyone from Ahab's family who was in Jezreel. He also killed all of Ahab's chief men. And he killed Ahab's close friends and his priests. He didn't leave anyone in Ahab's family alive.

¹²Then Jehu started out for Samaria. At Beth Eked of the Shepherds, ¹³he saw some people. They were relatives of Ahaziah, the king of Judah. Jehu asked them, "Who are you?"

They said, "We are Ahaziah's relatives. We've come down to visit the families of the king and of his mother."

¹⁴"Take them alive!" Jehu ordered. So his men took them alive. Then they killed them by the well of Beth Eked. They killed a total of 42 men. Jehu didn't leave anyone alive.

¹⁵After Jehu left there, he came upon Jehonadab. He was the son of Recab. Jehonadab was on his way to see Jehu. Jehu greeted him. He asked, "Are you my friend? You know I'm your friend."

"I am," Jehonadab answered.

"If that's true," said Jehu, "hold out your hand." So he did. Then Jehu helped him up into the chariot. ¹⁶Jehu said, "Come along with me. See how committed I am to serve the LORD." He had him ride along in his chariot.

¹⁷Jehu came to Samaria. He killed everyone who was left there from Ahab's family. And so he wiped out Ahab's royal house. That's what the LORD had said would happen. He had spoken that message to Elijah.

JEHU KILLS THOSE WHO SERVE BAAL

¹⁸Then Jehu brought all of the people together. He said to them, "Ahab served the god Baal a little. I will serve him a lot. ¹⁹Send for all of Baal's prophets. Also send for all of his priests and the others who serve him. Make sure that not a single one is missing. I'm going to hold a great sacrifice to honor Baal. Anyone who doesn't come will be killed." But Jehu was lying to them. He was planning to destroy those who served Baal.

²⁰Jehu said, "Call everyone together to honor Baal." So they did. ²¹Then he sent a message all through Israel. All of those who served Baal came. Not a single one of them stayed away. They crowded into Baal's temple. It was full from one end to the other.

²²Jehu spoke to the one who took care of the sacred robes. He told him, "Bring robes for everyone who serves Baal." So he brought the robes out for them.

²³Then Jehu went into Baal's temple. Jehonadab, the son of Recab, went with him. Jehu spoke to those who served Baal. He said, "Look around. Make sure that no one who serves the

LORD is here with you. Make sure only those who serve Baal are here." ²⁴So they went in to offer sacrifices and burnt offerings.

Jehu had stationed 80 men outside. He warned them, "I'm placing some men in your hands. Don't let a single one of them escape. If you do, you will pay for his life with yours."

²⁵Jehu finished sacrificing the burnt offering. As soon as he did, he gave an order to the guards and officers. He commanded them, "Go inside and kill everyone. Don't let a single one of them escape."

So they cut them down with their swords. The guards and officers threw the bodies outside. Then they entered the most sacred area inside Baal's temple. ²⁶They brought the sacred stone of Baal outside. They burned it up. ²⁷So they destroyed Baal's sacred stone. They also tore down Baal's temple. People have used it as a public toilet to this very day.

²⁸So Jehu destroyed the worship of the god Baal in Israel. ²⁹But he didn't turn away from the sins of Jeroboam, the son of Nebat. Jeroboam had caused Israel to commit those same sins. Jehu worshiped the golden calves at Bethel and Dan.

³⁰The LORD said to Jehu, "You have done well. You have accomplished what is right in my eyes. You have done to Ahab's royal house everything I wanted you to do. So your sons after you will sit on the throne of Israel. They will rule until the time of your children's grandchildren."

³¹But Jehu wasn't careful to obey the law of the LORD. He didn't obey the God of Israel with all his heart. He didn't turn away from the sins of Jeroboam. Jeroboam had caused Israel to commit those same sins.

³²In those days the LORD began to make the kingdom of Israel smaller. Hazael gained control over many parts of Israel. He gained control over all of their territory ³³east of the Jordan River. It included the whole land of Gilead from Aroer by the Arnon River valley all the way to Bashan. That was the territory of Gad, Reuben and Manasseh.

³⁴The other events of Jehu's rule are written down. Everything he did and accomplished is written down. All of those things are written in the official records of the kings of Israel.

³⁵Jehu joined the members of his family who had already died. His body was buried in Samaria. His son Jehoahaz became the next king after him. ³⁶Jehu had ruled over Israel in Samaria for 28 years.

ATHALIAH AND JOASH

11 Athaliah was Ahaziah's mother. She saw that her son was dead. So she began to wipe out the whole royal house of Judah.

²But Jehosheba went and got Joash, the son of Ahaziah. She was the daughter of King Jehoram and the sister of Ahaziah. She stole Joash away from among the royal princes. All of them were about to be murdered. She put Joash and his nurse in a bedroom. That's how she hid him from Athaliah. And that's why Athaliah didn't kill him. ³The child remained hidden with his nurse at the LORD's temple for six years. Athaliah ruled over the land during that time.

⁴In the seventh year the priest Jehoiada sent for the commanders of companies of 100 men. They were the commanders over the Carites and guards. He had them brought to him at the temple of the LORD. He made a covenant with them. He made them take an oath at the temple. Then he showed them the king's son.

⁵He gave them a command. He said, "Here's what you must do. There are five companies of you. Some of you are in the three companies that are going on duty on the Sabbath day. A third of you must guard the royal palace. ⁶A third of you must guard the Sur Gate. And a third of you must guard the gate that is behind the guard. All of you must take turns guarding the temple. ⁷"The rest of you are in the other two companies. Normally you are not on duty on the Sabbath. But you also must guard the temple for the king. ⁸Station yourselves around the king. Each man must have his weapon in his hand. Anyone else who approaches

your companies must be put to death. Stay close to the king no matter where he goes."

⁹The commanders of the companies did just as the priest Jehoiada ordered. Each commander got his men and came to Jehoiada. Some of the men were going on duty on the Sabbath day. Others were going off duty.

¹⁰Then Jehoiada gave weapons to the commanders. He gave them spears and shields. The weapons had belonged to King David. They had been in the LORD's temple.

¹¹The guards stationed themselves around the new king. Each man had his weapon in his hand. They were near the altar and the temple. They stood from the south side of the temple to its north side. Their line formed half of a circle.

¹²Jehoiada brought Ahaziah's son out. He put the crown on him. He gave him a copy of the covenant. And he announced that Joash was king. Jehoiada and his sons anointed him. The people clapped their hands. Then they shouted, "May the king live a long time!"

¹³Athaliah heard the noise the guards and the people were making. So she went to the people at the LORD's temple. ¹⁴She looked. And there was the king! He was standing next to the pillar. That was the usual practice. The officers and trumpet players were standing beside the king. All of the people of the land were filled with joy. They were blowing trumpets. Then Athaliah tore her royal robes. She called out, "Treason! It's treason!"

¹⁵The priest Jehoiada gave an order to the commanders of the companies. They were in charge of the troops. He said to them, "Bring her away from the temple between the line of guards. Use your swords to kill anyone who follows her." The priest had said, "She must not be put to death at the LORD's temple."

¹⁶So they grabbed hold of her as she reached the place where the horses enter the palace grounds. There she was put to death.

¹⁷Then Jehoiada made a covenant between the LORD and the king and people. He had the king and people promise that they would be the LORD's people. Jehoiada also made a covenant between the king and the people.

¹⁸All of the people of the land went to Baal's temple. They tore it down. They smashed to pieces the altars and the statues of gods. They killed Mattan in front of the altars. He was the priest of Baal.

Then the priest Jehoiada stationed guards at the temple of the LORD. ¹⁹He took with him the commanders of companies of 100 men. They were the commanders over the Carites and guards. He also took with him all of the people of the land. All of them brought the new king down from the LORD's temple. They went into the palace. They entered it by going through the gate of the guards. Then the king sat down on the royal throne.

²⁰All of the people of the land were filled with joy. And the city was quiet. That's because Athaliah had been killed with a sword at the palace.

²¹Joash was seven years old when he became king.

JOASH REPAIRS THE TEMPLE

12 Joash became king of Judah. It was in the seventh year of Jehu's rule. Joash ruled in Jerusalem for 40 years. His mother's name was Zibiah. She was from Beersheba.

²Joash did what was right in the eyes of the LORD. He lived that way as long as the priest Jehoiada was teaching him.

³But the high places weren't removed. The people continued to offer sacrifices and burn incense there.

⁴Joash spoke to the priests. He said, "Collect all of the money the people bring as sacred offerings to the LORD's temple. That includes the money that is collected when the men who are able to serve in the army are counted. It includes the money that is received from people who make a special promise to the LORD. It also includes the money people bring to the temple just because they want to.

⁵"Let each priest receive the money from one of the people who are in charge of the temple's treasures. Let all

of that money be used to repair the temple where it needs it."

⁶It was now the 23rd year of King Joash. And the priests still hadn't repaired the temple. ⁷So the king sent for the priest Jehoiada and the other priests. He asked them, "Why aren't you repairing the temple where it needs it? Don't take any more money from the people who are in charge of the treasures. Instead, hand it over so the temple can be repaired."

⁸The priests agreed that they wouldn't collect any more money from the people. They also agreed that they wouldn't repair the temple themselves.

⁹The priest Jehoiada got a chest. He drilled a hole in its lid. He placed the chest beside the altar for burnt offerings. The chest was on the right side as people enter the LORD's temple. Some priests guarded the entrance. They put into the chest all of the money the people brought to the temple.

¹⁰From time to time there was a large amount of money in the chest. When that happened, the royal secretary and the high priest came. They counted the money the people had brought to the temple. Then they put it into bags.

¹¹After they added it all up, they used it to repair the temple. They gave it to the men who had been put in charge of the work. Those men used it to pay the workers. They paid the builders and those who worked with wood. ¹²They paid those who cut stones and those who laid them. They bought lumber and blocks of stone. So they used the money to repair the LORD's temple. They also paid all of the other costs to make the temple like new again.

¹³The money the people brought to the LORD's temple wasn't used to make silver bowls. It wasn't used for wick cutters, sprinkling bowls or trumpets. And it wasn't used for any other articles made out of gold or silver. ¹⁴Instead, it was paid to the workers. They used it to repair the temple. ¹⁵The royal secretary and the high priest didn't require a report from those who were in charge of the work. That's because they were completely honest. They al-

ways paid the workers. ¹⁶Money was received from those who brought guilt offerings and sin offerings. But it wasn't taken to the LORD's temple. It belonged to the priests.

¹⁷About that time Hazael, the king of Aram, went up and attacked Gath. Then he captured it. After that, he turned back to attack Jerusalem. ¹⁸But Joash, the king of Judah, didn't want to go to war. So he got all of the sacred objects. They had been set apart to the LORD by the kings who had ruled over Judah before him. They were Jehoshaphat, Jehoram and Ahaziah. Joash got the gifts he himself had set apart. He got all of the gold that was among the temple treasures. He also got all of the gold from the royal palace. He sent all of those things to Hazael, the king of Aram. Then Hazael pulled his army back from Jerusalem.

¹⁹The other events of the rule of Joash are written down. Everything he did is written down. All of those things are written in the official records of the kings of Judah.

²⁰The officials of Joash made evil plans against him. They killed him at Beth Millo. It happened on the road that goes down to Silla. ²¹The officials who murdered him were Jozabad and Jehozabad. Jozabad was the son of Shimeath. Jehozabad was the son of Shomer.

After Joash died, his body was buried in the family tomb in the City of David. His son Amaziah became the next king after him.

JEHOAHAZ BECOMES KING OF ISRAEL

13 Jehoahaz became king of Israel in Samaria. It was in the 23rd year of Joash, the king of Judah. Jehoahaz ruled for 17 years. Joash was the son of Ahaziah. Jehoahaz was the son of Jehu.

²Jehoahaz did what was evil in the sight of the LORD. He committed the sins Jeroboam, the son of Nebat, had committed. Jeroboam had caused Israel to commit those same sins. Jehoahaz didn't turn away from them.

³So the LORD's anger burned against Israel. For a long time he kept them under the power of Hazael, the king of

Aram. He also kept them under the power of his son Ben-Hadad.

⁴Then Jehoahaz asked the LORD to show him his favor. The LORD listened to him. The LORD saw how badly the king of Aram was treating Israel. ⁵The LORD provided someone to save Israel. And they escaped from the power of Aram. So the people of Israel lived in their own homes, just as they had before.

⁶But the people didn't turn away from the sins of the royal house of Jeroboam. He had caused Israel to commit those same sins. The people continued to commit them. And the pole that was used to worship the goddess Asherah remained standing in Samaria.

⁷The army of Jehoahaz had almost nothing left. All it had was 50 horsemen, 10 chariots and 10,000 soldiers on foot. The king of Aram had destroyed the rest of them. He had made them like dust at threshing time.

⁸The other events of the rule of Jehoahaz are written down. Everything he did and accomplished is written down. All of those things are written in the official records of the kings of Israel.

⁹Jehoahaz joined the members of his family who had already died. His body was buried in Samaria. His son Jehoash became the next king after him.

JEHOASH BECOMES KING OF ISRAEL

¹⁰Jehoash became king of Israel in Samaria. It was in the 37th year that Joash was king of Judah. Jehoash

When we pray for someone not to die and then they die, does that mean that God didn't love them?

No, not at all. People die. That is part of life. When a person dies, it does not mean that God does not love the person or that God does not love the people who wanted that person to live. It also does not mean that someone lacked faith.

The Bible says God loves *all* people. That is why he sent Jesus to die on the cross. He loved people so much that he sent Jesus to take away people's sins.

God hates death, but death is not the end. God's people can look forward to eternal life in heaven with God.

It is OK to cry when our loved ones die. We miss them very much. But if they are Christians, they are going to heaven, and Jesus has made a special place for them.

checkout
2 Kings 13:14

Related verses:
Psalm 116:15;
John 3:16;
1 Thessalonians
4:13-18

JASON'S IMAGINATION

WELL DONE, GOOD AND FAITHFUL SERVANT. COME AND SHARE YOUR MASTER'S HAPPINESS.

GOD'S ROYAL ORDER OF SERVICE AWARD

ruled for 16 years. He was the son of Jehoahaz.

¹¹Jehoash did what was evil in the sight of the LORD. He didn't turn away from any of the sins of Jeroboam, the son of Nebat. Jeroboam had caused Israel to commit those same sins. And Jehoash continued to commit them.

¹²The other events of the rule of Jehoash are written down. Everything he did and accomplished is written down. That includes his war against Amaziah, the king of Judah. All of those things are written in the official records of the kings of Israel.

¹³Jehoash joined the members of his family who had already died. His body was buried in the royal tombs in Samaria. Jeroboam became the next king on Israel's throne after him.

¹⁴Elisha was suffering from a sickness. Later he would die from it. Jehoash, the king of Israel, went down to see him. He sobbed over him. "My father!" he cried. "You are like a father to me! You are the true chariots and horsemen of Israel!"

¹⁵Elisha said to Jehoash, "Get a bow and some arrows." So he did.

¹⁶"Hold the bow in your hands," Elisha said to the king of Israel. So Jehoash took hold of the bow. Then Elisha put his hands on the king's hands.

¹⁷"Open the east window," Elisha said. So he did. "Shoot!" Elisha said. So he shot.

"That's the LORD's arrow!" Elisha announced. "It means you will win the battle over Aram! You will completely destroy the men of Aram at Aphek."

¹⁸He continued, "Get some arrows." So the king did. Elisha told him, "Strike the ground." He struck it three times. Then he stopped.

¹⁹The man of God was angry with him. He said, "You should have struck the ground five or six times. Then you would have won the war over Aram. You would have completely destroyed them. But now you will win only three battles over them."

²⁰Elisha died. And his body was buried.

Some robbers from Moab used to enter the country of Israel every spring. ²¹One day some people of Israel were burying a man's body. Suddenly they saw a group of robbers. So they threw the man's body into Elisha's tomb. The body touched Elisha's bones. When it did, the man came back to life again. He stood up on his feet.

²²Hazael, the king of Aram, treated Israel badly. He did it the whole time Jehoahaz was king.

²³But the LORD showed his favor to Israel. He was tender and kind to them. He showed concern for them. He did all of those things because of the covenant he had made with Abraham, Isaac and Jacob. To this very day he hasn't been willing to destroy them. And he hasn't driven them out of his land.

²⁴Hazael, the king of Aram, died. His son Ben-Hadad became the next king after him. ²⁵Then Jehoash took some towns back from Ben-Hadad, the son of Hazael. Ben-Hadad had captured them in battle from Jehoahaz, the father of Jehoash. Jehoash won three battles over Ben-Hadad. So Jehoash took back the Israelite towns.

AMAZIAH BECOMES KING OF JUDAH

14 Amaziah began to rule as king over Judah. It was in the second year that Jehoash was king of Israel. He was the son of Jehoahaz. Amaziah was the son of Joash. ²Amaziah was 25 years old when he became king. He ruled in Jerusalem for 29 years. His mother's name was Jehoaddin. She was from Jerusalem.

³Amaziah did what was right in the eyes of the LORD. But he didn't do what King David had done. He always followed the example of his father Joash. ⁴The high places weren't removed. The people continued to offer sacrifices and burn incense there.

⁵The kingdom was firmly under his control. So he put to death the officials who had murdered his father, the king. ⁶But he didn't put their children to death. He obeyed what is written in the Scroll of the Law of Moses. There the LORD commanded, "Parents must not be put to death because of what their children do. And children must not be put to death because of what their par-

ents do. People must die because of their own sins." *(Deuteronomy 24:16)*

⁷Amaziah won the battle over 10,000 men of Edom. It happened in the Valley of Salt. During the battle he captured the town of Sela. He called it Joktheel. That's the name it still has to this very day.

⁸Then Amaziah sent messengers to Jehoash, the king of Israel. He was the son of Jehoahaz, the son of Jehu. The message said, "Come on. Meet me face to face in battle."

⁹But Jehoash, the king of Israel, answered Amaziah, the king of Judah. He said, "A thorn bush in Lebanon sent a message to a cedar tree there. It said, 'Give your daughter to be married to my son.' Then a wild animal in Lebanon came along. It walked all over the thorn bush. ¹⁰It's true that you have won the battle over Edom. So you are proud. Enjoy your success while you can. But stay home and enjoy it! Why ask for trouble? Why bring yourself crashing down? Why bring Judah down with you?"

¹¹But Amaziah wouldn't listen. So Jehoash, the king of Israel, attacked. He and Amaziah, the king of Judah, faced each other in battle. The battle took place at Beth Shemesh in Judah.

¹²Israel drove Judah away. Every man ran home. ¹³Jehoash king of Israel captured Amaziah king of Judah at Beth Shemesh. Amaziah was the son of Joash. Joash was the son of Ahaziah. Jehoash went to Jerusalem. He broke down part of its wall. It's the part that went from the Ephraim Gate to the Corner Gate. That part of the wall was 600 feet long.

¹⁴Jehoash took all of the gold, silver and articles that were in the LORD's temple. He also took all of those same kinds of things that were among the treasures of the royal palace. And he took the prisoners. Then he returned to Samaria.

¹⁵The other events of the rule of Jehoash are written down. Everything he did and accomplished is written down. That includes his war against Amaziah, the king of Judah. All of those things are written in the official records of the kings of Israel.

¹⁶Jehoash joined the members of his family who had already died. His body was buried in Samaria in the royal tombs of Israel. His son Jeroboam became the next king after him.

¹⁷Amaziah king of Judah lived for 15 years after Jehoash king of Israel died. Amaziah was the son of Joash. Jehoash was the son of Jehoahaz. ¹⁸The other events of Amaziah's rule are written down. They are written in the official records of the kings of Judah.

¹⁹Some people made evil plans against Amaziah in Jerusalem. So he ran away to Lachish. But they sent men to Lachish after him. There they killed him. ²⁰His body was brought back on a horse. Then he was buried in the family tomb in Jerusalem, the City of David.

²¹All of the people of Judah made Uzziah king. He was 16 years old. They made him king in place of his father Amaziah. ²²Uzziah rebuilt Elath. He brought it under Judah's control again. He did it after Amaziah joined the members of his family who had already died.

JEROBOAM II BECOMES KING OF ISRAEL

²³Jeroboam became king of Israel in Samaria. It was in the 15th year that Amaziah was king of Judah. Jeroboam ruled for 41 years. Amaziah was the son of Joash. Jeroboam was the son of Jehoash.

²⁴Jeroboam did what was evil in the sight of the LORD. He didn't turn away from any of the sins the earlier Jeroboam, the son of Nebat, had committed. That Jeroboam had caused Israel to commit those same sins.

²⁵Jeroboam, the son of Jehoash, made the borders of Israel the same as they were before. They reached from Lebo Hamath all the way to the Dead Sea. That's what the LORD, the God of Israel, had said would happen. He had spoken that message through his servant Jonah. The prophet Jonah was the son of Amittai. Jonah was from Gath Hepher.

²⁶The LORD had seen how much everyone in Israel was suffering. It didn't matter whether they were slaves or free. They didn't have anyone to help them. ²⁷The LORD hadn't said he would wipe

out Israel's name from the earth. So he saved them by using the powerful hand of Jeroboam, the son of Jehoash.

²⁸The other events of the rule of Jeroboam are written down. Everything he did is written down. What he and his army accomplished is written down. That includes how he brought Damascus and Hamath back under Israel's control. Damascus and Hamath had belonged to the territory of Yaudi. All of those things are written in the official records of the kings of Israel.

²⁹Jeroboam joined the members of his family who had already died. His body was buried in the royal tombs of Israel. His son Zechariah became the next king after him.

UZZIAH BECOMES KING OF JUDAH

15 Uzziah began to rule as king over Judah. It was in the 27th year that Jeroboam was king of Israel. Uzziah was the son of Amaziah. ²Uzziah was 16 years old when he became king. He ruled in Jerusalem for 52 years. His mother's name was Jecoliah. She was from Jerusalem.

³Uzziah did what was right in the eyes of the LORD, just as his father Amaziah had done. ⁴But the high places weren't removed. The people continued to offer sacrifices and burn incense there.

⁵The LORD caused King Uzziah to suffer from a skin disease until the day he died. He lived in a separate house. His son Jotham was in charge of the palace. Jotham ruled over the people of the land.

⁶The other events of the rule of Uzziah are written down. Everything he did is written down. All of those things are written in the official records of the kings of Judah.

⁷Uzziah joined the members of his family who had already died. His body was buried near them in the City of David. His son Jotham became the next king after him.

ZECHARIAH BECOMES KING OF ISRAEL

⁸Zechariah became king of Israel in Samaria. It was in the 38th year that Uzziah was king of Judah. Zechariah ruled for six months. He was the son of Jeroboam, the son of Jehoash.

⁹Zechariah did what was evil in the sight of the LORD. He did what the kings of Israel before him had done. He didn't turn away from the sins Jeroboam, the son of Nebat, had committed. Jeroboam had caused Israel to commit those same sins.

¹⁰Shallum made evil plans against Zechariah. He attacked Zechariah in front of the people and killed him. Then he became the next king after him. Shallum was the son of Jabesh.

¹¹The other events of the rule of Zechariah are written down. They are written in the official records of the kings of Israel. ¹²That's what the LORD had said would happen. He had spoken that message to Jehu. It had said, "Your sons after you will sit on the throne of Israel. They will rule until the time of your children's grandchildren." *(2 Kings 10:30)*

SHALLUM BECOMES KING OF ISRAEL

¹³Shallum became king of Israel. It was in the 39th year that Uzziah was king of Judah. Shallum ruled in Samaria for one month. He was the son of Jabesh.

¹⁴Menahem went from Tirzah up to Samaria. There he attacked Shallum, the son of Jabesh. He killed him and became the next king after him. Menahem was the son of Gadi.

¹⁵The other events of Shallum's rule are written down. The evil things he planned are written down. All of those things are written in the official records of the kings of Israel.

¹⁶At that time Menahem started out from Tirzah and attacked Tiphsah. He attacked everyone in the city and the area around it. That's because they refused to open their gates for him. He destroyed Tiphsah. He ripped open all of their pregnant women.

MENAHEM BECOMES KING OF ISRAEL

¹⁷Menahem became king of Israel. It was in the 39th year that Uzziah was king of Judah. Menahem ruled in Sa-

maria for ten years. He was the son of Gadi.

¹⁸Menahem did what was evil in the sight of the LORD. During his entire rule he didn't turn away from the sins Jeroboam, the son of Nebat, had committed. Jeroboam had caused Israel to commit those same sins.

¹⁹Then Tiglath-Pileser marched into the land of Israel. He was king of Assyria. Menahem gave him 37 tons of silver to get his help. He wanted to make his control over the kingdom stronger. ²⁰Menahem forced Israel to give him that money. Every wealthy person had to give him 20 ounces of silver. All of it went to the king of Assyria. So he pulled his troops back. He didn't stay in the land anymore.

²¹The other events of the rule of Menahem are written down. Everything he did is written down. All of those things are written in the official records of the kings of Israel. ²²Menahem joined the members of his family who had already died. His son Pekahiah became the next king after him.

PEKAHIAH BECOMES KING OF ISRAEL

²³Pekahiah became king of Israel in Samaria. It was in the 50th year that Uzziah was king of Judah. Pekahiah ruled for two years. He was the son of Menahem.

²⁴Pekahiah did what was evil in the sight of the LORD. He didn't turn away from the sins Jeroboam, the son of Nebat, had committed. Jeroboam had caused Israel to commit those same sins.

²⁵One of Pekahiah's chief officers was Pekah. He was the son of Remaliah. Pekah made evil plans against Pekahiah. He took 50 men of Gilead with him and killed Pekahiah. He also killed Argob and Arieh. He killed all of them in the safest place in the royal palace at Samaria. So Pekah killed Pekahiah. He became the next king after him.

²⁶The other events of the rule of Pekahiah are written down. Everything he did is written down. All of those things are written in the official records of the kings of Israel.

PEKAH BECOMES KING OF ISRAEL

²⁷Pekah became king of Israel in Samaria. It was in the 52nd year that Uzziah was king of Judah. Pekah ruled for 20 years. He was the son of Remaliah. ²⁸Pekah did what was evil in the sight of the LORD. He didn't turn away from the sins Jeroboam, the son of Nebat, had committed. Jeroboam had caused Israel to commit those same sins.

²⁹During the rule of Pekah, the king of Israel, Tiglath-Pileser marched into the land again. He was king of Assyria. He took the towns of Ijon, Abel Beth Maacah, Janoah, Kedesh and Hazor. He also took the lands of Gilead and Galilee. That included the whole territory of Naphtali. He took the people away from their own land. He sent them off to Assyria.

³⁰Then Hoshea made evil plans against Pekah, the son of Remaliah. Hoshea was the son of Elah. Hoshea attacked Pekah and killed him. Then Hoshea became the next king after him. It was in the 20th year of the rule of Jotham, the son of Uzziah.

³¹The other events of the rule of Pekah are written down. Everything he did is written down. All of those things are written in the official records of the kings of Israel.

JOTHAM BECOMES KING OF JUDAH

³²Jotham began to rule as king over Judah. It was in the second year that Pekah was king of Israel. He was the son of Remaliah. Jotham was the son of Uzziah. ³³Jotham was 25 years old when he became king. He ruled in Jerusalem for 16 years. His mother's name was Jerusha. She was the daughter of Zadok.

³⁴Jotham did what was right in the eyes of the LORD, just as his father Uzziah had done.

³⁵But the high places weren't removed. The people continued to offer sacrifices and burn incense there. Jotham rebuilt the Upper Gate of the LORD's temple.

³⁶The other events of the rule of Jotham are written down. Everything he

did is written down. All of those things are written in the official records of the kings of Judah.

[37]In those days the LORD began to send Rezin and Pekah against Judah. Rezin was king of Aram. Pekah was the son of Remaliah.

[38]Jotham joined the members of his family who had already died. His body was buried in the family tomb in the city of King David. His son Ahaz became the next king after him.

AHAZ BECOMES KING OF JUDAH

16 Ahaz began to rule as king over Judah. It was in the 17th year of the rule of Pekah, the son of Remaliah. Ahaz was the son of Jotham. [2]Ahaz was 20 years old when he became king. He ruled in Jerusalem for 16 years.

Ahaz didn't do what was right in the eyes of the LORD his God. He didn't do what King David had done. [3]He followed the ways of the kings of Israel. He even sacrificed his son in the fire to another god. He followed the practices of the nations. The LORD hated those practices. He had driven out those nations to make room for the people of Israel. [4]Ahaz offered sacrifices and burned incense at the high places. He also did it on the tops of hills and under every green tree.

[5]Rezin and Pekah marched up to Jerusalem and surrounded it. Rezin was king of Aram. Pekah, the son of Remaliah, was king of Israel. They attacked Ahaz. But they couldn't overpower him. [6]At that time Rezin, the king of Aram, got back Elath for Aram. He drove out the people of Judah. Then the people of Edom moved into Elath. And they still live there to this very day.

[7]Ahaz sent messengers to Tiglath-Pileser. He was king of Assyria. The message of Ahaz said, "I am your servant. You are my master. Come up and save me from the powerful hands of the kings of Aram and Israel. They are attacking me."

[8]Ahaz took the silver and gold that were in the LORD's temple. He also took the silver and gold that were among the treasures in the royal palace. He sent all of it as a gift to the king of Assyria.

[9]So the king of Assyria did what Ahaz asked him to do. He attacked the city of Damascus and captured it. He sent its people away to Kir. And he put Rezin to death.

[10]Then King Ahaz went to Damascus. He went there to see Tiglath-Pileser, the king of Assyria. Ahaz saw an altar in Damascus. He sent a drawing of it to the priest Uriah. He also sent him plans for building it.

[11]So the priest Uriah built an altar. He followed all of the plans King Ahaz had sent from Damascus. He finished it before Ahaz returned.

[12]The king came back from Damascus. When he saw the altar, he approached it. Then he offered sacrifices on it. [13]He offered up his burnt offering and grain offering. He poured out his drink offering. And he sprinkled blood from his friendship offerings on the altar.

[14]The bronze altar for burnt offerings stood in front of the LORD. It was between the new altar and the LORD's temple. Ahaz took it away from the front of the temple. He put it on the north side of the new altar.

[15]Then King Ahaz gave orders to the priest Uriah. He said, "Offer sacrifices on the large new altar. Offer the morning burnt offering and the evening grain offering. Offer my burnt offering and my grain offering. Offer the burnt offering of all of the people of the land. Offer their grain offering and their drink offering. Sprinkle on the altar all of the blood from the burnt offerings and sacrifices. But I will use the bronze altar to look for advice and direction."

[16]The priest Uriah did just as King Ahaz had ordered.

[17]Ahaz took away the sides of the bronze stands. He removed the bowls from the stands. He removed the huge bowl from the bronze bulls it stood on. He placed the bowl on a stone base. [18]He took away the covered area that had been used on the Sabbath day. It had been built at the LORD's temple. He removed the royal entrance that was outside the temple. Ahaz did all of that to honor the king of Assyria.

[19]The other events of the rule of

Ahaz are written down. Everything he did is written down. All of those things are written in the official records of the kings of Judah.

²⁰Ahaz joined the members of his family who had already died. His body was buried in the family tomb in the City of David. His son Hezekiah became the next king after him.

HOSHEA BECOMES THE LAST KING OF ISRAEL

17 Hoshea became king of Israel in Samaria. It was in the 12th year that Ahaz was king of Judah. Hoshea ruled for nine years. He was the son of Elah.

²Hoshea did what was evil in the sight of the LORD. But he wasn't as evil as the kings of Israel who ruled before him.

³Shalmaneser came up to attack Hoshea. Shalmaneser was king of Assyria. He had been Hoshea's master. He had forced Hoshea to bring him gifts. ⁴But the king of Assyria found out that Hoshea had turned against him. Hoshea had sent messengers to So, the king of Egypt. Hoshea didn't send gifts to the king of Assyria anymore. He had been sending them every year. So Shalmaneser grabbed hold of him and put him in prison.

⁵The king of Assyria marched into the whole land of Israel. He marched to Samaria and surrounded it for three years. From time to time he attacked it. ⁶Finally, the king of Assyria captured Samaria. It was in the ninth year of Hoshea. The king of Assyria took the people of Israel away from their own land. He sent them off to Assyria. He settled some of them in Halah. He settled others in Gozan on the Habor River. And he settled still others in the towns of the Medes.

ISRAEL IS FORCED TO GO AWAY TO ASSYRIA

⁷All of that took place because the people of Israel had committed sins against the LORD their God. He had brought them up out of Egypt. He had brought them out from under the power of Pharaoh, the king of Egypt. But they worshiped other gods. ⁸The LORD had driven out other na-

tions to make room for them. But they followed the evil practices of those nations. They also followed the practices that the kings of Israel had started. ⁹The people of Israel did things against the LORD their God in secret. What they did wasn't right. They built high places for worship in all of their towns. They built them at lookout towers. They also built them at cities that had high walls around them. ¹⁰They set up sacred stones. And they set up poles that were used to worship the goddess Asherah. They did that on every high hill and under every green tree.

¹¹The LORD had driven out nations to make room for Israel. But the people of Israel burned incense at every high place, just as those nations had done. The Israelites did evil things that made the LORD very angry. ¹²They worshiped statues of gods. They did it even though the LORD had said, "Do not do that."

¹³The LORD warned Israel and Judah through all of his prophets and seers. He said, "Turn from your evil ways. Keep my commands and rules. Obey every part of my Law. I commanded your people who lived long ago to obey it. And I gave it to you through my servants the prophets."

¹⁴But the people wouldn't listen. They were as stubborn as their people of long ago had been. Those people didn't trust in the LORD their God. ¹⁵They refused to obey his rules. They broke the covenant he had made with them. They didn't pay any attention to the warnings he had given them. They worshiped worthless statues of gods. Then they themselves became worthless. They followed the example of the nations that were around them. They did it even though the LORD had ordered them not to. He had said, "Do not do as they do." They did the very things the LORD had told them not to do.

¹⁶They turned away from all of the commands of the LORD their God. They made two statues of gods for themselves. The statues were shaped like calves. They made a pole that was used to worship the goddess Asherah. They bowed down to all of the stars. And they worshiped the god Baal.

[17]They sacrificed their sons and daughters in the fire. They practiced all kinds of evil magic. They gave themselves over to do what was evil in the sight of the LORD. All of those things made him very angry. [18]So the LORD was filled with anger against Israel. He removed them from his land. Only the tribe of Judah was left. [19]And even Judah didn't obey the commands of the LORD their God. They followed the practices Israel had started.

[20]So the LORD turned his back on all of the people of Israel. He made them suffer. He handed them over to people who stole everything they had. And finally he threw them out of his land. [21]He tore Israel away from the royal house of David. The people of Israel made Jeroboam, the son of Nebat, their king. Jeroboam tried to get Israel to stop following the LORD. He caused them to commit a terrible sin. [22]The people of Israel were stubborn. They continued to commit all of the sins Jeroboam had committed. They didn't turn away from them.

[23]So the LORD removed them from his land. That's what he had warned them he would do. He had given that warning through all of his servants the prophets. So the people of Israel were taken away from their country. They were forced to go to Assyria. And that's where they still are.

ASSYRIA BRINGS OTHER PEOPLE TO SAMARIA

[24]The king of Assyria brought people from Babylon. He also brought them from Cuthah, Avva, Hamath and Sepharvaim. He settled all of them in the towns of Samaria. They took the place of the people of Israel. They took over Samaria and lived in its towns. [25]When they first lived there, they didn't worship the LORD. So he sent lions among them. And the lions killed some of the people. [26]A report was given to the king of Assyria. He was told, "You forced people to leave their own homes. You settled them in the towns of Samaria. But they don't know what the god of that country requires. So he has sent lions among them. And the lions are killing

the people off. That's because the people don't know what that god requires."

[27]Then the king of Assyria gave an order. He said, "Get one of the priests you captured from Samaria. Send him back to live there. Have him teach the people what the god of that land requires."

[28]So one of the priests went back to live in Bethel. He was one of those who had been forced to leave Samaria. He taught the people there how to worship the LORD.

[29]In spite of that, the people from each nation made statues of their own gods. They made them in all of the towns where they had settled. They set up those statues in small temples. The people of Samaria had built the temples at the high places. [30]The people from Babylon made statues of the god Succoth Benoth. Those from Cuthah made statues of Nergal. Those from Hamath made statues of Ashima. [31]The Avvites made statues of Nibhaz and Tartak. The Sepharvites sacrificed their children in the fire to Adrammelech and Anammelech. They were the gods of Sepharvaim.

[32]So the people of Samaria worshiped the LORD. But they also appointed all kinds of their own people to serve them as priests. The priests served in the small temples at the high places. [33]The people worshiped the LORD. But they also served their own gods. They followed the evil practices of the nations from which they had been brought.

[34]They are still stubborn. They continue in their old practices to this very day. And now they don't even worship the LORD. They don't follow his directions and rules. They don't obey his laws and commands. The LORD had given all of those laws to the family of Jacob. He gave the name Israel to Jacob.

[35]The LORD made a covenant with the people of Israel. At that time he commanded them, "Do not worship any other gods. Do not bow down to them. Do not serve them or sacrifice to them. [36]I am the one you must worship. I brought you up out of Egypt by my great power. I saved you by reach-

ing out my mighty arm. You must bow down to me. You must offer sacrifices to me. ³⁷You must always be careful to follow my directions and rules. You must obey the laws and commands I wrote for you. Do not worship other gods.

³⁸"Do not forget the covenant I made with you. And remember, you must not worship other gods. ³⁹Instead, worship me. I will save you from the powerful hand of all of your enemies. I am the LORD your God."

⁴⁰But the people wouldn't listen. Instead, they were stubborn. They continued in their old practices. ⁴¹They worshiped the LORD. But at the same time, they served the statues of their gods. And to this very day their children and grandchildren continue to do what their people before them did.

HEZEKIAH BECOMES KING OF JUDAH

18 Hezekiah began to rule as king over Judah. It was in the third year that Hoshea was king of Israel. He was the son of Elah. Hezekiah was the son of Ahaz. ²Hezekiah was 25 years old when he became king. He ruled in Jerusalem for 29 years. His mother's name was Abijah. She was the daughter of Zechariah.

³Hezekiah did what was right in the eyes of the LORD, just as King David had done. ⁴Hezekiah removed the high places. He smashed the sacred stones. He cut down the poles that were used to worship the goddess Asherah. He broke into pieces the bronze snake Moses had made. Up to that time the people of Israel had been burning incense to it. They called it Nehushtan.

⁵Hezekiah trusted in the LORD, the God of Israel. There was no one like him among all of the kings of Judah. There was no king like him either before him or after him. ⁶Hezekiah remained true to the LORD. He didn't stop following him. He obeyed the commands the LORD had given Moses.

⁷The LORD was with Hezekiah. He was successful in everything he did. He refused to remain under the control of the king of Assyria. He didn't

serve him. ⁸He won the war against the Philistines. He won battles at their lookout towers. He won battles at their cities that had high walls around them. He won battles against the Philistines all the way to Gaza and its territory.

⁹Shalmaneser marched to Samaria and surrounded it. It was in the fourth year of King Hezekiah. That was the seventh year of Hoshea, the king of Israel. He was the son of Elah. Shalmaneser was king of Assyria.

¹⁰At the end of three years the army of Assyria took Samaria. So it was captured in the sixth year of Hezekiah. That was the ninth year of Hoshea, the king of Israel. ¹¹The king of Assyria took the people of Israel away from their own land. He sent them off to Assyria. He settled some of them in Halah. He settled others in Gozan on the Habor River. And he settled still others in the towns of the Medes.

¹²Those things happened because the Israelites hadn't obeyed the LORD their God. They had broken the covenant he had made with them. They had refused to do everything Moses, the servant of the LORD, had commanded. They hadn't paid any attention to those commands. They hadn't obeyed them.

¹³Sennacherib attacked and captured all of the cities of Judah that had high walls around them. It was in the 14th year of the rule of Hezekiah. Sennacherib was king of Assyria.

¹⁴Hezekiah, the king of Judah, sent a message to the king of Assyria at Lachish. It said, "I have done what is wrong. Pull your troops back from me. Then I'll pay you anything you ask me to."

The king of Assyria forced Hezekiah, the king of Judah, to give him 11 tons of silver. Hezekiah also had to give him a ton of gold. ¹⁵So Hezekiah gave him all of the silver that was in the LORD's temple. He also gave him all of the silver that was among the treasures in the royal palace.

¹⁶Hezekiah, the king of Judah, had covered the doors and doorposts of the LORD's temple with gold. But now he had to strip it off. He had to give it to the king of Assyria.

SENNACHERIB WARNS JERUSALEM

¹⁷The king of Assyria sent his highest commander from Lachish to King Hezekiah at Jerusalem. He also sent his chief officer and his field commander along with a large army. All of them came up to Jerusalem. They stopped at the channel that brings water from the Upper Pool. It was on the road to the Washerman's Field. ¹⁸They called for King Hezekiah. Eliakim, Shebna and Joah went out to them. Eliakim, the son of Hilkiah, was in charge of the palace. Shebna was the secretary. Joah, the son of Asaph, kept the records.

¹⁹The field commander said to them, "Give Hezekiah this message. Tell him,

" 'Sennacherib is the great king of Assyria. He says, "Why are you putting your faith in what your king says? ²⁰You say you have a military plan. You say you have a strong army. But your words don't mean anything. Who are you depending on? Why don't you want to stay under my control?

²¹" ' "You are depending on Egypt. Why are you doing that? Egypt is nothing but a broken papyrus stem. Try leaning on it. It will only cut your hand. Pharaoh, the king of Egypt, is just like that to everyone who depends on him.

²²" ' "Suppose you say to me, 'We are depending on the LORD our God.' Didn't Hezekiah remove your god's high places and altars? Didn't Hezekiah say to the people of Judah and Jerusalem, 'You must worship at the altar in Jerusalem'?

²³" ' "Come on. Make a deal with my master, the king of Assyria. I'll give you 2,000 horses. But only if you can put riders on them! ²⁴You are depending on Egypt for chariots and horsemen. You can't drive away even the least important officer among my master's officials.

²⁵" ' "Besides, do you think I've come without receiving a message from the LORD? Have I come to attack and destroy this place

without a message from him? The LORD himself told me to march out against your country. He told me to destroy it." ' "

²⁶Then Shebna, Joah and Eliakim, the son of Hilkiah, spoke to the field commander. They said, "Please speak to us in the Aramaic language. We understand it. Don't speak to us in Hebrew. If you do, the people who are on the wall will be able to understand you."

²⁷But the commander replied, "My master sent me to say these things. Are these words only for your master and you to hear? Aren't they also for the men who are sitting on the wall? They are going to suffer just like you. They'll have to eat their own waste. They'll have to drink their own urine."

²⁸Then the commander stood up and spoke in the Hebrew language. He called out, "Pay attention to what the great king of Assyria is telling you. ²⁹He says, 'Don't let Hezekiah trick you. He can't save you from my powerful hand. ³⁰Don't let Hezekiah talk you into trusting in the LORD. Don't believe him when he says, "You can be sure that the LORD will save us. This city will not be handed over to the king of Assyria." '

³¹"Don't listen to Hezekiah. The king of Assyria says, 'Make a peace treaty with me. Come over to my side. Then every one of you will eat fruit from your own vine and fig tree. Every one of you will drink water from your own well. ³²You will do that until I come back. Then I'll take you to a land that is just like yours. It's a land that has a lot of grain and fresh wine. It has plenty of bread and vineyards. It has olive trees and honey. So choose life! Don't choose death!'

"Don't pay any attention to Hezekiah. He's telling you a lie when he says, 'The LORD will save us.'

³³"Has the god of any nation ever saved his land from the powerful hand of the king of Assyria? ³⁴Where are the gods of Hamath and Arpad? Where are the gods of Sepharvaim, Hena and Ivvah? Have they saved Samaria from my power?

³⁵"Which one of all of the gods of

those countries has been able to save his land from me? So how can the LORD save Jerusalem from my power?"

³⁶But the people remained silent. They didn't say anything. That's because King Hezekiah had commanded, "Don't answer him."

³⁷Then Eliakim, the son of Hilkiah, went to Hezekiah. Eliakim was in charge of the palace. The secretary Shebna went with him. So did Joah, the son of Asaph. Joah kept the records. All of them went to Hezekiah with their clothes torn. They told him what the field commander had said.

ISAIAH PROPHESIES THAT JERUSALEM WILL BE SAVED

19 When King Hezekiah heard what the field commander had said, he tore his clothes. He put on black clothes. Then he went into the LORD's temple.

²Hezekiah sent Eliakim, who was in charge of the palace, to the prophet Isaiah, the son of Amoz. He also sent the leading priests and the secretary Shebna to him. All of them were wearing black clothes.

³They told Isaiah, "Hezekiah says, 'Today we're in great trouble. The LORD is warning us. He's bringing shame on us. Sometimes babies come to the moment when they should be born. But their mothers aren't strong enough to allow them to be born. Today we are like those mothers. We aren't strong enough to save ourselves. ⁴" 'Perhaps the LORD your God will hear everything the field commander has said. His master, the king of Assyria, has sent him to make fun of the living God. Maybe the LORD your God will punish him for what he has heard him say. So pray for the remaining people who are still alive here.' "

⁵King Hezekiah's officials came to Isaiah. ⁶Then Isaiah said to them, "Tell your master, 'The LORD says, "Do not be afraid of what you have heard. The officers who are under the king of Assyria have spoken evil things against me. ⁷Listen! I will send him news from his own country. It will upset him so much that he will return home. There I will have him cut down with a sword." ' "

⁸The field commander heard that

What language did they speak in Bible days?

At first everyone in the world spoke the same language. That is how it was when the world first began. But these people became proud and thought they were as good as God. They tried to build a tower to heaven. So God gave them all different languages. That caused them to get confused. They quit building and formed groups based on their language (Genesis 11:1–9). People have lived in these kinds of groups ever since. Most of the people you read about in the Bible spoke Hebrew, Aramaic or Greek.

checkout
2 Kings 18:26–28

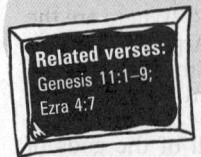

Related verses:
Genesis 11:1–9;
Ezra 4:7

the king of Assyria had left Lachish. So the commander pulled his troops back from Jerusalem. He went to join the king. He found out that the king was fighting against Libnah.

⁹During that time Sennacherib received a report. He was told that Tirhakah was marching out to fight against him. Tirhakah was the king of Egypt. He was from the land of Cush.

Sennacherib sent messengers again to Hezekiah with a letter. It said, ¹⁰"Tell Hezekiah, the king of Judah, 'Don't let the god you depend on trick you. He says, "Jerusalem will not be handed over to the king of Assyria." But don't believe him.

¹¹" 'I'm sure you have heard about what the kings of Assyria have done to all of the other countries. They have destroyed them completely. So do you think you will be saved? ¹²The kings who ruled before me destroyed many nations. Did the gods of those nations save them? Did the gods of Gozan, Haran or Rezeph save them? What about the gods of the people of Eden who were in Tel Assar? ¹³Where is the king of Hamath? Where is the king of Arpad? Where is the king of the city of Sepharvaim? Where are the kings of Hena or Ivvah?' "

HEZEKIAH PRAYS TO THE LORD

¹⁴When Hezekiah received the letter from the messengers, he read it. Then he went up to the LORD's temple. There he spread the letter out in front of the LORD.

¹⁵Hezekiah prayed to the LORD. He said, "LORD, you are the God of Israel. You sit on your throne between the cherubim. You alone are God over all of the kingdoms on earth. You have made heaven and earth. ¹⁶Listen, LORD. Hear us. Open your eyes, LORD. Look at the trouble we're in. Listen to what Sennacherib is saying. You are the living God. And he dares to make fun of you!

¹⁷"LORD, it's true that the kings of Assyria have completely destroyed many nations and their lands. ¹⁸They have thrown the statues of the gods of those nations into the fire. And they have destroyed them. That's because they

weren't really gods at all. They were nothing but statues that were made out of wood and stone. They were made by the hands of men.

¹⁹"LORD our God, save us from the powerful hand of Sennacherib. Then all of the kingdoms on earth will know that you alone are God."

ISAIAH PROPHESIES THAT SENNACHERIB WILL FALL FROM POWER

²⁰Isaiah sent a message to Hezekiah. Isaiah was the son of Amoz. Isaiah said, "The LORD is the God of Israel. He says, 'I have heard your prayer about Sennacherib, the king of Assyria.'

²¹"Here is the message the LORD has spoken against him. The LORD says,

" 'You will not win the battle over Zion.
    Its people hate you and make fun of you.
The people of Jerusalem lift up their heads proudly
    as you run away.
²²Who have you laughed at?
    Who have you spoken evil things against?
    Who have you raised your voice against?
Who have you looked at so proudly?
    You have done it against me.
    I am the Holy One of Israel!
²³Through your messengers
    you have laughed at me again and again.
And you have said,
    "I have many chariots.
With them I have climbed to the tops of the mountains.
    I've climbed the highest mountains in Lebanon.
I've cut down its tallest cedar trees.
    I've cut down the best of its pine trees.
I've reached its farthest parts.
    I've reached its finest forests.
²⁴I've dug wells in strange lands.
    I've drunk the water from them.
I've walked through all of Egypt's streams.
    I've dried up every one of them."

²⁵" 'But I, the LORD, say, "Haven't you heard what I have done?

Long ago I arranged for you to do
all of that.
In days of old I planned it.
Now I have made it happen.
You have turned cities with high
walls
into piles of stone.
²⁶ Their people do not have any
power left.
They are troubled and put to
shame.
They are like plants in the field.
They are like new green plants.
They are like grass that grows on a
roof.
It dries up before it is completely
grown.
²⁷ " ' "But I know where you live.
I know when you come and go.
I know how very angry you are
with me.
²⁸ You roar against me and brag.
And I have heard your bragging.
So I will put my hook in your nose.
I will put my bit in your mouth.
And I will make you go home
by the same way you came." ' "

²⁹ The LORD said, "Hezekiah, here is a
miraculous sign for you.

"This year you will eat what grows
by itself.
In the second year you will eat
what grows from that.
But in the third year you will plant
your crops and gather them
in.
You will plant your grapevines
and eat their fruit.
³⁰ The people of Judah who are still
alive will be like plants.
Once more they will put down
roots and produce fruit.
³¹ Out of Jerusalem will come those
who remain.
Out of Mount Zion will come
those who are still left alive.

"My great love will make sure that
happens.
I rule over all.

³² "Here is a message from me about
the king of Assyria. It says,

" 'He will not enter this city.
He will not even shoot an arrow
at it.

He will not come near it with a
shield.
He will not build a ramp in order
to climb over its walls.
³³ By the same way he came he will
go home.
He will not enter this city,'
announces the LORD.
³⁴ " 'I will guard this city and save it.
I will do it for myself. And I will
do it for my servant David.' "

³⁵ That night the angel of the LORD
went into the camp of the Assyrians.
He put to death 185,000 soldiers there.
The people of Jerusalem got up the
next morning. They looked out and
saw all of the dead bodies. ³⁶ So Sennacherib, the king of Assyria, took the
army tents down. Then he left. He returned to Nineveh and stayed there.

³⁷ One day Sennacherib was worshiping in the temple of his god
Nisroch. His sons Adrammelech and
Sharezer cut him down with their
swords. Then they escaped to the land
of Ararat. Esarhaddon became the
next king after his father Sennacherib.

HEZEKIAH BECOMES SICK

20 In those days Hezekiah became very sick. He knew he
was about to die.
The prophet Isaiah, the son of
Amoz, went to him. Isaiah told Hezekiah, "The LORD says, 'Put everything
in order. Make out your will. You are
going to die soon. You will not get well
again.' "
²Hezekiah turned his face toward
the wall. He prayed to the LORD. He
said, ³ "LORD, please remember how
faithful I've been to you. I've lived the
way you wanted me to. I've served you
with all my heart. I've done what is
good in your sight." And Hezekiah
cried bitterly.
⁴ Isaiah was leaving the middle
courtyard. Before he had left it, a message came to him from the LORD. He
said, ⁵ "Go back and speak to Hezekiah.
He is the leader of my people. Tell him,
'The LORD, the God of King David,
says, "I have heard your prayer. I have
seen your tears. And I will heal you. On
the third day from now you will go up
to my temple. ⁶ I will add 15 years to

your life. And I will save you and this city from the powerful hand of the king of Assyria. I will guard this city. I will do it for myself. And I will do it for my servant David.' ' "

⁷Then Isaiah said, "Press some figs together. Spread them on a piece of cloth." So that's what they did. Then they applied it to Hezekiah's boil. And he got well again.

⁸Hezekiah had said to Isaiah, "You say the LORD will heal me. You say that I'll go up to his temple on the third day from now. What will the miraculous sign be to prove he'll really do that?"

⁹Isaiah answered, "The LORD will do what he has promised. Here is his sign to you. Do you want the shadow the sun makes to go forward ten steps? Or do you want it to go back ten steps?"

¹⁰"It's easy for the shadow to go forward ten steps," said Hezekiah. "So have it go back ten steps."

¹¹Then the prophet Isaiah called out to the LORD. And the LORD made the shadow go back ten steps. It went back the ten steps it had gone down on the stairway Ahaz had made.

MESSENGERS COME FROM BABYLON TO HEZEKIAH

¹²At that time Merodach-Baladan, the king of Babylonia, sent Hezekiah letters and a gift. He had heard that Hezekiah had been sick. Merodach-Baladan was the son of Baladan.

¹³Hezekiah received the messengers. He showed them everything that was in his storerooms. He showed them the silver and gold. He showed them the spices and the fine olive oil. He showed them where he kept his weapons. And he showed them all of his treasures. In fact, he showed them everything that was in his palace and in his whole kingdom.

¹⁴Then Isaiah the prophet went to King Hezekiah. He asked him, "What did those men say? Where did they come from?"

"They came from a land far away," Hezekiah said. "They came from Babylon."

¹⁵The prophet asked, "What did they see in your palace?"

"They saw everything in my palace,"

Hezekiah said. "I showed them all of my treasures."

¹⁶Then Isaiah said to Hezekiah, "Listen to the LORD's message. He says, ¹⁷'You can be sure the time will come when everything in your palace will be carried off to Babylon. Everything the kings before you have stored up until this day will be taken away. There will not be anything left,' says the LORD. ¹⁸'Some of the members of your family line will be taken away. They will be your own flesh and blood. They will include the children who will be born into your family line in years to come. And they will serve the king of Babylonia in his palace.' "

¹⁹"The message the LORD has spoken through you is good," Hezekiah replied. He thought, "There will be peace and safety while I'm still living."

²⁰The other events of the rule of Hezekiah are written down. Everything he accomplished is written down. That includes how he made the pool and the tunnel. He used them to bring water into Jerusalem. All of those things are written in the official records of the kings of Judah.

²¹Hezekiah joined the members of his family who had already died. His son Manasseh became the next king after him.

MANASSEH BECOMES KING OF JUDAH

21 Manasseh was 12 years old when he became king. He ruled in Jerusalem for 55 years. His mother's name was Hephzibah.

²Manasseh did what was evil in the sight of the LORD. He followed the practices of the nations. The LORD hated those practices. He had driven those nations out to make room for the people of Israel.

³Manasseh rebuilt the high places. His father Hezekiah had destroyed them. Manasseh also set up altars to the god Baal. He made a pole that was used to worship the goddess Asherah. Ahab, the king of Israel, had done those same things. Manasseh even bowed down to all of the stars. And he worshiped them.

⁴He built altars in the LORD's temple.

The LORD had said about his temple, "I will put my Name there in Jerusalem." ⁵In both courtyards of the LORD's temple Manasseh built altars to honor all of the stars.

⁶He sacrificed his own son in the fire to another god. He practiced all kinds of evil magic. He got messages from those who had died. He talked to the spirits of the dead. He did many things that were evil in the sight of the LORD. He made him very angry.

⁷Manasseh had carved a pole for worshiping Asherah. He put it in the temple. The LORD had spoken to David and his son Solomon about the temple. He had said, "My Name will be in this temple and in Jerusalem forever. Out of all of the cities in the tribes of Israel I have chosen Jerusalem. ⁸I gave this land to your people who lived long ago. I will not make the Israelites wander away from it again. But they must be careful to do everything I commanded them. They must obey the whole Law that my servant Moses gave them."

⁹But the people didn't pay any attention. Manasseh led them down the wrong path. They did more evil things than the nations the LORD had destroyed to make room for the people of Israel.

¹⁰The LORD spoke through his servants the prophets. He said, ¹¹"Manasseh, the king of Judah, has committed terrible sins. I hate them. Manasseh has done more evil things than the Amorites who were in the land before him. And he has led Judah to commit sin by worshiping his statues of gods.

¹²"I am the God of Israel. I tell you, 'I am going to bring trouble on Jerusalem and Judah. It will be so horrible that the ears of everyone who hears about it will ring. ¹³I will measure out punishment against Jerusalem, just as I did against Samaria. I used a plumb line against the royal family of Ahab to prove that they did not measure up to my standards. I will use the same plumb line against Jerusalem. I will wipe out Jerusalem, just as someone wipes a dish. I will wipe it and turn it upside down. ¹⁴I will desert those who remain among my people. I will hand them over to their enemies. All of their enemies will rob them.

¹⁵" 'That is because my people have done what is evil in my sight. They have made me very angry. They have done that from the day their own people came out of Egypt until this very day.' "

¹⁶Manasseh also spilled the blood of many people who weren't guilty of doing anything wrong. He spilled so much blood that he filled Jerusalem with it from one end of the city to the other. And he caused Judah to commit sin. So they also did what was evil in the sight of the LORD.

¹⁷The other events of the rule of Manasseh are written down. Everything he did is written down. That includes the sin he committed. All of those things are written in the official records of the kings of Judah.

¹⁸Manasseh joined the members of his family who had already died. His body was buried in his palace garden. It was called the garden of Uzza. Manasseh's son Amon became the next king after him.

AMON BECOMES KING OF JUDAH

¹⁹Amon was 22 years old when he became king. He ruled in Jerusalem for two years. His mother's name was Meshullemeth. She was the daughter of Haruz. She was from Jotbah.

²⁰Amon did what was evil in the sight of the LORD, just as his father Manasseh had done. ²¹He lived the way his father had lived. He worshiped the statues of the gods his father had worshiped. He bowed down to them. ²²He deserted the LORD, the God of his people. He didn't live the way the LORD wanted him to.

²³Amon's officials made plans against him. They murdered the king in his palace. ²⁴Then the people of the land killed all those who had made plans against King Amon. They made his son Josiah king in his place.

²⁵The other events of the rule of Amon are written down. Everything he did is written down. All of those things are written in the official records of the kings of Judah. ²⁶Amon's body was buried in his grave in the garden of Uzza. His son Josiah became the next king after him.

HILKIAH FINDS THE SCROLL OF THE LAW

22 Josiah was eight years old when he became king. He ruled in Jerusalem for 31 years. His mother's name was Jedidah. She was the daughter of Adaiah. She was from Bozkath.

²Josiah did what was right in the eyes of the LORD. He lived the way King David had lived. He didn't turn away from it to the right or the left.

³King Josiah sent his secretary Shaphan to the LORD's temple. It was in the 18th year of Josiah's rule. Shaphan was the son of Azaliah. Azaliah was the son of Meshullam. Josiah said, ⁴"Go up to the high priest Hilkiah. Have him add up the money that has been brought into the LORD's temple. Those who guard the doors have collected it from the people.

⁵"Have them put all of the money in the care of the men who have been put in charge of the work on the LORD's temple. Have them pay the workers who repair it. ⁶Have them pay the builders and those who work with wood. Have them pay those who lay the stones. Also have them buy lumber and blocks of stone to repair the temple.

⁷"But they don't have to report how they use the money that is given to them. That's because they are completely honest."

⁸The high priest Hilkiah spoke to the secretary Shaphan. He said, "I've found the Scroll of the Law in the LORD's temple." He gave it to Shaphan, who read it.

⁹Then Shaphan went to King Josiah. He told him, "Your officials have paid out the money that was in the LORD's temple. They've put it in the care of the workers and directors there." ¹⁰Shaphan continued, "The priest Hilkiah has given me a scroll." Shaphan read some of it to the king.

¹¹The king heard the words of the Scroll of the Law. When he did, he tore his royal robes. ¹²He gave orders to the priest Hilkiah, Ahikam, Acbor, the secretary Shaphan and Asaiah. Ahikam was the son of Shaphan. Acbor was the son of Micaiah. And Asaiah was the king's attendant.

Josiah commanded them, ¹³"Go. Ask the LORD for advice. Ask him about what is written in this scroll that has been found. Do it for me. Also do it for the people and the whole nation of Judah. The LORD's anger is burning against us. That's because our people before us didn't obey the words of this scroll. They didn't do everything that is written there about us."

¹⁴The priest Hilkiah went to speak to the prophet Huldah. So did Ahikam, Acbor, Shaphan and Asaiah. Huldah was the wife of Shallum. Shallum was the son of Tikvah. Tikvah was the son of Harhas. Shallum took care of the sacred robes. Huldah lived in the New Quarter of Jerusalem.

¹⁵She said to them, "The LORD is the God of Israel. He says, 'Tell the man who sent you to me, ¹⁶"The LORD says, 'I am going to bring horrible trouble on this place and its people. Everything that is written in the scroll the king of Judah has read will take place.

¹⁷" ' "That is because the people have deserted me. They have burned incense to other gods. They have made me very angry because of the statues of gods their hands have made. So my anger will burn against this place. The fire of my anger will not be put out.' " '

¹⁸"The king of Judah sent you to ask the LORD for advice. Tell him, 'The LORD is the God of Israel. He has a message for you about the things you heard. He says, ¹⁹"Your heart was tender. You made yourself low in my sight. You heard what I spoke against this place and its people. I said they would be under a curse. I told them they would be destroyed. You tore your royal robes and sobbed. And I have heard you," announces the LORD.

²⁰" ' "You will join the members of your family who have already died. Your body will be buried in peace. Your eyes will not see all of the trouble I am going to bring on this place." ' "

Huldah's answer was taken back to the king.

JOSIAH PROMISES TO FOLLOW THE COVENANT

23 Then the king called together all of the elders of Judah and Jerusalem. ²He went up to the LORD's temple. The people of Judah and Jerusalem went with him. So did the priests and prophets. All of them went, from the least important of them to the most important.

The king had all of the words of the Scroll of the Covenant read to them. The scroll had been found in the LORD's temple.

³The king stood next to his pillar. He agreed to the terms of the covenant in front of the LORD. He promised to follow him and obey his commands, directions and rules. He promised to obey them with all his heart and with all his soul. So he agreed to the terms of the covenant that were written down in that scroll. Then all of the people committed themselves to the covenant.

⁴Certain articles that were in the LORD's temple had been made to honor the god Baal and the goddess Asherah and all of the stars in the sky. The king ordered the high priest Hilkiah to remove those articles. He ordered the priests who were under him and the men who guarded the doors to help Hilkiah. Josiah burned the articles outside Jerusalem. He burned them in the fields in the Kidron Valley. And he took the ashes to Bethel.

⁵He got rid of the priests who served other gods. The kings of Judah had appointed them to burn incense. They burned the incense on the high places of the towns of Judah. And they burned it on the high places around Jerusalem. They burned incense to honor Baal and the sun and moon. They burned it to honor all of the stars.

⁶Josiah removed the Asherah pole from the LORD's temple. It had been used to worship Asherah. He took it to the Kidron Valley outside Jerusalem. There he burned it. He ground it into powder. And he scattered it over the graves of the ordinary people.

⁷He also tore down the rooms where the male temple prostitutes stayed. Those rooms were in the LORD's temple. The women had made cloth for Asherah in them.

⁸Josiah brought all of the priests from the towns of Judah and destroyed the high places. He destroyed them from Geba all the way to Beersheba. The priests had burned incense on them. Josiah broke down the high places at the gates. That included the high place at the entrance of the Gate of Joshua. It was on the left side of one of Jerusalem's gates. Joshua was the city governor.

⁹The priests of the high places didn't serve at the LORD's altar in Jerusalem. In spite of that, they ate with the other priests. All of them ate bread that was made without yeast.

¹⁰Josiah destroyed the high places at Topheth in the Valley of Ben Hinnom. He didn't want anyone to use them to sacrifice his son or daughter in the fire to the god Molech.

¹¹He removed the statues of horses from the entrance to the LORD's temple. The kings of Judah had set them apart to honor the sun. The statues were in the courtyard. They were near the room of an official named Nathan-Melech. Josiah burned the chariots that had been set apart to honor the sun.

¹²He pulled down the altars the kings of Judah had set up. They had put them on the palace roof near the upstairs room of Ahaz. Josiah also pulled down the altars Manasseh had built. They were in the two courtyards of the LORD's temple. Josiah removed the altars from there. He smashed them to pieces. Then he threw the broken pieces into the Kidron Valley.

¹³The king also destroyed the high places that were east of Jerusalem. They were at the southern end of the Mount of Olives. They were the ones Solomon, the king of Israel, had built. He had built a high place for worshiping Ashtoreth. She was the evil goddess of the people of Sidon. Solomon had also built one for worshiping Chemosh. He was the evil god of Moab. And Solomon had built one for worshiping Molech. He was the god of the people of Ammon. The LORD hated that god.

¹⁴Josiah smashed the sacred stones. He cut down the poles that were used to worship the goddess Asherah. Then he covered all of those places with human bones.

¹⁵There was an altar at Bethel. It was

at the high place that had been made by Jeroboam, the son of Nebat. Jeroboam had caused Israel to commit sin. Even that altar and high place were destroyed by Josiah. He burned the high place. He ground it into powder. He also burned the Asherah pole.

¹⁶Then Josiah looked around. He saw the tombs that were on the side of the hill. He had the bones removed from them. And he burned them on the altar to make it "unclean." That's what the LORD had said would happen. He had spoken that message through a man of God. The man had announced those things long before they took place.

¹⁷The king asked, "What's that stone on the grave over there?"

The men of the city said, "It marks the tomb where the body of a man of God is buried. He came from Judah. He spoke against the altar at Bethel. He announced the very things you have done to it."

¹⁸"Leave it alone," Josiah said. "Don't let anyone touch his bones."

So they spared his bones. They also spared the bones of the prophet who had come from the northern kingdom of Israel.

¹⁹Josiah did in the rest of the northern kingdom the same things he had done at Bethel. He removed all of the small temples at the high places. He made them "unclean." The kings of Israel had built them in the towns of the northern kingdom. The people in those towns had made the LORD very angry.

²⁰Josiah killed all of the priests of those high places on the altars. He burned human bones on the altars. Then he went back to Jerusalem.

²¹The king gave an order to all of the people. He said, "Celebrate the Passover Feast to honor the LORD your God. Do what is written in this Scroll of the Covenant."

²²A Passover Feast like that one had not been held for a long time. There hadn't been any like it since the days of the judges who led Israel. And there hadn't been any like it during the whole time the kings of Israel and Judah were ruling.

²³King Josiah celebrated the Passover in Jerusalem to honor the LORD. It was in the 18th year of his rule.

²⁴And that's not all. Josiah got rid of those who got messages from people who had died. He got rid of those who talked to the spirits of the dead. He got rid of the statues of family gods and the statues of other gods. He got rid of everything else the LORD hates that was in Judah and Jerusalem. He did it to carry out what the law required. That law was written in the scroll the priest Hilkiah had found in the LORD's temple.

²⁵There was no king like Josiah either before him or after him. None of them turned to the LORD as he did. He followed the LORD with all his heart and all his soul. He followed him with all his strength. He did everything the Law of Moses required.

²⁶In spite of that, the LORD didn't turn away from his burning anger. It blazed out against Judah. That's because of everything Manasseh had done to make him very angry.

²⁷So the LORD said, "I will remove Judah from my land. I will do to them what I did to Israel. I will turn my back on Jerusalem. It is the city I chose. I will also turn my back on this temple. I spoke about it. I said, 'I will put my Name here.' " *(1 Kings 8:29)*

²⁸The other events of the rule of Josiah are written down. Everything he did is written down. All of those things are written in the official records of the kings of Judah.

²⁹Pharaoh Neco was king of Egypt. He marched up to the Euphrates River. He went there to help the king of Assyria. It happened while Josiah was king. Josiah marched out to meet Neco in battle. When Neco saw him at Megiddo, he killed him.

³⁰Josiah's servants brought his body in a chariot from Megiddo to Jerusalem. They buried his body in his own tomb. Then the people of the land went and got Jehoahaz. They anointed him as king in place of his father Josiah.

JEHOAHAZ BECOMES KING OF JUDAH

³¹Jehoahaz was 23 years old when he became king. He ruled in Jerusalem

for three months. His mother's name was Hamutal. She was the daughter of Jeremiah. She was from Libnah.

[32]Jehoahaz did what was evil in the sight of the LORD. He did just as the kings who had ruled before him had done. [33]Pharaoh Neco put him in chains at Riblah in the land of Hamath. That kept him from ruling in Jerusalem. Neco made the people of Judah pay him a tax of almost four tons of silver and 75 pounds of gold.

[34]Pharaoh Neco made Eliakim king in place of his father Josiah. He changed Eliakim's name to Jehoiakim. But he took Jehoahaz with him to Egypt. And that's where Jehoahaz died.

[35]Jehoiakim paid Pharaoh Neco the silver and gold he required. To get the money, Jehoiakim taxed the land. He forced the people to give him the silver and gold. He made each one pay him what he required.

JEHOIAKIM BECOMES KING OF JUDAH

[36]Jehoiakim was 25 years old when he became king. He ruled in Jerusalem for 11 years. His mother's name was Zebidah. She was the daughter of Pedaiah. She was from Rumah.

[37]Jehoiakim did what was evil in the sight of the LORD. He did just as the kings who had ruled before him had done.

24 During Jehoiakim's rule, Nebuchadnezzar marched into the land and attacked it. He was king of Babylonia. He became Jehoiakim's master for three years. But then Jehoiakim decided he didn't want to remain under Nebuchadnezzar's control.

[2]The LORD sent robbers against Jehoiakim from Babylonia, Aram, Moab and Ammon. He sent them to destroy Judah. That's what the LORD had said would happen. He had spoken that message through his servants the prophets.

[3]Those things happened to Judah in keeping with what the LORD had commanded. He brought enemies against his people in order to remove them from his land. He removed them because of all of the sins Manasseh had committed. [4]He had spilled the blood of many people who weren't guilty of doing anything wrong. In fact, he spilled so much of their blood that he filled Jerusalem with it. So the LORD refused to forgive him.

[5]The other events of the rule of Jehoiakim are written down. Everything he did is written down. All of those things are written in the official records of the kings of Judah.

[6]Jehoiakim joined the members of his family who had already died. His son Jehoiachin became the next king after him.

[7]The king of Egypt didn't march out from his own country again. That's because the king of Babylonia had taken so much of his territory. That territory reached from the Wadi of Egypt all the way to the Euphrates River.

JEHOIACHIN BECOMES KING OF JUDAH

[8]Jehoiachin was 18 years old when he became king. He ruled in Jerusalem for three months. His mother's name was Nehushta. She was the daughter of Elnathan. She was from Jerusalem.

[9]Jehoiachin did what was evil in the sight of the LORD. He did just as his father Jehoiakim had done.

[10]At that time the officers of Nebuchadnezzar, the king of Babylonia, marched to Jerusalem. They surrounded it and got ready to attack it. [11]Nebuchadnezzar himself came up to the city. He arrived while his officers were attacking it.

[12]Jehoiachin, the king of Judah, handed himself over to him. Jehoiachin's mother did the same thing. And so did all of his attendants, nobles and officials.

The king of Babylonia took Jehoiachin away as his prisoner. It was in the eighth year of Nebuchadnezzar's rule.

[13]He removed all of the treasures from the LORD's temple. He also removed all of the treasures from the royal palace. He took away all of the gold articles that Solomon, the king of Israel, had made for the temple. That's what the LORD had announced would happen.

[14]Nebuchadnezzar took all of the people of Jerusalem to Babylonia as

prisoners. That included all of the officers and fighting men. It also included all of the skilled workers. The total number of prisoners was 10,000. Only the poorest people were left in the land.

¹⁵Nebuchadnezzar took Jehoiachin to Babylon as his prisoner. He also took the king's mother from Jerusalem to Babylon. And he took Jehoiachin's wives, his officials and the most important men in the land.

¹⁶The king also forced the whole army of 7,000 soldiers to go away to Babylonia. Those men were strong and able to go to war. And the king forced 1,000 skilled workers to go to Babylonia.

¹⁷Nebuchadnezzar made Jehoiachin's uncle Mattaniah king in his place. And he changed Mattaniah's name to Zedekiah.

ZEDEKIAH BECOMES KING OF JUDAH

¹⁸Zedekiah was 21 years old when he became king. He ruled in Jerusalem for 11 years. His mother's name was Hamutal. She was the daughter of Jeremiah. She was from Libnah.

¹⁹Zedekiah did what was evil in the sight of the LORD. He did just as Jehoiakim had done. ²⁰The enemies of Jerusalem and Judah attacked them because the LORD was angry. In the end he threw them out of his land.

NEBUCHADNEZZAR DESTROYS JERUSALEM

Zedekiah also refused to remain under the control of Nebuchadnezzar.

25 Nebuchadnezzar was king of Babylonia. He marched out against Jerusalem. All of his armies went with him. It was in the ninth year of the rule of Zedekiah. It was on the tenth day of the tenth month. Nebuchadnezzar set up camp outside the city. He brought in war machines all around it. ²It was surrounded until the 11th year of King Zedekiah's rule.

³By the ninth day of the fourth month, there wasn't any food left in

Why did God send the Jews to Babylon?

The people of Judah did not listen to the prophets. They did not follow God, and they treated poor people very badly. So God allowed the Babylonian army to punish them. Many of Judah's people were taken to Babylon to be slaves. The Babylonians took the best young people from Judah and trained them to live like Babylonians. This made Babylon an even stronger nation. It made Judah a weaker nation. The Jews spent 70 years in Babylon, just as God had said they would.

checkout
2 Kings 24:14

Related verses:
Jeremiah
34:1–22;
Ezekiel 7:1–4

the city. So the people didn't have anything to eat.

[4]Then the Babylonians broke through the city wall. Judah's whole army ran away at night. They went out through the gate between the two walls that were near the king's garden. They escaped even though the Babylonians surrounded the city. Judah's army ran toward the Arabah Valley. [5]But the armies of Babylonia chased King Zedekiah. They caught up with him in the flatlands near Jericho. All of his soldiers were separated from him. They had scattered in every direction. [6]The king was captured. He was taken to the king of Babylonia at Riblah. That's where Nebuchadnezzar decided how he would be punished. [7]His men killed the sons of Zedekiah. They forced him to watch it with his own eyes. Then they poked out his eyes. They put him in bronze chains. And they took him to Babylon.

[8]Nebuzaradan was an official of the king of Babylonia. In fact, he was commander of the royal guard. He came to Jerusalem. It was in the 19th year that Nebuchadnezzar was king of Babylonia. It was on the seventh day of the fifth month. [9]Nebuzaradan set the LORD's temple on fire. He also set fire to the royal palace and all of the houses in Jerusalem. He burned down every important building. [10]The armies of Babylonia broke down the walls around Jerusalem. That's what the commander told them to do. [11]Some people still remained in the city. But the commander Nebuzaradan took them away as prisoners. He also took the rest of the people of the land. That included those who had joined the king of Babylonia. [12]But the commander left some of the poorest people of the land behind. He told them to work in the vineyards and fields.

[13]The armies of Babylonia destroyed the LORD's temple. They broke the bronze pillars into pieces. They broke up the bronze stands that could be moved around. And they broke up the huge bronze bowl. Then they carried the bronze away to Babylon. [14]They also took away the pots, shovels, wick cutters and dishes. They took away all of the bronze articles that were used for any purpose in the temple. [15]The commander of the royal guard took away the shallow cups for burning incense. He took away the sprinkling bowls. So he took away everything that was made out of pure gold or silver.

[16]The bronze was more than anyone could weigh. It included the bronze from the two pillars. It also included the bronze from the huge bowl and the stands. Solomon had made all of those things for the LORD's temple. [17]Each pillar was 27 feet high. The bronze top of one pillar was four and a half feet high. It was decorated with a set of bronze chains and pomegranates all around it. The other pillar was just like it. It also had a set of chains.

[18]The commander of the guard took some prisoners. They included the chief priest Seraiah and the priest Zephaniah who was under him. They also included the three men who guarded the temple doors. [19]Some people were still left in the city. The commander took as a prisoner the officer who was in charge of the fighting men. He took the five men who gave advice to the king. He also took the secretary who was the chief officer in charge of getting the people of the land to serve in the army. And he took 60 of the secretary's men who were still in the city. [20]The commander Nebuzaradan took all of them away. He brought them to the king of Babylonia at Riblah. [21]There the king had them put to death. Riblah was in the land of Hamath.

So the people of Judah were taken as prisoners. They were taken far away from their own land.

[22]Nebuchadnezzar, the king of Babylonia, appointed Gedaliah to be over the people he had left behind in Judah. Gedaliah was the son of Ahikam. Ahikam was the son of Shaphan. [23]All of Judah's army officers and their men heard about what had happened. They heard that the king had appointed Gedaliah as governor. So they came to Gedaliah at Mizpah. Ishmael, the son of Nethaniah, came. So did Johanan, the son of Kareah. Seraiah, the son of Tanhumeth, also came.

And so did Jaazaniah, the son of the Maacathite. All of their men came too. Seraiah was from Netophah.

²⁴Gedaliah took an oath to give hope to all of those men. He spoke in a kind way to them. He said, "Don't be afraid of the officials from Babylonia. Settle down in the land of Judah. Serve the king of Babylonia. Then things will go well with you."

²⁵But in the seventh month Ishmael, the son of Nethaniah, came with ten men. He killed Gedaliah. He also killed the people of Judah and Babylonia who were with Gedaliah at Mizpah. Nethaniah was the son of Elishama. Ishmael was a member of the royal family.

²⁶After he had killed Gedaliah, all of the people ran away to Egypt. Everyone from the least important of them to the most important ran away. The army officers went with them. All of them went to Egypt because they were afraid of the Babylonians.

JEHOIACHIN IS SET FREE

²⁷Evil-Merodach set Jehoiachin, the king of Judah, free from prison. It was in the 37th year after Jehoiachin had been taken away to Babylon. It was also the year Evil-Merodach became king of Babylonia. It was on the 27th day of the 12th month. ²⁸Evil-Merodach spoke kindly to Jehoiachin. He gave him a place of honor. Other kings were with Jehoiachin in Babylon. But his place was more important than theirs.

²⁹So Jehoiachin put his prison clothes away. For the rest of Jehoiachin's life the king provided what he needed. ³⁰The king did that for Jehoiachin day by day as long as he lived.

quest challenge

I Wonder . . .

Why is it important to remember what God has already done for me?

Real Life Challenge

Maybe you go to a new school because your family moved. That can be really scary. In those situations it's good to remember other times when God helped you get through difficulties. Then you can remember to stick with him when another challenge comes along.

Quest Clue

2 Kings 17 will give you a picture of what happened when the Israelites didn't remember what God had done for them and tried to do things their own way. Psalm 78 will encourage you to remember what God has done in your life and pass on the story to others.

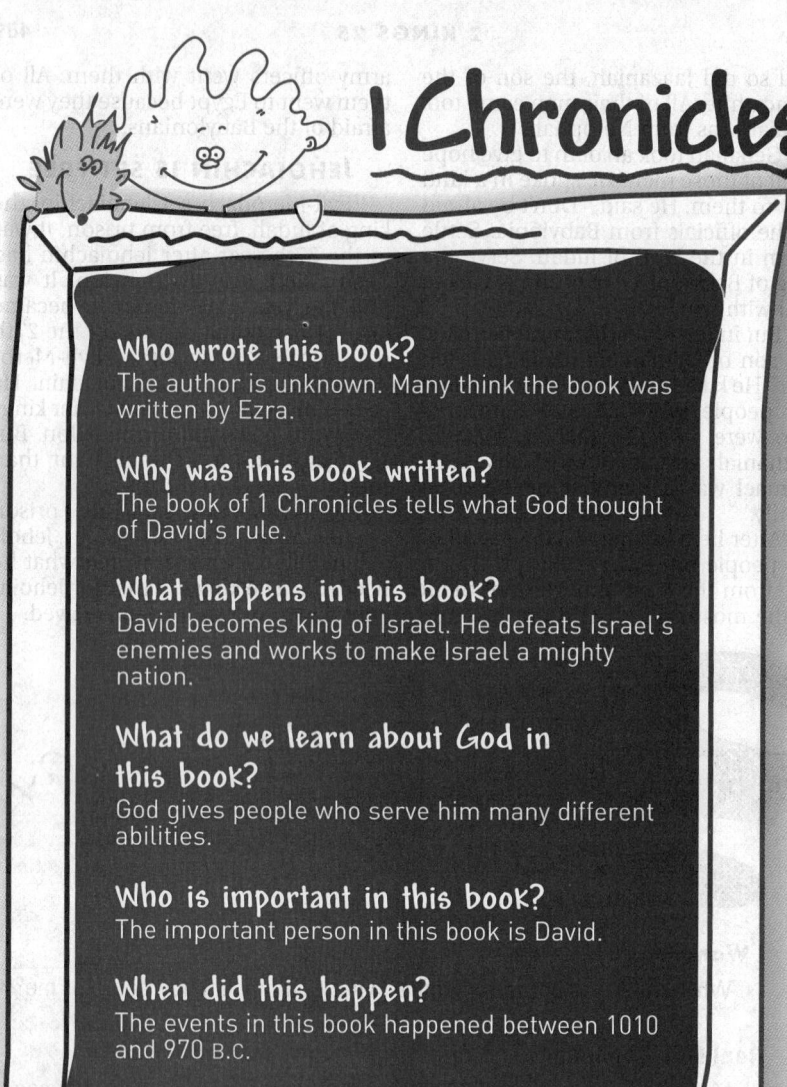

1 Chronicles

Who wrote this book?
The author is unknown. Many think the book was written by Ezra.

Why was this book written?
The book of 1 Chronicles tells what God thought of David's rule.

What happens in this book?
David becomes king of Israel. He defeats Israel's enemies and works to make Israel a mighty nation.

What do we learn about God in this book?
God gives people who serve him many different abilities.

Who is important in this book?
The important person in this book is David.

When did this happen?
The events in this book happened between 1010 and 970 B.C.

A LIST OF NAMES FROM ADAM TO ABRAHAM

A LIST OF NAMES FROM ADAM TO THE SONS OF NOAH

1 Adam, Seth, Enosh, ²Kenan, Mahalalel, Jared, ³Enoch, Methuselah, Lamech, Noah.

⁴The sons of Noah were Shem, Ham and Japheth.

THE SONS OF JAPHETH

⁵The sons of Japheth were Gomer, Magog, Madai, Javan, Tubal, Meshech and Tiras.

⁶The sons of Gomer were Ashkenaz, Riphath and Togarmah.

⁷The sons of Javan were Elishah, Tarshish, the Kittim and the Rodanites.

THE SONS OF HAM

⁸ The sons of Ham were
Cush, Egypt, Put and Canaan.
⁹ The sons of Cush were
Seba, Havilah, Sabta, Raamah
and Sabteca.
The sons of Raamah were
Sheba and Dedan.
¹⁰ Cush was the father of
Nimrod. Nimrod grew up to be
a mighty hero on the earth.
¹¹ Egypt was the father of
the Ludites, Anamites, Lehabites and Naphtuhites. ¹²He was
also the father of the Pathrusites, Casluhites and Caphtorites. The Philistines came from
the Casluhites.
¹³ Canaan was the father of Sidon.
Sidon was his oldest son.
Canaan was also the father of
the Hittites, ¹⁴Jebusites, Amorites and Girgashites. ¹⁵And he
was the father of the Hivites,
Arkites, Sinites, ¹⁶Arvadites,
Zemarites and Hamathites.

THE SONS OF SHEM

¹⁷ The sons of Shem were
Elam, Asshur, Arphaxad, Lud
and Aram.
The sons of Aram were
Uz, Hul, Gether and Meshech.
¹⁸ Arphaxad was the father of Shelah.
Shelah was the father of Eber.
¹⁹ Eber was the father of two sons.
One was named Peleg. The
earth was divided up in his
time. His brother was named
Joktan.
²⁰ Joktan was the father of
Almodad, Sheleph, Hazarmaveth and Jerah. ²¹He was also
the father of Hadoram, Uzal,
Diklah, ²²Obal, Abimael, Sheba,
²³Ophir, Havilah and Jobab. All
of them were sons of Joktan.

A LIST OF NAMES FROM SHEM TO ABRAHAM

²⁴ Shem, Arphaxad, Shelah,
²⁵ Eber, Peleg, Reu,
²⁶ Serug, Nahor, Terah,
²⁷ Abram. Abram was also called
Abraham.

THE FAMILY LINE OF ABRAHAM

²⁸ The sons of Abraham were
Isaac and Ishmael.

THE FAMILY LINE OF HAGAR

²⁹ Here are the members of the
family line of Hagar.
Nebaioth was Ishmael's oldest
son. Then came Kedar, Adbeel,
Mibsam, ³⁰Mishma, Dumah,
Massa, Hadad, Tema, ³¹Jetur,
Naphish and Kedemah. All of
them were Ishmael's sons.

THE FAMILY LINE OF KETURAH

³² Here are the sons that were born
to Abraham's concubine Ketu-
rah.
They were Zimran, Jokshan,
Medan, Midian, Ishbak and
Shuah.
The sons of Jokshan were
Sheba and Dedan.
³³ The sons of Midian were
Ephah, Epher, Hanoch, Abida
and Eldaah.
All of them came from Keturah.

THE FAMILY LINE OF SARAH

³⁴ Abraham was the father of Isaac.
The sons of Isaac were
Esau and Israel.

THE FAMILY LINE OF ESAU

³⁵ The sons of Esau were
Eliphaz, Reuel, Jeush, Jalam
and Korah.
³⁶ The sons of Eliphaz were
Teman, Omar, Zepho, Gatam
and Kenaz.
Timna had Amalek by Eliphaz.
³⁷ The sons of Reuel were
Nahath, Zerah, Shammah and
Mizzah.

THE PEOPLE OF SEIR IN EDOM

³⁸ The sons of Seir were
Lotan, Shobal, Zibeon, Anah,
Dishon, Ezer and Dishan.
³⁹ The sons of Lotan were
Hori and Homam. Timna was
Lotan's sister.
⁴⁰ The sons of Shobal were
Alvan, Manahath, Ebal, Shepho
and Onam.
The sons of Zibeon were

Aiah and Anah.
⁴¹The son of Anah was
Dishon.
The sons of Dishon were
Hemdan, Eshban, Ithran and
Keran.
⁴²The sons of Ezer were
Bilhan, Zaavan and Akan.
The sons of Dishan were
Uz and Aran.

THE RULERS OF EDOM

⁴³Before Israel had a king, there
were kings who ruled in Edom.
Bela was the son of Beor. Bela's
city was called Dinhabah.
⁴⁴When Bela died, Jobab became
the next king. Jobab was the son
of Zerah from Bozrah.
⁴⁵When Jobab died, Husham became the next king. Husham
was from the land of the people
of Teman.
⁴⁶When Husham died, Hadad became the next king. Hadad was
the son of Bedad. Hadad had
won the battle over Midian in
the country of Moab. Hadad's
city was called Avith.
⁴⁷When Hadad died, Samlah became the next king. Samlah was
from Masrekah.
⁴⁸When Samlah died, Shaul became the next king. Shaul was
from Rehoboth on the river.
⁴⁹When Shaul died, Baal-Hanan
became the next king. Baal-Hanan was the son of Acbor.
⁵⁰When Baal-Hanan died, Hadad
became the next king. Hadad's
city was called Pau. His wife's
name was Mehetabel. She was
the daughter of Matred. Matred
was the daughter of Me-Zahab.
⁵¹Hadad also died.

The chiefs of Edom were
Timna, Alvah, Jetheth, ⁵²Oholi-
bamah, Elah, Pinon, ⁵³Kenaz,
Teman, Mibzar, ⁵⁴Magdiel and
Iram. They were the chiefs of
Edom.

THE SONS OF ISRAEL

2 Here are the names of the sons
of Israel.

Reuben, Simeon, Levi, Judah,
Issachar, Zebulun, ²Dan, Jo-
seph, Benjamin, Naphtali, Gad,
Asher.

THE FAMILY LINE OF JUDAH

THE FAMILY LINE FROM JUDAH'S SONS TO HEZRON'S SONS

³The sons of Judah were
Er, Onan and Shelah. A woman
from Canaan had those three
sons by him. She was the
daughter of Shua. Er was
Judah's oldest son. He was evil
in the LORD's eyes. So the LORD
put him to death. ⁴Tamar was
Judah's daughter-in-law. She
had Perez and Zerah by him.
The total number of Judah's
sons was five.
⁵The sons of Perez were
Hezron and Hamul.
⁶The sons of Zerah were
Zimri, Ethan, Heman, Calcol
and Darda. The total number of
Zerah's sons was five.
⁷The son of Carmi was Achar.
He brought trouble on Israel.
He took some of the things that
had been set apart to the LORD
in a special way to be destroyed.
When he did that, he disobeyed
the LORD's command.
⁸The son of Ethan was
Azariah.
⁹Hezron was the father of
Jerahmeel, Ram and Caleb.

THE FAMILY LINE OF RAM

¹⁰Ram was the father of
Amminadab. Amminadab was
the father of Nahshon. Nahshon was the leader of the people of Judah. ¹¹Nahshon was the
father of Salmon. Salmon was
the father of Boaz. ¹²Boaz was
the father of Obed. And Obed
was the father of Jesse.
¹³Jesse's first son was
Eliab. His second son was Abinadab. The third was Shimea.
¹⁴The fourth was Nethanel. The
fifth was Raddai. ¹⁵The sixth
was Ozem. And the seventh was
David. ¹⁶Their sisters were Zer-

uiah and Abigail. Zeruiah's three sons were Abishai, Joab and Asahel. ¹⁷Abigail was the mother of Amasa. Amasa's father was Jether. Jether belonged to the family line of Ishmael.

THE FAMILY LINE OF CALEB

¹⁸Caleb was the son of Hezron. Caleb's wife Azubah had children by him. Jerioth also had children by him. Azubah's sons were Jesher, Shobab and Ardon. ¹⁹When Azubah died, Caleb got married to Ephrath. She had Hur by him. ²⁰Hur was the father of Uri. And Uri was the father of Bezalel.

²¹Later, Hezron made love to the daughter of Makir. He had gotten married to her when he was 60 years old. She had Segub by him. Makir was the father of Gilead. ²²Segub was the father of Jair. Jair controlled 23 towns in Gilead. ²³But Geshur and Aram captured Havvoth Jair. They also captured Kenath and the settlements that were around it. The total number of towns that were captured was 60. Hezron, Segub and Jair belonged to the family line of Makir. Makir was the father of Gilead.

²⁴Hezron died in Caleb Ephrathah. Abijah was Hezron's wife. She had Ashhur by him. Ashhur was born after Hezron died. Ashhur was the father of Tekoa.

THE FAMILY LINE OF JERAHMEEL

²⁵Here are the sons of Jerahmeel. He was the oldest son of Hezron. Ram was Jerahmeel's oldest son. Then came Bunah, Oren, Ozem and Ahijah. ²⁶Jerahmeel had another wife. Her name was Atarah. She was the mother of Onam.

²⁷Here are the sons of Ram. He was the oldest son of Jerahmeel. The sons of Ram were Maaz, Jamin and Eker.

²⁸The sons of Onam were

Will people write about us in a special Bible, too?

The Bible tells about many people. Their names are there for all to see. But the Bible was written long ago, and it is complete. It is more than a bunch of stories about people who lived a long time ago. It is God's message about Jesus, and it tells how you should live today. The Bible also tells us about the future, not just the past. The Bible tells you that those who believe in Jesus have their names written in the "Lamb's Book of Life." It is not a Bible, but it is another book that God has. It lists the name of everyone who will live with God in heaven. If you love Jesus, there is a place in that book for your name.

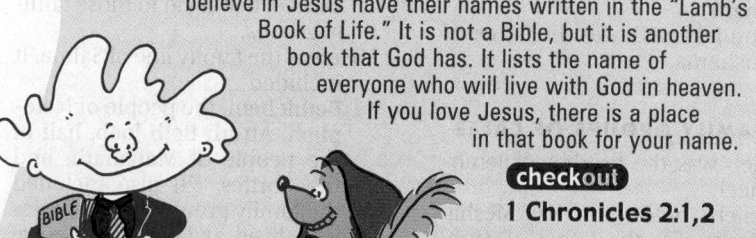

checkout

1 Chronicles 2:1,2

Related verse:
Revelation 21:27

Shammai and Jada.
The sons of Shammai were
Nadab and Abishur.
29 Abishur's wife was named Abihail. She had Ahban and Molid by him.
30 The sons of Nadab were
Seled and Appaim. Seled died without having any children.
31 The son of Appaim was
Ishi. Ishi was the father of Sheshan.
Sheshan was the father of Ahlai.
32 The sons of Jada were
Jether and Jonathan. Jada was Shammai's brother. Jether died without having any children.
33 The sons of Jonathan were
Peleth and Zaza.
They belonged to the family line of Jerahmeel.
34 Sheshan didn't have any sons. All he had was daughters.
He had a servant from Egypt named Jarha. 35 Sheshan gave his daughter to be married to his servant Jarha. She had Attai by Jarha.
36 Attai was the father of Nathan.
Nathan was the father of Zabad.
37 Zabad was the father of Ephlal.
Ephlal was the father of Obed.
38 Obed was the father of Jehu.
Jehu was the father of Azariah.
39 Azariah was the father of Helez.
Helez was the father of Eleasah.
40 Eleasah was the father of Sismai.
Sismai was the father of Shallum.
41 Shallum was the father of Jekamiah.
And Jekamiah was the father of Elishama.

THE FAMILY GROUPS OF CALEB

42 Caleb was the brother of Jerahmeel.
Caleb's oldest son was Mesha. Mesha was the father of Ziph. Caleb had another son named Mareshah. Mareshah was the father of Hebron.
43 The sons of Hebron were
Korah, Tappuah, Rekem and Shema. 44 Shema was the father

of Raham. Raham was the father of Jorkeam. Rekem was the father of Shammai. 45 The son of Shammai was Maon. Maon was the father of Beth Zur.
46 Caleb had a concubine named Ephah. She was the mother of Haran, Moza and Gazez. Haran was the father of Gazez.
47 The sons of Jahdai were
Regem, Jotham, Geshan, Pelet, Ephah and Shaaph.
48 Caleb had a concubine named Maacah. She was the mother of Sheber and Tirhanah. 49 She was also the mother of Shaaph and Sheva. Shaaph was the father of Madmannah. Sheva was the father of Macbenah and Gibea. Caleb's daughter was Acsah.
50 All of them belonged to the family line of Caleb.

Hur was the oldest son of Ephrathah.
Hur was the brother of Shobal. Shobal was the father of Kiriath Jearim. 51 Hur was the father of Salma. Salma was the father of Bethlehem. Hur was also the father of Hareph. Hareph was the father of Beth Gader.
52 Here is the family line of Shobal, the father of Kiriath Jearim. It included
Haroeh and half of the people of Manahath. 53 It also included the family groups of Kiriath Jearim. They were the Ithrites, Puthites, Shumathites and Mishraites. The people of Zorah and Eshtaol belonged to those family groups.
54 Here is the family line of Salma. It included
Bethlehem, the people of Netophah, Atroth Beth Joab, half of the people of Manahath, and the Zorites. 55 It also included the family groups of secretaries who lived at Jabez. They were the Tirathites, Shimeathites and Sucathites. They were the Kenites who belonged to the family line of Hammath. Hammath was the father of the family line of Recab.

THE SONS OF DAVID

3 Here are the sons of David who were born to him in Hebron. His first son was Amnon. Amnon's mother was Ahinoam from Jezreel.

The second son was Daniel. His mother was Abigail from Carmel.

2 The third son was Absalom. His mother was Maacah. She was the daughter of Talmai, the king of Geshur.

The fourth son was Adonijah. His mother was Haggith.

3 The fifth son was Shephatiah. His mother was Abital.

The sixth son was Ithream. David's wife Eglah had Ithream by him.

4 Those six sons were born to David in Hebron. He ruled there for seven and a half years.

After that, he ruled in Jerusalem for 33 years. 5 Children were born to him there.

They included Shammua, Shobab, Nathan and Solomon. The mother of those four sons was Bathsheba. She was the daughter of Ammiel. 6 David's children also included Ibhar, Elishua, Eliphelet, 7 Nogah, Nepheg, Japhia, 8 Elishama, Eliada and Eliphelet. There were nine of them. 9 David was the father of all of those sons. His concubines also had sons by him. David's sons had a sister named Tamar.

THE KINGS OF JUDAH

10 Solomon's son was Rehoboam.
Abijah was the son of Rehoboam.
Asa was the son of Abijah.
Jehoshaphat was the son of Asa.
11 Jehoram was the son of Jehoshaphat.
Ahaziah was the son of Jehoram.
Joash was the son of Ahaziah.
12 Amaziah was the son of Joash.
Azariah was the son of Amaziah.
Jotham was the son of Azariah.
13 Ahaz was the son of Jotham.
Hezekiah was the son of Ahaz.
Manasseh was the son of Hezekiah.
14 Amon was the son of Manasseh.
Josiah was the son of Amon.
15 Josiah's first son was Johanan.
Jehoiakim was his second son.
Zedekiah was the third son.
Shallum was the fourth son.
16 The next king after Jehoiakim was his son Jehoiachin.
After that, Josiah's son Zedekiah became king.

THE ROYAL FAMILY LINE AFTER JEHOIACHIN

17 Here are the members of the family line of Jehoiachin. He was taken as a prisoner to Babylon.
His sons were Shealtiel, 18 Malkiram, Pedaiah, Shenazzar, Jekamiah, Hoshama and Nedabiah.
19 The sons of Pedaiah were Zerubbabel and Shimei.
The sons of Zerubbabel were Meshullam and Hananiah.
Shelomith was their sister.
20 There were also five other sons. They were Hashubah, Ohel, Berekiah, Hasadiah and Jushab-Hesed.
21 The family line of Hananiah included
Pelatiah and Jeshaiah. It also included the sons of Rephaiah, Arnan, Obadiah and Shecaniah.
22 The family line of Shecaniah included
Shemaiah and his sons.
They were Hattush, Igal, Bariah, Neariah and Shaphat.
The total number of men was six.
23 The sons of Neariah were Elioenai, Hizkiah and Azrikam.
The total number of sons was three.
24 The sons of Elioenai were Hodaviah, Eliashib, Pelaiah, Akkub, Johanan, Delaiah and Anani. The total number of sons was seven.

OTHER FAMILY GROUPS OF JUDAH

4 The family line of Judah included Perez, Hezron, Carmi, Hur and Shobal.

[2] Reaiah was the son of Shobal and the father of Jahath. Jahath was the father of Ahumai and Lahad. Those were the family groups of the people of Zorah.

[3] The sons of Etam were Jezreel, Ishma and Idbash. Their sister was named Hazzelelponi. [4] Penuel was the father of Gedor. Ezer was the father of Hushah.

Those people belonged to the family line of Hur. He was the oldest son of Ephrathah and the father of Bethlehem.

[5] Ashhur was the father of Tekoa. Ashhur had two wives. Their names were Helah and Naarah.

[6] Naarah had Ahuzzam, Hepher, Temeni and Haahashtari by Ashhur. They belonged to the family line of Naarah.

[7] The sons of Helah were Zereth, Zohar, Ethnan [8] and Koz. Koz was the father of Anub and Hazzobebah. He was also the father of the family groups of Aharhel. Aharhel was the son of Harum.

[9] Jabez was more respected than his brothers. His mother had named him Jabez. She had said, "I was in a lot of pain when he was born."

[10] Jabez cried out to the God of Israel. He said, "I wish you would bless me. I wish you would give me more territory. Let your powerful hand be with me. Keep me from harm. Then I won't have any pain." God gave him what he asked for.

[11] Kelub was the brother of Shuhah and the father of Mehir. Mehir was the father of Eshton. [12] Eshton was the father of Beth Rapha, Paseah and Tehinnah. Tehinnah was the father of Ir Nahash. Those were the men of Recah.

[13] The sons of Kenaz were Othniel and Seraiah.

The sons of Othniel were Hathath and Meonothai. [14] Meonothai was the father of Ophrah.

Seraiah was the father of Joab. Joab was the father of Ge Harashim. Ge Harashim was called by that name because all of its people were skilled workers.

[15] The sons of Caleb were Iru, Elah and Naam. Caleb was the son of Jephunneh.

The son of Elah was Kenaz.

[16] The sons of Jehallelel were Ziph, Ziphah, Tiria and Asarel.

[17] The sons of Ezrah were Jether, Mered, Epher and Jalon. One of Mered's wives had Miriam, Shammai and Ishbah by him. Ishbah was the father of Eshtemoa. [18] Those were the children of Pharaoh's daughter Bithiah. Mered had gotten married to her. His wife from Judah had Jered, Heber and Jekuthiel by him. Jered was the father of Gedor. Heber was the father of Soco. Jekuthiel was the father of Zanoah.

[19] Hodiah's wife was the sister of Naham. Her sons were the father of Keilah the Garmite and Eshtemoa the Maacathite.

[20] The sons of Shimon were Amnon, Rinnah, Ben-Hanan and Tilon.

The family line of Ishi included Zoheth and Ben-Zoheth.

[21] Shelah was the son of Judah. The sons of Shelah were Er and Laadah. Er was the father of Lecah. Laadah was the father of Mareshah. He was also the father of the family groups of the linen workers who lived in Beth Ashbea. [22] Other sons of Shelah were Jokim, Joash, Saraph and the men of Cozeba. Moab and Jashubi Lehem were ruled by sons of Shelah. The records of all of those matters are very old. [23] Some of Shelah's sons were potters who lived in Netaim and Gederah. They stayed there and worked for the king.

THE FAMILY LINE OF SIMEON

24 The family line of Simeon included

Nemuel, Jamin, Jarib, Zerah and Shaul.
25 Shallum was Shaul's son. Mibsam was Shallum's son. Mishma was Mibsam's son.
26 The family line of Mishma included Hammuel. Hammuel was Mishma's son. Zaccur was Hammuel's son. Shimei was Zaccur's son.

27 Shimei had 16 sons and six daughters. But his brothers didn't have many children. So their whole family group didn't have as many people as Judah had. 28 Shimei's family group lived in Beersheba, Moladah, Hazar Shual, 29 Bilhah, Ezem, Tolad, 30 Bethuel, Hormah, Ziklag, 31 Beth Marcaboth, Hazar Susim, Beth Biri and Shaaraim. Those were their towns until David became king. 32 Five of the villages that were around those towns were Etam, Ain, Rimmon, Token and Ashan. 33 The territory of all of the villages that were around those towns reached all the way to Baalath. Those were their settlements. The tribe of Simeon kept its own family history.

34 Simeon's family line included Meshobab, Jamlech and Joshah. Joshah was the son of Amaziah. 35 Simeon's family line also included Joel and Jehu. Jehu was the son of Joshibiah. Joshibiah was the son of Seraiah. Seraiah was the son of Asiel. 36 And the family line included Elioenai, Jaakobah, Jeshohaiah, Asaiah, Adiel, Jesimiel, Benaiah 37 and Ziza. Ziza was the son of Shiphi. Shiphi was the son of Allon. Allon was the son of Jedaiah. Jedaiah was the son of Shimri. And Shimri was the son of Shemaiah.

38 The men whose names are listed above were leaders of their family groups. Their families greatly increased their numbers.
39 They spread out all the way to the edge of Gedor east of the valley. They looked for grasslands for their flocks.
40 They found grasslands that were rich and good. The land had plenty of room. It was peaceful and quiet. Some of the people of Ham had lived there before.
41 The men whose names are listed lived at the time when Hezekiah was king of Judah. They came and attacked the Hamites in their homes. They also attacked the Meunites who were there. And they completely destroyed them. What happened to them is clear even to this very day. The men of Simeon settled down where the Meunites had lived. They had enough grasslands for their flocks.
42 Five hundred of those men came into the hill country of Seir and attacked it. They were led by Pelatiah, Neariah, Rephaiah and Uzziel. Those four men were the sons of Ishi. 43 They killed the rest of the Amalekites who had escaped. And they still live there to this very day.

THE FAMILY LINE OF REUBEN

5 Here is a list of the sons of Reuben. First, here are a few things about him. Reuben was the oldest son of Israel. But he had sex with his father's concubine. He made his father's bed "unclean." That's why his rights as the oldest son were given to the sons of Joseph, the son of Israel. So Reuben isn't listed in the family history as the one who had the rights of the oldest son. 2 Judah was the leader among his brothers. A ruler came from his family line. But the rights of the oldest son belonged to Joseph. 3 Reuben was the oldest son of Israel. Reuben's sons were

Hanoch, Pallu, Hezron and Carmi.
4 The family line of Joel includes his son Shemaiah. Gog was the son of Shemaiah.
Shimei was the son of Gog.
5 Micah was the son of Shimei. Reaiah was the son of Micah. Baal was the son of Reaiah.
6 And Beerah was the son of Baal. Beerah was a leader of the people of Reuben. Tiglath-Pileser took Beerah as a prisoner to another country. Tiglath-Pileser was the king of Assyria.
7 Here are the relatives of the fam-

ily groups of Reuben. They are listed in their family history.

They include Chief Jeiel, Zechariah [8]and Bela. Bela was the son of Azaz. Azaz was the son of Shema. Shema was the son of Joel. All of them settled in the area from Aroer to Nebo and Baal Meon. [9]To the east they settled in the land up to the edge of the desert. That desert reaches all the way to the Euphrates River. They settled there because their livestock had increased their numbers in Gilead.

[10]While Saul was king, the people of Reuben went to war against the Hagrites. They won the battle over them. Then they settled down in their houses. They settled through the entire area east of Gilead.

THE FAMILY LINE OF GAD

[11]The people of Gad lived next to the people of Reuben in Bashan. They spread out all the way to Salecah.
[12]Joel was their chief. Shapham was next. Then came Janai and Shaphat in Bashan.
[13]Here are their relatives family by family. They included Michael, Meshullam, Sheba, Jorai, Jacan, Zia and Eber. The total number of them was seven.
[14]Those were the sons of Abihail. Abihail was the son of Huri. Huri was the son of Jaroah. Jaroah was the son of Gilead. Gilead was the son of Michael. Michael was the son of Jeshishai. Jeshishai was the son of Jahdo. And Jahdo was the son of Buz.
[15]Ahi was the leader of some of the families of Gad. Ahi was the son of Abdiel. Abdiel was the son of Guni.
[16]The people of Gad lived in the land of Gilead. They lived in the villages of Bashan. They also lived on all of the grasslands of Sharon as far as they reached.
[17]All of those names were written down in the family history. They were

written during the time when Jotham was king of Judah and Jeroboam was king of Israel.

[18]The tribes of Reuben and Gad and half of the tribe of Manasseh had 44,760 men who were able to serve in the army. They were able to handle a shield and sword. They were also able to use a bow. They were trained for battle. [19]They went to war against the Hagrites, Jetur, Naphish and Nodab. [20]God helped his people fight against the Hagrites and all who were helping them. He handed all of those enemies over to his people. That's because they cried out to him during the battle. He answered their prayers, because they trusted in him.

[21]They captured the livestock of the Hagrites. They captured 50,000 camels, 250,000 sheep and 2,000 donkeys. They also took 100,000 people as prisoners. [22]Many others were killed, because God won the battle over them. His people lived in the land until they themselves were taken as prisoners to other countries.

THE FAMILY LINE OF HALF OF THE TRIBE OF MANASSEH

[23]The people in half of the tribe of Manasseh greatly increased their numbers. They settled in the land from Bashan to Baal Hermon. Baal Hermon is also called Senir. Another name for it is Mount Hermon.

[24]Here are the leaders of their families. They included Epher, Ishi, Eliel, Azriel, Jeremiah, Hodaviah and Jahdiel. They were brave fighting men. They were famous. They were the leaders of their families. [25]But they weren't faithful to the God of their people. They joined themselves to the gods of the nations of the land and worshiped them. God had destroyed those nations to make room for his people.

[26]So the God of Israel stirred up the spirit of Pul. He was king of Assyria. He was also called Tiglath-Pileser. He took the tribes of Reuben and Gad and half of the tribe of Manasseh to other countries as his prisoners. He took them to Halah, Habor, Hara and the river of Gozan. And that's where they still are to this very day.

THE FAMILY LINE OF LEVI

6 The sons of Levi were Gershon, Kohath and Merari.
2 The sons of Kohath were Amram, Izhar, Hebron and Uzziel.
3 Aaron, Moses and Miriam were born in the family line of Amram.

The sons of Aaron were Nadab, Abihu, Eleazar and Ithamar.
4 Eleazar was the father of Phinehas.

Phinehas was the father of Abishua.
5 Abishua was the father of Bukki.

Bukki was the father of Uzzi.
6 Uzzi was the father of Zerahiah.

Zerahiah was the father of Meraioth.
7 Meraioth was the father of Amariah.

Amariah was the father of Ahitub.
8 Ahitub was the father of Zadok.

Zadok was the father of Ahimaaz.
9 Ahimaaz was the father of Azariah.

Azariah was the father of Johanan.
10 Johanan was the father of Azariah. Azariah served as priest in the temple Solomon built in Jerusalem.
11 Azariah was the father of Amariah.

Amariah was the father of Ahitub.
12 Ahitub was the father of Zadok.

Zadok was the father of Shallum.
13 Shallum was the father of Hilkiah.

Hilkiah was the father of Azariah.
14 Azariah was the father of Seraiah.

And Seraiah was the father of Jehozadak.
15 Jehozadak was taken away from his own land. The LORD took the people of Judah and Jerusalem to Babylonia. He used Nebuchadnezzar to take them there as prisoners.

16 The sons of Levi were Gershon, Kohath and Merari.
17 The names of the sons of Gershon were Libni and Shimei.
18 The sons of Kohath were Amram, Izhar, Hebron and Uzziel.
19 The sons of Merari were Mahli and Mushi.

Here are the members of the family groups of the Levites. They are listed under the names of their fathers.
20 Gershon was the father of Libni.

Jahath was Libni's son.

Zimmah was Jahath's son.
21 Joah was Zimmah's son.

Iddo was Joah's son.

Zerah was Iddo's son.

And Jeatherai was Zerah's son.
22 The family line of Kohath included his son Amminadab.

Korah was Amminadab's son.

Assir was Korah's son.
23 Elkanah was Assir's son.

Ebiasaph was Elkanah's son.

Assir was Ebiasaph's son.
24 Tahath was Assir's son.

Uriel was Tahath's son.

Uzziah was Uriel's son.

And Shaul was Uzziah's son.
25 The family line of Elkanah included his son Amasai.

Amasai was the father of Ahimoth.
26 Elkanah was Ahimoth's son.

Zophai was Elkanah's son.

Nahath was Zophai's son.
27 Eliab was Nahath's son.

Jeroham was Eliab's son.

Elkanah was Jeroham's son.

And Samuel was Elkanah's son.
28 The sons of Samuel were his first son Joel and his second son Abijah.
29 The family line of Merari included his son Mahli.

Libni was Mahli's son.

Shimei was Libni's son.

Uzzah was Shimei's son.
30 Shimea was Uzzah's son.

Haggiah was Shimea's son.

And Asaiah was Haggiah's son.

THE LEVITES WHO WERE IN CHARGE OF THE MUSIC

³¹Here are the Levites David put in charge of the music in the house of the LORD. He did it after the ark was placed there. ³²The men used their music to serve in front of the holy tent, the Tent of Meeting. They served there until Solomon built the temple of the LORD in Jerusalem. They did their work based on the rules they had been given.

³³Here are the men who served. The list also includes their sons.

The family line of Kohath included

Heman. He led the music.
He was the son of Joel.
Joel was the son of Samuel.
³⁴Samuel was the son of Elkanah.
Elkanah was the son of Jeroham.
Jeroham was the son of Eliel.
Eliel was the son of Toah.
³⁵Toah was the son of Zuph.
Zuph was the son of Elkanah.
Elkanah was the son of Mahath.
Mahath was the son of Amasai.
³⁶Amasai was the son of Elkanah.
Elkanah was the son of Joel.
Joel was the son of Azariah.
Azariah was the son of Zephaniah.
³⁷Zephaniah was the son of Tahath.
Tahath was the son of Assir.
Assir was the son of Ebiasaph.
Ebiasaph was the son of Korah.
³⁸Korah was the son of Izhar.
Izhar was the son of Kohath.
Kohath was the son of Levi.
And Levi was the son of Israel.
³⁹Heman had a relative named Asaph. Asaph served as Heman's helper at his right side.
Asaph was the son of Berekiah.
Berekiah was the son of Shimea.
⁴⁰Shimea was the son of Michael.
Michael was the son of Baaseiah.
Baaseiah was the son of Malkijah.
⁴¹Malkijah was the son of Ethni.
Ethni was the son of Zerah.
Zerah was the son of Adaiah.
⁴²Adaiah was the son of Ethan.
Ethan was the son of Zimmah.
Zimmah was the son of Shimei.
⁴³Shimei was the son of Jahath.
Jahath was the son of Gershon.
And Gershon was the son of Levi.
⁴⁴Here are the Levites in the family line of Merari who served as Heman's helpers at his left side. They were relatives of the Kohathites.
Ethan was the son of Kishi.
Kishi was the son of Abdi.
Abdi was the son of Malluch.
⁴⁵Malluch was the son of Hashabiah.
Hashabiah was the son of Amaziah.
Amaziah was the son of Hilkiah.
⁴⁶Hilkiah was the son of Amzi.
Amzi was the son of Bani.
Bani was the son of Shemer.
⁴⁷Shemer was the son of Mahli.
Mahli was the son of Mushi.
Mushi was the son of Merari.
And Merari was the son of Levi.

⁴⁸The rest of the Levites were appointed to do all of the other work at the holy tent. It was the house of God.

⁴⁹Aaron and his sons after him brought the offerings. They sacrificed them on the altar of burnt offering. They also burned incense on the altar of incense. That was part of what they did in the Most Holy Room. That's how they paid for the sin of Israel. They did everything just as Moses, the servant of God, had commanded.

⁵⁰Here are the members of the family line of Aaron.
Eleazar was Aaron's son.
Phinehas was Eleazar's son.
Abishua was Phinehas's son.
⁵¹Bukki was Abishua's son.
Uzzi was Bukki's son.
Zerahiah was Uzzi's son.
⁵²Meraioth was Zerahiah's son.
Amariah was Meraioth's son.
Ahitub was Amariah's son.
⁵³Zadok was Ahitub's son.
And Ahimaaz was Zadok's son.

⁵⁴Here were the places where they settled. They were given to them as their territory. Some were given to the

children of Aaron who were from the family group of Kohath. They were given out by using lots. The first lot was for Kohath.

⁵⁵The Kohathites were given Hebron in Judah. They also received the grasslands that were around Hebron. ⁵⁶But the fields and villages that were around the city were given to Caleb, the son of Jephunneh.

⁵⁷So the people in the family line of Aaron received Hebron. It was a city where people could go for safety. Aaron's family line received Libnah, Jattir, Eshtemoa, ⁵⁸Hilen and Debir. ⁵⁹They also received Ashan, Juttah and Beth Shemesh. They were given all of those towns together with their grasslands. ⁶⁰From the tribe of Benjamin they received Gibeon, Geba, Alemeth and Anathoth. They received those towns together with their grasslands.

All of those towns were handed out to the family groups of Kohath. The total number of towns was 13.

⁶¹The rest of the members of the family line of Kohath were given ten towns. The towns were from the family groups of half of the tribe of Manasseh.

⁶²The members of the family line of Gershon were given 13 towns. They received them family group by family group. Most of the towns were from the tribes of Issachar, Asher and Naphtali. The rest were from the other half of the tribe of Manasseh. It's in Bashan.

⁶³The members of the family line of Merari were given 12 towns. They received them family group by family group. The towns were from the tribes of Reuben, Gad and Zebulun.

⁶⁴So the people of Israel gave the Levites all of those towns and their grasslands. ⁶⁵They gave other towns to them from the tribes of Judah, Simeon and Benjamin.

⁶⁶Some of the family groups of Kohath were given towns from the tribe of Ephraim as their territory.

⁶⁷In the hill country of Ephraim they received Shechem. Shechem was a city where people could go

for safety. The Kohathites also received Gezer, ⁶⁸Jokmeam, Beth Horon, ⁶⁹Aijalon and Gath Rimmon. They were given all of those towns together with their grasslands.

⁷⁰From half of the tribe of Manasseh the people of Israel gave the towns of Aner and Bileam. They gave them to the rest of the family groups of Kohath. They gave them together with their grasslands.

⁷¹Here is what the members of the family line of Gershon were given.

They received Golan in Bashan and also Ashtaroth. They received them together with their grasslands.

They received them from half of the tribe of Manasseh.

⁷²From the tribe of Issachar they received Kedesh, Daberath, ⁷³Ramoth and Anem. They received them together with their grasslands.

⁷⁴From the tribe of Asher they received Mashal, Abdon, ⁷⁵Hukok and Rehob. They received them together with their grasslands.

⁷⁶From the tribe of Naphtali they received Kedesh in Galilee. They also received Hammon and Kiriathaim. They were given all of those towns together with their grasslands.

⁷⁷The members of the family line of Merari make up the rest of the Levites. Here is what they were given.

From the tribe of Zebulun they received Jokneam, Kartah, Rimmono and Tabor. They received them together with their grasslands.

⁷⁸The tribe of Reuben was across the Jordan River east of Jericho. From that tribe the Merarites received Bezer in the desert, Jahzah, ⁷⁹Kedemoth and Mephaath. They received them together with their grasslands.

⁸⁰From the tribe of Gad they received Ramoth in Gile-

ad. They also received Mahanaim, [81]Heshbon and Jazer. They
received all of those towns together with their grasslands.

THE FAMILY LINE OF ISSACHAR

7 The sons of Issachar were
Tola, Puah, Jashub and Shimron. The total number of sons
was four.
[2] The sons of Tola were
Uzzi, Rephaiah, Jeriel, Jahmai,
Ibsam and Samuel. They were
the leaders of their families.
The total number of fighting
men who were listed in the history of the family line of Tola
was 22,600. That was when David was king.
[3] The son of Uzzi was
Izrahiah.
The sons of Izrahiah were
Michael, Obadiah, Joel and Isshiah. All five of them were
chiefs. [4]Based on their family
history, 36,000 of their men
were ready for battle. That's because they had many wives and
children.
[5] The total number of fighting
men who belonged to all of the
family groups of Issachar was
87,000. The men were listed in
their family history.

THE FAMILY LINE OF BENJAMIN

[6] The three sons of Benjamin were
Bela, Beker and Jediael.
[7] The sons of Bela were
Ezbon, Uzzi, Uzziel, Jerimoth
and Iri. They were the leaders of
their families. The total number
of sons was five. Their family
history listed 22,034 fighting
men.
[8] The sons of Beker were
Zemirah, Joash, Eliezer, Elioenai, Omri, Jeremoth, Abijah,
Anathoth and Alemeth. All of
them were the sons of Beker.
[9]Their family history listed the
leaders of their families. It also
listed 20,200 fighting men.
[10] The son of Jediael was
Bilhan.

The sons of Bilhan were
Jeush, Benjamin, Ehud, Kenaanah, Zethan, Tarshish and
Ahishahar. [11]All of those sons of
Jediael were the leaders of their
families. There were 17,200
fighting men who were ready to
go to war.
[12] The Shuppites and Huppites belonged to the family line of Ir.
The Hushites belonged to the
family line of Aher.

THE FAMILY LINE OF NAPHTALI

[13] The sons of Naphtali were
Jahziel, Guni, Jezer and Shillem.
They belonged to the family
line of Bilhah.

THE FAMILY LINE OF MANASSEH

[14] Here is the family line of Manasseh.
He had a concubine who was
from the land of Aram. She had
Asriel and Makir by him. Makir
was the father of Gilead. [15]Makir
got married to a woman from
among the Huppites and Shuppites. He had a sister named
Maacah.
Another member of Manas-
seh's family line was Zelophehad. All he had was daughters.
[16]Makir's wife Maacah had a
son by him. She named the boy
Peresh. He had a brother
named Sheresh. The sons of
Sheresh were Ulam and Rakem.
[17] The son of Ulam was
Bedan.
Those were the members of the
family line of Makir, the son of
Manasseh. Gilead was the son
of Makir. [18]Gilead's sister was
Hammoleketh. She was the
mother of Ishhod, Abiezer and
Mahlah.
[19] The sons of Shemida were
Ahian, Shechem, Likhi and
Aniam.

THE FAMILY LINE OF EPHRAIM

[20] Here are the members of the
family line of Ephraim.

Shuthelah was Ephraim's son.
Bered was Shuthelah's son.
Tahath was Bered's son.
Eleadah was Tahath's son.
Tahath was Eleadah's son.
²¹ Zabad was Tahath's son.
And Shuthelah was Zabad's son.

Men from Gath killed Ezer and Elead when they went down to steal their livestock. ²²Their father Ephraim sobbed over them for many days. His relatives came to comfort him. ²³Then he made love to his wife. She became pregnant and had a baby boy. Ephraim named him Beriah. That's because something bad had happened in his family. ²⁴His daughter was Sheerah. She built Lower and Upper Beth Horon. She also built Uzzen Sheerah.

²⁵ Rephah was Beriah's son.
Resheph was Rephah's son.
Telah was Resheph's son.
Tahan was Telah's son.
²⁶ Ladan was Tahan's son.
Ammihud was Ladan's son.
Elishama was Ammihud's son.
²⁷ Nun was Elishama's son.
And Joshua was the son of Nun.

²⁸The lands and settlements of the members of Ephraim's line included Bethel and the villages that were around it. Naaran was on the east. Gezer and its villages were on the west. The lands and settlements included Shechem. They also included the villages that were around Shechem all the way to Ayyah and its villages. ²⁹Along the borders of Manasseh were Beth Shan, Taanach, Megiddo and Dor, together with their villages. The members of the family line of Joseph lived in those towns. Joseph was the son of Israel.

THE FAMILY LINE OF ASHER

³⁰ The sons of Asher were
Imnah, Ishvah, Ishvi and Beriah. They had a sister named Serah.
³¹ The sons of Beriah were
Heber and Malkiel. Malkiel was the father of Birzaith.
³² Heber was the father of Japhlet,
Shomer, Hotham and their sister Shua.
³³ The sons of Japhlet were
Pasach, Bimhal and Ashvath.
They were Japhlet's sons.
³⁴ The sons of Shomer were
Ahi, Rohgah, Hubbah and Aram.
³⁵ The sons of Shomer's brother Helem were
Zophah, Imna, Shelesh and Amal.
³⁶ The sons of Zophah were
Suah, Harnepher, Shual, Beri, Imrah, ³⁷Bezer, Hod, Shamma, Shilshah, Ithran and Beera.
³⁸ The sons of Jether were
Jephunneh, Pispah and Ara.
³⁹ The sons of Ulla were
Arah, Hanniel and Rizia.

⁴⁰All of them were members of the family line of Asher. They were the leaders of their families. They were fine men. They were brave fighting men. They were outstanding leaders. The total number of men who were ready for battle was 26,000. They were listed in their family history.

THE FAMILY HISTORY OF SAUL

8 Benjamin was the father of Bela. Bela was his first son. Ashbel was his second son. Aharah was the third.
² Nohah was the fourth. And Rapha was the fifth.
³ The sons of Bela were
Addar, Gera, Abihud, ⁴Abishua, Naaman, Ahoah, ⁵Gera, Shephuphan and Huram.
⁶ Here are the members of the family line of Ehud. They were the leaders of the families who were living in Geba. Later, they were taken away from their own land. They were forced to go to Manahath.
⁷ The sons of Ehud were Naaman, Ahijah and Gera. Gera took them away from their land. He was the father of Uzza and Ahihud.
⁸ Sons were born to Shaharaim in Moab. That happened after he had divorced his wives Hushim and Baara. ⁹His wife Hodesh

had sons by him. Their names were Jobab, Zibia, Mesha, Malcam, [10]Jeuz, Sakia and Mirmah. His sons were the leaders of their families. [11]His wife Hushim had Abitub and Elpaal by him.

[12]The sons of Elpaal were
Eber, Misham and Shemed. Shemed built Ono and Lod and the villages that were around it. [13]Beriah and Shema were also sons of Elpaal. They were the leaders of the families who were living in Aijalon. Beriah and Shema drove out the people who were living in Gath.

[14]Ahio, Shashak, Jeremoth, [15]Zebadiah, Arad, Eder, [16]Michael, Ishpah and Joha were the sons of Beriah.

[17]Zebadiah, Meshullam, Hizki, Heber, [18]Ishmerai, Izliah and Jobab were other sons of Elpaal.

[19]Jakim, Zicri, Zabdi, [20]Elienai, Zillethai, Eliel, [21]Adaiah, Beraiah and Shimrath were the sons of Shimei.

[22]Ishpan, Eber, Eliel, [23]Abdon, Zicri, Hanan, [24]Hananiah, Elam, Anthothijah, [25]Iphdeiah and Penuel were the sons of Shashak.

[26]Shamsherai, Shehariah, Athaliah, [27]Jaareshiah, Elijah and Zicri were the sons of Jeroham.

[28]All of those men were the leaders of their families. They were listed as chiefs in their family history. They lived in Jerusalem.

[29]Jeiel lived in the city of Gibeon. He was the father of Gibeon. Jeiel had a wife named Maacah. [30]His oldest son was Abdon. His other sons were Zur, Kish, Baal, Ner, Nadab, [31]Gedor, Ahio, Zeker [32]and Mikloth. Mikloth was the father of Shimeah. Mikloth and Shimeah also lived in Jerusalem. They lived near their relatives.

[33]Ner was the father of Kish. Kish was the father of Saul. Saul was the father of Jonathan, Malki-Shua, Abinadab and Esh-Baal.

[34]The son of Jonathan was Merib-Baal. Merib-Baal was the father of Micah.

[35]The sons of Micah were Pithon, Melech, Tarea and Ahaz.

[36]Ahaz was the father of Jehoaddah. Jehoaddah was the father of Alemeth, Azmaveth and Zimri. Zimri was the father of Moza.

[37]Moza was the father of Binea. Raphah was Binea's son. Eleasah was Raphah's son. And Azel was Eleasah's son.

[38]Azel had six sons. Their names were
Azrikam, Bokeru, Ishmael, Sheariah, Obadiah and Hanan. All of them were the sons of Azel.

[39]Here are the sons of Azel's brother Eshek.
Ulam was his first son. Jeush was the second. Eliphelet was the third. [40]The sons of Ulam were brave fighting men. They could handle a bow. They had many sons and grandsons. The total number of sons and grandsons was 150.

All of those men belonged to the family line of Benjamin.

9

The whole community of Israel was listed in their family histories. They were written down in the records of the kings of Israel.

THE PEOPLE WHO LIVED IN JERUSALEM

The people of Judah were taken away from their own land. They were taken as prisoners to Babylonia. That's because they weren't faithful to the LORD. [2]The first ones who came back from there were some Israelites, priests, Levites and temple servants. They settled down again in their own towns on their own property.

[3]Some of them lived in Jerusalem. They included people from Judah, Benjamin, Ephraim and Manasseh.

[4]They included Uthai. He was the son of Ammihud. Ammihud was the son of Omri. Omri was the son of Imri. Imri was the son of Bani. Bani belonged to the family line of Perez. Perez was the son of Judah.

5 The family line of Shelah included his oldest son Asaiah. It also included the sons of Asaiah.

6 The family line of Zerah included Jeuel.
The total number of the people of Judah was 690.

7 The family line of Benjamin included Sallu. He was the son of Meshullam. Meshullam was the son of Hodaviah. Hodaviah was the son of Hassenuah.

8 Ibneiah was the son of Jeroham. Elah was the son of Uzzi. Uzzi was the son of Micri. Meshullam was the son of Shephatiah. Shephatiah was the son of Reuel. Reuel was the son of Ibnijah.

9 The total number of the people of Benjamin was 956. They were listed in their family history. All of those men were the leaders of their families.

10 The family line of the priests included Jedaiah, Jehoiarib and Jakin.

11 It also included Azariah. He was the son of Hilkiah. Hilkiah was the son of Meshullam. Meshullam was the son of Zadok. Zadok was the son of Meraioth. Meraioth was the son of Ahitub. Azariah was the official who was in charge of the house of God.

12 Adaiah was the son of Jeroham. Jeroham was the son of Pashhur. Pashhur was the son of Malkijah. Maasai was the son of Adiel. Adiel was the son of Jahzerah. Jahzerah was the son of Meshullam. Meshullam was the son of Meshillemith. Meshillemith was the son of Immer.

13 The total number of priests was 1,760. They were the leaders of their families. They were able men. It was their duty to serve in the house of God.

14 The family line of the Levites included Shemaiah. He was the son of Hasshub. Hasshub was the son of Azrikam. Azrikam was the son of Hashabiah. Shemaiah belonged to the family line of Merari. 15 The family line

of the Levites also included Bakbakkar, Heresh, Galal and Mattaniah. Mattaniah was the son of Mica. Mica was the son of Zicri. Zicri was the son of Asaph. 16 Obadiah was the son of Shemaiah. Shemaiah was the son of Galal. Galal was the son of Jeduthun. Berekiah was the son of Asa. Asa was the son of Elkanah. He lived in the villages of the people of Netophah.

17 The men who guarded the gates were Shallum, Akkub, Talmon, Ahiman and other Levites. Shallum was their chief. 18 He was stationed at the King's Gate on the east side of the temple. That duty has continued to this very day. Those guards belonged to the camp of the Levites.

19 Shallum was the son of Kore. Kore was the son of Ebiasaph. Ebiasaph was the son of Korah. Shallum and the other Levites in his family belonged to the family line of Korah. They had the duty of guarding the entrances to the temple.
Their fathers had also had the duty of guarding the entrance to the house of the LORD. 20 Long ago Phinehas, the son of Eleazar, was in charge of those who guarded the gate. And the LORD was with him.

21 Zechariah guarded the entrance to the Tent of Meeting. He was the son of Meshelemiah.

22 The total number of the men who were chosen to guard the entrances was 212. They were listed in their family history in their villages. David and the prophet Samuel had appointed them to their positions. They appointed them because they trusted them.

23 Those Levites and their children after them were in charge of guarding the gates of the house of the LORD. The house of the LORD was also called the temple. 24 The men who guarded the gates were on the four sides of the temple. They were on the east, west, north and south sides. 25 From time to time, their relatives in their villages

had to come to the temple. They had to share their duties for a week at a time.

²⁶The four main men who guarded the gates were Levites. They were trusted with the duty of taking care of the storerooms and the other rooms in the house of God. ²⁷They spent the night in their positions around the house of God. That's because they had to guard it. They were in charge of the key that opened the temple each morning.

²⁸Some Levites were in charge of the articles that were used when they served at the temple. They counted the articles when they were brought in. They also counted them when they were taken out.

²⁹Other Levites were appointed to take care of all of the other articles that belonged to the temple. They also took care of the flour, wine, olive oil, incense and spices. ³⁰Some of the priests took care of mixing the spices.

³¹There was a Levite named Mattithiah. He was the oldest son of Shallum. Shallum belonged to the family line of Korah. Mattithiah was trusted with the duty of baking the offering bread. ³²The bread was placed on the table every Sabbath day. Some Levites in the family line of Kohath were in charge of preparing the bread.

³³Those who led the music lived in rooms in the temple. They were the leaders of their Levite families. Their only duty was to lead the music. They had to do that work day and night.

³⁴All of them were the leaders of their Levite families. They were listed as chiefs in their family history. They lived in Jerusalem.

THE FAMILY HISTORY OF SAUL

³⁵Jeiel lived in the city of Gibeon. He was the father of Gibeon. Jeiel had a wife named Maacah. ³⁶His oldest son was Abdon. His other sons were Zur, Kish, Baal, Ner, Nadab, ³⁷Gedor, Ahio, Zechariah and Mikloth. ³⁸Mikloth was the father of Shimeam. Mikloth and Shimeam lived in Jerusalem. They lived near their relatives.

³⁹Ner was the father of Kish. Kish was the father of Saul. Saul was the father of Jonathan, Malki-Shua, Abinadab and Esh-Baal.

⁴⁰The son of Jonathan was Merib-Baal. Merib-Baal was the father of Micah.

⁴¹The sons of Micah were Pithon, Melech, Tahrea and Ahaz.

⁴²Ahaz was the father of Jadah. Jadah was the father of Alemeth, Azmaveth and Zimri. Zimri was the father of Moza. ⁴³Moza was the father of Binea. Rephaiah was Binea's son. Eleasah was Rephaiah's son. And Azel was Eleasah's son.

⁴⁴Azel had six sons. Their names were Azrikam, Bokeru, Ishmael, Sheariah, Obadiah and Hanan. They were the sons of Azel.

SAUL TAKES HIS OWN LIFE

10 The Philistines fought against Israel. The men of Israel ran away from them. But many Israelites were killed on Mount Gilboa.

²The Philistines kept chasing Saul and his sons. They killed his sons Jonathan, Abinadab and Malki-Shua. ³The fighting was heavy around Saul. Men who were armed with bows and arrows caught up with him. They shot their arrows at him and wounded him badly.

⁴Saul spoke to the man who was carrying his armor. He said, "Pull out your sword. Stick it through me. If you don't, those men who aren't circumcised will come and hurt me badly."

But the man was terrified. He wouldn't do it. So Saul took his own sword and fell on it. ⁵The man saw that Saul was dead. So he fell on his own sword and died. ⁶Saul and his three sons died. All of them died together.

⁷All of the Israelites who lived in the valley saw that their army had run away. They saw that Saul and his sons were dead. So they left their towns and ran away. Then the Philistines came and settled down in them.

⁸The day after the Philistines had won the battle, they came to take what

they wanted from the dead bodies. They found Saul and his sons dead on Mount Gilboa. [9]So they took what they wanted from Saul's body. They took his head and his armor. Then they sent messengers through the whole land of the Philistines. They announced the news to the statues of their gods. They also announced it among their people. [10]They put Saul's armor in the temple of their gods. They hung his head up in the temple of their god Dagon.

[11]The people of Jabesh Gilead heard about everything the Philistines had done to Saul. [12]So all of their brave men went and got the bodies of Saul and his sons. They brought them to Jabesh. Then they buried the bones of Saul and his sons under the great tree that was there. They didn't eat anything for seven days.

[13]Saul died because he wasn't faithful to the LORD. He didn't obey the word of the LORD. He even asked for advice from a person who gets messages from those who have died. [14]He didn't ask the LORD for advice. So the LORD put him to death. He turned the kingdom over to David. David was the son of Jesse.

DAVID BECOMES KING OVER ISRAEL

11 The whole community of Israel came together to see David at Hebron. They said, "We are your own flesh and blood. [2]In the past, Saul was our king. But you led the men of Israel in battle. The LORD your God said to you, 'You will be the shepherd over my people Israel. You will become their ruler.' "

[3]All of the elders of Israel came to see King David at Hebron. There he made a covenant with them in the sight of the LORD. They anointed David as king over Israel. It happened just as the LORD had promised through Samuel.

DAVID CAPTURES JERUSALEM

[4]David and all of the men of Israel marched to Jerusalem. Jerusalem was also called Jebus.

The Jebusites who lived there [5]spoke to David. They said, "You won't get in here."

But David captured the fort of Zion. It became known as the City of David.

[6]David had said, "Anyone who leads the attack against the Jebusites will become the commander of Israel's army." Joab went up first. So he became the commander of the army. He was the son of Zeruiah.

[7]David moved into the fort. So it was called the City of David. [8]He built up the city around the fort. He filled in the low places. He built a wall around it. During that time, Joab built up the rest of the city.

[9]David became more and more powerful. That's because the LORD who rules over all was with him.

DAVID'S MIGHTY MEN

[10]The chiefs of David's mighty men and the whole community of Israel helped David greatly. They helped him become king over the entire land. That's exactly what the LORD had promised him. [11]Here is a list of David's mighty men.

Jashobeam was chief of the officers. He was a Hacmonite. He used his spear against 300 men. He killed all of them at one time.

[12]Next to him was Eleazar. He was one of the three mighty men. He was the son of Dodai, the Ahohite. [13]Jashobeam was with David at Pas Dammim. The Philistines had gathered there for battle. Israel's troops ran away from the Philistines. At the place where that happened, there was a field that was full of barley. [14]The three mighty men took their stand in the middle of the field. They didn't let the Philistines capture it. They struck them down. The LORD helped them win a great battle.

[15]David was near the rock at the cave of Adullam. Three of the 30 chiefs came down to him there. A group of Philistines was camped in the Valley of Rephaim. [16]At that time David was in his usual place of safety. Some Philistine troops were stationed at Bethlehem.

[17]David longed for water. He said, "I wish someone would get me a drink of water from the well that is near the gate of Bethlehem!"

[18]So the Three fought their way past

the Philistine guards. They got some water from the well that was near the gate of Bethlehem. They took the water back to David.

But David refused to drink it. Instead, he poured it out as a drink offering to the LORD. ¹⁹"I would never drink that water!" David said. "It would be like drinking the blood of these men. They put their lives in danger by going to Bethlehem." The men had put their lives in danger by bringing the water back. So David wouldn't drink it.

Those were some of the brave things the three mighty men did.

²⁰Abishai was chief over the Three. He was the brother of Joab. He used his spear against 300 men. He killed all of them. So he became as famous as the Three were. ²¹He was honored twice as much as the Three. He became their commander. But he wasn't included among them.

²²Benaiah was a great hero from Kabzeel. He was the son of Jehoiada. Benaiah did many brave things. He struck down two of Moab's best fighting men. He also went down into a pit on a snowy day. He killed a lion there. ²³And Benaiah struck down an Egyptian who was seven and a half feet tall. The Egyptian was holding a spear as big as a weaver's rod. Benaiah went out to fight against him with a club. He grabbed the spear out of the Egyptian's hand. Then he killed him with it. ²⁴Those were some of the brave things Benaiah, the son of Jehoiada, did. He too was as famous as the three mighty men were. ²⁵He was honored more than any of the Thirty. But he wasn't included among the Three. And David put him in charge of his own personal guards.

²⁶Here is a list of David's mighty men.

Asahel, the brother of Joab
Elhanan, the son of Dodo, from Bethlehem
²⁷Shammoth, the Harorite
Helez, the Pelonite
²⁸Ira, the son of Ikkesh, from Tekoa
Abiezer from Anathoth
²⁹Sibbecai, the Hushathite
Ilai, the Ahohite

³⁰Maharai from Netophah
Heled, the son of Baanah, from Netophah
³¹Ithai, the son of Ribai, from Gibeah in Benjamin
Benaiah from Pirathon
³²Hurai from the valleys of Gaash
Abiel, the Arbathite
³³Azmaveth, the Baharumite
Eliahba, the Shaalbonite
³⁴the sons of Hashem, the Gizonite
Jonathan, the son of Shagee, the Hararite
³⁵Ahiam, the son of Sacar, the Hararite
Eliphal, the son of Ur
³⁶Hepher, the Mekerathite
Ahijah, the Pelonite
³⁷Hezro from Carmel
Naarai, the son of Ezbai
³⁸Joel, the brother of Nathan
Mibhar, the son of Hagri
³⁹Zelek from Ammon
Naharai, from Beeroth, who carried the armor of Joab, the son of Zeruiah
⁴⁰Ira, the Ithrite
Gareb, the Ithrite
⁴¹Uriah, the Hittite
Zabad, the son of Ahlai
⁴²Adina, the son of Shiza, the Reubenite, who was chief of the Reubenites and the 30 men with him
⁴³Hanan, the son of Maacah
Joshaphat, the Mithnite
⁴⁴Uzzia, the Ashterathite
Shama and Jeiel, the sons of Hotham from Aroer
⁴⁵Jediael, the son of Shimri
his brother Joha, the Tizite
⁴⁶Eliel, the Mahavite
Jeribai and Joshaviah, the sons of Elnaam
Ithmah from Moab
⁴⁷Eliel
Obed
Jaasiel, the Mezobaite

FIGHTING MEN JOIN DAVID

12 Some fighting men came to David at Ziklag. They were among those who helped him in battle. David had been forced to hide from Saul, the son of Kish. ²The men were armed with bows.

They were able to shoot arrows or throw stones from a sling with either hand. They were relatives of Saul from the tribe of Benjamin. Here is a list of them.

³Their chief Ahiezer and Joash, the sons of Shemaah the Gibeathite
Jeziel and Pelet, the sons of Azmaveth
Beracah
Jehu from Anathoth
⁴Ishmaiah, the Gibeonite, who was a mighty man among the Thirty and a leader of the Thirty
Jeremiah
Jahaziel
Johanan
Jozabad from Gederah
⁵Eluzai
Jerimoth
Bealiah
Shemariah
Shephatiah, the Haruphite
⁶the Korahites Elkanah, Isshiah, Azarel, Joezer and Jashobeam
⁷Joelah and Zebadiah, the sons of Jeroham from Gedor

⁸Some men of Gad went over to David's side at his usual place of safety in the desert. They were brave fighting men. They were ready for battle. They were able to use shields and spears. Their faces were like the faces of lions. They could run as fast as antelopes in the mountains.
⁹Ezer was their chief.
Obadiah was next in command.
Eliab was third.
¹⁰Mishmannah was fourth. Jeremiah was fifth.
¹¹Attai was sixth. Eliel was seventh.
¹²Johanan was eighth. Elzabad was ninth.
¹³Jeremiah was tenth. And Macbannai was eleventh.
¹⁴All of those men of Gad were army commanders. The least important of them was equal to 100 men. The most important was equal to 1,000.
¹⁵They went across the Jordan River when it was flowing over its banks. That happened in the first month of spring. They chased away everyone who lived in the valleys. They chased them away from the east and west sides of the river.
¹⁶Some men from the territories of Benjamin and Judah also came to David at his usual place of safety.
¹⁷David went out to meet them. He said to them, "Have you come to me in peace? Have you come to help me? If you have, I'm ready to have you join me. But suppose you have come to hand me over to my enemies when I haven't even harmed anyone. Then may the God of our people see it and judge you."
¹⁸The Spirit of God came on Amasai. He was chief of the Thirty. He said,

"David, we belong to you!
Son of Jesse, we're on your side!
May you have great success.
May those who help you also
have success.
Your God will help you."

So David welcomed them. He made them leaders in his army.
¹⁹Some men of Manasseh went over to David's side when he marched out with the Philistines to fight against Saul.
But David and his men didn't help the Philistines. That's because after all of the Philistine rulers had discussed the matter, they sent him away. They said, "Suppose he deserts to his master Saul. Then our heads will be cut off!"
²⁰So David went to Ziklag. Here are the men of Manasseh who went over to his side. They were Adnah, Jozabad, Jediael, Michael, Jozabad, Elihu and Zillethai. They were leaders of companies of 1,000 men in Manasseh. ²¹They helped David fight against enemy armies. All of the men of Manasseh were brave fighting men. They were commanders in David's army.
²²Day after day men came to help him. Soon he had a large army. It was like the army of God.

OTHER FIGHTING MEN JOIN DAVID AT HEBRON

²³Large numbers of men came to David at Hebron. They were prepared for battle. They came to hand Saul's kingdom over to him, just as the LORD

had said. Here are the numbers of the men who came.

²⁴ The men from Judah carried shields and spears. They were prepared for battle. The total number of them was 6,800.
²⁵ The fighting men from Simeon were ready for battle. The total number of them was 7,100.
²⁶ The total number of men from Levi was 4,600. ²⁷ They included Jehoiada. He was the leader of the family of Aaron. He came with 3,700 men. ²⁸ They also included Zadok. He was a brave young fighter. He came with 22 officers from his family.
²⁹ The men from Benjamin were Saul's relatives. Most of them had remained faithful to Saul's family until that time. The total number of them was 3,000.
³⁰ The men from Ephraim were brave fighting men. They were famous in their own family groups. The total number of them was 20,800.
³¹ The men from half of the tribe of Manasseh had been chosen by name to come and make David king. The total number of them was 18,000.
³² The men from Issachar understood what was going on at that time. They knew what Israel should do. The total number of their chiefs was 200. They came with all of their relatives who were under their command.
³³ The men from Zebulun knew how to fight well. That's because they had done it many times before. They were prepared for battle. They had every kind of weapon. They came to help David with their whole heart. The total number of them was 50,000.
³⁴ The total number of officers from Naphtali was 1,000. They came with 37,000 men who carried shields and spears.
³⁵ The men from Dan were ready

for battle. The total number of them was 28,600.
³⁶ The men from Asher knew how to fight well. That's because they had done it many times before. They were prepared for battle. The total number of them was 40,000.
³⁷ The men from the tribes of Reuben and Gad and half of the tribe of Manasseh were armed with every kind of weapon. The men came from the east side of the Jordan River. The total number of them was 120,000.
³⁸ All of those fighting men offered to serve in the army. Before they came to Hebron, they had agreed completely to make David king over all of the people of Israel. All of the rest of the people also agreed to make David king.
³⁹ The men spent three days there with David. They ate and drank what their families had given them. ⁴⁰ Their neighbors also brought food. They brought it on donkeys, camels, mules and oxen. They came from as far away as the territories of Issachar, Zebulun and Naphtali. There was plenty of flour, fig cakes, raisin cakes, wine, olive oil, cattle and sheep. The people of Israel brought all of those things because they were so happy.

DAVID WANTS TO BRING THE ARK BACK

13 David talked with each of his officers. He wanted to get their advice. Some of them were commanders of thousands of men. Others were commanders of hundreds.
² David spoke to the whole community of Israel. He said, "Let's send word to the rest of our people no matter how far away they live. They live in all of the territories of Israel. Let's also send word to the priests and Levites who are with them in their towns and grasslands. Let's invite everyone to come and join us. Let's do it if it seems good to you and if that's what the LORD our God wants. ³ Let's bring the ark of our God back here to us. We didn't use it to ask God for advice during the whole time Saul was king."

[4]So that's what the whole community agreed to do. It seemed right to them.

[5]David gathered all of the people together. They came from the area between the Shihor River in Egypt and Lebo Hamath. They came to bring the ark of God from Kiriath Jearim to Jerusalem. [6]David went to Baalah of Judah. The whole community of Israel went with him. Baalah is also called Kiriath Jearim. All of the people went there to get the ark of God the LORD. He sits on his throne between the cherubim. The ark is named after the LORD.

[7]The ark of God was placed on a new cart. Then it was moved from Abinadab's house. Uzzah and Ahio were guiding it.

[8]David was celebrating with all his might in the sight of God. So was the whole community of Israel. All of them were singing songs. They were also playing harps, lyres, tambourines, cymbals and trumpets.

[9]They came to the threshing floor of Kidon. The oxen nearly fell there. So Uzzah reached out his hand to hold the ark steady.

[10]Then the LORD's anger burned against Uzzah. He struck him down because he had put his hand on the ark. So Uzzah died there in front of God.

[11]David was angry because the LORD's burning anger had broken out against Uzzah. That's why the place is still called Perez Uzzah to this very day.

[12]David was afraid of God that day. He asked, "How can I ever bring the ark of God back here to me?"

[13]So he didn't take the ark to be with him in the City of David. Instead, he took it to the house of Obed-Edom. Obed-Edom was from Gath. [14]The ark of God remained with the family of Obed-Edom. It stayed in his house for three months. And the LORD blessed his family. He also blessed everything that belonged to him.

DAVID'S PALACE AND FAMILY

14 Hiram was king of Tyre. He sent messengers to David. He sent cedar logs along with them. He also sent skilled workers to build a palace for David. They worked with stone and wood.

[2]David knew that the LORD had made his position as king secure. He knew that he had made him king over the whole nation of Israel. He knew that the LORD had greatly honored his kingdom. The LORD had done it because the Israelites were his people.

[3]In Jerusalem David got married to more women. He also became the father of more sons and daughters. [4]Here is a list of the children who were born to him in Jerusalem. Their names were Shammua, Shobab, Nathan, Solomon, [5]Ibhar, Elishua, Elpelet, [6]Nogah, Nepheg, Japhia, [7]Elishama, Beeliada and Eliphelet.

DAVID WINS THE BATTLE OVER THE PHILISTINES

[8]The Philistines heard that David had been anointed king over the entire nation of Israel. So their whole army went to look for him. But David heard about it. He went out to where they were. [9]The Philistines had come and attacked the people in the Valley of Rephaim.

[10]So David asked God for advice. He said, "Should I go and attack the Philistines? Will you hand them over to me?"

The LORD answered him, "Go. I will hand them over to you."

[11]So David and his men went up to Baal Perazim. There David won the battle over the Philistines. He said, "God has broken through against my enemies, just as water breaks through a dam." That's why the place was called Baal Perazim.

[12]The Philistines had left the statues of their gods there. So David gave orders to burn them up.

[13]Once more the Philistines attacked the people in the valley. [14]So David asked God for advice again.

God answered him, "Do not go straight up. Instead, circle around them. Attack them in front of the balsam trees. [15]Listen for the sound of marching in the tops of the trees. Then move out to fight. The sound will mean that I have gone out in front of you. I will strike down the Philistine army."

[16]So David did just as God had commanded him. He and his men struck down the Philistine army. They struck them down from Gibeon all the way to Gezer.

[17]So David became famous in every land. The LORD made all of the nations afraid of him.

DAVID BRINGS THE ARK TO JERUSALEM

15 David constructed buildings for himself in the City of David. Then he prepared a place for the ark of God. He set up a tent for it. [2]He said, "Only Levites can carry the ark of God. That's because the LORD chose them to carry his ark. He chose them to serve him forever in front of the place where his throne is."

[3]David gathered the whole community of Israel together in Jerusalem. He wanted to bring the ark of the LORD up to the place he had prepared for it. [4]He called together the members of the family line of Aaron. He also called the Levites together.

Here are the men who came from the families of the Levites.

[5]From the families of Kohath
    came the leader Uriel and 120
    relatives.
[6]From the families of Merari
    came the leader Asaiah and
    220 relatives.
[7]From the families of Gershon
    came the leader Joel and 130
    relatives.
[8]From the families of Elizaphan
    came the leader Shemaiah and
    200 relatives.
[9]From the families of Hebron
    came the leader Eliel and 80
    relatives.
[10]From the families of Uzziel
    came the leader Amminadab
    and 112 relatives.

[11]David sent for the priests Zadok and Abiathar. He also sent for Uriel, Asaiah, Joel, Shemaiah, Eliel and Amminadab. They were Levites. [12]He said to them, "You are the leaders of the families of Levi. You and the other Levites must set yourselves apart to serve the LORD and his people. You must bring up the ark of the LORD. He is the God of Israel. Put the ark in the place I've prepared for it.

[13]"Remember when the anger of the LORD our God broke out against us? It was because you Levites didn't bring the ark up the first time. We didn't ask the LORD how to do it in the way the law requires."

[14]So the priests and Levites set themselves apart. Then they brought up the ark of the LORD. He is the God of Israel. [15]This time the Levites used the poles to carry the ark of God on their shoulders. That's what Moses had commanded in keeping with the word of the LORD.

[16]David told the Levite leaders to appoint their relatives as singers. He wanted them to sing joyful songs. He also wanted them to play lyres, harps and cymbals along with their singing.

[17]So the Levites appointed Heman, the son of Joel. From his relatives they chose Asaph, the son of Berekiah. Other relatives were from the family of Merari. From them they chose Ethan, the son of Kushaiah. [18]Along with them they chose their relatives who were next in line. Their names were Zechariah, Jaaziel, Shemiramoth, Jehiel, Unni, Eliab, Benaiah, Maaseiah, Mattithiah, Eliphelehu, Mikneiah, Obed-Edom and Jeiel. They guarded the gates.

[19]Heman, Asaph and Ethan played the bronze cymbals. [20]Zechariah, Aziel, Shemiramoth, Jehiel, Unni, Eliab, Maaseiah and Benaiah played the high notes on the lyres. [21]Mattithiah, Eliphelehu, Mikneiah, Obed-Edom, Jeiel and Azaziah played the low notes on the harps.

[22]Kenaniah was the leader of the Levites. He was in charge of the singing because he was good at it.

[23]Berekiah and Elkanah guarded the ark. [24]Some of the priests blew trumpets in front of the ark of God. Their names were Shebaniah, Joshaphat, Nethanel, Amasai, Zechariah, Benaiah and Eliezer. Obed-Edom and Jehiah also helped guard the ark.

[25]David and the elders of Israel went to bring up the ark of the covenant of the LORD. So did the commanders of companies of 1,000 men. With great joy they brought the ark up from the house of Obed-Edom.

²⁶God had helped the Levites who were carrying the ark of the covenant of the LORD. So seven bulls and seven rams were sacrificed.

²⁷David was wearing a robe that was made out of fine linen. So were all of the Levites who were carrying the ark. And so were the singers and the choir director Kenaniah. David was also wearing a sacred linen apron.

²⁸So the whole community of Israel brought up the ark of the covenant of the LORD. They shouted. They blew rams' horns and trumpets. They played cymbals, lyres and harps.

²⁹The ark of the covenant of the LORD was brought into the City of David. Saul's daughter Michal was watching from a window. She saw King David dancing and celebrating. That made her hate him in her heart.

16

The ark of God was brought into Jerusalem. It was put in the tent David had set up for it. The priests brought burnt offerings and friendship offerings to God.

²After David finished sacrificing those offerings, he blessed the people in the name of the LORD. ³He gave to each Israelite man and woman a loaf of bread. He also gave each one a date cake and a raisin cake.

⁴He appointed some of the Levites to serve in front of the ark of the LORD. David wanted them to pray, give thanks and praise the LORD. He is the God of Israel. ⁵Asaph was the leader of those Levites. Zechariah was next. Then came Jeiel, Shemiramoth, Jehiel, Mattithiah, Eliab, Benaiah, Obed-Edom and Jeiel. They played the lyres and harps. Asaph played the cymbals. ⁶The priests Benaiah and Jahaziel blew the trumpets. They blew them at regular times in front of the ark of the covenant of God.

DAVID'S PSALM OF THANKS TO THE LORD

⁷That day was the first time David gave Asaph and his helpers this psalm of thanks to the LORD.

⁸Give thanks to the LORD. Worship him.
Tell the nations what he has done.

⁹Sing to him. Sing praise to him.
Tell about all of the wonderful things he has done.

¹⁰Praise him, because his name is holy.
Let the hearts of those who trust in the LORD be glad.

¹¹Look to the LORD and to his strength.
Always look to him.

¹²Remember the wonderful things he has done.
Remember his miracles and how he judged our enemies.

¹³Remember what he has done, you children of his servant Israel.
Remember it, you people of Jacob. You are God's chosen ones.

¹⁴He is the LORD our God.
He judges the whole earth.

¹⁵He will keep his covenant forever.
He will keep his promise for all time to come.

¹⁶He will keep the covenant he made with Abraham.
He will keep the oath he took when he made his promise to Isaac.

¹⁷He made it stand as a law for Jacob.
He made it stand as a covenant for Israel. It will last forever.

¹⁸He said, "I will give you the land of Canaan.
It will belong to you."

¹⁹At first there weren't very many of God's people.
There were only a few. And they were strangers in the land.

²⁰They wandered from nation to nation.
They wandered from one kingdom to another.

²¹But God didn't allow anyone to beat them down.
To keep them safe, he gave a command to kings.

²²He said to them, "Do not touch my anointed ones.
Do not harm my prophets."

²³All you people of the earth, sing to the LORD.
Day after day tell about how he saves us.

²⁴ Tell the nations about his glory.
　　Tell all people about the
　　　wonderful things he has done.
²⁵ The LORD is great. He is really
　　worthy of praise.
　　People should have respect for
　　　him as the greatest God of all.
²⁶ All of the gods of the nations are
　　like their statues.
　　They can't do anything.
　　But the LORD made the heavens.
²⁷ Glory and majesty are all around
　　him.
　　Strength and joy can be seen in
　　　the place where he lives.
²⁸ Praise the LORD, all you nations.
　　Praise the LORD for his glory and
　　　strength.
²⁹ Praise the LORD for the glory that
　　belongs to him.
　　Bring an offering and come to
　　　him.
　　Worship the LORD because of his
　　　beauty and holiness.
³⁰ All you people of the earth,
　　tremble when you are with
　　　him.
　　The world is firmly set in place. It
　　　can't be moved.

³¹ Let the heavens be filled with joy.
　　Let the earth be glad.
　　Let them say among the nations,
　　　"The LORD rules!"
³² Let the ocean and everything in it
　　roar.
　　Let the fields and everything in
　　　them be glad.
³³ Then the trees in the forest will
　　sing with joy.
　　They will sing to the LORD.
　　He will judge the people of the
　　　world.

³⁴ Give thanks to the LORD, because
　　he is good.
　　His faithful love continues forever.
³⁵ Cry out, "Save us, God our Savior.
　　Save us. Bring us back from
　　　among the nations.
　　Then we will give thanks to you,
　　　because your name is holy.
　　We will celebrate by praising
　　　you."
³⁶ Give praise to the LORD, the God of
　　Israel,
　　for ever and ever.

Then all of the people said, "Amen!"
They also said, "Praise the LORD."

Why do we worship God?

We worship God because it makes so much sense. God created us. God is good to us. God created the world. God is the only Lord and ruler of everything. Worship means praising and thanking God for who he is and for what he has done. If we love God, we enjoy him and want to worship him. And God does command us to worship him, since he is the one true God. We can worship God in many different ways. We can sing, read the Bible, give money, pray and help other people. Which one is your favorite?

checkout
1 Chronicles 16:29

Related verse:
Exodus 20:3

³⁷David left Asaph and his helpers to serve in front of the ark of the covenant of the LORD. They served there at regular times. They did it as they were required to do each day. ³⁸David also left Obed-Edom and his 68 helpers to serve with them. Obed-Edom and Hosah guarded the gates. Obed-Edom was the son of Jeduthun.

³⁹David left the priest Zadok and some other priests in front of the holy tent of the LORD. It was at the high place in Gibeon. ⁴⁰David left them there to sacrifice burnt offerings to the LORD on the altar every morning and evening. They did it in keeping with everything that is written in the Law of the LORD. That's the Law he had given to Israel.

⁴¹Heman and Jeduthun were with the priests. So were the rest of those who had been chosen by name and appointed to serve. They had been chosen to give thanks to the LORD, "because his faithful love continues forever." ⁴²It was the duty of Heman and Jeduthun to blow the trumpets. They also had the duty of playing the cymbals and other instruments for the sacred songs. The sons of Jeduthun were stationed at one of the gates.

⁴³All of the people left. Everyone went home. And David returned home to bless his family.

GOD MAKES A PROMISE TO DAVID

17 David settled down in his palace. Then he spoke to the prophet Nathan. He said, "Here I am, living in a palace that has beautiful cedar walls. But the ark of the covenant of the LORD is under a tent."

²Nathan replied to David, "Do what you want to. God is with you."

³That night a message came to Nathan from God. He said,

⁴"Go and speak to my servant David. Tell him, 'The LORD says, "You are not the one who will build me a house to live in. ⁵I have not lived in a house from the day I brought Israel up out of Egypt until now. I have moved my tent from one place to another. I have

moved my home from one place to another. ⁶I have moved from place to place with all of the people of Israel. I commanded their leaders to be shepherds over them. I never asked any of those leaders, 'Why haven't you built me a house that has beautiful cedar walls?' " '

⁷"So tell my servant David, 'The LORD who rules over all says, "I took you away from the grasslands. That is where you were taking care of your father's sheep and goats. I made you ruler over my people Israel. ⁸I have been with you everywhere you have gone. I cut off all of your enemies when you were attacking them. Now I will make you famous. Your name will be just as respected as the names of the most important people on earth.

⁹" ' "I will provide a place where my people Israel can live. I will plant them in the land. Then they will have a home of their own. They will not be bothered anymore. Sinful people will no longer crush them, as they did at first. ¹⁰That is what your enemies have done ever since I appointed leaders over my people Israel. But I will bring all of them under your control.

" ' "I tell you that I will build a royal house for your family. ¹¹Some day your life will come to an end. You will join the members of your family who have already died. Then I will give you one of your own sons to become the next king after you. I will make his kingdom secure.

¹²" ' "He is the one who will build me a house. I will set up his throne. It will last forever. ¹³I will be his father. And he will be my son. I took my love away from the man who ruled before you. But I will never take my love away from your son. ¹⁴I will place him over my house and my kingdom forever. His throne will last forever." ' "

¹⁵Nathan reported to David all of the words that the LORD had spoken to him.

DAVID PRAYS TO THE LORD

¹⁶Then King David went into the holy tent. He sat down in front of the LORD. He said,

"LORD God, who am I? My family isn't important. So why have you brought me this far? ¹⁷I would have thought that you had already done more than enough for me. But now, God, you have spoken about what is going to happen to my royal house in days to come. LORD God, you have treated me as if I were the most honored man of all.

¹⁸"What more can I say to you for honoring me? You know all about me. ¹⁹LORD, you have done a wonderful thing. You have given me many great promises. All of them are for my good. They are exactly what you wanted to give me.

²⁰"LORD, there isn't anyone like you. There isn't any God but you. We have heard about it with our own ears.

²¹"Who is like your people Israel? God, we are the one nation on earth you have saved. You have set us free for yourself. Your name has become famous. You have done great and wonderful things. You have driven nations out to make room for your people. You saved us when you set us free from Egypt. No other god has done any of those things for its people. ²²You made Israel your very own people forever. LORD, you have become our God.

²³"And now, LORD, let the promise you have made to me and my royal house stand forever. Do exactly as you promised. ²⁴When your promise comes true, your name will be honored forever. People will say, 'The LORD rules over all. He is the God over Israel. He is Israel's God.' My royal house will be made secure in your sight.

²⁵"My God, you have shown me that you will build me a royal house. So I can pray to you boldly. ²⁶LORD, you are God! You have promised many good things to me. ²⁷You have been pleased to bless my royal house. Now it will continue forever in your sight. LORD, you have blessed it. And it will be blessed forever."

DAVID WINS MANY BATTLES

18 While David was king of Israel, he won many battles over the Philistines. He brought them under his control. He took Gath away from the Philistines. He also captured the villages that were around Gath.

²David also won the battle over the people of Moab. They were brought under his rule. They gave him the gifts he required them to bring him.

³David fought against Hadadezer all the way to Hamath. Hadadezer was king of Zobah. He had gone to take complete control of the land along the Euphrates River. ⁴David captured 1,000 of Hadadezer's chariots, 7,000 chariot riders and 20,000 soldiers on foot. He cut the legs of all but 100 of the chariot horses.

⁵The Arameans of Damascus came to help Hadadezer, the king of Zobah. But David struck down 22,000 of them. ⁶He stationed some soldiers in the Aramean kingdom of Damascus. The people of Aram were brought under his rule. They gave him the gifts he required them to bring him. The LORD helped David win his battles everywhere he went.

⁷David took the gold shields that were carried by the officers of Hadadezer. He brought the shields to Jerusalem. ⁸He took a huge amount of bronze from Tebah and Cun. Those towns belonged to Hadadezer. Later, Solomon used the bronze to make the huge bronze bowl for washing. He also used it to make the pillars and many other bronze articles for the temple.

⁹Tou was king of Hamath. He heard that David had won the battle over the entire army of Hadadezer, the king of Zobah. ¹⁰So Tou sent his son Hadoram to King David. Hadoram greeted David. He praised him because he had won the battle over Hadadezer. Hadadezer had been at war with Tou. So Hadoram brought David all kinds of

articles that were made out of gold, silver and bronze.

[11] King David set those articles apart for the LORD. He had done the same thing with the silver and gold he had taken from other nations. The nations were Edom, Moab, Ammon, Philistia and Amalek.

[12] Abishai struck down 18,000 men of Edom in the Valley of Salt. Abishai was the son of Zeruiah. [13] He stationed some soldiers in Edom. The whole nation of Edom was brought under his rule. The LORD helped David win his battles everywhere he went.

DAVID'S OFFICIALS

[14] David ruled over the whole nation of Israel. He did what was fair and right for all of his people. [15] Joab, the son of Zeruiah, was commander over the army. Jehoshaphat, the son of Ahilud, kept the records. [16] Zadok, the son of Ahitub, was a priest. Ahimelech, the son of Abiathar, was also a priest. Shavsha was the secretary. [17] Benaiah, the son of Jehoiada, was commander over the Kerethites and Pelethites. And King David's sons were the chief officials who served at his side.

DAVID GOES TO WAR AGAINST THE PEOPLE OF AMMON

19 Nahash was king of Ammon. After he died, his son became the next king after him. [2] David thought, "I'm going to be kind to Hanun. His father Nahash was kind to me." So David sent messengers to Hanun. He wanted them to tell Hanun how sad he was that Hanun's father had died.

David's messengers went to the land of Ammon. They told Hanun how sad David was.

[3] The Ammonite nobles spoke to Hanun. They said, "David has sent messengers to tell you he is sad. They say he wants to honor your father. But the real reason they've come is to look the land over. They want to destroy it."

[4] So Hanun grabbed hold of David's men. He shaved them. He cut their clothes off just below the waist and left them half naked. Then he sent them away.

[5] Someone came and told David what had happened to his men. So David sent messengers to them because they were filled with shame. King David said to them, "Stay at Jericho until your beards grow out again. Then come back here."

[6] The Ammonites realized that what they had done had made David very angry with them. So Hanun and the Ammonites got 37 tons of silver. They used it to hire chariots and chariot riders from Aram Naharaim, Aram Maacah and Zobah. [7] They hired 32,000 chariots and riders. They also hired the king of Maacah and his troops. All of them came out and camped near Medeba. At the same time the Ammonites brought their troops together from their towns. Then they marched out to fight.

[8] David heard about it. So he sent Joab out with the entire army of Israel's fighting men. [9] The Ammonites marched out. They took up their battle positions at the entrance to their city. The kings who came to help them gathered their troops together in the open country.

[10] Joab saw that there were lines of soldiers in front of him and behind him. So he chose some of the best troops in Israel. He sent them to march out against the Arameans. [11] He put the rest of the men under the command of his brother Abishai. They were sent to march out against the Ammonites.

[12] Joab said, "Suppose the Arameans are too strong for me. Then you must come and help me. But suppose the Ammonites are too strong for you. Then I'll come and help you. [13] Be strong. Let's be brave as we fight for our people and the cities of our God. The LORD will do what he thinks is best."

[14] Then Joab and the troops who were with him marched out to attack the Arameans. They ran away from him. [15] The Ammonites saw that the Arameans were running away. So they also ran away from Joab's brother Abishai. They went inside the city. Then Joab went back to Jerusalem.

[16] The Arameans saw that they had been driven away by Israel. So they

sent messengers to get some Arameans from east of the Euphrates River. The Arameans were under the command of Shophach. He was the commander of Hadadezer's army.

¹⁷David was told about it. So he gathered the whole army of Israel together. They went across the Jordan River. David marched out against the Arameans. He lined up his soldiers opposite them. He lined them up to meet the Arameans in battle.

The Arameans began to fight against him. ¹⁸But then they ran away from Israel. David killed 7,000 of their chariot riders. He killed 40,000 of their soldiers who were on foot. He also killed Shophach, the commander of their army.

¹⁹The people who were under the rule of Hadadezer saw that Israel had won the battle over them. So they made a peace treaty with David. They were brought under his rule.

After that, the Arameans wouldn't help the Ammonites anymore.

JOAB CAPTURES THE CITY OF RABBAH

20 In the spring, Joab led Israel's army out. It was the time when kings go off to war. Joab destroyed the land of Ammon. He went to the city of Rabbah. He surrounded it and got ready to attack it. But David remained in Jerusalem. Later, Joab attacked Rabbah and completely destroyed it.

²David took the gold crown off the head of the king of Ammon. The crown weighed 75 pounds. It had jewels in it. It was placed on David's head. He took a huge amount of goods from the city. ³He brought out the people who were there. He made them work with saws and iron picks and axes. David did that to all of the towns in Ammon. Then he and his entire army returned to Jerusalem.

ISRAEL GOES TO WAR AGAINST THE PHILISTINES

⁴War broke out at Gezer against the Philistines. At that time Sibbecai killed Sippai. So the Philistines were brought under Israel's control. Sibbecai was a Hushathite. Sippai was from the family line of Rapha.

⁵In another battle against the Philistines, Elhanan killed Lahmi. Elhanan was the son of Jair. Lahmi was the brother of Goliath. Goliath was from the city of Gath. Lahmi's spear was as big as a weaver's rod.

⁶There was still another battle. It took place at Gath. A huge man lived there. He had six fingers on each hand and six toes on each foot. So the total number of his toes and fingers was 24. He was also from the family line of Rapha. ⁷He made fun of Israel. So Jonathan killed him. Jonathan was the son of David's brother Shimea.

⁸Those Philistine men lived in Gath. They were from the family line of Rapha. David and his men killed them.

DAVID COUNTS HIS FIGHTING MEN

21 Satan rose up against Israel. He stirred up David to count the men of Israel. ²So David spoke to Joab and the commanders of the troops. He said, "Go! Count the men of Israel from Beersheba all the way to Dan. Report back to me. Then I'll know how many there are."

³Joab replied, "May the LORD multiply his troops 100 times. King David, you are my master. Aren't all of the men under your control? Why would you want me to count them? Do you want to make Israel guilty?"

⁴In spite of what Joab said, the king's word had more authority than Joab's word did. So Joab left and went all through Israel. Then he came back to Jerusalem. ⁵Joab reported to David how many fighting men he had counted. In the whole land of Israel there were 1,100,000 men who could use a sword well. That included 470,000 men in Judah.

⁶But Joab didn't include the tribes of Levi and Benjamin in the total number. The king's command was sickening to Joab. ⁷It was also evil in the sight of God. So he punished Israel.

⁸Then David said to God, "I committed a great sin when I counted Israel's men. I beg you to take away my guilt. I've done a very foolish thing."

[9]The LORD spoke to David's prophet Gad. He said, [10]"Go and tell David, 'The LORD says, "I could punish you in three different ways. Choose one of them for me to use against you." ' "

[11]So Gad went to David. He said to him, "The LORD says, 'Take your choice. [12]You can have three years when there will not be enough food in the land. You can have three months when your enemies will sweep you away. They will catch up with you. They will cut you down with their swords. Or you can have three days when my sword will punish you. That means there would be three days of plague in the land. My angel would strike people down in every part of Israel.'

"So take your pick. Tell me how to answer the One who sent me."

[13]David said to Gad, "I'm suffering terribly. Let me fall into the hands of the LORD. His mercy is very great. But don't let me fall into the hands of men."

[14]So the LORD sent a plague on Israel. And 70,000 Israelites died. [15]God sent an angel to destroy Jerusalem. But as the angel was doing it, the LORD saw it. He was very sad because of the plague. So he spoke to the angel who was destroying the people. He said, "That is enough! Do not kill any more people!"

The angel of the LORD was standing at Araunah's threshing floor. Araunah was from the city of Jebus.

[16]David looked up. He saw the angel of the LORD standing between heaven and earth. The angel was holding out a sword over Jerusalem. David and the elders fell with their faces to the ground. They were wearing black clothes.

[17]David said to God, "I ordered the fighting men to be counted. I'm the one who has sinned. I'm the one who has done what is wrong. These people are like sheep. What have they done? LORD my God, let your powerful hand punish me and my family. But don't let this plague continue to strike your people."

DAVID BUILDS AN ALTAR

[18]Then the angel of the LORD ordered Gad to tell David to go up to the threshing floor of Araunah, the Jebusite. He wanted David to build an altar there to honor the LORD.

[19]So David went up and did it. He obeyed the message that Gad had spoken in the LORD's name.

[20]Araunah was threshing wheat. He turned and saw the angel. His four children were with him. They hid themselves. [21]David approached the threshing floor. Araunah looked up and saw him. So Araunah left the threshing floor. He bowed down to David with his face toward the ground.

[22]David said to him, "Let me have the property your threshing floor is on. I want to build an altar there to honor the LORD. When I do, the plague on the people will be stopped. Sell the threshing floor to me for the full price."

[23]Araunah said to David, "Take it! King David, you are my master. Do what you please. I'll even provide the oxen for the burnt offerings. Use boards from the threshing sleds for the wood. Use the wheat for the grain offering. I'll give all of it to you."

[24]But King David replied to Araunah, "No! I want to pay the full price. I won't take what belongs to you and give it to the LORD. I won't sacrifice a burnt offering that hasn't cost me anything."

[25]So David paid Araunah 15 pounds of gold for the property. [26]David built an altar there to honor the LORD. He sacrificed burnt offerings and friendship offerings. He called out to the LORD. The LORD answered him by sending fire from heaven on the altar for burnt offerings. [27]Then the LORD spoke to the angel. And the angel put his sword away. [28]When the angel did that, David was still at the threshing floor of Araunah, the Jebusite. David saw that the LORD had answered him. So he offered sacrifices there.

[29]At that time, the LORD's holy tent was at the high place in Gibeon. The altar for burnt offerings was there too. Moses had made the holy tent in the desert. [30]David couldn't go to the tent to pray to God. That's because he was afraid of the sword of the angel of the LORD.

22

David announced, "The house of the LORD God will be built here. Israel's altar for burnt offerings will also be here."

DAVID MAKES PLANS FOR BUILDING THE TEMPLE

2David gave orders to bring together the outsiders who were living in Israel. He appointed some of them to cut stones. He wanted them to prepare blocks of stone for building the house of God.

3David provided a large amount of iron to make nails. They were for the doors of the gates and for the fittings. He provided more bronze than anyone could weigh. 4He also provided more cedar logs than anyone could count. The people of Sidon and Tyre brought large numbers of logs to David.

5David said, "My son Solomon is young. He's never done anything like this before. The house that will be built for the LORD should be very grand and wonderful. It should be famous and beautiful in the eyes of all of the nations. I'll get things ready for it." So David got many things ready before he died.

6Then he sent for his son Solomon. He told him to build a house for the LORD, the God of Israel.

7David said to Solomon, "My son, with all my heart I wanted to build a house for the LORD my God. That's where his Name will be. 8But a message from the LORD came to me. It said, 'You have spilled the blood of many people. You have fought many wars. You are not the one who will build a house for my Name. That is because I have seen you spill the blood of many people on the earth.

9" 'But you are going to have a son. He will be a man of peace. And I will give him peace and rest from all of his enemies on every side. His name will be Solomon. I will give Israel peace and quiet while he is king. 10He will build a house for my Name. He will be my son. And I will be his father. I will make his kingdom secure over Israel. It will last forever.'

11"My son, may the LORD be with you. May you have success. May you

build the house of the LORD your God, just as he said you would. 12May the LORD give you good sense. May he give you understanding when he makes you king over Israel. Then you will keep the law of the LORD your God.

13"Be careful to obey the rules and laws the LORD gave Moses for Israel. Then you will have success. Be strong and brave. Don't be afraid. Don't lose hope.

14"I've tried very hard to provide for the LORD's temple. I've provided 3,750 tons of gold and 37,500 tons of silver. I've provided more bronze and iron than anyone can weigh. I've also given plenty of wood and stone. You can add to it.

15"You have a lot of workers. You have people who can cut stones and people who can lay the stones. You have people who can work with wood. You also have people who are skilled in every other kind of work. 16Some of them can work with gold and silver. Others can work with bronze and iron. There are more workers than anyone can count. So begin the work. May the LORD be with you."

17Then David ordered all of Israel's leaders to help his son Solomon. 18He said to them, "The LORD your God is with you. He's given you peace and rest on every side. He's handed the people who are living in the land over to me. The land has been brought under the control of the LORD and his people.

19"So look to the LORD your God with all your heart and soul. Start building the temple of the LORD God. Then bring the ark of the covenant of the LORD into it. Also bring in the sacred articles that belong to God. The temple will be built for the Name of the LORD."

THE FAMILY LINE OF LEVI

23

David had become very old. So he made his son Solomon king over Israel. 2He gathered together all of the leaders of Israel. He also gathered the priests and the Levites together. 3The Levites who were 30 years old or more were counted. The total number of men was 38,000.

⁴David said, "From them, 24,000 will direct the work of the LORD's temple. And 6,000 will be officials and judges. ⁵Another 4,000 will guard the gates. And 4,000 will praise the LORD with the instruments of music I've provided for that purpose."

⁶David separated the Levites into groups. He did it based on the sons of Levi. The sons were Gershon, Kohath and Merari.

THE FAMILY OF GERSHON

⁷Ladan and Shimei belonged to the family of Gershon.

⁸The sons of Ladan were Jehiel, Zetham and Joel. Jehiel was the oldest son. The total number of sons was three.

⁹The sons of Shimei were Shelomoth, Haziel and Haran. The total number of sons was three. They were the leaders of the families of Ladan.

¹⁰The sons of Shimei were Jahath, Ziza, Jeush and Beriah. The total number of the sons of Shimei was four.

¹¹Jahath was the first son. Ziza was the second son. But Jeush and Beriah didn't have many sons. So they were counted as one family. They had only one task.

THE FAMILY OF KOHATH

¹²The sons of Kohath were Amram, Izhar, Hebron and Uzziel. The total number of sons was four.

¹³Aaron and Moses belonged to Amram's family line.
Aaron and his family line were set apart forever as the LORD's priests.
They had the duty of setting the most holy things apart to the LORD. They offered sacrifices to the LORD. They served him. They gave blessings in his name forever. ¹⁴The sons of Moses, the man of God, were counted as part of the tribe of Levi.

¹⁵The sons of Moses were Gershom and Eliezer.

¹⁶Shubael was the oldest son in the family line of Gershom.

¹⁷Rehabiah was the oldest son in the family line of Eliezer.
Eliezer didn't have any other sons. But Rehabiah had a great many sons.

¹⁸Shelomith was the oldest son of Izhar.

¹⁹Jeriah was the first son of Hebron.
Amariah was his second son. Jahaziel was the third. Jekameam was the fourth.

²⁰Micah was the first son of Uzziel. Isshiah was his second son.

THE FAMILY OF MERARI

²¹The sons of Merari were Mahli and Mushi.
The sons of Mahli were Eleazar and Kish.

²²Eleazar died without having any sons. All he had was daughters. They got married to their cousins. The cousins were the sons of Kish.

²³The sons of Mushi were Mahli, Eder and Jerimoth. The total number of sons was three.

²⁴Those were the family lines of Levi. They were recorded under the names of the family leaders. Each worker who was 20 years old or more was counted. They served in the LORD's temple.

²⁵David had said, "The LORD is the God of Israel. He has given peace and rest to his people. He has come to Jerusalem to live there forever. ²⁶So the Levites don't need to carry the holy tent anymore. They don't need to carry any of its articles anymore. Those were the articles that were used to serve there."

²⁷The Levites who were 20 years old or more were counted. That was in keeping with David's final directions.

²⁸The Levites had the duty of helping the members of Aaron's family line. They helped them serve in the LORD's temple. They were in charge of the courtyards and the side rooms. They made all of the sacred things pure and clean.

They also had other duties at the house of God. ²⁹They were in charge of setting the holy bread out on the table. They prepared the flour for the grain offerings. They made the wafers without using any yeast. They did the baking and the mixing. They measured the amount and size of everything.

³⁰They stood every morning to thank and praise the LORD. They did the same thing every evening. ³¹They also did it every time burnt offerings were brought to the LORD. Those offerings were brought every Sabbath day. They were also brought at every New Moon Feast and during the appointed yearly feasts.

The Levites served in front of the LORD at regular times. The proper number of Levites was always used when they served. They served in the way the law required of them.

³²So the Levites carried out their duties for the Tent of Meeting and for the Holy Room. They worked under their relatives who were in the family line of Aaron. They helped them serve at the LORD's temple.

THE GROUPS OF PRIESTS

24 Here are the groups of priests the sons of Aaron were separated into.

The sons of Aaron were Nadab, Abihu, Eleazar and Ithamar. ²But Nadab and Abihu died before their father did. They didn't have any sons. So Eleazar and Ithamar served as the priests.

³With the help of Zadok and Ahimelech, David separated the priests into groups. Each group served in its appointed order and time. Zadok belonged to the family line of Eleazar. Ahimelech belonged to the family line of Ithamar. ⁴More leaders were found among Eleazar's family line than among Ithamar's. So the priests were separated into their groups based on that fact. There were 16 family leaders from Eleazar's line. There were eight family leaders from Ithamar's line.

⁵The priests were separated into their groups by using lots. That was the fair way to do it. The priests were officials of the temple and officials of God. They came from the family lines of Eleazar and Ithamar.

⁶Shemaiah was a Levite. He was the son of Nethanel. He was the writer who recorded the names of the priests. He wrote them down in front of the king and the officials. The officials included the priest Zadok and Ahimelech. Ahimelech was the son of Abiathar. They also included the leaders of the families of the priests and the Levites. One family was chosen by lot from Eleazar. Then one was chosen from Ithamar.

⁷The 1st lot that was drawn out was for Jehoiarib.
The 2nd was for Jedaiah.
⁸The 3rd was for Harim.
The 4th was for Seorim.
⁹The 5th was for Malkijah.
The 6th was for Mijamin.
¹⁰The 7th was for Hakkoz.
The 8th was for Abijah.
¹¹The 9th was for Jeshua.
The 10th was for Shecaniah.
¹²The 11th was for Eliashib.
The 12th was for Jakim.
¹³The 13th was for Huppah.
The 14th was for Jeshebeab.
¹⁴The 15th was for Bilgah.
The 16th was for Immer.
¹⁵The 17th was for Hezir.
The 18th was for Happizzez.
¹⁶The 19th was for Pethahiah.
The 20th was for Jehezkel.
¹⁷The 21st was for Jakin.
The 22nd was for Gamul.
¹⁸The 23rd was for Delaiah.
The 24th was for Maaziah.

¹⁹That was their appointed order for serving when they entered the LORD's temple. That order was based on the rules Aaron had given them long ago. Everything was done exactly as the LORD had commanded Aaron. The LORD is the God of Israel.

THE REST OF THE LEVITES

²⁰Here are the other members of the family line of Levi.
From the sons of Amram came Shubael.
From the sons of Shubael came Jehdeiah.
²¹From the sons of Rehabiah came Isshiah.
Isshiah was the oldest.
²²From the people of Izhar came Shelomoth.
From the sons of Shelomoth came Jahath.
²³Jeriah was the first son of Hebron. Amariah was his second

son. Jahaziel was the third. Jekameam was the fourth.

²⁴ The son of Uzziel was Micah.
From the sons of Micah came Shamir.

²⁵ The brother of Micah was Isshiah.
From the sons of Isshiah came Zechariah.

²⁶ The sons of Merari were Mahli and Mushi.
The son of Jaaziah was Beno.

²⁷ The sons of Merari
from Jaaziah were Beno, Shoham, Zaccur and Ibri.

²⁸ From Mahli came Eleazar. Eleazar didn't have any sons.

²⁹ From Kish came
Jerahmeel. Jerahmeel was the son of Kish.

³⁰ The sons of Mushi were Mahli, Eder and Jerimoth.

Those were the Levites, family by family. ³¹They cast lots, just as their relatives, the sons of Aaron, had done. They did it in front of King David, Zadok and Ahimelech. They did it in front of the family leaders of the priests. They also did it in front of the family leaders of the Levites. The families of the oldest brother were treated in the same way as the families of the youngest.

THE SINGERS

25 David and the commanders of the army set apart some of the sons of Asaph, Heman and Jeduthun. They set them apart to serve the LORD by prophesying while harps, lyres and cymbals were being played. Here is the list of the men who served in that way.

²From the sons of Asaph came Zaccur, Joseph, Nethaniah and Asarelah. The sons of Asaph were under the direction of Asaph. He prophesied under the king's direction.

³From the sons of Jeduthun came Gedaliah, Zeri, Jeshaiah, Shimei, Hashabiah and Mattithiah. The total number was six. They were under the direction of their father Jeduthun. He prophesied while playing the harp. He used it to thank and praise the LORD.

⁴From the sons of Heman came Bukkiah, Mattaniah, Uzziel, Shubael, Jerimoth, Hananiah, Hanani, Eliathah, Giddalti, Romamti-Ezer, Joshbekashah, Mallothi, Hothir and Mahazioth. ⁵All of them were sons of the king's prophet Heman. They were given to Heman to bring him honor. That's what God had promised. God gave him 14 sons and three daughters.

⁶All of them were under the direction of their fathers. They played music for the LORD's temple. They served at the house of God by playing cymbals, lyres and harps. Asaph, Jeduthun and Heman were under the king's direction.

⁷All of them were trained and skilled in playing music for the LORD. Their total number was 288. That included their relatives. ⁸Young and old alike cast lots for their duties. That was true for students as well as teachers.

⁹The 1st lot that was drawn out was for Asaph. It was for Joseph and his sons and relatives. The total number was 12.
The 2nd lot was for Gedaliah and his relatives and sons. The total number was 12.

¹⁰The 3rd was for Zaccur and his sons and relatives. The total number was 12.

¹¹The 4th was for Izri and his sons and relatives. The total number was 12.

¹²The 5th was for Nethaniah and his sons and relatives. The total number was 12.

¹³The 6th was for Bukkiah and his sons and relatives. The total number was 12.

¹⁴The 7th was for Jesarelah and his sons and relatives. The total number was 12.

¹⁵The 8th was for Jeshaiah and his sons and relatives. The total number was 12.

¹⁶The 9th was for Mattaniah and his sons and relatives. The total number was 12.

¹⁷The 10th was for Shimei

and his sons and relatives. The total number was 12.

¹⁸ The 11th was for Azarel and his sons and relatives. The total number was 12.

¹⁹ The 12th was for Hashabiah and his sons and relatives. The total number was 12.

²⁰ The 13th was for Shubael and his sons and relatives. The total number was 12.

²¹ The 14th was for Mattithiah and his sons and relatives. The total number was 12.

²² The 15th was for Jerimoth and his sons and relatives. The total number was 12.

²³ The 16th was for Hananiah and his sons and relatives. The total number was 12.

²⁴ The 17th was for Joshbekashah and his sons and relatives. The total number was 12.

²⁵ The 18th was for Hanani and his sons and relatives. The total number was 12.

²⁶ The 19th was for Mallothi and his sons and relatives. The total number was 12.

²⁷ The 20th was for Eliathah and his sons and relatives. The total number was 12.

²⁸ The 21st was for Hothir and his sons and relatives. The total number was 12.

²⁹ The 22nd was for Giddalti and his sons and relatives. The total number was 12.

³⁰ The 23rd was for Mahazioth and his sons and relatives. The total number was 12.

³¹ The 24th was for Romamti-Ezer and his sons and relatives. The total number was 12.

THE MEN WHO GUARDED THE GATES

26 Here are the groups of men who guarded the gates.

From the family of Korah came Meshelemiah, the son of Kore. Kore was one of the sons of Asaph.

² Meshelemiah had sons. Zechariah was his first son. Jediael was his second son.

Zebadiah was the third. Jathniel was the fourth.

³ Elam was the fifth. Jehohanan was the sixth. And Eliehoenai was the seventh.

⁴ Obed-Edom also had sons. Shemaiah was his first son. Jehozabad was his second son. Joah was the third. Sacar was the fourth. Nethanel was the fifth.

⁵ Ammiel was the sixth. Issachar was the seventh. And Peullethai was the eighth. God had blessed Obed-Edom.

⁶ His son Shemaiah also had sons. They were leaders in their family. That's because they were men of great ability. ⁷ The sons of Shemaiah were Othni, Rephael, Obed and Elzabad. Elzabad's brothers Elihu and Semakiah were also able men. ⁸ All of them belonged to the family line of Obed-Edom. They and their sons and relatives were men of ability. They were strong enough to do their work. The total number of men in the family line of Obed-Edom was 62.

⁹ Meshelemiah's sons and relatives were able men. Their total number was 18.

¹⁰ Hosah belonged to the family line of Merari. Hosah's first son was Shimri. But Shimri wasn't the oldest son. His father had made him the first. ¹¹ Hilkiah was Hosah's second son. Tabaliah was the third. Zechariah was the fourth. The total number of Hosah's sons and relatives was 13.

¹² Those groups of men guarded the gates. They worked under their chief men. They served at the LORD's temple, just as their relatives had served. ¹³ Lots were cast for each gate, family by family. Young and old alike were chosen.

¹⁴ The lot that was drawn out for the East Gate was for Shelemiah. Then lots were cast for his son Zechariah. He

gave wise advice. The lot that was drawn out for the North Gate was for him. [15]The lot for the South Gate was for Obed-Edom. The lot for the storeroom was for his sons. [16]Lots were drawn out for the West Gate and the Shalleketh Gate on the upper road. Those lots were for Shuppim and Hosah.

One guard stood next to another. [17]There were six Levites a day on the east. There were four a day on the north. There were four a day on the south. And there were two at a time at the storeroom. [18]Two Levite guards were at the courtyard to the west. And four were at the road.

[19]Those were the groups of the men who guarded the gates. They belonged to the family lines of Korah and Merari.

OTHER OFFICIALS

[20]The Levite relatives of the men who guarded the gates were in charge of the treasures in the house of God. They were also in charge of other treasures that had been set apart for God. [21]Ladan was from the family line of Gershon. Some leaders of families belonged to Ladan's family line. One of them was Jehieli. [22]The sons of Jehieli were Zetham and his brother Joel. They were in charge of the treasures in the LORD's temple.

[23]Here are the officials who were from the family lines of Amram, Izhar, Hebron and Uzziel.

[24]Shubael was from the family line of Moses' son Gershom. Shubael was the officer in charge of the treasures. [25]His relatives through Eliezer included his son Rehabiah. Jeshaiah was Rehabiah's son. Joram was Jeshaiah's son. Zicri was Joram's son. And Shelomith was Zicri's son. [26]Shelomith and his relatives were in charge of all of the treasures that had been set apart for God. King David had set those treasures apart. Some family leaders had also set them apart. They were the commanders of thousands of men and commanders of hundreds. The trea-

sures had also been set apart by other army commanders. [27]Some of the goods that had been taken in battle were set apart to repair the LORD's temple. [28]The prophet Samuel had set apart some things for God. Saul, the son of Kish, had set apart other things. So had Abner, the son of Ner. And so had Joab, the son of Zeruiah.

All of those things and all of the others that had been set apart were taken care of by Shelomith and his relatives.

[29]From the family line of Izhar came Kenaniah and his sons. They were given duties that were away from the temple. They were officials and judges over Israel.

[30]From the family line of Hebron came Hashabiah and his relatives. They were able men. The total number was 1,700. It was their duty to serve the king in Israel west of the Jordan River. It was also their duty to do all of the LORD's work there.

[31]Jeriah was the chief of the family line of Hebron. That's based on their family history. In the 40th year of David's rule, a search was made in the records. That's how men of ability were found in the family line of Hebron at Jazer in Gilead. [32]Jeriah had 2,700 relatives. They were able men. They were family leaders. King David had put them in charge of the tribes of Reuben and Gad and half of the tribe of Manasseh. They were in charge of matters having to do with God and the king.

THE COMPANIES IN THE KING'S ARMY

27 Here is the list of the Israelites who served in the king's army. They included leaders of families. They included commanders of thousands of men and commanders of hundreds. They also included other officers. All of them served the king in everything concerning the army companies that were on duty month by month all through the year. The total number of men in each company was 24,000.

2 Jashobeam was in charge of the first company for the first month. He was the son of Zabdiel. The total number of men in Jashobeam's company was 24,000. 3 He belonged to the family line of Perez. He was chief of all of the army officers for the first month.

4 Dodai was in charge of the second company for the second month. He belonged to the family line of Ahoah. Mikloth was the leader of Dodai's company. The total number of men in Dodai's company was 24,000.

5 The third army commander for the third month was the priest Benaiah, the son of Jehoiada. Benaiah was the chief. The total number of men in Benaiah's company was 24,000. 6 That same Benaiah was a mighty man among the Thirty. In fact, he was leader over the Thirty. His son Ammizabad was in charge of his company.

7 The fourth commander for the fourth month was Joab's brother Asahel. Asahel's son Zebadiah was the next commander after him. The total number of men in Asahel's company was 24,000.

8 The fifth commander for the fifth month was Shamhuth. He was an Izrahite. The total number of men in Shamhuth's company was 24,000.

9 The sixth commander for the sixth month was Ira. He was the son of Ikkesh from Tekoa. The total number of men in Ira's company was 24,000.

10 The seventh commander for the seventh month was Helez. He was a Pelonite from Ephraim. The total number of men in Helez's company was 24,000.

11 The eighth commander for the eighth month was Sibbecai. He was a Hushathite from Zerah. The total number of men in Sibbecai's company was 24,000.

12 The ninth commander for the ninth month was Abiezer. He was from Anathoth in Benjamin. The total number of men in Abiezer's company was 24,000.

13 The tenth commander for the tenth month was Maharai. He was a Netophathite from Zerah. The total number of men in Maharai's company was 24,000.

14 The 11th commander for the 11th month was Benaiah. He was from Pirathon in Ephraim. The total number of men in Benaiah's company was 24,000.

15 The 12th commander for the 12th month was Heldai. He was a Netophathite from the family line of Othniel. The total number of men in Heldai's company was 24,000.

THE OFFICERS OVER THE TRIBES

16 Here are the officers over the tribes of Israel.

Over the tribe of Reuben was Eliezer, the son of Zicri.
Over Simeon was Shephatiah, the son of Maacah.
17 Over Levi was Hashabiah, the son of Kemuel.
Over Aaron was Zadok.
18 Over Judah was Elihu. He was David's brother.
Over Issachar was Omri, the son of Michael.
19 Over Zebulun was Ishmaiah, the son of Obadiah.
Over Naphtali was Jerimoth, the son of Azriel.
20 Over Ephraim was Hoshea, the son of Azaziah.
Over half of the tribe of Manasseh was Joel, the son of Pedaiah.
21 Over the half of the tribe of Manasseh in Gilead was Iddo, the son of Zechariah.
Over Benjamin was Jaasiel, the son of Abner.
22 Over Dan was Azarel, the son of Jeroham.

Those were the officers over the tribes of Israel.

23 David didn't count the men who were 20 years old or less. That's because the LORD had promised to make the people of Israel as many as the

stars in the sky. [24]Joab, the son of Zeruiah, began to count the men. But he didn't finish. The LORD was angry with Israel because David had begun to count the men. So the number wasn't written down in the official records of King David.

OTHER OFFICIALS
OF THE KING

[25]Azmaveth was in charge of the royal storerooms. He was the son of Adiel.

Jonathan was in charge of the storerooms in the fields, towns, villages and lookout towers. He was the son of Uzziah.

[26]Ezri was in charge of the workers who farmed the land. He was the son of Kelub.

[27]Shimei was in charge of the vineyards. He was from Ramah.

Zabdi was in charge of the grapes from the vineyards. He was also in charge of storing the wine. He was a Shiphmite.

[28]Baal-Hanan was in charge of the olive trees and sycamore-fig trees in the western hills. He was from Geder.

Joash was in charge of storing the olive oil.

[29]Shitrai was in charge of the herds that ate grass in Sharon. He was from Sharon.

Shaphat was in charge of the herds in the valleys. He was the son of Adlai.

[30]Obil was in charge of the camels. He was from the family line of Ishmael.

Jehdeiah was in charge of the donkeys. He was from Meronoth.

[31]Jaziz was in charge of the flocks. He was a Hagrite.

All of those men were the officials in charge of King David's property.

[32]Jonathan was David's uncle. He gave good advice. He was a man of understanding. He was also a secretary. Jehiel took care of the king's sons. He was the son of Hacmoni.

[33]Ahithophel was the king's adviser. Hushai was the king's friend. He was an Arkite. [34]Jehoiada and Abiathar became the next advisers after Ahithophel. Jehoiada was the son of Benaiah. Joab was the commander of the royal army.

DAVID TALKS ABOUT HIS PLANS FOR THE TEMPLE

28 David asked all of the officials of Israel to come together at Jerusalem. He sent for the officers who were over the tribes. He sent for the commanders of the companies who served the king. He sent for the commanders of thousands of men and commanders of hundreds. He sent for the officials who were in charge of all of the royal property and livestock. They belonged to the king and his sons. He sent for the palace officials and the mighty men. He also sent for all of the brave fighting men.

[2]King David stood up. He said, "All of you, listen to me. With all my heart I wanted to build a house for the LORD. I wanted it to be a place of peace and rest for the ark of the covenant of the LORD. The ark is the stool for our God's feet. I made plans to build the LORD's house. [3]But God said to me, 'You are not the one who will build a house for my Name. That is because you are a fighting man. You have spilled people's blood.'

[4]"But the LORD chose me. He is the God of Israel. He chose me from my whole family to be king over Israel forever. He chose Judah to lead the tribes. From the families of Judah he chose my family. From my father's sons he chose me. He was pleased to make me king over the whole nation of Israel. [5]"The LORD has given me many sons. From all of them he has chosen my son Solomon. He wants Solomon to sit on the throne of the LORD's kingdom. He wants him to rule over Israel. [6]He said to me, 'Your son Solomon is the one who will build my house and my courtyards. I have chosen him to be my son. And I will be his father. [7]I will make his kingdom secure. It will last forever. That will happen if he does not turn away from my commands and laws. He must continue to obey them, just as he is doing now.'

[8]"So I'm giving you a command in the sight of all of the people of Israel. The LORD's community is watching. And our God is listening. I command you to be careful to follow all of the

commands of the LORD your God. Then you will own this good land. You will pass it on to your children after you as their share forever.

⁹"My son Solomon, always remember the God of your father. Serve him with all your heart. Do it with a mind that wants to obey him. The LORD looks deep down inside every heart. He understands the real reasons for everything you think. If you look to him, you will find him. But if you desert him, he will turn his back on you forever. ¹⁰Think about it. The LORD has chosen you to build a temple as a holy place where he can live. So be strong. Get to work."

¹¹Then David gave his son Solomon the plans for the porch of the temple. He gave him the plans for its buildings and its storerooms. He gave him the plans for its upper parts and its inside rooms. He gave him the plans for the place where sin is paid for and forgiven. ¹²He gave him the plans for everything the Spirit of the LORD had put in his mind. There were plans for the courtyards of the LORD's temple. There were plans for all of the rooms that were around it. There were plans for the places where the treasure of God's temple would be kept. There were plans for the places where the things that were set apart for God would be kept.

¹³David told Solomon how to separate the priests and Levites into groups. He gave him directions for all of the work they should do when they served in the LORD's temple.

He also showed him how all of the articles should be used at the temple. ¹⁴Different articles were used for different purposes.

David told Solomon how much gold should be used for each gold article. He also told him how much silver should be used for each silver article. ¹⁵He told him how much gold should be used to make each gold lampstand and its lamps. He told him how much silver should be used to make each

How do I become even closer to God than I am now?

Think of God as someone who wants to be your very best friend. You will need to spend time together. You can spend time with God by reading the Bible. You can also talk with God about your life by praying. Tell God about your feelings when you pray. Tell him that you are sorry for disobeying him. Ask him to help you to obey. Ask him to help you be close to him. You also get closer to God by praising him. Thank him for loving you and for giving you everything you need. Finally, ask another person to pray for you.

checkout
1 Chronicles 28:9

Walk closer to God!
stiltz $10.00

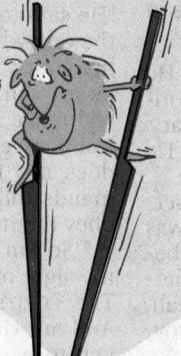

Related verses:
Colossians 1:9–14;
2 Timothy 3:16,17

silver lampstand and its lamps. The amount depended on how each lampstand would be used.

¹⁶David told Solomon how much gold should be used to make each table for holy bread. He told him how much silver should be used to make the silver tables. ¹⁷He told him how much pure gold should be used to make the forks, sprinkling bowls and pitchers. He told him how much gold should be used to make each gold dish. He told him how much silver should be used to make each silver dish.

¹⁸And he told him how much pure gold should be used to make the altar for burning incense. David also gave Solomon the plan for the chariot of the gold cherubim. They spread their wings over the ark of the covenant of the LORD.

¹⁹David said, "I have written everything down. The LORD's powerful hand helped me. He helped me understand every part of the plan."

²⁰David also said to his son Solomon, "Be strong and brave. Get to work. Don't be afraid. Don't lose hope. The LORD God is my God. He is with you. He won't fail you. He won't desert you until all of the work for serving in the LORD's temple is finished. ²¹The groups of the priests and Levites are ready to do all of the work on God's temple. Every worker who is willing and skilled can help you do all of the work. The officials and all of the people will obey every command you give them."

GIFTS ARE BROUGHT FOR THE TEMPLE

29 Then King David spoke to the whole community. He said, "God has chosen my son Solomon. But Solomon is young. He's never done anything like this before. The task is huge. This grand and wonderful temple won't be built for human beings. It will be built for the LORD God.

²"With all of my riches I've done everything I could for the temple of my God. I've provided gold for the gold work and silver for the silver work. I've provided bronze for the bronze work and iron for the iron work. I've given wood for the things that will be made out of wood. I've given onyx and turquoise for the settings. I've given stones of different colors and all kinds of fine stone and marble. I've provided everything in huge amounts.

³"With all my heart I want the temple of my God to be built. So I'm giving my personal treasures of gold and silver for it. I'm adding them to everything else I've provided for the holy temple. ⁴I'm giving 110 tons of gold and 260 tons of pure silver. Cover the walls of the buildings with it. ⁵Use it for the gold work and the silver work. Use it for everything the skilled workers will do. How many of you are willing to set yourselves apart to the LORD today?"

⁶Many people were willing to give. They included the leaders of families and the officers of the tribes of Israel. They included the commanders of thousands of men and commanders of hundreds. They also included the officials who were in charge of the king's work. ⁷All of them gave to the work on God's temple. They gave more than 190 tons of gold and 375 tons of silver. They also gave 675 tons of bronze and 3,750 tons of iron. ⁸Anyone who had valuable jewels added them to the treasure for the LORD's temple. Jehiel was in charge of the temple treasure. He was from the family line of Gershon.

⁹The people were happy when they saw what their leaders had been willing to give. The leaders had given freely. With their whole heart they had given everything to the LORD. King David was filled with joy.

DAVID PRAISES THE LORD

¹⁰David praised the LORD in front of the whole community. He said,

"LORD, we give you praise.
    You are the God of our father
      Israel.
    We give you praise for ever and
      ever.
¹¹LORD, you are great and powerful.
    Glory, majesty and beauty belong
      to you.
    Everything in heaven and on
      earth belongs to you.

LORD, the kingdom belongs to you. You are honored as the One who rules over all.

¹²Wealth and honor come from you. You are the ruler of all things. In your hands are strength and power. You can give honor and strength to everyone.

¹³Our God, we give you thanks. We praise your glorious name.

¹⁴"But who am I? And who are my people? Without your help we wouldn't be able to give this much. Everything comes from you. We've given back to you only what comes from you. ¹⁵We are outsiders and strangers in your sight. So were all of our people who lived long ago. Our days on this earth are like a shadow. We don't have any hope.

¹⁶"LORD our God, we've given more than enough. We've provided it to build you a temple where you will put your holy Name. But all of it comes from you. All of it belongs to you. ¹⁷My God, I know that you put our hearts to the test. And you are pleased when we are honest. I've given all of these things just because I wanted to. When I did it, I was completely honest with you. And I've been happy to see that your people who are here have also been willing to give to you.

¹⁸"LORD, you are the God of our fathers Abraham, Isaac and Israel. Keep this longing in the hearts of your people forever. Keep their hearts true to you. ¹⁹Help my son Solomon serve you with all his heart. Then he will keep your commands and rules. He will do what you require. He'll do everything to build the grand and wonderful temple I've provided for."

²⁰Then David spoke to the whole community. He said, "Praise the LORD your God." So all of them praised the LORD. He's the God of their people who lived long ago. The whole community bowed low. They fell down flat with their faces toward the ground. They did it in front of the LORD and the king.

SOLOMON BECOMES THE NEXT KING

²¹The next day they offered sacrifices to the LORD. They brought burnt

---

KIDS' QUESTION

Why are some people rich?

Some are rich because they were born into rich families. Others work hard, save and invest wisely. A few get their money as gifts or awards. Some cheat others.

Some people who *seem* rich have lots of nice things but no money. They are so far in debt that they may never get out. They are not really rich. They just *look* that way.

"Rich" and "poor" are just labels. Many people who live in poor countries would say that almost *everyone* in North America is rich. They have so little that almost everyone else seems rich to them.

You are truly rich only when you are content with what you have. You do not become content by being rich. You become content by being glad just to love and serve God.

checkout
1 Chronicles
29:12

Polite, young handsome boy seeks rich parents to pay his allowance

Related verses:
Philippians
4:11,12;
1 Timothy 6:6

offerings to him. They sacrificed 1,000 bulls, 1,000 rams and 1,000 male lambs. They also brought the required drink offerings. And they offered many other sacrifices for the whole community of Israel. ²²They ate and drank with great joy that day. They did it in the sight of the LORD.

Then they announced a second time that Solomon was king. He was the son of David. They anointed Solomon to be ruler in the sight of the LORD. They also anointed Zadok to be priest. ²³So Solomon sat on the throne of the LORD. He ruled as king in place of his father David. Things went well with him. All of the people of Israel obeyed him. ²⁴All of the officers and mighty men promised to be completely faithful to King Solomon. So did all of King David's sons.

²⁵The LORD greatly honored Solomon in the sight of all of the people. He gave him royal majesty. Solomon was given more glory than any king over Israel had ever had.

DAVID DIES

²⁶David was king over the whole nation of Israel. He was the son of Jesse. ²⁷He ruled over Israel for 40 years. He ruled for seven years in Hebron and for 33 years in Jerusalem. ²⁸He died when he was very old. He had enjoyed a long life. He had enjoyed wealth and honor. His son Solomon became the next king after him.

²⁹The events of King David's rule from beginning to end are written down. They are written in the records of the prophets Samuel, Nathan and Gad. ³⁰The records tell all about David's rule and power. They tell about what happened concerning him and Israel and the kingdoms of all of the other lands.

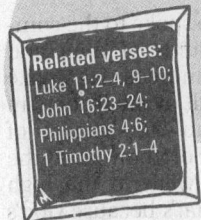

KIDS' QUESTION

What do we need to pray for?

We need to pray for three things: (1) our needs, (2) the needs of others and (3) God's will to be done. Many of the requests we bring to God will be one of these kinds of prayers. For example, we need food, clothing and shelter. So do other people. We also need forgiveness and help in resisting temptation, doing good, and becoming what God wants us to be.

There are many other types of prayers. We can praise and thank God, and tell him how wonderful he is. We can also pray for God's will to be done on earth. Jesus taught us to pray, "May your will be done here on earth, just as it is in heaven" (Matthew 6:10). God is our friend. He wants to hear from us.

checkout
1 Chronicles
29:18–20

Related verses:
Luke 11:2–4, 9–10;
John 16:23–24;
Philippians 4:6;
1 Timothy 2:1–4

DEAR GOD, I DON'T FEEL LIKE PRAYING FOR ALL THE USUAL STUFF TODAY. CAN WE JUST TALK?

2 Chronicles

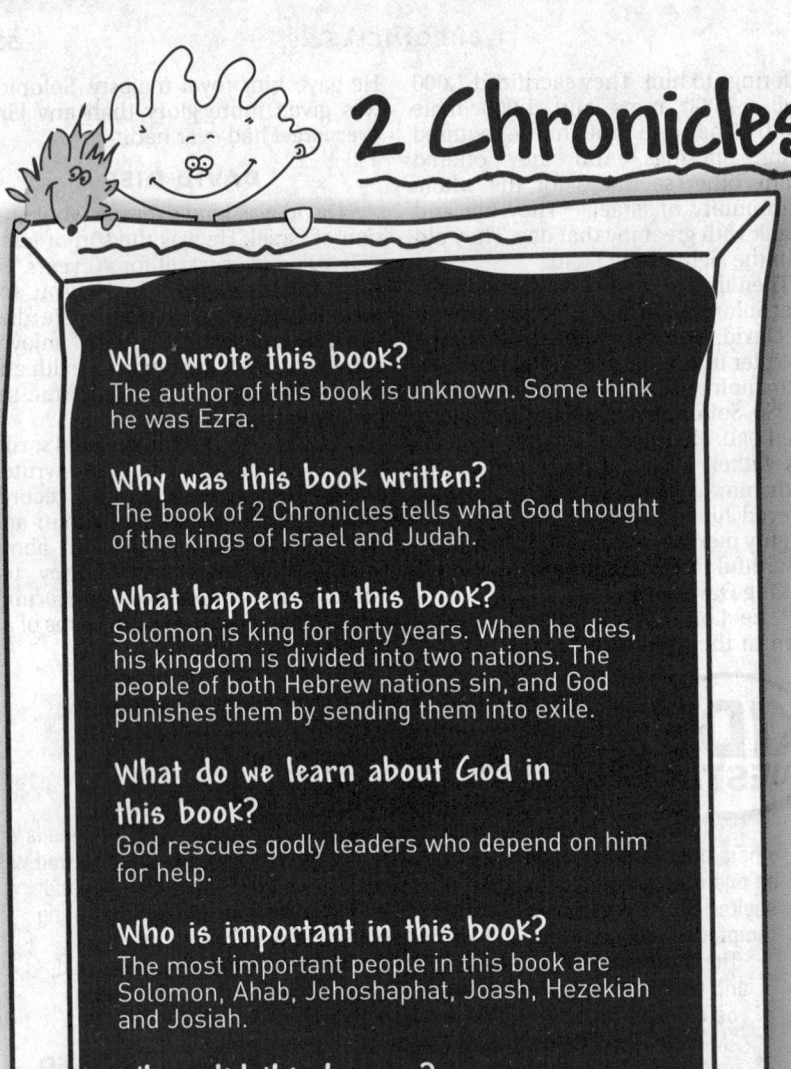

Who wrote this book?
The author of this book is unknown. Some think he was Ezra.

Why was this book written?
The book of 2 Chronicles tells what God thought of the kings of Israel and Judah.

What happens in this book?
Solomon is king for forty years. When he dies, his kingdom is divided into two nations. The people of both Hebrew nations sin, and God punishes them by sending them into exile.

What do we learn about God in this book?
God rescues godly leaders who depend on him for help.

Who is important in this book?
The most important people in this book are Solomon, Ahab, Jehoshaphat, Joash, Hezekiah and Josiah.

When did this happen?
The events in this book happened between 970 and 586 B.C.

SOLOMON ASKS GOD FOR WISDOM

1 Solomon was the son of David. Solomon made his position secure over his kingdom. The LORD his God was with him. He made Solomon very great.

²Solomon spoke to the whole community of Israel. He spoke to the commanders of thousands of men and commanders of hundreds. He spoke to the judges and all of the leaders in Israel. He spoke to the leaders of Israel's families. ³Solomon and the whole community went to the high place at Gibeon. That's because God's

Tent of Meeting was there. The LORD's servant Moses had made the tent in the desert.

⁴David had brought the ark of God up from Kiriath Jearim. He had brought it to the place he had prepared for it. He had set up a tent for it in Jerusalem.

⁵But the bronze altar that Bezalel had made was in Gibeon. Bezalel was the son of Uri. Uri was the son of Hur. The altar was in front of the LORD's holy tent. So Solomon and the whole community asked the LORD for advice there.

⁶Solomon went up to the bronze altar in front of the LORD at the Tent of Meeting. Solomon sacrificed 1,000 burnt offerings on the altar.

⁷That night God appeared to Solomon. He said to him, "Ask for anything you want me to give you."

⁸Solomon answered God, "You were very kind to my father David. Now you have made me king in his place. ⁹LORD God, let the promise you gave to my father David come true. You have made me king. My people are like the dust of the earth. They can't be counted. ¹⁰Give me wisdom and knowledge. Then I'll be able to lead these people. Without your help, who would be able to rule this great nation of yours?"

¹¹God said to Solomon, "I am glad that those are the things you really want. You have not asked for wealth, riches or honor. You have not even asked to have your enemies killed. You have not asked to live for a long time. Instead, you have asked for wisdom and knowledge. You want to be able to rule my people wisely. I have made you king over them.

¹²"So wisdom and knowledge will be given to you. I will also give you wealth, riches and honor. You will have more than any king before you ever had. And no king after you will have as much."

¹³Then Solomon left the high place at Gibeon. He went from the Tent of Meeting there to Jerusalem. And he ruled over Israel.

¹⁴Solomon had 1,400 chariots and 12,000 horses. He kept some of them in the chariot cities. He kept others with him in Jerusalem.

¹⁵The king made silver and gold as common in Jerusalem as stones. He made cedar wood as common there as sycamore-fig trees in the western hills.

¹⁶Solomon got horses from Egypt and Kue. The king's buyers purchased them from Kue. ¹⁷They could get a chariot from Egypt for 15 pounds of silver. They could get a horse for less than four pounds of silver. They sold horses and chariots to all of the Hittite and Aramean kings.

SOLOMON ASKS HIRAM TO HELP BUILD THE TEMPLE

2 Solomon gave orders to build a temple. That's where the LORD would put his Name. Solomon also gave orders to build a royal palace for himself. ²He chose 70,000 men to carry things. He chose 80,000 to cut stones in the hills. He put 3,600 men in charge of them.

³Solomon sent a message to Hiram. Hiram was king of Tyre. The message said,

"Send me cedar logs, just as you did for my father David. You sent him cedar to build a palace to live in. ⁴Now I'm about to build a temple. The Name of the LORD my God will be there. I'll set the temple apart for him.

"Sweet-smelling incense will be burned in front of him there. The holy bread will be set out at regular times. Burnt offerings will be sacrificed there every morning and evening. They will be sacrificed every Sabbath day. They will be sacrificed at every New Moon Feast. And they will be sacrificed at every yearly appointed feast of the LORD our God. That's a law for Israel that will last for all time to come.

⁵"The temple I'm going to build will be beautiful. That's because our God is greater than all other gods. ⁶So who is able to build a temple for him? After all, the heavens can't hold him. In fact, not even the highest heavens can hold him. So who am I to build a temple for him? It will only be a place to burn sacrifices to him.

[7]"Send me someone who is skilled at working with gold, silver, bronze and iron. He must also be able to work with purple, blue and bright red yarn. He must be skilled in the art of carving. Send him to work in Judah and Jerusalem with my skilled workers. My father David provided them to help me.

[8]"Also send me cedar, pine and algum logs from Lebanon. I know that your men are skilled in cutting wood there. My men will work with yours. [9]They'll provide me with plenty of lumber. That's because the temple I'm building must be large and beautiful.

[10]"I'll pay your servants. They will cut the wood. I'll pay them 125,000 bushels of wheat that has been ground up. I'll pay them 125,000 bushels of barley. I'll also pay them 115,000 gallons of wine and 115,000 gallons of olive oil."

[11]King Hiram of Tyre replied to Solomon. He wrote a letter to him. It said,

"The LORD loves his people. That's why he has made you their king."

[12]Hiram continued,

"I praise the LORD. He is the God of Israel. He made heaven and earth. He has given King David a wise son. You have good sense. You understand what is right. You will build a temple for the LORD. You will also build a palace for yourself.

[13]"I'm sending Huram-Abi to you. He is very skillful. [14]His mother was from Dan. His father was from Tyre. He is trained to work with gold, silver, bronze and iron. He knows how to work with stone and wood. He can also work with purple, blue and bright red yarn and fine linen. He's skilled in all kinds of carving. He can follow any pattern you give him. He'll work with your skilled workers. He'll also work with those of your father David. David was my master.

[15]"Now please send us what you promised. Send us the wheat, barley, olive oil and wine. [16]And we'll cut all of the logs from Lebanon you need. We'll make rafts out of them. We'll float them by sea down to Joppa. Then you can take them up to Jerusalem."

[17]Solomon counted all of the outsiders who were living in Israel. He did it after his father David had counted them. There were 153,600 of them. [18]He chose 70,000 to carry things. He chose 80,000 to cut stones in the hills. He put 3,600 men in charge of the people to keep them working.

SOLOMON BUILDS THE TEMPLE

3 Then Solomon began to build the temple of the LORD. He built it on Mount Moriah in Jerusalem. That's where the LORD had appeared to Solomon's father David. He had appeared at the threshing floor of Araunah. Araunah was from Jebus. David had provided the threshing floor. [2]Solomon began building the temple on the second day of the second month. It was in the fourth year of his rule.

[3]Solomon laid the foundation for God's temple. It was 90 feet long and 30 feet wide. Solomon's men followed the standard measure that was used at that time. [4]The porch in front of the temple was 30 feet across and 30 feet high.

Solomon covered the inside of the temple with pure gold. [5]He covered the inside of the main hall with pine boards. Then he covered the boards with fine gold. He decorated the hall with palm tree patterns and chain patterns. [6]He decorated the temple with valuable jewels. The gold he used came from Parvaim. [7]He covered the ceiling beams, doorframes, walls and doors of the temple with gold. He carved cherubim on the walls.

[8]He built the Most Holy Room. It was as long as the temple was wide. It was 30 feet long and 30 feet wide. He covered the inside of the Most Holy Room with 23 tons of fine gold. [9]He also covered the upper parts with gold. The gold on the nails weighed 20 ounces.

[10]For the Most Holy Room, Solomon made a pair of carved cherubim. He covered them with gold. [11]The total length of the cherubim's wings from tip to tip was 30 feet. One wing of the first cherub was seven and a half feet long. Its tip touched the temple wall. The other wing was also seven and a half feet long. Its tip touched the wing tip of the other cherub.

[12]In the same way one wing of the second cherub was seven and a half feet long. Its tip touched the other temple wall. The other wing was also seven and a half feet long. Its tip touched the wing tip of the first cherub. [13]So the total length of the wings of the two cherubim was 30 feet from tip to tip. The cherubim stood facing the main hall.

[14]Solomon made the curtain out of blue, purple and bright red yarn and fine linen. A skilled worker sewed cherubim into its pattern.

[15]In front of the temple, Solomon made two pillars. Each pillar was 26 feet tall. Each had a decorated top that was seven and a half feet high. [16]Solomon made chains that were linked together. He put them on top of the pillars. He also made 100 pomegranates. He fastened them to the chains.

[17]Solomon set the pillars up in front of the temple. One was on the south. The other was on the north. He named the one on the south Jakin. The one on the north he named Boaz.

MORE FACTS ABOUT THE TEMPLE

4 Solomon made a bronze altar that was 30 feet long, 30 feet wide and 15 feet high. [2]He made a huge metal bowl for washing. Its shape was round. It measured 15 feet from rim to rim. It was seven and a half feet high. And it was 45 feet around. [3]Below the rim there was a circle of bull figures around the bowl. In every 18 inches around the bowl there were ten bulls. The bulls were arranged in two rows. They were made as part of the bowl itself.

[4]The bowl stood on 12 bulls. Three of them faced north. Three faced west. Three faced south. And three faced east. The bowl rested on top of them.

Their rear ends were toward the center. [5]The bowl was three inches thick. Its rim was like the rim of a cup. The rim was shaped like the bloom of a lily. The bowl held 17,500 gallons of water.

[6]Solomon made ten smaller bowls for washing. He placed five of them on the south side of the huge bowl. He placed the other five on the north side.

The things that were used for the burnt offerings were rinsed in the smaller bowls. But the priests used the huge bowl for washing.

[7]Solomon made ten gold lampstands. He followed the pattern the LORD had given him. He placed the lampstands in the temple. He put five of them on the south side. He put the other five on the north side.

[8]He made ten tables. He placed them in the temple. He put five of them on the south side. He put the other five on the north side. He also made 100 gold sprinkling bowls.

[9]He made the courtyard of the priests. He also made the large courtyard. He made doors for it. He covered the doors with bronze.

[10]He placed the huge bowl on the south side of the courtyard. He put it at the southeast corner.

[11]He also made the pots, shovels and sprinkling bowls.

So Huram finished the work he had started for King Solomon. Here's what he made for God's temple.

[12]He made the two pillars.

He made the two tops for the pillars. The tops were shaped like bowls.

He made the two sets of chains that were linked together. They decorated the two bowl-shaped tops of the pillars.

[13]He made the 400 pomegranates for the two sets of chains. There were two rows of pomegranates for each chain. They decorated the bowl-shaped tops of the pillars.

[14]He made the stands and their bowls.

[15]He made the huge bowl. He made the 12 bulls that were under it.

[16]He made the pots, shovels and

meat forks. He also made all of the articles that were connected with them.

Huram-Abi made all of those objects for King Solomon for the LORD's temple. He made them out of bronze. Then he shined them up. ¹⁷The king had them made in clay molds. It was done on the flatlands of the Jordan River between Succoth and Zarethan. ¹⁸Solomon made huge numbers of those articles. There were too many of them to weigh. No one even tried to weigh the bronze they were made out of.

¹⁹Solomon also made all of the articles that were in God's temple.

He made the golden altar.
He made the tables for the holy bread.
²⁰He made the pure gold lampstands and their lamps. The lamps burned in front of the Most Holy Room, just as the law required.
²¹He made the gold flowers. He made the gold lamps and tongs. They were made out of solid gold.
²²He made the wick cutters, sprinkling bowls, dishes, and shallow cups for burning incense. All of them were made out of pure gold. He made the gold doors of the temple. They were the inner doors to the Most Holy Room and the doors of the main hall.

5 Solomon finished all of the work for the LORD's temple. Then he brought in the things his father David had set apart for the LORD. They included the silver and gold and all of the articles for God's temple. Solomon placed them with the other treasures that were there.

SOLOMON BRINGS THE ARK TO THE TEMPLE

²Then Solomon sent for the elders of Israel. He told them to come to Jerusalem. They included all of the leaders of the tribes. They also included the chiefs of the families of Israel. Solomon wanted them to bring up the ark of the LORD's covenant from Zion. Zion was the City of David. ³All of the men of Israel came together to where the king was. It was at the time of the Feast of Booths. The feast was held in the seventh month.

⁴All of the elders of Israel arrived. Then the Levites picked up the ark and carried it. ⁵They brought up the ark. They also brought up the Tent of Meeting and all of the sacred articles that were in the tent. The priests, who were Levites, carried everything up.

⁶The entire community of Israel had gathered around King Solomon. All of them were in front of the ark. They sacrificed huge numbers of sheep and cattle. There were so many that they couldn't be recorded. In fact, they couldn't even be counted.

⁷The priests brought the ark of the LORD's covenant to its place in the Most Holy Room of the temple. They put it under the wings of the cherubim.

⁸The cherubim's wings were spread out over the place where the ark was. They covered the ark. They also covered the poles that were used to carry it. ⁹The poles reached out from the ark. They were so long that their ends could be seen from in front of the Most Holy Room. But they couldn't be seen from outside the Holy Room. They are still there to this very day.

¹⁰There wasn't anything in the ark except the two tablets. Moses had placed them in it at Mount Horeb. That's where the LORD had made a covenant with the Israelites. He made it after they came out of Egypt.

¹¹The priests left the Holy Room. All of the priests who were there had set themselves apart to the LORD. It didn't matter what group they were in.

¹²All of the Levites who played music stood near the east side of the altar. They included Asaph, Heman, Jeduthun and their sons and relatives. They were dressed in fine linen. They were playing cymbals, harps and lyres. They were joined by 120 priests who were blowing trumpets.

¹³The trumpet players and singers made music together as if they were only one voice. They praised the LORD.

They gave thanks to him. Some of them played their trumpets, cymbals and other instruments. The others raised their voices to praise the LORD. They sang,

"He is good.
His faithful love continues forever."

Then a cloud filled the temple of the LORD. ¹⁴The priests couldn't do their work because of it. The glory of the LORD filled God's temple.

6 Then Solomon said, "LORD, you have said you would live in a dark cloud. ²I've built a beautiful temple for you. You can live in it forever."

³The whole community of Israel was standing there. The king turned around and gave them his blessing. ⁴Then he said,

"I praise the LORD. He is the God of Israel. With his mouth he made a promise to my father David. With his powerful hands he made it come true. He said, ⁵'I brought my people out of Egypt. Ever since I did that, I have not chosen a city in any tribe of Israel where a temple could be built for my Name. I have not chosen anyone to be the leader over my people Israel. ⁶But now I have chosen Jerusalem. I will put my Name there. And I have chosen David to rule over my people Israel.'

⁷"With all his heart my father David wanted to build a temple. He wanted to do it so the Name of the LORD could be there. The LORD is the God of Israel.

⁸"But the LORD spoke to my father David. He said, 'With all your heart you wanted to build a temple for my Name. It is good that you wanted to do that. ⁹But you will not build the temple. Instead, your son will build the temple for my Name. He is your own flesh and blood.'

¹⁰"The LORD has kept the promise he made. I've become the next king after my father David. Now I'm sitting on the throne of Israel. That's exactly what the LORD promised would happen. I've built the temple for the Name of the LORD. He is the God of Israel. ¹¹I've placed the ark there. The tablets of the LORD's covenant are inside it. He made that covenant with the people of Israel."

SOLOMON PRAYS TO SET THE TEMPLE APART TO THE LORD

¹²Then Solomon stood in front of the LORD's altar. He stood in front of the whole community of Israel. He spread out his hands to pray. ¹³He had made a bronze stage. It was seven and a half feet long and seven and a half feet wide. It was four and a half feet high. He had placed it in the center of the outer courtyard. He stood on the stage. Then he got down on his knees in front of the whole community of Israel. He spread out his hands toward heaven. ¹⁴He said,

"LORD, you are the God of Israel. There is no God like you in heaven or on earth. You keep the covenant you made with us. You show us your love. You do that when we follow you with all our hearts. ¹⁵You have kept your promise to my father David. He was your servant. With your mouth you made a promise. With your powerful hand you have made it come true. And today we can see it.

¹⁶"LORD, you are the God of Israel. Keep the promises you made to my father David. Do it for him. He was your servant. You said to him, 'You will always have a son to sit on the throne of Israel in my sight. That will be true only if your sons are careful in everything they do. They must live the way my law tells them to. That is the way you have lived.' ¹⁷LORD, you are the God of Israel. So let your promise to your servant David come true.

¹⁸"But will you really live on earth with human beings? After all, the heavens can't hold you. In fact, even the highest heavens can't hold you. So this temple I've built certainly can't hold you! ¹⁹"But please pay attention to

my prayer. LORD my God, show me your favor as I make my appeal to you. Listen to my cry for help. Hear the prayer I'm praying to you. ²⁰Let your eyes look toward this temple day and night. You said you would put your Name here. Listen to the prayer I'm praying toward this place.

²¹"Hear me when I ask you to show us your favor. Listen to your people Israel when they pray toward this place. Listen to us from heaven. It's the place where you live. When you hear us, forgive us.

²²"Suppose a man does something wrong to his neighbor. And he is required to take an oath and make a promise. He must come and do it in front of your altar in this temple. ²³When he does, listen to him from heaven. Take action. Judge between the man and his neighbor. Pay back the one who is guilty. Do to him what he has done to the other person. Tell everyone that the person who hasn't done anything wrong is free of blame. That will prove he isn't guilty.

²⁴"Suppose your people Israel have lost the battle against their enemies. And suppose they've sinned against you. But they turn back to you and praise your name. They pray to you in this temple. And they ask you to show them your favor. ²⁵Then listen to them from heaven. Forgive the sin of your people Israel. Bring them back to the land you gave to them and their people who lived long ago.

²⁶"Suppose your people have sinned against you. And because of that, the sky is closed up and there isn't any rain. But your people pray toward this place. They praise you by admitting they've sinned. And they turn away from their sin because you have made them suffer. ²⁷Then listen to them from heaven. Forgive the sin of your people Israel. Teach them the right way to live. Send rain on the land you gave them as their share.

²⁸"Suppose there isn't enough food in the land. And a plague strikes the land. The hot winds completely dry up our crops. Or locusts or grasshoppers come and eat them up. Or enemies surround one of our cities and get ready to attack it. Or trouble or sickness comes. ²⁹But suppose one of your people prays to you. He asks you to show him your favor. He is aware of how much he is suffering. And he spreads out his hands toward this temple to pray. ³⁰Then listen to him from heaven. It's the place where you live. Forgive him. Deal with him in keeping with everything he does. You know his heart. In fact, you are the only one who knows every human heart.

³¹"Your people will have respect for you. They will live the way you want them to. They'll live that way as long as they are in the land you gave our people long ago.

³²"Suppose a stranger who doesn't belong to your people Israel has come from a land far away. He has come because he's heard about your great name. He has heard that you reached out your mighty hand and powerful arm. So he comes and prays toward this temple. ³³Then listen to him from heaven. It's the place where you live. Do what that stranger asks you to do.

"Then all of the nations on earth will know you. They will have respect for you. They'll respect you just as your own people Israel do. They'll know that your Name is in this house I've built.

³⁴"Suppose your people go to war against their enemies. It doesn't matter where you send them. And suppose they pray to you toward this city you have chosen. They pray toward the temple I've built for your Name. ³⁵Then listen to them from heaven. Listen to their prayer. Listen to them when they ask you to show them your favor. Stand up for them.

³⁶"Suppose they sin against you.

After all, there isn't anyone who doesn't sin. And suppose you get angry with them. You hand them over to their enemies. They take them as prisoners to another land. It doesn't matter whether it's near or far away. [37]But suppose your people change their ways in the land where they are held as prisoners. They turn away from their sins. They beg you to help them in the land where they are prisoners. They say, 'We have sinned. We've done what is wrong. We've done what is evil.' [38]And they turn back to you with all their heart and soul. Suppose it happens in the land where they were taken as prisoners. There they pray toward the land you gave their people long ago. They pray toward the city you have chosen. And they pray toward the temple I've built for your Name. [39]Then listen to them from heaven. It's the place where you live. Listen to their prayer. Listen to them when they ask you to show them your favor. Stand up for them. Your people have sinned against you. Please forgive them.

[40]"My God, let your eyes see us. Let your ears pay attention to the prayers that are offered in this place.

[41] "LORD God, rise up and come to
    your resting place.
  Come in together with the ark.
  It's the sign of your power.
  LORD God, may your priests put
    on salvation as if it were
    their clothes.
  May your faithful people be glad
    because you are so good.
[42]LORD God, don't turn your back
    on your anointed king.
  Remember the great love you
    promised to your servant
    David."

SOLOMON SETS THE TEMPLE APART TO THE LORD

7 Solomon finished praying. Then fire came down from heaven. It burned up the burnt offering and the sacrifices. The glory of the LORD filled the temple. [2]The priests couldn't enter the temple of the LORD. His glory filled it.

[3]All of the people of Israel saw the fire coming down. They saw the glory of the LORD above the temple. So they got down on their knees in the courtyard with their faces toward the ground. They worshiped the LORD. They gave thanks to him. They said,

"He is good.
  His faithful love continues
    forever."

[4]Then the king and all of the people offered sacrifices to the LORD. [5]King Solomon sacrificed 22,000 head of cattle and 120,000 sheep and goats. So the king and all of the people set the temple of God apart.

[6]The priests and Levites took their positions. The Levites played the LORD's musical instruments. King David had made them for praising the LORD. They were used when he gave thanks to the LORD. He said, "His faithful love continues forever."

Across from where the Levites were, the priests blew their trumpets. All of the people of Israel were standing.

[7]Solomon set the middle area of the courtyard apart to the LORD. It was in front of the LORD's temple. There Solomon sacrificed burnt offerings. He also sacrificed the fat of the friendship offerings there. He did it there because the bronze altar he had made couldn't hold all of the burnt offerings, the grain offerings and the fat parts.

[8]At that time Solomon celebrated the Feast of Booths for seven days. The whole community of Israel was with him. It was a huge crowd. People came from as far away as Lebo Hamath and the Wadi of Egypt. [9]On the eighth day they held a service. For seven days they had celebrated by setting the altar apart to honor God. The feast continued for seven more days.

[10]Then Solomon sent the people home. It was the 23rd day of the seventh month. The people were glad. Their hearts were full of joy. That's because the LORD had done good things for David and Solomon and his people Israel.

THE LORD APPEARS TO SOLOMON

¹¹Solomon finished the LORD's temple and the royal palace. He had done everything he had planned to do in the LORD's temple and his own palace.

¹²The LORD appeared to him at night. He said,

"I have heard your prayer. I have chosen this place for myself. It is a temple where sacrifices will be offered.

¹³"Suppose I close up the sky and there isn't any rain. Suppose I command locusts to eat up the crops. And I send a plague among my people. ¹⁴But they make themselves low in my sight. They pray and look to me. And they turn from their evil ways. Then I will listen to them from heaven. I will forgive their sin. And I will heal their land. After all, they are my people.

¹⁵"Now my eyes will see them. My ears will pay attention to the prayers they offer in this place. ¹⁶I have chosen this temple. I have set it apart for myself. My Name will be there forever. My eyes and my heart will always be there.

¹⁷"But you must walk with me, just as your father David did. Do everything I command you to do. Obey my rules and laws. ¹⁸Then I will set up your royal throne. I made a covenant with your father David to do that. I said to him, 'You will always have a son to rule over Israel.'

¹⁹"But suppose all of you turn away from me. You refuse to obey the rules and commands I have given you. And you go off to serve other gods and worship them. ²⁰Then I will remove Israel from my land. It is the land I gave them. I will turn my back on this temple. I will do it even though I have set it apart for my Name to be there. I will make all of the nations hate it. They will laugh and joke about it.

²¹"This temple is now so grand and beautiful. But the time is coming when all those who pass by it will be shocked. They will say, 'Why has the LORD done a thing like this to this land and temple?'

²²"People will answer, 'Because they have deserted the LORD. He is the God of their people who lived long ago. He brought them out of Egypt. But they have been holding on to other gods. They've been worshiping them.

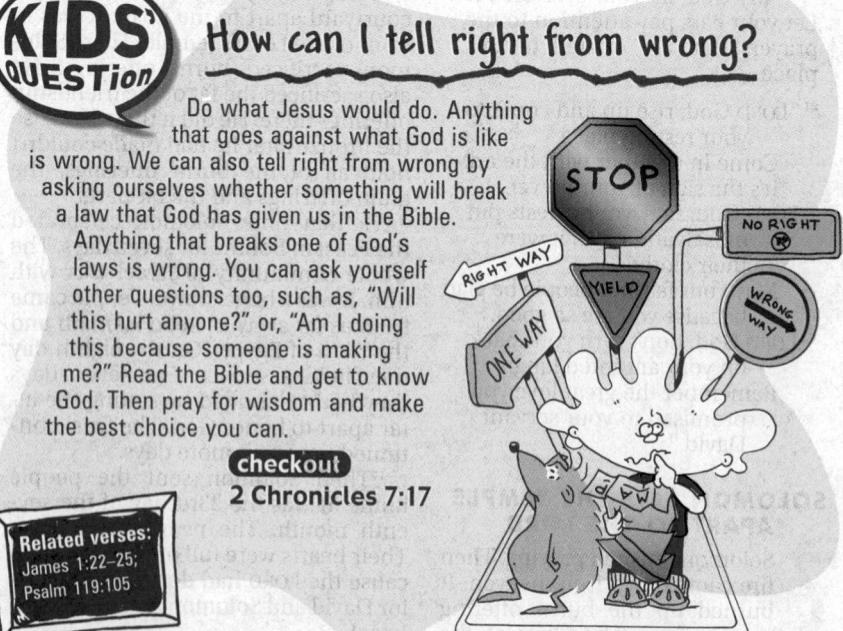

KIDS' QUESTION

How can I tell right from wrong?

Do what Jesus would do. Anything that goes against what God is like is wrong. We can also tell right from wrong by asking ourselves whether something will break a law that God has given us in the Bible. Anything that breaks one of God's laws is wrong. You can ask yourself other questions too, such as, "Will this hurt anyone?" or, "Am I doing this because someone is making me?" Read the Bible and get to know God. Then pray for wisdom and make the best choice you can.

checkout
2 Chronicles 7:17

Related verses:
James 1:22–25;
Psalm 119:105

They've been serving them. That's why he has brought all of this horrible trouble on them.' "

OTHER THINGS SOLOMON DID

8 Solomon built the LORD's temple and his own palace. It took him 20 years to build them. After that, ²Solomon rebuilt the villages Hiram had given him. He settled Israelites in them.

³Then Solomon went to Hamath Zobah. He captured it. ⁴He also built up Tadmor in the desert. He built up all of the cities in Hamath where he could store things. ⁵He rebuilt Lower Beth Horon and Upper Beth Horon. He put up high walls around them. He made their city gates secure with heavy metal bars. ⁶He rebuilt Baalath and all of the cities where he could store things. He also rebuilt all of the cities for his chariots and horses.

Solomon built anything he wanted to build in Jerusalem, Lebanon and all of the territory he ruled over.

⁷There were still many people left in the land who weren't Israelites. They included Hittites, Amorites, Perizzites, Hivites and Jebusites. ⁸They were children of the people who had lived in the land before the Israelites came. The people of Israel hadn't destroyed them. Solomon had forced them to work very hard as his slaves. And they still work for Israel to this very day.

⁹But Solomon didn't force the men of Israel to work as his slaves. Instead, some were his fighting men. Others were commanders of his captains, chariots and chariot drivers. ¹⁰Still others were King Solomon's chief officials. There were 250 officials in charge of the other men.

¹¹Solomon brought Pharaoh's daughter up from the City of David to the palace he had built for her. He said, "My wife must not live in the palace of David, who was the king of Israel. It's one of the places the ark of the LORD has entered. That makes it holy."

¹²Solomon had built the LORD's altar. It stood in front of the temple porch. On that altar Solomon sacrificed burnt offerings to the LORD. ¹³Each day he sacrificed what the Law of Moses required. He sacrificed the required offerings every Sabbath day. He also sacrificed them at each New Moon Feast and during the three yearly feasts. Those three were the Feast of Unleavened Bread, the Feast of Weeks and the Feast of Booths.

¹⁴Solomon followed the orders his father David had given him. He appointed the groups of priests for their duties. He appointed the Levites to lead the people in praising the LORD. They also helped the priests do their required tasks each day. Solomon appointed the groups of men who guarded all of the gates. That's what David, the man of God, had ordered. ¹⁵King David's commands were followed completely. They applied to the priests and Levites. They also applied to the temple treasure.

¹⁶All of Solomon's work was carried out. It started the day the foundation of the LORD's temple was laid. It ended when the LORD's temple was finished.

¹⁷Solomon went to Ezion Geber and Elath on the coast of Edom. ¹⁸Hiram sent him ships that his own officers commanded. They were men who knew the sea. Together with Solomon's men they sailed to Ophir. They brought back 17 tons of gold. They gave it to King Solomon.

THE QUEEN OF SHEBA VISITS SOLOMON

9 The queen of Sheba heard about how famous Solomon was. So she came to Jerusalem to test him with hard questions. She arrived with a very large group of attendants. Her camels were carrying spices, huge amounts of gold, and valuable jewels. She came to Solomon and asked him about everything she wanted to know.

²He answered all of her questions. There wasn't anything that was too hard for him to explain to her.

³So the queen of Sheba saw how wise Solomon was. She saw the palace he had built. ⁴She saw the food that was on his table. She saw his officials sitting there. She saw the robes of the servants who waited on everyone. She saw the robes the wine tasters were wearing. And she saw the burnt offer-

ings Solomon sacrificed at the LORD's temple. She could hardly believe everything she had seen.

⁵She said to the king, "Back in my own country I heard a report about you. I heard about how much you had accomplished. I also heard about how wise you are. Everything I heard is true. ⁶But I didn't believe what people were saying. So I came to see for myself. And now I believe it! You are twice as wise as people say you are. The report I heard doesn't even begin to tell the whole story about you.

⁷"How happy your men must be! How happy your officials must be! They always get to serve you and hear the wise things you say.

⁸"May the LORD your God be praised. He must take great delight in you. He placed you on his throne as king. He put you there to rule for him. Your God loves Israel very much. He longs to take good care of them forever. That's why he has made you king over them. He knows that you will do what is fair and right."

⁹She gave the king four and a half tons of gold. She also gave him huge amounts of spices and valuable jewels. There had never been as many spices as the queen of Sheba gave to King Solomon.

¹⁰The servants of Hiram and those of Solomon brought gold from Ophir. They also brought algumwood and valuable jewels. ¹¹The king used the algumwood to make steps for the LORD's temple and the royal palace. He also used it to make harps and lyres for those who played the music. No one had ever seen that much algumwood in Judah before.

¹²King Solomon gave the queen of Sheba everything she wanted and asked for. In fact, he gave her more than she had brought to him. Then she left. She returned to her own country with her attendants.

SOLOMON IN ALL OF HIS GLORY

¹³Each year Solomon received 25 tons of gold. ¹⁴That didn't include the money that was brought in by business and trade. All of the kings of Arabia also brought gold and silver to Solomon. So did the governors of Israel.

¹⁵King Solomon made 200 large shields out of hammered gold. Each one weighed seven and a half pounds. ¹⁶He also made 300 small shields out of hammered gold. Each one weighed almost four pounds. The king put all of the shields in the Palace of the Forest of Lebanon.

¹⁷Then he made a large throne. It was decorated with ivory. It was covered with pure gold. ¹⁸The throne had six steps. A gold stool for the king's feet was connected to it. The throne had armrests on both sides of the seat. A statue of a lion stood on each side of the throne. ¹⁹Twelve lions stood on the six steps. There was one at each end of each step. Nothing like that throne had ever been made for any other kingdom.

²⁰All of King Solomon's cups were made out of gold. All of the articles that were used in the Palace of the Forest of Lebanon were made out of pure gold. Nothing was made out of silver. When Solomon was king, silver wasn't considered to be worth very much.

²¹He had many ships that carried goods to be traded. The crews of those ships were made up of Hiram's men. Once every three years the ships returned. They brought gold, silver, ivory, apes and baboons.

²²King Solomon was richer than all of the other kings on earth. He was also wiser than they were.

²³All of these kings wanted to meet Solomon in person. They wanted to see for themselves how wise God had made him. ²⁴Year after year, everyone who came to him brought a gift. They brought articles that were made out of silver and gold. They brought robes, weapons and spices. They also brought horses and mules.

²⁵Solomon had 4,000 spaces where he kept his horses and chariots. He had 12,000 horses. He kept some of his horses and chariots in the chariot cities. He kept the others with him in Jerusalem.

²⁶Solomon ruled over all of the kings from the Euphrates River to the land of the Philistines. He ruled all the way to the border of Egypt.

²⁷The king made silver as common

in Jerusalem as stones. He made cedar wood as common there as sycamore-fig trees in the western hills.

²⁸Solomon got horses from Egypt. He also got them from many other countries.

SOLOMON DIES

²⁹The other events of Solomon's rule from beginning to end are written down. They are written in the records of the prophet Nathan. They are written in the prophecy of Ahijah. He was from Shiloh. They are also written in the records of the visions of the prophet Iddo about Jeroboam. Jeroboam was the son of Nebat.

³⁰Solomon ruled in Jerusalem over the whole nation of Israel for 40 years. ³¹Then he joined the members of his family who had already died. His body was buried in the city of his father David. Solomon's son Rehoboam became the next king after him.

ISRAEL REFUSES TO FOLLOW REHOBOAM

10 Rehoboam went to Shechem. All of the people of Israel had gone there to make him king.

²Jeroboam heard about it. He was the son of Nebat. Jeroboam was in Egypt at that time. He had gone there for safety. He wanted to get away from King Solomon. But now he returned from Egypt.

³So the people sent for Jeroboam. He and all of the people went to Rehoboam. They said to him, ⁴"Your father put a heavy load on our shoulders. But now make our hard work easier. Make the heavy load on us lighter. Then we'll serve you."

⁵Rehoboam answered, "Come back to me in three days." So the people went away.

⁶Then King Rehoboam asked the elders for advice. They had served his father Solomon while he was still living. Rehoboam asked them, "What advice can you give me? How should I answer these people?"

⁷They replied, "Be kind to them. Please them. Give them what they are asking for. Then they'll always serve you."

⁸But Rehoboam didn't accept the advice the elders gave him. He asked for advice from the young men who had grown up with him and were now serving him. ⁹He asked them, "What's your advice? How should I answer these people? They said to me, 'Make the load your father put on our shoulders lighter.' "

¹⁰The young men who had grown up with him gave their answer. They replied, "The people have said to you, 'Your father put a heavy load on our shoulders. Make it lighter.' Tell them, 'My little finger is stronger than my father's legs. ¹¹My father put a heavy load on your shoulders. But I'll make it even heavier. My father beat you with whips. But I'll beat you with bigger whips.' "

¹²Three days later Jeroboam and all of the people returned to Rehoboam. That's because the king had said, "Come back to me in three days."

¹³The king answered them in a mean way. He didn't accept the advice of the elders. ¹⁴Instead, he followed the advice of the young men. He said, "My father put a heavy load on your shoulders. But I'll make it even heavier. My father beat you with whips. But I'll beat you with bigger whips."

¹⁵So the king didn't listen to the people. That's because God had planned it that way. What the LORD had said through Ahijah came true. Ahijah had spoken the LORD's message to Jeroboam, the son of Nebat. Ahijah was from Shiloh.

¹⁶All of the people of Israel saw that the king refused to listen to them. So they answered the king. They said,

"We don't have any share in
    David's royal family.
We don't have any share in Jesse's
    son.
People of Israel, let's go back to
    our homes.
David's royal family, take care of
    your own kingdom!"

So all of the people of Israel went home.

¹⁷But Rehoboam still ruled over the Israelites who were living in the towns of Judah.

¹⁸Adoniram was in charge of those who were forced to work hard for King Rehoboam. The king sent him out among the Israelites. But they killed him by throwing stones at him. Rehoboam was able to get away in his chariot. He escaped to Jerusalem. ¹⁹Israel has refused to follow the royal family of David to this very day.

11 Rehoboam arrived in Jerusalem. He brought together 180,000 fighting men from the tribes of Judah and Benjamin. He had decided to make war against Israel. He wanted his fighting men to get the kingdom of Israel back for him.

²But a message came to Shemaiah from the LORD. He was a man of God. The LORD said to him, ³"Speak to Solomon's son Rehoboam, the king of Judah. Speak to all of the people of Israel in Judah and Benjamin. Tell them, ⁴'The LORD says, "Do not go up to fight against your relatives. I want every one of you to go back home. Things have happened exactly the way I planned them." ' "

So the fighting men obeyed the LORD's message. They turned back. They didn't march out against Jeroboam.

REHOBOAM BUILDS UP JUDAH'S TOWNS

⁵Rehoboam lived in Jerusalem. He made Judah more secure by building up their towns. ⁶He built up Bethlehem, Etam, Tekoa, ⁷Beth Zur, Soco and Adullam. ⁸He also built up Gath, Mareshah, Ziph, ⁹Adoraim, Lachish, Azekah, ¹⁰Zorah, Aijalon and Hebron. All of them were cities in Judah and Benjamin that had high walls around them.

¹¹Rehoboam made those cities even more secure. He put commanders in them. He gave them plenty of food, olive oil and wine. ¹²He put shields and spears in all of those cities. He made them very strong. So he ruled over Judah and Benjamin.

¹³The priests and Levites were on Rehoboam's side. They came from their territories all over Israel. ¹⁴The Levites even left their grasslands and other property behind. They came to Judah and Jerusalem. That's because Jeroboam and his sons had refused to accept them as priests of the LORD. ¹⁵Jeroboam appointed his own priests to serve at the high places. He had made statues of gods that looked like goats and calves. His priests served those gods.

¹⁶Some people from every tribe in Israel followed the Levites to Jerusalem. With all their hearts they wanted to worship the LORD. He is the God of Israel. They came to Jerusalem to offer sacrifices to him. He was the God of their people of long ago. ¹⁷All those who came to Jerusalem made the kingdom of Judah strong. They helped Solomon's son Rehoboam for three years. During that time they lived the way David and Solomon had lived.

REHOBOAM'S FAMILY

¹⁸Rehoboam got married to Mahalath. She was the daughter of David's son Jerimoth. Her mother was Abihail. Abihail was the daughter of Jesse's son Eliab. ¹⁹Mahalath had sons by Rehoboam. Their names were Jeush, Shemariah and Zaham. ²⁰Then Rehoboam married Maacah. She was the daughter of Absalom. She had sons by Rehoboam. Their names were Abijah, Attai, Ziza and Shelomith. ²¹Rehoboam loved Absalom's daughter Maacah. In fact, he loved her more than any of his other wives and concubines. He had a total of 18 wives and 60 concubines. And he had a total of 28 sons and 60 daughters.

²²Rehoboam appointed Maacah's son Abijah to be the chief prince among his brothers. He did it to make him king. ²³He acted wisely. He scattered some of his sons through all of the territories of Judah and Benjamin. He put them in all of the cities that had high walls around them. He gave them plenty of food and everything else they needed. He also gave them many wives.

SHISHAK ATTACKS JERUSALEM

12 Rehoboam had made his position as king secure. He had become very strong.

Then he turned away from the law of the LORD. So did all of the people of Judah.

²They hadn't been faithful to the LORD. So Shishak attacked Jerusalem. It was in the fifth year that Rehoboam was king. Shishak was king of Egypt. ³He came with 1,200 chariots and 60,000 horsemen. Troops of Libyans, Sukkites and Cushites came with him from Egypt. There were so many of them they couldn't be counted. ⁴Shishak captured the cities of Judah that had high walls around them. He came all the way to Jerusalem.

⁵Then the prophet Shemaiah came to Rehoboam and the leaders of Judah. They had gathered together in Jerusalem. They were afraid of Shishak. Shemaiah said to them, "The LORD says, 'You have left me. So now I am leaving you to Shishak.'"

⁶The king and the leaders of Israel made themselves low in the LORD's sight. They said, "The LORD does what is right and fair."

⁷The LORD saw they had made themselves low. So he gave a message to Shemaiah. It said, "They have made themselves low in my sight. So I will not destroy them. Instead, I will soon save them. I will not pour out my burning anger on Jerusalem through Shishak. ⁸But its people will be brought under his control. Then they will learn the difference between serving me and serving the kings of other lands."

⁹Shishak, the king of Egypt, attacked Jerusalem. He carried away the treasures of the LORD's temple. He also carried the treasures of the royal palace away. He took everything. That included the gold shields Solomon had made.

¹⁰So King Rehoboam made bronze shields to take their place. He gave them to the commanders of the guards who were on duty at the entrance to the royal palace. ¹¹Every time the king went to the LORD's temple, the guards went with him. They carried the shields. Later, they took them back to the room where they were kept.

¹²Rehoboam had made himself low in the LORD's sight. So the LORD turned his anger away from him. Rehoboam

wasn't totally destroyed. In fact, some good things happened in Judah.

¹³King Rehoboam had made his position secure in Jerusalem. He continued as king. He was 41 years old when he became king. He ruled for 17 years in Jerusalem. It was the city the LORD had chosen out of all of the cities in the tribes of Israel. He wanted to put his Name there. The name of Rehoboam's mother was Naamah from Ammon.

¹⁴Rehoboam did what was evil. That's because he hadn't worshiped the LORD with all his heart.

¹⁵The events of Rehoboam's rule from beginning to end are written down. They are written in the records of the prophets Shemaiah and Iddo. The records deal with family histories. Rehoboam and Jeroboam were always at war with each other.

¹⁶Rehoboam joined the members of his family who had already died. His body was buried in the City of David. His son Abijah became the next king after him.

ABIJAH BECOMES KING OF JUDAH

13 Abijah became king of Judah. It was in the 18th year of Jeroboam's rule over Israel. ²Abijah ruled in Jerusalem for three years. His mother's name was Maacah. She was a daughter of Uriel. Uriel was from Gibeah.

There was war between Abijah and Jeroboam. ³Abijah went into battle with an army of 400,000 able fighting men. Jeroboam lined up his soldiers against them. He had 800,000 able troops.

⁴Abijah stood on Mount Zemaraim. It's in the hill country of Ephraim. Abijah said, "Jeroboam and all you men of Israel, listen to me! ⁵The LORD is the God of Israel. Don't you know that he has placed David and his sons after him on Israel's throne forever? The LORD made a covenant of salt with David. The salt means the covenant will last for all time to come.

⁶"Jeroboam, the son of Nebat, was an official of David's son Solomon. But he refused to obey his master. ⁷Some worthless and evil men gathered around him. They opposed Solomon's

son Rehoboam. At that time Rehoboam was young. He couldn't make up his mind. He wasn't strong enough to stand up against those men.

8"Now you plan to stand up against the kingdom of the LORD. His kingdom is in the hands of men in David's family line. It's true that you have a huge army. You have the golden calves that Jeroboam made to be your gods.

9"But you drove out the priests of the LORD, the sons of Aaron. You also drove out the Levites. You appointed your own priests. That's what the people of other nations do. Anyone can come and set himself apart. All he has to do is sacrifice a young bull and seven rams. Then he becomes a priest of gods that aren't really gods at all!

10"But the LORD is our God. We haven't deserted him. The priests who serve the LORD belong to the family line of Aaron. The Levites help them. 11Every morning and evening the priests bring burnt offerings and sweet-smelling incense to the LORD. They set out the holy bread on the table. That table is 'clean.' They light the lamps on the gold lampstand every evening.

"We always do what the LORD our God requires in his law. But you have deserted him. 12God is with us. He's our leader. His priests will blow their trumpets. They will sound the battle cry against you. Men of Israel, don't fight against the LORD. He's the God of your people who lived long ago. You can't possibly succeed."

13Jeroboam had sent some troops behind Judah's battle lines. He told them to hide and wait there. He and his men stayed in front of Judah's lines. 14Judah turned and saw that they were being attacked from the front and from the back. Then they cried out to the LORD. The priests blew their trumpets. 15The men of Judah shouted the battle cry. When they did, God drove Jeroboam and all of Israel's men away from Abijah and Judah.

16The men of Israel ran away from them. God handed Israel over to Judah. 17Abijah and his men wounded and killed large numbers of them. In fact, 500,000 of Israel's able men lay dead or wounded.

18So at that time the men of Israel were brought under Judah's control. The men of Judah won the battle over them. That's because they trusted in the LORD. He's the God of their people.

19Abijah chased Jeroboam. He took from him the towns of Bethel, Jeshanah and Ephron. He also took the villages that were around them. 20Jeroboam didn't get his power back during the time of Abijah. In fact, the LORD struck him down. And he died.

21But Abijah grew stronger. He got married to 14 wives. He had 22 sons and 16 daughters.

22The other events of Abijah's rule are written down. The things he did and said are written in the notes of the prophet Iddo.

14 Abijah joined the members of his family who had already died. His body was buried in the City of David. His son Asa became the next king after him. While Asa was king, the country had peace and rest for ten years.

ASA BECOMES KING OF JUDAH

2Asa did what was good and right in the eyes of the LORD his God. 3He removed the altars where strange gods were worshiped. He took away the high places. He smashed the sacred stones. He cut down the poles that were used to worship the goddess Asherah. 4He commanded Judah to worship the LORD, the God of their people. He commanded them to obey the LORD's laws and commands.

5He removed the high places and incense altars from every town in Judah. The kingdom had peace and rest under him. 6He built up the cities of Judah that had high walls around them. The land was at peace. No one was at war with Asa during those years. That's because the LORD gave him peace and rest.

7"Let's build up our towns," Asa said to the people of Judah. "Let's put walls around them. Let's provide them with towers. Let's make them secure with gates that have heavy metal bars. The land still belongs to us. That's because we've trusted in the LORD our God. We trusted in him, and he has given us peace and rest on every side." So they built. And things went well for them.

⁸Asa had an army of 300,000 men from Judah. They carried spears and large shields. There were 280,000 men from Benjamin. They were armed with bows and small shields. All of those men were brave soldiers.

⁹Zerah marched out against them. He was from Cush. He had a huge army. He also had 300 chariots. They came all the way to Mareshah.

¹⁰Asa went out to meet Zerah in battle. They took up their positions in the Valley of Zephathah. It's near Mareshah.

¹¹Then Asa called out to the LORD his God. He said, "LORD, there isn't anyone like you. You help the weak against the strong. LORD our God, help us. We trust in you. In your name we have come out to fight against this huge army. LORD, you are our God. Don't let mere men win the battle over you."

¹²The LORD struck down the men of Cush for Asa and Judah. The Cushites ran away. ¹³Asa and his army chased them all the way to Gerar. A large number of Cushites fell down wounded or dead. So they couldn't fight back. The LORD and his army crushed them. The men of Judah carried off a large amount of goods.

¹⁴They attacked all of the villages around Gerar. The LORD had made the people in those villages afraid of him. The men of Judah took everything from all of the villages. ¹⁵They also attacked the camps of those who took care of the herds. They carried off large numbers of sheep, goats and camels. Then they returned to Jerusalem.

ASA MAKES JUDAH A BETTER NATION

15 The Spirit of God came on Azariah. He was the son of Oded. ²Azariah went out to meet Asa. He said to him, "Asa and all you people of Judah and Benjamin, listen to me. The LORD is with you when you are with him. If you really look for him, you will find him. But if you desert him, he will desert you.

³"For a long time Israel didn't worship the true God. They didn't have a priest who taught them. So they didn't know God's law. ⁴But when they were in trouble, they turned to the LORD, the God of Israel. When they did, they found him.

⁵"In those days it wasn't safe to travel around. The people who lived in all of the areas of the land were having a lot of trouble. ⁶One nation was crushing another. One city was crushing another. That's because God was causing them to suffer terribly.

⁷"But be strong. Don't give up. God will reward you for your work."

⁸Asa heard that prophecy. He paid attention to the words of the prophet Azariah, the son of Oded. So Asa became bolder than ever. He removed the statues of gods from the whole land of Judah and Benjamin. He also removed them from the towns he had captured in the hills of Ephraim. He did it because he hated those gods. He repaired the altar of the LORD. It was in front of the porch of the LORD's temple.

⁹Then he gathered all of the people of Judah and Benjamin together. He also gathered together the people from Ephraim, Manasseh and Simeon who had settled among them. Large numbers of people had come over to him from Israel. They came because they saw that the LORD his God was with him.

¹⁰They gathered in Jerusalem. It was the third month of the 15th year of Asa's rule. ¹¹At that time they sacrificed to the LORD 700 head of cattle and 7,000 sheep and goats. The animals were among the things they had taken after the battle.

¹²They made a covenant to look to the LORD, the God of their people. They looked to him with all their heart and soul. ¹³All those who wouldn't look to the LORD, the God of Israel, would be killed. It wouldn't matter how important they were. It wouldn't matter whether they were men or women. ¹⁴They took an oath and made a promise to the LORD. They praised him out loud. They shouted. They blew trumpets and horns.

¹⁵All of the people of Judah were happy about the promise they had made. They turned to God with all their heart. When they did, they found

him. So the LORD gave them peace and rest on every side.

[16]King Asa also removed his grandmother Maacah from her position as queen mother. That's because she had made a pole that was used to worship the goddess Asherah. The LORD hated it. So Asa cut it down. He broke it up. He burned it in the Kidron Valley.

[17]Asa didn't remove the high places from Israel. But he committed his whole life completely to the LORD. [18]He and his father had set apart silver, gold and other articles to the LORD. He brought them into God's temple.

[19]There weren't any more wars until the 35th year of Asa's rule.

THE LAST YEARS OF ASA'S RULE

16 Baasha was king of Israel. He marched out against Judah. It was in the 36th year of Asa's rule over Judah. Baasha built up the walls of Ramah. He did it to keep people from leaving or entering the territory of Asa, the king of Judah.

[2]Asa took the silver and gold from among the treasures of the LORD's temple and his own palace. He sent it to Ben-Hadad. Ben-Hadad was king of Aram. He was ruling in Damascus. [3]"Let's make a peace treaty between us," Asa said. "My father and your father had made a peace treaty between them. Now I'm sending you silver and gold. So break your treaty with Baasha, the king of Israel. Then he'll go back home."

[4]Ben-Hadad agreed with King Asa. He sent his army commanders against the towns of Israel. They attacked Ijon, Dan, Abel Maim and all of the cities in Naphtali where Baasha stored things. [5]Baasha heard about it. So he stopped building up Ramah. He stopped working there. [6]Then King Asa brought all of the men of Judah to Ramah. They carried away the stones and wood Baasha had been using. Asa used them to build up Geba and Mizpah.

[7]At that time the prophet Hanani came to Asa, the king of Judah. He said to him, "You trusted the king of Aram. You didn't trust in the LORD your God.

So the army of the king of Aram has escaped from you. [8]The people of Cush and Libya had a strong army. They had large numbers of chariots and horsemen. But you trusted in the LORD. So he handed them over to you. [9]The LORD looks out over the whole earth. He gives strength to those who commit their lives completely to him. You have done a foolish thing. From now on you will be at war."

[10]Asa was angry with the prophet because of what he had said. In fact, he was so angry he put him in prison. At the same time, Asa treated some of his own people very badly.

[11]The events of Asa's rule from beginning to end are written down. They are written in the records of the kings of Judah and Israel.

[12]In the 39th year of Asa's rule his feet began to hurt. The pain was terrible. But even though he was suffering, he didn't look to the LORD for help. All he did was go to the doctors.

[13]In the 41st year of Asa's rule he joined the members of his family who had already died. [14]His body was buried in a tomb. He had cut it out for himself in the City of David. His body was laid on a wooden frame. It was covered with spices and different mixes of perfume. A huge fire was made in his honor.

JEHOSHAPHAT BECOMES KING OF JUDAH

17 Jehoshaphat was the son of Asa. Jehoshaphat became the next king after him. He made his kingdom strong in case Israel would attack him. [2]He placed troops in all of the cities of Judah that had high walls around them. He stationed some soldiers in Judah. He also put some in the towns of Ephraim that his father Asa had captured.

[3]The LORD was with Jehoshaphat. That's because in his early years he lived the way King David had lived. He didn't ask for advice from the gods that were named after Baal. [4]Instead, he looked to the God of his father. He followed the LORD's commands instead of the practices of Israel.

[5]The LORD made the kingdom secure under Jehoshaphat's control. All

of the people of Judah brought gifts to Jehoshaphat. So he had great wealth and honor. ⁶His heart was committed to living the way the LORD wanted him to. He removed the high places from Judah. He also removed the poles that were used to worship the goddess Asherah.

⁷In the third year of his rule, he sent his officials to teach in the towns of Judah. The officials were Ben-Hail, Obadiah, Zechariah, Nethanel and Micaiah. ⁸Some Levites were with them. Their names were Shemaiah, Nethaniah, Zebadiah, Asahel, Shemiramoth, Jehonathan, Adonijah, Tobijah and Tob-Adonijah. The priests Elishama and Jehoram were also with them. ⁹They taught people all through Judah. They took the Scroll of the Law of the LORD with them. They went around to all of the towns of Judah. And they taught the people.

¹⁰All of the kingdoms of the lands around Judah became afraid of the LORD. So they didn't go to war against Jehoshaphat. ¹¹Some Philistines brought to Jehoshaphat the gifts and silver he required of them. The Arabs brought him their flocks. They brought him 7,700 rams and 7,700 goats. ¹²Jehoshaphat became more and

more powerful. He built forts in Judah. He also built cities in Judah where he could store things. ¹³He had large supplies in the towns of Judah. In Jerusalem he kept men who knew how to fight well. ¹⁴Here is a list of them, family by family.

From Judah there were commanders of companies of 1,000.
One of them was Adnah. He commanded 300,000 fighting men.
¹⁵Another was Jehohanan. He commanded 280,000.
¹⁶Another was Amasiah, the son of Zicri. Amasiah commanded 200,000. He had offered to serve the LORD.
¹⁷From Benjamin there were also commanders.
One of them was Eliada. He was a brave soldier. He commanded 200,000 men. They were armed with bows and shields.
¹⁸Another was Jehozabad. He commanded 180,000 men. They were prepared for battle.

¹⁹Those were the men who served the king. He stationed some other men in

KIDS' QUESTION

What's a casket?

A casket is a metal or wooden box in which a dead body is placed. Usually a casket is buried in the ground in a cemetery. People have used caskets to bury people for thousands of years. They do it to show respect for the dead person. It would be awful just to put the body in the garbage. Burying a dead body in a casket is also a part of what we do to show we are sad about the person's death.

checkout 2 Chronicles 16:14

DISPLAY CASKETS

HEAVEN'S DELIVERY BOX

Related verse:
Romans 12:15

the cities all through Judah. The cities had high walls around them.

MICAIAH PROPHESIES AGAINST AHAB

18 Jehoshaphat had great wealth and honor. He joined forces with Ahab by getting married to Ahab's daughter. ²Some years later he went down to visit Ahab in Samaria. Ahab killed a lot of sheep and cattle for him and the people who were with him. Ahab tried to get Jehoshaphat to attack Ramoth Gilead. ³Ahab was the king of Israel. He spoke to Jehoshaphat, the king of Judah. He asked, "Will you go with me to fight against Ramoth Gilead?"

Jehoshaphat replied, "Yes. I'll go with you. My men will also go with you. We'll join you in the war." ⁴He continued, "First ask the LORD for advice."

⁵So the king of Israel brought 400 prophets together. He asked them, "Should we go to war against Ramoth Gilead? Or should I stay here?"

"Go," they answered. "God will hand it over to you."

⁶But Jehoshaphat asked, "Isn't there a prophet of the LORD here? If there is, ask him what we should do."

⁷The king of Israel answered Jehoshaphat. He said, "There is still one other man we can go to. We can ask the LORD for advice through him. But I hate him. He never prophesies anything good about me. He only prophesies bad things. His name is Micaiah. He's the son of Imlah."

"You shouldn't say bad things about him," Jehoshaphat replied.

⁸So the king of Israel called for one of his officials. He told him, "Bring Micaiah, the son of Imlah, at once."

⁹The king of Israel and Jehoshaphat, the king of Judah, were wearing their royal robes. They were sitting on their thrones at the threshing floor. It was near the entrance of the gate of Samaria. All of the prophets were prophesying in front of them.

¹⁰Zedekiah was the son of Kenaanah. Zedekiah had made horns out of iron. They looked like animal horns. He announced, "The LORD says, 'With these horns you will drive back the men of Aram until they are destroyed.' "

¹¹All of the other prophets were prophesying the same thing. "Attack Ramoth Gilead," they said. "Win the battle over it. The LORD will hand it over to you."

¹²A messenger went to get Micaiah. He said to him, "Look. The other prophets agree. All of them are saying the king will have success. So agree with them. Say the same thing they do."

¹³But Micaiah said, "You can be sure that the LORD lives. And you can be just as sure that I can only tell the king what my God says."

¹⁴When Micaiah arrived, the king spoke to him. He asked, "Should we go to war against Ramoth Gilead? Or should I stay here?"

"Attack," he answered. "You will win. The people of Ramoth Gilead will be handed over to you."

¹⁵The king said to him, "I've made you promise to tell the truth many times before. So don't tell me anything but the truth in the name of the LORD."

¹⁶Then Micaiah answered, "I saw all of the people of Israel scattered on the hills. They were like sheep that didn't have a shepherd. The LORD said, 'These people do not have a master. Let each of them go home in peace.' "

¹⁷The king of Israel spoke to Jehoshaphat. He said, "Didn't I tell you he never prophesies anything good about me? He only prophesies bad things."

¹⁸Micaiah continued, "Listen to the LORD's message. I saw the LORD sitting on his throne. Some of the angels of heaven were standing at his right side. The others were standing at his left side. ¹⁹The LORD said, 'Who will try to get Ahab, the king of Israel, to attack Ramoth Gilead? I want him to die there.'

"One angel suggested one thing. Another suggested something else. ²⁰Finally, a spirit came forward and stood in front of the LORD. The spirit said, 'I'll try to get Ahab to do it.'

" 'How?' the LORD asked.

²¹"The spirit said, 'I'll go and put lies in the mouths of all of his prophets.'

" 'You will have success in getting

Ahab to attack Ramoth Gilead,' said the LORD. 'Go and do it.'

²²"So the LORD has put lies in the mouths of your prophets. He has said that great harm will come to you."

²³Then Zedekiah, the son of Kenaanah, went up and slapped Micaiah in the face. "So you think the spirit that was sent by the LORD went away from me to speak to you, do you?" he asked. "Which way did he go?"

²⁴Micaiah replied, "You will find out on the day you go to hide in an inside room to save your life."

²⁵Then the king of Israel gave an order. He said, "Take Micaiah away. Send him back to Amon. Amon is the ruler of the city of Samaria. And send him back to Joash. Joash is a member of the royal court. ²⁶Tell them, 'The king says, "Put this fellow in prison. Don't give him anything but bread and water until I return safely." ' "

²⁷Micaiah announced, "Do you really think you will return safely? If you do, the LORD hasn't spoken through me." He continued, "All of you people, remember what I've said!"

AHAB IS KILLED AT RAMOTH GILEAD

²⁸So the king of Israel went up to Ramoth Gilead. Jehoshaphat, the king of Judah, went there too.

²⁹The king of Israel spoke to Jehoshaphat. He said, "I'll go into battle wearing different clothes. Then people won't recognize me. But you wear your royal robes." So the king of Israel put on different clothes. Then he went into battle.

³⁰The king of Aram had given an order to his chariot commanders. He had said, "Fight only against the king of Israel. Don't fight against anyone else."

³¹The chariot commanders saw Jehoshaphat. They thought, "That's the king of Israel." So they turned to attack him. But Jehoshaphat cried out. And the LORD helped him. God drew the commanders away from him. ³²They saw he wasn't the king of Israel after all. So they stopped chasing him.

³³But someone shot an arrow without taking aim. The arrow hit the king of Israel between the parts of his armor. The king told the chariot driver, "Turn the chariot around. Get me out of this battle. I've been wounded."

³⁴All day long the battle continued. The king of Israel kept himself standing up by leaning against the inside of his chariot. He kept his face toward the men of Aram until evening. At sunset he died.

19

Jehoshaphat, the king of Judah, returned safely to his palace in Jerusalem. ²The prophet Jehu went out to meet him. He was the son of Hanani. Jehu said to the king, "You shouldn't help evil people. You shouldn't love those who hate the LORD. The LORD is angry with you. ³But there's some good in you. You have gotten rid of all of the poles in the land that are used to worship the goddess Asherah. And you have worshiped God with all your heart."

JEHOSHAPHAT APPOINTS JUDGES

⁴Jehoshaphat lived in Jerusalem. He went out again among the people. He went from Beersheba to the hill country of Ephraim. He turned the people back to the LORD, the God of Israel.

⁵Jehoshaphat appointed judges in the land. He put them in all of the cities of Judah that had high walls around them. ⁶He told the judges, "Think carefully about what you do. After all, you aren't judging for mere men. You are judging for the LORD. He's with you every time you make a decision. ⁷Have respect for the LORD. Judge carefully. He is always right. He treats everyone the same. He doesn't want his judges to take money from people who want special favors."

⁸In Jerusalem, Jehoshaphat chose some Levites and priests. He also chose some leaders of Israelite families. He appointed all of them to apply the law of the LORD fairly. He wanted them to decide cases. He wanted them to settle matters between people. All of those judges lived in Jerusalem.

⁹Here are the orders Jehoshaphat gave them. He said, "Have respect for the LORD. Serve him faithfully. Do it with all your heart. ¹⁰Cases will come to you from your fellow judges who

live in the other cities. The cases might be about murder or other matters that the law, commands, directions and rules deal with. Warn the judges not to sin against the LORD. If you don't warn them, he will be angry with you and your fellow judges. Do what I say. Then you won't sin.

¹¹"The chief priest Amariah will be over you in any matter that concerns the LORD. Zebadiah is the leader of the tribe of Judah. He is the son of Ishmael. Zebadiah will be over you in any matter that concerns the king. The Levites will serve as your officials. Be brave. And may the LORD be with those of you who do well."

JEHOSHAPHAT WINS THE BATTLE OVER MOAB AND AMMON

20 After that, the Moabites, Ammonites and some Meunites went to war against Jehoshaphat.

²Some people came and told him, "A huge army is coming from Edom to fight against you. They have come across the Dead Sea. They are already in Hazazon Tamar." Hazazon Tamar is also called En Gedi.

³Jehoshaphat was alarmed. So he decided to ask the LORD for advice. He told all of the people of Judah to go without eating. ⁴The people came together to ask the LORD for help. In fact, they came from every town in Judah to pray to him.

⁵Then Jehoshaphat stood up among the people of Judah and Jerusalem. He was in front of the new courtyard at the LORD's temple. ⁶He said,

"LORD, you are the God of our people. You are the God who is in heaven. You rule over all of the kingdoms of the nations. Your hands are strong and powerful. No one can fight against you and win.

⁷"Our God, you drove out the people who lived in this land. You drove them out to make room for your people Israel. You gave this land forever to those who belong to the family line of your friend Abraham.

⁸"They have lived in this land. They've built a temple here for your Name. They have said, ⁹'Suppose trouble comes on us. It doesn't matter whether it's a punishing sword, plague or hunger. We'll serve you. We'll stand in front of this temple where your Name is. We'll cry out to you when we're in trouble. Then you will hear us. You will save us.'

¹⁰"But here are men from Ammon, Moab and Mount Seir. You wouldn't allow Israel to march in and attack their territory when the Israelites came from Egypt. So Israel turned away from them. They didn't destroy them. ¹¹See how they are paying us back. They are coming to drive us out. They want to take over the land you gave us as our share.

¹²"Our God, won't you please judge them? We don't have the power to face this huge army that's attacking us. We don't know what to do. But we're looking to you to help us."

¹³All of the men of Judah stood there in front of the LORD. Their wives, children and little ones were with them.

¹⁴Then the Spirit of the LORD came on Jahaziel. He was standing among the people of Israel. He was the son of Zechariah. Zechariah was the son of Benaiah. Benaiah was the son of Jeiel. Jeiel was the son of Mattaniah. Jahaziel was a Levite. He was from the family line of Asaph.

¹⁵Jahaziel said, "King Jehoshaphat, listen! All you who live in Judah and Jerusalem, listen! The LORD says to you, 'Do not be afraid. Do not lose hope because of this huge army. The battle is not yours. It is mine.

¹⁶'Tomorrow march down against them. They will be climbing up by the Pass of Ziz. You will find them at the end of the valley in the Desert of Jeruel. ¹⁷You will not have to fight this battle. Take your positions. Stand firm. You will see how I will save you. Judah and Jerusalem, do not be afraid. Do not lose hope. Go out and face them tomorrow. I will be with you.' "

¹⁸Jehoshaphat bowed down with his

face toward the ground. All of the people of Judah and Jerusalem also bowed down. They worshiped the LORD.

¹⁹Then some Levites from the families of Kohath and Korah stood up. They praised the LORD, the God of Israel. They praised him with very loud voices.

²⁰Early in the morning all of the people left for the Desert of Tekoa. As they started out, Jehoshaphat stood up. He said, "Judah, listen to me! People of Jerusalem, listen to me! Have faith in the LORD your God. He'll take good care of you. Have faith in his prophets. Then you will have success."

²¹Jehoshaphat asked the people for advice. Then he appointed men to sing to the LORD. He wanted them to praise him because of his glory and holiness. They marched out in front of the army. They said,

"Give thanks to the LORD.
His faithful love continues
forever."

²²They began to sing and praise him. Then the LORD hid some men and told them to wait. He wanted them to attack the people of Ammon, Moab and Mount Seir. They had gone into Judah and attacked it. But they lost the battle. ²³The men of Ammon and Moab rose up against the men from Mount Seir. They destroyed them. They put an end to them. When they finished killing the men from Seir, they destroyed each other.

²⁴The men of Judah came to the place that looks out over the desert. They turned to look down at the huge army. But all they saw was dead bodies lying there on the ground. No one had escaped.

²⁵So Jehoshaphat and his men went down there to carry off anything of value. Among the dead bodies they found a lot of supplies, clothes and articles of value. There was more than they could take away. There was so much it took three days to collect all of it.

²⁶On the fourth day they gathered together in the Valley of Beracah. There they praised the LORD. That's why it's called the Valley of Beracah to this very day.

²⁷Then all of the men of Judah and Jerusalem returned to Jerusalem. They were filled with joy. Jehoshaphat led them. The LORD had made them happy because all of their enemies were dead. ²⁸They entered Jerusalem and went to the LORD's temple. They were playing harps, lutes and trumpets.

²⁹All of the kingdoms of the surrounding countries began to have respect for God. They had heard how the LORD had fought against Israel's enemies.

³⁰The kingdom of Jehoshaphat was at peace. His God had given him peace and rest on every side.

JEHOSHAPHAT'S RULE COMES TO AN END

³¹So Jehoshaphat ruled over Judah. He was 35 years old when he became Judah's king. He ruled in Jerusalem for 25 years. His mother's name was Azubah. She was the daughter of Shilhi. ³²Jehoshaphat followed the ways of his father Asa. He didn't wander away from them. He did what was right in the eyes of the LORD.

³³But the high places weren't removed. The people still hadn't worshiped the God of Israel with all their hearts.

³⁴The other events of Jehoshaphat's rule from beginning to end are written down. They are written in the official records of Jehu, the son of Hanani. They are written in the records of the kings of Israel.

³⁵Jehoshaphat king of Judah and Ahaziah king of Israel agreed to be friends. Ahaziah was guilty of doing what was evil. ³⁶Jehoshaphat agreed with him to build a lot of ships. They were built at Ezion Geber. They carried goods that were traded for other goods.

³⁷Eliezer was the son of Dodavahu from Mareshah. Eliezer prophesied against Jehoshaphat. He said, "You have joined forces with Ahaziah. So the LORD will destroy what you have made." The ships were wrecked. They were never able to sail or trade goods.

21 Jehoshaphat joined the members of his family who had already died. His body was buried in the family tomb in the

City of David. His son Jehoram became the next king after him.

²Jehoram's brothers, the sons of Jehoshaphat, were Azariah, Jehiel, Zechariah, Azariahu, Michael and Shephatiah. All of them were sons of Jehoshaphat, the king of Israel. ³Their father had given them many gifts. He had given them silver, gold and articles of value. He had also given them cities in Judah that had high walls around them. But he had made Jehoram king. That's because Jehoram was his oldest son.

JEHORAM BECOMES KING OF JUDAH

⁴Jehoram made his position secure over his father's kingdom. Then he killed all of his brothers with his sword. He also killed some of the princes of Israel.

⁵Jehoram was 32 years old when he became king. He ruled in Jerusalem for eight years. ⁶He followed the ways of the kings of Israel, just as the royal family of Ahab had done. In fact, he got married to a daughter of Ahab. Jehoram did what was evil in the sight of the LORD.

⁷But the LORD didn't want to destroy the royal family of David. That's because the LORD had made a covenant with him. He had promised to keep the lamp of David's kingdom burning brightly for him and his children after him forever.

⁸When Jehoram was king over Judah, Edom refused to remain under Judah's control. They set up their own king. ⁹So Jehoram went to Edom. He took his officers and all of his chariots with him. The men of Edom surrounded him and his chariot commanders. But he got up at night and fought his way out. ¹⁰To this very day Edom has refused to remain under Judah's control.

At that same time, Libnah also refused to remain under the control of Judah. That's because Jehoram had deserted the LORD, the God of his people. ¹¹He had also built high places on the hills of Judah. He had caused the people of Jerusalem to worship other gods. They weren't faithful to the LORD. Jehoram had led Judah down the wrong path.

¹²Jehoram received a letter from the prophet Elijah. It said,

"The LORD is the God of your father David. The LORD says, 'You have not followed the ways of your own father Jehoshaphat or of Asa, the king of Judah. ¹³Instead, you have followed the ways of the kings of Israel. You have led Judah and the people of Jerusalem to worship other gods, just as the royal family of Ahab did. Also, you have murdered your own brothers. They were members of your own family. They were better men than you are.

¹⁴ "'So now I am about to strike your people down with a heavy blow. I will strike down your sons, your wives and everything that belongs to you. ¹⁵And you yourself will be very sick for a long time. The sickness will finally cause your insides to come out.' "

¹⁶The LORD stirred up the anger of the Philistines against Jehoram. He also stirred up the anger of the Arabs. They lived near the people of Cush. ¹⁷The Philistines and Arabs attacked Judah. They went in and carried off all of the goods they found in the king's palace. They also took his sons and wives. The only son he had left was Ahaziah. He was the youngest son.

¹⁸After all of that, the LORD made Jehoram very sick. He couldn't be healed. ¹⁹After he had been sick for two years, the sickness caused his insides to come out. He died in great pain. His people didn't make a fire in his honor, as they had done for the kings who ruled before him.

²⁰Jehoram was 32 years old when he became king. He ruled in Jerusalem for eight years. No one was sorry when he passed away. His body was buried in the City of David. But it wasn't placed in the tombs of the kings.

AHAZIAH BECOMES KING OF JUDAH

22 The people of Jerusalem made Ahaziah king in place of Jehoram. Ahaziah was Jehoram's youngest son. Robbers had come with the Arabs into Jehoram's camp. The robbers had killed all of his older sons. So Ahaziah, the king of Judah, began to rule. He was the son of Jehoram.

²Ahaziah was 22 years old when he became king. He ruled in Jerusalem for one year. His mother's name was Athaliah. She was a granddaughter of Omri.

³Ahaziah also followed the ways of the royal family of Ahab. That's because Ahaziah's mother gave him bad advice. She told him to do what was wrong. ⁴So he did what was evil in the sight of the LORD, just as the family of Ahab had done.

After Ahaziah's father died, the members of Ahab's family became his advisers. That's what destroyed him. ⁵He also followed their advice when he joined forces with Joram, the king of Israel. They went to war against Hazael at Ramoth Gilead. Joram was the son of Ahab. Hazael was king of Aram. The soldiers of Aram wounded Joram. ⁶So he returned to Jezreel to give his wounds time to heal. His enemies had wounded him at Ramoth in his battle against Hazael, the king of Aram.

Ahaziah, the son of Jehoram, went down to Jezreel. He went there to see Joram. That's because Joram had been wounded. Ahaziah was king of Judah. Joram was the son of Ahab.

⁷Through Ahaziah's visit to Joram, God caused Ahaziah to fall from power. When Ahaziah arrived, he rode out with Joram to meet Jehu, the son of Nimshi. The LORD had anointed Jehu to destroy the royal family of Ahab. ⁸So Jehu punished Ahab's family, just as the LORD had told him to. While he was doing it, he found the princes of Judah and the sons of Ahaziah's relatives. They had been serving Ahaziah. So Jehu killed them.

⁹Then he went to look for Ahaziah. Jehu's men captured him while he was hiding in Samaria. Ahaziah was brought to Jehu and put to death. People buried his body, because they said, "He was a grandson of Jehoshaphat, who followed the LORD with all his heart."

So no one in the royal family of Ahaziah was powerful enough to keep the kingdom.

ATHALIAH AND JOASH

¹⁰Athaliah was Ahaziah's mother. She saw that her son was dead. So she began to wipe out the whole royal house of Judah.

¹¹But Jehosheba went and got Joash, the son of Ahaziah. She was the daughter of King Jehoram. She stole Joash away from among the royal princes. All of them were about to be murdered. She put Joash and his nurse in a bedroom. Jehosheba, the daughter of King Jehoram, was the wife of the priest Jehoiada. She was also Ahaziah's sister.

So Jehosheba hid the child from Athaliah. That's why Athaliah couldn't kill him. ¹²The child remained hidden with the priest and his wife at God's temple for six years. Athaliah ruled over the land during that time.

23 When Joash was seven years old, Jehoiada showed how strong he was. He made a covenant with the commanders of companies of 100 men. The commanders were Azariah son of Jeroham, Ishmael son of Jehohanan, Azariah son of Obed, Maaseiah son of Adaiah, and Elishaphat son of Zicri. ²They went all through Judah. They gathered together the Levites and the leaders of Israelite families from all of the towns. They came to Jerusalem. ³The whole community made a covenant with the new king at God's temple.

Jehoiada said to them, "Ahaziah's son will rule over Judah. That's what the LORD promised concerning the family line of David. ⁴Here's what I want you to do. A third of you priests and Levites who are going on duty on the Sabbath day must guard the doors. ⁵A third of you must guard the royal palace. And a third of you must guard the Foundation Gate. All of the other men must guard the courtyards of the LORD's temple.

⁶"Don't let anyone enter the temple except the priests and Levites who are on duty. They can enter because they are set apart to the LORD. But all of the other men must guard the places where the LORD has sent them. ⁷"The Levites must station them-

selves around the new king. Each man must have his weapons in his hand. Anyone else who enters the temple must be put to death. Stay close to the king no matter where he goes."

⁸The Levites did just as the priest Jehoiada ordered. So did all of the men of Judah. Each commander got his men. Some of the men were going on duty on the Sabbath day. Others were going off duty. Jehoiada didn't let any of the groups go. ⁹Then he gave weapons to the commanders of the companies. He gave them spears, large shields and small shields. The weapons had belonged to King David. They had been in God's temple.

¹⁰Jehoiada stationed all of the men around the new king. Each man had his weapon in his hand. They were standing near the altar and the temple. They stood from the south side of the temple to its north side. Their line formed half of a circle.

¹¹Jehoiada and his sons brought Ahaziah's son out. They put the crown on him. They gave him a copy of the covenant. And they announced that he was king. They anointed him. Then they shouted, "May the king live a long time!"

¹²Athaliah heard the noise of the people running and cheering the new king. So she went to them at the LORD's temple.

¹³She looked. And there was the king! He was standing next to his pillar at the entrance. The officers and trumpet players were standing beside the king. All of the people of the land were filled with joy. They were blowing trumpets. Singers with their musical instruments were leading the songs of praise.

Then Athaliah tore her royal robes. She shouted, "Treason! It's treason!"

¹⁴The priest Jehoiada sent out the commanders of the companies of 100 men. They were in charge of the troops. He said to them, "Bring her away from the temple between the line of guards. Use your swords to kill anyone who follows her." The priest had said, "Don't put her to death at the LORD's temple."

¹⁵So they grabbed hold of her as she reached the entrance of the Horse Gate on the palace grounds. There they put her to death.

¹⁶Then Jehoiada made a covenant. He promised that he, the people and the king would be the LORD's people.

¹⁷All of the people went to Baal's temple. They tore it down. They smashed the altars and the statues of gods. They killed Mattan in front of the altars. He was the priest of Baal.

¹⁸Then Jehoiada put the priests, who were Levites, in charge of the LORD's temple. David had given them their duties in the temple. He had appointed them to sacrifice burnt offerings to the LORD. He wanted them to do it in keeping with what was written in the Law of Moses. David wanted them to sing and be full of joy.

¹⁹Jehoiada stationed guards at the gates of the LORD's temple. No one who was "unclean" in any way could enter.

²⁰Jehoiada took with him the commanders of hundreds, the nobles, the rulers of the people, and all of the people of the land. He brought the new king down from the LORD's temple. They went into the palace through the Upper Gate. Then they seated the king on the royal throne.

²¹All of the people of the land were filled with joy. And the city was quiet. That's because Athaliah had been killed with a sword.

JOASH REPAIRS THE TEMPLE

24 Joash was seven years old when he became king. He ruled in Jerusalem for 40 years. His mother's name was Zibiah. She was from Beersheba.

²Joash did what was right in the eyes of the LORD. He lived that way as long as the priest Jehoiada was alive. ³Jehoiada chose two wives for Joash. They had sons and daughters by Joash.

⁴Some time later Joash decided to make the LORD's temple look like new again. ⁵He called together the priests and Levites. He said to them, "Go to the towns of Judah. Collect the money that the nation of Israel owes every year. Use it to repair the temple of your God. Do it now." But the Levites didn't do it right away.

⁶So the king sent for the chief priest

Jehoiada. He said to him, "Why haven't you required the Levites to bring in the tax from Judah and Jerusalem? It was set up by the LORD's servant Moses and the whole community of Israel. It was used for the tent where the tablets of the covenant were kept."

⁷The children of that evil woman Athaliah had broken into God's temple. They had used even its sacred objects for the gods that were named after Baal.

⁸King Joash commanded that a wooden chest be made. It was placed outside near the gate of the LORD's temple. ⁹Then a message went out in Judah and Jerusalem. It said that the people should bring the tax to the LORD. God's servant Moses had required Israel to pay that tax when they were in the desert.

¹⁰All of the officials and people gladly brought their money. They dropped it into the chest until it was full.

¹¹The chest was brought in by the Levites to the king's officials. Every time the officials saw there was a large amount of money in the chest, it was emptied out. The royal secretary and the officer of the chief priest came and emptied it. Then they carried it back to its place. They did it regularly. They collected a great amount of money.

¹²The king and Jehoiada gave it to the men who were doing the work on the LORD's temple. They hired people who could lay the stones and people who could work with wood. They also hired people who could work with iron and bronze. They hired all of them to repair the temple.

¹³The men who were in charge of the

Where does all the money in the bank machines come from?

Bank workers put it there. About once a week they open the machines and put the money in. They get the money from the bank's safe. Bank machines are called Automatic Teller Machines or ATMs. People can use ATMs to put money into their bank accounts, to find out how much they have in the bank or to take money out of their accounts. The bank workers put enough cash into the machines so that whoever needs to get some from their account can do so.

There were no ATMs in the time of King Joash, but the chest was a little bit like an ATM. The people put money into the chest, and the royal officials emptied it when it was full and used it to pay the temple workers.

checkout
2 Chronicles 24:10,11

WELCOME TO INSTANT BANKING

Related verse:
Proverbs 13:11

work did their best. The repairs went very well under them. They rebuilt God's temple. They did it in keeping with its original plans. They made it stronger. ¹⁴So they finished the work. Then they brought the rest of the money to the king and Jehoiada. It was used to pay for the articles that were made for the LORD's temple. The articles were used for serving at the temple. They were also used for the burnt offerings. The articles included dishes and other objects that were made out of gold and silver. As long as Jehoiada lived, burnt offerings were sacrificed continually at the LORD's temple.

¹⁵Jehoiada had become very old. He died at the age of 130. ¹⁶His body was buried with the kings in the City of David. That's because he had done so many good things in Israel for God and his temple.

THE EVIL THINGS JOASH DID

¹⁷After Jehoiada died, the officials of Judah came to King Joash. They bowed down to him. He listened to them. ¹⁸They turned their backs on the temple of the LORD, the God of their people. They worshiped poles that were made to honor the goddess Asherah. They also worshiped statues of other gods.

Because Judah and Jerusalem were guilty of sin, God became angry with them. ¹⁹The LORD sent prophets to the people to bring them back to him. The prophets gave witness against the people. But they wouldn't listen.

²⁰Then the Spirit of God came on the priest Zechariah. He was the son of Jehoiada. Zechariah stood in front of the people. He told them, "God says, 'Why do you refuse to obey my commands? You will not have success. You have deserted me. So I have deserted you.' "

²¹But the people made evil plans against Zechariah. The king ordered them to kill Zechariah by throwing stones at him. They did it in the courtyard of the LORD's temple. ²²King Joash didn't remember how kind Zechariah's father Jehoiada had been to him. So he killed Jehoiada's son.

As Zechariah was dying he said, "May the LORD see this. May he hold you accountable."

²³In the spring, the army of Aram marched into Judah and Jerusalem against Joash. They killed all of the leaders of the people. They took a large amount of goods from Judah. They sent it to their king in Damascus. ²⁴The army of Aram had come with only a few men. But the LORD allowed them to win the battle over a much larger army. Judah had deserted the LORD, the God of their people. That's why the LORD punished Joash.

²⁵The army of Aram pulled back. They left Joash badly wounded. His officials planned to do evil things to him. That's because he murdered the son of the priest Jehoiada. They killed Joash in his bed. So he died. His body was buried in the City of David. But it wasn't placed in the tombs of the kings.

²⁶Those who made the plans against Joash were Zabad and Jehozabad. Zabad was the son of Shimeath. She was from Ammon. Jehozabad was the son of Shimrith. She was from Moab. ²⁷The story of the sons of Joash is written in the notes on the records of the kings. The many prophecies about him are written there too. So is the record of how he made God's temple look like new again. His son Amaziah became the next king after him.

AMAZIAH BECOMES KING OF JUDAH

25 Amaziah was 25 years old when he became king. He ruled in Jerusalem for 29 years. His mother's name was Jehoaddin. She was from Jerusalem.

²Amaziah did what was right in the eyes of the LORD. But he didn't do it with all his heart. ³The kingdom was firmly under his control. So he put to death the officials who had murdered his father, the king.

⁴But he didn't put their children to death. He obeyed what is written in the Law, the Scroll of Moses. There the LORD commanded, "Parents must not be put to death because of what their children do. And children must not be put to death because of what their parents do. People must die because of their own sins." *(Deuteronomy 24:16)*

⁵Amaziah called the people of Judah

together. He arranged them by families under commanders of thousands and commanders of hundreds. He did it for all of the people of Judah and Benjamin. Then he brought together the men who were 20 years old or more. He found out there were 300,000 men who were able to serve in the army. They could handle spears and shields. ⁶He also hired 100,000 fighting men from Israel. He had to pay them almost four tons of silver.

⁷But a man of God came to him. He said, "King Amaziah, these troops from Israel must not march out with you. The LORD is not with Israel. He isn't with any of the people of Ephraim. ⁸Go and fight bravely in battle if you want to. But God will destroy you right in front of your enemies. God has the power to help you or destroy you."

⁹Amaziah asked the man of God, "But what about all of that silver I paid for these Israelite troops?"

The man of God replied, "The LORD can give you much more than that."

¹⁰So Amaziah let the troops go who had come to him from Ephraim. He sent them home. They were very angry with Judah. In fact, they were burning with anger when they went home.

¹¹Then Amaziah showed how strong he was. He led his army to the Valley of Salt. There he killed 10,000 men of Seir. ¹²The army of Judah also captured 10,000 men alive. They took them to the top of a cliff. Then they threw them down. All of them were smashed to pieces.

¹³The troops Amaziah had sent back attacked some towns in Judah. He hadn't allowed the troops to take part in the war. They attacked towns from Samaria to Beth Horon. They killed 3,000 people. They carried off huge amounts of goods.

¹⁴Amaziah returned from killing the men of Edom. He brought back the statues of the gods of Seir. He set them up as his own gods. He bowed down to them. He burned sacrifices to them. ¹⁵The LORD's anger burned against Amaziah. He sent a prophet to him. The prophet said, "Why do you ask the gods of those people for advice? They couldn't even save their own people from your power!"

¹⁶While the prophet was still speaking, the king spoke to him. He said, "Did I ask you for advice? Stop! If you don't, you will be struck down."

So the prophet stopped. But then he said, "I know that God has decided to destroy you. That's because you have worshiped other gods. You haven't listened to my advice."

¹⁷Amaziah, the king of Judah, spoke to his advisers. Then he sent a message to Jehoash, the king of Israel. Jehoash was the son of Jehoahaz. Jehoahaz was the son of Jehu. Amaziah dared Jehoash, "Come on. Meet me face to face in battle."

¹⁸But Jehoash, the king of Israel, answered Amaziah, the king of Judah. He said, "A thorn bush in Lebanon sent a message to a cedar tree there. It said, 'Give your daughter to be married to my son.' Then a wild animal in Lebanon came along. It walked all over the thorn bush. ¹⁹You brag that you have won the battle over Edom. You are very proud. But stay home! Why ask for trouble? Why bring yourself crashing down? Why bring Judah down with you?"

²⁰But Amaziah wouldn't listen. That's because God had planned to hand Judah over to Jehoash. After all, they had asked the gods of Edom for advice.

²¹So Jehoash, the king of Israel, attacked. He and Amaziah, the king of Judah, faced each other in battle. The battle took place at Beth Shemesh in Judah. ²²Israel drove Judah away. Every man ran home.

²³Jehoash king of Israel captured Amaziah king of Judah at Beth Shemesh. Amaziah was the son of Joash. Joash was the son of Ahaziah. Jehoash brought Amaziah to Jerusalem. He broke down part of its wall. It's the part that went from the Ephraim Gate to the Corner Gate. That part of the wall was 600 feet long. ²⁴Jehoash took all of the gold and silver. He took all of the articles he found in God's temple. Obed-Edom had been in charge of them. Jehoash also took the palace treasures and the prisoners. Then he returned to Samaria.

²⁵Amaziah king of Judah lived for 15 years after Jehoash king of Israel died.

Amaziah was the son of Joash. Jehoash was the son of Jehoahaz.

²⁶The other events of Amaziah's rule from beginning to end are written down. They are written in the records of the kings of Judah and Israel.

²⁷Amaziah turned away from following the LORD. From that time on, some people made evil plans against him in Jerusalem. So he ran away to Lachish. But they sent men to Lachish after him. There they killed him. ²⁸His body was brought back on a horse. Then he was buried in the family tomb in Jerusalem, the City of Judah.

UZZIAH BECOMES KING OF JUDAH

26 All of the people of Judah made Uzziah king. He was 16 years old. They made him king in place of his father Amaziah.

²Uzziah rebuilt Elath. He brought it under Judah's control again. He did it after Amaziah joined the members of his family who had already died.

³Uzziah was 16 years old when he became king. He ruled in Jerusalem for 52 years. His mother's name was Jecoliah. She was from Jerusalem.

⁴Uzziah did what was right in the eyes of the LORD, just as his father Amaziah had done. ⁵He looked to God during the days of Zechariah. Zechariah taught him to have respect for God. As long as Uzziah looked to the LORD, God gave him success.

⁶Uzziah went to war against the Philistines. He broke down the walls of Gath, Jabneh and Ashdod. Then he rebuilt some towns that were near Ashdod. He also rebuilt some other towns where Philistines lived. ⁷God helped him fight against the Philistines. He also helped him fight against the Meunites and against the Arabs who lived in Gur Baal. ⁸The Ammonites brought to Uzziah the gifts he required of them. He became famous all the way to the border of Egypt. That's because he had become very powerful.

⁹Uzziah built towers in Jerusalem. They were at the Corner Gate, the Valley Gate and the angle of the wall. He made the towers very strong. ¹⁰He also built towers in the desert.

He dug many wells, because he had a lot of livestock. The livestock were in the western hills and on the flatlands. Uzziah had people working in his fields and vineyards in the hills and in the rich lands. That's because he loved the soil.

¹¹Uzziah's army was well trained. It was ready to march out by companies in keeping with their numbers. Jeiel and Maaseiah brought them together. Jeiel was the secretary. Maaseiah was the officer. They were under the direction of Hananiah. He was one of the royal officials. ¹²The total number of family leaders who were over the fighting men was 2,600. ¹³An army of 307,500 men was under their command. The men were trained for war. They were a powerful force. They helped the king against his enemies. ¹⁴Uzziah provided the entire army with shields, spears, helmets, coats of armor, bows, and stones for their slings. ¹⁵In Jerusalem he made machines that were based on patterns that skilled men had drawn up. The machines were used on the towers and on the corners of walls. They could shoot arrows. They could also throw large stones.

Uzziah became famous everywhere. God greatly helped him until he became powerful.

¹⁶But after Uzziah became powerful, his pride brought him down. He wasn't faithful to the LORD his God. He entered the LORD's temple to burn incense on the altar for burning incense. ¹⁷The priest Azariah followed him in. So did 80 other brave priests of the LORD. ¹⁸They stood up to Uzziah. They said, "Uzziah, it isn't right for you to burn incense to the LORD. Only the priests are supposed to do that. They are members of the family line of Aaron. They have been set apart to burn incense. So get out of here. Leave the temple. You haven't been faithful. The LORD God won't honor you."

¹⁹Uzziah was holding a shallow cup. He was ready to burn incense. He became angry. He shouted at the priests in the LORD's temple. He did it near the altar for burning incense.

While he was shouting, a skin disease suddenly broke out on his forehead. ²⁰The chief priest Azariah looked at him. So did all of the other priests. They saw that Uzziah had a skin disease on his forehead. So they hurried him out of the temple. Actually, he himself really wanted to leave. He knew that the LORD was making him suffer.

²¹King Uzziah had the skin disease until the day he died. He lived in a separate house because he had the disease. And he wasn't allowed to enter the LORD's temple.

Uzziah's son Jotham was in charge of the palace. Jotham ruled over the people of the land.

²²The other events of Uzziah's rule from beginning to end were written down by the prophet Isaiah. Isaiah was the son of Amoz.

²³Uzziah joined the members of his family who had already died. His body was buried near theirs in a royal burial ground. People said, "He had a skin disease." His son Jotham became the next king after him.

JOTHAM BECOMES KING OF JUDAH

27 Jotham was 25 years old when he became king. He ruled in Jerusalem for 16 years. His mother's name was Jerusha. She was the daughter of Zadok.

²Jotham did what was right in the eyes of the LORD, just as his father Uzziah had done. But Jotham didn't enter the LORD's temple as Uzziah had done. In spite of that, the people continued to do very sinful things.

³Jotham rebuilt the Upper Gate of the LORD's temple. He did a lot of work on the wall at the hill of Ophel. ⁴He built towns in the hills of Judah. He also built forts and towers in areas that had a lot of trees in them.

⁵Jotham went to war against the king of Ammon. He won the battle over the people of Ammon. That year they paid Jotham almost four tons of silver. They paid him 62,000 bushels of wheat and 62,000 bushels of barley. They also brought him the same amount in the second and third years.

⁶Jotham became powerful. That's because he had worshiped the LORD his God with all his heart.

⁷The other events of Jotham's rule are written down. That includes all of his wars and the other things he did. All of those things are written in the records of the kings of Israel and Judah. ⁸Jotham was 25 years old when he became king. He ruled in Jerusalem for 16 years.

⁹Jotham joined the members of his family who had already died. His body was buried in the City of David. His son Ahaz became the next king after him.

AHAZ BECOMES KING OF JUDAH

28 Ahaz was 20 years old when he became king. He ruled in Jerusalem for 16 years.

He didn't do what was right in the eyes of the LORD. He didn't do what King David had done. ²He followed the ways of the kings of Israel. He also made metal statues of gods that were named after Baal. ³He burned sacrifices in the Valley of Ben Hinnom. He sacrificed his children in the fire to other gods. He followed the practices of the nations. The LORD hated those practices. He had driven out those nations to make room for the people of Israel. ⁴Ahaz offered sacrifices and burned incense at the high places. He also did it on the tops of hills and under every green tree.

⁵So the LORD his God handed him over to the king of Aram. The men of Aram won the battle over him. They took many of his people as prisoners. They brought them to Damascus.

God also handed Ahaz over to Pekah. His army wounded or killed many of the troops of Ahaz. Pekah was king of Israel. ⁶In one day Pekah killed 120,000 soldiers in Judah. That's because Judah had deserted the LORD, the God of their people. Pekah was the son of Remaliah.

⁷Zicri was a fighting man from Ephraim. He killed Maaseiah, Azrikam and Elkanah. Maaseiah was the king's son. Azrikam was the officer who was in charge of the palace. And Elkanah was next in command after the king. ⁸The men of Israel captured 200,000 wives, sons and daughters from their

relatives in Judah. They also took a large amount of goods. They carried all of it back to Samaria.

⁹But a prophet of the LORD was there. His name was Oded. When the army returned to Samaria, he went out to meet them. He said to them, "The LORD is the God of your people. He burned with anger against Judah. So he handed them over to you. But you have killed them. Your anger reached all the way to heaven.

¹⁰"Now you are planning to make the men and women of Judah and Jerusalem your slaves. But aren't you also guilty of sins against the LORD your God? ¹¹Listen to me! You have taken your relatives from Judah as prisoners. The LORD's anger is burning against you. So send your relatives back."

¹²Then some of the leaders in Ephraim stood up to those who were returning from the war. The leaders were Azariah, Berekiah, Jehizkiah and Amasa. Azariah was the son of Jehohanan. Berekiah was the son of Meshillemoth. Jehizkiah was the son of Shallum. And Amasa was the son of Hadlai. ¹³"Don't bring those prisoners here," they said. "If you do, we'll be guilty in the sight of the LORD. Do you really want to add to our sin and guilt? We're already very guilty. The LORD's anger is burning against Israel."

¹⁴So the soldiers gave up the prisoners and the goods they had taken. They did it in front of the officials and the whole community. ¹⁵Azariah, Berekiah, Jehizkiah and Amasa received the prisoners. From the goods that had been taken they gave clothes to all those who were naked. They gave them clothes, sandals, food, drink and healing lotion. They put all of the weak people on donkeys. They took them back to their relatives at Jericho. Then they returned to Samaria. Jericho was also known as the City of Palm Trees.

¹⁶At that time King Ahaz sent men to the king of Assyria to get help. ¹⁷The men of Edom had come again and attacked Judah. They had carried prisoners away. ¹⁸At the same time the Philistines had attacked towns in the western hills and in the Negev Desert of Judah. They had captured Beth Shemesh, Aijalon and Gederoth. They had also captured Soco, Timnah and Gimzo and the villages that were around them. They had settled down in all of them.

¹⁹The LORD had brought Judah down because of Ahaz, their king. Ahaz had stirred up the people of Judah to do evil things. He hadn't been faithful to the LORD at all.

²⁰Tiglath-Pileser came to Ahaz. But he gave Ahaz trouble instead of help. Tiglath-Pileser was king of Assyria. ²¹Ahaz took some things from the LORD's temple. He also took some from the royal palace and from the princes. He gave all of them to the king of Assyria. But that didn't help him.

²²When King Ahaz was in trouble, he became even more unfaithful to the LORD. ²³He offered sacrifices to the gods of Damascus. They had won the battle over him. He thought, "The gods of the kings of Aram have helped them. So I'll sacrifice to them. Then they'll help me." But they brought him down. In fact, they brought the whole nation of Israel down.

²⁴Ahaz gathered together everything that belonged to God's temple. He took all of it away. He shut the doors of the LORD's temple. He set up altars at every street corner in Jerusalem. ²⁵In every town in Judah he built high places. Sacrifices were burned there to other gods. That made the LORD, the God of his people, very angry.

²⁶The other events of the rule of Ahaz and all of his evil practices from beginning to end are written down. They are written in the records of the kings of Judah and Israel.

²⁷Ahaz joined the members of his family who had already died. His body was buried in the city of Jerusalem. But it wasn't placed in the tombs of the kings of Israel. His son Hezekiah became the next king after him.

HEZEKIAH PURIFIES THE TEMPLE

29 Hezekiah was 25 years old when he became king. He ruled in Jerusalem for 29 years. His mother's name was Abijah. She was the daughter of Zechariah. ²Hezekiah did what was right in the eyes of the LORD, just as King David had done.

³In the first month of Hezekiah's first year as king, he opened the doors of the LORD's temple. He repaired them. ⁴He brought the priests and Levites in. He gathered them together in the open area on the east side of the temple. ⁵He said, "Levites, listen to me! Set yourselves apart to the LORD. Set apart the temple of the LORD. He's the God of your people. Remove anything that is 'unclean' from the temple. ⁶Our people weren't faithful. They did what was evil in the sight of the LORD our God. They deserted him. They turned their faces away from the place where he lives. They turned their backs on him. ⁷They also shut the doors of the temple porch. They put the lamps out. They didn't burn incense at the temple. They didn't sacrifice burnt offerings to the God of Israel there.

⁸"So the LORD has become angry with Judah and Jerusalem. He has made them look so bad that everyone is shocked when they see them. They laugh at them. You can see it with your own eyes. ⁹That's why our people have been killed with swords. That's why our sons and daughters and wives have become prisoners.

¹⁰"So I'm planning to make a covenant with the LORD, the God of Israel. Then he'll turn his burning anger away from us.

¹¹"My sons, don't fail to obey the LORD. He has chosen you to stand in front of him and work for him. He wants you to serve him and burn incense to him."

¹²Here are the Levites who went to work.

Mahath and Joel were from the family line of Kohath.
Mahath was the son of Amasai.
Joel was the son of Azariah.
Kish and Azariah were from the family line of Merari.
Kish was the son of Abdi. Azariah was the son of Jehallelel.
Joah and Eden were from the family line of Gershon.
Joah was the son of Zimmah.
Eden was the son of Joah.
¹³Shimri and Jeiel were from the family line of Elizaphan.

Zechariah and Mattaniah were from
the family line of Asaph.
¹⁴Jehiel and Shimei were from
the family line of Heman.
Shemaiah and Uzziel were from
the family line of Jeduthun.

¹⁵All of those Levites gathered the other Levites together. They set themselves apart to the LORD. Then they went in to purify the LORD's temple. That's what the king had ordered them to do. They did what the LORD told them to. ¹⁶The priests went into the LORD's temple to make it pure. They brought out to the temple courtyard everything that was "unclean." They had found "unclean" things in the LORD's temple. The Levites took them and carried them out to the Kidron Valley.

¹⁷On the first day of the first month they began to set everything in the temple apart to the LORD. By the eighth day of the month they reached the LORD's porch. For eight more days they set the LORD's temple itself apart to him. They finished on the 16th day of the first month.

¹⁸Then they went to King Hezekiah. They reported, "We've purified the whole temple of the LORD. That includes the altar for burnt offerings and all of its tools. It also includes the table for the holy bread and all of its articles. ¹⁹We've prepared all of the articles King Ahaz had removed. We've set them apart to the LORD. Ahaz had removed them while he was king. He wasn't faithful to the LORD. The articles are now in front of the LORD's altar."

²⁰Early the next morning King Hezekiah gathered the city officials together. They went up to the LORD's temple. ²¹They brought seven bulls, seven rams, seven male lambs and seven male goats with them. They sacrificed the animals as a sin offering for the kingdom, for the temple and for Judah. The king commanded the priests to offer them on the LORD's altar. The priests were from the family line of Aaron. ²²They killed the bulls. Then they sprinkled the blood on the altar. Next they killed the rams and sprinkled the

blood on the altar. Then they killed the lambs and sprinkled the blood on the altar.

²³The goats for the sin offering were brought to the king and the whole community. They placed their hands on them. ²⁴Then the priests killed the goats. They put the blood on the altar as a sin offering. It paid for the sin of the whole nation of Israel. The king had ordered the burnt offering and the sin offering for the whole nation.

²⁵He stationed the Levites in the LORD's temple. They had cymbals, harps and lyres. They did everything in the way King David, his prophet Gad, and the prophet Nathan had required. The LORD had given commands about all of those things through his prophets. ²⁶So the Levites stood ready with David's musical instruments. And the priests had their trumpets ready.

²⁷Hezekiah gave the order to sacrifice the burnt offering on the altar. The offering began. Singing to the LORD also began. The singing was accompanied by the trumpets and by the instruments of David. He had been king of Israel. ²⁸The whole community bowed down. They worshiped the LORD. At the same time the singers sang. The priests blew their trumpets. All of that continued until the burnt offering had been sacrificed.

²⁹So the offerings were finished. King Hezekiah got down on his knees. He worshiped the LORD. So did everyone who was with him.

³⁰The king and his officials ordered the Levites to praise the LORD. They used the words of David and the prophet Asaph. They sang praises with joy. They bowed their heads and worshiped the LORD.

³¹Then Hezekiah said, "You have set yourselves apart to the LORD. Come and bring sacrifices and thank offerings to his temple."

So the whole community brought sacrifices and thank offerings. Everyone who wanted to brought burnt offerings.

³²The whole community brought 70 bulls, 100 rams and 200 male lambs. They brought all of them as burnt offerings to the LORD. ³³The total number of animals that were set apart as sacrifices to the LORD was 600 bulls and 3,000 sheep and goats.

³⁴But there weren't enough priests to skin all of the burnt offerings. So their brother Levites helped them. They worked until the task was finished. By that time other priests had been set apart to the LORD. The Levites had been more careful than the priests when they set themselves apart. ³⁵There were large numbers of burnt offerings, along with the drink offerings and the fat from the friendship offerings. They were offered along with the burnt offerings.

So the service of the LORD's temple was started up again. ³⁶Hezekiah and all of the people were filled with joy. That's because everything had been done so quickly. God had provided for his people in a wonderful way.

HEZEKIAH CELEBRATES THE PASSOVER FEAST

30 Hezekiah sent a message to all of the people of Israel and Judah. He also wrote letters to the tribes of Ephraim and Manasseh. He invited everyone to come to the LORD's temple in Jerusalem. He wanted them to celebrate the Passover Feast in honor of the LORD. He is the God of Israel.

²The king, his officials and the whole community in Jerusalem decided to celebrate the Passover in the second month. ³They hadn't been able to celebrate it at the regular time. That's because there weren't enough priests who had set themselves apart to the LORD. Also, the people hadn't gathered together in Jerusalem.

⁴The plan seemed good to the king and the whole community. ⁵They decided to send a message all through Israel. It was sent out from Beersheba all the way to Dan. The message invited the people to come to Jerusalem. It invited them to celebrate the Passover in honor of the LORD, the God of Israel.

The Passover hadn't been celebrated by large numbers of people for a long time. It hadn't been done in keeping with what was written in the law.

⁶Messengers went all through Israel and Judah. They carried letters from

the king and his officials. The king had ordered them to do that. The letters said,

"People of Israel, return to the LORD. He is the God of Abraham, Isaac and Israel. Return to him. Then he will return to you who are left in the land. You have escaped from the power of the kings of Assyria.

7"Don't be like the rest of your people and relatives. They weren't faithful to the LORD, the God of their people. That's why he punished them. He made them look so bad that everyone was shocked when they saw them. You can see it for yourselves.

8"Don't be stubborn. Don't be as your people were. Obey the LORD. Come to the temple. He has set it apart to himself forever. Serve the LORD your God. Then he'll turn his burning anger away from you.

9"Suppose you return to the LORD. Then those who captured your relatives and children will be kind to them. In fact, your relatives and children will come back to this land. The LORD your God is kind and tender. He won't turn away from you if you return to him."

10The messengers went from town to town in Ephraim and Manasseh. They went all the way to Zebulun. But the people made fun of them. They laughed at them. 11In spite of that, some men from Asher, Manasseh and Zebulun made themselves low in the LORD's sight. They went to Jerusalem. 12God's powerful hand helped the people of Judah. He helped them agree with one another. So they did what the king and his officials had ordered. They did what the LORD told them to do.

13A very large crowd of people gathered together in Jerusalem. They went there to celebrate the Feast of Unleavened Bread. It took place in the second month. 14They removed the altars in Jerusalem. They cleared away the altars for burning incense. They threw all of the altars into the Kidron Valley. 15They killed the Passover lamb on the 14th day of the second month. The priests and Levites were filled with shame. They set themselves apart to the LORD. They brought burnt offerings to his temple. 16Then they went to their regular positions. They did it just as the Law of Moses, the man of God, required. The Levites gave the blood of the animals to the priests. The priests sprinkled it on the altar.

17Many people in the crowd hadn't set themselves apart to the LORD. They weren't "clean." They couldn't set their lambs apart to him. So the Levites had to kill the Passover lambs for all of them.

18Many people came from Ephraim, Manasseh, Issachar and Zebulun. Most of them hadn't made themselves pure and clean. But they still ate the Passover meal. That was against what was written in the law. But Hezekiah prayed for them. He said, "The LORD is good. May he forgive everyone 19who wants to worship God with all his heart. God is the LORD, the God of their people. May God forgive them even if they aren't 'clean' in keeping with the rules of the temple."

20The LORD answered Hezekiah's prayer. He healed the people.

21The people of Israel who were in Jerusalem celebrated the Feast of Unleavened Bread. They celebrated for seven days with great joy.

The Levites and priests sang to the LORD every day. Their singing was accompanied by musical instruments. The instruments were used to praise the LORD.

22Hezekiah spoke words that gave hope to all of the Levites. They understood how to serve the LORD well. For the seven days of the Feast they ate the share that was given to them. They also sacrificed friendship offerings. They praised the LORD, the God of their people.

23Then the whole community agreed to celebrate the Feast for seven more days. So for another seven days they celebrated with joy.

24Hezekiah, the king of Judah, provided 1,000 bulls and 7,000 sheep and goats for the community. The officials provided 1,000 bulls and 10,000 sheep and goats for them. A large number of priests set themselves apart to the LORD.

²⁵The entire community of Judah was filled with joy. So were the priests and Levites. And so were all of the people who had gathered together from Israel. That included the outsiders who had come from Israel. It also included those who lived in Judah.

²⁶There was great joy in Jerusalem. There hadn't been anything like it in Israel since the days of Solomon, the son of David. Solomon had been king of Israel.

²⁷The priests and Levites gave their blessing to the people. God heard them. Their prayer reached all the way to heaven. It's the holy place where he lives.

31 The Feast came to an end. The people of Israel who were in Jerusalem went out to the towns of Judah. They smashed the sacred stones. They cut down the poles that were used to worship the goddess Asherah. They destroyed the high places and the altars. They did those things all through Judah and Benjamin. They also did them in Ephraim and Manasseh. They destroyed all of the objects that were used to worship other gods. Then the people returned to their own towns and property.

THE PEOPLE BRING GIFTS TO THE LORD

²Hezekiah put the priests and Levites in groups based on their duties. The priests sacrificed burnt offerings and friendship offerings. The Levites served the LORD by giving thanks and singing praises at the gates of his house.

³The king gave some of his own possessions to the temple. He gave them for the morning and evening burnt offerings. He gave them for the burnt offerings for every Sabbath day. He gave them for the burnt offerings for every New Moon feast. And he gave them for the burnt offerings for every yearly appointed feast. He did it in keeping with what is written in the Law of the LORD.

⁴Hezekiah gave an order to the people who were living in Jerusalem. He commanded them to give to the priests and Levites the share they owed them. Then the priests and Levites could give their full attention to the Law of the LORD.

⁵The order went out. Right away the people of Israel began to give freely. They gave the first share of the harvest of their grain, fresh wine, olive oil and honey. They also gave the first share of everything else their fields produced. They brought a large amount. It was a tenth of everything.

⁶The people of Israel and Judah who lived in the towns of Judah brought a tenth of their herds and flocks. They also brought a tenth of the holy things they had set apart to the LORD their God. They put them in piles. ⁷They began doing it in the third month. They finished in the seventh month. ⁸Hezekiah and his officials came and saw the piles. When they did, they praised the LORD. And they blessed his people Israel.

⁹Hezekiah asked the priests and Levites about the piles. ¹⁰The chief priest Azariah answered him. He said, "The people have been bringing their gifts to the LORD's temple. Ever since they began to bring them, we've had enough to eat. We have even had plenty to spare. That's because the LORD has blessed his people. So we have a large amount left over." Azariah was from the family line of Zadok.

¹¹Hezekiah gave orders to prepare storerooms in the LORD's temple. And it was done. ¹²The people were faithful. They brought in their offerings, a tenth of everything they produced, and the gifts they had set apart to the LORD. The Levite Conaniah was in charge of those things. His brother Shimei was next in command after him. ¹³Conaniah and his brother Shimei had directors who worked under them. Their names were Jehiel, Azaziah, Nahath, Asahel, Jerimoth, Jozabad, Eliel, Ismakiah, Mahath and Benaiah. King Hezekiah and Azariah had appointed them. Azariah was the official who was in charge of God's temple.

¹⁴The Levite Kore guarded the East Gate. He was in charge of the offerings people chose to give to God. He handed out the offerings that were made to

the LORD. He also handed out the gifts that had been set apart to the LORD. Kore was the son of Imnah. ¹⁵Eden, Miniamin, Jeshua, Shemaiah, Amariah and Shecaniah helped Kore. They were faithful in helping him in the towns of the priests. They handed out gifts to their brother priests, group by group. They gave the gifts to young men and old men alike.

¹⁶In addition to that, they handed out gifts to the males who were three years old or more. The names of those males were listed in their family history. All of them would enter the LORD's temple. They would carry out their duties each day. Each group did all of the different things it was supposed to do.

¹⁷Kore and his Levite companions also handed out gifts to the priests. The priests were listed by their families in their family history. Those Levites also handed out gifts to the Levites who were 20 years old or more. Each group did all of the different things it was supposed to do.

¹⁸Those groups included all of the little ones, the wives, and the sons and daughters of the whole community. All of them were listed in their family history. They were faithful in setting themselves apart to serve the LORD.

¹⁹Some of the priests, who were from the family line of Aaron, lived in other towns or on farms around their towns. Men were chosen by name to hand out shares to those priests. They gave a share to every male among them. They also gave a share to everyone whose name was written down in the family history of the Levites.

²⁰That's what Hezekiah did all through Judah. He did what was good and right. He was faithful to the LORD his God. ²¹He looked to his God. He worked for him with all his heart. That's the way he worked in everything he did to serve God's temple. He obeyed the law. He followed the LORD's commands. So he had success.

SENNACHERIB'S ARMY SURROUNDS JERUSALEM

32 Hezekiah had been completely faithful to the LORD. But in spite of that, Sennacherib came and marched into Judah. He was the king of Assyria. He surrounded the cities that had high walls around them. He got ready to attack them. He thought he could win the battle over them. He thought he could take them for himself.

²Hezekiah saw that Sennacherib had come to Jerusalem to make war against it. ³So he asked his officials and military leaders for advice. He asked them about blocking off the water from the springs that were outside the city. They gave him the advice he asked for.

⁴A large group of men gathered together. They blocked all of the springs. They also blocked the stream that flowed through the land. "Why should the kings of Assyria come and find plenty of water?" they asked.

⁵Then Hezekiah worked hard repairing all of the broken parts of the wall. He built towers on it. He built another wall outside that one. He built up the areas that had been filled in around the City of David. He also made large numbers of weapons and shields.

⁶He appointed military officers over the people. He gathered the officers together in front of him in the open area at the city gate. He gave them words of hope. He said, ⁷"Be strong. Be brave. Don't be afraid. Don't lose hope. The king of Assyria has a huge army with him. But there's a greater power with us than there is with him. ⁸The only thing he has is human strength. But the LORD our God is with us. He will help us. He'll fight our battles."

The people had great faith in what Hezekiah, the king of Judah, said.

⁹Later Sennacherib, the king of Assyria, and all of his forces surrounded Lachish. They got ready to attack it. At that time, he sent his officers to Jerusalem. They went there with a message for Hezekiah, the king of Judah. The message was also for all of the people of Judah who were there. The message said,

¹⁰"Sennacherib, the king of Assyria, says, 'Why are you putting your faith in what your king says? Why do you remain in Jerusalem when you are surrounded?

¹¹" 'Hezekiah says, "The LORD our God will save us from the powerful hand of the king of Assyria." But he isn't telling you the truth. If you listen to him, you will die of hunger and thirst.

¹²" 'Didn't Hezekiah himself remove your god's high places and altars? Didn't Hezekiah say to the people of Judah and Jerusalem, "You must worship at one altar. You must burn sacrifices on it"?

¹³" 'Don't you know what I and the kings who ruled before me have done? Don't you know what we've done to all of the peoples of the other lands? Were the gods of those nations ever able to save their lands from my power? ¹⁴The kings who ruled before me destroyed many nations. Which one of the gods of those nations has been able to save his people from me? So how can your god save you from my power?

¹⁵" 'Don't let Hezekiah trick you. He's telling you lies. Don't believe him. No god of any nation or kingdom has been able to save his people from my power. No god has been able to save his people from the power of the kings who ruled before me. So your god won't save you from my power either!' "

¹⁶Sennacherib's officers spoke even more things against the LORD God and his servant Hezekiah. ¹⁷The king also wrote letters against the LORD. His letters made fun of the God of Israel. They said, "The peoples of other lands have their gods. But those gods didn't save their people from my powerful hand. So the god of Hezekiah won't save his people from my powerful hand either."

¹⁸Then the officers called out in the Hebrew language to the people of Jerusalem who were on the wall. They were trying to scare them and make them afraid. That's because they wanted to capture the city. ¹⁹They were comparing the God of Jerusalem to the gods of the other nations of the world. But those gods were only statues. They had been made by the hands of men.

²⁰King Hezekiah cried out in prayer to God in heaven. He prayed about the problem Jerusalem was facing. So did the prophet Isaiah. He was the son of Amoz.

²¹The LORD sent an angel. The angel wiped out all of the enemy's fighting men, leaders and officers. He put an end to them right there in the camp of the Assyrian king.

So Sennacherib went back to his own land in shame. He went into the temple of his god. There some of his own sons cut him down with their swords.

²²So the LORD saved Hezekiah and the people of Jerusalem. He saved them from the power of Sennacherib, the king of Assyria. He also saved them from all of their other enemies. He took care of them on every side.

²³Many people brought offerings to Jerusalem for the LORD. They brought expensive gifts for Hezekiah, the king of Judah. From then on, all of the nations thought highly of him.

HEZEKIAH'S PRIDE, SUCCESS AND DEATH

²⁴In those days Hezekiah became sick. He knew he was about to die. So he prayed to the LORD. And the LORD answered him. He gave him a miraculous sign.

²⁵But Hezekiah's heart was proud. He didn't give thanks for the many kind things the LORD had done for him. So the LORD became angry with him. He also became angry with Judah and Jerusalem.

²⁶Then Hezekiah had a change of heart. He was sorry he had been proud. The people of Jerusalem were also sorry they had sinned. So the LORD wasn't angry with them as long as Hezekiah was king.

²⁷Hezekiah was very rich. He received great honor. He made storerooms for his silver and gold. He also made them for his jewels, spices, shields and all kinds of expensive things. ²⁸He made buildings to store the harvest of grain, fresh wine and olive oil. He made barns for all kinds of cattle. He made sheep pens for his flocks. ²⁹He built villages. He gained large numbers of flocks and herds. God had made him very rich.

³⁰Hezekiah blocked up the upper opening of the Gihon spring. He directed the water to flow down to the west side of the City of David. He had success in everything he did.

³¹The rulers of Babylon sent messengers to him. They asked him about the miraculous sign that had taken place in the land. Then God left him to put him to the test. He wanted to know everything that was in his heart.

³²Hezekiah did many things that showed he was faithful to the LORD. Those things and the other events of his rule are written down. They are written in the record of the vision of the prophet Isaiah, the son of Amoz. That record is part of the records of the kings of Judah and Israel.

³³Hezekiah joined the members of his family who had already died. His body was buried on the hill where the tombs of David's family are. The whole nation of Judah honored him when he died. So did the people of Jerusalem. Hezekiah's son Manasseh became the next king after him.

MANASSEH BECOMES KING OF JUDAH

33 Manasseh was 12 years old when he became king. He ruled in Jerusalem for 55 years.

²Manasseh did what was evil in the sight of the LORD. He followed the practices of the nations. The LORD hated those practices. He had driven those nations out to make room for the people of Israel.

³Manasseh rebuilt the high places. His father Hezekiah had destroyed them. Manasseh also set up altars to the gods that were named after Baal. He made poles that were used to worship the goddess Asherah. He even bowed down to all of the stars. And he worshiped them.

⁴He built altars in the LORD's temple. The LORD had said about his temple, "My Name will remain in Jerusalem forever." ⁵In both courtyards of the LORD's temple Manasseh built altars to honor all of the stars.

⁶He sacrificed his children in the fire

What should I say if someone makes fun of the Bible?

If a friend makes fun of the Bible, you can politely explain how you feel and ask that person to stop. Your friend may not know how special the Bible is to you. This might give you a chance to explain that the Bible comes from God, who created the whole universe, and it's very important to you. You might be the first one to help this person understand that the message in the Bible is for everyone in the world. If your friend doesn't want to listen, it's best to let it pass and then pray for him or her.

checkout
2 Chronicles 32:17

HEY, BIBLE BOY!

Related verses:
Proverbs 30:5;
John 17:17;
2 Timothy 3:16;
1 Peter 3:14–15

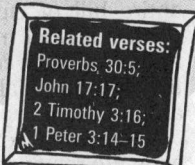

to other gods. He did it in the Valley of Ben Hinnom. He practiced all kinds of evil magic. He took part in worshiping evil powers. He got messages from those who had died. He talked to the spirits of the dead. He did many things that were evil in the sight of the LORD. He made him very angry.

[7]Manasseh had carved a statue of a god. He put it in God's temple. God had spoken to David and his son Solomon about the temple. He had said, "My Name will be in this temple and in Jerusalem forever. Out of all of the cities in the tribes of Israel I have chosen Jerusalem. [8]I gave this land to your people who lived long ago. I will not make the Israelites leave it again. But they must be careful to do everything I commanded them. They must follow all of the laws, directions, and rules I gave them through Moses."

[9]But Manasseh led Judah and the people of Jerusalem down the wrong path. They did more evil things than the nations the LORD had destroyed to make room for the people of Israel.

[10]The LORD spoke to Manasseh and his people. But they didn't pay any attention to him. [11]So the LORD brought the army commanders of the king of Assyria against them. They took Manasseh as a prisoner. They put a hook in his nose. They put him in bronze chains. And they took him to Babylon.

[12]When Manasseh was in trouble, he asked the LORD his God to show favor to him. He made himself very low in the sight of the God of his people. [13]Manasseh prayed to him. When he did, the LORD felt sorry for him. He answered his prayer. He brought him back to Jerusalem and his kingdom. Then Manasseh knew that the LORD is God.

[14]After that, Manasseh rebuilt the outer wall of the City of David. It was west of the Gihon spring in the valley. It reached all the way to the entrance of the Fish Gate. It went around the entire hill of Ophel. Manasseh also made the wall much higher. He stationed military commanders in all of the cities in Judah that had high walls around them.

[15]Manasseh got rid of the strange gods. He removed the statue of one of those gods from the LORD's temple. He also removed all of the altars he had built on the temple hill and in Jerusalem. He threw them out of the city. [16]Then he made the LORD's altar look like new again. He sacrificed friendship offerings and thank offerings on it. He told the people of Judah to serve the LORD, the God of Israel. [17]The people continued to offer sacrifices at the high places. But they offered them only to the LORD their God.

[18]The other events of Manasseh's rule are written down in the official records of the kings of Israel. They include his prayer to his God. They also include the words the prophets spoke to him in the name of the LORD, the God of Israel. [19]Everything about Manasseh is written in the records of the prophets. That includes his prayer and the fact that God felt sorry for him. It includes everything he did before he made himself low in the LORD's sight. It includes all of his sins and the fact that he wasn't faithful to the LORD. It includes the locations where he built high places. It includes the places where he set up poles that were used to worship the goddess Asherah. And it includes the places where he set up statues of other gods.

[20]Manasseh joined the members of his family who had already died. His body was buried in his palace. His son Amon became the next king after him.

AMON BECOMES KING OF JUDAH

[21]Amon was 22 years old when he became king. He ruled in Jerusalem for two years. [22]Amon did what was evil in the sight of the LORD, just as his father Manasseh had done. Amon worshiped and offered sacrifices to all of the statues of gods that Manasseh had made. [23]He didn't make himself low in the LORD's sight as his father Manasseh had done. So Amon became even more guilty. [24]Amon's officials made plans against him. They murdered him in his palace. [25]Then the people of the land killed all those who had made plans against King Amon. They made his son Josiah king in his place.

JOSIAH MAKES JUDAH A BETTER NATION

34 Josiah was eight years old when he became king. He ruled in Jerusalem for 31 years. ²He did what was right in the eyes of the LORD. He lived the way King David had lived. He didn't turn away from it to the right or the left.

³While he was still young, he began to worship the God of King David. It was the eighth year of Josiah's rule.

In his 12th year he began to get rid of the high places in Judah and Jerusalem. He removed the poles that were used to worship the goddess Asherah. He also removed the wooden and metal statues of gods. ⁴He ordered the altars of the gods that were named after Baal to be torn down. He cut to pieces the altars for burning incense that were above them. He smashed the Asherah poles. He also smashed the wooden and metal statues of gods. He broke all of them to pieces. He scattered the pieces over the graves of those who had offered sacrifices to those gods. ⁵He burned the bones of the priests on their altars. That's the way he made Judah and Jerusalem pure and clean.

⁶He went to the towns of Manasseh, Ephraim and Simeon. He went all the way to Naphtali. He also went to the destroyed places around all of those towns. ⁷Everywhere he went he tore down the altars and the Asherah poles. He crushed the statues of gods to powder. He cut to pieces all of the altars for burning incense. He destroyed all of those things everywhere in Israel. Then he went back to Jerusalem.

⁸In the 18th year of Josiah's rule, he decided to make the land and temple pure and clean. So he sent Shaphan, Maaseiah and Joah to repair the temple of the LORD his God. Shaphan was the son of Azaliah. Maaseiah was ruler of the city. And Joah, the son of Joahaz, kept the records.

⁹They went to the high priest Hilkiah. They gave him the money that had been brought into God's temple. The Levites who guarded the doors had collected it. They had received some of the money from the people of Manasseh, Ephraim and the others who remained in Israel. They had received the rest of it from the people of Judah and Benjamin and those who lived in Jerusalem.

¹⁰They put all of the money in the care of the men who had been appointed to direct the work on the LORD's temple. Those men paid the workers who repaired the temple and made it look like new again. ¹¹They also gave money to the builders and those who worked with wood. The workers used it to buy lumber and blocks of stone. The lumber was used for the supports and beams for the buildings. The kings of Judah had let the buildings fall down.

¹²The men were faithful in doing the work. Jahath and Obadiah directed them. They were Levites from the family line of Merari. Zechariah and Meshullam also directed them. They were from the family line of Kohath. The Levites were skilled in playing musical instruments. ¹³They were in charge of the laborers. They directed all of the workers from job to job. Some of the Levites were secretaries and writers. Others guarded the doors.

HILKIAH FINDS THE SCROLL OF THE LAW

¹⁴The money that had been taken into the LORD's temple was being brought out. At that time the priest Hilkiah found the Scroll of the Law of the LORD. It had been given through Moses. ¹⁵Hilkiah spoke to the secretary Shaphan. He said, "I've found the Scroll of the Law in the LORD's temple." He gave it to Shaphan.

¹⁶Then Shaphan took the scroll to King Josiah. He told him, "Your officials are doing everything they've been asked to do. ¹⁷They have paid out the money that was in the LORD's temple. They've put it in the care of the directors and workers." ¹⁸Shaphan continued, "The priest Hilkiah has given me a scroll." Shaphan read some of it to the king.

¹⁹The king heard the words of the Law. When he did, he tore his royal robes. ²⁰He gave orders to Hilkiah, Ahikam, Abdon, the secretary Shaphan

and Asaiah. Ahikam was the son of Shaphan. Abdon was the son of Micah. And Asaiah was the king's attendant. Josiah commanded them, 21"Go. Ask the LORD for advice. Ask him about what is written in this scroll that has been found. Do it for me. Also do it for those who remain in Israel and Judah. The LORD has poured out his burning anger on us. That's because our people before us didn't obey what the LORD had said. They didn't do everything that is written in this scroll."

22Hilkiah and those the king had sent with him went to speak to the prophet Huldah. She was the wife of Shallum. Shallum was the son of Tokhath. Tokhath was the son of Hasrah. Shallum took care of the sacred robes.

Huldah lived in the New Quarter of Jerusalem.

23She said to them, "The LORD is the God of Israel. He says, 'Tell the man who sent you to me, 24"The LORD says, 'I am going to bring horrible trouble on this place and its people. All of the curses that are written down in the scroll that has been read to the king of Judah will take place. 25That is because the people have deserted me. They have burned incense to other gods. They have made me very angry because of everything their hands have made. So I will pour out my burning anger on this place. The fire of my anger will not be put out.' " '

26"The king of Judah sent you to ask for advice. Tell him, 'The LORD is the

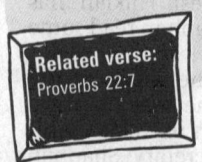

KIDS' QUESTION

What are accounts?

A bank account is a place to put your money in a bank. The money is set aside just for you. An account is like a piggy bank or an envelope with your name on it at the bank. It is a way for the bank to keep track of your money.

The bank keeps track of each person's money by using accounts. If three of your friends each gave you some money to keep for them, you could keep it in three separate places. Then you could put all the money in one place.

That is how accounts work at a bank.

Shaphan, Maaseiah, and Joah kept records for King Josiah of the money that had been collected to pay the workers who were repairing the temple. These records were like bank accounts today, because every worker needed to be paid just the right amount.

JASON'S IMAGINATION

checkout

2 Chronicles 34:9

Related verse:
Proverbs 22:7

God of Israel. He has a message for you about the things you heard. [27]He says, "Your heart was tender. You made yourself low in my sight. You heard what I spoke against this place and its people. So you made yourself low. You tore your royal robes and sobbed. And I have heard you," announces the LORD. [28]" ' "You will join the members of your family who have already died. Your body will be buried in peace. Your eyes will not see all of the trouble I am going to bring on this place and those who live here." ' "

Huldah's answer was taken back to the king.

[29]Then the king called together all of the elders of Judah and Jerusalem. [30]He went up to the LORD's temple. The people of Judah and Jerusalem went with him. So did the priests and Levites. All of them went, from the least important of them to the most important. The king had all of the words of the Scroll of the Covenant read to them. The scroll had been found in the LORD's temple.

[31]The king stood next to his pillar. He agreed to the terms of the covenant in front of the LORD. He promised to follow him and obey his commands, directions and rules. He promised to obey them with all his heart and with all his soul. So he promised to obey the terms of the covenant that were written down in that scroll.

[32]Then he had everyone in Jerusalem and in Benjamin commit themselves to the covenant. The people of Jerusalem did it in keeping with the covenant of the God of Israel.

[33]Josiah removed all of the statues of gods from the whole territory that belonged to the people of Israel. The LORD hated those statues. Josiah had everyone in Israel serve the LORD their God. As long as he lived, they didn't fail to follow the LORD, the God of their people.

JOSIAH CELEBRATES THE PASSOVER FEAST

35 Josiah celebrated the Passover Feast in Jerusalem in honor of the LORD. The Passover lamb was killed on the 14th day of the first month. [2]Josiah appointed the priests to their duties. He cheered them up as they served the LORD at his temple.

[3]The Levites taught all of the people of Israel. The Levites had been set apart to the LORD. Josiah said to them, "Put the sacred ark of the covenant in the temple Solomon built. He was the son of David and king of Israel. The ark must not be carried around on your shoulders. Serve the LORD your God. Serve his people Israel. [4]Prepare yourselves by families in your groups. Do it based on the directions that were written by David, the king of Israel, and by his son Solomon.

[5]"Stand at the temple. Stand there with a group of Levites for each group of families among your people. [6]Kill the Passover lambs. Set yourselves apart to the LORD. Prepare the lambs for your people. Do what the LORD commanded through Moses."

[7]Josiah provided animals for the Passover offerings. He gave them for all of the people who were there. He gave a total of 30,000 sheep and goats and 3,000 head of cattle. He gave all of them from his own possessions.

[8]His officials also gave freely. They gave to the people and the priests and Levites. Hilkiah, Zechariah and Jehiel were in charge of God's temple. They gave the priests 2,600 Passover lambs and 300 head of cattle. [9]Conaniah and his brothers Shemaiah and Nethanel also gave offerings. So did Hashabiah, Jeiel and Jozabad. All of them were the leaders of the Levites. They gave 5,000 Passover lambs and 500 head of cattle for the Levites.

[10]The Passover service was arranged. The priests stood in their places. The Levites were in their groups. That's what the king had ordered.

[11]The Passover lambs were killed. The priests sprinkled the blood that had been handed to them. The Levites skinned the animals.

[12]They set the burnt offerings to one side. Those offerings were for the smaller family groups of the people to offer to the LORD. That's what was written in the Scroll of Moses. The Levites did the same thing with the cattle.

[13]They cooked the Passover ani-

mals over the fire, just as the law required. They boiled the holy offerings in pots, large kettles and pans. They served the offerings quickly to all of the people.

[14]After that, they got things ready for themselves and the priests. That's because the priests, who were from the family line of Aaron, were busy until dark. They were sacrificing the burnt offerings and the fat parts. The Levites got things ready for themselves and for the priests, who belonged to Aaron's family line.

[15]Those who played music were from the family line of Asaph. They were in the places that had been set up by David, Asaph, Heman and Jeduthun. Jeduthun had been the king's prophet. The guards at each gate didn't have to leave their places. That's because their brother Levites got things ready for them.

[16]So at that time the entire service in honor of the LORD was carried out. The Passover Feast was celebrated. The burnt offerings were sacrificed on the LORD's altar. That's what King Josiah had ordered.

[17]The people of Israel who were there celebrated the Passover at that time. They observed the Feast of Unleavened Bread for seven days. [18]The Passover hadn't been observed like that in Israel since the days of the prophet Samuel. None of the kings of Israel had ever celebrated a Passover like Josiah's. He celebrated it with the priests and Levites. All of the people of Judah and Israel were there along with the people of Jerusalem. [19]That Passover Feast was celebrated in the 18th year of Josiah's rule.

JOSIAH DIES

[20]Josiah had put the temple in order. After all of that, Neco went up to fight at Carchemish. He was king of Egypt. Carchemish was on the Euphrates River. Josiah marched out to meet Neco in battle. [21]But Neco sent messengers to him. They said, "King Josiah, there isn't any trouble between you and me. I'm not attacking you at this time. I'm at war with another country. God told me to

hurry. He's with me. So stop opposing him. If you don't, he'll destroy you."

[22]But Josiah wouldn't turn away from Neco. He wore different clothes so people wouldn't recognize him. He wanted to go to war against Neco. He wouldn't listen to what God had commanded Neco to say. Instead, he went out to fight him on the flatlands of Megiddo.

[23]Men who had bows shot arrows at King Josiah. After he was hit, he told his officers, "Take me away. I'm badly wounded." [24]So they took him out of his chariot. They put him in his other chariot. They brought him to Jerusalem. There he died. His body was buried in the tombs of his family. All of the people of Judah and Jerusalem sobbed over him.

[25]Jeremiah wrote songs of sadness about Josiah. To this very day all of the male and female singers remember Josiah by singing those songs. That became a practice in Israel. The songs are written down in the Book of the Songs of Sadness.

[26]Josiah did many things that showed he was faithful to the LORD. Those things and the other events of Josiah's rule were in keeping with what is written in the Law of the LORD. [27]All of the events from beginning to end are written down. They are written in the records of the kings of Israel and Judah.

36

[1]The people of the land went and got Jehoahaz. He was the son of Josiah. The people made Jehoahaz king in Jerusalem in place of his father.

JEHOAHAZ BECOMES KING OF JUDAH

[2]Jehoahaz was 23 years old when he became king. He ruled in Jerusalem for three months. [3]The king of Egypt removed him from his throne in Jerusalem. The king of Egypt made the people of Judah pay him a tax of almost four tons of silver and 75 pounds of gold.

[4]Neco, the king of Egypt, made Eliakim king over Judah and Jerusalem. Eliakim was a brother of Jehoahaz. Neco changed Eliakim's name to Jehoiakim. But he took Eliakim's brother Jehoahaz with him to Egypt.

JEHOIAKIM BECOMES KING OF JUDAH

⁵Jehoiakim was 25 years old when he became king. He ruled in Jerusalem for 11 years. He did what was evil in the sight of the LORD his God.

⁶Nebuchadnezzar attacked him. Nebuchadnezzar was king of Babylonia. He put Jehoiakim in bronze chains. And he took him to Babylon. ⁷Nebuchadnezzar also took articles from the LORD's temple. He took them to Babylon. He put them in his own temple there.

⁸The other events of Jehoiakim's rule are written in the records of the kings of Israel and Judah. He did things the LORD hated. Those things and everything that happened to him are also written in those records. His son Jehoiachin became the next king after him.

JEHOIACHIN BECOMES KING OF JUDAH

⁹Jehoiachin was 18 years old when he became king. He ruled in Jerusalem for three months and ten days. He did what was evil in the sight of the LORD.

¹⁰In the spring, King Nebuchadnezzar sent for him. He brought him to Babylon. He also brought articles of value from the LORD's temple. He made Zedekiah king over Judah and Jerusalem. Zedekiah was Jehoiachin's uncle.

ZEDEKIAH BECOMES KING OF JUDAH

¹¹Zedekiah was 21 years old when he became king. He ruled in Jerusalem for 11 years.

¹²He did what was evil in the sight of the LORD his God. He didn't pay any attention to the message the LORD spoke through the prophet Jeremiah.

¹³Zedekiah also refused to remain under the control of King Nebuchadnezzar. The king had made him take an oath in God's name. But his heart became very stubborn. He wouldn't turn to the LORD, the God of Israel.

¹⁴And that's not all. The people and the leaders of the priests became more and more unfaithful. They followed all of the practices of the nations. The LORD hated those practices. The people and leaders made the LORD's temple "unclean." The LORD had set the temple in Jerusalem apart in a special way for himself.

NEBUCHADNEZZAR DESTROYS JERUSALEM

¹⁵The LORD, the God of Israel, sent word to his people through his messengers. He sent it to them again and again. He took pity on his people. He also took pity on the temple where he lived.

¹⁶But God's people made fun of his messengers. They hated his words. They laughed at his prophets. Finally the LORD's burning anger was stirred up against his people. Nothing could save them.

¹⁷The LORD brought the king of Babylonia against them. The Babylonian army killed their young people with their swords at the temple. They didn't spare young men or women. They didn't spare the old people either. God handed all of them over to Nebuchadnezzar.

¹⁸Nebuchadnezzar carried off to Babylon all of the articles from God's temple. Some of the articles were large. Others were small. He carried off the treasures of the temple. He also carried off the treasures that belonged to the king and his officials.

¹⁹The Babylonians set God's temple on fire. They broke down the wall of Jerusalem. They burned all of the palaces. They destroyed everything of value there.

²⁰Nebuchadnezzar took the rest of the people to Babylon as prisoners. They had escaped from being killed with swords. They served him and his sons. That lasted until the kingdom of Persia became stronger than Babylonia.

²¹The land of Israel enjoyed its sabbath years. It rested. That deserted land wasn't farmed for a full 70 years. What the LORD had spoken through Jeremiah came true.

²²It was the first year of the rule of Cyrus. He was king of Persia. The LORD stirred him up to send a message all through his kingdom. It happened so

that what the LORD had spoken through Jeremiah would come true. The message was written down. It said,

²³"Cyrus, the king of Persia, says,
" 'The LORD is the God of heaven. He has given me all of the kingdoms on earth. He has appointed me to build a temple for him at Jerusalem in Judah. Any one of his people among you can go up to Jerusalem. And may the LORD your God be with you.' "

quest challenge

I Wonder . . .

What does it mean to be humble?

Real Life Challenge

You get a test back from your teacher and it says 100 percent at the top in big, bold numbers and letters. What is your reaction? Do you dance around, waving it in the air for everyone to see? Do you study less for the next test because you don't think you need to? Or do you thank God for helping you prepare? Think about Jesus for a moment. What did he give up so that he could become human? (Hint: check out Philippians 2.) How could you follow Jesus' example?

Quest Clue

Look in 2 Chronicles 32 (after verse 23) to see how Hezekiah changed his heart. Then check out the description of Jesus' humility in Philippians 2 (up to verse 11).

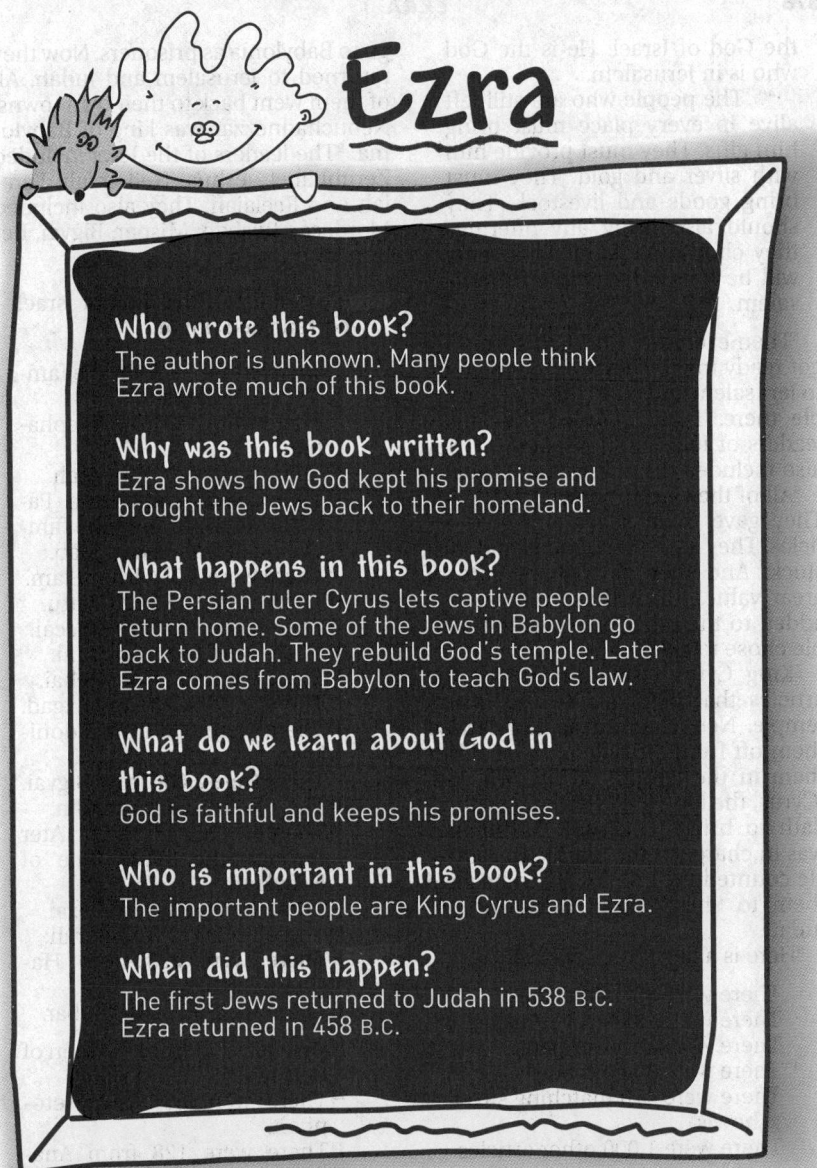

Ezra

Who wrote this book?
The author is unknown. Many people think Ezra wrote much of this book.

Why was this book written?
Ezra shows how God kept his promise and brought the Jews back to their homeland.

What happens in this book?
The Persian ruler Cyrus lets captive people return home. Some of the Jews in Babylon go back to Judah. They rebuild God's temple. Later Ezra comes from Babylon to teach God's law.

What do we learn about God in this book?
God is faithful and keeps his promises.

Who is important in this book?
The important people are King Cyrus and Ezra.

When did this happen?
The first Jews returned to Judah in 538 B.C. Ezra returned in 458 B.C.

CYRUS HELPS THE JEWS BUILD THE LORD'S TEMPLE

1 It was the first year of the rule of Cyrus. He was king of Persia. The LORD stirred him up to send a message all through his kingdom. It happened so that what the LORD had spoken through Jeremiah would come true. The message was written down. It said,

²"Cyrus, the king of Persia, says,

" 'The LORD is the God of heaven. He has given me all of the kingdoms on earth. He has appointed me to build a temple for him at Jerusalem in Judah.

³" 'Any one of his people among you can go up to Jerusalem. And may your God be with you. You can build the LORD's temple. He is

the God of Israel. He is the God who is in Jerusalem.

⁴" 'The people who are still left alive in every place must bring him gifts. They must provide him with silver and gold. They must bring goods and livestock. They should also bring any offerings they choose to. All of those gifts will be for God's temple in Jerusalem.' "

⁵Then everyone God had stirred up got ready to go. They wanted to go up to Jerusalem and build the LORD's temple there. They included the family leaders of Judah and Benjamin. They also included the priests and Levites.
⁶All of their neighbors helped them. They gave them silver and gold articles. They gave them goods and livestock. And they gave them gifts of great value. All of those things were added to the other offerings the people chose to give.
⁷King Cyrus also brought out the articles that belonged to the LORD's temple. Nebuchadnezzar had carried them off from Jerusalem. He had put them in the temple of his own god. ⁸Cyrus, the king of Persia, told Mithredath to bring them out. Mithredath was in charge of the temple treasures. He counted the articles. Then he gave them to Sheshbazzar, the prince of Judah.
⁹Here is a list of the articles.

There were 30 gold dishes.
There were 1,000 silver dishes.
There were 29 silver pans.
¹⁰There were 30 gold bowls.
There were 410 matching silver bowls.
There were 1,000 other articles.

¹¹The total number of gold and silver articles was 5,400. Sheshbazzar took all of them with him to Jerusalem. He brought them along when the Jews who had been forced to leave Judah came back from Babylon.

A LIST OF PEOPLE WHO RETURNED TO JUDAH

2 Nebuchadnezzar had taken many Jews away from the land of Judah. He had forced them to go to Babylonia as prisoners. Now they returned to Jerusalem and Judah. All of them went back to their own towns. Nebuchadnezzar was king of Babylonia. ²The leaders of the Jews included Zerubbabel, Jeshua, Nehemiah, Seraiah and Reelaiah. They also included Mordecai, Bilshan, Mispar, Bigvai, Rehum and Baanah.

Here is a list of the men of Israel who returned home.

³There were 2,172 from the family line of Parosh.
⁴There were 372 from Shephatiah.
⁵There were 775 from Arah.
⁶There were 2,812 from Pahath-Moab through the family line of Jeshua and Joab.
⁷There were 1,254 from Elam.
⁸There were 945 from Zattu.
⁹There were 760 from Zaccai.
¹⁰There were 642 from Bani.
¹¹There were 623 from Bebai.
¹²There were 1,222 from Azgad.
¹³There were 666 from Adonikam.
¹⁴There were 2,056 from Bigvai.
¹⁵There were 454 from Adin.
¹⁶There were 98 from Ater through the family line of Hezekiah.
¹⁷There were 323 from Bezai.
¹⁸There were 112 from Jorah.
¹⁹There were 223 from Hashum.
²⁰There were 95 from Gibbar.

²¹There were 123 from the men of Bethlehem.
²²There were 56 from Netophah.
²³There were 128 from Anathoth.
²⁴There were 42 from Azmaveth.
²⁵There were 743 from Kiriath Jearim, Kephirah and Beeroth.
²⁶There were 621 from Ramah and Geba.
²⁷There were 122 from Micmash.
²⁸There were 223 from Bethel and Ai.
²⁹There were 52 from Nebo.

³⁰There were 156 from Magbish.
³¹There were 1,254 from the other Elam.
³²There were 320 from Harim.
³³There were 725 from Lod, Hadid and Ono.
³⁴There were 345 from Jericho.
³⁵There were 3,630 from Senaah.

³⁶Here is a list of the priests.

There were 973 from the family line of Jedaiah through the line of Jeshua.
³⁷There were 1,052 from Immer.
³⁸There were 1,247 from Pashhur.
³⁹There were 1,017 from Harim.

⁴⁰Here is a list of the Levites.

There were 74 from the family lines of Jeshua and Kadmiel through the line of Hodaviah.

⁴¹Here is a list of the singers.

There were 128 from the family line of Asaph.

⁴²Here is a list of the men who guarded the temple gates.

There were 139 from the family lines of
Shallum, Ater, Talmon, Akkub, Hatita and Shobai.

⁴³Here is a list of the members of the family lines of the temple servants.

Ziha, Hasupha, Tabbaoth,
⁴⁴Keros, Siaha, Padon,
⁴⁵Lebanah, Hagabah, Akkub,
⁴⁶Hagab, Shalmai, Hanan,
⁴⁷Giddel, Gahar, Reaiah,
⁴⁸Rezin, Nekoda, Gazzam,
⁴⁹Uzza, Paseah, Besai,
⁵⁰Asnah, Meunim, Nephussim,
⁵¹Bakbuk, Hakupha, Harhur,
⁵²Bazluth, Mehida, Harsha,
⁵³Barkos, Sisera, Temah,
⁵⁴Neziah, Hatipha

⁵⁵Here is a list of the members of the family lines of the servants of Solomon.

Sotai, Hassophereth, Peruda,
⁵⁶Jaala, Darkon, Giddel,
⁵⁷Shephatiah, Hattil, Pokereth-Hazzebaim, Ami

⁵⁸The total number of the members of the family lines of the temple servants and the servants of Solomon was 392.

⁵⁹Many people came up to Judah from the towns of Tel Melah, Tel Harsha, Kerub, Addon and Immer. But they weren't able to prove that their families belonged to the people of Israel.

⁶⁰There were 652 of them from the family lines of
Delaiah, Tobiah and Nekoda.

⁶¹Here is a list of the members of the family lines of the priests.

They were Hobaiah, Hakkoz and Barzillai. Barzillai had married a daughter of Barzillai from Gilead. So he was also called Barzillai.
⁶²The priests looked for their family records. But they couldn't find them. So they weren't able to serve as priests. They weren't "clean."
⁶³The governor gave them an order. He told them not to eat any of the most sacred food. They had to wait until there was a priest who could use the Urim and Thummim to find out what the LORD wanted them to do.

⁶⁴The total number of the entire group that returned was 42,360. ⁶⁵That didn't include their 7,337 male and female slaves. There were also 200 male and female singers. ⁶⁶And there were 736 horses, 245 mules, ⁶⁷435 camels and 6,720 donkeys.

⁶⁸All of the people arrived at the LORD's temple in Jerusalem. Then some of the leaders of the families brought offerings they chose to give. They would be used for rebuilding the house of God. It would stand in the same place it had been before. ⁶⁹The people gave money for the work. It was based on how much they had.

They gave 1,100 pounds of gold. They also gave three tons of silver. And they gave 100 sets of clothes for the priests. All of that was added to the temple treasure.

⁷⁰The priests and Levites settled in their own towns. So did the singers, the men who guarded the gates, and the temple servants. The rest of the people of Israel also settled in their own towns.

THE PEOPLE REBUILD THE ALTAR

3 The people of Israel had settled down in their towns. In the seventh month all of them gathered together in Jerusalem.

²Then Jeshua began to build the altar for burnt offerings to honor the God of Israel. Jeshua was the son of Jehozadak. The other priests helped Jeshua. So did Zerubbabel and his men. They built the altar in keeping with what is written in the Law of Moses. Moses was a man of God. Zerubbabel was the son of Shealtiel.

³The people who built the altar were afraid of the nations that were around them. But they built it anyway. They set it up where it had stood before.

They sacrificed burnt offerings on it to the LORD. They offered the morning and evening sacrifices on it.

⁴Then they celebrated the Feast of Booths. They did it in keeping with what is written in the Law. They sacrificed the number of burnt offerings that were required for each day.

⁵After they celebrated the Feast of Booths, they sacrificed the regular burnt offerings. They offered the New Moon sacrifices. They also offered the sacrifices for all of the appointed sacred feasts of the LORD. And they sacrificed the offerings the people chose to give him. ⁶On the first day of the seventh month they began to offer burnt offerings to the LORD. They did it even though the foundation of the LORD's temple hadn't been finished yet.

THE PEOPLE BEGIN TO REBUILD THE TEMPLE

⁷The people gave money to those who worked with stone and those who worked with wood. They gave food and drink and olive oil to the people of Sidon and Tyre. Then those people brought cedar logs down from Lebanon to the Mediterranean Sea. They floated them down to Joppa. Cyrus,

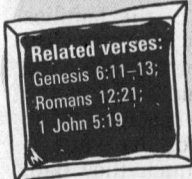

Why is the world so violent and evil?

Disobeying God is the root cause of all evil. Because people sin, the world is filled with evil. It has been this way since Adam and Eve's first sin in the Garden of Eden. They disobeyed God and ate the forbidden fruit.

In some ways it may seem that violence is worse today. Weapons are more destructive. There are more guns and knives and more ways of hurting people than ever before. But violence and evil come out of hearts that are separated from God, and the world has always had that. As long as people rebel against God, we will have violence and evil in the world.

checkout
Ezra 4:4,5

Related verses:
Genesis 6:11–13;
Romans 12:21;
1 John 5:19

the king of Persia, authorized them to do it.

[8]It was the second month of the second year after they had arrived at the house of God in Jerusalem. Zerubbabel, the son of Shealtiel, began the work. Jeshua, the son of Jehozadak, helped him. So did everyone else. That included the priests and Levites. It also included the rest of those who had returned to Jerusalem. They had been prisoners in Babylonia. Levites who were 20 years old or more were appointed to be in charge of building the LORD's house.

[9]Those who joined together to direct the work included Jeshua and his sons and brothers. They also included Kadmiel and his sons. And they included the sons of Henadad and all of their sons and brothers. All of those men were Levites. Kadmiel and his sons were members of the family line of Hodaviah.

[10]The builders laid the foundation of the LORD's temple. Then the priests came. They were wearing their special clothes. They brought their trumpets with them. The Levites who belonged to the family line of Asaph also came. They brought their cymbals with them. The priests and Levites took their places to praise the LORD. They did everything just as King David had required them to. [11]They sang to the LORD. They praised him. They gave thanks to him. They said,

"The LORD is good.
His faithful love to Israel
continues forever."

All of the people gave a loud shout. They praised the LORD. They were glad because the foundation of the LORD's temple had been laid.

[12]But many of the older priests and Levites and family leaders sobbed out loud. They had seen the first temple. So when they saw the foundation of the second temple being laid, they sobbed. Others shouted with joy. [13]No one could tell the difference between the shouts of joy and the sounds of sobbing. That's because the people made so much noise. The sound was heard far away.

ENEMIES OPPOSE THE REBUILDING OF THE TEMPLE

4 The enemies of Judah and Benjamin heard about what the people who had returned from Babylonia were doing. They heard that they were building a temple to honor the LORD. He is the God of Israel. [2]The enemies came to Zerubbabel. The family leaders of Israel were with him. The enemies said, "We want to help you build. We're just like you. We worship your God. We offer sacrifices to him. We've been doing that ever since the time of Esarhaddon. He was king of Assyria. He brought our people here."

[3]Zerubbabel and Jeshua answered them. So did the rest of the family leaders of Israel. They said, "You can't help us build a temple to honor our God. You aren't part of us. We'll build it ourselves. We'll do it to honor the LORD. He is the God of Israel. Cyrus, the king of Persia, commanded us to build it."

[4]Then the nations that were around Judah tried to make its people lose hope. They wanted to make them afraid to go on building. [5]So they hired advisers to work against them. They wanted their plans to fail. They did it during the whole time Cyrus was king of Persia. They kept doing it until Darius became king.

LATER ENEMIES ALSO OPPOSE THE JEWS

[6]The enemies of the Jews brought charges against the people of Judah and Jerusalem. It happened when Xerxes began to rule over Persia.

[7]Then Artaxerxes became king of Persia. During his rule, Bishlam, Mithredath, Tabeel and their friends wrote a letter to him. It was written in the Aramaic language. And it used the Aramaic alphabet.

[8]Rehum and Shimshai also wrote a letter to King Artaxerxes. Rehum was the commanding officer. Shimshai was the secretary. Their letter was against the people of Jerusalem. It said,

[9]We, Rehum and Shimshai, are writing this letter. Rehum is the

commanding officer. Shimshai is the secretary. Our friends join us in writing. They include the judges and officials who are in charge of the people from Tripolis, Persia, Erech and Babylon. They are also over the Elamites from Susa. [10]And they are over those who were forced to leave their countries. The great King Ashurbanipal, who is worthy of honor, forced them to leave. He settled them in the city of Samaria. He also settled them in other places west of the Euphrates River.

[11]Here is a copy of the letter that was sent to Artaxerxes.

We are sending this letter to you, King Artaxerxes.

It is from your servants who live west of the Euphrates River.

[12]We want you to know that the Jews who left you and came up to us have gone to Jerusalem. They are rebuilding that evil city. It has caused trouble for a long time. The Jews are making its walls like new again. They are repairing the foundations.

[13]Here is something else we want you to know. Suppose this city is rebuilt. And suppose its walls are made like new again. Then no more taxes, gifts or fees will be collected. And there will be less money for you.

[14]We owe a lot to you. We don't want to see dishonor brought on you. So we're sending this letter to tell you what is going on. [15]Then you can have a search made in the official records. Have someone check the records of the kings who ruled before you.

If you do, you will find out that Jerusalem is an evil city. It causes trouble for kings and countries. For a long time the city has refused to let anyone rule over it. That's why it was destroyed. [16]We want you to know that this city shouldn't be rebuilt. Its walls shouldn't be made like new again. If that happens, you won't have

anything left west of the Euphrates River.

[17]The king replied,

I am writing this letter to Rehum, the commanding officer. I am also writing it to Shimshai, the secretary. And I am writing it to your friends who are living in Samaria and in other places west of the Euphrates River.

I give you my greetings.

[18]The letter you sent us has been read to me. It has been explained to me in my language. [19]I gave an order. I had a search made. We found out that Jerusalem has a long history of turning against the kings of the countries that have ruled over it. It has refused to remain under their control. It is always stirring up trouble. [20]Jerusalem has had powerful kings. Some of them ruled over everything west of the Euphrates. Taxes, gifts and fees were paid to them. [21]So give an order to those men. Make them stop their work. Then the city won't be rebuilt until I give the order. [22]Pay careful attention to this matter. Why should we let this danger grow? That would not be in our best interests.

[23]The copy of the letter of King Artaxerxes was read to Rehum and the secretary Shimshai. It was also read to their friends. Right away they went to the Jews in Jerusalem. They forced them to stop their work.

[24]And so the work on the house of God in Jerusalem came to an end. Nothing more was done on it until the second year that Darius was king of Persia.

TATTENAI SENDS A LETTER TO KING DARIUS

5 The prophets Haggai and Zechariah prophesied to the Jews in Judah and Jerusalem. They spoke to them in the name of the God of Israel. He had spoken to those prophets. Zechariah belonged to the family line of Iddo.

²Zerubbabel, the son of Shealtiel, began to work. So did Jeshua, the son of Jehozadak. They began to rebuild the house of God in Jerusalem. The prophets of God were right there with them. They were helping them.

³At that time Tattenai was governor of the land west of the Euphrates River. He and Shethar-Bozenai and their friends went to the Jews. They asked them, "Who authorized you to rebuild this temple? Who told you that you could make this building like new again?" ⁴They also asked, "What are the names of the men who are putting up this building?"

⁵But the God of the Jews was watching over their elders. So they didn't have to stop their work. First a report would have to be sent to Darius. Then they would have to receive his answer in writing.

⁶Here is a copy of the letter that was sent to King Darius. It was from Tattenai, the governor of the land west of the Euphrates. Shethar-Bozenai joined him in writing it. So did their friends. They were officials of that land. ⁷The report they sent to the king said,

We are sending this letter to you, King Darius.

We give you our most friendly greetings.

⁸We want you to know that we went to the land of Judah. We went to the temple of the great God. The people are building it with large stones. They are putting wooden beams in the walls. The people are working hard. The work is moving ahead very quickly under the direction of the people.

⁹We asked the elders some questions. We said to them, "Who authorized you to rebuild this temple? Who told you that you could make this building like new again?" ¹⁰We also asked them their names. We wanted to write down the names of their leaders for your information.

¹¹Here is the answer they gave us. They said,

"We serve the God of heaven and earth. We are rebuilding the temple that was built many years ago. The great King Solomon built it and finished it. ¹²But our people made the God of heaven angry. So he handed them over to Nebuchadnezzar from Chaldea. He was king of Babylonia. He destroyed this temple. He forced the Jews to leave their own country. He took them away to Babylonia.

¹³"But King Cyrus gave an order to rebuild this house of God. He gave it in the first year he was king of Babylonia. ¹⁴He even removed some gold and silver articles from the temple of Babylon. Nebuchadnezzar had brought them there from the house of God in Jerusalem. He had taken them to the temple in Babylon.

"Then King Cyrus brought them out. He gave them to a man named Sheshbazzar. Cyrus had appointed him as governor. ¹⁵He told him, 'Take these articles with you. Go and put them in the temple in Jerusalem. Rebuild the house of God in the same place where it stood before.'

¹⁶"So Sheshbazzar made the trip to Jerusalem. He laid the foundations of the house of God there. From that day until now the people have been working on it. But they haven't finished it yet."

¹⁷If it pleases you, King Darius, let a search be made in the official records of the kings of Babylonia. Find out whether King Cyrus really did give an order to rebuild this house of God in Jerusalem. Then tell us what you decide to do.

KING DARIUS SENDS A REPLY TO TATTENAI

6 King Darius gave an order. He had a search made in the official records that were stored among the treasures at Babylon. ²A scroll was found in a safe storeroom at Ecbatana in the land of Media. Here is what was written on it.

This is my official reply to your letter.

³In the first year that Cyrus was king, he gave an order. It concerned God's temple in Jerusalem. It said,

Rebuild the temple. Then the Jews can offer sacrifices there. Lay its foundations. The temple must be 90 feet high and 90 feet wide. ⁴Its walls must have three layers of large stones. They must also have a layer of beautiful wood. Use money from the royal treasures to pay for everything.

⁵The gold and silver articles from the house of God must be returned. Nebuchadnezzar had taken them from the first temple in Jerusalem. And he had brought them to Babylon. Now they must be returned to their places in the temple at Jerusalem. They must be put in the house of God there.

⁶Tattenai, you are governor of the land west of the Euphrates River. I want you to stay away from the temple in Jerusalem. Shethar-Bozenai and the other officials of that area must also stay away from it. ⁷Don't try to stop the work on God's temple. Let the governor of the Jews and their elders rebuild the house of their God. Let them build it in the same place where it stood before.

⁸Here is what I want you to do for the elders of the Jews. Here is how you must help the men who build the house of their God.

Pay all of their expenses from the royal treasures. Use the money you collect from the people who live west of the Euphrates. Don't let the work on the temple stop. ⁹Don't fail to give the priests in Jerusalem what they ask for each day. Give them what they need. Give them young bulls, rams and male lambs. The priests can use them to sacrifice burnt offerings to the God of heaven. Also give them wheat, salt, wine and olive oil. ¹⁰Give them those things so they can offer sacrifices that please the God of heaven. And I want them to pray that things will go well for me and my sons.

¹¹Don't change this order. If a man tries to change it, he must be put to death. A pole must be pulled from his house. The pole must be stuck through his body. Then it must be set up where people can see it. Because the man tried to change my royal order, his house must be broken to pieces. ¹²God has chosen to put his Name in the temple at Jerusalem. May he wipe out any king or nation that lifts a hand to change this order. May he also wipe out anyone who tries to destroy the temple in Jerusalem.

That's what I have ordered. I am King Darius. Make sure you carry out my order.

THE TEMPLE IS COMPLETED AND SET APART TO GOD

¹³The governor Tattenai carried out the order King Darius had sent. So did Shethar-Bozenai and their friends.

¹⁴The elders of the Jews continued to build the temple. They enjoyed great success because of the preaching of the prophets Haggai and Zechariah. Zechariah belonged to the family line of Iddo.

The people finished building the temple. That's what the God of Israel had commanded them to do. Cyrus and Darius had given orders allowing them to do it. Later, Artaxerxes supplied many things that were needed in the temple. Those three men were kings of Persia.

¹⁵So the temple was completed on the third day of the month of Adar. It was in the sixth year that Darius was king.

¹⁶When the house of God was set apart, the people of Israel celebrated with joy. The priests and Levites joined them. So did the rest of those who had returned from Babylonia. ¹⁷When the house of God was set apart to him, the people sacrificed 100 bulls. They also sacrificed 200 rams and 400 male lambs. As a sin offering for the whole nation of Israel, the people sacrificed 12 male goats. One goat was sacrificed for each tribe in Israel.

¹⁸The priests were appointed to their companies. And the Levites were appointed to their groups. All of them served God at Jerusalem. They served him in keeping with what is written in the Scroll of Moses.

THE PEOPLE CELEBRATE THE PASSOVER FEAST

¹⁹Those who had returned from Babylonia celebrated the Passover Feast. It was on the 14th day of the first month. ²⁰The priests and Levites had made themselves pure and clean. The Levites killed the Passover lamb for everyone who had returned from Babylonia. They also did it for themselves and their relatives, the priests.

²¹So the people of Israel who had returned ate the Passover lamb. They ate it together with all those who had separated themselves from the practices of their neighbors who weren't Jews. Those practices were "unclean." The people worshiped the LORD. He is the God of Israel.

²²For seven days they celebrated the Feast of Unleavened Bread with joy. That's because the LORD had filled them with joy. They were glad because he had changed the mind of the king of Persia. So the king had helped them with the work on the house of the God of Israel.

EZRA COMES TO JERUSALEM

7 After all of those things had happened, Ezra came up to Jerusalem from Babylonia. It was during the rule of Artaxerxes. He was king of Persia. Ezra was the son of Seraiah. Seraiah was the son of Azariah. Azariah was the son of Hilkiah. ²Hilkiah was the son of Shallum. Shallum was the son of Zadok. Zadok was the son of Ahitub. ³Ahitub was the son of Amariah. Amariah was the son of Azariah. Azariah was the son of Meraioth. ⁴Meraioth was the son of Zerahiah. Zerahiah was the son of Uzzi. Uzzi was the son of Bukki. ⁵Bukki was the son of Abishua. Abishua was the son of Phinehas. Phinehas was the son of Eleazar. And Eleazar was the son of the chief priest Aaron.

⁶So Ezra came up from Babylonia. He was a teacher. He knew the Law of Moses very well. The LORD had given Israel that law. He is the God of Israel. The king had given Ezra everything he asked for. That's because the powerful hand of the LORD his God helped him.

⁷Some of the people of Israel came up to Jerusalem too. They included priests, Levites and singers. They also included the temple servants and those who guarded the temple gates. It was in the seventh year that Artaxerxes was king.

⁸Ezra arrived in Jerusalem in the fifth month of the seventh year of the king's rule. ⁹Ezra had begun his journey from Babylonia on the first day of the first month. He arrived in Jerusalem on the first day of the fifth month. That's because the gracious hand of his God helped him. ¹⁰Ezra had committed himself to study and obey the Law of the LORD. He also wanted to teach the LORD's rules and laws in Israel.

KING ARTAXERXES GIVES EZRA A LETTER

¹¹Ezra was a priest and teacher. He was an educated man. He knew the LORD's commands and rules for Israel very well. Here is a copy of a letter King Artaxerxes had given to Ezra. It said,

¹²I, Artaxerxes, am writing this letter. I am the greatest king of all.

I have given it to the priest Ezra. He is a teacher of the Law of the God of heaven.

I give you my greetings.

¹³Ezra, there are people from Israel in my kingdom. I am giving an order that any of them who want to go to Jerusalem with you can go. The order also allows priests and Levites to go with you. ¹⁴I and my seven advisers are sending you to see how things are going in Judah and Jerusalem. Find out whether the people there are obeying the Law of your God. You have a copy of that law with you. ¹⁵I and my advisers have freely given some silver and gold to the God of Israel. He lives in Jerusalem. Take the silver and gold with

you. ¹⁶Also take any other silver and gold you can get from the land of Babylonia. And take the offerings the people and priests choose to give for the temple of their God in Jerusalem. ¹⁷Make sure you use the money to buy bulls, rams and male lambs. Also buy their grain offerings and drink offerings. Then sacrifice them on the altar of the temple of your God in Jerusalem.

¹⁸You and the other Jews can do what you think is best with the rest of the silver and gold. Do what your God wants you to do. ¹⁹Give to the God of Jerusalem all of the articles you are accountable for. Use them for worshiping your God in his temple. ²⁰You might need to supply some other things for the temple of your God. If you do, take them from among the royal treasures.

²¹I, King Artaxerxes, also give this order. It applies to all those who are in charge of the treasures west of the Euphrates River. Make sure you provide anything the priest Ezra might ask you to give. He is a teacher of the Law of the God of heaven. ²²Give Ezra up to three and three-fourths tons of silver. Give him up to 600 bushels of wheat. Give him up to 600 gallons of wine. Also give him up to 600 gallons of olive oil. And give him as much salt as he needs.

²³Work hard for the temple of the God of heaven. Do everything he has required. I don't want him to be angry with my kingdom and the kingdom of my sons. ²⁴I want you to know that you don't have any authority to collect taxes, gifts or fees from these people. You can't collect them from the priests, Levites, singers or those who guard the temple gates. And you can't collect them from the temple servants or other workers at the house of God in Jerusalem.

²⁵Ezra, appoint judges and other court officials. When you do it, use the wisdom your God gives you. Those you appoint should do what is right and fair when they judge people. They should do it for everyone who lives west of the Euphrates. They should do it for everyone who knows the laws of your God. And I want you to teach the people who don't know those laws.

²⁶Anyone who doesn't obey the law of your God must be punished. The same thing applies to anyone who doesn't obey my law. The people must be punished in keeping with the laws they have broken. Some of them must be put to death. Others must be forced to leave the places where they live. Others must have their property taken away from them. Still others must be put in prison.

EZRA PRAISES THE LORD

²⁷People of Israel, give praise to the LORD. He is the God of our people who lived long ago. He has put it in the king's heart to bring honor to the LORD's temple in Jerusalem. The king has honored the LORD in his letter. ²⁸The LORD has shown his good favor to me. He has caused the king and his advisers to show me their favor. In fact, all of the king's powerful officials have shown favor to me. The strong hand of the LORD my God helped me. That gave me new strength. So I gathered together leaders from Israel to go up to Jerusalem with me.

THE FAMILY LEADERS WHO RETURNED TO JERUSALEM WITH EZRA

8 Many family leaders came up to Jerusalem with me from Babylonia. So did others who were listed with them. It was during the time when Artaxerxes was king. Here is a list of those who came.

²Gershom came from the family line of Phinehas.
Daniel came from the family line of Ithamar.
Hattush came from the family line of David. ³Hattush also belonged to the family of Shecaniah.

Zechariah came from the family line of Parosh. The total number of men who were listed with him was 150.
⁴Eliehoenai came from the family line of Pahath-Moab. Eliehoenai was the son of Zerahiah. The total number of men with him was 200.
⁵Shecaniah came from the family line of Zattu. Shecaniah was the son of Jahaziel. The total number of men with him was 300.
⁶Ebed came from the family line of Adin. Ebed was the son of Jonathan. The total number of men with him was 50.
⁷Jeshaiah came from the family line of Elam. Jeshaiah was the son of Athaliah. The total number of men with him was 70.
⁸Zebadiah came from the family line of Shephatiah. Zebadiah was the son of Michael. The total number of men with him was 80.
⁹Obadiah came from the family line of Joab. Obadiah was the son of Jehiel. The total number of men with him was 218.
¹⁰Shelomith came from the family line of Bani. Shelomith was the son of Josiphiah. The total number of men with him was 160.
¹¹Zechariah came from the family line of Bebai. Zechariah was the son of Bebai. The total number of men with him was 28.
¹²Johanan came from the family line of Azgad. Johanan was the son of Hakkatan. The total number of men with him was 110.
¹³Eliphelet, Jeuel and Shemaiah came from the family line of Adonikam. Some members of their family had gone up to Jerusalem before them. The total number of men with them was 60.
¹⁴Uthai and Zaccur came from the family line of Bigvai. The total number of men with them was 70.

EZRA LEADS MANY JEWS BACK TO JERUSALEM

¹⁵I gathered the people together at the waterway that flows toward Ahava. We camped there for three days. I looked for Levites among the people and priests. But I didn't find any. ¹⁶So I sent for Eliezer, Ariel, Shemaiah, Elnathan and Jarib. I also sent for Elnathan, Nathan, Zechariah and Meshullam. All of them were leaders. And I sent for Joiarib and Elnathan. They were very well educated.
¹⁷I sent all of those men to Iddo. He was the leader in Casiphia. He and his relatives were temple servants there. I told my men what to say to them. I wanted Iddo and his relatives to bring some attendants to us for the house of our God.
¹⁸The gracious hand of our God helped us. So they brought us Sherebiah. He was a man of ability. He came from the family line of Mahli. Mahli was the son of Levi. Levi was a son of Israel. They also brought us Sherebiah's sons and brothers. The total number of men was 18. ¹⁹And they brought Hashabiah and his brothers and nephews. They brought them together with Jeshaiah. He came from the family line of Merari. The total number of men was 20. ²⁰They also brought 220 of the temple servants. That was a special group David and his officials had established. They were supposed to help the Levites. All of them were listed by name.
²¹I announced a fast by the waterway that flows toward Ahava. I told the people not to eat any food. In that way, we made ourselves low in the sight of God. We prayed that he would give us and our children a safe journey. We asked him to keep safe everything we owned.
²²I was ashamed to ask King Artaxerxes for soldiers and horsemen. They could have kept us safe from enemies on the road. But we had told the king that our God would keep us safe. We had said, "The gracious hand of our God helps everyone who looks to him. But he becomes very angry with anyone who deserts him."
²³So we didn't eat anything. We

prayed to our God about all of those matters. And he answered our prayers. ²⁴Then I set 12 of the leading priests apart. I also set apart Sherebiah, Hashabiah and ten of their relatives.

²⁵I weighed out to them the offering of silver and gold and other articles. They had been given for the house of our God. The king, his advisers and officials, and all of the people of Israel who were there had given them. ²⁶I weighed out 25 tons of silver to those men. I weighed out almost four tons of silver articles. I weighed out almost four tons of gold. ²⁷I weighed out 20 gold bowls. They weighed 19 pounds. I also weighed out two fine articles. The bronze they were made out of was highly polished. They were as priceless as gold.

²⁸I said to those men, "You are set apart to the LORD. So are these articles. The silver and gold were offered to the LORD by those who chose to give them. He is the God of your people. ²⁹Guard all of those things carefully until you weigh them out. Weigh them in the special rooms of the LORD's temple in Jerusalem. Do it in front of the leading priests and the Levites. Make sure the family leaders of Israel are watching."

³⁰Then the priests and Levites received the silver and gold and sacred articles. All of them had been weighed out. They were going to take them to the house of our God in Jerusalem.

³¹On the 12th day of the first month we started out. We left the waterway that flows toward Ahava. And we headed for Jerusalem. The powerful hand of our God helped us. He kept us safe from enemies and robbers along the way. ³²So we arrived in Jerusalem. There we rested for three days.

³³On the fourth day we weighed out the silver and gold. We also weighed out the sacred articles. We weighed everything in the house of our God. We handed all of it over to the priest Meremoth. He was the son of Uriah. Eleazar, Jozabad and Noadiah were with him. Eleazar was the son of Phinehas. Jozabad was the son of Jeshua. Noadiah was the son of Binnui. Jozabad and Noadiah were Levites. ³⁴Everything was listed by number and weight. And the total weight was recorded at that time.

³⁵Then the people sacrificed burnt offerings to the God of Israel. They had returned from Babylonia. They offered 12 bulls for the whole nation of Israel. They offered 96 rams and 77 male lambs. All of that was a burnt offering to the LORD. They sacrificed 12 male goats as a sin offering.

³⁶They also handed over the king's orders. They gave them to the royal officials and governors who ruled over the land west of the Euphrates River. Then those men helped the people. They also did many things for the house of God.

EZRA PRAYS FOR THE PEOPLE

9 After all of those things had been done, the leaders came to me. They said, "The people of Israel have committed sins. Even the priests and Levites have sinned. They haven't kept themselves separate from the nations that are around them. The LORD hates the practices of those nations. He hates what the Canaanites, Hittites, Perizzites and Jebusites do. He also hates what the Ammonites, Moabites, Egyptians and Amorites do.

²"The men of Israel have gotten married to the daughters of some of those people. They've also taken some of those women for their sons to marry. So they've mixed our holy nation with the nations around us. By getting married to women who don't worship the LORD, we leaders and officials have led the way in breaking our covenant with him. We haven't been faithful to him."

³When I heard that, I tore my inner robe and my coat. I pulled hair from my head and beard. I was so shocked I sat down. ⁴Then everyone who trembled with fear because of what the God of Israel had said gathered around me. They came because the people who had returned from Babylonia had not been faithful. So I sat there in shock until the time of the evening sacrifice.

⁵Then I got up. I had been very sad for quite a while. My inner robe and my coat were torn. I fell down on my knees. I spread my hands out to the LORD my God. ⁶I prayed,

"You are my God. I'm filled with shame and dishonor. I can hardly look to you and pray. That's because our sins are piled up above our heads. Our guilt reaches all the way to the heavens. ⁷We are filled with it. It has been like that ever since the days of our people who lived long ago.

"Kings of other countries have killed many of us and our kings and priests with their swords. They've forced others to leave their own land. They've taken them away as prisoners. They've robbed others. They've made still others feel ashamed and dishonored.

"All of those things have happened to us because we've committed so many sins. And that's how things still are to this very day.

⁸"But you are the LORD our God. Now you have shown us your favor for a short time. You have allowed a few of us to remain here. Your temple has given us new hope. So you have made things easier for us. You have given us a little rest from our slavery. ⁹We are still slaves. But you are our God. You haven't deserted us. You haven't left us in our slavery. You have been kind to us. The kings of Persia have seen it. You have given us new life to repair your temple and rebuild it. You have given us a place of safety in Judah and Jerusalem.

¹⁰"You are our God. What can we say after the way you have blessed us? We said no to what you commanded us to do. ¹¹"You gave us your commands through your servants the prophets. You said, 'You are entering the land to take it as your own. The sinful practices of its people have polluted it. They have filled it with their unclean acts from one end to the other. The LORD hates all of their practices. ¹²So don't let your daughters get married to their sons. And don't let their daughters marry your sons. Don't make a peace treaty with them at any

time. Then you will be strong. You will eat the good things the land produces. And you will leave all of it to your children as their share. They and their children after them will enjoy it forever.'

¹³"Our evil acts and our terrible sins have brought about the things that have happened to us. You are our God. Because we sinned so much, you should have punished us even more than you have. But you have left many of your people alive. ¹⁴Suppose we don't obey your commands again. And suppose we continue to get married to people who commit sins that you hate. If we do, you will be so angry with us that you will destroy us. You won't leave us even a few people. You won't leave anyone alive.

¹⁵"LORD, you are the God of Israel. You are holy. You always do what is right. Today you have left many of your people alive. Here we are with all of our guilt. You see the guilt of our sin. Because we have sinned, not one of us can stand in front of you."

THE PEOPLE ADMIT THEY HAVE SINNED

10 Ezra was praying and admitting to God that his people had sinned. He was sobbing and throwing himself down in front of the house of God. Then a large crowd gathered around him. Men, women and children were there. They too sobbed bitterly.

²Shecaniah spoke to Ezra. Shecaniah was the son of Jehiel. He belonged to the family line of Elam. Shecaniah said, "We haven't been faithful to our God. We've gotten married to women from the nations that are around us. In spite of that, there is still hope for Israel. ³So let's make a covenant in the sight of our God. Let's promise to send away all of those women and their children. That's what you have advised us to do. Those who respect our God's commands have given us the same advice. We want to do what the Law says. ⁴"Get up, Ezra. This matter is in your hands. Do what you need to. We will be

behind you all the way. Be brave and do it."

⁵So Ezra got up. He made the leading priests and Levites and all of the people of Israel take an oath. He made them promise they would do what Shecaniah had suggested. And they took the oath.

⁶Then Ezra left the house of God. He went to Jehohanan's room. Jehohanan was the son of Eliashib. While Ezra was there, he didn't eat any food. He didn't drink any water. That's because he was filled with sadness. He sobbed because the people weren't faithful to the LORD's commands. Those people were the ones who had returned from Babylonia.

⁷Then an announcement was sent all through Judah and Jerusalem. All those who had returned were told to gather together in Jerusalem. ⁸They were supposed to come there before three days had passed. If they didn't, they would lose all of their property. They would also be removed from the community of those who had returned. That's what the officials and elders had decided.

⁹Before the three days were over, all of the men of Judah and Benjamin had gathered together in Jerusalem. It was the 20th day of the ninth month. They were sitting in the open area in front of the house of God. They were very upset by what they knew would happen. And they were upset because it was raining.

¹⁰Then the priest Ezra stood up. He said, "You haven't been faithful to the LORD. You have gotten married to women from other lands. So you have added to Israel's guilt. ¹¹Admit to the LORD that you have sinned. Tell the God of your people what you have done. Then do what he wants you to do. Separate yourselves from the nations that are around you. Send away your wives from other lands."

¹²The whole community answered with a loud voice. They said, "You are right! We must do as you say. ¹³But there are a lot of people here. And it's the rainy season. So we can't stand outside. Besides, this matter can't be taken care of in just a day or two. That's

because we have sinned terribly by what we've done.

¹⁴"Our officials can act for the whole community. Have everyone in our towns who has married a woman from another land come at a certain time. Tell them to come together with the elders and judges of each town. Then our God will turn his burning anger away from us concerning this whole matter."

¹⁵Only a few men opposed that. They included Jonathan and Jahzeiah. Meshullam and the Levite Shabbethai joined them. Jonathan was the son of Asahel. Jahzeiah was the son of Tikvah.

¹⁶So those who had returned did what had been suggested. The priest Ezra chose some family leaders. There was one from each family group. All of them were chosen by name. They sat down to check out each case. They started on the first day of the tenth month. ¹⁷By the first day of the first month they were finished. They had handled all of the cases of the men who had gotten married to women from other lands.

A LIST OF THOSE WHO HAD MARRIED WOMEN FROM OTHER LANDS

¹⁸Among the family lines of the priests, here are the men who had married women from other lands.

Maaseiah, Eliezer, Jarib and Gedaliah
came from the family line of Jeshua and his brothers. Jeshua was the son of Jehozadak. ¹⁹All of them made a firm promise to send their wives away. Each of those men brought a ram from his flock as a guilt offering.
²⁰Hanani and Zebadiah
came from the family line of Immer.
²¹Maaseiah and Elijah
came from the family line of Harim. So did Shemaiah, Jehiel and Uzziah.
²²Elioenai, Maaseiah and Ishmael
came from the family line of

Pashhur. So did Nethanel, Jozabad and Elasah.

23 Among the Levites, here are the men who had married women from other lands.

There were Jozabad, Shimei and Kelaiah. There were also Pethahiah, Judah and Eliezer. Kelaiah's other name was Kelita.

24 Eliashib came from the singers. Shallum, Telem and Uri came from the men who guarded the temple gates.

25 Among the other Israelites, here are the men who had married women from other lands.

Ramiah, Izziah, Malkijah and Mijamin came from the family line of Parosh. So did Eleazar, Malkijah and Benaiah.

26 Mattaniah, Zechariah and Jehiel came from the family line of Elam. So did Abdi, Jeremoth and Elijah.

27 Elioenai, Eliashib and Mattaniah came from the family line of Zattu. So did Jeremoth, Zabad and Aziza.

28 Jehohanan, Hananiah, Zabbai and Athlai came from the family line of Bebai.

29 Meshullam, Malluch and Adaiah came from the family line of Bani. So did Jashub, Sheal and Jeremoth.

30 Adna, Kelal, Benaiah and Maaseiah came from the family line of Pahath-Moab. So did Mattaniah, Bezalel, Binnui and Manasseh.

31 Eliezer, Ishijah, Malkijah, Shemaiah and Shimeon came from the family line of Harim. 32 So did Benjamin, Malluch and Shemariah.

33 Mattenai, Mattattah, Zabad and Eliphelet came from the family line of Hashum. So did Jeremai, Manasseh and Shimei.

34 Maadai, Amram and Uel came from the family line of Bani. 35 So did Benaiah, Bedeiah, Keluhi, 36 Vaniah, Meremoth, Eliashib, 37 Mattaniah, Mattenai and Jaasu.

38 Shimei came from the family line of Binnui. 39 So did Shelemiah, Nathan, Adaiah, 40 Macnadebai, Shashai, Sharai, 41 Azarel, Shelemiah, Shemariah, 42 Shallum, Amariah and Joseph.

43 Jeiel, Mattithiah, Zabad and Zebina came from the family line of Nebo. So did Jaddai, Joel and Benaiah.

44 All of those men had married women from other lands. Some of them had even had children by those wives.

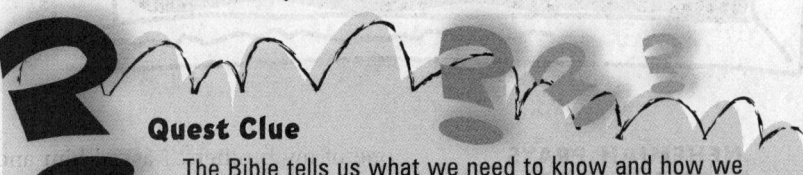

Quest Clue

The Bible tells us what we need to know and how we should live, but often people ignore it. Take a look at some verses that will help you understand why it's always a good idea to read the Bible.

Find Ezra 7 to learn about the secret of Ezra's success. Then find verses in Matthew 22 and Acts 17 that will give you more encouragement to find out what the Bible has to say.

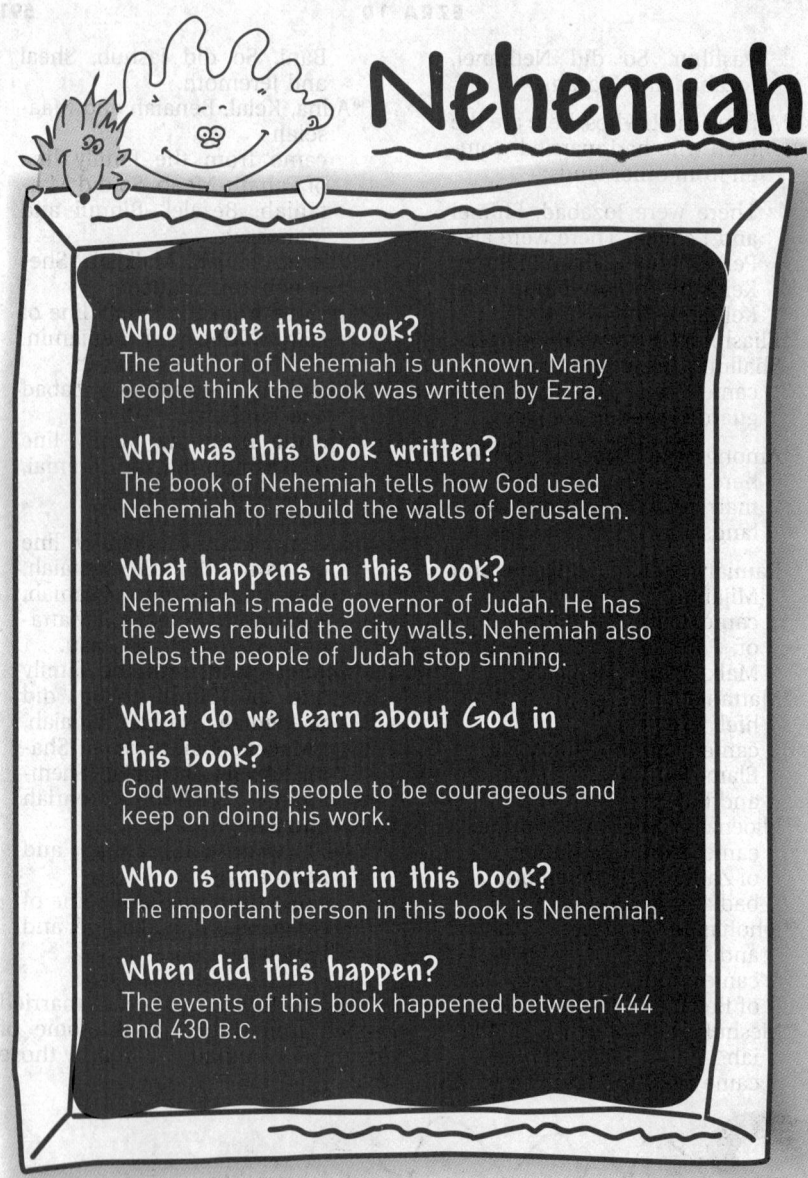

Nehemiah

Who wrote this book?
The author of Nehemiah is unknown. Many people think the book was written by Ezra.

Why was this book written?
The book of Nehemiah tells how God used Nehemiah to rebuild the walls of Jerusalem.

What happens in this book?
Nehemiah is made governor of Judah. He has the Jews rebuild the city walls. Nehemiah also helps the people of Judah stop sinning.

What do we learn about God in this book?
God wants his people to be courageous and keep on doing his work.

Who is important in this book?
The important person in this book is Nehemiah.

When did this happen?
The events of this book happened between 444 and 430 B.C.

NEHEMIAH PRAYS TO THE LORD

1 These are the words of Nehemiah. He was the son of Hacaliah.

I was in the safest place in Susa. I was there in the 20th year that Artaxerxes was king. It was in the month of Kislev. ²At that time Hanani came from Judah with some other men. He was one of my brothers. I asked him and the other men about the Jews who were left alive in Judah. They had returned from Babylonia. I also asked him about Jerusalem.

³He and the men who were with him said to me, "Some of the people who returned are still alive. They are back in the land of Judah. But they are having a hard time. People are making fun

of them. The wall of Jerusalem is broken down. Its gates have been burned with fire."

[4]When I heard about those things, I sat down and sobbed. For several days I was very sad. I didn't eat any food. And I prayed to the God of heaven. [5]I said,

"LORD, you are the God of heaven. You are a great and wonderful God. You keep the covenant you made with those who love you and obey your commands. You show them your love.

[6]"Please pay careful attention to my prayer. See how your people are suffering. Please listen to me. I'm praying to you day and night. I'm praying for the people of Israel. We Israelites have committed sins against you. All of us admit it. I and my family have also sinned against you. [7]We've done some very evil things. We haven't obeyed the commands, rules and laws you gave your servant Moses.

[8]"Remember what you told him. You said, 'If you people are not faithful, I will scatter you among the nations. [9]But if you return to me, I will bring you back. If you obey my commands, I will gather you together again. I will bring you back from the farthest places on earth. I will bring you to the special place where I have chosen to put my Name.'

[10]"LORD, they are your people. They serve you. You used your great strength and mighty hand to set them free from Egypt. [11]Lord, please pay careful attention to my prayer. Listen to the prayers of all of us. We take delight in bringing honor to your name. Give me success today. Help King Artaxerxes show me his favor."

I was the king's wine taster.

ARTAXERXES SENDS NEHEMIAH TO JERUSALEM

2 Wine was brought in for King Artaxerxes. It was the month of Nisan in the 20th year of his rule. I got the wine and gave it to him. I hadn't been sad in front of him before.

But now I was. [2]So the king asked me, "Why are you looking so sad? You aren't sick. You must be feeling sad deep down inside."

I was really afraid. [3]But I said to the king, "May you live forever! Why shouldn't I look sad? The city where my people of long ago are buried has been destroyed. And fire has burned up its gates."

[4]The king said to me, "What do you want?"

I prayed to the God of heaven. [5]Then I answered the king, "Are you pleased with me, King Artaxerxes? If it pleases you, send me to Judah. Let me go to the city of Jerusalem. That's where my people are buried. I want to rebuild it."

[6]The queen was sitting beside the king. He turned and asked me, "How long will your journey take? When will you get back?" It pleased the king to send me. So I chose a certain time.

[7]I also said to him, "If it pleases you, may I take some letters with me? I want to give them to the governors of the land west of the Euphrates River. Then they'll help me travel safely through their territory until I arrive in Judah.

[8]"May I also have a letter to Asaph? He takes care of your forest. I want him to give me some logs so I can make beams out of them. I want to use them for the gates of the fort that is by the temple. Some of the logs will be used in the city wall. And I'll need some for the house I'm going to live in." The gracious hand of my God helped me. So the king gave me what I asked for.

[9]Then I went to the governors of the land west of the Euphrates. I gave them the king's letters. He had also sent army officers and horsemen along with me.

[10]Sanballat and Tobiah heard about what was happening. They were very upset that someone had come to work for the good of Israel's people. Sanballat was a Horonite. Tobiah was an official from Ammon.

NEHEMIAH CHECKS OUT THE WALLS OF JERUSALEM

[11]I went to Jerusalem. I stayed there for three days. [12]Then at night I took a few men with me to check out the

walls. I hadn't told anyone what my God wanted me to do for Jerusalem. There weren't any donkeys with me except the one I was riding on.

[13]That night I went out through the Valley Gate. I went toward the Jackal Well and the Dung Gate. I checked out the walls of Jerusalem. They had been broken down. I also checked the city gates. Fire had burned them up. [14]I moved on toward the Fountain Gate and the King's Pool. But there wasn't enough room for my donkey to get through. [15]It was still night. I went up the Kidron Valley. I kept checking the wall. Finally, I turned back. I went back in through the Valley Gate.

[16]The officials didn't know where I had gone. They didn't know what I had done either. That's because I hadn't said anything to anyone yet. I hadn't told the priests or nobles or officials. And I hadn't spoken to any others who would be rebuilding the wall.

[17]I said to them, "You can see the trouble we're in. Jerusalem has been destroyed. Fire has burned up its gates. Come on. Let's rebuild the wall of Jerusalem. Then people won't make fun of us anymore." [18]I also told them how the gracious hand of my God was helping me. And I told them what the king had said to me.

They replied, "Let's start rebuilding." So they began that good work.

[19]But Sanballat, the Horonite, heard about it. So did Tobiah, the official from Ammon. Geshem, the Arab, heard about it too. All of them laughed at us. They made fun of us. "What do you think you are doing?" they asked. "Are you turning against the king?"

[20]I answered, "The God of heaven will give us success. We serve him. So we'll start rebuilding the walls. But you don't have any share in Jerusalem. You don't have any claim to it. You don't have any right to worship here."

How can we buy things with a check instead of money?

The letter Nehemiah carried to Asaph was like a check. It told Asaph that the king would pay for the materials Nehemiah needed. A check tells the bank to pay money from your account to someone else. If you look closely on a check you will see the words, "Pay to the order of" and then a blank line. This line means, "Give money to the person named on this line. Give this person the amount written on this check, and take the money from my account." There is a place for the person who wrote the check to sign it. This shows that the check really came from you.

Checks are easy to use and safer than cash.

A check allows you to pay someone without having to go to the bank or carry a lot of money. If you lose cash, anyone can find it and use it. That is why people tell you not to send cash through the mail. But if you write a check, only the person you wrote it to is allowed to cash it.

checkout
Nehemiah 2:7,8

Related verses:
Proverbs 7:21;
Jeremiah 32:9,10

A LIST OF THE PEOPLE WHO REPAIRED THE WALL

3 The high priest Eliashib and the other priests went to work. They rebuilt the Sheep Gate. They set it apart to God. They put its doors in place. They continued to rebuild the wall up to the Tower of the Hundred. They set the tower apart to God. Then they continued to rebuild the wall all the way to the Tower of Hananel. ²Some men from Jericho rebuilt the next part of the wall. And Zaccur rebuilt the next part. He was the son of Imri.

³The sons of Hassenaah rebuilt the Fish Gate. They laid its beams. They put its doors and metal bolts and bars in place. ⁴Meremoth repaired the next part of the wall. He was the son of Uriah. Uriah was the son of Hakkoz. Next to Meremoth, Meshullam made some repairs. He was the son of Berekiah. Berekiah was the son of Meshezabel. Next to Meshullam, Zadok also made some repairs. He was the son of Baana. ⁵Some men from Tekoa repaired the next part of the wall. But their nobles refused to do any work at all. They didn't pay any attention to the people who were in charge of the work.

⁶Joiada and Meshullam repaired the Jeshanah Gate. Joiada was the son of Paseah. Meshullam was the son of Besodeiah. Joiada and Meshullam laid the beams of the gate. They put its doors and metal bolts and bars in place. ⁷Next to them, some men from Gibeon and Mizpah made repairs. They included Melatiah from Gibeon and Jadon from Meronoth. Those places were under the authority of the governor of the land west of the Euphrates River.
⁸Uzziel repaired the next part of the wall. He made his living by working with gold. He was the son of Harhaiah. Hananiah made repairs on the next part. He made his living by making perfume. So the wall of Jerusalem was made like new again all the way to the Broad Wall. ⁹Rephaiah repaired the next part. He was the son of Hur. Rephaiah ruled over half of the territory where Jerusalem was located.

¹⁰Jedaiah repaired the part of the wall that was across from his house. He was the son of Harumaph. Hattush made repairs next to Jedaiah. Hattush was the son of Hashabneiah. ¹¹Malkijah and Hasshub repaired another part of the wall. They also repaired the Tower of the Ovens. Malkijah was the son of Harim. Hasshub was the son of Pahath-Moab.
¹²Shallum repaired the next part. His daughters helped him. He was the son of Hallohesh. Shallum ruled over the other half of the territory where Jerusalem was located.

¹³Hanun repaired the Valley Gate. Some people who lived in Zanoah helped him. They rebuilt it. They put its doors and metal bolts and bars in place. They also repaired 500 yards of the wall. They repaired it all the way to the Dung Gate.

¹⁴Malkijah repaired the Dung Gate. He was the son of Recab. Malkijah ruled over the territory where Beth Hakkerem was located. He rebuilt the gate. He put its doors and metal bolts and bars in place.

¹⁵Shallun repaired the Fountain Gate. He was the son of Col-Hozeh. Shallun ruled over the territory where Mizpah was located. He rebuilt the gate. He put a roof over it. And he put the doors and metal bolts and bars of the gate in place. He also repaired the wall by the Pool of Siloam. It was near the King's Garden. Shallun repaired the wall as far as the steps that go down from the City of David.
¹⁶Next to Shallun, Nehemiah made some repairs. He was the son of Azbuk. Nehemiah ruled over half of the territory where Beth Zur was located. He repaired the wall up to the part that was across from the tombs of David. He repaired it all the way to the man-made pool and the House of Heroes.
¹⁷Next to Nehemiah, some Levites made repairs. They worked under the direction of Rehum. He was the son of Bani. Next to Rehum, Hashabiah made repairs for his territory. He ruled over half of the territory where Keilah was located. ¹⁸Next to him, other people from that territory made some re-

pairs. They worked under the direction of Binnui. He was the son of Henadad. Binnui ruled over the other half of the territory where Keilah was located.

[19]Next to him, Ezer repaired another part of the wall. He was the son of Jeshua. Ezer ruled over the territory where Mizpah was located. He repaired the part that was across from the place that went up to the storeroom where the weapons were kept. He repaired the wall up to the angle.

[20]Next to him, Baruch worked hard to repair another part of the wall. He was the son of Zabbai. He repaired the part from the angle to the entrance to Eliashib's house. Eliashib was high priest. [21]Next to Baruch, Meremoth repaired another part. He was the son of Uriah. Uriah was the son of Hakkoz. Meremoth repaired the part from the entrance to Eliashib's house to the end of the house.

[22]Next to Meremoth, some priests from the surrounding area made repairs. [23]Next to them, Benjamin and Hasshub repaired the part of the wall that was in front of their house. Next to them, Azariah repaired the part that was beside his house. He was the son of Maaseiah. Maaseiah was the son of Ananiah.

[24]Next to Azariah, Binnui made repairs on another part. Binnui was the son of Henadad. Binnui repaired the wall from Azariah's house to the angle and the corner. [25]Palal worked across from the angle. He was the son of Uzai. Palal also worked across from the tower that was part of the upper palace. It was near the courtyard of the guard. Next to him, Pedaiah made some repairs. He was the son of Parosh.

[26]The temple servants who lived on the hill of Ophel helped him. They repaired the wall up to the part that was across from the Water Gate. It was toward the east and the palace tower. [27]Next to the temple servants, the men from Tekoa repaired another part. They made repairs from the large palace tower to the wall of Ophel.

[28]The priests made repairs above the Horse Gate. Each priest repaired the part of the wall that was in front of his own house. [29]Next to them, Zadok made repairs across from his house. He was the son of Immer. Next to Zadok, Shemaiah made some repairs. He was the son of Shecaniah. Shemaiah guarded the East Gate.

[30]Next to him, Hananiah and Hanun repaired another part of the wall. Hananiah was the son of Shelemiah. Hanun was the sixth son of Zalaph. Next to Hananiah and Hanun, Meshullam made some repairs. He was the son of Berekiah. Meshullam repaired the part that was across from where he lived.

[31]Next to him, Malkijah made some repairs. He made his living by working with gold. He repaired the wall up to the house of the temple servants and the traders. It was across from the Inspection Gate. He also repaired the wall as far as the room that was above the corner. [32]The traders and those who made their living by working with gold made some repairs. They repaired the wall from the room above the corner to the Sheep Gate.

NEHEMIAH'S ENEMIES OPPOSE HIM

4 Sanballat heard that we were rebuilding the wall. So he burned with anger. He became very upset. He made fun of the Jews. [2]He spoke to his friends and the army of Samaria. He said, "What are those Jews trying to do? Can they make their city wall like new again? Will they offer sacrifices? Can they finish everything in a single day? The stones from their city wall and buildings are piled up like trash. And everything has been badly burned. Can they use those stones to rebuild everything again?"

[3]Tobiah from Ammon was at Sanballat's side. He said, "What are they building? They're putting up a stone wall. But suppose a fox climbs on top of it. Even that will break it down!"

[4]I prayed to God. I said, "Our God, please listen to our prayer. Some people hate us. They're making fun of us. So let others make fun of them. Let them be carried off like stolen goods. Let them be taken to another country

as prisoners. [5]Don't hide your eyes from their guilt. Don't forgive their sins. They have made fun of the builders."

[6]So we rebuilt the wall. We repaired it until all of it was half as high as we wanted it to be. The people worked with all their heart.

[7]But Sanballat and Tobiah heard that Jerusalem's walls continued to be repaired. The Arabs and some people from Ammon heard the same thing. Some men from Ashdod heard about it too. They heard that the gaps in the wall were being filled in. So they burned with anger. [8]All of them made evil plans to come and fight against Jerusalem. They wanted to stir up trouble against it.

[9]But we prayed to our God. We put guards on duty day and night to watch out for danger.

[10]During that time, the people in Judah spoke up. They said, "The workers are getting weaker and weaker all the time. Broken stones are piled up everywhere. They are in our way. So we can't rebuild the wall."

[11]And our enemies said, "We will be right there among them. We'll kill them. We'll put an end to their work. We'll do it before they even know it or see us."

[12]Then the Jews who lived near our enemies came to us. They told us ten times, "No matter where you are, they'll attack us."

[13]So I stationed some people behind the lowest parts of the wall. That's where our enemies could easily attack us. I stationed the people family by family. They had their swords, spears and bows with them.

[14]I looked things over. Then I stood up and spoke to the nobles, the officials and the rest of the people. I said, "Don't be afraid of your enemies. Remember the Lord. He is great and powerful. So fight for your brothers and sisters. Fight for your sons and daughters. Fight for your wives and homes."

[15]Our enemies heard that we knew what they were trying to do. They heard that God had blocked their evil plans. So all of us returned to the wall. Each of us did our own work.

[16]From that day on, half of my men did the work. The other half were given spears, shields, bows and armor. The officers stationed themselves behind all of the people of Judah. [17]The people continued to build the wall. Those who carried supplies did their work with one hand. They held a weapon in the other hand. [18]Each of the builders wore his sword at his side as he worked. But the man who blew the trumpet stayed with me.

[19]Then I spoke to the nobles, the officials and the rest of the people. I said, "This is a big job. It covers a lot of territory. We're separated too far from one another along the wall. [20]When you hear the sound of the trumpet, join us at that location. Our God will fight for us!"

[21]So we continued the work. Half of the men held spears. We worked from the first light of sunrise until the stars came out at night. [22]At that time I also spoke to the people. I told them, "Have every man and his helper stay inside Jerusalem at night. Then they can guard us at night. And they can work during the day."

[23]My relatives and I didn't take our clothes off. My men and the guards didn't take theirs off either. Each man kept his weapon with him, even when he went to get water.

NEHEMIAH HELPS SOME POOR PEOPLE

5 Some men and their wives cried out against their Jewish brothers and sisters. [2]Some of them were saying, "We and our sons and daughters have increased our numbers. Now there are many of us. We have to get some grain so we can eat and stay alive."

[3]Others were saying, "We're being forced to sell our fields, vineyards and homes. We have to do it to buy grain. There isn't enough food for everyone."

[4]Still others were saying, "We've had to borrow money. We needed it to pay the king's tax on our fields and vineyards. [5]We belong to the same family lines as the rest of our people. Our sons and daughters are as good as theirs. But we've had to sell them off as slaves. Some of our daughters have al-

ready been made slaves. But we can't do anything about it. That's because our fields and vineyards now belong to others."

⁶I heard them when they cried out. And I burned with anger when I heard what they were saying. ⁷I thought it over for a while. Then I brought charges against the nobles and officials. I told them, "You are forcing your own people to pay too much interest!"

So I called together a large group of people to handle the matter. ⁸I said, "Our Jewish brothers and sisters were sold to other nations. We've done everything we could to buy them back and bring them home. But look at what you are doing! You are actually selling your own people! Now we'll have to buy them back too!"

The people kept quiet. They couldn't think of anything to say.

⁹So I continued, "What you are doing isn't right. Shouldn't you show respect for our God? Shouldn't you live in a way that will keep our enemies from making fun of us?

¹⁰"I'm lending the people money and grain. So are my relatives and my men. But you must stop charging too much interest!

¹¹"Give the people's fields back to them. Give them back their vineyards, olive groves and houses. Do it right away. You have charged them too much. Give everything back to them. Give them back the one percent on the money, grain, fresh wine and olive oil you have charged them."

¹²"We'll give it back," they said. "And we won't require anything more from them. We'll do exactly as you say."

Then I sent for the priests. I made the nobles and officials take an oath to do what they had promised. ¹³I also shook out my pockets and emptied them. I said, "Some of you might decide not to keep the promise you have made. If that happens, may God shake you out of your house! May he empty

KIDS' QUESTION

Why didn't the Jews ever change their clothes while they were rebuilding the walls?

Not everyone around Jerusalem wanted the walls to be rebuilt. Some people were trying hard to stop the workers. Because of this, the workers had to be on guard all the time. They also had to take turns working so that someone could work every hour of the day and night. Nehemiah and the workers wanted so much to rebuild the walls that they did not even change their clothes. Soon the walls were rebuilt.

checkout
Nehemiah 4:23

Related verses:
Nehemiah
1:1—2:20; 4:1–23

you of everything you own! May you be left with nothing at all!"

The whole community said, "Amen." They praised the LORD. And the leaders did what they had promised to do.

¹⁴And that's not all. I was appointed as governor of Judah in the 20th year that Artaxerxes was king of Persia. I remained in that position until his 32nd year. During those 12 years, I and my relatives didn't eat the food that was provided for my table.

¹⁵But there had been governors before me. They had put a heavy load on the people. They had taken a pound of silver from each of them. They had also taken food and wine from them. Their officials had acted like high and mighty rulers over them.

But I have great respect for God. So I didn't act like that. ¹⁶Instead, I spent all of my time working on this wall. All of my men were gathered there to work

on it too. We didn't receive any land for ourselves.

¹⁷Many people ate at my table. They included 150 Jews and officials. They also included leaders who came to us from the nations that were around us. ¹⁸Each day one ox, six of the best sheep and some birds were prepared for me. Every ten days plenty of wine of all kinds was brought in as well. In spite of all that, I never asked for the food that was provided for my table. That's because the people were already paying too many taxes.

¹⁹You are my God. Please remember me. Show me your favor. Keep in mind everything I've done for these people.

NEHEMIAH'S ENEMIES CONTINUE TO OPPOSE HIM

6 Sanballat, Tobiah and Geshem, the Arab, heard about what I had done. So did the rest of our enemies. All of them heard I had re-

Should I borrow money from the bank or from my friends?

It is better not to borrow at all. Save your money until you have enough for what you need. Or pray for a way to earn extra and look for work you can do. But if you must borrow, sign a written agreement. Do this even if the money comes from a friend. Then pay it back as soon as you can.

Try not to borrow from friends. Money can cause trouble between friends. It is better not to put your friends under the pressure of waiting for you to pay them back.

What if a friend wants to borrow from you? Either give the money as a gift or make a loan but think of it as a gift. That way you will never worry about whether it gets paid back. And anytime someone does not pay you back, forgive the person and forget it.

checkout

Nehemiah 5:4

Related verse:
Proverbs 18:19

I'D LIKE TO BORROW 53¢ FOR AN ICE CREAM CONE PLEASE

built the wall. In fact, they heard there weren't any gaps left in it. But up to that time I hadn't put up the gates at the main entrances to the city. ²Sanballat and Geshem sent me a message. They said, "Come. Let's talk with one another. Let's meet in one of the villages on the flatlands of Ono."

But they were planning to harm me. ³So I sent messengers to them with my answer. I replied, "I'm working on a huge project. So I can't get away. Why should the work stop while I leave it? Why should I go down and talk with you?"

⁴They sent me the same message four times. And I gave them the same answer each time.

⁵Sanballat sent his helper to me a fifth time. He brought the same message. He was carrying a letter that wasn't sealed. ⁶It said,

"A report is going around among the nations. Geshem says it's true. We hear that you and the other Jews are planning to turn against the Persian rulers. And that's why you are building the wall.

"It's also reported that you are about to become their king. ⁷People say that you have even appointed prophets to make an announcement about you. In Jerusalem they are going to say, 'Judah has a king!' That report will get back to the king of Persia. So come. Let's talk things over."

⁸I sent a reply to Sanballat. I said, "What you are saying isn't really happening. You are just making it up."

⁹All of them were trying to frighten us. They thought, "Their hands will get too weak to do the work. So it won't be completed."

But I prayed to God. I said, "Make my hands stronger."

¹⁰One day I went to Shemaiah's house. He was the son of Delaiah. Delaiah was the son of Mehetabel. Shemaiah had shut himself up in his home. He said, "Let's go to God's house. Let's meet inside the temple. Let's close the temple doors. Some people want to kill you. They will come at night."

¹¹But I said, "Should a man like me run away? Should someone like me go into the temple just to save his life? No! I won't go!"

¹²I realized that God hadn't sent Shemaiah. Tobiah and Sanballat had hired him. That's why he had prophesied lies about me. ¹³They had hired him to scare me. They wanted me to commit a sin by doing what he said. That would give me a bad name in the community. People would find fault with me and my work.

¹⁴You are my God. Remember what Tobiah and Sanballat have done. Also remember the prophet Noadiah. She and the rest of the prophets have been trying to scare me.

THE CITY WALL IS COMPLETED

¹⁵So the city wall was completed on the 25th day of the month of Elul. It was finished in 52 days. ¹⁶All of our enemies heard about it. All of the nations that were around us became afraid. They weren't sure of themselves anymore. They realized that our God had helped us finish the work.

¹⁷In those days the nobles of Judah sent many letters to Tobiah. And replies from Tobiah came back to them. ¹⁸Many people in Judah had taken an oath that they would be faithful to him. That's because he was Shecaniah's son-in-law. Shecaniah was the son of Arah. Tobiah's son Jehohanan had married Meshullam's daughter. Meshullam was the son of Berekiah. ¹⁹Tobiah's friends kept reporting to me the good things he did. They also kept telling him what I said. And Tobiah himself sent letters to scare me.

7 The wall had been rebuilt. I had put up the gates at the main entrances to the city. Those who guarded the gates were appointed to their positions. So were the singers and Levites. ²I put my brother Hanani in charge of Jerusalem. Hananiah helped him. Hananiah was commander of the fort that was by the temple. Hanani was an honest man. He had more respect for God than most people do. ³I said to Hanani and Hananiah,

"Don't open the gates of Jerusalem until the hottest time of the day. Tell the men who guard the gates to shut them before they go off duty. Make sure they lock them up tight. Also appoint as guards some people who live in Jerusalem. Station some of them at their appointed places. Station others near their own homes."

A LIST OF PEOPLE WHO RETURNED TO JUDAH

⁴Jerusalem was large. It had a lot of room. But only a few people lived there. The houses hadn't been rebuilt yet. ⁵So my God stirred me up to gather the people together. He also told me to gather the nobles and officials together with them. He wanted me to list them by families. I found the family history of those who had been the first to return. Here is what I found written in it.

⁶Nebuchadnezzar had taken many Jews away from the land of Judah. He had forced them to go to Babylonia as prisoners. Now they returned to Jerusalem and Judah. All of them went back to their own towns. Nebuchadnezzar was king of Babylonia. ⁷The leaders of the Jews included Zerubbabel, Jeshua, Nehemiah, Azariah, Raamiah and Nahamani. They also included Mordecai, Bilshan, Mispereth, Bigvai, Nehum and Baanah.

Here is a list of the men of Israel who returned home.

⁸There were 2,172 from the family line of Parosh.
⁹There were 372 from Shephatiah.
¹⁰There were 652 from Arah.
¹¹There were 2,818 from Pahath-Moab through the family line of Jeshua and Joab.
¹²There were 1,254 from Elam.
¹³There were 845 from Zattu.
¹⁴There were 760 from Zaccai.
¹⁵There were 648 from Binnui.
¹⁶There were 628 from Bebai.
¹⁷There were 2,322 from Azgad.
¹⁸There were 667 from Adonikam.
¹⁹There were 2,067 from Bigvai.

²⁰There were 655 from Adin.
²¹There were 98 from Ater through the family line of Hezekiah.
²²There were 328 from Hashum.
²³There were 324 from Bezai.
²⁴There were 112 from Hariph.
²⁵There were 95 from Gibeon.

²⁶There were 188 from the men of Bethlehem and Netophah.
²⁷There were 128 from Anathoth.
²⁸There were 42 from Beth Azmaveth.
²⁹There were 743 from Kiriath Jearim, Kephirah and Beeroth.
³⁰There were 621 from Ramah and Geba.
³¹There were 122 from Micmash.
³²There were 123 from Bethel and Ai.
³³There were 52 from Nebo.
³⁴There were 1,254 from the other Elam.
³⁵There were 320 from Harim.
³⁶There were 345 from Jericho.
³⁷There were 721 from Lod, Hadid and Ono.
³⁸There were 3,930 from Senaah.

³⁹Here is a list of the priests.

There were 973 from the family line of Jedaiah through the line of Jeshua.
⁴⁰There were 1,052 from Immer.
⁴¹There were 1,247 from Pashhur.
⁴²There were 1,017 from Harim.

⁴³The Levites belonged to the family line of Jeshua through Kadmiel through the line of Hodaviah. The total number of men was 74.

⁴⁴The singers belonged to the family line of Asaph. The total number of men was 148.

⁴⁵The men who guarded the temple gates belonged to the family lines of Shallum, Ater, Talmon, Akkub, Hatita and Shobai. The total number of men was 138.

⁴⁶Here is a list of the members of the family lines of the temple servants.

Ziha, Hasupha, Tabbaoth,
⁴⁷Keros, Sia, Padon,

48 Lebana, Hagaba, Shalmai,
49 Hanan, Giddel, Gahar,
50 Reaiah, Rezin, Nekoda,
51 Gazzam, Uzza, Paseah,
52 Besai, Meunim, Nephussim,
53 Bakbuk, Hakupha, Harhur,
54 Bazluth, Mehida, Harsha,
55 Barkos, Sisera, Temah,
56 Neziah, Hatipha

57 Here is a list of the members of the family lines of the servants of Solomon.

Sotai, Sophereth, Perida,
58 Jaala, Darkon, Giddel,
59 Shephatiah, Hattil,
Pokereth-Hazzebaim, Amon

60 The total number of the members of the family lines of the temple servants and the servants of Solomon was 392.

61 Many people came up to Judah from the towns of Tel Melah, Tel Harsha, Kerub, Addon and Immer. But they weren't able to prove that their families belonged to the people of Israel.

62 There were 642 of them from the family lines of
Delaiah, Tobiah and Nekoda.

63 Here is a list of the members of the family lines of the priests.

They were
Hobaiah, Hakkoz and Barzillai. Barzillai had married a daughter of Barzillai from Gilead. So he was also called Barzillai.

64 The priests looked for their family records. But they couldn't find them. So they weren't able to serve as priests. They weren't "clean."

65 The governor gave them an order. He told them not to eat any of the most sacred food. They had to wait until there was a priest who could use the Urim and Thummim to get decisions from the LORD.

66 The total number of the entire group that returned was 42,360. 67 That didn't include their 7,337 male and female slaves. There were also 245 male and female singers. 68 And there were 736 horses, 245 mules, 69 435 camels and 6,720 donkeys.

70 Some of the family leaders helped pay for the work. The governor gave 19 pounds of gold to be added to the temple treasure. He also gave 50 bowls and 530 sets of clothes for the priests. 71 Some of the family leaders gave 375 pounds of gold for the work. They also gave one and a third tons of silver. All of that was added to the temple treasure. 72 The rest of the people gave a total of 375 pounds of gold and one and a fourth tons of silver. They also gave 67 sets of clothes for the priests.

73 The priests and Levites settled down in their own towns. So did the singers, the temple servants and the men who guarded the gates. The rest of the people of Israel also settled in their own towns.

EZRA READS THE LAW TO THE PEOPLE

8 The people of Israel had settled down in their towns. In the seventh month, 1 all of them gathered together. They went to the open area in front of the Water Gate. They told Ezra to bring out the Scroll of the Law of Moses. The LORD had given Israel that law so they would obey him. Ezra was a teacher of the law.

2 The priest Ezra brought the Law out to the whole community. It was the first day of the seventh month. The group was made up of men and women and everyone who was old enough to understand what Ezra was going to read.

3 He read the Law to them from sunrise until noon. He did it as he faced the open area in front of the Water Gate. He read it to the men, women and others who could understand. And all of the people paid careful attention as Ezra was reading the Scroll of the Law.

4 Ezra, the teacher, stood on a high wooden stage. It had been built for the occasion. Mattithiah, Shema and Anaiah stood at his right side. So did Uriah, Hilkiah and Maaseiah. Pedaiah, Mishael and Malkijah stood at his left

side. So did Hashum, Hashbaddanah, Zechariah and Meshullam.

⁵Ezra opened the scroll. All of the people could see him. That's because he was standing above them. As he opened the scroll, the people stood up. ⁶Ezra praised the LORD. He is the great God. All of the people lifted up their hands. They said, "Amen! Amen!" Then they bowed down. They turned their faces toward the ground. And they worshiped the LORD.

⁷The Levites taught the Law to the people. They remained standing while the Levites taught them. The Levites who were there included Jeshua, Bani, Sherebiah, Jamin, Akkub, Shabbethai and Hodiah. They also included Maaseiah, Kelita, Azariah, Jozabad, Hanan and Pelaiah. ⁸All of those Levites read

parts of the Scroll of the Law of God to the people. They made it clear to them. They told them what it meant. So the people were able to understand what was being read.

⁹Then Nehemiah and Ezra spoke up. So did the Levites who were teaching the people. All of those men said to the people, "This day is set apart to honor the LORD your God. So don't sob. Don't be sad." All of the people had been sobbing as they listened to the words of the Law. Nehemiah was governor. Ezra was a priest and a teacher of the law.

¹⁰Nehemiah said, "Go and enjoy some good food and sweet drinks. Send some of it to those who don't have any. This day is set apart to honor our Lord. So don't be sad. The joy of the LORD makes you strong."

Why don't teachers just get to the point instead of going on and on about the subject?

Some kids find it more difficult to learn certain subjects than other kids. Good teachers take time to teach *all* the students in a class, not just the ones who understand the material right away. And good teachers take the time to add facts and reasons for what they are teaching. Listen and pay attention—you'll probably learn some interesting stuff!

checkout
Nehemiah 8:8

Related verses:
Joshua 8:34–35;
Ecclesiastes 12:11;
Philippians 3:1

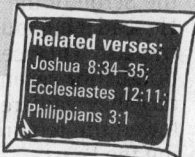

¹¹The Levites calmed all of the people down. They said, "Be quiet. This is a sacred day. So don't be sad."

¹²Then all of the people went away to eat and drink. They shared their food with others. They celebrated with great joy. Now they understood the words they had heard. That's because everything had been explained to them.

¹³All of the family leaders gathered around Ezra, the teacher. So did the priests and Levites. All of them paid attention to the words of the Law. It was the second day of the month.

¹⁴The LORD had given the Law through Moses. He wanted the people of Israel to obey it. It is written there that they were supposed to live in booths during the Feast of Booths. That Feast was celebrated in the seventh month. ¹⁵They were also supposed to spread the message all through their towns and in Jerusalem. They were supposed to announce, "Go out into the central hill country. Bring back some branches from olive and wild olive trees. Also bring some from myrtle, palm and shade trees. Use the branches to make booths."

¹⁶So the people went out and brought some branches back. They built themselves booths on their own roofs. They made them in their courtyards. They put them up in the courtyards of the house of God. They built them in the open area in front of the Water Gate. And they built them in the open area in front of the Gate of Ephraim.

¹⁷All those who had returned from Babylonia made booths. They lived in them during the Feast of Booths. They hadn't celebrated the Feast with so much joy for a long time. In fact, they had never celebrated it like that from the days of Joshua, the son of Nun, until that very day. So their joy was very great.

¹⁸Day after day, Ezra read parts of the Scroll of the Law of God to them. He read it out loud from the first day to the last. They celebrated the Feast of Booths for seven days. On the eighth day they gathered together. They followed the required rules for celebrating the Feast.

THE PEOPLE OF ISRAEL PRAY TO THE LORD

9 It was the 24th day of the seventh month. The people of Israel gathered together again. They didn't eat any food. They wore black clothes. They put dust on their heads. ²The people of Israel separated themselves from everyone else. They stood and admitted they had sinned. They also admitted that their people before them had done evil things.

³They stood where they were. They listened while the Levites read parts of the Scroll of the Law of the LORD their God. They listened for a fourth of the day. They spent another fourth of the day admitting their sins. They also worshiped the LORD their God.

⁴The Levites stood on the stairs. They included Jeshua, Bani, Kadmiel and Shebaniah. They also included Bunni, Sherebiah, Bani and Kenani. With loud voices they called out to the LORD their God. ⁵Then some Levites spoke up. They included Jeshua, Kadmiel, Bani and Hashabneiah. They also included Sherebiah, Hodiah, Shebaniah and Pethahiah. They said to the people, "Stand up. Praise the LORD your God. He lives for ever and ever!"

So the people said, "LORD, may your glorious name be praised. May it be lifted high above every other name that is blessed and praised. ⁶You are the one and only LORD. You made the heavens. You made even the highest heavens. You created all of the stars in the sky. You created the earth and everything that is on it. And you made the oceans and everything that is in them. You give life to everything. Every living being in heaven worships you.

⁷"You are the LORD God. You chose Abram. You brought him out of Ur in Babylonia. You named him Abraham. ⁸You knew that his heart was faithful to you. And you made a covenant with him. You promised to give to his children after him a land of their own. It was the land of the Canaanites, Hittites and Amorites. The Periz-

zites, Jebusites and Girgashites also lived there. You have kept your promise. That's because you always do what is right and fair.

⁹"You saw how our people suffered long ago in Egypt. You heard them cry out to you at the Red Sea. ¹⁰You did miraculous signs and wonders against Pharaoh. You sent plagues on all of his officials. In fact, you sent them on all of the people of Egypt. You knew how they treated our people. They looked down on them. But you made a name for yourself. That name remains to this very day. ¹¹"You parted the Red Sea for the people of Israel. They passed through it on dry ground. But you threw into the sea those who chased them. They sank down like a stone into the mighty waters. ¹²By day you led them with a pillar of cloud. At night you led them with a pillar of fire. It gave them light to show them the way you wanted them to go.

¹³"You came down on Mount Sinai. From heaven you spoke to our people. You gave them rules and laws. Those laws are right and fair. You gave them orders and commands that are good. ¹⁴You taught them about your holy Sabbath day. You gave them commands, orders and laws. You did it through your servant Moses.

¹⁵"When the people were hungry, you gave them bread from heaven. When they were thirsty, you brought them water out of a rock.

"You told them to go into the land of Canaan. You told them to take it as their own. It was the land you had promised to give them. You had even raised your hand and taken an oath to do it.

¹⁶"But our people before us became proud and stubborn. They didn't obey your commands. ¹⁷They refused to listen to you. They forgot the miracles you had done among them. So they became stubborn. When they refused to obey you, they appointed a leader for themselves. They wanted to go back to being slaves

in Egypt. But you are a God who forgives. You are gracious. You are tender and kind. You are slow to get angry. You are full of love. So you didn't desert them.

¹⁸"They made for themselves a metal statue of a god that looked like a calf. They said, 'Here is your god. He brought you up out of Egypt.' And they did evil things that dishonored you. But you still didn't desert them.

¹⁹"Because you loved them so much, you didn't leave them in the desert. During the day the pillar of cloud didn't stop guiding them on their path. At night the pillar of fire didn't stop shining on the way you wanted them to go. ²⁰You gave them your good Spirit to teach them. You didn't hold back your manna from their mouths. And you gave them water when they were thirsty. ²¹For 40 years you took good care of them in the desert. They had everything they needed. Their clothes didn't wear out. And their feet didn't swell up.

²²"You gave them kingdoms and nations. You even gave them lands far away. They took over the country of Sihon. He was king of Heshbon. They also took over the country of Og. He was king of Bashan. ²³You gave them as many children as there are stars in the sky. You told their parents to enter the land. You told them to take it over. And you brought their children into it. ²⁴Their children went into the land. They took it as their own. You brought the people of Canaan under Israel's control. The Canaanites lived in the land. But you handed them over to Israel. You also handed their kings and the other nations in the land over to Israel. You allowed Israel to deal with them just as they wanted to.

²⁵"Your people captured cities that had high walls around them. They also took over the rich land in Canaan. They took houses that were filled with all kinds of good things. They took over wells that

had already been dug. They took many vineyards, olive groves and fruit trees. They ate until they were very full and satisfied. They were filled with joy because you were so good to them.

²⁶"But they didn't obey you. Instead, they turned against you. They turned their backs on your law. They killed your prophets. The prophets had warned them to turn back to you. But they did very evil things that dishonored you.

²⁷"So you handed them over to their enemies, who beat them down. Then they cried out to you. From heaven you heard them. You loved them very much. So you sent leaders to help them. The leaders saved them from the powerful hand of their enemies.

²⁸"But as soon as the people were enjoying peace and rest again, they did what was evil in your sight. Then you handed them over to their enemies. So their enemies ruled over them. When they cried out to you again, you heard them from heaven. You loved them very much. So you saved them time after time.

²⁹"You warned them to obey your law again. But they became proud. They didn't obey your commands. They sinned against your rules. Anyone who obeys them will live by them. But the people didn't care about that. They turned their backs on you. They became very stubborn. They refused to listen to you.

³⁰"For many years you put up with them. By your Spirit you warned them through your prophets. In spite of that, they didn't pay any attention. So you handed them over to the nations that were around them. ³¹But you loved them very much. So you didn't put an end to them. You didn't desert them. That's because you are a gracious God. You are tender and kind.

³²"Our God, you are great, mighty and wonderful. You keep the covenant you made with us. You show us your love. So don't let all of our suffering seem like a small thing in your sight. We've suffered greatly. So have our kings and leaders. So have our priests and prophets. Our people who lived long ago also suffered. And all of your people are suffering right now. In fact, we've been suffering from the time of the kings of Assyria until today.

³³"In spite of everything that has happened to us, you have been fair. You have been faithful in what you have done. But we did what was wrong. ³⁴Our kings and leaders didn't follow your law. Our priests and our people before us didn't follow it either. They didn't pay any attention to your commands. They didn't listen to the warnings you gave them. ³⁵They didn't serve you. They didn't turn from their evil ways. They didn't obey you even when they had a kingdom. You were very good to them. And they enjoyed it. You gave them a rich land. It had plenty of room in it. But they still didn't serve you.

³⁶"Now look at us. We are slaves today. We're slaves in the land you gave our people long ago. You gave it to them so they could eat its fruit and the other good things it produces. ³⁷But we have sinned against you. So its great harvest goes to the kings of Persia. You have placed them over us. They rule over our bodies and cattle just as they please. And we are suffering terribly.

THE PEOPLE AGREE TO OBEY GOD'S LAW

³⁸"So we are making a firm agreement. We're writing it down. Our leaders are stamping it with their seals. And so are our Levites and priests."

10 Here are the names of those who stamped the agreement with their seals.

The governor Nehemiah, the son of Hacaliah

Zedekiah, ²Seraiah, Azariah, Jeremiah,

³Pashhur, Amariah, Malkijah,
⁴Hattush, Shebaniah, Malluch,
⁵Harim, Meremoth, Obadiah,
⁶Daniel, Ginnethon, Baruch,
⁷Meshullam, Abijah, Mijamin,
⁸Maaziah, Bilgai, Shemaiah

They were the priests.

⁹Here are the names of the Levites.

Jeshua, the son of Azaniah
Binnui, one of the sons of Hen-
    adad
Kadmiel

¹⁰Here are the names of those
    who helped them.

Shebaniah, Hodiah, Kelita, Pe-
    laiah, Hanan,
¹¹Mica, Rehob, Hashabiah,
¹²Zaccur, Sherebiah, Shebaniah,
¹³Hodiah, Bani, Beninu

¹⁴Here are the names of the leaders of
the people.

Parosh, Pahath-Moab, Elam,
    Zattu, Bani,
¹⁵Bunni, Azgad, Bebai,
¹⁶Adonijah, Bigvai, Adin,
¹⁷Ater, Hezekiah, Azzur,
¹⁸Hodiah, Hashum, Bezai,
¹⁹Hariph, Anathoth, Nebai,
²⁰Magpiash, Meshullam, Hezir,
²¹Meshezabel, Zadok, Jaddua,
²²Pelatiah, Hanan, Anaiah,
²³Hoshea, Hananiah, Hasshub,
²⁴Hallohesh, Pilha, Shobek,
²⁵Rehum, Hashabnah, Maaseiah,
²⁶Ahiah, Hanan, Anan,
²⁷Malluch, Harim, Baanah

²⁸The rest of the people gathered together. They included the
priests, the Levites and the men
who guarded the gates. They included the singers and temple
servants. They also included all
those who separated themselves
from the surrounding nations to
obey the Law of God. All of those
men brought their wives with
them. And they brought all of
their sons and daughters who
were old enough to understand
what was being agreed to. ²⁹All of
the men joined the nobles of their
people. They made a firm agree-

ment. They put themselves under
a curse and took an oath. They
promised to follow the Law of
God. It had been given through
Moses, the servant of God. They
promised to obey carefully all of
the commands, rules and laws of
the LORD our Lord.

³⁰The priests, Levites and people said, "We promise not to give
our daughters to be married to
men from the nations that are
around us. And we promise not to
let their daughters get married to
our sons.

³¹"The people around us will
bring goods and grain to sell on
the Sabbath day. But we won't buy
anything from them on the Sabbath. In fact, we won't buy anything from them on any holy day.
Every seventh year we won't farm
the land. And we'll forgive people
what they owe us.

³²"We will be accountable for
carrying out the commands for
serving in the house of our God.
Each of us will give an eighth of an
ounce of silver every year. ³³It will
pay for the holy bread that is
placed on the table in the temple.
It will pay for the regular grain offerings and burnt offerings. It will
pay for the offerings on the Sabbath days. It will pay for the offerings at the New Moon Feasts and
appointed feasts. It will pay for
the holy offerings. It will be used
for sin offerings to pay for the sin
of Israel. It will also pay for everything else that needs to be done at
the house of our God.

³⁴"We are the priests, Levites
and people. We have cast lots to
decide when each of our families
should bring a gift of wood to the
house of our God. They will bring
it at certain appointed times every year. The wood will be burned
on the altar of the LORD our God.
That's what the Law requires.

³⁵"We will also be accountable
for bringing the first share of our
crops each year. And we'll bring
the first share of every fruit tree.
We'll bring them to the LORD's
house.

[36]"Each of us will bring our oldest son to the priests who serve there. We'll also bring the male animals that were born first to their mothers among our cattle, herds and flocks. We'll bring them to the house of our God. That's what the Law requires.

[37]"We will also bring the first part of the meal we grind. We'll bring the first of our grain offerings. We'll bring the first share of fruit from all of our trees. And we'll bring the first share of our olive oil and fresh wine. We'll give all of those things to the priests. They'll put them in the storerooms of the house of our God.

"And we'll give a tenth of our crops to the Levites. They collect the tenth shares. They do it in all of the towns where we work. [38]A priest from Aaron's family line must go with the Levites when they receive the tenth shares. And the Levites must bring a tenth of those shares up to the house of our God. They must put it in the rooms where the treasures are stored.

[39]"The people of Israel, including the Levites, must bring their gifts. They must bring grain, olive oil and fresh wine. They must put them in the storerooms where the articles for the temple are kept. That's where the priests stay when they are serving at the temple. The singers and the men who guard the gates also stay there.

"We won't forget to take care of the house of our God."

PEOPLE ARE CHOSEN TO LIVE IN JERUSALEM

11 The leaders of the people settled down in Jerusalem. The rest of the people cast lots. They did it to choose one person out of every ten. That person was brought to live in the holy city of Jerusalem. The other nine had to stay in their own towns. [2]The people praised all those who agreed to live in Jerusalem.

[3]Here are the leaders from different parts of the country who settled down in Jerusalem. Some Israelites, priests and Levites lived in the towns of Judah. So did some temple servants and some members of the family lines of Solomon's servants. All of them lived on their own property in the towns of Judah. [4]At the same time, other people from the tribes of Judah and Benjamin lived in Jerusalem.

Here are the leaders from the family line of Judah.

There was Athaiah. He was the son of Uzziah. Uzziah was the son of Zechariah. Zechariah was the son of Amariah. Amariah was the son of Shephatiah. Shephatiah was the son of Mahalalel. Mahalalel belonged to the family line of Perez. [5]There was also Maaseiah. He was the son of Baruch. Baruch was the son of Col-Hozeh. Col-Hozeh was the son of Hazaiah. Hazaiah was the son of Adaiah. Adaiah was the son of Joiarib. Joiarib was the son of Zechariah. Zechariah belonged to the family line of Shelah. [6]Many able men who belonged to the family line of Perez lived in Jerusalem. The total number of them was 468.

[7]Here are the leaders from the family line of Benjamin.

There was Sallu. He was the son of Meshullam. Meshullam was the son of Joed. Joed was the son of Pedaiah. Pedaiah was the son of Kolaiah. Kolaiah was the son of Maaseiah. Maaseiah was the son of Ithiel. Ithiel was the son of Jeshaiah. [8]There were also Gabbai and Sallai. They were Sallu's followers. The total number of men was 928. [9]Joel was their chief officer. He was the son of Zicri. A man named Judah was in charge of the New Quarter of Jerusalem. He was the son of Hassenuah.

[10]Here are the leaders from among the priests.

There were Jedaiah, Jakin and the son of Joiarib. [11]There was also Seraiah. He was the son of Hilkiah. Hilkiah was the son of Meshullam. Meshullam was the son of

Zadok. Zadok was the son of Meraioth. Meraioth was the son of Ahitub. Ahitub was a ruler in God's house. [12]There were also those who helped them. They carried out the work for the temple. The total number of men was 822.

There was also Adaiah. He was the son of Jeroham. Jeroham was the son of Pelaliah. Pelaliah was the son of Amzi. Amzi was the son of Zechariah. Zechariah was the son of Pashhur. Pashhur was the son of Malkijah. [13]There were also those who helped Adaiah. They were family leaders. The total number of men was 242.

There was also Amashsai. He was the son of Azarel. Azarel was the son of Ahzai. Ahzai was the son of Meshillemoth. Meshillemoth was the son of Immer. [14]There were also those who helped Amashsai. They were able men. The total number of them was 128. Their chief officer was Zabdiel. He was the son of Haggedolim.

[15]Here are the leaders from among the Levites.

There was Shemaiah. He was the son of Hasshub. Hasshub was the son of Azrikam. Azrikam was the son of Hashabiah. Hashabiah was the son of Bunni. [16]There were also Shabbethai and Jozabad. They were two of the leaders of the Levites. They were in charge of the work that was done outside God's house.

[17]There was also Mattaniah. He led in prayer and in giving thanks. He was the son of Mica. Mica was the son of Zabdi. Zabdi was the son of Asaph. There was also Bakbukiah. He was second among those who helped Mattaniah. And there was Abda. He was the son of Shammua. Shammua was the son of Galal. Galal was the son of Jeduthun. [18]The total number of Levites in the holy city was 284.

[19]Here are the leaders from among the men who guarded the gates.

There were Akkub, Talmon and those who helped them. They stood guard at the gates. The total number of men was 172.

[20]The rest of the Israelites were in all of the towns of Judah. The priests and Levites were with them. All of them lived on their own family property.

[21]The temple servants lived on the hill of Ophel. Ziha and Gishpa were in charge of them.

[22]Uzzi was the chief officer of the Levites in Jerusalem. He was the son of Bani. Bani was the son of Hashabiah. Hashabiah was the son of Mattaniah. Mattaniah was the son of Mica. Uzzi was one of the members of Asaph's family line. They were singers. They were in charge of the worship services at God's house. [23]The singers received their orders from the Persian king. He told them what they should do every day.

[24]Pethahiah worked for the king in all matters that were connected with the people. He was the son of Meshezabel. Meshezabel belonged to the family line of Zerah. Zerah was the son of Judah.

[25]Many of the people of Judah lived in villages that had fields around them. Some of them lived in Kiriath Arba and the settlements that were around it. Others lived in Dibon and its settlements. Others lived in Jekabzeel and its villages. [26]Others lived in Jeshua, Moladah and Beth Pelet.

[27]Others lived in Hazar Shual and in Beersheba and its settlements. [28]Others lived in Ziklag and in Meconah and its settlements. [29]Others lived in En Rimmon and Zorah. Others lived in Jarmuth, [30]Zanoah and Adullam and their villages. Others lived in Lachish and its fields. Still others lived in Azekah and its settlements. So the people of Judah were living all the way from Beersheba to the Valley of Hinnom.

[31]Some of the members of the family line of Benjamin who were from Geba lived in Micmash. Others lived in Aija and in Bethel and its settlements. [32]Others lived in Anathoth, Nob and Ananiah. [33]Others lived in Hazor, Ramah and Gittaim. [34]Others lived in Hadid, Zeboim and Neballat. [35]Others lived in Lod and Ono. Still others lived in the Valley of Skilled Workers.

[36]Some of the groups of the Levites from Judah settled in the territory of Benjamin.

THE PRIESTS AND LEVITES WHO RETURNED TO JUDAH

12 Some priests and Levites returned to Judah with Zerubbabel and Jeshua. Zerubbabel was the son of Shealtiel. Here are the names of those priests and Levites.

Seraiah, Jeremiah, Ezra, [2]Amariah, Malluch, Hattush, [3]Shecaniah, Rehum, Meremoth, [4]Iddo, Ginnethon, Abijah, [5]Mijamin, Moadiah, Bilgah, [6]Shemaiah, Joiarib, Jedaiah, [7]Sallu, Amok, Hilkiah, Jedaiah

All of them were the leaders of the priests and those who helped them. They lived in the days of Jeshua.

[8]The Levites were Jeshua, Binnui, Kadmiel, Sherebiah and Judah. There were also Mattaniah and those who helped him. They were in charge of the songs for giving thanks. [9]Bakbukiah and Unni helped them. They stood and sang across from them during the services.

[10]Jeshua was the father of Joiakim. Joiakim was the father of Eliashib. Eliashib was the father of Joiada. [11]Joiada was the father of Jonathan. And Jonathan was the father of Jaddua.

[12]Here are the names of the family leaders of the priests. They were the leaders in the days of Joiakim.

Meraiah was from Seraiah's family.

Hananiah was from Jeremiah's family.

[13]Meshullam was from Ezra's family.

Jehohanan was from Amariah's family.

[14]Jonathan was from Malluch's family.

Joseph was from Shecaniah's family.

[15]Adna was from Harim's family.

Helkai was from Meremoth's family.

[16]Zechariah was from Iddo's family.

Meshullam was from Ginnethon's family.

[17]Zicri was from Abijah's family.

Piltai was from Miniamin's and Moadiah's family.

[18]Shammua was from Bilgah's family.

Jehonathan was from Shemaiah's family.

[19]Mattenai was from Joiarib's family.

Uzzi was from Jedaiah's family.

[20]Kallai was from Sallu's family.

Eber was from Amok's family.

[21]Hashabiah was from Hilkiah's family.

And Nethanel was from Jedaiah's family.

[22]The names of the family leaders of the Levites in the days of Eliashib, Joiada, Johanan and Jaddua were written down. So were the names of the family leaders of the priests. That happened while Darius ruled over Persia. [23]The names of the leaders in Levi's family line up to the time of Johanan were written down. They were written in the official records. Johanan was the son of Eliashib. [24]The leaders of the Levites were Hashabiah, Sherebiah and Jeshua. Jeshua was the son of Kadmiel.

Those who helped them stood across from them to sing praises and give thanks. One group would sing back to the other. That's what David, the man of God, had ordered.

[25]Mattaniah, Bakbukiah, Obadiah, Meshullam, Talmon and Akkub stood at the gates of the temple. They guarded the storerooms at the gates. [26]They served in the days of Joiakim. He was the son of Jeshua. Jeshua was the son of Jehozadak. They also served in the days of Nehemiah and Ezra. Nehemiah was governor. Ezra was a priest and a teacher of the law.

THE WALL OF JERUSALEM IS SET APART TO GOD

[27]The wall of Jerusalem was set apart to God. For that occasion, the Levites were gathered together from where they lived. They were brought to Jerusalem to celebrate that happy occasion. They celebrated the fact that the wall was being set apart to God. They

did it by singing and giving their thanks to him. They celebrated by playing music on cymbals, harps and lyres.

²⁸The singers were also brought together. Some of them came in from the area around Jerusalem. Others came from the villages where the people of Netophah lived. ²⁹Others came from Beth Gilgal. Still others came from the area of Geba and Azmaveth. The singers had built villages for themselves around Jerusalem.

³⁰The priests and Levites made themselves pure. Then they made the people, the gates and the wall pure and clean.

³¹I, Nehemiah, had the leaders of Judah go up on top of the wall. I also appointed two large choirs to sing and give thanks. I told one of them to walk south on top of the wall. That was toward the Dung Gate. ³²Hoshaiah and half of the leaders of Judah followed them. ³³Azariah, Ezra, Meshullam, ³⁴Judah, Benjamin, Shemaiah and Jeremiah also followed them.

³⁵Some priests who had trumpets followed them. So did Zechariah. He was the son of Jonathan. Jonathan was the son of Shemaiah. Shemaiah was the son of Mattaniah. Mattaniah was the son of Micaiah. Micaiah was the son of Zaccur. Zaccur was the son of Asaph. ³⁶Those who helped Zechariah also marched along. They were Shemaiah, Azarel, Milalai, Gilalai, Maai, Nethanel, Judah and Hanani. They brought instruments of music with them. That's what David, the man of God, had ordered. Ezra led the group that was marching south. He was a teacher of the law.

³⁷At the Fountain Gate they continued straight up the steps of the City of David that went up to the wall. Then the group passed above David's house. They continued on to the Water Gate on the east.

³⁸The second choir went north. I followed them on top of the wall. Half of the people went with me. They went past the Tower of the Ovens. They went to the Broad Wall. ³⁹They marched over the Gate of Ephraim. They went over the Jeshanah Gate and the Fish Gate. They went past the Tower of Hananel and the Tower of the Hundred. They continued on to the Sheep Gate. At the Gate of the Guard they stopped.

⁴⁰Then the two choirs that sang and gave thanks took their places in God's house. So did I. So did half of the officials. ⁴¹And so did the priests. They were Eliakim, Maaseiah, Miniamin, Micaiah, Elioenai, Zechariah and Hananiah. They had their trumpets with them. ⁴²Maaseiah, Shemaiah, Eleazar, Uzzi, Jehohanan, Malkijah, Elam and Ezer were also there. The choirs sang under the direction of Jezrahiah.

⁴³On that day large numbers of sacrifices were offered. The people were glad because God had given them great joy. The women and children were also very happy. The joyful sound in Jerusalem could be heard far away.

⁴⁴At that time some men were put in charge of the storerooms. That's where all of the gifts the people brought were placed. They included the first shares of their crops. They also included a tenth of everything the Law required. From the fields that were around the towns the people had to bring the shares of their crops that were required by the Law. They gave them to the priests and Levites. That's because the people of Judah were pleased with the priests and Levites who were serving God.

⁴⁵The priests and Levites did everything their God wanted them to do. They made things pure and clean. The singers and those who guarded the temple gates also served God. Everything was done just as David and his son Solomon had commanded. ⁴⁶A long time ago there had been directors for the singers. There had also been directors for the songs for giving thanks and praise to God. It was in the time of David and Asaph.

⁴⁷So now in the days of Zerubbabel and Nehemiah, all of the people of Israel brought their gifts. They gave the singers and those who guarded the gates what they were supposed to give them every day. They also set apart the shares for the other Levites. And the Levites set apart the shares for the priests in the family line of Aaron.

NEHEMIAH WARNS THE PEOPLE

13 On that same day the Scroll of Moses was read out loud. All of the people heard it. It was written there that no one from Ammon or Moab should ever be allowed to become a member of the community of God. ²That's because they hadn't given the people of Israel food and water. Instead, they had hired Balaam to call a curse down on them. But our God turned the curse into a blessing.

³When that law was read, the people of Judah obeyed it. They put out of Israel everyone who was from another nation.

⁴The priest Eliashib had been put in charge of the storerooms in the house of our God. He had worked closely with Tobiah. ⁵He had also provided a large room for Tobiah. It had been used to store the grain offerings. The incense and temple articles had been put there. And a tenth of the grain, olive oil and fresh wine had been kept there. That's what the Law required for the Levites. That's also what it required for the singers and those who guarded the temple gates. The gifts for the priests had been kept there too.

⁶But I wasn't in Jerusalem while all of that was going on. I had returned to the Persian King Artaxerxes, the king of Babylonia. I went to him in the 32nd year of his rule. Some time later I asked him to let me return to Jerusalem.

⁷When I got back, I learned about the evil thing Eliashib had done. He had provided a room for Tobiah. It was in the courtyards of God's house. ⁸So I was very unhappy. I threw all of Tobiah's things out of the room.

⁹I gave orders to make the rooms pure and clean again. Then I put the supplies from God's house back into them. That included the grain offerings and the incense.

¹⁰I also learned that the shares the Levites were supposed to receive hadn't been given to them. So all of the Levites and singers had to leave their regular temple duties. They had to go back and farm their own fields.

¹¹I gave a warning to the officials. I asked them, "Why aren't you taking care of God's house?" Then I brought them together. I stationed them in their proper places. I put them back to work.

¹²All of the people of Judah brought a tenth of the grain, olive oil and fresh wine. They took it to the storerooms.

¹³I put some men in charge of the storerooms. They were Shelemiah, Zadok and Pedaiah. Shelemiah was a priest. Zadok was a teacher of the law. And Pedaiah was a Levite. I made Hanan their assistant. He was the son of Zaccur. Zaccur was the son of Mattaniah. I knew that those men could be trusted. They were put in charge of handing out the supplies to their people.

¹⁴You are my God. Remember me because of what I've done. I've worked faithfully for your temple and its services. So please don't forget the good things I've done.

¹⁵In those days I saw some men of Judah stomping on grapes in winepresses. They were doing it on the Sabbath day. Others were bringing in grain. They were loading it on donkeys. Still others were loading up wine, grapes, figs and other kinds of things. They were bringing all of it into Jerusalem on the Sabbath. So I warned them not to sell food on that day. ¹⁶People from Tyre who lived in Jerusalem were bringing in fish. In fact, they were bringing in all kinds of goods. They were selling them in Jerusalem on the Sabbath. The people of Judah were buying them.

¹⁷I gave a warning to the nobles of Judah. I said, "Why are you doing such an evil thing? You are misusing the Sabbath day! ¹⁸Your people before you did the very same things. That's why our God has brought all of this trouble on us. That's why he's making this city suffer so much. Now you are stirring up even more of his anger against Israel. You are misusing the Sabbath day."

¹⁹Evening shadows fell on the gates of Jerusalem before the Sabbath started. So I ordered the gates to be shut. They had to remain closed until the

Sabbath was over. I stationed some of my own men at the gates. I told them not to let anything be brought in on the Sabbath day.

²⁰Once or twice some traders and sellers spent the night outside Jerusalem. They were hoping to sell all kinds of goods. ²¹But I gave them a warning. I said, "Why are you spending the night by the wall? If you do this again, I'll arrest you." So from that time on they didn't come on the Sabbath anymore.

²²I commanded the Levites to make themselves pure. Then I told them to go and guard the gates. I wanted the Sabbath day to be kept holy.

You are my God. Remember me because of the good things I've done. Be kind to me in keeping with your great love.

²³In those days I also saw that some men of Judah had gotten married to women from Ashdod. Others had married women from Ammon or Moab. ²⁴Half of their children spoke the language of Ashdod. Or they spoke the language of one of the other nations. They didn't even know how to speak the language of Judah.

²⁵So I gave them a warning. I called curses down on them. I beat some of them up. I pulled their hair out. I made them take an oath in God's name. I said, "You must promise not to give your daughters to be married to their sons. You must promise not to let their daughters marry your sons. And you must not marry their daughters either.

²⁶"That's how Solomon, the king of Israel, sinned. He married women from other nations. There wasn't a king like him anywhere. His God loved him. In fact, God made him king over the whole nation of Israel. But even he was led into sin by women from other lands. ²⁷Now I hear that you too are doing all of the same terrible and evil things. You aren't being faithful to our God. You are marrying women from other lands."

²⁸One of the sons of Joiada was the son-in-law of Sanballat. Joiada was the high priest. He was the son of Eliashib. I drove Joiada's son away from me. Sanballat was a Horonite.

²⁹You are my God. Remember what those priests have done. They have polluted their own work. They have also polluted the covenant that God made with the priests and Levites long ago.

³⁰So I made the priests and Levites pure. I made them pure from every practice that had come from other countries and had polluted them. I gave them their duties. Each one had his own job to do. ³¹I also made plans for gifts of wood to be brought at certain appointed times. And I made plans for the first share of the crops to be brought.

You are my God. Please remember me. Show me your favor.

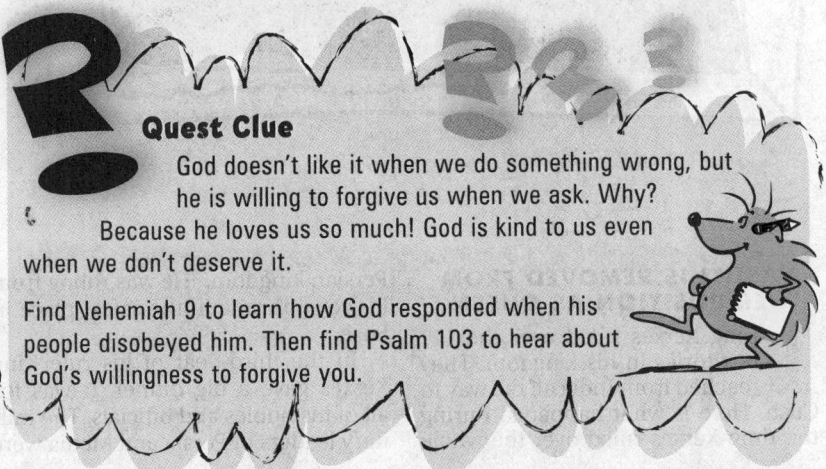

Quest Clue

God doesn't like it when we do something wrong, but he is willing to forgive us when we ask. Why? Because he loves us so much! God is kind to us even when we don't deserve it.

Find Nehemiah 9 to learn how God responded when his people disobeyed him. Then find Psalm 103 to hear about God's willingness to forgive you.

Esther

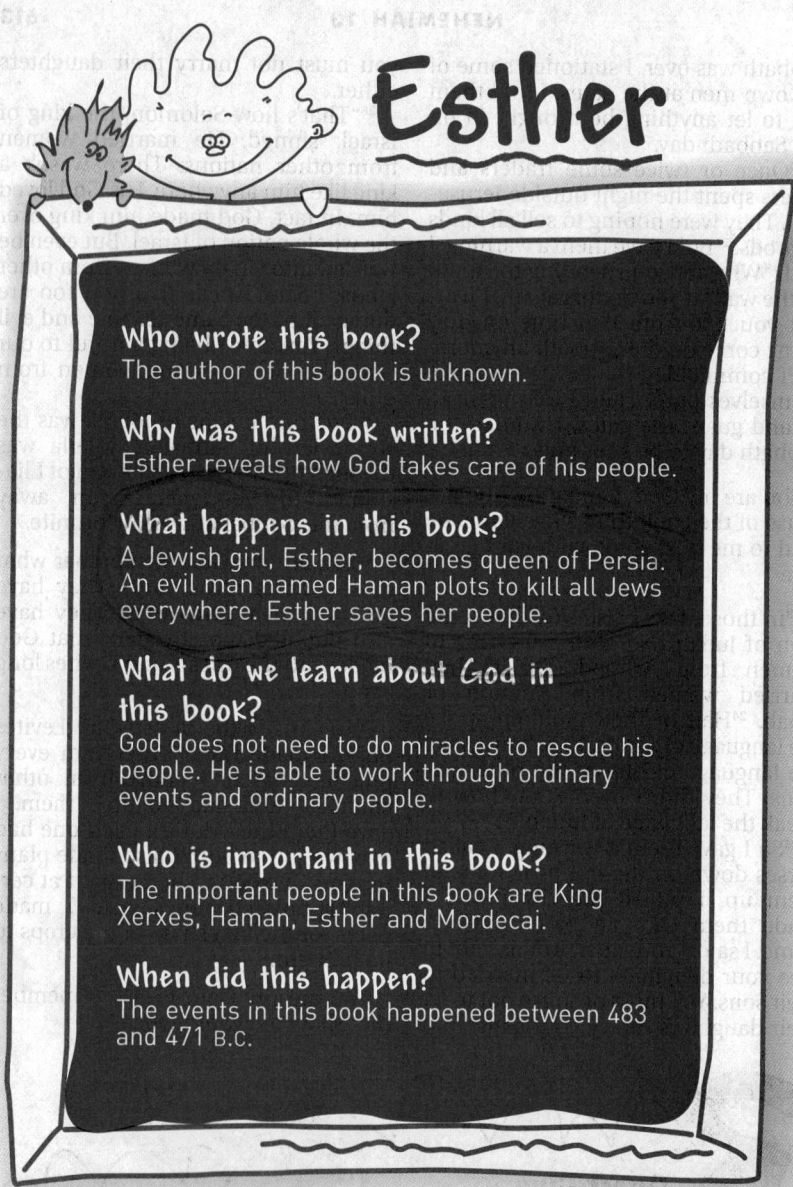

Who wrote this book?
The author of this book is unknown.

Why was this book written?
Esther reveals how God takes care of his people.

What happens in this book?
A Jewish girl, Esther, becomes queen of Persia. An evil man named Haman plots to kill all Jews everywhere. Esther saves her people.

What do we learn about God in this book?
God does not need to do miracles to rescue his people. He is able to work through ordinary events and ordinary people.

Who is important in this book?
The important people in this book are King Xerxes, Haman, Esther and Mordecai.

When did this happen?
The events in this book happened between 483 and 471 B.C.

VASHTI IS REMOVED FROM HER POSITION AS QUEEN

1 King Xerxes ruled over the 127 territories in his kingdom. They reached from India all the way to Cush. Here is what happened during the time Xerxes ruled over the whole Persian kingdom. ²He was ruling from his royal throne in the safest place in Susa.

³In the third year of his rule King Xerxes gave a big dinner. It was for all of his nobles and officials. The military leaders of Persia and Media were

there. So were the princes and the nobles of the territories he ruled over. ⁴Every day for 180 days he showed his guests the great wealth of his kingdom. He also showed them how glorious his kingdom was.

⁵When those days were over, the king gave another big dinner. It lasted for seven days. It was held in the garden of the king's courtyard. It was for all of the people who lived in the safest place in Susa. Everyone from the least important person to the most important was invited.

⁶The garden was decorated with white and blue linen banners. They hung from ropes that were made out of white linen and purple cloth. The ropes were connected to silver rings on marble pillars. There were gold and silver couches in the garden. They were placed on a floor that was made out of small stones. The floor had purple crystal, marble, mother-of-pearl and other stones of great value.

⁷Royal wine was served in gold cups. Each cup was different from all of the others. There was plenty of wine. The king always provided as much as his guests wanted. ⁸He commanded that they should be allowed to drink as much or as little as they wished. He directed all of his servants to give them what they asked for.

⁹Queen Vashti also gave a big dinner. Only women were invited. It was held in the royal palace of King Xerxes.

¹⁰On the seventh day Xerxes was in a good mood because he had drunk a lot of wine. So he gave a command to the seven officials who served him. They were Mehuman, Biztha, Harbona, Bigtha, Abagtha, Zethar and Carcas. ¹¹He told them to bring Queen Vashti to him. He wanted her to come wearing her royal crown. He wanted to show off her beauty to the people and nobles. She was lovely to look at.

¹²The attendants told Queen Vashti what the king had ordered her to do. But she refused to come. So the king became very angry. In fact, he burned with anger.

¹³It was the king's practice to ask advice from those who knew a lot about matters of law and fairness. So he spoke with the wise men who were supposed to understand what was going on at that time. ¹⁴They were the men who were closest to the king. They were Carshena, Shethar, Admatha, Tarshish, Meres, Marsena and Memucan. They were the seven nobles of Persia and Media. They were the king's special advisers. In fact, they were the most important men in the kingdom.

¹⁵"You know the law," the king said. "What should I do to Queen Vashti? She hasn't obeyed my command. The officials told her what I ordered her to do, didn't they?"

¹⁶Then Memucan gave a reply to the king and the nobles. He said, "Queen Vashti has done what is wrong. But she didn't do it only against you, King Xerxes. She did it also against all of the nobles. And she did it against the people in all of the territories you rule over.

¹⁷"All of the women will hear about what the queen has done. Then they will look down on their husbands. They'll say, 'King Xerxes commanded Queen Vashti to be brought to him. But she wouldn't come.' ¹⁸Starting today, the leading women in Persia and Media who have heard about the queen's actions will act in the same way. They'll disobey all of your nobles, just as she disobeyed you. They won't have any respect for their husbands. They won't honor them.

¹⁹"So if it pleases you, send out a royal order. Let it be written down in the laws of Persia and Media. They can never be changed. Let the royal order say that Vashti can never see you again. Also let her position as queen be given to someone who is better than she is.

²⁰"And let your order be announced all through your entire kingdom. Then all of the other women will have respect for their husbands from the least important of them to the most important."

²¹The king and his nobles were pleased with that advice. So he did what Memucan had suggested. ²²He sent messages out to every territory in the kingdom. He sent them to each territory in its own writing. He sent them to every nation in its own language. The messages announced in

each nation's language that every man should rule over his own family.

ESTHER BECOMES QUEEN OF PERSIA

2 Later, the anger of King Xerxes calmed down. Then he remembered Vashti and what she had done. He also remembered the royal order he had sent out concerning her. ²At that time the king's personal attendants made a suggestion. They said, "King Xerxes, let a search be made for some beautiful young virgins for you. ³Appoint some officials in every territory in your kingdom. Have them bring all of those beautiful virgins into the safest place in Susa. Put them in the special place where the virgins stay. Then put Hegai in charge of them. He's the eunuch who serves you. He's in charge of the virgins. Let beauty care be given to the new group of virgins. ⁴Then let the one who pleases you the most become queen in Vashti's place."

The king liked that advice. So he followed it.

⁵There was a Jew living in the safest place in Susa. He was from the tribe of Benjamin. His name was Mordecai. He was the son of Jair. Jair was the son of Shimei. Shimei was the son of Kish. ⁶Nebuchadnezzar had forced Mordecai to leave Jerusalem. He was among the prisoners who were carried off along with Jehoiachin. Jehoiachin had been king of Judah. Nebuchadnezzar was king of Babylonia.

⁷Mordecai had a cousin named Hadassah. He had brought her up in his own home. She didn't have a father or mother. Hadassah was also called Esther. She was very beautiful. Mordecai had adopted her as his own daughter. He had done it when her father and mother died.

⁸After the king's order and law were announced, many virgins were brought to the safest place in Susa. Hegai was put in charge of them. Esther was also taken to the king's palace. She was put under the control of Hegai. He was in charge of the place where the virgins stayed.

⁹Esther pleased him. He showed her his favor. Right away he provided her with her beauty care and special food. He appointed seven female attendants to help her. They were chosen from the king's palace. He moved her and her attendants into the best part of the place where the virgins stayed.

¹⁰Esther hadn't told anyone who her people were. She hadn't talked about her family. That's because Mordecai had told her not to.

¹¹Mordecai tried to find out how Esther was getting along. He wanted to know what was happening to her. So he walked back and forth near the courtyard by the place where the virgins stayed. He did it every day.

¹²Each virgin had to complete 12 months of beauty care. They used oil of myrrh for six months. And they used perfume and make-up for the other six months. A virgin's turn to go in to King Xerxes could come only after a full 12 months had passed.

¹³And here is how she would go to the king. She would be given anything she wanted from the place where the virgins stayed. She could take it with her to the king's palace. ¹⁴In the evening she would go there. In the morning she would leave. Then she would go to the special place where the king's concubines stayed. She would be put under the control of Shaashgaz. He was the king's eunuch who was in charge of the concubines. She would never return to the king unless he was pleased with her. He had to send for her by name before she could go to him again.

¹⁵Mordecai had adopted Esther. She had been the daughter of his uncle Abihail. Her turn came to go in to the king. She only asked for what Hegai suggested. He was the king's eunuch who was in charge of the place where the virgins stayed. Everyone who saw Esther was pleased with her. ¹⁶She was taken to King Xerxes in the royal house. It was now the tenth month. That was the month of Tebeth. It was the seventh year of the rule of Xerxes.

¹⁷The king liked Esther more than he liked any of the other women. She pleased him more than any of the other virgins. So he put a royal crown on her head. He made her queen in Vashti's place.

¹⁸Then the king gave a big dinner. It was in honor of Esther. All of his nobles and officials were invited. He announced a holiday all through the territories he ruled over. He freely gave many gifts in keeping with his royal wealth.

MORDECAI UNCOVERS A PLAN TO KILL THE KING

¹⁹The virgins were gathered together a second time. At that time Mordecai was sitting at the palace gate. ²⁰Esther had kept her family history a secret. She hadn't told anyone who her people were. Mordecai had told her not to. She continued to follow his directions. That's what she had always done when he was bringing her up.

²¹Bigthana and Teresh were two of the king's officers. They guarded the door of the royal palace. They became angry with King Xerxes. So they decided to kill him. They made their evil plans while Mordecai was sitting at the palace gate. ²²So he found out about it. And he told Queen Esther. Then she reported it to the king. She told him that Mordecai had uncovered the plans against him. ²³Some people checked Esther's report. And they found out it was true. So the two officials were put to death. Then poles were stuck through them. They were set up where people could see them. All of that was written in the official records. It was written down while the king was watching.

HAMAN PLANS TO DESTROY THE JEWS

3 After those events, King Xerxes honored Haman. Haman was the son of Hammedatha. He was from the family line of Agag. The king gave Haman a higher position than he had before. He gave him a seat of honor. It was higher than the positions any of the other nobles had. ²All of the royal officials at the palace gate got down on their knees. They gave honor to Haman. That's because the king had commanded them to do it.

But Mordecai refused to get down on his knees. He wouldn't give Haman any honor at all.

³The royal officials at the palace gate asked Mordecai a question. They said, "Why don't you obey the king's command?" ⁴Day after day they spoke to him. But he still refused to obey. So they told Haman about it. They wanted to see whether he would let Mordecai get away with what he was doing. Mordecai had told them he was a Jew.

⁵Haman noticed that Mordecai wouldn't get down on his knees. He wouldn't give Haman any honor. So Haman burned with anger. ⁶But he had found out who Mordecai's people were. So he decided not to kill just Mordecai. He also looked for a way to destroy all of Mordecai's people. They were Jews. He wanted to kill all of them everywhere in the kingdom of Xerxes.

⁷The lot was cast in front of Haman. That was done to choose a day and a month. It was the 12th year that Xerxes was king. It was in the first month. That was the month of Nisan. The lot chose the 12th month. That was the month of Adar. The lot was also called *pur.*

⁸Then Haman said to King Xerxes, "Certain people are scattered among the nations. They live in all of the territories in your kingdom. Their practices are different from the practices of all other people. They don't obey your laws. It really isn't good for you to put up with them.

⁹"If it pleases you, give the order to destroy them. I'll even add 375 tons of silver to the royal treasures. You can use it to pay the men who take care of the matter."

¹⁰So the king took his ring off his finger. The ring had his royal seal on it. He gave the ring to Haman. Haman was the son of Hammedatha, the Agagite. He was the enemy of the Jews.

¹¹"Keep the money," the king said to Haman. "Do what you want to with those people."

¹²The king sent for the royal secretaries. It was the 13th day of the first month. The secretaries wrote down all of Haman's orders. They wrote them down in the writing of each territory in the kingdom. They also wrote them in the language of each nation. The orders were sent to the royal officials. They were also sent to the governors of the territories. And they went out to

the nobles of the nations. The orders were written in the name of King Xerxes himself. And they were stamped with his own royal seal. [13]They were carried by messengers. They were sent to all of the king's territories.

The orders commanded people to destroy, kill and wipe out all of the Jews. That included young people and old people alike. It included women and little children. All of the Jews were supposed to be killed on a single day. That day was the 13th day of the 12th month. It was the month of Adar. The orders also commanded people to take the goods that belonged to the Jews.

[14]A copy of the order had to be sent out as law. It had to be sent to every territory in the kingdom. It had to be announced to the people of every nation. Then they would be ready for that day.

[15]The king commanded the messengers to go out. So they did. The order was sent out from the safest place in Susa. Then the king and Haman sat down to drink wine. But the people in the city were bewildered.

MORDECAI TALKS ESTHER INTO HELPING THE JEWS

4 Mordecai found out about everything that had been done. So he tore his clothes. He put on black clothes. He sat down in ashes. Then he went out into the city. He sobbed out loud. He cried bitter tears. [2]But he only went as far as the palace gate. That's because no one who was dressed in black clothes was allowed to go through it.

[3]All of the Jews were very sad. They didn't eat anything. They sobbed and cried. Many of them put on black clothes. They were lying down in ashes. They did all of those things in every territory where the king's order and law had been sent.

[4]Esther's eunuchs and female attendants came to her. They told her about Mordecai. So she became very troubled. She wanted him to take his black clothes off. So she sent him other clothes to wear. But he wouldn't accept them. [5]Then Esther sent for Hathach. He was one of the king's eu-

nuchs. He had been appointed to take care of her. She ordered him to find out what was troubling Mordecai. She wanted to know why he was so upset.

[6]So Hathach went out to see Mordecai. He was in the open area in front of the palace gate. [7]Mordecai told him everything that had happened to him. He told him about the exact amount of money Haman had promised to add to the royal treasures. He said Haman wanted it to be used to pay some men to destroy the Jews.

[8]Mordecai also gave Hathach a copy of the order. It commanded people to wipe out the Jews. The order had been sent from Susa.

Mordecai told Hathach to show the order to Esther. He wanted him to explain it to her. He told him to try and get her to go to the king. He wanted her to beg for mercy. He wanted her to make an appeal to the king for her people.

[9]Hathach went back. He reported to Esther what Mordecai had said. [10]Then Esther directed him to give an answer to Mordecai. She told him to say, [11]"There is a certain law that everyone knows about. All of the king's officials know about it. The people in the royal territories know about it. It applies to any man or woman who approaches the king in the inner courtyard without being sent for. It says they must be put to death. But there is a way out. Suppose the king reaches out his gold rod toward them. Then their lives will be spared. But 30 days have gone by since the king sent for me."

[12]Esther's words were reported to Mordecai. [13]Then he sent back an answer. He said, "You live in the king's palace. But don't think that just because you are there you will be the only Jew who will escape. [14]What if you don't say anything at this time? Then help for the Jews will come from another place. But you and your family will die. Who knows? It's possible that you became queen for a time just like this."

[15]Then Esther sent a reply to Mordecai. She said, [16]"Go. Gather together all of the Jews who are in Susa. And fast for my benefit. Don't eat or drink anything for three days. Don't do it night

or day. I and my attendants will fast just as you do. Then I'll go to the king. I'll do it even though it's against the law. And if I have to die, I'll die."

[17]So Mordecai went away. He carried out all of Esther's directions.

ESTHER INVITES THE KING AND HAMAN TO A BIG DINNER

5 On the third day Esther put her royal robes on. She stood in the inner courtyard of the palace. It was in front of the king's hall.

The king was sitting on his royal throne in the hall. He was facing the entrance. [2]He saw Queen Esther standing in the courtyard. He was pleased with her. So he reached out toward her the gold rod that was in his hand. Then Esther approached him. She touched the tip of the rod.

[3]The king asked, "What is it, Queen Esther? What do you want? I'll give it to you. I'll even give you up to half of my kingdom."

[4]Esther replied, "King Xerxes, if it pleases you, come to a big dinner today. I've prepared it for you. Please have Haman come with you."

[5]"Bring Haman at once," the king said to his servants. "Then we'll do what Esther asks."

So the king and Haman went to the big dinner Esther had prepared. [6]As they were drinking wine, the king asked Esther the same question again. He said, "What do you want? I'll give it to you. What do you want me to do for you? I'll even give you up to half of my kingdom."

[7]Esther replied, "Here is what I want. Here is my appeal to you. [8]I hope you will show me your favor. I hope you will be pleased to give me what I want. And I hope you will be pleased to listen to my appeal. If you are, I'd like you and Haman to come tomorrow to the big dinner I'll prepare for you. Then I'll answer your question."

HAMAN BRAGS ABOUT BEING INVITED TO ESTHER'S DINNER

[9]That day Haman was happy. So he left the palace in a good mood. But then he saw Mordecai at the palace gate. He noticed that Mordecai didn't stand up when he walked by. In fact, Mordecai didn't have any respect for him at all. So he burned with anger against him. [10]But Haman was able to control himself. He went on home.

Haman called his friends and his wife Zeresh together. [11]He bragged to them about how rich he was. He talked about how many sons he had. He spoke about all of the ways the king had honored him. He bragged about how the king had given him a higher position than any of the other nobles and officials had. [12]"And that's not all!" Haman added. "I'm the only person Queen Esther invited to come with the king to the big dinner she gave. Now she has invited me along with the king tomorrow.

[13]"But even all of that doesn't satisfy me. I won't be satisfied as long as I see that Jew Mordecai sitting at the palace gate."

[14]Haman's wife Zeresh and all of his friends spoke up. They said to him, "Get a pole. In the morning, ask the king to have Mordecai put to death. Have the pole stuck through his body. Set it up at a place where it will be 75 feet above the ground. Everyone will be able to see it there. Then go to the dinner with the king. Have a good time."

Haman was delighted with that suggestion. So he got the pole ready.

THE KING HONORS MORDECAI

6 That night the king couldn't sleep. So he ordered the official records of his rule to be brought in. He ordered someone to read them to him. [2]It was written there that Mordecai had uncovered the plans of Bigthana and Teresh against the king. They had been two of the king's officers who guarded the door of the royal palace. They had decided to kill King Xerxes.

[3]"What great honor has Mordecai received for doing that?" the king asked.

"Nothing has been done for him," his attendants answered.

[4]The king asked, "Who is in the courtyard?"

Haman had just entered the outer courtyard of the palace. He had come to speak to the king about putting Mordecai to death. He wanted to talk about putting Mordecai's body up on the pole he had gotten ready for him.

⁵The king's attendants said to him, "Haman is standing in the courtyard."

"Bring him in," the king ordered.

⁶Haman entered. Then the king asked him, "What should be done for the man I want to honor?"

Haman said to himself, "Is there anyone the king would rather honor than me?" ⁷So he answered the king. He said, "Here is what you should do for the man you want to honor. ⁸Have your servants get a royal robe you have worn. Have them bring a horse you have ridden on. Have a royal crest placed on its head. ⁹Then give the robe and horse to one of your most noble princes. Let the robe be put on the man you want to honor. Let him be led on the horse through the city streets. Let people announce in front of him, 'This is what is done for the man the king wants to honor!' "

¹⁰"Go right away," the king commanded Haman. "Get the robe. Bring the horse. Do exactly what you have suggested. Do it for the Jew Mordecai. He's sitting out there at the palace gate. Make sure you do everything you have suggested."

¹¹So Haman got the robe and the horse. He put the robe on Mordecai. And he led him on horseback through the city streets. He walked along in front of him and announced, "This is what is done for the man the king wants to honor!"

¹²After that, Mordecai returned to the palace gate. But Haman rushed home. He covered his head because he was very sad. ¹³He told his wife Zeresh everything that had happened to him. He also told all of his friends.

His advisers and his wife Zeresh spoke to him. They said, "Your fall from power started with Mordecai. He's a Jew. So now you can't stand up against him. You are going to be destroyed!" ¹⁴They were still talking with him when the king's officials arrived. They hurried Haman away to the big dinner Esther had prepared.

HAMAN IS PUT TO DEATH

7 So the king and Haman went to dine with Queen Esther. ²They were drinking wine on the second day. The king again asked, "What do you want, Queen Esther? I'll give it to you. What do you want me to do for you? I'll even give you up to half of my kingdom."

³Then Queen Esther answered, "King Xerxes, I hope you will show me your favor. I hope you will be pleased to let me live. That's what I want. Please spare my people. That's my appeal to you.

⁴"My people and I have been sold to be destroyed. We've been sold to be killed and wiped out. Suppose we had only been sold as male and female slaves. Then I wouldn't have said anything. That kind of suffering wouldn't be a good enough reason to bother you."

⁵King Xerxes asked Queen Esther, "Who is the man who has dared to do such a thing? And where is he?"

⁶Esther said, "The man hates us! He's our enemy! He's this evil Haman!"

Then Haman was terrified in front of the king and queen.

⁷The king got up. He was burning with anger. He left his wine and went out into the palace garden.

But Haman realized that the king had already decided what he was going to do to him. So he stayed behind to beg Queen Esther for his life.

⁸The king returned from the palace garden to the dinner hall. Just then he saw Haman falling on the couch where Esther was lying.

The king shouted, "Will he even molest the queen? Is he going to attack her while she's right here with me in the palace?"

As soon as the king finished speaking, his men covered Haman's face.

⁹Then Harbona said, "There's a pole standing near Haman's house. He has gotten it ready for Mordecai. Mordecai is the one who spoke up to help you. Haman had planned to have him put to death. He was going to have the pole stuck through his body. Then he was going to set it up at a place where it would be 75 feet above the ground."

Harbona was one of the officials who attended the king.

The king said to his men, "Put Haman to death! Stick the pole through his body! Set it up where everyone can see it!" [10]So they did. And they used the pole Haman had gotten ready for Mordecai. Then the king's anger calmed down.

THE KING ALLOWS THE JEWS TO FIGHT FOR THEIR LIVES

8 That same day King Xerxes gave Queen Esther everything Haman had owned. Haman had been the enemy of the Jews.

Esther had told the king that Mordecai was her cousin. So Mordecai came to see the king. [2]The king took his ring off. It had his royal seal on it. He had taken it back from Haman. Now he gave it to Mordecai. And Esther put Mordecai in charge of everything Haman had owned.

[3]Esther made another appeal to the king. She fell at his feet and sobbed. She begged him to put an end to the evil plan of Haman, the Agagite. He had decided to kill the Jews.

[4]The king reached out his gold rod toward Esther. She got up and stood in front of him.

[5]"King Xerxes, I hope you will show me your favor," she said. "I hope you will think that what I'm asking is the right thing to do. I hope you are pleased with me. If you are, and if it pleases you, let an order be written. Let it take the place of the messages Haman wrote. Haman was the son of Hammedatha, the Agagite. He planned to kill the Jews. He wrote orders to destroy us in all of your territories. [6]I couldn't stand by and see the horrible trouble that would fall on my people! I couldn't stand to see my family destroyed!"

[7]King Xerxes gave a reply to Queen Esther and the Jew Mordecai. He said, "Haman attacked the Jews. So I've given Esther everything he owned. My men have stuck a pole through his dead body. And they've set it up where everyone can see it.

[8]"Now write another order in my name. Do it for the benefit of the Jews. Do what seems best to you. Stamp the order with my royal seal. Nothing that is written in my name and stamped with my seal can ever be changed."

[9]Right away the king sent for the royal secretaries. It was the 23rd day of the third month. That was the month of Sivan. They wrote down all of Mordecai's orders to the Jews. They also wrote them to the royal officials, the governors and the nobles of the 127 territories in his kingdom. The territories reached from India all the way to Cush. The orders were written down in the writing of each territory. They were written in the language of each nation. They were also written to the Jews in their own writing and language.

[10]Mordecai wrote the orders in the name of King Xerxes. He stamped them with the king's royal seal. He sent them by messengers on horseback. They rode fast horses that were raised just for the king.

[11]The Jews in every city could now gather together and fight for their lives. The king's order gave them that right. But what if soldiers from any nation or territory attacked them? What if they attacked their women and children? Then the Jews could destroy, kill and wipe out those soldiers. They could also take the goods that belonged to their enemies. [12]A day was appointed for the Jews to do that in all of the king's territories. It was the 13th day of the 12th month. That was the month of Adar.

[13]A copy of the order was sent out as law in every territory. It was announced to the people of every nation. So the Jews would be ready on that day. They could pay their enemies back.

[14]The messengers rode on the royal horses. They raced along. That's what the king commanded them to do. The order was also sent out in the safest place in Susa.

[15]Mordecai left the king and went on his way. Mordecai was wearing royal clothes. They were blue and white. He was also wearing a large gold crown. And he was wearing a purple coat. It was made out of fine linen. The city of Susa celebrated with great joy.

[16]The Jews were filled with joy and

happiness. They were very glad because now they were being honored. [17]They celebrated and enjoyed good food. They were glad and full of joy. That was true everywhere the king's order went out. It was true in every territory and every city. Many people from other nations announced that they had become Jews. That's because they were so afraid of the Jews.

THE JEWS WIN THE BATTLE OVER THEIR ENEMIES

9 The king's order had to be carried out on the 13th day of the 12th month. That was the month of Adar. On that day the enemies of the Jews had hoped to win the battle over them. But now everything had changed. The Jews had gained the advantage over those who hated them.

[2]The Jews gathered together in their cities. They gathered in all of the territories King Xerxes ruled over. They came together to attack those who were trying to destroy them. No one could stand up against them. The people from all of the other nations were afraid of them.

[3]All of the nobles in the territories helped the Jews. So did the royal officials, the governors and the king's officers. That's because they were so afraid of Mordecai. [4]He was well known in the palace. His fame spread all through the territories. So he became more and more important.

[5]The Jews struck down all of their enemies with swords. They killed them and destroyed them. They did what they pleased to those who hated them. [6]The Jews killed 500 men. They destroyed them in the safest place in Susa.

[7]They also killed Parshandatha, Dalphon, Aspatha, [8]Poratha, Adalia, Aridatha, [9]Parmashta, Arisai, Aridai and Vaizatha. [10]They were the ten sons of Haman. He was the son of Hammedatha. Haman had been the enemy of the Jews. They didn't take anything that belonged to their enemies.

[11]A report was brought to the king that same day. He was told how many men had been killed in the safest place in Susa. [12]He said to Queen Esther,

"The Jews have killed 500 men. They destroyed them in the safest place in Susa. They also killed the ten sons of Haman there. What have they done in the rest of my territories? Now what do you want? I'll give it to you. What do you want me to do for you? I'll do that too."

[13]"If it pleases you," Esther answered, "let the Jews in Susa carry out today's order tomorrow also. Stick poles through the dead bodies of Haman's ten sons. Set them up where everyone can see them."

[14]So the king commanded that it be done. An order was sent out in Susa. And the king's men did to the bodies of Haman's sons everything they were told to do. [15]The Jews in Susa came together on the 14th day of the month of Adar. They put 300 men to death in Susa. But they didn't take anything that belonged to those men.

[16]During that time, the rest of the Jews also gathered together. They lived in the king's territories. They came together to fight for their lives. They didn't want their enemies to bother them anymore. They wanted to get some peace and rest. So they killed 75,000 of their enemies. But they didn't take anything that belonged to them. [17]It happened on the 13th of Adar. On the 14th day they rested. They made it a day to celebrate with great joy. And they enjoyed good food.

PURIM IS CELEBRATED

[18]But the Jews in Susa had gathered together on the 13th and 14th. Then on the 15th they rested. They made it a day to celebrate with great joy. And they enjoyed good food.

[19]That's why Jews who live out in the villages celebrate on the 14th of Adar. They celebrate that day with great joy. And they enjoy good food. They also give presents to each other on that day.

[20]Mordecai wrote down those events. He sent letters to all of the Jews all through the territories of King Xerxes. It didn't matter whether the Jews lived nearby or far away. [21]Mordecai told them to celebrate the 14th and 15th days of the month of Adar. He wanted them to do it every year.

²²Mordecai told the Jews to celebrate the time when they got rest from their enemies. That was the month when their sadness was turned into joy. It was when their sobbing turned into a day for celebrating. He wrote the letters to celebrate those days as times of joy. He wanted the people to enjoy good food. He told them to give presents of food to one another. He also wanted them to give gifts to those who were poor.

²³So the Jews agreed to continue the celebrating they had started. They kept doing what Mordecai had written to them.

²⁴Haman was the son of Hammedatha, the Agagite. He had been the enemy of all of the Jews. He had planned to destroy them. He had cast the lot to destroy them completely. The lot was also called *pur*. ²⁵But the king had found out about Haman's evil plan. So the king had sent out written orders. He had ordered that the evil plan Haman had made against the Jews should come back on his own head. He had also commanded that Haman and his sons should be put to death. Poles should be stuck through their dead bodies. Then they should be set up where everyone could see them.

²⁶The days the Jews were celebrating were called Purim. Purim comes from the word *pur*. *Pur* means "lot." Now the Jews celebrate those two days every year. They do it because of everything that was written in Mordecai's letter. They also do it because of what they had seen and what had happened to them.

²⁷So they established it as a regular practice. They decided they would always observe those two days of the year. They would celebrate in the required way. And they would celebrate at the appointed time. They and their children after them and everyone who joined them would always observe those days. ²⁸The days should be remembered and celebrated. They

should be remembered by every family for all time to come. They should be celebrated in every territory and in every city. The Jews should never stop celebrating the days of Purim. Their children after them should always remember those days.

²⁹So Queen Esther, the daughter of Abihail, wrote a second letter. She wrote it together with the Jew Mordecai. They wanted to give their full authority to this second letter about Purim. ³⁰Mordecai sent letters to all of the Jews in the 127 territories of the kingdom of Xerxes. The letters had messages of kindness and hope in them.

³¹The letters established the days of Purim at their appointed times. They spoke about what the Jew Mordecai and Queen Esther had ordered the people to do. Everything should be done in keeping with the directions the Jews had set up for themselves and their children after them. The directions applied to their times of fasting and sadness. ³²Esther's order established the rules about Purim. It was written down in the records.

THE GREATNESS OF MORDECAI

10 King Xerxes required people all through his kingdom to bring him gifts. He required gifts from its farthest shores. ²All of his powerful and mighty acts are written down. That includes the whole story of how important Mordecai was. The king had given him a position of great honor. All of those things are written in the official records of the kings of Media and Persia.

³The Jew Mordecai's position was second only to the position of King Xerxes. Mordecai was the most important Jew. All of the other Jews had the highest respect for him. That's because he worked for the good of his people. And he spoke up for the benefit of all of the Jews.

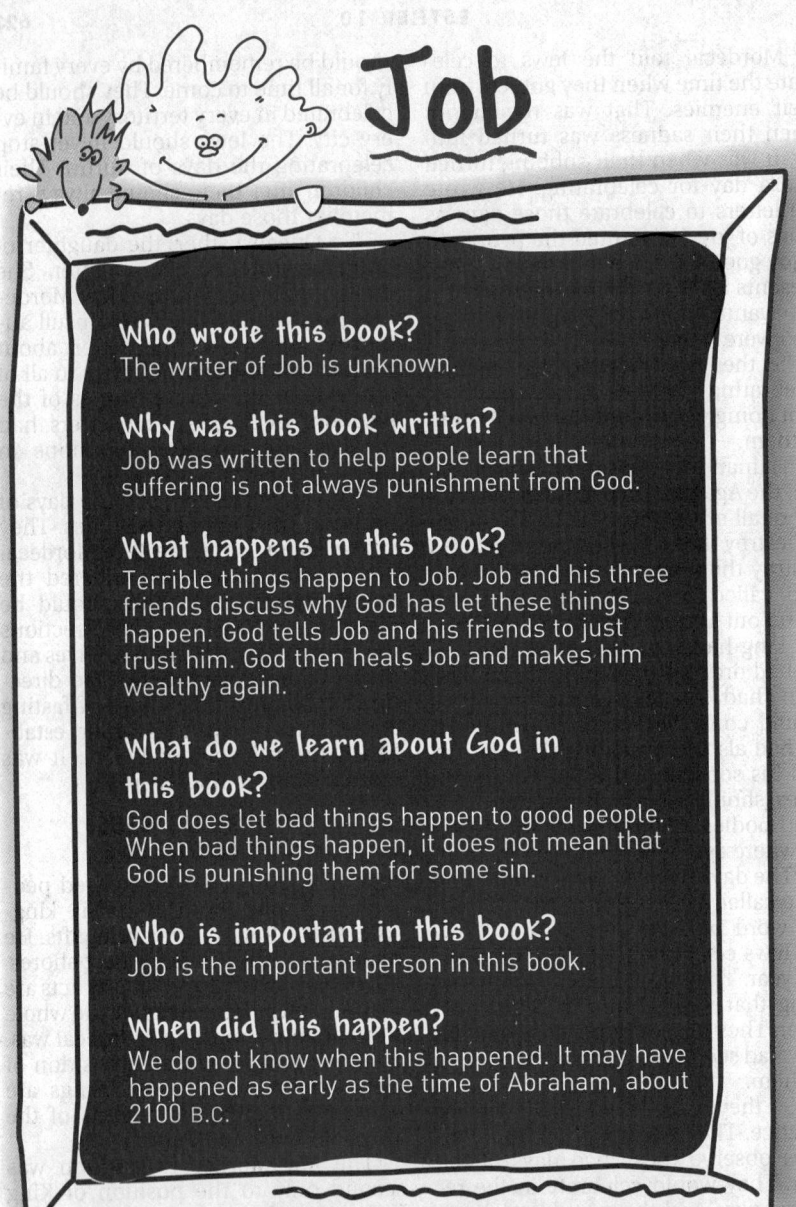

Job

Who wrote this book?
The writer of Job is unknown.

Why was this book written?
Job was written to help people learn that suffering is not always punishment from God.

What happens in this book?
Terrible things happen to Job. Job and his three friends discuss why God has let these things happen. God tells Job and his friends to just trust him. God then heals Job and makes him wealthy again.

What do we learn about God in this book?
God does let bad things happen to good people. When bad things happen, it does not mean that God is punishing them for some sin.

Who is important in this book?
Job is the important person in this book.

When did this happen?
We do not know when this happened. It may have happened as early as the time of Abraham, about 2100 B.C.

THE STORY BEGINS

1 There was a man who lived in the land of Uz. His name was Job. He was honest. He did what was right. He had respect for God and avoided evil.

²Job had seven sons and three daughters. ³He owned 7,000 sheep and 3,000 camels. He owned 500 pairs of oxen and 500 donkeys. He also had a large number of servants. He was the most important man among all of the people in the east.

⁴His sons used to take turns giving big dinners in their homes. They would invite their three sisters to eat and drink with them.

⁵When the time for enjoying good

food was over, Job would have his children made pure and clean. He would sacrifice a burnt offering for each of them. He would do it early in the morning. He would think, "Perhaps my children have sinned. Maybe they have spoken evil things against God in their hearts."

That's what Job always did for his children when he felt they had sinned.

JOB IS PUT TO THE TEST

⁶One day angels came to the LORD. Satan also came with them. ⁷The LORD said to Satan, "Where have you come from?"

Satan answered, "From traveling all around the earth. I've been going from one end of it to the other."

⁸Then the LORD said to Satan, "Have you thought about my servant Job? There isn't anyone on earth like him. He is honest. He does what is right. He has respect for me and avoids evil."

⁹"You always give Job everything he needs," Satan replied. "That's why he has respect for you. ¹⁰Haven't you guarded him and his family? Haven't you taken care of everything he has? You have blessed everything he does. His flocks and herds are spread all through the land.

¹¹"But reach out your hand and strike down everything he has. Then I'm sure he will speak evil things against you. In fact, he'll do it right in front of you."

¹²The LORD said to Satan, "All right. I am handing everything he has over to you. But do not touch the man himself."

Then Satan left the LORD and went on his way.

¹³One day Job's sons and daughters were at their oldest brother's house. They were enjoying good food and drinking wine.

¹⁴During that time a messenger came to Job. He said, "The oxen were plowing. The donkeys were eating grass near them. ¹⁵Then the Sabeans attacked us and carried the animals off. They killed some of the servants with their swords. I'm the only one who has escaped to tell you!"

¹⁶While he was still speaking, a second messenger came. He said, "God sent lightning from the sky. It struck the sheep and killed them. It burned up some of the servants. I'm the only one who has escaped to tell you!"

¹⁷While he was still speaking, a third messenger came. He said, "The Chaldeans separated themselves into three groups. They attacked your camels and carried them off. They killed the rest of the servants with their swords. I'm the only one who has escaped to tell you!"

¹⁸While he was still speaking, a fourth messenger came. He said, "Your sons and daughters were at their oldest brother's house. They were enjoying good food and drinking wine. ¹⁹Suddenly a strong wind blew in from the desert. It struck the four corners of the house. The house fell down on your children. Now all of them are dead. I'm the only one who has escaped to tell you!"

²⁰After Job heard all of those reports, he got up and tore his robe. He shaved his head. Then he fell to the ground and worshiped the LORD. ²¹He said,

"I was born naked.
  And I'll leave here naked.
You have given, and you have
    taken away.
  May your name be praised."

²²In spite of everything, Job didn't sin by blaming God for doing anything wrong.

JOB IS PUT TO THE TEST AGAIN

2 On another day angels came to the LORD. Satan also came to him along with them. ²The LORD said to Satan, "Where have you come from?"

Satan answered, "From traveling all around the earth. I've been going from one end of it to the other."

³Then the LORD said to Satan, "Have you thought about my servant Job? There isn't anyone on earth like him. He is honest. He does what is right. He has respect for me and avoids evil. You tried to turn me against him. You wanted me to destroy him without any reason. But he still continues to be faithful."

⁴Satan replied, "A man will give

everything he has to save himself. So Job is willing to give up the lives of his family to save his own life.

⁵"But reach out your hand and strike his flesh and bones. Then I'm sure he will speak evil things against you. In fact, he'll do it right in front of you."

⁶The LORD said to Satan, "All right. I am handing him over to you. But you must spare his life."

⁷Then Satan left the LORD and went on his way. He sent painful sores on Job. They covered him from the bottom of his feet to the top of his head. ⁸He got part of a broken pot. He used it to scrape his skin. He did it while he was sitting in ashes.

⁹His wife said to him, "Are you still continuing to be faithful to the LORD? Speak evil things against him and die!"

¹⁰Job replied, "You are talking like a foolish woman. We accept good things from God. So we should also accept trouble when he sends it."

In spite of everything, Job didn't say anything that was sinful.

JOB'S THREE FRIENDS COME TO COMFORT HIM

¹¹Job had three friends named Eliphaz the Temanite, Bildad the Shuhite, and Zophar the Naamathite. They heard about all of the troubles that had come to Job. So they started out from their homes. They had agreed to meet together. They wanted to go and show their concern for Job. They wanted to comfort him.

¹²When they got closer to where he lived, they could see him. But they could hardly recognize him. They began to sob out loud. They tore their robes and sprinkled dust on their heads.

¹³Then they sat down on the ground with him for seven days and seven nights. No one said a word to him. That's because they saw how much he was suffering.

JOB WISHES HE HAD NEVER BEEN BORN

3 After a while, Job opened his mouth to speak. He called down a curse on the day he had been born. ²He said,

³"May the day I was born be wiped out.
  May the night be wiped away
    when people said, 'A boy is
    born!'
⁴May that day turn into darkness.
  May God in heaven not care
    about it.
  May no light shine on it.
⁵May darkness and deep shadow
    take it back.
  May a cloud settle over it.
  May blackness cover up its light.
⁶May deep darkness take over the
    night I was born.
  May it not be included among
    the days of the year.
  May it never appear in any of the
    months.
⁷May no children ever have been
    born on that night.
  May no shout of joy be heard in
    it.
⁸May people call down a curse on
    that day.
  May those who are ready to wake
    up the sea monster Leviathan
    curse that day.
⁹May its morning stars become
    dark.
  May it lose all hope of ever
    seeing daylight.
  May it not see the first light of
    the morning sun.
¹⁰It didn't keep my mother from
    letting me be born.
  It didn't keep my eyes from
    seeing trouble.

¹¹"Why didn't I die when I was born?
  Why didn't I die as I came out of
    my mother's body?
¹²Why was I placed on her knees?
  Why did her breasts give me
    milk?
¹³If all of that hadn't happened,
  I would be lying down in peace.
  I'd be asleep and at rest in the
    grave.
¹⁴I'd be with the earth's kings and
    advisers.
  They had built for themselves
    places that are now destroyed.
¹⁵I'd be with rulers who used to have
    gold.
  They had filled their houses with
    silver.

16 Why wasn't I buried like a baby
　　who was born dead?
　　Why wasn't I buried like a child
　　who never saw the light of
　　day?
17 In the grave, sinful people don't
　　cause trouble anymore.
　　And there those who are tired
　　find rest.
18 Prisoners also enjoy peace there.
　　They don't hear a slave driver
　　shouting at them anymore.
19 The least important and most
　　important people are there.
　　And there the slaves are set free
　　from their owners.

20 "Why is the light that leads to life
　　given to those who suffer?
　　Why is it given to those whose
　　spirits are bitter?
21 Why is life given to those who long
　　for death that doesn't come?
　　Why is it given to those who
　　would rather search for death
　　than for hidden treasure?
22 Why is life given to those who are
　　actually happy and glad
　　when they reach the grave?
23 Why is life given to a man like me?
　　God hasn't told me what will
　　happen to me.
　　He has surrounded me with
　　nothing but trouble.
24 I sigh instead of eating food.
　　Groans pour out of me like water.
25 What I was afraid of has come on
　　me.
　　What I worried about has
　　happened to me.
26 I don't have any peace and quiet.
　　I can't find any rest. All I have is
　　trouble."

THE FIRST SPEECH
OF ELIPHAZ

4 Then Eliphaz the Temanite re-
　plied,

2 "Job, suppose someone tries to
　　talk to you.
　　Will that make you uneasy?
　　I can't keep from speaking up.
3 Look, you taught many people.
　　You made weak hands strong.
4 Your words helped those who had
　　fallen down.

　　You made shaky knees strong.
5 Now trouble comes to you. And
　　you are unhappy about it.
　　It strikes you down. And you are
　　afraid.
6 Shouldn't you worship God and
　　trust in him?
　　Shouldn't your honest life give
　　you hope?

7 "Here's something to think about.
　　Have blameless people ever been
　　wiped out?
　　Have honest people ever been
　　completely destroyed?
8 Here's what I've observed.
　　People gather a crop from what
　　they plant.
　　If they plant evil and trouble,
　　that's what they will harvest.
9 The breath of God destroys them.
　　The blast of his anger wipes
　　them out.
10 Powerful lions might roar and
　　growl.
　　But their teeth are broken.
11 Lions die because they don't have
　　any food.
　　Then their cubs are scattered.

12 "A message came to me in secret.
　　It was as quiet as a whisper.
13 I had a scary dream one night.
　　I was sound asleep.
14 Fear and trembling grabbed hold
　　of me.
　　That made every bone in my
　　body shake.
15 A spirit glided past my face.
　　The hair on my body stood on
　　end.
16 Then the spirit stopped.
　　But I couldn't tell what it was.
　　Something stood there in front of
　　me.
　　I heard a soft voice.
17 It said, 'Can a human being be
　　more right than God?
　　Can a mere man be more pure
　　than the One who made him?
18 God doesn't trust those who serve
　　him.
　　He even brings charges against
　　his angels.
19 So he'll certainly find fault with
　　human beings.
　　After all, they are made out of
　　dust.

They can be crushed more easily
　　than a moth.
²⁰ Between sunrise and sunset they
　　are broken to pieces.
　　Nobody even notices. They
　　disappear forever.
²¹ Like a tent that falls down, they get
　　weak.
　　They die because they didn't
　　follow God's wisdom.' "

5 Eliphaz continued,

"Call out if you want to, Job.
　　But who will answer you?
　　Which one of the holy angels will
　　you turn to?
² Anger kills foolish people.
　　Jealousy destroys those who are
　　childish.
³ I saw that foolish people were
　　having success.
　　But suddenly a curse came down
　　on their houses.

⁴ Their children aren't safe at all.
　　They lose their case in court.
　　No one speaks up for them.
⁵ Hungry people eat up the crops of
　　those who are foolish.
　　They even take the food that
　　grows among thorns.
　　Thirsty people long for the
　　wealth of the foolish.
⁶ Hard times don't just grow out of
　　the soil.
　　Trouble doesn't jump out of the
　　ground.
⁷ People are born to have trouble.
　　And that's just as sure as sparks
　　fly up.

⁸ "If I were you, I'd make my appeal
　　to God.
　　I'd bring my case to be judged by
　　him.
⁹ He does wonderful things that
　　can't be understood.

Do angels sin?

We do not know if angels can sin anymore. Satan was once an
angel who was thrown out of heaven because he wanted to take
God's place. And we know that some angels sinned in the past. But can other
angels sin now? We do not know. Eliphaz, Job's friend, pretended to know.
But later, God called Eliphaz a liar.

Human beings sin
because they have a deep
longing to sin. This has
been true ever since Adam
and Eve disobeyed God in
the Garden of Eden. Every
person ever born has been
born a sinner. Angels are
not like human beings in
that way. They do not have
a deep longing to sin. So it is
not natural for angels to
disobey God.

checkout Job 4:18

Related verses:
2 Peter 2:4;
Jude 6

JASON'S IMAGINATION

He does miracles that can't even
be counted.

¹⁰ He sends rain on the earth.
He sends water on the
countryside.

¹¹ He lifts up those who are lowly in
spirit.
He lifts up those who are sad.
He keeps them safe.

¹² He stops those who are tricky from
doing what they plan to do.
The work of their hands doesn't
succeed.

¹³ Some people think they are so
wise.
But God catches them in their
own tricks.
He sweeps away the evil plans of
sinful people.

¹⁴ Darkness covers them in the
daytime.
At noon they feel their way
around as if it were night.

¹⁵ God saves needy people from the
cutting words of their
enemies.
He saves them from their
powerful hands.

¹⁶ So those who are poor have hope.
And God shuts the mouths of
people who don't treat others
fairly.

¹⁷ "Blessed is the person God
corrects.
So don't hate the Mighty One's
training.

¹⁸ He wounds. But he also bandages
up those he wounds.
He harms. But his hands also
heal those he harms.

¹⁹ From six troubles he will save you.
Even if you are in trouble seven
times, no harm will come to
you.

²⁰ When there isn't enough food, God
will keep you from dying.
When you go into battle, he
won't let a sword strike you
down.

²¹ He will keep you safe from words
that can hurt you.
You won't need to be afraid
when everything is being
destroyed.

²² You will laugh when things are
being destroyed.

You will enjoy life even when
there isn't enough food.
You won't be afraid of wild
animals.

²³ You will make a covenant with the
stones in the fields.
They won't keep your crops from
growing.
Even wild animals will be at
peace with you.

²⁴ You will know that the tent you
live in is secure.
You will check out your
property.
You will see that nothing is
missing.

²⁵ You can be sure you will have a lot
of children.
They will be as many as the
blades of grass on the earth.

²⁶ You will go down to the grave
while you are still very strong.
You will be like a crop that is
gathered at the right time.

²⁷ "We have carefully studied all of
those things.
And they are true.
So pay attention to them.
Apply them to yourself."

JOB'S REPLY

6 Job replied,

² "I wish my great pain could be
weighed!
I wish all of my suffering could
be weighed on scales!

³ I'm sure they would weigh more
than the grains of sand on the
seashore.
No wonder I've been so quick to
speak!

⁴ The Mighty One has shot me with
his arrows.
I have to drink their poison.
God's terrors are aimed at me.

⁵ Does a wild donkey cry out when
it has enough grass?
Does an ox call out when it has
plenty of food?

⁶ Is food that doesn't have any taste
eaten without salt?
Is there any flavor in the white of
an egg?

⁷ I refuse to touch that kind of food.
It makes me sick.

8 "I wish I could have what I'm
    asking for!
  I wish God would give me what
    I'm hoping for!
9 I wish he would crush me!
  I wish his powerful hand would
    cut off my life!
10 Then I'd still have one thing to
    comfort me.
  It would be that I haven't said no
    to the Holy One's commands.
  That would give me joy in spite
    of my pain that never ends.

11 "I'm so weak that I no longer have
    any hope.
  Things have gotten so bad that I
    can't wait for help anymore.
12 Am I as strong as stone?
  Is my body made out of bronze?
13 I don't have the power to help
    myself.
  All hope of success has been
    taken away from me.

14 "A man's friends should love him
    when his hope is gone.
  They should be faithful to him
    even if he stops showing respect
    for the Mighty One.
15 But my friends aren't faithful to
    me.
  They are like streams that only
    flow for part of the year.
  They are like rivers that flow over
    their banks
16 when the ice begins to break up.
  The streams rise when the snow
    starts to melt.
17 But they stop flowing when the
    dry season comes.
  They disappear from their
    stream beds when the
    weather warms up.
18 Groups of traders turn away from
    their usual paths.
  They go up into the dry and
    empty land.
  And they die there.
19 Traders from Tema look for water.
  Traveling merchants from Sheba
    also hope to find it.
20 They become troubled because
    they had expected to find
    some.
  But when they arrive at the
    stream beds,
  they don't find any water at all.

21 And now, my friends, you haven't
    helped me either.
  You see the horrible condition
    I'm in.
  And that makes you afraid.
22 I've never said, 'Give me
    something to help me.
  Use your wealth to set me free.
23 Save me from the powerful hand
    of my enemy.
  Set me free from the power of
    mean people.'

24 "Teach me. Then I'll be quiet.
  Show me what I've done wrong.
25 Honest words are so painful!
  But your reasoning doesn't prove
    anything.
26 Are you trying to correct what I'm
    saying?
  You are treating the words of this
    hopeless man
  like nothing but wind.
27 You would even cast lots for those
    whose fathers have died.
  You would even trade away your
    closest friend.

28 "But now please look at me.
  Would I tell you a lie right here in
    front of you?
29 Stop what you are saying. Don't be
    so unfair.
  Think it over again.
  You are trying to take my honesty
    away from me.
30 Has my mouth spoken anything
    that is evil?
  Do my lips say things that are
    hateful?"

7 Job continued,

  "Doesn't every man have to
    work hard on this earth?
  Aren't his days like the days of a
    hired worker?
2 I've been like a slave
  who longs for the evening
    shadows to come.
  I've been like a hired worker
  who can hardly wait to get paid.
3 I've been given several months
    that were useless to me.
  My nights have been filled with
    suffering.
4 When I lie down I think,
  'How long will it be before I can
    get up?'

The night drags on.
I toss and turn until sunrise.
⁵ My body is covered with worms
     and sores.
   My skin is broken. It has boils all
     over it.

⁶ "My days pass by faster than a
     weaver can work.
   They come to an end. I don't
     have any hope.
⁷ God, remember that my life is only
     a breath.
   I'll never be happy again.
⁸ The eyes that see me now won't
     see me anymore.
   You will look for me. But I'll be
     gone.
⁹ When a cloud disappears, it's gone
     forever.
   And anyone who goes down to
     the grave never returns.
¹⁰ He never comes home again.
   Even his own family doesn't
     remember him.

¹¹ "So I won't keep quiet.
   When I'm suffering greatly, I'll
     speak out.
   When my spirit is bitter, I'll tell
     you how unhappy I am.
¹² Am I the ocean? Am I the sea
     monster?
   If I'm not, why do you guard me
     so closely?
¹³ Sometimes I think my bed will
     comfort me.
   I think my couch will keep me
     from being unhappy.
¹⁴ But even then you send me
     dreams that frighten me.
   You send me visions that terrify
     me.
¹⁵ So I would rather choke to
     death.
   That would be better than living
     in this body of mine.
¹⁶ I hate my life. I don't want to live
     forever.
   Leave me alone. My days don't
     mean anything to me.

¹⁷ "What are human beings that you
     think so much of them?
   What are they that you pay so
     much attention to them?
¹⁸ You check up on them every
     morning.

You put them to the test every
     moment.
¹⁹ Won't you ever look away from me?
   Won't you leave me alone even
     for one second?
²⁰ If I've really sinned, tell me what
     I've done to you.
   Why do you watch people so
     closely?
   Why do you shoot your arrows at
     me?
   Have I become a problem to you?
²¹ Why don't you forgive the wrong
     things I've done?
   Why don't you forgive me for my
     sins?
   I'll soon lie down in the dust of my
     grave.
   You will search for me. But I'll be
     gone."

THE FIRST SPEECH OF BILDAD

8 Then Bildad the Shuhite re-
     plied,

² "Job, how long will you talk like
     that?
   Your words don't have any
     meaning.
³ Does God ever treat people unfairly?
   Does the Mighty One make what
     is wrong
   appear to be right?
⁴ Your children sinned against him.
   So he punished them for their sin.
⁵ But look to God.
   Make your appeal to the Mighty
     One.
⁶ Be pure and honest.
   And he will rise up and help you
     now.
   He'll return you to the place
     where you belong.
⁷ In the past, things went well with
     you.
   But in days to come, things will
     get even better.

⁸ "Find out what your people who
     lived long ago taught.
   Discover what those who lived
     before them learned.
⁹ After all, we were born only
     yesterday.
   So we don't know anything.
   Our days on this earth are like a
     shadow that disappears.

¹⁰Won't your people of long ago
    teach you and tell you?
  Won't the things they said help
    you understand?
¹¹Can grass grow tall where there
    isn't any swamp?
  Can plants grow well where there
    isn't any water?
¹²While they are still growing and
    haven't been cut,
  they dry up faster than grass does.
¹³The same thing happens to
    everyone who forgets God.
  The hope of ungodly people dies
    out.
¹⁴What they trust in is very weak.
  What they depend on is like a
    spider's web.
¹⁵A person leans on it, but it falls
    apart.
  He holds on to it, but it gives
    way.
¹⁶He is like a plant in the sunshine
    that receives plenty of water.
  It spreads its new growth all over
    the garden.
¹⁷It wraps its roots around a pile of
    rocks.
  It tries to find places to grow
    among the stones.
¹⁸But when a plant is pulled up from
    its spot,
  that place says, 'I never saw you.'
¹⁹The life of that plant is sure to dry
    up.
  But from the same soil other
    plants will grow.

²⁰"I'm sure God doesn't turn his
    back on anyone who is honest.
  And he doesn't help those who
    do what is evil.
²¹He will fill your mouth with
    laughter.
  Shouts of joy will come from
    your lips.
²²Your enemies will put on shame as
    if it were clothes.
  The tents of sinful people will be
    gone."

JOB'S REPLY

9 Job replied,
²"I'm sure that what you have
    said is true.
  But how can human beings be
    right with God?

³They might wish to argue with
    him.
  But they couldn't answer him
    even once in a thousand times.
⁴His wisdom is deep. His power is
    great.
  No one opposes him and comes
    away unharmed.
⁵He moves mountains, and they
    don't even know it.
  When he is angry, he turns them
    upside down.
⁶He shakes the earth loose from its
    place.
  He makes its pillars tremble.
⁷When he tells the sun not to shine,
    it doesn't.
  He turns off the light of the stars.
⁸He's the only one who can spread
    the heavens out.
  He alone can walk on the waves
    of the ocean.
⁹He made the Big Dipper and Orion.
  He created the Pleiades and the
    southern stars.
¹⁰He does wonderful things that
    can't be understood.
  He does miracles that can't even
    be counted.
¹¹When he passes by me, I can't see
    him.
  When he goes past me, I can't
    recognize him.
¹²If he takes something, who can
    stop him?
  Who would dare to ask him,
    'What are you doing?'
¹³God doesn't hold back his anger.
  Even the helpers of the sea
    monster Rahab
  bowed in fear at his feet.

¹⁴"So how can I disagree with God?
  How can I possibly argue with
    him?
¹⁵Even if I hadn't done anything
    wrong,
  I couldn't answer him.
  I could only beg my Judge to
    have mercy on me.
¹⁶Suppose I called out to him and he
    answered.
  I don't believe he'd listen to me.
¹⁷He would send a storm to crush
    me.
  He'd increase my wounds
    without any reason.

¹⁸ He wouldn't let me catch my
  breath.
  He'd make my life very bitter.
¹⁹ If it's a matter of strength, he is
  mighty!
  And if it's a matter of being fair,
  who would dare to bring charges
  against him?
²⁰ Even if I hadn't sinned, what I said
  would prove me guilty.
  Even if I were honest, my words
  would show that I'm wrong.

²¹ "Even though I'm honest,
  I'm not concerned about myself.
  I hate my own life.
²² It all amounts to the same thing.
  That's why I say,
  'God destroys honest people and
  sinful people alike.'
²³ Suppose a plague brings sudden
  death.
  Then he laughs when those who
  haven't sinned lose hope.
²⁴ Suppose a nation falls into the
  power of sinful people.
  Then God makes its judges blind
  to the truth.
  If he isn't the one doing it, who is?

²⁵ "God, my days race by like a
  runner.
  They fly away without seeing any
  joy.
²⁶ They speed along like papyrus
  boats.
  They are like eagles swooping
  down on their food.
²⁷ Suppose I say, 'I'll forget about all
  of my problems.
  I'll change my frown into a
  smile.'
²⁸ Then I'd still be afraid I'd go on
  suffering.
  That's because I know you would
  say
  I had done something wrong.
²⁹ In fact, you have already said I'm
  guilty.
  So why should I struggle without
  any reason?
³⁰ Suppose I clean myself with soap.
  Suppose I wash my hands with
  cleanser.
³¹ Even then you would throw me
  into a muddy pit.
  And even my clothes would hate
  me.

³² "God isn't a man like me. I can't
  answer him.
  We can't take each other to court.
³³ I wish someone would settle
  matters between us.
  I wish someone would force us to
  work things out.
³⁴ I wish someone would keep God
  from punishing me.
  Then his terror wouldn't frighten
  me anymore.
³⁵ I would speak up without being
  afraid of him.
  But as things stand now, I can't
  do that.

10

"I'm sick of living.
  So I'll talk openly about
  my problems.
I'll speak out because my spirit is
  bitter.
² I'll say to God, 'Don't find me
  guilty.
  Instead, tell me what charges
  you are bringing against me.
³ Does it make you happy when you
  crush me?
  Does it please you to turn your
  back on what you have made?
  While you do those things,
  you smile on the plans of sinful
  people!
⁴ You don't have human eyes.
  You don't see as people see.
⁵ Your days aren't like the days of a
  human being.
  Your years aren't like the years of
  a mere man.
⁶ So you search for my mistakes.
  You look for my sin.
⁷ You already know I'm not guilty.
  No one can save me from your
  powerful hand.

⁸ " 'Your hands shaped me and
  made me.
  So are you going to destroy me
  now?
⁹ Remember, you molded me like
  clay.
  So are you going to turn me back
  into dust?
¹⁰ Didn't you pour me out like milk?
  Didn't you form me like cheese?
¹¹ Didn't you put skin and flesh on
  me?
  Didn't you sew me together with
  bones and muscles?

¹²You gave me life. You were kind to
    me.
  You took good care of me. You
    watched over me.
¹³ " 'But here's what you hid in your
    heart.
  Here's what you had on your
    mind.
¹⁴If I sinned, you would be watching
    me.
  You wouldn't let me go without
    punishing me.
¹⁵If I were guilty, how terrible that
    would be for me!
  Even if I haven't sinned,
  I can't be proud of what I've done.
  That's because I'm so full of
    shame.
  I'm drowning in my suffering.
¹⁶If I become proud, you hunt me
    down like a lion.
  You show your mighty power
    against me.
¹⁷You bring new witnesses against
    me.
  You become more and more
    angry with me.
  You use your power against me
    again and again.

¹⁸ " 'Why did you bring me out of my
    mother's body?
  I wish I had died before anyone
    saw me.
¹⁹I wish I'd never been born!
  I wish I'd been carried straight
    from my mother's body to the
    grave!
²⁰Aren't my few days almost over?
  Leave me so I can have a
    moment of joy.
²¹Turn away before I go to the place
    I can't return from.
  It's the land of darkness and deep
    shadow.
²²It's the land of darkest night
  and deep shadow and disorder.
  There even the light is like
    darkness.' "

THE FIRST SPEECH
OF ZOPHAR

11 Then Zophar the Naama-
    thite replied,

²"Don't all of your words require an
    answer?

I'm sure that what you are saying
    can't be right.
³Your useless talk won't keep us
    quiet.
  Someone has to correct you
    when you make fun of truth.
⁴You say to God, 'My beliefs are
    perfect.
  I'm pure in your sight.'
⁵I wish God would speak.
  I wish he'd answer you.
⁶I wish he'd show you the secrets of
    wisdom.
  After all, true wisdom has two
    sides.
  Here's what I want you to know.
  God has forgotten some of your
    sins.

⁷"Do you know how deep the
    mysteries of God are?
  Can you discover the limits of the
    Mighty One's knowledge?
⁸They are higher than the
    heavens.
  What can you do?
  They are deeper than the deepest
    grave.
  What can you know?
⁹They are longer than the earth.
  They are wider than the ocean.

¹⁰"Suppose God comes along and
    puts you in prison.
  Suppose he takes you to court.
  Then who can oppose him?
¹¹He certainly knows when people
    tell lies.
  When he sees evil, he pays
    careful attention to it.
¹²A wild donkey's colt can't be born
    a human being.
  And a man who doesn't have any
    sense can't become wise.

¹³"So commit yourself to God
    completely.
  Reach out your hands to him for
    help.
¹⁴Get rid of all of the sin you have.
  Don't let anything that is evil stay
    in your tent.
¹⁵Then you can face others without
    feeling any shame.
  You can stand firm without being
    afraid.
¹⁶You can be sure you will forget
    your troubles.

They will be like water that has
flowed on by.
¹⁷Life will be brighter than the sun
at noon.
And darkness will become like
morning.
¹⁸You will be secure, because there
is hope.
You will look around you and
find a safe place to rest.
¹⁹You will lie down, and no one will
make you afraid.
Many people will want you to
show them your favor.
²⁰But sinful people won't find what
they are looking for.
They won't be able to escape.
All they can hope for is to die."

JOB'S REPLY

12 Job replied,
²"You people think you
know everything,
don't you?
You are sure that wisdom will die
with you!
³But I have a brain, just like you.
I'm as clever as you are.
In fact, everyone knows as much
as you do.

⁴"My friends laugh at me all the
time,
even though I called out to God
and he answered.
My friends laugh at me,
even though I'm honest and
right.
⁵People who have an easy life look
down on those who have
problems.
They think trouble comes only to
those whose feet are slipping.
⁶Why doesn't anyone bother the
tents of robbers?
Why do those who make God
angry remain secure?
They carry the statues of their
gods in their hands!

⁷"But ask the animals what God
does.
They will teach you.
Or ask the birds of the air.
They will tell you.
⁸Or speak to the earth. It will teach
you.

Or let the fish of the ocean
educate you.
⁹Are there any of those creatures
that don't know
what the powerful hand of the
LORD has done?
¹⁰He holds the life of every creature
in his hand.
He controls the breath of every
human being.
¹¹Our tongues tell us what tastes
good and what doesn't.
And our ears tell us what's true
and what isn't.
¹²Old people are wise.
Those who live a long time have
understanding.

¹³"Wisdom and power belong to God.
Advice and understanding also
belong to him.
¹⁴What he tears down can't be
rebuilt.
Any man he puts in prison can't
be set free.
¹⁵If he holds back the water,
everything dries up.
If he lets the water loose, it floods
the land.
¹⁶Strength and success belong to
him.
Those who tell lies and those
who believe them also belong
to him.
¹⁷He removes the wisdom of
advisers and leads them away.
He makes judges look foolish.
¹⁸He sets people free from the
chains that kings put on them.
Then he dresses the kings in the
clothes of slaves.
¹⁹He removes the authority of
priests and leads them away.
He removes from their positions
those who have been in control
for a long time.
²⁰He shuts the mouths of trusted
advisers.
He takes away the understanding
of elders.
²¹He looks down on proud leaders.
He takes away the strength of
those who are mighty.
²²He tells people the secrets of
darkness.
He brings evil plans out into the
light.

²³ He makes nations great, and then
    he destroys them.
He makes nations grow, and then
    he scatters them.
²⁴ He takes away the understanding
    of the leaders of the earth.
He makes them wander in a
    desert where no one lives.
²⁵ Without any light, they feel their
    way along in darkness.
God makes them unsteady like
    those who get drunk.

13 "My eyes have seen
    everything God has
    done.
    My ears have heard it and
      understood it.
² What you know, I also know.
    I'm as clever as you are.
³ In fact, I long to speak to the
    Mighty One.
I want to argue my case with
    God.
⁴ But you spread lies about me and
    take away my good name.
If you are trying to heal me,
    you aren't very good doctors!
⁵ I wish you would keep your
    mouths shut!
Then people would think you
    were wise.
⁶ Listen to my case.
    Listen as I make my appeal.
⁷ Will you say evil things in order to
    help God?
Will you tell lies for him?
⁸ Do you want to be on God's side?
    Will you argue his case for him?
⁹ Would it turn out well if he looked
    you over carefully?
Could you fool him as you fool
    others?
¹⁰ He would certainly correct you
    if you took his side in secret.
¹¹ Wouldn't his glory terrify you?
    Wouldn't the fear of him fall on
    you?
¹² Your sayings are as useless as
    ashes.
The answers you give are as weak
    as clay.
¹³ "So be quiet and let me speak.
    Then I won't care what happens
    to me.
¹⁴ Why do I put myself in danger?
    Why do I take my life in my hands?

¹⁵ Even if God kills me, I'll still put
    my hope in him.
I'll argue my case in front of him.
¹⁶ No matter how things turn out,
    I'm sure I'll still be saved.
After all, no ungodly person
    would dare to come into his court.
¹⁷ Listen carefully to what I'm saying.
    Pay close attention to my words.
¹⁸ I've prepared my case.
    And I know I'll be proved right.
¹⁹ Can others bring charges against
    me?
If they can, I'll keep quiet and
    die.

²⁰ "God, I won't hide from you.
    Here are the only two things I
    want.
²¹ Keep your powerful hand far away
    from me.
And stop making me so afraid.
²² Then send for me, and I'll answer.
    Or let me speak, and you reply.
²³ How many things have I done
    wrong?
How many sins have I
    committed?
Show me my crime. Show me my
    sin.
²⁴ Why do you turn your face away
    from me?
Why do you think of me as your
    enemy?
²⁵ I'm already like a leaf that is blown
    by the wind.
Are you going to terrify me even
    more?
I'm already like dry straw.
Are you going to keep on chasing
    me?
²⁶ You write down bitter things
    against me.
You make me suffer for the sins
    I committed when I was young.
²⁷ You put my feet in chains.
    You watch every step I take.
You do it by putting marks on the
    bottom of my feet.

²⁸ "People waste away like
    something that is rotten.
They are like clothes that are
    eaten by moths.

14 "They have only a few
    days to live.
    Their lives are full of
    trouble.

²They grow like flowers, and then
  they dry up.
  They are like shadows that
  quickly disappear.

³"God, why do you keep looking at
  someone like me?
  Are you planning to take me to
  court?
⁴Who can bring what is pure from
  something that isn't pure?
  No one!
⁵You decide how long anyone will
  live.
  You have established the number
  of his months.
  You have set a limit to the
  number of his days.
⁶So look away from him. Leave him
  alone.
  Let him put in his time like a
  hired worker.

⁷"At least there is hope for a tree.
  If it's cut down, it will begin to
  grow again.
  New branches will appear on it.
⁸Its roots may grow old in the
  ground.
  Its stump may die in the soil.
⁹But when it smells water, it will
  begin to grow.
  It will send out new growth like a
  plant.
¹⁰No man is like that. When he dies,
  he is buried in a grave.
  He takes his last breath. Then he
  is gone.
¹¹Water disappears from lakes.
  Riverbeds become empty and
  dry.
¹²In the same way, a man lies down
  and never gets up.
  He won't wake up or rise from his
  sleep
  until the heavens are gone.

¹³"I wish you would hide me in a
  grave!
  I wish you would cover me up
  until your anger passes by!
  I wish you would set the time for
  me to spend in the grave
  and then bring me back up!
¹⁴If a man dies, will he live again?
  All the days of my hard work
  I will wait for the time when you
  give me new life.

¹⁵You will call out to me, and I will
  answer you.
  Your hands created me. So you
  will long for me.
¹⁶Then you will count every step I
  take.
  But you won't keep track of my
  sin.
¹⁷The wrong things I've done will be
  sealed up in a bag.
  You will wipe out my sins by
  forgiving them.

¹⁸"A mountain wears away and
  crumbles.
  A rock is moved from its place.
¹⁹Water wears stones away.
  Storms wash soil away.
  In the same way, you destroy our
  hope.
²⁰You overpower us completely, and
  then we're gone.
  You change the way we look and
  send us to our graves.
²¹If our children are honored, we
  don't even know it.
  If they are dishonored, we don't
  even see it.
²²All we feel is the pain of our own
  bodies.
  We are full of sadness only for
  ourselves."

THE SECOND SPEECH OF ELIPHAZ

15

Then Eliphaz the Temanite
replied,

²"Job, if you were wise,
  would you answer us with a lot of
  meaningless talk?
  Would you fill your stomach with
  the hot east wind?
³Would you argue with useless
  words?
  Would you give worthless
  speeches?
⁴But you even cause others to lose
  their respect for God.
  You make it hard for them to be
  faithful to him.
⁵Your sin makes you say evil things.
  You talk like people who twist the
  truth.
⁶Your own mouth judges you, not
  mine.
  Your own lips witness against you.

7 "Are you the first man who was
　　ever born?
　　Were you created before the
　　　hills?
8 Do you listen in when God speaks
　　with his angels?
　　Do you think you are the only
　　　wise person?
9 What do you know that we don't
　　know?
　　What understanding do you have
　　　that we don't have?
10 People who are old and gray are
　　on our side.
　　And they are even older than
　　　your parents!
11 Aren't God's words of comfort
　　enough for you?
　　He speaks them to you gently.
12 Why have you let your wild ideas
　　carry you away?
　　Why do your eyes flash with
　　　anger?
13 Why do you get so angry with God?
　　Why do words like those pour
　　　out of your mouth?

14 "Can human beings really be pure?
　　Can mere men really be right
　　　with God?
15 God doesn't trust his holy angels.
　　Even the heavens aren't pure in
　　　his sight.
16 So he'll certainly find fault with
　　human beings.
　　After all, they are evil and sinful.
　　They drink up evil as if it were
　　　water.

17 "Listen to me. I'll explain things to
　　you.
　　Let me tell you what I've seen.
18 I'll tell you what those who are
　　wise have said.
　　They don't hide anything they've
　　　received
　　from their people of long ago.
19 The land was given only to those
　　people.
　　Their wisdom didn't come from
　　　outsiders.
　　And here's what those who are
　　　wise have said.
20 Sinful people always suffer pain.
　　Mean people suffer all their lives.
21 Terrifying sounds fill their ears.
　　When everything seems to be
　　　going well,

robbers attack them.
22 They lose all hope of escaping the
　　darkness of death.
　　They will certainly be killed with
　　　swords.
23 They wander around. They are like
　　food for vultures.
　　They know that the day they will
　　　die is near.
24 Suffering and pain terrify them.
　　Their troubles overpower them,
　　like a king ready to attack his
　　　enemies.
25 They shake their fists at God.
　　They brag about themselves and
　　　oppose the Mighty One.
26 They boldly charge against him
　　with their thick, strong shields.

27 "Their faces are very fat.
　　Their stomachs hang out.
28 They'll live in towns that have
　　been destroyed.
　　They'll live in houses where no
　　　one else lives.
　　The houses will crumble to
　　　pieces.
29 They won't be rich anymore. Their
　　wealth won't last.
　　Their property will no longer
　　　spread out over the land.
30 They won't escape the darkness of
　　death.
　　A flame will dry up everything
　　　they have.
　　The breath of God will blow
　　　them away.
31 Don't let them fool themselves
　　by trusting in what is worthless.
　　They won't get anything out of it.
32 Even before they die, they'll be
　　paid back in full.
　　No matter what they do, it won't
　　　succeed.
33 They'll be like vines
　　that are stripped of their unripe
　　　grapes.
　　They'll be like olive trees
　　that drop their flowers.
34 People who are ungodly won't
　　have any children.
　　Fire will burn up the tents of
　　　people who accept money
　　from those who want special
　　　favors.
35 Instead of having children,
　　ungodly people create suffering.

All they produce is evil.
They are full of lies."

JOB'S REPLY

16
Job replied,

2 "I've heard many of those
things before.
You are terrible at comforting me!
3 Your speeches go on forever.
Won't they ever end?
What's wrong with you?
Why do you keep on arguing?
4 If you and I changed places,
I could say the same things you
are saying.
I could make fine speeches against
you.
I could shake my head at you.
5 But what I might say would give
you hope.
My words of comfort would help
you.

6 "If I speak, it doesn't help me.
And if I keep quiet, my pain
doesn't go away.
7 God has worn me out completely.
He has destroyed my whole
family.
8 People can see the condition he
has put me in.
My thin body stands as a witness
against me.
9 God is angry with me.
He attacks me and tears me up.
He grinds his teeth at me.
He stares at me as if he were my
enemy.
10 People make fun of me.
They slap my face and laugh at
me.
All of them join together against
me.
11 God has turned me over to sinful
people.
He has handed me over to them.
12 Everything was going well with
me.
But he broke me into pieces like
a clay pot.
He grabbed me by the neck and
crushed me.
He has taken aim at me.
13 He shoots his arrows at me from
all sides.
Without pity, he stabs me in the
kidneys.

He spills my insides on the
ground.
14 He smashes through me as if I
were a wall.
He rushes at me like a fighting
man.

15 "I've sewed black cloth over my
skin.
All I can do is sit here in the dust.
16 My face is red from crying.
I have deep circles under my
eyes.
17 But I haven't harmed anyone.
My prayers to God are pure.

18 "Earth, please don't cover up my
blood!
May God always hear my cry for
help!
19 Even now my witness is in heaven.
The one who speaks up for me is
there.
20 My go-between is my friend
as I pour out my tears to God.
21 He makes his appeal to God to
help me
as a man begs someone to help
his friend.

22 "Only a few years will pass by.
Then I'll go on a journey I won't
return from.

17
1 My strength is almost
gone.
I won't live much longer.
A grave is waiting for me.
2 People who make fun of me are all
around me.
I'm forced to watch as they
attack me with their words.

3 "God, please pay the price to have
me set free.
Who else would put up money
for me?
4 You have closed the minds of
those who are trying to
comfort me.
They don't understand that I
haven't done anything wrong.
So don't let them win the
argument.
5 Suppose a man tells lies about his
friends to get a reward.
Then his own children will suffer
for it.

6 "God has made everyone laugh at
　　me.
　People spit in my face.
7 My eyes have grown weak because
　　I'm so sad.
　My body is so thin it hardly casts
　　a shadow.
8 Those who claim to be honest
　are shocked when they see me.
Those who think they haven't
　　sinned
　are stirred up against me.
　They think I'm ungodly.
9 But godly people will keep doing
　　what is right.
　Those who have clean hands will
　　grow stronger.

10 "Come on, all of you! Try again!
　I can't find a wise person among
　　you.
11 My life is almost over. My plans are
　　destroyed.
　And so are the longings of my
　　heart.
12 People like you turn night into day.
　Even though it's dark you say,
　　'Light is nearby.'
13 Suppose the only home I can hope
　　for is a grave.
　And suppose I make my bed in
　　the darkness of death.
14 Suppose I say to the grave,
　　'You are like a father to me.'
　And suppose I say to its worms,
　　'You are like a mother or sister to
　　me.'
15 Then what hope do I have?
　Who can give me any hope?
16 Will hope go down to the gates of
　　death with me?
　Will we go down together into
　　the dust of the grave?"

THE SECOND SPEECH
OF BILDAD

18 Then Bildad the Shuhite
replied,

2 "Job, when will you stop these
　　speeches of yours?
　Be reasonable! Then we can talk.
3 Why do you look at us as if we
　　were cattle?
　Why do you think of us as being
　　stupid?
4 Your anger is tearing you to pieces.

Does the earth have to be
　deserted just to prove you are
　right?
Must all of the rocks be moved
　from their places?

5 "The lamps of sinful people are
　blown out.
　Their flames will never burn
　again.
6 The lights in their tents become
　dark.
　The lamps beside those who are
　evil go out.
7 They walk more slowly than they
　used to.
　Their own evil plans make them
　fall.
8 Their feet take them into a net.
　They wander right into it.
9 A trap grabs hold of their heels.
　It refuses to let them go.
10 A trap lies in their path.
　A rope to catch them is hidden
　on the ground.
11 Terrors alarm them on every side.
　They follow them every step of
　the way.
12 Trouble would like to eat them up.
　Danger waits for them when they
　fall.
13 It eats away parts of their skin.
　Death itself feeds on their arms
　and legs.
14 They are torn away from the safety
　of their tents.
　They are marched off to the one
　who rules over death.
15 Fire races through their tents.
　Burning sulfur is scattered over
　their homes.
16 Their roots dry up under them.
　Their branches dry up above
　them.
17 No one on earth remembers them.
　Their names are forgotten in the
　land.
18 They are driven from light into
　darkness.
　They are thrown out of the
　world.
19 Their family dies out among their
　people.
　No one is left where they used to
　live.
20 What has happened to them
　shocks the people in the west.

It terrifies the people in the east.
²¹ Now you know what the homes of
sinners are like.
Those who don't know God live
in places like that."

JOB'S REPLY

19

Job replied,

² "How long will you
people make me
suffer?
How long will you crush me with
your words?
³ You have already made fun of me
many times.
You have attacked me without
feeling any shame.
⁴ Suppose it's true that I've gone
down the wrong path.
Then it's my concern, not yours.
⁵ Suppose you want to place
yourselves above me.
Suppose you want to use my
shame to prove I'm wrong.
⁶ Then I want you to know that God
hasn't treated me right.
In fact, he has captured me in his
net.

⁷ "I cry out, 'Someone harmed me!'
But I don't get any reply.
I call out for help.
But I'm not treated fairly.
⁸ God has blocked my way, and I
can't get through.
He has made my paths so dark I
can't see where I'm going.
⁹ He has taken my wealth away from
me.
He has stripped me of my honor.
¹⁰ He tears me down on every side
until I'm gone.
He pulls up the roots of my hope
as if I were a tree.
¹¹ His anger burns against me.
He thinks I'm one of his enemies.
¹² His troops march toward me in
force.
They come at me from every
direction.
They camp around my tent.

¹³ "God has caused my brothers to
desert me.
The people I used to know are
now strangers to me.
¹⁴ My family has gone away.

My friends have forgotten me.
¹⁵ My guests and my female servants
think of me as a stranger.
They look at me as if I were an
outsider.
¹⁶ I send for my servant, but he
doesn't answer.
He doesn't come, even though I
beg him to.
¹⁷ My wife can't stand the way my
breath smells.
My own relatives won't have
anything to do with me.
¹⁸ Even little children laugh at me.
When I appear, they make fun of
me.
¹⁹ All of my close friends hate me.
Those I love have turned against
me.
²⁰ I'm nothing but skin and bones.
I've only escaped by the skin of
my teeth.

²¹ "Have pity on me, my friends!
Please have pity!
God has struck me down with his
powerful hand.
²² Why do you chase after me as he
does?
Aren't you satisfied with what
you have done to me
already?

²³ "I wish my words were written
down!
I wish they were written on a
scroll!
²⁴ I wish they were cut into lead with
an iron tool!
I wish they were carved in rock
forever!
²⁵ I know that my Redeemer lives.
In the end he will stand on the
earth.
²⁶ After my skin has been destroyed,
in my body I'll still see God.
²⁷ I myself will see him with my own
eyes.
I'll see him, and he won't be a
stranger to me.
How my heart longs for that day!

²⁸ "You might say, 'Let's keep
bothering Job.
After all, he's the cause of all of
his suffering.'
²⁹ But you should be afraid when
God comes to judge you.

He'll be angry. He'll punish you
with his sword.
Then you will know that he is the
Judge."

THE SECOND SPEECH
OF ZOPHAR

20 Then Zophar the Naamathite replied,

2 "My troubled thoughts force me to
answer you.
That's because I'm very upset.
3 What you have just said makes fun
of me.
So I really have to reply to you.

4 "I'm sure you must know how
things have always been.
They've been that way
ever since man was placed on
this earth.
5 Those who are evil are happy for
only a short time.
The joy of ungodly people lasts
only for a moment.
6 Their pride might reach all the
way up to the heavens.
Their heads might touch the
clouds.
7 But they will disappear forever,
like the waste from their own
bodies.
Anyone who has seen them will
say,
'Where did they go?'
8 Like a dream they will fly away.
They will never be seen again.
They will be driven away like
visions in the night.
9 The eyes that saw them won't see
them anymore.
Even their own families won't
remember them.
10 Their children must pay back what
they took from poor people.
Their own hands must give back
the wealth they stole.
11 They might feel young and very
strong.
But they will soon lie down in the
dust of their graves.

12 "Anything that is evil tastes sweet
to them.
They keep it under their tongues
for a while.

13 They can't stand to let it go.
So they hold it in their mouths.
14 But their food will turn sour in
their stomachs.
It will become like the poison of
a serpent inside them.
15 They will spit out the rich food
they swallowed.
God will make their stomachs
throw it up.
16 They will suck the poison of a
serpent.
The fangs of an adder will kill
them.
17 They won't enjoy streams that flow
with honey.
They won't enjoy rivers that flow
with cream.
18 What they worked for they must
give back
before they can eat it.
They won't enjoy what they have
earned.
19 They've crushed poor people and
left them with nothing.
They've taken over houses they
didn't even build.

20 "No matter how much they have,
they always long for more.
But their treasure can't save
them.
21 There isn't anything left for them
to eat up.
Their success won't last.
22 While they are enjoying the good
life,
trouble will catch up with them.
Terrible suffering will come on
them.
23 When they've filled their
stomachs,
God will pour out his burning
anger on them.
He'll strike them down with blow
after blow.
24 They might run away from iron
weapons.
But arrows that have bronze tips
will wound them.
25 They will pull the arrows out of
their backs.
They will remove the shining tips
from their livers.
They will be filled with terror.
26   Total darkness hides and waits
for their treasures.

God will send a fire that will
  destroy them.
It will burn up everything that's
  left in their tents.
[27] Heaven will show their guilt to
  everyone.
The earth will be a witness
  against them.
[28] A flood will carry their houses
  away.
Rushing water will wash them
  away
on the day when God judges.
[29] Now you know what God will do to
  sinful people.
Now you know what he has
  planned for them."

JOB'S REPLY

21 Job replied,
[2] "Listen carefully to what
  I'm saying.
Let that be the comfort you
  people give me.
[3] Put up with me while I speak.
After I've spoken, you can make
  fun of me!

[4] "I'm not arguing with mere human
  beings.
So why shouldn't I be angry and
  uneasy?
[5] Look at me and be amazed.
Put your hand over your mouth
  and stop talking!
[6] When I think about these things,
  I'm terrified.
My whole body trembles.
[7] Why do sinful people keep on
  living?
The older they grow, the richer
  they get.
[8] They see their children grow up
  around them.
They watch their family increase
  in number.
[9] Their homes are safe.
They don't have to be afraid.
God isn't punishing them.
[10] Every time their bulls mate, their
  cows become pregnant.
And the calves don't die before
  they are born.
[11] Sinful people send their children
  out like a flock of lambs.
Their little ones dance
  around.

[12] They sing to the music of
  tambourines and harps.
They have a good time while
  flutes are being played.
[13] Those who are evil spend their
  years living well.
They go down to their graves in
  peace.
[14] But they say to God, 'Leave us
  alone!
We don't want to know how you
  want us to live.
[15] Who is the Mighty One? Why
  should we serve him?
What would we get if we prayed
  to him?'
[16] But they aren't in control of their
  own success.
So I don't pay any attention to
  the advice they give.

[17] "How often are their lamps blown
  out?
How often does trouble come on
  them?
How often does God punish
  them when he's angry?
[18] How often are they like dried-up
  seed coverings blowing in the
  wind?
How often are they like straw
  swept away by a storm?
[19] People say, 'God punishes a man's
  children for his sins.'
But let him punish the man
  himself.
Then he'll learn a lesson from it.
[20] Let his own eyes see how he is
  destroyed.
Let him drink the wine of the
  Mighty One's anger.
[21] What does he care about the
  family he leaves behind?
What does he care about them
  when his life comes to an end?

[22] "Can anyone teach God
  anything?
After all, he judges even the
  angels in heaven.
[23] Some people die while they are
  still very strong.
They are completely secure. They
  have an easy life.
[24] They are well fed.
Their bodies are healthy.
[25] Others die while their spirits are
  bitter.

They've never enjoyed anything
good.
26 Side by side they lie in the dust of
death.
The worms in their graves cover
all of them.

27 "I know exactly what you people
are thinking.
I know you are planning to do
bad things to me.
28 You are saying to yourselves,
'Where is the great man's house
now?
Where are the tents where his
evil family lived?'
29 Haven't you ever asked questions
of those who travel?
Haven't you paid any attention to
their stories?
30 They'll tell you that sinful people
are spared from the day of
trouble.
They'll say that those people
are saved from the day when God
will judge.
31 Who speaks against them for the
way they act?
Who pays them back for what
they've done?
32 Their bodies will be carried to
their graves.
Guards will watch over their
tombs.
33 The soil in the valley will be
pleasant
to those who have died.
Many people will walk along
behind their bodies.
Many others will walk in front of
them.

34 "So how can you comfort me with
your speeches?
They don't make any sense at all.
Your answers are nothing but
lies!"

THE THIRD SPEECH
OF ELIPHAZ

22 Then Eliphaz the Temanite
replied,

2 "Can any man be of benefit to
God?
Can even a wise man be of any
help to him?

3 Job, what pleasure would it give
the Mighty One if you were
right?
What would he get if you were
completely honest?

4 "You say you have respect for
him.
Is that why he corrects you?
Is that why he brings charges
against you?
5 Haven't you done many evil
things?
Don't you sin again and again?
6 You took clothes away from your
relatives
just because they owed you some
money.
You left them naked for no
reason at all.
7 You didn't give any water to people
who were tired.
You held food back from those
who were hungry.
8 You did it even though you were
honored and powerful.
You owned land and lived on it.
9 But you sent widows away without
anything.
You mistreated children whose
fathers had died.
10 That's why traps have been set all
around you.
That's why sudden danger
terrifies you.
11 That's why it's so dark you can't
even see.
That's why a flood covers you up.

12 "Isn't God in the highest parts of
heaven?
See how high the highest stars
are!
13 But you still say, 'What does God
know?
Can he see through the darkest
clouds to judge us?
14 He goes around in the highest
heavens.
Thick clouds keep him from
seeing us.'
15 Will you stay on the old path
that sinful people have walked
on?
16 They were carried off even before
they died.
Their foundations were washed
away by a flood.

¹⁷They said to God, 'Leave us alone!
What can you do to us, you
Mighty One?'
¹⁸But he was the one who filled their
houses with good things.
So I don't pay any attention to
the advice they give.

¹⁹"Those who do what is right are
joyful
when they see sinners
destroyed.
Those who haven't done
anything wrong make fun of
them.
²⁰They say, 'Our enemies are
completely destroyed.
Fire has burned up their
wealth.'

²¹"Job, obey God and be at peace
with him.
Then he will help you succeed.
²²Do what he teaches you to do.
Keep his words in your heart.
²³If you return to the Mighty One,
you will have what you had
before.
But first you must remove
everything that is evil far from
your tent.
²⁴You must throw your gold nuggets
away.
You must toss your gold from
Ophir into a valley.
²⁵Then the Mighty One himself will
be your gold.
He'll be like the finest silver to
you.
²⁶You will find delight in the Mighty
One.
You will honor God and trust in
him.
²⁷You will pray to him, and he will
hear you.
You will keep the promises you
made to him.
²⁸What you decide to do will be
done.
Light will shine on the path you
take.
²⁹When people are brought low you
will say, 'Lift them up!'
Then God will help them.
³⁰He'll even save those who are
guilty.
He'll save them because your
hands are clean."

JOB'S REPLY

23

Job replied,
²"Even today my problems
are more than I can
handle.
In spite of my groans, God's hand
is heavy on me.
³I wish I knew where I could find
him!
I wish I could go to the place
where he lives!
⁴I would state my case to him.
I'd give him all of my arguments.
⁵I'd find out what his answers
would be.
I'd think about what he would
say.
⁶Would he oppose me with his
great power?
No. He wouldn't bring charges
against me.
⁷I'm an honest person. I could state
my case to him.
Then my Judge would tell me
once and for all that I'm not
guilty.

⁸"But if I go to the east, God isn't
there.
If I go to the west, I don't find
him.
⁹When he's working in the north, I
don't see him there.
When he turns to the south, I
don't see him there either.
¹⁰But he knows every step I take.
When he has put me to the test,
I'll come out as pure as gold.
¹¹My feet have closely followed his
steps.
I've stayed on his path without
turning away.
¹²I haven't disobeyed his
commands.
I've treasured his words more
than my daily bread.

¹³"But he's the only God. Who can
oppose him?
He does anything he wants to do.
¹⁴He carries out his plans against
me.
And he still has many other plans
just like them.
¹⁵That's why I'm so terrified.
When I think about all of this,
I'm afraid of him.

16 God has made my heart weak.
   The Mighty One has filled me
      with terror.
17 But even the darkness of death
      won't make me silent.
   When the darkness of the grave
      covers my face, I won't be
      quiet.

24

"Why doesn't the Mighty
One set a time for
judging sinful
people?
Why do those who know him
      have to keep waiting for that
      day?
2 People move their neighbor's
      boundary stones.
   They steal their neighbor's flocks.
3 They take away the donkeys
      that belong to children whose
      fathers have died.
   They take a widow's ox until she
      has paid what she owes.
4 They push those who are needy
      out of their way.
   They force all of the poor people
      in the land to go into hiding.
5 The poor are like wild donkeys in
      the desert.
   They have to go around looking
      for food.
   The dry and empty land provides
      the only food for their
      children.
6 The poor go to the fields and get a
      little grain.
   They gather up what is left in the
      vineyards of sinners.
7 The poor don't have any clothes.
   So they spend the night
      naked.
   They don't have anything to
      cover themselves in the cold.
8 They are soaked by mountain
      rains.
   They hug the rocks because they
      don't have anything to keep
      them warm.
9 Children whose fathers have died
      are torn away from their
      mothers.
   A poor person's baby is taken
      away to pay back what is
      owed.
10 The poor don't have any clothes.
   They go around naked.

They carry bundles of grain, but
      they still go hungry.
11 They work very hard as they crush
      olives.
   They stomp on grapes in
      winepresses,
   but they are still thirsty.
12 The groans of those who are dying
      are heard from the city.
   Those who are wounded cry out
      for help.
   But God doesn't charge anyone
      with doing what is wrong.

13 "Some people hate it when
      daylight comes.
   In the daytime they never walk
      outside.
14 When daylight is gone, murderers
      get up.
   They kill poor people and those
      who are in need.
   In the night they sneak around
      like robbers.
15 Those who commit adultery wait
      until the sun goes down.
   They think, 'No one will see us.'
   They keep their faces hidden.
16 In the dark, people break into
      houses.
   But by day they shut themselves
      in.
   They don't want anything to do
      with the light.
17 The deepest darkness is like
      morning to them.
   The terrors of darkness are their
      friends.

18 "But sinners are like bubbles on
      the surface of water.
   Their share of the land is under
      God's curse.
   So no one goes to their
      vineyards.
19 Melted snow disappears when the
      air is hot and dry.
   And sinners disappear when they
      go down into their graves.
20 Even their mothers forget them.
   The worms in their graves eat
      them up.
   No one remembers sinful people
      anymore.
   They are cut down like trees.
21 They mistreat women who aren't
      able to have children.
   They aren't kind to widows.

22 But God is powerful.
He even drags away people who
are strong.
When he rises up against them,
they can never be sure they are
safe.
23 God might let them rest and feel
secure.
But his eyes see how they live.
24 For a little while they are honored.
Then they are gone.
They are brought low.
And they die like everyone else.
They are cut off like heads of
grain.
25 "Who can prove that what I'm
saying is wrong?
Who can prove that my words
aren't true?"

THE THIRD SPEECH OF BILDAD

25 Then Bildad the Shuhite
replied,

2 "God is King. He should be feared.
He establishes peace in the
highest parts of heaven.
3 Can anyone count his troops?
Is there anyone his light doesn't
shine on?
4 How can human beings be right
with God?
How can mere people really be
pure?
5 Even the moon isn't bright
and the stars aren't pure in God's
eyes.
6 So how about human beings? They
are like maggots.
How about mere people? They
are like worms."

JOB'S REPLY

26 Job replied,

2 "Bildad, you haven't
helped people who
aren't strong!
You haven't saved people who
are weak!
3 You haven't offered advice to those
who aren't wise!
In fact, you haven't understood
anything at all!
4 Who helped you say those things?

Whose spirit was speaking
through you?
5 "The spirits of the dead are
suffering greatly.
So are those that are under the
waters.
And so are all those that live in
them.
6 Death is naked in the sight of
God.
The Grave lies open in front of
him.
7 He spreads out the northern skies
over empty space.
He hangs the earth over nothing.
8 He wraps up water in his clouds.
They are heavy, but they don't
burst.
9 He covers the face of the full
moon.
He spreads his clouds over it.
10 He marks out the place where the
sky meets the sea.
He marks out the boundary
between light and darkness.
11 The pillars of the heavens shake.
They are terrified when his anger
blazes out.
12 With his power he stirred up the
oceans.
In his wisdom he cut the sea
monster Rahab to pieces.
13 His breath made the skies bright
and clear.
His hand wounded the serpent
that glides through the sea.
14 Those are only on the edges of
what he does.
They are only the soft whispers
that we hear from him.
So who can understand how very
powerful he is?"

27 Job continued to speak. He
said,

2 "God hasn't treated me fairly.
The Mighty One has made my
spirit bitter.
You can be sure that God lives.
And here's something else you
can be sure of.
3 As long as I have life
and God gives me breath,
4 my mouth won't say evil things.
My lips won't tell lies.

5 I'll never admit you people are
right.
Until I die, I'll say I'm telling the
truth.
6 I'll continue to say I'm right.
I'll never let go of that.
I won't blame myself as long as I
live.

7 "May my enemies suffer like sinful
people!
May my attackers be punished
like those who aren't fair!
8 What hope do ungodly people
have when their lives are cut
off?
What hope do they have when
God takes away their lives?
9 God won't listen to their cry
when trouble comes on them.
10 They won't take delight in the
Mighty One.
They'll never call out to God.

11 "I'll teach all of you about God's
power.
I won't hide the things the
Mighty One does.
12 You have seen those things
yourselves.
So why do you continue your
useless talk?

13 "Here's what God does to sinful
people.
Here's what those who are mean
receive from the Mighty One.
14 All of their children will be killed
with swords.
They'll never have enough to eat.
15 A plague will kill those who are left
alive.
The widows of sinful men
won't even sob over their own
children.
16 Sinners might store up silver like
dust
and clothes like piles of clay.
17 But people who do what is right
will wear those clothes.
People who haven't done
anything wrong
will divide up that silver.
18 The house an evil person builds is
like a moth's cocoon.
It's like a hut that's made by
someone on guard duty.

19 Sinful people lie down wealthy,
but their wealth is taken away.
When they open their eyes,
everything is gone.
20 Terrors sweep over them like a
flood.
A storm takes them away during
the night.
21 The east wind carries them off,
and they are gone.
It sweeps them out of their
houses.
22 It blows against them without
mercy.
They try to escape from its power.
23 It claps its hands and makes fun of
them.
It hisses them out of their
houses.

28

"There are mines where
silver is found.
There are places where
gold is purified.
2 Iron is taken out of the earth.
Copper is melted down from ore.
3 A miner lights up the darkness.
He searches for ore in the
deepest pits.
He looks for it in the blackest
darkness.
4 Far from where people live he cuts
a tunnel.
He does it in places where others
don't go.
Far away from people he swings
back and forth on ropes.
5 Food grows on the surface of the
earth.
But far below, the earth is
changed as if by fire.
6 Sapphires are taken from its rocks.
Its dust contains nuggets of gold.
7 No bird knows the miner's hidden
path.
No falcon's eye has seen it.
8 Proud animals don't walk on it.
Lions don't prowl there.
9 The miner attacks the hardest rock.
His strong hands uncover the
base of the mountains.
10 He tunnels through the rock.
His eyes see all of its treasures.
11 He searches the places where the
rivers begin.
He brings hidden things out into
the light.

12 "And where can wisdom be found?
   Where does understanding live?
13 No one knows how much it's
      worth.
   It can't be found anywhere in the
      world.
14 The ocean says, 'It's not in me.'
   The sea says, 'It's not here either.'
15 It can't be bought with the finest
      gold.
   Its price can't be weighed out in
      silver.
16 It can't be bought with gold from
      Ophir.
   It can't be bought with priceless
      onyx or sapphires.
17 Gold or crystal can't compare with
      it.
   It can't be bought with jewels
      made of gold.
18 Don't bother to talk about coral
      and jasper.
   Wisdom is worth far more than
      rubies.
19 A topaz from Cush can't compare
      with it.
   It can't be bought with the purest
      gold.

20 "So where does wisdom come
      from?
   Where does understanding live?
21 It's hidden from the eyes of every
      living thing.
   Even the birds of the air can't
      find it.
22 Death and the Grave say,
   'Only reports about it have
      reached our ears.'
23 But God understands the way to it.
   He's the only one who knows
      where it lives.
24 He sees from one end of the earth
      to the other.
   He views everything in the world.
25 He made the mighty wind.
   He measured out the waters.
26 He gave orders for the rain to fall.
   He made paths for the
      thunderstorms.
27 Then he looked at wisdom and set
      its price.
   He established it and put it to the
      test.
28 He said to human beings,
   'Have respect for me. That will
      prove you are wise.

Avoid evil. That will show you
   have understanding.' "

29

Job continued to speak. He
said,

2 "How I long for the good old days!
   That's when God watched over
      me.
3 The light of his lamp shone on me.
   I walked through darkness by his
      light.
4 Those were the best days of my
      life.
   That's when God's friendship
      blessed my house.
5 The Mighty One was still with me.
   My children were all around me.
6 The path in front of me was like
      sweet cream.
   It was as if the rock poured out
      olive oil for me.

7 "In those days I went to the city
      gate.
   I took my seat as a member of
      the council.
8 Young people who saw me
      stepped to one side.
   Old people stood up as I
      approached.
9 The leaders stopped speaking.
   They covered their mouths with
      their hands.
10 The voices of the nobles became
      quiet.
   Their tongues stuck to the roofs
      of their mouths.
11 Everyone who heard me said good
      things about me.
   Those who saw me honored me.
12 That's because I saved poor people
      who cried out for help.
   I saved helpless children whose
      fathers had died.
13 Those who were dying gave me
      their blessing.
   I made the hearts of widows sing.
14 I put on a godly life as if it were my
      clothes.
   Fairness was my robe and my
      turban.
15 I was like eyes for those who were
      blind.
   I was like feet for those who
      couldn't walk.
16 I was like a father to needy people.

I stood up for strangers in court.
¹⁷ Sinners are like animals that have
powerful teeth.
But I took from their mouths the
people they had caught.

¹⁸ "I thought, 'I'll die in my own
house.
The days of my life will be as
many as the grains of sand.
¹⁹ My roots will reach down to the
water.
The dew will lie all night on my
branches.
²⁰ I will remain healthy and strong.
My bow will stay as good as new
in my hand.'

²¹ "People wanted to hear what I had
to say.
They waited silently for the
advice I gave them.
²² After I had spoken, they didn't
speak anymore.
My words fell gently on their
ears.
²³ They waited for me just as they
would wait for showers.
They drank my words just as they
would drink the spring rain.
²⁴ When I smiled at them, they could
hardly believe it.
The light of my face lifted their
spirits.
²⁵ I chose the way they should go. I
sat as their chief.
I lived as a king lives among his
troops.
I was like someone who comforts
those who are sad.

30

"But now those who are
younger than I am
make fun of me.
I wouldn't put even their parents
with my sheep dogs!
² Their strong hands couldn't give
me any help.
That's because their strength was
gone.
³ They were weak because they were
needy and hungry.
They wandered through dry and
empty deserts at night.
⁴ Among the bushes they gathered
salty plants.
They ate the roots of desert
trees.

⁵ They were driven away from
society.
They were shouted at as if they
were robbers.
⁶ They were forced to live in dry
stream beds.
They had to stay among rocks
and in holes in the ground.
⁷ Like donkeys they cried out
among the bushes.
There they crowded together and
hid.
⁸ They were so foolish that no one
respected them.
They were driven out of the land.

⁹ "Now their children laugh at me.
They make fun of me with their
songs.
¹⁰ They hate me. They stay away
from me.
They even dare to spit in my face.
¹¹ God has made my body weak.
It's like a tent that has fallen
down.
So those children do what they
want to in front of me.
¹² Many people attack me on my
right side.
They lay traps for my feet.
They come at me from every
direction.
¹³ They tear up the road I walk on.
They succeed in destroying me.
They do it without any help.
¹⁴ They attack me like troops
smashing through a wall.
Among the destroyed buildings
they come rolling in.
¹⁵ Terrors sweep over me.
My honor is driven away as if by
the wind.
My safety vanishes like a cloud.

¹⁶ "Now my life is slipping away.
Days of suffering grab hold of
me.
¹⁷ At night my bones hurt.
My gnawing pains never stop.
¹⁸ God's great power becomes like
clothes to me.
He chokes me like the neck of my
shirt.
¹⁹ He throws me down into the mud.
I'm nothing but dust and ashes.

²⁰ "God, I cry out to you. But you
don't answer me.

I stand up. But all you do is look
at me.
²¹ You do mean things to me.
Your mighty hand attacks me.
²² You pick me up and blow me away
with the wind.
You toss me around in the storm.
²³ I know that you will bring me
down to death.
That's what you have appointed
for everyone.
²⁴ "No one would crush people
when they cry out for help in
their trouble.
²⁵ Haven't I sobbed over those who
are in trouble?
Haven't I felt sorry for poor
people?
²⁶ I hoped good things would
happen, but something evil
came.
I looked for light, but all I saw
was darkness.
²⁷ My insides are always churning.
Nothing but days of suffering are
ahead of me.
²⁸ My skin has become dark, but the
sun didn't do it.
I stand up in the community and
cry out for help.
²⁹ I've become a brother to wild dogs.
Owls are my companions.
³⁰ My skin grows black and peels.
My body burns with fever.
³¹ My harp is tuned to sadness.
My flute makes a sound like
sobbing.

31 "I made an agreement with
my eyes.
I promised not to look at
another woman with
sexual longing.
² What do human beings receive
from God above?
What do they get from the
Mighty One in heaven?
³ Sinful people are destroyed.
Trouble comes to those who do
what is wrong.
⁴ Doesn't God see how I live?
Doesn't he count every step I
take?

⁵ "I haven't told any lies.
My feet haven't hurried to cheat
others.

⁶ So let God weigh me in honest
scales.
Then he'll know I haven't done
anything wrong.
⁷ Suppose my steps have turned
away from the right path.
Suppose my heart has longed for
what my eyes have seen.
Or suppose my hands have
become 'unclean.'
⁸ Then may others eat what I've
planted.
May my crops be pulled up by
the roots.

⁹ "Suppose my heart has been
tempted by a woman.
Or suppose I've prowled around
my neighbor's door.
¹⁰ Then may my wife grind another
man's grain.
May other men have sex with
her.
¹¹ Wanting another woman would
have been a shameful thing.
It would have been a sin that
should be judged.
¹² It's like a fire that burns down to
the grave.
It would have caused my crops to
be pulled up by the roots.

¹³ "Suppose I haven't treated my
male and female servants
fairly
when they've brought charges
against me.
¹⁴ Then what will I do when God
opposes me?
What answer will I give him
when he asks me to explain
myself?
¹⁵ Didn't he who made me make my
servants also?
Didn't the same God form us
inside our mothers?

¹⁶ "I haven't said no to what poor
people have wanted.
I haven't let widows lose their
hope.
¹⁷ I haven't kept my bread to myself.
I've shared it with children
whose fathers had died.
¹⁸ From the time I was young, I've
helped those widows.
I've raised those children as a
father would.

¹⁹Suppose I've seen people dying
because they didn't have any
clothes.
I've seen needy people
who had nothing to wear.
²⁰And they didn't give me their
blessing
when I warmed them with wool
from my sheep.
²¹Suppose I've raised my hand
against children whose fathers
have died.
And I did it because I knew
I had power in the courts.
²²Then let my arm fall from my
shoulder.
Let it be broken off at the joint.
²³I was afraid God would destroy
me.
His glory terrifies me.
So I'd never do things like that.

²⁴"Suppose I've put my trust in gold.
I've said to pure gold, 'You make
me feel secure.'
²⁵And I'm happy because I'm so
wealthy.
I'm glad because my hands have
earned so much.
²⁶Suppose I've worshiped the sun in
all of its glory.
I've bowed down to the moon in
all of its beauty.
²⁷My heart has been secretly
tempted.
My hand has thrown kisses to the
sun and moon.
²⁸Then those things would have
been sins that should be
judged.
And I wouldn't have been faithful
to God in heaven.

²⁹"I wasn't happy when hard times
came to my enemies.
I didn't enjoy seeing the trouble
they had.
³⁰I didn't allow my mouth to sin
by calling down curses on them.
³¹The workers in my house always
said,
'Job always gives plenty of food
to everyone.'
³²No stranger ever had to spend the
night in the street.
My door was always open to
travelers.
³³I didn't hide my sin as others do.

I didn't hide my guilt in my heart.
³⁴I was never afraid of the crowd.
I never worried that my relatives
might hate me.
I didn't have to keep quiet or stay
inside.

³⁵"I wish someone would listen to
me!
I'm signing my name to
everything I've said.
I hope the Mighty One will give
me his answer.
I hope the one who brings
charges against me will write
them down.
³⁶I'll wear them on my shoulder.
I'll put them on my head like a
crown.
³⁷I'll give that person a report of
every step I take.
I'll approach him like a prince.

³⁸"Suppose my land cries out
against me.
And all of its soil is wet with
tears.
³⁹Suppose I've used up its crops
without paying for them.
Or I've broken the spirit of its
renters.
⁴⁰Then let thorns grow instead of
wheat.
Let weeds come up instead of
barley."

The words of Job end here.

THE SPEECH OF ELIHU

32 So the three men stopped
answering Job, because he
thought he was right.
²But Elihu the Buzite burned with
anger against Job. That's because Job
said he himself was right instead of
God. Elihu was the son of Barakel. He
was from the family of Ram.

³Elihu's anger also burned against
Job's three friends. They hadn't found
any way to prove that Job was wrong.
But they still said he was guilty.

⁴Elihu had waited before he spoke to
Job. That's because the others were
older than he was. ⁵But he saw that the
three men didn't have anything more
to say. So he burned with anger.

⁶Elihu the Buzite, the son of Barakel,
said,

"I'm young, and you are old.
So I was afraid to tell you what I
know.
⁷ I thought, 'Those who are older
should speak first.
Those who have lived for many
years
should teach people how to be
wise.'
⁸ But the spirit in people gives them
understanding.
The breath of the Mighty One
gives them wisdom.
⁹ Older people aren't the only ones
who are wise.
They aren't the only ones who
understand what is right.

¹⁰ "So I'm saying you should listen to
me.
I'll tell you what I know.
¹¹ I waited while you men spoke.
I listened to your reasoning.
While you were searching for
words,
¹² I paid careful attention to you.
But not one of you has proved that
Job is wrong.
None of you has answered his
arguments.
¹³ Don't claim, 'We have enough
wisdom to answer Job.'
Let God, not a mere man, prove
that he's wrong.
¹⁴ Job hasn't directed his words
against me.
I won't answer him with your
arguments.

¹⁵ "Job, those men are afraid.
They don't have anything else to
say.
They've run out of words.
¹⁶ Do I have to keep on waiting, now
that they are silent?
They are just standing there with
nothing to say.
¹⁷ I too have something to say.
I too will tell what I know.
¹⁸ I'm full of words.
My spirit inside me forces me to
speak.
¹⁹ Inside I'm like wine that is bottled
up.
I'm like new wineskins ready to
burst.
²⁰ I must speak so I can feel better.
I must open my mouth and reply.

²¹ I'll treat everyone the same.
I won't praise anyone without
meaning it.
²² If I weren't honest when I praised
people,
my Maker would soon take me
from this life.

33

"Job, listen now to my
words.
Pay attention to
everything I say.
² I'm about to open my mouth.
My words are on the tip of my
tongue.
³ What I say comes from an honest
heart.
My lips speak only what I know is
true.
⁴ The Spirit of God has made me.
The breath of the Mighty One
gives me life.
⁵ So answer me if you can.
Prepare yourself to face me.
⁶ In God's sight I'm just like you.
I too have been made out of clay.
⁷ You don't have to be afraid of me.
My hand won't be too heavy on
you.

⁸ "But I heard what you said.
And here are the exact words I
heard.
⁹ You said, 'I'm pure. I haven't
sinned in the ways you have
charged.
I'm clean. I'm not guilty of doing
anything wrong.
¹⁰ But God has found fault with me.
He thinks I'm his enemy.
¹¹ He puts my feet in chains.
He watches every step I take.'

¹² "But I'm telling you that you aren't
right when you talk like that.
After all, God is greater than a
mere man.
¹³ Why do you claim that God
never answers any of our
questions?
¹⁴ He speaks in one way and then
another.
We might not even realize it.
¹⁵ He might speak in a dream or in a
vision at night.
That's when people are sound
asleep in their beds.
¹⁶ He might speak in their ears.

His warnings might terrify them.

17 He warns men in order to turn
   them away from sinning.
   He wants to keep them from
   being proud.

18 He wants to stop them from going
   down into the grave.
   He doesn't want them to be killed
   with swords.

19 Someone might be punished by
   suffering in bed.
   The pain in his bones might
   never go away.

20 He might feel so bad he can't eat
   anything.
   He might even hate the finest
   food.

21 His body might waste away to
   nothing.
   His bones might have been
   hidden.
   But now they stick out.

22 He might approach the very edge
   of the grave.
   The messengers of death might
   come for him.

23 "But suppose there is an angel
   who will speak up for him.
   The angel is very special. He's
   one out of a thousand.
   He will tell that person what is
   right for him.

24 He'll be gracious to him. He'll say
   to God,
   'Spare him from going down into
   the grave.
   I know a way that can set him free.'

25 Then his body is made like new
   again.
   He becomes as strong and
   healthy as when he was
   young.

26 He prays to God and finds favor
   with him.
   He sees God's face and shouts
   with joy.
   God makes him right with
   himself again.

27 Then the person comes to others
   and says,
   'I sinned. I made what was wrong
   appear to be right.
   But I wasn't punished as I should
   have been.

28 God set me free. He kept me from
   going down into the grave.

So I'll live to enjoy the light that
   leads to life.'

29 "God does all of those things to
   people.
   In fact, he does them again and
   again.

30 He wants to stop people from
   going down into the grave.
   Then the light that leads to life
   will shine on them.

31 "Pay attention, Job! Listen to me!
   Be quiet so I can speak.

32 If you have anything to say, answer
   me.
   Speak up. I want to help you be
   cleared of all charges.

33 But if you don't have anything to
   say, listen to me.
   Be quiet so I can teach you how
   to be wise."

34

Elihu continued,

2 "Hear what I'm saying,
   you wise men.
   Listen to me, you who have
   learned so much.

3 Our tongues tell us what tastes
   good and what doesn't.
   And our ears tell us what's true
   and what isn't.

4 So let's choose for ourselves what
   is right.
   Let's learn together what is
   good.

5 "Job says, 'I'm not guilty of doing
   anything wrong.
   But God doesn't treat me fairly.

6 Even though I'm right,
   he thinks I'm a liar.
   Even though I'm not guilty,
   his arrows give me wounds that
   can't be healed.'

7 Is there any other man like Job?
   He laughs at God and makes fun
   of him.

8 He's a companion of those who do
   evil.
   He spends his time with sinful
   people.

9 He asks, 'What good is it
   to try to please God?'

10 "So listen to me, you men who
   have understanding.
   God would never do what is evil.

The Mighty One would never do
   what is wrong.
¹¹ He pays a man back for what he's
   done.
   He gives him exactly what he
      should get.
¹² It isn't possible for God to do
   wrong.
   The Mighty One would never
      treat people unfairly.
¹³ Who appointed him to rule over
   the earth?
   Who put him in charge of the
      whole world?
¹⁴ If he really wanted to,
   he could hold back his spirit and
      breath.
¹⁵ Then everyone would die together.
   They would return to the dust.

¹⁶ "Job, if you have understanding,
   listen to me.
   Pay attention to what I'm saying.
¹⁷ Can someone who hates to be fair
   govern?
   Will you bring charges against
      the holy and mighty One?
¹⁸ He says to kings, 'You are
   worthless.'
   He says to nobles, 'You are evil.'
¹⁹ He doesn't favor princes.
   He treats rich people and poor
      people the same.
   His hands created all of them.
²⁰ They die suddenly in the middle of
   the night.
   God strikes them down, and they
      pass away.
   Those who are mighty are
      removed, but not by human
      hands.

²¹ "His eyes see how people live.
   He watches every step they
      take.
²² There isn't a dark place or deep
   shadow
   where those who do what is evil
      can hide.
²³ God doesn't need to bring charges
   against men.
   He knows they are guilty.
   So he doesn't need to have them
      appear in his court to be
      judged.
²⁴ He destroys the mighty without
   asking them questions in
   court.

Then he sets others up in their
   places.
²⁵ He knows what they do.
   So he crushes them during the
      night.
²⁶ He punishes them for the sins they
   commit.
   He does it where everyone can
      see them.
²⁷ That's because they turned away
   from following him.
   They didn't have respect for
      anything he does.
²⁸ They caused poor people to cry
   out to him.
   He heard the cries of those who
      were in need.
²⁹ But if he remains silent, who can
   judge him?
   If he turns his face away, who
      can see him?
   He rules over people and nations
      alike.
³⁰   He keeps those who are ungodly
      from ruling.
   He keeps them from laying traps
      for others.

³¹ "Someone might say to God,
   'I'm guilty of sinning,
   but I won't do it anymore.
³² Show me my sins that I'm not
   aware of.
   If I've done what is wrong,
   I won't do it again.'
³³ But you refuse to turn away from
   your sins.
   So God won't treat you the way
      you want to be treated.
   You must decide, Job. I can't do it
      for you.
   So tell me what you know.

³⁴ "You men who have
   understanding have spoken.
   You wise men who hear me have
      said to me,
³⁵ 'Job doesn't know what he's talking
   about.
   The things he has said don't
      make any sense.'
³⁶ I wish Job would be put to the
   hardest test!
   He answered like someone who
      is evil.
³⁷ To his sin he adds even more sin.
   He claps his hands and makes
      fun of us.

He multiplies his words against
God."

35

Elihu continued,

² "Job, do you think it's fair
for you to say,
'God will clear me of all
charges'?
³ You ask him, 'What good is it for
me not to sin?
What do I get by not sinning?'

⁴ "I'd like to reply to you
and to your friends who are with
you.
⁵ Look up at the heavens.
Observe the clouds that are high
above you.
⁶ If you sin, what does that mean to
God?
If you sin many times, what does
that do to him?
⁷ If you do what is right, how does
that help him?
What does he get from you?
⁸ The evil things you do only hurt
someone like yourself.
The right things you do only help
other human beings.

⁹ "People cry out when they are
beaten down.
They beg to be set free from the
power of those who are over
them.
¹⁰ But no one says, 'Where is the God
who made me?
He gives us songs even during
the night.
¹¹ He teaches more to us than to wild
animals.
He makes us wiser than the birds
of the air.'
¹² He doesn't answer sinful people
when they cry out to him.
That's because they are so proud.
¹³ In fact, God doesn't listen to their
empty cries.
The Mighty One doesn't pay any
attention to them.
¹⁴ So he certainly won't listen to you.
When you say you don't see him,
he won't hear you.
He won't listen when you state
your case to him.
He won't pay attention even if
you wait for him.

¹⁵ When you say his anger never
punishes sin, he won't hear
you.
He won't listen when you say he
doesn't pay any attention to
evil.
¹⁶ So you say things that don't mean
anything.
You use a lot of words,
but you don't know what you are
talking about."

36

Elihu continued,

² "Put up with me a little
longer.
I'll show you I can speak up for
God even more.
³ I get my knowledge from far away.
I'll announce that the One who
made me is fair.
⁴ You can be sure that my words are
true.
One who has perfect knowledge
is talking to you.

⁵ "God is mighty, but he doesn't hate
people.
He's mighty, and he knows
exactly what he's going to do.
⁶ He doesn't keep alive those who
are evil.
Instead, he gives suffering
people their rights.
⁷ He watches over those who do
what is right.
He puts them on thrones as if
they were kings.
He honors them forever.
⁸ But some people are held by
chains.
They are tied up with painful
ropes.
⁹ God tells them what they've done.
He tells them they've become
proud and sinned against
him.
¹⁰ He makes them listen when he
corrects them.
He commands them to turn
away
from the evil things they've done.
¹¹ If they obey him and serve him,
they'll enjoy a long and happy
life.
Things will go well with them.
¹² But if they don't listen to him,
they'll be killed with swords.

They'll die because they didn't want to know anything about him.

¹³ "Those whose hearts are ungodly are always angry.
Even when God puts them in chains,
they don't cry out for help.
¹⁴ They die while they are still young.
They die among the male prostitutes at the temples.
¹⁵ But God saves suffering people while they are suffering.
He speaks to them while they are hurting.

¹⁶ "Job, he wants to take you out of the jaws of trouble.
He wants to bring you to a wide and safe place.
He'd like to seat you at a table that is loaded with the best food.
¹⁷ But now you are loaded down with the punishment sinners will receive.
You have been judged fairly.
¹⁸ Be careful that no one tempts you with riches.
Don't take money from people who want special favors,
no matter how much it is.
¹⁹ Can your wealth keep you out of trouble?
Can all of your mighty efforts keep you going?
²⁰ Don't long for the night to come so you can drag people away from their homes.
²¹ Be careful not to do what is evil.
You seem to like evil better than suffering!

²² "God is honored because he is so powerful.
He has no equal as a teacher.
²³ Who has told him what he can do?
Who has said to him, 'You have done what is wrong'?
²⁴ Remember to thank him for what he's done.
People have praised him with their songs.
²⁵ Every human being has seen his work.
People can see it from far away.

²⁶ How great God is! We'll never completely understand him.
We'll never find out how long he has lived.

²⁷ "He makes mist rise from the water.
Then it falls as rain into the streams.
²⁸ The clouds pour down their moisture.
Rain showers fall on people everywhere.
²⁹ Who can understand how God spreads out the clouds?
Who can explain how he thunders from his home in heaven?
³⁰ See how he scatters his lightning around him!
He lights up the deepest parts of the ocean.
³¹ The rain he sends makes things grow for the nations.
He provides them with plenty of food.
³² He holds lightning bolts in his hands.
He commands them to strike their marks.
³³ His thunder announces that a storm is coming.
Even the cattle let us know it's approaching.

37 "When I hear the thunder, my heart pounds.
It beats faster inside me.
² Listen! Listen to the roar of his voice!
Listen to the thunder that comes from him!
³ He sends his lightning across the sky.
It reaches from one end of the earth to the other.
⁴ Next comes the sound of his roaring thunder.
He thunders with his majestic voice.
When his voice fills the air, he doesn't hold anything back.
⁵ God's voice thunders in wonderful ways.
We'll never understand the great things he does.

⁶He says to the snow, 'Fall on the earth.'
He tells the rain, 'Pour down your mighty waters.'
⁷He stops everyone from working.
He wants them to see his work.
⁸The animals go inside.
They remain in their dens.
⁹The storm comes out of its storeroom in the heavens.
The cold comes from the driving winds.
¹⁰The breath of God produces ice.
The shallow water freezes over.
¹¹He loads the clouds with moisture.
He scatters his lightning through them.
¹²He directs the clouds to circle above the surface of the whole earth.
They do everything he commands them to do.
¹³He tells the clouds to punish people.
Or he brings them to water his earth and show his love.

¹⁴"Job, listen to me.
Stop and think about the wonderful things God does.
¹⁵Do you know how he controls the clouds?
Do you understand how he makes his lightning flash?
¹⁶Do you know how the clouds stay up in the sky?
Do you understand the wonders of the One who has perfect knowledge?
¹⁷Even your clothes are too hot for you
when the land lies quiet under the south wind.
¹⁸Can you help God spread out the skies?
They are as hard as a mirror that's made out of bronze.

¹⁹"Job, tell us what we should say to God.
We can't prepare our case because our minds are dark.

How come God makes storms with lightning and thunder?

God made laws that control how the weather works. Thunderstorms are part of our weather. Without rain, the grass, flowers and crops would not grow. The lightning and thunder in those storms comes from the electricity in the air and on the earth. Of course God can interrupt his laws of nature. But he made those laws so the earth would work and be beautiful. God does not send storms to scare us or hurt us. But storms do bring danger, so we should stay out of their way and find cover when they come.

checkout Job 36:29—37:13

Related verses:
1 Kings 18:5–45;
Psalm 77:17,18

JASON'S IMAGINATION

²⁰Should he be told that I want to speak?
   Would any man ask to be destroyed by him?
²¹No one can look at the sun.
   It's too bright after the wind has swept the skies clean.
²²Out of the north, God comes in his shining glory.
   He comes in all of his wonderful majesty.
²³We can't reach up to the Mighty One.
   He is lifted high because of his power.
   Everything he does is fair and right.
   So he doesn't crush people.
²⁴That's why they have respect for him.
   He cares about all those who are wise."

THE FIRST SPEECH OF THE LORD

38
The LORD spoke to Job out of a storm. He said,

²"Who do you think you are to disagree with my plans?
   You do not know what you are talking about.
³Get ready to stand up for yourself.
   I will ask you some questions.
   Then I want you to answer me.

⁴"Where were you when I laid the earth's foundation?
   Tell me, if you know.
⁵Who measured it? I am sure you know!
   Who stretched a measuring line across it?
⁶What was it built on?
   Who laid its most important stone?
⁷When it happened, the morning stars sang together.
   All of the angels shouted with joy.

⁸"Who created the ocean?
   Who caused it to be born?
⁹I put clouds over it as if they were its clothes.
   I wrapped it in thick darkness.
¹⁰I set limits for it.

   I put its doors and metal bars in place.
¹¹I said, 'You can come this far.
   But you can't come any farther.
   Here is where your proud waves have to stop.'

¹²"Job, have you ever commanded the morning to come?
   Have you ever shown the sun where to rise?
¹³The daylight takes the earth by its edges
   as if it were a blanket.
   Then it shakes sinful people out of it.
¹⁴The earth takes shape like clay under a seal.
   Its features stand out
   like the different parts of your clothes.
¹⁵Sinners would rather have darkness than light.
   When the light comes, their power is broken.

¹⁶"Have you traveled to the springs at the bottom of the ocean?
   Have you walked in its deepest parts?
¹⁷Have the gates of death been shown to you?
   Have you seen the gates of darkness?
¹⁸Do you understand how big the earth is?
   Tell me, if you know all of those things.

¹⁹"Where does light come from?
   And where does darkness live?
²⁰Can you take them to their places?
   Do you know the paths to their houses?
²¹I am sure you know! After all, you were already born!
   You have lived so many years!

²²"Have you entered the places where the snow is kept?
   Have you seen the storerooms for the hail?
²³I store up snow and hail for times of trouble.
   I keep them for days of war and battle.
²⁴Where does lightning come from?
   Where do the east winds that blow across the earth live?

²⁵ Who tells the rain where it should
  fall?
  Who makes paths for the
    thunderstorms?
²⁶ They bring water to places where
  no one lives.
  They water deserts that do not
    have anyone in them.
²⁷ They satisfy the needs of dry and
  empty lands.
  They make grass start growing
    there.
²⁸ Does the rain have a father?
  Who is the father of the drops of
    dew?
²⁹ Does the ice have a
  mother?
  Who is the mother of the frost
    from the heavens?
³⁰ The waters become as hard as
  stone.
  The surface of the ocean freezes
    over.

³¹ "Can you tie up the beautiful
  Pleiades?
  Can you untie the ropes that
    hold Orion together?
³² Can you bring out all of the stars
  in their seasons?
  Can you lead out the Big Dipper
    and the Little Dipper?
³³ Do you know the laws that govern
  the heavens?
  Can you rule over the earth the
    way I do?

³⁴ "Can you give orders to the
  clouds?
  Can you make them pour rain
    down on you?
³⁵ Do you send the lightning bolts on
  their way?
  Do they report to you, 'Here we
    are'?
³⁶ Who put wisdom in people's
  hearts?
  Who gave understanding to their
    minds?
³⁷ Who is wise enough to count the
  clouds?
  Who can tip over the water jars
    of the heavens?
³⁸ I tip them over when the ground
  becomes hard.
  I do it when the dirt sticks
    together.

³⁹ "Do you hunt for food for mother
  lions?
  Do you satisfy the hunger of their
    cubs?
⁴⁰ Some of them lie low in their dens.
  Others lie waiting in the bushes.
⁴¹ Who provides food for ravens
  when their babies cry out to me?
  They wander around because
    they do not have anything to
    eat.

39

"Job, do you know when
  mountain goats
  have their babies?
Do you watch when female deer
  give birth?
² Do you count the months until the
  animals have their babies?
  Do you know the time when they
    give birth?
³ They bend their back legs and
  have their babies.
  Then their labor pains stop.
⁴ Their little ones grow strong and
  healthy in the wild.
  They leave and do not come
    home again.

⁵ "Who let the wild donkeys go
  free?
  Who untied their ropes?
⁶ I gave them the dry and empty
  land as their home.
  I gave them salt flats to live in.
⁷ They laugh at all of the noise in
  town.
  They do not hear the shouts of
    the donkey drivers.
⁸ They wander over the hills to look
  for grass.
  They search for anything green
    to eat.

⁹ "Job, will wild oxen agree to serve
  you?
  Will they stay by your feed box at
    night?
¹⁰ Can you keep them in straight
  rows with harnesses?
  Will they plow the valleys behind
    you?
¹¹ Will you depend on them for their
  great strength?
  Will you let them do your heavy
    work?
¹² Can you trust them to bring in
  your grain?

Will they take it to your threshing floor?

13 "The wings of ostriches flap with joy.
But they can't compare with the wings and feathers of storks.
14 Ostriches lay their eggs on the ground.
They let them get warm in the sand.
15 They do not know that something might step on them.
A wild animal might walk all over them.
16 Ostriches are mean to their little ones.
They treat them as if they did not belong to them.
They do not care that their work was useless.
17 I did not provide ostriches with wisdom.
I did not give them good sense.
18 But when they spread their feathers to run,
they laugh at a horse and its rider.

19 "Job, do you give horses their strength?
Do you put flowing manes on their necks?
20 Do you make them jump like locusts?
They terrify others with their proud snorting.
21 They paw the ground wildly.
They are filled with joy.
They charge at their enemies.
22 They laugh at fear. They are not afraid of anything.
They do not run away from swords.
23 Many arrows rattle at their sides.
Flashing spears and javelins are also there.
24 They are so stirred up that they eat up the ground.
They can't stand still when trumpets are blown.
25 When they hear the trumpets they snort, 'Aha!'
They catch the smells of battle far away.
They hear the shouts of commanders and the battle cries.

26 "Job, are you wise enough to teach hawks where to fly?
They spread their wings and fly toward the south.
27 Do you command eagles to fly so high?
They build their nests as high as they can.
28 They live on cliffs and stay there at night.
High up on the rocks they think they are safe.
29 From there they look for their food.
They can see it from far away.
30 Their little ones like to eat blood.
Eagles gather where they see dead bodies."

40

The LORD continued,

2 "I am the Mighty One.
Will the man who argues with me correct me?
Let him who brings charges against me answer me!"

JOB'S REPLY

3 Job replied to the LORD,

4 "I'm not worthy. How can I reply to you?
I'm putting my hand over my mouth. I'll stop talking.
5 I spoke once. But I really don't have any answer.
I spoke twice. But I won't say anything else."

THE SECOND SPEECH OF THE LORD

6 Then the LORD spoke to Job out of the storm. He said,

7 "Get ready to stand up for yourself.
I will ask you some more questions.
Then I want you to answer me.
8 "Would you dare to claim that I am not being fair?
Would you judge me in order to make yourself seem right?
9 Is your arm as powerful as mine is?
Can your voice thunder as mine does?

¹⁰Then put on glory and beauty as if
they were your clothes.
  Also put honor and majesty on.
¹¹Let loose your great anger.
  Look at those who are proud and
  bring them low.
¹²Look at proud people and bring
them down.
  Crush those who are evil right
  where they are.
¹³Bury their bodies in the dust
together.
  Cover their faces in the grave.
¹⁴Then I myself will admit
to you
  that your own right hand can
  save you.

¹⁵"Look at the behemoth. It is a
huge animal.
  I made both of you.
  It eats grass like an ox.
¹⁶Look at the strength it has in its
hips!
  What power it has in the muscles
  of its stomach!

¹⁷Its tail sways back and forth like a
cedar tree.
  The tendons of its thighs are
  close together.
¹⁸Its bones are like tubes made out
of bronze.
  Its legs are like rods made out of
  iron.
¹⁹It ranks first among my works.
  I made it. I can approach it with
  my sword.
²⁰The hills produce food for it.
  All of the other wild animals play
  near it.
²¹It lies under lotus plants.
  It hides in tall grass in the
  swamps.
²²The lotus plants hide it in their
shade.
  Poplar trees near streams
  surround it.
²³It is not afraid when the river
roars.
  It is secure even when the Jordan
  River rushes against its
  mouth.

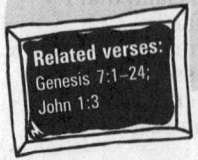

Were there dinosaurs on the ark?

Dinosaurs are popular today. We even have stuffed dinosaur toys. Scientists say that these unusual animals lived more than a hundred million years ago. So it's natural to wonder where they fit into the Bible. Most Bible experts believe that dinosaurs died out many years before the great flood that we read about in Genesis. So there wouldn't have been any dinosaurs to put on the ark. But the behemoth was a "huge animal," like many dinosaurs. Remember that the Bible tells us mainly about people, God's creation of all things and God's plan for our lives. It does not tell us *everything*.

checkout Job 40:15–19

Related verses:
Genesis 7:1–24;
John 1:3

JASON'S IMAGINATION

—moo

²⁴ Can anyone capture it by its eyes?
   Can anyone trap it and poke a
   hole through its nose?

41
"Job, can you pull the
leviathan out of the
sea with a fish hook?
Can you tie down its tongue with
   a rope?
² Can you put a rope through its
   nose?
   Can you stick a hook through its
   jaw?
³ Will it keep begging you for
   mercy?
   Will it speak gently to you?
⁴ Will it make an agreement with
   you?
   Can you make it your slave for
   life?
⁵ Can you make a pet out of it like a
   bird?
   Can you put it on a leash for your
   young women?
⁶ Will traders offer you something
   for it?
   Will they divide it up among the
   merchants?
⁷ Can you fill its body with
   harpoons?
   Can you throw fishing spears
   into its head?
⁸ If you touch it, it will fight you.
   Then you will remember never to
   touch it again!
⁹ No one can possibly control the
   leviathan.
   Just looking at it will terrify you.
¹⁰ No one dares to wake it up.
   So who can possibly stand up to
   me?
¹¹ Who has a claim against me that I
   must pay?
   Everything on earth belongs to
   me.
¹² "Now I will speak about the
   leviathan's legs.
   I will talk about its strength and
   its graceful body.
¹³ Who can strip off its outer coat?
   Who would try to put a bridle on
   it?
¹⁴ Who dares to open its jaws?
   Its mouth is filled with terrifying
   teeth.
¹⁵ Its back has rows of shields
   that are close together.

¹⁶ Each one is so close to the next
   one
   that not even air can pass
   between them.
¹⁷ They are joined tightly to one
   another.
   They stick together and can't be
   forced apart.
¹⁸ The leviathan's snorting throws
   out flashes of light.
   Its eyes shine like the first light of
   day.
¹⁹ Fire seems to spray out of its
   mouth.
   Sparks of fire shoot out.
²⁰ Smoke pours out of its nose.
   It is like smoke from a boiling pot
   over burning grass.
²¹ Its breath sets coals on fire.
   Flames fly out of its mouth.
²² Its neck is very strong.
   People run to get out of its way.
²³ Its rolls of fat are close together.
   They are firm and can't be
   moved.
²⁴ Its chest is as hard as rock.
   It is as hard as a lower millstone.
²⁵ When the leviathan rises up,
   even mighty people are
   terrified.
   They run away when it moves
   around wildly.
²⁶ A sword that strikes it has no
   effect.
   Neither does a spear or dart or
   javelin.
²⁷ It treats iron as if it were straw.
   It crushes bronze as if it were
   rotten wood.
²⁸ Arrows do not make it run away.
   Stones that are thrown from
   slings are like straw hitting it.
²⁹ A club seems like a piece of straw
   to it.
   It laughs when it hears a javelin
   rattling.
³⁰ Its undersides are like broken
   pieces of pottery.
   It leaves a trail in the mud like a
   threshing sled.
³¹ It makes the ocean churn like a
   boiling pot.
   It stirs up the sea like perfume
   someone is making.
³² It leaves a shiny trail behind it.
   You would think the ocean had
   white hair.

³³Nothing on earth is equal to the
leviathan.
    That creature is not afraid of
anything.
³⁴It looks down on proud people.
    It rules over all those who are
proud."

JOB'S REPLY

42 Job replied to the LORD,
²"I know that you can do
anything.
No one can keep you from doing
what you plan to do.
³You asked me, 'Who do you think
you are to disagree with my
plans?
You do not know what you are
talking about.'
I spoke about things I didn't
completely understand.
I talked about things that were
too wonderful for me to know.

⁴"You said, 'Listen now, and I will
speak.
I will ask you some questions.
Then I want you to answer me.'
⁵My ears had heard about you.
    But now my own eyes have seen
you.
⁶So I hate myself.
    I'm really sorry for what I said
about you.
    That's why I'm sitting in dust and
ashes."

THE STORY ENDS

⁷After the LORD finished speaking to Job, he spoke to Eliphaz the Temanite. He said, "I am angry with you and your two friends. You have not said what is true about me, as my servant Job has.

⁸"So now get seven bulls and seven rams. Go to my servant Job. Then sacrifice a burnt offering for yourselves. My servant Job will pray for you. And I will accept his prayer. I will not punish you for saying the foolish things you said. You have not said what is true about me, as my servant Job has."

⁹So Eliphaz the Temanite, Bildad the Shuhite, and Zophar the Naamathite did what the LORD told them to do. And the LORD accepted Job's prayer.

¹⁰After Job had prayed for his friends, the LORD made him successful again. He gave him twice as much as he had before. ¹¹All of his brothers and sisters and everyone who had known him before came to see him. They ate with him in his house. They showed their concern for him. They comforted him because of all of the troubles the LORD had brought on him. Each one gave him a piece of silver and a gold ring.

¹²The LORD blessed the last part of Job's life even more than the first part. He gave Job 14,000 sheep and 6,000 camels. He gave him 1,000 pairs of oxen and 1,000 donkeys.

¹³Job also had seven sons and three daughters. ¹⁴He named the first daughter Jemimah. He named the second Keziah. And he named the third Keren-Happuch. ¹⁵Job's daughters were more beautiful than any other women in the whole land. Their father gave them a share of property along with their brothers.

¹⁶After all of that happened, Job lived for 140 years. He saw his children, his grandchildren and his great-grandchildren. ¹⁷And so he died. He had lived for a very long time.

Quest Clue

In Job chapter 42, we find out that when bad things happened to Job, he didn't handle it very well. He questioned God's goodness, but later he felt sorry about it. At the end of the book of Lamentations, a Quest Challenge will give you ideas for what to do when bad things happen to you.

Psalms

Who wrote this book?
David wrote 73 of the 150 psalms. Several people wrote the others.

Why was this book written?
The psalms show God's people how to talk to him and to worship him.

What kinds of psalms are there?
There are seven kinds of psalms:

1. Praise psalms like Psalms 33 and 103 show us how to thank God for who he is.

2. History psalms like Psalms 68 and 106 tell what God has done for his people.

3. Friendship psalms like Psalms 8 and 23 remind us that God loves us and tell us how we can show our love to him.

4. Anger psalms like Psalms 35 and 137 ask God to punish evil people.

5. Confession psalms like Psalms 32 and 51 show us how to talk to God about our sins.

6. Messiah psalms like Psalms 22 and 89 tell us about the coming of Jesus.

7. Worship psalms like Psalms 30 and 120 were used on special religious holidays and show us how to worship God with other people.

BOOK I

Psalms 1–41

PSALM 1

¹Blessed is the one who obeys the law of the LORD.
He doesn't follow the advice of evil people.
He doesn't make a habit of doing what sinners do.
He doesn't join those who make fun of the LORD and his law.
²Instead, he takes delight in the law of the LORD.

He thinks about his law day and
   night.
[3] He is like a tree that is planted
   near a stream of water.
   It always bears its fruit at the
      right time.
   Its leaves don't dry up.
   Everything godly people do turns
      out well.

[4] Sinful people are not like that at
   all.
   They are like straw
   that the wind blows away.
[5] When the LORD judges them, their
   life will come to an end.
   Sinners won't have any place
      among those who are godly.

[6] The LORD watches over the lives of
   those who are godly.
   But the lives of sinful people will
      lead to their death.

PSALM 2

[1] Why do the nations plan evil
   together?
   Why do they make useless plans?
[2] The kings of the earth take their
   stand against the LORD.
   The rulers of the earth gather
      together against his anointed
      king.
[3] "Let us break free from their
   chains," they say.
   "Let us throw off their ropes."

[4] The One who sits on his throne in
   heaven laughs.
   The Lord makes fun of those
      rulers and their plans.
[5] When he is angry, he warns them.
   When his anger blazes out, he
      terrifies them.
[6] He says to them,
   "I have placed my king on my
      holy mountain of Zion."

[7] I will announce what the LORD has
promised.

   He said to me, "You are my son.
      Today I have become your father.
[8] Ask me, and I will give the nations
      to you.
   All nations on earth will belong
      to you.
[9] You will rule them with an iron
      rod.
   You will break them to pieces like
      clay pots."

[10] Kings, be wise!
   Rulers of the earth, be warned!
[11] Serve the LORD and have respect
      for him.
   Serve him with joy and
      trembling.
[12] Obey the son completely, or he
      will be angry.
   Your way of life will lead to your
      death.
   His anger can blaze out at any
      moment.

Does God have a sense of humor?

Yes. People love to laugh, and
God created us in his image. But
that does not mean that he likes
all our jokes. Some people use humor to
hurt or disgust other people. God would
never do that because God is holy. It
might sound cruel for God to laugh at
the evil plans of wicked rulers, but this
really means that God is in control of the
situation.

checkout Psalm 2:4

Related verses:
Psalm 37:13;
Ecclesiastes 3:4

Blessed are all those who go to
    him for safety.

PSALM 3

A psalm of David when he ran away
from his son Absalom.

[1] LORD, I have so many enemies!
    So many people are rising up
      against me!
[2] Many are saying about me,
    "God will not save him."   *Selah*

[3] LORD, you are like a shield that
      keeps me safe.
    You honor me. You help me win
      the battle.
[4] I call out to the LORD.
    He answers me from his holy hill.
                                Selah

[5] I lie down and sleep.
    I wake up again, because the
      LORD takes care of me.
[6] I won't be afraid of the tens of
      thousands
    who are lined up against me on
      every side.

[7] LORD, rise up!
    My God, save me!
  Strike all my enemies in the face.
  Break the teeth of sinful people.

[8] LORD, you are the one who saves.
    May your blessing be on your
      people.   *Selah*

PSALM 4

For the director of music.
A psalm of David to be played
on stringed instruments.

[1] My faithful God,
    answer me when I call out to
      you.
  Give me rest from my trouble.
  Show me your favor. Hear my
    prayer.

[2] How long will you people turn my
      glory into shame?
    How long will you love what will
      certainly fail you?
    How long will you pray to statues
      of gods?   *Selah*
[3] Remember that the LORD has set
      his faithful people apart for
      himself.
    The LORD will hear me when I
      call out to him.

[4] When you are angry, do not sin.
    When you are in bed,
    look deep down inside you and
      be silent.   *Selah*
[5] Offer sacrifices to the LORD in the
      right way.
    Trust in him.

[6] Many are asking, "Who can show
      us anything good?"
    LORD, let us see your face smiling
      on us with favor.

KIDS' QUESTION

Why did I have a bad dream when I prayed before I went to sleep?

God does not say that Christians will never have bad dreams. He says
he will be with you and protect you when you are afraid. A lot of
things can cause bad dreams. You may be worried or scared.
You may feel sick or be too warm. Maybe you saw a
scary movie or heard a scary noise. It is good to pray
before falling asleep at night. Ask God to help you
sleep. Ask him to help you be brave, and thank him
for keeping you safe. Remember that he is there with
you no matter what happens.

checkout Psalm 3:5

Related verses:
Psalms 23:4;
34:17–19

7 You have filled my heart with great
    joy.
  It is greater than the joy of
    people who have lots of grain
    and fresh wine.
8 I will lie down and sleep in peace.
  LORD, you alone keep me safe.

PSALM 5

For the director of music. A psalm
of David to be played on flutes.

1 LORD, listen to my words.
  Pay attention when I sigh.
2 My King and my God,
  listen to me when I cry for help.
  I pray to you.
3 LORD, in the morning you hear my
    voice.
  In the morning I pray to you.
  I wait for you in hope.

4 God, you aren't happy with
    anything that is evil.
  Those who do what is wrong
    can't live where you are.
5 Those who are proud can't stand
    in front of you.
  You hate everyone who does
    what is evil.

6 You destroy those who tell lies.
  LORD, you hate murderers and
    those who cheat others.

7 Because of your great love
  I will come into your house.
  With deep respect I will bow down
    toward your holy temple.
8 LORD, I have many enemies.
  Lead me in your right path.
  Make your way smooth and
    straight for me.

9 Not a word from their mouths can
    be trusted.
  Their hearts are filled with plans
    to destroy others.
  Their throats are like open graves.
  With their tongues they tell lies.
10 God, show that they are guilty.
  Let their evil plans bring them
    down.
  Send them away because of their
    many sins.
  They have refused to obey you.

11 But let all those who go to you for
    safety be glad.
  Let them always sing with joy.
  Spread your cover over them and
    keep them safe.

KIDS' QUESTioN

Is it OK to cheat at a game when the game is called "Cheat" and that's what you're supposed to do?

It is too bad that this game is called Cheat, because it gives the idea that
cheating is all right. God doesn't like cheating because it requires you
to lie and take advantage of people. Still, you should play by the
rules of the game no matter what it is called. For example, a game
might call for players to make up stories about themselves to trick
people. That would not be wrong because it is a game, and
everyone knows that the stories are made up. Games with funny
rules like that can be fun. You can have fun in
a game as long as everyone understands
the rules and follows them. Play by the
    rules of every game
    unless they break
    God's rules.

checkout
Psalm 5:6

Related verses:
Deuteronomy
25:16;
Hosea 12:7

CHEAT
THE GAME

Then those who love you will be
  glad because of you.
¹²LORD, you bless those who do what
    is right.
  Like a shield, your loving care
    keeps them safe.

PSALM 6

For the director of music.
For *sheminith*. A psalm of David
to be played on stringed instruments.

¹LORD, don't correct me when you
    are angry.
  Don't punish me when you are
    burning with anger.
²LORD, have mercy on me. I'm so
    weak.
  LORD, heal me. My body is full of
    pain.
³My soul is very troubled.
  LORD, how long will it be until
    you save me?

⁴LORD, turn to me and help me.
  Save me. Your love never fails.
⁵People can't remember you when
    they are dead.
  How can they praise you when
    they are in the grave?

⁶My groaning has worn me out.
  All night long my tears flood my
    bed.
  My bed is wet because of my
    crying.
⁷I'm so sad I can't see very well.
  My eyesight gets worse because
    of all of my enemies.

⁸Get away from me, all of you who
    do evil.
  The LORD has heard my sobbing.
⁹The LORD has heard my cry for his
    favor.
  The LORD accepts my prayer.
¹⁰All of my enemies will be troubled
    and put to shame.
  They will turn back in dishonor.
  It will happen suddenly.

PSALM 7

A *shiggaion* of David.
He sang it to the LORD about Cush,
who was from the tribe of Benjamin.

¹LORD my God, I go to you for
    safety.
  Help me. Save me from all those
    who are chasing me.
²If you don't, they will tear me apart
    as if they were lions.

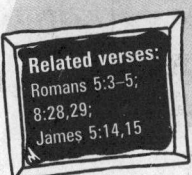

Why does God let us get sick?

Sickness is part of being human. Sometimes sickness is the
body's way of telling us that we should stop living a certain way.
Maybe we ate too much or ate something bad. Or maybe we did not get
enough sleep. Sickness first came into the
world through sin. But all kinds of
people get sick: good and bad,
rich and poor, old and young.
God wants us to take care of
ourselves and be healthy so
we can live for him. And
when we are sick, we can
pray to God and ask him to
make us better.

checkout
Psalm 6:2

Related verses:
Romans 5:3-5;
8:28,29;
James 5:14,15

They will rip me to pieces so that
  no one can save me.

³LORD my God, suppose I have
  done something wrong.
  Suppose I am guilty.
⁴I have done evil to my friend.
  Or I have robbed my enemy
    without any reason.
⁵If I have done any of those things,
  let my enemy chase me and
    catch me.
  Let him walk all over me.
  Let him bury me in the dust.
                Selah

⁶LORD, rise up in your anger.
  Rise up against the great anger of
    my enemies.
  My God, wake up. Command
    that the right thing be done.
⁷Let all the people of the earth
  gather around you.
  Rule over them from your throne
    in heaven.
⁸ LORD, judge all people.
  LORD, judge me. But remember
    that I have done what is right.
  Most High God, remember that I
    am honest.
⁹God, you always do what is right.
  You look deep down inside the
    hearts and minds of people.
  Bring to an end the terrible things
    sinful people do.
  Make godly people safe.

¹⁰The Most High God is like a shield
  that keeps me safe.

He saves those whose hearts are
  honest.
¹¹God judges fairly.
  He shows his anger every day.
¹²If evil people don't change their
    ways,
  God will sharpen his sword.
  He will get his bow ready to use.
¹³He has prepared his deadly
    weapons.
  He has made his flaming arrows
    ready.

¹⁴Anyone who is full of evil
  plans trouble and ends up telling
    lies.
¹⁵Anyone who digs a hole and
    shovels it out
  falls into the pit he has made.
¹⁶The trouble he causes comes back
    on him.
  The terrible things he does come
    down on his own head.

¹⁷I will give thanks to the LORD
  because he does what is right.
  I will sing praise to the LORD
    Most High.

PSALM 8

For the director of music. For *gittith.*
    A psalm of David.

¹LORD, our Lord,
  how majestic is your name in the
    whole earth!

You have made your glory
  higher than the heavens.

If we went high enough in the sky would we find heaven?

No. No one but God knows exactly where heaven is. We describe its location by saying it is "up." But no one can see it or find it the way we might find a park or a house. We could ride a spaceship way out into space, but we would not find heaven. Only God can take us there. And that's what he does after we die if we have trusted in Jesus as our Savior.

Related verses:
John 3:13;
Luke 24:50,51

checkout
Psalm 8:1

2 You have made sure that children and infants praise you.
You have done it because of your enemies.
You have done it to put a stop to their talk.

3 I think about the heavens.
I think about what your fingers have created.
I think about the moon and stars that you have set in place.

4 What is a human being that you think about him?
What is a son of man that you take care of him?

5 You made him a little lower than the heavenly beings.
You placed on him a crown of glory and honor.

6 You made human beings the rulers over all that your hands have created.
You put everything under their control.

7 They rule over all flocks and herds and over the wild animals.

8 They rule over the birds of the air and over the fish in the ocean.
They rule over everything that swims in the oceans.

9 LORD, our Lord,
how majestic is your name in the whole earth!

PSALM 9

For the director of music.
A psalm of David to the tune of "The Death of the Son."

1 LORD, I will praise you with all my heart.
I will tell about all of the miracles you have done.

2 I will be glad and full of joy because of you.
Most High God, I will sing praise to you.

3 My enemies turn back.
They fall down and die right in front of you.

4 You have proved that I haven't done anything wrong.
You have sat on your throne and judged fairly.

5 You have punished the nations.
You have destroyed evil people.
You have erased their names from your book for ever and ever.

6 The enemy has been destroyed forever.
You have leveled their cities to the ground.
Even the memory of them is gone.

7 The LORD rules forever.

When I die, will I become an angel?

No. Angels are different from human beings. God created them separately from us. But you are a little like an angel because you too have a spirit. In other words, you have a soul and will live forever and can know God. But you also have a body.

When you die you will leave your body behind and get a new and perfect body in heaven. We do not know exactly what this perfect body will be like, but we know that other people in heaven will be able to recognize us. You will be you, only better.

Related verse:
2 Corinthians 5:1

checkout

Psalm 8:5

He has set up his throne so that
   he can judge people.
8 He will judge the world in keeping
      with what is right.
   He will rule over all of its people
      fairly.
9 The LORD is a place of safety for
      those who have been beaten
      down.
   He keeps them safe in times of
      trouble.
10 LORD, those who know you will
      trust in you.
   You have never deserted those
      who look to you.

11 Sing praises to the LORD. He rules
      from his throne in Zion.
   Tell among the nations what he
      has done.
12 The One who pays back murderers
      remembers.
   He doesn't forget the cries of
      those who are hurting.

13 LORD, see how badly my enemies
      treat me!
   Show me your favor. Don't let me
      go down to the gates of death.
14 Then I can give praise to you
   at the gates of the city of Zion.
   There I will be full of joy
      because you have saved me.

15 The nations have fallen into the
      pit they have dug.
   Their feet are caught in the net
      they have hidden.
16 The LORD is known to be fair.
   Evil people are trapped by what
      they have done.
                           Higgaion. Selah
17 Sinful people go down to the
      grave.
   So do all the nations that forget
      God.
18 But those who are in need will
      always be remembered.
   The hope of those who are
      hurting will never die.

19 LORD, rise up. Don't let people win
      the battle.
   Let the nations come to you and
      be judged.
20 LORD, strike them with terror.
   Let the nations know they are
      only human.   *Selah*

PSALM 10

1 LORD, why are you so far away?
   Why do you hide yourself in
      times of trouble?

2 An evil person is proud and hunts
   down those who are weak.

Why do people litter?

Some people litter because it is a habit for them. Others are just careless or do not care. No matter why people litter, it is against the law and hurts our world. Littering shows a lack of respect for others and their property, including God's. It makes everything look ugly and dirty. But God tells us to be respectful of other people, their property, God's creation and the law. So we should not litter.

checkout **Psalm 8:6**

Related verses:
Genesis 1:26;
Psalm 24:1

He catches weak people by
　making clever plans.
³ He brags about what his heart
　longs for.
He speaks well of those who
　always want more.
He attacks the LORD with his
　words.
⁴ Because he is proud, that evil
　person doesn't turn to the
　LORD.
There is no room for God in any
　of his thoughts.
⁵ Everything always goes well for him.
So he is proud.
He doesn't want to have anything
　to do with God's laws.
He makes fun of all of his
　enemies.
⁶ He says to himself, "I will always
　be secure.
I will always be happy. I'll never
　have any trouble."
⁷ His mouth is full of curses and lies
　and warnings.
With his tongue he speaks evil
　and makes trouble.
⁸ Sinful people hide and wait near
　the villages.
From their hiding places they
　murder those who aren't
　guilty of doing anything
　wrong.
They watch in secret for those
　they want to attack.
⁹ They hide and wait like a lion in
　the bushes.
From their hiding places they
　wait to catch those who are
　helpless.
They catch them and drag them
　off in their nets.
¹⁰ Those they have attacked are
　beaten up. They fall to the
　ground.
They fall because their attackers
　are too strong for them.
¹¹ Sinful people say to themselves,
　"God doesn't pay any
　attention.
He covers his face. He never sees
　us."

¹² LORD, rise up! God, show your
　power!
Don't forget those who are
　helpless.

¹³ Why do sinful people attack you
　with their words?
Why do they say to themselves,
　"He won't hold us accountable"?
¹⁴ God, you see trouble and sadness.
You take note of it. You do
　something about it.
So those who are attacked place
　themselves in your care.
You help children whose fathers
　have died.
¹⁵ Take away the power of bad and
　sinful people.
Hold them accountable for the
　evil things they do.
Uncover all the evil they have
　done.

¹⁶ The LORD is King for ever and ever.
The nations will disappear from
　his land.
¹⁷ LORD, you hear the longings of
　those who are hurting.
You cheer them up and give
　them hope.
You listen to their cries.
¹⁸ You stand up for those whose
　fathers have died
and for those who have been
　beaten down.
You do it so that no one made of
　dust
may terrify others anymore.

PSALM 11

For the director of music.
A psalm of David.

¹ I run to the LORD for safety.
So how can you say to me,
　"Fly away like a bird to your
　mountain.
² Look! Evil people are bending their
　bows.
They are placing their arrows
　against the strings.
They are planning to shoot from
　the shadows
at those who have honest hearts.
³ When law and order are being
　destroyed,
what can godly people do?"

⁴ The LORD is in his holy temple.
The LORD is on his throne in
　heaven.
He watches all people.
His eyes study them.

⁵The LORD watches over those who
    do what is right.
But he hates sinful people and
    those who love to hurt others.
⁶He will pour out flaming coals and
    burning sulfur
on those who do what is wrong.
A hot and dry wind will destroy
    them.
⁷The LORD always does what is
    right.
So he loves it when people do
    what is fair.
Those who are honest will enjoy
    his blessing.

PSALM 12

For the director of music.
For *sheminith*. A psalm of David.

¹Help, LORD! Those who do what is
    right are gone.
Those who are faithful have
    disappeared from the earth.
²Everyone tells lies to his
    neighbors.
With his lips he praises others,
    but he doesn't really mean it.

³May the LORD cut off all lips that
    don't mean what they say.

May he cut out every tongue that
    brags.
⁴They say, "We will win the battle
    with our tongues.
Our lips belong to us. No one else
    is in charge of us."

⁵The LORD says, "The weak are
    beaten down.
Those who are in need groan.
So I will stand up to help them.
I will keep them safe from those
    who tell lies about them."
⁶The words of the LORD are perfect.
They are like silver made pure in
    a clay furnace.
They are like silver made pure
    seven times over.

⁷LORD, you will keep us safe.
You will always keep sinners
    from hurting us.
⁸Proud and sinful people walk
    around openly
when the evil they do is praised
    by others.

PSALM 13

For the director of music.
A psalm of David.

¹LORD, how long must I wait? Will
    you forget me forever?

Why does God have rules?

God has rules to protect us and to help us. God's rules protect
us just like a wall that protects us from danger. The wall stops
us from going any further than we should and getting into trouble. God's
rules also help us the way older people take care of
a baby. The baby may not always like baby
food, but we know that she needs it.
Sometimes God tells us what to do to help
us. God loves us more than anyone else
does, and he knows what is best for us.
His rules are for our good. That is why we
need to trust him and obey him.

checkout Psalm 11:7

Related verses:
Deuteronomy
5:33; 7:8

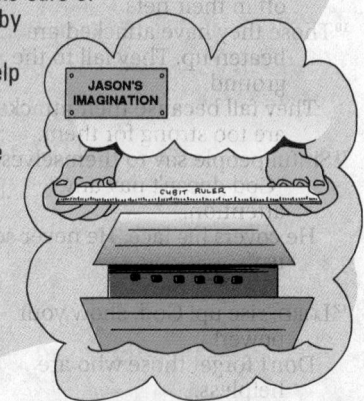

JASON'S
IMAGINATION

CUBIT RULER

How long will you turn your face
away from me?
²How long must I struggle with my
thoughts?
How long must my heart be sad
day after day?
How long will my enemies keep
winning the battle over me?

³LORD my God, look at me and
answer me.
Give me new life, or I will die.
⁴Then my enemies will say, "We
have beaten him."
They will be filled with joy when
I die.

⁵But I trust in your faithful love.
My heart is filled with joy
because you will save me.
⁶I will sing to the LORD.
He has been so good to me.

PSALM 14

For the director of music.
A psalm of David.

¹Foolish people say in their hearts,
"There is no God."
They do all kinds of horrible and
evil things.
No one does anything good.

²The LORD looks down from heaven
on all people.

He wants to see if there are any
who understand.
He wants to see if there are any
who trust in God.
³All of them have turned away.
They have all become evil.
No one does anything good,
no one at all.

⁴Won't those who do evil ever
learn?
They eat up my people as if they
were eating bread.
They don't call out to the LORD
for help.
⁵Just look at them! They are filled
with terror
because God is among those who
do right.
⁶You who do evil make it hard for
poor people to do what they
plan to do.
But the LORD is their place of
safety.

⁷How I pray that the One who saves
Israel will come out of Zion!
Then the LORD will bless his
people with great success
again.
So let the people of Jacob be
filled with joy! Let Israel be
glad!

KIDS' QUESTION

Do all people lie?

All people sin. One of the most
common sins is lying. There are
even people in the world who forget the
difference between truth and lies
because they lie so much. But
that is not the way it is with
most people. Everyone lies at
some time. But hardly
anyone lies all the time.

checkout Psalm 12:2

Related verse:
Romans 3:13

PSALM 15

A psalm of David.

¹LORD, who can live in your sacred
    tent?
  Who can stay on your holy hill?

²Anyone who lives without blame
    and does what is right.
  He speaks the truth from his
    heart.
³ He doesn't tell lies about others.
  He doesn't do wrong to his
    neighbors.
  He doesn't say anything bad
    about them.
⁴He hates sinful people.
  He honors those who have
    respect for the LORD.
  He keeps his promises
    even when it hurts.
⁵He lends his money without
    charging too much interest.
  He doesn't accept money to
    harm those who aren't guilty.

Anyone who lives like that
  will always be secure.

PSALM 16

A *miktam* of David.

¹God, keep me safe.
  I go to you for safety.

²I said to the LORD, "You are my
    Lord.
  Without you, I don't have
    anything that is good."
³God's people who live in our land
    are glorious.
  I take great delight in them.
⁴Those who run after other gods
    will have nothing but trouble.
  I will not pour out offerings of
    blood to those gods.
  My lips will not speak their
    names.

⁵LORD, everything you have given
    me is good.
  You have made my life secure.

KIDS' QUESTION

Would God send nice people to hell if they are not Christians?

Some people are nice and some are mean. But all people do bad things, even nice people. And even one bad deed is too many. Imagine one huge piece of glass with one tiny broken corner. Even though most of it is OK, the whole piece is broken as long as the corner is chipped. That is how we are. God is perfect and we are not. To be fair, God has to punish sin. So all people need to be forgiven of their sins.

God does not *want* to send anyone to hell. That is why he sent Jesus. Jesus died on the cross to pay the price for our sins. God wants everyone to trust in Jesus and be forgiven, so they can go to heaven. But some people do not want to admit that they sin. They won't ask for forgiveness because they don't think they need it. Or they are unwilling to obey God. They do not believe that Jesus paid for their sins. So God lets the painful results of their choice come into their lives.

checkout
Psalm 14:2,3

Related verse:
Romans 5:16

⁶I am very pleased with what you
  have given me.
I am very happy with what I've
  received from you.
⁷I will praise the LORD. He gives me
  good advice.
Even at night my heart teaches
  me.
⁸I know that the LORD is always
  with me.
He is at my right hand.
I will always be secure.

⁹So my heart is glad. Joy is on my
  tongue.
My body also will be secure.
¹⁰You will not leave me in the grave.
You will not let your faithful one
  rot away.
¹¹You always show me the path that
  leads to life.
You will fill me with joy when I
  am with you.
You will give me endless
  pleasures at your right hand.

PSALM 17

A prayer of David.

¹LORD, hear me when I ask you to
  treat me fairly.

Listen to my cry for help.
Hear my prayer.
  It doesn't come from lips that tell
    lies.
²When you hand down your
  sentence, may it be in my
  favor.
May your eyes see what is right.

³Look deep down into my heart.
Study me carefully at night.
Put me to the test.
You won't find anything wrong.
I have made up my mind
  that my mouth won't say sinful
    things.
⁴I don't do the things other people
  do.
By obeying your word
I have kept myself from acting
  like those who try to hurt others.
⁵My steps have stayed on your paths.
My feet have not slipped.

⁶God, I call out to you because you
  will answer me.
Listen to me. Hear my prayer.
⁷Show the wonder of your great
  love.
By using your powerful right
  hand,

Is there church in heaven?

We will not have churches in heaven like the ones we have on
earth. Everyone in heaven will be a believer, and we will all be
together with God. We will be able
to talk, laugh, pray and have fun
together all the time. We will not
need church buildings either.
We will see Jesus in person.
We will be able to be with him
all the time. There will also be
angels in heaven praising God
with us.

checkout Psalm 16:11

Related verses:
1 John 3:2;
Revelation
21:1–27

JASON'S
IMAGINATION

CHURCH
OF HEAVEN
TODAY'S GUEST SPEAKERS:
Moses and the Apostle Paul

you save those who go to you for
  safety from their enemies.
⁸Take good care of me, just as you
  would take care of your own
  eyes.
Hide me in the shadow of your
  wings.
⁹Save me from the sinful people
  who attack me.
Save me from my deadly
  enemies who are all around
  me.
¹⁰They make their hearts hard and
  stubborn.
Their mouths speak with pride.
¹¹They have tracked me down. They
  are all around me.
Their eyes watch for a chance to
  throw me to the ground.
¹²They are like a hungry lion,
  waiting to attack.
They are like a powerful lion,
  hiding in the bushes.

¹³LORD, rise up. Oppose them and
  bring them down.
With your sword, save me from
  those evil people.
¹⁴LORD, by your power save me from
  people like that.
They belong to this world. They
  get their reward in this life.

You satisfy the hunger of those you
  love.
Their children have plenty.
And those children store up
  wealth for their children.
¹⁵Because I do what is right, I will
  enjoy your blessing.
When I wake up, I will be
  satisfied because I will see
  you.

PSALM 18

For the director of music.
A psalm of David, the servant of the LORD.
  He sang the words of this song
  to the LORD. He sang them when
  the LORD saved him from the
  powerful hand of all of his
  enemies and of Saul. He said,

¹I love you, LORD.
  You give me strength.

²The LORD is my rock and my fort.
  He is the One who saves me.

My God is my rock. I go to him
  for safety.
He is like a shield to me. He's the
  power that saves me. He's my
  place of safety.
³I call out to the LORD. He is worthy
  of praise.
He saves me from my enemies.

⁴The ropes of death were almost
  wrapped around me.
A destroying flood swept over
  me.
⁵The ropes of the grave were tight
  around me.
Death set its trap in front of me.
⁶When I was in trouble, I called out
  to the LORD.
I cried to my God for help.
From his temple he heard my
  voice.
My cry for help reached his ears.

⁷The earth trembled and shook.
The base of the mountains
  rocked back and forth.
It trembled because the LORD
  was angry.
⁸Smoke came out of his nose.
Flames of fire came out of his
  mouth.
Burning coals blazed out of it.
⁹He opened the heavens and came
  down.
Dark clouds were under his feet.
¹⁰He got on the cherubim and flew.
The wings of the wind lifted him
  up.
¹¹He covered himself with darkness.
The dark rain clouds of the sky
  were like a tent around him.
¹²Clouds came out of the brightness
  that was all around him.
They came with hailstones and
  flashes of lightning.
¹³The LORD thundered from heaven.
The voice of the Most High God
  was heard.
¹⁴He shot his arrows and scattered
  our enemies.
He sent great flashes of lightning
  and chased the enemies away.
¹⁵The bottom of the sea could be
  seen.
The foundations of the earth
  were uncovered.
LORD, it happened when your
  anger blazed out.

It came like a blast of breath
  from your nose.

¹⁶ He reached down from heaven. He
  took hold of me.
  He lifted me out of deep waters.
¹⁷ He saved me from my powerful
  enemies.
  He set me free from those who
  were too strong for me.
¹⁸ They stood up to me when I was in
  trouble.
  But the LORD helped me.
¹⁹ He brought me out into a wide
  and safe place.
  He saved me because he was
  pleased with me.

²⁰ The LORD has been good to me
  because I do what is right.
  He has rewarded me because I
  lead a pure life.
²¹ I have lived the way the LORD
  wanted me to.

I haven't done evil by turning
  away from my God.
²² I keep all of his laws in mind.
  I haven't turned away from his
  commands.
²³ He knows that I am without
  blame.
  He knows I've kept myself from
  sinning.
²⁴ The LORD has rewarded me for
  doing what is right.
  He has rewarded me because I
  haven't done anything wrong.

²⁵ LORD, to those who are faithful you
  show that you are faithful.
  To those who are without blame
  you show that you are without
  blame.
²⁶ To those who are pure you show
  that you are pure.
  But to those whose paths are
  crooked you show that you are
  clever.

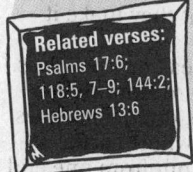

Why should we go to God for help?

We should ask God for help because we need him. Asking why we should go to God for help is like asking, "Why should I go to the gas station for gas?" God is the one who gives us life, the one who makes us able to walk, talk and move; he is the one who gives us knowledge and the one who gives us all we need. In a sense, he is the *only* one who can help us. That is why we should go to God for help. But if someone is physically or mentally hurting you, immediately tell a teacher, principal or other trusted adult.

checkout

Psalm 18:6

Related verses:
Psalms 17:6;
118:5, 7–9; 144:2;
Hebrews 13:6

²⁷You save those who aren't proud.
　But you bring down those whose
　eyes are proud.
²⁸LORD, you keep the lamp of my life
　burning brightly.
　You are my God. You bring light
　into my darkness.
²⁹With your help I can attack a troop
　of soldiers.
　With the help of my God I can
　climb over a wall.

³⁰God's way is perfect.
　The word of the LORD doesn't
　have any flaws.
　He is like a shield
　to all who go to him for safety.
³¹Who is God except the LORD?
　Who is the Rock except our God?
³²God gives me strength for the
　battle.
　He makes my way perfect.
³³He makes my feet like the feet of a
　deer.
　He helps me stand on the highest
　places.
³⁴He trains my hands to fight every
　battle.
　My arms can bend a bow of
　bronze.
³⁵LORD, you are like a shield that
　keeps me safe. You help me
　win the battle.
　Your strong right hand keeps me
　going.
　You bend down to make me
　great.
³⁶You give me a wide path to walk on
　so that I don't twist my ankles.

³⁷I chased my enemies and caught
　them.
　I didn't turn back until they were
　destroyed.
³⁸I crushed them so that they
　couldn't get up.
　They fell under my feet.
³⁹LORD, you gave me strength to
　fight the battle.
　You made my enemies bow down
　at my feet.
⁴⁰You made them turn their backs
　and run away.
　So I destroyed my enemies.
⁴¹They cried out for help. But there
　was no one to save them.
　They called out to you. But you
　didn't answer them.

⁴²I beat them as fine as dust blown
　by the wind.
　I poured them out like mud in
　the streets.

⁴³You saved me when my own
　people attacked me.
　You made me the ruler over
　nations.
　People I didn't know serve me
　now.
⁴⁴As soon as they hear me, they obey
　me.
　People from other lands bow
　down to me in fear.
⁴⁵All of them give up hope.
　They come trembling out of their
　hiding places.

⁴⁶The LORD lives! Give praise to my
　Rock!
　Give honor to God my Savior!
⁴⁷He is the God who pays my
　enemies back.
　He brings the nations under my
　control.
⁴⁸　He saves me from my enemies.
　You have honored me more than
　them.
　You have saved me from men
　who want to hurt me.
⁴⁹LORD, I will praise you among the
　nations.
　I will sing praises to you.
⁵⁰The LORD helps his king win great
　battles.
　He shows his faithful love to his
　anointed king.
　He shows it to me and my family
　forever.

PSALM 19

For the director of music.
A psalm of David.

¹The heavens tell about the glory of
　God.
　The skies show that his hands
　created them.
²Day after day they speak about it.
　Night after night they make it
　known.
³But they don't speak or use words.
　No sound is heard from them.
⁴At the same time, their voice goes
　out into the whole earth.
　Their words go out from one end
　of the world to the other.

God has set up a tent in the
heavens for the sun.

5 The sun is like a groom coming
out of the room where he
spent his wedding night.
The sun is like a great runner
who takes delight in running a
race.

6 It rises at one end of the heavens.
Then it moves across to the other
end.
Nothing can hide from its heat.

7 The law of the LORD is perfect.
It gives us new strength.
The laws of the LORD can be
trusted.
They make childish people wise.

8 The rules of the LORD are right.
They give joy to our hearts.
The commands of the LORD shine
brightly.
They give light to our minds.

9 The law that brings respect for the
LORD is pure.
It lasts forever.
The directions the LORD gives are
true.
All of them are completely right.

10 They are more priceless than gold.
They have greater value than
huge amounts of pure gold.
They are sweeter than honey
that is taken from the
honeycomb.

11 I am warned by them.
When I obey them, I am greatly
rewarded.

12 Can I know my mistakes?
Forgive my hidden faults.

13 Keep me also from the sins I want
to commit.
May they not be my master.
Then I will be without blame.
I will not be guilty of any great
sin against your law.

14 LORD, may the words of my mouth
and the thoughts of my heart
be pleasing in your eyes.
You are my Rock and my
Redeemer.

PSALM 20

For the director of music.
A psalm of David.

1 May the LORD answer you when
you are in trouble.
May the God of Jacob keep you
safe.

2 May he send you help from the
sacred tent.
May he give you aid from Zion.

3 May he remember all of your
sacrifices.
May he accept your burnt
offerings.   *Selah*

4 May he give you what your heart
longs for.

Why did God create the world?

We don't know exactly why God created the world and the
heavens. But we do
know that he enjoys making things.
And we know that he enjoys
having friends. He enjoys
sharing his love with men,
women, boys and girls. The
beauty of this world reminds us
of God's greatness every day.

checkout
Psalm 19:1

Related verses:
Genesis 1:1—2:1;
Isaiah 45:7

**JASON'S
IMAGINATION**

May he make all of your plans
    succeed.
⁵We will shout with joy when you
    win the battle.
We will lift up our flags in the
    name of our God.
May the LORD give you
    everything you ask for.

⁶Now I know that the LORD saves
    his anointed king.
He answers him from his holy
    heaven.
The power of God's right hand
    saves the king.
⁷Some trust in chariots. Some trust
    in horses.
But we trust in the LORD our God.
⁸They are brought to their knees
    and fall down.
But we get up and stand firm.

⁹LORD, save the king!
    Answer us when we call out to
    you!

PSALM 21

For the director of music.
A psalm of David.

¹LORD, the king is filled with joy
    because you are strong.
How great is his joy because you
    help him win his battles!
²You have given him what his heart
    longed for.
You haven't kept back from him
    what his lips asked for.   *Selah*
³You welcomed him with rich
    blessings.
You placed a crown of pure gold
    on his head.
⁴He asked you for life, and you gave
    it to him.
You promised him days that
    would never end.
⁵His glory is great because you
    helped him win his battles.
You have honored him with glory
    and majesty.

KIDS' QUESTion

Why do so many people keep translating the Bible?

The Bible was not written in English. The Old Testament was written in the Hebrew language, and the New Testament was written in the Greek language. Over the years men and women have worked hard to put the Bible into different languages. Putting the Bible into another language is called "translation."

    There are many English translations. This is because people keep trying to translate the Hebrew and Greek into words that are just right for people who speak English. Some people still do not have the Bible in their own language.

    God wants us to take the message about Jesus to everyone all over the world. This means that translating the Bible into other languages is a very important job.

checkout Psalm 19:7–10

Related verses:
Isaiah 6:8;
Matthew 28:19,20

⁶You have given him blessings that
will last forever.
You have made him glad and
joyful because you are with
him.
⁷The king trusts in the LORD.
The faithful love of the Most
High God
will keep the king secure.
⁸You, the king, will capture all of
your enemies.
Your right hand will take hold of
them.
⁹When you appear,
you will be like a flaming furnace
to them.
The LORD will swallow them up in
his anger.
His fire will burn them up.
¹⁰You will wipe their children from
the face of the earth.
You will remove them from the
human race.
¹¹Your enemies make evil plans
against you.
They think up evil things to do.
But they can't succeed.
¹²You will make them turn their
backs and run away
when you aim your arrows at
them.

¹³LORD, may you be honored
because you are strong.
We will sing and praise your
might.

PSALM 22

For the director of music.
A psalm of David to the tune
of "The Doe of the Morning."

¹My God, my God, why have you
deserted me?
Why do you seem to be so far
away when I need you to save
me?
Why do you seem to be so far
away that you can't hear my
groans?
²My God, I cry out in the daytime.
But you don't answer.
I cry out at night. I can't keep
quiet.

³But you rule from your throne as
the Holy One.

You are the God Israel praises.
⁴Our people of long ago put their
trust in you.
They trusted in you, and you
saved them.
⁵They cried out to you and were
saved.
They trusted in you, and you
didn't let them down.

⁶People treat me like a worm and
not a man.
They hate me and look down on
me.
⁷All those who see me laugh at me.
They shout at me and make fun
of me.
They shake their heads at me.
⁸They say, "He trusts in the LORD.
Let the LORD help him.
If the LORD is pleased with him,
let him save him."

⁹But you brought me out of my
mother's body.
You made me trust in you
even when I was at my mother's
breast.
¹⁰From the time I was born, you
took good care of me.
Ever since I came out of my
mother's body, you have been
my God.
¹¹Don't be far away from me.
Trouble is near,
and there is no one to help me.

¹²Many enemies are all around me.
They are like strong bulls from
the land of Bashan.
¹³They are like roaring lions that
tear to pieces what they kill.
They open their mouths wide to
attack me.
¹⁴My strength is like water that is
poured out on the ground.
I feel as if my bones aren't
connected.
My heart has turned to wax.
It has melted away inside me.
¹⁵My strength is dried up like a piece
of broken pottery.
My tongue sticks to the roof of
my mouth.
You bring me down to the edge
of the grave.
¹⁶A group of sinful people has
closed in on me.

They are all around me like a
   pack of dogs.
They have pierced my hands and
   my feet.
¹⁷ I can see all of my bones right
   through my skin.
People stare at me. They laugh
   when I suffer.
¹⁸ They divide up my clothes among
   them.
They cast lots for what I am
   wearing.

¹⁹ LORD, don't be so far away.
You give me strength. Come
   quickly to help me.
²⁰ Save me from the sword.
Save the only life I have. Save me
   from the power of those dogs.
²¹ Save me from the mouths of those
   lions.
Save me from the horns of those
   wild oxen.

²² I will announce your name to my
   brothers and sisters.
I will praise you among those
   who worship you.
²³ You who have respect for the
   LORD, praise him!
All you people of Jacob, honor
   him!
All you people of Israel, worship
   him!
²⁴ He has not forgotten the one who
   is hurting.
He has not turned away from his
   suffering.
He has not turned his face away
   from him.
He has listened to his cry for help.

²⁵ Because of what you have done,
I will praise you in the whole
   community of those who
   worship you.
In front of those who respect you,
I will keep my promises.
²⁶ Those who are poor will eat and
   be satisfied.
Those who look to the LORD will
   praise him.
May their hearts be filled with
   new hope!
²⁷ People from one end of the earth
   to the other
will remember and turn to the
   LORD.

The people of all the nations
will bow down before him.
²⁸ The LORD is King.
He rules over the nations.

²⁹ All the rich people of the earth will
   worship God and take part in
   his feasts.
All those who go down to the
   edge of the grave will fall on
   their knees in front of him.
I'm talking about those who can
   hardly keep themselves alive.
³⁰ Those who are not yet born will
   serve him.
Those who are born later will be
   told about the Lord.
³¹ And they will tell people who have
   not yet been born
   that he has done what is right.

PSALM 23

A psalm of David.

¹ The LORD is my shepherd. He gives
   me everything I need.
²   He lets me lie down in fields of
   green grass.
He leads me beside quiet waters.
³   He gives me new strength.
He guides me in the right paths
   for the honor of his name.
⁴ Even though I walk
   through the darkest valley,
I will not be afraid.
   You are with me.
Your shepherd's rod and staff
   comfort me.

⁵ You prepare a feast for me
   right in front of my enemies.
You pour oil on my head.
   My cup runs over.
⁶ I am sure that your goodness and
   love will follow me
all the days of my life.
And I will live in the house of the
   LORD
   forever.

PSALM 24

A psalm of David.

¹ The earth belongs to the LORD.
   And so does everything in it.
The world belongs to him. And
   so do all those who live in it.
² He set it firmly on the oceans.
He made it secure on the waters.

³Who can go up to the temple on
    the hill of the LORD?
Who can stand in his holy place?
⁴Anyone who has clean hands and
    a pure heart.
He does not worship the statue
    of a god.
He doesn't use the name of that
    god when he makes a
    promise.
⁵People like that will receive the
    LORD's blessing.
When God their Savior hands
    down his sentence, it will be
    in their favor.
⁶The people who look to God are
    like that.
God of Jacob, they look to you.
                Selah

⁷Open wide, you gates.
Open up, you age-old doors.
Then the King of glory will come
    in.
⁸Who is the King of glory?
The LORD, who is strong and
    mighty.
The LORD, who is mighty in
    battle.
⁹Open wide, you gates.
Open wide, you age-old doors.
Then the King of glory will come
    in.
¹⁰Who is he, this King of glory?
The LORD who rules over all.
He is the King of glory.   *Selah*

PSALM 25

A psalm of David.

¹LORD, I worship you.
² My God, I trust in you.
Don't let me be put to shame.
    Don't let my enemies win the
    battle over me.
³Those who put their hope in you
    will never be put to shame.
But those who can't be trusted
    will be put to shame. They have
    no excuse.

⁴LORD, show me your ways.
    Teach me how to follow you.
⁵Guide me in your truth. Teach me.
    You are God my Savior.
I put my hope in you all day long.
⁶LORD, remember your great mercy
    and love.
You have shown them to your
    people for a long time.
⁷Don't remember the sins I
    committed when I was young.
Don't remember how often I
    refused to obey you.
Remember me because you love
    me.
LORD, you are good.

⁸The LORD is honest and good.
    He teaches sinners to walk in his
    ways.
⁹He shows those who aren't proud
    how to do what is right.
He teaches them his ways.

KIDS' QUESTION

Will my pet go to heaven when it dies?

We do not know what happens to animals when they die. But God does know, and we know that his plan is good. Only he knows whether they will join us in heaven. Sometimes we may get the idea that animals think and understand as we do. But God created animals different from people. They do not have souls, and they cannot enjoy God as a friend the way we can. But God still cares about animals on earth. Part of the job God gave to people is to care for animals. Just as a shepherd takes care of all the needs of sheep, God cares for us as our shepherd.

Related verses:
Psalm 104:27,28;
Isaiah 11:6–9

checkout   Psalm 23:1

10 All of the LORD's ways are loving
and faithful
   for those who obey what his
      covenant commands.
11 LORD, be true to your name.
   Forgive my sin, even though it is
      great.
12 Who is the man who has respect
for the LORD?
   God will teach him the way he
      has chosen for him.
13 Things will always go well for
him.
   His children will be given the
      land.
14 The LORD shares his plans with
those who have respect for
him.
   He makes his covenant known to
      them.
15 My eyes always look to the LORD.
   He alone can set my feet free
      from the trap.

16 Turn to me and show me your
favor.
   I am lonely and hurting.
17 The troubles of my heart have
increased.
   Set me free from my great pain.
18 Look at how I'm hurting! See how
much I suffer!
   Take away all of my sins.
19 Look at how many enemies I have!
   See how terrible their hatred is
      for me!
20 Guard my life. Save me.
   Don't let me be put to shame.
   I go to you for safety.
21 May my honest and good life keep
me safe.
   I have put my hope in you.

22 God, set Israel free
   from all of their troubles!

PSALM 26

A psalm of David.

1 LORD, when you hand down your
sentence, let it be in my favor.
   I have lived without blame.
   I have trusted in the LORD.
   I have never doubted him.
2 LORD, test me. Try me out.
   Look deep down into my heart
      and mind.
3 Your love is always with me.

I have always lived by your truth.
4 I don't spend time with people
who tell lies.
   I don't keep company with
      pretenders.
5 I hate to be with a group of sinful
people.
   I refuse to spend time with those
      who are evil.
6 I wash my hands to show that I'm
not guilty.
   LORD, I come near your altar.
7 I shout my praise to you.
   I tell about all the wonderful
      things you have done.
8 LORD, I love the house where you
live.
   I love the place where your glory
      is.
9 Don't destroy me together with
sinners.
   Don't take my life away along
      with murderers.
10 Their hands are always planning
to do evil.
   Their right hands are full of
      money that bought them off.
11 But I live without blame.
   Set me free and show me your
      favor.
12 My feet stand on level ground.
   In the whole community I will
      praise the LORD.

PSALM 27

A psalm of David.

1 The LORD gives me light and saves
me.
   Why should I fear anyone?
   The LORD is my place of safety.
   Why should I be afraid?
2 My enemies are evil.
   They will trip and fall
when they attack me
   and try to eat me alive.
3 Even if an army attacks me,
   my heart will not be afraid.
   Even if war breaks out against me,
   I will still trust in God.
4 I'm asking the LORD for only one
thing.
   Here is what I want.
   I want to live in the house of the
      LORD
      all the days of my life.

I want to look at the beauty of the
LORD.
I want to worship him in his
temple.
⁵When I'm in trouble,
he will keep me safe in his house.
He will hide me in the safety of his
holy tent.
He will put me on a rock that is
very high.
⁶Then I will win the battle
over my enemies who are all
around me.
At his holy tent I will offer my
sacrifice with shouts of joy.
I will sing and make music to the
LORD.
⁷LORD, hear my voice when I call
out to you.
Show me your favor and answer
me.
⁸My heart says, "Look to him!"
LORD, I will look to you.
⁹Don't turn your face away from
me.
Don't turn me away because you
are angry.
You have helped me.
God my Savior, don't say no to me.
Don't desert me.
¹⁰My father and mother may desert
me,
but the LORD will accept me.
¹¹LORD, teach me your ways.
Lead me along a straight path.
There are many people who beat
me down.
¹²My enemies want to harm me. So
don't turn me over to them.
Witnesses who tell lies are rising
up against me.
They are trying to destroy me.

¹³Here is something I am still sure
of.
I will see the LORD's goodness
while I'm still alive.
¹⁴Wait for the LORD.
Be strong and don't lose hope.
Wait for the LORD.

PSALM 28

A psalm of David.

¹LORD, my Rock, I call out to you.
Pay attention to me.
If you remain silent, I will die.

I will be like those who have
gone down into the grave.
²Hear my cry for your favor
when I call out to you for help.
Hear me when I lift up my hands
in prayer
toward your Most Holy Room.

³Don't drag me away with sinners.
Don't drag me away with those
who do evil.
They speak in a friendly way to
their neighbors.
But their hearts are full of hatred.
⁴Pay them back for their evil
actions.
Pay them back for what their
hands have done.
Give them exactly what they
should get.
⁵They don't care about the LORD's
mighty acts.
They don't care about what his
hands have done.
So he will tear them down.
He will never build them up
again.

⁶Give praise to the LORD.
He has heard my cry for his favor.
⁷The LORD gives me strength. He is
like a shield that keeps me
safe.
My heart trusts in him, and he
helps me.
My heart jumps for joy.
I will sing and give thanks to
him.

⁸The LORD gives strength to his
people.
He guards and saves his anointed
king.
⁹Save your people. Bless those who
belong to you.
Be their shepherd. Take care of
them forever.

PSALM 29

A psalm of David.

¹Praise the LORD, you mighty
angels.
Praise the LORD for his glory and
strength.
²Praise the LORD for the glory that
belongs to him.
Worship the LORD because of his
beauty and holiness.

³The voice of the LORD is heard over
the waters.
The God of glory thunders.
The LORD thunders over the
mighty waters.
⁴The voice of the LORD is powerful.
The voice of the LORD is majestic.
⁵The voice of the LORD breaks the
cedar trees.
The LORD breaks the cedars of
Lebanon into pieces.
⁶He makes the mountains of
Lebanon skip like a calf.
He makes Mount Hermon jump
like a young wild ox.
⁷The voice of the LORD strikes
with flashes of lightning.
⁸The voice of the LORD shakes the
desert.
The LORD shakes the Desert of
Kadesh.
⁹The voice of the LORD twists the
oak trees.
It strips the forests bare.
And in his temple everyone cries
out, "Glory!"

¹⁰The LORD on his throne rules over
the flood.
The LORD rules from his throne
as King forever.
¹¹The LORD gives strength to his
people.
The LORD blesses his people with
peace.

PSALM 30

A psalm of David. A song for committing
the completed temple to God.

¹LORD, I will give you honor.
You brought me out of deep
trouble.
You didn't give my enemies the
joy of seeing me die.
²LORD my God, I called out to you
for help.
And you healed me.
³LORD, you brought me up from the
edge of the grave.
You kept me from going down
into the pit.

⁴Sing to the LORD, you who are
faithful to him.
Praise him, because his name is
holy.
⁵His anger lasts for only a moment.

But his favor lasts for a person's
whole life.
Sobbing can remain through the
night.
But joy comes in the morning.

⁶When I felt safe, I said,
"I will always be secure."
⁷LORD, when you showed me your
favor,
you made my mountain stand
firm.
But when you turned your face
away from me,
I was terrified.
⁸LORD, I called out to you.
I cried to you for your favor.
⁹I said, "What good will come if I
die?
What good will come if I go down
into the grave?
Can the dust of my dead body
praise you?
Can it tell how faithful you are?
¹⁰LORD, hear me. Show me your
favor.
LORD, help me."

¹¹You turned my loud crying into
dancing.
You removed my black clothes
and dressed me with joy.
¹²So my heart will sing to you. I can't
keep silent.
LORD, my God, I will give you
thanks forever.

PSALM 31

For the director of music.
A psalm of David.

¹LORD, I have gone to you for safety.
Don't let me ever be put to
shame.
Save me, because you do what is
right.
²Pay attention to me.
Come quickly to help me.
Be the rock I go to for safety.
Be the strong fort that saves me.
³You are my rock and my fort.
Lead me and guide me for the
honor of your name.
⁴Free me from the trap that is set
for me.
You are my place of safety.
⁵Into your hands I commit my very
life.

LORD, set me free. You are my
   faithful God.

⁶ I hate those who worship
      worthless statues of gods.
   I trust in the LORD.
⁷ I will be glad and full of joy
      because you love me.
   You saw that I was hurting.
   You took note of my great pain.
⁸ You have not handed me over to
      the enemy.
   You have put me in a wide and
      safe place.

⁹ LORD, show me your favor. I'm in
      deep trouble.
   I'm so sad I can hardly see.
   My whole body grows weak with
      sadness.
¹⁰ Pain has taken over my life.
   My years are spent in groaning.

I have no strength because I'm
   hurting so much.
My body is getting weaker and
   weaker.
¹¹ My neighbors make fun of me
      because I have so many enemies.
   My friends are afraid of me.
   Those who see me on the street
      run away from me.
¹² They have forgotten me. I might as
      well be dead.
   I have become like broken
      pottery.
¹³ I hear the lies many people tell
      about me.
   There is terror all around me.
   Many have joined together against
      me.
   They plan to kill me.
¹⁴ But I trust in you, LORD.
   I say, "You are my God."

In heaven, we won't just sing and worship all day, will we?

We will be happy all the time in heaven. We read in the Bible about angels
singing and praising God all the time. That may sound boring, but remember
that people in heaven sing because they are *glad*. Even though we don't know
exactly what we'll be doing, we do know that life with God will be happy,
joyful and exciting.

Imagine that you are a tadpole. All your life you have lived only in the
water. You know that someday you will become a frog and you will
get to live on land. But you have no
idea what life on land is really like.
And it does not sound very good
when the frogs explain it to you
because there is no water and you
cannot swim. That is the way it is
with heaven. It will always be hard for
us to understand what is so great
about heaven until we get there. But
once we're there, it will be hard to
imagine ever wanting to stay on earth!

checkout **Psalm 30:12**

Related verses:
1 Corinthians 2:9;
13:12

JASON'S
IMAGINATION

¹⁵ My whole life is in your hands.
Save me from my enemies.
Save me from those who are
chasing me.
¹⁶ Let your face smile on me with
favor.
Save me because your love is
faithful.
¹⁷ LORD, I have cried out to you.
Don't let me be put to shame.
But let sinners be put to shame.
Let them lie silent in the grave.
¹⁸ Their lips tell lies. Let them be
silenced.
They speak with pride against
those who do right.
They make fun of them.

¹⁹ How great your goodness is!
You have stored it up for those
who have respect for you.
While other people watch, you
give it to those who run to you
for safety.
²⁰ They are safe because you are with
them.
You hide them from the evil
plans of their enemies.
In your house you keep them safe
from those who bring charges
against them.

²¹ Give praise to the LORD.
He showed me his wonderful
love
when my enemies attacked the
city I was in.
²² I was afraid and said,
"I've been cut off from you!"
But you heard my cry for your
favor.
You heard me when I called out
to you for help.

²³ Love the LORD, all of you who are
faithful to him!
The LORD watches over the
faithful.
But he completely pays back
those who are proud.
²⁴ Be strong, all of you who put your
hope in the LORD.
Never give up.

PSALM 32

A *maskil* of David.

¹ Blessed is the one whose lawless
acts are forgiven.

His sins have been taken away.
² Blessed is the man whose sin the
LORD never counts against
him.
He doesn't want to cheat anyone.

³ When I kept silent about my sin,
my body became weak
because I groaned all day long.
⁴ Day and night
your heavy hand punished me.
I became weaker and weaker
as I do in the heat of summer.
Selah

⁵ Then I admitted my sin to you.
I didn't cover up the wrong I had
done.
I said, "I will admit my lawless acts
to the LORD."
And you forgave the guilt of my
sin.   *Selah*

⁶ Let everyone who is godly pray to
you
while they can still look to you.
When troubles come like a flood,
they certainly won't reach those
who are godly.
⁷ You are my hiding place.
You will keep me safe from
trouble.
You will surround me with songs
sung by those who praise you
because you save your people.
Selah

⁸ I will guide you and teach you the
way you should go.
I will give you good advice and
watch over you.
⁹ Don't be like the horse or the
mule.
They can't understand anything.
They have to be controlled by bits
and bridles.
If they aren't, they won't come to
you.
¹⁰ Sinful people have all kinds of
trouble.
But the LORD's faithful love
is all around those who trust in
him.

¹¹ Be glad because of what the LORD
has done for you.
Be joyful, you who do what is
right!
Sing, all of you whose hearts are
honest!

PSALM 33

¹You who are godly, sing with joy to the LORD.
  It is right for honest people to praise him.
²Praise the LORD with the harp.
  Make music to him on the lyre that has ten strings.
³Sing a new song to him.
  Play with skill, and shout with joy.

⁴What the LORD says is right and true.
  He is faithful in everything he does.
⁵The LORD loves what is right and fair.
  The earth is full of his faithful love.

⁶The heavens were made when the LORD commanded it to happen.
  All of the stars were created by the breath of his mouth.
⁷He gathers the waters of the sea together.
  He puts the oceans in their places.
⁸Let the whole earth have respect for the LORD.

  Let all of the people in the world honor him.
⁹He spoke, and the world came into being.
  He commanded, and it stood firm.
¹⁰The LORD blocks the sinful plans of the nations.
  He keeps them from doing what they want to do.
¹¹But the plans of the LORD stand firm forever.
  What he wants to do will last for all time.

¹²Blessed is the nation whose God is the LORD.
  Blessed are the people he chose to be his own.
¹³From heaven the LORD looks down and sees everyone.
¹⁴From his throne he watches all those who live on the earth.
¹⁵He creates the hearts of all people.
  He is aware of everything they do.
¹⁶A king isn't saved just because his army is big.
  A soldier doesn't escape just because he is very strong.
¹⁷People can't trust a horse to save them either.

KIDS' QUESTION

Where does all the money from fountains and wishing wells go?

Many people who have fountains or wishing wells give the money away to help needy people. If you do throw change into a fountain or wishing well, do not bother to make a wish. Instead, pray for the people who will be helped by your money.

checkout
Psalm 32:10

WISHING WELL

RIVER BANK

Related verses:
Psalm 125:1;
Isaiah 26:4

Though it is very strong, it can't
save them.
¹⁸ But the LORD looks with favor on
those who respect him.
He watches over those who put
their hope in his faithful love.
¹⁹ He watches over them to save
them from death.
He wants to keep them alive
when there is no food in the
land.

²⁰ We wait in hope for the LORD.
He helps us. He is like a shield
that keeps us safe.
²¹ Our hearts are full of joy because
of him.
We trust in him, because he is
holy.
²² LORD, may your faithful love rest
on us.
We put our hope in you.

PSALM 34

A psalm of David when he was
in front of Abimelech and pretended
to be out of his mind. Abimelech
drove him away, and he left.

¹ I will thank the LORD at all times.
My lips will always praise him.
² I will honor the LORD.

Let those who are hurting hear
and be joyful.
³ Join me in giving glory to the
LORD.
Let us honor him together.

⁴ I looked to the LORD, and he
answered me.
He saved me from everything I
was afraid of.
⁵ Those who look to him beam with
joy.
They are never put to shame.
⁶ This poor man called out, and the
LORD heard him.
He saved him out of all of his
troubles.
⁷ The angel of the LORD stands
guard
around those who have respect
for him.
And he saves them.

⁸ Taste and see that the LORD is
good.
Blessed is the man who goes to
him for safety.
⁹ You people of God, have respect
for the LORD.
Those who respect him have
everything they need.
¹⁰ The lions may grow weak and
hungry.

Are angels our imaginary friends?

Angels are real and not imaginary. Some people think they can
talk to angels or that they have special angels who guide them.
But the Bible teaches that angels are God's messengers. They serve him
and do what he says. Often, God tells them to help us. But they are not
our friends the way people
are or even the way God
can be. Angels are God's
servants and are not
people. But they are as
real as God is.

checkout Psalm 34:7

EXCUSE ME, COULD I
GET A SECOND SPOON
FOR MY FRIEND HERE?

Related verse:
Hebrews 1:14

But those who look to the LORD
have every good thing they
need.

[11] My children, come. Listen to me.
I will teach you to have respect
for the LORD.

[12] Do you love life
and want to see many good days?

[13] Then keep your tongues from
speaking evil.
Keep your lips from telling lies.

[14] Turn away from evil, and do good.
Look for peace, and go after it.

[15] The LORD looks with favor on
those who are godly.
His ears are open to their cry.

[16] The LORD doesn't look with favor
on those who do evil.
He removes all memory of them
from the earth.

[17] Godly people cry out, and the
LORD hears them.
He saves them from all of their
troubles.

[18] The LORD is close to those whose
hearts have been broken.

He saves those whose spirits
have been crushed.

[19] Anyone who does what is right
may have many troubles.
But the LORD saves him from all
of them.

[20] The LORD watches over all of his
bones.
Not one of them will be broken.

[21] Sinners will be killed by their own
evil.
The enemies of godly people will
be judged.

[22] The LORD sets those who serve
him free.
No one who goes to him for
safety will be judged.

PSALM 35

A psalm of David.

[1] LORD, stand up against those who
stand up against me.
Fight against those who fight
against me.

[2] Pick up your large shields and
your small shields.

Why do we have to pray instead of just talking with God?

Prayer does not have to be very formal and serious. Prayer can be natural, like having a talk with a friend. We can talk to God whenever we need to. We can tell him what we are excited about, tell him what worries us or ask him for help. So when we pray, we *are* just talking with God. We are talking to our best friend.

We can pray about anything—anytime, anywhere—because God loves us.

checkout
Psalm 34:3

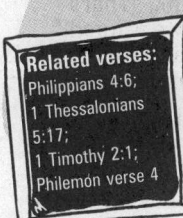

Related verses:
Philippians 4:6;
1 Thessalonians
5:17;
1 Timothy 2:1;
Philemon verse 4

GOD, THERE'S SOMETHING I WANT TO TALK TO YOU ABOUT. IT'S NOT A BIG DEAL, SO I DON'T NEED TO PRAY ABOUT IT. BUT I JUST WANTED TO TALK TO YOU ABOUT IT.

Rise up and help me.
³ Get your spear and javelin ready to
    fight
    against those who are chasing me.
    Say to me, "I will save you."
⁴ Let those who are trying to kill me
    be brought down in dishonor.
    Let those who plan to destroy me
    be turned back in terror.
⁵ Let them be like straw blowing in
    the wind,
    while the angel of the LORD
    drives them away.
⁶ Let their path be dark and
    slippery,
    while the angel of the LORD
    chases them.
⁷ They set a trap for me without any
    reason.
    Without any reason they dug a
    pit to catch me.
⁸ So let them be destroyed without
    warning.
    Let the trap they set for me catch
    them.
    Let them fall into the pit and be
    destroyed.
⁹ Then I will be full of joy because of
    what the LORD has done.
    I will be glad because he has
    saved me.
¹⁰ My whole being will cry out,
    "Who is like you, LORD?
    You save poor people from those
    who are too strong for them.
    You save poor and needy people
    from those who rob them."
¹¹ Mean people come forward to give
    witness against me.
    They ask me things I don't know
    anything about.
¹² They pay me back with evil, even
    though I was good to them.
    They leave me without hope.
¹³ But when they were sick, I put on
    black clothes.
    I made myself low by going
    without food.
    My prayers for them weren't
    always answered.
¹⁴ So I went around crying
    as if I were crying over my friend
    or relative.
    I bowed my head in sadness
    as if I were sobbing over my
    mother.

¹⁵ But when I tripped and fell, they
    were all very happy.
    Attackers gathered against me
    when I didn't even know it.
    They kept on telling lies about
    me.
¹⁶ They were like ungodly people.
    They made fun of me.
    They ground their teeth at me in
    hate.
¹⁷ Lord, how much longer will you
    just look on?
    Save me from their deadly
    attacks.
    Save the only life I have.
    Save me from those lions.
¹⁸ I will give you thanks in the whole
    community.
    Among all of your people I will
    praise you.

¹⁹ Don't let those who are my
    enemies without any reason
    laugh at me and make fun of me.
    Don't let those who hate me
    without any reason
    wink at me with an evil purpose.
²⁰ They don't speak words of peace.
    They make up false charges
    against those who live quietly in
    the land.
²¹ They open their mouths wide at
    me. They make fun of me.
    They say, "With our own eyes we
    have seen what you did."

²² LORD, you have seen this. Don't be
    silent.
    Lord, don't be far away from me.
²³ Wake up! Rise up to help me!
    My God and Lord, stand up for
    me.
²⁴ LORD my God, when you hand
    down your sentence, let it be
    in my favor.
    You always do what is right.
    Don't let my enemies have the
    joy of seeing me fall.
²⁵ Don't let them think, "That's
    exactly what we wanted!"
    Don't let them say, "We have
    swallowed him up."

²⁶ Let all those who laugh at me
    because I'm in trouble
    be ashamed and bewildered.
    Let all who think they are better
    than I am

put on shame and dishonor as if
they were clothes.
27 Let those who are happy when my
name is cleared
shout with joy and gladness.
Let them always say, "May the
LORD be honored.
He is pleased when everything
goes well with the one who
serves him."
28 You always do what is right. My
tongue will speak about it
and praise you all day long.

PSALM 36

For the director of music.
A psalm of David,
the servant of the LORD.

1 Here are the words God has given
me to say
about the evil ways of anyone
who sins.
He doesn't have any respect for
God.
2 He praises himself so much
that he can't see his sin or
hate it.
3 His mouth speaks words that are
evil and false.
He has stopped being wise. He
has stopped doing good.
4 Even as he lies in bed he makes
evil plans.
He commits himself to a sinful
way of life.
He never says no to what is
wrong.
5 LORD, your love is as high as the
heavens.
Your faithful love reaches up to
the skies.
6 You are as holy as the mountains
are high.
You are as honest as the oceans
are deep.
LORD, you keep people and
animals safe.
7 How priceless your faithful
love is!
Important and ordinary people
alike
find safety in the shadow of your
wings.
8 They eat well because there is
more than enough in your
house.

You let them drink from your
river that flows with good
things.
9 You have the fountain of life.
We are filled with light because
you give us light.
10 Keep on loving those who know
you.
Keep on doing right to those
whose hearts are honest.
11 Don't let the feet of those who are
proud step on me.
Don't let the hands of those who
are evil drive me away.
12 See how those who do evil have
fallen!
They are thrown down. They
aren't able to get up.

PSALM 37

A psalm of David.

1 Don't be upset because of sinful
people.
Don't be jealous of those who do
wrong.
2 Like grass, they will soon dry up.
Like green plants, they will soon
die.
3 Trust in the LORD and do good.
Then you will live in the land and
enjoy its food.
4 Find your delight in the LORD.
Then he will give you everything
your heart really wants.
5 Commit your life to the LORD.
Here is what he will do if you
trust in him.
6 He will make your godly ways
shine like the dawn.
He will make your honest life
shine like the sun at noon.
7 Be still. Be patient. Wait for the
LORD to act.
Don't be upset when other
people succeed.
Don't be upset when they carry
out their evil plans.
8 Keep from being angry. Turn away
from anger.
Don't be upset. That only leads to
evil.
9 Sinful people will be cut off from
the land.

But it will be given to those who
put their hope in the LORD.

¹⁰ In a little while, there won't be any
more sinners.
Even if you look for them, you
won't be able to find them.
¹¹ But those who are free of pride will
be given the land.
They will enjoy great peace.

¹² Sinful people make plans to harm
those who do what is right.
They grind their teeth at them.
¹³ But the Lord laughs at those who
do evil.
He knows the day is coming
when he will judge them.

¹⁴ Sinners pull out their swords.
They bend their bows.
They want to kill poor and needy
people.
They plan to murder those who
lead honest lives.
¹⁵ But they will be killed with their
own swords.
Their own bows will be broken.

¹⁶ Those who do what is right may
have very little.
But it's better than the wealth of
many sinners.
¹⁷ The power of those who are evil
will be broken.
But the LORD takes good care of
those who do what is right.
¹⁸ Every day the LORD watches over
those who are without blame.
What he has given them will last
forever.
¹⁹ When trouble comes to them, they
will have what they need.
When there is little food in the
land, they will still have
plenty.

²⁰ But sinful people will die.
The LORD's enemies will be like
flowers in the field.
They will disappear like smoke.

²¹ Sinful people borrow and don't
pay back.
But those who are godly give
freely to others.

KIDS' QUESTION

Why can't friends just get along instead of fighting and arguing with each other?

You'd think that friends would get along great all the time. But conflicts
happen because everyone has ups and downs, and sometimes a friend is
just in a bad mood. No two people agree on everything all the time.
When people disagree they should talk it through and work
together to solve the problem instead of fighting. If your friends
are always arguing, you can be a good example yourself and help
them resolve the issue. You can also set a good example for your
friends by spending more
time with kids who are
learning to get along with
each other.

checkout Psalm 37:8

Related verses:
Proverbs 17:4;
20:3

²²The LORD will give the land to
those he blesses.
But he will cut off those he puts a
curse on.

²³If the LORD is pleased with the way
a man lives,
he makes his steps secure.
²⁴Even if the man trips, he won't fall.
The LORD'S hand takes good care
of him.

²⁵I once was young, and now I'm
old.
But I've never seen godly people
deserted.
I've never seen their children
begging for bread.
²⁶The godly are always giving and
lending freely.
Their children will be blessed.

²⁷Turn away from evil and do good.
Then you will live in the land
forever.
²⁸The LORD loves those who are
honest.
He will not desert those who are
faithful to him.

They will be kept safe forever.
But the children of sinners will
be cut off from the land.
²⁹Those who do what is right will be
given the land.
They will live in it forever.

³⁰The mouths of those who do what
is right speak words of
wisdom.
They say what is honest.
³¹God's law is in their hearts.
Their feet do not slip.

³²Those who are evil hide and wait
for godly people.
They are trying to kill them.
³³But the LORD will not leave the
godly in their power.
He will not let them be found
guilty when they are brought
into court.

³⁴Wait for the LORD to act.
Live as he wants you to.
He will honor you by giving you
the land.
When sinners are cut off from it,
you will see it.

³⁵I saw a mean and sinful
person.
He was doing well, like a green
tree in its own soil.
³⁶But he soon passed away and was
gone.
Even though I looked for him, I
couldn't find him.

³⁷Think about those who are
without blame. Look at those
who are honest.

Why do we have to be good and obey in school?

Teachers have rules for how students should act in school so the school
will be safe and students will be able to learn. Just think of the chaos if
all the kids did whatever they wanted,
whenever they wanted. No one would
learn anything, except how to be rowdy.
In class, for example, if everyone talked
at the same time, no one would hear the
teacher. And if kids were
allowed to run, push and
shove in the hall, people
would get hurt.

checkout
Psalm 37:27–28

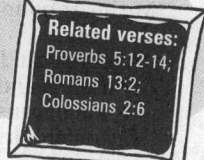

Related verses:
Proverbs 5:12-14;
Romans 13:2;
Colossians 2:6

A man who loves peace will have
a tomorrow.
³⁸But all sinners will be destroyed.
Those who are evil won't have a
tomorrow.
They will be cut off from the land.

³⁹The LORD saves those who do what
is right.
He is their place of safety when
trouble comes.
⁴⁰The LORD helps them and saves
them.
He saves them from sinful
people
because they go to him for safety.

PSALM 38

A psalm of David. A prayer.

¹LORD, don't correct me when you
are angry.
Don't punish me when you are
burning with anger.
²You have wounded me with your
arrows.
You have struck me with your
hand.
³Because of your anger, my whole
body is sick.
Because of my sin, I'm not
healthy.
⁴My guilt has become too much for
me.
It is a load too heavy to carry.

⁵My wounds are ugly. They stink.
I've been foolish. I have sinned.
⁶I am bent over. I've been brought
very low.
All day long I go around sobbing.
⁷My back is filled with burning
pain.
My whole body is sick.
⁸I am weak. I feel as if I've been
broken in pieces.
I groan because of the great pain
in my heart.

⁹Lord, everything I really want is
clearly known to you.
You always hear me when I sigh.
¹⁰My heart pounds. My strength is
gone.
My eyes can hardly see.
¹¹My friends and companions avoid
me because of my wounds.
My neighbors stay far away from
me.

¹²Those who are trying to kill me set
their traps.
Those who want to harm me talk
about destroying me.
All day long they plan ways to
trick me.

¹³I'm like a deaf person. I can't
hear.
I'm like someone who can't
speak, who can't say a word.
¹⁴I'm like a man who doesn't hear.
I'm like someone whose mouth
can't make any reply.
¹⁵LORD, I wait for you to help me.
LORD my God, I know you will
answer.
¹⁶I said, "Don't let my enemies have
the joy of seeing me fall.
Don't let them brag when my
foot slips."

¹⁷I am about to fall.
My pain never leaves me.
¹⁸I admit that I have done wrong.
I am troubled by my sin.
¹⁹I have many powerful enemies.
They are strong and healthy.
They hate me without any
reason.
²⁰They pay me back with evil, even
though I was good to them.
They tell lies about me because I
try to do what is good.

²¹LORD, don't desert me.
My God, don't be far away from
me.
²²Lord my Savior,
come quickly to help me.

PSALM 39

For the director of music.
For Jeduthun. A psalm of David.

¹I said, "I will be careful about how
I live.
I will not sin by what I say.
I will keep my mouth closed
when sinful people are near me."
²I was silent and kept quiet.
I didn't even say anything good.
But the pain inside me grew
worse.
³My heart was deeply troubled.
As I thought about what was
happening to me,
I became even more troubled.
Then I spoke out.

⁴I said, "LORD, show me when my
life will end.
  Show me how many days I have
  left.
  Tell me how short my life will be.
⁵You have given me only a few days
to live.
  My whole life doesn't seem like
  anything to you.
  No man's life lasts any longer
  than a breath.   *Selah*
⁶People are only shadows as they
go here and there.
  They rush around, but it doesn't
  mean anything.
  They pile up wealth, but they
  don't know who will get it.

⁷"Lord, what can I look forward to
now?
  You are the only hope I have.
⁸Save me from all the wrong things
I've done.
  Don't let foolish people make fun
  of me.
⁹I keep silent. I don't open my
mouth.
  You are the one who has caused
  all of this to happen.
¹⁰Please stop beating me.
  I'm about to die from the blows
  of your hand.

¹¹You correct and punish people for
their sin.
  Just as a moth eats cloth, you
  destroy their wealth.
  No one's life lasts any longer than
  a breath.   *Selah*

¹²"LORD, hear my prayer.
  Listen to my cry for help.
  Pay attention to my sobbing.
  I'm like a guest in your home.
  I'm only a visitor, like all of my
  family who lived before me.
¹³Leave me alone.
  Let me be full of joy again before
  I die."

PSALM 40

For the director of music.
A psalm of David.

¹I was patient while I waited for the
LORD.
  He turned to me and heard my
  cry for help.
²I was sliding down into the pit of
death, and he pulled me out.
  He brought me up out of the
  mud and dirt.
  He set my feet on a rock.
  He gave me a firm place to stand
  on.
³He gave me a new song to sing.

Is it wrong to stop telling my friends about Jesus even when they won't listen?

It is good that you want to tell your friends about Jesus. But it is also good to respect them as people. Sometimes your friends will not seem interested. And sometimes they may tell you that they do not want to talk about it anymore. Whenever that happens you need to respect their wishes and stop talking to them about it.

They will still learn about Jesus from you by watching how you live. Your friends will notice if you live like a Christian. They will see that you are loving and kind and that you do not do bad things all the time. They will see Jesus in you and learn about him as they watch.

Related verses:
Ecclesiastes 3:1;
Matthew 5:15,16

checkout Psalm 40:3

It is a hymn of praise to our God.
Many people will see what he has
    done and will worship him.
They will put their trust in the
    LORD.

⁴Blessed is the man
    who trusts in the LORD.
He doesn't look to proud people
    for help.
    He doesn't turn away to worship
      statues of gods.
⁵LORD my God,
    no one can compare with you.
You have done many miracles.
    And you plan to do many more
      for us.
There are too many of them
    for me to talk about.

⁶You didn't want sacrifices and
    offerings.
You weren't pleased with burnt
    offerings and sin offerings.

You gave me ears to hear you and
    obey you.
⁷Then I said, "Here I am.
    It is written about me in the
      scroll.
⁸My God, I have come to do what
    you want.
Your law is in my heart."

⁹I have told the whole community
    of those who worship you
    that what you do is right.
LORD, you know
    that I haven't kept quiet.
¹⁰I haven't kept to myself that what
    you did for me was right.
I have spoken about how faithful
    you were when you saved me.
I haven't hidden your love and
    truth
    from the whole community.
¹¹LORD, don't hold back your mercy
    from me.

KIDS' QUESTion

Where did they get the scrolls from?

Today, we use pencils and pens to write, and we write on paper.
But the Bible was written before these things were invented. Instead
of using paper, people would write on long strips of *papyrus* or *parchment*.
Papyrus was made from a plant that grows in Bible lands. Parchment was made
from animal skins. Both papyrus and parchment could be sewn together and
rolled up from one end to the other into long scrolls. Museums have some of
these ancient scrolls. People read from these scrolls like books. But there
wasn't a lot of them because
each one had to be copied
by hand. Today, everyone
can have his or her own
Bible to read. But in those
days, most temples and
churches would have only
one copy. Because of this,
the scrolls were very
valuable, and the priests
took good care of them.

checkout Psalm 40:7

Related verse:
2 Timothy 4:13

JASON'S IMAGINATION

scrolls 10 talents

10 talents

scrolls

May your love and truth always
keep me safe.

¹²There are more troubles all around
me than I can count.
My sins have caught up with me,
and I can't see any longer.
My sins are more than the hairs of
my head.
I have lost all hope.

¹³LORD, please save me.
LORD, come quickly to help me.
¹⁴Let all those who are trying to kill
me be put to shame.
Let them not be honored.
Let all those who want to destroy
me
be turned back in shame.
¹⁵Some people make fun of me.
Let them be shocked when their
plans fail.
¹⁶But let all those who look to you
be joyful and glad because of
what you have done.
Let those who love you because
you save them always say,
"May the LORD be honored!"

¹⁷But I am poor and needy.
May the Lord be concerned
about me.
You are the One who helps me and
saves me.
My God, please don't wait any
longer.

PSALM 41

For the director of music.
A psalm of David.

¹Blessed is the one who cares about
weak people.
When he is in trouble, the LORD
saves him.
²The LORD will guard him and keep
him alive.
He will bless him in the land.
He won't hand him over to the
wishes of his enemies.
³The LORD will take care of him
when he is lying sick in
bed.
He will make him well again.
⁴I said, "LORD, show me your favor.
Heal me. I have sinned against
you."
⁵My enemies are saying bad things
about me.

They say, "When will he die and
be forgotten?"
⁶When anyone comes to see me,
he says things he doesn't mean.
At the same time, he thinks up lies
to tell against me.
Then he goes out and spreads
those lies around.

⁷All of my enemies whisper to each
other about me.
They want something terrible to
happen to me.
⁸They say, "He is sick and will die
very soon.
He will never get up from his bed
again."
⁹Even my close friend, whom I
trusted, has deserted me.
I even shared my bread with him.

¹⁰But LORD, show me your favor.
Make me well, so I can pay them
back.
¹¹Then I will know that you are
pleased with me,
because my enemies haven't won
the battle over me.
¹²You will take good care of me
because I've been honest.
You will let me be with you
forever.

¹³Give praise to the LORD, the God of
Israel,
for ever and ever.
Amen and Amen.

BOOK II

Psalms 42–72

PSALM 42

For the director of music.
A *maskil* of the Sons of Korah.

¹A deer longs for streams of water.
God, I long for you in the same
way.
²I am thirsty for God. I am thirsty
for the living God.
When can I go and meet with
him?
³My tears have been my food
day and night.

All day long people say to me,
　"Where is your God?"
⁴When I remember what has
　　happened,
　I tell God all of my troubles.
I remember how I used to walk
　　along with the crowd of
　　worshipers.
　I led them to the house of God.
We shouted with joy and gave
　　thanks
　as we went to the holy feast.

⁵My spirit, why are you so sad?
　Why are you so upset deep down
　　inside me?
　Put your hope in God.
　Once again I will have reason to
　　praise him.
　He is my Savior and ⁶my God.

My spirit is very sad deep down
　　inside me.
　So I will remember you here
　　where the Jordan River begins.
I will remember you here on the
　　Hermon mountains
　and on Mount Mizar.
⁷You have sent wave upon wave of
　　trouble over me.
　It roars down on me like a
　　waterfall.
All of your waves and breakers
　　have rolled over me.

⁸During the day the LORD sends his
　　love to me.
　During the night I sing about
　　him.
　I say a prayer to the God who
　　gives me life.

⁹I say to God my Rock,
　"Why have you forgotten me?
Why must I go around in sorrow?
　Why am I beaten down by my
　　enemies?"
¹⁰My body suffers deadly pain
　as my enemies make fun of me.
All day long they say to me,
　"Where is your God?"

¹¹My spirit, why are you so sad?
　Why are you so upset deep down
　　inside me?
　Put your hope in God.
　Once again I will have reason to
　　praise him.
　He is my Savior and my God.

PSALM 43

¹God, when you hand down your
　　decision, let it be in my favor.
Stand up for me against an
　　ungodly nation.
Save me from those lying and
　　sinful people.
²You are God, my place of safety.
　Why have you turned your back
　　on me?
Why must I go around in sorrow?
　Why am I beaten down by my
　　enemies?
³Send out your light and your truth.
　Let them guide me.
Let them bring me back to your
　　holy mountain,
　to the place where you live.
⁴Then I will go to the altar of God.
　I will go to God. He is my joy and
　　my delight.
God, you are my God.
　I will praise you by playing the
　　harp.

⁵My spirit, why are you so sad?
　Why are you so upset deep down
　　inside me?
　Put your hope in God.
　Once again I will have reason to
　　praise him.
　He is my Savior and my God.

PSALM 44

For the director of music.
A *maskil* of the Sons of Korah.

¹God, we have heard what you did.
　Those who came before us have
　　told us
what you did in their days,
　in days long ago.
²With your powerful hand you
　　drove out the nations.
　You settled our people in the
　　land.
You crushed the people who were
　　there.
　And you made our people do
　　well.
³They didn't win the land with their
　　swords.
　They didn't gain success with
　　their powerful arms.
Your powerful right hand and your
　　mighty arm gave them
　　success.

You looked on them with favor.
You loved them.

4 You are my King and my God.
You give success to the people of
Jacob.
5 With your help we push our
enemies back.
By your power we walk all over
them.
6 I don't trust in my bow.
My sword doesn't bring me
success.
7 But you give us success over our
enemies.
You put them to shame.
8 All day long we talk about how
great God is.
We will praise your name forever.
Selah

9 But now you have turned your
back on us and made us low.
You don't march out with our
armies anymore.
10 You made us turn and run from
our enemies.
They have taken what belongs to
us.
11 You handed us over to be eaten up
like sheep.
You have scattered us among the
nations.
12 You sold your people for very little.
You didn't gain anything when
you sold them.

13 You have made us something that
our neighbors laugh at.
Those who live around us make
fun of us and tease us.
14 The nations make jokes about us.
They shake their heads at us.
15 All day long I am reminded of my
shame.
My face is covered with it
16 because of those who laugh at me
and attack me with their
words.
They want to get even with me.

17 All of this happened to us,
even though we had not
forgotten you.
We had been true to the
covenant you made with us.
18 Our hearts had not turned away
from you.

Our feet had not wandered from
your path.
19 But you crushed us and left us to
the wild dogs.
You covered us over with deep
darkness.

20 We didn't forget our God.
We didn't spread out our hands
in prayer to a strange god.
21 If we had, God would have
discovered it.
He knows the secrets of our
hearts.
22 But because of you, we face death
all day long.
We are considered as sheep to be
killed.

23 Lord, wake up! Why are you
sleeping?
Get up! Don't say no to us
forever.
24 Why do you turn your face away
from us?
Why do you forget our pain and
troubles?

25 We are brought down to the dust.
Our bodies lie flat on the ground.
26 Rise up and help us.
Save us because of your faithful
love.

PSALM 45

For the director of music.
A *maskil* of the Sons of Korah.
A wedding song to the tune of "Lilies."

1 My heart is full of beautiful words
as I say my poem for the king.
My tongue is like the pen of a
skillful writer.

2 You are the most excellent of men.
Your lips have been given the
ability to speak gracious
words.
God has blessed you forever.
3 Mighty one, put your sword at
your side.
Put on glory and majesty as if
they were your clothes.
4 In your majesty ride out with
power
in honor of what is true and
right.
Do it in honor of all those who are
not proud.

Let your right hand do wonderful
things.
5 Shoot your sharp arrows into the
hearts of your enemies.
Let the nations come under your
control.
6 Your throne is the very throne of
God.
Your kingdom will last for ever
and ever.
You will rule by treating everyone
fairly.
7 You love what is right and hate
what is evil.
So your God has placed you
above your companions.
He has filled you with joy by
pouring the sacred oil on your
head.
8 Myrrh and aloes and cassia make
all of your robes smell good.
In palaces decorated with ivory
the music played on stringed
instruments makes you glad.
9 Daughters of kings are among the
women you honor.
At your right hand is the royal
bride dressed in gold from
Ophir.
10 Royal bride, listen. Think about
this and pay attention to it.
Forget about your people and the
home you came from.
11 The king is charmed by your
beauty.
Honor him. He is now your
master.
12 The people of Tyre will come with
gifts.
Wealthy people will try to gain
your favor.
13 The princess comes into the
palace in all her glory.
Her gown has gold threads
running through it.
14 Dressed in beautiful clothes, she is
led to the king.
Her virgin companions follow
her
and are brought to him.
15 They are led in with joy and
gladness.
They enter the palace of the king.

16 Your sons will rule just as your
father and grandfather did.
You will make them princes
through the whole land.
17 I will make sure that people will
always remember you.
The nations will praise you for
ever and ever.

PSALM 46

For the director of music.
A song of the Sons of Korah.
For *alamoth.*

1 God is our place of safety. He gives
us strength.
He is always there to help us in
times of trouble.
2 The earth may fall apart.
The mountains may fall into the
middle of the sea.
But we will not be afraid.
3 The waters of the sea may roar and
foam.
The mountains may shake when
the waters rise.
But we will not be afraid.   *Selah*

4 God's blessings are like a river.
They fill the city of God with
joy.
That city is the holy place where
the Most High God lives.
5 Because God is there, the city will
not fall.
God will help it at the beginning
of the day.
6 Nations are in disorder. Kingdoms
fall.
God speaks, and the people of
the earth melt in fear.

7 The LORD who rules over all is with
us.
The God of Jacob is like a fort to
us.   *Selah*

8 Come and see what the LORD has
done.
See the places he has destroyed
on the earth.
9 He makes wars stop from one end
of the earth to the other.
He breaks every bow. He snaps
every spear.
He burns every shield with fire.
10 He says, "Be still, and know that I
am God.
I will be honored among the
nations.
I will be honored in the earth."

¹¹The LORD who rules over all is with
us.
The God of Jacob is like a fort to
us. *Selah*

For the director of music.
A psalm of the Sons of Korah.

¹Clap your hands, all you nations.
Shout to God with cries of joy.
²How wonderful is the LORD Most
High!
He is the great King over the
whole earth.
³He brought nations under our
control.
He made them fall under us.
⁴He chose our land for us.
The people of Jacob are proud of
their land,
and God loves them. *Selah*

⁵God went up to his throne while
his people were shouting with
joy.
The LORD went up while
trumpets were playing.
⁶Sing praises to God. Sing praises.
Sing praises to our King. Sing
praises.

⁷God is the King of the whole earth.
Sing a psalm of praise to him.
⁸God rules over the nations.
He is seated on his holy throne.
⁹The nobles of the nations come
together.
They are now part of the people
of the God of Abraham.
The kings of the earth belong to
God.
He is greatly honored.

A song. A psalm of the Sons of Korah.

¹The LORD is great. He is really
worthy of praise.
Praise him in the city of our God,
his holy mountain.
²Mount Zion is high and beautiful.
It brings joy to everyone on
earth.
Mount Zion is like the highest
parts of Mount Zaphon.
It is the city of the Great King.
³God is there to keep it safe.

He has shown himself to be like a
fort to the city.

⁴Many kings joined forces.
They entered Israel together.
⁵But when they saw Mount Zion,
they were amazed.
They ran away in terror.
⁶Trembling took hold of them.
They felt pain like a woman
giving birth to a baby.
⁷LORD, you destroyed them like
ships of Tarshish
that were torn apart by an east
wind.

⁸What we heard we have also seen.
We have seen it
in the city of the LORD who rules
over all.
We have seen it in the city of our
God.
We have heard and seen that God
makes her secure forever.
Selah

⁹God, inside your temple
we think about your faithful love.
¹⁰God, your fame reaches from one
end of the earth to the other.
In the same way, people praise
you from one end of the earth
to the other.
You use your power to do what is
right.
¹¹Mount Zion is filled with joy.
The villages of Judah are glad.
That's because you judge fairly.

¹²Walk around Zion. Go all around
it.
Count its towers.
¹³Think carefully about its outer
walls.
Just look at how safe it is!
Then you can tell its people that
God keeps them safe.
¹⁴This God is our God for ever and
ever.
He will be our guide to the very
end.

For the director of music.
A psalm of the Sons of Korah.

¹Hear this, all you nations.
Listen, all you who live in this
world.

² Listen, ordinary and important
people alike.
Listen, those of you who are rich
or poor.
³ My mouth will speak wise words.
What I say from my heart will
give understanding.
⁴ I will pay attention to a proverb.
I will explain my riddle as I play
the harp.

⁵ Why should I be afraid when
trouble comes?
Why should I fear when sinners
are all around me?
They are the kind of people who
want to take advantage of me.
⁶ They trust in their wealth.
They brag about how rich they
are.
⁷ No man can pay for the life of
anyone else.
No one can give God what that
would cost.
⁸ The price for a life is very high.
No payment is ever enough.
⁹ No one can pay enough to live
forever
and not rot in the grave.

¹⁰ Everyone can see that even wise
people die.
Foolish and dumb people also
pass away.
All of them leave their wealth to
others.
¹¹ Their graves will remain their
houses forever.
Their graves will be their homes
for all time to come.
Naming lands after themselves
won't help either.

¹² Even though people may be very
rich, they don't live on and on.
They are like the animals. They
die.

¹³ That's what happens to those who
trust in themselves.
It also happens to their followers,
who agree with what they say.
Selah
¹⁴ Like sheep they will end up in the
grave.
Death will swallow them up.
When honest people come to
power, a new day will dawn.

The bodies of sinners will waste
away in the grave.
They will end up far away from
their princely houses.
¹⁵ But God will save me from the
grave.
He will certainly take me to
himself.   *Selah*

¹⁶ Don't be upset when someone
becomes rich.
Don't be troubled when he
becomes more and more
wealthy.
¹⁷ He won't take anything with him
when he dies.
His riches won't go down to the
grave with him.
¹⁸ While he lived, he believed he was
blessed.
People praised him when things
were going well for him.
¹⁹ But he will die, like his people of
long ago.
He will never again see the light
that leads to life.

²⁰ People who have riches but don't
understand
are like the animals. They die.

PSALM 50

A psalm of Asaph.

¹ The Mighty One, God, the LORD,
speaks.
He calls out to the earth
from the sunrise in the east
to the sunset in the west.
² From Zion, perfect and beautiful,
God's glory shines out.
³ Our God comes, and he won't be
silent.
A burning fire goes ahead of him.
A terrible storm is all around
him.
⁴ He calls out to heaven and earth to
be his witnesses.
Then he judges his people.
⁵ He says, "Gather my holy people
around me.
They made a covenant with me
by offering a sacrifice."
⁶ The heavens announce that what
God decides is right.
He himself is the Judge.   *Selah*

⁷ God says, "Listen, my people, and
I will speak.

Listen, Israel, and I will give
witness against you.
I am God, your God.
⁸I don't find fault with you because
of your sacrifices.
I don't find fault with the burnt
offerings you always bring me.
⁹I don't need a bull from your barn.
I don't need goats from your
pens.
¹⁰Every animal in the forest already
belongs to me.
And so do the cattle on a
thousand hills.
¹¹I own every bird in the mountains.
The creatures of the field belong
to me.
¹²If I were hungry, I wouldn't tell
you.
The world belongs to me. And so
does everything in it.
¹³Do I eat the meat of bulls?
Do I drink the blood of goats?
¹⁴Bring me thank offerings, because
I am your God.
Carry out the promises you made
to me, because I am the Most
High God.

¹⁵Call out to me when trouble
comes.
I will save you. And you will
honor me."

¹⁶But here is what God says to sinful
people.

"What right do you have to speak
the words of my laws?
How dare you speak the words of
my covenant!
¹⁷You hate my teaching.
You turn your back on what I say.
¹⁸When you see a thief, you join
him.
You make friends with those who
commit adultery.
¹⁹You use your mouth to speak evil.
You use your tongue to spread
lies.
²⁰You always speak against your
brother.
You always tell lies about your
own mother's son.
²¹You have done those things, and I
kept silent.
So you thought I was just like
you.

KIDS' QUESTion

Why are animals becoming extinct?

One reason some animals are becoming extinct is their habitats are being disrupted. People move in and take away the land used by the animals. Some people don't care what happens to plants and animals. They just do whatever they want, without thinking about how it affects nature. But God has given people the job of taking care of the world. That means taking good care of *all* of it, plants and animals included.

Remember that you can make a difference. Could you and your family recycle paper and aluminum cans? Or volunteer to clean up litter at a park? Or how about join a nature club? We can all do our part to take care of God's earth.

checkout
Psalm 50:10

Related verses:
Genesis 1:28–31;
Proverbs 12:10;
Ezekiel 34:25

BEEF $6.99lb
CHICKEN SOLD OUT

EXTINCT

But now I'm going to correct you.
I will bring charges against you.

²² "You who forget God, think about
this.
If you don't, I will tear you to
pieces.
No one will be able to save you.
²³ Anyone who sacrifices thank
offerings to me honors me.
He makes it possible for me to
show him
that I am the God who saves."

PSALM 51

For the director of music.
A psalm of David when the prophet
Nathan came to him after David had
committed adultery with Bathsheba.

¹ God, show me your favor
in keeping with your faithful
love.
Because your love is so tender and
kind,
wipe out my lawless acts.
² Wash away all of the evil things
I've done.
Make me pure from my sin.

³ I know the lawless acts I've
committed.
I can't forget my sin.
⁴ You are the one I've really sinned
against.
I've done what is evil in your
sight.
So you are right when you
sentence me.
You are fair when you judge me.
⁵ I know I've been a sinner ever
since I was born.
I've been a sinner ever since my
mother became pregnant with
me.
⁶ I know that you want truth to be in
my heart.
You teach me wisdom deep
down inside me.

⁷ Make me pure by sprinkling me
with hyssop plant. Then I will
be clean.
Wash me. Then I will be whiter
than snow.
⁸ Let me hear you say, "Your sins are
forgiven."
That will bring me joy and
gladness.

Why didn't God give us money right away when my dad lost his job?

We do not always know why God does what he does. But we know that he loves us and has a plan for us. He has a plan even for the hard times in our lives.

Sometimes God is working out something that we do not know about. Maybe it is even better than what we wanted or had before. God can use times like this to teach us to trust him.

If your dad has lost his job, do whatever you can to help. Pitch in with any money you can spare. Say good and cheerful words to him. Donate your allowance. Do odd jobs for neighbors to earn more money if you can. Ask God to provide what you need and trust him to do it.

Related verses:
Psalm 138:7,8;
Philippians
4:6,7,19

checkout
Psalm 50:15

Answer Booth

The opinions of this child do not reflect the views of this household

Let the body you have broken be
glad.
⁹ Take away all of my sins.
Wipe away all of the evil things
I've done.

¹⁰ God, create a pure heart in me.
Give me a new spirit that is
faithful to you.
¹¹ Don't send me away from you.
Don't take your Holy Spirit away
from me.
¹² Give me back the joy that comes
from being saved by you.
Give me a spirit that obeys you.
That will keep me going.

¹³ Then I will teach your ways to
those who commit lawless
acts.
And sinners will turn back to
you.
¹⁴ You are the God who saves me.
I have committed murder.
Take away my guilt.
Then my tongue will sing about
how right you are
no matter what you do.
¹⁵ Lord, open my lips so that I can
speak.
Then my mouth will praise you.
¹⁶ You don't take delight in sacrifice.
If you did, I would bring it.

You don't take pleasure in burnt
offerings.
¹⁷ The greatest sacrifice you want is a
broken spirit.
God, you will gladly accept a
heart
that is broken because of sadness
over sin.

¹⁸ May you be pleased to give Zion
success.
Build up the walls of Jerusalem.
¹⁹ Then holy sacrifices will be offered
in the right way.
Whole burnt offerings will bring
delight to you.
And bulls will be offered on your
altar.

PSALM 52

For the director of music.
A *maskil* of David when Doeg, who was
from Edom, had gone to Saul. Doeg had
told Saul, "David has gone to the house
of Ahimelech."

¹ You think you are such a big,
strong man!
Why do you brag about the evil
things you've done?
You are a dishonor to God all the
time.
² You plan ways to destroy others.

Is it wrong to tell someone your parents are home when they're not?

It would be a lie to say you are not home alone when you are. But your
parents probably do not want you to tell strangers that you are home alone.
You can think of something to say that is
the truth. You could say something like,
"They can't come to the phone right
now," or "They are not available," or
"Please let me take a message, and they
will get back to you." Talk with your mom
or dad about what you can say without
lying. Write it down and leave it by
the phone if you
need to. Each lie you
tell makes it easier
to tell other lies.

MY PARENTS ARE TIED
UP AT THE MOMENT
COULD I HAVE THEM
RETURN YOUR CALL?

Related verse:
Proverbs 12:17

checkout

Psalm 51:6

Your tongue is like a blade that
　　has a sharp edge.
You are always telling lies.
³ You love evil instead of good.
　　You would rather lie than tell the
　　truth.　　　　　　*Selah*
⁴ You love to harm others with
　　your words, you liar!

⁵ So God will destroy you forever.
　　He will grab hold of you and
　　　throw you out of your tent.
　　He will remove you from this life.
　　　　　　　　　　　Selah

⁶ Those who do what is right will see
　　it and learn a lesson from it.
　　They will laugh at you and say,
⁷ "Just look at this fellow!
　　He didn't depend on God for his
　　safety.
　　He put his trust in all his wealth.
　　He grew strong by destroying
　　others!"

⁸ But I am like a healthy olive tree.
　　My roots are deep in the house of
　　God.
　I trust in your faithful love
　　for ever and ever.
⁹ I will praise you forever for what
　　you have done.
　　I will put my hope in you
　　　because you are good.
　　I will praise you when I'm with
　　your faithful people.

PSALM 53

For the director of music.
For *mahalath*. A *maskil* of David.

¹ Foolish people say in their hearts,
　　"There is no God."
They do all kinds of horrible and
　　evil things.
No one does anything good.

² God looks down from heaven
　　on all people.
He wants to see if there are any
　　who understand.
He wants to see if there are any
　　who trust in God.
³ All of them have turned away.
　　They have all become evil.
No one does anything good,
　　no one at all.

⁴ Won't those who do evil ever
　　learn?

They eat up my people as if they
　　were eating bread.
They don't call out to God for
　　help.
⁵ Just look at them! They are filled
　　with terror
even when there is nothing to be
　　afraid of!
People of Israel, God will scatter
　　the bones of those who attack
　　you.
You will put them to shame,
　　because God hates them.

⁶ How I pray that the One who saves
　　Israel will come out of Zion!
God will bless his people with
　　great success again.
So let the people of Jacob be
　　filled with joy! Let Israel be
　　glad!

PSALM 54

For the director of music.
To be played on stringed instruments.
A *maskil* of David when the men from
Ziph had gone to Saul. They had said,
　　"Isn't David hiding among us?"

¹ God, save me by your power.
　　Set me free by your might.
² God, hear my prayer.
　　Listen to what I'm saying.

³ Strangers are attacking me.
　　Mean people are trying to kill
　　me.
　　They don't care about God.
　　　　　　　　　　　Selah

⁴ But I know that God helps me.
　　The Lord is the one who keeps
　　me going.

⁵ My enemies tell lies about me.
　　Do to them the evil things they
　　planned against me.
　　God, be faithful and destroy
　　them.

⁶ I will sacrifice an offering to you
　　just because I choose to.
LORD, I will praise your name
　　because it is good.
⁷ You have saved me from all of my
　　troubles.
　　With my own eyes I have seen
　　you win the battle over my
　　enemies.

PSALM 55

For the director of music.
A *maskil* of David to be played
on stringed instruments.

¹God, listen to my prayer.
  Pay attention to my cry for help.
² Hear me and answer me.
My thoughts upset me. I'm very
  troubled.
³ I'm troubled by what my
  enemies say about me.
I'm upset because sinful people
  stare at me.
They cause me all kinds of
  suffering.
When they are angry, they attack
  me with their words.

⁴I feel great pain deep down inside
  me.
  The terrors of death are crushing
  me.
⁵Fear and trembling have taken
  hold of me.
  Panic has overpowered me.
⁶I said, "I wish I had wings like a
  dove!
  Then I would fly away and be at
  rest.
⁷I would escape to a place far away.
I would stay out in the desert.
                              Selah
⁸I would hurry to my place of
  safety.
  It would be far away from the
  winds and storms I'm facing."

⁹Lord, destroy the plans of sinners.
  Keep them from
  understanding one another.
I see people destroying things
  and fighting in the city.
¹⁰Day and night they prowl around
  on top of its walls.
  The city is full of crime and
  trouble.
¹¹Forces that destroy are at work
  inside it.
  Its streets are full of people who
  cheat others and take
  advantage of them.

¹²If an enemy were making fun of me,
  I could stand it.
If he were looking down on me,
  I could hide from him.
¹³But it's you, someone like myself.

It's my companion, my close
  friend.
¹⁴We used to enjoy good friendship
  as we walked with the crowds at
  the house of God.

¹⁵Let death take my enemies by
  surprise.
  Let them be buried alive,
  because their hearts and homes
  are full of evil.

¹⁶But I call out to God.
  And the LORD saves me.
¹⁷Evening, morning and noon
  I groan and cry out.
  And he hears my voice.
¹⁸Even though many enemies are
  fighting against me,
  he brings me safely back from
  the battle.
¹⁹God sits on his throne forever.
  He hears my prayers and makes
  my enemies suffer.   *Selah*
  They never change their ways.
  They don't have any respect for
  God.

²⁰My companion attacks his friends.
  He breaks his promise.
²¹His talk is as smooth as butter.
  But he has war in his heart.
His words flow like olive oil.
  But they are like swords ready for
  battle.
²²Turn your worries over to the
  LORD.
  He will keep you going.
  He will never let godly people
  fall.
²³God, you will bring sinners
  down to the grave.
Murderers and liars
  won't live out even half of their
  lives.

But I trust in you.

PSALM 56

For the director of music.
A *miktam* of David after the Philistines
had captured him in Gath. To the tune
of "A Dove on Distant Oak Trees."

¹God, show me your favor. Men are
  chasing me.
  All day long they keep attacking
  me.

2 Those who tell lies about me chase
　　me all day long.
　Many proud people are attacking
　　me.

3 When I'm afraid,
　　I will trust in you.
4 I trust in God. I praise his word.
　I trust in God. I will not be afraid.
　What can people do to me?

5 All day long they twist my words.
　They are always making plans to
　　harm me.
6 They get together and hide.
　They watch my steps.
　They hope to kill me.

7 Make sure you don't let them
　　escape.
　God, bring down the nations in
　　your anger.
8 Write down my poem of sadness.
　List my tears on your scroll.
　Aren't you making a record of
　　them?

9 My enemies will turn back
　　when I call out to you for help.
　Then I will know that God is on
　　my side.
10 I trust in God. I praise his word.
　I trust in the LORD. I praise his
　　word.
11 I trust in God. I will not be afraid.
　What can mere men do to me?

12 God, I have made promises to you.
　I will bring my thank offerings to
　　you.
13 You have saved me from death.
　You have kept me from tripping
　　and falling.
　Now I can live with you
　　in the light that leads to life.

PSALM 57

For the director of music.
A *miktam* of David when he had run
　away from Saul into the cave.
To the tune of "Do Not Destroy."

1 Show me your favor, God. Show
　　me your favor.
　I go to you for safety.
　I will find safety in the shadow of
　　your wings.
　There I will stay until the danger
　　is gone.

2 I cry out to God Most High.
　I cry out to God, and he carries
　　out his plan for me.
3 He answers from heaven and saves
　　me.
　He puts to shame those who
　　chase me.　　　　　*Selah*
　He shows me his love and his
　　truth.

4 Men who are like lions are all
　　around me.
　I am lying down among hungry
　　animals.
　Their teeth are like spears and
　　arrows.
　Their tongues are like sharp
　　swords.

5 God, may you be honored above
　　the heavens.
　Let your glory be over the whole
　　earth.

6 My enemies spread a net to catch
　　me by the feet.
　I felt helpless.
　They dug a pit in my path.
　But they fell into it themselves.
　　　　　　　　　　　Selah

7 God, my heart feels secure.
　My heart feels secure.
　I will sing and make music to
　　you.
8 My spirit, wake up!
　Harp and lyre, wake up!
　I want to sing and make music
　　before the sun rises.

9 Lord, I will praise you among the
　　nations.
　I will sing about you among the
　　people of the earth.
10 Great is your love. It reaches to the
　　heavens.
　Your truth reaches to the skies.

11 God, may you be honored above
　　the heavens.
　Let your glory be over the whole
　　earth.

PSALM 58

For the director of music.
A *miktam* of David to the tune
　of "Do Not Destroy."

1 Are you rulers really fair when you
　　speak?

Do you judge people honestly?
² No, in your hearts you plan to be
    unfair.
  With your hands you do terrible
    things on the earth.
³ Even from birth those who are evil
    go down the wrong path.
  From the day they are born they
    go the wrong way and speak
    lies.
⁴ Their words are like the poison of
    a snake.
  They are like the poison of a
    cobra that has covered up its
    ears.
⁵ It won't listen to any tune of a
    snake charmer,
  even if the charmer really plays
    well.

⁶ God, break the teeth in the
    mouths of those sinners!
  LORD, tear out the sharp teeth of
    those lions!
⁷ Let those people disappear like
    water that flows away.
  When they draw their bows, let
    their arrows be dull.
⁸ Let them be like a slug that melts
    away as it moves along.
  Let them be like a baby that is
    born dead and never sees the
    sun.

⁹ Evil people will be swept away
    quicker than a pot can feel the
    heat of thorns burning under it.
  And it doesn't matter if the
    thorns are green or dry.
¹⁰ Godly people will be glad when
    those who have hurt them are
    paid back.
  They will wash their feet in the
    blood of those who do evil.
¹¹ Then people will say,
  "The godly will get their reward.
  There really is a God who judges
    the earth."

PSALM 59

For the director of music. A *miktam* of
David when Saul had sent men to watch
  David's house in order to kill him.
  To the tune of "Do Not Destroy."

¹ God, save me from my enemies.
  Keep me safe from those who
    rise up against me.

² Save me from those who do evil.
  Save me from murderers.
³ See how they hide and wait for
    me!
  LORD, angry people plan to harm
    me,
  even though I haven't hurt them
    in any way or sinned against
    them.
⁴ I haven't done anything wrong to
    them. But they are ready to
    attack me.
  Rise up and help me! Look at
    what I'm up against!
⁵ LORD God who rules over all, rise
    up. God of Israel,
  punish all of the nations.
  Don't show any mercy to those
    sinful people
  who have turned against me.
                                        Selah

⁶ My enemies are like a pack of
    barking dogs
  that come back to the city in the
    evening.
  They prowl around the city.
⁷ Listen to what pours out of their
    mouths.
  The words from their lips are like
    swords.
  They think, "Who can hear us?"
⁸ But you laugh at them, LORD.
  You make fun of all those
    nations.

⁹ You give me strength. I look to
    you.
  God, you are like a fort to me.
  ¹⁰ You are my loving God.

God will march out in front of me.
  He will let me look down on
    those who tell lies about me.
¹¹ Lord, you are like a shield that
    keeps us safe.
  Don't kill my enemies all at once.
  If you do, my people will forget
    about it.
  Use your power to make my
    enemies wander around.
  Destroy them.
¹² They have sinned with their
    mouths.
  Their lips have spoken evil
    words.
  They have called down a curse on
    me and lied.

Let them be caught in their
pride.
¹³Burn them up in your anger.
Burn them up until there isn't
anything left of them.
Then everyone from one end of
the earth to the other will
know
that God rules over the people of
Jacob. *Selah*

¹⁴My enemies are like a pack of
barking dogs
that come back into the city in
the evening.
They prowl around the city.
¹⁵They wander around looking for
food.
They groan if they don't find
something that will satisfy
them.
¹⁶But I will sing about your strength.
In the morning I will sing about
your love.
You are like a fort to me.
You keep me safe in times of
trouble.

¹⁷You give me strength. I sing praise
to you.
God, you are like a fort to me.
You are my loving God.

PSALM 60

For the director of music. For teaching.
A *miktam* of David when he fought
against Aram Naharaim and Aram Zobah.
That was when Joab returned and
struck down 12,000 people from Edom
in the Valley of Salt. To the tune
of "The Lily of the Covenant."

¹God, you have turned away from
us. You have attacked us.
You have been angry. Now turn
back to us!
²You have shaken the land and torn
it open.
Fix its cracks, because it is falling
apart.
³You have shown your people hard
times.
You have made us drink the wine
of your anger.
Now we can't even walk straight.

⁴But you lead into battle those who
have respect for you.

You give them a flag to wave
against the enemy's weapons.
Selah

⁵Save us. Help us with your
powerful right hand,
so that those you love may be
saved.
⁶God has spoken from his temple.
He has said, "I will win the battle.
Then I will divide up the land
around Shechem.
I will divide up the Valley of
Succoth.
⁷Gilead belongs to me.
So does the land of Manasseh.
Ephraim is the strongest tribe.
It is like a helmet for my head.
Judah is the royal tribe.
It is like a ruler's staff.
⁸Moab serves me like one who
washes my feet.
I toss my sandal on Edom to
show that I own it.
I shout to Philistia that I have
won the battle."

⁹Who will bring me to the city that
has high walls around it?
Who will lead me to the land of
Edom?
¹⁰God, isn't it you, even though you
have now turned away from
us?
Isn't it you, even though you
don't lead our armies into
battle anymore?
¹¹Help us against our enemies.
The help people give doesn't
amount to anything.
¹²With your help we will win the
battle.
You will walk all over our
enemies.

PSALM 61

For the director of music.
A psalm of David to be played
on stringed instruments.

¹God, hear my cry for help.
Listen to my prayer.

²From a place far away I call out to
you.
I call out as my heart gets
weaker.
Lead me to the safety of a rock
that is high above me.

³You have always kept me safe from
my enemies.
You are like a strong tower to me.

⁴I long to live in your holy tent
forever.
There I find safety in the shadow
of your wings.   *Selah*

⁵God, you have heard my promises.
You have given me what belongs
to those who worship you.

⁶Add many days to the king's life.
Let him live on and on for many
years.

⁷May he always enjoy your blessing
as he rules.
Let your love and truth keep him
safe.

⁸Then I will always sing praise to
you.
I will keep my promises day after
day.

PSALM 62

For the director of music.
For Jeduthun. A psalm of David.

¹I find my rest in God alone.
He is the One who saves me.

²He alone is my rock. He is the One
who saves me.
He is like a fort to me. I will
always be secure.

³How long will you enemies attack
me?
Will all of you throw me down?
I'm like a leaning wall.
I'm like a fence that is about to
fall.

⁴You only want to pull me down
from my place of honor.
You take delight in telling lies.
You bless me with what you say.
But in your hearts you call down
curses on me.   *Selah*

⁵I will find my rest in God alone.
He is the One who gives me
hope.

⁶He alone is my rock. He is the One
who saves me.
He is like a fort to me. I will
always be secure.

⁷I depend on God to save me and
to honor me.
He is my mighty rock. He is my
place of safety.

⁸Trust in him at all times, you
people.
Tell him all of your troubles.
God is our place of safety.   *Selah*

⁹Ordinary people are only a breath.
Important people are not what
they seem to be.
If they were weighed on a scale,
they wouldn't amount to
anything.
Together they are only a breath.

¹⁰Don't trust in money you have
taken from others.
Don't be proud of things you
have stolen.
Even if your riches grow,
don't put your trust in them.

¹¹God, I have heard you say two
things.
One is that you, God, are strong.

¹² The other is that you, Lord, are
loving.
I'm sure you will reward each
person
in keeping with what he has done.

PSALM 63

A psalm of David when he was
in the Desert of Judah.

¹God, you are my God.
I greatly long for you.
With all my heart I thirst for you
in this dry desert
where there isn't any water.

²I have seen you in the sacred tent.
There I have seen your power
and your glory.

³Your love is better than life.
I will bring glory to you with my
lips.

⁴I will praise you as long as I live.
I will lift up my hands when I
pray to you.

⁵I will be as satisfied as if I had
eaten the best food there is.
I will sing praise to you with my
mouth.

⁶As I lie on my bed I remember
you.
I think of you all night long.

⁷Because you have helped me,
I sing in the shadow of your
wings.

⁸I hold on to you.

Your powerful right hand takes
good care of me.

9 Those who are trying to kill me
will be destroyed.
They will go down into the grave.
10 They will be killed with swords.
They will become food for wild
dogs.
11 But the king will be filled with joy
because of what God has
done.
All those who take an oath in
God's name will praise him.
But the mouths of liars will be
shut.

PSALM 64

For the director of music.
A psalm of David.

1 God, hear me as I tell you my
problem.
Don't let my enemies kill me.
2 Hide me from those who make evil
plans against me.
Hide me from that crowd of
people who are doing evil.

3 They make their tongues like
sharp swords.
They aim their words like deadly
arrows.
4 They shoot from their hiding
places at people who aren't
guilty of doing anything
wrong.
They shoot quickly. They aren't
afraid of being caught.

5 They help each other make evil
plans.
They talk about hiding their
traps.
They say, "Who can see what we
are doing?"
6 They make plans to do what is
evil.
They say, "We have thought up a
perfect plan!"
The hearts and minds of people
are so clever!

7 But God will shoot my enemies
with his arrows.
He will suddenly strike them
down.
8 He will turn their own words
against them.

He will destroy them.
All those who see them will shake
their heads
and look down on them.

9 Everyone will respect God.
They will tell about his works.
They will think about what he
has done.
10 Let godly people be full of joy
because of what the LORD has
done.
Let them go to him for safety.
Let all those whose hearts are
honest praise him.

PSALM 65

For the director of music.
A psalm of David. A song.

1 God, we look forward to praising
you in Zion.
We will keep our promises to
you.
2 All people will come to you,
because you hear and answer
prayer.
3 When our sins became too much
for us,
you forgave our lawless acts.
4 Blessed are those you choose
and bring near to worship you.
You bring us into the courtyards of
your holy temple.
There in your house we are filled
with all kinds of good things.

5 God our Savior, you answer us by
doing wonderful things.
You save us by your power.
People all over the world and
beyond the farthest oceans
put their hope in you.
6 You formed the mountains by your
power.
You showed how strong you are.
7 You calmed the oceans and their
roaring waves.
You calmed the angry words and
actions of the nations.
8 Those who live far away are
amazed at the miracles you
have done.
What you do makes people from
one end of the
earth to the other sing for joy.

9 You take care of the land and
water it.

You make it very rich.
You fill your streams with water.
  You provide the people with
    grain.
  That's how you prepare the land.
¹⁰ You water its rows.
  You smooth out its bumps.
  You soften it with showers.
  And you bless its crops.
¹¹ You bring the year to a close with
    huge crops.
  You provide more than enough
    food.
¹² The grass grows thick even in the
    desert.
  The hills are dressed with
    gladness.
¹³ The meadows are covered with
    flocks and herds.
  The valleys are dressed with
    grain.
  They sing and shout with joy.

PSALM 66

For the director of music.
A song. A psalm.

¹ Shout to God with joy, everyone
    on earth!
²   Sing about the glory of his name!
  Give him glorious praise!
³ Say to God, "What wonderful
    things you do!
  Your power is so great
  that your enemies bow down to
    you in fear.
⁴ Everyone on earth bows down to
    you.
  They sing praise to you.
  They sing praise to your name."
                    Selah

⁵ Come and see what God has done.
  See what wonderful things he
    has done for his people!
⁶ He turned the Red Sea into dry
    land.
  The people of Israel passed
    through the waters on foot.
  Come, let us be full of joy
    because of what he did.
⁷ He rules by his power forever.
  His eyes watch the nations.
  Let no one who refuses to obey
    him rise up against him.
                    Selah

⁸ Praise our God, you nations.

Let the sound of the praise you
    give him be heard.
⁹ He has kept us alive.
  He has kept our feet from
    slipping.
¹⁰ God, you have put us to the test.
  You put us through fire to make
    us like silver.
¹¹ You put us in prison.
  You placed heavy loads on our
    backs.
¹² You let people run over our heads.
  We went through fire and water.
  But you brought us to a place
    where we have everything we
    need.

¹³ I will come to your temple with
    burnt offerings.
  I will keep my promises to you.
¹⁴ I made them with my lips.
  My mouth spoke them when I
    was in trouble.
¹⁵ I will sacrifice fat animals to you as
    burnt offerings.
  I will offer rams, bulls and goats
    to you.   *Selah*

¹⁶ Come and listen, all of you who
    have respect for God.
  Let me tell you what he has done
    for me.
¹⁷ I cried out to him with my mouth.
  I praised him with my tongue.
¹⁸ If I had enjoyed having sin in my
    heart,
  the Lord would not have
    listened.
¹⁹ But God has listened.
  He has heard my prayer.
²⁰ Give praise to God.
  He has accepted my prayer.
  He has not held his love back
    from me.

PSALM 67

For the director of music.
A psalm. A song to be played
on stringed instruments.

¹ God, show us your favor. Bless us.
  May you smile on us with your
    favor.   *Selah*
² Then your ways will be known on
    earth.
  All nations will see that you have
    the power to save.
³ God, may the nations praise you.

May all of the people on earth
  praise you.
[4] May the nations be glad and sing
  with joy.
  You rule the people of the earth
    fairly.
  You guide the nations of the
    earth.   *Selah*
[5] God, may the nations praise you.
  May all of the people on earth
    praise you.

[6] Then the land will produce its
    crops.
  God, our God, will bless us.
[7] God will bless us.
  People from one end of the earth
    to the other
  will have respect for him.

PSALM 68

For the director of music.
A psalm of David. A song.

[1] May God rise up and scatter his
    enemies.
  May they turn and run away
    from him.
[2] As wind blows smoke away,
  so may God blow them away.
As fire melts wax,
  so may he destroy sinful people.
[3] But may those who do what is
    right be glad
  and filled with joy when they are
    with him.
  May they be happy and joyful.

[4] Sing to God. Sing praise to his
    name.
  Lift up a song to the One who
    rides on the clouds.
His name is the LORD.
  Be glad when you are with him.
[5] God is in his holy temple.
  He is a father to those whose
    fathers have died.
  He takes care of women whose
    husbands have died.
[6] God gives lonely people a family.
  He sets prisoners free, and they
    go out singing.
But those who refuse to obey him
  live in a land that is baked by the
    sun.

[7] God, you led your people out.
  You marched through a dry and
    empty land.   *Selah*

[8] The ground shook
  when you, the God of Sinai,
    appeared.
The heavens poured down rain
  when you, the God of Israel,
    appeared.
[9] God, you gave us plenty of rain.
  You renewed your worn-out
    land.
[10] God, your people settled in it.
  From all of your riches, you
    provided for those who were
    poor.

[11] The Lord gave a message.
  Many people made it widely
    known.
[12] They said, "Kings and armies are
    running away.
  In the camps, Israel's soldiers are
    dividing up
  the things they have taken from
    their enemies.
[13] Even while the soldiers sleep near
    the campfires,
  God wins the battle for them.
  He gives the enemy's silver and
    gold
  to Israel, his dove."
[14] The Mighty One has scattered the
    kings around the land.
  It was like snow falling on Mount
    Zalmon.

[15] The mountains of Bashan are
    majestic.
  The mountains of Bashan are
    very rocky.
[16] You rocky mountains are jealous
    of Mount Zion, aren't you?
  That's where God chooses to rule.
  That's where the LORD himself
    will live forever.
[17] God has come with tens of
    thousands of his chariots.
  He has come with thousands and
    thousands of them.
  The Lord has come from Mount
    Sinai.
  He has entered his holy place.
[18] When he went up to his place on
    high,
  he led a line of prisoners.
  He received gifts from people,
    even from those who refused to
    obey him.
  The LORD God went up to live on
    Mount Zion.

¹⁹ Give praise to the Lord. Give
    praise to God our Savior.
He carries our heavy loads day
    after day.   *Selah*
²⁰ Our God is a God who saves.
He is the King and the LORD. He
    saves us from death.

²¹ God will certainly smash the heads
    of his enemies.
He will break the hairy heads of
    those who keep on sinning.
²² The Lord says, "I will bring your
    enemies from Bashan.
I will bring them up from the
    bottom of the sea.
²³ Then your feet can wade in their
    blood.
The tongues of your dogs can lick
    up all the blood they want."

²⁴ God, those who worship you come
    marching into view.
My God and King, those who
    follow you have entered the
    sacred tent.
²⁵ The singers are walking in front.
Next come those who play the
    music.
Young women playing
    tambourines are with them.
²⁶ The leaders sing, "Praise God
    among all those who worship
    him.
Praise the LORD in the
    community of Israel."
²⁷ The little tribe of Benjamin leads
    the worshipers.
Next comes the great crowd of
    Judah's princes.
Then come the princes of
    Zebulun and the princes of
    Naphtali.

²⁸ God, show us your power.
Show us your strength.
God, do as you have done before.
²⁹ Do it from your temple at
    Jerusalem,
where kings will bring you gifts.
³⁰ Give a strong warning to Egypt,
    that beast among the tall
    grass.
Warn the leaders of the nations,
    who are like bulls among the
    calves.
May they bow down before you
    with gifts of silver.

Scatter the nations who like to
    make war.
³¹ Messengers will come from Egypt.
The people of Cush will be quick
    to bring gifts to you.

³² Sing to God, you kingdoms of the
    earth.
Sing praise to the Lord.   *Selah*
³³ He rides in the age-old skies
    above.
He thunders with his mighty
    voice.
³⁴ Tell how powerful God is.
He rules as king over Israel.
The skies show how powerful he
    is.
³⁵ How wonderful is God in his holy
    place!
The God of Israel gives power
    and strength to his people.

Give praise to God!

PSALM 69

For the director of music.
A psalm of David to the tune of "Lilies."

¹ God, save me.
My troubles are like a flood.
I'm up to my neck in them.
² I'm sinking in deep mud.
I have no firm place to stand.
I am out in deep water.
The waves roll over me.
³ I'm worn out from calling for help.
My throat is very dry.
My eyes grow tired
    looking for my God.
⁴ Those who hate me without any
    reason
are more than the hairs on my
    head.
Many people who don't have any
    reason to be my enemies
are trying to destroy me.
They force me to give back
    what I didn't steal.

⁵ God, you know how foolish I've
    been.
My guilt is not hidden from you.

⁶ Lord, you are the LORD who rules
    over all.
May those who put their hope in
    you not be dishonored
    because of me.
You are the God of Israel.

May those who worship you not
  be put to shame because of me.
⁷Because of you, people laugh at me.
  My face is covered with shame.
⁸I'm a stranger to my brothers.
  I'm an outsider to my own
    mother's sons.
⁹My great love for your house
    destroys me.
  Those who make fun of you
    make fun of me also.
¹⁰When I sob and go without eating,
  they laugh at me.
¹¹When I put on black clothes to
    show how sad I am,
  people make jokes about me.
¹²Those who gather in public places
    make fun of me.
  Those who get drunk make up
    songs about me.

¹³But LORD, I pray to you.
  May this be the time you show
    me your favor.
  God, answer me because you love
    me so much.
  Save me, as you always do.
¹⁴Save me from the trouble I'm in.
  It's like slippery mud. Don't let
    me sink in it.
  Save me from those who hate me.
  Save me from the deep water I'm
    in.
¹⁵Don't let the floods cover me.
  Don't let the deep water swallow
    me up.
  Don't let the grave close its
    mouth over me.
¹⁶LORD, answer me because your
    love is so good.
  Turn to me because you are so
    kind.
¹⁷Don't turn your face away from me.
  Answer me quickly. I'm in
    trouble.
¹⁸Come near and save me.
  Set me free from my enemies.

¹⁹You know how they make fun of
    me.
  They dishonor me and put me to
    shame.
  You know all about my enemies.
²⁰They have broken my heart by
    saying evil things about me.
  It has left me helpless.
  I looked for pity, but I didn't find
    any.

I looked for someone to comfort
    me, but I didn't find anyone.
²¹They put bitter spices in my food.
  They gave me vinegar when I was
    thirsty.

²²Let their feast be a trap and a snare.
  Let my enemies get what's
    coming to them.
²³Let their eyes grow weak so they
    can't see.
  Let their backs be bent forever.
²⁴Pour out your anger on them.
  Let them feel its burning heat.
²⁵May their homes be deserted.
  May no one live in their tents.
²⁶They attack those you have
    wounded.
  They talk about the pain of those
    you have hurt.
²⁷Charge them with one crime after
    another.
  Don't save them.
²⁸May their names be erased from
    the Book of Life.
  Don't include them in the list of
    those who do right.

²⁹I'm in pain. I'm in deep trouble.
  God, save me and keep me safe.

³⁰I will praise God's name by singing
    to him.
  I will bring him glory by giving
    him thanks.
³¹That will please the LORD more
    than offering him an ox.
  It will please him more than
    offering him a bull with its
    horns and hoofs.
³²Poor people will see it and be glad.
  The hearts of those who worship
    God will be strengthened.
³³The LORD hears those who are in
    need.
  He doesn't forget his people in
    prison.

³⁴Let heaven and earth praise him.
  Let the oceans and everything
    that moves in them praise
    him.
³⁵God will save Zion.
  He will build the cities of Judah
    again.
  Then people will live in them and
    own the land.
³⁶ The children of those who serve
    God will receive it.

Those who love him will live
there.

PSALM 70

For the director of music.
A prayer of David.

¹ God, hurry and save me.
  LORD, come quickly and help me.
² Let those who are trying to kill me
    be put to shame.
  Let them not be honored.
  Let all those who want to destroy
    me
    be turned back in shame.
³ Some people make fun of me.
  Let them be turned back when
    their plans fail.
⁴ But let all those who look to you
  be joyful and glad because of
    what you have done.
  Let those who love you because
    you save them always say,
  "May God be honored!"

⁵ But I am poor and needy.
  God, come quickly to me.
  You are the One who helps me and
    saves me.
  LORD, please don't wait any
    longer.

PSALM 71

¹ LORD, I have gone to you for safety.
  Let me never be put to shame.
² You do what is right. Save me and
    help me.
  Pay attention to me and save me.
³ Be my rock of safety
  that I can always go to.
  Give the command to save me.
  You are my rock and my fort.
⁴ My God, save me from the power
    of sinners.
  Save me from the hands of those
    who are mean and evil.

⁵ You are the King and the LORD. You
    have always been my hope.
  I have trusted in you ever since I
    was young.
⁶ From the time I was born I have
    depended on you.
  You brought me out of my
    mother's body.
  I will praise you forever.
⁷ To many people I am an example
    of how much you care.

You are strong. You are my place
    of safety.
⁸ My mouth is filled with praise for
    you.
  All day long I will talk about your
    glory.

⁹ Don't push me away when I'm old.
  Don't desert me when my
    strength is gone.
¹⁰ My enemies speak against me.
  Those who want to kill me get
    together and make evil plans.
¹¹ They say, "God has deserted him.
  Go after him and grab him.
  No one will save him."
¹² God, don't stay so far away from
    me.
  My God, come quickly and help
    me.
¹³ May those who bring charges
    against me die in shame.
  May those who want to harm me
    be covered with shame and
    dishonor.

¹⁴ But I will always have hope.
  I will praise you more and more.
¹⁵ I will say that what you have done
    is right.
  All day long I will talk about how
    you have saved your people.
  It is more than I can understand.
¹⁶ LORD and King, I will come and
    announce your mighty acts.
  I will announce that you alone
    do what is right.
¹⁷ God, ever since I was young you
    have taught me about what
    you have done.
  To this very day I tell about your
    wonderful acts.
¹⁸ God, don't leave me
  even when I'm old and have gray
    hair.
  Let me live to tell my children
    about your power.
  Let me tell all of them about your
    mighty acts.

¹⁹ God, your saving acts reach to the
    skies.
  You have done great things.
  God, who is like you?
²⁰ You have sent many bitter troubles
    my way.
  But you will give me new life.
  Even if I'm almost in the grave,

you will bring me back.
21 You will honor me more and more.
You will comfort me once again.

22 My God, I will use the harp to
praise you
because you are always faithful.
Holy One of Israel,
I will use the lyre to sing praise to
you.
23 My lips will shout with joy
when I sing praise to you.
You have saved me.
24 All day long my tongue will say
that you have done what is right.
Those who wanted to harm me
have been put to shame.
They have not been honored.

PSALM 72

A psalm of Solomon.

1 God, give the king the ability to
judge fairly.
He is your royal son. Help him to
do what is right.
2 Then he will rule your people in
the right way.
He will be fair to those among
your people who are hurting.
3 The mountains and the hills will
produce rich crops,
because the people will do what
is right.
4 The king will stand up for those
who are hurting.
He will save the children of those
who are in need.
He will crush those who beat
others down.

5 He will rule as long as the sun
shines
and the moon gives its light.
He will rule for all time to come.
6 He will be like rain falling on the
fields.
He will be like showers watering
the earth.
7 Godly people will do well as long
as he rules.
They will have more than they
need as long as the moon
lasts.

8 He will rule from ocean to ocean.
His kingdom will reach from the
Euphrates River to the ends of
the earth.

9 The desert tribes will bow down to
him.
His enemies will lick the dust.
10 The kings of Tarshish and of places
far away
will bring him gifts.
The kings of Sheba and Seba
will give him presents.
11 All kings will bow down to him.
All nations will serve him.

12 People who are in need will cry
out, and he will save them.
He will save those who are
hurting.
They don't have anyone else who
can help them.
13 He will take pity on those who are
weak and in need.
He will save them from death.
14 He will save them from people
who beat others down.
He will save them from people
who do mean things to them.
Their lives are very special to
him.

15 May he live a long time!
May gold from Sheba be given to
him.
May people always pray for him.
May they ask the LORD to bless
him all day long.
16 Let there be plenty of grain
everywhere in the land.
May it sway in the wind on the
tops of the hills.
Let crops grow well, like those in
Lebanon.
Let them grow like the grass of
the field.
17 May the king's name be
remembered forever.
May his fame last as long as the
sun shines.

All nations will be blessed because
of him.
They will call him blessed.

18 Give praise to the LORD God, the
God of Israel.
Only he can do wonderful things.
19 Give praise to his glorious name
forever.
May his glory fill the whole earth.
Amen and Amen.

²⁰ The prayers of David, the son of Jesse, end here.

BOOK III

Psalms 73–89

PSALM 73

A psalm of Asaph.

¹ God is truly good to Israel.
He is good to those who have pure hearts.

² But my feet had almost slipped.
I had almost tripped and fallen.
³ I saw that proud and sinful people were doing well.
And I began to long for what they had.

⁴ They don't have any troubles.
Their bodies are healthy and strong.
⁵ They don't have the problems others have.
They don't suffer as other people do.
⁶ Their pride is like a necklace.
They put on meanness as if it were their clothes.
⁷ Many sins come out of their hard and stubborn hearts.
There is no limit to their proud and evil thoughts.
⁸ They laugh at others and speak words of hatred.
They are proud. They warn others about the harm they can do to them.
⁹ They brag as if they owned heaven itself.
They talk as if they controlled the earth.
¹⁰ So people listen to them.
They lap up their words like water.
¹¹ They say, "How can God know what we're doing?
Does the Most High God really know that much?"

¹² Here is what sinful people are like.
They don't have a care in the world.
They keep getting richer and richer.

¹³ It seems as if I have kept my heart pure without any reason.
It didn't do me any good to wash my hands
to show that I wasn't guilty of doing anything wrong.
¹⁴ Day after day I've been in pain.
God has punished me every morning.

¹⁵ What if I had said, "I will speak as evil people do"?
Then I wouldn't have been faithful to God's children.
¹⁶ I tried to understand it all.
But it was more than I could handle.
¹⁷ It troubled me until I entered God's temple.
Then I understood what will happen to bad people in the end.

¹⁸ God, I'm sure you will make them slip and fall.
You will throw them down and destroy them.
¹⁹ It will happen very suddenly.
A terrible death will take them away completely.
²⁰ A dream goes away when a person wakes up.
Lord, it will be like that when you rise up.
It will be as if those people were only a dream.

²¹ At one time my heart was sad and my spirit was bitter.
²² I didn't have any sense. I didn't know anything.
I acted like a wild animal toward you.
²³ But I am always with you.
You hold me by my right hand.
²⁴ You give me wise advice to guide me.
And when I die, you will take me away
into the glory of heaven.
²⁵ I don't have anyone in heaven but you.
I don't want anything on earth besides you.
²⁶ My body and my heart may grow weak.
God, you give strength to my heart.

You are everything I will ever
need.

27 Those who don't want anything to
do with you will die.
You destroy all those who aren't
faithful to you.
28 But I am close to you. And that's
good.
Lord and King, I have made you
my place of safety.
I will talk about everything you
have done.

PSALM 74

A maskil of Asaph.

1 God, why have you turned your
back on us for so long?
Why does your anger burn
against us? We are your very
own sheep.
2 Remember that you chose us to be
your own people a long time
ago.
Remember that you set us free
from slavery to be your very
own tribe.
Remember Mount Zion, where
you lived.
3 Walk through this place that has
been torn down beyond
repair.
See how completely your
enemies have destroyed the
temple!

4 In the place where you used to
meet with us,
your enemies have shouted,
"We've won the battle!"
They have set up their flags to
show they have beaten us.
5 They acted like people cutting
down a forest with axes.
6 They smashed all of the beautiful
wooden walls
with their axes and hatchets.
7 They burned your temple to the
ground.
They polluted the place where
your Name is.
8 They had said in their hearts, "We
will crush them completely!"
They burned every place where
you were worshiped in the
land.

9 You don't give us miraculous signs
anymore.
There aren't any prophets left.
None of us knows how long that
will last.

10 God, how long will your enemies
make fun of you?
Will they attack you with their
words forever?
11 Why don't you help us? Why do
you hold back your powerful
right hand?
Use your strong arms to destroy
your enemies!

12 God, you have been my king for a
long time.
The whole earth has seen you
save us over and over again.
13 You parted the Red Sea by your
power.
You broke the heads of that sea
monster in Egypt.
14 You crushed the heads of the sea
monster Leviathan.
You fed it to the creatures of the
desert.
15 You opened up streams and
springs.
You dried up rivers that flow all
year long.
16 You rule over the day and the
night.
You created the sun and the
moon.
17 You decided where the borders of
the earth would be.
You made both summer and
winter.

18 Lord, remember how your
enemies have made fun of
you.
Remember how foolish people
have attacked you with their
words.
19 Don't hand Israel, your dove, over
to those wild animals.
Don't forget your suffering
people forever.
20 Honor the covenant you made
with us.
Horrible things are happening in
every dark corner of the land.
21 Don't let your suffering people be
put to shame.

May those who are poor and
needy praise you.

22 God, rise up. Stand up for your
cause.
Remember how foolish people
make fun of you all day long.
23 Pay close attention to the shouts
of your enemies.
The trouble they cause never
stops.

PSALM 75

For the director of music.
A psalm of Asaph. A song to the
tune of "Do Not Destroy."

1 God, we give thanks to you.
We give thanks because your
Name is near.
People talk about the wonderful
things you have done.

2 You say, "I choose the appointed
time to judge people.
And I judge them fairly.
3 When the earth and all of its
people tremble,
I keep everything from falling to
pieces.   Selah
4 To the proud I say, 'Don't brag
anymore.'
To sinners I say, 'Don't show off
your power.
5 Don't show it off against me.
Don't speak with your noses in
the air.' "

6 No one from east or west or north
or south
can act as judge.
7 God is the One who judges.
He says to one person, "You are
guilty."
To another he says, "You are not
guilty."
8 In the hand of the LORD is a cup.
It is full of wine mixed with
spices.
It is the wine of his anger.
He pours it out. All of the evil
people on earth
drink it down to the very last
drop.

9 I will speak about this forever.
I will sing praise to the God of
Jacob.

10 God will destroy the power of all
sinful people.
But he will make godly people
more powerful.

PSALM 76

For the director of music.
A psalm of Asaph. A song to be
played on stringed instruments.

1 In the land of Judah, God is
known.
His name is great in Israel.
2 His tent is in Jerusalem.
The place where he lives is on
Mount Zion.
3 There he broke the deadly arrows
of his enemies.
He broke their shields and
swords.
He broke their weapons of war.
                                   Selah

4 God, you shine like a very bright
light.
You are more majestic than
mountains full of wild
animals.
5 Brave soldiers have been robbed
of everything they had.
Now they lie there, sleeping in
death.
Not one of them can even lift his
hands.
6 God of Jacob, at your command
both horse and chariot lie still.
7 People should have respect for you
alone.
Who can stand in front of you
when you are angry?
8 From heaven you handed down
your sentence.
The land was afraid and became
quiet.
9 God, that happened when you
rose up to judge.
It happened when you came to
save all of your suffering
people in the land.   Selah
10 Your anger against sinners brings
you praise.
Those who live through your
anger gather to worship you.

11 Make promises to the LORD your
God and keep them.

Let all of the neighboring nations bring gifts to the One who should be respected.
¹²He breaks the proud spirit of rulers.
The kings of the earth have respect for him.

PSALM 77

For the director of music.
For Jeduthun. A psalm of Asaph.

¹I cried out to God for help.
I cried out to God to hear me.
²When I was in trouble, I looked to the Lord.
During the night I lifted up my hands in prayer.
But I refused to be comforted.

³God, I remembered you, and I groaned.
I thought about you, and I became weak.   *Selah*
⁴You kept me from going to sleep.
I was so troubled I couldn't speak.
⁵I thought about days gone by.
I thought about the years of long ago.
⁶I remembered how I used to sing praise to you in the night.
I thought about it, and here is what I asked myself.

⁷"Will the Lord turn away from us forever?
Won't he ever show us his kindness again?
⁸Has his faithful love disappeared forever?
Has his promise failed for all time?
⁹Has God forgotten to show us his favor?
Has he held back his tender love because he was angry?" *Selah*

¹⁰Then I thought, "Here is what I will make my appeal to.
For many years the Most High God showed how powerful his right hand is."
¹¹LORD, I will remember what you did.
Yes, I will remember your miracles of long ago.
¹²I will spend time thinking about everything you have done.
I will consider all of your mighty acts.

¹³God, everything you do is holy.
What god is so great as our God?
¹⁴You are the God who does miracles.
You show your power among the nations.
¹⁵With your mighty arm you set your people free.
You set the children of Jacob and Joseph free.   *Selah*

¹⁶God, the water of the Red Sea saw you.
It saw you and boiled up.
The deepest waters were stirred up.
¹⁷The clouds poured down rain.
The skies rumbled with thunder.
Lightning flashed back and forth like arrows.
¹⁸Your thunder was heard in the windstorm.
Your lightning lit up the world.
The earth trembled and shook.
¹⁹Your path led through the Red Sea.
You walked through the mighty waters.
But your footprints were not seen.

²⁰You led your people like a flock.
You led them by the hands of Moses and Aaron.

PSALM 78

A *maskil* of Asaph.

¹My people, listen to my teaching.
Pay attention to what I say.
²I will open my mouth and tell stories.
I will speak about things that were hidden.
They happened a long time ago.
³We have heard about them and we know them.
Our people who lived before us have told us about them.
⁴We won't hide them from our children.
We will tell them to those who live after us.
We will tell them about what the LORD has done that is worthy of praise.

We will talk about his power and
the wonderful things he has
done.
⁵He gave laws to the people of
Jacob.
He gave Israel their law.
He commanded our people who
lived before us
to teach his laws to their
children.
⁶Then those born later would know
his laws.
Even their children yet to come
would know them.
And they in turn would tell their
children.
⁷Then they would put their trust in
God.
They would not forget what he
had done.
They would obey his commands.
⁸They would not be like their
people who lived before them.
Those people were stubborn.
They refused to obey God.
Their hearts were not true to him.
Their spirits were not faithful to
him.

⁹The soldiers of Ephraim were
armed with bows.
But they ran away on the day of
battle.
¹⁰They didn't keep the covenant God
had made with them.
They refused to live by his law.
¹¹They forgot what he had done.
They didn't remember the
wonders he had shown them.
¹²He did miracles right in front of
our people who lived long
ago.
At that time they were living in
the land of Egypt, in the area
of Zoan.
¹³God parted the Red Sea and led
them through it.
He made the water stand up like
a wall.
¹⁴He guided them with the cloud
during the day.
He led them with the light of a
fire all night long.
¹⁵He broke the rocks open in the
desert.
He gave them as much water as
there is in the oceans.

¹⁶He brought streams out of a rocky
cliff.
He made water flow down like
rivers.
¹⁷But they continued to sin against
him.
In the desert they refused to obey
the Most High God.
¹⁸They were stubborn and put God
to the test.
They ordered him to give them
the food they longed for.
¹⁹They spoke against God. They
said,
"Can God put food on a table in
the desert?
²⁰When he struck the rock, streams
of water poured out.
Huge amounts of water flowed
down.
But can he also give us food?
Can he supply meat for his
people?"
²¹When the LORD heard what they
said, he was very angry.
His anger broke out like fire
against the people of Jacob.
He became very angry with
Israel.
²²That was because they didn't
believe in God.
They didn't trust in his power to
save them.
²³But he gave a command to the
skies above.
He opened the doors of the
heavens.
²⁴He rained down manna for the
people to eat.
He gave them the grain of
heaven.
²⁵Mere men ate the bread of angels.
He sent them all of the food they
could eat.
²⁶He made the east wind blow from
the heavens.
By his power he caused the south
wind to blow.
²⁷He rained meat down on them like
dust.
He sent them birds like sand on
the seashore.
²⁸He made the birds come down
inside their camp.
The birds fell all around their
tents.

29 People ate until they had more
than enough.
He gave them what they had
longed for.
30 But even before they had finished
eating, God acted.
He did it while the food was still
in their mouths.
31 His anger rose up against them.
He put to death the strongest
among them.
He struck down Israel's young
men.

32 But even after all that, they kept
on sinning.
Even after they had seen the
miracles he did, they still
didn't believe.
33 So he brought their days to an end
like a puff of smoke.
He ended their years with terror.
34 Every time God killed some of
them, the others would look
to him.
They gladly turned back to him
again.
35 They remembered that God was
their Rock.
They remembered that God Most
High had set them free.
36 But they didn't mean it when they
praised him.
They lied to him when they
spoke.
37 Their hearts were not true to him.
They weren't faithful to the
covenant he had made with
them.
38 But he was full of tender love.
He forgave their sins
and didn't destroy his people.
Time after time he held back his
anger.
He didn't let all of his burning
anger blaze out.
39 He remembered that they were
only human.
He remembered they were only a
breath of air
that drifts by and doesn't return.

40 How often they refused to obey
him in the desert!
How often they caused him
sorrow in that dry and empty
land!

41 Again and again they put God to
the test.
They made the Holy One of Israel
sad and angry.
42 They didn't remember his power.
They forgot the day he set them
free
from those who had beaten them
down.
43 They forgot how he had shown
them his miraculous signs in
Egypt.
They forgot his miracles in the
area of Zoan.
44 He turned the rivers of Egypt into
blood.
The people of Egypt couldn't
drink water from their
streams.
45 He sent large numbers of flies that
bit them.
He sent frogs that destroyed their
land.
46 He gave their crops to the
grasshoppers.
He gave their food to the locusts.
47 He destroyed their vines with
hail.
He destroyed their fig trees with
sleet.
48 He killed their cattle with hail.
Their livestock were struck by
lightning.
49 He brought great trouble on Egypt
by pouring out his blazing
anger.
In his hot anger he sent
destroying angels against
them.
50 God prepared a path for his anger.
He didn't spare their lives.
He gave them over to the plague.
51 He killed the oldest son of each
family in Egypt.
He struck down the oldest son in
every house in the land of
Ham.
52 But he brought his people out like
a flock.
He led them like sheep through
the desert.
53 He guided them safely, and they
weren't afraid.
But the Red Sea swallowed up
their enemies.
54 He brought his people to the
border of his holy land.

He led them to the central hill
country he had taken by his
power.
⁵⁵ He drove the nations out to make
room for his people.
He gave to each family a piece of
land to pass on to their
children.
He settled the tribes of Israel in
their homes.

⁵⁶ But they put God to the test.
They refused to obey the Most
High God.
They didn't keep his laws.
⁵⁷ Like their people who lived before
them,
they turned away from him and
were not faithful.
They were like a bow that doesn't
shoot straight.
They couldn't be trusted.
⁵⁸ They made God angry by going to
their high places.
They made him jealous by
worshiping the statues of their
gods.
⁵⁹ When God saw what the people
were doing, he was very
angry.
He turned away from them
completely.
⁶⁰ He deserted the holy tent at
Shiloh.
He left the tent he had set up
among his people.
⁶¹ He allowed the ark to be captured.
Into the hands of his enemies he
sent the ark where his glory
rested.
⁶² He let his people be killed with
swords.
He was very angry with them.
⁶³ Fire destroyed their young men.
Their young women had no one
to get married to.
⁶⁴ Their priests were killed with
swords.
Their widows weren't able to cry.

⁶⁵ Then the Lord woke up as if he
had been sleeping.
He was like a man waking up
from the deep sleep caused by
wine.
⁶⁶ He drove his enemies back.
He put them to shame that will
last forever.

⁶⁷ He turned his back on the tents of
the people of Joseph.
He didn't choose to live in the
tribe of Ephraim.
⁶⁸ Instead, he chose to live in the
tribe of Judah.
He chose Mount Zion, which he
loved.
⁶⁹ There he built his holy place as
secure as the heavens.
He built it to last forever, like the
earth.
⁷⁰ He chose his servant David.
He took him from the sheep
pens.
⁷¹ He brought him from tending
sheep
to be the shepherd of his people
Jacob.
He made him the shepherd of
Israel, his special people.
⁷² David cared for them with a
faithful and honest heart.
With skilled hands he led them.

PSALM 79

A psalm of Asaph.

¹ God, an army from the nations has
attacked your land.
They have polluted your holy
temple.
They have completely destroyed
Jerusalem.
² They have given the dead bodies
of your people
as food to the birds of the air.
They have given the bodies of your
faithful people
to the animals of the earth.
³ They have poured out the blood of
your people like water
all around Jerusalem.
No one is left to bury the dead.
⁴ We are something our neighbors
joke about.
The nations around us laugh at
us and make fun of us.

⁵ LORD, how long will you be angry
with us? Will it be forever?
How long will your jealousy burn
like fire?
⁶ Pour out your burning anger on
the nations
that don't pay any attention to
you.

Pour it out on the kingdoms
that don't worship you.
7 They have swallowed up the
people of Jacob.
They have destroyed Israel's
homeland.
8 Don't hold against us the sins of
our people who lived before
us.
May you be quick to show us
your tender love.
We are in great need.

9 God our Savior, help us.
Then glory will come to you.
Be true to your name.
Save us and forgive our sins.
10 Why should the nations say,
"Where is their God?"
Show the nations that you punish
those who kill your people.
We want to see it happen.
11 Listen to the groans of the
prisoners.
Use your powerful arm
to save the lives of those who
have been sentenced to death.

12 Lord, our neighbors have laughed
at you.
Pay them back seven times for
what they have done.
13 We are your people. We are your
very own sheep.
We will praise you forever.
For all time to come
we will keep on praising you.

PSALM 80

For the director of music.
A psalm of Asaph to the tune of
"The Lilies of the Covenant."

1 Shepherd of Israel, hear us.
You lead the people of Joseph
like a flock.
You sit on your throne between
the cherubim.
Show your glory
2   to the people of Ephraim,
Benjamin and Manasseh.
Call your strength into action.
Come and save us.

3 God, make us new again.
Let your face smile on us with
favor.
Then we will be saved.

4 LORD God who rules over all,
how long will your anger burn
against the prayers of your
people?
5 You have given us tears as our
food.
You have made us drink tears by
the bowlful.
6 You have let our neighbors fight
against us.
Our enemies laugh at us.

7 God who rules over all, make us
new again.
Let your face smile on us with
favor.
Then we will be saved.

8 You brought Israel out of Egypt.
Israel was like a vine.
After you drove the nations out of
Canaan,
you planted the vine in their
land.
9 You prepared the ground for it.
It took root and spread out over
the whole land.
10 The mountains were covered with
its shade.
The shade of its branches
covered the mighty cedar
trees.
11 Your vine sent its branches out all
the way to the Mediterranean
Sea.
They reached as far as the
Euphrates River.

12 Why have you broken down the
walls around your vine?
Now all who pass by it can pick
its grapes.
13 Wild pigs from the forest destroy
it.
The creatures of the field feed on
it.
14 God who rules over all, return to
us!
Look down from heaven and see
us!
Watch over your vine.
15   Guard the root you have planted
with your powerful right
hand.
Take care of the branch you have
raised up for yourself.
16 Your vine has been cut down. Fire
has burned it up.

You have been angry with us, and
we are dying.

¹⁷ May you honor the people at your
right hand.

May you honor the nation you
have raised up for yourself.

¹⁸ Then we won't turn away from
you.

Give us new life. We will worship
you.

¹⁹ LORD God who rules over all, make
us new again.

Let your face smile on us with
favor.

Then we will be saved.

PSALM 81

For the director of music.
For *gittith*. A psalm of Asaph.

¹ Sing joyfully to God! He gives us
strength.

Give a loud shout to the God of
Jacob!

² Let the music begin. Play the
tambourines.

Play sweet music on harps and
lyres.

³ Blow the ram's horn on the day of
the New Moon Feast.

Blow it again when the moon is
full and the Feast of Booths
begins.

⁴ This is an order given to Israel.

It is a law of the God of Jacob.

⁵ He gave it as a covenant law for
the people of Joseph

when God went out to punish
Egypt.

There we heard a language we
didn't understand.

⁶ God said, "I removed the load
from your shoulders.

I set your hands free from
carrying heavy baskets.

⁷ You called out when you were in
trouble, and I saved you.

I answered you out of a
thundercloud.

I put you to the test at the waters
of Meribah.   *Selah*

⁸ "My people, listen and I will warn
you.

Israel, I wish you would listen to
me!

⁹ Don't have anything to do with the
gods of other nations.

Don't bow down and worship
strange gods.

¹⁰ I am the LORD your God.

I brought you up out of Egypt.

Open your mouth wide, and I
will fill it with good things.

¹¹ "But my people wouldn't listen to
me.

Israel wouldn't obey me.

¹² So I let them go their own
stubborn way.

I let them follow their own sinful
plans.

¹³ "I wish my people would listen to
me!

I wish Israel would live as I want
them to live!

¹⁴ Then I would quickly bring their
enemies under control.

I would use my power against
their attackers.

¹⁵ Those who hate me would bow
down to me in fear.

They would be punished forever.

¹⁶ But you would be fed with the
finest wheat.

I would satisfy you with the
sweetest honey."

PSALM 82

A psalm of Asaph.

¹ God takes his place at the head of
a large gathering of rulers and
judges.

He announces his decisions
among them.

² He says, "How long will you stand
up for those who aren't fair to
others?

How long will you show favor to
sinful people?   *Selah*

³ Stand up for those who are weak
and for those whose fathers
have died.

See to it that those who are poor
and those who are beaten
down are treated fairly.

⁴ Save the weak and those who are
in need.

Save them from the power of
sinful people.

⁵ "You rulers and judges don't know
      anything.
   You don't understand anything.
   You are in the dark about what is
      right.
   Law and order have been
      destroyed all over the world.
⁶ "I said, 'Rulers and judges, you are
      "gods."
   You are all children of the Most
      High God.'
⁷ But you will die, just like everyone
      else.
   You will die like every other
      ruler."

⁸ God, rise up. Judge the earth.
   All of the nations belong to you.

PSALM 83

A song. A psalm of Asaph.

¹ God, don't keep silent.
   God, don't keep quiet. Don't be
      still.
² See how your enemies are getting
      ready for action.
   See how they are rising up
      against you.
³ They make clever plans against
      your people.
   They make evil plans against
      those you love.
⁴ "Come," they say. "Let's destroy
      that whole nation.
   Then the name of Israel won't be
      remembered anymore."

⁵ All of them agree on the evil plans
      they have made.
   They join forces against you.
⁶ Their forces include the people of
      Edom,
   Ishmael, Moab and Hagar.
⁷ They also include the people of
      Byblos, Ammon, Amalek,
   Philistia and Tyre.
⁸ Even Assyria has joined them
   to give strength to the people of
      Moab and Ammon.   *Selah*

⁹ Do to them what you did to the
      people of Midian.
   Do to them what you did to
      Sisera and Jabin at the Kishon
      River.
¹⁰ Sisera and Jabin died near the
      town of Endor.

Their bodies were left to rot on
      the ground.
¹¹ Do to the nobles of your enemies
   what you did to Oreb and
      Zeeb.
   Do to all of their princes what
      you did to Zebah and
      Zalmunna.
¹² They said, "Let's take over
   the grasslands that belong to
      God."

¹³ My God, make them like straw
   that the wind blows away.
   Make them like tumbleweed.
¹⁴ Destroy them as fire burns up a
      forest.
   Destroy them as a flame sets
      mountains on fire.
¹⁵ Chase them with your mighty
      winds.
   Terrify them with your storm.
¹⁶ LORD, put them to shame
   so that people will worship you.
¹⁷ May they always be filled with
      terror and shame.
   May they die in dishonor.
¹⁸ Your name is the LORD. Let them
      know
   that you alone are the Most High
      God over the whole earth.

PSALM 84

For the director of music. For *gittith*.
A psalm of the Sons of Korah.

¹ LORD who rules over all,
   how lovely is the place where you
      live!
² I long to be in the courtyards of
      the LORD's temple.
   I deeply long to be there.
   My whole being cries out
      for the living God.

³ LORD who rules over all,
   even the sparrow has found a
      home near your altar.
   My King and my God,
      the swallow also has a nest there,
   where she may have her young.
⁴ Blessed are those who live in your
      house.
   They are always praising you.
                              Selah

⁵ Blessed are those whose strength
      comes from you.

They have decided to travel to
    your temple.
⁶As they pass through the dry Valley
    of Baca,
    they make it a place where water
        flows.
    The rain in the fall covers it with
        pools.
⁷Those people get stronger as they
    go along,
    until each of them appears in
        Zion, where God lives.

⁸LORD God who rules over all, hear
    my prayer.
    God of the people of Jacob, listen
        to me.   *Selah*
⁹God, look with favor on your
    anointed king.
    You appointed him to be like a
        shield that keeps us safe.

¹⁰A single day in your courtyards is
    better
    than a thousand anywhere else.
    I would rather guard the door of
        the house of my God
    than live in the tents of sinful
        people.
¹¹The LORD God is like the sun that
    gives us light.
    He is like a shield that keeps us
        safe.
    The LORD blesses us with favor
        and honor.
    He doesn't hold back anything
        good
    from those whose lives are
        without blame.

¹²LORD who rules over all,
    blessed is everyone who trusts in
        you.

PSALM 85

For the director of music.
A psalm of the Sons of Korah.

¹LORD, you showed favor to your
    land.
    You blessed the people of Jacob
        with great success again.
²You forgave the evil things your
    people did.
    You took away all of their sins.
                                Selah
³You stopped being angry with
    them.

You turned your burning anger
    away from them.
⁴God our Savior, make us new
    again.
    Stop being unhappy with us.
⁵Will you be angry with us forever?
    Will you be angry for all time to
        come?
⁶Won't you give us new life again?
    Then we'll be joyful because of
        what you have done.
⁷LORD, show us your faithful love.
    Save us.

⁸I will listen to what God the LORD
    will say.
    He promises peace to his faithful
        people.
    But they must not return to their
        foolish ways.
⁹I know he's ready to save those
    who have respect for him.
    Then his glory can be seen in our
        land.

¹⁰God's truth and faithful love join
    together.
    His peace and holiness kiss each
        other.
¹¹His truth springs up from the
    earth.
    His holiness looks down from
        heaven.
¹²The LORD will certainly give what
    is good.
    Our land will produce its crops.
¹³God's holiness leads the way in
    front of him.
    It prepares the way for his
        coming.

PSALM 86

A prayer of David.

¹LORD, hear me and answer me.
    I am poor and needy.
²Keep my life safe. I am faithful to
    you.
    You are my God. Save me.
    I trust in you.
³Lord, show me your favor.
    I call out to you all day long.
⁴Bring joy to me.
    Lord, I worship you.
⁵Lord, you are good. You are
    forgiving.

You are full of love for all who call
out to you.
⁶LORD, hear my prayer.
Listen to my cry for your favor.
⁷When I'm in trouble, I will call out
to you.
And you will answer me.

⁸Lord, there's no one like you
among the gods.
No one can do what you do.
⁹Lord, all of the nations you have
made
will come and worship you.
They will bring glory to you.
¹⁰You are great. You do wonderful
things.
You alone are God.

¹¹LORD, teach me how you want me
to live.
Then I will follow your truth.
Give me a heart that doesn't want
anything
more than to worship you.
¹²Lord my God, I will praise you
with all my heart.
I will bring glory to you forever.
¹³Great is your love for me.
You have kept me from going
down into the grave.

¹⁴God, proud people are attacking
me.
A gang of mean people is trying
to kill me.
They don't care about you.
¹⁵But Lord, you are a God who is
tender and kind.
You are gracious.
You are slow to get angry.
You are faithful and full of love.
¹⁶Turn to me and show me your
favor.
Give me strength and save me.
¹⁷Prove your goodness to me.
Then my enemies will see it and
be put to shame.
LORD, you have helped me and
given me comfort.

PSALM 87

A psalm of the Sons of Korah. A song.

¹The LORD has built his city
on the holy mountain.
²He loves the city of Zion
more than all of the other places
where the people of Jacob live.

³City of God,
the LORD says glorious things
about you.   *Selah*
⁴He says, "I will include Egypt and
Babylon
in a list of those who recognize
me as king.
I will also include Philistia and
Tyre, along with Cush.
I will say about them, 'They were
born in Zion.' "

⁵Certainly it will be said about
Zion,
"This nation and that nation
were born in her.
The Most High God himself will
make her secure."
⁶Here is what the LORD will write in
his list of the nations.
"Each of them was born in Zion."
          Selah
⁷As they make music they will
sing,
"Zion, all of our blessings come
from you."

PSALM 88

For the director of music.
For *mahalath leannoth*. A song.
A psalm of the Sons of Korah.
A *maskil* of Heman the Ezrahite.

¹LORD, you are the God who saves
me.
Day and night I cry out to you.
²Please hear my prayer.
Pay attention to my cry for help.

³I have so many troubles
I'm about to die.
⁴People think my life is over.
I'm like someone who doesn't
have any strength.
⁵People treat me as if I were dead.
I'm like those who have been
killed and are now in the
grave.
You don't even remember them
anymore.
They are cut off from your care.

⁶It seems as if you have put me
deep down in the grave,
that deep and dark place.
⁷Your burning anger lies heavy on
me.
All the waves of your anger have
crashed over me.   *Selah*

⁸You have taken my closest friends
away from me.
You have made me sickening to
them.
I feel trapped. I can't escape.
⁹ I'm crying so much I can't see
very well.

LORD, I call out to you every day.
I lift up my hands to you in
prayer.
¹⁰Do you work miracles for those
who are dead?
Do dead people rise up and
praise you?   *Selah*
¹¹Do those who are dead speak
about your love?
Do those who are in the grave tell
how faithful you are?
¹²Are your miracles known in that
dark place?
Are your holy acts known in that
land where the dead are
forgotten?

¹³LORD, I cry out to you for help.
In the morning I pray to you.
¹⁴LORD, why do you say no to me?
Why do you turn your face away
from me?

¹⁵I've been in pain ever since I was
young.
I've been close to death.
You have made me suffer terrible
things.
I have lost all hope.
¹⁶Your burning anger has swept over
me.
Your terrors have destroyed me.
¹⁷All day long they surround me like
a flood.
They have closed in all around
me.
¹⁸You have taken my companions
and loved ones away from me.
The darkness is my closest
friend.

PSALM 89

A *maskil* of Ethan the Ezrahite.

¹LORD, I will sing about your great
love forever.
For all time to come, I will tell
how faithful you are.
²I will tell everyone that your love
stands firm forever.

I will tell them that you are
always faithful, even in
heaven itself.
³You said, "Here is the covenant I
have made with my chosen
one.
Here is the promise I have made
to my servant David.
⁴'I will make your family line
continue forever.
I will make your kingdom secure
for all time to come.'"   *Selah*

⁵LORD, the heavens praise you for
your miracles.
When your holy angels gather
together,
they praise you for how faithful
you are.
⁶Who in the skies above can
compare with the LORD?
Who among the angels is like the
LORD?
⁷God is highly respected among his
holy angels.
He's more wonderful than all
those who are around him.
⁸LORD God who rules over all, who
is like you?
LORD, you are mighty. You are
faithful in everything you do.

⁹You rule over the stormy sea.
When its waves rise up, you calm
them down.
¹⁰You crushed Egypt and killed her
people.
With your powerful arm you
scattered your enemies.
¹¹The heavens belong to you. The
earth is yours also.
You made the world and
everything that is in it.
¹²You created everything from north
to south.
Mount Tabor and Mount
Hermon sing to you with joy.
¹³Your arm is powerful.
Your hand is strong.
Your right hand is mighty.

¹⁴Your kingdom is built on what is
right and fair.
Your truth and faithful love lead
the way in front of you.
¹⁵Blessed are those who have
learned to shout praise to you.

LORD, they live in the light of
      your favor.
¹⁶ All day long they are full of joy
      because of who you are.
    They praise you because you do
      what is right.
¹⁷ You are their glory. You give them
      strength.
    You favor them by honoring our
      king.
¹⁸ Our king is like a shield that keeps
      us safe.
    He belongs to the LORD.
    He belongs to the Holy One of
      Israel.

¹⁹ You once spoke to your faithful
      people in a vision.
    You said, "I have given strength
      to a soldier.
    I have raised up a young man
      from among the people.
²⁰ I have found my servant David.
    I have poured my sacred oil on
      his head.
²¹ My powerful hand will keep him
      going.
    My mighty arm will give him
      strength.
²² No enemies will require him to
      bring gifts to them.
    No evil person will beat him
      down.

²³ I will crush the king's enemies.
    I will completely destroy them.
²⁴ I will love him and be faithful to
      him.
    Because of me his power will
      increase.
²⁵ I will give him a great kingdom.
    It will reach from the
      Mediterranean Sea to the
      Euphrates River.
²⁶ He will call out to me, 'You are my
      Father.
    You are my God. You are my Rock
      and Savior.'
²⁷ I will also make him my oldest
      son.
    Among all the kings of the earth,
      he will be the most important
      one.
²⁸ I will continue to love him
      forever.
    I will never break my covenant
      with him.
²⁹ I will make his family line
      continue forever.
    His kingdom will last as long as
      the heavens.
³⁰ "What if his sons turn away from
      my laws
    and do not follow them?
³¹ What if they disobey my orders
      and fail to keep my commands?

Why do I need two fathers, my dad and God?

We call God "our Father" because he
created us, watches over us and
provides everything we need. The
Bible even tells us that God has
adopted us as his very own
children. But God has also given
us human fathers and mothers to
take care of us on earth.

checkout Psalm 89:26

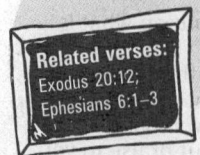
Related verses:
Exodus 20:12;
Ephesians 6:1–3

³²Then I will punish them for their
    sins.
    I will strike them with the rod.
    I will whip them for their evil
      acts.
³³But I will not stop loving David.
    I will always be faithful to him.
³⁴I will not break my covenant.
    I will not go back on my word.
³⁵Once and for all, I have made a
      promise with an oath.
    It is based on my holiness.
    And I will not lie to David.
³⁶His family line will continue
      forever.
    His kingdom will last as long as
      the sun.
³⁷It will last forever like the moon,
    that faithful witness in the sky."
                            Selah

³⁸But you have turned your back on
      your anointed king.
    You have been very angry with
      him.
³⁹You have broken the covenant you
      made with him.
    You have thrown your servant's
      crown into the dirt.
⁴⁰You have broken through the walls
      around his city.
    You have completely destroyed
      his secure places.
⁴¹All those who pass by have carried
      off what belonged to him.
    His neighbors make fun of him.
⁴²You have made his enemies
      strong.
    You have made all of them
      happy.
⁴³You have made his sword useless.
    You have not helped him in
      battle.
⁴⁴You have put an end to his glory.
    You have knocked his throne to
      the ground.
⁴⁵You have cut short the days of his
      life.
    You have covered him with
      shame.   *Selah*

⁴⁶LORD, how long will you hide
      yourself? Will it be forever?
    How long will your anger burn
      like fire?
⁴⁷Remember how short my life is.
    You have created all people for
      such a useless purpose!

⁴⁸What man can live and not die?
    Who can escape the power of the
      grave?   *Selah*
⁴⁹Lord, where is the great love you
      used to have?
    You faithfully promised it to
      David.
⁵⁰Lord, remember how my enemies
      have made fun of me.
    I've had to put up with mean
      words from all of the nations.
⁵¹LORD, your enemies have said
      mean things.
    They have laughed at everything
      your anointed king has done.

⁵²Give praise to the LORD forever!
    Amen and Amen.

BOOK IV

Psalms 90–106

PSALM 90

A prayer of Moses, the man of God.

¹Lord, from the very beginning
    you have been like a home to us.
²Before you created the world and
      the mountains were made,
    from the beginning to the end
      you are God.

³You turn human beings back to
      dust.
    You say to them, "Return to
      dust."
⁴To you a thousand years
    are like a day that has just gone
      by.
    They are like a few hours of the
      night.
⁵You sweep people away, and they
      die.
    They are like new grass that
      grows in the morning.
⁶In the morning it springs up new,
    but by evening it's all dried up.

⁷Your anger destroys us.
    Your burning anger terrifies us.
⁸You have put our sins right in front
      of you.
    You have placed our secret sins
      where you can see them
      clearly.

⁹You have been angry with us all of
   our days.
   We groan as we come to the end
    of our lives.
¹⁰We live to be about 70.
   Or we may live to be 80, if we
    stay healthy.
   But all that time is filled with
    trouble and sorrow.
   The years quickly pass, and we
    are gone.
¹¹Who knows how powerful your
    anger is?
   It's as great as the respect we
    should have for you.
¹²Teach us to realize how short our
    lives are.
   Then our hearts will become
    wise.

¹³LORD, please stop punishing us!
   How long will you keep it up?
   Be kind to us.
¹⁴Satisfy us with your faithful love
    every morning.
   Then we can sing with joy and be
    glad all of our days.
¹⁵Make us glad for as many days as
    you have made us suffer.
   Give us joy for as many years as
    we've had trouble.
¹⁶Show us your mighty acts.
   Let our children see your
    glorious power.

¹⁷May the Lord our God show us his
   favor.
   Lord, make what we do succeed.
   Please make what we do
    succeed.

PSALM 91

¹The person who rests in the
    shadow of the Most High God
   will be kept safe by the Mighty
    One.
²I will say about the LORD,
   "He is my place of safety.
   He is like a fort to me.
   He is my God. I trust in him."

³He will certainly save you from
    hidden traps
   and from deadly sickness.
⁴He will cover you with his wings.
   Under the feathers of his wings
    you will find safety.
   He is faithful. He will keep you
    safe like a shield or a tower.
⁵You won't have to be afraid of the
    terrors that come during the
    night.
   You won't have to fear the arrows
    that come at you during the
    day.
⁶You won't have to be afraid of the
    sickness that attacks in the
    darkness.
   You won't have to fear the plague
    that destroys at noon.

Who created God?

No one created God. He has always existed. This is hard to
understand because everything else that we know about has a
beginning and an end.
Each day has a morning and
night. Basketball games have an
opening tip-off and a final
buzzer. People are born and they
die. But God has no beginning or
end. He always was and always
will be.

checkout
Psalm 90:1,2

Related verse:
Hebrews 13:8

7 A thousand may fall dead at your
　　side.
　Ten thousand may fall near your
　　right hand.
　But no harm will come to you.
8 You will see with your own eyes
　　how God punishes sinful people.

9 The LORD is the one who keeps
　　you safe.
　So let the Most High God be like
　　a home to you.
10 Then no harm will come to you.
　No terrible plague will come near
　　your tent.
11 The LORD will command his angels
　　to take good care of you.
12 They will lift you up in their
　　hands.
　Then you won't trip over a stone.
13 You will walk all over lions and
　　cobras.
　You will crush mighty lions and
　　poisonous snakes.
14 The LORD says, "I will save the one
　　who loves me.
　I will keep him safe, because he
　　trusts in me.
15 He will call out to me, and I will
　　answer him.
　I will be with him in times of
　　trouble.

I will save him and honor him.
16 I will give him a long and full life.
　I will save him."

PSALM 92

A psalm. A song for the Sabbath day.

1 LORD, it is good to praise you.
　Most High God, it is good to
　　make music to honor you.
2 It is good to sing every morning
　　about your love.
　It is good to sing every night
　　about how faithful you are.
3 I sing about it to the music of the
　　lyre that has ten strings.
　I sing about it to the music of the
　　harp.
4 LORD, you make me glad by what
　　you have done.
　I sing with joy about the works of
　　your hands.
5 LORD, how great are the things you
　　do!
　How wise your thoughts are!
6 Here is something a man who isn't
　　wise doesn't know.
　Here is what a foolish person
　　doesn't understand.
7 Those who are evil spring up like
　　grass.
　Those who do wrong succeed.

Sometimes I'm afraid to go to school. What should I do?

Talk to your parents or guardian about your fears. They can help. If there is a specific reason why you are afraid, tell them about it. Teachers and school counselors can also help. Or call up a friend or two. Who knows, they might have the same fears.
Also, you can ask your Sunday school teacher and pastor to pray for you to be brave. Remember, you can always talk to God. Tell him your fears and ask him for courage.

checkout
Psalm 91:5

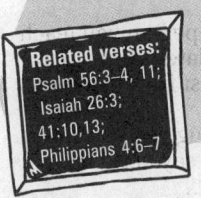

Related verses:
Psalm 56:3–4, 11;
Isaiah 26:3;
41:10,13;
Philippians 4:6–7

I'M ON
'STRESS LEAVE'
FROM SCHOOL
TODAY.

But they will be destroyed
forever.

⁸ But LORD, you are honored forever.

⁹ LORD, your enemies will certainly
die.
All those who do evil will be
scattered.
¹⁰ You have made me as strong as a
wild ox.
You have poured the finest olive
oil on me.
¹¹ I've seen my evil enemies
destroyed.
I've heard that they have lost the
battle.

¹² Those who do what is right will
grow like a palm tree.
They will grow strong like a cedar
tree in Lebanon.
¹³ Their roots will be firm in the
house of the LORD.
They will grow strong and
healthy in the courtyards of
our God.
¹⁴ When they get old, they will still
bear fruit.
Like young trees they will stay
fresh and strong.
¹⁵ They will say to everyone, "The
LORD is honest.
He is my Rock. There is no evil in
him."

PSALM 93

¹ The LORD rules.
He puts on majesty as if it were
clothes.
The LORD puts on majesty and
strength.
The world is firmly set in place.
It can't be moved.
² LORD, you began to rule a long
time ago.
You have always existed.

³ LORD, the seas have lifted up their
voice.
They have lifted up their
pounding waves.
⁴ But LORD, you are more powerful
than the roar of the ocean.
You are stronger than the waves
of the sea.
LORD, you are powerful in
heaven.

⁵ Your laws do not change.
LORD, your temple will be holy
for all time to come.

PSALM 94

¹ LORD, you are the God who
punishes.
Since you are the one who
punishes, come and show
your anger.
² Judge of the earth, rise up.
Pay back proud people for what
they have done.
³ LORD, how long will those who are
evil be glad?
How long will they be full of joy?

⁴ Proud words pour out of their
mouths.
All those who do evil are always
bragging.
⁵ LORD, they crush your people.
They beat down those who
belong to you.
⁶ They kill outsiders. They kill
widows.
They murder children whose
fathers have died.
⁷ They say, "The LORD doesn't see
what's happening.
The God of Jacob doesn't pay any
attention to it."

⁸ You who aren't wise, pay attention.
You foolish people, when will
you become wise?
⁹ Does he who made the ear not
hear?
Does he who formed the eye not
see?
¹⁰ Does he who corrects nations not
punish?
Does he who teaches human
beings not know anything?
¹¹ The LORD knows what people
think.
He knows that their thoughts
don't amount to anything.

¹² LORD, blessed is the man you
correct.
Blessed is the person you teach
from your law.
¹³ You give him rest from times of
trouble,
until a pit is dug to trap sinners.
¹⁴ The LORD won't say no to his
people.

He will never desert those who
  belong to him.
¹⁵ He will again judge people in
  keeping with what is right.
  All those who have honest hearts
  will follow the right way.

¹⁶ Who will rise up for me against
  sinful people?
  Who will stand up for me against
  those who do evil?
¹⁷ Suppose the LORD had not helped
  me.
  Then I would soon have been
  lying quietly in the grave.
¹⁸ I said, "My foot is slipping."
  But LORD, your love kept me from
  falling.
¹⁹ I was very worried.
  But your comfort brought joy to
  my heart.

²⁰ Can you have anything to do with
  rulers who aren't fair?
  Can those who make laws that
  cause suffering be friends of
  yours?
²¹ They join together against those
  who do what is right.
  They sentence to death those
  who aren't guilty of doing
  anything wrong.
²² But the LORD has become like a
  fort to me.
  My God is my rock. I go to him
  for safety.
²³ He will pay them back for their
  sins.
  He will destroy them for their evil
  acts.
  The LORD our God will destroy
  them.

PSALM 95

¹ Come, let us sing with joy to the
  LORD.
  Let us give a loud shout to the
  Rock who saves us.
² Let us come to him and give him
  thanks.
  Let us praise him with music and
  song.

³ The LORD is the great God.
  He is the greatest King.
  He rules over all of the gods.
⁴ He owns the deepest parts of the
  earth.

The mountain peaks belong to
  him.
⁵ The ocean is his, because he
  made it.
  He formed the dry land with his
  hands.

⁶ Come, let us bow down and
  worship him.
  Let us fall on our knees in front
  of the LORD our Maker.
⁷ He is our God.
  We are the sheep belonging to
  his flock.
  We are the people he takes good
  care of.

Listen to his voice today.
⁸ If you hear it, don't be stubborn
  as you were at Meribah.
  Don't be stubborn as you were
  that day at Massah in the
  desert.
⁹ There your people of long ago
  really put me to the test.
  They did it even though they had
  seen what I had done for
  them.
¹⁰ For 40 years I was angry with
  them.
  I said, "Their hearts are always
  going down the wrong path.
  They do not know how I want
  them to live."
¹¹ So when I was angry, I took an
  oath.
  I said, "They will never enjoy the
  rest I planned for them."

PSALM 96

¹ Sing a new song to the LORD.
  All you people of the earth, sing
  to the LORD.
² Sing to the LORD. Praise him.
  Day after day tell about how he
  saves us.
³ Tell the nations about his glory.
  Tell all people about the
  wonderful things he has done.

⁴ The LORD is great. He is really
  worthy of praise.
  People should have respect for
  him as the greatest God of all.
⁵ All of the gods of the nations are
  like their statues.
  They can't do anything.
  But the LORD made the heavens.

⁶Glory and majesty are all around
  him.
    Strength and glory can be seen in
    his temple.

⁷Praise the LORD, all you nations.
    Praise the LORD for his glory and
    strength.
⁸Praise the LORD for the glory that
  belongs to him.
    Bring an offering and come into
    the courtyards of his temple.
⁹Worship the LORD because of his
  beauty and holiness.
    All you people of the earth,
    tremble when you are with
    him.

¹⁰Say to the nations, "The LORD
  rules."
    The world is firmly set in place. It
    can't be moved.
    The LORD will judge the people of
    the world fairly.
¹¹Let the heavens be full of joy. Let
  the earth be glad.
    Let the ocean and everything in
    it roar.

¹²Let the fields and everything in
  them be glad.
    Then all of the trees in the forest
    will sing with joy.
¹³They will sing to the LORD,
  because he is coming to judge
  the earth.
    He will judge the people of the
    world
    in keeping with what is right and
    true.

PSALM 97

¹The LORD rules. Let the earth be
  glad.
    Let countries that are far away be
    full of joy.

²Clouds and thick darkness
  surround him.
    His rule is built on what is right
    and fair.
³The LORD sends fire ahead of him.
    It burns up his enemies all
    around him.
⁴His lightning lights up the world.
    The earth sees it and trembles.

Why do some people believe that trees, plants and animals have spirits?

Some people do believe that trees, plants and animals have spirits, and many false religions teach that they do. But only *people* have souls that live forever.

Still, God does want us to respect the world he created. God created all plants and all animals. He told Adam and Eve to rule the world and take care of it. People have the job of taking care of it now just as much as Adam and Eve did then.

The Bible says that all of nature praises God. That means that nature shows God's glory. But plants and animals do not have spirits. And we must be sure never to worship nature. We should worship only God.

Related verse:
Deuteronomy 5:7

checkout
Psalm 96:12

⁵The mountains melt like wax
 when the LORD is near.
He is the Lord of the whole earth.
⁶The heavens announce that what
 he does is right.
All people everywhere see his
 glory.

⁷All who worship statues of gods or
 brag about them are put to
 shame.
All you gods, worship the LORD!

⁸Zion hears about it and is filled
 with joy.
LORD, the villages of Judah are
 glad
because of how you judge.
⁹LORD, you are the Most High God.
You rule over the whole earth.
You are honored much more
 than all gods.

¹⁰Let those who love the LORD hate
 evil.
He guards the lives of those who
 are faithful to him.

He saves them from the power of
 sinful people.
¹¹The light of his favor shines on
 those who do what is right.
Joy comes to those whose hearts
 are honest.
¹²You who are godly, be glad
 because of what the LORD has
 done.
Praise him, because his name is
 holy.

PSALM 98

A psalm.

¹Sing a new song to the LORD.
 He has done wonderful things.
By the power of his right hand and
 his holy arm
 he has saved his people.
²The LORD has made known his
 power to save.
He has shown the nations that he
 does what is right.
³He has shown his faithful love
 to the people of Israel.

Doesn't God ever get tired of answering prayers?

Nope. God never gets even a little bit tired of answering prayers. He loves to hear from us because he loves us. Jesus died for our sins so that we would be forgiven for the wrong things we've done—and to be friends with him. Those things never change. No matter how often we ask things of him, he will listen.

God wants to work in our lives to change our behavior, thoughts, and habits. We should never fear that we are wearing him out with our prayers. It is even OK to pray the same thing over and over because God wants to keep being a part of our lives.

checkout
Psalm 98:1-3

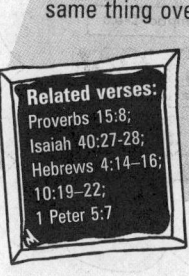

Related verses:
Proverbs 15:8;
Isaiah 40:27-28;
Hebrews 4:14-16;
10:19-22;
1 Peter 5:7

JASON'S IMAGINATION

GOD'S OFFICE

ANSWERED PRAYERS

People from one end of the earth
to the other
have seen that our God has saved
us.

⁴Shout to the LORD with joy,
everyone on earth.
Burst into joyful songs and make
music.
⁵Make music to the LORD with the
harp.
Sing and make music with the
harp.
⁶Blow the trumpets. Give a blast on
the ram's horn.
Shout to the LORD with joy. He is
the King.
⁷Let the ocean and everything in it
roar.
Let the world and all who live in
it shout.
⁸Let the rivers clap their hands.
Let the mountains sing together
with joy.
⁹Let them sing to the LORD,
because he is coming to judge
the earth.
He will judge the nations of the
world
in keeping with what is right and
fair.

PSALM 99

¹The LORD rules.
Let the nations tremble.
He sits on his throne between the
cherubim.
Let the earth shake.
²Great is the LORD in Zion.
He is honored over all of the
nations.
³Let them praise his great and
wonderful name.
He is holy.

⁴The King is mighty. He loves what
is fair.
He has set up the rules for
fairness.
He has done what is right and fair
for the people of Jacob.
⁵Honor the LORD our God.
Worship at his feet.
He is holy.

⁶Moses and Aaron were two of his
priests.
Samuel was one of those who
worshiped him.
They called out to the LORD.
And he answered them.
⁷He spoke to them from the pillar
of cloud.

Did people in Bible times have music?

People had music in Bible times, and they loved it. They did not have compact
discs, tapes, pianos or electric guitars. Their instruments included harps,
tambourines, flutes and several kinds of horns. They also loved to sing.
They sang a lot of songs to God.
They also sang songs to express
their feelings. They sang sad
songs called "dirges" when they
were very unhappy. King David
wrote a lot of songs. He played
the harp and wrote the music and
words to play on it. Many of his
songs are right
here in the book
of Psalms.

JASON'S
IMAGINATION

Not-so-compact Discs

NEW RELEASES

Related verses:
Exodus 15:1–21

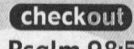

checkout
Psalm 98:5,6

They obeyed his laws and the
orders he gave them.
⁸ LORD our God, you answered
them.
You showed Israel that you are a
God who forgives.
But when they did wrong, you
punished them.
⁹ Honor the LORD our God.
Worship at his holy mountain.
The LORD our God is holy.

PSALM 100

A psalm for giving thanks.

¹ Shout to the LORD with joy,
everyone on earth.
² Worship the LORD with gladness.
Come to him with songs of joy.
³ I want you to realize that the LORD
is God.
He made us, and we belong to
him.
We are his people.
We are the sheep belonging to
his flock.
⁴ Give thanks as you enter the gates
of his temple.
Give praise as you enter its
courtyards.
Give thanks to him and praise his
name.
⁵ The LORD is good. His faithful love
continues forever.
It will last for all time to come.

PSALM 101

A psalm of David.

¹ I will sing about your love and
fairness.
LORD, I will sing praise to you.
² I will be careful to lead a life
that is without blame.
When will you come and help
me?

I will lead a life
that is without blame in my
house.
³ I won't look at anything that is
evil.

I hate the acts of people who aren't
faithful to you.
I don't even want people like that
around me.

⁴ I will stay away from those whose
hearts are twisted.
I don't want to have anything to
do with evil.
⁵ I will get rid of anyone
who tells lies about his neighbor
in secret.
I won't put up with anyone
whose eyes and heart are proud.
⁶ I will look with favor on the
faithful people in the land.
They will live with me.
Those whose lives are without
blame will serve me.
⁷ No one who lies and cheats
will live in my house.
No one who tells lies
will serve me.
⁸ Every morning I will get rid of
all the sinful people in the land.
I will remove from the city of the
LORD
everyone who does what is evil.

PSALM 102

A prayer of a suffering man when
he is weak and pours out his
problems to the LORD.

¹ LORD, hear my prayer.
Listen to my cry for help.
² Don't turn your face away from me
when I'm in trouble.
Pay attention to me.
When I call out for help, answer
me quickly.

³ My days are disappearing like
smoke.
My body burns like glowing
coals.
⁴ My strength has dried up like
grass.
I even forget to eat my food.
⁵ I groan out loud because of my
suffering.
I'm nothing but skin and bones.
⁶ I'm like a desert owl.
I'm like an owl among destroyed
buildings.
⁷ I can't sleep. I've become
like a bird alone on a roof.
⁸ All day long my enemies laugh at
me.
Those who make fun of me use
my name as a curse.

⁹I eat ashes as my food.
My tears fall into what I'm
drinking.
¹⁰You were very angry with me.
So you picked me up and threw
me away.
¹¹The days of my life are like an
evening shadow.
I dry up like grass.

¹²But LORD, you are seated on your
throne forever.
Your fame will continue for all
time to come.
¹³You will rise up and show deep
concern for Zion.
The time has come for you to
show favor to it.
¹⁴The stones of your destroyed city
are priceless to us.
Even its dust brings deep
concern to us.
¹⁵The nations will worship the LORD.
All of the kings on earth will
respect his glorious power.
¹⁶The LORD will build Zion again.
He will appear in his glory.

¹⁷He will answer the prayer of those
who don't have anything.
He won't say no to their cry for
help.
¹⁸Let this be written down for those
born after us.
Then people who are not yet
born can praise the LORD.
¹⁹Here is what should be written.
"The LORD looked down from his
temple in heaven.
From heaven he viewed the
earth.
²⁰He heard the groans of the
prisoners.
He set free those who were
sentenced to death."
²¹So people will talk about him in
Zion.
They will praise him in
Jerusalem.
²²Nations and kingdoms
will gather there to worship the
LORD.
²³When I was still young, he took
away my strength.

Where did God live before heaven was made?

The word *heaven* refers to three places: (1) wherever God is, (2) the New Jerusalem or (3) the sky. We read in the Bible that God is in heaven. He did not make heaven. It is a "place" only in the sense that it is where God is. Wherever God sits on his great throne, there is heaven.

Someday God will make a new place called "heaven" or "the New Jerusalem." But that place will be for us.

checkout Psalm 102:12

Related verses:
Deuteronomy
26:15;
1 Kings 8:30

He wasn't going to let me live
much longer.
²⁴ So I said, "My God, don't let me die
in the middle of my life.
You will live for all time to come.
²⁵ In the beginning you made the
earth secure.
You placed it on its foundations.
Your hands created the heavens.
²⁶ They will pass away. But you will
remain.
They will all wear out like a piece
of clothing.
You will make them like clothes
that are taken off and thrown
away.
²⁷ But you remain the same.
Your years will never end.
²⁸ Our children will live with you.
Their sons and daughters will be
safe in your care."

PSALM 103

A psalm of David.

¹ I will praise the LORD.
Deep down inside me, I will
praise him.
I will praise him, because his
name is holy.
² I will praise the LORD.
I won't forget anything he does
for me.

³ He forgives all my sins.
He heals all my sicknesses.
⁴ He saves my life from going down
into the grave.
His faithful and tender love
makes me feel like a king.
⁵ He satisfies me with the good
things I long for.
Then I feel young and strong
again, just like an eagle.

⁶ The LORD does what is right and
fair
for all who are beaten down.

⁷ He told Moses all about his plans.
He let the people of Israel see his
mighty acts.
⁸ The LORD is tender and kind. He is
gracious.
He is slow to get angry. He is full
of love.
⁹ He won't keep bringing charges
against us.
He won't stay angry with us
forever.
¹⁰ He doesn't punish us for our sins
as much as we should be
punished.
He doesn't pay us back in
keeping with the evil things
we've done.
¹¹ His love for those who have
respect for him

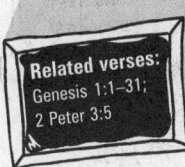

How did God create the earth?

Whenever we make something, we have to start with something else. We need to use clay, string, glue, paper, crayons, sand or materials like that. We can't even imagine creating something out of *nothing*. How could we just say the words and make something appear? But God is so powerful that he can do what is impossible for us. He can make anything he wants, even from nothing. That's what it means to be God.

Related verses:
Genesis 1:1–31;
2 Peter 3:5

checkout
Psalm 102:25

is as high as the heavens are
  above the earth.
¹²He has removed our lawless acts
  from us
  as far as the east is from the west.
¹³A father is tender and kind to his
  children.
  In the same way, the LORD is
  tender and kind
  to those who have respect for
  him.
¹⁴He knows what we are made of.
  He remembers that we are dust.
¹⁵People's lives are like grass.
  People grow like the flowers in
  the field.
¹⁶When the wind blows on them,
  they are gone.
  No one can tell that they had
  ever been there.
¹⁷But the LORD's love
  for those who have respect for
  him
  lasts for ever and ever.
  Their children's children will know
  that he always does what is right.
¹⁸He always loves those who keep
  his covenant.
  He always does what is right for
  those who remember to obey
  his commands.
¹⁹The LORD has set up his throne in
  heaven.
  His kingdom rules over all.
²⁰Praise the LORD, you angels of his.
  Praise him, you mighty ones

who carry out his orders and
  obey his word.
²¹Praise the LORD, all you angels in
  heaven.
  Praise him, all you who serve
  him and do what he wants.
²²Let everything the LORD has made
  praise him
  everywhere in his kingdom.

I will praise the LORD.

PSALM 104

¹I will praise the LORD.

LORD my God, you are very great.
  You are dressed in glory and
  majesty.
²You wrap yourself in light as if it
  were a robe.
  You spread the heavens out like a
  tent.
³ You build your palace high in the
  heavens.
  You make the clouds serve as your
  chariot.
  You ride on the wings of the
  wind.
⁴You make the winds serve as your
  messengers.
  You make flashes of lightning
  serve you.

⁵You placed the earth on its
  foundations.
  It can never be moved.
⁶You covered it with the oceans like
  a blanket.

Why do people wait until the last minute to pray?

Some people wait until the last minute to pray because they
forget or because they do not think they need God's help. They
think they can do almost anything on their own. Or maybe they forgot
about God. Then, when things get worse, they cry
out to God for help as a last resort. Of course, we
should not wait until we have a huge
problem to pray. Remember that we
need God's help all the time, 24/7.
We should talk with him *first* in
every situation we face.

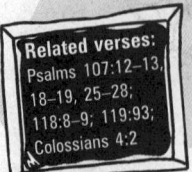
Related verses:
Psalms 107:12–13,
18–19, 25–28;
118:8–9; 119:93;
Colossians 4:2

checkout Psalm 103:2

The waters covered the
mountains.

⁷ But you commanded the waters,
and they ran away.

At the sound of your thunder
they rushed off.

⁸ They flowed down the mountains.
They went into the valleys.
They went to the place you
appointed for them.

⁹ You drew a line they can't cross.
They will never cover the earth
again.

¹⁰ You make springs pour water into
the valleys.
It flows between the mountains.

¹¹ The springs give water to all of the
wild animals.
The wild donkeys satisfy their
thirst.

¹² The birds of the air build nests by
the waters.
They sing among the branches.

¹³ You water the mountains from
your palace high in the
clouds.
The earth is filled with the things
you have made.

¹⁴ You make grass grow for the cattle
and plants for people to take care
of.
That's how they get food from
the earth.

¹⁵ There is wine to make people glad.
There is olive oil to make them
healthy.
And there is bread to make them
strong.

¹⁶ The cedar trees of Lebanon belong
to the LORD.
You planted them and gave them
plenty of water.

¹⁷ There the birds make their nests.
The stork has its home in the
pine trees.

¹⁸ The high mountains belong to the
wild goats.
The cliffs are a safe place for the
rock badgers.

¹⁹ The moon serves to mark off the
seasons.
The sun knows when to go down.

²⁰ You bring darkness, and it
becomes night.
Then all the animals of the forest
prowl around.

KIDS' QUESTiON

Is it OK to complain to God?

Yes, it is all right to complain to God. We should be honest
about our feelings; besides, it's impossible to hide them from
God. As we see in Psalms and the book of Job, the people who prayed told
God how they really felt. They respected God. They told him that they
believed in his goodness. That is how we should pray too.

We can and should tell God how we
feel. Also, we should tell him
that we know he is God and
has our best interests in mind.
Remember, he loves us!

God is on our side. He will
come alongside and
help us if we trust
him.

checkout
Psalm 103:17-22

Related verses:
Job 3:1–10;
Psalms 77:1–20;
102:1–28;
Ecclesiastes
7:13–14;
Habakkuk 1:1—2:1;
1 Peter 5:7

DEAR GOD, PLEASE HELP MY MOM,
SHE'S GOING CLEAN CRAZY. IT'S
"CLEAN YOUR ROOM, CLEAN YOUR
HANDS"... I CAN UNDERSTAND THAT,
BUT "CLEAN OUT YOUR GARBAGE
CAN"? THAT'S WHAT A GARBAGE
CAN IS FOR!

²¹ The lions roar while they hunt.
   All of their food comes from God.
²² The sun rises, and they slip away.
   They return to their dens and lie
      down.
²³ Then a man gets up and goes to
      work.
   He keeps working until evening.

²⁴ LORD, you have made so many
      things!
   How wise you were when you
      made all of them!
   The earth is full of your
      creatures.
²⁵ Look at the ocean, so big and
      wide!
   It is filled with more creatures
      than people can count.
   It is filled with living things, from
      the largest to the smallest.
²⁶ Ships sail back and forth on it.
   The leviathan, the sea monster
      you made, plays in it.

²⁷ All of those creatures depend on
      you
   to give them their food when
      they need it.
²⁸ When you give it to them,
   they eat it.
   When you open your hand,

they are satisfied with good
   things.
²⁹ When you turn your face away
      from them,
   they are terrified.
   When you take away their breath,
   they die and turn back into dust.
³⁰ When you send your Spirit,
   you create them.
   You give new life to the earth.

³¹ May the glory of the LORD
      continue forever.
   May the LORD be happy with
      what he has made.
³² When he looks at the earth, it
      trembles.
   When he touches the mountains,
      they pour out smoke.

³³ I will sing to the LORD all my life.
   I will sing praise to my God as
      long as I live.
³⁴ May these thoughts of mine please
      him.
   I find my joy in the LORD.
³⁵ But may those who sin be gone
      from the earth.
   May evil people disappear.

I will praise the LORD.

Praise the LORD.

Do I really have to eat my vegetables, or are my parents just making sure I clean my plate?

God has said that children must obey their parents. So you should eat whatever food your parents say you have to eat. And you should eat it even if you do not like it. Parents tell children to eat vegetables because our bodies need them. The Bible also tells us that we should take care of our bodies because God lives in us and wants to use us. We should do what we can to stay healthy. That means eating good food. It means eating vegetables!

Related verses:
1 Corinthians 6:19;
Ephesians 6:1–3

checkout
Psalm 104:14

PSALM 105

¹ Give thanks to the LORD. Worship
  him.
  Tell the nations what he has done.
² Sing to him. Sing praise to him.
  Tell about all of the wonderful
    things he has done.
³ Praise him, because his name is
    holy.
  Let the hearts of those who trust
    in the LORD be glad.
⁴ Look to the LORD and to his
    strength.
  Always look to him.

⁵ Remember the wonderful things
    he has done.
  Remember his miracles and how
    he judged our enemies.
⁶ Remember what he has done, you
    children of his servant
    Abraham.
  Remember it, you people of
    Jacob, God's chosen ones.
⁷ He is the LORD our God.
  He judges the whole earth.

⁸ He will keep his covenant forever.
  He will keep his promise for all
    time to come.
⁹ He will keep the covenant he
    made with Abraham.
  He will keep the oath he took
    when he made his promise to
    Isaac.
¹⁰ He made it stand as a law for
    Jacob.
  He made it stand as a covenant
    for Israel. It will last forever.
¹¹ He said, "I will give you the land of
    Canaan.
  It will belong to you."

¹² At first there weren't very many of
    God's people.
  There were only a few. And they
    were strangers in the land.
¹³ They wandered from nation to
    nation.
  They wandered from one
    kingdom to another.
¹⁴ But God didn't allow anyone to
    beat them down.
  To keep them safe, he gave a
    command to kings.
¹⁵ He said to them, "Do not touch my
    anointed ones.
  Do not harm my prophets."

¹⁶ He made the people in the land go
    hungry.
  He destroyed all their food
    supplies.
¹⁷ He sent a man ahead of them into
    Egypt.
  That man was Joseph. He had
    been sold as a slave.
¹⁸ The Egyptians put his feet in
    chains.
  They put an iron collar around
    his neck.
¹⁹ He was in prison until what he
    said would happen came true.
  The word of the LORD proved
    that he was right.
²⁰ The king of Egypt sent for Joseph
    and let him out of prison.
  The ruler of many nations set
    him free.
²¹ He put Joseph in charge of his
    palace.
  He made him ruler over
    everything he owned.
²² Joseph was in charge of teaching
    the princes.
  He taught the elders how to think
    and live wisely.

²³ Then the rest of Jacob's family
    went to Egypt.
  The people of Israel lived as
    outsiders in the land of Ham.
²⁴ The LORD gave his people so many
    children
  that there were too many of them
    for their enemies.
²⁵ He made the Egyptians hate his
    people.
  The Egyptians made evil plans
    against them.
²⁶ The LORD sent his servant Moses
    to the king of Egypt.
  He sent Aaron, his chosen one,
    along with him.
²⁷ The LORD gave them the power to
    do miraculous signs among
    the Egyptians.
  They did his wonders in the land
    of Ham.
²⁸ He sent darkness over the land.
  He did it because the Egyptians
    had refused to obey his words.
²⁹ He turned their rivers and streams
    into blood.
  He caused the fish in them to
    die.

³⁰ Their land was covered with frogs.
　Frogs even went into the
　　bedrooms of the rulers.
³¹ The LORD spoke, and large
　　numbers of flies came.
　Gnats filled the whole country.
³² He turned their rain into hail.
　Lightning flashed all through
　　their land.
³³ He destroyed their vines and fig
　　trees.
　He broke down the trees in
　　Egypt.
³⁴ He spoke, and the locusts came.
　There were so many of them they
　　couldn't be counted.
³⁵ They ate up every green thing in
　　the land.
　They ate up what the land
　　produced.
³⁶ Then he killed the oldest son of
　　every family in Egypt.
　He struck down the oldest of all
　　of their sons.
³⁷ He brought the people of Israel
　　out of Egypt.
　The Egyptians loaded them
　　down with silver and gold.
　From among the tribes of Israel
　　no one got tired or fell down.
³⁸ The Egyptians were glad when the
　　people of Israel left.
　They were terrified because of
　　Israel.
³⁹ The LORD spread out a cloud to
　　cover his people.
　He gave them a fire to light up
　　the night.
⁴⁰ They asked for meat, and he
　　brought them quail.
　He satisfied them with manna,
　　the bread of heaven.
⁴¹ He broke open a rock, and streams
　　of water poured out.
　They flowed like a river in the
　　desert.
⁴² He remembered the holy promise
　　he had made to his servant
　　Abraham.
⁴³ His chosen people shouted for joy
　　as he brought them out of
　　Egypt.
⁴⁴ He gave them the lands of other
　　nations.
　He let them take over what
　　others had worked for.

⁴⁵ He did it so they might obey his
　　rules
　and follow his laws.

Praise the LORD.

PSALM 106

¹ Praise the LORD.

Give thanks to the LORD, because
　he is good.
His faithful love continues forever.
² Who can speak enough about the
　　mighty acts of the LORD?
　Who can praise him as much as
　　he should be praised?
³ Blessed are those who always do
　　what is fair.
　Blessed are those who keep
　　doing what is right.
⁴ LORD, remember me when you
　　show favor to your people.
　Help me when you save them.
⁵ Then I will enjoy the good things
　　you give your chosen ones.
　I will be joyful together with your
　　people.
　I will join them when they praise
　　you.

⁶ We have sinned, just as our people
　　of long ago did.
　We too have done what is evil
　　and wrong.
⁷ When our people were in Egypt,
　　they forgot about the LORD's
　　miracles.
　They didn't remember his many
　　kind acts.
　At the Red Sea they refused to
　　obey him.
⁸ But he saved them for the honor of
　　his name.
　He did it to make his mighty
　　power known.
⁹ He ordered the Red Sea to dry up,
　　and it did.
　He led his people through it as if
　　it were a desert.
¹⁰ He saved them from the power of
　　their enemies.
　He set them free from their
　　control.
¹¹ The waters covered their enemies.
　Not one of them escaped alive.
¹² Then his people believed his
　　promises
　and sang praise to him.

¹³ But they soon forgot what he had
    done.
    They didn't wait for his advice.
¹⁴ In the desert they longed for food.
    In that dry and empty land they
    put God to the test.
¹⁵ So he gave them what they asked
    for.
    But he also sent a sickness that
    killed many of them.
¹⁶ In their camp some of them
    became jealous of Moses.
    They were also jealous of Aaron.
    He had been set apart to serve
    the LORD.
¹⁷ The ground opened up and
    swallowed Dathan.
    It buried Abiram and his
    followers.
¹⁸ Fire blazed among all of them.
    Flames destroyed those evil
    people.

¹⁹ At Mount Horeb they made a
    metal statue of a bull calf.
    They worshiped that statue of a
    god.
²⁰ They traded their glorious God
    for a statue of a bull that eats
    grass.
²¹ They forgot the God who saved
    them.
    They forgot the One who had
    done great things in Egypt.
²² They forgot the miracles he did in
    the land of Ham.
    They forgot the wonderful things
    he did by the Red Sea.
²³ So he said he would destroy them.
    But Moses, his chosen one,
stood up for them.
    He kept God's anger from
    destroying them.

²⁴ Later on, they refused to enter the
    pleasant land of Canaan.
    They didn't believe God's promise.
²⁵ In their tents they told the LORD
    how unhappy they were.
    They didn't obey him.
²⁶ So he lifted up his hand and
    promised with an oath
    that he would make them die in
    the desert.
²⁷ He promised he would scatter
    their children's children
    among the nations.

He would make them die in
    other lands.

²⁸ They joined in worshiping the
    Baal that was worshiped at
    Peor.
    They ate food that had been
    offered to gods that aren't
    even alive.
²⁹ Their evil ways made the LORD
    angry.
    So a plague broke out among
    them.
³⁰ But Phinehas stood up and took
    action.
    Then the plague stopped.
³¹ What Phinehas did made him
    right with the LORD.
    It will be remembered for all
    time to come.

³² By the waters of Meribah the
    LORD's people made him
    angry.
    Moses got in trouble because of
    them.
³³ They refused to obey the Spirit of
    God.
    So Moses spoke without
    thinking.

³⁴ They didn't destroy the nations in
    Canaan
    as the LORD had commanded
    them.
³⁵ Instead, they mixed with those
    nations
    and adopted their ways.
³⁶ They worshiped statues of their
    gods.
    That became a trap for them.
³⁷ They sacrificed their sons and
    daughters
    as offerings to demons.
³⁸ They killed those who weren't
    guilty of doing anything
    wrong.
    They killed their own sons and
    daughters.
    They sacrificed them as offerings
    to statues of the gods of
    Canaan.
    The land became "unclean"
    because of the blood of their
    children.
³⁹ The people polluted themselves by
    what they had done.
    They weren't faithful to the LORD.

⁴⁰ So the LORD became angry with
his people.
He turned away from his own
children.
⁴¹ He handed them over to the
nations.
Their enemies ruled over them.
⁴² They beat them down
and kept them under their
power.
⁴³ Many times the LORD saved them.
But they refused to obey him.
So he destroyed them because of
their sins.
⁴⁴ But he heard them when they
cried out.
He paid special attention to their
suffering.
⁴⁵ Because they were his people, he
remembered his covenant.
Because of his great love, he felt
sorry for them.
⁴⁶ He made all those who held them
as prisoners
show concern for them.
⁴⁷ LORD our God, save us.
Bring us back from among the
nations.
Then we will give thanks to you,
because your name is holy.
We will celebrate by praising you.

⁴⁸ Give praise to the LORD, the God of
Israel,
for ever and ever.
Let all of the people say, "Amen!"

Praise the LORD.

BOOK V

Psalms 107–150

PSALM 107

¹ Give thanks to the LORD, because
he is good.
His faithful love continues
forever.
² That's what those who have been
set free by the LORD should
say.
He set them free from the power
of the enemy.
³ He brought them back from other
lands.

He brought them back from east
and west, from north and
south.

⁴ Some of them wandered in deserts
that were dry and empty.
They couldn't find their way to a
city where they could settle
down.
⁵ They were hungry and thirsty.
Their lives were slipping away.
⁶ Then they cried out to the LORD
because of their problems.
And he saved them from their
troubles.
⁷ He led them straight
to a city where they could settle
down.
⁸ Let them give thanks to the LORD
for his faithful love.
Let them give thanks for the
miracles he does for his
people.
⁹ He gives those who are thirsty all
of the water they want.
He gives those who are hungry all
of the good food they can eat.

¹⁰ Others lived in the deepest
darkness.
They suffered as prisoners in
iron chains.
¹¹ That's because they hadn't obeyed
the words of God.
They had refused to follow the
advice of the Most High God.
¹² So he made them do work that
was hard and bitter.
They tripped and fell, and there
was no one to help them.
¹³ Then they cried out to the LORD
because of their problems.
And he saved them from their
troubles.
¹⁴ He brought them out of the
deepest darkness.
He broke their chains off.
¹⁵ Let them give thanks to the LORD
for his faithful love.
Let them give thanks for the
miracles he does for his people.
¹⁶ He breaks down gates that are
made of bronze.
He cuts through bars that are
made of iron.
¹⁷ Others were foolish. They suffered
because of their sins.

They suffered because they
wouldn't obey the LORD.
[18] They refused to eat anything.
They came close to passing
through the gates of death.
[19] Then they cried out to the LORD
because of their problems.
And he saved them from their
troubles.
[20] He gave his command and healed
them.
He saved them from the grave.
[21] Let them give thanks to the LORD
for his faithful love.
Let them give thanks for the
miracles he does for his
people.
[22] Let them sacrifice thank
offerings.
Let them talk about what he has
done as they sing with joy.

[23] Others sailed out on the ocean in
ships.
They traded goods on the mighty
waters.
[24] They saw the works of the LORD.
They saw the miracles he did on
the ocean.
[25] He spoke and stirred up a storm.
It lifted the waves high.
[26] They rose up to the heavens. Then
they went down deep into the
ocean.
In that kind of danger the
people's boldness melted
away.
[27] They were unsteady like those
who get drunk.
They didn't know what to do.
[28] Then they cried out to the LORD
because of their problems.
And he brought them out of their
troubles.
[29] He made the storm as quiet as a
whisper.
The waves of the ocean calmed
down.
[30] The people were glad when the
ocean became calm.
Then he guided them to the
harbor they were looking for.
[31] Let them give thanks to the LORD
for his faithful love.
Let them give thanks for the
miracles he does for his
people.

[32] Let them honor him among his
people who gather for
worship.
Let them praise him in the
meeting of the elders.

[33] He turned rivers into a desert.
He turned flowing springs into
thirsty ground.
[34] He turned land that produced
crops into a salty land where
nothing could grow.
He did it because the people who
lived there were evil.
[35] He turned the desert into pools of
water.
He turned the dry and cracked
ground into flowing springs.
[36] He brought hungry people there to
live.
They built a city where they
could settle down.
[37] They planted fields and vineyards
that produced large crops.
[38] He blessed the people, and they
greatly increased their
numbers.
He kept their herds from getting
smaller.
[39] Then the number of God's people
got smaller.
They were brought low by
trouble, suffering and sorrow.
[40] The One who looks down on
proud nobles
made them wander in a desert
where no one lives.
[41] But he lifted needy people out of
their suffering.
He made their families increase
like flocks of sheep.
[42] Honest people see it and are filled
with joy.
But no one who is evil has
anything to say.
[43] Let those who are wise pay
attention to these things.
Let them think about the LORD's
great love.

PSALM 108

A song. A psalm of David.

[1] God, my heart feels secure.
I will sing and make music to you
with all my heart.

2 Harp and lyre, wake up!
     I want to sing and make music
       before the sun rises.
3 LORD, I will praise you among the
       nations.
     I will sing about you among the
       people of the earth.
4 Great is your love. It is higher than
       the heavens.
     Your truth reaches to the skies.
5 God, may you be honored above
       the heavens.
     Let your glory be over the whole
       earth.

6 Save us. Help us with your
       powerful right hand,
     so that those you love may be
       saved.
7 God has spoken from his temple.
     He has said, "I will win the
       battle.
   Then I will divide up the land
       around Shechem.
   I will divide up the Valley of
       Succoth.
8 Gilead belongs to me. So does the
       land of Manasseh.
     Ephraim is the strongest tribe.
     It is like a helmet for my
       head.
     Judah is the royal tribe. It is like a
       ruler's staff.
9 Moab serves me like one who
       washes my feet.
     I toss my sandal on Edom to
       show that I own it.
     I shout to Philistia that I have
       won the battle."

10 Who will bring me to the city that
       has high walls around it?
     Who will lead me to the land of
       Edom?
11 God, isn't it you, even though you
       have now turned away from
       us?
     Isn't it you, even though you
       don't lead our armies into
       battle anymore?
12 Help us against our enemies.
     The help people give doesn't
       amount to anything.
13 With your help we will win the
       battle.
     You will walk all over our
       enemies.

PSALM 109

For the director of music.
A psalm of David.

1 God, I praise you.
     Don't remain silent.
2 Sinful people who lie and cheat
       have spoken against me.
     They have used their tongues to
       tell lies about me.
3 They gather all around me with
       their words of hatred.
     They attack me without any
       reason.
4 They bring charges against me,
       even though I love them
     and pray for them.
5 They pay me back with evil for the
       good things I do.
     They pay back my love with
       hatred.

6 Appoint an evil person to take my
       enemies to court.
     Let him stand at their right hand
       and bring charges against
       them.
7 When they are tried, let them be
       found guilty.
     May even their prayers judge
       them.
8 May their days be few.
     Let others take their places as
       leaders.
9 May their children's fathers die.
     May their wives become widows.
10 May their children be driven from
       their destroyed homes.
     May they wander around like
       beggars.
11 May everything those people own
       be taken away to pay for what
       they owe.
     May strangers rob them of
       everything they've worked for.
12 May no one be kind to them
     or take pity on the children they
       leave behind.
13 May their family line come to an
       end.
     May their names be forgotten by
       those who live after them.
14 May the LORD remember the evil
       things their fathers have
       done.
     May he never erase the sins of
       their mothers.

¹⁵ May the LORD never forget their sins.
Then he won't let people remember those sinners anymore.
¹⁶ They never thought about doing anything kind.
Instead, they drove those who were poor and needy to their deaths.
They did the same thing to those whose hearts were broken.
¹⁷ They loved to call down curses on others.
May their curses come back on them.
They didn't find any pleasure in giving anyone their blessing.
May no blessing ever come to them.
¹⁸ They called down curses on others as easily as they put on clothes.
Cursing was as natural to them as getting a drink of water
or putting olive oil on their bodies.
¹⁹ May their curses cover them like coats.
May their curses be wrapped around them like a belt forever.
²⁰ May that be the LORD's way of paying back
those who bring charges against me.
May it happen to those who say evil things about me.

²¹ But LORD and King,
be true to your name. Treat me well.
Because your love is so good, save me.
²² I am poor and needy.
My heart is wounded deep down inside me.
²³ I fade away like an evening shadow.
I'm like a locust that someone brushes off.
²⁴ My knees are weak because I've gone without food.
My body is very thin.
²⁵ Those who bring charges against me laugh at me.
When they see me, they shake their heads at me.

²⁶ LORD my God, help me.
Save me because you love me.
²⁷ LORD, let my enemies know that you yourself have saved me.
You have done it with your own hand.
²⁸ They may call down a curse on me.
But you will give me your blessing.
When they attack me, they will be put to shame.
But I will be filled with joy.
²⁹ Those who bring charges against me will be clothed with dishonor.
They will be wrapped in shame as if it were a coat.

³⁰ With my mouth I will continually praise the LORD.
I will praise him when all of his people gather for worship.
³¹ He stands ready to help those who need it.
He saves them from those who have sentenced them to death.

PSALM 110

A psalm of David.

¹ The LORD says to my Lord,
"Sit at my right hand
until I put your enemies
under your control."

² The LORD will make your royal authority spread out from Zion to other lands.
You will rule over your enemies who are all around you.
³ Your troops will be willing to fight for you
on the day of battle.
You will be wrapped in holy majesty.
Just as the dew falls fresh early in the morning,
you will always be young and strong.

⁴ The LORD has taken an oath and made a promise.
He will not change his mind.
He has said, "You are a priest forever,
just like Melchizedek."

5 The Lord is at your right hand.
  He will crush kings on the day
    when he is angry.
6 He will judge the nations. He will
    pile up dead bodies on the
    field of battle.
  He will crush the rulers of the
    whole earth.
7 He will drink from a brook along
    the way and receive new
    strength.
  And so he will win the battle.

PSALM 111

1 Praise the LORD.

I will praise the LORD with all my
  heart.
I will praise him where honest
  people gather for worship.

2 The LORD has done great things.
  All who take delight in what he
    has done will spend time
    thinking about it.
3 What he does shows his glory and
    majesty.
  He will always do what is right.
4 The LORD causes his miracles to be
    remembered.
  He is kind and tender.
5 He provides food for those who
    have respect for him.
  He remembers his covenant
    forever.
6 He has shown his people what his
    power can do.
  He has given them the lands of
    other nations.
7 He is faithful and right in
    everything he does.
  All his rules can be trusted.
8 They will stand firm for ever and
    ever.
  They were given by the LORD.
  He is faithful and honest.
9 He set his people free.
  He made a covenant with them
    that will last forever.
  His name is holy and wonderful.

10 If you really want to become wise,
    you must begin by having
    respect for the LORD.
  All those who follow his rules have
    good understanding.
  People should praise him forever.

PSALM 112

1 Praise the LORD.

Blessed is the one who has respect
  for the LORD.
He finds great delight when he
  obeys God's commands.

2 His children will be powerful in
    the land.
  Because he is honest, his
    children will be blessed.
3 His family will have wealth and
    riches.
  He will always be blessed for
    doing what is right.
4 Even in the darkness light shines
    on honest people.
  It shines on those who are kind
    and tender and godly.
5 Good things will come to those
    who are willing to lend freely.
  Good things will come to those
    who are fair in everything they
    do.
6 They will always be secure.
  Those who do what is right will
    be remembered forever.
7 They aren't afraid when bad news
    comes.
  They stand firm because they
    trust in the LORD.
8 Their hearts are secure. They aren't
    afraid.
  In the end they will see their
    enemies destroyed.
9 They have spread their gifts
    around to poor people.
  Their good works continue
    forever.
  They will be powerful and
    honored.
10 Evil people will see it and be
    upset.
  They will grind their teeth and
    become weaker and weaker.
  What evil people long to do can't
    succeed.

PSALM 113

1 Praise the LORD.

Praise him, you who serve the
  LORD.
  Praise the name of the LORD.
2 Let us praise the name of the
  LORD,

both now and forever.

³ From the sunrise in the east to the
sunset in the west,
may the name of the LORD be
praised.

⁴ The LORD is honored over all of the
nations.
His glory reaches to the highest
heavens.
⁵ Who is like the LORD our God?
He sits on his throne in heaven.
⁶ He bends down to look
at the heavens and the earth.

⁷ He raises poor people up from the
trash pile.
He lifts needy people out of the
ashes.
⁸ He lets them sit with princes.
He lets them sit with the princes
of their own people.
⁹ He gives children to the woman
who doesn't have any
children.
He makes her a happy mother in
her own home.

Praise the LORD.

PSALM 114

¹ The people of Israel came out of
Egypt.
The people of Jacob left a land
where a different language
was spoken.
² Then Judah became the holy place
where God lived.
Israel became the land he ruled
over.

³ The Red Sea saw him and parted.
The Jordan River stopped
flowing.
⁴ The mountains leaped like rams.
The hills skipped like lambs.

⁵ Red Sea, why did you part?
Jordan River, why did you stop
flowing?
⁶ Why did you mountains leap like
rams?
Why did you hills skip like
lambs?

⁷ Earth, tremble with fear when the
Lord comes.
Tremble when the God of Jacob
is near.
⁸ He turned the rock into a pool.

He turned the hard rock into
springs of water.

PSALM 115

¹ LORD, may glory be given to you,
not to us.
You are loving and faithful.

² Why do the nations ask,
"Where is their God?"
³ Our God is in heaven.
He does anything he wants to do.
⁴ But the statues of their gods are
made out of silver and gold.
They are made by the hands of
men.
⁵ They have mouths, but they can't
speak.
They have eyes, but they can't see.
⁶ They have ears, but they can't
hear.
They have noses, but they can't
smell.
⁷ They have hands, but they can't
feel.
They have feet, but they can't
walk.
They have throats, but they can't
say anything.
⁸ Those who make statues of gods
will be like them.
So will all those who trust in
them.

⁹ People of Israel, trust in the LORD.
He helps you. He is like a shield
that keeps you safe.
¹⁰ Priests of Aaron, trust in the LORD.
He helps you. He is like a shield
that keeps you safe.
¹¹ You who have respect for the
LORD, trust in him.
He helps you. He is like a shield
that keeps you safe.

¹² The LORD remembers us and will
bless us.
He will bless the people of Israel.
He will bless the priests of Aaron.
¹³ The LORD will bless those who
have respect for him.
He will bless important and
unimportant people alike.

¹⁴ May the LORD give you many
children.
May he give them to you and to
your children after you.
¹⁵ May the LORD bless you.

He is the Maker of heaven and
earth.

16 The highest heavens belong to the
LORD.
But he has given the earth to
human beings.
17 Dead people don't praise the LORD.
Those who lie quietly in the
grave don't praise him.
18 But we who are alive praise the
LORD,
both now and forever.

Praise the LORD.

PSALM 116

1 I love the LORD, because he heard
my voice.
He heard my cry for his favor.
2 Because he paid attention to me,
I will call out to him as long as I
live.
3 The ropes of death were wrapped
around me.
The horrors of the grave came
over me.
I was overcome by trouble and
sorrow.
4 Then I called out to the LORD.
I cried out, "LORD, save me!"

5 The LORD is holy and kind.
Our God is full of tender love.
6 The LORD takes care of those who
are as helpless as children.
When I was in great need, he
saved me.

7 I said to myself, "Be calm.
The LORD has been good to me."

8 LORD, you have saved me from
death.
You have dried the tears from my
eyes.
You have kept me from tripping
and falling.
9 So now I can enjoy life here with
you
while I'm still living.
10 I believed in you even when I said
to myself,
"I'm in great pain."
11 When I was terrified, I said to
myself,
"No one tells the truth."

12 The LORD has been so good to me!
How can I ever pay him back?
13 I will bring an offering of wine to
the LORD
and thank him for saving me.
I will worship him.
14 In front of all of the LORD's people,
I will do what I promised him.

15 The LORD pays special attention
when his faithful people die.
16 LORD, I serve you.
I serve you just as my mother
did.
You have set me free from the
chains of my suffering.

17 LORD, I will sacrifice a thank
offering to you.
I will worship you.
18 In front of all of the LORD's people,
I will do what I promised him.
19 I will keep my promise in the
courtyards of the LORD's
temple.
I will keep my promise in
Jerusalem itself.

Praise the LORD.

PSALM 117

1 All you nations, praise the LORD.
All you people on earth, praise
him.
2 Great is his love for us.
The LORD is faithful forever.

Praise the LORD.

PSALM 118

1 Give thanks to the LORD, because
he is good.
His faithful love continues
forever.

2 Let the people of Israel say,
"His faithful love continues
forever."
3 Let the priests of Aaron say,
"His faithful love continues
forever."
4 Let those who have respect for the
LORD say,
"His faithful love continues
forever."

5 When I was in great pain, I cried
out to the LORD.
He answered me and set me free.

⁶The LORD is with me. I will not be
afraid.
What can mere men do to me?
⁷The LORD is with me. He helps me.
I will win the battle over my
enemies.

⁸It is better to go to the LORD for
safety
than to trust in mere men.
⁹It is better to go to the LORD for
safety
than to trust in human leaders.

¹⁰The nations were all around me.
But by the LORD's power I
destroyed them.
¹¹They were around me on every side.
But by the LORD's power I
destroyed them.
¹²They attacked me like large
numbers of bees.
But they died out as quickly as
burning thorns.
By the LORD's power I destroyed
them.

¹³I was pushed back. I was about to
be killed.
But the LORD helped me.
¹⁴The LORD gives me strength. I sing
about him.
He has saved me.

¹⁵Shouts of joy ring out in the tents
of godly people.
They praise him for his help in
battle.
They shout, "The LORD's powerful
right hand has done mighty
things!
¹⁶ The LORD's powerful right hand
has won the battle!
The LORD's powerful right hand
has done mighty things!"

¹⁷I will not die. I will live.
I will talk about what the LORD
has done.
¹⁸The LORD has really punished
me.
But he didn't let me die.

Why did God take Grandpa to heaven?

Every person has to die. We do not like to think about this fact, but it is true.
Sometimes people die when they are young because of an accident, disease
or another sad thing. But even the
healthiest person will die some day.
Every person gets older. Our
bodies get weaker and weaker
and then they finally wear out.
No one wants a special
grandfather or grandmother to die.
But sometimes older people are
suffering so much that death
brings them relief. Certainly it is
better to be with God in heaven
than to be suffering on earth. If our
grandparents believe in Jesus, then
someday we will see them again.

Psalm 116:15

JASON'S
IMAGINATION

GRANDPA'S
STORY TELLING
CORNER

Related verses:
2 Samuel 12:22,23

¹⁹ Open the gates of the temple for me.
I will enter and give thanks to the
LORD.
²⁰ This is the gate of the LORD.
Only those who do what is right
can go through it.
²¹ LORD, I will give thanks to you,
because you answered me.
You have saved me.
²² The stone the builders didn't
accept
has become the most important
stone of all.
²³ The LORD has done it.
It is wonderful in our eyes.
²⁴ The LORD has done it on this day.
Let us be joyful and glad in it.

²⁵ LORD, save us.
LORD, give us success.
²⁶ Blessed is the one who comes in
the name of the LORD.
From the temple of the LORD we
bless you.
²⁷ The LORD is God.
He has made the light of his
favor shine on us.
Take branches in your hands. Join
in the march on the day of the
feast.
March up to the corners of the
altar.
²⁸ You are my God, and I will give
thanks to you.
You are my God, and I will honor
you.
²⁹ Give thanks to the LORD, because
he is good.
His faithful love continues
forever.

PSALM 119

א Aleph

¹ Blessed are those who live without
blame.
They live in keeping with the law
of the LORD.
² Blessed are those who obey his
covenant laws.
They trust in him with all their
hearts.
³ They don't do anything wrong.
They live as he wants them to
live.
⁴ You have given me rules

that I must obey completely.
⁵ I hope I will always stand firm
in following your orders.
⁶ Then I won't be put to shame
when I think about all of your
commands.
⁷ I will praise you with an honest
heart
as I learn about how fair your
decisions are.
⁸ I will obey your orders.
Please don't leave me all alone.

ב Beth

⁹ How can a young person keep his
life pure?
By living in keeping with your
word.
¹⁰ I trust in you with all my heart.
Don't let me wander away from
your commands.
¹¹ I have hidden your word in my
heart
so that I won't sin against you.
¹² LORD, I give praise to you.
Teach me your orders.
¹³ With my lips I talk about
all of the decisions you have
made.
¹⁴ Following your covenant laws
gives me joy
just as great riches give joy to
others.
¹⁵ I spend time thinking about your
rules.
I consider how you want me to
live.
¹⁶ I take delight in your orders.
I won't fail to obey your word.

ג Gimel

¹⁷ Be good to me, and I will live.
I will obey your word.
¹⁸ Open my eyes so that I can see
the wonderful truths in your law.
¹⁹ I'm a stranger on earth.
Don't hide your commands from
me.
²⁰ My heart is filled with longing
for your laws at all times.
²¹ You correct proud people. They
are under your curse.
They wander away from your
commands.
²² I obey your covenant laws.
So don't let evil people laugh at
me or hate me.

23 Even if rulers sit together and tell
    lies about me,
   I will spend time thinking about
    your orders.
24 Your covenant laws are my delight.
   They give me wise advice.

ד Daleth

25 I lie in the dust. I'm about to die.
   Keep me alive as you have
    promised.
26 I told you how I've lived, and you
    gave me your answer.
   Teach me your orders.
27 Help me understand what your
    rules can teach me.
   Then I'll spend time thinking
    about the miracles you have
    done.
28 My sadness has worn me out.
   Give me strength as you have
    promised.
29 Keep me from cheating and telling
    lies.
   Be kind and teach me your law.
30 I have chosen to be faithful to you.
   I put my trust in your laws.

31 LORD, I'm careful to obey your
    covenant laws.
   Don't let me be put to shame.
32 I am quick to follow your
    commands,
   because you have set my heart
    free.

ה He

33 LORD, teach me to follow your
    orders.
   Then I will obey them to the very
    end.
34 Help me understand your law.
   Then I will follow it
   and obey it with all my heart.
35 Teach me to live as you command,
   because that makes me very
    happy.
36 Make me want to follow your
    covenant laws
   instead of wanting to gain things
    only for myself.
37 Turn my eyes away from things
    that are worthless.
   Keep me alive as you have
    promised.

Why don't parents let us watch certain TV shows?

Many TV shows give the idea that we should go
against what God says. Many of the people
who make television shows are not Christians. They do not know God and often
show programs that are not good for us
to watch. Some shows even come right
out and tell us to do wrong things. But
we should always try to do what is
right. That includes the kind of television
shows we watch. So it is good to turn off
the set or change the channel when a bad
show comes on.

checkout Psalm 119:9

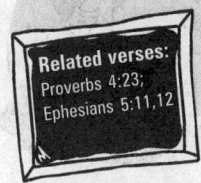

Related verses:
Proverbs 4:23;
Ephesians 5:11,12

³⁸ Keep your promise to me.
   Then other people will have
      respect for you.
³⁹ Please don't let me be put to
      shame.
   Your laws are good.
⁴⁰ I really want to follow your rules.
   Keep me alive, because you do
      what is right.

                ٦   Waw

⁴¹ LORD, show me your faithful love.
   Save me as you have promised.
⁴² Then I will answer those who
      make fun of me,
   because I trust in your word.
⁴³ Help me always to tell the truth
      about how faithful you are.
   I have put my hope in your laws.
⁴⁴ I will always obey your law,
   for ever and ever.
⁴⁵ I will lead a full and happy life,
   because I've tried to obey your
      rules.
⁴⁶ I will talk about your covenant
      laws to kings.
   I will not be put to shame.
⁴⁷ I take delight in obeying your
      commands
   because I love them.

⁴⁸ I praise your commands, and I
      love them.
   I spend time thinking about your
      orders.

                ז   Zayin

⁴⁹ Remember what you have said to
      me.
   You have given me hope.
⁵⁰ Even when I suffer, I am
      comforted
   because you promised to keep
      me alive.
⁵¹ Proud people are always making
      fun of me.
   But I don't turn away from your
      law.
⁵² LORD, I remember the laws you
      gave long ago.
   I find comfort in them.
⁵³ I am very angry
   because evil people have turned
      away from your law.
⁵⁴ No matter where I live,
   I sing about your orders.
⁵⁵ LORD, during the night I remember
      who you are.
   That's why I keep your law.
⁵⁶ I have really done my best
   to obey your rules.

Why do we memorize verses?

We memorize
Bible verses
because we want to remember
what God has told us. If we
have a verse memorized, it
will be with us all the time.
That means when we are
out playing or doing
anything else, the verse is
with us wherever we go.
That is important when
we have a problem and
need to remember a
verse right now.

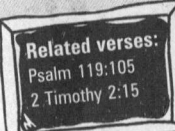

checkout
Psalm 119:11

Related verses:
Psalm 119:105
2 Timothy 2:15

ת Heth

⁵⁷ LORD, you are everything I need.
I have promised to obey your
words.
⁵⁸ I have looked to you with all my
heart.
Be kind to me as you have
promised.
⁵⁹ I have thought about the way I
live.
And I have decided to follow
your covenant laws.
⁶⁰ I won't waste any time.
I will be quick to obey your
commands.
⁶¹ Evil people may tie me up with
ropes.
But I won't forget to obey your
law.
⁶² At midnight I get up to give you
thanks
because your decisions are very
fair.
⁶³ I'm a friend to everyone who has
respect for you.
I'm a friend to everyone who
follows your rules.
⁶⁴ LORD, the earth is filled with your
love.
Teach me your orders.

ט Teth

⁶⁵ LORD, be good to me
as you have promised.
⁶⁶ Increase my knowledge and give
me good sense,
because I believe in your
commands.
⁶⁷ Before I went through suffering, I
went down the wrong path.
But now I obey your word.
⁶⁸ You are good, and what you do is
good.
Teach me your orders.
⁶⁹ Proud people have spread lies
about me and have taken
away my good name.
But I follow your rules with all
my heart.
⁷⁰ Their hearts are hard and
stubborn. They don't feel
anything.
But I take delight in your law.
⁷¹ It was good for me to suffer.
That's what helped me to
understand your orders.

⁷² The law you gave is worth more to
me
than thousands of pieces of silver
and gold.

י Yodh

⁷³ You made me and formed me with
your own hands.
Give me understanding so that I
can learn your commands.
⁷⁴ May those who have respect for
you be filled with joy when
they see me.
I have put my hope in your word.
⁷⁵ LORD, I know that your laws are
right.
You were faithful to your promise
when you made me suffer.
⁷⁶ May your faithful love comfort me
as you have promised me.
⁷⁷ Show me your tender love so that I
can live.
I take delight in your law.
⁷⁸ Proud people have treated me
badly without any reason.
May they be put to shame.
I will spend time thinking about
your rules.
⁷⁹ May those who have respect for
you come to me.
Then I can teach them your
covenant laws.
⁸⁰ May my heart be without blame as
I follow your orders.
Then I won't be put to shame.

כ Kaph

⁸¹ I deeply long for you to save me.
I have put my hope in your word.
⁸² My eyes grow tired looking for
what you have promised.
I say, "When will you comfort
me?"
⁸³ I'm as useless as a wineskin that
smoke has dried up.
But I don't forget to follow your
orders.
⁸⁴ How long do I have to wait?
When will you punish those who
attack me?
⁸⁵ Proud people do what is against
your law.
They dig pits for me to fall into.
⁸⁶ All of your commands can be
trusted.
Help me, because people attack
me without any reason.

[87] They almost wiped me off the face
of the earth.
But I have not turned away from
your rules.
[88] Keep me alive, because you love
me.
Then I will obey the covenant
laws you have given.

ל   Lamedh

[89] LORD, your word lasts forever.
It stands firm in the heavens.
[90] You will be faithful for all time to
come.
You made the earth, and it
continues to exist.
[91] Your laws continue to this very
day,
because all things serve you.
[92] If I had not taken delight in your
law,
I would have died because of my
suffering.
[93] I will never forget your rules.
You have kept me alive, because I
obey them.
[94] Save me, because I belong to you.
I've tried to obey your rules.
[95] Sinful people are waiting to
destroy me.
But I will spend time thinking
about your covenant laws.
[96] I've learned that everything has its
limits.
But your commands are perfect.
They are always there when I
need them.

מ   Mem

[97] LORD, I really love your law!
All day long I spend time
thinking about it.
[98] Your commands make me wiser
than my enemies,
because your commands are
always in my heart.
[99] I know more than all of my
teachers do,
because I spend time thinking
about your covenant laws.
[100] I understand more than the elders
do,
because I obey your rules.
[101] I've kept my feet from every path
that sinners take
so that I might obey your word.

[102] I haven't turned away from your
laws,
because you yourself have taught
me.
[103] Your words are very sweet to my
taste!
They are sweeter than honey to
me.
[104] I gain understanding from your
rules.
So I hate every path that sinners
take.

נ   Nun

[105] Your word is like a lamp that
shows me the way.
It is like a light that guides me.
[106] I have taken an oath. I have
promised
to follow your laws, because they
are right.
[107] I have suffered very much.
LORD, keep me alive as you have
promised.
[108] LORD, accept the praise I freely
give you.
Teach me your laws.
[109] I keep putting my life in danger.
But I won't forget to obey your
law.
[110] Evil people have set a trap for me.
But I haven't wandered away
from your rules.
[111] Your covenant laws are your gift to
me forever.
They fill my heart with joy.
[112] I have decided to obey your orders
to the very end.

ס   Samekh

[113] I hate people who can't make up
their minds.
But I love your law.
[114] You are my place of safety.
You are like a shield that keeps
me safe.
I have put my hope in your word.
[115] Get away from me, you who do
evil!
Then I can do what my God
commands me to do.
[116] Keep me going as you have
promised. Then I will live.
Don't let me lose all hope.
[117] Take good care of me, and I will be
saved.
I will always honor your orders.

¹¹⁸ You turn your back on all those
who wander away from your
orders.
They lie and cheat, but it doesn't
amount to anything.
¹¹⁹ You throw away all of the sinners
on earth as if they were trash.
So I love your covenant laws.
¹²⁰ My body trembles because I have
respect for you.
I have great respect for your
laws.

ע   Ayin

¹²¹ I have done what is right and fair.
So don't leave me to those who
beat me down.
¹²² Make sure that everything goes
well with me.
Don't let proud people beat me
down.
¹²³ My eyes grow tired as I look to you
to save me.
Please save me as you have
promised.
¹²⁴ Be good to me, because you love
me.
Teach me your orders.
¹²⁵ I serve you. Help me to
understand what is right.
Then I will understand your
covenant laws.
¹²⁶ LORD, it's time for you to act.
People are breaking your law.

¹²⁷ I love your commands more than
gold.
I love them more than pure gold.
¹²⁸ I consider all of your rules to be
right.
So I hate every path that sinners
take.

פ   Pe

¹²⁹ Your covenant laws are wonderful.
So I obey them.
¹³⁰ When your words are made clear,
they bring light.
They bring understanding to
childish people.
¹³¹ I open my mouth and pant like a
dog,
because I long to know your
commands.
¹³² Turn to me and show me your
favor.
That's what you've always done
for those who love you.
¹³³ Teach me how to live as you have
promised.
Don't let any sin be my master.
¹³⁴ Set me free from men who beat
me down.
Then I will obey your rules.
¹³⁵ Let your face smile on me with
favor.
Teach me your orders.
¹³⁶ Streams of tears flow from my
eyes,

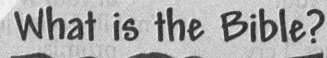

What is the Bible?

The Bible is God's message to us. The name "Bible" means
"book." The Bible is not just one book. It's a group of books that
have been put together. The Bible tells us how to live the way God wants
us to. It tells us what's right and what's wrong. The Bible tells us all this
through stories and lessons and interesting
facts. It tells us about God's wonderful plan of
salvation. To find out what God wants
you to do, look in the Bible.

checkout
Psalm
119:105

→ instruction manuel
→ plan of Salvation
→ HIS story
→ the truth
→ Lifes map

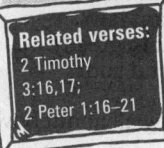

Related verses:
2 Timothy
3:16,17;
2 Peter 1:16–21

because people don't obey your
law.

צ Tsadhe

137 LORD, you do what is fair.
And your laws are right.
138 The laws you have made are fair.
They can be completely trusted.
139 My anger is wearing me out,
because my enemies don't pay
any attention to your words.
140 Your promises have proved to be
true.
I love them.
141 I'm not important. People look
down on me.
But I don't forget to obey your
rules.
142 You always do what is right.
And your law is true.
143 I've had my share of trouble and
suffering.
But I take delight in your
commands.
144 Your covenant laws are always
right.
Help me to understand them.
Then I will live.

ק Qoph

145 LORD, I call out to you with all my
heart.
Answer me, and I will obey your
orders.
146 I call out to you.
Save me, and I will keep your
covenant laws.
147 I get up before the sun rises. I cry
out for help.
I've put my hope in your word.
148 My eyes stay open all night long.
I spend my time thinking about
your promises.
149 Listen to me, because you love me.
LORD, keep me alive as you have
promised.
150 Those who think up evil plans are
near.
They have wandered far away
from your law.
151 But LORD, you are near.
All your commands are true.
152 Long ago I learned from your
covenant laws
that you made them to last
forever.

ר Resh

153 Look at how I'm suffering!
Save me, because I haven't
forgotten to obey your law.
154 Stand up for me and set me
free.
Keep me alive as you have
promised.
155 Those who are evil are far from
being saved.
They don't want to obey your
orders.
156 LORD, you have deep concern for
me.
Keep me alive as you have
promised.
157 Many enemies attack me.
But I haven't turned away from
your covenant laws.
158 I get very angry when I see
people who aren't faithful to
you.
They don't obey your word.
159 See how I love your rules!
LORD, keep me alive, because you
love me.
160 All your words are true.
All your laws are right. They last
forever.

ש Sin and Shin

161 Rulers attack me without any
reason.
But my heart trembles because
of your word.
162 I'm filled with joy because of your
promise.
It's like finding a great fortune.
163 I hate lies with a deep hatred.
But I love your law.
164 Seven times a day I praise you
for your laws, because they are
right.
165 Those who love your law enjoy
great peace.
Nothing can make them trip and
fall.
166 LORD, I wait for you to save me.
I follow your commands.
167 I obey your covenant laws,
because I love them greatly.
168 I obey your rules and your
covenant laws,
because you know all about how
I live.

ת Taw

169 LORD, may you hear my cry.
     Give me understanding, just as
          you said you would.
170 May you hear my prayer.
     Save me, just as you promised.
171 May my lips pour out praise to
          you,
     because you teach me your
          orders.
172 May my tongue sing about your
          word,
     because all of your commands
          are right.
173 May your hand be ready to
          help me,
     because I have chosen to obey
          your rules.
174 LORD, I long for you to save me.
     I take delight in your law.
175 Let me live so that I can praise
          you.
     May your laws keep me going.
176 Like a lost sheep, I've gone down
          the wrong path.
     Come and look for me,
     because I haven't forgotten to
          obey your commands.

PSALM 120

A song for those who go up
to Jerusalem to worship the LORD.

1 I call out to the LORD when I'm in
          trouble,
     and he answers me.
2 LORD, save me from people whose
          lips tell lies.
     Save me from people whose
          tongues don't tell the truth.

3 What will the LORD do to you, you
          lying tongue?
     And what more will he do?
4 He will punish you with the sharp
          arrows of a soldier.
     He will punish you with burning
          wood from a desert tree.

5 How terrible it is for me to live in
          the tents of the people of
          Meshech!
     How terrible to live in the tents
          of the people of Kedar!
6 I have lived too long
     among those who hate peace.
7 I want peace.
     But when I speak, they want war.

If Jesus has already won, why is everyone still fighting?

Jesus beat sin and death when he rose from the dead. But people still fight because all people, even Christians, are sinners. Jesus died for our sins, but we still have sin in our hearts. We need to love and follow Jesus, and he will help us to fight against our sinful desires.

Jesus will not *make* us live at peace with each other. He will only show us how to do it and leave the choice to us. The more we love him, the more we will live at peace and not fight.

checkout
Psalm 120:6,7

Related verses:
James 3:16; 4:1–6

PSALM 121

A song for those who go up
to Jerusalem to worship the LORD.

¹ I look up to the hills.
   Where does my help come from?
² My help comes from the LORD.
   He is the Maker of heaven and
      earth.

³ He won't let your foot slip.
   He who watches over you won't
      get tired.
⁴ In fact, he who watches over Israel
   won't get tired or go to sleep.

⁵ The LORD watches over you.
   The LORD is like a shade tree at
      your right hand.
⁶ The sun won't harm you during
      the day.
   The moon won't harm you
      during the night.

⁷ The LORD will keep you from every
      kind of harm.
   He will watch over your life.
⁸ The LORD will watch over your life
      no matter where you go,
      both now and forever.

PSALM 122

A song for those who go up
to Jerusalem to worship the LORD.
A psalm of David.

¹ I was very glad when they said to
      me,
   "Let us go up to the house of the
      LORD."
² Jerusalem, our feet are standing
      inside your gates.
³ Jerusalem is built like a city
   where everything is close
      together.
⁴ The tribes of the LORD go there to
      praise his name.
   They do it in keeping with the
      law he gave to Israel.
⁵ The thrones of the family line of
      David are there.
   That's where the people are
      judged.
⁶ Pray for the peace of Jerusalem.
      Say,
   "May those who love you be
      secure.
⁷ May there be peace inside your
      walls.

Do angels stay in the car or fly beside?

God watches over us. He uses angels to help us. If God wants an angel to be with us in the car, that is where the angel will be. If God wants the angel to be outside the car while it is moving, that is where the angel will be. Angels go wherever God tells them to go. They do whatever God tells them to do.

checkout

Psalm 121:1,2

Related verses:
Revelation 22:8,9

May your people be kept safe."
[8] I'm concerned for my family and
friends.
So I say to Jerusalem, "May you
enjoy peace."
[9] I'm concerned about the house of
the LORD our God.
So I pray that things will go well
with Jerusalem.

PSALM 123

A song for those who go up
to Jerusalem to worship the LORD.

[1] I look up and pray to you.
Your throne is in heaven.
[2] Slaves depend on their masters.
Maids depend on the women
they work for.
In the same way, we depend on
the LORD our God.
We wait for him to show us his
favor.

[3] LORD, show us your favor. Show us
your favor,
because people have made so
much fun of us.
[4] We have had to put up with a lot
from those who are proud.
They were always laughing at us.

PSALM 124

A song for those who go up
to Jerusalem to worship the LORD.
A psalm of David.

[1] Here is what Israel should say.
Suppose the LORD had not been
on our side.
[2] Suppose the LORD had not been on
our side
when our enemies attacked us.
[3] Suppose he had not been on our
side
when their anger blazed out
against us.
Then they would have swallowed
us alive.
[4] They would have been like a flood
that drowned us.
They would have swept over us
like a rushing river.
[5] They would have washed us away
like a swollen stream.

[6] Give praise to the LORD.
He has not let our enemies chew
us up.
[7] We have escaped like a bird
from a hunter's trap.
The trap has been broken,
and we have escaped.

KIDS' QUESTION

Does God sleep, or does he just rest?

God does not have a body like we do, so he doesn't need
to sleep or eat. When the Bible says God "rests," it
means he has stopped doing something. To us,
that is like rest. But God does not get
tired or worn out. So he doesn't
need to rest the way we do.
And when we go to sleep at
night God stays awake. He
watches over us all through
the night.

checkout Psalm 121:3,4

Related verse:
Genesis 2:2

8 Our help comes from the LORD.
   He is the Maker of heaven and
     earth.

PSALM 125

A song for those who go up
to Jerusalem to worship the LORD.

1 Those who trust in the LORD are
     like Mount Zion.
   They will always be secure. They
     will last forever.
2 Like the mountains around
     Jerusalem,
   the LORD is all around his people
     both now and forever.

3 Evil people will not always rule
     the land the LORD gave to those
     who do right.
   If they did, those who do right
     might do what is evil.

4 LORD, do good to those who are
     good.
   Do good to those whose hearts
     are honest.
5 But what about those who have
     taken paths that are crooked?
   The LORD will drive them out,
     along with those who do what
     is evil.

May Israel enjoy peace.

PSALM 126

A song for those who go up
to Jerusalem to worship the LORD.

1 Our enemies took us away from
     Zion.
   But when the LORD brought us
     home,
   it seemed like a dream to us.
2 Our mouths were filled with
     laughter.
   Our tongues sang with joy.
   Then the people of other nations
     said,
   "The LORD has done great things
     for them."
3 The LORD has done great things for
     us.
   And we are filled with joy.

4 LORD, bless us with great success
     again,
   as rain makes streams flow in the
     Negev Desert.

5 Those who cry as they plant their
     crops
   will sing with joy when they
     gather them in.
6 Those who go out sobbing
   as they carry seeds to plant
   will come back singing with joy.
   They will bring the new crop
     back with them.

PSALM 127

A song for those who go up
to Jerusalem to worship the LORD.
A psalm of Solomon.

1 If the LORD doesn't build a house,
   the work of its builders is useless.
   If the LORD doesn't watch over a
     city,
   it's useless for those on guard
     duty to stand watch over it.
2 It's useless for you to work from
     early morning
   until late at night
   just to get food to eat.
   God provides for those he loves
     even while they sleep.

3 Children are a gift from the LORD.
   They are a reward from him.
4 Children who are born to people
     when they are young
   are like arrows in the hands of a
     soldier.
5 Blessed are those
   who have many children.
   They won't be put to shame
   when they go up against their
     enemies in court.

PSALM 128

A song for those who go up
to Jerusalem to worship the LORD.

1 Blessed are all those who have
     respect for the LORD.
   They live as he wants them to
     live.
2 Your work will give you what you
     need.
   Blessings and good things will
     come to you.
3 As a vine bears a lot of fruit,
   so your wife will have many
     children by you.
   They will sit around your table
   like young olive trees.

⁴Only a man who has respect for
the LORD
will be blessed like that.

⁵May the LORD bless you from Zion.
May you enjoy the good things
that come to Jerusalem
all the days of your life.
⁶   May you live to see your
grandchildren.

May Israel enjoy peace.

PSALM 129

A song for those who go up
to Jerusalem to worship the LORD.

¹Here is what Israel should say.
Many times my enemies have
beaten me down ever
since I was a young nation.
²Many times my enemies have
beaten me down ever
since I was a young nation,
but they haven't won the battle.
³They have made deep wounds in
my back.
It looks like a field a farmer has
plowed.
⁴The LORD does what is right.
Sinners had tied me up with
ropes. But the LORD has set
me free.

⁵May all those who hate Zion
be driven back in shame.
⁶May they be like grass that grows
on the roof of a house.
It dries up before it can grow.
⁷There isn't enough of it to fill a
person's hand.
There isn't enough to tie up and
carry away.
⁸May no one who passes by say to
those who hate Zion,
"May the blessing of the LORD be
on you.
We bless you in the name of the
LORD."

PSALM 130

A song for those who go up
to Jerusalem to worship the LORD.

¹LORD, I cry out to you
because I'm suffering so deeply.
²Lord, listen to me.
Pay attention to my cry for your
favor.

³LORD, suppose you kept a record of
sins.
Lord, who then wouldn't be
found guilty?
⁴But you forgive.
So people have respect for you.

Does God have things to do at nighttime?

God does not need to sleep
because he does not have
a body like yours. God is
also everywhere and
lives forever. So there is
no night or day to him.
God is always working
when you are sleeping.
When you go to sleep, you
can be sure that God is
awake, watching over you
and taking
care of you.

Related verse:
Psalm 4:8

checkout

Psalm 127:2

...PLEASE HELP US NOT HAVE TO WAKE UP
AT NIGHT, AND DON'T LET LOUD NOISES HAPPEN,
AND HELP THE CAT CATCH ALL THE MICE,
AND DON'T LET MY DAD SNORE SO LOUD
THAT HE WAKES UP MY MOM, AND HELP
OUR BRAINS TO KEEP ON WORKING EVEN
THOUGH WE HAVE THEM TURNED OFF, AND...

5 With all my heart I wait for the
    LORD to help me.
  I put my hope in his word.
6 I wait for the Lord to help me.
  I wait with more longing than
    those on guard duty wait for
    the morning.
  I'll say it again.
  I wait with more longing than
    those on guard duty wait for
    the morning.

7 Israel, put your hope in the LORD,
    because the LORD's love never
    fails.
  He sets his people completely
    free.
8 He himself will set Israel
    free from all of their sins.

PSALM 131

A song for those who go up
to Jerusalem to worship the LORD.
A psalm of David.

1 LORD, my heart isn't proud.
  My eyes aren't proud either.
  I don't concern myself with
    important matters.
  I don't concern myself with
    things that are too wonderful
    for me.
2 I have made myself calm and
    content
  like a young child in its mother's
    arms.
  Deep down inside me, I am as
    content as a young child.

3 Israel, put your hope in the LORD
    both now and forever.

PSALM 132

A song for those who go up
to Jerusalem to worship the LORD.

1 LORD, remember David
  and all of the hard times he went
    through.

2 LORD, he took an oath.
  Mighty One of Jacob, he made a
    promise to you.
3 He said, "I won't enter my house
    or go to bed.
4 I won't let my eyes sleep.
  I won't close my eyelids
5 until I find a place for the LORD.

I want to build a house for the
    Mighty One of Jacob."

6 Here are the words we heard in
    Ephrathah.
  We heard them again in the fields
    of Kiriath Jearim.
7 "Let us go to the LORD's house.
  Let us worship at his feet.
8 LORD, rise up and come to your
    resting place.
  Come in together with the ark.
  It's the sign of your power.
9 May your priests put on godliness
    as if it were their clothes.
  May your faithful people sing
    with joy."

10 In honor of your servant David,
    don't turn your back on your
    anointed king.

11 The LORD took an oath and made a
    promise to David.
  It is a firm promise that he will
    never break.
  He said, "After you die,
  I will place one of your own sons
    on your throne.
12 If your sons keep my covenant
    and the laws I teach them,
  then their sons will sit
  on your throne for ever and
    ever."

13 The LORD has chosen Zion.
  That's the place where he wants
    to live.
14 He has said, "This will be my
    resting place for ever and ever.
  Here I will sit on my throne,
    because that's what I want.
15 I will greatly bless Zion with
    everything it needs.
  I will give plenty of food to the
    poor people living there.
16 I will put salvation on its priests as
    if it were their clothes.
  God's faithful people will always
    sing with joy.

17 "Here in Jerusalem I will raise up a
    mighty king from the family of
    David.
  I will set up the lamp of David's
    kingdom for my anointed
    king.
  Its flame will burn brightly
    forever.

¹⁸ I will put shame on his enemies as
   if it were their clothes.
   But the royal crown he wears will
   shine with glory."

PSALM 133

A song for those who go up
to Jerusalem to worship the LORD.
A psalm of David.

¹ How good and pleasant it is
   when God's people live together
   in peace!
² It's like the special olive oil
   that was poured on Aaron's head.
   It ran down on his beard
   and on the collar of his robe.
³ It's as if the dew of Mount Hermon
   were falling on Mount Zion.
   There the LORD gives his blessing.
   He gives life that never ends.

PSALM 134

A song for those who go up
to Jerusalem to worship the LORD.

¹ All of you who serve the LORD,
   praise the LORD.
   All of you who serve at night in
   the house of the LORD, praise
   him.
² Lift up your hands in the temple
   and praise the LORD.

³ May the LORD bless you from Zion.
   He is the Maker of heaven and
   earth.

PSALM 135

¹ Praise the LORD.

Praise the name of the LORD.
   You who serve the LORD, praise
   him.
² You who serve in the house of the
   LORD, praise him.
   You who serve in the courtyards
   of the temple of our God,
   praise him.

³ Praise the LORD, because he is
   good.
   Sing praise to his name, because
   that is pleasant.
⁴ The LORD has chosen the people of
   Jacob to be his own.
   He has chosen Israel to be his
   special treasure.

⁵ I know that the LORD is great.
   I know that our Lord is greater
   than all gods.
⁶ The LORD does anything he wants
   to do
   in the heavens and on the earth.
   He does it even in the deepest
   parts of the oceans.
⁷ He makes clouds rise from one
   end of the earth to the other.
   He sends lightning with the rain.
   He brings the wind out of his
   storerooms.

⁸ He killed the oldest son of each
   family in Egypt.
   He struck down the oldest males
   that were born to people and
   animals.
⁹ He did miraculous signs in Egypt.
   He did wonders against Pharaoh
   and everyone who served him.
¹⁰ He destroyed many nations.
   He killed mighty kings.
¹¹ He killed Sihon, the king of the
   Amorites,
   and Og, the king of Bashan.
   He killed all of the kings of
   Canaan.
¹² He gave their land as a gift
   to his people Israel.

¹³ LORD, your name continues
   forever.
   LORD, your fame will last for all
   time to come.
¹⁴ When the LORD hands down his
   sentence, it will be in his
   people's favor.
   He will show deep concern for
   those who serve him.

¹⁵ The statues of the gods of the
   nations are made of silver and
   gold.
   They are made by the hands of
   men.
¹⁶ They have mouths, but they can't
   speak.
   They have eyes, but they can't see.
¹⁷ They have ears, but they can't
   hear.
   They have mouths, but they can't
   breathe.
¹⁸ Those who make statues of gods
   will be like them.
   So will all those who trust in
   them.

¹⁹ People of Israel, praise the LORD.
Priests of Aaron, praise the LORD.
²⁰ Tribe of Levi, praise the LORD.
You who have respect for the
LORD, praise him.
²¹ Give praise to the LORD in Zion.
Give praise to the One who lives
in Jerusalem.

Praise the LORD.

PSALM 136

¹ Give thanks to the LORD, because
he is good.
His faithful love continues forever.
² Give thanks to the greatest God of
all.
His faithful love continues forever.
³ Give thanks to the most powerful
Lord of all.
His faithful love continues forever.

⁴ Give thanks to the only one who
can do great miracles.
His faithful love continues forever.
⁵ By his understanding he made the
heavens.
His faithful love continues forever.
⁶ He spread out the earth on the
waters.
His faithful love continues forever.
⁷ He made the great lights in the sky.
His faithful love continues forever.
⁸ He made the sun to rule over the
day.
His faithful love continues forever.
⁹ He made the moon and stars to
rule over the night.
His faithful love continues forever.

¹⁰ Give thanks to the One who killed
the oldest son of each family
in Egypt.
His faithful love continues forever.
¹¹ He brought the people of Israel
out of Egypt.
His faithful love continues forever.
¹² He did it by reaching out his
mighty hand and powerful
arm.
His faithful love continues forever.

¹³ Give thanks to the One who parted
the Red Sea.
His faithful love continues forever.
¹⁴ He brought Israel through the
middle of it.
His faithful love continues forever.

¹⁵ But he swept Pharaoh and his
army into the Red Sea.
His faithful love continues forever.

¹⁶ Give thanks to the One who led his
people through the desert.
His faithful love continues forever.
¹⁷ He killed great kings.
His faithful love continues forever.
¹⁸ He struck down mighty kings.
His faithful love continues forever.
¹⁹ He killed Sihon, the king of the
Amorites.
His faithful love continues forever.
²⁰ He killed Og, the king of Bashan.
His faithful love continues forever.
²¹ He gave their land as a gift.
His faithful love continues forever.
²² He gave it as a gift to his servant
Israel.
His faithful love continues forever.

²³ Give thanks to the One who
remembered us when
things were going badly for us.
His faithful love continues forever.
²⁴ He set us free from our enemies.
His faithful love continues forever.
²⁵ He gives food to every creature.
His faithful love continues forever.

²⁶ Give thanks to the God of heaven.
His faithful love continues forever.

PSALM 137

¹ We were sitting by the rivers of
Babylon.
We cried when we remembered
what had happened to Zion.
² On the nearby poplar trees
we hung up our harps.
³ Those who held us as prisoners
asked us to sing.
Those who enjoyed hurting us
ordered us to sing joyful
songs.
They said, "Sing one of the songs
of Zion to us!"

⁴ How can we sing the songs of the
LORD
while we are in another land?
⁵ Jerusalem, if I forget you,
may my right hand never be able
to play the harp again.
⁶ If I don't remember you,
may my tongue stick to the roof
of my mouth so I can't sing.

May it happen if I don't consider
  Jerusalem
    to be my greatest joy.

⁷ LORD, remember what the people
    of Edom did
  on the day Jerusalem fell.
  "Tear it down!" they cried.
  "Tear it down to the ground!"

⁸ People of Babylon, you are
    sentenced to be destroyed.
  Happy are those who pay you
    back
  for what you have done to us.
⁹ Happy are those who grab your
    babies
  and smash them against the rocks.

PSALM 138

A psalm of David.

¹ LORD, I will praise you with all my
    heart.
  In front of those who think they
    are gods
  I will sing praise to you.
² I will bow down facing your holy
    temple.
  I will praise your name,
  because you are loving and
    faithful.
  You have honored your name and
    your word
  more than anything else.
³ When I called out to you, you
    answered me.
  You made me strong and brave.

⁴ LORD, may all of the kings on earth
    praise you
  when they hear about what you
    have promised.
⁵ LORD, may they sing about what
    you have done,
  because your glory is great.

⁶ The LORD is in heaven. But he
    watches over those who are
    free of pride.
  He knows those who are proud
  and stays far away from them.
⁷ Trouble is all around me,
  but you keep me alive.
  You reach out your hand to put a
    stop to the anger of my
    enemies.
  With your powerful right hand
    you save me.

⁸ LORD, you will do everything you
    have planned for me.
  LORD, your faithful love
    continues forever.
  You have done so much for us.
  Don't stop now.

PSALM 139

For the director of music.
A psalm of David.

¹ LORD, you have seen what is in my
    heart.
  You know all about me.
² You know when I sit down and
    when I get up.
  You know what I'm thinking even
    though you are far away.
³ You know when I go out to work
    and when I come back home.
  You know exactly how I live.
⁴ LORD, even before I speak a word,
  you know all about it.

⁵ You are all around me. You are
    behind me and in front of me.
  You hold me in your power.
⁶ I'm amazed at how well you know
    me.
  It's more than I can understand.

⁷ How can I get away from your
    Spirit?
  Where can I go to escape from
    you?
⁸ If I go up to the heavens, you are
    there.
  If I lie down in the deepest parts
    of the earth, you are also
    there.
⁹ Suppose I were to rise with the sun
    in the east
  and then cross over to the west
  where it sinks into the ocean.
¹⁰ Your hand would always be there
    to guide me.
  Your right hand would still be
    holding me close.

¹¹ Suppose I were to say, "I'm sure
    the darkness will hide me.
  The light around me will become
    as dark as night."
¹² Even that darkness would not be
    dark to you.
  The night would shine like the
    day,
  because darkness is like light to
    you.

¹³You created the deepest parts of
my being.
You put me together inside my
mother's body.
¹⁴How you made me is amazing and
wonderful.
I praise you for that.
What you have done is
wonderful.
I know that very well.
¹⁵None of my bones was hidden
from you
when you made me inside my
mother's body.
That place was as dark as the
deepest parts of the earth.
When you were putting me
together there,
¹⁶ your eyes saw my body even
before it was formed.
You planned how many days I
would live.
You wrote down the number of
them in your book
before I had lived through even
one of them.

¹⁷God, your thoughts about me are
priceless.
No one can possibly add them all
up.

¹⁸If I could count them,
they would be more than the
grains of sand.
If I were to fall asleep counting
and then wake up,
you would still be there with me.

¹⁹God, I wish you would kill the
people who are evil!
I wish those murderers would get
away from me!
²⁰They are your enemies. They
misuse your name.
They misuse it for their own evil
purposes.
²¹LORD, I really hate those who hate
you!
I really hate those who rise up
against you!
²²I have nothing but hatred for
them.
I consider them to be my
enemies.

²³God, see what is in my heart.
Know what is there.
Put me to the test.
Know what I'm thinking.
²⁴See if there's anything in my life
you don't like.
Help me live in the way that is
always right.

Did God Know Adam and Eve were going to sin?

Yes. God knows everything even before it happens. He knew that Adam
and Eve were going to sin. Still he did not want them to, and
he was disappointed with their choice. But God loved
them, so he made a way for the sin to be
forgiven. God's plan was to send
Jesus to die on the cross for
everyone's sins. When Jesus died
and rose again, he paid for the sins
of the whole world. He paid for
Adam's sins, Eve's sins and your sins,
all at once. Anyone who wants it can
have eternal life just by
trusting in Jesus.

Related verses:
John 2:23–25;
Acts 17:27

checkout
Psalm 139:4

PSALM 140

For the director of music.
A psalm of David.

[1] LORD, save me from sinful men.
Keep me safe from those who
want to hurt me.
[2] They make evil plans in their
hearts.
They are always starting fights.
[3] Their tongues are as deadly as the
tongue of a serpent.
The words from their lips are like
the poison of a snake.   *Selah*

[4] LORD, keep me out of the hands of
sinful people.
Keep me safe from men who
want to hurt me.
They plan to trip me up and
make me fall.
[5] Proud people have hidden their
traps to catch me.
They have spread out their nets.
They have set traps for me along
my path.   *Selah*

[6] LORD, I say to you, "You are my
God."
LORD, hear my cry for your favor.
[7] LORD and King, you save me
because you are strong.

You are like a shield that keeps
me safe in the day of battle.
[8] LORD, don't give sinners what they
want.
Don't let their plans succeed.
If you do, they will become
proud.   *Selah*

[9] Those who are all around me have
caused me trouble
by what their lips have said.
Let that trouble fall on their own
heads.
[10] Let burning coals fall on people
like that.
May they be thrown into the fire.
May they be thrown into muddy
pits and never get out.
[11] Don't let men who tell lies about
me settle down in the land.
May trouble hunt down those
who want to hurt me.

[12] I know that the LORD makes sure
that poor people are treated
fairly.
He stands up for those who are
in need.
[13] I'm sure that those who do right
will praise your name.
Those who are honest will live
with you.

Do babies stay in heaven until they are born?

God creates each person as a new
soul. He creates a new person who
never existed before each time a
baby starts growing inside a
mother's body. Babies do not live
in heaven while waiting to be born
here on earth. The starting place
for every person is right inside a
mother's womb.

checkout Psalm 139:13

Related verses:
John 3:6,7

JASON'S IMAGINATION

HEAVEN'S
STORK STATION
EARTH BOUND

PSALM 141

A psalm of David.

¹ LORD, I call out to you. Come
quickly to help me.
Listen to me when I call out to
you.
² May my prayer come to you like
the sweet smell of incense.
When I lift up my hands in
prayer, may it be like the
evening sacrifice.

³ LORD, guard my mouth.
Keep watch over the door of my
lips.
⁴ Don't let my heart be drawn to
what is evil.
Don't let me join men who do
evil.
They don't do what is right.
Don't let me join them and eat
their fancy food.

⁵ If a person who does what is right
were to strike me, it would be
an act of kindness.
If that person were to correct me,
it would be like pouring olive
oil on my head.
I wouldn't say no to it.

But I always pray against the
things that sinful people do.
⁶ When their rulers are thrown
down from the rocky cliffs,
those evil people will realize that
my words were true.
⁷ They will say, "As clumps of dirt
are left from plowing up the
ground,
so our bones will be scattered
near an open grave."

⁸ But LORD and King, I keep looking
to you.
I go to you for safety. Don't let me
die.
⁹ Keep me from the traps of those
who do evil.
Save me from the traps they have
set for me.
¹⁰ Let evil people fall into their own
nets.
But let me go safely on my way.

PSALM 142

A prayer of David when he was
in the cave. A *maskil*.

¹ I call out to the LORD.
I pray to him for his favor.

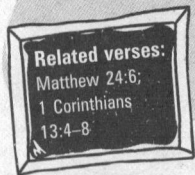

Why does God let wars happen?

God *could* stop all wars and fights in the
world. But God wants human beings to
choose to live in peace with each other. People
are not perfect, and sometimes they get
angry with each other. Wars start when
leaders of countries get so angry that
they decide to fight. If these people
followed God's commands for living,
there would be no wars. But because
we ignore God and break his rules,
we suffer. God has told us to forgive
each other rather than fight back.

checkout Psalm 140:1,2

Related verses:
Matthew 24:6;
1 Corinthians
13:4–8

²I pour out my problem to him.
  I tell him about my trouble.

³When I grow weak,
  you know what I'm going
    through.
 In the path where I walk,
  people have hidden a trap to
    catch me.
⁴Look around me, and you will see
  that no one is concerned
    about me.
 I have no place of safety.
  No one cares whether I live
    or die.

⁵LORD, I cry out to you.
  I say, "You are my place of safety.
  You are everything I need in this
    life."
⁶Listen to my cry.
  I am in great need.
 Save me from those who are
    chasing me.
  They are too strong for me.
⁷My troubles are like a prison.
  Set me free so I can praise your
    name.

 Then those who do what is right
  will gather around me
 because you have been good to
    me.

PSALM 143

A psalm of David.

¹LORD, hear my prayer.
  Listen to my cry for your favor.
 You are faithful and right.
  Come and help me.
²Don't take me to court and judge
    me,
  because in your eyes no living
    person does what is right.

³My enemies chase me.
  They crush me down to the
    ground.
 They make me live in darkness
  like those who died long ago.
⁴So I grow weak.
  Deep down inside me, I'm afraid.

⁵I remember what happened long
    ago.
  I spend time thinking about all of
    your acts.
  I consider what your hands have
    done.

⁶I spread out my hands to you in
    prayer.
  I'm thirsty for you, just as dry
    ground is thirsty for rain.
        Selah

⁷LORD, answer me quickly.
  I'm growing weak.
 Don't turn your face away from me,
  or I will be like those who go
    down into the grave.
⁸In the morning let me hear about
    your faithful love,
  because I've put my trust in you.
 Show me the way I should live,
  because I pray to you.
⁹LORD, save me from my enemies,
  because I go to you for safety.
¹⁰Teach me to do what you want,
  because you are my God.
 May your good Spirit
  lead me on a level path.

¹¹LORD, be true to your name. Keep
    me alive.
  Because you do what is right, get
    me out of trouble.
¹²Because your love is faithful, put
    an end to my enemies.
  Destroy all of them, because I
    serve you.

PSALM 144

A psalm of David.

¹Give praise to the LORD. He is my
    rock.
  He trains my hands for war.
  He trains my fingers for battle.
²He is my loving God. He is like a
    fort to me.
  He is my place of safety and the
    One who saves me.
  He is like a shield that keeps me
    safe. I go to him for safety.
  He brings nations under my
    control.

³LORD, what is a human being that
    you take care of him?
  What is a son of man that you
    think about him?
⁴His life doesn't last any longer
    than a breath.
  His days are like a shadow that
    quickly disappears.

⁵LORD, open up your heavens and
    come down.

Touch the mountains, and they
will pour out smoke.
⁶Send flashes of lightning and
scatter my enemies.
Shoot your arrows and chase
them away.
⁷My enemies are like a mighty
flood.
Reach down from heaven and
save me.
Save me from strangers who
attack me.
⁸They tell all kinds of lies with their
mouths.
Even when they make a promise
by raising their right hands,
they don't mean it.

⁹God, I will sing a new song to you.
I will make music to you on a
harp that has ten strings.
¹⁰You are the One who helps kings
win battles.
You save your servant David
from dying by the sword.

¹¹Save me. Set me free
from strangers who attack me.
They tell all kinds of lies with their
mouths.
Even when they make a promise
by raising their right hands,
they don't mean it.

¹²While our sons are young,
they will be like healthy plants.
Our daughters will be like pillars
that have been made to decorate
a palace.
¹³Our storerooms will be filled
with every kind of food.
The sheep in our fields will
increase by thousands.
They will increase by tens of
thousands.
¹⁴ Our oxen will pull heavy loads.
None of our city walls will be
broken down.
No one will be carried off as a
prisoner.
No cries of pain will be heard in
our streets.

¹⁵Blessed are the people about
whom all of those things are
true.
Blessed are the people whose
God is the LORD.

PSALM 145

A psalm of praise. A psalm
of David.

¹I will honor you, my God the King.
I will praise your name for ever
and ever.
²Every day I will praise you.
I will praise your name for ever
and ever.

³LORD, you are great. You are really
worthy of praise.
No one can completely
understand how great you are.
⁴Parents will praise your works to
their children.
They will tell about your mighty
acts.
⁵They will speak about your
glorious majesty.
I will spend time thinking about
your miracles.
⁶They will speak about the
powerful and wonderful
things you do.
I will talk about the great things
you have done.
⁷They will celebrate your great
goodness.
They will sing with joy about
your holy acts.

⁸The LORD is gracious. He is kind
and tender.
He is slow to get angry. He is full
of love.
⁹The LORD is good to all.
He shows deep concern for
everything he has made.
¹⁰LORD, every living thing you have
made will praise you.
Your faithful people will praise
you.
¹¹They will tell about your glorious
kingdom.
They will speak about your
power.
¹²Then all people will know about
the mighty things you have
done.
They will know about the
glorious majesty of your
kingdom.
¹³Your kingdom is a kingdom that
will last forever.
Your rule will continue for all
time to come.

The LORD is faithful and will keep
all of his promises.
He is loving toward everything he
has made.
[14] The LORD takes good care of all
those who fall.
He lifts up all those who feel
helpless.
[15] Every living thing looks to you for
food.
You give it to them exactly when
they need it.
[16] You open your hand
and satisfy the needs of every
living creature.

[17] The LORD is right in everything he
does.
He is loving toward everything he
has made.
[18] The LORD is ready to help all those
who call out to him.
He helps those who really mean
it when they call out to him.
[19] He satisfies the needs of those
who have respect for him.
He hears their cry and saves
them.
[20] The LORD watches over all those
who love him.
But he will destroy all sinful
people.

[21] I will praise the LORD with my
mouth.
Let every creature praise his holy
name
for ever and ever.

PSALM 146

[1] Praise the LORD.

I will praise the LORD.
[2]   I will praise the LORD all my life.
I will sing praise to my God as
long as I live.

[3] Don't put your trust in human
leaders.
Don't trust in people. They can't
save you.
[4] When they die, they return to the
ground.
On that very day their plans are
bound to fail.

[5] Blessed are those who depend on
the God of Jacob for help.
Blessed are those who put their
hope in the LORD their God.
[6] He is the Maker of heaven and
earth and the ocean.
He made everything in them.
The LORD remains faithful
forever.

Does God know about people who are hungry?

God knows everything. He even knows how many hairs you have on your head. God knows about all the hungry people in the world, and it makes him sad. Remember, he put us in charge of the world. God wants us to care about people and help those who need it. This includes helping to feed those who are hungry. Think about what you can do to feed the hungry people in your community.

checkout Psalm 146:6,7

Related verses:
Matthew 10:29,30;
James 2:14–17

⁷He stands up for those who are
    beaten down.
  He gives food to hungry people.
  The LORD sets prisoners free.
⁸ The LORD gives sight to those
    who are blind.
  The LORD lifts up those who feel
    helpless.
  The LORD loves those who do
    what is right.
⁹The LORD watches over the
    outsiders who live in our land.
  He takes good care of children
    whose fathers have died.
  He also takes good care of
    widows.
  But he causes evil people to fail
    in everything they do.
¹⁰The LORD rules forever.
  The God of Zion will rule for all
    time to come.

  Praise the LORD.

PSALM 147

¹Praise the LORD.

How good it is to sing praises to
    our God!
  How pleasant and right it is to
    praise him!

²The LORD builds up Jerusalem.
  He gathers the scattered people
    of Israel.
³He heals those who have broken
    hearts.
  He takes care of their wounds.

⁴He decides how many stars there
    should be.
  He gives each one of them a
    name.
⁵Great is our Lord. His power is
    mighty.
  There is no limit to his
    understanding.
⁶The LORD gives strength to those
    who aren't proud.
  But he throws evil people down
    to the ground.

⁷Sing to the LORD and give thanks
    to him.
  Make music to our God on the
    harp.
⁸He covers the sky with clouds.
  He supplies the earth with rain.
  He makes grass grow on the hills.

⁹He provides food for the cattle.
  He provides for the young ravens
    when they cry out.
¹⁰He doesn't take pleasure in the
    strength of horses.
  He doesn't take delight in the
    strong legs of men.
¹¹The LORD takes delight in those
    who have respect for him.
  They put their hope in his
    faithful love.

¹²Jerusalem, praise the LORD.
  Zion, praise your God.
¹³He makes the bars of your gates
    stronger.
  He blesses the people who live
    inside you.
¹⁴He keeps your borders safe and
    secure.
  He satisfies you with the finest
    wheat.

¹⁵He sends his command to the
    earth.
  His word arrives there quickly.
¹⁶He spreads the snow like wool.
  He scatters the frost like ashes.
¹⁷He throws down his hail like small
    stones.
  No one can stand his icy blast.
¹⁸He gives his command, and the ice
    melts.
  He stirs up his winds, and the
    waters flow.

¹⁹He has made his word known to
    the people of Jacob.
  He has made his laws and rules
    known to Israel.
²⁰He hasn't done that for any other
    nation.
  They don't know his laws.

  Praise the LORD.

PSALM 148

¹Praise the LORD.

Praise the LORD from the heavens.
  Praise him in the heavens above.
²Praise him, all his angels.
  Praise him, all his angels in
    heaven.
³Praise him, sun and moon.
  Praise him, all you shining stars.
⁴Praise him, you highest heavens.
  Praise him, you waters above the
    skies.

⁵Let all of them praise the name of
the LORD,
because he gave a command and
they were created.
⁶He set them in place for ever and
ever.
He gave them laws they will
always have to obey.

⁷Praise the LORD from the earth,
you great sea creatures and all of
the deepest parts of the
ocean.
⁸Praise him, lightning and hail,
snow and clouds.
Praise him, you stormy winds
that obey him.
⁹Praise him, all you mountains and
hills.
Praise him, all you fruit trees and
cedar trees.
¹⁰Praise him, all you wild animals
and cattle.
Praise him, you small creatures
and flying birds.
¹¹Praise him, you kings of the earth
and all nations.

Praise him, all you princes and
rulers on earth.
¹²Praise him, young men and young
women.
Praise him, old people and
children.

¹³Let them praise the name of the
LORD.
His name alone is honored.
His glory is higher than the earth
and the heavens.
¹⁴He has given his people a strong
king.
All of his faithful people praise
him for that gift.
All of the people of Israel are
close to his heart.

Praise the LORD.

PSALM 149

¹Praise the LORD.

Sing a new song to the LORD.
Sing praise to him in the
community of his faithful
people.

Where did angels come from?

God created everything, and that includes angels. The Bible
does not say, "God created angels." And it does not tell *when*
God created angels. But we know he
did because the Bible explains that
God created everything that
exists. We also do not know if
God created all the angels at
once or if he creates them as he
needs them. Angels take orders
from God and serve him. They
are not equal with God, and they
do not have the same powers as
God.

checkout Psalm 148:2,5

Related verses:
Nehemiah 9:6;
Colossians 1:15,16

JASON'S IMAGINATION

²Let Israel be filled with joy because
　God is their Maker.
Let the people of Zion be glad
　because he is their King.
³Let them praise his name with
　dancing.
Let them make music to him
　with harps and tambourines.
⁴The LORD takes delight in his
　people.
He saves those who aren't proud.
He makes them feel like kings.
⁵Let his faithful people be filled
　with joy because of that
　honor.
Let them sing with joy even when
　they are lying in bed.
⁶May they praise God with their
　mouths.
May they hold in their hands a
　sword that has two edges.
⁷Let them pay the nations back.
Let them punish the people of
　the earth.
⁸Let them put the kings of those
　nations in chains.
Let them put their nobles in iron
　chains.

⁹Let them carry out God's sentence
　against the nations.
That will bring glory to all of his
　faithful people.

Praise the LORD.

PSALM 150

¹Praise the LORD.

Praise God in his holy temple.
Praise him in his mighty
　heavens.
²Praise him for his powerful acts.
Praise him because he is greater
　than anything else.
³Praise him by blowing trumpets.
Praise him with harps and lyres.
⁴Praise him with tambourines and
　dancing.
Praise him with stringed
　instruments and flutes.
⁵Praise him with clashing cymbals.
Praise him with clanging
　cymbals.
⁶Let everything that has breath
　praise the LORD.

Praise the LORD.

How does God make the sun and moon go up and down?

God made powerful laws to rule nature. These laws control the sun, moon, earth, and other planets and stars. One law, gravity, draws objects toward each other. Other natural laws control the weather. Many forces determine whether the day will be sunny or cloudy, or warm or cold. The heat from the sun, the currents in the ocean, and the wind do a lot of the work. God set up the rules that make all these forces work together. And because God controls all creation, he can interrupt the laws if he wants to. The planets and stars move as God directs. God is very powerful.

checkout
Psalm 148:3,6

Related verses:
Hebrews 1:2,3

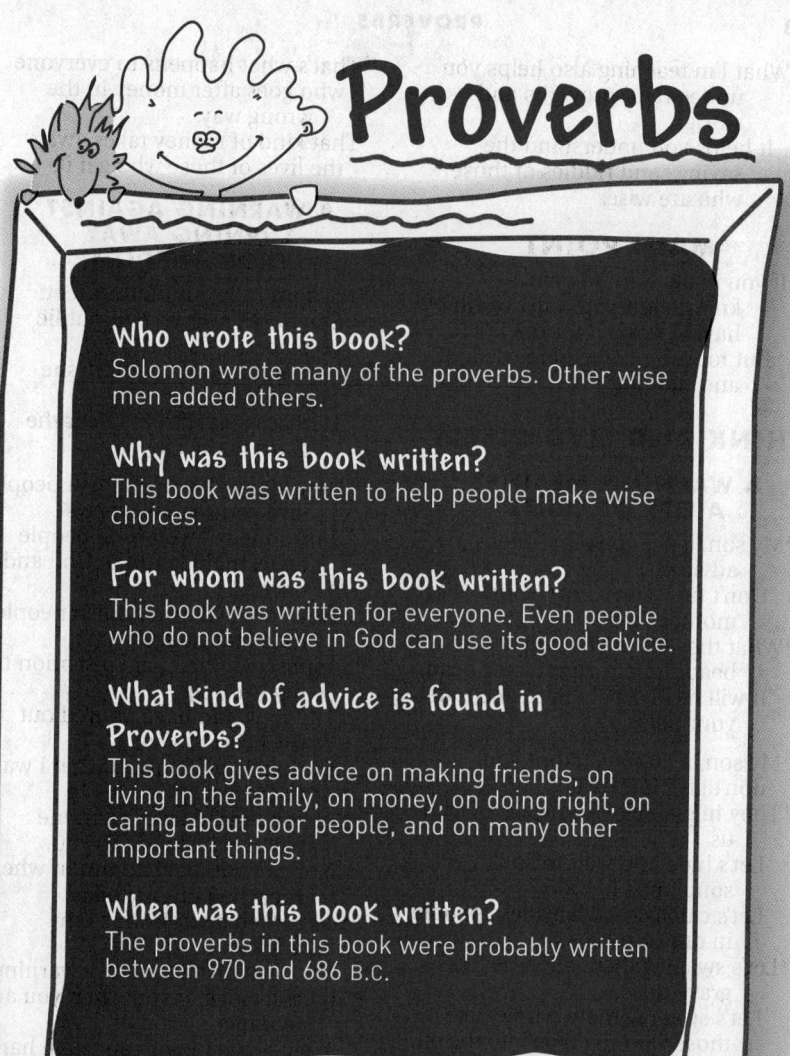

Proverbs

Who wrote this book?
Solomon wrote many of the proverbs. Other wise men added others.

Why was this book written?
This book was written to help people make wise choices.

For whom was this book written?
This book was written for everyone. Even people who do not believe in God can use its good advice.

What kind of advice is found in Proverbs?
This book gives advice on making friends, on living in the family, on money, on doing right, on caring about poor people, and on many other important things.

When was this book written?
The proverbs in this book were probably written between 970 and 686 B.C.

PURPOSE

1 These are the proverbs of Solomon. He was the son of David and the king of Israel.

² Proverbs teach you wisdom and train you.
They help you understand wise sayings.
³ They provide you with training and help you live wisely.
They lead to what is right and honest and fair.
⁴ They give understanding to childish people.
They give knowledge and good sense to those who are young.
⁵ Let wise people listen and add to what they have learned.
Let those who understand what is right get guidance.

⁶What I'm teaching also helps you
understand proverbs and
stories.
It helps you understand the
sayings and riddles of those
who are wise.

MAIN POINT

⁷If you really want to gain
knowledge, you must begin by
having respect for the LORD.
But foolish people hate wisdom
and training.

THINK AND LIVE WISELY

A WARNING AGAINST
A LIFE OF CRIME

⁸My son, listen to your father's
advice.
Don't turn away from your
mother's teaching.
⁹What they teach you will be like a
beautiful crown on your head.
It will be like a chain to decorate
your neck.

¹⁰My son, if sinners tempt you,
don't give in to them.
¹¹They might say, "Come along with
us.
Let's hide and wait to spill
someone's blood.
Let's catch some harmless people
in our trap.
¹²Let's swallow them alive, as the
grave does.
Let's swallow them whole, like
those who go down into the pit.
¹³We'll get all kinds of valuable
things.
We'll fill our houses with what we
steal.
¹⁴Come and join our gang.
We'll share everything we have."
¹⁵My son, don't go along with them.
Don't even set your feet on their
paths.
¹⁶They are always in a hurry to sin.
They are quick to spill someone's
blood.
¹⁷How useless it is to spread a net
while all the birds are watching!
¹⁸Those who hide and wait will spill
their own blood.
They will be caught in their own
trap.

¹⁹That's what happens to everyone
who goes after money in the
wrong way.
That kind of money takes away
the lives of those who get it.

A WARNING AGAINST
TURNING AWAY
FROM WISDOM

²⁰Wisdom calls out in the street.
She raises her voice in public
places.
²¹At the noisy street corners she
cries out.
Here is what she says near the
gates of the city.

²²"How long will you childish people
love your childish ways?
How long will you rude people
enjoy making fun of God and
others?
How long will you foolish people
hate knowledge?
²³Suppose you had paid attention to
my warning.
Then I would have poured out
my heart to you.
I would have told you what I was
thinking.
²⁴But you turned away from me
when I called out to you.
None of you paid attention when
I reached out my hand.
²⁵You turned away from all my
advice.
You wouldn't accept my warning.
²⁶So I will laugh at you when you are
in danger.
I will make fun of you when hard
times come.
²⁷I will laugh when hard times hit
you like a storm.
I will laugh when danger comes
your way like a windstorm.
I will make fun of you when
suffering and trouble come.

²⁸"Then you will call to me. But I
won't answer.
You will look for me. But you
won't find me.
²⁹You hated knowledge.
You didn't choose to have respect
for the LORD.
³⁰You wouldn't accept my advice.
You turned your backs on my
warnings.

³¹ So you will eat the fruit of the way
   you have lived.
   You will choke on the fruit of
   what you have planned.

³² "Childish people go down the
   wrong path. They will die.
   Foolish people are satisfied with
   the way they live. They will be
   destroyed.

³³ But those who listen to me will live
   in safety.
   They will not worry. They won't
   be afraid of getting hurt."

GOOD THINGS COME
FROM WISDOM

2 My son, accept my words.
   Store up my commands inside
   you.
² Let your ears listen to wisdom.
   Apply your heart to
   understanding.
³ Call out for the ability to be wise.
   Cry out for understanding.
⁴ Look for it as you would look for
   silver.
   Search for it as you would search
   for hidden treasure.
⁵ Then you will understand how to
   have respect for the LORD.
   You will find out how to know
   God.
⁶ The LORD gives wisdom.
   Knowledge and understanding
   come from his mouth.
⁷ He stores up success for honest
   people.
   He is like a shield to those who
   live without blame. He keeps
   them safe.
⁸ He guards the path of those who
   are honest.
   He watches over the way of his
   faithful ones.

⁹ You will understand what is right
   and honest and fair.
   You will understand the right
   way to live.
¹⁰ Your heart will become wise.
   Your mind will delight in
   knowledge.
¹¹ Good sense will keep you safe.
   Understanding will guard you.

¹² Wisdom will save you from the
   ways of evil men.

It will save you from men who
   twist their words.
¹³ Men like that leave the straight
   paths
   to walk in dark ways.
¹⁴ They take delight in doing what is
   wrong.
   They take joy in twisting
   everything around.
¹⁵ Their paths are crooked.
   Their ways are not straight.

¹⁶ Wisdom will save you from a
   woman who commits
   adultery.
   It will save you from a sinful wife
   and her tempting words.
¹⁷ She leaves the man she married
   when she was young.
   She breaks the promise she
   made to her God.
¹⁸ Her house leads down to death.
   Her paths lead to the spirits of
   the dead.
¹⁹ No one who goes to her comes
   back
   or reaches the paths of life.

²⁰ You will walk in the ways of good
   people.
   You will follow the paths of those
   who do right.
²¹ Honest people will live in the land.
   Those who are without blame
   will remain in it.
²² But sinners will be cut off from the
   land.
   Those who aren't faithful will be
   torn away from it.

MORE GOOD THINGS COME
FROM WISDOM

3 My son, do not forget my
   teaching.
   Keep my commands in your
   heart.
² They will help you live for many
   years.
   They will bring you success.

³ Don't let love and truth ever leave
   you.
   Tie them around your neck.
   Write them on the tablet of your
   heart.
⁴ Then you will find favor and a
   good name
   in the eyes of God and people.

⁵Trust in the LORD with all your heart.
Do not depend on your own understanding.
⁶In all your ways remember him.
Then he will make your paths smooth and straight.

⁷Don't be wise in your own eyes.
Have respect for the LORD and avoid evil.
⁸That will bring health to your body.
It will make your bones strong.

⁹Honor the LORD with your wealth.
Give him the first share of all your crops.
¹⁰Then your storerooms will be so full they can't hold everything.
Your huge jars will spill over with fresh wine.

¹¹My son, do not hate the LORD's training.
Do not object when he corrects you.

¹²The LORD trains those he loves.
He is like a father who trains the son he is pleased with.

¹³Blessed is the one who finds wisdom.
Blessed is the one who gains understanding.
¹⁴Wisdom pays better than silver does.
She earns more than gold does.
¹⁵She is worth more than rubies.
Nothing you want can compare with her.
¹⁶Long life is in her right hand.
In her left hand are riches and honor.
¹⁷Her ways are pleasant ways.
All her paths lead to peace.
¹⁸She is a tree of life to those who hold her close.
Those who hold on to her will be blessed.

¹⁹By wisdom the LORD laid the earth's foundations.

KIDS' QUESTION

How will I know what I want to do when I grow up?

God has made you good at doing certain things. He has given you talents, interests and abilities. You will learn more about these gifts as you get older. Your parents and friends will help you discover and develop them.

But do not wait for someone to tell you what to do. Whenever you get interested in something or do well in something, find out more about it. Ask questions about it. Read books about it. Take an extra class.

And ask God to guide you. God has a plan for your life. He created you and loves you. He knows what you will be best at. He will guide you if you ask him.

checkout Proverbs 3:5,6

CAREER CHOICES FAIR

RADIO DJ

JOIN THE MARINES

SURGEON

SPACE RESEARCH

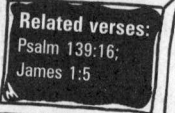

Related verses:
Psalm 139:16;
James 1:5

Through understanding he set
the heavens in place.
20 By his knowledge the seas were
separated,
and the clouds dropped their dew.

21 My son, hold on to good sense and
the understanding of what is
right.
Don't let them out of your sight.
22 They will be life for you.
They will be like a gracious
necklace around your neck.
23 Then you will go on your way in
safety.
You will not trip and fall.
24 When you lie down, you won't be
afraid.
When you lie down, you will
sleep soundly.
25 Don't be terrified by sudden
trouble.
Don't be afraid when sinners are
destroyed.

26 The LORD is the one you will trust
in.
He will keep your feet from being
caught in a trap.

27 Don't hold back good from those
who are worthy of it.
Don't hold it back when you can
help.
28 Suppose you have something to
give.
Don't say to your neighbor,
"Come back later.
I'll give it to you tomorrow."

29 Don't plan to harm your
neighbor.
He lives near you and trusts you.
30 Don't bring charges against a man
without any reason.
He has not harmed you.

31 Don't be jealous of a man who
hurts others.
Don't choose any of his ways.

KIDS' QUESTioN

Why do I have to give money to church?

It is part of God's plan for Christians to give money to the church. Churches have bills to pay just like families and businesses. They have electric bills, phone bills, water bills and many other bills. Churches also have to pay the pastors and secretaries. They pay for church school supplies, missions and special events. This is how God's people are able to worship God, do his work and help others learn how to follow him.

God's people have always given money to those who lead in worship and service to God. Abraham did it. The Israelites did it. Jesus did it. The apostles did it. Everyone who loves God does it. They know it is a lot of work to lead God's people, so they pitch in and help pay for it.

Related verses:
1 Timothy
5:17,18;
Haggai 1:1–15

checkout
Proverbs 3:9,10

[32] The LORD really hates sinful
people.
But he makes honest people his
closest friends.

[33] The LORD puts a curse on the
houses of sinners.
But he blesses the homes of
those who do what is right.

[34] He laughs at proud people who
make fun of others.
But he gives grace to those who
are not proud.

[35] Wise people receive honor.
But the LORD puts foolish people
to shame.

WISDOM IS BEST

4 My children, listen to a father's
teaching.
Pay attention and gain
understanding.

[2] I give you good advice.
So don't turn away from what I
teach you.

[3] I was once a young boy in my
father's house.
I was my mother's only child.

[4] My father taught me.
He said, "Hold on to my words
with all your heart.
Keep my commands. Then you
will live.

[5] Get wisdom. Get understanding.
Don't forget my words. Don't turn
away from them.

[6] Stay close to wisdom, and she will
keep you safe.
Love her, and she will watch over
you.

[7] Wisdom is best. So get wisdom.
No matter what it costs, get
understanding.

[8] Value wisdom, and she will lift you
up.
Hold her close, and she will
honor you.

[9] She will set a beautiful crown on
your head.
She will give you a glorious
crown."

[10] My son, listen. Accept what
I say.
Then you will live for many
years.

[11] I guide you in the way of
wisdom.

I lead you along straight paths.

[12] When you walk, nothing will slow
you down.
When you run, you won't trip
and fall.

[13] Hold on to my teaching. Don't let
it go.
Guard it well. It is your life.

[14] Don't take the path of evil people.
Don't live the way sinners do.

[15] Stay away from their path. Don't
travel on it.
Turn away from it. Go on your
way.

[16] Sinners can't sleep until they do
what is evil.
They can't rest until they make
someone fall.

[17] They do evil just as easily as they
eat food.
They hurt others as easily as they
drink wine.

[18] The path of those who do what is
right is like the first gleam of
dawn.
It shines brighter and brighter
until the full light of day.

[19] But the way of those who do what
is wrong is like deep darkness.
They don't know what makes
them trip and fall.

[20] My son, pay attention to what I
say.
Listen closely to my words.

[21] Don't let them out of your sight.
Keep them in your heart.

[22] They are life to those who find
them.
They are health to your whole
body.

[23] Above everything else, guard your
heart.
It is where your life comes from.

[24] Don't speak with twisted words.
Keep evil talk away from your
lips.

[25] Let your eyes look straight
ahead.
Keep looking right in front of
you.

[26] Make level paths for your feet to
walk on.
Only go on ways that are firm.

[27] Don't turn to the right or left.
Keep your feet from the path of
evil.

A WARNING AGAINST COMMITTING ADULTERY

5 My son, pay attention to my
wisdom.
Listen carefully to my wise
sayings.
² Then you will continue to have
good sense.
Your lips will keep on speaking
words of knowledge.
³ A woman who commits adultery
has lips that drip honey.
What she says is smoother than
oil.
⁴ But in the end she is like bitter
poison.
She cuts like a sword that has
two edges.
⁵ Her feet go down to death.
Her steps lead straight to the
grave.
⁶ She doesn't give any thought to
her way of life.
Her paths are crooked, but she
doesn't realize it.

⁷ My sons, listen to me.
Don't turn away from what
I say.
⁸ Stay on a path far away from that
evil woman.
Don't even go near the door of
her house.
⁹ If you do, you will give your best
strength to others.
You will give the best years of
your life to someone who is
mean.
¹⁰ Strangers will use up all of your
wealth.
Your hard work will make
someone else rich.
¹¹ At the end of your life you will
groan.
Your skin and your body will be
worn out.
¹² You will say, "How I hated to take
advice!
How my heart refused to be
corrected!
¹³ I would not obey my teachers.

Is it all right to laugh at dirty jokes?

Some jokes are funny but not good. Avoid laughing at a joke that uses bad words or talks about sex in a wrong way. Dirty jokes are called dirty even by people who do not know God because even they know they are bad. Jokes that make fun of other people's skin color or religion are also bad. Why? Because God is holy and pure, and he wants us to be holy and pure too. Being involved in dirty jokes fills our minds with wrong thoughts and may cause others to feel bad. Get away from someone who is telling jokes that are bad. They will just tell you more of those kinds of jokes if you stick around and laugh. There are plenty of good, clean jokes. Listen to those, tell those and have fun!

checkout
Proverbs 4:14,15

Related verses:
Psalm 1:1,2;
Ephesians 5:4

GIANT MUD PIT

I wouldn't listen to those who
taught me.
¹⁴ I was almost totally destroyed.
It happened right in front of the
whole community."

¹⁵ Drink water from your own well.
Drink running water from your
own spring.
¹⁶ Should your springs pour out into
the streets?
Should your streams of water
pour out in public places?
¹⁷ No! Let them belong to you alone.
Never share them with strangers.
¹⁸ May your fountain be blessed.
May the wife you married when
you were young make you
happy.
¹⁹ She is like a loving doe, a graceful
deer.
May her breasts always satisfy
you.
May you always be captured by
her love.
²⁰ My son, why be captured by a
woman who commits
adultery?
Why hug the wife of another
man?

²¹ The LORD watches a man's ways.
He studies all of his paths.
²² A sinner is trapped by his own evil
acts.
He is held tight by the ropes of
his sins.
²³ He will die because he refused to
be corrected.
His sins will capture him because
he was very foolish.

WARNINGS AGAINST FOOLISH ACTS

6 My son, don't put up money
for what your neighbor
owes.
Don't agree to pay up for
someone else.
² Don't be trapped by what you have
said.
Don't be caught by the words of
your mouth.
³ Instead, my son, do something to
free yourself.
Don't fall into your neighbor's
hands.
Don't be proud.
Hurry and make your appeal to
your neighbor.

KIDS' QUESTION

Why do we have to learn to save money?

It is important to save money because you will need money in the future. For example, someday you will want to buy something that costs a lot. You may want to buy a special gift for a friend, you may have an emergency and need money quickly or you may want to go to college. People who do not save for these things have to borrow money to pay for them. But then they have to pay back the loan plus interest. That is foolish. It is wiser to save up for what you will need so that when you need the money it is there.

Jason for President
in 2044

checkout

Proverbs 6:6–8

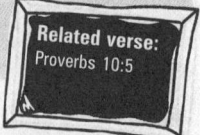

Related verse:
Proverbs 10:5

⁴Don't let your eyes go to sleep.
  Don't let your eyelids close.
⁵As a deer frees itself from a hunter,
    free yourself.
  As a bird frees itself from a
    trapper, free yourself.

⁶You people who don't want to
    work, think about the ant!
  Consider its ways and be wise!
⁷It has no commander.
  It has no leader or ruler.
⁸But it stores up its food in
    summer.
  It gathers its food at harvest time.

⁹You lazy people, how long will you
    lie there?
  When will you get up from your
    sleep?
¹⁰You might sleep a little or take a
    little nap.
  You might even fold your hands
    and rest.
¹¹Then you would be poor, as if
    someone had robbed you.
  You would have little, as if
    someone had stolen from you.

¹²A worthless and evil man
    goes around saying twisted
    things with his mouth.
¹³ He winks with his eyes.
  He makes signals with his feet.
  He motions with his fingers.
¹⁴ His plans are evil. He has lies in
    his heart.
  He is always stirring up
    fights.
¹⁵Trouble will catch up with him in
    an instant.
  He will suddenly be destroyed.
  Nothing can save him.

¹⁶There are six things the LORD
    hates.
  In fact, he hates seven things.
¹⁷   The LORD hates proud eyes,
    a lying tongue,
  and hands that kill those
    who aren't guilty.
¹⁸   He also hates hearts that
    make evil plans,
  feet that are quick to do evil,
¹⁹   any witness who pours out
    lies,

Is it wrong to leave your homework till the last minute so that you can watch TV?

School is important because that is where we learn information that can help us live in this world. Homework is a part of school. Teachers give homework to help students learn what is being taught in class. Remember that God wants us to do our best at everything we do. That includes school. TV is all right if we watch good programs. But school is more important. Do your homework first and do the best you can at it. Then do your family jobs and responsibilities. *Then* take time for playing, watching TV and other activities. You will have a better time playing when you know that all your work is done.

Related verses:
Colossians
3:23,24;
1 Timothy 4:12

checkout
Proverbs 6:9–11

and anyone who stirs up
family fights.

A WARNING AGAINST COMMITTING ADULTERY

²⁰ My son, keep your father's
commands.
Don't turn away from your
mother's teaching.
²¹ Tie them to your heart forever.
Put them around your neck.
²² When you walk, they will guide
you.
When you sleep, they will watch
over you.
When you wake up, they will
speak to you.
²³ Your father's commands are like a
lamp.
Your mother's teaching is like a
light.

And the training that corrects you
leads to life.
²⁴ It keeps you from a sinful woman.
It keeps you from the smooth
tongue of a woman who
commits adultery.
²⁵ Don't hunger in your heart after
her beauty.
Don't let her eyes capture you.
²⁶ A prostitute leaves you with only a
loaf of bread.
Another man's wife hunts your
very life.
²⁷ You can't shovel fire into your lap
without burning your clothes.
²⁸ You can't walk on hot coals
without burning your feet.
²⁹ It's the same for anyone who has
sex with another man's wife.
Anyone who touches her will be
punished.

KIDS' QUESTion

What if one parent says you can watch a certain movie and then the other one says you can't?

Some kids go back and forth between parents until one gives in and says OK.
That is wrong because it dishonors what the first parent said. It is also unwise
because your parents protect you and provide for you. You may regret it if
you get your parents into a fight or if you pit one against the other. Nicely
ask why if you really must know
their reasons for saying no.
But do not argue,
complain or whine
about it. And do not
ask your other
parent, hoping for a
different answer.
Accept what the
first parent says.
They are a team.

checkout

Proverbs 6:20,21

JASON'S IMAGINATION

SOLOMON

Related verses:
Exodus 20:12;
Ephesians 6:1-3

³⁰ People don't hate a thief who steals
   to fill his empty stomach.
³¹ But when he is caught, he must
   pay seven times as much as
   he stole.
   It may even cost him everything
   he has.
³² A man who commits adultery has
   no sense.
   Anyone who does it destroys
   himself.
³³ He will be beaten up and
   dishonored.
   His shame will never be wiped
   away.
³⁴ Jealousy stirs up a husband's
   anger.
   He will show no mercy when he
   gets even.
³⁵ He won't accept any payment.
   He won't take any money, no
   matter how much he is
   offered.

A WARNING AGAINST A WOMAN WHO COMMITS ADULTERY

7 My son, obey my words.
   Store up my commands inside
   you.
² Obey my commands and you will
   live.
   Guard my teachings as you
   would your own eyes.
³ Tie them on your fingers.
   Write them on the tablet of your
   heart.
⁴ Say to wisdom, "You are my sister."
   Call understanding a member of
   your family.
⁵ They will keep you from a woman
   who commits adultery.
   They will keep you from the
   smooth talk of a sinful wife.

⁶ I stood at the window of my
   house.
   I looked out through it.
⁷ Among those who were childish
   I saw a young man who had no
   sense.
⁸ He went down the street near that
   sinful woman's corner.
   He walked toward her house.
⁹ The sun had gone down. Day was
   fading.
   The darkness of night was falling.

¹⁰ A woman came out to meet him.
   She was dressed like a prostitute
   and had a clever plan.
¹¹ She was a loud and pushy woman.
   She never stayed at home.
¹² Sometimes in the streets,
   sometimes at other places,
   at every corner she would wait.
¹³ She took hold of the young man
   and kissed him.
   With a bold face she spoke to
   him.

¹⁴ She said, "At home I have meat left
   over from my offerings.
   Today I offered what I had
   promised I would.
¹⁵ So I came out to meet you.
   I looked for you. And I have
   found you!
¹⁶ I have covered my bed
   with colored sheets from Egypt.
¹⁷ I've perfumed my bed with spices.
   I used myrrh, aloes and
   cinnamon.
¹⁸ Come, let's drink our fill of love
   until morning.
   Let's enjoy ourselves by having
   sex!
¹⁹ My husband isn't home.
   He's gone on a long journey.
²⁰ He took his bag full of money.
   He won't be home for several
   days."

²¹ She led him down the wrong path
   with her clever words.
   She charmed him with her
   smooth talk.
²² All at once he followed her.
   He was like an ox going to be
   killed.
   He was like a deer stepping into a
   trap
²³   until an arrow struck its liver.
   He was like a bird rushing into a
   trap.
   Little did he know it would cost
   him his life!

²⁴ My sons, listen to me.
   Pay attention to what I say.
²⁵ Don't let your hearts turn to her
   ways.
   Don't step onto her paths.
²⁶ She has brought down a lot of
   men.
   She has killed a huge crowd.

²⁷ Her house is a road to the grave.
　It leads down to the place of the dead.

WISDOM IS WORTH MORE THAN ANYTHING

8 Doesn't wisdom call out?
　Doesn't understanding raise her voice?
² On the high roads along the way,
　she takes her place where the paths meet.
³ Beside the gates leading into the city,
　she cries out at the entrances.
⁴ She says, "Men, I call out to you.
　I raise my voice to all human beings.
⁵ You who are childish, get some good sense.
　You who are foolish, gain understanding.
⁶ Listen! I have worthy things to say.
　I open my lips to speak what is right.
⁷ My mouth speaks what is true.
　My lips hate evil.
⁸ All the words of my mouth are honest.
　None of them is twisted or sinful.
⁹ To those who have understanding, all my words are right.
　To those who have knowledge, they are true.
¹⁰ Choose my teaching instead of silver.
　Choose knowledge rather than fine gold.
¹¹ Wisdom is worth more than rubies.
　Nothing you want can compare with her.

¹² "I, wisdom, live together with understanding.
　I have knowledge and good sense.
¹³ To have respect for the LORD is to hate evil.
　I hate pride and bragging.
　I hate evil ways and twisted words.
¹⁴ I have good sense and give good advice.
　I have understanding and power.
¹⁵ By me kings rule.
　Leaders make laws that are fair.
¹⁶ By me princes govern.
　By me all nobles rule on earth.
¹⁷ I love those who love me.
　Those who look for me find me.
¹⁸ With me are riches and honor.
　With me are lasting wealth and success.
¹⁹ My fruit is better than fine gold.
　My gifts are better than the finest silver.
²⁰ I walk in ways that are honest.
　I take paths that are right.
²¹ I leave riches to those who love me.
　I give them more than they have room for.

²² "The LORD created me as the first of his works,
　before his acts of long ago.
²³ I was formed at the very beginning.
　I was formed before the world began.
²⁴ Before there were any oceans, I was born.
　There weren't any springs of water at that time.
²⁵ Before the mountains were settled in place, I was born.
　Before there were any hills, I was born.
²⁶ It happened before the LORD made the earth and its fields.
　It was before he made the dust of the world.
²⁷ I was there when he set the heavens in place.
　When he marked out the place where the sky meets the sea, I was there.
²⁸ That was when he put the clouds above.
　It was when he fixed the ocean springs in place.
²⁹ It was when he set limits for the sea
　so that the waters had to obey his command.
　When he marked out the foundations of the earth, I was there.
³⁰ I was the skilled worker at his side.
　I was filled with delight day after day.
　I was always happy to be with him.

[31] His whole world filled me with joy.
  I took delight in all human
    beings.

[32] "My children, listen to me.
  Blessed are those who keep my
    ways.
[33] Listen to my teaching and be wise.
  Don't turn away from it.
[34] Blessed is the one who listens
    to me.
  He watches every day at my
    doors.
  He waits beside my doorway.
[35] Those who find me find life.
  They receive favor from the
    LORD.
[36] But those who don't find me harm
    only themselves.
  Everyone who hates me loves
    death."

WISDOM AND FOOLISHNESS CALL OUT

9 Wisdom has built her house.
  She has made its seven pillars.
  [2] She has prepared her meat
    and mixed her wine.
  She has also set her table.
[3] She has sent out her female
    servants.
  She calls out from the highest
    point of the city.
[4] She says, "Let all who are childish
    come in here!"
  She speaks to those who have no
    sense.
[5] "Come and eat my food.
  Drink the wine I have mixed.
[6] Leave your childish ways and you
    will live.
  Walk in the way that leads to
    understanding.

[7] "When you correct someone who
    makes fun of others,
  you might be laughed at.
  When you warn a sinner, you
    might get hurt.
[8] Don't warn those who make fun of
    others. They will hate you.
  Warn those who are wise. They
    will love you.
[9] Teach a wise man. He will become
    even wiser.
  Teach a person who does right.
  He will learn even more.

[10] "If you really want to become wise,
  you must begin by
    having respect for the LORD.
  To know the Holy One is to gain
    understanding.
[11] Through me, you will live a long
    time.
  Years will be added to your life.
[12] If you are wise, your wisdom will
    reward you.
  If you make fun of others, you
    alone will suffer."

[13] The woman called Foolishness is
    loud.
  She doesn't control herself. She
    doesn't know anything.
[14] She sits at the door of her
    house.
  She sits at the highest point of
    the city.
[15] She calls out to those who pass by.
  She calls out to those who go
    straight on their way.
[16] She says, "Let all who are childish
    come in here!"
  She speaks to those who have no
    sense.
[17] She says, "Stolen water is sweet.
  Food eaten in secret tastes
    good!"
[18] But they don't know that dead
    people are there.
  They don't know that her guests
    are in the deepest parts of the
    grave.

THE PROVERBS OF SOLOMON

10 These are the proverbs of
  Solomon.

A wise son makes his father
    glad.
  But a foolish son brings sorrow
    to his mother.

[2] Riches that are gained by sinning
    aren't worth anything.
  But doing what is right saves you
    from death.

[3] The LORD gives those who do right
    the food they need.
  But he lets those who do wrong
    go hungry.

[4] Hands that don't want to work
    make you poor.

But hands that work hard bring
wealth to you.

⁵A child who gathers crops in
summer is wise.
But a child who sleeps at harvest
time brings shame.

⁶Blessings are like crowns on the
heads of those who do right.
But the trouble caused by what
sinners say destroys them.

⁷To remember those who do right is
a blessing.
But the names of those who do
wrong will rot.

⁸A wise heart accepts commands.
But foolish chattering destroys
you.

⁹Anyone who lives without blame
walks safely.
But anyone who takes a crooked
path will get caught.

¹⁰An evil wink gets you into trouble.
And foolish chattering destroys
you.

¹¹The mouths of those who do right
are a fountain of life.
But the trouble caused by what
sinners say destroys them.

¹²Hate stirs up fights.
But love erases all sins by
forgiving them.

¹³Wisdom is found on the lips of
those who understand what is
right.
But those who have no sense are
punished.

¹⁴Wise people store up
knowledge.
But the mouths of foolish people
destroy them.

¹⁵The wealth of rich people is like a
city that makes them feel safe.

What is the quickest way to save money?

The easiest and quickest way to save money is to set some aside *every time* you get some. You may want to begin by putting some in a jar. After you have saved a few dollars, you can put them in the bank.

Some people do not save, because they think it is not worthwhile. But it may surprise you how fast the money adds up. If you are eight years old and save 50 cents a week at eight percent interest until you are 65, you will have more than $25,000! Just remember to write down:

• *Why.* Example: "I want to buy _____."

• *When.* Example: "I will set aside half of my allowance and any other money I get."

• *How.* Example: "I will put the cash in a jar every week and then take it to the bank once a month."

checkout **Proverbs 10:4**

Related verses:
Proverbs 21:17,20

But having nothing destroys
those who are poor.

¹⁶ People who do what is right earn
life.
But what sinners earn causes
them to be punished.

¹⁷ Anyone who pays attention to his
training
is on his way to life.
But anyone who refuses to be
corrected
leads others down the wrong
path.

¹⁸ Anyone who hides hatred has
lying lips.
And anyone who spreads lies is
foolish.

¹⁹ Those who talk a lot are likely to sin.
But those who control their
tongues are wise.

²⁰ The tongues of those who do right
are like fine silver.
But the hearts of those who do
wrong aren't worth very
much.

²¹ The words of those who do right
benefit many people.
But those who are foolish die
because they have no sense.

²² The blessing of the LORD brings
wealth.
Trouble doesn't come with it.

²³ A foolish person finds pleasure in
doing evil things.
But a man who has
understanding takes delight
in wisdom.

²⁴ What sinners are afraid of will
catch up with them.
But those who do right will get
what they want.

²⁵ When the storm is over, sinners
are gone.
But those who do right stand
firm forever.

²⁶ Anyone who doesn't want to work
hurts those who send him.
He is like vinegar on the teeth or
smoke in the eyes.

KIDS' QUESTION

Is it OK to beg for things from your parents?

It is OK to *ask* your parents for things but not to beg. For example, you could ask for a special treat, Christmas presents or permission to go to a friend's house or to stay up late. But you should accept their answer with a good attitude even if they say no. Do not beg. Do not ask over and over and over to try to get them to give you what they really do not want to give you. God gave you parents to protect you and provide for you. They gave their answer because they thought it was best for you. You might be sorry if you talk them into going against their first answer. Respect and obey your mom and dad.

checkout
Proverbs 10:10

Related verses:
Ephesians 6:1–3;
Colossians 3:20

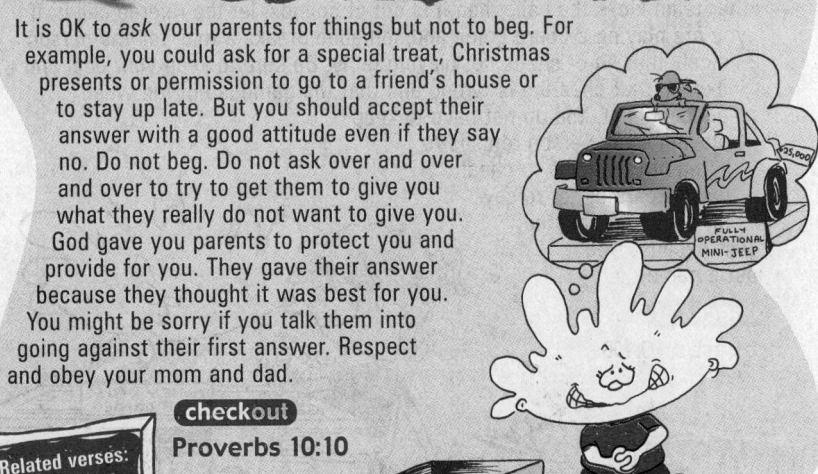

[27] Having respect for the LORD leads to a longer life.
But the years of evil people are cut short.

[28] Those who do right can expect joy.
But the hopes of sinners are bound to fail.

[29] The way of the LORD leads to a safe place for those who do right.
But it destroys those who do evil.

[30] Those who do right will never be removed from the land.
But those who do wrong will not remain in it.

[31] The mouths of those who do right produce wisdom.
But tongues that speak twisted words will be cut out.

[32] Those who do right know the proper thing to say.
But those who do wrong speak only twisted words.

11 The LORD hates it when people use scales to cheat others.
But he is delighted when people use honest weights.

[2] When pride comes, shame follows.
But wisdom comes to those who are not proud.

[3] Those who do what is right are guided by their honest lives.
But those who aren't faithful are destroyed by their trickery.

[4] Wealth isn't worth anything when God judges you.
But doing what is right saves you from death.

[5] The ways of honest people are made straight because they do what is right.
But those who do what is wrong are brought down by their own sins.

KIDS' QUESTion

What should I do if someone cheats me?

If an adult cheats you out of money at a store, you should tell your parents and let them deal with it. If you are playing a sport like soccer and someone on the other team kicks the ball when it is out of bounds, let the referee call it. If you are playing a board game and someone breaks a rule, tell the person nicely that he or she is not playing fairly. Be sure to keep your cool and explain that cheating is wrong and that the game is not fun when people cheat. You do not have to keep playing if the person refuses to listen or continues to cheat. Just be careful not to say that someone cheated just because you lost a game.

checkout
Proverbs 10:12

Related verses:
Proverbs 3:30;
Luke 3:14

MONEY BAGS the game

⁶Godly people are saved by doing
what is right.
But those who aren't faithful are
trapped by evil longings.

⁷When an evil man dies, his hope
dies with him.
Everything he expected to
gain from his power will be
lost.

⁸Those who do right are saved from
trouble.
But trouble comes on those who
do wrong.

⁹With their words ungodly people
destroy their neighbors.
But those who do what is right
escape because of their
knowledge.

¹⁰When those who do right succeed,
their city is glad.
When those who do wrong die,
people shout for joy.

¹¹The blessing of honest people
builds up a city.
But the words of sinners
destroy it.

¹²A person who has no sense makes
fun of his neighbor.
But a man who has
understanding controls his
tongue.

¹³Those who talk about others tell
secrets.
But those who can be trusted
keep things to themselves.

¹⁴Without the guidance of good
leaders a nation falls.
But many good advisers can
save it.

¹⁵Anyone who puts up money for
what someone else owes will
certainly suffer.
But a person who doesn't agree
to pay up for someone else is
safe.

¹⁶A woman who has a kind heart
gains respect.
But men who are not kind gain
only wealth.

¹⁷A kind man benefits himself.
But a mean person brings
trouble on himself.

KIDS' QUESTION

Is it OK to tell secrets to parents?

Yes. In fact, unless the secret involves a
surprise for a parent, it is often best to tell *only*
your parents. You should not tell secrets to anybody else
unless you have permission from the person who told you.
Think of your parents as your bigger and wiser
partners. God gave you your parents to
teach you, guide you, help you learn and
help you make wise choices. They
are part of you. They are there *for
you*. That is why it is fine to tell
them a secret. If the secret is
something fun just between you
and a friend, though, you do not
have to tell anyone, not even
your mom or dad.

checkout
Proverbs 11:13

Related verses:
Proverbs 20:19;
2 Corinthians 4:2

¹⁸Those who do what is wrong really
earn nothing.
But those who plant what is right
will certainly be rewarded.

¹⁹Right living leads to life.
But anyone who runs after evil
will die.

²⁰The LORD hates those whose
hearts are twisted.
But he is pleased with those who
live without blame.

²¹You can be sure that sinners will
be punished.
And you can also be sure that
godly people will go free.

²²A beautiful woman who has no
sense
is like a gold ring in a pig's
nose.

²³What godly people long for ends
only in what is good.
But what sinners hope for ends
only in God's anger.

²⁴Some give freely but get even
richer.
Others don't give what they
should but get even poorer.

²⁵Anyone who gives a lot will succeed.
Anyone who renews others will
be renewed.

²⁶People call down curses on those
who store up grain for
themselves.
But blessing makes those who
are willing to sell feel like
kings.

²⁷Anyone who looks for what is good
finds favor.
But bad things happen to a
person who plans to do evil.

²⁸Those who trust in their riches will
fall.
But those who do right will be as
healthy as a green leaf.

²⁹Those who bring trouble on their
families will receive nothing
but wind.
And foolish people will serve
wise people.

³⁰The fruit that godly people bear is
like a tree of life.

And those who lead others to do
what is right are wise.

³¹Godly people get what they should
get on earth.
So ungodly people and sinners
will certainly get what they
should get!

12

Anyone who loves to be
trained loves
knowledge.
Anyone who hates to be
corrected is stupid.

²The LORD blesses anyone who
does good.
But he judges any man who is
tricky.

³If a man does what is evil, he can't
become strong and steady.
But if people do what is right,
they can't be removed from
the land.

⁴A noble wife is her husband's
crown.
But a wife who brings shame is
like sickness in his bones.

⁵The plans of godly people are
right.
But the advice of sinners will
lead you the wrong way.

⁶The words of those who are evil
hide and wait to spill people's
blood.
But the speech of those who are
honest saves them from traps
like that.

⁷Sinners are destroyed and taken
away.
But the houses of godly people
stand firm.

⁸A man is praised for how wise he is.
But people hate those who have
twisted minds.

⁹Being nobody and having a
servant
is better than pretending to be
somebody and having no
food.

¹⁰Those who do what is right take
good care of their animals.
But the kindest acts of those who
do wrong are mean.

¹¹ Anyone who farms his land will
    have plenty of food.
  But a person who chases dreams
    has no sense.

¹² Those who do what is wrong want
    to steal from others.
  But those who do what is right
    bear good fruit because of
    their deep roots.

¹³ A sinner is trapped by his sinful talk.
  But a godly person escapes
    trouble.

¹⁴ Many good things come from
    what a man says.
  And the work of his hands
    rewards him.

¹⁵ The way of a foolish person seems
    right to him.
  But a wise person listens to advice.

¹⁶ Foolish people are easily upset.
  But wise people pay no attention
    to hurtful words.

¹⁷ An honest witness tells the truth.
  But a dishonest witness tells lies.

¹⁸ Thoughtless words cut like a
    sword.
  But the tongue of wise people
    brings healing.

¹⁹ Truthful words last forever.
  But lies last for only a moment.

²⁰ There are lies in the hearts of
    those who plan evil.
  But there is joy for those who
    work to bring peace.

²¹ No harm comes to godly people.
  But sinners have all the trouble
    they can handle.

²² The LORD hates those whose lips
    tell lies.
  But he is pleased with people
    who tell the truth.

²³ Wise people keep their knowledge
    to themselves.
  But the hearts of foolish people
    shout foolish things.

²⁴ Hands that work hard will rule.
  But people who don't want to
    work will become slaves.

KIDS' QUESTION

If God made spiders, why do people squish them?

God created spiders just as he made all the other animals. But there's a big difference between animals and human beings. People are created in God's image and are supposed to take care of all creation. That includes all animals and plants. This means we do not have permission to harm or kill for fun. We can't just destroy anything we please. We can kill animals and plants for food and to control their population. We can remove or kill spiders, insects and other bugs that threaten us. We can stop bugs from spreading disease. But we should be kind to animals whenever possible. And we should take good care of the world.

checkout
Proverbs 12:10

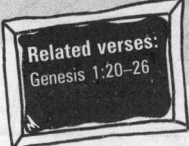

Related verses:
Genesis 1:20–26

²⁵ Worry makes a man's heart heavy.
But a kind word cheers him up.

²⁶ Godly people are careful about the
friends they choose.
But the way of sinners leads
them down the wrong path.

²⁷ Anyone who refuses to work
doesn't even cook what he
catches.
But a man who works hard
values what he has.

²⁸ There is life in doing what is right.
Along that path you will never die.

13

A wise child pays
attention to what
his father teaches
him.
But anyone who makes fun of
others doesn't listen to
warnings.

² The good things a man says
benefit him.
But a liar loves to hurt others.

³ Anyone who guards what he says
guards his life.
But anyone who speaks without
thinking will be destroyed.

⁴ People who refuse to work want
things and get nothing.
But the longings of people who
work hard are completely
satisfied.

⁵ Those who do right hate what is
false.
But those who do wrong bring
shame and dishonor.

⁶ Doing right guards those who are
honest.
But evil destroys those who are
sinful.

KIDS' QUESTION

Why is it wrong to look at someone's spelling test and write the words down?

Think about what you are doing. Whenever you take answers from another person's test or copy stuff from another person's homework, you are stealing that person's work. You are also lying because you are telling the teacher that you took the answers from your own head when you did not. In other words, you are taking someone else's work without permission and then pretending that it is yours. You are stealing from another student and lying to the teacher. God tells us not to lie, steal or cheat. We only hurt ourselves when we do. Learn what you need to learn and resist the temptation to cheat.

checkout
Proverbs 12:19

Related verses:
Luke 16:10;
Ephesians 4:25

7 Some people pretend to be rich
   but have nothing.
  Others pretend to be poor but
   have great wealth.

8 A man who is rich might have to
   pay to save his life.
  But a poor person is not in
   danger of that.

9 The lights of godly people shine
   brightly.
  But the lamps of sinners are
   blown out.

10 Pride only leads to arguing.
   But those who take advice are
    wise.

11 Money that is gained in the wrong
    way disappears.
   But money that is gathered little
    by little grows.

12 Hope that is put off makes one
    sick at heart.
   But a longing that is met is like a
    tree of life.

13 Anyone who hates what he is
    taught will pay for it later.

But a person who respects a
 command will be rewarded.

14 The teaching of wise people is like
    a fountain that gives life.
   It turns those who listen to it
    away from the jaws of death.

15 Good understanding wins favor.
   But the way of liars doesn't last.

16 Wise people act in keeping with
    the knowledge they have.
   But foolish people show how
    foolish they are.

17 An evil messenger gets into
    trouble.
   But a messenger who is trusted
    brings healing.

18 Those who turn away from their
    training become poor and
    ashamed.
   But those who accept warnings
    are honored.

19 A longing that is met is like
    something that tastes sweet.
   But foolish people hate to turn
    away from evil.

KIDS' QUESTION

Sometimes when I hang around with my friends, they do something bad. What should I do?

If the kids you are with begin to talk about or plan something that is not right, tell them not to do it. Don't yell or get angry—just explain that what they are doing is wrong.
You can suggest doing something else. If that doesn't work, you should leave. If those kids don't want to be friends anymore, then they aren't very good friends or the type of friends you would want to have anyway. When something like this happens, talk about it with your parents.

Related verses:
John 17:15;
Ephesians 5:11;
3 John 1:11

checkout
Proverbs 13:20

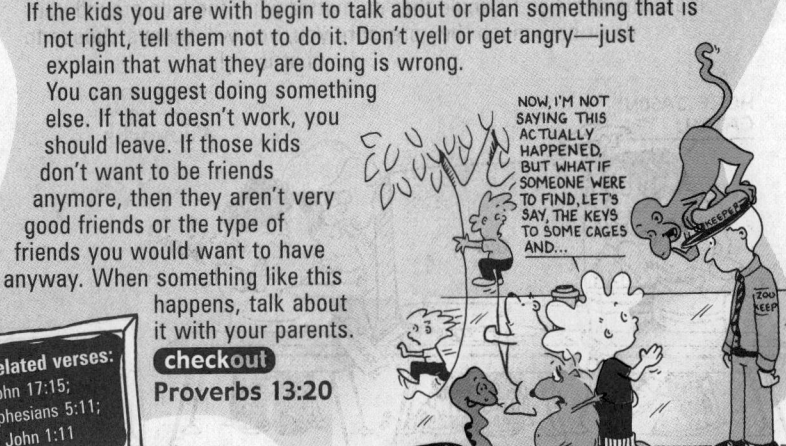

20 Anyone who walks with wise people grows wise.
But a companion of foolish people suffers harm.

21 Hard times chase those who are sinful.
But success is the reward of those who do right.

22 A good person leaves what he owns to his children and grandchildren.
But a sinner's wealth is stored up for those who do right.

23 The fields of poor people might produce a lot of food.
But those who beat them down destroy it all.

24 Those who don't correct their children hate them.
But those who love them are careful to train them.

25 Those who do right eat until they are full.

But the stomachs of those who do wrong go hungry.

14 A wise woman builds her house.
But a foolish woman tears hers down with her own hands.

2 An honest person has respect for the LORD.
But a person whose paths are crooked hates him.

3 Foolish people are punished for what they say.
But the things wise people say keep them safe.

4 Where there are no oxen, the feed box is empty.
But a strong ox brings in a great harvest.

5 An honest witness does not lie.
But a dishonest witness pours out lies.

The kids around me keep getting me into trouble. What can I do?

First, you can ignore them. If you don't pay attention to them, they probably will stop trying to get you into trouble. If this doesn't work, ask the teacher to change your seat. Remember, no one can *make* you do something wrong or break the rules. Other kids can *pressure* you, but in the end *you* always make the decision. Decide that no matter what the kids around you do or how much they pressure you, you will always choose to do what is right.

checkout
Proverbs 14:7

HERE, JASON! CATCH!

PSSST! JASON!

Related verse:
Psalm 35:11

⁶Those who make fun of others
   look for wisdom and don't
   find it.
 But knowledge comes easily to
   those who understand what is
   right.

⁷Stay away from a foolish man.
 You won't find knowledge in
   what he says.

⁸People are wise and
   understanding when they
   think about the way they live.
 But people are foolish when their
   foolish ways trick them.

⁹Foolish people laugh at making
   things right when they sin.
 But honest people try to do the
   right thing.

¹⁰Each heart knows its own sadness.
 And no one else can share its joy.

¹¹The houses of sinners will be
   destroyed.
 But the tents of honest people
   will stand firm.

¹²There is a way that may seem right
   to a man.
 But in the end it leads to death.

¹³Even when you laugh, your heart
   can be hurting.
 And your joy can end in sadness.

¹⁴Those who aren't faithful will be
   paid back
 for what they've done.
 And good men will receive
   rewards
 for how they've lived.

¹⁵A childish person believes
   anything.
 But a wise person thinks about
   how he lives.

¹⁶A wise person has respect for the
   LORD and avoids evil.
 But a foolish person gets mad
   and is thoughtless.

¹⁷Anyone who gets angry quickly
   does foolish things.
 And a man who is tricky is
   hated.

KIDS' QUESTION

If I'm supposed to love everybody, why am I supposed to stay away from certain kids?

God wants us to be loving and kind to everyone. But that does not mean we have to be a *close friend* to everyone. Some people try to get us in trouble. If we spend too much time with them, we can find ourselves doing what we should not do. Your closest friends should be those who help you become a better person. They should be those who have the same attitudes as you do about serving God. Try to be close to kids who love God and want to serve him. Talk with your parents about this. If they tell you to stay away from certain kids, do what they say. Parents can really help you learn to pick good friends.

checkout Proverbs 13:20

Related verses:
Proverbs 27:17;
John 17:15

¹⁸ Childish people act in keeping
   with their foolish ways.
   But knowledge makes wise
   people feel like kings.

¹⁹ Evil people will bow down in front
   of good people.
   And those who do wrong will
   bow down at the gates of
   those who do right.

²⁰ Poor people are avoided even by
   their neighbors.
   But rich people have many
   friends.

²¹ Anyone who hates his neighbor
   commits sin.
   But blessed is the person who is
   kind to those in need.

²² Those who plan evil go down the
   wrong path.
   But those who plan good find
   love and truth.

²³ All hard work pays off.
   But if all you do is talk, you will
   be poor.

²⁴ The wealth of wise people is their
   crown.
   But the foolish ways of foolish
   people lead to what is foolish.

²⁵ An honest witness saves lives.
   But a dishonest witness tells lies.

²⁶ Anyone who shows respect for the
   LORD has a strong tower.
   It will be a safe place for his
   children.

²⁷ Respect for the LORD is like a
   fountain that gives life.
   It turns you away from the jaws
   of death.

²⁸ A large population is a king's
   glory.
   But a prince without followers is
   destroyed.

Why can't poor people make more money?

It is hard for poor people to make money because they don't have jobs or their jobs pay very little. Most jobs that pay well require education or special training. But that costs money, which poor people do not have. Some people live in a poor country where almost *all* the jobs pay low wages.

Being poor tends to make people stay poor, because people need money for opportunities to make their lives better. This is where the saying comes from, "The rich get richer and the poor get poorer."

That is why we should try to help. We can give to groups that teach people skills so they can get better jobs. We can pray for them, too.

checkout
Proverbs 13:23

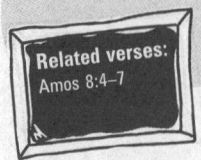

Related verses:
Amos 8:4–7

Jason's Mowing
$$$
managing

²⁹Anyone who is patient has great understanding.
But anyone who gets angry quickly shows how foolish he is.

³⁰A peaceful heart gives life to the body.
But jealousy rots the bones.

³¹Anyone who crushes poor people makes fun of their Maker.
But anyone who is kind to those in need honors God.

³²When trouble comes, sinners are brought down.
But godly people have a safe place even when they die.

³³Wisdom rests in the hearts of those who understand what is right.
And even among foolish people she makes herself known.

³⁴Doing what is right lifts people up.
But sin brings shame to any nation.

³⁵A king is pleased with a wise servant.
But a servant who is full of shame invites the king's anger.

15 A gentle answer turns anger away.
But mean words stir up anger.

²The tongues of wise people use knowledge well.
But the mouths of foolish people pour out foolish words.

³The eyes of the LORD are everywhere.
They watch those who are evil and those who are good.

⁴A tongue that brings healing is like a tree of life.

Why is it not good to talk to strangers?

Because there are a lot of bad people in the world. It is sad but true. Some people want to do bad things to children. And that is why parents and teachers tell children not to talk to strangers. God does not have a rule against it in the Bible, so it is not *wrong*. But it could be dangerous. Your parents do not want you to put yourself in a place where a bad person could hurt you. If a stranger asks you for help or you see someone in trouble, get an adult to help him or her. Do not just go with any stranger.

checkout
Proverbs 14:15

MASQUERADE PARTY

Related verses:
Romans 16:17,18

But a tongue that tells lies
produces a broken spirit.

⁵A foolish person turns his back on
how his father has trained
him.
But anyone who accepts being
corrected shows
understanding.

⁶The houses of those who do what
is right hold great wealth.
But those who do what is wrong
earn only trouble.

⁷The lips of wise people spread
knowledge.
But that's not true of the hearts
of foolish people.

⁸The LORD hates the sacrifice of
sinful people.
But the prayers of honest people
please him.

⁹The LORD hates how sinners live.
But he loves those who run after
what is right.

¹⁰Hard training is in store for anyone
who leaves the right path.
A person who hates to be
corrected will die.

¹¹Death and the Grave lie open in
front of the LORD.
So the hearts of mere men
certainly lie open to him!

¹²Anyone who makes fun of others
doesn't like to be corrected.
He won't ask wise people for
advice.

¹³A happy heart makes a face look
cheerful.
But a sad heart produces a
broken spirit.

¹⁴A heart that understands what is
right looks for knowledge.
But the mouths of foolish people
feed on what is foolish.

¹⁵All the days of those who are
crushed are filled with pain
and suffering.

How are kids supposed to earn money?

Kids can earn money by doing work for their parents and neighbors. Ask your parents what you can do around the house. Ask neighbors how you can earn money from them. Maybe you can clean up the yard, wash dishes, wash the car or run errands. Most adults like to pay kids for doing those kinds of jobs.

You can also start your own business. Make something that you can sell, or provide a service such as gardening, lawn care or delivery. Ask your parents and God for ideas and for good opportunities. If you really want to earn money, do every job well.

Think about what you are doing, keep going until you are done and never complain.

checkout
**Proverbs
14:23**

Related verses:
Philippians 2:14;
Colossians
3:23,24

But a cheerful heart enjoys a
   good time that never ends.

16 It is better to have respect for the
   LORD and have little
than to be rich and have trouble.

17 A meal of vegetables where there
   is love
is better than the finest meat
   where there is hatred.

18 A man who burns with anger stirs
   up fights.
But a person who is patient
   calms things down.

19 The way of people who don't want
   to work is blocked with
   thorns.
But the path of honest people is
   a wide road.

20 A wise son makes his father
   glad.
But a foolish son hates his
   mother.

21 A person who has no sense enjoys
   doing foolish things.
But a man who has
   understanding walks straight
   ahead.

22 Plans fail without good advice.
But they succeed when there are
   many advisers.

23 Joy is found in giving the right
   answer.
And how good is a word spoken
   at the right time!

24 The path of life leads up for those
   who are wise.
It keeps them from going down
   to the grave.

25 The LORD tears down the proud
   person's house.
But he keeps the widow's
   property safe.

26 The LORD hates the thoughts of
   sinful people.

Is it OK to tell people to shut up if they are being jerks?

We do not have to like it when someone does something annoying or wrong.
But we should not do something bad to them in return either. God wants us
to be loving and kind to others. So the rule is to be respectful, not bossy
or rude. Say something kind if the person will listen to your opinion.
Sometimes it is good to tell friends that they are not being
nice or that they are being mean.
You may make a new friend if
you respond to cruelty
with kindness. You will
make an enemy if
you respond with
more cruelty.

checkout
Proverbs 15:1

Related verses:
Proverbs 4:24;
1 Peter 2:17

But the thoughts of pure people
are pleasing to him.

27 Anyone who always wants more
brings trouble to his family.
But a person who refuses to be
paid off will live.

28 The hearts of those who do right
think about how they will
answer.
But the mouths of those who do
wrong pour out evil.

29 The LORD is far away from those
who do wrong.
But he hears the prayers of those
who do right.

30 A cheerful look brings joy to your
heart.
And good news gives health to
your body.

31 If you listen to a warning, you will
live.

You will be at home among those
who are wise.

32 Anyone who turns away from his
training hates himself.
But anyone who accepts being
corrected gains understanding.

33 Having respect for the LORD
teaches you how to live wisely.
So don't be proud if you want to
be honored.

16 People make plans in
their hearts.
But the LORD controls
what they say.

2 Everything a man does might
seem right to him.
But the LORD knows what that
man is thinking.

3 Commit to the LORD everything
you do.
Then your plans will succeed.

Why do parents sometimes not let kids buy what they want, even when they have enough money for it?

Usually it is because they love their children. Sometimes you want something that is not good for you. Your parents know this and forbid it. When you were a baby, you may have wanted to drink drain cleaner. You did not know any better, and you thought it would be good. Your parents stopped you because they knew the drain cleaner would badly hurt you.

Your parents also want you to learn to control your desires. You cannot buy *everything* you want. You have to make the choice to buy some things and not others. You also have to learn to give and to save money for later. Your parents are trying to help you learn these skills.

checkout Proverbs 15:5

Related verses:
Proverbs 13:1;
1 Timothy 4:12

⁴The LORD works everything out for his own purposes.
Even those who do wrong were made for a day of trouble.

⁵The LORD hates all those who have proud hearts.
You can be sure that they will be punished.

⁶Through love and truth sin is paid for.
People avoid evil when they have respect for the LORD.

⁷When the way you live pleases the LORD,
he makes even your enemies live at peace with you.

⁸It is better to have a little and do right
than to have a lot and be unfair.

⁹In your heart you plan your life.
But the LORD decides where your steps will take you.

¹⁰A king might speak as if his words come from God.

But what he says should not turn right into wrong.

¹¹Honest scales and balances come from the LORD.
He made all of the weights in the bag.

¹²A king hates it when his people do what is wrong.
A ruler is made secure when they do what is right.

¹³Kings are pleased when what you say is honest.
They value people who speak the truth.

¹⁴An angry king can order your death.
But a wise man will try to calm him down.

¹⁵When a king's face is happy, it means life.
His favor is like rain in the spring.

¹⁶It is much better to get wisdom than gold.

Why can't I have all the things I want?

There are at least three reasons. First, you do not ask God for them. Second, you ask God but you want them only for yourself, so he says no. Third, they cost too much or are bad for you, so your parents say no. God wants you to love him, help others, give to his work and be content. Thinking about money gets in the way of all that. You cannot spend every day shopping from morning till night and also love God, help others, give to his work and be content. Sooner or later you have to stop *getting* and start *giving*.

checkout Proverbs 15:27

Related verses:
Proverbs 21:17;
James 4:1–3

JASON'S IMAGINATION

It is much better to choose
understanding than silver.

17 The path of honest people takes
them away from evil.
Those who guard their ways
guard their lives.

18 If you are proud, you will be
destroyed.
If you are proud, you will fall.

19 Suppose you are lowly in spirit
and are with those who are
beaten down.
That's better than sharing stolen
goods with those who are
proud.

20 If anyone pays attention to what
he is taught, he will succeed.
Blessed is the person who puts
his trust in the LORD.

21 Wise hearts are known for
understanding what is right.

Pleasant words make people
want to learn more.

22 Understanding is like a fountain of
life to those who have it.
But foolish people are punished
for the foolish things they do.

23 The hearts of wise people guide
their mouths.
Their words make people want
to learn more.

24 Pleasant words are like honey.
They are sweet to the spirit and
bring healing to the body.

25 There is a way that may seem right
to a man.
But in the end it leads to death.

26 The hunger of a worker makes him
work.
His hunger drives him on.

27 A worthless man plans to do evil
things.

Is it wrong to spread rumors?

A rumor is a story about someone that many people have heard but that no one can prove. Rumors almost always do much more harm than good. Do not just pass along a story about someone as soon as you hear it. First try to find out if it is true. If the story is true, you have two good choices: (1) You can forget the whole thing.

(2) You can talk to the person that the story is about and try to help him or her.

God wants us to be loving and kind to others. It is not loving or kind to pass along a story that might not be true or to pass along a true story if someone might get hurt.

checkout
Proverbs 16:28

Related verse:
Proverbs 20:19

His words are like a burning
fire.

28 A twisted person stirs up fights.
Anyone who talks about others
comes between close friends.

29 A man who wants to hurt others
tries to get them to sin.
He leads them down a path that
isn't good.

30 When he winks with his eyes,
he is planning to do
wrong.
When his lips are tightly closed,
he is up to no good.

31 Gray hair is a glorious crown.
You get it by living the right
way.

32 It is better to be patient than to
fight.
It is better to control your temper
than to take a city.

33 Lots are cast into the lap to make
decisions.
But everything they decide
comes from the LORD.

17

It is better to eat a dry
crust of bread in
peace and quiet
than to eat a big dinner in a
house that is full of fighting.

2 A wise servant will rule over a
shameful child.
He will be given part of the
property as if he were a family
member.

3 Fire tests silver. Heat tests gold.
But the LORD tests our hearts.

4 An evil person listens to evil
words.
A liar pays attention to words
that are harmful.

5 Anyone who laughs at those who
are poor makes fun of their
Maker.
Anyone who is happy when
others suffer will be punished.

6 Grandchildren are like a crown to
older people.
And children are proud of their
parents.

Is it OK to slam the door when you're mad?

No. God wants us to control our emotions, not to let them control us. Emotions are good. We need to understand what we are feeling. It is OK to be angry. But we should also think about why we are angry, talk about it and work at getting over the anger. We have to be careful about how we express our anger. It does not help to yell, scream, call people names, hit or slam doors. It can even hurt someone or something and make matters worse. People will be more likely to listen to our feelings if we can talk calmly. The Bible says that we can and should control our anger.

checkout
Proverbs 16:32

Related verses:
Proverbs 25:28;
James 1:19,20

⁷It isn't proper for foolish people to
    brag.
    And it certainly isn't proper for
      rulers to tell lies!

⁸Money buys favors for those who
    give it.
    No matter where they turn, they
      succeed.

⁹Those who erase a sin by forgiving
    it show love.
    But those who talk about it come
      between close friends.

¹⁰A person who understands what is
    right learns more from just a
    warning
    than a foolish person learns from
      100 strokes with a whip.

¹¹An evil person never wants to
    obey.
    An official who shows no mercy
      will be sent against him.

¹²It is better to meet a bear whose
    cubs have been stolen
    than to meet a foolish person
      who is acting foolishly.

¹³Evil will never leave the house
    of anyone who pays back evil for
      good.

¹⁴Starting to argue is like making a
    crack in a dam.
    So drop the matter before a fight
      breaks out.

¹⁵The LORD hates two things.
    He hates it when the guilty are
      set free.
    He also hates it when those who
      aren't guilty are punished.

¹⁶What good is money in the hands
    of a foolish person?
    He doesn't want to become wise.

¹⁷A friend loves at all times.
    He is there to help when trouble
      comes.

¹⁸A man who has little sense agrees
    to pay what other people owe.
    It isn't wise to put up money for
      others.

¹⁹The one who loves to argue loves
    to sin.
    The one who builds a high gate is
      just asking to be destroyed.

²⁰If your heart is twisted, you won't
    succeed.
    If your tongue tells lies, you will
      get into trouble.

²¹It is sad to have a foolish child.
    The parents of a foolish person
      have no joy.

²²A cheerful heart makes you
    healthy.
    But a broken spirit dries you up.

²³Anyone who does wrong accepts
    favors in secret.
    Then he turns what is right into
      wrong.

²⁴Anyone who understands what is
    right keeps wisdom in view.
    But the eyes of a foolish person
      look everywhere else.

²⁵A foolish child makes his father
    sad
    and his mother sorry.

²⁶It isn't good to punish those who
    aren't guilty.
    It isn't good to whip officials just
      because they are honest.

²⁷Anyone who has knowledge
    controls his words.
    A man who has understanding is
      not easily upset.

²⁸We think even a foolish person is
    wise if he keeps silent.
    We think he understands what is
      right if he controls his tongue.

18

A person who isn't friendly
looks out only for
himself.
He opposes all good sense.

²A foolish person doesn't want to
    understand.
    He takes delight in saying only
      what he thinks.

³People hate it when evil comes.
    And they refuse to honor those
      who bring shame.

⁴The words of a person's mouth are
    like deep water.
    But the fountain of wisdom is
      like a flowing stream.

⁵It isn't good to favor those who do
    wrong.

And it isn't good to hold back
   what is fair from those who
   aren't guilty.

⁶What a foolish person says leads to
   arguing.
   He is just asking for a beating.

⁷The words of a foolish person drag
   him down.
   He is trapped by what he says.

⁸The words of anyone who talks
   about others are like tasty
   bites of food.
   They go deep down inside you.

⁹Anyone who doesn't want to
   work
   is like someone who destroys.

¹⁰The name of the LORD is like a
   strong tower.
   Godly people run to it and are
   safe.

¹¹The wealth of rich people is like
   a city that makes them feel
   safe.
   They think of it as a city with
   walls that can't be climbed.

¹²If a man's heart is proud, he will be
   destroyed.
   So don't be proud if you want to
   be honored.

¹³To answer before listening
   is foolish and shameful.

¹⁴A man's cheerful heart gives him
   strength when he is sick.
   You can't keep going if you have a
   broken spirit.

¹⁵Those whose hearts understand
   what is right get knowledge.
   The ears of those who are wise
   listen for it.

¹⁶A gift opens the way for the one
   who gives it.
   It helps him meet important
   people.

¹⁷The first one to tell his case seems
   right.
   Then someone else comes
   forward and questions him.

¹⁸Casting lots will put a stop to
   arguing.

It will keep the strongest enemies
   apart.

¹⁹A broken friendship is harder to
   deal with than a city that has
   high walls around it.
   And arguing is like the locked
   gates of a mighty city.

²⁰A man can fill his stomach with
   what he says.
   The words from his lips can
   satisfy him.

²¹Your tongue has the power of life
   and death.
   Those who love to talk will eat
   the fruit of their words.

²²The one who finds a wife finds
   what is good.
   He receives favor from the
   LORD.

²³Poor people beg for mercy.
   But rich people answer in a
   mean way.

²⁴Even a man who has many
   companions can be
   destroyed.
   But there is a friend who sticks
   closer than a brother.

19

It is better to be poor and
   to live without
   blame
than to be foolish and to twist
   words around.

²It isn't good to get all stirred up
   without knowledge.
   And it isn't good to be in a hurry
   and miss the way.

³A man's own foolish acts destroy
   his life.
   But his heart is angry with the
   LORD.

⁴Wealth brings many friends.
   But the friends of poor people
   leave them alone.

⁵A dishonest witness will be
   punished.
   And those who pour out lies will
   not go free.

⁶Many try to win the favor of
   rulers.
   And everyone is the friend of a
   man who gives gifts.

⁷A poor person is avoided by his
   whole family.
   His friends avoid him even more.
   The poor person runs after them
      to beg.
   But he can't find them.

⁸Anyone who gets wisdom loves
   himself.
   Anyone who values
      understanding succeeds.

⁹A dishonest witness will be
   punished.
   And those who pour out lies will
      die.

¹⁰It isn't proper for a foolish person
   to live in great comfort.
   And it is much worse when a
      slave rules over princes!

¹¹A man's wisdom makes him
   patient.
   He will be honored if he forgives
      someone who sins against him.

¹²A king's anger is like a lion's roar.
   But his favor is like dew on the
      grass.

¹³If a child is foolish, he destroys his
   father.
   A nagging wife is like dripping
      that never stops.

¹⁴You will receive houses and wealth
   from your parents.
   But a wise wife is given by the
      LORD.

¹⁵Anyone who doesn't want to work
   sleeps his life away.
   And a person who refuses to
      work goes hungry.

¹⁶Those who obey what they are
   taught guard their lives.
   But those who don't care how
      they live will die.

¹⁷Anyone who is kind to poor people
   lends to the LORD.
   God will reward him for what he
      has done.

¹⁸Train your child. Then there is
   hope.
   Don't do anything to bring about
      his death.

¹⁹Anyone who burns with anger
   must pay for it.

If you save him, you will have to
   do it again.

²⁰Listen to advice and accept what
   you are taught.
   In the end you will be wise.

²¹A man may have many plans in his
   heart.
   But the LORD's purpose wins out
      in the end.

²²Every man longs for love that
   never fails.
   It is better to be poor than to be a
      liar.

²³Having respect for the LORD leads
   to life.
   Then you will be content and
      free from trouble.

²⁴A person who doesn't want to
   work leaves his hand in the
      dish.
   He won't even bring it back up to
      his mouth!

²⁵If you whip a person who makes
   fun of others,
   childish people will learn to be
      wise.
   If you warn someone who already
      understands what is right,
   he will gain even more
      knowledge.

²⁶A child who robs his father and
   drives out his mother
   brings shame and dishonor.

²⁷My son, if you stop listening to
   what I teach you,
   you will wander away from the
      words of knowledge.

²⁸A dishonest witness makes fun of
   what is right.
   The mouths of those who do
      wrong gulp down evil.

²⁹Those who make fun of others will
   be judged.
   Foolish people will be punished.

20 Wine causes you to make
   fun of others, and
   beer causes you to
      start fights.
   Anyone who is led down the
      wrong path by them is not
      wise.

² A king's anger is like a lion's roar.
  Anyone who makes him angry
    may lose his life.

³ Avoiding a fight brings honor to a
    man.
  But every foolish person is quick
    to argue.

⁴ Anyone who refuses to work
    doesn't plow in the right
    season.
  When he looks for a crop at
    harvest time, he doesn't find it.

⁵ The purposes of a man's heart are
    like deep water.
  But a man who has
    understanding brings them
    out.

⁶ Many claim to have love that
    never fails.
  But who can find a faithful man?

⁷ Anyone who does what is right
    lives without blame.

  Blessed are his children after
    him.

⁸ A king sits on his throne to judge.
  He gets rid of all evil when he
    sees it.

⁹ No one can say, "I have kept my
    heart pure.
  I'm clean. I haven't sinned."

¹⁰ The LORD hates two things.
  He hates weights that weigh
    things heavier or lighter than
    they really are.
  He also hates measures that
    measure things larger or
    smaller than they really are.

¹¹ A child is known by his
    actions.
  He is known by whether his
    conduct is pure and right.

¹² The LORD has made two things.
  He has made ears that hear.
  He has also made eyes that see.

Can you have more than one best friend?

Sure. God wants you to be loving and kind to everyone. You will probably know many kids who like you and want to be your friend if you are doing that. Friends are great, and it is fun to have a lot of them. You can have many good friends, and you do not have to put them in order of who is best. You might have one or two friends who are closer than all the others. But be careful about saying that one person is your *very best* friend. That may make the others feel bad. You do not *have* to have a favorite friend the way you have a favorite food.

checkout
Proverbs 19:22

Related verses:
Proverbs 17:17;
Galatians 6:10

¹³ Don't love sleep, or you will
      become poor.
   Stay awake, and you will have
      more food than you need.

¹⁴ "It's no good. It's no good!" says a
      buyer.
   Then off he goes and brags about
      what he bought.

¹⁵ There is gold. There are plenty of
      rubies.
   But lips that speak knowledge are
      a priceless jewel.

¹⁶ Take the coat of one who puts up
      money for what a stranger
      owes.
   Hold it until you get paid back if
      he does it for a
      woman who commits
      adultery.

¹⁷ Food gained by cheating tastes
      sweet to a man.
   But he will end up with a mouth
      full of sand.

¹⁸ Make plans by asking for
      guidance.
   If you go to war, get good advice.

¹⁹ A person who talks about others
      tells secrets.
   So avoid anyone who talks too
      much.

²⁰ If anyone calls down curses on his
      father or mother,
   his lamp will be blown out in
      total darkness.

²¹ Property you gain quickly at the
      beginning
   will not be blessed in the end.

²² Don't say, "I'll get even with you
      for the wrong you did to me!"
   Wait for the LORD, and he will
      save you.

²³ The LORD hates weights that weigh
      things heavier or lighter than
      they really are.
   Scales that are not honest don't
      please him.

Is it OK to use Canadian coins in American vending machines?

Many vending machines have signs that say, "No foreign coins." Money from other countries might get jammed in the machine. But even if the coins work, they may not be worth the same amount. If you put foreign coins into the machine you would cheat the owner of the machine. That would be wrong. In King Solomon's day, people did not have vending machines. But they would sometimes cheat by using scales that did not measure fairly. That too was wrong.

Do not look for ways to "save money" by being dishonest. Instead, be honest all the time and trust God. God owns everything. He can help you with the extra few cents you think you would gain from cheating the vending machine.

checkout
Proverbs 20:10,11

Related verses:
Proverbs 13:11;
Romans 13:1–7

24 The LORD directs a man's steps.
So how can anyone understand his own way?

25 A man is trapped if he makes a hasty promise to God
and only later thinks about what he said.

26 A wise king gets rid of evil people.
He runs the threshing wheel over them.

27 The lamp of the LORD searches a man's heart.
It searches deep down inside him.

28 Love and truth keep a king safe.
Faithful love makes his throne secure.

29 Young men are proud of their strength.
Gray hair brings honor to old men.

30 Blows and wounds wash evil away.
And beatings make you pure deep down inside.

21 The king's heart is in the hand of the LORD.
He directs it like a stream of water anywhere he pleases.

2 Everything a man does might seem right to him.
But the LORD knows what he is thinking.

3 Do what is right and fair.
The LORD accepts that more than sacrifices.

4 Proud eyes and a proud heart are the lamp of sinful people.
But those things are evil.

5 The plans of people who work hard succeed.
You can be sure that those in a hurry will become poor.

6 A fortune made by people who tell lies
amounts to nothing and leads to death.

Is it OK to keep secrets from your friends?

Most of the time it is all right to keep secrets. You do not have to tell *everything* you know to *everyone* who asks. Sometimes secrets can be fun, like with birthday presents. Sometimes secrets are important, because it is better for you not to give out certain information to just anyone. But you should *not* keep something a secret if it means that someone will get hurt or get in trouble. For example, a boy might say that he is going to beat up somebody, or a girl might say that she is going to steal something. Tell someone who can help if you hear a secret like that. Do not promise to keep a secret before you hear what it is.

checkout
Proverbs 20:19

Related verses:
Matthew 6:3–6

⁷The harmful things that evil
    people do will drag them
    away.
  They refuse to do what is right.

⁸The path of those who are guilty is
    crooked.
  But the conduct of those who are
    not guilty is honest.

⁹It is better to live on a corner of a
    roof
  than to share a house with a
    nagging wife.

¹⁰A sinful person longs to do evil.
  He doesn't show his neighbor
    any mercy.

¹¹When you punish someone who
    makes fun of others, childish
    people get wise.
  If you teach a person who is
    already wise, he will get even
    more knowledge.

¹²The Blameless One knows where
    sinners live.
  And he destroys them.

¹³If you refuse to listen to the cries
    of poor people,
  you too will cry out and not be
    answered.

¹⁴A secret gift calms anger down.
  A hidden favor softens great
    anger.

¹⁵When you do what is fair, you
    make godly people glad.
  But you terrify those who do
    what is evil.

¹⁶A man who leaves the path of
    understanding
  ends up with those who are dead.

¹⁷Anyone who loves pleasure will
    become poor.
  Anyone who loves wine and oil
    will never be rich.

KIDS' QUESTION

Why can't most parents afford a lot of things?

Usually it is because they have a limited amount of money to spend. A lot of that money has to go toward bills that *must* be paid. Your parents have to buy food, clothes, toothpaste and soap. They have to pay for the home in which you live. They have to pay for gas, electricity and other utilities. They have to pay taxes to the government. After all these bills, most parents have little left for other things.

That may sound unfair, but it is really wise planning. We should say no to some things so we can have enough for the things we need and want. God will provide for us if we do.

checkout
Proverbs 21:17

Related verses:
Matthew 6:33;
Hebrews 13:5

¹⁸ Those who do what is evil pay the
price for setting godly people
free.
Those who aren't faithful pay the
price for honest people.

¹⁹ It is better to live in a desert
than to live with a nagging, angry
wife.

²⁰ The best food and olive oil are
stored up in the houses of
wise people.
But a foolish man eats up
everything he has.

²¹ Anyone who wants to be godly and
loving
finds life, success and honor.

²² Those who are wise can attack a
strong city.
They can pull down the
place of safety its people
trust in.

²³ Anyone who is careful about what
he says
keeps himself out of trouble.

²⁴ A proud person is called a
"mocker."
He thinks much too highly of
himself.

²⁵ Some people will die while they
are still hungry.
That's because their hands refuse
to work.

²⁶ All day long they hunger for more.
But godly people give without
holding back.

²⁷ God hates sacrifices that are
brought by evil people.
He hates it even more when they
bring them for the wrong
reason.

²⁸ Witnesses who aren't honest
will die.

Why do people have to budget their money?

People should budget their money so they will have enough for all the bills they must pay. Everyone has big bills that will come due in the future. It is good to write them down as a reminder so you will not be surprised when the bills come. The budget tells you how much to set aside each week or month so that you will have the money to pay the bills when they come.

Every day brings opportunities to spend money. A budget helps you know whether you can afford to spend it.

You do not *have* to budget your money. You can just go and spend it. But that would be foolish because you would run out of money too soon. Then you would not have enough for the things you need, and you would never get to spend your money on the things you really want. Everyone should have a plan for how to spend his or her money.

Related verses:
Proverbs 22:3;
23:21

checkout
Proverbs 21:20

And anyone who listens to them
will be destroyed forever.

29 A sinful man tries to look as if he
were bold.
But an honest person thinks
about how he lives.

30 No wisdom, wise saying or plan
can succeed against the LORD.

31 You can prepare a horse for the
day of battle.
But the power to win comes from
the LORD.

22

You should want a good
name more than
you want great
riches.
To be highly respected is better
than having silver or gold.

2 The LORD made rich people and
poor people.
That's what they have in
common.

3 Wise people see danger and go to
a safe place.

But childish people keep going
and suffer for it.

4 Have respect for the LORD and
don't be proud.
That will bring you wealth and
honor and life.

5 Thorns and traps lie in the paths
of evil people.
But those who guard themselves
stay far away from them.

6 Train a child in the way he should
go.
When he is old, he will not turn
away from it.

7 Rich people rule over those who
are poor.
Borrowers are slaves to
lenders.

8 Anyone who plants evil gathers a
harvest of trouble.
His power to beat others down
will be destroyed.

9 Anyone who gives freely will be
blessed.

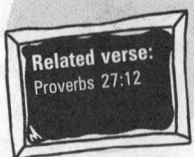

Why do sharks eat people?

Sharks attack people because they are meat-eaters. When they
are hungry, they will attack anything that looks good to eat. But
sharks don't go looking for people to attack. They just react to what comes
near them. The smart thing to do is to stay away from sharks. When you
go where you shouldn't go,
you get into trouble. You
can get hurt walking
through poison ivy or
playing in a thunder-
storm. Smart people
know this and stay out
of the way. There are
dangers in the world. Be
careful to avoid them.

checkout

Proverbs 22:3

Related verse:
Proverbs 27:12

That's because he shares his food with those who are poor.

¹⁰ If you drive away those who make fun of others, fighting also goes away.
Arguing and unkind words will stop.

¹¹ Have a pure and loving heart, and speak kindly.
Then you will be a friend of the king.

¹² The eyes of the LORD keep watch over knowledge.
But he does away with the words of those who aren't faithful.

¹³ People who don't want to work say, "There's a lion outside!"
Or they say, "I'll be murdered if I go out into the streets!"

¹⁴ The mouth of a woman who commits adultery is like a deep pit.
Any man the LORD is angry with will fall into it.

¹⁵ A child is going to do foolish things.
But correcting him will drive his foolishness far away from him.

¹⁶ One person may beat poor people down in order to get rich.
Another person may give gifts to rich people. Both of them will become poor.

SAYINGS OF THOSE WHO ARE WISE

¹⁷ Pay attention and listen to the sayings of those who are wise.
Apply your heart to the sayings I teach.

¹⁸ It is pleasing when you keep them in your heart.
Have all of them ready on your lips.

¹⁹ You are the one I am teaching today.
I want you to trust in the LORD.

²⁰ I have written 30 sayings for you.

How do credit cards work?

A credit card lets you borrow money from a bank whenever you want to buy something. The bank gives you the card and says you can borrow a certain amount of money.

Imagine that you want to buy a pair of jeans with a credit card. You hand the card to the sales clerk. The sales clerk then checks to make sure that you have permission to borrow that much money. If so, the *bank* pays for the item. The bank loans you the money. The store lets you take home what you wanted to buy.

A little while later, a bill for the amount you borrowed comes in the mail. If you do not pay the bill by the due date, the bank charges you interest. This is how most people get in trouble with credit cards. They borrow more than they can pay back. Then the credit card becomes like a trap. Wise people borrow only as much as they can afford to pay back.

checkout Proverbs 22:5

Related verses:
Luke 16:10–13

They will give you knowledge
and good advice.
²¹ I am teaching you words that are
completely true.
Then you can give the right
answers to the one who
sent you.

1.

²² Don't take advantage of poor
people just because they are
poor.
Don't beat down those who are
in need by taking them to
court.
²³ The LORD will stand up for them in
court.
He will take back the stolen
goods from those who have
robbed them.

2.

²⁴ Don't be a friend with anyone who
burns with anger.

Don't go around with a person
who gets angry easily.
²⁵ You might learn his habits.
And then you will be trapped by
them.

3.

²⁶ Don't agree to pay for
what someone else owes.
²⁷ Don't put up money for him.
If you don't have the money to
pay,
your bed will be taken right out
from under you!

4.

²⁸ Don't move old boundary stones
that your people set up long ago.

5.

²⁹ Do you see a man who does good
work?
He will serve kings.
He won't serve ordinary people.

Why are some children suspended from school?

Students learn best in safe places.
Weapons, illegal drugs, and fighting
have no place in schools. That's why
schools have rules against these
things. Those who break the rules
put themselves and others in
danger. When that happens,
principals may tell students that
they may not return to school.
That means they are 'suspended'
until they can follow the rules.
This helps them learn to cooperate.
It also helps keep schools safe
places for everyone to learn.

checkout Proverbs 22:10

DID YOU KNOW
THAT TOMMY
WAS SUSPENDED
FROM SCHOOL?

Related verses:
Proverbs 19:25;
21:11

23

6.

When you sit down to eat
  with a ruler,
look carefully at what's in
  front of you.
2 Put a knife to your throat
  if you like to eat too much.
3 Don't long for his fancy food.
  It can fool you.

7.

4 Don't wear yourself out to get rich.
  Be wise enough to say no.
5 When you take even a quick look
  at riches, they are gone.
They grow wings and fly away
  into the sky like an eagle.

8.

6 Don't eat the food of anyone who
  won't share it.
Don't long for his fancy food.
7 He is the kind of person
  who is always thinking about
  how much it costs.
"Eat and drink," he says to you.

But he doesn't mean it.
8 You will throw up what little you
  have eaten.
You will have wasted your words
  of praise.

9.

9 Don't speak to a foolish person.
  He will laugh at your wise
  words.

10.

10 Don't move old boundary stones.
  Don't try to take over the fields of
  children whose fathers have
  died.
11 The One who guards them is
  strong.
  He will stand up for them in
  court against you.

11.

12 Apply your heart to what you are
  taught.
Listen carefully to words of
  knowledge.

KIDS' QUESTION

Why do you have to do whatever your friends want or they get mad?

Your friends may get mad when you don't do something they want you to do. But that's not the way friendship should work. Sometimes a compromise is the way for everyone to be happy. Other times making everyone happy means taking turns doing what each friend wants. If friends always want things their way, or if they get angry when you don't always go along with them, talk with them about it. Friendship should be a good thing for everyone.

checkout
Proverbs 22:24,25

JASON, WHAT ARE YOU DOING? GET BACK IN THE GOAL!

-YAY!

JASON! GET BACK IN THE GOAL!

HOT DOGS

Related verses:
Ecclesiastes 7:9;
1 Corinthians
13:4–5

12.

¹³Don't hold back training from a
　　child.
　　If you correct him, he won't
　　　die.
¹⁴So correct him.
　　Then you will save him from
　　　death.

13.

¹⁵My child, if your heart is wise,
　　my heart will be glad.
¹⁶Deep down inside, I will be happy
　　when you say what is right.

14.

¹⁷Do not long for what sinners have.
　　But always show great respect for
　　the LORD.
¹⁸There really is hope for you
　　tomorrow.
　　So your hope will not be cut off.

15.

¹⁹My child, listen and be
　　wise.
　　Keep your heart on the right
　　　path.
²⁰Don't join those who drink too
　　much wine.
　　Don't join those who stuff
　　themselves with meat.
²¹Those who drink or eat too much
　　will become poor.
　　If they sleep too much, they'll
　　have to wear rags.

16.

²²Listen to your father, who gave
　　you life.
　　Don't hate your mother when she
　　is old.
²³Buy the truth. Don't sell it.
　　Get wisdom, training and
　　understanding.

Should I hang out with popular people to become popular?

This may seem like the way to be popular, but it probably won't last. It's OK to be friends with the popular kids, but it's not OK to do whatever they say to be accepted by them. Instead, be the kind of person who others will want to hang around with. Be confident that God loves you.

Remember that the Bible teaches us to think about the needs of others, not just our own. Spend some time with kids who aren't very popular and help them feel good about themselves. You'll be amazed at how good *you* will feel when you make others feel good.

checkout

Proverbs 23:19

BOOST YOUR POPULARITY! GET YOUR PICTURE TAKEN WITH MAX AND THE "CHILLY RAPPER"! ONLY $1 A PHOTO!

Related verses:
Psalm 119:5;
Proverbs 13:20;
1 John 3:18–19

²⁴The father of a godly child is very
happy.
Anyone who has a wise child is
glad.
²⁵May your father and mother be
glad.
May the woman who gave birth
to you be happy.

17.

²⁶My son, give me your heart.
Keep your eyes on the way I live.
²⁷A prostitute is like a deep pit.
A wife who commits adultery is
like a narrow well.
²⁸She hides and waits like a thief.
She causes many men to sin.

18.

²⁹Who has trouble? Who has sorrow?
Who argues? Who has problems?
Who has wounds for no reason?
Who has red eyes?

³⁰Those who spend too much time
with wine.
Or those who like to taste wine
that is mixed with spices.
³¹Don't look at wine when it is red.
Don't look at it when it bubbles
in the cup.
And don't look at it when it goes
down smoothly.
³²In the end it bites like a snake.
It bites like a poisonous serpent.
³³Your eyes will see strange sights.
Your mind will imagine weird
things.
³⁴You will feel like someone sleeping
on the ocean.
You will think you are lying
among the ropes in a boat.
³⁵"They hit me," you will say. "But
I'm not hurt!
They beat me. But I don't feel it!
When will I wake up
so I can find another drink?"

Why do parents dislike your friends just because they have green hair or something?

Parents want the best for their children. They know that friends have a big
influence. So when they see green hair, they may be surprised and not
know what to think. They know that having green hair may be one way
kids express themselves or get attention. But if your friends have
green hair to make their parents angry, then your parents might
worry that you might pick up that attitude.

Your mom and dad
probably won't assume
that you will want to
have green hair too, but
they may think you might
pick up a bad attitude. It's
not the clothes or hair that
your parents don't like—it's
what they think the clothes
mean to that person.

MY PARENTS WON'T
LET ME BRING MY
FRIENDS HOME, SO
CAN WE COME TO
YOUR HOUSE?

checkout
**Proverbs
23:24,25**

Related verse:
Romans 12:2

24

19.

Do not want what evil
men have.
Don't long to be with
them.
²In their hearts they plan to hurt
others.
With their lips they talk about
making trouble.

20.

³By wisdom a house is built.
Through understanding it is
made secure.
⁴Through knowledge its rooms are
filled
with priceless and beautiful
things.

21.

⁵A wise man has great power.
A man who has knowledge
increases his strength.
⁶If you go to war, you need
guidance.
If you want to win, you need
many good advisers.

22.

⁷Wisdom is too high for anyone
who is foolish.
He has nothing to say when
people meet at the city gate to
conduct business.

23.

⁸Anyone who thinks up sinful
things to do
will be known as one who plans
evil.
⁹Foolish plans are sinful.
People hate those who make fun
of others.

24.

¹⁰If you grow weak when trouble
comes,
your strength is very small!

25.

¹¹Save those who are being led away
to death.
Hold back those who are about
to be killed.
¹²Don't say, "But we didn't know
anything about this."

The One who knows what you
are thinking sees it.
The One who guards your life
knows it.
He will pay each person back for
what he has done.

26.

¹³Eat honey, my child. It is good.
Honey from a honeycomb has a
sweet taste.
¹⁴I want you to know that wisdom is
sweet to you.
If you find it, there is hope for
you tomorrow.
So your hope will not be cut off.

27.

¹⁵Don't hide and wait like a
burglar at a godly person's
house.
Don't rob his home.
¹⁶Even if godly people fall down
seven times, they always get
up.
But those who are evil are
brought down by trouble.

28.

¹⁷Don't be happy when your enemy
falls.
When he trips, don't let your
heart be glad.
¹⁸The LORD will see it, but he won't
be pleased.
He might turn his anger away
from your enemy.

29.

¹⁹Don't be upset because of evil
people.
Don't long for what sinners
have.
²⁰Tomorrow evil people won't have
any hope.
The lamps of sinners will be
blown out.

30.

²¹My son, have respect for the LORD
and the king.
Don't join those who disobey
them.
²²The LORD and the king will
suddenly destroy them.
Who knows what trouble those
two can bring?

MORE SAYINGS OF THOSE WHO ARE WISE

²³Here are more sayings of those who are wise.

Taking sides in court is not good.
²⁴ A curse will fall on those who say
        the guilty are not guilty.
    Nations will call down curses on
        them.
    People will speak against them.
²⁵But it will go well with those who
        sentence guilty people.
    Rich blessings will come to them.

²⁶An honest answer
    is like a kiss on the lips.

²⁷Finish your outdoor work.
    Get your fields ready.
    After that, build your house.

²⁸Don't give witness against your
        neighbor without any reason.
    Don't use your lips to tell lies.
²⁹Don't say, "I'll do to him what he
        did to me.
    I'll get even with that man for
        what he did."

³⁰I went past the field of someone
        who didn't want to work.
    I went past the vineyard of a man
        who didn't have any sense.
³¹Thorns had grown up everywhere.
    The ground was covered with
        weeds.
    The stone wall had fallen down.
³²I applied my heart to what I
        observed.
    I learned a lesson from what I
        saw.
³³You might sleep a little or take a
        little nap.
    You might even fold your hands
        and rest.
³⁴Then you would be poor, as if
        someone had robbed you.
    You would have little, as if
        someone had stolen
        from you.

MORE PROVERBS OF SOLOMON

25 These are more proverbs of Solomon. They were copied down by the men of Hezekiah, the king of Judah.

²When God hides a matter, he gets
        glory.
    When kings figure out a matter,
        they get glory.

³The heavens are high and the
        earth is deep.
    In the same way, the minds of
        kings are hard to figure out.

⁴Remove the scum from the silver.
    Then the master worker can
        make something.
⁵Remove sinful people from where
        the king is.
    When he does what is right, his
        kingdom will be secure.

⁶Don't brag in front of the king.
    Don't claim a place among great
        people.
⁷Let the king say to you, "Come up
        here."
    That's better than for him to
        shame you in front of nobles.

What you have seen with your own
        eyes
⁸ don't bring too quickly to court.
    What will you do in the end
        if your neighbor puts you to
        shame?

⁹If you talk about a matter with
        your neighbor,
    don't tell others what was said.
¹⁰If you do, someone might hear it
        and put you to shame.
    Then no one will ever respect
        you again.

¹¹The right word at the right time
    is like golden apples in silver
        jewelry.

¹²A wise person's warning to a
        listening ear
    is like a gold earring or jewelry
        made of fine gold.

¹³A messenger trusted by those who
        send him
    is like cool snow at harvest
        time.
    He renews the spirit of his
        masters.

¹⁴A man who brags about gifts he
        doesn't give
    is like wind and clouds that don't
        produce rain.

¹⁵If you are patient, you can win an
official over to your side.
And gentle words can break a
bone.

¹⁶If you find honey, eat just
enough.
If you eat too much of it, you will
throw up.
¹⁷Don't go to your neighbor's home
very often.
If he sees too much of you, he
will hate you.

¹⁸A man who gives false witness
against his neighbor
is like a club, a sword or a sharp
arrow.

¹⁹Trusting someone who is not
faithful when trouble
comes
is like a bad tooth or a disabled
foot.

²⁰You may sing songs to a troubled
heart.
But that's like taking a coat away
on a cold day.
It's like pouring vinegar on
baking soda.

²¹If your enemy is hungry, give him
food to eat.
If he is thirsty, give him water to
drink.
²²By doing those things, you will
pile up burning coals on his
head.
And the LORD will reward
you.

²³The north wind brings rain.
And a crafty tongue brings angry
looks.

²⁴It is better to live on a corner of a
roof
than to share a house with a
nagging wife.

²⁵Hearing good news from a land far
away
is like drinking cold water when
you are tired.

²⁶Sometimes a godly person gives in
to those who are evil.
Then he becomes like a muddy
spring of water or a polluted
well.

²⁷It isn't good for you to eat too
much honey.
And you shouldn't try to get
others to honor you.

²⁸A man who can't control himself
is like a city whose walls are
broken down.

26

It isn't proper to honor a
foolish person.
That's like having snow in
summer or rain at
harvest time.

²A curse given for no reason is like
a wandering bird or a flying
sparrow.
It doesn't go anywhere.

³A whip is for a horse. A harness is
for a donkey.
And a beating is for the backs of
foolish people.

⁴Don't answer a foolish person in
keeping with his foolish acts.
If you do, you will be like him
yourself.

⁵Answer a foolish person in
keeping with his foolish acts.
If you do, he won't be wise in his
own eyes.

⁶Sending a message in the hand of
a foolish person
is like cutting off your feet or
drinking something harmful.

⁷A proverb in the mouth of a
foolish person
is like disabled legs that are
useless.

⁸Giving honor to a foolish
person
is like tying a stone in a
slingshot.

⁹A proverb in the mouth of a
foolish person
is like a thorn in the hand of
someone who is drunk.

¹⁰Anyone who hires a foolish
person or someone who is
passing by
is like a person who shoots
arrows at just anybody.

¹¹A foolish person who does the
same foolish things again

is like a dog that returns to where
it has thrown up.

¹²Do you see a man who is wise in
his own eyes?
There is more hope for a foolish
person than for him.

¹³A person who doesn't want to
work says, "There's a lion in
the road!
There's an angry lion wandering
in the streets!"

¹⁴A person who doesn't want to
work turns over in bed
just like a door that swings back
and forth.

¹⁵A person who doesn't want to work
leaves his hand in the dish.
He acts as if he is too tired to
bring it back up to his mouth.

¹⁶A person who doesn't want to
work is wiser in his own eyes
than seven people who give
careful answers.

¹⁷Don't get mixed up in someone
else's fight as you are
passing by.

That's like picking a dog up by its
ears.

¹⁸Suppose a crazy person shoots
flaming arrows that can kill.

¹⁹A man who lies to his neighbor
and says, "I was only joking!" is
just like that person.

²⁰If you don't have wood, your fire
goes out.
If you don't talk about others,
arguing dies down.

²¹Coal glows. Wood burns.
And a man who argues stirs up
fights.

²²The words of anyone who talks
about others are like tasty
bites of food.
They go deep down inside you.

²³Warm words that come from an
evil heart
are like shiny paint on a clay pot.

²⁴Someone who wants to hurt you
uses his words to hide his
hatred.
But his heart is full of lies that
cover up his evil plans.

If my parents are arguing, is it OK to tell them to stop?

Sometimes parents disagree, and they need to talk it out. Even people who love each other very much will disagree from time to time. It is not wrong to disagree. It is not hateful to argue either. And it is not your job as a child to keep your parents from arguing. But you should always feel free to tell them how you feel. Tell them that you do not like it when they argue. But do not try to tell them what to do. Pray for your parents every day. Ask God to help them get along and to give them wisdom. Tell another adult who can help your mom and dad if the arguing leads to yelling, screaming and hitting.

checkout **Proverbs 26:17**

Related verse:
Philippians 4:2

²⁵What a person says can be charming. But don't believe him.
Seven things that God hates can fill that person's heart.

²⁶Hatred can be hidden by lies.
But what is evil will be shown to everyone.

²⁷If anyone digs a pit, he will fall into it.
If he rolls a big stone, it will roll back on him.

²⁸A tongue that tells lies hates the people it hurts.
And words that seem to praise you destroy you.

27

Don't brag about tomorrow.
You don't know what a day will bring.

²Let another person praise you, and not your own mouth.
Let someone else praise you, and not your own lips.

³Stones are heavy. Sand weighs a lot.
But letting a foolish person make you angry is a heavier load than both of them.

⁴Anger is mean. Great anger overpowers you.
But who can face jealousy?

⁵Being warned openly is better than being loved in secret.

⁶Wounds from a friend can be trusted.
But an enemy kisses you many times.

⁷When you are full, you even hate honey.
When you are hungry, even what is bitter tastes sweet.

⁸A man who wanders away from his home
is like a bird that wanders from its nest.

⁹Perfume and incense bring joy to your heart.

Is it OK to lie knowing you will tell the truth later?

Sometimes people lie when they are joking around. They make up a story so that someone will laugh. It is OK to joke and to kid around, but it is not OK to lie. Be careful not to make an excuse for lying. Sometimes people will cover up a lie with an excuse such as, "It was just a joke" or "I was going to tell the truth later." But that is a sure way to lose people's trust. After a while people do not know when you are telling the truth and when you are not. It is always best to tell the truth.

checkout
Proverbs 26:18, 19

Related verse:
Ephesians 4:25

And a friend is sweeter when he
gives you honest advice.

¹⁰Don't desert your friend or your
father's friend.
And don't go to your family when
trouble strikes you.
A neighbor nearby is better
than a family member far
away.

¹¹My child, be wise and bring joy to
my heart.
Then I can answer anyone who
makes fun of me.

¹²Wise people see danger and go to
a safe place.
But childish people keep on
going and suffer for it.

¹³Take the coat of one who puts up
money for what a stranger
owes.
Hold it until you get paid back if
he does it for a woman who
commits adultery.

¹⁴Suppose you loudly bless your
neighbor early in the
morning.
Then you might as well be calling
down a curse on him.

¹⁵A nagging wife is like
dripping that never stops on a
rainy day.

¹⁶Stopping her is like trying to stop
the wind.
It's like trying to grab oil with
your hand.

¹⁷As iron sharpens iron,
so one person sharpens another.

¹⁸A person who takes good care of a
fig tree will eat its fruit.
And a person who looks after his
master will be honored.

¹⁹When you look into water, you see
a likeness of your face.
When you look into your heart,
you see what you are really
like.

Should I tell the truth to someone even if they won't like it?

If telling the truth will help the person, you should tell the truth even if it hurts
at first. Imagine that a friend is starting to hang around with troublemakers.
You will tell your friend the truth about what he or she is doing if you really
are a good friend. Your friend may not like what you have to say. But it is
still the truth, and he or she needs to hear it. You do not have to be
cruel, though. You do not have to tell someone, "You have a long
nose" or "You don't play basketball very well" or "Your house sure
needs to be painted" or "Your clothes are old and worn out."
Sometimes kindness means
that you keep your
thoughts to yourself.

checkout
Proverbs 27:6

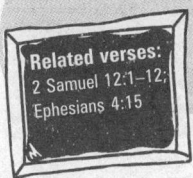

Related verses:
2 Samuel 12:1–12;
Ephesians 4:15

²⁰ Death and the Grave are never
satisfied.
A man's eyes are never satisfied
either.

²¹ Fire tests silver. Heat tests gold.
But a man is tested by the praise
he receives.

²² You can grind a foolish person in a
mill.
You can grind him as you would
grind grain with a tool.
But you can't remove his
foolishness from him.

²³ Be sure you know how your flocks
are doing.
Pay careful attention to your
herds.

²⁴ Riches don't last forever.
And a crown is not secure for all
time to come.

²⁵ The hay is removed, and new
growth appears.
The grass from the hills is
gathered in.

²⁶ Then your lambs will provide you
with clothes.

And the money from selling your
goats will buy you a field.

²⁷ You will have plenty of goats' milk.
It will feed you and your family.
It will also feed your female
servants.

28 Sinners run away even
when no one is
chasing them.
But those who do what is right
are as bold as lions.

² A country has many rulers when
its people don't obey.
But an understanding king
knows how to keep order.

³ A ruler who beats poor people
down
is like a pounding rain that
leaves no crops.

⁴ Those who turn away from the law
praise sinners.
But those who obey the law
oppose them.

⁵ Sinful men don't understand what
is fair.

What is budgeting?

A budget is a plan for your money. It is a good idea to have a
budget no matter how much money you have. For example, let's
say you have $10. You could plan to give $1 to church and put $2 in your
savings account. You might also decide to set aside $4 for a church
camping trip. The final $3 you
could spend.

The Israelites were told to
pay careful attention to their
herds. Their animals were like
money to them. We should
pay careful attention to our
spending too.

checkout
Proverbs 27:23

Related verses:
Proverbs 21:20;
22:3

But those who worship the LORD
understand it completely.

6 It is better to be poor and live
without blame
than to be rich and follow a
crooked path.

7 A child who obeys the law
understands what is right.
But a child who likes to eat too
much brings shame on his
father.

8 A person who increases his wealth
by charging high interest
piles it up for someone who will
be kind to poor people.

9 If you don't pay attention to the
law,
even your prayers are hated.

10 Those who lead honest people
down an evil path
will fall into their own trap.
But those who are without
blame
will receive good things.

11 Rich people may be wise in their
own eyes.
But a poor person who
understands what is right
knows what they are really
like.

12 When godly people win, everyone
is very happy.
But when sinners take charge,
everyone hides.

13 Anyone who hides his sins doesn't
succeed.
But anyone who admits his sins
and gives them up finds mercy.

14 Blessed is the one who always has
respect for the LORD.
But anyone who is stubborn will
get into trouble.

15 An evil person who rules over
helpless people
is like a roaring lion or an angry
bear.

16 A ruler who is mean to his people
doesn't have any sense.
But anyone who hates money
gained in the wrong way will
enjoy a long life.

17 A man who is troubled because he
is guilty of murder
will be on the run until the day
he dies.
No one should give him any
help.

18 Anyone who lives without blame is
kept safe.
But anyone whose path is
crooked will suddenly fall.

19 Anyone who farms his land will
have plenty of food.
But anyone who chases dreams
will be very poor.

20 A faithful man will be richly
blessed.
But anyone who wants to get rich
will be punished.

21 Favoring one person over another
is not good.
But some men will do wrong for
a piece of bread.

22 A man who won't share what he
has wants to get rich.
He doesn't know he is going to be
poor.

23 It is better to warn a man than to
pretend to praise him.
In the end he will be more
pleased with you.

24 Anyone who steals from his
parents and says, "It's not
wrong,"
is just like a man who destroys.

25 A person who always wants more
stirs up fights.
But anyone who trusts in the
LORD will succeed.

26 Anyone who trusts in himself is
foolish.
But a person who lives wisely is
kept safe.

27 Those who give to poor people
will have everything they need.
But those who close their eyes to
the poor
will be under many curses.

28 When those who are evil take
charge, other people hide.
But when those who are evil die,
godly people grow stronger.

29

A man who still won't obey after being warned many times will suddenly be destroyed. Nothing can save him.

2 When those who do right grow stronger, the people are glad.
But when those who do wrong become rulers, the people groan.

3 A man who loves wisdom makes his father glad.
But a man who spends time with prostitutes wastes his father's wealth.

4 By doing what is fair, a king makes a country secure.
But the one who wants to be paid off tears it down.

5 A man who only pretends to praise his neighbor
is spreading a net to catch him by the feet.

6 A sinful man is trapped by his own sin.
But a godly person can sing and be glad.

7 Those who do what is right want to treat poor people fairly.
But those who do what is wrong don't care about the poor.

8 Those who make fun of others stir up a city.
But wise people turn anger away.

9 Suppose a wise man goes to court with a foolish person.
Then the foolish person gets mad and pokes fun. And there is no peace.

10 Murderers hate honest people. They try to kill those who do what is right.

11 A foolish person lets his anger run wild.
But a wise person keeps himself under control.

Why doesn't the government just print more money in factories and give it to the poor?

Some governments have tried to print money and just give it to the poor. It did not work because very soon the money was worth very little.

Money is not just printed paper. It gets its value from something else. In our country, money gets its value from all the goods and services that people make. Each dollar means that someone somewhere did one dollar's worth of work. The more work we all do, the more money we have. The less work we do, the less money we have.

The best way to get more money to poor people is to help them get jobs. That way, they get paid while they also create more goods and services.

checkout
Proverbs 28:19

Related verses:
Proverbs 20:21;
28:22

¹²If rulers listen to lies,
 all their officials become evil.

¹³The LORD gives sight to the eyes of
 poor people and those who
 beat others down.
 That's what they both have in
 common.

¹⁴If a king judges poor people fairly,
 his throne will always be secure.

¹⁵If a child is corrected, he becomes
 wise.
 But a child left to himself brings
 shame to his mother.

¹⁶When those who do wrong grow
 stronger, so does sin.
 But those who do right will see
 them destroyed.

¹⁷If you train your children, they will
 give you peace.
 They will bring delight to you.

¹⁸Where there is no message from
 God, the people don't control
 themselves.
 But blessed are those who obey
 the law.

¹⁹A servant can't be corrected only
 by words.
 Even if he understands, he won't
 obey.

²⁰Have you seen a man who speaks
 without thinking?
 There is more hope for foolish
 people than for him.

²¹If you spoil your servant while he
 is young,
 he will bring you sorrow later
 on.

²²An angry man stirs up fights.
 And a person who burns with
 anger commits many sins.

Why do people play the lottery if they probably won't win?

People gamble and play the lottery because they *hope* to win. They think that having a lot of money will solve all their problems. After all, the cost of one lottery ticket is very low. People figure they aren't losing much.

Jesus warned us against loving money. Many people who win millions in lotteries end up worse off than they were before. They spend everything and have more problems than ever. That is because people cannot solve their money problems by having lots of it. We need to be content with what God has given us and spend it wisely.

checkout
Proverbs 28:20

Related verses:
Matthew 6:24;
Luke 12:21

²³ If a man is proud, he will be made
low.
But if he isn't proud, he will be
honored.

²⁴ Anyone who helps a thief is his
own enemy.
When he is put under oath, he
doesn't dare give witness.

²⁵ If you are afraid of people, it will
trap you.
But if you trust in the LORD, he
will keep you safe.

²⁶ Many people want to meet a ruler.
But only the LORD sees that
people are treated fairly.

²⁷ Those who do what is right hate
dishonest people.
Those who do what is wrong
hate honest people.

THE SAYINGS OF AGUR

30 These sayings are the
words of Agur, son of Ja-
keh. He spoke them as if
they came from God.

He spoke them to Ithiel
and to Ucal.

² He said, "I know less than anyone.
I don't understand as other men do.
³ I haven't learned wisdom.
And I don't know the Holy One.
⁴ Who has gone up to heaven and
come down?
Who has gathered up the wind in
the palms of his hands?
Who has wrapped up the waters in
his coat?
Who has set all the boundaries of
the earth in place?
What is his name? What is his son's
name?
Tell me if you know!

⁵ "Every word of God is perfect.
He is like a shield to those who
trust in him.
He keeps them safe.
⁶ Don't add to his words.
If you do, he will correct you.
He will prove that you are a liar.

⁷ "LORD, I ask you for two things.

What does the government do with all the taxes we pay?

The national government collects taxes to pay for highways, bridges, courtrooms, judges, soldiers, assistance for the poor, national parks and things like that. Local governments collect taxes to pay for police protection, libraries, public health, fire protection, schools and things like that. The government uses money from taxes to provide things that the citizens need and want.

checkout Proverbs 29:4

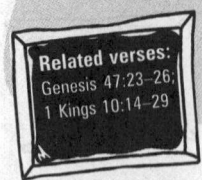

Related verses:
Genesis 47:23–26;
1 Kings 10:14–29

Don't refuse me before I die.

[8] Keep lies far away from me.
Don't make me either poor or
rich,
but give me only the bread I need
each day.

[9] If you don't, I might have too
much.
Then I might say I don't know
you.
I might say, 'Who is the LORD?'
Or I might become poor and steal.
Then I would bring shame to the
name of my God.

[10] "Don't tell lies about a servant
when you talk to his master.
If you do, he will call down
curses on you. And you will
pay for it.

[11] "Some people call down curses on
their fathers.
Others don't bless their mothers.

[12] Some are pure in their own
eyes.
But their dirty sins haven't been
washed away.

[13] Some have eyes that are very
proud.

They look down on others.

[14] Some people have teeth like
swords.
The teeth in their jaws are as
sharp as knives.
They are ready to eat up the poor
people of the earth.
They are ready to eat up those
who are the most needy.

[15] "A bloodsucking worm has two
daughters.
They cry out, 'Give! Give!'

"Three things are never satisfied.
Four things never say, 'Enough!'

[16] The first is the grave.
The second is a woman who can't
have a baby.
The third is land. It never gets
enough water.
And the fourth is fire. It never
says, 'Enough!'

[17] "Some make fun of their fathers.
Others laugh about obeying their
mothers.
The ravens of the valley will peck
their eyes out.
Then the vultures will eat them.

KIDS' QUESTION

What if I told a lie and didn't know it was a lie? Is it still a lie?

To pass on information that you *think* is true is not lying. But people do make mistakes. That is why it is so important to check out the facts before you tell something to others. Suppose you heard from a friend that the school concert would begin at 8:00 P.M. It would be good to find out for sure before telling your parents about the concert. Just think how they would feel if they showed up and found out it had started a half hour earlier. It is better for everybody if people know that they can rely on what you say.

checkout Proverbs 29:20

wrongfully accused
unjustly punished
FREE Jason!

Related verses:
Proverbs 17:28;
18:21

18 "Three things are too amazing
   for me.
   There are four things I don't
   understand.
19 The first is the way of an eagle in
   the sky.
   The second is the way of a snake
   on a rock.
   The third is the way of a ship on
   the ocean.
   And the fourth is the way of a
   man with a young woman.

20 "This is the way of a woman who
   commits adultery.
   She eats. She wipes her
   mouth.
   Then she says, 'I haven't done
   anything wrong.'

21 "Under three things the earth
   shakes.
   Under four things it can't
   stand up.
22 The first is a servant who becomes
   a king.
   The second is a foolish person
   who is full of food.

23 The third is a woman who is
   married but not loved by her
   husband.
   And the fourth is a woman
   servant who takes the
   place of the woman she works for.

24 "Four things on earth are small.
   But they are very wise.
25 The first are ants. They aren't very
   strong.
   But they store up their food in
   the summer.
26 The second are rock badgers. They
   aren't very powerful.
   But they make their home
   among the rocks.
27 The third are locusts. They don't
   have a king.
   But they all march forward in
   ranks.
28 And the fourth are lizards. Your
   hand can catch them.
   But you will find them in kings'
   palaces.

29 "Three things walk as if they were
   kings.

Is it stealing if a poor person takes food?

Yes. No matter what a person steals or why he or she steals it, it is stealing. The Bible says a lot about poor people. God told the nation of Israel to help the poor. Hungry people were allowed to gather leftover grain from the fields. But the poor were never told that they were allowed to steal food. There are many poor and hungry people in the world today, too. We should do whatever we can to help them so that they will not be tempted to steal food.

PRE-KINGDOM
FOOD STORE

COOKIES

checkout
Proverbs 30:7–9

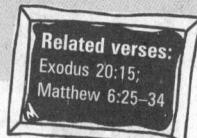

Related verses:
Exodus 20:15;
Matthew 6:25–34

Four things move as kings do.
³⁰ The first is a lion. It is mighty
among the animals.
It doesn't back away from
anything.
³¹ The second is a rooster that walks
proudly.
The third is a billy goat.
And the fourth is a king who has
his army around him.

³² "Have you been foolish?
Have you thought you were
better than others?
Have you planned evil?
If you have, put your hand over
your mouth and stop
talking!
³³ If you churn cream, you will
produce butter.
If you twist a nose, you will
produce blood.
And if you stir up anger, you will
produce a fight."

THE SAYINGS OF KING LEMUEL

31 These are the sayings of King Lemuel. His mother taught them to him. She spoke them as if they came from God.

² She said, "My son! My very own
son!
The son I prayed for!
³ Don't waste your strength on
women.
Don't waste it on those who
destroy kings.

⁴ "Lemuel, it isn't good for kings to
drink wine.
It isn't good for rulers to long for
beer.
⁵ If they do, they might drink and
forget what the law
commands.
They might take away the rights
of all those who are beaten
down.
⁶ Give beer to those who are dying.
Give wine to those who are sad
and troubled.
⁷ Let them drink and forget how
poor they are.
Let them forget their suffering.

⁸ "Speak up for those who can't
speak for themselves.

Speak up for the rights of all
those who are poor.
⁹ Speak up and judge fairly.
Speak up for the rights of those
who are poor and needy."

THE NOBLE WIFE

¹⁰ Who can find a noble wife?
She is worth far more than
rubies.
¹¹ Her husband trusts her
completely.
She gives him all the important
things he needs.
¹² She brings him good, not harm,
all the days of her life.
¹³ She chooses wool and flax.
She loves to work with her
hands.
¹⁴ She is like the ships of traders.
She brings her food from far
away.
¹⁵ She gets up while it is still dark.
She provides food for her
family.
She also gives some to her
female servants.
¹⁶ She considers a field and buys it.
She uses some of the money she
earns to plant a vineyard.
¹⁷ She gets ready to work hard.
Her arms are strong.
¹⁸ She sees that her trading earns a
lot of money.
Her lamp doesn't go out at night.
¹⁹ With one hand she holds the
wool.
With the other she spins the
thread.
²⁰ She opens her arms to those who
are poor.
She reaches out her hands to
those who are needy.
²¹ When it snows, she's not afraid for
her family.
All of them are dressed in the
finest clothes.
²² She makes her own bed coverings.
She is dressed in fine linen and
purple clothes.
²³ Her husband is respected at the
city gate.
There he takes his seat among
the elders of the land.
²⁴ She makes linen clothes and sells
them.
She supplies belts to the traders.

²⁵ She puts on strength and honor as
     if they were her clothes.
  She can laugh at the days that are
     coming.
²⁶ She speaks wisely.
  She teaches faithfully.
²⁷ She watches over family matters.
  She is busy all the time.
²⁸ Her children stand up and call her
     blessed.
  Her husband also rises up, and
     he praises her.

²⁹ He says, "Many women do noble
     things.
  But you are better than all the
     others."
³⁰ Charm can fool you. Beauty fades.
  But a woman who has respect for
     the LORD should be praised.
³¹ Give her the reward she has
     earned.
  Let everything she has done
     bring praise to her at the city
     gate.

I Wonder . . .

How can I make my faith stronger?

Real Life Challenge

When you're having a bad day, it helps to have a friend offer a
listening ear. The people you hang out with can have a big influence
on you—and on your faith. It's important to make sure you have
people in your life who will cheer you on as you walk through
each day.

Quest Clue

Look at Proverbs 3 to see how important it is to God that
you make friends with people who can encourage you.
Check Romans 1 to see what Paul thought about the
role of friends in our lives. Then find 1 Thessalonians 1 to see what a community of faithful friends
should look like.

Ecclesiastes

Who wrote this book?
This book was probably written by Solomon.

Why was this book written?
Ecclesiastes shows that no one can have a happy life without God.

For whom was this book written?
Ecclesiastes was written for anyone who thinks that God is not important.

What do we learn about God in this book?
God is more important than money, pleasure, work or anything else in life.

When was this book written?
If Solomon wrote Ecclesiastes, it was written sometime during the tenth century B.C. If it was written by someone else, the date is unknown.

What are some important passages in this book?
Pleasure can't make people happy. Ecclesiastes 2:1–11
Success can't make people happy. Ecclesiastes 2:17–26

NOTHING HAS ANY MEANING

1 These are the words of the Teacher. He was the son of David. He was also king in Jerusalem.

2 "Meaningless! Everything is meaningless!"
says the Teacher.
"Everything is completely meaningless!
Nothing has any meaning."

3 What does a man get for all of his work?
Why does he work so hard on this earth?

⁴People come and people go.
　But the earth remains forever.
⁵The sun rises. Then it sets.
　And then it hurries back to where
　　it rises.
⁶The wind blows to the south.
　Then it turns to the north.
　Around and around it goes.
　It always returns to where it
　　started.
⁷Every stream flows into the ocean.
　But the ocean never gets full.
　The streams return
　　to the place they came from.
⁸All things are tiresome.
　They are more tiresome than
　　anyone can say.
　But our eyes never see enough of
　　anything.
　Our ears never hear enough.
⁹Everything that has ever been will
　　come back again.
　Everything that has ever been
　　done will be done again.
　Nothing is new on earth.
¹⁰There isn't anything about which
　　someone can say,
　"Look! Here's something new."
　It was already here long ago.
　It was here before we were.
¹¹No one remembers the men of
　　long ago.
　Even those who haven't been
　　born yet
　won't be remembered
　　by those who will be born after
　　them.

WISDOM DOESN'T HAVE ANY MEANING

¹²I, the Teacher, was king over Israel in Jerusalem. ¹³I spent all of my time studying. I used my wisdom to check everything out. I looked into everything that is done on earth. What a heavy load God has put on men!

¹⁴I've seen what is done on this earth. It doesn't have any meaning. It's like chasing the wind.

¹⁵People can't straighten things that
　　are twisted.
　They can't count things that don't
　　even exist.

¹⁶I said to myself, "Look, my wisdom has really been growing. In fact, I'm now wiser than anyone who ruled over Jerusalem in the past. I have a lot of wisdom and knowledge."

¹⁷Then I used my mind to understand what it really means to be wise. And I wanted to know what foolish pleasure is all about. But I found out that that's also like chasing the wind.

¹⁸A lot of human wisdom leads to a
　　lot of sorrow.
　More knowledge only brings
　　more sadness.

PLEASURE DOESN'T HAVE ANY MEANING

2 I said to myself, "Come on. I'll put pleasure to the test. I want to find out what is good." But that also proved to be meaningless.

²"Laughter is foolish," I said. "And what can pleasure do for me?" ³I tried cheering myself up by drinking wine. I even tried living in a foolish way. But wisdom was still guiding my mind. I wanted to see what was really important for men to do on earth during the few days of their lives.

⁴So I started some large projects. I built houses for myself. I planted vineyards. ⁵I made gardens and parks. I planted all kinds of fruit trees in them. ⁶I made lakes to water groves of healthy trees.

⁷I bought male and female slaves. And I had other slaves who were born in my house. I also owned more herds and flocks than anyone in Jerusalem ever had before. ⁸I stored up silver and gold for myself. I gathered up the treasures of kings and their kingdoms. I got some male and female singers. I also got many women for myself. Women delight the hearts of men.

⁹I became far more important than anyone in Jerusalem had ever been before. And in spite of everything, I didn't lose my wisdom.

¹⁰I gave myself everything my eyes
　　wanted.
　There wasn't any pleasure that I
　　refused to give myself.
　I took delight in everything I did.
　And that was what I got for all of
　　my work.
¹¹But then I looked over everything
　　my hands had done.

I saw what I had worked so hard
   to get.
And nothing had any meaning.
It was like chasing the wind.
Nothing was gained on this
   earth.

WISDOM AND FOOLISH PLEASURE DON'T HAVE ANY MEANING

¹²I decided to think about wisdom.
   I also thought about foolish
      pleasure.
What more can a new king do?
   Can he do anything more than
      others have already done?
¹³I saw that wisdom is better than
      foolishness,
   just as light is better than
      darkness.
¹⁴The eyes of a wise man see things
      clearly.
   A person who is foolish lives in
      darkness.
But I finally realized that death
      catches up
   with both of them.

¹⁵Then I thought,

"What happens to a foolish
      person will catch up with me
      too.
   So what do I gain by being wise?"
I said to myself,
   "That doesn't have any meaning
      either."
¹⁶Like a foolish person, a wise man
      won't be remembered very
      long.
   In days to come, both of them
      will be forgotten.
Like a person who is foolish,
   a wise man must die too!

WORK DOESN'T HAVE ANY MEANING

¹⁷So I hated life. That's because the
work that is done on this earth made
me sad. None of it has any meaning.
It's like chasing the wind.
¹⁸I hated everything I had worked
for on earth. I'll have to leave all of it to
someone who lives after me. ¹⁹And who
knows whether he will be wise or foolish? Either way, he'll take over everything on earth I've worked so hard for.
That doesn't have any meaning either.

²⁰So I began to lose hope because of
all of my hard work on this earth. ²¹A
man might use wisdom, knowledge
and skill to do his work. But then he
has to leave everything he owns to
someone who hasn't worked for it.
That doesn't have any meaning either.
In fact, it isn't fair.
²²What does a man get for all of his
hard work on earth? What does he get
for all of his worries? ²³As long as he
lives, his work is nothing but pain and
sorrow. Even at night his mind can't rest.
That doesn't have any meaning either.
²⁴A man can't do anything better
than eat and drink and be satisfied
with his work. I'm finally seeing that
those things also come from the hand
of God. ²⁵Without his help, who can
eat or find pleasure?
²⁶God gives wisdom, knowledge and
happiness to a man who pleases him.
But to a sinner he gives the task of
gathering and storing up wealth. Then
the sinner must hand it over to the one
who pleases God. That doesn't have
any meaning either. It's like chasing
the wind.

THERE IS A TIME FOR EVERYTHING

3 There is a time for everything.
There's a time for everything
      that is done on earth.

²There is a time to be born.
   And there's a time to die.
There is a time to plant.
   And there's a time to pull up
      what is planted.
³There is a time to kill.
   And there's a time to heal.
There is a time to tear down.
   And there's a time to build up.
⁴There is a time to cry.
   And there's a time to laugh.
There is a time to be sad.
   And there's a time to dance.
⁵There is a time to scatter stones.
   And there's a time to gather
      them.
There is a time to hug.
   And there's a time not to hug.
⁶There is a time to search.
   And there's a time to stop
      searching.
There is a time to keep.

And there's a time to throw away.
⁷There is a time to tear.
    And there's a time to mend.
    There is a time to be silent.
    And there's a time to speak.
⁸There is a time to love.
    And there's a time to hate.
    There is a time for war.
    And there's a time for peace.

⁹What does the worker get for his hard work? ¹⁰I've seen the heavy load God has put on men. ¹¹He has made everything beautiful in its time. He has also given men a sense of what he's been doing down through the ages. But they can't completely figure out what he's done from the beginning to the end.

¹²They should be happy and do good while they live. I know there's nothing better for them to do than that. ¹³Everyone should eat and drink. People should be satisfied with all of their hard work. That is God's gift to them.

¹⁴I know that everything God does will last forever. Nothing can be added to it. And nothing can be taken from it.

God does that so men will have respect for him.

¹⁵Everything that now exists has
    already been.
    And what is coming has existed
        before.
    God will judge those who treat
        others badly.

¹⁶Here's something else I saw on earth.

    Where people should be treated
        right,
        they are treated wrong.
    Where people should be treated
        fairly,
        they are treated unfairly.

¹⁷I said to myself,

    "God will judge
        godly and sinful people alike.
    He has a time for every act.
        He has a time for everything that
            is done."

¹⁸I also thought, "God puts human beings to the test. Then they can see they are just like animals. ¹⁹What hap-

Why do some people die before they are old?

Death entered the world when Adam and Eve first sinned. Ever since then, pain and death have been part of life. Everything that is alive in our world has to die. Plants die. Animals die. People die. Death can come from automobile accidents, sickness, old age and many other causes. And life is short no matter how long a person lives. Just ask someone who is 60 or 70 or 80. Remember that because life is short, we should make the most of every day we are alive. Each breath is a gift from God. But also remember that this life on earth is not all there is. After we die we can live forever with God.

checkout Ecclesiastes 3:1,2

Related verses:
2 Corinthians 5:6;
Philippians
1:23,24

pens to animals happens to people too. Death waits for people and animals alike. People die, just as animals do. All of them have the same breath. People don't have any advantage over animals. Nothing has any meaning.

[20]"People and animals go to the same place. All of them come from dust. And all of them return to dust. [21]Who can know whether the spirit of a man goes up? Who can tell whether the spirit of an animal goes down into the earth?"

[22]So man should enjoy his work. That's what God made him for. I saw that there's nothing better for him to do than that. After all, who can show him what will happen after he is gone?

SUFFERING, HARD WORK AND FRIENDSHIP

4 I looked and saw how much people were suffering on this earth.

I saw the tears of those who are
　suffering.
　They don't have anyone to
　　comfort them.
Power is on the side of those who
　beat them down.
　Those who are suffering don't
　　have anyone to comfort
　　them.
[2]Then I announced that those
　who have already died
are happier than those
　who are still alive.
[3]But someone who hasn't been
　born yet
　is better off than the dead or the
　　living.
　That's because he hasn't seen the
　　evil things
　　that are done on earth.

[4]I also saw that man works hard and accomplishes a lot. But he does it only because he wants what his neighbor has. That doesn't have any meaning either. It's like chasing the wind.

[5]A foolish person folds his hands
　and doesn't work.
　And that destroys him.
[6]One handful with peace and
　quiet

is better than two handfuls with
　hard work.
　Working too hard is like chasing
　　the wind.

[7]Again I saw something on earth that didn't mean anything.

[8]A man lived all by himself.
　He didn't have any sons or
　　brothers.
　His hard work never ended.
　But he wasn't happy with what
　　he had.
　"Who am I working so hard for?"
　　he asked.
　"Why don't I get the things I
　　enjoy?"
　That doesn't have any meaning
　　either.
　In fact, it's a very bad deal!

[9]Two people are better than one.
　They can help each other in
　　everything they do.
[10]Suppose someone falls down.
　Then his friend can help him up.
　But suppose the man who falls
　　down doesn't have anyone to
　　help him up.
　Then feel sorry for him!
[11]Or suppose two people lie down
　　together.
　Then they'll keep warm.
　But how can one person keep
　　warm alone?
[12]One person could be
　　overpowered.
　But two people can stand up for
　　themselves.
　And a rope made out of three
　　cords isn't easily broken.

GETTING AHEAD DOESN'T HAVE ANY MEANING

[13]A poor but wise young man is better off than an old but foolish king. That king doesn't pay attention to a warning anymore. [14]The young man might have come from prison to become king. Or he might have been born poor within the kingdom but still became king. [15]I saw that everyone was following the young man who had become the new king.

[16]At first, all of the people served him when he became king. But those who came later weren't pleased with

the way he was ruling. That doesn't have any meaning either. It's like chasing the wind.

HAVE RESPECT FOR GOD

5 Be careful what you say when you go to God's house. Go there to listen. Don't be like foolish people when you offer your sacrifice. They do what is wrong and don't even know it.

² Don't be too quick to speak.
   Don't be in a hurry to say
      anything to God.
   He is in heaven. You are on earth.
   So use only a few words when
      you speak.
³ Dreams come to people when they
      worry a lot.
   When foolish people talk, they
      use too many words.

⁴When you make a promise to God, don't wait too long to carry it out. He isn't pleased with foolish people. So do what you have promised. ⁵It is better to make no promise at all than to make a promise and not keep it.

⁶Don't let your mouth cause you to sin. Don't object to the temple messenger. Don't say, "My promise was a mistake." Why should God be angry with what you say? Why should he destroy what you have done? ⁷Dreaming too much and talking too much are meaningless. So have respect for God.

RICHES DON'T HAVE ANY MEANING

⁸Suppose you see poor people being mistreated somewhere. And what is being done to them isn't right or fair. Don't be surprised by that. One official is watched by a higher one. Others who are even higher are watching both of them. ⁹All of them take what the land produces. And the king himself takes his share from the fields.

Is it OK if we pray really fast or slow?

The speed of a prayer is not important. What matters is that we mean what we pray. Sometimes we pray fast because we are excited. That is fine. But people who pray *very* fast may just be repeating a memorized prayer or saying certain words out of habit and trying to finish quickly. Whenever we pray, God is listening right then, and he does not want us to just speed through some words we always say.

Sometimes we pray slowly because we are really thinking about what we want to tell God. Other times we pray slowly because we are letting our thoughts wander. It is always best to keep our attention on God. Fast, medium or slow, prayer should be a real talk with God.

checkout
**Ecclesiastes
5:1,2**

Related verses:
1 Kings 8:54–55;
Ecclesiastes 5:3,7;
Matthew 6:7;
Hebrew 10:22

THANK YOU
GOD, AMEN.

¹⁰Anyone who loves money never
has enough.
Anyone who loves wealth is never
satisfied with what he gets.
That doesn't have any meaning
either.

¹¹As more and more goods are
made,
more and more people use them
up.
So how can those goods benefit
their owner?
All he can do is look at them with
longing.

¹²The sleep of a worker is sweet.
It doesn't matter whether he eats
a little or a lot.
But the wealth of a rich man
keeps him awake at night.

¹³I've seen something very evil on
earth.
It's when wealth is stored up
and then brings harm to its
owner.

¹⁴It's also when wealth is lost
because of an unwise business
deal.
Then there won't be anything left
for the owner's son.
¹⁵A man is born naked.
He comes into the world with
nothing.
And he goes out of it with
nothing.
He doesn't get anything from his
work
that he can take with him.

¹⁶Here's something else that is very
evil.

A man is born, and a man dies.
And what does he get for his work?
Nothing. It's like working for the
wind.
¹⁷All his life he eats in darkness.
His life is full of trouble, suffering
and anger.

¹⁸I realized that it's good and proper
for a man to eat and drink. It's good for

How do poor people get poor?

Most people become poor by being born into poor families.
In fact, many people in the world live in a poor country where
almost everyone is poor. It is not their fault that they are poor.
There are many other reasons for poverty. Some people get hurt in
accidents or in war and then cannot get good jobs. Some people get
a lot of big bills and have to spend all their money paying those bills.
Some do not have a family to help them get started in life. Some are
poor because they have been cheated by other people. And some
people become poor because they have made bad choices. No
matter what makes someone
poor, we must try to help.
God is kind to us even though
we make mistakes. So we
should be kind to others.

checkout

Ecclesiastes 5:8,9

Related verses:
Proverbs 22:2;
James 2:1–5

him to be satisfied with his hard work on this earth. That's what he should do during the few days of life God has given him. That's what God made him for.

¹⁹Sometimes God gives a man wealth and possessions. He makes it possible for him to enjoy them. He helps him accept the life he has given him. He helps him to be happy in his work. All of those things are gifts from God. ²⁰A man like that doesn't have to think about how his life is going. That's because God fills his heart with joy.

6 I've seen another evil thing on this earth. And it's a heavy load on men. ²God gives a man wealth, possessions and honor. He has everything his heart longs for. But God doesn't let him enjoy those things. Instead, strangers enjoy them. That doesn't have any meaning. It's a very evil thing.

³A man might have a hundred children. He might live a long time. But suppose he can't enjoy his wealth. And suppose he isn't buried in the proper way. Then it doesn't matter how long he lives.

I'm telling you that a baby that is born dead is better off than he is. ⁴That kind of birth doesn't have any meaning. The baby dies in darkness and leaves this world. And in darkness it is forgotten. ⁵It didn't even see the sun. It didn't know anything at all. But it has more rest than that man does. ⁶And that's true even if he lives for 2,000 years but doesn't get to enjoy his wealth. All people die and go to the grave, don't they?

⁷Man eats up everything he works
    to get.
    But he is never satisfied.
⁸What advantage does a wise man
    have
    over someone who is
      foolish?
    What does a poor man gain

Is it OK to pray to get something that our friends have?

It is good to tell God what is on our mind, but it is not good to think that we need to have certain things to be happy. Sure, maybe we feel happy at first. But it won't last. Happiness that lasts comes from knowing God and obeying him.

    Wanting what others have is called envy. God tells us not to envy because people who envy are never satisfied; they never think they have enough, even after they get all that they want. Instead of envying, God tells us to be content with what we have.

    But we should still tell God how we feel. When a friend has something that we would like, we should talk with God about it, especially if it is something we need. We can trust that God will give us what is best for us.

checkout
Ecclesiastes 6:7

Related verses:
Genesis 11:8–9;
1 Samuel 8:5–20;
James 4:1–3

DEAR GOD, PLEASE GIVE ME FREDA'S SENSE OF HUMOR, GOOD VALUES LIKE SUSIE'S, AND A BASEBALL CARD COLLECTION LIKE TOMMY'S.

by knowing how to act toward
others?

⁹Being satisfied with what you have
is better than always wanting
more.
That doesn't have any meaning
either.
It's like chasing the wind.

¹⁰God has already planned what
now exists.
He has already decided what
man is.
A man can't argue with the One
who is stronger than he is.

¹¹The more words people use,
the less meaning there is.
And that doesn't help anyone.

¹²Who knows what's good for a man?
He lives for only a few meaningless
days. He passes through life like a
shadow. Who can tell him what will
happen on earth after he is gone?

GOOD ADVICE ABOUT
HOW TO LIVE

7 A good name is better than
fine perfume.
People can learn more from
sobbing when someone
dies

than from being happy when
someone is born.

²So it's better to go where people
are sobbing
than to go where people are
having a good time.
Everyone will die someday.
Those who are still living
should really think about that.

³Sadness is good for the heart.
That's why sorrow is better than
laughter.

⁴Those who are wise are found
where there is sorrow.
But foolish people are found
where there is pleasure.

⁵Pay attention to a wise man's
warning.
That's better than listening to the
songs of those who are
foolish.

⁶A foolish person's laughter
is like the crackling of thorns
burning under a pot.
That doesn't have any meaning
either.

⁷When a wise man takes wealth by
force, he becomes foolish.
It is sinful to take money from
people who want special
favors.

Is it bad to ask God for something
we don't really need?

It is not the *best* way to pray, but it is not bad. God invites us to come to him
with our needs and concerns. He invites us to tell him how we feel. He
promises to meet our needs, to care about our cares and to work out his
good plans in our lives. Sometimes we ask God for things we *think* we
need, but really we do not need them at
all. It is OK to tell God we wish we had
this or that thing.

Whenever we pray, we should be honest
and tell God our real feelings. But we should
also accept his answers and be content with
what he gives us.

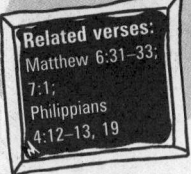

Related verses:
Matthew 6:31–33;
7:1;
Philippians
4:12–13, 19

checkout
Ecclesiastes 6:9

THANK YOU, GOD,
FOR BLESSING MY
VEGETABLE GARDEN.

VEGETABLES

⁸The end of a matter is better than
　　its beginning.
　So it's better to be patient than
　　proud.
⁹Don't become angry quickly.
　Anger lives in the hearts of
　　foolish people.
¹⁰Don't say, "Why were things better
　　in the good old days?"
　It isn't wise to ask that kind of
　　question.
¹¹Wisdom is a good thing.
　It's like getting a share of the
　　family wealth.
　It benefits those who live on this
　　earth.
¹²Wisdom provides safety,
　just as money provides safety.
　But here's the advantage of
　　wisdom.
　It guards the lives of those who
　　have it.
¹³Think about what God has done.

Who can make straight
　what he has made crooked?
¹⁴When times are good, be happy.
　But when times are bad, here's
　　something to think about.

God has made bad times.
　He has also made good times.
So a man can't find out anything
　about what's ahead for him.

¹⁵In my meaningless life here's what
I've seen.

I've seen a godly man dying
　even though he is godly.
And I've seen a sinful man living a
　　long time
　even though he is sinful.
¹⁶Don't claim to be better than you
　　are.
　And don't claim to be wiser than
　　you are.
　Why destroy yourself?
¹⁷Don't be too sinful.
　And don't be foolish.
　Why die before your time comes?
¹⁸It's good to hold on to both of
　　those things.
　Don't let go of either one.
A man who has respect for God
　　will avoid
　going too far in either direction.

¹⁹Wisdom makes one wise man
　　more powerful
　than ten rulers in a city.

How come the olden days and these days are different?

First, people change the way they dress, the style of their homes and the kinds of foods they eat. Second, technology keeps changing. Every year, engineers and inventors create new products. Some of these things improve our lives, and others make things a little harder, but all of them bring change.

Automobiles, airplanes, telephones, microwave ovens, antibiotics, computers, and CD players have changed our lives. But many things stay the same. People still laugh and cry and are born young and grow old. People still have to work, and each person still needs God's love.

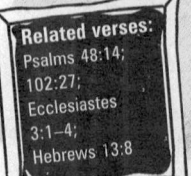

Related verses:
Psalms 48:14;
102:27;
Ecclesiastes
3:1–4;
Hebrews 13:8

checkout
Ecclesiastes 7:10

WHEN I WAS
A BOY... WE
DIDN'T HAVE
A T.V.

²⁰There isn't anyone on earth
　who does only what is right and
　never sins.

²¹Don't pay attention to everything
　people say.
　If you do, you might hear your
　servant calling down a curse
　on you.
²²Many times you yourself have
　called down curses on others.
　Deep down inside, you know
　that's true.

²³I used wisdom to put all of those
things to the test. I said,

　"I've made up my mind to be
　wise."
　But it was more than I could
　accomplish.
²⁴No matter what else wisdom may
　be,
　it's far away and very deep.
　Who can find it?
²⁵So I tried to understand wisdom
　more completely.
　I wanted to study it and figure it
　out.
　I tried to find out everything I
　could about it.
　I tried to understand why it's
　foolish to be evil.
　I wanted to see why choosing
　foolishness is so unwise.
²⁶A woman who hunts a man down
　is more painful than death.
　Her heart is like a trap.
　Her hands are like chains.
　A man who pleases God will try to
　get away from her.
　But she will trap a sinner.

²⁷"Look," says the Teacher. "Here's
what I've discovered.

　"I added one thing to another to
　find out
　everything I could about wisdom.
²⁸I searched and searched
　but found very little.
　I did find one honest man among
　a thousand.
　But I didn't find one honest
　woman among a thousand.
²⁹Here's the only other thing I found.
　God made men honest.
　But they've made many evil
　plans."

8

Who is like a wise man?
Who knows how to explain
　things?
Wisdom makes a man's face
　bright.
　It softens the look on his face.

OBEY THE KING

²I'm telling you to obey the king's
command. You took an oath to serve
him. You made a promise to God.
³Don't be in a hurry to quit your job in
the palace. Don't stand up for something the king doesn't like. He'll do
anything he wants to. ⁴He has the final
word. So who can ask him, "What are
you doing?"

⁵No one who obeys his command
　will be harmed.
　Those who are wise will know the
　proper time and way to
　approach him.
⁶There's a proper time and way for
　people to do everything.
　That's true even though a man
　might be suffering greatly.

⁷No one knows what lies
　ahead.
　So who can tell a person what's
　going to happen?
⁸He can't stop the wind from
　blowing.
　And he doesn't have the power to
　decide when he will die.
　No one is let out of the army in
　times of war.
　And evil won't let go of those who
　practice it.

⁹I understood all of those things. I
used my mind to study everything
that's done on earth. A man sometimes makes life hard for others. But
he ends up hurting himself.
¹⁰I also saw sinful people being buried. They used to come and go from
the place of worship. And others
praised them in the city where they
worshiped. That doesn't have any
meaning either.
¹¹Sometimes the sentence for a
crime isn't carried out quickly. So people make plans to commit even more
crimes.
¹²An evil man may be guilty of a hundred crimes and still live a long time.

But I know that things will go better with men who have great respect for God. [13]Sinful people don't respect God. So things won't go well with them. Like a shadow, they won't be around very long.

[14]Here's something else on this earth that doesn't have any meaning. Sometimes godly men get what sinful people should receive. And sinful men get what godly people should receive. Here's what I'm telling you. That doesn't have any meaning either.

[15]So I advise everyone to enjoy life. A man on this earth can't do anything better than eat and drink and be glad. Then he will enjoy his work. He'll be happy all the days of the life God has given him on earth.

[16]I used my mind to understand what it really means to be wise. I wanted to observe the hard work man does on earth. He doesn't close his eyes and go to sleep day or night.

[17]I saw everything God has done. No one can understand what happens on earth. Man might try very hard to figure it out. But he still can't discover what it all means. A wise man might claim he knows. But he can't really understand it either.

EVERYONE DIES

9 I thought about all of those things. I realized that those who are wise and do what is right are under God's control. What they do is also under his control.

But a man doesn't know whether God will show favor to him. [2]Everyone will die someday. Death comes to godly and sinful people alike. It comes to good and bad people alike. It comes to "clean" and "unclean" people alike. Those who offer sacrifices and those who don't offer them also die.

A good person dies,
   and so does a sinner.
Those who take oaths die.
   So do those who are afraid to
     take them.

[3]Here's what is so bad about everything that happens on this earth. Death catches up with all of us. Also, the hearts of people are full of evil.

They live in foolish pleasure. After that, they join those who have already died.

[4]Anyone who is living still has hope. Even a live dog is better off than a dead lion!

[5]People who are still alive know
   they'll die.
But those who have died don't
   know anything.
They don't receive any more
   rewards.
And they are soon forgotten.
[6]Their love, hate and jealousy
   disappear.
They will never share again
   in anything that happens on
   earth.

[7]Go and enjoy your food. Be joyful as you drink your wine. Now is the time God favors what you do. [8]Always wear white clothes to show you are happy. Anoint your head with olive oil.

[9]You love your wife. So enjoy life with her. Do it all the days of this meaningless life God has given you on earth. That's what he made you for. That's what you get for all of your hard work on earth.

[10]No matter what you do, work at it with all your might. Remember, you are going to your grave. And there isn't any work or planning or knowledge or wisdom there.

[11]Here's something else I've seen on this earth.

Races aren't always won by those
   who run fast.
Battles aren't always won by
   those who are strong.
Wise people don't always have
   plenty of food.
Clever people aren't always
   wealthy.
Those who have learned a lot
   aren't always favored.
God controls the timing of every
   event.
He also controls how things turn
   out.

[12]A man doesn't know when trouble will come to him.

Fish are caught in nets.
Birds are taken in traps.

And people are trapped by hard
times
that come when they don't
expect them.

BEING WISE IS BETTER THAN BEING FOOLISH

¹³Here's something else I saw on this
earth. I saw an example of wisdom
that touched me deeply. ¹⁴There was
once a small city. Only a few people
lived there. A powerful king attacked
it. He brought in war machines all
around it.

¹⁵A certain man lived in that city. He
was poor but wise. He used his wisdom to save the city. But no one remembered that poor man. ¹⁶So I said,
"It's better to be wise than to be powerful." But people looked down on the
poor man's wisdom. No one paid any
attention to what he said.

¹⁷People should listen to the quiet
words
of those who are wise.
That's better than paying attention
to the shouts

of a ruler of foolish people.
¹⁸Wisdom is better than weapons of
war.
But one sinner destroys a lot of
good.

10 Dead flies give perfume a
bad smell.
And a little foolishness
can make a lot of
wisdom useless.
²The hearts of wise people lead
them on the right path.
But the hearts of foolish people
take them down the wrong
path.
³A foolish person doesn't have any
sense at all.
He shows everyone he is foolish.
He does it even when he is
walking along the road.
⁴Suppose a ruler gets very angry
with you.
If he does, don't quit your job in
the palace.
Stay calm. That will overcome
the effects of your big
mistakes.

Why do athletes get paid so much money to do something that's fun?

Because millions of people pay a lot of money to see them play. Television
networks pay millions of dollars for the right to show games. Sports fans
spend millions on tickets, shirts, caps and other things. That is why sports
stars ask for big salaries and usually get them.

But it is not all fun. To be excellent in a sport takes years of hard
work and training. And most athletes suffer cuts, bruises and
broken bones.

It may not seem right that athletes get paid so much for playing
a game. But life is not always fair. And many professional athletes
are broke when they retire from
sports. They sometimes spend their
money as fast as they get it.

checkout
Ecclesiastes 9:11

Related verse:
Ecclesiastes 8:14

⁵Here's something evil I've seen on
   this earth.
   And it's the kind of mistake that
   rulers make.
⁶Foolish people are given many
   important jobs.
   Rich people are given
   unimportant ones.
⁷I've seen slaves on horseback.
   I've also seen princes who were
   forced to walk as if they were
   slaves.

⁸Anyone who digs a pit might fall
   into it.
   Anyone who breaks through a
   wall might be bitten by a
   snake.
⁹Anyone who removes stones from
   rock pits might get hurt.
   Anyone who cuts logs might get
   wounded.

¹⁰Suppose the blade of an ax is dull.
   And its edge hasn't been
   sharpened.
   Then more effort is needed to use
   it.
   But skill will bring success.
¹¹Suppose a snake bites before it is
   charmed.
   Then there isn't any benefit in
   being a snake charmer.

¹²A man who is wise says gracious
   things.
   But a foolish person is destroyed
   by what his own lips speak.
¹³At first what he says is foolish.
   In the end his words are very evil.
¹⁴   He talks too much.

No one knows what lies ahead for
   him.
   Who can tell him what will
   happen after he is gone?

¹⁵The work a foolish person does
   makes him tired.
   He doesn't even know the way to
   town.

¹⁶How terrible it is for a land whose
   king used to be a servant!
   How terrible if its princes get
   drunk in the morning!
¹⁷How blessed is the land whose
   king was born into the royal
   family!

How blessed if its princes eat and
   drink at the proper time!
   How blessed if they eat and drink
   to become strong and not to
   get drunk!

¹⁸When a man won't work, the roof
   falls down.
   When his hands aren't busy, the
   house leaks.

¹⁹People laugh at a dinner party.
   And wine makes life happy.
   People think money can buy
   everything.

²⁰Don't call down curses on the king.
   Don't even think about doing it.
   Don't call down curses on rich
   people.
   Don't even do it in your
   bedroom.
   A bird might fly away and carry
   your words.
   It might report what you said.

BE BOLD

11 Put your money into trade
   across the ocean.
   After a while you will earn
   something from it.
²Give shares of what you earn to a
   lot of people.
   After all, you don't know what
   great trouble might come on
   the land.

³Clouds that are full of water
   pour rain down on the earth.
   A tree might fall to the south or the
   north.
   It will stay in the place where it
   falls.
⁴Anyone who keeps on watching
   the wind won't plant seeds.
   Anyone who keeps looking at the
   clouds won't gather crops.

⁵You don't know the path the wind
   takes.
   You don't know how a baby is
   made inside its mother.
   So you can't understand how God
   works either.
   He made everything.

⁶In the morning plant your seeds.
   In the evening keep your hands
   busy.
   You don't know what will succeed.

It may be one or the other.
Or both might do equally well.

REMEMBER THE ONE WHO CREATED YOU

⁷ Light is sweet.
People enjoy being out in the sun.
⁸ No matter how many years a man might live,
let him enjoy all of them.
But let him remember the dark days.
There will be many of them.
Nothing that's going to happen will have any meaning.

⁹ Young man, be happy while you are still young.
Let your heart be joyful while you are still strong.
Do what your heart tells you to do.
Go after what your eyes look at.
But I want you to know
that God will judge you for everything you do.
¹⁰ So drive worry out of your heart.
Get rid of all of your troubles.
Being young and strong doesn't have any meaning.

12 Remember the One who created you.
Remember him while you are still young.
Think about him before your times of trouble come.
The years will come when you will say,
"I don't find any pleasure in them."
² That's when the sunlight will become dark.
The moon and the stars will also grow dark.
And the clouds will return after it rains.
³ Remember your Creator before those who guard the house tremble with old age.
That's when strong men will be bent over.
The women who grind grain will stop because there are so few of them left.
Those who look through the windows won't be able to see very well.
⁴ Remember your Creator before the front doors are closed.

If it's wrong to steal, why do they call it "stealing bases" in baseball?

Games are just part of what makes life enjoyable. Ecclesiastes 11:9 tells kids to be happy while they are young but also reminds them that God will judge everything people do. So it is important to follow God's rules even while playing a game.

"Stealing bases" in baseball, though, is not really stealing. This is just a word used to describe a certain kind of play. Baseball has other words that can be confusing too. Batters are "walked" by the pitcher, the game is played on a "diamond" and fourth base is called "home plate." In order to play any game the right way, it is important to know what the special words mean. It is not wrong to "steal" second base unless you pick it up and take it home!

JASON'S IMAGINATION

WORLD RECORD for STEALING BASES

checkout
Ecclesiastes 11:9

Related verses:
Ecclesiastes
11:7,8; 12:1

That's when the sound of
grinding will fade away.
Old men will rise up when they
hear birds singing.
But they will barely hear any of
their songs.
⁵Remember your Creator before
you become afraid of places
that are too high.
You will also be terrified because
of danger in the streets.
Remember your Creator before
the almond trees have buds
on them.
That's when grasshoppers will
drag themselves along.
Old men will not want to make
love anymore.
Man will go to his dark home in
the grave.
And those who sob over the dead
will walk around in the streets.

⁶Remember your Creator before
the silver cord is cut.
That's when the golden bowl will
be broken.
The wheel will be broken at the
well.
The pitcher will be smashed at
the spring.
⁷Remember your Creator before
you return to the dust you
came from.
That's when your spirit will go
back to God who gave it.

⁸"Meaningless! Everything is
meaningless!"
says the Teacher.
"Nothing has any meaning."

HAVE RESPECT FOR GOD

⁹The Teacher was wise. He gave
knowledge to people. He put many
proverbs to the test. He thought about

Does your body stay in the grave when you go to heaven?

The body you have here on earth
is not made to last. It will
decay after you die. When God
creates a new heaven and a
new earth, he will give you
a new body that will last
forever. What happens to
your earthly body during
your life or in the grave will
not affect your forever life
with God in any way. Your
new body will be perfect
and healthy, and it will never
wear out.

checkout

Ecclesiastes 12:7

Related verses:
Psalm 49:15;
1 Corinthians
15:35–44

JASON'S
IMAGINATION

NEW HEAVENLY
BODIES

them carefully. Then he wrote them down in order. ¹⁰He did his best to find just the right words. And what he wrote was honest and true.

¹¹The sayings of those who are wise move people to take action. Their collected sayings really nail things down. They are given to us by one Shepherd. ¹²My son, be careful not to pay attention to anything that is added to them.

Books will never stop being written. Too much studying makes people tired.

¹³Everything has now been heard.
And here's the final thing I want to say.
Have respect for God and obey his commandments.
That's what everyone should do.
¹⁴God will judge everything people do.
That includes everything they try to hide.
He'll judge everything, whether it's good or evil.

Is it all right to say bad things if there is no one there to hear you?

Wrong is wrong even if no one else ever finds out about it. It is wrong to swear, lie and say bad things about others even if nobody hears you do it. Try hard to speak and think what is good and right, because that is what really matters. Even what you *think about* counts. God knows every one of our thoughts. And remember that *he* is always there to hear your words, too!

checkout
Ecclesiastes 12:13,14

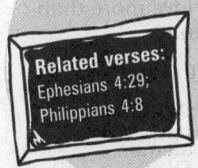

Related verses:
Ephesians 4:29;
Philippians 4:8

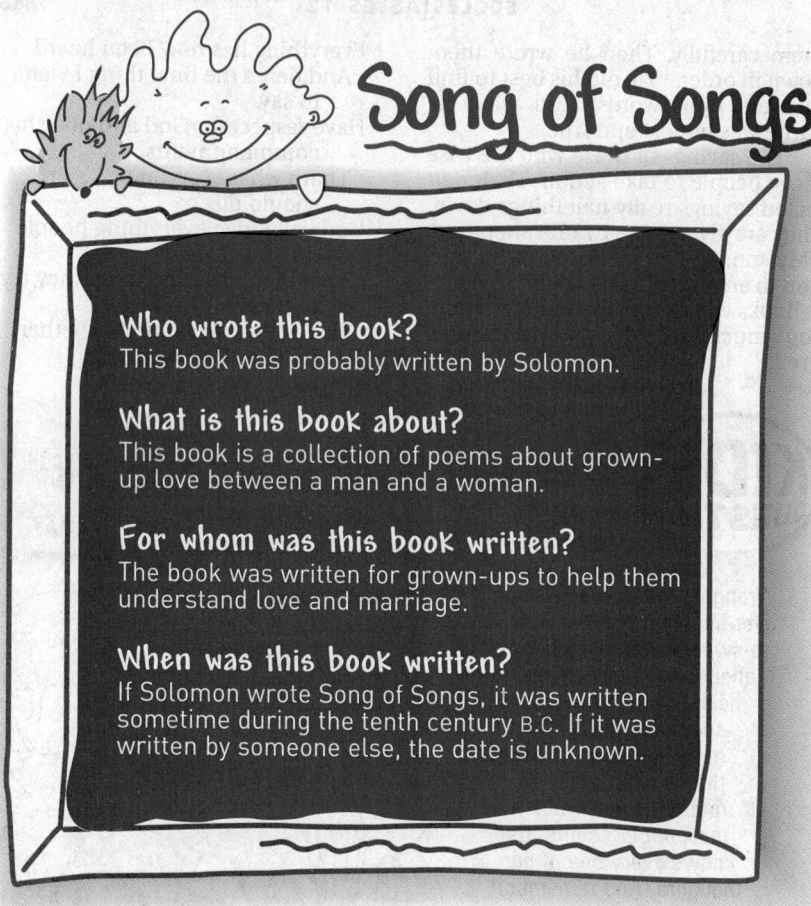

Song of Songs

Who wrote this book?
This book was probably written by Solomon.

What is this book about?
This book is a collection of poems about grown-up love between a man and a woman.

For whom was this book written?
The book was written for grown-ups to help them understand love and marriage.

When was this book written?
If Solomon wrote Song of Songs, it was written sometime during the tenth century B.C. If it was written by someone else, the date is unknown.

1 This is the greatest song Solomon ever wrote.

A Shulammite woman says to King Solomon,

2 "I long for your lips to kiss me!
  Your love makes me happier than wine does.
3 The lotion you have on pleases me.
  Your name is like perfume that is poured out.
  No wonder the young women love you!
4 Take me away with you. Let us hurry!
  King Solomon, bring me into your palace."

The other women say,

"King Solomon, you fill us with joy.
  You make us happy.
  We praise your love more than we praise wine."

The woman says to the king,

"It is right for them to love you!

5 "Women of Jerusalem,
  my skin is dark but lovely.
  It is dark like the tents in Kedar.
  It's like the curtains of Solomon's tent.
6 Don't stare at me because I'm dark.
  The sun has made my skin look like this.
  My brothers burned with anger against me.
  They made me take care of the vineyards.

I haven't even taken care of my
own vineyard.

[7] "King Solomon, I love you.
So tell me where you take care of
your flock.
Tell me where you rest your
sheep at noon.
Why should I have to act like a
prostitute
near the flocks of your friends?"

The other women say,

[8] "You are the most beautiful
woman of all.
Don't you know where to find the
king?
Follow the tracks the sheep
make.
Take care of your young goats
near the tents of the shepherds."

King Solomon says to the Shulammite woman,

[9] "You are my love.
You are like a mare that pulls one
of Pharaoh's chariots.
[10] Your earrings make your cheeks
even more beautiful.
Your strings of jewels make your
neck even more lovely."

The other women say to her,

[11] "We will make gold earrings for
you.
We'll decorate them with silver."

The woman says,

[12] "The king was at his table.
My perfume gave off a sweet
smell.
[13] The one who loves me is like a
small bag of myrrh
resting between my breasts.
[14] He is like henna flowers
from the vineyards of En Gedi."

The king says,

[15] "You are so beautiful, my love!
So beautiful!
Your eyes are like doves."

The woman says,

[16] "You are so handsome, my love!
So charming!
The green field is our bed.
[17] Cedar trees above us are the

beams of our house.
Fir trees overhead are its rafters.

2 "I am like a rose on the coast
of Sharon.
I'm like a lily in the valleys."

The king says,

[2] "My love, among the young
women
you are like a lily among thorns."

The woman says,

[3] "My love, among the young men
you are like an apple tree among
the trees of the forest.
I'm happy to sit in your shade.
Your fruit tastes so sweet to me.
[4] You have taken me to the dinner
hall.
Your banner of love is lifted high
above me.
[5] Give me some raisins to make me
strong.
Give me some apples to make
me feel like new again.
Our love has made me weak.
[6] Your left arm is under my head.
Your right arm is around me.
[7] Women of Jerusalem, take an oath
and make me a promise.
Let the antelopes and the does
serve as witnesses.
Don't stir up love.
Don't wake it up until it's ready.

[8] "Listen! I hear my love!
Look! Here he comes!
He's leaping across the
mountains.
He's coming over the hills.
[9] The one who loves me is like an
antelope or a young deer.
Look! There he stands behind
our wall.
He's gazing through the window.
He's peering through the screen.
[10] He said to me, 'Rise up, my love.
Come with me, my beautiful one.
[11] Look! The winter is past.
The rains are over and gone.
[12] Flowers are appearing on the
earth.
The season for singing has come.
The cooing of doves
is heard in our land.
[13] The fig trees are producing their
early fruit.

The flowers on the vines are
　　giving off their sweet smell.
Rise up and come, my love.
Come with me, my beautiful
　　one.' "

The king says,

14 "You are like a dove in an opening
　　in the rocks.
You are like a dove in a hiding
　　place on a mountainside.
Show me your face.
Let me hear your voice.
Your voice is so sweet.
Your face is so lovely.
15 Catch the foxes for us.
Catch the little foxes.
They destroy our vineyards.
The vineyards are in bloom."

The woman says,

16 "My love belongs to me, and I
　　belong to him.
Like an antelope, he eats among
　　the lilies.
17 Until the day begins
and the shadows fade away,
turn to me, my love.
Be like an antelope
or like a young deer
on the rocky hills.

3 "All night long on my bed
I searched for the one my heart
　　loves.
I looked for him but didn't find
　　him.
2 I will get up. I'll go around in the
　　city.
I'll look through all of its streets.
I'll search for the one my heart
　　loves.
So I looked for him but didn't
　　find him.
3 Those on guard duty found me
as they were walking around in
　　the city.
'Have you seen the one my heart
　　loves?' I asked.
4 As soon as I had passed by them
I found the one my heart loves.
I threw my arms around him. I
　　didn't let him go
until I had brought him to my
　　mother's house.
I took him to my mother's
　　room.

5 Women of Jerusalem, take an oath
　　and make me a promise.
Let the antelopes and the does
　　serve as witnesses.
Don't stir up love.
Don't wake it up until it's ready."

The other women say,

6 "Who is this man coming up from
　　the desert
like a column of smoke?
He smells like myrrh and incense
　　made from all of the spices of the
　　trader.
7 Look! There's Solomon's movable
　　throne.
Sixty soldiers accompany it.
They have been chosen from the
　　best warriors in Israel.
8 All of them are wearing swords.
They have fought many battles.
Each one has his sword at his side.
Each is prepared for the terrors
　　of the night.
9 King Solomon made the movable
　　throne for himself.
He made it out of wood from
　　Lebanon.
10 He formed its posts out of silver.
He made its base out of gold.
Its seat was covered with purple
　　cloth.
It was decorated inside with
　　loving care
by the women of Jerusalem.
11 Women of Zion, come out.
Look at King Solomon wearing
　　his crown.
His mother placed it on him.
She did it on his wedding day.
His heart was full of joy."

4 The king says to the Shulammite
woman,

"You are so beautiful, my love!
So beautiful!
Your eyes behind your veil are
　　like doves.
Your hair flows like a flock of black
　　goats
coming down from Mount Gilead.
2 Your teeth are as clean as a flock of
　　sheep.
Their wool has just been clipped.
They have just come up from
　　being washed.

Each of your teeth has its twin.
  Not one of them is alone.
³Your lips are like a bright red
    ribbon.
  Your mouth is so lovely.
  Your cheeks behind your veil
    are like the halves of a
    pomegranate.
⁴Your neck is strong and beautiful
    like the tower of David.
  That tower is built with beautiful
    stones.
  A thousand shields are hanging on
    it.
  All of them belong to mighty
    soldiers.
⁵Your two breasts are lovely.
  They are like two young
    antelopes
  that eat among the lilies.
⁶I will go to the mountain of myrrh.
  I'll go to the hill of incense.
  I'll stay there until the day begins
    and the shadows fade away.

⁷Every part of you is so beautiful,
    my love.
  There is no flaw in you.

⁸"Come with me from Lebanon, my
    bride.
  Come with me from Lebanon.
  Come down from the top of
    Mount Amana.
  Come down from the top of
    Senir.
  Come to me from the peak of
    Mount Hermon.
  Leave the dens where the lions
    live.
  Leave the places in the
    mountains where the leopards
    stay.
⁹My bride, you have stolen my
    heart
  with one glance of your eyes.
  My sister, you have stolen my
    heart
  with one jewel in your necklace.

Why do I have to brush my teeth?

God has given us bodies to use for serving him. It is our job to take care of our bodies and to use them well. This means we should eat the right foods, get enough sleep, watch our weight, exercise, dress warmly in cold weather and not hurt ourselves with drugs, alcohol or tobacco. It also means we should brush our teeth and keep ourselves clean. It would not be a sin to skip brushing our teeth for one day. But God does want us to take care of our teeth. It is not a sin to eat candy. But God doesn't want us to eat only candy and destroy our health. God wants us to take care of the bodies he gave us.

checkout
Song of Songs 4:2

Related verse:
1 Corinthians 6:19

[10] My bride, your love is so
　　delightful.
　My sister, your love makes me
　　happier than wine does.
　Your perfume smells better than
　　any spice.
[11] Your lips are as sweet as a
　　honeycomb, my bride.
　Milk and honey are under your
　　tongue.
　Your clothes smell like the cedar
　　trees in Lebanon.
[12] My bride, you are like a garden
　　that is locked up.
　My sister, you are like a spring of
　　water that has a fence around
　　it.
　You are like a fountain that is
　　sealed up.
[13] You are like trees whose branches
　　are loaded
　with pomegranates, fine fruits,
　　henna and nard,
[14] 　with saffron, cane and
　　cinnamon.
　You are like every kind of incense
　　tree.

You have myrrh, aloes
　and all of the finest spices.
[15] You are like a fountain in a
　　garden.
　You are like a well of flowing
　　water
　streaming down from Lebanon."

The woman says,

[16] "Wake up, north wind!
　Come, south wind!
　Blow on my garden.
　Then its sweet smell will spread
　　everywhere.
　Let my love come into his
　　garden.
　Let him taste its fine fruits."

5 The king says,

"My bride, I have come into my
　　garden.
　My sister, I've gathered my myrrh
　　and my spice.
　I've eaten my honeycomb and my
　　honey.
　I've drunk my wine and my
　　milk."

Why did people go to wells instead of using the water at home?

People who lived in Bible times did not have pipes or sinks in their houses. They had to go to rivers, streams, wells and cisterns for their water. A well was a deep hole they dug all the way to the water in the ground. A cistern was a big hole in the ground that held rainwater. Many people today still use wells. Water from wells and cisterns is very clean. A well provides plenty of refreshing, clean water. That is why Solomon spoke of a well in his poetry.

checkout
Song of Songs 4:15

JASON'S IMAGINATION

PLEASE DON'T USE! (not invented yet)

Related verses:
Genesis 24:45;
John 4:4–7,13,14

The other women say to the Shulammite woman and to Solomon,

> "Friends, eat and drink.
> Lovers, drink all you want."

The woman says,

2 "I slept, but my heart was awake.
  Listen! The one who loves me is
    knocking.
  He says, 'My sister, I love you.
  Open up so I can come in.
  You are my dove.
    You are perfect in every way.
  My head is soaked with dew.
    The night air has made my hair
      wet.'
3 "But I've taken my robe off.
    Must I put it on again?
  I've washed my feet.
    Must I get them dirty again?
4 My love put his hand through the
    opening.
  My heart began to pound for
    him.
5 I got up to open the door for my
    love.
  My hands dripped with myrrh.
  It flowed from my fingers
    onto the handles of the lock.
6 I opened the door for my love.
  But he had left. He was gone.
  My heart sank because he had
    left.
  I looked for him but didn't find
    him.
  I called out to him, but he didn't
    answer.
7 Those on guard duty found me
    as they were walking around in
      the city.
  They beat me. They hurt me.
  Those on guard duty at the walls
    took my coat away from me.
8 Women of Jerusalem, take an oath
    and make me a promise.
  If you find the one who
    loves me,
    tell him our love has made me
      weak."

The other women say,

9 "You are the most beautiful
    woman of all.
  How is the one you love better
    than others?
  How is he better than anyone else?

Why do you ask us to make you a
  promise?"

The woman says,

10 "The one who loves me is tanned
    and handsome.
  He's the finest man among
    10,000.
11 His head is like the purest gold.
  His hair is wavy and as black as a
    raven.
12 His eyes are like doves
    by streams of water.
  They look as if they've been
    washed in milk.
  They are set like jewels in his
    head.
13 His cheeks are like beds of spice
    that give off perfume.
  His lips are like lilies
    that drip with myrrh.
14 His arms are like gold
    that are set with chrysolite.
  His body is like polished ivory
    that is decorated with
      sapphires.
15 His legs are like pillars of marble
    that are set on bases of pure gold.
  He looks like the finest cedar tree
    in the mountains of Lebanon.
16 His mouth is very sweet.
  Everything about him is
    delightful.
  That's what the one who loves me
    is like.
  That's what my friend is like,
    women of Jerusalem."

6 The other women say,
  "You are the most beautiful
    woman of all.
  Where has the one who loves you
    gone?
  Which way did he turn?
  We'll help you look for him."

The woman says,

2 "My love has gone down to his
    garden.
  He's gone to the beds of spices.
  He's eating in the gardens.
  He's gathering lilies.
3 I belong to my love, and he
    belongs to me.
  He's eating among the lilies."

The king says,

4 "My love, you are as beautiful as
    the city of Tirzah.
  You are as lovely as Jerusalem.
  You are as majestic as troops
    carrying their banners.
5 Turn your eyes away from me.
    They overpower me.
  Your hair flows like a flock of black
    goats
  coming down from Mount
    Gilead.
6 Your teeth are as clean as a flock of
    sheep
  coming up from being
    washed.
  Each of your teeth has its twin.
  Not one of them is alone.
7 Your cheeks behind your veil
  are like the halves of a
    pomegranate.
8 There might be 60 queens and 80
    concubines.
  There might be more virgins
    than anyone can count.
9 But you are my perfect dove.
  There isn't anyone like you.
  You are your mother's favorite
    daughter.
  The young women see you and
    call you blessed.
  The queens and concubines
    praise you."

The other women say,

10 "Who is this woman?
  She is like the sunrise in all of its
    glory.
  She is as beautiful as the moon.
  She is as bright as the sun.
  She is as majestic as troops
    carrying their banners."

The king says,

11 "I went down to a grove of nut
    trees.
  I wanted to look at the new
    plants growing in the valley.
  I wanted to find out whether the
    vines had budded.
  I wanted to see if the
    pomegranate trees had
    bloomed.
12 Before I realized it,
  I was among the royal chariots of
    my people."

The other women say,

13 "Come back to us.
  Come back, Shulammite woman.
  Come back to us.
  Come back. Then we can look at
    you."

The woman says,

"Why do you want to look at me
  as you would watch a dancer at
  Mahanaim?"

7 The king says to the Shulammite
  woman,

"You are like a prince's daughter.
  Your feet in sandals are so
    beautiful.
  Your graceful legs are like jewels.
  The hands of a skilled worker
    must have shaped them.
2 Your navel is like a round bowl
  that always has mixed wine
    in it.
  Your waist is like a mound of
    wheat
  that is surrounded by lilies.
3 Your two breasts are lovely.
  They are like two young
    antelopes.
4 Your neck is smooth and beautiful
  like an ivory tower.
  Your eyes are like the pools of
    Heshbon
  by the gate of Bath Rabbim.
  Your nose is like the towering
    mountains of Lebanon
  that face the city of Damascus.
5 Your head is like a crown on you.
  It is as beautiful as Mount
    Carmel.
  Your hair is as smooth as purple
    silk.
  I am captured by your flowing
    curls.
6 You are so beautiful! You please
    me so much!
  You are so delightful, my love!
7 You are as graceful as a palm
    tree.
  Your breasts are as sweet as the
    freshest fruit.
8 I said, 'I will climb the palm tree.
  I'll take hold of its fruit.'
  May your breasts be as sweet as
    the fruit on the vine.
  May your breath smell like the
    tastiest apples.

⁹ May your lips be like the finest
  wine."

The woman says,

"May my wine go straight to you,
  my love.
  May it flow gently over our lips as
  we sleep.

¹⁰ "I belong to you, my love.
  And you long for me.
¹¹ Come, my love. Let's go to the
  country.
  Let's spend the night in the
  villages.
¹² Let's go out to the vineyards
  early.
  Let's go and see if the vines have
  budded.
  Let's find out whether their flowers
  have opened.
  Let's see if the pomegranate trees
  are blooming.
  I'll make love to you in the
  vineyards.
¹³ The mandrake flowers give off
  their strong smell.
  All of the best things are waiting
  for us,
new and old alike.
  I've stored them up for you, my
  love.

8 "I wish you were like a brother
  to me.
  I wish my mother's breasts had
  nursed you.
Then if I found you outside,
  I could kiss you.
  No one would look down on me.
² I'd bring you to my mother's
  house.
  She taught me everything
  I know.
  I'd give you spiced wine to drink.
  It's the juice of my
  pomegranates.
³ Your left arm is under my head.
  Your right arm is around me.
⁴ Women of Jerusalem, take an oath
  and make me a promise.
  Don't stir up love.
  Don't wake it up until it's
  ready."

The other women say,

⁵ "Who is this woman coming up
  from the desert?

She's leaning on the one who
  loves her."

The woman says to the king,

"Under the apple tree I woke you
  up.
  That's where your mother
  became pregnant with you.
  She went into labor, and you
  were born there.
⁶ Hold me close to your heart like
  the seal around your neck.
  Keep me close to yourself like the
  ring on your finger.
  My love for you is so strong it
  won't let you go.
  Love is as powerful as death.
  Love's jealousy is as strong as the
  grave.
  Love is like a blazing fire.
  It burns like a mighty flame.
⁷ No amount of water can put
  it out.
  Rivers can't drown it.
  Suppose someone offers
  all of his wealth to buy love.
  That won't even come close to
  being enough."

The woman's brothers say,

⁸ "We have a little sister.
  Her breasts are still small.
  What should we do for our sister
  when she gets engaged?
⁹ If she were a wall,
  we'd build silver towers on her.
  If she were a door,
  we'd cover her with cedar
  boards."

The woman says to the king,

¹⁰ "I am a wall.
  My breasts are like well-built
  towers.
  So in your eyes I've become
  like someone who makes you
  happy.
¹¹ Solomon, you had a vineyard in
  Baal Hamon.
  You rented your vineyard to
  others.
  They had to pay 25 pounds
  of silver for its fruit.
¹² But I can give my own vineyard to
  anyone I want to.
  So I give my 25 pounds of silver
  to you, Solomon.

Give 5 pounds to those who take
    care of its fruit."

The king says,

[13]"My love, you live in the gardens.
    My friends listen for your voice.
    But let me hear it now."

The woman says,

[14]"Come away with me, my love.
    Be like an antelope
  or like a young deer
    on mountains that are full of
      spices."

quest challenge

I Wonder ...

Why is it important for me to praise God?

Real Life Challenge

Sometimes there are days when everything seems to go wrong. You miss the bus, your locker gets jammed, someone says something mean to you—the list is endless. When you're feeling down, what would happen if you started to think about God and what he has done for you?

Quest Clue

As you look at Isaiah 25 and 26 and Revelation 5, think about how your mood changes as you read about how much God loves and protects you.

I Wonder ...

When I'm sad, how can God help me?

Real Life Challenge

Have you ever felt sad because you didn't get invited to a party or because a friend sat at a different table at lunch. When we feel sad, God wants to be there to comfort us and reassure us of the hope we always have in him.

Quest Clue

Look for some encouraging words in Isaiah 61 and Hosea 14. Take time to think about the pictures the writers give in these chapters—they show how much God wants to help you with the things that hurt you.

Isaiah

Who wrote this book?
The prophet Isaiah.

Why was this book written?
Isaiah warns the people of Judah that God will punish them, just as he is punishing Israel, if they keep on doing wicked things. Isaiah also promises that God will comfort his people after punishing them, and he will make their nation strong again.

What do we learn about God in this book?
Isaiah uses many special names for God. These names show that God is holy, God is a judge and God is our salvation.

What is special about this book?
Isaiah gives many wonderful prophecies about Jesus, the coming Savior.

What are some important passages?
God's holiness. Isaiah 6
Who Jesus is. Isaiah 9:1–7
What Jesus will do. Isaiah 11
Jesus' death on the cross. Isaiah 53
A new heaven and earth. Isaiah 65:17–25

1 Here is the vision about Judah and Jerusalem that Isaiah had. It came to him when Uzziah, Jotham, Ahaz and Hezekiah were ruling. They were kings of Judah. Isaiah was the son of Amoz.

ISRAEL REFUSES TO OBEY THE LORD

²Listen to me, heavens! Pay attention to me, earth!

The LORD has said,
"I raised children. I brought them up.
But they have refused to obey me.
³The ox knows its master.
The donkey knows where its owner feeds it.
But Israel does not know me.
My people do not understand me."

4 They are a sinful nation.
  They are loaded down with guilt.
  They are people who do nothing
    but evil.
  They are children who are always
    sinning.
  They have deserted the LORD.
  They have turned against the
    Holy One of Israel.
  They have turned their backs on
    him.

5 Israel, why do you want to be
    beaten all the time?
  Why do you always refuse to
    obey the LORD?
  Your head is covered with wounds.
  Your whole heart is weak.
6 There isn't a healthy spot on your
    body
  from the bottom of your feet to
    the top of your head.
  There are only wounds, cuts
    and open sores.
  They haven't been cleaned up or
    bandaged
  or treated with olive oil.

7 Your country has been deserted.
  Your cities have been burned
    down.
  The food from your fields is being
    eaten up by outsiders.
  They are doing it right in front of
    you.
  Your land has been completely
    destroyed.
  It looks as if strangers have taken
    it over.
8 The city of Zion is left like a hut
  where someone stands guard in a
    vineyard.
  It is left like an empty cabin in a
    melon field.
  It's like a city that is being
    attacked.
9 The LORD who rules over all
  has let some people live through
    that time of trouble.
  If he hadn't, we would have
    become like Sodom.
  We would have been like
    Gomorrah.

10 Rulers of Sodom,
  hear the LORD's message.
  People of Gomorrah,
  listen to the law of our God.

11 "Do you think I need any more of
    your sacrifices?"
  asks the LORD.
  "I have more than enough of your
    burnt offerings.
  I have more than enough of rams
  and the fat of your fattest
    animals.
  I do not find any pleasure
  in the blood of your bulls, lambs
    and goats.
12 Who asked you to bring all of
    those animals
  when you come to worship me?
  Who asked you and your animals
  to walk all over my courtyards?
13 Stop bringing offerings that do not
    mean anything to me!
  I hate your incense.
  I can't stand your evil gatherings.
  I can't stand the way you
    celebrate your New Moon
    Feasts,
  Sabbath days and special
    services.
14 I hate your New Moon Feasts
  and your other appointed feasts.
  They have become a heavy load to
    me.
  I am tired of carrying it.
15 You might spread out your hands
    toward me when you pray.
  But I will not look at you.
  You might even offer many
    prayers.
  But I will not listen to them.
  Your hands are covered with the
    blood of the people you have
    murdered.
16   So wash your hands. Make
    yourselves clean.
  Get your evil actions out of my
    sight!
  Stop doing what is wrong!
17   Learn to do what is right!
  Treat people fairly.
  Give hope to those who are
    beaten down.
  Cheer them up.
  Stand up in court for children
    whose fathers have died.
  And do the same thing for
    widows.

18 "Come. Let us talk some more
    about this matter,"
  says the LORD.

"Even though your sins are bright
    red,
  they will be as white as snow.
  Even though they are deep red,
    they will be white like wool.
¹⁹ But you have to be willing to
    change and obey me.
  If you are, you will eat the best
    food that grows on the land.
²⁰ You must follow me. You must
    obey me.
  If you do not, you will be killed
    with swords."
                The Lᴏʀᴅ has spoken.

²¹ See how the faithful city of
    Jerusalem
  has become like a prostitute!
  Once it was full of people who
    treated others fairly.
  Those who did what was right
    used to live in it.
  But now murderers live there!
²² Jerusalem, your silver isn't pure
    anymore.
  Your best wine has been made
    weak with water.
²³ Your rulers refuse to obey the
    Lᴏʀᴅ.
  They are companions of robbers.
  All of them love to accept money
    from those who want special
    favors.
  They are always looking for gifts
    from other people.
  They don't stand up in court for
    children whose fathers have
    died.
  They don't do it for widows
    either.
²⁴ The Lord is the Mighty One of
    Israel.
  The Lᴏʀᴅ who rules over all
    announces,
  "Israel, you have become my
    enemies.
  I will pay you back for what you
    have done.
  Then you will not trouble me
    anymore.
²⁵ I will turn my powerful hand
    against you.
  I will make you completely clean.
  I will remove everything that is
    not pure.
²⁶ I will give judges to you like the
    ones you had long ago.

I will give you advisers like those
    you had at the beginning.
  Then you will be called
  The City That Does What Is Right.
  You will also be called The
    Faithful City."

²⁷ Zion will be saved when others are
    treated fairly.
  Those who are sorry for their sins
    will be saved
  when what is right is done.
²⁸ But sinners and those who refuse
    to obey the Lᴏʀᴅ will be
    destroyed.
  And those who desert the Lᴏʀᴅ
    will die.

²⁹ Israel, you take delight in
    worshiping among the sacred
    oak trees.
  You will be full of shame for
    doing that.
  You have chosen to worship in the
    sacred gardens.
  You will be dishonored for doing
    that.
³⁰ You will be like an oak tree whose
    leaves are dying.
  You will be like a garden that
    doesn't have any water.
³¹ Your strongest men will become
    like dry pieces of wood.
  Their worship of other gods will
    be the spark that lights the
    fire.
  Everything will be burned up.
  No one will be there to put the
    fire out.

PEOPLE FROM MANY NATIONS WILL WORSHIP AT MOUNT ZION

2 Here is a vision that Isaiah, the
son of Amoz, had about Judah
and Jerusalem.

² In the last days

the mountain where the Lᴏʀᴅ's
    temple is located will be
    famous.
  It will be the most important
    mountain of all.
  It will stand out above the hills.
  All of the nations will go to it.

³ People from many nations will go
there. They will say,

"Come. Let us go up to the Lord's
mountain.
Let's go to the house of Jacob's
God.
He will teach us how we should
live.
Then we will live the way he
wants us to."
The law of the Lord will be taught
at Zion.
His message will go out from
Jerusalem.
⁴He will judge between the nations.
He'll settle problems among
many of them.
They will hammer their swords
into plows.
They'll hammer their spears into
pruning tools.
Nations will not go to war against
one another.
They won't even train to fight
anymore.
⁵People of Jacob, come.
Let us live the way the Lord has
taught us to.

THE DAY OF THE LORD
IS COMING

⁶Lord, you have deserted the
people of Jacob.
They are your people.
The land is full of false beliefs
from the east.
The people practice evil magic,
just as the Philistines do.
They make ungodly people their
friends.
⁷Their land is full of silver and
gold.
There is no end to their
treasures.
Their land is full of horses.
There is no end to their chariots.
⁸Their land is full of statues of gods.
They bow down to what their
own hands have made.
They bow down to what their
fingers have shaped.
⁹So man will be brought low.
People will be put to shame.
Do not forgive them.

¹⁰Go and hide in caves in the rocks,
you people!
Hide in holes in the ground.
Hide from the terror of the Lord!

Hide when he comes in glory and
majesty!
¹¹A man who brags will be brought
low.
Men who are proud will be put to
shame.
The Lord alone will be honored
at that time.
¹²The Lord who rules over all has
set apart a day when he will
judge.
He has set it apart for all those
who are proud and think they
are important.
He has set it apart for all those
who brag about themselves.
All of them will be brought low.
¹³The Lord has set that day apart for
all of the cedar trees in
Lebanon.
They are very tall.
He has set it apart for all of the
oak trees in Bashan.
¹⁴He has set it apart for all of the
towering mountains.
He has set it apart for all of the
high hills.
¹⁵He has set it apart for every high
tower
and every strong wall.
¹⁶He has set it apart for every
trading ship
and every beautiful boat.
¹⁷A man who brags will be brought
low.
Men who are proud will be put to
shame.
The Lord alone will be honored at
that time.
¹⁸　And the statues of gods will
totally disappear.

¹⁹People will run and hide in caves
in the rocks.
They will go into holes in the
ground.
They will run away from the terror
of the Lord.
They will run when he comes in
glory and majesty.
When he comes, he will shake
the earth.
²⁰Men had made some statues of
gods out of silver.
They had made others out of
gold.
Then they worshiped them.

But when the LORD comes,
  they will throw the statues away
    to the rodents and bats.
²¹ They will run and hide in caves in
    the rocks.
  They will go into holes in the cliffs.
  They will run away from the terror
    of the LORD.
  They will run when he comes in
    glory and majesty.
  When he comes, he will shake
    the earth.

²² Stop trusting man. He can't help
    you.
  He only lives for a little while.
  What good is he?

THE LORD WILL JUDGE JERUSALEM AND JUDAH

3 Here is what
  the LORD who rules over all is
    about to do.
The Lord will take away from
    Jerusalem and Judah
  supplies and help alike.
He will take away all of the
    supplies of food and water.
² He'll take away heroes and
    soldiers.
  He'll take away judges and
    prophets.
  He'll take away fortune tellers
    and elders.
³ He'll take away captains of
    companies of 50 men.
  He'll take away government
    leaders.
  He'll take away advisers, skilled
    workers
  and those who are clever at
    doing evil magic.
⁴ The LORD will make young boys
    rule over all of them.
  Mere children will govern them.
⁵ People will crush one another.
  They will fight against each
    other.
  They will fight against their
    neighbors.
  Young people will attack old
    people.
  Ordinary people will attack those
    who are more important.

⁶ A man will grab hold of one of his
    brothers

at his father's home. He will say,
  "You have a coat. So you be our
    leader.
  Take charge of all of these
    broken-down buildings!"
⁷ But at that time the brother will
    cry out,
  "I can't help you.
  I don't have any food or clothing in
    my house.
  Don't make me the leader of
    these people."

⁸ Jerusalem is about to fall.
  And so is Judah.
  They say and do things against the
    LORD.
  They dare to disobey him to his
    very face.
⁹ The look on their faces is a witness
    against them.
  They show off their sin, just as
    the people of Sodom did.
  They don't even try to hide it.
  How terrible it will be for them!
  They have brought trouble on
    themselves.

¹⁰ Tell those who do what is right
    that things will go well with
    them.
  They will enjoy the results of the
    good things they've done.
¹¹ But how terrible it will be for those
    who do what is evil!
  Trouble is about to fall on them.
  They will be paid back for the
    evil things they've done.

¹² Those who are young crush my
    people.
  Women rule over them.
  My people, your leaders have
    taken you down the wrong
    path.
  They have turned you away from
    the right path.

¹³ The LORD takes his place in court.
  He stands up to judge the
    people.
¹⁴ He judges the elders and leaders of
    his people.
  He says to them,
  "My people are like a vineyard.
  You have destroyed them.
  The things you have taken from
    poor people are in your
    houses.

15 What do you mean by crushing my
people?
Why are you grinding the faces of
the poor into the dirt?"
announces the Lord.
He is the LORD who rules over all.

16 The LORD continues,
"The women in Zion are very
proud.
They walk along with their noses
in the air.
They tease men with their eyes.
They walk with quick, short steps.
Little chains jingle on their
ankles.
17 So I will put sores on the heads of
Zion's women.
And I will remove the hair from
their heads."

18 At that time the Lord will take away
the beautiful things they wear. He will
take away their decorations, headbands and moon-shaped necklaces.
19 He'll take away their earrings, bracelets and veils. 20 He'll remove their
headdresses, ankle chains and belts.
He'll take away their perfume bottles
and charms. 21 He'll remove the rings
they wear on their fingers and in their
noses. 22 He'll take away their fine
robes and their capes and coats. He'll
take away their purses 23 and mirrors.
And he'll take away their linen clothes,
turbans and shawls.

24 Instead of smelling sweet,
the women will smell bad.
Instead of wearing belts,
they will wear ropes.
Instead of having beautiful hair,
they won't have any hair at all.
Instead of wearing fine clothes,
they'll wear black clothes to
show how sad they are.
Instead of being beautiful,
they'll have the brands of slaves
on their bodies.
25 Jerusalem, your men will be killed
with swords.
Your soldiers will die in battle.
26 The city of Zion will be very sad.
Like a widow, she will lose
everything.
She will sit on the ground and
sob.

4 At that time seven women
will grab hold of one man.
They'll say to him, "We will eat
our own food.
We'll provide our own clothes.
Just let us become your wives.
Take away our shame!"

THE BRANCH OF THE LORD

2 At that time Israel's king will be
beautiful and glorious. He will be
called The Branch of the LORD. The
fruit of the land will be the pride and
glory of those who are still left alive in
Israel.
3 Those who are left in Zion will be
called holy. They will be recorded
among those who are alive in Jerusalem. 4 The Lord will wash away the
sin of the women in Zion. He will clean
up the blood that was spilled there.
He will judge those who spilled that
blood. His burning anger will blaze
out at them.
5 Then the LORD will create over Jerusalem a cloud of smoke by day. He will
also create a glow of flaming fire at
night. They will appear over all of
Mount Zion and those who gather together there. The LORD's glory will be
like a tent over them. 6 It will cover
them and give them shade from the
hot sun all day long. It will be a safe
place where they can hide from
storms and rain.

THE SONG OF THE VINEYARD

5 I will sing a song for the LORD.
He is the one I love.
It's a song about his vineyard
Israel.
The one I love had a vineyard.
It was on a hillside that had rich
soil.
2 He dug up the soil and removed its
stones.
He planted the very best vines in
it.
He built a lookout tower there.
He also cut out a winepress for it.
Then he kept looking for a crop of
good grapes.
But the vineyard produced only
bad fruit.

3 So the LORD said, "People of
Jerusalem and Judah,

you be the judge between me
and my vineyard.
⁴ What more could I have done for
my vineyard?
I did everything I could.
I kept looking for a crop of good
grapes.
So why did it produce only bad
ones?
⁵ Now I will tell you
what I am going to do to my
vineyard.
I will take away its fence.
And it will be destroyed.
I will break down its wall.
And people will walk all over it.
⁶ I will turn my vineyard into a dry
and empty desert.
It will not be pruned or taken
care of.
Thorns and bushes will grow
there.
I will command the clouds
not to rain on it."

⁷ The vineyard of the LORD who
rules over all
is the nation of Israel.
The people of Judah
are the garden he takes delight in.
He kept looking for them to do
what is fair.
But all he saw was blood being
spilled.
He kept looking for them to do
what is right.
But all he heard were cries of
suffering.

THE LORD JUDGES
HIS VINEYARD

⁸ How terrible it will be for you who
get too many houses!
How terrible for you who get too
many fields!
Finally there won't be any space
left in the land.
Then you will live all alone.

⁹ I heard the LORD who rules over all
announce a message. He said,

"You can be sure that the great
houses will become empty.
The fine homes will be left with
no one living in them.
¹⁰ A ten-acre vineyard will produce
only six gallons of wine.

Six bushels of seeds will produce
less than a bushel of grain."

¹¹ How terrible it will be for those
who get up early in the
morning
to start drinking!
How terrible for those who stay up
late at night
until they are drunk with wine!
¹² They have harps and lyres at their
big dinners.
They have tambourines, flutes
and wine.
But they don't have any concern
for the mighty acts of the
LORD.
They don't have any respect for
what his powerful hands have
done.
¹³ So my people will be taken away
as prisoners.
That's because they don't
understand what the LORD has
done.
Their government leaders will die
of hunger.
The rest of the people won't have
any water to drink.
¹⁴ So the grave is hungry to receive
them.
Its mouth is open wide to
swallow them up.
Their nobles and the rest of the
people will go down into it.
They will go there together with
all those who have wild
parties.
¹⁵ So man will be brought low.
People will be put to shame.
Those who brag will be brought
down.
¹⁶ But the LORD who rules over all
will be honored
because he judges fairly.
The holy God will show that he is
holy
by doing what is right.
¹⁷ Then sheep will graze as if they
were in their own
grasslands.
Lambs will eat grass among the
destroyed buildings
where rich people used to live.
¹⁸ How terrible it will be for those
who continue to sin
and lie about it!

How terrible for those who keep
　on doing what is evil
　as if they were tied to it!
¹⁹ How terrible for those who say,
　"Let God hurry up and do what
　　he says he will.
　We want to see it happen.
　Let the Holy One of Israel carry
　　out his plan soon.
　We want to know what it is."

²⁰ How terrible it will be for those
　who say
　that what is evil is good!
　How terrible for those who say
　that what is good is evil!
　How terrible for those who say
　that darkness is light
　and light is darkness!
　How terrible for those who say
　that what is bitter is sweet
　and what is sweet is bitter!

²¹ How terrible it will be for those
　who think they are wise!
　How terrible for those who think
　they are really clever!

²² How terrible it will be for those
　who are heroes at drinking wine!
　How terrible for those
　who are heroes at mixing drinks!
²³ How terrible for those
　who take money to set guilty
　　people free!
　How terrible for those
　who don't treat good people
　　fairly!
²⁴ Flames of fire burn up straw.
　Dry grass sinks down into those
　　flames.
　Evil people will be like plants
　　whose roots rot away.
　They will be like flowers that are
　　blown away like dust.
　That's because they have said no
　　to the law of the LORD who
　　rules over all.
　They have turned against the
　　message of the Holy One of
　　Israel.
²⁵ So the LORD's anger burns against
　his people.
　He raises his hand against them.
　He strikes them down.
　The mountains shake.
　The bodies of dead people lie in
　　the streets like trash.

Even then, the LORD is still angry.
　His hand is still raised against
　　them.

²⁶ He lifts up a banner to gather the
　nations that are far away.
　He whistles for them to come
　　from the farthest places on earth.
　Here they come.
　They are moving very quickly.
²⁷ None of them grows tired.
　None of them falls down.
　None of them sleeps or even
　　takes a nap.
　All of them are ready for battle.
　Every belt is pulled tight.
　Not a single sandal strap is broken.
²⁸ The enemies' arrows are sharp.
　All of their bows are ready.
　The hoofs of their horses are as
　　hard as rock.
　Their chariot wheels turn like a
　　twister.
²⁹ The sound of their army is like the
　roar of lions.
　It's like the roar of young lions.
　They growl as they capture what
　　they were chasing.
　They carry it off.
　No one can take it away from
　　them.
³⁰ At that time the enemy army will
　roar over Israel.
　It will sound like the roaring of
　　the ocean.
　If someone looks at the land of
　　Israel,
　he will see darkness and trouble.
　The clouds will make even the
　　light become dark.

THE LORD APPOINTS ISAIAH TO SPEAK FOR HIM

6 In the year that King Uzziah died, I saw the Lord. He was seated on his throne. His long robe filled the temple. He was highly honored. ²Above him were seraphs. Each of them had six wings. With two wings they covered their faces. With two wings they covered their feet. And with two wings they were flying. ³They were calling out to one another. They were saying,

"Holy, holy, holy is the LORD who
　rules over all.

The whole earth is full of his
  glory."

⁴The sound of their voices caused the stone doorframe to shake. The temple was filled with smoke.

⁵"How terrible it is for me!" I cried out. "I'm about to be destroyed! My mouth speaks sinful words. And I live among people who speak sinful words. Now I have seen the King with my own eyes. He is the LORD who rules over all."

⁶A seraph flew over to me. He was holding a hot coal. He had used tongs to take it from the altar. ⁷He touched my mouth with the coal. He said, "This has touched your lips. Your guilt has been taken away. Your sin has been paid for."

⁸Then I heard the voice of the Lord. He said, "Who will I send? Who will go for us?"

I said, "Here I am. Send me!"

⁹So he said, "Go and speak to these people. Tell them,

" 'You will hear but never
    understand.
  You will see but never know what
    you are seeing.'

¹⁰Make the hearts of these people
    stubborn.
  Plug up their ears.
  Close their eyes.
  Otherwise they might see with
    their eyes.
  They might hear with their ears.
  They might understand with
    their hearts.
  And they might turn to me and be
    healed."

¹¹Then I said, "Lord, how long will it be like that?"

He answered,

"It will last until the cities of Israel
    are destroyed
  and no one is living in them.
  It will last until the houses are
    deserted.
  The fields will be completely
    destroyed.
¹²It will last until I have sent
    everyone far away.
  The land will be totally deserted.
¹³Even if a tenth of the people
    remain there,
  the land will be completely
    destroyed again.

Why are some Kids bullies?

Usually bullies are bigger and stronger than other kids. They have learned to get what they want by force. Bullies are all ages—some never outgrow it. You can find them everywhere you go. No one should get away with bullying others. If you see it happening or get bullied yourself, tell a teacher, the principal or your mom or dad right away.

checkout
Isaiah 5:23

Related verses:
1 Samuel
17:41–42;
Ecclesiastes 4:1

But when oak trees and terebinth
    trees
are cut down, stumps are left.
And my holy people will be like
    stumps
    that begin to grow again."

THE MIRACULOUS SIGN
OF IMMANUEL

7 Ahaz was king of Judah. Rezin
was king of Aram. And Pekah
was king of Israel. Rezin and Pekah marched up to fight against Jerusalem. But they couldn't overpower it.
Ahaz was the son of Jotham and the
grandson of Uzziah. Pekah was the
son of Remaliah.

²The royal family of Ahaz was told,
"The army of Aram has joined forces
with Ephraim's army." So the hearts of
Ahaz and his people trembled with
fear. They shook just as trees in the forest shake when the wind blows
through them.

³The LORD said to me, "Go out and
see Ahaz. Take your son Shear-Jashub
with you. Meet Ahaz at the end of the
channel that brings water from the
Upper Pool. It is on the road to the
Washerman's Field.

⁴"Tell Ahaz, 'Be careful. Stay calm.
Do not be afraid. Do not lose hope because of the burning anger of Rezin,
Aram and the son of Remaliah. After
all, they are nothing but a couple of
pieces of smoking firewood. ⁵Aram,
Ephraim and Remaliah's son have
planned to destroy you. They said,
⁶"Let's march into Judah and attack it.
Let's tear everything down. Then we
can share the land among ourselves.
And we can make Tabeel's son king
over it."

⁷" 'But I am the LORD and King. I say,

" ' "That will not happen.
    It will not take place.
⁸The capital of Aram is Damascus.
    And the ruler of Damascus is
        only Rezin.
Do not worry about the people of
    Ephraim.
    They will be too crushed to be
        considered a people.
    That will happen before 65 years
        are over.
⁹The capital of Ephraim is Samaria.

And the ruler of Samaria is only
    Remaliah's son.
If you do not stand firm in your
    faith,
    you will not stand at all." ' "

¹⁰The LORD spoke to Ahaz through
me again. He said, ¹¹"I am the LORD
your God. Ask me to give you a miraculous sign. It can be anything in the
deepest grave or in the highest heaven."
¹²But Ahaz said, "I won't ask. I won't
put the LORD to the test."
¹³Then I said, "Listen, you members
of the royal family of Ahaz! Isn't it
enough for you to test the patience of
men? Are you also going to test the patience of my God? ¹⁴The LORD himself
will give you a miraculous sign. The
virgin is going to have a baby. She will
give birth to a son. And he will be
called Immanuel.
¹⁵"The time will come when he is old
enough to decide between what is
wrong and what is right. By that time
he will have only butter and honey to
eat. ¹⁶But even before that happens,
the lands of the two kings you are
afraid of will be completely destroyed.
¹⁷"The LORD will also bring the king
of Assyria against you. And he will
bring him against your people and the
whole royal family. That will be a time
of trouble unlike any since the people
of Ephraim broke away from Judah."
¹⁸At that time the LORD will whistle
for the Egyptians. They will come like
flies from the streams of Egypt. He will
also whistle for the Assyrians. They
will come from their country like bees.
¹⁹All of them will come and camp in
the deep valleys. They will camp in
caves in the rocks. And they'll camp
near bushes and water holes.
²⁰At that time the Lord will use the
Assyrians to punish you. Ahaz had
hired them earlier from east of the Euphrates River. Now their king will be
like a razor in the Lord's hand. He will
shave the hair from your head and
legs. He will also shave off your beards.
²¹At that time a man will only be able
to keep one young cow and two goats
alive. ²²But they will give enough milk
and butter to live on. Everyone who is
left alive in the land will have nothing
but butter and honey to eat.

²³The land used to have vineyards with 1,000 vines worth 25 pounds of silver. But soon the whole land will be covered with thorns and bushes. ²⁴Men will go there to hunt with bows and arrows. That's because it will be covered with bushes and thorns. ²⁵All of the hills used to be plowed with hoes. But you won't go there anymore. That's because you will be afraid of the thorns and bushes. Cattle will be turned loose on those hills. And sheep will run there.

THE LORD USES ASSYRIA TO JUDGE JUDAH

8 The LORD said to me, "Get a large scroll. Write 'Maher-Shalal-Hash-Baz' on it with a pen. ²I will send for Zechariah and the priest Uriah. They can be trusted. They will be witnesses for me. Zechariah is the son of Jeberekiah."

³Then I went and made love to my wife, who was a prophet. She became pregnant and had a baby boy. The LORD said to me, "Name him Maher-Shalal-Hash-Baz.

⁴"The king of Assyria will carry off the wealth of Damascus. He will also carry away the goods that were taken from Samaria. That will happen before the boy knows how to say 'My father' or 'My mother.' "

⁵The LORD continued,

⁶ "I am like the gently flowing
    stream of Siloam.
But the people of Judah have
    turned their backs on me.
They are filled with joy because of
    the fall of Rezin
and the son of Remaliah.
⁷So I am about to bring against
    these people
    the king of Assyria and his whole
    army.
The Assyrians will be like the
    mighty Euphrates River
when it is flooding.
They will run over everything in
    their path.
⁸They will sweep on into Judah like
    a flood.
They will pass through Judah
    and reach all the way to
    Jerusalem.

Immanuel, they will attack your
    land like an eagle.
Their wings will spread out and
    cover it."

⁹Sound the battle cry, you nations!
    But you will be torn apart.
Listen, all of you lands far away!
Prepare for battle! But you will be
    torn apart.
Prepare for battle! But you will be
    torn apart.
¹⁰Make your battle plans! But you
    won't succeed.
Give your orders! But they won't
    be carried out.
That's because God is with us.

HAVE RESPECT FOR GOD

¹¹The LORD put his powerful hand on me and spoke to me. He warned me not to live the way these people live. He said,

¹² "People of Judah, do not agree
    with those who say
    Isaiah is guilty of treason.
Do not fear what they fear.
    Do not be afraid.
¹³I am the LORD who rules over all.
You must think about me as holy.
You must have respect for me.
    You must fear me.
¹⁴Then I will be a holy place of
    safety for you.
But for many people in Israel and
    Judah I will be
a stone that causes them to trip.
I will be a rock that makes them
    fall.
And for the people of Jerusalem I
    will be
a trap and a snare.
¹⁵Many of them will trip.
They will fall and be broken.
They will be trapped and
    captured."

¹⁶Keep safe what the LORD said to
    you through me.
Seal up among my followers
    what he taught you through
    me.
¹⁷I will wait for the LORD.
He is turning his face away from
    Jacob's people.
I will put my trust in him.

¹⁸Here I am. Here are the children the LORD has given me. We are signs and reminders to Israel from the LORD who rules over all. He lives on Mount Zion.

¹⁹Some will tell you to ask for advice from people who get messages from those who have died. Others will tell you to ask for advice from people who talk to the spirits of the dead. But those people only whisper. Their words are barely heard. So shouldn't you ask for advice from your God? Why should you get advice from dead people to help those who are alive?

²⁰Follow what the LORD taught you and said to you through me. People who don't speak in keeping with those words won't have any hope in the morning. ²¹They will suffer and be hungry. They'll wander through the land. When they are very hungry, they will become angry. They'll look up toward heaven. They'll call down curses on their king and their God. ²²Then they will look at the earth. They'll see nothing but suffering and darkness. They'll see terrible sadness. They'll be driven into total darkness.

A SON WILL BE GIVEN TO US

9 But there won't be any more sadness for those who were suffering. In the past the LORD brought shame on the land of Zebulun. He also brought shame on the land of Naphtali. But in days to come he will honor Galilee, where people from other nations live. He will honor the land along the Mediterranean Sea. And he will honor the territory east of the Jordan River.

²The people who are now living in darkness
will see a great light.
They are now living in a very dark land.
But a light will shine on them.
³LORD, you will make our nation larger.
You will increase their joy.
They will show you how glad they are.
They will be as glad as people are at harvest time.
They will be as glad as soldiers are

when they share the things
they've taken after a battle.
⁴You set Israel free from Midian long ago.
In the same way, you will break the heavy yoke that weighs Israel down.
You will break the wooden beams that are on their shoulders.
You will break the rods of those who strike them down.
⁵Every fighting man's boot that is used in battle will be burned up.
So will every piece of clothes that is covered with blood.
All of them will be thrown into the fire.
⁶A child will be born to us.
A son will be given to us.
He will rule over us.
And he will be called
Wonderful Adviser and Mighty God.
He will also be called Father Who Lives Forever
and Prince Who Brings Peace.
⁷The authority of his rule will continue to grow.
The peace he brings will never end.
He will rule on David's throne and over his kingdom.
He will make the kingdom strong and secure.
His rule will be based on what is fair and right.
It will last forever.
The LORD's great love will make sure that happens.
He rules over all.

THE LORD IS ANGRY WITH ISRAEL

⁸The Lord has sent a message against Jacob's people.
He will punish Israel.
⁹All of the people will know about it.
Ephraim's people and those who live in Samaria will know about it.
Their hearts are very proud.
They say,
¹⁰"The brick buildings have fallen down.

But we will rebuild them with
  blocks of stone.
The fig trees have been chopped
  down.
But we'll plant cedar trees in
  place of them."
¹¹In spite of that, the LORD has made
  Rezin's enemies stronger.
He has stirred up Assyria to fight
  against Israel.
¹²Arameans from the east
  have opened their mouths and
    swallowed Israel up.
So have Philistines from the
  west.

Even then, the LORD is still
  angry.
His hand is still raised against
  them.

¹³But his people have not returned
  to the One who struck them
    down.
They haven't turned for help
  to the LORD who rules over all.
¹⁴So he will cut off from Israel heads
  and tails alike.
In a single day he will cut off
  palm branches and tall grass
    alike.
The palm branches are the people
  who rule over others.
The tall grass is the people who
  bow down to them.
¹⁵The elders and important leaders
  are the heads.
The prophets who teach lies are
  the tails.
¹⁶Those who guide the people of
  Israel are leading them down
    the wrong path.
So those who follow them aren't
  on the right road.
¹⁷The Lord will not be pleased with
  the young men.
He won't take pity on widows
  and on children whose fathers
    have died.
All of them are ungodly and evil.
They say sinful things with their
  mouths.

Even then, the LORD is still angry.
His hand is still raised against
  them.

¹⁸What is evil burns like a fire.
It burns up bushes and thorns.

It sets the forest on fire.
It sends up a huge column of
  smoke.
¹⁹The LORD rules over all.
When he gets angry, he will burn
  up the land.
The people will die.
Men will eat their brothers.
²⁰People will eat up everything they
  can find on their right.
But they'll still be hungry.
They will eat everything they can
  find on their left.
But they won't be satisfied.
So they will eat the dead bodies of
  their children.
²¹ That's what Manasseh's people
    will do to Ephraim.
And that's what Ephraim's people
  will do to Manasseh.
Together they will turn against
  Judah.

Even then, the LORD is still angry.
His hand is still raised against
  them.

10

How terrible it will be for
  you
who make laws that aren't
  fair!
How terrible for you
  who write laws that make life
    hard for others!
²You take away the rights of poor
  people.
You hold back what is fair
  from my people who are
    suffering.
You take for yourselves what
  belongs to widows.
You rob children whose fathers
  have died.
³What will you do on the day when
  the LORD punishes you?
On that day trouble will come
  from far away.
Who will you run to for help?
Who will you trust your riches
  with?
⁴All you can do is bow down in fear
  among the prisoners.
All you can do is fall among those
  who have died in battle.

Even then, the LORD is still angry.
His hand is still raised against
  them.

THE LORD WILL JUDGE ASSYRIA

⁵The LORD says, "How terrible it will
    be for the people of Assyria!
    They are the war club that carries
        out my anger.
⁶I will send them against the
        ungodly nation of Judah.
    I will order them to fight against
        my own people.
    They make me angry.
    I will order them to take their
        goods and carry them away.
    I will order them to walk on my
        people
    as if they were walking on mud.
⁷But that is not what the king of
        Assyria plans.
    It is not what he has in mind.
    His purpose is to destroy many
        nations.
    His purpose is to put an end to
        them.
⁸'Aren't all of my commanders
        kings?' he says.
⁹ 'I took over Calno just as I took
        Carchemish.
    I took over Hamath just as I did
        Arpad.
    I took Samaria just as I did
        Damascus.
¹⁰My powerful hand grabbed hold of
        kingdoms
    whose people worship statues of
        gods.
    They had more gods than
        Jerusalem and Samaria did.
¹¹I took over Samaria and its statues
        of gods.
    In the same way, I will take
        Jerusalem and its gods.' "

¹²The Lord will finish everything he
has planned to do against Mount Zion
and Jerusalem. Then he'll say, "Now I
will punish the king of Assyria. I will
punish him because his heart and his
eyes are so proud.
¹³"The king of Assyria says,

" 'I have used my powerful hand
        to take over all of those nations.
    I am very wise.
    I have great understanding.
    I have wiped out the borders
        between nations.
    I've taken their treasures.

Like a great hero I've brought
        their kings under my control.
¹⁴I've taken the wealth of the
        nations.
    It was as easy as reaching into a
        bird's nest.
    I've gathered the riches of all of
        those countries.
    It was as easy as gathering eggs
        that have been left in a nest.
    Not a single baby bird flapped its
        wings.
    Not one of them opened its
        mouth to chirp.' "

¹⁵Does an ax claim to be more
        important
    than the one who swings it?
    Does a saw brag that it is better
    than the one who uses it?
    That would be like a stick
    swinging someone who picks it
        up!
    It would be like a war club
    waving the one who carries it!
¹⁶So the LORD who rules over all will
        send a sickness.
    The Lord will send it on the king
        of Assyria's strong fighting
        men.
    It will make them weaker and
        weaker.
    The army he was so proud of will
        be completely destroyed.
    It will be as if it had been burned
        up in a fire.
¹⁷The LORD is the light of Israel.
    He will become a fire.
    Israel's Holy One will become a
        flame.
    In a single day he will burn up all
        of Assyria's bushes.
    He will destroy all of their thorns.
¹⁸He will completely destroy the
        beauty
    of their forests and rich farm
        lands.
    The Assyrian army will be like a
        sick man
    who becomes weaker and
        weaker.
¹⁹It will be like the trees of their
        forests.
    So few of them will be left
        standing
    that even a child could count
        them.

ISRAEL WILL RETURN TO THE LORD

²⁰ In days to come, some people will
still be left alive in Israel.
They will be from Jacob's family
line.
But they won't depend any longer
on
the nation that struck them
down.
Instead, they will truly depend on
the LORD.
He is the Holy One of Israel.
²¹ The people of Jacob who are still
alive
will return to the Mighty God.
²² Israel, your people might be as
many as the grains of sand by
the sea.
But only a few of them will
return.
The LORD has handed down a
death sentence.
He will destroy his people.
What he does is right.
²³ The LORD who rules over all will
carry out his sentence.
The Lord will destroy the whole
land.

²⁴ The LORD rules over all. The Lord
says,

"My people who live in Zion,
do not be afraid of the Assyrian
army.
They beat you with rods.
They lift up war clubs against
you,
just as the Egyptians did.
²⁵ Very soon I will not be angry with
you anymore.
I will turn my anger against the
Assyrians.
I will destroy them."

²⁶ The LORD who rules over all will
beat them with a whip.
He will strike them down as he
struck Midian down at the
rock of Oreb.
And he will reach his wooden staff
out over the waters.
That's what he did in Egypt.
²⁷ People of Zion, in days to come he
will lift
the heavy load of the Assyrians
from your shoulders.

He will remove their yokes from
your necks.
They will be broken
because you have become so
strong.
²⁸ The Assyrian army has entered the
town of Aiath.
They have passed through
Migron.
They have stored up supplies at
Micmash.
²⁹ They have marched through the
pass there. They said,
"Let's camp for the night at
Geba."
The people of Ramah tremble with
fear.
Those who live in Gibeah of Saul
run away.
³⁰ Town of Gallim, cry out!
Laishah, listen!
Poor Anathoth!
³¹ The people of Madmenah are
running away.
Those who live in Gebim are
hiding.
³² Today the Assyrians have stopped
at Nob.
They are shaking their fists
at Mount Zion in the city of
Jerusalem.

³³ The Assyrian soldiers are like trees
in a forest.
The LORD who rules over all
will chop them down.
The Lord will cut off their
branches
with his great power.
He will chop the tall trees down.
He will cut down even the
highest ones.
³⁴ The Mighty One will chop down
the forest with his ax.
He will cut down the cedar trees
in Lebanon.

A BRANCH WILL COME FROM JESSE'S FAMILY LINE

11 Jesse's family is like a tree
that has been cut
down.
A new little tree will grow from
its stump.
From its roots a Branch will grow
and produce fruit.

² The Spirit of the LORD will rest on
　　that Branch.
　　He will help him to be wise and
　　　understanding.
　　He will help him make wise plans
　　　and carry them out.
　　He will help him know the LORD
　　　and have respect for him.
³ The Branch will take delight
　　in respecting the LORD.

　　He will not judge things only by
　　　the way they look.
　　He won't make decisions based
　　　simply on what people say.
⁴ He will always do what is right
　　when he judges those who are in
　　　need.
　　He'll be completely fair
　　when he makes decisions about
　　　poor people.
　　When he commands that people
　　　be punished,
　　it will happen.
　　When he orders that evil people be
　　　put to death,
　　it will take place.
⁵ He will put godliness on as if it
　　were his belt.
　　He'll wear faithfulness around
　　his waist.

⁶ Wolves will live with lambs.
　　Leopards will lie down with
　　　goats.
　　Calves and lions will eat together.
　　And little children will lead them
　　　around.
⁷ Cows will eat with bears.
　　Their little ones will lie down
　　　together.
　　And lions will eat straw like oxen.
⁸ A baby will play near a hole where
　　cobras live.
　　A young child will put his hand
　　　into a nest
　　where poisonous snakes live.
⁹ None of those animals will harm
　　　or destroy anything or anyone
　　on my holy mountain of Zion.
　　The oceans are full of water.
　　In the same way, the earth will be
　　　filled
　　with the knowledge of the LORD.

¹⁰ At that time the man who is called
the Root from Jesse's family line will be
like a banner that brings nations together. They will come to him. And the
place where he rules will be glorious.
¹¹ At that time the Lord will reach out
his hand to gather his people a second
time. He will bring back those who are

KIDS' QUESTION

Are there animals in heaven?

After Christ comes again, God will create new heavens and the
new earth. That includes the animal kingdom. But keep in mind
that the animals will not be just like they are here on earth. They will not be
dangerous. They will not attack people or be afraid of us. And all of them
will get along with each other. They will not
need to eat other animals. The Bible also
says that there will be trees and other
plant life in heaven. We do not know
whether we'll see our own pets who
have died. But the Bible does say that
there will be animals.

checkout Isaiah 11:6

Related verses:
Isaiah 55:12,13

left alive. He'll bring them back from Assyria, Lower Egypt, Upper Egypt and Cush. He'll bring them from Elam, Babylonia and Hamath. He will also bring them from the islands of the Mediterranean Sea.

¹²He will lift up a banner.
It will show the nations that he is
gathering the people of Israel.
He'll bring back those who had
been taken away as prisoners.
He'll gather together the scattered
people of Judah.
He'll bring them back from all
four directions.
¹³Ephraim's people won't be jealous
anymore.
Judah's attackers will be cut off.
Ephraim won't be jealous of Judah.
And Judah won't attack Ephraim.
¹⁴Together they will rush down the
slopes of Philistia to the west.
They'll take what belongs to the
people of the east.
They'll take over Edom and Moab.
The people of Ammon will be
under their control.
¹⁵The LORD will dry up
the Red Sea in Egypt.
With his powerful hand he'll send
a burning wind
to sweep over the Euphrates
River.
He will break it up into many
streams.
Then people will be able to go
across it wearing sandals.
¹⁶There was a road the people of
Israel used
when they came up from Egypt.
In the same way, there will be a
wide road coming out of
Assyria.
It will be used by the LORD's
people who are left alive
there.

TWO SONGS OF PRAISE

12 In days to come, the people of Israel will sing,

"LORD, we will praise you.
You were angry with us.
But now your anger has turned
away from us.
And you have brought us comfort.

²God, you are the one who saves us.
We will trust in you.
Then we won't be afraid.
LORD, you give us strength.
We sing about you.
LORD, you have saved us."
³People of Israel, he will save you.
That will bring you joy like water
that is brought up from wells.

⁴In days to come, the people of Israel
will sing,

"Give thanks to the LORD. Worship
him.
Tell the nations what he has
done.
Announce how honored he is.
⁵Sing to the LORD. He has done
glorious things.
Let it be known all over the
world.
⁶People of Zion, give a loud shout!
Sing with joy!
The Holy One of Israel is among
you.
And he is great."

A MESSAGE ABOUT BABYLONIA

13 Here is the vision about Babylonia that Isaiah, the son of Amoz, saw.

²Lift up a banner on the top of a
bare hill.
Shout to the enemy soldiers.
Wave for them to enter the gates
that are used by the nobles of
Babylon.
³The LORD has set those soldiers
apart to fight for him.
He has sent for them to carry out
his anger against Babylon.
They will be happy when he wins
the battle for them.

⁴Listen! I hear a noise in the
mountains.
It sounds like a huge crowd.
Listen! I hear a loud noise among
the kingdoms.
It sounds like nations gathering
together.
The LORD who rules over all is
bringing
an army together for war.
⁵They come from lands far away.

They come from the farthest
places on earth.
The LORD and those weapons of
his anger
are coming to destroy the whole
country of Babylonia.

⁶Cry out! The day of the LORD is
near.
The Mighty One is coming to
destroy them.
⁷Their hands won't be able to help
them.
Everyone's heart will melt away
in fear.
⁸The people will be filled with
terror.
Pain and suffering will grab hold
of them.
They will groan with pain like a
woman having a baby.
They'll look at one another in
terror.
Their faces will burn with
shame.

⁹The day of the LORD is coming.
It will be a terrible day.
The LORD's burning anger will
blaze out.
He will make the land dry and
empty.
He'll destroy the sinners in it.
¹⁰All of the stars in the sky
will stop giving their light.
The sun will be darkened as soon
as it rises.
The moon will not shine.
¹¹The LORD will punish the world
because it is so evil.
He will punish evil people for
their sins.
He'll put an end to the bragging of
those who are proud.
He'll bring down the pride of
those who don't show any
pity.
¹²He'll make men harder to find
than pure gold.
They will be harder to find than
gold from Ophir.
¹³He will make the heavens tremble.
He'll shake the earth out of its
place.
The LORD who rules over all will
show how angry he is.
At that time his burning anger
will blaze out.

¹⁴Outsiders who live in Babylonia
will scatter
like antelope that are chased by a
hunter.
They are like sheep that don't
have a shepherd.
All of them will return to their own
people.
They will run back to their own
countries.
¹⁵Those who are captured will have
spears stuck through them.
Those who are caught will be
killed with swords.
¹⁶Their babies will be smashed to
pieces
right in front of their eyes.
Their houses will be robbed.
Their wives will be raped.

¹⁷The LORD will stir up the Medes to
attack the Babylonians.
They aren't interested in getting
silver.
They don't delight in gold.
¹⁸Instead, they will use their bows
and arrows
to strike the young men down.
They won't even show any mercy
to babies.
They won't take pity on children.
¹⁹The city of Babylon is the jewel of
kingdoms.
It is the glory and pride of the
Babylonians.
But God will destroy it
just as he did Sodom and
Gomorrah.
²⁰No one will ever live in Babylon
again.
No one will live there for all time
to come.
Arabs will never set up their tents
there.
Shepherds will never rest their
flocks there.
²¹But desert creatures will lie down
there.
Wild dogs will fill its houses.
Owls will live there.
Wild goats will jump around in it.
²²Hyenas will cry out in its forts.
Wild dogs will bark in its
beautiful palaces.
The time for Babylon to be
punished is near.
Its days are numbered.

14

The LORD will show
tender love toward
Jacob's people.
Once again he will choose Israel.
He'll settle them in their own
land.
Outsiders will join them.
They and the people of Jacob will
become one people.
² Nations will help Israel
return to their own land.
People from other nations will
belong to Israel.
They will serve them as male and
female servants in the LORD's
land.
The Israelites will make prisoners
of those who had held them
as prisoners.
They will rule over those who
had crushed them.

³ The LORD will put an end to Israel's
suffering and trouble. They won't be
slaves anymore. ⁴ They will make fun of
the king of Babylonia. They will say,

"See how the one who crushed
others has fallen!
See how his anger has come to
an end!
⁵ The LORD has taken away the
authority of evil people.
He has broken the power of
rulers.
⁶ When they became angry, they
struck nations down.
Their blows never stopped.
In their anger they brought
nations under their control.
They attacked them again and
again.
⁷ All of the lands now enjoy peace
and rest.
They break out into singing.
⁸ Even the pine trees are glad.
The cedar trees of Lebanon are
happy too.
They say, 'Babylon, you have fallen.
Now no one comes and cuts us
down.'

⁹ "King of Babylonia, many people
in the grave are really excited
about meeting you when you go
down there.
The spirits of the dead get up to
welcome you.

At one time all of them were
leaders in the world.
They were kings over the nations.
They get up from their thrones.
¹⁰ All of them call out to you.
They say,
'You have become weak, just as we
are.
You have become like us.'
¹¹ Your grand show of power has
been brought down to the
grave.
The noise of your harps has
come down here along with
your power.
Maggots are spread out under you.
Worms cover you.

¹² "King of Babylonia, you thought
you were the bright morning
star.
But now you have fallen from
heaven!
You once brought nations down.
But now you have been thrown
down to the earth!
¹³ You said in your heart,
'I will go up to heaven.
I'll raise my throne
above the stars of God.
I'll sit as king on the mountain
where the gods meet.
I'll set up my throne on the
highest slopes of the sacred
mountain.
¹⁴ I will rise above the tops of the
clouds.
I'll make myself like the Most
High God.'
¹⁵ But now you have been brought
down to the grave.
You have been thrown into the
deepest part of the pit.

¹⁶ "Those who see you stare at you.
They think about what has
happened to you.
They say to themselves,
'Is this the man who shook the
earth?
Is he the one who made
kingdoms tremble with fear?
¹⁷ Did he turn the world into a
desert?
Did he destroy its cities?
Did he refuse to let his prisoners
go home?'

¹⁸ "All of the kings of the nations are
    buried with honor.
  Each of them lies in his own tomb.
¹⁹ But you have been thrown out of
    your tomb.
  You are like a branch that is cut
    off and thrown away.
  You are covered with the bodies
    of those who have been killed
    with swords.
  You have been tossed into a
    stony pit along with them.
  You are like a dead body that
    people have walked on.
²⁰ You won't be buried like other
    kings.
  That's because you have destroyed
    your land.
  You have killed your people.

  "The children of that evil man will
    be killed.
  None of them will be left to carry
    on the family name.
²¹ So prepare a place to kill his
    children.
  Kill them because of the sins of
    the rulers
  who lived before them.
  They must not rise to power.
  They must not rule over the
    world.
  They must not cover the earth
    with their cities."

²² "I will rise up against them,"
    announces the LORD who rules
    over all.
  "I will destroy Babylon.
  It will not be remembered
    anymore.
  No one will be left alive there.
  I will destroy its people and their
    children after them,"
               announces the LORD.
²³ "I will turn it into a place where
    nothing but owls can live.
  I will turn it into a swamp.
  I will sweep through it like a
    broom and destroy
    everything,"
  announces the LORD who rules
    over all.

A MESSAGE ABOUT ASSYRIA

²⁴ The LORD who rules over all has
taken an oath. He has said,

"You can be sure that what I have
    planned will happen.
  What I have decided will take
    place.
²⁵ I will crush the Assyrians in my
    land.
  On my mountains I will walk all
    over them.
  The yokes they put on my people
    will be removed.
  The heavy load they put on their
    shoulders will be taken away."

²⁶ That's how the LORD carries out his
    plan all over the world.
  That's how he reaches out his
    powerful hand to punish all of
    the nations.
²⁷ The LORD who rules over all has
    planned it.
  Who can stop him?
  He has reached out his powerful
    hand.
  Who can keep him from using it?

A MESSAGE ABOUT
THE PHILISTINES

²⁸ A message came to me from the
LORD in the year King Ahaz died. The
LORD said,

²⁹ "The rod of Assyria has struck all
    of you Philistines.
  But do not be glad that it is
    broken.
  That rod is like a snake that will
    produce an even more
    poisonous snake.
  It will produce a darting,
    poisonous serpent.
³⁰ Even the poorest people in Israel
    will have plenty to eat.
  Those who are in need will lie
    down in safety.
  But I will destroy your families.
  They will die of hunger.
  I will kill any of them who are
    still left alive.

³¹ "Cities of Philistia, cry out for help!
    Scream in pain!
  All of you Philistines, melt away
    in fear!
  An army is coming from the north
    in a cloud of dust.
  No one in its ranks is falling
    behind.
³² What answer should be given

to the messengers from that
　　nation?
Tell them, 'The LORD has made
　　Zion secure.
　　His suffering people will find
　　　safety there.' "

A MESSAGE ABOUT MOAB

15 Here is a message the LORD
gave me about Moab.

The city of Ar in Moab is
　　destroyed.
　It happened in a single night.
Kir in Moab is also destroyed.
　It happened in a single night.
2 The people of Dibon go up to their
　　temple to worship.
　They go to their high places to
　　sob.
　The people of Moab cry over the
　　cities of Nebo and Medeba.
　All of their heads are shaved.
　All of their beards have been cut
　　off.
3 In the streets they wear black
　　clothes.
　On their roofs and in the market
　　places
　all of them are crying.
　They fall down flat with their faces
　　toward the ground.
　And they sob.
4 The people of Heshbon and
　　Elealeh cry out.
　Their voices are heard all the way
　　to Jahaz.
　So the fighting men of Moab cry
　　out.
　Their hearts are weak.

5 My heart cries out over Moab.
　Some who run away get as far as
　　Zoar.
　Others run all the way to Eglath
　　Shelishiyah.
　Others go up the road to Luhith.
　They are sobbing as they go.
　Still others travel the road to
　　Horonaim.
　They sing a song of sadness
　　because their town is being
　　destroyed.
6 The waters at Nimrim are dried up.
　And so is the grass.
　The plants have died.
　Nothing green is left.

7 The people are trying to escape
　　through the Valley of the Poplar
　　Trees.
　They are carrying with them the
　　wealth
　they have collected and stored up.
8 Their loud cries echo along the
　　border of Moab.
　They reach as far as Eglaim.
　Their songs of sadness reach all
　　the way to Beer Elim.
9 The waters of the city of Dimon
　　are full of blood.
　But the LORD will bring even
　　more trouble on Dimon.
　He will bring lions against those
　　who run away from Moab.
　They will also attack those who
　　remain in the land.

16 People of Moab, send
lambs as a gift
to the ruler of Judah.
Send them from Sela.
　Send them across the desert.
　Send them to Mount Zion in the
　　city of Jerusalem.
2 The women of Moab are at the
　　places
　where people go across the
　　Arnon River.
　They are like birds that flap their
　　wings
　when they are pushed from their
　　nest.

3 The Moabites say to the rulers of
　　Judah,
　"Give us advice. Make a decision.
Cover us with your shadow.
　Make it like night even at noon.
Hide those of us who are running
　　away.
　Don't turn them over to their
　　enemies.
4 Let those who have run away from
　　Moab stay with you.
　Keep them safe from those who
　　are trying to destroy them."

Those who crush others will be
　　destroyed.
　The killing will stop.
　The attackers will disappear
　　from the earth.
5 A man from the royal house of
　　David will sit on Judah's
　　throne.

He will rule with faithful love.
When he judges he will do what is
    fair.
He will be quick to do what is
    right.
⁶We have heard all about Moab's
    pride.
We have heard how very proud
    they are.
They think they are so much
    better than others.
They brag about themselves.
But all of their bragging is
    nothing but empty words.

⁷So the people of Moab cry out.
All of them cry over their
    country.
Sing a song of sadness.
Sob over the men of Kir
    Hareseth.
⁸The vineyards of Heshbon dry up.
So do the vines of Sibmah.
The rulers of the nations
    have walked all over its finest
    vines.
Those vines once reached as far as
    Jazer.
They spread out toward the
    desert.
Their new growth went
    all the way to the Dead Sea.
⁹Jazer sobs over the vines of Sibmah.
And so do I.
Heshbon and Elealeh,
I soak you with my tears!
There isn't any ripe fruit for people
    to shout about.
There isn't any harvest to make
    them happy.
¹⁰Joy and gladness are taken away
    from the orchards.
No one sings or shouts in the
    vineyards.
No one stomps on grapes at the
    winepresses.
That's because the LORD has put
    an end to the shouting.
¹¹My heart sobs over Moab like a
    song of sadness played on a
    harp.
Deep down inside me I sob over
    Kir Hareseth.
¹²Moab's people go to their high
    place to pray.
But all they do is wear
    themselves out.

Their god Chemosh can't help
    them at all.

¹³That's the message the LORD has
already spoken about Moab. ¹⁴But now
he says, "In exactly three years, people
will look down on Moab's glory. Now
Moab has many people. But by that
time only a few of them will be left
alive. And even they will be weak."

MESSAGES ABOUT DAMASCUS AND ISRAEL

17 Here is a message the LORD
gave me about Damascus.
He said,

"Damascus will not be a city
    anymore.
Instead, all of its buildings will be
    knocked down.
²The cities of Aroer will be
    deserted.
They will be left to the flocks that
    lie down there.
No one will make them afraid.
³Ephraim's people will no longer
    have cities with high walls
    around them.
Royal power will disappear from
    Damascus.
Those who are left alive in Aram
    will be like the glory of the
    people of Israel,"
            announces the LORD
            who rules over all.

⁴"In days to come, the glory of
    Jacob's people will fade.
Their strength will get weaker
    and weaker.
⁵It will be as when a worker cuts
    and gathers grain
    in the Valley of Rephaim.
He gathers up stalks with his
    arms.
Only a few heads of grain are left.
⁶In the same way, only a few people
    will be left alive.
It will be as when workers knock
    olives off the trees.
Only two or three olives are left on
    the highest branches.
Four or five at most are left on
    the limbs that produce fruit,"
            announces the LORD,
            the God of Israel.

⁷In days to come, men will look to
their Maker for help.
They will turn their eyes to the
Holy One of Israel.
⁸They won't trust in the altars
they made with their own hands.
They won't pay any attention to
the poles they used
to worship the goddess Asherah.
And they won't depend on the
incense altars
they made with their own fingers.

⁹At that time the strong cities in
Israel will be deserted. They will be as
they were when the Israelites drove
the Canaanites out of them. They will
be like places that are taken over by
bushes and weeds. The whole land will
become dry and empty.

¹⁰Israel, you have forgotten God,
who saves you.
You have not remembered the
Rock, who keeps you safe.
You might set out the finest plants.
You might plant vines from other
lands.
¹¹The plants might start to grow on
the day you set them out.
The vines might begin to bud on
the morning you plant them.
But even if they do, there won't be
any harvest.
Instead, there will be sickness
and pain that won't go away.

¹²How terrible it looks for us!
Many nations are marching
against us.
The noise of their armies is like
the sound of the ocean.
They are making a lot of noise.
It sounds like huge waves
crashing on the shore.
¹³It sounds like the roar of rushing
waters.
But when the LORD speaks out
against them, they run far
away.
The wind blows them away like
straw on the hills.
A strong wind drives them along
like tumbleweeds.
¹⁴In the evening, the nations terrify
us.
But before morning comes, they
are gone.

That's what happens to those who
steal our goods.
That's what happens to those
who take what belongs to us.

A MESSAGE ABOUT CUSH

18 How terrible it will be for
the land
whose armies are like
large numbers of
flying insects!
That land is along the rivers of
Cush.
²Its people send messengers on the
Nile River.
They travel over the water in
papyrus boats.

Messengers, hurry back home!
Go back to your people,
who are tall and have smooth
skin.
Everyone is afraid of them.
They are warriors.
Their language is different from
ours.
Their land is divided up by rivers.

³Pay attention, all you people of the
world!
Listen, all you who live on earth!
Banners will be lifted up on the
mountains.
And you will see them.
Trumpets will be blown.
And you will hear them.
⁴The LORD says to me,
"I will look down from heaven,
where I live.
I will be as quiet as summer heat
in the sunshine.
I will be as quiet as a cloud of
dew in the heat of harvest."
⁵A farmer cuts off new growth with
pruning knives.
He cuts down spreading
branches and takes them
away.
He does it before the grapes are
harvested.
That's when the blooms are gone
and the grapes are ripe.
In the same way, the LORD will cut
off the nations
that are gathered against his
people.
⁶Their dead bodies will be left for the
birds of the mountains to eat.

They will be left for the wild
   animals.
The birds will eat the dead bodies
   all summer long.
The wild animals will eat them
   all through the winter.

⁷At that time gifts will be brought to
the LORD who rules over all.

The people who are tall and have
   smooth skin will bring them.
Everyone is afraid of those
   people.
They are warriors. Their language
   is different from ours.
Their land is divided up by rivers.

They will bring their gifts to Mount
Zion. That's where the LORD who rules
over all has put his Name.

A MESSAGE ABOUT EGYPT

19 Here is a message the LORD
gave me about Egypt.

The LORD is coming to Egypt.
   He's riding on a cloud that moves
   very fast.
The statues of the gods in Egypt
   tremble with fear because of
   him.
The hearts of the people there
   melt away inside them.

²The LORD says, "I will stir up one
   Egyptian against another.
Relatives will fight against
   relatives.
Neighbors will fight against one
   another.
Cities will fight against cities.
Kingdoms will fight against one
   another.
³The people of Egypt will lose hope.
   I will keep them from doing what
   they plan to do.
They will ask their gods for advice.
   They will turn to the spirits of
   dead people for help.
They will go to people who get
   messages from those who
   have died.
They will ask for advice from
   people who talk to the spirits
   of the dead.
⁴I will hand the Egyptians over
   to a mean and unkind master.

A powerful king will rule over
   them," announces the Lord.
He is the LORD who rules over all.

⁵The waters of the Nile River will
   dry up.
The bottom of it will be cracked
   and dry.
⁶Its waterways will stink.
   And the streams of Egypt will get
   smaller and smaller
until they dry up.
The tall grass that grows along the
   river will dry up.
⁷ So will the plants along the banks
   of the Nile.
Even the planted fields along the
   Nile will dry up.
Everything that grows there will
   blow away and disappear.
⁸The fishermen will moan.
   All those who drop hooks into
   the Nile will sob.
Those who throw their nets on the
   water
will become very sad.
⁹Those who make clothes out of
   flax will lose hope.
So will those who weave fine
   linen.
¹⁰Those who work with cloth will be
   unhappy.
And all those who work for
   money will be sick at heart.

¹¹The officials of the city of Zoan are
   very foolish.
Pharaoh's wise men give advice
   that doesn't make any sense.
How can they dare to say to
   Pharaoh,
"We're among the wise men"?
How can they say to him,
"We're like the advisers to the
   kings of long ago"?

¹²Pharaoh, where are your wise men
   now?
Let them tell you
what the LORD who rules over all
   has planned against Egypt.
¹³The officials of Zoan have become
   foolish.
The leaders of Memphis have
   been lied to.
The most important leaders in
   Egypt

have led its people down the
wrong path.
¹⁴The LORD has given them
a spirit that makes them feel dizzy.
They make Egypt unsteady in
everything it does.
Egypt is like a person who drinks
too much.
He throws up and then walks
around in the mess he's
made.
¹⁵No one in Egypt can do anything
to help them.
Its elders and important leaders
can't help them.
Its prophets and priests can't do
anything.
Those who rule over others can't
help.
And those who bow down to
them can't help either.

¹⁶In days to come, the people of
Egypt will be as terrified as women.
The LORD who rules over all will raise
his hand against them. Then they will
tremble with fear. ¹⁷The people of Judah will bring terror to the Egyptians.
Everyone in Egypt who hears the
name of Judah will be terrified. That's
because of what the LORD who rules
over all is planning to do to them.
¹⁸At that time the people of five
cities in Egypt will use the Hebrew
language when they worship the LORD
who rules over all. They will take an
oath. And they will promise to be
faithful to him. One of those cities is
called The City of the Sun.
¹⁹At that time there will be an altar to
the LORD in the middle of Egypt. There
will be a monument to him at its border. ²⁰They will remind people that the
LORD who rules over all is worshiped
in Egypt. The people there will cry out
to the LORD because of those who treat
them badly. He will send someone to
stand up for them and save them. And
he will set them free.
²¹So the LORD will make himself
known to the people of Egypt. At that
time they will recognize that he is the
LORD. They will worship him by bringing sacrifices and grain offerings to
him. They will make promises to the
LORD. And they will keep them. ²²The
LORD will strike Egypt with a plague.

But then he will heal them. They will
turn to the LORD. And he will answer
their prayers and heal them.
²³At that time there will be a wide
road from Egypt to Assyria. The people
of Assyria will go to Egypt. And the
people of Egypt will go to Assyria. The
people of Egypt and Assyria will worship the LORD together.
²⁴At that time Egypt, Assyria and Israel will be a blessing to the whole
earth. ²⁵The LORD who rules over all
will bless those three nations. He will
say, "Let the Egyptians be blessed.
They are my people. Let the Assyrians
be blessed. My hands created them.
And let the Israelites be blessed. They
are my very own people."

A MESSAGE ABOUT EGYPT AND CUSH

20 Sargon sent his highest
commander to the city of
Ashdod. He attacked it and
captured it. Sargon was king of Assyria. ²Three years earlier the LORD
had spoken to me. He had said, "Take
off the black clothes you are wearing.
And take your sandals off." So I did. I
went around barefoot. I didn't have
anything on but my underwear.
³After Ashdod was captured, the
LORD said, "My servant Isaiah has gone
around barefoot for three years. He
has not worn anything but his underwear. He is a sign and reminder to
Egypt and Cush about what will happen to them.
⁴"The king of Assyria will lead prisoners away from Egypt and Cush.
Young people and old people alike will
be taken away. Like Isaiah, they will be
barefoot. They will not be wearing
anything but their underwear. And
their backsides will be bare. So the
Egyptians will be put to shame.
⁵"People trusted in Cush to help
them. They bragged about what Egypt
could do for them. But they will be
afraid and put to shame. ⁶At that time
the people who live on the coast of
Philistia will speak up. They will say,
'See what has happened to those we
depended on! We ran to them for help.
We wanted them to save us from the
king of Assyria. Now how can we
escape?' "

A MESSAGE ABOUT BABYLONIA

21 Here is a message the LORD gave me about Babylonia. It is known as the Desert by the Two Rivers.

An attack is coming through the
     desert.
It is coming from a land of terror.
It's sweeping along like a
     windstorm blowing across the
     Negev Desert.

²I have seen a vision about
     something terrible that will
     happen.
People are turning against
     Babylon.
Robbers are taking its goods.
Elamites, attack the city! Medes,
     surround it!
The LORD will put an end to all of
     the suffering Babylon has
     caused.

³The vision fills my body with pain.
     Pains take hold of me.
They are like the pains of a
     woman having a baby.
I am shaken by what I hear.
     I'm terrified by what I see.
⁴My heart grows weak.
     Fear makes me tremble.
I longed for evening to come.
But it brought me horror instead
     of rest.

⁵In my vision the Babylonians set
     the tables.
They spread the rugs out.
They eat. They drink.
Get up, you officers!
Rub your shields with oil!

⁶The Lord said to me,

"Go. Put a guard on duty on
     Jerusalem's walls.
Have him report what he sees.
⁷Tell him to watch for chariots
     that are pulled by teams of horses.
Tell him to watch for men riding
     on donkeys or camels.
Make sure he stays awake.
Make sure he stays wide awake."

⁸"My master!" the guard shouts
back.

"Day after day I stand here on the
     lookout tower.
Every night I stay here on duty.
⁹Look! Here comes a man in a
     chariot!
It's being pulled by a team of
     horses.
He's calling out the news,
     'Babylon has fallen! It has fallen!
All of the statues of its gods
     lie broken in pieces on the
     ground!' "

¹⁰My people, you have been crushed
     like grain on a threshing floor.
But now I'm telling you the good
     news I've heard.
It comes from the LORD who
     rules over all.
He is the God of Israel.

A MESSAGE ABOUT EDOM

¹¹Here is a message the LORD gave me about Edom.

Someone is calling out to me from
     the land of Seir. He says,
"Guard, when will the night be
     over?
Guard, how soon will it end?"
¹²The guard answers,
"Morning is coming. But the
     night will return.
If you want to ask again,
     come back and ask."

A MESSAGE ABOUT ARABIA

¹³Here is a message the LORD gave me about Arabia.

He told me to give orders to
     traders from Dedan.
They were camping in the
     bushes of Arabia.
¹⁴ I told them to bring water for
     those who are thirsty.
I also gave orders to those who live
     in Tema.
I told them to bring food for
     those who are running away.
¹⁵They are running away from
     where the fighting is heaviest.
That's where the swords are
     ready to strike.
That's where the bows are ready
     to shoot.

¹⁶The Lord says to me, "In exactly
one year, Kedar's grand show of power

will come to an end. [17]Only a few of Kedar's soldiers who shoot arrows will be left alive." The LORD has spoken. He is the God of Israel.

A MESSAGE ABOUT JERUSALEM

22 Here is a message the LORD gave me about the Valley of Vision.

People of Jerusalem, what's the matter with you?
Why have all of you gone up on the roofs of your houses?
[2]Why is your town so full of noise?
Why is your city so full of the sound of wild parties?
Those among you who died weren't killed with swords.
They didn't die in battle.
[3]All of your leaders have run away.
They've been captured without a single arrow being shot.
All those who were caught were taken away as prisoners.
They ran off while your enemies were still far away.
[4]So I said, "Leave me alone.
Let me sob bitter tears.
Don't try to comfort me.
My people have been destroyed."

[5]The LORD who rules over all sent the noise of battle against you.
The Lord brought disorder and terror
to the Valley of Vision.
The walls of the city were knocked down.
Cries for help were heard in the mountains.
[6]Soldiers from Elam came armed with bows and arrows.
They came with their chariots and horses.
Soldiers from Kir got their shields ready.
[7]Your rich valleys filled up with chariots.
Horsemen took up their battle positions at your city gates.
[8] Judah wasn't a safe place to live in anymore.

When all of that happened, you depended
on the weapons in the Palace of the Forest of Lebanon.
[9]You saw that the City of David had many holes in its walls.
They needed to be repaired.
You stored up water in the Lower Pool.
[10]You picked out the weaker buildings in Jerusalem.
You tore them down and used their stones
to strengthen the city walls against attack.
[11]You built a pool between the two walls.
You used it to save the water that was running down from the Old Pool.
But you didn't look to the One who made it all possible.
You didn't pay any attention to the One
who planned everything long ago.

[12]The LORD who rules over all called out to you at that time.
The Lord told you to sob and cry.
He told you to tear your hair out.
And he told you to put black clothes on.
[13]Instead, you are enjoying yourselves at wild parties!
You are killing cattle and sheep.
You are eating their meat and drinking wine.
You are saying, "Let's eat and drink,
because tomorrow we'll die."

[14]I heard the LORD who rules over all speaking. "Your sin can never be paid for as long as you people live," says the Lord.

[15]The LORD who rules over all speaks. The Lord says,

"Go. Speak to the head servant Shebna.
He is in charge of the palace. Tell him,
[16]'What are you doing here outside the city?
Who allowed you to cut out a tomb for yourself here?
Who said you could carve out your grave on the hillside?
Who allowed you to cut out your resting place in the rock?

17 " 'Watch out, you mighty man!
　　The LORD is about to grab hold of
　　　you.
　　He is about to throw you away.
18 He will roll you up tightly like a
　　　ball.
　　He will throw you into a very
　　　large country.
　　There you will die.
　　And there the chariots you are so
　　　proud of will remain.
　　You bring shame on your
　　　master's family!
19 The LORD will remove you from
　　　your job.
　　You will be brought down from
　　　your high position.

20 " 'At that time he will send for his
servant Eliakim. He is the son of Hilkiah. 21 The LORD will put your robe on
Eliakim. He will tie your belt around
him. He will hand your authority over
to him. Eliakim will be like a father to
the people of Jerusalem and Judah.
22 " 'The LORD will give Eliakim the
key of authority in David's royal house.
No one can shut what he opens. And
no one can open what he shuts. 23 The
LORD will set him firmly in place like a
peg that is driven into a wall. He will
hold a position of honor in his family.
24 The good name of his whole family
will depend on him. They will be like
bowls and jars hanging on a peg.

25 " 'But a new day is coming,' " announces the LORD who rules over all.
" 'At that time the peg that was driven
into the wall will give way. It will break
off and fall down. And the heavy load
hanging on it will also fall.' " The LORD
has spoken.

A MESSAGE ABOUT TYRE

23 Here is a message the LORD
gave me about Tyre.

Men in the ships of Tarshish, cry
　　out!
　　The city of Tyre is destroyed.
　　Its houses and harbor are gone.
　　That's the message you have
　　　received
　　from the island of Cyprus.

2 People on the island of Tyre, be
　　silent.

Traders from the city of Sidon, be
　　quiet.
　　Those who sail on the
　　　Mediterranean Sea have made
　　　you rich.
3 Grain from Egypt
　　came across the mighty waters.
　　The harvest of the Nile River
　　　brought wealth to Tyre.
　　It became the market place of
　　　the nations.

4 Sidon, be ashamed. Mighty Tyre
　　out in the sea, be ashamed.
　　The sea has spoken. It has said,
　"It's as if I had never felt labor
　　　pains or had children.
　　It's as if I had never brought up
　　　sons or daughters.
　　It's as if the city of Tyre had never
　　　existed."
5 The Egyptians will hear about
　　what has happened to Tyre.
　　They'll be very sad and troubled.

6 People of the island of Tyre, cry out!
　　Go across the sea to Tarshish.
7 Just look at Tyre.
　　It's no longer the old, old city
　　　that was known for its wild
　　　parties.
　　It no longer sends its people out
　　　to settle in lands far away.
8 Tyre was a city that produced
　　　kings.
　　Its traders were princes.
　　They were honored all over the
　　　earth.
　　So who planned to destroy such
　　　a city?
9 The LORD who rules over all
　　　planned to do it.
　　He wanted to bring down all of
　　　its pride and glory.
　　He wanted to put to shame those
　　　who were honored all over the
　　　earth.

10 People of Tarshish, spread out over
　　　your land
　　like the waters of the Nile.
　　There isn't anything to hold you
　　　back anymore.
11 The LORD has reached his
　　　powerful hand out over the
　　　sea.
　　He has made its kingdoms
　　　tremble with fear.

He has given a command
concerning Phoenicia.
He has ordered that its forts be
destroyed.
¹²He said, "No more wild parties for
you!
People of Sidon, you are now
destroyed!

"Leave your city. Go across the sea
to Cyprus.
Even there you will not find any
rest."
¹³Look at the land of the Babylonians.
No one lives there anymore.
The Assyrians have turned it
into a place for desert creatures.
They built their towers in order to
attack it.
They took everything out of its
forts.
They knocked all of its buildings
down.
¹⁴Men in the ships of Tarshish, cry
out!
Mighty Tyre is destroyed!

¹⁵A time is coming when people will
forget about Tyre for 70 years. That's
the length of a king's life. But at the
end of those 70 years, Tyre will be like
the prostitute that people sing about.
They say,

¹⁶"Forgotten prostitute, pick up a
harp.
Walk through the city.
Play the harp well. Sing many
songs.
Then you will be remembered."

¹⁷At the end of the 70 years, the LORD
will punish Tyre. He will let it return to
its way of life as a prostitute. It will
earn its living with all of the kingdoms
on the face of the earth. ¹⁸But the money it earns will be set apart for the
LORD. The money won't be stored up or
kept for Tyre. Instead, it will go to
those who live the way the LORD wants
them to. It will pay for plenty of food
and fine clothes for them.

THE LORD WILL DESTROY
THE EARTH

24 The LORD is going to
completely destroy
everything on earth.

He will twist its surface.
He'll scatter those who live on it.
²Priests and people alike will suffer.
So will masters and their
servants.
And so will women and their
female servants.
Sellers and buyers alike will suffer.
So will those who borrow and
those who lend.
And so will those who owe
money and those who lend it.
³The earth will be completely
destroyed.
Everything of value will be taken
out of it.
That's what the LORD
has said.

⁴The earth will dry up completely.
The world will dry up and waste
away.
The most important people on
earth will fade away.
⁵The earth is polluted by its people.
They haven't obeyed the laws of
the LORD.
They haven't done what he told
them to do.
They've broken the covenant
that will last forever.
⁶So the LORD will send a curse on
the earth.
Its people will pay for what
they've done.
They will be burned up.
Very few of them will be left.
⁷The vines and fresh wine will dry
up completely.
Those who used to have a good
time will groan.
⁸The happy sounds of tambourines
will be gone.
The noise of those who enjoy
wild parties will stop.
The joyful music of harps will
become silent.
⁹People will no longer sing as they
drink wine.
Beer will taste bitter to those
who drink it.
¹⁰Destroyed cities will lie empty.
People will lock themselves
inside their houses.
¹¹In the streets people will cry out
for wine.
All joy will turn into sadness.

All happiness will be driven out
of the earth.
¹²All of the buildings will be
knocked down.
Every city gate will be smashed
to pieces.
¹³That's how it will be on the earth.
And that's how it will be among
the nations.
It will be as when workers knock
all but a few olives off the
trees.
It will be like a vine that has only
a few grapes left after the
harvest.

¹⁴Those who are left alive will shout
with joy.
People from the west will praise
the LORD because he is the
King.
¹⁵So give glory to him, you who live
in the east.
Honor the name of the LORD, you
who are in the islands of the
sea.
He is the God of Israel.
¹⁶From one end of the earth to the
other we hear singing.
People are saying,
"Give glory to the One who
always does what is right."

But I said, "I feel very bad.
I'm getting weaker and weaker.
How terrible it is for me!
People turn against one another.
They can't be trusted.
So they turn against each other."
¹⁷People of the earth,
terror, a pit and a trap are
waiting for you.
¹⁸Anyone who runs away from the
terror
will fall into the pit.
Anyone who climbs out of the pit
will be caught in the trap.

The LORD will open the windows
of the skies.
He will flood the land.
The foundations of the earth will
shake.
¹⁹The earth will be broken up.
It will split open.
It will be shaken to pieces.
²⁰The earth will be unsteady like
someone who is drunk.

It will sway like a tent in the
wind.
Its sin will weigh so heavily on it
that it will fall.
It will never get up again.

²¹At that time the LORD will punish
the spiritual forces of evil in the
heavens above.
He will also punish the kings on
the earth below.
²²They will be brought together
like prisoners in chains.
They'll be locked up in prison.
After many days the LORD will
punish them.
²³The LORD who rules over all will
rule
on Mount Zion in Jerusalem.
The elders of the city will be there.
They will see his glory.
His rule will be so glorious that the
sun and moon
will be too ashamed to shine.

A SONG OF PRAISE

25 LORD, you are my God.
I will honor you.
I will praise your name.
You have been perfectly faithful.
You have done wonderful things.
You had planned them long ago.
²You have turned cities into piles of
trash.
You have pulled down the high
walls that were around them.
You have destroyed our enemies'
forts.
They will never be rebuilt.
³Powerful nations will honor you.
Even sinful people from their
cities will have respect for you.
⁴Poor people have come to you for
safety.
You have kept needy people safe
when they were in trouble.
You have been a place to hide
when storms came.
You have been a shade from the
heat of the sun.
Evil people attack us.
They are like a storm beating
against a wall.
⁵ They are like the heat of the
desert.
You stopped the noisy shouts of
our enemies.

You kept them from winning the
battle over us and singing
about it.
You are like the shadow of a
cloud that cools the earth.

⁶On Mount Zion the LORD who
rules over all will prepare
a feast for all of the nations.
The best and richest foods
and the finest aged wines will be
served.

⁷On that mountain the LORD will
destroy
the veil of sadness that covers all
of the nations.
He will destroy the gloom that is
spread over everyone.

⁸ He will swallow up death forever.
The LORD and King will wipe away
the tears
from everyone's face.
He will remove the shame of his
people
from the whole earth.
The LORD has spoken.

⁹At that time they will say,

"He is our God.
We trusted in him, and he saved
us.

He is the LORD. We trusted in him.
Let us be filled with joy because
he saved us."

¹⁰The LORD's powerful hand will
keep Mount Zion safe.
But he will walk all over Moab.
Its people will be crushed,
just as straw is crushed in animal
waste.

¹¹They will try to swim their way out
of it.
They will spread their hands out
in it,
just as a swimmer spreads his
hands out to swim.
But God will bring down Moab's
pride.
None of their skill will help them.

¹²He will pull down their high,
strong walls.
He will bring them down to the
ground.
He'll bring them right down to
the dust.

ANOTHER SONG OF PRAISE

26 At that time a song will be
sung in the land of Judah.
It will say,

Will we eat in heaven?

We will be *able* to
eat in heaven. But we
will not *have* to eat to live the
way we do on earth. Jesus said
he would eat with his people
there. But no one in heaven
will ever go hungry.

 Isaiah 25:6

Related verse:
Matthew 26:29

JASON'S
IMAGINATION

"We have a strong city.
　　God's saving power surrounds it
　　　like walls and towers.
² Open its gates
　　so that those who do what is
　　　right can enter.
　　They are the people who remain
　　　faithful to God.
³ LORD, you will give perfect peace
　　to anyone who commits himself
　　　to be faithful to you.
　　That's because he trusts in you.
⁴ "Trust in the LORD forever.
　　The LORD is the Rock.
　　The LORD will keep us safe
　　　forever.
⁵ He brings down those who are
　　　proud.
　　He pulls down cities that have
　　　high walls.
　　They fall down flat on the ground.
　　He throws them down to the
　　　dust.
⁶ The feet of those who were
　　　crushed stomp on them.
　　Those who were helpless walk all
　　　over them."

⁷ LORD, you are honest and fair.
　　You guide those who do what is
　　　right.
　　You lead them on a straight path.
　　You make their way smooth.
⁸ LORD, we are living the way your
　　　laws command us to live.
　　We are waiting for you to act.
　　Our hearts long for you to be true
　　　to your name.
　　That's what you are known for.
⁹ My heart longs for you at night.
　　My spirit longs for you in the
　　　morning.
　　You will come and judge the
　　　earth.
　　Then the people of the world will
　　　learn to do what is right.
¹⁰ Grace is shown to sinful people.
　　But they still don't learn to do
　　　what is right.
　　They keep on doing evil even in a
　　　land where others are honest
　　　and fair.
　　They don't have any respect for
　　　the majesty of the LORD.
¹¹ LORD, you have raised your hand
　　　high to punish them.
　　But they don't even see it.

Let them see how much you love
　　　your people.
　　Then they will be put to shame.
　　Let the fire you are saving for
　　　your enemies burn them up.
¹² LORD, you give us peace.
　　You are the one who has done
　　　everything we've
　　　accomplished.
¹³ LORD, you are our God.
　　Other masters besides you have
　　　ruled over us.
　　But your name is the only one we
　　　honor.
¹⁴ Those other masters are now dead.
　　They will never live again.
　　Their spirits won't rise from the
　　　dead.
　　You punished them and destroyed
　　　them.
　　You wiped out all memory of
　　　them.
¹⁵ LORD, you have made our nation
　　　grow.
　　You have made it larger.
　　You have gained glory for yourself.
　　You have increased the size of
　　　our land.

¹⁶ LORD, when your people were
　　　suffering, they came to you.
　　When you punished them,
　　　they could barely whisper a
　　　prayer.
¹⁷ LORD, you made us like a woman
　　　who is having a baby.
　　She groans and cries out in pain.
¹⁸ We were pregnant. We groaned
　　　with pain.
　　But nothing was born.
　　We didn't bring your saving power
　　　to the earth.
　　We didn't give life to the people
　　　of the world.

¹⁹ Israel, those among you who have
　　　died will live again.
　　Their bodies will rise from the
　　　dead.
　　You who lie in the grave,
　　　wake up and shout with joy.
　　The dew of the morning gives life
　　　to the earth.
　　So the earth will give up its dead
　　　people.

²⁰ My people, go into your houses.
　　Shut the doors behind you.

Hide yourselves for a little while.
Do it until the LORD's anger is
over.
²¹ He is coming from the place where
he lives.
He will punish the people of the
earth for their sins.
The blood that has been spilled on
the earth will be
brought out into the open.
The ground will no longer hide
those who have been killed.

ISRAEL WILL BE SAVED

27 At that time

the LORD will punish
Leviathan with his
sword.
His great, powerful and deadly
sword will punish
the serpent that glides through the
sea.
He will kill that twisting sea
monster.

² At that time the LORD will sing
about his fruitful vineyard. He will say,

³ "I am the LORD. I watch over my
vineyard.
I water it all the time.
I guard it day and night.
I do it so no one can harm it.
⁴ I am not angry with my vineyard.
I wish thorns and bushes would
come up in it.
Then I would march out against
them in battle.
I would set all of them on fire.
⁵ So the enemies of my people had
better come to me for safety.
They should make peace with
me.
I will say it again.
They should make peace with
me."

⁶ In days to come, Jacob's people
will put down roots like a vine.
Israel will bud and bloom.
They will fill the whole world
with fruit.

⁷ The LORD struck down those who
struck Israel down.
But he hasn't punished Israel as
much.

The LORD killed those who killed
many of his people.
But he hasn't punished his
people as much.
⁸ The LORD will use war to punish
Israel.
He will make them leave their
land.
With a strong blast of his anger he
will drive them out.
It will be as if the east wind were
blowing.
⁹ The people of Jacob will have to
pay for their sin.
That must happen in order for
their sin to be taken away.
They will make all of the altar
stones like chalk.
They will crush them to pieces.
No poles that had been used to
worship the goddess
Asherah will be left standing.
No incense altars will be left
either.
¹⁰ Cities that have high walls around
them will become empty.
They will be deserted
settlements.
They will be like a desert.
Calves will eat and lie down in
them.
They will strip the branches of
their trees bare.
¹¹ When their twigs are dry, they will
be broken off.
Then women will come and
make fires with them.
The people of Jacob don't
understand the LORD.
So the One who made them
won't be concerned about
them.
Their Creator won't show them
his favor.

¹² At that time the LORD will separate
Israel from other people. He will gather the Israelites together. He will gather
them one by one from the Euphrates
River all the way to the Wadi of Egypt.
¹³ At that time a loud trumpet will
be blown. Those who were dying in
Assyria will come and worship the
LORD. So will those who were taken
away to Egypt. All of them will worship
the LORD on his holy mountain in Jerusalem.

THE LORD WILL JUDGE ISRAEL

28 How terrible it will be for
the city of Samaria!
It sits on a hill like a crown
of flowers.
The leaders of Ephraim are drunk.
They take pride in their city.
It sits above a valley that has rich
soil.
How terrible it will be for the
glorious beauty of that fading
flower!
² The Lord will bring the strong and
powerful king of Assyria
against Samaria.
The Lord will throw that city
down to the ground with great
force.
It will be like a hailstorm.
It will be like a wind that destroys
everything.
It will be like a driving rain and a
flooding storm.
³ That city is like a crown.
The leaders of Ephraim are
drunk.
They take pride in their city.
But its enemies will walk all over
it.
⁴ It sits on a hill above a rich valley.
It's like a crown of flowers whose
glorious beauty is fading
away.
But it will become like a fig that is
ripe before harvest.
As soon as someone sees it,
he picks it and swallows it.

⁵ At that time the LORD who rules
over all
will be like a glorious crown.
He will be like a beautiful wreath
for those of his people who will
be left alive.
⁶ He will help those
who are fair when they judge.
He will give strength to those
who turn back their enemies at
the city gate.

⁷ Israel's leaders are drunk from
wine.
They can't walk straight.
They are drunk from beer.
They are unsteady on their feet.
Priests and prophets drink beer.
They can't walk straight.
They are mixed up from drinking
too much wine.
They drink too much beer.
They are unsteady on their feet.
The prophets see visions but don't
really understand them.
The priests aren't able to make
good decisions.
⁸ They throw up. All of the tables are
covered
with the mess they've made.
There isn't one spot on the tables
that isn't smelly and dirty.

⁹ My people are making fun of me.
They say,
"Who does he think he's trying to
teach?
Who does he think he's
explaining his message to?
Is it to children who do not need
their mother's milk anymore?
Is it to those who have just been
taken from her breast?
¹⁰ Here is how he teaches.
Do this and do that.
Do that and do this.
Obey this rule and obey that rule.
Obey that rule and obey this rule.
Learn a little here and learn a
little there."

¹¹ All right then, these people won't
listen to me.
So God will speak to them.
He will speak by using people who
speak unfamiliar languages.
He will speak by using the
mouths of strangers.
¹² He said to his people,
"I am offering you a resting
place.
Let those who are tired rest."
He continued, "I am offering you a
place of peace and quiet."
But they wouldn't listen.
¹³ So then, here is what the LORD's
message will become to them.
Do this and do that.
Do that and do this.
Obey this rule and obey that rule.
Obey that rule and obey this rule.
Learn a little here and learn a
little there.
So when they try to go forward,
they'll fall back and be wounded.
They'll be trapped and captured.

¹⁴Listen to the LORD's message,
  you who make fun of the truth.
  Listen, you who rule over these
    people in Jerusalem.
¹⁵You brag, "We have entered into a
    covenant with death.
  We have made an agreement
    with the grave.
  When a terrible plague comes to
    punish us,
    it can't touch us.
  That's because we depend on lies
    to keep us safe.
  We hide behind what isn't true."

¹⁶So the LORD and King speaks. He
says,

  "Look! I am laying a stone in Zion.
    It is a stone that has been tested.
  It is the most important stone for a
    firm foundation.
    The one who trusts in that stone
      will never be shaken.
¹⁷I will use a measuring line to prove
    that you have not been fair.
  I will use a plumb line to prove
    that you have not done what
    is right.
  Hail will sweep away the lies you
    depend on to keep you safe.
  Water will flood your hiding
    place.
¹⁸Your covenant with death will be
    called off.
  The agreement you made with
    the grave will not stand.
  When the terrible plague comes to
    punish you,
  you will be beaten down by it.
¹⁹As often as it comes, it will carry
    you away.
  Morning after morning, day and
    night,
    it will come to punish you."

If you understand this message,
  it will bring you absolute terror.
²⁰You will be like someone whose
    bed is too short to lie down
    on.
  You will be like those whose
    blankets are too small to wrap
    themselves in.
²¹The LORD will rise up to judge, just
    as he did at Mount Perazim.
  He will get up to act, just as he
    did in the Valley of Gibeon.

He'll do his work, but it will be
    strange work.
  He'll carry out his task, but it will
    be an unexpected one.
²²Now stop making fun of me.
  If you don't, your chains will
    become heavier.
  The LORD who rules over all has
    spoken to me.
  The Lord has told me he has
    ordered that the whole land
    be destroyed.

²³Listen and hear my voice.
  Pay attention to what I'm
    saying.
²⁴When a farmer plows in order to
    plant, does he plow without
    stopping?
  Does he keep on breaking up the
    soil and making the field
    level?
²⁵When he's made the surface even,
    doesn't he plant caraway
    seeds?
  Doesn't he scatter cummin?
  Doesn't he plant wheat in its
    proper place?
  Doesn't he plant barley where it
    belongs?
  Doesn't he plant spelt along the
    edge of the field?
²⁶His God directs him.
  He teaches him the right way to
    do his work.

²⁷Caraway seeds are beaten out with
    a rod.
  They aren't separated out under
    a threshing sled.
  Cummin seeds are beaten out with
    a stick.
  The wheel of a cart isn't rolled
    over them.
²⁸Grain must be ground up to make
    bread.
  A farmer separates it out.
  But he doesn't go on doing it
    forever.
  He drives the wheels of a
    threshing cart over it.
  But he doesn't let the horses
    grind it to dust.
²⁹All of those insights come from the
    LORD who rules over all.
  His advice is wonderful. His
    wisdom is glorious.

THE LORD WILL JUDGE JERUSALEM

29 Jerusalem, how terrible it
will be for you!
Ariel, you are the city
where David settled.
The years will come and go.
Keep on celebrating your regular
feasts.
² The LORD says, "Ariel, I will
surround you.
Jerusalem, I will get ready to
attack you.
Your people will sob.
They will sing songs of sadness.
I will make you like the front of an
altar
that is covered with blood.
³ I will be like an army that is camped
against you on all sides.
I will surround you with towers
in order to attack you.
I will build my ramps all around
you and set up my ladders.
⁴ You will be brought down to the
grave.
You will speak from deep down
inside the ground.
Your words will be barely heard
out of the dust.
Your voice will sound like the
voice of a ghost
coming from under the ground.
Your words will sound like a
whisper out of the dust."

⁵ Jerusalem, all of your enemies will
become like fine dust.
Their terrifying armies will
become like straw
that the wind blows away.
All of a sudden, in an instant,
⁶ the LORD who rules over all will
come.
He will come with thunder,
earthquakes and a lot of noise.
He'll bring windstorms and
rainstorms with him.
He'll send a blazing fire that will
burn everything up.

⁷ Armies from all of the nations will
fight against Ariel.
They will attack it and its fort.
They'll surround it completely.
But suddenly those armies will
disappear like a dream.

They will vanish like a vision in
the night.
⁸ They will be like a hungry person
who dreams he is eating.
But when he wakes up, he's still
hungry.
They will be like a thirsty person
who dreams he is drinking.
But when he wakes up, he is
weak.
His thirst hasn't been satisfied.
In the same way, the armies from
all of the nations
that fight against Mount Zion
will disappear.

⁹ People of Jerusalem, be shocked
and amazed.
Make yourselves blind so you
can't see anything.
Get drunk, but not from wine.
Be unsteady on your feet, but not
because of beer.
¹⁰ The LORD has made you fall into a
deep sleep.
He has closed the eyes of your
prophets.
He has covered the heads of your
seers so they can't see.

¹¹ For you, this whole vision is like
words that are sealed up in a scroll.
Suppose you give it to someone who
can read. And suppose you say to him,
"Please read this for us." Then he'll answer, "I can't. It's sealed up." ¹² Or suppose you give the scroll to someone
who can't read. And suppose you say,
"Please read this for us." Then he'll answer, "I don't know how to read."

¹³ The Lord says,

"These people worship me only
with their words.
They honor me by what they
say.
But their hearts are far away
from me.
Their worship doesn't mean
anything to me.
They teach nothing but human
rules.
¹⁴ So once more I will shock these
people
with many wonderful acts.
I will destroy the wisdom of those
who think they are so wise.

I will do away with the cleverness
  of those who think they are so
  smart."
15 How terrible it will be for people
  who do everything they can
  to hide their plans from the
  LORD!
They do their work in darkness.
  They think, "Who sees us? Who
  will know?"
16 They turn everything upside
  down.
How silly they are to think that
  potters are like the clay they
  work with!
Can what is made say to the one
  who made it,
"You didn't make me"?
Can the pot say to the potter,
  "You don't know anything"?

17 In a very short time, Lebanon will
  be turned into rich farm
  lands.
The rich farm lands will seem
  like a forest.
18 At that time those who can't hear
  will hear what is read from the
  scroll.
Those who are blind will come
  out of gloom and darkness.
They will be able to see.
19 Those who aren't proud will once
  again find their joy in the
  LORD.
And those who are in need will
  find their joy in the Holy One
  of Israel.
20 Those who don't show any pity
  will vanish.
Those who make fun of others
  will disappear.
All those who look for ways to do
  what is evil will be cut off.
21 Without any proof, they claim that
  a man is guilty.
In court they try to trap
  the one who speaks up for others.
By using dishonest witnesses they
  keep those who aren't guilty
  from being treated fairly.

22 Long ago the LORD saved Abraham
from trouble. Now he says to Jacob's
people,

"You will not be ashamed
  anymore.

Your faces will no longer grow
  pale with fear.
23 You will see your children living
  among you.
I myself will give you those
  children.
Then you will honor my name.
  You will recognize how holy I am.
I am the Holy One of Jacob.
You will have great respect for me.
  I am the God of Israel.
24 I will give understanding to you
  who find yourselves going down
  the wrong path.
You who are always speaking
  against others
will accept what I teach you."

THE LORD WILL JUDGE HIS STUBBORN PEOPLE

30 "How terrible it will be
          for these stubborn
          children of mine!"
announces the LORD.
"How terrible for those who carry
  out plans that did not come
  from me!
Their agreement with Egypt did
  not come from my Spirit.
So they pile up one sin on top of
  another.
2 They go down to Egypt
  without asking me for advice.
They look to Pharaoh to help
  them.
They ask Egypt to keep them
  safe.
3 But looking to Pharaoh will only
  bring them shame.
Asking Egypt for help will bring
  them dishonor.
4 Their officials have gone to the
  city of Zoan.
Their messengers have arrived in
  Hanes.
5 But the people of Judah will be put
  to shame
because they are trusting in a
  nation that is useless to them.
Egypt will not bring them any help
  or advantage.
Instead, it will bring them shame
  and dishonor."

6 Here is a message the LORD gave
me about the animals in the Negev
Desert.

Judah's messengers carry their
    riches on the backs of
    donkeys.
They carry their treasures on the
    humps of camels.
They travel through a land of
    danger and suffering.
It's a land that is filled with lions.
Poisonous snakes are also there.
The messengers travel to a nation
    that can't do them any good.
⁷They travel to Egypt, whose help is
    totally useless.
That's why I call it Rahab the
    Do-Nothing.

⁸The LORD said to me, "Go now.
Write on a tablet for the people
    of Judah
what I am about to say.
Also write it on a scroll.
In days to come
it will be a witness that lasts
    forever.
⁹The people of Judah refuse to obey
    me.
They are children who tell lies.
They will not listen to what I
    want to teach them.
¹⁰They say to the seers,
    'Don't see any more visions!'
They say to the prophets,
    'Don't give us any more visions of
    what is right!
Tell us pleasant things.
Prophesy things we want to hear
    even if they aren't true.
¹¹Get out of our way!
Get off our path!
Keep the Holy One of Israel away
    from us!' "

¹²So the Holy One of Israel speaks.
He says,

"You have turned your backs on
    what I have said.
You have depended on telling
    people lies.
You have crushed others.
¹³Those sins are like cracks in a high
    wall.
They get bigger and bigger.
Suddenly the wall breaks apart.
Then it quickly falls down.
¹⁴It breaks into small pieces like a
    clay pot.
It breaks up completely.

Not one piece is left big enough
    for taking coals from a fireplace.
Not one piece is left for dipping
    water out of a well."

¹⁵The LORD and King is the Holy One
of Israel. He says,

"You will find peace and rest
    when you turn away from your
    sins and depend on me.
You will receive the strength you
    need
    when you stay calm and trust in
    me.
But you do not want to do what I
    tell you to.
¹⁶You said, 'No. We'll escape on
    horses.'
So you will have to escape!
You said, 'We'll ride off on fast
    horses.'
So those who chase you will use
    faster horses!
¹⁷When one of them dares you to
    fight,
    a thousand of you will run
    away.
When five of them dare you,
    all of you will run away.
So few of you will be left that you
    will be
like a flagpole on top of a
    mountain.
You will be like only one banner
    on a hill."

¹⁸But the LORD longs to show you his
    favor.
He wants to give you his tender
    love.
The LORD is a God who is always
    fair.
Blessed are all those who wait for
    him to act!

¹⁹People of Zion, who live in Jerusalem, you won't sob anymore. When you cry out to the Lord for help, he will show you his favor. As soon as he hears you, he'll answer you. ²⁰He might treat you like prisoners. You might eat the bread of trouble. You might drink the water of suffering. But he will be your Teacher. He won't hide himself anymore. You will see him with your own eyes. ²¹You will hear your Teacher's voice behind you. You will hear it whether you turn to the right or the

left. It will say, "Here is the path I want you to take. So walk on it."

²²Then you will get rid of the silver statues of your gods. You won't have anything to do with the gold statues either. All of them are "unclean." So you will throw them away like dirty rags. You will say to them, "Get away from us!"

²³The LORD will send rain on the seeds you plant in the ground. The crops that grow will be rich and plentiful. At that time your cattle will eat grass in rolling meadows. ²⁴The oxen and donkeys that work the soil will eat the finest feed and crushed grain. The farmers will use pitchforks and shovels to separate it from the straw.

²⁵At that time the towers of your enemies will fall down. Their soldiers will die. Streams of water will flow on every high mountain and hill. ²⁶The moon will shine like the sun. And the sunlight will be seven times brighter than usual. It will be like the light of seven full days. That will happen when the LORD bandages and heals the wounds and bruises he has brought on his people.

²⁷The LORD will come from far away
  in all of his power and glory.
He will show his burning anger.
  Thick clouds of smoke will be all
    around him.
His mouth will speak angry words.
  The words from his tongue will
    be like a destroying fire.
²⁸His breath will be like a rushing
    flood
  that rises up to the neck.
He'll separate out the nations he is
    going to destroy.
He'll place a bit in their jaws.
  It will lead them down the road
    to death.
²⁹You will sing
  as you do on the night you
    celebrate a holy feast.
Your hearts will be filled with joy.
  You will be as joyful as people
    playing their flutes
as they go up to the mountain of
    the LORD.
  He is the Rock of Israel.
³⁰The LORD will cause people to hear
    his powerful voice.

He will make them see his arm
    coming down to punish them.
It will come down with burning
    anger and destroying fire.
It will come down with rain,
    thunderstorms and hail.
³¹The voice of the LORD will tear the
    Assyrians apart.
He will strike them down with
    his mighty rod.
³²He will strike them
  with his rod to punish them.
Each time he does, his people will
    celebrate
  with the music of harps and
    tambourines.
He will use his powerful arm
  to strike the Assyrians down in
    battle.
³³In the Valley of Ben Hinnom,
    Topheth has been prepared
    for a long time.
It has been made ready for the
    king of Assyria.
Its fire pit has been made deep
    and wide.
It has plenty of wood for the fire.
The breath of the LORD
  will be like a stream of burning
    sulfur.
It will set the wood on fire.

THE LORD WILL JUDGE THOSE WHO DEPEND ON EGYPT

31

How terrible it will be for those who go down to Egypt for help!
How terrible for those who
    depend on horses!
They trust in how many chariots
    they have.
They trust in how strong their
    horsemen are.
But they don't look to the Holy
    One of Israel.
They don't ask the LORD for his
    help.
²He too is wise. He can bring
    horrible trouble.
He does what he says he'll do.
He'll rise up against everyone who
    does what is evil.
He'll fight against those who help
    them.
³The men of Egypt are only
    human.
They aren't God.

Their horses are only flesh and
blood.
They aren't spirits.
The LORD will reach out his
powerful hand
to punish everyone.
The Egyptians provide help.
But they will be tripped up.
The people of Judah receive the
help.
But they will fall down.
All of them will be destroyed.

4 The LORD says to me,

"A powerful lion stands over its
food and growls.
A lot of shepherds can be
brought together to drive it
away.
But the lion is not frightened by
their shouts.
It is not upset by the noise they
make.
In the same way, I will come down
from heaven.
I will fight on Mount Zion and on
its hills.
Nothing will drive me away.
I am the LORD who rules over all.
5 Like a bird hovering over its nest, I
will guard Jerusalem.
I will keep it safe.
I will pass over it and save it.
I am the LORD who rules over
all."

6 People of Israel, return to the LORD.
He's the one you have so strongly opposed. 7 The time will come when every one of you will turn your backs on
your gods of silver and gold. You
sinned when you made them with
your own hands.

8 The LORD says, "The Assyrians will
be killed with swords.
But it will not be men who use
them.
The swords that kill them will not
be used by human beings.
The Assyrians will run away from
those swords.
But their young men will be
caught
and forced to work hard.
9 Their hiding places will be
destroyed
when terror strikes them.

When their commanders see their
enemy's battle flags,
they will be filled with panic,"
announces the LORD.
His fire blazes out from Mount
Zion.
His furnace burns in Jerusalem.

THE KING WHO WILL DO WHAT IS RIGHT

32 A king will come who will
do what is right.
His officials will govern
fairly.
2 Each man will be like a place to get
out of the wind.
He will be like a place to hide
from storms.
He'll be like streams of water
flowing in the desert.
He'll be like the shadow of a
huge rock in a dry and thirsty
land.

3 Then the eyes of those who see
won't be closed anymore.
The ears of those who hear will
listen to the truth.
4 The minds of thoughtless people
will know and understand.
Tongues that stutter will speak
clearly.
5 Foolish people won't be
considered noble anymore.
Those who are worthless won't
be highly respected.
6 A foolish person says foolish
things.
His mind is full of evil thoughts.
He doesn't do what is right.
He tells lies about the LORD.
He doesn't give hungry people any
food.
He doesn't let thirsty people have
any water.
7 The one who is worthless uses
sinful methods.
He makes evil plans against poor
people.
He destroys them with his lies.
He does it even when those
people are right.
8 But the man who is noble makes
noble plans.
And by doing noble things he
succeeds.

THE SINFUL WOMEN IN JERUSALEM

⁹You women who are so contented,
  pay attention to me.
You who feel so secure,
  listen to what I have to say.
¹⁰You feel secure now.
  But in a little over a year you will
    tremble with fear.
  The grape harvest will fail.
  There won't be any fruit.
¹¹So tremble, you contented
    women.
  Tremble with fear, you who feel
    so secure.
  Take your fine clothes off.
  Put black clothes on.
¹²Beat your chests to show how sad
    you are.
  The pleasant fields have been
    destroyed.
  The fruitful vines have dried up.
¹³My people's land is overgrown
    with thorns and bushes.
  Sob over all of the houses that
    were once filled with joy.
  Cry over this city that used to be
    full of wild parties.
¹⁴The royal palace will be left empty.
  The noisy city will be deserted.
  The fort and lookout tower will
    become
  a dry and empty desert forever.
  Donkeys will enjoy being there.
  Flocks will eat there.
¹⁵That will continue until the Holy
    Spirit
  is poured out on us from heaven.
  Then the desert will be turned into
    rich farm lands.
  The rich farm lands will seem
    like a forest.
¹⁶In the desert and the rich farm
    lands
  people will do what is right.
  And they will treat one another
    fairly.
¹⁷Doing what is right will bring
    peace and rest.
  When my people do that, they
    will stay calm
  and trust in the LORD forever.
¹⁸They will live in a peaceful land.
  Their homes will be secure.
  They will enjoy peace and quiet.
¹⁹Hail might strip the forests bare.

Cities might be completely
  destroyed.
²⁰But how blessed you people will be!
  You will plant your seeds by
    every stream.
  You will let your cattle and
    donkeys
  wander anywhere they want to.

THE LORD WILL JUDGE ASSYRIA

33 How terrible it will be
  for you, you who
  destroy others!
Assyria, you haven't been
  destroyed yet.
How terrible for you, you who turn
  against others!
  Others haven't turned against
    you yet.
When you stop destroying,
  you will be destroyed.
When you stop turning against
    others,
  others will turn against you.

²LORD, show us your favor.
  We long for you to help us.
  Make us strong every morning.
  Save us when we're in trouble.
³When the nations hear you
    thunder, they run away.
  When you rise up against them,
    they scatter.
⁴Nations, what you have taken in
    battle is destroyed.
  It's as if young locusts had eaten
    it up.
  Like large numbers of locusts,
    people rush to get it.
⁵The LORD is honored. He lives in
    heaven.
  He will fill Zion's people with
    what is fair and right.
⁶He will be the firm foundation for
    their entire lives.
  He will give them all of the
    wisdom, knowledge and
    saving power they will ever
    need.
  Respect for the LORD is the key to
    that treasure.

⁷Look! Judah's brave men cry out
    loud in the streets.
  The messengers who were sent
    to bring peace sob bitter tears.

⁸The wide roads are deserted.
No one travels on them.
Our peace treaty with Assyria is
broken.
Those who witnessed it are
looked down on.
No one is respected.
⁹The land is filled with sadness and
wastes away.
Lebanon is full of shame and
dries up.
The rich land of Sharon is like the
Arabah Desert,
The trees of Bashan and Carmel
drop their leaves.

¹⁰ "Now I will take action," says the
LORD.
"Now I will be honored.
Now I will be respected.
¹¹Assyria, your plans and actions are
like straw.
Your anger is a fire that will
destroy you.
¹²The nations will be burned to
ashes.
They will be like bushes that are
cut down and set on fire.

¹³ "You nations far away, listen to
what I have done!
My people who are near,
recognize how powerful I am!
¹⁴The sinners in Zion are terrified.
They tremble with fear.
They say, 'Who of us can live
through the LORD's destroying
fire?
Who of us can live through the
fire that burns forever?'
¹⁵A person must do what is right.
He must be honest and tell the
truth.
He must not get rich by cheating
others.
His hands must not receive
money from those who want
special favors.
He must not let his ears listen to
plans to commit murder.
He must close his eyes to even
thinking about doing what is
evil.
¹⁶A person like that will be kept safe.
It will be as if he were living on
high mountains.
It will be as if he were living in a
mountain fort.

He will have all of the food he
needs.
And he will never run out of
water."

¹⁷People of Judah, you will see the
king in all of his glory and
majesty.
You will view his kingdom
spreading far and wide.
¹⁸You will think about what used to
terrify you.
You will say to yourself,
"Where is that chief officer of
Assyria?
Where is the one who forced us to
send gifts to his king?
Where is the officer in charge of
the towers
that were used when we were
attacked?"
¹⁹You won't see those proud people
anymore.
They spoke a strange language.
None of us could understand it.

²⁰Just look at Zion! It's the city
where we celebrate our regular
feasts.
Turn your eyes toward Jerusalem.
It will be a peaceful place to live
in.
It will be like a tent that will
never be moved.
Its stakes will never be pulled up.
None of its ropes will be broken.
²¹There the LORD will be our Mighty
One.
It will be like a place of wide
rivers and streams.
No boat with oars will travel on
them.
No mighty ship will sail on them.
²²That's because the LORD is our
judge.
The LORD gives us our law.
The LORD is our king.
He will save us.

²³The ropes on your ship hang
loose.
The mast isn't very secure.
The sail isn't spread out.
But the LORD will strike the
Assyrians down.
Then a large amount of goods
will be taken from them and
divided up.

Even people who are disabled
will carry off what was taken.
24 No one living in Zion will ever say
again, "I'm sick."
And the sins of those who live
there will be forgiven.

THE LORD WILL JUDGE THE NATIONS

34 Nations, come near and
listen to me!
Pay attention to what I'm
about to say.
Let the earth and everything in it
listen.
Let the world and everything that
comes out of it pay attention.
2 The LORD is angry with all of the
nations.
His anger burns against all of
their armies.
He will totally destroy them.
He will have them killed.
3 Those who are killed won't be
buried.
Their dead bodies will be thrown
on the ground.
They will give off a very bad smell.
Their blood will cover the
mountains.
4 All of the stars in the heavens will
vanish.
The sky will be rolled up like a
scroll.
All of the stars in the sky will fall
like dried-up leaves from a
vine.
They will drop like wrinkled figs
from a fig tree.

5 The sword of the LORD will finish
its deadly work in the sky.
Then it will come down to strike
Edom.
He will totally destroy that
nation.
6 His sword will be red with blood.
It will be covered with fat.
The blood will flow like the blood
of lambs and goats being
sacrificed.
The fat will be like the fat
taken from the kidneys of rams.
That's because the LORD will offer
a sacrifice
in the city of Bozrah.
He will kill many people in Edom.

7 The people and their leaders will
be killed
like wild oxen and young bulls.
Their land will be wet with their
blood.
The dust will be covered with
their fat.

8 That's because the LORD has set
aside a day to pay Edom back.
He has set aside a year to pay
them back for what they did
to the city of Zion.
9 The streams of Edom will be
turned into tar.
Its dust will be turned into
blazing sulfur.
Its land will become burning tar.
10 The fire will keep burning night
and day.
It can't be put out.
Its smoke will go up forever.
Edom will lie empty for all time to
come.
No one will ever travel through it
again.
11 The desert owl and screech owl
will make it their home.
The great owl and the raven will
build their nests there.
God will use his measuring line
to show how completely Edom
will be destroyed.
He will use his plumb line
to show how empty Edom will
become.
12 Edom's nobles won't have
anything left there
that can be called a kingdom.
All of its princes will vanish.
13 Thorns will cover its forts.
Bushes and weeds will cover its
safest places.
It will become a home for wild
dogs.
It will become a place where owls
live.
14 Desert creatures will meet with
hyenas.
Wild goats will call out to each
other.
Night creatures will also sleep
there.
They will find places where they
can rest.
15 Owls will make their nests and lay
their eggs there.

And they will hatch them.
They will take care of their little
ones
under the shadow of their wings.
Male and female falcons will also
gather there.

¹⁶Look in the scroll of the LORD.
There you will read that

none of those animals will be
missing.
Male and female alike will be
there.
The LORD himself has commanded
it.
And his Spirit will gather them
together.
¹⁷The LORD will decide what part of
the land goes to each animal.
Then he will give each one its
share.
It will belong to them forever.
And they will live there for all
time to come.

THE LORD WILL SET HIS PEOPLE FREE

35 The desert and the dry
ground will be glad.
The dry places will be full
of joy.
Flowers will grow there.
Like the first crocus in the spring,
2 the desert will bloom with
flowers.
It will be very glad and shout
with joy.
The glorious beauty of Lebanon
will be given to it.
It will be as beautiful as the rich
lands
of Carmel and Sharon.
Everyone will see the glory of the
LORD.
They will see the beauty of our
God.

³Strengthen the hands of those who
are weak.
Help those whose knees give
way.
⁴Say to those whose hearts are
afraid,
"Be strong. Do not fear.
Your God will come.
He will pay your enemies back.
He will come to save you."

⁵Then the eyes of those who are
blind will be opened.
The ears of those who can't hear
will be unplugged.
⁶Those who can't walk will leap like
a deer.
And those who can't speak will
shout with joy.
Water will pour out in dry places.
Streams will flow in the desert.
⁷The burning sand will become a
pool of water.
The thirsty ground will become
bubbling springs.
In the places where wild dogs once
lay down,
tall grass and papyrus will grow.

⁸A wide road will go through the
land.
It will be called The Way of
Holiness.
Only those who are pure and clean
can travel on it.
Only those who lead a holy life
can use it.
Evil and foolish people can't walk
on it.
⁹No lions will use it.
No wild animals will be on it.
None of them will be there.
Only people who have been set
free will walk on it.
10 Those the LORD has saved will
return to their land.
They will sing as they enter the
city of Zion.
Joy that lasts forever will be
like beautiful crowns on their
heads.
They will be filled with gladness
and joy.
Sorrow and sighing will be
gone.

SENNACHERIB WARNS JERUSALEM

36 Sennacherib attacked and
captured all of the cities of
Judah that had high walls
around them. It was in the 14th year of
the rule of Hezekiah. Sennacherib was
king of Assyria. ²He sent his field commander from Lachish to King Hezekiah at Jerusalem. He sent him along
with a large army. The commander
stopped at the channel that brings

water from the Upper Pool. It was on the road to the Washerman's Field.

³Eliakim, Shebna and Joah went out to him. Eliakim, the son of Hilkiah, was in charge of the palace. Shebna was the secretary. Joah, the son of Asaph, kept the records.

⁴The field commander said to them, "Give Hezekiah this message. Tell him,

" 'Sennacherib is the great king of Assyria. He says, "Why are you putting your faith in what your king says? ⁵You say you have a military plan. You say you have a strong army. But your words don't mean anything. Who are you depending on? Why don't you want to stay under my control?

⁶ ' "You are depending on Egypt. Why are you doing that? Egypt is nothing but a broken papyrus stem. Try leaning on it. It will only cut your hand. Pharaoh, the king of Egypt, is just like that to everyone who depends on him.

⁷ ' "Suppose you say to me, 'We are depending on the LORD our God.' Didn't Hezekiah remove your god's high places and altars? Didn't Hezekiah say to the people of Judah and Jerusalem, 'You must worship at the altar in Jerusalem'?

⁸ ' "Come on. Make a deal with my master, the king of Assyria. I'll give you 2,000 horses. But only if you can put riders on them! ⁹You are depending on Egypt for chariots and horsemen. You can't drive away even the least important officer among my master's officials.

¹⁰ ' "Besides, do you think I've come without being sent by the LORD? Have I come to attack and destroy this land without receiving a message from him? The LORD himself told me to march out against your country. He told me to destroy it." ' "

¹¹Then Eliakim, Shebna and Joah spoke to the field commander. They said, "Please speak to us in the Aramaic language. We understand it. Don't speak to us in Hebrew. If you do, the people who are on the wall will be able to understand you."

¹²But the commander replied, "My master sent me to say these things. Are these words only for your master and you to hear? Aren't they also for the men who are sitting on the wall? They are going to suffer just like you. They'll have to eat their own waste. They'll have to drink their own urine."

¹³Then the commander stood up

Will there be toys in heaven?

We like toys because they bring us fun. But we get tired of toys, too. Boys and girls stop playing with baby toys. That is because they have outgrown them. After kids become teenagers they stop playing with kid toys. Grownups have "toys" too.

A grownup toy might be a snowmobile or a computer. But by the time we get to heaven, no matter how old we are, we will have outgrown our "earthly" toys. God will give us everything we need for true and lasting joy.

checkout Isaiah 35:10

Related verses:
1 Corinthians
13:11,12; 14:20

and spoke in the Hebrew language. He called out, "Pay attention to what the great king of Assyria is telling you. [14]He says, 'Don't let Hezekiah trick you. He can't save you! [15]Don't let Hezekiah talk you into trusting in the LORD. Don't believe him when he says, "You can be sure that the LORD will save us. This city will not be handed over to the king of Assyria." '

[16]"Don't listen to Hezekiah. The king of Assyria says, 'Make a peace treaty with me. Come over to my side. Then every one of you will eat fruit from your own vine and fig tree. Every one of you will drink water from your own well. [17]You will do that until I come back. Then I'll take you to a land that is just like yours. It's a land that has a lot of grain and fresh wine. It has plenty of bread and vineyards.

[18]" 'Don't let Hezekiah fool you. He's telling you a lie when he says, "The LORD will save us." Has the god of any nation ever saved his land from the powerful hand of the king of Assyria? [19]Where are the gods of Hamath and Arpad? Where are the gods of Sepharvaim? Have they saved Samaria from my power? [20]Which one of all of the gods of those countries has been able to save his land from me? So how can the LORD save Jerusalem from my power?' "

[21]But the people remained silent. They didn't say anything. That's because King Hezekiah had commanded, "Don't answer him."

[22]Then Eliakim, the son of Hilkiah, went to Hezekiah. Eliakim was in charge of the palace. The secretary Shebna went with him. So did Joah, the son of Asaph. Joah kept the records. All of them went to Hezekiah with their clothes torn. They told him what the field commander had said.

ISAIAH PROPHESIES THAT JERUSALEM WILL BE SAVED

37 When King Hezekiah heard what the field commander had said, he tore his clothes. He put on black clothes. Then he went into the LORD's temple. [2]Hezekiah sent Eliakim, who was in charge of the palace, to me. He also sent the leading priests and the secretary Shebna to me. All of them were wearing black clothes.

[3]They told me, "Hezekiah says, 'Today we're in great trouble. The LORD is warning us. He's bringing shame on us. Sometimes babies come to the moment when they should be born. But their mothers aren't strong enough to allow them to be born. Today we are like those mothers. We aren't strong enough to save ourselves.

[4]" 'Perhaps the LORD your God will hear everything the field commander has said. His master, the king of Assyria, has sent him to make fun of the living God. Maybe the LORD your God will punish him for what he has heard him say. So pray for the remaining people who are still alive here.' "

[5]King Hezekiah's officials came to me. [6]Then I said to them, "Tell your master, 'The LORD says, "Do not be afraid of what you have heard. The officers who are under the king of Assyria have spoken evil things against me. [7]Listen! I will send him news from his own country. It will upset him so much that he will return home. There I will have him cut down with a sword." ' "

[8]The field commander heard that the king of Assyria had left Lachish. So the commander pulled his troops back from Jerusalem. He went to join the king. He found out that the king was fighting against Libnah.

[9]During that time Sennacherib received a report. He was told that Tirhakah was marching out to fight against him. Tirhakah was king of Egypt. He was from the land of Cush.

When Sennacherib heard the report, he sent messengers again to Hezekiah with a letter. It said, [10]"Tell Hezekiah, the king of Judah, 'Don't let the god you depend on trick you. He says, "Jerusalem will not be handed over to the king of Assyria." But don't believe him. [11]I'm sure you have heard about what the kings of Assyria have done to all of the other countries. They have destroyed them completely. So do you think you will be saved? [12]" 'The kings who ruled before me destroyed many nations. Did the gods of those nations save them? Did the gods of Gozan, Haran or Rezeph save them? What about the gods of the people of Eden who were in Tel Assar? ¹³Where is the king of Hamath? Where is the king of Arpad? Where is the king of the city of Sepharvaim? Where are the kings of Hena or Ivvah?' "

HEZEKIAH PRAYS TO THE LORD

¹⁴When Hezekiah received the letter from the messengers, he read it. Then he went up to the LORD's temple. There he spread the letter out in front of the LORD.

¹⁵Hezekiah prayed to the LORD. He said, ¹⁶"LORD who rules over all, you are the God of Israel. You sit on your throne between the cherubim. You alone are God over all of the kingdoms on earth. You have made heaven and earth. ¹⁷Listen, LORD. Hear us. Open your eyes, LORD. Look at the trouble we're in. Listen to what Sennacherib is saying. You are the living God. And he dares to make fun of you!

¹⁸"LORD, it's true that the kings of Assyria have completely destroyed many nations and their lands. ¹⁹They have thrown the statues of the gods of those nations into the fire. And they have destroyed them. That's because they weren't really gods at all. They were nothing but statues that were made out of wood and stone. They were made by human hands.

²⁰"LORD our God, save us from the powerful hand of Sennacherib. Then all of the kingdoms on earth will know that you alone are God."

SENNACHERIB FALLS FROM POWER

²¹I sent a message to Hezekiah. I said, "The LORD is the God of Israel. He says, 'You have prayed to me about Sennacherib, the king of Assyria. ²²So here is the message I have spoken against him. I am telling him,

" ' "You will not win the battle over Zion.
Its people hate you and make fun of you.
The people of Jerusalem lift up their heads proudly
as you run away.
²³Who have you laughed at?

Who have you spoken evil things against?
Who have you raised your voice against?
Who have you looked at so proudly?
You have done it against me.
I am the Holy One of Israel!
²⁴Through your messengers
you have laughed at me again and again.
And you have said,
'I have many chariots.
With them I have climbed to the tops of the mountains.
I've climbed the highest mountains in Lebanon.
I've cut down its tallest cedar trees.
I've cut down the best of its pine trees.
I've reached its farthest mountains.
I've reached its finest forests.
²⁵I've dug wells in strange lands.
I've drunk the water from them.
I've walked through all of Egypt's streams.
I've dried up every one of them.'
²⁶" ' "But I, the LORD, say, 'Haven't you heard what I have done?
Long ago I arranged for you to do all of that.
In days of old I planned it.
Now I have made it happen.
You have turned cities with high walls
into piles of stone.
²⁷Their people do not have any power left.
They are troubled and put to shame.
They are like plants in the field.
They are like new green plants.
They are like grass that grows on a roof.
It dries up before it is completely grown.
²⁸" ' " 'But I know where you live.
I know when you come and go.
I know how very angry you are with me.
²⁹You roar against me and brag.
And I have heard your bragging.
So I will put my hook in your nose.
I will put my bit in your mouth.
And I will make you go home by the same way you came.' " ' "

³⁰The LORD said, "Hezekiah, here is a miraculous sign for you.

"This year you will eat what grows by itself.
Next year you will eat what grows from that.
But in the third year you will plant your crops and gather them in.
You will plant your grapevines and eat their fruit.
³¹The people of Judah who are still alive will be like plants.
Once more they will put down roots and produce fruit.
³²Out of Jerusalem will come those who remain.
Out of Mount Zion will come those who are still left alive.
My great love will make sure that happens.
I rule over all.

³³"Here is a message from me about the king of Assyria. It says,

" 'He will not enter this city.
He will not even shoot an arrow at it.
He will not come near it with a shield.
He will not build a ramp in order to climb over its walls.
³⁴By the way that he came he will go home.
He will not enter this city,'
announces the LORD.
³⁵ "I will guard this city and save it.
I will do it for myself.
And I will do it for my servant David."

³⁶Then the angel of the LORD went into the camp of the Assyrians. He put to death 185,000 soldiers there. The people of Jerusalem got up the next morning. They looked out and saw all of the dead bodies. ³⁷So Sennacherib, the king of Assyria, took the army tents down. Then he left. He returned to Nineveh and stayed there. ³⁸One day Sennacherib was worshiping in the temple of his god Nisroch. His sons Adrammelech and Sharezer cut him down with their swords. Then they escaped to the land of Ararat. Esarhaddon became the next king after his father Sennacherib.

HEZEKIAH PRAISES THE LORD FOR HEALING HIM

38

In those days Hezekiah became very sick. He knew he was about to die. I went to see him. I told him, "The LORD says, 'Put everything in order. Make out your will. You are going to die soon. You will not get well again.' "

²Hezekiah turned his face toward the wall. He prayed to the LORD. He said, ³"LORD, please remember how faithful I've been to you. I've lived the way you wanted me to. I've served you with all my heart. I've done what is good in your sight." And Hezekiah cried bitterly.

⁴A message came to me from the LORD. He said, ⁵"Go and speak to Hezekiah. Tell him, 'The LORD, the God of King David, says, "I have heard your prayer. I have seen your tears. I will add 15 years to your life. ⁶And I will save you and this city from the powerful hand of the king of Assyria. I will guard this city.

⁷" ' "Here is a miraculous sign from me. It will show you that I will heal you, just as I promised I would. ⁸The shadow that was made by the sun has gone down ten steps on the stairway of Ahaz. I will make it go back up those ten steps." ' " So the shadow went back up the ten steps it had gone down.

⁹Here is a song of praise that was written by Hezekiah, the king of Judah. He wrote it after he was sick and had gotten well again.

¹⁰I said, "I'm enjoying the best years of my life.
Must I now go through the gates of death?
Will the rest of my years be taken away from me?"
¹¹I said, "LORD, I'll never see you again
while I'm still alive.
I'll never see people anymore.
I'll never again be with those who live in this world.
¹²My body is like a shepherd's tent.
It has been pulled down and carried off.
My life is like a piece of cloth that I've rolled up.

You have cut it off from the loom.
In a short period of time you
have brought my life to an
end.
¹³ I waited patiently until sunrise.
But like a lion you broke all of my
bones.
In a short period of time you
have brought my life to an
end.
¹⁴ I cried softly like a weak little bird.
I groaned like a sad dove.
My eyes grew tired as I looked up
toward heaven.
Lord, I'm in trouble. Please come
and help me!

¹⁵ "But what can I say?
You have promised to heal me.
And you yourself have done it.
Once I was proud and bitter.
But now I will live the rest of my
life free of pride.

¹⁶ Lord, people find the will to live
because you keep your
promises.
And my spirit also finds life in
your promises.
You brought me back to health.
You let me live.
¹⁷ I'm sure it was for my benefit
that I suffered such great pain.
You love me. You kept me
from going down into the pit of
death.
You have put all of my sins
behind your back.
¹⁸ People in the grave can't praise
you.
Dead people can't sing praise to
you.
Those who go down to the grave
can't hope for you to be faithful
to them.
¹⁹ It is those who are alive who praise
you.

Why are cemeteries so creepy?

Death is a scary thing because it is final. A person who dies does not come back ever again. It is like going on a trip and *never* coming back. People who die can never come back to talk to their friends and relatives. They can never undo what they did wrong on this earth. Death also scares us because it can happen so fast. One second the person is awake and talking and the next second the person cannot talk or live with us ever again.

That is why graveyards or cemeteries can be so creepy. No one wants to die, and cemeteries are where dead bodies are buried. Also, movies and television shows picture cemeteries as places where ghosts and other spooky things hang out. But Christians do not have to be afraid of death because they know that they will go to heaven when they die.

checkout ▶ Isaiah 38:18

Related verses:
Romans 8:38,39

And that's what I'm doing today.
Fathers tell their children
　about how faithful you are.

20 "You will save me.
So we will sing and play music
　on stringed instruments.
We will sing all the days of our
　lives
　in your temple."

21When Hezekiah was sick, I had said, "Press some figs together. Spread them on a piece of cloth. Apply them to Hezekiah's boil. Then he'll get well again."

22At that time Hezekiah had asked me, "What will the miraculous sign be to prove I'll go up to the LORD's temple?" That's when the LORD had made the shadow go back ten steps.

MESSENGERS COME FROM BABYLON TO HEZEKIAH

39 At that time Merodach-Baladan, the king of Babylonia, sent Hezekiah letters and a gift. He had heard that Hezekiah had been sick but had gotten well again. Merodach-Baladan was the son of Baladan.

2Hezekiah gladly received the messengers. He showed them what was in his storerooms. He showed them the silver and gold. He took them to where the spices and the fine olive oil were kept. He showed them where he kept all of his weapons. And he showed them all of his treasures. In fact, he showed them everything that was in his palace and in his whole kingdom.

3Then I went to King Hezekiah. I asked him, "What did those men say? Where did they come from?"

"They came from a land far away," Hezekiah said. "They came to me from Babylon."

4I asked, "What did they see in your palace?"

"They saw everything in my palace," Hezekiah said. "I showed them all of my treasures."

5Then I said to Hezekiah, "Listen to the message of the LORD who rules over all. He says, 6'You can be sure the time will come when everything in your palace will be carried off to Babylon. Everything the kings before you

have stored up until this day will be taken away. There will not be anything left,' says the LORD.

7 'Some of the members of your family line will be taken away. They will be your own flesh and blood. They will include the children who will be born into your family line in years to come. And they will serve the king of Babylonia in his palace.' "

8"The message the LORD has spoken through you is good," Hezekiah replied. He thought, "There will be peace and safety while I'm still living."

GOD COMFORTS HIS PEOPLE

40 "Comfort my people,"
　　　says your God.
"Comfort them.
2Speak tenderly to the people of
　Jerusalem.
Announce to them
that their hard service has been
　completed.
Tell them that their sin has been
　paid for.
Tell them I have punished them
　enough
　for all of their sins."

3A messenger is calling out,
"In the desert prepare
　the way for the LORD.
Make a straight road through it
　for our God.
4Every valley will be filled in.
Every mountain and hill will be
　made level.
The rough ground will be
　smoothed out.
The rocky places will be made
　flat.
5Then the glory of the LORD will
　appear.
And everyone will see it.
　　　The LORD has spoken."

6Another messenger says, "Cry
　out."
And I said, "What should I cry?"

"Cry out, 'All people are like grass.
They don't last any longer than
　flowers in the field.
7The grass dries up. The flowers fall
　to the ground.
That happens when the LORD
　makes his wind blow on them.

So people are just like grass.
8 The grass dries up. The flowers fall
to the ground.
But what our God says will stand
forever.' "

9 Zion, you are bringing good news
to your people.
Go up on a high mountain and
announce it.
Jerusalem, you are bringing good
news to them.
Shout the message loudly.
Shout it out loud. Don't be afraid.
Say to the towns of Judah,
"Your God is coming!"
10 The LORD and King is coming with
power.
His powerful arm will rule for him.
He has set his people free.
He is bringing them back as his
reward.
He has won the battle over their
enemies.
11 He takes care of his flock like a
shepherd.
He gathers the lambs in his arms.
He carries them close to his heart.
He gently leads those that have
little ones.

12 Who has measured the oceans by
using the palm of his hand?
Who has used the width of his
hand to mark off the sky?
Who has measured out the dust of
the earth in a basket?
Who has weighed the mountains
on scales?
Who has weighed the hills in a
balance?
13 Who can ever understand what is
in the LORD's mind?
Who can ever give him advice?
14 Did the LORD have to ask anyone
to help him understand?
Did he have to ask someone to
teach him the right way?
Who taught him what he knows?
Who showed him how to
understand?

15 The nations are only a drop in a
bucket to him.
He considers them as nothing
but dust on the scales.
He weighs the islands as if they
were only fine dust.

16 Lebanon doesn't have enough
trees to keep his altar fires
burning.
It doesn't have enough animals
to sacrifice as burnt offerings
to him.
17 To him, all of the nations don't
amount to anything.
He considers them to be
worthless.
In fact, they are less than nothing
in his sight.

18 So who will you compare God to?
Is there any other god like him?
19 Will you compare him to a statue
of a god?
Any skilled worker can make a
statue.
Then another worker covers it
with gold
and makes silver chains for it.
20 But someone who is too poor to
bring that kind of offering
will choose some wood that
won't rot.
Then he looks for a skilled worker.
He pays the worker to make a
statue of a god that won't fall
over.

21 Don't you know who made
everything?
Haven't you heard about him?
Hasn't it been told to you from the
beginning?
Haven't you understood it ever
since the earth was made?
22 God sits on his throne high above
the earth.
Its people look like grasshoppers
to him.
He spreads the heavens out like a
cover.
He sets it up like a tent to live in.
23 He takes the power of princes
away from them.
He reduces the rulers of this
world to nothing.
24 They are planted.
They are scattered like seeds.
They put down roots in the
ground.
But as soon as that happens, God
blows on them and they dry up.
Then a windstorm sweeps them
away like straw.

25 "So who will you compare me to?
    Who is equal to me?" says the
        Holy One.
26 Look up toward the sky.
    Who created everything you see?
    The LORD causes the stars to come
        out at night one by one.
    He gives each one of them a
        name.
    His power and strength are great.
    So none of the stars is missing.

27 Family of Jacob, why do you say,
    "The LORD doesn't notice our
        condition"?
    People of Israel, why do you say,
    "Our God doesn't pay any
        attention to our rightful
        claims"?
28 Don't you know who made
        everything?
    Haven't you heard about him?
    The LORD is the God who lives
        forever.
    He created everything on earth.
    He won't become worn out or get
        tired.
    No one will ever know how great
        his understanding is.
29 He gives strength to those who are
        tired.
    He gives power to those who are
        weak.
30 Even young people become worn
        out and get tired.
    Even the best of them trip and
        fall.
31 But those who trust in the LORD
        will receive new strength.
    They will fly as high as eagles.
    They will run and not get tired.
    They will walk and not grow
        weak.

THE LORD HELPS ISRAEL

41

The LORD says, "People
who live on the
islands,
come and stand quietly in front
    of me.
Let the nations gain new strength
    in order to state their case.
Let them come forward and speak.
Let us go to court and find out
    who is right.

2 "Who has stirred up a king from
    the east?

Who has helped him win his
    battles?
I hand nations over to him.
I bring kings under his control.
He turns them into dust with his
    sword.
With his bow he turns them into
    straw blowing in the wind.
3 He hunts them down. Then he
    moves on unharmed.
He travels so fast that his feet
    don't seem to touch the ground.
4 Who has made that happen? Who
    has carried it out?
Who has created all of the people
    who have ever lived?
I, the LORD, have done it.
I was with the first of them.
And I will be with the last of
    them."

5 The people on the islands have
    seen that king coming.
And it has made them afraid.
People tremble with fear from
    one end of the earth to the
    other.
They come and gather together.
6   They help each other.
They say to one another, "Be
    strong!"
7 One skilled worker makes a statue
    of a god.
Another covers it with gold.
The first worker says to the
    second,
    "You have done a good job."
Another worker smooths out the
    metal with a hammer.
Still another gives the statue its
    final shape.
The third worker says to the last
    one,
    "You have done a good job."
Then they nail the statue down
    so it won't fall over.

8 The LORD says, "People of Israel,
    you are my servants.
Family of Jacob, I have chosen
    you.
You are the children of my friend
    Abraham.
9 I gathered you from one end of the
    earth to the other.
From the farthest places on earth
    I brought you together.
I said, 'You are my servants.'

I have chosen you.
I have not turned my back on you.
¹⁰ So do not be afraid. I am with you.
Do not be terrified. I am your
God.
I will make you strong and help
you.
My powerful right hand will take
good care of you.
I always do what is right.

¹¹ "All those who are angry with you
will be put to shame.
And they will be dishonored.
Those who oppose you will be
destroyed.
And they will vanish.
¹² You might search for your
enemies.
But you will not find them.
Those who go to war against you
will completely disappear.
¹³ I am the LORD your God.
I take hold of your right hand.
I say to you, 'Do not be afraid.
I will help you.'
¹⁴ Family of Jacob, you are as weak as
a worm.
But do not be afraid.
People of Israel, there are only a
few of you.
But do not be afraid.
I myself will help you," announces
the LORD.
He is the one who sets his people
free.
He is the Holy One of Israel.
¹⁵ He says, "I will make you into a
threshing sled.
It will be new and sharp.
It will have many teeth.
You will grind the mountains
down and crush them.
You will turn the hills into
nothing but straw.
¹⁶ You will toss them in the air.
A strong wind will catch them
and blow them away.
You will be glad because I will
make that happen.
You will praise me.
I am the Holy One of Israel.

¹⁷ "Those who are poor and needy
search for water.
But there isn't any.
Their tongues are dry because
they are thirsty.

But I will help them. I am the
LORD.
I will not desert them.
I am Israel's God.
¹⁸ I will make streams flow on the
bare hilltops.
I will make springs come up in
the valleys.
I will turn the desert into pools of
water.
I will turn the dry and cracked
ground into flowing springs.
¹⁹ I will make trees grow in the
desert.
I will plant cedar and acacia trees
there.
I will plant myrtle and olive trees
there.
I will make pine trees grow in the
dry and empty desert.
I will plant fir and cypress trees
there.
²⁰ Then people will see and know
that my powerful hand has done
it.
They will consider and understand
that I have created it.
I am the Holy One of Israel."

²¹ The LORD says to the nations and
their gods,
"State your case."
Jacob's King says to them,
"Prove your case to me.
²² Show me your facts. Tell me and
my people
what is going to happen.
Tell us what happened in the past.
Then we can check it out
and see if it is really true.
Or announce to us the things that
will take place.
²³ Tell us what will happen in the
days ahead.
Then we will know that you are
gods.
Do something. It does not matter
whether it is good or bad.
Then we will be terrified and
filled with fear.
²⁴ But you are less than nothing.
Your actions are completely
worthless.
I hate it when people worship
you.

²⁵ "I have stirred up a king
who will come from the north.

He lives in the east.
He will bring honor to me.
He walks all over rulers as if they
were mud.
He steps on them just as a potter
stomps on clay.
26 Which one of you gods said those
things
would happen before they did?
Who told us about them
so we could know them?
Who told us ahead of time?
Who told us so we could say,
'You are right'?
None of you told us about them.
None of you told us ahead of
time.
In fact, no one heard you say
anything at all.
27 I was the first to tell Zion.
I said, 'Look! The people of Israel
are coming back!'
I sent a prophet to Jerusalem
with the good news.
28 I look, but there is no one
among the gods that can give me
advice.
None of them can answer
when I ask them the simplest
question.
29 So they are not really gods at all.
What they do does not amount
to anything.
They are as useless as wind.

THE LORD'S CHOSEN
SERVANT

42 "Here is my servant. I
take good care of
him.
I have chosen him. I am very
pleased with him.
I will put my Spirit on him.
He will make everything right
among the nations.
2 He will not shout or cry out.
He will not raise his voice in the
streets.
3 He will not break a bent twig.
He will not put out a dimly
burning flame.
He will be faithful and make
everything right.
4 He will not grow weak or lose
hope.
He will not give up until he makes
everything right on the earth.

The islands will put their hope in
his law."

5 God created the heavens and
spread them out.
The LORD made the earth and
everything that grows on it.
He gives breath to its people.
He gives life to those who walk on
it.
He says to his servant,
6 "I, the LORD, have chosen you to
do what is right.
I will take hold of your hand.
I will keep you safe.
You will put my covenant with
the people of Israel into effect.
And you will be a light for the
other nations.
7 You will open eyes that can't see.
You will set prisoners free.
Those who sit in darkness will
come out of their cells.

8 "I am the LORD. That is my name!
I will not let any other god share
my glory.
I will not let statues of gods share
my praise.
9 What I said would happen has
taken place.
Now I announce new things to
you.
Before they even begin to happen,
I announce them to you."

A SONG OF PRAISE
TO THE LORD

10 Sing a new song to the LORD.
Sing praise to him from one end
of the earth to the other.
Sing, you who sail out on the
ocean.
Sing, all of you creatures in it.
Sing, you islands.
Sing, all of you who live there.
11 Let the desert and its towns raise
their voices.
Let those who live in the
settlements of Kedar be glad.
Let the people of Sela sing with joy.
Let them shout from the tops of
the mountains.
12 Let them give glory to the LORD.
Let them praise him in the
islands.
13 The LORD will march out like a
mighty warrior.

He will stir up his anger like a
soldier getting ready to fight.
He will shout the battle cry.
And he will win the battle over
his enemies.

¹⁴The LORD says, "For a long time I
have kept silent.
I have been calm and quiet.
But now, like a woman having a
baby,
I cry out. I am struggling to
breathe.
¹⁵I will completely destroy the
mountains and hills.
I will dry up everything that
grows there.
I will turn rivers into dry land.
I will dry up the pools.
¹⁶Israel is blind.
So I will lead them along paths
they had not known before.
I will guide them on roads they are
not familiar with.
I will turn the darkness into light
as they travel.
I will make the rough places
smooth.
Those are the things I will do.
I will not desert my people.
¹⁷Some people trust in statues of
gods.
They say to them, 'You are our
gods.'
But they will be dishonored.
They will be put to shame.

ISRAEL CAN'T SEE OR HEAR

¹⁸"Israel, listen to me! You can hear,
but you do not understand.
Look to me! You can see,
but you do not know what you
are seeing.
¹⁹The people of Israel serve me. But
who is more blind than they
are?
Who is more deaf than the
messengers I send?
Who is more blind than those who
have committed themselves
to be faithful to me?
Who is more blind than my
servants?
²⁰Israel, you have seen many things.
But you have not paid any
attention to me.
Your ears are open.

But you do not hear anything I
say."
²¹The LORD wanted his people to see
how great and glorious his law is.
He wanted to show them
that he always does what is right.
²²Enemies have carried off
everything they own.
All of my people are trapped in
pits
or hidden away in prisons.
They themselves have become like
stolen goods.
No one can save them.
They have been carried off.
And there is no one who will say,
"Send them back."

²³Family of Jacob, who among you
will listen to what I'm saying?
People of Israel, which one of
you will pay close attention in
days to come?
²⁴Who allowed you to be carried off
like stolen goods?
Who handed you over to
robbers?
The LORD did it!
We have sinned against him.
Israel, you wouldn't follow his
ways.
You didn't obey his law.
²⁵So he poured his burning anger
out on you.
He had many of you killed off in
battle.
You were surrounded by flames.
But you didn't realize what was
happening.
Many of you were destroyed.
But you didn't learn anything
from it.

THE LORD SAVES ISRAEL

43 Family of Jacob, the LORD
created you.
People of Israel, he
formed you.
He says, "Do not be afraid.
I will set you free.
I will send for you by name.
You belong to me.
²You will pass through deep waters.
But I will be with you.
You will pass through the rivers.
But their waters will not sweep
over you.

You will walk through fire.
But you will not be burned.
The flames will not harm you.
³I am the LORD your God.
I am the Holy One of Israel.
I am the one who saves you.
I will give up Egypt to set you free.
I will give up Cush and Seba for
you.
⁴You are priceless to me.
I love you and honor you.
So I will trade other people for
you.
I will give up other nations to
save your lives.
⁵Do not be afraid. I am with you.
I will bring your people back
from the east.
I will gather you from the west.
⁶I will say to the north, 'Let them
go!'
And I will say to the south, 'Do
not hold them back.'
Bring my sons from far away.
Bring my daughters from the
farthest places on earth.
⁷Bring back everyone who belongs
to me.
I created them to bring glory to
me.
I formed them and made them."

⁸Lead my people into court.
They have eyes but can't see.
Bring those who have ears but
can't hear.
⁹All of the nations are gathering
together.
All of them are coming.
Which one of their gods said
ahead of time
that the people of Israel would
return?
Which of them told us anything
at all about the past?
Let them bring in their witnesses
to prove they were right.
Then others will hear them. And
they will say,
"What they said is true."
¹⁰"People of Israel, you are my
witnesses," announces the
LORD.
"I have chosen you to be my
servants.
I wanted you to know me and
believe in me.

I wanted you to understand that
I am the one and only God.
Before me, there was no other god
at all.
And there will not be any god
after me.
¹¹I am the one and only LORD.
I am the only one who can save
you.
¹²I have made known what would
happen.
I told you about it. And I saved
you.
I did it. It was not some other god
you worship.
You are my witnesses that I am
God," announces the LORD.
¹³"And that is not all! I have always
been God,
and I always will be.
No one can save people from my
powerful hand.
When I do something, who can
undo it?"

THE LORD FORGIVES ISRAEL BUT ALSO PUNISHES THEM

¹⁴The LORD sets his people free.
He is the Holy One of Israel. He
says,
"People of Israel, I will send an
army to Babylon to save you.
I will cause all of the Babylonians
to run away.
They will try to escape in the
ships they were so proud of.
¹⁵I am your LORD and King.
I am your Holy One.
I created you."

¹⁶Long ago the LORD opened
a way for his people to go
through the Red Sea.
He made a path through the
mighty waters.
¹⁷He caused Egypt to send out its
chariots and horses.
He sent its entire army to its
death.
Its soldiers lay down there.
They never got up again.
They were destroyed.
They were blown out like a dimly
burning flame.
But the LORD says,
¹⁸"Forget the things that happened
in the past.

Do not keep on thinking about
them.
19 I am about to do something new.
It is beginning to happen even
now.
Don't you see it coming?
I am going to make a way for you
to go through the desert.
I will make streams of water in
the dry and empty land.
20 Even wild dogs and owls honor me.
That is because I provide water
in the desert
for my people to drink.
I cause streams to flow in the dry
and empty land
for my chosen ones.
21 I do it for the people I made for
myself.
I want them to sing praise to me.

22 "Family of Jacob, you have not
prayed to me as you should.
People of Israel, you have not
even begun to get tired while
doing it.
23 You have not brought me sheep
for burnt offerings.
You have not honored me with
your sacrifices.
I have not loaded you down
by requiring grain offerings.
I have not made you tired
by requiring you to burn incense.
24 But you have not bought any
sweet-smelling cane for me.
You have not given me the fattest
parts
of your animal sacrifices.
Instead, you have loaded me down
with your sins.
You have made me tired with the
wrong things you have done.

25 "I am the one who wipes out your
lawless acts.
I do it because of who I am.
I will not remember your sins
anymore.
26 But let us go to court together.
Remind me of what you have
done.
State your case.
Prove to me that you are not
guilty.
27 Your father Jacob sinned.
Your priests and prophets
refused to obey me.

28 So I will put the high officials of
your temple to shame.
I will let Jacob's family be totally
destroyed.
And I will let people make fun of
Israel.

THE LORD CHOOSES ISRAEL

44 "Family of Jacob, listen to
me. You are my
servants.
People of Israel, I have chosen
you.
2 I made you. I formed you when
you were born as a nation.
I will help you.
So listen to what I am saying.
Family of Jacob, do not be afraid.
You are my servants.
People of Israel, I have chosen
you.
3 I will pour water out on the thirsty
land.
I will make streams flow on the
dry ground.
I will pour out my Spirit on your
children.
I will pour out my blessing on
their children after them.
4 They will spring up like grass in a
meadow.
They will grow like poplar trees
near flowing streams.
5 Some will say, 'We belong to the
LORD.'
Others will call themselves by
Jacob's name.
Still others will write on their
hands,
'We belong to the Lord.'
And they will be called by the
name of Israel.

WORSHIP THE LORD, NOT OTHER GODS

6 "I am Israel's King. I set them free.
I am the LORD who rules over all.
So listen to what I am saying.
I am the First and the Last.
I am the one and only God.
7 Who is like me? Let him come
forward and speak boldly.
Let him tell me everything that
has happened
since I created my people long
ago.

And let him tell me what has not
    happened yet.
Let him announce ahead of
    time what is going to take
    place.
⁸ Do not tremble with fear. Do not
    be afraid.
Didn't I announce everything
    that has happened?
Didn't I tell you about it long
    ago?
You are my witnesses. Is there any
    other God but me?
No! There is no other Rock. I do
    not know even one."

⁹ Those who make statues of gods
    don't amount to anything.
And the statues they think so
    much of are worthless.
Those who would speak up for
    them are blind.
They don't know anything.
So they will be put to shame.
¹⁰ People make statues of gods.
But those gods can't do them any
    good.
¹¹ People like that will be put to
    shame.
Those who make statues of gods
    are mere men.
Let all of them come together and
    state their case.
They will be terrified and put to
    shame.

¹² A blacksmith gets his tool.
He uses it to shape metal over
    the burning coals.
He uses his hammers to make a
    statue of a god.
He forms it with his powerful
    arm.
He gets hungry and loses his
    strength.
He doesn't drink any water.
He gets weaker and weaker.
¹³ A carpenter measures a piece of
    wood with a line.
He draws a pattern on it with a
    marker.
He cuts out a statue with sharp
    tools.
He marks it with compasses.
He shapes it into the form of a
    handsome man.
He does all of that so he can put
    it in a temple.

¹⁴ He cuts down a cedar tree.
Or perhaps he takes a cypress or
    an oak tree.
It might be a tree that grew in the
    forest.
Or it might be a pine tree he
    planted.
And the rain made it grow.
¹⁵ Man gets wood from trees for
    fuel.
He uses some of it to warm
    himself.
He starts a fire and bakes
    bread.
But he also uses some of it to
    make a god and worship it.
He makes a statue of a god and
    bows down to it.
¹⁶ He burns half of the wood in the
    fire.
He prepares a meal over it.
He cooks meat over it.
He eats until he is full.
He also warms himself. He says,
    "Good! I'm getting warm.
The fire is nice and hot."
¹⁷ From the rest of the wood he
    makes a statue.
It becomes his god.
He bows down and worships it.
He prays to it. He says,
    "Save me. You are my god."
¹⁸ People like that don't even know
    what they are doing.
Their eyes are shut so that they
    can't see the truth.
Their minds are closed so that
    they can't understand it.
¹⁹ No one even stops to think about
    this.
No one has any sense or
    understanding.
If anyone did, he would say,
    "I used half of the wood for fuel.
I even baked bread over the
    fire.
I cooked meat. Then I ate it.
Should I now make a statue of a
    god
out of the wood that's left over?
Should I bow down to a block of
    wood?
The LORD would hate that."
²⁰ That's as foolish as eating ashes!
The mind of someone like that
has led him down the wrong
    path.

He can't save himself.
He can't bring himself to say,
"This thing I'm holding in my right hand
isn't really a god at all."

21 The LORD says, "Family of Jacob,
remember those things.
People of Israel, you are my
servants.
I have made you. You are my
servants.
Israel, I will not forget you.
22 I will sweep your sins away as if
they were a cloud.
I will blow them away as if they
were the morning mist.
Return to me.
Then I will set you free."

23 Sing with joy, you heavens!
The LORD does wonderful things.
Shout out loud, you earth!
Burst into song, you mountains!
Sing, you forests and all of your
trees!
The LORD sets the family of Jacob
free.
He shows his glory in Israel.

PEOPLE WILL LIVE IN JERUSALEM AGAIN

24 The LORD says,
"People of Israel, I set you free.
I formed you when you were
born as a nation.

"I am the LORD. I have made
everything.
I alone spread out the heavens.
I formed the earth by myself.

25 "Some prophets are not really
prophets at all.
I show that their miraculous
signs are fake.
I make those who practice evil
magic look foolish.
I destroy the learning of those who
think they are wise.
Their knowledge does not make
any sense at all.
26 I make the words of my servants
the prophets come true.
I carry out what my messengers
say will happen.

"I say about Jerusalem,
'My people will live there again.'
I say about the towns of Judah,
'They will be rebuilt.'
I say about their broken-down
buildings,
'I will make them like new
again.'
27 I say to the deep waters,
'Dry up. Let your streams
become dry.'
28 I say about Cyrus,
'He is my shepherd.
He will accomplish everything I
want him to.
He will say about Jerusalem,
"Let it be rebuilt."
And he will say about the temple,
"Let its foundations be laid." '

45

"Cyrus is my anointed
king.
I take hold of his right
hand.
I give him the power
to bring nations under his
control.
I help him strip kings of their
power
to go to war against him.
I break city gates open so he can
go through them.
I say to him,
2 'I will march out ahead of you.
I will make the mountains level.
I will break down bronze gates.
I will cut through their heavy
iron bars.
3 I will give you treasures that are
hidden away in dark places.
I will give you riches that are
stored up in secret places.
Then you will know that I am the
LORD.
I am the God of Israel.
I am sending for you by name.
4 Cyrus, I am sending for you by
name.
I am doing it for the good of the
family of Jacob.
They are my servants.
I am doing it for Israel.
They are my chosen people.
You do not know anything about
me.
But I am giving you a title of
honor.
5 I am the LORD. There is no other
LORD.

I am the one and only God.
You do not know anything about
  me.
But I will make you strong.
⁶Then people will know there is no
  God but me.
Everyone from where the sun
  rises in the east
to where it sets in the west will
  know it.
I am the LORD.
There is no other LORD.
⁷I cause light to shine. I also create
  darkness.
I bring good times. I also create
  hard times.
I do all of those things. I am the
  LORD.

⁸" 'Rain down godliness, you
  heavens above.
Let the clouds shower it down.
Let the earth open wide to receive
  it.
Let freedom spring to life.
Let godliness grow along with it.
I have created all of those things.
I am the LORD.' "

⁹How terrible it will be for anyone
  who argues with his Maker!
He is like a broken piece of
  pottery lying on the ground.
Does clay say to a potter,
"What are you making?"
Does a pot say,
"You don't have any skill"?
¹⁰How terrible it will be for anyone
  who says to his father,
"Why did you give me life?"
How terrible for anyone who says
  to his mother,
"Why have you brought me into
  the world?"

¹¹The LORD is the Holy One of
  Israel.
He made them.
He says to them,
"Are you asking me about what
  will happen to my children?
Are you telling me what I should
  do with what my hands have
  made?
¹²I made the earth.
I created man to live there.
My own hands spread out the
  heavens.

I put all of the stars in their
  places.
¹³I will stir up Cyrus and help him
  win his battles.
I will make all of his roads
  straight.
He will rebuild Jerusalem.
My people have been taken away
  from their country.
But he will set them free.
I will not pay him to do it.
He will not receive a reward for
  it,"
says the LORD who rules over all.

¹⁴The LORD says to the people of Jerusalem,

"You will get everything Egypt
  produces.
You will receive everything the
  people of Cush
and the tall Sabeans get in trade.
All of it will belong to you.
And all of those people will walk
  behind you as slaves.
They will be put in chains and
  come over to you.
They will bow down to you.
They will admit,
'God is with you.
There is no other God.' "

¹⁵You are a God who hides
  yourself.
You are the God of Israel. You
  save us.
¹⁶All those who make statues of gods
  will be put to shame.
They will be dishonored.
They will be led away in shame
  together.
¹⁷But the LORD will save Israel.
He will save them forever.
They will never be put to shame or
  dishonored.
That will be true for all time to
  come.

¹⁸The LORD created the heavens.
He is God.
He formed the earth and made it.
He set it firmly in place.
He didn't create it to be empty.
Instead, he formed it for people
  to live on.
He says, "I am the LORD.
There is no other LORD.
¹⁹I have not spoken in secret.

I have not spoken from a dark
place.
I have not said to Jacob's
people,
'It is useless to look for me.'
I am the LORD. I always speak the
truth.
I always say what is right.

20 "Come together, you people of the
nations
who escaped from Babylonia.
Gather together and come into
court.
Only people who do not know
anything
would carry around gods that are
made out of wood.
They pray to gods that can't save
them.
21 Tell me what will happen. State
your case.
Talk it over together.
Who spoke long ago about what
would happen?
Who said it a long time ago?
I did. I am the LORD.
I am the one and only God.
I always do what is right.
I am the one who saves.
There is no God but me.

22 "All of you who live anywhere on
earth,
turn to me and be saved.
I am God. There is no other God.
23 I have made a promise with an
oath in my own name.
I have spoken with complete
honesty.
I will not take back a single word.
I said,
'Everyone's knee will bow down to
me.
Everyone's mouth will take an
oath in my name.'
24 They will say, 'The LORD always
does what is right.
Only he can make us strong.' "
All those who have been angry
with the LORD will come to
him.
And they will be put to shame.
25 But the LORD will help all of the
people of Israel.
He will make them right with
himself.
And they will praise him.

THERE IS NO OTHER GOD

46 The gods Bel and Nebo
are brought down in
shame.
The statues of them are being
carried away on the backs of
animals.
They used to be carried around by
the people who worshiped
them.
But now they've become a heavy
load for tired animals.
2 Bel and Nebo are brought down in
shame together.
They aren't able to save their own
statues.
They themselves are carried off
as prisoners.

3 The LORD says, "Family of Jacob,
listen to me.
Pay attention, you people of
Israel who are left alive.
I have taken good care of you
since your life began.
I have carried you since you were
born as a nation.
4 I will continue to carry you even
when you are old.
I will take good care of you even
when your hair is gray.
I have made you. And I will carry
you.
I will take care of you. And I will
save you.
I am the LORD.

5 "Who will you compare me to?
Who is equal to me?
What am I like?
Who can you compare me to?
6 Some people pour gold out of
their bags.
They weigh out silver on the
scales.
They hire someone who works
with gold to make it into a
god.
They bow down to it and worship
it.
7 They lift it up on their shoulders
and carry it.
They set it up in its place. And
there it stands.
It can't move from that spot.
Someone might cry out to it.
But it does not answer him.

It can't save him from his troubles.
[8] So remember that, you who refuse to obey me.
Keep it in your minds and hearts.

[9] "Remember what happened in the past.
Think about what took place long ago.
I am God. There is no other God.
I am God. There is no one like me.
[10] Before something even happens, I announce how it will end.
In fact, from times long ago I announced what was still to come.
I say, 'My plan will succeed.
I will do anything I want to do.'
[11] I will send for a man from the east to carry out my plan.
From a land far away, he will come like a bird that eats dead bodies.
I will bring about what I have said.
I will do what I have planned.
[12] Listen to me, you stubborn people.
Pay attention, you who refuse to do what is right.
[13] The time is almost here for me to make everything right.
It is not far away.
The time for me to save you will not be put off.
I will save the city of Zion.
I will bring honor to Israel.

BABYLON WILL FALL

47 "City of Babylon, go down and sit in the dust.
Leave your throne and sit on the ground.
City of the Babylonians, your life will not be comfortable and easy anymore.
[2] Get millstones and grind some flour like a female slave.
Take your veil off.
Lift your skirts up. Make your legs bare.
Wade through the streams.
[3] Everyone will see your naked body.
Everyone will see your shame.
I will pay you back for what you did.
I will not spare any of your people."

[4] The one who sets us free is the Holy One of Israel.
His name is The LORD Who Rules Over All.

[5] The LORD says, "City of the Babylonians,
go into a dark prison and sit there quietly.
You will not be called the queen of kingdoms anymore.
[6] I was angry with my people.
I treated them as if they did not belong to me.
I handed them over to you.
And you did not show them any pity.
You even placed heavy loads on their old people.
[7] You said, 'I will continue to be queen forever!'
But you did not think about what you were doing.
You did not consider how things might turn out.

[8] "So listen, you who love pleasure.
You think you are safe and secure.
You say to yourself,
'I am like a god.
No one is greater than I am.
I'll never be a widow.
And my children will never be taken away from me.'
[9] But both of those things will happen to you in a moment.
They will take place on a single day.
You will lose your children.
And you will become a widow.
That is what will happen to you.
All of your evil magic and powerful spells will not save you.
[10] You have felt secure in your evil ways.
You have said, 'No one sees what I'm doing.'
Your wisdom and knowledge lead you down the wrong path.
You say to yourself,
'I am like a god. No one is greater than I am.'

¹¹ So horrible trouble will come on
you.
You will not know how to use
your evil magic to make it go
away.
Great trouble will fall on you.
No amount of money can keep it
away.
Something terrible will happen to
you all at once.
You will not see it coming ahead
of time.

¹² "So keep on casting your magic
spells.
Keep on practicing your evil
magic.
You have been doing those
things ever since you were a
child.
Perhaps they will help you.
Maybe they will scare your
enemies away.
¹³ All of the advice you have received
has only worn you out!
Let those who study the heavens
come forward.
They claim to know what is going
to happen
by watching the stars every
month.
So let them save you from the
trouble
that is coming on you.
¹⁴ They are just like straw.
Fire will burn them up.
They can't even save themselves
from the powerful flames.
They are not like coals that can
warm anyone.
They are not like a fire to sit by.
¹⁵ They can't do you any good.
You have done business with
them ever since you were a
child.
You have always asked them for
advice.
All of them are bewildered and
continue in their own ways.
None of them can save you."

ISRAEL IS STUBBORN

48 People of Jacob, listen to
me.
You are called by the
name of Israel.

You come from the family line of
Judah.
You take oaths in the name of the
LORD.
You pray to Israel's God.
But you aren't honest.
You don't mean what you say.
² You call yourselves citizens of the
holy city of Jerusalem.
You say you depend on Israel's
God.
His name is The LORD Who Rules
Over All. He says,
³ "Long ago I told you ahead of time
what would happen.
I announced it and made it
known.
Then all of a sudden I acted.
And those things took place.
⁴ I knew how stubborn you were.
Your neck was as unbending as
iron.
Your forehead was as hard as
bronze.
⁵ So I told you those things long
ago.
Before they happened I
announced them to you.
I did it so you would not be able to
say,
'My statues of gods did them.
My wooden and metal gods
made them happen.'
⁶ You have heard me tell you those
things.
Think about all of them.
Won't you admit they have taken
place?

"From now on I will tell you about
new things that will happen.
I have not made them known to
you before.
⁷ Those things are taking place right
now.
They did not happen long ago.
You have not heard of them
before today.
So you can't say,
'Oh, yes. I already knew about
them.'
⁸ You have not heard or understood
what I said.
Your ears have been plugged up
for a long time.
I knew very well that you would
turn against me.

From the day you were born, you
 have refused to obey me.
⁹For the honor of my own name I
 put off showing my anger.
I hold it back from you so people
 will continue to praise me.
I do not want to destroy you.
¹⁰I have put you to the test in the
 furnace of suffering.
I have tried to make you pure.
But I did not use as much heat as
 it takes to make silver pure.
¹¹I tried to purify you for my own
 honor.
I did it for the honor of my
 name.
How can I let myself be
 dishonored?
I will not give up my glory to any
 other god.

ISRAEL IS SET FREE

¹²"Family of Jacob, listen to me.
 People of Israel, pay attention.
I have chosen you.
I am the First and the Last.
I am the LORD.
¹³With my own hand I laid the
 foundations of the earth.
With my right hand I spread out
 the heavens.
When I send for them,
 they come and stand ready to
 obey me.

¹⁴"People of Israel, come together
 and listen to me.
What other god has said ahead of
 time that certain things would
 happen?
I have chosen Cyrus.
He will carry out my plans
 against Babylon.
He will use his powerful arm
 against the Babylonians.
¹⁵I myself have spoken.
I have chosen him to carry out
 my purpose.
I will bring him to Babylon.
He will succeed in what I tell him
 to do.

¹⁶"Come close and listen to me.

"From the first time I said Cyrus
 was coming,
I did not do it in secret.
When he comes, I will be there."

The LORD and King has filled me
 with his Spirit.
People of Israel, he has sent me
 to you.

¹⁷The LORD is the Holy One of Israel.
 He sets his people free. He says
 to them,
"I am the LORD your God.
I teach you what is best for you.
I direct you in the way you
 should go.
¹⁸I wish you would pay attention to
 my commands.
If you did, peace would flow over
 you like a river.
Holiness would sweep over you
 like the waves of the ocean.
¹⁹Your family would be like the
 sand.
Your children after you would be
 as many as the grains of sand
 by the sea.
It would be impossible to count
 them.
I would always accept the
 members of your family line.
They would never be cut off or
 destroyed."

²⁰People of Israel, leave Babylon!
 Hurry up and get away from the
 Babylonians!
Here is what I want you to
 announce.
Make it known with shouts of joy.
Send the news out from one end
 of the earth to the other.
Say, "The LORD has set Jacob's
 people free.
They are his servants."
²¹They didn't get thirsty when he led
 them through the deserts.
He made water flow out of the
 rock for them.
He broke the rock open,
 and water came out of it.

²²"There is no peace for those who
are evil," says the LORD.

THE SERVANT OF THE LORD

49 People who live on the
 islands, listen to me.
 Pay attention, you nations
 far away.
Before I was born the LORD chose
 me to serve him.

He appointed me by name.
²He made my words like a sharp
  sword.
He hid me in the palm of his
  hand.
He made me into a sharpened
  arrow.
He took good care of me and
  kept me safe.
³He said to me, "You are my true
  servant Israel.
I will show my glory through
  you."
⁴But I said, "In spite of my hard
  work,
I feel as if I haven't accomplished
  anything.
I've used up all of my strength.
It seems as if everything I've
  done is worthless.
But the LORD will give me what I
  should receive.
My God will reward me."

⁵The LORD formed me in my
  mother's body to be his
  servant.
He wanted me to bring the
  family of Jacob back to him.
He wanted me to gather the
  people of Israel to himself.
The LORD will honor me.
My God will give me strength.

⁶The LORD says to me,

"It is not enough for you as my
  servant
to bring the tribes of Jacob back
  to their land.
It is not enough for you to bring
  back
the people of Israel I have kept
  alive.
I will also make you a light for
  other nations.
Then you will make it possible
  for the whole world to be
  saved."

⁷The LORD sets his people free.
He is the Holy One of Israel.
He speaks to his servant, who is
  looked down on and hated by
  the nations.
He speaks to the servant of
  rulers. He says to him,
"Kings will see you and rise up to
  honor you.

Princes will see you and bow
  down to show you their
  respect.
I am the LORD. I am faithful.
I am the Holy One of Israel.
I have chosen you."

ISRAEL IS BROUGHT BACK TO THEIR LAND

⁸The LORD says to his servant,

"When it is time to show you my
  favor, I will answer your
  prayers.
When it is time to save you, I will
  help you.
I will keep you safe.
You will put my covenant with
  the people of Israel into
  effect.
Then their land will be made like
  new again.
Each tribe will be sent back to its
  territory that was left empty.
⁹I want you to say to the prisoners,
  'Come out.'
Tell those who are in their dark
  cells, 'You are free!'

"On their way home they will eat
  beside the roads.
They will find plenty to eat on
  every bare hill.
¹⁰They will not get hungry or
  thirsty.
The heat from the desert sun will
  not beat down on them.
The One who shows his tender
  love to them will guide them.
Like a shepherd, he will lead
  them beside springs of water.
¹¹I will make roads across the
  mountains.
I will build wide roads for my
  people.
¹²They will come from far away.
Some of them will come from the
  north.
Others will come from the west.
Still others will come from Aswan
  in the south."

¹³Shout with joy, you heavens!
Be glad, you earth!
Burst into song, you mountains!
The LORD will comfort his people.
He will show his tender love to
  those who are suffering.

¹⁴But the city of Zion said, "The
 LORD has deserted me.
 The Lord has forgotten me."

¹⁵The LORD answers, "Can a mother
 forget the baby
 who is nursing at her breast?
 Can she stop showing her tender
 love
 to the child who was born to her?
 She might forget her child.
 But I will not forget you.
¹⁶I have written your name on the
 palms of my hands.
 Your walls are never out of my
 sight.
¹⁷Your people will hurry back.
 Those who destroyed you so
 completely will leave you.
¹⁸Look up. Look all around you.
 All of your people are getting
 together
 to come back to you.
 You can be sure that I live,"
 announces the LORD.
 "And you can be just as sure that
 your people
 will be like decorations you will
 wear.
 Like a bride, you will wear them
 proudly.

¹⁹"Zion, you were destroyed. Your
 land was left empty.
 It was turned into a dry and
 empty desert.
 But now you will be too small to
 hold all of your people.
 And those who destroyed you
 will be far away.
²⁰The children who were born
 during your time of sorrow
 will speak to you. They will say,
 'This city is too small for us.
 Give us more space to live in.'
²¹Then you will say to yourself,
 'Whose children are these?
 I lost my children.
 And I couldn't have any more.
 My children were taken far away
 from me.
 And no one wanted them.
 Who brought these children up?
 I was left all alone.
 So where have these children
 come from?' "
²²The LORD and King continues,

"I will call out to the nations.
 I will give a signal to them.
 They will bring back your sons in
 their arms.
 They will carry your daughters
 on their shoulders.
²³Their kings will become like
 fathers to you.
 Their queens will be like mothers
 who nurse you.
 They will bow down to you with
 their faces toward the ground.
 They will kiss the dust at your
 feet to show you their respect.
 Then you will know that I am the
 LORD.
 Those who put their hope in me
 will not be ashamed."

²⁴Can goods that were stolen by
 soldiers be taken away from
 them?
 Can prisoners be set free from
 the powerful Babylonians?

²⁵"Yes, they can," the LORD answers.

"Prisoners will be taken away from
 soldiers.
 Stolen goods will be taken back
 from the powerful
 Babylonians.
 Zion, I will fight against those who
 fight against you.
 And I will save your people.
²⁶I will make those who beat you
 down eat the flesh of others.
 They will drink blood and get
 drunk on it as if it were wine.
 Then everyone on earth will know
 that I am the one who saves you.
 I am the LORD. I set you free.
 I am the Mighty One of Jacob."

THE LORD'S SERVANT OBEYS HIM

50 The LORD says to the people in Jerusalem,

"Do you think I divorced your
 people before you?
 Is that why I sent them away?
 If it is, show me the letter of
 divorce.
 I did not sell you into slavery to
 pay someone I owe.
 You were sold because you sinned
 against me.

Your people were sent away
  because of their lawless acts.
² When I came to save you, why
  didn't anyone welcome me?
  When I called out to you, why
  didn't anyone answer me?
  Wasn't my arm powerful enough to
  set you free?
  Wasn't I strong enough to save
  you?
  I dry up the sea with a single
  command.
  I turn rivers into a desert.
  Then fish rot because they do not
  have any water.
  They die because they are thirsty.
³ I make the sky turn dark.
  It looks as if it is dressed in black
  clothes."

⁴ The LORD and King has taught me
  what to say.
  He has taught me how to help
  those who are tired.
  He wakes me up every morning.
  He makes me want to listen like a
  good student.
⁵ The LORD and King has unplugged
  my ears.
  I've always obeyed him.
  I haven't turned away from him.
⁶ I let my enemies beat me on my
  bare back.
  I let them pull the hair out of my
  beard.
  I didn't turn my face away
  when they made fun of me and
  spit on me.
⁷ The LORD and King helps me.
  He won't let me be dishonored.
  So I've made up my mind to keep
  on serving him.
  I know he won't let me be put to
  shame.
⁸ He is near. He will prove I haven't
  done anything wrong.
  So who will bring charges against
  me?
  Let's face each other in court!
  Who can bring charges against
  me?
  Let him come and face me!
⁹ The LORD and King helps me.
  So who will judge me?
  My enemies will be like clothes
  that moths have eaten up.
  They will disappear.

¹⁰ Does anyone among you have
  respect for the LORD?
  Does anyone obey the message
  of the LORD's servant?
  Let the person who walks in the
  dark
  trust in the LORD.
  Let the one who doesn't have any
  light to guide him
  depend on his God.
¹¹ But all of you sinners who light fires
  should go ahead and walk in
  their light.
  You who carry flaming torches
  should walk in their light.
  Here's what I'm going to do to you.
  I'll make you lie down in great
  pain.

ZION WILL BE SAVED

51 The LORD says, "Listen to
  me, you who want to
  do what is right.
  Pay attention, you who look to me.
  Consider the rock you were cut
  out of.
  Think about the rock pit you
  were dug from.
² Consider Abraham. He is the
  father of your people.
  Think about Sarah. She is your
  mother.
  When I chose Abraham, he did not
  have any children.
  But I blessed him and gave him
  many of them.
³ You can be sure that I will comfort
  Zion's people.
  I will look with loving concern on
  all of their destroyed
  buildings.
  I will make their deserts like Eden.
  I will make their dry and empty
  land like my very own
  garden.
  Joy and gladness will be there.
  People will sing and give thanks
  to me.

⁴ "Listen to me, my people.
  Pay attention, my nation.
  My law will go out to the nations.
  I make everything right.
  That will be a guiding light for
  them.
⁵ The time for me to set you free is
  near.

I will soon save you.
My powerful arm will make
    everything right among the
    nations.
The islands will put their hope in
    me.
They will wait for my powerful
    arm to act.
⁶ Look up toward the heavens.
Then look at the earth.
The heavens will vanish like
    smoke.
The earth will wear out like
    clothes.
Those who live there will die like
    flies.
But I will save you forever.
My saving power will never
    end.

⁷ "Listen to me, you who know what
    is right.
Pay attention, you who have my
    law in your hearts.
Do not be afraid when mere
    people make fun of you.
Do not be terrified when they
    laugh at you.
⁸ They will be like clothes that
    moths have eaten up.
They will be like wool that
    worms have chewed up.
But my saving power will last
    forever.
I will save you for all time to
    come."

⁹ Wake up! LORD, wake up! Dress
    your powerful arm with
    strength
as if it were your clothes.
Wake up, just as you did in the
    past.
Wake up, as you did long ago.
Didn't you cut Rahab to pieces?
Didn't you stab that sea monster
    to death?
¹⁰ Didn't you dry up the Red Sea?
Didn't you dry up those deep
    waters?
You made a road on the bottom of
    that sea.
Then those who were set free
    went across.
¹¹ Those the LORD has saved will
    return to their land.
They will sing as they enter the
    city of Zion.

Joy that lasts forever will be like
    beautiful crowns on their
    heads.
They will be filled with gladness
    and joy.
Sorrow and sighing will be
    gone.

¹² The LORD says to his people,
    "I comfort you because of who I
    am.
Why are you afraid of mere men?
They are only human beings.
They are like grass that dries up.
¹³ How can you forget me? I made
    you.
I spread out the heavens.
I laid the foundations of the
    earth.
Why are you terrified every day?
Is it because those who are angry
    with you are crushing you?
Is it because they are trying to
    destroy you?
Their anger can't harm you
    anymore.
¹⁴ You prisoners who are so afraid
    will soon be set free.
You will not die in your prison
    cells.
You will not go without food.
¹⁵ I am the LORD your God.
I stir up the ocean. I make its
    waves roar.
My name is The LORD Who Rules
    Over All.
¹⁶ I have put my words in your
    mouth.
I have kept you safe in the palm
    of my hand.
I set the heavens in place.
I laid the foundations of the
    earth.
I say to Zion, 'You are my
    people.' "

THE CUP OF THE LORD'S BURNING ANGER

¹⁷ Wake up, Jerusalem!
Wake up! Get up!
The LORD has handed you the cup
    of his burning anger.
And you have drunk from it.
That cup makes men unsteady on
    their feet.
And you have drunk from it to
    the very last drop.

¹⁸None of the children who were
 born to you
 are left to guide you.
None of the children you brought
 up
 are left to lead you by the hand.
¹⁹Nothing but trouble has come to
 you.
You have been wiped out and
 destroyed.
And you have suffered hunger
 and war.
No one feels sorry for you.
No one can comfort you.
²⁰Your children have fainted.
They lie helpless at every street
 corner.
They are like antelope that have
 been caught in a net.
They have felt the full force of the
 LORD's burning anger.
Jerusalem, your God had to warn
 them strongly.

²¹So listen to me, you suffering
 people of Jerusalem.
You have been made drunk, but
 not by drinking wine.
²²Your LORD and King speaks.
He is your God.
He stands up for his people. He says,
 "I have taken from you the cup of
 my burning anger.
It made you unsteady on your
 feet.
But you will never drink
 from that cup again.
²³Instead, I will give it to those who
 made you suffer.
They said to you,
'Fall down flat on the ground.
Then we can walk all over you.'
And that is exactly what you did.
You made your back like a street
 to be walked on."

52

Wake up! Zion, wake up!
Dress yourself with
 strength as if it were
 your clothes.
Holy city of Jerusalem,
 put on your clothes of glory.
Those who haven't been
 circumcised will never enter
 you again.
Neither will those who are
 "unclean."

²Get up, Jerusalem! Shake off your
 dust.
Take your place on your throne.
Captured people of Zion,
 remove the chains from your
 neck.

³The LORD says,

"When you were sold as slaves, no
 one paid anything for you.
Now no one will pay any money
 to set you free."

⁴The LORD and King continues,

"Long ago my people went down
 to Egypt.
They lived there for a while.
Later, Assyria crushed them
 without any reason.

⁵"Now look at what has happened to
them," announces the LORD.

"Once again my people have been
 taken away.
And no one paid anything for
 them.
Those who rule over them brag
 about it,"
 announces the LORD.
"All day long without stopping,
 people speak evil things against
 my name.
⁶So the day will come when my
 people will really know the
 meaning of my name.
They will know what kind of God
 I am.
They will know that I told them
 ahead of time they would
 return to their land.
They will know that it was I."

⁷What a beautiful sight it is
 to see messengers coming with
 good news!
How beautiful to see them coming
 down from the mountains
 with a message about peace!
How wonderful it is when they
 bring the good news
 that we are saved!
How wonderful when they say to
 Zion,
 "Your God rules!"
⁸Listen! Those on guard duty are
 shouting out the message.

With their own eyes
they see the LORD returning to Zion.
So they shout with joy.
⁹ Burst into songs of joy together,
you broken-down buildings in
Jerusalem.
The LORD has comforted his
people.
He has set Jerusalem free.
¹⁰ The LORD will use the power of his
holy arm to save his people.
All of the nations will see him do
it.
Everyone from one end of the
earth to the other will see it.

¹¹ You who carry the articles that
belong to the LORD's temple,
leave Babylon!
Leave it! Get out of there!
Don't touch anything that isn't
pure and clean.
Come out of Babylon and be
pure.
¹² But this time you won't have to
leave in a hurry.
You won't have to rush away.
The LORD will go ahead of you and
lead you.
The God of Israel will follow
behind you and guard you.

THE SUFFERING AND GLORY OF THE LORD'S SERVANT

¹³ The LORD says, "My servant will
act wisely and accomplish his
task.
He will be highly honored. He
will be greatly respected.
¹⁴ Many people were shocked when
they saw him.
He was so scarred that he did not
look like a man at all.
His body was so twisted that he
did not look like a human
being anymore.
¹⁵ But many nations will be surprised
when they see what he has
done.
Kings will be so amazed that they
will not be able to say
anything.
They will understand things they
were never told about.
They will know the meaning of
things they never heard
about."

53 Who has believed what
we've been saying?
Who has seen the LORD's
saving power?
² His servant grew up like a tender
young plant.
He grew like a root coming up
out of dry ground.
He didn't have any beauty or
majesty that made us notice
him.
There wasn't anything special
about the way he
looked that drew us to him.
³ Men looked down on him. They
didn't accept him.
He knew all about sorrow and
suffering.
He was like someone people turn
their faces away from.
We looked down on him. We
didn't have any respect for
him.

⁴ He suffered the things we should
have suffered.
He took on himself the pain that
should have been ours.
But we thought God was
punishing him.
We thought God was wounding
him and making him suffer.
⁵ But the servant was pierced
because we had sinned.
He was crushed because we had
done what was evil.
He was punished to make us
whole again.
His wounds have healed us.
⁶ All of us are like sheep. We have
wandered away from God.
All of us have turned to our own
way.
And the LORD has placed on his
servant
the sins of all of us.

⁷ He was beaten down and made to
suffer.
But he didn't open his mouth.
He was led away like a sheep to be
killed.
Lambs are silent while their wool
is being cut off.
In the same way, he didn't open
his mouth.
⁸ He was arrested and sentenced to
death.

Then he was taken away.
He was cut off from this life.
He was punished for the sins of
my people.
Who among those who were
living at that time
could have understood those
things?
⁹He was given a grave with those
who were evil.
But his body was buried in the
tomb of a rich man.
He was killed even though he
hadn't harmed anyone.
And he had never lied to
anyone.

¹⁰The LORD says, "It was my plan to
crush him
and cause him to suffer.
I made his life a guilt offering to
pay for sin.
But he will see all of his children
after him.
In fact, he will continue to live.
My plan will be brought about
through him.
¹¹After he suffers, he will see the
light that leads to life.
And he will be satisfied.

My godly servant will make many
people godly
because of what he will
accomplish.
He will be punished for their
sins.
¹²So I will give him a place of honor
among those who are great.
He will be rewarded just like
others who win the battle.
That is because he was willing to
give his life as a sacrifice.
He was counted among those
who had committed crimes.
He took the sins of many people
on himself.
And he gave his life for those
who had done what is wrong."

JERUSALEM WILL BE GLORIOUS

54 "Jerusalem, sing!
You are now like a woman
who never had a
child.
Burst into song! Shout with joy!
You who have never had labor
pains,
you are now all alone.

Why did they beat up Jesus?

Some people got very angry at Jesus because he spoke against
the bad things they were doing. They tried to get Jesus to be
quiet. They even tried to get him to sin. But they were mostly angry because
he claimed to be the Son of God. The Jews were waiting for a Messiah, or
Savior, but they were expecting a proud and
mighty king. They thought the Savior
would defeat the Romans and drive
them out of Israel. They did not
expect a man who wanted to be a
servant to people. Finally, the
people got so angry that they asked
to have Jesus beat up and killed.
Even though the people meant to hurt
Jesus, God made good come from bad.
Jesus' suffering and death
were part of God's great
plan to save us from sin.

Related verses:
Matthew
26:57–68

checkout

Isaiah 53:10

But you will have more children
than a woman who still has a
husband,"
                              says the LORD.

2 "Make a large area for your tent.
Spread out its curtains.
Go ahead and make your tent
wider.
Make its ropes longer.
Drive the stakes down deeper.

3 You will spread out to the right
and the left.
Your children after you will drive
out the nations that are now
living in your land.
They will settle down in the
deserted cities of those
nations.

4 "Do not be afraid. You will not be
put to shame anymore.
Do not be afraid of being
dishonored.
People will no longer make fun
of you.
You will forget the time when you
suffered as slaves in Egypt.
You will no longer remember the
shame
of being a widow in Babylonia.

5 I made you. I am now your
husband.
My name is The LORD Who Rules
Over All.
I am the Holy One of Israel.
I have set you free.
I am the God of the whole earth.

6 You were like a wife who was
deserted.
And her heart was broken.
You were like a wife who married
young.
And her husband sent her away.
But now I am calling you to come
back," says your God.

7 "For a brief moment I left you.
But because I love you so much, I
will bring you back.

8 For a moment I turned my face
away from you.
I was very angry with you.
But I will show you my loving
concern.
My faithful love will continue
forever,"
says the LORD. He is the one who
set you free.

9 "During Noah's time I took an oath
and made a promise.
I said I would never cover the
earth with water again.
In the same way, I have promised
not to be angry with you.
I will never punish you again.

10 The mountains might shake.
The hills might be removed.
But my faithful love for you will
never be shaken.
And my covenant that promises
peace to you will never be
broken,"
says the LORD. He shows you his
loving concern.

11 "Suffering city, you have been
beaten by storms.
You have not been comforted.
I will rebuild you with turquoise
stones.
I will rebuild your foundations
with sapphires.

12 I will line the top of your city wall
with rubies.
I will make your gates out of
gleaming jewels.
And I will make all of your walls
out of precious stones.

13 I will teach all of your children.
And they will enjoy great peace.

14 When you do what is right,
you will be made secure.
Your leaders will not be mean to
you.
You will not have anything to be
afraid of.
You will not be terrified anymore.
Terror will not come near you.

15 People might attack you. But I will
not be the cause of it.
Those who attack you will give
themselves up to you.

16 "I created blacksmiths.
They fan the coals into flames of
fire.
They make weapons that are fit for
their work.
I also created those who destroy
others.

17 But no weapon that is used
against you will succeed.
People might bring charges
against you.
But you will prove that they are
wrong.

Those are the things I do for my
servants.
I make everything right for
them,"
announces the LORD.

THE LORD INVITES HIS PEOPLE TO COME TO HIM

55 "Come, all of you who are
thirsty.
Come and drink the water
I offer to you.
You who do not have any money,
come.
Buy and eat the grain I give you.
Come and buy wine and milk.
You will not have to pay anything
for it.
² Why spend money on what is not
food?
Why work for what does not
satisfy you?
Listen carefully to me.
Then you will eat what is good.
You will enjoy the richest food
there is.
³ Listen and come to me.

Pay attention to me.
Then you will live.
I will make a covenant with you
that will last forever.
I will give you my faithful love.
I promised it to David.
⁴ I made him a witness to the
nations.
He became a leader and
commander over them.
⁵ You too will send for nations you
do not know.
Even though they do not know
you,
they will hurry and come to you.
That is what I will do. I am the
LORD your God.
I am the Holy One of Israel.
I have honored you."

⁶ Turn to the LORD before it's too
late.
Call out to him while he's still
ready to help you.
⁷ Let the one who is evil stop doing
evil things.
And let him quit thinking evil
thoughts.

KIDS' QUESTION: Will God give children toys if they ask him for them?

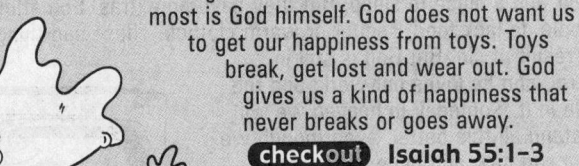

Some people think God is there to give us toys and other things we want. But God does not just hand out stuff. His purpose is to make us into people who are like Christ. God really cares about us, and he knows what we need. Toys seem important sometimes, but there are other things that we need more. What we need most is God himself. God does not want us to get our happiness from toys. Toys break, get lost and wear out. God gives us a kind of happiness that never breaks or goes away.

checkout Isaiah 55:1–3

GOD
the real
North Pole

Related verses:
Philippians 4:4–7;
James 4:2,3

Let him turn to the LORD.
The LORD will show him his
tender love.
Let him turn to our God.
He is always ready to forgive.

8 "My thoughts are not like your
thoughts.
And your ways are not like my
ways,"
announces the LORD.
9 "The heavens are higher than the
earth.
And my ways are higher than
your ways.
My thoughts are higher than
your thoughts.
10 The rain and the snow
come down from the sky.
They do not return to it
without watering the earth.
They make plants come up and
grow.
The plants produce seeds for
farmers.

They also produce food for
people to eat.
11 The words I speak are like that.
They will not return to me
without producing results.
They will accomplish what I want
them to.
They will do exactly what I sent
them to do.
12 "My people, you will leave
Babylonia with joy.
You will be led out of it in peace.
The mountains and hills
will burst into song as you go.
And all of the trees in the fields
will clap their hands.
13 Pine trees will grow where there
used to be bushes that had
thorns on them.
And myrtle trees will grow where
there used to be thorns.
That will bring me great fame.
It will be a lasting reminder of
what I can do.
It will not be forgotten."

Why doesn't God just give us money when we need it?

God often does give us money when we need it. He meets our needs. But sometimes we do not see God's work in our lives. God usually provides for us through jobs, people and other ordinary means. Even though we do not think of these as miracles, they still come from God. He wants us to work, plan, be responsible and use well what we have.

People often want a lot of things that they do not really need. Many people in our world receive something to eat, something to wear and a place to sleep. But they have no extras. Sometimes people do lack food, shelter or warm clothes. These sad things are the result of sin. But God is still in control, and he loves our world and the people in it. Someday in heaven we will understand all this better, even though we may feel sad now and have big questions when we see hurting people.

checkout
Isaiah 55:8,9

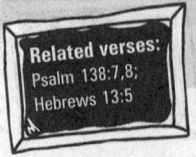

Related verses:
Psalm 138:7,8;
Hebrews 13:5

THE LORD WILL SAVE THOSE WHO COME TO HIM

56 The LORD says,
"Do what is fair and right.
I will soon come and save you.
Soon everyone will know that
what I do is right.

2 Blessed is the man who does what
I want him to.
He is faithful in keeping the
Sabbath day.
He does not misuse it.
He does not do what is evil on
that day."

3 Suppose an outsider wants to
follow the LORD.
Then he shouldn't say,
"The LORD won't accept me as
one of his people."
And a eunuch shouldn't say,
"I'm like a dry tree
that doesn't bear any fruit."

4 The LORD says,

"Suppose some eunuchs keep my
Sabbath days.
They choose to do what pleases
me.
And they are faithful in keeping
my covenant.

5 Then I will set up a monument in
the area of my temple.
Their names will be written on it.
That will be better for them
than having sons and
daughters.
The names of the eunuchs will be
remembered forever.
They will never be forgotten.

6 "Suppose outsiders want to follow
me
and serve me.
They want to love me
and worship me.
They keep the Sabbath day and do
not misuse it.
And they are faithful in keeping
my covenant.

7 Then I will bring them to my holy
mountain of Zion.
I will give them joy in my house.
They can pray there.
I will accept their burnt offerings
and sacrifices on my altar.

My house will be called
a house where people from all
nations can pray."

8 The LORD and King will gather
those who were taken away from
their homes in Israel.
He announces, "I will gather them
to myself.
And I will gather others to join
them."

THE LORD JUDGES ISRAEL'S EVIL LEADERS

9 Come, all of you enemy nations!
Come like wild animals.
Come and destroy like animals in
the forest.

10 Israel's prophets are blind.
They don't know the LORD.
All of them are like watchdogs that
can't even bark.
They just lie around and dream.
They love to sleep.

11 They are like dogs that love to eat.
They never get enough.
They are like shepherds who don't
have any understanding.
All of them do as they please.
They only look for what they can
get for themselves.

12 "Come!" they shout. "Let's get
some wine!
Let's drink all the beer we can!
Tomorrow we'll do the same thing.
And that will be even better than
today."

57 Those who are right with
God die.
And no one really cares
about it.
Men who are faithful to the LORD
are swept away by trouble.
And no one understands why
that happens
to those who do what is right.

2 Those who lead honest lives
will enjoy peace and rest when
they die.

3 The LORD says, "Come here,
you children of women who
practice evil magic!
You are children of prostitutes
and those who commit
adultery.

4 Who are you making fun of?

Who are you laughing at?
Who are you sticking your
    tongue out at?
You are people who refuse to obey
    me.
You are just a bunch of liars!
⁵You burn with sinful longing
    among the oak trees.
You worship your gods by having
    sex under every green tree.
You sacrifice your children in the
    valleys.
You also do it under the cliffs.
⁶You have chosen some of the
    smooth stones in the valleys
    to be your gods.
You have joined yourselves to
    them.
You have even poured out drink
    offerings to them.
You have given grain offerings to
    them.
So why should I take pity on you?
⁷You have made your bed to have
    sex on a very high hill.
You went up there to offer your
    sacrifices.
⁸You have set up statues to remind
    you of your gods.
You have put them behind your
    doors and doorposts.
You deserted me. You invited other
    lovers into your bed.
You climbed into it and
    welcomed them.
You made a deal with them.
And you looked at their naked
    bodies.
⁹You went to the god Molech with
    olive oil.
You took a lot of perfume along
    with you.
You sent your messengers to
    places far away.
You even sent them down to the
    place of the dead.
¹⁰All of your efforts wore you out.
But you would not say, 'It's
    hopeless.'
You received new strength.
So you did not give up.

¹¹ "Who are you so afraid of
    that you have not been true to
    me?
You have not remembered me.
You do not even care about me.

I have not punished you for a long
    time.
That is why you are not afraid of
    me.
¹²You have not done what is right or
    good.
I will let everyone know about it.
And that will not be of any
    benefit to you.
¹³Go ahead and cry out for help to
    all of the statues of your gods.
See if they can save you!
The wind will carry them off.
Just a puff of air will blow them
    away.
But anyone who comes to me for
    safety
will receive the land.
He will possess my holy
    mountain of Zion."

THE LORD COMFORTS THOSE WHO AREN'T PROUD

¹⁴A messenger says,

"Build up the road! Build it up! Get
    it ready!
Remove anything that would
    keep my people from coming
    back."
¹⁵The One who is highly honored
    lives forever.
His name is holy. He says,
"I live in a high and holy place.
But I also live with anyone who
    turns away from his sins.
I live with anyone who is not
    proud.
I give new life to him.
I give it to anyone who turns
    away from his sins.
¹⁶I will not find fault with my people
    forever.
I will not always be angry with
    them.
If I were, I would cause their
    spirits to grow weak.
The very breath of life would go
    out of the people I created.
¹⁷I was very angry with them.
They always longed for more and
    more of everything.
So I punished them for that sin.
I turned my face away from them
    because I was angry.
But they kept on wanting their
    own way.

¹⁸I have seen what they have done.
But I will heal them.
I will guide them.
And I will comfort them just as I
did before.
¹⁹ Then the people of Israel who are
sorry for their sins will praise
me.
I will give perfect peace to those
who are far away and those
who are near.
And I will heal them," says the
LORD.
²⁰But those who are evil are like the
rolling sea.
It never rests.
Its waves toss up mud and sand.

²¹"There is no peace for those who
are evil," says my God.

WHAT TRUE WORSHIP IS ALL ABOUT

58

The LORD told me,
"Shout out loud. Do not
hold back.
Raise your voice like a trumpet.
Tell my people that they have
refused to obey me.
Tell the family of Jacob how
much they have sinned.
²Day after day they worship me.
They seem ready and willing to
know how I want them to live.
They act as if they were a nation
that does what is right.
They act as if they have not
turned away from my
commands.
They claim to want me to give
them fair decisions.
They seem ready and willing to
come near and worship me.
³'We have gone without food,' they
say.
'Why haven't you noticed it?
We have made ourselves suffer.
Why haven't you paid any
attention to us?'

"On the day when you fast, you do
as you please.
You take advantage of all of your
workers.
⁴When you fast, it ends in arguing
and fighting.

You hit one another with your
fists.
That is an evil thing to do.
The way you are now fasting
keeps your prayers from being
heard in heaven.
⁵Do you think that is the way I want
you to fast?
Is it only a time for a man to
make himself suffer?
Is it only for people to bow their
heads like tall grass that is
bent by the wind?
Is it only for people to lie down
on black cloth and ashes?
Is that what you call a fast?
Do you think I can accept that?

⁶"Here is the way I want you to fast.

"Set free those who are held by
chains without any reason.
Untie the ropes that hold people
as slaves.
Set free those who are crushed.
Break every evil chain.
⁷Share your food with hungry
people.
Provide homeless people with a
place to stay.
Give naked people clothes to
wear.
Provide for the needs of your
own family.
⁸Then the light of my blessing will
shine on you like the rising
sun.
I will heal you quickly.
I will march out ahead of you.
And my glory will follow behind
you and guard you.
That is because I always do what
is right.
⁹You will call out to me for help.
And I will answer you.
You will cry out.
And I will say, 'Here I am.'

"Get rid of the chains you use to
hold others down.
Stop pointing your finger at
others as if they had done
something wrong.
Stop saying harmful things about
them.
¹⁰Work hard to feed hungry people.
Satisfy the needs of those who
are crushed.

Then my blessing will light up
　　your darkness.
And the night of your suffering
　　will become as bright as the
　　noonday sun.
¹¹ I will always guide you.
I will satisfy your needs in a land
　　that is baked by the sun.
I will make you stronger.
You will be like a garden that has
　　plenty of water.
You will be like a spring whose
　　water never runs dry.
¹² Your people will rebuild the cities
　　that were destroyed long ago.
And you will build again on the
　　old foundations.
You will be called The One Who
　　Repairs Broken Walls.
You will be called The One Who
　　Makes City Streets Like New
　　Again.

¹³ "Do not work on the Sabbath day.
Do not do just anything you want
　　to on my holy day.
Make the Sabbath a day you can
　　enjoy.
Honor my holy day.
Do not work on it.
Do not do just anything you want
　　to.

Do not talk about things that are
　　worthless.
¹⁴ Then you will find your joy in me.
I will give you control over the
　　most important places in the
　　land.
And you will enjoy all of the good
　　things
in the land I gave your father
　　Jacob."

　　　　　　The LORD has spoken.

THE LORD SETS HIS PEOPLE FREE

59 People of Israel, the LORD's
　　arm is not too weak to
　　save you.
His ears aren't too deaf to hear
　　your cry for help.
² But your sins have separated you
　　from your God.
They have caused him to turn his
　　face away from you.
So he won't listen to you.
³ Your hands and fingers are stained
　　with blood.
You are guilty of committing
　　murder.
Your mouth has told lies.
Your tongue says evil things.
⁴ People aren't fair when they
　　present their cases in court.

Why didn't God just forgive everybody?

It would not be right or fair for God just to forgive everyone. Every wrong deed must be punished. But God loved us so much that he sent his Son Jesus to take the punishment for us. Jesus died on the cross in our place so that we would not have to go to hell. Now everyone can be forgiven. All we have to do is trust in Jesus.

checkout Isaiah 59:1,2

Related verse:
John 3:16

They aren't honest when they
    state their case.
They depend on weak arguments.
    They tell lies.
They plan to make trouble.
Then they carry it out.
⁵The plans they make are like the
    eggs of poisonous snakes.
Anyone who eats those eggs will
    die.
When one of them is broken, a
    snake comes out.
⁶Those people weave their evil
    plans together like a spider's
    web.
But the webs they make can't be
    used as clothes.
They can't cover themselves with
    what they make.
Their acts are evil.
They do things to harm others.
⁷They are always in a hurry to sin.
They run quickly to murder
    those who aren't guilty.
Their thoughts are evil.
They leave a trail of suffering and
    pain.
⁸They don't know how to live at
    peace with others.
What they do isn't fair.
They lead twisted lives.
No one who lives like that will
    enjoy peace and rest.

⁹We aren't being treated fairly.
We haven't been set free yet.
The God who always does what is
    right
hasn't come to help us.
We look for light. But we see
    nothing but darkness.
We look for brightness. But we
    walk in deep shadows.
¹⁰Like blind people we feel our way
    along the wall.
We are like those who can't see.
At noon we trip and fall as if the
    sun had already set.
Compared to those who are
    healthy, we are like dead
    people.
¹¹All of us growl like hungry bears.
We cry like sad doves.
We want the LORD to do what is
    fair and save us.
But he doesn't do it.
We long for him to set us free.

But the time for that seems far
    away.

¹²That's because we've done so
    many things he considers
    wrong.
Our sins prove that we are guilty.
The wrong things we've done are
    always troubling us.
We admit that we have sinned.
¹³We've refused to obey the LORD.
We've made evil plans against
    him.
We've turned our backs on our
    God.
We've stirred up trouble and
    refused to follow him.
We've told lies that came from
    our own minds.
¹⁴So people stop others from doing
    what is fair.
They keep them from doing what
    is right.
No one tells the truth in court
    anymore.
No one is honest there.
¹⁵In fact, truth can't be found
    anywhere.
Those who refuse to do evil are
    attacked.

The LORD sees that people aren't
    treating others fairly.
That makes him unhappy.
¹⁶He sees that there is no one who
    helps his people.
He is shocked that no one stands
    up for them.
So he will use his own powerful
    arm to save them.
He has the strength to do it
    because he is holy.
¹⁷He will put the armor of holiness
    on his chest.
He'll put the helmet of salvation
    on his head.
He'll pay people back for the
    wrong things they do.
He'll wrap himself in anger as if it
    were a coat.
¹⁸He will pay his enemies back for
    what they have done.
He'll pour his anger out on them.
He'll punish those who attack him.
He'll give the people in the
    islands what they have
    coming to them.

¹⁹People in the west will show
    respect for the LORD's name.
People in the east will worship
    him because of his glory.
The LORD will come like a rushing
    river that was held back.
His breath will drive it along.

²⁰"I set my people free. I will come
    to Mount Zion.
I will come to those in Jacob's
    family who turn away from
    their sins,"
                announces the LORD.

²¹"Here is the covenant I will make
with them," says the LORD. "My Spirit
is on you. I have put my words in your
mouth. They will never leave your
mouth. And they will never leave the
mouths of your children or their children after them. That will be true for
all time to come," says the LORD.

ZION WILL BE GLORIOUS

60 "People of Jerusalem, get
    up.
Shine, because your light
    has come.
My glory will shine on you.
²Darkness covers the earth.
    Thick darkness spreads over the
        nations.
But I will rise and shine on you.
My glory will appear over you.
³Nations will come to your light.
    Kings will come to the brightness
        of your new day.

⁴"Look up. Look all around you.
All of your people are getting
    together to come back to you.
Your sons will come from far away.
Your daughters will be carried
    like little children.
⁵Then your face will glow with joy.
Your heart will beat fast because
    you are so happy.
Wealth from across the ocean will
    be brought to you.
The riches of the nations will
    come to you.
⁶Herds of young camels will cover
    your land.
They will come from Midian and
    Ephah.
They will also come from Sheba.
They'll carry gold and incense.

And people will shout praises to
    me.
⁷All of Kedar's flocks will be
    gathered to you.
The rams of Nebaioth will serve
    as your sacrifices.
I will accept them as offerings on
    my altar.
That is how I will bring honor to
    my glorious temple.

⁸"Whose ships are these that sail
    along like clouds?
They fly like doves to their nests.
⁹People from the islands are
    coming to me.
The ships of Tarshish are out in
    front.
They are bringing your children
    back from far away.
Your children are bringing their
    silver and gold with them.
They are coming to honor me.
I am the LORD your God.
I am the Holy One of Israel.
I have honored you.

¹⁰"People from other lands will
    rebuild your walls.
Their kings will serve you.
When I was angry with you, I
    struck you.
But now I will show you my
    tender love.
¹¹Your gates will always stand open.
They will never be shut, day or
    night.
Then people can bring you the
    wealth of the nations.
Their kings will come along with
    them.
¹²The nation or kingdom that will
    not serve you will be
    destroyed.
It will be completely wiped out.

¹³"Lebanon's glorious trees will be
    brought to you.
Its pines, firs and cypress trees
    will be brought.
They will be used to make my
    temple beautiful.
And I will bring glory to the place
    where my throne is.
¹⁴The children of those who crush
    you will come and bow down
    to you.

All those who hate you will kneel
down at your feet.
Jerusalem, they will call you The
City of the LORD.
They will name you Zion, the
City of the Holy One of Israel.

15 "You have been deserted and
hated.
No one even travels through
you.
But I will make you into
something to be proud of
forever.
You will be a place of joy for all
time to come.
16 You will get everything you need
from kings and nations.
You will be like children who are
nursing
at their mother's breasts.
Then you will know that I am the
one who saves you.
I am the LORD. I set you free.
I am the Mighty One of Jacob.
17 Instead of bronze I will bring you
gold.
In place of iron I will give you
silver.
Instead of wood I will bring you
bronze.
In place of stones I will give you
iron.
I will make peace govern you.
I will make godliness rule over
you.
18 People will no longer harm one
another in your land.
They will not wipe out or destroy
anything inside your borders.
You will call your walls Salvation.
And you will name your gates
Praise.
19 You will not need the light of the
sun by day anymore.
The bright light of the moon will
no longer have to shine on
you.
I will be your light forever.
My glory will shine on you.
I am the LORD your God.
20 Your sun will never set again.
Your moon will never lose its
light.
I will be your light forever.
Your days of sorrow will come to
an end.

21 Then all of your people will do
what is right.
The land will belong to them
forever.
They will be like a young tree I
have planted.
My hands have created them.
They will show how glorious I
am.
22 The smallest family among you
will become a tribe.
The smallest tribe will become a
mighty nation.
I am the LORD.
When it is the right time, I will
act quickly."

THE LORD'S SERVANT ACCOMPLISHES HIS WORK

61 The Spirit of the LORD and
King is on me.
The LORD has anointed
me
to tell the good news to poor
people.
He has sent me to comfort
those whose hearts have been
broken.
He has sent me to announce
freedom
for those who have been
captured.
He wants me to set prisoners free
from their dark prisons.
2 He has sent me to announce the
year
when he will set his people free.
He wants me to announce the day
when he will pay his enemies
back.
Our God has sent me to comfort
all those who are sad.
3 He wants me to help those in
Zion who are filled with
sorrow.
I will put beautiful crowns on their
heads
in place of ashes.
I will anoint them with oil to give
them gladness
instead of sorrow.
I will give them a spirit of praise
in place of a spirit of sadness.
They will be like oak trees that are
strong and straight.
The LORD himself will plant them
in the land.

That will show how glorious he
is.

⁴They will rebuild the places that
were destroyed long ago.
They will repair the buildings
that have been broken down
for many years.
They will make the destroyed
cities like new again.
They have been broken down for
a very long time.
⁵Outsiders will serve you by taking
care of your flocks.
People from other lands will
work in your fields and
vineyards.
⁶You will be called priests of the
LORD.
You will be named workers for
our God.
You will enjoy the wealth of nations.
You will brag about getting their
riches.
⁷Instead of being put to shame
my people will receive a double
share of wealth.
Instead of being dishonored
they will be glad to be in their
land.
They will receive a double share of
riches there.
And they'll be filled with joy that
will last forever.

⁸The LORD says, "I love those who
do what is right.
I hate it when people steal and
do other sinful things.
So I will be faithful to those who
do what is right.
And I will bless them.
I will make a covenant with them
that will last forever.
⁹Their children after them will be
famous among the nations.
Their families will be praised by
people everywhere.
All those who see them will agree
that I have blessed them."

¹⁰The people of Jerusalem will say,
"We take great delight in the
LORD.
We are joyful because we belong
to our God.
He has dressed us with salvation
as if it were our clothes.

He has put robes of godliness on
us.
We are like a groom who is dressed
up for his wedding.
We are like a bride who decorates
herself with her jewels.
¹¹The soil makes the young plant
come up.
A garden causes seeds to grow.
In the same way, the LORD and
King will make godliness
grow.
And all of the nations will praise
him."

THE LORD GIVES ZION A NEW NAME

62 The LORD says, "For the
good of Zion I will
not keep silent.
For Jerusalem's benefit I will not
remain quiet.
I will not keep silent until its
people's godliness
shines like the sunrise.
I will not remain quiet until they
are saved
and shine like a blazing torch.
²Jerusalem, the nations will see
that I have made everything right
for you.
All of their kings will see your
glory.
You will be called by a new name.
I myself will give it to you.
³You will be like a glorious crown in
my strong hand.
You will be like a royal crown in
my powerful hand.
⁴People will not call you Deserted
anymore.
They will no longer name your
land Empty.
Instead, you will be called The One
the LORD Delights In.
Your land will be named The
Married One.
I will take delight in you.
And your land will be like a bride.
⁵As a young man gets married to a
young woman,
your people will marry you.
As a groom is happy with his bride,
I will be full of joy over you."

⁶Jerusalem, I have stationed guards
on your walls.

They must never be silent day or
night.
You who call out to the LORD
must not give yourselves any
rest.
7 And don't give him any rest
until he makes Jerusalem
secure.
Don't give him any peace
until people all over the earth
praise that city.

8 The LORD has taken an oath and
made a promise.
He has lifted up his right hand
and mighty arm.
He has promised, "I will never give
your grain
to your enemies for food again.
Outsiders will never again drink
the fresh wine
you have worked so hard for.
9 Instead, those who gather the
grain will eat it themselves.
And they will praise me.
Those who gather grapes to make
the wine will enjoy it.
They will drink it in the
courtyards of my temple."

10 Go out through your gates, people
of Jerusalem! Go out!
Prepare the way for the rest of
your people to return.
Build up the road! Build it up!
Remove the stones.
Raise a banner over the city
for the nations to see.

11 The LORD has announced a
message
from one end of the earth to the
other.
He has said, "Tell the people of
Zion,
'Look! Your Savior is coming!
He is bringing his people back as
his reward.
He has won the battle over their
enemies.' "
12 They will be called The Holy
People.
The LORD will set them free.
And Jerusalem will be named
The City the LORD Cares
About.
It won't be deserted anymore.

GOD WILL SAVE HIS PEOPLE AND PUNISH THEIR ENEMIES

63 Who is this man coming
from the city of
Bozrah in Edom?
His clothes are stained bright
red.
Who is he? He is dressed up in all
of his glory.
He is marching toward us with
great strength.

The LORD answers, "It is I.
I have won the battle.
I am mighty.
I have saved my people."

2 Why are your clothes red?
They look as if you have been
stomping
on grapes in a winepress.

3 The LORD answers, "I have been
stomping on the nations
as if they were grapes.
No one was there to help me.
I walked all over the nations
because I was angry.
That is why I stomped on them.
Their blood splashed all over my
clothes.
So my clothes were stained
bright red.
4 I decided it was time to pay Israel's
enemies back.
The year for me to set my people
free had come.
5 I looked around, but no one was
there to help me.
I was shocked that no one gave
me any help.
So I used my own powerful arm to
save my people.
I had the strength to do it
because I was angry.
6 I walked all over the nations
because I was angry with
them.
I made them drink from the cup
of my burning anger.
I poured their blood out on the
ground."

ISAIAH PRAYS TO THE LORD

7 I will talk about the kind things the
LORD has done.
I'll praise him for everything he's
done for us.

He has done many good things
for the nation of Israel.
That's because he loves us and is
very kind to us.
[8] In the past he said, "They are my
people.
They will not turn against me."
So he saved them.
[9] When they suffered, he suffered
with them.
He sent his angel to save them.
He set them free because he is
loving and kind.
He lifted them up and carried
them.
He did it again and again in days
long ago.
[10] But they refused to obey him.
They made his Holy Spirit sad.
So he turned against them and
became their enemy.
He himself fought against them.

[11] Then his people remembered
what he did long ago.
They recalled the days of Moses
and his people.
They asked, "Where is the One
who brought
Israel through the Red Sea?
Moses led them as the shepherd
of his flock.
Where is the One who put
his Holy Spirit among them?
[12] He used his glorious and powerful
arm
to help Moses.
He parted the waters of the sea in
front of them.
That mighty act made him
famous forever.
[13] He led them through that deep
sea.
Like a horse in open country,
they didn't trip and fall.
[14] Like cattle that are taken down to
the flatlands,
they were given rest by the Spirit
of the LORD."
That's how he guided his people.
So he made a glorious name for
himself.

[15] LORD, look down from heaven.
Look down from your holy and
glorious throne.
Where is your great love for us?
Where is your power?

Why don't you show us
your tender love and concern?
[16] You are our Father.
Abraham might not accept us as
his children.
Jacob might not recognize us as
his family.
But you are our Father, LORD.
Your name is The One Who
Always Sets Us Free.
[17] LORD, why do you let us wander
away from you?
Why do you let us become so
stubborn
that we don't respect you?
Come back and help us.
We are the tribes that belong to
you.
[18] For a little while your holy people
possessed the land.
But now our enemies have torn
your temple down.
[19] We are like people you never ruled
over.
We are like those who don't
belong to you.

64 I wish you would open
up your heavens
and come down to us!
I wish the mountains would
tremble
when you show your power!
[2] Be like a fire that causes twigs to
burn.
It also makes water boil.
So come down and make yourself
known to your enemies.
Cause the nations to shake with
fear
when they see your power!
[3] Long ago you did some wonderful
things we didn't expect.
You came down, and the
mountains trembled
when you showed your power.
[4] No one's ears have ever heard of a
God like you.
No one's eyes have ever seen a
God who is greater than you.
No God but you acts for the good
of those who trust in him.
[5] You come to help those who enjoy
doing what is right.
You help those who thank you
for teaching them how to
live.

But when we continued to disobey
you,
you became angry with us.
So how can we be saved?
⁶ All of us have become like
someone who is "unclean."
All of the good things we do are
like polluted rags to you.
All of us are like leaves that have
dried up.
Our sins sweep us away like the
wind.
⁷ No one prays to you.
No one asks you for help.
You have turned your face away
from us.
You have let us waste away
because we have sinned so much.

⁸ LORD, you are our Father.
We are the clay. You are the
potter.
Your hands made all of us.
⁹ Don't be so angry with us, LORD.
Don't remember our sins
anymore.
Please show us your favor.
All of us belong to you.
¹⁰ Your sacred cities have become a
desert.
Even Zion is a desert.
Jerusalem is a dry and empty
place.
¹¹ Our people used to praise you in
our holy and glorious temple.
But now it has been burned
down.
Everything we treasured has
been destroyed.
¹² LORD, won't you help us even after
everything that's happened?
Will you keep silent and punish
us more than we can stand?

THE LORD ANSWERS
ISAIAH'S PRAYER

65 The LORD says, "I made
myself known to
those who were not
asking for me.
I was found by those who were
not trying to find me.
I spoke to a nation that did not
pray to me.
'Here I am,' I said. 'Here I am.'
² All day long I have held out my
hands

to welcome a stubborn nation.
They lead sinful lives.
They go where their evil thoughts
take them.
³ They are always making me very
angry.
They do it right in front of me.
They offer sacrifices in the gardens
of other gods.
They burn incense on altars that
are made out of bricks.
⁴ They sit among the graves.
They spend their nights talking
to the spirits of the dead.
They eat the meat of pigs.
Their cooking pots hold soup
that has 'unclean' meat in it.
⁵ They say, 'Keep away! Don't come
near us!
We are too sacred for you!'
Those people are like smoke in my
nose.
They are like a fire that keeps
burning all day.

⁶ "I will judge them. I have even
written it down.
I will not keep silent.
Instead, I will pay them back for
all of their sins.
⁷ I will punish them for their sins
and the sins of their people
before them,"
says the LORD.
"They burned sacrifices on the
mountains.
They disobeyed me by
worshiping other gods on the
hills.
So I will really punish them
for all of the sins they have
committed."

⁸ The LORD says,

"Sometimes juice is still left in
grapes that have been crushed.
So people say, 'Don't destroy
them.
Some good juice is still left in
them.'
That is what I will do for the good
of those who serve me.
I will not destroy all of my
people.
⁹ I will give children
to the families of Jacob and
Judah.

They will possess my entire land.
My chosen people will be given all
   of it.
Those who serve me will live
   there.
[10] Their flocks will eat in the rich
   grasslands of Sharon.
Their herds will rest in the Valley
   of Achor.
That is what I will do for my
   people who follow me.

[11] "But some of you have deserted
   me.
You no longer worship on my
   holy mountain of Zion.
You spread a table for the god that
   is called Good Fortune.
You offer bowls of mixed wine to
   the god named Fate.
[12] So I will make it your fate to be
   killed with swords.
Each of you will die a horrible
   death.
That is because I called out to you,
   but you did not answer me.
I spoke to you, but you did not
   listen.
You did what is evil in my sight.
You chose to do what does not
   please me."

[13] So the LORD and King says,

"Those who serve me will have
   food to eat.
But you will be hungry.
My servants will have plenty to
   drink.
But you will be thirsty.
Those who serve me will be full of
   joy.
But you will be put to shame.
[14] My servants will sing
   with joy in their hearts.
But you will cry out
   because of the great pain in your
   hearts.
You will cry because your spirits
   are sad.
[15] My chosen ones will use your
   names
   when they call down curses on
   others.
I am your LORD and King.
I will put you to death.
But I will give new names to
   those who serve me.

[16] They will ask me to bless their
   land.
They will do it in my name.
I am the God of truth.
They will take oaths and make
   promises in their land.
They will do it in my name.
I am the God of truth.
The troubles of the past will be
   forgotten.
They will be hidden from my
   eyes.

THE LORD WILL CREATE NEW HEAVENS AND A NEW EARTH

[17] "I will create new heavens and a
   new earth.
The things that have happened
   before will not be
   remembered.
They will not even enter your
   minds.
[18] So be glad and full of joy forever
   because of what I will create.
I will cause others to take delight
   in Jerusalem.
They will be filled with joy
   when they see its people.
[19] And I will be full of joy because of
   Jerusalem.
I will take delight in my people.
Sobbing and crying
   will not be heard there anymore.

[20] "Babies in Jerusalem will no longer
   live only a few days.
Old people will not fail
   to live for a very long time.
Those who live to the age of 100
   will be thought of as still being
   young when they die.
Those who die before they are 100
   will be considered as having
   been under God's curse.
[21] My people will build houses and
   live in them.
They will plant vineyards and eat
   their fruit.
[22] They will no longer build houses
   only to have others live in them.
They will no longer plant crops
   only to have others eat them.
My people will live to be as old as
   trees.
My chosen ones will enjoy for a
   long time
   the things they have worked for.

²³ Their work will not be worthless
   anymore.
  They will not have children who
   are sure to face sudden terror.
Instead, I will bless them.
  I will also bless their children
   after them.
²⁴ Even before they call out to me, I
   will answer them.
  While they are still speaking, I
   will hear them.
²⁵ Wolves and lambs will eat
   together.
  Lions will eat straw like oxen.
  Serpents will not bite anyone.
They will eat nothing but dust.
  None of those animals will harm
   or destroy
  anything or anyone on my holy
   mountain of Zion,"
            says the LORD.

THE LORD JUDGES SOME PEOPLE AND BLESSES OTHERS

66
The LORD says,
"Heaven is my throne.
The earth is under my control.
So how could you ever build a
  house for me?
Where would my resting place
  be?

² Didn't my powerful hand make
   everything?
  That is how all things were
   created,"
          announces the LORD.

"The person I value is not proud.
  He is sorry for the wrong things
   he has done.
  He has great respect for what I
   say.
³ But others are not like that.
  They sacrifice bulls to me,
  but at the same time they kill
   people.
They offer lambs to me,
  but they also sacrifice dogs to
   other gods.
They bring grain offerings to me,
  but they also offer pig's blood to
   other gods.
They burn incense to me,
  but they also worship statues of
   gods.
They have chosen to go their own
   way.
  They take delight in things I hate.
⁴ So I have also made a choice.
  I will make them suffer greatly.
  I will bring on them what they
   are afraid of.
When I called out to them, no one
   answered me.

Will all people be nice in heaven?

All the people in heaven will be nice because everyone there will love God and love one another. No one will hurt anyone or be mean to anyone in heaven. There will be no crying or pain. There will be no pushing or shoving or name-calling in heaven. The Bible says that even animals will not hurt other animals. Wolves will not chase lambs and dogs will not chase cats. The Bible says that in heaven we will know God as he knows us. We do not want to hurt anyone when we know and understand God's love.

checkout Isaiah 65:25

Related verse:
Revelation 21:4

When I spoke to them, no one
listened.
They did what is evil in my sight.
They chose to do what displeases
me."

5 Listen to the word of the LORD.
Listen, you who tremble with
fear when he speaks. He says,
"Some of your own people hate
you.
They turn their backs on you
because you are faithful to
me.
They make fun of you and say,
'Let the LORD show his glory by
saving you.
Then we can see how happy you
are.'
But they will be put to shame.
6 Hear the loud sounds coming
from the city!
Listen to the noise coming from
the temple!
I am the one who is causing it.
I am paying my enemies back for
everything they have done.

7 "Zion is like a woman who has a
baby
before she goes into labor.
She has a son
even before her labor pains
begin.
8 Who has ever heard of anything
like that?
Who has ever seen such a thing?
Can a country be born in a day?
Can a nation be created in a
moment?
But as soon as Zion goes into
labor,
her people increase their
numbers.
9 Zion, would I bring you to the
moment of birth
and not let it happen?" says the
LORD.
"Would I close up a mother's body
when it is time for her baby to be
born?" says your God.
10 "Be glad along with Jerusalem, all
you who love her.
Be filled with joy because of her.
Take great delight in her,
all you who sob over her.
11 You will nurse at her comforting
breasts.

And you will be satisfied.
You will drink until you are full.
And you will delight in her rich
and plentiful supply."

12 The LORD continues,

"I will cause peace to flow over her
like a river.
I will make the wealth of nations
sweep over her like a flooding
stream.
You will nurse and be carried in
her arms.
You will play on her lap.
13 As a mother comforts her child,
I will comfort you.
You will find comfort in
Jerusalem."

14 When you see that happen, your
hearts will be filled with joy.
Just as grass grows quickly, you
will succeed.
The LORD will show his power to
those who serve him.
But he will pour out his anger on
his enemies.
15 The LORD will judge them with
fire.
His chariots are coming like a
windstorm.
He will pour out his burning anger
on his enemies.
It will blaze out like flames of
fire.
16 The LORD will bring everyone into
court.
He will use fire and his sword to
punish those he finds guilty.
He will put many people to
death.

17 "Some people set themselves apart
and make themselves pure. They do
it so they can go into the gardens to
worship other gods. They do what the
worship leader tells them to do. They
eat the meat of pigs and rats. They also
eat other things I hate. All of those
people will come to a horrible end,"
announces the LORD.
18 "They have done many evil things.
And they plan to do even more. So I
will come and gather the people of every nation and language. They will see
my glory when I act.
19 "I will do a miracle among them. I
will send to the nations some of those

who are left alive. I will send some of them to the people of Tarshish, Libya and Lydia, who are famous for using bows. I will send others to Tubal and Greece. And I will send still others to islands far away. The people who live there have not heard about my fame. They have not seen my glory. Those I send will tell the nations about my glory when I act.

²⁰"And they will bring back all of the people of Israel from all of those nations. They will bring them to my holy mountain in Jerusalem. My people will ride on horses, mules and camels. They will come in chariots and wagons," says the LORD. "Those messengers will bring my people as an offering to me. They will bring them to my temple, just as the Israelites bring their grain offerings in bowls that are 'clean.' ²¹And I will choose some of them to be priests and Levites," says the LORD.

²²"I will make new heavens and a new earth. And they will last forever," announces the LORD. "In the same way, your name and your children after you will last. ²³Everyone will come and bow down to me. They will do it at every New Moon Feast and on every Sabbath day," says the LORD.

²⁴"When they go out of Jerusalem, they will see the dead bodies of those who refused to obey me. The worms that eat the bodies will not die. The fire that burns them will not be put out. It will make everyone sick just to look at them."

quest challenge

I Wonder . . .

What's the first step I should take when I'm facing a problem?

Real Life Challenge

Problems are like a bunch of tangled hangers. If we jump right in, we end up pulling and yanking them apart. It's better to separate each hanger one by one. In the same way, we might be tempted to jump right in and try to fix our problems, but God wants us to ask him what to do first. Then we can proceed with his wisdom.

Quest Clue

Look at Psalm 32 and Isaiah 30 to see why our first step toward solving a problem should be asking God for help.

Jeremiah

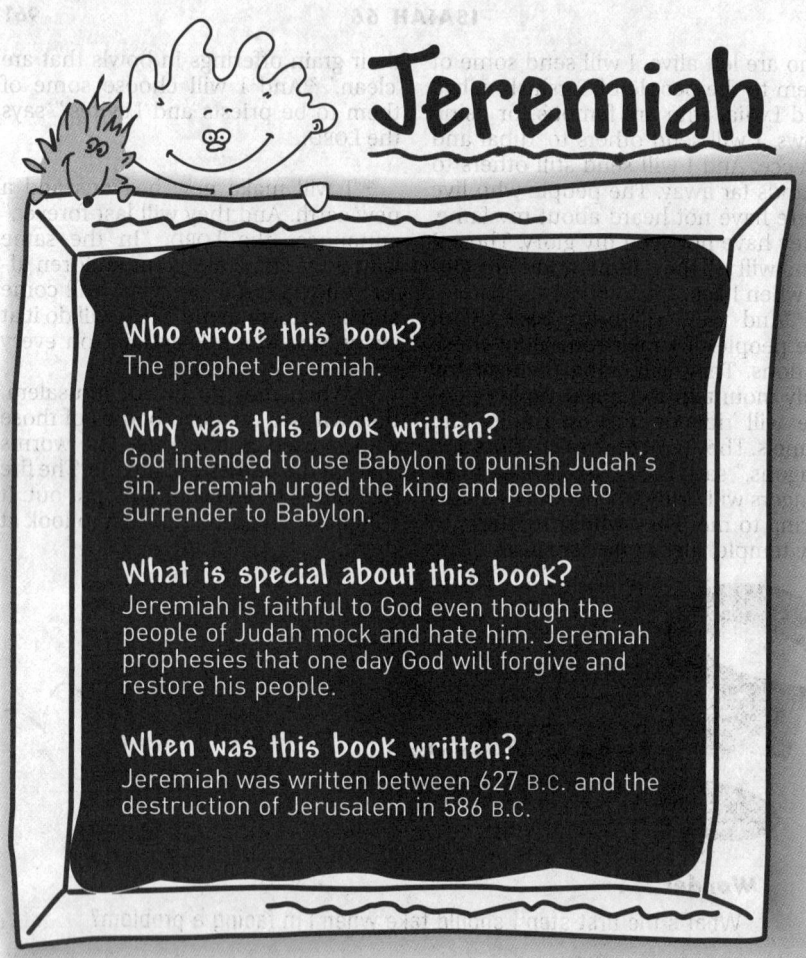

Who wrote this book?
The prophet Jeremiah.

Why was this book written?
God intended to use Babylon to punish Judah's sin. Jeremiah urged the king and people to surrender to Babylon.

What is special about this book?
Jeremiah is faithful to God even though the people of Judah mock and hate him. Jeremiah prophesies that one day God will forgive and restore his people.

When was this book written?
Jeremiah was written between 627 B.C. and the destruction of Jerusalem in 586 B.C.

1 These are the words Jeremiah received from the LORD. He was the son of Hilkiah. Jeremiah was one of the priests at Anathoth. That's a town in the territory of Benjamin. ²A message came to Jeremiah from the LORD. It came in the 13th year that Josiah was king over Judah. Josiah was the son of Amon.

³The LORD's message also came to Jeremiah during the whole time Jehoiakim was king over Judah. Jehoiakim was the son of Josiah. The LORD continued to speak to Jeremiah until the fifth month of the 11th year that Zedekiah was king over Judah. That's when the people of Jerusalem were forced to leave their country. Zedekiah was the son of Josiah. Here is what Jeremiah said.

THE LORD CHOOSES JEREMIAH

⁴A message came to me from the LORD. He said,

⁵ "Before I formed you in your
    mother's body I chose you.
  Before you were born I set you
    apart to serve me.
  I appointed you to be a prophet
    to the nations."

⁶ "You are my LORD and King," I said. "I don't know how to speak. I'm only a child."

⁷But the LORD said to me, "Do not

say, 'I'm only a child.' You must go to everyone I send you to. You must say everything I command you to say. [8]Do not be afraid of the people I send you to. I am with you. I will save you," announces the LORD.

[9]Then the LORD reached out his hand. He touched my mouth and spoke to me. He said, "I have put my words in your mouth. [10]Today I am appointing you to speak to nations and kingdoms. I want you to pull them up by the roots and tear them down. I want you to destroy them and crush them. But I also want you to build them up and plant them."

[11]A message came to me from the LORD. He asked me, "What do you see, Jeremiah?"

"The branch of an almond tree," I replied.

[12]The LORD said to me, "You have seen correctly. I am watching to see that my word comes true."

[13]Another message came to me from the LORD. He asked me, "What do you see?"

"A pot that has boiling water in it," I answered. "It's leaning toward us from the north."

[14]The LORD said to me, "Something very bad will be poured out on everyone who lives in this land. It will come from the north. [15]I am about to send for all of the armies in the northern kingdoms," announces the LORD.

"Their kings will come to
    Jerusalem.
They will set up their thrones at
    the very gates of the city.
They will attack all of the walls
    that surround the city.
They will go to war against all of
    the towns of Judah.
[16]I will judge my people.
They have done many evil
    things.
They have deserted me.
They have burned incense to other
    gods.
They have worshiped the gods
    their own hands have made.

[17]"So get ready! Stand up! Tell them everything I command you to. Do not let them terrify you. If you do, I will terrify you in front of them. [18]Today I have made you like a city that has a high wall around it. I have made you like an iron pillar and a bronze wall. Now you can stand up against the whole land. You can stand against the kings and officials of Judah. You can stand against its priests and its people. [19]They will fight against you. But they will not overcome you. I am with you. I will save you," announces the LORD.

ISRAEL DESERTS THE LORD

2 A message came to me from the LORD. He said, [2]"Go. Announce my message to the people in Jerusalem. I want everyone to hear it. Tell them,

" 'I remember how faithful you
        were to me when you were
        young.
    You loved me as if you were my
        bride.
    You followed me through the
        desert.
    Nothing had been planted there.
[3]Your people were holy to me.
    They were the first share of my
        harvest.
All those who destroyed them
        were held guilty.
    And trouble came to their
        enemies,' "
                announces the LORD.

[4]People of Jacob, hear the LORD's
        message.
    Listen, all you tribes of Israel.

[5]The LORD says,

"What did your people find wrong
        with me?
    Why did they wander so far away
        from me?
    They worshiped worthless statues
        of gods.
    Then they themselves became
        worthless.
[6]They did not ask, 'Where is the
        LORD?
    He brought us up out of Egypt.
    He led us through a dry and empty
        land.
    He guided us through deserts
        and deep valleys.
    It was a land of darkness where
        there wasn't any rain.
    No one lived or traveled there.'

[7] But I brought you into a land that
　　has rich soil.
　I gave you its fruit and its finest
　　　food.
　In spite of that, you polluted my
　　land.
　You turned it into something I
　　hate.
[8] The priests did not ask,
　　'Where is the LORD?'
　Those who taught my law did not
　　know me.
　The leaders refused to obey me.
　The prophets prophesied in the
　　name of Baal.
　They worshiped worthless
　　statues of gods.

[9] "So I am bringing charges against
　　you again,"
　　　　　announces the LORD.
　"And I will bring charges against
　　your children's children.
[10] Go over to the coasts of the
　　western nations and look.
　Send people to the land of Kedar
　　and have them look closely.
　See if there has ever been
　　anything like this.
[11] Has a nation ever changed its
　　gods?
　Actually, they are not even gods
　　at all.
　But my people have traded away
　　their glorious God.
　They have traded me for
　　worthless statues of gods.
[12] Sky above, be shocked over that.
　Tremble with horror,"
　　　　　announces the LORD.
[13] "My people have sinned twice.
　They have deserted me,
　　even though I am the spring of
　　water that gives life.
　And they have dug their own wells.
　But those wells are broken.
　They can't hold any water.
[14] Are you people of Israel servants?
　You were not born as slaves, were
　　you?
　Then why have you been carried
　　off like stolen goods?
[15] Lions have roared.
　They have growled at you.
　They have destroyed your land.
　Your towns are burned and
　　deserted.

[16] The men of Memphis and
　　Tahpanhes
　have shaved your heads to
　　dishonor you.
[17] Haven't you brought that on
　　yourselves?
　I am the LORD your God, but you
　　deserted me.
　You left me even while I was
　　leading you.
[18] Why do you go to Egypt
　　to drink water from the Shihor
　　River?
　Why do you go to Assyria
　　to drink from the Euphrates
　　River?
[19] You will be punished because you
　　have sinned.
　You will be corrected for turning
　　away from me.
　I am the LORD your God.
　If you desert me, bad things will
　　happen to you.
　If you do not respect me, you will
　　suffer bitterly.
　I want you to understand that,"
　　　　　announces the LORD
　　　　　who rules over all.

[20] "Long ago you broke off the yoke I
　　put on you.
　You tore off the ropes I tied you
　　up with.
　You said, 'I won't serve you!'
　In fact, on every high hill
　　you lay down like a prostitute.
　You worshiped other gods under
　　every green tree.
[21] You were like a good vine when I
　　planted you.
　You were a healthy plant.
　Then how did you turn against
　　me?
　How did you become a bad, wild
　　vine?
[22] You might wash yourself with
　　baking soda.
　You might use plenty of soap.
　But I can still see the stains your
　　guilt covers you with,"
　　announces the LORD and King.
[23] "You say, 'I am "clean."
　I haven't followed the gods that
　　are named after Baal.'
　How can you say that?
　Remember how you acted in the
　　valley.

Consider what you have done.
  You are like a female camel
    running quickly here and
    there.
24 You are like a wild donkey that
    lives in the desert.
  She smells the wind when she
    longs for a mate.
  Who can hold her back?
  The males that run after her do
    not need to wear themselves
    out.
  At mating time they will easily
    find her.
25 Do not run after other gods
    until your sandals are worn out
    and your throat is dry.
  But you said, 'It's no use!
  I love those gods.
  I must go after them.'

26 "A thief is dishonored when he is
    caught.
  And you people of Israel are
    filled with shame.
  Your kings and officials are
    dishonored.
  So are your priests and your
    prophets.
27 You say to a piece of wood, 'You
    are my father.'
  You say to a stone, 'You are my
    mother.'
  You have turned your backs
    to me.
  You refuse to look at me.
  But when you are in trouble, you
    say,
  'Come and save us!'
28 So where are the gods you made
    for yourselves?
  Let them come when you are in
    trouble!
  Let them save you if they can!
  Judah, you have as many gods
    as you have towns.

29 "Why do you bring charges against
    me?
  All of you have refused to obey
    me,"
            announces the LORD.
30 "I punished your people. But it did
    not do them any good.
  They did not pay attention when
    they were corrected.
  You have killed your prophets with
    swords.

  You have swallowed them up like
    a hungry lion.

31 "You who are now living, consider
my message. I am saying,

  "Have I been like a desert to Israel?
  Have I been like a land of deep
    darkness?
  Why do my people say, 'We are
    free to wander.
  We won't come to you anymore'?
32 Does a young woman forget all
    about her jewelry?
  Does a bride forget her wedding
    jewels?
  But my people have forgotten me
    more days than anyone can
    count.
33 You are very skilled at chasing
    after love!
  Even the worst of women can
    learn from how you act.
34 The blood of those you have killed
    is on your clothes.
  You have destroyed poor people
    who were not guilty.
  You did not catch them in the act
    of breaking in.
  In spite of all of that,
35 you say, 'I'm not guilty of doing
    anything wrong.
  The LORD isn't angry with me.'
  But I will judge you.
  That is because you say, 'I haven't
    sinned.'
36 Why do you keep on
    changing your ways so much?
  Assyria did not help you.
  And Egypt will not help you
    either.
37 So you will also leave Egypt
    with your hands tied together
    above your heads.
  I have turned my back on those
    you trust.
  They will not help you.

3 "Suppose a man divorces his
    wife.
  What if she then gets married
    to another man?
  Should her first husband return to
    her again?
  If he does, won't the land
    become completely 'unclean'?
  People of Israel, you have lived like
    a prostitute.

You have loved many other gods.
So do you think you can return to
   me now?"
           announces the LORD.
² "Look up at the bare hilltops.
Is there any place where you
   have not committed adultery
   with other gods?
By the side of the road you sat
   waiting for lovers.
You sat there like someone who
   wanders in the desert.
You have polluted the land.
You are like a sinful prostitute.
³ So I have held the showers back.
I have kept the spring rains from
   falling.
But you still have the bold face of a
   prostitute.
You refuse to blush with shame.
⁴ You have just now called out to
   me.
You said,
'My Father, you have been my
   friend
ever since I was young.
⁵ Will you always be angry with me?
Will your anger continue
   forever?'
That is how you talk.
But you do all of the evil things
   you can."

ISRAEL IS NOT FAITHFUL TO THE LORD

⁶ During the time Josiah was king, the LORD spoke to me. He said, "Have you seen what the people of Israel have done? They have not been faithful to me. They have committed adultery with other gods. They worshiped them on every high hill and under every green tree.
⁷ "I thought that after they had done all of those things, they would return to me. But they did not. Their sister nation Judah saw it. And they were not faithful to me either.
⁸ "I gave Israel their letter of divorce. I sent them away because they were unfaithful to me so many times. But I saw that their sister nation Judah did not have any respect for me. They were not faithful to me either. They also went out and committed adultery with other gods.
⁹ "Israel was not faithful to me, but

that did not bother them at all. They made the land 'unclean.' They worshiped gods that were made out of stone and wood. ¹⁰ In spite of all that, their sister Judah did not come back to me. They were not faithful to me either. They did not return with all their heart. They only pretended to," announces the LORD.

¹¹ The LORD said to me, "Israel and Judah have not been faithful to me. But Israel was not as bad as Judah was. ¹² "Go. Announce this message to the people in the north. Tell them,

" 'Israel, you have not been
   faithful,' announces the LORD.
'Return to me. Then I will look on
   you with favor again.
My love is faithful,' announces the
   LORD.
'I will not be angry with you
   forever.
¹³ Admit that you are guilty of doing
   what is wrong.
You have refused to obey me. I
   am the LORD your God.
You have committed adultery with
   other gods.
You worshiped them under every
   green tree.
And you have not obeyed me,' "
         announces the LORD.

¹⁴ "You people have not been faithful," announces the LORD. "Return to me. I am your husband. I will choose one of you from each town. I will choose two from each territory. And I will bring you to the city of Zion. ¹⁵ "Then I will give you shepherds who are dear to my heart. Their knowledge and understanding will help them lead you. ¹⁶ In those days your numbers will increase greatly in the land," announces the LORD.

"Then people will not talk about the ark of the covenant of the LORD anymore. It will never enter their minds. They will not remember it. The ark will not be missed. And another one will not be made.

¹⁷ "At that time they will call Jerusalem The Throne of the LORD. All of the nations will gather together there. They will go there to honor me. They will no longer do what their stubborn and evil hearts want them to do.

18"In those days the people of Judah will join the people of Israel. Together they will come from a land in the north. They will come to the land I gave to your people long ago. I wanted them to have it as their very own.

19"I myself said,

" 'I would gladly treat you like my children.
I would give you a pleasant land.
It is the most beautiful land any nation could have.'
I thought you would call me 'Father.'
I hoped you would always follow me.
20But you people are like a woman who is not faithful to her husband.
Israel, you have not been faithful to me,"
announces the LORD.

21A cry is heard on the bare hilltops.
The people of Israel are sobbing and praying.
That's because their lives are so twisted.
They've forgotten the LORD their God.

22"You have not been faithful,"
says the LORD.
"Return to me. I will heal you.
Then you will not turn away from me anymore."

"Yes," the people say. "We will come to you.
You are the LORD our God.
23The gods we worship on the hills and mountains are useless.
You are the LORD our God.
You are the only one who can save us.
24From our earliest years shameful gods have eaten up everything our people worked for.
They have eaten up our flocks and herds.
They've destroyed our sons and daughters.
25Let us lie down in our shame.
Let our dishonor cover us.
You are the LORD our God. But we have sinned against you.

We and our people before us have sinned.
We haven't obeyed you from our earliest years until now."

4 "If you will return, Israel, return to me,"
announces the LORD.
"Put the statues of your gods out of my sight.
I hate them.
Stop going down the wrong path.
2Take all of your oaths in my name.
Say, 'You can be sure that the LORD is alive.'
Let all of your promises be truthful, fair and honest.
Then I will bless the nations.
And they will take delight in me."

3Here is what the LORD is telling the people of Judah and Jerusalem. He says,

"Your hearts are as hard as a field that has not been plowed.
So change your ways and produce good crops.
Do not plant seeds among thorns.
4People of Judah and Jerusalem, obey me.
Do not let your hearts be stubborn.
If you do, my anger will blaze out against you.
It will burn like fire because of the evil things you have done.
No one will be able to put it out.

TROUBLE WILL COME FROM THE NORTH

5"Announce my message in Judah.
Tell it in Jerusalem.
Say, 'Blow trumpets all through the land!'
Give a loud shout and say,
'Gather together!
Let's run to cities that have high walls around them!'
6Warn everyone to go to Zion!
Run for safety! Do not wait!
I am bringing trouble from the north.
Everything will be totally destroyed."

⁷Lions have come out of their den.
  Those who destroy nations have
    begun to march out.
They have left their place
  to destroy your land completely.
Your towns will be broken to
    pieces.
  No one will live in them.
⁸So put on black clothes.
  Sob and cry over what has
    happened.
The LORD hasn't turned
  his burning anger away from us.

⁹"A dark day is coming," announces
    the LORD.
  "The king and his officials will
    lose hope.
The priests will be shocked.
  And the prophets will be
    terrified."

¹⁰Then I said, "You are my LORD and King. You have completely tricked the people of Judah and Jerusalem. You have told them, 'You will have peace and rest.' But swords are pointed at our throats."

¹¹At that time the people of Judah and Jerusalem will be warned. They will be told, "A hot and dry wind is coming, my people. It is blowing toward you from the bare hilltops in the desert. But it does not separate straw from grain. ¹²It is much too strong for that. The wind is coming from me. I am making my decision against you."

¹³Look! Our enemies are
    approaching like the clouds.
  Their chariots are coming like a
    strong wind.
Their horses are faster than eagles.
  How terrible it will be for us!
  We'll be destroyed!
¹⁴People of Jerusalem, wash your
    sins from your hearts and be
    saved.
  How long will you hold on to
    your evil thoughts?
¹⁵A voice is speaking all the way
    from the city of Dan.

Is thinking something bad the same as doing it or saying it?

No. It would be bad to wish that someone were dead. But it would be a *lot worse* to kill the person. Thoughts and actions are different.

It is still a good idea to try to think good thoughts, though. It is bad to think about doing bad things because sometimes we end up doing what we think about doing. Suppose your mother told you not to eat any cookies before dinner. But you see the cookies on the counter and keep thinking about how good they would taste. If you keep thinking about it you will soon want to eat the cookies really badly. You might even disobey your mom and take one. It will be a lot easier to do good things if you think good thoughts.

checkout Jeremiah 4:14

CLEANSING POOL

Related verses:
1 Chronicles 28:9;
James 1:14,15

From the hills of Ephraim it
announces
that trouble is coming.
16 "Tell the nations.
Warn Jerusalem.
Say, 'An army will attack you.
It is coming from a land far away.
It will shout a war cry
against the cities of Judah.
17 It will surround them like people
who guard a field.
Judah has refused to obey me,' "
announces the LORD.
18 "The army will attack you
because of your conduct and
actions.
That is how you will be punished.
It will be so bitter!
It will cut deep down into your
hearts!"

19 I'm suffering! I'm really suffering!
I'm hurting badly.
My heart is suffering so much!
It's pounding inside me.
I can't keep silent.
I've heard the sound of trumpets.
I've heard the battle cry.
20 One trouble follows another.
The whole land is destroyed.
In an instant my tents are gone.
My home disappears in a
moment.
21 How long must I look at our
enemy's battle flag?
How long must I hear the sound
of the trumpets?

22 The LORD says, "My people are
foolish.
They do not know me.
They are children who do not have
any sense.
They have no understanding
at all.
They are skilled in doing what
is evil.
They do not know how to do
what is good."

23 I looked at the earth.
It didn't have any shape. And it
was empty.
I looked at the sky.
Its light was gone.
24 I looked at the mountains.
They were shaking.
All of the hills were swaying.

25 I looked. And there weren't any
people.
Every bird in the sky had flown
away.
26 I looked. And the fruitful land had
become a desert.
All of its towns were destroyed.
The LORD had done all of that
because of his burning anger.

27 The LORD says,

"The whole land will be destroyed.
But I will not destroy it
completely.
28 So the earth will be filled with
sadness.
The sky above will grow dark.
I have spoken, and I will not take
pity on them.
I have made my decision, and I
will not change my mind."

29 People can hear the sound of
horsemen.
Men who are armed with bows
are coming.
The people in every town run
away.
Some of them go into the
bushes.
Others climb up among the
rocks.
All of the towns are deserted.
No one is living in them.

30 What are you doing, you who are
destroyed?
Why do you dress yourself in
bright red clothes?
Why do you put on jewels of
gold?
Why do you put makeup on your
eyes?
You make yourself beautiful for
no reason at all.
Your lovers hate you.
They are trying to kill you.

31 I hear a cry like the cry of a woman
having a baby.
I hear a groan like someone
having her first child.
It's the cry of the people of Zion
struggling to breathe.
They reach out their hands
and say,
"Help us! We're fainting!
Murderers are about to kill us!"

NO ONE IS HONEST

5 The LORD says, "Go up and down the streets of Jerusalem.
Look around.
Think about what you see.
Search through the market places.
See if you can find one honest person who tries to be truthful.
If you can, I will forgive this city.
² They take all of their oaths in my name.
They say, 'You can be sure that the LORD is alive.'
But their oaths can't be trusted."

³ LORD, don't your eyes look for truth?
You struck your people down.
But they didn't feel any pain.
You crushed them.
But they refused to be corrected.
They made their faces harder than stone.
They refused to turn away from their sins.
⁴ I thought, "The people of Jerusalem are foolish.
They don't know how the LORD wants them to live.
They don't know what their God requires of them.
⁵ So I will go to the leaders.
I'll speak to them.
They should know how the LORD wants them to live.
They must know what their God requires of them."
But all of them had broken off the yoke the LORD had put on them.
They had torn off the ropes he had tied them up with.
⁶ So a lion from the forest will attack them.
A wolf from the desert will destroy them.
A leopard will hide and wait near their towns.
It will tear to pieces anyone who dares to go out.
Again and again they have refused to obey the LORD.
They have turned away from him many times.

⁷ The LORD says, "Jerusalem, why should I forgive you?
Your people have deserted me.
They have taken their oaths in the names of gods
that are not really gods at all.
I supplied everything they needed.
But they committed adultery.
Large crowds went to the houses of prostitutes.
⁸ Your people are like stallions that have plenty to eat.
Their sinful longings are out of control.
Each of them goes after another man's wife.
⁹ Shouldn't I punish them for that?" announces the LORD.
"Shouldn't I pay back the nation that does those things?

¹⁰ "Armies of Babylonia, go through their vineyards and destroy them.
But do not destroy them completely.
Strip off their branches.
Those people do not belong to me.
¹¹ The people of Israel and Judah have not been faithful to me at all,"
announces the LORD.

¹² They have told lies about the LORD.
They said, "He won't do anything!
No harm will come to us.
We will never see war or be hungry.
¹³ The prophets are nothing but wind.
Their message doesn't come from the LORD.
So let what they say will happen be done to them."

¹⁴ The LORD God rules over all. He says to me,

"The people have spoken those words.
So my words will be like fire in your mouth.
I will make the people like wood.
And the fire will burn them up."

¹⁵ "People of Israel, listen to me,"
    announces the LORD.
"I am bringing against you
    a nation from far away.
It is an old nation. And it will last
    for a long time.
    Its people speak a language you
        do not know.
    You can't understand what they
        are saying.
¹⁶ The bags they carry their arrows in
    are like an open grave.
    All of their soldiers are mighty.
¹⁷ They will eat up your crops and
        your food.
    They will strike down your sons
        and daughters.
    They will kill your sheep and
        cattle.
    They will destroy your vines and
        fig trees.
    You trust in your cities that have
        high walls around them.
    But the people in them will be
        killed with swords.

¹⁸ "In spite of that, even in those days
I will not destroy you completely," announces the LORD.
¹⁹ " 'Jeremiah,' the people will ask,
'Why has the LORD our God done all of
this to us?'
"Then you will tell them, 'You have
deserted the LORD. You have served
other gods in your own land. So now
you will serve another nation in a land
that is not your own.'

²⁰ "Here is what I want you to
        announce
    to the people of Jacob.
    Tell it in Judah.
    Tell them I say,
²¹ 'Listen to this, you foolish people,
    who do not have any sense.
    You have eyes, but you do not see.
    You have ears, but you do not
        hear.
²² Shouldn't you have respect for
        me?' announces the LORD.
    'Shouldn't you tremble with fear
        in front of me?
    I made the sand to hold the ocean
        back.
    It will do that forever.
    The ocean can't go past it.
    The waves might roll, but they
        can't sweep over it.

They might roar, but they can't
    go across it.
²³ But you people have stubborn
    hearts.
    You refuse to obey me.
    You have turned away from me.
    You have gone down the wrong
        path.
²⁴ You do not say to yourselves,
    "Let us have respect for the LORD
        our God.
    He sends rain in the fall and the
        spring.
    He promises us that the harvest
        will come
    at the same time each year."
²⁵ But the things you have done
        wrong
    have robbed you of those gifts.
    Your sins have kept those good
        things
    far away from you.'

²⁶ "Jeremiah, some of my people are
        evil.
    They hide and wait just as people
        hide to catch birds.
    They set traps for men.
²⁷ A hunter uses tricks to fill his cage
        with birds.
    And my people have filled their
        houses with a lot of goods.
    They have become rich and
        powerful.
²⁸   They have grown fat and heavy.
    There is no limit to the evil
        things they do.
    In court they do not state the
        case
    of children whose fathers have
        died.
    They do not stand up for poor
        people.
²⁹ Shouldn't I punish them
        for that?"
    announces the LORD.
    "Shouldn't I pay back the
        nation that does those things?

³⁰ "Something horrible and
        shocking
    has happened in the land.
³¹ The prophets prophesy lies.
    The priests rule by their own
        authority.
    And my people love it that way.
    But what will they do in the
        end?"

BABYLONIA WILL ATTACK JERUSALEM

6 The LORD says, "People of Benjamin, run for safety! Run away from Jerusalem!
Blow trumpets in Tekoa!
Warn everyone in Beth Hakkerem!
Horrible trouble is coming from the north.
The Babylonians will destroy everything with awful power.
² I will destroy the city of Zion, even though it is very beautiful.
³ Shepherds will come against it with their flocks.
They will set up their tents around it.
All of them will take care of their own sheep."

⁴ The Babylonians say, "Prepare for battle against Judah!
Get up! Let's attack them at noon!
But the daylight is fading.
The shadows of evening are getting longer.
⁵ So get up! Let's attack them at night!
Let's destroy their strongest forts!"

⁶ The LORD who rules over all speaks to the Babylonians. He says,

"Cut some trees down.
Use the wood to build ramps against Jerusalem's walls.
I must punish that city.
It is filled with people who treat others badly.
⁷ Wells keep giving fresh water.
And Jerusalem keeps on sinning.
Its people are always fighting and causing trouble.
When I look at them,
I see nothing but sickness and wounds.
⁸ Jerusalem, listen to my warning.
If you do not, I will turn away from you.
Your land will become a desert.
No one will be able to live there."

⁹ The LORD rules over all. He says to me,

"People gather the few grapes that are left on a vine.
So let Israel's enemies gather the few people
who are left alive in the land.
Look carefully at the branches again.
Do it like someone who gathers the last few grapes."

¹⁰ Who can I speak to? Who can I warn?
Who will even listen to me?
Their ears are closed
so they can't hear.
The LORD's message displeases them.
They don't take any delight in it.
¹¹ But the LORD's anger burns inside me.
I can no longer hold it in.

The LORD says to me, "Pour out my anger on the children in the street.
Pour it out on the young people who are gathered together.
Husband and wife alike will be caught in it.
So will those who are very old.
¹² I will reach out my hand against those who live in the land,"

announces the LORD.
"Then their houses will be turned over to others.
So will their fields and their wives.
¹³ Everyone wants to get richer and richer,
from the least important of them to the most important.
Prophets and priests alike
try to fool everyone they can.
¹⁴ They bandage the wounds of my people
as if they were not very deep.
'Peace, peace,' they say.
But there isn't any peace.
¹⁵ Are they ashamed of their hateful actions?
No. They do not feel any shame at all.
They do not even know how to blush.
So they will fall like others who have already fallen.

They will be brought down when
  I punish them,"
                    says the LORD.

¹⁶The LORD tells the people of Judah,

"Stand where the roads cross, and
  look around.
Ask where the old paths are.
Ask for the good path, and walk
  on it.
Then your hearts will find rest
  in me.
But you said, 'We won't walk
  on it.'
¹⁷I appointed prophets to warn you.
  I said,
'Listen to the sound of the
  trumpets!'
But you said, 'We won't listen.'
¹⁸So pay attention, you nations.
  Be witnesses for me.
Watch what will happen to my
  people.
¹⁹Earth, pay attention.
  I am going to bring trouble on
  them.
I will punish them because of the
  evil things they have done.
They have not listened to my words.
They have said no to my law.
²⁰What do I care about incense from
  the land of Sheba?
Why should I bother with sweet-
  smelling cane from a land far
  away?
I do not accept your burnt
  offerings.
Your sacrifices do not please
  me."

²¹So the LORD says,

"I will bring an army against the
  people of Judah.
Parents and children alike will
  trip and fall.
Neighbors and friends will die."

²²The LORD says to Jerusalem,

"Look! An army is coming
  from the land of the north.
I am stirring up a great nation.
Its army is coming from a land
  that is very far away.
²³Its soldiers are armed with bows
  and spears.
They are mean. They do not
  show any mercy at all.

They come riding in on their
  horses.
They sound like the roaring
  ocean.
They are lined up for battle.
They are marching out
  to attack you, city of Zion."

²⁴We have heard reports about
  them.
And our hands can't help us.
We are suffering greatly.
It's like the pain of a woman
  having a baby.
²⁵Don't go out to the fields.
  Don't walk on the roads.
Our enemies have swords.
And there is terror on every side.
²⁶Put on black clothes, my people.
  Roll among the ashes.
Cry with bitter sobbing
  just as you would cry for an only
  child.
The one who is going to destroy us
  will come suddenly.

²⁷The LORD says to me, "I have made
  you like one who tests metals.
My people are the ore.
I want you to watch them
  and test the way they live.
²⁸All of them are used to disobeying
  me.
They go around telling lies about
  others.
They are like bronze mixed with
  iron.
All of them do very sinful things.
²⁹The fire is made very hot
  so the lead will burn away.
But it is impossible to make those
  people pure.
Those who are evil are not
  removed.
³⁰They are like silver that is thrown
  away.
That is because I have not
  accepted them."

WORSHIPING OTHER GODS IS WORTHLESS

7 A message came to me from the
LORD. He said, ²"Stand at the
gate of my house. Announce my
message to the people there. Say,
" 'Listen to the LORD's message, all of
you people of Judah. You always come
through these gates to worship the

LORD. ³The God of Israel is speaking to you. He is the LORD who rules over all. He says, "Change the way you live and act. Then I will let you live in this place.

⁴" ' "Do not trust in lies. Do not say, 'This is the temple of the LORD! This is the temple of the LORD! This is the temple of the LORD!'

⁵" ' "You must really change the way you live and act. Treat each other fairly. ⁶Do not treat outsiders or widows badly in this place. Do not take advantage of children whose fathers have died. Do not kill those who are not guilty of doing anything wrong. Do not worship other gods. That will only bring harm to you.

⁷" ' "If you obey me, I will let you live in this place. It is the land I gave your people who lived long ago. It was promised to them for ever and ever.

⁸" ' "But look! You are trusting in worthless lies.

⁹" ' "You continue to steal and commit murder. You commit adultery and tell lies. You burn incense to Baal. You worship other gods you have not known anything about before.

¹⁰" ' "Then you come and stand in front of me. You keep coming to this house where I have put my Name. You say, 'We are safe.' You think you are safe when you do so many things I hate. ¹¹My Name is in this house. But you have made it a den for robbers! I have been watching you!" announces the LORD.

¹²" ' "Go now to the town of Shiloh. Go to the place where I first made a home for my Name. See what I did to it because of the evil things my people Israel were doing.

¹³" ' "I spoke to you again and again," announces the LORD. "I warned you while you were doing all of those things. But you did not listen. I called out to you. But you did not answer. ¹⁴So what I did to Shiloh I will now do to the house where my Name is. It is the temple you trust in. It is the place I gave to you and your people of long ago.

¹⁵" ' "But I will throw you out of my land. That is exactly what I did to the people of Ephraim. And they are your relatives." '

¹⁶"Jeremiah, do not pray for those people. Do not make any appeal or request for them. Do not beg me. I will not listen to you.

¹⁷"Don't you see what they are doing? They are worshiping other gods in the towns of Judah. They are offering sacrifices to them in the streets of Jerusalem. ¹⁸The children go out and gather wood. The fathers light the fire. The women mix the dough. They make flat cakes of bread for the goddess who is called the Queen of Heaven. They pour out drink offerings to other gods. That makes me very angry. ¹⁹"But am I the one they are hurting?" announces the LORD. "Aren't they only harming themselves? They should be ashamed of it."

²⁰So the LORD and King says, "I will pour out my burning anger on this place. It will strike people and animals alike. It will destroy the trees and the crops in the fields. It will burn, and no one will be able to put it out."

²¹The LORD who rules over all is the God of Israel. He says, "Go ahead! Add your burnt offerings to your other sacrifices. Eat the meat yourselves! ²²When I brought your people out of Egypt, I spoke to them. But I did not just give them commands about burnt offerings and sacrifices. ²³I also gave them another command. I said, 'Obey me. Then I will be your God. And you will be my people. Live the way I command you to live. Then things will go well with you.'

²⁴"But they did not listen. They refused to pay any attention to me. Instead, they did what their stubborn and evil hearts wanted them to do. They went backward and not forward.

²⁵"Again and again I sent my servants the prophets to you. They came to you day after day. They prophesied from the time your people left Egypt until now.

²⁶"But the people did not listen. They refused to pay any attention to me. They were stubborn. They did more evil things than their people who lived before them.

²⁷"Jeremiah, when you tell them all of that, they will not listen to you. When you call out to them, they will not answer.

²⁸"So say to them, 'You are a nation

that has not obeyed the LORD your God. You did not pay attention when you were corrected. Truth has died out. You do not tell the truth anymore.' "

²⁹The LORD says to the people of Jerusalem, "Cut off your hair. Throw it away. Sing a song of sadness on the bare hilltops. I am very angry with you. I have turned my back on you. I have deserted you.

THE VALLEY OF DEATH

³⁰"The people of Judah have done what is evil in my eyes," announces the LORD. "They have set up statues of their gods. They have worshiped them in the house where my Name is. They have made my house 'unclean.' I hate those statues. ³¹The people have built the high places of Topheth in the Valley of Ben Hinnom. There they worship other gods. And there they sacrifice their children in the fire. That is something I did not command. It did not even enter my mind.

³²"So watch out!" announces the LORD. "The days are coming when people will not call it Topheth anymore. And they will not call it the Valley of Ben Hinnom either. Instead, they will call it the Valley of Death. They will bury the dead bodies of some people in Topheth. But they will run out of room. ³³Then they will not be able to bury the bodies of other people there. So the bodies will become food for the birds of the air and the wild animals. And no one will scare them away.

³⁴"I will put an end to the sounds of joy and gladness. The voices of brides and grooms will not be heard anymore. There will not be any sounds of joy in the towns of Judah and the streets of Jerusalem. The land will become a desert.

8 "At that time the tombs will be opened," announces the LORD. "The bones of the kings and officials of Judah will be brought out. The bones of the priests and prophets will be removed. So will the bones of the people of Jerusalem. ²They will lie outside under the sun, moon and all of the stars.

"All of those people had loved and

served those things. They had followed them and worshiped them. They had asked them for advice. So the bones of those people will not be gathered up or buried again. Instead, they will be like trash lying there on the ground.

³"Everyone who is left alive in this evil nation will want to die rather than live. That is what they will long for in the lands where I force them to go," announces the LORD who rules over all.

THE LORD PUNISHES HIS SINFUL PEOPLE

⁴"Jeremiah, tell them, 'The LORD says,

" ' "When people fall down, don't
     they get up again?
When someone turns away,
     doesn't he come back?
⁵Then why have the people of
     Jerusalem turned away
     from me?
Why do they always turn away?
They keep on telling lies.
     They refuse to come back to me.
⁶I have listened carefully.
     But they do not say what is right.
They refuse to turn away from
     their sins.
No one says, 'What have I done?'
All of them go their own way.
     They are like horses charging
     into battle.
⁷Storks know when to fly south.
     So do doves, swifts and thrushes.
But my people do not know
     what I require them to do.

⁸" ' "How can you people say, 'We
     are wise.
We have the law of the LORD'?
Actually, the teachers of the law
     have told lies about it.
     Their pens have not written what
     is true.
⁹Those who think they are wise will
     be put to shame.
They will become terrified. They
     will be trapped.
They have not accepted my
     message.
So what kind of wisdom do they
     have?
¹⁰I will give their wives to other men.

I will give their fields to new
　　owners.
Everyone wants to get richer and
　　richer,
from the least important of them
　　to the most important.
Prophets and priests alike
　　try to fool everyone they can.
¹¹ They bandage the wounds of my
　　people
　　as if they were not very deep.
'Peace, peace,' they say.
　　But there isn't any peace.
¹² Are they ashamed of their hateful
　　actions?
No. They do not feel any shame
　　at all.
They do not even know how to
　　blush.
So they will fall like others who
　　have already fallen.
They will be brought down when
　　I punish them,"
　　　　　　　　　　says the LORD.
¹³ " ' "I will take away their harvest,"
　　　　　　announces the LORD.
"There will not be any grapes on
　　the vines.
The trees will not bear any figs.
The leaves on the trees will dry up.
What I have given them
　　will be taken away from
　　them." ' "

¹⁴ Why are we sitting here?
　　Let's gather together!
Let's run to the cities that have
　　high walls around them!
Let's die there!
The LORD our God has sentenced
　　us to death.
He has given us poisoned water
　　to drink.
That's because we've sinned
　　against him.
¹⁵ We hoped peace would come.
　　But nothing good has happened
　　to us.
We hoped we would finally be
　　healed.
But all we got was terror.
¹⁶ When our enemy's horses snort,
　　the noise is heard all the way
　　from Dan.
When their stallions neigh,
　　the whole land trembles with
　　fear.

They have come to destroy
　　the land and everything in it.
The city and everyone who lives
　　there will be destroyed.

¹⁷ "People of Judah, I will send
　　poisonous snakes among you.
No one will be able to charm
　　them.
And they will bite you,"
　　　　　announces the LORD.

¹⁸ LORD, my heart is weak inside me.
　　You comfort me when I'm sad.
¹⁹ Listen to the cries of my people
　　from a land far away.
They cry out, "Isn't the LORD in
　　Zion?
Isn't its King there anymore?"

The LORD says, "Why have they
　　made me so angry
by worshiping their wooden
　　gods?
Why have they made me angry
　　with their worthless statues
　　of gods from other lands?"

²⁰ The people say, "The harvest is
　　over.
The summer has ended.
And we still haven't been saved."

²¹ My people are crushed, so I am
　　crushed.
I sob, and I am filled with horror.
²² Isn't there any healing lotion in
　　Gilead?
Isn't there a doctor there?
Then why doesn't someone heal
　　the wounds of my people?

9 ¹ I wish my head were a spring
　　of water!
I wish my eyes were a fountain
　　of tears!
I would sob day and night
　　over my people who have been
　　killed.
² I wish I had somewhere to go in
　　the desert
where a traveler could stay!
Then I could leave my people.
I could get away from them.
All of them commit adultery by
　　worshiping other gods.
They aren't faithful to the LORD.

³ "They get ready to use
　　their tongues like bows,"
　　　　　　announces the LORD.

"Their mouths shoot out lies like
	arrows.
	They tell lies to gain power in the
		land.
	They go from one sin to another.
	They do not pay any attention
		to me.
⁴Be on guard against your friends.
	Do not trust the members of
		your own family.
	Every one of them cheats.
	Every friend tells lies.
⁵One friend cheats another.
	No one tells the truth.
	They have taught their tongues
		how to lie.
	They wear themselves out
		sinning.
⁶Jeremiah, you live among people
		who tell lies.
	When they lie, they refuse to pay
		any attention to me,"
			announces the LORD.

⁷So the LORD who rules over all says,

	"I will put them through the fire to
		test them.
	What else can I do?
	My people are so sinful!
⁸Their tongues are like deadly
		arrows.
	They tell lies.
	With their mouths all of them
		speak kindly to their
		neighbors.
	But in their hearts they set traps
		for them.
⁹Shouldn't I punish them for that?"
	announces the LORD.
	"Shouldn't I pay back the nation
		that does those things?"

¹⁰I will cry and sob over the fields in
		the hills.
	I will sing a song of sadness
		about the desert grasslands.
	They are dry and empty. No one
		travels through them.
	The mooing of cattle isn't heard
		there.
	The birds of the air have flown
		away.
	All of the animals are gone.

¹¹The LORD says, "I will knock all of
	Jerusalem's buildings down.
	I will make it a home for wild
		dogs.

The towns of Judah will be
		completely destroyed.
	No one will be able to live in
		them."

¹²Who is wise enough to understand those things? Who has been taught by the LORD? Who can explain them? Why has the land been destroyed so completely? Why has it become like a desert that no one can go across?

¹³The LORD answered me, "Because my people have turned away from my law. I gave it to them. But they have not kept it. They have not obeyed me. ¹⁴Instead, they have done what their stubborn hearts wanted them to do. They have worshiped the gods that are named after Baal. They have done what their people have taught them to do down through the years."

¹⁵So now the LORD who rules over all speaks. He is the God of Israel. He says, "I will make these people eat bitter food. I will make them drink poisoned water. ¹⁶I will scatter them among the nations. They and their people before them have not had anything to do with those nations before. I will chase these people with swords. I will hunt them down until I have destroyed them."

¹⁷The LORD rules over all. He says,

	"Here is something I want you to
		think about.
	Send for the women who sob
		over the dead.
	Send for the most skilled among
		them."

¹⁸Let them come quickly
		and sob over us.
	Let them cry until tears flow from
		our eyes.
	Let them sob until water pours
		out of our eyes.
¹⁹People are heard sobbing in Zion.
	They are saying, "We are
		destroyed!
	We are filled with shame!
	We must leave our land.
	Our houses have been torn
		down."

²⁰Women, hear the LORD's message.
	Listen to what he's saying.
	Teach your daughters how to sob
		over the dead.

Teach one another a song of
   sadness.
²¹ Death has climbed in through our
   windows.
   It has entered our forts.
   It has removed the children from
     the streets.
   It has taken the young people out
     of the market places.

²²Say, "The LORD announces,

" 'The dead bodies of men will be
   like trash
   lying in the open fields.
They will lie there like grain
   that is cut down at harvest time.
   No one will gather them up.' "

²³The LORD says,

"Do not let a wise man brag about
   how wise he is.
Do not let a strong man boast
   about how strong he is.
Do not let a rich person brag
   about how rich he is.
²⁴ But here is what the one who
   brags should boast about.

He should brag that he has
   understanding and knows me.
I want him to know that I am the
   LORD.
No matter what I do on earth,
   I am always kind, fair and
     right.
And I take delight in that,"
           announces the LORD.

²⁵"The days are coming when I will
judge people," announces the LORD. "I
will punish all those who are circumcised only in their bodies. ²⁶That includes the people of Egypt, Judah,
Edom, Ammon and Moab. It also includes all those who live in the desert
in places far away. None of the people
in those nations is really circumcised.
And not even the people of Israel are
circumcised in their hearts."

THE LORD IS THE ONLY TRUE GOD

10 People of Israel, listen to
what the LORD is telling
you. ²He says,

KIDS' QUESTION

Is outer space hot or cold?

Most of outer space is very cold; only the stars and the space
right around them are hot. God created the universe with count-
less stars. The stars give out a lot of heat, but there is a lot more space than
stars. So anything not close to a star has almost no heat at all. The heat
produced by the Sun, the star that's closest
to Earth, produces just the right
amount of light and heat for us to
live on our planet. The air on Earth
keeps the heat in. God created
Earth with just the right climate
so that human beings, his
special creations, could live
here. Earth is our home.

checkout
Jeremiah 10:12

JASON'S IMAGINATION

NASA

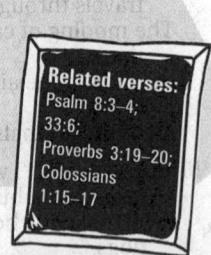

Related verses:
Psalm 8:3–4;
33:6;
Proverbs 3:19–20;
Colossians
1:15–17

"Do not follow the practices of other nations.
Do not be terrified by warnings in the sky.
Do not be afraid, even though the nations are terrified by them.
³ The practices of those nations are worthless.
People cut a tree out of the forest.
A skilled worker shapes the wood with a sharp tool.
⁴ Others decorate it with silver and gold.
They use a hammer to nail it to the floor.
They want to keep it from falling down.
⁵ The statues of their gods can't speak.
They are like scarecrows in a field of melons.
They have to be carried around because they can't walk.
So do not worship them.
They can't do you any harm.
And they can't do you any good either."

⁶ LORD, no one is like you.
You are great.
You are mighty and powerful.
⁷ King of the nations,
everyone should have respect for you.
That's what people should give you.
Among all of the wise people in the nations
there is no one like you.
No one can compare with you in all of their kingdoms.
⁸ All of them are foolish. They don't have any sense.
They think they are taught by worthless wooden gods.
⁹ Hammered silver is brought from Tarshish.
Gold is brought from Uphaz.
People who are skilled in working with wood and gold make a statue.
Then they put blue and purple clothes on it.
The whole thing is made by skilled workers.

¹⁰ But you are the only true God.
You are the only living God.
You are the King who rules forever.
When you are angry, the earth trembles with fear.
The nations can't stand up under your anger.

¹¹ The LORD says to the Jews who are living in Babylonia, "Tell the people of the nations, 'Your gods did not make the heavens and the earth. In fact, those gods will disappear from the earth. They will vanish from under the heavens.' "

¹² But God used his power to make the earth.
His wisdom set the world in place.
His understanding spread the heavens out.
¹³ When he thunders, the waters in the heavens roar.
He makes clouds rise from one end of the earth to the other.
He sends lightning along with the rain.
He brings the wind out from his storerooms.

¹⁴ No one has any sense. No one knows anything at all.
Everyone who works with gold is put to shame by his wooden gods.
The metal gods he worships are fakes.
They can't even breathe.
¹⁵ They are worthless. People make fun of them.
When the LORD judges them, they will be destroyed.
¹⁶ The God of Jacob is not like them.
He gives his people everything they need.
He made everything that exists.
And that includes Israel.
It's the nation that belongs to him.
His name is The LORD Who Rules Over All.

THE LAND WILL BE DESTROYED

¹⁷ People of Jerusalem, your enemies have surrounded you.
They are attacking you.

So gather up what belongs to you.
Then leave the land.
¹⁸ The LORD says,
"I am about to throw out of this
land
everyone who lives in it.
I will bring trouble on them.
They will be captured."

¹⁹ How terrible it will be for me!
I've been wounded!
And my wound can't be healed!
In spite of that, I said to myself,
"I'm sick. But I'll have to put up
with it."
²⁰ Jerusalem is like a tent that has
been destroyed.
All of its ropes have snapped.
My people have gone away from
me.
Now no one is left to set up my
tent.
I have no one to set it up for me.
²¹ The leaders of my people are like
shepherds
who don't have any sense.
They don't ask the LORD for
advice.
That's why they don't succeed.
And that's why their whole flock
is scattered like sheep.
²² Listen! A message is coming!
I hear the sound of a great army
marching down from the north!
It will turn Judah's towns into a
desert.
They will become a home for
wild dogs.

JEREMIAH PRAYS
TO THE LORD

²³ LORD, I know that a man doesn't
control his own life.
He doesn't direct his own steps.
²⁴ Correct me, LORD. But please be
fair.
Don't correct me when you are
angry.
If you do, nothing will be left of
me.
²⁵ Pour out your burning anger on
the nations.
They don't pay any attention to
you.
They refuse to worship you.
They have destroyed the people of
Jacob.

They've wiped them out
completely.
They've also destroyed the land
they lived in.

THE LORD'S PEOPLE HAVE
BROKEN HIS COVENANT

11 A message came to me
from the LORD. He said,
² "Listen to the terms of the
covenant I made with my people long
ago. Tell Judah the terms still apply to
them. Tell those who live in Jerusalem
that they must obey them too.
³ "I am the God of Israel. So let the
people know what I want them to do.
Tell them I am saying, 'May the man
who does not obey the terms of the
covenant be under my curse. ⁴ I gave
those terms to your people long ago.
That was when I brought them out of
Egypt. I saved them out of that furnace
that melts iron down and makes it
pure.' I said, 'Obey me. Do everything I
command you to do. Then you will be
my people. And I will be your God.
⁵ " 'I raised my hand and made an
oath to your people long ago. I promised them I would give them a land
that had plenty of milk and honey.' It is
the land you own today. I kept my
promise."
I replied, "Amen, LORD."
⁶ The LORD said to me, "Here is what I
want you to announce in the towns of
Judah. Say it also in the streets of Jerusalem. Tell the people, 'Listen to the
terms of my covenant. Obey them.
⁷ Long ago I brought your people up
from Egypt. From that time until today, I warned them again and again. I
said, "Obey me."
⁸ " 'But they did not listen. They did
not pay any attention to me. Instead,
they did what their stubborn and
evil hearts wanted them to do. So I
brought down on them all of the
curses of the covenant. I commanded
them to obey it. But they refused.' "
⁹ The LORD continued, "The people
of Judah have made some evil plans.
So have those who live in Jerusalem.
¹⁰ All of them have returned to the sins
their people committed long ago.
Those people refused to listen to what
I told them. And now the people of Israel and Judah alike have worshiped

other gods and served them. They have broken the covenant I made with their people who lived before them.

¹¹"So I say, 'I will bring trouble on them. They will not be able to escape it. They will cry out to me. But I will not listen to them.

¹²" 'The people of Jerusalem and of the towns of Judah will cry out to the gods they burn incense to. But those gods will not help them at all when trouble strikes them. ¹³Judah, you have as many gods as you have towns. And in Jerusalem you have set up as many altars as there are streets. You are burning incense to that shameful god Baal.'

¹⁴"Jeremiah, do not pray for those people. Do not make any appeal or request for them. They will call out to me when they are in trouble. But I will not listen to them.

¹⁵ "I love the people of Judah.
    But they are working out their
       evil plans along with many
       others.
    So what are they doing in my
       temple?
    Can meat that is offered to me
       keep me from punishing
       you?
    When you do evil things, you get
       a lot of pleasure from them."

¹⁶ People of Judah, the LORD once
       called you a healthy olive tree.
    He thought its fruit was
       beautiful.
    But now he will come with the
       roar of a mighty storm.
    He will set the tree on fire.
    And its branches will be broken.

¹⁷The LORD who rules over all planted you. But now he has ordered your enemies to destroy you. The people of Israel and Judah have done what is evil. They have made the LORD very angry by burning incense to Baal.

JEREMIAH'S ENEMIES MAKE EVIL PLANS AGAINST HIM

¹⁸The LORD told me about the evil plans of my enemies. That's how I knew about them. He showed me what they were doing. ¹⁹I had been like a gentle lamb that was led off to be killed. I didn't realize they had made plans against me. They had said,

    "Let's destroy the tree and its fruit.
    Let's cut him off while he's still
       living.
    Then his name won't be
       remembered anymore."
²⁰ But LORD, you rule over all.
    You always judge fairly.
    You put people's hearts and
       minds to the test.
    So pay them back for what they've
       done.
    I've committed my cause to you.

²¹The LORD says, "Jeremiah, here is what I am telling you about the men of Anathoth. They want to kill you. They are saying, 'Don't prophesy in the LORD's name. If you do, we will kill you with our own hands.' "

²²So the LORD who rules over all says, "I will punish them. Their young men will be killed with swords. Their sons and daughters will die of hunger. ²³Only a few people will be left alive. I will judge the men of Anathoth. I will destroy them when the time to punish them comes."

JEREMIAH ARGUES WITH THE LORD

12

LORD, when I bring a
    matter to you,
you always do what is
    right.
But now I would like to speak with
    you
about whether you are being fair.
Why are sinful people successful?
Why do those who can't be
    trusted have an easy life?
² You have planted them.
    Their roots are deep in the
       ground.
    They grow and produce fruit.
    They honor you by what they say.
    But their hearts are far away from
       you.
³ LORD, you know me and see me.
    You test my thoughts about you.
    Drag those people off like sheep to
       be killed!
    Set them apart for the day of
       their death!
⁴ How long will the land be thirsty
    for water?

How long will the grass in every
    field be dry?
The people who live in the land
    are evil.
So the animals and birds have
    died.
And that's not all. The people are
    saying,
"The LORD won't see what
    happens to us."

THE LORD REPLIES
TO JEREMIAH

5 The LORD says, "Suppose you
    have run in a race with other
    men.
And suppose they have worn you
    out.
Then how would you be able to
    race against horses?
Suppose you feel safe only in open
    country.
Then how would you get along in
    the bushes near the Jordan
    River?
6 Even your own family has turned
    against you.
They have shouted loudly at you.
They might say nice things about
    you.
But do not trust them.

7 "I will turn my back on my
    people.
I will desert my land.
I love the people of Judah.
In spite of that, I will hand them
    over to their enemies.
8 My land has become to me
    like a lion in the forest.
It roars at me.
So I hate it.
9 My own land has become like a
    spotted hawk.
And other hawks surround it and
    attack it.
Come, all of you wild animals!
Gather together!
Come together to eat up my
    land.
10 Many shepherds will destroy my
    vineyard.
They will walk all over it.
They will turn my pleasant
    vineyard
into a dry and empty land.
11 My vineyard will become a desert.

It will be dry and empty in my
    sight.
The whole land will be completely
    destroyed.
And no one even cares.
12 Many will come to destroy it.
They will gather on the bare
    hilltops in the desert.
I will use them as my sword to
    destroy my people.
They will kill them from one end
    of the land to the other.
No one will be safe.
13 People will plant wheat. But all
    they will gather is thorns.
They will wear themselves out.
But they will not
    have anything to show for it.
My anger is burning against you.
So you will be ashamed of the
    crop you gather."

14 The LORD continues, "All of my evil
neighbors have taken over the land I
gave my people Israel. So I will pull
them up by their roots from the lands
they live in. And I will pull up the roots
of the people of Judah from among
them.

15 "But after I pull those nations up, I
will show my tender love to them
again. I will bring all of them back to
their own lands. I will take all of them
back to their own countries.

16 "Suppose they learn to follow the
practices of my people. And they take
an oath and make a promise in my
name. They say, 'You can be sure that
the LORD is alive.' They do it just as
they once taught my people to take
oaths in Baal's name. Then I will give
them a place among my people.

17 "But what if one of those nations
does not listen? Then you can be sure I
will pull it up by the roots and destroy
it," announces the LORD.

A LINEN BELT

13 The LORD said to me, "Go
and buy a linen belt. Put it
around your waist. But do
not let it get wet."

2 So I bought a belt, just as the LORD
had told me to do. And I put it around
my waist.

3 Then another message came to me
from the LORD. He said, 4 "Take off the

belt you bought and are wearing around your waist. Go to Perath. Hide the belt there in a crack in the rocks."

⁵So I went and hid it at Perath. I did just as the LORD had told me to do.

⁶Many days later the LORD spoke to me again. He told me, "Go to Perath. Get the belt I told you to hide there."

⁷So I went to Perath. I dug up the belt. I took it from the place where I had hidden it. But it had rotted. It was completely useless.

⁸Then another message came to me from the LORD. He said, ⁹"In the same way, I will destroy Judah's pride. And I will destroy the great pride of Jerusalem.

¹⁰"Those people are evil. They refuse to listen to what I say. They do what their stubborn hearts want them to do. They chase after other gods. They serve them and worship them. So they will be like this belt. They will be completely useless. ¹¹A belt is tied around a man's waist. In the same way, I tied all of the people of Israel and Judah to me," announces the LORD. "I wanted them to be my people. They should have brought me fame and praise and honor. But they have not listened to me.

WINESKINS

¹²"Tell them, 'The LORD is the God of Israel. He says, "Every wineskin should be filled with wine." '

"The people might say to you, 'Don't we know that every wineskin should be filled with wine?'

¹³"If they do, tell them, 'The LORD says, "I am going to fill with wine everyone who lives in this land. I will make the kings who sit on David's throne drunk. And I will fill with wine the priests, the prophets and everyone who lives in Jerusalem. ¹⁴I will smash them against one another. I will punish parents and children alike," announces the LORD. "I will not feel sorry for them. I will not show them any kindness. My tender love for them will not keep me from destroying them." ' "

JUDAH WILL BE TAKEN AWAY FROM THEIR LAND

¹⁵People of Judah, listen to me. Pay attention. Don't be proud.

The LORD has spoken.
¹⁶Give glory to the LORD your God.
  Honor him before he sends
    darkness to cover the land.
Do it before you trip and fall
    on the darkened hills.
You hope that light will come.
  But he will turn it into thick
    darkness.
He will change it to deep
    shadows.
¹⁷If you don't listen,
  I will sob in secret.
Because you are so proud,
I will sob bitterly.
  Tears will flow from my eyes.
The LORD's flock will be taken
    away as prisoners.

¹⁸Speak to the king and his mother.
  Tell them,
  "Come down from your thrones.
Your glorious crowns
    are about to fall from your
    heads."
¹⁹The gates of the cities in the Negev
    Desert will be shut tight.
  There won't be anyone to open
    them.
You will be carried away as
    prisoners.
  You will be taken away completely.

²⁰Jerusalem, look up!
  Your enemies are coming from
    the north.
Where is the flock you were
    supposed to take care of?
  Where are the sheep you were so
    proud of?
²¹You have worked hard to make
    special friends.
  But the LORD will let them rule
    over you.
Then what will you say?
Suffering will take hold of you.
  It will be like the pain of a
    woman having a baby.
²²Suppose you ask yourself,
  "Why has this happened to me?"
It's because you have committed
    so many sins.
  That's the reason your skirt has
    been torn off.
That's why your body has been
    treated so badly.
²³Can people from Ethiopia change
    their skin?

Can leopards change their spots?
It's the same with you.
You have always done what is
evil.
So how can you do what is good?

²⁴The LORD says, "I will scatter you
like straw
that the desert wind blows away.
²⁵That is what will happen to you.
I have appointed it for you,"
announces the LORD.
"You have forgotten me.
You have trusted in other gods.
²⁶So I will pull your skirt up over
your face.
Then people will see the shame
of your naked body.
²⁷They will see that you have not
been faithful to me.
You have committed adultery
with other gods.
And you have acted like a
prostitute
who does not have any shame.
I have seen what you did
on the hills and in the fields.
And I hate it.
How terrible it will be for you,
Jerusalem!
How long will you choose to be
'unclean'?"

WAR AND HUNGER

14 A message came to me
from the LORD. He told me
there wouldn't be any rain
in the land. He said,

²"Judah is filled with sadness.
Its cities are wasting away.
The people sob over the land.
Crying is heard in Jerusalem.
³The nobles send their servants to
get water.
They go to the wells.
But they do not find any water.
They return with empty jars.
They are terrified. They do not
have any hope.
They cover their heads.
⁴The ground is dry and cracked.
There isn't any rain in the land.
The farmers are terrified.
They cover their heads.
⁵Even the does in the fields
desert their newborn fawns.
There isn't any grass to eat.

⁶Wild donkeys stand on the bare
hilltops.
They long for water as wild dogs
do.
Their eyesight fails
because they do not have any
grass to eat."

⁷Our sins are a witness against us.
LORD, do something for the
honor of your name.
We have completely turned away
from you.
We've sinned against you.
⁸You are Israel's only hope.
You save us when we're in
trouble.
Why are you like a stranger to us?
Why are you like a traveler who
stays for only one night?
⁹Why are you like a man who is
taken by surprise?
Why are you like a soldier who
can't save anyone?
LORD, you are among us.
And we are your people.
Please don't desert us!

¹⁰The LORD has given me a message
about these people. He says,

"They really love to wander away
from me.
Their feet go down the wrong
path.
I do not accept these people.
I will remember the evil things
they have done.
I will punish them for their sins."

¹¹The LORD continued, "Do not pray
that things will go well with them.
¹²Even if they go without food, I will
not listen to their cry for help. They
might sacrifice burnt offerings and
grain offerings. But I will not accept
them. Instead, I will destroy them with
war, hunger and plague."
¹³But I said, "LORD and King, the
prophets keep telling them something
else. They say, 'You won't have to suffer
from war or hunger. Instead, the LORD
will give you peace and rest in this
place.' "
¹⁴Then the LORD said to me, "The
prophets are prophesying lies in my
name. I have not sent them or appointed them. I have not even spoken
to them. Everything they tell you about

their visions or secret knowledge is a lie. They pretend to bring you messages from other gods. They try to get you to believe their own mistaken ideas.

[15] "So here is what I am saying about the prophets who are prophesying in my name. I did not send them. But they are saying, 'No war or hunger will come to this land.' Those same prophets will die because of war and hunger. [16] And the people they are prophesying to will be thrown out into the streets of Jerusalem. They will die because of hunger and war. No one will bury their bodies. No one will bury their wives or children. I will pour trouble out on them. That is exactly what they should get.

[17] "Jeremiah, give them this message. Tell them,

" 'Let tears flow from my eyes.
  Let them pour out night and day.
  Never let them stop.
The people of my own nation
  have suffered a terrible wound.
  They have been crushed.
[18] Suppose I go into the country.
  Then I see people who have been
    killed with swords.
  Or suppose I go into the city.
  Then I see people who have died
    of hunger.
Prophet and priest alike have gone
    to a land
  they hadn't had anything to do
    with before.' "

[19] LORD, have you turned your back
    on Judah completely?
  Do you hate the city of Zion?
Why have you made us suffer?
  We can't be healed.
We hoped peace would come.
  But nothing good has happened
    to us.
We hoped we would finally be
    healed.
  But all we got was terror.
[20] LORD, we admit we've done evil
    things.
  We also admit that our people of
    long ago were guilty.
  It's true that we've sinned against
    you.
[21] For the honor of your name, don't
    turn your back on us.

Don't bring shame on your
    glorious throne in the
    temple.
Remember the covenant you
    made with us.
  Please don't break it.
[22] Do any of the worthless gods of
    the nations bring rain?
  Do the skies send down showers
    all by themselves?
No. LORD our God, you send the
    rain.
  So we put our hope in you.
  You are the one who does all of
    those things.

15 Then the LORD said to me, "Suppose Moses and Samuel were standing in front of me. Even then my heart would not feel sorry for these people. Send them away from me! Let them go! [2] "Suppose they ask you, 'Where should we go?'

"Then tell them, 'The LORD says,

" ' "Those I have appointed to die
    will die.
Those I have appointed to be
    killed with swords
  will be killed with swords.
Those I have appointed to die of
    hunger
  will die of hunger.
Those I have appointed to be
    taken away as prisoners
  will be taken away." ' "

[3] "I will send four kinds of destroyers against them," announces the LORD. "Swords will kill them. Dogs will drag them away. Birds of the air will eat them up. And wild animals will destroy them. [4] "I will make all of the kingdoms on earth hate them. That will happen because of what Manasseh did in Jerusalem. He was king of Judah and the son of Hezekiah.

[5] "Jerusalem, who will have pity on
    you?
  Who will sob over you?
  Who will stop to ask how you are
    doing?
[6] You have said no to me,"
    announces the LORD.
  "You keep on turning away from
    me.

So I will destroy you with my own
hands.
  I can't show you my tender love
anymore.
⁷I will stand at the city gates of the
land.
  I will separate the straw from the
grain.
I will destroy my people. I will
bring great sorrow on them.
  They have not changed their
ways.
⁸I will increase the number of their
widows.
  They will be more than the
grains of sand on the
seashore.
At noon I will bring a destroyer
against the mothers of the young
men among my people.
All at once I will bring down on
them
great suffering and terror.
⁹Mothers who have many children
will grow weak.
  They will take their last breath.
The sun will set on them while it is
still day.
  They will be dishonored and put
to shame.
All those who are left alive I will
kill with swords.
  I will have their enemies do it,"
           announces the LORD.

¹⁰My mother, I wish I had never
been born!
  The whole land opposes me.
  They fight against me.
I haven't made loans to anyone.
And I haven't borrowed anything.
But everyone still calls down
curses on me.

¹¹The LORD said,

"Jeremiah, I will keep you safe for
a good purpose.
  I will make your enemies ask you
to pray for them.
They will make their appeal to you
when they are in great trouble.

¹²"People of Judah, the armies of
Babylonia
will come from the north.
  They are as strong as iron and
bronze.
  Can anyone break their power?

¹³I will give away your wealth and
your treasures.
  Your enemies will carry off
everything.
  And they will not pay anything
for it.
That will happen because you
have sinned so much.
  You have done it all through your
country.
¹⁴I will make you slaves to your
enemies.
  You will serve them in a land
you have not had anything to do
with before.
  My anger will start a fire
that will burn you up."

¹⁵LORD, you understand how much
I'm suffering.
  Show concern for me. Take care
of me.
  Pay back those who are trying to
harm me.
You are patient. Don't take my life
away from me.
  Think about how much shame I
suffer because of you.
¹⁶When I received your words, I ate
them.
  They filled me with joy.
  My heart took delight in them.
LORD God who rules over all,
  I belong to you.
¹⁷I never sat around with those who
go to wild parties.
  I never had a good time with
them.
I sat alone because you had put
your powerful hand on me.
  Your anger against sin was
burning inside me.
¹⁸Why does my pain never end?
  Why is my wound so deep?
  Why can't I ever get well?
To me you are like a stream that
runs dry.
  You are like a spring that doesn't
have any water.

¹⁹So the LORD says,

"Turn away from your sins. Then I
will heal you.
  And then you will be able to
serve me.
Speak words that are worthy, not
worthless.

Then you will be speaking
    for me.
Let these people turn to you.
    But you must not turn to them.
²⁰ I will make you like a wall to them.
I will make you like a strong
    bronze wall.
The people will fight against you.
    But they will not overcome you.
I am with you.
I will save you,"
              announces the LORD.
²¹ "I will save you from the hands of
    evil people.
I will set you free from those who
    treat you badly."

TIMES OF TROUBLE ARE COMING

16 A message came to me from the LORD. He said, ²"You must not get married. You must not have any sons or daughters in this land."

³Here is the LORD's message about the children who are born in this place. He says about them and their parents, ⁴"Some of them will die of deadly sicknesses. No one will sob over them. Their bodies will not be buried. Instead, they will be like trash lying there on the ground. Others will die because of war and hunger. Their bodies will not be buried. Instead, they will become food for the birds of the air and the wild animals."

⁵The LORD says, "Jeremiah, do not enter a house where a meal is being served because someone has died. Do not go there to sob or to comfort the family. I will not bless these people anymore. I have taken my love and pity away from them," announces the LORD.

⁶"Important and ordinary people alike will die in this land. Their bodies will not be buried. No one will sob over them. No one will cut himself or shave his head because of them. ⁷No one will offer food or drink to comfort those who sob over the dead. No one will do it even if someone's father or mother has died.

⁸"Do not enter a house where a big dinner party is being held. Do not sit down there to eat and drink. ⁹I am the LORD who rules over all. I am the God of Israel. I am telling you, 'In your days I will judge your people. You will see it with your own eyes. I will put an end to the sounds of joy and gladness here in Jerusalem. The voices of brides and grooms will not be heard anymore.'

¹⁰"Tell these people all of those things. They will ask you, 'Why has the LORD decided to send so much trouble on us? We haven't done anything wrong. We haven't committed any sins against the LORD our God.' ¹¹"When they say that, tell them, 'I did it because your people of long ago deserted me,' announces the LORD. 'They followed other gods. They served them and worshiped them. They deserted me. They did not obey my law. ¹²'But you have done more evil things than they did. All of you are doing what your stubborn and evil hearts want you to do. You are not obeying me. ¹³'So I will throw you out of this land. I will send you away to a land that you and your people have not had anything to do with before. There you will serve other gods day and night. And I will not show you any favor.'

¹⁴"But a new day is coming," announces the LORD. "At that time people will no longer say, 'The LORD brought the people of Israel up out of Egypt. And that's just as sure as he is alive.' ¹⁵"Instead, they will say, 'The LORD brought the people of Israel up out of the land of the north. He gathered them out of all of the countries where he had forced them to go. And that's just as sure as he is alive.' I will bring them back to the land I gave their people long ago.

¹⁶"But now I will send for many fishermen," announces the LORD. "They will catch some of these people. After that, I will send for many hunters. They will hunt the others down on every mountain and hill. They will bring them out of the cracks in the rocks. ¹⁷My eyes see everything these people do. What they do is not hidden from me. I always see their sin. ¹⁸I will pay them back double for their sin and the evil things they have done. They have made my land 'unclean.' They have set

up lifeless statues of their evil gods.
They have filled my land with them. I
hate those gods."

¹⁹LORD, you give me strength.
   You are like a fort to me.
When I'm in trouble,
   I go to you for safety.
The nations will come to you
   from one end of the earth to the
      other.
They will gather together and
   say,
"Our people of long ago didn't own
   anything
except statues of gods.
The statues were worthless.
   They didn't do them any good.
²⁰Do men really make their own
   gods?
Yes. But they aren't really gods at
   all!"

²¹The LORD says, "So I will teach
   them about myself.
This time I will show them
   how powerful and mighty I am.
Then they will know
   that I am the LORD.

17

"Judah's sin is carved
   with an iron tool.
   It is written with a sharp
      stone.
It is carved on the tablets of their
   hearts.
It is written on the horns that
   stick out
from the corners of their altars.
²Even their children offer sacrifices
   to other gods on those altars.
They use the poles that were made
   to worship the goddess Asherah.
They worship strange gods beside
   the green trees
   and on the high hills.
³I will give away my holy Mount
   Zion to the Babylonians.
Your enemies will carry off your
   wealth
   and all of your treasures.
I will give away your high places.
That will happen because you
   have sinned.
You have done it all through your
   country.
⁴You will lose the land I gave you.
   And it will be your own fault.

I will make you slaves to your
   enemies.
You will serve them in a land you
   have not had anything to do
   with before.
You have set my anger on fire.
   It will burn forever."

⁵The LORD says,

"Those who trust in man are
   under my curse.
They depend on human
   strength.
   Their hearts turn away from me.
⁶They will be like a bush in a dry
   and empty land.
They will not enjoy success when
   it comes.
They will live in dry places in the
   desert.
It is a land of salt where no one
   else lives.

⁷"But I will bless any man who
   trusts in me.
I will show my favor to the one
   who depends on me.
⁸He will be like a tree that is
   planted near water.
It sends out its roots beside a
   stream.
It is not afraid when heat
   comes.
   Its leaves are always green.
It does not worry when there is no
   rain.
   It always bears fruit."

⁹A human heart is more dishonest
   than anything else.
It can't be healed.
   Who can understand it?

¹⁰The LORD says, "I look deep down
   inside human hearts.
I see what is in people's minds.
I reward a man in keeping with his
   conduct.
I bless him based on what he has
   done."

¹¹Some people get rich in the wrong
   way.
They are like a partridge that
   hatches eggs it didn't lay.
When their lives are half over, their
   riches will desert them.
In the end they will prove how
   foolish they have been.

¹²Our temple is where the LORD's
glorious throne is.
From the beginning it has been
high and lifted up.
¹³LORD, you are Israel's only hope.
Everyone who deserts you will be
put to shame.
The names of those who turn
away from you will be listed
among the dead.
LORD, they have deserted you.
You are the spring of water that
gives life.

¹⁴LORD, heal me. Then I will be
healed.
Save me from my enemies. Then
I will be saved.
You are the one I praise.
¹⁵They keep saying to me,
"What has happened to the
message the LORD gave you?
Let it come true right now!"
¹⁶I haven't run away from being the
shepherd of your people.
You know I haven't wanted the
day of Jerusalem's fall to
come.
You are aware of every word that
comes from my lips.
¹⁷Don't be a terror to me.
When I'm in trouble, I go to you
for safety.
¹⁸Let those who attack me be put to
shame.
But keep me from shame.
Let them be terrified.
But keep me from terror.
Bring the day of trouble on them.
Destroy them once and for all.

KEEP THE SABBATH DAY HOLY

¹⁹The LORD said to me, "Go. Stand at
the city gate where the people gather
together. That is where the kings of Judah go in and out. Also go to all of the
other gates of Jerusalem. ²⁰Say, 'Listen
to the LORD's message, you kings of Judah and all of you people of Judah and
Jerusalem. You always come through
these gates.
²¹" 'The LORD says, "Make sure you
do not carry a load on the Sabbath day.
Do not bring it through the gates of Jerusalem. ²²Do not bring a load out of
your houses on the Sabbath. Do not do
any work on that day. Instead, keep

the Sabbath day holy. Do as I commanded your people long ago. ²³But
they did not listen. They did not pay
any attention to me. They were stubborn. They would not listen or pay attention when I corrected them.
²⁴" ' "Be careful to obey me," announces the LORD. "Do not bring a
load through the gates of this city
on the Sabbath. Instead, keep the
Sabbath day holy. Do not do any work
on it.
²⁵" ' "Then kings who sit on David's
throne will come through the gates of
this city. They and their officials will
come riding in chariots and on horses.
The people of Judah and Jerusalem
will come along with them. And this
city will always have people living in it.
²⁶Some will come from the towns of
Judah. And some will come in from the
villages around Jerusalem. Others will
come from the territory of Benjamin.
And others will come in from the western hills. Still others will come from
the central hill country and the Negev
Desert. All of them will bring burnt offerings and sacrifices. They will come
bringing grain offerings, incense and
thank offerings. They will take all of
those offerings to my house.
²⁷" ' "But what if you do not obey
me? Suppose you do not keep the Sabbath day holy. And suppose you carry
a load through the gates of Jerusalem
on the Sabbath. Then I will start a fire
that can't be put out. It will begin at the
gates of Jerusalem. It will destroy its
mighty towers." ' "

THE LORD SENDS JEREMIAH
TO THE POTTER'S HOUSE

18 A message came to me
from the LORD. He said,
²"Go down to the potter's
house. I will give you my message
there."
³So I went down to the potter's
house. I saw him working at his wheel.
⁴His hands were shaping a pot out of
clay. But he saw that something was
wrong with it. So he formed it into another pot. He shaped it in the way that
seemed best to him.
⁵Then the LORD's message came to
me. He said, ⁶"People of Israel, I can do
with you just as this potter does," an-

nounces the LORD. "The clay is in the potter's hand. And you are in my hand, people of Israel.

⁷"Suppose at any time I announce that a nation or kingdom is going to be pulled up by the roots. And I tell it that it will be torn down and destroyed. ⁸But suppose the nation I warned turns away from its sins. Then I will not do what I said I would. I will not bring trouble on it as I had planned.

⁹"Suppose at another time I announce that a nation or kingdom is going to be built up and planted. ¹⁰But it does what is evil in my sight. It does not obey me. Then I will think again about the good things I had wanted to do for it.

¹¹"So speak to the people of Judah and Jerusalem. Tell them, 'The LORD says, "Look! I am making plans against you. I am going to bring trouble on you. So each one of you must turn from your evil ways. Change the way you live and act."'

¹²"But they will reply, 'It's no use. We will continue to do what we've already planned. All of us will do what our stubborn and evil hearts want us to do.'"

¹³So the LORD says,

"Ask the nations a question. Say to them,
    'Who has ever heard anything like this?
The people of Israel have done a very horrible thing.
¹⁴Does the snow ever disappear from Lebanon's rocky slopes?
Do its cool waters ever stop flowing from places far away?
¹⁵But my people have forgotten me. They burn incense to worthless gods.
Their gods made them trip and fall as they walked on the old paths.
They made them use side roads instead of roads that were built up.

KIDS' QUESTION

How come there are no Bible stories that take place in winter?

Events in the Bible took place at all times of the year. Many of them took place in winter. But Bible lands are too warm in the winter for snow. That is why you do not hear much about it. There is some snow on some of the northern mountains of Israel. But mostly it rains in the winter. In fact, the winter is called the rainy season in that part of the world.

checkout
Jeremiah 18:14

Related verses:
Psalm 51:7;
Isaiah 55:10

¹⁶So their land will be completely
destroyed.
People will make fun of it again
and again.
All those who pass by it will be
shocked.
They will shake their heads.
¹⁷I will sweep over my people like a
wind from the east.
I will use the Babylonians to
scatter them.
I will show them my back and not
my face.
I will desert them when their day
of trouble comes.' "

¹⁸They said, "Come on. Let's make
plans against Jeremiah. We'll still have
priests to teach us the law. We'll always
have wise people to give us advice.
We'll have prophets to bring us messages from the LORD. So come on.
Let's speak out against Jeremiah. We
shouldn't pay any attention to what
he says."

¹⁹LORD, please listen to me!
Hear what my enemies are
saying about me!
²⁰Should the good things I've done
be paid back with evil?
But my enemies have dug a pit
for me.
Remember that I stood in front of
you
and spoke up for them.
I tried to turn your anger away
from them.
²¹So let their children die of hunger.
Let my enemies be killed in war.
Let their wives lose their children
and husbands.
Let their men be put to death.
Let their young men be killed in
battle.
²²Bring their enemies against them
without warning.
Let cries be heard from their
houses.
They have dug a pit to capture me.
They have hidden traps for my
feet.
²³But LORD, you know
all about their plans to kill me.
Don't forgive their crimes.
Don't erase their sins from your
sight.
Destroy my enemies.

Punish them when the time to
show your anger comes.

19 The LORD said to me, "Go
and buy a clay jar from a
potter. Take along some of
the elders of the people. Also tell some
of the priests to go with you. ²Go out to
the Valley of Ben Hinnom. Stand near
the entrance of the gate where broken
pieces of pottery are thrown away.
"There announce the message I give
you. ³Tell the people, 'Listen to the
LORD's message, you kings of Judah
and people of Jerusalem. The LORD
who rules over all is the God of Israel.
He says, "Listen! I am going to bring
trouble on Jerusalem. It will be so horrible that it will make the ears of everyone who hears about it ring.
⁴" ' "My people have deserted me.
They have made this city a place
where other gods are worshiped. They
have burned sacrifices to them here.
They and their people and the kings of
Judah had never had anything to do
with those gods before. My people
have also filled this place with the
blood of those who are not guilty of
anything. ⁵They have built the high
places where they worship Baal. There
they sacrifice their children in the fire
as offerings to Baal. That is something
I did not command or talk about. It did
not even enter my mind.
⁶" ' "So watch out!" announces the
LORD. "The days are coming when
people will not call this place Topheth
anymore. And they will not call it the
Valley of Ben Hinnom either. Instead,
they will call it the Valley of Death.
⁷" ' "In this place I will make the
plans of Judah and Jerusalem as useless as a broken jar. I will use their enemies to kill my people with swords.
They will die at the hands of those who
want to take their lives. I will give their
dead bodies as food to the birds of the
air and the wild animals.
⁸" ' "I will destroy this city completely. People will make fun of it. All
those who pass by it will be shocked.
They will laugh at its people because
of all of their wounds. ⁹I will make the
people of this city eat the dead bodies
of their sons and daughters. And they
will eat one another. They will do it

because things will be so bad during the attack. The enemies who want to take their lives will bring all of that trouble on them." '

¹⁰"Jeremiah, break the jar while those who go with you are watching. ¹¹Tell them, 'The LORD who rules over all says, "This potter's jar is smashed and can't be repaired. And I will smash this nation and this city. People will bury their dead in Topheth. But they will run out of room. ¹²Here is what I will do to Jerusalem and those who live here," announces the LORD. "I will make this city like Topheth. ¹³The houses in Jerusalem will be made 'unclean' like Topheth. So will the houses of the kings of Judah. All of those people burned incense on their roofs to all of the stars. They poured out drink offerings to other gods." ' "

¹⁴Then I returned from Topheth. That's where the LORD had sent me to prophesy. I stood in the courtyard of the LORD's temple. I spoke to all of the people. I said, ¹⁵"The LORD who rules over all is the God of Israel. He says, 'Listen! I am going to punish this city and the villages that are around it. I am going to bring against them all of the trouble I have announced. That is because my people were stubborn. They would not listen to what I said.' "

JEREMIAH AND PASHHUR

20 The priest Pashhur was chief officer in the LORD's temple. He was the son of Immer. Pashhur heard me prophesying that Jerusalem would be destroyed. ²So he had me beaten. Then he put me in prison at the Upper Gate of Benjamin at the LORD's temple.

³The next day Pashhur set me free. I said to him, "The LORD's name for you isn't Pashhur. It's Magor-Missabib. That name means Terror on Every Side.

⁴"The LORD says to you, 'I will make you a terror to yourself. You will also be a terror to all of your friends. With your own eyes you will see them die. Their enemies will kill them with swords. I will hand all of the people of Judah over to the king of Babylonia. He will carry them away to Babylonia or kill them with swords.

⁵" 'I will hand all of the wealth of this city over to Judah's enemies. I will give them all of its products and everything of value. I will turn over to them all of the treasures that belonged to the kings of Judah. They will take those things and carry them off to Babylon.

⁶" 'Pashhur, you and everyone who lives in your house will also be forced to go there. You have prophesied lies to all of your friends. So all of you will die in Babylonia. And that's where your bodies will be buried.' "

JEREMIAH ARGUES WITH THE LORD

⁷LORD, you tricked me, and I was
   tricked.
   You overpowered me and won.
People make fun of me all day
   long.
   Everyone laughs at me.

⁸Every time I speak, I cry out.
   All you ever tell me to talk
      about
   is fighting and trouble.
Your message has brought me
   nothing but dishonor.
   It has made me suffer shame all
      day long.
⁹Sometimes I think, "I won't talk
      about him anymore.
   I'll never speak in his name
      again."
But then your message burns in
   my heart.
   It's like a fire inside my very
      bones.
I'm tired of holding it in.
   In fact, I can't.
¹⁰I hear many people whispering,
   "There is terror on every side!
   Report Jeremiah! Let's report him
      to the authorities!"
All of my friends
   are waiting for me to slip.
They are saying, "Perhaps he will
      be tricked
   into making a mistake.
Then we'll win out over him.
   We'll get even with him."

¹¹But you are with me like a mighty
      warrior.
   So those who are trying to harm
      me will trip and fall.
   They won't win out over me.

They will fail. They'll be totally put
    to shame.
Their dishonor will never be
    forgotten.

¹²LORD, you rule over all.
    You test those who do what is
      right.
You see what is in people's hearts
    and minds.
So pay them back for what they've
    done.
I've committed my cause to you.

¹³Sing to the LORD, you people!
    Give praise to him!
He saves the lives of those who are
    in need.
He saves them from the powerful
    hands of sinful people.

¹⁴May the day I was born be under a
    curse!
May the day I was born to my
    mother not be blessed!
¹⁵May the man who brought my
    father the news be under a
    curse!
He's the one who made my father
    very glad.
He said, "You have had a baby!
    It's a boy!"
¹⁶May that man be like the towns
    the LORD destroyed without
    pity.
May that man hear loud sobs in
    the morning.
May he hear a battle cry
    at noon.
¹⁷He should have killed me in my
    mother's body.
He should have made my mother
    my grave.
He should have let her body stay
    large forever.
¹⁸Why did I ever come out of my
    mother's body?
I've seen nothing but trouble and
    sorrow.
My days will end in shame.

THE LORD REFUSES ZEDEKIAH'S APPEAL

21 A message came to me
from the LORD. It came
when King Zedekiah sent
Pashhur to me. Pashhur was the son of
Malkijah. Zedekiah sent the priest
Zephaniah along with him. Zephaniah
was the son of Maaseiah. They said to
me, ²"Ask the LORD to help us. Nebuchadnezzar is attacking us. He is king
of Babylonia. In the past the LORD did
wonderful things for us. Maybe he'll
do them again. Then Nebuchadnezzar
will pull his armies back from us."

³But I answered them, "Tell Zedeki-
ah and his people, ⁴'The LORD is the
God of Israel. He says, "The king of
Babylonia and his armies are all
around this city. They are getting ready
to attack you. You have weapons of
war in your hands to fight against
them. But I am about to turn your
weapons against you. And I will bring
your enemies inside this city.

⁵" ' "I myself will fight against you. I
will reach out my powerful hand and
mighty arm. I will come against you
with all of my burning anger. ⁶I will
strike down those who live in this city.
I will kill people and animals alike.
They will die of a terrible plague.

⁷" ' "After that, I will hand you over
to your enemies who want to kill you,"
announces the LORD. "I will hand over
Zedekiah, the king of Judah. I will
hand over his officials and the people
in this city who live through the
plague, war and hunger. All of them
will be turned over to Nebuchadnezzar, the king of Babylonia. He will kill
them with swords. He will not show
them any kindness. He will not feel
sorry for them. In fact, he will not have
any concern for them at all." ' '

⁸"Tell the people, 'The LORD says, "I
am offering you a choice. You can
choose the way that leads to life. Or
you can choose the way that leads to
death. ⁹Those who stay in this city will
die of war, hunger or plague. But those
who go out and give themselves up to
the Babylonians who are attacking you
will live. They will escape with their
lives.

¹⁰" ' "I have decided to do this city
harm and not good," announces the
LORD. "It will be handed over to the
king of Babylonia. And he will destroy
it with fire." '

¹¹"Also speak to Judah's royal family.
Tell them, 'Listen to the LORD's message. ¹²The LORD says to you who belong to David's royal house,

" ' "Every morning do what is right
   and fair.
Save those who have been
   robbed.
Set them free from the people
   who have treated them badly.
If you do not, my anger will blaze
   out against you.
It will burn like fire because of
   the evil things you have done.
No one will be able to put it out.
¹³Jerusalem, I am against you,"
            announces the LORD.
"You live above this valley.
You are on a high, rocky
   flatland.
And you say, 'Who can come
   against us?
Who can enter our place of
   safety?'
¹⁴But I will punish you in keeping
   with what you have done,"
            announces the LORD.
"I will start a fire in your forests.
It will burn up everything around
   you." ' "

THE LORD JUDGES EVIL KINGS

22 The LORD said to me, "Jeremiah, go down to the pal-
ace of the king of Judah.
Announce my message there. Tell him,
²'King of Judah, listen to the LORD's
message. You are sitting on David's
throne. You and your officials and your
people come through these gates.
³The LORD says, "Do what is fair and
right. Save those who have been
robbed. Set them free from the people
who have treated them badly. Do not
do anything wrong to outsiders or
widows in this place. Do not harm
children whose fathers have died. Do
not kill those who are not guilty of doing anything wrong.
⁴" ' "Be careful to obey those com-
mands. Then kings who sit on David's
throne will come through the gates of
this palace. They will come riding in
chariots and on horses. Their officials
and their people will come along with
them.
⁵" ' "But suppose you do not obey
those commands," announces the
LORD. "Then I promise you that this
palace will be destroyed. I make that

promise by taking an oath in my own
name." ' "
⁶The LORD speaks about the palace
of the king of Judah. He says,

"You are like the land of Gilead to
   me.
You are like the highest
   mountain in Lebanon.
But I will make you like a desert.
You will become like towns that
   no one lives in.
⁷I will send destroyers against you.
All of them will come with their
   weapons.
They will cut up your fine cedar
   beams.
They will throw them into the
   fire.

⁸"People from many nations will
pass by this city. They will ask one another, 'Why has the LORD done such a
thing to this great city?'
⁹"And the answer will be, 'Because
its people have turned away from the
covenant the LORD their God made
with them. They have worshiped other
gods. And they have served them.' "

¹⁰Don't sob over dead King Josiah.
   Don't be sad because he's gone.
Instead, sob bitterly over King
   Jehoahaz.
He was forced to leave his
   country.
He will never return.
He'll never see his own land
   again.

¹¹Jehoahaz became king of Judah after
his father Josiah. But he has gone away
from this place. That's because the
LORD says about him, "He will never
return. ¹²He will die in Egypt. That is
where he was taken as a prisoner. He
will not see this land again."

¹³The LORD says, "How terrible it will
   be for King Jehoiakim!
He builds his palace
by mistreating his people.
He builds its upstairs rooms
   with money that was gained by
   sinning.
He makes his own people work for
   nothing.
He does not pay them for what
   they do.

¹⁴He says, 'I will build myself a great
palace.
It will have large rooms upstairs.'
So he makes big windows in it.
He covers its walls with cedar
boards.
He decorates it with red paint.

¹⁵"Jehoiakim, does having more and
more cedar boards
make you a king?
Your father Josiah had enough to
eat and drink.
He did what was right and fair.
So everything went well with
him.
¹⁶He stood up for those who were
poor or needy.
So everything went well with
him.
That is what it means to know
me,"
announces the LORD.
¹⁷"Jehoiakim, the only thing on your
mind
is to get rich by cheating others.
You would even kill people who
are not guilty
of doing anything wrong.
You would mistreat them.
You would take everything they
own."

¹⁸So the LORD speaks about King Jehoiakim, the son of Josiah. He says,

"His people will not sob over him.
They will not say,
'My poor brother! My poor
sister!'
They will not sob over him.
They will not say,
'My poor master! How sad that
his glory is gone!'
¹⁹In fact, he will be buried like a
donkey.
His body will be dragged away
and thrown
outside the gates of Jerusalem."

²⁰The LORD says, "People of
Jerusalem, go up to Lebanon.
Cry out for help.
Let your voice be heard in the
land of Bashan.
Cry out from the mountains of
Abarim.
All those who were going to help
you are crushed.

²¹When you felt secure, I warned you.
But you said, 'I won't listen!'
You have acted like that ever since
you were young.
You have not obeyed me.
²²The wind will drive all of your
shepherds away.
All those who were going to help
you will be carried off as
prisoners.
Then you will be dishonored and
put to shame.
That will happen because you
have been so sinful.
²³Some of you live in Jerusalem in
the Palace of the Forest of
Lebanon.
You are comfortable in your
cedar buildings.
But you will groan when pain
comes on you.
It will be like the pain of a
woman having a baby.

²⁴"King Jehoiachin, you are the son
of Jehoiakim," announces the LORD.
"Suppose you were a ring on my right
hand. And suppose the ring even had
my royal seal on it. Then I would still
pull you off my finger. And that is just
as sure as I am alive.
²⁵"I will hand you over to those who
are trying to kill you. I will turn you
over to people you are afraid of. I will
give you to Nebuchadnezzar, the king
of Babylonia. I will hand you over to
his armies.
²⁶"I will throw you out into another
country. I will throw your mother out.
Neither of you was born in that country. But both of you will die there. ²⁷You
will never come back to the land you
long to return to."

²⁸This man Jehoiachin is like a
broken pot.
Everyone hates him. No one
wants him.
Why will he and his children be
thrown out of this land?
Why will they be sent to a land
they didn't have anything to do
with before?
²⁹Land, land, land,
listen to the LORD's message!
³⁰The LORD says,
"Let the record say that this man
did not have any children.

Let it report that he did not have
 any success in life.
None of his children will have
 success either.
None of them will sit on David's
 throne.
None of them will ever rule over
 Judah.

THE TRUE AND
RIGHTFUL BRANCH

23 "How terrible it will be for
 the shepherds who lead
 my people down the wrong
path!" announces the LORD. "They are
destroying and scattering the sheep
that belong to my flock."

²So the LORD, the God of Israel,
speaks to the shepherds who take care
of my people. He tells them, "You have
scattered my sheep. You have driven
them away. You have not taken good
care of them. So I will punish you for
the evil things you have done," announces the LORD.

³"I myself will gather together those
who are left alive in my flock. I will
gather them out of all of the countries
where I have driven them. And I will
bring them back to their own land.
There my sheep will have many lambs.
Their numbers will increase.

⁴"I will place shepherds over them
who will take good care of them. My
sheep will not be afraid or terrified
anymore. And none of them will be
missing," announces the LORD.

⁵"A new day is coming," announces
 the LORD.
"At that time I will raise up from
 David's royal line
a true and rightful Branch.
He will be a King who will rule
 wisely.
He will do what is fair and right
 in the land.
⁶In his days Judah will be saved.
Israel will live in safety.
And the Branch will be called
 The LORD Who Makes Us Right
 With Himself.

⁷"Other days are also coming," announces the LORD. "At that time people
will no longer say, 'The LORD brought
the people of Israel up out of Egypt.
And that's just as sure as he is alive.'

⁸"Instead, they will say, 'The LORD
brought the people of Israel up out of
the land of the north. He gathered
them out of all of the countries where
he had forced them to go. And that's
just as sure as he is alive.' Then they
will live in their own land."

PROPHETS WHO TELL LIES

⁹Here is my message about the
prophets.

My heart is broken inside me.
 All of my bones tremble with
 fear.
I am like a man who is drunk.
 I am like someone who has had
 too much wine.
That's what the LORD's holy words
 have done to me.
¹⁰The land is full of people
 who aren't faithful to the LORD.
Now the land is under his curse.
 And that's why it is thirsty for
 water.
 That's why the grasslands in the
 desert are dry.
The prophets are leading sinful
 lives.
 They don't use their power in the
 right way.

¹¹"Prophets and priests alike are
 ungodly,"
 announces the LORD.
"Even in my temple I find them
 sinning.
¹²So their path will become
 slippery.
They will be thrown out into
 darkness.
There they will fall.
I will bring trouble on them
 when the time to punish them
 comes,"
 announces the LORD.

¹³"Among the prophets of Samaria
 I saw something I can't stand.
They were prophesying in the
 name of Baal.
They were leading my people
 Israel down the wrong path.
¹⁴I have also seen something
 horrible among Jerusalem's
 prophets.
They are not faithful to me.
They are not living by the truth.

They strengthen the hands of
  those who do evil.
So the people do not turn from
  their sinful ways.
All of them are like the people of
  Sodom to me.
They are just like the people of
  Gomorrah."

¹⁵So the LORD who rules over all
speaks about the prophets. He says,

"I will make them eat bitter
  food.
I will make them drink poisoned
  water.
The prophets of Jerusalem have
  spread
  their ungodly ways all through
  the land."

¹⁶The LORD who rules over all says to
the people of Judah,

"Do not listen to what the
  prophets are saying to you.
They fill you with false hopes.
They talk about visions that come
  from their own minds.
What they say does not come
  from my mouth.
¹⁷They keep speaking to those who
  hate me. They say,
'The LORD says you will have
  peace.'
They speak to all those who do
  what their stubborn hearts want
  them to do.
They tell them, 'No harm will
  come to you.'
¹⁸But which of them has ever stood
  in my courts?
Have they been there to see a
  vision or hear my message?
Who has listened and heard my
  message there?
¹⁹A storm will burst out
  because of my burning anger.
A windstorm will sweep down
  on the heads of sinful people.
²⁰My anger will not turn back.
I will accomplish everything
  I plan to do.
In days to come
  you will understand it clearly.
²¹I did not send those prophets.
But they have run to tell you
  their message anyway.
I did not speak to them.

But they have still prophesied.
²²Suppose they had stood in my
  courts.
Then they would have
  announced my message to my
  people.
They would have turned my
  people from their evil ways.
They would have turned them
  away from their sins.

²³"Am I only a God who is nearby?"
                    announces the LORD.
"Am I not a God who is also far
  away?
²⁴Can anyone hide in secret places
  so that I can't see him?"
                    announces the LORD.
"Don't I fill heaven and earth?"
                    announces the LORD.

²⁵"I have heard what the prophets
are saying. They prophesy lies in my
name. They say, 'I had a dream! The
LORD has given me a dream!' ²⁶How
long will that continue in the hearts of
those prophets who tell lies? They try
to get others to believe their own mistaken ideas. ²⁷They tell one another
their dreams. They think that will
make my people forget my name. In
the same way, their people of long ago
forgot my name when they worshiped
Baal.
²⁸"Let the prophet who has a dream
tell his dream. But let the one who
has my message speak it faithfully.
Your prophets have given you straw to
eat instead of grain," announces the
LORD.
²⁹"My message is like fire," announces the LORD. "It is like a hammer
that breaks a rock in pieces.
³⁰"So I am against those prophets,"
announces the LORD. "I am against
those who steal messages from one
another. They claim that the messages
come from me.
³¹"Yes," announces the LORD. "I am
against the prophets who wag their
own tongues but still say, 'Here is what
the LORD says.' ³²I am against prophets
who talk about dreams that did not
come from me," announces the LORD.
"They tell foolish lies. Their lies lead
my people down the wrong path.
"But I did not send those prophets. I
did not appoint them. They do not

help my people in the least," announces the LORD.

PROPHETS WHO GIVE MESSAGES THAT ARE NOT FROM THE LORD

³³"Jeremiah, those people might ask you a question. Or a prophet or priest might do it. They might ask, 'What message have you received from the LORD?'

"Then tell them, 'You ask, "What message?" Here it is. "I will desert you," announces the LORD.'

³⁴"A prophet or priest might make a claim. Or someone else might do it. He might claim, 'I have received a message from the LORD.' Then I will punish him and his family.

³⁵"Here is what each of you people keeps on saying to your friend or relative. You ask, 'What is the LORD's answer?' Or you ask, 'What has the LORD spoken?' ³⁶But you must not talk about 'a message from the LORD' again. That is because your message becomes your own message. And so you twist my words. I am the living God. I am the LORD who rules over all. And I am your God.

³⁷"Here is what you keep saying to a prophet. You ask, 'What is the LORD's answer to you?' Or you ask, 'What has the LORD spoken?' ³⁸You claim, 'I have received a message from the LORD.' But I really say, 'You used the words, "I have received a message from the LORD." But I told you that you must not claim, "I have received a message from the LORD." '

³⁹"So you can be sure I will forget you. I will throw you out of my sight. I will also destroy the city I gave you and your people. ⁴⁰I will bring shame on you that will last forever. It will never be forgotten."

JUDAH IS LIKE TWO BASKETS OF FIGS

24 King Jehoiachin was forced to leave Jerusalem. He was the son of Jehoiakim. Jehoiachin was taken to Babylon by Nebuchadnezzar, the king of Babylonia. The officials and all of the skilled workers were forced to leave with him.

After they left, the LORD showed me two baskets of figs. They were in front of his temple. ²One basket had very good figs in it. They were like figs that ripen early. The other basket had figs that weren't good at all. In fact,

How can God hear everyone's prayers at once?

God can hear everyone's prayers at once because he is everywhere and all-powerful. People are not like that. People can be in only one place at a time. And usually we cannot listen to more than one person at a time. But God is not like us. He is not limited. He can hear and understand everyone who is praying to him in many different languages all at once. He can also give each person his full attention all at the same time. It all seems amazing to us, but it is easy to God.

checkout
Jeremiah 23:23,24

Related verses:
Luke 1:13;
Acts 10:31

they were so bad they couldn't even be eaten.

³Then the LORD asked me, "What do you see, Jeremiah?"

"Figs," I answered. "The good ones are very good. But the others are so bad they can't be eaten."

⁴Then a message came to me from the LORD. He said, ⁵"I am the LORD, the God of Israel. I say, 'I consider the people who were forced to leave Judah to be like those good figs. I sent them away from this place. I forced them to go to Babylonia. ⁶My eyes will watch over them. I will be good to them. And I will bring them back to this land. I will build them up. I will not tear them down. I will plant them. I will not pull them up by the roots.

⁷" 'I will change their hearts. Then they will know that I am the LORD. They will be my people. And I will be their God. They will return to me with all their heart.

⁸" 'But there are also figs that are not very good. In fact, they are so bad they can't be eaten,' says the LORD. 'Zedekiah, the king of Judah, is like those bad figs. So are his officials and the people of Jerusalem who are still left alive. I will punish them whether they remain in this land or live in Egypt.

⁹" 'I will make all of the kingdoms on earth displeased with them. In fact, they will hate them a great deal. They will laugh and joke about them. They will call down curses on them. All of that will happen no matter where I force them to go. ¹⁰I will send war, hunger and plague against them. They will be destroyed from the land I gave them and their people of long ago.' "

SEVENTY YEARS IN BABYLONIA

25 A message about all of the people of Judah came to me from the LORD. It came in the fourth year that Jehoiakim was king of Judah. It was the first year that Nebuchadnezzar was king of Babylonia. Jehoiakim was the son of Josiah.

²I, the LORD's prophet, spoke to all of the people of Judah and Jerusalem. I said, ³"For 23 years the LORD's messages have been coming to me. They began to come in the 13th year that Josiah was king of Judah. He was the son of Amon. The LORD's messages still come to me today. I've spoken to you people again and again. But you haven't listened to me.

⁴"The LORD has sent all of his servants the prophets to you. They've come to you again and again. But you haven't listened. You haven't paid any attention to them.

⁵"They said, 'Each of you must turn from your evil ways and practices. Then you can stay in the land forever. It's the land the LORD gave you and your people long ago. ⁶Don't follow other gods. Don't serve them or worship them. Don't make the LORD angry with the gods your own hands have made. Then he won't harm you.'

⁷" 'But you did not listen to me,' announces the LORD. 'You have made me very angry with the gods your hands have made. And you have brought harm on yourselves.'

⁸"The LORD who rules over all says, 'You have not listened to my words. ⁹So I will send for all of the nations in the north. And I will send for my servant Nebuchadnezzar, the king of Babylonia,' announces the LORD.

" 'I will bring all of them against this land and against you who live here. They will march out against all of the nations that are around this land. I will set them apart in a special way to be destroyed. People will be shocked because of them. And they will make fun of them. Those nations will be destroyed forever.

¹⁰" 'I will put an end to the sounds of joy and gladness. I will put an end to the voices of brides and grooms. The sound of grinding millstones will not be heard anymore. And lamps will not be lit anymore. ¹¹This whole country will become dry and empty. And those nations will serve the king of Babylonia for 70 years.

¹²" 'But I will punish that king and his nation because they are guilty. I will do it when the 70 years are over,' announces the LORD. 'I will make that land a desert forever.

¹³" 'I have spoken against that land. And I will make all of those things happen to it. Everything will happen that is written in this scroll. And I will

make everything Jeremiah prophesied against all of the nations come true. [14]The people of Babylonia will become slaves of many other nations and great kings. I will pay them back for what their hands have done.' "

THE LORD JUDGES THE NATIONS

[15]The LORD is the God of Israel. He said to me, "Take this cup from my hand. It is filled with the wine of my burning anger. Make all of the nations to which I send you drink it. [16]When they drink it, they will not even be able to walk straight. It will drive them out of their minds. I am going to send war against them."

[17]So I took the cup from the LORD's hand. I made all of the nations to which he sent me drink from it. [18]He sent me to Judah's kings and officials. He told me to go to Jerusalem and the towns of Judah. He wanted me to tell them they would be destroyed. Then people would be shocked because of them. They would make fun of them. They would call down curses on them. And that's how things still are today.

[19]Here is a list of the other kings and nations he sent me to.

Pharaoh, the king of Egypt
his attendants, his officials, all
of his people
[20]all of the people from other
lands who lived there
all of the kings of Uz
the Philistine kings of Ashkelon, Gaza and Ekron
the Philistines who were still
living in Ashdod
[21]Edom, Moab, Ammon
[22]all of the kings of Tyre and Sidon
the kings of the islands and other lands along the Mediterranean Sea
[23]Dedan, Teman, Buz
all of the other places far away
in the east
[24]all of the kings of Arabia
all of the other kings of people
who live in the desert
[25]all of the kings of Zimri, Elam
and Media
[26]all of the kings in the north,
near and far

So he sent me to all of the kingdoms on the face of the earth, one after the other. After all of them drink from the cup of the LORD's anger, the king of Babylonia will drink from it too.

[27]The LORD says, "Tell them, 'The LORD who rules over all is the God of Israel. He says, "Drink from this cup. Get drunk and throw up. Fall down and do not get up again. I am going to send war against you." '

[28]"But they might refuse to take the cup from your hand. They might not want to drink from it. Then tell them, 'The LORD who rules over all says, "You have to drink from it! [29]I am beginning to bring trouble on the city where I have put my Name. You might think you will not be punished. But you will certainly be punished. I am sending war against everyone who lives on earth," announces the LORD who rules over all.'

[30]"Jeremiah, prophesy against them. Tell them,

" 'The LORD will roar from heaven
like a lion.
His voice will sound like thunder
from his holy temple there.
He will roar loudly against his
land.
He will shout like those who
stomp on grapes in
winepresses.
He will shout against everyone
who lives on earth.
[31]The noise of battle will be heard
from one end of the earth to the
other.
That's because the LORD will
bring charges against the
nations.
He will judge every human being.
He will kill sinful people with his
sword,' "
announces the LORD.

[32]The LORD who rules over all says,

"Look! Horrible trouble is
spreading
from one nation to another.
A mighty storm is rising.
It is coming from a place
that is very far away."

[33]At that time those the LORD kills will be lying around everywhere. They will

be found from one end of the earth to the other. No one will sob over them. Their dead bodies will not be gathered up or buried. Instead, they will be like trash lying there on the ground.

³⁴ Sob and cry, you shepherds.
   Roll in the dust, you leaders of
      the flock.
   Your time to be killed has come.
   You will fall and be broken to
      pieces like fine clay pots.
³⁵ The shepherds won't have any
      place to run to.
   The leaders of the flock won't be
      able to escape.
³⁶ Listen to the cries of the
      shepherds.
   Hear the sobs of the leaders of
      the flock.
   The LORD is destroying their
      grasslands.
³⁷ Their peaceful meadows will be
      completely destroyed
   because of the LORD's burning
      anger.
³⁸ Like a lion he will leave his den.
   The land of those leaders will
      become a desert.
   That's because the sword of the
      LORD brings great harm.
   His anger will burn against them.

JEREMIAH'S ENEMIES TRY TO HAVE HIM KILLED

26 A message came to me from the LORD. It was shortly after Jehoiakim became king of Judah. He was the son of Josiah. ²The LORD said, "Stand in the courtyard of my house. Speak to the people of the towns in Judah. Speak to all those who come to worship in my house. Tell them everything I command you. Do not leave out a single word. ³Perhaps they will listen. Maybe they will turn from their evil ways. Then I will not do what I said I would. I will not bring trouble on them. I had planned to punish them because of the evil things they had done.

⁴"Tell them, 'The LORD says, "Listen to me. Obey my law that I gave you. ⁵And listen to the words my servants the prophets are speaking. I have sent them to you again and again. But you have not listened to them. ⁶So I will make this house like Shiloh. All of the nations on earth will call down curses on this city." ' "

⁷I spoke those words in the LORD's house. The priests, the prophets and all of the people heard me. ⁸I finished telling all of the people everything the LORD had commanded me to say.

But as soon as I did, the priests, the prophets and all of the people grabbed hold of me. They said, "You must die! ⁹Why do you prophesy those things in the LORD's name? Why do you say that this house will become like Shiloh? Why do you say that this city will be empty and deserted?" And all of the people crowded around me in the LORD's house.

¹⁰The officials of Judah heard what had happened. So they went up from the royal palace to the LORD's house. There they took their places at the entrance of the New Gate. ¹¹Then the priests and prophets spoke to the officials and all of the people. They said, "This man should be sentenced to death. He has prophesied against this city. You have heard it with your own ears!"

¹²Then I spoke to all of the officials and people. I said, "The LORD sent me to prophesy against this house and this city. He told me to say everything you have heard. ¹³So change the way you live and act. Obey the LORD your God. Then he won't do what he said he would. He won't bring on you the trouble he said he would bring.

¹⁴"As for me, I'm in your hands. Do to me what you think is good and right. ¹⁵But you can be sure of one thing. If you put me to death, you will be held accountable for spilling my blood. And I haven't even done anything wrong. You will bring guilt on yourselves and this city and those who live in it. The LORD has sent me to you. He wanted me to say all of those things so you could hear them. And that's the truth."

¹⁶Then the officials and all of the people spoke to the priests and prophets. They said, "This man shouldn't be sentenced to death! He has spoken to us in the name of the LORD our God."

¹⁷Some of the elders of the land stepped forward. They spoke to the

whole community that was gathered there. They said, [18]"Micah from Moresheth prophesied. It was during the time Hezekiah was king over Judah. Micah spoke to all of the people of Judah. He told them, 'The LORD who rules over all says,

" ' "Zion will be plowed up like a
        field.
    Jerusalem will be turned into a
        pile of trash.
    The temple hill will be covered
        with bushes and weeds." '

(Micah 3:12)

[19]"Did King Hezekiah or anyone else in Judah put Micah to death? Hezekiah had respect for the LORD. He asked the LORD to show him his favor. And the LORD didn't judge Jerusalem as he said he would. He didn't bring on it the trouble he said he would bring. But we are about to bring horrible trouble on ourselves!"

[20]Uriah was another man who prophesied in the name of the LORD. He was from Kiriath Jearim. He was the son of Shemaiah. Uriah prophesied against this city and this land. He said the same things I did.

[21]King Jehoiakim and all of his officers and officials heard Uriah's words. So the king tried to have him put to death.

But Uriah heard about it. He was afraid. And he ran away to Egypt. [22]So King Jehoiakim sent Elnathan to Egypt. He also sent some other men along with him. Elnathan was the son of Acbor. [23]Those men brought Uriah out of Egypt. They took him to King Jehoiakim. Then the king had Uriah struck down with a sword. He had Uriah's body thrown into one of the graves of the ordinary people.

[24]In spite of that, Ahikam stood up for me. He was the son of Shaphan. Because of Ahikam, I wasn't handed over to the people to be put to death.

JUDAH WILL SERVE NEBUCHADNEZZAR

27 A message came to me from the LORD. It was shortly after Zedekiah became king of Judah. He was the son of Josiah. [2]The LORD said, "Make a yoke

out of ropes and wooden boards. Put it on your neck.

[3]"Then write down a message for the kings of Edom, Moab, Ammon, Tyre and Sidon. Give it to their messengers who have come to Jerusalem. They have come to see Zedekiah, the king of Judah. [4]Give them a message for the kings who sent them. It should say, 'The LORD who rules over all is the God of Israel. He says, "Here is what I want you to tell your masters. [5]I reached out my great and powerful arm. I made the earth. I made its people and animals. And I can give the earth to anyone I please.

[6]" ' "Now I will hand all of your countries over to my servant Nebuchadnezzar. He is king of Babylonia. I will put even the wild animals under his control. [7]All of the nations will serve him and his son and grandson. After that, I will judge his land. Then many nations and great kings will make him serve them.

[8]" ' "But suppose any nation or kingdom will not serve Nebuchadnezzar, the king of Babylonia. And suppose it refuses to put its neck under his yoke. Then I will punish that nation with war, hunger and plague," announces the LORD. "I will punish it until his powerful hand destroys it.

[9]" ' "So do not listen to your prophets. Do not listen to those who claim to have secret knowledge. Do not listen to those who try to explain your dreams. Do not listen to those who get messages from people who have died. Do not listen to those who practice evil magic. All of them will tell you, 'You won't serve the king of Babylonia.'

[10]" ' "But they prophesy lies to you. If you listen to them, you will be removed far away from your lands. I will drive you away from them. And you will die.

[11]" ' "But suppose any nation will put its neck under the yoke of the king of Babylonia. And suppose it serves him. Then I will let that nation remain in its own land. I will let its people plow the land and live there," ' " announces the LORD.

[12]I gave the same message to Zedekiah, the king of Judah. I said, "Put

your neck under the yoke of the king of Babylonia. Obey him. Serve his people. Then you will live. [13]Why should you and your people die? Why should you die of war, hunger and plague? That's what the LORD said would happen to any nation that won't serve the king of Babylonia.

[14]"Don't listen to the words of the prophets who say to you, 'You won't serve the king of Babylonia.' They are prophesying lies to you. [15]'I have not sent them,' announces the LORD. 'They are prophesying lies in my name. So I will drive you away from your land. And you will die. So will the prophets who prophesy to you.' "

[16]Then I spoke to the priests and all of those people. I said, "The LORD says, 'Do not listen to the prophets who say, "Very soon the articles from the LORD's house will be brought back from Babylon." They are prophesying lies to you. [17]Do not listen to them. Serve the king of Babylonia. Then you will live. Why should this city be destroyed?

[18]" 'If they are prophets and have received a message from me, let them pray to me. I am the LORD who rules over all. Those prophets should pray that what is still in Jerusalem will remain here. They should pray that the articles in my house and the king's palace will not be taken to Babylon.

[19]" 'I am the LORD who rules over all. Do you know what those articles are? They include the two pillars in front of the temple. They include the huge metal bowl. They include the bronze stands that can be moved around. And they include the other articles that are left in this city. [20]Nebuchadnezzar, the king of Babylonia, did not take those things away at first. That was when he took King Jehoiachin from Jerusalem to Babylon. He also took all of the nobles of Judah and Jerusalem along with him. Jehoiachin is the son of Jehoiakim.

[21]" 'I am the LORD who rules over all. I am the God of Israel. Here is what will happen to the things that are left in my house, the king's palace and Jerusalem. [22]They will be taken to Babylon. They will remain there until the day I come for them,' announces the LORD.

'Then I will bring them back. I will return them to this place.' "

HANANIAH OPPOSES JEREMIAH

28 The prophet Hananiah spoke to me in the LORD's house. It was shortly after Zedekiah became king of Judah. It was in the fifth month of his fourth year. Hananiah was from Gibeon. He was the son of Azzur. In front of the priests and all of the people Hananiah said to me, [2]"The LORD who rules over all is the God of Israel. He says, 'I will break the yoke of the king of Babylonia. [3]Nebuchadnezzar, the king of Babylonia, removed all of the articles that belong to my house. He took them to Babylon. Before two years are over, I will bring them back to this place.

[4]" 'I will also bring King Jehoiachin back. He is the son of Jehoiakim. And I will bring back all of the others who were taken from Judah to Babylon,' announces the LORD. 'I will break the yoke of the king of Babylonia.' "

[5]Then I, the prophet Jeremiah, replied to the prophet Hananiah. I spoke to him in front of the priests and all of the people. They were standing in the LORD's house. [6]I said, "Amen, Hananiah! May the LORD do those things! May he make the words you have prophesied come true. May he bring back from Babylon the articles that belong to the LORD's house. May he bring back to this place all of the people who were taken away.

[7]"But listen to what I have to say. I want you and all of the people to hear it. [8]There have been prophets long before you and I were ever born. They have prophesied against many countries and great kingdoms. They have spoken about war, trouble and plague. [9]But what if a prophet says peace will come? Only if it comes true will he be recognized as one who has been truly sent by the LORD."

[10]The prophet Hananiah took the yoke off my neck. Then he broke it. [11]In front of all of the people he said, "The LORD says, 'In the same way, I will break the yoke of Nebuchadnezzar, the king of Babylonia. Before two years are over, I will remove it from the

necks of all of the nations.' " When I heard that, I went on my way.

¹²A message came to me from the LORD. It was shortly after the prophet Hananiah had broken the yoke off my neck. The message said, ¹³"Go. Tell Hananiah, 'The LORD says, "You have broken a wooden yoke. But in its place you will get an iron yoke." ¹⁴The LORD who rules over all is the God of Israel. He says, "I will put an iron yoke on the necks of all of those nations. I will make them serve Nebuchadnezzar, the king of Babylonia. So they will serve him. I will even give him control over the wild animals." ' "

¹⁵Then I, the prophet Jeremiah, spoke to the prophet Hananiah. I said, "Listen, Hananiah! The LORD hasn't sent you. But you have tricked these people. Now they trust in lies. ¹⁶So the LORD says, 'I am about to remove you from the face of the earth. Before this year is over, you will die. You have taught the people to turn against me.' "

¹⁷In the seventh month of that very year, the prophet Hananiah died.

JEREMIAH'S LETTER TO THE JEWS IN BABYLONIA

29 I, the prophet Jeremiah, sent a letter from Jerusalem to Babylonia. It was for the Jewish elders who were still alive there. It was also for the priests and prophets in Babylonia. And it was for all of the other people Nebuchadnezzar had taken from Jerusalem to Babylon. ²It was sent to them after King Jehoiachin had been forced to leave Jerusalem. His mother and the court officials were taken with him. The leaders of Judah and Jerusalem and all of the skilled workers had also been forced to go to Babylon.

³I gave the letter to Elasah and Gemariah. Zedekiah, the king of Judah, had sent them to King Nebuchadnezzar in Babylon. Elasah was the son of Shaphan. Gemariah was the son of Hilkiah. Here is what the letter said.

⁴The LORD who rules over all is the God of Israel. He speaks to all those he forced to go from Jerusalem to Babylon. He says, ⁵"Build houses and settle down. Plant gardens and eat what they produce. ⁶Get married. Have sons and daughters. Find wives for your sons. Give your daughters to be married. Then they too can have sons and daughters. Increase your numbers there. Do not let the number of your people get smaller.

⁷"Also work for the success of the city I have sent you to. Pray to the LORD for that city. If it succeeds, you too will enjoy success."

⁸The LORD who rules over all is the God of Israel. He says, "Do not let the prophets trick you. Do not be fooled by those who claim to have secret knowledge. Do not listen to people who try to explain their dreams to you. ⁹All of them are prophesying lies to you in my name. I have not sent them," announces the LORD.

¹⁰The LORD says, "You will be forced to live in Babylonia for 70 years. After they are over, I will come to you. My gracious promise to you will come true. I will bring you back home.

¹¹"I know the plans I have for you," announces the LORD. "I want you to enjoy success. I do not plan to harm you. I will give you hope for the years to come. ¹²Then you will call out to me. You will come and pray to me. And I will listen to you. ¹³When you look for me with all your heart, you will find me.

¹⁴"I will be found by you," announces the LORD. "And I will bring you back from where you were taken as prisoners. I will gather you from all of the nations. I will gather you from the places where I have forced you to go," announces the LORD. "I will bring you back to the place from which I sent you away."

¹⁵You might say, "The LORD has given us prophets in Babylonia." ¹⁶But here is what the LORD says about the king who now sits on David's throne. He also says it about all of the people who remain in this city. And he says it about all those who did not go

with you to Babylon. ¹⁷The LORD who rules over all says, "I will send war, hunger and plague against them. I will make them like bad figs. They are so bad they can't be eaten. ¹⁸I will hunt them down with war, hunger and plague. I will make all of the kingdoms on earth displeased with them. They will call down curses on them. All of the nations where I drive them will be shocked at them. They will make fun of them. And they will bring shame on them.

¹⁹"That is because they have not listened to my words," announces the LORD. "I sent messages to them again and again. I sent them through my servants the prophets. And you who were taken to Babylon have not listened either," announces the LORD.

²⁰So listen to the LORD's message. Listen, all of you whom he has sent away from Jerusalem to Babylon. ²¹The LORD who rules over all is the God of Israel. He speaks about Ahab and Zedekiah. They are prophesying lies to you in my name. Ahab is the son of Kolaiah. Zedekiah is the son of Maaseiah. The LORD says about Ahab and Zedekiah, "I will hand them over to Nebuchadnezzar, the king of Babylonia. He will put them to death. You will see it with your own eyes.

²²"Because of what happens to them, people will use their names when they call down curses on someone. All those who have been taken from Judah to Babylon will use their names in that way. They will say, 'May the LORD treat you like Zedekiah and Ahab. The king of Babylonia burned them in the fire.'

²³"That will happen because they have done awful things in Israel. They have committed adul-

KIDS' QUESTION

If we talk to God, does he always hear us?

Yes, God *always* hears us, no matter where we are or what we are doing. He is never asleep or far away. Nothing can stop him from hearing what we say. God knows our thoughts too. We do not have to talk out loud. Even if we barely whisper or just think our prayer, God hears us.

But we also need to know that God hates sin, which is disobeying God. If we keep sin in our hearts and try to hide it, God will want us to tell him.

God loves us more than we could possibly imagine. He *wants* to hear from us. He is always available and always listening. We can talk to him anytime.

checkout
Jeremiah 29:12

Related verses:
Psalm 66:18–20;
Proverbs 15:29;
Isaiah 55:6–7;
59:1–2;
1 Peter 3:12

POSSIBLE REASONS JASON DIDN'T GET A JEEP:
1. OUT OF STOCK
2. POSTAL STRIKE
3. REQUEST FULFILLMENT POSTPONED TILL I'M OLD ENOUGH FOR A DRIVER'S LICENSE.

DECEMBER
26

tery with their neighbors' wives. They have spoken lies in my name. I did not tell them to do that. I know what they have done. And I am a witness to it," announces the LORD.

SHEMAIAH OPPOSES JEREMIAH

²⁴Tell Shemaiah, the Nehelamite, ²⁵"The LORD who rules over all is the God of Israel. He says, 'You sent letters in your own name to all of the people in Jerusalem. You also sent them to the priest Zephaniah, the son of Maaseiah. And you sent them to all of the other priests.

" 'You said to Zephaniah, ²⁶"The LORD has appointed you priest in place of Jehoiada. He has put you in charge of the LORD's house. You are supposed to arrest any crazy person who claims to be a prophet. You should put him in prison. You should put iron bands around his neck.

²⁷" ' "So why haven't you punished Jeremiah from Anathoth? He claims to be a prophet among you. ²⁸He has sent a message to us in Babylon. It says, 'You will be there a long time. So build houses and settle down. Plant gardens and eat what they produce.' " ' "

²⁹But the priest Zephaniah read the letter to me. ³⁰Then a message came to me from the LORD. He said, ³¹"Send a message to all of the people who were taken away. Tell them, 'The LORD speaks about Shemaiah, the Nehelamite. He says, "Shemaiah has prophesied to you. But I did not send him. He has made you believe a lie.

³²" ' "So I say, 'I will certainly punish Shemaiah, the Nehelamite. I will also punish his children after him. He will not have any children left among these people. I will do good things for my people. But he will not see them,' " ' " announces the LORD. " ' " That is because he has taught people to turn against me.' " ' "

ISRAEL WILL RETURN TO THE LORD

30 A message came to me from the LORD. He said, ²"I am the LORD. I am the God of Israel. I say, 'Write on a scroll all of the words I have spoken to you. ³A new day is coming,' " announces the LORD. " 'At that time I will bring my people Israel and Judah back from where they have been taken as prisoners. I will bring them back to this land. Long ago I gave it to their people to have as their own,' " says the LORD.

⁴Here are the words the LORD spoke about Israel and Judah. He said, ⁵"I am the LORD. I say,

" 'Cries of fear are heard.
There is terror. There isn't any peace.
⁶Ask and see.
Can a man give birth to children?
Then why do I see every strong man
with his hands on his stomach?
Each of them is acting like a woman having a baby.
Every face is as pale as death.
⁷How awful that day will be!
No other day will be like it.
It will be a time of trouble for the people of Jacob.
But they will be saved out of it.

⁸" 'At that time I will break the yoke off their necks,'
announces the LORD who rules over all.
'I will tear off the ropes that hold them.
People from other lands will not make them slaves anymore.
⁹Instead, they will serve me.
And they will serve David their king.
I will raise him up for them.
I am the LORD their God.

¹⁰" 'People of Jacob, do not be afraid.
You are my servant.
Israel, do not be terrified,' "
announces the LORD.
" 'You can be sure that I will save you.
I will bring you out of a place far away.
I will bring your children back
from the land where they were taken.
Your people will have peace and security again.

And no one will make them
 afraid.
[11] I am with you. I will save you,' "
 announces the LORD.
" 'I will completely destroy all of
 the nations
 among which I scatter you.
 But I will not completely destroy
 you.
 I will correct you. But I will be fair.
 I will punish you in a way that is
 fair and right.' "

[12] The LORD says,

"Your wound can't be cured.
 Your pain can't be healed.
[13] No one will stand up for you.
 There isn't any medicine for your
 sore.
 There isn't any healing for you.
[14] All those who were going to help
 you have forgotten you.
 They do not care about you.
 I have struck you as if I were your
 enemy.
 I have punished you as if I were
 very mean.
 That is because your guilt is so
 great.
 You have sinned so much.
[15] Why do you cry out about your
 wound?
 Your pain can't be healed.
 Your guilt is very great.
 And you have committed many
 sins.
 That is why I have done all of
 those things to you.

[16] "But everyone who destroys you
 will be destroyed.
 All of your enemies will be forced
 to leave their countries.
 Those who steal from you will be
 stolen from.
 I will take the belongings
 of those who take things from
 you.
[17] But I will make you healthy again.
 I will heal your wounds,"
　　　　　announces the LORD.
"That is because you have been
 thrown out.
 You are called Zion, the one no
 one cares about."

[18] The LORD says,

"I will bless Jacob's people with
 great success again.
 I will show tender love to
 Israel.
 Jerusalem will be rebuilt where it
 was destroyed.
 The palace will stand in its
 proper place.
[19] From those places the songs of
 people giving thanks will be
 heard.
 The sound of great joy will come
 from there.
 I will increase the numbers of my
 people.
 Their numbers will not become
 smaller.
 I will bring them honor.
 People will have respect for
 them.
[20] Things will be as they used to be
 for Jacob's people.
 I will make their community firm
 and secure.
 I will punish everyone who treats
 them badly.
[21] Their leader will be one of their
 own people.
 Their ruler will rise up from
 among them.
 I will bring him near.
 And he will come close to me.
 He will commit himself to serve
 me,"
　　　　　announces the LORD.
[22] "So you will be my people.
 And I will be your God."

[23] A storm will burst out
 because of the LORD's burning
 anger.
 A strong wind will sweep down
 on the heads of evil people.
[24] The LORD's burning anger won't
 turn back.
 He will accomplish everything
 his heart plans to do.
 In days to come
 you will understand that.

31

"At that time I will be the
God of all of the tribes
of Israel," announces the
LORD. "And they will be my people."
[2] The LORD says,

"Some of my people will live
 through

them.
They will find help in the desert.
  I will come to give peace and rest
    to Israel."

[3] The LORD appeared to us in the past. He said,

  "I have loved you with a love that
    lasts forever.
  I have kept on loving you with
    faithful love.
[4] I will build you up again.
  Nation of Israel, you will be
    rebuilt.
  Once again you will use your
    tambourines to celebrate.
  You will go out and dance with joy.
[5] Once again you will plant
    vineyards
  on the hills of Samaria.
  Farmers will plant them.
  They will enjoy their fruit.
[6] There will be a day when those on
    guard duty will cry out.
  They will stand on the hills of
    Ephraim.
  And they will shout,
  'Come! Let's go up to Zion.
  Let's go up to where the LORD our
    God is.' "

[7] The LORD says,

  "Sing with joy because the people
    of Jacob are blessed.
  Shout because the LORD has
    made them the greatest
    nation.
  Make your praises heard.
  Say, 'LORD, save your people.
  Save the people who are left alive
    in Israel.'
[8] I will bring them from the land of
    the north.
  I will gather them from one end
    of the earth to the other.
  Even those who are blind and
    those who can't walk
  will be among them.
  Pregnant women and women
    having their babies
  will be among them also.
  A large number will return.
[9] Their eyes will be filled with tears
    as they come.
  They will pray as I bring them
    back.

  I will lead them beside streams of
    water.
  I will lead them on a level path
  where they will not trip or fall.
  I am Israel's father.
  And Ephraim is my oldest son.

[10] "Listen to my message, you nations.
  Announce it on shores far away.
  Say, 'He who scattered Israel will
    gather them.
  He will watch over his flock like a
    shepherd.'
[11] I will set the people of Jacob free.
  I will save them from those who
    are stronger than they are.
[12] They will come and shout for joy
    on Mount Zion.
  They will be joyful because of
    everything I give them.
  I give them grain, olive oil and
    fresh wine.
  I give them the young animals in
    their flocks and herds.
  Israel will be like a garden that has
    plenty of water.
  And they will not be sad
    anymore.
[13] Then young women will dance
    and be glad.
  And so will the men, young and
    old alike.
  I will turn their sobbing into
    gladness.
  I will comfort them.
  And I will give them joy instead
    of sorrow.
[14] I will satisfy the priests. I will give
    them more than enough.
  And my people will be filled with
    the good things I give them,"
      announces the LORD.

[15] The LORD says,

  "A voice is heard in Ramah.
  It is the sound of crying and deep
    sadness.
  Rachel is crying over her children.
  She refuses to be comforted,
  because they are gone."

[16] The LORD says,

  "Do not sob anymore.
  Do not let tears fall from your
    eyes.
  I will reward you for your work,"
      announces the LORD.

"Your children will return from the land of the enemy.
¹⁷ So I am giving you hope for the years to come,"
announces the LORD.
"Your children will return to their own land.

¹⁸ "I have heard the groans of Ephraim's people. They say,
'You corrected us like a calf you were training.
And we have been trained.
Bring us back to you, and we will come back.
You are the LORD our God.
¹⁹ After we wandered away from you, we turned away from our sins.
After we learned our lesson, we beat our chests in sorrow.
We were full of shame.
What we did when we were young brought dishonor on us.'

²⁰ Aren't the people of Ephraim my dear children?
Aren't they the children I take delight in?
I often speak against them.
But I still remember them.
So my heart longs for them.
I love them with a tender love,"
announces the LORD.

²¹ The LORD says, "Put up road signs.
Set up stones to show the way.
Look carefully for the highway.
Look for the road you will take.
Return, people of Israel.
Return to your towns.
²² How long will you wander, you people who are not faithful to me?
I will create a new thing on earth.
A woman will guard a man."

²³ The LORD who rules over all is the God of Israel. He says, "I will bring

---

Will I still have feelings in heaven?

Yes! People in heaven will have lots of feelings, all good ones. People in heaven will be filled with joy. You will be busy smiling, whistling, singing for joy and kicking your heels and jumping. No one knows exactly how we will spend our days, but you can be sure you will always be happy and never bored. You will be happy because you will be with God and because all sin, death and sadness will be gone forever. And think of the joy when you see your family and friends who have died before you. Heaven will be a place of great joy, gladness and positive feelings all around.

checkout

Jeremiah 31:13

Related verses:
John 16:20–22

JASON'S IMAGINATION

them back from the place where they were taken. The people in Judah and its towns will say once again, 'Holy temple in Jerusalem, may the LORD bless you. Sacred mountain, may he bless you.'

²⁴"People will live together in Judah and all of its towns. Farmers and shepherds will live there. ²⁵I will give rest to those who are tired. I will satisfy those who are weak."

²⁶When I heard that, I woke up and looked around. My sleep had been pleasant.

²⁷The LORD announces, "The days are coming when I will plant the nation of Israel and Judah again. I will plant it with children and young animals.

²⁸"I watched over Israel and Judah to pull them up by the roots. I tore them down. I crushed them. I destroyed them. I brought horrible trouble on them. But now I will watch over them to build them up and plant them," announces the LORD.

²⁹"In those days people will no longer say,

'The fathers have eaten sour grapes.
But the children have a bitter taste in their mouths.'

³⁰Instead, everyone will die for his own sin. The one who eats sour grapes will taste how bitter they are.

³¹"A new day is coming," announces the LORD.
"I will make a new covenant with the people of Israel.
I will also make it with the people of Judah.
³²It will not be like the covenant I made with their people long ago.
That was when I took them by the hand.
I led them out of Egypt.
But they broke my covenant.
They did it even though I was like a husband to them,"
          announces the LORD.
³³"This is the covenant I will make with Israel
after that time," announces the LORD.

Why do people cry at funerals?

People cry at funerals because they are very sad. They miss the person who has died. They want to see the person again and talk with him or her. They may know that their friend or loved one is now in heaven with Jesus. But still it hurts because they are not all together enjoying each other's company. We have funerals so we can say good-by and remember what the person meant to everyone. It is OK to cry at funerals. It helps everybody feel better and shows respect for the person who has died.

checkout
Jeremiah 31:15

Related verses:
John 11:35,36;
Romans 12:15

"I will put my law in their minds.
I will write it on their hearts.
I will be their God.
And they will be my people.
³⁴A man will not need to teach his
neighbor anymore.
And he will not need to teach his
friend anymore.
He will not say, 'Know the
LORD.'
Everyone will know me.
From the least important of
them to the most important,
all of them will know me,"
announces the LORD.
"I will forgive their evil ways.
I will not remember their sins
anymore."

³⁵The LORD speaks.

He makes the sun
shine by day.
He orders the moon and stars
to shine at night.
He stirs up the ocean.
He makes its waves roar.
His name is The LORD Who Rules
Over All.
³⁶"Suppose my orders for creation
disappear from my sight,"
announces the LORD.
"Only then will the people of Israel
stop being
a nation in my sight."

³⁷The LORD says,

"Suppose the sky above could be
measured.
Suppose the foundations of the
earth below could be
completely discovered.
Only then would I turn the people
of Israel away.
Even though they have
committed many sins,
I will still accept them,"
announces the LORD.

³⁸"A new day is coming," announces
the LORD. "At that time Jerusalem will
be rebuilt for me. It will be rebuilt from
the Tower of Hananel to the Corner
Gate. ³⁹The measuring line will reach
out from there. It will go straight to the
hill of Gareb. Then it will turn and
reach as far as Goah.
⁴⁰"There is a valley where dead bodies and ashes are thrown. That whole
valley will be holy to me. The side of
the Kidron Valley east of the city will be
holy to me. It will be holy all the way to
the corner of the Horse Gate. The city
will never again be pulled up by the
roots. It will never be destroyed."

JEREMIAH BUYS A FIELD

32 A message came to me
from the LORD. It came in
the 10th year that Zedeki-
ah was king of Judah. It was in the 18th
year of the rule of Nebuchadnezzar.
²The armies of the king of Babylonia
were getting ready to attack Jerusalem. I, the prophet Jeremiah, was being held as a prisoner. I was kept in the
courtyard of the guard. It was part of
Judah's royal palace.

³Zedekiah, the king of Judah, had
made me a prisoner there. He had said
to me, "Why do you prophesy as you
do? You say, 'The LORD says, "I am
about to hand this city over to the king
of Babylonia. He will capture it.

⁴" ' "Zedekiah, the king of Judah,
will not escape from the powerful
hands of the armies of Babylonia. He
will certainly be handed over to the
king of Babylonia. Zedekiah will speak
with him face to face. He will see him
with his own eyes. ⁵Nebuchadnezzar
will take Zedekiah to Babylon. Zedekiah will remain there until I deal with
him," announces the LORD. "Suppose
you fight against the armies of Babylonia. If you do, you will not succeed." ' "

⁶I said, "A message came to me from
the LORD. He said, ⁷'Hanamel is going
to come to you. He is the son of your
uncle Shallum. Hanamel will say, "Buy
my field at Anathoth. You are my closest relative. So it's your right and duty
to buy it." '

⁸"Then my cousin Hanamel came to
me. I was in the courtyard of the guard.
It happened just as the LORD had said
it would. Hanamel said, 'Buy my field
at Anathoth. It is in the territory of
Benjamin. It is your right to buy it and
own it. So buy it for yourself.'

"I knew that this was the LORD's
message. ⁹So I bought the field at Anathoth from my cousin Hanamel. I
weighed out seven ounces of silver for
him. ¹⁰I signed and sealed the deed of

purchase. I had some people witness everything. And I weighed out the silver on the scales.

¹¹"There were two copies of the deed. One was sealed and the other wasn't. The deed included the terms and conditions of the sale. ¹²I gave Baruch the copies of the deed. My cousin Hanamel saw me do it. The witnesses who had signed the deed were there too. So were all of the Jews who were sitting in the courtyard of the guard. Baruch was the son of Neriah. Neriah was the son of Mahseiah.

¹³"I gave Baruch directions in front of all of them. I said, ¹⁴'The LORD who rules over all is the God of Israel. He says, "Take this deed of purchase. Take the sealed and unsealed copies. Put them in a clay jar. Then they will last a long time." ¹⁵The LORD who rules over all is the God of Israel. He says, "Houses, fields and vineyards will again be bought in this land." '

¹⁶"I gave the deed of purchase to Baruch, the son of Neriah. Then I prayed to the LORD. I said,

¹⁷" 'LORD and King, you have reached out your great and powerful arm. You have made the heavens and the earth. Nothing is too hard for you.

¹⁸" 'You show your love to thousands of people. But you punish children for the sins of their fathers. Great and powerful God, your name is The LORD Who Rules Over All. ¹⁹Your purposes are great. Your acts are mighty. Your eyes see everything people do. You reward each one of them in keeping with his conduct. You do it based on what he has done.

²⁰" 'You performed miraculous signs and wonders in Egypt. And you have continued to do them to this very day. You have done them in Israel and among all people. You are still known for doing them. ²¹You brought your people Israel out of Egypt. You did it with miraculous signs and wonders. You reached out your mighty hand and powerful arm. You did great and wonderful things. ²²" 'You gave Israel this land.

Long before that, you took an oath. You promised to give their people a land that had plenty of milk and honey. ²³They came in and took it over. But they did not obey you. They didn't follow your law. They didn't do what you commanded them to do. So you brought all of this trouble on them.

²⁴" 'See how ramps are built up against Jerusalem's walls to attack it. The city will be handed over to the armies of Babylonia. They are attacking it. It will fall because of war, hunger and plague. What you said would happen is now happening, as you can see. ²⁵LORD and King, the city will be handed over to the armies of Babylonia. In spite of that, you tell me to buy a field. You say, "Pay for it with silver. And have the sale witnessed." ' "

²⁶Then a message came to me from the LORD. He said, ²⁷"I am the LORD. I am the God of all people. Is anything too hard for me?"

²⁸So the LORD says, "I am about to hand this city over to the armies of Babylonia. I will give it to Nebuchadnezzar, the king of Babylonia. He will capture it. ²⁹The armies of Babylonia are now attacking this city. They will come in and set it on fire. They will burn it down. They will burn up the houses where the people made me very angry. They burned incense on their roofs to the god Baal. And they poured out drink offerings to other gods.

³⁰"The people of Israel and Judah have done nothing but evil in my sight. They have done it since the nation was young. In fact, they have done nothing but make me very angry. They have worshiped statues of gods their own hands have made," announces the LORD. ³¹"This city has always stirred up my burning anger. It has done it since the day it was built. Now I must remove it from my sight. ³²"The people of Israel and Judah have made me very angry. They have done many evil things. They, their kings and officials have sinned. So

have their priests and prophets. And the people of Judah and Jerusalem have also sinned. ³³They turned their backs to me. They would not face me. I taught them again and again. But they would not listen or pay attention when they were corrected.

³⁴"They set up statues of their gods. They did it in the house where I have put my Name. They made my house 'unclean.' I hate those statues.

³⁵"The people built high places for Baal in the Valley of Ben Hinnom. That is where they sacrifice their children to Molech in the fire. That is something I did not command. It did not even enter my mind. They did something I hate. They made Judah sin."

³⁶You people of Judah are saying about this city, "By war, hunger and plague it will be handed over to the king of Babylonia."

But the LORD, the God of Israel, says, ³⁷"You can be sure that I will gather my people again. I will bring them from all of the lands where I send them when my burning anger blazes out against them. I will bring them back to this place. And I will let them live in safety.

³⁸"They will be my people. And I will be their God. ³⁹I will give them a single purpose in life. Then, they will always have respect for me. I will do it for their own good. And it will be for the good of their children after them.

⁴⁰"I will make a covenant with them that will last forever. I promise that I will never stop doing good to them. I will cause them to respect me. Then they will never turn away from me again. ⁴¹I will take pleasure in doing good things for them. I will certainly plant them in this land. I will do those things with all my heart and soul."

⁴²The LORD says, "I have brought all of this horrible trouble on these people. But now I will give them all of the good things I have promised them.

⁴³"Once more fields will be bought in this land. It is the land about which you now say, 'It is a dry and empty desert. It doesn't have any people or animals in it. It has been handed over to the armies of Babylonia.' ⁴⁴Fields will be bought with silver. Deeds will be signed, sealed and witnessed. That will be done in the territory of Benjamin. It will be done in the villages

How can God hear our prayers from heaven?

God can do anything. He is all-powerful and unlimited. He is everywhere all the time. He also knows everything. He knows what we think as well as what we say. So God can hear everyone's prayers from all over the world all the time.

Sometimes people think that God is "out there in heaven," far away. But God is not far away; he is always right here with us, and he knows exactly what's going on in our lives.

checkout
Jeremiah 32:27

JASON'S IMAGINATION

around Jerusalem and in the towns of Judah. It will also be done in the towns of the central hill country. And it will be done in the towns of the western hills and the Negev Desert. I will bless their people with great success again," announces the LORD.

THE LORD KEEPS HIS PROMISES

33 I was still being held as a prisoner. I was kept in the courtyard of the guard. Then another message came to me from the LORD. He said, ²"I made the earth. I formed it. And I set it in place. The LORD is my name. ³Call out to me. I will answer you. I will tell you great things you do not know. You will not be able to understand them."

⁴The LORD is the God of Israel. He speaks about the houses in Jerusalem. He talks about the royal palaces of Judah. The people had torn many of them down. They had used their stones to strengthen the city walls against attack. ⁵That was during their fight with the armies of Babylonia. The LORD says, "The houses will be filled with dead bodies. They will be the bodies of the men I will kill when my anger burns against them. I will hide my face from this city. That is because its people have committed so many sins.

⁶"But now I will bring health and healing to Jerusalem. I will heal my people. I will let them enjoy great peace and security. ⁷I will bring Judah and Israel back from the places where they have been taken. I will build up the nation again. It will be just as it was before.

⁸"I will wash from its people all of the sins they have committed against me. And I will forgive all of the sins they committed when they turned away from me.

⁹"Then this city will bring me fame, joy, praise and honor. All of the nations on earth will hear about the good things I do for this city. They will see the great success and peace I give it. Then they will be filled with wonder. And they will tremble with fear."

¹⁰The LORD says, "You say about this place, 'It's a dry and empty desert. It doesn't have any people or animals in it.' The towns of Judah and the streets of Jerusalem are now deserted. So they

KIDS' QUESTION

When did "Bible times" stop?

The last book in the Bible was written about 70 years after Jesus lived on earth. That is a very long time ago, almost 2,000 years. You might say that is when Bible times stopped. But in other ways, we are still in Bible times. God still speaks to us through the Bible. He still cares about us, and he still does miracles. We may not see God divide a sea as he did for Moses. And we may not see anyone walk on water the way Jesus did. But God still answers prayer, and he still changes the people who love him.

JASON'S IMAGINATION

LATEST STYLES

checkout
Jeremiah 32:40

Related verses:
John 20:30,31;
Hebrews 1:1–3

do not have any people or animals living in them. But happy sounds will be heard there once more. [11]They will be the sounds of joy and gladness. The voices of brides and grooms will fill the streets.

"And the voices of those who bring thank offerings to my house will be heard there. They will say,

'Give thanks to the LORD who rules
    over all,
  because he is good.
  His faithful love continues
    forever.'

That is because I will bless this land with great success again. It will be as it was before," says the LORD.

[12]The LORD who rules over all says, "This place is a desert. It does not have any people or animals in it. But there will again be grasslands near all of its towns. Shepherds will rest their flocks there. [13]Flocks will again pass under the hands of shepherds as they count their sheep," says the LORD. "That will be done in the towns of the central hill country. It will be done in the western hills and the Negev Desert. It will be done in the territory of Benjamin. And it will be done in the villages around Jerusalem and in the towns of Judah.

[14]"A new day is coming," announces the LORD. "At that time my gracious promise to my people will come true. I made it to the people of Israel and the people of Judah.

[15]"In those days and at that time
  I will make a true and rightful
    Branch grow from David's
    royal line.
  He will do what is fair and right
    in the land.
[16]In those days Judah will be saved.
  Jerusalem will live in safety.
  And it will be called
  The LORD Who Makes Us Right
    With Himself."

[17]The LORD says, "David will always have a son to sit on the throne of the nation of Israel. [18]"The priests, who are Levites, will always have a man to serve me. He will sacrifice burnt offerings. He will burn grain offerings. And he will offer sacrifices."

[19]A message came to me from the LORD. [20]He said, "Could you ever break my covenant with the day? Could you ever break my covenant with the night? Could you ever stop day and night from coming at their appointed times? [21]Only then could my covenant with my servant David be broken. Only then could my covenant with the Levites who serve me as priests be broken. Only then would David no longer have someone from his family line to rule on his throne.

[22]"Here is what I will do for my servant David. And here is what I will do for the Levites who serve me. I will make their children after them as many as the stars in the sky. And I will make them as many as the grains of sand on the seashore. It will be impossible to count them."

[23]A message came to me from the LORD. He said, [24]"Haven't you noticed what these people are saying? They say, 'The LORD once chose the two kingdoms of Israel and Judah. But now he has turned his back on them.' So they hate my people. They do not think of them as a nation anymore.

[25]"I say, 'What if I had not made my covenant with day and night? What if I had not established the laws of heaven and earth? [26]Only then would I turn my back on the children of Jacob and my servant David. Only then would I not choose one of David's sons to rule over the children of Abraham, Isaac and Jacob. But I will bless my people with great success again. I will love them with tender love.' "

ZEDEKIAH IS WARNED

34 Nebuchadnezzar, the king of Babylonia, and all of his armies were fighting against Jerusalem. They were also fighting against all of the towns that were around it. All of the kingdoms and nations Nebuchadnezzar ruled over were helping him.

At that time a message came to me from the LORD. He said, [2]"I am the LORD, the God of Israel. Go to Zedekiah, the king of Judah. Tell him, 'The LORD says, "I am about to hand this city over to the king of Babylonia. He will burn it down. [3]You will not escape from his powerful hand. You will certainly be captured. You will be handed over to him. You will see the king of Babylonia with your own eyes. He will speak with you face to face. And you will go to Babylon.

⁴" ' "But listen to my promise, Zedekiah. Listen, king of Judah. I say that you will not be killed with a sword. ⁵You will die in a peaceful way. People made fires to honor the kings who died before you. In the same way, they will make a fire in your honor. They will sob over you. They will say, 'My poor master!' I myself make this promise," announces the LORD.' "

⁶Then I, the prophet Jeremiah, told all of that to King Zedekiah in Jerusalem. ⁷At that time Nebuchadnezzar's armies were fighting against Jerusalem. They were also fighting against Lachish and Azekah. Those two cities were still holding out. They were the only cities left in Judah that had high walls around them.

THE PEOPLE SET THEIR SLAVES FREE

⁸A message came to me from the LORD. King Zedekiah had made a covenant with all of the people in Jerusalem. He had told them to set their Hebrew slaves free. ⁹All of them had to do it. That applied to male and female slaves alike. No one was allowed to hold another Jew as a slave.

¹⁰So all of the officials and people entered into that covenant. They agreed to set their male and female slaves free. They agreed not to hold them as slaves anymore. Instead, they set them free. ¹¹But later they changed their minds. They took back the people they had set free. They made them slaves again.

¹²Then a message came to me from the LORD. ¹³The LORD is the God of Israel. He says, "I made a covenant with your people long ago. I brought them out of Egypt. That is the land where they were slaves. I said, ¹⁴'Every seventh year you must set your people free. You must set free all of the Hebrews who have sold themselves to you. Let them serve you for six years. Then you must let them go free.' *(Deuteronomy 15:12)* But your people did

not listen to me. They did not pay any attention to me.

¹⁵"Recently you turned away from your sins. You did what is right in my eyes. Each of you set your Hebrew slaves free. You even made a covenant in front of me. You did it in the house where I have put my Name. ¹⁶But now you have turned around. You have treated my name as if it were not holy. Each of you has taken back your male and female slaves. You had set them free to go where they wished. But now you have forced them to become your slaves again."

¹⁷So the LORD says, "You have not obeyed me. You have not set your Hebrew slaves free. So now I will set you free," announces the LORD. "I will set you free to be destroyed by war, plague and hunger. I will make all of the kingdoms on earth displeased with you.

¹⁸"The men who have broken my covenant will be punished. They have not lived up to the terms of the covenant they made in front of me. When you made that covenant, you cut a calf in two. Then you walked between its pieces. Now I will cut you to pieces. ¹⁹That includes all of you who walked between the pieces of the calf. It includes the leaders of Judah and Jerusalem, the court officials and the priests. It also includes some of the people of the land.

²⁰"So I will hand all of those people over to their enemies who are trying to kill them. Their dead bodies will become food for the birds of the air and the wild animals.

²¹"I will hand King Zedekiah and his officials over to their enemies. I will hand them over to those who want to kill them. I will give them over to the armies of the king of Babylonia. They have now pulled back from you. ²²But I am going to give an order," announces the LORD. "I will bring them back to this city. They will fight against it. They will take it and burn it down. And I will completely destroy the towns of Judah. No one will be able to live there."

THE FAMILY OF RECAB

35 A message came to me from the LORD. It came during the time Jehoiakim was king over Judah. He was the son of Josiah. The message said, ²"Go to the members of the family line of Recab. Invite them to come to one of the side rooms in my house. Then give them wine to drink."

³So I went to get Jaazaniah. He was the son of Jeremiah. Jeremiah was the son of Habazziniah. I also went to get Jaazaniah's brothers and all of his sons. That included all of the members of the family line of Recab. ⁴I brought them into the LORD's house. I took them into the room of the sons of Hanan. He was the son of Igdaliah. He was also a man of God. His room was next to the room of the officials. Their room was above the room of Maaseiah. He was the son of Shallum. He also was one of those who guarded the temple doors. ⁵Then I got bowls full of wine and some cups. I set them down in front of the men from the family line of Recab. I said to them, "Drink some wine."

⁶But they replied, "We don't drink wine. That's because Jonadab gave us a command. He was the son of Recab. He was also one of our own people from long ago. He commanded, 'You and your children after you must never drink wine. ⁷Also you must never build houses. You must never plant crops or vineyards. You must never have any of those things. Instead, you must always live in tents. Then you will live a long time in the land where you are wandering around.'

⁸"We have done everything Jonadab, the son of Recab, commanded us to do. So we and our wives and our children have never drunk wine. ⁹We have never built houses to live in. We've never had vineyards, fields or crops. ¹⁰We've always lived in tents. We've completely obeyed everything Jonadab commanded our people of long ago.

¹¹"But Nebuchadnezzar, the king of Babylonia, marched into this land. Then we said, 'Come. We must go to Jerusalem. There we can escape the armies of Babylonia and Aram.' So we have remained in Jerusalem."

¹²Then a message came to me from the LORD. It said, ¹³"The LORD who rules over all is the God of Israel. He says, 'Go. Speak to the people of Judah and Jerusalem. Tell them, "Won't you ever learn a lesson? Won't you ever obey my words?" announces the LORD. ¹⁴' "Jonadab, the son of Recab, ordered his children not to drink wine. And they have kept his command. To this very day they do not drink wine. They obey the command Jonadab gave their people long ago. But I have spoken to you again and again. In spite of that, you have not obeyed me.

¹⁵" ' "Again and again I sent all of my servants the prophets to you. They said, 'Each of you must turn from your evil ways. You must change the way you act. Do not worship other gods. Do not serve them. Then you will live in the land. I gave it to you and your people long ago.' But you have not paid any attention. You have not listened to me.

¹⁶" ' "The children of Jonadab, the son of Recab, have obeyed the command Jonadab gave them long ago. But the people of Judah have not obeyed me." ' "

¹⁷So the LORD God who rules over all speaks. The God of Israel says, "Listen! I am going to bring horrible trouble on Judah. I will also bring it on everyone who lives in Jerusalem. I will bring on them every trouble I said I would. I spoke to them. But they did not listen. I called out to them. But they did not answer."

¹⁸Then I spoke to the members of the family line of Recab. I said, "The LORD who rules over all is the God of Israel. He says, 'You have obeyed the command Jonadab gave your people long ago. You have followed all of his directions. You have done everything he ordered.' ¹⁹So the LORD who rules over all speaks. The God of Israel says, 'Jonadab, the son of Recab, will always have a man from his family to serve me.' "

JEHOIAKIM BURNS UP JEREMIAH'S SCROLL

36 A message came to me from the LORD. It came in the fourth year that Jehoiakim was king of Judah. He was the son of Josiah. The message said, ²"Get a scroll. Write on it all of the words I have spoken to you. Write down what I have said about Israel, Judah and all of the other nations. Write what I have said to you from the time of King Josiah until now. ³The people of Judah will hear about all of the trouble I plan to bring on them. Maybe then all of them will turn from their evil ways. If they do, I will forgive their sins and the evil things they have done."

⁴So I sent for Baruch, the son of Neriah. I told him to write down all of the words the LORD had spoken to me. And Baruch wrote them on the scroll.

⁵Then I said to him, "I'm not allowed to go to the LORD's temple. ⁶So you go there. Go on a day when the people are fasting. Read to them from the scroll. Read the words of the LORD you wrote down as I gave them to you. Read them to all of the people of Judah who come in from their towns. ⁷They will hear what the LORD will do to them when his burning anger blazes out against them. Then perhaps they will pray to him. And maybe all of them will turn from their evil ways."

⁸Baruch, the son of Neriah, did ev-erything I told him to do. He went to the LORD's temple. There he read the words of the LORD from the scroll. ⁹It was in the fifth year that Jehoiakim, the son of Josiah, was king of Judah. It was the ninth month of that year. A time of fasting at the LORD's temple had been ordered. All of the people in Jerusalem were told to take part in it. So were those who had come in from the towns of Judah.

¹⁰Baruch read to all of the people who were at the LORD's temple. He read my words from the scroll. He was in the room of the secretary Gemariah. It was located in the upper courtyard at the entrance of the New Gate of the temple. Gemariah was the son of Shaphan.

¹¹Micaiah was the son of Gemariah, the son of Shaphan. Micaiah heard Baruch reading all of the LORD's words that were written on the scroll.

¹²Then he went down to the secretary's room in the royal palace. All of the officials were sitting there. They included the secretary Elishama and Delaiah, the son of Shemaiah. Elna-

KIDS' QUESTION

Who wrote the Bible?

The words in the Bible came from God. That is why the Bible is called "God's Word." God used people to write down the ideas, thoughts, teachings and words that he wanted to put in the Bible. God chose the writers for this very important task. And God used many people over many, many years. These people wrote in their own styles and in their own languages. But they wrote God's Word. God guided their thoughts as they wrote. And God made sure that what they wrote was exactly what he wanted. He kept them from making any mistakes.

checkout
Jeremiah 36:1,2

Related verses:
Exodus 31:18;
2 Peter 1:20,21

than, the son of Acbor, was also there. So was Gemariah, the son of Shaphan. Zedekiah, the son of Hananiah, was there too. And so were all of the other officials. [13]Micaiah told all of them what he had heard. He told them everything Baruch had read to the people from the scroll.

[14]All of the officials sent Jehudi to speak to Baruch, the son of Neriah. Jehudi was the son of Nethaniah. Nethaniah was the son of Shelemiah. Shelemiah was the son of Cushi. Jehudi said to Baruch, "Come. Bring the scroll you have read to the people."

So Baruch went to them. He carried the scroll with him. [15]The officials said to him, "Please sit down. Read the scroll to us."

So Baruch read it to them. [16]They heard all of its words. Then they looked at each other in fear. They said to Baruch, "We must report all of these words to the king."

[17]They said to Baruch, "Tell us. How did you happen to write all of these things? Did Jeremiah tell you to do it?"

[18]"Yes," Baruch replied. "He told me to write down all of these words. So I wrote them in ink on the scroll."

[19]Then the officials spoke to Baruch. They said, "You and Jeremiah must go and hide. Don't let anyone know where you are."

[20]The officials put the scroll in the room of the secretary Elishama. Then they went to the king in the courtyard. They reported everything to him.

[21]The king sent Jehudi to get the scroll. Jehudi brought it from the room of the secretary Elishama. He read it to the king. All of the officials were standing beside the king. So they heard it too. [22]It was the ninth month. The king was sitting in his winter apartment. A fire was burning in the fire pot in front of him. [23]Jehudi read three or four columns from the scroll. Then the king cut them off with a secretary's knife. He threw them into the fire pot. He did that until the entire scroll was burned up in the fire. [24]The king and some of his attendants heard all of those words. But they weren't afraid. They didn't tear their clothes.

[25]Elnathan, Delaiah and Gemariah begged the king not to burn the scroll.

But he wouldn't listen to them. [26]Instead, the king commanded three men to arrest the secretary Baruch and the prophet Jeremiah. But the LORD had hidden them. The three were Jerahmeel, Seraiah and Shelemiah. Jerahmeel was a member of the royal court. Seraiah was the son of Azriel. And Shelemiah was the son of Abdeel.

[27]A message came to me from the LORD. It came after the king burned the scroll that had the words Baruch had written down. I had told him to write them. The message said, [28]"Get another scroll. Write on it all of the words that were on the first one. King Jehoiakim burned that one up.

[29]"Also tell King Jehoiakim, 'The LORD says, "You burned that scroll. You said to Baruch, 'Why did you write that the king of Babylonia would certainly come? Why did you write that he would destroy this land? Why did you write that he would cut off people and animals alike from it?' "

[30]" 'So now the LORD has something to say about Jehoiakim, the king of Judah. He says, "No one from Jehoiakim's family line will sit on David's throne. Jehoiakim's body will be thrown out. It will lie outside in the heat by day and in the frost at night. [31]I will punish him and his children and his attendants. I will punish them for their sinful ways. I will bring on them all of the trouble I said I would. And I will bring it on the people of Jerusalem and Judah. They have not listened to me." ' "

[32]So I got another scroll. I gave it to the secretary Baruch, the son of Neriah. I told him what to write on it. He wrote down all of the words that were on the scroll King Jehoiakim had burned up in the fire. And he added many more words the LORD had given to me. They were similar to those that had already been written.

JEREMIAH IS PUT IN PRISON

37 Nebuchadnezzar, the king of Babylonia, appointed Zedekiah to be king of Judah. He was the son of Josiah. Zedekiah ruled in place of Jehoiachin, the son of Jehoiakim. [2]Zedekiah and his attendants didn't pay any attention to what the LORD had said through me.

And the people of the land didn't pay any attention either.

³But King Zedekiah sent Jehucal to me. He sent the priest Zephaniah along with him. Jehucal was the son of Shelemiah. Zephaniah was the son of Maaseiah. Jehucal and Zephaniah brought the king's message to me. It said, "Please pray to the LORD our God for us."

⁴At that time I was free to come and go among the people. I had not yet been put in prison. ⁵The armies of Babylonia were attacking Jerusalem. They received a report that Pharaoh's army had marched out of Egypt to help Zedekiah. So they pulled back from Jerusalem.

⁶A message came to me from the LORD. ⁷The LORD is the God of Israel. He says, "The king of Judah has sent you to ask me for advice. Tell him, 'Pharaoh's army has marched out to help you. But it will go back to its own land. It will return to Egypt. ⁸Then the armies of Babylonia will come back here. They will attack this city. They will capture it. Then they will burn it down.'

⁹"The LORD says, 'Do not fool yourselves. You think, "The Babylonians will leave us alone." But they will not! ¹⁰Suppose you destroy all of the armies of Babylonia that are attacking you. Suppose only wounded men are left in their tents. Even then they will come out and burn this city down.' "

¹¹The armies of Babylonia had pulled back from Jerusalem because of Pharaoh's army. ¹²So I started to leave the city. I was planning to go to the territory of Benjamin. I wanted to get my share of the property among the people there. ¹³I got as far as the Benjamin Gate. But the captain of the guard arrested me. He said, "You are going over to the side of the Babylonians!" The captain's name was Irijah, the son of Shelemiah. Shelemiah was the son of Hananiah.

How did they write the Old Testament if there weren't any paper or pencils?

When the oldest books in the Bible were written, there were no typewriters, computers or printing presses. There were no ballpoint pens, felt-tipped markers or pencils. But the people who lived back then did have other writing tools. The paper they used was different, too. Some people wrote on stone or pottery. Others wrote on paper made from *papyrus* or *parchment.* Papyrus paper was made from a plant that grows in the Bible lands. Parchment was made of animal skin. Either of these could be sewn into long pieces and rolled up into scrolls. Museums have some of these ancient scrolls. You may want to visit a museum and see one.

checkout
Jeremiah 36:27,28

Related verses:
Exodus 24:12;
2 Timothy 4:13

¹⁴I said to Irijah, "That isn't true! I'm not going to the side of the Babylonians."

But Irijah wouldn't listen to me. Instead, he arrested me. He brought me to the officials. ¹⁵They were angry with me. So they had me beaten. Then they took me to the house of the secretary Jonathan. It had been made into a prison. That's where they put me.

¹⁶I was put into a prison cell that was below ground level. I remained there a long time. ¹⁷Then King Zedekiah sent for me. He had me brought to the palace. There he spoke to me in private. He asked, "Do you have a message from the LORD for me?"

"Yes," I replied. "You will be handed over to the king of Babylonia."

¹⁸Then I continued, "Why have you put me in prison? What crime have I committed against you? What have I done to your officials or these people? ¹⁹Where are your prophets who prophesied to you? They said, 'The king of Babylonia won't attack you. He won't march into this land.'

²⁰"But now please listen, my king and master. Let me make my appeal to you. Please don't send me back to the house of the secretary Jonathan. If you do, I'll die there."

²¹Then King Zedekiah gave the order. His men put me in the courtyard of the guard. They gave me bread from the street of the bakers. They did it every day until all of the bread in the city was gone. So I remained in the courtyard of the guard.

JEREMIAH IS THROWN INTO AN EMPTY WELL

38 Shephatiah, Gedaliah, Jehucal and Pashhur heard what I was telling all of the people. Shephatiah was the son of Mattan. Gedaliah was the son of Pashhur. Jehucal was the son of Shelemiah. And Pashhur was the son of Malkijah. Those four men heard me say, ²"The LORD says, 'Those who stay in this city will die of war, hunger or plague. But those who go over to the side of the Babylonians will live. They will escape with their lives. They will remain alive.' ³The LORD also says, 'This city will certainly be handed over to the ar-mies of the king of Babylonia. They will capture it.' "

⁴Then those officials said to the king, "That man should be put to death. What he says is making the soldiers who are left in this city lose hope. It's making all of the people lose hope too. He isn't interested in what is best for the people. In fact, he's trying to destroy them."

⁵"He's in your hands," King Zedekiah answered. "I can't do anything to oppose you."

⁶So they took me and put me into an empty well. It belonged to Malkijah. He was a member of the royal court. His well was in the courtyard of the guard. Zedekiah's men lowered me by ropes into the well. It didn't have any water in it. All it had was mud. And I sank down into the mud.

⁷Ebed-Melech was an official in the royal palace. He was from the land of Cush. He heard that I had been put into the well. The king was sitting by the Benjamin Gate at that time. ⁸Ebed-Melech went out of the palace. He said to the king, ⁹"My king and master, everything those men have done to the prophet Jeremiah is evil. They have thrown him into an empty well. Soon there won't be any more bread in the city. Then he'll starve to death."

¹⁰So the king gave an order to Ebed-Melech from Cush. He said, "Take 30 men from here with you. Lift the prophet Jeremiah out of the well before he dies."

¹¹Then Ebed-Melech took the men with him. He went to a room under the place in the palace where the treasures were stored. He got some old rags and worn-out clothes from there. Then he let them down with ropes to me in the well.

¹²Ebed-Melech from Cush told me what to do. He said, "Put these old rags and worn-out clothes under your arms. They'll pad the ropes." So I did. ¹³Then the men pulled me up with the ropes. They lifted me out of the well. And I remained in the courtyard of the guard.

ZEDEKIAH QUESTIONS JEREMIAH AGAIN

¹⁴Then King Zedekiah sent for me. He had me brought to the third en-

trance to the LORD's temple. "I want to ask you something," the king said to me. "Don't hide anything from me."

[15]I said to Zedekiah, "Suppose I give you an answer. You will kill me, won't you? Suppose I give you good advice. You won't listen to me, will you?"

[16]But King Zedekiah took an oath. He promised me secretly, "I won't kill you. And I won't hand you over to those who want to take your life. That's just as sure as the LORD is alive. He's the one who has given us breath."

[17]So I said to Zedekiah, "The LORD God who rules over all is the God of Israel. He says, 'Give yourself up to the officers of the king of Babylonia. Then your life will be spared. And this city will not be burned down. You and your family will remain alive.

[18]" 'But what if you do not give yourself up to them? Then this city will be handed over to the Babylonians. They will burn it down. And you yourself will not escape from their powerful hands.' "

[19]King Zedekiah said to me, "I'm afraid of some of the Jews. They are the ones who have gone over to the side of the Babylonians. The Babylonians might hand me over to them. And those Jews will treat me badly."

[20]"They won't hand you over to them," I replied. "Obey the LORD. Do what I tell you to do. Then things will go well with you. Your life will be spared.

[21]"Don't refuse to give yourself up. The LORD has shown me what will happen if you do. [22]All of the women who are left in your palace will be brought out. They'll be given to the officials of the king of Babylonia. Those women will say to you,

" 'Your trusted friends have tricked you.
They have gotten the best of you.
Your feet are sunk down in the mud.
Your friends have deserted you.'

[23]"All of your wives and children will be brought out to the Babylonians. You yourself won't escape from their powerful hands. You will be captured by the king of Babylonia. And this city will be burned down."

[24]Then Zedekiah said to me, "Don't let anyone know about the talk we've had. If you do, you might die. [25]Suppose the officials find out that I've talked with you. And suppose they come to you and say, 'Tell us what you said to the king. Tell us what the king said to you. Don't hide it from us. If you do, we'll kill you.' [26]Then tell them, 'I was begging the king not to send me back to Jonathan's house. I don't want to die there.' "

[27]All of the officials came to me. And they questioned me. I told them everything the king had ordered me to say. None of them had heard what I told the king. So they didn't say anything else to me.

[28]I remained in the courtyard of the guard. I stayed there until the day Jerusalem was captured.

JERUSALEM IS DESTROYED

39 Here is how Jerusalem was captured. [1]Nebuchadnezzar, the king of Babylonia, marched out against it. He came with all of his armies and attacked it. It was in the ninth year that Zedekiah was king of Judah. It was in the tenth month. [2]The city wall was broken through. It happened on the ninth day of the fourth month. It was in the 11th year of Zedekiah's rule.

[3]All of the officials of the king of Babylonia came. They took seats near the Middle Gate. Nergal-Sharezer from Samgar was there. Nebo-Sarsekim, a chief officer, was also there. So was Nergal-Sharezer, a high official. And all of the other officials of the king of Babylonia were there too.

[4]King Zedekiah and all of the soldiers saw them. Then they ran away. They left the city at night. They went by way of the king's garden. They went out through the gate between the two walls. And they headed toward the Arabah Valley.

[5]But the armies of Babylonia chased them. They caught up with Zedekiah in the flatlands near Jericho. They captured him there. And they took him to Nebuchadnezzar, the king of Babylonia. He was at Riblah in the land of Hamath. That's where Nebuchadnezzar decided how he would be pun-

ished. ⁶The king of Babylonia killed the sons of Zedekiah at Riblah. He forced Zedekiah to watch it with his own eyes. He also killed all of the nobles of Judah. ⁷Then he poked out Zedekiah's eyes. He put him in bronze chains. And he took him to Babylon.

⁸The Babylonians set the royal palace on fire. They also set fire to the houses of the people. And they broke down the walls of Jerusalem.

⁹Nebuzaradan was commander of the royal guard. Some people still remained in the city. But he took them away to Babylon as prisoners. He also took along those who had gone over to his side. And he took the rest of the people.

¹⁰Nebuzaradan, the commander of the guard, left some of the poor people of Judah behind. They didn't own anything. So at that time he gave them vineyards and fields.

¹¹Nebuchadnezzar, the king of Babylonia, had given orders about me. He had given them to Nebuzaradan, the commander of the royal guard. Nebuchadnezzar had said, ¹²"Take him. Look after him. Don't harm him. Do for him anything he asks."

¹³So that's what Nebuzaradan, the commander of the guard, did. Nebushazban and Nergal-Sharezer were with him. So were all of the other officers of the king of Babylonia. Nebushazban was a chief officer. Nergal-Sharezer was a high official. All of those men ¹⁴sent for me. They had me taken out of the courtyard of the guard. They turned me over to Gedaliah. They told him to take me back to my home. So I remained among my own people. Gedaliah was the son of Ahikam, the son of Shaphan.

¹⁵A message came to me from the LORD. It came while I was being kept in the courtyard of the guard. He said, ¹⁶"Go. Speak to Ebed-Melech from Cush. Tell him, 'The LORD who rules over all is the God of Israel. He says, "I am about to make the words I spoke against this city come true. I will not give success to it. Instead, I will bring horrible trouble on it. At that time my words will come true. You will see it with your own eyes.

¹⁷"'"But I will save you on that day,"

announces the LORD. "You will not be handed over to those you are afraid of. ¹⁸I will save you. You will not be killed with a sword. Instead, you will escape with your life. That is because you trust in me," announces the LORD.'"

JEREMIAH IS SET FREE FROM HIS CHAINS

40 A message came to me from the LORD. It came after Nebuzaradan, the commander of the royal guard, had set me free at Ramah. I was being held by chains when he found me. I was among all of the prisoners from Jerusalem and Judah. We were being taken to Babylon.

²But the commander of the guard found me. He said to me, "The LORD your God ordered that this place be destroyed. ³And now he has brought it about. He has done exactly what he said he would do. All of these things have happened because you people sinned against the LORD. You didn't obey him. ⁴But today I'm setting you free from the chains that are on your wrists. Come with me to Babylon if you want to. I'll take good care of you there. But if you don't want to come, then don't. The whole country lies in front of you. Go anywhere you want to."

⁵But before I turned to go, Nebuzaradan continued, "Go back to Gedaliah, the son of Ahikam. The king of Babylonia has appointed Gedaliah to be over the towns of Judah. Go and live with him among your people. Or go anywhere else you want to." Ahikam was the son of Shaphan.

The commander gave me food and water. He also gave me a gift. Then he let me go. ⁶So I went to Mizpah to see Gedaliah, the son of Ahikam. I stayed with him. I lived among the people who were left behind in the land.

GEDALIAH IS MURDERED

⁷Some of Judah's army officers and their men were still in the open country. They heard that the king of Babylonia had appointed Gedaliah, the son of Ahikam, as governor over Judah. He had put him in charge of the men, women and children who were still

there. They were the poorest people in the land. They hadn't been taken to Babylon.

[8]When the army officers and their men heard those things, they came to Gedaliah at Mizpah. Ishmael, the son of Nethaniah, came. So did Johanan and Jonathan, the sons of Kareah. Seraiah, the son of Tanhumeth, also came. The sons of Ephai from Netophah came too. And so did Jaazaniah, the son of the Maacathite. All of their men came with them.

[9]Gedaliah son of Ahikam, the son of Shaphan, took an oath to give hope to all of those men. He spoke in a kind way to them. He said, "Don't be afraid to serve the Babylonians. Settle down in the land of Judah. Serve the king of Babylonia. Then things will go well with you. [10]I myself will stay at Mizpah. I'll speak for you to the officials of Babylonia who come to us. But you must harvest the wine, summer fruit and olive oil. Put them in your jars. Store them up. And live in the towns you have taken over."

[11]All of the Jews in Moab, Ammon and Edom heard what had happened. So did the Jews in all of the other countries. They heard that the king of Babylonia had left some people behind in Judah. They also heard that he had appointed Gedaliah, the son of Ahikam, as governor over them. Ahikam was the son of Shaphan.

[12]When they heard those things, all of them came back to the land of Judah. They went to Gedaliah at Mizpah. They came from all of the countries where they had been scattered. And they harvested a large amount of wine and summer fruit.

[13]Johanan and all of the other army officers who were still in the open country came to Gedaliah at Mizpah. Johanan was the son of Kareah. [14]The officers said to Gedaliah, "Don't you know that Baalis, the king of Ammon, has sent someone to take your life? It's Ishmael, the son of Nethaniah." But Gedaliah, the son of Ahikam, didn't believe them.

[15]Then Johanan, the son of Kareah, spoke in private to Gedaliah in Mizpah. He said, "Let me go and kill Ishmael, the son of Nethaniah. No one

will know about it. Why should he take your life? Why should he cause all of the Jews who are gathered around you to be scattered? Why should he cause the people who remain in Judah to die?"

[16]But Gedaliah, the son of Ahikam, spoke to Johanan, the son of Kareah. He said, "Don't do an awful thing like that! What you are saying about Ishmael isn't true."

41

In the seventh month Ishmael, the son of Nethaniah, came with ten men to Gedaliah, the son of Ahikam, at Mizpah. Nethaniah was the son of Elishama. Ishmael was a member of the royal family. He had been one of the king's officers. Ishmael and his ten men were eating together at Mizpah.

[2]They got up and struck down Gedaliah, the son of Ahikam, with their swords. They killed him even though the king of Babylonia had appointed him as governor over Judah. Ahikam was the son of Shaphan. [3]Ishmael also killed all of the Jews who were with Gedaliah at Mizpah. And he killed the Babylonian soldiers who were there.

[4]On the next day, people still hadn't found out that Gedaliah had been murdered. [5]On that day 80 men came from Shechem, Shiloh and Samaria. They had shaved off their beards. They had torn their clothes. And they had cut themselves. They brought grain offerings and incense with them. They took them to the LORD's house.

[6]Ishmael, the son of Nethaniah, went out from Mizpah to meet them. He was sobbing as he went. When he met them, he said, "Come to Gedaliah, the son of Ahikam."

[7]They went with him into the city. Then Ishmael, the son of Nethaniah, and the men who were with him killed them. And they threw them into an empty well.

[8]But ten of the men had spoken to Ishmael. They had said, "Don't kill us! We have some wheat and barley. We also have olive oil and honey. We've hidden all of it in a field." So he let them alone. He didn't kill them along with the others.

[9]But he had thrown all of the bodies of the men he had killed into the emp-

ty well. That included Gedaliah's body. The well was the one King Asa had made. He had made it when he strengthened Mizpah against attack by Baasha, the king of Israel. Ishmael, the son of Nethaniah, filled it with the bodies of those he had killed.

¹⁰Ishmael made prisoners of all the rest of the people who were in Mizpah. That included women who were members of the royal court. It also included all of the others who were left there. Nebuzaradan had appointed Gedaliah, the son of Ahikam, over them. Ishmael, the son of Nethaniah, took them as prisoners. Then he started out to go across the Jordan River to the land of Ammon. Nebuzaradan was the commander of the royal guard.

¹¹Johanan, the son of Kareah, and all of the other army officers who were with him were told what had happened. They heard about all of the crimes Ishmael, the son of Nethaniah, had committed. ¹²So they brought all of their men together. Then they went to fight against Ishmael, the son of Nethaniah. They caught up with him near the large pool in Gibeon. ¹³Ishmael had many people with him. They saw Johanan, the son of Kareah. And they saw the other army officers who were with him. So the people who had been forced to go with Ishmael were glad. ¹⁴All those whom Ishmael had taken as prisoners at Mizpah turned and went over to the side of Johanan, the son of Kareah. ¹⁵But Ishmael, the son of Nethaniah, and eight of his men escaped from Johanan. They ran away to the land of Ammon.

SOME JEWS TAKE JEREMIAH TO EGYPT

¹⁶Then Johanan, the son of Kareah, led away all of the people from Mizpah who were still alive. All of the other army officers who were with Johanan helped him do it. He had taken them away from Ishmael, the son of Nethaniah. That happened after Ishmael had murdered Gedaliah, the son of Ahikam. The people Johanan had taken away included the soldiers, women, children and court officials he had brought from Gibeon.

¹⁷They went on their way. They stopped at Geruth Kimham near Bethlehem. They were going to Egypt. ¹⁸They wanted to get away from the Babylonians. They were afraid of them because Ishmael, the son of Nethaniah, had killed Gedaliah, the son of Ahikam. The king of Babylonia had appointed Gedaliah as governor over Judah.

42 Then all of the army officers approached me. They included Johanan, the son of Kareah, and Jezaniah, the son of Hoshaiah. All of the people from the least important of them to the most important also came. ²All of them said to me, "Please listen to our appeal. Pray to the LORD your God. Pray for all of us who are left here. Once there were many of us. But as you can see, only a few of us are left now. ³So pray to the LORD your God. Pray that he'll tell us where we should go. Pray that he'll tell us what we should do."

⁴"I've heard you," I replied. "I'll certainly pray to the LORD your God. I'll do what you have asked me to do. In fact, I'll tell you everything the LORD says. I won't keep anything back from you."

⁵Then they said to me, "We'll do everything the LORD your God sends you to tell us to do. If we don't, may he be a true and faithful witness against us. ⁶It doesn't matter whether what you say is in our favor or not. We're asking you to pray to the LORD our God. And we'll obey him. Things will go well with us. That's because we will obey the LORD our God."

⁷Ten days later a message came to me from the LORD. ⁸So I sent for Johanan, the son of Kareah, and all of the other army officers who were with him. I also gathered together all of the people from the least important of them to the most important.

⁹I said to all of them, "The LORD is the God of Israel. You asked me to present your appeal to him. ¹⁰He told me, 'Stay in this land. Then I will build you up. I will not tear you down. I will plant you. I will not pull you up by the roots. I am very sad that I had to bring all of this trouble on you. ¹¹ 'Do not be afraid of the king of

Babylonia. You are afraid of him now. Do not be,' announces the LORD. 'I am with you. I will keep you safe. I will save you from his powerful hands. [12]I will show you my loving concern. Then he will have concern for you. And he will let you return to your land.'

[13]"But suppose you say, 'We won't stay in this land.' If you do, you will be disobeying the LORD your God. [14]And suppose you say, 'No! We'll go and live in Egypt. There we won't have to face war anymore. We won't hear the trumpets of war. And we won't get hungry.'

[15]"Then listen to what the LORD says to you who are left in Judah. He is the LORD who rules over all. He is the God of Israel. He says, 'Have you already made up your minds to go to Egypt? Are you going to settle down there?

[16]" 'Then the war you fear will catch up with you there. The hunger you are afraid of will follow you into Egypt. And you will die there. [17]In fact, that will happen to all those who go and settle in Egypt. All of them will die of war, hunger and plague. Not one of them will live. None of them will escape the trouble I will bring on them.'

[18]"He is the LORD who rules over all. He is the God of Israel. He says, 'My burning anger has been poured out on those who used to live in Jerusalem. In the same way, it will be poured out on you when you go to Egypt. People will call down curses on you. They will be shocked at you. They will say bad things about you. And they will bring shame on you. You will never see this place again.'

[19]"The LORD has spoken to you who are left in Judah. He has said, 'Do not go to Egypt.' Here is something you can be sure of. I am warning you about it today. [20]You made a big mistake when you asked me to pray to the LORD your God. You said, 'Pray to the LORD our God for us. Tell us everything he says. We'll do it.'

[21]"I have told you today what the LORD your God wants you to do. But you still haven't obeyed him. You haven't done anything he sent me to tell you to do. [22]So here is something else you can be sure of. You will die of war, hunger and plague. You want to go and settle down in Egypt. But you will die there."

43

I finished telling the people everything the LORD their God had said. I told them everything he had sent me to tell them. [2]After that, Azariah, the son of Hoshaiah, and Johanan, the son of Kareah, spoke to me. And all of the proud men joined them. They said, "You are lying! The LORD our God hasn't sent you to speak to us. He hasn't told you to say, 'You must not go to Egypt and settle down there.' [3]But Baruch, the son of Neriah, is turning you against us. He wants us to be handed over to the Babylonians. Then they can kill us. Or they can take us away to Babylon."

[4]So Johanan, the son of Kareah, disobeyed the LORD's command. So did all of the other army officers and all of the people. They didn't stay in the land of Judah.

[5]Instead Johanan, the son of Kareah, and all of the other army officers led away all of the people who were left in Judah. Those people had returned to Judah from all of the nations where they had been scattered. [6]Johanan and the other officers also led away many people Nebuzaradan had left in Mizpah. They included men, women and children. They also included women who were members of the royal court. Nebuzaradan had left them with Gedaliah, the son of Ahikam. He had also left them with the prophet Jeremiah and Baruch, the son of Neriah. Nebuzaradan was commander of the royal guard. Ahikam was the son of Shaphan.

[7]So the Jewish leaders disobeyed the LORD. They took everyone to Egypt. They went all the way to Tahpanhes.

[8]In Tahpanhes a message came to me from the LORD. He said, [9]"Make sure the Jews are watching you. Then get some large stones. Go to the entrance to Pharaoh's house in Tahpanhes. Bury the stones in the clay under the brick walkway there. [10]Then tell the Jews, 'The LORD who rules over all is the God of Israel. He says, "I will send for my servant Nebuchadnezzar, the king of Babylonia. And I will set his throne over these stones that are buried here. He will set

up his royal tent over them. [11]He will come and attack Egypt. He will bring death to those I have appointed to die. He will take away as prisoners those I have appointed to be taken away. And he will kill with swords those I have appointed to be killed.

[12]" ' "He will set the temples of the gods of Egypt on fire. He will burn their temples down. He will take the statues of their gods away. Nebuchadnezzar will be like a shepherd who wraps his coat around himself. He will wrap Egypt around himself. And he will leave there unharmed. [13]At Heliopolis in Egypt he will smash the sacred pillars to pieces. And he will burn down the temples of the gods of Egypt." ' "

DON'T WORSHIP OTHER GODS

44 A message came to me from the LORD about all of the Jews who were living in Lower Egypt. They were living in Migdol, Tahpanhes and Memphis. It was also about all of the Jews who were living in Upper Egypt. [2]The LORD who rules over all is the God of Israel. He said, "You saw all of the trouble I brought on Jerusalem. I also brought it on all of the towns in Judah. Today they lie there deserted and destroyed. [3]That is because of the evil things their people did. They made me very angry. They burned incense to other gods. And they worshiped them. They and you and your people of long ago never had anything to do with those gods before.

[4]"Again and again I sent my servants the prophets. They said, 'Don't worship other gods! The LORD hates it!'

[5]"But the people didn't listen. They didn't pay any attention. They didn't turn from their sinful ways. They didn't stop burning incense to other gods.

[6]"So my burning anger was poured out. It blazed out against the towns of Judah and the streets of Jerusalem. It made them the dry and empty places they are today."

[7]The LORD God who rules over all is the God of Israel. He says, "Why do you want to bring all of this trouble on yourselves? You are cutting off from Judah its men and women. You are cutting off the children and babies. Not one of you will be left. [8]Why do you want to make me angry with the gods your hands have made? Why do you burn incense to the gods of Egypt, where you have come to live? You will destroy yourselves. All of the nations on earth will call down curses on you. They will bring shame on you.

[9]"Have you forgotten the evil things your people did long ago? The kings and queens of Judah did those same things. So did you and your wives. They were done in the land of Judah and the streets of Jerusalem.

[10]"To this very day the people of Judah have not made themselves low in my sight. They have not shown any respect for me. They have not obeyed my law. They have not followed the rules I gave you and your people long ago."

[11]The LORD who rules over all is the God of Israel. He says, "I have decided to bring horrible trouble on you. I will destroy the whole land of Judah. [12]I will destroy the people of Judah who are left. They had decided to go to Egypt and settle down there. But all of them will die in Egypt. They will die of war or hunger. All of them will die, from the least important of them to the most important. They will die of war or hunger. People will call down curses on them. They will be shocked at them. They will say bad things about them. And they will bring shame on them. [13]I will use war, hunger and plague to punish the Jews who live in Egypt. I punished Jerusalem in the same way.

[14]"None of the people of Judah who have gone to live in Egypt will escape. Not one of them will live to return to Judah. They long to return and live there. But only a few will escape from Egypt and go back."

[15]All of the Jews who were living in Lower and Upper Egypt gathered to give me their answer. A large crowd had come together. It included men who knew that their wives were burning incense to other gods. Their wives were there with them.

All of them said to me, [16]"We won't

listen to the message you have spoken to us in the LORD's name! [17]We will certainly do everything we said we would. We'll burn incense to the goddess who is called the Queen of Heaven. We'll pour out drink offerings to her. We'll do just as we and our people before us did. Our kings and our officials also did it. All of us did it in the towns of Judah and the streets of Jerusalem. At that time we had plenty of food. We were well off. We didn't suffer any harm.

[18]"But then we stopped burning incense to the Queen of Heaven. We stopped pouring out drink offerings to her. And ever since that time we haven't had anything. Instead, we've been dying of war and hunger."

[19]The women added, "We burned incense to the Queen of Heaven. We poured out drink offerings to her. And our husbands knew we were making cakes that looked like her. They knew we were pouring out drink offerings to her."

[20]Then I spoke to all of the people who were answering me. I spoke to men and women alike. I said, [21]"Didn't the LORD know you were burning incense in the towns of Judah? Didn't he care that you were also doing it in the streets of Jerusalem? You and your people before you were doing it. Your kings and officials were doing it too. So were the rest of the people in the land.

[22]"The LORD couldn't put up with the evil things you were doing anymore. He hated the things you did. So people called down curses on your land. It became a dry and empty desert. No one lived there. And that's the way it still is today.

[23]"You have burned incense to other gods. You have sinned against the LORD. You haven't obeyed him or his law. You haven't followed his rules. You haven't lived up to the terms of the covenant he made with you. That's why all of this trouble has come on you. You have seen it with your own eyes."

[24]Then I spoke to all of the people. That included the women. I said, "All you people of Judah in Egypt, listen to the LORD's message. [25]The LORD who rules over all is the God of Israel. He says, 'You and your wives have done what you promised you would do. You said, "We will certainly keep the promises we made to the Queen of Heaven. We'll burn incense to her. We'll pour out drink offerings to her." '

"Go ahead then. Do what you said you would! Keep your promises! [26]But listen to the LORD's message. Listen, all you Jews living in Egypt. 'I take an oath in my own great name,' says the LORD. 'I promise that no one from Judah who lives anywhere in Egypt will ever again pray in my name. None of them will ever take an oath and say, "You can be sure that the LORD and King is alive."

[27]" 'I am watching over them to do them harm and not good. The Jews in Egypt will die of war and hunger until all of them are destroyed. [28]Some will not be killed. They will return to Judah from Egypt. But they will be very few. Then all of the people of Judah who came to live in Egypt will know the truth. They will know whether what I say or what they say will come true.

[29]" 'I will give you a miraculous sign that I will punish you in this place,' announces the LORD. 'Then you can be sure that my warnings of harm against you will come true.' [30]The LORD says, 'I am going to hand Pharaoh Hophra over to his enemies who want to take his life. In the same way, I handed King Zedekiah over to Nebuchadnezzar, the king of Babylonia. He was the enemy who wanted to take Zedekiah's life.' " Hophra was king of Egypt.

THE LORD SPEAKS TO BARUCH

45 I, the prophet Jeremiah, talked to Baruch, the son of Neriah. It was in the fourth year that Jehoiakim, the son of Josiah, was king of Judah. But it was after Baruch had written down on a scroll the words I was telling him to write. I said, [2]"The LORD is the God of Israel. Baruch, he says to you, [3]'You have said, "How terrible it is for me! The LORD has added sorrow to my pain. I'm worn out from all of my groaning. I can't find any rest." ' "

[4]The LORD said, "Tell Baruch, 'I say, "I will destroy what I have built up. I will pull up by the roots what I have

planted. I will do it all through the earth. ⁵So should you long for great things for yourself? Do not long for them. I will bring trouble on everyone," announces the LORD. "But no matter where you go, I will let you escape with your life." ' "

THE LORD'S MESSAGE ABOUT THE NATIONS

46 A message came to me from the LORD. It was about the nations.

A MESSAGE ABOUT EGYPT

²Here is what the LORD says about Egypt.

Here is his message against the army of Pharaoh Neco. He was king of Egypt. Nebuchadnezzar, the king of Babylonia, won the battle over his army. That happened at Carchemish on the Euphrates River. It was in the fourth year that Jehoiakim was king of Judah. He was the son of Josiah.

The message says,

³"Egyptians, prepare your shields!
　Prepare large and small shields
　　alike!
　March out for battle!
⁴Get the horses and chariots ready
　　to ride!
　Take up your battle positions!
　Put your helmets on!
Shine up your spears!
　Put on your armor!
⁵What do I see?
　The Egyptians are terrified.
They are pulling back.
　Their soldiers are losing.
They run away as fast as they
　　can.
　They do not look back.
　There is terror on every side,"
　　　　　　announces the LORD.
⁶"Those who run fast can't get
　　away.
　Those who are strong can't
　　escape.
In the north by the Euphrates
　　River
　they trip and fall.

⁷"Who is this that rises like the Nile
　　River?

Who rises like rivers of rushing
　　waters?
⁸Egypt rises like the Nile River.
　It rises like rivers of rushing
　　waters.
Egypt says, 'I will rise and cover
　　the earth.
　I'll destroy cities and their
　　people.'
⁹Charge, you horses!
　Drive fast, you chariot drivers!
March on, you soldiers!
　March on, you men of Cush and
　　Put who carry shields.
　March on, you men of Lydia who
　　draw bows.
¹⁰But that day belongs to me.
　I am the LORD who rules
　　over all.
　It is a day for me to pay back my
　　enemies.
The sword will eat until it is
　　satisfied.
　It will drink until it has no more
　　thirst for blood.
I am the Lord. I am the LORD who
　　rules over all.
　I will offer a sacrifice.
I will offer it in the land of the
　　north
　by the Euphrates River.

¹¹"People of Egypt,
　go up to Gilead and get some
　　healing lotion.
But no matter what you try, you
　　will not be healed.
　There isn't any healing for you.
¹²The nations will hear about your
　　shame.
　Your cries of pain will fill the
　　earth.
One soldier will trip over
　　another.
　Both of them will fall down
　　together."

¹³Nebuchadnezzar, the king of Babylonia, was coming to attack Egypt. Here is the message the LORD spoke to me about it. He said,

¹⁴"Egyptians, here is what I want
　　you to announce in your
　　land.
　Announce it in Migdol.
　Also announce it in Memphis
　　and Tahpanhes.

Say, 'Take up your battle positions!
　Get ready!
　The sword eats up those who are
　　around you.'
¹⁵ Why are your soldiers lying on the
　　ground?
　They can't stand, because I bring
　　them down.
¹⁶ They will trip again and again.
　They will fall over one another.
　They will say, 'Get up. Let's go back
　　home.
　Let's return to our own people
　　and our own lands.
　Let's get away from the swords
　　that will bring us great harm.'
¹⁷ The Egyptian soldiers will cry out,
　'Pharaoh is our king. But he's
　　only a loud noise.
　He has missed his chance to win
　　the battle.'

¹⁸ "I am the King.
　My name is The LORD Who Rules
　　Over All.
　Someone will come who is like
　　Mount Tabor among the
　　mountains.
　He is like Mount Carmel by the
　　Mediterranean Sea.
　And that is just as sure as I am
　　alive,"
　announces the King.
¹⁹ "So pack your belongings, you
　　who live in Egypt.
　You will be taken away from your
　　land.
　Memphis will be completely
　　destroyed.
　Its buildings will be broken
　　down.
　No one will live there.

²⁰ "Egypt is like a beautiful young
　　cow.
　But Nebuchadnezzar is coming
　　against her from the north.
　He will bite her like a fly.
²¹ Hired soldiers are in Egypt's army.
　They are like fat calves.
　All of them will turn and run
　　away.
　They will not hold their
　　positions.
　The day of trouble is coming on
　　them.
　The time for them to be
　　punished is near.

²² The Egyptians will hiss like a snake
　　that is trying to get away.
　A powerful army will advance
　　against them.
　Their enemies will come against
　　them with axes.
　They will be like those who cut
　　down trees.
²³ Egypt is like a thick forest.
　But they will chop it down,"
　　　　　announces the LORD.
　"There are more of them than
　　there are locusts.
　In fact, they can't even be
　　counted.
²⁴ The nation of Egypt will be put to
　　shame.
　It will be handed over to the
　　people of the north."

²⁵ The LORD who rules over all is the
God of Israel. He says, "I am about to
punish Amon, the god of Thebes. I will
also punish Pharaoh. I will punish
Egypt and its gods and kings. And I
will punish those who depend on
Pharaoh. ²⁶ I will hand them over to
those who are trying to kill them. I will
give them to Nebuchadnezzar, the
king of Babylonia, and his officers. But
later, many people will live in Egypt
again as in times past," announces the
LORD.

²⁷ "People of Jacob, do not be afraid.
　You are my servant.
　Israel, do not be terrified.
　I will bring you safely out of a
　　place far away.
　I will bring your children back
　　from the land where they were
　　taken.
　Your people will have peace and
　　security again.
　And no one will make them
　　afraid.
²⁸ People of Jacob, do not be afraid.
　You are my servant.
　I am with you," announces the
　　LORD.
　"I will completely destroy all of the
　　nations
　　among which I scatter you.
　But I will not completely destroy
　　you.
　I will correct you. But I will be fair.
　I will punish you in a way that is
　　fair and right."

A MESSAGE ABOUT THE PHILISTINES

47 A message came to me from the LORD. It was about the Philistines before Pharaoh attacked Gaza.

2 The LORD said,

"The armies of Babylonia are like
    waters rising in the north.
They will become a great flood.
They will flow over the land and
    everything in it.
They will flow over the towns and
    those who live in them.
The people will cry out.
All those who live in the land will
    sob.
3 They will sob when they hear
    galloping horses.
They will sob at the noise of
    enemy chariots.
They will sob at the rumble of
    their wheels.
Fathers will not even try to help
    their children.
Their hands will not be able to
    help them.
4 The day has come
    to destroy all of the Philistines.
The time has come to cut off all
    those
    who could help Tyre and Sidon.
I am about to destroy the
    Philistines.
I will not leave anyone alive
    who came from the coasts of
    Crete.
5 The people of Gaza will be so sad
    they will shave their heads.
And Ashkelon's people will be
    silent.
You who remain on the flatlands,
    how long will you cut yourselves?

6 " 'Sword of the LORD!' you cry out.
'How long will it be until you
    rest?
Return to the place you came
    from.
Stop killing us! Be still!'
7 But how can my sword rest
    when I have given it a
    command?
I have ordered it
    to attack Ashkelon and the
    Philistine coast."

A MESSAGE ABOUT MOAB

48 Here is what the LORD says about Moab.

The LORD who rules over all is the God of Israel. He says,

"How terrible it will be for Nebo!
    It will be destroyed.
Kiriathaim will be captured.
    It will be put to shame.
Its fort will be broken down.
    It will be put to shame.
2 Moab will not be praised
    anymore.
In Heshbon people will plan its
    fall from power.
They will say, 'Come. Let's put an
    end to that nation.'
City of Madmen, you too will be
    silent because you are sad.
My sword will hunt you down.
3 Listen to the cries from
    Horonaim.
The town is being completely
    destroyed.
4 Moab will be broken.
Her little ones will cry out.
5 The people go up the road to
    Luhith.
They are sobbing bitterly as
    they go.
Loud cries are heard on the road
    down to Horonaim.
People cry out because the town
    is being destroyed.
6 People of Moab run away! Run for
    your lives!
Become like a lonely bush in the
    desert.
7 You trust in the things you can do.
You trust in your riches.
So you too will be taken away as
    prisoners.
Your god Chemosh will be carried
    away.
So will its priests and officials.
8 The one who is going to destroy
    you
    will come against every town.
Not even one of them will
    escape.
The valley and the high flatlands
    will be destroyed.
I, the LORD, have spoken.
9 Sprinkle salt all over Moab.
It will be completely destroyed.

Its towns will be a dry and empty
  desert.
No one will live in them.

10 "May a person who is lazy when
    he does my work
  be under my curse!
May anyone who keeps his sword
    from killing
  be under my curse!

11 "Moab has been at peace and rest
    from its earliest days.
It is like wine that has not been
    shaken up.
It has not been poured from one
    jar to another.
Moab's people have not been
    taken away from their land.
They are like wine that tastes as it
    always did.
Its smell has not changed at all.
12 But other days are coming,"
    announces the LORD.
"At that time I will send people
    who pour wine from jars.
They will pour Moab out like wine.
They will empty its jars.
They will smash its jugs.
13 Then Moab's people will be
    ashamed of their god
    Chemosh.
They will be ashamed just as the
    people of Israel were
when they trusted in their god at
    Bethel.

14 "How can you say, 'We are soldiers.
We are men who are brave in
    battle'?
15 Moab will be destroyed.
Its enemies will march into its
    towns.
Her finest young men will die in
    battle,"
  announces the King.
His name is The LORD Who Rules
    Over All.
16 "The fall of Moab is near.
Its time of trouble will come
    quickly.
17 All you who live around it, sob
    over its people.
Be sad, you who know how
    famous Moab is.
Say, 'Its powerful ruler's rod is
    broken!
His glorious staff is smashed.'

18 "Come down from your glorious
    city, you who live in Dibon.
Come and sit on the thirsty
    ground.
The one who destroys your
    country
  will come up and attack you.
Your enemies will destroy your
    cities
  that have high walls around
    them.
19 Stand by the road and watch,
  you who live in Aroer.
Ask the men who are running
    away.
Ask the women who are
    escaping.
Ask them, 'What has happened?'
20 Moab has been put to shame.
It has been destroyed.
Sob and cry out!
Tell everyone Moab has been
    destroyed.
Announce it by the Arnon River.
21 The high flatlands have been
    judged.
So have Holon, Jahzah and
    Mephaath.
22 Dibon, Nebo and Beth Diblathaim
    have been judged.
23   So have Kiriathaim, Beth Gamul
    and Beth Meon.
24 Kerioth and Bozrah have also been
    judged.
And so have all of the towns of
    Moab, far and near alike.
25 Moab's power is gone.
Its strength is broken,"
              announces the LORD.

26 "Moab's people think they are
    better than I am.
So let their enemies make them
    drunk.
Let the people get sick and throw
    up.
Let them roll around in the mess
    they have made.
Let people laugh at them.
27 Moab, you laughed at Israel, didn't
    you?
Were Israel's people caught
    among robbers?
Is that why you shake your head at
    them?
Is that why you make fun of
    them

every time you talk about them?
²⁸ Leave your towns,
    you who live in Moab.
  Go and live among the rocks.
  Be like a dove that makes its nest
    at the mouth of a cave.

²⁹ "We have heard all about Moab's
    pride.
  We have heard how very proud
    they are.
  They think they are so much
    better than others.
  Their pride reaches deep down
    inside their hearts.
³⁰ I know how rude they are.
  But it will not get them
    anywhere,"
              announces the LORD.
  "Their bragging does not
    accomplish anything.
³¹ So I cry out over Moab.
  I cry for all of Moab's people.
  I groan for the men of Kir
    Hareseth.
³² I sob over you as Jazer sobs,
    you vines of Sibmah.
  Your branches used to spread out.
    They went all the way down to
      the Dead Sea.
    They reached as far as the sea of
      Jazer.
  The one who destroys your
    country
    has taken away your grapes and
      ripe fruit.
³³ Joy has left your orchards.
  Gladness is gone from your
    fields.
  I have stopped the flow of juice
    from your winepresses.
  No one stomps on your grapes
    with shouts of joy.
  There are shouts.
  But they are not shouts of joy.

³⁴ "The sound of their cry rises from
    Heshbon.
  It rises as far as Elealeh and
    Jahaz.
  It rises from Zoar.
  It goes all the way to Horonaim
    and Eglath Shelishiyah.
  Even the waters at Nimrim are
    dried up.
³⁵ In Moab people sacrifice offerings
    on the high places.
  They burn incense to their gods.

But I will put an end to those
    people,"
              announces the LORD.
³⁶ "Like a flute my heart sings a song
    of sadness for Moab.
  It sings like a flute for the men of
    Kir Hareseth.
  The wealth they had gotten is
    gone.
³⁷ Every head is shaved.
  Every beard is cut off.
  Every hand is cut.
  And every waist is covered with
    black cloth.
³⁸ Sobbing is the only sound in
    Moab.
  It is heard on all of its roofs.
  It is heard in the market places.
  I have broken Moab
    like a jar that no one wants,"
              announces the LORD.
³⁹ "How broken Moab is! How the
    people sob!
  They turn away from others
    because they are so ashamed.
  All those who are around them
    laugh at them.
  They are shocked at them."

⁴⁰ The LORD says,

  "Look! Nebuchadnezzar is like an
    eagle diving down.
  He is spreading his wings over
    Moab.
⁴¹ Kerioth will be captured.
  Its forts will be taken.
  At that time the hearts of Moab's
    soldiers will tremble in fear.
  They will be like the heart of a
    woman having a baby.
⁴² Moab will be destroyed as a
    nation.
  That is because its people
    thought
    they were better than I am.
⁴³ You people of Moab,"
              announces the LORD,
  "terror, a pit and a trap are
    waiting for you.
⁴⁴ Anyone who runs away from the
    terror
    will fall into the pit.
  Anyone who climbs out of the pit
    will be caught in the trap.
  The time is coming
    when I will punish Moab,"
              announces the LORD.

45 "In the shadow of Heshbon
　　those who are trying to escape
　　　stand helpless.
　A fire has blazed out from
　　Heshbon.
　Flames have come out from
　　Sihon's city.
　It burns the foreheads of Moab's
　　people.
　It burns the skulls of those who
　　brag loudly.
46 How terrible it will be for you,
　　Moab!
　Those who worship Chemosh are
　　destroyed.
　Your sons are being taken to
　　another country.
　Your daughters are taken away as
　　prisoners.

47 "But in days to come
　I will bless Moab with great
　　success again,"
　　　　　announces the LORD.

That's the report about how the
LORD said he would judge Moab.

A MESSAGE ABOUT AMMON

49 Here is what the LORD says
about the people of Am-
mon.

He says,

　"Doesn't Israel have any sons?
　Doesn't Israel have anyone
　to take over the family property?
　Then why has the god Molech
　　taken over Gad?
　Why do those who worship him
　　live in its towns?
2 But a new day is coming,"
　announces the LORD.
　"At that time I will sound the battle
　　cry.
　I will sound it against Rabbah in
　　the land of Ammon.
　It will become a pile of broken-
　　down buildings.
　The villages that are around it
　　will be set on fire.
　Then Israel will drive out
　　those who drove her out,"
　　　　　says the LORD.
3 "Heshbon, sob over Ai! It is
　　destroyed!
　Cry out, you who live in Rabbah!
　Put on black clothes and sob.

　Run here and there inside the
　　walls.
　Your god Molech will be carried
　　away.
　So will its priests and officials.
4 Why do you brag about your
　　valleys?
　You brag that they produce so
　　many crops.
　You are an unfaithful country.
　You trust in your riches. You say,
　　'Who will attack me?'
5 I will bring terror on you.
　It will come from all those who
　　are around you,"
　　　　　announces the Lord.
　　　　　He is the LORD
　　　　　who rules over all.
　"Every one of you will be driven
　　away.
　No one will bring back those who
　　escape.

6 "But after that, I will bless the
　　people of Ammon
　with great success again,"
　　　　　announces the LORD.

A MESSAGE ABOUT EDOM

7 Here is what the LORD says about
Edom.

The LORD who rules over all says,

　"Isn't there wisdom in the town of
　　Teman anymore?
　Can't those who are wise give
　　advice?
　Has their wisdom disappeared
　　completely?
8 Turn around and run away, you
　　who live in Dedan.
　Hide in deep caves.
　I will bring trouble on Esau's
　　family line.
　I will do it at the time I punish
　　them.
9 Edom, suppose grape pickers
　　came to harvest your vines.
　They would still leave a few grapes.
　Suppose robbers came at night.
　They would steal only as much as
　　they wanted.
10 But I will strip everything away
　　from Esau's people.
　I will uncover their hiding places.
　They will not be able to hide
　　anywhere.

Their children, relatives and
    neighbors will die.
Then Esau's people will be gone.
¹¹ Leave your children whose fathers
    have died.
I will watch over them.
    Your widows can also trust in me."

¹² The LORD says, "What if those who
do not have to drink the cup must
drink it anyway? Then shouldn't you
be punished? You will certainly be
punished. You must drink the cup. ¹³ I
make a promise with an oath in my
own name. Bozrah will be destroyed,"
announces the LORD. "People will be
shocked at it. They will bring shame
on it. They will call down curses on it.
And all of its towns will be destroyed
forever."

¹⁴ I've heard a message from the
    LORD.
A messenger was sent to the
    nations. The LORD told him to
    say,
"Gather yourselves together to
    attack Edom!
Prepare for battle!"

¹⁵ The LORD says to Edom, "I will
    make you weak among the
    nations.
They will look down on you.
¹⁶ You live in the safety of the rocks.
You live on top of the hills.
But the terror you stir up has now
    turned against you.
Your proud heart has tricked you.
You build your nest as high as an
    eagle does.
But I will bring you down from
    there,"
           announces the LORD.
¹⁷ "People of Edom,
all those who pass by you will be
    shocked.
They will make fun of you
    because of all of your wounds.
¹⁸ Sodom and Gomorrah were
    destroyed.
So were the towns that were near
    them,"
           says the LORD.
"You will be just like them.
No one will live in your land.
No one will stay there even for a
    short time.

¹⁹ "I will be like a lion coming up
    from the bushes by the Jordan
    River.
I will hunt in rich grasslands.
I will chase you from your land in
    an instant.
What nation will I choose to
    do it?
Which one will I appoint?
Is anyone like me?
Who would dare to argue
    with me?
What leader can stand against
    me?"
²⁰ So listen to what the LORD has
    planned
    against the people of Edom.
Hear what he has planned
    against those who live in
    Teman.
Edom's young people will be
    dragged away.
The LORD will completely destroy
    their grasslands because of them.
²¹ When the earth hears Edom fall, it
    will shake.
The people's cries will be heard
    all the way to the Red Sea.
²² Look! An enemy is coming.
It's like an eagle diving down.
It will spread its wings over
    Bozrah.
At that time the hearts of Edom's
    soldiers
will tremble in fear.
They'll be like the heart of a
    woman having a baby.

A MESSAGE ABOUT DAMASCUS

²³ Here is what the LORD says about
Damascus. He says,

"The people of Hamath and Arpad
    are terrified.
They have heard bad news.
They have lost all hope.
They are troubled like the rolling
    sea.
²⁴ The people of Damascus have
    become weak.
They have turned to run away.
Panic has taken hold of them.
Suffering and pain have taken
    hold of them.
Their pain is like the pain of a
    woman having a baby.

²⁵ Why hasn't the famous city been
deserted?
It is the town I take delight in.
²⁶ You can be sure its young men will
fall dead in the streets.
All of its soldiers will be put to
death at that time,"
announces the LORD
who rules over all.
²⁷ "I will set the walls of Damascus
on fire.
It will burn up the strong towers
of King Ben-Hadad."

A MESSAGE ABOUT KEDAR AND HAZOR

²⁸ Here is what the LORD says about
the land of Kedar and the kingdoms of
Hazor. Nebuchadnezzar, the king of
Babylonia, was planning to attack
them.

The LORD says to the armies of Babylonia,

"Prepare for battle. Attack Kedar.
Destroy the people of the east.
²⁹ Their tents and flocks will be taken
away from them.
Their tents will be carried off.
All of their goods and camels will
be stolen.
People will shout to them,
'There is terror on every side!'

³⁰ "Run away quickly!
You who live in Hazor, stay in
deep caves,"
announces the LORD.
"Nebuchadnezzar, the king of
Babylonia,
has made plans against you.
He has decided to attack you.

³¹ "Armies of Babylonia, prepare for
battle.
Attack a nation that feels
secure.
Its people do not have any
worries,"
announces the LORD.
"That nation does not have gates
or heavy metal bars.
Its people live all alone.
³² Their camels will be stolen.
Their large herds will be taken
away.
I will scatter to the winds those
who are in places far away.

I will bring trouble on them from
every side,"
announces the LORD.
³³ "Hazor will become a home for
wild dogs.
It will be a dry and empty desert
forever.
No one will live in that land.
No one will stay there even for a
short time."

A MESSAGE ABOUT ELAM

³⁴ A message came to me from the
LORD. It was about Elam. It came
shortly after Zedekiah became king of
Judah.

³⁵ The LORD who rules over all said,

"Elam's bow is the secret of its
strength.
But I will break it.
³⁶ I will bring the four winds against
Elam.
I will bring them from all four
directions.
I will scatter Elam's people to the
four winds.
They will be taken away
to every nation on earth.
³⁷ I will use Elam's enemies to smash
them.
Those who are trying to take
their lives will kill them.
I will bring trouble on Elam's
people.
My anger will burn against
them,"
announces the LORD.
"I will chase them with swords.
I will hunt them down
until I have destroyed them.
³⁸ I will set up my throne in Elam.
I will destroy its king and
officials,"
announces the LORD.
³⁹ "But in days to come I will bless
Elam
with great success again,"
announces the LORD.

A MESSAGE ABOUT BABYLONIA

50 Here is the message the
LORD spoke through me
about the city of Babylon
and the land of Babylonia. He said,

² "Announce this message among
    the nations.
  Lift up a banner.
Let the nations hear the message.
  Do not keep anything back.
Say, 'Babylon will be captured.
  The god Bel will be put to shame.
  Marduk will be filled with terror.
Babylon's gods will be put to
    shame.
  The gods its people made will be
    filled with terror.'
³ A nation from the north will
    attack it.
  That nation will destroy
    Babylonia.
No one will live there.
  People and animals alike will run
    away.

⁴ "A new day is coming,"
    announces the LORD.
  "At that time the people of Israel
    and Judah will gather
    together.
  They will come in tears to me.
  I am the LORD their God.
⁵ They will ask how to get to Zion.
  Then they will turn their faces
    toward it.
  They will come and join
    themselves to me.
  They will enter into the covenant
    I make with them.
  It will last forever.
  It will never be forgotten.

⁶ "My people have been like lost
    sheep.
  Their shepherds have led them
    down the wrong path.
  They have caused them to
    wander in the mountains.
  They have wandered over
    mountains and hills.
  They have forgotten that I am
    their true resting place.
⁷ Everyone who found them
    destroyed them.
  Their enemies said, 'We aren't
    guilty.
  They sinned against the LORD.
  He gave them everything they
    needed.
  He has always been Israel's hope.'

⁸ "People of Judah, run away from
    Babylon.

Leave the land of Babylonia.
  Be like the goats that lead the
    flock.
⁹ I will stir up great nations
    that will join forces against
    Babylon.
  I will bring them from the land of
    the north.
They will take up their battle
    positions against Babylon.
  They will come from the north
    and capture it.
  Their arrows will be like skilled
    soldiers.
  They will not miss their mark.
¹⁰ So the riches of Babylonia will be
    taken away.
  All those who steal from it will
    have more than enough,"
                announces the LORD.

¹¹ "People of Babylonia, you have
    stolen what belongs to me.
  That has made you glad and full
    of joy.
  You dance around like a young
    cow on a threshing floor.
  You neigh like stallions.
¹² Because of that, you will bring
    great shame on your land.
  Your whole nation will be
    dishonored.
  It will become the least important
    of the nations.
  It will become a dry and empty
    desert.
¹³ Because I am angry with it, no one
    will live there.
  It will be completely deserted.
  All those who pass by it will be
    shocked.
  They will make fun of it because
    of all of its wounds.

¹⁴ "All you who draw the bow,
    take up your battle positions
    around Babylon.
  Shoot at it! Do not spare any
    arrows!
  Its people have sinned against me.
¹⁵ Shout against them on every side!
    They are giving up.
  The towers of the city are falling.
  Its walls are being pulled down.
  I am paying its people back.
  So pay them back yourselves.
  Do to them what they have done
    to others.

¹⁶Do not leave anyone in Babylonia
to plant the fields.
Do not leave anyone to harvest
the grain.
Let each of them return to his own
people.
Let him run away to his own
land.
If he doesn't, his enemy's
sword will bring him great
harm.

¹⁷"Israel is like a scattered flock
that lions have chased away.
The first lion that ate them up
was the king of Assyria.
The last one that broke their
bones
was Nebuchadnezzar, the king of
Babylonia."

¹⁸The LORD who rules over all is the
God of Israel. He says,

"I punished the king of Assyria.
In the same way, I will punish
the king of Babylonia and his
land.
¹⁹But I will bring Israel back to their
own grasslands.
I will feed them on Mount
Carmel and in Bashan.
I will satisfy their hunger
on the hills of Ephraim and
Gilead.
²⁰A new day is coming,"
announces the LORD.
"At that time people will search for
Israel's guilt.
But they will not find any.
They will search for Judah's sins.
But they will not find any.
That is because I will forgive the
people I have spared.

²¹"Enemies of Babylonia, attack
their land of Merathaim.
Make war against those who live
in Pekod.
Chase them and kill them. Destroy
them completely,"
announces the LORD.
"Do everything I have
commanded you to do.
²²The noise of battle is heard in the
land.
It is the noise of a great city being
destroyed!
²³It has been broken to pieces.

It was the hammer that broke the
whole earth.
How empty Babylonia is among
the nations!
²⁴Babylonia, I set a trap for you.
And you were caught before you
knew it.
You were found and captured.
That is because you opposed me.
²⁵I have opened up my storeroom.
I have brought out the weapons I
use when I am angry.
I am the LORD and King who rules
over all.
I have work to do in the land of
the Babylonians.
²⁶So come against it from far away.
Open up its storerooms.
Stack everything up like piles of
grain.
Completely destroy that country.
Do not leave anyone alive there.
²⁷Kill all of its people.
Let them die in battle.
How terrible it will be for them!
Their time to be judged has
come.
Now they will be punished.
²⁸Listen to those who have escaped.
Listen to those who have
returned from Babylonia.
They are announcing in Zion
how I have paid Babylonia back.
I have paid it back for destroying
my temple.

²⁹"Send for men who are armed
with bows and arrows.
Send them against Babylon.
Set up camp all around it.
Do not let anyone escape.
Pay it back for what its people
have done.
Do to them what they have done
to others.
They have dared to disobey me.
I am the Holy One of Israel.
³⁰You can be sure its young men will
fall dead in the streets.
All of its soldiers will be put to
death at that time,"
announces the LORD.
³¹"Proud Babylonians, I am against
you,"
announces the Lord.
The LORD who rules over all says,
"Your day to be judged has come.

It is time for you to be punished.
³²You proud people will trip and fall.
No one will help you up.
I will start a fire in your towns.
It will burn up everyone who is
    around you."

³³The LORD who rules over all says,

"The people of Israel are being
    treated badly.
So are the people of Judah.
Those who have captured them
    are holding them.
They refuse to let them go.
³⁴But I am strong and will save them.
My name is The LORD Who Rules
    Over All.
I will stand up for them.
I will bring peace and rest to
    their land.
But I will bring trouble to those
    who live in Babylonia.

³⁵"A sword is coming against the
    Babylonians!"
announces the LORD.
"It is coming against those who
    live in Babylonia.
It is coming against their officials
    and wise men.
³⁶A sword is coming against their
    prophets.
But they are not really prophets
    at all!
So they will look foolish.
A sword is coming against their
    soldiers!
They will be filled with terror.
³⁷A sword is coming against their
    horses and chariots!
It is coming against all of the
    hired soldiers in their armies.
They will become like weak
    women.
A sword is coming against their
    treasures!
They will be stolen.
³⁸There will not be any rain for their
    rivers.
So they will dry up.
Those things will happen because
    their land is full of statues of
    gods.
Those gods will go crazy with
    terror.

³⁹"Desert creatures and hyenas will
    live in Babylon.

And so will owls.
People will never live there again.
It will not be lived in for all time
    to come.
⁴⁰I destroyed Sodom and Gomorrah.
I also destroyed the towns that
    were near them,"
                    announces the LORD.
"Babylonia will be just like them.
No one will live there.
No one will stay there even for a
    short time.

⁴¹"Look! An army is coming from the
    north.
I am stirring up a great nation
    and many kings.
They are coming from a land that
    is very far away.
⁴²Their soldiers are armed with
    bows and spears.
They are mean.
They do not show any mercy
    at all.
They come riding in on their
    horses.
They sound like the roaring
    ocean.
They are lined up for battle.
They are coming to attack you,
    city of Babylon.
⁴³The king of Babylonia has heard
    reports about them.
His hands can't help him.
He is in great pain.
It is like the pain of a woman
    having a baby.
⁴⁴I will be like a lion coming up from
    the bushes by the Jordan
    River.
I will hunt in rich grasslands.
I will chase the people of Babylon
    from their land in an instant.
What nation will I choose to
    do it?
Which one will I appoint?
Is anyone like me? Who would
    dare to argue with me?
What leader can stand against
    me?"
⁴⁵So listen to what the LORD has
    planned against Babylon.
Hear what he has planned
    against the land of the
    Babylonians.
Their young people will be
    dragged away.

The LORD will completely destroy
their grasslands because of
them.
⁴⁶ When the earth hears that
Babylonia has been captured,
it will shake.
The people's cries will be heard
among the nations.

51

The LORD says,

"I will stir up the spirits of
destroyers.
They will march out against
Babylonia and its people.
² I will send other nations against it
to separate the straw from the
grain.
I will send them to destroy
Babylonia completely.
They will oppose it on every side.
At that time it will be destroyed.
³ Do not let its soldiers get their
bows ready to use.
Do not let them put on their
armor.
Do not spare their young men.
Destroy their armies completely.
⁴ They will fall down dead in
Babylon.
They will receive deadly wounds
in its streets.
⁵ The land of Israel and Judah is full
of guilt.
Its people have sinned against
me.
But I have not deserted them. I am
their God.
I am the LORD who rules over all.
I am the Holy One of Israel.

⁶ "People of Judah, run away from
Babylonia!
Run for your lives!
Do not be destroyed because of
the sins of its people.
It is time for me to pay them back.
I will punish them for what they
have done.
⁷ Babylon was like a gold cup in my
hand.
That city made the whole earth
drunk.
The nations drank its wine.
So now they have gone crazy.
⁸ Babylon will suddenly fall and be
broken.
Sob over it!

Get healing lotion for its pain.
Perhaps it can be healed.
⁹ "The nations say, 'We would have
healed Babylon.
But it can't be healed.
So let's leave it. Let's each go to our
own land.
Babylon's sins reach all the way
to the skies.
They rise up as high as the
clouds.'
¹⁰ "The people of Judah say,
'The LORD has made things right
for us again.
So come. Let's tell in Zion
what the LORD our God has
done.'
¹¹ "I have stirred up you kings of the
Medes.
So sharpen your arrows!
Get your shields!
I plan to destroy Babylon.
I will pay the Babylonians back.
They have destroyed my temple.
¹² Lift up a banner! Attack Babylon's
walls!
Put more guards on duty!
Station more of them to watch
over you!
Hide and wait to attack them!
I will do what I have planned.
I will do what I have decided to
do
against the people of Babylon.
¹³ You who live by the rivers of
Babylon,
your end has come.
You who are rich in treasures,
it is time for you to be
destroyed.
¹⁴ I am the LORD who rules over all.
I have made a promise with an
oath in my own name.
I have said, 'I will certainly fill your
land with soldiers.
They will be as many as a huge
number of locusts.
They will win the battle over you.
They will shout for joy.'
¹⁵ "I used my power to make the
earth.
I used my wisdom to set the
world in place.
I used my understanding to
spread the heavens out.

¹⁶ When I thunder, the waters in the
  heavens roar.
  I make clouds rise from one
    end of the earth to the
    other.
  I send lightning with the rain.
  I bring out the wind from my
    storerooms.
¹⁷ "No one has any sense.
  No one knows anything.
  Everyone who works with gold is
    put to shame
  by his wooden gods.
  His metal gods are fakes.
  They can't even breathe.
¹⁸ They are worthless. People make
    fun of them.
  When I judge them, they will be
    destroyed.
¹⁹ I am not like them. I am the God
    of Jacob.
  I give my people everything they
    need.
  I can do it because I made
    everything, including Israel.
  It is the nation that belongs to me.
  My name is The LORD Who Rules
    Over All.

²⁰ "Babylonia, you are my war club.
  You are my weapon for battle.
  I use you to destroy nations.
  I use you to wipe out kingdoms.
²¹ I use you to destroy horses and
    their riders.
  I use you to destroy chariots and
    their drivers.
²² I use you to destroy men and
    women.
  I use you to destroy old people
    and young people.
  I use you to destroy young men
    and young women.
²³ I use you to destroy shepherds and
    their flocks.
  I use you to destroy farmers and
    their oxen.
  I use you to destroy governors
    and officials.

²⁴ "Judah, I will pay Babylon back.
You will see it with your own eyes. I will
pay back all those who live in Babylonia. I will pay them back for all of the
wrong things they have done in Zion,"
announces the LORD.

²⁵ "Babylonia, I am against you.

Your kingdom is like a destroying
  mountain.
You have destroyed the whole
  earth,"
          announces the LORD.
"I will reach out my hand against
  you.
  I will roll you off the cliffs.
  I will make you like a mountain
    that has been burned up.
²⁶ No rock will be taken from you to
    be used
  as the most important stone for a
    building.
  No stones will be taken from you
    to be used for a foundation.
  Your land will be empty forever,"
          announces the LORD.

²⁷ "Nations, lift up a banner in the
    land of Babylonia!
  Blow a trumpet among
    yourselves!
  Prepare yourselves for battle
    against Babylonia.
  Send the kingdoms
    of Ararat, Minni and Ashkenaz
    against it.
  Appoint a commander against it.
  Send many horses against it.
  Let them be as many as a huge
    number of locusts.
²⁸ Prepare yourselves for battle
    against Babylonia.
  Prepare the kings of the
    Medes.
  Prepare their governors and all of
    their officials.
  Prepare all of the countries they
    rule over.
²⁹ The Babylonians tremble and
    shake with fear.
  My plans against them stand firm.
  I plan to destroy their land
    completely.
  Then no one will live there.
³⁰ Babylon's soldiers have stopped
    fighting.
  They remain in their forts.
  Their strength is all gone.
  They have become like weak
    women.
  Their buildings are set on fire.
  The heavy metal bars on their
    gates are broken.
³¹ One messenger after another
  comes to the king of Babylonia.

All of them announce that
his entire city is captured.
³² The places where people go across
the Euphrates River have been
captured.
The swamps have been set on
fire.
And the soldiers are terrified."

³³ The LORD who rules over all is the
God of Israel. He says,

"The city of Babylon is like a
threshing floor
when cattle are walking on it.
The time to destroy it will soon
come."

³⁴ The people of Jerusalem say,
"Nebuchadnezzar, the king of
Babylonia, has destroyed us.
He has thrown us into a panic.
He has emptied us out like a jar.
Like a snake he has swallowed us
up.
He has filled his stomach with
our rich food.
Then he has spit us out of his
mouth."
³⁵ The people continue, "May the
people of Babylon
pay for the harmful things they
have done to us.
May those who live in Babylonia
pay for spilling the blood of our
people."
That's what the people who live
in Zion say.

³⁶ So the LORD says,

"I will stand up for you.
I will pay the Babylonians back
for what they did to you.
I will dry up their water supply.
I will make their springs run dry.
³⁷ Babylon will have all of its
buildings knocked down.
It will be a home for wild dogs.
No one will live there.
People will be shocked at it.
They will make fun of it.
³⁸ All of its people roar like young
lions.
They growl like lion cubs.
³⁹ They are stirred up.
So I will set a big dinner in front
of them.
I will make them drunk.

And they will shout and laugh.
But then they will lie down and
die.
They will never wake up,"
announces the LORD.
⁴⁰ "I will lead them down like lambs
to be put to death.
They will be like rams and goats
that have been killed.

⁴¹ "Babylon will be captured!
The whole earth was very proud
of it.
But it will be taken over by others!
The nations will be shocked
when it falls.
⁴² Babylon's enemies will sweep over
it like an ocean.
Like roaring waves they will
cover it.
⁴³ The towns of Babylonia will be
empty.
It will become a dry and desert
land.
No one will live there.
No one will even travel through
it.
⁴⁴ I will punish the god Bel in
Babylon.
I will make Bel spit out what it
has swallowed.
The nations will not come and
worship it anymore.
And Babylon's walls will fall
down.

⁴⁵ "Come out of there, my people!
Run for your lives!
Run away from my burning
anger.
⁴⁶ You will hear about terrible things
that are happening in
Babylonia.
But do not lose hope. Do not be
afraid.
You will hear one thing this year.
And you will hear something else
next year.
You will hear about awful things in
the land.
You will hear about one ruler
fighting against another.
⁴⁷ I will punish the gods of Babylon.
That time will certainly come.
Then the whole land will be full of
shame.
Its people will lie down and die
there.

⁴⁸ So heaven and earth and
  everything in them will shout
  for joy.
They will be glad because of
  what will happen to Babylon.
Armies will attack it from the north.
And they will destroy it,"
           announces the LORD.

⁴⁹ "Babylon's people have killed my
  people Israel.
They have also killed people all
  over the earth.
So now Babylon itself must fall.
⁵⁰ You who have not been killed in
  the war against Babylon,
leave! Do not wait!
In a land far away remember me.
And think about Jerusalem."

⁵¹ The people of Judah reply, "No one
  honors us anymore.
People make fun of us.
Our faces are covered with shame.
People from other lands have
  entered
  the holy places of the LORD's
  house."

⁵² "But a new day is coming,"
  announces the LORD.
"At that time I will punish the
  gods of Babylon.
And all through its land
  wounded people will groan.
⁵³ What if Babylon reached all the
  way to the sky?
What if it made its high walls
  even stronger?
I would still send destroyers
  against it,"
           announces the LORD.

⁵⁴ "The noise of people screaming
  comes from Babylon.
A terrible sound comes from its
  land.
It is the sound of a mighty city
  being destroyed.
⁵⁵ I will destroy Babylon.
I will put an end to all of its noise.
Waves of enemies will sweep
  through it like great waters.
The roar of their voices will fill
  the air.
⁵⁶ A destroying army will come
  against Babylon.
The soldiers in the city will be
  captured.

Their bows will be broken.
I am the LORD God who pays
  people back.
I will pay them back in full.
⁵⁷ I will make Babylon's officials and
  wise men drunk.
I will do the same thing to its
  governors, officers and
  soldiers.
They will lie down and die. They
  will never wake up,"
  announces the King. His name is
  The LORD Who Rules Over All.

⁵⁸ The LORD who rules over all says,

"Babylon's thick walls will fall
  down flat.
Its high gates will be set on fire.
The nations wear themselves out
  for no reason at all.
Their hard work will only be
  burned up in the flames."

⁵⁹ I gave a message to the staff officer
Seraiah, the son of Neriah. I told him
to take it with him to Babylon. He went
there with Zedekiah, the king of Judah.
He left in the fourth year of Zedekiah's
rule. Neriah was the son of Mahseiah.
⁶⁰ I had written about all of the trouble
that would come on Babylon. I had
written it down on a scroll. It included
everything that had been recorded
about Babylon. ⁶¹ I said to Seraiah, "When you get to
Babylon, here's what I want you to do.
Make sure that you read all of these
words out loud. ⁶² Then say, 'LORD, you
have said you will destroy this place.
You have said that no people or animals will live here. It will be empty forever.'
⁶³ "Finish reading the scroll. Tie a
stone to it. Throw it into the Euphrates
River. ⁶⁴ Then say, 'In the same way,
Babylon will sink down. It will never
rise again. That is because I will bring
such horrible trouble on it. And its
people will fall along with it.' "

The words of Jeremiah end here.

NEBUCHADNEZZAR
DESTROYS JERUSALEM

52 Zedekiah was 21 years old
when he became king. He
ruled in Jerusalem for 11
years. His mother's name was Hamu-

tal. She was the daughter of Jeremiah. She was from Libnah.

²Zedekiah did what was evil in the sight of the LORD. He did just as Jehoiakim had done. ³The enemies of Jerusalem and Judah attacked them because the LORD was angry. In the end he threw them out of his land.

Zedekiah refused to obey the king of Babylonia.

⁴Nebuchadnezzar was king of Babylonia. He marched out against Jerusalem. All of his armies went with him. It was in the ninth year of the rule of Zedekiah. It was on the tenth day of the tenth month. The armies set up camp outside the city. They set up ladders and built ramps and towers all around it. ⁵It was surrounded until the 11th year of King Zedekiah's rule.

⁶By the ninth day of the fourth month, there wasn't any food left in the city. So the people didn't have anything to eat. ⁷Then the Babylonians broke through the city wall.

Judah's whole army ran away. They left the city at night. They went out through the gate between the two walls that were near the king's garden. They escaped even though the Babylonians surrounded the city. Judah's army ran toward the Arabah Valley.

⁸But the armies of Babylonia chased King Zedekiah. They caught up with him in the flatlands near Jericho. All of his soldiers were separated from him. They had scattered in every direction. ⁹The king was captured.

He was taken to the king of Babylonia at Riblah. Riblah was in the land of Hamath. That's where Nebuchadnezzar decided how he would be punished. ¹⁰At Riblah the king of Babylonia killed the sons of Zedekiah. He forced him to watch it with his own eyes. Nebuchadnezzar also killed all of the officials of Judah. ¹¹Then he poked out Zedekiah's eyes. He put him in bronze chains. And he took him to Babylon. There he put Zedekiah in prison until the day he died.

¹²Nebuzaradan served the king of Babylonia. In fact, he was commander of the royal guard. He came to Jerusalem. It was in the 19th year that Nebuchadnezzar was king of Babylonia.

It was on the tenth day of the fifth month.

¹³Nebuzaradan set the LORD's temple on fire. He also set fire to the royal palace and all of the houses in Jerusalem. He burned down every important building. ¹⁴The armies of Babylonia broke down all of the walls around Jerusalem. That's what the commander told them to do.

¹⁵Some of the poorest people still remained in the city along with the others. But the commander Nebuzaradan took them away as prisoners. He also took the rest of the skilled workers. That included the people who had joined the king of Babylonia. ¹⁶But Nebuzaradan left the rest of the poorest people of the land behind. He told them to work in the vineyards and fields.

¹⁷The armies of Babylonia destroyed the LORD's temple. They broke the bronze pillars into pieces. They broke up the bronze stands that could be moved around. And they broke up the huge bronze bowl. Then they carried all of the bronze away to Babylon. ¹⁸They also took away the pots, shovels, wick cutters, sprinkling bowls and dishes. They took away all of the bronze articles that were used for any purpose in the temple. ¹⁹The commander of the royal guard took away the bowls and the shallow cups for burning incense. He took away the sprinkling bowls, the pots, the lampstands and the dishes. He took away the bowls that were used for drink offerings. So he took away everything that was made out of pure gold or silver.

²⁰The bronze was more than anyone could weigh. It included the bronze from the two pillars. It included the bronze from the huge bowl and the 12 bronze bulls that were under it. It also included the stands. King Solomon had made all of those things for the LORD's temple.

²¹Each of the pillars was 27 feet high and 18 feet around. The pillars were hollow. The metal in each of them was three inches thick. ²²The bronze top of one pillar was seven and a half feet high. It was decorated with a set of bronze chains and pomegranates all

around it. The other pillar was just like it. It also had pomegranates. ²³There were 96 pomegranates on the sides of each of the two tops. The total number of pomegranates above the bronze chains around each top was 100.

²⁴The commander of the guard took many prisoners. They included the chief priest Seraiah and the priest Zephaniah who was under him. They also included the three men who guarded the temple doors. ²⁵Some people were still left in the city. The commander took as a prisoner the officer who was in charge of the fighting men. He took the seven men who gave advice to the king. He also took the secretary who was the chief officer in charge of getting the people of the land to serve in the army. And he took 60 of the secretary's men who were still in the city.

²⁶The commander Nebuzaradan took all of them away. He brought them to the king of Babylonia at Riblah. ²⁷There the king had them put to death. Riblah was in the land of Hamath.

So the people of Judah were taken as prisoners. They were taken far away from their own land. ²⁸Here is the number of the people Nebuchadnezzar took to Babylon as prisoners.

In the seventh year of his rule, he took 3,023 Jews.
²⁹In his 18th year,
he took 832 people from Jerusalem.
³⁰In Nebuchadnezzar's 23rd year, Nebuzaradan, the commander of the royal guard, took 745 Jews to Babylon.
The total number of people who were taken to Babylon was 4,600.

JEHOIACHIN IS SET FREE

³¹Evil-Merodach set Jehoiachin, the king of Judah, free from prison. It was in the 37th year after Jehoiachin had been taken away to Babylon. It was also the year Evil-Merodach became king of Babylonia. It was on the 25th day of the 12th month. ³²Evil-Merodach spoke kindly to Jehoiachin. He gave him a place of honor. Other kings were with Jehoiachin in Babylon. But his place was more important than theirs.

³³So Jehoiachin put his prison clothes away. For the rest of Jehoiachin's life the king of Babylonia provided what he needed. ³⁴The king did that for Jehoiachin day by day as long as he lived. He did it until the day Jehoiachin died.

quest challenge

I Wonder . . .

What have I made more important than knowing and following God?

Real Life Challenge

Anything in our life that is more important than God is an idol. Idols can be familiar things like the desire to be popular or to have a lot of stuff. We need to be careful to not allow any part of our lives—such as sports, grades or friends—to become more important to us than God.

Quest Clue

Look at Exodus 20 and 32 to see how God feels when you make something more important than him. Then find Jeremiah 2, 7 and 44 to see how much it hurts you and God when you worship an idol.

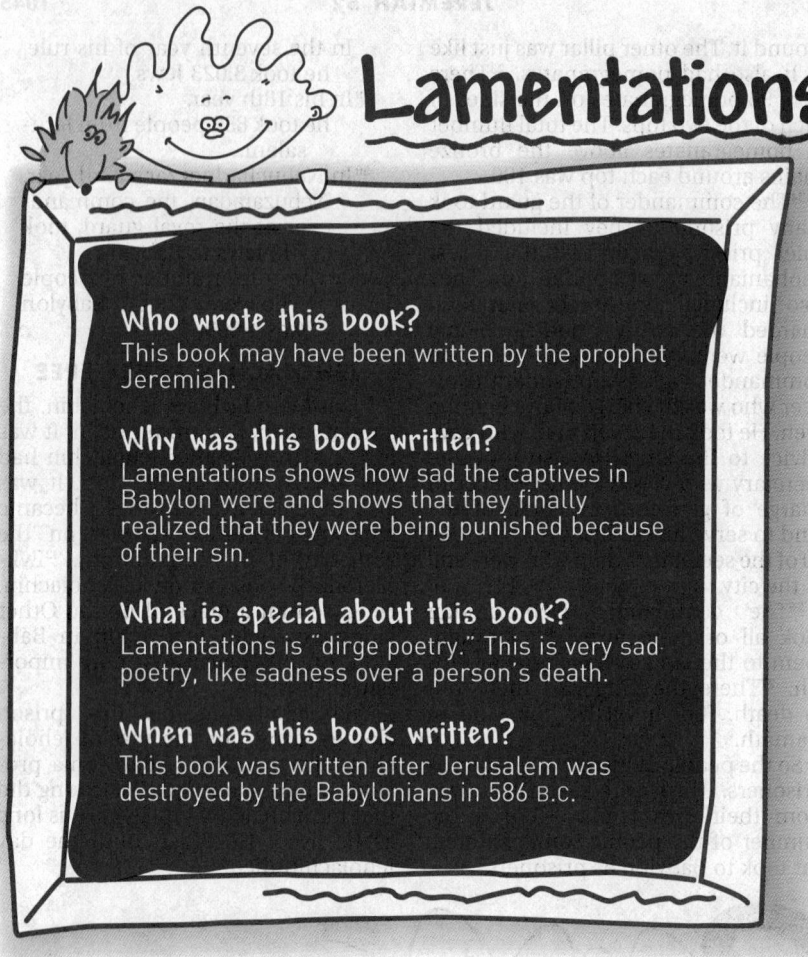

Lamentations

Who wrote this book?
This book may have been written by the prophet Jeremiah.

Why was this book written?
Lamentations shows how sad the captives in Babylon were and shows that they finally realized that they were being punished because of their sin.

What is special about this book?
Lamentations is "dirge poetry." This is very sad poetry, like sadness over a person's death.

When was this book written?
This book was written after Jerusalem was destroyed by the Babylonians in 586 B.C.

1 The city of Jerusalem is so
   empty!
   It used to be full of people.
But now it's like a woman whose
   husband has died.
   She used to be great among the
      nations.
She was like a queen among the
   kingdoms.
   But now she is a slave.

² Jerusalem sobs bitterly at night.
   Tears run down her cheeks.
   None of her friends comforts her.
All those who were going to
   help her
have turned against her.
   They have become her enemies.

³ After Judah's people had suffered
   greatly,
   they were taken away as
      prisoners.
Now they live among the nations.
   They can't find any place to rest.
All those who were chasing them
   have caught up with them.
   And they can't get away.

⁴ The roads to Zion are empty.
   No one travels to its appointed
      feasts.
All of the public places near its
   gates are deserted.
   Its priests groan.
Its young women are sad.
   And Zion itself sobs bitterly.

⁵Its enemies have become its
   masters.
   They have an easy life.
The LORD has brought suffering to
   Jerusalem
   because its people have
      committed so many sins.
Its children have been taken away
   as prisoners.
   Their enemies have forced them
      to leave their homes.

⁶The city of Zion used to be full of
   glory.
   But now its glory has faded away.
Its princes are like deer.
   They can't find anything to eat.
They are almost too weak to get
   away
   from those who hunt them down.

⁷Jerusalem's people are suffering
   and wandering.
   They remember all of the
      treasures
   they used to have.
But they fell into the hands of their
   enemies.
   And no one was there to help
      them.
Their enemies looked at them.
   They laughed because Jerusalem
      had been destroyed.

⁸Its people have committed many
   sins.
   They have become polluted.
All those who honored Jerusalem
   now look down on it.
   They look at it as if it were a
      naked woman.
The city groans and turns away
   in shame.

⁹Her skirts are dirty.
   She didn't think about how
      things might turn out.
Her fall from power amazed
   everyone.
   And no one was there to comfort
      her.
She said, "LORD, please pay
   attention to how much I'm
   suffering.
   My enemies have won the battle
      over me."

¹⁰Jerusalem's enemies took away
   all of its treasures.

Its people saw strangers
   enter its temple.
The LORD had commanded them
   not to do that.

¹¹All of Jerusalem's people groan
   as they search for bread.
They trade their treasures for food
   just to stay alive.
They say, "LORD, look at us.
   Think about our condition.
   Everyone looks down on us."

¹²They also say, "All of you who are
   passing by,
   don't you care about what has
      happened to us?
Just look at our condition.
   Has anyone suffered the way we
      have?
The LORD has brought all of this
   on us.
He has made us suffer.
   His anger has burned against us.

¹³"He sent fire down from heaven.
   It went deep down into our very
      bones.
He spread a net to catch us by the
   feet.
He stopped us right where we
   were.
He made our city empty.
   We are sick all the time.

¹⁴"We must carry the heavy load of
   our sins.
   He tied it on us with his hands.
Our sins are heavy on our necks.
   The Lord has taken away our
      strength.
He has handed us over to our
   enemies.
   We can't win the battle over them.

¹⁵"The Lord has refused to accept
   any of our soldiers.
He has sent for an army
   to crush our young men.
We are like grapes in the Lord's
   winepress.
   He has stomped on us,
   even though we are his very own
      people.

¹⁶"That's why we are sobbing.
   Tears are flowing from our eyes.
No one is near to comfort us.
   No one can heal our spirits.
   Our children don't have anything.

Our enemies are much too
strong for us."

¹⁷Zion reaches out its hands.
But no one is there to comfort its
people.
The LORD has ordered that
the neighbors of Jacob's people
would become their enemies.
Jerusalem has become polluted
among them.

¹⁸Its people say, "The LORD always
does what is right.
But we refused to obey his
commands.
Listen, all of you nations.
Pay attention to how much we're
suffering.
Our young women and young men
have been taken away as
prisoners.

¹⁹"We called out to those who were
going to help us.
But they turned against us.
Our priests and elders
died in the city.
They were searching for food
just to stay alive.

²⁰"LORD, see how upset we are!
We are suffering deep down
inside.
Our hearts are troubled.
Again and again we have refused
to obey you.
Outside the city, people are being
killed with swords.
Inside, there is nothing but
death.

²¹"People have heard us groan.
But no one is here to comfort us.
Our enemies have heard about all
of our troubles.
What you have done makes them
happy.
So please judge them, just as you
said you would.
Let them become like us.

²²"Please pay attention to all of their
sinful ways.
Punish them as you have
punished us.
You judged us because we had
committed so many sins.
We groan all the time.
And our hearts are weak."

2 See how the Lord covered the
city of Zion
with the cloud of his anger!
He threw Israel's glory down
from heaven to earth.
When he was angry, he turned
his back
on his own city.

²Without pity the Lord swallowed
up
all of the homes of Jacob's
people.
When he was angry, he tore
down
the forts of the people of Judah.
He brought their kingdom and its
princes
down to the ground in dishonor.

³When he burned with anger,
he took away Israel's power.
He pulled back his powerful right
hand
as the enemy approached.
His burning anger blazed out in
Jacob's land.
It burned up everything that was
near it.

⁴Like an enemy the Lord got his
bow ready to use.
He had a sword in his right hand.
Like an enemy he destroyed
everything that used to be
pleasing to him.
His anger blazed out like fire.
It burned up the homes in the
city of Zion.

⁵The Lord was like an enemy.
He swallowed up Israel.
He swallowed up all of its palaces.
He destroyed its forts.
He filled the people of Judah
with sorrow and sadness.

⁶The LORD's temple was like a
garden.
But he completely destroyed it.
He destroyed the place
where he used to meet with his
people.
He made Zion's people forget
their appointed feasts and
Sabbath days.
When he was very angry, he
turned his back on
king and priest alike.

⁷The Lord deserted his altar.
    He left his temple.
He handed the walls of Jerusalem's
        palaces
    over to its enemies.
They shouted loudly in the house
        of the LORD.
    You would have thought it was
        the day
    of an appointed feast.

⁸The LORD decided to tear down
    the walls around the city
        of Zion.
He measured out what he wanted
        to destroy.
    Then he destroyed it with his
        powerful hand.
He made even its towers and walls
        sing songs of sadness.
    All of them fell down.

⁹Its gates sank down into the
        ground.
    He broke their metal bars and
        destroyed them.
Its king and princes were taken
        away to other nations.
    There is no law anymore.
Jerusalem's prophets no longer
        receive
    visions from the LORD.

¹⁰The elders of the city of Zion
    sit silently on the ground.
They have sprinkled dust on their
        heads.
    They've put on black clothes to
        show how sad they are.
The young women of Jerusalem
    have bowed their heads toward
        the ground.

¹¹I've cried so much I can't see very
        well.
    I'm suffering deep down inside.
My heart is broken
    because my people are
        destroyed.
Children and babies are fainting
    in the streets of the city.

¹²They say to their mothers,
    "Where can we find something to
        eat and drink?"
They faint like wounded soldiers
    in the streets of the city.
Their lives are slipping away
    in their mothers' arms.

¹³City of Jerusalem, what can I say
        about you?
    What can I compare you to?
People of Zion, what are you like?
    I want to comfort you.
Your wound is as deep as the ocean.
    Who can heal you?

¹⁴The visions of your prophets were
        lies.
    They weren't worth anything.
They didn't show you the sins you
        had committed.
    So that's why you were captured.
The messages they gave you
        were lies.
    They led you down the wrong
        path.

¹⁵All those who pass by
    clap their hands and make fun of
        you.
They laugh at you and shake their
        heads
    at the city of Jerusalem.
They say, "Could that be the city
    that was called perfect and
        beautiful?
    Is that the city that brought joy to
        everyone on earth?"

¹⁶All of your enemies open their
        mouths
    wide against you.
They laugh at you and grind their
        teeth.
    They say, "We have swallowed
        Jerusalem's people up.
This is the day we've waited for.
    And we've lived to see it."

¹⁷The LORD has done what he
        planned to do.
    He has made what he said come
        true.
He gave the command long ago.
    He has destroyed you without pity.
He has let your enemies laugh
        at you.
    He has made them stronger than
        you are.

¹⁸People in the city of Zion,
    cry out from your heart to the
        Lord.
Let your tears flow like a river
    day and night.
Don't stop at all.
    Don't give your eyes any rest.

¹⁹ Get up. Cry out as the night begins.
Tell the Lord all of your troubles.
Lift up your hands to him.
Pray that the lives of your
children will be spared.
At every street corner they faint
because they are so hungry.

²⁰ Jerusalem says, "LORD, look at me.
Think about my condition.
Have you ever treated anyone
else like this?
Should women have to eat their
babies?
Should they eat the children
they've taken care of?
Should priests and prophets be
killed
in your own temple?

²¹ "Young people and old people
alike
lie dead in the dust of my streets.
My young women and young men
have been killed with swords.
You killed them when you were
angry.
You put them to death without
pity.

²² "You sent for terrors to come
against me on every side.
It was as if you were inviting
people to enjoy a feast day.
Because you were angry, no one
escaped.
No one was left alive.
I took good care of my children
and brought them up.
But my enemies have destroyed
them."

3 I am a man who has suffered
greatly.
The Lord has used the
Babylonians
to punish our people.
² He has driven me away. He has
made me walk
in darkness instead of light.
³ He has turned his powerful hand
against me.
He has done it again and again,
all day long.

⁴ He has worn my body out.
He has broken my bones.
⁵ He has surrounded me and
attacked me.

He has made me suffer bitterly.
He has made things hard for me.
⁶ He has made me live in darkness
like those who are dead and gone.

⁷ He has built walls around me. I
can't escape.
He has put heavy chains on me.
⁸ I call out and cry for help.
But he won't listen to me when I
pray.
⁹ He has put up a stone wall to block
my way.
He has made my paths crooked.

¹⁰ He has been like a bear waiting to
attack me.
He has been like a lion hiding in
the bushes.
¹¹ He has dragged me off the path.
He has torn me to pieces.
And he has left me helpless.
¹² He has gotten his bow ready
to use.
He has shot his arrows at me.

¹³ The arrows from his bag
have gone through my heart.
¹⁴ My people laugh at me all the
time.
They sing and make fun of me all
day long.
¹⁵ The LORD has made my life bitter.
He has made me suffer bitterly.

¹⁶ He made me chew stones that
broke my teeth.
He has walked all over me in the
dust.
¹⁷ I have lost all hope of ever having
any peace.
I've forgotten what good times
are like.
¹⁸ So I say, "My glory has faded away.
My hope in the LORD is gone."

¹⁹ I remember how I suffered and
wandered.
I remember how bitter my life
was.
²⁰ I remember it very well.
My spirit is very sad deep down
inside me.
²¹ But here is something else I
remember.
And it gives me hope.

²² The LORD loves us very much.
So we haven't been completely
destroyed.

His loving concern never fails.
²³ His great love is new every
        morning.
    LORD, how faithful you are!
²⁴ I say to myself, "The LORD is
        everything I will ever need.
    So I will put my hope in him."

²⁵ The LORD is good to those who put
        their hope in him.
    He is good to those who look to
        him.
²⁶ It is good when people wait
        quietly
    for the LORD to save them.
²⁷ It is good for a man to carry a
        heavy load of suffering
    while he is young.

²⁸ Let him sit alone and not say
        anything.
    The LORD has placed that load on
        him.
²⁹ Let him bury his face in the dust.
    There might still be hope for
        him.
³⁰ Let him turn his cheek toward
        those who would slap him.
    Let him be filled with shame.

³¹ The Lord doesn't turn his back
        on people forever.
³² He might bring suffering.
    But he will also show loving
        concern.
    How great his faithful love is!
³³ He doesn't want to bring pain
        or suffering to people.

³⁴ Every time people crush prisoners
        under their feet,
    the Lord knows all about it.
³⁵ When people refuse to give a man
        his rights,
    the Most High God knows it.
³⁶ When people don't treat a man
        fairly,
    the Lord knows it.

³⁷ Suppose people order something
        to happen.
    It won't happen unless the Lord
        has planned it.
³⁸ Troubles and good things alike
        come to people
    because the Most High God has
        commanded them to come.
³⁹ A man who is still alive shouldn't
        blame God

when God punishes him for his
        sins.
⁴⁰ Let's take a good look at the way
        we're living.
    Let's return to the LORD.
⁴¹ Let's lift up our hands to God in
        heaven.
    Let's pray to him with all our
        hearts.
⁴² Let's say, "We have sinned.
    We've refused to obey you.
    And you haven't forgiven us.

⁴³ "You have covered yourself with
        the cloud of your anger.
    You have chased us.
    You have killed our people
        without pity.
⁴⁴ You have covered yourself with the
        cloud of your anger.
    Our prayers can't get through to
        you.
⁴⁵ You have made us become like
        trash and garbage
    among the nations.

⁴⁶ "All of our enemies have opened
        their mouths wide
    to swallow us up.
⁴⁷ We are terrified and trapped.
    We are broken and destroyed."
⁴⁸ Streams of tears flow from my
        eyes.
    That's because my people are
        destroyed.

⁴⁹ Tears will never stop flowing from
        my eyes.
    My eyes can't get any rest.
⁵⁰ I'll sob until the LORD looks down
        from heaven.
    I'll cry until he notices my tears.
⁵¹ What I see brings pain to my
        spirit.
    All of the people in my city are
        suffering so much.

⁵² Those who were my enemies for
        no reason at all
    hunted me down as if I were a
        bird.
⁵³ They tried to end my life
    by throwing me into a deep pit.
    They threw stones down at me.
⁵⁴ The water rose and covered my
        head.
    I thought I was going to die.

⁵⁵ LORD, I called out to you.

I called out from the bottom of
the pit.

⁵⁶ I prayed, "Please don't close your
ears
to my cry for help."
And you heard my appeal.

⁵⁷ You came near when I called out
to you.
You said, "Do not be afraid."

⁵⁸ Lord, you stood up for me in
court.
You saved my life and set me free.

⁵⁹ LORD, you have seen the wrong
things
people have done to me.
Stand up for me again!

⁶⁰ You have seen how my enemies
have tried to get even with me.
You know all about their plans
against me.

⁶¹ LORD, you have heard them laugh
at me.
You know all about their plans
against me.

⁶² You have heard my enemies
whispering among themselves.
They speak against me all day
long.

⁶³ Just look at them sitting and
standing there!
They sing and make fun of me.

⁶⁴ LORD, pay them back.
Punish them for what their
hands have done.

⁶⁵ Cover their minds with a veil.
Put a curse on them!

⁶⁶ LORD, get angry with them and
hunt them down.
Wipe them off the face of the
earth.

4 Look at how the gold has lost
its brightness!
See how dull the fine gold has
become!
The sacred jewels are scattered
at every street corner.

² The priceless children of Zion
were worth their weight in gold.
But now they are thought of as
clay pots
made by the hands of a potter.

³ Even wild dogs
nurse their young pups.

But my people are as mean
as ostriches in the desert.

⁴ When our babies get thirsty,
their tongues stick to the roofs of
their mouths.
When our children beg for bread,
no one gives them any.

⁵ Those who once ate fine food
are dying in the streets.
Those who wore fancy clothes
are now lying on piles of trash.

⁶ My people have been punished
more than Sodom was.
It was destroyed in a moment.
No one offered it a helping hand.

⁷ Jerusalem's princes were brighter
than snow.
They were whiter than milk.
Their bodies were redder than
rubies.
They looked like sapphires.

⁸ But now they are blacker than
coal.
No one even recognizes them in
the streets.
Their skin is wrinkled on their
bones.
It has become as dry as a stick.

⁹ Those who have been killed with
swords are better off
than those who have to die of
hunger.
Those who are hungry waste away
to nothing.
They don't have any food from
the fields.

¹⁰ With their own hands, loving
mothers
have had to cook even their own
children.
They ate their children
when my people were destroyed.

¹¹ The LORD has become very angry.
He has poured out his burning
anger.
He started a fire in Zion.
It burned up the very
foundations.

¹² The kings of the earth couldn't
believe what was happening.
Neither could any of the world's
people.

Enemies actually attacked and
    entered
    the gates of Jerusalem.

13 It happened because Jerusalem's
    prophets had sinned.
    Its priests had done evil things.
All of them spilled the blood
    of those who did what was right.

14 Now those prophets and priests
    have to feel their way along the
    streets
    like people who are blind.
The blood of those they killed has
    made them "unclean."
So no one dares even to touch
    their clothes.

15 "Go away! You are 'unclean'!"
    people cry out to them.
"Go away! Get out of here!
    Don't touch us!"
So they run away and wander
    around.
    Then people among the nations
    say,
    "They can't stay here anymore."

16 The LORD himself has scattered
    them.
    He doesn't watch over them
    anymore.
No one shows the priests any
    respect.
No one honors the elders.

17 And that's not all. Our eyes grew
    tired.
    We looked for help that never
    came.
We watched from our towers.
    We kept looking for a nation that
    couldn't save us.

18 People hunted us down no matter
    where we went.
    We couldn't even walk in our
    streets.
Our end was near. We only had a
    few days to live.
Our end had come.

19 Those who were hunting us down
    were faster
    than eagles in the sky.
They chased us over the
    mountains.
    They hid and waited for us in the
    desert.

20 Zedekiah, the LORD's anointed
    king, was our last hope.
    But he was caught in their traps.
We thought he would keep
    us safe.
We expected to continue living
    among the nations.

21 People of Edom, be joyful.
    You who live in the land of Uz,
    be glad.
But the cup of the LORD's anger
    will also be passed to you.
Then you will become drunk.
    Your clothes will be stripped off.

22 People of Zion, the time for you to
    be punished
    will come to an end.
The LORD won't keep you away
    from your land any longer.
But he will punish your sin, people
    of Edom.
    He will show you the evil things
    you have done.

5 LORD, think about what has
    happened to us.
    Look at the shame our enemies
    have brought on us.
2 The land you gave us has been
    turned over to outsiders.
    Our homes have been given to
    strangers.
3 Our fathers have been killed.
    Our mothers don't have
    husbands.
4 We have to buy the water we
    drink.
    We have to pay for the wood
    we use.
5 Those who chase us are right
    behind us.
    We're tired. We can't get any rest.
6 We put ourselves under the
    control of Egypt and Assyria
    just to get enough bread.
7 Our people before us sinned.
    And they are now dead.
    We are being punished because
    of their sins.
8 Slaves rule over us.
    No one can set us free
    from their powerful hands.
9 We put our lives in danger just to
    get some bread to eat.
    Robbers in the desert might kill
    us with their swords.

¹⁰Our skin is as hot as an oven.
    We are so hungry we're burning
        up with fever.
¹¹Our women have been raped in
        Zion.
    Our virgins have been raped in
        the towns of Judah.
¹²Our princes have been hung up by
        their hands.
    No one shows our elders any
        respect.
¹³Our young men are forced to grind
        grain at the mill.
    Our boys almost fall down
        as they carry heavy loads of wood.
¹⁴Our elders don't go to the city gate
        anymore.
    Our young men have stopped
        playing their music.
¹⁵There isn't any joy in our hearts.
    Our dancing has turned into
        sobbing.

¹⁶All of our honor is gone.
    How terrible it is for us! We have
        sinned.
¹⁷So our hearts are weak.
    Our eyes can't see very clearly.
¹⁸Mount Zion has been deserted.
    Wild dogs are prowling all
        around on it.

¹⁹LORD, you rule forever.
    Your throne will last for all time
        to come.
²⁰Why do you always forget us?
    Why have you deserted us for so
        long?
²¹LORD, please bring us back to you.
    Then we can return.
    Make our lives like new again.
²²Or have you completely turned
        away from us?
    Are you really that angry with
        us?

quest challenge

I Wonder . . .

What should I do when bad things happen?

Real Life Challenge

Perhaps your best friend moved away, or you lost someone you loved.
Maybe your parents told you they were getting a divorce. You may
want to blame God or ask him why it happened. But he loves you and
will help you. Tell him what's on your mind—even if you're really
angry. He understands how you feel.

Quest Clue

Lamentations 3 (after verse 18) gives a great picture of hope in the
middle of problems. The beginning of Job 42 shows us how Job felt
when bad things happened to him. Paul describes how he responded
to hard times in 2 Corinthians 1. Romans 8 and James 1 will give you
hope about the tough times you face.

Ezekiel

Who wrote this book?
The prophet Ezekiel.

Why was this book written?
The first part of Ezekiel shows why God must punish the wicked people still in Judah. The second part shows that God will bring his people back to their land and that a new temple will be built in Jerusalem.

What do we learn about God in this book?
God is holy. He will not live among a wicked people.

What is special about this book?
Ezekiel acts out many of his prophecies. Ezekiel also describes a great temple to be built in Jerusalem after the captives return from Babylon.

When was this book written?
Ezekiel was written between 593 and 571 B.C.

Where was this book written?
Ezekiel was a captive in Babylon when he wrote this book.

THE LORD GIVES EZEKIEL VISIONS OF HIS GLORY

1 I was 30 years old. I was with my people who had been taken away from their country. We were by the Kebar River in the land of Babylonia. On the fifth day of the fourth month, the heavens were opened. I saw visions of God.

²It was the fifth day of the month. Jehoiachin had been king of Judah. It was the fifth year since he had been brought to Babylon as a prisoner. ³A message came to me from the LORD. I was by the Kebar River in Babylonia. The LORD put his strong hand on me there. I am Ezekiel, the son of Buzi. I'm a priest.

⁴I looked up and saw a windstorm coming from the north. I saw a huge cloud. The fire of lightning was flashing out of it. Bright light surrounded it. The center of the fire looked like glowing metal.

⁵I saw in the fire something that looked like four living creatures. They appeared to have the shape of a man. ⁶But each of them had four faces and four wings. ⁷Their legs were straight. Their feet looked like the feet of a calf. They were as bright as polished bronze.

⁸The creatures had a man's hands under their wings on their four sides. All four of them had faces and wings. ⁹Their wings touched one another. Each of the creatures went straight ahead. They didn't change their direction as they moved.

¹⁰Here's what their faces looked like. Each of the four creatures had a man's face. On the right side each had the face of a lion. On the left each had the face of an ox. Each one also had an eagle's face. ¹¹That's what their faces looked like.

Two of their wings were spread out and lifted up. Each one touched the wing of another creature on either side. The other two wings covered their bodies. ¹²All of the creatures went straight ahead. Anywhere their spirits would lead them to go, they would go. They didn't change their direction as they went.

¹³The living creatures looked like burning coals of fire or like torches. Fire moved back and forth among the creatures. It was bright. Lightning flashed out of it. ¹⁴The creatures raced back and forth like flashes of lightning.

¹⁵As I looked at the living creatures, I saw wheels on the ground beside them. Each creature had four faces. ¹⁶Here's how the wheels looked and worked. They gleamed like chrysolite. All four of them looked alike. Each one seemed to be made like a wheel inside another wheel at right angles.

¹⁷The wheels could go in any one of the four directions the creatures faced. The wheels didn't change their direction as the creatures moved. ¹⁸Their rims were high and terrifying. All four rims were full of eyes all the way around them.

KIDS' QUESTion

Why do angels light up and get bright?

The main reason is that they reflect the glory of God. God is light, and the angels are God's messengers. The angels that came to tell about Jesus' birth certainly glowed brightly with God's glory. But angels do not always appear that way. When angels appeared to Abraham he thought they were ordinary men. He even offered them supper!

checkout Ezekiel 1:5–7

Related verses:
Genesis 19:1,2;
Luke 2:9

[19]When the creatures moved, the wheels beside them moved. When the living creatures rose from the ground, the wheels also rose. [20]Anywhere their spirits would lead them to go, they would go. And the wheels would rise along with them. That's because the spirits of the living creatures were in the wheels.

[21]When the creatures moved, the wheels also moved. When the creatures stood still, they also stood still. When the creatures rose from the ground, the wheels rose along with them. That's because the spirits of the living creatures were in the wheels.

[22]Something that looked like a huge space was spread out above the heads of the living creatures. It gleamed like ice. It was terrifying. [23]The wings of the creatures were spread out under the space. They reached out toward one another. Each creature had two wings covering its body.

[24]When the creatures moved, I heard the sound of their wings. It was like the roar of rushing waters. It sounded like the thundering voice of the Mighty One. It was like the loud noise an army makes. When the creatures stood still, they lowered their wings.

[25]Then a voice came from above the huge space over their heads. They stood with their wings lowered. [26]Above the space over their heads was something that looked like a throne made out of sapphire.

On the throne high above was a figure that appeared to be human. [27]From his waist up he looked like glowing metal that was full of fire. From his waist down he looked like fire. Bright light surrounded him. [28]The glow around him looked like a rainbow in the clouds on a rainy day.

That's what the glory of the LORD looked like. When I saw it, I fell with my face toward the ground. Then I heard the voice of someone speaking.

THE LORD CHOOSES EZEKIEL

2 He said to me, "Son of man, stand up on your feet. I will speak to you." [2]As he spoke, the Spirit of the LORD came into me. He raised me to my feet. I heard him speaking to me.

[3]He said, "Son of man, I am sending

KIDS' QUESTION

What do angels really look like?

The word *angel* means "messenger." Angels are God's messengers. They can also be God's warriors. In the Bible we read about people who saw angels. Sometimes the people knew that they were looking at angels, and sometimes they did not know it. Cherubim and seraphim are described in the Bible as having wings. But the angels who appeared to people on earth looked like normal people, sometimes shining brightly and sometimes not. We do not know what angels look like in heaven.

checkout
Ezekiel 1:10,11

Related verse:
Hebrews 13:2

you to the people of Israel. That nation has refused to obey me. They have turned against me. They and their people before them have been against me to this very day. ⁴The people I am sending you to are very stubborn. Tell them, 'Here is what the LORD and King says.'

⁵"They might listen, or they might not. After all, they refuse to obey me. But whether they listen or not, they will know that a prophet was among them.

⁶"Son of man, do not be afraid of them or of what they say. Do not be afraid, even if thorns and bushes are all around you and you live among scorpions. Do not be afraid of what they say. Do not be terrified by them. They always refuse to obey me.

⁷"You must give them my message. They might listen, or they might not. After all, they refuse to obey me. ⁸Son of man, listen to what I tell you. Do not be like those who refuse to obey me. Open your mouth. Eat what I give you."

⁹Then I looked up. I saw a hand reach out to me. A scroll was in it. ¹⁰He unrolled it in front of me. Both sides had words written on them. They spoke about sadness, sorrow and trouble.

3 He said to me, "Son of man, eat what is in front of you. Eat this scroll. Then go and speak to the people of Israel." ²So I opened my mouth. And he gave me the scroll to eat.

³Then he said to me, "Son of man, eat this scroll I am giving you. Fill your stomach with it." So I ate it. And it tasted as sweet as honey in my mouth.

⁴Then he said to me, "Son of man, go to the people of Israel. Give them my message.

⁵"I am not sending you to people who speak another language that is hard to learn. Instead, I am sending you to the people of Israel. ⁶You are not being sent to many nations whose people speak other languages that are hard to learn. You would not be able to understand them. Suppose I had sent you to them. Then they certainly would have listened to you. ⁷But the people of Israel do not want to listen to

you. That is because they do not want to listen to me.

"All of the people of Israel are very stubborn. ⁸But I will make you just as stubborn as they are. ⁹I will make you very brave. So do not be afraid of them. Do not let them terrify you, even though they refuse to obey me."

¹⁰He continued, "Son of man, listen carefully. Take to heart everything I tell you. ¹¹Go now to your own people who were brought here as prisoners. Speak to them. Tell them, 'Here is what the LORD and King says.' Speak to them whether they listen or not."

¹²Then the Spirit of the LORD lifted me up. I heard a loud rumbling sound behind me. May the glory of the LORD be praised in the place where he lives! ¹³The sound was made by the wings of the living creatures. They were brushing against one another. The sound was also made by the wheels beside them. It was a loud rumbling sound.

¹⁴Then the Spirit lifted me up and took me away. My spirit was bitter. I was burning with anger. The strong hand of the LORD was on me. ¹⁵I came to my people who had been brought as prisoners to Tel Abib. It was near the Kebar River. I went to where they were living. There I sat among them for seven days. I was shocked by everything that had happened.

THE LORD WARNS ISRAEL

¹⁶After seven days, a message came to me from the LORD. ¹⁷He said, "Son of man, I have appointed you as a prophet to warn the people of Israel. So listen to my message. Give them a warning from me.

¹⁸"Suppose I say to a sinful person, 'You can be sure you will die.' And you do not warn him. You do not try to get him to change his evil ways in order to save his life. Then he will die because he has sinned. And I will hold you accountable for his death.

¹⁹"But suppose you do warn that sinful person. And he does not turn away from his sin or his evil ways. Then he will die because he has sinned. But you will have saved yourself.

²⁰"Or suppose a godly person turns away from his godliness and does

what is evil. And suppose I put something in his way that will trip him up. Then he will die. Since you did not warn him, he will die for his sin. The godly things he did will not be remembered. And I will hold you accountable for his death.

²¹"But suppose you do warn a godly person not to sin. And he does not sin. Then you can be sure that he will live because he listened to your warning. And you will have saved yourself."

²²The strong hand of the LORD was on me. He said, "Get up. Go out to the flatlands. I will speak to you there."

²³So I got up and went out to the flatlands. The glory of the LORD was standing there. It was just like the glory I had seen by the Kebar River. So I fell with my face toward the ground.

²⁴Then the Spirit of the LORD came into me. He raised me to my feet. He said to me, "Go, son of man. Shut yourself inside your house. ²⁵Some people will tie you up with ropes. So you will not be able to go out among your people. ²⁶I will make your tongue stick to the roof of your mouth. Then you will be silent. You will not be able to correct them. They always refuse to obey me.

²⁷"But later I will speak to you. I will open your mouth. Then you will tell them, 'Here is what the LORD and King says.' Those who listen will listen. And those who refuse to listen will refuse. They always refuse to obey me.

AN ATTACK ON JERUSALEM IS PICTURED

4 "Son of man, get a clay tablet. Put it in front of you. Draw the city of Jerusalem on it. ²Then pretend to surround it and attack it. Make some little models of war machines. Build a ramp up to it. Set camps up around it. Surround it with models of logs to be used for knocking down its gates. ³Then get an iron pan. Put it between you and the city. Pretend it is an iron wall. Turn your face toward the city. It will be under attack when you begin to attack it. That will show the people of Israel what is going to happen to Jerusalem.

⁴"Next, lie down on your left side. Pretend that you are putting Israel's sin on yourself. Keep their sin on you

for the number of days you lie on your side. ⁵Let each day you lie there stand for one year of their sin. So you will keep Israel's sin on you for 390 days.

⁶"After you have finished that, lie down again. This time lie on your right side. Pretend that you are putting Judah's sin on yourself. Lie there for 40 days. That is one day for each year of their sin.

⁷"Next, turn your face toward the model of Jerusalem under attack. Uncover your arm as if you were a soldier ready to fight. Prophesy against the city.

⁸"I will tie you up with ropes. Then you will not be able to turn from one side to the other. You will stay that way until you have finished attacking Jerusalem.

⁹"Get some wheat and barley. Also get some beans and lentils. And get some millet and spelt. Put everything in a storage jar. Use it to make some bread for yourself. Eat it during the 390 days you are lying down on your side. ¹⁰Weigh out eight ounces of food to eat each day. Eat it at your regular mealtimes. ¹¹Also measure out two thirds of a quart of water. Drink it at your regular mealtimes.

¹²"Eat your food as you would eat a barley cake. Bake it over human waste in front of the people." ¹³The LORD said, "That is how the people of Israel will eat 'unclean' food. They will eat it in the nations where I will drive them."

¹⁴Then I said, "No, LORD and King! I won't do it! I've never eaten anything that was 'unclean.' From the time I was young until now, I've never eaten anything that was found dead. And I've never eaten anything that was torn apart by wild animals. 'Unclean' meat has never entered my mouth."

¹⁵"All right," he said. "I will let you bake your bread over waste from cows. You can use that instead of human waste."

¹⁶He continued, "Son of man, I will cut off the food supply in Jerusalem. The people will be worried as they eat their tiny share of food. They will not have any hope as they drink their tiny share of water. ¹⁷There will be very little food and water. The people will be shocked as they look at one another.

They will become weaker and weaker because of their sin.

5 "Son of man, get a sharp sword. Use it as a barber's razor. Shave your head and beard with it. Then get a set of scales and weigh the hair. Separate it into three piles.

²"Burn up a third of the hair inside the city. Do it when you stop attacking the model of Jerusalem. Next, get another third of the hair. Strike it with a sword all around the city. Then scatter the last third to the winds. That is because I will chase the people with a sword that is ready to strike them down. ³But save a few of the hairs. Tuck them away in the clothes you are wearing.

⁴"Next, get a few more hairs. Throw them into the fire. Burn them up. The fire will spread to all of the people of Israel."

⁵The LORD and King says, "This little model stands for Jerusalem. I have placed that city in the center of the nations. Countries are all around it. ⁶But its people are sinful. They have refused to obey my laws and rules. They have turned their backs on my laws. They have not followed my rules. Those people are worse than the nations and countries around them."

⁷The LORD and King continues, "You people have been worse than the nations around you. You have not lived by my rules or kept my laws. You have not even lived up to the standards of the nations around you."

⁸The LORD and King continues, "Jerusalem, I myself am against you. I will punish you in the sight of the nations. ⁹I will do to you what I have never done before and will never do again. That is because you worship statues of gods. I hate them. ¹⁰So parents will eat their own children inside the city. And children will eat their parents. I will punish you. And I will scatter to the winds anyone who is left alive.

¹¹"You have made my temple 'unclean.' You have set up statues of all of your evil gods. You have done other things I hate. So I will not show you my favor anymore. I will not spare you or feel sorry for you. And that is just as sure as I am alive," announces the LORD and King.

¹²"A third of your people will die of the plague inside your walls. Or they will die of hunger there. Another third will be killed with swords outside your walls. And I will scatter the last third of your people to the winds. I will chase them with a sword that is ready to strike them down.

¹³"Then I will not be angry anymore. My burning anger against them will die down. And I will be satisfied. Then they will know that I have spoken with strong feelings. And my burning anger toward them will come to an end. I am the LORD.

¹⁴"I will destroy you. I will bring shame on you in the sight of the nations that are around you. All those who pass by will see it. ¹⁵You will be put to shame. The nations will make fun of you. You will serve as a warning to others. They will be shocked when they see you. So I will punish you because my anger burns against you. You will feel the sting of my warning. I have spoken. I am the LORD.

¹⁶"I will shoot at you with my deadly, destroying arrows of hunger. I will shoot to kill. I will bring more and more hunger on you. I will cut off your food supply. ¹⁷I will send hunger and wild animals against you. They will destroy all of your children. Plague and murder will sweep over you. And I will send swords to kill you. I have spoken. I am the LORD."

EZEKIEL PROPHESIES AGAINST THE MOUNTAINS OF ISRAEL

6 A message came to me from the LORD. He said, ²"Son of man, turn your attention to the mountains of Israel. Prophesy against them. ³Say, 'Mountains of Israel, listen to the message of the LORD and King. Here is what he says to the mountains and hills. And here is what he says to the canyons and valleys. He tells them, "I will send swords to kill your people. I will destroy the high places where you worship other gods.

⁴" 'Your altars will be torn down. Your incense altars will be smashed. And I will kill your people in front of the statues of your gods. ⁵I will put the

dead bodies of Israelites in front of those statues. I will scatter your bones around your altars.

⁶" ' "No matter where you live, the towns will be destroyed. The high places will be torn down. So your altars will be completely destroyed. The statues of your gods will be smashed to pieces. Your incense altars will be broken down. And everything you have made will be wiped out. ⁷Your people will fall down dead among you. Then you will know that I am the LORD.

⁸" ' "But I will spare some of you. Some will escape from being killed with swords. You will be scattered among other lands and nations. ⁹You will be taken away to those nations as prisoners. Those of you who escape will remember me. You will recall how much pain your unfaithful hearts gave me. You turned away from me. Your eyes longed to see the statues of your gods. You will hate yourselves because of all of the evil things you have done. I hate those things too. ¹⁰You will know that I am the LORD. I said I would bring trouble on you. And my warning came true." ' "

¹¹The LORD and King said to me, "Clap your hands. Stamp your feet. Cry out, 'How sad!' Do it because the people of Israel have done so many evil things. I hate those things. Israel will be destroyed by war, hunger and plague. ¹²Those who are far away will die of the plague. Those who are near will be killed with swords. Those who are left alive and are spared will die of hunger. And my burning anger toward them will come to an end.

¹³"Then they will know that I am the LORD. Their people will lie dead among the statues of their gods around their altars. Their bodies will lie on every high hill and every mountaintop. They will lie under every green tree and leafy oak tree. They used to offer sweet-smelling incense to all of their gods at those places. ¹⁴I will reach out my powerful hand against them. The land will become dry and empty. Those people will live from the desert all the way to Diblah. They will know that I am the LORD."

THE END HAS COME

7 A message came to me from the LORD. He said, ²"Son of man, I am the LORD and King. I say to the land of Israel, 'The end has come! It has come on the four corners of the land. ³The end has now come for you. I will pour out my anger on you. I will judge you based on how you have lived. I will pay you back for all of your evil practices. I hate them.

⁴" 'I will not spare you or feel sorry for you. You can be sure that I will pay you back in keeping with how you have lived. I will judge you for your evil practices. I hate them. You will know that I am the LORD.'

⁵"I am the LORD and King. I say, 'Horrible trouble is coming! No one has ever heard of anything like it.

⁶" 'The end has come! The end has come! It has stirred itself up against you. It is here! ⁷Death has come on you who live in the land. The time for you to be destroyed has come. The day when it will happen is near. There is no joy on your mountains. There is nothing but panic.

⁸" 'I am about to pour out all of my burning anger on you. I will judge you based on how you have lived. I will pay you back for all of your evil practices. I hate them.

⁹" 'I will not spare you or feel sorry for you. I will pay you back based on how you have lived. I will judge you for your evil practices. I hate them. You will know that I am the one who strikes you down. I am the LORD.

¹⁰" 'The day for me to punish you is here! It has come! Death has arrived. The time is ripe for you to be judged. Your pride has grown so much that you will be destroyed. ¹¹Your mean and harmful acts have become like a rod. I will use it to punish you for your sins. None of you will be left. No wealth or anything of value will remain.

¹²" 'The time has come! The day has arrived! I will soon pour out my burning anger on the whole crowd of you. Do not let the buyer be happy. Do not let the seller be sad. ¹³The seller will not get back the land that was sold as long as both of them are alive.

" 'Ezekiel, the vision I gave you about that whole crowd will come true. They have committed many sins. So none of them will remain alive. ¹⁴They might blow trumpets. They might get everything ready. But no one will go into battle. I will soon pour out my burning anger on the whole crowd.

¹⁵" 'There is trouble everywhere. War is outside the city. Plague and hunger are inside it. Those who are out in the country will die in battle. Those in the city will be destroyed by hunger and plague. ¹⁶All those who escape and are left alive will run to the mountains. They have committed many sins. So they will cry like sad doves in the valleys.

¹⁷" 'Their hands will be powerless to help them. Their knees will become as weak as water. ¹⁸They will put on black clothes. They will put on terror as if it were their clothes. Their faces will be covered with shame. Their heads will be shaved.

¹⁹" 'They will throw their silver into the streets. Their gold will be like an "unclean" thing. Their silver and gold will not be able to save them on the day I pour out my anger on them. They will not be able to satisfy their hunger. Their stomachs will not be full. Their silver and gold have tripped them up. They have made them fall into sin. ²⁰My people were so proud of their beautiful jewelry. They used it to make statues of their evil gods. I hate those gods. So I will turn their statues into an "unclean" thing for them.

²¹" 'I will hand everything over to strangers. I will turn it over to sinful people in other countries. They will pollute it. ²²I will turn my face away from my people. Their enemies will pollute my beautiful temple. Robbers will enter it and pollute it.

²³" 'Ezekiel, get ready to put my people in chains. The land is full of murderers. They are harming one another all over Jerusalem. ²⁴I will bring the most evil nations against them. They will take over the houses in the city. I will put an end to the pride of those who are mighty. Their holy places will be polluted.

²⁵" 'When terror comes, they will look for peace. But there will not be any. ²⁶Trouble after trouble will come. One report will follow another. But they will not be true. The people will try to get visions from the prophets. But there will not be any. The teaching of the law by the priests will be gone. So will advice from the elders.

²⁷" 'The king will be filled with sadness. The princes will lose all hope. The hands of the people of the land will tremble. I will punish them based on how they have lived. I will judge them by their own standards. Then they will know that I am the LORD.' "

THE PEOPLE WORSHIP OTHER GODS IN THE TEMPLE

8 It was the sixth year since King Jehoiachin had been brought to Babylon as a prisoner. On the fifth day of the sixth month, I was sitting in my house. The elders of Judah were sitting there with me. The LORD and King put his powerful hand on me there.

²I looked up and saw a figure that appeared to be human. From his waist down he looked like fire. From his waist up he looked as bright as glowing metal. ³He reached out what appeared to be a hand. He took hold of me by the hair of my head. The Spirit of the LORD lifted me up between earth and heaven. In visions God gave me, the Spirit took me to Jerusalem. He brought me to the entrance of the north gate of the inner courtyard. The statue of a god was standing there. It made God very angry. ⁴There in front of me was the glory of the God of Israel. It looked just as it did in the vision I had seen on the flatlands.

⁵Then the LORD said to me, "Son of man, look toward the north." So I did. I saw a statue that made God angry. It was in the entrance of the gate north of the altar.

⁶He said to me, "Son of man, do you see what the people of Israel are doing here? They are doing things I hate very much. Those things will cause me to go far away from my temple. But you will see things I hate even more."

⁷Then he brought me to the en-

trance to the courtyard. I looked up and saw a hole in the wall. [8]He said to me, "Son of man, dig into the wall." So I did. And I saw a door there.

[9]He continued, "Go through it. Look at the evil things they are doing here. I hate those things."

[10]So I went in and looked. All over the walls were pictures of all kinds of crawling things and other animals. The LORD hates it when people worship those things. There were also carvings of all of the gods of the people of Israel.

[11]In front of them stood 70 elders of Israel. Jaazaniah was standing there among them. He is the son of Shaphan. Each elder was holding a shallow cup. A sweet-smelling cloud of incense was rising from the cups.

[12]The LORD said to me, "Son of man, do you see what the elders of Israel are doing in the dark? Each of them is in his own room worshiping his own god. They say, 'The LORD doesn't see us. He has deserted the land.'" [13]He continued, "You will see them doing things I hate even more."

[14]Then he brought me to the entrance of the north gate of the LORD's house. I saw women sitting there. They were sobbing over the god Tammuz. [15]The LORD said to me, "Son of man, do you see what they are doing? You will see things I hate even more."

[16]Then he brought me into the inner courtyard of the LORD's house. About 25 men were there. They were at the entrance to the LORD's temple between the porch and the altar. Their backs were turned toward the temple. Their faces were turned toward the east. And they were bowing down to the sun.

[17]He said to me, "Son of man, have you seen all of that? The people of Judah are doing things here that I hate. This is a very serious matter. They are harming one another all through the land. They continue to make me very angry. Just look at them making fun of me! [18]So I am angry with them. I will punish them. I will not spare them or feel sorry for them. They might even shout in my ears. But I will not listen to them."

THE LORD JUDGES THOSE WHO WORSHIP OTHER GODS

9 Then I heard the LORD call out in a loud voice. He said, "Bring those who guard the city here. Make sure each of them has a weapon." [2]I saw six men coming from the direction of the upper gate. It faces north. Each of them had a deadly weapon. A man who was wearing linen clothes came along with them. He was carrying a writing kit at his side. They came in and stood beside the bronze altar.

[3]The glory of the God of Israel had been above the cherubim. It moved from there to the doorway of the temple.

Then the LORD called to the man who was dressed in linen clothes. He had the writing kit. [4]The LORD said to him, "Go all through Jerusalem. Look for those who are sad and sorry about all of the things that are being done there. I hate those things. Put a mark on the foreheads of those people."

[5]I heard him speak to the six men. He said, "Follow him through the city. Do not show any pity or concern. [6]Kill old men and women, young men and women, and children. But do not touch anyone who has the mark. Start at my temple." So they began with the elders who were in front of the temple.

[7]Then he said to the men, "Make the temple 'unclean.' Fill the courtyards with dead bodies. Go!" So they went out and started killing people all through the city.

[8]While they were doing it, I was left alone. I fell with my face toward the ground. I cried out, "LORD and King, are you going to destroy all of the Israelites who are still left alive? Will you pour out your burning anger on all those who remain in Jerusalem?"

[9]He answered me, "The sin of Israel and Judah is very great. The land is full of murderers. They are not being fair to one another anywhere in Jerusalem. They say, 'The LORD has deserted the land. He doesn't see us.' [10]So I will not spare them or feel sorry for them. Anything that happens to them will be their own fault."

[11]Then the man who was wearing

linen clothes returned. He had the writing kit. He reported, "I've done what you commanded."

THE GLORY OF THE LORD MOVES OUT OF THE TEMPLE

10 I looked up and saw something that appeared to be a throne made out of sapphire. It was above the huge space that was spread out over the heads of the cherubim. ²The LORD spoke to the man who was wearing linen clothes. He said, "Go in among the wheels beneath the cherubim. Fill your hands with burning coals from the fire that is among the cherubim. Scatter the coals over the city." As I watched, he went in.

³The cherubim were standing on the south side of the temple when the man went in. A cloud filled the inner courtyard. ⁴Then the glory of the LORD rose from above the cherubim. It moved to the doorway of the temple. The cloud filled the temple. And the courtyard was full of the brightness of the glory of the LORD. ⁵The sound the wings of the cherubim made could be heard as far away as the outer courtyard. It was like the voice of the Mighty God when he speaks.

⁶The LORD gave a command to the man who was dressed in linen clothes. He said, "Get some coals of fire from among the wheels. Take them from among the cherubim." So the man went in and stood beside a wheel. ⁷Then one of the cherubim reached out his hand. He picked up some of the burning coals that were among the wheels. He handed them to the man who was wearing linen clothes. The man took them and left. ⁸I saw what looked like a man's hands. They were under the wings of the cherubim.

⁹I looked up and saw four wheels beside the cherubim. One wheel was beside each of them. The wheels gleamed like chrysolite. ¹⁰All four of them looked alike. Each wheel appeared to be inside another wheel at right angles. ¹¹The wheels could go in any one of the four directions the cherubim faced. The wheels didn't change their direction as the cherubim moved. The cherubim went in the direction their heads faced. They didn't change their direction as they moved.

¹²Their whole bodies were completely covered with eyes. That included their backs, hands and wings. Their four wheels were covered with eyes too. ¹³I heard someone tell the wheels to start spinning around. ¹⁴Each of the cherubim had four faces. One face was the face of a cherub. The second was a man's face. The third was the face of a lion. And the fourth was an eagle's face.

¹⁵The cherubim rose from the ground. They were the same living creatures I had seen by the Kebar River. ¹⁶When the cherubim moved, the wheels beside them moved. The cherubim spread their wings to rise from the ground. As they did, the wheels didn't leave their side. ¹⁷When the cherubim stood still, the wheels also stood still. When the cherubim rose, the wheels rose along with them. That's because the spirits of the living creatures were in the wheels.

¹⁸Then the glory of the LORD moved away from the doorway of the temple. It stopped above the cherubim. ¹⁹While I watched, they spread their wings. They rose from the ground. As they went, the wheels went along with them. They stopped at the entrance of the east gate of the LORD's house. And the glory of the God of Israel was above them.

²⁰Those were the same living creatures I had seen by the Kebar River. I had seen them beneath the God of Israel. I realized that they were cherubim. ²¹Each one had four faces and four wings. Under their wings was what looked like a man's hands. ²²Their faces looked the same as the ones I had seen by the Kebar River. Each of the cherubim went straight ahead.

THE LORD PUNISHES ISRAEL'S LEADERS

11 Then the Spirit of the LORD lifted me up. He brought me to the east gate of the LORD's house. There were 25 men at the entrance of the gate. I saw Jaazaniah and Pelatiah among them. They were leaders of the people. Jaazaniah is the son of Azzur. Pelatiah is the son of Benaiah.

²The LORD said to me, "Son of man, these men are making evil plans. They are giving bad advice to the city. ³They say, 'This is not the time to build houses. The city is like a cooking pot. And we are the meat.' ⁴So prophesy against them. Prophesy, son of man."

⁵Then the Spirit of the LORD came on me. He told me to tell them, "The LORD says, 'People of Israel, that is what you are saying. But I know what you are thinking. ⁶You have killed many people in this city. In fact, you have filled its streets with dead bodies.'

⁷"So the LORD and King says, 'The bodies you have thrown there are the meat. And the city is the cooking pot. But I will drive you out of it. ⁸You are afraid of the swords of war. But I will bring them against you,' announces the LORD and King.

⁹" 'I will drive you out of the city. I will hand you over to strangers. And I will punish you. ¹⁰You will be killed with swords. I will judge you at the borders of Israel. Then you will know that I am the LORD.

¹¹" 'This city will not be a pot for you. And you will not be the meat in it. I will judge you at the borders of Israel. ¹²Then you will know that I am the LORD. You have not followed my rules. You have not kept my laws. Instead, you have lived by the standards of the nations that are around you.' "

¹³Pelatiah, the son of Benaiah, died as I was prophesying. Then I fell with my face toward the ground. I cried out in a loud voice. I said, "LORD and King, will you destroy all of the Israelites who are still left alive?"

¹⁴A message came to me from the LORD. He said, ¹⁵"Son of man, the people of Jerusalem have spoken about your relatives. They have also spoken about all of the other people of Israel. They have said, 'Stay far away from the LORD. This land was given to us. And it belongs to us.'

THE LORD WILL BRING HIS PEOPLE BACK HOME

¹⁶"So tell them, 'The LORD and King says, "I sent some of my people far away among the nations. I scattered them among the countries. But for a little while I have been their temple in

Why do governments do wrong things?

Governments do wrong things for the same reason that individual persons do wrong things. People are naturally selfish and try to live their lives without God. We call this sin. Governments are made up of people, so they will sometimes do wrong things. That is why many governments have a system of "checks and balances," which lets one part of government stop the actions of another.

The good news is that God watches over those who are leaders in government. Pray that God will make your country's leaders just and wise.

checkout
Ezekiel 11:1-4

Related Verses:
1 Kings 2:1–3;
Psalm 53:3;
94:20–25;
1 Timothy 2:2

the countries where they have gone." '

¹⁷"Tell them, 'The LORD and King says, "I will gather you from the nations. I will bring you back from the countries where you have been scattered. I will give you back the land of Israel." '

¹⁸"They will return to it. They will remove all of its statues of evil gods. I hate those gods. ¹⁹I will give my people hearts that are completely committed to me. I will give them a new spirit that is faithful to me. I will remove their stubborn hearts from them. And I will give them hearts that obey me. ²⁰Then they will follow my rules. They will be careful to keep my laws. They will be my people. And I will be their God.

²¹"But some people have hearts that are committed to worshiping the statues of their evil gods. I hate those gods. Anything that happens to those people will be their own fault," announces the LORD and King.

²²Then the cherubim spread their wings. The wheels were beside them. The glory of the God of Israel was above them. ²³The glory of the LORD went up from the city. It stopped above the Mount of Olives east of it. ²⁴The Spirit of God lifted me up. He took me to those who had been brought to Babylonia as prisoners. Those are the things that happened in the visions the Spirit gave me.

Then the visions I had seen were gone. ²⁵I told my people everything the LORD had shown me.

MANY PEOPLE WILL BE TAKEN TO BABYLONIA

12 A message came to me from the LORD. He said, ²"Son of man, you are living among people who refuse to obey

Is it OK to stay up late on school nights if your friends do?

You should follow your own family's rules no matter what your friends do. Every family has its own rules. Your friends do not get to say what is OK for you. It is important for *you* to obey *your* parents. So if your parents tell you to go to bed at a certain time, do it, no matter what your friends do. God has given your parents the job of raising you. Your parents have a good reason for wanting you not to stay up late on a school night. You will be sleepy the next day if you stay up late. You will not do your best in school if you are sleepy. Your mom and dad know that. They know how important it is for you to do well in school. Listen to your parents so you can learn to get the sleep you need.

checkout Ezekiel 11:12

Related verses:
Deuteronomy 5:16;
Colossians 3:20

me. They have eyes that can see. But they do not really see. They have ears that can hear. But they do not really hear. They refuse to obey me.

³"Son of man, pack your belongings as if you were going on a long trip. Leave in the daytime. Let the people see you. Start out from where you are. Go to another place. Perhaps they will understand the meaning of what you are doing. But they will still refuse to obey me. ⁴Bring out your belongings packed for a long trip. Do it during the daytime. Let the people see you. Then in the evening, pretend you are being forced to leave home. Let the people see you.

⁵"While the people are watching, dig through the mud bricks of your house. Then take your belongings out through the hole in the wall. ⁶Put them on your shoulder. Carry them out at sunset. Let the people see you. Cover your face so you can't see the land. All of that will show the people of Israel what is going to happen to them."

⁷So I did just as he commanded me. During the day I brought out my things as if I were going on a long trip. In the evening I dug through the wall of my house with my hands. At sunset I took my belongings out. I put them on my shoulders. The people watched what I was doing.

⁸In the morning a message came to me from the LORD. He said, ⁹"Son of man, didn't the people of Israel ask you, 'What are you doing?' They always refuse to obey me.

¹⁰"Tell them, 'The LORD and King says, "This message is about Zedekiah, the prince in Jerusalem. It is also about all of the people of Israel who still live there." ' ¹¹Tell them, 'The things I've done are a picture of what's going to happen to you. So what I've done will

KIDS' QUESTION

Do people live in the land of Israel today?

Many thousands of people live in the places where Bible events took place. Egypt, Iraq, Jordan and Israel are some of the places where Abraham, Joseph, Moses, David, Solomon, Jonah and Jesus lived. The cities that Paul visited are in Turkey, Greece and Italy. People go to these lands every year to visit places they read about in the Bible. Some of the people there still dress like they did in Bible times. But the bigger cities are very modern. They have tall buildings, telephones, fax machines and computers.

checkout
Ezekiel 11:16,17

Related verse:
Jeremiah 23:3

Departing for ISRAEL

PAGING JASON PLEASE REPORT TO LOST AND FOUND!

AIRPORT LOST & FOUND

CLASS 103

happen to you. You will be forced to leave home. You will be taken to Babylonia as prisoners.'

¹²"The prince among them will put his things on his shoulder and leave. He will do it at sunset. Someone will dig a hole in a wall for him to go through. He will cover his face so he can't see the land. ¹³I will spread out my net to catch him. He will be caught in my trap. I will bring him to Babylonia. It is the land where the Chaldeans live. But he will not see it. He will die there. ¹⁴I will scatter to the winds all those who are around him. I will scatter his officials and all of his troops. And I will chase them with a sword that is ready to strike them down.

¹⁵"They will know that I am the LORD when I scatter them among the nations. I will send them to other countries. ¹⁶But I will spare a few of them. I will save them from war, hunger and plague. In those countries they will admit they have done all kinds of evil things. I hate those things. They will know that I am the LORD."

¹⁷A message came to me from the LORD. He said, ¹⁸"Son of man, tremble with fear as you eat your food. Tremble as you drink your water. ¹⁹Speak to the people of the land. Say to them, 'Here is what the LORD and King says about those who live in Jerusalem and Israel. He tells them, "They will be worried as they eat their food. They will not have any hope as they drink their water. Their land will be stripped of everything in it because all those who live there are harming one another. ²⁰The towns where people live will be completely destroyed. The land will become a dry and empty desert. Then you will know that I am the LORD." ' "

²¹A message came to me from the LORD. He said, ²²"Son of man, you have a proverb in the land of Israel. It says, 'The days go by, and not even one vision comes true.' ²³Tell them, 'The LORD and King says, "I am going to put an end to that proverb. They will not use that saying in Israel anymore." ' Tell them, 'The days are coming soon when every vision will come true. ²⁴There will be no more false visions. People will no longer use magic to find out whether good things are going to

happen in Israel. ²⁵I am the LORD. So I will say what I want to. And it will come true when I want it to. In your days I will do everything I say I will. But you people always refuse to obey me,' announces the LORD and King."

²⁶A message came to me from the LORD. He said, ²⁷"Son of man, the people of Israel are saying, 'The vision Ezekiel sees won't come true for many years. He is prophesying about a time that is a long way off.'

²⁸"So tell them, 'The LORD and King says, "Everything I say will come true. It will happen when I want it to," announces the LORD and King.' "

THE LORD PUNISHES THOSE WHO PRETEND TO BE TRUE PROPHETS

13 A message came to me from the LORD. He said, ²"Son of man, prophesy against those who are now prophesying in Israel. What they prophesy comes out of their own minds. Tell them, 'Listen to the LORD's message! ³The LORD and King says, "How terrible it will be for you foolish prophets! You say what your own minds tell you to. Your visions did not come from me.

⁴" ' "Israel, your prophets are like wild dogs that live among broken-down buildings. ⁵You have not repaired the cracks in the city wall for the people of Israel. So it will not stand firm in the battle on the day I judge you. ⁶The visions of those prophets are false. They use magic to try to find out what is going to happen. But their magic tricks are lies. They say, 'The LORD announces.' But I have not sent them. In spite of that, they expect their words to come true.

⁷" ' "You prophets have seen false visions. You have used magic to try to find out what is going to happen. But your magic tricks are lies. So you lied when you said, 'The LORD announces.' I did not even speak to you at all."

⁸" 'The LORD and King says, "I am against you prophets. Your messages are false. Your visions do not come true," announces the LORD and King.

⁹" ' "Israel, my powerful hand will be against the prophets who see false visions. Their magic tricks are lies.

They will not be among the leaders of my people. They will not be listed in the records of Israel. In fact, they will not even enter the land. Then you will know that I am the Lord and King.

10" ' "They lead my people away from me. They say, 'Peace.' But there isn't any peace. They are like people who build a weak wall. They try to cover up the weakness by painting the wall white. 11Tell those who do it that their wall is going to fall. Heavy rains will come. I will send hailstones crashing down. Powerful winds will blow. 12The wall will fall down. Then people will ask them, 'Now where is the paint you covered it with?' "

13" 'So the Lord and King speaks. He says, "When I am burning with anger, I will send a powerful wind. Hailstones and heavy rains will come. They will fall with great force. 14I will tear down the wall you prophets painted over. I will knock it down. The only thing left will be its foundation. When it falls, you will be destroyed along with it. Then you will know that I am the Lord.

15" ' "So I will pour out all of my burning anger on the wall. I will also send it against you prophets who painted it. I will say to you, 'The wall is gone. You who painted it will be gone too. 16You prophets of Israel prophesied to Jerusalem. You saw visions of peace for its people. But there wasn't any peace,' announces the Lord and King." '

17"Son of man, turn your attention to the daughters of your people. What they prophesy comes out of their own minds. So prophesy against them. 18Tell them, 'The Lord and King says, "How terrible it will be for you women who sew magic charms to put around your wrists! You make veils of different lengths to put on your heads. You do those things to trap people. You trap my people. But you will also be trapped. 19You have treated me as if I were not holy. You did it among my very own people. You did it for a few handfuls of barley and scraps of bread. You told lies to my people. They like to listen to lies. You killed those who should have lived. And you spared those who should have died."

20" 'So the Lord and King says, "I am against your magic charms. You use them to trap people as if they were birds. I will tear them off your arms. I will set free the people you trap like birds. 21I will tear your veils off your heads. I will save my people from your powerful hands. They will no longer be under your control. Then you will know that I am the Lord.

22" ' "I had not made godly people sad. But when you told them lies, you made them lose all hope. You advised sinful people not to turn from their evil ways. You did not want them to save their lives. 23So you will never see false visions again. You will not use your magic tricks anymore. I will save my people from your powerful hands. Then you will know that I am the Lord." ' "

THE LORD JUDGES THOSE WHO WORSHIP OTHER GODS

14 Some of the elders of Israel came to see me. They sat down with me. 2Then a message came to me from the Lord. He said, 3"Son of man, these men have thought about nothing but other gods. They have fallen into the evil trap of worshiping them. Should I let those men ask me for any advice?

4"Speak to them. Tell them, 'The Lord and King says, "Suppose an Israelite thinks about other gods. And he falls into the evil trap of worshiping them. Then he goes to a prophet to ask for advice. If he does, I myself will tell the prophet to answer him in keeping with his worship of many gods. 5I will win back the hearts of the people of Israel. All of them have deserted me for their other gods." '

6"So speak to the people of Israel. Tell them, 'The Lord and King says, "Turn away from your sins! Also turn away from your gods. Give up all of the evil things you have done. I hate them.

7" ' "Suppose an Israelite or outsider who lives in Israel separates himself from me. And he thinks about other gods. He falls into the evil trap of worshiping them. Then he goes to a prophet to ask me for advice. If he does, I myself will tell the prophet to answer him. 8I will turn against him. I will make an example out of him. People will laugh at him. I will cut him off from you. Then you will know that I am the LORD.

[9] ' "Suppose that prophet is stirred up to give a prophecy. Then I am the one who has stirred him up. And I will reach out my powerful hand against him. I will destroy him from among my people Israel. [10]The prophet will be as much to blame as the one who asks him for advice. Both of them will be guilty. [11]Then the people of Israel will no longer wander away from me. And they will not pollute themselves anymore with their many sins. They will be my people. And I will be their God," ' announces the LORD and King."

THE LORD PUNISHES ALL SINNERS

[12]A message came to me from the LORD. He said, [13]"Son of man, suppose the people in a certain country sin against me. And they are not faithful to me. So I reach out my powerful hand against them. I cut off their food supply. I make them very hungry. I kill them and their animals. [14]And suppose Noah, Daniel and Job were in that country. Then those three men could save only themselves by doing what is right," announces the LORD and King.

[15]"Or suppose I send wild animals through that country. And they kill all of its children. It becomes a dry and empty desert. No one can pass through it because of the animals. [16]And suppose those three men were in that country. Then they could not save their own sons or daughters. They alone would be saved. But the land would become a dry and empty desert. And that is just as sure as I am alive," announces the LORD and King.

[17]"Or suppose I send swords to kill the people in that country. And I say, 'Let swords sweep all through the land.' And I kill its people and their animals. [18]And suppose those three men were in that country. Then they could not save their own sons or daughters. They alone would be saved. And that is just as sure as I am alive," announces the LORD and King.

[19]"Or suppose I send a plague into that land. And I pour out my burning anger on it by spilling blood. I kill its people and their animals. [20]And suppose Noah, Daniel and Job were in that land. Then they could not save their own sons or daughters. They could save only themselves by doing what is right. And that is just as sure as I am alive," announces the LORD and King.

[21]The LORD and King says, "It will get much worse. I will punish Jerusalem in four horrible ways. There will be war, hunger, wild animals and plague. They will destroy the people and their animals.

[22]"But some people will be left alive. Some children will be brought out of the city. They will come to you. You will see how they act and the way they live. And you will be comforted in spite of all of the trouble I brought on Jerusalem. [23]You will be comforted when you see how they act and the way they live. Then you will know that I did not do anything there without a reason," announces the LORD and King.

JERUSALEM IS LIKE A USELESS VINE

15 A message came to me from the LORD. He said, [2]"Son of man, is the wood of a vine better than the wood of any of the trees in the forest? [3]Can its wood ever be made into anything useful? Can pegs be made from it to hang things on?

[4]"Suppose it is thrown in the fire to be burned. And the fire burns both ends and blackens the middle. Then is it useful for anything? [5]It was not useful when it was whole. So how can it be made into something useful now? The fire has burned it and blackened it."

[6]The LORD and King says, "Instead of the wood of any tree in the forest, I have given the vine to burn in the fire. I will treat the people who live in Jerusalem the same way. [7]I will turn against them. They might have come out of the fire. But the fire will destroy them anyway. I will turn against them. Then they will know that I am the LORD. [8]I will make the land a dry and empty desert. My people have not

been faithful to me," announces the LORD and King.

A STORY THAT PICTURES UNFAITHFUL JERUSALEM

16 A message came to me from the LORD. He said, ²"Son of man, tell the people of Jerusalem the evil things they have done. I hate those things.

³"Tell them, 'The LORD and King speaks to Jerusalem. He says, "Your history in the land of Canaan goes back a long way. Your father was an Amorite. Your mother was a Hittite. ⁴On the day you were born your cord was not cut. You were not washed with water to clean you up. You were not rubbed with salt. And you were not wrapped in large strips of cloth. ⁵No one took pity on you. No one was concerned enough to do any of those things for you. Instead, you were thrown out into an open field. You were hated on the day you were born.

⁶" ' "I was passing by. I saw you kicking around in your blood. As you were lying there, I said to you, 'Live!' ⁷I made you grow like a plant in a field. Soon you had grown up. You became the most beautiful jewel of all. Your breasts had formed. Your hair had grown. But you were naked and bare.

⁸" ' "Later, I was passing by again. I looked at you. I saw that you were old enough for love. So I got married to you and took good care of you. I covered your naked body. I took an oath and made a firm promise to you. I entered into a covenant with you. And you became mine," announces the LORD and King.

⁹" ' "I bathed you with water. I washed the blood off you. And I put lotions on you. ¹⁰I put a beautiful dress on you. I gave you leather sandals. I dressed you in fine linen. I covered you with expensive clothes. ¹¹I decorated you with jewelry. I put bracelets on your arms. I gave you a necklace for your neck. ¹²I put rings on your nose and ears. And I gave you a beautiful crown for your head.

¹³" ' "So you were decorated with gold and silver. Your clothes were made out of fine linen. They were made of expensive and beautiful cloth. Your food was made out of fine flour, honey and olive oil. You became very beautiful. You became a queen. ¹⁴You were so beautiful that your fame spread among the nations. The glory I had given you made your beauty perfect," announces the LORD and King.

¹⁵" ' "But you trusted in your beauty. You used your fame to become a prostitute. You offered your body freely to anyone who passed by. In fact, you gave yourself to anyone who wanted you. ¹⁶You used some of your clothes to make high places colorful. That is where people worshiped other gods. You were a prostitute there. Things like that should never happen. They should never take place.

¹⁷" ' "I had given you fine jewelry. It was made out of gold and silver. You used it to make for yourself statues of male gods. You worshiped those gods. You were not faithful to me. ¹⁸You put your beautiful clothes on them. You offered my oil and incense to them. ¹⁹You also offered them the food that was made out of fine flour, olive oil and honey. I had given it to you to eat. You offered it as sweet-smelling incense to them. That is what you did," announces the LORD and King.

²⁰" ' "Then you got your sons and daughters who belonged to me. And you sacrificed them as food to other gods. Wasn't it enough for you to be a prostitute? ²¹You killed my children. You sacrificed them to other gods.

²²" ' "You did not remember the days when you were young. At that time you were naked and bare. You were kicking around in your blood. But now you have done evil things. I hate them. You have worshiped other gods. You have not been faithful to me.

²³" ' "How terrible it will be for you!" announces the LORD and King. "How terrible for you! You continued to sin against me. ²⁴Your people built up mounds for themselves in every market place. They put little places of worship on them. ²⁵They set them up at every street corner. Jerusalem, you misused your beauty. You offered your body to anyone who passed by. You did it again and again.

²⁶" ' "You committed shameful acts with the people of Egypt. They were

your neighbors, and they were filled with longing for their lovers. You offered yourself to others again and again. That made me very angry. ²⁷So I reached out my powerful hand against you. I made your territory smaller. I handed you over to your Philistine enemies. The people in their towns were shocked by your impure conduct.

²⁸" ' "You also committed shameful acts with the people of Assyria. Nothing ever seemed to satisfy you. You could never get enough. ²⁹Then you offered yourself to the people of Babylonia. But that did not satisfy you either. There are many traders in the land of Babylonia.

³⁰" ' "You can't control yourself," announces the LORD and King. "Just look at all of the things you are doing! You are acting like a prostitute who has no shame at all. ³¹Your people built up mounds at every street corner. You put little places of worship on them in every market place. But you did not really act like a prostitute. You refused to let your lovers pay you anything.

³²" ' "You unfaithful wife! You would rather be with strangers than with your own husband! ³³Every prostitute gets paid. But you give gifts to all of your lovers. You offer them money to come to you from everywhere. You want them to make love to you. You are not faithful to me. ³⁴As a prostitute, you are the opposite of others. No one runs after you to make love to you. You are exactly the opposite. You pay them. They do not pay you." ' "

³⁵You prostitute, listen to the LORD's message. ³⁶The LORD and King says, "You poured out your wealth on your lovers. You took your clothes off and made love to them. You did it again and again. You worshiped other gods. I hate them. You even sacrificed your children to them.

³⁷"So I am going to gather together all of the lovers you found pleasure with. They include those you loved and those you hated. I will gather them against you from everywhere. I will take your clothes off right in front of them. Then they will see you completely naked. ³⁸I will hand down my sentence against you. You will be punished like women who commit adultery and sacrifice their children to other gods. My anger burns against you so much that I will sentence you to death for everything you have done.

³⁹"Then I will hand you over to your lovers. They will tear down those mounds you built. They will destroy the little places of worship you put on them. They will take your clothes off. They will remove your fine jewelry. And they will leave you naked and bare.

⁴⁰"They will bring a crowd against you. The crowd will put you to death by throwing stones at you. And they will chop you to pieces with their swords. ⁴¹They will burn your houses down and punish you. Many women will see it.

"I will not let you be a prostitute anymore. You will no longer pay your lovers. ⁴²Then my burning anger against you will die down. My jealous anger will turn away from you. I will be calm. I will not be angry anymore.

⁴³"You did not remember the days when you were young. The things you did made me very angry. So anything that happens to you will be your own fault," announces the LORD and King. "You added impure conduct to all of the other evil things you did. I hate all of those things.

⁴⁴"All those who use proverbs will use this one about you. They will say, 'Like mother, like daughter.' ⁴⁵You are a true daughter of your mother. She hated her husband and children. And you are a true sister of your sisters. They hated their husbands and children.

"Your mother was a Hittite. Your father was an Amorite. ⁴⁶Your older sister was Samaria. She lived north of you with her daughters. Your younger sister was Sodom. She lived south of you with her daughters. ⁴⁷You lived exactly the way they did. You copied their evil practices. I hate those practices. Everything you did was so sinful that you soon became even worse than they were.

⁴⁸"Your sister Sodom and her daughters never did what you and your daughters have done. And that is just as sure as I am alive," announces the LORD and King.

⁴⁹"Here is the sin your sister Sodom committed. She and her daughters were proud. They ate too much. They were not concerned about others. They did not help those who were poor and in need. ⁵⁰They were very proud. They did many things that were evil in my sight. I hated those things. So I got rid of Sodom and her daughters, just as you have seen.

⁵¹"Samaria did not commit half the sins you did. You sinned even more than they did. I hate those sins. Compared to what you did, you made your sisters seem godly. ⁵²So you will be dishonored. You have given your sisters an excuse for what they did. Your sins were far worse than theirs. In fact, your sisters appear to be more godly than you. So then, be ashamed. You will be dishonored. You have made them appear to be godly.

⁵³"I will not only give you back what you had before. I will also do the same thing for Sodom and her daughters. And I will do the same for Samaria and her daughters. ⁵⁴That will make you feel dishonored. You will be ashamed of everything you have done. You have made them feel better because you sinned more and were punished more than they were. ⁵⁵Your sisters Sodom and Samaria and their daughters will return to what they were before. And you and your daughters will return to what you were before.

⁵⁶"In the past you would not even mention your sister Sodom. You were proud at that time. ⁵⁷That was before your sin was uncovered. Now the daughters of Edom make fun of you. So do all of her neighbors and the daughters of the Philistines. Everyone who lives around you looks down on you. ⁵⁸You will be punished for your impure conduct. I will also punish you for the other evil things you have done. I hate all of those things," announces the LORD.

⁵⁹The LORD and King says, "I will punish you in keeping with what you have done. I sealed with an oath the covenant I made with you. You hated that oath. And you broke my covenant. ⁶⁰"But I will remember my covenant with you. I made it with you when you were young. Now I will make a new covenant with you. It will last forever. ⁶¹Then you will remember how you have lived. You will be ashamed when I give you Samaria and Sodom. Samaria is your older sister. Sodom is your younger one. I will give them and their daughters to you as daughters. That can't happen based on my old covenant with you. ⁶²So I will make my new covenant with you. Then you will know that I am the LORD.

⁶³"I will pay for all of the sins you have committed. Then you will remember what you have done. You will be ashamed of it. Because of your shame, you will never speak against me again," announces the LORD and King.

TWO EAGLES AND A VINE

17 A message came to me from the LORD. He said, ²"Son of man, tell the people of Israel a story about their kings. Let them know what will happen to them. ³Tell them, 'The LORD and King says, "A great eagle came to the city of 'Lebanon.' It had powerful wings and a lot of long feathers. The feathers were colorful and beautiful. The eagle landed in the top of a cedar tree. ⁴It broke off the highest twig. It carried it away to Babylonia. There are many traders in that land. The eagle planted the twig in the city of Babylon.

⁵" ' "Then it got a seed from your land. It put it in rich soil near plenty of water. It planted the seed like a willow tree. ⁶The seed grew into a low, spreading vine. Its branches turned toward the eagle. And its roots remained under the eagle. So the seed became a vine. It produced branches and put out leaves.

⁷" ' "But there was another great eagle. It also had powerful wings and a lot of feathers. The vine now sent its roots out toward that eagle. It sent them out from the place where it was planted. And it reached out its branches to the eagle for water. ⁸The seed had been planted in good soil near plenty of water. Then it could produce branches and bear fruit. It could become a beautiful vine." '

⁹"Ezekiel, tell the Israelites, 'The LORD and King asks, "Will the vine

grow? Won't it be pulled up by its roots? Won't all of its fruit be stripped off? Won't it dry up? All of its new growth will dry up. It will not take a strong arm or many people to pull it up. ¹⁰It will not grow even if it is pulled up and planted somewhere else. It will dry up completely when the east wind strikes it. It will dry up in the place where it grew." ' "

¹¹A message came to me from the LORD. He said, ¹²"These people refuse to obey me. Ask them, 'Don't you know what these things mean?' Tell them, 'Nebuchadnezzar went to Jerusalem. He was king of Babylonia. He carried off King Jehoiachin and the nobles. He brought them back with him to the city of Babylon.

¹³" 'Then Nebuchadnezzar made a peace treaty with Zedekiah. He was a member of Jerusalem's royal family. Nebuchadnezzar made him take an oath and promise he would keep the treaty. He also took the leading men of the land away as prisoners. ¹⁴He did it to bring their kingdom down. It would not rise again. In fact, it would be able to last only by keeping his treaty.

¹⁵" 'But Zedekiah turned against him. He sent messengers to Egypt. They went there to get horses and a large army. Will he succeed? Will he who does things like that escape? Can he break the peace treaty and still escape?

¹⁶" 'Zedekiah will die in Babylon,' announces the LORD and King. 'And that is just as sure as I am alive. He will die in the land of King Nebuchadnezzar, who put him on the throne. He is the king whose oath Zedekiah hated. He also broke Nebuchadnezzar's treaty.

¹⁷" 'So Nebuchadnezzar will build ramps against the walls of Jerusalem. He will set up war machines to destroy many lives. Pharaoh will not be able to help Zedekiah during the war. The huge and mighty army of Egypt will not be of any help.

¹⁸" 'Zedekiah hated Nebuchadnezzar's oath and broke his treaty. He had made a firm promise to keep it. But he broke it anyway. So he will not escape.

¹⁹" 'The LORD and King says, "Zedekiah hated the oath he took in my name. He broke the treaty. So I will pay him back. And that is just as sure as I am alive. ²⁰I will spread out my net to catch him. He will be caught in my trap. I will bring him to Babylon. I will judge him there because he was not faithful to me.

²¹" ' "All of Zedekiah's troops will be killed with swords when they try to run away. Those who are left alive will be scattered to the winds. Then you will know that I have spoken. I am the LORD.

²²" 'The LORD and King says, "I myself will get a twig from the very top of a cedar tree and plant it. I will break off the highest twig. I will plant it on a very high mountain. ²³I will plant it on the high mountains of Israel. It will produce branches and bear fruit. It will become a beautiful cedar tree. All kinds of birds will make their nests in it. They will live in the shade of its branches. ²⁴All of the trees in the fields will know that I bring tall trees down. I make short trees grow tall. I dry up green trees. And I make dry trees green."

" 'I have spoken. I will do it. I am the LORD.' "

PEOPLE WILL DIE BECAUSE OF THEIR OWN SINS

18 A message came to me from the LORD. He said, ²"You people have a proverb about the land of Israel. What do you mean by it? It says,

" 'The parents eat sour grapes.
But the children have a bitter
taste in their mouths.'

³"You will not use that proverb in Israel anymore," announces the LORD and King. "And that is just as sure as I am alive. ⁴Everyone belongs to me. Father and son alike belong to me. People will die because of their own sins.

⁵"Suppose a godly man
does what is fair and right.
⁶And he does not eat at the
mountain temples.
He does not worship the statues
of Israel's gods.

He does not have sex with another
man's wife.

He does not make love to his own
wife

during her monthly period.

[7] He does not treat anyone badly.
Instead, he always gives back
what he took as security for a loan.

He does not steal.

Instead, he gives his food to
hungry people.

He provides clothes for those
who are naked.

[8] He does not lend money and
charge too much interest.

He keeps himself from doing
what is wrong.

He judges cases fairly.

[9] He follows my rules.

He is faithful in keeping my laws.

He always does what is right.

You can be sure he will live,"

announces the LORD
and King.

[10] "But suppose he has a mean son
who harms other people. The son
commits murder. Or he does some
other things that are wrong. [11] Suppose
he does those things even though his
father never did.

"Suppose he eats at the mountain
temples.

And he has sex with another
man's wife.

[12] He treats poor and needy people
badly.

He steals.

He does not pay back what he
owes.

He worships statues of gods.

He does other things I hate.

[13] He lends money and charges too
much interest.

Will a man like that live? He will not!
You can be sure he will be put to death.
And what happens to him will be his
own fault. He did many things I hate.

[14] "But suppose that son has a son of
his own. And the son sees all of the sins
his father commits. He sees them, but
he does not do them.

[15] "Suppose he does not eat at the
mountain temples.

And he does not worship the
statues of Israel's gods.

He does not have sex with
another man's wife.

[16] He does not treat anyone badly.

He does not make people give
him something

to prove they will pay back what
they owe him.

He does not steal.

Instead, he gives his food to
hungry people.

He provides clothes for those
who are naked.

[17] He keeps himself from committing
sins.

He does not lend money and
charge too much interest.

He keeps my laws and follows my
rules.

He will not die because of his father's
sin. You can be sure he will live. [18] But
his father will die because of his own
sin. He got rich by cheating others. He
robbed his relatives. He also did what
was wrong among his people.

[19] "But you still ask, 'Is the son guilty
along with his father?' No! The son did
what was fair and right. He was careful
to keep all of my rules. So you can be
sure he will live. [20] People will die because of their own sins. The son will
not be guilty because of what his father did. And the father will not be
guilty because of what his son did. The
right things a godly person does will
be added to his account. The wrong
things a sinful person does will be
charged against him.

[21] "But suppose a sinful person turns
away from all of the sins he has committed. And he keeps all my rules. He
does what is fair and right. Then you
can be sure he will live. He will not die.
[22] None of the sins he has committed
will be held against him. Because of
the godly things he has done, he will
live.

[23] "When sinful people die, it does
not give me any joy," announces the
LORD and King. "But when they turn
away from their sins and live, that
makes me very happy.

[24] "Suppose a godly person stops doing what is right. And he commits sin.
He does the same evil things a sinful
person does. He does things I hate.
Then he will not live. I will not remem-

ber any of the right things he has done. He has not been faithful to me. He has also committed many other sins. So he is guilty. He will die.

²⁵"But you say, 'What the Lord does isn't fair.' Listen to me, people of Israel. What I do is always fair. What you do is not.

²⁶"Suppose a godly person stops doing what is right. And he commits sin. Then he will die because of it. He will die because of the sin he has committed.

²⁷"But suppose a sinful person turns away from the evil things he has done. And he does what is fair and right. Then he will save his life. ²⁸He thinks about all of the evil things he has done. And he turns away from them. So you can be sure he will live. He will not die.

²⁹"But the people of Israel still say, 'What the Lord does isn't fair.' People of Israel, what I do is always fair. What you do is not.

³⁰"So I will judge you people. I will judge each of you in keeping with what you have done," announces the LORD and King.

"Turn away from your sins! Turn away from all of the evil things you have done. Then sin will not bring you down. ³¹Get rid of all of the evil things you have done. Let me give you a new heart and a new spirit. Then you will be faithful to me. Why should you die, people of Israel? ³²When anyone dies, it does not give me any joy," announces the LORD and King. "So turn away from your sins. Then you will live!

A SONG OF SADNESS ABOUT ISRAEL'S PRINCES

19 "Sing a song of sadness about Israel's princes. ²Say to Israel,

" 'You were like a mother lion to your princes.
　　She lay down among the young lions.
　　She brought up her cubs.
³One of them was Jehoahaz.
　　He became a strong lion.
　　He learned to tear apart what he caught.
　　And he ate men up.

⁴The nations heard about him.
　　They trapped him in their pit.
　　They put hooks in his face.
　　And they led him away to Egypt.

⁵" 'The mother lion looked and waited.
　　But all of her hope was gone.
　　So she got another one of her cubs.
　　She made him into a strong lion.
⁶He prowled with the lions.
　　He became very strong.
　　He learned to tear apart what he caught.
　　And he ate men up.
⁷He broke down their forts.
　　He completely destroyed their towns.
　　The land and all those who were in it
　　were terrified when he roared.
⁸Then nations came against him.
　　They came from all around him.
　　They spread out their net to catch him.
　　He was trapped in their pit.
⁹They used hooks to pull him into a cage.
　　They brought him to the king of Babylonia.
　　They put him in prison.
　　So his roar was not heard anymore
　　on the mountains of Israel.

¹⁰" 'Israel, you were like a vine in a vineyard.
　　It was planted near water.
　　It had a lot of fruit and many branches.
　　There was plenty of water.
¹¹Its branches were strong.
　　Each was good enough to be made into a ruler's rod.
　　The vine grew high
　　above all of the leaves.
　　It stood out because it was so tall
　　and had so many branches.
¹²But Nebuchadnezzar became angry.
　　He pulled it up by its roots.
　　He threw it to the ground.
　　The east wind dried it up.
　　Its fruit was stripped off.
　　Its strong branches dried up.
　　And fire destroyed them.

¹³Now it is planted in the
Babylonian desert.
It is in a dry and thirsty land.
¹⁴One of its main branches was
Zedekiah.
Fire spread from it and burned
up its fruit.
None of its branches is good
enough
to be made into a ruler's rod.'

"That is a song of sadness. And that is
how it should be used."

ISRAEL REFUSES TO OBEY THE LORD

20 It was the seventh year since King Jehoiachin had been brought to Babylon as a prisoner. On the tenth day of the fifth month, some of the elders of Israel came to ask the LORD for advice. They sat down with me.

²Then a message came to me from the LORD. He said, ³"Son of man, speak to the elders of Israel. Tell them, 'The LORD and King says, "Have you come to ask me for advice? I will not let you do that," announces the LORD and King. "And that is just as sure as I am alive." '

⁴"Are you going to judge them, son of man? Will you judge them? Tell them the evil things their people did long ago. I hate those things. ⁵Tell them, 'The LORD and King says, "I chose Israel. On that day I raised my hand and took an oath. I made a promise to the members of Jacob's family line. I made myself known to them in Egypt. I raised my hand and told them, 'I am the LORD your God.'

⁶" ' "On that day I promised I would bring them out of Egypt. I told them I would take them to a land I had found for them. It had plenty of milk and honey. It was the most beautiful land of all. ⁷I said to them, 'Each of you must get rid of the statues of the evil gods you worship. Do not pollute yourselves by worshiping the gods of Egypt. I am the LORD your God.'

⁸" ' "But they refused to obey me. They would not listen to me. They did not get rid of the evil gods they worshiped. And they did not turn away from Egypt's gods. So I said I would pour out all of my burning anger on them in Egypt.

⁹" ' "But I wanted my name to be honored. I kept it from being treated as if it were not holy. I did not want that to happen in front of the nations my people lived among. I had made myself known to Israel in the sight of those nations. I had brought my people out of Egypt.

¹⁰" ' "So I led them out of Egypt. I brought them into the Desert of Sinai. ¹¹I gave them my rules. I made my laws known to them. The one who obeys them will live by them. ¹²I also told them to observe my Sabbath days. That is the sign of the covenant I made with them. I wanted them to know that I made them holy. I am the LORD.

¹³" ' "But the people of Israel refused to obey me in the desert. They did not follow my rules. They turned their backs on my laws. The one who obeys them will live by them. They totally misused my Sabbath days. So I said I would pour out my burning anger on them. I would destroy them in the desert.

¹⁴" ' "But I wanted my name to be honored. I kept it from being treated as if it were not holy. I did not want that to happen in front of the nations. They had seen me bring Israel out of Egypt.

¹⁵" ' "I also raised my hand and took an oath in the desert. I told my people I would not bring them into the land I had given them. It had plenty of milk and honey. It was the most beautiful land of all. ¹⁶But they turned their backs on my laws. They did not follow my rules. They misused my Sabbaths. Their hearts were committed to worshiping the statues of their gods.

¹⁷" ' "Then I felt sorry for them. So I did not destroy them. I did not put an end to them in the desert. ¹⁸I spoke to their children there. I said, 'Do not follow the rules your parents gave you. Do not obey their laws. Do not pollute yourselves by worshiping their gods. ¹⁹I am the LORD your God. So follow my rules. Be careful to obey my laws. ²⁰Keep my Sabbath days holy. That is the sign of the covenant I made with you. You will know that I am the LORD your God.'

²¹" ' "But their children refused to obey me. They did not follow my rules. They were not careful to keep my laws. The one who obeys them will live by them. They misused my Sabbaths. So I said I would pour out all of my burning anger on them in the desert.

²²" ' "But I kept myself from punishing them at that time. I wanted my name to be honored. So I kept it from being treated as if it were not holy. I did not want that to happen in front of the nations. They had seen me bring Israel out of Egypt.

²³" ' "I also raised my hand and took an oath in the desert. I told my people I would scatter them among the nations. I would send them to other countries. ²⁴They had not obeyed my laws. They had turned their backs on my rules. They had misused my Sabbaths. Their eyes longed to see the statues of their parents' gods.

²⁵" ' "I even let them follow rules that were not good. I let them have laws they could not live by. ²⁶I let them become polluted by offering sacrifices to other gods. They even sacrificed the first male child who was born in each family. I wanted to fill them with horror. Then they would know that I am the LORD." '

²⁷"Son of man, speak to the people of Israel. Tell them, 'The LORD and King says, "Your people spoke evil things against me long ago. They deserted me. ²⁸But I brought them into the land. I had taken an oath and promised to give the land to them. Then they offered sacrifices that made me very angry. They did it on every high hill and under every green tree. There they brought their sweet-smelling incense. And there they poured out their drink offerings. ²⁹Then I said to them, 'What? You are going to a high place?' " ' " That high place is called Bamah to this very day.

THE LORD JUDGES ISRAEL AND BLESSES THEM

³⁰The LORD said to me, "Speak to the people of Israel. Tell them, 'The LORD and King says, "Are you going to pollute yourselves the way your people did? Do you long to see the statues of their evil gods? ³¹You pollute yourselves by offering sacrifices to other gods. You even sacrifice your children in the fire. You continue to do those things to this very day. People of Israel, should I let you ask me for advice? I will not let you do that," announces the LORD and King. "And that is just as sure as I am alive.

³²" ' "You say, 'We want to be like the other nations. We want to be like all of the other people in the world. They serve gods that are made out of wood and stone.' But what you have in mind will never happen. ³³I will rule over you by reaching out my mighty hand and powerful arm. I will pour my burning anger out on you," announces the LORD and King. "And that is just as sure as I am alive.

³⁴" ' "I will bring you back from the nations. I will gather you together from the countries where you have been scattered. I will reach out my mighty hand and powerful arm. I will pour my burning anger out on you. ³⁵I will send you among the nations. There I will judge you face to face. It will be as if I were judging you in the desert again. ³⁶Long ago, I judged your people in the desert of Egypt. In the same way, I will judge you," announces the LORD and King.

³⁷" ' "I will take note of you as you pass under my shepherd's rod. I will separate those who obey me from those who do not. And I will give the blessings of the new covenant to those of you who obey me. ³⁸I will get rid of those among you who turn against me and refuse to obey me. I will bring them out of the land where they are living. But they will not enter the land of Israel. Then you will know that I am the LORD.

³⁹" ' "People of Israel, the LORD and King says, 'Go, every one of you! Serve your gods. But later you will listen to me. You will no longer treat my name as if it were not holy. You will not offer sacrifices to other gods anymore.

⁴⁰" ' ' "People of Israel, you will serve me,' announces the LORD and King. 'You will serve me on my high and holy mountain in Jerusalem. There I will accept you. I will require your offerings and your finest gifts. I want you to bring them along with all of your other

holy sacrifices. [41]I will bring you back from the nations. I will gather you together from the countries where you have been scattered. Then I will accept you as if you were sweet-smelling incense. I will show that I am holy among you. The nations will see it.

[42]" ' " 'I will bring you into the land of Israel. Then you will know that I am the LORD. Long ago I raised my hand and took an oath. I promised to give that land to your people. [43]There you will remember your conduct. You will think about everything you did that polluted you. And you will hate yourselves because of all of the evil things you have done.

[44]" ' " 'People of Israel, I will deal with you for the honor of my name. I will not deal with you based on your evil conduct and sinful practices. Then you will know that I am the LORD,' announces the LORD and King." ' "

EZEKIEL PROPHESIES AGAINST THE SOUTH

[45]A message came to me from the LORD. He said, [46]"Son of man, turn your attention to Judah in the south. Preach against it. Prophesy against its forests. [47]Tell them, 'Listen to the LORD's message. The LORD and King says, "I am about to set you on fire. The fire will destroy all of your trees. It will burn up green trees and dry trees alike. The blazing flame will not be put out. The faces of everyone from south to north will be burned by it. [48]Everyone will see that I started the fire. It will not be put out. I am the LORD." ' "

[49]Then I said, "LORD and King, people are talking about me. They are saying, 'Isn't he just telling stories?' "

GOD USES BABYLONIA TO JUDGE ISRAEL

21 A message came to me from the LORD. He said, [2]"Son of man, turn your attention to Jerusalem. Preach against the temple. Prophesy against the land of Israel. [3]Tell them, 'The LORD says, "I am against you. I will pull out my sword. I will cut off from you godly people and sinful people alike. [4]Because I am going to cut them off, my sword will be ready to use. I will strike everyone down from south to north. [5]Then all people will know that I have pulled out my sword. I will not put it back. I am the LORD." '

[6]"Groan, son of man! Groan in front of your people with a broken heart and bitter sorrow. [7]They will ask you, 'Why are you groaning?'

"Then you will say, 'Because of the news that is coming. The hearts of all of the people will melt away in fear. Their hands will not be able to help them. Their spirits will grow weak. And their knees will become as weak as water.'

"The news is coming! You can be sure those things will happen," announces the LORD and King.

[8]A message came to me from the LORD. He said, [9]"Son of man, prophesy. Say, 'The Lord says,

" ' "A sword! A sword!
A sharp and shiny sword is
    coming from Babylonia!
[10]It is sharpened to kill people.
    It flashes like lightning." ' "

The people say, "Should we take delight in the rod of the ruler of the LORD's son Judah? The sword looks down on every stick like that."

[11]The LORD says,

"I have told Nebuchadnezzar to
    shine his sword.
It is in his hand.
It has been sharpened and shined.
    It is ready for the killer's hand.
[12]Son of man, cry out and sob.
    The sword is against my people.
It is against all of the princes of
    Israel.
It will kill them
    along with the rest of my people.
So beat your chest in sorrow.

[13]"You can be sure that testing will come. Why does the sword look down on the rod? Because the rod will not continue to rule," announces the LORD and King.

[14]"Son of man, prophesy.
    Clap your hands.
Let the sword strike twice.
    Let it strike even three times.
It is a sword to kill people.

It is a sword to kill many people.
It is closing in on them from
    every side.
15 People's hearts will melt away in
    fear.
Many will be wounded or killed.
I have prepared the sword to kill
    people
    at all of their city gates.
It flashes like lightning.
It is in the killer's hand.
16 Sword, cut to the right.
Then cut to the left.
Strike people down everywhere
    your blade is turned.
17 I too will clap my hands.
My burning anger will calm down.
I have spoken. I am the LORD."

18 A message came to me from the LORD. He said, 19 "Son of man, mark out on a map two roads for the sword to take. The sword belongs to the king of Babylonia. Both roads start from the same country. Put up a sign where the road turns off to the city of Rabbah. 20 Mark out one road for the sword to take against Rabbah in Ammon. Mark out another against Judah and the walls of Jerusalem.

21 "The king of Babylonia will stop at the place where the two roads meet. He will ask his gods to tell him which way to go. He will cast lots by pulling arrows out of a bag. And he will look carefully at the liver of a sheep.

22 "His right hand will pull out the arrow for Jerusalem. There he will get huge logs ready to knock down its gates. He will give the command to kill its people. He will sound the battle cry. He will build a ramp up to the city wall. He will bring in his war machines.

23 "The decision to attack Jerusalem will seem like the wrong advice to those who made a treaty with Nebuchadnezzar. But he will remind them that they are guilty. And he will take them away as prisoners."

24 So the LORD and King says, "You people have reminded everyone of how guilty you are. You have done it by refusing to obey me or any other authority. Everything you do clearly shows how sinful you are. So you will be taken away as prisoners."

25 King Zedekiah, the day for you to be punished has finally come. You are an unholy and evil prince in Israel. Your time is up. 26 The LORD and King says, "Take off your turban. Remove your crown. Things will not be as they were in the past. Those who are not important will be honored. And those who are honored will be brought down. 27 Jerusalem will fall. I will destroy it. It will not be rebuilt until the true king comes. After all, the kingdom belongs to him. I will give it to him.

28 "Son of man, prophesy. Say, 'The LORD and King speaks about the Ammonites. He also talks about the way they laugh because of Jerusalem's fall. He says,

" ' "A sword! A sword!
Nebuchadnezzar's sword is ready
    to kill you.
It is shined to destroy you.
It flashes like lightning.
29 The visions of your prophets are
    false.
They use magic to try to find out
    what is going to happen to you.
But their magic tricks are lies.
The sword will strike the necks of
    you sinful people.
You will be killed.
The day for you to be punished
    has finally come.
Your time is up.
30 Ammon, return your sword to its
    place.
In the land where you were
    created, I will judge you.
That is where you came from.
31 I will pour out my anger on you.
I will breathe out my burning
    anger against you.
I will hand you over to mean people.
They are skilled at destroying
    others.
32 You will be burned in the fire.
Your blood will be spilled in your
    land.
You will not be remembered
    anymore.
I have spoken. I am the LORD." ' "

JERUSALEM SINS AGAINST THE LORD

22 A message came to me from the LORD. He said, 2 "Son of man, are you go-

ing to judge Jerusalem? Will you judge this city that has so many murderers in it? Then tell its people they have done many evil things. I hate those things. ³Tell them, 'The LORD and King says, "Your city brings death on itself. You spill blood inside its walls. You pollute yourselves by making statues of gods. ⁴You are guilty of spilling blood. The statues you have made have polluted you.

" ' "You have brought your days to a close. The end of your years has come. So the nations will make fun of you. All of the countries will laugh at you. ⁵Those who are near you will tell jokes about you. So will those who are far away. Trouble fills the streets of your sinful city.

⁶" ' "The princes of Israel are in your city. All of them use their power to spill blood. ⁷They have made fun of fathers and mothers alike. They have crushed outsiders. They have treated badly the children whose fathers have died. They have done the same thing to widows.

⁸" ' "You have looked down on the holy things that were set apart to me. You have misused my Sabbath days. ⁹You have spread lies about others so you can spill someone's blood. You eat at the mountain temples. You commit impure acts.

¹⁰" ' "You bring shame on your fathers by having sex with their wives. You have sex with women during their monthly period. That is when they are 'unclean.' ¹¹One of you has sex with another man's wife. I hate that sin. Another brings shame on his daughter-in-law by having sex with her. Still another has sex with his sister, even though she is his own father's daughter.

¹²" ' "You accept money from people who want special favors. You do it to spill someone's blood. You charge too much interest when you lend money. You get rich by cheating your neighbors. And you have forgotten me," announces the LORD and King.

¹³" ' "I will clap my hands because I am so angry. You got rich by cheating others. You spilled blood inside the walls of your city. ¹⁴Will you be brave on the day I deal with you? Will you be strong at that time? I have spoken. I will do it. I am the LORD.

¹⁵" ' "I will scatter you among the nations. I will send you to other countries. I will put an end to your 'uncleanness.' ¹⁶You will be polluted in the sight of the nations. Then you will know that I am the LORD." ' "

¹⁷A message came to me from the LORD. He said, ¹⁸"Son of man, the people of Israel have become like scum to me. All of them are like the copper, tin, iron and lead that are left inside a furnace. They are only the scum that is removed from silver."

¹⁹So the LORD and King says, "People of Israel, all of you have become like scum. So I will gather you together in Jerusalem. ²⁰Men put silver, copper, iron, lead and tin into a furnace. They melt it with a blazing fire. In the same way, I will gather you. I will pour out my burning anger on you. I will put you inside the city and melt you. ²¹I will gather you together. My burning anger will blaze out at you. And you will be melted inside Jerusalem. ²²Silver is melted in a furnace. And you will be melted inside the city. Then you will know that I have poured out my burning anger on you. I am the LORD."

²³Another message came to me from the LORD. He said, ²⁴"Son of man, speak to the land. Tell it, 'You have not had any rain or showers. That is because I am angry with you.'

²⁵"Ezekiel, the princes of the land are like a roaring lion that tears its food apart. They eat people up. They take treasures and other valuable things. They cause many women in the land to become widows.

²⁶"Its priests break my law. They treat things that are set apart to me as if they were not holy. They treat holy and common things as if they were the same. They teach that there is no difference between things that are 'clean' and things that are not. They refuse to keep my Sabbath days. So they treat me as if I were not holy.

²⁷"The officials in the land are like wolves that tear their food apart. They spill blood and kill people to get rich. ²⁸The prophets cover up those acts for them. The visions of those prophets

are false. They use magic to try to find out what is going to happen. But their magic tricks are lies. They say, 'The LORD and King says,' But I have not spoken to them.

²⁹"The people of the land get rich by cheating others. They steal. They crush those who are poor and in need. They treat outsiders badly. They refuse to be fair to them.

³⁰"I looked for a man among them who would stand up for Jerusalem. I tried to find someone who would pray to me for the land. Then I would not have to destroy it. But I could not find anyone who would pray for it. ³¹So I will pour out my anger on its people. I will destroy them because my anger burns against them. And anything that happens to them will be their own fault," announces the LORD and King.

SAMARIA AND JERUSALEM ARE LIKE TWO IMPURE SISTERS

23 A message came to me from the LORD. He said, ²"Son of man, once there were two women. They had the same mother. ³They became prostitutes in Egypt. They have been unfaithful to me since they were young. In that land they allowed their breasts to be touched. They permitted their virgin breasts to be kissed.

⁴"The older sister was named Oholah. The younger one was Oholibah. They belonged to me. Sons and daughters were born to them. Oholah stands for Samaria. And Oholibah stands for Jerusalem.

⁵"Oholah was unfaithful to me even while she still belonged to me. She longed for her Assyrian lovers. ⁶They included soldiers who wore blue uniforms. They also included governors and commanders. All of them were young and handsome. They rode horses. ⁷She gave herself as a prostitute to all of Assyria's finest warriors. She polluted herself with the statues of the gods of everyone she longed for. ⁸"She started being a prostitute in Egypt. And she never stopped. When she was young, men had sex with her.

They kissed her virgin breasts. They used up all of their sinful longings on her.

⁹"So I handed her over to her Assyrian lovers. She longed for them. ¹⁰They stripped her naked. They took her sons and daughters away. And they killed her with their swords. Other women laughed when that happened. I was the one who had punished her.

¹¹"Her sister Oholibah saw it. But her evil longing for sexual sin was worse than her sister's. ¹²She too longed for the men of Assyria. They included governors and commanders. They included soldiers who wore uniforms. They also included men who rode horses. All of them were young and handsome. ¹³I saw that she too polluted herself. So both sisters did the same evil things.

¹⁴"But Oholibah went even further with her sexual sins. She saw pictures of men drawn on a wall. They were figures of Babylonians drawn in red. ¹⁵They had belts around their waists. They wore flowing turbans on their heads. All of them looked like Babylonian chariot officers. They were from the land of the Chaldeans. ¹⁶"As soon as she saw the pictures, she longed for the men. So she sent messengers to them in Babylonia. ¹⁷Then the Babylonians came to her. They went to bed with her. They made love to her. They polluted her when they had sex with her. After they did it, she became sick of them. So she turned away from them.

¹⁸"She acted like a prostitute who had no shame at all. She openly showed her naked body. I became sick of what she was doing. So I turned away from her. I had also turned away from her sister.

¹⁹"But Oholibah offered her body to her lovers again and again. She remembered the days when she was a young prostitute in Egypt. ²⁰There she had longed for her lovers. Their private parts seemed as big as those of donkeys. And their flow of semen appeared to be as much as that of horses. ²¹So you wanted to return to the days when you were young. You longed for the time when you first became impure in Egypt. That was when you al-

lowed your breasts to be kissed. And you permitted your young breasts to be touched."

²²So the LORD and King says, "Oholibah, I will stir up your lovers against you. You became sick of them. You turned away from them. But I will bring them against you from every side. ²³They include the Babylonians and all of the Chaldeans. They include the men from Pekod, Shoa and Koa. They also include all of the Assyrians. They are young and handsome. Some of them are governors and commanders. Others are chariot officers. Still others are very high officials. All of them ride horses.

²⁴"So a huge army will come against you with weapons, chariots and wagons. They will take up positions against you on every side. They will carry large and small shields. They will wear helmets. I will turn you over to them to be punished. They will punish you in their own way.

²⁵"I will pour out my jealous anger on you. And the army's anger will burn against you. They will cut off your noses and ears. Some of you who are left will be killed with swords. They will take your sons and daughters away. Others of you who are left will be burned up. ²⁶The army will also strip your clothes off. They will take your fine jewelry away from you.

²⁷"You became an impure prostitute in Egypt. But I will put a stop to all of that. You will no longer want to do any of it. You will not remember Egypt anymore."

²⁸The LORD and King says, "I am about to hand you over to people you hate. You became sick of them. You turned away from them. ²⁹They will punish you because they hate you so much. They will take everything you have worked for away from you. They will leave you naked and bare. Then everyone will see that you are a prostitute who has no shame at all. You were impure. You offered your body to your lovers again and again.

³⁰"That is why you will be punished. You longed for lovers in other nations. You polluted yourself by worshiping their gods. ³¹You did the same things your sister Oholah did. So I will put her

cup in your hand. It is filled with the wine of my anger."

³²The LORD and King says to Oholibah,

"You will drink from your sister's cup.
It is large and deep.
It is filled with the wine of my anger.
So others will laugh at you.
They will make fun of you.
³³You will become drunk and sad.
The cup of my anger will completely destroy you.
It is the same cup your sister Samaria drank from.
³⁴You will drink from it until it is empty.
Then you will throw it down and break it in pieces.
And you will claw at your breasts.

I have spoken," announces the LORD and King.

³⁵So the LORD and King says, "You have forgotten me. You have pushed me behind your back. You have been impure. You have acted like a prostitute. So I will punish you."

³⁶The LORD said to me, "Son of man, are you going to judge Oholah and Oholibah? Then tell them they have done many evil things. I hate those things. ³⁷They have committed adultery. Their hands are covered with the blood of the people they have murdered. They have worshiped other gods. They have not been faithful to me. They have even sacrificed their children as food to other gods. Those children belonged to me.

³⁸"Here are some other things the sisters have done to me. They have polluted my temple. They have misused my Sabbath days. ³⁹They have sacrificed their children to their gods. On that same day they entered my temple and polluted it. That is what they have done in my house.

⁴⁰"They even sent messengers to bring men from far away. When the men arrived, Oholibah took a bath. She put makeup on her eyes. She put her jewelry on. ⁴¹She sat down on a beautiful couch. A table was in front of it. There she put the incense and olive oil that belonged to me.

⁴²"The noise of a carefree crowd was all around her. Sabeans were brought from the desert. Other men were brought along with them. They put bracelets on the arms of the two sisters. They put beautiful crowns on their heads.

⁴³"Then I spoke about Oholibah. She was worn out by adultery. I said, 'Let them use her as a prostitute. After all, that is what she is.' ⁴⁴So they had sex with her. In fact, they had sex with both of those impure women, Oholah and Oholibah. It was just like having sex with prostitutes.

⁴⁵"But men who are right with God will sentence the sisters to be punished. They will be punished in the same way as women who commit adultery and murder. After all, they have committed adultery. And their hands are covered with the blood of the people they have murdered."

⁴⁶The LORD and King says, "Bring an angry crowd against the sisters. Hand them over to those who will terrify them and steal everything they have. ⁴⁷The crowd will kill them by throwing stones at them. They will cut them down with their swords. They will kill their sons and daughters. And they will burn their houses down.

⁴⁸"So I will put an end to impurity in the land. Then all of its women will be warned. They will not want to be like the sisters. ⁴⁹Those sisters will be punished because of the impure things they have done. They will be judged because they have worshiped other gods. Then they will know that I am the LORD and King."

JERUSALEM IS LIKE A COOKING POT

24 It was the ninth year since King Jehoiachin had been brought to Babylon as a prisoner. On the tenth day of the tenth month, a message came to me from the LORD. He said, ²"Son of man, write down today's date. The king of Babylonia has surrounded Jerusalem and attacked it this very day.

³"Your people refuse to obey me. So tell them a story. Say to them, 'The LORD and King told me,

" ' "Put a cooking pot on the fire.
  Pour water into it.
⁴Put pieces of meat in it.
  Use all of the best pieces.
Use the leg and shoulder.
  Fill it with the best bones.
⁵Pick the finest animal in the flock.
  Pile wood under the pot to cook
    the bones.
Bring the water to a boil.
  Cook the bones in it." ' "

⁶The LORD and King says,

"How terrible it will be for this city!
  It has so many murderers in it.
How terrible for the pot that is
    coated with scum!
The scum on it will not go away.
Take the meat and bones out of
    the pot piece by piece.
Do not cast lots for them.

⁷"The blood Jerusalem's people
    spilled is inside its walls.
They poured it out on a bare
    rock.
They did not pour it on the
    ground.
If they had, dust would have
    covered it up.
⁸So I put their blood on the bare
    rock.
I did not want it to be covered
    up.
I poured my burning anger out on
    them.
I paid them back."

⁹So the LORD and King said to me,

"How terrible it will be for this city!
  It has so many murderers in it.
I too will pile the wood high.
¹⁰So pile on the wood.
  Light the fire.
Cook the meat well.
  Mix in the spices.
Let the bones be blackened.
¹¹Then set the empty pot on the
    coals.
Let it get hot. Let its copper glow.
Then what is not pure in it will
    melt.
Its scum will be burned away.
¹²But it can't be cleaned up.
  Its thick scum has not been
    removed.
Even fire can't burn it off.

[13]"Jerusalem, you are really impure. I tried to clean you up. But you would not let me make you pure. So you will not be clean again until my burning anger against you has calmed down.

[14]"I have spoken. The time has come for me to act. I will not hold back. I will not feel sorry for you. I will do what I said I would do. You will be judged for your conduct and actions. I am the LORD," announces the LORD and King.

EZEKIEL'S WIFE DIES

[15]A message came to me from the LORD. He said, [16]"Son of man, I will take away from you the wife you delight in. It will happen very soon. But do not sing songs of sadness. Do not let any tears flow from your eyes. [17]Groan quietly. Do not sob out loud over your wife when she dies. Keep your turban on your head. Keep your sandals on your feet. Do not cover the lower part of your face. Do not eat the food people eat to comfort them when someone dies."

[18]So I spoke to my people in the morning. And in the evening my wife died. The next morning I did what I had been commanded to do.

[19]Then the people said to me, "Tell us what these things have to do with us."

[20]So I told them. I said, "A message came to me from the LORD. He said, [21]'Speak to the people of Israel. Tell them, "The LORD and King says, 'I am about to pollute my temple. I will let the Babylonians burn it down. It is the beautiful building you are so proud of. You take delight in it. You love it. The sons and daughters you left behind will be killed with swords.

[22]" ' "So do what Ezekiel did. Do not cover the lower part of your face. Do not eat the food people eat to comfort them when someone dies. [23]Keep your turbans on your heads. Keep your sandals on your feet. Do not cry or sob. You will waste away because you have sinned so much. You will groan among yourselves.

[24]" ' "What Ezekiel has done will show you what is going to happen to you. You will do just as he has done. Then you will know that I am the LORD and King.' " '

[25]"Son of man, I will take away their beautiful temple. It is their joy and glory. They take delight in it. Their hearts long for it. I will also take away their sons and daughters. [26]On the day I destroy everything, a man will escape. He will come and tell you the news.

[27]"At that time I will open your mouth. Then you will no longer be silent. You will speak with the man. That will show them what will happen to them. And they will know that I am the LORD."

A MESSAGE ABOUT AMMON

25 A message came to me from the LORD. He said, [2]"Son of man, turn your attention to the Ammonites. Prophesy against them. [3]Tell them, 'Listen to the message of the LORD and King. He says, "You laughed when my temple was polluted. You also laughed when the land of Israel was completely destroyed. You made fun of the people of Judah when they were taken away as prisoners. [4]So I am going to hand you over to the people of the east. They will set up their tents in your land. They will camp among you. They will eat your fruit. They will drink your milk. [5]I will turn the city of Rabbah into grasslands for camels. Ammon will become a resting place for sheep. Then you will know that I am the LORD." ' "

[6]The LORD and King says, "You clapped your hands. You stamped your feet. You hated the land of Israel deep down inside you. You were glad because of what happened to it. [7]So I will reach out my powerful hand against you. I will give you and everything you have to the nations. I will cut you off from them. I will wipe you out. I will destroy you. Then you will know that I am the LORD."

A MESSAGE ABOUT MOAB

[8]The LORD and King says, "Moab and Edom said, 'Look! The people of Judah have become like all of the other nations.' [9]So I will let Moab's enemies attack its lower hills. They will begin at the border towns. Those towns include Beth Jeshimoth, Baal Meon and Kiriathaim. They are the glory of that

land. ¹⁰I will hand Moab over to the people of the east. I will also give the Ammonites to them. And the Ammonites will no longer be remembered among the nations. ¹¹I will punish Moab. Then they will know that I am the LORD."

A MESSAGE ABOUT EDOM

¹²The LORD and King says, "Edom got even with the people of Judah. That made them very guilty." ¹³He continues, "I will reach out my hand against Edom. I will kill its people and their animals. I will completely destroy it. They will be killed with swords from Teman all the way to Dedan. ¹⁴I will use my people Israel to pay Edom back. They will punish Edom because my anger burns against it. They will know how I pay my enemies back," announces the LORD and King.

A MESSAGE ABOUT THE PHILISTINES

¹⁵The LORD and King says, "The Philistines hated Judah deep down inside them. So they tried to get even with them. They had been Judah's enemies for many years. So they tried to destroy them." ¹⁶He continues, "I am about to reach out my hand against the Philistines. I will cut off the Kerethites. I will destroy those who remain along the coast. ¹⁷You can be sure that I will pay them back. I will punish them because my anger burns against them. When I pay them back, they will know that I am the LORD."

A MESSAGE ABOUT TYRE

26 It was the first day of a month near the end of the 11th year since King Jehoiachin had been brought to Babylon as a prisoner. A message came to me from the LORD. He said, ²"Son of man, Tyre laughed because of what happened to Jerusalem. The people of Tyre said, 'Jerusalem is the gateway to the nations. But the gate is broken. Its doors have swung open to us. Jerusalem has been destroyed. So now we will succeed.'"

³The LORD and King says, "But I am against you, Tyre. I will bring many nations against you. They will come in like the waves of the sea. ⁴They will destroy your walls. They will pull your towers down. I will clear away the stones of your broken-down buildings. I will turn you into nothing but a bare rock.

⁵"Out in the Mediterranean Sea your island city will become a place to spread fishnets. I have spoken," announces the LORD and King. "The nations will take you and everything you have. ⁶Your settlements on the coast will be destroyed by war. Then you will know that I am the LORD."

⁷The LORD and King says, "From the north I am going to bring Nebuchadnezzar against Tyre. He is king of Babylonia. He is the greatest king of all. He will come with horses and chariots. Horsemen and a great army will be brought along with him.

⁸"He will go to war against you. He will destroy your settlements on the coast. He will bring in war machines to attack you. A ramp will be built up to your walls. He will use his shields against you. ⁹He will use huge logs to knock your walls down. He will destroy your towers with his weapons.

¹⁰"He will have so many horses that they will cover you with dust. Your walls will shake because of the noise of his war horses, wagons and chariots. He will enter your gates, just as men enter a city whose walls have been broken through. ¹¹The hoofs of his horses will pound in your streets. He will kill your people with swords. Your strong pillars will fall to the ground.

¹²"His men will take away from you your wealth and anything else you have. They will pull your walls down. They will completely destroy your fine houses. They will throw the stones and lumber of your broken-down buildings into the sea.

¹³"I will put an end to your noisy songs. No one will hear the music of your harps anymore. ¹⁴I will turn you into nothing but a bare rock. You will become a place to spread fishnets. You will never be rebuilt. I have spoken. I am the LORD," announces the LORD and King.

¹⁵The LORD and King speaks to Tyre. He says, "The lands along the coast will shake because of the sound of

your fall. Wounded people will groan because so many are dying there.

¹⁶"Then all of the princes along the coast will step down from their thrones. They will put their robes away. They will take off their beautiful clothes. They will sit on the ground. They will put on terror as if it were their clothes. They will tremble with fear all the time. They will be shocked because of what has happened to you.

¹⁷"Then they will sing a song of sadness about you. They will say to you,

" 'Famous city, you have been
   completely destroyed!
You were filled with sea traders.
You and your citizens
   were a mighty power on the seas.
You terrified everyone
   who lived in you.
¹⁸The lands along the coast
   trembled with fear
   when you fell.
The islands in the sea
   were terrified when you were
   destroyed.' "

¹⁹The LORD and King says to Tyre, "I will turn you into an empty city. You will be like cities where no one lives anymore. I will cause the ocean to sweep over you. Its mighty waters will cover you. ²⁰So I will bring you down together with those who go down into the grave. The people who are there lived long ago. You will have to live in the earth below. It will be like living in buildings that were destroyed many years ago. You will go down into the grave along with others. And you will never come back. You will not take your place in this world again. ²¹I will bring you to a horrible end. You will be gone forever. People will look for you. But they will never find you," announces the LORD and King.

A SONG OF SADNESS ABOUT TYRE

27 A message came to me from the LORD. He said, ²"Son of man, sing a song of sadness about Tyre. ³It is located at the gateway to the Mediterranean Sea. It does business with nations on many coasts. Say to it, 'The LORD and King says,

" ' "Tyre, you say,
'I am perfect and beautiful.'
⁴You were like a ship that ruled over
   the high seas.
Your builders made you perfect
   and beautiful.
⁵They cut all of your lumber
   from pine trees on Mount
      Hermon.
They used a cedar tree from
      Lebanon
   to make a mast for you.
⁶They made your oars
   out of oak trees from Bashan.
They made your deck out of
   cypress wood
   from the coasts of Cyprus.
They decorated it with ivory.
⁷Your sail was made out of
   beautiful, Egyptian linen.
It served as your banner.
Your shades were made out of blue
   and purple cloth.
They were from the coasts of
      Elishah.
⁸Men from Sidon and Arvad
   manned your oars.
Tyre, your sailors were skillful.
⁹Very skilled workers from Byblos
   were on board.
They kept you waterproof.
All of the ships on the sea and
   their sailors
   came up beside you.
They brought their goods to
   trade for yours.

¹⁰" ' "City of Tyre, men from Persia,
      Lydia and Put
   served as soldiers in your army.
They hung their shields and
   helmets on your walls.
That brought glory to you.
¹¹Men from Arvad and Cilicia
   guarded your walls on every side.
Men from Gammad
   were in your towers.
They hung their shields around
   your walls.
They made you perfect and
   beautiful.

¹²" ' "Tarshish did business with you because you had so much wealth. They traded silver, iron, tin and lead for your goods.

¹³" ' "Greece, Tubal and Meshech did business with you. They traded

slaves and bronze articles for your products.

¹⁴" ' "Men from Beth Togarmah traded work horses, war horses and mules for your goods.

¹⁵" ' "Men from Rhodes did business with you. Many lands along the coast bought goods from you. They paid you with ivory tusks and ebony wood.

¹⁶" ' "Aram did business with you because you had so many products for sale. They traded turquoise, purple cloth and needlework for your goods. They also traded fine linen, coral and rubies for them.

¹⁷" ' "Judah and Israel did business with you. They traded wheat from Minnith, sweets, honey, olive oil and lotion for your products.

¹⁸" ' "Damascus traded wine from Helbon and wool from Zahar to you. They did business with you because you had so many products and so much wealth.

¹⁹" ' "Danites and Greeks from Uzal bought goods from you. They traded wrought iron, cassia and cane for your products.

²⁰" ' "Dedan traded saddle blankets to you.

²¹" ' "Arabia and all of the princes of Kedar bought goods from you. They traded you lambs, rams and goats for them.

²²" ' "Traders from Sheba and Raamah did business with you. They traded the finest spices, jewels and gold for your goods.

²³" ' "Haran, Canneh and Eden did business with you. So did traders from Sheba, Asshur and Kilmad. ²⁴In your market place they traded beautiful clothes, blue cloth, and needlework to you. They also traded colorful rugs that had twisted cords and tight knots.

²⁵" ' "The ships of Tarshish
carry your products.
You are like a ship filled with a
heavy load
in the middle of the sea.
²⁶The sailors who man your oars
take you
out to the high seas.
But the east wind will break you in
pieces
in the middle of the sea.

²⁷You will be wrecked on that day.
Your wealth, goods and products
will sink deep into the sea.
So will your sailors, officers,
carpenters,
traders and all of your soldiers.
Anyone else on board will sink
too.
²⁸The lands along the coast will
shake
when your officers cry out.
²⁹All those who man the oars
will desert their ships.
The sailors and all of the officers
will stand on the shore.
³⁰They will raise their voices.
They will cry bitterly over you.
They will sprinkle dust on their
heads.
They will roll in ashes.
³¹They will shave their heads
because of you.
And they will put on black
clothes.
They will sob over you.
Their spirits will be greatly
troubled.
They will be very sad.
³²As they sob and cry over you,
they will sing a song of sadness
about you.
They will say, 'Who was ever like
Tyre?
It was destroyed in the sea.'
³³Your goods went out on the seas.
You supplied many nations with
what they needed.
You had so much wealth and so
many products.
You made the kings of the earth
rich.
³⁴Now the sea has torn you apart.
You have sunk deep down into it.
Your products and all of your
people
have gone down with you.
³⁵All those who live in the lands
along the coast
are shocked because of what has
happened to you.
Their kings tremble with fear.
Their faces are twisted in horror.
³⁶The traders among the nations
hiss at you.
You have come to a horrible
end.
And you will be gone forever." ' "

A MESSAGE ABOUT THE KING OF TYRE

28

A message came to me from the LORD. He said, ²"Son of man, speak to Ethbaal. He is the ruler of Tyre. Tell him, 'The LORD and King says,

" ' "In your proud heart
  you say, 'I am a god.
I sit on the throne of a god
  in the Mediterranean Sea.'
But you are only a man. You are
  not a god.
In spite of that, you think you are
  as wise as a god.
³Are you wiser than Daniel?
  Isn't even one secret hidden from
    you?
⁴You are wise and understanding.
  So you have become very
    wealthy.
You have piled up gold and silver
  among your treasures.
⁵You have used your great skill in
    trading
  to increase your wealth.
You are very rich.
  So your heart has become
    proud." ' "

⁶The LORD and King says,

"You think you are wise.
  In fact, you claim to be as wise as
    a god.
⁷So I am going to bring strangers
    against you.
  They will not show you any pity
    at all.
They will use their swords against
    your beauty and wisdom.
  They will strike down your
    shining glory.
⁸They will bring you down to the
    grave.
  You will die a horrible death
  in the middle of the sea.
⁹Then will you say, 'I am a god'?
  Will you say that to those who
    kill you?
You will be only a man to those
    who kill you.
  You will not be a god to them.
¹⁰You will die just like those who
    have not been circumcised.
  Strangers will kill you.

I have spoken," announces the LORD
and King.

¹¹A message came to me from the
LORD. He said, ¹²"Son of man, sing a
song of sadness about the king of Tyre.
Tell him, 'The LORD and King says,

" ' "You were the model of
    perfection.
  You were full of wisdom.
  You were perfect and beautiful.
¹³You were in Eden.
  It was my garden.
All kinds of jewels decorated you.
  Here is a list of them.

  ruby, topaz and emerald
  chrysolite, onyx and jasper
  sapphire, turquoise and beryl

Your settings and mountings were
    made out of gold.
  On the day you were created,
  they were prepared.
¹⁴I appointed you to be like a
    guardian cherub.
  I anointed you for that purpose.
You were on my holy mountain.
  You walked among the gleaming
    jewels.
¹⁵Your conduct was without blame
    from the day you were created.
  But soon you began to sin.
¹⁶You traded with many nations.
  You harmed people everywhere.
  And you sinned.
So I sent you away from my
    mountain in shame.
  Guardian cherub, I drove you
    away
  from among the gleaming jewels.
¹⁷You thought you were so
    handsome
  that it made your heart proud.
You thought you were so glorious
  that it spoiled your wisdom.
So I threw you down to the earth.
  I made an example out of you in
    front of kings.
¹⁸Your many sins and dishonest trade
    polluted your temple.
So I made you go up in flames.
  I turned you into nothing but
    ashes on the ground.
  I let everyone see it.
¹⁹All of the nations that knew you
  are shocked because of what
    happened to you.

You have come to a horrible end.
And you will be gone forever." ' "

A MESSAGE ABOUT SIDON

²⁰A message came to me from the LORD. He said, ²¹"Son of man, turn your attention to the city of Sidon. Prophesy against it. ²²Say, 'The LORD and King says,

" ' "Sidon, I am against your
    people.
I will gain glory for myself inside
    your city walls.
I will punish your people.
I will show that I am holy among
    them.
Then they will know that I am
    the LORD.
²³I will send a plague on them.
I will make blood flow in your
    streets.
Those who are killed will fall
    inside you.
Swords will strike your people on
    every side.
Then they will know that I am
    the LORD.

²⁴" ' "The people of Israel will no longer have neighbors who hate them. Those neighbors will not be like sharp and painful thorns anymore. Then Israel will know that I am the LORD and King." ' "

²⁵The LORD and King says, "I will gather the people of Israel together from the nations where they have been scattered. I will show that I am holy among them. I will let the nations see it. Then Israel will live in their own land. I gave it to my servant Jacob. ²⁶My people will live there in safety. They will build houses. They will plant vineyards. They will live in safety. I will punish all of their neighbors who told lies about them. Then Israel will know that I am the LORD their God."

A MESSAGE ABOUT EGYPT

29 It was the tenth year since King Jehoiachin had been brought to Babylon as a prisoner. On the 12th day of the tenth month, a message came to me from the LORD. He said, ²"Son of man, turn

How come the devil wants us to be bad?

Satan is proud. He wants to make us disobey God and be part of his own kingdom instead. He does not want us to serve God. He wants to hurt our faith in God and make us doubt God's love and goodness. If Satan had his way, Christians would just sit around, do nothing good and tell no one about Jesus.

Satan is proud like the king of Tyre described in this part of Ezekiel. Because Satan refused to obey God, he was thrown out of God's kingdom. He wants to keep others out of God's kingdom too.

checkout
Ezekiel 28:17

Related verses:
1 Peter 5:8,9

Satan's Destruction Program

TEMPTATION

SIN

ROAD TO DESTRUCTION

ETERNAL SUFFERING

your attention to Pharaoh Hophra. He is king of Egypt. Prophesy against him and the whole land of Egypt. ³Tell him, 'The LORD and King says,

" ' "Pharaoh Hophra, I am against you.
King of Egypt, you are like a huge monster
lying among your streams.
You say, 'The Nile River belongs to me.
I made it for myself.'
⁴But I will put hooks in your jaws.
I will make the fish in your streams stick to your scales.
I will pull you out from among your streams.
All of the fish will stick to your scales.
⁵I will leave you out in the desert.
All of the fish in your streams will be there with you.
You will fall down in an open field.
You will not be picked up.
I will feed you to the wild animals and to the birds of the air.

⁶Then everyone who lives in Egypt will know that I am the LORD.

" ' "You have been like a walking stick made out of a papyrus stem. The people of Israel tried to lean on you. ⁷They took hold of you. But you broke under their weight. You tore their shoulders open. They leaned on you. But you snapped in two. And their backs were broken." ' "

⁸So the LORD and King says, "I will send Nebuchadnezzar's sword against you. He will kill your people and their animals. ⁹Egypt will become a dry and empty desert. Then your people will know that I am the LORD.

"You said, 'The Nile River belongs to me. I made it for myself.' ¹⁰So I am against you and your streams. I will destroy the land of Egypt. I will turn it into a dry and empty desert from Migdol all the way to Aswan. I will destroy everything as far as the border of Cush. ¹¹"No people or animals will travel through Egypt. No one will even live there for 40 years. ¹²Egypt will be more empty than any other land. Its destroyed cities will lie empty for 40 years. I will scatter the people of Egypt

among the nations. I will send them to other countries."

¹³But the LORD and King says, "At the end of 40 years I will gather the Egyptians together from the nations where they were scattered. ¹⁴I will bring them back from where they were taken as prisoners. I will return them to Upper Egypt. That is where they came from. There they will be an unimportant kingdom.

¹⁵"Egypt will be the least important kingdom of all. It will never place itself above the other nations again. I will make it very weak. Then it will never again rule over the nations. ¹⁶The people of Israel will no longer trust in Egypt. Instead, Egypt will remind them of how they sinned when they turned to it for help. Then they will know that I am the LORD and King."

¹⁷It was the 27th year since King Jehoiachin had been brought to Babylon as a prisoner. On the first day of the first month, a message came to me from the LORD. He said, ¹⁸"Son of man, Nebuchadnezzar, the king of Babylonia, drove his army in a hard military campaign against Tyre. Their helmets rubbed their heads bare. The heavy loads they carried made their shoulders raw. But he and his army did not gain anything from the campaign he led against Tyre.

¹⁹"So I am going to give Egypt to Nebuchadnezzar, the king of Babylonia. He will carry off its wealth. He will take away anything else you have. He will give it to his army. ²⁰I have given Egypt to him as a reward for his efforts. After all, he and his army attacked Egypt because I told them to," announces the LORD and King.

²¹"When Nebuchadnezzar wins the battle over Egypt, I will make the people of Israel strong again. Ezekiel, I will open your mouth. And you will be able to speak to them. Then they will know that I am the LORD."

A SONG OF SADNESS ABOUT EGYPT

30 A message came to me from the LORD. He said, ²"Son of man, prophesy. Say, 'The LORD and King says,

" ' "Cry out,
   'A terrible day is coming!'
³The day is near.
   The day of the LORD is coming.
   It will be a cloudy day.
   The nations have been
     sentenced to die.
⁴I will send Nebuchadnezzar's
     sword against Egypt.
   Cush will suffer terribly.
   Many will die in Egypt.
   Then its wealth will be carried
     away.
   Its foundations will be torn
     down.

⁵The people of Cush, Put, Lydia, Libya and the whole land of Arabia will be killed with swords. So will the Jews who live in Egypt. They went there from the covenant land of Israel. And the Egyptians will die too." ' "

⁶The LORD says,

"Those who were going to help
     Egypt will die.
   The strength Egypt was so proud
     of will fail.
   Its people will be killed with swords
     from Migdol all the way to
     Aswan,"
              announces the LORD
                   and King.
⁷ "Egypt will be more empty than
     any other land.
   Its cities will be completely
     destroyed.
⁸I will set Egypt on fire.
   All those who came to help it will
     be crushed.
   Then they will know that I am
     the LORD.

⁹"At that time I will send messengers out in ships. They will terrify the people of Cush who are so contented. Cush will suffer greatly when Egypt falls. And you can be sure it will fall."

¹⁰The LORD and King says,

"I will put an end to the huge
     armies of Egypt.
   I will use Nebuchadnezzar, the
     king of Babylonia, to do it.
¹¹He and his armies will attack the
     land and destroy it.
   They will not show its people any
     pity at all.

   They will use their swords against
     Egypt.
   They will fill the land with dead
     bodies.
¹²I will dry up the streams of the
     Nile River.
   I will sell the land to evil men.
   I will use the powerful hands of
     strangers
   to destroy the land and
     everything in it.

"I have spoken. I am the LORD."

¹³The LORD and King says,

"I will destroy the statues of
     Egypt's gods.
   I will put an end to the gods
   the people in Memphis worship.
   Egypt will not have princes
     anymore.
   I will spread fear all through the
     land.
¹⁴I will completely destroy Upper
     Egypt.
   I will set Zoan on fire.
   I will punish Thebes.
¹⁵I will pour out my burning anger
     on Pelusium.
   It is a fort in eastern Egypt.
   I will cut off the huge army of
     Thebes.
¹⁶I will set Egypt on fire.
   Pelusium will groan with terrible
     pain.
   Thebes will be ripped apart.
   Memphis will suffer greatly
     because of everything that
     happens.
¹⁷The young men of Heliopolis and
     Bubastis
   will be killed with swords.
   Their people will be taken away
     as prisoners.
¹⁸I will break Egypt's power over
     other lands.
   That will be a dark day for
     Tahpanhes.
   There the strength Egypt was so
     proud of
   will come to an end.
   Egypt will be covered with clouds.
   The people in its villages
     will be taken away as prisoners.
¹⁹So I will punish Egypt.
   Then they will know that I am
     the LORD."

²⁰It was the 11th year since King Jehoiachin had been brought to Babylon as a prisoner. On the seventh day of the first month, a message came to me from the LORD. He said, ²¹"Son of man, I have broken the powerful arm of Pharaoh Hophra, the king of Egypt. No bandages have been put on his arm to heal it. It has not been put in a cast. So his arm will not be strong enough to use a sword. ²²I am against Pharaoh, the king of Egypt. I will break both of his arms. I will break his healthy arm and his broken one. His sword will fall from his hand. ²³I will scatter the people of Egypt among the nations. I will send them to other countries.

²⁴"I will make the arms of the king of Babylonia stronger. I will put my sword in his hand. But I will break the arms of Pharaoh. And he will groan in front of Nebuchadnezzar. He will cry out like someone dying from his wounds. ²⁵I will make the arms of the king of Babylonia stronger. But the arms of Pharaoh will not be able to help Egypt. I will put my sword in Nebuchadnezzar's hand. He will get ready to use it against Egypt. Then they will know that I am the LORD.

²⁶"I will scatter the Egyptians among the nations. I will send them to other countries. Then they will know that I am the LORD."

A CEDAR TREE IN LEBANON

31 It was the 11th year since King Jehoiachin had been brought to Babylon as a prisoner. On the first day of the third month, a message came to me from the LORD. He said, ²"Son of man, speak to Pharaoh Hophra, the king of Egypt. Also speak to his huge army. Tell him,

" 'Who can be compared with your majesty?
³ Think about what happened to Assyria.
  Once it was like a cedar tree in Lebanon.
It had beautiful branches
  that provided shade for the forest.
It grew very high.
  Its top was above all of the leaves.

⁴ The waters fed it.
  Deep springs made it grow tall.
Their streams flowed
  all around its base.
They made their way
  to all of the trees in the fields.
⁵ So it grew higher
  than any other tree in the fields.
It grew more limbs.
  Its branches grew long.
They spread because they had
  plenty of water.
⁶ All of the birds of the air
  made their nests in its limbs.
All of the wild animals
  had their babies under its branches.
All of the great nations
  lived in its shade.
⁷ Its spreading branches
  made it majestic and beautiful.
Its roots went down deep
  to where there was plenty of water.
⁸ The cedar trees in my garden
  were no match for it.
The pine trees
  could not equal its limbs.
The plane trees
  could not compare with its branches.
No tree in my garden
  could match its beauty.
⁹ I gave it many branches.
  They made it beautiful.
All of the trees in my Garden of Eden
  were jealous of it.' "

¹⁰So the LORD and King says, "The cedar tree grew very high. Its top was above all of the leaves. It was proud of how tall it was. ¹¹So I handed it over to the Babylonian ruler of the nations. I wanted him to punish it because it was so evil. I decided to get rid of it.

¹²"The Babylonians cut it down and left it there. They did not show it any pity at all. Some of its branches fell on the mountains. Others fell in all of the valleys. They lay broken in all of the stream beds in the land. All of the nations on earth came out from under its shade. And they went on their way. ¹³All of the birds of the air settled on the fallen tree. All of the wild animals moved among its branches.

¹⁴"So trees that receive plenty of water must never grow so high that it makes them proud. Their tops must never be above the rest of the leaves. No other trees that receive a lot of water must ever grow that high. They are appointed to die and go down into the earth below. They will join the other nations that go down into the grave."

¹⁵The LORD and King says, "Assyria was like a cedar tree. But I brought it down to the grave. On that day I dried up the deep springs of water and covered them. I held its streams back. I shut off its rich supply of water. Because of that, Lebanon was dressed in darkness as if it were clothes. All of the trees in the fields dried up.

¹⁶"I brought the cedar tree down to the grave. It joined the other nations that go down there. I made the nations on earth shake because of the sound of its fall. Then all of the trees of Eden were comforted in the earth below. That included the finest and best trees in Lebanon. And it included all the trees that received plenty of water. ¹⁷Others also went down into the grave along with it. That included those that lived in its shade. And it included those nations that were going to help it. They joined those who had been killed with swords.

¹⁸"Which one of the trees of Eden can be compared with you? What tree is as glorious and majestic as you are? But you too will be brought down to the earth below. There you will join the trees of Eden. You will lie down with those who have not been circumcised. You will be among those who were killed with swords.

"That is what will happen to Pharaoh and his huge armies," announces the LORD and King.

A SONG OF SADNESS ABOUT PHARAOH

32 It was the 12th year since King Jehoiachin had been brought to Babylon as a prisoner. On the first day of the 12th month, a message came to me from the LORD. He said, ²"Son of man, sing a song of sadness about Pharaoh Hophra, the king of Egypt. Tell him,

" 'You are like a lion among the nations.
You are like a monster in the sea.
You move around wildly in your rivers.
You churn the water with your feet.
You make the streams muddy.' "

³The LORD and King says,

"I will use a large crowd of people to throw my net over you.
They will pull you up in it.
⁴Then I will throw you on the land.
I will toss you into an open field.
I will let all of the birds of the air settle on you.
I will let all of the wild animals eat you up.
⁵I will scatter the parts of your body all over the mountains.
I will fill the valleys with your remains.
⁶I will soak the land with your blood.
It will flow all the way to the mountains.
The valleys will be filled with the parts of your body.
⁷When I wipe you out,
I will put a cover over the heavens.
I will darken the stars.
I will cover the sun with a cloud.
The moon will stop shining.
⁸I will darken all of the bright lights in the sky above you.
I will bring darkness over your land,"

announces the LORD
and King.

⁹"The hearts of many people will be troubled.
That is because I will destroy you among the nations.
You had never known anything about those lands before.
¹⁰Many nations will be shocked when they see what has happened to you.
Their kings will tremble with fear when they find out about it.
I will get ready to use Nebuchadnezzar
as my sword against them.
On the day you fall from power, each of the kings will tremble with fear.

Each will be afraid he is the next to die."

[11]The LORD and King says,

"I will send against you
      the sword of the king of
         Babylonia.
[12]I will destroy your huge army.
   They will be killed with the
      swords
   of Babylonia's mighty soldiers.
   The soldiers will not show them
      any pity.
   They will bring Egypt down in all
      of its pride.
   Its huge armies will be thrown
      down.
[13]I will destroy all of its cattle
   from the places where they have
      plenty of water.
   Human feet will never stir the
      water up again.
   The hoofs of cattle will not make
      it muddy anymore.
[14]I will let the waters of Egypt settle.
   I will make its streams flow like
      olive oil,"
            announces the LORD
                  and King.
[15]"I will turn Egypt into an empty
      land.
   I will strip away everything in it.
   I will strike down everyone who
      lives there.
   Then they will know that I am
      the LORD.

[16]"That is the song of sadness people will sing about Egypt. Women from other nations will sing it. They will sob over Egypt and its huge armies," announces the LORD and King.

[17]It was the 15th day of a month near the end of the 12th year since King Jehoiachin had been brought to Babylon as a prisoner. A message came to me from the LORD. He said, [18]"Son of man, sob over the huge army of Egypt. Tell the Egyptians they will go down into the earth below. The women singers from the other mighty nations will go down into the grave along with them and others.
[19]"Tell them, 'Are you any better than others? Since you are not, go down there. Lie down with those who have not been circumcised.'

[20]"They will fall dead among those who were killed with swords. Nebuchadnezzar is ready to use his sword against them. Let Egypt be dragged off together with its huge armies.
[21]"The mighty leaders who are already in the grave will talk about Egypt. They will also speak about the nations that were going to help it. They will say, 'They have come down here. They are lying down with those who had not been circumcised. They are here with those who were killed with swords.'

[22]"Assyria is there with its whole army. Its king is surrounded by the graves of all of its people who were killed with swords. [23]Their graves are deep down in the pit. Assyria's army lies around the grave of its king. All those who spread terror while they were alive are now dead. They were killed with swords.

[24]"Elam is also there. Its huge armies lie around the grave of its king. All those who spread terror while they were alive are now dead. They were killed with swords. They had not been circumcised. They went down into the earth below. Their shame is like the shame of others who go down into the grave.

[25]"A bed is made for Elam's king among the dead. His huge armies lie around his grave. They had not been circumcised. They were killed with swords. They had spread terror while they were alive. So now their shame is like the shame of others who go down into the grave. They lie down among the dead.

[26]"Meshech and Tubal are also there. Their huge armies lie around the graves of their kings. They had not been circumcised. They had spread their terror while they were alive. So they were killed with swords.

[27]"They lie down with the other dead soldiers who had not been circumcised. They and their weapons had gone down into the grave. Their swords had been placed under their heads. They had spread their terror while they were alive. But now the shame of their sin covers their bones.

[28]"Pharaoh Hophra, you too will be broken. You will lie down among those

who had not been circumcised. You will be there with those who were killed with swords.

²⁹"Edom is also there. So are its kings and all of its princes. In spite of their power, they lie down with those who were killed with swords. They lie down with those who had not been circumcised. They are there with others who went down into the grave.

³⁰"All of the princes of the north are there too. So are all of the people of Sidon. They went down into the grave in dishonor. While they were alive, they used their power to spread terror. They had never been circumcised. But now they lie down there with those who were killed with swords. Their shame is like the shame of others who go down into the grave.

³¹"Pharaoh and his whole army will see all of them. That will comfort him in spite of the fact that his huge armies were killed with swords," announces the LORD and King. ³²"I let Pharaoh spread terror while he was alive. But now he and his huge armies will be buried with those who had not been circumcised. They will lie down there with those who were killed with swords," announces the LORD and King.

THE LORD WARNS ISRAEL

33 A message came to me from the LORD. He said, ²"Son of man, speak to the people of your own country. Tell them, 'Suppose I send enemies against a land. And its people choose one of their men to stand guard. ³He sees the enemies coming against the land. He blows a trumpet to warn the people.

⁴" 'Someone hears the trumpet. But he does not pay any attention to the warning. The enemies come and kill him. Then what happens to him will be his own fault. ⁵He heard the sound of the trumpet. But he did not pay any attention to the warning. So what happened to him was his own fault. If he had paid attention, he would have saved himself.

⁶" 'But suppose the guard sees the enemies coming. And he does not blow the trumpet to warn the people. The enemies come and kill one of them. Then his life has been taken away from him because he sinned. But I will hold the guard accountable for his death.'

⁷"Son of man, I have appointed you as a prophet to warn the people of Israel. So listen to my message. Give them a warning from me.

⁸"Suppose I say to a sinful person, 'You can be sure that you will die.' And suppose you do not try to get him to change his ways. Then he will die because he has sinned. And I will hold you accountable for his death.

⁹"But suppose you do warn that sinful person. You tell him to change his ways. But he does not do it. Then he will die because he has sinned. But you will have saved yourself.

¹⁰"Son of man, speak to the people of Israel. Tell them, 'You are saying, "Our sins and the wrong things we have done weigh us down. We are wasting away because we have sinned so much. So how can we live?" '

¹¹"Tell them, 'When sinful people die, it does not give me any joy. But when they turn away from their sins and live, that makes me very happy. And that is just as sure as I am alive,' announces the LORD and King. 'So turn away from your sins! Change your evil ways! Why should you die, people of Israel?'

¹²"Son of man, speak to the people of your own country. Tell them, 'The right things a godly person does will not save him when he does not obey the LORD. The wrong things a sinful person does will not destroy him when he turns away from them. If a godly person sins, he will not be allowed to live just because he used to do what is right.'

¹³"Suppose I tell someone who is godly that he will live. And he trusts in the fact that he used to do what was right. But now he does what is evil. Then I will not remember any of the right things he has done. He will die because he has done so many evil things.

¹⁴"Suppose I say to a sinful person, 'You can be sure you will die.' And then he turns away from his sin. He does what is fair and right. ¹⁵He gives back what he took as security for a loan. He

returns what he has stolen. He follows my rules that give life. He does not do what is evil. Then you can be sure he will live. He will not die. ¹⁶None of the sins he has committed will be held against him. He has done what is fair and right. So you can be sure he will live.

¹⁷"In spite of that, your people say, 'What the Lord does isn't fair.' But it is what you do that is not fair.

¹⁸"Suppose someone who is godly stops doing what is right. And he does what is evil. Then he will die because of it. ¹⁹But suppose a sinful person turns away from the evil things he has done. And he does what is fair and right. Then he will live by doing that.

²⁰"In spite of that, you people of Israel say, 'What the Lord does isn't fair.' But I will judge each of you based on how you have lived."

THE LORD EXPLAINS WHY JERUSALEM FELL

²¹It was the 12th year since we had been brought to Babylonia as prisoners. On the fifth day of the tenth month, a man who had escaped from Jerusalem came to bring me a report. He said, "The city has fallen!"

²²The evening before the man arrived, the LORD put his strong hand on me. He opened my mouth before the man came to me in the morning. So my mouth was opened. I was no longer silent.

²³Then a message came to me from the LORD. He said, ²⁴"Son of man, the people who live in those broken-down buildings in Israel are saying, 'Abraham was only one man. But he owned the land. We are many people. The land must certainly belong to us.'

²⁵"So tell them, 'The LORD and King says, "You eat meat that still has blood in it. You worship your gods. You commit murder. So should you still possess the land? ²⁶You depend on your swords. You do things I hate. Each one of you has sex with your neighbor's wife. So should you still possess the land?" '

²⁷"Tell them, 'The LORD and King says, "The people who are left in those broken-down buildings will be killed with swords. Wild animals will eat up those who are out in the country. Those who are in caves and other safe places will die of a plague. And that is just as sure as I am alive.

²⁸" ' "I will turn the land into a dry

KIDS' QUESTION

Why doesn't God just zap the bad people?

God loves people so much that he is giving them time to turn away from being bad and turn to him. God is very patient. He loves even the worst people in the world. But some day he will stop waiting, and everyone who refuses to live God's way will be punished. That will be a very sad day, but it will come.

checkout Ezekiel 33:11

Related verse: 2 Peter 3:9

and empty desert. The strength Jerusalem is so proud of will come to an end. The mountains of Israel will be deserted. No one will travel across them. ²⁹So I will turn the land into a dry and empty desert. I will punish my people because of all of the evil things they have done. I hate those things. They will know that I am the LORD." '

³⁰"Son of man, your people are talking about you. They are getting together by the walls of their houses and at their doors. They are saying to one another, 'Come. Listen to the LORD's message.'

³¹"My people come to you, just as they usually do. They sit in front of you. They listen to what you say. But they do not put it into practice. With their mouths they claim to be faithful to me. But in their hearts they want what belongs to others. They try to get rich by cheating them. ³²You are nothing more to them than someone who sings love songs. They say you have a beautiful voice. They think you play an instrument well. They listen to what you say. But they do not put it into practice.

³³"Everything I have told you will come true. You can be sure of it. Then the people will know that a prophet has been among them."

THE LORD IS THE SHEPHERD OF HIS PEOPLE

34

A message came to me from the LORD. He said, ²"Son of man, prophesy against the shepherds of Israel. Tell them, 'The LORD and King says, "How terrible it will be for you shepherds of Israel! You only take care of yourselves. You should take good care of your flocks. ³Instead, you eat the butter. You dress yourselves with the wool. You kill the finest animals. But you do not take care of your flocks. ⁴You have not made the weak ones in the flock stronger. You have not healed the sick. You have not bandaged those that are hurt. You have not brought back those that have wandered away. You have not searched for the lost. When you ruled over them, you were mean to them. You treated them badly.

⁵" ' "So they were scattered because they did not have a shepherd. They became food for all of the wild animals. ⁶My sheep wandered all over the mountains and high hills. They were scattered over the whole earth. No one searched for them. No one looked for them."

⁷" 'Shepherds, listen to the LORD's message. ⁸He says, "My flock does not have a shepherd. Many of my sheep have been stolen. They have become food for all of the wild animals. My shepherds did not care for my sheep. They did not even search for them. Instead, they only took care of themselves. And that is just as sure as I am alive," announces the LORD and King.

⁹" 'Shepherds, listen to the LORD's message. ¹⁰The LORD and King says, "I am against the shepherds. I will hold them accountable for my flock. I will stop them from taking care of the flock. Then they will not be able to feed themselves anymore. I will save my flock from their mouths. My sheep will no longer be food for them." ' "

¹¹The LORD and King says, "I myself will search for my sheep. I will look after them. ¹²A shepherd looks after his scattered flock when he is with them. And I will look after my sheep. I will save them from all of the places where they were scattered on a dark and cloudy day.

¹³"I will bring them out from among the nations. I will gather them together from other countries. I will bring them into their own land. They will eat grass on the mountains of Israel. I will also let them eat in the valleys and in all of the places in the land where people live. ¹⁴I will take care of them in the best grasslands. They will eat grass on the high mountains of Israel. There they will lie down in the finest grasslands. They will eat grass in the best places on Israel's mountains.

¹⁵"I myself will take care of my sheep. I will let them lie down in safety," announces the LORD and King. ¹⁶"I will search for the lost. I will bring back those that have wandered away. I will bandage the ones that are hurt. I will make the weak ones stronger. But I will destroy those that are fat and strong. I will take good care of my sheep. I will treat them fairly."

17The LORD and King says, "You are my flock. I will judge between one sheep and another. I will judge between rams and goats. 18You already eat in the best grasslands. Must you also stomp all over the other fields? You already drink clear water. Must you also make the rest of the water muddy with your feet? 19Must my flock have to eat the grass you have stomped on? Must they drink the water you have made muddy?"

20So the LORD and King speaks to them. He says, "I myself will judge between the fat sheep and the skinny sheep. 21You push the other sheep around with your hips and shoulders. You use your horns to butt all of the weak sheep. Finally, you drive them away. 22But I will save my sheep. They will not be carried off anymore. I will judge between one sheep and another.

23"I will place one shepherd over them. He will belong to the family line of my servant David. He will take good care of them. He will look after them. He will be their shepherd. 24I am the LORD. I will be their God. And my servant from David's line will be prince among them. I have spoken. I am the LORD.

25"I will make a covenant with them. It promises to give them peace. I will get rid of the wild animals in the land. Then my sheep can live safely in the desert. They can sleep in the forests. 26"I will bless them. I will also bless the places surrounding my holy mountain of Zion. I will send down rain at the right time. There will be showers of blessing. 27The trees in the fields will bear their fruit. And the ground will produce its crops. The people will be secure in their land. I will break the chains that hold them. I will save them from the powerful hands of those who made them slaves. Then they will know that I am the LORD. 28"The nations will not carry them off anymore. Wild animals will no longer eat them up. They will live in safety. And no one will make them afraid. 29I will give them a land that is famous for its crops. They will never be hungry there again. The nations will not make fun of them anymore.

30"Then they will know that I am with them. I am the LORD their God. And they will know that they are my people Israel," announces the LORD and King. 31"You are the sheep belonging to my flock. You are my people. And I am your God," announces the LORD and King.

A MESSAGE ABOUT EDOM

35

A message came to me from the LORD. He said, 2"Son of man, turn your attention to Mount Seir. Prophesy against it. 3Tell it, 'The LORD and King says, "Mount Seir, I am against you. I will reach out my powerful hand against you. I will turn you into a dry and empty desert. 4I will destroy your towns. Your land will become empty. Then you will know that I am the LORD.

5" "People of Edom, you have been Israel's enemies for a long time. You let many Israelites be killed with swords when they were in great trouble. At that time I used Nebuchadnezzar to punish them and destroy them completely. 6Now I will hand you over to murderers. They will hunt you down. You murdered others. So murderers will chase you. And that is just as sure as I am alive," announces the LORD and King.

7" "I will turn Mount Seir into a dry and empty desert. No one will be able to go anywhere or do anything there. 8I will fill your mountains with dead bodies. Some of those who are killed with swords will fall down dead on your hills. Others will die in your valleys and in all of your canyons. 9I will make your land empty forever. No one will live in your towns. Then you will know that I am the LORD.

10" "You said, 'The nations of Israel and Judah will belong to us. We will take them over.' You said that, even though I was there. I am the LORD. 11You were full of anger, jealousy and hatred toward my people. So I will punish you. When I judge you, they will know that I am the LORD. And that is just as sure as I am alive," announces the LORD and King.

12" "You will know that I have heard all of the terrible things you said about those who live in the mountains of Israel. You made fun of them. You said, 'They have been destroyed. They've been handed over to us. Let's wipe them out.' [13]You bragged that you were better than I am. You spoke against me. You did not hold anything back. But I heard it.' ' "

[14]The LORD and King says, "The whole earth will be glad. But I will make your land empty. [15]You were happy when the land of Israel became empty. So I will treat you in the same way. Mount Seir, you will be empty. So will the whole land of Edom. Then you will know that I am the LORD."

A MESSAGE ABOUT ISRAEL

36 "Son of man, prophesy to the mountains of Israel. Tell them, 'Mountains of Israel, listen to the LORD's message. [2]The LORD and King says, "Your enemies made fun of you. They bragged, 'The hills you lived in for a long time belong to us now.' " '

[3]"Ezekiel, prophesy. Say, 'The LORD and King says, "Your enemies destroyed you. They hunted you down from every side. So the rest of the nations took over your land. People talked about you. They told lies about you." ' "

[4]Mountains of Israel, listen to the message of the LORD and King. He speaks to you mountains, hills, canyons and valleys. He speaks to you destroyed cities and deserted towns. The rest of the nations around you took everything of value away from you. They made fun of you. [5]So the LORD and King says, "My anger burns against those nations. I have spoken against them and the whole land of Edom. They were very happy when they took over my land. Deep down inside them they hated Israel. They wanted to take its grasslands.

[6]"Ezekiel, prophesy about the land of Israel. Speak to the mountains, hills, canyons and valleys. Tell them, 'The LORD and King says, "My jealous anger burns against the nations. They have laughed at you." [7]So the LORD and King says, "I raise my hand and take an oath. I promise that the nations around you will also be laughed at.

[8]" ' "Mountains of Israel, you will produce branches and bear fruit for my people Israel. They will come home soon. [9]I am concerned about you. I will look on you with favor. Farmers will plow your ground. They will plant seeds in it.

[10]" ' "I will multiply the number of people who live in Israel. The towns will no longer be empty. Their broken-down houses will be rebuilt. [11]I will increase the number of your people and animals. They will have many babies. I will settle people in your towns, just as I did in the past. I will help you succeed more than ever before. Then you will know that I am the LORD.

[12]" ' "I will let my people Israel walk there again. They will possess you. They will receive you as their own. You will never take their children away from them again." ' "

[13]The LORD and King says, "People say to you mountains, 'You destroy people. You let your nation's children be taken away.' [14]But I will not let you destroy people anymore. I will no longer let your nation's children be taken away," announces the LORD and King.

[15]"You will not have to listen to the nations laughing at you anymore. People will no longer make fun of you. You will not let your nation fall," announces the LORD and King.

[16]Another message came to me from the LORD. He said, [17]"Son of man, the people of Israel used to live in their own land. But they polluted it because of how they acted and the way they lived. To me they were 'unclean' like a woman who was having her monthly period.

[18]"They spilled people's blood in the land. They polluted the land by worshiping other gods. So I poured out my burning anger on them. [19]I scattered them among the nations. I sent them to other countries. I judged them based on how they acted and the way they lived.

[20]"They treated my name as if it were not holy. They did it everywhere they went among the nations. People said about them, 'They are the LORD's people. But they were forced to leave his land.' [21]I was concerned about my holy

name. The people of Israel treated it as if it were not holy. They did it everywhere they went among the nations.

²²"But tell the people of Israel, 'The LORD and King speaks. He says, "People of Israel, I will not take action for your benefit. Instead, I will act for the honor of my holy name. You have treated it as if it were not holy. You did it everywhere you went among the nations. ²³But I will show everyone how holy my great name is. You have treated it as if it were not holy. So I will use you to show the nations how holy I am. Then they will know that I am the LORD," announces the LORD and King.

²⁴" ' "I will take you out of the nations. I will gather you together from all of the countries. I will bring you back into your own land.

²⁵" ' "I will sprinkle pure water on you. Then you will be 'clean.' I will make you completely pure and clean. I will take all of the statues of your gods away from you. ²⁶I will give you new hearts. I will give you a new spirit that is faithful to me. I will remove your stubborn hearts from you. I will give you hearts that obey me.

²⁷" ' "I will put my Spirit in you. I will move you to follow my rules. I want you to be careful to keep my laws. ²⁸You will live in the land I gave your people long ago. You will be my people. And I will be your God.

²⁹" ' "I will save you from all of your 'uncleanness.' I will give you plenty of grain. You will have more than enough. So you will never be hungry again. ³⁰I will multiply the fruit on your trees. I will increase the crops in your fields. Then the nations will no longer make fun of you because you are hungry.

³¹" ' "You will remember your evil ways and the sinful things you have done. You will hate yourselves because you have sinned so much. I also hate your evil practices. ³²I want you to know that I am not doing those things for your benefit," announces the LORD and King. "People of Israel, you should be ashamed of yourselves! Your conduct has brought dishonor to you." ' "

³³The LORD and King says, "I will make you pure from all of your sins. On that day I will settle you in your towns again. Your broken-down houses will be rebuilt. ³⁴The dry and empty land will be farmed again.

"Everyone who passes through it will see that it is no longer empty. ³⁵They will say, 'This land was completely destroyed. But now it's like the Garden of Eden. The cities were full of broken-down buildings. They were destroyed and empty. But now they have high walls around them. And people live in them.'

³⁶"Then the nations that remain around you will know that I have rebuilt what was once destroyed. I have planted again the fields that were once empty. I have spoken. And I will do it. I am the LORD."

³⁷The LORD and King says, "Once again I will answer the prayers of the people of Israel. Here is what I will do for them. I will multiply them as if they were sheep. ³⁸Large flocks of animals are sacrificed at Jerusalem during the appointed feasts there. In the same way, the destroyed cities will be filled with flocks of people. Then they will know that I am the LORD."

ISRAEL'S DRY BONES WILL COME TO LIFE AGAIN

37 The LORD put his strong hand on me. His Spirit brought me away from my home. He put me down in the middle of a valley. It was full of bones. ²He led me back and forth among them. I saw a huge number of bones in the valley. The bones were very dry.

³The LORD asked me, "Son of man, can these bones live?"

I said, "LORD and King, you are the only one who knows."

⁴Then he said to me, "Prophesy to these bones. Tell them, 'Dry bones, listen to the LORD's message. ⁵The LORD and King speaks to you. He says, "I will put breath in you. Then you will come to life again. ⁶I will attach tendons to you. I will put flesh on you. I will cover you with skin. So I will put breath in you. And you will come to life again. Then you will know that I am the LORD." ' "

⁷So I prophesied just as the LORD commanded me to. As I was prophesying, I heard a noise. It was a rattling

sound. The bones came together. One bone connected itself to another. [8]I saw tendons and flesh appear on them. Skin covered them. But there was no breath in them.

[9]Then the LORD said to me, "Prophesy to the breath. Prophesy, son of man. Tell it, 'The LORD and King says, "Breath, come from all four directions. Go into these dead bodies. Then they can live." ' "

[10]So I prophesied just as he commanded me to. And the breath entered them. Then they came to life again. They stood up on their feet. They were like a huge army.

[11]Then the LORD said to me, "Son of man, these bones stand for all of the people of Israel. The people say, 'Our bones are dried up. We've lost all hope. We are cut off.'

[12]So prophesy. Tell them, 'The LORD and King says, "My people, I am going to open up your graves. I am going to bring you out of them. I will take you back to the land of Israel. [13]So I will open up your graves and bring you out of them. Then you will know that I am the LORD. You are my people. [14]I will put my Spirit in you. And you will live again. I will settle you in your own land. Then you will know that I have spoken. I have done it," announces the LORD.' "

ISRAEL WILL BE ONE NATION UNDER ONE KING

[15]A message came to me from the LORD. He said, [16]"Son of man, get a stick of wood. Write on it, 'Belonging to the tribe of Judah and the Israelites who are connected with it.' Then get another stick. Write on it, 'Ephraim's stick. Belonging to the tribes of Joseph and all of the Israelites connected with them.' [17]Join them together into one stick in your hand.

[18]"The people of your own country will ask you, 'What do you mean by this?' [19]Tell them, 'The LORD and King says, "I am going to get the stick of Joseph and the Israelites connected with it. That stick is in Ephraim's hand. I am going to join it to Judah's stick. They will become a single stick of wood in my hand." '

[20]"Show them the sticks you wrote on. [21]Tell them, 'The LORD and King says, "I will take the Israelites out of the nations where they have gone. I will gather them together from all around. I will bring them back to their own land. [22]There I will make them one nation. They will live on the mountains of Israel. All of them will have one king. They will never be two nations again. They will never again be separated into two kingdoms.

[23]" ' "They will no longer pollute themselves by worshiping any of their evil gods. They will not do wrong things anymore. They always turn away from me. But I will save them from that sin. I will make them pure and clean. They will be my people. And I will be their God.

[24]" ' "A man who belongs to the family line of my servant David will be their king. All of them will have one shepherd. They will follow my laws. And they will be careful to keep my rules. [25]They will live in the land I gave to my servant Jacob. That is where your people lived long ago. They, their children, their children's children, and their children after them will live there forever. And my servant from David's line will be their prince forever.

[26]" ' "I will make a covenant with them. It promises to give them peace. The covenant will last forever. I will make them my people. And I will increase their numbers. I will put my temple among them forever. [27]I will live with them. I will be their God. And they will be my people. [28]My temple will be among them forever. Then the nations will know that I make Israel holy. I am the LORD." ' "

A MESSAGE ABOUT GOG

38 A message came to me from the LORD. He said, [2]"Son of man, turn your attention to Gog. He is from the land of Magog. He is the chief prince of Meshech and Tubal. Prophesy against him.

[3]"Tell him, 'The LORD and King says, "Gog, I am against you. You are the chief prince of Meshech and Tubal. [4]But I will turn you around. I will put hooks in your jaws. I will bring you out of your land along with your whole

army. Your horses will come with you. Your horsemen will be completely armed. Your huge army will carry large and small shields. All of them will be ready to use their swords.

5" ' "The men of Persia, Cush and Put will march out with them. All of them will have shields and helmets. 6Gomer and all of its troops will be there too. Beth Togarmah from the far north will also come with all of its troops. Many nations will help you.

7" ' "Get ready. Be prepared. Take command of the huge armies that are gathered around you. 8After many years you will be called together to fight. Later, you will march into a land that has not had war for a while. Its people were gathered together from many nations. They came to the mountains of Israel. No one had lived in those mountains for a long time. So the people had been brought back from other nations. Now all of the people live in safety. 9You, all of your troops and the many nations with you will march up to attack them. All of you will advance like a storm. You will be like a cloud covering their land."

10" 'The LORD and King says, "At that time some ideas will come to you. You will make evil plans. 11You will say, 'I will march out against a land whose villages don't have walls around them. I'll attack those peaceful people. I'll do it when they aren't expecting it. None of their villages has walls or gates with heavy metal bars on them.

12" ' " 'I will rob those people. I'll steal everything they have. Then I'll turn my attention to the destroyed houses where people are living again. They have returned there from other nations. Now they are rich. They have plenty of livestock and all kinds of goods. They are living in Israel. It is the center of the earth.'

13" ' "The people of Sheba and Dedan will speak to you. So will the traders of Tarshish and all of its villages. They will say, 'Have you come to rob us? Have you gathered your huge army together to steal our silver and gold? Are you going to take our livestock and goods away from us? Do you plan to carry off everything we have?' " '

14"Son of man, prophesy. Tell Gog,

'The LORD and King says, "A time is coming when my people Israel will be living in safety. You will see that it is a good time to attack them. 15So you will come from your place in the far north. Many nations will join you. All of their men will be riding on horses. You will have a huge and mighty army. 16They will advance against my people Israel. They will be like a cloud covering their land. Gog, in days to come I will bring you against my land. Then the nations will know me. I will use you to show them how holy I am." '

17" 'The LORD and King says to Gog, "In the past I spoke about you through my servants, the prophets of Israel. At that time they prophesied for years that I would bring you against them. 18Here is what will happen in days to come. You will attack the land of Israel. That will stir up my hot anger," announces the LORD and King.

19" ' "At that time my burning anger will blaze out at you. There will be a great earthquake in the land of Israel. 20The fish in the sea, the birds of the air and the wild animals will tremble with fear because of what I will do. So will every creature that moves along the ground. And so will all of the people on earth. The mountains will come crashing down. The cliffs will break into pieces. Every wall will fall to the ground.

21" ' "I will punish you on all of my mountains," announces the LORD and King. "Your men will use their swords against one another. 22I will judge you. I will send a plague against you. A lot of blood will be spilled. I will send heavy rain, hailstones and burning sulfur down to the earth. They will fall on you and your troops. They will also come down on the many nations that are helping you. 23That will show how great and holy I am. I will make myself known to many nations. Then they will know that I am the LORD." '

39 "Son of man, prophesy against Gog. Tell him, 'The LORD and King says, "Gog, I am against you. You are the chief prince of Meshech and Tubal. 2But I will turn you around. I will drag you along. I will bring you from the far north. I will send you against the

mountains of Israel. ³Then I will knock your bow out of your left hand. I will make your arrows drop from your right hand.

⁴" ' "You will fall dead on the mountains of Israel. You and all of your troops will die there. So will the nations that join you. I will feed you to all kinds of birds that eat dead bodies. So they and the wild animals will eat you up. ⁵You will fall dead in the open fields. I have spoken," announces the LORD and King.

⁶" ' "I will send fire on the land of Magog. It will burn up the people who live in safety on the coast. So they will know that I am the LORD.

⁷" ' "I will make my holy name known among my people Israel. I will no longer let them treat my name as if it were not holy. Then the nations will know that I am the Holy One in Israel. I am the LORD. ⁸The day I will judge you is coming. You can be sure of it," announces the LORD and King. "It is the day I have spoken about.

⁹" ' "At that time those who live in the towns of Israel will go out and light a fire. They will use it to burn up the weapons. That includes small and large shields. It also includes bows and arrows, war clubs and spears. It will take seven years to burn all of them up. ¹⁰People will not gather wood from the fields. They will not cut the forests down. Instead, they will burn the weapons. And they will rob those who robbed them. They will steal from those who stole from them," announces the LORD and King.

¹¹" ' "Gog, at that time I will bury you in a grave in Israel. It will be in the valley where people travel east of the Dead Sea. It will block the path of travelers. That is because you and your huge armies will be buried there. So it will be called The Valley of Gog's Armies.

¹²" ' "It will take seven months for the people of Israel to bury the bodies. They will do it to make the land 'clean' again. ¹³All of the people in the land will bury them. That will bring glory to me. It will be a time to remember," announces the LORD and King.

¹⁴" ' "After the seven months are over, men will be hired to finish the job of making the land 'clean' again. Some will go all through it. They will look for any remaining human bones on the ground. Other people will bury the bones. ¹⁵So some will go through the land. When they see a bone, they will put a marker beside it. Then those who dig the graves will take it to The Valley of Gog's Armies. There they will bury it. ¹⁶That is how they will make the land 'clean' again." ' " Also a town called Gog's Armies will be located there.

¹⁷The LORD and King said to me, "Son of man, speak to every kind of bird. Call out to all of the wild animals. Tell them, 'Gather together. Come from everywhere. Gather around the sacrifice I am preparing for you. It is the great sacrifice on the mountains of Israel. There you will eat human bodies and drink human blood.

¹⁸" 'You will eat the bodies of mighty men. You will drink the blood of the princes of the earth. You will eat their bodies and drink their blood as if they were rams and lambs, goats and bulls. You will enjoy it as if you were eating the fattest animals from Bashan.

¹⁹" 'So I am preparing a sacrifice for you. You will eat fat until you are completely full. You will drink blood until you are drunk. ²⁰At my table you will eat horses, riders, mighty men and soldiers until you are full,' announces the LORD and King.

²¹" 'I will show all of the nations my glory. They will see how I punish them when I use my powerful hand against them. ²²From that time on, the people of Israel will know that I am the LORD their God.

²³" 'The nations will know that the people of Israel were taken away as prisoners because they sinned against me. They were not faithful to me. So I turned my face away from them. I handed them over to their enemies. All of them were killed with swords. ²⁴I punished them because they were "unclean." They did many things that were wrong. So I turned my face away from them.' "

²⁵The LORD and King says, "I will now bring the people of Jacob back home again. I will show my tender love for all of the people of Israel. I will make sure that my name is kept holy.

26"My people will forget the shameful things they have done. They will not remember all of the ways they were unfaithful to me. They used to live in safety in their land. At that time no one made them afraid.

27"So I will bring them back from the nations. I will gather them from the countries of their enemies. And I will use them to show many nations how holy I am. 28Then they will know that I am the LORD their God. I let the nations take my people away as prisoners. But now I will bring them back to their own land. I will not leave anyone behind. 29I will no longer turn my face away from the people of Israel. I will pour out my Spirit on them," announces the LORD and King.

THE NEW TEMPLE AREA

40 It was the 14th year after Jerusalem had been captured. It was the tenth day of a month near the beginning of the 25th year since we had been brought to Babylonia as prisoners. On that very day the LORD put his strong hand on me. He took me back to my land. 2In visions God gave me, he brought me to the land of Israel. He set me on a very high mountain. Some buildings were on the south side of it. They looked like a city.

3He took me there. I saw a man who appeared to be made out of bronze. He was standing at the gate of the outer courtyard. He was holding a linen measuring tape and a measuring rod. 4The man said to me, "Son of man, look with your eyes. Listen with your ears. Pay attention to everything I show you. That is why the LORD brought you here. Tell the people of Israel everything you see."

THE EAST GATE TO THE OUTER COURTYARD

5I saw a wall that completely surrounded the temple area. The measuring rod in the man's hand was ten and a half feet long. He measured the wall with it. The wall was as thick and as high as one measuring rod. 6Then the man went to the gate that faced east. He climbed its steps. He measured the gateway. It was one rod

wide. 7The rooms where the guards stood were one rod long and one rod wide. The walls between the rooms were almost nine feet thick. The gateway next to the porch was one rod wide. The porch faced the front of the temple.

8Then the man measured the porch of the gateway. 9It was 14 feet wide. Each of its doorposts was three and a half feet thick. The porch of the gateway faced the front of the temple.

10Inside the east gate were three rooms on each side. All of the rooms were the same size. The walls on each side of the rooms had the same thickness.

11Then the man measured the entrance of the gateway. It was 17 and a half feet wide and almost 23 feet long. 12In front of each room was a wall. It was 21 inches high. The rooms measured ten and a half feet on each side. 13Then he measured the gateway from the back wall of one room to the back wall of the room across from it. It was almost 44 feet from the top of one wall to the top of the other.

14He measured along the front of the side walls that were all around the inside of the gateway. The total was 105 feet. That didn't include the porch that faced the courtyard. 15It was 87 and a half feet from the entrance of the gateway to the far end of its porch. 16The rooms and their side walls inside the gateway had narrow openings on top of them. So did the porch. All of the openings faced the inside. The front of each side wall was decorated with a palm tree.

THE OUTER COURTYARD

17Then the man brought me into the outer courtyard. There I saw some rooms and a sidewalk. They had been built all around the courtyard. Along the sidewalk were 30 rooms. 18The sidewalk went all the way up to the sides of the gateways. It was as wide as they were long. That was the lower sidewalk.

19Then he measured from the inside of the lower gateway to the outside of the inner courtyard. The east side measured 175 feet. So did the north side.

THE NORTH GATE

²⁰Then the man measured the gate that faced north. He wanted to show me how long and wide it was. The gate led into the outer courtyard. ²¹It had three rooms on each side. Their side walls and porch measured the same as the ones at the first gateway. They measured 87 and a half feet long and almost 44 feet wide. ²²Its openings, porch and palm tree decorations measured the same as the ones at the east gate. Seven steps led up to the north gate. Its porch was across from them.

²³The inner courtyard had a gate. It faced the gate on the north. It was just like the east gate. He measured from one gate to the one across from it. The total was 175 feet.

THE SOUTH GATE

²⁴Then the man led me to the south side of the courtyard. There I saw a gate that faced south. He measured its doorposts and porch. They measured the same as the others. ²⁵The gateway and its porch had narrow openings all around. The openings were the same as the others had. The side walls and porch measured 87 and a half feet long and almost 44 feet wide. ²⁶Seven steps led up to it. Its porch was across from them. The front of each side wall was decorated with a palm tree.

²⁷The inner courtyard also had a gate that faced south. The man measured from that gate to the outer gate on the south side. The total was 175 feet.

THE GATES TO THE INNER COURTYARD

²⁸Then the man brought me into the inner courtyard. We went through the south gate. He measured it. It was the same size as the others. ²⁹Its rooms, side walls and porch measured the same as the ones at the other gateways. The gateway and its porch had openings all around. The side walls and porch measured 87 and a half feet long and almost 44 feet wide. ³⁰The porches of the gateways around the inner courtyard were almost 44 feet wide and 9 feet long. ³¹Its porch faced the outer courtyard. Palm trees decorated its doorposts. Eight steps led up to it.

³²Then the man brought me to the east side of the inner courtyard. There he measured the gateway. It was the same size as the others. ³³Its rooms, side walls and porch measured the same as the ones at the other gateways. The gateway and its porch had openings all around. The side walls and porch measured 87 and a half feet long and almost 44 feet wide. ³⁴Its porch faced the outer courtyard. Each doorpost was decorated with a palm tree. Eight steps led up to the porch.

³⁵Then the man brought me to the north gate. He measured it. It was the same size as the others. ³⁶Its rooms, side walls and porch measured the same as the ones at the other gateways. It had openings all around. The side walls and the porch measured 87 and a half feet long and almost 44 feet wide. ³⁷The porch faced the outer courtyard. Each doorpost was decorated with a palm tree. Eight steps led up to the porch.

THE ROOMS FOR PREPARING SACRIFICES

³⁸A room with a doorway was by the porch of each inner gateway. The burnt offerings were washed there. ³⁹On each side of the porch of the gateway were two tables. The burnt offerings were killed on them. So were the sin offerings and guilt offerings.

⁴⁰Two more tables were by the outer wall of the gateway porch. They were near the steps at the entrance of the north gateway. Two more tables were on the other side of the steps. ⁴¹So there were four tables on each side of the gateway. The total number of tables was eight. Animals for sacrifice were killed on all of them.

⁴²There were also four other tables for the burnt offerings. They were made out of blocks of stone. Each table was two and a half feet long and two and a half feet wide. And each was almost two feet high. The tools for killing the burnt offerings and other sacrifices were placed on them. ⁴³Large hooks hung on the walls all around. Each was three inches long. The meat of the offerings was placed on the tables.

THE ROOMS FOR THE PRIESTS

⁴⁴Near the inner gates were two rooms. They were in the inner courtyard. One room was next to the north gate. It faced south. The other one was next to the south gate. It faced north. ⁴⁵The man said to me, "The room that faces south is for the priests who are in charge of the temple. ⁴⁶The one that faces north is for the priests who are in charge of the altar. All of those priests are the sons of Zadok. They are the only Levites who can approach the LORD to serve him."

⁴⁷Then the man measured the courtyard. It was square. It measured 175 feet long and 175 feet wide. And the altar was in front of the temple.

THE TEMPLE

⁴⁸The man brought me to the porch of the temple. He measured the doorposts of the porch. Each of them was almost nine feet wide. The entrance was 24 and a half feet wide. Each of the side walls was a little over five feet wide. ⁴⁹The porch was 35 feet wide. It was 21 feet from front to back. It was reached by some stairs. Pillars were on each side of the doorposts.

41 Then the man brought me to the Holy Room in the temple. There he measured the doorposts. Each of them was ten and a half feet wide. ²The entrance was 17 and a half feet wide. Each of its side walls was almost nine feet wide. He also measured the Holy Room. It was 70 feet long and 35 feet wide.

³Then he went into the Most Holy Room. There he measured the doorposts at the entrance. Each one of them was three and a half feet wide. The entrance itself was ten and a half feet wide. Each of its side walls was a little over 12 feet wide.

⁴He also measured the Most Holy Room. It was 35 feet long and 35 feet wide. He said to me, "This is the Most Holy Room." It was beyond the back wall of the Holy Room.

⁵Then the man measured the wall of the temple. It was ten and a half feet thick. Each side room around the temple was seven feet wide. ⁶The side rooms were on three floors. There were 30 rooms on each floor. Ledges had been built all around the wall of the temple. So the floor beams of the side rooms rested on the ledges. The beams didn't go into the temple wall. ⁷The side rooms of the temple were wider as we went up floor by floor. A stairway went from the lowest floor all the way up to the top floor. It passed through the middle floor.

⁸I saw that the temple had a raised base all around it. The base formed the foundation of the side rooms. It was as long as one measuring rod. So it was ten and a half feet long. ⁹The outer wall of each side room was almost nine feet thick. The open area between the side rooms of the temple ¹⁰and the priests' rooms was 35 feet wide all around the temple. ¹¹The side rooms had entrances from the open area. One was on the north side. Another was on the south. The base next to the open area was almost nine feet wide all around.

¹²There was a large building right behind the temple. It was on the west side of the outer courtyard. It was 122 and a half feet wide. Its wall was almost nine feet thick all around. And it was 157 and a half feet long.

¹³Then the man measured the temple. It was 175 feet long. The open area and the large building behind the temple also measured 175 feet. ¹⁴The east side of the inner courtyard was 175 feet wide. That included the front of the temple.

¹⁵Then the man measured the building that was on the west side of the outer courtyard. It was behind the temple. It was 175 feet long. That included the walkways of the building on each side.

The Holy Room, the Most Holy Room and the porch that faced the inner courtyard ¹⁶were covered with wood. So were the gateways, narrow openings and walkways around those three places. The gateways and everything beyond them were covered with wood. The floor, the wall up to the openings, and the openings themselves were also covered.

¹⁷The area above the outside of the entrance to the Most Holy Room was decorated. There were also decorations all around the walls of the Most

Holy Room. [18]Carved cherubim and palm trees were used in the decorations. Each cherub had a palm tree next to it. And each palm tree had a cherub next to it.

Each cherub had two faces. [19]One was a man's face. It looked toward the palm tree on one side. The other was the face of a lion. It looked toward the palm tree on the other side. The decorations were carved all around the whole temple.

[20]Cherubim and palm trees decorated the wall of the Holy Room. They were carved from the floor all the way up to the area above the entrance.

[21]The Holy Room had a doorframe that was shaped like a rectangle. So did the Most Holy Room. [22]A wooden altar stood in the Holy Room. It was a little over five feet high. It was three and a half feet long and three and a half feet wide. Its corners, base and sides were made out of wood. The man said to me, "This is the table that stands in front of the LORD."

[23]The Holy Room had double doors. So did the Most Holy Room. [24]Each door had two parts that could swing back and forth. [25]Cherubim and palm trees were carved on the doors of the Holy Room. The decorations were like the ones on the walls. A wooden roof went out beyond the front of the porch. [26]The side walls of the porch had narrow openings on top of them. Palm trees were carved on each side. A wooden roof went out beyond the entrance to each side room of the temple.

THE ROOMS FOR THE PRIESTS

42 Then the man led me north into the outer courtyard of the temple. He brought me to the rooms that were across from the inner courtyard. They were across from the outer wall of the temple on the north side. [2]The rooms were in a building north of the temple. The building had a door that faced north. It was 175 feet long. It was 87 and a half feet wide.

[3]One row of rooms was next to the inner courtyard. The other row was across from the sidewalk of the outer courtyard. Each room was 35 feet long. Walkways in front of each row faced each other on all three floors. [4]Between the two rows was an inner sidewalk. It was 17 and a half feet wide and 175 feet long. Each of the rooms had a door on the north side.

[5]The rooms on the top floor were narrower than the others. The walkways took up more space from them than they did from the rooms on the other two floors. [6]The courtyards had pillars. But the rooms on the third floor didn't. So their floor space was smaller than the space in the rooms on the other floors.

[7]The building had an outer wall that was even with the outer row of rooms and with the outer courtyard. The wall continued east of the outer row for 87 and a half feet. [8]So there were two rows of rooms. The row next to the outer courtyard was 87 and a half feet long. The one closest to the temple was 175 feet long. [9]The first floor of the building had an entrance on the east side. It led to the outer courtyard.

[10]There were also two rows of rooms in a building next to the south side of the inner courtyard. The building was across from the south wall of the outer courtyard. [11]Between the two rows was an inner sidewalk. The rooms were like the ones in the north building. They were as long and wide as the rooms on the north. The doorways of the rooms on the south were like the ones on the north. [12]People entered the south rooms through the doorway at the east end of the inner sidewalk. The south wall continued east of the outer row of rooms.

[13]The man said to me, "The north and south rooms face the inner courtyard. They are the priests' rooms. That is where the priests who approach the LORD will eat the very holy offerings. They will also store them there. That includes the grain offerings, sin offerings and guilt offerings. This place is holy.

[14]"The priests who enter these holy rooms must leave behind the clothes they served in. Then they can go into the outer courtyard. The clothes they served in are holy. So they must put other clothes on. They have to do that before they go near the places where other people go."

¹⁵The man finished measuring what was inside the temple area. Then he led me out through the east gate. He measured all around the area. ¹⁶He measured the east side with his measuring rod. It was 875 feet long. ¹⁷He measured the north side. It was 875 feet long. ¹⁸He measured the south side. It was 875 feet long. ¹⁹Finally, he turned and measured the west side. It was 875 feet long. ²⁰So he measured the area on all four sides. It had a wall around it. The wall was 875 feet long and 875 feet wide. It separated what was holy from what was not.

THE GLORY OF THE LORD RETURNS TO THE TEMPLE

43 Then the man brought me to the east gate. ²There I saw the glory of the God of Israel. He was coming from the east. His voice was like the roar of rushing waters. His glory made the land shine brightly.

³The vision I saw was like the one I had when he came to destroy the city. It was also like the visions I had seen by the Kebar River. I fell with my face toward the ground. ⁴The glory of the LORD entered the temple through the east gate. ⁵Then the Spirit lifted me up. He brought me into the inner courtyard. The glory of the LORD filled the temple.

⁶The man was standing beside me. I heard someone speaking to me from inside the temple. ⁷He said, "Son of man, this is the place where my throne is. The stool for my feet is also here. I will live here among the people of Israel forever. They will never again treat my name as if it were not holy. They and their kings will not serve other gods anymore. The people will no longer worship the lifeless gods of their kings at their high places.

⁸"The people of Israel placed their own doorway next to my holy doorway. They put their doorposts right beside mine. Nothing but a thin wall separated us. They treated my name as if it were not holy. I hated it when they did that. So I became angry with them and destroyed them. ⁹Now let them stop serving other gods. Let them quit worshiping the lifeless gods of their

kings. If they obey me, I will live among them forever.

¹⁰"Son of man, tell the people of Israel about the temple. Then they will be ashamed of their sins. Let them think carefully about the plan of the temple. ¹¹What if they are ashamed of everything they have done? Then show them all of the plans of the temple. Explain to them how it is laid out. Tell them about its exits and entrances. Show them exactly what it will look like. Give them all of its rules and laws. Write everything down so they can see it. Then they will be faithful to its plan. And they will obey all of its rules.

¹²"Here is the law of the temple. The whole area on top of Mount Zion will be very holy. That is the law of the temple."

THE ALTAR

¹³The man said, "Here is the size of the altar. The standard measurement I am using is 21 inches. The base of the altar is 21 inches high. The base has a ledge that is 21 inches wide. It also has a rim that is nine inches wide around the edge. Here is how high the altar is. ¹⁴The lower part is three and a half feet high. It has a ledge that is 21 inches wide. The middle part is seven feet high. It has a ledge that is 21 inches wide.

¹⁵"The top part is where the sacrifices are burned. It is seven feet high. A horn sticks out from each of its upper four corners. ¹⁶The top part of the altar is square. It is 21 feet long and 21 feet wide. ¹⁷The middle part is also square. It is 24 and a half feet long. It is 24 and a half feet wide. Its rim is ten and a half inches wide. The base of the altar is 21 inches high all the way around. The steps leading up to the top of the altar face east."

¹⁸Then the man said to me, "Son of man, the LORD and King speaks. He says, 'Here are the rules for the altar when it is built. Follow them when you sacrifice burnt offerings and sprinkle blood on it. ¹⁹Give a young bull to the priests as a sin offering. They are Levites from the family of Zadok. They approach me to serve me,' announces the LORD and King. ²⁰'Get some of the

bull's blood. Put it on the four horns. Also put it on the four corners of the middle part of the altar and all around the rim. That will make the altar pure and clean. ²¹Use the bull for the sin offering. Burn it in the proper place outside the temple.

²²" 'On the second day offer a male goat. It must not have any flaws. It is a sin offering to make the altar pure and clean. So do as you did with the bull. ²³When you finish making the altar pure, offer a young bull and a ram from the flock. They must not have any flaws. ²⁴Offer them to me. The priests must sprinkle salt on them. Then they must sacrifice them as a burnt offering to me.

²⁵" 'Provide a male goat each day for seven days. It is a sin offering. Also provide a young bull and a ram from the flock. They must not have any flaws. ²⁶For seven days the priests must make the altar pure and clean. That is how they will set it apart to me. ²⁷" 'From the eighth day on, the priests must bring your burnt offerings and friendship offerings. They must sacrifice them on the altar. Then I will accept you,' announces the LORD and King."

THE PRINCE, THE LEVITES AND THE PRIESTS

44 Then the man brought me back to the outer gate of the temple. It was the one that faced east. It was shut. ²The LORD said to me, "This gate must remain shut. It must not be opened. No one can enter through it. It must remain shut because I have entered through it. I am the God of Israel. ³The prince is the only one who can sit in the gateway. There he can eat in front of me. He must enter through the porch of the gateway. And he must go out the same way."

⁴Then the man brought me through the north gate. He took me to the front of the temple. I looked up and saw the glory of the LORD. It filled his temple. I fell with my face toward the ground.

⁵The LORD said to me, "Son of man, pay attention. Look carefully. Listen closely to everything I tell you about all of the rules concerning my temple.

Pay attention to the entrance to the temple and to all of its exits.

⁶"Speak to the people of Israel. They refuse to obey me. Tell them, 'The LORD and King says, "People of Israel, I have had enough of your evil practices. I hate them. ⁷You brought strangers into my temple. They were not circumcised. Their hearts were stubborn. You polluted my temple. But you offered me food, fat and blood anyway. When you did all of those things, you broke the covenant I made with you. I hated all of the evil things you did.

⁸" ' "You did not do what I told you to. You did not take care of my holy things. Instead, you put other people in charge of my temple." ' " ⁹The LORD and King says, "No stranger whose heart is stubborn can enter my temple. They have not been circumcised. Even if they live among the people of Israel they can't enter it.

¹⁰"Some Levites wandered far away from me when Israel went down the wrong path. They worshiped the statues of their gods. So they will be punished because they have sinned. ¹¹They might serve in my temple. They might be in charge of its gates. They might kill the burnt offerings and sacrifices for the people. And they might stand in front of the people and serve them in other ways.

¹²"But they served the people of Israel while they were worshiping their gods. They made the people fall into sin. So I raised my hand and took an oath. I warned them that I would punish them because of their sin," announces the LORD and King. ¹³"They must not approach me to serve me as priests. They must not come near any of my holy things. They must stay away from my very holy offerings. They did many things they should have been ashamed of. I hated those things.

¹⁴"But I will still put them in charge of the temple duties. They can do all of the work that has to be done there.

¹⁵"But the priests must approach me to serve me. They are Levites from Zadok's family line. They faithfully carried out their duties in my temple. They obeyed me when the people of

Israel turned away from me. Those priests must serve me by offering sacrifices of fat and blood," announces the LORD and King. ¹⁶"They are the only ones who can enter my temple. Only they can come near to serve me and do my work.

¹⁷"They will enter the gates of the inner courtyard. When they do, they must wear linen clothes. They will serve at the gates of the inner courtyard or inside the temple. When they do, they must not wear any clothes that are made out of wool. ¹⁸They must have linen turbans on their heads. They must wear linen underwear around their waists. They must not put anything on that makes them sweat.

¹⁹"They will go into the outer courtyard where the people are. When they do, they must take off the clothes they have been serving in. They must leave them in the sacred rooms. And they must put other clothes on. Then they will not make the people holy if the people happen to touch their clothes.

²⁰"The priests must not shave their heads. They must not let their hair grow long. They must keep it cut short. ²¹No priest can drink wine when he enters the inner courtyard. ²²They must not get married to widows or divorced women. They can only marry Israelite virgins or the widows of priests.

²³"The priests must teach my people the difference between what is holy and what is not. They must show them how to tell the difference between what is 'clean' and what is not.

²⁴"When people do not agree, the priests must serve as judges between them. They must make their decisions based on my laws. They must obey my laws and rules for all of my appointed feasts. And they must keep my Sabbath days holy.

²⁵"A priest must not make himself 'unclean' by going near a dead person. But suppose the dead person was his father or mother. Or suppose it was his son or daughter or brother or unmarried sister. Then the priest can make himself 'unclean.' ²⁶After he is pure and clean again, he must wait seven days. ²⁷Then he can go to the inner courtyard to serve in the temple. But

when he does, he must sacrifice a sin offering for himself," announces the LORD and King.

²⁸"The priests will not receive any part of the land of Israel. I myself will be their only share. ²⁹They will eat the grain offerings, sin offerings and guilt offerings. Everything in Israel that is set apart to me in a special way will belong to them. ³⁰The best of every first share of the people's crops will belong to the priests. So will all of their special gifts. The people must give the priests the first share of their ground meal. Then I will bless my people's families.

³¹"The priests must not eat any bird or animal that is found dead. They must not eat anything that wild animals have torn apart.

DIVIDING UP THE LAND

45 "People of Israel, you will divide up the land you will receive. When you do, give me my share of it. It will be a sacred area. It will be eight and a fourth miles long and six and a half miles wide. The entire area will be holy. ²The temple area in it will be 875 feet long and 875 feet wide. An 87-and-a-half-foot strip around it will be open land.

³"In the sacred area, measure off a large strip of land. It will be eight and a fourth miles long and three and a third miles wide. The temple will be in it. It will be the most holy place of all. ⁴The large strip will be the sacred share of land for the priests. There they will serve in the temple. And they will approach me to serve me there. Their houses will be built on that land. The holy temple will also be located there.

⁵"So the Levites will serve in the temple. They will have an area eight and a fourth miles long and three and a third miles wide. The towns they live in will be located there.

⁶"Give the city an area one and two thirds miles wide and eight and a fourth miles long. It will be right next to the sacred area. It will belong to all of the people of Israel.

⁷"The prince will have land on both sides of the sacred area and the city. Its border will run east and west along the land of one of the tribes. ⁸The prince

will own that land in Israel. And my princes will not crush my people anymore. Instead, they will allow the people of Israel to receive their own share of land. It will be divided up based on their tribes."

⁹The LORD and King says, "Princes of Israel, you have gone far enough! Stop hurting others. Do not crush them. Do what is fair and right. Stop taking my people's land away from them," announces the LORD and King.

¹⁰"Use weights and measures that are honest and exact. ¹¹Use the same standard to measure dry and liquid products. Use a 6-bushel measure for dry products. And use a 60-gallon measure for liquids. ¹²Every amount of money must be weighed out in keeping with the standard weights.

OFFERINGS AND HOLY DAYS

¹³"You must offer a special gift. It must be 13 and a third cups out of every six bushels of grain. ¹⁴Give two and a half quarts out of every 60 gallons of olive oil. ¹⁵Also give one sheep from every flock of 200 sheep. Get them from the grasslands of Israel that receive plenty of water. Use them for grain offerings, burnt offerings and friendship offerings. They will be used to pay for the sin of the people," announces the LORD and King.

¹⁶"All of the people in the land will take part in that special gift. The prince in Israel will use it. ¹⁷He must provide the burnt offerings, grain offerings and drink offerings. They will be for the yearly feasts, New Moon Feasts and Sabbath days. So they will be for all of the appointed feasts of the people of Israel. The prince will provide the sin offerings, grain offerings, burnt offerings and friendship offerings. They will be used to pay for the sin of the people."

¹⁸The LORD and King says, "Get a young bull. It must not have any flaws. Use it to make the temple pure and clean. Do it on the first day of the first month. ¹⁹The priest must get some of the blood from the sin offering. He must put some on the doorposts of the temple. He must apply some to the four corners of the middle part of the

altar. He must put the rest on the gateposts of the inner courtyard.

²⁰"Do the same thing on the seventh day of the month. Do it for those who sin without meaning to. And do it for those who sin without realizing what they are doing. So you will make the temple pure and clean.

²¹"Keep the Passover Feast on the 14th day of the first month. It will last for seven days. During that time you must eat bread that is made without yeast.

²²"The prince must provide a bull as a sin offering. It will be for him and all of the people of the land. ²³For each of the seven days of the Feast he must provide seven bulls and seven rams. They must not have any flaws. They will be a burnt offering to me. The prince must also provide a male goat for a sin offering. ²⁴He must bring a little over half a bushel for each bull or ram. He must also provide four quarts of olive oil for each of them.

²⁵"The seven days of the Feast begin on the 15th day of the seventh month. During those days the prince must provide the same sin offerings, burnt offerings, grain offerings and olive oil."

46 The LORD and King says, "On the six working days of each week you must keep the east gate of the inner courtyard of the temple shut. But open it on Sabbath days and during New Moon Feasts. ²The prince must enter the temple area through the porch of the gateway. He must stand by the gatepost. The priests must sacrifice his burnt offering and friendship offerings. He must worship at the entrance of the gateway. Then he must leave. But the gate will not be shut until evening.

³"On Sabbath days and during New Moon Feasts the people of the land must gather together at the entrance of the temple gateway. That is where they must worship me.

⁴"The prince must bring a burnt offering to me on the Sabbath. It will be six male lambs and a ram. They must not have any flaws. ⁵He must offer a little over half a bushel of grain along with the ram. The grain he offers along with the lambs can be as much as he

wants to give. He must also offer four quarts of olive oil for every half bushel of grain.

6"On the day of the New Moon Feast the prince must also offer a young bull, six lambs and a ram. They must not have any flaws. 7He must offer a little over half a bushel of grain along with the bull or ram. The grain he offers along with the lambs can be as much as he wants to give. He must also offer four quarts of olive oil for every half bushel of grain.

8"When the prince enters the temple area, he must go in through the porch of the gateway. He must leave the same way.

9"The people of the land must worship me at the appointed feasts. Those who enter through the north gate must leave through the south gate. Those who enter through the south gate must leave through the north gate. They must not leave through the same gate they entered. Each one must go out the opposite gate. 10The prince must be among them. He must go in when they go in. And he must leave when they leave.

11"At the yearly feasts and other appointed feasts there must be grain offerings. The prince must offer a little over half a bushel of grain along with a bull or ram. The grain he offers along with the lambs can be as much as he wants to give. He must also offer four quarts of olive oil for every half bushel of grain. 12He can also bring another offering to me because he chooses to. It might be a burnt offering or friendship offering. When he brings it, the east gate must be opened for him. He will bring his offering just as he does on the Sabbath day. Then he will leave. After he has gone out, the gate must be shut.

13"Every day you must provide a lamb that is a year old. It must not have any flaws. It is a burnt offering to me. You must provide it every morning. 14You must also offer grain along with it every morning. Bring 13 and a third cups of grain. Also bring one and a third quarts of olive oil to make the flour a little wet. So you will give the grain offering to me. That will be a law that will last for all time to come. 15Pro-

vide the lamb, grain offering and oil every morning. They will be used for a regular burnt offering."

16The LORD and King says, "Suppose the prince makes a gift from his share of land. And he gives it to one of his sons. Then the property will also belong to his sons after him. It will be handed down to them.

17"But suppose he makes a gift from his share of land to one of his servants. Then the servant can keep it until the Year of Jubilee. After that, it will be returned to the prince. His property can be handed down only to his sons. It belongs to them.

18"The prince must not take any share of land that belongs to the people. He must not drive them off their property. He must give his sons their share out of his own property. Then my people will not be separated from their property."

19The man brought me through the entrance at the side of the north building. That's where the priests' sacred rooms were located. He showed me a place west of the building. 20He said to me, "This is where the priests will cook the guilt offerings and sin offerings. They will also bake the grain offerings here. Then they will not have to bring the offerings into the outer courtyard. That will keep the people from touching the offerings and becoming holy."

21Then the man brought me to the outer courtyard. He led me around to its four corners. In each corner I saw another smaller courtyard. 22So in the four corners of the outer courtyard were walled courtyards. Each one was 70 feet long and 52 and a half feet wide. All of them were the same size. 23Around the inside of each of the four courtyards was a stone ledge. Places for fire were built all around under each ledge. 24The man said to me, "These are the kitchens. Those who serve at the temple will cook the people's sacrifices here."

A RIVER WILL FLOW FROM THE TEMPLE

47 The man brought me back to the entrance to the temple. I saw water flowing east from under a temple gateway. The temple faced east. The water was coming down from under the south side of the temple. It was flowing south of the altar.

²Then he brought me out through the north gate of the outer courtyard. He led me around the outside to the outer gate that faced east. The water was flowing from the south side of the east gate.

³Then the man went toward the east. He had a measuring line in his hand. He measured off 1,750 feet. He led me through water that was up to my ankles. ⁴Then he measured off another 1,750 feet. He led me through water that was up to my knees. Then he measured off another 1,750 feet. He led me through water that was up to my waist. ⁵Then he measured off another 1,750 feet. But now it was a river that I could not go across. The water had risen so high that it was deep enough to swim in. ⁶He asked me, "Son of man, do you see this?"

Then he led me back to the bank of the river. ⁷When I arrived there, I saw a large number of trees. They were on both sides of the river.

⁸The man said to me, "This water flows toward the eastern territory. It goes down into the Arabah Valley. There it enters the Dead Sea. When it empties into it, the water there becomes fresh. ⁹Large numbers of creatures will live where the river flows. It will have huge numbers of fish. This water flows there and makes the salt water fresh. So where the river flows everything will live.

¹⁰"People will stand along the shore to fish. From En Gedi all the way to En Eglaim there will be places for spreading fishnets. The Dead Sea will have many kinds of fish. They will be like the fish in the Mediterranean Sea.

¹¹"But none of the swamps will have fresh water in them. They will stay salty.

¹²"Fruit trees of all kinds will grow on both banks of the river. Their leaves will not dry up. The trees will always have fruit on them. Every month they will bear fruit. The water from the temple will flow to them. Their fruit will be used for food. And their leaves will be used for healing."

THE BORDERS OF THE LAND

¹³The LORD and King says, "People of Israel, here are the borders you will have after you divide up the land. Each of the 12 tribes will receive a share. But the family of Joseph will have two shares. ¹⁴Divide the land into equal parts. Long ago I raised my hand and took an oath. I promised to give the land to your people. So all of it will belong to you.

¹⁵"Here are the borders of the land.

"On the north side the border will start at the Mediterranean Sea. It will go by the Hethlon road past Lebo Hamath. Then it will continue on to Zedad, ¹⁶Berothah and Sibraim. Sibraim is between Damascus and Hamath. The border will reach all the way to Hazer Hatticon. It is right next to Hauran. ¹⁷The border will go from the sea to Hazar Enan. It will run north of Damascus and south of Hamath. That will be the north border.

¹⁸"On the east side the border will run between Hauran and Damascus. It will continue along the Jordan River between Gilead and the land of Israel. It will reach to the Dead Sea and all the way to Tamar. That will be the east border.

¹⁹"On the south side the border will start at Tamar. It will reach all the way to the waters of Meribah Kadesh. Then it will run along the Wadi of Egypt. It will end at the Mediterranean Sea. That will be the south border.

²⁰"On the west side, the Mediterranean Sea will be the border. It will go to a point across from Lebo Hamath. That will be the west border.

²¹"You must divide up this land among yourselves. Do it based on the number of men in your tribes. ²²Each of the tribes must receive a share of the land.

"You must also give some land to the outsiders who have settled among you and who have children. Treat them as if they had been born in Israel. Let them have some land among your tribes. ²³Outsiders can settle in any tribe. There you must give them their share," announces the LORD and King.

THE LAND WILL BE DIVIDED UP

48 "Here are the tribes. They are listed by their names. Dan will receive one share of land. It will be at the northern border of Israel. The border will follow the Hethlon road to Lebo Hamath. Hazar Enan will be part of the border. So will the northern border of Damascus next to Hamath. Dan's northern border will run from east to west.

²"Asher will receive one share. It will border the territory of Dan from east to west.

³"Naphtali will receive one share. It will border the territory of Asher from east to west.

⁴"Manasseh will receive one share. It will border the territory of Naphtali from east to west.

⁵"Ephraim will receive one share. It will border the territory of Manasseh from east to west.

⁶"Reuben will receive one share. It will border the territory of Ephraim from east to west.

⁷"Judah will receive one share. It will border the territory of Reuben from east to west.

⁸"You must give one share as a special gift to me. It will border the territory of Judah from east to west. It will be eight and a fourth miles wide. It will be as long as the border of each of the territories of the tribes. Its border will run from east to west. The temple will be in the center of that strip of land.

⁹"Give that special share of land to me. It will be eight and a fourth miles long and three and a third miles wide. ¹⁰It will be the sacred share of land for the priests. It will be eight and a fourth miles long on the north side. It will be three and a third miles wide on the west side. It will be three and a third miles wide on the east side. And it will be eight and a fourth miles long on the south side. My temple will be in the center of it.

¹¹"This share of land will be for the priests who are set apart to me. They

will come from the family line of Zadok. The members of that family served me faithfully. They did not go down the wrong path as the Levites and other Israelites did. ¹²Their share of land will be a special gift to them. It will be part of the sacred share of the land. It will be very holy. Its border will run along the territory of the Levites.

¹³"The Levites will receive a share. It will be next to the territory of the priests. The Levites' share will be eight and a fourth miles long and three and a third miles wide. ¹⁴They must not sell or trade any of it. It is the best part of the land. It must not be handed over to anyone else. It is set apart to me.

¹⁵"The area that remains is one and two thirds miles wide. It is eight and a fourth miles long. It will not be holy. The people in Jerusalem can build houses there. They can use some of it as grasslands. The city will be in the center of it. ¹⁶Each of the four sides of the city will be one and a half miles long. ¹⁷Each of the four sides of the city's grasslands will be 437 and a half feet long.

¹⁸"What remains of the area will be three and a third miles long on the east and west sides. Its border will run along the border of the sacred share. Its crops will supply food for the city workers. ¹⁹They will farm the area. They will come from all of the tribes of Israel. ²⁰The entire area will be a square. Each of its four sides will be eight and a fourth miles long. Set the sacred share apart as a special gift to me. Do the same thing with the property of the city.

²¹"The area that remains on both sides will belong to the prince. So his land does not include the sacred share and the city property. The eastern part of his land will reach from the sacred share all the way to the eastern border. The western part will reach from the sacred share to the western border. The sacred share itself is eight and a fourth miles long on its east and west sides. Both of those areas will be right next to the borders of the two tribes on the north and south sides. They will belong to the prince. The sacred share will be in the center of them. It will have the temple in it.

²²"The property of the Levites will lie in the center of the prince's share. So will the property of the city. The prince's land will lie between the borders of the tribes of Judah and Benjamin.

²³"Here is the land for the rest of the tribes. Benjamin will receive one share. It will reach from the eastern border to the western border.

²⁴"Simeon will receive one share. It will border the territory of Benjamin from east to west.

²⁵"Issachar will receive one share. It will border the territory of Simeon from east to west.

²⁶"Zebulun will receive one share. It will border the territory of Issachar from east to west.

²⁷"Gad will receive one share. It will border the territory of Zebulun from east to west.

²⁸"The southern border of Gad will run south from Tamar to the waters of Meribah Kadesh. It will continue along the Wadi of Egypt. It will end at the Mediterranean Sea.

²⁹"That is the land you must divide among the tribes of Israel. And those will be the shares they will receive," announces the Lord and King.

THE GATES OF THE CITY

³⁰"Here is a list of the gates of the city. Start with its north side. It will be a mile and a half long. ³¹The city gates will be named after the tribes of Israel. The north side will have three gates. They will be the gates of Reuben, Judah and Levi.

³²"The east side will be a mile and a half long. It will have three gates. They will be the gates of Joseph, Benjamin and Dan.

³³"The south side will be a mile and a half long. It will have three gates. They will be the gates of Simeon, Issachar and Zebulun.

³⁴"The west side will be a mile and a half long. It will have three gates. They will be the gates of Gad, Asher and Naphtali.

³⁵"The city will be six miles around. "From that time on, its name will be

THE LORD IS THERE."

quest challenge

I Wonder . . .

Why is it wrong to cheat?

Real Life Challenge

During your math test, you notice that the boy sitting next to you has his paper out in plain view. You have a decision to make: keep your eyes on your own paper or get a little "help" from your classmate. A lot of kids would go ahead and look, but God wants you to honestly earn your grades. He will help you so you don't have to be dishonest.

Quest Clue

Read Leviticus 6, Ezekiel 22 and 1 Corinthians 6 to find out more about how God feels about cheating.

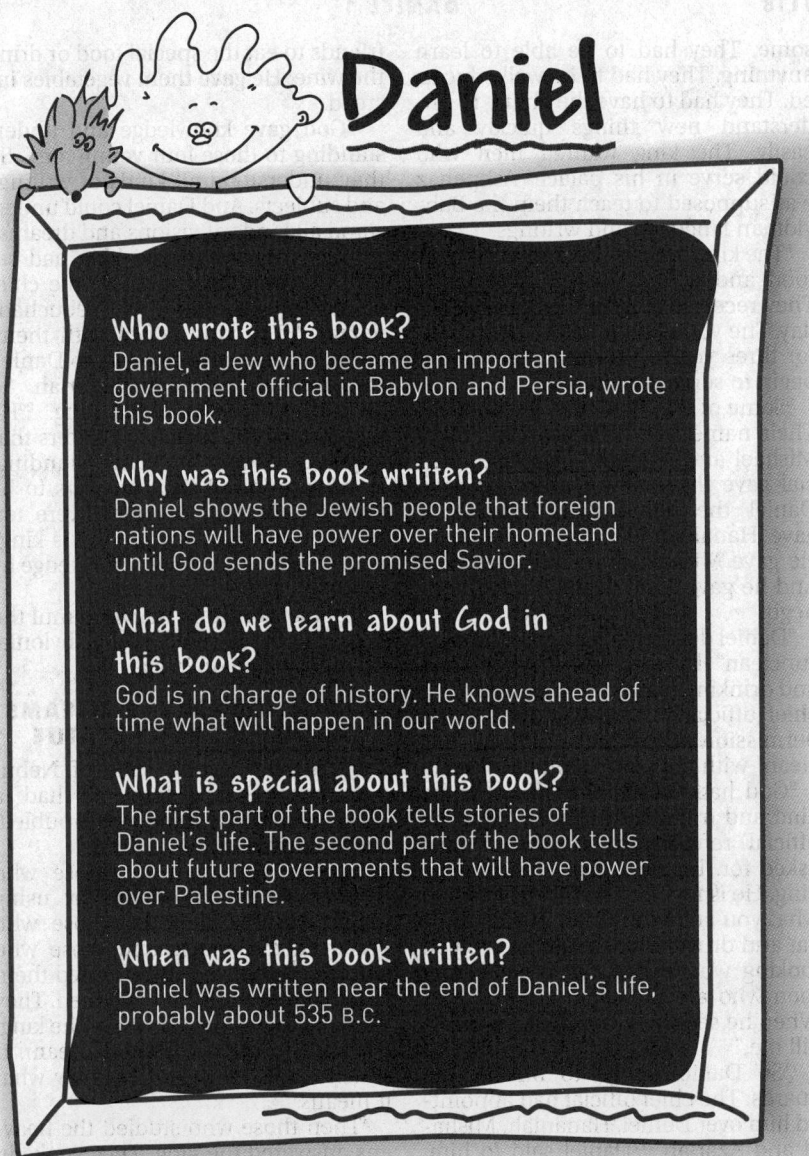

Daniel

Who wrote this book?

Daniel, a Jew who became an important government official in Babylon and Persia, wrote this book.

Why was this book written?

Daniel shows the Jewish people that foreign nations will have power over their homeland until God sends the promised Savior.

What do we learn about God in this book?

God is in charge of history. He knows ahead of time what will happen in our world.

What is special about this book?

The first part of the book tells stories of Daniel's life. The second part of the book tells about future governments that will have power over Palestine.

When was this book written?

Daniel was written near the end of Daniel's life, probably about 535 B.C.

DANIEL IS TRAINED IN BABYLON

1 It was the third year that Jehoiakim was king of Judah. Nebuchadnezzar came to Jerusalem. His armies surrounded the city and attacked it. Nebuchadnezzar was king of Babylonia.

²The LORD handed Jehoiakim, the king of Judah, over to him. Nebuchadnezzar also took some of the articles from God's temple. He carried them off to the temple of his god in Babylonia. He put them among the treasures of his god.

³The king gave Ashpenaz an order. Ashpenaz was the chief of Nebuchadnezzar's court officials. The king told him to bring in some of the Israelites. He wanted nobles and men from the royal family. ⁴He was looking for young men who were healthy and hand-

some. They had to be able to learn anything. They had to be well educated. They had to have the ability to understand new things quickly and easily. The king wanted men who could serve in his palace. Ashpenaz was supposed to teach them the Babylonian language and writings.

⁵The king had his servants give them food and wine from his own table. They received a certain amount every day. The young men had to be trained for three years. After that, they could begin to serve the king.

⁶Some of the men were from Judah. Their names were Daniel, Hananiah, Mishael and Azariah. ⁷The chief official gave them new names. He gave Daniel the name Belteshazzar. He gave Hananiah the name Shadrach. He gave Mishael the name Meshach. And he gave Azariah the name Abednego.

⁸Daniel decided not to make himself "unclean" by eating the king's food and drinking his wine. So he asked the chief official for a favor. He wanted permission not to make himself "unclean" with the king's food and wine.

⁹God had caused the official to be kind and friendly to Daniel. ¹⁰But the official refused to do what Daniel asked for. He said, "I'm afraid of the king. He is my master. He has decided what you and your three friends must eat and drink. Why should he see you looking worse than the other young men who are the same age you are? When he sees how you look, he might kill me."

¹¹So Daniel spoke to one of the guards. The chief official had appointed him over Daniel, Hananiah, Mishael and Azariah. ¹²Daniel said to him, "Please test us for ten days. Give us nothing but vegetables to eat. And give us only water to drink. ¹³Then compare us with the young men who eat the king's food. See how we look. After that, do what you want to."

¹⁴So the guard agreed. He tested them for ten days.

¹⁵After the ten days they looked healthy and well fed. In fact, they looked better than any of the young men who ate the king's food. ¹⁶So the guard didn't require Daniel and his friends to eat the special food or drink the wine. He gave them vegetables instead.

¹⁷God gave knowledge and understanding to those four young men. So they understood all kinds of writings and subjects. And Daniel could understand all kinds of visions and dreams.

¹⁸The three years the king had set for their training ended. So the chief official brought them to Nebuchadnezzar. ¹⁹The king talked with them. He didn't find anyone equal to Daniel, Hananiah, Mishael and Azariah. So they began to serve the king. ²⁰He asked them for advice in matters that required wisdom and understanding. He always found their answers to be the best. In fact, the men were ten times better than anyone in his kingdom who claimed to get knowledge by using magic.

²¹Daniel served in Babylon until the first year Cyrus ruled over Babylonia. Cyrus was king of Persia.

NEBUCHADNEZZAR DREAMS ABOUT A LARGE STATUE

2 In the second year of Nebuchadnezzar's rule, he had a dream. His mind was troubled. He couldn't sleep.

²So the king sent for those who claimed to get knowledge by using magic. He also sent for those who practiced evil magic and those who studied the heavens. He wanted them to tell him what he had dreamed. They came in and stood in front of the king. ³He said to them, "I had a dream. It troubles me. So I want to know what it means."

⁴Then those who studied the heavens answered the king. They spoke in Aramaic. They said, "King Nebuchadnezzar, may you live forever! Tell us what you dreamed. Then we'll explain what it means."

⁵The king replied to them, "I have made up my mind. You must tell me what I dreamed. And you must tell me what it means. If you don't, I'll have you cut to pieces. And I'll have your houses turned into piles of trash.

⁶"So tell me what I dreamed. Explain it to me. Then I'll give you gifts. I'll reward you. I'll give you great honor. So

tell me the dream. And tell me what it means."

[7]Once more they replied, "King Nebuchadnezzar, tell us what you dreamed. Then we'll tell you what it means."

[8]The king answered, "I know what you are doing. You are trying to gain more time. You realize that I've made up my mind. [9]You must tell me the dream. If you don't, you will pay for it. You have gotten together and made evil plans. You hope things will change. So you are telling me lies. But I want you to tell me what I dreamed. Then I'll know that you can tell me what it means."

[10]They answered the king, "There isn't a man on earth who can do what you are asking! No king has ever asked for anything like that. Not even a king as great and mighty as you has asked for it. Those who get knowledge by using magic have never been asked to do what you are asking. And those who study the heavens haven't been asked to do it either. [11]What you are asking is much too hard. No one can tell you what you dreamed except the gods. And they don't live among human beings."

[12]That made the king very angry. He ordered that all of the wise men in Babylon be put to death. [13]So the order was given to kill them. Men were sent out to look for Daniel and his friends. They were also supposed to be put to death.

[14]Arioch was the commander of the king's guard. He went out to put the wise men of Babylon to death. So Daniel spoke to him wisely and carefully. [15]He asked the king's officer, "Why did Nebuchadnezzar give a terrible order like that?" Then Arioch explained to Daniel what was going on.

[16]When Daniel heard that, he went to the king. He told him he would explain the dream to him. But he needed more time.

[17]Then Daniel returned to his house. He explained everything to his friends Hananiah, Mishael and Azariah. [18]He asked them to pray that the God of heaven would give him mercy. He wanted God to help him understand the mystery of the king's dream. Then

he and his friends wouldn't be killed along with the other wise men in Babylon.

[19]During that night, God gave Daniel a vision. He showed him what the mystery was all about. Then Daniel praised the God of heaven. [20]He said,

"May God be praised for ever and ever!
He is wise and powerful.
[21]He changes times and seasons.
He sets up kings.
He removes them from power.
The wisdom of those who are wise comes from him.
He gives knowledge to those who have understanding.
[22]He explains deep and hidden things.
He knows what happens in the darkest places.
And where he is, everything is light.
[23]God of my people, I thank and praise you.
You have given me wisdom and power.
You have made known to me what we asked you for.
You have shown us the king's dream."

DANIEL TELLS THE KING WHAT HIS DREAM MEANS

[24]Then Daniel went to Arioch. The king had appointed him to put the wise men of Babylon to death. Daniel said to him, "Don't kill the wise men of Babylon. Take me to the king. I'll tell him what his dream means."

[25]So Arioch took Daniel to the king at once. Arioch said, "I have found a man among those you brought here from Judah. He can tell you what your dream means."

[26]Nebuchadnezzar spoke to Daniel, who was also called Belteshazzar. The king asked him, "Are you able to tell me what I saw in my dream? And can you tell me what it means?"

[27]Daniel replied, "You have asked us to explain a mystery to you. But no wise man can do that. And those who try to figure things out by using magic can't do it either. [28]"But there is a God in heaven who

can explain mysteries. Nebuchadnezzar, he has shown you what is going to happen. Here is what you dreamed. And here are the visions that passed through your mind while you were lying on your bed.

²⁹"My king, while you were still in bed your mind thought about things that haven't happened yet. The One who explains mysteries showed those things to you.

³⁰"Now the mystery has been explained to me. But it isn't because I have greater wisdom than anyone else. It's because God wants you to know what the mystery means, my king. He wants you to understand what went through your mind.

³¹"King Nebuchadnezzar, you looked up and saw a large statue standing in front of you. It was huge. It shone brightly. And it terrified you. ³²The head of the statue was made out of pure gold. Its chest and arms were made of silver. Its stomach and thighs were bronze. ³³Its legs were made out of iron. And its feet were partly iron and partly baked clay.

³⁴"While you were watching, a rock was cut out. But human hands didn't do it. It struck the statue on its feet of iron and clay. It smashed them. ³⁵Then the iron and clay were broken to pieces. So were the bronze, silver and gold. All of them were broken to pieces at the same time. They became like straw on a threshing floor at harvest time. The wind blew them away without leaving a trace. But the rock that struck the statue became a huge mountain. It filled the whole earth.

³⁶"That was your dream. Now I will tell you what it means. ³⁷Nebuchadnezzar, you are the greatest king of all. The God of heaven has given you authority and power. He has given you might and glory. ³⁸He has put everyone under your control. He has also given you authority over the wild animals and the birds of the air. It doesn't matter where they live. He has made you ruler over all of them. You are that head of gold.

³⁹"After you, another kingdom will take over. It won't be as powerful as yours. Next, a third kingdom will rule over the whole earth. The bronze part of the statue stands for that kingdom.

⁴⁰"Finally, there will be a fourth kingdom. It will be as strong as iron. Iron breaks and smashes everything to pieces. And the fourth kingdom will crush and break all of the others. ⁴¹You saw that the feet and toes were made out of iron and baked clay. And the fourth kingdom will be divided up. But it will still be almost as strong as iron. That's why you saw iron mixed with clay. ⁴²The toes were partly iron and partly clay. And the fourth kingdom will be partly strong and partly weak. ⁴³You saw the iron mixed with baked clay. And the fourth kingdom will be made up of all kinds of people. They won't hold together any more than iron mixes with clay.

⁴⁴"In the time of those kings, the God of heaven will set up a kingdom. It will never be destroyed. And no other nation will ever take it over. It will crush all of those other kingdoms. It will bring them to an end. But it will last forever. ⁴⁵That's what the vision of the rock cut out of a mountain means. Human hands didn't cut the rock out. It broke the statue to pieces. It smashed the iron, bronze, clay, silver and gold.

"The great God has shown you what will take place in days to come. The dream is true. And you can trust the meaning I have given you for it."

⁴⁶Then King Nebuchadnezzar bowed low in front of Daniel. He wanted to honor him. So he ordered that an offering and incense be offered up to him.

⁴⁷The king said to Daniel, "I'm sure your God is the greatest God of all. He is the Lord of kings. He explains mysteries. That's why you were able to explain the mystery of my dream."

⁴⁸Then the king put Daniel in a position of authority. He gave him many gifts. He made him ruler over the city of Babylon and the towns around it. He put him in charge of all of its other wise men.

⁴⁹The king also did what Daniel asked him to. He appointed Shadrach, Meshach and Abednego to help Daniel govern Babylon and the towns around it. Daniel himself remained at the royal court.

DANIEL'S FRIENDS ARE THROWN INTO A BLAZING FURNACE

3 King Nebuchadnezzar made a statue that was covered with gold. It was 90 feet tall and 9 feet wide. He set it up on the flatlands of Dura near the city of Babylon.

²Then the king sent for the royal rulers, high officials and governors. He sent for the advisers, treasurers, judges and court officers. And he sent for all of the other officials of Babylon. He asked them to come to a special gathering to honor the statue he had set up.

³So the royal rulers, high officials and governors came together. So did the advisers, treasurers, judges and court officers. All of the other officials joined them. They came to honor the statue that King Nebuchadnezzar had set up. They stood in front of it.

⁴Then a messenger called out loudly, "Listen, you people who come from every nation! Pay attention, you who speak other languages! Here is what the king commands you to do. ⁵You will soon hear the sound of horns and flutes. You will hear zithers, lyres, harps and pipes. In fact, you will hear all kinds of music. When you do, you must fall down and worship the gold statue that King Nebuchadnezzar has set up. ⁶If you don't, you will be thrown into a blazing furnace right away."

⁷All of the people heard the sound of the horns and flutes. They heard the zithers, lyres, harps and other musical instruments. As soon as they did, they fell down and worshiped Nebuchadnezzar's gold statue. They had come from every nation and language.

⁸At that time some people who studied the heavens came forward. They spoke against the Jews. ⁹They said, "King Nebuchadnezzar, may you live forever! ¹⁰You commanded everyone to fall down and worship the gold statue. You told them to do it when they heard the horns, flutes, zithers, lyres, harps, pipes and other musical instruments. ¹¹If they didn't, they would be thrown into a blazing furnace. ¹²But you have appointed some Jews to help Daniel govern Babylon and the towns around it. Their names are Shadrach, Meshach and Abednego. They don't pay any attention to you, King Nebuchadnezzar. They don't serve your gods. And they refuse to worship the gold statue you have set up."

¹³Nebuchadnezzar burned with anger. He sent for Shadrach, Meshach and Abednego. So they were brought to him.

¹⁴The king said to them, "Shadrach, Meshach and Abednego, is what I heard about you true? Don't you serve my gods? Don't you worship the gold statue I set up? ¹⁵You will hear the horns, flutes, zithers, lyres, harps, pipes and other musical instruments. When you do, fall down and worship the statue I made. If you will, that's very good. But if you won't, you will be thrown at once into a blazing furnace. Then what god will be able to save you from my powerful hand?"

¹⁶Shadrach, Meshach and Abednego replied to the king. They said, "King Nebuchadnezzar, we don't need to talk about this anymore. ¹⁷We might be thrown into the blazing furnace. But the God we serve is able to bring us out of it alive. He will save us from your powerful hand.

¹⁸"But we want you to know this. Even if we knew that our God wouldn't save us, we still wouldn't serve your gods. We wouldn't worship the gold statue you set up."

¹⁹Then Nebuchadnezzar's anger burned against Shadrach, Meshach and Abednego. The look on his face changed. And he ordered that the furnace be heated seven times hotter than usual. ²⁰He also gave some of the strongest soldiers in his army a command. He ordered them to tie up Shadrach, Meshach and Abednego. Then he told his men to throw them into the blazing furnace. ²¹So they were tied up. Then they were thrown into the furnace. They were wearing their robes, pants, turbans and other clothes.

²²The king's command was carried out quickly. The furnace was so hot that its flames killed the soldiers who threw Shadrach, Meshach and Abednego into it. ²³So the three men were firmly tied up. And they fell into the blazing furnace.

²⁴Then King Nebuchadnezzar leaped to his feet. He was so amazed he asked his advisers, "Didn't we tie three men up? Didn't we throw three men into the fire?"

"Yes, we did," they replied.

²⁵The king said, "Look! I see four men walking around in the fire. They aren't tied up. And the fire hasn't even harmed them. The fourth man looks like a son of the gods."

²⁶Then the king approached the opening of the blazing furnace. He shouted, "Shadrach, Meshach and Abednego, come out! You who serve the Most High God, come here!"

So they came out of the fire. ²⁷The royal rulers, high officials, governors and advisers crowded around them. They saw that the fire hadn't harmed their bodies. Not one hair on their heads was burned. Their robes weren't burned either. And they didn't even smell like smoke.

²⁸Then Nebuchadnezzar said, "May the God of Shadrach, Meshach and Abednego be praised! He has sent his angel and saved his servants. They trusted in him. They refused to obey my command. They were willing to give up their lives. They would rather die than serve or worship any god except their own God.

²⁹"No other god can save people that way. So I'm giving an order. No one from any nation or language can say anything against the God of Shadrach, Meshach and Abednego. If they do, they'll be cut to pieces. And their houses will be turned into piles of trash."

³⁰Then the king honored Shadrach, Meshach and Abednego. He gave them higher positions in the city of Babylon and the towns around it.

NEBUCHADNEZZAR DREAMS ABOUT A TREE

4 I, King Nebuchadnezzar, am writing this letter.

I am sending it to you people from every nation and language in the whole world.

May you have great success!

²I am pleased to tell you what has happened. The Most High God has done miraculous signs and wonders for me.

³His miraculous signs are great.
  His wonders are mighty.
His kingdom will last forever.
  His rule will never end.

⁴I was at home in my palace. I was content and very successful. ⁵But I had a dream that made me afraid. I was lying on my bed. Then dreams and visions passed through my mind. They terrified me.

⁶So I commanded that all of the wise men in Babylon be brought to me. I wanted them to tell me what my dream meant. ⁷Those who try to figure things out by using magic came. So did those who study the heavens. I told all of them what I had dreamed. But they couldn't tell me what it meant.

⁸Finally, Daniel came to me. He is called Belteshazzar, after the name of my god. The spirit of the holy gods is in him. I told him my dream.

⁹I said, "Belteshazzar, you are chief of the magicians. I know that the spirit of the holy gods is in you. No mystery is too hard for you to figure out. Here is my dream. Tell me what it means.

¹⁰"Here are the visions I saw while I was lying on my bed. I looked up and saw a tree standing in the middle of the land. It was very tall. ¹¹It had grown to be large and strong. Its top touched the sky. It could be seen anywhere on earth. ¹²Its leaves were beautiful. It had a lot of fruit on it. It provided enough food for people and animals. Under the tree, the wild animals found shade. The birds of the air lived in its branches. Every creature was fed from that tree.

¹³"While I was still lying on my bed, I looked up. In my visions, I saw a holy messenger. He was coming down from heaven. ¹⁴He called out in a loud voice. He said, 'Cut the tree down. Break off its branches. Strip its leaves off. Scatter its fruit. Let the animals that

are under it run away. Let the birds that are in its branches fly off. [15]But leave the stump with its roots in the ground. Let it stay in the field. Put a band of iron and bronze around it.

" 'Let King Nebuchadnezzar become wet with the dew of heaven. Let him live like the animals among the plants of the earth. [16]Let him no longer have the mind of a man. Instead, let him be given the mind of an animal. Let him stay that way until seven periods of time pass by.

[17]" 'The decision is announced by holy messengers. So all who are alive will know that the Most High God is King. He rules over all of the kingdoms of men. He gives them to anyone he wants. Sometimes he puts the least important men in charge of them.'

[18]"That's the dream I, King Nebuchadnezzar, had. Now tell me what it means, Belteshazzar. None of the wise men in my kingdom can explain it to me. But you can. After all, the spirit of the holy gods is in you."

DANIEL EXPLAINS NEBUCHADNEZZAR'S DREAM

[19]Daniel, who was also called Belteshazzar, was very bewildered for a while. His thoughts terrified him. So the king said, "Belteshazzar, don't let the dream or its meaning make you afraid."

Belteshazzar answered, "My master, I wish the dream were about your enemies! I wish its meaning had to do with them! [20]You saw a tree. It grew to be large and strong. Its top touched the sky. It could be seen from anywhere on earth. [21]Its leaves were beautiful. It had a lot of fruit on it. It provided enough food for people and animals. Under the tree, the wild animals found shade. The birds of the air lived in its branches.

[22]"My king, you are that tree! You have become great and strong. Your greatness has grown until it reaches the sky. Your

rule has spread to all parts of the earth.

[23]"My king, you saw a holy messenger. He came down from heaven. He said, 'Cut the tree down. Destroy it. But leave the stump with its roots in the ground. Let it stay in the field. Put a band of iron and bronze around it. Let King Nebuchadnezzar become wet with the dew of heaven. Let him live like the wild animals. Let him stay that way until seven periods of time pass by.'

[24]"My king and master, here is what your dream means. The Most High God has given an order against you. [25]You will be driven away from people. You will live like the wild animals. You will eat grass just as cattle do. You will become wet with the dew of heaven. Seven periods of time will pass by for you. Then you will recognize that the Most High God rules over all of the kingdoms of men. He gives them to anyone he wants.

[26]"But he gave a command to leave the stump of the tree along with its roots. That means your kingdom will be given back to you. It will happen when you recognize that the God of heaven rules.

[27]"So, my king, I hope you will accept my advice. Stop being sinful. Do what is right. Give up your evil practices. Show kindness to those who are being treated badly. Then perhaps things will continue to go well with you."

NEBUCHADNEZZAR'S DREAM COMES TRUE

[28]All of that happened to me. [29]It took place twelve months later. I was walking on the roof of my palace in Babylon. [30]I said, "Isn't this the great Babylon I have built as a place for my royal palace? I used my mighty power to build it. It shows how glorious my majesty is."

[31]I was still speaking when a voice was heard from heaven. It said, "King Nebuchadnezzar, here is what has been ordered concerning you. Your royal authority has been taken from you. [32]You

will be driven away from people. You will live like the wild animals. You will eat grass just as cattle do. Seven periods of time will pass by for you. Then you will recognize that the Most High God rules over all of the kingdoms of men. He gives them to anyone he wants."

³³What had been said about me came true at once. I was driven away from people. I ate grass just as cattle do. My body became wet with the dew of heaven. I stayed that way until my hair grew like the feathers of an eagle. My nails became like the claws of a bird.

³⁴At the end of that time I, Nebuchadnezzar, looked up toward heaven. My mind became clear again. Then I praised the Most High God. I gave honor and glory to the One who lives forever.

His rule will last forever.
    His kingdom will never end.
³⁵He considers all of the nations on
    earth
    to be nothing.
He does as he pleases
    with the powers of heaven.
He does what he wants
    with the nations of the earth.
No one can hold his hand back.
    No one can say to him,
    "What have you done?"

³⁶My honor and glory were returned to me when my mind became clear again. The glory of my kingdom was given back to me. My advisers and nobles came to me. And I was put back on my throne. I became even greater than I had been before.

³⁷Now I, Nebuchadnezzar, give praise and honor and glory to the King of heaven. Everything he does is right. All of his ways are fair. He is able to bring down those who live proudly.

A HAND WRITES ON THE PALACE WALL

5 King Belshazzar gave a big dinner. He invited a thousand of his nobles to it. He drank wine with them.

²While Belshazzar was drinking his wine, he gave orders to his servants. He commanded them to bring in some gold and silver cups. They were the cups his father Nebuchadnezzar had taken from the temple in Jerusalem. Belshazzar had them brought in so everyone could drink from them. That included the king himself, his nobles, his wives and his concubines.

³So the servants brought in the gold cups that had been taken from God's temple in Jerusalem. The king and his nobles drank from them. So did his wives and concubines. ⁴As they drank the wine, they praised their gods. The statues of those gods were made out of gold, silver, bronze, iron, wood or stone.

⁵Suddenly the fingers of a human hand appeared. They wrote something on the plaster of the palace wall. It happened near the lampstand. The king watched the hand as it wrote. ⁶His face turned pale. He became so afraid that his knees knocked together. His legs couldn't hold him up any longer.

⁷The king sent for those who try to figure things out by using magic. He also sent for those who study the heavens. All of them were wise men in Babylon. He ordered that they be brought to him. He said to them, "I want one of you to read this writing and tell me what it means. If you do, you will be dressed in purple clothes. A gold chain will be put around your neck. And you will be made the third highest ruler in the kingdom."

⁸Then all of the king's wise men came in. But they couldn't read the writing. They couldn't tell him what it meant. ⁹So King Belshazzar became even more terrified. His face grew more pale. And his nobles were bewildered.

¹⁰The queen heard the king and his nobles talking. So she came into the dining hall. "King Belshazzar, may you live forever!" she said. "Don't be afraid! Don't look so pale! ¹¹I know a man in your kingdom who has the spirit of the holy gods in him. He has understanding and wisdom and good sense just like the gods. That was discovered when your father Nebuchadnezzar

was king. Nebuchadnezzar appointed him chief of those who tried to figure things out by using magic. He also put him in charge of those who studied the heavens.

[12] "The man's name is Daniel. Your father called him Belteshazzar. He has a clever mind and knowledge and understanding. He is also able to tell what dreams mean. He can explain riddles and solve hard problems. Send for him. He'll tell you what the writing means."

[13] So Daniel was brought to the king. The king said to him, "Are you Daniel? Are you one of the prisoners my father the king brought here from Judah? [14] I have heard that the spirit of the gods is in you. I've also heard that you have understanding and good sense and special wisdom.

[15] "The wise men and those who practice magic were brought to me. They were asked to read this writing and tell me what it means. But they couldn't.

[16] "I have heard that you are able to explain things and solve hard problems. I hope you can read this writing and tell me what it means. If you can, you will be dressed in purple clothes.

A gold chain will be put around your neck. And you will be made the third highest ruler in the kingdom."

[17] Then Daniel answered the king. He said, "You can keep your gifts for yourself. You can give your rewards to someone else. But I will read the writing for you. I'll tell you what it means.

[18] "King Belshazzar, the Most High God was good to your father Nebuchadnezzar. He gave him authority and greatness and glory and honor. [19] God gave him a high position. Then all of the people from every nation and language became afraid of the king. He put to death anyone he wanted to. He spared anyone he wanted to spare. He gave high positions to anyone he wanted to. And he brought down anyone he wanted to bring down.

[20] "But his heart became very stubborn and proud. So he was removed from his royal throne. His glory was stripped away from him. [21] He was driven away from people. He was given the mind of an animal. He lived like the wild donkeys. He ate grass just as cattle do. His body became wet with the dew of heaven. He stayed that way until he recognized that the Most High

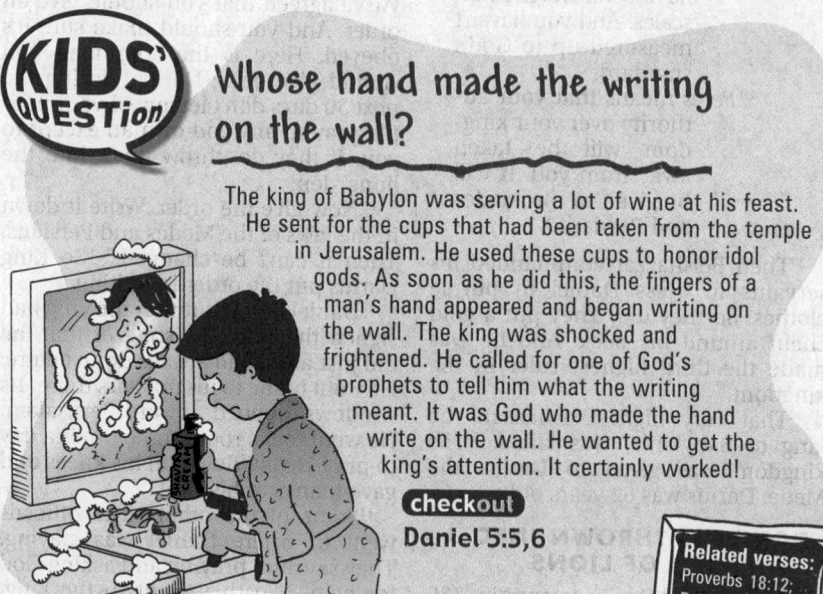

KIDS' QUESTION

Whose hand made the writing on the wall?

The king of Babylon was serving a lot of wine at his feast. He sent for the cups that had been taken from the temple in Jerusalem. He used these cups to honor idol gods. As soon as he did this, the fingers of a man's hand appeared and began writing on the wall. The king was shocked and frightened. He called for one of God's prophets to tell him what the writing meant. It was God who made the hand write on the wall. He wanted to get the king's attention. It certainly worked!

checkout
Daniel 5:5,6

Related verses:
Proverbs 18:12;
Daniel 5:1–31

God rules over all of the kingdoms of men. He puts anyone he wants to in charge of them.

²²"But you knew all of that, Belshazzar. After all, you are Nebuchadnezzar's son. In spite of that, you are still proud. ²³You have taken your stand against the Lord of heaven. You had your servants bring cups from his temple to you. You and your nobles drank wine from them. So did your wives and concubines. You praised your gods. The statues of those gods are made out of silver, gold, bronze, iron, wood or stone. They can't see or hear or understand anything. But you didn't honor the God who holds in his hand your very life and everything you do. ²⁴So he sent the hand that wrote on the wall.

²⁵"Here is what was written.

MENE, MENE, TEKEL, PARSIN

²⁶"And here is what those words mean.

> *Mene* means that God has limited the time of your rule. He has brought it to an end.
> ²⁷*Tekel* means that you have been weighed on scales. And you haven't measured up to God's standard.
> ²⁸*Peres* means that your authority over your kingdom will be taken away from you. It will be given to the Medes and Persians."

²⁹Then Belshazzar commanded his servants to dress Daniel in purple clothes. So they did. They put a gold chain around his neck. And he was made the third highest ruler in the kingdom.

³⁰That very night Belshazzar, the king of Babylonia, was killed. ³¹His kingdom was given to Darius the Mede. Darius was 62 years old.

DANIEL IS THROWN INTO A DEN OF LIONS

6 It pleased Darius to appoint 120 royal rulers over his entire kingdom. ²He placed three leaders over them. One of the leaders was Daniel. The royal rulers were made accountable to the three leaders. Then the king wouldn't lose any of his wealth. ³Daniel did a better job than the other two leaders or any of the royal rulers. He was an unusually good and able man. So the king planned to put him in charge of the whole kingdom.

⁴But the other two leaders and the royal rulers heard about it. So they looked for a reason to bring charges against Daniel. They tried to find something wrong with the way he ran the government. But they weren't able to. They couldn't find any fault with his work. He could always be trusted. He never did anything wrong. And he always did what he was supposed to.

⁵Finally those men said, "It's almost impossible for us to come up with a reason to bring charges against this man Daniel. If we do, it will have to be in connection with the law of his God."

⁶So the two leaders and the royal rulers went as a group to the king. They said, "King Darius, may you live forever! ⁷All of the royal leaders, high officials, royal rulers, advisers and governors want to make a suggestion. We've agreed that you should give an order. And you should make sure it's obeyed. Here is the command you should give. King Darius, during the next 30 days don't let any of your people pray to any god or man except to you. If they do, throw them into the lions' den.

⁸"Now give the order. Write it down in the laws of the Medes and Persians. Then it can't be changed." ⁹So King Darius put the order in writing.

¹⁰Daniel found out that the king had signed the order. In spite of that, he did just as he had always done before. He went home to his upstairs room. Its windows opened toward Jerusalem. He went to his room three times a day to pray. He got down on his knees and gave thanks to his God.

¹¹Some of the other royal officials went to where Daniel was staying. They saw him praying and asking God for help. ¹²So they went to the king. They spoke to him about his royal order. They said, "King Darius, didn't you

sign an official order? It said that for the next 30 days none of your people could pray to any god or man except to you. If they did, they would be thrown into the lions' den.''

The king answered, "The order must still be obeyed. It's one of the laws of the Medes and Persians. So it can't be changed.''

¹³Then they spoke to the king again. They said, "Daniel is one of the prisoners from Judah. He doesn't pay any attention to you, King Darius. He doesn't obey the order you put in writing. He still prays to his God three times a day.''

¹⁴When the king heard that, he was very upset. He didn't want Daniel to be harmed in any way. Until sunset, he did everything he could to save him.

¹⁵Then the men went as a group to the king. They said to him, "King Darius, remember that no order or law you make can be changed. That's what the laws of the Medes and Persians require.''

¹⁶So the king gave the order. Daniel was brought out and thrown into the lions' den. The king said to him, "You always serve your God faithfully. So may he save you!''

¹⁷A stone was brought and placed over the opening of the den. The king sealed it with his own special ring. He also sealed it with the rings of his nobles. Then nothing could be done to help Daniel.

¹⁸The king returned to his palace. He didn't eat anything that night. He didn't ask for anything to be brought to him for his enjoyment. And he couldn't sleep.

¹⁹As soon as the sun began to rise, the king got up. He hurried to the lions' den. ²⁰When he got near it, he called out to Daniel. His voice was filled with great concern. He said, "Daniel! You serve the living God. You always serve him faithfully. So has he been able to save you from the lions?''

²¹Daniel answered, "My king, may you live forever! ²²My God sent his angel. And his angel shut the mouths of the lions. They haven't hurt me at all. That's because I haven't done anything wrong in God's sight. I've never done anything wrong to you either, my king.''

²³The king was filled with joy. He ordered his servants to lift Daniel out of the den. So they did. They didn't see any wounds on him. That's because he had trusted in his God.

²⁴Then the king gave another order. The men who had said bad things about Daniel were brought in. They were thrown into the lions' den. So were their wives and children. Before they hit the bottom of the den, the lions attacked them. And the lions crushed all of their bones.

²⁵Then King Darius wrote to the people from every nation and language in the whole world. He said,

How did Daniel sleep with the lions without being afraid?

The Bible does not say that Daniel was not afraid. It says that Daniel was willing to face the lions because he trusted God. Daniel believed that obeying God was right even if it meant being in danger. Even if Daniel was afraid, he faced the lions with confidence because of his trust in God.

checkout **Daniel 6:22**

Related verses:
Daniel 6:1–28

"May you have great success!

26"I order people in every part of my kingdom to respect and honor Daniel's God.

"He is the living God.
He will live forever.
His kingdom will not be destroyed.
His rule will never end.
27 He sets people free and saves
them.
He does miraculous signs and
wonders.
He does them in the heavens and
on the earth.
He has saved Daniel
from the power of the lions."

28So Daniel had success while Darius was king. Things went well with him during the rule of Cyrus, the Persian.

DANIEL HAS A VISION ABOUT FOUR ANIMALS

7 It was the first year that Belshazzar was king of Babylon. Daniel had a dream. He was lying on his bed. In his dream, visions passed through his mind. He wrote down what he saw.

2Daniel said, "I had a vision at night. I looked up and saw the four winds of heaven. They were stirring up the Mediterranean Sea. 3Four large animals came up out of the sea. Each one was different from the others.

4"The first animal was like a lion. It had the wings of an eagle. I watched until its wings were torn off. Then it was lifted up from the ground. It stood on two feet like a man. And a man's heart was given to it.

5"I saw a second animal. It looked like a bear. It was raised up on one of its sides. And it had three ribs between its teeth. It was told, 'Get up! Eat meat until you are full!'

6"After that, I saw another animal. It looked like a leopard. On its back were four wings like the wings of a bird. It had four heads. And it was given authority to rule.

7"After that, in my vision I looked up and saw a fourth animal. It was terrifying and very powerful. It had large iron teeth. It crushed those it attacked and

ate them up. It stomped on anything that was left. It was different from the other animals. And it had ten horns.

8"I thought about the horns. Then I saw another horn. It was a little one. It grew up among the other horns. Three of the first horns were pulled up by their roots to make room for it. The little horn had eyes like the eyes of a man. Its mouth was always bragging.

9"As I watched,

"thrones were set in place.
The Eternal God took his seat.
His clothes were as white as snow.
The hair on his head was white
like wool.
His throne was blazing with fire.
And flames were all around its
wheels.
10 A river of fire was flowing.
It was coming out from in front
of God.
Thousands and thousands of
angels served him.
Millions of them stood in front of
him.
The court was seated.
And the books were opened.

11"Then I continued to watch because of the way the horn was bragging. I kept looking until the fourth animal was killed. I watched until its body was destroyed. It was thrown into the blazing fire. 12The authority of the other animals had been stripped away from them. But they were allowed to live for a period of time.

13"In my vision I saw One who looked like a son of man. He was coming with the clouds of heaven. He approached the Eternal God. He was led right up to him. 14And he was given authority, glory and a kingdom. People from every nation and language worshiped him. His authority will last forever. It will not pass away. His kingdom will never be destroyed.

AN ANGEL TELLS DANIEL WHAT HIS DREAM MEANS

15"My spirit was troubled. The visions that passed through my mind upset me. 16I approached an angel who was standing there. I asked him what all of those things really meant.

"So he explained everything to me.

He told me what it meant. He said, [17]"The four large animals stand for four kingdoms. The kingdoms will appear on the earth. [18]But the holy people of the Most High God will receive the kingdom. They will possess it forever. It will belong to them for ever and ever.'

[19]"Then I wanted to know what the fourth animal stood for. It was different from the others. It was the most terrifying of all. It had iron teeth and bronze claws. It crushed those it attacked and ate them up. It stomped on anything that was left.

[20]"I also wanted to know about the ten horns on its head. And I wanted to know about the other horn that grew up later. It caused three of the ten horns to fall out. It appeared to be stronger than the others. It had eyes. And its mouth was always bragging.

[21]"I saw that the horn was at war with God's people. It was winning the battle over them. [22]But then the Eternal God came. He decided in favor of his holy people. So the time came when the kingdom was given to them.

[23]"Here's how the angel explained it to me. He said, 'The fourth animal stands for a fourth kingdom. It will appear on earth. It will be different from the other kingdoms. It will eat up the whole earth. It will stomp on it and crush it. [24]The ten horns stand for ten kings. They will come from the fourth kingdom.

" 'After them another king will appear. He will be different from the earlier ones. He'll bring three kings under his control. [25]He'll speak against the Most High God. He'll treat God's people badly. He will try to change the times and laws that were given by God. God's people will be handed over to him for three and a half years.

[26]" 'But the court will open. And the power of that king will be taken away from him. It will be completely destroyed forever. [27]Then the authority, power and greatness of all of the kingdoms on earth will be handed over to the people of the Most High God. His kingdom will last forever. Every ruler will worship and obey him.'

[28]"That's all I saw. My thoughts deeply troubled me. My face turned pale. But I kept those things to myself."

DANIEL HAS A VISION ABOUT A RAM AND A GOAT

8 It was the third year of King Belshazzar's rule. After the vision that had already appeared to me, I had another one. [2]In my vision I saw myself in the city of Susa. It has high walls around it. It is in the land of Elam. In the vision I was beside the Ulai Waterway.

[3]I looked up and saw a ram that had two horns. He was standing beside the waterway. His horns were long. One of them was longer than the other. But it grew up later. [4]I watched the ram as he charged toward the west. He also charged toward the north and the south. No animal could stand up against him. Not one of them could save anyone from his power. He did as he pleased. And he became great.

[5]I was thinking about all of that. Then a goat suddenly came from the west. He had a large horn between his eyes. He raced across the whole earth without even touching the ground. [6]He came toward the ram that had the two horns. It was the ram I had seen standing beside the waterway. The goat was burning with anger. He charged at the ram. [7]I saw him attack the ram with mighty force. He struck the ram and broke his two horns. The ram didn't have the power to stand up against him. The goat knocked him to the ground and stomped on him. No one could save the ram from his power.

[8]The goat became very great. But when his power was at its greatest, his large horn was broken off. In its place four large horns grew up toward the four winds of heaven.

[9]Out of one of the four horns came another horn. It started small but became more and more powerful. It grew to the south and to the east and toward the beautiful land of Israel. [10]It grew until it reached the stars in the sky. It threw some of them down to the earth. And it stomped on them.

[11]It set itself up to be as great as God. He is the Prince of the heavenly army. It took the daily sacrifices away from

him. And his temple in Jerusalem was brought low. [12]Because many of God's people refused to obey him, they were handed over to the horn. The daily sacrifices were also given over to it. It was successful no matter what it did. And the true worship of God was thrown down to the ground.

[13]Then I heard a holy angel speaking. Another holy angel spoke to him. He asked, "How long will it take for the vision to come true? The daily sacrifices will be stopped. Those who refuse to obey God will be destroyed. The temple will be handed over to an enemy. And some of the stars will be stomped on."

[14]One of the holy angels said to me, "It will take 2,300 evenings and mornings. Then the temple will be made holy again."

GABRIEL TELLS DANIEL WHAT HIS VISION MEANS

[15]I was watching the vision. And I was trying to understand it. Then I saw someone who looked like a man. [16]I heard a voice from the Ulai Waterway. It called out, "Gabriel, tell Daniel what his vision means."

[17]Gabriel came close to where I was standing. I was terrified and fell down flat with my face toward the ground. He said to me, "Son of man, I want you to understand that the vision tells about the time of the end."

[18]While he was speaking to me, I was sound asleep. I lay with my face toward the ground. Then he touched me. He raised me to my feet.

[19]He said, "I am going to tell you what will happen later. It will take place when God is angry. The vision tells about the appointed time of the end. [20]You saw a ram that had two horns. It stands for the kings of Media and Persia. [21]The goat stands for the king of Greece. The large horn between his eyes is the first king. [22]Four horns took its place when it was broken off. They stand for four kingdoms that will come from his nation. But those kingdoms will not be as powerful as his.

[23]"Toward the end of their rule, those who refuse to obey God will become completely evil. Then another king will appear. He will have a mean-looking face. He will be a master at making clever plans. [24]He will become very strong. But he will not get that way by his own power. People will be amazed at the way he destroys everything. He will be successful no matter what he does. He will destroy the mighty men and the holy people.

[25]"He will tell lies in order to succeed. He will think he is more important than anyone else. When people feel safe, he will destroy many of them. He will stand up against the greatest Prince of all. Then he will be destroyed. But he will not be killed by human beings.

[26]"The vision of the evenings and mornings that has been given to you is true. But seal up the vision. It tells about a time far off."

[27]I was worn out. I lay sick for several days. Then I got up and returned to my work for the king. The vision bewildered me. I couldn't understand it.

DANIEL PRAYS TO THE LORD

9 It was the first year that Darius was king of Babylonia. He was from Media and was the son of Xerxes. [2]In that year I learned from the Scriptures that Jerusalem would remain destroyed for 70 years. That was what the LORD had told the prophet Jeremiah. [3]So I prayed to the Lord God. I begged him. I made many appeals to him. I didn't eat anything. I put on black clothes. And I sat down in ashes.

[4]I prayed to the LORD my God. I admitted that we had sinned. I said,

"Lord, you are a great and wonderful God. You keep the covenant you made with all those who love you and obey your commands. You show them your love.
[5]"We have sinned and done what is wrong. We have been evil. We have refused to obey you. We have turned away from your commands and laws. [6]We haven't listened to your servants the prophets. They spoke in your name to our kings and princes. They also brought your message to all of our people in the land.
[7]"Lord, you always do what is

right. But we are covered with shame today. We are the people of Judah and Jerusalem. All of us are Israelites, no matter where we live. We are now living in many countries. You scattered us among the nations because we weren't faithful to you. [8]LORD, we and our kings and princes and people are covered with shame. We have sinned against you.

[9]"You are the Lord our God. You show us your tender love. You forgive us. But we have turned against you. [10]You are the LORD our God. But we haven't obeyed you. We haven't kept the laws you gave us through your servants the prophets. [11]All of the people of Israel have broken your law and turned away from it. They have refused to obey you.

"Curses and warnings are written down in the Law of Moses. He was your servant. Those curses have been poured out on us. That's because we have sinned against you. [12]The warnings you gave us and our rulers have come true. You have brought great trouble on us. Nothing like what has been done to Jerusalem has ever happened anywhere else on earth.

[13]"The curses that are written in the Law of Moses have fallen on us. We have received nothing but trouble. You are the LORD our God. But we haven't asked for your favor. We haven't turned away from our sins. We've refused to pay attention to the laws you gave us. [14]LORD, you didn't hold back from bringing this trouble on us. You always do what is right. But we haven't obeyed you.

[15]"Lord our God, you used your mighty hand to bring your people out of Egypt. You made a name for yourself. It is still great to this very day. But we have sinned. We've done what is wrong. [16]Lord, you saved your people before. So turn your burning anger away from Jerusalem again. After all, it is your city. It's your holy mountain. All those who live around us laugh

at Jerusalem and your people. That's because we have sinned. Our people before us did evil things too.

[17]"Our God, hear my prayers. Pay attention to the appeals I make to you. Look with favor on your temple that has been destroyed. Do it for your own honor. [18]Our God, please listen to us. The city that belongs to you has been destroyed. Open your eyes and see it. We aren't asking you to answer our prayers because we are godly. Instead, we're asking you to do it because you love us so much.

[19]"Lord, please listen! Lord, please forgive us! Lord, hear our prayers! Take action for your own honor. Our God, please don't wait. Your city and your people belong to you."

GABRIEL TELLS DANIEL ABOUT SEVENTY "WEEKS"

[20]I was speaking and praying. I was admitting that I and my people Israel had sinned. I was making my appeal to the LORD my God concerning his holy mountain of Zion. [21]While I was still praying, Gabriel came to me. I had seen him in my earlier vision. He flew over to me very quickly. It was about the time when the evening sacrifice is offered. [22]He helped me understand. He said, "Daniel, I have come now to give you a good knowledge and understanding of these things. [23]You are highly respected. So as soon as you began to pray, the LORD gave you an answer. I have come to tell you what it is. Here is how you must understand the vision.

[24]"The LORD has appointed 70 'weeks' for your people and your holy city. During that time, acts against God's law will be stopped. Sin will come to an end. And the evil things people do will be paid for. Then everyone will always do what is right. Everything that has been made known in visions and prophecies will come true. And the Most Holy Room in the temple will be anointed.

[25]"Here is what I want you to know and understand. There will be seven

'weeks.' Then there will be 62 'weeks.' The seven 'weeks' will begin when an order is given to rebuild Jerusalem and make it like new again.

"At the end of the 62 'weeks,' the Anointed King will come. Jerusalem will have streets and a water system when it is rebuilt. But that will be done in times of trouble. 26After the 62 'weeks,' the Anointed King will be cut off. His followers will desert him. And everything he has will be taken away from him. The army of the ruler who will come will destroy the city and the temple. The end will come like a flood. War will continue until the end. The LORD has ordered that many places be destroyed.

27"A covenant will be put into effect with many people for one 'week.' In the middle of the 'week' sacrifices and offerings will come to an end. In one part of the temple a hated thing that destroys will be set up. It will remain until the LORD brings the end he has ordered."

DANIEL HAS A VISION ABOUT WHAT WILL HAPPEN TO ISRAEL

10 It was the third year that Cyrus, the king of Persia, ruled over Babylonia. At that time I was living in Babylon. There the people called me Belteshazzar. A message came to me from God. It was true. It was about a great war. I had a vision that showed me what it meant.

2At that time I was very sad for three weeks. 3I didn't eat any rich food. No meat or wine touched my lips. I didn't use any lotions at all until the three weeks were over.

4I was standing on the bank of the great Tigris River. It was the 24th day of the first month. 5I looked up and saw a man who was dressed in linen clothes. A belt that was made out of the finest gold was around his waist. 6His body gleamed like chrysolite. His face shone like lightning. His eyes

Why are nuclear weapons even around?

Nuclear weapons were invented during World War II to gain an advantage over the enemy nations and make the Japanese surrender.

Because these weapons can kill hundreds of thousands of people at once, people all over the world have been working to get rid of them. They feel that we will only destroy ourselves if we use them.

In this present evil world countries feel that they need to protect themselves against evil dictators and other powerful nations. Since some countries already have nuclear weapons, other countries feel they must have the same amount of power to protect their nation.

As long as rulers and nations put their trust in their own strength rather than in God, there will always be weapons to fight a war. That is why we need to pray for peace and for our leaders who need to make wise decisions.

checkout
Daniel 9:26

Related verses:
Proverbs 3:25–26;
15:1;
Romans 1:28–29

were like flaming torches. His arms and legs were as bright as polished bronze. And his voice was like the sound of a large crowd.

[7]I was the only one who saw the vision. The men who were there with me didn't see it. But they were so terrified that they ran and hid. [8]So I was left alone as I was watching that great vision. I felt very weak. My face turned as pale as death. And I was helpless.

[9]Then I heard the man speak. As I listened to him, I fell sound asleep. My face was toward the ground.

[10]A hand touched me. It pulled me up on my hands and knees. I began to tremble with fear. [11]The man said, "Daniel, you are highly respected. Think carefully about what I am going to say to you. And stand up. God has sent me to you." When he said that, I trembled as I stood up.

[12]He continued, "Do not be afraid, Daniel. You decided to get more understanding. You went without food as you worshiped your God. Since the first day you did those things, your words were heard. I have come to give you an answer. [13]But the prince of Persia opposed me for 21 days. Then

Michael came to help me. He is one of the leaders of the angels. He helped me win the battle over the king of Persia.

[14]"Now I have come to explain the vision to you. I will tell you what will happen to your people. The vision shows what will take place in days to come."

[15]While he was telling me those things, I bowed with my face toward the ground. I wasn't able to speak. [16]Then someone who looked like a man touched my lips. I opened my mouth. I began to speak to the one who was standing in front of me. I said, "My master, I'm greatly troubled because of the vision I've seen. And I'm helpless. [17]How can I talk with you? I feel very weak. In fact, I can hardly breathe."

[18]The one who looked like a man touched me again. He gave me strength. [19]"Do not be afraid," he said. "You are highly respected. May peace be with you! Be strong now. Be strong."

When he spoke to me, I became stronger. I said, "Speak, my master. You have given me strength."

[20]So he said, "Do you know why I

Why doesn't God answer prayers right away?

God knows more than we know. He has more wisdom than we have. So he gives the answer at the time that is best. Sometimes we do not have to wait at all—God answers our prayers even before we put them into words. At other times we must wait.

God has good reasons for his timing. Sometimes God is using people and circumstances to answer, bringing them all together like a big team. And sometimes God waits to answer in order to test our faith and help us learn to trust in him. When we decide to keep trusting, our faith becomes stronger.

Related verses:
Genesis 21:1–2;
Psalm 40:1;
Isaiah 55:8–9;
Matthew 7:7,11

checkout
Daniel 10:12,13

YES, OPERATOR – COULD YOU TELL ME THE TIME DIFFERENCE BETWEEN HERE AND HEAVEN? I AM EXPECTING AN IMPORTANT ANSWER TO PRAYER AND...

have come to you? Soon I will return to fight against the prince of Persia. When I go, the prince of Greece will come. [21]But first I will tell you what is written in the Book of Truth. No one gives me any help against those princes except Michael. He is your leader. [1]I stepped forward to help him and keep him safe. It was the first year that Darius, the Mede, was king.

THE KINGS OF EGYPT AND SYRIA

[2]"Now then, what I'm about to tell you is true. Three more kings will appear in Persia. Then a fourth one will rule. He will be much richer than all of the others. He will use his wealth to gain power. And he will stir up everyone against the kingdom of Greece.

[3]"After him, a mighty king will appear. He will rule with great power. He will do as he pleases. [4]Not long after his rule ends, his kingdom will be broken up. It will be divided up into four parts. His children will not receive it when he dies. And it will not be as strong as his kingdom. It will be pulled up by the roots. And it will be given to others.

[5]"The king of Egypt will become strong. But one of his commanders will become even stronger. He will rule over his own kingdom with great power. [6]After many years, the two kingdoms will join forces. The daughter of the next king of Egypt will go to the king of Syria. She will join forces with him. But she will not hold on to her power. And he and his power will not last either. In those days she and her attendants will be put to death. Her father will die. So will the one who helped her.

[7]"Someone from her family line will take her place. He will attack the army of the next king of Syria. Then he will enter his fort. He will fight against that army and win. [8]He will take the metal statues of their gods. He will also take away their priceless articles of silver and gold. He will carry everything off to Egypt. For many years he will leave the king of Syria alone.

[9]"That king will march into territory that was controlled by Egypt. Then he will return to his own country. [10]His sons will prepare for war. They will gather a huge army. It will sweep along like a mighty flood. It will fight its way as far as one of the Egyptian forts.

[11]"Another king of Egypt will march out with mighty force. He will fight against the next king of Syria. That king will gather a huge army. But it will lose the battle. [12]His soldiers will be carried off. Then the king of Egypt will be filled with pride. He will kill many thousands of soldiers. But his success will not last.

[13]"The king of Syria will bring another army together. It will be larger than the first one. After several years, he will march out with a huge army. It will have everything it needs for battle.

[14]"In those times many people will rise up against the next king of Egypt. Lawless men in your own nation will refuse to obey him. That is what you saw in your vision. But they will not succeed.

[15]"Then the king of Syria will go to a certain city that has high walls around it. He will build ramps against them. And he will capture that city. The forces of Egypt will not have the power to stop him. Even their best troops will not be strong enough to stand up against him. [16]He will do anything he wants to. No one will be able to stand up against him. He will take over the beautiful land of Israel. And he will have the power to destroy it.

[17]"He will decide to come with the might of his entire kingdom. He will join forces with the king of Egypt. And he will give him his daughter to become his wife. He will do it in order to take control of Egypt. But his plans will not succeed. They will not help him.

[18]"Then he will turn his attention to the lands along the Mediterranean coast. He will take over many of them. But a commander will put an end to his proud actions. He will turn his pride back on him. [19]After that, the king of Syria will return to the forts in his own country. But he will trip and fall. And he will never be seen again. [20]"The next king after him will send someone out to collect taxes. The taxes will help maintain the glory of

his kingdom. But in a few years the king will be destroyed. It will not happen because someone becomes angry with him or kills him in battle.

²¹"Another king will take his place. Many people will hate him. He will not be honored as a king should be. He will lead an army into the kingdom when its people feel secure. He will make clever plans to capture it. ²²Then he will sweep away a huge army. The army and a prince of the covenant will be destroyed.

²³"The king of Syria will make an agreement with that prince. But then he will not keep his word. He will rise to power with the help of only a few people. ²⁴When the people in the richest areas feel secure, he will attack them. He will do what the kings before him could not do. And he will reward his followers with the goods and wealth he takes. He will make clever plans to take over the forts. But that will last for only a short time.

²⁵"He will stir up his strength and courage. With a large army he will go to war against the next king of Egypt. That king will fight against him with a huge and very powerful army. But he will not be able to stand up against him. So the plans of the king of Syria will succeed. ²⁶The trusted advisers of the king of Egypt will try to destroy him. His army will be swept away. Many of his soldiers will be wounded or killed.

²⁷"The kings of Syria and Egypt will sit at the same table. But in their hearts they will plan to do what is evil. And they will tell lies to each other. But it will not do them any good. God will put an end to their plans at his appointed time.

²⁸"The king of Syria will return to his own country. He will go back there with great wealth. But he will make evil plans against the holy temple in Jerusalem. He will do a lot of harm to the temple and the people who worship there. Then he will return to his own country.

²⁹"At God's appointed time, the king of Syria will march south again. But this time things will turn out differently. ³⁰Roman ships will oppose him. He will lose hope. Then he will turn back.

He will take out his anger against the holy temple. And he will show favor to the Jews who desert it.

³¹"His army will come and make the temple area 'unclean.' They will put a stop to the daily sacrifices. Then they will set up a hated thing that destroys. ³²He will pretend to praise those who have broken the covenant. He will lead them to do what is evil. But the people who know their God will firmly oppose him.

³³"Those who are wise will teach many others. But for a while, some of the wise will be killed with swords. Others will be burned to death. Still others will be made prisoners. Or they will be robbed of everything they have. ³⁴When that happens, they will receive a little help. Many who are not honest will join them.

³⁵"So some of the wise people will suffer. They will be made pure in the fire. They will be made spotless until the time of the end. It will still come at God's appointed time.

A KING WILL HONOR HIMSELF

³⁶"A certain king will do as he pleases. He will honor himself. He will put himself above every god. He will say things that have never been heard before against the greatest God of all. He will have success until God is not angry anymore. What God has decided to do must take place.

³⁷"The king will not show any respect for the gods his people have always worshiped. He will not respect the one women long for. He will not have respect for any god. Instead, he will put himself above all of them. ³⁸In place of them, he will worship a god of war. He will honor a god his people have not had anything to do with before. He will give gold and silver to that god. He will bring jewels and expensive gifts to it.

³⁹"He will attack the strongest forts. A new god will help him do it. He will greatly honor those who recognize him as their leader. He will make them rulers over many people. And he will give them land as a reward.

⁴⁰"A king in the south will go to war against him. It will happen at the time of the end. The king who will honor

himself will rush out against him. He will come with chariots and horsemen. He will attack with a lot of ships. He will lead his army into many countries. He will sweep through them like a flood.

⁴¹"He will also march into the beautiful land of Israel. Many countries will fall. But Edom, Moab and the leaders of Ammon will be saved from his mighty hand. ⁴²His power will reach out into many countries. Even Egypt will not escape. ⁴³He will gain control of all of Egypt's riches. He will take their gold and silver treasures. The people of Libya and Cush will be under his control.

⁴⁴"But reports from the east and the north will terrify him. He will burn with anger and march out to destroy many people and wipe them out. ⁴⁵He will set up his royal tents. He will put them between the Mediterranean Sea and the beautiful holy mountain of Zion. But his end will come. And no one will help him.

THE TIME OF THE END

12 "At that time Michael will appear. He is the great leader of the angels who guards your people. There will be a time of terrible suffering. Things will be worse than at any time since nations began. But at that time of suffering your people will be saved. Their names are written in the Book of Life.

²"Huge numbers of people who lie dead in their graves will wake up. Some will rise up to life that will never end. Others will rise up to shame that will never end. ³Those who are wise will shine like the brightness of the sky. Those who lead many others to do

what is right will be like the stars for ever and ever.

⁴"But I want you to roll up the scroll, Daniel. Seal it until the time of the end. Many people will go here and there to increase their knowledge."

⁵Then I looked up and saw two other angels. One was on this side of the Tigris River. And one was on the other side. ⁶The man who was dressed in linen was above the waters of the river. One of the angels said to him, "How long will it be before these amazing things come true?"

⁷The man raised both hands toward heaven. I heard him take an oath in the name of the One who lives forever. He answered me, "Three and a half years. Then the power of the holy people will be broken at last. And all of those things will come true."

⁸I heard what he said. But I didn't understand it. So I asked, "My master, what will come of all of this?"

⁹He answered, "Go on your way, Daniel. The scroll is rolled up. It is sealed until the time of the end. ¹⁰Many people will be made pure in the fire. They will be made spotless. But sinful people will continue to be evil. Not one sinful person will understand. But those who are wise will.

¹¹"The daily sacrifices will be stopped. And the hated thing that destroys will be set up. After that, there will be 1,290 days. ¹²Blessed are those who wait for the 1,335 days and reach the end of them.

¹³"Daniel, go on your way until the end. Your body will rest in the grave. Then at the end of the days you will rise from the dead. And you will receive what God has appointed for you."

Quest Clue

Daniel and his friends show a lot of courage in chapters 3 and 6 of this book. To learn more about facing tough situations, find the Quest Challenge at the end of 2 Timothy.

Hosea

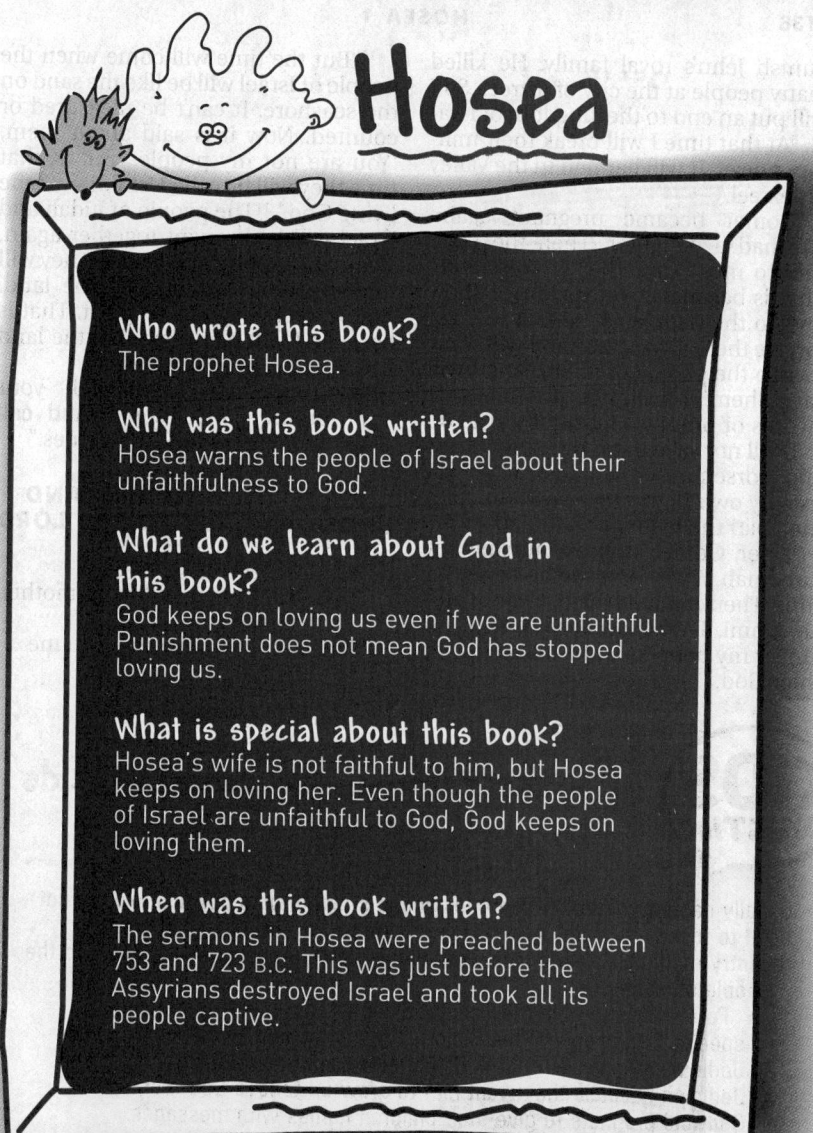

Who wrote this book?
The prophet Hosea.

Why was this book written?
Hosea warns the people of Israel about their unfaithfulness to God.

What do we learn about God in this book?
God keeps on loving us even if we are unfaithful. Punishment does not mean God has stopped loving us.

What is special about this book?
Hosea's wife is not faithful to him, but Hosea keeps on loving her. Even though the people of Israel are unfaithful to God, God keeps on loving them.

When was this book written?
The sermons in Hosea were preached between 753 and 723 B.C. This was just before the Assyrians destroyed Israel and took all its people captive.

1 A message came to Hosea from the LORD. He was the son of Beeri. The message came while Uzziah, Jotham, Ahaz and Hezekiah were kings of Judah. It also came while Jeroboam was king of Israel. He was the son of Jehoash. Here is what Hosea said.

HOSEA'S WIFE AND CHILDREN

²The LORD began to speak through me. He said to me, "Go. Get married to a woman who will commit adultery. Take as your own the children who will be born as a result of her adultery. Marry her because the people of the land are guilty of the worst kind of adultery. They have not been faithful to me." ³So I married Gomer. She was the daughter of Diblaim. Gomer became pregnant. And she had a son by me.

⁴Then the LORD said to me, "Name him Jezreel. That is because I will soon

punish Jehu's royal family. He killed many people at the city of Jezreel. So I will put an end to the kingdom of Israel. ⁵At that time I will break their military power. It will happen in the Valley of Jezreel."

⁶Gomer became pregnant again. She had a daughter. Then the LORD said to me, "Name her Lo-Ruhamah. That is because I will no longer show love to the people of Israel. I will not forgive them anymore. ⁷But I will show love to the people of Judah. And I will save them. I will not use bows or swords or other weapons of war to do it. I will not save them by using horses and horsemen either. Instead, I will use my own power to save them. I am the LORD their God."

⁸Later, Gomer stopped nursing Lo-Ruhamah. After that, she had another son. ⁹Then the LORD said, "Name him Lo-Ammi. That is because Israel is no longer my people. And I am no longer their God.

¹⁰"But the time will come when the people of Israel will be like the sand on the seashore. It can't be measured or counted. Now it is said about them, 'You are not my people.' But at that time they will be called 'children of the living God.' ¹¹The people of Judah and Israel will be brought together again. They will appoint one leader. They will increase their numbers in the land. And Jezreel's day will be great. That is because I will plant Israel in the land again.

2 "People of Israel, call your brothers My People. And call your sisters My Loved Ones."

ISRAEL IS PUNISHED AND BROUGHT BACK TO THE LORD

²I said to my children,

"Talk things over with your mother. Talk to her.
She isn't acting like a wife to me anymore.

Why did Bible people give their kids such funny names?

Usually names from other countries sound strange to us because we are not used to them. The names may sound funny to us, but the people in that country think they sound nice. Your name would probably sound funny to the people of Israel.

Parents like to give their children names that mean something special. The people of the Bible felt this way. For example, the name Jedidiah means "lover of God." Parents might name their son Jedidiah because they want him to grow up to love God. Sometimes God told prophets to give their children names with messages.

Hosea named his children Lo-Ruhamah and Lo-Ammi for that reason. Lo-Ruhamah means "not loved," and Lo-Ammi means "not my people." These unusual names gave a special message to God's people.

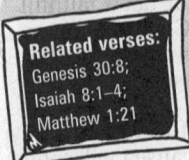 **checkout** Hosea 1:6–9

Related verses:
Genesis 30:8;
Isaiah 8:1–4;
Matthew 1:21

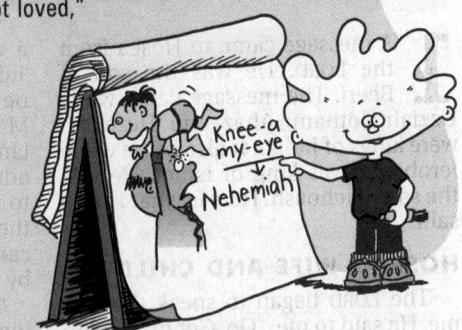

She no longer treats me as her
    husband.
Tell her to stop looking and acting
    like a prostitute.
Tell her not to let her lovers
    lie on her breasts anymore.
³If she doesn't stop it, I will strip
    her naked.
    I'll make her as bare as she was
        on the day she was born.
I'll make her like a desert.
    She will become like dry land.
    And I'll let her die of thirst."

⁴I won't show my love to Gomer's
    children.
    They are the children of other
        men.
⁵Their mother hasn't been faithful
    to me.
    She who became pregnant with
        them
    has brought shame on herself.
    She said, "I will chase after my
        lovers.
    They give me my food and
        water.
    They provide me with wool and
        linen.
    They give me olive oil and wine."
⁶So I will block her path with
    bushes that have thorns.
    I'll build a wall around her.
    Then she can't go to her lovers.
⁷She will still chase after her lovers.
    But she won't catch them.
    She'll look for them.
    But she won't find them.
    Then she'll say,
    "I'll go back to my husband.
    That's where I was at first.
    I was better off then than I am
        now."
⁸She wouldn't admit that I was the
    one
    who gave her everything she had.
    I provided her with grain, olive
        oil and fresh wine.
    I gave her plenty of silver and gold.
    But she used it to make statues of
        Baal.
⁹So I will take away my grain when
    it gets ripe.
    I'll take my fresh wine when it's
        ready.
    I'll take back my wool and my
        linen.

I gave them to her to cover her
    naked body.
¹⁰So now I'll uncover her body.
    All of her lovers will see it.
    No one can stop me from
        punishing her.
¹¹I will put a stop to the special
    times she celebrates.
    I'll bring an end to the feasts she
        celebrates each year.
    I'll stop her New Moon Feasts and
        her Sabbath days.
    I'll bring all of her appointed
        feasts to an end.
¹²I will destroy her vines and her fig
    trees.
    She said they were her pay from
        her lovers.
    I'll make them like clumps of
        bushes and weeds.
    Wild animals will eat them up.

¹³The LORD announces,

"Israel burned incense to the gods
    that were named after Baal.
I will punish her
    for all of the times she did that.
She decorated herself with rings
    and jewelry.
    Then she went after her lovers.
    But she forgot all about me.

¹⁴"So now I am going to draw her
    back to me.
    I will lead her into the desert.
    There I will speak tenderly to her.
¹⁵I will give her back her vineyards.
    I will make the Valley of Achor a
        door of hope for her.
Then she will love me, as she did
    when she was young.
    She will love me just as she did
        when she came up out of Egypt.
¹⁶"A new day is coming," announces
    the LORD.
    "Israel will call me My Husband.
    She will no longer call me My
        Master.
¹⁷She will no longer speak about the
    gods
    that are named after Baal.
    She will not pray to them for help
        anymore.
¹⁸At that time I will make a covenant
    for the good of my people.
    I will make it with the wild
        animals

and the birds of the air.
It will also be made with the
      creatures
   that move on the ground.
I will remove bows and swords
   and other weapons of war from
      the land.
Then my people can lie down in
   safety.
[19] I will make Israel my own.
   She will belong to me forever.
I will do to her what is right and
   fair.
   I will love her tenderly.
[20] I will be faithful to her.
   And she will recognize me as
      the LORD.

[21] "So at that time I will answer her,"
   announces the LORD.
"I will command the skies
   to send rain on the earth.
[22] Then the earth will produce grain,
   olive oil and fresh wine.
   And Israel will be called Jezreel.
   That is because I will answer her
      prayers.
[23] I will plant her in the land for
      myself.
   I will show my love to the one I
      called Not My Loved One.
   I will say, 'You are my people'
      to those who were called
      Not My People.
   And they will say, 'You are
      my God.' "

HOSEA BRINGS HIS WIFE BACK TO HIMSELF

3 The LORD said to me, "Go. Show
your love to your wife again. She
is loved by another man. And
she has committed adultery. But I
want you to love her just as I love the
people of Israel. They turn to other
gods. And they love to offer raisin
cakes to Baal and eat them. In spite of
that, I love my people."

[2] So I bought Gomer for six ounces of
silver and about ten bushels of barley.
[3] Then I told her, "You must wait for me
for a long time. You must not be a prostitute. You must not have sex with any
man. And I will wait for you."

[4] So the people of Israel will live for a
long time without a king or prince.
They won't have sacrifices or sacred

stones. They won't have sacred linen
aprons or statues of family gods. [5] After
that, the people of Israel will return to
the LORD their God. They will look to
him and to a king from the family line
of David. In the last days, they will
tremble with fear as they come to the
LORD. And they will receive his full
blessing.

THE LORD BRINGS CHARGES AGAINST ISRAEL

4 People of Israel, listen to the
   LORD's message.
   He is bringing charges
against you who live in Israel.
He says, "There is no faithfulness
   or love in the land.
   No one recognizes me as God.
[2] People call down curses on others.
   They tell lies and commit
      murder.
   They steal and commit adultery.
They break all of my laws.
   They keep on spilling the blood
      of others.
[3] That is why the land is drying up.
   All those who live in it
   are getting weaker and weaker.
The wild animals and the birds of
   the air are dying.
   So are the fish in the ocean.

[4] "But you priests should not blame
      the people.
   You should not find fault with
      one another.
After all, your people
   could also bring charges against
      you.
[5] You trip and fall day and night.
   And the prophets fall down along
      with you.
So I will destroy your nation.
   She is the one who gave birth to
      you.
[6] My people are destroyed
   because they do not know me.

"You priests have refused to obey
      me.
   So I will refuse to accept you as
      my priests.
You have not paid any attention to
   my law.
   So I will not let your children be
      my priests.
[7] The more priests there are,

the more they sin against me.
They have traded their glorious
God for that shameful god
Baal.
[8] They live off the sins of my people.
And they want them to keep on
sinning.
[9] So here is what I will do.
I will punish people and priests
alike.
I will judge them because of their
sinful lives.
I will pay them back
for the evil things they have
done.
[10] "My people will eat.
But they will not have enough.
They will have sex with
prostitutes.
But they will not have any
children.
That is because they have
deserted me.
[11] They have sex with prostitutes.
They drink old wine and fresh
wine.
When they do those things,
it destroys their ability to
understand.
[12] They ask a wooden statue of a god
for advice.
They expect to get answers from
a stick of wood.
They act like prostitutes.
That leads them down the wrong
path.
I am their God.
But they are not faithful to me.
[13] They offer sacrifices on the
mountaintops.
They burn offerings on the hills.
They worship under oak, poplar
and terebinth trees.
The trees provide plenty of
shade.
So your daughters become
prostitutes.
And your daughters-in-law
commit adultery.
[14] "I will not punish your daughters
when they become prostitutes.
I will not judge your daughters-in-
law
when they commit adultery.
After all, the men themselves have
sex with sinful women.

They offer sacrifices where
temple prostitutes earn their
living.
People who can't understand will
be destroyed!

[15] "Israel, you are not faithful to me.
But I do not want Judah to
become guilty too.

"My people, do not go to Gilgal to
offer sacrifices.
Do not go up to Bethel to
worship other gods.
Do not take an oath and say,
'You can be sure that the LORD is
alive.'
[16] The people of Israel are stubborn.
They are as stubborn as a young
cow.
So how can I take care of them
like lambs in a meadow?
[17] The people of Ephraim have
joined themselves to other
gods.
And nothing can be done to help
them.
[18] They continue to be unfaithful
to me
even when their drinks are gone.
And their rulers love to do
shameful things.
[19] A windstorm will blow all of them
away.
And their sacrifices will bring
shame on them.

THE LORD JUDGES ISRAEL

5 "Listen to me, you priests!
Pay attention, people of Israel!
Listen, you members of the
royal family!
Here is my decision against you.
You have been like a trap at
Mizpah.
You have been like a net spread
out on Mount Tabor.
[2] You refuse to obey me.
You offer sacrifices to other
gods.
So I will punish all of you.
[3] People of Ephraim, I know all
about you.
What you are doing is not hidden
from me.
Now you have joined yourselves to
other gods.

You have made yourselves
'unclean.'

⁴ "You can't return to me
because you have done so many
evil things.
In your hearts you long to act like
prostitutes.
You do not recognize me as the
LORD.
⁵ Israel, your pride witnesses that
you are guilty.
People of Ephraim, you trip and
fall because you have sinned.
Judah, you fall down along with
them.
⁶ Israel, you will come to worship me.
You will bring your animals to
offer as sacrifices.
But you will not find me.
I have turned away from you.
⁷ You are not faithful to me.
Your children do not belong to
me.
The way you act at your New
Moon Feasts
will destroy you and your fields.

⁸ "My people, blow trumpets in
Gibeah!
Blow horns in Ramah!
Shout the battle cry in Bethel!
Say to Benjamin, 'The Assyrian
army is coming!'
⁹ People of Ephraim, you will be
completely destroyed
when it is time for me to punish
you.
You can be sure it will happen.
I am announcing it among your
tribes.
¹⁰ Judah, your leaders have stolen
some land.
They have moved their borders
farther north.
So I will pour out my anger on you
like a flood of water.
¹¹ Ephraim, you will soon be
crushed.
The Assyrians will stomp all over
you.
It will happen because you have
made up your minds
to chase after other gods.
¹² Ephraim, I will be like a moth to
you.
Judah, I will cause you to rot
away.

¹³ "Ephraim, you saw how sick you
were.
Judah, you saw that you were
wounded.
Ephraim, you turned to Assyria for
help.
You sent gifts to the great King
Tiglath-Pileser.
But he is not able to make you well.
He can't heal your wounds.
¹⁴ Ephraim, I will be like a lion to
you.
Judah, I will attack you like a
powerful lion.
I will tear you to pieces.
I will drag you off.
Then I will leave you.
No one will be able to save you.
¹⁵ I will go back to my home in
heaven.
I will stay there until you admit
you have sinned.
Then you will turn to me.
You will suffer so much
that you will really want me to
help you."

ISRAEL REFUSES TO TURN AWAY FROM THEIR SINS

6 The people say, "Come.
Let us return to the LORD.
He has torn us to pieces.
But he will heal us.
He has wounded us.
But he'll bandage our wounds.
² After two days he will give us new
life.
On the third day he'll make us
like new again.
Then we will enjoy his blessing.
³ Let's recognize him as the LORD.
Let's keep trying to really know
him.
You can be sure the sun will rise.
And you can be just as sure the
LORD will appear.
He will come to renew us like the
winter rains.
He will be like the spring rains
that water the earth."

⁴ The LORD says, "Ephraim, what
can I do with you?
And what can I do with you,
Judah?
Your love for me vanishes like the
morning mist.

It soon disappears like the early
   dew.
⁵ So I used the words of my
   prophets to cut you in pieces.
I used my words to put you to
   death.
When I judged you, I struck you
   like lightning.
⁶ I want mercy and not sacrifice.
I want you to recognize me as
   God
instead of bringing me burnt
   offerings.
⁷ Just as Adam disobeyed me,
   you have broken the covenant I
     made with you.
You were not faithful to me in the
   land I gave you.
⁸ Ramoth Gilead is a city where
   sinful people live.
It is stained with footprints of
   blood.
⁹ On the road to Shechem, groups of
   priests act like robbers.
They hide and wait to attack
   people.
They murder them
   and commit other shameful
     crimes.
¹⁰ People of Israel, I have seen
   a horrible thing in your land.
People of Ephraim, you have
     joined yourselves to other
     gods.
You have made yourselves
   'unclean.'

¹¹ "People of Judah, I have appointed
   a time
for you to be destroyed.

"My people, I would like to bless
   you
with great success again."

7 The LORD says,

"I would like to heal Israel.
But when I try to, Ephraim's sins
   are brought out into the open.
The crimes of Samaria
   are made known to everyone.
The people tell lies.
   They break into houses and steal.
   They rob others in the streets.
² But they do not realize
   that I remember all of the evil
     things they do.

Their sins pile up and cover them.
I am always aware of those sins.

³ "Their evil conduct even makes
   the king glad.
Their lies make the princes
   happy.
⁴ But all of the people are unfaithful
   to the king.
Their anger against him burns
   like the coals in an oven.
The baker does not even need to
   stir up the fire
until the dough is ready."

⁵ On special days to honor our king,
   the princes get drunk with wine.
And the king enjoys the party.
   He joins hands with those
who pretend to be faithful to
   him.
⁶ Their hearts are as hot as an oven.
   They make evil plans to get rid of
     him.
Their anger burns like a slow fire
   all night.
In the morning it blazes out like
   a flaming fire.
⁷ All of them are as hot as an oven.
They destroy their rulers.
All of their kings fall from power.
But none of them calls on the
   LORD for help.

⁸ The people of Ephraim mix with
   the nations.
They are like a flat cake
   that is baked on only one side.
⁹ People from other lands make
     them weaker and weaker.
But they don't realize it.
Their hair is becoming gray.
   But they don't even notice it.
¹⁰ The pride of Israel witnesses that
   they are guilty.
But in spite of everything,
they don't return to the LORD their
   God.
They don't go to him for help.

¹¹ The LORD says,

"The people of Ephraim are like a
   dove.
They are easily tricked.
   They do not have any sense at
     all.
First they call out to Egypt for
   help.

Then they turn to Assyria.
¹²When they send for help,
I will throw my net over
them.
I will capture them like birds of
the air.
I will punish them,
just as I warned them I would.
¹³How terrible it will be for them!
They have wandered away
from me.
So they will be destroyed.
They have refused to obey me.
I long to save them.
But they tell lies about me.
¹⁴They do not cry out to me from
their hearts.
Instead, they just lie on their
beds and sob.
They cut themselves when they
pray to Baal
for grain and fresh wine.
So they turn away from me.
¹⁵I brought them up and made them
strong.
But they make evil plans against
me.
¹⁶I am the Most High God. But they
do not turn to me.
They are like a bow that does not
shoot straight.
Their leaders will be killed with
swords.
They will die because they have
spoken too proudly.
The people of Egypt
will make fun of them."

ISRAEL WILL HARVEST A WINDSTORM

8 The LORD said to me,

"Put a trumpet to your lips!
Give a warning to my people!
Assyria is like an eagle.
It is ready to attack my land.
My people have broken the
covenant I made with them.
They have refused to obey my
law.
²Israel shouts to me,
'We recognize you as our God!'
³But they have turned away from
what is good.
So an enemy will chase them.
⁴My people appoint kings I do not
want.

They choose princes without my
permission.
They use their silver and gold
to make statues of gods.
That is how they destroy
themselves."
⁵The LORD says, "People of Samaria,
throw out your god that looks
like a calf!
My anger burns against you.
How long will it be until you are
able
to remain faithful to me?
⁶Your calf is not God.
A skilled worker from Israel
made it.
But it will be broken to pieces."

⁷The LORD says,

"Worshiping other gods is like
worshiping the wind.
It is like planting worthless
seeds.
Assyria is like a windstorm.
That is all my people will harvest.
There are no heads of grain
on the stems that will come up.
So they will not produce any
flour.
Even if they did produce grain,
the Assyrians would eat all of it
up.
⁸So the people of Israel are
swallowed up.
Now they are like a worthless pot
to me
among the nations.
⁹They have gone up to Assyria for
help.
They are like a wild donkey
that wanders around by itself.
Ephraim's people have sold
themselves
to their Assyrian lovers.
¹⁰They have sold themselves to the
nations
to get their help.
But now I will gather them
together.
They will get weaker and weaker.
The mighty kings of Assyria will
crush them.

¹¹"Ephraim built many altars where
they sacrificed
sin offerings to other gods.
So their altars have become

places where they commit sin.
¹²I wrote down many things in my
    law for their good.
  But they considered my laws as
    something strange.
¹³They offer sacrifices to me.
  They eat the meat of the animals
    they bring.
  But I am not pleased with any of
    that.
  I will remember the evil things
    they have done.
  I will punish them for their sins.
  And they will return to Egypt.
¹⁴Israel has forgotten the One who
    made them.
  They have built palaces for
    themselves.
  Judah has built forts in many
    towns.
  But I will send fire down on their
    cities.
  It will burn up their forts."

ISRAEL WILL BE PUNISHED

9 Israel, don't be joyful.
  Don't be glad as the other
    nations are.
You haven't been faithful to your
    God.
  You love to get paid for being a
    prostitute.
  Your pay is the grain at every
    threshing floor.
²But soon there won't be any grain
    or wine to feed you.
  There won't even be any fresh
    wine.
³You won't remain in the LORD's
    land.
  Ephraim, you will return to Egypt.
  You will eat "unclean" food in
    Assyria.
⁴You won't pour out wine offerings
    to the LORD.
  Your sacrifices won't please him.
  They'll be like the bread people
    eat when someone dies.
  Everyone who eats those
    sacrifices will be "unclean."
  They themselves will have to eat
    that kind of food.
  They can't bring it into the LORD's
    temple.

⁵What will you do when your
    appointed feasts come?

What will you do on the LORD's
    special days?
⁶Some of you will escape without
    being destroyed.
  But you will die in Egypt.
  Your bodies will be buried at
    Memphis.
  Weeds will cover your treasures of
    silver.
  Thorns will grow up in your
    tents.
⁷The time when God will punish
    you is coming.
  The day when he will judge you
    is near.
  I want you to know that.
  You have committed many sins.
  And you hate me very much.
  That's why you think I'm foolish.
  You think I'm crazy.
  But the LORD speaks through me.
⁸People of Ephraim, I'm a true
    prophet.
  My God is warning you through
    me.
  But you set traps for me
    everywhere I go.
  You hate me so much
  you even wait for me in God's
    house.
⁹You have sunk very deep into sin,
  just as our people did at Gibeah
    long ago.
  God will remember the evil things
    you have done.
  He will punish you for your sins.

¹⁰The LORD says,

"When I first found Israel,
  it was like finding grapes in the
    desert.
When I saw your people long
    ago,
  it was like seeing the early fruit
    on a fig tree.
But then they went to Baal Peor.
  There they gave themselves to
    that shameful god Baal.
  They became as evil as the god
    they loved.
¹¹Ephraim's greatness and glory will
    be gone.
  It will fly away like a bird.
Women will no longer have
    children.
  They will not be able to get
    pregnant.

¹²But suppose they do have
children.
Then I will kill every one of them.
How terrible it will be for them
when I turn away from them!"

¹³Tyre is planted in a pleasant place.
And so is Ephraim.
But the Assyrians will kill
Ephraim's children.
¹⁴LORD, what should you do to
Ephraim's people?
Give them women whose babies
die before they are born.
Give them women whose breasts
don't have any milk.

¹⁵The LORD says,

"My people did many evil things
in Gilgal.
That is why I hated them there.
They committed many sins.
So I will drive them out of my
land.
I will not love them anymore.
All of their leaders refuse to obey
me.
¹⁶Ephraim is like a worthless plant.
Its roots are dried up.
It does not produce any fruit.
Suppose Ephraim's people have
children.
Then I will kill the children they
love so much."

¹⁷My God will turn his back on his
people.
They have not obeyed him.
So they will wander among other
nations.

10 Israel was like a
spreading vine.
They produced fruit for
themselves.
As they grew more fruit,
they built more altars.
As their land became richer,
they made the sacred stones they
worshiped more beautiful.
²Their hearts are dishonest.
So now they must pay for their
sins.
The LORD will tear their altars
down.
He'll destroy their sacred stones.

³Then they'll say, "We don't have a
king.

That's because we didn't have
any respect for the LORD.
But suppose we did have a king.
What could he do for us?"
⁴They make a lot of promises.
They make agreements among
themselves.
They take oaths they don't mean
to keep.
So court cases spring up
like poisonous weeds in a plowed
field.
⁵The people who live in Samaria
are filled with fear.
They are afraid their god that
looks like a calf
will be carried off from Bethel.
They will sob over it.
So will the priests who lead them
to worship it.
The priests were full of joy
because their statue was so
glorious.
But it will be captured
and taken far away from them.
⁶It will be carried off to Assyria.
The people of Ephraim will be
forced
to give it to the great king.
They will be dishonored.
Israel will be ashamed
that all they have left to worship
is a wooden god.
⁷Samaria's king will be carried off.
He will be like a twig floating
away in a river.
⁸The high places where Israel
worshiped other gods
will be destroyed.
That's where they sinned against
the LORD.
Thorns and weeds will grow up
there.
They will cover the altars.
Then the people will say to the
mountains, "Cover us!"
They'll say to the hills, "Fall
on us!"

⁹The LORD says,

"Israel, you have done evil
things
ever since your people sinned at
Gibeah long ago.
And you are still doing what is
evil.
War caught up

with those who sinned at
   Gibeah.
¹⁰ So I will punish you when I
   want to.
Nations will gather together to
   fight against you.
They will put you in chains
   because you have committed so
   many sins.
¹¹ Ephraim, you were like a well-
   trained young cow.
It loved to thresh grain.
I spared its pretty neck
   from pulling heavy loads.
But now I will make you do hard
   work.
Judah also must plow.
So all of the people of Jacob
   must break up the ground.
¹² Your hearts are as hard as a field
   that has not been plowed.
If you change your ways,
   you will produce good crops.
So plant the seeds of doing what is
   right.
   Then you will harvest the fruit of
      your faithful love.
It is time to turn to me.
   When you do, I will come
and shower my blessings
   on you.
¹³ But you have planted the seeds of
   doing what is wrong.
So you have harvested the fruit
   of your evil conduct.
You have had to eat the fruit of
   your lies.
You have trusted in your own
   strength.
   You have depended on your
      many soldiers.
¹⁴ But the roar of battle will come
   against you.
All of your forts will be
   completely destroyed.
It will happen just as Shalman
   destroyed Beth Arbel in a battle.
Mothers and their children
   were smashed on the ground.
¹⁵ People of Bethel, that will happen
   to you.
   You have committed far too
      many sins.
When the time for me to punish
   you comes,
   your king will be completely
      destroyed."

THE LORD LOVES ISRAEL

11

The LORD continues,

"When Israel was a young
     nation, I loved them.
I chose to bring my son out of
   Egypt.
² But the more I called out to Israel,
   the further they went away from
   me.
They brought sacrifices to the
   statues of the gods
   that were named after Baal.
And they burned incense to
   them.
³ I taught Israel to walk.
I took them up in my arms.
But they did not realize
   I was the one who took care of
   them.
⁴ I led them with kindness and love.
I did not lead them with ropes.
I lifted the heavy loads from their
   shoulders.
I bent down and fed them.

⁵ "But they refuse to turn away from
   their sins.
So they will return to Egypt.
And Assyria will rule over them.
⁶ Swords will flash in their cities.
The heavy metal bars on their
   gates will be destroyed.
Their plans will come to an end.
⁷ My people have made up their
   minds
   to turn away from me.
Even if they call out to me,
   I will certainly not honor them.
I am the Most High God."

⁸ The LORD continues,

"People of Ephraim, how can I give
     you up?
   Israel, how can I hand you over
     to your enemies?
Can I destroy you as I did the town
   of Admah?
   Can I treat you like Zeboiim?
My heart is stirred inside me.
   It is filled with pity for you.
⁹ My anger will not burn against you
   anymore.
   I will not completely destroy you.
After all, I am God.
   I am not a mere man.
I am the Holy One among you.

My burning anger will not come
    against you.
[10] I will roar like a lion against my
    enemies.
    You will follow me.
    When I roar, my children will
    come home trembling with
    fear.
    You will return from the west.
[11] You will come trembling like birds
    from Egypt.
    You will return like doves from
    Assyria.
    I will settle you again in your
    homes,"
    announces the LORD.

ISRAEL HAS SINNED

[12] The people of Ephraim tell
    nothing but lies.
    Israel has not been honest with
    me.
    And Judah continues to wander
    away from God.
    They have deserted the faithful
    Holy One.

12 [1] The people of Ephraim
    look to others for
    help.
    It's like chasing the wind.
    The wind they keep chasing
    is hot and dry.
    They tell more and more lies.

They are always hurting
    others.
    They make a peace treaty with
    Assyria.
    They send olive oil to Egypt to
    get help.
[2] The LORD is bringing charges
    against Judah.
    He will punish Jacob's people
    because of how they act.
    He'll pay them back
    for the evil things they've done.
[3] Even before Jacob was born,
    he was holding on to his
    brother's heel.
    When he became a man,
    he struggled with God.
[4] At Peniel he struggled with the
    angel and won.
    He sobbed and begged for his
    blessing.
    God also met with him at Bethel.
    He talked with him there.
[5] He is the LORD God who rules
    over all.
    He wants us to remember
    that his name is The LORD.
[6] People of Jacob, you must return
    to your God.
    You must hold on to love and do
    what is fair.
    You must trust in your God
    always.

KIDS' QUESTION

Why does God love people?

God loves us because that is what he decided to do. God does
not love us because we are good or nice. In fact no one could
ever be good enough to be worthy of God's love. God loves us
because it is his will. And he *is* love.
He promises that nothing
anywhere will ever make him
stop. He loves us so much
that he sent his son Jesus
to die for our sins.

checkout Hosea 11:8

Related verses:
John 3:16
Romans 8:38,39

⁷You are like a trader who uses
  dishonest scales.
  You love to cheat others.
⁸People of Ephraim, you brag,
  "We are very rich.
  We've become wealthy.
  And no one can prove we sinned
  to gain all of this wealth."

⁹The Lord says,

"I am the Lord your God.
  I brought you out of Egypt.
  But I will make you live in tents
  again.
  That is what you did when you
  celebrated
  the Feast of Booths in the desert.
¹⁰I spoke to the prophets.
  They saw many visions.
  I gave you warnings through
  them."

¹¹The people of Gilead are evil!
  They aren't worth anything!
  Gilgal's people sacrifice bulls to
  other gods.
  Their altars will become like piles
  of stones
  on a plowed field.
¹²Jacob ran away to the country of
  Aram.
  There Israel served Laban to get
  a wife.
  He took care of sheep to pay for
  her.
¹³The prophet Moses brought Israel
  up from Egypt.
  The Lord used him to take care
  of them.
¹⁴But Ephraim's people have made
  the Lord very angry.
  Their Lord will hold them
  accountable for the blood
  they've spilled.
  He'll pay them back for the
  shameful things they've done.

THE LORD IS ANGRY
WITH ISRAEL

13 When the tribe of
  Ephraim spoke,
  the other tribes
  trembled with fear.
  Ephraim was honored in Israel.
  But its people sinned by
  worshiping Baal.
  So they were as good as dead.

²Now they sin more and more.
  They use their silver
  to make statues of gods for
  themselves.
  The statues come from their own
  clever ideas.
  Skilled workers make all of them.
  The people pray to those gods.
  They offer human sacrifices to
  them.
  They kiss the gods that look like
  calves.
³So those people will vanish like
  the morning mist.
  They will soon disappear like the
  early dew.
  They will be like straw
  that the wind blows around on a
  threshing floor.
  They will be like smoke
  that escapes through a window.

⁴The Lord says,

"People of Israel, I am the Lord
  your God.
  I brought you out of Egypt.
  You must not recognize any God
  but me.
  You must not have any Savior
  except me.
⁵I took care of you in the desert.
  It was a land of burning heat.
⁶I fed you until you were satisfied.
  Then you became proud.
  You forgot all about me.
⁷So I will leap on you like a lion.
  I will hide and wait
  beside the road like a leopard.
⁸I will attack you like a bear
  that is robbed of her cubs.
  I will rip you wide open.
  Like a lion I will eat you up.
  Like a wild animal I will tear you
  apart.

⁹"Israel, you will be destroyed.
  I helped you. But you turned
  against me.
¹⁰Where is your king?
  Wasn't he supposed to save you?
  Where are the rulers in all of your
  towns?
  You said, 'Give us a king and
  princes.'
¹¹So I became angry and gave you a
  king.
  Then I took him away from you.

¹²Ephraim, your guilt is piling up.
    I am keeping a record of all of
        your sins.
¹³You will suffer pain like a woman
        having a baby.
    You are like a foolish child.
    It is time for you to be born.
    But you refuse to come out of
        your mother's body.

¹⁴"I will set you free from the power
        of the grave.
    I will save you from death.
    Death, where are your plagues?
    Grave, where is your power to
        destroy?

"Ephraim, I will no longer pity
        you.
¹⁵ Even though you are doing well
        among the other tribes,
    trouble will come to you.
    I will send a hot and dry wind
        from the east.
    It will blow in from the desert.
    Your springs will not have any
        water.
    Your wells will dry up.

All of your treasures
    will be taken out of your
        storerooms.
¹⁶People of Samaria, you must pay
        for your sins.
    You have refused to obey me.
    You will be killed with swords.
    Your little children will be
        smashed on the ground.
    Your pregnant women will be
        ripped wide open."

THE LORD BLESSES THOSE WHO TURN AWAY FROM SIN

14 Israel, return to the LORD
        your God.
    Your sins have destroyed
        you!
²Tell the LORD you are turning away
        from your sins.
    Return to him.
    Say to him,
    "Forgive us for all of our sins.
    Please be kind to us.
    Welcome us back to you.
    Then our lips will offer you our
        praise.

Why do people do wrong when they know that it's wrong?

People sin because of their sinful nature and because they forget about God. God created Adam and Eve perfect. But Adam and Eve sinned. They disobeyed God. You can read about it in Genesis 3:1–24. Sin came into the world the instant Adam and Eve disobeyed God. Since that time, everyone is born with a sinful nature. It seems *natural* to us to do what is wrong. It is not that everything we do is wrong. We can do good and make right choices too. But we find it natural and easy to make the wrong choices.

checkout Hosea 13:6

Related verses:
Isaiah 53:6;
Romans 3:11

³Assyria can't save us.
We won't trust in our war horses.
Our own hands have made statues
of gods.
But we will never call them our
gods again.
We are like children whose fathers
have died.
But you show us your tender
love."

⁴Then the LORD will answer,

"My people always wander away
from me.
But I will put an end to that.
My anger has turned away from
them.
Now I will love them freely.
⁵I will be like the dew to Israel.
They will bloom like a lily.
They will send their roots down
deep
like a cedar tree in Lebanon.
⁶They will spread out like new
branches.
They will be as beautiful as an
olive tree.

They will smell as sweet as the
cedar trees in Lebanon.
⁷Once again my people will live
in the safety of my shade.
They will grow like grain.
They will bloom like vines.
And they will be as famous
as wine from Lebanon.
⁸Ephraim will have nothing more to
do with other gods.
I will answer the prayers of my
people.
I will take good care of them.
I will be like a green pine tree to
them.
All of the fruit they bear will
come from me."

⁹If you are wise, you will realize
that what I've said is true.
If you have understanding,
you will know what it means.
The ways of the LORD are right.
People who are right with God
live the way he wants them to.
But those who refuse to obey
him trip and fall.

quest challenge

I Wonder . . .

How can I share what God has done for me?

Real Life Challenge

You encourage others when you tell them about what God is doing in
your life. Maybe you prayed that God would help you not to get mad
at your sister. The next time she borrows something without asking,
you handle it calmly instead of blowing up. When God teaches you
something or helps you, tell someone!

Quest Clue

Find Jeremiah 31 to see when God shares what he is going to do for
his people. Then look at Joel 1 for tips on passing it on.

Joel

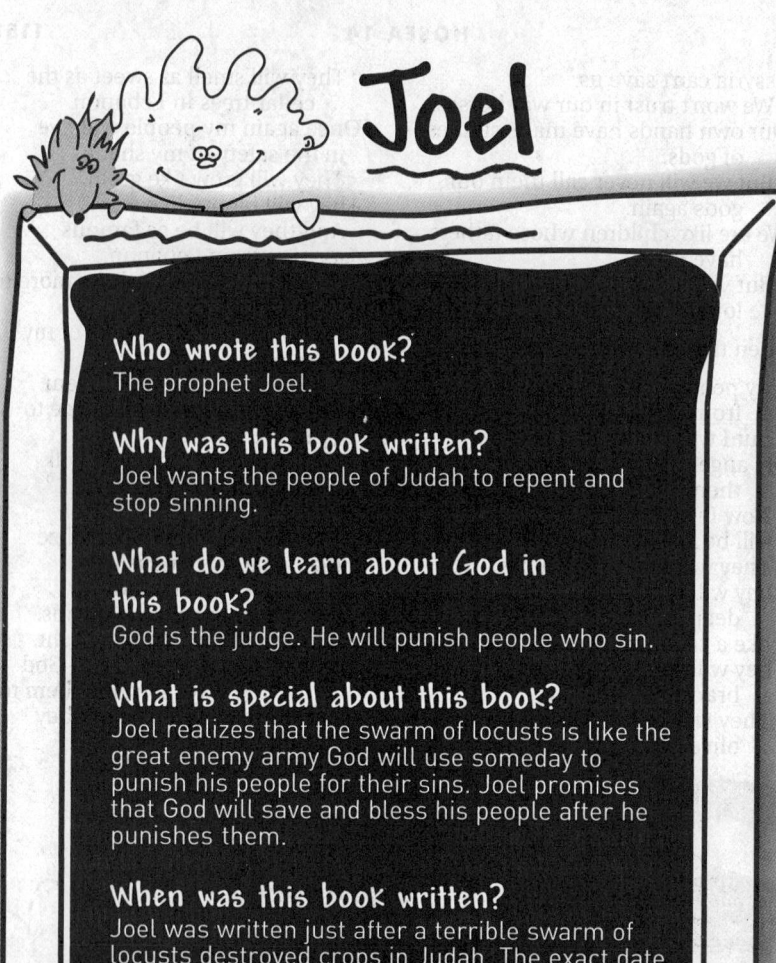

Who wrote this book?
The prophet Joel.

Why was this book written?
Joel wants the people of Judah to repent and stop sinning.

What do we learn about God in this book?
God is the judge. He will punish people who sin.

What is special about this book?
Joel realizes that the swarm of locusts is like the great enemy army God will use someday to punish his people for their sins. Joel promises that God will save and bless his people after he punishes them.

When was this book written?
Joel was written just after a terrible swarm of locusts destroyed crops in Judah. The exact date is not known.

1 A message came to Joel from the LORD. He was the son of Pethuel. Here is what Joel said.

LOCUSTS ATTACK THE LAND

² Elders, listen to me.
  Pay attention, all you who live in the land.
Has anything like this ever happened in your whole life?
  Did it ever happen to your people
  who lived long ago?
³ Tell your children about it.
  Let them tell their children.
And let their children tell it
  to those who live after them.
⁴ The giant locusts have eaten
  what the common locusts have left.
The young locusts have eaten
  what the giant locusts have left.
And other locusts have eaten
  what the young locusts have left.

⁵ Get up and sob, you people who drink too much!

Cry, all you who drink wine!
Cry because the fresh wine
   has been taken away from you.
⁶The locusts are like an army
   that has marched into our land.
There are so many of them
   they can't even be counted.
Their teeth are as sharp as a lion's
   teeth.
They are like the fangs of a
   female lion.
⁷The locusts have completely
   destroyed our vines.
They have wiped out our fig
   trees.
They've stripped off the bark and
   thrown it away.
They've left the branches bare.

⁸My people, sob like a virgin
   who is dressed in black clothes.
She is sad because she has lost
   the young man she was going to
   marry.
⁹No one brings grain offerings and
   drink offerings
   to the LORD's house anymore.
So the priests who serve the LORD
   are filled with sorrow.
¹⁰Our fields are wiped out.
   The ground is dried up.
The grain is destroyed.
   The fresh wine is gone.
And there isn't any more olive oil.
¹¹Farmers, be sad.
   Cry, you who grow vines.
Sob because the wheat and barley
   are gone.
The crops in the fields are
   destroyed.
¹²The vines and fig trees are dried up.
   The pomegranate, palm and
   apple trees
   don't have any fruit on them.
In fact, all of the trees in the fields
   are dried up.
And my people's joy has faded
   away.

TURN AWAY FROM SIN

¹³Priests, put on black clothes and
   sob.
Cry, you who serve at the altar.
Come, you who serve my God in
   the temple.
   Spend the night dressed in black
   clothes.

Sob because no one brings grain
   offerings and drink offerings
   to the house of your God
   anymore.
¹⁴Announce a holy fast.
   Tell the people not to eat
   anything.
   Gather them together for a
   special service.
Send for all of the elders
   who live in the land.
Have them come to the house of
   the LORD your God.
   And pray to him.

¹⁵The day of the LORD is near.
   How sad it will be on that day!
   The Mighty One is coming to
   destroy you.

¹⁶Our food has been taken away
   right in front of our eyes.
There isn't any joy or gladness
   in the house of our God.
¹⁷The seeds have dried up in the
   ground.
   The grain is also gone.
The storerooms have been
   destroyed.
   The barns are broken down.
¹⁸Listen to the cattle groan!
   The herds wander around.
They don't have any grass to eat.
   The flocks of sheep are also
   suffering.

¹⁹LORD, I call out to you.
   Fire has burned up the
   grasslands.
   Flames have destroyed all of the
   trees in the fields.
²⁰Even the wild animals cry out to
   you for help.
The streams of water have dried
   up.
Fire has burned up the
   grasslands.

THE LORD SENDS AN ARMY
OF LOCUSTS

2 Priests, blow the trumpets in
   Zion.
   Give a warning on my holy
   mountain.
Let everyone who lives in the land
   tremble with fear.
The day of the LORD is coming.
   It is very near.

²That day will be dark and sad.
  It will be black and cloudy.
A huge army of locusts is coming.
  They will spread across the
    mountains
  like the sun when it rises.
There has never been an army like
    it.
  And there will never be another
  for all time to come.

³Like fire they eat up everything in
    their path.
  Behind them it looks as if flames
    have burned the land.
In front of them the land is like the
    Garden of Eden.
  Behind them it is a dry and
    empty desert.
  Nothing escapes them.
⁴They look like horses.
  Like war horses they charge
    ahead.
⁵They sound like chariots as they
    leap over the mountaintops.
  They crackle like fire burning up
    dry weeds.
  They are like a mighty army
  that is ready for battle.

⁶When people see them, they
    tremble with fear.
  All of their faces turn pale.
⁷The locusts charge ahead like
    warriors.
  They climb over walls like
    soldiers.
  All of them march in line.
  They don't turn to the right or
    the left.
⁸They don't bump into one another.
  Each of them marches straight
    ahead.
  They charge through everything
    that tries to stop them.
  But they still stay in line.
⁹They attack a city.
  They run along its wall.
  They climb into houses.
  They enter through windows like
    robbers.
¹⁰As they march forward, the earth
    shakes.
  The sky trembles as they
    approach.
  The sun and moon grow dark.
  And the stars stop shining.

¹¹The LORD thunders with his
    mighty voice
  as he leads his army.
He has so many forces they can't
  even be counted.
  Those who obey his commands
    are great in number.
The day of the LORD is great and
    terrifying.
  Who can live through it?

LET YOUR HEARTS BE BROKEN

¹²The Lord announces to his people,

  "Return to me with all your heart.
    There is still time.
  Do not eat any food.
    Sob and cry."

¹³Don't just tear your clothes to
    show how sad you are.
  Let your hearts be broken.
Return to the LORD your God.
  He is gracious.
  He is tender and kind.
  He is slow to get angry.
  He is full of love.
  He takes pity on you.
  He won't destroy you.
¹⁴Who knows? He might turn toward
    you
  and have pity on you.
  He might even give you his
    blessing.
Then you can bring grain offerings
    and drink offerings
  to the LORD your God.

¹⁵Priests, blow the trumpets in Zion.
  Announce a holy fast.
Tell the people not to eat anything.
  Gather them together for a
    special service.
¹⁶Bring them together.
  Set all of them apart to me.
Bring together the elders.
  Gather the children and the
    babies
  who are still nursing.
Let the groom leave his bedroom.
  Let the bride leave their marriage
    bed.
¹⁷Let the priests who serve the LORD
    sob.
  Let them cry between the temple
    porch and the altar.
Let them say, "LORD, spare your
    people.

Don't let others make fun of
them.
Don't let the nations laugh at
them.
Don't let them tease your people
and say,
'Where is their God?' "

THE LORD ANSWERS THE PRAYER OF HIS PEOPLE

¹⁸ Then the LORD will show concern
for his land.
He will take pity on his people.

¹⁹ He will reply,

"I will send you grain, olive oil and
fresh wine.
It will be enough to satisfy you
completely.
I will never allow other nations
to make fun of you again.

²⁰ "I will drive far away from you
the army that comes from the
north.
I will send some of its forces
into a dry and empty land.
Those in front will be pushed into
the Dead Sea.
The ones in back will be driven
into the Mediterranean Sea.
Their dead bodies will give off a
bad smell."

The LORD has done great things.
²¹ Land, don't be afraid.
Be glad and full of joy.
The LORD has done great things.
²² Wild animals, don't be afraid.
The grasslands are turning green
again.
The trees are bearing their fruit.
The vines and fig trees are
producing rich crops.
²³ People of Zion, be glad.
Be joyful because of what the
LORD your God has done.
He has given you the right amount
of rain in the fall.
He has sent you plenty of
showers.
He has sent fall and spring rains
alike,
just as he did before.
²⁴ Your threshing floors will be
covered with grain.
Olive oil and fresh wine will spill
over

from the places where they are
stored.

²⁵ The LORD says,

"I sent a great army of locusts to
attack you.
They included common locusts,
giant locusts,
young locusts and other locusts.
I will make up for the years
they ate your crops.
²⁶ You will have plenty to eat.
It will satisfy you completely.
Then you will praise me.
I am the LORD your God.
I have done wonderful miracles
for you.
My people will never be put to
shame again.
²⁷ You will know that I am with you
in Israel.
I am the LORD your God.
There is no other God.
So my people will never be put to
shame again.

THE DAY OF THE LORD IS COMING

²⁸ "After that, I will pour out my
Spirit on all people.
Your sons and daughters will
prophesy.
Your old men will have dreams.
Your young men will have
visions.
²⁹ In those days I will pour out my
Spirit
on those who serve me, men and
women alike.
³⁰ I will show wonders in the heavens
and on the earth.
There will be blood and fire and
clouds of smoke.
³¹ The sun will become dark.
The moon will turn red like
blood.
It will happen before the great
and terrible day of the LORD
comes.
³² Everyone who calls out to me will
be saved.
On Mount Zion and in
Jerusalem
some of my people will be left
alive.
I have chosen them.
That is what I have promised.

THE LORD JUDGES THE NATIONS

3 "At that time I will bless Judah and Jerusalem
with great success again.
²I will gather all of the nations together.
I will bring them down to the Valley of Jehoshaphat.
There I will judge them.
I will punish them for what they have done
to my people Israel.
They scattered them among the nations.
They divided up my land among themselves.
³They cast lots for my people.
They sold boys into slavery to get prostitutes.
They sold girls to buy some wine to drink.

⁴"Tyre and Sidon, why are you doing things like that to me? And why are you doing them, all of you people in Philistia? Are you trying to get even with me for something I have done? If you are, I will pay you back for it in a quick and speedy way. ⁵You took my silver and gold. You carried off my finest treasures to your temples. ⁶You sold the people of Judah and Jerusalem to the Greeks. You wanted to send them far away from their own country.

⁷"But now I will stir them up into action. I will bring them back from the places you sold them to. And I will do to you what you did to them. ⁸I will sell your sons and daughters to the people of Judah. And they will sell them to the Sabeans far away." The LORD has spoken.

⁹Announce this among the nations.
Tell them to prepare for battle.
Nations, get your soldiers ready!
Bring all of your fighting men together
and march out to attack.
¹⁰Hammer your plows into swords.
Hammer your pruning tools into spears.
Let those who are weak say,
"We are soldiers!"
¹¹Come quickly, all of you surrounding nations.

Gather together in the Valley of Jehoshaphat.

LORD, send your soldiers down from heaven!

¹²The LORD says,

"Stir up the nations into action!
Let them march into the valley where I will judge them.
I will take my seat in court.
I will judge all of the surrounding nations.
¹³My soldiers, swing your sickles.
The nations are ripe for harvest.
Come. Stomp on them as if they were grapes.
Crush them until the winepress of my anger is full.
Do it until the wine spills over from the places where it is stored.
The nations have committed far too many sins!"

¹⁴Huge numbers of soldiers are gathered in the valley
where the LORD will hand down his sentence.
The day of the LORD is near in that valley.
¹⁵The sun and moon will become dark.
The stars won't shine anymore.
¹⁶The LORD will roar like a lion from Jerusalem.
His voice will sound like thunder from Zion.
The earth and sky will tremble.
But the LORD will keep the people of Israel safe.
He will be a place of safety for them.

THE LORD BLESSES HIS PEOPLE

¹⁷The LORD says,

"You will know that I am the LORD your God.
I live in Zion.
It is my holy mountain.
Jerusalem will be my holy city.
People from other lands will never attack it again.
¹⁸"At that time fresh wine will drip from the mountains.

Milk will flow down from the
　hills.
Water will run through all of
　Judah's valleys.
A fountain will flow out of my
　temple.
It will water the places where
　acacia trees grow.
[19] But Egypt will be deserted.
　Edom will become a dry and
　　empty desert.
They did terrible harm to the
　people of Judah.

My people were not guilty of
　doing anything wrong.
But Egypt and Edom spilled their
　blood anyway.
[20] My people will live in Judah and
　Jerusalem forever.
The land will be their home for
　all time to come.
[21] Egypt and Edom have spilled my
　people's blood.
I will punish them for it."

　The LORD lives in Zion!

quest challenge

I Wonder . . .

How can I have hope when bad things happen?

Real Life Challenge

Have you ever lost a friend? That can be really painful. For awhile you might really miss that person and wonder if a new friend could ever be as good. But God gives us a reason to have hope—we are not alone. He is always with us.

Quest Clue

Psalm 42 will encourage you when you feel down. Joel 2 and 3 will show you what God promised his people after they went through a hard time. Finally, Romans 8 will give you hope in any situation.

I Wonder . . .

What does it mean to follow God in everyday life?

Real Life Challenge

When you and another classmate have a disagreement, it's tempting to want your own way. But think differently. God asks us to be fair and kind to others. He can help you find a way to work out your disagreement in a way that works for both of you.

Quest Clue

Take a look at Amos 5 to see how God wants you to live every day. Then look at Romans 12 for more encouragement to live in a way that pleases God.

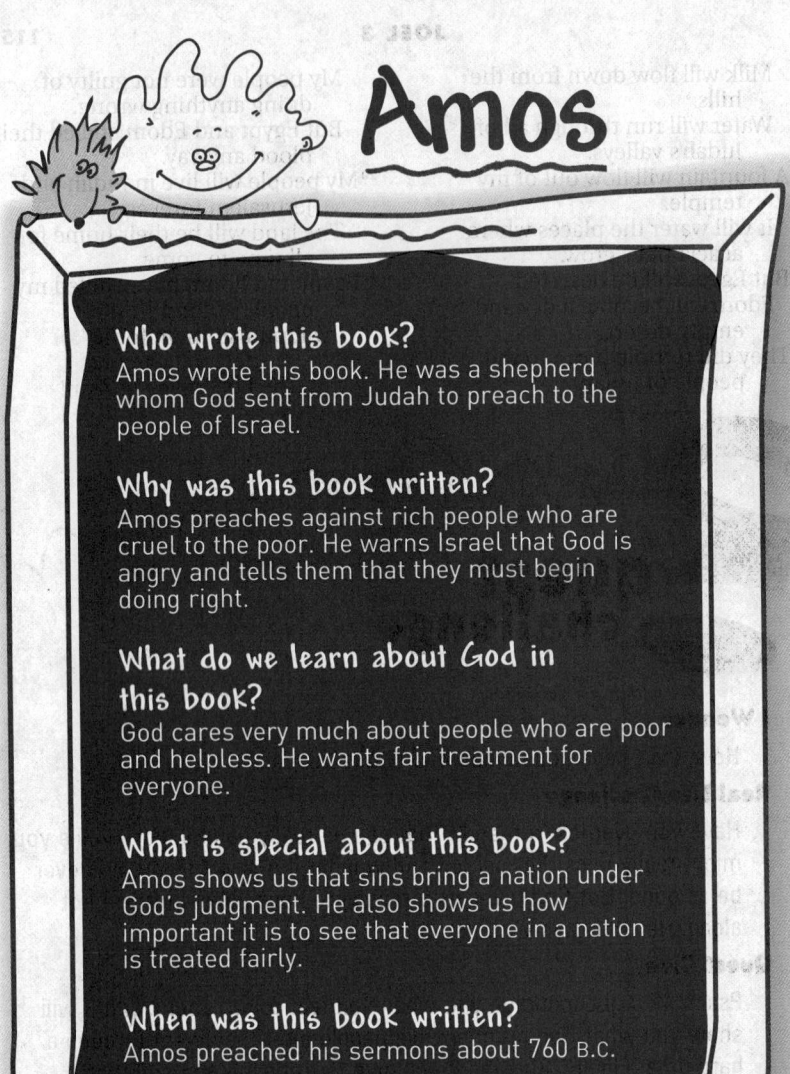

Amos

Who wrote this book?
Amos wrote this book. He was a shepherd whom God sent from Judah to preach to the people of Israel.

Why was this book written?
Amos preaches against rich people who are cruel to the poor. He warns Israel that God is angry and tells them that they must begin doing right.

What do we learn about God in this book?
God cares very much about people who are poor and helpless. He wants fair treatment for everyone.

What is special about this book?
Amos shows us that sins bring a nation under God's judgment. He also shows us how important it is to see that everyone in a nation is treated fairly.

When was this book written?
Amos preached his sermons about 760 B.C.

1 These are the words of Amos. He was a shepherd from the town of Tekoa. Here is the vision he saw concerning Israel. It came to him two years before the earthquake. At that time Uzziah was king of Judah. Jeroboam was king of Israel. He was the son of Jehoash. Here are the words of Amos.

²I said,

"The LORD roars like a lion from Jerusalem.

His voice sounds like thunder from Zion.
The grasslands of the shepherds turn brown.
The top of Mount Carmel dries up."

THE LORD PUNISHES ISRAEL'S NEIGHBORS

³The LORD says,

"The people of Damascus have sinned again and again.

So I will punish them.
They used threshing sleds with
  iron teeth
to crush Gilead's people.
⁴ So I will send fire to destroy the
  palace of King Hazael.
It will burn up the forts of his son
  Ben-Hadad.
⁵ I will break down the city gate of
  Damascus.
I will cut off the king
who lives in the Valley of Aven.
He holds the ruler's rod in Beth
  Eden.
The people of Aram will be taken
  away to Kir as prisoners,"
  says the LORD.

⁶ The LORD says,

"The people of Gaza have sinned
  again and again.
So I will punish them.
They captured whole
  communities.
They sold them to Edom.
⁷ So I will send fire to destroy the
  walls of Gaza.
It will burn up its forts.
⁸ I will cut off the king of Ashdod.
He holds the ruler's rod in
  Ashkelon.
I will use my powerful hand
  against Ekron.
Every single Philistine will die,"
  says the LORD and King.

⁹ The LORD says,

"The people of Tyre have sinned
  again and again.
So I will punish them.
They captured whole
  communities.
They sold them to Edom.
They did not honor the treaty
of friendship they had made.
¹⁰ So I will send fire to destroy the
  walls of Tyre.
It will burn up its forts."

¹¹ The LORD says,

"The people of Edom have sinned
  again and again.
So I will punish them.
They chased Israel with swords
that were ready to strike them
  down.
They did not show them any pity.

They were angry all the time.
Their anger blazed out.
It could not be stopped.
¹² So I will send fire to destroy the
  city of Teman.
It will burn up Bozrah's forts."

¹³ The LORD says,

"The people of Ammon have
  sinned again and again.
So I will punish them.
They ripped open the pregnant
  women in Gilead.
They wanted to add land to their
  territory.
¹⁴ So I will set fire to destroy the
  walls of Rabbah.
It will burn up its forts.
War cries will be heard on that day
  of battle.
Strong winds will blow on that
  stormy day.
¹⁵ Ammon's god Molech will be
  carried away.
So will its officials,"
  says the LORD.

2 The LORD says,

"The people of Moab have
  sinned again and again.
So I will punish them.
They burned the bones
of Edom's king to ashes.
² So I will send fire to destroy Moab.
It will burn up Kerioth's forts.
Moab will come crashing down
  with a loud noise.
War cries will be heard.
So will the blast of trumpets.
³ I will cut off Moab's ruler.
I will also kill all of its officials,"
  says the LORD.

⁴ The LORD says,

"The people of Judah have sinned
  again and again.
So I will punish them.
They have refused to obey my law.
They have not kept my rules.
Other gods have led them down
  the wrong path.
Their people before them
  worshiped those gods.
⁵ So I will send fire to destroy Judah.
It will burn up Jerusalem's forts."

THE LORD PUNISHES ISRAEL

⁶The LORD says,

"The people of Israel have sinned
  again and again.
So I will punish them.
They sell into slavery those who
  do what is right.
They trade needy people
  for a mere pair of sandals.
⁷They grind the heads of the poor
  into the dust of the ground.
They refuse to be fair to those
  who are crushed.
A father and his son have sex with
  the same girl.
They treat my name as if it were
  not holy.
⁸They lie down beside every altar
  on clothes they had taken
  until the owner paid back what
  was owed.
In the house of their God
  they drink wine that was taken as
  fines.

⁹"I destroyed the Amorites to make
  room
  for my people in the land.
The Amorites were as tall as cedar
  trees.
  They were as strong as oak trees.
But I cut off their fruit above the
  ground
  and their roots below it.

¹⁰"People of Israel, I brought you up
  out of Egypt.
I led you in the desert for 40 years.
I gave you the land of the
  Amorites.
¹¹I raised up prophets from among
  your children.
I also set some of your young
  people apart to me as
  Nazirites.
Isn't that true, people of Israel?"
              announces the LORD.
¹²"But you made the Nazirites drink
  wine.
You commanded the prophets
  not to prophesy.

¹³"A cart that is loaded with grain
  crushes anything it runs over.
In the same way, I will crush you.
¹⁴Your fastest runners will not
  escape.

The strongest people will not get
  away.
Even soldiers will not be able
  to save their own lives.
¹⁵Men who are armed with bows will
  lose the battle.
Soldiers who are quick on their
  feet will not escape.
Horsemen will not be able
  to save their own lives.
¹⁶Even your bravest soldiers
  will run away naked on that day,"
              announces the LORD.

THE LORD JUDGES HIS CHOSEN PEOPLE

3 People of Israel, listen to the
LORD's message. It is against
you. It is against the whole
family he brought up out of Egypt. He
says,

²"Out of all of the families on earth
  I have chosen only you.
So I will punish you
  because you have committed so
  many sins."

³Do two people walk together
  unless they've agreed to do so?
⁴Does a lion roar in the bushes
  when it doesn't have any food?
Does it growl in its den
  when it hasn't caught anything?
⁵Does a bird fall into a trap on the
  ground
  where no one has set a trap for it?
Does a net spring up from the
  earth
  when there isn't anything for it to
  catch?
⁶When someone blows a trumpet
  in a city,
  don't the people tremble with
  fear?
When trouble comes to a city,
  hasn't the LORD caused it?

⁷The LORD and King never does
  anything
  without telling his servants the
  prophets about it.

⁸A lion has roared.
  Who isn't afraid?
The LORD and King has spoken.
  Who can do anything but
  prophesy?

⁹Speak to the people in the forts of
    Ashdod and Egypt.
Tell them, "Gather together
    on the mountains of Samaria.
Look at the great trouble in that
    city.
Its people are committing many
    crimes."

¹⁰"They do not know how to do
    what is right,"
    announces the LORD.
    "They pile up stolen goods in
    their forts."

¹¹So the LORD and King says,

"Enemies will take over your land.
    They will pull down your places
    of safety.
    They will rob your forts."

¹²The LORD says,

"Suppose a shepherd saves only
    two leg bones
    from a lion's mouth.
Or he might save only a piece of
    an ear.
    That is how the Israelites will be
    saved.
They sit in Samaria
    on the edge of their beds.

They lie down in Damascus
    on their couches."

¹³"Listen to me," announces the
LORD. "Witness against the people of
Jacob," says the LORD God who rules
over all.

¹⁴"I will punish Israel for their sins.
    When I do, I will destroy their
    altars at Bethel.
The horns that stick out from the
    upper corners
    of their main altar will be cut off.
    They will fall to the ground.
¹⁵I will tear their winter houses down.
    I will also pull down their
    summer houses.
The houses they have decorated
    with ivory will be destroyed.
And their princely houses will be
    torn down,"
                announces the LORD.

ISRAEL HAS NOT RETURNED TO THE LORD

4 Listen to the LORD's message,
    you women who live on the hill
    of Samaria.
You treat poor people badly.
You crush those who are in need.

Were there any crimes in the Bible?

KIDS' QUESTION

Yes, many of them. Crime has been in the world ever since
Adam and Eve first sinned against God. Noah built an ark
because there was so much crime. God sent the prophet Amos because
there was so much crime. Jesus died because there was so much crime.
Many stories in the Bible tell about a crime and its results. People do
crimes because of sin. That is why God sent Jesus. Only Jesus can
take away our sins. Only Jesus can help
us stop doing crimes and start
obeying God. If everyone
followed Jesus, there
would be a lot less crime
in the world.

checkout Amos 3:9

Related verses:
Genesis 6:1–11;
Luke 23:38–43

You say to your husbands,
    "Bring us some drinks!"
But you are already as fat
    as the cows in Bashan.
² The LORD and King has taken an
    oath
    in his own holy name.
He says, "You can be sure
    that the time will come
when your enemies will put hooks
    in your faces.
    They will lead every one of you
    away with fishhooks.
³ Each of you will go straight out
    through a gap in the wall.
You will be thrown out of the city
    on the hill where you crush
    others,"
               announces the LORD.
⁴ "People of Samaria, go to Bethel
    and sin!
    Go to Gilgal! Sin there even more!
Bring your sacrifices every
    morning.
    Every third year, bring a tenth
    of everything you produce.
⁵ Bake some bread with yeast.
    Burn it as a thank offering.
Brag about the offerings you freely
    give.
    That is what you Israelites love to
    do,"
               announces the LORD
                    and King.

⁶ "I made sure your stomachs were
    empty in every city.
You did not have enough bread
    in any of your towns.
In spite of that, you still have not
    returned to me,"
               announces the LORD.

⁷ "I also held rain back from you.
    The time to harvest crops
    was still three months away.
I sent rain on one town.
    But I held it back from another.
One field had rain.
    Another did not. So it dried up.
⁸ People wandered from town to
    town to look for water.
But they did not get enough to
    drink.
In spite of that, you still have not
    returned to me,"
               announces the LORD.

⁹ "Many times I struck your gardens
    and vineyards.
I sent hot winds to dry them up
    completely.
Locusts ate up your fig and olive
    trees.
In spite of that, you still have not
    returned to me,"
               announces the LORD.
¹⁰ "I sent plagues on you,
    just as I did on Egypt.
I killed your young men with
    swords.
I also let the horses you had
    captured be killed.
I filled your noses with the bad
    smell of your camps.
In spite of that, you still have not
    returned to me,"
               announces the LORD.
¹¹ "I destroyed some of you,
    just as I did Sodom and
    Gomorrah.
You were like a burning stick that
    was pulled out of the fire.
In spite of that, you still have not
    returned to me,"
               announces the LORD.
¹² "People of Israel, I will punish you.
Because I will do that to you,
    prepare to meet your God!"
¹³ The LORD forms the mountains.
    He creates the wind.
He makes his thoughts known to
    human beings.
He turns sunrise into darkness.
He rules over the highest places
    on earth.
His name is The LORD God Who
    Rules Over All.

LOOK TO THE LORD AND LIVE

5 People of Israel, listen to the
LORD's message. Hear my song
of sadness about you. I say,

² "The people of Israel have fallen.
    They will never get up again.
They are deserted in their own
    land.
    No one can lift them up."

³ The LORD and King says,

"A thousand soldiers will march
    out from a city in Israel.

But only a hundred will return.
A hundred soldiers will march out
    from a town.
But only ten will come back."

[4] The LORD speaks to the people of
Israel. He says,

"Look to me and live.
[5]   Do not look to Bethel.
Do not go to Gilgal.
Do not travel to Beersheba.
The people of Gilgal will be taken
    away as prisoners.
Nothing will be left of Bethel."

[6] Israel, look to the LORD and live.
If you don't, he will sweep
    through
    the people of Joseph like a fire.
It will burn everything up.
And Bethel won't have anyone to
    put it out.

[7] You turn what is fair into
    something bitter.

What is right you throw down to
    the ground.
[8] The LORD made the Pleiades and
    Orion.
He turns darkness into sunrise.
He makes the day fade into
    night.
He sends for the waters in the
    clouds.
Then he pours them out on the
    surface of the land.
His name is The LORD.
[9] He destroys places of safety.
He tears down cities
that have high walls around
    them.
[10] Israel, you hate those who do what
    is right in court.
You can't stand those who tell the
    truth.

[11] You walk all over poor people.
You make them give you grain.
You have built stone houses.

Why do we give flowers after someone has died?

Many people bring flowers to funerals and gravesides or send them to the families of people who have died. This is to show respect and to show that they miss the person. It is also to honor the family of the person who has died and to let them know that the person giving the flowers is sorry about their loss. Flowers also remind us of life. If the person who died was a Christian, the flowers remind the person's family that their loved one is enjoying new life in heaven. God wants us to show respect for the dead.

Amos 5:1 talks about God's song of sadness about the people of Israel who have fallen and will never get up again. Even though these people have not died, their lives have been crushed because of the wrong choices which they have made. God cares about all people and is sad when people are hurting or die. Jesus even cried at the funeral of his friend Lazarus.

checkout
Amos 5:1,2

Related verses:
Romans 12:15;
1 Peter 2:17

But you won't live in them.
You have planted fruitful
    vineyards.
But you won't drink the wine
    they produce.
¹² I know how many crimes you have
    committed.
You have sinned far too much.

You crush those who do what is
    right.
You accept money from people
    who want special favors.
You take away the rights of poor
    people in the courts.
¹³ So those who are wise keep quiet
    in times like these.
That's because the times are evil.

¹⁴ Look to what is good, not to what
    is evil.
Then you will live.
And the LORD God who rules over
    all
will be with you,
    just as you say he is.
¹⁵ Hate what is evil. Love what is
    good.
Do what is fair in the courts.
Perhaps the LORD God who rules
    over all
will show you his favor.
After all, you are the only ones left
    in the family line of Joseph.

¹⁶ The LORD God rules over all. The
Lord says,

"People will sob in all of the
    streets.
They will be very sad in every
    market place.
Even farmers will be told to cry
    loudly.
People will sob over the dead.
¹⁷ Workers will cry in all of the
    vineyards.
That is because I will punish
    you,"

                says the LORD.

THE DAY OF THE LORD IS COMING

¹⁸ How terrible it will be for you
    who long for the day of the LORD!
Why do you want it to come?
    That day will be dark, not light.
¹⁹ It will be like a man running away
    from a lion

only to meet a bear.
He enters his house and rests his
    hand on a wall
only to be bitten by a snake.
²⁰ The day of the LORD will be dark,
    not light.
It will be very black.
There won't be a ray of sunlight
    anywhere.

²¹ The LORD says,

"I hate your holy feasts.
I can't stand them.
I hate it when you gather
    together.
²² You bring me burnt offerings and
    grain offerings.
But I will not accept them.
You bring your best friendship
    offerings.
But I will not even look at them.
²³ Take the noise of your songs away!
I will not listen to the music of
    your harps.
²⁴ I want you to treat others fairly.
So let fair treatment roll on
    just as a river does!
Always do what is right.
Let right living flow along
    like a stream that never runs dry!

²⁵ "People of Israel, did you bring me
    sacrifices and offerings
for 40 years in the desert?
²⁶ Yes. But you have honored the place
    where your king worshiped other
    gods.
You have carried the stands
    the statues of your gods were on.
You have lifted up the banners
    of the stars you worship as gods.
You made all of those things for
    yourselves.
²⁷ So I will send you away
    as prisoners beyond Damascus,"
says the LORD.
His name is God Who Rules Over
    All.

THE LORD JUDGES ISRAEL'S PRIDE

6 How terrible it will be for you
    men
who are so contented on
    Mount Zion!
How terrible for you who feel
    secure

on the hill of Samaria!
You are famous men from the
   greatest nation.
The people of Israel come to you
   for help and advice.
²Go to the city of Calneh. Look at it.
Go from there to the great city of
   Hamath.
Then go down to Gath in
   Philistia.
Are those places better off than
   your two kingdoms?
Is their land larger than yours?
³You are trying to avoid the time
   when trouble will come.
But you are only bringing closer
   the Assyrian rule of terror.
⁴You lie down on beds
   that are decorated with ivory.
You rest on your couches.
You eat the best lambs
   and the fattest calves.
⁵You pluck away on your harps as
   David did.
You play new songs on musical
   instruments.
⁶You drink wine by the bowlful.
You use the finest lotions.
But Joseph's people will soon be
   destroyed.
And you aren't even sad about it.
⁷So you will be among the first
   to be taken away as prisoners.
You won't be able to enjoy good
   food.
You won't lie around on couches
   anymore.

⁸The LORD and King has taken an
oath in his own name. He is the LORD
God who rules over all. He announces,

"I hate the pride of Jacob's people.
I can't stand their forts.
I will hand the city of Samaria
   and everything in it over to their
   enemies."

⁹Ten men might be left in one house.
If they are, they will die there. ¹⁰Relatives might come to burn the dead
bodies. If they do, they'll have to carry
them out of the house first. They
might ask someone still hiding there,
"Is anyone here with you?" If the answer is no, the relatives will say, "Be
quiet! We must not pray in the LORD's
name."

¹¹The LORD has already given an
   order.
He will smash large houses to
   pieces.
He will crush small houses to
   bits.
¹²Horses don't run on rocky ground.
People don't plow there with
   oxen.
But you have turned fair treatment
   into poison.
You have turned the fruit of right
   living into bitterness.
¹³You are happy because you
   captured the town of Lo
   Debar.
You say, "We were strong enough
   to take Karnaim too."
¹⁴But the LORD God rules over all.
He announces, "People of
   Israel,
I will stir up a nation against you.
They will crush you from Lebo
   Hamath
all the way down to the Arabah
   Valley."

THE LORD GIVES AMOS THREE VISIONS

7 The LORD and King gave me a
vision. He was bringing large
numbers of locusts on the land.
The king's share of the first crop had
already been harvested. Now the second crop was coming up. ²The locusts
stripped the land clean. Then I cried
out, "LORD and King, forgive Israel!
How can Jacob's people continue?
They are such a weak nation!"
³So the LORD had pity on them.
"I will let them continue for now," he
said.
⁴The LORD and King gave me a second vision. He was using fire to punish
his people. It dried up the deep waters.
It burned the land up. ⁵Then I cried
out, "LORD and King, please stop! How
can Jacob's people continue? They are
such a weak nation!"
⁶So the LORD had pity on them.
"I will let them continue for now,"
the LORD and King said.
⁷Then the Lord gave me a third vision. He was standing by a wall. It had
been built very straight, all the way up

and down. He was holding a plumb line. [8]The LORD asked me, "What do you see, Amos?"

"A plumb line," I replied.

Then the Lord said, "Look at what I am doing. I am hanging a plumb line next to my people Israel. It will show how crooked they are. I will no longer spare them.

[9] "The high places where Isaac's
    people worship other gods
    will be destroyed.
The other places of worship in
    Israel will also be torn down.
I will use my sword
    to attack Jeroboam's royal
    family."

AMAZIAH TELLS AMOS TO STOP PROPHESYING

[10]Amaziah was priest of Bethel. He sent a message to Jeroboam, the king of Israel. He said, "Amos is making evil plans against you right here in Israel. The people in the land can't stand to listen to what he's saying. [11]Amos is telling them,

" 'Jeroboam will be killed with a
    sword.
The people of Israel will be taken
    away as prisoners.
They will be carried off from
    their own land.' "

[12]Then Amaziah said to Amos, "Get out of Israel, you prophet! Go back to the land of Judah. Earn your living there. Do your prophesying there. [13]Don't prophesy here at Bethel anymore. This is where the king worships. The main temple in the kingdom is located here."

[14]Amos answered Amaziah, "I was not a prophet. I wasn't even a prophet's son. I was a shepherd. I also took care of sycamore-fig trees. [15]But the LORD took me away from taking care of the flock. He said to me, 'Go. Prophesy to my people Israel.' [16]Now then, listen to the LORD's message. You say,

" 'Don't prophesy against Israel.
Stop preaching against the
    people of Isaac.'

[17]"But the LORD says,

" 'Your wife will become a
    prostitute
    in the city of Bethel.
Your sons and daughters will be
    killed with swords.
Your land will be measured and
    divided up.
And you yourself will die in
    another country.
The people of Israel will be taken
    away as prisoners.
They will be carried off from
    their own land.' "

THE LORD GIVES AMOS ANOTHER VISION

8 The LORD and King gave me a vision. He showed me a basket of ripe fruit. [2]"What do you see, Amos?" he asked.

"A basket of ripe fruit," I replied.

Then the LORD said to me, "The time is ripe for my people Israel. I will no longer spare them.

[3]"The time is coming when the songs in the temple will turn to crying," announces the LORD and King. "Many, many bodies will be thrown everywhere! So be quiet!"

[4]Listen to me, you who walk all
    over needy people.
You crush those who are poor in
    the land.

[5]You say,

"When will the New Moon Feast
    be over?
Then we can sell our grain.
When will the Sabbath day come
    to an end?
Then people can buy our
    wheat."
But you don't measure out the
    right amount.
You raise your prices.
You cheat others by using
    dishonest scales.
[6]You buy poor people to make
    slaves out of them.
You buy those who are in need
    for a mere pair of sandals.
You even sell the worthless parts
    of your wheat.

[7]People of Jacob, you are proud that the LORD is your God. But he has taken an oath in his own name. He says, "I

will never forget anything Israel has done.

8 "The land will tremble because of
  what will happen.
  Everyone who lives in it will sob.
So the whole land will rise like the
  Nile River.
  It will be stirred up.
Then it will settle back down again
  like that river in Egypt."

9 The LORD and King announces,

"At that time I will make the sun go
  down at noon.
  The earth will become dark in
  the middle of the day.
10 I will turn your holy feasts into
  times for sobbing.
  I will turn all of your songs into
  crying.
You will have to wear black clothes.
  You will shave your heads.
I will make you sob as if your only
  son had died.
  The end of that time will be like a
  bitter day."

11 The LORD and King announces,

"The days are coming
  when I will send hunger through
  the land.
But people will not be hungry for
  food.
  They will not be thirsty for water.
Instead, they will be hungry
  to hear a message from me.
12 People will wander from the Dead
  Sea to the Mediterranean.
  They will travel from north to east.
They will look for a message from
  me.
  But they will not find it.

13 "At that time

"the lovely young women and
  strong young men
  will faint because they are so
  thirsty.
14 Some people take oaths in the
  name
  of Samaria's shameful god.
Others say, 'People of Dan, you
  can be sure
  that your god is alive.'
Still others say, 'You can be sure
  that Beersheba's god is alive.'

But all of those people will fall
  dead.
  They will never get up again."

THE LORD GIVES AMOS A FINAL VISION

9 I saw the Lord standing next to
  the altar in the temple. He said
  to me,

"Strike the tops of the temple
  pillars.
  Then the heavy stones at the
  base of the entrance will
  shake.
Bring everything down on the
  heads of everyone there.
  I will kill with my swords
  those who are left alive.
Not one of them will escape.
  None will get away.
2 They might dig down to the
  deepest parts of the grave.
  But my powerful hand will take
  them out of there.
They might climb up to the
  heavens.
  But I will bring them down from
  there.
3 They might hide on top of Mount
  Carmel.
  But I will hunt them down
  and grab hold of them.
They might hide from me at the
  bottom of the ocean.
  But I will command the serpent
  to bite them.
4 Their enemies might take them
  away
  as prisoners to another country.
But I will command their enemies
  to kill them with their swords.
I will turn my eyes toward them to
  harm them.
  I will not help them."

5 The LORD rules over all.
  The Lord touches the earth, and
  it melts.
  Everyone who lives in it sobs.
The whole land rises like the Nile
  River.
  Then it settles back down again
  like that river in Egypt.
6 The LORD builds his palace high in
  the heavens.
  He lays its foundation on the
  earth.

He sends for the waters in the
   clouds.
Then he pours them out on the
   surface of the land.
His name is The LORD.

7 "You Israelites are just like
   the people of Cush to me,"
      announces the LORD.
"I brought Israel up from Egypt.
I also brought the Philistines
   from Crete
and the Arameans from Kir.

8 "I am the LORD and King.
   My eyes are watching the sinful
     kingdom of Israel.
I will wipe it off the face of the
   earth.
   But I will not totally destroy the
     people of Jacob,"
      announces the LORD.
9 "I will give an order.
   I will shake the people of Israel
     among all of the nations.
They will be like grain that is
   shaken through a screen.
Not a pebble will fall to the
   ground.
10 All of the sinners among my
   people
will be killed with swords.
They say, 'Nothing bad will ever
   happen to us.'

ISRAEL WILL BE MADE LIKE NEW AGAIN

11 "The time will come when I will
   rebuild
David's fallen tent.
I will repair its broken places.

I will rebuild what was destroyed.
I will make it what it used to be.
12 Then my people will take control
   of those
   who are left alive in Edom.
They will also possess all of the
   nations
   that belong to me,"
      announces the LORD.
He will do all of those things.

13 "A new day is coming," announces
the LORD.

"At that time those who plow the
   land
   will catch up with those who
     harvest the crops.
Those who stomp on grapes
   will catch up with those who
     plant the vines.
Fresh wine will drip from the
   mountains.
   It will flow down from all of the
     hills.
14 I will bring my people Israel back
   home.
I will bless them with great
   success again.
They will rebuild the destroyed
   cities and live in them.
They will plant vineyards and
   drink the wine they produce.
They will make gardens and eat
   their fruit.
15 I will plant Israel in their own land.
They will never again be
   removed
from the land I have given
   them,"

      says the LORD your God.

Quest Clue

The book of Amos predicts a lot of scary events. But
chapter 5 gives some good instructions on how to live
your life each day. To learn more about this, take the Quest
Challenge at the end of Joel.

Obadiah

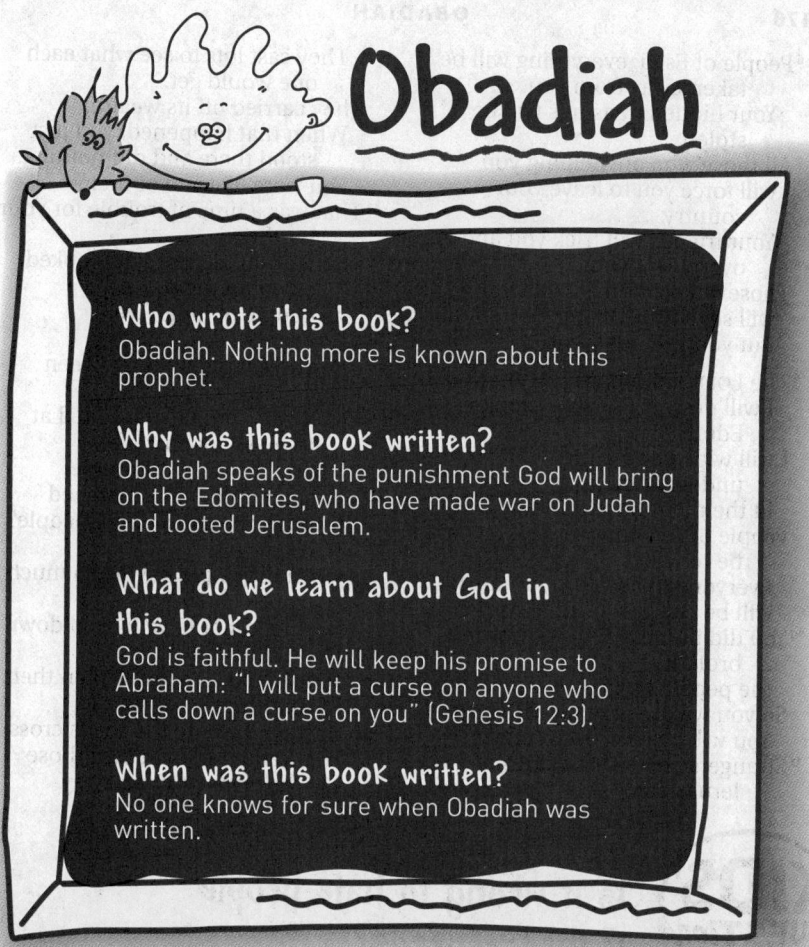

Who wrote this book?
Obadiah. Nothing more is known about this prophet.

Why was this book written?
Obadiah speaks of the punishment God will bring on the Edomites, who have made war on Judah and looted Jerusalem.

What do we learn about God in this book?
God is faithful. He will keep his promise to Abraham: "I will put a curse on anyone who calls down a curse on you" (Genesis 12:3).

When was this book written?
No one knows for sure when Obadiah was written.

¹This is the vision about Edom that Obadiah had. Here is what he said.

We've heard a message from the
    LORD and King.
  A messenger was sent to the
    nations.
The LORD told him to say,
  "Get up! Let us go and make war
    against Edom."

²The LORD says to Edom,

"I will make you weak among the
    nations.
  They will look down on you.
³You live in the safety of the rocks.
  You make your home high up in
    the mountains.
  But your proud heart has tricked
    you.

So you say to yourself,
  'No one can bring me down to
    the ground.'
⁴You have built your home as high
    as an eagle does.
  You have made your nest among
    the stars.
  But I will bring you down from
    there,"
           announces the LORD.
⁵"Edom, suppose robbers came to
    you at night.
  They would steal only as much as
    they wanted.
Suppose grape pickers came to
    harvest your vines.
  They would still leave a few
    grapes.
  But you are facing horrible
    trouble!

⁶People of Esau, everything will be
  taken away from you.
  Your hidden treasures will be
    stolen.
⁷All those who are helping you
  will force you to leave your
    country.
  Your friends will trick you and
    overpower you.
Those who eat bread with you
  will set a trap for you.
  But you will not see it."

⁸The LORD announces, "At that time
  I will destroy the wise men of
    Edom.
I will wipe out the men of
    understanding
  in the mountains of Esau.
⁹People of Teman, your soldiers will
  be terrified.
  Everyone in Esau's mountains
    will be cut down with swords.
¹⁰You did harmful things to your
  brothers,
  the people of Jacob.
So you will be covered with shame.
  You will be destroyed forever.
¹¹Strangers entered the gates of
  Jerusalem.

They cast lots to see what each
  one would get.
They carried off its wealth.
When that happened, you just
  stood there and did nothing.
You were like one of them.
¹²That was a time of trouble for your
  brothers.
  So you should not have looked
    down on them.
The people of Judah were
  destroyed.
  So you should not have been
    happy about it.
You should not have laughed at
  them so much
  when they were in trouble.
¹³You should not have marched
  through the gates of my people's
    city
  when they were having so much
    trouble.
You should not have looked down
  on them.
You should not have stolen their
  wealth.
¹⁴You waited where the roads cross.
  You wanted to cut down those
    who were running away.

Is it wrong to hate people if they're nerds?

Yes. Some people get called "nerds" or "jerks" for no good reason. We should think the best of them and try to get to know them instead of believing every bad thing we hear about them. Sometimes we do meet people who say bad things and are mean to us. But we should not *hate* them or be mean back to them. God wants us to be loving and kind to others. So we should not hurt others or make fun of them.

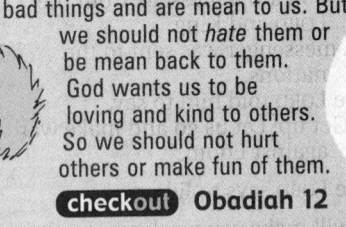

checkout Obadiah 12

Related verses:
Matthew 5:43,44

You should not have done that.
You handed over to their enemies
those who were still left alive.
You should not have done that.
They were in trouble.

¹⁵ "The day of the LORD is near
for all of the nations.
Others will do to you
what you have done to them.
You will be paid back
for what you have done.
¹⁶ You Edomites polluted my holy
mountain of Zion
by drinking and celebrating
there.
So all of the nations will drink
from the cup of my anger.
And they will keep on drinking
from it.
They will vanish.
It will be as if they had never
existed.
¹⁷ But on Mount Zion some of my
people will be left alive.
I will save them.
Zion will be my holy mountain
once again.
And the people of Jacob
will again receive the land as
their own.
¹⁸ They will be like a fire.
Joseph's people will be like a
flame.

The nation of Esau will be like
straw.
Jacob's people will set Edom on
fire and burn it up.
No one will be left alive
among Esau's people."
The LORD has spoken.

¹⁹ Israelites from the Negev Desert
will take over Esau's
mountains.
Israelites from the western hills
will possess Philistia.
They'll take over the territories
of Ephraim and Samaria.
Israelites from the tribe of
Benjamin
will possess the land of Gilead.
²⁰ Some Israelites were forced to
leave their homes.
They'll come back to Canaan and
possess
it all the way to the town of
Zarephath.
Some people from Jerusalem were
taken
to the city of Sepharad.
They'll return and possess
the towns of the Negev Desert.
²¹ Leaders from Mount Zion will go
and rule over the mountains of
Esau.
And the kingdom will belong to
the LORD.

quest challenge

I Wonder . . .

Who can I count on?

Real Life Challenge

Sometimes we think we should be able to accomplish our tasks by ourselves. Are you weak when you need help? No, God looks at it differently. The next time you're tempted to do it yourself, remember God wants to help.

Quest Clue

Take a look at Exodus 18. Who does Israel count on for help? What advice does Moses get? Finally, look at Habakkuk 3 to see that God wants to help.

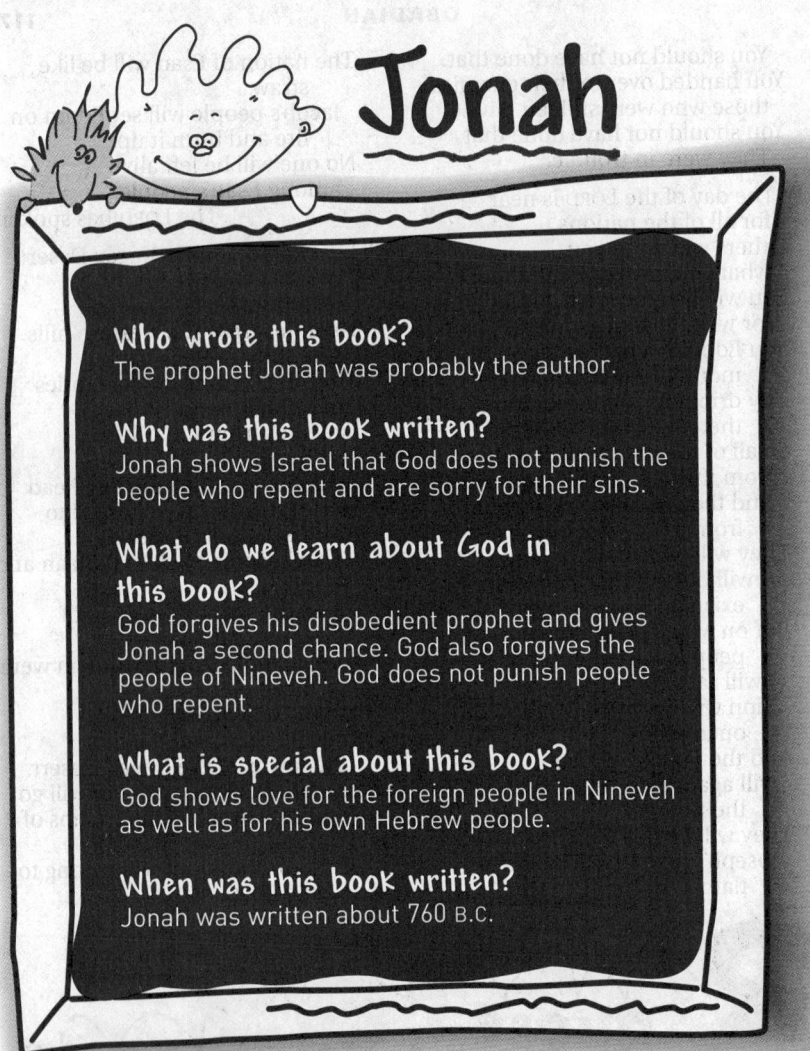

Jonah

Who wrote this book?
The prophet Jonah was probably the author.

Why was this book written?
Jonah shows Israel that God does not punish the people who repent and are sorry for their sins.

What do we learn about God in this book?
God forgives his disobedient prophet and gives Jonah a second chance. God also forgives the people of Nineveh. God does not punish people who repent.

What is special about this book?
God shows love for the foreign people in Nineveh as well as for his own Hebrew people.

When was this book written?
Jonah was written about 760 B.C.

JONAH RUNS AWAY FROM THE LORD

1 A message from the LORD came to Jonah. He was the son of Amittai. The LORD said, ²"Go to the great city of Nineveh. Preach against it. The sins of its people have come to my attention."

³But Jonah ran away from the LORD. He headed for Tarshish. So he went down to the port of Joppa. There he found a ship that was going to Tarshish. He paid the fare and went on board. Then he sailed for Tarshish. He was running away from the LORD.

⁴But the LORD sent a strong wind over the Mediterranean Sea. A wild storm came up. It was so wild that the ship was in danger of breaking apart. ⁵All of the sailors were afraid. Each one cried out to his own god for help. They threw the ship's contents into the sea. They were trying to make the ship lighter.

But Jonah had gone below deck. There he lay down and fell into a deep sleep. ⁶The captain went down to him and said, "How can you sleep? Get up and call out to your god for help! Maybe he'll pay attention to what's happening to us. Then we won't die."

⁷The sailors said to one another,

"Come. Let's cast lots to find out who is to blame for getting us into all of this trouble." So they did. And Jonah was picked.

⁸They asked him, "What terrible thing have you done to bring all of this trouble on us? Tell us. What do you do for a living? Where do you come from? What is your country? What people do you belong to?"

⁹He answered, "I'm a Hebrew. I worship the LORD. He is the God of heaven. He made the sea and the land."

¹⁰They found out he was running away from the LORD. That's because he had told them. Then they became terrified. So they asked him, "How could you do a thing like that?"

¹¹The sea was getting rougher and rougher. So they asked him, "What should we do to you to make the sea calm down?"

¹²"Pick me up and throw me into the sea," he replied. "Then it will become calm. I know it's my fault that this terrible storm has come on you."

¹³Instead of doing what he said, the men did their best to row back to land. But they couldn't. The sea got even rougher than before.

¹⁴Then they cried out to the LORD. They prayed, "LORD, please don't let us die for taking this man's life. After all, he might not be guilty of doing anything wrong. So don't hold us accountable for killing him. LORD, you always do what you want to." ¹⁵Then they took Jonah and threw him overboard. And the stormy sea became calm.

¹⁶When the men saw what had happened, they began to have great respect for the LORD. They offered a sacrifice to him. And they made promises to him.

¹⁷But the LORD sent a huge fish to swallow Jonah. And Jonah was inside the fish for three days and three nights.

JONAH PRAYS TO THE LORD

2 From inside the fish Jonah prayed to the LORD his God. ²He said,

"When I was in trouble, I called out to you.
And you answered me.
When I had almost drowned,
I called out for help.
And you listened to my cry.

KIDS' QUESTion

Why isn't everyone a Christian?

Not everyone wants to be a Christian. And God doesn't force people to obey him. Some people reject Jesus and also act mean to Christians. That's because they don't accept the love that God has for them. Other people just don't know the truth. They have not heard about Jesus and what he did for them. We should try to tell these people about God's love.

checkout Jonah 1:3

Related verses:
Matthew 7:13,14;
John 15:9

³You threw me into the
Mediterranean Sea.
I was in the middle of its waters.
They were all around me.
All of your rolling waves
were sweeping over me.
⁴I said, 'I have been driven away
from you.
But I will look again
toward your holy temple in
Jerusalem.'
⁵I had almost drowned in the
waves.
The deep waters were all around
me.
Seaweed was wrapped around
my head.
⁶I sank down to the bottom of the
mountains.
I thought I had died
and gone down into the grave
forever.
But you brought my life up
from the very edge of the pit.
You are the LORD my God.

⁷"When my life was nearly over,
I remembered you, LORD.
My prayer rose up to you.
It reached you in your holy
temple in heaven.

⁸"Some people worship the
worthless statues of their
gods.
They turn away from the grace
you want to give them.
⁹But I will sacrifice a thank offering
to you.
And I will sing a song of thanks.
I will do what I have promised.
LORD, you are the one who
saves."

¹⁰The LORD gave the fish a command. And it spit Jonah up onto dry land.

JONAH GOES TO NINEVEH

3 A message came to Jonah from the LORD a second time. He said, ²"Go to the great city of Nineveh. Announce to its people the message I give you."

³Jonah obeyed the LORD. He went to Nineveh. It was a very important city. In fact, it took about three days to see all of it. ⁴On the first day, Jonah started into the city. He announced, "In 40 days Nineveh will be destroyed."

⁵The people of Nineveh believed God's warning. They decided not to eat any food for a while. All of them put on black clothes. That's what everyone from the least important of them to the most important did.

⁶The news reached the king of Nineveh. He got up from his throne. He took his royal robes off and dressed himself in black clothes. He sat down in the dust. ⁷Then he sent out a message to the people of Nineveh. He said,

"I and my nobles give this order.

"Don't let any person or animal taste anything. That includes your herds and flocks. People and animals must not eat or drink anything. ⁸Let people and animals alike be covered with black cloth. All of you must call out to God with all your hearts. Stop doing what is evil. Don't harm others. ⁹Who knows? God might take pity on us. He might turn away from his burning anger. Then we won't die."

¹⁰God saw what they did. They stopped doing what was evil. So he took pity on them. He didn't destroy them as he had said he would.

THE LORD SHOWS CONCERN FOR NINEVEH

4 But Jonah was very upset. He became angry. ²He prayed to the LORD and said, "LORD, isn't this exactly what I thought would happen when I was still at home? That's why I was so quick to run away to Tarshish. I knew that you are gracious. You are tender and kind. You are slow to get angry. You are full of love. You are a God who takes pity on people. You don't want to destroy them. ³LORD, take away my life. I'd rather die than live."

⁴But the LORD replied, "Do you have any right to be angry?"

⁵Jonah left the city. He sat down at a place east of it. There he put some branches over his head. He sat in their shade. He waited to see what would happen to the city.

⁶Then the LORD God sent a vine and

made it grow up over Jonah. It gave him more shade for his head. It made him more comfortable. Jonah was very happy he had the vine. ⁷But before sunrise the next day, God sent a worm. It chewed the vine so much that it dried up.

⁸When the sun rose, God sent a burning east wind. The sun beat down on Jonah's head. It made him very weak. He wanted to die. So he said, "I'd rather die than live."

⁹But God said to Jonah, "Do you have any right to be angry about what happened to the vine?"

"I do," he said. "In fact, I'm angry enough to die."

¹⁰But the LORD said, "You have been concerned about this vine. But you did not take care of it. You did not make it grow. It grew up in one night and died the next. ¹¹Nineveh has more than 120,000 people. They can't tell right from wrong. Nineveh also has a lot of cattle. So shouldn't I show concern for that great city?"

quest challenge

I Wonder . . .

What happens if I disobey God?

Real Life Challenge

If you ever disobeyed your parents, you probably found out it can only lead to trouble. That's because God tells us not to disobey. When we do something he doesn't want us to do, we are in danger of getting hurt and hurting others.

Quest Clue

Read Jonah chapter 1 for a dramatic story about what happened to Jonah when he disobeyed God. Then read the end of Luke 6 for a picture of what happens when we don't follow God's guidelines.

I Wonder . . .

Why should I be kind to mean people?

Real Life Challenge

It's easy to be kind to people who are nice to you. But it's harder to be kind to people who have been mean to you. And yet God expects you to be kind to them.

Quest Clue

Read chapter 4 of Jonah to see how God showed mercy on the Ninevites. Then look at Matthew 5 to see God's answer for why you should be kind to mean people.

Micah

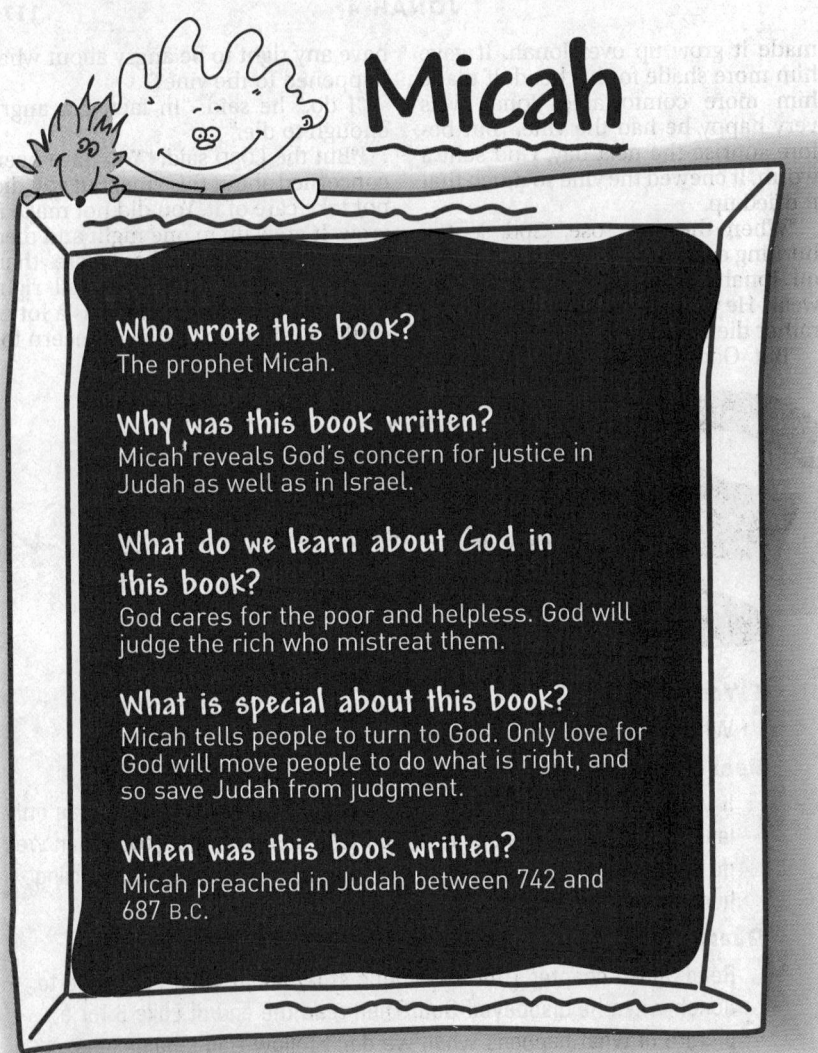

Who wrote this book?
The prophet Micah.

Why was this book written?
Micah reveals God's concern for justice in Judah as well as in Israel.

What do we learn about God in this book?
God cares for the poor and helpless. God will judge the rich who mistreat them.

What is special about this book?
Micah tells people to turn to God. Only love for God will move people to do what is right, and so save Judah from judgment.

When was this book written?
Micah preached in Judah between 742 and 687 B.C.

---

1 A message came to Micah from the LORD. He was from the town of Moresheth. The message came while Jotham, Ahaz and Hezekiah were kings of Judah. This is the vision Micah saw concerning Samaria and Jerusalem. Here is what he said.

² Listen to me, all of you nations!
Earth and everyone who lives in it, pay attention!
The LORD and King will be a witness against you.
The Lord will speak from his holy temple in heaven.

THE LORD WILL JUDGE SAMARIA AND JERUSALEM

³ The LORD is about to come down from his home in heaven.
He rules over the highest places on earth.
⁴ The mountains will melt under him
like wax near a fire.
The valleys will be broken apart by water rushing down a slope.
⁵ All of that will happen because Jacob's people have done what is wrong.

The people of Israel
have committed many sins.
Who is to blame
for the wrong things Jacob has
done?
Samaria!
Who is to blame for the high
places
where Judah's people worship
other gods?
Jerusalem!

⁶So the LORD says,

"I will turn Samaria into a pile of
trash.
It will become a place for
planting vineyards.
I will dump its stones down into
the valley.
And I will destroy it
down to its very foundations.
⁷All of the statues of Samaria's gods
will be broken to pieces.
All of the gifts its people gave to
temple prostitutes
will be burned with fire.

I will destroy all of the statues of
its gods.
Samaria collected gifts that were
paid to temple prostitutes.
So the Assyrians will use the gifts
to pay their own temple
prostitutes."

MICAH SOBS OVER HIS PEOPLE

⁸I will sob and cry because Samaria
will be destroyed.
I'll walk around barefoot.
I won't have anything on but my
underwear.
I'll bark like a wild dog.
I'll hoot like an owl.
⁹Samaria's wounds can't be
healed.
The LORD will also judge Judah.
Enemies will march up to the very
gate of my people.
They will reach Jerusalem itself.
¹⁰Don't tell the people of Gath
about it.
Don't let them see you sob.

KIDS' QUESTION

When did all this happen?

Everything in the Bible happened almost 2,000 years ago or more. That is hundreds and hundreds of years before your grandparents were born. Some events in the Old Testament happened 3,000 years ago. For example, Micah spoke to the Israelites some 2,700 years ago. Many, many years also separate the Old Testament from the New Testament. There are 400 years between the last event in the Old Testament and the first event in the New Testament. People who lived that long ago did not have televisions, cars and computers. But they were a lot like us, too. That is why the Bible has so much to say to us today. *People* have not changed even though the way people travel, what they eat and what they do in their spare time has changed.

GRAMPA, WERE YOU ALIVE WHEN JESUS WAS HERE?

checkout Micah 1:1

Related verse:
Hebrews 4:2

People in Beth Ophrah, roll in
the dust.
[11] You who live in the town of
Shaphir,
leave in shame and without your
clothes.
Those who live in Zaanan
won't come out to help you.
The people in Beth Ezel will sob.
They won't be able to help keep
you safe.
[12] Those who live in Maroth will
groan with pain
as they wait for help.
That's because the LORD will bring
trouble on them.
It will reach the very gate of
Jerusalem.
[13] You who live in Lachish,
get your horses ready to pull
their chariots.
You trust in military power.
That was the beginning of sin
for the people of Zion.
The wrong things Israel did
were also done by you.
[14] People of Judah, you might as well
say good-by
to Moresheth near Gath.
The town of Aczib won't give any
help
to the kings of Israel.
[15] An enemy will attack
you who live in Mareshah.
Israel's glorious leaders will have
to run away
and hide in the cave of Adullam.
[16] The children you enjoy so much
will be taken away as prisoners.
So shave your heads and sob.
Make them as bare as the head of
a vulture.

PEOPLE'S PLANS AND GOD'S PLANS

2 How terrible it will be for
those
who plan to harm others!
How terrible for those who make
evil plans
before they even get out of bed!
As soon as daylight comes,
they carry them out.
That's because they have the
power to do it.
[2] If they want fields or houses,
they take them.

They cheat men out of
their homes and property.
[3] So the LORD says to them,

"I am planning to send trouble on
you.
You will not be able to save
yourselves from it.
You will not live so proudly
anymore.
It will be a time of trouble.
[4] At that time people will make fun
of you.
They will tease you by singing a
song of sadness.
They will pretend to be you and
say,
'We are totally destroyed.
Our enemies have divided up our
land.
The LORD has taken it away from
us!
He has given our fields to those
who turned against us.' "

[5] So you won't even have anyone left
in the LORD's community
who can divide up the land for
you.

SOME PROPHETS AREN'T REALLY PROPHETS AT ALL

[6] "Don't prophesy," the people's
prophets say.
"Don't prophesy about bad
things.
Nothing shameful is going to
happen to us."
[7] People of Jacob, should others say,
"The LORD isn't angry with us.
He doesn't do things like that"?

The LORD replies, "What I promise
brings good things
to those who lead honest lives.
[8] But lately my people have attacked
one another
as if they were enemies.
You strip the rich robes off
those who happen to pass by.
They thought they were as safe as
men
returning from a battle they had
won.
[9] You drive the women among my
people
out of their pleasant homes.
You take my blessing away

from their children forever.
¹⁰ Get up! Leave this land!
It is no longer your resting place.
You have made it 'unclean.'
You have completely destroyed
it.
¹¹ Suppose a prophet goes around
telling lies.
And he prophesies that you will
have
plenty of wine and beer.
Then that kind of prophet would be
just right for this nation!

THE LORD PROMISES HE WILL SAVE HIS PEOPLE

¹² "People of Jacob, I will gather all of
you.
I will bring together
you who are still left alive in
Israel.
I will gather you together like
sheep in a pen.
You will be like a flock in its
grasslands.
Your country will be filled with
people.
¹³ I will open the way for you to
return.
I will march in front of you.
You will break through the city
gates and go free.
I am your King. I will pass through
the gates
in front of you.
I will lead the way."

THE LORD WARNS ISRAEL'S LEADERS AND PROPHETS

3 Then I said,

"Listen, you leaders of Jacob's
people!
Pay attention, you rulers of
Israel!
You should know how to judge
others fairly.
² But you hate what is good.
And you love what is evil.
You are like someone
who tears the skin off my people.
You pull the meat off their bones.
³ You eat my people's bodies.
You strip their skin off.
You break their bones in pieces.
You chop them up like meat.
You put them in a cooking pot."

⁴ The time will come when Israel
will cry out to the LORD.
But he won't answer them.
In fact, he'll turn his face away
from them.
They have done what is evil.

⁵ The LORD says,

"You prophets are leading my
people
down the wrong path.
If they feed you,
you promise them peace.
If they do not,
you prepare to go to war against
them.
⁶ So night will come on you.
But you will not have any visions.
Darkness will cover you.
But you will not be able
to figure out what is going to
happen.
The sun will set on you prophets.
The day will become dark for
you.
⁷ You who see visions will be put to
shame.
You who try to figure out what is
going to happen
will be dishonored.
All of you will cover your faces.
I will not answer you."

⁸ The Spirit of the LORD
has filled me with power.
He helps me do what is fair.
He makes me brave.
Now I'm prepared to tell Jacob's
people
what they've done wrong.
I'm ready to tell Israel they've
sinned.
⁹ Listen to me, you leaders of Jacob's
people!
Pay attention, you rulers of
Israel!
You hate to do what is fair.
You twist everything that is right.
¹⁰ You build up Zion by spilling the
blood of others.
You build Jerusalem by doing
what is evil.
¹¹ Your judges take money from
people
who want special favors.
Your priests teach only if they get
paid for it.

Your prophets won't tell fortunes
　　unless they receive money.
But you still claim to depend on
　　the LORD.
You say, "The LORD is with us.
　　No trouble will come on us."
[12] So because of what you have done,
　　Zion will be plowed up like a
　　field.
Jerusalem will be turned into a
　　pile of trash.
The temple hill will be covered
　　with bushes and weeds.

PEOPLE FROM MANY NATIONS WILL WORSHIP AT MOUNT ZION

4 In the last days
　　the mountain where the LORD's
　　　temple is located will be
　　　famous.
It will be the most important
　　mountain of all.
It will stand out above the hills.
And nations will go to it.

[2] People from many nations will go
there. They will say,

"Come, let us go up to the LORD's
　　mountain.
Let's go to the house of Jacob's
　　God.
He will teach us how we should
　　live.
Then we will live the way he
　　wants us to."
The law of the LORD will be taught
　　at Zion.
His message will go out from
　　Jerusalem.
[3] He will judge between people
　　from many nations.
He'll settle problems among
　　strong nations everywhere.
They will hammer their swords
　　into plows.
They'll hammer their spears into
　　pruning tools.
Nations will not go to war against
　　one another.
They won't even train to fight
　　anymore.
[4] Every man will have
　　his own vine and fig tree.
And no one will make them
　　afraid.

That's what the LORD who rules
　　over all has promised.
[5] Other nations worship and trust in
　　their gods.
But we will worship and obey the
　　LORD.
He will be our God for ever and
　　ever.

THE LORD'S KINGDOM WILL COME

[6] "The time is coming
　　when I will gather those who are
　　　disabled,"
announces the LORD.
"I will bring together those
who were taken away as
　　prisoners.
I will gather those I have allowed
　　to suffer.
[7] I will make the disabled my
　　faithful people.
I will make those who were
　　driven away from their homes
　　a strong nation.
I will rule over them on Mount
　　Zion.
I will be their King from that time
　　on and forever.
[8] Jerusalem, you used to be
　　like a guard tower for my flock.
City of Zion, you used to be
　　a place of safety for my
　　people.
The glorious kingdom you had
　　before
will be given back to you.
Once again a king will rule over
　　your people."

[9] Why are you crying out so loudly
　　now?
Don't you have a king?
Have your advisers died?
Is that why pain comes on you
like the pain of a woman having
　　a baby?
[10] People of Zion, groan with pain.
Cry out like a woman having a
　　baby.
Soon you must leave your city.
You must camp in the open
　　fields.
You will have to go to Babylonia.
But that's where the LORD will
　　save you.
There he will set you free

from the powerful hand of your
enemies.

¹¹ But now many nations
have gathered together to attack
you.
They say, "Let Jerusalem be
polluted.
We want to see others laugh
when Zion suffers!"
¹² But those nations don't know
what the LORD has in mind.
They don't understand his plan.
He will gather them up like
bundles of grain.
He will take them to his
threshing floor.

¹³ The LORD says,

"People of Zion, get up
and crush your enemies.
I will make you like a threshing
ox.
I will give you iron horns and
bronze hoofs.
So you will crush many
nations."

They got their money in the wrong
way.
But you will set it apart to the
LORD.
You will give their wealth
to the LORD of the whole earth.

A RULER WILL COME FROM BETHLEHEM

5 Jerusalem, you are being
attacked.
So bring your troops
together.
Our enemies have surrounded us.
They want to slap the face of
Israel's ruler.

² The LORD says,

"Bethlehem, you might not be
an important town in the nation
of Judah.
But out of you will come
a ruler over Israel for me.
His family line goes back
to the early years of your
nation.
It goes all the way back
to days of long ago."
Bethlehem was also called
Ephrathah.

³ The LORD will hand his people
over to their enemies.
That will last until the promised
ruler is born.
Then his relatives in Judah
will return to their land.
The LORD will rule over them
and the people of Israel.

⁴ The promised ruler will stand firm
and take care of his flock.
The LORD will give him the
strength to do it.
The LORD his God will give him
the authority to rule.
His people will live safely.
His greatness will reach
from one end of the earth to the
other.
⁵ And he will bring them peace.

THE LORD WILL SAVE HIS PEOPLE FROM THEIR ENEMIES

The Assyrians will attack our land.
Enemies will march through our
forts.
But we will raise up many
shepherds against them.
We'll send out against them
as many leaders as we need to.
⁶ They will use their swords to rule
over Assyria.
They'll rule the land of Nimrod
with swords that are ready to
strike.
The Assyrians will march across
our borders
and attack our land.
But the promised ruler will save
us from them.

⁷ Jacob's people who are still left
alive
will be scattered among many
nations.
They will be like dew the LORD has
sent.
It doesn't wait for a man's
command.
They will be like rain that falls on
the grass.
Rain doesn't wait for someone to
give it orders.
⁸ So Jacob's people will be scattered
among many nations.
They will be like a lion
among the animals in the forest.
They'll be like a young lion

among flocks of sheep.
Lions attack and tear as they move
    along.
No one can keep them
    from killing what they want.
⁹ LORD, your powerful hand will win
    the battle
    over your enemies.
All of them will be destroyed.

¹⁰ "At that time I will destroy
    your war horses," announces the
    LORD.
"I will smash your chariots.
¹¹ I will destroy the cities in your
    land.
    I will tear down all of your forts.
¹² I will destroy your worship of evil
    powers.
    You will no longer be able
    to put a spell on anyone.
¹³ I will destroy the statues of your
    gods.
    I will take your sacred stones
    away from you.
You will no longer bow down
    to the gods your hands have
    made.
¹⁴ I will pull down the poles you used
    to worship the goddess Asherah.
    And I will destroy your cities
    completely.
¹⁵ I will pay back the nations
    that have not obeyed me.
    My anger will burn against
    them."

THE LORD BRINGS
CHARGES AGAINST ISRAEL

6 Israel, listen to the LORD's mes-
    sage. He says to me,

"Stand up in court.
    Let the mountains serve as
    witnesses.
    Let the hills hear what you have
    to say."

² Hear the LORD's case, you
    mountains.
    Listen, you age-old foundations
    of the earth.
The LORD has a case against his
    people Israel.
    He is bringing charges against
    them.

³ The LORD says,

"My people, what have I done to
    you?
    Have I made things too hard for
    you? Answer me.
⁴ I brought your people up out of
    Egypt.
    I set them free from the land
    where they were slaves.
I sent Moses to lead them.
    Aaron and Miriam helped him.
⁵ Remember how Balak, the king of
    Moab,
    planned to put a curse on your
    people.
But Balaam, the son of Beor,
    gave them a blessing instead.
Remember their journey from
    Shittim to Gilgal.
    I want you to know
    that I always do what is right."

⁶ The people of Israel say,

"What should we bring with us
    when we go to worship the LORD?
What should we offer the God of
    heaven
    when we bow down to him?
Should we take burnt offerings to
    him?
    Should we sacrifice calves
    that are a year old?
⁷ Will the LORD be pleased with
    thousands of rams?
    Will he take delight in 10,000
    rivers of olive oil?
Should we offer our oldest sons
    for the wrong things we've done?
Should we sacrifice our own
    children
    to pay for our sins?"

⁸ The LORD has shown you what is
    good.
    He has told you what he requires
    of you.
You must treat people fairly.
    You must love others faithfully.
And you must be very careful to
    live
    the way your God wants you to.

THE LORD WILL PUNISH
HIS PEOPLE

⁹ The LORD is calling out to
    Jerusalem.
    And it would be wise to pay
    attention to him.

He says, "Listen, tribe of Judah
and you people who are gathered
in the city.

¹⁰You sinful people, should I forget
that you got your treasures by
stealing them?

You use dishonest measures to
cheat others.

I have placed a curse on that
practice.

¹¹Should I forgive you who use
dishonest scales?

You use weights that weigh
things heavier
or lighter than they really are.

¹²The rich people among you harm
others.

You are always telling lies.

You try to fool others by what
you say.

¹³So I will strike you down.

I will destroy you
because you have sinned so
much.

¹⁴You will eat. But you will not be
satisfied.

Your stomachs will still be empty.

You will try to save what you can.

But you will not be able to.

If you do save something,
it will be destroyed in battle.

¹⁵You will plant seeds.

But you will not harvest any
crops.

You will press olives.

But you will not use the oil for
yourselves.

You will crush grapes.

But you will not drink the wine
that is made from them.

¹⁶You have followed the evil
practices
of King Omri of Israel.

You have done what the family
of King Ahab did.

You have followed their bad
example.

So I will let you be destroyed.

Others will make fun of you.

The nations will laugh at you."

MICAH IS SAD BECAUSE ISRAEL HAS SINNED

7 I'm suffering very much!
I'm like someone who gathers
summer fruit in a
vineyard
after the good fruit has already
been picked.

No grapes are left to eat.

None of the early figs I long for
remain.

²Faithful people have disappeared
from the land.

Those who are honest are
gone.

All men hide and wait
to spill the blood of others.

What does God want us to do?

God tells us in the Bible what he
wants us to do. There are a lot of
messages in the Bible. But God has four
main ones:

(1) Believe in Jesus. Trust him
every day.

(2) Obey Jesus. Do what he says.

(3) Love God and others.

(4) Be fair and honest and live for
God without acting like a big shot.

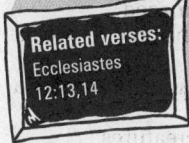
checkout
Micah 6:8

Related verses:
Ecclesiastes
12:13,14

They use nets to try and trap one
     another.
³They are very good at doing what
     is evil.
Rulers require gifts.
Judges accept money from people
     who want special favors.
Those who are powerful
     always get what they want.
All of them make evil plans
     together.
⁴The best of them are as harmful as
     thorns.
The most honest of them are
     even worse.
The time your prophets warned
     you about has come.
God is about to punish you.
Panic has taken hold of you.
⁵Don't trust your neighbors.
Don't put your faith in your
     friends.
Be careful of what you say
     even to your own wife.
⁶Sons don't honor their fathers.
Daughters refuse to obey their
     mothers.
Daughters-in-law are against their
     mothers-in-law.
A man's enemies are the
     members of his own family.

⁷So I will look to the LORD.
I'll put my trust in God my
     Savior.
He will hear me.

JERUSALEM WILL BE REBUILT

⁸The people of Jerusalem say,

"Don't laugh when we suffer,
     you enemies of ours!
We have fallen.
     But we'll get up.
Even though we sit in the dark,
     the LORD will give us light.
⁹We've sinned against the LORD.
     So he is angry with us.
That will continue until he takes
     up our case.
Then he'll do what is right for us.
He'll bring us out into the light.
Then we'll see him save us.
¹⁰The people of Nineveh will see it
     too.
And they will be put to shame.
After all, they said to us,
     'Where is the LORD your God?'

But we will see them destroyed.
Soon they will be stomped on
     like mud in the streets."
¹¹People of Jerusalem, the time will
     come
when your walls will be rebuilt.
Land will be added to your
     territory.
¹²At that time your people will come
     back to you.
They'll return from Assyria
     and the cities of Egypt.
They'll come from the countries
     between Egypt and the
     Euphrates River.
They'll return from the lands
     between the seas.
They'll come back from the
     countries
between the mountains.
¹³But the rest of the earth will be
     deserted.
The people who live in it
     have done many evil things.

PRAYER AND PRAISE

¹⁴LORD, be like a shepherd to your
     people.
Take good care of them.
They are your flock.
They live by themselves
     in the safety of a forest.
Rich grasslands are all around
     them.
Let them eat grass in Bashan and
     Gilead
just as they did long ago.

¹⁵The LORD says to his people,

"I showed your people my
     wonders
when they came out of Egypt
     long ago.
In the same way, I will show
     them to you."

¹⁶When the nations see those
     wonders,
they will be put to shame.
All of their power will be taken
     away from them.
They will be so amazed
     that they won't be able to speak
     or hear.
¹⁷They'll be forced to eat dust like a
     snake.
They'll be like creatures

that have to crawl on the ground.
They'll come out of their dens
trembling with fear.
They'll show respect for the LORD
our God.
They will also have respect for
his people.
[18] LORD, who is a God like you?
You forgive sin.
You forgive your people
when they do what is wrong.
You don't stay angry forever.
Instead, you take delight in
showing

your faithful love to them.
[19] Once again you will show loving
concern for us.
You will completely wipe out
the evil things we've done.
You will throw all of our sins
into the bottom of the sea.
[20] You will be true to Jacob's
people.
You will show your faithful love
to Abraham's children.
You will do what you promised to
do for our people
when you took an oath long ago.

quest challenge

I Wonder . . .

How can I please God?

Real Life Challenge

Perhaps you have to share games, toys or a computer with your
siblings or classmates. Sometimes you might not feel like sharing
what you own with others. But God wants you to care about others
as much as *he* cares about them. He wants you to show others
kindness and forgiveness, which the Bible calls mercy. Ask him to
help you be fair and generous with the kids around you.

Quest Clue

Read Genesis 6 about a man who pleased God. Then
look at Micah 6 to learn more about how you can
please him by caring about others.

Nahum

Who wrote this book?
The prophet Nahum.

Why was this book written?
Nahum assures the people of Judah that God will destroy Nineveh, the capital city of their great enemy, Assyria.

What do we learn about God in this book?
God will punish the enemies of the people he loves.

When was this book written?
Nahum probably preached between 663 and 655 B.C.

1 Here is a message the LORD gave Nahum in a vision about Nineveh. It is written on a scroll. Nahum was from the town of Elkosh. Here is what he said.

THE LORD IS ANGRY WITH NINEVEH

² The LORD is a jealous God who punishes people.
He pays them back for the evil things they do.
His anger burns against them.
The LORD punishes his enemies.
He holds his anger back until the right time to use it.
³ The LORD is slow to get angry.
He is very powerful.
The LORD will not let guilty people go

without punishing them.
When he marches out, he stirs up winds and storms.
Clouds are the dust kicked up by his feet.
⁴ He controls the seas. He dries them up.
He makes all of the rivers run dry.
Bashan and Mount Carmel dry up.
The flowers in Lebanon fade.
⁵ He causes the mountains to shake.
The hills melt away.
The earth trembles because he is there.
So do the world and all those who live in it.
⁶ Who can stand firm when his anger burns?
Who can live when he is angry?

His anger blazes out like fire.
  He smashes the rocks to pieces.

[7] The LORD is good.
  When people are in trouble,
    they can go to him for safety.
  He takes good care of those
    who trust in him.
[8] But he will destroy Nineveh
    with a powerful flood.
  He will chase his enemies
    into the darkness of punishment.

[9] The LORD will put an end
    to anything they plan against
    him.
  He won't allow Assyria to win the
    battle
  over his people a second time.
[10] His enemies will be tangled up
    among thorns.
  Their wine will make them
    drunk.
  They'll be burned up like dry
    straw.

[11] Nineveh, a king has marched out
    from you.
  He makes evil plans against the
    LORD.
  He gives harmful advice.

[12] The LORD says,

  "His army has many soldiers.
    Other nations are helping them.
  But they will be cut off and pass
    away.
  Judah, I punished you.
    But I will not do it anymore.
[13] Now I will break Assyria's yoke off
    your neck.
  I will tear off the ropes that hold
    you."

[14] Nineveh, the LORD has given an
    order concerning you.
  He has said, "You will not have
    any children
    to carry on your name.
  I will destroy the wooden and
    metal statues

How come when I pray to God he doesn't always answer?

God answers all our prayers, but not always the way we want him to. Sometimes his answer is *no* or *wait*. God knows a lot more about everything than we do. Sometimes he has plans that we do not know about. He answers the way that he knows is best, even if we do not understand it. Part of trusting God means trusting that his answers are good. God hears and answers all our prayers.

Hello - you've reached heaven's 1-800 number. There isn't anyone here to take your call right now, but if you leave a long message at the sound of the choir, we will return your call. This is a recording...

checkout
Nahum 1:7

Related verse:
2 Corinthians
2:8,9

that are in the temple of your
gods.
I will get your grave ready for you.
You are worthless."

¹⁵ Look at the mountains of Judah!
I see a messenger running to
bring good news!
He's telling us that peace has
come!
People of Judah, celebrate your
feasts.
Carry out your promises.
The evil Assyrians won't attack you
again.
They'll be completely destroyed.

THE LORD WILL DESTROY NINEVEH

2 Nineveh, armies are coming to
attack you.
Guard the forts!
Watch the roads!
Get ready!
Gather all of your strength!

² Assyria once took everything of
value from God's people.
Its army destroyed all of their
vines.
But the LORD will bring back
the glory of Jacob's people.
He'll make Israel glorious again.

³ The shields of the soldiers
attacking Nineveh are red.
The armies are dressed in bright
red uniforms.
The metal on their chariots
flashes
when they are prepared for war.
Their spears are ready to use.
⁴ The chariots race through the
main streets.
They rush back and forth
through them.
They look like flaming torches.
They dart around like lightning.

⁵ The commander of the attackers
sends for his special troops.
But they trip and fall on their way.
They run toward the city wall.
They keep their shield in front of
them.
⁶ They open the gates that hold
back
the waters of the river.
And the palace falls down.

⁷ The attackers order that the city's
people
be taken away as prisoners.
The female slaves cry like sad
doves.
They beat their chests.
⁸ Nineveh is like a pool.
Its water is draining away.
"Stop running away!" someone
cries out.
But no one turns back.
⁹ "Steal the silver!" the attackers
shout.
"Grab the gold!"
The supply is endless.
There is plenty of wealth
among all of the city's treasures.
¹⁰ Nineveh is destroyed, robbed and
stripped!
Hearts melt away in fear.
Knees give way.
Bodies tremble with fear.
Everyone's face turns pale.

¹¹ Assyria is like a lion.
Where is the lions' den now?
Where did they feed their cubs?
Where did all of the lions go?
In their den they had nothing to
fear.
¹² The lion killed enough for his cubs
to eat.
He choked what he caught for his
mate.
He filled his home with what he
had killed.
He brought to his dens what he
had caught.

¹³ "Nineveh, I am against you,"
announces the LORD who rules
over all.
"I will burn up your chariots with
fire.
Your young lions will be killed
with swords.
I will leave you nothing on earth
to catch.
The voices of your messengers
will no longer be heard."

THE LORD WILL JUDGE NINEVEH

3 How terrible it will be for
Nineveh!
It is a city of murderers!
It is full of liars!
It's filled with stolen goods!

The killing never stops!
² Whips crack!
  Wheels clack!
Horses charge!
  Chariots rumble!
³ Horsemen attack!
  Swords flash!
  Spears gleam!
Many people die.
  Dead bodies pile up.
They can't even be counted.
  People trip over them.
⁴ All of that was caused by the evil
    longings
  of the prostitute Nineveh.
That woman who practiced evil
    magic
  was very beautiful.
She used her sinful charms
  to make slaves out of the nations.
She worshiped evil powers
  in order to trap others.

⁵ "Nineveh, I am against you,"
  announces the LORD who rules
    over all.
  "I will pull your skirts up over your
    face.
  I will show the nations your
    naked body.
  Kingdoms will make fun of your
    shame.
⁶ I will throw garbage at you.
  I will look down on you.
  I will make an example out of
    you.
⁷ All those who see you will run
    away from you.
  They will say, 'Nineveh is
    destroyed.
  Who will sob over it?'
Where can I find someone
  to comfort your people?"

⁸ Nineveh, are you better than
    Thebes
  on the Nile River?
There was water all around that
    city.
  The river helped to keep it safe.
  The waters were like a wall
    around it.
⁹ Cush and Egypt gave it all of the
    strength it needed.
  Put and Libya also helped it.
¹⁰ But Thebes was captured anyway.
  Its people were taken away as
    prisoners.

Its babies were smashed to pieces
  at every street corner.
The Assyrian soldiers cast lots
  for all of its great leaders.
They put them in chains
  and made slaves out of them.
¹¹ People of Nineveh, you too will get
    drunk.
  You will try to hide from your
    enemies.
  You will look for a place of safety.

¹² All of your forts are like fig trees
    that have their first ripe fruit on
    them.
  When the trees are shaken,
    the figs fall into the mouths
    of those who eat them.
¹³ Look at your troops.
  All of them are weak.
The gates of your forts
  are wide open to your enemies.
  Fire has destroyed their heavy
    metal bars.

¹⁴ Prepare for the attack by storing
    up water!
  Make your walls as strong as you
    can!
  Make some bricks out of clay!
  Mix the mud to hold them
    together!
  Use them to repair the walls!
¹⁵ In spite of all of your hard work,
    fire will burn you up inside your
    city.
Your enemies will cut you down
    with their swords.
  They will destroy you
  just as grasshoppers eat up
    crops.
Multiply like grasshoppers!
  Increase your numbers like
    locusts!
¹⁶ You have more traders
    than the number of stars in the
    sky.
  But like locusts they strip the land.
  Then they fly away.
¹⁷ Your guards are like grasshoppers.
  Your officials are like large
    numbers of locusts.
  They settle in the walls on a cold
    day.
But when the sun appears, they fly
    away.
  And no one knows where
    they go.

¹⁸King of Assyria, your leaders are
   asleep.
Your nobles lie down to rest.
Your people are scattered on the
   mountains.
No one is left to gather them
   together.
¹⁹Nothing can heal your wounds.

You will die of them.
All those who hear the news about
   you clap their hands
because you have fallen from
   power.
All of them suffered
because you never showed them
   any pity.

quest challenge

I Wonder . . .

How does God protect me?

Real Life Challenge

If you see a scary movie, you might have a hard time falling asleep
that night. This is a good time to remember that God is in charge and
that he keeps you safe. He will protect you from harm—even if it is
only in your imagination!

Quest Clue

Read Psalm 9 for some helpful verses on God's protection. Then find
Nahum 1 for more encouragement not to be afraid.

I Wonder . . .

How can I be more confident?

Real Life Challenge

You are assigned to give a report in front of the entire class, and you
are completely terrified. God can help you even in situations like
this. He promises to help you with the scary things you
have to do when you rely on him.

Quest Clue

Find Jeremiah 17 to learn how God helps people who
depend on him. Then look at Habakkuk 3 for more
encouragement about what God will do for you.

Habakkuk

Who wrote this book?
The prophet Habakkuk.

Why was this book written?
Habakkuk shows that people never get away with being wicked but will be punished by God.

What do we learn about God in this book?
God is too holy to let people get away with sin. He punishes everyone who sins, even people like the Babylonians, who seemed to get rich by being wicked.

What is special about this book?
Habakkuk is afraid when he learns that God will send the Babylonians against Judah. But in the end Habakkuk decides to trust God anyway.

When was this book written?
Habakkuk was written during the reign of good King Josiah, who ruled Judah from 639 to 597 B.C.

1 This is a vision the prophet Habakkuk received from the LORD. Here is what Habakkuk said.

HABAKKUK ASKS THE LORD A QUESTION

²LORD, how long do I have to call
    out for help?
  Why don't you listen to me?
 How long must I keep telling you
    that things are terrible?
  Why don't you save us?
³Why do you make me watch while
    people treat others so unfairly?

Why do you put up with the wrong
    things
  they are doing?
I have to look at death.
  People are harming others.
  They are arguing and fighting all
    the time.
⁴The law can't do what it's
    supposed to do.
  Fairness never comes out on top.
Sinful people surround those
  who do what is right.
  So people are never treated
    fairly.

THE LORD GIVES HIS ANSWER

⁵The LORD replies,

"Look at the nations. Watch them.
    Be totally amazed at what you
      see.
I am going to do something in
    your days
    that you would never believe.
You would not believe it
    even if someone told you about
      it.
⁶I am going to send the armies of
    Babylonia to attack you.
    They are very mean. They move
      quickly.
They sweep across the whole
    earth.
    They take over places
    that do not belong to them.
⁷They terrify others.
    They do not recognize any laws
      but their own.
    That is how proud they are.
⁸Their horses are faster than
    leopards.
    They are meaner than wolves in
      the dark.
Their horsemen charge straight
    into battle.
    They ride in from far away.
They come down like an eagle
    diving for its food.
⁹All of them are ready to destroy
    others.
    Their huge armies advance like a
      wind out of the desert.
    They gather prisoners like sand.
¹⁰They laugh at kings
    and make fun of rulers.
They laugh at all of the cities
    that have high walls around
      them.
They build dirt ramps against the
    walls
    and capture the cities.
¹¹They sweep past like the wind.
    Then they go on their way.
They are guilty.
    They worship their own
      strength."

HABAKKUK ASKS THE LORD ANOTHER QUESTION

¹²LORD, haven't you existed forever?
    You are my holy God.
    So we won't die, will we?

LORD, you have appointed the
    Babylonians
    to punish your people.
My Rock, you have chosen them
    to judge us.
¹³Your eyes are too pure to look at
    what is evil.
You can't put up with the wrong
    things people do.
So why do you put up
    with those who can't be trusted?
The evil Babylonians swallow up
    those who are more godly than
      themselves.
So why are you silent?
¹⁴You have made men as if they
    were only fish in the sea.
They are like sea creatures that
    don't have a ruler.
¹⁵The evil Babylonians pull all of
    them up with hooks.
They catch them in their nets.
They gather them up.
So they celebrate.
They are glad.
¹⁶They offer sacrifices to their nets.
    They burn incense to them.
Their nets allow them to live in
    great comfort.
    They enjoy the finest food.
¹⁷Are you going to let them
    keep on emptying their nets?
Will they go on destroying nations
    without showing them any mercy?

2 I will go up to the lookout
    tower.
    I'll station myself on the city
      wall.
I'll wait to see how the LORD will
    reply to me.
Then I'll try to figure out how to
    answer him.

THE LORD GIVES HIS ANSWER

²The LORD replies,

"Write down the message I am
    showing you in a vision.
Write it clearly on the tablets you
    use.
Then a messenger can read it
    and run to announce it.
³The message I give you
    waits for the time I have
      appointed.
It speaks about what is going to
    happen.

And all of it will come true.
It might take a while.
   But wait for it.
You can be sure it will come.
   It will happen when I want it to.

4 "The Babylonians are very proud.
   What they want is not good.

"But the one who is right with God
   will live by faith.

5 "Wine makes the Babylonians do
    foolish things.
   They are proud. They never rest.
Like the grave, they are always
    hungry for more.
Like death, they are never
    satisfied.
They gather all of the nations to
    themselves.
They take their people away as
    prisoners.

6 "Won't those people laugh at the
Babylonians? Won't they make fun of
them? They will say to them,

" 'How terrible it will be for you
   who pile up stolen goods!
You get rich by cheating others.
   How long will that go on?
7 Those who owe you money will
    suddenly rise up.
   You charge them too much
    interest.
So they will wake up
   and make you tremble with
    fear.
Then they will take away
   everything you have.
8 You have robbed many nations.
   So the nations that are left will
    rob you.
You have spilled man's blood.
   You have destroyed lands and
    cities
   and everyone in them.'

9 "How terrible it will be for the
   Babylonians!
They build their kingdom with
   money
   they gained by cheating others.

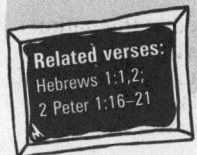

When was the Bible made?

God spent many, many years having the Bible written. He started a long time before computers or cars or even books. The people who wrote down God's words used long pieces of paper made from big leaves or animal skins. God had people writing for him for more than 1,000 years. They were writing when Moses was born and they were still writing after Jesus' death. We should read the Bible even though it was written before any of us was born. When we read the stories and understand what God is saying, we learn how we should live today.

checkout
Habakkuk 2:2

Related verses:
Hebrews 1:1,2;
2 Peter 1:16–21

JASON'S IMAGINATION

IN THE BEGINNING

They have tried to make the
     kingdom
  as secure as possible.
  After all, they did not want to be
     destroyed.
¹⁰ They have planned to wipe out
     many nations.
  But they have brought shame on
     their own kingdom.
  So they must pay with their own
     lives.
¹¹ The stones in the walls of their
     homes will cry out.
  And the wooden beams will echo
     that cry.

¹² "How terrible it will be for the
     Babylonians!
  They build cities by spilling the
     blood of others.
  They establish towns by
     committing crimes.
¹³ I am the LORD who rules over all.
  Human effort is no better than
     wood that feeds a fire.
  So the nations wear themselves
     out for nothing.
¹⁴ The oceans are full of water.
  In the same way, the earth will be
     filled
  with the knowledge of my glory.

¹⁵ "How terrible it will be for the
     Babylonians!
  They give drinks to their
     neighbors.
  They pour the drinks from
     wineskins
  until their neighbors are drunk.
  They want to look at their naked
     bodies.
¹⁶ But the Babylonians will be filled
     with shame instead of glory.
  So now it is their turn to drink
   and be stripped of their
     clothes.
  The cup of anger in my powerful
     right hand
   is going to punish them.
  They will be covered with shame
     instead of glory.
¹⁷ The harm they have done to
     Lebanon
  will bring them down.
  Because they have killed so many
     animals,
   animals will terrify them.
  They have spilled man's blood.

They have destroyed lands and
     cities
  and everyone in them.

¹⁸ "If someone carves a statue of a
     god, what is it worth?
  What value is there in a god
     that teaches lies?
  The one who trusts in another god
     worships his own creation.
  He makes statues of gods that
     can't speak.
¹⁹ How terrible it will be for the
     Babylonians!
  They say to a wooden god, 'Come
     to life!'
  They say to a stone god, 'Wake up!'
  Can those gods give advice?
  They are covered with gold and
     silver.
  They can't even breathe.
²⁰ But I am in my holy temple.
  Let the whole earth be silent in
     front of me."

HABAKKUK PRAYS TO
THE LORD

3 This is a prayer of the prophet
Habakkuk. It is on *shigionoth*.
Here is what he said.

² LORD, I know how famous you are.
  I have great respect for you
  because of your mighty acts.
  Do them again for us.
  Make them known in our time.
  When you are angry,
     please show us your tender love.

³ God, you came from Teman.
  You, the Holy One, came from
     Mount Paran.   *Selah*
  Your glory covered the heavens.
  Your praise filled the earth.
⁴ Your glory was like the sunrise.
  Rays of light flashed from your
     mighty hand.
  Your power was hidden there.
⁵ You sent plagues ahead of you.
  Sickness followed behind you.
⁶ When you stood up, the earth
     shook.
  When you looked at the nations,
     they trembled with fear.
  The age-old mountains crumbled.
  The ancient hills fell down.
  Your mighty acts will last
     forever.

⁷I saw the tents of Cushan in
  trouble.
The people of Midian were
  suffering greatly.

⁸LORD, did your anger burn against
  the rivers?
Were you angry with the
  streams?
Were you angry with the Red Sea?
  You rode your horses and
    chariots
  to overcome it.
⁹You got your bow ready to use.
  You asked for many arrows.
                    Selah

You broke up the surface
  of the earth with rivers.
¹⁰The mountains saw you and
  shook.
  Floods of water swept by.
The sea roared.
  It lifted its waves high.

¹¹The sun and moon stood still in
  the sky.
  They stopped because your
    flying arrows flashed by.
  Your gleaming spear shone like
    lightning.
¹²When you were angry, you
  marched across the earth.
  Because of your anger you
    destroyed the nations.
¹³You came out to set your people
  free.
  You saved your chosen ones.
You crushed Pharaoh, the leader
  of that evil land of Egypt.
You stripped him from head to
  foot.   *Selah*
¹⁴His soldiers rushed out to scatter
  us.
  They were laughing at us.

They thought they would easily
  destroy us.
They saw us as weak people who
  were trying to hide.
So you wounded Pharaoh's head
  with his own spear.
¹⁵Your horses charged into the Red
  Sea.
  They stirred up the great waters.

¹⁶I listened and my heart pounded.
  My lips trembled at the sound.
My bones seemed to rot.
  And my legs shook.
But I will be patient.
  I'll wait for the day of trouble to
    come on Babylonia.
  It's the nation that is attacking
    us.
¹⁷The fig trees might not bud.
  The vines might not produce any
    grapes.
  The olive crop might fail.
  The fields might not produce any
    food.
  There might not be any sheep in
    the pens.
  There might not be any cattle in
    the barns.
¹⁸But I will still be glad
  because of what the LORD has
    done.
  God my Savior fills me with joy.

¹⁹The LORD and King gives me
  strength.
  He makes my feet like the feet of
    a deer.
  He helps me walk on the highest
    places.

This prayer is for the director of music. It should be sung while being accompanied by stringed instruments.

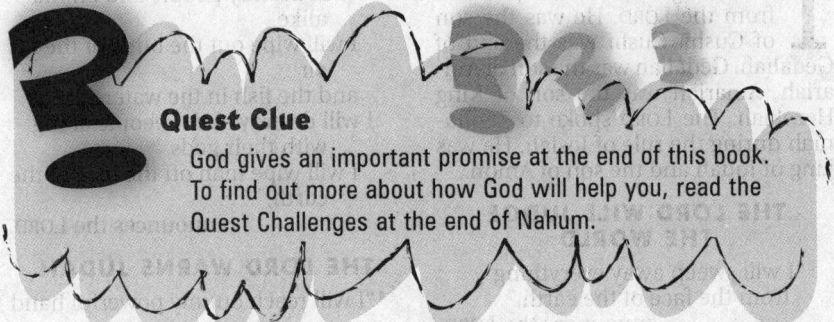

Quest Clue

God gives an important promise at the end of this book.
To find out more about how God will help you, read the
Quest Challenges at the end of Nahum.

Zephaniah

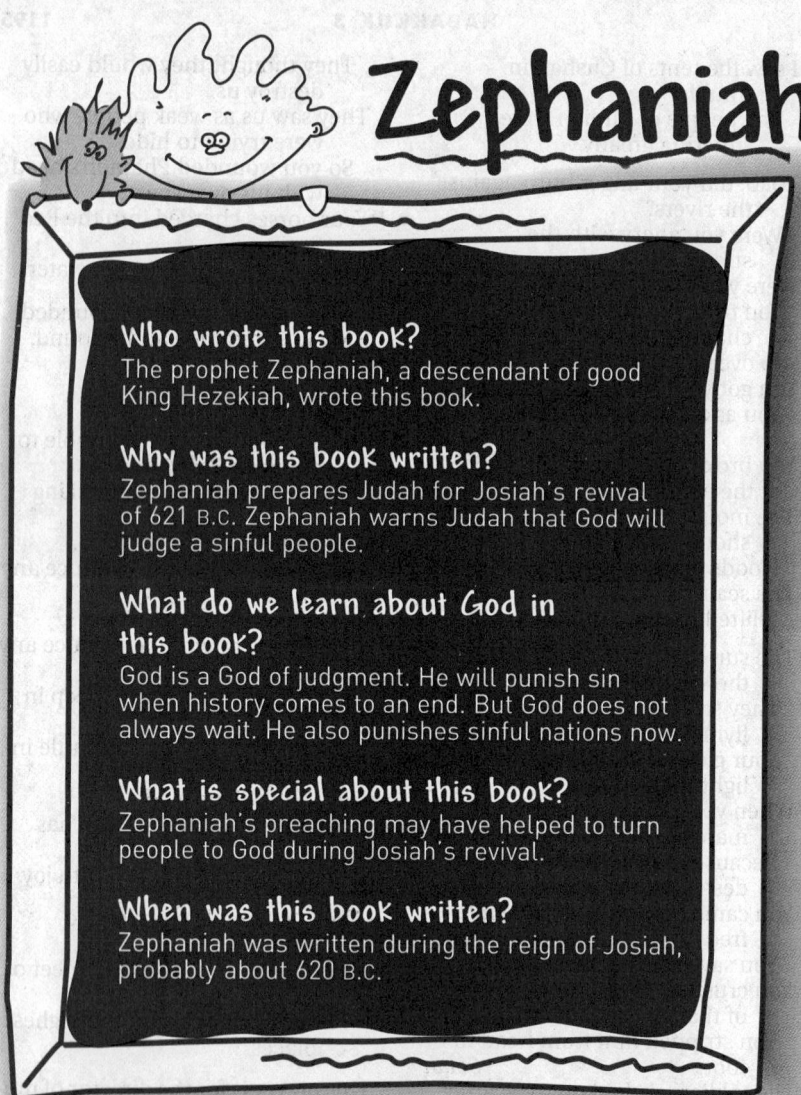

Who wrote this book?
The prophet Zephaniah, a descendant of good King Hezekiah, wrote this book.

Why was this book written?
Zephaniah prepares Judah for Josiah's revival of 621 B.C. Zephaniah warns Judah that God will judge a sinful people.

What do we learn about God in this book?
God is a God of judgment. He will punish sin when history comes to an end. But God does not always wait. He also punishes sinful nations now.

What is special about this book?
Zephaniah's preaching may have helped to turn people to God during Josiah's revival.

When was this book written?
Zephaniah was written during the reign of Josiah, probably about 620 B.C.

1 A message came to Zephaniah from the LORD. He was the son of Cushi. Cushi was the son of Gedaliah. Gedaliah was the son of Amariah. Amariah was the son of King Hezekiah. The LORD spoke to Zephaniah during the rule of Josiah. He was king of Judah and the son of Amon.

THE LORD WILL JUDGE THE WORLD

² "I will sweep away everything
from the face of the earth,"
announces the LORD.

³ "I will destroy people and animals
alike.
I will wipe out the birds of the
air
and the fish in the waters.
I will destroy sinful people along
with their gods.
I will wipe man off the face of the
earth,"
announces the LORD.

THE LORD WARNS JUDAH

⁴ "I will reach out my powerful hand
against Judah.

I will punish all those who live in
Jerusalem.
I will cut off from that place
what is left of Baal worship.
The officials and priests who serve
other gods
will be removed.
[5] I will wipe out those who bow
down on their roofs
to worship all of the stars.
I will destroy those who take oaths
not only in my name but also in
the name of Molech.
[6] I will cut off those who stop
following me.
They no longer look to me or ask
me for advice.
[7] Be silent in front of me.
I am the LORD and King.
The day of the LORD is near.
I have prepared a sacrifice.
I have set apart for myself
the people I invited.
[8] When my sacrifice is ready to be
offered,
I will punish the princes and the
king's sons.
I will also judge all those who
follow
the practices of other nations.
[9] At that time I will punish
all those who worship other
gods.
They fill the temples of their gods
with lies and other harmful
things.

[10] "At that time people at the Fish
Gate in Jerusalem
will cry out," announces the
LORD.
"So will those at the New Quarter.
The buildings on the hills will
come crashing down
with a loud noise.
[11] Cry out, you who live in the
market places.
All of your merchants will be
wiped out.
Those who trade in silver will be
destroyed.
[12] At that time I will search Jerusalem
with lamps.
I will punish those who are so
contented.
They are like wine that has not
been shaken up.

They think, 'The LORD won't do
anything.
It doesn't matter whether it's
good or bad.'
[13] Their wealth will be stolen.
Their houses will be destroyed.
They will build houses.
But they will not live in them.
They will plant vineyards.
But they will not drink the wine
they produce.

THE DAY OF THE LORD IS COMING

[14] "The great day of the LORD is
near.
In fact, it is coming quickly.
Listen! The cries on that day will
be bitter.
Even soldiers will cry out in fear.
[15] At that time I will pour out my
anger.
There will be great suffering and
pain.
It will be a day of horrible trouble.
It will be a time of darkness and
gloom.
It will be filled with the blackest
clouds.
[16] Trumpet blasts and battle cries
will be heard.
Soldiers will attack cities
that have forts and corner
towers.
[17] I will bring trouble on the people.
They will trip and fall as if they
were blind.
They have sinned against me.
Their blood will be poured out like
dust.
Their bodies will lie rotting on
the ground.
[18] Their silver and gold
will not be able to save them
on the day I pour out my anger.
The whole world will be burned up
when my jealous anger blazes
out.
Everyone who lives on earth
will come to a sudden end."

2 Gather your people together,
you shameful nation of Judah!
Gather them together!
[2] Come together before the
appointed time arrives.
The day of the LORD will sweep in

like straw blown by the wind.
Soon the LORD's anger will burn
against you.
The day of his anger will come
on you.
³ So look to him, all of you people in
the land
who worship him faithfully.
You always do what he
commands you to do.
Continue to do what is right.
Don't be proud.
Then perhaps the LORD will keep
you safe
on the day he pours out his anger
on the world.

A MESSAGE ABOUT PHILISTIA

⁴ Gaza will be deserted.
Ashkelon will be destroyed.
Ashdod will be emptied out at
noon.
Ekron will be pulled up by its
roots.
⁵ How terrible it will be for you
Kerethites
who live by the Mediterranean
Sea!
Philistia, the LORD has spoken
against you.
What happened to Canaan will
happen to you.
The LORD says, "I will destroy you.
No one will be left."
⁶ The Kerethites live in the land by
the sea.
It will become a place for
shepherds and sheep pens.
⁷ It will belong to those who are still
left alive
among the people of Judah.
They will find grasslands there.
They will take over
the houses in Ashkelon and live
in them.
The LORD their God will take care
of them.
He will bless them with great
success again.

A MESSAGE ABOUT MOAB AND AMMON

⁸ The LORD says,

"I have heard Moab make fun of
my people.

The Ammonites also laughed at
them.
They told them that bad things
would happen to their land.
⁹ So Moab will become like Sodom,"
announces the LORD who rules
over all.
"Ammon will be like Gomorrah.
Weeds and salt pits will cover
those countries.
They will be dry and empty
deserts forever.
Those who are still left alive
among my people
will take all of their valuable
things.
So they will receive those lands
as their own.
And that is just as sure as I am
alive."
The LORD is the God of Israel.

¹⁰ Moab and Ammon will be judged
because they are so proud.
They made fun of the LORD's
people.
They laughed at them.
¹¹ The LORD who rules over all will
terrify Moab and Ammon.
He will destroy all of the gods on
earth.
Then the nations on every shore
will worship him.
All of them will serve him in their
own lands.

A MESSAGE ABOUT CUSH

¹² The LORD says, "People of Cush,
you too will be killed with my
sword."

A MESSAGE ABOUT ASSYRIA

¹³ The LORD will reach out his
powerful hand against the
north.
He will destroy Assyria.
He'll leave Nineveh totally empty.
It will be as dry as a desert.
¹⁴ Flocks and herds will lie down
there.
So will creatures of every kind.
Desert owls and screech owls
will rest on its pillars.
Their cries will echo through the
windows.
The doorways will be full of
trash.

The cedar beams will be
showing.
¹⁵ Nineveh is a carefree city.
It lived in safety.
It said to itself,
"I am like a god.
No one is greater than I am."
But it has been destroyed.
Wild animals make their home
there.
All those who pass by laugh
and shake their fists at it.

THE LORD WILL SAVE
JERUSALEM

3 How terrible it will be for
Jerusalem!
Its people crush others.
They refuse to obey the LORD.
They are "unclean."
² They don't obey anyone.
They don't accept the LORD's
warnings.
They don't trust in him.
They don't ask their God for his
help.
³ Their officials are like roaring
lions.
Their rulers are like wolves that
hunt in the evening.
They don't leave anything to eat
in the morning.
⁴ Their prophets are proud.
They can't be trusted.
Their priests pollute the temple.
They break the law they teach
others to obey.
⁵ In spite of that, the LORD is good to
Jerusalem.
He never does anything that is
wrong.
Every morning he does what is
fair.
Each new day he does the right
thing.
But those who do what is wrong
aren't even ashamed of it.

⁶ The LORD says to his people,

"I have cut off other nations.
I have wiped out their forts.
I have left their streets deserted.
No one walks along them.
Their cities are destroyed.
Not even one person is left.
⁷ I said to you people of Jerusalem,
'Because I cut off other nations,

you will have respect for me.
Now you will accept my
warning.'
I wish you had returned to me.
Then your homes would not
have been torn down.
And I would not have had to
punish you so much.
But you still wanted to go on
sinning
in every way you could.
⁸ So wait for me to come as judge,"
announces the LORD.
"Wait for the day I will stand up
to witness against all sinners.
I have decided to gather the
nations.
I will bring the kingdoms
together.
And I will pour out all of my
burning anger on them.
The fire of my jealous anger
will burn the whole world up.

⁹ "But then I will purify what all of
the nations say.
And they will use their words to
worship me.
They will serve me together.
¹⁰ My scattered people, you will
come to me
from beyond the rivers of Cush.
You will worship me.
You will bring me offerings.
¹¹ You have done many wrong things
to me.
But at that time you will not be
put to shame anymore.
Then I will remove from this city
those who take delight in their
pride.
You will never be proud again
on my holy mountain of Zion.
¹² But inside your city I will leave
those who are not proud at all.
They trust in me.
¹³ Those who are still left alive in
Israel
will not do anything wrong.
They will not tell any lies.
They will not say anything to fool
others.
They will eat and lie down in peace.
And no one will make them
afraid."

¹⁴ People of Zion, sing!
Israel, shout loudly!

People of Jerusalem, be glad!
Let your hearts be full of joy.
¹⁵ The LORD has stopped punishing
you.
He has made your enemies turn
away from you.
The LORD is the King of Israel.
He is with you.
You will never again be afraid
that others will harm you.
¹⁶ The time is coming when people
will say to Jerusalem,
"Zion, don't be afraid.
Don't give up.
¹⁷ The LORD your God is with you.
He is mighty enough to save you.
He will take great delight in you.
The quietness of his love will
calm you down.
He will sing with joy because of
you."

¹⁸ The LORD says to his people,

"You used to celebrate my
appointed feasts in Jerusalem.

You are sad because you can't do
that anymore.
So others make fun of those
feasts.
That was a heavy load for you to
carry.
But I will bring you back to your
city.
¹⁹ At that time I will punish
all those who crushed you.
I will save those among you who
are disabled.
I will gather those who have
been scattered.
I will give you praise and honor
in every land where you were put
to shame.
²⁰ At that time I will gather you
together.
And I will bring you home.
I will give you honor and praise
among all of the nations on earth.
I will bless you with great success
again,"
says the LORD.

I Wonder . . .

What can I do when I feel like a "loser"?

Real Life Challenge

As you walk down the hall you might notice what other kids are
wearing, who they're talking to, or how they're acting. Sometimes
you might think you just don't measure up. Don't believe the lie that
you're not good enough. Your father is God, and he has provided a
plan for how to fight against the lies the devil tells you. God loves you
and will teach you how to spot a lie and get rid of it.

Quest Clue

Find out how much God loves you in Zephaniah 3:17. Then look in
Ephesians 6 for God's recipe for overcoming lies with God's truth.
Copy these verses down and carry them in your backpack. This is
your battle plan.

Haggai

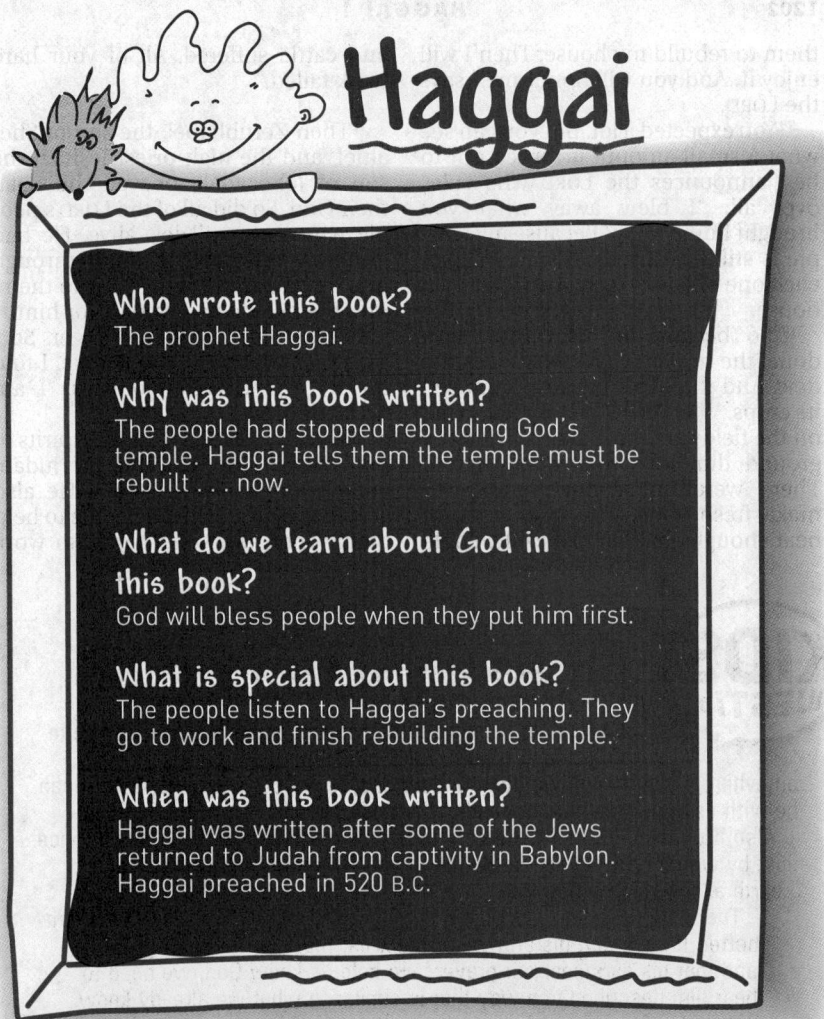

Who wrote this book?
The prophet Haggai.

Why was this book written?
The people had stopped rebuilding God's temple. Haggai tells them the temple must be rebuilt . . . now.

What do we learn about God in this book?
God will bless people when they put him first.

What is special about this book?
The people listen to Haggai's preaching. They go to work and finish rebuilding the temple.

When was this book written?
Haggai was written after some of the Jews returned to Judah from captivity in Babylon. Haggai preached in 520 B.C.

HAGGAI TELLS HIS PEOPLE TO REBUILD THE LORD'S TEMPLE

1 A message came to the prophet Haggai from the LORD. Haggai gave it to Zerubbabel and Jeshua. It came on the first day of the sixth month of the second year that Darius was king of Persia. Zerubbabel was governor of Judah and the son of Shealtiel. Jeshua was high priest and the son of Jehozadak. Here is what Haggai said.

²The LORD who rules over all says, "The people of Judah are saying, 'The time hasn't come yet for the LORD's temple to be rebuilt.' "

³So the message came to me from the LORD. He said, ⁴"My temple is still destroyed. In spite of that, you are living in your houses that have beautiful wooden walls."

⁵The LORD who rules over all says, "Think carefully about how you are living. ⁶You have planted many seeds. But the crops you have gathered are small. So you eat. But you never have enough. You drink. But you are never full. You put your clothes on. But you are not warm. You earn your pay. But it will not buy everything you need."

⁷He continues, "Think carefully about how you are living. ⁸Go up into the mountains. Bring logs down. Use

them to rebuild my house. Then I will enjoy it. And you will honor me," says the LORD.

9"You expected a lot. But you can see what a small amount it turned out to be," announces the LORD who rules over all. "I blew away what you brought home. Why? Because my temple is still destroyed. In spite of that, each one of you is busy with your own house.

10"So because of what you have done, the heavens have held back the dew. And the earth has not produced its crops. 11I ordered the rain not to fall on the fields and mountains. Then the ground did not produce any grain. There were not enough grapes to make fresh wine. The trees did not bear enough olives to make oil. People

and cattle suffered. All of your hard work failed."

12Then Zerubbabel, the son of Shealtiel, and the high priest Jeshua, the son of Jehozadak, obeyed the LORD their God. So did all of the LORD's people who were still left alive. He had given his message to them through me. He had sent me to speak to them. And the people had respect for him.

13I was the LORD's messenger. So I gave his message to the people. I told them, "The LORD announces, 'I am with you.' "

14So the LORD stirred up the spirits of Zerubbabel, the governor of Judah, and the high priest Jeshua. He also stirred up the rest of the people to help them. Then everyone began to work

How can God be everywhere?

We human beings have physical bodies; we can only be in one place at a time. But God is not like that. God can be anywhere, even though we don't understand how. God is a spirit, and he can be with us in our hearts and minds. The Bible says so.

Also, God is *all-powerful*. He can do anything. He can be all places at once just by wanting to. He can be on his throne in heaven and be with us on earth at the same time.

The Bible describes God like a human being to help us understand him better. It says that his arm will protect us, that his hand will guide us, and that his ears hear our prayers. To help us know God, we need to hear him described in a way that is similar to what we already know. But God is far greater than any human being.

God is with us no matter where we go. He is always there to love us, help us and listen to our prayers. God wants us to know this so we will never be afraid to come to him.

checkout
Haggai 1:13

Related verses:
2 Chronicles 2:6;
Job 42:2–3;
Psalm 103:22;
139:2–3, 7–8;
Proverbs 15:3

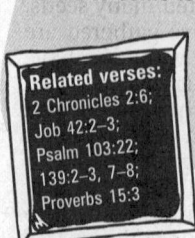

on the temple of the LORD who rules over all. He is their God. ¹⁵It was the 24th day of the sixth month of the second year that Darius was king.

THE NEW TEMPLE WILL BE BEAUTIFUL

2 A second message came to me from the LORD. It came on the 21st day of the seventh month. The LORD said, ²"Speak to Zerubbabel, the governor of Judah and the son of Shealtiel. Also speak to the high priest Jeshua, the son of Jehozadak. And speak to all of my people who are still left alive. Ask them, ³'Did any of you who are here see how beautiful this temple used to be? How does it look to you now? It doesn't look so good, does it?

⁴" 'But be strong, Zerubbabel,' announces the LORD. 'Be strong, Jeshua. Be strong, all of you people in the land,' announces the LORD. 'Start rebuilding. I am with you,' announces the LORD who rules over all. ⁵'That is what I promised you when you came out of Egypt. My Spirit continues to be with you. So do not be afraid.' "

⁶The LORD says, "In a little while I will shake the heavens and the earth once more. I will also shake the ocean and the dry land. ⁷I will shake all of the nations. Then what they consider to be priceless will come to my temple. And I will fill the temple with glory," says the LORD who rules over all.

⁸"The silver belongs to me. So does the gold," announces the LORD. ⁹"The new temple will be more beautiful than the first one was," says the LORD. "And in this place I will give peace to my people," announces the LORD who rules over all.

THE LORD WILL MAKE HIS PEOPLE PURE AND CLEAN

¹⁰A third message came to me from the LORD. It came on the 24th day of the ninth month of the second year that Darius was king. ¹¹The LORD who rules over all speaks. He says, "Ask the priests what the law says. ¹²Suppose someone carries holy meat in the clothes he is wearing. And the clothes touch some bread or stew. Or they touch some wine, olive oil or other

food. Then do those things also become holy?"

The priests answered, "No."

¹³So I said, "Suppose someone is made 'unclean' by touching a dead body. And then he touches one of those things. Does it become 'unclean' too?"

"Yes," the priests replied. "It does."

¹⁴Then I said, "The LORD announces, 'That is how I look at these people and this nation. Anything they do and anything they sacrifice on the altar is "unclean."

¹⁵" 'Now think carefully about the time before one stone was laid on top of another in my temple. ¹⁶People went to get 20 measures of grain. But they could find only 10. They went to where the wine was stored to get 50 measures. But only 20 were there. ¹⁷You worked very hard to produce all of those things. But I struck them with rot, mold and hail. And you still did not turn to me,' announces the LORD.

¹⁸" 'It is the 24th day of the ninth month. From this day on, think carefully about the day when the foundation of my temple was laid. Think about it carefully. ¹⁹Are any seeds still left in your barns? Until now, your vines and fig trees have not produced any fruit. Your pomegranate and olive trees have not produced any either.

" 'But from this day on I will bless you.' "

THE LORD COMPARES ZERUBBABEL TO HIS ROYAL RING

²⁰A final message came to me from the LORD. It also came on the 24th day of the ninth month. He said, ²¹"Speak to Zerubbabel, the governor of Judah. Tell him I will shake the heavens and the earth. ²²I will throw down royal thrones. I will smash the power of other kingdoms. I will destroy chariots and their drivers. Horses and their riders will fall. They will be killed with the swords of their relatives.

²³" 'Zerubbabel, at that time I will pick you,' announces the LORD. 'You are my servant,' announces the LORD. 'You will be like a ring that has my royal seal on it. I have chosen you,' announces the LORD who rules over all."

Zechariah

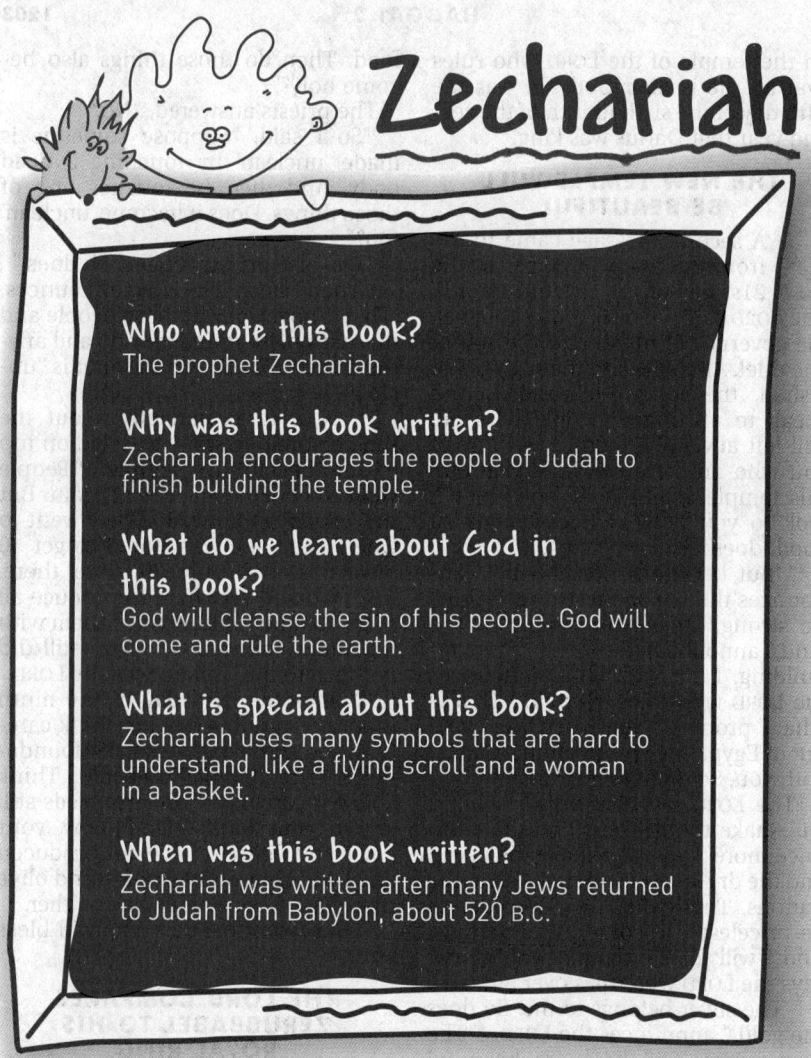

Who wrote this book?
The prophet Zechariah.

Why was this book written?
Zechariah encourages the people of Judah to finish building the temple.

What do we learn about God in this book?
God will cleanse the sin of his people. God will come and rule the earth.

What is special about this book?
Zechariah uses many symbols that are hard to understand, like a flying scroll and a woman in a basket.

When was this book written?
Zechariah was written after many Jews returned to Judah from Babylon, about 520 B.C.

THE LORD WANTS HIS PEOPLE TO RETURN TO HIM

1 A message came to the prophet Zechariah from the LORD. It was the eighth month of the second year that Darius was king of Persia. Zechariah was the son of Berekiah. Berekiah was the son of Iddo. Here is what Zechariah said.

² The LORD who rules over all was very angry with our people years ago. ³ And now he says to us, "Return to me. Then I will return to you," announces the LORD. ⁴ "Do not be like your people years ago. The earlier prophets gave them my message. I said, 'Stop doing what is evil. Turn away from your sinful practices.' But they would not listen to me. They would not pay any attention," announces the LORD.

⁵ "Where are those people now? And what about my prophets? Do they live forever? ⁶ I commanded my servants the prophets what to say. I told them what I planned to do. But your people refused to obey me. So I had to punish them.

"Then they had a change of heart. They said, 'The LORD who rules over all has punished us because of how we have lived. He was fair and right to do that. He has done to us just what he decided to do.' "

A VISION OF A HORSEMAN AMONG SOME MYRTLE TREES

[7]During the second year that Darius was king, a message came to me from the LORD. It was the 24th day of the 11th month. That's the month of Shebat.

[8]I had a vision at night. I saw a man riding a red horse. He was standing among the myrtle trees in a valley. Behind him were red, brown and white horses.

[9]An angel was talking with me. I asked him, "Sir, what are these?"

He answered, "I will show you what they are."

[10]Then the man who was standing among the myrtle trees said, "They are the messengers the LORD has sent out. He told them to go all through the earth."

[11]They brought a report to the angel of the LORD. He was standing among the myrtle trees. They said to him, "We have gone all through the earth. We've found the whole world enjoying peace and rest."

[12]Then the angel of the LORD spoke up. He said, "LORD, you rule over all. How long will you keep from showing your tender love to Jerusalem? How long will you keep it from the towns of Judah? You have been angry with them for 70 years."

[13]So the LORD replied with kind and comforting words. He spoke them to the angel who talked with me.

[14]Then the angel said, "Announce this message. Say, 'The LORD who rules over all says, "I am very jealous for my people in Jerusalem and Zion. [15]But I am very angry with the nations that feel secure. I was only a little angry with my people. But the nations went too far and tried to wipe them out."

[16]" 'So the LORD says, "I will return to Jerusalem. I will show its people my tender love. My temple will be rebuilt there. Workers will use a measuring line when they rebuild Jerusalem," announces the LORD.

[17]" 'He says, "My towns will be filled with good things once more. I will comfort Zion. And I will choose Jerusalem again." ' "

A VISION OF FOUR HORNS AND FOUR SKILLED WORKERS

[18]Then I looked up and saw four animal horns. [19]I spoke to the angel who was talking with me. "What are these horns?" I asked.

He said, "They are the powerful nations that scattered Judah, Israel and Jerusalem."

[20]Then the LORD showed me four skilled workers. [21]I asked, "What are they coming to do?"

He answered, "They are the powerful nations that scattered the people of Judah. That made them helpless. But the workers have come to terrify the horns. They will destroy the power of those nations. They had used their power to scatter Judah's people."

A VISION OF A MAN HOLDING A MEASURING LINE

2 Then I looked up and saw a man. He was holding a measuring line. [2]"Where are you going?" I asked.

"To measure Jerusalem," he answered. "I want to find out how wide and how long it is."

[3]Then the angel who was talking with me left. Another angel came over to him. [4]He said to him, "Run! Tell that young man Zechariah, 'Jerusalem will be like a city that does not have any walls around it. It will have huge numbers of people and animals in it. [5]And I myself will be like a wall of fire around it,' announces the LORD. 'I will be the city's glory.' "

[6]"Israel, I have scattered you in all four directions," announces the LORD. "Come quickly! Run away from the land of the north," announces the LORD.

[7]"Come, people of Zion who are in Babylonia! Escape, you who live in the city of Babylon!" [8]The LORD rules over all. His angel says to Israel, "The LORD has sent me to honor him. He wants me to punish the nations that have robbed you of everything. After all, anyone who hurts you hurts those the LORD loves and guards. [9]So I will raise my powerful hand to strike your ene-

mies down. Their own slaves will rob them of everything. Then you will know that the LORD who rules over all has sent me.

¹⁰" 'People of Zion, shout and be glad! I am coming to live among you,' announces the LORD. ¹¹At that time many nations will join themselves to me. And they will become my people. I will live among you.' says the LORD. Then you will know that the LORD who rules over all has sent me to you.

¹²"He will receive Judah as his share in the holy land. And he will choose Jerusalem again.

¹³"All you people of the world, be still because the LORD is coming. He is getting ready to come down from his holy temple in heaven."

A VISION OF THE HIGH PRIEST DRESSED IN FINE CLOTHES

3 Then the LORD showed me the high priest Jeshua. He was standing in front of the angel of the LORD. Satan was standing to the right of Jeshua. He was there to bring charges against the high priest. ²The LORD said to Satan, "May the LORD correct you! He has chosen Jerusalem. So may he correct you! Isn't this man Jeshua like a burning stick pulled out of the fire?"

³Jeshua stood in front of the angel. He was wearing clothes that were very dirty. ⁴The angel spoke to those who were standing near him. He said, "Take his dirty clothes off."

He said to Jeshua, "I have taken your sin away. I will put fine clothes on you."

⁵I added, "Put a clean turban on his head." So they did. And they dressed him while the angel of the LORD stood by.

⁶Then the angel spoke to Jeshua. He said, ⁷"The LORD who rules over all says, 'You must live the way I want you to. And you must do what I want you to do. Then you will rule in my temple. You will be in charge of my courtyards.

KIDS' QUESTION

Who is the devil?

The devil is Satan. The word *devil* means "liar" or "accuser." Satan used to be an angel. But he wanted to be like God, so he fought against God. God kicked him out of heaven. Ever since then Satan has been trying to stop God from having his way. He tries to stop God's people from believing in God and obeying him. But God is far stronger than Satan. In the end Satan will be thrown into hell and suffer forever. He will not win.

checkout

Zechariah 3:1

Related verses:
Ephesians 6:11;
Hebrews 2:14;
Revelation 20:10

GREEN DYE

BIBLE

memory verses

And I will give you a place among these who are standing here.

8"'High priest Jeshua, pay attention! I want you other priests who are sitting with Jeshua to listen also. All of you men are signs of things to come. I am going to bring my servant the Branch. 9Look at the stone I have put in front of Jeshua! There are seven eyes on that one stone. I will carve a message on it,' says the LORD who rules over all. 'And I will remove the sin of this land in one day.

10"'At that time each of you will invite your neighbors to visit you. They will sit under your vines and fig trees,' announces the LORD."

A VISION OF THE GOLD LAMPSTAND AND TWO OLIVE TREES

4 Then the angel who was talking with me returned. He woke me up. It was as if I had been asleep. 2"What do you see?" he asked me.

"I see a solid gold lampstand," I answered. "It has a bowl on top of it. There are seven lamps on it. Seven tubes lead to each of them. 3There are two olive trees by the lampstand. One is on its right side. The other is on its left."

4I asked the angel who was talking with me, "Sir, what are these?"

5He answered, "Don't you know what they are?"

"No, sir," I replied.

6So he said to me, "A message came to Zerubbabel from the LORD. He said, 'Your strength will not get my temple rebuilt. Your power will not do it either. Only the power of my Spirit will do it,' says the LORD who rules over all. 7"So nothing can stop Zerubbabel from completing the temple. Even a mountain of problems will be smoothed out by him. When the temple is finished, he will put its most important stone in place. Then the people will shout, 'God bless it! God bless it!'"

8A message came to me from the LORD. His angel said, 9"The hands of Zerubbabel have laid the foundation of this temple. His hands will also complete it. Then you will know that the LORD who rules over all has sent me to you.

10"Do not look down on the small amount of work done on the temple so far. People will be filled with joy when they see Zerubbabel holding the most important stone.

"The seven eyes on the stone are the eyes of the LORD himself. He looks out over the whole earth."

11Then I said to the angel, "I see two olive trees. One is on the right side of the lampstand. The other is on the left. What are those trees?"

12I continued, "I also see two olive branches. They are next to the two gold pipes that pour out golden olive oil. What are those branches?"

13He answered, "Don't you know what they are?"

"No, sir," I said.

14So he told me, "They are Zerubbabel and Jeshua. The Lord of the whole earth has anointed them to serve him."

A VISION OF A FLYING SCROLL

5 I looked up again and saw a flying scroll. 2"What do you see?" the angel asked me.

"A flying scroll," I replied. "It's 30 feet long and 15 feet wide."

3He said to me, "A curse sent by the LORD is written on it. It is going out over the whole land. Every thief will be driven out of the land. That is what it says on one side of the scroll. Everyone who lies when taking an oath to tell the truth will also be driven out. That is what it says on the other side. 4The LORD who rules over all announces, 'I will send the curse out. It will enter the house of the thief. It will also enter the house of anyone who lies when taking an oath in my name. It will remain in that house and destroy it. It will pull down its beams and stones.'"

A VISION OF A WOMAN IN A BASKET

5Then the angel who was talking with me came forward. He said to me, "Look at what is coming."

6"What is it?" I asked.

"A measuring basket," he replied. "The sins of the people all through the land are in it."

⁷Then the basket's cover was lifted up. It was made out of lead. A woman was sitting in the basket! ⁸The angel said, "She stands for everything that is evil." Then he pushed her down into the basket. He put the lead cover back over its opening.

⁹I looked up and saw two other women. They had wings like the wings of a stork. A wind sent by the LORD carried them along. They lifted the basket up between heaven and earth.

¹⁰"Where are they taking the basket?" I asked the angel.

¹¹He replied, "To the country of Babylonia. A temple will be built for it. When the temple is ready, the basket will be set there in its place."

A VISION OF FOUR CHARIOTS

6 I looked up again and saw four chariots. They were coming out from between two mountains. The mountains were made out of bronze.

²The first chariot was pulled by red horses. The second one had black horses. ³The third had white horses. And the fourth had spotted horses. All of the horses were powerful.

⁴I asked the angel who was talking with me, "Sir, what are these?"

⁵The angel answered, "The four spirits of heaven. They are going out to serve the Lord of the whole world. ⁶The chariot pulled by the black horses is going toward the north country. The one with the white horses is going toward the west. And the one with the spotted horses is going toward the south."

⁷The powerful horses went out. They were in a hurry to go all over the earth. The angel said, "Go all through the earth!" So they did.

⁸Then the LORD called out to me, "Look! The horses going toward the north have given my Spirit rest in the north country."

A CROWN IS GIVEN TO JESHUA

⁹A message came to me from the LORD. His angel said, ¹⁰"Get some silver and gold from Heldai, Tobijah and Jedaiah. They have just come back from Babylonia. On that same day

go to Josiah's house. He is the son of Zephaniah. ¹¹Use the silver and gold to make a crown. Set it on the head of the high priest Jeshua. He is the son of Jehozadak.

¹²"Give Jeshua a message from the LORD who rules over all. He says, 'Here is the man whose name is The Branch. He will branch out and build my temple. ¹³That is what he will do. He will be dressed in majesty as if it were his royal robe. He will sit as king on his throne. He will also be a priest there. So he will combine the positions of king and priest in himself.'

¹⁴"The crown will be given to Heldai, Tobijah, Jedaiah and Zephaniah's son Hen. The crown will be kept in the LORD's temple. It will remind everyone that the LORD's promises will come true.

¹⁵"Those who are far away will come to Jerusalem. They will help build the LORD's temple. Then his people will know that the LORD who rules over all has sent me to them. It will happen if they are careful to obey the LORD their God."

TREAT EVERYONE FAIRLY

7 During the fourth year that Darius was king, a message came to me from the LORD. It was the fourth day of the ninth month. That's the month of Kislev.

²The people of Bethel wanted to ask the LORD to show them his favor. So they sent Sharezer and Regem-Melech and their men. ³They went to the prophets and priests at the LORD's temple. They asked them, "Should we sob and go without eating in the fifth month? That's what we've done for many years."

⁴Then the message came to me from the LORD who rules over all. He said, ⁵"Ask the priests and all of the people in the land a question for me. Say to them, 'You sobbed and fasted in the fifth and seventh months. You did it for the past 70 years. But did you really do it for me? ⁶And when you were eating and drinking, weren't you just enjoying good food for yourselves?

⁷" 'Didn't I tell you the same thing through the earlier prophets? That was when Jerusalem and the towns

around it were at rest and enjoyed success. People lived in the Negev Desert and the western hills at that time.' "

⁸Another message came to me from the LORD. ⁹He rules over all. He says to his people, "Treat everyone fairly. Show faithful love and tender concern to one another. ¹⁰Do not take advantage of widows. Do not mistreat children whose fathers have died. Do not crush strangers or poor people. Do not make evil plans against one another."

¹¹But they refused to pay attention to the LORD. They were stubborn. They turned their backs and covered up their ears. ¹²They made their hearts as hard as the hardest stone. They wouldn't listen to the law. They wouldn't pay attention to the LORD's messages.

So the LORD who rules over all was very angry. After all, his Spirit had spoken to his people through the earlier prophets.

¹³"When I called, they did not listen," says the LORD. "So when they called, I would not listen. ¹⁴I used a windstorm to scatter them among all of the nations. They were strangers there. The land they left behind became dry and empty. No one could even travel through it. That is how they turned the pleasant land into a dry and empty desert."

THE LORD PROMISES TO BLESS JERUSALEM

8 Another message came to me from the LORD who rules over all. He said, ²"I am very jealous for my people in Zion. In fact, I am burning with jealousy for them."

³He continued, "I will return to Zion. I will live among my people in Jerusalem. Then Jerusalem will be called The City of Truth. And my mountain will be called The Holy Mountain."

⁴He continued, "Once again old men and women will sit in the streets of Jerusalem. All of them will be using canes because they are old. ⁵The city streets will be filled with boys and girls. They will be playing there."

⁶He continued, "All of that might seem wonderful to the people who are living at that time. But it will not seem wonderful to me."

⁷He continued, "I will save my people. I will gather them from the countries of the east and the west. ⁸I will bring them back to live in Jerusalem. They will be my people. I will be their

KIDS' QUESTion

Is it OK to bug my sister?

God wants us to be kind and not mean. He wants us to respect people. It can be fun to tease and tickle each other. But we should stop if the person asks us to stop. Sometimes we may not even know we are doing something that bothers people or makes them angry with us. We should stop as soon as we find out. It is easy for brothers and sisters to get on each other's nerves. That is because they spend so much time together. We need to work hard to make our families places of love and kindness.

checkout
Zechariah 7:9

Related verses:
Romans 12:9,10;
Galatians 5:26

faithful God. I will keep my promises to them."

⁹The LORD who rules over all says to his people, "Listen to the words that were spoken by the prophets Haggai and Zechariah. They spoke to you when the work on my temple started up again. Let your hands be strong so that you can rebuild the temple.

¹⁰"Before the work was started again, there was no pay for the people or food for the animals. People could not go about their business safely because of their enemies. I had turned all of them against one another. ¹¹But now I will not punish you who are living at this time. I will not treat you as I treated your people before you," announces the LORD who rules over all.

¹²"Your seeds will grow well. Your vines will bear fruit. The ground will produce crops for you. And the heavens will drop their dew on your land. I will give all of those things to those who are still left alive here.

¹³"Judah and Israel, in the past the nations called down curses on you. But now I will save you. You will be a blessing to others. Do not be afraid. Let your hands be strong so that you can do my work."

¹⁴The LORD who rules over all says, "Years ago your people made me angry. So I decided to bring trouble on them. I did not show them any pity. ¹⁵But now I plan to do good things to Jerusalem and Judah again. So do not be afraid.

¹⁶"Here is what you must do. Speak the truth to one another. Make true and wise decisions in your courts. ¹⁷Do not make evil plans against your neighbors. When you take an oath to tell the truth, do not lie. Many people love to do that. But I hate all of those things," announces the LORD.

¹⁸Another message came to me from the LORD who rules over all. He said, ¹⁹"You have established special times to go without eating. They are your fasts in the fourth, fifth, seventh and tenth months. They will become days of joy. They will be happy times for Judah. It will happen if you take delight in telling the truth and bringing about peace."

²⁰He continued, "Many nations will still come to you. And those who live in many cities will also come. ²¹The people who live in one city will go to another city. They will say, 'Let's go right away to ask the LORD to show us his

---

KIDS' QUESTION

Did children in Bible times color?

Children in Bible times did not color with crayons like the ones we have today. But they did draw pictures and play games. People who study old cities have found some of the games. Children back then dressed differently from the way we do. Their houses and schools were made differently. They had different kinds of games. But they were just like kids today in many ways. They liked to have fun. They had family chores to do. Their parents corrected them. They learned things. They were happy sometimes and sad sometimes. They were real kids.

checkout Zechariah 8:5

Related verses:
Matthew 18:2–5

favor. Let's look to him as our God. We ourselves are going.' ²²Large numbers of people and nations will come to Jerusalem. They will look to me. They will ask me to show them my favor."

²³He continued, "At that time many men from all nations and languages will take hold of one Jew. They will grab hold of the hem of his robe. And they will say, 'We want to go to Jerusalem with you. We've heard that God is with you.' "

THE LORD DESTROYS ISRAEL'S ENEMIES

9 This is the LORD's message against the land of Hadrach.
He will judge Damascus.
That's because all of the tribes of Israel look to him.
So do other people.
²The LORD will judge Hamath too.
It's next to Damascus.
He will also punish Tyre and Sidon even though they are very clever.

³Tyre's people have built a fort for themselves.
They've piled up silver like dust.
They have as much gold as the dirt in the streets.
⁴But the Lord will take away everything they have.
He'll destroy their power on the Mediterranean Sea.
And Tyre will be completely burned up.
⁵Ashkelon will see it and become afraid.
Gaza will groan with pain.
So will Ekron. Its hope will vanish.
Gaza will no longer have a king.
Ashkelon will be deserted.
⁶Strangers will take over Ashdod.
The LORD says, "I will take away everything the Philistines are so proud of.
⁷They will no longer drink the blood of their animal sacrifices.

KIDS' QUESTION

If I cheated and I won, do I have to tell?

You should not cheat in the first place. But if you do cheat, you should admit what you did and make it right whether you won or lost. In a game that is very important to you, you might think about cheating to get ahead. Just remember that winning is not all that matters. It is more important to do what God wants. When you do something wrong and realize it, the best response is to confess. You may also need to pay back or give back what you got. Do not think you can cheat and then laugh about it later. God wants you to be an honest person.

checkout
Zechariah 8:16

Related verse:
James 5:16

MONEY BAGS
(the game)

I will remove the 'unclean' food
from between their teeth.
The Philistines who are left will
belong to our God.
They will become leaders in
Judah.
And Ekron will be like the
Jebusites.
So the Philistines will become
part of Israel.
⁸ But I will guard my temple
against enemy armies.
No one will ever crush my people
again.
I will make sure it does not
happen.

A KING COMES TO ZION

⁹ "City of Zion, be full of joy!
People of Jerusalem, shout!
See, your king comes to you.
He always does what is right.
He has the power to save.
He is gentle and riding on a
donkey.
He is sitting on a donkey's colt.
¹⁰ I will take the chariots away from
Ephraim.
I will remove the war horses from
Jerusalem.
I will break the bows that are
used in battle.
Your king will announce peace to
the nations.
He will rule from ocean to ocean.
His kingdom will reach from the
Euphrates River
to the ends of the earth.
¹¹ I will set your prisoners free
from where their enemies are
keeping them.
I will do it because of the blood
that put my covenant with you
into effect.
¹² Return to your place of safety,
you prisoners who still have
hope.
Even now I announce that I will
give you back
much more than you had before.
¹³ I will bend Judah as I bend my
bow.
I will make Ephraim's people my
arrows.
Zion, I will stir up your sons.
Greece, they will attack your
sons.

My people, I will use you as my
sword."

THE LORD WILL APPEAR

¹⁴ Then the LORD will appear over his
people.
His arrows will flash like
lightning.
The LORD and King will blow the
trumpet of his thunder.
He'll march out like a storm in
the south.
¹⁵ The LORD who rules over all
will be like a shield to his
people.
They will destroy their enemies.
They'll use slings to throw stones
at them.
They'll drink the blood of their
enemies
as if it were wine.
They'll be full like the bowl that is
used
for sprinkling the corners of the
altar.
¹⁶ The LORD their God will save his
people on that day.
They will be like sheep that
belong to his flock.
They will gleam in his land
like jewels in a crown.
¹⁷ How very beautiful they will be!
Grain and fresh wine
will make the young men and
women strong.

THE LORD WILL TAKE CARE OF JUDAH

10 People of Judah, ask the
LORD
to send rain in the spring.
He is the one who makes the
storm clouds.
He sends down showers of rain on
all people.
He gives everyone the plants in
the fields.
² Other gods tell lies.
Those who practice magic
see visions that aren't true.
They tell dreams that fool people.
They give comfort that doesn't do
any good.
So the people wander around like
sheep.
They are crushed because they
don't have a shepherd.

³The LORD who rules over all says,

"My anger burns against the
    shepherds.
I will punish the leaders.
I will take care of my flock.
    They are the people of Judah.
    I will make them like a proud
        horse in battle.
⁴The most important building
        stone
    will come from the tribe of Judah.
    The tent stake will also come
        from it.
And the bow that is used in battle
    will come from it.
    In fact, every ruler will come
        from it.
⁵Together they will be like soldiers
        in battle.
    They will fight their way
        through the muddy streets.
I will be with them.
    So they will fight against the
        horsemen
    and destroy them.

⁶"I will make the family of Judah
        strong.
    I will save the people of Joseph.
I will bring them back
    because I have tender love for
        them.
It will be as if
    I had not sent them away.
I am the LORD their God.
    I will help them.
⁷The people of Ephraim will
        become like mighty men.
    Their hearts will be glad
        as if they were drinking wine.
    Their children will see it
        and be filled with joy.
    I will make their hearts glad.
⁸I will whistle for my people
    and gather them in.
I will set them free.
    There will be as many of them as
        before.
⁹I have scattered them among the
        nations.
    But in lands far away they will
        remember me.
    They and their children will be
        kept alive.
    And they will return.
¹⁰I will bring them back from Egypt.
    I will gather them from Assyria.

I will bring them to Gilead and
    Lebanon.
    There will not be enough room
        for them.
¹¹They will pass through a sea of
        trouble.
    The stormy sea will calm down.
    All of the deep places in the Nile
        River will dry up.
Assyria's pride will be brought
    down.
    Egypt's right to rule will
        disappear.
¹²I will make my people strong.
    They will worship and obey me,"
                announces the LORD.

11 Lebanon, open your
        doors!
    Then fire can burn up your
        cedar trees.
²Pine trees, cry out!
    The cedar trees have fallen down.
    The majestic trees are destroyed.
Cry out, you oak trees of Bashan!
    The thick forest has been cut
        down.
³Listen to the shepherds cry out!
    Their rich grasslands are
        destroyed.
Listen to the lions roar!
    The trees and bushes along the
        Jordan River are gone.

THE TWO SHEPHERDS

⁴The LORD my God says, "Take care
of the sheep that are set apart to be
sacrificed. ⁵Those who buy them kill
them. And they are not punished for it.
Those who sell them say, 'Praise the
LORD! We're rich!' And their own shepherds do not spare them.

⁶"I will no longer have pity on the
people in the land," announces the
LORD. "I will hand all of them over to
their neighbors and their king. They
will crush the people in the land. And I
will not save them from their powerful
hands."

⁷So I took care of the sheep set apart
to be sacrificed. I took special care of
those that had been crushed. Then I
got two shepherd's staffs. I called one
of them Favor. I called the other one
Union. And I took care of the flock. ⁸In
one month I got rid of three worthless
shepherds.

The sheep hated me. And I got tired of them. ⁹So I said, "I won't be your shepherd anymore. Let those of you who are dying die. Let those who are passing away pass away. Let those who are left eat one another up."

¹⁰Then I got my staff called Favor. I broke it. That meant the covenant the LORD had made with all of the nations was broken. ¹¹It happened that very day. The sheep that had been crushed were watching me. They knew it was the LORD's message.

¹²I told them, "If you think it is best, give me my pay. But if you don't think so, you keep it." So they paid me 30 silver coins.

¹³The LORD said to me, "Throw the coins to the potter." What a good price they had set for me! So I threw the 30 silver coins to the potter in the LORD's temple.

¹⁴Then I broke my second staff called Union. That broke the union between Judah and Israel.

¹⁵The LORD said to me, "Now pretend to be a foolish shepherd. Get the things you need. ¹⁶I am going to raise up a shepherd over the land. He will not take care of those that are wounded. He will not look for the young ones. He will not heal those that are hurt. He will not feed the healthy ones. Instead, he will eat the best sheep. He will even tear their hoofs off.

¹⁷ "How terrible it will be for that
    worthless shepherd!
He deserts the flock.
May a sword strike his arm and his
    right eye!
May his powerful arm become
    weak!
May his right eye be totally
    blinded!"

THE LORD WILL DESTROY JERUSALEM'S ENEMIES

12 This is the LORD's message about Israel. The LORD spread out the heavens. He laid the foundation of the earth. He created the spirits of all men. He says, ²"Jerusalem will be like a cup in my hand. It will make all of the surrounding nations drunk from the wine of my anger. Judah will be attacked by its enemies. So will Jerusalem.

³"At that time all of the nations on earth will gather together against Jerusalem. Then it will become like a rock that can't be moved. All of the nations that try to move it will only hurt themselves. ⁴On that day I will fill every horse with panic. I will make every rider crazy," announces the LORD. "I will watch over the people of Judah. But I will make all of the horses of the nations blind.

⁵"Then the leaders of Judah will say in their hearts, 'The people of Jerusalem are strong. That's because the LORD who rules over all is their God.'

⁶"At that time Judah's leaders will be like a fire pot in a pile of wood. They will be like a burning torch among bundles of grain. They will destroy all of the surrounding nations on every side. But Jerusalem will remain unharmed in its place.

⁷"I will save the houses in Judah first. The honor of David's family line is great. So is the honor of those who live in Jerusalem. But their honor will not be greater than the honor of the rest of Judah.

⁸"At that time I will be like a shield to those who live in Jerusalem. Then even the weakest among them will be great warriors like David. And David's family line will be like the Angel of the LORD who leads them. ⁹On that day I will begin to destroy all of the nations that attack Jerusalem.

ISRAEL'S PEOPLE WILL SOB OVER THE ONE THEY PIERCED

¹⁰"I will pour out a spirit of grace and prayer on David's family line. I will also send it on those who live in Jerusalem. They will look to me. I am the one they have pierced. They will sob over me as someone sobs over an only child who has died. They will be full of sorrow over me, just like someone who is full of sorrow over an oldest son.

¹¹"At that time there will be a lot of crying in Jerusalem. It will sound like the sobs of the people at Hadad Rimmon over Josiah's death in the Valley of Megiddo. ¹²Everyone in the land will sob. Each family will cry by themselves

and their wives by themselves. That will include the family lines of David, Nathan, ¹³Levi, Shimei and ¹⁴all of the others.

THE LORD MAKES ISRAEL PURE AND CLEAN

13 "At that time a fountain will be opened for the benefit of David's family line. It will also bless the others who live in Jerusalem. It will wash away their sins. It will make them pure and clean.

²"On that day I will remove the names of other gods from the land. They will not even be remembered anymore," announces the LORD who rules over all. "I will drive the evil prophets out of the land. I will get rid of the spirit that put lies in their mouths. ³Some people might still prophesy. But their own fathers and mothers will speak to them. They will tell them, 'You must die. You have told lies in the LORD's name.' When they prophesy, their own parents will stab them.

⁴"At that time every prophet will be ashamed of his vision. He will no longer pretend to be a true prophet. He will not put on clothes that are made out of hair in order to trick people. ⁵In fact, he will say, 'I'm not really a prophet. I'm a farmer. I've farmed the land since I was young.' ⁶Suppose someone asks him, 'What are those wounds on your body?' Then he will answer, 'I was given these wounds at the house of my friends.'

THE GOOD SHEPHERD IS KILLED AND THE SHEEP ARE SCATTERED

⁷"My sword, wake up! Attack my shepherd!
Attack the man who is close to me,"
announces the LORD who rules over all.
"Strike the shepherd down.
Then the sheep will be scattered.
And I will turn my hand against their little ones.
⁸Here is what will happen in the whole land,"
announces the LORD.
"Two-thirds of the people will be struck down and die.

But one-third will be left.
⁹I will put that third in the fire.
I will make them as pure as silver.
I will test them like gold.
They will call out to me.
And I will answer them.
I will say, 'They are my people.'
And they will say, 'The LORD is our God.' "

THE LORD WILL BE KING OVER THE WHOLE EARTH

14 The day of the LORD is coming. At that time Jerusalem's enemies will steal everything its people have. They will divide it up right in front of them.

²The LORD will gather all of the nations together. They will fight against Jerusalem. They'll capture the city. Its houses will be robbed. Its women will be raped. Half of the people will be taken away as prisoners. But the rest of them won't be taken.

³Then the LORD will march out and fight against those nations. He will go to war against them.

⁴On that day he will stand on the Mount of Olives. It's east of Jerusalem. It will be split in two from east to west. Half of the mountain will move north. The other half will move south. A large valley will be formed. ⁵The people will run away through that mountain valley. It will reach all the way to Azel. They'll run away just as they ran from the earthquake when Uzziah was king of Judah. Then the LORD my God will come. All of the holy ones will come with him.

⁶There won't be any light on that day. The sun, moon and stars will not shine. ⁷It will be a day unlike any other. It won't be separated into day and night. It will be a day known only to the LORD. After that day is over, there will be light again.

⁸At that time water that gives life will flow out from Jerusalem. Half of it will run into the Dead Sea. The other half will go to the Mediterranean Sea. The water will flow in summer and winter.

⁹The LORD will be king over the whole earth. On that day there will be one LORD. His name will be the only name.

¹⁰The whole land south of Jerusalem will be changed. From Geba to Rimmon it will become like the Arabah Valley. But Jerusalem will be raised up. It will remain in its place. From the Benjamin Gate to the First Gate to the Corner Gate nothing will be changed. From the Tower of Hananel to the royal winepress the city will remain the same. ¹¹People will live in it. Jerusalem will never be destroyed again. It will be secure.

¹²The LORD will punish all of the nations that fought against Jerusalem. He'll strike them with a plague. It will make their bodies rot while they are still standing on their feet. Their eyes will rot in their heads. Their tongues will rot in their mouths. ¹³On that day the LORD will fill people with great panic. They will grab one another by the hand. And they'll attack each other. ¹⁴Judah will also fight at Jerusalem. The wealth of all of the surrounding nations will be collected. Huge amounts of gold, silver and clothes will be gathered up. ¹⁵The same kind of plague will strike the horses, mules, camels and donkeys. In fact, it will strike all of the animals in the army camps.

¹⁶But some people from all of the nations that have attacked Jerusalem will still be left alive. All of them will go up there to worship the King. He is the LORD who rules over all. Year after year they will celebrate the Feast of Booths.

¹⁷Some nations might not go up to Jerusalem to worship the King. If they don't, they won't have any rain. ¹⁸The people of Egypt might not go up there to take part. Then they won't have any rain either. That's the plague the LORD will send on the nations that don't go to celebrate the Feast of Booths. ¹⁹Egypt will be punished. So will all of the other nations that don't celebrate the Feast.

²⁰On that day HOLY TO THE LORD will be carved on the bells of the horses. The cooking pots in the LORD's temple will be just like the sacred bowls in front of the altar for burnt offerings. ²¹Every pot in Jerusalem and Judah will be set apart to the LORD. All those who come to offer sacrifices will get some of the pots and cook in them. At that time there won't be any Canaanites in the LORD's temple. He is the LORD who rules over all.

quest challenge

I Wonder...

Why does God allow difficult events to happen in my life?

Real Life Challenge

It's natural to ask why God allows difficult things to happen: serious illness, death or divorce. There's no easy answer to this question. But we do know this: God is with us through whatever we face.

Quest Clue

Look at Zechariah 13 for a verse that compares the tough times to the process of making gold and silver pure. Romans 5 and James 1 show how you can benefit from difficult situations.

Malachi

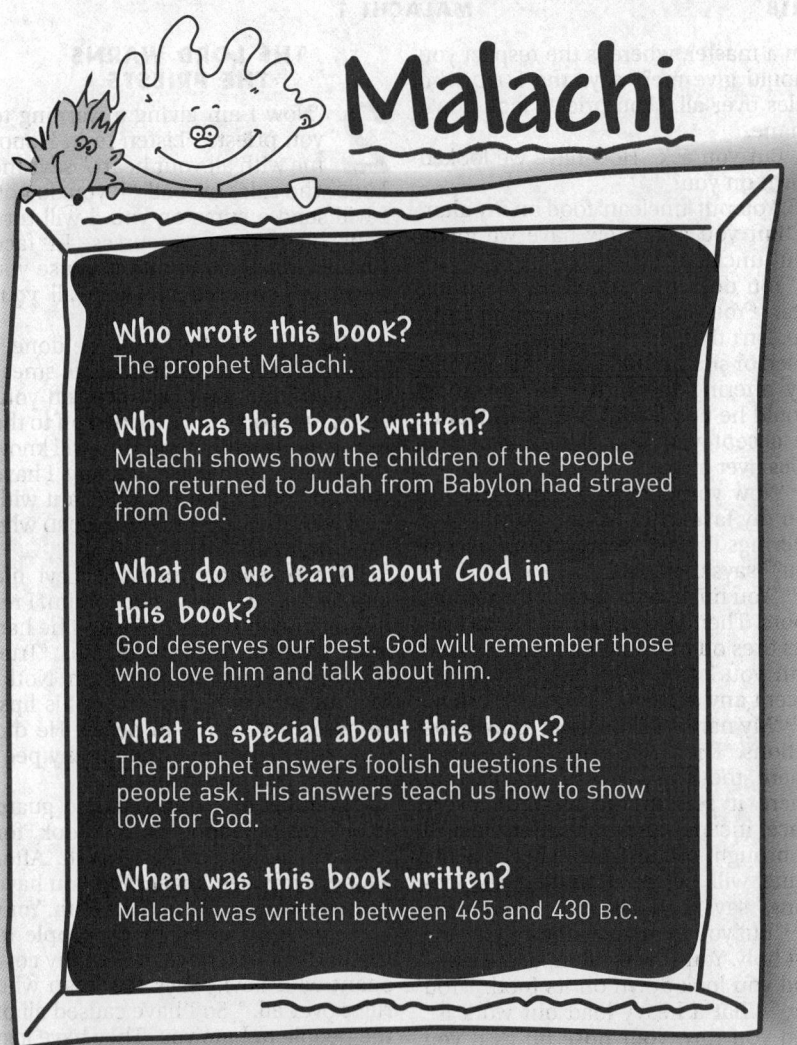

Who wrote this book?
The prophet Malachi.

Why was this book written?
Malachi shows how the children of the people who returned to Judah from Babylon had strayed from God.

What do we learn about God in this book?
God deserves our best. God will remember those who love him and talk about him.

What is special about this book?
The prophet answers foolish questions the people ask. His answers teach us how to show love for God.

When was this book written?
Malachi was written between 465 and 430 B.C.

1 This is the LORD's message to Israel through Malachi.

THE LORD CHOOSES JACOB INSTEAD OF ESAU

²"Israel, I have loved you," says the LORD.

"But you ask, 'How have you loved us?'

"Wasn't Esau Jacob's brother?" says the LORD. "But I chose Jacob ³instead of Esau. I turned Esau's mountains into a dry and empty land. I left that land of Edom to the wild dogs in the desert."

⁴Edom might say, "We have been crushed. But we'll rebuild our cities."

The LORD who rules over all says, "They might rebuild their cities. But I will destroy them. They will be called The Evil Land. My anger will always remain on them. ⁵You will see it with your own eyes. You will say, 'The LORD is great! He rules even beyond the borders of Israel!'

GIVE YOUR BEST TO THE LORD

⁶"A son honors his father. A servant honors his master. If I am a father, where is the honor I should have? If I

am a master, where is the respect you should give me?" says the LORD who rules over all. "You priests look down on me.

"But you ask, 'How have we looked down on you?'

⁷"You put 'unclean' food on my altar.

"But you ask, 'How have we made you "unclean?" '

"You do it by looking down on my altar. ⁸You sacrifice blind animals to me. Isn't that wrong? You sacrifice disabled or sick animals. Isn't that wrong? Try offering them to your governor! Would he be pleased with you? Would he accept you?" says the LORD who rules over all.

⁹"Now you dare to ask me to show you my favor! But as long as you give offerings like those, how can I accept you?" says the LORD.

¹⁰"You might as well shut the temple doors! Then you would not light useless fires on my altar. I am not pleased with you," says the LORD. "I will not accept any of the offerings you bring.

¹¹"My name will be great among the nations. They will worship me from where the sun rises in the east to where it sets in the west. In every place, incense and pure offerings will be brought to me. That is because my name will be great among the nations," says the LORD.

¹²"But you treat my name as if it were not holy. You say my altar is 'unclean.' And you look down on its food. ¹³You say, 'What a heavy load our work is!' And you turn your nose up as if you hate working for me," says the LORD who rules over all.

"You bring animals that have been hurt. Or you bring disabled or sick animals. Then you dare to offer them to me as sacrifices! Should I accept them from you?" says the LORD.

¹⁴"Suppose you have a male sheep or goat that does not have any flaws. And you promise to offer it to me. But then you sacrifice an animal that has flaws. When you do that, you cheat me. And anyone who cheats me is under my curse. After all, I am a great king," says the LORD who rules over all. "The other nations have respect for my name. So why don't you respect it?

THE LORD WARNS THE PRIESTS

2 "Now I am giving a warning to you priests. ²Listen to it. Honor me with all your heart," says the LORD who rules over all. "If you do not, I will send a curse on you. I will turn your blessings into curses. In fact, I have already done that because you have not honored me with all your heart.

³"Because of what you have done, I will punish your children. I will smear the guts from your sacrifices on your faces. And you will be carried off to the dump along with them. ⁴You will know that I have given you a warning. I have warned you so that my covenant with Levi will continue," says the LORD who rules over all.

⁵"My covenant promised Levi life and peace. So I gave them to him. I required him to respect me. And he had great respect for my name. ⁶True teaching came from his mouth. Nothing but the truth came from his lips. He walked with me in peace. He did what was right. He turned many people away from their sins.

⁷"The lips of a priest should guard knowledge. People should look for true teaching from his mouth. After all, he is my messenger. ⁸But you have turned away from the right path. Your teaching has caused many people to trip and fall. You have broken my covenant with Levi," says the LORD who rules over all. ⁹"So I have caused all of the people to hate you. They have lost respect for you. You have not done what I told you to do. Instead, you have favored one person over another in matters of the law."

JUDAH IS NOT FAITHFUL TO THE LORD

¹⁰People of Judah, all of us have one Father. One God created us. So why do we break the covenant the LORD made with our people long ago? We don't even keep our promises to one another.

¹¹You have broken your promises. A hateful thing has been done in Israel and Jerusalem. The LORD loves his temple. But you have polluted it. You

men have married women who worship other gods.

¹²May the LORD punish you who do that. It doesn't matter who you are. May the LORD who rules over all cut you off from the tents of Jacob's people. May he remove you even if you bring offerings to him.

¹³Here's something else you do. You flood the LORD's altar with your tears. You sob and cry because he doesn't pay attention to your offerings anymore. He doesn't accept them from your hands with pleasure.

¹⁴You ask, "Why?" It's because the LORD is holding you accountable. He watches how you treat the wife you married when you were young. You have broken your promise to her. You did it even though she's your partner. You promised to stay married to her. And the LORD was a witness to it.

¹⁵Hasn't he made the two of you one? Both of you belong to him in body and spirit. And why has he made you one? Because he was looking for godly children. So guard yourself in your spirit. Don't break your promise to the wife you married when you were young.

¹⁶"I hate divorce," says the LORD God of Israel. "I hate it when people do anything that harms others," says the LORD who rules over all.

So guard yourself in your spirit. And don't break your promises.

THE LORD WILL JUDGE HIS PEOPLE

¹⁷You have worn the LORD out by what you keep saying.

"How have we worn him out?" you ask.

You have done it by saying, "All those who do evil things are good in the LORD'S sight. And he is pleased with them." Or you ask, "Is God really fair?"

3 The LORD who rules over all says, "I will send my messenger. He will prepare my way for me. Then suddenly the Lord you are looking for will come to his temple. The messenger of the covenant will come. He is the one you long for."

²But who can live through the day when he comes? Who will be left standing when he appears? He will be like a fire that makes things pure. He will be like soap that makes things clean. ³He will act like one who makes silver pure. And he will purify the Levites, just as gold and silver are purified with fire.

Then the LORD's people will bring proper offerings. ⁴And the offerings of Judah and Jerusalem will be acceptable to him. It will be as it was in days and years gone by.

⁵"So I will come and judge you. I will be quick to bring charges against all of you," says the LORD who rules over all. "I will bring charges against you sinful people who do not have any respect for me. That includes those who practice evil magic. It includes those who commit adultery and those who tell lies in court. It includes those who cheat workers out of their pay. It includes those who crush widows. It also includes those who mistreat children whose fathers have died. And it includes those who take away the rights of outsiders in the courts.

DO NOT STEAL FROM GOD

⁶"I am the LORD. I do not change. That is why I have not destroyed you members of Jacob's family. ⁷You have turned away from my rules. You have not obeyed them. You have lived that way ever since the days of your people long ago. Return to me. Then I will return to you," says the LORD who rules over all.

"But you ask, 'How can we return?'

⁸"Will a man dare to steal from me? But you rob me!

"You ask, 'How do we rob you?'

"By holding back your offerings. You also steal from me when you do not bring me a tenth of everything you produce. ⁹So you are under my curse. In fact, your whole nation is under it. That is because you are robbing me.

¹⁰"Bring the entire tenth to the storerooms in my temple. Then there will be plenty of food. Put me to the test," says the LORD. "Then you will see that I will throw open the windows of heaven. I will pour out so many blessings that you will not have enough room for them. ¹¹I will keep bugs from eating up your crops. And your grapes

will not drop from the vines before they are ripe," says the LORD.

¹²"Then all of the nations will call you blessed. Your land will be delightful," says the LORD who rules over all.

¹³"You have spoken bad things against me," says the LORD.

"But you ask, 'What have we spoken against you?'

¹⁴"You have said, 'It is useless to serve God. What did we gain by obeying his laws? And what did we get by pretending to be sad in front of the LORD? ¹⁵But now we call proud people blessed. Things go well with those who do what is evil. And God doesn't even punish those who argue with him.' "

¹⁶Those who had respect for the LORD talked with one another. They cheered each other up. And the LORD heard them. A list of people and what they did was written on a scroll in front of him. It included the names of those who respected the LORD and honored him.

¹⁷"They will belong to me," says the LORD who rules over all. "They will be my special treasure. I will spare them just as a loving father spares his son who serves him. ¹⁸Then once again you will see the difference between godly people and sinful people. And you will see the difference between those who serve me and those who do not.

THE DAY OF THE LORD IS COMING

4 "You can be sure the day of the LORD is coming. My anger will burn like a furnace. All those who are proud will be like straw. So will all those who do what is evil. The day that is coming will set them on fire," says the LORD who rules over all. "Not even a root or a branch will be left to them.

²"But here is what will happen for you who have respect for me. The sun

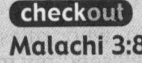

What is tithing?

Tithe means "a tenth." In Old Testament times, God commanded the Israelites to give a tithe of everything they produced. They gave sheep, grain, cows and other animals to the priests. These tithes were like a paycheck for the priests. If a person had ten sheep, a tithe would be one of those sheep. Because of the tithe the priests were able to work full-time leading the people in worship and taking care of God's house. Sometimes people gave even more than that as a way of thanking God.

Many Christians today use the word *tithe* to describe the giving they do. Usually they mean that they give a part of their money to God. Sometimes they give ten percent, sometimes they give less or more. Whenever we give gladly, we show that we trust God to take care of us.

checkout
Malachi 3:8

Related verses:
Haggai 1:1–15;
1 Corinthians
16:1,2

that brings life will rise. Its rays will bring healing to my people. You will go out and leap like calves that have just been let out of the barn.

³"Then you will stomp on sinful people. They will be like ashes under your feet. That will happen on the day I act," says the LORD.

⁴"Remember the law my servant Moses gave you. Remember the rules and laws I gave him at Mount Horeb.

They were for the whole nation of Israel.

⁵"I will send you the prophet Elijah. He will come before the day of the LORD arrives. It will be a great and terrifying day. ⁶Elijah will teach parents how to love their children. He will also teach children how to honor their parents. If that does not happen, I will come. And I will put a curse on the land."

quest challenge

I Wonder . . .

How can I give to others?

Real Life Challenge

Perhaps your church or school has a program at Christmas to help provide gifts to needy people in your area. Although you might not have a lot of money, you can still find ways to be generous. You might have a toy or piece of clothing you don't want anymore. Or you might be willing to give up one of your own presents to a kid who might not get any. God loves it when we help others, and we feel good about ourselves, too!

Quest Clue

Find Malachi 3 to learn about how God feels when we give to him and to others. Then find 2 Corinthians 9 for more encouragement to be generous.

New Testament

THE BOOKS
OF THE BIBLE
from MATTHEW
to REVELATION

Matthew

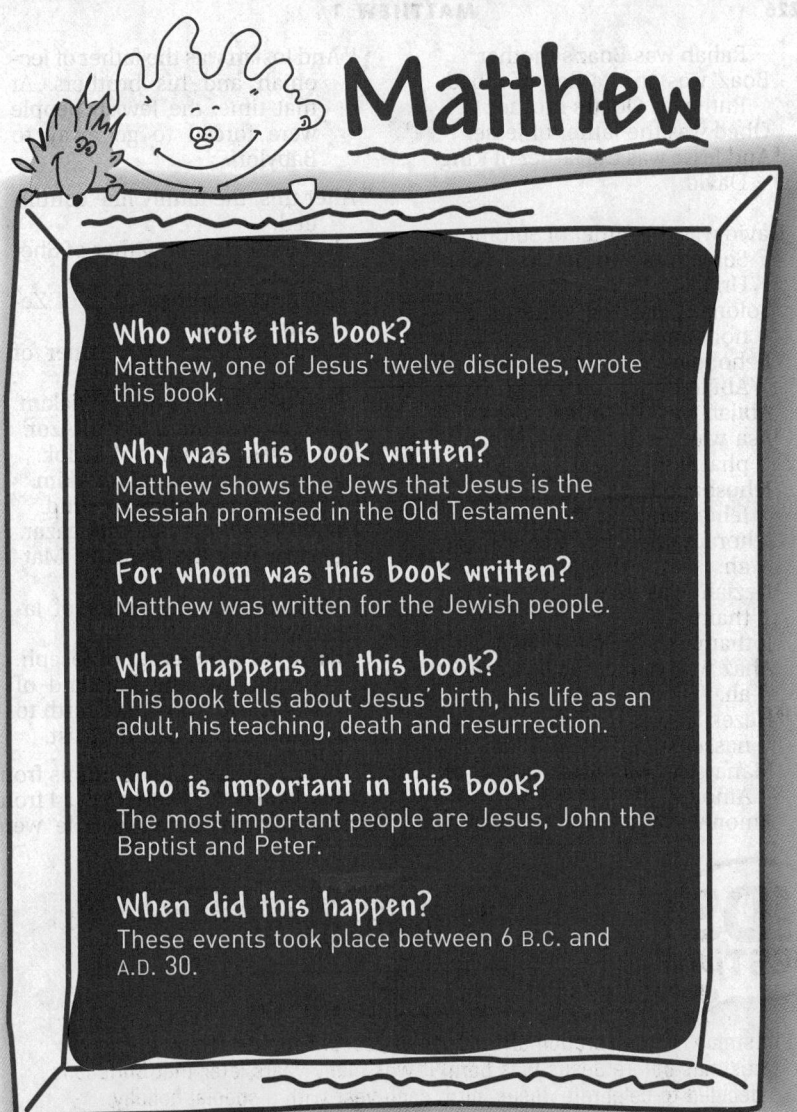

Who wrote this book?
Matthew, one of Jesus' twelve disciples, wrote this book.

Why was this book written?
Matthew shows the Jews that Jesus is the Messiah promised in the Old Testament.

For whom was this book written?
Matthew was written for the Jewish people.

What happens in this book?
This book tells about Jesus' birth, his life as an adult, his teaching, death and resurrection.

Who is important in this book?
The most important people are Jesus, John the Baptist and Peter.

When did this happen?
These events took place between 6 B.C. and A.D. 30.

THE FAMILY LINE OF JESUS

1 This is a record of the family line of Jesus Christ. He is the son of David. He is also the son of Abraham.

² Abraham was the father of Isaac.
Isaac was the father of Jacob.
Jacob was the father of Judah and his brothers.
³ Judah was the father of Perez and Zerah. Tamar was their mother.
Perez was the father of Hezron.
Hezron was the father of Ram.
⁴ Ram was the father of Amminadab.
Amminadab was the father of Nahshon.
Nahshon was the father of Salmon.
⁵ Salmon was the father of Boaz.

Rahab was Boaz's mother.
Boaz was the father of Obed.
Ruth was Obed's mother.
Obed was the father of Jesse.
⁶And Jesse was the father of King David.

David was the father of Solomon. Solomon's mother had been Uriah's wife.
⁷Solomon was the father of Rehoboam.
Rehoboam was the father of Abijah.
Abijah was the father of Asa.
⁸Asa was the father of Jehoshaphat.
Jehoshaphat was the father of Jehoram.
Jehoram was the father of Uzziah.
⁹Uzziah was the father of Jotham.
Jotham was the father of Ahaz.
Ahaz was the father of Hezekiah.
¹⁰Hezekiah was the father of Manasseh.
Manasseh was the father of Amon.
Amon was the father of Josiah.

¹¹And Josiah was the father of Jeconiah and his brothers. At that time, the Jewish people were forced to go away to Babylon.

¹²After this, the family line continued.
Jeconiah was the father of Shealtiel.
Shealtiel was the father of Zerubbabel.
¹³Zerubbabel was the father of Abiud.
Abiud was the father of Eliakim.
Eliakim was the father of Azor.
¹⁴Azor was the father of Zadok.
Zadok was the father of Akim.
Akim was the father of Eliud.
¹⁵Eliud was the father of Eleazar.
Eleazar was the father of Matthan.
Matthan was the father of Jacob.
¹⁶Jacob was the father of Joseph. Joseph was the husband of Mary. And Mary gave birth to Jesus, who is called Christ.

¹⁷So there were 14 generations from Abraham to David. There were 14 from David until the Jewish people were

Did people in the Bible have Christmas?

Christmas is a celebration of the birth of Jesus. People did not celebrate Christmas before Jesus was born. It was many years later that Christians decided to celebrate Jesus' birth each year with a special holiday. They chose December 25. That day is probably not the exact day Jesus was born, but that's OK. What matters is that we have a day to remember the day Jesus was born and to celebrate that he came to save us from our sins.

checkout Matthew 2:1

Related verses:
Isaiah 9:6,7;
Luke 2:1-20

forced to go away to Babylon. And there were 14 from that time to the Christ.

JESUS CHRIST IS BORN

¹⁸This is how the birth of Jesus Christ came about. His mother Mary and Joseph had promised to get married. But before they started to live together, it became clear that she was going to have a baby. She became pregnant by the power of the Holy Spirit. ¹⁹Her husband Joseph was a godly man. He did not want to put her to shame in public. So he planned to divorce her quietly.

²⁰But as Joseph was thinking about this, an angel of the Lord appeared to him in a dream. The angel said, "Joseph, son of David, don't be afraid to take Mary home as your wife. The baby inside her is from the Holy Spirit. ²¹She is going to have a son. You must give him the name Jesus. That is because he will save his people from their sins."

²²All of this took place to bring about what the Lord had said would happen. He had said through the prophet, ²³"The virgin is going to have a baby. She will give birth to a son. And he will be called Immanuel." *(Isaiah 7:14)* The name Immanuel means "God with us."

²⁴Joseph woke up. He did what the angel of the Lord commanded him to do. He took Mary home as his wife. ²⁵But he did not make love to her until after she gave birth to a son. And Joseph gave him the name Jesus.

THE WISE MEN VISIT JESUS

2 Jesus was born in Bethlehem in Judea. This happened while Herod was king of Judea.

After Jesus' birth, Wise Men from the east came to Jerusalem. ²They asked, "Where is the child who has been born to be king of the Jews? When we were in the east, we saw his star. Now we have come to worship him."

³When King Herod heard about it, he was very upset. Everyone in Jerusalem was troubled too. ⁴So Herod called together all the chief priests of the people. He also called the teachers of the law. He asked them where the Christ was going to be born.

⁵"In Bethlehem in Judea," they replied. "This is what the prophet has written. He said,

⁶" 'But you, Bethlehem, in the land of Judah,
are certainly not the least important among the towns of Judah.
A ruler will come out of you.
He will be the shepherd of my people Israel.' " *(Micah 5:2)*

⁷Then Herod called for the Wise Men secretly. He found out from them exactly when the star had appeared. ⁸He sent them to Bethlehem. He said, "Go! Make a careful search for the child. As soon as you find him, bring me a report. Then I can go and worship him too."

⁹After the Wise Men had listened to the king, they went on their way. The star they had seen when they were in the east went ahead of them. It finally stopped over the place where the child was. ¹⁰When they saw the star, they were filled with joy. ¹¹The Wise Men went to the house. There they saw the child with his mother Mary. They bowed down and worshiped him. Then they opened their treasures. They gave him gold, incense and myrrh.

¹²But God warned them in a dream not to go back to Herod. So they returned to their country on a different road.

JESUS' FAMILY ESCAPES TO EGYPT

¹³When the Wise Men had left, Joseph had a dream. In the dream an angel of the Lord appeared to him. "Get up!" the angel said. "Take the child and his mother and escape to Egypt. Stay there until I tell you to come back. Herod is going to search for the child. He wants to kill him."

¹⁴Joseph got up. During the night, he left for Egypt with the child and his mother Mary. ¹⁵They stayed there until King Herod died. So the words the Lord had spoken through the prophet came true. He had said, "I chose to bring my son out of Egypt." *(Hosea 11:1)*

¹⁶Herod realized that the Wise Men had tricked him. So he became very

angry. He gave orders concerning Bethlehem and the area around it. All the boys two years old and under were to be killed. This agreed with the time when the Wise Men had seen the star.

[17]In this way, the words the prophet Jeremiah spoke came true. He had said,

[18] "A voice is heard in Ramah.
  It's the sound of crying and deep
    sadness.
  Rachel is crying over her children.
  She refuses to be comforted,
  because they are gone."

(Jeremiah 31:15)

JESUS' FAMILY RETURNS TO NAZARETH

[19]After Herod died, Joseph had a dream while he was still in Egypt. In the dream an angel of the Lord appeared to him. [20]The angel said, "Get up! Take the child and his mother. Go to the land of Israel. Those who were trying to kill the child are dead."

[21]So Joseph got up. He took the child and his mother Mary back to the land of Israel. [22]But then he heard that Archelaus was king of Judea. Archelaus was ruling in place of his father Herod. This made Joseph afraid to go there. Warned in a dream, Joseph went back to the land of Galilee instead. [23]There he lived in a town called Nazareth. So what the prophets had said about Jesus came true. They had said, "He will be called a Nazarene."

JOHN THE BAPTIST PREPARES THE WAY

3 In those days John the Baptist came and preached in the Desert of Judea. [2]He said, "Turn away from your sins! The kingdom of heaven is near."

[3]John is the one the prophet Isaiah had spoken about. He had said,

  "A messenger is calling out in the
    desert,
  'Prepare the way for the Lord.
  Make straight paths for him.' "

(Isaiah 40:3)

[4]John's clothes were made out of camel's hair. He had a leather belt around his waist. His food was locusts and wild honey. [5]People went out to him from Jerusalem and all of Judea. They also came from the whole area around the Jordan River. [6]When they admitted they had sinned, John baptized them in the Jordan.

[7]John saw many Pharisees and Sadducees coming to where he was baptizing. He said to them, "You are like a nest of poisonous snakes! Who warned you to escape the coming of God's anger? [8]Produce fruit that shows you have turned away from your sins. [9]Don't think you can say to yourselves, 'Abraham is our father.' I tell you, God can raise up children for Abraham even from these stones. [10]The ax is already lying at the roots of the trees. All the trees that don't produce good fruit will be cut down. They will be thrown into the fire.

[11]"I baptize you with water, calling you to turn away from your sins. But after me, one will come who is more powerful than I am. And I'm not fit to carry his sandals. He will baptize you with the Holy Spirit and with fire. [12]His pitchfork is in his hand to clear the straw from his threshing floor. He will gather his wheat into the storeroom. But he will burn up the husks with fire that can't be put out."

JESUS IS BAPTIZED

[13]Jesus came from Galilee to the Jordan River. He wanted to be baptized by John. [14]But John tried to stop him. He told Jesus, "I need to be baptized by you. So why do you come to me?"

[15]Jesus replied, "Let it be this way for now. It is right for us to do this. It carries out God's holy plan." Then John agreed.

[16]As soon as Jesus was baptized, he came up out of the water. At that moment heaven was opened. Jesus saw the Spirit of God coming down on him like a dove.

[17]A voice from heaven said, "This is my Son, and I love him. I am very pleased with him."

JESUS IS TEMPTED

4 The Holy Spirit led Jesus into the desert. There the devil tempted him. [2]After 40 days and 40 nights

of going without eating, Jesus was hungry.

³The tempter came to him. He said, "If you are the Son of God, tell these stones to become bread."

⁴Jesus answered, "It is written, 'Man doesn't live only on bread. He also lives on every word that comes from the mouth of God.' " *(Deuteronomy 8:3)*

⁵Then the devil took Jesus to the holy city. He had him stand on the highest point of the temple. ⁶"If you are the Son of God," he said, "throw yourself down. It is written,

" 'The Lord will command his
　　angels to take good care of
　　you.
　They will lift you up in their
　　hands.
　Then you won't trip over a
　　stone.' " 　　　　*(Psalm 91:11,12)*

⁷Jesus answered him, "It is also written, 'Do not put the Lord your God to the test.' " *(Deuteronomy 6:16)*

⁸Finally, the devil took Jesus to a very high mountain. He showed him all the kingdoms of the world and their glory.

⁹"If you bow down and worship me," he said, "I will give you all of this."

¹⁰Jesus said to him, "Get away from me, Satan! It is written, 'Worship the Lord your God. He is the only one you should serve.' " *(Deuteronomy 6:13)*

¹¹Then the devil left Jesus. Angels came and took care of him.

JESUS BEGINS TO PREACH

¹²John had been put in prison. When Jesus heard about this, he returned to Galilee.

¹³Jesus left Nazareth. He went to live in the city of Capernaum. It was by the lake in the area of Zebulun and Naphtali. ¹⁴In that way, what the prophet Isaiah had said came true. He had said,

¹⁵"Land of Zebulun! Land of
　　Naphtali!
　Galilee, where non-Jewish
　　people live!
　Land along the Mediterranean
　　Sea! Territory east of the
　　Jordan River!
¹⁶The people who are now living in
　　darkness

KIDS' QUESTION

How can God be three persons and one person at the same time?

We don't know *how* God can be three persons at the same time. But we know that he is because the Bible tells us he is. The idea of three-in-one is called the Trinity. The word *trinity* is not in the Bible, but some passages talk about God in this way. One God is Father, Son and Holy Spirit all at once. It's a little bit like water. Water can be a liquid, gas or solid. We use liquid water to take a drink or take a bath. Water becomes a gas when we boil it. And we get water as a solid when we freeze it. But all three are water. Just remember that we do not have three Gods or that God acts three different ways at three different times. He really is three persons in one, and all three have always existed.

checkout Matthew 3:16,17

Related verse:
Deuteronomy 6:4

will see a great light.
They are now living in a very dark
    land.
But a light will shine on them."

(Isaiah 9:1,2)

¹⁷From that time on Jesus began to preach. "Turn away from your sins!" he said. "The kingdom of heaven is near."

JESUS CHOOSES THE FIRST DISCIPLES

¹⁸One day Jesus was walking beside the Sea of Galilee. There he saw two brothers. They were Simon Peter and his brother Andrew. They were throwing a net into the lake. They were fishermen. ¹⁹"Come. Follow me," Jesus said. "I will make you fishers of people."

²⁰At once they left their nets and followed him.

²¹Going on from there, he saw two other brothers. They were James, son of Zebedee, and his brother John. They were in a boat with their father Zebedee. As they were preparing their nets, Jesus called out to them.

²²Right away they left the boat and their father and followed Jesus.

JESUS HEALS SICK PEOPLE

²³Jesus went all over Galilee. There he taught in the synagogues. He preached the good news of God's kingdom. He healed every illness and sickness the people had.

²⁴News about him spread all over Syria. People brought to him all who were ill with different kinds of sicknesses. Some were suffering great pain. Others were controlled by demons. Some were shaking wildly. Others couldn't move at all. And Jesus healed all of them.

²⁵Large crowds followed him. Some people came from Galilee, from the area known as the Ten Cities, and from Jerusalem and Judea. Others came from the area across the Jordan River.

JESUS GIVES BLESSINGS

5 Jesus saw the crowds. So he went up on a mountainside and sat down. His disciples came to him. ²Then he began to teach them. He said,

³"Blessed are those who are
    spiritually needy.
The kingdom of heaven belongs
    to them.

Why do we study the Bible?

The Bible is God's message to us. That is why it is important to study it. It helps us know and understand God. When we study the Bible we find out how God wants us to live. To study something is different from just reading it. When we only read a verse once or twice we may not see its meaning. We need to read the Bible many, many times so we can understand it and remember what God is saying to us.

checkout
Matthew 4:4

Related verses:
Psalm 119:4–6

⁴Blessed are those who are sad.
　　They will be comforted.
⁵Blessed are those who are free of
　　pride.
　　They will be given the earth.
⁶Blessed are those who are hungry
　　and thirsty for what is right.
　　They will be filled.
⁷Blessed are those who show
　　mercy.
　　They will be shown mercy.
⁸Blessed are those whose hearts are
　　pure.
　　They will see God.
⁹Blessed are those who make
　　peace.
　　They will be called sons
　　　of God.
¹⁰Blessed are those who suffer for
　　doing what is right.
　　The kingdom of heaven belongs
　　　to them.

¹¹"Blessed are you when people make fun of you and hurt you because of me. You are also blessed when they tell all kinds of evil lies about you be-cause of me. ¹²Be joyful and glad. Your reward in heaven is great. In the same way, people hurt the prophets who lived long ago.

SALT AND LIGHT

¹³"You are the salt of the earth. But suppose the salt loses its saltiness. How can it be made salty again? It is no longer good for anything. It will be thrown out. People will walk all over it.

¹⁴"You are the light of the world. A city on a hill can't be hidden. ¹⁵Also, people do not light a lamp and put it under a bowl. Instead, they put it on its stand. Then it gives light to everyone in the house.

¹⁶"In the same way, let your light shine in front of others. Then they will see the good things you do. And they will praise your Father who is in heaven.

JESUS GIVES FULL MEANING TO THE LAW

¹⁷"Do not think I have come to get rid of what is written in the Law or in

Does Satan Know about the Bible?

Satan knows all about the Bible. He even knows what it says. But Satan certainly does not follow what the Bible teaches. In fact, he does everything he can to stop people from obeying God's commands. Just because someone knows the truth does not mean he or she will do it. Satan is a liar and the father of lies. He has lied and twisted the truth so much that he believes some of his own lies. For example, Satan thinks that he can beat God and escape his punishment. But the Bible tells the truth. Some day God will totally wipe out Satan and his demons.

checkout **Matthew 4:5,6**

Related verses:
James 2:19;
Revelation 20:10

the Prophets. I have not come to do that. Instead, I have come to give full meaning to what is written. ¹⁸What I'm about to tell you is true. Heaven and earth will disappear before the smallest letter disappears from the Law. Not even the smallest stroke of a pen will disappear from the Law until everything is completed.

¹⁹"Do not break even one of the least important commandments. And do not teach others to break them. If you do, you will be called the least important person in the kingdom of heaven. Instead, practice and teach these commands. Then you will be called important in the kingdom of heaven. ²⁰"Here is what I tell you. You must be more godly than the Pharisees and the teachers of the law. If you are not, you will certainly not enter the kingdom of heaven.

MURDER

²¹"You have heard what was said to people who lived long ago. They were told, 'Do not commit murder. *(Exodus 20:13)* Anyone who murders will be judged for it.' ²²But here is what I tell you. Do not be angry with your broth-er. Anyone who is angry with his brother will be judged. Again, anyone who says to his brother, 'Raca,' must stand trial in the Sanhedrin. But anyone who says, 'You fool!' will be in danger of the fire in hell.

²³"Suppose you are offering your gift at the altar. And you remember that your brother has something against you. ²⁴Leave your gift in front of the altar. First go and make peace with your brother. Then come back and offer your gift.

²⁵"Suppose someone has a claim against you and is taking you to court. Settle the matter quickly. Do it while you are still with him on your way. If you don't, he may hand you over to the judge. The judge may hand you over to the officer. And you may be thrown into prison. ²⁶What I'm about to tell you is true. You will not get out until you have paid the very last penny!

ADULTERY

²⁷"You have heard that it was said, 'Do not commit adultery.' *(Exodus 20:14)* ²⁸But here is what I tell you. Do not even look at a woman in the wrong way. Anyone who does has already

Are beatitudes short for bad attitudes?

The word *beatitude* means "blessed" or "happy." Jesus once made a list of things that make people truly happy. We call this list "the beatitudes." It has a lot of surprises in it. It is not the kind of list we would expect of things to make us happy. It describes the kind of people God wants us to be. Sometimes people think that they will become rich or famous or powerful by following Jesus. Maybe they will; maybe they won't. In the beatitudes Jesus tells us that we should expect our rewards in heaven.

Following him is better than being rich, famous or powerful.

checkout Matthew 5:1,2

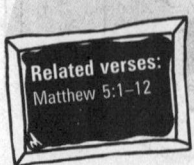

Related verses:
Matthew 5:1-12

committed adultery with her in his heart.

²⁹"If your right eye causes you to sin, poke it out and throw it away. Your eye is only one part of your body. It is better to lose it than for your whole body to be thrown into hell.

³⁰"If your right hand causes you to sin, cut it off and throw it away. Your hand is only one part of your body. It is better to lose it than for your whole body to go into hell.

DIVORCE

³¹"It has been said, 'Suppose a man divorces his wife. If he does, he must give her a letter of divorce.' *(Deuteronomy 24:1)* ³²But here is what I tell you. Anyone who divorces his wife causes her to commit adultery. And anyone who gets married to the divorced woman commits adultery. A man may divorce his wife only if she has not been faithful to him.

OATHS

³³"Again, you have heard what was said to your people long ago. They were told, 'Do not break the promises you make to the Lord. Keep the oaths you have made to him.' ³⁴But here is what I tell you. Do not make any promises like that at all. Do not make them in the name of heaven. That is God's throne. ³⁵Do not make them in the name of the earth. That is the stool for God's feet. Do not make them in the name of Jerusalem. That is the city of the Great King. ³⁶And do not take an oath in the name of your head. You can't make even one hair white or black.

³⁷"Just let your 'Yes' mean 'Yes.' Let your 'No' mean 'No.' Anything more than this comes from the evil one.

BE KIND TO OTHERS

³⁸"You have heard that it was said, 'An eye must be put out for an eye. A tooth must be knocked out for a tooth.' *(Exodus 21:24; Leviticus 24:20; Deuteronomy 19:21)* ³⁹But here is what I tell you. Do not fight against an evil person.

"Suppose someone hits you on your right cheek. Turn your other cheek to him also. ⁴⁰Suppose someone takes you to court to get your shirt. Let him have your coat also. ⁴¹Suppose someone forces you to go one mile. Go two miles with him.

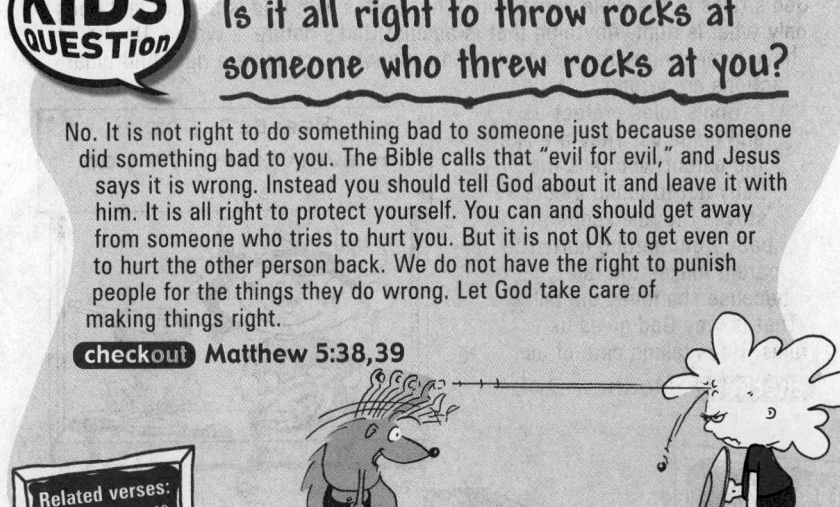

KIDS' QUESTION

Is it all right to throw rocks at someone who threw rocks at you?

No. It is not right to do something bad to someone just because someone did something bad to you. The Bible calls that "evil for evil," and Jesus says it is wrong. Instead you should tell God about it and leave it with him. It is all right to protect yourself. You can and should get away from someone who tries to hurt you. But it is not OK to get even or to hurt the other person back. We do not have the right to punish people for the things they do wrong. Let God take care of making things right.

checkout Matthew 5:38,39

Related verses:
Matthew 5:43–48;
Romans 12:17–21

DAVID & GOLIATH PLAY KIT

⁴²"Give to the one who asks you for something. Don't turn away from the one who wants to borrow something from you.

LOVE YOUR ENEMIES

⁴³"You have heard that it was said, 'Love your neighbor. *(Leviticus 19:18)* Hate your enemy.' ⁴⁴But here is what I tell you. Love your enemies. Pray for those who hurt you. ⁴⁵Then you will be sons of your Father who is in heaven.

"He causes his sun to shine on evil people and good people. He sends rain on those who do right and those who don't.

⁴⁶"If you love those who love you, what reward will you get? Even the tax collectors do that. ⁴⁷If you greet only your own people, what more are you doing than others? Even people who are ungodly do that. ⁴⁸So be perfect, just as your Father in heaven is perfect.

GIVING TO NEEDY PEOPLE

6 "Be careful not to do 'good works' in front of others. Don't do them to be seen by others. If you do, your Father in heaven will not reward you.

²"When you give to needy people, do not announce it by having trumpets blown. Do not be like those who only pretend to be holy. They announce what they do in the synagogues and on the streets. They want to be honored by others. What I'm about to tell you is true. They have received their complete reward.

³"When you give to the needy, don't let your left hand know what your right hand is doing. ⁴Then your giving will be done secretly. Your Father will reward you. He sees what you do secretly.

PRAYER

⁵"When you pray, do not be like those who only pretend to be holy. They love to stand and pray in the syn-

How did God decide what was wrong and what was right?

God's rules in the Bible come from what God is like. God is perfect and does only what is right. Anything that is against God's nature is wrong. He did not have a meeting with the angels to decide what actions are right and what actions are wrong.

God's rules protect us and guide us. They are like the parent who tells the baby not to touch a hot stove. The rule keeps the baby from getting hurt. The parent makes the rule because she loves the baby. That is why God gives us rules. He is taking care of us.

checkout Matthew 5:48

Related verses:
1 Peter 1:15,16

REFLECT GOD
in everything you do
$5.00

MIRRORS

agogues and on the street corners. They want to be seen by others. What I'm about to tell you is true. They have received their complete reward.

⁶"When you pray, go into your room. Close the door and pray to your Father, who can't be seen. He will reward you. Your Father sees what is done secretly.

⁷"When you pray, do not keep talking on and on the way ungodly people do. They think they will be heard because they talk a lot. ⁸Do not be like them. Your Father knows what you need even before you ask him.

⁹"This is how you should pray.

" 'Our Father in heaven,
    may your name be honored.
¹⁰May your kingdom come.
    May what you want to happen be
        done
        on earth as it is done in heaven.
¹¹Give us today our daily bread.
¹²Forgive us our sins,
        just as we also have forgiven
            those who sin against us.

¹³Keep us from falling into sin when
    we are tempted.
    Save us from the evil one.'

¹⁴"Forgive people when they sin against you. If you do, your Father who is in heaven will also forgive you. ¹⁵But if you do not forgive people their sins, your Father will not forgive your sins.

FASTING

¹⁶"When you go without eating, do not look gloomy like those who only pretend to be holy. They make their faces very sad. They want to show people they are fasting. What I'm about to tell you is true. They have received their complete reward.

¹⁷"But when you go without eating, put olive oil on your head. Wash your face. ¹⁸Then others will not know that you are fasting. Only your Father, who can't be seen, will know it. He will reward you. Your Father sees what is done secretly.

Why do we have to pray when God already knows what we are going to pray?

One of the most important reasons for praying is that it changes the person who is praying. When we pray, we become more like God wants us to be. *We* learn something from *God*!

Also, God wants to have a friendship with us. No one would say, "Why do we have to talk to our friends?" Talking with God just grows out of loving him and being cared for by him.

checkout
Matthew 6:7,8

Related verses:
Psalm 32:5–6;
139:4;
Ephesians 6:18;
Philippians 4:6;
Colossians 4:2

THANK YOU FOR YOU KNOW WHAT AND FORGIVE ME FOR SCARING YOU KNOW WHO WITH A FROG AND...

PUT AWAY RICHES IN HEAVEN

19"Do not put away riches for yourselves on earth. Moths and rust can destroy them. Thieves can break in and steal them. 20Instead, put away riches for yourselves in heaven. There, moths and rust do not destroy them. There, thieves do not break in and steal them. 21Your heart will be where your riches are.

22"The eye is like a lamp for the body. Suppose your eyes are good. Then your whole body will be full of light. 23But suppose your eyes are bad. Then your whole body will be full of darkness. If the light inside you is darkness, then it is very dark!

24"No one can serve two masters at the same time. He will hate one of them and love the other. Or he will be faithful to one and dislike the other. You can't serve God and Money at the same time.

DO NOT WORRY

25"I tell you, do not worry. Don't worry about your life and what you will eat or drink. And don't worry about your body and what you will wear. Isn't there more to life than eating? Aren't there more important things for the body than clothes?

26"Look at the birds of the air. They don't plant or gather crops. They don't put away crops in storerooms. But your Father who is in heaven feeds them. Aren't you worth much more than they are?

27"Can you add even one hour to your life by worrying?

28"And why do you worry about clothes? See how the wild flowers grow. They don't work or make clothing. 29But here is what I tell you. Not even Solomon in all of his glory was dressed like one of those flowers.

30"If that is how God dresses the wild

What should I say to God when I pray?

Tell him whatever is on your mind. Some kids think you always have to pray the same thing. It is easy to pray the same words you prayed last time. And that is OK. But you do not have to say the same thing every time. You can think about what you are saying and be honest with God. Do not show off. The Lord's Prayer can be a guide for what to talk to God about. Here is a short list: (1) Thank God for what he has done. (2) Confess your sins. Tell him you are sorry for the bad things you have done. (3) Ask him to help others, guide you and give you strength to do what is right. Talk to God about anything that is on your mind.

checkout
Matthew 6:9–13

Related verses:
James 5:16;
1 Peter 5:7

grass, won't he dress you even better? After all, the grass is here only today. Tomorrow it is thrown into the fire. Your faith is so small!

[31]"So don't worry. Don't say, 'What will we eat?' Or, 'What will we drink?' Or, 'What will we wear?' [32]People who are ungodly run after all of those things. Your Father who is in heaven knows that you need them.

[33]"But put God's kingdom first. Do what he wants you to do. Then all of those things will also be given to you.

[34]"So don't worry about tomorrow. Tomorrow will worry about itself. Each day has enough trouble of its own.

BE FAIR WHEN YOU JUDGE OTHERS

7 "Do not judge others. Then you will not be judged. [2]You will be judged in the same way you judge others. You will be measured in the same way you measure others.

[3]"You look at the bit of sawdust in your friend's eye. But you pay no attention to the piece of wood in your own eye. [4]How can you say to your friend, 'Let me take the bit of sawdust out of your eye'? How can you say this while there is a piece of wood in your own eye?

[5]"You pretender! First take the piece of wood out of your own eye. Then you will be able to see clearly to take the bit of sawdust out of your friend's eye.

[6]"Do not give holy things to dogs. Do not throw your pearls to pigs. If you do, they might walk all over them. Then they might turn around and tear you to pieces.

ASK, SEARCH, KNOCK

[7]"Ask, and it will be given to you. Search, and you will find. Knock, and the door will be opened to you. [8]Everyone who asks will receive. He who searches will find. The door will be opened to the one who knocks.

[9]"Suppose your son asks for bread. Which of you will give him a stone? [10]Or suppose he asks for a fish. Which of you will give him a snake? [11]Even though you are evil, you know how to give good gifts to your children. How

What's so bad about wanting to wear clothes that are in style?

It is all right to wear clothes that are in style. We should take care of ourselves. But we should not think that having the latest clothes will make us happy and get us friends. Remember, wearing nice clothes does not make a person nice. It is what is on the inside of the person that really counts. People who make and sell clothes are trying to make money. They place ads on TV and radio to make people want to buy their clothes. They change the styles and say that everyone should wear the latest style. Often the most stylish clothes are also the most expensive. Ask your parents to buy only what they can afford.

checkout Matthew 6:31–33

Related verses:
Philippians
4:11,12;
1 Timothy 6:6–8

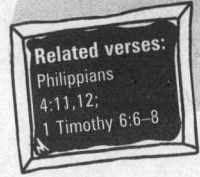

much more will your Father who is in heaven give good gifts to those who ask him!

¹²"In everything, do to others what you would want them to do to you. This is what is written in the Law and in the Prophets.

THE LARGE AND SMALL GATES

¹³"Enter God's kingdom through the narrow gate. The gate is large and the road is wide that lead to death and hell. Many people go that way. ¹⁴But the gate is small and the road is narrow that lead to life. Only a few people find it.

A TREE AND ITS FRUIT

¹⁵"Watch out for false prophets. They come to you pretending to be sheep. But on the inside they are hungry wolves. ¹⁶You can tell what they really are by what they do.

"Do people pick grapes from bushes? Do they pick figs from thorns? ¹⁷In the same way, every good tree bears good fruit. But a bad tree bears bad fruit. ¹⁸A good tree can't bear bad fruit. And a bad tree can't bear good fruit. ¹⁹Every tree that does not bear good fruit is cut down. It is thrown into the fire. ²⁰You can tell each tree by its fruit.

²¹"Not everyone who says to me, 'Lord, Lord,' will enter the kingdom of heaven. Only those who do what my Father in heaven wants will enter.

²²"Many will say to me on that day, 'Lord! Lord! Didn't we prophesy in your name? Didn't we drive out demons in your name? Didn't we do many miracles in your name?' ²³Then I

What happens to my money if the bank gets robbed?

The money in the bank is insured. The government promises that you will always be able to get your money even if someone steals all the money in the bank. So you should not worry about your money in the bank. It is safe. Very few banks get robbed, and most bank robbers get caught. The few thieves who get away get very little money. Even thieves who steal a lot of money will not get *your* money. Even though your money is safe in the bank, though, your faith in God and love for Jesus are your real treasures. You can take them with you when you die!

checkout

Matthew 6:19,20

Related verses:
Luke 12:33,34

will tell them clearly, 'I never knew you. Get away from me, you who do evil!'

THE WISE AND FOOLISH BUILDERS

²⁴"So then, everyone who hears my words and puts them into practice is like a wise man. He builds his house on the rock. ²⁵The rain comes down. The water rises. The winds blow and beat against that house. But it does not fall. It is built on the rock.

²⁶"But everyone who hears my words and does not put them into practice is like a foolish man. He builds his house on sand. ²⁷The rain comes down. The water rises. The winds blow and beat against that house. And it falls with a loud crash."

²⁸Jesus finished saying all these things. The crowds were amazed at his teaching. ²⁹He taught like one who had authority. He did not speak like their teachers of the law.

JESUS HEALS A MAN WHO HAD A SKIN DISEASE

8 Jesus came down from the mountainside. Large crowds followed him. ²A man who had a skin disease came and got down on his knees in front of Jesus. He said, "Lord, if you are willing to make me 'clean,' you can do it."

³Jesus reached out his hand and touched the man. "I am willing to do it," he said. "Be 'clean'!"

Right away the man was healed of his skin disease.

⁴Then Jesus said to him, "Don't tell anyone. Go and show yourself to the priest. Offer the gift Moses commanded. It will be a witness to them."

A ROMAN COMMANDER HAS FAITH

⁵When Jesus entered Capernaum, a Roman commander came to him. He asked Jesus for help. ⁶"Lord," he said,

I want to have nice friends, but how do I know if kids are nice?

You can get an idea of what a person is like by reputation, especially if the reputation is good. If you hear from a lot of people that someone is nice, that's probably a good sign that the person really *is* nice. Sometimes, however, a person's reputation is not always accurate. Someone may say that a boy is stuck-up when, instead, he is only shy. Be careful not to judge kids before you know them—give them a chance.

The best way to know if the kids are nice is to get to know them yourself. Start talking with them. The Bible teaches that a person's words show what is in that person's heart. If people talk about bad things, swear or tell dirty jokes, that is a sign of what they are really like. Watch kids in action with others. Pretty soon you will know if they're nice or not.

checkout Matthew 7:16–20

Related verses:
Proverbs 17:17;
20:6

"my servant lies at home and can't move. He is suffering terribly."

[7]Jesus said, "I will go and heal him."

[8]The commander replied, "Lord, I am not good enough to have you come into my house. But just say the word, and my servant will be healed. [9]I myself am a man under authority. And I have soldiers who obey my orders. I tell this one, 'Go,' and he goes. I tell that one, 'Come,' and he comes. I say to my servant, 'Do this,' and he does it."

[10]When Jesus heard this, he was amazed. He said to those following him, "What I'm about to tell you is true. In Israel I have not found anyone whose faith is so strong.

[11]"I say to you that many will come from the east and the west. They will take their places at the feast in the kingdom of heaven. They will sit with Abraham, Isaac and Jacob. [12]But those who think they belong to the kingdom will be thrown outside, into the darkness. There they will sob and grind their teeth."

[13]Then Jesus said to the Roman commander, "Go! It will be done just as you believed it would."

And his servant was healed at that very hour.

JESUS HEALS MANY PEOPLE

[14]When Jesus came into Peter's house, he saw Peter's mother-in-law. She was lying in bed. She had a fever. [15]Jesus touched her hand, and the fever left her. She got up and began to wait on him.

[16]When evening came, many people controlled by demons were brought to Jesus. He drove out the spirits with a word. He healed all who were sick. [17]He did it to make what the prophet Isaiah had said come true. He had said,

If I break something that belongs to someone else but fix it, do I have to tell what I did?

Tell the person the truth. That is what God would want you to do and it shows that you respect the person who owns what you broke. How would *you* feel if a friend broke something of yours and did not tell you? You would probably want to know what happened even if your friend fixed it. You probably would not like it if he tried to keep a secret from you. And you would probably not like it if you found out later. If you break something that belongs to someone else, fix it or pay to have it fixed. But also let the person know what you did and do not try to hide the truth. Treat other people the way you would like them to treat you. That is what Jesus told his disciples to do.

checkout Matthew 7:12

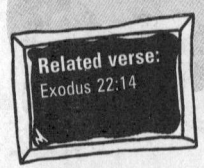

Related verse:
Exodus 22:14

JASON'S IMAGINATION

HIDDEN OASIS

"He suffered the things we should
have suffered.
He took on himself the
sicknesses that should have
been ours."   *(Isaiah 53:4)*

IT COSTS TO FOLLOW JESUS

¹⁸Jesus saw the crowd around him.
So he gave his disciples orders to go to
the other side of the Sea of Galilee.
¹⁹Then a teacher of the law came to
him. He said, "Teacher, I will follow
you no matter where you go."
²⁰Jesus replied, "Foxes have holes.
Birds of the air have nests. But the Son
of Man has no place to lay his head."
²¹Another follower said to him,
"Lord, first let me go and bury my father."
²²But Jesus told him, "Follow me. Let
the dead bury their own dead."

JESUS CALMS THE STORM

²³Jesus got into a boat. His disciples
followed him. ²⁴Suddenly a terrible
storm came up on the lake. The waves
crashed over the boat. But Jesus was
sleeping.
²⁵The disciples went and woke him
up. They said, "Lord! Save us! We're
going to drown!"

²⁶He replied, "Your faith is so small!
Why are you so afraid?"
Then Jesus got up and ordered the
winds and the waves to stop. It became completely calm.
²⁷The disciples were amazed. They
asked, "What kind of man is this? Even
the winds and the waves obey him!"

JESUS HEALS TWO MEN
CONTROLLED BY DEMONS

²⁸Jesus arrived at the other side of
the lake in the area of the Gadarenes.
Two men controlled by demons met
him. They came from the tombs. The
men were so wild that no one could
pass that way.
²⁹"Son of God, what do you want
with us?" they shouted. "Have you
come here to punish us before the
time for us to be judged?"
³⁰Not very far away, a large herd of
pigs was feeding. ³¹The demons
begged Jesus, "If you drive us out, send
us into the herd of pigs."
³²Jesus said to them, "Go!"
So the demons came out of the men
and went into the pigs. The whole herd
rushed down the steep bank. They
ran into the lake and drowned in the
water.

KIDS' QUESTION

Why is hell dark if they have fires?

The Bible uses a lot of words to describe hell. *Fire* is one of
them. *Dark* is another. Fire means that in hell there is a lot of
burning and pain. Do you remember having a fever? You felt like
you were burning up, but there was no flame. Darkness means
loneliness. Can you imagine anything
more lonely than sitting by
yourself in total
darkness? Hell is a
terrible place.

checkout

Matthew 8:12

Related verses:
Luke 16:24–28;
Revelation 20:15

[33]Those who were tending the pigs ran off. They went into the town and reported all this. They told the people what had happened to the men who had been controlled by demons. [34]Then the whole town went out to meet Jesus. When they saw him, they begged him to leave their area.

JESUS HEALS A MAN WHO COULD NOT WALK

9 Jesus stepped into a boat. He went over to the other side of the lake and came to his own town. [2]Some men brought to him a man who could not walk. He was lying on a mat. Jesus saw that they had faith. So he said to the man, "Don't lose hope, son. Your sins are forgiven."

[3]Then some teachers of the law said to themselves, "This fellow is saying a very evil thing!"

[4]Jesus knew what they were thinking. So he said, "Why do you have evil thoughts in your hearts? [5]Is it easier to say, 'Your sins are forgiven'? Or to say, 'Get up and walk'? [6]I want you to know that the Son of Man has authority on earth to forgive sins."

Then he spoke to the man who could not walk. "Get up," he said. "Take your mat and go home." [7]The man got up and went home.

[8]When the crowd saw this, they were filled with wonder. They praised God for giving that kind of authority to men.

JESUS CHOOSES MATTHEW

[9]As Jesus went on from there, he saw a man named Matthew. He was sitting at the tax collector's booth.

"Follow me," Jesus told him. Matthew got up and followed him.

[10]Later Jesus was having dinner at Matthew's house. Many tax collectors and "sinners" came. They ate with Jesus and his disciples.

[11]The Pharisees saw this. So they asked the disciples, "Why does your teacher eat with tax collectors and 'sinners'?"

[12]Jesus heard that. So he said, "Those who are healthy don't need a doctor. Sick people do. [13]Go and learn what this means, 'I want mercy and not sacrifice.' (Hosea 6:6) I have not come to get those who think they are right with God to follow me. I have come to get sinners to follow me."

JESUS IS ASKED ABOUT FASTING

[14]One day John's disciples came. They said to Jesus, "We and the Pharisees go without eating. Why don't your disciples go without eating?"

[15]Jesus answered, "How can the guests of the groom be sad while he is with them? The time will come when the groom will be taken away from them. Then they will fast.

[16]"People don't sew a patch of new cloth on old clothes. The new piece will pull away from the old. That will make the tear worse.

[17]"People don't pour new wine into old wineskins. If they do, the skins will burst. The wine will run out, and the wineskins will be destroyed. No, everyone pours new wine into new wineskins. Then both are saved."

A DEAD GIRL AND A SUFFERING WOMAN

[18]While Jesus was saying this, a ruler came. He got down on his knees in front of Jesus. He said, "My daughter has just died. But come and place your hand on her. Then she will live again."

[19]Jesus got up and went with him. So did his disciples.

[20]Just then a woman came up behind Jesus. She had a sickness that made her bleed. It had lasted for 12 years. She touched the edge of his clothes. [21]She thought, "I only need to touch his clothes. Then I will be healed."

[22]Jesus turned and saw her. "Dear woman, don't give up hope," he said. "Your faith has healed you." The woman was healed at that very moment.

[23]When Jesus entered the ruler's house, he saw the flute players there. And he saw the noisy crowd. [24]He said, "Go away. The girl is not dead. She is sleeping." But they laughed at him.

[25]After the crowd had been sent outside, Jesus went in. He took the girl by the hand, and she got up. [26]News about what Jesus had done spread all over that area.

JESUS HEALS TWO BLIND MEN

27As Jesus went on from there, two blind men followed him. They called out, "Have mercy on us, Son of David!" 28When Jesus went indoors, the blind men came to him. He asked them, "Do you believe that I can do this?"

"Yes, Lord," they replied.

29Then he touched their eyes. He said, "It will happen to you just as you believed." 30They could now see again. Jesus strongly warned them, "Be sure that no one knows about this." 31But they went out and spread the news. They talked about him all over that area.

32While they were going out, another man was brought to Jesus. A demon controlled him, and he could not speak. 33When the demon was driven out, the man spoke.

The crowd was amazed. They said, "Nothing like this has ever been seen in Israel." 34But the Pharisees said, "He drives out demons by the power of the prince of demons."

THERE ARE ONLY A FEW WORKERS

35Jesus went through all the towns and villages. He taught in their synagogues. He preached the good news of the kingdom. And he healed every illness and sickness. 36When he saw the crowds, he felt deep concern for them. They were beaten down and helpless, like sheep without a shepherd.

37Then Jesus said to his disciples, "The harvest is huge. But there are only a few workers. 38So ask the Lord of the harvest to send workers out into his harvest field."

JESUS SENDS OUT THE TWELVE DISCIPLES

10 Jesus called for his 12 disciples to come to him. He gave them authority to drive out evil spirits and to heal every illness and sickness.

2Here are the names of the 12 apostles. First are Simon Peter and his brother Andrew. Then come James, son of Zebedee, and his brother John. 3Next are Philip and Bartholomew, and also Thomas and Matthew the tax collector. Two more are James, son of Alphaeus, and Thaddaeus. 4The last are Simon the Zealot and Judas Iscariot. Judas is the one who was later going to hand Jesus over to his enemies.

5Jesus sent these 12 out with the following orders. "Do not go among those who aren't Jews," he said. "Do not enter any town of the Samaritans. 6Instead, go to the people of Israel. They are like sheep that have become lost. 7As you go, preach this message, 'The kingdom of heaven is near.' 8Heal those who are sick. Bring those who are dead back to life. Make those who have skin diseases 'clean' again. Drive out demons. You have received freely, so give freely.

9"Do not take along any gold, silver or copper in your belts. 10Do not take a bag for the journey. Do not take extra clothes or sandals or walking sticks. A worker should be given what he needs.

11"When you enter a town or village, look for someone who is willing to welcome you. Stay at that person's house until you leave. 12As you enter the home, greet those who live there. 13If that home welcomes you, give it your blessing of peace. If it does not, don't bless it.

14"Some people may not welcome you or listen to your words. If they don't, shake the dust off your feet when you leave that home or town. 15What I'm about to tell you is true. On judgment day it will be easier for Sodom and Gomorrah than for that town.

16"I am sending you out like sheep among wolves. So be as wise as snakes and as harmless as doves.

17"Watch out! Men will hand you over to the local courts. They will whip you in their synagogues. 18You will be brought to governors and kings because of me. You will be witnesses to them and to those who aren't Jews.

19"But when they arrest you, don't worry about what you will say or how you will say it. At that time you will be given the right words to say. 20It will not be you speaking. The Spirit of your Father will be speaking through you.

21"Brothers will hand over brothers

to be killed. Fathers will hand over their children. Children will rise up against their parents and have them put to death. ²²Everyone will hate you because of me. But anyone who stands firm to the end will be saved.

²³"When people attack you in one place, escape to another. What I'm about to tell you is true. You will not finish going through the cities of Israel before the Son of Man comes.

²⁴"A student is not better than his teacher. A servant is not better than his master. ²⁵It is enough for the student to be like his teacher. And it is enough for the servant to be like his master. If the head of the house has been called Beelzebub, what can the others who live there expect?

²⁶"So don't be afraid of your enemies. Everything that is secret will be brought out into the open. Everything that is hidden will be uncovered. ²⁷What I tell you in the dark, speak in the daylight. What is whispered in your ear, shout from the rooftops. ²⁸Do not be afraid of those who kill the body but can't kill the soul. Instead, be afraid of the One who can destroy both soul and body in hell.

²⁹"Aren't two sparrows sold for only a penny? But not one of them falls to the ground without your Father knowing it. ³⁰He even counts every hair on your head! ³¹So don't be afraid. You are worth more than many sparrows.

³²"What about someone who says in front of others that he knows me? I will also say in front of my Father who is in heaven that I know him. ³³But what about someone who says in front of others that he doesn't know me? I will say in front of my Father who is in heaven that I don't know him.

³⁴"Do not think that I came to bring peace to the earth. I didn't come to bring peace. I came to bring a sword. ³⁵I have come to turn

> " 'sons against their fathers.
> Daughters will refuse to obey
>   their mothers.
> Daughters-in-law will be against
>   their mothers-in-law.
> ³⁶ A man's enemies will be the
>   members of his own family.'
> *(Micah 7:6)*

³⁷"Anyone who loves his father or mother more than me is not worthy of me. Anyone who loves his son or daughter more than me is not worthy of me. ³⁸And anyone who does not pick up his cross and follow me is not worthy of me. ³⁹If anyone finds his life, he will lose it. If anyone loses his life because of me, he will find it.

⁴⁰"Anyone who welcomes you welcomes me. And anyone who welcomes me welcomes the One who sent me. ⁴¹Suppose someone welcomes a prophet as a prophet. That one will receive a prophet's reward. And suppose someone welcomes a godly person as a godly person. That one will receive a godly person's reward. ⁴²Suppose someone gives even a cup of cold water to a little one who follows me. What I'm about to tell you is true. That one will certainly be rewarded."

JESUS AND JOHN THE BAPTIST

11 Jesus finished teaching his 12 disciples. Then he went on to teach and preach in the towns of Galilee.

²John was in prison. When he heard what Christ was doing, he sent his disciples to him. ³They asked Jesus, "Are you the one who was supposed to come? Or should we look for someone else?"

⁴Jesus replied, "Go back to John. Report to him what you hear and see. ⁵Blind people receive sight. Disabled people walk. Those who have skin diseases are healed. Deaf people hear. Those who are dead are raised to life. And the good news is preached to those who are poor. ⁶Blessed are those who do not give up their faith because of me."

⁷As John's disciples were leaving, Jesus began to speak to the crowd about John. He said, "What did you go out into the desert to see? Tall grass waving in the wind? ⁸If not, what did you go out to see? A man dressed in fine clothes? No. People who wear fine clothes are in kings' palaces. ⁹Then what did you go out to see? A prophet? Yes, I tell you, and more than a prophet. ¹⁰He is the one written about in Scripture. It says,

" 'I will send my messenger ahead
   of you.
He will prepare your way for
   you.'   *(Malachi 3:1)*

¹¹"What I'm about to tell you is true.
No one more important than John the
Baptist has ever been born. But the
least important person in the kingdom of heaven is more important than
he is. ¹²Since the days of John the Baptist, the kingdom of heaven has been
advancing with force. And forceful
people are taking hold of it. ¹³All the
Prophets and the Law prophesied until John came. ¹⁴If you are willing to accept it, John is the Elijah who was
supposed to come. ¹⁵Those who have
ears should listen.

¹⁶"What can I compare today's people to? They are like children sitting in
the market places and calling out to
others. They say,

¹⁷" 'We played the flute for you.
   But you didn't dance.
We sang a funeral song.
   But you didn't become sad.'

¹⁸When John came, he didn't eat or
drink as you do. And people say, 'He
has a demon.' ¹⁹But when the Son of
Man came, he ate and drank as you do.
And people say, 'This fellow is always
eating and drinking far too much. He's
a friend of tax collectors and "sinners." ' Those who act wisely prove
that wisdom is right."

CITIES THAT DO NOT TURN
AWAY FROM SIN

²⁰Jesus began to speak against the
cities where he had done most of his
miracles. The people there had not
turned away from their sins. So he
said, ²¹"How terrible it will be for you,
Korazin! How terrible for you, Bethsaida! Suppose the miracles done in you
had been done in Tyre and Sidon. They
would have turned away from their
sins long ago. They would have put on
black clothes. They would have sat
down in ashes. ²²But I tell you this. On
judgment day it will be easier for Tyre
and Sidon than for you.

²³"And what about you, Capernaum?
Will you be lifted up to heaven? No!
You will go down to the place of the

dead. Suppose the miracles done in
you had been done in Sodom. It would
still be here today. ²⁴But I tell you this.
On judgment day it will be easier for
Sodom than for you."

REST FOR ALL WHO
ARE TIRED

²⁵At that time Jesus said, "I praise
you, Father. You are Lord of heaven
and earth. You have hidden these
things from the wise and educated.
But you have shown them to little children. ²⁶Yes, Father. This is what you
wanted.

²⁷"My Father has given all things to
me. The Father is the only one who
knows the Son. And the only ones who
know the Father are the Son and those
to whom the Son chooses to make him
known.

²⁸"Come to me, all of you who are
tired and are carrying heavy loads. I
will give you rest. ²⁹Become my servants and learn from me. I am gentle
and free of pride. You will find rest for
your souls. ³⁰Serving me is easy, and
my load is light."

JESUS IS LORD OF THE
SABBATH DAY

12 One Sabbath day Jesus
walked through the grain-
fields. His disciples were
hungry. So they began to break off
some heads of grain and eat them.
²The Pharisees saw this. They said to
Jesus, "Look! It is against the Law to do
this on the Sabbath. But your disciples
are doing it anyway!"

³Jesus answered, "Haven't you read
about what David did? He and his men
were hungry. ⁴So he entered the house
of God. He and his men ate the holy
bread. Only priests were allowed to eat
it. ⁵Haven't you read the Law? It tells
how every Sabbath day the priests in
the temple have to do their work on
that day. But they are not considered
guilty.

⁶"I tell you that one who is more important than the temple is here.
⁷Scripture says, 'I want mercy and not
sacrifice.' *(Hosea 6:6)* You don't know
what those words mean. If you did,
you would not bring charges against

those who are not guilty. [8]The Son of Man is Lord of the Sabbath day."

[9]Going on from that place, Jesus went into their synagogue. [10]A man with a weak and twisted hand was there. The Pharisees were trying to find fault with Jesus. So they asked him, "Does the Law allow us to heal on the Sabbath day?"

[11]He said to them, "What if one of your sheep falls into a pit on the Sabbath? Won't you take hold of it and lift it out? [12]A man is worth more than sheep! So the Law allows us to do good on the Sabbath day."

[13]Then Jesus said to the man, "Stretch out your hand." So he stretched it out. It was as good as new, just as good as the other hand. [14]But the Pharisees went out and planned how to kill Jesus.

GOD'S CHOSEN SERVANT

[15]Jesus knew all about the Pharisees' plans. So he left that place. Many followed him, and he healed all their sick people. [16]But he warned them not to tell who he was. [17]This was to make what was spoken through the prophet Isaiah come true. It says,

[18]"Here is my servant. I have chosen him.
　He is the one I love. I am very pleased with him.
　I will put my Spirit on him.
　He will announce to the nations that everything will be made right.
[19]He will not argue or cry out.
　No one will hear his voice in the streets.
[20]He will not break a bent twig.
　He will not put out a dimly burning flame.
　He will make everything right.
[21]　The nations will put their hope in him." *(Isaiah 42:1–4)*

JESUS AND BEELZEBUB

[22]A man controlled by demons was brought to Jesus. The man was blind and could not speak. Jesus healed him. Then the man could speak and see. [23]All the people were amazed. They said, "Could this be the Son of David?"

[24]The Pharisees heard this. So they said, "This fellow drives out demons by the power of Beelzebub, the prince of demons."

[25]Jesus knew what they were thinking. So he said to them, "Every kingdom that fights against itself will be destroyed. Every city or family that is divided against itself will not stand. [26]If Satan drives out Satan, he fights against himself. Then how can his kingdom stand? [27]You say I drive out demons by the power of Beelzebub. Then by whose power do your people drive them out? So then, they will be your judges. [28]But suppose I drive out demons by the Spirit of God. Then God's kingdom has come to you.

[29]"Or think about this. How can you enter a strong man's house and just take what the man owns? You must first tie him up. Then you can rob his house.

[30]"Anyone who is not with me is against me. Anyone who does not gather sheep with me scatters them. [31]So here is what I tell you. Every sin and every evil word spoken against God will be forgiven. But speaking evil things against the Holy Spirit will not be forgiven. [32]Anyone who speaks a word against the Son of Man will be forgiven. But anyone who speaks against the Holy Spirit will not be forgiven. A person like that won't be forgiven either now or in days to come.

[33]"If you make a tree good, its fruit will be good. If you make a tree bad, its fruit will be bad. You can tell a tree by its fruit.

[34]"You nest of poisonous snakes! How can you who are evil say anything good? Your mouths say everything that is in your hearts. [35]A good man says good things. These come from the good that is put away inside him. An evil man says evil things. These come from the evil that is put away inside him. [36]But here is what I tell you. On judgment day, people will have to account for every careless word they have spoken. [37]By your words you will be found guilty or not guilty."

THE MIRACULOUS SIGN OF JONAH

[38]Some of the Pharisees and the teachers of the law came to Jesus. They

said, "Teacher, we want to see a miraculous sign from you."

³⁹He answered, "Evil and unfaithful people ask for a miraculous sign! But none will be given except the sign of the prophet Jonah. ⁴⁰Jonah was in the stomach of a huge fish for three days and three nights. Something like that will happen to the Son of Man. He will spend three days and three nights in the grave.

⁴¹"The men of Nineveh will stand up on judgment day with the people now living. And the Ninevites will prove that those people are guilty. The men of Nineveh turned away from their sins when Jonah preached to them. And now one who is more important than Jonah is here.

⁴²"The Queen of the South will stand up on judgment day with the people now living. And she will prove that they are guilty. She came from very far away to listen to Solomon's wisdom. And now one who is more important than Solomon is here.

⁴³"What happens when an evil spirit comes out of a man? It goes through dry areas looking for a place to rest. But it doesn't find it. ⁴⁴Then it says, 'I will return to the house I left.' When it arrives there, it finds the house empty. The house has been swept clean and put in order. ⁴⁵Then the evil spirit goes and takes with it seven other spirits more evil than itself. They go in and live there. That man is worse off than before. That is how it will be with the evil people of today."

JESUS' MOTHER AND BROTHERS

⁴⁶While Jesus was still talking to the crowd, his mother and brothers stood outside. They wanted to speak to him. ⁴⁷Someone told him, "Your mother and brothers are standing outside. They want to speak to you."

⁴⁸Jesus replied to him, "Who is my mother? And who are my brothers?" ⁴⁹Jesus pointed to his disciples. He said, "Here is my mother! Here are my brothers! ⁵⁰Anyone who does what my Father in heaven wants is my brother or sister or mother."

THE STORY OF THE FARMER

13 That same day Jesus left the house and sat by the Sea of Galilee. ²Large crowds gathered around him. So he got into a boat. He sat down in it. All the people stood on the shore. ³Then he told them many things by using stories.

He said, "A farmer went out to plant his seed. ⁴He scattered the seed on the ground. Some fell on a path. Birds came and ate it up. ⁵Some seed fell on rocky places, where there wasn't much soil. The plants came up quickly, because the soil wasn't deep. ⁶When the sun came up, it burned the plants. They dried up because they had no roots. ⁷Other seed fell among thorns. The thorns grew up and crowded out the plants. ⁸Still other seed fell on good soil. It produced a crop 100, 60 or 30 times more than what was planted. ⁹Those who have ears should listen."

¹⁰The disciples came to him. They asked, "Why do you use stories when you speak to the people?"

¹¹He replied, "You have been given the chance to understand the secrets of the kingdom of heaven. It has not been given to outsiders. ¹²Everyone who has that kind of knowledge will be given more. In fact, they will have very much. If anyone doesn't have that kind of knowledge, even what little he has will be taken away from him. ¹³Here is why I use stories when I speak to the people. I say,

"They look, but they don't really see.
    They listen, but they don't really
        hear or understand.

¹⁴"In them the words of the prophet Isaiah come true. He said,

" 'You will hear but never
        understand.
    You will see but never know what
        you are seeing.
¹⁵The hearts of these people have
        become stubborn.
    They can barely hear with their
        ears.
    They have closed their eyes.
Otherwise they might see with
        their eyes.
    They might hear with their ears.

They might understand with
  their hearts.
They might turn to the Lord, and
  then he would heal them.'

(Isaiah 6:9,10)

¹⁶"But blessed are your eyes because they see. And blessed are your ears because they hear. ¹⁷What I'm about to tell you is true. Many prophets and godly people wanted to see what you see. But they didn't see it. They wanted to hear what you hear. But they didn't hear it.

¹⁸"Listen! Here is the meaning of the story of the farmer. ¹⁹People hear the message about the kingdom but do not understand it. Then the evil one comes. He steals what was planted in their hearts. Those people are like the seed planted on a path. ²⁰Others received the seed that fell on rocky places. They are those who hear the message and at once receive it with joy. ²¹But they have no roots. So they last only a short time. They quickly fall away from the faith when trouble or suffering comes because of the message. ²²Others received the seed that fell among the thorns. They are those who hear the message. But then the worries of this life and the false promises of wealth crowd it out. They keep it from producing fruit. ²³But still others received the seed that fell on good soil. They are those who hear the message and understand it. They produce a crop 100, 60 or 30 times more than the farmer planted."

THE STORY OF THE WEEDS

²⁴Jesus told the crowd another story. "Here is what the kingdom of heaven is like," he said. "A man planted good seed in his field. ²⁵But while everyone was sleeping, his enemy came. The enemy planted weeds among the wheat and then went away. ²⁶The wheat began to grow and form grain. At the same time, weeds appeared. ²⁷"The owner's servants came to him. They said, 'Sir, didn't you plant good seed in your field? Then where did the weeds come from?'

²⁸" 'An enemy did this,' he replied.

"The servants asked him, 'Do you want us to go and pull the weeds up?'

²⁹" 'No,' the owner answered. 'While you are pulling up the weeds, you might pull up the wheat with them. ³⁰Let both grow together until the harvest. At that time I will tell the workers what to do. Here is what I will say to them. First collect the weeds. Tie them in bundles to be burned. Then gather the wheat. Bring it into my storeroom.' "

THE STORIES OF THE MUSTARD SEED AND THE YEAST

³¹Jesus told the crowd another story. He said, "The kingdom of heaven is like a mustard seed. Someone took the seed and planted it in a field. ³²It is the smallest of all your seeds. But when it grows, it is the largest of all garden plants. It becomes a tree. Birds come and rest in its branches."

³³Jesus told them still another story. "The kingdom of heaven is like yeast," he said. "A woman mixed it into a large amount of flour. The yeast worked its way all through the dough."

³⁴Jesus spoke all these things to the crowd by using stories. He did not say anything to them without telling a story. ³⁵So the words spoken by the prophet came true. He had said,

"I will open my mouth and tell
  stories.
I will speak about things that
  were hidden since the world
  was made."   (Psalm 78:2)

JESUS EXPLAINS THE STORY OF THE WEEDS

³⁶Then Jesus left the crowd and went into the house. His disciples came to him. They said, "Explain to us the story of the weeds in the field."

³⁷He answered, "The one who planted the good seed is the Son of Man. ³⁸The field is the world. The good seed stands for the people who belong to the kingdom. The weeds are the people who belong to the evil one. ³⁹The enemy who plants them is the devil. The harvest is judgment day. And the workers are angels.

⁴⁰"The weeds are pulled up and burned in the fire. That is how it will be on judgment day. ⁴¹The Son of Man

will send out his angels. They will weed out of his kingdom everything that causes sin. They will also get rid of all who do evil. ⁴²They will throw them into the blazing furnace. There people will sob and grind their teeth. ⁴³Then God's people will shine like the sun in their Father's kingdom. Those who have ears should listen.

THE STORIES OF THE HIDDEN TREASURE AND THE PEARL

⁴⁴"The kingdom of heaven is like treasure that was hidden in a field. When a man found it, he hid it again. He was very happy. So he went and sold everything he had. And he bought that field.

⁴⁵"Again, the kingdom of heaven is like a trader who was looking for fine pearls. ⁴⁶He found one that was very valuable. So he went away and sold everything he had. And he bought that pearl.

THE STORY OF THE NET

⁴⁷"Again, the kingdom of heaven is like a net. It was let down into the lake. It caught all kinds of fish. ⁴⁸When it was full, the fishermen pulled it up on the shore. Then they sat down and gathered the good fish into baskets. But they threw the bad fish away. ⁴⁹This is how it will be on judgment day. The angels will come. They will separate the people who did what is wrong from those who did what is right. ⁵⁰They will throw the evil people into the blazing furnace. There the evil ones will sob and grind their teeth.

⁵¹"Do you understand all these things?" Jesus asked.

"Yes," they replied.

⁵²He said to them, "Every teacher of the law who has been taught about the kingdom of heaven is like the owner of a house. He brings new treasures out of his storeroom as well as old ones."

A PROPHET WITHOUT HONOR

⁵³Jesus finished telling these stories. Then he moved on from there. ⁵⁴He came to his hometown of Nazareth. There he began teaching the people in their synagogue. They were amazed.

"Where did this man get this wisdom? Where did he get this power to do miracles?" they asked. ⁵⁵"Isn't this the carpenter's son? Isn't his mother's name Mary? Aren't his brothers James, Joseph, Simon and Judas? ⁵⁶Aren't all his sisters with us? Then where did this man get all these things?" ⁵⁷They were not pleased with him at all.

But Jesus said to them, "A prophet is not honored in his hometown. He doesn't receive any honor in his own home."

⁵⁸He did only a few miracles there because they had no faith.

JOHN THE BAPTIST'S HEAD IS CUT OFF

14 At that time Herod, the ruler of Galilee and Perea, heard reports about Jesus. ²He said to his attendants, "This is John the Baptist. He has risen from the dead! That is why he has the power to do miracles."

³Herod had arrested John. He had tied him up and put him in prison because of Herodias. She was the wife of Herod's brother Philip. ⁴John had been saying to Herod, "It is against the Law for you to have her." ⁵Herod wanted to kill John. But he was afraid of the people, because they thought John was a prophet.

⁶On Herod's birthday the daughter of Herodias danced for Herod and his guests. She pleased Herod very much. ⁷So he promised with an oath to give her anything she asked for. ⁸Her mother told her what to say. So the girl said to Herod, "Give me the head of John the Baptist on a big plate."

⁹The king was very upset. But he thought of his promise and his dinner guests. So he told one of his men to give her what she asked for. ¹⁰Herod had John's head cut off in the prison. ¹¹His head was brought in on a big plate and given to the girl. She then carried it to her mother.

¹²John's disciples came and took his body and buried it. Then they went and told Jesus.

JESUS FEEDS THE FIVE THOUSAND

¹³Jesus heard what had happened to John. He wanted to be alone. So he went in a boat to a quiet place. The

crowds heard about this. They followed him on foot from the towns. [14]When Jesus came ashore, he saw a large crowd. He felt deep concern for them. He healed their sick people.

[15]When it was almost evening, the disciples came to him. "There is nothing here," they said. "It's already getting late. Send the crowds away. They can go and buy some food in the villages."

[16]Jesus replied, "They don't need to go away. You give them something to eat."

[17]"We have only five loaves of bread and two fish," they answered.

[18]"Bring them here to me," he said. [19]Then Jesus directed the people to sit down on the grass. He took the five loaves and the two fish. He looked up to heaven and gave thanks. He broke the loaves into pieces. Then he gave them to the disciples. And the disciples gave them to the people.

[20]All of them ate and were satisfied. The disciples picked up 12 baskets of leftover pieces. [21]The number of men who ate was about 5,000. Women and children also ate.

JESUS WALKS ON THE WATER

[22]Right away Jesus made the disciples get into the boat. He had them go on ahead of him to the other side of the Sea of Galilee. Then he sent the crowd away. [23]After he had sent them away, he went up on a mountainside by himself to pray. When evening came, he was there alone. [24]The boat was already a long way from land. It was being pounded by the waves because the wind was blowing against it.

[25]Early in the morning, Jesus went out to the disciples. He walked on the lake. [26]They saw him walking on the lake and were terrified. "It's a ghost!" they said. And they cried out in fear.

[27]Right away Jesus called out to them, "Be brave! It is I. Don't be afraid."

Would God make a friendly ghost like Casper?

No. Some people in the Bible thought they saw a ghost or a spirit. The disciples thought they were seeing a ghost when they saw Jesus walking on the water. When Jesus appeared to his disciples after he rose from the dead, he said he was not a ghost. And some Bible translations use the word *ghost* to mean "spirit." But the Bible does not teach that spirits fly around visiting people. Many people have believed that people come back as ghosts after death. But that is not taught in the Bible at all.

What some people call the Holy Ghost is the Holy Spirit. When Jesus left the earth, he sent the Holy Spirit to live within us. He is the one who comforts, guides and protects us.

checkout Matthew 14:26

Related verse:
Luke 24:39

[28] "Lord, is it you?" Peter asked. "If it is, tell me to come to you on the water."

[29] "Come," Jesus said.

So Peter got out of the boat. He walked on the water toward Jesus. [30] But when Peter saw the wind, he was afraid. He began to sink. He cried out, "Lord! Save me!"

[31] Right away Jesus reached out his hand and caught him. "Your faith is so small!" he said. "Why did you doubt me?"

[32] When they climbed into the boat, the wind died down. [33] Then those in the boat worshiped Jesus. They said, "You really are the Son of God!"

[34] They crossed over the lake and landed at Gennesaret. [35] The men who lived there recognized Jesus. So they sent a message all over the nearby countryside. People brought all their sick to Jesus. [36] They begged him to let those who were sick just touch the edge of his clothes. And all who touched him were healed.

WHAT MAKES PEOPLE "UNCLEAN"?

15 Some Pharisees and some teachers of the law came from Jerusalem to see Jesus. They asked, [2] "Why don't your disciples obey what the elders teach? Your disciples don't wash their hands before they eat!"

[3] Jesus replied, "And why don't you obey God's command? You would rather follow your own teachings! [4] God said, 'Honor your father and mother.' *(Exodus 20:12; Deuteronomy 5:16)* He also said, 'If anyone calls down a curse on his father or mother, he will be put to death.' *(Exodus 21:17; Leviticus 20:9)* [5] But you allow people to say to their parents, 'Any help you might have received from us is a gift set apart for God.' [6] So they do not need to honor their parents with their gift. You make the word of God useless in order to follow your own teachings.

[7] "You pretenders! Isaiah was right when he prophesied about you. He said,

[8] " 'These people honor me by what they say.

But their hearts are far away
    from me.
[9] Their worship doesn't mean
    anything to me.
They teach nothing but human
    rules.' "   *(Isaiah 29:13)*

[10] Jesus called the crowd to him. He said, "Listen and understand. [11] What goes into your mouth does not make you 'unclean.' It's what comes out of your mouth that makes you 'unclean.' "

[12] Then the disciples came to him. They asked, "Do you know that the Pharisees were angry when they heard this?"

[13] Jesus replied, "There are plants that my Father in heaven has not planted. They will be pulled up by the roots. [14] Leave them. The Pharisees are blind guides. If a blind person leads another who is blind, both of them will fall into a pit."

[15] Peter said, "Explain this to us."

[16] "Don't you understand yet?" Jesus asked them. [17] "Don't you see? Everything that enters the mouth goes into the stomach. Then it goes out of the body. [18] But the things that come out of the mouth come from the heart. Those are the things that make you 'unclean.' [19] Evil thoughts come out of the heart. So do murder, adultery, and other sexual sins. And so do stealing, false witness, and telling lies about others. [20] Those are the things that make you 'unclean.' But eating without washing your hands does not make you 'unclean.' "

THE FAITH OF A WOMAN FROM CANAAN

[21] Jesus left Galilee and went to the area of Tyre and Sidon. [22] A woman from Canaan lived near Tyre and Sidon. She came to him and cried out, "Lord! Son of David! Have mercy on me! A demon controls my daughter. She is suffering terribly."

[23] Jesus did not say a word. So his disciples came to him. They begged him, "Send her away. She keeps crying out after us."

[24] Jesus answered, "I was sent only to the people of Israel. They are like lost sheep."

²⁵Then the woman fell to her knees in front of him. "Lord! Help me!" she said.

²⁶He replied, "It is not right to take the children's bread and throw it to their dogs."

²⁷"Yes, Lord," she said. "But even the dogs eat the crumbs that fall from their owners' table."

²⁸Then Jesus answered, "Woman, you have great faith! You will be given what you are asking for." And her daughter was healed at that very moment.

JESUS FEEDS THE FOUR THOUSAND

²⁹Jesus left there. He walked along the Sea of Galilee. Then he went up on a mountainside and sat down. ³⁰Large crowds came to him. They brought blind people and those who could not walk. They also brought disabled people, those who could not speak, and many others. They laid them at his feet, and he healed them.

³¹The people were amazed. Those who could not speak were speaking. The disabled were made well. Those not able to walk were walking. Those who were blind could see. So the people praised the God of Israel.

³²Then Jesus called for his disciples to come to him. He said, "I feel deep concern for these people. They have already been with me three days. They don't have anything to eat. I don't want to send them away hungry. If I do, they will become too weak on their way home."

³³His disciples answered him. "There is nothing here," they said. "Where could we get enough bread to feed this large crowd?"

³⁴"How many loaves do you have?" Jesus asked.

"Seven," they replied, "and a few small fish."

³⁵Jesus told the crowd to sit down on the ground. ³⁶He took the seven loaves and the fish and gave thanks. Then he broke them and gave them to the disciples. And the disciples passed them out to the people. ³⁷All of them ate and were satisfied. After that, the disciples picked up seven baskets of leftover pieces. ³⁸The number of men who ate was 4,000. Women and children also ate.

³⁹After Jesus had sent the crowd

Why do some people make music with bad words?

Some music writers and performers do not love God or try to obey him. They write and sing angry songs. Other music has bad words because the writers and singers want to shock their listeners. They want to get everyone's attention with really, really awful words. But much of the time music has bad words because the writers, singers, producers and stores know that people will buy that kind of music. Music people will keep making bad songs as long as people keep buying bad music.

checkout Matthew 15:18

Related verses:
Ephesians 4:29;
Philippians 4:8

Editing Booth
when we're done, it
may be short, but it
will be decent!

away, he got into the boat. He went to the area near Magadan.

JESUS IS ASKED FOR A MIRACULOUS SIGN

16 The Pharisees and Sadducees came to put Jesus to the test. They asked him to show them a miraculous sign from heaven.

²He replied, "In the evening you look at the sky. You say, 'It will be good weather. The sky is red.' ³And in the morning you say, 'Today it will be stormy. The sky is red and cloudy.' You know the meaning of what you see in the sky. But you can't understand the signs of what is happening right now. ⁴An evil and unfaithful people look for a miraculous sign. But none will be given to them except the sign of Jonah."

Then Jesus left them and went away.

THE YEAST OF THE PHARISEES AND SADDUCEES

⁵The disciples crossed over to the other side of the lake. They had forgotten to take bread. ⁶"Be careful," Jesus said to them. "Watch out for the yeast of the Pharisees and Sadducees."

⁷The disciples talked about this among themselves. They said, "He must be saying this because we didn't bring any bread."

⁸Jesus knew what they were saying. So he said, "Your faith is so small! Why are you talking to each other about having no bread? ⁹Don't you understand yet? Don't you remember the five loaves for the 5,000? Don't you remember how many baskets of pieces you gathered? ¹⁰Don't you remember the seven loaves for the 4,000? Don't you remember how many baskets of pieces you gathered? ¹¹How can you possibly not understand? I wasn't talking to you about bread. But watch out for the yeast of the Pharisees and Sadducees."

¹²Then the disciples understood that Jesus was not telling them to watch out for the yeast used in bread. He was warning them against what the Pharisees and Sadducees taught.

PETER SAYS THAT JESUS IS THE CHRIST

¹³Jesus went to the area of Caesarea Philippi. There he asked his disciples, "Who do people say the Son of Man is?"

¹⁴They replied, "Some say John the Baptist. Others say Elijah. Still others say Jeremiah, or one of the prophets."

¹⁵"But what about you?" he asked. "Who do you say I am?"

¹⁶Simon Peter answered, "You are the Christ. You are the Son of the living God."

¹⁷Jesus replied, "Blessed are you, Simon, son of Jonah! No mere man showed this to you. My Father in heaven showed it to you. ¹⁸Here is what I tell you. You are Peter. On this rock I will build my church. The gates of hell will not be strong enough to destroy it. ¹⁹I will give you the keys to the kingdom of heaven. What you lock on earth will be locked in heaven. What you unlock on earth will be unlocked in heaven."

²⁰Then Jesus warned his disciples not to tell anyone that he was the Christ.

JESUS TELLS ABOUT HIS COMING DEATH

²¹From that time on Jesus began to explain to his disciples what would happen to him. He told them he must go to Jerusalem. There he must suffer many things from the elders, the chief priests and the teachers of the law. He must be killed and on the third day rise to life again.

²²Peter took Jesus to one side and began to scold him. "Never, Lord!" he said. "This will never happen to you!"

²³Jesus turned and said to Peter, "Get behind me, Satan! You are standing in my way. You do not have in mind the things of God. Instead, you are thinking about human things."

²⁴Then Jesus spoke to his disciples. He said, "If anyone wants to follow me, he must say no to himself. He must pick up his cross and follow me. ²⁵If he wants to save his life, he will lose it. But if he loses his life for me, he will find it. ²⁶"What good is it if someone gains

the whole world but loses his soul? Or what can anyone trade for his soul? ²⁷The Son of Man is going to come in his Father's glory. His angels will come with him. And he will reward everyone in keeping with what they have done.

²⁸"What I'm about to tell you is true. Some who are standing here will not die before they see the Son of Man coming in his kingdom."

JESUS' APPEARANCE IS CHANGED

17 After six days Jesus took Peter, James, and John the brother of James with him. He led them up a high mountain. They were all alone. ²There in front of them his appearance was changed. His face shone like the sun. His clothes became as white as the light. ³Just then Moses and Elijah appeared in front of them. Moses and Elijah were talking with Jesus.

⁴Peter said to Jesus, "Lord, it is good for us to be here. If you wish, I will put up three shelters. One will be for you, one for Moses, and one for Elijah."

⁵While Peter was still speaking, a bright cloud surrounded them. A voice from the cloud said, "This is my Son, and I love him. I am very pleased with him. Listen to him!"

⁶When the disciples heard this, they were terrified. They fell with their faces to the ground. ⁷But Jesus came and touched them. "Get up," he said. "Don't be afraid." ⁸When they looked up, they saw no one except Jesus.

⁹They came down the mountain. On the way down, Jesus told them what to do. "Don't tell anyone what you have seen," he said. "Wait until the Son of Man has been raised from the dead."

¹⁰The disciples asked him, "Why do the teachers of the law say that Elijah has to come first?"

¹¹Jesus replied, "That's right. Elijah is supposed to come and make all things new again. ¹²But I tell you, Elijah has already come. People didn't recognize him. They have done to him everything they wanted to do. In the same way, they are going to make the Son of Man suffer."

¹³Then the disciples understood that Jesus was talking to them about John the Baptist.

JESUS HEALS A BOY WHO HAD A DEMON

¹⁴When they came near the crowd, a man approached Jesus. He got on his knees in front of him. ¹⁵"Lord," he said, "have mercy on my son. He shakes wildly and suffers a great deal. He of-

KIDS' QUESTion

Why does Jesus want us to follow him?

Jesus told us to follow him because he is the way to God, heaven and eternal life. When Jesus was on earth the disciples and others spent a lot of time with him and listened to his words. They went everywhere he went and learned from him. Today we follow Jesus by copying his example and by doing what he commanded

checkout Matthew 16:26,27

Related verse:
Matthew 4:19

ten falls into the fire or into the water. [16]I brought him to your disciples. But they couldn't heal him."

[17]"You unbelieving and evil people!" Jesus replied. "How long do I have to stay up with you? How long do I have to put up with you? Bring the boy here to me."

[18]Jesus ordered the demon to leave the boy, and it came out of him. He was healed at that very moment.

[19]Then the disciples came to Jesus in private. They asked, "Why couldn't we drive out the demon?"

[20/21]He replied, "Because your faith is much too small. What I'm about to tell you is true. If you have faith as small as a mustard seed, it is enough. You can say to this mountain, 'Move from here to there.' And it will move. Nothing will be impossible for you."

[22]They came together in Galilee. Then Jesus said to them, "The Son of Man is going to be handed over to men. [23]They will kill him. On the third day he will rise from the dead."

Then the disciples were filled with deep sadness.

JESUS PAYS THE TEMPLE TAX

[24]Jesus and his disciples arrived in Capernaum. There the tax collectors came to Peter. They asked him, "Doesn't your teacher pay the temple tax?"

[25]"Yes, he does," he replied.

When Peter came into the house, Jesus spoke first. "What do you think, Simon?" he asked. "Who do the kings of the earth collect taxes and fees from? Do they collect from their own sons or from others?"

[26]"From others," Peter answered.

"Then the sons don't have to pay," Jesus said to him. [27]"But we don't want to make them angry. So go to the lake and throw out your fishing line. Take the first fish you catch. Open its mouth. There you will find the exact coin you need. Take it and give it to them for my tax and yours."

WHO IS THE MOST IMPORTANT PERSON IN THE KINGDOM?

18 At that time the disciples came to Jesus. They asked him, "Who is the most important person in the kingdom of heaven?"

[2]Jesus called a little child over to him. He had the child stand among them. [3]Jesus said, "What I'm about to tell you is true. You need to change and become like little children. If you don't, you will never enter the kingdom of heaven. [4]Anyone who becomes as free of pride as this child is the most important in the kingdom of heaven.

[5]"Anyone who welcomes a little

Will God let me visit Grandpa in heaven?

One of the great things about going to heaven will be getting to see the people you love. If they have trusted in Jesus, they will be there. If your grandpa is in heaven, you will be able to see him when you go there. You will be able to visit with him just the way Moses and Elijah visited with Jesus on the mountain.

BEAM ME UP - SIR

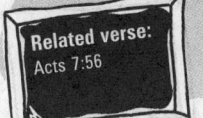

Related verse: Acts 7:56

checkout
Matthew 17:1-3

child like this in my name welcomes me.

⁶"But what if someone leads one of these little ones who believe in me to sin? If he does, it would be better for him to have a large millstone hung around his neck and be drowned at the bottom of the sea.

⁷"How terrible it will be for the world because of the things that lead people to sin! Things like that must come. But how terrible for those who cause them!

⁸"If your hand or foot causes you to sin, cut it off and throw it away. It would be better for you to enter the kingdom of heaven with only one hand or one foot than to go into hell with two hands and two feet. In hell the fire burns forever. ⁹If your eye causes you to sin, poke it out and throw it away. It would be better for you to enter the kingdom of heaven with one eye than to have two eyes and be thrown into the fire of hell.

THE STORY OF THE LOST SHEEP

¹⁰/¹¹"See that you don't look down on one of these little ones. Here is what I tell you. Their angels in heaven can go at any time to see my Father who is in heaven.

¹²"What do you think? Suppose a man owns 100 sheep and one of them wanders away. Won't he leave the 99 sheep on the hills? Won't he go and look for the one that wandered off? ¹³What I'm about to tell you is true. If he finds that sheep, he is happier about the one than about the 99 that didn't wander off. ¹⁴It is the same with your Father in heaven. He does not want any of these little ones to be lost.

WHEN SOMEONE SINS AGAINST YOU

¹⁵"If your brother sins against you, go to him. Tell him what he did wrong.

If Jesus doesn't want us to get hurt, why did he tell us to chop our hands off and poke our eyes out?

Jesus does not want people to cut off a hand or poke out an eye. He was using a very bold statement to make a point. It is like saying, "I would give *anything* to have an ice cream cone right now." You would not actually give *anything*. You just want everyone to know how badly you want ice cream. Jesus wanted to make people realize how bad sin is. When Jesus said it that way, it showed people how important it is to stop anything that causes sin.

checkout

Matthew 18:8

LAST WEEK'S LESSON
Hands and Eyes

Related verses:
Matthew 5:29,30

Keep it between the two of you. If he listens to you, you have won him back.

¹⁶"But what if he won't listen to you? Then take one or two others with you. Scripture says, 'Every matter must be proved by the words of two or three witnesses.' *(Deuteronomy 19:15)* ¹⁷But what if he also refuses to listen to the witnesses? Then tell it to the church. And what if he refuses to listen even to the church? Then don't treat him as your brother. Treat him as you would treat an ungodly person or a tax collector.

¹⁸"What I'm about to tell you is true. What you lock on earth will be locked in heaven. What you unlock on earth will be unlocked in heaven.

¹⁹"Again, here is what I tell you. Suppose two of you on earth agree about anything you ask for. My Father in heaven will do it for you. ²⁰Where two or three people meet together in my name, I am there with them."

THE SERVANT WHO HAD NO MERCY

²¹Peter came to Jesus. He asked, "Lord, how many times should I for-give my brother when he sins against me? Up to seven times?"

²²Jesus answered, "I tell you, not seven times, but 77 times.

²³"The kingdom of heaven is like a king who wanted to collect all the money his servants owed him. ²⁴As the king began to do it, a man who owed him millions of dollars was brought to him. ²⁵The man was not able to pay. So his master gave an order. The man, his wife, his children, and all he owned had to be sold to pay back what he owed.

²⁶"The servant fell on his knees in front of him. 'Give me time,' he begged. 'I'll pay everything back.'

²⁷"His master felt sorry for him. He forgave him what he owed and let him go.

²⁸"But then that servant went out and found one of the other servants who owed him a few dollars. He grabbed him and began to choke him. 'Pay back what you owe me!' he said.

²⁹"The other servant fell on his knees. 'Give me time,' he begged him. 'I'll pay you back.'

³⁰"But the first servant refused. In-

KIDS' QUESTION
Why does God want us to pray together?

God enjoys it when his people pray together. It is one of the ways we can help and support one another. The Bible calls Christians a "body." This means they work best when they work together, like the different parts of a body. When believers pray together, they strengthen and encourage each other.

checkout
Matthew 18:19,20

Related verses:
2 Chronicles 7:14;
Psalm 34:3

PRAYER MEETING IN JASON'S ROOM AT BEDTIME. ALL WELCOME

stead, he went and had the man thrown into prison. The man would be held there until he could pay back what he owed. ³¹The other servants saw what had happened. It troubled them greatly. They went and told their master everything that had happened. ³²"Then the master called the first servant in. 'You evil servant,' he said. 'I forgave all that you owed me because you begged me to. ³³Shouldn't you have had mercy on the other servant just as I had mercy on you?' ³⁴In anger his master turned him over to the jailers. He would be punished until he paid back everything he owed.

³⁵"This is how my Father in heaven will treat each of you unless you forgive your brother from your heart."

JESUS TEACHES ABOUT DIVORCE

19 When Jesus finished saying these things, he left Galilee. He went into the area of Judea on the other side of the Jordan River. ²Large crowds followed him. He healed them there.

³Some Pharisees came to put him to the test. They asked, "Does the Law allow a man to divorce his wife for any reason at all?"

⁴Jesus replied, "Haven't you read that in the beginning the Creator 'made them male and female'? *(Genesis 1:27)* ⁵He said, 'That's why a man will leave his father and mother and be joined to his wife. The two will become one.' *(Genesis 2:24)* ⁶They are no longer two, but one. So a man must not separate what God has joined together."

⁷They asked, "Then why did Moses command that a man can give his wife a letter of divorce and send her away?"

⁸Jesus replied, "Moses let you divorce your wives because you were stubborn. But it was not this way from the beginning. ⁹Here is what I tell you. Anyone who divorces his wife and gets married to another woman commits adultery. A man may divorce his wife only if she has not been faithful to him."

¹⁰The disciples said to him, "If that's the way it is between a husband and wife, it is better not to get married."

Why do some moms and dads divorce?

When a man and a woman get married, they promise to stay with each other for life. They know it won't always be easy, but they want to work out their problems and stay together. When the arguments and other troubles come, some people don't know how to handle them. Usually the problems start small. Eventually, these problems can become so big that the husband or the wife or both decide to end their marriage. Sometimes a marriage ends because one partner is not a Christian or one partner is unfaithful.

God wants Christians to stay married and work things out if possible. He knows that if they do, their lives will almost always be better.

checkout
Matthew 19:8–9

Related verses:
Proverbs 18:22;
Matthew 19:3–12;
Romans 3:23;
1 Corinthians
7:10–11, 26–28

¹¹Jesus replied, "Not everyone can accept the idea of staying single. Only those who have been helped to live without getting married can accept it. ¹²Some men are not able to have children because they were born that way. Some have been made that way by other people. Others have made themselves that way in order to serve the kingdom of heaven. The one who can accept living that way should do it."

LITTLE CHILDREN ARE BROUGHT TO JESUS

¹³Some people brought little children to Jesus. They wanted him to place his hands on the children and pray for them. But the disciples told the people to stop.

¹⁴Jesus said, "Let the little children come to me. Don't keep them away. The kingdom of heaven belongs to people like them." ¹⁵Jesus placed his hands on them. Then he went on from there.

JESUS AND THE RICH YOUNG MAN

¹⁶A man came up to Jesus. He asked, "Teacher, what good thing must I do to receive eternal life?"

¹⁷"Why do you ask me about what is good?" Jesus replied. "There is only One who is good. If you want to enter the kingdom, obey the commandments."

¹⁸"Which ones?" the man asked.

Jesus said, " 'Do not commit murder. Do not commit adultery. Do not steal. Do not give false witness. ¹⁹Honor your father and mother.' *(Exodus 20:12–16; Deuteronomy 5:16–20)* And 'love your neighbor as you love yourself.' " *(Leviticus 19:18)*

²⁰"I have obeyed all those com-

After our parents pray with us, do we still need to pray on our own later?

Your parents pray with you each day to help learn how to pray. The prayers that you say with them are your prayers and are about you talking to God. Whoever is praying with you probably also has their own time when they talk to God. If there is something that you want to talk to God about on your own, after praying with your parents or at any other time, go ahead. God loves to hear from you. Your parents will also be happy to know that you are learning so well and praying on your own.

The whole reason that your parents are teaching you to pray is that when you are older you will be able to pray all by yourself and get to know God better without them being there.

NOW THAT MY PARENTS HAVE GONE, THERE ARE A FEW OTHER ITEMS I'D LIKE TO DISCUSS...

checkout
Matthew 19:14, 15

Related verses:
Luke 18:15–17

mandments," the young man said. "What else do I need to do?"

²¹Jesus answered, "If you want to be perfect, go and sell everything you have. Give the money to those who are poor. You will have treasure in heaven. Then come and follow me."

²²When the young man heard this, he went away sad. He was very rich.

²³Then Jesus said to his disciples, "What I'm about to tell you is true. It is hard for rich people to enter the kingdom of heaven. ²⁴Again I tell you, it is hard for a camel to go through the eye of a needle. But it is even harder for the rich to enter God's kingdom."

²⁵When the disciples heard this, they were really amazed. They asked, "Then who can be saved?"

²⁶Jesus looked at them and said, "With man, that is impossible. But with God, all things are possible."

²⁷Peter answered him, "We have left everything to follow you! What reward will be given to us?"

²⁸"What I'm about to tell you is true," Jesus said to them. "When all things are made new, the Son of Man will sit on his glorious throne. Then you who have followed me will also sit on 12 thrones. You will judge the 12 tribes of Israel. ²⁹Everyone who has left houses or families or fields because of me will receive 100 times as much. They will also receive eternal life. ³⁰But many who are first will be last. And many who are last will be first.

THE STORY OF THE WORKERS IN THE VINEYARD

20 "The kingdom of heaven is like a man who owned land. He went out early in the morning to hire people to work in his vineyard. ²He agreed to give them the usual pay for a day's work. Then he sent them into his vineyard.

³"About nine o'clock in the morning he went out again. He saw others standing in the market place doing nothing. ⁴He told them, 'You also go and work in my vineyard. I'll pay you what is right.' ⁵So they went.

"He went out again about noon and at three o'clock and did the same thing. ⁶About five o'clock he went out and found still others standing around. He asked them, 'Why have you been standing here all day long doing nothing?'

⁷"'Because no one has hired us,' they answered.

KIDS' QUESTion

Why do we have marriage?

God invented marriage because every person needs someone to be close to and to love. He also created marriage as the way for bringing children into the world. God knows what is best for us. He knows that it is best for babies and children to have a mother and father to protect and care for them. Marriage is good. In fact, God brought the first husband and wife together in the Garden of Eden before any sin came into the world. Husbands and wives should stay together, work out their problems and be good parents. That is God's plan.

checkout Matthew 19:5

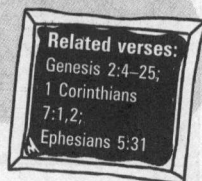

Related verses:
Genesis 2:4–25;
1 Corinthians 7:1,2;
Ephesians 5:31

"He said to them, 'You also go and work in my vineyard.'

8"When evening came, the owner of the vineyard spoke to the person who was in charge of the workers. He said, 'Call the workers and give them their pay. Begin with the last ones I hired. Then go on to the first ones.'

9"The workers who were hired about five o'clock came. Each received the usual day's pay. 10So when those who were hired first came, they expected to receive more. But each of them also received the usual day's pay.

11"When they received it, they began to complain about the owner. 12'These people who were hired last worked only one hour,' they said. 'You have paid them the same as us. We have done most of the work and have been in the hot sun all day.'

13"The owner answered one of them. 'Friend,' he said, 'I'm being fair to you. Didn't you agree to work for the usual day's pay? 14Take your money and go. I want to give the ones I hired last the same pay I gave you. 15Don't I have the right to do what I want with my own money? Do you feel cheated because I gave so freely to the others?'

16"So those who are last will be first. And those who are first will be last."

JESUS AGAIN TELLS ABOUT HIS COMING DEATH

17Jesus was going up to Jerusalem. On the way, he took the 12 disciples to one side to talk to them.

18"We are going up to Jerusalem," he said. "The Son of Man will be handed over to the chief priests and the teachers of the law. They will sentence him to death. 19Then they will turn him over to people who are not Jews. The people will make fun of him and whip him. They will nail him to a cross. On the third day, he will rise from the dead!"

A MOTHER ASKS A FAVOR OF JESUS

20The mother of Zebedee's sons came to Jesus. Her sons came with her. Getting on her knees, she asked a favor of him.

21"What do you want?" Jesus asked.

She said, "Promise me that one of my two sons may sit at your right hand in your kingdom. Promise that the other one may sit at your left hand."

22"You don't know what you're asking for," Jesus said to them. "Can you drink the cup of suffering I am going to drink?"

Why did the disciples tell the people Jesus was too busy to see the kids?

Many parents brought their children to see Jesus. Jesus always welcomed them. The disciples did try to keep kids away from Jesus. They did not understand how much Jesus loved children. Maybe they thought the kids would be too loud. Maybe they thought the kids would be in the way. The disciples did not quite understand that Jesus wanted all people to come to him. He especially wanted children to feel welcome. Jesus thinks kids are very important.

Related verses:
Matthew 18:1–6

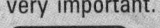

Matthew 19:13,14

"We can," they answered.

²³Jesus said to them, "You will certainly drink from my cup. But it is not for me to say who will sit at my right or left hand. These places belong to those my Father has prepared them for."

²⁴The other ten disciples heard about this. They became angry at the two brothers.

²⁵Jesus called them together. He said, "You know about the rulers of the nations. They hold power over their people. Their high officials order them around. ²⁶Don't be like that. Instead, anyone who wants to be important among you must be your servant. ²⁷And anyone who wants to be first must be your slave.

²⁸"Be like the Son of Man. He did not come to be served. Instead, he came to serve others. He came to give his life as the price for setting many people free."

TWO BLIND MEN RECEIVE THEIR SIGHT

²⁹Jesus and his disciples were leaving Jericho. A large crowd followed him. ³⁰Two blind men were sitting by the side of the road. They heard that Jesus was going by. So they shouted, "Lord! Son of David! Have mercy on us!"

³¹The crowd commanded them to stop. They told them to be quiet. But the two men shouted even louder, "Lord! Son of David! Have mercy on us!"

³²Jesus stopped and called out to them. "What do you want me to do for you?" he asked.

³³"Lord," they answered, "we want to be able to see."

³⁴Jesus felt deep concern for them. He touched their eyes. Right away they could see. And they followed him.

JESUS ENTERS JERUSALEM

21 As they all approached Jerusalem, they came to Bethphage. It was on the Mount of Olives. Jesus sent out two disciples. ²He said to them, "Go to the village ahead of you. As soon as you get there, you will find a donkey tied up. Her colt will be with her. Untie

Why do some kids get their allowances free and others have to earn it?

Every family is different. In some families children earn their allowances by doing chores. In other families children receive money just for being part of the family. And in some families kids do not get any allowance at all. It is all up to the parents.

Be thankful for the opportunity to help at home. Learn how to be a good worker and how to be a member of the team. You will always find a reason to complain if you compare your family with others. But if you remember that God put you and your family together, you will be thankful.

checkout
Matthew
20:11,12

Related verses:
Deuteronomy 5:16;
Ecclesiastes
7:11,12

them and bring them to me. ³If anyone says anything to you, say that the Lord needs them. The owner will send them right away."

⁴This took place so that what was spoken through the prophet would come true. It says,

⁵ "Say to the city of Zion,
  'See, your king comes to you.
He is gentle and riding on a
    donkey.
He is riding on a donkey's
    colt.' "   *(Zechariah 9:9)*

⁶The disciples went and did what Jesus told them to do. ⁷They brought the donkey and the colt. They placed their coats on them. Then Jesus sat on the coats. ⁸A very large crowd spread their coats on the road. Others cut branches from the trees and spread them on the road. ⁹Some of the people went ahead of him, and some followed. They all shouted,

"Hosanna to the Son of David!"

"Blessed is the one who comes in the name of the Lord!"
                    (Psalm 118:26)

"Hosanna in the highest heaven!"

¹⁰When Jesus entered Jerusalem, the whole city was stirred up. The people asked, "Who is this?"

¹¹The crowds answered, "This is Jesus. He is the prophet from Nazareth in Galilee."

JESUS CLEARS OUT THE TEMPLE

¹²Jesus entered the temple area. He began chasing out all those who were buying and selling there. He turned over the tables of the people who were exchanging money. He also turned over the benches of those who were selling doves. ¹³He said to them, "It is written that the Lord said, 'My house will be called a house where people can pray.' *(Isaiah 56:7)* But you are making it a 'den for robbers.' " *(Jeremiah 7:11)*

¹⁴Blind people and those who were disabled came to Jesus at the temple. There he healed them. ¹⁵The chief priests and the teachers of the law saw the wonderful things he did. They also

saw the children in the temple area shouting, "Hosanna to the Son of David!" But when they saw all of this, they became angry.

¹⁶"Do you hear what these children are saying?" they asked him.

"Yes," replied Jesus. "Haven't you ever read about it in Scripture? It says,

" 'You have made sure that
    children and infants
    praise you.' "   *(Psalm 8:2)*

¹⁷Then Jesus left the people and went out of the city to Bethany. He spent the night there.

THE FIG TREE DRIES UP

¹⁸Early in the morning, Jesus was on his way back to Jerusalem. He was hungry. ¹⁹He saw a fig tree by the road. He went up to it but found nothing on it except leaves. Then he said to it, "May you never bear fruit again!" Right away the tree dried up.

²⁰When the disciples saw this, they were amazed. "How did the fig tree dry up so quickly?" they asked.

²¹Jesus replied, "What I'm about to tell you is true. You must have faith and not doubt. Then you can do what was done to the fig tree. And you can say to this mountain, 'Go and throw yourself into the sea.' It will be done. ²²If you believe, you will receive what you ask for when you pray."

THE AUTHORITY OF JESUS IS QUESTIONED

²³Jesus entered the temple court-yard. While he was teaching there, the chief priests and the elders of the people came to him. "By what authority are you doing these things?" they asked. "Who gave you this authority?"

²⁴Jesus replied, "I will also ask you one question. If you answer me, I will tell you by what authority I am doing these things. ²⁵Where did John's baptism come from? Was it from heaven? Or did it come from men?"

They talked to each other about it. They said, "If we say, 'From heaven,' he will ask, 'Then why didn't you believe him?' ²⁶But what if we say, 'From men?' We are afraid of the people. Everyone believes that John was a prophet."

²⁷So they answered Jesus, "We don't know."

Jesus said, "Then I won't tell you by what authority I am doing these things either.

THE STORY OF THE TWO SONS

²⁸"What do you think about this? A man had two sons. He went to the first and said, 'Son, go and work today in the vineyard.'

²⁹" 'I will not,' the son answered. But later he changed his mind and went.

³⁰"Then the father went to the other son. He said the same thing. The son answered, 'I will, sir.' But he did not go.

³¹"Which of the two sons did what his father wanted?"

"The first," they answered.

Jesus said to them, "What I'm about to tell you is true. Tax collectors and prostitutes will enter the kingdom of God ahead of you. ³²John came to show you the right way to live. And you did not believe him. But the tax collectors and the prostitutes did. You saw this. But even then you did not turn away from your sins and believe him.

THE STORY OF THE RENTERS

³³"Listen to another story. A man who owned some land planted a vineyard. He put a wall around it. He dug a pit for a winepress in it. He also built a lookout tower. He rented the vineyard out to some farmers. Then he went away on a journey. ³⁴When harvest time approached, he sent his servants to the renters. He told the servants to collect his share of the fruit.

³⁵"But the renters grabbed his servants. They beat one of them. They killed another. They threw stones at the third to kill him. ³⁶Then the man sent other servants to the renters. He sent more than he did the first time. The renters treated them the same way.

³⁷"Last of all, he sent his son to them. 'They will respect my son,' he said.

³⁸"But the renters saw the son coming. They said to each other, 'This is the one who will receive all the owner's property someday. Come, let's kill him. Then everything will be ours.'

³⁹So they took him and threw him out of the vineyard. Then they killed him.

⁴⁰"When the owner of the vineyard comes back, what will he do to those renters?"

⁴¹"He will destroy those evil people," they replied. "Then he will rent the vineyard out to other renters. They will give him his share of the crop at harvest time."

⁴²Jesus said to them, "Haven't you ever read what the Scriptures say,

" 'The stone the builders didn't
     accept
has become the most important
     stone of all.
The Lord has done it.
It is wonderful in our eyes'?
(Psalm 118:22,23)

⁴³"So here is what I tell you. The kingdom of God will be taken away from you. It will be given to people who will produce its fruit. ⁴⁴Everyone who falls on that stone will be broken to pieces. But the stone will crush anyone it falls on."

⁴⁵The chief priests and the Pharisees heard Jesus' stories. They knew he was talking about them. ⁴⁶So they looked for a way to arrest him. But they were afraid of the crowd. The people believed that Jesus was a prophet.

THE STORY OF THE WEDDING DINNER

22 Jesus told them more stories. He said, ²"Here is what the kingdom of heaven is like. A king prepared a wedding dinner for his son. ³He sent his servants to those who had been invited to the dinner. The servants told them to come. But they refused.

⁴"Then he sent some more servants. He said, 'Tell those who were invited that I have prepared my dinner. I have killed my oxen and my fattest cattle. Everything is ready. Come to the wedding dinner.'

⁵"But the people paid no attention. One went away to his field. Another went away to his business. ⁶The rest grabbed his servants. They treated them badly and then killed them.

⁷"The king became very angry. He sent his army to destroy them. They

killed those murderers and burned their city.

8"Then the king said to his servants, 'The wedding dinner is ready. But those I invited were not fit to come. 9Go to the street corners. Invite to the dinner anyone you can find.' 10So the servants went out into the streets. They gathered all the people they could find, both good and bad. Soon the wedding hall was filled with guests.

11"The king came in to see the guests. He noticed a man there who was not wearing wedding clothes. 12'Friend,' he asked, 'how did you get in here without wedding clothes?' The man couldn't think of anything to say.

13"Then the king told his servants, 'Tie up his hands and feet. Throw him outside into the darkness. Out there people will sob and grind their teeth.' 14"Many are invited, but few are chosen."

IS IT RIGHT TO PAY TAXES TO CAESAR?

15The Pharisees went out. They made plans to trap Jesus with his own words. 16They sent their followers to him. They sent the Herodians with them.

"Teacher," they said, "we know you are a man of honor. You teach the way of God truthfully. You don't let others tell you what to do or say. You don't care how important they are. 17Tell us then, what do you think? Is it right to pay taxes to Caesar or not?"

18But Jesus knew their evil plans. He said, "You pretenders! Why are you trying to trap me? 19Show me the coin people use for paying the tax."

They brought him a silver coin.

20He asked them, "Whose picture is this? And whose words?"

21"Caesar's," they replied.

Then he said to them, "Give to Caesar what belongs to Caesar. And give to God what belongs to God."

KIDS' QUESTION

If you know a friend is going to do something wrong, should you try to stop the person?

Yes, definitely. First, try to talk your friend out of doing what is wrong. Explain that you care about him or her and that is why you want to help. Use your friendship to encourage this friend to do what is right. If he or she won't listen, talk with your parents. If your friend starts doing something wrong, it may be best to leave.

checkout
Matthew 22:15

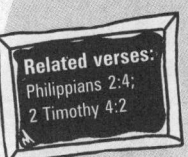
Related verses: Philippians 2:4; 2 Timothy 4:2

²²When they heard this, they were amazed. So they left him and went away.

MARRIAGE WHEN THE DEAD RISE

²³That same day the Sadducees came to Jesus with a question. They do not believe that people rise from the dead.

²⁴"Teacher," they said, "here is what Moses told us. If a man dies without having children, his brother must get married to the widow. He must have children to carry on his brother's name. ²⁵There were seven brothers among us. The first one got married and died. Since he had no children, he left his wife to his brother. ²⁶The same thing happened to the second and third brothers. It happened right on down to the seventh brother. ²⁷Finally, the woman died. ²⁸Now then, when the dead rise, whose wife will she be? All seven of them were married to her."

²⁹Jesus replied, "You are mistaken, because you do not know the Scriptures. And you do not know the power of God. ³⁰When the dead rise, they won't get married. And their parents won't give them to be married. They will be like the angels in heaven.

³¹"What about the dead rising? Haven't you read what God said to you? ³²He said, 'I am the God of Abraham. I am the God of Isaac. And I am the God of Jacob.' *(Exodus 3:6)* He is not the God of the dead. He is the God of the living."

³³When the crowds heard this, they were amazed by what he taught.

THE MOST IMPORTANT COMMANDMENT

³⁴The Pharisees heard that the Sadducees weren't able to answer Jesus. So the Pharisees got together. ³⁵One of them was an authority on the law. So he tested Jesus with a question. ³⁶"Teacher," he asked, "which is the most important commandment in the Law?"

³⁷Jesus replied, " 'Love the Lord your God with all your heart and with all your soul. Love him with all your mind.' *(Deuteronomy 6:5)* ³⁸This is the first and most important commandment. ³⁹And the second is like it. 'Love your neighbor as you love yourself.' *(Leviticus 19:18)* ⁴⁰Everything that is written in the

KIDS' QUESTION

Are angels boys or girls?

People are either male or female. You are a boy or girl because of how your body was made. But angels do not have bodies, so they are neither boys nor girls. There are no man or woman angels. The two angels Michael and Gabriel do have male names. And angels who visited people in human form usually appeared as a man. But that does not mean that they are men.

checkout
Matthew 22:30

ANGEL IN DISGUISE

Related verses:
Hebrews 1:13,14

Law and the Prophets is based on these two commandments."

WHOSE SON IS THE CHRIST?

⁴¹The Pharisees were gathered together. Jesus asked them, ⁴²"What do you think about the Christ? Whose son is he?"

"The son of David," they replied.

⁴³He said to them, "Then why does David call him 'Lord'? The Holy Spirit spoke through David himself. David said,

⁴⁴ " 'The Lord said to my Lord,
"Sit at my right hand
until I put your enemies
under your control." '

(Psalm 110:1)

⁴⁵So if David calls him 'Lord,' how can he be David's son?"

⁴⁶No one could answer him with a single word. From that day on, no one dared to ask him any more questions.

JESUS JUDGES THE PHARISEES AND THE TEACHERS OF THE LAW

23 Jesus spoke to the crowds and to his disciples. ²"The teachers of the law and the Pharisees sit in Moses' seat," he said. ³"So you must obey them. Do everything they tell you. But don't do what they do. They don't practice what they preach. ⁴They tie up heavy loads and put them on other people's shoulders. But they themselves aren't willing to lift a finger to move them.

⁵"Everything they do is done for others to see. On their foreheads and arms they wear little boxes that hold Scripture verses. They make the boxes very wide. And they make the tassels on their coats very long.

⁶"They love to sit down in the place of honor at dinners. They also love to have the most important seats in the synagogues. ⁷They love to be greeted in the market places. They love it when people call them 'Rabbi.'

⁸"But you shouldn't be called 'Rabbi.' You have only one Master, and you are all brothers. ⁹Do not call anyone on earth 'father.' You have one Father, and he is in heaven. ¹⁰You shouldn't be called 'teacher.' You have one Teacher, and he is the Christ. ¹¹The most important person among you will be your servant. ¹²Anyone who lifts himself up will be brought down. And any-

What are God's rules for right and wrong?

God has given us the Bible to tell us about himself and how he wants us to live. We need to do our best to obey what God tells us in his Word. Jesus said that the most important rule is to love God with all our heart. He says the next most important rule is to love our neighbor as ourselves. We should love God first and then other people. God also wants us to choose the *best* way to live. Some things are poor choices even though they are not wrong. We should say yes to the *best* things if we want to make the right choices.

checkout Matthew 22:37–40

Related verses:
Exodus 20:1–17;
1 Corinthians
10:23,24

one who is brought down will be lifted up.

13/14"How terrible it will be for you, teachers of the law and Pharisees! You pretenders! You shut the kingdom of heaven in people's faces. You yourselves do not enter. And you will not let those enter who are trying to.

15"How terrible for you, teachers of the law and Pharisees! You pretenders! You travel everywhere to win one person to your faith. Then you make him twice as much a son of hell as you are.

16"How terrible for you, blind guides! You say, 'If anyone takes an oath in the name of the temple, it means nothing. But anyone who takes an oath in the name of the gold of the temple must keep the oath.' 17You are blind and foolish! Which is more important? Is it the gold? Or is it the temple that makes the gold holy?

18"You also say, 'If anyone takes an oath in the name of the altar, it means nothing. But anyone who takes an oath in the name of the gift on it must keep the oath.' 19You blind men! Which is more important? Is it the gift? Or is it the altar that makes the gift holy?

20"So anyone who takes an oath in the name of the altar takes an oath in the name of it and of everything on it. 21And anyone who takes an oath in the name of the temple takes an oath in the name of it and of the One who lives in it. 22And anyone who takes an oath in the name of heaven takes an oath in the name of God's throne and of the One who sits on it.

23"How terrible for you, teachers of the law and Pharisees! You pretenders! You give God a tenth of your spices, like mint, dill and cummin. But you have not practiced the more important things of the law, like fairness, mercy and faithfulness. You should have practiced the last things without failing to do the first. 24You blind guides! You remove the smallest insect from your food. But you swallow a whole camel!

25"How terrible for you, teachers of the law and Pharisees! You pretenders! You clean the outside of the cup and dish. But on the inside you are full of greed. You only want to satisfy yourselves. 26Blind Pharisee! First clean the inside of the cup and dish. Then the outside will also be clean.

27"How terrible for you, teachers of the law and Pharisees! You pretenders! You are like tombs that are painted white. They look beautiful on the outside. But on the inside they are full of the bones of the dead. They are also full of other things that are not pure and clean. 28It is the same with you. On the outside you seem to be doing what is right. But on the inside you are full of what is wrong. You pretend to be what you are not.

29"How terrible for you, teachers of the law and Pharisees! You pretenders! You build tombs for the prophets. You decorate the graves of the godly. 30And you say, 'If we had lived in the days of those who lived before us, we wouldn't have done what they did. We wouldn't have helped to kill the prophets.' 31So you give witness against yourselves. You admit that you are the children of those who murdered the prophets. 32So finish the sins that those who lived before you started!

33"You nest of poisonous snakes! How will you escape from being sentenced to hell? 34So I am sending you prophets, wise men, and teachers. You will kill some of them. You will nail some to a cross. Others you will whip in your synagogues. You will chase them from town to town.

35"So you will pay for all the godly people's blood spilled on earth. I mean from the blood of godly Abel to the blood of Zechariah, the son of Berekiah. Zechariah was the one you murdered between the temple and the altar. 36What I'm about to tell you is true. All this will happen to those who are now living.

37"Jerusalem! Jerusalem! You kill the prophets and throw stones in order to kill those who are sent to you. Many times I have wanted to gather your people together. I have wanted to be like a hen who gathers her chicks under her wings. But you would not let me! 38Look, your house is left empty. 39I tell you, you will not see me again until you say, 'Blessed is the one who comes in the name of the Lord.' "
(Psalm 118:26)

SIGNS OF THE END

24 Jesus left the temple. He was walking away when his disciples came up to him. They wanted to call his attention to the temple buildings. ²"Do you see all these things?" Jesus asked. "What I'm about to tell you is true. Not one stone here will be left on top of another. Every stone will be thrown down."

³Jesus was sitting on the Mount of Olives. There the disciples came to him in private. "Tell us," they said. "When will this happen? And what will be the sign of your coming? What will be the sign of the end?"

⁴Jesus answered, "Keep watch! Be careful that no one fools you. ⁵Many will come in my name. They will claim, 'I am the Christ!' They will fool many people.

⁶"You will hear about wars. You will also hear people talking about future wars. Don't be alarmed. Those things must happen. But the end still isn't here. ⁷Nation will fight against nation. Kingdom will fight against kingdom. People will go hungry. There will be earthquakes in many places. ⁸All these are the beginning of birth pains.

⁹"Then people will hand you over to be treated badly and killed. All nations will hate you because of me. ¹⁰At that time, many will turn away from their faith. They will hate each other. They will hand each other over to their enemies. ¹¹Many false prophets will appear. They will fool many people. ¹²Because evil will grow, most people's love will grow cold. ¹³But the one who stands firm to the end will be saved. ¹⁴This good news of the kingdom will be preached in the whole world. It will be a witness to all nations. Then the end will come.

¹⁵"The prophet Daniel spoke about 'the hated thing that destroys.' *(Daniel 9:27; 11:31; 12:11)* Someday you will see it standing in the holy place. The reader should understand this. ¹⁶Then those who are in Judea should escape to the mountains. ¹⁷No one on the roof should go down into his house to take anything out. ¹⁸No one in the field should go back to get his coat. ¹⁹How awful it will be in those days for pregnant women! How awful for nursing mothers! ²⁰Pray that you will not have to escape in winter or on the Sabbath day. ²¹There will be terrible suffering in those days. It will be worse than any other from the beginning of the world until now. And there will never be anything like it again. ²²If the time had not been cut short, no one would live. But because of God's chosen people, it will be shortened.

²³"At that time someone may say to you, 'Look! Here is the Christ!' Or, 'There he is!' Do not believe it. ²⁴False Christs and false prophets will appear. They will do great signs and miracles. They will try to fool God's chosen people if possible. ²⁵See, I have told you ahead of time.

²⁶"So if anyone tells you, 'He is far out in the desert,' do not go out there. Or if anyone says, 'He is deep inside the house,' do not believe it. ²⁷Lightning that comes from the east can be seen in the west. It will be the same when the Son of Man comes. ²⁸The vultures will gather wherever there is a dead body.

²⁹"Right after the terrible suffering of those days,

" 'The sun will be darkened.
The moon will not shine.
The stars will fall from the sky.
The heavenly bodies will be
      shaken.'   *(Isaiah 13:10; 34:4)*

³⁰"At that time the sign of the Son of Man will appear in the sky. All the nations on earth will be sad. They will see the Son of Man coming on the clouds of the sky. He will come with power and great glory. ³¹He will send his angels with a loud trumpet call. They will gather his chosen people from all four directions. They will bring them from one end of the heavens to the other.

³²"Learn a lesson from the fig tree. As soon as its twigs get tender and its leaves come out, you know that summer is near. ³³In the same way, when you see all those things happening, you know that the end is near. It is right at the door. ³⁴What I'm about to tell you is true. The people living at that time will certainly not pass away until all those things have happened.

³⁵Heaven and earth will pass away. But my words will never pass away.

THE DAY AND HOUR ARE NOT KNOWN

³⁶"No one knows about that day or hour. Not even the angels in heaven know. The Son does not know. Only the Father knows.

³⁷"Remember how it was in the days of Noah. It will be the same when the Son of Man comes.

³⁸"In the days before the flood, people were eating and drinking. They were getting married. They were giving their daughters to be married. They did all those things right up to the day Noah entered the ark. ³⁹They knew nothing about what would happen until the flood came and took them all away. That is how it will be when the Son of Man comes.

⁴⁰"Two men will be in the field. One will be taken and the other left. ⁴¹Two women will be grinding with a hand mill. One will be taken and the other left.

⁴²"So keep watch. You do not know on what day your Lord will come. ⁴³You must understand something. Suppose the owner of the house knew what time of night the robber was coming. Then he would have kept watch. He would not have let his house be broken into. ⁴⁴So you also must be ready. The Son of Man will come at an hour when you don't expect him.

⁴⁵"Suppose a master puts one of his servants in charge of the other servants in his house. The servant's job is to give them their food at the right time. The master wants a faithful and wise servant for this. ⁴⁶It will be good for the servant if the master finds him doing his job when the master returns. ⁴⁷What I'm about to tell you is true. The master will put that servant in charge of everything he owns.

⁴⁸"But suppose that servant is evil. Suppose he says to himself, 'My master is staying away a long time.' ⁴⁹Suppose he begins to beat the other servants. And suppose he eats and drinks with those who drink too much. ⁵⁰The master of that servant will

Why hasn't God told us when Jesus is coming back?

Jesus told his disciples that he would return to earth some day. But when they asked when, he told them that these things were not for them to know. Jesus did not want them to be concerned with *when* he would return. He wanted them to stay alert and live just as God wanted them to *until* he returned. God did not say exactly when Jesus would return. He *did* say that certain things need to happen before Jesus comes back. One of those things is that Jesus will not come back until the good news about him has been told to the whole world.

checkout Matthew 24:36,42

Related verses:
1 Thessalonians
5:23;
James 5:7,8

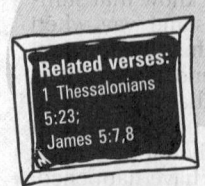

come back on a day the servant doesn't expect him. He will return at an hour the servant does not know. ⁵¹Then the master will cut him to pieces. He will send him to the place where pretenders go. There people will sob and grind their teeth.

THE STORY OF TEN BRIDESMAIDS

25 "Here is what the kingdom of heaven will be like at that time. Ten bridesmaids took their lamps and went out to meet the groom. ²Five of them were foolish. Five were wise. ³The foolish ones took their lamps but didn't take any olive oil with them. ⁴The wise ones took oil in jars along with their lamps. ⁵The groom did not come for a long time. So the bridesmaids all grew tired and fell asleep.

⁶"At midnight someone cried out, 'Here's the groom! Come out to meet him!'

⁷"Then all the bridesmaids woke up and got their lamps ready. ⁸The foolish ones said to the wise ones, 'Give us some of your oil. Our lamps are going out.'

⁹" 'No,' they replied. 'There may not be enough for all of us. Instead, go to those who sell oil. Buy some for yourselves.'

¹⁰"So they went to buy the oil. But while they were on their way, the groom arrived. The bridesmaids who were ready went in with him to the wedding dinner. Then the door was shut.

¹¹"Later, the other bridesmaids also came. 'Sir! Sir!' they said. 'Open the door for us!'

¹²"But he replied, 'What I'm about to tell you is true. I don't know you.'

¹³"So keep watch. You do not know the day or the hour that the groom will come.

THE STORY OF THREE SERVANTS

¹⁴"Again, here is what the kingdom of heaven will be like. A man was going on a journey. He sent for his servants and put them in charge of his property. ¹⁵He gave $10,000 to one. He gave $4,000 to another. And he gave $2,000 to the third. The man gave each ser-

vant the amount of money he knew the servant could take care of. Then he went on his journey.

¹⁶"The servant who had received the $10,000 went at once and put his money to work. He earned $10,000 more. ¹⁷The one with the $4,000 earned $4,000 more. ¹⁸But the man who had received $2,000 went and dug a hole in the ground. He hid his master's money in it.

¹⁹"After a long time the master of those servants returned. He wanted to collect all the money they had earned. ²⁰The man who had received $10,000 brought the other $10,000. 'Master,' he said, 'you trusted me with $10,000. See, I have earned $10,000 more.'

²¹"His master replied, 'You have done well, good and faithful servant! You have been faithful with a few things. I will put you in charge of many things. Come and share your master's happiness!'

²²"The man with $4,000 also came. 'Master,' he said, 'you trusted me with $4,000. See, I have earned $4,000 more.'

²³"His master replied, 'You have done well, good and faithful servant! You have been faithful with a few things. I will put you in charge of many things. Come and share your master's happiness!'

²⁴"Then the man who had received $2,000 came. 'Master,' he said, 'I knew that you are a hard man. You harvest where you have not planted. You gather crops where you have not scattered seed. ²⁵So I was afraid. I went out and hid your $2,000 in the ground. See, here is what belongs to you.'

²⁶"His master replied, 'You evil, lazy servant! So you knew that I harvest where I have not planted? You knew that I gather crops where I have not scattered seed? ²⁷Well then, you should have put my money in the bank. When I returned, I would have received it back with interest.'

²⁸"Then his master commanded the other servants, 'Take the $2,000 from him. Give it to the one who has $20,000. ²⁹Everyone who has will be given more. He will have more than enough. And what about anyone who doesn't have? Even what he has will be

taken away from him. ³⁰Throw that worthless servant outside. There in the darkness, people will sob and grind their teeth.'

THE SHEEP AND THE GOATS

³¹"The Son of Man will come in all his glory. All the angels will come with him. Then he will sit on his throne in the glory of heaven. ³²All the nations will be gathered in front of him. He will separate the people into two groups. He will be like a shepherd who separates the sheep from the goats. ³³He will put the sheep to his right and the goats to his left.

³⁴"Then the King will speak to those on his right. He will say, 'My Father has blessed you. Come and take what is yours. It is the kingdom prepared for you since the world was created. ³⁵I was hungry. And you gave me something to eat. I was thirsty. And you gave me something to drink. I was a stranger. And you invited me in. ³⁶I needed clothes. And you gave them to me. I was sick. And you took care of me. I was in prison. And you came to visit me.'

³⁷"Then the people who have done what is right will answer him. 'Lord,' they will ask, 'when did we see you hungry and feed you? When did we see you thirsty and give you something to drink? ³⁸When did we see you as a stranger and invite you in? When did we see you needing clothes and give them to you? ³⁹When did we see you sick or in prison and go to visit you?'

⁴⁰"The King will reply, 'What I'm about to tell you is true. Anything you did for one of the least important of these brothers of mine, you did for me.'

⁴¹"Then he will say to those on his left, 'You are cursed! Go away from me into the fire that burns forever. It has been prepared for the devil and his angels. ⁴²I was hungry. But you gave me

---

Is the stock market a place where you buy animals?

Sometimes animals are called "stock" or "livestock." But the stock market is a place where people trade in companies, not animals. People who buy stock own shares of the company. They can sell their shares or stock to other people if they want to. Meanwhile, the company gets to spend the money on supplies and workers that help the company grow.

This is one way to put your money to work. The shares of a company are worth money. If a company does well, its stock price will go up. People who own the stock can sell it at the higher price. But if the company does not do well, the price will go down. People who sell their stock at the lower price will lose money. The man in Jesus' parable probably invested or loaned his money. His investment did well, and he earned more money.

checkout

Matthew 25:16

Related verses:
Proverbs 13:11;
Matthew 6:19–21

nothing to eat. I was thirsty. But you gave me nothing to drink. ⁴³I was a stranger. But you did not invite me in. I needed clothes. But you did not give me any. I was sick and in prison. But you did not take care of me.'

⁴⁴"They also will answer, 'Lord, when did we see you hungry or thirsty and not help you? When did we see you as a stranger or needing clothes or sick or in prison and not help you?'

⁴⁵"He will reply, 'What I'm about to tell you is true. Anything you didn't do for one of the least important of these, you didn't do for me.'

⁴⁶"Then they will go away to be punished forever. But those who have done what is right will receive eternal life."

THE PLAN TO KILL JESUS

26 Jesus finished saying all these things. Then he said to his disciples, ²"As you know, the Passover Feast is two days away. The Son of Man will be handed over to be nailed to a cross."

³Then the chief priests met with the elders of the people. They met in the palace of Caiaphas, the high priest.

⁴They made plans to arrest Jesus in a clever way. They wanted to kill him. ⁵"But not during the Feast," they said. "The people may stir up trouble."

A WOMAN POURS PERFUME ON JESUS

⁶Jesus was in Bethany. He was in the home of a man named Simon, who had a skin disease. ⁷A woman came to Jesus with a special sealed jar of very expensive perfume. She poured the perfume on his head while he was at the table.

⁸When the disciples saw this, they became angry. "Why this waste?" they asked. ⁹"The perfume could have been sold at a high price. The money could have been given to poor people."

¹⁰Jesus was aware of this. So he said to them, "Why are you bothering this woman? She has done a beautiful thing to me. ¹¹You will always have poor people with you. But you will not always have me. ¹²She poured the perfume on my body to prepare me to be buried. ¹³What I'm about to tell you is true. What she has done will be told anywhere this good news is preached

If someone isn't popular, how come others think less of him or her as a person?

Popular kids aren't better than others just because they are popular, especially if they are popular for the wrong reasons. Each person, including you, is a valuable creation of God. Looking down on others is never right; the Bible says that all people are important to God and valuable in his sight. God wants us to treat everyone well and with respect. If you're wondering why more popular kids don't pay more attention to you, be careful that you aren't busy ignoring other kids who seem even less popular. Go out of your way to make others feel good and respected, whether they are popular or not.

checkout

Matthew 25:37–40

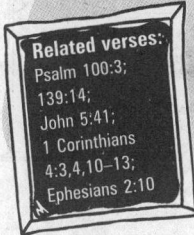

Related verses:
Psalm 100:3;
139:14;
John 5:41;
1 Corinthians
4:3,4,10–13;
Ephesians 2:10

all over the world. It will be told in memory of her."

JUDAS AGREES TO HAND JESUS OVER

[14]One of the Twelve went to the chief priests. His name was Judas Iscariot. [15]He asked, "What will you give me if I hand Jesus over to you?" So they counted out 30 silver coins for him. [16]From then on, Judas watched for the right time to hand Jesus over to them.

THE LORD'S SUPPER

[17]It was the first day of the Feast of Unleavened Bread. The disciples came to Jesus. They asked, "Where do you want us to prepare for you to eat the Passover meal?"

[18]He replied, "Go into the city to a certain man. Tell him, 'The Teacher says, "My time is near. I am going to celebrate the Passover at your house with my disciples." ' "

[19]So the disciples did what Jesus had told them to do. They prepared the Passover meal.

[20]When evening came, Jesus was at the table with the Twelve. [21]While they were eating, he said, "What I'm about to tell you is true. One of you will hand me over to my enemies."

[22]The disciples became very sad. One after the other, they began to say to him, "It's not I, Lord, is it?"

[23]Jesus replied, "The one who has dipped his hand into the bowl with me will hand me over. [24]The Son of Man will go just as it is written about him. But how terrible it will be for the one who hands over the Son of Man! It would be better for him if he had not been born."

[25]Judas was the one who was going to hand him over. He said, "It's not I, Rabbi, is it?"

Jesus answered, "Yes. It is you."

[26]While they were eating, Jesus took bread. He gave thanks and broke it. He handed it to his disciples and said, "Take this and eat it. This is my body."

[27]Then he took the cup. He gave thanks and handed it to them. He said, "All of you drink from it. [28]This is my blood of the new covenant. It is poured out to forgive the sins of many. [29]Here is what I tell you. From now on, I won't drink wine with you again until the day I drink it with you in my Father's kingdom."

How does God get the money that I give to him?

When people say that they are giving money to God, they mean that they are giving it *in service to God.* They are giving it to the church, to a missionary, to the poor or to other people who have a need. In other words, they give money to people because God wants them to. And they are giving it for the purpose of helping God's people. We do not give money directly to God. Instead we give money to people in God's name and for God's work.

This is exactly the way God wants it. We show our love for God by loving others.

Related verses:
1 John 2:9–11;
4:20,21

checkout

Matthew 25:40

³⁰Then they sang a hymn and went out to the Mount of Olives.

JESUS SAYS THAT PETER WILL FAIL

³¹Jesus told them, "This very night you will all turn away because of me. It is written that the Lord said,

" 'I will strike the shepherd down.
Then the sheep of the flock will
be scattered.'   (Zechariah 13:7)

³²But after I rise from the dead, I will go ahead of you into Galilee."

³³Peter replied, "All the others may turn away because of you. But I never will."

³⁴"What I'm about to tell you is true," Jesus answered. "It will happen this very night. Before the rooster crows, you will say three times that you don't know me."

³⁵But Peter said, "I may have to die with you. But I will never say I don't know you." And all the other disciples said the same thing.

JESUS PRAYS IN GETHSEMANE

³⁶Then Jesus went with his disciples to a place called Gethsemane. He said to them, "Sit here while I go over there and pray."

³⁷He took Peter and the two sons of Zebedee along with him. He began to be sad and troubled. ³⁸Then he said to them, "My soul is very sad. I feel close to death. Stay here. Keep watch with me."

³⁹He went a little farther. Then he fell with his face to the ground. He prayed, "My Father, if it is possible, take this cup of suffering away from me. But let what you want be done, not what I want."

⁴⁰Then he returned to his disciples and found them sleeping. "Couldn't you men keep watch with me for one hour?" he asked Peter. ⁴¹"Watch and pray. Then you won't fall into sin when you are tempted. The spirit is willing. But the body is weak."

⁴²Jesus went away a second time. He

Will Jesus come into my house in heaven for a visit?

Jesus always visits those who let him in. Jesus often visited his friends Mary, Martha and Lazarus while he was on earth. Jesus once went to a friend's wedding. And just before Jesus went to the cross, he told his disciples that he would eat and drink with them in heaven. Jesus will visit all of his friends in heaven. He will visit you too if you have asked him to take away your sins. Everyone who loves him will finally get to see him face to face!

checkout Matthew 26:29

Related verse:
Revelation 3:20

JASON'S IMAGINATION

JESUS!

prayed, "My Father, is it possible for this cup to be taken away? But if I must drink it, may what you want be done."

⁴³Then he came back. Again he found them sleeping. They couldn't keep their eyes open. ⁴⁴So he left them and went away once more. For the third time he prayed the same thing.

⁴⁵Then he returned to the disciples. He said to them, "Are you still sleeping and resting? Look! The hour is near. The Son of Man is about to be handed over to sinners. ⁴⁶Get up! Let us go! Here comes the one who is handing me over to them!"

JESUS IS ARRESTED

⁴⁷While Jesus was still speaking, Judas arrived. He was one of the Twelve. A large crowd was with him. They were carrying swords and clubs. The chief priests and the elders of the people had sent them.

⁴⁸Judas, who was going to hand Jesus over, had arranged a signal with them. "The one I kiss is the man," he said. "Arrest him."

⁴⁹So Judas went to Jesus at once. He said, "Greetings, Rabbi!" And he kissed him.

⁵⁰Jesus replied, "Friend, do what you came to do."

Then the men stepped forward. They grabbed Jesus and arrested him. ⁵¹At that moment, one of Jesus' companions reached for his sword. He pulled it out and struck the servant of the high priest with it. He cut off the servant's ear.

⁵²"Put your sword back in its place," Jesus said to him. "All who use the sword will die by the sword. ⁵³Do you think I can't ask my Father for help? He would send an army of more than 70,000 angels right away. ⁵⁴But then how would the Scriptures come true? They say it must happen in this way."

⁵⁵At that time Jesus spoke to the crowd. "Am I leading a band of armed men against you?" he asked. "Do you have to come out with swords and clubs to capture me? Every day I sat in the temple courtyard teaching. And you didn't arrest me. ⁵⁶But all this has happened so that the words of the prophets would come true."

Then all the disciples left him and ran away.

JESUS IS TAKEN TO THE SANHEDRIN

⁵⁷Those who had arrested Jesus took him to Caiaphas, the high priest. The teachers of the law and the elders had come together there. ⁵⁸Not too far away, Peter followed Jesus. He went right up to the courtyard of the high priest. He entered and sat down with the guards to see what would happen.

⁵⁹The chief priests and the whole Sanhedrin were looking for something to use against Jesus. They wanted to put him to death. ⁶⁰But they did not find any proof, even though many false witnesses came forward.

Finally, two other witnesses came forward. ⁶¹They said, "This fellow claimed, 'I am able to destroy the temple of God. I can build it again in three days.' "

⁶²Then the high priest stood up. He asked Jesus, "Aren't you going to answer? What are these charges that these men are bringing against you?"

⁶³But Jesus remained silent.

The high priest said to him, "I command you under oath by the living God. Tell us if you are the Christ, the Son of God."

⁶⁴"Yes. It is just as you say," Jesus replied. "But here is what I say to all of you. In days to come, you will see the Son of Man sitting at the right hand of the Mighty One. You will see the Son of Man coming on the clouds of heaven."

⁶⁵Then the high priest tore his clothes. He said, "He has spoken a very evil thing against God! Why do we need any more witnesses? You have heard him say this evil thing. ⁶⁶What do you think?"

"He must die!" they answered.

⁶⁷Then they spit in his face. They hit him with their fists. Others slapped him. ⁶⁸They said, "Prophesy to us, Christ! Who hit you?"

PETER SAYS HE DOES NOT KNOW JESUS

⁶⁹Peter was sitting out in the courtyard. A female servant came to him. "You also were with Jesus of Galilee," she said.

⁷⁰But in front of all of them, Peter said he was not. "I don't know what you're talking about," he said.

⁷¹Then he went out to the gate leading into the courtyard. There another woman saw him. She said to the people, "This fellow was with Jesus of Nazareth."

⁷²Again he said he was not. With an oath he said, "I don't know the man!"

⁷³After a little while, those standing there went up to Peter. "You must be one of them," they said. "The way you talk gives you away."

⁷⁴Then Peter began to call down curses on himself. He took an oath and said to them, "I don't know the man!"

Right away a rooster crowed. ⁷⁵Then Peter remembered what Jesus had said. "The rooster will crow," Jesus had told him. "Before it does, you will say three times that you don't know me." Peter went outside. He broke down and sobbed.

JUDAS HANGS HIMSELF

27 It was early in the morning. All the chief priests and the elders of the people decided to put Jesus to death. ²They tied him up and led him away. Then they handed him over to Pilate, who was the governor.

³Judas, who had handed him over, saw that Jesus had been sentenced to die. He felt deep shame and sadness for what he had done. So he returned the 30 silver coins to the chief priests and the elders. ⁴"I have sinned," he said. "I handed over a man who is not guilty."

"What do we care?" they replied. "That's your problem."

⁵So Judas threw the money into the temple and left. Then he went away and hanged himself.

⁶The chief priests picked up the coins. They said, "It's against the law to put this money into the temple fund. It is blood money. It has paid for a man's death." ⁷So they decided to use the money to buy a potter's field. People from other countries would be buried there. ⁸That is why it has been called The Field of Blood to this very day. ⁹Then the words spoken by Jeremiah

the prophet came true. He had said, "They took the 30 silver coins. That price was set for him by the people of Israel. ¹⁰They used the coins to buy a potter's field, just as the Lord commanded me." *(Zechariah 11:12,13; Jeremiah 19:1–13; 32:6–9)*

JESUS IS BROUGHT TO PILATE

¹¹Jesus was standing in front of the governor. The governor asked him, "Are you the king of the Jews?"

"Yes. It is just as you say," Jesus replied.

¹²But when the chief priests and the elders brought charges against him, he did not answer. ¹³Then Pilate asked him, "Don't you hear the charges they are bringing against you?"

¹⁴But Jesus made no reply, not even to a single charge. The governor was really amazed.

¹⁵It was the governor's practice at the Passover Feast to let one prisoner go free. The people could choose the one they wanted. ¹⁶At that time they had a well-known prisoner named Barabbas. ¹⁷So when the crowd gathered, Pilate asked them, "Which one do you want me to set free? Barabbas? Or Jesus who is called Christ?" ¹⁸Pilate knew that the leaders were jealous. He knew this was why they had handed Jesus over to him.

¹⁹While Pilate was sitting on the judge's seat, his wife sent him a message. It said, "Don't have anything to do with that man. He is not guilty. I have suffered a great deal in a dream today because of him."

²⁰But the chief priests and the elders talked the crowd into asking for Barabbas and having Jesus put to death.

²¹"Which of the two do you want me to set free?" asked the governor.

"Barabbas," they answered.

²²"Then what should I do with Jesus who is called Christ?" Pilate asked.

They all answered, "Crucify him!"

²³"Why? What wrong has he done?" asked Pilate.

But they shouted even louder, "Crucify him!"

²⁴Pilate saw that he wasn't getting anywhere. Instead, the crowd was starting to get angry. So he took water and washed his hands in front of

them. "I am not guilty of this man's death," he said. "You are accountable for that!"

[25]All the people answered, "We and our children will accept the guilt for his death!"

[26]Pilate let Barabbas go free. But he had Jesus whipped. Then he handed him over to be nailed to a cross.

THE SOLDIERS MAKE FUN OF JESUS

[27]The governor's soldiers took Jesus into the palace, which was called the Praetorium. All the rest of the soldiers gathered around him. [28]They took off his clothes and put a purple robe on him. [29]Then they twisted thorns together to make a crown. They placed it on his head. They put a stick in his right hand. Then they fell on their knees in front of him and made fun of him. "We honor you, king of the Jews!" they said. [30]They spit on him. They hit him on the head with the stick again and again.

[31]After they had made fun of him, they took off the robe. They put his own clothes back on him. Then they led him away to nail him to a cross.

JESUS IS NAILED TO A CROSS

[32]On their way out of the city, they met a man from Cyrene. His name was Simon. They forced him to carry the cross.

[33]They came to a place called Golgotha. The word Golgotha means The Place of the Skull. [34]There they mixed wine with bitter spices and gave it to Jesus to drink. After tasting it, he refused to drink it.

[35]When they had nailed him to the cross, they divided up his clothes by casting lots. [36]They sat down and kept watch over him there.

[37]Above his head they placed the written charge against him. It read, THIS IS JESUS, THE KING OF THE JEWS.

[38]Two robbers were crucified with him. One was on his right and one was on his left.

[39]Those who passed by shouted at Jesus and made fun of him. They shook their heads [40]and said, "So you are going to destroy the temple and build it again in three days? Then save yourself! Come down from the cross, if you are the Son of God!"

[41]In the same way the chief priests, the teachers of the law and the elders made fun of him. [42]"He saved others," they said. "But he can't save himself! He's the King of Israel! Let him come down now from the cross! Then we will believe in him. [43]He trusts in God. Let God rescue him now if he wants him. He's the one who said, 'I am the Son of God.' "

[44]In the same way the robbers who were being crucified with Jesus also made fun of him.

JESUS DIES

[45]From noon until three o'clock, the whole land was covered with darkness. [46]About three o'clock, Jesus cried out in a loud voice. He said, *"Eloi, Eloi, lama sabachthani?"* This means "My God, my God, why have you deserted me?" *(Psalm 22:1)*

[47]Some of those standing there heard Jesus cry out. They said, "He's calling for Elijah."

[48]Right away one of them ran and got a sponge. He filled it with wine vinegar and put it on a stick. He offered it to Jesus to drink. [49]The rest said, "Leave him alone. Let's see if Elijah comes to save him."

[50]After Jesus cried out again in a loud voice, he died.

[51]At that moment the temple curtain was torn in two from top to bottom. The earth shook. The rocks split. [52]Tombs broke open. The bodies of many holy people who had died were raised to life. [53]They came out of the tombs. After Jesus was raised to life, they went into the holy city. There they appeared to many people.

[54]The Roman commander and those guarding Jesus saw the earthquake and all that had happened. They were terrified. They exclaimed, "He was surely the Son of God!"

[55]Not very far away, many women were watching. They had followed Jesus from Galilee to take care of his needs. [56]Mary Magdalene was among them. Mary, the mother of James and Joses, was also there. So was the mother of Zebedee's sons.

JESUS IS BURIED

⁵⁷As evening approached, a rich man came from the town of Arimathea. His name was Joseph. He had become a follower of Jesus. ⁵⁸He went to Pilate and asked for Jesus' body. Pilate ordered that it be given to him.

⁵⁹Joseph took the body and wrapped it in a clean linen cloth. ⁶⁰He placed it in his own new tomb that he had cut out of the rock. He rolled a big stone in front of the entrance to the tomb. Then he went away.

⁶¹Mary Magdalene and the other Mary were sitting there across from the tomb.

THE GUARDS AT THE TOMB

⁶²The next day was the day after Preparation Day. The chief priests and the Pharisees went to Pilate. ⁶³"Sir," they said, "we remember something that liar said while he was still alive. He claimed, 'After three days I will rise again.' ⁶⁴So give the order to make the tomb secure until the third day. If you don't, his disciples might come and steal the body. Then they will tell the people that Jesus has been raised from the dead. This last lie will be worse than the first."

⁶⁵"Take some guards with you," Pilate answered. "Go. Make the tomb as secure as you can." ⁶⁶So they went and made the tomb secure. They put a seal on the stone and placed some guards on duty.

JESUS RISES FROM THE DEAD

28 The Sabbath day was now over. It was dawn on the first day of the week. Mary Magdalene and the other Mary went to look at the tomb.

²There was a powerful earthquake. An angel of the Lord came down from heaven. The angel went to the tomb. He rolled back the stone and sat on it. ³His body shone like lightning. His

Why doesn't God take us to heaven as soon as we get saved?

God does not take his people to heaven right away because he wants us to learn and grow up in our faith. He wants us to tell others about Jesus, to help others and to make the world better. God has work for his people to do. He has work for *you* to do.

checkout
Matthew 28:19,20

SEE, THIS IS WHAT JESUS DID FOR US.

JESUS

Related verses:
John 9:4;
2 Peter 3:9

clothes were as white as snow. [4]The guards were so afraid of him that they shook and became like dead men.

[5]The angel said to the women, "Don't be afraid. I know that you are looking for Jesus, who was crucified. [6]He is not here! He has risen, just as he said he would! Come and see the place where he was lying. [7]Go quickly! Tell his disciples, 'He has risen from the dead. He is going ahead of you into Galilee. There you will see him.' Now I have told you."

[8]So the women hurried away from the tomb. They were afraid, but they were filled with joy. They ran to tell the disciples.

[9]Suddenly Jesus met them. "Greetings!" he said.

They came to him, took hold of his feet and worshiped him.

[10]Then Jesus said to them, "Don't be afraid. Go and tell my brothers to go to Galilee. There they will see me."

THE GUARDS REPORT TO THE CHIEF PRIESTS

[11]While the women were on their way, some of the guards went into the city. They reported to the chief priests all that had happened.

[12]When the chief priests met with the elders, they came up with a plan. They gave the soldiers a large amount of money. [13]They told the soldiers, "We want you to say, 'His disciples came during the night. They stole his body while we were sleeping.' [14]If the governor hears this report, we will pay him off. That will keep you out of trouble."

[15]So the soldiers took the money and did as they were told. This story has spread all around among the Jews to this very day.

JESUS' FINAL ORDERS TO HIS DISCIPLES

[16]Then the 11 disciples went to Galilee. They went to the mountain where Jesus had told them to go. [17]When they saw him, they worshiped him. But some still had their doubts.

[18]Then Jesus came to them. He said, "All authority in heaven and on earth has been given to me. [19]So you must go and make disciples of all nations. Baptize them in the name of the Father and of the Son and of the Holy Spirit. [20]Teach them to obey everything I have commanded you. And you can be sure that I am always with you, to the very end."

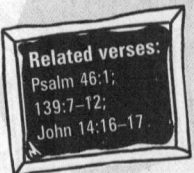

KIDS' QUESTION

How is God always there?

God can always be with us because he does not have a physical body. God does not have to stay in one place the way we do. We don't know exactly how this works, but that's OK. God is much, much greater and more amazing than we can imagine. Isn't it great to know that God is there . . . and here?

checkout

Matthew 28:20

Related verses:
Psalm 46:1;
139:7–12;
John 14:16–17

GOD @ EVERYWHERE.IAM

Mark

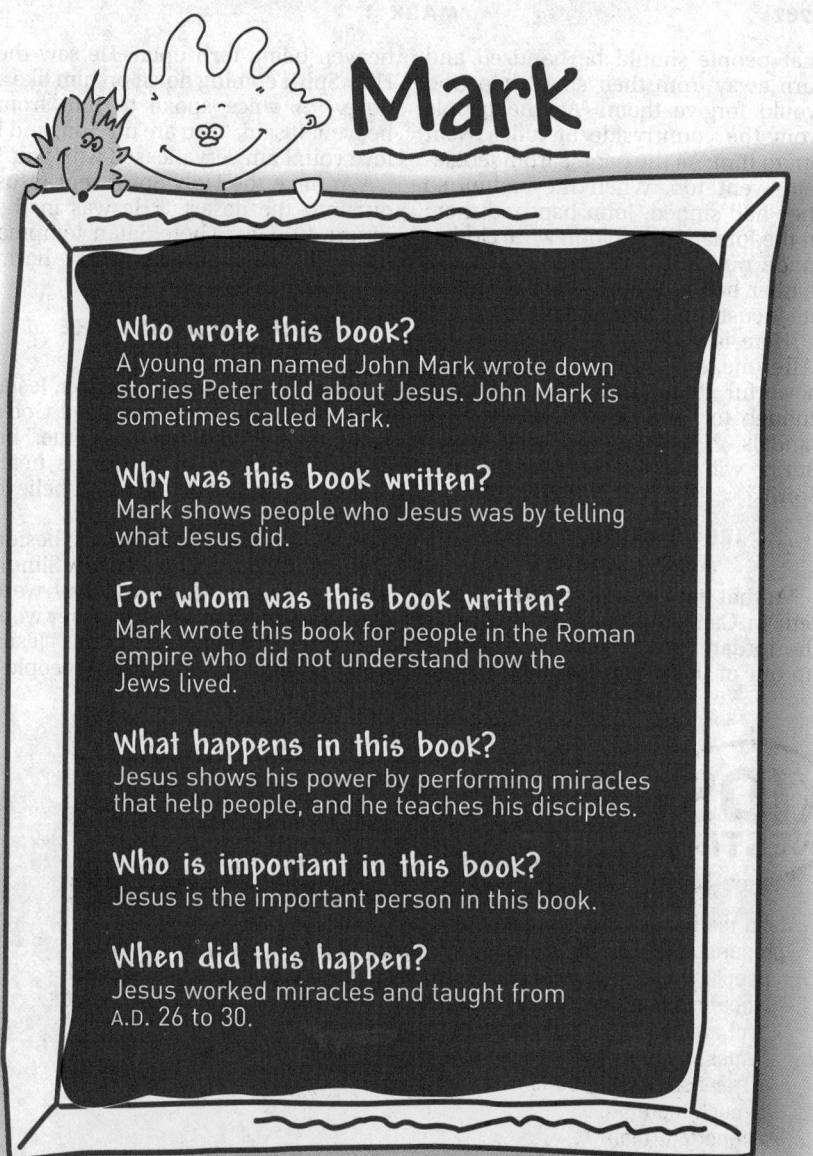

Who wrote this book?
A young man named John Mark wrote down stories Peter told about Jesus. John Mark is sometimes called Mark.

Why was this book written?
Mark shows people who Jesus was by telling what Jesus did.

For whom was this book written?
Mark wrote this book for people in the Roman empire who did not understand how the Jews lived.

What happens in this book?
Jesus shows his power by performing miracles that help people, and he teaches his disciples.

Who is important in this book?
Jesus is the important person in this book.

When did this happen?
Jesus worked miracles and taught from A.D. 26 to 30.

JOHN THE BAPTIST PREPARES THE WAY

1 This is the beginning of the good news about Jesus Christ, the Son of God.

²Long ago Isaiah the prophet wrote,

"I will send my messenger ahead of you.

He will prepare your way."

(Malachi 3:1)

³ "A messenger is calling out in the desert,
'Prepare the way for the Lord.
Make straight paths for him.' "

(Isaiah 40:3)

⁴And so John came. He baptized people in the desert. He also preached

that people should be baptized and turn away from their sins. Then God would forgive them. ⁵All the people from the countryside of Judea went out to him. All the people from Jerusalem went too. When they admitted they had sinned, John baptized them in the Jordan River. ⁶John wore clothes made out of camel's hair. He had a leather belt around his waist. And he ate locusts and wild honey.

⁷Here is what John was preaching. "After me, one will come who is more powerful than I am. I'm not good enough to bend down and untie his sandals. ⁸I baptize you with water. But he will baptize you with the Holy Spirit."

JESUS IS BAPTIZED AND TEMPTED

⁹At that time Jesus came from Nazareth in Galilee. John baptized him in the Jordan River. ¹⁰Jesus was coming up out of the water. Just then he saw heaven being torn open. He saw the Holy Spirit coming down on him like a dove. ¹¹A voice spoke to him from heaven. It said, "You are my Son, and I love you. I am very pleased with you."

¹²At once the Holy Spirit sent Jesus out into the desert. ¹³He was in the desert 40 days. There Satan tempted him. The wild animals didn't harm Jesus. Angels took care of him.

JESUS CHOOSES THE FIRST DISCIPLES

¹⁴After John was put in prison, Jesus went into Galilee. He preached God's good news. ¹⁵"The time has come," he said. "The kingdom of God is near. Turn away from your sins and believe the good news!"

¹⁶One day Jesus was walking beside the Sea of Galilee. There he saw Simon and his brother Andrew. They were throwing a net into the lake. They were fishermen. ¹⁷"Come. Follow me," Jesus said. "I will make you fishers of people."

Why did John the Baptist live in the desert?

John the Baptist was a prophet. God had given him the important job of preparing the way for Jesus. John wanted to preach away from where people were living. That way they would have to go out to see him and hear his message. Living in the desert also kept him from having a lot of arguments with the leaders in Jerusalem. They did not like his message very much. John was also showing that a person's friendship with God is much more important than having a nice comfortable place to stay.

checkout

Mark 1:4

Related verses:
John 1:19–34

¹⁸At once they left their nets and followed him.

¹⁹Then Jesus walked a little farther. As he did, he saw James, son of Zebedee, and his brother John. They were in a boat preparing their nets. ²⁰Right away he called out to them. They left their father Zebedee in the boat with the hired men. Then they followed Jesus.

JESUS DRIVES OUT AN EVIL SPIRIT

²¹Jesus and those with him went to Capernaum. When the Sabbath day came, he went into the synagogue. There he began to teach. ²²The people were amazed at his teaching. He taught them like one who had authority. He did not talk like the teachers of the law.

²³Just then a man in their synagogue cried out. He was controlled by an evil spirit. He said, ²⁴"What do you want with us, Jesus of Nazareth? Have you come to destroy us? I know who you are. You are the Holy One of God!"

²⁵"Be quiet!" said Jesus firmly. "Come out of him!"

²⁶The evil spirit shook the man wildly. Then it came out of him with a scream.

²⁷All the people were amazed. So they asked each other, "What is this? A new teaching! And with so much authority! He even gives orders to evil spirits, and they obey him." ²⁸News about Jesus spread quickly all over Galilee.

JESUS HEALS MANY PEOPLE

²⁹Jesus and those with him left the synagogue. Right away they went with James and John to the home of Simon and Andrew. ³⁰Simon's mother-in-law was lying in bed. She had a fever. They told Jesus about her. ³¹So he went to her. He took her hand and helped her up. The fever left her. Then she began to serve them.

³²That evening after sunset, the people brought to Jesus all who were sick. They also brought all who were controlled by demons. ³³All the people in town gathered at the door. ³⁴Jesus healed many of them. They had all kinds of sicknesses. He also drove out many demons. But he would not let the demons speak, because they knew who he was.

JESUS PRAYS IN A QUIET PLACE

³⁵It was very early in the morning and still dark. Jesus got up and left the

Why did the Holy Spirit come down on Jesus like a dove?

The Holy Spirit is a spirit and does not have a body. So he took a form that people could see. A dove was a great form to take because when people see doves they think of peace and purity. That is exactly what the Holy Spirit brings to us. After Jesus left the earth he sent the Holy Spirit. The Holy Spirit stays with all Christians now that Jesus is in heaven. The Holy Spirit lives inside God's people.

checkout

Mark 1:10

Related verse:
1 Corinthians 6:19

PET STORE

DOVE

house. He went to a place where he could be alone. There he prayed. [36]Simon and his friends went to look for Jesus. [37]When they found him, they called out, "Everyone is looking for you!"

[38]Jesus replied, "Let's go somewhere else. I want to go to the nearby towns. I must preach there also. That is why I have come." [39]So he traveled all around Galilee. He preached in their synagogues. He also drove out demons.

JESUS HEALS A MAN WHO HAD A SKIN DISEASE

[40]A man who had a skin disease came to Jesus. On his knees he begged Jesus. He said, "If you are willing to make me 'clean,' you can do it."

[41]Jesus was filled with deep concern. He reached out his hand and touched the man. "I am willing to do it," he said. "Be 'clean'!" [42]Right away the disease left him. He was healed.

[43]Jesus sent him away at once. He gave the man a strong warning. [44]"Don't tell this to anyone," he said. "Go and show yourself to the priest. Offer the sacrifices that Moses commanded. It will be a witness to the priest and the people that you are 'clean.' "

[45]But the man went out and started talking right away. He spread the news to everyone. So Jesus could no longer enter a town openly. He stayed outside in lonely places. But people still came to him from everywhere.

JESUS HEALS A MAN WHO COULD NOT WALK

2 A few days later, Jesus entered Capernaum again. The people heard that he had come home. [2]So many people gathered that there was no room left. There was not even room outside the door. And Jesus preached the word to them.

[3]Four of those who came were carrying a man who could not walk. [4]But they could not get him close to Jesus because of the crowd. So they made a hole in the roof above Jesus. Then they lowered the man through it on a mat. [5]Jesus saw their faith. So he said to the man, "Son, your sins are forgiven." [6]Some teachers of the law were sit-

ting there. They were thinking, [7]"Why is this fellow talking like that? He's saying a very evil thing! Only God can forgive sins!"

[8]Right away Jesus knew what they were thinking. So he said to them, "Why are you thinking these things? [9]Is it easier to say to this man, 'Your sins are forgiven'? Or to say, 'Get up, take your mat and walk'? [10]I want you to know that the Son of Man has authority on earth to forgive sins."

Then Jesus spoke to the man who could not walk. [11]"I tell you," he said, "get up. Take your mat and go home." [12]The man got up and took his mat. Then he walked away while everyone watched. All the people were amazed. They praised God and said, "We have never seen anything like this!"

JESUS CHOOSES LEVI

[13]Once again Jesus went out beside the Sea of Galilee. A large crowd came to him. He began to teach them. [14]As he walked along he saw Levi, son of Alphaeus. Levi was sitting at the tax collector's booth. "Follow me," Jesus told him. Levi got up and followed him.

[15]Later Jesus was having dinner at Levi's house. Many tax collectors and "sinners" were eating with him and his disciples. They were part of the large crowd following Jesus.

[16]Some teachers of the law who were Pharisees were there. They saw Jesus eating with "sinners" and tax collectors. So they asked his disciples, "Why does he eat with tax collectors and 'sinners'?"

[17]Jesus heard that. So he said to them, "Those who are healthy don't need a doctor. Sick people do. I have not come to get those who think they are right with God to follow me. I have come to get sinners to follow me."

JESUS IS ASKED ABOUT FASTING

[18]John's disciples and the Pharisees were going without eating. Some people came to Jesus. They said to him, "John's disciples are fasting. The disciples of the Pharisees are also fasting. But your disciples are not. Why aren't they?"

[19]Jesus answered, "How can the guests of the groom go without eating while he is with them? They will not fast as long as he is with them. [20]But the time will come when the groom will be taken away from them. On that day they will go without eating.

[21]"People don't sew a patch of new cloth on old clothes. If they do, the new piece will pull away from the old. That will make the tear worse. [22]People don't pour new wine into old wineskins. If they do, the wine will burst the skins. Then the wine and the wineskins will both be destroyed. No, everyone pours new wine into new wineskins."

JESUS IS LORD OF THE SABBATH DAY

[23]One Sabbath day Jesus was walking with his disciples through the grainfields. The disciples began to break off some heads of grain. [24]The Pharisees said to Jesus, "Look! It is against the Law to do this on the Sabbath. Why are your disciples doing it?"

[25]He answered, "Haven't you ever read about what David did? He and his men were hungry. They needed food. [26]It was when Abiathar was high priest. David entered the house of God and ate the holy bread. Only priests were allowed to eat it. David also gave some to his men."

[27]Then Jesus said to them, "The Sabbath day was made for man. Man was not made for the Sabbath day. [28]So the Son of Man is Lord even of the Sabbath day."

3 Another time Jesus went into the synagogue. A man with a weak and twisted hand was there. [2]Some Pharisees were trying to find fault with Jesus. They watched him closely. They wanted to see if he would heal the man on the Sabbath day.

[3]Jesus spoke to the man with the weak and twisted hand. "Stand up in front of everyone," he said.

[4]Then Jesus asked them, "What does the Law say we should do on the Sabbath day? Should we do good? Or should we do evil? Should we save life? Or should we kill?" But no one answered.

[5]Jesus looked around at them in anger. He was very upset because their hearts were stubborn. Then he said to the man, "Stretch out your hand." He stretched it out, and his hand was as good as new.

[6]Then the Pharisees went out and began to make plans with the Herodians. They wanted to kill Jesus.

CROWDS FOLLOW JESUS

[7]Jesus went off to the Sea of Galilee with his disciples. A large crowd from Galilee followed. [8]People heard about all that Jesus was doing. And many came to him. They came from Judea, Jerusalem, and Idumea. They came from the lands east of the Jordan River. And they came from the area around Tyre and Sidon.

[9]Because of the crowd, Jesus told his disciples to get a small boat ready for him. This would keep the people from crowding him. [10]Jesus had healed many people. So those who were sick were pushing forward to touch him.

[11]When people with evil spirits saw him, they fell down in front of him. The spirits shouted, "You are the Son of God!" [12]But Jesus ordered them not to tell who he was.

JESUS APPOINTS THE TWELVE APOSTLES

[13]Jesus went up on a mountainside. He called for certain people to come to him, and they came. [14]He appointed 12 of them and called them apostles. From that time on they would be with him. He would also send them out to preach. [15]They would have authority to drive out demons.

[16]So Jesus appointed the Twelve. Simon was one of them. Jesus gave him the name Peter. [17]There were James, son of Zebedee, and his brother John. Jesus gave them the name Boanerges. Boanerges means Sons of Thunder. [18]There were also Andrew, Philip, Bartholomew, Matthew, Thomas, and James, son of Alphaeus. And there were Thaddaeus and Simon the Zealot. [19]Judas Iscariot was one of them too. He was the one who was later going to hand Jesus over to his enemies.

JESUS AND BEELZEBUB

²⁰Jesus entered a house. Again a crowd gathered. It was so large that Jesus and his disciples were not even able to eat. ²¹His family heard about this. So they went to take charge of him. They said, "He is out of his mind."

²²Some teachers of the law were there. They had come down from Jerusalem. They said, "He is controlled by Beelzebub! He is driving out demons by the power of the prince of demons."

²³So Jesus called them over and spoke to them by using stories. He said, "How can Satan drive out Satan? ²⁴If a kingdom fights against itself, it can't stand. ²⁵If a family is divided, it can't stand. ²⁶And if Satan fights against himself, and his helpers are divided, he can't stand. That is the end of him. ²⁷In fact, none of you can enter a strong man's house and just take what the man owns. You must first tie him up. Then you can rob his house.

²⁸"What I'm about to tell you is true. Everyone's sins and evil words against God will be forgiven. ²⁹But anyone who speaks evil things against the Holy Spirit will never be forgiven. His guilt will last forever."

³⁰Jesus said this because the teachers of the law were saying, "He has an evil spirit."

JESUS' MOTHER AND BROTHERS

³¹Jesus' mother and brothers came and stood outside. They sent someone in to get him. ³²A crowd was sitting around Jesus. They told him, "Your mother and your brothers are outside. They are looking for you."

³³"Who is my mother? Who are my brothers?" he asked.

³⁴Then Jesus looked at the people sitting in a circle around him. He said, "Here is my mother! Here are my brothers! ³⁵Anyone who does what God wants is my brother or sister or mother."

THE STORY OF THE FARMER

4 Again Jesus began to teach by the Sea of Galilee. The crowd that gathered around him was very large. So he got into a boat. He sat down in it out on the lake. All the people were along the shore at the water's edge. ²He taught them many things by using stories.

In his teaching he said, ³"Listen! A farmer went out to plant his seed. ⁴He scattered the seed on the ground. Some fell on a path. Birds came and ate it up. ⁵Some seed fell on rocky places, where there wasn't much soil. The plants came up quickly, because the soil wasn't deep. ⁶When the sun came up, it burned the plants. They dried up because they had no roots. ⁷Other seed fell among thorns. The thorns grew up and crowded out the plants. So the plants did not bear grain. ⁸Still other seed fell on good soil. It grew up and produced a crop 30, 60, or even 100 times more than the farmer planted."

⁹Then Jesus said, "Those who have ears should listen."

¹⁰Later Jesus was alone. The Twelve asked him about the stories. So did the others around him. ¹¹He told them, "The secret of God's kingdom has been given to you. But to outsiders everything is told by using stories. ¹²In that way,

" 'They will see but never know
     what they are seeing.
They will hear but never
     understand.
Otherwise they might turn and be
     forgiven!' "   *(Isaiah 6:9,10)*

¹³Then Jesus said to them, "Don't you understand this story? Then how will you understand any stories of this kind? ¹⁴The seed the farmer plants is God's message. ¹⁵What is seed scattered on a path like? The message is planted. The people hear the message. Then Satan comes. He takes away the message that was planted in them. ¹⁶And what is seed scattered on rocky places like? The people hear the message. At once they receive it with joy. ¹⁷But they have no roots. So they last only a short time. They quickly fall away from the faith when trouble or suffering comes because of the message. ¹⁸And what is seed scattered among thorns like? The people hear the message. ¹⁹But then the worries of this life come to them. Wealth comes

with its false promises. The people also long for other things. All of those are the kinds of things that crowd out the message. They keep it from producing fruit. ²⁰And what is seed scattered on good soil like? The people hear the message. They accept it. They produce a good crop 30, 60, or even 100 times more than the farmer planted."

A LAMP ON A STAND

²¹Jesus said to them, "Do you bring in a lamp to put it under a large bowl or a bed? Don't you put it on its stand? ²²What is hidden is meant to be seen. And what is put out of sight is meant to be brought out into the open. ²³Everyone who has ears should listen."

²⁴"Think carefully about what you hear," he said. "As you give, so you will receive. In fact, you will receive even more. ²⁵If you have something, you will be given more. If you have nothing, even what you have will be taken away from you."

THE STORY OF THE GROWING SEED

²⁶Jesus also said, "Here is what God's kingdom is like. A farmer scatters seed on the ground. ²⁷Night and day the seed comes up and grows. It happens whether the farmer sleeps or gets up. He doesn't know how it happens. ²⁸All by itself the soil produces grain. First the stalk comes up. Then the head appears. Finally, the full grain appears in the head. ²⁹Before long the grain ripens. So the farmer cuts it down, because the harvest is ready."

THE STORY OF THE MUSTARD SEED

³⁰Again Jesus said, "What can we say God's kingdom is like? What story can we use to explain it? ³¹It is like a mustard seed, which is the smallest seed planted in the ground. ³²But when you plant the seed, it grows. It becomes the largest of all garden plants. Its branches are so big that birds can rest in its shade."

³³Using many stories like those, Jesus spoke the word to them. He told them as much as they could understand. ³⁴He did not say anything to them without using a story. But when he was alone with his disciples, he explained everything.

JESUS CALMS THE STORM

³⁵When evening came, Jesus said to his disciples, "Let's go over to the other side of the lake." ³⁶They left the crowd

KIDS' QUESTION: What's a parable?

A "parable" is a story that teaches a lesson. Jesus told many parables. Sometimes his parables hid the truth from people who were not really interested in obeying him.

Sometimes parables taught the truth to people who were interested and wanted to learn. People who wanted to learn asked Jesus to explain the story. As soon as he did, they understood the lesson.

checkout Mark 4:33

Related verses: Matthew 13:34,35

GLUE STICK

Good Samaritan PAIR APPLE

behind. And they took him along in a boat, just as he was. There were also other boats with him.

³⁷A wild storm came up. Waves crashed over the boat. It was about to sink. ³⁸Jesus was in the back, sleeping on a cushion. The disciples woke him up. They said, "Teacher! Don't you care if we drown?"

³⁹He got up and ordered the wind to stop. He said to the waves, "Quiet! Be still!" Then the wind died down. And it was completely calm.

⁴⁰He said to his disciples, "Why are you so afraid? Don't you have any faith at all yet?"

⁴¹They were terrified. They asked each other, "Who is this? Even the wind and the waves obey him!"

JESUS HEALS A MAN CONTROLLED BY DEMONS

5 They went across the Sea of Galilee to the area of the Gerasenes. ²Jesus got out of the boat. A man with an evil spirit came from the tombs to meet him. ³The man lived in the tombs. No one could keep him tied up anymore. Not even a chain could hold him. ⁴His hands and feet had often been chained. But he tore the chains apart. And he broke the iron cuffs on his ankles. No one was strong enough to control him. ⁵Night and day he screamed among the tombs and in the hills. He cut himself with stones.

⁶When he saw Jesus a long way off, he ran to him. He fell on his knees in front of him. ⁷He shouted at the top of his voice, "Jesus, Son of the Most High God, what do you want with me? Promise before God that you won't hurt me!" ⁸This was because Jesus had said to him, "Come out of this man, you evil spirit!"

⁹Then Jesus asked the demon, "What is your name?"

"My name is Legion," he replied. "There are many of us." ¹⁰And he begged Jesus again and again not to send them out of the area.

¹¹A large herd of pigs was feeding on the nearby hillside. ¹²The demons begged Jesus, "Send us among the pigs. Let us go into them." ¹³Jesus allowed it. The evil spirits came out of the man and went into the pigs. There were about 2,000 pigs in the herd. The whole herd rushed down the steep bank. They ran into the lake and drowned.

¹⁴Those who were tending the pigs

KIDS' QUESTION

What are demons?

Demons are bad angels. They followed Satan when he turned against God. Demons are beings who work and fight against God. Demons are Satan's helpers. There is only one devil, but there are thousands of demons. They are all over the world trying to keep people from following Jesus and obeying God. But God is more powerful than all the demons and the devil put together. God will keep us safe from demons if we trust in him.

At the end of time, all demons will be thrown into the lake of fire with the devil.

checkout

Mark 5:9

SHHHHHH...
Demon
trapp!

Related verses:
Luke 4:41;
Revelation 18:2

ran off. They told the people in the town and countryside what had happened. The people went out to see for themselves.

¹⁵Then they came to Jesus. They saw the man who had been controlled by many demons. He was sitting there. He was now dressed and thinking clearly. All this made the people afraid. ¹⁶Those who had seen it told them what had happened to the man. They told about the pigs as well. ¹⁷Then the people began to beg Jesus to leave their area.

¹⁸Jesus was getting into the boat. The man who had been controlled by demons begged to go with him. ¹⁹Jesus did not let him. He said, "Go home to your family. Tell them how much the Lord has done for you. Tell them how kind he has been to you."

²⁰So the man went away. In the area known as the Ten Cities, he began to tell how much Jesus had done for him. And all the people were amazed.

A DYING GIRL AND A SUFFERING WOMAN

²¹Jesus went across the Sea of Galilee in a boat. It landed at the other side. There a large crowd gathered around him. ²²Then a man named Jairus came. He was a synagogue ruler. Seeing Jesus, he fell at his feet. ²³He begged Jesus, "Please come. My little daughter is dying. Place your hands on her to heal her. Then she will live." ²⁴So Jesus went with him.

A large group of people followed. They crowded around him. ²⁵A woman was there who had a sickness that made her bleed. It had lasted for 12 years. ²⁶She had suffered a great deal, even though she had gone to many doctors. She had spent all the money she had. But she was getting worse, not better. ²⁷Then she heard about Jesus. She came up behind him in the crowd and touched his clothes. ²⁸She thought, "I just need to touch his clothes. Then I will be healed." ²⁹Right away her bleeding stopped. She felt in her body that her suffering was over.

³⁰At once Jesus knew that power had gone out from him. He turned around in the crowd. He asked, "Who touched my clothes?"

³¹"You see the people," his disciples answered. "They are crowding against you. And you still ask, 'Who touched me?' "

³²But Jesus kept looking around. He wanted to see who had touched him. ³³Then the woman came and fell at his feet. She knew what had happened to her. She was shaking with fear. But she told him the whole truth. ³⁴He said to her, "Dear woman, your faith has healed you. Go in peace. You are free from your suffering."

³⁵While Jesus was still speaking, some people came from the house of Jairus. He was the synagogue ruler. "Your daughter is dead," they said. "Why bother the teacher anymore?"

³⁶But Jesus didn't listen to them. He told the synagogue ruler, "Don't be afraid. Just believe."

³⁷He let only Peter, James, and John, the brother of James, follow him. ³⁸They came to the home of the synagogue ruler. There Jesus saw a lot of confusion. People were crying and sobbing loudly. ³⁹He went inside. Then he said to them, "Why all this confusion and sobbing? The child is not dead. She is only sleeping." ⁴⁰But they laughed at him.

He made them all go outside. He took only the child's father and mother and the disciples who were with him. And he went in where the child was. ⁴¹He took her by the hand. Then he said to her, *Talitha koum!* This means, "Little girl, I say to you, get up!" ⁴²The girl was 12 years old. Right away she stood up and walked around. They were totally amazed at this. ⁴³Jesus gave strict orders not to let anyone know what had happened. And he told them to give her something to eat.

A PROPHET WITHOUT HONOR

6 Jesus left there and went to his hometown of Nazareth. His disciples went with him. ²When the Sabbath day came, he began to teach in the synagogue. Many who heard him were amazed.

"Where did this man get these things?" they asked. "What's this wisdom that has been given to him? He even does miracles! ³Isn't this the carpenter? Isn't this Mary's son? Isn't this the brother of James, Joseph, Judas and Simon? Aren't his sisters here with us?" They were not pleased with him at all.

[4]Jesus said to them, "A prophet is not honored in his hometown. He doesn't receive any honor among his relatives. And he doesn't receive any in his own home."

[5]Jesus laid his hands on a few sick people and healed them. But he could not do any other miracles there. [6]He was amazed because they had no faith.

JESUS SENDS OUT THE TWELVE DISCIPLES

Jesus went around teaching from village to village. [7]He called the Twelve to him. Then he sent them out two by two. He gave them authority to drive out evil spirits.

[8]Here were his orders. "Take only a walking stick for your trip. Do not take bread or a bag. Take no money in your belts. [9]Wear sandals. But do not take extra clothes. [10]When you are invited into a house, stay there until you leave town. [11]Some places may not welcome you or listen to you. If they don't, shake the dust off your feet when you leave. That will be a witness against the people living there."

[12]They went out. And they preached that people should turn away from their sins. [13]They drove out many demons. They poured olive oil on many sick people and healed them.

JOHN THE BAPTIST'S HEAD IS CUT OFF

[14]King Herod heard about this. Jesus' name had become well known. Some were saying, "John the Baptist has been raised from the dead! That is why he has the power to do miracles."

[15]Others said, "He is Elijah."

Still others claimed, "He is a prophet. He is like one of the prophets of long ago."

[16]But when Herod heard this, he said, "I had John's head cut off. And now he has been raised from the dead!"

[17]In fact, it was Herod himself who had given orders to arrest John. He had him tied up and put in prison. He did this because of Herodias. She was the wife of Herod's brother Philip. But now Herod was married to her. [18]John had been saying to Herod, "It is against the Law for you to have your brother's wife." [19]Herodias held that against John. She wanted to kill him. But she could not, [20]because Herod was afraid of John. So he kept John safe. Herod knew John was a holy man who did what was right. When Herod heard him, he was very puzzled. But he liked to listen to him.

[21]Finally the right time came. Herod gave a big dinner on his birthday. He invited his high officials and military leaders. He also invited the most important men in Galilee. [22]Then the daughter of Herodias came in and danced. She pleased Herod and his dinner guests.

The king said to the girl, "Ask me for anything you want. I'll give it to you." [23]And he promised her with an oath, "Anything you ask for I will give you. I'll give you up to half of my kingdom."

[24]She went out and said to her mother, "What should I ask for?"

"The head of John the Baptist," she answered.

[25]At once the girl hurried to ask the king. She said, "I want you to give me the head of John the Baptist on a big plate right now."

[26]The king was very upset. But he thought of his promise and his dinner guests. So he did not want to say no to the girl. [27]He sent a man right away to bring John's head. The man went to the prison and cut off John's head. [28]He brought it back on a big plate. He gave it to the girl, and she gave it to her mother.

[29]John's disciples heard about this. So they came and took his body. Then they placed it in a tomb.

JESUS FEEDS THE FIVE THOUSAND

[30]The apostles gathered around Jesus. They told him all they had done and taught. [31]But many people were coming and going. So they did not even have a chance to eat.

Then Jesus said to his apostles, "Come with me by yourselves to a quiet place. You need to get some rest." ³²So they went away by themselves in a boat to a quiet place.

³³But many people who saw them leaving recognized them. They ran from all the towns and got there ahead of them. ³⁴When Jesus came ashore, he saw a large crowd. He felt deep concern for them. They were like sheep without a shepherd. So he began teaching them many things.

³⁵By that time it was late in the day. His disciples came to him. "There is nothing here," they said. "It's already very late. ³⁶Send the people away. They can go and buy something to eat in the nearby countryside and villages."

³⁷But Jesus answered, "You give them something to eat."

They said to him, "That would take eight months of a person's pay! Should we go and spend that much on bread? Are we supposed to feed them?"

³⁸"How many loaves do you have?" Jesus asked. "Go and see."

When they found out, they said, "Five loaves and two fish."

³⁹Then Jesus directed them to have all the people sit down in groups on the green grass. ⁴⁰So they sat down in groups of 100s and 50s.

⁴¹Jesus took the five loaves and the two fish. He looked up to heaven and gave thanks. He broke the loaves into pieces. Then he gave them to his disciples to set in front of the people. He also divided the two fish among them all.

⁴²All of them ate and were satisfied. ⁴³The disciples picked up 12 baskets of broken pieces of bread and fish. ⁴⁴The number of men who had eaten was 5,000.

JESUS WALKS ON THE WATER

⁴⁵Right away Jesus made his disciples get into the boat. He had them go on ahead of him to Bethsaida. Then he sent the crowd away. ⁴⁶After leaving them, he went up on a mountainside to pray.

⁴⁷When evening came, the boat was in the middle of the Sea of Galilee. Jesus was alone on land. ⁴⁸He saw the disciples pulling hard on the oars. The wind was blowing against them.

Early in the morning, he went out to them. He walked on the lake. When he was about to pass by them, ⁴⁹they saw him walking on the lake. They thought he was a ghost. They cried out. ⁵⁰They all saw him and were terrified.

Right away he said to them, "Be brave! It is I. Don't be afraid."

Why do some people believe in ghosts?

A ghost is the spirit of a person separated from the body. Some people believe that ghosts come back from the dead to visit people. They have seen television shows, movies or cartoons that have ghosts. Or they believe in ghosts because many other people believe in ghosts. Some people believe in them because they have had strange experiences that they cannot explain. They figure that ghosts are the only answer.

The Bible does not say that people come back to earth without their bodies. God takes your spirit from earth forever as soon as you die. Believers go to be with God. Unbelievers go to a place of suffering. People do not come back as ghosts.

Related verse:
Hebrews 9:27

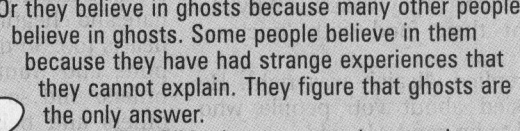

checkout Mark 6:49

⁵¹Then he climbed into the boat with them. The wind died down. And they were completely amazed. ⁵²They had not understood about the loaves. They were stubborn.

⁵³They crossed over the lake and landed at Gennesaret. There they tied up the boat. ⁵⁴As soon as Jesus and his disciples got out, people recognized him. ⁵⁵They ran through that whole area to bring to him those who were sick. They carried them on mats to where they heard he was.

⁵⁶He went into the villages, the towns and the countryside. Everywhere he went, the people brought the sick to the market places. Those who were sick begged him to let them touch just the edge of his clothes. And all who touched him were healed.

WHAT MAKES PEOPLE "UNCLEAN"?

7 The Pharisees gathered around Jesus. So did some of the teachers of the law. All of them had come from Jerusalem. ²They saw some of his disciples eating food with "unclean" hands. That means they were not washed.

³The Pharisees and all the Jews do not eat unless they wash their hands to make them pure. That's what the elders teach. ⁴When they come from the market place, they do not eat unless they wash. And they follow many other teachings. For example, they wash cups, pitchers, and kettles in a special way.

⁵So the Pharisees and the teachers of the law questioned Jesus. "Why don't your disciples live by what the elders teach?" they asked. "Why do they eat their food with 'unclean' hands?"

⁶He replied, "Isaiah was right. He prophesied about you people who pretend to be good. He said,

" 'These people honor me by what
    they say.
But their hearts are far away
    from me.
⁷Their worship doesn't mean
    anything to me.
They teach nothing but human
    rules.'   (Isaiah 29:13)

⁸You have let go of God's commands. And you are holding on to the teachings that men have made up."

⁹Jesus then said to them, "You have a fine way of setting aside God's commands! You do this so you can follow your own teachings. ¹⁰Moses said, 'Honor your father and mother.' (Exodus 20:12; Deuteronomy 5:16) He also said, 'If anyone calls down a curse on his father or mother, he will be put to death.' (Exodus 21:17; Leviticus 20:9) ¹¹But you allow people to say to their parents, 'Any help you might have received from us is Corban.' (Corban means 'a gift set apart for God.') ¹²So you no longer let them do anything for their parents. ¹³You make the word of God useless by putting your own teachings in its place. And you do many things like that."

¹⁴Again Jesus called the crowd to him. He said, "Listen to me, everyone. Understand this. ¹⁵/¹⁶Nothing outside of you can make you 'unclean' by going into you. It is what comes out of you that makes you 'unclean.' "

¹⁷Then he left the crowd and entered the house. His disciples asked him about this teaching.

¹⁸"Don't you understand?" Jesus asked. "Don't you see? Nothing that enters people from the outside can make them 'unclean.' ¹⁹It doesn't go into the heart. It goes into the stomach. Then it goes out of the body." In saying this, Jesus was calling all foods "clean."

²⁰He went on to say, "What comes out of people makes them 'unclean.' ²¹Evil thoughts come from the inside, from people's hearts. So do sexual sins, stealing and murder. Adultery, ²²greed, hate and cheating come from people's hearts too. So do desires that are not pure, and wanting what belongs to others. And so do telling lies about others and being proud and being foolish. ²³All those evil things come from inside a person. They make him 'unclean.' "

THE FAITH OF A GREEK WOMAN

²⁴Jesus went from there to a place near Tyre. He entered a house. He did not want anyone to know where he

was. But he could not keep it a secret.

²⁵Soon a woman heard about him. An evil spirit controlled her little daughter. The woman came to Jesus and fell at his feet. ²⁶She was a Greek, born in Syrian Phoenicia. She begged Jesus to drive the demon out of her daughter.

²⁷"First let the children eat all they want," he told her. "It is not right to take the children's bread and throw it to their dogs."

²⁸"Yes, Lord," she replied. "But even the dogs under the table eat the children's crumbs."

²⁹Then he told her, "That was a good reply. You may go. The demon has left your daughter."

³⁰So she went home and found her child lying on the bed. And the demon was gone.

JESUS HEALS A MAN WHO COULD NOT HEAR OR SPEAK

³¹Then Jesus left the area of Tyre and went through Sidon. He went down to the Sea of Galilee and into the area known as the Ten Cities.

³²There some people brought a man to him. The man was deaf and could hardly speak. They begged Jesus to place his hand on him.

³³Jesus took the man to one side, away from the crowd. He put his fingers into the man's ears. Then he spit and touched the man's tongue. ³⁴Jesus looked up to heaven. With a deep sigh, he said to the man, *"Ephphatha!"* That means "Be opened!" ³⁵The man's ears were opened. His tongue was freed up, and he began to speak clearly.

³⁶Jesus ordered the people not to tell anyone. But the more he did so, the more they kept talking about it.

³⁷People were really amazed. "He has done everything well," they said. "He even makes deaf people able to hear. And he makes those who can't speak able to talk."

JESUS FEEDS THE FOUR THOUSAND

8 During those days another large crowd gathered. They had nothing to eat. So Jesus called for his disciples to come to him. He said, ²"I feel deep concern for these people. They have already been with me three days. They don't have anything to eat. ³If I send them away hungry, they will become too weak on their way home. Some of them have come from far away."

⁴His disciples answered him. "There is nothing here," they said. "Where can anyone get enough bread to feed them?"

⁵"How many loaves do you have?" Jesus asked.

"Seven," they replied.

⁶He told the crowd to sit down on the ground. He took the seven loaves and gave thanks to God. Then he broke them and gave them to his disciples. They set the loaves down in front of the people. ⁷The disciples also had a few small fish. Jesus gave thanks for them too. He told the disciples to pass them around. ⁸The people ate and were satisfied.

After that, the disciples picked up seven baskets of leftover pieces. ⁹About 4,000 men were there. Jesus sent them away. ¹⁰Then he got into a boat with his disciples. He went to the area of Dalmanutha.

¹¹The Pharisees came and began to ask Jesus questions. They wanted to put him to the test. So they asked him for a miraculous sign from heaven. ¹²He sighed deeply. He said, "Why do you people ask for a sign? What I'm about to tell you is true. No sign will be given to you."

¹³Then he left them. He got back into the boat and crossed to the other side of the lake.

THE YEAST OF THE PHARISEES AND HEROD

¹⁴The disciples had forgotten to bring bread. They had only one loaf with them in the boat.

¹⁵"Be careful," Jesus warned them. "Watch out for the yeast of the Pharisees. And watch out for the yeast of Herod."

¹⁶They talked about this with each other. They said, "He must be saying this because we don't have any bread."

¹⁷Jesus knew what they were saying. So he asked them, "Why are you talking about having no bread? Why can't you see or understand? Are you stub-

born? ¹⁸Do you have eyes and still don't see? Do you have ears and still don't hear? And don't you remember? ¹⁹Earlier I broke five loaves for the 5,000. How many baskets of pieces did you pick up?"

"Twelve," they replied.

²⁰"Later I broke seven loaves for the 4,000. How many baskets of pieces did you pick up?"

"Seven," they answered.

²¹He said to them, "Can't you understand yet?"

JESUS HEALS A BLIND MAN

²²Jesus and his disciples came to Bethsaida. Some people brought a blind man. They begged Jesus to touch him.

²³He took the blind man by the hand. Then he led him outside the village. He spit on the man's eyes and put his hands on him.

"Do you see anything?" Jesus asked.

²⁴The man looked up. He said, "I see people. They look like trees walking around."

²⁵Once more Jesus put his hands on the man's eyes. Then his eyes were opened so that he could see again. He saw everything clearly.

²⁶Jesus sent him home. He told him, "Don't go into the village."

PETER SAYS THAT JESUS IS THE CHRIST

²⁷Jesus and his disciples went on to the villages around Caesarea Philippi. On the way he asked them, "Who do people say I am?"

²⁸They replied, "Some say John the Baptist. Others say Elijah. Still others say one of the prophets."

²⁹"But what about you?" he asked. "Who do you say I am?"

Peter answered, "You are the Christ."

³⁰Jesus warned them not to tell anyone about him.

JESUS TELLS ABOUT HIS COMING DEATH

³¹Jesus then began to teach his disciples. He taught them that the Son of Man must suffer many things. He taught them that the elders would not accept him. The chief priests and the teachers of the law would not accept him either. He must be killed and after

Why didn't an angel take Jesus off the cross?

It was God's will for Jesus to suffer and die on the cross. Jesus could have called on thousands of angels to rescue him. But he did not do that. Why? He was taking the punishment for our sins. If angels had stepped in and rescued Jesus, he would not have died for us. Then we could not be forgiven. Jesus' disciple named Peter tried to stop Jesus from being arrested. But Jesus told him not to do that because it was God's plan for him.

Jesus said something very important just before he died. He said, "My God, my God, why have you deserted me?" (Mark 15:34). God had left him totally alone. No one was there to help him or comfort him, not even the angels. This was part of his suffering for our sins.

checkout Mark 8:31

Related verses:
Matthew 26:51–54

three days rise again. [32]He spoke clearly about this.

Peter took Jesus to one side and began to scold him.

[33]Jesus turned and looked at his disciples. He scolded Peter. "Get behind me, Satan!" he said. "You are not thinking about the things of God. Instead, you are thinking about human things."

[34]Jesus called the crowd to him along with his disciples. He said, "If anyone wants to come after me, he must say no to himself. He must pick up his cross and follow me. [35]If he wants to save his life, he will lose it. But if he loses his life for me and for the good news, he will save it. [36]What good is it if someone gains the whole world but loses his soul? [37]Or what can anyone trade for his soul?

[38]"Suppose you are ashamed of me and my words among these adulterous and sinful people. Then the Son of Man will be ashamed of you when he comes in his Father's glory with the holy angels."

9 Jesus said to them, "What I'm about to tell you is true. Some who are standing here will not die before they see God's kingdom coming with power."

JESUS' APPEARANCE IS CHANGED

[2]After six days Jesus took Peter, James and John with him. He led them up a high mountain. They were all alone. There in front of them his appearance was changed. [3]His clothes became so white they shone. They were whiter than anyone in the world could bleach them. [4]Elijah and Moses appeared in front of Jesus and his disciples. The two of them were talking with Jesus.

[5]Peter said to Jesus, "Rabbi, it is good for us to be here. Let us put up three shelters. One will be for you, one for Moses, and one for Elijah." [6]Peter didn't really know what to say, because they were so afraid.

[7]Then a cloud appeared and surrounded them. A voice came from the cloud. It said, "This is my Son, and I love him. Listen to him!"

[8]They looked around. Suddenly they no longer saw anyone with them except Jesus.

[9]They came down the mountain. On the way down, Jesus ordered them not to tell anyone what they had seen. He told them to wait until the Son of Man had risen from the dead. [10]So they kept the matter to themselves. But they asked each other what "rising from the dead" meant.

[11]Then they asked Jesus, "Why do the teachers of the law say that Elijah has to come first?"

[12]Jesus replied, "That's right. Elijah does come first. He makes all things new again. So why is it written that the Son of Man must suffer much and not be accepted? [13]I tell you, Elijah has come. They have done to him everything they wanted to do. They did it just as it is written about him."

JESUS HEALS A BOY WHO HAD AN EVIL SPIRIT

[14]When Jesus and those who were with him came to the other disciples, they saw a large crowd around them. The teachers of the law were arguing with them. [15]When all the people saw Jesus, they were filled with wonder. And they ran to greet him.

[16]"What are you arguing with them about?" Jesus asked.

[17]A man in the crowd answered. "Teacher," he said, "I brought you my son. He is controlled by a spirit. Because of this, my son can't speak anymore. [18]When the spirit takes hold of him, it throws him to the ground. He foams at the mouth. He grinds his teeth. And his body becomes stiff. I asked your disciples to drive out the spirit. But they couldn't do it."

[19]"You unbelieving people!" Jesus replied. "How long do I have to stay with you? How long do I have to put up with you? Bring the boy to me."

[20]So they brought him. As soon as the spirit saw Jesus, it threw the boy into a fit. He fell to the ground. He rolled around and foamed at the mouth.

[21]Jesus asked the boy's father, "How long has he been like this?"

"Since he was a child," he answered. [22]"The spirit has often thrown him into fire or water to kill him. But if you can do anything, take pity on us. Please help us."

²³" 'If you can'?" said Jesus. "Everything is possible for the one who believes."

²⁴Right away the boy's father cried out, "I do believe! Help me overcome my unbelief!"

²⁵Jesus saw that a crowd was running over to see what was happening. Then he ordered the evil spirit to leave the boy. "You spirit that makes him unable to hear and speak!" he said. "I command you, come out of him. Never enter him again."

²⁶The spirit screamed. It shook the boy wildly. Then it came out of him. The boy looked so lifeless that many people said, "He's dead." ²⁷But Jesus took him by the hand. He lifted the boy to his feet, and the boy stood up.

²⁸Jesus went indoors. Then his disciples asked him in private, "Why couldn't we drive out the evil spirit?"

²⁹He replied, "This kind can come out only by prayer."

³⁰They left that place and passed through Galilee. Jesus did not want anyone to know where they were. ³¹That was because he was teaching his disciples.

He said to them, "The Son of Man is going to be handed over to men. They will kill him. After three days he will rise from the dead." ³²But they didn't understand what he meant. And they were afraid to ask him about it.

WHO IS THE MOST IMPORTANT PERSON?

³³Jesus and his disciples came to a house in Capernaum. There he asked them, "What were you arguing about on the road?" ³⁴But they kept quiet. On the way, they had argued about which one of them was the most important person.

³⁵Jesus sat down and called for the Twelve to come to him. Then he said, "If you want to be first, you must be the very last. You must be the servant of everyone."

³⁶Jesus took a little child and had the child stand among them. Then he took the child in his arms. He said to them, ³⁷"Anyone who welcomes one of these little children in my name welcomes me. And anyone who welcomes me doesn't welcome only me but also the One who sent me."

ANYONE WHO IS NOT AGAINST US IS FOR US

³⁸"Teacher," said John, "we saw a man driving out demons in your name. We told him to stop, because he was not one of us."

³⁹"Do not stop him," Jesus said. "No one who does a miracle in my name can in the next moment say anything bad about me. ⁴⁰Anyone who is not against us is for us.

⁴¹"What I'm about to tell you is true. Suppose someone gives you a cup of water in my name because you belong to me. That one will certainly not go without a reward.

LEADING PEOPLE TO SIN

⁴²"What if someone leads one of these little ones who believe in me to sin? If he does, it would be better for him to be thrown into the sea with a large millstone tied around his neck. ⁴³/⁴⁴"If your hand causes you to sin, cut it off. It would be better for you to enter God's kingdom with only one hand than to go into hell with two hands. In hell the fire never goes out. ⁴⁵/⁴⁶"If your foot causes you to sin, cut it off. It would be better for you to enter God's kingdom with only one foot than to have two feet and be thrown into hell. ⁴⁷"If your eye causes you to sin, poke it out. It would be better for you to enter God's kingdom with only one eye than to have two eyes and be thrown into hell. ⁴⁸In hell,

" 'The worms do not die.
   The fire is not put out.'

(Isaiah 66:24)

⁴⁹Everyone will be salted with fire.

⁵⁰"Salt is good. But suppose it loses its saltiness. How can you make it salty again? Have salt in yourselves. And be at peace with each other."

JESUS TEACHES ABOUT DIVORCE

10 Jesus left that place and went into the area of Judea and across the Jordan River. Again crowds of people came to him. As usual, he taught them.

²Some Pharisees came to put him to the test. They asked, "Does the Law allow a man to divorce his wife?"

³"What did Moses command you?" he replied.

⁴They said, "Moses allowed a man to write a letter of divorce and send her away."

⁵"You were stubborn. That's why Moses wrote you this law," Jesus replied. ⁶"But at the beginning of creation, God 'made them male and female.' *(Genesis 1:27)* ⁷That's why a man will leave his father and mother and be joined to his wife. ⁸The two of them will become one.' *(Genesis 2:24)* They are no longer two, but one. ⁹So a man must not separate what God has joined together."

¹⁰When they were in the house again, the disciples asked Jesus about this.

¹¹He answered, "What if a man divorces his wife and gets married to another woman? He commits adultery against her. ¹²And what if she divorces her husband and gets married to another man? She commits adultery."

LITTLE CHILDREN ARE BROUGHT TO JESUS

¹³People were bringing little children to Jesus. They wanted him to touch them. But the disciples told the people to stop.

¹⁴When Jesus saw this, he was angry. He said to his disciples, "Let the little children come to me. Don't keep them away. God's kingdom belongs to people like them. ¹⁵What I'm about to tell you is true. Anyone who will not receive God's kingdom like a little child will never enter it."

¹⁶Then he took the children in his arms. He put his hands on them and blessed them.

JESUS AND THE RICH YOUNG MAN

¹⁷As Jesus started on his way, a man ran up to him. He fell on his knees before Jesus. "Good teacher," he said, "what must I do to receive eternal life?"

¹⁸"Why do you call me good?" Jesus answered. "No one is good except God. ¹⁹You know what the commandments say. 'Do not commit murder. Do not commit adultery. Do not steal. Do

How come my friends go to a different church?

In most families, parents decide where children will go to church. Some people go to a certain church because they grew up going to that church. Even after moving across town, they might drive there every Sunday to be with friends and family. Some people choose a church because they enjoy a certain style of worship. Others go to a certain church because of its teachings. People choose churches for many different reasons. It is best to choose a church that honors Jesus, studies the Bible, helps people obey God and helps people in need.

checkout
Mark 9:40

Related verses:
Acts 2:1;
Hebrews 10:24,25

not give false witness. Do not cheat. Honor your father and mother.' "
(Exodus 20:12–16; Deuteronomy 5:16–20)

²⁰"Teacher," he said, "I have obeyed all those commandments since I was a boy."

²¹Jesus looked at him and loved him. "You are missing one thing," he said. "Go and sell everything you have. Give the money to those who are poor. You will have treasure in heaven. Then come and follow me."

²²The man's face fell. He went away sad, because he was very rich.

²³Jesus looked around. He said to his disciples, "How hard it is for rich people to enter God's kingdom!"

²⁴The disciples were amazed at his words. But Jesus said again, "Children, how hard it is to enter God's kingdom! ²⁵Is it hard for a camel to go through the eye of a needle? It is even harder for the rich to enter God's kingdom!"

²⁶The disciples were even more amazed. They said to each other, "Then who can be saved?"

²⁷Jesus looked at them and said, "With man, that is impossible. But not with God. All things are possible with God."

²⁸Peter said to him, "We have left everything to follow you!"

²⁹"What I'm about to tell you is true," Jesus replied. "Has anyone left home or family or fields for me and the good news? ³⁰They will receive 100 times as much in this world. They will have homes and families and fields. But they will also be treated badly by others. In the world to come they will live forever. ³¹But many who are first will be last. And the last will be first."

JESUS AGAIN TELLS ABOUT HIS COMING DEATH

³²They were on their way up to Jerusalem. Jesus was leading the way. The disciples were amazed. Those who followed were afraid.

Again Jesus took the Twelve to one side. He told them what was going to happen to him. ³³"We are going up to

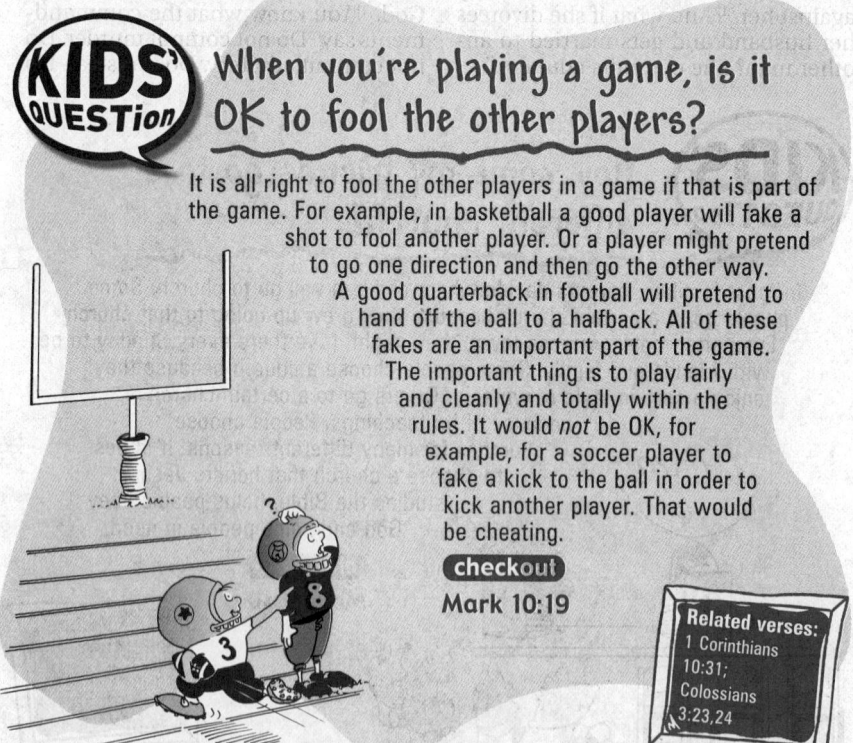

KIDS' QUESTION

When you're playing a game, is it OK to fool the other players?

It is all right to fool the other players in a game if that is part of the game. For example, in basketball a good player will fake a shot to fool another player. Or a player might pretend to go one direction and then go the other way. A good quarterback in football will pretend to hand off the ball to a halfback. All of these fakes are an important part of the game. The important thing is to play fairly and cleanly and totally within the rules. It would *not* be OK, for example, for a soccer player to fake a kick to the ball in order to kick another player. That would be cheating.

checkout

Mark 10:19

Related verses:
1 Corinthians 10:31;
Colossians 3:23,24

Jerusalem," he said. "The Son of Man will be handed over to the chief priests and the teachers of the law. They will sentence him to death. Then they will hand him over to people who are not Jews. ³⁴The people will make fun of him and spit on him. They will whip him and kill him. Three days later he will rise from the dead!"

JAMES AND JOHN ASK A FAVOR OF JESUS

³⁵James and John came to Jesus. They were the sons of Zebedee. "Teacher," they said, "we would like to ask a favor of you."

³⁶"What do you want me to do for you?" he asked.

³⁷They replied, "Let one of us sit at your right hand in your glorious kingdom. Let the other one sit at your left hand."

³⁸"You don't know what you're asking for," Jesus said. "Can you drink the cup of suffering I drink? Or can you go through the baptism of suffering I must go through?"

³⁹"We can," they answered.

Jesus said to them, "You will drink the cup I drink. And you will go through the baptism I go through. ⁴⁰But it is not for me to say who will sit at my right or left hand. These places belong to those they are prepared for."

⁴¹The other ten disciples heard about it. They became angry at James and John.

⁴²Jesus called them together. He said, "You know about those who are rulers of the nations. They hold power over their people. Their high officials order them around. ⁴³Don't be like that. Instead, anyone who wants to be important among you must be your servant. ⁴⁴And anyone who wants to be first must be the slave of everyone. ⁴⁵Even the Son of Man did not come to be served. Instead, he came to serve others. He came to give his life as the price for setting many people free."

BLIND BARTIMAEUS RECEIVES HIS SIGHT

⁴⁶Jesus and his disciples came to Jericho. They were leaving the city. A large crowd was with them.

Did Jesus know that he would come to life again?

He sure did! He not only knew he would come to life again, but he also told his disciples about it at least three times. They must not have understood because they were so surprised when he rose from the grave. They did not expect Jesus to come back to life. When they saw him, they did not recognize him at first. But then Jesus came up close, talked with them and ate with them. Then they realized it really was him. And they remembered that he had told them all about it!

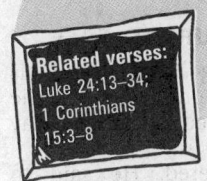

checkout

Mark 10:32-34

Related verses:
Luke 24:13–34;
1 Corinthians
15:3–8

JASON'S IMAGINATION

BACK IN 3 DAYS

A blind man was sitting by the side of the road begging. His name was Bartimaeus. Bartimaeus means Son of Timaeus. [47]He heard that Jesus of Nazareth was passing by. So he began to shout, "Jesus! Son of David! Have mercy on me!"

[48]Many people commanded him to stop. They told him to be quiet. But he shouted even louder, "Son of David! Have mercy on me!"

[49]Jesus stopped and said, "Call for him."

So they called out to the blind man, "Cheer up! Get up on your feet! Jesus is calling for you."

[50]He threw his coat to one side. Then he jumped to his feet and came to Jesus.

[51]"What do you want me to do for you?" Jesus asked him.

The blind man said, "Rabbi, I want to be able to see."

[52]"Go," said Jesus. "Your faith has healed you."

Right away he could see. And he followed Jesus along the road.

JESUS ENTERS JERUSALEM

11 As they all approached Jerusalem, they came to Bethphage and Bethany at the Mount of Olives. Jesus sent out two of his disciples. [2]He said to them, "Go to the village ahead of you. Just as you enter it, you will find a donkey's colt tied there. No one has ever ridden it. Untie it and bring it here. [3]Someone may ask you, 'Why are you doing this?' If so, say, 'The Lord needs it. But he will send it back here soon.' "

[4]So they left. They found a colt out in the street. It was tied at a doorway. They untied it. [5]Some people standing there asked, "What are you doing? Why are you untying that colt?" [6]They answered as Jesus had told them to. So the people let them go.

[7]They brought the colt to Jesus. They threw their coats over it. Then he sat on it.

[8]Many people spread their coats on the road. Others spread branches they had cut in the fields. [9]Those in front and those in back shouted,

"Hosanna!"

"Blessed is the one who comes in the name of the Lord!"

(Psalm 118:25,26)

[10]"Blessed is the coming kingdom of our father David!"

"Hosanna in the highest heaven!"

[11]Jesus entered Jerusalem and went to the temple. He looked around at everything. But it was already late. So he went out to Bethany with the Twelve.

JESUS CLEARS THE TEMPLE

[12]The next day as Jesus and his disciples were leaving Bethany, they were hungry. [13]Not too far away, he saw a fig tree. It was covered with leaves. He went to find out if it had any fruit. When he reached it, he found nothing but leaves. It was not the season for figs.

[14]Then Jesus said to the tree, "May no one ever eat fruit from you again!" And his disciples heard him say it.

[15]When Jesus reached Jerusalem, he entered the temple area. He began chasing out those who were buying and selling there. He turned over the tables of the people who were exchanging money. He also turned over the benches of those who were selling doves. [16]He would not allow anyone to carry items for sale through the temple courtyards.

[17]Then he taught them. He told them, "It is written that the Lord said,

" 'My house will be called
a house where people from all
   nations can pray.'   *(Isaiah 56:7)*

But you have made it a 'den for robbers.' " *(Jeremiah 7:11)*

[18]The chief priests and the teachers of the law heard about this. They began looking for a way to kill Jesus. They were afraid of him, because the whole crowd was amazed at his teaching.

[19]When evening came, Jesus and his disciples left the city.

THE DRIED-UP FIG TREE

[20]In the morning as Jesus and his disciples walked along, they saw the fig tree. It was dried up all the way down to the roots.

[21]Peter remembered. He said to

Jesus, "Rabbi, look! The fig tree you put a curse on has dried up!"

²²"Have faith in God," Jesus said. ²³"What I'm about to tell you is true. Suppose one of you says to this mountain, 'Go and throw yourself into the sea.' You must not doubt in your heart. You must believe that what you say will happen. Then it will be done for you.

²⁴"So I tell you, when you pray for something, believe that you have already received it. Then it will be yours. ²⁵/²⁶And when you stand praying, forgive anyone you have anything against. Then your Father in heaven will forgive your sins."

THE AUTHORITY OF JESUS IS QUESTIONED

²⁷Jesus and his disciples arrived again in Jerusalem. He was walking in the temple courtyards. Then the chief priests came to him. The teachers of the law and the elders came too.

²⁸"By what authority are you doing these things?" they asked. "Who gave you authority to do this?"

²⁹Jesus replied, "I will ask you one question. Answer me, and I will tell you by what authority I am doing these things. ³⁰Was John's baptism from heaven? Or did it come from men? Tell me!"

³¹They talked to each other about it. They said, "If we say, 'From heaven,' he will ask, 'Then why didn't you believe him?' ³²But what if we say, 'From men'?" They were afraid of the people. Everyone believed that John really was a prophet.

³³So they answered Jesus, "We don't know."

Jesus said, "Then I won't tell you by what authority I am doing these things either."

THE STORY OF THE RENTERS

12 Jesus began to speak to the people by using stories. He said, "A man planted a vineyard. He put a wall around it. He dug a pit for a winepress. He also built a lookout tower. He rented the vineyard out to some farmers. Then he went away on a journey.

²"At harvest time he sent a servant to the renters. He told the servant to collect from them some of the fruit of the vineyard. ³But they grabbed the servant and beat him up. Then they sent him away with nothing. ⁴So the man sent another servant to the renters. They hit this one on the head and treated him badly. ⁵The man sent still another servant. The renters killed him. The man sent many others. The renters beat up some of them. They killed the others.

⁶"The man had one person left to send. It was his son, and he loved him. He sent him last of all. He said, 'They will respect my son.'

⁷"But the renters said to each other, 'This is the one who will receive all the owner's property someday. Come, let's kill him. Then everything will be ours.' ⁸So they took him and killed him. They threw him out of the vineyard.

⁹"What will the owner of the vineyard do then? He will come and kill those renters. He will give the vineyard to others.

¹⁰"Haven't you read what Scripture says,

" 'The stone the builders didn't accept
has become the most important stone of all.
¹¹The Lord has done it.
It is wonderful in our eyes'?"

(Psalm 118:22,23)

¹²Then the religious leaders looked for a way to arrest Jesus. They knew he had told the story against them. But they were afraid of the crowd. So they left him and went away.

IS IT RIGHT TO PAY TAXES TO CAESAR?

¹³Later the religious leaders sent some of the Pharisees and Herodians to Jesus. They wanted to trap him with his own words.

¹⁴They came to him and said, "Teacher, we know you are a man of honor. You don't let others tell you what to do or say. You don't care how important they are. But you teach the way of God truthfully. Is it right to pay taxes to Caesar or not? ¹⁵Should we pay or shouldn't we?"

But Jesus knew what they were trying to do. So he asked, "Why are you trying to trap me? Bring me a silver coin. Let me look at it."

[16]They brought the coin.

He asked them, "Whose picture is this? And whose words?"

"Caesar's," they replied.

[17]Then Jesus said to them, "Give to Caesar what belongs to Caesar. And give to God what belongs to God."

They were amazed at him.

MARRIAGE WHEN THE DEAD RISE

[18]The Sadducees came to Jesus with a question. They do not believe that people rise from the dead. [19]"Teacher," they said, "Moses wrote for us about a man who died and didn't have any children. But he did leave a wife behind. That man's brother must get married to the widow. He must have children to carry on his dead brother's name.

[20]"There were seven brothers. The first one got married. He died without leaving any children. [21]The second one got married to the widow. He also died and left no child. It was the same with the third one. [22]In fact, none of the seven left any children. Last of all, the woman died too. [23]When the dead rise, whose wife will she be? All seven of them were married to her."

[24]Jesus replied, "You are mistaken because you do not know the Scriptures. And you do not know the power of God. [25]When the dead rise, they won't get married. And their parents won't give them to be married. They will be like the angels in heaven.

[26]"What about the dead rising? Haven't you read in the scroll of Moses the story of the bush? God said to Moses, 'I am the God of Abraham. I am the God of Isaac. And I am the God of Jacob.' *(Exodus 3:6)* [27]He is not the God of the dead. He is the God of the living. You have made a big mistake!"

THE MOST IMPORTANT COMMANDMENT

[28]One of the teachers of the law came and heard the Sadducees argu-

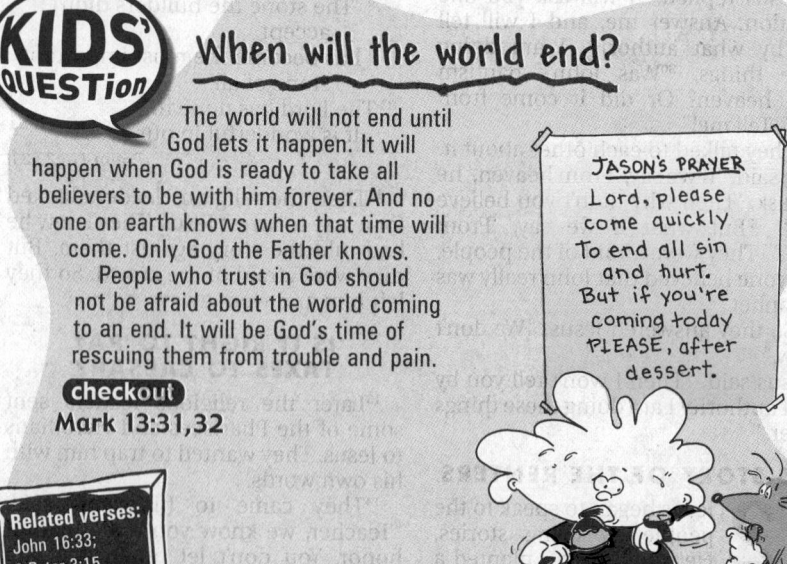

KIDS' QUESTION

When will the world end?

The world will not end until God lets it happen. It will happen when God is ready to take all believers to be with him forever. And no one on earth knows when that time will come. Only God the Father knows.

People who trust in God should not be afraid about the world coming to an end. It will be God's time of rescuing them from trouble and pain.

checkout
Mark 13:31,32

Related verses:
John 16:33;
2 Peter 3:15

JASON'S PRAYER
Lord, please come quickly
To end all sin and hurt.
But if you're coming today
PLEASE, after dessert.

ing. He noticed that Jesus had given the Sadducees a good answer. So he asked him, "Which is the most important of all the commandments?"

²⁹Jesus answered, "Here is the most important one. Moses said, 'Israel, listen to me. The Lord is our God. The Lord is one. ³⁰Love the Lord your God with all your heart and with all your soul. Love him with all your mind and with all your strength.' *(Deuteronomy 6:4,5)* ³¹And here is the second one. 'Love your neighbor as you love yourself.' *(Leviticus 19:18)* There is no commandment more important than these."

³²"You have spoken well, teacher," the man replied. "You are right in saying that God is one. There is no other God but him. ³³To love God with all your heart and mind and strength is very important. So is loving your neighbor as you love yourself. These things are more important than all burnt offerings and sacrifices."

³⁴Jesus saw that the man had answered wisely. He said to him, "You are not far from God's kingdom."

From then on, no one dared to ask Jesus any more questions.

WHOSE SON IS THE CHRIST?

³⁵Jesus was teaching in the temple courtyard. He asked, "Why do the teachers of the law say that the Christ is the son of David? ³⁶The Holy Spirit spoke through David himself. David said,

" 'The Lord said to my Lord,
"Sit at my right hand
until I put your enemies
under your control." '

(Psalm 110:1)

³⁷David himself calls him 'Lord.' So how can he be David's son?"

The large crowd listened to Jesus with delight.

³⁸As he taught, he said, "Watch out for the teachers of the law. They like to walk around in long robes. They like to be greeted in the market places. ³⁹They love to have the most important seats in the synagogues. They also love to have the places of honor at dinners. ⁴⁰They take over the houses of widows. They say long prayers to show off. God will punish those men very much."

THE WIDOW'S OFFERING

⁴¹Jesus sat down across from the place where people put their temple offerings. He watched the crowd putting their money into the offering boxes. Many rich people threw large amounts into them.

⁴²But a poor widow came and put in two very small copper coins. They were worth much less than a penny.

⁴³Jesus asked his disciples to come to him. He said, "What I'm about to tell you is true. That poor widow has put more into the offering box than all the others. ⁴⁴They all gave a lot because they are rich. But she gave even though she is poor. She put in everything she had. She gave all she had to live on."

SIGNS OF THE END

13 Jesus was leaving the temple. One of his disciples said to him, "Look, Teacher! What huge stones! What wonderful buildings!"

²"Do you see these huge buildings?" Jesus asked. "Not one stone here will be left on top of another. Every stone will be thrown down."

³Jesus was sitting on the Mount of Olives, across from the temple. Peter, James, John and Andrew asked him a question in private. ⁴"Tell us," they said. "When will these things happen? And what will be the sign that they are all about to come true?"

⁵Jesus said to them, "Keep watch! Be careful that no one fools you. ⁶Many will come in my name. They will claim, 'I am he.' They will fool many people.

⁷"You will hear about wars. You will also hear people talking about future wars. Don't be alarmed. Those things must happen. But the end still isn't here. ⁸Nation will fight against nation. Kingdom will fight against kingdom. There will be earthquakes in many places. People will go hungry. All of those things are the beginning of birth pains.

⁹"Watch out! You will be handed over to the local courts. You will be whipped in the synagogues. You will stand in front of governors and kings because of me. In that way you will be

witnesses to them. [10]The good news has to be preached to all nations before the end comes. [11]You will be arrested and brought to trial. But don't worry ahead of time about what you will say. Just say what God brings to your mind at the time. It is not you speaking, but the Holy Spirit.

[12]"Brothers will hand over brothers to be killed. Fathers will hand over their children. Children will rise up against their parents and have them put to death. [13]Everyone will hate you because of me. But the one who stands firm to the end will be saved.

[14]"You will see 'the hated thing that destroys.' *(Daniel 9:27; 11:31; 12:11)* It will stand where it does not belong. The reader should understand this. Then those who are in Judea should escape to the mountains. [15]No one on the roof should go down into his house to take anything out. [16]No one in the field should go back to get his coat. [17]How awful it will be in those days for pregnant women! How awful for nursing mothers! [18]Pray that this will not happen in winter.

[19]"Those days will be worse than any others from the time God created the world until now. And there will never be any like them again. [20]If the Lord had not cut the time short, no one would live. But because of God's chosen people, he has shortened it.

[21]"At that time someone may say to you, 'Look! Here is the Christ!' Or, 'Look! There he is!' Do not believe it. [22]False Christs and false prophets will appear. They will do signs and miracles. They will try to fool God's chosen people if possible. [23]Keep watch! I have told you everything ahead of time.

[24]"So in those days there will be terrible suffering. After that, Scripture says,

" 'The sun will be darkened.
    The moon will not shine.
[25]The stars will fall from the sky.
    The heavenly bodies will be
        shaken.'   *(Isaiah 13:10; 34:4)*

[26]"At that time people will see the Son of Man coming in clouds. He will come with great power and glory. [27]He will send his angels. He will gather his chosen people from all four directions. He will bring them from the ends of the earth to the ends of the heavens.

[28]"Learn a lesson from the fig tree. As soon as its twigs get tender and its leaves come out, you know that summer is near. [29]In the same way, when you see those things happening, you know that the end is near. It is right at the door. [30]What I'm about to tell you is true. The people living at that time will certainly not pass away until all those things have happened. [31]Heaven and earth will pass away. But my words will never pass away.

THE DAY AND HOUR ARE NOT KNOWN

[32]"No one knows about that day or hour. Not even the angels in heaven know. The Son does not know. Only the Father knows.

[33]"Keep watch! Stay awake! You do not know when that time will come. [34]It's like a man going away. He leaves his house and puts his servants in charge. Each one is given a task to do. He tells the one at the door to keep watch.

[35]"So keep watch! You do not know when the owner of the house will come back. It may be in the evening or at midnight. It may be when the rooster crows or at dawn. [36]He may come suddenly. So do not let him find you sleeping.

[37]"What I say to you, I say to everyone. 'Watch!' "

A WOMAN POURS PERFUME ON JESUS

14 The Passover and the Feast of Unleavened Bread were only two days away. The chief priests and the teachers of the law were looking for a clever way to arrest Jesus. They wanted to kill him. [2]"But not during the Feast," they said. "The people may stir up trouble."

[3]Jesus was in Bethany. He was at the table in the home of a man named Simon, who had a skin disease. A woman came with a special sealed jar of very expensive perfume. It was made out of pure nard. She broke the jar

open and poured the perfume on Jesus' head.

⁴Some of the people there became angry. They said to one another, "Why waste this perfume? ⁵It could have been sold for more than a year's pay. The money could have been given to poor people." So they found fault with the woman.

⁶"Leave her alone," Jesus said. "Why are you bothering her? She has done a beautiful thing to me. ⁷You will always have poor people with you. You can help them any time you want to. But you will not always have me. ⁸She did what she could. She poured perfume on my body to prepare me to be buried. ⁹What I'm about to tell you is true. What she has done will be told anywhere the good news is preached all over the world. It will be told in memory of her."

¹⁰Judas Iscariot was one of the Twelve. He went to the chief priests to hand Jesus over to them. ¹¹They were delighted to hear that he would do this. They promised to give Judas money. So he watched for the right time to hand Jesus over to them.

THE LORD'S SUPPER

¹²It was the first day of the Feast of Unleavened Bread. That was the time to sacrifice the Passover lamb.

Jesus' disciples asked him, "Where do you want us to go and prepare for you to eat the Passover meal?"

¹³So he sent out two of his disciples. He told them, "Go into the city. A man carrying a jar of water will meet you. Follow him. ¹⁴He will enter a house. Say to its owner, 'The Teacher asks, "Where is my guest room? Where can I eat the Passover meal with my disciples?"' ¹⁵He will show you a large upstairs room. It will have furniture and will be ready. Prepare for us to eat there."

¹⁶The disciples left and went into the city. They found things just as Jesus had told them. So they prepared the Passover meal.

¹⁷When evening came, Jesus arrived with the Twelve. ¹⁸While they were at the table eating, Jesus said, "What I'm about to tell you is true. One of you who is eating with me will hand me over to my enemies."

¹⁹The disciples became sad. One by one they said to him, "It's not I, is it?"

When is Jesus coming back to Earth?

When Jesus ascended into heaven, angels promised he would return, just as he said. But Jesus said he would return when people least expect it. So no one knows exactly when he is coming back. It could be today; it could be far, far in the future. That is why Jesus told us to be ready for his return all the time. We should stay close to God and always do what is right.

Although no one knows when Jesus will return, we do know that every day brings his return closer. And when he comes, it will be a wonderful day for those who love him.

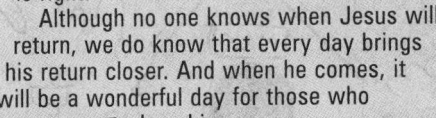

Related verses:
1 Corinthians
15:51–58;
1 Thessalonians
4:15—5:11;
2 Thessalonians
1:7–10; 2:1–6

checkout
Mark
13:33-37

SHOW & TELL
Next Week's
Topic:
Your Best
Friend

²⁰"It is one of the Twelve," Jesus replied. "It is the one who dips bread into the bowl with me. ²¹The Son of Man will go just as it is written about him. But how terrible it will be for the one who hands over the Son of Man! It would be better for him if he had not been born."

²²While they were eating, Jesus took bread. He gave thanks and broke it. He handed it to his disciples and said, "Take it. This is my body."

²³Then he took the cup. He gave thanks and handed it to them. All of them drank from it.

²⁴"This is my blood of the new covenant," he said to them. "It is poured out for many. ²⁵What I'm about to tell you is true. I won't drink wine with you again until the day I drink it in God's kingdom."

²⁶Then they sang a hymn and went out to the Mount of Olives.

JESUS SAYS THAT PETER WILL FAIL

²⁷"You will all turn away," Jesus told the disciples. "It is written,

" 'I will strike the shepherd down.
  Then the sheep will be
    scattered.'   *(Zechariah 13:7)*

²⁸But after I rise from the dead, I will go ahead of you into Galilee."

²⁹Peter said, "All the others may turn away. But I will not."

³⁰"What I'm about to tell you is true," Jesus answered. "It will happen today, this very night. Before the rooster crows twice, you yourself will say three times that you don't know me."

³¹But Peter would not give in. He said, "I may have to die with you. But I will never say I don't know you." And all the others said the same thing.

JESUS PRAYS IN GETHSEMANE

³²Jesus and his disciples went to a place called Gethsemane. Jesus said to them, "Sit here while I pray."

³³He took Peter, James and John along with him. He began to be very upset and troubled. ³⁴"My soul is very sad. I feel close to death," he said to them. "Stay here. Keep watch."

³⁵He went a little farther. Then he fell

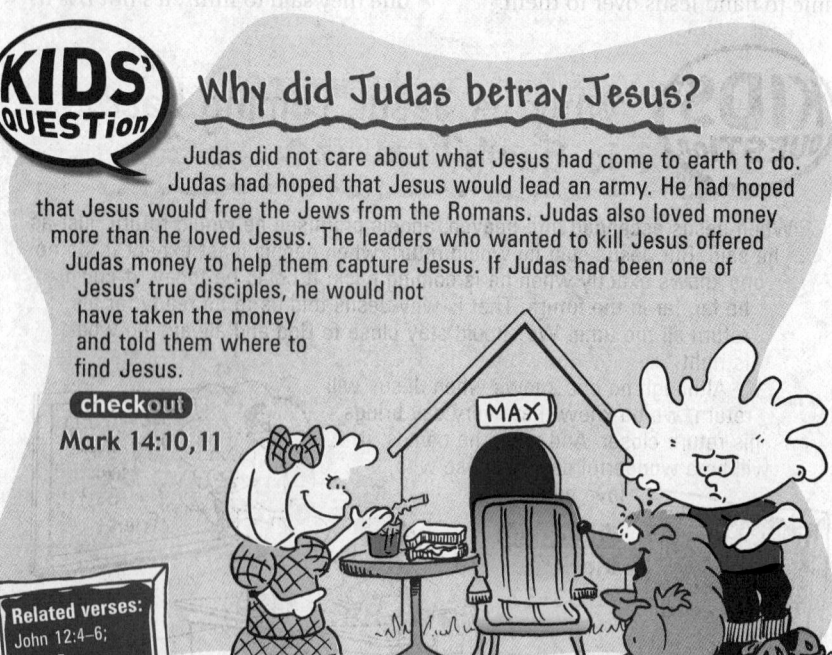

KIDS' QUESTION

Why did Judas betray Jesus?

Judas did not care about what Jesus had come to earth to do. Judas had hoped that Jesus would lead an army. He had hoped that Jesus would free the Jews from the Romans. Judas also loved money more than he loved Jesus. The leaders who wanted to kill Jesus offered Judas money to help them capture Jesus. If Judas had been one of Jesus' true disciples, he would not have taken the money and told them where to find Jesus.

checkout
Mark 14:10,11

Related verses:
John 12:4–6;
18:2–5

MAX

to the ground. He prayed that, if possible, the hour might pass by him. [36]"*Abba*," he said, "everything is possible for you. Take this cup of suffering away from me. But let what you want be done, not what I want." *Abba* means Father.

[37]Then he returned to his disciples and found them sleeping. "Simon," he said to Peter, "are you asleep? Couldn't you keep watch for one hour? [38]Watch and pray. Then you won't fall into sin when you are tempted. The spirit is willing. But the body is weak."

[39]Once more Jesus went away and prayed the same thing. [40]Then he came back. Again he found them sleeping. They couldn't keep their eyes open. They did not know what to say to him.

[41]Jesus returned the third time. He said to them, "Are you still sleeping and resting? Enough! The hour has come. Look! The Son of Man is about to be handed over to sinners. [42]Get up! Let us go! Here comes the one who is handing me over to them!"

JESUS IS ARRESTED

[43]Just as Jesus was speaking, Judas appeared. He was one of the Twelve. A crowd was with him. They were carrying swords and clubs. The chief priests, the teachers of the law, and the elders had sent them.

[44]Judas, who was going to hand Jesus over, had arranged a signal with them. "The one I kiss is the man," he said. "Arrest him and have the guards lead him away."

[45]So Judas went to Jesus at once. He said, "Rabbi!" And he kissed him.

[46]The men grabbed Jesus and arrested him.

[47]Then one of those standing nearby pulled his sword out. He struck the servant of the high priest and cut off his ear.

[48]"Am I leading a band of armed men against you?" asked Jesus. "Do you have to come out with swords and clubs to capture me? [49]Every day I was with you. I taught in the temple courtyard, and you didn't arrest me. But the Scriptures must come true."

[50]Then everyone left him and ran away.

[51]A young man was following Jesus. The man was wearing nothing but a piece of linen cloth. When the crowd grabbed him, [52]he ran away naked. He left his clothing behind.

JESUS IS TAKEN TO THE SANHEDRIN

[53]The crowd took Jesus to the high priest. All of the chief priests, the elders, and the teachers of the law came together.

[54]Not too far away, Peter followed Jesus. He went right into the courtyard of the high priest. There he sat with the guards. He warmed himself at the fire.

[55]The chief priests and the whole Sanhedrin were looking for something to use against Jesus. They wanted to put him to death. But they did not find any proof. [56]Many witnesses lied about him. But their stories did not agree.

[57]Then some stood up. They gave false witness about him. [58]"We heard him say, 'I will destroy this temple made by human hands. In three days I will build another temple, not made by human hands.' " [59]But what they said did not agree.

[60]Then the high priest stood up in front of them. He asked Jesus, "Aren't you going to answer? What are these charges these men are bringing against you?"

[61]But Jesus remained silent. He gave no answer.

Again the high priest asked him, "Are you the Christ? Are you the Son of the Blessed One?"

[62]"I am," said Jesus. "And you will see the Son of Man sitting at the right hand of the Mighty One. You will see the Son of Man coming on the clouds of heaven."

[63]The high priest tore his clothes. "Why do we need any more witnesses?" he asked. [64]"You have heard him say a very evil thing against God. What do you think?"

They all found him guilty and said he must die.

[65]Then some began to spit at him. They blindfolded him. They hit him with their fists. They said, "Prophesy!" And the guards took him and beat him.

PETER SAYS HE DOES NOT KNOW JESUS

66Peter was below in the courtyard. One of the high priest's female servants came by. 67When she saw Peter warming himself, she looked closely at him.

"You also were with Jesus, that Nazarene," she said.

68But Peter said he had not been with him. "I don't know or understand what you're talking about," he said. He went out to the entrance to the courtyard.

69The servant saw him there. She said again to those standing around, "This fellow is one of them."

70Again he said he was not.

After a little while, those standing nearby said to Peter, "You must be one of them. You are from Galilee."

71He began to call down curses on himself. He took an oath and said to them, "I don't know this man you're talking about!"

72Right away the rooster crowed the second time. Then Peter remembered what Jesus had spoken to him. "The rooster will crow twice," he had said. "Before it does, you will say three times that you don't know me." Peter broke down and sobbed.

JESUS IS BROUGHT TO PILATE

15 It was very early in the morning. The chief priests, with the elders, the teachers of the law, and the whole Sanhedrin, made a decision. They tied Jesus up and led him away. Then they handed him over to Pilate.

2"Are you the king of the Jews?" asked Pilate.

"Yes. It is just as you say," Jesus replied.

3The chief priests brought many charges against him. 4So Pilate asked him again, "Aren't you going to answer? See how many things they charge you with."

5But Jesus still did not reply. Pilate was amazed.

6It was the usual practice at the Passover Feast to let one prisoner go free. The people could choose the one they wanted. 7A man named Barabbas was in prison. He was there with some other people who had fought against the country's rulers. They had committed murder while they were fighting against the rulers. 8The crowd came up and asked Pilate to do for them what he usually did.

9"Do you want me to let the king of the Jews go free?" asked Pilate. 10He knew that the chief priests had handed Jesus over to him because they were jealous. 11But the chief priests stirred up the crowd. So the crowd asked Pilate to let Barabbas go free instead.

12"Then what should I do with the one you call the king of the Jews?" Pilate asked them.

13"Crucify him!" the crowd shouted.

14"Why? What wrong has he done?" asked Pilate.

But they shouted even louder, "Crucify him!"

15Pilate wanted to satisfy the crowd. So he let Barabbas go free. He ordered that Jesus be whipped. Then he handed him over to be nailed to a cross.

THE SOLDIERS MAKE FUN OF JESUS

16The soldiers led Jesus away into the palace. It was called the Praetorium. They called together the whole company of soldiers.

17The soldiers put a purple robe on Jesus. Then they twisted thorns together to make a crown. They placed it on his head. 18They began to call out to him, "We honor you, king of the Jews!" 19Again and again they hit him on the head with a stick. They spit on him. They fell on their knees and pretended to honor him.

20After they had made fun of him, they took off the purple robe. They put his own clothes back on him. Then they led him out to nail him to a cross.

JESUS IS NAILED TO A CROSS

21A man named Simon from Cyrene was passing by. He was the father of Alexander and Rufus. Simon was on his way in from the country. The soldiers forced him to carry the cross.

22They brought Jesus to the place called Golgotha. The word Golgotha means The Place of the Skull. 23Then they gave him wine mixed with spices. But he did not take it.

²⁴They nailed him to the cross. Then they divided up his clothes. They cast lots to see what each of them would get.

²⁵It was nine o'clock in the morning when they crucified him. ²⁶They wrote out the charge against him. It read, THE KING OF THE JEWS.

²⁷/²⁸They crucified two robbers with him. One was on his right and one was on his left.

²⁹Those who passed by shouted at Jesus and made fun of him. They shook their heads and said, "So you are going to destroy the temple and build it again in three days? ³⁰Then come down from the cross! Save yourself!"

³¹In the same way the chief priests and the teachers of the law made fun of him among themselves. "He saved others," they said. "But he can't save himself! ³²Let this Christ, this King of Israel, come down now from the cross! When we see that, we will believe."

Those who were being crucified with Jesus also made fun of him.

JESUS DIES

³³At noon, darkness covered the whole land. It lasted three hours. ³⁴At three o'clock Jesus cried out in a loud voice, *"Eloi, Eloi, lama sabachthani?"* This means "My God, my God, why have you deserted me?" *(Psalm 22:1)*

³⁵Some of those standing nearby heard Jesus cry out. They said, "Listen! He's calling for Elijah."

³⁶One of them ran and filled a sponge with wine vinegar. He put it on a stick. He offered it to Jesus to drink. "Leave him alone," he said. "Let's see if Elijah comes to take him down."

³⁷With a loud cry, Jesus took his last breath.

³⁸The temple curtain was torn in two from top to bottom.

³⁹A Roman commander was standing there in front of Jesus. He heard his cry and saw how Jesus died. Then he said, "This man was surely the Son of God!"

⁴⁰Not very far away, some women were watching. Mary Magdalene was among them. Mary, the mother of the younger James and of Joses, was also there. So was Salome. ⁴¹In Galilee those women had followed Jesus. They had taken care of his needs.

Many other women were also there. They had come up with him to Jerusalem.

JESUS IS BURIED

⁴²It was the day before the Sabbath. That day was called Preparation Day. As evening approached, ⁴³Joseph went boldly to Pilate and asked for Jesus' body. Joseph was from the town of Arimathea. He was a leading member of the Jewish Council. He was waiting for God's kingdom.

⁴⁴Pilate was surprised to hear that Jesus was already dead. So he called for the Roman commander. He asked him if Jesus had already died. ⁴⁵The commander said it was true. So Pilate gave the body to Joseph.

⁴⁶Then Joseph bought some linen cloth. He took the body down and wrapped it in the linen. He put it in a tomb cut out of rock. Then he rolled a stone against the entrance to the tomb.

⁴⁷Mary Magdalene and Mary the mother of Joses saw where Jesus' body had been placed.

JESUS RISES FROM THE DEAD

16 The Sabbath day ended. Mary Magdalene, Mary the mother of James, and Salome bought spices. They were going to apply them to Jesus' body.

²Very early on the first day of the week, they were on their way to the tomb. It was just after sunrise. ³They asked each other, "Who will roll the stone away from the entrance to the tomb?"

⁴Then they looked up and saw that the stone had been rolled away. The stone was very large.

⁵They entered the tomb. As they did, they saw a young man dressed in a white robe. He was sitting on the right side. They were alarmed.

⁶"Don't be alarmed," he said. "You are looking for Jesus the Nazarene, who was crucified. But he has risen! He is not here! See the place where they had put him. ⁷Go! Tell his disci-

ples and Peter, 'He is going ahead of you into Galilee. There you will see him. It will be just as he told you.' "

[8]The women were shaking and confused. They went out and ran away from the tomb. They said nothing to anyone, because they were afraid.

———————————

[9]Jesus rose from the dead early on the first day of the week. He appeared first to Mary Magdalene. He had driven seven demons out of her. [10]She went and told those who had been with him. She found them crying. They were very sad. [11]They heard that Jesus was alive and that she had seen him. But they did not believe it.

[12]After that, Jesus appeared in a different form to two of them. This happened while they were walking out in the country. [13]The two returned and told the others about it. But the others did not believe them either.

[14]Later Jesus appeared to the Eleven as they were eating. He spoke firmly to them because they had no faith. They would not believe those who had seen him after he rose from the dead.

[15]He said to them, "Go into all the world. Preach the good news to everyone. [16]Anyone who believes and is baptized will be saved. But anyone who does not believe will be punished. [17]Here are the miraculous signs that those who believe will do. In my name they will drive out demons. They will speak in languages they had not known before. [18]They will pick up snakes with their hands. And when they drink deadly poison, it will not hurt them at all. They will place their hands on sick people. And the people will get well."

[19]When the Lord Jesus finished speaking to them, he was taken up into heaven. He sat down at the right hand of God.

[20]Then the disciples went out and preached everywhere. The Lord worked with them. And he backed up his word by the signs that went with it.

quest challenge

I Wonder . . .

How can I show God that I love him?

Real Life Challenge

Showing that you love God may be easier than you think. Picture this situation: You're walking down the hall at school, and you see that another kid has tripped. His books and papers are in a mess all over the floor. Other kids are pushing past him and walking on his stuff. In this situation, you can show that you love God—how?

Quest Clue

Look through Mark 12 to discover what Jesus had to say about loving God. You'll find more clues in Matthew 25 and John 14.

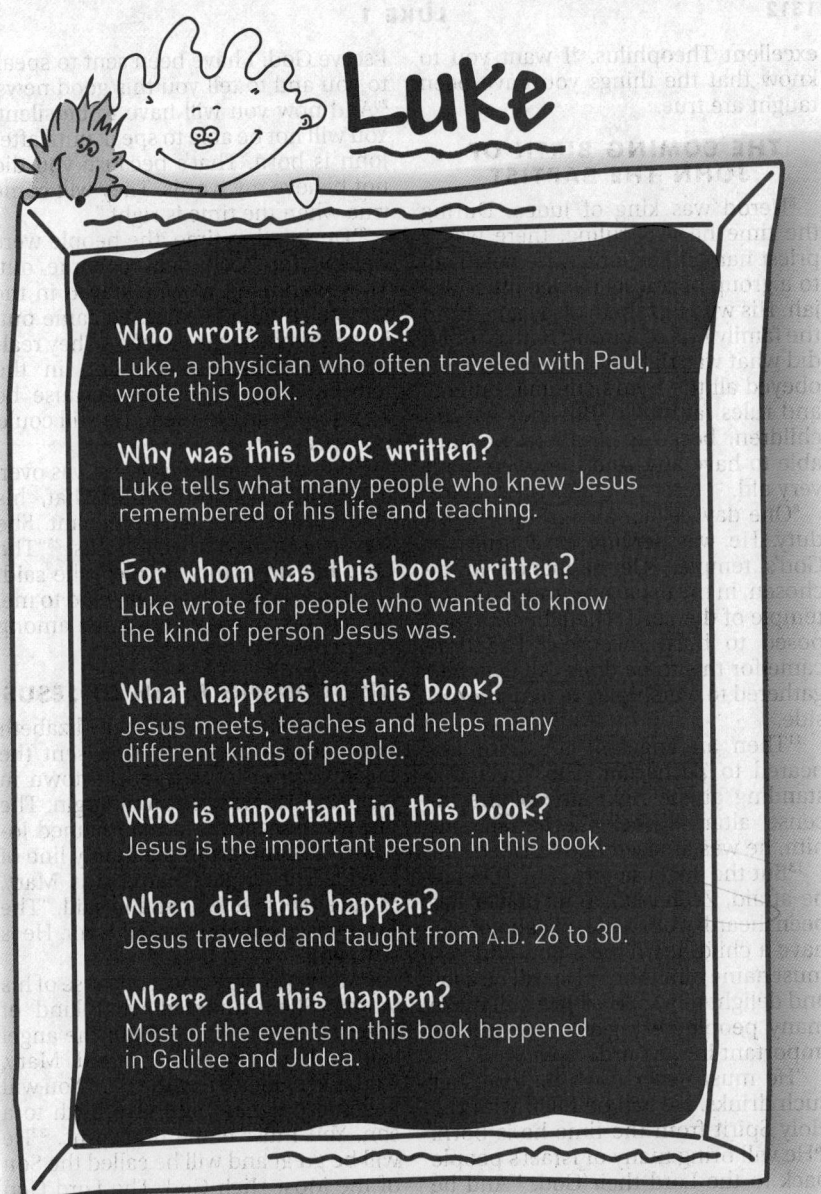

Luke

Who wrote this book?
Luke, a physician who often traveled with Paul, wrote this book.

Why was this book written?
Luke tells what many people who knew Jesus remembered of his life and teaching.

For whom was this book written?
Luke wrote for people who wanted to know the kind of person Jesus was.

What happens in this book?
Jesus meets, teaches and helps many different kinds of people.

Who is important in this book?
Jesus is the important person in this book.

When did this happen?
Jesus traveled and taught from A.D. 26 to 30.

Where did this happen?
Most of the events in this book happened in Galilee and Judea.

LUKE WRITES AN ORDERLY REPORT

1 Many people have attempted to write about the things that have taken place among us. ²Reports of these things were handed down to us. There were people who saw these things for themselves from the beginning and then passed the word on.

³I myself have carefully looked into everything from the beginning. So it seemed good also to me to write down an orderly report of exactly what happened. I am doing this for you, most

excellent Theophilus. ⁴I want you to know that the things you have been taught are true.

THE COMING BIRTH OF JOHN THE BAPTIST

⁵Herod was king of Judea. During the time he was ruling, there was a priest named Zechariah. He belonged to a group of priests named after Abijah. His wife Elizabeth also came from the family line of Aaron. ⁶Both of them did what was right in God's eyes. They obeyed all the Lord's commandments and rules faithfully. ⁷But they had no children, because Elizabeth was not able to have any. And they were both very old.

⁸One day Zechariah's group was on duty. He was serving as a priest in God's temple. ⁹He happened to be chosen, in the usual way, to go into the temple of the Lord. There he was supposed to burn incense. ¹⁰The time came for this to be done. All who had gathered to worship were praying outside.

¹¹Then an angel of the Lord appeared to Zechariah. The angel was standing at the right side of the incense altar. ¹²When Zechariah saw him, he was amazed and terrified.

¹³But the angel said to him, "Do not be afraid, Zechariah. Your prayer has been heard. Your wife Elizabeth will have a child. It will be a boy, and you must name him John. ¹⁴He will be a joy and delight to you. His birth will make many people very glad. ¹⁵He will be important in the Lord's eyes.

"He must never use wine or other such drinks. He will be filled with the Holy Spirit from the time he is born. ¹⁶He will bring many of Israel's people back to the Lord their God. ¹⁷And he will prepare the way for the Lord. He will have the same spirit and power that Elijah had. He will teach parents how to love their children. He will also teach people who don't obey to be wise and do what is right. In this way, he will prepare a people who are ready for the Lord."

¹⁸Zechariah asked the angel, "How can I be sure of this? I am an old man, and my wife is old too."

¹⁹The angel answered, "I am Gabriel.

I serve God. I have been sent to speak to you and to tell you this good news. ²⁰And now you will have to be silent. You will not be able to speak until after John is born. That's because you did not believe my words. They will come true when the time is right."

²¹During that time, the people were waiting for Zechariah to come out. They wondered why he stayed in the temple so long. ²²When he came out, he could not speak to them. They realized he had seen a vision in the temple. They knew this because he kept motioning to them. He still could not speak.

²³When his time of service was over, he returned home. ²⁴After that, his wife Elizabeth became pregnant. She stayed at home for five months. ²⁵"The Lord has done this for me," she said. "In these days, he has been kind to me. He has taken away my shame among the people."

THE COMING BIRTH OF JESUS

²⁶In the sixth month after Elizabeth had become pregnant, God sent the angel Gabriel to Nazareth, a town in Galilee. ²⁷He was sent to a virgin. The girl was engaged to a man named Joseph. He came from the family line of David. The virgin's name was Mary. ²⁸The angel greeted her and said, "The Lord has given you special favor. He is with you."

²⁹Mary was very upset because of his words. She wondered what kind of greeting this could be. ³⁰But the angel said to her, "Do not be afraid, Mary. God is very pleased with you. ³¹You will become pregnant and give birth to a son. You must name him Jesus. ³²He will be great and will be called the Son of the Most High God. The Lord God will make him a king like his father David of long ago. ³³He will rule forever over his people, who came from Jacob's family. His kingdom will never end."

³⁴"How can this happen?" Mary asked the angel. "I am a virgin."

³⁵The angel answered, "The Holy Spirit will come to you. The power of the Most High God will cover you. So the holy one that is born will be called the Son of God. ³⁶Your relative Eliza-

beth is old. And even she is going to have a child. People thought she could not have children. But she has been pregnant for six months now. ³⁷Nothing is impossible with God."

³⁸"I serve the Lord," Mary answered. "May it happen to me just as you said it would." Then the angel left her.

MARY VISITS ELIZABETH

³⁹At that time Mary got ready and hurried to a town in Judea's hill country. ⁴⁰There she entered Zechariah's home and greeted Elizabeth. ⁴¹When Elizabeth heard Mary's greeting, the baby inside her jumped. And Elizabeth was filled with the Holy Spirit. ⁴²In a loud voice she called out, "God has blessed you more than other women. And blessed is the child you will have! ⁴³But why is God so kind to me? Why has the mother of my Lord come to me? ⁴⁴As soon as I heard the sound of your voice, the baby inside me jumped for joy. ⁴⁵You are a woman God has blessed. You have believed that what the Lord has said to you will be done!"

MARY'S SONG

⁴⁶Mary said,

"My soul gives glory to the Lord.
⁴⁷ My spirit delights in God my Savior.
⁴⁸He has taken note of me
even though I am not important.
From now on all people will call me blessed.
⁴⁹ The Mighty One has done great things for me.
His name is holy.
⁵⁰He shows his mercy to those who have respect for him,
from parent to child down through the years.
⁵¹He has done mighty things with his arm.
He has scattered those who are proud in their deepest thoughts.
⁵²He has brought down rulers from their thrones.
But he has lifted up people who are not important.
⁵³He has filled those who are hungry with good things.

How come Zechariah couldn't talk until his son was born?

Zechariah was a priest who worked in the temple. One day he went into a part of the temple where only the priest could go. The angel Gabriel appeared and told him that he was going to have a son. Zechariah did not believe the angel's promise. Because of this, God took away Zechariah's voice. This was a sign to Zechariah that the angel's message was true. It was also a sign to the people that Zechariah had met with God. About nine months later Zechariah's son was born. Zechariah asked for a tablet to write down his son's name. As soon as he wrote the name "John" as Gabriel had told him to, Zechariah could talk again.

checkout
Luke 1:22

Related verses: Luke 1:5–23

But he has sent those who are
　　rich away empty.
⁵⁴He has helped the people of Israel,
　　who serve him.
　　He has always remembered to be
　　　kind
⁵⁵to Abraham and his children down
　　through the years.
　　He has done it just as he said to
　　　our people of long ago."

⁵⁶Mary stayed with Elizabeth about
three months. Then she returned
home.

JOHN THE BAPTIST IS BORN

⁵⁷The time came for Elizabeth to
have her baby. She gave birth to a son.
⁵⁸Her neighbors and relatives heard
that the Lord had been very kind to
her. They shared her joy.
⁵⁹On the eighth day, they came to
have the child circumcised. They were
going to name him Zechariah, like his
father. ⁶⁰But his mother spoke up. "No!"
she said. "He must be called John."
⁶¹They said to her, "No one among
your relatives has that name."
⁶²Then they motioned to his father.

They wanted to find out what he
would like to name the child. ⁶³He
asked for something to write on. Then
he wrote, "His name is John." Everyone was amazed.
⁶⁴Right away Zechariah could speak
again. His first words gave praise to
God. ⁶⁵The neighbors were all filled
with fear and wonder. All through
Judea's hill country, people were talking about all these things. ⁶⁶Everyone
who heard this wondered about it.
And because the Lord was with John,
they asked, "What is this child going
to be?"

ZECHARIAH'S SONG

⁶⁷His father Zechariah was filled
with the Holy Spirit. He prophesied,

⁶⁸"Give praise to the Lord, the God
　　of Israel!
　　He has come and set his people
　　　free.
⁶⁹He has acted with great power and
　　has saved us.
　　He did it for those who are from
　　the family line of his servant
　　David.

KIDS' QUESTION

Why did an angel come to Mary?

An angel came to
Mary to tell her
God's message. God wanted
Mary to know that she would be
the mother of Jesus, God's
Son. Mary was scared when
she first heard the news. But
she was also very glad. She
wanted to obey God more
than anything else. And she
felt very honored to be
Jesus' mother.

checkout Luke 1:26,27

Related verses:
Luke 1:26–38

JASON'S IMAGINATION

I'LL GO!

SPECIAL ASSIGNMENT
ANNOUNCEMENT!
God is considering using
an angel to take a very
special message to Mary!

PICK ME! PICK ME!

ASSIGNMENT DESK

70 Long ago holy prophets said he would do it.
71 He has saved us from our enemies. We are rescued from all who hate us.
72 He has been kind to our people. He has remembered his holy covenant.
73 He made an oath to our father Abraham.
74 He promised to save us from our enemies, so that we could serve him without fear.
75 He wants us to be holy and godly as long as we live.
76 "And you, my child, will be called a prophet of the Most High God. You will go ahead of the Lord to prepare the way for him.
77 You will tell his people how they can be saved. You will tell them that their sins can be forgiven.
78 All of that will happen because our God is tender and caring. His kindness will bring the rising sun to us from heaven.
79 It will shine on those living in darkness and in the shadow of death. It will guide our feet on the path of peace."
80 The child grew up, and his spirit became strong. He lived in the desert until he appeared openly to Israel.

JESUS IS BORN

2 In those days, Caesar Augustus made a law. It required that a list be made of everyone in the whole Roman world. ²It was the first time a list was made of the people while Quirinius was governor of Syria. ³All went to their own towns to be listed.

⁴So Joseph went also. He went from the town of Nazareth in Galilee to Judea. That is where Bethlehem, the town of David, was. Joseph went there because he belonged to the family line of David. ⁵He went there with Mary to be listed. Mary was engaged to him. She was expecting a baby.

⁶While Joseph and Mary were there, the time came for the child to be born. ⁷She gave birth to her first baby. It was

Why was Jesus born in a stinky stable?

There was nowhere else for Mary and Joseph to go. Many people had come to Bethlehem to write their names in the record books. The Romans had told everyone to go to their hometowns and be counted. The city was very crowded, and all the inns were full. Jesus' parents could not find a room anywhere. The only place they could find was out where the animals stayed. This was all part of God's plan, though. Jesus' plain birth lets us know that he laid aside his glory and came for *all* people, not just the rich and famous.

checkout Luke 2:6,7

Related verses: Luke 2:1–12; Philippians 2:5–8

a boy. She wrapped him in large strips of cloth. Then she placed him in a manger. There was no room for them in the inn.

ANGELS APPEAR TO THE SHEPHERDS

[8]There were shepherds living out in the fields nearby. It was night, and they were looking after their sheep. [9]An angel of the Lord appeared to them. And the glory of the Lord shone around them. They were terrified. [10]But the angel said to them, "Do not be afraid. I bring you good news of great joy. It is for all the people. [11]Today in the town of David a Savior has been born to you. He is Christ the Lord. [12]Here is how you will know I am telling you the truth. You will find a baby wrapped in strips of cloth and lying in a manger."

[13]Suddenly a large group of angels from heaven also appeared. They were praising God. They said,

[14]"May glory be given to God in the highest heaven!

And may peace be given to those he is pleased with on earth!"

[15]The angels left and went into heaven. Then the shepherds said to one another, "Let's go to Bethlehem. Let's see this thing that has happened, which the Lord has told us about."

[16]So they hurried off and found Mary and Joseph and the baby. The baby was lying in the manger. [17]After the shepherds had seen him, they told everyone. They reported what the angel had said about this child. [18]All who heard it were amazed at what the shepherds said to them.

[19]But Mary kept all these things like a secret treasure in her heart. She thought about them over and over. [20]The shepherds returned. They gave glory and praise to God. Everything they had seen and heard was just as they had been told.

JOSEPH AND MARY TAKE JESUS TO THE TEMPLE

[21]When the child was eight days old, he was circumcised. At the same time

Do people keep their culture when they move to a different country?

People who move from one country to another often try hard to keep the customs and traditions of their home country. But sometimes they are the only family in the neighborhood who are from that country.

For example, if the people want to speak their native language, they have to talk with others who also speak their language. If they want to eat the food of their homeland, they need to know where they can buy the ingredients. If they celebrate the holidays they grew up with, they may be the only ones doing so. Or the people in their new country may celebrate the same holiday, such as Christmas, but they may celebrate it in a different way.

Moving to another country or culture can be a struggle. But new friends and neighbors can help by making them feel welcome.

checkout
Luke 2:6-20

Related verses:
Genesis 12:1;
Romans 12:13;
Hebrews 13:2;
1 Peter 4:9

he was named Jesus. This was the name the angel had given him before his mother became pregnant.

²²The time for making them pure came as it is written in the Law of Moses. So Joseph and Mary took Jesus to Jerusalem. There they presented him to the Lord. ²³In the Law of the Lord it says, "The first boy born in every family must be set apart for the Lord." (Exodus 13:2,12) ²⁴They also offered a sacrifice. They did it in keeping with the Law, which says, "a pair of doves or two young pigeons." (Leviticus 12:8)

²⁵In Jerusalem there was a man named Simeon. He was a good and godly man. He was waiting for God's promise to Israel to happen. The Holy Spirit was with him. ²⁶The Spirit had told Simeon that he would not die before he had seen the Lord's Christ. ²⁷The Spirit led him into the temple courtyard.

Then Jesus' parents brought the child in. They came to do for him what the Law required.

²⁸Simeon took Jesus in his arms and praised God. He said,

²⁹ "Lord, you are the King over all.
    Now let me, your servant, go in
        peace.
    That is what you promised.
³⁰ My eyes have seen your
        salvation.
³¹   You have prepared it in the sight
        of all people.
³² It is a light to be given to those
        who aren't Jews.
    It will bring glory to your people
        Israel."

³³The child's father and mother were amazed at what was said about him. ³⁴Then Simeon blessed them. He said to Mary, Jesus' mother, "This child is going to cause many people in Israel to fall and to rise. God has sent him. But many will speak against him. ³⁵The thoughts of many hearts will be known. A sword will wound your own soul too."

³⁶There was also a prophet named Anna. She was the daughter of Penuel from the tribe of Asher. Anna was very old. After getting married, she lived with her husband seven years. ³⁷Then she was a widow until she was 84. She never left the temple. She worshiped night and day, praying and going without eating.

³⁸Anna came up to Jesus' family at that very moment. She gave thanks to God. And she spoke about the child to all who were looking forward to the time when Jerusalem would be set free.

³⁹Joseph and Mary did everything the Law of the Lord required. Then they returned to Galilee. They went to their own town of Nazareth. ⁴⁰And the child grew and became strong. He was very wise. He was blessed by God's grace.

THE BOY JESUS AT THE TEMPLE

⁴¹Every year Jesus' parents went to Jerusalem for the Passover Feast. ⁴²When he was 12 years old, they went up to the Feast as usual.

⁴³After the Feast was over, his parents left to go back home. The boy Jesus stayed behind in Jerusalem. But they were not aware of it. ⁴⁴They thought he was somewhere in their group. So they traveled on for a day.

Then they began to look for him among their relatives and friends. ⁴⁵They did not find him. So they went back to Jerusalem to look for him. ⁴⁶After three days they found him in the temple courtyard. He was sitting with the teachers. He was listening to them and asking them questions. ⁴⁷Everyone who heard him was amazed at how much he understood. They also were amazed at his answers.

⁴⁸When his parents saw him, they were amazed. His mother said to him, "Son, why have you treated us like this? Your father and I have been worried about you. We have been looking for you everywhere."

⁴⁹"Why were you looking for me?" he asked. "Didn't you know I had to be in my Father's house?" ⁵⁰But they did not understand what he meant by that.

⁵¹Then he went back to Nazareth with them, and he obeyed them. But his mother kept all these things like a secret treasure in her heart. ⁵²Jesus became wiser and stronger. He also became more and more pleasing to God and to people.

JOHN THE BAPTIST PREPARES THE WAY

3 Tiberius Caesar had been ruling for 15 years. Pontius Pilate was governor of Judea. Herod was the ruler of Galilee. His brother Philip was the ruler of Iturea and Traconitis. Lysanias was ruler of Abilene. ²Annas and Caiaphas were high priests. At that time God's word came to John, son of Zechariah, in the desert. ³He went into all the countryside around the Jordan River. There he preached that people should be baptized and turn away from their sins. Then God would forgive them.

⁴Here is what is written in the scroll of the prophet Isaiah. It says,

"A messenger is calling out in the desert,
'Prepare the way for the Lord.
Make straight paths for him.
⁵Every valley will be filled in.
Every mountain and hill will be made level.
The crooked roads will become straight.
The rough ways will become smooth.
⁶And everyone will see God's salvation.' "   *(Isaiah 40:3–5)*

⁷John spoke to the crowds coming to be baptized by him. He said, "You are like a nest of poisonous snakes! Who warned you to escape the coming of God's anger? ⁸Produce fruit that shows you have turned away from your sins. And don't start saying to yourselves, 'Abraham is our father.' I tell you, God can raise up children for Abraham even from these stones. ⁹The ax is already lying at the roots of the trees. All the trees that don't produce good fruit will be cut down. They will be thrown into the fire."

¹⁰"Then what should we do?" the crowd asked.

¹¹John answered, "If you have extra clothes, you should share with those who have none. And if you have extra food, you should do the same."

¹²Tax collectors also came to be baptized. "Teacher," they asked, "what should we do?"

¹³"Don't collect any more than you are required to," John told them.

¹⁴Then some soldiers asked him, "And what should we do?"

John replied, "Don't force people to give you money. Don't bring false charges against people. Be happy with your pay."

¹⁵The people were waiting. They were expecting something. They were all wondering in their hearts if John might be the Christ.

¹⁶John answered them all, "I baptize you with water. But One who is more powerful than I am will come. I'm not good enough to untie the straps of his sandals. He will baptize you with the Holy Spirit and with fire. ¹⁷His pitchfork is in his hand to toss the straw away from his threshing floor. He will gather the wheat into his storeroom. But he will burn up the husks with fire that can't be put out."

¹⁸John said many other things to warn the people. He also preached the good news to them.

¹⁹But John found fault with Herod, the ruler of Galilee, because of Herodias. She was the wife of Herod's brother. John also spoke strongly to Herod about all the other evil things he had done. ²⁰So Herod locked him up in prison. He added this sin to all his others.

THE BAPTISM AND FAMILY LINE OF JESUS

²¹When all the people were being baptized, Jesus was baptized too. And as he was praying, heaven was opened. ²²The Holy Spirit came down on him in the form of a dove. A voice came from heaven. It said, "You are my Son, and I love you. I am very pleased with you."

²³Jesus was about 30 years old when he began his special work for God and others. It was thought that he was the son of Joseph.

Joseph was the son of Heli.
²⁴Heli was the son of Matthat.
Matthat was the son of Levi.
Levi was the son of Melki.
Melki was the son of Jannai.
Jannai was the son of Joseph.
²⁵Joseph was the son of Mattathias.

Mattathias was the son of Amos.

Amos was the son of Nahum.

Nahum was the son of Esli.

Esli was the son of Naggai.

²⁶Naggai was the son of Maath.

Maath was the son of Mattathias.

Mattathias was the son of Semein.

Semein was the son of Josech.

Josech was the son of Joda.

²⁷Joda was the son of Joanan.

Joanan was the son of Rhesa.

Rhesa was the son of Zerubbabel.

Zerubbabel was the son of Shealtiel.

Shealtiel was the son of Neri.

²⁸Neri was the son of Melki.

Melki was the son of Addi.

Addi was the son of Cosam.

Cosam was the son of Elmadam.

Elmadam was the son of Er.

²⁹Er was the son of Joshua.

Joshua was the son of Eliezer.

Eliezer was the son of Jorim.

Jorim was the son of Matthat.

Matthat was the son of Levi.

³⁰Levi was the son of Simeon.

Simeon was the son of Judah.

Judah was the son of Joseph.

Joseph was the son of Jonam.

Jonam was the son of Eliakim.

³¹Eliakim was the son of Melea.

Melea was the son of Menna.

Menna was the son of Mattatha.

Mattatha was the son of Nathan.

Nathan was the son of David.

³²David was the son of Jesse.

Jesse was the son of Obed.

Obed was the son of Boaz.

Boaz was the son of Salmon.

Salmon was the son of Nahshon.

³³Nahshon was the son of Amminadab.

Amminadab was the son of Ram.

Ram was the son of Hezron.

Hezron was the son of Perez.

Perez was the son of Judah.

³⁴Judah was the son of Jacob.

Jacob was the son of Isaac.

Isaac was the son of Abraham.

Abraham was the son of Terah.

Terah was the son of Nahor.

³⁵Nahor was the son of Serug.

Serug was the son of Reu.

Reu was the son of Peleg.

Peleg was the son of Eber.

Eber was the son of Shelah.

³⁶Shelah was the son of Cainan.

Cainan was the son of Arphaxad.

Arphaxad was the son of Shem.

Shem was the son of Noah.

Noah was the son of Lamech.

³⁷Lamech was the son of Methuselah.

Methuselah was the son of Enoch.

Enoch was the son of Jared.

Jared was the son of Mahalalel.

Mahalalel was the son of Kenan.

³⁸Kenan was the son of Enosh.

Enosh was the son of Seth.

Seth was the son of Adam.

Adam was the son of God.

JESUS IS TEMPTED

4 Jesus, full of the Holy Spirit, returned from the Jordan River. The Spirit led him into the desert. ²There the devil tempted him for 40 days.

Jesus ate nothing during that time. At the end of the 40 days, he was hungry.

³The devil said to him, "If you are the Son of God, tell this stone to become bread."

⁴Jesus answered, "It is written, 'Man doesn't live only on bread.' " *(Deuteronomy 8:3)*

⁵Then the devil led Jesus up to a high place. In an instant, he showed Jesus all the kingdoms of the world. ⁶He said to him, "I will give you all their authority and glory. It has been given to me, and I can give it to anyone I want to. ⁷So if you worship me, it will all be yours."

⁸Jesus answered, "It is written, 'Worship the Lord your God. He is the only one you should serve.' " *(Deuteronomy 6:13)*

⁹Then the devil led Jesus to Jerusalem. He had him stand on the highest point of the temple. "If you are the Son of God," he said, "throw yourself down from here. ¹⁰It is written,

" 'The Lord will command his
        angels to take good care of
        you.
[11] They will lift you up in their hands.
        Then you won't trip over a
        stone.' "   *(Psalm 91:11,12)*

[12]Jesus answered, "Scripture says,
'Do not put the Lord your God to the
test.' "   *(Deuteronomy 6:16)*
[13]When the devil finished all this
tempting, he left Jesus until a better
time.

JESUS IS NOT ACCEPTED
IN NAZARETH

[14]Jesus returned to Galilee in the
power of the Holy Spirit. News about
him spread through the whole countryside. [15]He taught in their synagogues, and everyone praised him.
[16]Jesus went to Nazareth, where he
had been brought up. On the Sabbath
day he went into the synagogue as he
usually did. And he stood up to read.
[17]The scroll of the prophet Isaiah
was handed to him. He unrolled it and
found the right place. There it is written,

[18] "The Spirit of the Lord is on me.
        He has anointed me
     to tell the good news to poor
        people.
   He has sent me to announce
        freedom for prisoners.
   He has sent me so that the blind
        will see again.
   He wants me to free those who are
        beaten down.
[19]   And he has sent me to announce
        the year when he will set his
        people free."   *(Isaiah 61:1,2)*

[20]Then Jesus rolled up the scroll. He
gave it back to the attendant and sat
down. The eyes of everyone in the synagogue were staring at him.
[21]He began by saying to them, "Today this passage of Scripture is coming
true as you listen."
[22]Everyone said good things about
him. They were amazed at the gracious words they heard from his lips.
"Isn't this Joseph's son?" they asked.
[23]Jesus said, "Here is a saying you
will certainly apply to me. 'Doctor,
heal yourself! Do the things here in

your hometown that we heard you did
in Capernaum.' "
[24]"What I'm about to tell you is true,"
he continued. "A prophet is not accepted in his hometown. [25]I tell you for
sure that there were many widows in
Israel in the days of Elijah. And there
had been no rain for three and a half
years. There wasn't enough food to eat
anywhere in the land. [26]But Elijah was
not sent to any of those widows. Instead, he was sent to a widow in Zarephath near Sidon. [27]And there were
many in Israel who had skin diseases
in the days of Elisha the prophet. But
not one of them was healed except
Naaman the Syrian."
[28]All the people in the synagogue
were very angry when they heard that.
[29]They got up and ran Jesus out of
town. They took him to the edge of the
hill on which the town was built. They
planned to throw him down the cliff.
[30]But Jesus walked right through the
crowd and went on his way.

JESUS DRIVES OUT
AN EVIL SPIRIT

[31]Then Jesus went to Capernaum, a
town in Galilee. On the Sabbath day he
began to teach the people. [32]They were
amazed at his teaching, because his
message had authority.
[33]In the synagogue there was a man
controlled by a demon, an evil spirit.
He cried out at the top of his voice.
[34]"Ha!" he said. "What do you want
with us, Jesus of Nazareth? Have you
come to destroy us? I know who you
are. You are the Holy One of God!"
[35]"Be quiet!" Jesus said firmly.
"Come out of him!"
   Then the demon threw the man
down in front of everybody. And it
came out without hurting him.
[36]All the people were amazed. They
said to each other, "What is this teaching? With authority and power he gives
orders to evil spirits. And they come
out!"
[37]The news about Jesus spread
throughout the whole area.

JESUS HEALS MANY PEOPLE

[38]Jesus left the synagogue and went
to the home of Simon. At that time,

Simon's mother-in-law was suffering from a high fever. So they asked Jesus to help her. ³⁹He bent over her and commanded the fever to leave, and it left her. She got up at once and began to serve them.

⁴⁰At sunset, people brought to Jesus all who were sick. He placed his hands on each one and healed them. ⁴¹Also, demons came out of many people. The demons shouted, "You are the Son of God!" But he commanded them to be quiet. He would not allow them to speak, because they knew he was the Christ.

⁴²At dawn, Jesus went out to a place where he could be by himself. The people went to look for him. When they found him, they tried to keep him from leaving them. ⁴³But he said, "I must announce the good news of God's kingdom to the other towns also. That is why I was sent." ⁴⁴And he kept on preaching in the synagogues of Judea.

JESUS CHOOSES THE FIRST DISCIPLES

5 One day Jesus was standing by the Sea of Galilee. The people crowded around him and listened to the word of God. ²Jesus saw two boats at the edge of the water. They had been left there by the fishermen, who were washing their nets. ³He got into the boat that belonged to Simon. Jesus asked him to go out a little way from shore. Then he sat down in the boat and taught the people.

⁴When he finished speaking, he turned to Simon. He said, "Go out into deep water. Let the nets down so you can catch some fish."

⁵Simon answered, "Master, we've worked hard all night and haven't caught anything. But because you say so, I will let down the nets."

⁶When they had done so, they caught a large number of fish. There were so many that their nets began to break. ⁷So they motioned to their partners in the other boat to come and help them. They came and filled both boats so full that they began to sink.

⁸When Simon Peter saw this, he fell at Jesus' knees. "Go away from me, Lord!" he said. "I am a sinful man!"

⁹He and everyone with him were amazed at the number of fish they had caught. ¹⁰So were James and John, the sons of Zebedee, who worked with Simon.

Then Jesus said to Simon, "Don't be afraid. From now on you will catch people."

¹¹So they pulled their boats up on shore. Then they left everything and followed him.

JESUS HEALS A MAN WITH A SKIN DISEASE

¹²While Jesus was in one of the towns, a man came along. He had a skin disease all over his body. When he saw Jesus, he fell with his face to the ground. He begged him, "Lord, if you are willing to make me 'clean,' you can do it."

¹³Jesus reached out his hand and touched the man. "I am willing to do it," he said. "Be 'clean'!" Right away the disease left him.

¹⁴Then Jesus ordered him, "Don't tell anyone. Go and show yourself to the priest. Offer the sacrifices that Moses commanded. It will be a witness to the priest and the people that you are 'clean.' "

¹⁵But the news about Jesus spread even more. So crowds of people came to hear him. They also came to be healed of their sicknesses. ¹⁶But Jesus often went away to be by himself and pray.

JESUS HEALS A MAN WHO COULD NOT WALK

¹⁷One day Jesus was teaching. Pharisees and teachers of the law were sitting there. They had come from every village of Galilee and from Judea and Jerusalem. They heard that the Lord had given Jesus the power to heal the sick.

¹⁸Some men came carrying a man who could not walk. He was lying on a mat. They tried to take him into the house to place him in front of Jesus. ¹⁹They could not find a way to do this because of the crowd. So they went up on the roof. Then they lowered the man on his mat through the opening in the roof tiles. They lowered him into

the middle of the crowd, right in front of Jesus.

[20]When Jesus saw that they had faith, he said, "Friend, your sins are forgiven."

[21]The Pharisees and the teachers of the law began to think, "Who is this fellow who says such an evil thing? Who can forgive sins but God alone?"

[22]Jesus knew what they were thinking. So he asked, "Why are you thinking these things in your hearts? [23]Is it easier to say, 'Your sins are forgiven'? Or to say, 'Get up and walk'? [24]I want you to know that the Son of Man has authority on earth to forgive sins." So he spoke to the man who could not walk. "I tell you," he said, "get up. Take your mat and go home."

[25]Right away, the man stood up in front of them. He took his mat and went home praising God. [26]Everyone was amazed and gave praise to God. They were filled with wonder. They said, "We have seen unusual things today."

JESUS CHOOSES LEVI

[27]After this, Jesus left the house. He saw a tax collector sitting at the tax booth. The man's name was Levi.

"Follow me," Jesus said to him.

[28]Levi got up, left everything and followed him.

[29]Then Levi gave a huge dinner for Jesus at his house. A large crowd of tax collectors and others were eating with them. [30]But the Pharisees and their teachers of the law complained to Jesus' disciples. They said, "Why do you eat and drink with tax collectors and 'sinners'?"

[31]Jesus answered them, "Those who are healthy don't need a doctor. Sick people do. [32]I have not come to get those who think they are right with God to follow me. I have come to get sinners to turn away from their sins."

JESUS IS ASKED ABOUT FASTING

[33]Some of the people who were there said to Jesus, "John's disciples often pray and go without eating. So do the disciples of the Pharisees. But yours go on eating and drinking."

[34]Jesus answered, "Can you make the guests of the groom go without eating while he is with them? [35]But the time will come when the groom will be taken away from them. In those days they will fast."

[36]Then Jesus gave them an example. He said, "People don't tear a patch from new clothes and sew it on old clothes. If they do, they will tear the new clothes. Also, the patch from the new clothes will not match the old clothes. [37]People don't pour new wine into old wineskins. If they do, the new wine will burst the skins. The wine will run out, and the wineskins will be destroyed. [38]No, new wine must be poured into new wineskins. [39]After people drink old wine, they don't want the new. They say, 'The old wine is better.'"

JESUS IS LORD OF THE SABBATH DAY

6 One Sabbath day Jesus was walking through the grainfields. His disciples began to break off some heads of grain. They rubbed them in their hands and ate them.

[2]Some of the Pharisees said, "It is against the Law to do this on the Sabbath. Why are you doing it?"

[3]Jesus answered them, "Haven't you ever read about what David did? He and his men were hungry. [4]He entered the house of God and took the holy bread. He ate the bread that only priests were allowed to eat. David also gave some to his men."

[5]Then Jesus said to them, "The Son of Man is Lord of the Sabbath day."

[6]On another Sabbath day, Jesus went into the synagogue and was teaching. A man whose right hand was weak and twisted was there. [7]The Pharisees and the teachers of the law were trying to find fault with Jesus. So they watched him closely. They wanted to see if he would heal on the Sabbath.

[8]But Jesus knew what they were thinking. He spoke to the man who had the weak and twisted hand. "Get up and stand in front of everyone," he said. So the man got up and stood there.

[9]Then Jesus said to them, "What does the Law say we should do on the

Sabbath day? Should we do good? Or should we do evil? Should we save life? Or should we destroy it?"

[10]He looked around at all of them.

Then he said to the man, "Stretch out your hand."

He did, and his hand was as good as new.

[11]But the Pharisees and the teachers of the law were very angry. They began to talk to each other about what they might do to Jesus.

JESUS CHOOSES THE TWELVE APOSTLES

[12]On one of those days, Jesus went out to a mountainside to pray. He spent the night praying to God. [13]When morning came, he called for his disciples to come to him. He chose 12 of them and made them apostles.

[14]Simon was one of them. Jesus gave him the name Peter. There were also Simon's brother Andrew, James, John, Philip and Bartholomew. [15]And there were Matthew, Thomas, and James, son of Alphaeus. There were also Simon who was called the Zealot [16]and Judas, son of James. Judas Iscariot was one of them too. He was the one who would later hand Jesus over to his enemies.

JESUS GIVES BLESSINGS AND WARNINGS

[17]Jesus went down the mountain with them and stood on a level place. A large crowd of his disciples was there. A large number of other people were there too. They came from all over Judea, including Jerusalem. They also came from the coast of Tyre and Sidon.

[18]They had all come to hear Jesus and to be healed of their sicknesses. People who were troubled by evil spirits were made well. [19]Everyone tried to touch Jesus. Power was coming from him and healing them all.

[20]Jesus looked at his disciples. He said to them,

"Blessed are you who are needy.
God's kingdom belongs to you.
[21]Blessed are you who are hungry now.
You will be satisfied.

Blessed are you who are sad now.
You will laugh.
[22]Blessed are you when people hate you,
when they have nothing to do with you
and say bad things about you,
and when they treat your name as something evil.
They do all this because you are followers of the Son of Man.

[23]"Their people treated the prophets the same way long ago. When these things happen to you, be glad and jump for joy. You will receive many blessings in heaven.

[24]"But how terrible it will be for you who are rich!
You have already had your easy life.
[25]How terrible for you who are well fed now!
You will go hungry.
How terrible for you who laugh now!
You will cry and be sad.
[26]How terrible for you when everyone says good things about you!
Their people treated the false prophets the same way long ago.

LOVE YOUR ENEMIES

[27]"But here is what I tell you who hear me. Love your enemies. Do good to those who hate you. [28]Bless those who call down curses on you. And pray for those who treat you badly.

[29]"Suppose someone hits you on one cheek. Turn your other cheek to him also. Suppose someone takes your coat. Don't stop him from taking your shirt.

[30]"Give to everyone who asks you. And if anyone takes what belongs to you, don't ask to get it back. [31]Do to others as you want them to do to you.

[32]"Suppose you love those who love you. Should anyone praise you for that? Even 'sinners' love those who love them. [33]And suppose you do good to those who are good to you. Should anyone praise you for that? Even 'sinners' do that. [34]And suppose you lend money to those who can pay you back.

Should anyone praise you for that? Even a 'sinner' lends to 'sinners,' expecting them to pay everything back. ³⁵"But love your enemies. Do good to them. Lend to them without expecting to get anything back. Then you will receive a lot in return. And you will be sons of the Most High God. He is kind to people who are evil and are not thankful. ³⁶So have mercy, just as your Father has mercy.

BE FAIR WHEN YOU JUDGE OTHERS

³⁷"If you do not judge others, then you will not be judged. If you do not find others guilty, then you will not be found guilty. Forgive, and you will be forgiven. ³⁸Give, and it will be given to you. A good amount will be poured into your lap. It will be pressed down, shaken together, and running over. The same amount you give will be measured out to you."

³⁹Jesus also gave them another example. He asked, "Can a blind person lead another blind person? Won't they both fall into a pit? ⁴⁰Students are not better than their teachers. But everyone who is completely trained will be like his teacher.

⁴¹"You look at the bit of sawdust in your friend's eye. But you pay no attention to the piece of wood in your own eye. ⁴²How can you say to your friend, 'Let me take the bit of sawdust out of your eye'? How can you say this while there is a piece of wood in your own eye? You pretender! First take the piece of wood out of your own eye. Then you will be able to see clearly to take the bit of sawdust out of your friend's eye.

A TREE AND ITS FRUIT

⁴³"A good tree doesn't bear bad fruit. And a bad tree doesn't bear good fruit. ⁴⁴You can tell each tree by the kind of fruit it bears. People do not pick figs from thorns. And they don't pick grapes from bushes. ⁴⁵"A good man says good things.

Is it stealing to borrow someone else's stuff without asking?

As long as the person has given permission for you to take his or her stuff without asking, no. But try to show respect for the owner of everything you want to borrow. What if the owner needed it right away or had promised it to someone else? Leave a note if the person has told you something like, "Use it anytime you want," and he or she is not around to ask. You want the person to know that it was not stolen and that *you* borrowed it. Again, this shows respect for your friend. Also, do not steal something and then make the excuse that you were "just borrowing it." Be an honest person who respects others and their property.

checkout Luke 6:31

JASON'S IMAGINATION

HEY! THAT'S MY SUIT

Related verse: 1 Peter 2:17

These come from the good that is put away in his heart. An evil man says evil things. These come from the evil that is put away in his heart. Their mouths say everything that is in their hearts.

THE WISE AND FOOLISH BUILDERS

46"Why do you call me, 'Lord, Lord,' and still don't do what I say? 47Some people come to me and listen to me and do what I say. I will show you what they are like. 48They are like someone who builds a house. He digs down deep and sets it on solid rock. When a flood comes, the river rushes against the house. But the water can't shake it. The house is well built.

49"But here is what happens when people listen to my words and do not obey them. They are like someone who builds a house on soft ground instead of solid rock. The moment the river rushes against that house, it falls down. It is completely destroyed."

A ROMAN COMMANDER HAS FAITH

7 Jesus finished saying all those things to the people. Then he entered Capernaum. 2There the servant of a Roman commander was sick and about to die. His master thought highly of him. 3The commander heard about Jesus. So he sent some elders of the Jews to him. He told them to ask Jesus to come and heal his servant.

4They came to Jesus and begged him, "This man deserves to have you do this. 5He loves our nation and has built our synagogue." 6So Jesus went with them.

When Jesus came near the house, the Roman commander sent friends to him. He told them to say, "Lord, don't trouble yourself. I am not good enough to have you come into my house. 7That is why I did not even think I was fit to come to you. But just say the word, and my servant will be

KIDS' QUESTION

How can I love my enemies?

Do kind things for them, wish them well and pray for them. Forgive them and do not curse them when they do mean things to you. Treat them like a friend rather than fighting back or trying to hurt them. If that sounds hard to do, you are right. But that is how you turn enemies into friends. Enemies do not like us. They are out to hurt us. They may push us, hit us, call us names and try to get us into trouble. We do not have to like what they do to us. But we can love them with the help of God's Holy Spirit. After all, that is what God did for us. Who knows what may happen? Your enemies today may turn out to be your friends tomorrow.

checkout Luke 6:35,36

Related verses:
Romans 12:17–21;
1 John 3:16–19

healed. [8]I myself am a man who is under authority. And I have soldiers who obey my orders. I tell this one, 'Go,' and he goes. I tell that one, 'Come,' and he comes. I say to my servant, 'Do this,' and he does it."

[9]When Jesus heard this, he was amazed at him. He turned to the crowd that was following him. He said, "I tell you, even in Israel I have not found anyone whose faith is so strong."

[10]Then the men who had been sent to Jesus returned to the house. They found that the servant was healed.

JESUS RAISES A WIDOW'S SON FROM THE DEAD

[11]Some time later, Jesus went to a town called Nain. His disciples and a large crowd went along with him. [12]He approached the town gate. Just then, a dead person was being carried out. He was the only son of his mother. She was a widow. A large crowd from the town was with her.

[13]When the Lord saw her, he felt sorry for her. So he said, "Don't cry."

[14]Then he went up and touched the coffin. Those carrying it stood still. Jesus said, "Young man, I say to you, get up!"

[15]The dead man sat up and began to talk. Then Jesus gave him back to his mother.

[16]The people were all filled with wonder and praised God. "A great prophet has appeared among us," they said. "God has come to help his people." [17]This news about Jesus spread all through Judea and the whole country.

JESUS AND JOHN THE BAPTIST

[18]John's disciples told him about all these things. So he chose two of them. [19]He sent them to the Lord. They were

Why should I give money to the church to pay for the things I don't exactly need?

Other people have needs that you do not have. It is important for you to give so they can have their needs met. Churches give money, food and clothing to missions and to people in need. If you walk to church, you do not need a parking lot. But the people who drive to church do need it. If your family does not have any babies, you do not need the nursery. But the families that have babies do. Maybe, though, you would really miss a program or service if your church didn't offer it anymore. Or maybe you do not need it right now but you will in the future.

Support the church with your prayers, money and work. That way, everybody will have their needs met.

Related verse:
2 Corinthians 9:12

checkout
Luke 6:38

PLEASE GIVE FOR THE NEW BIRD SANCTUARY

to ask Jesus, "Are you the one who was supposed to come? Or should we look for someone else?"

20The men came to Jesus. They said, "John the Baptist sent us to ask you, 'Are you the one who was supposed to come? Or should we look for someone else?' "

21At that very time Jesus healed many people. They had illnesses, sicknesses and evil spirits. He also gave sight to many who were blind. 22So Jesus replied to the messengers, "Go back to John. Tell him what you have seen and heard. Blind people receive sight. Disabled people walk. Those who have skin diseases are healed. Deaf people hear. Those who are dead are raised to life. And the good news is preached to those who are poor. 23Blessed are those who do not give up their faith because of me."

24So John's messengers left. Then Jesus began to speak to the crowd about John. He said, "What did you go out into the desert to see? Tall grass waving in the wind? 25If not, what did you go out to see? A man dressed in fine clothes? No. Those who wear fine clothes and have many expensive things are in palaces. 26Then what did you go out to see? A prophet? Yes, I tell you, and more than a prophet.

27"He is the one written about in Scripture. It says,

" 'I will send my messenger ahead of you.
He will prepare your way for you.' *(Malachi 3:1)*

28I tell you, no one more important than John has ever been born. But the least important person in God's kingdom is more important than he is."

29All the people who heard Jesus' words agreed that God's way was right. Even the tax collectors agreed. These people had all been baptized by John.

Why do we have to respect teachers?

The Bible says that God expects his people to respect those in authority over them. That includes teachers. To do their best, teachers need the respect of their students. This means being polite and kind to them, listening and doing what they say. If you don't respect your teacher, you probably won't learn as much.

checkout
Luke 6:40

Related verse:
Romans 13:3

GOOD MORNING, SIR!

[30]But the Pharisees and the authorities on the law did not accept God's purpose for themselves. They had not been baptized by John.

[31]"What can I compare today's people to?" Jesus asked. "What are they like? [32]They are like children sitting in the market place and calling out to each other. They say,

" 'We played a flute for you.
But you didn't dance.
We sang a funeral song.
But you didn't cry.'

[33]"That is how it has been with John the Baptist. When he came to you, he didn't eat bread or drink wine. And you say, 'He has a demon.' [34]But when the Son of Man came, he ate and drank as you do. And you say, 'This fellow is always eating and drinking far too much. He's a friend of tax collectors and "sinners." ' [35]All who follow wisdom prove that wisdom is right."

A SINFUL WOMAN POURS PERFUME ON JESUS

[36]One of the Pharisees invited Jesus to have dinner with him. So he went to the Pharisee's house. He took his place at the table. [37]There was a woman in that town who had lived a sinful life. She learned that Jesus was eating at the Pharisee's house. So she came with a special sealed jar of perfume. [38]She stood behind Jesus and cried at his feet. She began to wet his feet with her tears. Then she wiped them with her hair. She kissed them and poured perfume on them.

[39]The Pharisee who had invited Jesus saw this. He said to himself, "If this man were a prophet, he would know who is touching him. He would know what kind of woman she is. She is a sinner!"

[40]Jesus answered him, "Simon, I have something to tell you."

"Tell me, teacher," he said.

[41]"Two people owed money to a certain lender. One owed him 500 silver coins. The other owed him 50 silver coins. [42]Neither of them had the money to pay him back. So he let them go without paying. Which of them will love him more?"

[43]Simon replied, "I suppose the one who owed the most money."

"You are right," Jesus said.

[44]Then he turned toward the woman. He said to Simon, "Do you see this woman? I came into your house. You did not give me any water to wash my feet. But she wet my feet with her tears and wiped them with her hair. [45]You did not give me a kiss. But this woman has not stopped kissing my feet since I came in. [46]You did not put any olive oil on my head. But she has poured perfume on my feet. [47]So I tell you this. Her many sins have been forgiven. She has loved a lot. But the one who has been forgiven little loves only a little."

[48]Then Jesus said to her, "Your sins are forgiven."

[49]The other guests began to talk about this among themselves. They said, "Who is this who even forgives sins?"

[50]Jesus said to the woman, "Your faith has saved you. Go in peace."

THE STORY OF THE FARMER

8 After this, Jesus traveled around from one town and village to another. He announced the good news of God's kingdom. The Twelve were with him. [2]So were some women who had been healed of evil spirits and sicknesses. One was Mary Magdalene. Seven demons had come out of her. [3]Another was Joanna, the wife of Cuza. He was the manager of Herod's household. Susanna and many others were there also. These women were helping to support Jesus and the Twelve with their own money.

[4]A large crowd gathered together. People came to Jesus from town after town. As they did, he told a story. He said, [5]"A farmer went out to plant his seed. He scattered the seed on the ground. Some fell on a path. People walked on it, and the birds of the air ate it up. [6]Some seed fell on rocky places. When it grew, the plants dried up because they had no water. [7]Other seed fell among thorns. The thorns grew up with it and crowded out the plants. [8]Still other seed fell on good soil. It grew up and produced a crop 100 times more than the farmer planted."

When Jesus said this, he called out, "Those who have ears should listen."

⁹His disciples asked him what the story meant.

¹⁰He said, "You have been given the chance to understand the secrets of God's kingdom. But to outsiders I speak by using stories. In that way,

" 'They see, but they will not know what they are seeing.
They hear, but they will not understand what they are hearing.'   *(Isaiah 6:9)*

¹¹"Here is what the story means. The seed is God's message. ¹²People on the path are those who hear. But then the devil comes. He takes away the message from their hearts. He does it so they won't believe. Then they can't be saved. ¹³Those on the rock are the ones who hear the message and receive it with joy. But they have no roots. They believe for a while. But when they are put to the test, they fall away from the faith. ¹⁴The seed that fell among thorns stands for those who hear the message. But as they go on their way, they are choked by life's worries, riches and pleasures. So they do not reach full growth.

¹⁵"But the seed on good soil stands for those with an honest and good heart. They hear the message. They keep it in their hearts. They remain faithful and produce a good crop.

A LAMP ON A STAND

¹⁶"People do not light a lamp and then hide it in a jar or put it under a bed. Instead, they put it on a stand. Then those who come in can see its light. ¹⁷What is hidden will be seen. And what is out of sight will be brought into the open and made known.

¹⁸"So be careful how you listen. If you have something, you will be given more. If you have nothing, even what you think you have will be taken away from you."

JESUS' MOTHER AND BROTHERS

¹⁹Jesus' mother and brothers came to see him. But they could not get near

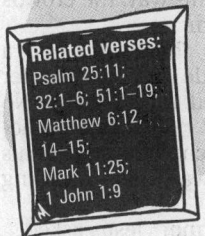

Do we have to pray to be forgiven?

We have God's promise that he will always forgive us if we come to him truly sorry for what we have done. That is what the word *confession* means—that we tell God what we have done wrong to forgive us. Because only God can forgive sins, we need to confess them to him in order to be truly forgiven.

checkout

Luke 7:47–49

Related verses:
Psalm 25:11;
32:1–6; 51:1–19;
Matthew 6:12,
14–15;
Mark 11:25;
1 John 1:9

DEAR GOD, PLEASE FORGIVE ME FOR THE THINGS I DID WRONG TODAY. AND WOULD IT BE TOO MUCH TO ASK YOU TO FORGIVE ME IN ADVANCE FOR ALL THE MISTAKES I'LL PROBABLY MAKE TOMORROW?

him because of the crowd. ²⁰Someone told him, "Your mother and brothers are standing outside. They want to see you."

²¹He replied, "My mother and brothers are those who hear God's word and do what it says."

JESUS CALMS THE STORM

²²One day Jesus said to his disciples, "Let's go over to the other side of the lake." So they got into a boat and left.

²³As they sailed, Jesus fell asleep. A storm came down on the lake. It was so bad that the boat was about to sink. They were in great danger.

²⁴The disciples went and woke Jesus up. They said, "Master! Master! We're going to drown!"

He got up and ordered the wind and the huge waves to stop. The storm quieted down. It was completely calm.

²⁵"Where is your faith?" he asked his disciples.

They were amazed and full of fear. They asked one another, "Who is this? He commands even the winds and the waves, and they obey him."

JESUS HEALS A MAN CONTROLLED BY DEMONS

²⁶Jesus and his disciples sailed to the area of the Gerasenes across the lake from Galilee. ²⁷When Jesus stepped on shore, he was met by a man from the town. The man was controlled by demons. For a long time he had not worn clothes or lived in a house. He lived in the tombs.

²⁸When he saw Jesus, he cried out and fell at his feet. He shouted at the top of his voice, "Jesus, Son of the Most High God, what do you want with me? I beg you, don't hurt me!"

²⁹This was because Jesus had commanded the evil spirit to come out of the man. Many times the spirit had taken hold of him. His hands and feet were chained, and he was kept under guard. But he had broken his chains. And then the demon had forced him to go out into lonely places in the countryside.

³⁰Jesus asked him, "What is your name?"

"Legion," he replied, because many demons had gone into him. ³¹And they begged Jesus again and again not to order them to go into the Abyss.

³²A large herd of pigs was feeding there on the hillside. The demons begged Jesus to let them go into the pigs. And he allowed it.

³³When the demons came out of the man, they went into the pigs. Then the herd rushed down the steep bank. They ran into the lake and drowned.

³⁴Those who were tending the pigs saw what had happened. They ran off and reported it in the town and countryside. ³⁵The people went out to see what had happened.

Then they came to Jesus. They found the man who was now free of the demons. He was sitting at Jesus' feet. He was dressed and thinking clearly. All this made the people afraid.

³⁶Those who had seen it told the others how the man who had been controlled by demons was now healed. ³⁷Then all the people who lived in the area of the Gerasenes asked Jesus to leave them. They were filled with fear. So he got into the boat and left.

³⁸The man who was now free of the demons begged to go with him. But Jesus sent him away. He said to him, ³⁹"Return home and tell how much God has done for you."

So the man went away. He told people all over town how much Jesus had done for him.

A DYING GIRL AND A SUFFERING WOMAN

⁴⁰When Jesus returned, a crowd welcomed him. They were all expecting him.

⁴¹Then a man named Jairus came. He was a synagogue ruler. He fell at Jesus' feet. He begged Jesus to come to his house. ⁴²His only daughter was dying. She was about 12 years old.

As Jesus was on his way, the crowds almost crushed him.

⁴³A woman was there who had a sickness that made her bleed. Her sickness had lasted for 12 years. No one could heal her. ⁴⁴She came up behind Jesus and touched the edge of his clothes. Right away her bleeding stopped.

⁴⁵"Who touched me?" Jesus asked.

They all said they didn't do it. Then Peter said, "Master, the people are crowding and pushing against you."

⁴⁶But Jesus said, "Someone touched me. I know that power has gone out from me."

⁴⁷The woman realized that people would notice her. Shaking with fear, she came and fell at his feet. In front of everyone, she told why she had touched him. She also told how she had been healed in an instant.

⁴⁸Then he said to her, "Dear woman, your faith has healed you. Go in peace."

⁴⁹While Jesus was still speaking, someone came from the house of Jairus. Jairus was the synagogue ruler. "Your daughter is dead," the messenger said. "Don't bother the teacher anymore."

⁵⁰Hearing this, Jesus said to Jairus, "Don't be afraid. Just believe. She will be healed."

⁵¹When he arrived at the house of Jairus, he did not let everyone go in with him. He took only Peter, John and James, and the child's father and mother.

⁵²During this time, all the people were crying and sobbing loudly over the child. "Stop crying!" Jesus said. "She is not dead. She is sleeping."

⁵³They laughed at him. They knew she was dead.

⁵⁴But he took her by the hand and said, "My child, get up!"

⁵⁵Her spirit returned, and right away she stood up. Then Jesus told them to give her something to eat. ⁵⁶Her parents were amazed. But Jesus ordered them not to tell anyone what had happened.

JESUS SENDS OUT THE TWELVE DISCIPLES

9 Jesus called the Twelve together. He gave them power and authority to drive out all demons and to heal sicknesses. ²Then he sent them out to preach about God's kingdom and to heal those who were sick.

³He told them, "Don't take anything for the journey. Do not take a walking stick or a bag. Do not take any bread, money or extra clothes. ⁴When you are invited into a house, stay there until you leave town. ⁵Some people may not welcome you. If they don't, shake the dust off your feet when you leave their town. This will be a witness against the people living there."

⁶So the Twelve left. They went from village to village. They preached the good news and healed people everywhere.

⁷Now Herod, the ruler of Galilee, heard about everything that was going on. He was bewildered, because some were saying that John the Baptist had been raised from the dead. ⁸Others were saying that Elijah had appeared. Still others were saying that a prophet of long ago had come back to life. ⁹But Herod said, "I had John's head cut off. So who is it that I hear such things about?" And he tried to see Jesus.

JESUS FEEDS THE FIVE THOUSAND

¹⁰The apostles returned. They told Jesus what they had done. Then he took them with him. They went off by themselves to a town called Bethsaida. ¹¹But the crowds learned about it and followed Jesus. He welcomed them and spoke to them about God's kingdom. He also healed those who needed to be healed.

¹²Late in the afternoon the Twelve came to him. They said, "Send the crowd away. They can go to the nearby villages and countryside. There they can find food and a place to stay. There is nothing here."

¹³Jesus replied, "You give them something to eat."

The disciples answered, "We have only five loaves of bread and two fish. We would have to go and buy food for all this crowd." ¹⁴About 5,000 men were there.

But Jesus said to his disciples, "Have them sit down in groups of about 50 each." ¹⁵The disciples did so, and everyone sat down.

¹⁶Jesus took the five loaves and the two fish. He looked up to heaven and gave thanks. He broke them into pieces. Then he gave them to the disciples to set in front of the people. ¹⁷All of them ate and were satisfied. The disciples picked up 12 baskets of leftover pieces.

PETER SAYS THAT JESUS IS THE CHRIST

[18]One day Jesus was praying alone. Only his disciples were with him. He asked them, "Who do the crowds say I am?"

[19]They replied, "Some say John the Baptist. Others say Elijah. Still others say that one of the prophets of long ago has come back to life."

[20]"But what about you?" he asked. "Who do you say I am?"

Peter answered, "The Christ of God."

[21]Jesus strongly warned them not to tell this to anyone. [22]He said, "The Son of Man must suffer many things. The elders will not accept him. The chief priests and teachers of the law will not accept him either. He must be killed and on the third day rise from the dead."

[23]Then he said to all of them, "If anyone wants to follow me, he must say no to himself. He must pick up his cross every day and follow me. [24]If he wants to save his life, he will lose it. But if he loses his life for me, he will save it. [25]What good is it if someone gains the whole world but loses or gives up his very self?

[26]"Suppose you are ashamed of me and my words. The Son of Man will come in his glory and in the glory of the Father and the holy angels. Then he will be ashamed of you.

[27]"What I'm about to tell you is true. Some who are standing here will not die before they see God's kingdom."

JESUS' APPEARANCE IS CHANGED

[28]About eight days after Jesus said this, he went up on a mountain to pray. He took Peter, John and James with him.

[29]As he was praying, the appearance of his face changed. His clothes became as bright as a flash of lightning. [30]Two men, Moses and Elijah, [31]appeared in shining glory. Jesus and the two of them talked together. They spoke about his coming death. He was going to die soon in Jerusalem.

[32]Peter and his companions had been very sleepy. But then they became completely awake. They saw Jesus' glory and the two men standing with him.

[33]As the men were leaving Jesus, Peter spoke up. "Master," he said to him, "it is good for us to be here. Let us put up three shelters. One will be for you, one for Moses, and one for Elijah." He didn't really know what he was saying.

[34]While Jesus was speaking, a cloud appeared. It surrounded them. The disciples were afraid as they entered the cloud. [35]A voice came from the cloud. It said, "This is my Son, and I have chosen him. Listen to him." [36]When the voice had spoken, they found that Jesus was alone.

The disciples kept quiet about this. They didn't tell anyone at that time what they had seen.

JESUS HEALS A BOY WHO HAD AN EVIL SPIRIT

[37]The next day Jesus and those who were with him came down from the mountain. A large crowd met Jesus.

[38]A man in the crowd called out. "Teacher," he said, "I beg you to look at my son. He is my only child. [39]A spirit takes hold of him, and he suddenly screams. It throws him into fits so that he foams at the mouth. It hardly ever leaves him. It is destroying him. [40]I begged your disciples to drive it out. But they couldn't do it."

[41]"You unbelieving and evil people!" Jesus replied. "How long do I have to stay with you? How long do I have to put up with you?"

Then he said to the man, "Bring your son here."

[42]Even while the boy was coming, the demon threw him into a fit. The boy fell to the ground. But Jesus ordered the evil spirit to leave the boy. Then Jesus healed him and gave him back to his father. [43]They were all amazed at God's greatness.

Everyone was wondering about all that Jesus did. Then Jesus said to his disciples, [44]"Listen carefully to what I am about to tell you. The Son of Man is going to be handed over to men." [45]But they didn't understand what this meant. That was because it was hidden from them. And they were afraid to ask Jesus about it.

WHO IS THE MOST IMPORTANT PERSON?

⁴⁶The disciples began to argue about which one of them would be the most important person. ⁴⁷Jesus knew what they were thinking. So he took a little child and had the child stand beside him.

⁴⁸Then he spoke to them. "Anyone who welcomes this little child in my name welcomes me," he said. "And anyone who welcomes me welcomes the One who sent me. The least important person among all of you is the most important."

⁴⁹"Master," said John, "we saw a man driving out demons in your name. We tried to stop him, because he is not one of us."

⁵⁰"Do not stop him," Jesus said. "Anyone who is not against you is for you."

THE SAMARITANS DO NOT WELCOME JESUS

⁵¹The time grew near for Jesus to be taken up to heaven. So he made up his mind to go to Jerusalem. ⁵²He sent messengers on ahead. They went into a Samaritan village to get things ready for him. ⁵³But the people there did not welcome Jesus. That was because he was heading for Jerusalem.

⁵⁴The disciples James and John saw this. They asked, "Lord, do you want us to call down fire from heaven to destroy them?"

⁵⁵But Jesus turned and commanded them not to do it. ⁵⁶They went on to another village.

IT COSTS TO FOLLOW JESUS

⁵⁷Once Jesus and those who were with him were walking along the road. A man said to Jesus, "I will follow you no matter where you go."

⁵⁸Jesus replied, "Foxes have holes. Birds of the air have nests. But the Son of Man has no place to lay his head."

⁵⁹He said to another man, "Follow me."

But the man replied, "Lord, first let me go and bury my father."

⁶⁰Jesus said to him, "Let dead people bury their own dead. You go and tell others about God's kingdom."

⁶¹Still another man said, "I will follow you, Lord. But first let me go back and say good-by to my family."

⁶²Jesus replied, "Suppose you start to plow and then look back. If you do,

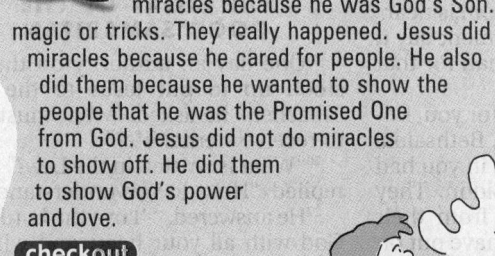

How did Jesus do miracles?

A miracle is something only God can do. Jesus was able to do miracles because he was God's Son. Jesus' miracles were not magic or tricks. They really happened. Jesus did miracles because he cared for people. He also did them because he wanted to show the people that he was the Promised One from God. Jesus did not do miracles to show off. He did them to show God's power and love.

checkout
Luke 9:42,43

Related verses:
John 20:30,31

you are not fit for service in God's kingdom."

JESUS SENDS OUT THE SEVENTY-TWO

10 After this the Lord appointed 72 others. He sent them out two by two ahead of him. They went to every town and place where he was about to go.

²He told them, "The harvest is huge, but the workers are few. So ask the Lord of the harvest to send out workers into his harvest field.

³"Go! I am sending you out like lambs among wolves. ⁴Do not take a purse or bag or sandals. And don't greet anyone on the road.

⁵"When you enter a house, first say, 'May this house be blessed with peace.' ⁶If someone there loves peace, your blessing of peace will rest on him. If not, it will return to you. ⁷Stay in that house. Eat and drink anything they give you. Workers are worthy of their pay. Do not move around from house to house.

⁸"When you enter a town and are welcomed, eat what is set down in front of you. ⁹Heal the sick people who are there. Tell them, 'God's kingdom is near you.'

¹⁰"But what if you enter a town and are not welcomed? Then go into its streets and say, ¹¹'We wipe off even the dust of your town that sticks to our feet. We do it to show that God isn't pleased with you. But here is what you can be sure of. God's kingdom is near.'

¹²"I tell you this. On judgment day it will be easier for Sodom than for that town.

¹³"How terrible it will be for you, Korazin! How terrible for you, Bethsaida! Suppose the miracles done in you had been done in Tyre and Sidon. They would have turned away from their sins long ago. They would have put on black clothes. They would have sat down in ashes. ¹⁴On judgment day it will be easier for Tyre and Sidon than for you.

¹⁵"And what about you, Capernaum? Will you be lifted up to heaven? No! You will go down to the place of the dead.

¹⁶"Anyone who listens to you listens to me. Anyone who does not accept you does not accept me. And anyone who does not accept me does not accept the One who sent me."

¹⁷The 72 returned with joy. They said, "Lord, even the demons obey us when we speak in your name."

¹⁸Jesus replied, "I saw Satan fall like lightning from heaven. ¹⁹I have given you authority to walk all over snakes and scorpions. You will be able to destroy all the power of the enemy. Nothing will harm you. ²⁰But do not be glad when the evil spirits obey you. Instead, be glad that your names are written in heaven."

²¹At that time Jesus was full of joy through the Holy Spirit. He said, "I praise you, Father. You are Lord of heaven and earth. You have hidden these things from the wise and educated. But you have shown them to little children. Yes, Father. This is what you wanted.

²²"My Father has given all things to me. The Father is the only one who knows who the Son is. And the only ones who know the Father are the Son and those to whom the Son chooses to make the Father known."

²³Then Jesus turned to his disciples. He said to them in private, "Blessed are the eyes that see what you see. ²⁴I tell you, many prophets and kings wanted to see what you see. But they didn't see it. They wanted to hear what you hear. But they didn't hear it."

THE STORY OF THE GOOD SAMARITAN

²⁵One day an authority on the law stood up to put Jesus to the test. "Teacher," he asked, "what must I do to receive eternal life?"

²⁶"What is written in the Law?" Jesus replied. "How do you understand it?"

²⁷He answered, " 'Love the Lord your God with all your heart and with all your soul. Love him with all your strength and with all your mind.' *(Deuteronomy 6:5)* And, 'Love your neighbor as you love yourself.' " *(Leviticus 19:18)*

²⁸"You have answered correctly," Jesus replied. "Do that, and you will live."

²⁹But the man wanted to make him-

self look good. So he asked Jesus, "And who is my neighbor?"

³⁰Jesus replied, "A man was going down from Jerusalem to Jericho. Robbers attacked him. They stripped off his clothes and beat him. Then they went away, leaving him almost dead. ³¹A priest happened to be going down that same road. When he saw the man, he passed by on the other side. ³²A Levite also came by. When he saw the man, he passed by on the other side too.

³³But a Samaritan came to the place where the man was. When he saw the man, he felt sorry for him. ³⁴He went to him, poured olive oil and wine on his wounds and bandaged them. Then he put the man on his own donkey. He took him to an inn and took care of him. ³⁵The next day he took out two silver coins. He gave them to the owner of the inn. 'Take care of him,' he said. 'When I return, I will pay you back for any extra expense you may have.'

³⁶"Which of the three do you think was a neighbor to the man who was attacked by robbers?"

³⁷The authority on the law replied, "The one who felt sorry for him."

Jesus told him, "Go and do as he did."

JESUS AT THE HOME OF MARTHA AND MARY

³⁸Jesus and his disciples went on their way. Jesus came to a village where a woman named Martha lived. She welcomed him into her home. ³⁹She had a sister named Mary.

Mary sat at the Lord's feet listening to what he said. ⁴⁰But Martha was busy with all the things that had to be done. She came to Jesus and said, "Lord, my sister has left me to do the work by myself. Don't you care? Tell her to help me!"

⁴¹"Martha, Martha," the Lord answered. "You are worried and upset about many things. ⁴²But only one thing is needed. Mary has chosen what is better. And it will not be taken away from her."

Why did God make Satan if God knew Satan would make sin?

God created all people and all angels with the ability to choose whether to obey him. God is praised when people and angels obey him. Satan chose to disobey God and fight against Jesus' good work in this world. God makes everything good. That includes the people and angels who have the choice of whether to serve God.

Satan tries to get people to choose to disobey. God has allowed Satan to have freedom now. But in the end God will defeat Satan and punish him.

checkout Luke 10:18

Related verses:
Revelation
20:7–10

JESUS TEACHES ABOUT PRAYER

11 One day Jesus was praying in a certain place. When he finished, one of his disciples spoke to him. "Lord," he said, "teach us to pray, just as John taught his disciples."

²Jesus said to them, "When you pray, this is what you should say.

" 'Father,
may your name be honored.
May your kingdom come.
³Give us each day our daily bread.
⁴Forgive us our sins,
    as we also forgive everyone who
       sins against us.
Keep us from falling into sin when
    we are tempted.' "

⁵Then Jesus said to them, "Suppose someone has a friend. He goes to him at midnight. He says, 'Friend, lend me three loaves of bread. ⁶A friend of mine on a journey has come to stay with me. I have nothing for him to eat.'

⁷"Then the one inside answers, 'Don't bother me. The door is already locked. My children are with me in bed. I can't get up and give you anything.'

⁸"I tell you, that person will not get up. And he won't give the man bread just because he is his friend. But because the man keeps on asking, he will get up. He will give him as much as he needs.

⁹"So here is what I say to you. Ask, and it will be given to you. Search, and you will find. Knock, and the door will be opened to you. ¹⁰Everyone who asks will receive. He who searches will find. And the door will be opened to the one who knocks.

¹¹"Fathers, suppose your son asks for a fish. Which of you will give him a snake instead? ¹²Or suppose he asks for an egg. Which of you will give him a scorpion? ¹³Even though you are evil, you know how to give good gifts to your children. How much more will your Father who is in heaven give the Holy Spirit to those who ask him!"

JESUS AND BEELZEBUB

¹⁴Jesus was driving out a demon. The man who had the demon could not speak. When the demon left, the man began to speak. The crowd was amazed.

¹⁵But some of them said, "Jesus is driving out demons by the power of

KIDS' QUESTion

Will I ever get a demon?

It is true that some people have demons in them. But demons can only enter people who let them and who are not close to God. It is easy to get the idea from watching television and hearing kids talk that demons can take over people's lives whenever they want. But that is not true. And never forget that God is much more powerful than Satan or any of the demons. He loves us and will protect us.

checkout
Luke 10:19,20

Related verses:
Romans 8:38,39;
1 John 3:8

Beelzebub, the prince of demons."
[16]Others put Jesus to the test by asking for a miraculous sign from heaven.

[17]Jesus knew what they were thinking. So he said to them, "Any kingdom that fights against itself will be destroyed. A family that is divided against itself will fall. [18]If Satan fights against himself, how can his kingdom stand?

"I say this because of what you claim. You say I drive out demons by the power of Beelzebub. [19]Suppose I do drive out demons with Beelzebub's help. With whose help do your followers drive them out? So then, they will be your judges. [20]But suppose I drive out demons with the help of God's powerful finger. Then God's kingdom has come to you.

[21]"When a strong man is completely armed and guards his house, what he owns is safe. [22]But when someone stronger attacks, he is overpowered. The attacker takes away the armor the man had trusted in. Then he divides up what he has stolen.

[23]"Anyone who is not with me is against me. Anyone who does not gather sheep with me scatters them.

[24]"What happens when an evil spirit comes out of a man? It goes through dry areas looking for a place to rest. But it doesn't find it. Then it says, 'I will return to the house I left.' [25]When it arrives there, it finds the house swept clean and put in order. [26]Then the evil spirit goes and takes seven other spirits more evil than itself. They go in and live there. That man is worse off than before."

[27]As Jesus was saying these things, a woman in the crowd called out. She shouted, "Blessed is the mother who gave you birth and nursed you."

[28]He replied, "Instead, blessed are those who hear God's word and obey it."

THE MIRACULOUS SIGN OF JONAH

[29]As the crowds grew larger, Jesus spoke to them. "The people of today are evil," he said. "They ask for a miraculous sign from God. But none will be given except the sign of Jonah. [30]He was a sign from God to the people of Nineveh. In the same way, the Son of Man will be a sign from God to the people of today.

[31]"The Queen of the South will stand up on judgment day with the men now living. And she will prove that they are guilty. She came from very far away to listen to Solomon's wisdom. And now one who is more important than Solomon is here.

[32]"The men of Nineveh will stand up on judgment day with the people now living. And the Ninevites will prove that those people are guilty. The men of Nineveh turned away from their sins when Jonah preached to them. And now one who is more important than Jonah is here.

THE EYE IS THE LAMP OF THE BODY

[33]"No one lights a lamp and hides it. No one puts it under a bowl. Instead, people put a lamp on its stand. Then those who come in can see the light.

[34]"Your eye is like a lamp for your body. Suppose your eyes are good. Then your whole body also is full of light. But suppose your eyes are bad. Then your body also is full of darkness. [35]So make sure that the light inside you is not darkness.

[36]"Suppose your whole body is full of light. And suppose no part of it is dark. Then your body will be completely lit up. It will be as when the light of a lamp shines on you."

SIX WARNINGS

[37]Jesus finished speaking. Then a Pharisee invited him to eat with him. So Jesus went in and took his place at the table. [38]But the Pharisee noticed that Jesus did not wash before the meal. He was surprised.

[39]Then the Lord spoke to him. "You Pharisees clean the outside of the cup and dish," he said. "But inside you are full of greed and evil. [40]You foolish people! Didn't the one who made the outside make the inside also? [41]Give to poor people what is inside the dish. Then everything will be clean for you.

[42]"How terrible it will be for you Pharisees! You give God a tenth of your garden plants, such as mint and rue. But you have forgotten to be fair and

to love God. You should have practiced the last things without failing to do the first.

⁴³"How terrible for you Pharisees! You love the most important seats in the synagogues. You love having people greet you in the market places.

⁴⁴"How terrible for you! You are like graves that are not marked. People walk over them without knowing it."

⁴⁵An authority on the law spoke to Jesus. He said, "Teacher, when you say things like that, you say bad things about us too."

⁴⁶Jesus replied, "How terrible for you authorities on the law! You put such heavy loads on people that they can hardly carry them. But you yourselves will not lift one finger to help them.

⁴⁷"How terrible for you! You build tombs for the prophets. It was your people of long ago who killed them. ⁴⁸So you give witness that you agree with what your people did long ago. They killed the prophets, and now you build the prophets' tombs.

⁴⁹"So God in his wisdom said, 'I will send prophets and apostles to them. They will kill some. And they will try to hurt others.' ⁵⁰So the people of today will be punished. They will pay for all

the prophets' blood spilled since the world began. ⁵¹I mean from the blood of Abel to the blood of Zechariah, who was killed between the altar and the temple. Yes, I tell you, the people of today will be punished for all these things.

⁵²"How terrible for you authorities on the law! You have taken away the key to the door of knowledge. You yourselves have not entered. And you have stood in the way of those who were entering."

⁵³When Jesus left there, the Pharisees and the teachers of the law strongly opposed him. They threw a lot of questions at him. ⁵⁴They set traps for him. They wanted to catch him in something he might say.

JESUS GIVES WORDS OF WARNING AND HOPE

12 During that time a crowd of many thousands had gathered. There were so many people that they were stepping on one another.

Jesus spoke first to his disciples. "Be on your guard against the yeast of the Pharisees," he said. "They just pretend to be godly. ²Everything that is secret

KIDS' QUESTION

Does the devil have power like God does?

The devil has great powers. But he is not even close to being as powerful as God. Satan can do fake miracles, lie, make bad look good and good look bad and trick people into doing wrong. But he also has many limits. He cannot be everywhere at the same time. He cannot create anything. He cannot even touch you without God's permission. And he has no power over Jesus. The Bible tells us we have nothing to fear from Satan.

checkout
Luke 12:4,5

Related verses: Job 1:6–12; 2:1–7

RUMBLE RUMBLE

will be brought out into the open. Everything that is hidden will be uncovered. ³What you have said in the dark will be heard in the daylight. What you have whispered to someone behind closed doors will be shouted from the rooftops.

⁴"My friends, listen to me. Don't be afraid of those who kill the body but can't do any more than that. ⁵I will show you whom you should be afraid of. Be afraid of the One who can kill the body and also has the power to throw you into hell. Yes, I tell you, be afraid of him.

⁶"Aren't five sparrows sold for two pennies? But God does not forget even one of them. ⁷In fact, he even counts every hair on your head! So don't be afraid. You are worth more than many sparrows.

⁸"What about someone who says in front of others that he knows me? I tell you, the Son of Man will say that he knows that person in front of God's angels. ⁹But what about someone who says in front of others that he doesn't know me? I, the Son of Man, will say that I don't know him in front of God's angels.

¹⁰"Everyone who speaks a word against the Son of Man will be forgiven. But anyone who speaks evil things against the Holy Spirit will not be forgiven.

¹¹"You will be brought before synagogues, rulers and authorities. But do not worry about how to stand up for yourselves or what to say. ¹²The Holy Spirit will teach you at that time what you should say."

THE STORY OF THE RICH MAN

¹³Someone in the crowd spoke to Jesus. "Teacher," he said, "tell my brother to divide the family property with me."

¹⁴Jesus replied, "Friend, who made me a judge or umpire between you?"

¹⁵Then he said to them, "Watch out! Be on your guard against wanting to have more and more things. Life is not

When you want something you see on a TV commercial, why doesn't your mom let you have it?

Many times the products advertised on television look much better than they really are, and your parents know it. Your parents have the responsibility to guide and protect you. Their job is to teach you God's ways and God's wisdom. They may not let you have something that looks exciting on TV because they know that it isn't going to be as great as it seems. Or they may know you do not need it or that it costs too much. Or they know it would actually be bad for you, even if you can't imagine how.

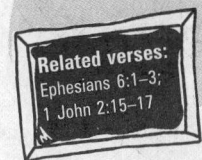 **checkout** Luke 12:15

Related verses:
Ephesians 6:1–3;
1 John 2:15–17

made up of how much a person has."

¹⁶Then Jesus told them a story. He said, "A certain rich man's land produced a good crop. ¹⁷He thought to himself, 'What should I do? I don't have any place to store my crops.'

¹⁸"Then he said, 'This is what I'll do. I will tear down my storerooms and build bigger ones. I will store all my grain and my other things in them. ¹⁹I'll say to myself, "You have plenty of good things stored away for many years. Take life easy. Eat, drink and have a good time." '

²⁰"But God said to him, 'You foolish man! This very night I will take your life away from you. Then who will get what you have prepared for yourself?'

²¹"That is how it will be for anyone who stores things away for himself but is not rich in God's eyes."

DO NOT WORRY

²²Then Jesus spoke to his disciples. He said, "I tell you, do not worry. Don't worry about your life and what you will eat. And don't worry about your body and what you will wear. ²³There is more to life than eating. There are more important things for the body than clothes.

²⁴"Think about the ravens. They don't plant or gather crops. They don't have any storerooms at all. But God feeds them. You are worth much more than birds!

²⁵"Can you add even one hour to your life by worrying? ²⁶You can't do that very little thing. So why worry about the rest?

²⁷"Think about how the lilies grow. They don't work or make clothing. But here is what I tell you. Not even Solomon in all of his glory was dressed like one of those flowers. ²⁸If that is how God dresses the wild grass, how much better will he dress you! After all, the grass is here only today. Tomorrow it is thrown into the fire. Your faith is so small!

²⁹"Don't spend time thinking about what you will eat or drink. Don't worry about it. ³⁰People who are ungodly run after all of those things. Your Father knows that you need them.

³¹"But put God's kingdom first. Then those other things will also be given to you.

³²"Little flock, do not be afraid. Your Father has been pleased to give you the kingdom. ³³Sell what you own. Give to those who are poor. Provide

Why doesn't God give us some things we pray for?

God is much wiser than we are. He knows what will happen if we get some of the things we pray for. He wants the very best for us. He has plans for our lives. Sometimes God does not give us what we pray for because it might hurt us. At other times God doesn't give us something right away. He wants us to wait patiently. And sometimes God has plans we cannot understand, so he waits or works something out that we cannot see. We can always trust in God's great care for us—whether the answer is yes, no or wait.

Related verses:
Psalms 17:6;
Proverbs 3:5–6;
Jeremiah 21:11;
4:3;
1 Peter 5:7

checkout
Luke 12:29–31

purses for yourselves that will not wear out. Put away riches in heaven that will not be used up. There, no thief can come near it. There, no moth can destroy it. [34]Your heart will be where your riches are.

BE READY

[35]"Be dressed and ready to serve. Keep your lamps burning. [36]Be like servants waiting for their master to return from a wedding dinner. When he comes and knocks, they can open the door for him at once.

[37]"It will be good for those servants whose master finds them ready when he comes. What I'm about to tell you is true. The master will then dress himself so he can serve them. He will have them take their places at the table. And he will come and wait on them. [38]It will be good for those servants whose master finds them ready. It will even be good if he comes very late at night.

[39]"But here is what you must understand. Suppose the owner of the house knew at what hour the robber was coming. He would not have let his house be broken into. [40]You also must be ready. The Son of Man will come at an hour when you don't expect him."

[41]Peter asked, "Lord, are you telling this story to us, or to everyone?"

[42]The Lord answered, "Suppose a master puts one of his servants in charge of his other servants. The servant's job is to give them the food they are to receive at the right time. The master wants a faithful and wise manager for this. [43]It will be good for the servant if the master finds him doing his job when the master returns. [44]What I'm about to tell you is true. The master will put that servant in charge of everything he owns.

[45]"But suppose the servant says to himself, 'My master is taking a long time to come back.' Suppose he begins to beat the other servants. Suppose he feeds himself. And suppose he drinks until he gets drunk. [46]The master of that servant will come back on a day the servant doesn't expect him. He will return at an hour the servant doesn't know. Then the master will cut him to pieces. He will send him to the place where unbelievers go.

[47]"Suppose a servant knows his master's wishes. But he doesn't get ready. And he doesn't do what his master wants. That servant will be beaten with many blows. [48]But suppose the servant does not know his master's wishes. And suppose he does things for which he should be punished. He will be beaten with only a few blows.

"Much will be required of everyone who has been given much. Even more will be asked of the person who is supposed to take care of much.

JESUS WILL SEPARATE PEOPLE FROM ONE ANOTHER

[49]"I have come to bring fire on the earth. How I wish the fire had already started! [50]But I have a baptism of suffering to go through. And I will be very troubled until it is completed.

[51]"Do you think I came to bring peace on earth? No, I tell you. I have come to separate people. [52]From now on there will be five members in a family, each one against the other. There will be three against two and two against three. [53]They will be separated. Father will turn against son and son against father. Mother will turn against daughter and daughter against mother. Mother-in-law will turn against daughter-in-law and daughter-in-law against mother-in-law."

UNDERSTANDING WHAT IS HAPPENING

[54]Jesus spoke to the crowd. He said, "You see a cloud rising in the west. Right away you say, 'It's going to rain.' And it does. [55]The south wind blows. So you say, 'It's going to be hot.' And it is. [56]You pretenders! You know how to understand the appearance of the earth and the sky. Why can't you understand the meaning of what is happening right now?

[57]"Why don't you judge for yourselves what is right? [58]Suppose someone has a claim against you, and you are on your way to court. Try hard to settle the matter on the way. If you don't, that person may drag you off to the judge. The judge may turn you over to the officer. And the officer may

throw you into prison. [59]I tell you, you will not get out until you have paid the very last penny!"

JESUS GIVES A WARNING

13 Some people who were there at that time told Jesus about certain Galileans. Pilate had mixed their blood with their sacrifices.

[2]Jesus said, "These people from Galilee suffered greatly. Do you think they were worse sinners than all the other Galileans? [3]I tell you, no! But unless you turn away from your sins, you will all die too. [4]Or what about the 18 people in Siloam? They died when the tower fell on them. Do you think they were more guilty than all the others living in Jerusalem? [5]I tell you, no! But unless you turn away from your sins, you will all die too."

[6]Then Jesus told a story. "A man had a fig tree," he said. "It had been planted in his vineyard. When he went to look for fruit on it, he didn't find any. [7]So he went to the man who took care of the vineyard. He said, 'For three years now I've been coming to look for fruit on this fig tree. But I haven't found any. Cut it down! Why should it use up the soil?'

[8]"'Sir,' the man replied, 'leave it alone for one more year. I'll dig around it and feed it. [9]If it bears fruit next year, fine! If not, then cut it down.'"

JESUS HEALS A DISABLED WOMAN ON THE SABBATH DAY

[10]Jesus was teaching in one of the synagogues on a Sabbath day. [11]A woman there had been disabled by an evil spirit for 18 years. She was bent over and could not stand up straight.

[12]Jesus saw her. He asked her to come to him. He said to her, "Woman, you will no longer be disabled. I am about to set you free." [13]Then he put his hands on her.

Right away she stood up straight and praised God.

[14]Jesus had healed the woman on the Sabbath day. This made the synagogue ruler angry. He told the people, "There are six days for work. So come

and be healed on those days. But do not come on the Sabbath."

[15]The Lord answered him, "You pretenders! Doesn't each of you go to the barn and untie his ox or donkey on the Sabbath day? Then don't you lead it out to give it water? [16]This woman is a member of Abraham's family line. But Satan has kept her disabled for 18 long years. Shouldn't she be set free on the Sabbath day from what was keeping her disabled?"

[17]When Jesus said this, all those who opposed him were put to shame. But the people were delighted. They loved all the wonderful things he was doing.

THE STORIES OF THE MUSTARD SEED AND THE YEAST

[18]Then Jesus asked, "What is God's kingdom like? What can I compare it to? [19]It is like a mustard seed. Someone took the seed and planted it in a garden. It grew and became a tree. The birds sat in its branches."

[20]Again he asked, "What can I compare God's kingdom to? [21]It is like yeast that a woman used. She mixed it into a large amount of flour. The yeast worked its way all through the dough."

THE NARROW DOOR

[22]Then Jesus went through the towns and villages, teaching the people. He was on his way to Jerusalem. [23]Someone asked him, "Lord, are only a few people going to be saved?"

He said to them, [24]"Try very hard to enter through the narrow door. I tell you, many will try to enter and will not be able to. [25]The owner of the house will get up and close the door. Then you will stand outside knocking and begging. You will say, 'Sir, open the door for us.'

"But he will answer, 'I don't know you. And I don't know where you come from.'

[26]"Then you will say, 'We ate and drank with you. You taught in our streets.'

[27]"But he will reply, 'I don't know you. And I don't know where you come from. Get away from me, all you who do evil!'

[28]"You will sob and grind your teeth

when you see those who are in God's kingdom. You will see Abraham, Isaac and Jacob and all the prophets there. But you yourselves will be thrown out. ²⁹People will come from east and west and north and south. They will take their places at the feast in God's kingdom. ³⁰Then the last will be first. And the first will be last."

JESUS' SADNESS OVER JERUSALEM

³¹At that time some Pharisees came to Jesus. They said to him, "Leave this place. Go somewhere else. Herod wants to kill you."

³²He replied, "Go and tell that fox, 'I will drive out demons. I will heal people today and tomorrow. And on the third day I will reach my goal.' ³³In any case, I must keep going today and tomorrow and the next day. Certainly no prophet can die outside Jerusalem!

³⁴"Jerusalem! Jerusalem! You kill the prophets and throw stones in order to kill those who are sent to you. Many times I have wanted to gather your people together. I have wanted to be like a hen who gathers her chicks under her wings. But you would not let me!

³⁵"Look, your house is left empty. I tell you, you will not see me again until you say, 'Blessed is the one who comes in the name of the Lord.' " *(Psalm 118:26)*

JESUS EATS AT A PHARISEE'S HOUSE

14 One Sabbath day, Jesus went to eat in the house of a well-known Pharisee. While he was there, he was being carefully watched. ²In front of him was a man whose body was badly swollen.

³Jesus turned to the Pharisees and the authorities on the law. He asked them, "Is it breaking the Law to heal on the Sabbath?"

⁴But they remained silent.

So Jesus took hold of the man and healed him. Then he sent him away.

⁵He asked them another question. He said, "Suppose one of you has a son or an ox that falls into a well on the Sabbath day. Wouldn't you pull him out right away?" ⁶And they had nothing to say.

⁷Jesus noticed how the guests picked the places of honor at the table. So he told them a story. ⁸He said, "Suppose someone invites you to a wedding feast. Do not take the place of honor. A person more important than you may have been invited. ⁹If so, the host who invited both of you will come to you. He will say, 'Give this person your seat.' Then you will be filled with shame. You will have to take the least important place.

¹⁰"But when you are invited, take the lowest place. Then your host will come over to you. He will say, 'Friend, move up to a better place.' Then you will be honored in front of all the other guests. ¹¹Anyone who lifts himself up will be brought down. And anyone who is brought down will be lifted up."

¹²Then Jesus spoke to his host. "Suppose you give a lunch or a dinner," he said. "Do not invite your friends, your brothers or sisters, or your relatives, or your rich neighbors. If you do, they may invite you to eat with them. So you will be paid back.

¹³"But when you give a big dinner, invite those who are poor. Also invite those who can't walk, the disabled and the blind. ¹⁴Then you will be blessed. Your guests can't pay you back. But you will be paid back when those who are right with God rise from the dead."

THE STORY OF THE BIG DINNER

¹⁵One of the people at the table with Jesus heard him say those things. So he said to Jesus, "Blessed is the one who will eat at the feast in God's kingdom."

¹⁶Jesus replied, "A certain man was preparing a big dinner. He invited many guests. ¹⁷Then the day of the dinner arrived. He sent his servant to those who had been invited. The servant told them, 'Come. Everything is ready now.'

¹⁸"But they all had the same idea. They began to make excuses. The first one said, 'I have just bought a field. I have to go and see it. Please excuse me.'

¹⁹"Another said, 'I have just bought five pairs of oxen. I'm on my way to try them out. Please excuse me.'

²⁰"Still another said, 'I just got married, so I can't come.'

²¹"The servant came back and reported this to his master.

"Then the owner of the house became angry. He ordered his servant, 'Go out quickly into the streets and lanes of the town. Bring in those who are poor. Also bring those who can't walk, the blind and the disabled.'

²²"'Sir,' the servant said, 'what you ordered has been done. But there is still room.'

²³"Then the master told his servant, 'Go out to the roads. Go out to the country lanes. Make the people come in. I want my house to be full. ²⁴I tell you, not one of those men who were invited will get a taste of my dinner.' "

IT COSTS TO BE A DISCIPLE

²⁵Large crowds were traveling with Jesus. He turned and spoke to them. He said, ²⁶"Anyone who comes to me must hate his father and mother. He must hate his wife and children. He must hate his brothers and sisters. And he must hate even his own life. Unless he does, he can't be my disciple. ²⁷Anyone who doesn't carry his cross and follow me can't be my disciple.

²⁸"Suppose someone wants to build a tower. Won't he sit down first and figure out how much it will cost? Then he will see whether he has enough money to finish it. ²⁹Suppose he starts building and is not able to finish. Then everyone who sees what he has done will laugh at him. ³⁰They will say, 'This fellow started to build. But he wasn't able to finish.'

³¹"Or suppose a king is about to go to war against another king. And suppose he has 10,000 men, while the other has 20,000 coming against him. Won't he first sit down and think about whether he can win?

³²"And suppose he decides he can't win. Then he will send some men to ask how peace can be made. He will do this while the other king is still far away.

³³"In the same way, you must give up everything you have. If you don't, you can't be my disciple.

³⁴"Salt is good. But suppose it loses its saltiness. How can it be made salty

Why is it so hard to find things in my desk?

Is it jammed with a lot of stuff? It's a good idea to go through your desk and take out all the notes, wrappers, old papers, stale food, broken pencils and other extra stuff you don't need. Next, make sure that everything you do need is in there. Then organize everything—put each item in a certain place so you know where it is and can find it when you need it. Try cleaning up your desk at the beginning or end of each day. That will keep you from filling it with junk.

(checkout)

Luke 15:8,9

Related verse:
Proverbs 16:3

again? ³⁵It is not good for the soil. And it is not good for the trash pile. It will be thrown out.

"Those who have ears should listen."

THE STORY OF THE LOST SHEEP

15 The tax collectors and "sinners" were all gathering around to hear Jesus. ²But the Pharisees and the teachers of the law were whispering among themselves. They said, "This man welcomes sinners and eats with them."

³Then Jesus told them a story. ⁴He said, "Suppose one of you has 100 sheep and loses one of them. Won't he leave the 99 in the open country? Won't he go and look for the one lost sheep until he finds it? ⁵When he finds it, he will joyfully put it on his shoulders ⁶and go home. Then he will call his friends and neighbors together. He will say, 'Be joyful with me. I have found my lost sheep.'

⁷"I tell you, it will be the same in heaven. There will be great joy when one sinner turns away from sin. Yes, there will be more joy than for 99 godly people who do not need to turn away from their sins.

THE STORY OF THE LOST COIN

⁸"Or suppose a woman has ten silver coins and loses one. She will light a lamp and sweep the house. She will search carefully until she finds the coin. ⁹And when she finds it, she will call her friends and neighbors together. She will say, 'Be joyful with me. I have found my lost coin.'

¹⁰"I tell you, it is the same in heaven. There is joy in heaven over one sinner who turns away from sin."

THE STORY OF THE LOST SON

¹¹Jesus continued, "There was a man who had two sons. ¹²The younger son spoke to his father. He said, 'Father,

If we prayed to find something we lost, would we really find it?

No job is too small for God. It is good to pray for what matters to us, even something small that is lost. God may help us find it right away, or he may help us remember where we put it. He also might have us retrace our steps to find it so we will be more careful next time.

But prayer is not a substitute for being careful. We should not be careless and think, "Oh, well, if I lose it, I can just ask God to find it for me." That is not the right way to use prayer.

checkout Luke 15:9

Related verses:
2 Kings 6:5–6;
Psalm 139:1–2;
Matthew 10:29–31;
Luke 15:8

JASON'S IMAGINATION

LITTLE BO PEEP HAS LOST HER SHEEP AND DOESN'T KNOW WHERE TO FIND THEM. SHE PRAYED ON HER OWN THAT THEY WOULD COME HOME DRAGGING THEIR TAILS BEHIND THEM.

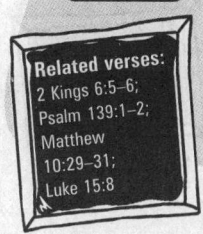

give me my share of the family property.' So the father divided his property between his two sons.

[13] "Not long after that, the younger son packed up all he had. Then he left for a country far away. There he wasted his money on wild living. [14] He spent everything he had.

"Then the whole country ran low on food. So the son didn't have what he needed. [15] He went to work for someone who lived in that country, who sent him to the fields to feed the pigs. [16] The son wanted to fill his stomach with the food the pigs were eating. But no one gave him anything.

[17] "Then he began to think clearly again. He said, 'How many of my father's hired workers have more than enough food! But here I am dying from hunger! [18] I will get up and go back to my father. I will say to him, "Father, I have sinned against heaven. And I have sinned against you. [19] I am no longer fit to be called your son. Make me like one of your hired workers." ' [20] So he got up and went to his father.

"While the son was still a long way off, his father saw him. He was filled with tender love for his son. He ran to him. He threw his arms around him and kissed him.

[21] "The son said to him, 'Father, I have sinned against heaven and against you. I am no longer fit to be called your son.'

[22] "But the father said to his servants, 'Quick! Bring the best robe and put it on him. Put a ring on his finger and sandals on his feet. [23] Bring the fattest calf and kill it. Let's have a big dinner and celebrate. [24] This son of mine was dead. And now he is alive again. He was lost. And now he is found.'

KIDS' QUESTion

Do angels have hearts?

Angels have feelings just as people do and just as God does. Bible passages tell of angels being very happy whenever a person first believes in Jesus. The Bible also tells of angels singing songs of gladness and praise to God.

It says that angels care about us and that they helped Jesus. But angels do not have real hearts because they do not have bodies.

checkout

Luke 15:10

To my Guardian angel my very special valentine! xoxoxo from Jason + Max

Related verses:
Hebrews 12:22,23

"So they began to celebrate.

25"The older son was in the field. When he came near the house, he heard music and dancing. 26So he called one of the servants. He asked him what was going on.

27"'Your brother has come home,' the servant replied. 'Your father has killed the fattest calf. He has done this because your brother is back safe and sound.'

28"The older brother became angry. He refused to go in. So his father went out and begged him.

29"But he answered his father, 'Look! All these years I've worked like a slave for you. I have always obeyed your orders. You never gave me even a young goat so I could celebrate with my friends. 30But this son of yours wasted your money with some prostitutes. Now he comes home. And for him you kill the fattest calf!'

31"'My son,' the father said, 'you are always with me. Everything I have is yours. 32But we had to celebrate and be glad. This brother of yours was dead. And now he is alive again. He was lost. And now he is found.'"

THE STORY OF THE CLEVER MANAGER

16 Jesus told his disciples another story. He said, "There was a rich man who had a manager. Some said that the manager was wasting what the rich man owned. 2So the rich man told him to come in. He asked him, 'What is this I hear about you? Tell me exactly how you have handled what I own. You can't be my manager any longer.'

3"The manager said to himself, 'What will I do now? My master is taking away my job. I'm not strong enough to dig. And I'm too ashamed to beg. 4I know what I'm going to do. I'll do something so that when I lose my job here, people will welcome me into their houses.'

5"So he called in each person who owed his master something. He asked

Why don't sisters and brothers get along sometimes?

Most arguments between brothers and sisters are normal. When you live with somebody, sometimes you disagree about how to do things. This happens in every family—even families where people love each other very much.

The next time you have a fight with your brother or sister, try to talk about your differences without yelling or hitting. If you are upset, calm down and lower your voice. Tell the person how you feel. It also helps to try to see things from the other person's point of view. Listen to each other without interrupting. Then as you talk it out, you can suggest a way to solve the problem. Maybe you can give up a little of what you wanted. Remember that you're both on the same team. Every conflict is an opportunity for you to learn one of life's most valuable skills— how to get along with others.

checkout
Luke 15:27–31

Related verses:
Proverbs 15:1;
Romans 12:17–18;
Ephesians 4:32

the first one, 'How much do you owe my master?'

⁶" 'I owe 800 gallons of olive oil,' he replied.

"The manager told him, 'Take your bill. Sit down quickly and change it to 400 gallons.'

⁷"Then he asked the second one, 'And how much do you owe?'

" 'I owe 1,000 bushels of wheat,' he replied.

"The manager told him, 'Take your bill and change it to 800 bushels.'

⁸"The manager had not been honest. But the master praised him for being clever. The people of this world are clever in dealing with those who are like themselves. They are more clever than God's people.

⁹"I tell you, use the riches of this world to help others. In that way, you will make friends for yourselves. Then when your riches are gone, you will be welcomed into your eternal home in heaven.

¹⁰"Suppose you can be trusted with very little. Then you can be trusted with a lot. But suppose you are not honest with very little. Then you will not be honest with a lot.

¹¹"Suppose you have not been worthy of trust in handling worldly wealth. Then who will trust you with true riches? ¹²Suppose you have not been worthy of trust in handling someone else's property. Then who will give you property of your own?

¹³"No servant can serve two masters at the same time. He will hate one of them and love the other. Or he will be faithful to one and dislike the other. You can't serve God and Money at the same time."

¹⁴The Pharisees loved money. They heard all that Jesus said and made fun of him. ¹⁵Jesus said to them, "You try to make yourselves look good in the eyes of other people. But God knows your hearts. What is worth a great deal among people is hated by God.

MORE TEACHINGS

¹⁶"The teachings of the Law and the Prophets were preached until John

---

KIDS' QUESTION

Is it OK to say you tagged someone in tag when you really didn't?

It would be a lie to say that you tagged someone when you really did not. God says that lying is wrong. Lying is wrong even in a fun game like tag. Rules make a game fun. In fact, no one would know how to play if there were no rules. You would never know who won or lost. Think of how silly it would be if everyone cheated all the time in a game of tag. It would not be any fun and it certainly would not be a good way to play tag. In a good game, all the players follow the rules. The Bible says that if you are true and honest in little ways you will be true and honest in big ways. Be honest in everything you do, even in tag.

Related verses: Proverbs 11:1; Matthew 25:23

(checkout)

Luke 16:10

came. Since then, the good news of God's kingdom is being preached. And everyone is trying very hard to enter it. ¹⁷It is easier for heaven and earth to disappear than for the smallest part of a letter to drop out of the Law.

¹⁸"Anyone who divorces his wife and gets married to another woman commits adultery. Also, the man who gets married to a divorced woman commits adultery.

THE RICH MAN AND LAZARUS

¹⁹"Once there was a rich man. He was dressed in purple cloth and fine linen. He lived an easy life every day. ²⁰A man named Lazarus was placed at his gate. Lazarus was a beggar. His body was covered with sores. ²¹Even dogs came and licked his sores. All he wanted was to eat what fell from the rich man's table.

²²"The time came when the beggar died. The angels carried him to Abraham's side. The rich man also died and was buried. ²³In hell, the rich man was suffering terribly. He looked up and saw Abraham far away. Lazarus was by his side. ²⁴So the rich man called out, 'Father Abraham! Have pity on me! Send Lazarus to dip the tip of his finger in water. Then he can cool my tongue with it. I am in terrible pain in this fire.'

²⁵"But Abraham replied, 'Son, remember what happened in your lifetime. You received your good things. Lazarus received bad things. Now he is comforted here, and you are in terrible pain. ²⁶Besides, a wide space has been placed between us and you. So those who want to go from here to you can't go. And no one can cross over from there to us.'

²⁷"The rich man answered, 'Then I beg you, father. Send Lazarus to my family. ²⁸I have five brothers. Let Lazarus warn them. Then they will not come to this place of terrible suffering.'

²⁹"Abraham replied, 'They have the teachings of Moses and the Prophets. Let your brothers listen to them.'

³⁰" 'No, father Abraham,' he said. 'But if someone from the dead goes to them, they will turn away from their sins.'

³¹"Abraham said to him, 'They do not listen to Moses and the Prophets. So they will not be convinced even if someone rises from the dead.' "

KIDS' QUESTION

What is hell like?

Hell is very dark and very painful. It is a lonely place of suffering. The worst thing about hell is that it means being separated forever from God and from all that is good. There is no love, joy, fun, laughter or celebration in hell. Some people make jokes about hell and say that they want to go there to be with their friends. But no one will have any friends in hell. No one will have any fun in hell. No one should joke about wanting to go there.

checkout Luke 16:23

Related verses:
Matthew 25:41;
Revelation 20:10

SIN, FAITH AND DUTY

17 Jesus spoke to his disciples. "Things that make people sin are sure to come," he said. "But how terrible it will be for the person who brings them! ²Suppose people lead one of these little ones to sin. It would be better for those people to be thrown into the sea with a millstone tied around their neck. ³So watch what you do.

"If your brother sins, tell him he is wrong. Then if he turns away from his sins, forgive him. ⁴Suppose he sins against you seven times in one day. And suppose he comes back to you each time and says, 'I'm sorry.' Forgive him."

⁵The apostles said to the Lord, "Give us more faith!"

⁶He replied, "Suppose you have faith as small as a mustard seed. Then you can say to this mulberry tree, 'Be pulled up. Be planted in the sea.' And it will obey you.

⁷"Suppose one of you had a servant plowing or looking after the sheep. And suppose the servant came in from the field. Would you say to him, 'Come along now and sit down to eat'? ⁸No. Instead, you would say, 'Prepare my supper. Get yourself ready. Wait on me while I eat and drink. Then after that you can eat and drink.' ⁹Would you thank the servant because he did what he was told to do?

¹⁰"It's the same with you. Suppose you have done everything you were told to do. Then you should say, 'We are not worthy to serve you. We have only done our duty.' "

JESUS HEALS TEN MEN

¹¹Jesus was on his way to Jerusalem. He traveled along the border between Samaria and Galilee. ¹²As he was going into a village, ten men met him. They had a skin disease. They were standing close by. ¹³And they called out in a loud voice, "Jesus! Master! Have pity on us!"

¹⁴Jesus saw them and said, "Go. Show yourselves to the priests." While they were on the way, they were healed.

¹⁵When one of them saw that he was healed, he came back. He praised God

KIDS' QUESTION

Why can't we go to heaven and just see it and then come back?

This is a little bit like asking, "Can I become a teenager and then come back to my age right now?" You have to grow up before you can be a teenager. You cannot simply jump there and come back. In the same way, heaven is more than a place that you can visit. It is a time at the end of this life. God has to make us ready to go there. We have to change in order to go there. We know that heaven exists because God has told us about it in the Bible. But if you wanted just to see it and then come back, God would have to do a miracle.

checkout Luke 16:26

Related verses:
2 Corinthians 12:2–4;
Revelation 4:1

in a loud voice. [16]He threw himself at Jesus' feet and thanked him. The man was a Samaritan.

[17]Jesus asked, "Weren't all ten healed? Where are the other nine? [18]Didn't anyone else return and give praise to God except this outsider?"

[19]Then Jesus said to him, "Get up and go. Your faith has healed you."

THE COMING OF GOD'S KINGDOM

[20]Once the Pharisees asked Jesus when God's kingdom would come. He replied, "The coming of God's kingdom is not something you can see just by watching for it carefully. [21]People will not say, 'Here it is.' Or, 'There it is.' God's kingdom is among you."

[22]Then Jesus spoke to his disciples. "The time is coming," he said, "when you will long to see one of the days of the Son of Man. But you won't see it. [23]People will tell you, 'There he is!' Or, 'Here he is!' Don't go running off after them.

[24]"When the Son of Man comes, he will be like the lightning. It flashes and lights up the sky from one end to the other. [25]But first the Son of Man must suffer many things. He will not be accepted by the people of today.

[26]"Remember how it was in the days of Noah. It will be the same when the Son of Man comes. [27]People were eating and drinking. They were getting married. They were giving their daughters to be married. They did all those things right up to the day Noah entered the ark. Then the flood came and destroyed them all.

[28]"It was the same in the days of Lot. People were eating and drinking. They were buying and selling. They were planting and building. [29]But on the day Lot left Sodom, fire and sulfur rained down from heaven. And all the people were destroyed.

[30]"It will be just like that on the day the Son of Man is shown to the world. [31]Suppose someone is on the roof of his house on that day. And suppose his goods are inside the house. He should not go down to get them. No one in the field should go back for anything either. [32]Remember Lot's wife! [33]Anyone who tries to keep his life will lose

it. Anyone who loses his life will keep it.

[34]"I tell you, on that night two people will be in one bed. One person will be taken and the other left. [35/36]Two women will be grinding grain together. One will be taken and the other left."

[37]"Where, Lord?" his disciples asked.

He replied, "The vultures will gather where there is a dead body."

THE STORY OF THE WIDOW WHO WOULD NOT GIVE UP

18 Jesus told his disciples a story. He wanted to show them that they should always pray and not give up. [2]He said, "In a certain town there was a judge. He didn't have any respect for God or care about people. [3]A widow lived in that town. She came to the judge again and again. She kept begging him, 'Make things right for me. Someone is doing me wrong.'

[4]"For some time the judge refused. But finally he said to himself, 'I don't have any respect for God. I don't care about people. [5]But this widow keeps bothering me. So I will see that things are made right for her. If I don't, she will wear me out by coming again and again!' "

[6]The Lord said, "Listen to what the unfair judge says.

[7]"God's chosen people cry out to him day and night. Won't he make things right for them? Will he keep putting them off? [8]I tell you, God will see that things are made right for them. He will make sure it happens quickly.

"But when the Son of Man comes, will he find people on earth who have faith?"

THE STORY OF THE PHARISEE AND THE TAX COLLECTOR

[9]Jesus told a story to some people who were sure they were right with God. They looked down on everybody else. [10]He said to them, "Two men went up to the temple to pray. One was a Pharisee. The other was a tax collector.

[11]"The Pharisee stood up and prayed about himself. 'God, I thank you that I am not like other people,' he

said. 'I am not like robbers or those who do other evil things. I am not like those who commit adultery. I am not even like this tax collector. [12]I fast twice a week. And I give a tenth of all I get.'

[13]"But the tax collector stood not very far away. He would not even look up to heaven. He beat his chest and said, 'God, have mercy on me. I am a sinner.'

[14]"I tell you, the tax collector went home accepted by God. But not the Pharisee. Everyone who lifts himself up will be brought down. And anyone who is brought down will be lifted up."

LITTLE CHILDREN ARE BROUGHT TO JESUS

[15]People were also bringing babies to Jesus. They wanted him to touch them. When the disciples saw this, they told the people to stop.

[16]But Jesus asked the children to come to him. "Let the little children come to me," he said. "Don't keep them away. God's kingdom belongs to people like them. [17]What I'm about to tell you is true. Anyone who will not receive God's kingdom like a little child will never enter it."

JESUS AND THE RICH RULER

[18]A certain ruler asked Jesus a question. "Good teacher," he said, "what must I do to receive eternal life?"

[19]"Why do you call me good?" Jesus answered. "No one is good except God. [20]You know what the commandments say. 'Do not commit adultery. Do not commit murder. Do not steal. Do not give false witness. Honor your father and mother.' " *(Exodus 20:12–16; Deuteronomy 5:16–20)*

[21]"I have obeyed all those commandments since I was a boy," the ruler said.

[22]When Jesus heard this, he said to him, "You are still missing one thing. Sell everything you have. Give the money to those who are poor. You will have treasure in heaven. Then come and follow me."

[23]When the ruler heard this, he became very sad. He was very rich.

[24]Jesus looked at him. Then he said, "How hard it is for rich people to enter God's kingdom! [25]Is it hard for a camel to go through the eye of a needle? It is even harder for the rich to enter God's kingdom!"

[26]Those who heard this asked, "Then who can be saved?"

[27]Jesus replied, "Things that are impossible with people are possible with God."

[28]Peter said to him, "We have left everything we had in order to follow you!"

[29]"What I'm about to tell you is true," Jesus said to them. "Has anyone left home or family for God's kingdom? [30]They will receive many times as much in this world. In the world to come they will live forever."

JESUS AGAIN TELLS ABOUT HIS COMING DEATH

[31]Jesus took the Twelve to one side. He told them, "We are going up to Jerusalem. Everything that the prophets wrote about the Son of Man will come true. [32]He will be handed over to people who are not Jews. They will make fun of him. They will laugh at him and spit on him. They will whip him and kill him. [33]On the third day, he will rise from the dead!"

[34]The disciples did not understand any of this. Its meaning was hidden from them. So they didn't know what Jesus was talking about.

A BLIND BEGGAR RECEIVES HIS SIGHT

[35]Jesus was approaching Jericho. A blind man was sitting by the side of the road begging. [36]The blind man heard the crowd going by. He asked what was happening. [37]They told him, "Jesus of Nazareth is passing by."

[38]So the blind man called out, "Jesus! Son of David! Have mercy on me!"

[39]Those who led the way commanded him to stop. They told him to be quiet. But he shouted even louder, "Son of David! Have mercy on me!"

[40]Jesus stopped and ordered the man to be brought to him. When the man came near, Jesus spoke to him. [41]"What do you want me to do for you?" Jesus asked.

"Lord, I want to be able to see," the blind man replied.

⁴²Jesus said to him, "Receive your sight. Your faith has healed you."
⁴³Right away he could see. He followed Jesus, praising God. When all the people saw it, they also praised God.

ZACCHAEUS THE TAX COLLECTOR

19 Jesus entered Jericho and was passing through. ²A man named Zacchaeus lived there. He was a chief tax collector and was very rich.

³Zacchaeus wanted to see who Jesus was. But he was a short man. He could not see Jesus because of the crowd. ⁴So he ran ahead and climbed a sycamore-fig tree. He wanted to see Jesus, who was coming that way.

⁵Jesus reached the spot where Zacchaeus was. He looked up and said, "Zacchaeus, come down at once. I must stay at your house today." ⁶So Zacchaeus came down at once and welcomed him gladly.

⁷All the people saw this. They began to whisper among themselves. They said, "Jesus has gone to be the guest of a 'sinner.' "

⁸But Zacchaeus stood up. He said, "Look, Lord! Here and now I give half of what I own to those who are poor. And if I have cheated anybody out of anything, I will pay it back. I will pay back four times the amount I took."

⁹Jesus said to Zacchaeus, "Today salvation has come to your house. You are a member of Abraham's family line. ¹⁰The Son of Man came to look for the lost and save them."

THE STORY OF THREE SERVANTS

¹¹While the people were listening to these things, Jesus told them a story. He was near Jerusalem. The people thought that God's kingdom was going to appear right away.

¹²Jesus said, "A man from an important family went to a country far away. He went there to be made king and then return home. ¹³So he sent for ten of his servants. He gave them each

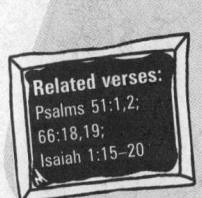

When we're bad, can we still pray?

Yes. A person can pray at any time. When people do bad things or make mistakes, they need God more than ever. When we do something wrong, we need to talk with God about it. We need to admit that what we did was wrong, say we're sorry and ask him to forgive us. Then God can help us do better next time. If we wait until we are good enough to pray, we will never pray!

check out

Luke 18:13,14

Related verses:
Psalms 51:1,2;
66:18,19;
Isaiah 1:15–20

about three months' pay. 'Put this money to work until I come back,' he said.

¹⁴"But those he ruled over hated him. They sent some messengers after him. They were sent to say, 'We don't want this man to be our king.'

¹⁵"But he was made king and returned home. Then he sent for the servants he had given the money to. He wanted to find out what they had earned with it.

¹⁶"The first one came to him. He said, 'Sir, your money has earned ten times as much.'

¹⁷" 'You have done well, my good servant!' his master replied. 'You have been faithful in a very small matter. So I will put you in charge of ten towns.'

¹⁸"The second servant came to his master. He said, 'Sir, your money has earned five times as much.'

¹⁹"His master answered, 'I will put you in charge of five towns.'

²⁰"Then another servant came. He said, 'Sir, here is your money. I have kept it hidden in a piece of cloth.

²¹I was afraid of you. You are a hard man. You take out what you did not put in. You harvest what you did not plant.'

²²"His master replied, 'I will judge you by your own words, you evil servant! So you knew that I am a hard man? You knew that I take out what I did not put in? You knew that I harvest what I did not plant? ²³Then why didn't you put my money in the bank? When I came back, I could have collected it with interest.'

²⁴"Then he said to those standing by, 'Take his money away from him. Give it to the one who has ten times as much.'

²⁵" 'Sir,' they said, 'he already has ten times as much!'

²⁶"He replied, 'I tell you that everyone who has will be given more. But here is what will happen to anyone who has nothing. Even what he has will be taken away from him. ²⁷And what about my enemies who did not want me to be king over them? Bring them here! Kill them in front of me!' "

How much should a person give to the church?

Christians are free to give as much as they want to the church. Zacchaeus gave half of what he owned! But many people like to start with ten percent of their income. This means one dime from every dollar. That is their tithe.

Christians should try to give at least ten percent of their money and time to help with God's work and support their church. Those who are able should give even more. Even if you start small, you should pray that God will help you to give more someday. It is more important that you give *something* than that you give only if you have a lot.

checkout Luke 19:8

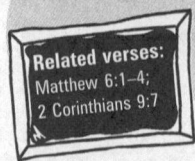

Related verses:
Matthew 6:1–4;
2 Corinthians 9:7

JESUS ENTERS JERUSALEM

²⁸After Jesus had said this, he went on ahead. He was going up to Jerusalem.

²⁹He approached Bethphage and Bethany. The hill there was called the Mount of Olives. Jesus sent out two of his disciples. He said to them, ³⁰"Go to the village ahead of you. As soon as you get there, you will find a donkey's colt tied up. No one has ever ridden it. Untie it and bring it here. ³¹Someone may ask you, 'Why are you untying it?' If so, say, 'The Lord needs it.' "

³²Those who were sent ahead went and found the young donkey. It was there just as Jesus had told them. ³³They were untying the colt when its owners came. The owners asked them, "Why are you untying the colt?"

³⁴They replied, "The Lord needs it."

³⁵Then the disciples brought the colt to Jesus. They threw their coats on the young donkey and put Jesus on it. ³⁶As he went along, people spread their coats on the road.

³⁷Jesus came near the place where the road goes down the Mount of Olives. There the whole crowd of disciples began to praise God with joy. In loud voices they praised him for all the miracles they had seen. They shouted,

³⁸"Blessed is the king who comes in the name of the Lord!"

(Psalm 118:26)

"May there be peace and glory in the highest heaven!"

³⁹Some of the Pharisees in the crowd spoke to Jesus. "Teacher," they said, "tell your disciples to stop!"

⁴⁰"I tell you," he replied, "if they keep quiet, the stones will cry out."

⁴¹He approached Jerusalem. When he saw the city, he began to sob. ⁴²He said, "I wish you had known today what would bring you peace! But now it is hidden from your eyes. ⁴³The days will come when your enemies will arrive. They will build a wall of dirt up against your city. They will surround you and close you in on every side. ⁴⁴You didn't recognize the time when God came to you. So your enemies will smash you to the ground. They will destroy you and all the people inside your walls. They will not leave one stone on top of another."

JESUS CLEARS OUT THE TEMPLE

⁴⁵Then Jesus entered the temple area. He began chasing out those who were selling there. ⁴⁶He told them, "It is

Is Jesus sad when I do something wrong?

Jesus is very sad whenever we do bad things. He is more upset over the sins of the world than anyone else is. The Bible says that he once sobbed when he came near to Jerusalem, because he felt so bad about the sins of the people there. Jesus is sad because he knows and sees how much sin hurts us and others. But Jesus realizes that we make mistakes. He keeps on forgiving if we ask him to. He loves us so much that he will not give up on us.

checkout
Luke 19:41

Related verses:
Psalm 78:40,41;
Matthew 23:37

written that the Lord said, 'My house will be a house where people can pray.' *(Isaiah 56:7)* But you have made it a 'den for robbers.' " *(Jeremiah 7:11)*

⁴⁷Every day Jesus was teaching at the temple. But the chief priests and the teachers of the law were trying to kill him. So were the leaders among the people. ⁴⁸But they couldn't find any way to do it. All the people were paying close attention to his words.

THE AUTHORITY OF JESUS IS QUESTIONED

20 One day Jesus was teaching the people in the temple courtyard. He was preaching the good news to them.

The chief priests and the teachers of the law came up to him. The elders came with them. ²"Tell us by what authority you are doing these things," they all said. "Who gave you this authority?"

³Jesus replied, "I will also ask you a question. Tell me, ⁴was John's baptism from heaven? Or did it come from men?"

⁵They talked to each other about it. They said, "If we say, 'From heaven,' he will ask, 'Why didn't you believe him?' ⁶But if we say, 'From men,' all the people will throw stones at us and kill us. They believe that John was a prophet."

⁷So they answered Jesus, "We don't know where John's baptism came from."

⁸Jesus said, "Then I won't tell you by what authority I am doing these things either."

THE STORY OF THE RENTERS

⁹Jesus went on to tell the people a story. "A man planted a vineyard," he said. "He rented it out to some farmers. Then he went away for a long time. ¹⁰At harvest time he sent a servant to the renters. They were supposed to give him some of the fruit of the vineyard. But the renters beat the servant. Then they sent him away with nothing. ¹¹So the man sent another servant. They beat that one and treated him badly. They also sent him away with nothing. ¹²The man sent a third ser-

vant. The renters wounded him and threw him out.

¹³"Then the owner of the vineyard said, 'What should I do? I have a son, and I love him. I will send him. Maybe they will respect him.'

¹⁴"But when the renters saw the son, they talked the matter over. 'This is the one who will receive all the owner's property someday,' they said. 'Let's kill him. Then everything will be ours.' ¹⁵So they threw him out of the vineyard. And they killed him.

"What will the owner of the vineyard do to the renters? ¹⁶He will come and kill them. He will give the vineyard to others."

When the people heard this, they said, "We hope this never happens!"

¹⁷Jesus looked right at them and said, "Here is something I want you to explain the meaning of. It is written,

" 'The stone the builders didn't accept
has become the most important stone of all.' *(Psalm 118:22)*

¹⁸Everyone who falls on that stone will be broken to pieces. But the stone will crush anyone it falls on."

¹⁹The teachers of the law and the chief priests looked for a way to arrest Jesus at once. They knew he had told that story against them. But they were afraid of the people.

IS IT RIGHT TO PAY TAXES TO CAESAR?

²⁰The religious leaders sent spies to keep a close watch on Jesus. The spies pretended to be honest. They hoped they could trap Jesus with something he would say. Then they could hand him over to the power and authority of the governor. ²¹So the spies questioned Jesus. "Teacher," they said, "we know that you speak and teach what is right. We know you don't favor one person over another. You teach the way of God truthfully. ²²Is it right for us to pay taxes to Caesar or not?"

²³Jesus saw they were trying to trick him. So he said to them, ²⁴"Show me a silver coin. Whose picture and words are on it?"

²⁵"Caesar's," they replied.

He said to them, "Then give to Caesar what belongs to Caesar. And give to God what belongs to God."

²⁶They were not able to trap him with what he had said there in front of all the people. Amazed by his answer, they became silent.

MARRIAGE WHEN THE DEAD RISE

²⁷The Sadducees do not believe that people rise from the dead. Some of them came to Jesus with a question. ²⁸"Teacher," they said, "Moses wrote for us about a man's brother who dies. Suppose the brother leaves a wife but has no children. Then the man must get married to the widow. He must have children to carry on his dead brother's name. ²⁹"There were seven brothers. The first one got married to a woman. He died without leaving any children. ³⁰The second one got married to her. ³¹And then the third one got married to her. One after another, the seven brothers got married to her. They all died. None left any children. ³²Finally, the woman died too. ³³Now then, when the dead rise, whose wife will she be? All seven brothers were married to her."

³⁴Jesus replied, "People in this world get married. And their parents give them to get married. ³⁵But it will not be like that when the dead rise. Those who are considered worthy to take part in what happens at that time won't get married. And their parents won't give them to be married. ³⁶They can't die anymore. They are like the angels. They are God's children. They will be given a new form of life when the dead rise.

³⁷"Remember the story of Moses and the bush. Even Moses showed that the dead rise. The Lord said to him, 'I am the God of Abraham. I am the God of Isaac. And I am the God of Jacob.' *(Exodus 3:6)* ³⁸He is not the God of the dead. He is the God of the living. In his eyes, everyone is alive."

³⁹Some of the teachers of the law replied, "You have spoken well, teacher!" ⁴⁰And no one dared to ask him any more questions.

Is God happy for one country and sad for the other at the end of a war?

All sin and death makes God sad. In wars, people from both sides are hurt and killed. Countries, cities, neighborhoods and families are torn apart. God is sad about all the destruction caused by sin, including war.

But sometimes God does send war as a punishment for evil. In the Old Testament we read that some nations suffered in wars as a punishment for their sins against others. And sometimes war seems to be the only way to stop an evil dictator or an evil government. But that doesn't mean God is happy to see nations go to war.

Related verses:
Amos 5:6–7,
14–15;
Micah 4:3

(checkout) Luke 21:10

WHOSE SON IS THE CHRIST?

⁴¹Jesus said to them, "Why do people say that the Christ is the Son of David? ⁴²David himself says in the Book of Psalms,

" 'The Lord said to my Lord,
    "Sit at my right hand
⁴³until I put your enemies
    under your control." ' *(Psalm 110:1)*

⁴⁴David calls him 'Lord.' So how can he be David's son?"

⁴⁵All the people were listening. Jesus said to his disciples, ⁴⁶"Watch out for the teachers of the law. They like to walk around in long robes. They love to be greeted in the market places. They love to have the most important seats in the synagogues. They also love to have the places of honor at dinners. ⁴⁷They take over the houses of widows. They say long prayers to show off. God will punish those men very much."

THE WIDOW'S OFFERING

21 As Jesus looked up, he saw rich people putting their gifts into the temple offering boxes. ²He also saw a poor widow put in two very small copper coins.

³"What I'm about to tell you is true," Jesus said. "That poor widow has put in more than all the others. ⁴All of those other people gave a lot because they are rich. But even though she is poor, she put in everything. She had nothing left to live on."

SIGNS OF THE END

⁵Some of Jesus' disciples were talking about the temple. They spoke about how it was decorated with beautiful stones and with gifts that honored God. But Jesus asked, ⁶"Do you see all this? The time will come when not one stone will be left on top of another. Every stone will be thrown down."

⁷"Teacher," they asked, "when will these things happen? And what will be the sign that they are about to take place?"

⁸Jesus replied, "Keep watch! Be careful that you are not fooled. Many will come in my name. They will claim, 'I am he!' And they will say, 'The time is near!' Do not follow them. ⁹Do not be afraid when you hear about wars and about fighting against rulers. Those things must happen first. But the end will not come right away."

¹⁰Then Jesus said to them, "Nation will fight against nation. Kingdom will fight against kingdom. ¹¹In many places there will be powerful earthquakes. People will go hungry. There will be terrible sicknesses. Things will happen that will make people afraid. There will be great and miraculous signs from heaven.

¹²"But before all this, people will arrest you and treat you badly. They will hand you over to synagogues and prisons. You will be brought to kings and governors. All this will happen to you because of my name. ¹³In that way you will be witnesses to them. ¹⁴But make up your mind not to worry ahead of time about how to stand up for yourselves. ¹⁵I will give you words of wisdom. None of your enemies will be able to withstand them or oppose them.

¹⁶"Even your parents, brothers, sisters, relatives and friends will hand you over to the authorities. They will put some of you to death. ¹⁷Everyone will hate you because of me. ¹⁸But not a hair on your head will be harmed. ¹⁹If you stand firm, you will gain life.

²⁰"A time is coming when you will see armies surround Jerusalem. Then you will know that it will soon be destroyed. ²¹Those who are in Judea should then escape to the mountains. Those in the city should get out. Those in the country should not enter the city. ²²This is the time when God will punish Jerusalem. Everything will come true, just as it has been written. ²³"How awful it will be in those days for pregnant women! How awful for nursing mothers! There will be terrible suffering in the land. There will be great anger against those people. ²⁴Some will be killed by the sword. Others will be taken as prisoners to all the nations. Jerusalem will be overrun by those who aren't Jews until the times of the non-Jews come to an end.

²⁵"There will be miraculous signs in the sun, moon and stars. The nations

of the earth will be in terrible pain. They will be puzzled by the roaring and tossing of the sea. ²⁶Terror will make people faint. They will be worried about what is happening in the world. The sun, moon and stars will be shaken from their places.

²⁷"At that time people will see the Son of Man coming in a cloud. He will come with power and great glory. ²⁸When these things begin to take place, stand up. Hold your head up with joy and hope. The time when you will be set free will be very close."

²⁹Jesus told them a story. "Look at the fig tree and all the trees," he said. ³⁰"When you see leaves appear on the branches, you know that summer is near. ³¹In the same way, when you see these things happening, you will know that God's kingdom is near.

³²"What I'm about to tell you is true. The people living at that time will certainly not pass away until all these things have happened. ³³Heaven and earth will pass away. But my words will never pass away.

³⁴"Be careful. If you aren't, your hearts will be loaded down with wasteful living, drunkenness and the worries of life. Then the day the Son of Man returns will close on you like a trap. You will not be expecting it. ³⁵That day will come upon every person who lives on the whole earth. ³⁶"Always keep watching. Pray that you will be able to escape all that is about to happen. Also, pray that you will not be judged guilty when the Son of Man comes."

³⁷Each day Jesus taught at the temple. And each evening he went to spend the night on the hill called the Mount of Olives. ³⁸All the people came to the temple early in the morning. They wanted to hear Jesus speak.

JUDAS AGREES TO HAND JESUS OVER

22 The Feast of Unleavened Bread, called the Passover, was near. ²The chief priests and the teachers of the law were looking for a way to get rid of Jesus. They were afraid of the people.

³Then Satan entered Judas, who was called Iscariot. Judas was one of the Twelve. ⁴He went to the chief priests and the officers of the temple guard. He talked with them about how he could hand Jesus over to them. ⁵They were delighted and agreed to give him money.

⁶Judas accepted their offer. He watched for the right time to hand Jesus over to them. He wanted to do it when no crowd was around.

THE LAST SUPPER

⁷Then the day of Unleavened Bread came. That was the time the Passover lamb had to be sacrificed. ⁸Jesus sent Peter and John on ahead. "Go," he told them. "Prepare for us to eat the Passover meal."

⁹"Where do you want us to prepare for it?" they asked.

¹⁰Jesus replied, "When you enter the city, a man carrying a jar of water will meet you. Follow him to the house he enters. ¹¹Then say to the owner of the house, 'The Teacher asks, "Where is the guest room? Where can I eat the Passover meal with my disciples?" ' ¹²He will show you a large upstairs room with furniture in it. Prepare for us to eat there."

¹³Peter and John left. They found things just as Jesus had told them. So they prepared the Passover meal.

¹⁴When the hour came, Jesus and his apostles took their places at the table. ¹⁵He said to them, "I have really looked forward to eating this Passover meal with you. I wanted to do this before I suffer. ¹⁶I tell you, I will not eat the Passover meal again until it is celebrated in God's kingdom."

¹⁷After Jesus took the cup, he gave thanks. He said, "Take this cup and share it among yourselves. ¹⁸I tell you, I will not drink wine with you again until God's kingdom comes."

¹⁹Then Jesus took bread. He gave thanks and broke it. He handed it to them and said, "This is my body. It is given for you. Every time you eat it, do it in memory of me."

²⁰In the same way, after the supper he took the cup. He said, "This cup is the new covenant in my blood. It is poured out for you. ²¹But someone here is going to hand me over to my enemies. His hand is with mine on the

table. ²²The Son of Man will go to his death, just as God has already decided. But how terrible it will be for the one who hands him over!"

²³The apostles began to ask each other about this. They wondered which one of them would do it.

²⁴They also started to argue. They disagreed about which of them was thought to be the most important person.

²⁵Jesus said to them, "The kings of the nations hold power over their people. And those who order them around call themselves Protectors. ²⁶But you must not be like that. Instead, the most important among you should be like the youngest. The one who rules should be like the one who serves.

²⁷"Who is more important? Is it the one at the table, or the one who serves? Isn't it the one who is at the table? But I am among you as one who serves. ²⁸You have stood by me during my troubles. ²⁹And I give you a kingdom, just as my Father gave me a kingdom. ³⁰Then you will eat and drink at my table in my kingdom. And you will sit on thrones, judging the 12 tribes of Israel.

³¹"Simon, Simon! Satan has asked to sift you disciples like wheat. ³²But I have prayed for you, Simon. I have prayed that your faith will not fail. When you have turned back, help your brothers to be strong."

³³But Simon replied, "Lord, I am ready to go with you to prison and to death."

³⁴Jesus answered, "I tell you, Peter, you will say three times that you don't know me. And you will do it before the rooster crows today."

³⁵Then Jesus asked the disciples, "Did you need anything when I sent you without a purse, bag or sandals?"

"Nothing," they answered.

³⁶He said to them, "But now if you have a purse, take it. And also take a bag. If you don't have a sword, sell your coat and buy one. ³⁷It is written, 'He was counted among those who had committed crimes.' *(Isaiah 53:12)* I tell you that what is written about me must come true. Yes, it is already coming true."

³⁸The disciples said, "See, Lord, here are two swords."

"That is enough," he replied.

JESUS PRAYS ON THE MOUNT OF OLIVES

³⁹Jesus went out as usual to the Mount of Olives. His disciples followed him. ⁴⁰When they reached the place, Jesus spoke. "Pray that you won't fall into sin when you are tempted," he said to them.

⁴¹Then he went a short distance away from them. There he got down on his knees and prayed. ⁴²He said, "Father, if you are willing, take this cup of suffering away from me. But do what you want, not what I want."

⁴³An angel from heaven appeared to Jesus and gave him strength. ⁴⁴Because he was very sad and troubled, he prayed even harder. His sweat was like drops of blood falling to the ground.

⁴⁵After that, he got up from prayer and went back to the disciples. He found them sleeping. They were worn out because they were very sad.

⁴⁶"Why are you sleeping?" he asked them. "Get up! Pray that you won't fall into sin when you are tempted."

JESUS IS ARRESTED

⁴⁷While Jesus was still speaking, a crowd came up. The man named Judas was leading them. He was one of the Twelve. Judas approached Jesus to kiss him.

⁴⁸But Jesus asked him, "Judas, are you handing over the Son of Man with a kiss?"

⁴⁹Jesus' followers saw what was going to happen. So they said, "Lord, should we use our swords against them?" ⁵⁰One of them struck the servant of the high priest and cut off his right ear.

⁵¹But Jesus answered, "Stop this!" And he touched the man's ear and healed him.

⁵²Then Jesus spoke to the chief priests, the officers of the temple guard, and the elders. They had all come for him. "Am I leading a band of armed men against you?" he asked. "Do you have to come with swords and clubs? ⁵³Every day I was with you in the temple courtyard. And you

didn't lay a hand on me. But this is your hour. This is when darkness rules."

PETER SAYS HE DOES NOT KNOW JESUS

⁵⁴Then the men arrested Jesus and led him away. They took him into the high priest's house. Peter followed from far away. ⁵⁵They started a fire in the middle of the courtyard. Then they sat down together. Peter sat down with them.

⁵⁶A female servant saw him sitting there in the firelight. She looked closely at him. Then she said, "This man was with Jesus."

⁵⁷But Peter said he had not been with him. "Woman, I don't know him," he said.

⁵⁸A little later someone else saw Peter. "You also are one of them," he said.

"No," Peter replied. "I'm not!"

⁵⁹About an hour later, another person spoke up. "This fellow must have been with Jesus," he said. "He is from Galilee."

⁶⁰Peter replied, "Man, I don't know what you're talking about!"

Just as he was speaking, the rooster crowed. ⁶¹The Lord turned and looked right at Peter. Then Peter remembered what the Lord had spoken to him. "The rooster will crow today," Jesus had said. "Before it does, you will say three times that you don't know me." ⁶²Peter went outside. He broke down and sobbed.

THE GUARDS MAKE FUN OF JESUS

⁶³There were men guarding Jesus. They began laughing at him and beating him. ⁶⁴They blindfolded him. They said, "Prophesy! Who hit you?" ⁶⁵They also said many other things to make fun of him.

JESUS IS BROUGHT TO PILATE AND HEROD

⁶⁶At dawn the elders of the people met together. These included the chief priests and the teachers of the law. Jesus was led to them. ⁶⁷"If you are the Christ," they said, "tell us."

Jesus answered, "If I tell you, you will not believe me. ⁶⁸And if I asked you, you would not answer. ⁶⁹But from now on, the Son of Man will be seated at the right hand of the mighty God."

⁷⁰They all asked, "Are you the Son of God then?"

He replied, "You are right in saying that I am."

Why were the Roman soldiers so mean?

The Roman soldiers were mean for the same reason people are mean today. They did not love God or care about his ways. Roman soldiers were trained to keep people in line and even kill if they had to. The Roman soldiers were mean to Jesus because they treated all prisoners that way and they thought Jesus had done crimes just like the other prisoners.

They also egged each other on. One would make fun of Jesus and the others would join in. The soldiers were just going along with the crowd.

checkout

Luke 22:63–65

Related verses: Matthew 27:1–37

[71]Then they said, "Why do we need any more witnesses? We have heard it from his own lips."

23

Then the whole group got up and led Jesus off to Pilate. [2]They began to bring charges against Jesus. They said, "We have found this man misleading our people. He is against paying taxes to Caesar. And he claims to be Christ, a king."

[3]So Pilate asked Jesus, "Are you the king of the Jews?"

"Yes. It is just as you say," Jesus replied.

[4]Then Pilate spoke to the chief priests and the crowd. He announced, "I find no basis for a charge against this man."

[5]But they kept it up. They said, "His teaching stirs up the people all over Judea. He started in Galilee and has come all the way here."

[6]When Pilate heard this, he asked if the man was from Galilee. [7]He learned that Jesus was from Herod's area of authority. So Pilate sent Jesus to Herod. At that time Herod was also in Jerusalem.

[8]When Herod saw Jesus, he was very pleased. He had been wanting to see Jesus for a long time. He had heard much about him. He hoped to see Jesus do a miracle.

[9]Herod asked him many questions, but Jesus gave him no answer. [10]The chief priests and the teachers of the law were standing there. With loud shouts they brought charges against him.

[11]Herod and his soldiers laughed at him and made fun of him. They dressed him in a beautiful robe. Then they sent him back to Pilate. [12]That day Herod and Pilate became friends. Before this time they had been enemies.

[13]Pilate called together the chief priests, the rulers and the people. [14]He said to them, "You brought me this man. You said he was turning the people against the authorities. I have questioned him in front of you. I have found no basis for your charges against him. [15]Herod hasn't either. So he sent Jesus back to us. As you can see, Jesus has done nothing that is worthy of death. [16/17]So I will just have him whipped and let him go."

[18]With one voice the crowd cried out, "Kill this man! Give Barabbas to us!" [19]Barabbas had been thrown into prison. He had taken part in a struggle in the city against the authorities. He had also committed murder.

[20]Pilate wanted to let Jesus go. So he made an appeal to the crowd again. [21]But they kept shouting, "Crucify him! Crucify him!"

[22]Pilate spoke to them for the third time. "Why?" he asked. "What wrong has this man done? I have found no reason to have him put to death. So I will just have him whipped and let him go."

[23]But with loud shouts they kept calling for Jesus to be crucified. The people's shouts won out. [24]So Pilate decided to give them what they wanted. [25]He set free the man they asked for. The man had been thrown in prison for murder and for fighting against the authorities. Pilate gave Jesus over to them so they could carry out their plans.

JESUS IS NAILED TO A CROSS

[26]As they led Jesus away, they took hold of Simon. Simon was from Cyrene. He was on his way in from the country. They put a wooden cross on his shoulders. Then they made him carry it behind Jesus.

[27]A large number of people followed Jesus. Some were women whose hearts were filled with sorrow. They cried loudly because of him.

[28]Jesus turned and said to them, "Daughters of Jerusalem, do not cry for me. Cry for yourselves and for your children. [29]The time will come when you will say, 'Blessed are the women who can't have children! Blessed are those who never gave birth or nursed babies!' [30]It is written,

" 'The people will say to the
      mountains, "Fall on us!"
  They'll say to the hills,
      "Cover us!" '   *(Hosea 10:8)*

[31]People do these things when trees are green. So what will happen when trees are dry?"

[32]Two other men were also led out with Jesus to be killed. Both of them had broken the law. [33]The soldiers

brought them to the place called The Skull. There they nailed Jesus to the cross. He hung between the two criminals. One was on his right and one was on his left.

³⁴Jesus said, "Father, forgive them. They don't know what they are doing." The soldiers divided up his clothes by casting lots.

³⁵The people stood there watching. The rulers even made fun of Jesus. They said, "He saved others. Let him save himself if he is the Christ of God, the Chosen One."

³⁶The soldiers also came up and poked fun at him. They offered him wine vinegar. ³⁷They said, "If you are the king of the Jews, save yourself."

³⁸A written sign had been placed above him. It read, THIS IS THE KING OF THE JEWS.

³⁹One of the criminals hanging there made fun of Jesus. He said, "Aren't you the Christ? Save yourself! Save us!"

⁴⁰But the other criminal scolded him. "Don't you have any respect for God?" he said. "Remember, you are under the same sentence of death. ⁴¹We are being punished fairly. We are getting just what our actions call for. But this man hasn't done anything wrong."

⁴²Then he said, "Jesus, remember me when you come into your kingdom."

⁴³Jesus answered him, "What I'm about to tell you is true. Today you will be with me in paradise."

JESUS DIES

⁴⁴It was now about noon. The whole land was covered with darkness until three o'clock. ⁴⁵The sun had stopped shining. The temple curtain was torn in two. ⁴⁶Jesus called out in a loud voice, "Father, into your hands I commit my very life." After he said this, he took his last breath.

⁴⁷The Roman commander saw what had happened. He praised God and said, "Jesus was surely a man who did what was right."

⁴⁸The people had gathered to watch that sight. When they saw what hap-

Why did the people tell Jesus to come down from the cross?

Gallery Exhibit

The people who said this did not believe in Jesus or understand God's plan. They teased Jesus because he said he was God's son. They thought the Son of God would surely not let himself be killed on a cross. They did not realize that Jesus had the power to come down from the cross. He did not come down because he loved us and wanted to pay for our sins. If Jesus had saved himself and come down from the cross, we would not be saved from our sins.

checkout Luke 23:35,37

Related verses:
Mark 15:29,30

pened, they beat their chests and went away. ⁴⁹But all those who knew Jesus stood not very far away, watching those things. They included the women who had followed him from Galilee.

JESUS IS BURIED

⁵⁰A man named Joseph was a member of the Jewish Council. He was a good and honest man. ⁵¹He had not agreed with what the leaders had decided and done. He was from Arimathea, a town in Judea. He was waiting for God's kingdom.

⁵²Joseph went to Pilate and asked for Jesus' body. ⁵³He took it down and wrapped it in linen cloth. Then he put it in a tomb cut in the rock. No one had ever been buried there. ⁵⁴It was Preparation Day. The Sabbath was about to begin.

⁵⁵The women who had come with Jesus from Galilee followed Joseph. They saw the tomb and how Jesus' body was placed in it. ⁵⁶Then they went home. There they prepared spices and perfumes. But they rested on the Sabbath day in order to obey the Law.

JESUS RISES FROM THE DEAD

24 It was very early in the morning on the first day of the week. The women took the spices they had prepared. Then they went to the tomb. ²They found the stone rolled away from it. ³When they entered the tomb, they did not find the body of the Lord Jesus. ⁴They were wondering about this.

Suddenly two men in clothes as bright as lightning stood beside them. ⁵The women were terrified. They bowed down with their faces to the ground.

Then the men said to them, "Why do you look for the living among the dead? ⁶Jesus is not here! He has risen! Remember how he told you he would rise. It was while he was still with you in Galilee. ⁷He said, 'The Son of Man must be handed over to sinful people. He must be nailed to a cross. On the third day he will rise from the dead.' "

⁸Then the women remembered Jesus' words.

⁹They came back from the tomb. They told all these things to the Eleven and to all the others. ¹⁰Mary Magda-

Is there any other place you can go to besides heaven or hell when you die?

You may have heard people talk about Purgatory, "Limbo," or some other place for people to go after they die. But the Bible does not teach anything about a place like that. The Bible teaches that death is the end of life on earth and the start of life in either heaven or hell. People do not have a second chance after they die. There is no chance after death to accept Jesus' sacrifice for your sins. The Bible also makes it clear that Christians immediately go to be with God after they die.

checkout Luke 23:42,43

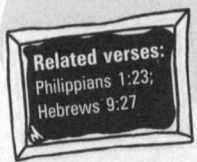

Related verses:
Philippians 1:23;
Hebrews 9:27

lene, Joanna, Mary the mother of James, and the others with them were the ones who told the apostles. ¹¹But the apostles did not believe the women. Their words didn't make any sense to them.

¹²But Peter got up and ran to the tomb. He bent over and saw the strips of linen lying by themselves. Then he went away, wondering what had happened.

ON THE ROAD TO EMMAUS

¹³That same day two of Jesus' followers were going to a village called Emmaus. It was about seven miles from Jerusalem. ¹⁴They were talking with each other about everything that had happened.

¹⁵As they talked about those things, Jesus himself came up and walked along with them. ¹⁶But God kept them from recognizing him.

¹⁷Jesus asked them, "What are you talking about as you walk along?"

They stood still, and their faces were sad. ¹⁸One of them was named Cleopas. He said to Jesus, "You must be a visitor to Jerusalem. If you lived there, you would know the things that have happened there in the last few days."

¹⁹"What things?" Jesus asked.

"About Jesus of Nazareth," they replied. "He was a prophet. He was powerful in what he said and did in the eyes of God and all of the people. ²⁰The chief priests and our rulers handed Jesus over to be sentenced to death. They nailed him to a cross. ²¹But we had hoped that he was the one who was going to set Israel free. Also, it is the third day since all this happened.

²²"Some of our women amazed us too. Early this morning they went to the tomb. ²³But they didn't find his body. So they came and told us what they had seen. They saw angels, who said Jesus was alive. ²⁴Then some of our friends went to the tomb. They saw it was empty, just as the women had said. They didn't see Jesus' body there."

²⁵Jesus said to them, "How foolish you are! How long it takes you to believe all that the prophets said! ²⁶Didn't the Christ have to suffer these things and then receive his glory?"

²⁷Jesus explained to them what was said about himself in all the Scriptures. He began with Moses and all the Prophets.

²⁸The two men approached the village where they were going. Jesus acted as if he were going farther. ²⁹But they tried hard to keep him from leaving. They said, "Stay with us. It is nearly evening. The day is almost over." So he went in to stay with them.

³⁰He joined them at the table. Then he took bread and gave thanks. He broke it and began to give it to them. ³¹Their eyes were opened, and they recognized him. But then he disappeared from their sight.

³²They said to each other, "He talked with us on the road. He opened the Scriptures to us. Weren't our hearts burning inside us during that time?"

³³They got up and returned at once to Jerusalem. There they found the Eleven and those with them. They were all gathered together. ³⁴They were saying, "It's true! The Lord has risen! He has appeared to Simon!"

³⁵Then the two of them told what had happened to them on the way. They told how they had recognized Jesus when he broke the bread.

JESUS APPEARS TO THE DISCIPLES

³⁶The disciples were still talking about this when Jesus himself suddenly stood among them. He said, "May peace be with you!"

³⁷They were surprised and terrified. They thought they were seeing a ghost.

³⁸Jesus said to them, "Why are you troubled? Why do you have doubts in your minds? ³⁹Look at my hands and my feet. It is really I! Touch me and see. A ghost does not have a body or bones. But you can see that I do."

⁴⁰After he said that, he showed them his hands and feet. ⁴¹But they still did not believe it. They were amazed and filled with joy.

So Jesus asked them, "Do you have anything here to eat?"

⁴²They gave him a piece of cooked fish. ⁴³He took it and ate it in front of them.

⁴⁴Jesus said to them, "This is what I

told you while I was still with you. Everything written about me must happen. Everything written about me in the Law of Moses, the Prophets and the Psalms must come true."

⁴⁵Then he opened their minds so they could understand the Scriptures. ⁴⁶He told them, "This is what is written. The Christ will suffer. He will rise from the dead on the third day. ⁴⁷His followers will preach in his name. They will tell others to turn away from their sins and be forgiven. People from every nation will hear it, beginning at Jerusalem. ⁴⁸You have seen these things with your own eyes.

⁴⁹"I am going to send you what my Father has promised. But for now, stay in the city. Stay there until you have received power from heaven."

JESUS IS TAKEN UP INTO HEAVEN

⁵⁰Jesus led his disciples out to the area near Bethany. Then he lifted up his hands and blessed them. ⁵¹While he was blessing them, he left them. He was taken up into heaven.

⁵²Then they worshiped him. With great joy, they returned to Jerusalem. ⁵³Every day they went to the temple, praising God.

Is there a McDonald's in heaven?

No. In heaven we will not need to eat to stay alive. We will have perfect bodies that live forever. But those bodies will be very real too. We will be able to taste good food just like we can now. Jesus did that after he rose from the dead. He ate some fresh fish right out of the pan to show his disciples that he was not a ghost. In other words, we will *enjoy* the good things in heaven. It will be great!

checkout
Luke 24:41–43

Related verses:
1 Corinthians
15:35–44

HEAVEN
FROM JASON'S
PERSPECTIVE

Fly-Thru

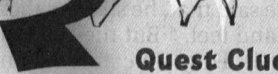

Quest Clue

Do you worry about whether you'll get the things you need? Jesus says he will meet our needs. We never need to worry! Read Matthew 6 and Luke 11 and 12 to hear Jesus' comforting words to you.

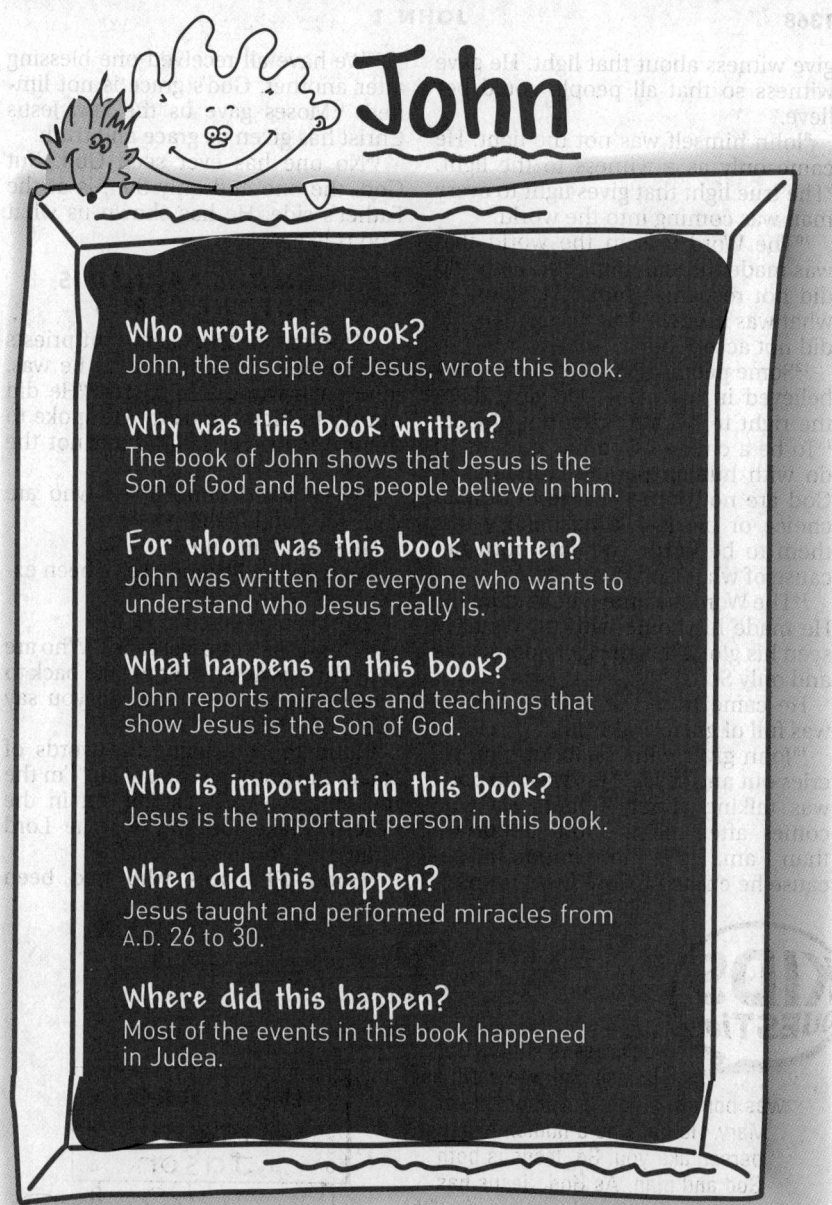

John

Who wrote this book?
John, the disciple of Jesus, wrote this book.

Why was this book written?
The book of John shows that Jesus is the Son of God and helps people believe in him.

For whom was this book written?
John was written for everyone who wants to understand who Jesus really is.

What happens in this book?
John reports miracles and teachings that show Jesus is the Son of God.

Who is important in this book?
Jesus is the important person in this book.

When did this happen?
Jesus taught and performed miracles from A.D. 26 to 30.

Where did this happen?
Most of the events in this book happened in Judea.

THE WORD BECAME HUMAN

1 In the beginning, the Word was already there. The Word was with God, and the Word was God. ²He was with God in the beginning.

³All things were made through him. Nothing that has been made was made without him. ⁴Life was in him, and that life was the light for all people. ⁵The light shines in the darkness. But the darkness has not understood it.

⁶A man came who was sent from God. His name was John. ⁷He came to

give witness about that light. He gave witness so that all people could believe.

[8]John himself was not the light. He came only as a witness to the light. [9]The true light that gives light to every man was coming into the world.

[10]The Word was in the world that was made through him. But the world did not recognize him. [11]He came to what was his own. But his own people did not accept him.

[12]Some people did accept him. They believed in his name. He gave them the right to become children of God. [13]To be a child of God has nothing to do with human parents. Children of God are not born because of human choice or because a husband wants them to be born. They are born because of what God does.

[14]The Word became a human being. He made his home with us. We have seen his glory. It is the glory of the one and only Son.

He came from the Father. And he was full of grace and truth.

[15]John gives witness about him. He cries out and says, "This was the one I was talking about. I said, 'He who comes after me is more important than I am. He is more important because he existed before I was born.' "

[16]We have all received one blessing after another. God's grace is not limited. [17]Moses gave us the law. Jesus Christ has given us grace and truth.

[18]No one has ever seen God. But God, the one and only Son, is at the Father's side. He has shown us what God is like.

JOHN THE BAPTIST IS NOT THE CHRIST

[19]The Jews of Jerusalem sent priests and Levites to ask John who he was. John gave witness to them. [20]He did not try to hide the truth. He spoke to them openly. He said, "I am not the Christ."

[21]They asked him, "Then who are you? Are you Elijah?"

He said, "I am not."

"Are you the Prophet we've been expecting?" they asked.

"No," he answered.

[22]They asked one last time, "Who are you? Give us an answer to take back to those who sent us. What do you say about yourself?"

[23]John replied, using the words of Isaiah the prophet. John said, "I'm the messenger who is calling out in the desert, 'Make the way for the Lord straight.' " *(Isaiah 40:3)*

[24]Some Pharisees who had been

Is Jesus God?

Yes, Jesus is fully God. He also came to earth and was born to a young woman named Mary. He became a human being, a person like you. So Jesus is both God and man. As God, Jesus has always existed. John called him "the Word" (See John 1:1). He was not created when he was born. Instead he *chose* to take on a human body.

checkout John 1:1,2

Related verses:
John 1:14;
Philippians 2:6–8

theolojikal answers jason

sent ²⁵asked him, "If you are not the Christ, why are you baptizing people? Why are you doing that if you aren't Elijah or the Prophet we've been expecting?"

²⁶"I baptize people with water," John replied. "But One is standing among you whom you do not know. ²⁷He is the One who comes after me. I am not good enough to untie his sandals."

²⁸This all happened at Bethany on the other side of the Jordan River. That was where John was baptizing.

JESUS IS THE LAMB OF GOD

²⁹The next day John saw Jesus coming toward him. John said, "Look! The Lamb of God! He takes away the sin of the world! ³⁰This is the One I was talking about. I said, 'A man who comes after me is more important than I am. That's because he existed before I was born.' ³¹I did not know him. But God wants to make it clear to Israel who this person is. That's the reason I came baptizing with water."

³²Then John told them, "I saw the Holy Spirit come down from heaven like a dove. The Spirit remained on Jesus. ³³I would not have known him. But the One who sent me to baptize with water told me, 'You will see the Spirit come down and remain on someone. He is the One who will baptize with the Holy Spirit.' ³⁴I have seen it happen. I give witness that this is the Son of God."

JESUS CHOOSES THE FIRST DISCIPLES

³⁵The next day John was again with two of his disciples. ³⁶He saw Jesus walking by. John said, "Look! The Lamb of God!"

³⁷The two disciples heard him say this. So they followed Jesus. ³⁸Then Jesus turned around and saw them following. He asked, "What do you want?"

They said, "Rabbi, where are you staying?" *Rabbi* means Teacher.

³⁹"Come," he replied. "You will see."

So they went and saw where he was staying. They spent the rest of the day with him. It was about four o'clock in the afternoon.

⁴⁰Andrew was Simon Peter's brother. Andrew was one of the two disciples who heard what John had said. He had also followed Jesus. ⁴¹The first thing Andrew did was to find his brother Simon. He told him, "We have found the Messiah." Messiah means Christ. ⁴²And he brought Simon to Jesus.

Jesus looked at him and said, "You are Simon, son of John. You will be called Cephas." Cephas means Peter (or rock).

JESUS CHOOSES PHILIP AND NATHANAEL

⁴³The next day Jesus decided to leave for Galilee. He found Philip and said to him, "Follow me."

⁴⁴Philip was from the town of Bethsaida. So were Andrew and Peter. ⁴⁵Philip found Nathanael and told him, "We have found the One that Moses wrote about in the Law. The prophets also wrote about him. He is Jesus of Nazareth, the son of Joseph."

⁴⁶"Nazareth! Can anything good come from there?" Nathanael asked.

"Come and see," said Philip.

⁴⁷Jesus saw Nathanael approaching. Here is what Jesus said about him. "He is a true Israelite. There is nothing false in him."

⁴⁸"How do you know me?" Nathanael asked.

Jesus answered, "I saw you while you were still under the fig tree. I saw you there before Philip called you."

⁴⁹Nathanael replied, "Rabbi, you are the Son of God. You are the King of Israel."

⁵⁰Jesus said, "You believe because I told you I saw you under the fig tree. You will see greater things than that." ⁵¹Then he said to the disciples, "What I'm about to tell you is true. You will see heaven open. You will see the angels of God going up and coming down on the Son of Man."

JESUS CHANGES WATER INTO WINE

2 On the third day there was a wedding. It took place at Cana in Galilee. Jesus' mother was there. ²Jesus and his disciples had also been invited to the wedding. ³When the wine was gone, Jesus' mother said to him, "They have no more wine."

⁴"Dear woman, why do you bring me into this?" Jesus replied. "My time has not yet come."

⁵His mother said to the servants, "Do what he tells you."

⁶Six stone water jars stood nearby. The Jews used water from that kind of jar for special washings to make themselves pure. Each jar could hold 20 to 30 gallons.

⁷Jesus said to the servants, "Fill the jars with water." So they filled them to the top.

⁸Then he told them, "Now dip some out. Take it to the person in charge of the dinner."

They did what he said. ⁹The person in charge tasted the water that had been turned into wine. He didn't realize where it had come from. But the servants who had brought the water knew.

Then the person in charge called the groom to one side. ¹⁰He said to him, "Everyone brings out the best wine first. They bring out the cheaper wine after the guests have had too much to drink. But you have saved the best until now."

¹¹That was the first of Jesus' miraculous signs. He did it at Cana in Galilee. Jesus showed his glory by doing it. And his disciples put their faith in him.

JESUS CLEARS OUT THE TEMPLE

¹²After this, Jesus went down to Capernaum. His mother and brothers and disciples went with him. They all stayed there for a few days.

¹³It was almost time for the Jewish Passover Feast. So Jesus went up to Jerusalem. ¹⁴In the temple courtyard he found people who were selling cattle, sheep and doves. Others were sitting at tables exchanging money.

¹⁵So Jesus made a whip out of ropes. He chased all the sheep and cattle from the temple area. He scattered the coins of the people exchanging money. And he turned over their tables. ¹⁶He told those who were selling

Why is being good not enough to get someone into heaven?

It is impossible to be good enough to get into heaven. Every person has sinned, and even one sin is too many to get into heaven. Heaven is perfect because God is perfect—there is no sin at all.

That is why we need Jesus. Only through Jesus can we be in God's presence because Jesus forgives our sins.

We are each like a pane of glass in a window. If even one tiny corner of it is broken, it is broken. We need a miracle to make us whole again. We need to believe in Jesus and invite him to save us. Then we can have our sins forgiven and be ready for heaven.

checkout
John 3:5-7, 16-18

Related verses:
Psalm 14:1-3;
Isaiah 1:18;
Romans 3:9-18,
3:23

JASON'S IMAGINATION

WELCOME TO HEAVEN

FAITH

doves, "Get these out of here! How dare you turn my Father's house into a market!"

[17]His disciples remembered what had been written. It says, "My great love for your house will destroy me." *(Psalm 69:9)*

[18]Then the Jews asked him, "What miraculous sign can you show us? Can you prove your authority to do all of this?"

[19]Jesus answered them, "Destroy this temple. I will raise it up again in three days."

[20]The Jews replied, "It has taken 46 years to build this temple. Are you going to raise it up in three days?"

[21]But the temple Jesus had spoken about was his body.

[22]His disciples later remembered what he had said. That was after he had been raised from the dead. Then they believed the Scriptures. They also believed the words that Jesus had spoken.

[23]Meanwhile, he was in Jerusalem at the Passover Feast. Many people saw the miraculous signs he was doing. And they believed in his name. [24]But Jesus did not fully trust them. He knew what people are like. [25]He didn't need others to tell him what people are like. He already knew what was in the human heart.

JESUS TEACHES NICODEMUS

3 There was a Pharisee named Nicodemus. He was one of the Jewish rulers. [2]He came to Jesus at night and said, "Rabbi, we know you are a teacher who has come from God. We know that God is with you. If he weren't, you couldn't do the miraculous signs you are doing."

[3]Jesus replied, "What I'm about to tell you is true. No one can see God's kingdom without being born again."

[4]"How can I be born when I am old?" Nicodemus asked. "I can't go back inside my mother! I can't be born a second time!"

[5]Jesus answered, "What I'm about to tell you is true. No one can enter God's kingdom without being born through water and the Holy Spirit. [6]People give birth to people. But the Spirit gives birth to spirit. [7]You should not be sur-

prised when I say, 'You must all be born again.'

[8]"The wind blows where it wants to. You hear the sound it makes. But you can't tell where it comes from or where it is going. It is the same with everyone who is born through the Spirit."

[9]"How can this be?" Nicodemus asked.

[10]"You are Israel's teacher," said Jesus. "Don't you understand these things?

[11]"What I'm about to tell you is true. We speak about what we know. We give witness to what we have seen. But still you people do not accept our witness. [12]I have spoken to you about earthly things, and you do not believe. So how will you believe if I speak about heavenly things?

[13]"No one has ever gone into heaven except the One who came from heaven. He is the Son of Man. [14]Moses lifted up the snake in the desert. The Son of Man must be lifted up also. [15]Then everyone who believes in him can live with God forever.

[16]"God loved the world so much that he gave his one and only Son. Anyone who believes in him will not die but will have eternal life.

[17]"God did not send his Son into the world to judge the world. He sent his Son to save the world through him. [18]Anyone who believes in him is not judged. But anyone who does not believe is judged already. He has not believed in the name of God's one and only Son.

[19]"Here is the judgment. Light has come into the world, but people loved darkness instead of light. They loved darkness because what they did was evil.

[20]"Everyone who does evil things hates the light. They will not come into the light. They are afraid that what they do will be seen. [21]But anyone who lives by the truth comes into the light. He does this so that it will be easy to see that what he has done is with God's help."

JOHN THE BAPTIST GIVES WITNESS ABOUT JESUS

[22]After this, Jesus and his disciples went out into the countryside of Ju-

dea. There he spent some time with them. And he baptized people there.

²³John was also baptizing. He was at Aenon near Salim, where there was plenty of water. People were coming all the time to be baptized. ²⁴That was before John was put in prison.

²⁵Some of John's disciples and a certain Jew began to argue. They argued about special washings to make people "clean." ²⁶They came to John and said to him, "Rabbi, that man who was with you on the other side of the Jordan River is baptizing people. He is the one you gave witness about. Everyone is going to him."

²⁷John replied, "A person can receive only what God gives him from heaven. ²⁸You yourselves are witnesses that I said, 'I am not the Christ. I was sent ahead of him.' ²⁹The bride belongs to the groom. The friend who helps the groom waits and listens for him. He is full of joy when he hears the groom's voice. That joy is mine, and it is now complete. ³⁰He must become more important. I must become less important.

³¹"The One who comes from above is above everything. The one who is from the earth belongs to the earth and speaks like someone from the earth. The One who comes from heaven is above everything. ³²He gives witness to what he has seen and heard. But no one accepts what he says. ³³Anyone who has accepted it has said, 'Yes. God is truthful.' ³⁴The One whom God has sent speaks God's words. God gives the Holy Spirit without limit.

³⁵"The Father loves the Son and has put everything into his hands. ³⁶Anyone who believes in the Son has eternal life. Anyone who says no to the Son will not have life. God's anger remains on him."

JESUS TALKS WITH A WOMAN FROM SAMARIA

4 The Pharisees heard that Jesus was winning and baptizing more disciples than John. ²But in fact Jesus was not baptizing. His disciples were. ³When the Lord found out about all this, he left Judea. He went back to Galilee again.

⁴Jesus had to go through Samaria. ⁵He came to a town in Samaria called

How do you get permission to go to heaven?

There is only one way to get to heaven and that is through Jesus Christ. Only people who trust in Jesus go to heaven. We can place our trust in Jesus by praying to God and telling him that we want to be his child. Here is one way to pray that kind of prayer: *"I am sorry for disobeying you. I believe that Jesus came to earth, died for my sins and rose from the dead. Please take away my sins and come live inside me."* The Bible says that whoever does this becomes a new person, a child of God. And all of God's children go to be with him in heaven when they die.

checkout
John 3:16

Related verses:
Romans 10:9,10

Sychar. It was near the piece of land Jacob had given his son Joseph. [6]Jacob's well was there. Jesus was tired from the journey. So he sat down by the well. It was about noon.

[7]A woman from Samaria came to get some water. Jesus said to her, "Will you give me a drink?" [8]His disciples had gone into the town to buy food.

[9]The Samaritan woman said to him, "You are a Jew. I am a Samaritan woman. How can you ask me for a drink?" She said this because Jews don't have anything to do with Samaritans.

[10]Jesus answered her, "You do not know what God's gift is. And you do not know who is asking you for a drink. If you did, you would have asked him. He would have given you living water."

[11]"Sir," the woman said, "you don't have anything to get water with. The well is deep. Where can you get this living water?

[12]"Our father Jacob gave us the well. He drank from it himself. So did his sons and his flocks and herds. Are you more important than he is?"

[13]Jesus answered, "All who drink this water will be thirsty again. [14]But anyone who drinks the water I give him will never be thirsty. In fact, the water I give him will become a spring of water in him. It will flow up into eternal life."

[15]The woman said to him, "Sir, give me this water. Then I will never be thirsty. And I won't have to keep coming here to get water."

[16]He told her, "Go. Get your husband and come back."

[17]"I have no husband," she replied.

Jesus said to her, "You are right when you say you have no husband. [18]The fact is, you have had five husbands. And the man you have now is not your husband. What you have just said is very true."

[19]"Sir," the woman said, "I can see that you are a prophet. [20]Our people have worshiped on this mountain for a long time. But you Jews claim that the place where we must worship is in Jerusalem."

[21]Jesus said, "Believe me, woman. A time is coming when you will not worship the Father on this mountain or in Jerusalem. [22]You Samaritans worship what you do not know. We worship what we do know. Salvation comes from the Jews.

[23]"But a new time is coming. In fact, it is already here. True worshipers will worship the Father in spirit and in truth. They are the kind of worshipers the Father is looking for.

[24]"God is spirit. His worshipers must worship him in spirit and in truth."

[25]The woman said, "I know that

Why can't we see God?

We can't see God because he is spirit. He has no body. But we can see what he does. Balloons are filled with air that we can't see, but we see the balloon get big as the air is put in. We can't see radio waves, but we hear music on the radio. Many things happen that our eyes can't see. God is like that. He is real even though our eyes don't see him. And we believe in him even though our eyes don't see him. That's called faith. Some day in heaven we will see God face to face. We *will* be able to see him.

checkout John 4:24

Related verse:
Hebrews 11:6

Messiah is coming." (He is called Christ.) "When he comes, he will explain everything to us."

²⁶Then Jesus said, "I, the one speaking to you, am he."

THE DISCIPLES JOIN JESUS AGAIN

²⁷Just then Jesus' disciples returned. They were surprised to find him talking with a woman. But no one asked, "What do you want from her?" No one asked, "Why are you talking with her?"

²⁸The woman left her water jar and went back to the town. She said to the people, ²⁹"Come. See a man who told me everything I've ever done. Could this be the Christ?"

³⁰The people came out of the town and made their way toward Jesus.

³¹His disciples were saying to him, "Rabbi, eat something!"

³²But he said to them, "I have food to eat that you know nothing about."

³³Then his disciples asked each other, "Did someone bring him food?"

³⁴Jesus said, "My food is to do what my Father sent me to do. My food is to finish his work.

³⁵"You say, 'Four months more, and then it will be harvest time.' But I tell you, open your eyes! Look at the fields! They are ripe for harvest right now. ³⁶Those who gather the crop are already getting paid. They are already harvesting the crop for eternal life. So those who plant and those who gather can now be glad together.

³⁷"Here is a true saying. 'One plants and another gathers.' ³⁸I sent you to gather what you have not worked for. Others have done the hard work. You have gathered the benefits of their work."

MANY SAMARITANS BELIEVE IN JESUS

³⁹Many of the Samaritans from the town of Sychar believed in Jesus. They believed because of the woman's witness. She said, "He told me everything I've ever done."

⁴⁰Then the Samaritans came to him and tried to get him to stay with them. So he stayed two days. ⁴¹Because of his words, many more people became believers.

⁴²They said to the woman, "We no longer believe just because of what you said. We have now heard for ourselves. We know that this man really is the Savior of the world."

JESUS HEALS THE OFFICIAL'S SON

⁴³After the two days, Jesus left for Galilee. ⁴⁴He himself had pointed out that a prophet is not respected in his own country. ⁴⁵When he arrived in Galilee, the people living there welcomed him. They had seen everything he had done in Jerusalem at the Passover Feast. That was because they had also been there.

⁴⁶Once more, Jesus visited Cana in Galilee. Cana is where he had turned the water into wine. A royal official was there. His son was sick in bed at Capernaum. ⁴⁷The official heard that Jesus had arrived in Galilee from Judea. So he went to Jesus and begged him to come and heal his son. The boy was close to death.

⁴⁸Jesus told him, "You people will never believe unless you see miraculous signs and wonders."

⁴⁹The royal official said, "Sir, come down before my child dies."

⁵⁰Jesus replied, "You may go. Your son will live."

The man believed what Jesus said, and so he left. ⁵¹While he was still on his way home, his servants met him. They gave him the news that his boy was living. ⁵²He asked what time his son got better. They said to him, "The fever left him yesterday afternoon at one o'clock."

⁵³Then the father realized what had happened. That was the exact time Jesus had said to him, "Your son will live." So he and all his family became believers.

⁵⁴This was the second miraculous sign that Jesus did after coming from Judea to Galilee.

JESUS HEALS A DISABLED MAN

5 Some time later, Jesus went up to Jerusalem for a Jewish feast. ²In Jerusalem near the Sheep Gate is a pool. In the Aramaic language it is called Bethesda. It is surrounded

by five rows of columns with a roof over them. ³/⁴Here a great number of disabled people used to lie down. Among them were those who were blind, those who could not walk, and those who could hardly move.

⁵One person who was there had been disabled for 38 years. ⁶Jesus saw him lying there. He knew that the man had been in that condition for a long time. So he asked him, "Do you want to get well?"

⁷"Sir," the disabled man replied, "I have no one to help me into the pool when an angel stirs the water up. I try to get in, but someone else always goes down ahead of me."

⁸Then Jesus said to him, "Get up! Pick up your mat and walk."

⁹At once the man was healed. He picked up his mat and walked.

The day this happened was a Sabbath. ¹⁰So the Jews said to the man who had been healed, "It is the Sabbath. The law does not allow you to carry your mat."

¹¹But he replied, "The one who made me well said to me, 'Pick up your mat and walk.' "

¹²They asked him, "Who is this fellow? Who told you to pick it up and walk?"

¹³The one who was healed had no idea who it was. Jesus had slipped away into the crowd that was there.

¹⁴Later Jesus found him at the temple. Jesus said to him, "See, you are well again. Stop sinning, or something worse may happen to you." ¹⁵The man went away. He told the Jews it was Jesus who had made him well.

LIFE BECAUSE OF THE SON

¹⁶Jesus was doing these things on the Sabbath day. So the Jews began to oppose him.

¹⁷Jesus said to them, "My Father is always doing his work. He is working right up to this very day. I am working too."

¹⁸For this reason the Jews tried even harder to kill him. Jesus was not only breaking the Sabbath. He was even calling God his own Father. He was making himself equal with God.

¹⁹Jesus answered, "What I'm about to tell you is true. The Son can do noth-ing by himself. He can do only what he sees his Father doing. What the Father does, the Son also does. ²⁰This is because the Father loves the Son. He shows him everything he does. Yes, you will be amazed! The Father will show him even greater things than these.

²¹"The Father raises the dead and gives them life. In the same way, the Son gives life to anyone he wants to.

²²"Also, the Father does not judge anyone. He has given the Son the task of judging. ²³Then all people will hon-or the Son just as they honor the Fa-ther. Those who do not honor the Son do not honor the Father, who sent him.

²⁴"What I'm about to tell you is true. Anyone who hears my word and be-lieves him who sent me has eternal life. He will not be found guilty. He has crossed over from death to life.

²⁵"What I'm about to tell you is true. A time is coming for me to give life. In fact, it has already begun. The dead will hear the voice of the Son of God. Those who hear it will live.

²⁶"The Father has life in himself. He has also allowed the Son to have life in himself. ²⁷And the Father has given him the authority to judge. This is be-cause he is the Son of Man.

²⁸"Do not be amazed at this. A time is coming when all who are in the grave will hear his voice. ²⁹They will all come out of their graves. Those who have done good will rise and live again. Those who have done evil will rise and be found guilty.

³⁰"I can do nothing by myself. I judge only as I hear. And my judging is fair. I do not try to please myself. I try only to please the One who sent me.

GIVING WITNESS
ABOUT JESUS

³¹"If I give witness about myself, it doesn't count. ³²There is someone else who gives witness in my favor. And I know that his witness about me counts.

³³"You have sent people to John. He has given witness to the truth. ³⁴I do not accept human witness. I only talk about it so you can be saved. ³⁵John was like a lamp that burned and gave

light. For a while you chose to enjoy his light.

36"The witness I have is more important than John's. I am doing the very work the Father gave me to finish. It gives witness that the Father has sent me.

37"The Father who sent me has himself given witness about me. You have never heard his voice. You have never seen what he really looks like. 38And his word does not live in you. This is because you do not believe the One he sent.

39"You study the Scriptures carefully. You study them because you think they will give you eternal life. The Scriptures you study give witness about me. 40But you refuse to come to me and receive life.

41"I do not accept praise from people. 42But I know you. I know that you do not have love for God in your hearts. 43I have come in my Father's name, and you do not accept me. But if someone else comes in his own name, you will accept him.

44"You accept praise from one another. But you make no effort to receive the praise that comes from the only God. So how can you believe? 45Do not think I will bring charges against you in front of the Father. Moses is the one who does that. And he is the one you build your hopes on.

46"Do you believe Moses? Then you should believe me. He wrote about me. 47But you do not believe what he wrote. So how are you going to believe what I say?"

JESUS FEEDS THE FIVE THOUSAND

6 Some time after this, Jesus crossed over to the other side of the Sea of Galilee. It is also called the Sea of Tiberias. 2A large crowd of people followed him. They had seen the miraculous signs he had done on those who were sick.

3Then Jesus went up on a mountainside. There he sat down with his disciples. 4The Jewish Passover Feast was near.

Why is the Bible in two parts instead of in one part?

The two parts of the Bible are called the Old Testament and the New Testament. The Old Testament tells about the beginning of the world. It tells about how the people of Israel obeyed and disobeyed God over many, many years. In the Old Testament God told people that Jesus was coming. Jesus himself told the Jews that the Old Testament pointed to his work. On the other hand, the New Testament tells about Jesus, about the very first Christians and about the future. You can think of the Old Testament and New Testament as "before Christ" and "after Christ." But remember that the Bible is all one book even though it has two main parts.

checkout
John 5:39

SUPER SPECIAL TESTAMENTS
two for the price of one!

Related verses: Hebrews 1:1,2

⁵Jesus looked up and saw a large crowd coming toward him. So he said to Philip, "Where can we buy bread for these people to eat?" ⁶He asked this only to put Philip to the test. He already knew what he was going to do.

⁷Philip answered him, "Eight months' pay would not buy enough bread for each one to have a bite!"

⁸Another of his disciples spoke up. It was Andrew, Simon Peter's brother. ⁹He said, "Here is a boy with five small loaves of barley bread. He also has two small fish. But how far will that go in such a large crowd?"

¹⁰Jesus said, "Have the people sit down." There was plenty of grass in that place, and they sat down. The number of men among them was about 5,000.

¹¹Then Jesus took the loaves and gave thanks. He handed out the bread to those who were seated. He gave them as much as they wanted. And he did the same with the fish.

¹²When all of them had enough to eat, Jesus spoke to his disciples. "Gather the leftover pieces," he said. "Don't waste anything."

¹³So they gathered what was left over from the five barley loaves. They filled 12 baskets with the pieces left by those who had eaten.

¹⁴The people saw the miraculous sign that Jesus did. Then they began to say, "This must be the Prophet who is supposed to come into the world." ¹⁵But Jesus knew that they planned to come and force him to be their king. So he went away again to a mountain by himself.

JESUS WALKS ON THE WATER

¹⁶When evening came, Jesus' disciples went down to the Sea of Galilee. ¹⁷There they got into a boat and headed across the lake toward Capernaum. By now it was dark. Jesus had not yet joined them.

¹⁸A strong wind was blowing, and the water became rough. ¹⁹They rowed three or three and a half miles. Then they saw Jesus coming toward the boat. He was walking on the water. They were terrified. ²⁰But he said to them, "It is I. Don't be afraid."

²¹Then they agreed to take him into the boat. Right away the boat reached the shore where they were heading.

²²The next day the crowd that had stayed on the other side of the lake realized something. They saw that only one boat had been there. They knew that Jesus had not gotten into it with his disciples. And they knew that the disciples had gone away alone. ²³Then some boats from Tiberias

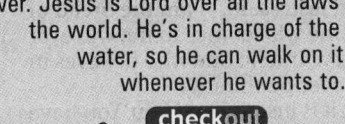

How did Jesus walk on water?

Jesus did a lot of miracles. We do not know how he did them. Jesus is God, so he can do anything. Walking on the water was not the way Jesus got around all the time. He did this miracle to teach his disciples that they could trust him in any situation. It showed them his power. Jesus is Lord over all the laws in the world. He's in charge of the water, so he can walk on it whenever he wants to.

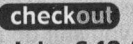
John 6:19,20

Related verses:
Job 38:8;
Matthew 14:26

landed. It was near the place where the people had eaten the bread after the Lord gave thanks. ²⁴The crowd realized that Jesus and his disciples were not there. So they got into boats and went to Capernaum to look for Jesus.

JESUS IS THE BREAD OF LIFE

²⁵They found him on the other side of the lake. They asked him, "Rabbi, when did you get here?"

²⁶Jesus answered, "What I'm about to tell you is true. You are not looking for me because you saw miraculous signs. You are looking for me because you ate the loaves until you were full. ²⁷Do not work for food that spoils. Work for food that lasts forever. That is the food the Son of Man will give you. God the Father has put his seal of approval on him."

²⁸Then they asked him, "What does God want from us? What works does he want us to do?"

²⁹Jesus answered, "God's work is to believe in the One he has sent."

³⁰So they asked him, "What miraculous sign will you give us? What will you do so we can see it and believe you? ³¹Long ago our people ate the manna in the desert. It is written in Scripture, 'The Lord gave them bread from heaven to eat.' " *(Exodus 16:4; Nehemiah 9:15; Psalm 78:24,25)*

³²Jesus said to them, "What I'm about to tell you is true. It is not Moses who has given you the bread from heaven. It is my Father who gives you the true bread from heaven. ³³The bread of God is the One who comes down from heaven. He gives life to the world."

³⁴"Sir," they said, "give us this bread from now on."

³⁵Then Jesus said, "I am the bread of life. No one who comes to me will ever go hungry. And no one who believes in me will ever be thirsty.

³⁶"But it is just as I told you. You have seen me, and you still do not believe. ³⁷Everyone the Father gives me will come to me. I will never send away anyone who comes to me.

³⁸"I have not come down from heaven to do what I want to do. I have come to do what the One who sent me wants me to do. ³⁹The One who sent me doesn't want me to lose anyone he has given me. He wants me to raise them up on the last day. ⁴⁰My Father wants all who look to the Son and believe in him to have eternal life. I will raise them up on the last day."

⁴¹Then the Jews began to complain about Jesus. That was because he said, "I am the bread that came down from heaven." ⁴²They said, "Isn't this Jesus, the son of Joseph? Don't we know his father and mother? How can he now say, 'I came down from heaven'?"

⁴³"Stop complaining among yourselves," Jesus answered. ⁴⁴"No one can come to me unless the Father who sent me brings him. Then I will raise him up on the last day.

⁴⁵"It is written in the Prophets, 'God will teach all of them.' *(Isaiah 54:13)* Everyone who listens to the Father and learns from him comes to me.

⁴⁶"No one has seen the Father except the One who has come from God. Only he has seen the Father. ⁴⁷What I'm about to tell you is true. Everyone who believes has life forever.

⁴⁸"I am the bread of life. ⁴⁹Long ago your people ate the manna in the desert, and they still died. ⁵⁰But here is the bread that comes down from heaven. A person can eat it and not die. ⁵¹I am the living bread that came down from heaven. Everyone who eats some of this bread will live forever. The bread is my body. I will give it for the life of the world."

⁵²Then the Jews began to argue sharply among themselves. They said, "How can this man give us his body to eat?"

⁵³Jesus said to them, "What I'm about to tell you is true. You must eat the Son of Man's body and drink his blood. If you don't, you have no life in you. ⁵⁴Anyone who eats my body and drinks my blood has eternal life. I will raise him up on the last day.

⁵⁵"My body is real food. My blood is real drink. ⁵⁶Anyone who eats my body and drinks my blood remains in me. And I remain in him.

⁵⁷"The living Father sent me, and I live because of him. In the same way, those who feed on me will live because of me. ⁵⁸This is the bread that came down from heaven. Long ago your peo-

ple ate manna and died. But those who feed on this bread will live forever."

⁵⁹He said this while he was teaching in the synagogue in Capernaum.

MANY DISCIPLES LEAVE JESUS

⁶⁰Jesus' disciples heard this. Many of them said, "This is a hard teaching. Who can accept it?"

⁶¹Jesus was aware that his disciples were complaining about his teaching. So he said to them, "Does this upset you? ⁶²What if you see the Son of Man go up to where he was before? ⁶³The Holy Spirit gives life. The body means nothing at all. The words I have spoken to you are from the Spirit. They give life. ⁶⁴But there are some of you who do not believe."

Jesus had known from the beginning which of them did not believe. And he had known who was going to hand him over to his enemies. ⁶⁵So he continued speaking. He said, "This is why I told you that no one can come to me unless the Father helps him."

⁶⁶From this time on, many of his disciples turned back. They no longer followed him.

⁶⁷"You don't want to leave also, do you?" Jesus asked the Twelve.

⁶⁸Simon Peter answered him, "Lord, who can we go to? You have the words

of eternal life. ⁶⁹We believe and know that you are the Holy One of God."

⁷⁰Then Jesus replied, "Didn't I choose you, the 12 disciples? But one of you is a devil!" ⁷¹He meant Judas, the son of Simon Iscariot. Judas was one of the Twelve. But later he was going to hand Jesus over to his enemies.

JESUS GOES TO THE FEAST OF BOOTHS

7 After this, Jesus went around in Galilee. He stayed away from Judea on purpose. He knew that the Jews there were waiting to kill him. ²The Jewish Feast of Booths was near. ³Jesus' brothers said to him, "You should leave here and go to Judea. Then your disciples will see the kinds of things you do. ⁴No one who wants to be well known does things in secret. Since you are doing these things, show yourself to the world." ⁵Even Jesus' own brothers did not believe in him.

⁶So Jesus told them, "The right time has not yet come for me. For you, any time is right. ⁷The people of the world can't hate you. But they hate me. This is because I give witness that what they do is evil.

⁸"You go to the Feast. I am not yet going up to this Feast. For me, the right time has not yet come."

Will I go to heaven when I die?

Every person who trusts in Jesus gets to go to heaven. You will go to heaven, too, if you have trusted in Jesus to take away your sins. That is God's promise. Nothing can take away God's promise of heaven. When you die as a Christian, you go straight to live with God. You do not need to fear death.

checkout John 6:39,40

Related verses: Romans 8:38,39; 1 John 5:13

⁹After he said this, he stayed in Galilee.

¹⁰When his brothers had left for the Feast, he went also. But he went secretly, not openly. ¹¹At the Feast the Jews were watching for him. They were asking, "Where is he?"

¹²Many people in the crowd were whispering about him. Some said, "He is a good man."

Others replied, "No. He fools the people."

¹³But no one would say anything about him openly. They were afraid of the Jews.

JESUS TEACHES AT THE FEAST

¹⁴Jesus did nothing until halfway through the Feast. Then he went up to the temple courtyard and began to teach. ¹⁵The Jews were amazed. They asked, "How did this man learn so much without studying?"

¹⁶Jesus answered, "What I teach is not my own. It comes from the One who sent me. ¹⁷Anyone who chooses to do what God wants him to do will find out whether my teaching comes from God or from me. ¹⁸Someone who speaks on his own does it to get honor for himself. But someone who works for the honor of the One who sent him is truthful. There is nothing false about him.

¹⁹"Didn't Moses give you the law? But not one of you keeps the law. Why are you trying to kill me?"

²⁰"You are controlled by demons," the crowd answered. "Who is trying to kill you?"

²¹Jesus said to them, "I did one miracle, and you are all amazed. ²²Moses gave you circumcision, and so you circumcise a child on the Sabbath day. But circumcision did not really come from Moses. It came from Abraham. ²³You circumcise a child on the Sabbath day. You think that if you do, you won't break the law of Moses. Then why are you angry with me? I healed a whole man on the Sabbath!

²⁴"Stop judging only by what you see. Judge correctly."

IS JESUS THE CHRIST?

²⁵Then some of the people of Jerusalem began asking questions. They said, "Isn't this the man some people are trying to kill? ²⁶Here he is! He is speaking openly. They aren't saying a word to him. Have the authorities really decided that he is the Christ? ²⁷But we know where this man is from. When the Christ comes, no one will know where he is from."

²⁸Jesus was still teaching in the temple courtyard. He cried out, "Yes, you know me. And you know where I am from. I am not here on my own. The One who sent me is true. You do not know him. ²⁹But I know him. I am from him, and he sent me."

³⁰When he said this, they tried to arrest him. But no one laid a hand on him. His time had not yet come.

³¹Still, many people in the crowd put their faith in him. They said, "How will it be when the Christ comes? Will he do more miraculous signs than this man?"

³²The Pharisees heard the crowd whispering things like this about him. Then the chief priests and the Pharisees sent temple guards to arrest him.

³³Jesus said, "I am with you for only a short time. Then I will go to the One who sent me. ³⁴You will look for me, but you won't find me. You can't come where I am going."

³⁵The Jews said to one another, "Where does this man plan to go? Does he think we can't find him? Will he go where our people live scattered among the Greeks? Will he go there to teach the Greeks? ³⁶What did he mean when he said, 'You will look for me, but you won't find me'? And, 'You can't come where I am going'?"

³⁷It was the last and most important day of the Feast. Jesus stood up and spoke in a loud voice. He said, "Let anyone who is thirsty come to me and drink. ³⁸Does anyone believe in me? Then, just as Scripture says, streams of living water will flow from inside him."

³⁹When he said this, he meant the Holy Spirit. Those who believed in Jesus would receive the Spirit later. Up to that time, the Spirit had not been given. This was because Jesus had not yet received glory.

⁴⁰When some of the people heard

his words, they said, "This man must be the Prophet we've been expecting."

⁴¹Others said, "He is the Christ."

Still others asked, "How can the Christ come from Galilee? ⁴²Doesn't Scripture say that the Christ will come from David's family? Doesn't it say that he will come from Bethlehem, the town where David lived?"

⁴³So the people did not agree about who Jesus was. ⁴⁴Some wanted to arrest him. But no one laid a hand on him.

THE JEWISH LEADERS DO NOT BELIEVE

⁴⁵Finally the temple guards went back to the chief priests and the Pharisees. They asked the guards, "Why didn't you bring him in?"

⁴⁶"No one ever spoke the way this man does," the guards replied.

⁴⁷"You mean he has fooled you also?" the Pharisees asked. ⁴⁸"Have any of the rulers or Pharisees believed in him? ⁴⁹No! But this mob knows nothing about the law. There is a curse on them."

⁵⁰Then Nicodemus, a Pharisee, spoke. He was the one who had gone to Jesus earlier. He asked, ⁵¹"Does our law find someone guilty without hearing him first? Doesn't it want to find out what he is doing?"

⁵²They replied, "Are you from Galilee too? Look into it. You will find that a prophet does not come out of Galilee."

---

⁵³Then each of them went home.

8 But Jesus went to the Mount of Olives. ²At sunrise he arrived in the temple courtyard again. All the people gathered around him there. He sat down to teach them.

³The teachers of the law and the Pharisees brought in a woman. She had been caught in adultery. They made her stand in front of the group. ⁴They said to Jesus, "Teacher, this woman was caught in the act of adultery. ⁵In the Law, Moses commanded us to kill such women by throwing stones at them. Now what do you say?" ⁶They were trying to trap Jesus with that

question. They wanted to have a reason to bring charges against him.

But Jesus bent down and started to write on the ground with his finger. ⁷They kept asking him questions. So he stood up and said to them, "Has any one of you not sinned? Then you be the first to throw a stone at her."

⁸He bent down again and wrote on the ground.

⁹Those who heard what he had said began to go away. They left one at a time, the older ones first. Soon only Jesus was left. The woman was still standing there.

¹⁰Jesus stood up and asked her, "Woman, where are they? Hasn't anyone found you guilty?"

¹¹"No one, sir," she said.

"Then I don't find you guilty either," Jesus said. "Go now and leave your life of sin."

JESUS' WITNESS IS TRUE

¹²Jesus spoke to the people again. He said, "I am the light of the world. Those who follow me will never walk in darkness. They will have the light that leads to life."

¹³The Pharisees argued with him. "Here you are," they said, "appearing as your own witness. But your witness does not count."

¹⁴Jesus answered, "Even if I give witness about myself, my witness does count. I know where I came from. And I know where I am going. But you have no idea where I come from or where I am going. ¹⁵You judge by human standards. I don't judge anyone. ¹⁶But if I do judge, what I decide is right. This is because I am not alone. I stand with the Father, who sent me. ¹⁷Your own Law says that the witness of two is what counts. ¹⁸I give witness about myself. My other witness is the Father, who sent me."

¹⁹Then they asked him, "Where is your father?"

"You do not know me or my Father," Jesus replied. "If you knew me, you would know my Father also."

²⁰He spoke these words while he was teaching in the temple area. He was

near the place where the offerings were put. But no one arrested him. His time had not yet come.

²¹Once more Jesus spoke to them. "I am going away," he said. "You will look for me, and you will die in your sin. You can't come where I am going."

²²This made the Jews ask, "Will he kill himself? Is that why he says, 'You can't come where I am going'?"

²³But Jesus said, "You are from below. I am from heaven. You are from this world. I am not from this world. ²⁴I told you that you would die in your sins. Do you believe that I am the one I claim to be? If you don't, you will certainly die in your sins."

²⁵"Who are you?" they asked.

"Just what I have been claiming all along," Jesus replied. ²⁶"I have a lot to say that will judge you. But the One who sent me can be trusted. And I tell the world what I have heard from him."

²⁷They did not understand that Jesus was telling them about his Father. ²⁸So Jesus said, "You will lift up the Son of Man. Then you will know that I am the one I claim to be. You will also know that I do nothing on my own. I speak just what the Father has taught me. ²⁹The One who sent me is with me. He has not left me alone, because I always do what pleases him."

³⁰Even while Jesus was speaking, many people put their faith in him.

THE CHILDREN OF ABRAHAM

³¹Jesus spoke to the Jews who had believed him. "If you obey my teaching," he said, "you are really my disciples. ³²Then you will know the truth. And the truth will set you free."

³³They answered him, "We are Abraham's children. We have never been slaves of anyone. So how can you say that we will be set free?"

³⁴Jesus replied, "What I'm about to tell you is true. Everyone who sins is a slave of sin. ³⁵A slave has no lasting place in the family. But a son belongs to the family forever. ³⁶So if the Son of Man sets you free, you will really be free.

³⁷"I know you are Abraham's children. But you are ready to kill me. You have no room for my word. ³⁸I am telling you what I saw when I was with my Father. You do what you have heard from your father."

³⁹"Abraham is our father," they answered.

Jesus said, "Are you really Abraham's children? If you are, you will do the things Abraham did. ⁴⁰But you have decided to kill me. I am a man who has told you the truth I heard from God. Abraham didn't do the things you want to do. ⁴¹You are doing the things your own father does."

"We are not children of people who weren't married to each other," they objected. "The only Father we have is God himself."

THE CHILDREN OF THE DEVIL

⁴²Jesus said to them, "If God were your Father, you would love me. I came from God, and now I am here. I have not come on my own. He sent me.

⁴³"Why aren't my words clear to you? Because you can't really hear what I say. ⁴⁴You belong to your father, the devil. You want to obey your father's wishes.

"From the beginning, the devil was a murderer. He has never obeyed the truth. There is no truth in him. When he lies, he speaks his natural language. He does this because he is a liar. He is the father of lies.

⁴⁵"But because I tell the truth, you don't believe me! ⁴⁶Can any of you prove I am guilty of sinning? Am I not telling the truth? Then why don't you believe me?

⁴⁷"Everyone who belongs to God hears what God says. The reason you don't hear is that you don't belong to God."

JESUS MAKES CLAIMS ABOUT HIMSELF

⁴⁸The Jews answered Jesus, "Aren't we right when we say you are a Samaritan? Aren't you controlled by a demon?"

⁴⁹"I am not controlled by a demon," said Jesus. "I honor my Father. You do not honor me. ⁵⁰I am not seeking glory for myself. But there is One who brings glory to me. He is the judge. ⁵¹What I'm about to tell you is true. Anyone who obeys my word will never die."

⁵²Then the Jews cried out, "Now we know you are controlled by a demon! Abraham died. So did the prophets. But you say that anyone who obeys your word will never die. ⁵³Are you greater than our father Abraham? He died. So did the prophets. Who do you think you are?"

⁵⁴Jesus replied, "If I bring glory to myself, my glory means nothing. You claim that my Father is your God. He is the one who brings glory to me. ⁵⁵You do not know him. But I know him. If I said I did not, I would be a liar like you. But I do know him. And I obey his word.

⁵⁶"Your father Abraham was filled with joy at the thought of seeing my day. He saw it and was glad."

⁵⁷"You are not even 50 years old," the Jews said to Jesus. "And you have seen Abraham?"

⁵⁸"What I'm about to tell you is true," Jesus answered. "Before Abraham was born, I am!"

⁵⁹When he said this, they picked up stones to kill him. But Jesus hid himself. He slipped away from the temple area.

JESUS HEALS A MAN BORN BLIND

9 As Jesus went along, he saw a man who was blind. He had been blind since he was born. ²Jesus' disciples asked him, "Rabbi, who sinned? Was this man born blind because he sinned? Or did his parents sin?"

³"It isn't because this man sinned," said Jesus. "It isn't because his parents sinned. This happened so that God's work could be shown in his life. ⁴While it is still day, we must do the work of the One who sent me. Night is coming. Then no one can work. ⁵While I am in the world, I am the light of the world."

⁶After he said this, he spit on the ground. He made some mud with the spit. Then he put the mud on the man's eyes.

⁷"Go," he told him. "Wash in the Pool of Siloam." Siloam means Sent.

So the man went and washed. And he came home able to see.

⁸His neighbors and those who had earlier seen him begging asked questions. "Isn't this the same man who used to sit and beg?" they asked.

Why is the devil after us?

Satan is God's enemy. He is against anyone who is on God's side. Satan does not like our friendship with God. He hates it when we spend time with the Lord. And he wants to stop us from obeying God and from doing good. The devil hates God, so he hates us because we love God. Staying close to God helps us to close our ears to Satan's lies and evil suggestions.

checkout
John 8:44

Related verses:
1 Peter 5:8,9;
Revelation 12:9

[9]Some claimed that he was.

Others said, "No. He only looks like him."

But the man who had been blind kept saying, "I am the man."

[10]"Then how were your eyes opened?" they asked.

[11]He replied, "The man they call Jesus made some mud and put it on my eyes. He told me to go to Siloam and wash. So I went and washed. Then I could see."

[12]"Where is this man?" they asked him.

"I don't know," he said.

THE PHARISEES WANT TO KNOW WHAT HAPPENED

[13]They brought to the Pharisees the man who had been blind. [14]The day Jesus made the mud and opened the man's eyes was a Sabbath. [15]So the Pharisees also asked him how he was able to see.

"He put mud on my eyes," the man replied. "Then I washed. And now I can see."

[16]Some of the Pharisees said, "Jesus has not come from God. He does not keep the Sabbath day."

But others asked, "How can a sinner do such miraculous signs?"

So the Pharisees did not agree with each other.

[17]Finally they turned again to the blind man. "What do you have to say about him?" they asked. "It was your eyes he opened."

The man replied, "He is a prophet."

[18]The Jews still did not believe that the man had been blind and now could see. So they sent for his parents. [19]"Is this your son?" they asked. "Is this the one you say was born blind? How is it that now he can see?"

[20]"We know he is our son," the parents answered. "And we know he was born blind. [21]But we don't know how he can now see. And we don't know who opened his eyes. Ask him. He is an adult. He can speak for himself."

[22]His parents said this because they were afraid of the Jews. The Jews had already decided that anyone who said Jesus was the Christ would be put out of the synagogue. [23]That was why the man's parents said, "He is an adult. Ask him."

[24]Again they called the man who had been blind to come to them. "Give glo-

Why are some people different from others?

Jesus' disciples thought that people have disabilities because of their sin. But Jesus told them that they were wrong. Life is not perfect and just about everyone gets hurt or is limited in some way. Some people get hurt in accidents. Some are injured in sports. Some are born with poor hearing or crippling diseases. You can probably think of many ways that people can be harmed. Many doctors, nurses and other people can help us when we are hurt or need help. Scientists are always working on new glasses, wheel chairs, hearing aids, medicines and other wonderful things that help us.

Also, we can rely on God's strength, even when our bodies are weak.

checkout John 9:2,3

Related verses:
2 Corinthians
11:30; 12:9,10

ry to God by telling the truth!" they said. "We know that the man who healed you is a sinner."

²⁵He replied, "I don't know if he is a sinner or not. I do know one thing. I was blind, but now I can see!"

²⁶Then they asked him, "What did he do to you? How did he open your eyes?"

²⁷He answered, "I have already told you. But you didn't listen. Why do you want to hear it again? Do you want to become his disciples too?"

²⁸Then they began to attack him with their words. "You are this fellow's disciple!" they said. "We are disciples of Moses! ²⁹We know that God spoke to Moses. But we don't even know where this fellow comes from."

³⁰The man answered, "That is really surprising! You don't know where he comes from, and yet he opened my eyes. ³¹We know that God does not listen to sinners. He listens to godly people who do what he wants them to do. ³²Nobody has ever heard of anyone opening the eyes of a person born blind. ³³If this man had not come from God, he could do nothing."

³⁴Then the Pharisees replied, "When you were born, you were already deep in sin. How dare you talk like that to us!" And they threw him out of the synagogue.

THE BLIND WILL SEE

³⁵Jesus heard that the Pharisees had thrown the man out. When he found him, he said, "Do you believe in the Son of Man?"

³⁶"Who is he, sir?" the man asked. "Tell me, so I can believe in him."

³⁷Jesus said, "You have now seen him. In fact, he is the one speaking with you."

³⁸Then the man said, "Lord, I believe." And he worshiped him.

³⁹Jesus said, "I have come into this world to judge it. I have come so that the blind will see and those who see will become blind."

⁴⁰Some Pharisees who were with him heard him say this. They asked, "What? Are we blind too?"

⁴¹Jesus said, "If you were blind, you would not be guilty of sin. But since you claim you can see, you remain guilty.

THE SHEPHERD AND THE FLOCK

10 "What I'm about to tell you is true. What if someone does not enter the sheep pen through the gate but climbs in another way? That person is a thief and a robber. ²The one who enters through the gate is the shepherd of the sheep. ³The gatekeeper opens the gate for him. The sheep listen to his voice. He calls his own sheep by name and leads them out. ⁴When he has brought all of his own sheep out, he goes on ahead of them. His sheep follow him because they know his voice. ⁵But they will never follow a stranger. In fact, they will run away from him. They don't recognize a stranger's voice."

⁶Jesus used this story. But the Jews who were there didn't understand what he was telling them.

⁷So Jesus said again, "What I'm about to tell you is true. I am like a gate for the sheep. ⁸All those who ever came before me were thieves and robbers. But the sheep did not listen to them. ⁹I'm like a gate. Anyone who enters through me will be saved. He will come in and go out. And he will find plenty of food. ¹⁰The thief comes only to steal and kill and destroy. I have come so they can have life. I want them to have it in the fullest possible way.

¹¹"I am the good shepherd. The good shepherd gives his life for the sheep. ¹²The hired man is not the shepherd who owns the sheep. So when the hired man sees the wolf coming, he leaves the sheep and runs away. Then the wolf attacks the flock and scatters it. ¹³The man runs away because he is a hired man. He does not care about the sheep.

¹⁴"I am the good shepherd. I know my sheep, and my sheep know me. ¹⁵They know me just as the Father knows me and I know the Father. And I give my life for the sheep.

¹⁶"I have other sheep that do not belong to this sheep pen. I must bring them in too. They also will listen to my voice. Then there will be one flock and one shepherd.

¹⁷"The reason my Father loves me is that I give up my life. But I will take it back again. ¹⁸No one takes it from me. I give it up myself. I have the authority to give it up. And I have the authority to take it back again. I received this command from my Father."

¹⁹After Jesus spoke these words, the Jews again could not agree with each other. ²⁰Many of them said, "He is controlled by a demon. He has gone crazy! Why should we listen to him?"

²¹But others said, "A person controlled by a demon does not say things like this. Can a demon open the eyes of someone who is blind?"

THE JEWS DO NOT BELIEVE

²²Then came the Feast of Hanukkah at Jerusalem. It was winter. ²³Jesus was in the temple area walking in Solomon's Porch. ²⁴The Jews gathered around him. They said, "How long will you keep us waiting? If you are the Christ, tell us plainly."

²⁵Jesus answered, "I did tell you. But you do not believe. The kinds of things I do in my Father's name speak for me.

²⁶But you do not believe, because you are not my sheep.

²⁷"My sheep listen to my voice. I know them, and they follow me. ²⁸I give them eternal life, and they will never die. No one can steal them out of my hand. ²⁹My Father, who has given them to me, is greater than anyone. No one can steal them out of my Father's hand. ³⁰I and the Father are one."

³¹Again the Jews picked up stones to kill him.

³²But Jesus said to them, "I have shown you many miracles from the Father. Which one of these are you throwing stones at me for?"

³³"We are not throwing stones at you for any of these," replied the Jews. "We are stoning you for saying a very evil thing. You are only a man. But you claim to be God."

³⁴Jesus answered them, "Didn't God say in your Law, 'I have said you are gods'? *(Psalm 82:6)* ³⁵We know that Scripture is always true. God spoke to some people and called them 'gods.' ³⁶If that is true, what about the One the Father set apart as his very own and sent into

What's Hanukkah?

The Maccabees were a brave family of Jews. They lived between the time of the Old Testament and the time of the New Testament. The Jews were ruled by other nations at that time. Most of the rulers were mean to them. The Jews decided to fight against these rulers. Judas Maccabeus led the fight. The Maccabees led the Jews to win many battles and fix up the temple. When the temple was finished they had a big party and feast. They called it Hanukkah, which means "Feast of Lights" or "Feast of Dedication." Every year Jewish people still observe this feast in December. It lasts eight days. The Bible tells us about other Jewish feasts too. We are most familiar with the Feast of Unleavened Bread, which is also called the Passover.

checkout
John 10:22

Related verse:
Matthew 26:17

the world? Why do you charge me with saying a very evil thing? Is it because I said, 'I am God's Son'?

[37]"Don't believe me unless I do what my Father does. [38]But what if I do it? Even if you don't believe me, believe the miracles. Then you will know and understand that the Father is in me and I am in the Father."

[39]Again they tried to arrest him. But he escaped from them.

[40]Then Jesus went back across the Jordan River. He went to the place where John had been baptizing in the early days. There he stayed. [41]Many people came to him. They said, "John never did a miraculous sign. But everything he said about this man was true." [42]And in that place many believed in Jesus.

LAZARUS DIES

11 A man named Lazarus was sick. He was from Bethany, the village where Mary and her sister Martha lived. [2]Mary would later pour perfume on the Lord. She would also wipe his feet with her hair. Her brother Lazarus was sick in bed. [3]So the sisters sent a message to Jesus. "Lord," they told him, "the one you love is sick."

[4]When Jesus heard this, he said, "This sickness will not end in death. No, it is for God's glory. God's Son will receive glory because of it."

[5]Jesus loved Martha and her sister and Lazarus. [6]But after he heard Lazarus was sick, he stayed where he was for two more days.

[7]Then he said to his disciples, "Let us go back to Judea."

[8]"But Rabbi," they said, "a short time ago the Jews tried to kill you with stones. Are you still going back there?"

[9]Jesus answered, "Aren't there 12 hours of daylight? A person who walks during the day won't trip and fall. He can see because of this world's light. [10]But when he walks at night, he'll trip and fall. He has no light."

[11]After he said this, Jesus went on speaking to them. "Our friend Lazarus has fallen asleep," he said. "But I am going there to wake him up."

[12]His disciples replied, "Lord, if he's sleeping, he will get better."

[13]Jesus had been speaking about the death of Lazarus. But his disciples thought he meant natural sleep.

[14]So then he told them plainly, "Lazarus is dead. [15]For your benefit, I am glad I was not there. Now you will believe. But let us go to him."

[16]Then Thomas, who was called Didymus, spoke to the rest of the disciples. "Let us go also," he said. "Then we can die with Jesus."

JESUS COMFORTS THE SISTERS

[17]When Jesus arrived, he found out that Lazarus had already been in the tomb for four days. [18]Bethany was less than two miles from Jerusalem. [19]Many Jews had come to Martha and Mary. They had come to comfort them because their brother was dead.

[20]When Martha heard that Jesus was coming, she went out to meet him. But Mary stayed at home.

[21]"Lord," Martha said to Jesus, "I wish you had been here! Then my brother would not have died. [22]But I know that even now God will give you anything you ask for."

[23]Jesus said to her, "Your brother will rise again."

[24]Martha answered, "I know he will rise again. This will happen when people are raised from the dead on the last day."

[25]Jesus said to her, "I am the resurrection and the life. Anyone who believes in me will live, even if he dies. [26]And those who live and believe in me will never die. Do you believe this?"

[27]"Yes, Lord," she told him. "I believe that you are the Christ, the Son of God. I believe that you are the One who was supposed to come into the world."

[28]After she said this, she went back home. She called her sister Mary to one side to talk to her. "The Teacher is here," Martha said. "He is asking for you."

[29]When Mary heard this, she got up quickly and went to him. [30]Jesus had not yet entered the village. He was still at the place where Martha had met him. [31]Some Jews had been comforting Mary in the house. They noticed how quickly she got up and went out. So they followed her. They thought she was going to the tomb to cry there.

³²Mary reached the place where Jesus was. When she saw him, she fell at his feet. She said, "Lord, I wish you had been here! Then my brother would not have died."

³³Jesus saw her crying. He saw that the Jews who had come along with her were crying also. His spirit became very sad, and he was troubled.

³⁴"Where have you put him?" he asked.

"Come and see, Lord," they replied.

³⁵Jesus sobbed.

³⁶Then the Jews said, "See how much he loved him!"

³⁷But some of them said, "He opened the eyes of the blind man. Couldn't he have kept this man from dying?"

JESUS RAISES LAZARUS FROM THE DEAD

³⁸Once more Jesus felt very sad. He came to the tomb. It was a cave with a stone in front of the entrance.

³⁹"Take away the stone," he said.

"But, Lord," said Martha, the sister of the dead man, "by this time there is a bad smell. Lazarus has been in the tomb for four days."

⁴⁰Then Jesus said, "Didn't I tell you that if you believed, you would see God's glory?"

⁴¹So they took away the stone. Then Jesus looked up. He said, "Father, I thank you for hearing me. ⁴²I know that you always hear me. But I said this for the benefit of the people standing here. I said it so they will believe that you sent me."

⁴³Then Jesus called in a loud voice. He said, "Lazarus, come out!"

⁴⁴The dead man came out. His hands and feet were wrapped with strips of linen. A cloth was around his face.

Jesus said to them, "Take off the clothes he was buried in and let him go."

THE PLAN TO KILL JESUS

⁴⁵Many of the Jews who had come to visit Mary saw what Jesus did. So they put their faith in him.

⁴⁶But some of them went to the Pharisees. They told the Pharisees what Jesus had done. ⁴⁷Then the chief priests and the Pharisees called a meeting of the Sanhedrin.

"What can we do?" they asked. "This man is doing many miraculous signs. ⁴⁸If we let him keep on doing this, everyone will believe in him. Then the Romans will come. They will take away our temple and our nation."

⁴⁹One of them spoke up. His name

KIDS' QUESTION

Do God and Jesus cry?

While he lived on earth, Jesus cried real tears when he was sad. God the Father may not shed tears that way, but he does feel sad. He feels sad whenever people hurt. He feels sad whenever they disobey him. He feels sad whenever they don't believe in him. We can bring God joy by doing three things. We can believe in Jesus. We can show love to others. And we can tell people about Jesus.

checkout
John 11:33–35

Related verses:
Psalm 78:40,41;
Ephesians 4:30

was Caiaphas. He was high priest at that time. He said, "You don't know anything at all! ⁵⁰You don't realize what is good for you. It is better if one man dies for the people than if the whole nation is destroyed."

⁵¹He did not say this on his own. But he was high priest at that time. So he told ahead of time that Jesus would die for the Jewish nation. ⁵²He also prophesied that Jesus would die for God's children scattered everywhere. He would die to bring them together and make them one.

⁵³So from that day on, the Jewish rulers planned to kill Jesus.

⁵⁴Jesus no longer moved around openly among the Jews. Instead, he went away to an area near the desert. He went to a village called Ephraim. There he stayed with his disciples.

⁵⁵It was almost time for the Jewish Passover Feast. Many people went up from the country to Jerusalem. They went there for the special washing that would make them pure before the Passover Feast. ⁵⁶They kept looking for Jesus as they stood in the temple area. They asked one another, "What do you think? Isn't he coming to the Feast at all?"

⁵⁷But the chief priests and the Pharisees had given orders. They had commanded anyone who found out where Jesus was staying to report it. Then they could arrest him.

MARY POURS PERFUME ON JESUS

12 It was six days before the Passover Feast. Jesus arrived at Bethany, where Lazarus lived. Lazarus was the one Jesus had raised from the dead. ²A dinner was given at Bethany to honor Jesus. Martha served the food. Lazarus was among those at the table with Jesus.

³Then Mary took about a pint of pure nard. It was an expensive perfume. She poured it on Jesus' feet and wiped them with her hair. The house was filled with the sweet smell of the perfume.

⁴But Judas Iscariot didn't like what Mary did. He was one of Jesus' disciples. Later he was going to hand Jesus

over to his enemies. Judas said, ⁵"Why wasn't this perfume sold? Why wasn't the money given to poor people? It was worth a year's pay."

⁶He didn't say this because he cared about the poor. He said it because he was a thief. Judas was in charge of the money bag. He used to help himself to what was in it.

⁷"Leave her alone," Jesus replied. "The perfume was meant for the day I am buried. ⁸You will always have the poor among you. But you won't always have me."

⁹Meanwhile a large crowd of Jews found out that Jesus was there, so they came. But they did not come only because of Jesus. They also came to see Lazarus. After all, Jesus had raised him from the dead.

¹⁰So the chief priests made plans to kill Lazarus too. ¹¹Because of Lazarus, many of the Jews were starting to follow Jesus. They were putting their faith in him.

JESUS ENTERS JERUSALEM

¹²The next day the large crowd that had come for the Feast heard that Jesus was on his way to Jerusalem. ¹³So they took branches from palm trees and went out to meet him. They shouted,

"Hosanna!"

"Blessed is the one who comes in the name of the Lord!"

(Psalm 118:25,26)

"Blessed is the King of Israel!"

¹⁴Jesus found a young donkey and sat on it. This is just as it is written in Scripture. It says,

¹⁵ "City of Zion, do not be afraid.
See, your king is coming.
He is sitting on a donkey's colt."

(Zechariah 9:9)

¹⁶At first, Jesus' disciples did not understand all this. They realized it only after he had received glory. Then they realized that these things had been written about him. They realized that the people had done these things to him.

¹⁷A crowd had been with Jesus when he called Lazarus from the tomb and

raised him from the dead. So they continued to tell everyone about what had happened. [18]Many people went out to meet him. They had heard that he had done this miraculous sign.

[19]So the Pharisees said to one another, "This isn't getting us anywhere. Look how the whole world is following him!"

JESUS TELLS ABOUT HIS COMING DEATH

[20]There were some Greeks among the people who went up to worship during the Feast. [21]They came to ask Philip for a favor. Philip was from Bethsaida in Galilee.

"Sir," they said, "we would like to see Jesus."

[22]Philip went to tell Andrew. Then Andrew and Philip told Jesus.

[23]Jesus replied, "The hour has come for the Son of Man to receive glory. [24]What I'm about to tell you is true. Unless a grain of wheat falls to the ground and dies, it remains only one seed. But if it dies, it produces many seeds.

[25]"Anyone who loves his life will lose it. But anyone who hates his life in this world will keep it and have eternal life. [26]Anyone who serves me must follow me. And where I am, my servant will also be. My Father will honor the one who serves me.

[27]"My heart is troubled. What should I say? 'Father, save me from this hour'? No. This is the very reason I came to this hour. [28]Father, bring glory to your name!"

Then a voice came from heaven. It said, "I have brought glory to my name. I will bring glory to it again."

[29]The crowd there heard the voice. Some said it was thunder. Others said an angel had spoken to Jesus.

[30]Jesus said, "This voice was for your benefit, not mine. [31]Now it is time for the world to be judged. Now the prince of this world will be thrown out. [32]But I am going to be lifted up from the earth. When I am, I will bring all people to myself." [33]He said this to show them how he was going to die.

[34]The crowd spoke up. "The Law tells us that the Christ will remain forever," they said. "So how can you say,

'The Son of Man must be lifted up'? Who is this 'Son of Man'?"

[35]Then Jesus told them, "You are going to have the light just a little while longer. Walk while you have the light. Do this before darkness catches up with you. Anyone who walks in the dark does not know where he is going. [36]While you have the light, put your trust in it. Then you can become sons of light."

When Jesus had finished speaking, he left and hid from them.

THE JEWS STILL DO NOT BELIEVE

[37]Jesus had done all these miraculous signs in front of them. But they still would not believe in him. [38]This happened as Isaiah the prophet had said it would. He had said,

"Lord, who has believed what
    we've been saying?
Who has seen the Lord's saving
    power?"   *(Isaiah 53:1)*

[39]For this reason, they could not believe. As Isaiah says in another place,

[40]"The Lord has blinded their eyes.
    He has closed their minds.
So they can't see with their eyes.
    They can't understand with their
    minds.
They can't turn to the Lord. If
    they could, he would heal
    them."   *(Isaiah 6:10)*

[41]Isaiah said this because he saw Jesus' glory and spoke about him.

[42]At the same time that Jesus did those miracles, many of the leaders believed in him. But because of the Pharisees, they would not admit they believed. They were afraid they would be thrown out of the synagogue. [43]They loved praise from people more than praise from God.

[44]Then Jesus cried out, "Anyone who believes in me does not believe in me only. He also believes in the One who sent me. [45]When he looks at me, he sees the One who sent me. [46]I have come into the world to be a light. No one who believes in me will stay in darkness.

[47]"I don't judge a person who hears my words but does not obey them. I

didn't come to judge the world. I came to save it. [48]But there is a judge for anyone who does not accept me and my words. The very words I have spoken will judge him on the last day. [49]"I did not speak on my own. The Father who sent me commanded me what to say. He also told me how to say it. [50]I know that his command leads to eternal life. So everything I say is just what the Father has told me to say."

JESUS WASHES HIS DISCIPLES' FEET

13 It was just before the Passover Feast. Jesus knew that the time had come for him to leave this world. It was time for him to go to the Father. Jesus loved his disciples who were in the world. So he now showed them how much he really loved them.

[2]The evening meal was being served. The devil had already tempted Judas Iscariot, son of Simon. He had told Judas to hand Jesus over to his enemies. [3]Jesus knew that the Father had put everything under his power. He also knew he had come from God and was returning to God.

[4]So he got up from the meal and took off his outer clothes. He wrapped a towel around his waist. [5]After that, he poured water into a large bowl. Then he began to wash his disciples' feet. He dried them with the towel that was wrapped around him.

[6]He came to Simon Peter.

"Lord," Peter said to him, "are you going to wash my feet?"

[7]Jesus replied, "You don't realize now what I am doing. But later you will understand."

[8]"No," said Peter. "You will never wash my feet."

Jesus answered, "Unless I wash you, you can't share life with me."

[9]"Lord," Simon Peter replied, "not just my feet! Wash my hands and my head too!"

[10]Jesus answered, "A person who has had a bath needs to wash only his feet. The rest of his body is clean. And you are clean. But not all of you are."

[11]Jesus knew who was going to hand him over to his enemies. That was why he said not every one was clean.

[12]When Jesus finished washing their feet, he put on his clothes. Then he returned to his place.

"Do you understand what I have done for you?" he asked them. [13]"You call me 'Teacher' and 'Lord.' You are right. That is what I am. [14]I, your Lord and Teacher, have washed your feet. So you also should wash one another's feet. [15]I have given you an example. You should do as I have done for you.

[16]"What I'm about to tell you is true. A servant is not more important than his master. And a messenger is not more important than the one who sends him. [17]Now you know these things. So you will be blessed if you do them.

JESUS TELLS WHAT JUDAS WILL DO

[18]"I am not talking about all of you. I know those I have chosen. But this will happen so that Scripture will come true. It says, 'The one who shares my bread has deserted me.' *(Psalm 41:9)*

[19]"I am telling you now, before it happens. When it does happen, you will believe that I am he. [20]What I'm about to tell you is true. Anyone who accepts someone I send accepts me. And anyone who accepts me accepts the One who sent me."

[21]After he had said this, Jesus' spirit was troubled. Here is the witness he gave. "What I'm about to tell you is true," he said. "One of you is going to hand me over to my enemies."

[22]His disciples stared at one another. They had no idea which one of them he meant. [23]The disciple Jesus loved was next to him at the table. [24]Simon Peter motioned to that disciple. He said, "Ask Jesus which one he means."

[25]The disciple was leaning back against Jesus. He asked him, "Lord, who is it?"

[26]Jesus answered, "It is the one I will give this piece of bread to. I will give it to him after I have dipped it in the dish."

He dipped the piece of bread. Then he gave it to Judas Iscariot, son of Simon. [27]As soon as Judas took the bread, Satan entered into him.

"Do quickly what you are going to do," Jesus told him. [28]But no one at the meal understood why Jesus said this to him. ²⁹Judas was in charge of the money. So some of the disciples thought Jesus was telling him to buy what was needed for the Feast. Others thought Jesus was talking about giving something to poor people.

³⁰As soon as Judas had taken the bread, he went out. And it was night.

JESUS SAYS THAT PETER WILL FAIL

³¹After Judas was gone, Jesus spoke. He said, "Now the Son of Man receives glory. And he brings glory to God. ³²If the Son brings glory to God, God himself will bring glory to the Son. God will do it at once.

³³"My children, I will be with you only a little longer. You will look for me. Just as I told the Jews, so I am telling you now. You can't come where I am going.

³⁴"I give you a new command. Love one another. You must love one another, just as I have loved you. ³⁵If you love one another, everyone will know you are my disciples."

³⁶Simon Peter asked him, "Lord, where are you going?"

Jesus replied, "Where I am going you can't follow now. But you will follow me later."

³⁷"Lord," Peter asked, "why can't I follow you now? I will give my life for you."

³⁸Then Jesus answered, "Will you really give your life for me? What I'm about to tell you is true. Before the rooster crows, you will say three times that you don't know me!

JESUS COMFORTS HIS DISCIPLES

14 "Do not let your hearts be troubled. Trust in God. Trust in me also.

²"There are many rooms in my Father's house. If this were not true, I would have told you. I am going there to prepare a place for you. ³If I go and do that, I will come back. And I will take you to be with me. Then you will also be where I am.

⁴"You know the way to the place where I am going."

JESUS IS THE WAY TO THE FATHER

⁵Thomas said to him, "Lord, we don't know where you are going. So how can we know the way?"

⁶Jesus answered, "I am the way and the truth and the life. No one comes to the Father except through me. ⁷If you really knew me, you would know my Father also. From now on, you do know him. And you have seen him."

How do I trust God for everything, including money?

First, pray. Tell God what you need, what you would like and how you feel. But also tell him that you trust him to take care of you and to do what is best for you. Then put your mind at ease and do not worry. God promises to provide for his people. He also tells us to be content with what we have. You can be sure that God is doing what is best for you.

checkout
John 14:1

Related verses:
Psalm 125:1;
Proverbs 3:5

⁸Philip said, "Lord, show us the Father. That will be enough for us."

⁹Jesus answered, "Don't you know me, Philip? I have been among you such a long time! Anyone who has seen me has seen the Father. So how can you say, 'Show us the Father'?

¹⁰"Don't you believe that I am in the Father? Don't you believe that the Father is in me? The words I say to you are not just my own. The Father lives in me. He is the One who is doing his work. ¹¹Believe me when I say I am in the Father. Also believe that the Father is in me. Or at least believe what the miracles show about me.

¹²"What I'm about to tell you is true. Anyone who has faith in me will do what I have been doing. In fact, he will do even greater things. That is because I am going to the Father.

¹³"And I will do anything you ask in my name. Then the Son will bring glory to the Father. ¹⁴You may ask me for anything in my name. I will do it.

THE FATHER WILL SEND THE HOLY SPIRIT

¹⁵"If you love me, you will obey what I command. ¹⁶I will ask the Father. And he will give you another Friend to help you and to be with you forever. ¹⁷The Friend is the Spirit of truth. The world can't accept him. That is because the world does not see him or know him. But you know him. He lives with you, and he will be in you.

¹⁸"I will not leave you like children who don't have parents. I will come to you.

¹⁹"Before long, the world will not see me anymore. But you will see me. Because I live, you will live also. ²⁰On that day you will realize that I am in my Father. You will know that you are in me, and I am in you.

²¹"Anyone who has my commands and obeys them loves me. My Father will love the one who loves me. I too will love him. And I will show myself to him."

Will I have a bedroom when I live with Jesus forever?

Jesus told his disciples that his Father lives where there are many rooms. He said that he was going to prepare a place for them. We do not know exactly what that place or house will be like. But we do know that after Jesus has come again and God has created the new heavens and new earth, our bodies will be different from what they are now. We will not need food or sleep. We will not need bedrooms like the ones we have here. But we will have very nice places set aside for each of us, prepared especially for us by Jesus. And we will not have to worry about the weather. The temperature will always be perfect. We will not even have to be concerned about what to wear. God will give us new clothes.

JASON'S IMAGINATION

checkout **John 14:2**

Related verses:
Revelation 21:1-27

²²Then Judas spoke. "Lord," he said, "why do you plan to show yourself only to us? Why not also to the world?" The Judas who spoke those words was not Judas Iscariot.

²³Jesus replied, "Anyone who loves me will obey my teaching. My Father will love him. We will come to him and make our home with him. ²⁴Anyone who does not love me will not obey my teaching. The words you hear me say are not my own. They belong to the Father who sent me.

²⁵"I have spoken all these things while I am still with you. ²⁶But the Father will send the Friend in my name to help you. The Friend is the Holy Spirit. He will teach you all things. He will remind you of everything I have said to you.

²⁷"I leave my peace with you. I give my peace to you. I do not give it to you as the world does. Do not let your hearts be troubled. And do not be afraid.

²⁸"You heard me say, 'I am going away. And I am coming back to you.' If you loved me, you would be glad I am going to the Father. The Father is greater than I am. ²⁹I have told you now before it happens. Then when it does happen, you will believe.

³⁰"I will not speak with you much longer. The prince of this world is coming. He has no power over me. ³¹But the world must learn that I love the Father. They must also learn that I do exactly what my Father has commanded me to do.

"Come now. Let us leave.

THE VINE AND THE BRANCHES

15 "I am the true vine. My Father is the gardener. ²He cuts off every branch joined to me that does not bear fruit. He trims every branch that does bear fruit. Then it will bear even more fruit.

³"You are already clean because of the word I have spoken to you. ⁴Remain joined to me, and I will remain joined to you. No branch can bear fruit by itself. It must remain joined to the

Is Jesus the only way to heaven?

Yes, Jesus is the only way to heaven. He said, "No one comes to the Father except through me." Jesus is the only answer to our need for forgiveness. He is the only one who has the *right* to take away our sins because he died for us. He is the only one who has the *power* to take them away because he is God. And he is the only one who can be perfectly fair to every single person because only he is a perfect and just judge.

checkout John 14:6

Related verses:
John 6:68;
Revelation 22:17

vine. In the same way, you can't bear fruit unless you remain joined to me.

⁵"I am the vine. You are the branches. If anyone remains joined to me, and I to him, he will bear a lot of fruit. You can't do anything without me. ⁶If anyone does not remain joined to me, he is like a branch that is thrown away and dries up. Branches like those are picked up. They are thrown into the fire and burned.

⁷"If you remain joined to me and my words remain in you, ask for anything you wish. And it will be given to you. ⁸When you bear a lot of fruit, it brings glory to my Father. It shows that you are my disciples.

⁹"Just as the Father has loved me, I have loved you. Now remain in my love. ¹⁰If you obey my commands, you will remain in my love. In the same way, I have obeyed my Father's commands and remain in his love. ¹¹I have told you this so that my joy will be in you. I also want your joy to be complete.

¹²"Here is my command. Love each other, just as I have loved you. ¹³No one has greater love than the one who gives his life for his friends. ¹⁴You are my friends if you do what I command.

¹⁵"I do not call you servants anymore. Servants do not know their master's business. Instead, I have called you friends. I have told you everything I learned from my Father.

¹⁶"You did not choose me. Instead, I chose you. I appointed you to go and bear fruit. It is fruit that will last. Then the Father will give you anything you ask for in my name.

¹⁷"Here is my command. Love each other.

THE WORLD HATES THE DISCIPLES

¹⁸"Does the world hate you? Remember that it hated me first. ¹⁹If you belonged to the world, it would love you like one of its own. But you do not belong to the world. I have chosen you out of the world. That is why the world hates you.

²⁰"Remember the words I spoke to you. I said, 'A servant is not more important than his master.' *(John 13:16)* If

Does God have friends or is he alone?

God has many friends. He counts every person who loves and knows him as a friend. God doesn't have other "gods" to be friends with. He is the only God there is and wants people to know that. But God wants to have friendship with us. In fact, God wants to be our closest friend. He wants us to know him. So he has done a lot to make friends with us and to have our friendship. That's why he created us, sent Jesus to save us and gave us the Bible.

checkout John 15:12-15

Related verse:
Matthew 23:37

people hated me and tried to hurt me, they will do the same to you. If they obeyed my teaching, they will obey yours also. ²¹They will treat you like that because of my name. They do not know the One who sent me.

²²"If I had not come and spoken to them, they would not be guilty of sin. But now they have no excuse for their sin. ²³Those who hate me hate my Father also.

²⁴"I did miracles among them that no one else did. If I hadn't, they would not be guilty of sin. But now they have seen those miracles. And still they have hated both me and my Father. ²⁵This has happened so that what is written in their Law would come true. It says, 'They hated me without any reason.' *(Psalms 35:19; 69:4)*

²⁶"I will send the Friend to you from the Father. He is the Spirit of truth, who comes out from the Father. When the Friend comes to help you, he will give witness about me.

²⁷"You also must give witness. This is because you have been with me from the beginning.

16

"I have told you all of this so that you will not go down the wrong path. ²You will be thrown out of the synagogue. In fact, a time is coming when those who kill you will think they are doing God a favor. ³They will do things like that because they do not know the Father or me.

⁴"Why have I told you this? So that when the time comes, you will remember that I warned you. I didn't tell you this at first because I was with you.

WHAT THE HOLY SPIRIT WILL DO

⁵"Now I am going to the One who sent me. But none of you asks me, 'Where are you going?' ⁶Because I have said these things, you are filled with sadness.

⁷"But what I'm about to tell you is true. It is for your good that I am going away. Unless I go away, the Friend will not come to help you. But if I go, I will send him to you. ⁸When he comes, he will prove that the world's people are guilty. He will prove their guilt concerning sin and godliness and judgment.

⁹"The world is guilty as far as sin is concerned. That is because people do not believe in me. ¹⁰The world is guilty as far as godliness is concerned. That is because I am going to the Father, where you can't see me anymore. ¹¹The world is guilty as far as judgment is concerned. That is because the devil,

Can I do whatever I want when I'm older?

Some kids think that when they grow up they will be able to do anything they want. Some adults think they can do whatever they want too. But it is not true. We have to obey rules and laws all our lives. When God gave the Ten Commandments, he gave them to all people, of all ages, for all time. No one outgrows the need to obey God. We should always do what God says.

checkout **John 15:14**

Related verse:
Revelation 22:12

JASON'S IMAGINATION

the prince of this world, has already been judged.

¹²"I have much more to say to you. It is more than you can handle right now. ¹³But when the Spirit of truth comes, he will guide you into all truth. He will not speak on his own. He will speak only what he hears. And he will tell you what is still going to happen.

¹⁴"He will bring me glory by receiving something from me and showing it to you. ¹⁵Everything that belongs to the Father is mine. That is why I said the Holy Spirit will receive something from me and show it to you.

¹⁶"In a little while, you will no longer see me. Then after a little while, you will see me."

THE DISCIPLES' SADNESS WILL TURN INTO JOY

¹⁷Some of his disciples spoke to one another. They said, "What does he mean by saying, 'In a little while, you will no longer see me. Then after a little while, you will see me'? And what does he mean by saying, 'I am going to the Father'?" ¹⁸They kept asking, "What does he mean by 'a little while'? We don't understand what he is saying."

¹⁹Jesus saw that they wanted to ask him about those things. So he said to them, "Are you asking one another what I meant? Didn't you understand when I said, 'In a little while, you will no longer see me. Then after a little while, you will see me'? ²⁰What I'm about to tell you is true. You will cry and be full of sorrow while the world is full of joy. You will be sad, but your sadness will turn into joy.

²¹"A woman giving birth to a baby has pain. This is because her time to give birth has come. But when her baby is born, she forgets the pain. She forgets because she is so happy that a baby has been born into the world.

²²"That's the way it is with you. Now it's your time to be sad. But I will see you again. Then you will be full of joy. And no one will take your joy away.

²³"When that day comes, you will no longer ask me for anything. What I'm about to tell you is true. My Father will give you anything you ask for in my name. ²⁴Until now you have not asked for anything in my name. Ask, and you will receive what you ask for. Then your joy will be complete.

²⁵"I have not been speaking to you plainly. But a time is coming when I will speak clearly. Then I will tell you plainly about my Father. ²⁶When that

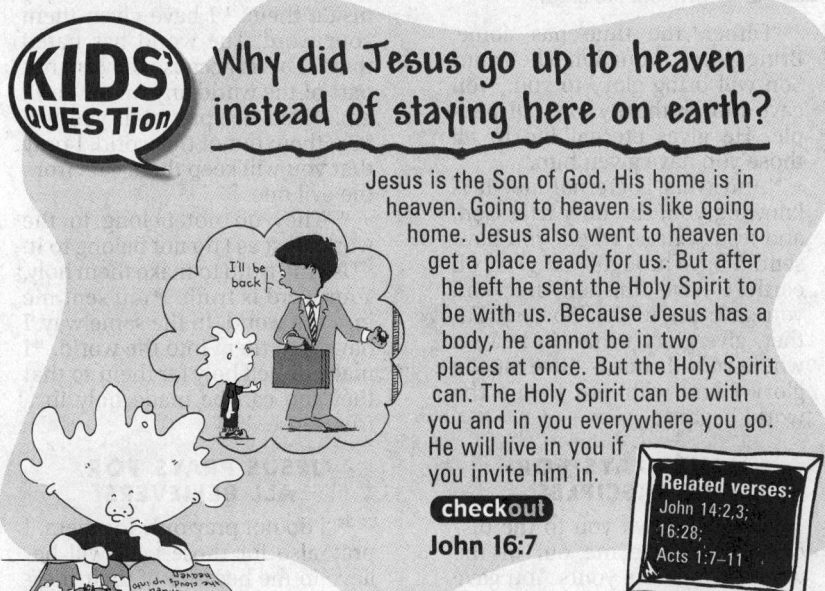

KIDS' QUESTION

Why did Jesus go up to heaven instead of staying here on earth?

Jesus is the Son of God. His home is in heaven. Going to heaven is like going home. Jesus also went to heaven to get a place ready for us. But after he left he sent the Holy Spirit to be with us. Because Jesus has a body, he cannot be in two places at once. But the Holy Spirit can. The Holy Spirit can be with you and in you everywhere you go. He will live in you if you invite him in.

I'll be back

checkout

John 16:7

Related verses:
John 14:2,3;
16:28;
Acts 1:7-11

day comes, you will ask for things in my name. I am not saying I will ask the Father instead of you asking him. ²⁷No, the Father himself loves you because you have loved me. He also loves you because you have believed that I came from God.

²⁸"I came from the Father and entered the world. Now I am leaving the world and going back to the Father."

²⁹Then Jesus' disciples said, "Now you are speaking plainly. You are using examples that are clear. ³⁰Now we can see that you know everything. You don't even need anyone to ask you questions. This makes us believe that you came from God."

³¹"At last you believe!" Jesus said. ³²"But a time is coming when you will be scattered and go to your own homes. In fact, that time is already here. You will leave me all alone. But I am not really alone. My Father is with me.

³³"I have told you these things, so that you can have peace because of me. In this world you will have trouble. But cheer up! I have won the battle over the world."

JESUS PRAYS FOR HIMSELF

17 After Jesus said this, he looked toward heaven and prayed. He said,

"Father, the time has come. Bring glory to your Son. Then your Son will bring glory to you. ²You gave him authority over all people. He gives eternal life to all those you have given him.

³"And what is eternal life? It is knowing you, the only true God, and Jesus Christ, whom you have sent. ⁴I have brought you glory on earth. I have finished the work you gave me to do. ⁵So now, Father, give glory to me in heaven where your throne is. Give me the glory I had with you before the world began.

JESUS PRAYS FOR HIS DISCIPLES

⁶"I have shown you to the disciples you gave me out of the world. They were yours. You gave them to me. And they have

obeyed your word. ⁷Now they know that everything you have given me comes from you. ⁸I gave them the words you gave me. And they accepted them. They knew for certain that I came from you. They believed that you sent me.

⁹"I pray for them. I am not praying for the world. I am praying for those you have given me, because they are yours. ¹⁰All I have is yours, and all you have is mine. Glory has come to me because of my disciples.

¹¹"I will not remain in the world any longer. But they are still in the world, and I am coming to you. Holy Father, keep them safe by the power of your name. It is the name you gave me. Keep them safe so they can be one, just as you and I are one.

¹²"While I was with them, I guarded them. I kept them safe through the name you gave me. None of them has been lost, except the one who was sentenced to be destroyed. It happened so that Scripture would come true.

¹³"I am coming to you now. But I say these things while I am still in the world. I say them so that those you gave me can have all my joy inside them. ¹⁴I have given them your word. The world has hated them. This is because they are not part of the world any more than I am. ¹⁵I do not pray that you will take them out of the world. I pray that you will keep them safe from the evil one.

¹⁶"They do not belong to the world, just as I do not belong to it. ¹⁷Use the truth to make them holy. Your word is truth. ¹⁸You sent me into the world. In the same way, I have sent them into the world. ¹⁹I make myself holy for them so that they too can be made holy in a true sense.

JESUS PRAYS FOR ALL BELIEVERS

²⁰"I do not pray only for them. I pray also for those who will believe in me because of their message. ²¹Father, I pray that all of

them will be one, just as you are in me and I am in you. I want them also to be in us. Then the world will believe that you have sent me.

²²"I have given them the glory you gave me. I did this so they would be one, just as we are one. ²³I will be in them, just as you are in me. I want them to be brought together perfectly as one. This will let the world know that you sent me. It will also show the world that you have loved those you gave me, just as you have loved me.

²⁴"Father, I want those you have given me to be with me where I am. I want them to see my glory, the glory you have given me. You gave it to me because you loved me before the world was created. ²⁵"Father, you are holy. The world does not know you, but I know you. Those you have given me know you have sent me. ²⁶I have shown you to them. And I will continue to show you to them. Then the love you have for me will be in them. I myself will be in them."

JESUS IS ARRESTED

18 When Jesus had finished praying, he left with his disciples. They crossed the Kidron Valley. On the other side there was a grove of olive trees. Jesus and his disciples went into it.

²Judas knew the place. He was going to hand Jesus over to his enemies. Jesus had often met in that place with his disciples. ³So Judas came to the grove. He was guiding a group of soldiers and some officials. The chief priests and the Pharisees had sent them. They were carrying torches, lanterns and weapons.

⁴Jesus knew everything that was going to happen to him. So he went out and asked them, "Who is it that you want?"

⁵"Jesus of Nazareth," they replied.

"I am he," Jesus said.

Judas, who was going to hand Jesus over, was standing there with them. ⁶When Jesus said, "I am he," they moved back. Then they fell to the ground.

⁷He asked them again, "Who is it that you want?"

They said, "Jesus of Nazareth."

⁸"I told you I am he," Jesus answered. "If you are looking for me, then let these men go." ⁹This happened so that the words Jesus had spoken would come true. He had said, "I have not lost anyone God has given me." *(John 6:39)*

¹⁰Simon Peter had a sword and pulled it out. He struck the high priest's servant and cut off his right ear. The servant's name was Malchus.

¹¹Jesus commanded Peter, "Put your sword away! Shouldn't I drink the cup of suffering the Father has given me?"

JESUS IS TAKEN TO ANNAS

¹²Then the group of soldiers, their leader and the Jewish officials arrested Jesus. They tied him up ¹³and brought him first to Annas. He was the father-in-law of Caiaphas, the high priest at that time. ¹⁴Caiaphas had advised the Jews that it would be good if one man died for the people.

PETER SAYS HE IS NOT JESUS' DISCIPLE

¹⁵Simon Peter and another disciple were following Jesus. The high priest knew the other disciple. So that disciple went with Jesus into the high priest's courtyard. ¹⁶But Peter had to wait outside by the door.

The other disciple came back. He was the one the high priest knew. He spoke to the woman who was on duty there. Then he brought Peter in.

¹⁷The woman at the door spoke to Peter. "You are not one of Jesus' disciples, are you?" she asked him.

"I am not," he replied.

¹⁸It was cold. The servants and officials stood around a fire. They had made it to keep warm. Peter was also standing with them. He was warming himself.

THE HIGH PRIEST QUESTIONS JESUS

¹⁹Meanwhile, the high priest questioned Jesus. He asked him about his disciples and his teaching.

²⁰"I have spoken openly to the world," Jesus replied. "I always taught in synagogues or at the temple, where all the Jews come together. I didn't say anything in secret. ²¹Why question me? Ask the people who heard me. They certainly know what I said."

²²When Jesus said that, one of the officials nearby hit him in the face. "Is this any way to answer the high priest?" he asked.

²³"Have I said something wrong?" Jesus replied. "If I have, give witness to it. But if I spoke the truth, why did you hit me?"

²⁴While Jesus was still tied up, Annas sent him to Caiaphas, the high priest.

PETER AGAIN SAYS HE IS NOT JESUS' DISCIPLE

²⁵Simon Peter stood there. He was warming himself. Then someone asked him, "You aren't one of Jesus' disciples, are you?"

He said, "I am not."

²⁶One of the high priest's servants was a relative of the man whose ear Peter had cut off. He said to Peter, "Didn't I see you with Jesus in the olive grove?"

²⁷Again Peter said no.

At that very moment a rooster began to crow.

JESUS IS BROUGHT TO PILATE

²⁸Then the Jews led Jesus from Caiaphas to the palace of the Roman governor. By now it was early morning. The Jews did not want to be made "unclean." They wanted to be able to eat the Passover meal. So they did not enter the palace.

²⁹Pilate came out to them. He asked, "What charges are you bringing against this man?"

³⁰"He has committed crimes," they replied. "If he hadn't, we would not have handed him over to you."

³¹Pilate said, "Take him yourselves. Judge him by your own law."

"But we don't have the right to put anyone to death," the Jews complained. ³²This happened so that the words Jesus had spoken about how he was going to die would come true.

³³Then Pilate went back inside the palace. He ordered Jesus to be brought to him. Pilate asked him, "Are you the king of the Jews?"

³⁴"Is that your own idea?" Jesus asked. "Or did others talk to you about me?"

³⁵"Am I a Jew?" Pilate replied. "It was your people and your chief priests who handed you over to me. What have you done?"

³⁶Jesus said, "My kingdom is not part of this world. If it were, those who serve me would fight. They would try to keep the Jews from arresting me. My kingdom is from another place."

³⁷"So you are a king, then!" said Pilate.

Jesus answered, "You are right to say I am a king. In fact, that's the reason I was born. I came into the world to give witness to the truth. Everyone who is on the side of truth listens to me."

³⁸"What is truth?" Pilate asked.

Then Pilate went out again to the Jews. He said, "I find no basis for any charge against him. ³⁹But it is your practice for me to set one prisoner free for you at Passover time. Do you want me to set 'the king of the Jews' free?"

⁴⁰They shouted back, "No! Not him! Give us Barabbas!" Barabbas had taken part in an armed struggle against the country's rulers.

JESUS IS SENTENCED TO BE CRUCIFIED

19 Then Pilate took Jesus and had him whipped. ²The soldiers twisted thorns together to make a crown. They put it on Jesus' head. Then they put a purple robe on him. ³They went up to him again and again. They kept saying, "We honor you, king of the Jews!" And they hit him in the face.

⁴Once more Pilate came out. He said to the Jews, "Look, I am bringing Jesus out to you. I want to let you know that I find no basis for a charge against him."

⁵Jesus came out wearing the crown of thorns and the purple robe. Then Pilate said to them, "Here is the man!"

⁶As soon as the chief priests and their officials saw him, they shouted, "Crucify him! Crucify him!"

But Pilate answered, "You take him

and crucify him. I myself find no basis for a charge against him."

[7]The Jews replied, "We have a law. That law says he must die. He claimed to be the Son of God."

[8]When Pilate heard that, he was even more afraid. [9]He went back inside the palace. "Where do you come from?" he asked Jesus.

But Jesus did not answer him.

[10]"Do you refuse to speak to me?" Pilate said. "Don't you understand? I have the power to set you free or to nail you to a cross."

[11]Jesus answered, "You were given power from heaven. If you weren't, you would have no power over me. So the one who handed me over to you is guilty of a greater sin."

[12]From then on, Pilate tried to set Jesus free. But the Jews kept shouting, "If you let this man go, you are not Caesar's friend! Anyone who claims to be a king is against Caesar!"

[13]When Pilate heard that, he brought Jesus out. Pilate sat down on the judge's seat. It was at a place called The Stone Walkway. In the Aramaic language it was called Gabbatha. [14]It was about noon on Preparation Day in Passover Week.

"Here is your king," Pilate said to the Jews.

[15]But they shouted, "Kill him! Kill him! Crucify him!"

"Should I crucify your king?" Pilate asked.

"We have no king but Caesar," the chief priests answered.

[16]Finally, Pilate handed Jesus over to them to be nailed to a cross.

JESUS IS NAILED TO A CROSS

So the soldiers took charge of Jesus. [17]He had to carry his own cross. He went out to a place called The Skull. In the Aramaic language it was called Golgotha. [18]There they nailed Jesus to the cross. Two other men were crucified with him. One was on each side of him. Jesus was in the middle.

[19]Pilate had a notice prepared. It was fastened to the cross. It read, JESUS OF NAZARETH, THE KING OF THE JEWS. [20]Many of the Jews read the sign. The place where Jesus was crucified was near the city. The sign was written in the Aramaic, Latin and Greek languages.

[21]The chief priests of the Jews argued with Pilate. They said, "Do not write 'The King of the Jews.' Write that this man claimed to be king of the Jews."

[22]Pilate answered, "I have written what I have written."

[23]When the soldiers crucified Jesus, they took his clothes. They divided them into four parts. Each soldier got one part. Jesus' long, inner robe was left. It did not have any seams. It was made out of one piece of cloth from top to bottom.

[24]"Let's not tear it," they said to one another. "Let's cast lots to see who will get it."

This happened so that Scripture would come true. It says,

"They divided up my clothes
    among them.
They cast lots for what I was
    wearing."   *(Psalm 22:18)*

So that is what the soldiers did.

[25]Jesus' mother stood near his cross. So did his mother's sister, Mary the wife of Clopas, and Mary Magdalene.

[26]Jesus saw his mother there. He also saw the disciple he loved standing nearby. Jesus said to his mother, "Dear woman, here is your son." [27]He said to the disciple, "Here is your mother." From that time on, the disciple took her into his home.

JESUS DIES

[28]Later Jesus said, "I am thirsty." He knew that everything was now finished. He knew that what Scripture said must come true. [29]A jar of wine vinegar was there. So they soaked a sponge in it. They put the sponge on a stem of the hyssop plant. Then they lifted it up to Jesus' lips.

[30]After Jesus drank he said, "It is finished." Then he bowed his head and died.

[31]It was Preparation Day. The next day would be a special Sabbath. The Jews did not want the bodies left on the crosses during the Sabbath. So they asked Pilate to have the legs broken and the bodies taken down. [32]The soldiers came and broke the legs of the

first man who had been crucified with Jesus. Then they broke the legs of the other man.

³³But when they came to Jesus, they saw that he was already dead. So they did not break his legs. ³⁴Instead, one of the soldiers stuck his spear into Jesus' side. Right away, blood and water flowed out. ³⁵The man who saw it has given witness. And his witness is true. He knows that he tells the truth. He gives witness so that you also can believe.

³⁶These things happened in order that Scripture would come true. It says, "Not one of his bones will be broken." *(Exodus 12:46; Numbers 9:12; Psalm 34:20)* ³⁷Scripture also says, "They will look to the one they have pierced." *(Zechariah 12:10)*

JESUS IS BURIED

³⁸Later Joseph asked Pilate for Jesus' body. Joseph was from the town of Arimathea. He was a follower of Jesus. But he followed Jesus secretly because he was afraid of the Jews. After Pilate gave him permission, Joseph came and took the body away.

³⁹Nicodemus went with Joseph. He was the man who had earlier visited Jesus at night. Nicodemus brought some mixed spices, about 75 pounds.

⁴⁰The two men took Jesus' body. They wrapped it in strips of linen cloth, along with the spices. That was the way the Jews buried people's bodies.

⁴¹At the place where Jesus was crucified, there was a garden. A new tomb was there. No one had ever been put in it before. ⁴²That day was the Jewish Preparation Day, and the tomb was nearby. So they placed Jesus there.

THE TOMB IS EMPTY

20 Early on the first day of the week, Mary Magdalene went to the tomb. It was still dark. She saw that the stone had been moved away from the entrance. ²So she ran to Simon Peter and another disciple, the one Jesus loved. She said, "They have taken the Lord out of the tomb! We don't know where they have put him!"

³So Peter and the other disciple started out for the tomb. ⁴Both of them were running. The other disciple ran faster than Peter. He reached the tomb first. ⁵He bent over and looked in at the strips of linen lying there. But he did not go in.

⁶Then Simon Peter, who was behind him, arrived. He went into the tomb. He saw the strips of linen lying there. ⁷He also saw the burial cloth that had

Why did Jesus' clothes look so different from ours?

The clothes worn by Jesus and his friends look different to us today. But they were in style at the time he lived. His clothes were just right for the weather and tastes of the day. You might look at pictures from your mom's or dad's photo album and notice the different styles when they were younger. Styles and tastes change quickly, and they are different depending on the country or climate that people live in, too.

checkout
John 19:23,24

Related verse:
Matthew 27:35

been around Jesus' head. The cloth was folded up by itself. It was separate from the linen.

[8]The disciple who had reached the tomb first also went inside. He saw and believed. [9]They still did not understand from Scripture that Jesus had to rise from the dead.

JESUS APPEARS TO MARY MAGDALENE

[10]Then the disciples went back to their homes. [11]But Mary stood outside the tomb crying. As she cried, she bent over to look into the tomb. [12]She saw two angels dressed in white. They were seated where Jesus' body had been. One of them was where Jesus' head had been laid. The other sat where his feet had been placed.

[13]They asked her, "Woman, why are you crying?"

"They have taken my Lord away," she said. "I don't know where they have put him."

[14]Then she turned around and saw Jesus standing there. But she didn't realize that it was Jesus.

[15]"Woman," he said, "why are you crying? Who are you looking for?"

She thought he was the gardener. So she said, "Sir, did you carry him away? Tell me where you put him. Then I will go and get him."

[16]Jesus said to her, "Mary."

She turned toward him. Then she cried out in the Aramaic language, "Rabboni!" Rabboni means Teacher.

[17]Jesus said, "Do not hold on to me. I have not yet returned to the Father. Instead, go to those who believe in me. Tell them, 'I am returning to my Father and your Father, to my God and your God.' "

[18]Mary Magdalene went to the disciples with the news. She said, "I have seen the Lord!" And she told them that he had said these things to her.

JESUS APPEARS TO HIS DISCIPLES

[19]On the evening of that first day of the week, the disciples were together. They had locked the doors because they were afraid of the Jews.

Jesus came in and stood among them. He said, "May peace be with you!" [20]Then he showed them his hands and his side. The disciples were very happy when they saw the Lord.

[21]Again Jesus said, "May peace be with you! The Father has sent me. So now I am sending you." [22]He then breathed on them. He said, "Receive the Holy Spirit. [23]If you forgive anyone's sins, they are forgiven. If you do not forgive them, they are not forgiven."

JESUS APPEARS TO THOMAS

[24]Thomas was one of the Twelve. He was called Didymus. He was not with the other disciples when Jesus came. [25]So they told him, "We have seen the Lord!"

But he said to them, "First I must see the nail marks in his hands. I must put my finger where the nails were. I must put my hand into his side. Only then will I believe what you say."

[26]A week later, Jesus' disciples were in the house again. Thomas was with them. Even though the doors were locked, Jesus came in and stood among them.

He said, "May peace be with you!" [27]Then he said to Thomas, "Put your finger here. See my hands. Reach out your hand and put it into my side. Stop doubting and believe."

[28]Thomas said to him, "My Lord and my God!"

[29]Then Jesus told him, "Because you have seen me, you have believed. Blessed are those who have not seen me but still have believed."

[30]Jesus did many other miraculous signs in front of his disciples. They are not written down in this book. [31]But these are written down so that you may believe that Jesus is the Christ, the Son of God. If you believe this, you will have life because you belong to him.

JESUS DOES A MIRACLE AT THE SEA

21 After this, Jesus appeared to his disciples again. It was by the Sea of Galilee. Here is what happened.

[2]Simon Peter and Thomas, who was called Didymus, were there together. Nathanael from Cana in Galilee and

the sons of Zebedee were with them. So were two other disciples.

³"I'm going out to fish," Simon Peter told them. They said, "We'll go with you." So they went out and got into the boat. That night they didn't catch anything.

⁴Early in the morning, Jesus stood on the shore. But the disciples did not realize that it was Jesus.

⁵He called out to them, "Friends, don't you have any fish?"

"No," they answered.

⁶He said, "Throw your net on the right side of the boat. There you will find some fish."

When they did, they could not pull the net into the boat. There were too many fish in it.

⁷Then the disciple Jesus loved said to Simon Peter, "It is the Lord!" As soon as Peter heard that, he put his coat on. He had taken it off earlier. Then he jumped into the water.

⁸The other disciples followed in the boat. They were towing the net full of fish. The shore was only about 100 yards away. ⁹When they landed, they saw a fire of burning coals. There were fish on it. There was also some bread.

¹⁰Jesus said to them, "Bring some of the fish you have just caught."

¹¹Simon Peter climbed into the boat. He dragged the net to shore. It was full of large fish. There were 153 of them. But even with that many fish the net was not torn.

¹²Jesus said to them, "Come and have breakfast."

None of the disciples dared to ask him, "Who are you?" They knew it was the Lord.

¹³Jesus came, took the bread and gave it to them. He did the same thing with the fish. ¹⁴This was the third time Jesus appeared to his disciples after he was raised from the dead.

JESUS TAKES PETER BACK

¹⁵When Jesus and the disciples had finished eating, Jesus spoke to Simon Peter. He asked, "Simon, son of John, do you really love me more than these others do?"

"Yes, Lord," he answered. "You know that I love you."

Jesus said, "Feed my lambs."

Why are there four books about Jesus in the Bible?

The Gospels are the four books in the Bible that tell us the most about Jesus' life on earth. God used *four* books because each book shows us something different about Jesus. Together these books tell about Jesus' birth, life, death and resurrection.

The Gospels are all named after their writers: Matthew, Mark, Luke and John. Matthew and John were close friends of Jesus. They were two of the twelve disciples. Matthew was a tax collector. John was a fisherman. Mark was a friend of the twelve disciples. Luke was a doctor.

checkout John 20:30,31

Just One Gospel

BENEFITS
• Bibles will be more compact
• easier to read

Related verses:
Luke 1:1–4

¹⁶Again Jesus asked, "Simon, son of John, do you really love me?"

He answered, "Yes, Lord. You know that I love you."

Jesus said, "Take care of my sheep."

¹⁷Jesus spoke to him a third time. He asked, "Simon, son of John, do you love me?"

Peter felt bad because Jesus asked him the third time, "Do you love me?" He answered, "Lord, you know all things. You know that I love you."

Jesus said, "Feed my sheep. ¹⁸What I'm about to tell you is true. When you were younger, you dressed yourself. You went wherever you wanted to go. But when you are old, you will stretch out your hands. Someone else will dress you. Someone else will lead you where you do not want to go."

¹⁹Jesus said this to point out how Peter would die. His death would bring glory to God.

Then Jesus said to him, "Follow me!"

²⁰Peter turned around. He saw that the disciple Jesus loved was following them. He was the one who had leaned back against Jesus at the supper. He had said, "Lord, who is going to hand you over to your enemies?" ²¹When Peter saw that disciple, he asked, "Lord, what will happen to him?"

²²Jesus answered, "Suppose I want him to remain alive until I return. What does that matter to you? You must follow me."

²³Because of what Jesus said, a false report spread among the believers. The story was told that the disciple Jesus loved wouldn't die. But Jesus did not say he would not die. He only said, "Suppose I want him to remain alive until I return. What does that matter to you?"

²⁴This is the disciple who gives witness to these things. He also wrote them down. We know that his witness is true.

²⁵Jesus also did many other things. What if every one of them were written down? I suppose that even the whole world would not have room for the books that would be written.

I Wonder . . .

How can I be sure that I'll be with Jesus in heaven?

Real Life Challenge

Sometimes you may wonder if it's really possible to know that someday you'll be with Jesus in heaven. You may question whether you have acted the right way, said the right words, or believed the right things. But Jesus is very clear about what you need to do in order to be with him in heaven, so you don't ever have to worry about it. He wants you to know for sure that you will be with him!

Quest Clue

Read John 3 and 14 for Jesus' teaching about what you need to do to be with him in heaven. It may be simpler than you think!

Acts

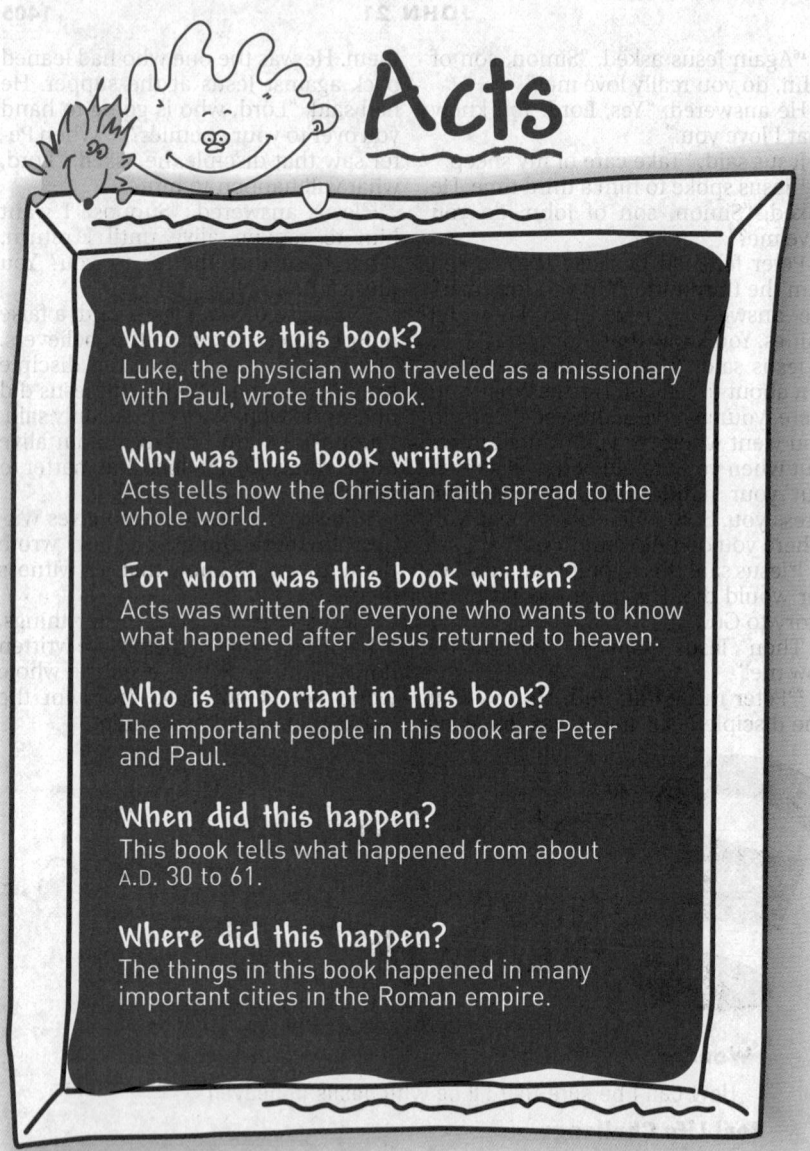

Who wrote this book?
Luke, the physician who traveled as a missionary with Paul, wrote this book.

Why was this book written?
Acts tells how the Christian faith spread to the whole world.

For whom was this book written?
Acts was written for everyone who wants to know what happened after Jesus returned to heaven.

Who is important in this book?
The important people in this book are Peter and Paul.

When did this happen?
This book tells what happened from about A.D. 30 to 61.

Where did this happen?
The things in this book happened in many important cities in the Roman empire.

JESUS IS TAKEN UP INTO HEAVEN

1 Theophilus, I wrote about Jesus in my earlier book. I wrote about all he did and taught ²until the day he was taken up to heaven. Before Jesus left, he gave orders to the apostles he had chosen. He did this through the Holy Spirit. ³After his suffering and death, he appeared to them. In many ways he proved that he was alive. He appeared to them over a period of 40 days. During that time he spoke about God's kingdom.

⁴One day Jesus was eating with them. He gave them a command. "Do not leave Jerusalem," he said. "Wait for the gift my Father promised. You have heard me talk about it. ⁵John baptized with water. But in a few days you will be baptized with the Holy Spirit."

⁶When the apostles met together,

they asked Jesus a question. "Lord," they said, "are you going to give the kingdom back to Israel now?"

[7]He said to them, "You should not be concerned about times or dates. The Father has set them by his own authority. [8]But you will receive power when the Holy Spirit comes on you. Then you will be my witnesses in Jerusalem. You will be my witnesses in all Judea and Samaria. And you will be my witnesses from one end of the earth to the other."

[9]After Jesus said this, he was taken up to heaven. They watched until a cloud hid him from their sight.

[10]While he was going up, they kept on looking at the sky. Suddenly two men dressed in white clothing stood beside them. [11]"Men of Galilee," they said, "why do you stand here looking at the sky? Jesus has been taken away from you into heaven. But he will come back in the same way you saw him go."

MATTHIAS IS CHOSEN TO TAKE THE PLACE OF JUDAS

[12]The apostles returned to Jerusalem from the Mount of Olives. It is almost a mile from the city. [13]When they arrived, they went upstairs to the room where they were staying. Peter, John, James and Andrew were there. Philip, Thomas, Bartholomew and Matthew were there too. So were James, son of Alphaeus, Simon the Zealot, and Judas, son of James. [14]They all came together regularly to pray. The women joined them too. So did Jesus' mother Mary and his brothers.

[15]In those days Peter stood up among the believers. About 120 of them were there. [16]Peter said, "Brothers, a long time ago the Holy Spirit spoke through David's mouth about Judas. What he said in Scripture had to come true. Judas was the guide for the men who arrested Jesus. [17]But Judas was one of us. He shared with us in our work for God."

[18]Judas bought a field with the reward he got for the evil thing he had done. He fell down headfirst in the field. His body burst open. All his insides spilled out. [19]Everyone in Jerusalem heard about this. So they called that field Akeldama. In their language, Akeldama means The Field of Blood.

[20]Peter said, "Here is what is written in the book of Psalms. It says,

" 'May his home be deserted.
   May no one live in it.'
(Psalm 69:25)

The Psalms also say,

" 'Let someone else take his place
   as leader.'   (Psalm 109:8)

[21]So we need to choose someone to take his place. It will have to be a man who was with us the whole time the Lord Jesus lived among us. [22]That time began when John was baptizing. It ended when Jesus was taken up from us. The one we choose must join us in giving witness that Jesus rose from the dead."

[23]So they suggested two men. One was Joseph, who was called Barsabbas. He was also called Justus. The other man was Matthias. [24]Then they prayed. "Lord," they said, "you know everyone's heart. Show us which of these two you have chosen. [25]Show us who should take the place of Judas as an apostle. He gave up being an apostle to go where he belongs." [26]Then they cast lots. Matthias was chosen. So he was added to the 11 apostles.

THE HOLY SPIRIT COMES AT PENTECOST

2 The day of Pentecost came. The believers all gathered in one place. [2]Suddenly a sound came from heaven. It was like a strong wind blowing. It filled the whole house where they were sitting. [3]They saw something that looked like tongues of fire. The flames separated and settled on each of them. [4]All of them were filled with the Holy Spirit. They began to speak in languages they had not known before. The Spirit gave them the ability to do this.

[5]Godly Jews from every country in the world were staying in Jerusalem. [6]A crowd came together when they heard the sound. They were bewildered because they each heard the believers speaking in their own language. [7]The crowd was really amazed.

They asked, "Aren't all these people from Galilee? [8]Why, then, do we each hear them speaking in our own native language? [9]We are Parthians, Medes and Elamites. We live in Mesopotamia, Judea and Cappadocia. We are from Pontus, Asia, [10]Phrygia and Pamphylia. Others of us are from Egypt and the parts of Libya near Cyrene. Still others are visitors from Rome. [11]Some of the visitors are Jews. Others have accepted the Jewish faith. Also, Cretans and Arabs are here. We hear all these people speaking about God's wonders in our own languages!" [12]They were amazed and bewildered. They asked one another, "What does this mean?"

[13]But some people in the crowd made fun of the believers. "They've had too much wine!" they said.

PETER SPEAKS TO THE CROWD

[14]Then Peter stood up with the Eleven. In a loud voice he spoke to the crowd. "My Jewish friends," he said, "let me explain this to you. All of you who live in Jerusalem, listen carefully to what I say. [15]You think these people are drunk. But they aren't. It's only nine o'clock in the morning! [16]No, here is what the prophet Joel meant. [17]He said,

" 'In the last days, God says,
    I will pour out my Holy Spirit on
        all people.
Your sons and daughters will
    prophesy.
    Your young men will see visions.
    Your old men will have dreams.
[18]In those days I will pour out my
        Spirit
    even on those who serve me,
        both men and women.
    When I do, they will prophesy.
[19]I will show wonders in the heavens
        above.
    I will show miraculous signs on
        the earth below.
    There will be blood and fire and
        clouds of smoke.
[20]The sun will become dark.
    The moon will turn red like blood.
    This will happen before the
        coming of the great and
        glorious day of the Lord.
[21]Everyone who calls
    on the name of the Lord will be
        saved.'
                              (Joel 2:28–32)

Didn't the tongues of fire on the apostles' heads burn them?

They were not real tongues of fire but something that looked like tongues of fire. It was a sign that God had sent the Holy Spirit just as Jesus had promised. The appearance of the fire meant that the Holy Spirit had come into the lives of Jesus' followers. Now the Holy Spirit lived inside them. And everyone watching knew that something very special was happening.

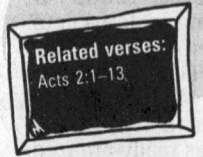

Related verses:
Acts 2:1–13

checkout
Acts 2:3,4

[22]"Men of Israel, listen to this! Jesus of Nazareth was a man who had God's approval. God did miracles, wonders and signs among you through Jesus. You yourselves know this. [23]Long ago God planned that Jesus would be handed over to you. With the help of evil people, you put Jesus to death. You nailed him to the cross. [24]But God raised him from the dead. He set him free from the suffering of death. It wasn't possible for death to keep its hold on Jesus. [25]David spoke about him. He said,

" 'I know that the Lord is always
    with me.
  He is at my right hand.
  I will always be secure.
[26]So my heart is glad. Joy is on my
    tongue.
  My body also will be full of hope.
[27]You will not leave me in the grave.
  You will not let your Holy One rot
    away.
[28]You always show me the path that
    leads to life.
  You will fill me with joy when I
    am with you.'   (Psalm 16:8–11)

[29]"Brothers, you can be sure that King David died. He was buried. His tomb is still here today. [30]But David was a prophet. He knew that God had made a promise to him. He had taken an oath that someone in David's family line would be king after him. [31]David saw what was ahead. So he spoke about the Christ rising from the dead. He said that the Christ would not be left in the grave. His body wouldn't rot in the ground. [32]God has raised this same Jesus back to life. We are all witnesses of this. [33]Jesus has been given a place of honor at the right hand of God. He has received the Holy Spirit from the Father. This is what God had promised. It is Jesus who has poured out what you now see and hear. [34]David did not go up to heaven. But he said,

" 'The Lord said to my Lord,
  "Sit at my right hand.
[35]I will put your enemies
    under your control." '   (Psalm 110:1)

[36]"So be sure of this, all you people of Israel. You nailed Jesus to the cross.

But God has made him both Lord and Christ."

[37]When the people heard this, their hearts were filled with shame. They said to Peter and the other apostles, "Brothers, what should we do?"

[38]Peter replied, "All of you must turn away from your sins and be baptized in the name of Jesus Christ. Then your sins will be forgiven. You will receive the gift of the Holy Spirit. [39]The promise is for you and your children. It is also for all who are far away. It is for all whom the Lord our God will choose."

[40]Peter said many other things to warn them. He begged them, "Save yourselves from these evil people." [41]Those who accepted his message were baptized. About 3,000 people joined the believers that day.

THE BELIEVERS SHARE LIFE TOGETHER

[42]The believers studied what the apostles taught. They shared life together. They broke bread and ate together. And they prayed. [43]Everyone felt that God was near. The apostles did many wonders and miraculous signs. [44]All the believers were together. They shared everything they had. [45]They sold what they owned. They gave each other everything they needed. [46]Every day they met together in the temple courtyard. In their homes they broke bread and ate together. Their hearts were glad and honest and true. [47]They praised God. They were respected by all the people. Every day the Lord added to their group those who were being saved.

PETER HEALS THE DISABLED BEGGAR

3 One day Peter and John were going up to the temple. It was three o'clock in the afternoon. It was the time for prayer. [2]A man unable to walk was being carried to the temple gate called Beautiful. He had been that way since he was born. Every day someone put him near the gate. There he would beg from people going into the temple courtyards.

[3]He saw that Peter and John were about to enter. So he asked them for money. [4]Peter looked straight at him,

and so did John. Then Peter said, "Look at us!" [5]So the man watched them closely. He expected to get something from them.

[6]Peter said, "I don't have any silver or gold. But I'll give you what I have. In the name of Jesus Christ of Nazareth, get up and walk." [7]Then Peter took him by the right hand and helped him up. At once the man's feet and ankles became strong. [8]He jumped to his feet and began to walk. He went with Peter and John into the temple courtyards. He walked and jumped and praised God. [9]All the people saw him walking and praising God. [10]They recognized him as the same man who used to sit and beg at the temple gate called Beautiful. They were filled with wonder. They were amazed at what had happened to him.

PETER SPEAKS TO THE JEWS

[11]The beggar was holding on to Peter and John. All the people were amazed. They came running to them at Solomon's Porch. [12]When Peter saw this, he said, "Men of Israel, why does this surprise you? Why do you stare at us? We haven't made this man walk by our own power or godliness. [13]The God of our fathers, Abraham, Isaac and Jacob, has done this. He has brought glory to Jesus, who serves him. But you handed Jesus over to be killed. Pilate had decided to let him go. But you spoke against Jesus when he was in Pilate's court. [14]You spoke against the Holy and Blameless One. You asked for a murderer to be set free instead. [15]You killed the one who gives life. But God raised him from the dead. We are witnesses of this. [16]This man whom you see and know was made strong because of faith in Jesus' name. Faith in Jesus has healed him completely. You can see it with your own eyes.

[17]"My friends, I know you didn't realize what you were doing. Neither did your leaders. [18]But God had given a promise through all the prophets. And this is how he has made his promise come true. He said that his Christ would suffer. [19]So turn away from your sins. Turn to God. Then your sins will

Why do people get baptized?

People get baptized to follow Jesus' example and because Jesus told his followers to baptize every new believer. The water of baptism reminds us that Jesus washes away our sins. It also reminds us of "drowning" our old, sinful natures and becoming "new" people through Jesus. Christians still sin, but their lives are pointed in a new direction, away from sin.

Some Christians believe that babies from Christian families should be baptized to show that they belong to Jesus. Some Christians think that only believers in Jesus should be baptized, to show that Jesus is their Savior. Either way, baptism is a very important event in a Christian's life.

checkout Acts 2:38,39

Related verses:
Matthew 3:13–17;
28:19

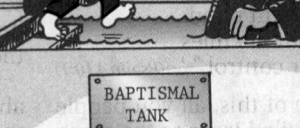

BAPTISMAL
TANK

be wiped away. The time will come when the Lord will make everything new. [20]He will send the Christ. Jesus has been appointed as the Christ for you. [21]He must remain in heaven until the time when God makes everything new. He promised this long ago through his holy prophets. [22]Moses said, 'The Lord your God will raise up for you a prophet like me. He will be one of your own people. You must listen to everything he tells you. [23]Those who do not listen to him will be completely cut off from their people.'
(Deuteronomy 18:15,18,19)

[24]"Samuel and all the prophets after him spoke about this. They said these days would come. [25]What the prophets said was meant for you. The covenant God made with your people long ago is yours also. He said to Abraham, 'All nations on earth will be blessed through your children.' *(Genesis 22:18; 26:4)* [26]God raised up Jesus, who serves him. God sent him first to you. He did it to bless you. He wanted to turn each of you from your evil ways."

PETER AND JOHN ARE TAKEN TO THE SANHEDRIN

4 Peter and John were speaking to the people. The priests, the captain of the temple guard, and the Sadducees came up to the apostles. [2]They were very upset by what the apostles were teaching the people. The apostles were saying that because Jesus rose from the dead, people can be raised from the dead. [3]So the temple authorities arrested Peter and John. It was already evening, so they put them in prison until the next day. [4]But many who heard the message believed. The number of men who believed grew to about 5,000.

[5]The next day the rulers, the elders and the teachers of the law met in Jerusalem. [6]Annas, the high priest, was there. So were Caiaphas, John, Alexander and others in the high priest's family. [7]They had Peter and John brought to them. They wanted to question them. "By what power did you do this?" they asked. "And through whose name?"

[8]Peter was filled with the Holy Spirit. He said to them, "Rulers and elders of the people! [9]Are you asking us to explain our actions today? Do you want to know why we were kind to a disabled man? Are you asking how he was healed? [10]Then listen to this, you and all the people of Israel! You nailed Jesus Christ of Nazareth to the cross. But God raised him from the dead. It is through Jesus' name that this man stands healed in front of you. [11]Scripture says that Jesus is

" 'the stone you builders did not accept.
But it has become the most important stone of all.'
(Psalm 118:22)

[12]You can't be saved by believing in anyone else. God has given us no other name under heaven that will save us."

[13]The leaders saw how bold Peter and John were. They also realized that Peter and John were ordinary men with no training. This surprised the leaders. They realized that these men had been with Jesus. [14]The leaders could see the man who had been healed standing there with them. So there was nothing they could say. [15]They ordered Peter and John to leave the Sanhedrin. Then they talked things over. [16]"What can we do with these men?" they asked. "Everybody in Jerusalem knows they have done an outstanding miracle. We can't say it didn't happen. [17]We have to stop this thing. It must not spread any further among the people. We have to warn these men. They must never speak to anyone in Jesus' name again."

[18]Once again the leaders called in Peter and John. They commanded them not to speak or teach at all in Jesus' name. [19]But Peter and John replied, "Judge for yourselves. Which is right from God's point of view? Should we obey you? Or God? [20]There's nothing else we can do. We have to speak about the things we've seen and heard."

[21]The leaders warned them again. Then they let them go. They couldn't decide how to punish Peter and John. They knew that all the people were praising God for what had happened. [22]The man who had been healed by the miracle was over 40 years old.

THE BELIEVERS PRAY

²³Peter and John were allowed to leave. They went back to their own people. They reported everything the chief priests and the elders had said to them. ²⁴When the believers heard this, they raised their voices together in prayer to God. "Lord and King," they said, "you made the heavens, the earth and the sea. You made everything in them. ²⁵Long ago you spoke by the Holy Spirit through the mouth of our father David, who served you. You said,

" 'Why are the nations angry?
    Why do the people make useless
        plans?
²⁶ The kings of the earth take their
        stand against the Lord.
    The rulers of the earth gather
        together
    against his Anointed King.'
                            (Psalm 2:1,2)

²⁷"In fact, Herod and Pontius Pilate met together in this city with those who weren't Jews. They also met with the people of Israel. All of them made plans against your holy servant Jesus.

He is the one you anointed. ²⁸They did what your power and purpose had already decided should happen. ²⁹Now, Lord, consider the bad things they say they are going to do. Help us to be very bold when we speak your word. ³⁰Stretch out your hand to heal. Do miraculous signs and wonders through the name of your holy servant Jesus."

³¹After they prayed, the place where they were meeting was shaken. They were all filled with the Holy Spirit. They were bold when they spoke God's word.

THE BELIEVERS SHARE WHAT THEY OWN

³²All the believers were agreed in heart and mind. They didn't claim that anything they had was their own. They shared everything they owned. ³³With great power the apostles continued their teaching. They gave witness that the Lord Jesus had risen from the dead. And they were greatly blessed by God.

³⁴There were no needy persons among them. From time to time, those who owned land or houses sold them.

KIDS' QUESTION

Will all of my friends go to heaven?

God loves your friends just as he loves you. But only God knows who will go to heaven and who will go to hell. Nobody else knows. There is only one way to heaven, and that is Jesus. We can go to heaven only if we trust Christ. If your friends do not follow Jesus, you can tell them about how he died for their sins. That will help them understand. God wants all people to be saved, but he leaves the choice to us. It is worth going to heaven even if your friends do not. No one will have any fun in hell.

checkout Acts 4:12

Related verse:
1 John 2:23

They brought the money from the sales. ³⁵They put it down at the apostles' feet. It was then given out to anyone who needed it.

³⁶Joseph was a Levite from Cyprus. The apostles called him Barnabas. The name Barnabas means Son of Help. ³⁷Barnabas sold a field he owned. He brought the money from the sale. He put it down at the apostles' feet.

ANANIAS AND SAPPHIRA

5 A man named Ananias and his wife, Sapphira, also sold some land. ²He kept part of the money for himself. Sapphira knew he had kept it. He brought the rest of it and put it down at the apostles' feet.

³Then Peter said, "Ananias, why did you let Satan fill your heart? He made you lie to the Holy Spirit. You have kept some of the money you received for the land. ⁴Didn't the land belong to you before it was sold? After it was sold, you could have used the money as you wished. What made you think of doing such a thing? You haven't lied to just anyone. You've lied to God."

⁵When Ananias heard this, he fell down and died. All who heard what had happened were filled with fear. ⁶Some young men came and wrapped up his body. They carried him out and buried him.

⁷About three hours later, the wife of Ananias came in. She didn't know what had happened. ⁸Peter asked her, "Tell me. Is this the price you and Ananias sold the land for?"

"Yes," she said. "That's the price."

⁹Peter asked her, "How could you agree to test the Spirit of the Lord? Listen! You can hear the steps of the men who buried your husband. They are at the door. They will carry you out also."

¹⁰At that very moment she fell down at his feet and died. Then the young men came in. They saw that Sapphira was dead. So they carried her out and buried her beside her husband. ¹¹The whole church and all who heard about these things were filled with fear.

THE APOSTLES HEAL MANY PEOPLE

¹²The apostles did many miraculous signs and wonders among the people. All the believers used to meet together at Solomon's Porch. ¹³No outsider dared to join them. But the people thought highly of them. ¹⁴More and more men and women believed in the Lord. They joined the other believers. ¹⁵So people brought those who were sick into the streets. They placed them on beds and mats. They hoped that at least Peter's shadow might fall on some of them as he walked by. ¹⁶Crowds even gathered from the towns around Jerusalem. They brought their sick. They also brought those who were suffering because of evil spirits. All of them were healed.

AN ANGEL OPENS THE PRISON DOORS

¹⁷The high priest and all his companions were Sadducees. They were very jealous of the apostles. ¹⁸So they arrested them and put them in the public prison. ¹⁹But during the night an angel of the Lord came. He opened the prison doors and brought the apostles out. ²⁰"Go! Stand in the temple courtyard," the angel said. "Tell the people all about this new life."

²¹Early the next day they did as they had been told. They entered the temple courtyard. There they began to teach the people.

The high priest and his companions arrived. They called the Sanhedrin together. The Sanhedrin was a gathering of all the elders of Israel. They sent for the apostles who were in prison. ²²The officers arrived at the prison. But they didn't find the apostles there. So they went back and reported it. ²³"We found the prison locked up tight," they said. "The guards were standing at the doors. But when we opened the doors, we didn't find anyone inside." ²⁴When the captain of the temple guard and the chief priests heard this report, they were bewildered. They wondered what would happen next.

²⁵Then someone came and said, "Look! The men you put in prison are standing in the temple courtyard. They are teaching the people." ²⁶So the captain went with his officers and brought the apostles back. But they didn't use force. They were afraid the

people would kill them by throwing stones at them.

²⁷They brought the apostles to be judged by the Sanhedrin. The high priest questioned them. ²⁸"We gave you clear orders not to teach in Jesus' name," he said. "But you have filled Jerusalem with your teaching. You want to make us guilty of this man's death."

²⁹Peter and the other apostles replied, "We must obey God instead of people! ³⁰You had Jesus killed by nailing him to a cross. But the God of our people raised Jesus from the dead. ³¹Now Jesus is Prince and Savior. God has proved this by giving him a place of honor at his own right hand. He did it so that he could turn Israel away from their sins and forgive them. ³²We are witnesses of these things. And so is the Holy Spirit. God has given the Spirit to those who obey him."

³³When the leaders heard this, they became very angry. They wanted to put the apostles to death. ³⁴But a Pharisee named Gamaliel stood up in the Sanhedrin. He was a teacher of the law. He was honored by all the people. He ordered the men to be taken outside for a little while. ³⁵Then he spoke to the Sanhedrin. "Men of Israel," he said, "think carefully about what you plan to do to these men. ³⁶Some time ago Theudas appeared. He claimed he was really somebody. About 400 people followed him. But he was killed. All his followers were scattered. So they accomplished nothing. ³⁷After this, Judas from Galilee came along. This was in the days when the Romans made a list of all the people. Judas led a gang of men against the Romans. He too was killed. All his followers were scattered. ³⁸So let me give you some advice. Leave these men alone! Let them go! If their plans and actions are only human, they will fail. ³⁹But if their plans come from God, you won't be able to stop these men. You will only find yourselves fighting against God."

⁴⁰His speech won the leaders over. They called the apostles in and had

KIDS' QUESTION

If the law says something is right but God says it's wrong, who's right?

God. The Bible tells us to obey the government. But we should obey God instead of the government whenever a government law goes against God's law. God is in charge of everything. The government is *not* the highest authority. We should pray even if the government were to pass a law against it. We should worship, read the Bible and tell others about Jesus even if the government were to say we cannot. And we should never lie or steal even if the government were to say it was OK, because God has laws against lying and stealing. God created and rules the universe. No one can have higher authority. So we must always obey God first.

checkout
Acts 5:29

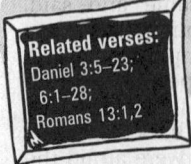
Related verses:
Daniel 3:5–23;
6:1–28;
Romans 13:1,2

them whipped. The leaders ordered them not to speak in Jesus' name. Then they let the apostles go.

[41]The apostles were full of joy as they left the Sanhedrin. They considered it an honor to suffer shame for the name of Jesus. [42]Day after day, they kept teaching in the temple courtyards and from house to house. They never stopped telling the good news that Jesus is the Christ.

SEVEN LEADERS ARE CHOSEN

6 In those days the number of believers was growing. The Jews who followed Greek practices complained against the Jews who followed only Jewish practices. They said that the widows of men who followed Greek practices were not being taken care of. They weren't getting their fair share of food each day. [2]So the Twelve gathered all the believers together. They said, "It wouldn't be right for us to give up teaching God's word in order to wait on tables. [3]Brothers, choose seven of your men. They must be known as men who are wise and full of the Holy Spirit. We will turn this important work over to them. [4]Then we can give our attention to prayer and to teaching the word."

[5]This plan pleased the whole group. They chose Stephen. He was full of faith and of the Holy Spirit. Philip, Procorus, Nicanor, Timon and Parmenas were chosen too. The group also chose Nicolas from Antioch. He had accepted the Jewish faith. [6]The group brought them to the apostles. Then the apostles prayed and placed their hands on them.

[7]So God's word spread. The number of believers in Jerusalem grew quickly. Also, a large number of priests began to obey Jesus' teachings.

STEPHEN IS ARRESTED

[8]Stephen was full of God's grace and power. He did great wonders and miraculous signs among the people. [9]But members of the group called the Synagogue of the Freedmen began to oppose him. Some of them were Jews from Cyrene and Alexandria. Others were Jews from Cilicia and Asia Minor. They all began to argue with Stephen.

[10]But he was too wise for them. They couldn't stand up against the Holy Spirit who spoke through him.

[11]Then in secret they talked some men into lying about Stephen. They said, "We heard Stephen speak evil things against Moses. He also spoke evil things against God."

[12]So the people were stirred up. The elders and the teachers of the law were stirred up too. They arrested Stephen and brought him to the Sanhedrin. [13]They found people who were willing to tell lies. The false witnesses said, "This fellow never stops speaking against this holy place. He also speaks against the law. [14]We have heard him say that this Jesus of Nazareth will destroy this place. He says Jesus will change the practices that Moses handed down to us."

[15]All who were sitting in the Sanhedrin looked right at Stephen. They saw that his face was like the face of an angel.

STEPHEN SPEAKS TO THE SANHEDRIN

7 Then the high priest questioned Stephen. "Is what these people are saying true?" he asked.

[2]"Brothers and fathers, listen to me!" Stephen replied. "The God of glory appeared to our father Abraham. At that time Abraham was still in Mesopotamia. He had not yet begun living in Haran. [3]'Leave your country and your people,' God said. 'Go to the land I will show you.' *(Genesis 12:1)*

[4]"So Abraham left the land of Babylonia. He settled in Haran. After his father died, God sent Abraham to this land where you are now living. [5]God didn't give him any property here. He didn't give him even a foot of land. But God made a promise to him and to all his family after him. He said they would possess the land. The promise was made even though at that time Abraham had no child.

[6]"Here is what God said to him. 'Your family after you will be strangers in a country that is not their own. They will be slaves and will be treated badly for 400 years. [7]But I will punish the nation that makes them slaves,' God said. 'After that, they will leave that

country and worship me here.' *(Genesis 15:13,14)*

8"Then God made a covenant with Abraham. God told him that circumcision would show who the members of the covenant were. Abraham became Isaac's father. He circumcised Isaac eight days after he was born. Later, Isaac became Jacob's father. Jacob had 12 sons. They became the founders of the 12 tribes of Israel.

9"Jacob's sons were jealous of their brother Joseph. So they sold him as a slave. He was taken to Egypt. But God was with him. 10He saved Joseph from all his troubles. God made Joseph wise. He helped him to become the friend of Pharaoh, the king of Egypt. So Pharaoh made Joseph ruler over Egypt and his whole palace.

11"There was not enough food for all Egypt and Canaan. This brought great suffering. Jacob and his sons couldn't find food. 12But Jacob heard that there was grain in Egypt. So he sent his sons on their first visit. 13On their second visit, Joseph told his brothers who he was. Pharaoh learned about Joseph's family.

14"After this, Joseph sent for his father Jacob and his whole family. The total number of people was 75. 15Then Jacob went down to Egypt. There he and his family died. 16Some of their bodies were brought back to Shechem. They were placed in a tomb Abraham had bought. He had purchased it from Hamor's sons at Shechem for a certain amount of money.

17"In Egypt the number of our people grew and grew. It was nearly time for God to make his promise to Abraham come true. 18Another king became ruler of Egypt. He knew nothing about Joseph. 19He was very evil and dishonest with our people. He beat them down. He forced them to throw out their newborn babies to die.

20"At that time Moses was born. He was not an ordinary child. For three months he was taken care of by his family. 21Then he was placed outside. But Pharaoh's daughter took him home. She brought him up as her own son. 22Moses was taught all the knowledge of the people of Egypt. He became a powerful speaker and a man of action.

23"When Moses was 40 years old, he decided to visit the people of Israel. They were his own people. 24He saw one of them being treated badly by a man of Egypt. So he went to help him. He got even by killing the man. 25Moses thought his own people would realize that God was using him to save them. But they didn't.

26"The next day Moses saw two men of Israel fighting. He tried to make peace between them. 'Men, you are both of Israel,' he said. 'Why do you want to hurt each other?'

27"But the man who was treating the other one badly pushed Moses to one side. He said, 'Who made you ruler and judge over us? 28Do you want to kill me as you killed the Egyptian yesterday?' *(Exodus 2:14)* 29When Moses heard this, he escaped to Midian. He lived there as a stranger. He became the father of two sons there.

30"Forty years passed. Then an angel appeared to Moses in the flames of a burning bush. This happened in the desert near Mount Sinai. 31When Moses saw the bush, he was amazed. He went over for a closer look. There he heard the Lord's voice. 32'I am the God of your fathers,' the Lord said. 'I am the God of Abraham, Isaac and Jacob.' *(Exodus 3:6)* Moses shook with fear. He didn't dare to look.

33"Then the Lord said to him, 'Take off your sandals. The place you are standing on is holy ground. 34I have seen my people beaten down in Egypt. I have heard their groans. I have come down to set them free. Now come. I will send you back to Egypt.' *(Exodus 3:5,7,8,10)*

35"This is the same Moses the two men of Israel would not accept. They had said, 'Who made you ruler and judge?' But God himself sent Moses to rule the people of Israel and set them free. He spoke to Moses through the angel who had appeared to him in the bush. 36So Moses led them out of Egypt. He did wonders and miraculous signs in Egypt, at the Red Sea, and for 40 years in the desert.

37"This is the same Moses who spoke to the people of Israel. 'God will send you a prophet,' he said. 'He will be like me. He will come from your own people.' *(Deuteronomy 18:15)* ³⁸Moses was with the Israelites in the desert. He was with the angel who spoke to him on Mount Sinai. Moses was with our people of long ago. He received living words to pass on to us.

³⁹"But our people refused to obey Moses. They would not accept him. In their hearts, they wished they were back in Egypt. ⁴⁰They told Aaron, 'Make us a god who will lead us. This fellow Moses led us out of Egypt. But we don't know what has happened to him!' *(Exodus 32:1)* ⁴¹That was the time they made a statue to be their god. It looked like a calf. They brought sacrifices to it. They were glad because of what they had made with their own hands. ⁴²But God turned away from them. He left them to worship the sun, moon and stars. This agrees with what is written in the book of the prophets. There it says,

" 'People of Israel, did you bring
    me sacrifices and offerings
  for 40 years in the desert?
⁴³You lifted up the place where
    Molech was worshiped.
  You lifted up the star of your god
    Rephan.
  You made statues of them to
    worship.
  So I will send you away from your
    country.'   *(Amos 5:25–27)*
  God sent them to Babylon and
    even farther.

⁴⁴"Long ago our people had with them in the desert the holy tent where the tablets of the covenant were kept. Moses had made the holy tent as God had commanded him. It was made like the pattern he had seen. ⁴⁵Our people received the tent from God. They brought it with them when they took the land of Canaan. God drove out the nations that were in their way. At that time Joshua was Israel's leader.

"The tent remained in the land until David's time. ⁴⁶David was blessed by God. So David asked if he could build a house for the God of Jacob. ⁴⁷Instead, it was Solomon who built it for him.

⁴⁸"But the Most High God does not live in houses made by human hands. As God says through the prophet,

⁴⁹" 'Heaven is my throne.
  The earth is under my control.
  What kind of house will you build
    for me?
                    says the Lord.
  Where will my resting place be?
⁵⁰Didn't my hand make all these
    things?'   *(Isaiah 66:1,2)*

⁵¹"You people! You won't obey! You are stubborn! You won't listen! You are just like your people of long ago! You always oppose the Holy Spirit! ⁵²Was there ever a prophet your people didn't try to hurt? They even killed those who told about the coming of the Blameless One. And now you have handed him over to his enemies. You have murdered him. ⁵³The law you received was brought by angels. But you haven't obeyed it."

STEPHEN IS KILLED

⁵⁴When the Sanhedrin heard this, they became very angry. They ground their teeth at Stephen. ⁵⁵But he was full of the Holy Spirit. He looked up to heaven and saw God's glory. He saw Jesus standing at God's right hand. ⁵⁶"Look!" he said. "I see heaven open. The Son of Man is standing at God's right hand."

⁵⁷When the Sanhedrin heard this, they covered their ears. They yelled at the top of their voices. They all rushed at him. ⁵⁸They dragged him out of the city. They began to throw stones at him to kill him. The witnesses took off their coats. They placed them at the feet of a young man named Saul.

⁵⁹While the members of the Sanhedrin were throwing stones at Stephen, he prayed. "Lord Jesus, receive my spirit," he said. ⁶⁰Then he fell on his knees. He cried out, "Lord! Don't hold this sin against them!" When he had said this, he died.

8 Saul was there. He had agreed that Stephen should die.

THE CHURCH IS SCATTERED

On that day the church in Jerusalem began to be attacked and treated badly. All except the apostles were scattered throughout Judea and Samaria.

²Godly Jews buried Stephen. They sobbed and sobbed over him.

[3]But Saul began to destroy the church. He went from house to house. He dragged men and women away and put them in prison.

PHILIP GOES TO SAMARIA

[4]The believers who had been scattered preached the word everywhere they went. [5]Philip went down to a city in Samaria. There he preached about the Christ. [6]The crowds listened to Philip. They saw the miraculous signs he did. They all paid close attention to what he said. [7]Evil spirits screamed and came out of many people. Many who were disabled or who couldn't walk were healed. [8]So there was great joy in that city.

SIMON THE EVIL MAGICIAN

[9]A man named Simon lived in the city. For quite a while he had practiced evil magic there. He amazed all the people of Samaria. He claimed to be someone great. [10]All of the people listened to him, from the least important of them to the most important. They exclaimed, "This man is known as the Great Power of God!" [11]He had amazed them for a long time with his magic. So they followed him.

[12]But Philip preached the good news of God's kingdom. He preached the name of Jesus Christ. So men and women believed and were baptized. [13]Simon himself believed and was baptized. He followed Philip everywhere. He was amazed by the great signs and miracles he saw.

[14]The apostles in Jerusalem heard that people in Samaria had accepted God's word. So they sent Peter and John to them. [15]When they arrived there, they prayed that the believers would receive the Holy Spirit. [16]The Holy Spirit had not yet come on any of them. They had only been baptized in the name of the Lord Jesus. [17]Then Peter and John placed their hands on them. And they received the Holy Spirit.

[18]Simon watched as the apostles placed their hands on them. He saw that the Spirit was given to them. So he offered money to Peter and John. [19]He said, "Give me this power too. Then everyone I place my hands on will receive the Holy Spirit."

[20]Peter answered, "May your money be destroyed with you! Do you think you can buy God's gift with money? [21]You have no part or share in this holy work. Your heart is not right with God. [22]Turn away from this evil sin of yours. Pray to the Lord. Perhaps he will forgive you for having such a thought in your heart. [23]I see that you are very bitter. You are a prisoner of sin."

[24]Then Simon answered, "Pray to the Lord for me. Pray that nothing you have said will happen to me."

[25]Peter and John gave witness and

Does Jesus live with God in heaven or does he live by himself?

When Jesus left the earth, he went to heaven to live with God the Father. That is where he is right now. He sits at the Father's right hand. That is the place of highest honor.

checkout Acts 7:55,56

Related verse:
Colossians 3:1

preached the Lord's word. Then they returned to Jerusalem. On the way they preached the good news in many villages in Samaria.

PHILIP AND THE MAN FROM ETHIOPIA

26An angel of the Lord spoke to Philip. "Go south to the desert road," he said. "It's the road that goes down from Jerusalem to Gaza." 27So Philip started out. On his way he met an Ethiopian official. The man had an important position. He was in charge of all the wealth of Candace. She was the queen of Ethiopia. He had gone to Jerusalem to worship. 28On his way home he was sitting in his chariot. He was reading the book of Isaiah the prophet. 29The Holy Spirit told Philip, "Go to that chariot. Stay near it."

30So Philip ran up to the chariot. He heard the man reading Isaiah the prophet. "Do you understand what you're reading?" Philip asked.

31"How can I?" he said. "I need someone to explain it to me." So he invited Philip to come up and sit with him.

32Here is the part of Scripture the official was reading. It says,

"He was led like a sheep to be
     killed.
Just as lambs are silent while
     their wool is being cut off,
he did not open his mouth.
33When he was treated badly, he was
     refused a fair trial.
Who can say anything about his
     children?
His life was cut off from the
     earth."   *(Isaiah 53:7,8)*

34The official said to Philip, "Tell me, please. Who is the prophet talking about? Himself, or someone else?" 35Then Philip began with that same part of Scripture. He told him the good news about Jesus.

36/37As they traveled along the road, they came to some water. The official said, "Look! Here is water! Why shouldn't I be baptized?" 38He gave orders to stop the chariot. Then both

KIDS' QUESTION

Why can't I see angels?

Angels are spirits. They do not have bodies as we do. Angels appear with bodies only when God sends them to speak to people like Philip. We know of only a few times when angels appeared to people. That includes the exodus from Egypt, the time of Elijah and the time of the early church. God does not show off his angels. He has angels appear only at times when people really need to see them. Angels can do their work without being seen. Some of the jobs that people want angels to do have been given to God's people. Angels do not need to hang around doing what we are supposed to be doing.

checkout Acts 8:26

Related verse:
Hebrews 1:14

Philip and the official went down into the water. Philip baptized him. ³⁹When they came up out of the water, the Spirit of the Lord suddenly took Philip away. The official did not see him again. He went on his way full of joy. ⁴⁰Philip was seen next at Azotus. From there he traveled all around. He preached the good news in all the towns. Finally he arrived in Caesarea.

SAUL BECOMES A BELIEVER

9 Meanwhile, Saul continued to oppose the Lord's followers. He said they would be put to death. He went to the high priest. ²He asked the priest for letters to the synagogues in Damascus. He wanted to find men and women who belonged to the Way of Jesus. The letters would allow him to take them as prisoners to Jerusalem. ³On his journey, Saul approached Damascus. Suddenly a light from heaven flashed around him. ⁴He fell to the ground. He heard a voice speak to him. "Saul! Saul!" the voice said. "Why are you opposing me?"

⁵"Who are you, Lord?" Saul asked.

"I am Jesus," he replied. "I am the one you are opposing. ⁶Now get up and go into the city. There you will be told what you must do."

⁷The men traveling with Saul stood there. They weren't able to speak. They had heard the sound. But they didn't see anyone. ⁸Saul got up from the ground. He opened his eyes, but he couldn't see. So they led him by the hand into Damascus. ⁹For three days he was blind. He didn't eat or drink anything.

¹⁰In Damascus there was a believer named Ananias. The Lord called out to him in a vision. "Ananias!" he said.

"Yes, Lord," he answered.

¹¹The Lord told him, "Go to the house of Judas on Straight Street. Ask for a man from Tarsus named Saul. He is praying. ¹²In a vision he has seen

Why did Jesus appear to Saul?

At first Saul was against Jesus and anyone who followed him. Saul hated Christians so much that he got permission to capture them and put them in jail. One day Saul was traveling to another city to look for Christians. All of a sudden a bright light blinded him. God used the light to get Saul's attention. Then Jesus appeared to him and talked to him, and Saul believed in Jesus. He became a follower of Jesus and a missionary. He went all over the world helping people become Christians instead of trying to get rid of Christians. Some of his letters to Christians are in our Bibles today.

checkout

Acts 9:3–6

Related verses:
Galatians 1:13–15

a man named Ananias. The man has come and placed his hands on him. Now he will be able to see again."

[13] "Lord," Ananias answered, "I've heard many reports about this man. They say he has done great harm to God's people in Jerusalem. [14] Now he has come here to arrest all those who worship you. The chief priests have given him authority to do this."

[15] But the Lord said to Ananias, "Go! I have chosen this man to work for me. He will carry my name to those who aren't Jews and to their kings. He will bring my name to the people of Israel. [16] I will show him how much he must suffer for me."

[17] Then Ananias went to the house and entered it. He placed his hands on Saul. "Brother Saul," he said, "you saw the Lord Jesus. He appeared to you on the road as you were coming here. He has sent me so that you will be able to see again. You will be filled with the Holy Spirit."

[18] Right away something like scales fell from Saul's eyes. And he could see again. He got up and was baptized. [19] After eating some food, he got his strength back.

SAUL IN DAMASCUS AND JERUSALEM

Saul spent several days with the believers in Damascus. [20] At once he began to preach in the synagogues. He taught that Jesus is the Son of God. [21] All who heard him were amazed. They asked, "Isn't he the man who caused great trouble in Jerusalem for those who worship Jesus? Hasn't he come here to take them as prisoners to the chief priests?" [22] But Saul grew more and more powerful. The Jews living in Damascus couldn't believe what was happening. Saul proved to them that Jesus is the Christ.

[23] After many days, the Jews had a meeting. They planned to kill Saul. [24] But he learned about their plan. Day and night they watched the city gates closely in order to kill him. [25] But his followers helped him escape by night. They lowered him in a basket through an opening in the wall.

[26] When Saul came to Jerusalem, he tried to join the believers. But they were all afraid of him. They didn't believe he was really one of Jesus' followers. [27] But Barnabas took him to the apostles. He told them about Saul's journey. He said that Saul had seen the Lord. He told how the Lord had spoken to Saul. Barnabas also said that Saul had preached without fear in Jesus' name in Damascus.

[28] So Saul stayed with the believers. He moved about freely in Jerusalem. He spoke boldly in the Lord's name. [29] He talked and argued with Jews who followed Greek practices. But they tried to kill him. [30] The other believers heard about this. They took Saul down to Caesarea. From there they sent him off to Tarsus.

[31] Then the church throughout Judea, Galilee and Samaria enjoyed a time of peace. The Holy Spirit gave the church strength and boldness. So they grew in numbers. And they worshiped the Lord.

PETER GOES TO LYDDA AND JOPPA

[32] As Peter traveled around the country, he went to visit God's people in Lydda. [33] There he found a disabled man named Aeneas. For eight years the man had spent most of his time in bed. [34] "Aeneas," Peter said to him, "Jesus Christ heals you. Get up! Take care of your mat!" So Aeneas got up right away. [35] Everyone who lived in Lydda and Sharon saw him. They turned to the Lord.

[36] In Joppa there was a believer named Tabitha. Her name in the Greek language was Dorcas. She was always doing good and helping poor people. [37] About that time she became sick and died. Her body was washed and placed in a room upstairs. [38] Lydda was near Joppa. The believers heard that Peter was in Lydda. So they sent two men to him. They begged him, "Please come at once!"

[39] Peter went with them. When he arrived, he was taken upstairs to the room. All the widows stood around him crying. They showed him the robes and other clothes Dorcas had made while she was still alive. [40] Peter sent them all out of the room. Then he got down on his knees

and prayed. He turned toward the dead woman. He said, "Tabitha, get up." She opened her eyes. When she saw Peter, she sat up. ⁴¹He took her by the hand and helped her to her feet. Then he called the believers and the widows. He brought her to them. They saw that she was alive. ⁴²This became known all over Joppa. Many people believed in the Lord. ⁴³Peter stayed in Joppa for some time. He stayed with Simon, a man who worked with leather.

CORNELIUS CALLS FOR PETER

10 A man named Cornelius lived in Caesarea. He was a Roman commander in the Italian Regiment. ²Cornelius and all his family were faithful and worshiped God. He gave freely to people who were in need. He prayed to God regularly. ³One day about three o'clock in the afternoon he had a vision. He saw an angel of God clearly. The angel came to him and said, "Cornelius!"

⁴Cornelius was afraid. He stared at the angel. "What is it, Lord?" he asked.

The angel answered, "Your prayers and gifts to poor people have come up like an offering to God. So he has remembered you. ⁵Now send men to Joppa. Have them bring back a man named Simon. He is also called Peter. ⁶He is staying with another Simon, a man who works with leather. His house is by the sea."

⁷The angel who spoke to him left. Then Cornelius called two of his servants. He also called a godly soldier who was one of his attendants. ⁸He told them everything that had happened. Then he sent them to Joppa.

PETER HAS A VISION

⁹It was about noon the next day. The men were on their journey and were approaching the city. Peter went up on the roof to pray. ¹⁰He became hungry. He wanted something to eat. While the meal was being prepared, Peter had a

How could Peter kill and eat animals that were in a vision?

Peter did not actually eat the animals he saw in his vision. Before this, God had allowed the Jews to eat other kinds of animals, but not these. God was just telling him it was OK now to eat them. Soon after this vision Peter learned its meaning. Three men who were not Jews came to the door and asked Peter to come and talk to their leader. Before his vision Peter would not have had anything to do with people who were not Jews, because the Jewish religious leaders would not allow it. But the vision made him realize that it was OK for him to go with these men. Peter obeyed God and went to see their leader Cornelius. Cornelius wanted to hear about Jesus. Peter told him. And soon Cornelius, his family and his servants all became Christians.

checkout
Acts 10:12, 13

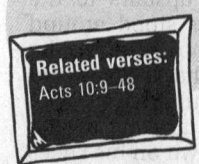

Related verses:
Acts 10:9–48

vision. ¹¹He saw heaven open up. There he saw something that looked like a large sheet. It was being let down to earth by its four corners. ¹²It had all kinds of four-footed animals in it. It also had reptiles of the earth and birds of the air. ¹³Then a voice told him, "Get up, Peter. Kill and eat."

¹⁴"No, Lord! I will not!" Peter replied. "I have never eaten anything that is not pure and 'clean.' "

¹⁵The voice spoke to him a second time. "Do not say anything is not pure that God has made 'clean,' " it said.

¹⁶This happened three times. Right away the sheet was taken back up to heaven.

¹⁷Peter was wondering what the vision meant. At that very moment the men sent by Cornelius found Simon's house. They stopped at the gate ¹⁸and called out. They asked if Simon Peter was staying there.

¹⁹Peter was still thinking about the vision. The Holy Spirit spoke to him. "Simon," he said, "three men are looking for you. ²⁰Get up and go downstairs. Don't let anything keep you from going with them. I have sent them."

²¹Peter went down and spoke to the men. "I'm the one you're looking for," he said. "Why have you come?"

²²The men replied, "We have come from Cornelius, the Roman commander. He is a good man who worships God. All the Jewish people respect him. A holy angel told him to invite you to his house. Cornelius wants to hear what you have to say." ²³Then Peter invited the men into the house to be his guests.

PETER GOES TO THE HOUSE OF CORNELIUS

The next day Peter went with the three men. Some of the believers from Joppa went along. ²⁴The following day he arrived in Caesarea. Cornelius was expecting them. He had called together er his relatives and close friends.

²⁵When Peter entered the house, Cornelius met him. As a sign of respect, he fell at Peter's feet. ²⁶But Peter made him get up. "Stand up," he said. "I am only a man myself."

²⁷Talking with Cornelius, Peter went inside. There he found a large group of people. ²⁸He said to them, "You know that it is against our law for a Jew to

Why was it against the law to make friends with a Gentile?

A Gentile was anyone who was not a Jew. It was *not* against the law for a Jew to make friends with a Gentile. God just did not want the Jewish people to *copy* the Gentiles. The Gentiles did not follow the Jewish laws and did not believe in the true God. Some Jews would not even walk through Gentile towns. Jews did accept some Gentiles into their religion. These Gentiles were called "God-fearers."

Acts 10:28

Related verses:
Galatians 2:11–14

have anything to do with those who aren't Jews. But God has shown me that I should not say anyone is not pure and 'clean.' [29] So when you sent for me, I came without asking any questions. May I ask why you sent for me?"

[30] Cornelius answered, "Four days ago at this very hour I was in my house praying. It was three o'clock in the afternoon. Suddenly a man in shining clothes stood in front of me. [31] He said, 'Cornelius, God has heard your prayer. He has remembered your gifts to poor people. [32] Send someone to Joppa to get Simon Peter. He is a guest in the home of another Simon, who works with leather. He lives by the sea.' [33] So I sent for you right away. It was good of you to come. Now we are all here. And God is here with us. We are ready to listen to everything the Lord has commanded you to tell us."

[34] Then Peter began to speak. "I now realize how true it is that God treats everyone the same," he said. [35] "He accepts people from every nation. He accepts all who have respect for him and do what is right.

[36] "You know the message God sent to the people of Israel. It is the good news of peace through Jesus Christ. He is Lord of all. [37] You know what has happened all through Judea. It started in Galilee after John preached about baptism. [38] You know how God anointed Jesus of Nazareth with the Holy Spirit and with power. Jesus went around doing good. He healed all who were under the devil's power. God was with him.

[39] "We are witnesses of everything he did in the land of the Jews and in Jerusalem. They killed him by nailing him to a cross. [40] But on the third day God raised him from the dead. God allowed Jesus to be seen. [41] But he wasn't seen by all the people. He was seen only by us. We are witnesses whom God had already chosen. We ate and drank with him after he rose from the dead.

[42] "He commanded us to preach to the people. He told us to give witness that he is the one appointed by God to judge the living and the dead. [43] All the prophets give witness about him.

They say that all who believe in him have their sins forgiven through his name."

[44] While Peter was still saying these things, the Holy Spirit came on all who heard the message. [45] Some Jewish believers had come with Peter. They were amazed because the gift of the Holy Spirit had been poured out even on those who weren't Jews. [46] They heard them speaking in languages they had not known before. They also heard them praising God.

Then Peter said, [47] "Can anyone keep these people from being baptized with water? They have received the Holy Spirit just as we have." [48] So he ordered that they be baptized in the name of Jesus Christ. Then they asked Peter to stay with them for a few days.

PETER EXPLAINS HIS ACTIONS

11 The apostles and the believers all through Judea heard that people who were not Jews had also received God's word. [2] Peter went up to Jerusalem. There the Jewish believers found fault with him. [3] They said, "You went into the house of those who aren't Jews. You ate with them."

[4] Peter explained everything to them. He told them exactly what had happened. [5] "I was in the city of Joppa praying," he said. "There I had a vision. I saw something that looked like a large sheet. It was being let down from heaven by its four corners. It came down to where I was. [6] I looked into it and saw four-footed animals of the earth. There were also wild animals, reptiles and birds. [7] Then I heard a voice speaking to me. 'Get up, Peter,' the voice said. 'Kill and eat.'

[8] "I replied, 'No, Lord! I will not! Nothing that is not pure and "clean" has ever entered my mouth.'

[9] "A second time the voice spoke from heaven. 'Do not say anything is not pure that God has made "clean,"' the voice said. [10] This happened three times. Then the sheet was pulled up into heaven.

[11] "Just then three men stopped at the house where I was staying. They had been sent to me from Caesarea. [12] The Holy Spirit told me not to let

anything keep me from going with them. These six brothers here went with me. We entered the man's house. [13]He told us how he had seen an angel appear in his house. The angel said, 'Send to Joppa for Simon Peter. [14]He has a message to bring to you. You and your whole family will be saved through it.'

[15]"As I began to speak, the Holy Spirit came on them. He came just as he had come on us at the beginning. [16]Then I remembered the Lord's words. 'John baptized with water,' he had said. 'But you will be baptized with the Holy Spirit.' [17]God gave them the same gift he gave those of us who believed in the Lord Jesus Christ. So who was I to think that I could oppose God?"

[18]When they heard this, they didn't object anymore. They praised God. They said, "So then, God has allowed even those who aren't Jews to turn away from their sins and live."

BELIEVERS ARE CALLED CHRISTIANS FOR THE FIRST TIME

[19]Some believers had been scattered by the suffering that came to them after Stephen's death. They traveled as far as Phoenicia, Cyprus and Antioch. But they told the message only to Jews. [20]Some believers from Cyprus and Cyrene went to Antioch. There they began to speak to Greeks also. They told them the good news about the Lord Jesus. [21]The Lord's power was with them. Large numbers of people believed and turned to the Lord.

[22]The church in Jerusalem heard about this. So they sent Barnabas to Antioch. [23]When he arrived and saw what the grace of God had done, he was glad. He told them all to remain true to the Lord with all their hearts. [24]Barnabas was a good man. He was full of the Holy Spirit and of faith. Large numbers of people came to know the Lord.

[25]Then Barnabas went to Tarsus to look for Saul. [26]He found him there. Then he brought him to Antioch. For a whole year Barnabas and Saul met with the church. They taught large numbers of people. At Antioch the believers were called Christians for the first time.

[27]In those days some prophets came down from Jerusalem to Antioch. [28]One of them was named Agabus. He stood up and spoke through the Spirit. He said there would not be nearly enough food anywhere in the Roman world. This happened while Claudius was the emperor. [29]The believers decided to provide help for the brothers and sisters living in Judea. All of them helped as much as they could. [30]They sent their gift to the elders through Barnabas and Saul.

AN ANGEL HELPS PETER ESCAPE FROM PRISON

12 About this time, King Herod arrested some people who belonged to the church. He planned to make them suffer greatly. [2]He had James killed with a sword. James was John's brother. [3]Herod saw that the death of James pleased the Jews. So he arrested Peter also. This happened during the Feast of Unleavened Bread. [4]After Herod arrested Peter, he put him in prison. Peter was placed under guard. He was watched by four groups of four soldiers each. Herod planned to put Peter on public trial. It would take place after the Passover Feast.

[5]So Peter was kept in prison. But the church prayed hard to God for him.

[6]It was the night before Herod was going to bring him to trial. Peter was sleeping between two soldiers. Two chains held him there. Lookouts stood guard at the entrance. [7]Suddenly an angel of the Lord appeared. A light shone in the prison cell. The angel struck Peter on his side. Peter woke up. "Quick!" the angel said. "Get up!" The chains fell off Peter's wrists.

[8]Then the angel said to him, "Put on your clothes and sandals." Peter did so. "Put on your coat," the angel told him. "Follow me." [9]Peter followed him out of the prison. But he had no idea that what the angel was doing was really happening. He thought he was seeing a vision. [10]They passed the first and second guards. Then they came to the iron gate leading to the city. It opened for them by itself. They

went through it. They walked the length of one street. Suddenly the angel left Peter.

¹¹Then Peter realized what had happened. He said, "Now I know for sure that the Lord sent his angel. He set me free from Herod's power. He saved me from everything the Jewish people were hoping for."

¹²When Peter understood what had happened, he went to Mary's house. Mary was the mother of John Mark. Many people had gathered in her home. They were praying there. ¹³Peter knocked at the outer entrance. A servant named Rhoda came to answer the door. ¹⁴She recognized Peter's voice. She was so excited that she ran back without opening the door. "Peter is at the door!" she exclaimed.

¹⁵"You're out of your mind," they said to her. But she kept telling them it was true. So they said, "It must be his angel."

¹⁶Peter kept on knocking. When they opened the door and saw him, they were amazed. ¹⁷Peter motioned with his hand for them to be quiet. He explained how the Lord had brought him out of prison. "Tell James and the others about this," he said. Then he went to another place.

¹⁸In the morning the soldiers were bewildered. They couldn't figure out what had happened to Peter. ¹⁹So Herod had them look everywhere for Peter. But they didn't find him. Then Herod questioned the guards closely. He ordered that they be put to death.

HEROD DIES

Herod went from Judea to Caesarea. He stayed there awhile. ²⁰He had been quarreling with the people of Tyre and Sidon. So they got together and asked for a meeting with him. This was because they depended on the king's country to supply them with food.

How could the angel unlock Peter and let him out of jail without keys?

Jesus told his followers to begin telling everyone about him. Peter, John and others were preaching in the temple. But the leaders did not like this at all. They told Peter not to talk about Jesus any more. Then they had Peter and the other disciples arrested and thrown in jail. The next day the leaders sent for the apostles to take them to trial. But the jail was empty. With God's power, an angel had opened the jail door the night before and let them out. This was a miracle. The Christians knew that God had come to their rescue. They knew that what they were doing was right.

checkout

Acts 12:6,7

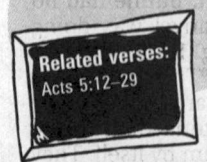

Related verses: Acts 5:12–29

They gained the support of Blastus and asked for peace. Blastus was a trusted personal servant of the king.

²¹The appointed day came. Herod was seated on his throne. He was wearing his royal robes. He made a speech to the people. ²²Then they shouted, "This is the voice of a god. It's not the voice of a man." ²³Right away an angel of the Lord struck Herod down. Herod had not given praise to God. So he was eaten by worms and died.

²⁴But God's word continued to increase and spread.

²⁵Barnabas and Saul finished their task. Then they returned from Jerusalem. They took John Mark with them.

BARNABAS AND SAUL ARE SENT OFF

13 In the church at Antioch there were prophets and teachers. Among them were Barnabas, Simeon, and Lucius from Cyrene. Simeon was also called Niger. Another was Manaen. He had been brought up with Herod, the ruler of Galilee. Saul was among them too. ²While they were worshiping the Lord and fasting, the Holy Spirit spoke. "Set apart Barnabas and Saul for me," he said. "I have appointed them to do special work." ³The prophets and teachers fasted and prayed. They placed their hands on Barnabas and Saul. Then they sent them off.

EVENTS ON CYPRUS

⁴Barnabas and Saul were sent on their way by the Holy Spirit. They went down to Seleucia. From there they sailed to Cyprus. ⁵They arrived at Salamis. There they preached God's word in the Jewish synagogues. John was with them as their helper.

⁶They traveled all across the island until they came to Paphos. There they met a Jew named Bar-Jesus. He was an evil magician and a false prophet. ⁷He was an attendant of Sergius Paulus, the governor. Paulus was a man of understanding. He sent for Barnabas and Saul. He wanted to hear God's word.

How big were the worms that ate King Herod?

Many people still believed that Jesus was a fake and a liar. They were waiting for a king, but they were expecting a very different kind of king! King Herod had become very popular with many of the people because he had been hurting the Christians. Some people even told him that he looked and sounded like a god. Herod liked that. He let them treat him as though he really was a god. Because Herod did this, God caused him to be filled with tiny worms that ate him from the inside out.

JASON'S IMAGINATION

checkout Acts 12:23

Related verse: James 4:6

[8]But Elymas, the evil magician, opposed them. The name Elymas means "magician." He tried to keep the governor from becoming a believer. [9]Saul was also known as Paul. He was filled with the Holy Spirit. He looked straight at Elymas. He said to him, [10]"You are a child of the devil! You are an enemy of everything that is right! You cheat people. You use all kinds of tricks. Won't you ever stop twisting the right ways of the Lord? [11]Now the Lord's hand is against you. You are going to go blind. You won't be able to see the light of the sun for a while."

Right away mist and darkness came over him. He tried to feel his way around. He wanted to find someone to lead him by the hand. [12]When the governor saw what had happened, he believed. He was amazed at what Paul was teaching about the Lord.

PAUL PREACHES IN PISIDIAN ANTIOCH

[13]From Paphos, Paul and his companions sailed to Perga in Pamphylia. There John left them and returned to Jerusalem. [14]From Perga they went on to Pisidian Antioch. On the Sabbath day they entered the synagogue and sat down. [15]The Law and the Prophets were read aloud. Then the synagogue rulers sent word to Paul and his companions. They said, "Brothers, do you have a message of hope for the people? If you do, please speak."

[16]Paul stood up and motioned with his hand. Then he said, "Men of Israel, and you non-Jews who worship God, listen to me! [17]The God of Israel chose our people who lived long ago. He blessed them greatly while they were in Egypt. With his mighty power he led them out of that country. [18]He put up with them for about 40 years in the desert. [19]He destroyed seven nations in Canaan. Then he gave the land to his people as their rightful share. [20]All of this took about 450 years.

"After this, God gave them judges until the time of Samuel the prophet. [21]Then the people asked for a king. He gave them Saul, son of Kish. Saul was from the tribe of Benjamin. He ruled for 40 years. [22]God removed him and made David their king. Here is God's witness about him. 'David, son of Jesse, is a man dear to my heart,' he said. 'He will do everything I want him to do.'

[23]"From this man's family line God has brought to Israel the Savior Jesus. This is what he had promised. [24]Before Jesus came, John preached that we should turn away from our sins and be baptized. He preached this to all Israel. [25]John was coming to the end of his work. 'Who do you think I am?' he said. 'I am not the one you are looking for. No, he is coming after me. I am not good enough to untie his sandals.'

[26]"Listen, brothers, you children of Abraham! Listen, you non-Jews who worship God! This message of salvation has been sent to us. [27]The people of Jerusalem and their rulers did not recognize Jesus. By finding him guilty, they made the prophets' words come true. These are read every Sabbath day. [28]The people and their rulers had no reason at all for sentencing Jesus to death. But they asked Pilate to have him killed. [29]They did everything that had been written about Jesus. Then they took him down from the cross. They laid him in a tomb. [30]But God raised him from the dead. [31]For many days he was seen by those who had traveled with him from Galilee to Jerusalem. Now they are his witnesses to our people.

[32]"We are telling you the good news. What God promised our people long ago [33]he has done for us, their children. He has raised up Jesus. This is what is written in the second Psalm. It says,

> " 'You are my Son.
> Today I have become your
> Father.'　　　*(Psalm 2:7)*

[34]God raised Jesus from the dead. He will never rot in the grave. This is what is written in Scripture. It says,

> " 'Holy and sure blessings were
> promised to David.
> I will give them to you.'
> 　　　*(Isaiah 55:3)*

[35]In another place it says,

> " 'You will not let your Holy One
> rot away.'　　*(Psalm 16:10)*

[36]"David carried out God's purpose while he lived. Then he died. He was buried with his people. His body rotted away. [37]But the One whom God raised from the dead did not rot away.

[38]"My brothers, here is what I want you to know. I announce to you that your sins can be forgiven because of what Jesus has done. [39]Through him everyone who believes is made right with God. Moses' law could not make you right in God's eyes. [40]Be careful! Don't let what the prophets spoke about happen to you. They said,

[41] " 'Look, you who make fun of the
          truth!
     Wonder and die!
     I am going to do something in
          your days
     that you would never believe.
     You wouldn't believe it even if
          someone told you.' "

(Habakkuk 1:5)

[42]Paul and Barnabas started to leave the synagogue. The people invited them to say more about these things on the next Sabbath day. [43]The people were told they could leave the service. Many Jews followed Paul and Barnabas. Many non-Jews who faithfully worshiped the God of the Jews did the same. Paul and Barnabas talked with them. They tried to get them to keep living in God's grace.

[44]On the next Sabbath day, almost the whole city gathered to hear the word of the Lord. [45]When the Jews saw the crowds, they became very jealous. They said evil things against what Paul was saying.

[46]Then Paul and Barnabas answered them boldly. "We had to speak God's word to you first," they said. "But you don't accept it. You don't think you are good enough for eternal life. So now we are turning to those who aren't Jews. [47]This is what the Lord has commanded us to do. He said,

     " 'I have made you a light for those
          who aren't Jews.
     You will bring salvation to the
          whole earth.' "   (Isaiah 49:6)

[48]When the non-Jews heard this, they were glad. They honored the word of the Lord. All who were appointed for eternal life believed.

[49]The word of the Lord spread through the whole area. [50]But the Jews stirred up the important women who worshiped God. They also stirred up the men who were leaders in the city. They tried to get them to attack Paul and Barnabas. They threw them out of that area. [51]Paul and Barnabas didn't like this. So they shook the dust from their feet. They went on to Iconium. [52]The believers were filled with joy and with the Holy Spirit.

PAUL AND BARNABAS PREACH IN ICONIUM

14 At Iconium, Paul and Barnabas went into the Jewish synagogue as usual. They spoke there with great power. Large numbers of Jews and non-Jews became believers. [2]But the Jews who refused to believe stirred up those who weren't Jews. They poisoned their minds against the two men and the new believers. [3]So Paul and Barnabas spent a lot of time there. They spoke boldly for the Lord. He gave them the ability to do miraculous signs and wonders. In this way the Lord showed that they were telling the truth about his grace.

[4]The people of the city did not agree with each other. Some were on the side of the Jews. Others were on the side of the apostles. [5]Jews and non-Jews alike planned to treat Paul and Barnabas badly. Their leaders agreed. They planned to kill them by throwing stones at them. [6]But Paul and Barnabas found out about the plan. They escaped to the Lycaonian cities of Lystra and Derbe and to the surrounding area. [7]There they continued to preach the good news.

PAUL PREACHES IN LYSTRA

[8]In Lystra there sat a man who couldn't walk. He hadn't been able to use his feet since the day he was born. [9]He listened as Paul spoke. Paul looked right at him. He saw that the man had faith to be healed. [10]So he called out, "Stand up on your feet!" Then the man jumped up and began to walk.

[11]The crowd saw what Paul had done. They shouted in the Lycaonian language. "The gods have come down to us in human form!" they exclaimed. [12]They called Barnabas Zeus. Paul was the main speaker. So they called him Hermes. [13]Just outside the city was the temple of the god Zeus. The priest of Zeus brought bulls and wreaths to the city gates. He and the crowd wanted to offer sacrifices to Paul and Barnabas.

[14]But the apostles Barnabas and Paul heard about this. So they tore their clothes. They rushed out into the crowd. They shouted, [15]"Why are you men doing this? We are only human, just like you. We are bringing you good news. Turn away from these worthless things. Turn to the living God. He is the one who made the heavens and the earth and the sea. He made everything in them. [16]In the past, he let all nations go their own way. [17]But he has given proof of what he is like. He has shown kindness by giving you rain from heaven. He gives you crops in their seasons. He provides you with plenty of food. He fills your hearts with joy." [18]Paul and Barnabas told them all these things. But they had trouble keeping the crowd from offering sacrifices to them.

[19]Then some Jews came from Antioch and Iconium. They won the crowd over to their side. They threw stones at Paul. They thought he was dead, so they dragged him out of the city. [20]The believers gathered around Paul. Then he got up and went back into the city. The next day he and Barnabas left for Derbe.

PAUL AND BARNABAS RETURN TO ANTIOCH

[21]Paul and Barnabas preached the good news in the city of Derbe. They won large numbers of followers. Then they returned to Lystra, Iconium and Antioch. [22]There they helped the believers gain strength. They told them to remain true to what they had been taught. "We must go through many hard times to enter God's kingdom," they said. [23]Paul and Barnabas appointed elders for them in each church. The elders had trusted in the Lord. Paul and Barnabas prayed and fasted. They placed the elders in the Lord's care.

[24]After going through Pisidia, Paul and Barnabas came into Pamphylia. [25]They preached the word in Perga. Then they went down to Attalia. [26]From Attalia they sailed back to Antioch. That was where they had been committed to God's grace. They had now completed the work God had given them to do. [27]When they arrived at Antioch, they gathered the church together. They reported all that God had done through them. They told how he had opened the way for non-Jews to believe. [28]And they stayed there a long time with the believers.

CHURCH LEADERS MEET IN JERUSALEM

15 Certain people came down from Judea to Antioch. Here is what they were teaching the believers. "Moses commanded you to be circumcised," they said. "If you aren't, you can't be saved." [2]But Paul and Barnabas didn't agree with this. They argued strongly with them. So Paul and Barnabas were appointed to go up to Jerusalem. Some other believers were chosen to go with them. They were supposed to see the apostles and elders about this question.

[3]The church sent them on their way. As they traveled through Phoenicia and Samaria, they told how those who weren't Jews had turned to God. This news made all the believers very glad. [4]When they arrived in Jerusalem, the church welcomed them. The apostles and elders welcomed them too. Then Paul and Barnabas reported everything God had done through them.

[5]Some of the believers were Pharisees. They stood up and said, "Those who aren't Jews must be circumcised. They must obey the law of Moses."

[6]The apostles and elders met to consider this question. [7]After they had talked it over, Peter got up and spoke to them.

"Brothers," he said, "you know that some time ago God chose me to take the good news to those who aren't Jews. He wanted them to hear the good news and believe. [8]God knows the human heart. By giving the Holy Spirit to non-Jews, he showed that he accepted them. He did the same for them as he had done for us. [9]He showed that there is no difference between us and them. He made their hearts pure because of their faith.

[10]"Now then, why are you trying to test God? You test him when you put a heavy load on the believers' shoulders. Our people of long ago couldn't carry that load. We can't either. [11]No! We believe we are saved through the grace of our Lord Jesus. Those who aren't Jews are saved in the same way."

[12]Everyone became quiet as they listened to Barnabas and Paul. They were telling about the miraculous signs and wonders God had done through them among non-Jews.

[13]When they finished, James spoke up. "Brothers," he said, "listen to me. [14]Simon Peter has explained to us how God first showed his concern for those who aren't Jews. He chose some of them to be his very own people. [15]The prophets' words agree with that. They say,

[16] " 'After this I will return
    and rebuild David's fallen tent.
I will rebuild what was destroyed.
    I will make it what it used to be.
[17]Then the rest of the people can
    look to the Lord.
This means all the non-Jews who
    belong to me.
The Lord says this. He is the one
    who does these things.'

(Amos 9:11,12)

[18]   The Lord does things that have
    been known for a long time.

[19]"Now here is my opinion. We should not make it hard for the non-Jews who are turning to God. [20]Here is what we should write to them. They must not eat food polluted by being offered to statues of gods. They must not commit sexual sins. They must not eat the meat of animals that have been choked to death. And they must not drink blood. [21]These laws of Moses have been preached in every city from the earliest times. They are read out loud in the synagogues every Sabbath day."

A LETTER IS WRITTEN TO NON-JEWISH BELIEVERS

[22]Then the apostles, the elders and the whole church decided what to do. They would choose some of their own men. They would send them to Antioch with Paul and Barnabas. So they chose two leaders among the believers. Their names were Judas Barsabbas and Silas. [23]Here is the letter they sent with them.

The apostles and elders, your brothers, are writing this letter.

We are sending it to the non-Jewish believers in Antioch, Syria and Cilicia.

Greetings.

[24]We have heard that some of our people came to you and caused trouble. You were upset by what they said. But we had given them no authority to go. [25]So we all agreed to send our dear friends Barnabas and Paul to you. We chose some others to go with them. [26]Barnabas and Paul have put their lives in danger for the name of our Lord Jesus Christ. [27]So we are sending Judas and Silas with them. What they say will agree with this letter.

[28]It seemed good to the Holy Spirit and to us not to give you a load that is too heavy. So here are a few basic rules. [29]Don't eat food that has been offered to statues of gods. Don't drink blood. Don't eat the meat of animals that have been choked to death. And don't commit sexual sins. You will do well to keep away from these things.

Farewell.

[30]The men were sent down to Antioch. There they gathered the church together. They gave the letter to them. [31]The people read it. They were glad for its message of hope. [32]Judas and Silas were prophets. They said many things to give strength and hope to the believers. [33/34]Judas and Silas stayed there for some time. Then the believers sent them away with the blessing

of peace. They sent them back to those who had sent them out.

[35]Paul and Barnabas remained in Antioch. There they and many others taught and preached the word of the Lord.

PAUL AND BARNABAS DO NOT AGREE

[36]Some time later Paul spoke to Barnabas. "Let's go back to all the towns where we preached the word of the Lord," he said. "Let's visit the believers and see how they are doing." [37]Barnabas wanted to take John Mark with them. [38]But Paul didn't think it was wise to take him. Mark had deserted them in Pamphylia. He hadn't continued with them in their work. [39]Barnabas and Paul strongly disagreed with each other. So they went their separate ways. Barnabas took Mark and sailed for Cyprus. [40]But Paul chose Silas. The believers asked the Lord to give his grace to Paul and Silas as they went. [41]Paul traveled through Syria and Cilicia. He gave strength to the churches there.

TIMOTHY JOINS PAUL AND SILAS

16 Paul came to Derbe. Then he went on to Lystra. A believer named Timothy lived there. His mother was Jewish and a believer. His father was a Greek. [2]The believers at Lystra and Iconium said good things about Timothy. [3]Paul wanted to take him along on the journey. So he circumcised Timothy because of the Jews who lived in that area. They all knew that Timothy's father was a Greek. [4]Paul and his companions traveled from town to town. They reported what the apostles and elders in Jerusalem had decided. The people were supposed to obey what was in the report. [5]So the churches were made strong in the faith. The number of believers grew every day.

PAUL'S VISION OF THE MAN FROM MACEDONIA

[6]Paul and his companions traveled all through the area of Phrygia and Galatia. The Holy Spirit had kept them from preaching the word in Asia Minor. [7]They came to the border of Mysia. From there they tried to enter Bithynia. But the Spirit of Jesus would not let them. [8]So they passed by Mysia. Then they went down to Troas.

[9]During the night Paul had a vision. He saw a man from Macedonia standing and begging him. "Come over to Macedonia!" the man said. "Help us!" [10]After Paul had seen the vision, we got ready at once to leave for Macedonia. We decided that God had called us to preach the good news there.

LYDIA BECOMES A BELIEVER

[11]At Troas we got into a boat. We sailed straight for Samothrace. The next day we went on to Neapolis. [12]From there we traveled to Philippi, a Roman colony. It is an important city in that part of Macedonia. We stayed there several days.

[13]On the Sabbath day we went outside the city gate. We walked down to the river. There we expected to find a place of prayer. We sat down and began to speak to the women who had gathered together. [14]One of those listening was a woman named Lydia. She was from the city of Thyatira. Her business was selling purple cloth. She was a worshiper of God. The Lord opened her heart to accept Paul's message. [15]She and her family were baptized. Then she invited us to her home. "Do you consider me a believer in the Lord?" she asked. "If you do, come and stay at my house." She succeeded in getting us to go home with her.

PAUL AND SILAS ARE THROWN INTO PRISON

[16]One day we were going to the place of prayer. On the way we were met by a female slave. She had a spirit that helped her to tell ahead of time what was going to happen. She earned a lot of money for her owners by telling fortunes. [17]The woman followed Paul and the rest of us around. She shouted, "These men serve the Most High God. They are telling you how to be saved." [18]She kept this up for many days. Finally Paul became upset. Turning around, he spoke to the spirit. "In the name of Jesus Christ," he said, "I com-

mand you to come out of her!" At that very moment the spirit left her.

¹⁹The female slave's owners realized that their hope of making money was gone. So they grabbed Paul and Silas. They dragged them into the market place to face the authorities. ²⁰They brought them to the judges. "These men are Jews," her owners said. "They are making trouble in our city. ²¹They are suggesting practices that are against Roman law. These are practices we can't accept or take part in."

²²The crowd joined the attack against Paul and Silas. The judges ordered that Paul and Silas be stripped and beaten. ²³They were whipped without mercy. Then they were thrown into prison. The jailer was commanded to guard them carefully. ²⁴When he received his orders, he put Paul and Silas deep inside the prison. He fastened their feet so they couldn't get away.

²⁵About midnight Paul and Silas were praying. They were also singing hymns to God. The other prisoners were listening to them. ²⁶Suddenly there was a powerful earthquake. It shook the prison from top to bottom. All at once the prison doors flew open. Everybody's chains came loose.

²⁷The jailer woke up. He saw that the prison doors were open. He pulled out his sword and was going to kill himself. He thought the prisoners had escaped. ²⁸"Don't harm yourself!" Paul shouted. "We are all here!"

²⁹The jailer called out for some lights. He rushed in, shaking with fear. He fell down in front of Paul and Silas. ³⁰Then he brought them out. He asked, "Sirs, what must I do to be saved?"

³¹They replied, "Believe in the Lord Jesus. Then you and your family will be saved." ³²They spoke the word of the Lord to him. They also spoke to all the others in his house.

³³At that hour of the night, the jailer took Paul and Silas and washed their wounds. Right away he and his whole family were baptized. ³⁴The jailer brought them into his house. He set a meal in front of them. He and his whole family were filled with joy. They had become believers in God.

³⁵Early in the morning the judges sent their officers to the jailer. They ordered him, "Let those men go." ³⁶The jailer told Paul, "The judges have ordered me to set you and Silas free. You can leave now. Go in peace."

³⁷But Paul replied to the officers. "They beat us in public," he said. "We weren't given a trial. And we are Roman citizens! They threw us into prison. And now do they want to get rid of us quietly? No! Let them come themselves and personally lead us out."

³⁸The officers reported this to the judges. When the judges heard that Paul and Silas were Roman citizens, they became afraid. ³⁹So they came and said they were sorry. They led them out of the prison. Then they asked them to leave the city. ⁴⁰After Paul and Silas came out of the prison, they went to Lydia's house. There they met with the believers. They told them to be brave. Then they left.

PAUL AND SILAS ARRIVE IN THESSALONICA

17 Paul and Silas passed through Amphipolis and Apollonia. They came to Thessalonica. A Jewish synagogue was there. ²Paul went into the synagogue as he usually did. For three Sabbath days in a row he talked about the Scriptures with the Jews. ³He explained and proved that the Christ had to suffer and rise from the dead. "This Jesus I am telling you about is the Christ!" he said. ⁴His words won some of the Jews over. They joined Paul and Silas. A large number of Greeks who worshiped God joined them too. So did quite a few important women.

⁵But the Jews were jealous. So they rounded up some evil fellows from the market place. Forming a crowd, they started all kinds of trouble in the city. The Jews rushed to Jason's house. They were looking for Paul and Silas. They wanted to bring them out to the crowd. ⁶But they couldn't find them. So they dragged Jason and some other believers to the city officials. "These men have caused trouble all over the world," they shouted. "Now they have come here. ⁷Jason has welcomed them into his house. They are all disobeying

Caesar's commands. They say there is another king. He is called Jesus."

⁸When the crowd and the city officials heard this, they became very upset. ⁹They made Jason and the others give them money. They wanted to make sure they would return to the court. Then they let them go.

PAUL AND SILAS ARE SENT TO BEREA

¹⁰As soon as it was night, the believers sent Paul and Silas away to Berea. When they arrived, they went to the Jewish synagogue.

¹¹The Bereans were very glad to receive Paul's message. They studied the Scriptures carefully every day. They wanted to see if what Paul said was true. So they were more noble than the Thessalonians. ¹²Many of the Jews believed. A number of important Greek women also became believers. And so did many Greek men.

¹³The Jews in Thessalonica found out that Paul was preaching God's word in Berea. So they went there too. They stirred up the crowds and got them all worked up.

¹⁴Right away the believers sent Paul to the coast. But Silas and Timothy stayed in Berea. ¹⁵The men who went with Paul took him to Athens. Then they returned with orders that Silas and Timothy were supposed to join him as soon as they could.

PAUL PREACHES IN ATHENS

¹⁶Paul was waiting for Silas and Timothy in Athens. He was very upset to see that the city was full of statues of gods. ¹⁷So he went to the synagogue. There he talked with Jews and with Greeks who worshiped God. Each day he spoke with anyone who happened to be in the market place.

¹⁸A group of Epicurean and Stoic thinkers began to argue with him. Some of them asked, "What is this fellow chattering about?" Others said, "He seems to be telling us about gods we've never heard of." They said this because Paul was preaching the good news about Jesus. He was telling them that Jesus had risen from the dead.

¹⁹They took him to a meeting of the Areopagus. There they said to him, "What is this new teaching you're giv-

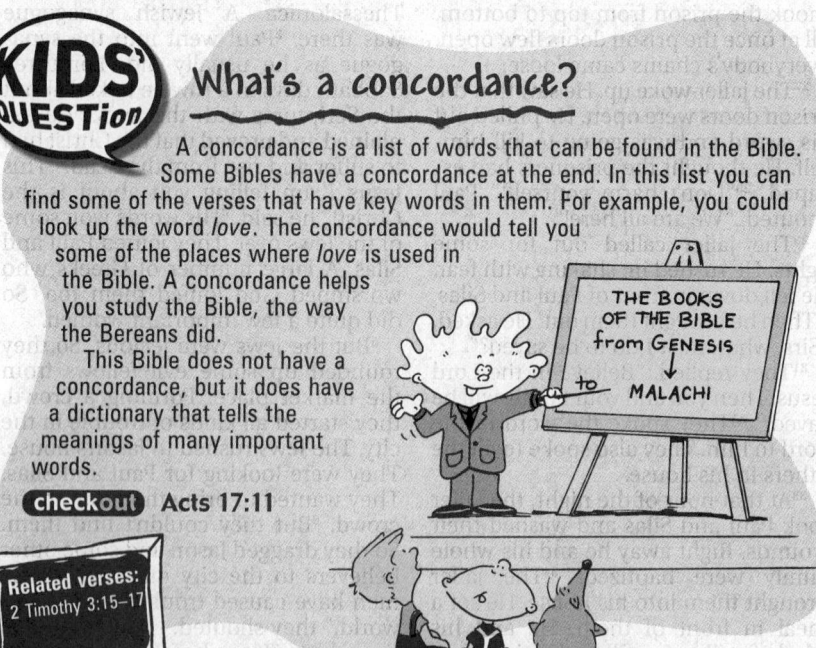

KIDS' QUESTION

What's a concordance?

A concordance is a list of words that can be found in the Bible. Some Bibles have a concordance at the end. In this list you can find some of the verses that have key words in them. For example, you could look up the word *love*. The concordance would tell you some of the places where *love* is used in the Bible. A concordance helps you study the Bible, the way the Bereans did.

This Bible does not have a concordance, but it does have a dictionary that tells the meanings of many important words.

checkout Acts 17:11

THE BOOKS OF THE BIBLE from GENESIS ↓ to MALACHI

Related verses: 2 Timothy 3:15–17

ing us? [20]You have some strange ideas. We've never heard them before. We want to know what they mean."

[21]All the people of Athens spent their time talking about and listening to the latest ideas. People from other lands who lived there did the same.

[22]Then Paul stood up in the meeting of the Areopagus. He said, "Men of Athens! I see that you are very religious in every way. [23]As I walked around, I looked carefully at the things you worship. I even found an altar with TO AN UNKNOWN GOD written on it. Now I am going to tell you about this 'unknown god' that you worship.

[24]"He is the God who made the world. He also made everything in it. He is the Lord of heaven and earth. He doesn't live in temples built by hands. [25]He is not served by human hands. He doesn't need anything. He himself gives life and breath to all people. He also gives them everything else they have. [26]From one man he made all the people of the world. Now they live all over the earth. He decided exactly when they should live. And he decided exactly where they should live. [27]God did this so that people would seek him. Then perhaps they would reach out for him and find him. They would find him even though he is not far from any of us. [28]'In him we live and move and exist.' As some of your own poets have also said, 'We are his children.'

[29]"Yes, we are God's children. So we shouldn't think that God is made out of gold or silver or stone. He isn't a statue planned and made by clever people. [30]In the past, God didn't judge people for what they didn't know. But now he commands all people everywhere to turn away from their sins. [31]He has set a day when he will judge the world fairly. He has appointed a man to be its judge. God has proved this to all people by raising that man from the dead."

[32]When they heard Paul talk about the dead rising, some of them made fun of it. But others said, "We want to hear you speak about this again." [33]So Paul left the meeting of the Areopagus. [34]A few men became followers of Paul and believed in Jesus. Dionysius was one of them. He was a member of the Areopagus. A woman named Damaris also became a believer. And so did some others.

PAUL GOES TO CORINTH

18 After this, Paul left Athens and went to Corinth. [2]There he met a Jew named Aquila, who was a native of Pontus. Aquila had recently come from Italy with his wife Priscilla. The emperor Claudius had ordered all the Jews to leave Rome. Paul went to see Aquila and Priscilla. [3]They were tentmakers, just as he was. So he stayed and worked with them. [4]Every Sabbath day he went to the synagogue. He was trying to get both Jews and Greeks to believe in the Lord.

[5]Silas and Timothy came from Macedonia. Then Paul spent all his time preaching. He gave witness to the Jews that Jesus was the Christ. [6]But the Jews opposed Paul. They treated him badly. He didn't like this. So he shook out his clothes. Then he said to them, "Anything that happens to you will be your own fault! Don't blame me for it! From now on I will go to people who are not Jews."

[7]Then Paul left the synagogue. He went next door to the house of Titius Justus, a man who worshiped God. [8]Crispus was the synagogue ruler. He and his whole family came to believe in the Lord. Many others who lived in Corinth heard Paul. They too believed and were baptized.

[9]One night the Lord spoke to Paul in a vision. "Don't be afraid," he said. "Keep on speaking. Don't be silent. [10]I am with you. No one will attack you and harm you. I have many people in this city." [11]So Paul stayed there for a year and a half. He taught them God's word.

[12]At that time Gallio was governor of Achaia. The Jews got together and attacked Paul. They brought him into court. [13]"This man," they charged, "is trying to talk people into worshiping God in ways that are against the law."

[14]Paul was about to speak up for himself. But just then Gallio spoke to the Jews. "You Jews are not claiming that Paul has committed a crime, whether large or small," he said. "If

you were, it would make sense for me to listen to you. [15]But this is about your own law. It is a question of words and names. Settle the matter yourselves. I will not be a judge of such things." [16]So he had them thrown out of the court. [17]Then all the Jews turned against Sosthenes. He was the synagogue ruler. They beat him up in front of the court. But Gallio didn't care at all.

PRISCILLA AND AQUILA TEACH APOLLOS

[18]Paul stayed in Corinth for some time. Then he left the believers and sailed for Syria. Priscilla and Aquila went with him. Before he sailed, he had his hair cut off at Cenchrea. He did this because he had made a promise to God. [19]They arrived at Ephesus. There Paul said good-by to Priscilla and Aquila. He himself went into the synagogue and talked with the Jews. [20]The Jews asked him to spend more time with them. But he said no. [21]As he left, he made them a promise. "If God wants me to," he said, "I will come back." Then he sailed from Ephesus. [22]When he landed at Caesarea, he went up to Jerusalem. There he greeted the church. He then went down to Antioch.

[23]Paul spent some time in Antioch. Then he left and traveled all over Galatia and Phrygia. He gave strength to all the believers there.

[24]At that time a Jew named Apollos came to Ephesus. He was an educated man from Alexandria. He knew the Scriptures very well. [25]Apollos had been taught the way of the Lord. He spoke with great power. He taught the truth about Jesus. But he only knew about John's baptism. [26]He began to speak boldly in the synagogue. Priscilla and Aquila heard him. So they invited him to their home. There they gave him a better understanding of the way of God.

[27]Apollos wanted to go to Achaia. The brothers agreed with him. They wrote to the believers there. They asked them to welcome him. When he arrived, he was a great help to those who had become believers by God's grace. [28]He argued strongly against the Jews in public meetings. He proved from the Scriptures that Jesus was the Christ.

PAUL GOES TO EPHESUS

19 While Apollos was at Corinth, Paul took the road to Ephesus. When he arrived, he found some believers there. [2]He asked them, "Did you receive the Holy Spirit when you became believers?"

"No," they answered. "We haven't even heard that there is a Holy Spirit."

[3]So Paul asked, "Then what baptism did you receive?"

"John's baptism," they replied.

[4]Paul said, "John baptized people, calling them to turn away from their sins. He told them to believe in the one who was coming after him. Jesus is that one." [5]After hearing this, they were baptized in the name of the Lord Jesus. [6]Paul placed his hands on them. Then the Holy Spirit came on them. They spoke in languages they had not known before. They also prophesied. [7]There were about 12 of them in all.

[8]Paul entered the synagogue. There he spoke boldly for three months. He tried to talk the people into accepting his teaching about God's kingdom. [9]But some of them wouldn't listen. They refused to believe. In public they said evil things about the Way of Jesus. So Paul left them. He took the believers with him. Each day he talked with people in the lecture hall of Tyrannus. [10]This went on for two years. So all the Jews and Greeks who lived in Asia Minor heard the word of the Lord.

[11]God did amazing miracles through Paul. [12]Even handkerchiefs and aprons that had touched him were taken to those who were sick. When this happened, their sicknesses were healed and evil spirits left them.

[13]Some Jews went around driving out evil spirits. They tried to use the name of the Lord Jesus to set free those who were controlled by demons. They said, "In Jesus' name I command you to come out. He is the Jesus that Paul is preaching about." [14]Seven sons of Sceva were doing this. Sceva was a Jewish chief priest. [15]One day the evil spirit answered them, "I know Jesus. And I know about Paul. But who are you?" [16]Then the man who had the evil

spirit jumped on Sceva's sons. He overpowered them all. He gave them a terrible beating. They ran out of the house naked and bleeding.

[17]The Jews and Greeks living in Ephesus heard about this. They were all overcome with fear. They held the name of the Lord Jesus in high honor. [18]Many who believed now came and openly admitted the evil they had done. [19]A number of those who had practiced evil magic brought their scrolls together. They set them on fire out in the open. They added up the value of the scrolls. They found that it would take more than two lifetimes to earn what the scrolls were worth.

[20]The word of the Lord spread everywhere. It became more and more powerful.

[21]After all this had happened, Paul decided to go to Jerusalem. He went through Macedonia and Achaia. "After I have been to Jerusalem," he said, "I must visit Rome also." [22]He sent Timothy and Erastus, two of his helpers, to Macedonia. But he stayed a little longer in Asia Minor.

TROUBLE IN EPHESUS

[23]At that time many people became very upset about the Way of Jesus. [24]There was a man named Demetrius who made things out of silver. He made silver models of the temple of the goddess Artemis. He brought in a lot of business for the other skilled workers. [25]One day he called them together. He also called others who were in the same kind of business. "Men," he said, "you know that we make good money from our work. [26]You have seen and heard what this fellow Paul is doing. He has talked to large numbers of people here in Ephesus. Almost everywhere in Asia Minor he has led people away from our gods. He says that the gods we make are not gods at all. [27]Our work is in danger of losing its good name. People's faith in the temple of the great goddess Artemis will be weakened. Now she is worshiped through all of Asia Minor and the whole world. But soon she will be robbed of her greatness."

[28]When they heard this, they became very angry. They began shout-ing, "Great is Artemis of the Ephesians!" [29]Soon people were making trouble in the whole city. They all rushed into the theater. They dragged Gaius and Aristarchus along with them. These two men had come with Paul from Macedonia. [30]Paul wanted to appear in front of the crowd. But the believers wouldn't let him. [31]Some of the officials in Asia Minor were friends of Paul. They sent him a message, begging him not to go into the theater.

[32]The crowd didn't know what was going on. Some were shouting one thing and some another. Most of the people didn't even know why they were there. [33]The Jews pushed Alexander to the front. Some of the crowd tried to tell him what to say. But he motioned for them to be quiet. He wanted to speak up for himself in front of the people. [34]But then they realized that he was a Jew. So they all shouted the same thing for about two hours. "Great is Artemis of the Ephesians!" they yelled.

[35]The city clerk quieted the crowd down. "Men of Ephesus!" he said. "The whole world knows that the city of Ephesus guards the temple of the great Artemis. They know that Ephesus guards her statue, which fell from heaven. [36]These facts can't be questioned. So calm down. Don't do anything foolish.

[37]"These men haven't robbed any temples. They haven't said evil things against our goddess. But you have brought them here anyhow. [38]Demetrius and the other skilled workers may feel they have been wronged by someone. Let them bring charges. The courts are open. We have our governors. [39]Is there anything else you want to bring up? Settle it in a court of law. [40]As it is, today we are in danger of being charged with causing all this trouble. But there is no reason for it. We wouldn't be able to explain what has happened." [41]After he said this, he sent the people away.

PAUL TRAVELS THROUGH MACEDONIA AND GREECE

20 All the trouble came to an end. Then Paul sent for the believers. After cheering them up, he said good-by. He then left for Macedonia. ²He traveled through that area, speaking many words of hope to the people. Finally he arrived in Greece. ³There he stayed for three months. He was just about to sail for Syria. But the Jews were making plans against him. So he decided to go back through Macedonia. ⁴Sopater, son of Pyrrhus, from Berea went with him. Aristarchus and Secundus from Thessalonica, Gaius from Derbe, and Timothy went too. Tychicus and Trophimus from Asia Minor also went with him. ⁵These men went on ahead. They waited for us at Troas. ⁶But we sailed from Philippi after the Feast of Unleavened Bread. Five days later we joined the others at Troas. We stayed there for seven days.

EUTYCHUS IS RAISED FROM THE DEAD

⁷On the first day of the week we met to break bread and eat together. Paul spoke to the people. He kept on talking until midnight because he planned to leave the next day. ⁸There were many lamps in the room upstairs where we were meeting. ⁹A young man named Eutychus was sitting in a window. He sank into a deep sleep as Paul talked on and on. Sound asleep, Eutychus fell from the third floor. When they picked him up from the ground, he was dead. ¹⁰Paul went down and threw himself on the young man. He put his arms around him. "Don't be alarmed," he told them. "He's alive!" ¹¹Then Paul went upstairs again. He broke bread and ate with them. He kept on talking until daylight. Then he left. ¹²The people took the young man home. They were greatly comforted because he was alive.

PAUL SAYS GOOD-BY TO THE EPHESIAN ELDERS

¹³We went on ahead to the ship. We sailed for Assos. There we were going to take Paul on board. He had planned it this way because he wanted to go there by land. ¹⁴So he met us at Assos. We took him on board and went on to Mitylene. ¹⁵The next day we sailed from there.

We arrived near Kios. The day after that we crossed over to Samos. We arrived at Miletus the next day. ¹⁶Paul had decided to sail past Ephesus. He didn't want to spend time in Asia Minor. He was in a hurry to get to Jerusalem. If he could, he wanted to be there by the day of Pentecost.

¹⁷From Miletus, Paul sent for the elders of the church at Ephesus. ¹⁸When they arrived, he spoke to them. "You know how I lived the whole time I was with you," he said. "From the first day I came into Asia Minor, ¹⁹I was free of pride. I served the Lord with tears. I served him even though I was greatly tested by the evil plans of the Jews. ²⁰You know I haven't let anyone keep me from preaching anything that would be helpful to you. I have taught you in public and from house to house. ²¹I have told both Jews and Greeks that they must turn away from their sins to God. They must have faith in our Lord Jesus.

²²"Now I am going to Jerusalem. The Holy Spirit compels me. I don't know what will happen to me there. ²³I only know that in every city the Spirit warns me. He tells me that I will face prison and suffering. ²⁴But my life means nothing to me. I only want to finish the race. I want to complete the work the Lord Jesus has given me. He wants me to give witness to others about the good news of God's grace.

²⁵"I have spent time with you preaching about the kingdom. I know that none of you will ever see me again. ²⁶So I tell you today that I am not guilty if anyone has not believed. ²⁷I haven't let anyone keep me from telling you everything God wants you to do.

²⁸"Keep watch over yourselves. Keep watch over all the believers. The Holy Spirit has made you leaders over them. Be shepherds of God's church. He bought it with his own blood. ²⁹I know that after I leave, wild wolves will come in among you. They won't spare any of the sheep. ³⁰Even men from your own people will rise up and twist the truth. They want to get the believers to follow them. ³¹So be on your guard! Remember that for three years I never stopped warning you.

Night and day I warned each of you with tears. ³²"Now I commit you to God's care. I commit you to the word of his grace. It can build you up. Then you will share in what God plans to give all his people. ³³I haven't longed for anyone's silver or gold or clothing. ³⁴You yourselves know that I have used my own hands to meet my needs. I have also met the needs of my companions. ³⁵In everything I did, I showed you that we must work hard and help the weak. We must remember the words of the Lord Jesus. He said, 'It is more blessed to give than to receive.' "

³⁶When Paul had said this, he got down on his knees with all of them and prayed. ³⁷They all cried as they hugged and kissed him. ³⁸What hurt them the most was that he had said they would never see his face again. Then they went with him to the ship.

PAUL CONTINUES HIS JOURNEY

21 After we had torn ourselves away from the Ephesian elders, we headed out to sea. We sailed straight to Cos. The next day we went to Rhodes. From there we continued on to Patara. ²We found a ship crossing over to Phoenicia. So we went on board and headed out to sea. ³We came near Cyprus and passed to the south of it. Then we sailed on to Syria. We landed at Tyre. There our ship was supposed to unload. ⁴We found the believers there and stayed with them for seven days. Led by the Holy Spirit, they tried to get Paul not to go on to Jerusalem. ⁵But when it was time to leave, we continued on our way. All the believers and their families went with us out of the city. There on the beach we got down on our knees to pray. ⁶We said good-by to each other. Then we went on board the ship. And they returned home.

⁷Continuing on from Tyre, we landed at Ptolemais. There we greeted the brothers and sisters. We stayed with them for a day. ⁸The next day we left and arrived at Caesarea. We stayed at the house of Philip the evangelist. He was one of the seven deacons. ⁹He had four unmarried daughters who prophesied.

¹⁰We stayed there several days. Then a prophet named Agabus came down from Judea. ¹¹He came over to us. Then he took Paul's belt and tied his own hands and feet with it. He said, "The Holy Spirit says, 'This is how the Jews of Jerusalem will tie up the owner of this belt. They will hand him over to people who are not Jews.' "

¹²When we heard this, we all begged Paul not to go up to Jerusalem. ¹³He asked, "Why are you crying? Why are you breaking my heart? I'm ready to be put in prison. In fact, I'm ready to die in Jerusalem for the Lord Jesus." ¹⁴We couldn't change his mind. So we gave up. We said, "May what the Lord wants to happen be done."

¹⁵After this, we got ready and went up to Jerusalem. ¹⁶Some of the believers from Caesarea went with us. They brought us to Mnason's home. We were supposed to stay there. Mnason was from Cyprus. He was one of the first believers.

PAUL ARRIVES IN JERUSALEM

¹⁷When we arrived in Jerusalem, the brothers and sisters gave us a warm welcome. ¹⁸The next day Paul and the rest of us went to see James. All the elders were there. ¹⁹Paul greeted them. Then he reported everything God had done among the non-Jews through his work.

²⁰When they heard this, they praised God. Then they spoke to Paul. "Brother," they said, "you see that thousands of Jews have become believers. All of them try very hard to obey the law. ²¹They have been told that you teach all the Jews who live among the non-Jews to turn away from Moses. They think that you teach them not to circumcise their children. They think that you teach them to give up our Jewish ways.

²²"What should we do? They will certainly hear that you have come. ²³So do what we tell you. There are four men with us who have made a promise to God. ²⁴Take them with you. Join them in the Jewish practice that makes people pure and clean. Pay their expenses so they can have their heads shaved. Then everybody will know that these reports about you are not true in any

way. They will know that you yourself obey the law.

²⁵"We have already given written directions to the believers who are not Jews. They must not eat food that has been offered to statues of gods. They must not drink blood. They must not eat the meat of animals that have been choked to death. And they must not commit sexual sins."

²⁶The next day Paul took the men with him. They all made themselves pure and clean in the usual way. Then Paul went to the temple. There he reported the date when the days of cleansing would end. At that time the proper offering would be made for each of them.

PAUL IS ARRESTED

²⁷The seven days of cleansing were almost over. Some Jews from Asia Minor saw Paul at the temple. They stirred up the whole crowd. They arrested Paul. ²⁸"Men of Israel, help us!" they shouted. "This is the man who teaches everyone in all places against our people. He speaks against our law and against this holy place. Besides, he has brought Greeks into the temple area. He has made this holy place unclean." ²⁹They said this because they had seen Trophimus the Ephesian in the city with Paul. They thought Paul had brought him into the temple area.

³⁰The whole city was stirred up. People came running from all directions. They grabbed Paul and dragged him out of the temple. Right away the temple gates were shut. ³¹The people were trying to kill Paul. But news reached the commander of the Roman troops. He heard that people were making trouble in the whole city of Jerusalem. ³²At once he took some officers and soldiers with him. They ran down to the crowd. The people causing the trouble saw the commander and his soldiers. So they stopped beating Paul.

³³The commander came up and arrested Paul. He ordered him to be held with two chains. Then he asked who Paul was and what he had done. ³⁴Some in the crowd shouted one thing, some another. But the commander couldn't get the facts because

of all the noise. So he ordered that Paul be taken into the fort. ³⁵Paul reached the steps. But then the mob became so wild that he had to be carried by the soldiers. ³⁶The crowd that followed kept shouting, "Kill him!"

PAUL SPEAKS TO THE CROWD

³⁷The soldiers were about to take Paul into the fort. Then he asked the commander, "May I say something to you?"

"Do you speak Greek?" he replied. ³⁸"Aren't you the Egyptian who turned some of our people against their leaders? Didn't you lead 4,000 terrorists out into the desert some time ago?"

³⁹Paul answered, "I am a Jew from Tarsus in Cilicia. I am a citizen of an important city. Please let me speak to the people."

⁴⁰The commander told him he could. So Paul stood on the steps and motioned to the crowd. When all of them were quiet, he spoke to them in the Aramaic language. **22** ¹"Brothers and fathers," Paul began, "listen to me now. I want to speak up for myself."

²When they heard that he was speaking to them in Aramaic, they became very quiet.

Then Paul said, ³"I am a Jew. I was born in Tarsus in Cilicia. But I grew up here in Jerusalem. I was well trained by Gamaliel in the law of our people. I wanted to serve God as much as any of you do today. ⁴I hurt the followers of the Way of Jesus. I sent many of them to their death. I arrested men and women. I threw them into prison. ⁵The high priest and the whole Council can give witness to this. I even had some official letters they had written to their friends in Damascus. So I went there to bring these people as prisoners to Jerusalem to be punished.

⁶"I had almost reached Damascus. About noon a bright light from heaven suddenly flashed around me. ⁷I fell to the ground and heard a voice speak to me. 'Saul! Saul!' it said. 'Why are you opposing me?'

⁸" 'Who are you, Lord?' I asked.

" 'I am Jesus of Nazareth,' he replied. 'I am the one you are opposing.'

⁹"The light was seen by my compan-

ions. But they didn't understand the voice of the one speaking to me.

[10] " 'What should I do, Lord?' I asked.

" 'Get up,' the Lord said. 'Go into Damascus. There you will be told everything you have been given to do.' [11]The brightness of the light had blinded me. So my companions led me by the hand into Damascus.

[12]"A man named Ananias came to see me. He was a godly Jew who obeyed the law. All the Jews living there respected him very much. [13]He stood beside me and said, 'Brother Saul, receive your sight!' At that very moment I was able to see him.

[14]"Then he said, 'The God of our people has chosen you. He wanted to tell you his plans for you. You have seen the Blameless One. You have heard words from his mouth. [15]Now you will give witness to all people about what you have seen and heard. [16]So what are you waiting for? Get up and call on his name. Be baptized. Have your sins washed away.'

[17]"I returned to Jerusalem and was praying at the temple. Then it seemed to me that I was dreaming. [18]I saw the Lord speaking to me. 'Quick!' he said. 'Leave Jerusalem at once. These people will not accept your witness about me.'

[19]" 'Lord,' I replied, 'these people know what I used to do. I went from one synagogue to another and put believers in prison. I also beat them. [20]Stephen was a man who gave witness to others about you. I stood there when he was killed. I had agreed that he should die. I even guarded the coats of those who were killing him.'

[21]"Then the Lord said to me, 'Go. I will send you far away to people who are not Jews.' "

PAUL THE ROMAN CITIZEN

[22]The crowd listened to Paul until he said this. Then they shouted, "Kill him! He isn't fit to live!"

[23]They shouted and threw off their coats. They threw dust into the air. [24]So the commanding officer ordered Paul to be taken into the fort. He gave orders for Paul to be whipped and questioned. He wanted to find out why the people were shouting at him like this.

[25]A commander was standing there as they stretched Paul out to be whipped. Paul said to him, "Does the law allow you to whip a Roman citizen who hasn't even been found guilty?"

[26]When the commander heard this, he went to the commanding officer and reported it. "What are you going to do?" the commander asked. "This man is a Roman citizen."

[27]So the commanding officer went to Paul. "Tell me," he asked. "Are you a Roman citizen?"

"Yes, I am," Paul answered.

[28]Then the officer said, "I had to pay a lot of money to become a citizen."

"But I was born a citizen," Paul replied.

[29]Right away those who were about to question him left. Even the officer was alarmed. He realized that he had put Paul, a Roman citizen, in chains.

PAUL IS TAKEN TO THE SANHEDRIN

[30]The commanding officer wanted to find out exactly what the Jews had against Paul. So the next day he let Paul out of prison. He ordered a meeting of the chief priests and all the Sanhedrin. Then he brought Paul and had him stand in front of them.

23 Paul looked straight at the Sanhedrin. "My brothers," he said, "I have always done my duty to God. To this very day I feel that I have done nothing wrong."

[2]Ananias the high priest heard this. So he ordered the men standing near Paul to hit him on the mouth.

[3]Then Paul said to him, "You pretender! God will hit you! You sit there and judge me by the law. But you yourself broke the law when you commanded them to hit me!"

[4]Those who were standing near Paul said, "How dare you talk like that to God's high priest!"

[5]Paul replied, "Brothers, I didn't realize he was the high priest. It is written, 'Do not speak evil about the ruler of your people.' " *(Exodus 22:28)*

[6]Paul knew that some of them were Sadducees and the others Pharisees. So he called out in the Sanhedrin. "My brothers," he said, "I am a Pharisee. I am the son of a Pharisee. I believe

that people will rise from the dead. That's why I am on trial."

⁷When he said this, the Pharisees and the Sadducees started to argue. They began to take sides. ⁸The Sadducees say that people will not rise from the dead. They don't believe there are angels or spirits either. But the Pharisees believe all these things.

⁹People were causing trouble and making a lot of noise. Some of the teachers of the law who were Pharisees stood up. They argued strongly. "We find nothing wrong with this man," they said. "What if a spirit or an angel has spoken to him?" ¹⁰The arguing got out of hand. The commanding officer was afraid that Paul would be torn to pieces by those who were arguing. So he ordered the soldiers to go down and take him away from them by force. They were supposed to bring him into the fort.

¹¹The next night the Lord stood near Paul. He said, "Be brave! You have given witness about me in Jerusalem. You must do the same in Rome."

THE PLAN TO KILL PAUL

¹²The next morning the Jews gathered secretly to make plans against Paul. They took an oath that they would not eat or drink anything until they had killed him. ¹³More than 40 men took part in this plan. ¹⁴They went to the chief priests and the elders. They said, "We have taken a strong oath. We have made a special promise to God. We will not eat anything until we have killed Paul. ¹⁵Now then, you and the Sanhedrin must make an appeal to the commanding officer. Ask him to bring Paul to you. Pretend you want more facts about his case. We are ready to kill him before he gets here."

¹⁶But Paul's nephew heard about this plan. So he went into the fort and told Paul.

¹⁷Then Paul called one of the commanders. He said to him, "Take this young man to the commanding officer. He has something to tell him." ¹⁸So the commander took Paul's nephew to the officer.

KIDS' QUESTION

Why did Paul want to tell the Romans about Jesus?

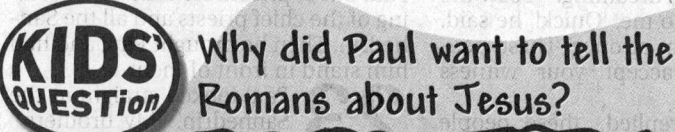

Many people in Rome had become followers of Jesus after hearing the disciples' message in Jerusalem. Some had become Christians in other cities and had then moved to Rome. Paul wanted to meet these believers and to cheer them on in their faith. Rome was the most important city in the world at that time. Paul knew that Jesus wanted him to preach the message all over the world, including Rome. He knew that a city like Rome could help spread the message of Jesus. Paul was also a Roman citizen. He knew people would listen to him there.

checkout
Acts 23:11

Related verse:
Acts 19:21

JASON'S IMAGINATION

Paul's Stuff

ROME ROME ROME ROME ROME

The commander said, "Paul, the prisoner, sent for me. He asked me to bring this young man to you. The young man has something to tell you." [19]The commanding officer took the young man by the hand. He spoke to him in private. "What do you want to tell me?" the officer asked.

[20]He said, "The Jews have agreed to ask you to bring Paul to the Sanhedrin tomorrow. They will pretend they want more facts about him. [21]Don't give in to them. More than 40 of them are waiting in hiding to attack him. They have taken an oath that they will not eat or drink anything until they have killed him. They are ready now. All they need is for you to bring Paul to the Sanhedrin."

[22]The commanding officer let the young man go. But he gave him a warning. "Don't tell anyone you have reported this to me," he said.

PAUL IS TAKEN TO CAESAREA

[23]Then the commanding officer called for two of his commanders. He ordered them, "Gather a company of 200 soldiers, 70 horsemen and 200 men armed with spears. Get them ready to go to Caesarea at nine o'clock tonight. [24]Provide horses for Paul so that he may be taken safely to Governor Felix."

[25]Here is the letter the officer wrote.

[26]I, Claudius Lysias, am writing this letter.

I am sending it to His Excellency, Governor Felix.

Greetings.

[27]The Jews grabbed Paul. They were about to kill him. But I came with my soldiers and saved him. I had learned that he is a Roman citizen. [28]I wanted to know why they were bringing charges against him. So I brought him to their Sanhedrin. [29]I found out that the charge against him was based on questions about their law. But there was no charge against him worthy of death or prison. [30]Then I was told about a plan against the man. So I sent him to you at once.

I also ordered those bringing charges against him to tell you their case.

[31]The soldiers followed their orders. During the night they took Paul with them. They brought him as far as Antipatris. [32]The next day they let the horsemen go on with him. The soldiers returned to the fort. [33]The horsemen arrived in Caesarea. They gave the letter to the governor. Then they handed Paul over to him. [34]The governor read the letter. He asked Paul where he was from. He learned that Paul was from Cilicia. [35]So he said, "I will hear your case when those bringing charges against you get here." Then he ordered that Paul be kept under guard in Herod's palace.

PAUL'S TRIAL IN FRONT OF FELIX

24 Five days later Ananias the high priest went down to Caesarea. Some elders and a lawyer named Tertullus went with him. They brought their charges against Paul to the governor. [2]So Paul was called in. Tertullus began to bring the charges against Paul. He said to Felix, "We have enjoyed a long time of peace while you have been ruling. You are a wise leader. You have made this a better nation. [3]Most excellent Felix, we gladly admit this everywhere and in every way. And we are very thankful. [4]I don't want to bother you. But would you be kind enough to listen to us for a short time?

[5]"We have found that Paul is a troublemaker. He stirs up trouble among Jews all over the world. He is a leader of those who follow Jesus of Nazareth. [6/7]He even tried to pollute our temple. So we arrested him. [8]Question him yourself. Then you will learn the truth about all these charges we are bringing against him."

[9]The Jews said the same thing. They agreed that the charges were true.

[10]The governor motioned for Paul to speak. Paul said, "I know that you have been a judge over this nation for quite a few years. So I am glad to stand up for myself. [11]About 12 days ago I went up to Jerusalem to worship. You can

easily check on this. [12]Those bringing charges against me did not find me arguing with anyone at the temple. I wasn't stirring up a crowd in the synagogues or anywhere else in the city. [13]They can't prove to you any of the charges they are making against me.

[14]"It is true that I worship the God of our people. I am a follower of the Way of Jesus. Those bringing charges against me call it a cult. I believe everything that agrees with the Law. I believe everything written in the Prophets. [15]I have the same hope in God that these men have. I believe that both the godly and the ungodly will rise from the dead. [16]So I always try not to do anything wrong in the eyes of God and man.

[17]"I was away for several years. Then I came to Jerusalem to bring my people gifts for those who were poor. I also came to offer sacrifices. [18]They found me doing this in the temple courtyard. I had already been made pure and clean in the usual way. There was no crowd with me. I didn't stir up any trouble.

[19]"But there are some other Jews who should be here in front of you. They are from Asia Minor. They should bring charges if they have anything against me. [20]Let the Jews who are here tell you what crime I am guilty of. After all, I was put on trial by the Sanhedrin. [21]Perhaps they blame me for what I said when I was on trial. I shouted, 'I believe that people will rise from the dead. That is why I am on trial here today.' "

[22]Felix knew all about the Way of Jesus. So he put off the trial for the time being. "Lysias the commanding officer will come," he said. "Then I will decide your case." [23]He ordered the commander to keep Paul under guard. He told him to give Paul some freedom. He also told him to allow Paul's friends to take care of his needs.

[24]Several days later Felix came with his wife Drusilla. She was a Jew. Felix sent for Paul and listened to him speak about faith in Christ Jesus. [25]Paul talked about how to live right. He talked about how people should control themselves. He also talked about the time when God will judge everyone. Then Felix became afraid. "That's enough for now!" he said. "You may leave. When I find the time, I will send for you." [26]He was hoping that Paul would offer him some money to let him go. So he often sent for Paul and talked with him.

[27]Two years passed. Porcius Festus took the place of Felix. But Felix wanted to do the Jews a favor. So he left Paul in prison.

PAUL'S TRIAL IN FRONT OF FESTUS

25 Three days after Festus arrived, he went up from Caesarea to Jerusalem. [2]There the chief priests and Jewish leaders came to him and brought their charges against Paul. [3]They tried to get Festus to have Paul taken to Jerusalem. They asked for this as a favor. They were planning to hide and attack Paul along the way. They wanted to kill him. [4]Festus answered, "Paul is being held at Caesarea. Soon I'll be going there myself. [5]Let some of your leaders come with me. If the man has done anything wrong, they can bring charges against him there."

[6]Festus spent eight or ten days in Jerusalem with them. Then he went down to Caesarea. The next day he called the court together. He ordered Paul to be brought to him. [7]When Paul arrived, the Jews who had come down from Jerusalem stood around him. They brought many strong charges against him. But they couldn't prove them.

[8]Then Paul spoke up for himself. He said, "I've done nothing wrong against the law of the Jews or against the temple. I've done nothing wrong against Caesar."

[9]But Festus wanted to do the Jews a favor. So he said to Paul, "Are you willing to go up to Jerusalem? Are you willing to go on trial there? Are you willing to face these charges in my court?"

[10]Paul answered, "I'm already standing in Caesar's court. This is where I should go on trial. I haven't done anything wrong to the Jews. You yourself know that very well. [11]If I am guilty of anything worthy of death, I'm willing to die. But the charges brought against

me by these Jews are not true. No one has the right to hand me over to them. I make my appeal to Caesar!"

[12]Festus talked it over with the members of his court. Then he said, "You have made an appeal to Caesar. To Caesar you will go!"

FESTUS TALKS WITH KING AGRIPPA

[13]A few days later King Agrippa and Bernice arrived in Caesarea. They came to pay a visit to Festus. [14]They were spending many days there. So Festus talked with the king about Paul's case. He said, "There's a man here that Felix left as a prisoner. [15]When I went to Jerusalem, the Jewish chief priests and the elders brought charges against the man. They wanted him to be found guilty.

[16]"I told them that this is not the way Romans do things. We don't judge people before they have faced those bringing charges against them. They must have a chance to speak up for themselves. [17]When the Jews came back with me, I didn't waste any time. I called the court together the next day. I ordered the man to be brought in. [18]Those bringing charges against him got up to speak. But they didn't charge him with any of the crimes I had expected. [19]Instead, they argued with him about their own beliefs. They didn't agree about a dead man named Jesus. Paul claimed Jesus was alive.

[20]"I had no idea how to look into such matters. So I asked Paul if he would be willing to go to Jerusalem. There he could be tried on these charges. [21]But Paul made an appeal to have the Emperor decide his case. So I ordered him to be held until I could send him to Caesar."

[22]Then Agrippa said to Festus, "I would like to hear this man myself."

Festus replied, "Tomorrow you will hear him."

PAUL SPEAKS TO AGRIPPA

[23]The next day Agrippa and Bernice arrived. They acted like very important people. They entered the courtroom. The most important officers and the leading men of the city came with them. When Festus gave the command, Paul was brought in. [24]Festus said, "King Agrippa, and all who are here with us, take a good look at this man! Both in Jerusalem and here in Caesarea a large number of Jews have come to me about him. They keep shouting that he shouldn't live any longer. [25]I have found that he hasn't done anything worthy of death. But he made his appeal to the Emperor. So I decided to send him to Rome.

[26]"I don't have anything certain to write about him to His Majesty. So I have brought him here today. Now all of you will be able to hear him. King Agrippa, it will also be very good for you to hear him. As a result of this hearing, I will have something to write. [27]It doesn't make sense to send a prisoner to Rome without listing the charges against him."

26 Agrippa said to Paul, "You may now speak for yourself."

So Paul motioned with his hand. Then he began to stand up for himself. [2]"King Agrippa," he said, "I am happy to be able to stand here today. I will speak up for myself against all the charges brought by the Jews. [3]I am very pleased that you are familiar with Jewish ways. You know the kinds of things they argue about. So I beg you to be patient as you listen to me.

[4]"The Jews all know how I have lived ever since I was a child. They know all about me from the beginning of my life. They know how I lived in my own country and in Jerusalem. [5]They have known me for a long time. So if they wanted to, they could give witness that I lived by the rules of the Pharisees. Those rules are harder to obey than the rules of any other group in the Jewish faith.

[6]"Today I am on trial because of the hope I have. I believe in what God promised our people long ago. [7]It is the promise that our 12 tribes are hoping to see come true. Because of this hope they serve God with a true and honest heart day and night. King Agrippa, it is also because of this hope that the Jews are bringing charges against me. [8]Why should any of you think it is impossible for God to raise the dead?

[9]"I myself believed that I should do everything I could to oppose the name of Jesus of Nazareth. [10]That's just what I was doing in Jerusalem. On the authority of the chief priests, I put many of God's people in prison. I agreed that they should die. [11]I often went from one synagogue to another to have them punished. I tried to force them to speak evil things against Jesus. I hated them so much that I even went to cities in other lands to hurt them.

[12]"On one of these journeys I was on my way to Damascus. I had the authority and commission of the chief priests. [13]About noon, King Agrippa, I was on the road. I saw a light coming from heaven. It was brighter than the sun. It was shining around me and my companions. [14]We all fell to the ground. I heard a voice speak to me in the Aramaic language. 'Saul! Saul!' it said. 'Why are you opposing me? It is hard for you to go against what you know is right.'

[15]"Then I asked, 'Who are you, Lord?'

" 'I am Jesus,' the Lord replied. 'I am the one you are opposing. [16]Now get up. Stand on your feet. I have appeared to you to appoint you to serve me and be my witness. You will tell others that you have seen me today. You will also tell them that I will show myself to you again.

[17]" 'I will save you from your own people and from those who aren't Jews. I am sending you to them [18]to open their eyes. I want you to turn them from darkness to light. I want you to turn them from Satan's power to God. I want their sins to be forgiven. They will be forgiven when they believe in me. They will have their place among God's people.'

[19]"So then, King Agrippa, I obeyed the vision that appeared from heaven. [20]First I preached to people in Damascus. Then I preached in Jerusalem and in all Judea. I preached also to people who are not Jews. I told them to turn away from their sins to God. The way they live must prove that they have turned away from their sins. [21]That's why the Jews grabbed me in the temple courtyard and tried to kill me. [22]"But God has helped me to this very day. So I stand here and give witness to both small and great. I have been saying nothing different from what the prophets and Moses said would happen. [23]They said the Christ would suffer. He would be the first to rise from the dead. He would announce the light of life to his own people and to those who aren't Jews."

[24]While Paul was still speaking up for himself, Festus interrupted. "You are out of your mind, Paul!" he shouted. "Your great learning is driving you crazy!"

[25]"I am not crazy, most excellent Festus," Paul replied. "What I am saying is true and reasonable. [26]The king is familiar with these things. So I can speak openly to him. I am certain he knows everything that has been going on. After all, it was not done in secret. [27]King Agrippa, do you believe the prophets? I know you do."

[28]Then Agrippa spoke to Paul. "Are you trying to talk me into becoming a Christian?" he said. "Do you think you can do that in such a short time?"

[29]Paul replied, "I don't care if it takes a short time or a long time. I pray to God for you and all who are listening to me today. I pray that you may become like me, except for these chains."

[30]The king stood up. The governor and Bernice and those sitting with them stood up too. [31]They left the room and began to talk with one another. "Why should this man die or be put in prison?" they said. "He has done nothing worthy of that!"

[32]Agrippa said to Festus, "This man could have been set free. But he has made an appeal to Caesar."

PAUL SAILS FOR ROME

27 It was decided that we would sail for Italy. Paul and some other prisoners were handed over to a Roman commander named Julius. He belonged to the Imperial Guard. [2]We boarded a ship from Adramyttium. It was about to sail for ports along the coast of Asia Minor. We headed out to sea. Aristarchus was with us. He was a Macedonian from Thessalonica.

[3]The next day we landed at Sidon.

There Julius was kind to Paul. He let Paul visit his friends so they could give him what he needed. [4]From there we headed out to sea again. We passed the calmer side of Cyprus because the winds were against us.

[5]We sailed across the open sea off the coast of Cilicia and Pamphylia. Then we landed at Myra in Lycia. [6]There the commander found a ship from Alexandria sailing for Italy. He put us on board. [7]We moved along slowly for many days. We had trouble getting to Cnidus. The wind did not let us stay on course. So we passed the calmer side of Crete, opposite Salmone. [8]It was not easy to sail along the coast. Then we came to a place called Fair Havens. It was near the town of Lasea.

[9]A lot of time had passed. Sailing had already become dangerous. By now it was after the Day of Atonement, a day of fasting. So Paul gave them a warning. [10]"Men," he said, "I can see that our trip is going to be dangerous. The ship and everything in it will be lost. Our own lives will be in danger also."

[11]But the commander didn't listen to what Paul said. Instead, he followed the advice of the pilot and the ship's owner. [12]The harbor wasn't a good place for ships to stay during winter. So most of the people decided we should sail on. They hoped we would reach Phoenix. They wanted to spend the winter there. Phoenix was a harbor in Crete. It faced both southwest and northwest.

THE STORM

[13]A gentle south wind began to blow. They thought that this was what they had been waiting for. So they pulled up the anchor and sailed along the shore of Crete. [14]Before very long, a wind blew down from the island. It had the force of a hurricane. It was called a "northeaster." [15]The ship was caught by the storm. We could not keep it sailing into the wind. So we gave up and were driven along. [16]We passed the calmer side of a small island called Cauda. We almost lost the lifeboat. [17]So the men lifted it on board. Then they tied ropes under the ship itself to hold it together. They were afraid it would get stuck on the sandbars of Syrtis. They lowered the sea anchor and let the ship be driven along.

[18]We took a very bad beating from the storm. The next day the crew began to throw the ship's contents overboard. [19]On the third day, they even threw the ship's gear overboard with their own hands. [20]The sun and stars didn't appear for many days. The storm was terrible. So we gave up all hope of being saved.

[21]The men had not eaten for a long time. Paul stood up in front of them. "Men," he said, "you should have taken my advice not to sail from Crete. Then you would have avoided this harm and loss.

[22]"Now I beg you to be brave. Not one of you will die. Only the ship will be destroyed. [23]I belong to God and serve him. Last night his angel stood beside me. [24]The angel said, 'Do not be afraid, Paul. You must go on trial in front of Caesar. God has shown his grace by sparing the lives of all those sailing with you.'

[25]"Men, continue to be brave. I have faith in God. It will happen just as he told me. [26]But we must run the ship onto the beach of some island."

THE SHIP IS DESTROYED

[27]On the 14th night we were still being driven across the Sea of Adria. About midnight the sailors had a feeling that they were approaching land. [28]They measured how deep the water was. They found that it was 120 feet deep. A short time later they measured the water again. This time it was 90 feet deep. [29]They were afraid we would crash against the rocks. So they dropped four anchors from the back of the ship. They prayed that daylight would come.

[30]The sailors wanted to escape from the ship. So they let the lifeboat down into the sea. They pretended they were going to lower some anchors from the front of the ship. [31]But Paul spoke to the commander and the soldiers. "These men must stay with the ship," he said. "If they don't, you can't be saved." [32]So the soldiers cut the ropes

that held the lifeboat. They let it drift away. [33]Just before dawn Paul tried to get them all to eat. "For the last 14 days," he said, "you have wondered what would happen. You have gone without food. You haven't eaten anything. [34]Now I am asking you to eat some food. You need it to live. Not one of you will lose a single hair from your head."

[35]After Paul said this, he took some bread and gave thanks to God. He did this where they all could see him. Then he broke it and began to eat. [36]All of them were filled with hope. So they ate some food. [37]There were 276 of us on board. [38]They ate as much as they wanted. They needed to make the ship lighter. So they threw the rest of the grain into the sea.

[39]When daylight came, they saw a bay with a sandy beach. They didn't recognize the place. But they decided to run the ship onto the beach if they could. [40]So they cut the anchors loose and left them in the sea. At the same time, they untied the ropes that held the rudders. They lifted the sail at the front of the ship to the wind. Then they headed for the beach. [41]But the ship hit a sandbar. So the front of it got stuck and wouldn't move. The back of the ship was broken to pieces by the pounding of the waves.

[42]The soldiers planned to kill the prisoners. They wanted to keep them from swimming away and escaping. [43]But the commander wanted to save Paul's life. So he kept the soldiers from carrying out their plan. He ordered those who could swim to jump overboard first and swim to land. [44]The rest were supposed to get there on boards or other pieces of the ship. That is how everyone reached land safely.

ON SHORE AT MALTA

28 When we were safe on shore, we found out that the island was called Malta. [2]The people of the island were unusually kind. It was raining and cold. So they built a fire and welcomed all of us.

[3]Paul gathered some sticks and put them on the fire. A poisonous snake was driven out by the heat. It fastened itself on Paul's hand. [4]The people of the island saw the snake hanging from his hand. They said to each other, "This man must be a murderer. He escaped from the sea. But Justice won't let him live." Justice was the name of a goddess.

[5]Paul shook the snake off into the fire. He was not harmed. [6]The people expected him to swell up. They thought he would suddenly fall dead. They waited for a long time. But they didn't see anything unusual happen to him. So they changed their minds. They said he was a god.

[7]Publius owned property nearby. He was the chief official on the island. He welcomed us to his home. For three days he took care of us. He treated us with kindness. [8]His father was sick in bed. The man suffered from fever and dysentery. So Paul went in to see him. Paul prayed for him. He placed his hands on him and healed him.

[9]Then the rest of the sick people on the island came. They too were healed. [10]The people of the island honored us in many ways. When we were ready to sail, they gave us the supplies we needed.

PAUL ARRIVES IN ROME

[11]After three months we headed out to sea. We sailed in a ship that had stayed at the island during the winter. It was a ship from Alexandria. On the front of it the figures of twin gods were carved. Their names were Castor and Pollux. [12]We landed at Syracuse and stayed there for three days.

[13]From there we sailed to Rhegium. The next day the south wind came up. The day after that, we reached Puteoli. [14]There we found some believers. They invited us to spend a week with them.

At last we came to Rome. [15]The brothers and sisters there had heard we were coming. They traveled as far as the Forum of Appius and the Three Taverns to meet us. When Paul saw these people, he thanked God and was cheered up. [16]When we got to Rome, Paul was allowed to live by himself. But a soldier guarded him.

PAUL PREACHES IN ROME

¹⁷Three days later Paul called a meeting of the Jewish leaders. So they came. Paul said to them, "My brothers, I have done nothing against our people. I have also done nothing against what our people of long ago practiced. But I was arrested in Jerusalem. I was handed over to the Romans.

¹⁸"They questioned me. And they wanted to let me go. They saw I wasn't guilty of any crime worthy of death. ¹⁹But the Jews objected. So I had to make an appeal to Caesar.

"It wasn't that I had anything against my own people. ²⁰I share Israel's hope. That is why I am held with this chain. So I have asked to see you and talk with you."

²¹They replied, "We have not received any letters from Judea about you. None of our companions who came from there has reported or said anything bad about you. ²²But we want to hear what your ideas are. We know that people everywhere are talking against those who believe as you do."

²³They decided to meet Paul on a certain day. At that time even more people came to the place where he was staying. From morning until evening, he told them about God's kingdom and explained it to them. Using the Law of Moses and the Prophets, he tried to get them to believe in Jesus.

²⁴Some believed what he said. Others did not. ²⁵They didn't agree with each other. They began to leave after Paul had made a final statement. He said, "The Holy Spirit was right when he spoke to your people long ago. Through Isaiah the prophet the Spirit said,

²⁶ " 'Go to your people. Say to them,
"You will hear but never
understand.
You will see but never know what
you are seeing."
²⁷These people's hearts have
become stubborn.
They can barely hear with their
ears.
They have closed their eyes.
Otherwise they might see with
their eyes.
They might hear with their ears.
They might understand with
their hearts.
They might turn, and then I would
heal them.' *(Isaiah 6:9,10)*

²⁸/²⁹"Here is what I want you to know. God has sent his salvation to people who are not Jews. And they will listen!"

³⁰For two whole years Paul stayed there in a house he rented. He welcomed all who came to see him. ³¹He preached boldly about God's kingdom. No one could keep him from teaching people about the Lord Jesus Christ.

Quest Clue

Maybe you feel uncomfortable telling your friends about God because they might not like you anymore. God asked many people in the Bible to share their faith, and sometimes they went through difficult times to do so. But God always gave them strength to do it.

Read Acts 21 to see what happened to Paul as a result of talking to others about God. Then find 2 Corinthians 11 to hear Paul's description of what he went through for God. Finally, read Philippians 3 to see why Paul was willing to suffer for his faith.

Romans

Who wrote this book?
Paul wrote this book to the church in Rome.

Why was this book written?
Romans shows how Jesus' death makes us right with God and how Jesus will help us to live a good life.

For whom was this book written?
This book is a letter Paul sent to Christians in Rome.

When was this book written?
This book was written about A.D. 57 from the city of Corinth.

1 I, Paul, am writing this letter. I serve Christ Jesus. I have been appointed to be an apostle. God set me apart to tell others his good news. ²He promised the good news long ago. He announced it through his prophets in the Holy Scriptures.

³The good news is about God's Son. As a human being, the Son of God belonged to King David's family line. ⁴By the power of the Holy Spirit, he was appointed to be the mighty Son of God because he rose from the dead. He is Jesus Christ our Lord.

⁵I received God's grace because of what Jesus did so that I could bring glory to him. He made me an apostle to all those who aren't Jews. I must invite them to have faith in God and obey him. ⁶You also are among those who are appointed to belong to Jesus Christ.

⁷I am sending this letter to all of you in Rome who are loved by God and appointed to be his people.

May God our Father and the Lord Jesus Christ give you grace and peace.

PAUL LONGS TO VISIT ROME

⁸First, I thank my God through Jesus Christ for all of you. People all over the world are talking about your faith. ⁹I serve God with my whole heart. I preach the good news about his Son. God knows that I always remember you ¹⁰in my prayers. I pray that now at last it may be God's plan to open the way for me to visit you.

¹¹I long to see you. I want to make you strong by giving you a gift from the Holy Spirit. ¹²I want us to cheer each other up by sharing our faith.

¹³Brothers and sisters, I want you to

know that I planned many times to visit you. But until now I have been kept from coming. My work has produced results among others who are not Jews. In the same way, I want to see results among you.

[14]I have a duty both to Greeks and to non-Greeks. I have a duty both to wise people and to foolish people. [15]So I really want to preach the good news also to you who live in Rome.

[16]I am not ashamed of the good news. It is God's power. And it will save everyone who believes. It is meant first for the Jews. It is meant also for those who aren't Jews.

[17]The good news shows how God makes people right with himself. From beginning to end, becoming right with God depends on a person's faith. It is written, "Those who are right with God will live by faith."

(Habakkuk 2:4)

GOD'S ANGER AGAINST SINNERS

[18]God shows his anger from heaven. It is against all the godless and evil things people do. They are so evil that they say no to the truth. [19]The truth about God is plain to them. God has made it plain.

[20]Ever since the world was created it has been possible to see the qualities of God that are not seen. I'm talking about his eternal power and about the fact that he is God. Those things can be seen in what he has made. So people have no excuse for what they do.

[21]They knew God. But they didn't honor him as God. They didn't thank him. Their thinking became worthless. Their foolish hearts became dark. [22]They claimed to be wise. But they made fools of themselves. [23]They would rather have statues of gods than the glorious God who lives forever. Their statues of gods are made to look like people, birds, animals and reptiles.

[24]So God let them go. He allowed them to do what their sinful hearts wanted to. He let them commit sexual sins. They polluted one another's bodies by what they did.

[25]They chose a lie instead of God's truth. They worshiped and served created things. They didn't worship the Creator. But he must be praised forever. Amen.

[26]So God let them go. They were filled with shameful longings. Their women committed sexual acts that were not natural. [27]In the same way, the men turned away from their natural love for women. They burned with

Is it all right to lie if you are embarrassed or scared?

No. It is wrong to lie, because God is truth and he has told us not to lie. Sometimes it is hard to tell the truth. It can be really hard when you feel ashamed or fear getting in trouble. But you should do what is right even when it is not easy. People will think "Wow!" if you tell the truth when it is hard. They will trust you more than ever and know that you are a dependable person. Don't ever be ashamed of the truth, including the truth about Jesus.

checkout
Romans 1:16

Related verses:
Zephaniah 3:13;
1 Peter 2:1

sexual longing for each other. Men did shameful things with other men. They suffered in their bodies for all the twisted things they did.

²⁸They didn't think it was important to know God. So God let them go. He allowed them to have dirty minds. They did things they shouldn't do.

²⁹They are full of every kind of sin, evil and ungodliness. They want more than they need. They commit murder. They want what belongs to other people. They fight and cheat. They hate others. They say mean things about other people. ³⁰They tell lies about them. They hate God. They are rude and proud. They brag. They think of new ways to do evil. They don't obey their parents. ³¹They are foolish. They can't be trusted. They are not loving and kind.

³²They know that God's commands are right. They know that those who do evil things should die. But they continue to do those very things. They also approve of others who do them.

GOD JUDGES FAIRLY

2 If you judge someone else, you have no excuse for it. When you judge another person, you are judging yourself. You do the same things you blame others for doing.

²We know that when God judges those who do evil things, he judges fairly. ³Though you are only a human being, you judge others. But you yourself do the same things. So how do you think you will escape when God judges you?

⁴Do you make fun of God's great kindness and favor? Do you make fun of God when he is patient with you? Don't you realize that God's kindness is meant to turn you away from your sins?

⁵But you are stubborn. In your heart you are not sorry for your sins. You are storing up anger against yourself. The day of God's anger is coming. Then his way of judging fairly will be shown. ⁶God "will give to each person in keeping with what he has done." *(Psalm 62:12; Proverbs 24:12)*

⁷God will give eternal life to those who keep on doing good. They want glory, honor, and life that never ends. ⁸But there are others who only look out for themselves. They don't accept the truth. They go down an evil path. God will pour out his burning anger on them. ⁹There will be trouble and suffering for everyone who does evil. That is meant first for the Jews. It is also meant for the non-Jews. ¹⁰But there will be glory, honor and peace for ev-

On TV, why do people who aren't married live together?

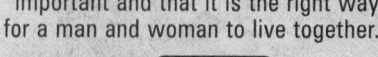

Many of the people who make TV shows do not love God. They do not care about what God wants. They do not understand that his way is the best way. They might have heard about Jesus but not opened their hearts to him. The Bible says that the foolish hearts of people like this have become dark. Some television programs try to show that marriage is not important. But God created marriage. And he says that it is important and that it is the right way for a man and woman to live together.

checkout
Romans 1:21

Related verse:
Hebrews 13:4

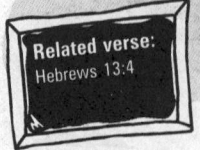

eryone who does good. That is meant first for the Jews. It is also meant for the non-Jews. [11]God treats everyone the same.

[12]Some people do not know God's law when they sin. They will not be judged by the law when they die. Others do know God's law when they sin. They will be judged by the law. [13]Hearing the law does not make a person right with God. People are considered to be right with God only when they obey the law.

[14]Those who aren't Jews do not have the law. Sometimes they just naturally do what the law requires. They are a law for themselves. This is true even though they don't have the law. [15]They show that what the law requires is written on their hearts. The way their minds judge them gives witness to that fact. Sometimes their thoughts find them guilty. At other times their thoughts find them not guilty.

[16]People will be judged on the day God appoints Jesus Christ to judge their secret thoughts. That's part of my good news.

THE JEWS AND THE LAW

[17]Suppose you call yourself a Jew. You trust in the law. You brag that you are close to God. [18]You know what God wants. You agree with what is best because the law teaches you. [19]You are sure you can lead people who are blind. You are sure you are a light for those who are in the dark. [20]You claim to be able to teach foolish people. You can even teach babies. You think that in the law you have all knowledge and truth.

[21]You teach others. But you don't teach yourself! You preach against stealing. But you steal! [22]You say that people should not commit adultery. But you commit adultery! You hate statues of gods. But you rob temples! [23]You brag about the law. But when you break it, you rob God of his honor! [24]It is written, "Those who aren't Jews say evil things against God's name

What happens to people who don't go to church?

They miss out on a very important part of God's plan for them. Going to church does not get a person into heaven. And not going to church does not send a person to hell. A person becomes a Christian by believing in Jesus, not by doing good deeds. But people who love God want to worship him and meet with other Christians. At church you can find friends and help for your problems. You can learn from God's Word and help others. And you can worship, sing and pray. People who do not go to church miss all that. They miss a very important meeting with God and with God's people. Also, when you get out of the habit of worshiping God, you are in danger of starting to worship something or someone else!

checkout Romans 1:25

Related verses: Hebrews 10:24,25

SERVICE 10:00A.M.

because of you." *(Isaiah 52:5; Ezekiel 36:22)*

²⁵Circumcision has value if you obey the law. But if you break the law, it is just as if you hadn't been circumcised.

²⁶Sometimes those who aren't circumcised do what the law requires. Won't God accept them as if they had been circumcised? ²⁷Many are not circumcised physically, but they obey the law. They will prove that you are guilty. You are breaking the law, even though you have the written law and are circumcised.

²⁸A man is not a Jew if he is a Jew only on the outside. And circumcision is more than just something done to the outside of a man's body.

²⁹No, a man is a Jew only if he is a Jew on the inside. And true circumcision means that the heart has been circumcised. It is done by the Holy Spirit. It is more than just obeying the written Law. Then a man's praise will not come from others. It will come from God.

GOD IS FAITHFUL

3 Is there any advantage in being a Jew? Is there any value in being circumcised? ²There is great value in every way!

First of all, the Jews have been given the very words of God.

³What if some Jews did not believe? Will the fact that they don't have faith keep God from being faithful? ⁴Not at all! God is true, even though every human being is a liar. It is written,

> "You are right when you sentence me.
> You are fair when you judge me."
> *(Psalm 51:4)*

⁵Doesn't the fact that we are wrong prove more clearly that God is right? Then what can we say? Can we say that God is not fair when he brings his anger down on us? As you can tell, I am just using human ways of thinking. ⁶God is certainly fair! If he weren't, how could he judge the world?

⁷Someone might argue, "When I lie, it becomes clearer that God is truthful. It makes his glory shine more brightly. Why then does he find me guilty of sin?"

⁸Why not say, "Let's do evil things so that good things will happen"? Some people actually lie by reporting that this is what we say. They are the ones who should be found guilty.

What is a conscience?

It is something God built into us to help us tell right from wrong. We need to learn to listen to it. It makes us feel bad when we are thinking about doing something wrong. It also makes us feel good when we are thinking about doing something right.

God gave us our conscience to help us decide what to do. We can get into the habit of ignoring it if we don't listen to it. After a while we won't hear it at all. That can lead to trouble. Listen carefully to your conscience.

checkout Romans 2:15

Related verses:
Acts 24:16;
1 Peter 3:16

NO ONE IS RIGHT WITH GOD

⁹What should we say then? Are we Jews any better? Not at all! We have already claimed that Jews are sinners. The same is true of those who aren't Jews.

¹⁰It is written,

> "No one is right with God, no one at all.
¹¹   No one understands.
>   No one trusts in God.
¹²All of them have turned away.
>   They have all become worthless.
> No one does anything good,
>   no one at all."
>
> *(Psalms 14:1–3; 53:1–3; Ecclesiastes 7:20)*

¹³ "Their throats are like open graves.
>   With their tongues they tell lies."
>
> *(Psalm 5:9)*

> "The words from their lips are like the poison of a snake."
>
> *(Psalm 140:3)*
¹⁴ "Their mouths are full of curses and bitterness." *(Psalm 10:7)*
¹⁵ "They run quickly to commit murder.
¹⁶   They leave a trail of failure and pain.
¹⁷ They do not know the way of peace." *(Isaiah 59:7,8)*
¹⁸ "They don't have any respect for God." *(Psalm 36:1)*

¹⁹What the law says, it says to those who are ruled by the law. Its purpose is to shut every mouth and make the whole world accountable to God. ²⁰So it can't be said that anyone will be made right with God by obeying the law. Not at all! The law makes us more aware of our sin.

If lots of different people in different places wrote the Bible, how did it get together in one big book?

The first books of the Bible, the Old Testament, were written to the Jewish people. The Jews protected these books and spent hour after hour carefully copying them again and again. Jesus often used verses from the Old Testament. He said that the verses in the Old Testament were the words of God. The books that we find in the New Testament were written by people who had seen Jesus or who were close to those who traveled with him. Their stories about Jesus and their letters were read in the local churches. For nearly 2,000 years now, all these Bible books have been together.

checkout Romans 3:2

JASON'S IMAGINATION

OVERNIGHT SCROLL

OVERNIGHT SCROLL

Related verses:
Matthew 5:17–20

BECOMING RIGHT WITH GOD

²¹But now God has shown us how to become right with him. The Law and the Prophets give witness to this. It has nothing to do with obeying the law. ²²We are made right with God by putting our faith in Jesus Christ. That happens to all who believe.

It is no different for the Jews than for anyone else. ²³Everyone has sinned. No one measures up to God's glory. ²⁴The free gift of God's grace makes all of us right with him. Christ Jesus paid the price to set us free. ²⁵God gave him as a sacrifice to pay for sins. So he forgives the sins of those who have faith in his blood.

God did all of that to prove that he is fair. Because of his mercy he did not punish people for the sins they had committed before Jesus died for them. ²⁶God did that to prove in our own time that he is fair. He proved that he is right. He also made right with himself those who believe in Jesus.

²⁷So who can brag? No one! Are people saved by obeying the law? Not at all! They are saved because of their faith. ²⁸We firmly believe that people are made right with God because of their faith. They are not saved by obeying the law.

²⁹Is God the God of Jews only? Isn't he also the God of those who aren't Jews? Yes, he is their God too. ³⁰There is only one God. When those who are circumcised believe in him, he makes them right with himself. When those who are not circumcised believe in him, he also makes them right with himself. ³¹Does faith make the law useless? Not at all! We agree with the law.

ABRAHAM'S FAITH MADE HIM RIGHT WITH GOD

4 What should we say about those things? What did our father Abraham discover about being right with God? ²Did he become right with God because of something he did? If so, he could brag about it. But he couldn't brag to God. ³What do we find in Scripture? It says, "Abraham believed God. God accepted Abraham's faith, and so his faith made him right with God." *(Genesis 15:6)*

⁴When a man works, his pay is not considered a gift. It is owed to him. ⁵But things are different with God. He makes evil people right with himself. If people trust in him, their faith is accepted even though they do not work. Their faith makes them right with God.

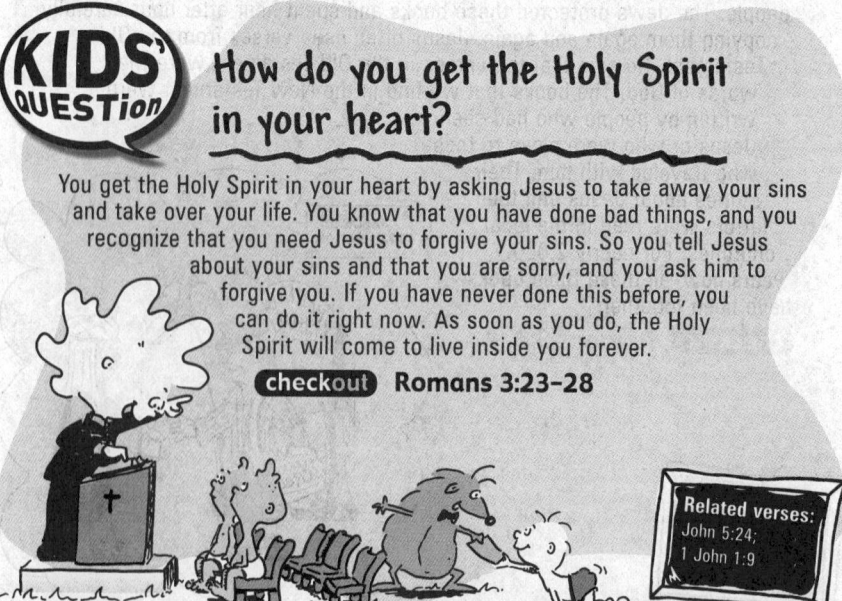

KIDS' QUESTION

How do you get the Holy Spirit in your heart?

You get the Holy Spirit in your heart by asking Jesus to take away your sins and take over your life. You know that you have done bad things, and you recognize that you need Jesus to forgive your sins. So you tell Jesus about your sins and that you are sorry, and you ask him to forgive you. If you have never done this before, you can do it right now. As soon as you do, the Holy Spirit will come to live inside you forever.

checkout Romans 3:23–28

Related verses:
John 5:24;
1 John 1:9

[6]King David says the same thing. He tells us how blessed some people are. God makes those people right with himself. But they don't have to do anything in return. David says,

[7]"Blessed are those
  whose lawless acts are forgiven.
Blessed are those
  whose sins are taken away.
[8]Blessed is the man
  whose sin the Lord never counts
    against him." *(Psalm 32:1,2)*

[9]Is that blessing only for those who are circumcised? Or is it also for those who are not circumcised? We have been saying that God accepted Abraham's faith, and so his faith made him right with God. [10]When did it happen? Was it after Abraham was circumcised, or before? It was before he was circumcised, not after! [11]He was circumcised as a sign of the covenant God had made with him. It showed that his faith had made him right with God before he was circumcised.

So Abraham is the father of all believers who have not been circumcised. God accepts their faith. So their faith makes them right with him. [12]Abraham is also the father of the circumcised who believe. So just being circumcised is not enough. Those who are circumcised must also follow the steps of our father Abraham. He had faith before he was circumcised.

[13]Abraham and his family received a promise. God promised that Abraham would receive the world. It would not come to him because he obeyed the law. It would come because of his faith, which made him right with God. [14]Do those who obey the law receive the promise? If they do, faith would have no value. God's promise would be worthless. [15]The law brings God's anger. Where there is no law, the law can't be broken.

[16]The promise is based on God's grace. The promise comes by faith. All of Abraham's children will certainly receive the promise. And it is not only for those who are ruled by the law. Those who have the same faith that Abraham had are also included. He is the father of us all.

[17]It is written, "I have made you a father of many nations." *(Genesis 17:5)* God considers Abraham to be our father. The God that Abraham believed in gives life to the dead. Abraham's God also speaks of things that do not exist as if they do exist.

[18]When there was no reason for hope, Abraham believed because he had hope. He became the father of many nations, exactly as God had promised. God said, "That is how many children you will have." *(Genesis 15:5)*

[19]Without becoming weak in his faith, Abraham accepted the fact that he was past the time when he could have children. At that time he was about 100 years old. He also realized that Sarah was too old to have children. [20]But he kept believing in God's promise. He became strong in his faith. He gave glory to God. [21]He was absolutely sure that God had the power to do what he had promised. [22]That's why "God accepted Abraham because he believed. So his faith made him right with God."

[23]The words "God accepted Abraham's faith" were written not only for Abraham. [24]They were written also for us. We believe in the God who raised Jesus our Lord from the dead. So God will accept our faith and make us right with himself.

[25]Jesus was handed over to die for our sins. He was raised to life in order to make us right with God.

PEACE AND JOY

5 We have been made right with God because of our faith. Now we have peace with him because of our Lord Jesus Christ. [2]Through faith in Jesus we have received God's grace. In that grace we stand. We are full of joy because we expect to share in God's glory.

[3]And that's not all. We are full of joy even when we suffer. We know that our suffering gives us the strength to go on. [4]The strength to go on produces character. Character produces hope. [5]And hope will never let us down. God has poured his love into our hearts. He did it through the Holy Spirit, whom he has given to us.

[6]At just the right time Christ died for ungodly people. He died for us when we had no power of our own. [7]It is unusual for anyone to die for a godly person. Maybe someone would be willing to die for a good person. [8]But here is how God has shown his love for us. While we were still sinners, Christ died for us.

[9]The blood of Christ has made us right with God. So we are even more sure that Jesus will save us from God's anger. [10]Once we were God's enemies. But we have been brought back to him because his Son has died for us. Now that God has brought us back, we are even more secure. We know that we will be saved because Christ lives.

[11]And that is not all. We are full of joy in God because of our Lord Jesus Christ. Because of him, God has brought us back to himself.

DEATH THROUGH ADAM, LIFE THROUGH CHRIST

[12]Sin entered the world because one man sinned. And death came because of sin. Everyone sinned, so death came to all people.

[13]Before the law was given, sin was in the world. But sin is not judged when there is no law. [14]Death ruled from the time of Adam to the time of Moses. Death ruled even over those who did not sin as Adam did. He broke God's command. But he also became a pattern of the One who was going to come.

[15]God's gift is different from Adam's sin. Many people died because of the sin of that one man. But it was even more sure that God's grace would also come through one man. That man is Jesus Christ. God's gift of grace was more than enough for the whole world.

[16]The result of God's gift is different from the result of Adam's sin. God judged one sin. That brought guilt. But after many sins, God's gift made people right with him.

[17]One man sinned, and death ruled because of his sin. But we are even more sure of what will happen because of what the one man, Jesus Christ, has done. Those who receive the rich supply of God's grace will rule with Christ in his kingdom. They have received God's gift and have been made right with him.

Why do people die?

People die because of sin. People would have lived forever if Adam and Eve had not sinned. But they disobeyed God and brought sin into the world. Now every person is born as a sinner in a sinful world. With sin came death. Plants and animals also die because of the sin that people brought into the world.

Every person's earthly body has to die. But people can live forever in heaven with God if they trust in Jesus and ask God to forgive their sins. Someday Jesus will return and raise his people to life. He will make his people new so their bodies will not ever break down again.

checkout Romans 5:12

Related verses:
Romans 6:23;
1 Corinthians
15:22

[18]One man's sin brought guilt to all people. So also one right act made all people right with God. And all who are right with God will live. [19]Many people were made sinners because one man did not obey. But one man did obey. That is why many people will be made right with God.

[20]The law was given so that sin would increase. But where sin increased, God's grace increased even more. [21]Sin ruled because of death. So also grace rules in the lives of those who are right with God. The grace of God brings eternal life because of what Jesus Christ our Lord has done.

LIVING A NEW LIFE

6 What should we say then? Should we keep on sinning so that God's grace can increase? [2]Not at all! As far as sin is concerned, we are dead. So how can we keep on sinning? [3]All of us were baptized into Christ Jesus. Don't you know that we were baptized into his death? [4]By be-

ing baptized, we were buried with Christ into his death. Christ has been raised from the dead by the Father's glory. And like Christ we also can live a new life.

[5]By being baptized, we have been joined with him in his death. We will certainly also be joined with him in his resurrection. [6]We know that what we used to be was nailed to the cross with him. That happened so our sinful bodies would lose their power. We are no longer slaves of sin. [7]Those who have died have been set free from sin.

[8]We died with Christ. So we believe that we will also live with him. [9]We know that Christ was raised from the dead and will never die again. Death doesn't control him anymore. [10]When he died, he died once and for all time as far as sin is concerned. Now that he lives, he lives as far as God is concerned.

[11]In the same way, consider yourselves to be dead as far as sin is concerned. Now that you believe in Christ

Why did Adam die when God said he wouldn't?

Two things died after Adam and Eve sinned. One part that died was their perfect bodies. They would have lived forever if they had not sinned. But once they had sinned their bodies changed and could not live forever. That meant that every plant, animal and person would also die one day. The second part that died was their perfect friendship with God. All of a sudden they were cut off from their close relationship with God. Both kinds of death came to Adam and Eve the moment they first disobeyed God. Everybody else born since then is like that, too, all because of sin. The only way out is to trust in Jesus. He came to earth to take away our sin so that we can have life.

checkout Romans 5:14,15

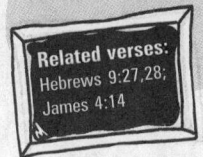

Related verses:
Hebrews 9:27,28;
James 4:14

Jesus, consider yourselves to be alive as far as God is concerned.

¹²So don't let sin rule your body, which is going to die. Don't obey its evil longings. ¹³Don't give the parts of your body to serve sin. Don't let them be used to do evil. Instead, give yourselves to God. You have been brought from death to life. Give the parts of your body to him to do what is right.

¹⁴Sin will not be your master. Law does not rule you. God's grace has set you free.

SLAVES TO RIGHT LIVING

¹⁵What should we say then? Should we sin because we are not ruled by law but by God's grace? Not at all!

¹⁶Don't you know that when you give yourselves to obey someone you become that person's slave? You can be slaves of sin. Then you will die. Or you can be slaves who obey God. Then you will live a godly life. ¹⁷You used to be slaves of sin. But thank God that with your whole heart you obeyed the teachings you were given! ¹⁸You have been set free from sin. You have become slaves to right living.

¹⁹Because you are human, you find this hard to understand. So I have said it in a way that will help you understand it. You used to give the parts of your body to be slaves to unclean living. You were becoming more and more evil. Now give your bodies to be slaves to right living. Then you will become holy.

²⁰Once you were slaves of sin. At that time right living did not control you. ²¹What benefit did you gain from doing the things you are now ashamed of? Those things lead to death! ²²You have been set free from sin. God has made you his slaves. The benefit you gain leads to holy living. And the end result is eternal life. ²³When you sin, the pay you get is death. But God gives you the gift of eternal life because of what Christ Jesus our Lord has done.

AN EXAMPLE FROM MARRIAGE

7 Brothers and sisters, I am speaking to you who know the law. Don't you know that the law has authority over us only as long as we are

KIDS' QUESTION

What is the Bible's biggest story?

The Bible's biggest story is the story of Jesus. The writers of the Old Testament told us that Jesus would come. They told how Jesus would be born, die and come to life again. The writers of the New Testament told us about Jesus' life, about God's plan to save us through Jesus and about the first Christians who believed in him. No matter where you look in the Bible, you can learn about Jesus.

checkout Romans 6:23

Related verses: John 3:16; Acts 4:12

alive? ²For example, by law a married woman is joined to her husband as long as he is living. But suppose her husband dies. Then the marriage law no longer applies to her. ³But suppose that married woman gets married again while her husband is still alive. Then she is called a woman who commits adultery. But suppose her husband dies. Then she is free from that law. She is not guilty of adultery even if she marries another man.

⁴My brothers and sisters, when Christ died you also died as far as the law is concerned. Then it became possible for you to belong to him. He was raised from the dead. Now our lives can be useful to God. ⁵Our sinful nature used to control us. The law stirred up sinful longings in our bodies. So the things we did resulted in death.

⁶But now we have died to what used to control us. We have been set free from the law. Now we serve in the new way of the Holy Spirit. We no longer serve in the old way of the written law.

STRUGGLING WITH SIN

⁷What should we say then? That the law is sin? Not at all! I wouldn't have known what sin was unless the law had told me. The law said, "Do not want what belongs to other people." (Exodus 20:17; Deuteronomy 5:21) If the law hadn't said that, I would not have known what it was like to want what belonged to others. ⁸But the commandment gave sin an opportunity. Sin caused me to want all kinds of things that belonged to others. No one can break a law that doesn't exist.

⁹Before I knew about the law, I was alive. But then the commandment came. Sin came to life, and I died. ¹⁰I found that the commandment that was supposed to bring life actually brought death. ¹¹When the commandment gave sin the opportunity, sin tricked me. It used the commandment to put me to death. ¹²So the law is holy. The commandment also is holy and right and good.

¹³Did what is good cause me to die? Not at all! Sin had to be recognized for what it really is. So it produced death in me through what was good. Be-

cause of the commandment, sin became totally sinful.

¹⁴We know that the law is holy. But I am not. I have been sold to be a slave of sin. ¹⁵I don't understand what I do. I don't do what I want to do. Instead, I do what I hate to do. ¹⁶I do what I don't want to do. So I agree that the law is good. ¹⁷As it is, I am no longer the one who does these things. It is sin living in me that does them.

¹⁸I know there is nothing good in my sinful nature. I want to do what is good, but I can't. ¹⁹I don't do the good things I want to do. I keep on doing the evil things I don't want to do. ²⁰I do what I don't want to do. But I am not really the one who is doing it. It is sin living in me.

²¹Here is the law I find working in me. When I want to do good, evil is right there with me. ²²Deep inside me I find joy in God's law. ²³But I see another law working in the parts of my body. It fights against the law of my mind. It makes me a prisoner of the law of sin. That law controls the parts of my body.

²⁴What a terrible failure I am! Who will save me from this sin that brings death to my body? ²⁵I give thanks to God. He will do it through Jesus Christ our Lord.

So in my mind I am a slave to God's law. But in my sinful nature I am a slave to the law of sin.

THE HOLY SPIRIT GIVES LIFE

8 Those who belong to Christ Jesus are no longer under God's sentence. ²I am now controlled by the law of the Holy Spirit. That law gives me life because of what Christ Jesus has done. It has set me free from the law of sin that brings death.

³The written law was made weak by our sinful nature. But God did what the written law could not do. He made his Son to be like those who have a sinful nature. He sent him to be an offering for sin. In that way, he judged sin in his Son's human body. ⁴Now we can do everything the law requires. Our sinful nature no longer controls the way we live. The Holy Spirit now controls the way we live.

⁵Don't live under the control of your sinful nature. If you do, you will think

about what your sinful nature wants. Live under the control of the Holy Spirit. If you do, you will think about what the Spirit wants.

[6]The way a sinful person thinks leads to death. But the mind controlled by the Spirit brings life and peace. [7]The sinful mind is at war with God. It does not obey God's law. It can't. [8]Those who are controlled by their sinful nature can't please God.

[9]But your sinful nature does not control you. The Holy Spirit controls you. The Spirit of God lives in you. Anyone who does not have the Spirit of Christ does not belong to Christ.

[10]Christ lives in you. So your body is dead because of sin. But your spirit is alive because you have been made right with God. [11]The Spirit of the One who raised Jesus from the dead is living in you. So the God who raised Christ from the dead will also give life to your bodies, which are going to die. He will do this by the power of his Spirit, who lives in you.

[12]Brothers and sisters, we have a duty. Our duty is not to live under the control of our sinful nature. [13]If you live under the control of your sinful nature, you will die. But by the power of the Holy Spirit you can put to death the sins your body commits. Then you will live.

[14]Those who are led by the Spirit of God are children of God. [15]You didn't receive a spirit that makes you a slave to fear once again. Instead you received the Holy Spirit, who makes you God's child. By the Spirit's power we call God *"Abba." Abba* means Father. [16]The Spirit himself joins with our spirits. Together they give witness that we are God's children.

[17]As his children, we will receive all that he has for us. We will share what Christ receives. But we must share in his sufferings if we want to share in his glory.

THE HOPE OF FUTURE GLORY

[18]What we are suffering now is nothing compared with the glory that will be shown in us. [19]Everything God created looks forward to the time when his children will appear in their full and final glory. [20]The created world was bound to fail. But that was not the

KIDS' QUESTION

Why do my parents get mad at me if they have Jesus in their hearts?

Not all anger is wrong. We should be angry with the bad things in the world. And we should try to make them right. When children disobey their parents and do other things that are wrong, sometimes their parents get angry. Good parents want their children to do what is right. And so they try to teach children right from wrong. But sometimes parents get angry at children for the wrong reasons. Maybe the parents are grouchy because they have had a bad day. Or maybe they misunderstand what their child has done. Parents are human too. They can make mistakes. Even Christian parents do what is wrong at times. That happens when they do not do what God wants them to do. No matter how your parents act, try to love them and pray for them.

Related verses:
Ephesians 4:26,27;
James 1:19,20

checkout
Romans 7:14,15

BIBLE
STORIES
OF
JESUS

result of its own choice. It was planned that way by the One who made it. God planned [21]to set the created world free. He didn't want it to rot away completely. Instead, he wanted it to have the same glorious freedom that his children have.

[22]We know that all that God created has been groaning. It is in pain as if it were giving birth to a child. The created world continues to groan even now. [23]And that's not all. We have the Holy Spirit as the promise of future blessing. But we also groan inside ourselves as we look forward to the time when God will adopt us as full members of his family. Then he will give us everything he has for us. He will raise our bodies and give glory to them.

[24]That's the hope we had when we were saved. But hope that can be seen is no hope at all. Who hopes for what he already has? [25]We hope for what we don't have yet. So we are patient as we wait for it.

[26]In the same way, the Holy Spirit helps us when we are weak. We don't know what we should pray for. But the Spirit himself prays for us. He prays with groans too deep for words. [27]God, who looks into our hearts, knows the mind of the Spirit. And the Spirit prays for God's people just as God wants him to pray.

WE WILL WIN

[28]We know that in all things God works for the good of those who love him. He appointed them to be saved in keeping with his purpose.

[29]God planned that those he had chosen would become like his Son. In that way, Christ will be the first and most honored among many brothers. [30]And those God has planned for, he has also appointed to be saved. Those he has appointed, he has made right with himself. To those he has made right with himself, he has given his glory.

[31]What should we say then? Since God is on our side, who can be against us? [32]God did not spare his own Son. He gave him up for us all. Then won't he also freely give us everything else?

[33]Who can bring any charge against God's chosen ones? God makes us right with himself. [34]Who can sentence us to death? Christ Jesus is at the right hand of God and is also praying for us. He died. More than that, he was raised to life.

KIDS' QUESTion

If Adam and Eve hadn't sinned, would people sin today?

We really do not know what would have happened if Adam and Eve had not sinned. They were given a very important test in the Garden of Eden. When they failed the test, sin entered the world once and for all. The world became broken and dirty. Every person after them has been a sinner. The wrong they did changed our world forever. Now, just like Paul, every one of us has to decide between good and evil.

checkout Romans 7:21

Related verses: Romans 5:12–19

GARDEN of EDEN   STAIN REMOVER   TIME MACHINE   STAIN REMOVER

35Who can separate us from Christ's love? Can trouble or hard times or harm or hunger? Can nakedness or danger or war? 36It is written,

"Because of you, we face death all day long.
We are considered as sheep to be killed." *(Psalm 44:22)*

37No! In all these things we will do even more than win! We owe it all to Christ, who has loved us.

38I am absolutely sure that not even death or life can separate us from God's love. Not even angels or demons, the present or the future, or any powers can do that. 39Not even the highest places or the lowest, or anything else in all creation can do that. Nothing at all can ever separate us from God's love because of what Christ Jesus our Lord has done.

GOD'S FREE CHOICE

9 I speak the truth in Christ. I am not lying. My mind tells me that what I say is true. It is guided by the Holy Spirit. 2My heart is full of sor-

row. My sadness never ends. 3I am so concerned about my people, who are members of my own race. I am ready to be cursed, if that would help them. I am even willing to be separated from Christ.

4They are the people of Israel. They have been adopted as God's children. God's glory belongs to them. So do the covenants. They received the law. They were taught to worship in the temple. They were given the promises. 5The founders of our nation belong to them. Christ comes from their family line. He is God over all. May he always be praised! Amen.

6Their condition does not mean that God's word has failed. Not everyone in the family line of Israel really belongs to Israel. 7Not everyone in Abraham's family line is really his child. Not at all! Scripture says, "Your family line will continue through Isaac." *(Genesis 21:12)*

8In other words, God's children are not just Abraham's natural children. Instead, they are the children God promised to him. They are the ones considered to be Abraham's children. 9God promised, "I will return at the

What made the Garden of Eden prettier than other gardens today?

The Garden of Eden was more beautiful than any garden today because God made it perfect. God was there, and there was no sin. It was only after Adam and Eve sinned that things got worse. Sin hurt the world and took away some of its beauty. Thorns and weeds started to grow. Growing vegetables and flowers started taking a lot of work. The whole world changed because of sin. It has been groaning in pain that way ever since.

checkout
Romans 8:22

Related verses: Genesis 3:17–19

JASON'S IMAGINATION
Garden of Eden
no thorns or thistles grow here

appointed time. Sarah will have a son." *(Genesis 18:10,14)*

¹⁰And that's not all. Rebekah's children had the same father. He was our father Isaac.

¹¹Here is what happened. Rebekah's twins had not even been born. They hadn't done anything good or bad yet. So they show that God's purpose is based firmly on his free choice. ¹²It was not because of anything they did but because of God's choice. So Rebekah was told, "The older son will serve the younger one." *(Genesis 25:23)* ¹³It is written, "I chose Jacob instead of Esau." *(Malachi 1:2,3)*

¹⁴What should we say then? Is God unfair? Not at all! ¹⁵He said to Moses,

"I will have mercy on whom I have mercy.
I will show love to those I love."
(Exodus 33:19)

¹⁶So it doesn't depend on what we want or do. It depends on God's mercy. ¹⁷In Scripture, God says to Pharaoh, "I had a special reason for making you king. I decided to use you to show my power. I wanted my name to become known everywhere on earth." *(Exodus 9:16)* ¹⁸So God does what he wants to do. He shows mercy to one person and makes another stubborn.

¹⁹One of you will say to me, "Then why does God still blame us? Who can oppose what he wants to do?" ²⁰But you are a mere man. So who are you to talk back to God? Scripture says, "Can what is made say to the one who made it, 'Why did you make me like this?' " *(Isaiah 29:16; 45:9)* ²¹Isn't the potter free to make different kinds of pots out of the same lump of clay? Some are for special purposes. Others are for ordinary use.

²²What if God chose to show his great anger? What if he chose to make his power known? That is why he put up with people he was angry with. They had been made to be destroyed. ²³What if he did that to show the riches of his glory to others? Those are the people he shows his mercy to. He had prepared them to receive his glory. ²⁴We are those people. He has chosen us. We do not come only from the Jewish race. Many of us are not Jews. ²⁵God says in Hosea,

"I will call those who are not my people 'my people.'
I will call the one who is not my loved one 'my loved one.' "
(Hosea 2:23)

²⁶He also says,

"Once it was said to them,
'You are not my people.'

KIDS' QUESTION

Can God help us pray?

Yes. Many times we want to talk with God but just don't know what to say or how to put our feelings into words. The Holy Spirit can help us think of the right words and say them. But even if we still don't know what to say, God knows what we are feeling and thinking. He understands what we *would* say if we could. The best way to pray is to just speak to God from the heart as best we can. He will understand what we mean even if we get the words messed up.

SORRY DAD, I WAS ON A ROLL. THAT LAST HALF HOUR WASN'T EVEN ON MY LIST.

Related verses:
Hebrews 7:25;
1 Peter 5:7

checkout
Romans 8:26,27

In that very place they will be
called 'children of the living
God.' " *(Hosea 1:10)*

[27]Isaiah cries out concerning Israel.
He says,

"The number of people from Israel
may be like the sand by the
sea.
But only a few of them will be
saved.
[28]The Lord will carry out his
sentence.
He will be quick to carry it out on
earth, once and for all."
(Isaiah 10:22,23)

[29]Earlier Isaiah had said,

"The Lord who rules over all
left us children and
grandchildren.
If he hadn't, we would have
become like Sodom.
We would have been like
Gomorrah." *(Isaiah 1:9)*

ISRAEL DOES NOT BELIEVE

[30]What should we say then? Those
who aren't Jews did not look for a way
to be right with God. But they found it
by having faith. [31]Israel did look for a
law that could make them right with
God. But they didn't find it. [32]Why not? Because they didn't look
for it by faith. They tried to get it by
working for it. They tripped over the
stone that causes people to trip and
fall. [33]It is written,

"Look! In Zion I am laying a stone
that causes people to trip.
It is a rock that makes them fall.
The one who trusts in him will
never be put to shame."
(Isaiah 8:14; 28:16)

10

Brothers and sisters, with
all my heart I long for the
people of Israel to be
saved. I pray to God for them. [2]I can
give witness about them that they
really want to serve God. But how they
are trying to do it is not based on what
they know.

[3]They didn't know how God makes
people right with himself. They tried
to get right with God in their own way.
They didn't do it in God's way.

[4]Christ has completed the law. So
now everyone who believes can be
right with God.

[5]Moses explained how the law could
help a person do what God requires.
He said, "The one who does those
things will live by them." *(Leviticus 18:5)*

[6]But the way to do what God requires must begin by having faith in
him. Scripture says, "Do not say in
your heart, 'Who will go up into heav-
en?' " *(Deuteronomy 30:12)* That means to
go up into heaven and bring Christ
down. [7]"And do not say, 'Who will go
down into the grave?' " *(Deuteronomy
30:13)* That means to bring Christ up
from the dead.

[8]But what does it say? "The word is
near you. It's in your mouth and in
your heart." *(Deuteronomy 30:14)* That
means the word we are preaching. You
must put your faith in it.

[9]Say with your mouth, "Jesus is
Lord." Believe in your heart that God
raised him from the dead. Then you
will be saved. [10]With your heart you
believe and are made right with God.
With your mouth you say that Jesus
is Lord. And so you are saved. [11]Scrip-
ture says, "The one who trusts in him
will never be put to shame." *(Isaiah
28:16)*

[12]There is no difference between
those who are Jews and those who are
not. The same Lord is Lord of all. He
richly blesses everyone who calls on
him. [13]Scripture says, "Everyone who
calls on the name of the Lord will be
saved." *(Joel 2:32)*

[14]How can they call on him unless
they believe in him? How can they believe in him unless they hear about
him? How can they hear about him
unless someone preaches to them?
[15]And how can anyone preach without
being sent? It is written, "How beautiful are the feet of those who bring
good news!" *(Isaiah 52:7)*

[16]But not all the people of Israel accepted the good news. Isaiah says,
"Lord, who has believed our mes-
sage?" *(Isaiah 53:1)* [17]So faith comes from
hearing the message. And the message
that is heard is the word of Christ.

[18]But I ask, "Didn't the people of Israel hear?" Of course they did. It is
written,

"Their voice has gone out into the
  whole earth.
Their words have gone out from
  one end of the world to the
  other."   *(Psalm 19:4)*

¹⁹Again I ask, "Didn't Israel understand?" First, Moses says,

"I will use people who are not a
  nation to make you jealous.
I will use a nation that has no
  understanding to make you
  angry."   *(Deuteronomy 32:21)*

²⁰Then Isaiah boldly speaks about
what God says. God said,

"I was found by those who were
  not trying to find me.
I made myself known to those
  who were not asking for me."
                        (Isaiah 65:1)

²¹But Isaiah also speaks about what
God says concerning Israel. God said,

"All day long I have held out my
  hands.
I have held them out to a
  stubborn people who do not
  obey me."   *(Isaiah 65:2)*

GOD'S FAITHFUL PEOPLE IN ISRAEL

11 So here is what I ask. Did
God turn his back on his
people? Not at all! I myself
belong to Israel. I am one of Abraham's
children. I am from the tribe of Benjamin. ²God didn't turn his back on his
people. After all, he chose them.

Don't you know what Scripture says
about Elijah? He complained to God
about Israel. ³He said, "Lord, they have

If God says that salvation is free, why do we have to buy a Bible?

We pay for Bibles because it costs money to make them. Publishers publish them. Printers print them. Stores sell them. These companies all need to pay their workers. The price we pay for a Bible pays the workers' wages. Paul, for instance, preached the gospel but worked hard to pay his bills by making tents.

But salvation does not cost us anything. It comes from God and *is* free. The punishment for sin is death. That means separation from God forever. But God sent his Son Jesus to die in our place. Jesus did not have to die because he did not sin. But he chose to die in our place. If we ask God to forgive our sins and accept that Jesus died in our place, God will forgive us. So salvation is free for us because we do not have to pay the penalty for our sins.

checkout

Romans 10:9,10

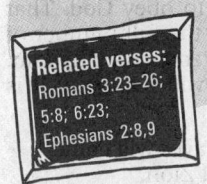

Related verses:
Romans 3:23–26;
5:8; 6:23;
Ephesians 2:8,9

killed your prophets. They have torn down your altars. I'm the only one left. And they are trying to kill me." *(1 Kings 19:10,14)*

[4]How did God answer him? God said, "I have kept 7,000 people for myself. They have not bowed down to Baal." *(1 Kings 19:18)*

[5]Some are also faithful today. They have been chosen by God's grace. [6]And if they are chosen by grace, it is no longer a matter of working for it. If it were, grace wouldn't be grace anymore.

[7]What should we say then? Israel did not receive what they wanted so badly. But those who were chosen did. God made the rest of them stubborn.

[8]It is written,

"God made it hard for them to understand.
He gave them eyes that could not see.
He gave them ears that could not hear.
And they are still like that today."
(Deuteronomy 29:4; Isaiah 29:10)

[9]David says,

"Let their feast be a trap and a snare.
Let it make Israel trip and fall.
Let Israel get what's coming to them.
[10]Let their eyes grow dark so they can't see.
Let their backs be bent forever."
(Psalm 69:22,23)

TWO KINDS OF OLIVE BRANCHES

[11]Again, here is what I ask. They didn't trip and fall once and for all time, did they? Not at all! Because Israel sinned, those who aren't Jews can be saved. That will make Israel jealous of them. [12]Israel's sin brought riches to the world. Their loss brought riches to the non-Jews. What greater riches will come when all Israel turns to God!

[13]I am talking to you who are not Jews. I am the apostle to the non-Jews. So I think the work I do for God and others is very important. [14]I hope somehow to stir up my own people to want what you have. Perhaps I can save some of them. [15]When they were not accepted, it became possible for the whole world to be brought back to God. So what will happen when they are accepted? It will be like life from the dead.

[16]The first handful of dough that is offered is holy. This makes all of the dough holy.

If the root is holy, so are the branches.

[17]Some of the natural branches have been broken off. You are a wild olive branch. But you have been joined to the tree with the other branches. Now you enjoy the life-giving sap of the olive tree root. [18]So don't think you are better than the other branches. Remember, you don't give life to the root. The root gives life to you.

[19]You will say, "Some branches were broken off so that I could be joined to the tree." [20]That's true. But they were broken off because they didn't believe. You stand only because you do believe. So don't be proud. Be afraid. [21]God didn't spare the natural branches. He won't spare you either.

[22]Think about how kind God is! Also think about how firm he is! He was hard on those who stopped following him. But he is kind to you. So you must continue to live in his kindness. If you don't, you also will be cut off.

[23]If the people of Israel do not continue in their unbelief, they will again be joined to the tree. God is able to join them to the tree again.

[24]After all, weren't you cut from a wild olive tree? Weren't you joined to an olive tree that was taken care of? And wasn't that the opposite of how things should be done? How much more easily will the natural branches be joined to their own olive tree!

ALL ISRAEL WILL BE SAVED

[25]Brothers and sisters, here is a mystery I want you to understand. It will keep you from being proud. Part of Israel has refused to obey God. That will continue until the full number of non-Jews has entered God's kingdom. [26]And so all Israel will be saved. It is written,

"The One who saves will come
from Mount Zion.

He will remove sin from Jacob.
²⁷ Here is my covenant with them.
I will take away their sins."

(Isaiah 59:20,21; 27:9;
Jeremiah 31:33,34)

²⁸ As far as the good news is concerned, the people of Israel are enemies. That is for your good. But as far as God's choice is concerned, the people of Israel are loved. That is because of God's promises to the founders of our nation. ²⁹ God does not take back his gifts. He does not change his mind about those he has chosen.

³⁰ At one time you did not obey God. But now you have received mercy because Israel did not obey. ³¹ In the same way, Israel has not been obeying God. But now they receive mercy because of God's mercy to you. ³² God has found everyone guilty of not obeying him. So now he can have mercy on everyone.

PRAISE TO GOD

³³ How very rich are God's wisdom and knowledge!
How he judges is more than we can understand!

The way he deals with people is more than we can know!
³⁴ "Who can ever know what is in the Lord's mind?
Or who can ever give him advice?"   *(Isaiah 40:13)*
³⁵ "Has anyone ever given anything to God,
so that God has to pay him back?"   *(Job 41:11)*
³⁶ All things come from him.
All things are directed by him.
All things are for his good.
May God be given the glory forever! Amen.

LIVING FOR GOD

12 Brothers and sisters, God has shown you his mercy. So I am asking you to offer up your bodies to him while you are still alive. Your bodies are a holy sacrifice that is pleasing to God. When you offer your bodies to God, you are worshiping him. ² Don't live any longer the way this world lives. Let your way of thinking be completely changed. Then you will be able to test what God

Is it OK to listen to bad music groups if you only listen to the music?

How can you listen to bad songs without hearing the words? That would be like trying to watch a video with your eyes closed. It does not make sense. You will hear the words and be affected by them even if you do not think you are listening to them. You will also set a bad example for others. Do you think others should listen to that music? You will be saying yes if *you* listen to it. Do you want to give money to the musicians who perform that music? You will if you buy their CDs. Of course, not all music is bad. Many songs have good words and are fun to listen to. Fill your mind with what is good.

checkout
Romans 12:2

Related verses:
1 Corinthians 10:31;
Philippians 4:8

wants for you. And you will agree that what he wants is right. His plan is good and pleasing and perfect.

³God's grace has been given to me. So here is what I say to every one of you. Don't think of yourself more highly than you should. Be reasonable when you think about yourself. Keep in mind the amount of faith God has given you.

⁴Each of us has one body with many parts. And the parts do not all have the same purpose. ⁵So also we are many persons. But in Christ we are one body. And each part of the body belongs to all the other parts.

⁶We all have gifts. They differ in keeping with the grace that God has given each of us. Do you have the gift of prophecy? Then use it in keeping with the faith you have. ⁷Is it your gift to serve? Then serve. Is it teaching? Then teach. ⁸Is it telling others how they should live? Then tell them. Is it giving to those who are in need? Then give freely. Is it being a leader? Then

work hard at it. Is it showing mercy? Then do it cheerfully.

LOVE

⁹Love must be honest and true. Hate what is evil. Hold on to what is good. ¹⁰Love each other deeply. Honor others more than yourselves. ¹¹Never let the fire in your heart go out. Keep it alive. Serve the Lord.

¹²When you hope, be joyful. When you suffer, be patient. When you pray, be faithful. ¹³Share with God's people who are in need. Welcome others into your homes.

¹⁴Bless those who hurt you. Bless them, and do not call down curses on them. ¹⁵Be joyful with those who are joyful. Be sad with those who are sad. ¹⁶Agree with each other. Don't be proud. Be willing to be a friend of people who aren't considered important. Don't think that you are better than others.

¹⁷Don't pay back evil with evil. Be careful to do what everyone thinks is

Is it OK to steal something back from someone who stole it from you?

It is always wrong to steal. If you think that someone stole something from you, politely ask the person about the item. You could say something like, "I see you found my pen. Thank you for finding it."

But you might be wrong. The person might have something that only *looks* like yours. If you catch someone stealing, ask the person to return what he or she stole. You can talk to a parent or teacher about the problem if that does not seem to help. But whatever you do, do not take anything without permission for any reason. You may end up taking something that really does not belong to you.

Romans 12:17,18

Related verses:
Exodus 20:15,16;
Romans 2:21

right. ¹⁸If possible, live in peace with everyone. Do that as much as you can.

¹⁹My friends, don't try to get even. Leave room for God to show his anger. It is written, "I am the One who judges people. I will pay them back," *(Deuteronomy 32:35)* says the Lord. ²⁰Do just the opposite. Scripture says,

"If your enemies are hungry, give
    them food to eat.
If they are thirsty, give them
    something to drink.
By doing those things, you will pile
    up burning coals on their
    heads."   *(Proverbs 25:21,22)*

²¹Don't let evil overcome you. Overcome evil by doing good.

OBEY THOSE IN AUTHORITY

13 All of you must be willing to obey completely those who rule over you. There are no authorities except the ones God has chosen. Those who now rule have been chosen by God. ²So when you oppose the authorities, you are opposing those whom God has appointed. Those who do that will be judged.

³If you do what is right, you won't need to be afraid of your rulers. But watch out if you do what is wrong! You don't want to be afraid of those in authority, do you? Then do what is right. The one in authority will praise you. ⁴He serves God and will do you good. But if you do wrong, watch out! The ruler doesn't carry a sword for no reason at all. He serves God. And God is carrying out his anger through him. The ruler punishes anyone who does wrong.

⁵You must obey the authorities. Then you will not be punished. You must also obey them because you know it is right.

⁶That's also why you pay taxes. The authorities serve God. Ruling takes up all their time. ⁷Give to everyone what you owe. Do you owe taxes? Then pay them. Do you owe anything else to the government? Then pay it. Do you owe respect? Then give it. Do you owe honor? Then show it.

What are taxes?

Taxes are money given to the government by the citizens of a country. This is the main way most governments get money. They use the money to run the country and provide all the services the government provides. The elected officials in the government decide how much tax we have to pay. We pay income taxes on the money we earn. We pay property taxes on the homes and land we own. We pay sales taxes on the items we buy in stores. The Bible tells us that we should not try to cheat the government out of taxes we owe.

checkout Romans 13:6

Related verses:
Mark 12:17;
1 Peter 2:13,14

MAP OF "TAXES"

LOVE, BECAUSE THE DAY IS NEAR

[8]Pay everything you owe. But you can never pay back all the love you owe each other. Those who love others have done everything the law requires. [9]Here are some commandments to think about. "Do not commit adultery." "Do not commit murder." "Do not steal." "Do not want what belongs to others." *(Exodus 20:13–15,17; Deuteronomy 5:17–19,21)* These and other commandments are all included in one rule. Here's what it is. "Love your neighbor as you love yourself." *(Leviticus 19:18)* [10]Love does not harm its neighbor. So love does everything the law requires.

[11]When you do those things, keep in mind the times we are living in. The hour has come for you to wake up from your sleep. Our full salvation is closer now than it was when we first believed in Christ. [12]The dark night of evil is nearly over. The day of Christ's return is almost here. So let us get rid of the works of darkness. Let us put on the armor of light.

[13]Let us act as we should, like people living in the daytime. Have nothing to do with wild parties. Don't get drunk. Don't take part in sexual sins or evil conduct. Don't fight with each other. Don't be jealous of anyone.

[14]Instead, put on the Lord Jesus Christ as your clothing. Don't think about how to satisfy what your sinful nature wants.

THE WEAK AND THE STRONG

14 Accept those whose faith is weak. Don't judge them where you have differences of opinion.

[2]The faith of some people allows them to eat anything. But others eat only vegetables because their faith is weak. [3]People who eat everything must not look down on those who do not. And people who don't eat everything must not judge those who do. God has accepted them.

[4]Who are you to judge someone else's servants? Whether they are faithful or not is their own master's concern. They will be faithful, because the Lord has the power to make them faithful.

[5]Some people consider one day to be more holy than another. Others think all days are the same. Each person should be absolutely sure in his own mind. [6]Those who think one day is special do it to honor the Lord. Those who eat meat do it to honor the Lord. They give thanks to God. Those who don't eat meat do it to honor the Lord. They also give thanks to God.

[7]We don't live for ourselves alone. And we don't die all by ourselves. [8]If we live, we live to honor the Lord. If we die, we die to honor the Lord. So whether we live or die, we belong to the Lord.

[9]Christ died and came back to life. He did this to become the Lord of both the dead and the living.

[10]Now then, who are you to judge your brother or sister? Why do you look down on them? We will all stand in God's courtroom to be judged. [11]It is written,

" 'You can be sure that I live,' says
    the Lord.
'And you can be just as sure that
    every knee will bow down in
    front of me.
Every tongue will tell the truth to
    God.' "   *(Isaiah 45:23)*

[12]So we will all have to explain to God the things we have done.

[13]Let us stop judging one another. Instead, make up your mind not to put anything in your brother's way that would make him trip and fall.

[14]I am absolutely sure that no food is "unclean" in itself. I say this as one who belongs to the Lord Jesus. But some people may consider a thing to be "unclean." If they do, it is "unclean" for them. [15]Your brothers and sisters may be upset by what you eat. If they are, you are no longer acting as though you love them. So don't destroy them by what you eat. Christ died for them. [16]Don't let something you consider good be spoken of as if it were evil.

[17]God's kingdom has nothing to do with eating or drinking. It is a matter of being right with God. It brings the peace and joy the Holy Spirit gives.

¹⁸Those who serve Christ in this way are pleasing to God. They are pleasing to people too.

¹⁹So let us do all we can to live in peace. And let us work hard to build each other up.

²⁰Don't destroy the work of God because of food. All food is "clean." But it is wrong for you to eat anything that causes someone else to trip and fall. ²¹Don't eat meat if it will cause your brothers and sisters to fall. Don't drink wine or do anything else that will make them fall.

²²No matter what you think about those things, keep it between yourself and God. Blessed are those who do not have to feel guilty for what they allow. ²³But those who have doubts are guilty if they eat. Their eating is not based on faith. Everything that is not based on faith is sin.

15 We who have strong faith should help the weak with their problems. We should not please only ourselves. ²We should all please our neighbors. Let us do

what is good for them. Let us build them up.

³Even Christ did not please himself. It is written, "Those who make fun of you have made fun of me also." *(Psalm 69:9)* ⁴Everything that was written in the past was written to teach us. The Scriptures give us strength to go on. They cheer us up and give us hope.

⁵Our God is a God who strengthens you and cheers you up. May he help you agree with each other as you follow Christ Jesus. ⁶Then you can give glory to God with one heart and voice. He is the God and Father of our Lord Jesus Christ.

⁷Christ has accepted you. So accept one another in order to bring praise to God.

⁸I tell you that Christ has become a servant of the Jews. He teaches us that God is true. He shows us that God will keep the promises he made to the founders of our nation. ⁹Jesus became a servant of the Jews so that people who are not Jews could give glory to God for his mercy. It is written,

Is it a sin if you're not sure if something is wrong but you still go along with it?

It is best not to do it until you find out for sure. Sometimes you do not know whether something is right or wrong. It may be a sin and you do not know it. It is still a sin even if you do not know about it. That is how it will be sometimes. You cannot know everything. Read the Bible every day so you can learn God's ways. Ask your parents or someone you trust if you are wondering about something and do not know what the Bible says about it. Do not assume that something is wrong just because you do not know about it. But do not take a chance either. Make sure something is OK to do before doing it.

checkout
Romans 14:23

Related verse:
1 Corinthians 4:4

"I will praise you among those
who aren't Jews.
I will sing praises to you."
(2 Samuel 22:50; Psalm 18:49)

[10]Again it says,

"You non-Jews, be full of joy.
Be joyful together with God's
people." *(Deuteronomy 32:43)*

[11]And again it says,

"All you non-Jews, praise the Lord.
All you nations, sing praises to
him." *(Psalm 117:1)*

[12]And Isaiah says,

"The Root of Jesse will grow up
quickly.
He will rule over the nations.
Those who aren't Jews will put
their hope in him." *(Isaiah 11:10)*

[13]May the God who gives hope fill you with great joy. May you have perfect peace as you trust in him. May the power of the Holy Spirit fill you with hope.

PAUL SERVES THE NON-JEWS

[14]My brothers and sisters, I am sure that you are full of goodness. What you know is complete. You are able to teach one another.

[15]I have written to you very boldly about some things. I wanted you to think about them again. The grace of God has allowed me [16]to serve Christ Jesus among those who aren't Jews. My duty as a priest is to preach God's good news. Then the non-Jews will become an offering that pleases God. The Holy Spirit will make the offering holy.

[17]Because I belong to Christ Jesus, I can take pride in my work for God. [18]I will not try to speak of anything except what Christ has done through me. He has been leading those who aren't Jews to obey God. He has been doing this by what I have said and done.

[19]He has given me power to do signs and miracles. He has given me the power of the Holy Spirit.

From Jerusalem all the way around to Illyricum I have finished preaching the good news about Christ. [20]I have always wanted to preach the good news where Christ was not known. I don't want to build on what someone else has started. [21]It is written,

"Those who were not told about
him will understand.
Those who have not heard will
know what it all means."
(Isaiah 52:15)

[22]That's why I have often been kept from coming to you.

PAUL PLANS TO VISIT ROME

[23]Now there is no more place for me to work in those areas. For many years I have been longing to see you. [24]So I plan to see you when I go to Spain. I hope to visit you while I am passing through. And I hope you will help me on my journey there. But first I want to enjoy being with you for a while.

[25]Now I am on my way to Jerusalem to serve God's people there. [26]The believers in Macedonia and Achaia were pleased to take an offering for those who were poor among God's people in Jerusalem. [27]They were happy to do it. And of course they owe it to them. Those who aren't Jews have shared from the Jews' spiritual blessings. So the non-Jews should share their earthly blessings with the Jews.

[28]I want to finish my task. I want to make sure that the poor in Jerusalem have received the offering. Then I will go to Spain. On my way I will visit you. [29]I know that when I come to you, I will come with the full blessing of Christ.

[30]Brothers and sisters, I am asking you through the authority of our Lord Jesus Christ to join me in my struggle by praying to God for me. Pray for me with the love the Holy Spirit provides. [31]Pray that I will be saved from those in Judea who do not believe. Pray that my work in Jerusalem will be accepted by God's people there. [32]Then, as God has planned, I will come to you with joy. Together we will be renewed.

[33]May the God who gives peace be with you all. Amen.

PERSONAL GREETINGS

16 I would like you to welcome our sister Phoebe. She serves the church in Cenchrea. [2]I ask you to receive her as one who belongs to the Lord. Receive her in the way God's people should. Give her any help she may need from you. She has been a great help to many people, including me.

³Greet Priscilla and Aquila. They work together with me in serving Christ Jesus. ⁴They have put their lives in danger for me. I am thankful for them. So are all the non-Jewish churches.

⁵Greet also the church that meets in the house of Priscilla and Aquila.

Greet my dear friend Epenetus. He was the first person in Asia Minor to become a believer in Christ.

⁶Greet Mary. She worked very hard for you.

⁷Greet Andronicus and Junias, my relatives. They have been in prison with me. They are leaders among the apostles. They became believers in Christ before I did.

⁸Greet Ampliatus. I love him as a brother in the Lord.

⁹Greet Urbanus. He works together with me in serving Christ. And greet my dear friend Stachys.

¹⁰Greet Apelles. Even though he was put to the test, he remained faithful as one who belonged to Christ.

Greet those who live in the house of Aristobulus.

¹¹Greet Herodion, my relative.

Greet the believers who live in the house of Narcissus.

¹²Greet Tryphena and Tryphosa. Those women work hard for the Lord.

Greet my dear friend Persis. She is another woman who has worked very hard for the Lord.

¹³Greet Rufus. He is a choice believer in the Lord. And greet his mother. She has been like a mother to me too.

¹⁴Greet Asyncritus, Phlegon and Hermes. Greet Patrobas, Hermas and the believers with them.

¹⁵Greet Philologus, Julia, Nereus and his sister. Greet Olympas and all of God's people with them.

¹⁶Greet one another with a holy kiss. All the churches of Christ send their greetings.

¹⁷I am warning you, brothers and sisters, to watch out for those who try to keep you from staying together. They want to trip you up. They teach you things opposite to what you have learned. Stay away from them. ¹⁸People like that are not serving Christ our Lord. They are serving only themselves. With smooth talk and with words they don't mean they fool people who don't know any better.

¹⁹Everyone has heard that you obey God. So you have filled me with joy. I want you to be wise about what is good. And I want you to have nothing to do with what is evil.

²⁰The God who gives peace will soon crush Satan under your feet.

May the grace of our Lord Jesus be with you.

²¹Timothy works together with me. He sends his greetings to you. So do Lucius, Jason and Sosipater, my relatives.

²²I, Tertius, wrote down this letter. I greet you as a believer in the Lord.

²³/²⁴Gaius sends you his greetings. He has welcomed me and the whole church here into his house.

Erastus is the director of public works here in the city. He sends you his greetings. Our brother Quartus also greets you.

²⁵May God receive glory. He is able to strengthen your faith because of the good news I preach. It is the message about Jesus Christ. It is in keeping with the mystery that was hidden for a very long time. ²⁶The mystery has now been made known through the writings of the prophets. The eternal God commanded that it be made known. He wanted all nations to believe and obey him. ²⁷May the only wise God receive glory forever through Jesus Christ. Amen.

1 Corinthians

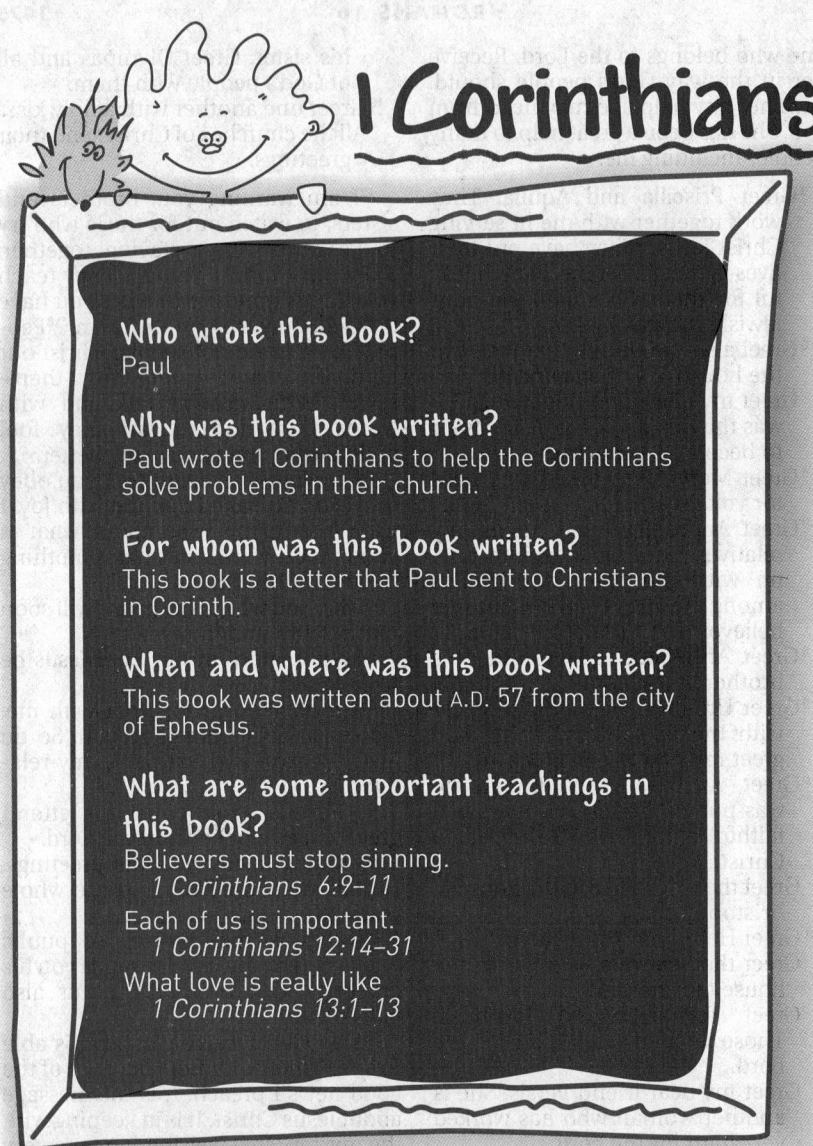

Who wrote this book?
Paul

Why was this book written?
Paul wrote 1 Corinthians to help the Corinthians solve problems in their church.

For whom was this book written?
This book is a letter that Paul sent to Christians in Corinth.

When and where was this book written?
This book was written about A.D. 57 from the city of Ephesus.

What are some important teachings in this book?
Believers must stop sinning.
1 Corinthians 6:9–11

Each of us is important.
1 Corinthians 12:14–31

What love is really like
1 Corinthians 13:1–13

---

1 I, Paul, am writing this letter. I have been chosen to be an apostle of Christ Jesus just as God planned. Our brother Sosthenes joins me in writing.

²We are sending this letter to you, the members of God's church in Corinth. You have been made holy because you belong to Christ Jesus. God has chosen you to be his holy people. He has done the same for all those everywhere who pray to our Lord Jesus Christ. Jesus is their Lord and ours.

³May God our Father and the Lord Jesus Christ give you grace and peace.

PAUL GIVES THANKS

⁴I always thank God for you. I thank him because of the grace he has given to you who belong to Christ Jesus. ⁵You have been blessed in every way because of him. All your teaching of the truth is better. Your understanding of

it is more complete. ⁶Our witness about Christ has been proved to be true in you.

⁷There is no gift of the Holy Spirit that you don't have. You are full of hope as you wait for our Lord Jesus Christ to come again. ⁸God will keep you strong to the very end. Then you will be without blame on the day our Lord Jesus Christ returns.

⁹God is faithful. He has chosen you to share life with his Son, Jesus Christ our Lord.

TAKING SIDES IN THE CHURCH

¹⁰Brothers and sisters, I ask all of you to agree with one another. I make my appeal in the name of our Lord Jesus Christ. Then you won't take sides. You will be in complete agreement in all that you think.

¹¹My brothers and sisters, some people who live in Chloe's house have told me you are arguing with each other. ¹²Here is what I mean. One of you says, "I follow Paul." Another says, "I follow Apollos." Another says, "I follow Peter." And still another says, "I follow Christ."

¹³Does Christ take sides? Did Paul die on the cross for you? Were you baptized in the name of Paul? ¹⁴I'm thankful that I didn't baptize any of you except Crispus and Gaius. ¹⁵No one can say that you were baptized in my name.

¹⁶It's true that I also baptized those who live in the house of Stephanas. Besides that, I don't remember if I baptized anyone else.

¹⁷Christ did not send me to baptize. He sent me to preach the good news. He commanded me not to use the kind of wisdom that people commonly use. That would take all the power away from the cross of Christ.

CHRIST IS GOD'S POWER AND WISDOM

¹⁸The message of the cross seems foolish to those who are lost and dying. But it is God's power to us who are being saved. ¹⁹It is written,

> "I will destroy the wisdom of those
> who are wise.

> I will do away with the cleverness
> of those who think they are so
> smart." *(Isaiah 29:14)*

²⁰Where is the wise person? Where is the educated person? Where are the great thinkers of this world? Hasn't God made the wisdom of the world foolish? ²¹God wisely planned that the world would not know him through its own wisdom. It pleased God to use the foolish things we preach to save those who believe.

²²Jews require miraculous signs. Greeks look for wisdom. ²³But we preach about Christ and his death on the cross. That is very hard for Jews to accept. And everyone else thinks it's foolish.

²⁴But there are those God has chosen, both Jews and others. To them Christ is God's power and God's wisdom. ²⁵The foolish things of God are wiser than human wisdom. The weakness of God is stronger than human strength.

²⁶Brothers and sisters, think of what you were when God chose you. Not many of you were considered wise by human standards. Not many of you were powerful. Not many of you belonged to important families.

²⁷But God chose the foolish things of the world to shame the wise. He chose the weak things of the world to shame the strong. ²⁸God chose the things of this world that are common and looked down on. He chose what is not considered to be important to do away with what is considered to be important. ²⁹So no one can brag to God.

³⁰Because of what God has done, you belong to Christ Jesus. He has become God's wisdom for us. He makes us right with God. He makes us holy and sets us free. ³¹It is written, "The one who brags should brag about what the Lord has done." *(Jeremiah 9:24)*

2 Brothers and sisters, when I came to you I didn't come with fancy words or great wisdom. I preached to you the truth about God's love. ²I made up my mind to pay attention to only one thing while I was with you. That one thing was Jesus Christ and his death on the cross.

³When I came to you, I was weak and

afraid and trembling all over. [4]I didn't preach my message with clever and compelling words. As I preached, the Holy Spirit showed his power. [5]That was so you would believe not because of human wisdom but because of God's power.

WISDOM FROM THE HOLY SPIRIT

[6]The words we speak to those who have grown in the faith are wise. Our words are different from the words of the wise people or rulers of this world. People like that aren't going anywhere. [7]No, we speak about God's secret wisdom. His wisdom has been hidden. But before time began, God planned that his wisdom would bring us heavenly glory.

[8]None of the rulers of this world understood God's wisdom. If they had, they would not have nailed the Lord of glory to the cross. [9]It is written,

"No eye has seen,
 no ear has heard,
 no mind has known
  what God has prepared for those
  who love him."　　*(Isaiah 64:4)*

[10]But God has shown it to us through his Spirit.

The Spirit understands all things. He understands even the deep things of God. [11]Who can know the thoughts of another person? Only a person's own spirit can know them. In the same way, only the Spirit of God knows God's thoughts.

[12]We have not received the spirit of the world. We have received the Spirit who is from God. The Spirit helps us understand what God has freely given us.

[13]That is what we speak about. We don't use words taught to us by people. We use words taught to us by the Holy Spirit. We use the words of the Spirit to teach the truths of the Spirit.

[14]Some people don't have the Holy Spirit. They don't accept the things that come from the Spirit of God. Things like that are foolish to them. They can't understand them. In fact, such things can't be understood without the Spirit's help.

[15]Everyone who has the Spirit can judge all things. But no one can judge those who have the Spirit. It is written,

[16]"Who can ever know what is in the
  Lord's mind?
 Can anyone ever teach him?"
　　　　　　　　(Isaiah 40:13)

But we have the mind of Christ.

TAKING SIDES IN THE CHURCH

3 Brothers and sisters, I couldn't speak to you as if you were guided by the Holy Spirit. I had to speak to you as if you were following the ways of the world. You aren't growing as Christ wants you to. You are still like babies. [2]The words I spoke to you were like milk, not like solid food. You weren't ready for solid food yet. And you still aren't ready for it.

[3]You are still following the ways of the world. Some of you are jealous. Some of you argue. So aren't you following the ways of the world? Aren't you acting like ordinary human beings? [4]One of you says, "I follow Paul." Another says, "I follow Apollos." Aren't you acting like ordinary human beings?

[5]After all, what is Apollos? And what is Paul? We are only people who serve. We helped you to believe. The Lord has given each of us our own work to do. [6]I planted the seed. Apollos watered it. But God made it grow.

[7]So the one who plants is not important. The one who waters is not important. It is God who makes things grow. He is the One who is important. [8]The one who plants and the one who waters have the same purpose. The Lord will give each of us a reward for our work. [9]We work together with God. You are like God's field. You are like his building.

[10]God has given me the grace to lay a foundation as a master builder. Now someone else is building on it. But each one should build carefully. [11]No one can lay any other foundation than the one that has already been laid. That foundation is Jesus Christ.

[12]A person may build on it using gold, silver, jewels, wood, hay or straw. [13]But each person's work will be shown for what it is. On judgment day it will

be brought to light. It will be put through fire. The fire will test how good everyone's work is. ¹⁴If the building doesn't burn up, God will give the builder a reward for his work. ¹⁵If the building burns up, the builder will lose everything. The builder will be saved, but only like one escaping through the flames.

¹⁶Don't you know that you yourselves are God's temple? God's Spirit lives in you. ¹⁷If anyone destroys God's temple, God will destroy him. God's temple is holy. And you are that temple.

¹⁸Don't fool yourselves. Suppose some of you think you are wise by the standards of the world. Then you should become a "fool" so that you can become wise.

¹⁹The wisdom of this world is foolish in God's eyes. It is written, "God catches wise people in their own tricks." *(Job 5:13)* ²⁰It is also written, "The Lord knows that the thoughts of the wise don't amount to anything." *(Psalm 94:11)*

²¹So no more bragging about human beings! All things are yours. ²²That means Paul or Apollos or Peter or the world or life or death or the present or the future. All are yours. ²³You are joined to Christ and belong to him. And Christ is joined to God.

APOSTLES OF CHRIST

4 Here is how you should think of us. We serve Christ. We are trusted with God's secret truth. ²Those who have been given a trust must prove that they are faithful.

³I care very little if I am judged by you or by any human court. I don't even judge myself. ⁴I don't feel I have done anything wrong. But that doesn't mean I'm not guilty. The Lord judges me.

⁵So don't judge anything before the appointed time. Wait until the Lord returns. He will bring to light what is hidden in the dark. He will show the real reasons why people do what they do. At that time each person will receive praise from God.

⁶Brothers and sisters, I have used myself and Apollos as examples to help you. You can learn from us the meaning of the saying, "Don't go beyond what is written." Then you won't be proud that you follow one person instead of another.

⁷Who makes you different from anyone else? What do you have that you

How does God know what we're saying if we're praying in our head?

God knows everything, even when we keep it to ourselves. He knows every thought of every person on earth. He knows what is in everyone's head. Nothing that anyone thinks or feels is hidden from God.

Praying silently means focusing our thoughts on God and talking to him in our head. He hears every silent prayer.

Of course, sometimes it is better to pray out loud, like when we are praying with another person. And praying out loud can help us concentrate when we are praying on our own. But God hears us either way, whether we say the words or just think them.

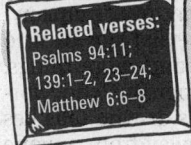

Related verses:
Psalms 94:11;
139:1–2, 23–24;
Matthew 6:6–8

checkout
1 Corinthians 2:11

did not receive? And if you did receive it, why do you brag as though you did not?

⁸You already have everything you want, don't you? Have you already become rich? Have you begun to rule as kings? And did you do that without us? I wish that you really had begun to rule. Then we could rule with you!

⁹It seems to me that God has put us apostles on display at the end of a parade. We are like men sentenced to die in front of a crowd. We have been made a show for the whole creation to see. Angels and people are staring at us.

¹⁰We are fools for Christ. But you are so wise in Christ! We are weak. But you are so strong! You are honored. But we are looked down on! ¹¹Up to this very hour we are hungry and thirsty. We are dressed in rags. We are being treated badly. We have no homes. ¹²We work hard with our own hands. When others call down a curse on us, we bless them. When we are attacked, we put up with it. ¹³When others say bad things about us, we answer kindly. Up to this moment we have become the world's garbage. We are everybody's trash.

¹⁴I am not writing this to shame you. You are my dear children, and I want to warn you. ¹⁵You may have 10,000 believers in Christ watching over you. But you don't have many fathers. I became your father by serving Christ Jesus and telling you the good news. ¹⁶So I'm asking you to follow my example.

¹⁷That's the reason I'm sending Timothy to you. He is like a son to me, and I love him. He is faithful in serving the Lord. He will remind you of my way of life in serving Christ Jesus. And that agrees with what I teach everywhere in every church.

¹⁸Some of you have become proud. You act as if I weren't coming to you. ¹⁹But I will come very soon, if that's what the Lord wants. Then I will find out how those proud people are talking. I will also find out what power they have. ²⁰The kingdom of God is not a matter of talk. It is a matter of power. ²¹Which do you want? Should I come to you with a whip? Or should I come in love and with a gentle spirit?

THROW THE EVIL PERSON OUT!

5 It is actually reported that there is sexual sin among you. I'm told that a man is living with his father's wife and is having sex with her. Even people who do not know God don't commit that sin. ²And you are proud! Shouldn't you be filled with sadness instead? Shouldn't you have put the man who did that out of your church?

³Even though I am not right there with you, I am with you in spirit. And I have already judged the one who did that, just as if I were there.

⁴When you come together in the name of our Lord Jesus, I will be with you in spirit. The power of our Lord Jesus will also be with you. ⁵When you come together like that, hand that man over to Satan. Then his sinful nature will be destroyed. His spirit will be saved on the day the Lord returns.

⁶Your bragging is not good. It is like yeast. Don't you know that just a little yeast works its way through the whole batch of dough? ⁷Get rid of the old yeast. Be like a new batch of dough without yeast. That is what you really are, because Christ has been offered up for us. He is our Passover lamb.

⁸So let us keep the Feast, but not with the old yeast. I'm talking about yeast that is full of hatred and evil. Let us keep the Feast with bread made without yeast. Let us do it with bread that is honest and true.

⁹I wrote a letter to you to tell you to stay away from people who commit sexual sins. ¹⁰I didn't mean the people of this world who sin that way or who always want more and more. I didn't mean those who cheat or who worship statues of gods. In that case you would have to leave this world!

¹¹But here is what I am writing to you. You must stay away from anyone who claims to be a believer but who does those things. Stay away from anyone who commits sexual sins or who always wants more and more things. Stay away from a person who worships statues of gods or who tells lies about others. Stay away from anyone

who gets drunk or who cheats. Don't even eat with a person like that.

¹²Is it my business to judge those outside the church? Aren't you supposed to judge those inside the church? ¹³God will judge those outside. Scripture says, "Get rid of that evil person!" *(Deuteronomy 17:7; 19:19; 21:21; 22:21,24; 24:7)*

DO NOT TAKE BELIEVERS TO COURT

6 Suppose one of you wants to bring a charge against another believer. Should you take it to the ungodly to be judged? Why not take it to God's people?

²Don't you know that God's people will judge the world? And if you are going to judge the world, aren't you able to judge small cases? ³Don't you know that we will judge angels? Then we should be able to judge the things of this life even more!

⁴So if you want to press charges in matters like that, appoint as judges members of the church who aren't very important! ⁵I say this to shame

you. Is it possible that no one among you is wise enough to judge matters between believers? ⁶Instead, one believer goes to court against another. And this happens in front of unbelievers!

⁷The very fact that you take another believer to court means you have lost the battle already. Why not be treated wrongly? Why not be cheated? ⁸Instead, you yourselves cheat and do wrong. And you do it to your brothers and sisters.

⁹Don't you know that evil people will not receive God's kingdom? Don't be fooled. Those who commit sexual sins will not receive the kingdom. Neither will those who worship statues of gods or commit adultery. Neither will men who are prostitutes or who commit homosexual acts. ¹⁰Neither will thieves or those who always want more and more. Neither will those who are often drunk or tell lies or cheat. People who live like that will not receive God's kingdom.

¹¹Some of you used to do those things. But your sins were washed

What should I do when kids are mean to me?

You may think that you'll feel better by getting even, but you won't. This will be difficult, but you should not be mean back. Instead, you should pray for them. That's what God expects his people to do. God's way always works out best. If you respond God's way, you'll feel better about yourself, and you may even help those kids change when they see your good example. If you have to, avoid them. Don't let their meanness get to you. If they threaten to hurt you physically, you should tell an adult right away.

checkout 1 Corinthians 4:12,13

Related verses:
Romans 12:20–21;
1 Peter 2:21–23

away. You were made holy. You were made right with God. All of that was done in the name of the Lord Jesus Christ and by the Spirit of our God.

SEXUAL SINS

[12]Some of you say, "Everything is permitted for me." But not everything is good for me. Again some of you say, "Everything is permitted for me." But I will not be controlled by anything. [13]Some of you say, "Food is for the stomach. And the stomach is for food." But God will destroy both of them.

The body is not meant for sexual sins. The body is meant for the Lord. And the Lord is meant for the body. [14]By his power God raised the Lord from the dead. He will also raise us up.

[15]Don't you know that your bodies belong to the body of Christ? Should I take what belongs to Christ and join it to a prostitute? Never! [16]Don't you know that when you join yourself to a prostitute, you become one with her in body? Scripture says, "The two will become one." *(Genesis 2:24)* [17]But anyone who is joined to the Lord becomes one with him in spirit.

[18]Keep far away from sexual sins. All the other sins a person commits are outside his body. But sexual sins are sins against one's own body.

[19]Don't you know that your bodies are temples of the Holy Spirit? The Spirit is in you. You have received him from God. You do not belong to yourselves. [20]Christ has paid the price for you. So use your bodies in a way that honors God.

MARRIAGE

7 Now I want to deal with the things you wrote me about. Some of you say, "It is good for a man not to have sex with a woman." [2]But since there is so much sexual sin, each man should have his own wife. And each woman should have her own husband. [3]A husband should satisfy his wife's sexual needs. And a wife should satisfy her husband's sexual needs.

[4]The wife's body does not belong only to her. It also belongs to her husband. In the same way, the husband's body does not belong only to him. It also belongs to his wife. [5]You shouldn't stop giving yourselves to each other except when you both agree to do so. And that should be only to give your-

KIDS' QUESTION

What are morals?

Morals are standards for right and wrong living. A person's morals are the rules that he or she follows for doing one thing and not another. People live by many different moral rules. But only God can say what is right for all people everywhere all the time. God has only one set of moral rules that he wants everyone to follow. Wise people live by God's morals. For example, they do not wonder whether they should steal things. They obey the rule against stealing because they know that God says it is wrong

checkout 1 Corinthians 6:9,10

Related verses:
Ephesians 5:1;
James 1:21

selves time to pray for a while. Then you should come together again. In that way, Satan will not tempt you when you can't control yourselves.

⁶I say those things to you as my advice, not as a command. ⁷I wish all of you were like me. But you each have your own gift from God. One has this gift. Another has that.

⁸I speak to those who are not married. I also speak to widows. It is good for you to stay single like me. ⁹But if you can't control yourselves, you should get married. It is better to get married than to burn with sexual longing.

¹⁰I give a command to those who are married. It is a direct command from the Lord, not from me. A wife must not leave her husband. ¹¹But if she does, she must not get married again. Or she can go back to her husband. And a husband must not divorce his wife.

¹²I also have something to say to ev-eryone else. It is from me, not a direct command from the Lord. Suppose a brother has a wife who is not a believer. If she is willing to live with him, he must not divorce her. ¹³And suppose a woman has a husband who is not a believer. If he is willing to live with her, she must not divorce him. ¹⁴The unbelieving husband has been made holy through his wife. The unbelieving wife has been made holy through her believing husband. If that were not the case, your children would not be pure and clean. But as it is, they are holy.

¹⁵If the unbeliever leaves, let that person go. In that case, a believing man or woman does not have to stay married. God wants us to live in peace. ¹⁶Wife, how do you know if you can save your husband? Husband, how do you know if you can save your wife?

¹⁷But each of you should remain in the place in life that the Lord has given you. Stay as you were when God chose

Why shouldn't we take drugs?

It is OK to take drugs that a doctor gives us as long as we take them as he or she says we should. Those kinds of drugs are called prescription medicine. Doctors give us these kinds of drugs to help us get well when we are sick. But there are many other drugs that are not medicines at all. They are bad for us. They affect our brains so that we cannot think right. They can even kill us. Some people use these drugs because they make them feel good for a little while. But often they get hooked and the drugs take over their lives. These drugs are so bad for us that they are against the law. We should not put anything into our bodies that will hurt us or control us because our bodies are the temple of the Holy Spirit. And we should not break the law either. That is why we should not take illegal drugs.

checkout
1 Corinthians 6:19,20

Related verses:
Romans 13:1;
Ephesians 5:18

you. That's the rule all the churches must follow.

¹⁸Was a man already circumcised when God chose him? Then he should not become uncircumcised. Was he uncircumcised when God chose him? Then he should not be circumcised. ¹⁹Being circumcised means nothing. Being uncircumcised means nothing. Doing what God commands is what counts.

²⁰Each of you should stay as you were when God chose you.

²¹Were you a slave when God chose you? Don't let it trouble you. But if you can get your master to set you free, do it. ²²Those who were slaves when the Lord chose them are now the Lord's free people. Those who were free when God chose them are now slaves of Christ. ²³Christ has paid the price for you. Don't become slaves of human beings.

²⁴Brothers and sisters, you are accountable to God. So all of you should stay as you were when God chose you.

²⁵Now I want to say something about virgins. I have no direct command from the Lord. But I give my opinion. Because of the Lord's mercy, I give it as one who can be trusted.

²⁶Times are hard for you right now. So I think it's good for you to stay as you are. ²⁷Are you married? Then don't get a divorce. Are you single? Then don't look for a wife. ²⁸But if you get married, you have not sinned. And if a virgin gets married, she has not sinned. But those who get married will have many troubles in this life. I want to save you from that.

²⁹Brothers and sisters, what I mean is that the time is short. From now on, those who have a husband or wife should live as if they did not. ³⁰Those who are sad should live as if they were not. Those who are happy should live as if they were not. Those who buy something should live as if it were not theirs to keep. ³¹Those who use the things of the world should not become all wrapped up in them. The world as it now exists is passing away.

³²I don't want you to have anything to worry about. A single man is concerned about the Lord's matters. He wants to know how he can please the Lord. ³³But a married man is concerned about the matters of this world. He wants to know how he can please his wife. ³⁴His concerns pull him in two directions.

A single woman or a virgin is concerned about the Lord's matters. She wants to serve the Lord with both body and spirit. But a married woman is concerned about the matters of this world. She wants to know how she can please her husband.

³⁵I'm saying those things for your own good. I'm not trying to hold you back. I want you to be free to live in a way that is right. I want you to give yourselves completely to the Lord.

³⁶Suppose a man thinks he is not acting properly toward the virgin he has promised to marry. Suppose she is getting old, and he feels that he should marry her. He should do as he wants. He is not sinning. They should get married.

³⁷But suppose the man has decided not to marry the virgin. And suppose he has no compelling need to get married and can control himself. If he has made up his mind not to get married, he also does the right thing.

³⁸So then, the man who marries the virgin does the right thing. But the man who doesn't marry her does an even better thing.

³⁹A woman has to stay married to her husband as long as he lives. If he dies, she is free to marry anyone she wants to. But the one she marries must belong to the Lord. ⁴⁰In my opinion, she is happier if she stays single. And I also think that I am led by the Spirit of God in saying that.

FOOD OFFERED TO STATUES OF GODS

8 Now I want to deal with food offered to statues of gods.

We know that we all have knowledge. Knowledge makes people proud. But love builds them up. ²Those who think they know something still don't know as they should. ³But those who love God are known by God.

⁴So then, here is what I say about eating food that is offered to statues of gods. We know that a god made by hu-

man hands is really nothing at all in the world. We know there is only one God. ⁵There may be so-called gods either in heaven or on earth. In fact, there are many "gods" and many "lords." ⁶But for us there is only one God. He is the Father. All things came from him, and we live for him. And there is only one Lord. He is Jesus Christ. All things came because of him, and we live because of him.

⁷But not everyone knows that. Some people still think that statues of gods are real gods. When they eat food that was offered to statues of gods, they think of it as food that was offered to real gods. And because they have a weak sense of what is right and wrong, they feel guilty. ⁸But food doesn't bring us close to God. We are no worse if we don't eat. We are no better if we do eat.

⁹But be careful how you use your freedom. Be sure it doesn't trip up someone who is weaker than you.

¹⁰Suppose you who have that knowledge are eating in a temple of one of those gods. And suppose someone who has a weak sense of what is right and wrong sees you. Won't that person become bold and eat what has been offered to statues of gods? ¹¹If so, then your knowledge destroys that weak brother or sister for whom Christ died.

¹²When you sin against other believers in that way, you harm their weak sense of what is right and wrong. By doing that you sin against Christ.

¹³So what should I do if what I eat causes my brother or sister to fall into sin? I will never eat meat again. In that way, I will not cause them to fall.

THE RIGHTS OF AN APOSTLE

9 Am I not free? Am I not an apostle? Haven't I seen Jesus our Lord? Aren't you the result of my work for the Lord? ²Even though others may not think of me as an apostle, I am certainly one to you! You are the proof that I am the Lord's apostle. ³That is what I say to stand up for myself when people judge me.

⁴Don't we have the right to eat and drink? ⁵Don't we have the right to take a believing wife with us when we trav-el? The other apostles do. The Lord's brothers do. Peter does. ⁶Or are Barnabas and I the only ones who have to work for a living?

⁷Who serves as a soldier but doesn't get paid? Who plants a vineyard but doesn't eat any of its grapes? Who takes care of a flock but doesn't drink any of the milk? ⁸Do I say that from only a human point of view? The Law says the same thing.

⁹Here is what is written in the Law of Moses. "Do not stop an ox from eating while it helps separate the grain from the straw." *(Deuteronomy 25:4)* Is it oxen that God is concerned about? ¹⁰Doesn't he say that for us? Yes, it was written for us. When a farmer plows and separates the grain, he does it because he hopes to share in the crop.

¹¹We have planted spiritual seed among you. Is it too much to ask that we receive from you some of the things we need? ¹²Others have the right to receive help from you. Don't we have even more right to do so?

But we didn't use that right. No, we have put up with everything. We didn't want to keep the good news of Christ from spreading.

¹³Don't you know that those who work in the temple get their food from the temple? Don't you know that those who serve at the altar eat from what is offered on the altar? ¹⁴In the same way, those who preach the good news should receive their living from their work. That is what the Lord has commanded.

¹⁵But I haven't used any of those rights. And I'm not writing because I hope you will do things like that for me. I would rather die than have anyone take away my pride in my work. ¹⁶But when I preach the good news, I can't brag. I have to preach it. How terrible it will be for me if I do not preach the good news!

¹⁷If I preach because I want to, I get a reward. If I preach because I have to, I'm only doing my duty. ¹⁸Then what reward do I get? Here is what it is. I am able to preach the good news free of charge. And I can do it without making use of my rights when I preach it.

¹⁹I am free. I don't belong to anyone. But I make myself a slave to every-

one. I do it to win as many as I can to Christ.

²⁰To the Jews I became like a Jew. That was to win the Jews. To those under the law I became like one who was under the law, even though I myself am not under the law. That was to win those under the law. ²¹To those who don't have the law I became like one who doesn't have the law. I am not free from God's law. I am under Christ's law. Now I can win those who don't have the law. ²²To those who are weak I became weak. That was to win the weak.

I have become all things to all people so that in all possible ways I might save some. ²³I do all of that because of the good news. And I want to share in its blessings.

²⁴In a race all the runners run. But only one gets the prize. You know that, don't you? So run in a way that will get you the prize. ²⁵All who take part in the games train hard. They do it to get a crown that will not last. But we do it to get a crown that will last forever.

²⁶So I do not run like someone who doesn't run toward the finish line. I do not fight like a boxer who hits nothing but air. ²⁷No, I train my body and bring it under control. Then after I have preached to others, I myself will not break the rules and fail to win the prize.

WARNINGS FROM ISRAEL'S HISTORY

10 Brothers and sisters, here is what I want you to know about our people who lived long ago. They were all led by the cloud. They all walked through the Red Sea. ²They were all baptized into Moses in the cloud and in the sea. ³They all ate the same supernatural food. ⁴They all drank the same supernatural water. They drank from the supernatural rock that went with them. That rock was Christ.

Where does the money I give to the church go?

It goes to the church's bank account, and it stays there until the church treasurer writes checks to pay the church's expenses. The church gives money to missions and needy people and has to pay for the building, heat, light, phone bills, postage, church school supplies, pastors' salaries, staff salaries and other things.

In most churches, people put their money in the offering plate when it is passed. After every offering, the money is collected, counted and put in a bank.

A gift to God's people is a gift to God. We should give because we are thankful for all God has given us.

checkout **1 Corinthians 9:14**

JASON'S IMAGINATION

HEAVEN BOUND

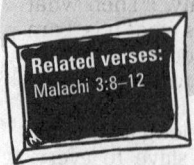

Related verses: Malachi 3:8–12

⁵But God was not pleased with most of them. Their bodies were scattered all over the desert.

⁶Now those things happened as examples for us. They are supposed to keep us from longing for evil things, as the people of Israel did.

⁷So don't worship statues of gods, as some of them did. It is written, "The people sat down to eat and drink. Then they got up to dance wildly in front of their god." *(Exodus 32:6)* ⁸We should not commit sexual sins, as some of them did. In one day 23,000 of them died. ⁹We should not put the Lord to the test, as some of them did. They were killed by snakes. ¹⁰Don't tell your leaders how unhappy you are with them. That's what some of the people of Israel did. And they were killed by the destroying angel.

¹¹Those things happened to them as examples for us. They were written down to warn us who are living at the time when God's work is being com-pleted. ¹²So be careful. When you think you are standing firm, you might fall.

¹³You are tempted in the same way all other human beings are. God is faithful. He will not let you be tempted any more than you can take. But when you are tempted, God will give you a way out so that you can stand up under it.

SHARING IN THE BODY AND BLOOD OF CHRIST

¹⁴My dear friends, run away from statues of gods. Don't worship them. ¹⁵I'm talking to people who are reasonable. Judge for yourselves what I say.

¹⁶When we give thanks for the cup at the Lord's Supper, aren't we sharing in the blood of Christ? When we break the bread, aren't we sharing in the body of Christ? ¹⁷Just as there is one loaf, so we who are many are one body. We all eat from the one loaf.

¹⁸Think about the people of Israel. Don't those who eat the offerings

Why did God put scary stories in the Bible?

The Bible tells true stories about real people. Some of the stories tell about bad things that can happen when we choose to do wrong. Sometimes those stories are scary. The Bible has stories like that to teach us, not to make us afraid. They tell us what to avoid. God wants to show us what we should do and how we should live.

And when we disobey him or do something bad, the results can be quite scary.

checkout
1 Corinthians 10:11

Related verses:
Deuteronomy
30:19,20

share in the altar? ¹⁹Do I mean that what is offered to a statue of a god is anything? Do I mean that a statue of a god is anything? ²⁰No! But what is offered by those who worship statues of gods is really offered to demons. It is not offered to God. I don't want you to be sharing with demons.

²¹You can't drink the cup of the Lord and the cup of demons too. You can't have a part in both the Lord's table and the table of demons. ²²Are we trying to make the Lord jealous? Are we stronger than he is?

THE BELIEVER'S FREEDOM

²³You say, "Everything is permitted." But not everything is good for us. Again you say, "Everything is permitted." But not everything builds us up. ²⁴We should not look out for our own interests. Instead, we should look out for the interests of others.

²⁵Eat anything that is sold in the meat market. Don't ask if it's right or wrong. ²⁶Scripture says, "The earth belongs to the Lord. And so does everything in it." *(Psalm 24:1)*

²⁷Suppose an unbeliever invites you to a meal and you want to go. Then eat anything that is put in front of you. Don't ask if it's right or wrong.

²⁸But suppose someone says to you, "This food has been offered to a statue of a god." Then don't eat it. Keep in mind the good of the one who told you. And don't eat because of a sense of what is right and wrong. ²⁹I'm talking about the other person's sense of what is right and wrong, not yours.

Why should my freedom be judged by what someone else thinks? ³⁰Suppose I give thanks when I eat. Then why should I be blamed for eating food I thank God for?

³¹So eat and drink and do everything else for the glory of God. ³²Don't do anything that causes another person to trip and fall. It doesn't matter if that person is a Jew or a Greek or a member of God's church.

³³Follow my example. I try to please everyone in every way. I'm not looking out for what is good for me. I'm looking out for the interests of others. I do it so that they might be saved.

Is it OK to lie to stop a friend from getting hurt?

You do not have to lie to stop your friends from getting hurt. You can usually think of better ways. For example, you can get the help of an adult who knows and cares about your friend. If the friend is worried about getting into trouble, the adult may be able to help. There are many other ways to help a friend besides lying. God will not force you to lie. You may think that lying will keep someone from getting hurt. But actually it will make many things worse.

checkout

1 Corinthians 10:13

Related verses:
Zephaniah 3:13;
Colossians 3:9

11

Follow my example, just as I follow the example of Christ.

PROPER WORSHIP

²I praise you for being faithful in remembering me. I also praise you for staying true to all my teachings, just as I gave them to you.

³Now I want you to know that the head of every man is Christ. The head of the woman is the man. And the head of Christ is God. ⁴Every man who prays or prophesies with his head covered brings shame on his head. ⁵And every woman who prays or prophesies with her head uncovered brings shame on her head. It is just as if her head were shaved.

⁶What if a woman does not cover her head? She should have her hair cut off. But it is shameful for her to cut her hair or shave it off. So she should cover her head.

⁷A man should not cover his head. He is the likeness and glory of God. But the woman is the glory of the man. ⁸The man did not come from the woman. The woman came from the man.

⁹Also, the man was not created for the woman. The woman was created for the man. ¹⁰That's why a woman should have her head covered. It shows that she is under authority. She should also cover her head because of the angels.

¹¹But here is how things are for those who belong to the Lord. The woman is not independent of the man. And the man is not independent of the woman. ¹²The woman came from the man, and the man is born from the woman. But everything comes from God.

¹³You be the judge. Is it proper for a woman to pray to God without covering her head? ¹⁴Suppose a man has long hair. Doesn't the very nature of things teach you that it is shameful? ¹⁵And suppose a woman has long hair. Doesn't the very nature of things teach you that it is her glory? Long hair is given to her as a covering.

¹⁶If anyone wants to argue about

Are things always either right or wrong?

Not every choice you make is either right or wrong. Sometimes you just like certain things more than others. It is not right or wrong to like strawberry ice cream more than chocolate. It is just a preference. Or you might have two toys to choose from. You choose one even though either one would have been all right to choose. Sometimes you have to choose between what is *good* and what is *better*. Parents and other wise people can give you good advice about those kinds of choices. Not *all* choices are either right or wrong.

checkout

1 Corinthians 10:23,24

Related verses:
Galatians 5:13,14;
James 1:5

that, we don't have any other practice. And God's churches don't either.

THE LORD'S SUPPER

[17]In the following matters, I don't praise you. Your meetings do more harm than good. [18]First, here is what people are telling me. When you come together as a church, you take sides. And in some ways I believe it. [19]No doubt you need to take sides in order to show which of you God agrees with! [20]When you come together, it is not the Lord's Supper you eat. [21]As you eat, each of you goes ahead without waiting for anyone else. One remains hungry and another gets drunk. [22]Don't you have homes to eat and drink in? Or do you think so little of God's church that you shame those in it who have nothing? What should I say to you? Should I praise you for that? Certainly not!

[23]I passed on to you what I received from the Lord. On the night the Lord Jesus was handed over to his enemies, he took bread. [24]When he had given thanks, he broke it. He said, "This is my body. It is given for you. Every time you eat it, do it in memory of me." [25]In the same way, after supper he took the cup. He said, "This cup is the new covenant in my blood. Every time you drink it, do it in memory of me."

[26]When you eat the bread and drink the cup, you are announcing the Lord's death until he comes again.

[27]So do not eat the bread or drink the cup of the Lord in a way that isn't worthy of him. If you do, you will be guilty of sinning against the body and blood of the Lord.

[28]A person should take a careful look at himself before he eats the bread and drinks from the cup. [29]Anyone who eats and drinks must recognize the body of the Lord. If he doesn't, God will judge him for it. [30]That is why many of you are weak and sick. That is why a number of you have died.

[31]We should judge ourselves. Then we would not be found guilty. [32]When the Lord judges us, he corrects us. Then we will not be judged along with the rest of the world.

[33]My brothers and sisters, when you come together to eat, wait for each other. [34]Those who are hungry should eat at home. Then when you come together, you will not be judged.

When I come, I will give you more directions.

GIFTS OF THE HOLY SPIRIT

12 Brothers and sisters, I want you to know about the gifts of the Holy Spirit. [2]You know that at one time you were unbelievers. You were somehow drawn away to worship statues of gods that couldn't even speak. [3]So I tell you that no one who is speaking with the help of God's Spirit says, "May Jesus be cursed." And without the help of the Holy Spirit no one can say, "Jesus is Lord."

[4]There are different kinds of gifts. But they are all given by the same Spirit. [5]There are different ways to serve. But they all come from the same Lord. [6]There are different ways to work. But the same God makes it possible for all of us to have all those different things.

[7]The Holy Spirit is given to each of us in a special way. That is for the good of all. [8]To some people the Spirit gives the message of wisdom. To others the same Spirit gives the message of knowledge. [9]To others the same Spirit gives faith. To others that one Spirit gives gifts of healing. [10]To others he gives the power to do miracles. To others he gives the ability to prophesy. To others he gives the ability to tell the spirits apart. To others he gives the ability to speak in different kinds of languages they had not known before. And to still others he gives the ability to explain what was said in those languages.

[11]All of the gifts are produced by one and the same Spirit. He gives them to each person, just as he decides.

ONE BODY BUT MANY PARTS

[12]There is one body. But it has many parts. Even though it has many parts, they make up one body. It is the same with Christ. [13]We were all baptized by one Holy Spirit into one body. It didn't matter whether we were Jews or Greeks, slaves or free people. We were all given the same Spirit to drink.

¹⁴The body is not made up of just one part. It has many parts. ¹⁵Suppose the foot says, "I am not a hand. So I don't belong to the body." It is still part of the body. ¹⁶And suppose the ear says, "I am not an eye. So I don't belong to the body." It is still part of the body. ¹⁷If the whole body were an eye, how could it hear? If the whole body were an ear, how could it smell? ¹⁸God has placed each part in the body just as he wanted it to be. ¹⁹If all the parts were the same, how could there be a body? ²⁰As it is, there are many parts. But there is only one body.

²¹The eye can't say to the hand, "I don't need you!" The head can't say to the feet, "I don't need you!" ²²In fact, it is just the opposite. The parts of the body that seem to be weaker are the ones we can't do without. ²³The parts that we think are less important we treat with special honor. The private parts aren't shown. But they are treated with special care. ²⁴The parts that

can be shown don't need special care.

But God has joined together all the parts of the body. And he has given more honor to the parts that didn't have any. ²⁵In that way, the parts of the body will not take sides. All of them will take care of each other. ²⁶If one part suffers, every part suffers with it. If one part is honored, every part shares in its joy.

²⁷You are the body of Christ. Each one of you is a part of it. ²⁸First, God has appointed apostles in the church. Second, he has appointed prophets. Third, he has appointed teachers. Then he has appointed people who do miracles and those who have gifts of healing. He also appointed those able to help others, those able to direct things, and those who can speak in different kinds of languages they had not known before.

²⁹Is everyone an apostle? Is everyone a prophet? Is everyone a teacher? Do all work miracles? ³⁰Do all have gifts of

What part of the body of Christ am I?

You are the part that does what you can do well. The Bible uses several different words to explain how Christians relate to each other. We are a *family* with brothers and sisters in Christ. We are a *building* with Christ as the cornerstone. We are a *body* with each person as a different part. God calls us a body to show how we should treat each other and work together. Like a body part, each of us can do something important. God gives each person at least one talent or ability so that person can help other believers. Not everybody has the same gifts. And like the parts of a body, we all need each other. All of our gifts are important. Do not worry too much about saying "I am a hand" or "I am a knee." Just help out in any way you can.

checkout

1 Corinthians 12:27

Related verses:
Romans 12:4–8;
1 Corinthians
12:1–30

healing? Do all speak in languages they had not known before? Do all explain what is said in those languages? ³¹But above all, you should want the more important gifts.

LOVE

And now I will show you the best way of all.

13 Suppose I speak in the languages of human beings and of angels. If I don't have love, I am only a loud gong or a noisy cymbal. ²Suppose I have the gift of prophecy. Suppose I can understand all the secret things of God and know everything about him. And suppose I have enough faith to move mountains. If I don't have love, I am nothing at all. ³Suppose I give everything I have to poor people. And suppose I give my body to be burned. If I don't have love, I get nothing at all.

⁴Love is patient. Love is kind. It does not want what belongs to others. It does not brag. It is not proud. ⁵It is not rude. It does not look out for its own interests. It does not easily become angry. It does not keep track of other people's wrongs.

⁶Love is not happy with evil. But it is full of joy when the truth is spoken. ⁷It always protects. It always trusts. It always hopes. It never gives up.

⁸Love never fails. But prophecy will pass away. Speaking in languages that had not been known before will end. And knowledge will pass away.

⁹What we know now is not complete. What we prophesy now is not perfect. ¹⁰But when what is perfect comes, the things that are not perfect will pass away.

¹¹When I was a child, I talked like a child. I thought like a child. I had the understanding of a child. When I became a man, I put childish ways behind me.

¹²Now we see only a dim likeness of things. It is as if we were seeing them in a mirror. But someday we will see clearly. We will see face to face. What I know now is not complete. But someday I will know completely, just as God knows me completely.

¹³The three most important things

Do I have to let little kids in my room to play when I have special stuff?

Sometimes. God is loving and kind. He wants us to be loving and kind, too. Let other kids play with your toys if it is safe and if their parents say it is OK. Your toys, clothes and other belongings are not more important than your friends and family.

But also take good care of your stuff. You can and should ask everyone playing in your room to respect your things. Try to let other kids have a turn with your stuff whenever you can. But you can say no if something is too hard for them or they might hurt it. Just be nice about it.

checkout   1 Corinthians 13:4,5

Related verses:
Galatians 5:22,23;
James 4:17

to have are faith, hope and love. But the greatest of them is love.

THE GIFTS THE HOLY SPIRIT GIVES

14 Follow the way of love. You should also want the gifts the Holy Spirit gives. Most of all, you should want the gift of prophecy.

²Anyone who speaks in a language he had not known before doesn't speak to people. He speaks only to God. In fact, no one understands that person. What he says with his spirit remains a mystery. ³But anyone who prophesies speaks to people. He says things to make them stronger, to give them hope and to comfort them. ⁴Those who speak in other languages build themselves up. But those who prophesy build up the church.

⁵I would like all of you to speak in other languages. But I would rather have you prophesy. Those who prophesy are more helpful than those who speak in other languages. But that is not the case if those who speak in other languages explain what they have said. Then the whole church can be built up.

⁶Brothers and sisters, suppose I were to come to you and speak in other languages. What good would I be to you? None! I would need to come with new truth or knowledge, or a prophecy or a teaching.

⁷Here are some examples. Certain objects make sounds. Take a flute or a harp. No one will know what the tune is unless different notes are played. ⁸Also, if the trumpet call isn't clear, who will get ready for battle?

⁹It's the same with you. You must speak words that people understand. If you don't, no one will know what you are saying. You will just be speaking into the air.

¹⁰It is true that there are all kinds of languages in the world. And they all have meaning. ¹¹But if I don't understand what someone is saying, I am a stranger to that person. And that person is a stranger to me.

Why do kids think something is cool one day and stupid the next?

People change, so those kids may just have changed their minds. Think about times when you did the same thing. What was your favorite TV show last year? How about your favorite music group? Your favorites are probably different now. As kids grow up, they outgrow the things they liked a year ago or even a few months before. Also remember that fads change quickly. Something is "in" one day and "out" the next. That's a good reason not to get too carried away trying to follow every fad that comes along.

JASON, THOSE SHOES WENT OUT OF STYLE 3:00 YESTERDAY AFTERNOON.

OH GREAT! "COOL" HAS AN EXPIRATION DATE.

checkout
1 Corinthians 13:11

Related verse:
1 Peter 1:24

¹²It's the same with you. You want to have gifts of the Spirit. So try to do your best in using gifts that build up the church.

¹³For that reason, those who speak in languages they had not known before should pray that they can explain what they say. ¹⁴If I pray in another language, my spirit prays. But my mind does not pray. ¹⁵So what should I do? I will pray with my spirit. But I will also pray with my mind. I will sing with my spirit. But I will also sing with my mind.

¹⁶Suppose you are praising God with your spirit. And suppose there are visitors among you who don't understand what's going on. How can they say "Amen" when you give thanks? They don't know what you are saying. ¹⁷You might be giving thanks well enough. But the others are not being built up.

¹⁸I thank God that I speak in other languages more than all of you do. ¹⁹But in the church I would rather speak five words that people can understand than 10,000 words in another language. Then I would be teaching others.

²⁰Brothers and sisters, stop thinking like children. Be like babies as far as evil is concerned. But be grown up in your thinking. ²¹In the Law it is written,

"Through people who speak
    unfamiliar languages
and through the lips of strangers
I will speak to these people.
But even then they will not listen
    to me."   *(Isaiah 28:11,12)*

That is what the Lord says.

²²So speaking in other languages is a sign for those who don't believe. It is not a sign for those who do believe. But prophecy is for believers. It is not for those who don't believe.

²³Suppose the whole church comes together and everyone speaks in other languages. And suppose visitors or unbelievers come in. Won't they say you are out of your minds? ²⁴But suppose unbelievers or visitors come in while everyone is prophesying. Then they will be shown by all who speak that

KIDS' QUESTION
Will we pray in heaven or just talk to God face to face?

We will be able to talk to God face to face. Moses talked with God face to face on earth. But that was unusual. God wants to be our friend. Right now we are separated from him a little because we can't see him. We have to pray to talk to God. But in heaven we will be able to go right up to God and talk to him. In heaven we will see God just as he is.

checkout

1 Corinthians 13:12

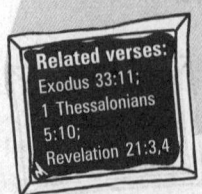

Related verses:
Exodus 33:11;
1 Thessalonians 5:10;
Revelation 21:3,4

JASON'S IMAGINATION

MAY GOD BE GRACIOUS TO US AND BLESS US AND MAKE HIS FACE SHINE UPON US. PSALM 67:1

they are sinners. They will be judged by all. [25]The secrets of their hearts will be brought out into the open. They will fall down and worship God. They will exclaim, "God is really here among you!"

PROPER WORSHIP

[26]Brothers and sisters, what should we say then? When you come together, every one of you brings something. You bring a hymn or a teaching or a word from God. You bring a message in another language or explain what was said. All of those things must be done to make the church strong.

[27]No more than two or three people should speak in another language. And they should speak one at a time. Then someone must explain what was said. [28]If there is no one to explain, the speakers should keep quiet in the church. They can speak to themselves and to God.

[29]Only two or three prophets are supposed to speak. Others should decide if what is being said is true. [30]What if a message from God comes to someone else who is sitting there? Then the one who is speaking should stop.

[31]Those who prophesy can all take turns. In that way, everyone can be taught and be given hope. [32]Those who prophesy should control their speaking. [33]God is not a God of disorder. He is a God of peace.

As in all the churches of God's people, [34]women should remain silent in the meetings. They are not allowed to speak. They must follow the lead of those who are in authority, as the Law says. [35]If they have a question about something, they should ask their own husbands at home. It is shameful for women to speak in church meetings.

[36]Did the word of God begin with you? Or are you the only people it has reached? [37]Suppose some think they are prophets or have gifts of the Holy Spirit. They should agree that what I am writing to you is the Lord's command. [38]Anyone who does not recognize that will not be recognized.

[39]Brothers and sisters, you should want to prophesy. And don't stop people from speaking in languages they had not known before. [40]But every-

thing should be done in a proper and orderly way.

PAUL EXPLAINS THE GOOD NEWS

15 Brothers and sisters, I want to remind you of the good news I preached to you. You received it and have put your faith in it. [2]Because you believed the good news, you are saved. But you must hold firmly to the message I preached to you. If you don't, you have believed it for nothing.

[3]What I received I passed on to you. And it is the most important of all. Here is what it is. Christ died for our sins, just as Scripture said he would. [4]He was buried. He was raised from the dead on the third day, just as Scripture said he would be. [5]He appeared to Peter.

Then he appeared to the Twelve. [6]After that, he appeared to more than 500 believers at the same time. Most of them are still living. But some have died. [7]He appeared to James. Then he appeared to all the apostles. [8]Last of all, he also appeared to me. I was like someone who wasn't born at the right time or in a normal way.

[9]I am the least important of the apostles. I'm not even fit to be called an apostle. I tried to destroy God's church. [10]But because of God's grace I am what I am. And his grace was not wasted on me. No, I have worked harder than all the other apostles. But I didn't do the work. God's grace was with me.

[11]So whether it was I or the other apostles who preached to you, that is what we preach. And that is what you believed.

BELIEVERS WILL RISE FROM THE DEAD

[12]We have preached that Christ has been raised from the dead. So how can some of you say that no one rises from the dead? [13]If no one rises from the dead, then not even Christ has been raised. [14]And if Christ has not been raised, what we preach doesn't mean anything. Your faith doesn't mean anything either. [15]More than that, we would be lying about God. We have

given witness that God raised Christ from the dead. But he did not raise him if the dead are not raised.

[16]If the dead are not raised, then Christ has not been raised either. [17]And if Christ has not been raised, your faith doesn't mean anything. Your sins have not been forgiven. [18]Those who have died believing in Christ are also lost.

[19]Do we have hope in Christ only for this life? Then people should pity us more than anyone else.

[20]But Christ really has been raised from the dead. He is the first of all those who will rise.

[21]Death came because of what a man did. Rising from the dead also comes because of what a man did. [22]Because of Adam, all people die. So because of Christ, all will be made alive.

[23]But here is the order of events. Christ is the first of those who rise from the dead. When he comes back, those who belong to him will be raised. [24]Then the end will come. Christ will destroy all rule, authority and power. He will hand over the kingdom to God the Father.

[25]Christ must rule until he has put all his enemies under his control. [26]The last enemy that will be destroyed is death. [27]Scripture says that God "has put everything under his control." (Psalm 8:6) It says that "everything" has been put under him. But it is clear that this does not include God himself, who puts everything under Christ. [28]When he has done that, the Son also will be under God's rule. God puts everything under the Son. In that way, God will be all in all.

[29]Suppose no one rises from the dead. Then what will people do who are baptized for the dead? Suppose the dead are not raised at all. Then why are people baptized for them? [30]And why would we put ourselves in danger every hour?

[31]I die every day. I really mean that, brothers and sisters. Here is something you can be sure of. I take pride in what Christ Jesus our Lord has done for you through my work. [32]Did I fight wild animals in Ephesus for only hu-

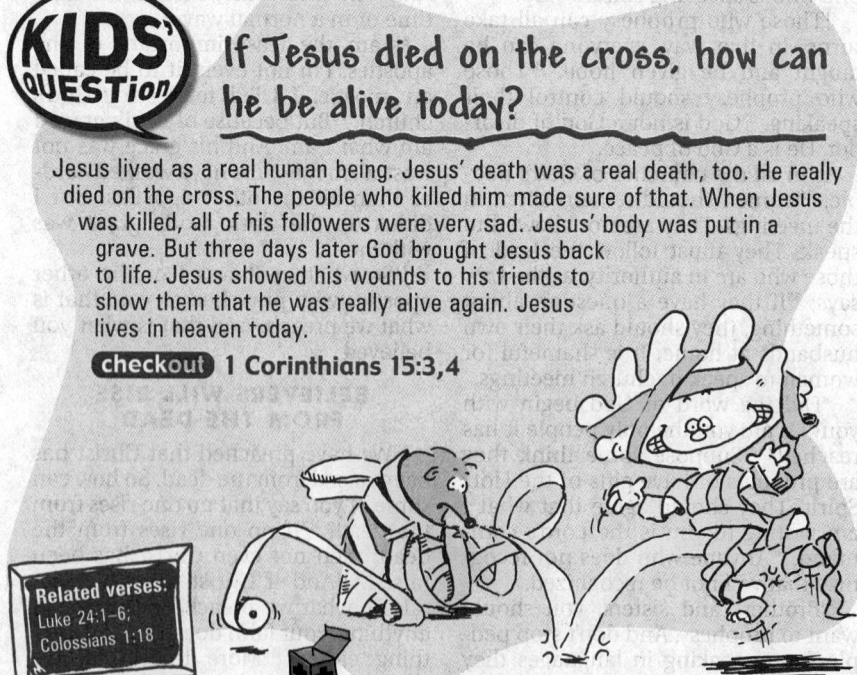

KIDS' QUESTION

If Jesus died on the cross, how can he be alive today?

Jesus lived as a real human being. Jesus' death was a real death, too. He really died on the cross. The people who killed him made sure of that. When Jesus was killed, all of his followers were very sad. Jesus' body was put in a grave. But three days later God brought Jesus back to life. Jesus showed his wounds to his friends to show them that he was really alive again. Jesus lives in heaven today.

checkout 1 Corinthians 15:3,4

Related verses:
Luke 24:1-6;
Colossians 1:18

man reasons? Then what have I gotten for it? If the dead are not raised,

"Let us eat and drink,
  because tomorrow we will die."
  (Isaiah 22:13)

³³Don't let anyone fool you. "Bad companions make a good person bad." ³⁴You should come back to your senses and stop sinning. Some of you don't know anything about God. I say this to make you ashamed.

THE BODY THAT RISES FROM THE DEAD

³⁵But someone might ask, "How are the dead raised? What kind of body will they have?" ³⁶How foolish! What you plant doesn't come to life unless it dies. ³⁷When you plant something, it isn't a completely grown plant that you put in the ground. You only plant a seed. Maybe it's wheat or something else. ³⁸But God gives the seed a body just as he has planned. And to each kind of seed he gives its own body.

³⁹All earthly creatures are not the same. People have one kind of body. Animals have another. Birds have another kind. Fish have still another.

⁴⁰There are also heavenly bodies as well as earthly bodies. Heavenly bodies have one kind of glory. Earthly bodies have another. ⁴¹The sun has one kind of glory. The moon has another kind. The stars have still another. And one star's glory is different from that of another star.

⁴²It will be like that with bodies that are raised from the dead. The body that is planted does not last forever. The body that is raised from the dead lasts forever. ⁴³It is planted without honor. But it is raised in glory. It is planted in weakness. But it is raised in power. ⁴⁴It is planted as an earthly body. But it is raised as a spiritual body.

Just as there is an earthly body, there is also a spiritual body. ⁴⁵It is written, "The first man Adam became a living person." *(Genesis 2:7)* The last Adam became a spirit that gives life. ⁴⁶What is spiritual did not come first. What is earthly came first. What is spiritual came after that. ⁴⁷The first man came from the dust of the earth. The second man came from heaven.

⁴⁸Those who belong to the earth are like the one who came from the earth. And those who are spiritual are like the

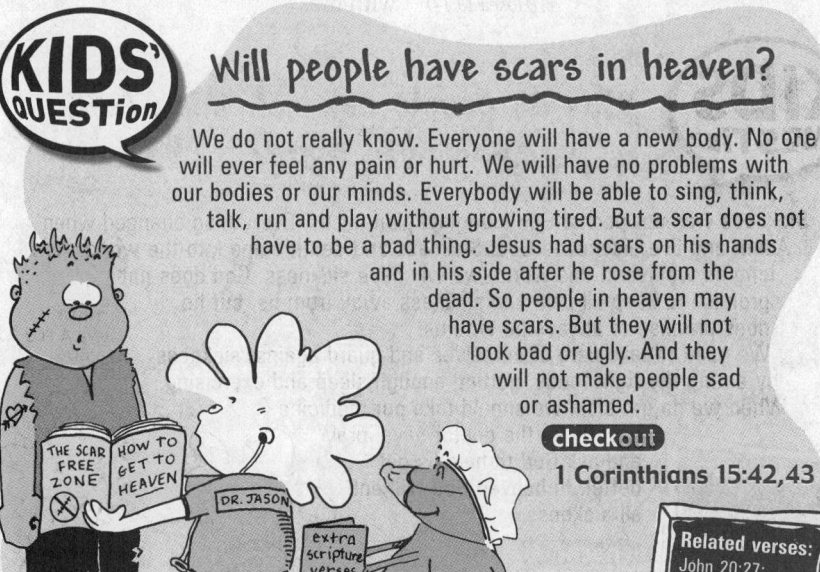

KIDS' QUESTION

Will people have scars in heaven?

We do not really know. Everyone will have a new body. No one will ever feel any pain or hurt. We will have no problems with our bodies or our minds. Everybody will be able to sing, think, talk, run and play without growing tired. But a scar does not have to be a bad thing. Jesus had scars on his hands and in his side after he rose from the dead. So people in heaven may have scars. But they will not look bad or ugly. And they will not make people sad or ashamed.

checkout
1 Corinthians 15:42,43

THE SCAR FREE ZONE Ⓧ

HOW TO GET TO HEAVEN

DR. JASON

extra scripture verses

Related verses:
John 20:27;
2 Corinthians
4:16—5:5

one who came from heaven. ⁴⁹We are like the earthly man. And we will be like the man from heaven.

⁵⁰Brothers and sisters, here is what I'm telling you. Bodies made of flesh and blood can't share in the kingdom of God. And what dies can't share in what never dies.

⁵¹Listen! I am telling you a mystery. We will not all die. But we will all be changed. ⁵²That will happen in a flash, as quickly as you can wink an eye. It will happen when the last trumpet sounds. The trumpet will sound, and the dead will be raised to live forever. And we will be changed.

⁵³Our natural bodies don't last forever. They must be dressed with what does last forever. What dies must be dressed with what does not die. ⁵⁴In fact, that is going to happen. What does not last will be dressed with what lasts forever. What dies will be dressed with what does not die. Then what is written will come true. It says, "Death has been swallowed up. It has lost the battle." *(Isaiah 25:8)*

⁵⁵ "Death, where is the battle you
　　thought you were winning?
Death, where is your sting?"
(Hosea 13:14)

⁵⁶The sting of death is sin. And the power of sin is the law. ⁵⁷But let us give thanks to God! He wins the battle for us because of what our Lord Jesus Christ has done.

⁵⁸My dear brothers and sisters, stand firm. Don't let anything move you. Always give yourselves completely to the work of the Lord. Because you belong to the Lord, you know that your work is not worthless.

THE OFFERING FOR GOD'S PEOPLE

16 Now I want to deal with the offering of money for God's people.

Do what I told the churches in Galatia to do. ²On the first day of every week, each of you should put some money away. The amount should be in keeping with how much money you make. Save the money so that you won't have to take up an offering when I come. ³When I arrive, I will send some people with your gift to Jerusalem. They will be people you consider to be good. And I will give them letters that explain who they are. ⁴If it seems good for me to go also, they will go with me.

Why do people get sick when God is watching over them?

Sickness was not part of God's original plan for us. Everything changed when Adam and Eve disobeyed God. Sickness and death came into the world. As long as we live in this world, we will have sickness. God does not promise to keep all pain and sickness away from us, but he does promise to always be with us.

We need to take care of ourselves and guard against sickness by eating the right foods, getting enough sleep and exercising. When we do get sick, we should take our medicine exactly as the doctor says, pray and ask God to help us get better. In heaven God will end all sickness.

Related verses:
Psalm 41:3;
Romans 8:18–25;
2 Corinthians 12:8–10;
James 5:14–15;
Revelation 21:4

checkout
1 Corinthians 15:43, 51

I THINK I HAVE A FLU BUG.

SNUFFLE SNUFFLE

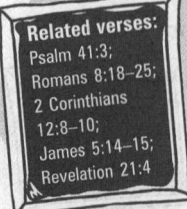

BUG SPRAY

WHAT PAUL ASKS FOR HIMSELF

[5]After I go through Macedonia, I will come to you. I will only be passing through Macedonia. [6]But I might stay with you for a while. I might even spend the winter. Then you can help me on my journey everywhere I go.

[7]I don't want to see you now while I am just passing through. I hope to spend some time with you, if the Lord allows it. [8]But I will stay at Ephesus until the day of Pentecost. [9]A door has opened wide for me to do some good work here. There are many people who oppose me.

[10]Timothy might come to you. Make sure he has nothing to worry about while he is with you. He is doing the work of the Lord, just as I am. [11]No one should refuse to accept him. Send him safely on his way so he can return to me. I'm expecting him to come back along with the others.

[12]I want to say something about our brother Apollos. I tried my best to get him to go to you with the others. But he didn't want to go right now. He will go when he can.

[13]Be on your guard. Stand firm in the faith. Be brave. Be strong. [14]Be loving in everything you do.

[15]You know that the first believers in Achaia were from the family of Stephanas. They have spent all their time serving God's people. Brothers and sisters, I am asking you [16]to follow the lead of people like them. Follow everyone who joins in the task and works hard at it.

[17]I was glad when Stephanas, Fortunatus and Achaicus arrived. They have supplied me with what you couldn't give me. [18]They renewed my spirit, and yours also. People like that are worthy of honor.

FINAL GREETINGS

[19]The churches in Asia Minor send you greetings. Aquila and Priscilla greet you warmly because of the Lord's love. So does the church that meets in their house. [20]All the brothers and sisters here send you greetings. Greet one another with a holy kiss.

[21]I, Paul, am writing this greeting with my own hand.

[22]If anyone does not love the Lord, let a curse be on that person! Come, Lord!

[23]May the grace of the Lord Jesus be with you.

[24]I give my love to all of you who belong to Christ Jesus. Amen.

quest challenge

I Wonder . . .

Why is it so important to take good care of my body?

Real Life Challenge

You probably see a lot of commercials on TV that advertise yummy-looking foods so you might be upset when your mom puts carrots and celery sticks in your lunch. Why won't she let you eat lots of "junk food"? It's because she knows that our bodies belong to God, and what you eat is really important.

Quest Clue

Read 1 Corinthians 3 to find out why eating junk food all the time isn't good. Then look in 1 Corinthians 6 and Hebrews 3 to find out how important it is to take care of your body.

2 Corinthians

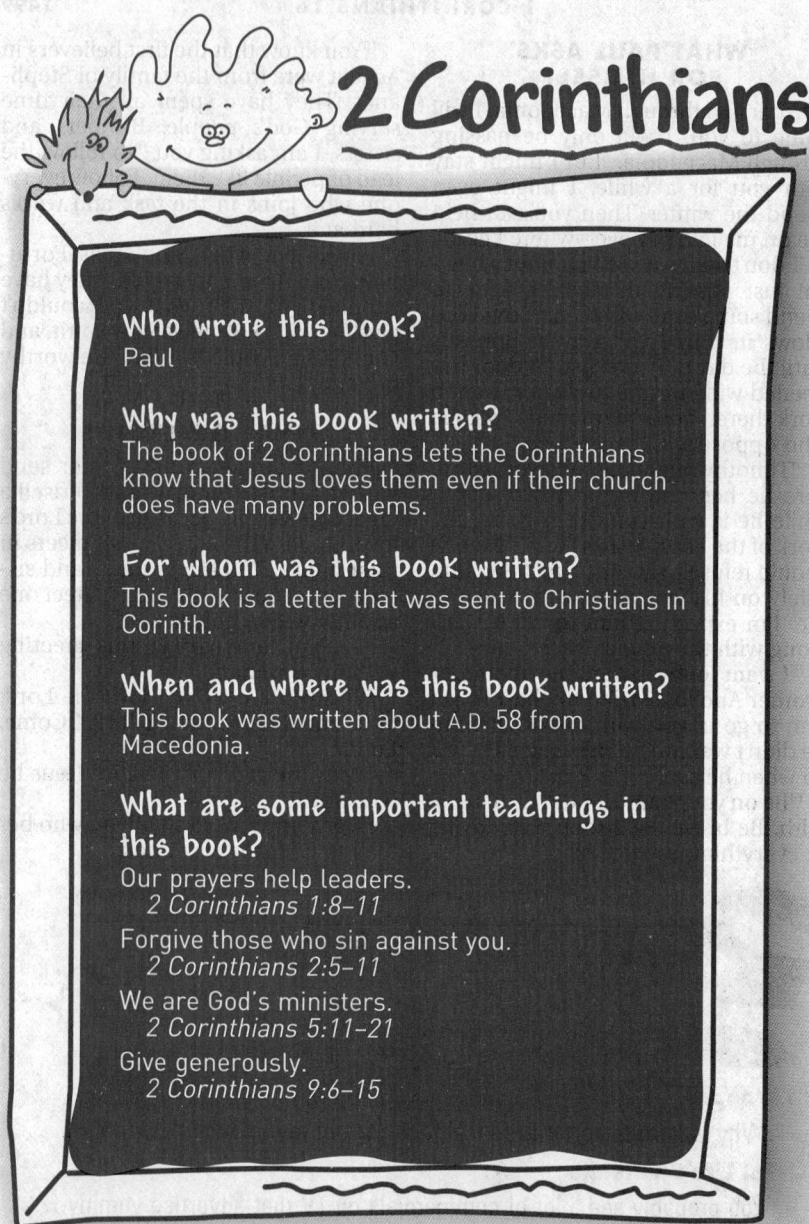

Who wrote this book?
Paul

Why was this book written?
The book of 2 Corinthians lets the Corinthians know that Jesus loves them even if their church does have many problems.

For whom was this book written?
This book is a letter that was sent to Christians in Corinth.

When and where was this book written?
This book was written about A.D. 58 from Macedonia.

What are some important teachings in this book?
Our prayers help leaders.
2 Corinthians 1:8–11

Forgive those who sin against you.
2 Corinthians 2:5–11

We are God's ministers.
2 Corinthians 5:11–21

Give generously.
2 Corinthians 9:6–15

---

1 I, Paul, am writing this letter. I am an apostle of Christ Jesus just as God planned. Timothy our brother joins me in writing.

We are sending this letter to you, the members of God's church in Corinth. It is also for all of God's people everywhere in Achaia.

[2] May God our Father and the Lord Jesus Christ give you grace and peace.

GOD GIVES COMFORT

[3] Give praise to the God and Father of our Lord Jesus Christ! He is the Father who gives tender love. All comfort comes from him. [4] He comforts us in all

our troubles. Now we can comfort others when they are in trouble. We ourselves have received comfort from God. [5]We share the sufferings of Christ. We also share his comfort.

[6]If we are having trouble, it is so that you will be comforted and renewed. If we are comforted, it is so that you will be comforted. Then you will be able to put up with the same suffering we have gone through. [7]Our hope for you remains firm. We know that you suffer just as we do. In the same way, God comforts you just as he comforts us.

[8]Brothers and sisters, we want you to know about the hard times we suffered in Asia Minor. We were having a lot of trouble. It was far more than we could stand. We even thought we were going to die. [9]In fact, in our hearts we felt as if we were under the sentence of death.

But that happened so that we would not depend on ourselves but on God. He raises the dead to life. [10]God has saved us from deadly dangers. And he will continue to do it. We have put our hope in him. He will continue to save us.

[11]You must help us by praying for us. Then many people will give thanks because of what will happen to us. They will thank God for his kindness to us in answer to the prayers of many.

PAUL CHANGES HIS PLANS

[12]Here is what we take pride in. Our sense of what is right and wrong gives witness that we have acted in God's holy and honest ways. That is how we live in the world. We live that way most of all when we are dealing with you. Our way of living is not wise in the eyes of the world. But it is in keeping with God's grace.

[13]We are writing only what you can read and understand. And here is what I hope. [14]Up to this point you have understood some of the things we have said. But now I hope that someday you will be able to take pride in us, just as we will take pride in you on the day the Lord Jesus returns. When you are able to do that, you will understand us completely.

[15]I was sure of those things. So I planned to visit you first. Here is how I thought you would be helped twice. [16]I planned to visit you on my way to Macedonia. I would have come back to you from there. Then you would have sent me on my way to Judea.

[17]When I planned all of that, did I do it without much thought? No. I don't make my plans the way the world makes theirs. In the same breath the world says, "Yes! Yes!" and "No! No!"

[18]But just as sure as God is faithful, our message to you is not "Yes" and "No." [19]Silas, Timothy and I preached to you about the Son of God, Jesus Christ. Our message did not say "Yes" and "No" at the same time. The message of Christ has always been "Yes."

[20]God has made a great many promises. They are all "Yes" because of what Christ has done. So through Christ we say "Amen." We want God to receive glory.

[21]He makes both us and you stand firm because we belong to Christ. He anointed us. [22]He put his Spirit in our hearts and marked us as his own. We can now be sure that he will give us everything he promised us.

[23]I call God as my witness. I wanted to spare you. So I didn't return to Corinth. [24]Your faith is not under our control. You stand firm in your own faith. But we work together with you for your joy.

2 So I made up my mind that I would not make another painful visit to you. [2]If I make you sad, who is going to make me glad? Only you, the one I made sad.

[3]I wrote what I did for a special reason. When I came, I didn't want to be troubled by those who should make me glad. I was sure that all of you would share my joy. [4]I was very troubled when I wrote to you. My heart was sad. My eyes were full of tears. I didn't want to make you sad. I wanted to let you know that I love you very deeply.

FORGIVE THOSE WHO MAKE YOU SAD

[5]Suppose someone has made us sad. In some ways, he hasn't made me sad so much as he has made all of you sad. But I don't want to put this too strongly. [6]He has been punished be-

cause most of you decided he should be. That is enough for him.

⁷Now you should forgive him and comfort him. Then he won't be sad more than he can stand. ⁸So I'm asking you to tell him again that you still love him.

⁹I wrote to you for a special reason. I wanted to see if you could stand the test. I wanted to see if you could obey everything that was asked of you.

¹⁰Anyone you forgive I also forgive. Was there anything to forgive? If so, I have forgiven it for your benefit, knowing that Christ is watching. ¹¹We don't want Satan to outsmart us. We know how he does his evil work.

SERVING UNDER THE NEW COVENANT

¹²I went to Troas to preach the good news about Christ. There I found that the Lord had opened a door of opportunity for me. ¹³But I still had no peace of mind. I couldn't find my brother Titus there. So I said good-by to the believers at Troas and went on to Macedonia.

¹⁴Give thanks to God! He, always leads us in the winners' parade because we belong to Christ. Through us, God spreads the knowledge of Christ everywhere like perfume. ¹⁵God considers us to be the sweet smell that Christ is spreading among people who are being saved and people who are dying. ¹⁶To the one, we are the smell of death. To the other, we are the perfume of life. Who is able to do that work?

¹⁷Unlike many people, we aren't selling God's word to make money. In fact, it is just the opposite. Because of Christ we speak honestly before God. We speak like people God has sent.

3 Are we beginning to praise ourselves again? Some people need letters that speak well of them. Do we need those kinds of letters, either to you or from you?

²You yourselves are our letter. You are written on our hearts. Everyone knows you and reads you. ³You make it clear that you are a letter from Christ. You are the result of our work for God. You are a letter written not with ink but with the Spirit of the living God.

You are a letter written not on tablets made out of stone but on human hearts.

⁴Through Christ, we can be sure of this because of our faith in God's power. ⁵In ourselves we are not able to claim anything for ourselves. The power to do what we do comes from God. ⁶He has given us the power to serve under a new covenant. The covenant is not based on the written Law of Moses. It comes from the Holy Spirit. The written Law kills, but the Spirit gives life.

THE GLORY OF THE NEW COVENANT

⁷The Law was written in letters on stone. Even though it was a way of serving God, it led to death. But even that way of serving God came with glory. And even though the glory was fading, the people of Israel couldn't look at Moses' face very long.

⁸Since all of that is true, won't the work of the Holy Spirit be even more glorious? ⁹The Law that sentences people to death is glorious. How much more glorious is the work of the Spirit! His work makes people right with God.

¹⁰The glory of the old covenant is nothing compared with the far greater glory of the new. ¹¹The glory of the old is fading away. How much greater is the glory of the new! It will last forever.

¹²Since we have that kind of hope, we are very bold. ¹³We are not like Moses. He used to cover his face with a veil. That was to keep the people of Israel from looking at his face while the brightness was fading away.

¹⁴But their minds were made stubborn. To this very day, the same veil remains when the old covenant is read. The veil has not been removed. Only faith in Christ can take it away. ¹⁵To this very day, when the Law of Moses is read, a veil covers the minds of those who hear it.

¹⁶But when anyone turns to the Lord, the veil is taken away. ¹⁷Now the Lord is the Holy Spirit. And where the Spirit of the Lord is, freedom is also there.

¹⁸Our faces are not covered with a veil. We all display the Lord's glory. We

are being changed to become more like him so that we have more and more glory. And the glory comes from the Lord, who is the Holy Spirit.

A TREASURE IN CLAY JARS

4 So because of God's mercy, we have work to do. He has given it to us. And we don't give up. ²Instead, we have given up doing secret and shameful things. We don't twist God's word. In fact, we do just the opposite. We present the truth plainly. In the sight of God, we make our appeal to everyone's sense of what is right and wrong.

³Suppose our good news is covered with a veil. Then it is veiled to those who are dying. ⁴The god of this world has blinded the minds of those who don't believe. They can't see the light of the good news of Christ's glory. He is the likeness of God.

⁵We do not preach about ourselves. We preach about Jesus Christ. We say that he is Lord. And we serve you because of him.

⁶God said, "Let light shine out of darkness." *(Genesis 1:3)* He made his light shine in our hearts. It shows us the light of God's glory in the face of Christ.

⁷Treasure is kept in clay jars. In the same way, we have the treasure of the good news in these earthly bodies of ours. That shows that the mighty power of the good news comes from God. It doesn't come from us.

⁸We are pushed hard from all sides. But we are not beaten down. We are bewildered. But that doesn't make us lose hope. ⁹Others make us suffer. But God does not desert us. We are knocked down. But we are not knocked out. ¹⁰We always carry around the death of Jesus in our bodies. In that way, the life of Jesus can be shown in our bodies.

¹¹We who are alive are always in danger of death because we are serving Jesus. So his life can be shown in our earthly bodies. ¹²Death is at work in us. But life is at work in you.

¹³It is written, "I believed, and so I have spoken." *(Psalm 116:10)* With that same spirit of faith we also believe. And we also speak.

¹⁴We know that God raised the Lord Jesus from the dead. And he will also raise us up with Jesus. He will bring us with you to God in heaven. ¹⁵All of that is for your benefit. God's grace is reaching more and more people. So they will become more and more thankful. They will give glory to God.

¹⁶We don't give up. Our bodies are becoming weaker and weaker. But our spirits are being renewed day by day. ¹⁷Our troubles are small. They last only

KIDS' QUESTiON

Why is it good to exercise?

Your body needs exercise, just as it needs food, air and water. Muscles need to be stretched and strengthened. The lungs need to breathe fresh, clean air. Joints need to be moved around. Blood needs to get moving.

Some people today don't get enough exercise—they sit around watching TV, playing video games or surfing the Internet for a long time. You need to get out and use your body. Good exercise comes from working around the house, working in the yard, riding bikes, running, walking and playing sports.

God gave us wonderful bodies and he wants us to take care of them.

Related verses:
1 Corinthians
6:19–20;
1 Timothy 4:8;
5:23

checkout
2 Corinthians 4:7

for a short time. But they are earning for us a glory that will last forever. It is greater than all our troubles. [18]So we don't spend all our time looking at what we can see. Instead, we look at what we can't see. What can be seen lasts only a short time. But what can't be seen will last forever.

OUR HOME IN HEAVEN

5 We know that the earthly tent we live in will be destroyed. But we have a building made by God. It is a house in heaven that lasts forever. Human hands did not build it.

[2]During our time on earth we groan. We long to put on our house in heaven as if it were clothing. [3]Then we will not be naked.

[4]While we live in this tent of ours, we groan under our heavy load. We don't want to be naked. We want to be dressed with our house in heaven. What must die will be swallowed up by life.

[5]God has made us for that very purpose. He has given us the Holy Spirit as a down payment. The Spirit makes us sure of what is still to come.

[6]So here is what we can always be certain about. As long as we are at home in our bodies, we are away from the Lord. [7]We live by believing, not by seeing. [8]We are certain about that. We would rather be away from our bodies and at home with the Lord. [9]So we try our best to please him. We want to please him whether we are at home in our bodies or away from them.

[10]We must all stand in front of Christ to be judged. Each one of us will be judged for the good things and the bad things we do while we are in our bodies. Then each of us will receive what we are supposed to get.

CHRIST BRINGS US BACK TO GOD

[11]We know what it means to have respect for the Lord. So we try to help other people to understand it.

What we are is plain to God. I hope it is also plain to your way of thinking. [12]We are not trying to make an appeal to you again. But we are giving you a chance to take pride in us. Then you can answer those who take pride in

how people look rather than in what is really in their hearts.

[13]Are we out of our minds? That is because we want to serve God. Does what we say make sense? That is because we want to serve you.

[14]Christ's love controls us. We are sure that one person died for everyone. And so everyone died.

[15]Christ died for everyone. He died so that those who live should not live for themselves anymore. They should live for Christ. He died for them and was raised again.

[16]So from now on we don't look at anyone the way the world does. At one time we looked at Christ in that way. But we don't anymore.

[17]Anyone who believes in Christ is a new creation. The old is gone! The new has come! [18]It is all from God. He brought us back to himself through Christ's death on the cross. And he has given us the task of bringing others back to him through Christ.

[19]God was bringing the world back to himself through Christ. He did not hold people's sins against them. God has trusted us with the message that people may be brought back to him. [20]So we are Christ's official messengers. It is as if God were making his appeal through us. Here is what Christ wants us to beg you to do. Come back to God!

[21]Christ didn't have any sin. But God made him become sin for us. So we can be made right with God because of what Christ has done for us.

6 We work together with God. So we are asking you not to receive God's grace and then do nothing with it. [2]He says,

"When I showed you my favor, I heard you.
On the day I saved you, I helped you."
                            (Isaiah 49:8)

I tell you, now is the time God shows his favor. Now is the day he saves.

PAUL'S SUFFERINGS

[3]We don't put anything in anyone's way. So no one can find fault with our work for God. [4]Instead, we make it clear that we serve God in every way. We serve him by holding steady. We

stand firm in all kinds of trouble, hard times and suffering.

⁵We don't give up when we are beaten or put in prison. When people stir up trouble in the streets, we continue to serve God. We work hard for him. We go without sleep and food. ⁶We remain pure. We understand completely what it means to serve God. We are patient and kind. We serve him in the power of the Holy Spirit. We serve him with true love. ⁷We speak the truth. We serve in the power of God. We hold the weapons of godliness in the right hand and in the left. ⁸We serve God in times of glory and shame. We serve him whether the news about us is bad or good. We are true to our calling.

But people treat us as if we were pretenders. ⁹We are known, but people treat us as if we were unknown. We are dying, but we continue to live. We are beaten, but we are not killed. ¹⁰We are sad, but we are always full of joy. We are poor, but we make many people rich. We have nothing, but we own everything.

¹¹Believers at Corinth, we have spoken freely to you. We have opened our hearts wide to you. ¹²We are not holding back our love from you. But you are holding back your love from us. ¹³I speak to you as if you were my children. It is only fair that you open your hearts wide to us also.

DO NOT BE JOINED TO UNBELIEVERS

¹⁴Do not be joined to unbelievers. What do right and wrong have in common? Can light and darkness be friends? ¹⁵How can Christ and Satan agree? What does a believer have in common with an unbeliever? ¹⁶How can the temple of the true God and the statues of other gods agree?

We are the temple of the living God. God has said, "I will live with them. I will walk among them. I will be their God. And they will be my people."

(Leviticus 26:12; Jeremiah 32:38; Ezekiel 37:27)

¹⁷"So come out from among them
    and be separate,
                    says the Lord.
Do not touch anything that is not
    pure and clean.

Then I will receive you."
                    (Isaiah 52:11; Ezekiel 20:34,41)
¹⁸"I will be your Father.
    You will be my sons and
        daughters,
                    says the Lord
            who rules over all."
                    (2 Samuel 7:14; 7:8)

7 Dear friends, we have these promises from God. So let us make ourselves pure from everything that pollutes our bodies and spirits. Let us be completely holy. We want to honor God.

PAUL'S JOY

²Make room for us in your hearts. We haven't done anything wrong to anyone. We haven't caused anyone to sin. We haven't taken advantage of anyone.

³I don't say this to judge you. I have told you before that you have an important place in our hearts. We would live or die with you. ⁴I have great faith in you. I am very proud of you. I am very happy. Even with all our troubles, my joy has no limit.

⁵When I came to Macedonia, my body wasn't able to rest. I was attacked no matter where I went. I had battles on the outside and fears on the inside.

⁶But God comforts those who are sad. He comforted me when Titus came. ⁷I was comforted not only when he came but also by the comfort you had given him. He told me how much you longed for me. He told me about your deep sadness and concern for me. That made my joy greater than ever.

⁸Even if my letter made you sad, I'm not sorry I sent it. At first I was sorry. I see that my letter hurt you, but only for a little while. ⁹Now I am happy. I'm not happy because you were made sad. I'm happy because your sadness led you to turn away from your sins. You became sad just as God wanted you to. So you were not hurt in any way by us.

¹⁰Godly sadness causes us to turn away from our sins and be saved. And we are certainly not sorry about that! But worldly sadness brings death. ¹¹Look at what that godly sadness

has produced in you. You are working hard to clear yourselves. You are angry and alarmed. You are longing to see me. You are concerned. You are ready to make sure that the right thing is done. In every way you have proved that you are not guilty in that matter. ¹²So even though I wrote to you, it wasn't because of the one who did the wrong. It wasn't because of the one who was hurt. Instead, I wrote you so that in the sight of God you could see for yourselves how faithful you are to us. ¹³All of that cheers us up.

We were also very glad to see how happy Titus was. You have all renewed his spirit. ¹⁴I had bragged about you to him. And you have not let me down. Everything we said to you was true. In the same way, our bragging about you to Titus has also turned out to be true. ¹⁵His love for you is even greater when he remembers that you all obeyed his teaching. You received him with fear and trembling. ¹⁶I am glad I can have complete faith in you.

GIVING FREELY TO OTHERS

8 Brothers and sisters, we want you to know about the grace that God has given to the churches in Macedonia. ²They have

suffered a great deal. But their joy was more than full. Even though they were very poor, they gave very freely.

³I give witness that they gave as much as they could. In fact, they gave even more than they could. Completely on their own, ⁴they begged us for the chance to share in serving God's people in that way. ⁵They did more than we expected. First they gave themselves to the Lord. Then they gave themselves to us in keeping with what God wanted.

⁶Titus had already started collecting money from you. So we asked him to get you to finish making your kind gift. ⁷You do well in everything else. You do well in faith and in speaking. You do well in knowledge and in complete commitment. And you do well in your love for us. So make sure that you also do well in the grace of giving to others.

⁸I am not commanding you to do it. But I want to put you to the test. I want to find out if you really love God. I want to compare your love with that of others.

⁹You know the grace shown by our Lord Jesus Christ. Even though he was rich, he became poor to help you. Because he became poor, you can become rich.

Why do I feel bad when I do something wrong?

That is your conscience talking. Maybe you did something you knew was wrong, or you hurt someone, or you did not do what was best, or you let God down. God built this warning system into us to alert us when we are about to do something wrong. It also helps us realize we should confess our sins so we can be forgiven. God created us to do good, and he wants us to do right. Our conscience makes us feel bad about doing wrong things so we will do good things instead.

checkout
2 Corinthians 7:10

Related verse:
1 Peter 3:16

[10]Here is my advice about what is best for you in that matter. Last year you were the first to give. You were also the first to want to give. [11]So finish the work. Then your longing to do it will be matched by your finishing it. Give on the basis of what you have.

[12]Do you really want to give? Then the gift is received in keeping with what you have, not with what you don't have.

[13]We don't want others to have it easy at your expense. We want things to be equal. [14]Right now you have plenty in order to take care of what they need. Then they will have plenty to take care of what you need. That will make things equal. [15]It is written, "Those who gathered a lot didn't have too much. And those who gathered a little had enough." *(Exodus 16:18)*

PAUL SENDS TITUS TO CORINTH

[16]God put into the heart of Titus the same concern I have for you. I am thankful to God for this. [17]Titus welcomed our appeal. He is also excited about coming to you. It was his own idea.

[18]Along with Titus, we are sending another brother. All the churches praise him for his service in telling the good news. [19]He was also chosen by the churches to go with us as we bring the offering. We are in charge of it. We want to honor the Lord himself. We want to show how ready we are to help.

[20]We want to keep anyone from blaming us for how we take care of that large gift. [21]We are trying hard to do what is right in the Lord's eyes and in the eyes of people.

[22]We are also sending another one of our brothers with them. He has often proved to us in many ways that he is very committed. He is now even more committed because he has great faith in you.

[23]Titus is my helper. He and I work together among you. Our brothers are messengers from the churches. They honor Christ. [24]So show them that you really love them. Show them why we are proud of you. Then the churches can see it.

9 I don't need to write to you about giving to God's people. [2]I know how much you want to

KIDS' QUESTION

If I tithe ten percent of my money, should I give more?

You can give as much as you like. God loves to receive a freely given gift. Jesus pointed out a widow who gave her last penny (Mark 12:42,43). The apostle Paul wrote about some very poor Christians who still gave richly (2 Corinthians 8:2). It is not the amount that matters. God cares about the person's motivation and willingness, too. Just be careful not to brag about your giving. Jesus scolded the Pharisees for boasting about what they gave (Matthew 23:23). He said, "When you give to the needy, don't let your left hand know what your right hand is doing. Then your giving will be done secretly. Your Father will reward you. He sees what you do secretly" (Matthew 6:3,4).

checkout
2 Corinthians 9:7

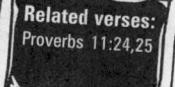

Related verses:
Proverbs 11:24,25

help. I have been bragging about it to the people in Macedonia. I have been telling them that since last year you who live in Achaia were ready to give. You are so excited that it has stirred up most of them to take action. ³But I am sending the brothers. Then our bragging about you in this matter will have a good reason. You will be ready, just as I said you would be.

⁴Suppose people from Macedonia come with me and find out that you are not prepared. Then we, as well as you, would be ashamed of being so certain. ⁵So I thought I should try to get the brothers to visit you ahead of time. They will finish the plans for the large gift you had promised. Then it will be ready as a gift that is freely given. It will not be given by force.

PLANTING MANY SEEDS

⁶Here is something to remember. The one who plants only a little will gather only a little. And the one who plants a lot will gather a lot. ⁷You should each give what you have decided in your heart to give. You shouldn't give if you don't want to. You shouldn't give because you are forced to. God loves a cheerful giver.

⁸And God is able to shower all kinds of blessings on you. In all things and at all times you will have everything you need. You will do more and more good works. ⁹It is written,

> "They have spread their gifts
>   around to poor people.
> Their good works continue
>   forever."   *(Psalm 112:9)*

¹⁰God supplies seed to the planter. He supplies bread for food. God will also supply and increase the amount of your seed. He will increase the results of your good works. ¹¹You will be made rich in every way. Then you can always give freely. We will take your many gifts to the people who need them. And they will give thanks to God.

¹²Your gifts meet the needs of God's people. And that's not all. Your gifts also cause many people to thank God. ¹³You have shown yourselves to be worthy by what you have given. So people will praise God because you obey him. That proves that you really

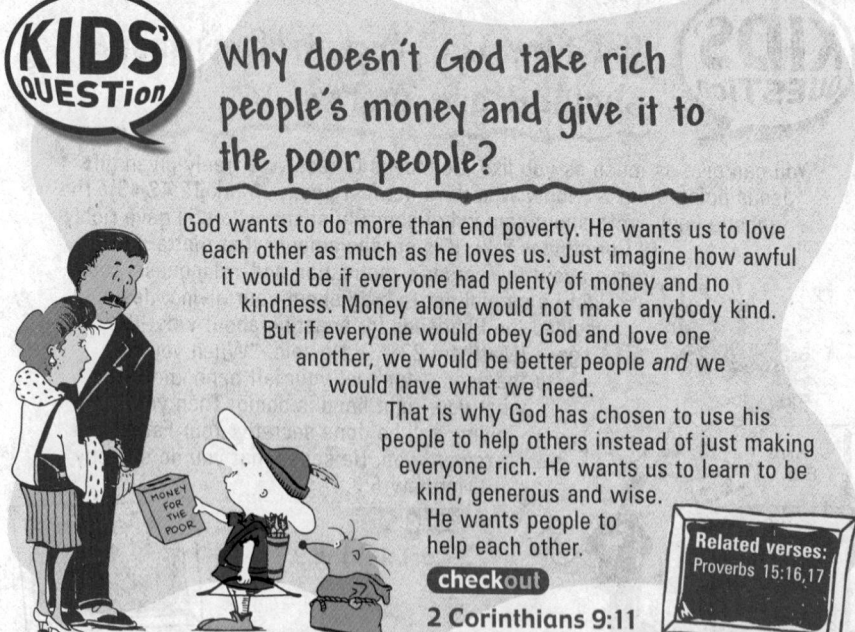

KIDS' QUESTION

Why doesn't God take rich people's money and give it to the poor people?

God wants to do more than end poverty. He wants us to love each other as much as he loves us. Just imagine how awful it would be if everyone had plenty of money and no kindness. Money alone would not make anybody kind. But if everyone would obey God and love one another, we would be better people *and* we would have what we need.

That is why God has chosen to use his people to help others instead of just making everyone rich. He wants us to learn to be kind, generous and wise. He wants people to help each other.

checkout

2 Corinthians 9:11

Related verses:
Proverbs 15:16,17

believe the good news about Christ. They will also praise God because you share freely with them and with everyone else. ¹⁴Their hearts will be filled with longing for you when they pray for you. God has given you grace that is better than anything.

¹⁵Let us give thanks to God for his gift. It is so great that no one can tell how wonderful it really is!

PAUL SPEAKS UP FOR HIMSELF

10 Christ is gentle and free of pride. So I make my appeal to you. I, Paul, am the one you call shy when I am face to face with you. But when I am away from you, you call me bold. ²I beg you that when I come I won't have to be as bold as I expect to be toward some people. They think that I live the way the people of this world live.

³I do live in the world. But I don't fight my battles the way the people of the world do. ⁴The weapons I fight with are not the weapons the world uses. In fact, it is just the opposite. My weapons have the power of God to destroy the camps of the enemy.

⁵I destroy every claim and every reason that keeps people from knowing God. I keep every thought under control in order to make it obey Christ. ⁶Until you have obeyed completely, I will be ready to punish you every time you don't obey.

⁷You are looking only at what appears on the surface of things. Suppose you are sure you belong to Christ. Then you should consider again that I belong to Christ just as much as you do.

⁸Do I brag too much about the authority the Lord gave me? If I do, it's because I want to build you up, not pull you down. And I'm not ashamed of that kind of bragging.

⁹Don't think that I'm trying to scare you with my letters. ¹⁰Some say, "His letters sound important. They are powerful. But in person he doesn't seem like much. And what he says doesn't amount to anything." ¹¹People like that have a lot to learn. What I say in my letters when I'm away from you,

I will do in my actions when I'm with you.

¹²I don't dare to compare myself with those who praise themselves. I'm not that kind of person. They measure themselves by themselves. They compare themselves with themselves. When they do that, they are not wise.

¹³But I won't brag more than I should. Instead, I will brag only about what I have done in the area God has given me. It is an area that reaches all the way to you. ¹⁴I am not going too far in my bragging. I would be going too far if I hadn't come to where you live. But I did get there with the good news about Christ.

¹⁵And I won't brag about work done by others. If I did, I would be bragging more than I should. As your faith continues to grow, I hope that my work among you will greatly increase. ¹⁶Then I will be able to preach the good news in the areas beyond you. I don't want to brag about work already done in someone else's territory.

¹⁷But, "The one who brags should brag about what the Lord has done." *(Jeremiah 9:24)* ¹⁸Those who praise themselves are not accepted. Those the Lord praises are accepted.

PAUL AND THOSE WHO PRETEND TO BE APOSTLES

11 I hope you will put up with a little of my foolish bragging. But you are already doing that.

²My jealousy for you comes from God himself. I promised to give you to only one husband. That husband is Christ. I wanted to be able to give you to him as if you were a pure virgin. ³But Eve was tricked by the snake's clever lies. And I'm afraid that in the same way your minds will somehow be led down the wrong path. They will be led away from your true and pure love for Christ.

⁴Suppose someone comes to you and preaches about a Jesus different from the Jesus we preached about. Or suppose you receive a spirit different from the one you received before. Or suppose you receive a message of good news different from the one you

accepted earlier. You put up with those kinds of things easily enough.

⁵But I don't think I'm in any way less important than those "super-apostles." ⁶I may not be a trained speaker. But I do have knowledge. I've made that very clear to you in every way.

⁷When I preached God's good news to you free of charge, I put myself down in order to lift you up. Was that a sin? ⁸Did I rob other churches when I received help from them so that I could serve you? ⁹When I was with you and needed something, I didn't cause you any expense. The believers who came from Macedonia gave me what I needed. I haven't caused you any expense at all. And I won't ever do it.

¹⁰I'm sure that the truth of Christ is in me. And I'm just as sure that nobody in Achaia will keep me from bragging. ¹¹Why? Because I don't love you? No! God knows I do! ¹²And I will keep on doing what I'm doing. That will stop those who claim they have things to brag about. They think they have a chance to be considered equal with us.

¹³People like that are false apostles. They work hard to trick others. They only pretend to be apostles of Christ.

¹⁴That comes as no surprise. Even Satan himself pretends to be an angel of light. ¹⁵So it doesn't surprise us that those who serve Satan pretend to be serving God. They will finally get exactly what they should.

PAUL BRAGS ABOUT HIS SUFFERINGS

¹⁶I will say it again. Don't let anyone think I'm a fool. But if you do, receive me just as you would receive a fool. Then I can do a little bragging.

¹⁷When I brag about myself like this, I'm not talking the way the Lord would. I'm talking like a fool. ¹⁸Many are bragging the way the people of the world do. So I will brag like that too.

¹⁹You are so wise! You gladly put up with fools! ²⁰In fact, you even put up with anyone who makes you a slave or uses you. You put up with those who take advantage of you. You put up with those who claim to be better than you. You put up with those who slap you in the face.

²¹I'm ashamed to have to say that I was too weak for that!

What anyone else dares to brag about, I also dare to brag about. I'm speaking like a fool! ²²Are they He-

KIDS' QUESTion

Why did Eve disobey God when she knew she would die?

She believed the devil's lies. God had said that Adam and Eve would die if they ate fruit from the "tree of the knowledge of good and evil." The devil told Eve that God did not really mean "die," and Eve believed him. She was no longer sure what would happen. Another trick the devil used was to promise that the fruit would do great things for her. He said that she would be like God if she ate it. That sounded good to Eve, so she ate it.

checkout
2 Corinthians 11:3

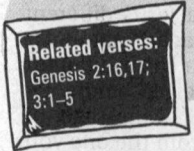

Related verses: Genesis 2:16,17; 3:1–5

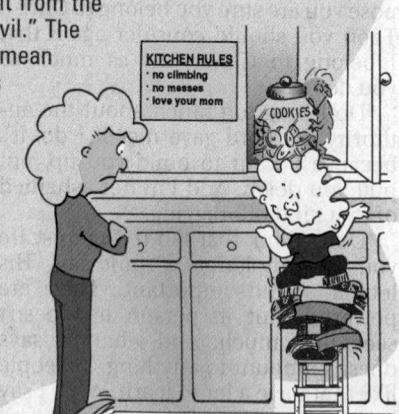

KITCHEN RULES
· no climbing
· no messes
· love your mom

COOKIES

brews? So am I. Do they belong to the people of Israel? So do I. Are they Abraham's children? So am I. [23]Are they serving Christ? I am serving him even more. I'm out of my mind to talk like this!

I have worked much harder. I have been in prison more often. I have suffered terrible beatings. Again and again I almost died. [24]Five times the Jews gave me 39 strokes with a whip. [25]Three times I was beaten with sticks. Once they tried to kill me by throwing stones at me. Three times I was shipwrecked. I spent a night and a day in the open sea.

[26]I have had to keep on the move. I have been in danger from rivers. I have been in danger from robbers. I have been in danger from people from my own country. I have been in danger from those who aren't Jews. I have been in danger in the city, in the country, and at sea. I have been in danger from people who pretended they were believers.

[27]I have worked very hard. Often I have gone without sleep. I have been hungry and thirsty. Often I have gone without food. I have been cold and naked.

[28]Besides everything else, every day I am concerned about all the churches. It is a very heavy load. [29]If anyone is weak, I feel weak. If anyone is led into sin, I burn on the inside.

[30]If I have to brag, I will brag about the things that show how weak I am. [31]I am not lying. The God and Father of the Lord Jesus knows this. May God be praised forever. [32]In Damascus the governor who served under King Aretas had their city guarded. He wanted to arrest me. [33]But I was lowered in a basket from a window in the wall. So I slipped through the governor's hands.

PAUL'S VISION AND HIS PAINFUL PROBLEM

12 We can't gain anything by bragging. But I have to do it anyway. I am going to tell you what I've seen. I want to talk about what the Lord has shown me.

[2]I know a believer in Christ who was taken up to the third heaven 14 years ago. I don't know if his body was taken up or not. Only God knows. [3]I don't

Does the devil have claws?

The devil can take many forms. When he appeared to Adam and Eve, he was a snake. But remember that Satan is also called an angel of light. He usually tries to look like something good and beautiful. And Satan is a liar, so he is usually trying to trick us. Satan works hard at trying to get us to do wrong things so he can show God how bad we are. He will say that we are not good enough to be God's children and that we are not forgiven. But always remember that God is much stronger than Satan. And God can keep us safe.

checkout

2 Corinthians 11:14

Related verses:
John 8:44;
Romans 8:38,39

know if that man was in his body or out of it. Only God knows. But I do know that ⁴he was taken up to paradise. He heard things that couldn't be put into words. They were things that people aren't allowed to talk about.

⁵I will brag about a man like that. But I won't brag about myself. I will brag only about how weak I am.

⁶Suppose I decide to brag. That would not make me a fool, because I would be telling the truth. But I don't do it. Then no one will think more of me than he should because of what I do or say.

⁷I could have become proud of myself because of the amazing and wonderful things God has shown me. So I was given a problem that caused pain in my body. It is a messenger from Satan to make me suffer. ⁸Three times I begged the Lord to take it away from me. ⁹But he said to me, "My grace is all you need. My power is strongest when you are weak."

So I am very happy to brag about how weak I am. Then Christ's power can rest on me. ¹⁰Because of how I suffered for Christ, I'm glad that I am weak. I am glad in hard times. I am glad when people say mean things about me. I am glad when things are difficult. And I am glad when people make me suffer. When I am weak, I am strong.

PAUL'S CONCERN FOR THE PEOPLE OF CORINTH

¹¹I have made a fool of myself. But you made me do it. You should have praised me. Even though I am nothing, I am in no way less important than the "super-apostles." ¹²You can recognize apostles by the signs, wonders and miracles they do. Those things were faithfully done among you no matter what happened.

¹³How were you less important than the other churches? The only difference was that I didn't cause you any expense. Forgive me for that wrong!

¹⁴Now I am ready to visit you for the third time. I won't cause you any expense. I don't want what you have. What I really want is you. After all, children shouldn't have to save up for their parents. Parents should save up for their children. ¹⁵So I will be very happy to spend everything I have for you. I will even spend myself. If I love you more, will you love me less?

¹⁶In any case, I haven't caused you

KIDS' QUESTiON

If God gives us everything we ask for then how come we don't have everything?

God does not give us everything we ask for. He gives us everything we *need*. Sometimes he gives us good things that we want. But sometimes we ask God to give us things that he is not willing to let us have because they would hurt us or make our lives worse. He is like a loving father who will not let a baby drink poison or play with fire. Sometimes we may hurt a little bit, like Paul with his painful problem. But God has a loving plan for us. His grace is all we need.

Related verses:
Matthew 7:7–11;
1 John 5:14,15

checkout
2 Corinthians
12:7–9

any expense. But I'm such a tricky fellow! I have caught you by tricking you!

[17]Did I take advantage of you through any of the men I sent to you? [18]I asked Titus to go to you. And I sent our brother with him. Titus didn't take advantage of you, did he? Didn't I act in the same spirit? Didn't I follow the same path?

[19]All this time, have you been thinking that I've been speaking up for myself? No, I've been speaking with God as my witness. I've been speaking like a believer in Christ. Dear friends, everything I do is to help you become stronger.

[20]I'm afraid that when I come I won't find you as I want you to be. I'm afraid that you won't find me as you want me to be. I'm afraid there will be arguing, jealousy and fits of anger. I'm afraid you will separate into your own little groups. Then you will tell lies about each other. You will talk about each other. I'm afraid you will be proud and cause trouble.

[21]I'm afraid that when I come again my God will put me to shame in front of you. Then I will be sad about many who sinned earlier and have not turned away from it. They have not turned away from uncleanness, sexual sins and wild living. They have done all those things.

FINAL WARNINGS

13 This will be my third visit to you. Scripture says, "Every matter must be proved by the words of two or three witnesses." *(Deuteronomy 19:15)* [2]I already warned you during my second visit. I now say it again while I'm away. When I return, I won't spare those who sinned earlier. I won't spare any of the others either.

[3]You are asking me to prove that Christ is speaking through me. He is not weak in dealing with you. He is powerful among you. [4]It is true that Christ was nailed to the cross because he was weak. But he lives by God's power. In the same way, I share his weakness. But by God's power I will live with him to serve you.

[5]Take a good look at yourselves to see if you are really believers. Test yourselves. Don't you realize that Christ Jesus is in you? Unless, of course, you fail the test! [6]I hope you will discover that I haven't failed the test.

[7]I pray to God that you won't do anything wrong. I don't pray so that people will see that I have passed the test. Instead, I pray so that you will do what is right, even if it seems I have failed. [8]I can't do anything to stop the truth. I can only work for the truth.

[9]I'm glad when I am weak but you are strong. I pray that you will become perfect. [10]That's why I write these things before I come to you. Then when I do come, I won't have to be hard on you when I use my authority.

The Lord gave me the authority to build you up. He didn't give it to me to tear you down.

FINAL GREETINGS

[11]Finally, brothers and sisters, goodby. Try to be perfect. Pay attention to what I'm saying. Agree with one another. Live in peace. And the God who gives love and peace will be with you.

[12]Greet one another with a holy kiss. [13]All of God's people send their greetings.

[14]May the grace shown by the Lord Jesus Christ, and the love that God has given us, and the sharing of life brought about by the Holy Spirit be with you all.

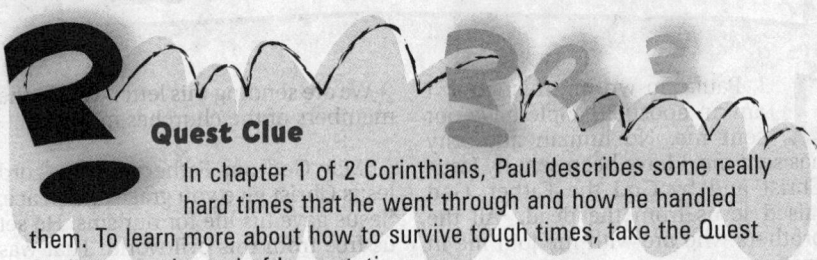

Quest Clue

In chapter 1 of 2 Corinthians, Paul describes some really hard times that he went through and how he handled them. To learn more about how to survive tough times, take the Quest Challenge at the end of Lamentations.

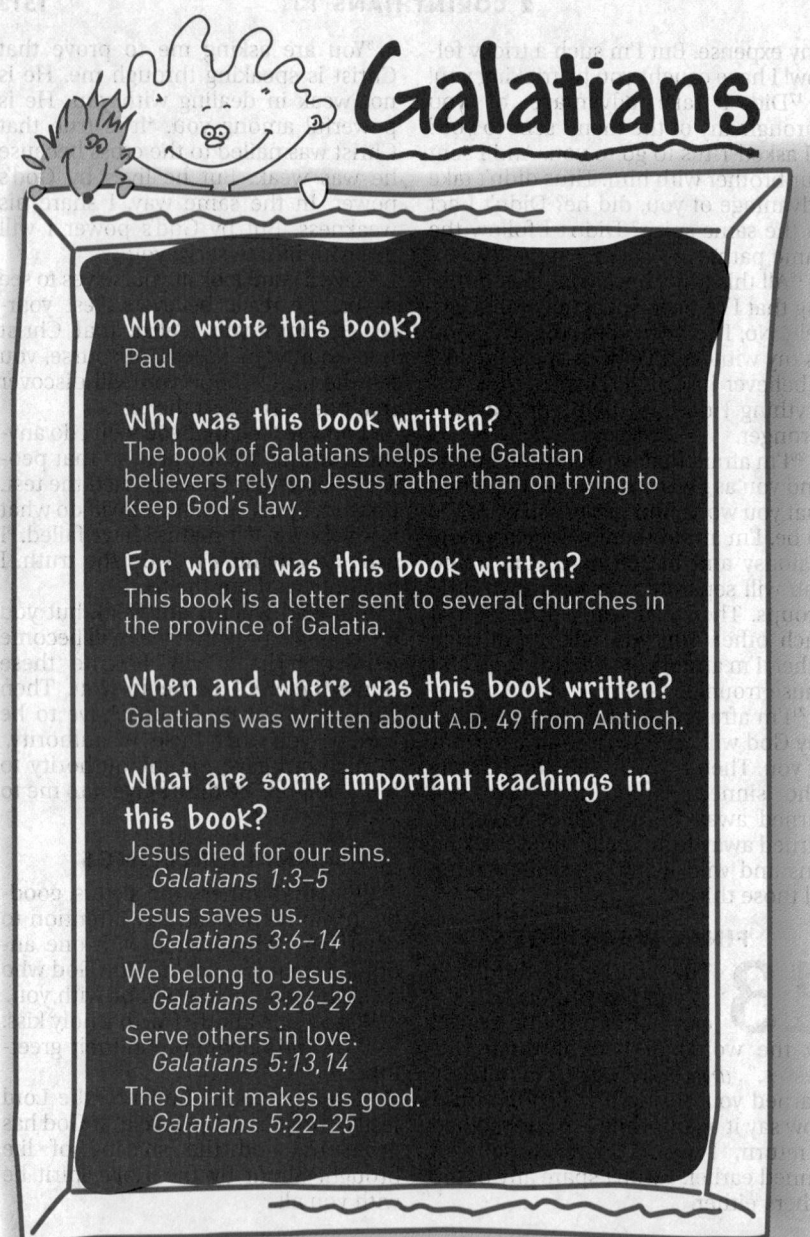

Galatians

Who wrote this book?
Paul

Why was this book written?
The book of Galatians helps the Galatian believers rely on Jesus rather than on trying to keep God's law.

For whom was this book written?
This book is a letter sent to several churches in the province of Galatia.

When and where was this book written?
Galatians was written about A.D. 49 from Antioch.

What are some important teachings in this book?
Jesus died for our sins.
  Galatians 1:3–5

Jesus saves us.
  Galatians 3:6–14

We belong to Jesus.
  Galatians 3:26–29

Serve others in love.
  Galatians 5:13,14

The Spirit makes us good.
  Galatians 5:22–25

1 I, Paul, am writing this letter. I am an apostle. People have not sent me. No human authority has sent me. I have been sent by Jesus Christ and by God the Father. God raised Jesus from the dead. ²All the brothers who are with me join me in writing.

We are sending this letter to you, the members of the churches in Galatia.

³May God our Father and the Lord Jesus Christ give you grace and peace. ⁴Jesus gave his life for our sins. He set us free from this evil world. That was what our God and Father wanted.

[5]Give glory to God for ever and ever. Amen.

THERE IS NO OTHER GOOD NEWS

[6]I am amazed. You are so quickly deserting the One who chose you because of the grace that Christ has provided. You are turning to a different "good news." [7]What you are accepting is really not the good news at all.

It seems that some people have gotten you all mixed up. They are trying to twist the good news about Christ.

[8]But suppose even we should preach a different "good news." Suppose even an angel from heaven should preach it. I'm talking about a different one than the good news we gave you. Let anyone who does that be judged by God forever. [9]I have already said it. Now I will say it again. Anyone who preaches a "good news" that is different from the one you accepted should be judged by God forever.

[10]Am I now trying to get people to think well of me? Or do I want God to think well of me? Am I trying to please people? If I were, I would not be serving Christ.

PAUL WAS APPOINTED BY GOD

[11]Brothers and sisters, here is what I want you to know. The good news I preached is not something a human being made up. [12]No one gave it to me. No one taught it to me. Instead, I received it from Jesus Christ. He showed it to me.

[13]You have heard of my earlier way of life as a Jew. With all my strength I attacked the church of God. I tried to destroy it. [14]I was moving ahead in my Jewish way of life. I went beyond many Jews who were my own age. I held firmly to the teachings passed down by my people.

[15]But God set me apart from the time I was born. He showed me his grace by appointing me. He was pleased [16]to show his Son in my life. He wanted me to preach about Jesus among those who aren't Jews.

When God appointed me, I didn't talk to anyone. [17]I didn't go up to Jerusalem to see those who were apostles before I was. Instead, I went at once into Arabia. Later I returned to Damascus.

[18]Then after three years I went up to Jerusalem. I went there to get to know Peter. I stayed with him for 15 days. [19]I didn't see any of the other apostles. I only saw James, the Lord's brother. [20]Here is what you can be sure of. And God gives witness to it. What I am writing you is not a lie.

[21]Later I went to Syria and Cilicia. [22]The members of Christ's churches in Judea did not know me in a personal way. [23]They only heard others say, "The man who used to attack us has changed. He is now preaching the faith he once tried to destroy." [24]And they praised God because of me.

PAUL IS ACCEPTED BY THE APOSTLES

2 Fourteen years later I went up again to Jerusalem. This time I went with Barnabas. I took Titus along also. [2]I went because God showed me what he wanted me to do. I told the people there the good news that I preach among those who aren't Jews. But I spoke in private to those who seemed to be leaders. I was afraid that I was running or had run my race for nothing.

[3]Titus was with me. He was a Greek. But even he was not forced to be circumcised.

[4]That matter came up because some who pretended to be believers had slipped in among us. They wanted to find out about the freedom we have because we belong to Christ Jesus. They wanted to make us slaves again.

[5]We didn't give in to them for a moment. We wanted the truth of the good news to remain with you.

[6]Some people in Jerusalem seemed to be important. It makes no difference to me what they were. God does not judge by what he sees on the outside. Those people added nothing to my message.

[7]In fact, it was just the opposite. They saw that I had been trusted with the task of preaching the good news just as Peter had been. My task was to preach to the non-Jews. Peter's task was to preach to the Jews. [8]God was

working through Peter as an apostle to the Jews. He was also working through me as an apostle to the non-Jews.

[9]James, Peter and John are considered to be pillars in the church. They recognized the special grace that was given to me. So they shook my hand and the hand of Barnabas. They wanted to show they accepted us. They agreed that we should go to the non-Jews. They would go to the Jews. [10]They asked only one thing. They wanted us to continue to remember poor people. That was what I really wanted to do anyway.

PAUL OPPOSES PETER

[11]When Peter came to Antioch, I told him to his face that I was against what he was doing. He was clearly wrong. [12]He used to eat with those who weren't Jews. But certain men came from the group that was led by James. When they arrived, Peter began to draw back. He separated himself from the non-Jews. He was afraid of the circumcision group.

[13]Peter's actions were not honest. The other Jews joined him. Even Barnabas was led down the wrong path.

[14]I saw what they were doing. It was not in line with the truth of the good news. So I spoke to Peter in front of them all. "You are a Jew," I said. "But you live like one who is not. So why do you force non-Jews to follow Jewish ways?"

GOD'S GRACE AND OUR FAITH

[15]We are Jews by birth. We are not "non-Jewish sinners." [16]We know that no one is made right with God by obeying the law. It is by believing in Jesus Christ. So we too have put our faith in Christ Jesus. That is so we can be made right with God by believing in Christ, not by obeying the law. No one can be made right with God by obeying the law.

[17]We are trying to be made right with God through Christ. But it is clear that we are sinners. So does that mean that Christ causes us to sin? Certainly not! [18]Suppose I build again what I had destroyed. Then I prove that I break the Law.

[19]Because of the law, I died as far as the law is concerned. I died so that I might live for God. [20]I have been crucified with Christ. I don't live any longer. Christ lives in me. My faith in the Son of God helps me to live my life in my body. He loved me. He gave himself for me.

[21]I do not get rid of the grace of God. What if a person could become right with God by obeying the law? Then Christ died for nothing!

FAITH OR OBEYING THE LAW

3 You foolish people of Galatia! Who has put you under an evil spell? When I preached, I clearly showed you that Jesus Christ had been nailed to the cross.

[2]I would like to learn just one thing from you. Did you receive the Holy Spirit by obeying the law? Or did you receive the Spirit by believing what you heard? [3]Are you so foolish? You began with the Holy Spirit. Are you now trying to complete God's work in you by your own strength?

[4]Have you suffered so much for nothing? And was it really for nothing? [5]Why does God give you his Spirit? Why does he work miracles among you? Is it because you do what the law says? Or is it because you believe what you have heard?

[6]Think about Abraham. Scripture says, "Abraham believed God. God accepted Abraham because he believed. So his faith made him right with God." (Genesis 15:6) [7]So you see, those who have faith are children of Abraham.

[8]Long ago, Scripture knew that God would make non-Jews right with himself by believing in him. He announced the good news ahead of time to Abraham. He said, "All nations will be blessed because of you." (Genesis 12:3; 18:18; 22:18) [9]So those who have faith are blessed along with Abraham. He was the man of faith.

[10]All who depend on obeying the law are under a curse. It is written, "May everyone who doesn't continue to do everything that is written in the Book of the Law be under God's curse." (Deuteronomy 27:26) [11]We know that no one is made right with God by keeping the law. Scripture says, "Those who

are right with God will live by faith."
(Habakkuk 2:4)

¹²The law is not based on faith. In fact, it is just the opposite. It teaches that "the one who does those things will live by them." *(Leviticus 18:5)*

¹³Christ set us free from the curse of the law. He did it by becoming a curse for us. It is written, "Everyone who is hung on a pole is under God's curse." *(Deuteronomy 21:23)* ¹⁴Christ Jesus set us free so that the blessing given to Abraham would come to non-Jews through Christ. He did it so that we might receive the promise of the Holy Spirit by believing in Christ.

THE LAW AND THE PROMISE

¹⁵Brothers and sisters, let me give you an example from everyday life. No one can get rid of an official agreement between people. No one can add to it. It can't be changed after it has been made. It is the same with God's covenant. ¹⁶The promises were given to Abraham. They were also given to his seed. Scripture does not say, "and to seeds." That means many people. It says, "and to your seed." *(Genesis 12:7; 13:15; 24:7)* That means one person. And that one person is Christ.

¹⁷Here is what I mean. The law came 430 years after the promise. But the law does not get rid of God's covenant and promise. The covenant had already been made by God. So the law does not do away with the promise. ¹⁸The great gift that God has for us does not depend on the law. If it did, it would no longer depend on a promise. But God gave it to Abraham as a free gift through a promise. ¹⁹Then what was the purpose of the law? It was added because of human sin. And it was supposed to control us until the promised Seed had come. The law was put into effect through angels by a go-between. ²⁰A go-between does not take sides. God didn't use a go-between when he made his promise to Abraham. But the same God was at work in both the law and the promise.

²¹So is the law opposed to God's promises? Certainly not! What if a law had been given that could give life? Then people could become right with

God by obeying the law. ²²But Scripture announces that the whole world is a prisoner because of sin. It does so in order that what was promised might be given to those who believe. The promise comes through faith in Jesus Christ.

²³Before faith in Christ came, we were held prisoners by the law. We were locked up until faith was made known. ²⁴So the law was put in charge until Christ came. He came so that we might be made right with God by believing in Christ. ²⁵But now faith in Christ has come. So we are no longer under the control of the law.

CHILDREN OF GOD

²⁶You are all children of God by believing in Christ Jesus. ²⁷All of you who were baptized into Christ have put on Christ as if he were your clothes. ²⁸There is no Jew or Greek. There is no slave or free person. There is no male or female. Because you belong to Christ Jesus, you are all one. ²⁹You who belong to Christ are Abraham's seed. You will receive what God has promised.

4 Here is what I have been saying. As long as your own children are young, they are no different from slaves in your house. They are no different, even though they own all of the property. ²They are under the care of guardians and those who manage the property. They are under their care until the time when their fathers give them the property. ³It is the same with us. When we were children, we were slaves to the basic things the people of the world believe.

⁴But then the right time came. God sent his Son. A woman gave birth to him. He was born under the authority of the law. ⁵He came to set free those who were under the law. He wanted us to be adopted as children with all the rights children have.

⁶Because you are his children, God sent the Spirit of his Son into our hearts. He is the Holy Spirit. By his power we call God "Abba." *Abba* means Father.

⁷So you aren't slaves any longer. You are God's children. Because you are his

children, he gives you what he promised to give his people.

PAUL'S CONCERN FOR THE BELIEVERS IN GALATIA

⁸At one time you didn't know God. You were slaves to gods that are really not gods at all. ⁹But now you know God. Even better, God knows you. So why are you turning back to those weak and worthless beliefs? Do you want to be slaves to them all over again?

¹⁰You are observing special days and months and seasons and years! ¹¹I am afraid for you. I am afraid that somehow I have wasted my efforts on you.

PAUL'S APPEAL TO THE BELIEVERS

¹²I make my appeal to you, brothers and sisters. I'm asking you to become like me. After all, I became like you. You didn't do anything wrong to me. ¹³As you know, it was because I was sick that I first preached the good news to you. ¹⁴My sickness was hard on you. But you didn't put me off. You didn't make fun of me. Instead, you welcomed me as if I were an angel of God. You welcomed me as if I were Christ Jesus himself.

¹⁵What has happened to all of your joy? If you could have torn out your own eyes and given them to me, you would have. I can give witness to that. ¹⁶Have I become your enemy now by telling you the truth?

¹⁷Those people are trying hard to win you over. But it is not for your good. They want to take you away from us. They want you to commit yourselves to them. ¹⁸It is fine to be committed to something, if the purpose is good. And you shouldn't be committed only when I am with you. You should always be committed.

¹⁹My dear children, I am in pain for you. Once again I have pain like a woman giving birth. And my pain will continue until Christ makes you like himself.

²⁰I wish I could be with you now. I

Why do some white people and black people hate each other?

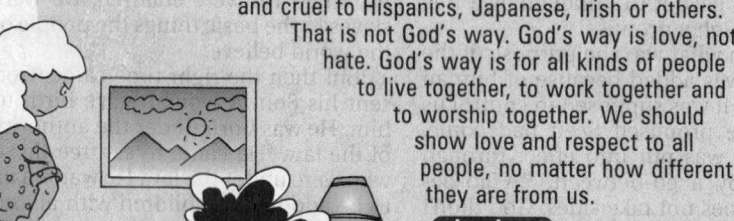

Hate is a problem that comes from sin. Some people hate others for very silly reasons. They may not like another person's religion, nationality, neighborhood, school or skin color. Many white people have hated black people just because they are black. And many black people have hated white people just because they are white. Other people have been mean and cruel to Hispanics, Japanese, Irish or others. That is not God's way. God's way is love, not hate. God's way is for all kinds of people to live together, to work together and to worship together. We should show love and respect to all people, no matter how different they are from us.

checkout

Galatians 3:26-28

Related verses:
Acts 17:26;
Colossians
3:11—14

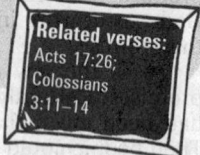

Topical Index

wish I could change my tone of voice. As it is, you bewilder me.

HAGAR AND SARAH

21You who want to be under the authority of the law, tell me something. Don't you know what the law says? 22It is written that Abraham had two sons. The slave woman gave birth to one of them. The free woman gave birth to the other one. 23Abraham's son by the slave woman was born in the usual way. But his son by the free woman was born because of God's promise.

24Those things can be taken as examples. The two women stand for two covenants. One covenant comes from Mount Sinai. It gives birth to children who are going to be slaves. It is Hagar. 25Hagar stands for Mount Sinai in Arabia. She stands for the present city of Jerusalem. That's because she and her children are slaves.

26But the Jerusalem that is above is free. She is our mother. 27It is written,

"Be glad, woman,
  you who have no children.
Start shouting,
  you who have no labor pains.
The woman who is all alone has
    more children
  than the woman who has a
    husband."   *(Isaiah 54:1)*

28Brothers and sisters, you are children because of God's promise just as Isaac was. 29At that time, the son born in the usual way tried to hurt the son born by the power of the Holy Spirit. It is the same now.

30But what does Scripture say? "Get rid of the slave woman. Get rid of her son. The slave woman's son will never have a share of the family's property with the free woman's son." *(Genesis 21:10)*

31Brothers and sisters, we are not the slave woman's children. We are the free woman's children.

CHRIST SETS US FREE

5 Christ has set us free. He wants us to enjoy freedom. So stand firm. Don't let the chains of slavery hold you again.

2Here is what I, Paul, say to you. Don't let yourselves be circumcised. If you do, Christ won't be of any value to you. 3I say it again. Every man who lets himself be circumcised must obey the whole law.

4Some of you are trying to be made right with God by obeying the law. You have been separated from Christ. You have fallen away from God's grace.

5But we expect to be made completely holy because of our faith in Christ. Through the Holy Spirit we wait in hope. 6Circumcision and uncircumcision aren't worth anything to those who believe in Christ Jesus. The only thing that really counts is faith that shows itself through love.

7You were running a good race. Who cut in on you and kept you from obeying the truth? 8The One who chooses you does not keep you from obeying the truth. 9You should know that "just a little yeast works its way through the whole batch of dough."

10The Lord makes me certain that you will not think in any other way. The one who has gotten you all mixed up will pay the price. It doesn't matter who that may be.

11Brothers and sisters, I am not still preaching that people must be circumcised. If I were, why am I still being opposed? If that were what I preach, then the cross wouldn't upset anyone.

12So then, what about troublemakers who try to get others to be circumcised? I wish they would go the whole way! I wish they would cut off everything that marks them as men!

CHOSEN TO BE FREE

13My brothers and sisters, you were chosen to be free. But don't use your freedom as an excuse to live in sin. Instead, serve one another in love. 14The whole law can be found in a single command. "Love your neighbor as you love yourself." *(Leviticus 19:18)*

15You must not keep on biting each other. You must not keep eating each other up. Watch out! You might destroy each other.

LIVING BY THE HOLY SPIRIT'S POWER

16So I say, live by the Holy Spirit's power. Then you will not do what your sinful nature wants you to do.

¹⁷The sinful nature does not want what the Spirit delights in. And the Spirit does not want what the sinful nature delights in. The two are at war with each other. That's what makes you do what you don't want to do. ¹⁸But if you are led by the Spirit, you are not under the authority of the law. ¹⁹What the sinful nature does is clear. It enjoys sexual sins, impure acts and wild living. ²⁰It worships statues of gods. It also worships evil powers. It is full of hatred and fighting. It is full of jealousy and fits of anger. It is interested only in getting ahead. It stirs up trouble. It separates people into their own little groups. ²¹It wants what others have. It gets drunk and takes part in wild parties. It does many things of that kind. I warn you now as I did before. People who live like that will not receive God's kingdom.

²²But the fruit the Holy Spirit produces is love, joy and peace. It is being patient, kind and good. It is being faithful ²³and gentle and having control of oneself. There is no law against things of that kind.

²⁴Those who belong to Christ Jesus have nailed their sinful nature to his cross. They don't want what their sinful nature loves and longs for.

²⁵Since we live by the Spirit, let us march in step with the Spirit. ²⁶Let us not become proud. Let us not make each other angry. Let us not want what belongs to others.

DO GOOD TO EVERYONE

6 Brothers and sisters, what if someone is caught in a sin? Then you who are guided by the Spirit should correct that person. Do it in a gentle way. But be careful. You could be tempted too. ²Carry each other's heavy loads. If you do, you will give the law of Christ its full meaning.

³If you think you are somebody when you are nobody, you are fooling yourselves. ⁴Each of you should put

KIDS' QUESTion

Is it cheating when you let the other team win when their team wasn't playing that well?

No. You must break a rule to cheat. It is not wrong to do the other team a favor. There are times when you might want to play easier to give the other team a chance in the game. That is a kind thing to do. But do not do it to make fun of them. Do it so the game will be fun for them. Maybe you can adjust the rules or change the teams to make it more even instead. Then you can all play your best and it will be more fun for everyone. Remember that God wants you to treat others with respect and love more than anything else. He does not care so much whether your team wins.

checkout
Galatians 5:22,23

Related verse: Luke 6:31

appointed me to share his grace with you. ³I'm talking about the mystery God showed me. I have already written a little about it. ⁴By reading it you will be able to understand what I know about the mystery of Christ.

⁵The mystery was not made known to people of other times. But now the Holy Spirit has made it known to God's holy apostles and prophets.

⁶Here is the mystery. Because of the good news, God's promises are for non-Jews as well as for Jews. Both groups are parts of one body. They share in the promise. It belongs to them because they belong to Christ Jesus.

⁷I now serve the good news because God gave me his grace. His power is at work in me. ⁸I am by far the least important of all of God's people. But he gave me the grace to preach to the non-Jews about the wonderful riches that Christ gives.

⁹God told me to make clear to everyone how the mystery came about. In times past it was kept hidden in the mind of God, who created all things. ¹⁰He wanted the rulers and authorities in the heavenly world to come to know his great wisdom. The church would make it known to them.

¹¹That was God's plan from the beginning. He has worked it out through Christ Jesus our Lord. ¹²Through him and through faith in him we can approach God. We can come to him freely. We can come without fear.

¹³So here is what I'm asking you to do. Don't lose hope because I am suffering for you. It will lead to the time when God will give you his glory.

PAUL PRAYS FOR GOD'S PEOPLE

¹⁴I bow in prayer to the Father because of my work among you. ¹⁵From the Father his whole family in heaven and on earth gets its name.

¹⁶I pray that he will use his glorious riches to make you strong. May his Holy Spirit give you his power deep down inside you. ¹⁷Then Christ will live in your hearts because you believe in him.

And I pray that your love will have deep roots. I pray that it will have a strong foundation. ¹⁸May you have power with all God's people to understand Christ's love. May you know how wide and long and high and deep it is. ¹⁹And may you know his love, even though it can't be known completely. Then you will be filled with everything God has for you.

²⁰God is able to do far more than we could ever ask for or imagine. He does everything by his power that is working in us. ²¹Give him glory in the church and in Christ Jesus. Give him glory through all time and for ever and ever. Amen.

THE BODY OF CHRIST IS ONE

4 I am a prisoner because of the Lord. So I am asking you to live a life worthy of what God chose you for.

²Don't be proud at all. Be completely gentle. Be patient. Put up with one another in love. ³The Holy Spirit makes you one in every way. So try your best to remain as one. Let peace keep you together.

⁴There is one body. There is one Spirit. You were appointed to one hope when you were chosen. ⁵There is one Lord. There is one faith and one baptism. ⁶There is one God and Father of all. He is over everything. He is through everything. He is in everything.

⁷But each one of us has received a gift of grace, just as Christ wanted us to have it. ⁸That is why Scripture says,

"When he went up to his place on high,
he led a line of prisoners.
He gave gifts to people."

(Psalm 68:18)

⁹What does "he went up" mean? It can only mean that he also came down to the lower, earthly places. ¹⁰The One who came down is the same as the One who went up higher than all the heavens. He did it in order to fill all of creation. ¹¹He is the One who gave some the gift to be apostles. He gave some the gift to be prophets. He gave some the gift of preaching the good news. And he gave some the gift to be pastors and teachers. ¹²He did it so that they might prepare God's people to serve. If they

good things. Long ago God prepared them for us to do.

GOD'S NEW FAMILY

[11]You who are not Jews by birth, here is what I want you to remember. You are called "uncircumcised" by those who call themselves "circumcised." But they have only been circumcised in their bodies by human hands.

[12]Before you believed in Christ, you were separated from him. You were not considered to be citizens of Israel. You were not included in what the covenants promised. You were without hope and without God in the world. [13]At one time you were far away from God. But now you belong to Christ Jesus. He spilled his blood for you. That has brought you near to God.

[14]Christ himself is our peace. He has made Jews and non-Jews into one group of people. He has destroyed the hatred that was like a wall between us. [15]Through his body on the cross, Christ put an end to the law with all its commands and rules. He wanted to create one new group of people out of the two. He wanted to make peace between them. [16]He planned to bring both of them as one body back to God because of

the cross. Christ put their hatred to death on that cross.

[17]He came and preached peace to you who were far away. He also preached peace to those who were near. [18]Through Christ we both come to the Father by the power of one Holy Spirit.

[19]So you are no longer strangers and outsiders. You are citizens together with God's people. You are members of God's family.

[20]You are a building that is built on the apostles and prophets. They are the foundation. Christ Jesus himself is the most important stone in the building. [21]The whole building is held together by him. It rises to become a holy temple because it belongs to the Lord.

[22]And because you belong to him, you too are being built together. You are being made into a house where God lives through his Spirit.

PAUL IS THE MESSENGER TO NON-JEWS

3 I, Paul, am a prisoner because of Christ Jesus. I am in prison because of my work among you who are not Jews.

[2]I am sure you have heard that God

Why is it wrong to be bad?

It is wrong to be bad because God created you to be good. Think about your bicycle. It was made for riding. Your bike exists so that you can go from one place to another. It would be foolish of you to use your bike for shoveling snow or for cooking. It was not made for those things. In the same way, God designed us to do what is good and right and to bring honor to him. God created everything. He knows what works and what doesn't. When we do bad things, we do what we were not created to do. He knows what will make us happy and what will hurt us. We go against God's design for us when we do bad.

checkout
Ephesians 2:10

Related verses:
2 Corinthians
5:15–17

dom and understanding that come from the Holy Spirit. I want you to know God better.

[18] I also pray that your mind might see more clearly. Then you will know the hope God has chosen you to receive. You will know that the things God's people will receive are rich and glorious. [19] And you will know his great power. It can't be compared with anything else. It is at work for us who believe. It is like the mighty strength [20] God showed when he raised Christ from the dead.

He seated him at his right hand in his heavenly kingdom. [21] There Christ sits far above all who rule and have authority. He also sits far above all powers and kings. He is above every title that can be given in this world and in the world to come.

[22] God placed all things under Christ's rule. He appointed him to be ruler over everything for the church. [23] The church is Christ's body. It is filled by Christ. He fills everything in every way.

GOD HAS GIVEN US NEW LIFE THROUGH CHRIST

2 You were living in your sins and lawless ways. But in fact you were dead. [2] You used to live as sinners when you followed the ways of this world. You served the one who rules over the spiritual forces of evil. He is the spirit who is now at work in those who don't obey God.

[3] At one time we all lived among them. We tried to satisfy what our sinful nature wanted to do. We followed its longings and thoughts. God was angry with us and everyone else because of the kind of people we were.

[4] But God loves us deeply. He is full of mercy. [5] So he gave us new life because of what Christ has done. He gave us life even when we were dead in sin. God's grace has saved you.

[6] God raised us up with Christ. He has seated us with him in his heavenly kingdom because we belong to Christ Jesus. [7] He has done it to show the riches of his grace for all time to come. His grace can't be compared with anything else. He has shown it by being kind to us because of what Christ Jesus has done.

[8] God's grace has saved you because of your faith in Christ. Your salvation doesn't come from anything you do. It is God's gift. [9] It is not based on anything you have done. No one can brag about earning it.

[10] God made us. He created us to belong to Christ Jesus. Now we can do

If I swear, will I go to hell when I die?

It is important to watch what we say, but God does not decide who goes to hell just by that person's speech. Forgiveness and eternal life depend on trusting Jesus Christ. If we say we are sorry and trust Jesus to save us, God forgives us. And if God forgives us, we will not go to hell. That does not make it all right to swear. We should always try to speak and do what is right.

Related verses:
Romans 3:14,18;
James 3:10

checkout
Ephesians 2:8,9

us with every spiritual blessing. Those blessings come from the heavenly world. They belong to us because we belong to Christ.

⁴God chose us to belong to Christ before the world was created. He chose us to be holy and without blame in his eyes. He loved us. ⁵So he decided long ago to adopt us as his children. He did it because of what Jesus Christ has done. It pleased God to do it. ⁶All those things bring praise to his glorious grace. God freely gave us his grace because of the One he loves.

⁷We have been set free because of what Christ has done. Through his blood our sins have been forgiven. We have been set free because God's grace is so rich. ⁸He poured his grace on us by giving us great wisdom and understanding.

⁹He showed us the mystery of his plan. It was in keeping with what he wanted to do. It was what he had planned through Christ. ¹⁰It will all come about when history has been completed. God will then bring together all things in heaven and on earth under one ruler. The ruler is Christ.

¹¹We were also chosen to belong to him. God decided to choose us long ago in keeping with his plan. He works out everything to fit his plan and purpose. ¹²We were the first to put our hope in Christ. We were chosen to bring praise to his glory.

¹³You also became believers in Christ. That happened when you heard the message of truth. It was the good news about how you could be saved. When you believed, he marked you with a seal. The seal is the Holy Spirit that he promised.

¹⁴The Spirit marks us as God's own. We can now be sure that someday we will receive all that God has promised. That will happen after God sets all of his people completely free. All of those things will bring praise to his glory.

PAUL PRAYS AND GIVES THANKS

¹⁵I have heard about your faith in the Lord Jesus. I have also heard about your love for all of God's people. That is why ¹⁶I have not stopped thanking God for you. I always remember you in my prayers.

¹⁷I pray to the God of our Lord Jesus Christ. God is the glorious Father. I keep asking him to give you the wis-

KIDS' QUESTION

Why did God let bad people hurt Jesus?

Jesus could have called on angels to save him. He did not have to let bad people hurt him. After all, he is God's Son. But Jesus chose to suffer and die for us. He knew he had to do this if we were to have our sins forgiven. So he did not ask for help or for God's angels to rescue him. He loved us so much that he paid for our sins with his suffering.

checkout

Ephesians 1:7–10

Related verses:
Matthew 26:53,54
1 John 2:2

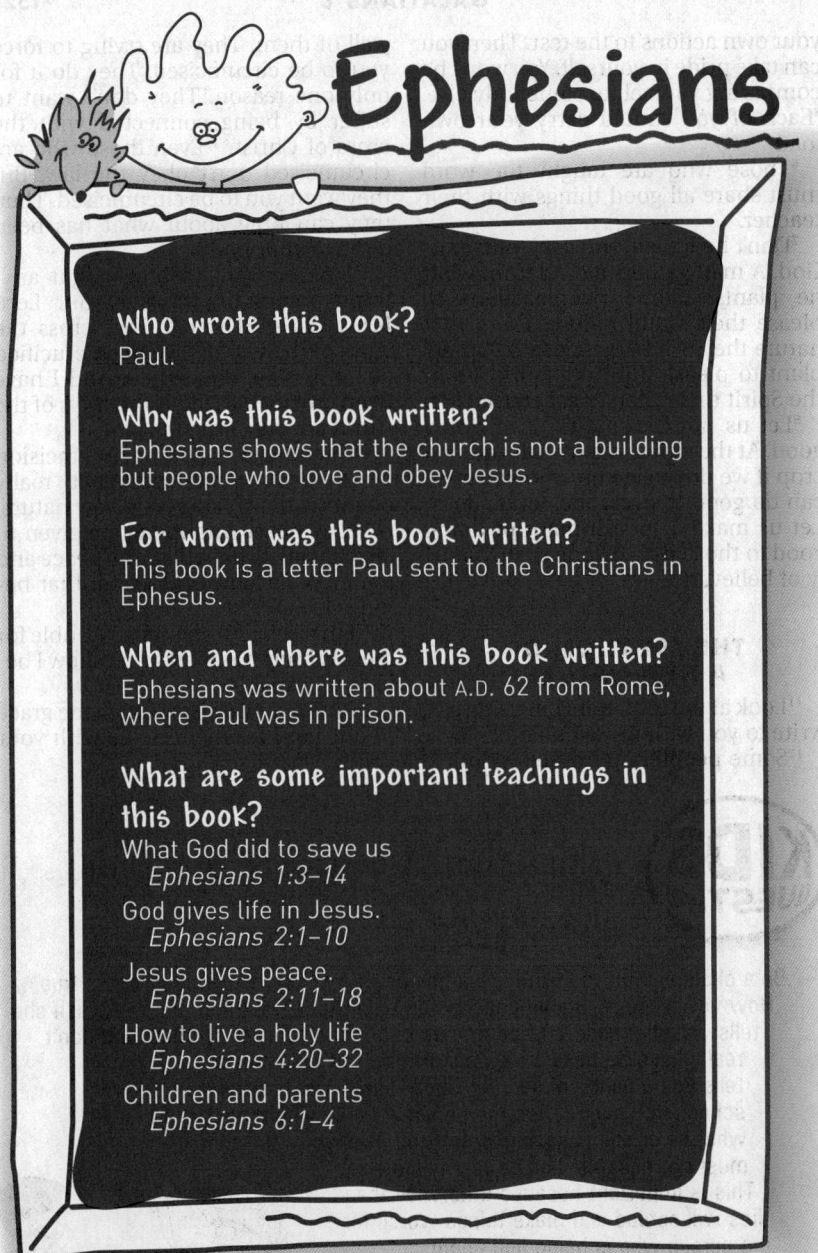

Ephesians

Who wrote this book?
Paul.

Why was this book written?
Ephesians shows that the church is not a building but people who love and obey Jesus.

For whom was this book written?
This book is a letter Paul sent to the Christians in Ephesus.

When and where was this book written?
Ephesians was written about A.D. 62 from Rome, where Paul was in prison.

What are some important teachings in this book?
What God did to save us
Ephesians 1:3–14

God gives life in Jesus.
Ephesians 2:1–10

Jesus gives peace.
Ephesians 2:11–18

How to live a holy life
Ephesians 4:20–32

Children and parents
Ephesians 6:1–4

1 I, Paul, am writing this letter. I am an apostle of Christ Jesus just as God planned.

I am sending this letter to you, God's people in Ephesus. Because you belong to Christ Jesus, you are faithful.

[2]May God our Father and the Lord Jesus Christ give you grace and peace.

GOD GIVES SPIRITUAL BLESSINGS

[3]Give praise to the God and Father of our Lord Jesus Christ. He has blessed

your own actions to the test. Then you can take pride in yourself. You won't be comparing yourself to somebody else. ⁵Each of you should carry your own load.

⁶Those who are taught the word must share all good things with their teacher.

⁷Don't be fooled. You can't outsmart God. A man gathers a crop from what he plants. ⁸Some people plant to please their sinful nature. From that nature they will harvest death. Others plant to please the Holy Spirit. From the Spirit they will harvest eternal life.

⁹Let us not become tired of doing good. At the right time we will gather a crop if we don't give up. ¹⁰So when we can do good to everyone, let us do it. Let us make a special point of doing good to those who belong to the family of believers.

THE CREATION OF A NEW NATURE

¹¹Look at the big letters I'm using as I write to you with my own hand! ¹²Some people want others to think well of them. They are trying to force you to be circumcised. They do it for only one reason. They don't want to suffer by being connected with the cross of Christ. ¹³Even those who are circumcised don't obey the law. But they want you to be circumcised. Then they can brag about what has been done to your body.

¹⁴I never want to brag about anything except the cross of our Lord Jesus Christ. Through that cross the ways of the world have been crucified as far as I am concerned. And I have been crucified as far as the ways of the world are concerned.

¹⁵Circumcision and uncircumcision don't mean anything. What really counts is the creation of a new nature.

¹⁶May peace and mercy be given to all who follow this rule. May peace and mercy be given to the Israel that belongs to God.

¹⁷Finally, let no one cause trouble for me. My body has marks that show I belong to Jesus.

¹⁸Brothers and sisters, may the grace of our Lord Jesus Christ be with your spirit. Amen.

What should you do if someone lies to you?

Be a champion for the truth. Be a boy or girl who stands up for what is true. How you respond to a lie depends on who it affects. If a friend lies when she tells you she made 20 free throws in a row playing basketball, you don't really have to make a big deal of that. But if someone tells you a bunch of bad lies about another kid at school, you need to tell the person who is lying that what he or she is saying is not true. And you must not pass the lies on to anyone else. This is important because otherwise the lies will spread and make things worse for the person who is being lied about. Remember, stick up for the truth, and when you tell others that lying is wrong, be sure to do it in a kind manner.

Related verses:
Romans 14:16;
Ephesians 5:11

checkout
Galatians 6:1

do, the body of Christ will be built up.

¹³That will continue until we all become one in the faith and in the knowledge of God's Son. Then we will be grown up in the faith. We will receive everything that Christ has for us.

¹⁴We will no longer be babies in the faith. We won't be like ships tossed around by the waves. We won't be blown here and there by every new teaching. We won't be blown around by the cleverness and tricks of people who try to hide their evil plans. ¹⁵Instead, we will speak the truth in love. We will grow up into Christ in every way.

He is the Head. ¹⁶He makes the whole body grow and build itself up in love. Under the control of Christ, each part of the body does its work. It supports the other parts. In that way, the body is joined and held together.

LIVING AS CHILDREN OF LIGHT

¹⁷Here is what I'm telling you. I am speaking for the Lord as I warn you. You must no longer live like those who aren't Jews. Their thoughts don't have any purpose. ¹⁸They can't understand the truth. They are separated from the life of God. That is because they don't know him. And they don't know him because their hearts are stubborn.

¹⁹They have lost all feeling for what is right. They have given themselves over to the evil pleasures of their bodies. They take part in every kind of unclean act. And they always long for more.

²⁰But that is not what you have learned about Christ. ²¹I'm sure you heard of him. I'm sure you were taught by him. What you learned was the truth about Jesus.

²²You were taught not to live the way you used to. You must get rid of your old way of life. That's because it is polluted by longing for things that lead you down the wrong path.

²³You were taught to be made new in your thinking. ²⁴You were taught to start living a new life. It is created to be truly good and holy, just as God is.

²⁵So each of you must get rid of your lying. Speak the truth to your neighbor. We are all parts of one body.

²⁶Scripture says, "When you are an-

Is it all right to tell a lie once in a while?

You should always tell the truth because God always tells the truth. God wants you to tell the truth because he is truth. Lies also cause trouble. Usually one lie leads to another. It is much simpler to tell the truth than to have to remember all the lies you have told and keep them covered up. People want you to tell the truth so they can trust you and know that you are a dependable person. They may even look to you for advice and leadership if they know you never lie. Get into the habit of telling the truth. Your friends, classmates, family and neighbors want to be able to trust what you say.

checkout
Ephesians 4:25

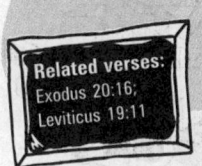
Related verses:
Exodus 20:16;
Leviticus 19:11

WANTED
FULL-TIME CHRISTIANS
NO PART-TIME
POSITIONS AVAILABLE

gry, do not sin." *(Psalm 4:4)* Do not let the sun go down while you are still angry. ²⁷Don't give the devil a chance.

²⁸Those who have been stealing must never steal again. Instead, they must work. They must do something useful with their own hands. Then they will have something to give to people in need.

²⁹Don't let any evil talk come out of your mouths. Say only what will help to build others up and meet their needs. Then what you say will help those who listen.

³⁰Do not make God's Holy Spirit sad. He marked you with a seal for the day when God will set you completely free.

³¹Get rid of all hard feelings, anger and rage. Stop all fighting and lying. Put away every form of hatred. ³²Be kind and tender to one another. Forgive each other, just as God forgave you because of what Christ has done.

5 You are the children that God dearly loves. So be just like him. ²Lead a life of love, just as Christ did. He loved us. He gave himself up for us. He was a sweet-smelling offering and sacrifice to God.

³There should not be even a hint of sexual sin among you. Don't do anything unclean. And do not always want more and more. Things like that are not what God's holy people should do.

⁴There must not be any unclean speech or foolish talk or dirty jokes. All of them are out of place. Instead, you should give thanks.

⁵Here is what you can be sure of. Those who give themselves over to sexual sins are lost. So are people whose lives are not pure. The same is true of those who always want more and more. People who do those things might as well worship statues of gods. No one who does them will receive a share in the kingdom of Christ and of God.

⁶Don't let anyone fool you with words that don't mean anything. Because of things like that, God is angry with those who don't obey. ⁷So don't go along with people like that.

⁸At one time you were in the dark. But now you are in the light because of what the Lord has done. Live like children of the light. ⁹The light produces

Is it wrong to copy computer games?

If a computer game is *copyrighted*, yes. "Copyright" means that the person or company who created it is the only one with the right to copy it. People who write books, songs and computer software often copyright their work so that other people cannot sell it or get a copy without paying for it. The law says that you have to get permission before you can copy or sell someone else's copyrighted work. If you do not, you are stealing information. Some people make illegal copies of computer games, other software, videos, songs or recipes but do not realize they are breaking the law. But that does not make it right.

Remember that wrong is wrong even if everybody does it.

checkout Ephesians 4:28

Related verses:
1 Peter 2:13,14

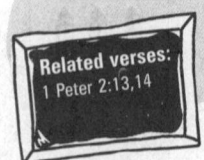

what is completely good, right and true. ¹⁰Find out what pleases the Lord.

¹¹Have nothing to do with the acts of darkness. They don't produce anything good. Show what they are really like. ¹²It is shameful even to talk about what people who don't obey do in secret.

¹³But everything the light shines on can be seen. ¹⁴Light makes everything clear. That is why it is said,

"Wake up, sleeper.
   Rise from the dead.
Then Christ will shine on you."

¹⁵So be very careful how you live. Do not live like people who aren't wise. Live like people who are wise. ¹⁶Make the most of every opportunity. The days are evil. ¹⁷So don't be foolish. Instead, understand what the Lord wants.

¹⁸Don't fill yourself up with wine. Getting drunk will lead to wild living. Instead, be filled with the Holy Spirit.

¹⁹Speak to each other with psalms, hymns and spiritual songs. Sing and make music in your heart to the Lord. ²⁰Always give thanks to God the Father for everything. Give thanks to him in the name of our Lord Jesus Christ.

²¹Follow the lead of one another because of your respect for Christ.

WIVES AND HUSBANDS

²²Wives, follow the lead of your husbands as you follow the Lord. ²³The husband is the head of the wife, just as Christ is the head of the church. The church is Christ's body. He is its Savior. ²⁴The church follows the lead of Christ. In the same way, wives should follow the lead of their husbands in everything.

²⁵Husbands, love your wives. Love them just as Christ loved the church. He gave himself up for her. ²⁶He did it to make her holy. He made her clean by washing her with water and the word. ²⁷He did it to bring her to himself as a brightly shining church. He wants a church that has no stain or wrinkle or any other flaw. He wants a church that is holy and without blame.

Does God get angry when I spend my money foolishly?

He doesn't get angry. But God does want us to be wise, and he is sad when we are foolish.

Think of it this way. God is your biggest fan. More than anyone else, he wants you to win. That is why he cares about how you use your money. If you keep wasting it and ignoring wise advice from everybody all the time, things will not go well for you. You will not have enough to give. You will not have the things you need and really want. You will be very unhappy. *Of course* God will be sad about that!

checkout
Ephesians 4:30

Related verse:
Joel 2:13

²⁸In the same way, husbands should love their wives. They should love them as they love their own bodies. Any man who loves his wife loves himself. ²⁹After all, people have never hated their own bodies. Instead, they feed and care for their bodies. And that is what Christ does for the church. ³⁰We are parts of his body. ³¹Scripture says, "That's why a man will leave his father and mother and be joined to his wife. The two will become one." *(Genesis 2:24)* ³²That is a deep mystery. But I'm talking about Christ and the church.

³³A husband also must love his wife. He must love her just as he loves himself. And a wife must respect her husband.

CHILDREN AND PARENTS

6 Children, obey your parents as believers in the Lord. Obey them because it's the right thing to do. ²Scripture says, "Honor your father and mother." That is the first commandment that has a promise. ³"Then things will go well with you. You will live a long time on the earth." *(Deuteronomy 5:16)*

⁴Fathers, don't make your children angry. Instead, train them and teach them the ways of the Lord as you raise them.

SLAVES AND MASTERS

⁵Slaves, obey your masters here on earth. Respect them and honor them with a heart that is true. Obey them just as you would obey Christ. ⁶Don't obey them only to please them when they are watching. Do it because you are slaves of Christ. Be sure your heart does what God wants.

⁷Serve your masters with all your heart. Work as if you were not serving people but the Lord. ⁸You know that the Lord will give you a reward. He will

If some of my friends are doing something that I think is bad, should I tell my parents?

Perhaps. It is great to be able to tell your parents about what is going on in your life. They want to know about things that bother you and will often have good advice on what to do. But you have to decide whether it is worth telling them about something that your friends are doing. If your friends are doing something that you think is bad, you can talk to your friends yourself. You do not need to tell your parents. But if your friends are breaking the law, or if someone could get hurt, you *should* tell your parents. If you are at school, you should tell a teacher or another grownup. If you aren't sure what to do, ask your parents for advice. They will probably be glad to help.

Most of all, *show* your friends what is *good*. Set a good example, rather than telling on every little bad thing you see someone do. That is what it really means to "have nothing to do with the acts of darkness."

checkout
Ephesians 5:11

Related verses:
Matthew 5:16;
John 3:19–21

give to each of you in keeping with the good you do. It doesn't matter whether you are slaves or free.

⁹Masters, treat your slaves in the same way. When you warn them, don't be too hard on them. You know that the One who is their Master and yours is in heaven. And he treats everyone the same.

GOD'S ARMOR

¹⁰Finally, let the Lord make you strong. Depend on his mighty power. ¹¹Put on all of God's armor. Then you can stand firm against the devil's evil plans. ¹²Our fight is not against human beings. It is against the rulers, the authorities and the powers of this dark world. It is against the spiritual forces of evil in the heavenly world.

¹³So put on all of God's armor. Evil days will come. But you will be able to stand up to anything. And after you have done everything you can, you will still be standing.

¹⁴So stand firm. Put the belt of truth around your waist. Put the armor of godliness on your chest. ¹⁵Wear on your feet what will prepare you to tell the good news of peace. ¹⁶Also, pick up the shield of faith. With it you can put out all of the flaming arrows of the evil one. ¹⁷Put on the helmet of salvation. And take the sword of the Holy Spirit. The sword is God's word.

¹⁸At all times, pray by the power of the Spirit. Pray all kinds of prayers. Be watchful, so that you can pray. Always keep on praying for all of God's people.

¹⁹Pray also for me. Pray that when I open my mouth, the right words will be given to me. Then I can be bold as I tell the mystery of the good news. ²⁰Because of the good news, I am being

Why do I have to obey my parents?

The most important reason for children to obey their parents is that God said to. God knows that children need to be safe and that they need to learn. He gives them parents to be in charge of the home and to teach them right from wrong. Living God's way means obeying moms and dads.

We know that some parents hurt or even abandon their children. It is hard to think of honoring and obeying parents like this. All children should try to love and honor their parents. But they should report the problem if their parents are not keeping them safe or if they are asking them to do something that is against God's law.

God promises long life to those who obey their parents. We know that God's promises can always be trusted. But we also know that some children die young, even if they have been obedient to good parents. Someday after Jesus comes again we will understand this better. We do know that we will live eternally with God in heaven if we trust Jesus, obey God's law and honor our parents.

checkout
Ephesians 6:1-3

Related verses:
Exodus 20:12;
Colossians 3:20

held by chains as the Lord's messenger. So pray that I will be bold as I preach the good news. That's what I should do.

FINAL GREETINGS

²¹Tychicus is a dear brother. He is faithful in serving the Lord. He will tell you everything about me. Then you will know how I am and what I am do-ing. ²²That's why I am sending him to you. I want you to know how we are. And I want him to cheer you up.

²³May God the Father and the Lord Jesus Christ give peace to the brothers and sisters. May they also give them love and faith.

²⁴May grace be given to everyone who loves our Lord Jesus Christ with a love that will never die.

Are Satan and Jesus still at war?

Jesus and Satan are bitter enemies. But Jesus will win. When Jesus says to love your enemies, he is not talking about loving the devil. He is talking about loving people. The devil will do everything in his power to try to stop people from believing in Jesus and living for Jesus. But we do not have to be afraid of Satan because God protects his people against Satan's power. Jesus never loses.

checkout

Ephesians 6:11,12

Related verse:
1 John 2:14

JASON'S IMAGINATION

Philippians

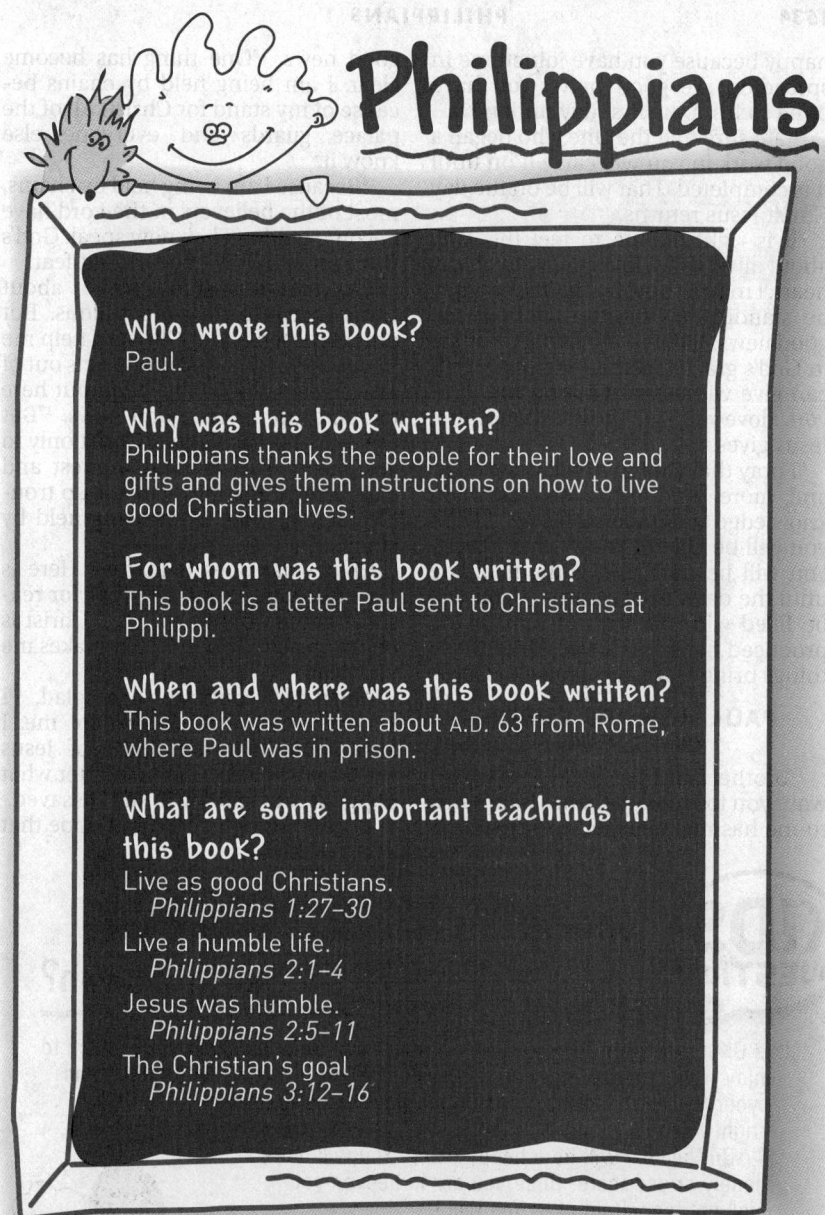

Who wrote this book?
Paul.

Why was this book written?
Philippians thanks the people for their love and gifts and gives them instructions on how to live good Christian lives.

For whom was this book written?
This book is a letter Paul sent to Christians at Philippi.

When and where was this book written?
This book was written about A.D. 63 from Rome, where Paul was in prison.

What are some important teachings in this book?
Live as good Christians.
Philippians 1:27–30

Live a humble life.
Philippians 2:1–4

Jesus was humble.
Philippians 2:5–11

The Christian's goal
Philippians 3:12–16

1 We, Paul and Timothy, are writing this letter. We serve Christ Jesus.

We are sending this letter to you, all of God's people in Philippi. You belong to Christ Jesus. We are also sending this letter to your leaders and deacons. ²May God our Father and the Lord Jesus Christ give you grace and peace.

PAUL PRAYS AND GIVES THANKS

³I thank my God every time I remember you. ⁴In all my prayers for all of you, I always pray with joy. ⁵I am

happy because you have joined me in spreading the good news. You have done so from the first day until now.

⁶I am sure that the One who began a good work in you will carry it on until it is completed. That will be on the day Christ Jesus returns.

⁷It is right for me to feel this way about all of you. I love you with all my heart. I may be held by chains, or I may be standing up for the truth of the good news. Either way, all of you share in God's grace together with me. ⁸God can give witness that I long for all of you. I love you with the love that Christ Jesus gives.

⁹I pray that your love will grow more and more. And let it be based on knowledge and understanding. ¹⁰Then you will be able to know what is best. You will be pure and without blame until the day Christ returns. ¹¹You will be filled with the fruit of right living produced by Jesus Christ. All of those things bring glory and praise to God.

PAUL HONORS CHRIST IN PRISON

¹²Brothers and sisters, here is what I want you to know. What has happened to me has really helped to spread the good news. ¹³One thing has become clear. I am being held by chains because of my stand for Christ. All of the palace guards and everyone else know it.

¹⁴Because I am being held by chains, most of the believers in the Lord have become bolder. They now speak God's word more boldly and without fear.

¹⁵It's true that some preach about Christ because they are jealous. But others preach about Christ to help me in my work. ¹⁶The last group acts out of love. They know I have been put here to stand up for the good news. ¹⁷But the others preach about Christ only to get ahead. They are not honest and true. They think they can stir up trouble for me while I am being held by chains.

¹⁸But what does it matter? Here is the important thing. Whether for reasons that are right or wrong, Christ is being preached about. That makes me very glad.

And I will continue to be glad. ¹⁹I know that you are praying for me. I also know that the Spirit of Jesus Christ will help me. So no matter what happens, I'm sure I will still be saved. ²⁰I completely expect and hope that

What if I don't want to leave my friends and family to go to heaven?

It is OK not to want to go to heaven right now. God has given you a place to enjoy right here and now on this earth. He has given you your home and your family and friends. You do not have to go to heaven right away.

But heaven will be a happy place. You will not be lonely or sad there. Once you are in heaven you will not feel afraid of it. You will be glad. And if your family and friends know Jesus, too, you all will be in heaven together.

checkout Philippians 1:21

Related verses: Revelation 21:3–5

I won't be ashamed in any way. I'm sure I will be brave enough. Now as always Christ will be lifted high through my body. He will be lifted up whether I live or die.

²¹For me, life finds all of its meaning in Christ. Death also has its benefits.

²²Suppose I go on living in my body. Then I will be able to carry on my work. It will bear a lot of fruit. But what should I choose? I don't know. ²³I can't decide between the two. I long to leave this world and be with Christ. That is better by far.

²⁴But it is more important for you that I stay alive. ²⁵I'm sure of that. So I know I will remain with you. And I will continue with all of you to help you grow and be joyful in what you have been taught. ²⁶I'm sure I will be with you again. Then your joy in Christ Jesus will be greater than ever because of me.

²⁷No matter what happens, live in a way that brings honor to the good news about Christ. Then I will know that you stand firm with one purpose. I may come and see you or only hear about you. But I will know that you work together as one person. And I will know that you work to spread the teachings of the good news.

²⁸So don't be afraid in any way of those who oppose you. That will show them that they will be destroyed and that you will be saved. That's what God will do.

²⁹Here is what he has given you to do for Christ. You must not only believe in him. You must also suffer for him.

³⁰You are going through the same struggle you saw me go through. As you have heard, I am still struggling.

THINKING LIKE CHRIST

2 Are you cheerful because you belong to Christ? Does his love comfort you? Is the Holy Spirit

If I die when I'm a kid, will I miss out on doing fun things on earth?

Your life on earth ends as soon as you die. That is true no matter how young or old you are when you die. But will you miss your fun on earth? Will you be sad up in heaven because of all the fun things you did not get to do before you died? Not at all! You will be in the presence of God. That is the most enjoyable thing a person can do. It is what we were created for. That is hard to understand right now. But it is still true.

Do not worry about missing out on fun. God has a wonderful plan for your life here on earth. Enjoy the life God has given you. You will not be sorry you went to heaven when the time comes for you to go. You will be very happy.

checkout Philippians 1:23,24

JASON'S IMAGINATION

Related verses:
1 Peter 1:3,4

your companion? Has Christ been gentle and loving toward you? ²Then make my joy complete by agreeing with each other. Have the same love. Be one in spirit and purpose.

³Don't do anything only to get ahead. Don't do it because you are proud. Instead, be free of pride. Think of others as better than yourselves.

⁴None of you should look out just for your own good. You should also look out for the good of others.

⁵You should think in the same way Christ Jesus does.

⁶In his very nature he was God.
But he did not think that
being equal with God was
something he should hold
on to.
⁷Instead, he made himself nothing.
He took on the very nature of a
servant.
He was made in human form.
⁸He appeared as a man.
He came down to the lowest
level.
He obeyed God completely, even
though it led to his death.

In fact, he died on a cross.
⁹So God lifted him up to the
highest place.
He gave him the name that is
above every name.
¹⁰When the name of Jesus is spoken,
everyone's knee will bow to
worship him.
Every knee in heaven and on
earth and under the earth will
bow to worship him.
¹¹Everyone's mouth will say that
Jesus Christ is Lord.
And God the Father will receive
the glory.

LIVING LIKE CHRIST

¹²My dear friends, you have always obeyed God. You obeyed while I was with you. And you have obeyed even more while I am not with you. So continue to work out your own salvation. Do it with fear and trembling. ¹³God is working in you. He wants your plans and your acts to be in keeping with his good purpose.

¹⁴Do everything without finding fault or arguing. ¹⁵Then you will be

---

KIDS' QUESTion

Is it OK to think that you are better than somebody else if you really are better?

Who says you are better than someone else? Sometimes people think they are better than they really are and become filled with pride. Remember that all of your abilities and talents come from God. Everyone needs to depend on God. There is nothing wrong with being glad that you did a good job at something like sports or grades. You do not have to pretend that you are lousy at it or apologize for being good. But do not compare yourself to others or think of yourself as better than they are. You may be a better basketball player, but that does not make you a better person. Remember that God gives important talents to *everybody*.

checkout
Philippians 2:3

Related verses:
Luke 18:9–14;
Romans 12:3,4,
6–8

pure and without blame. You will be children of God without fault in a sinful and evil world. Among the people of the world you shine like stars in the heavens. [16]You shine as you hold out to them the word of life. So I can brag about you on the day Christ returns. I can be happy that I didn't run or work for nothing.

[17]But my life might even be poured out like a drink offering on your sacrifices. I'm talking about the way you serve because you believe. Even so, I am glad. I am joyful with all of you. [18]So you too should be glad and joyful with me.

TIMOTHY AND EPAPHRODITUS

[19]I hope to send Timothy to you soon if the Lord Jesus allows it. Then I will be cheered up when I receive news about you. [20]I have no one else like Timothy. He truly cares about how you are doing.

[21]All the others are looking out for their own interests. They are not looking out for the interests of Jesus Christ.

[22]But you know that Timothy has proved himself. He has served with me like a son with his father in spreading the good news.

[23]So I hope to send him as soon as I see how things go with me. [24]And I'm sure I myself will come soon if the Lord allows it.

[25]But I think it's necessary to send Epaphroditus back to you. He is my brother in the Lord. He is a worker and a soldier of Christ together with me. He is also your messenger. You sent him to take care of my needs. [26]He longs for all of you. He is troubled because you heard he was sick.

[27]He was very sick. In fact, he almost died. But God had mercy on him. He also had mercy on me. God spared me sadness after sadness. [28]So I want even more to send him to you. Then when you see him again, you will be glad. And I won't worry so much.

[29]Welcome him as a brother in the Lord with great joy. Honor people like him. [30]He almost died for the work of Christ. He put his life in danger to make up for the help you couldn't give me.

KIDS' QUESTION

Is it really "finders keepers"?

No. "Finders keepers, losers weepers!" is an excuse for keeping something that belongs to someone else. If you find something valuable, try to find the owner. If you find money in a parking lot, take it to a police station. If you find a wallet, look for a name inside and let the owner come and get it. If you find a ten dollar bill in a classroom, take it to the teacher. If you find a basketball on the playground, take it to the gym teacher. Try to find the owner if you can.

checkout Philippians 2:4

Related verses:
Exodus 23:4;
Luke 6:31

DO NOT TRUST HUMAN NATURE

3 Finally, my brothers and sisters, be joyful because you belong to the Lord. It is no trouble for me to write about some important matters to you again. If you know about them, you will have a safe path to follow.

²Watch out for those dogs. They do evil things. When they circumcise, it is nothing more than a useless cutting of the body.

³But we have been truly circumcised. We worship God by the power of his Spirit. We brag about what Christ Jesus has done. We don't put our trust in our weak human nature.

⁴I have many reasons to trust in my human nature. Others may think they have reasons to trust in theirs. But I have even more. ⁵I was circumcised on the eighth day. I am part of the people of Israel. I am from the tribe of Benjamin. I am a pure Hebrew. As far as the law is concerned, I am a Pharisee. ⁶As far as being committed is concerned, I opposed and attacked the church. As far as keeping the Law is concerned, I kept it perfectly.

⁷I thought things like that were for my benefit. But now I consider them to be nothing because of Christ. ⁸Even more, I consider everything to be nothing compared to knowing Christ Jesus my Lord. To know him is the best thing of all. Because of him I have lost everything. But I consider all of it to be garbage so I can get to know Christ. ⁹I want to be joined to him.

For me, being right with God does not come from the law. It comes because I believe in Christ. It comes from God. It is received by faith.

¹⁰I want to know Christ better. I want to know the power that raised him from the dead. I want to share in his sufferings. I want to become like him by sharing in his death. ¹¹Then by God's grace I will rise from the dead.

MOVING ON TOWARD THE GOAL

¹²I have not yet received all of those things. I have not yet been made perfect. But I move on to take hold of what Christ Jesus took hold of me for.

¹³Brothers and sisters, I don't consider that I have taken hold of it yet. But here is the one thing I do. I forget what is behind me. I push hard toward

Will we look like we do now when we get new bodies?

No one knows *exactly* what we will look like. But the Bible makes it clear that we will have new and perfect bodies. We will be different. But we surely will not be strangers to each other. We will be able to recognize each other and enjoy each other's company, just as we do here on earth. But it will be better because we will never fight with each other!

Philippians 3:21

Related verses:
1 Corinthians 15:35–58

HOUSE OF MIRRORS

what is ahead of me. [14]I move on toward the goal to win the prize. God has appointed me to win it. The heavenly prize is Christ Jesus himself.

[15]All of us who are grown up in the faith should see things that way. Maybe you think differently about something. But God will make it clear to you. [16]Only let us live up to what we have already reached.

[17]Brothers and sisters, join with others in following my example. Pay close attention to those who live in keeping with the pattern we gave you.

[18]I have told you those things many times before. Now I say it again with tears in my eyes. Many people live like enemies of the cross of Christ. [19]The only thing they have coming to them is death. Their stomach is their god. They brag about what they should be ashamed of. They think only about earthly things.

[20]But we are citizens of heaven. And we can hardly wait for a Savior from there. He is the Lord Jesus Christ. [21]He has the power to bring everything under his control. By his power he will change our earthly bodies. They will become like his glorious body.

4 My brothers and sisters, that is how you should stand firm in the Lord's strength. I love you and long for you. Dear friends, you are my joy and my crown.

DO WHAT IS BEST

[2]Here is what I'm asking Euodia and Syntyche to do. I want them to agree with each other because they belong to the Lord.

[3]My true companion, here is what I ask you to do. Help those women. They have served at my side. They have helped me spread the good news. So have Clement and the rest of those who have worked together with me. Their names are all written in the Book of Life.

[4]Always be joyful because you belong to the Lord. I will say it again. Be joyful. [5]Let everyone know how gentle you are. The Lord is coming soon.

[6]Don't worry about anything. Instead, tell God about everything. Ask and pray. Give thanks to him. [7]Then

KIDS' QUESTION

Why do we pray?

Prayer is how we talk to God. It is a lot like talking to a good friend. When we have a good friend, we talk to that person about all sorts of things. That is just part of being a friend. In the same way, we talk to God about what is happening in our lives. God wants us to share our lives with him. He wants us to tell him about how we feel and what we need. He knows us, but he wants us to know him too. When we pray we get to know him better. Then God can make changes in us.

checkout
Philippians 4:6,7

Related verses:
Luke 6:12;
1 Thessalonians
5:17

God's peace will watch over your hearts and your minds because you belong to Christ Jesus. God's peace can never be completely understood.

⁸Finally, my brothers and sisters, always think about what is true. Think about what is noble, right and pure. Think about what is lovely and worthy of respect. If anything is excellent or worthy of praise, think about those kinds of things. ⁹Do what you have learned or received or heard from me. Follow my example.

The God who gives peace will be with you.

PAUL GIVES THANKS FOR HELP RECEIVED

¹⁰At last you are concerned about me again. That makes me very happy. We belong to the Lord. I know that you have been concerned. But you had no chance to show it.

¹¹I'm not saying that because I need anything. I have learned to be content no matter what happens to me. ¹²I know what it's like not to have what I need. I also know what it's like to have more than I need. I have learned the secret of being content no matter what happens. I am content whether I am well fed or hungry. I am content whether I have more than enough or not enough. ¹³I can do everything by the power of Christ. He gives me strength.

¹⁴But it was good of you to share in my troubles. ¹⁵And you believers at Philippi know what happened when I left Macedonia. Not one church helped me in the matter of giving and receiving. You were the only one that did. That was in the early days when you first heard the good news. ¹⁶Even when I was in Thessalonica, you sent me help when I needed it. You did it again and again.

¹⁷I'm not looking for a gift. I'm looking for what is best for you. ¹⁸I have received my full pay, and even more than that. I have everything I need.

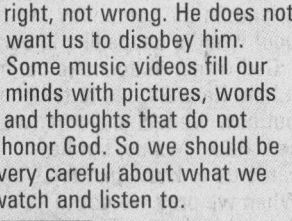

Is it wrong to watch music videos?

It is not wrong to watch television, listen to the radio, watch videos or listen to music. But God wants us to be wise about what we think about, watch or listen to. A lot of the stuff on shows, movies, music and radio is not good. Often the people on them use bad language, do bad things and make bad look good. We know that God wants us to do what is right, not wrong. He does not want us to disobey him. Some music videos fill our minds with pictures, words and thoughts that do not honor God. So we should be very careful about what we watch and listen to.

checkout
Philippians 4:8

Related verse:
Ephesians 5:11

That's because Epaphroditus brought me the gifts you sent. They are a sweet-smelling offering. They are a gift that God accepts. He is pleased with it.

[19]My God will meet all your needs. He will meet them in keeping with his wonderful riches that come to you because you belong to Christ Jesus.

[20]Give glory to our God and Father for ever and ever. Amen.

FINAL GREETINGS

[21]Greet all of God's people. They belong to Christ Jesus. The brothers who are with me send greetings. [22]All of God's people here send you greetings. Most of all, those who live in the palace of Caesar send you greetings.

[23]May the grace of the Lord Jesus Christ be with your spirit. Amen.

Why should we always have to rescue our friends when they get in trouble?

God says that we should help those who are in trouble, even our *enemies*. That's what it means to love, and helping others this way is how we can show them God's love. You can help your friends when they are in trouble. That's being a very good friend to them. However, there's a limit to what you can do—parents and other adults may need to help. You shouldn't lie for friends or make excuses for them. Sometimes letting friends learn to solve their own problems is the best thing to do.

checkout Philippians 4:14–16

Related verses:
Psalm 107:6;
Proverbs 19:19;
John 15:13

FROG CATCHING CLUB
SMELLY SWAMP BRANCH

Quest Clue

Philippians 2 tells us that Jesus was willing to become human even though he was God. To learn more about how you can follow Jesus' example and be humble like him, find the Quest Challenge at the end of 2 Chronicles.

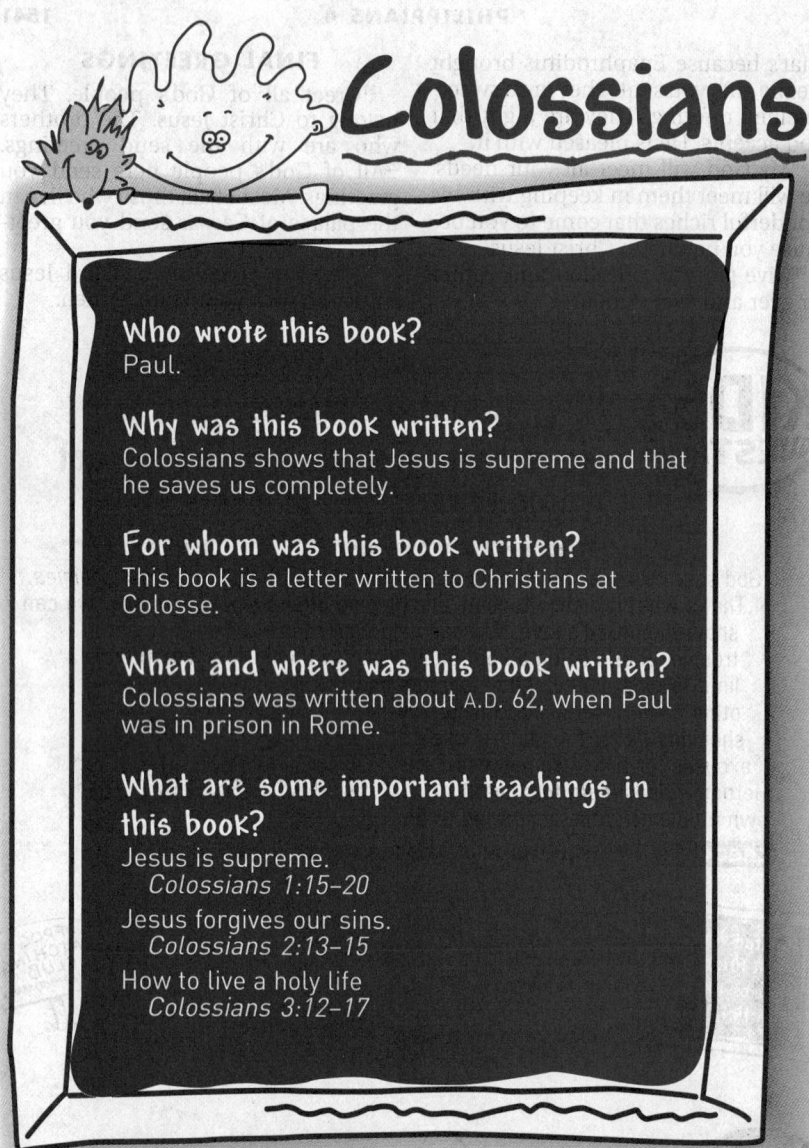

Colossians

Who wrote this book?
Paul.

Why was this book written?
Colossians shows that Jesus is supreme and that he saves us completely.

For whom was this book written?
This book is a letter written to Christians at Colosse.

When and where was this book written?
Colossians was written about A.D. 62, when Paul was in prison in Rome.

What are some important teachings in this book?
Jesus is supreme.
Colossians 1:15–20

Jesus forgives our sins.
Colossians 2:13–15

How to live a holy life
Colossians 3:12–17

---

1 I, Paul, am writing this letter. I am an apostle of Christ Jesus just as God planned. Our brother Timothy joins me in writing.

²We are sending this letter to you, our brothers and sisters in Colosse. You belong to Christ. You are holy and faithful.

May God our Father give you grace and peace.

PAUL PRAYS AND GIVES THANKS

³We always thank God, the Father of our Lord Jesus Christ, when we pray for you. ⁴We thank him because we have heard about your faith in Christ Jesus. We have also heard that you love all of God's people.

⁵Your faith and love are based on the hope you have. What you hope for is stored up for you in heaven. You have

already heard about it. You were told about it when the message of truth was given to you. I'm talking about the good news ⁶that has come to you.

All over the world the good news is bearing fruit and growing. It has been doing that among you since the day you heard it. That is when you understood God's grace in all its truth.

⁷You learned the good news from Epaphras. He is dear to us. He serves Christ together with us. He faithfully works for Christ and for us among you. ⁸He also told us about your love that comes from the Holy Spirit.

⁹That's why we have not stopped praying for you. We have been praying for you since the day we heard about you. We have been asking God to fill you with the knowledge of what he wants. We pray that he will give you spiritual wisdom and understanding.

¹⁰We pray that you will lead a life that is worthy of the Lord. We pray that you will please him in every way. So we want you to bear fruit in every good thing you do. We want you to grow to know God better. ¹¹We want you to be very strong, in keeping with his glorious power. We want you to be patient. Never give up. Be joyful ¹²as you give thanks to the Father.

He has made you fit to share with all his people. You will all receive a share in the kingdom of light.

¹³He has saved us from the kingdom of darkness. He has brought us into the kingdom of the Son he loves. ¹⁴Because of what the Son has done, we have been set free. Because of him, all of our sins have been forgiven.

CHRIST IS FAR ABOVE EVERYTHING

¹⁵Christ is the exact likeness of God, who can't be seen. He is first, and he is over all of creation. ¹⁶All things were created by him. He created everything in heaven and on earth. He created everything that can be seen and everything that can't be seen. He created kings, powers, rulers and authorities. Everything was created by him and for him. ¹⁷Before anything was created, he was already there. He holds everything together.

¹⁸And he is the head of the body, which is the church. He is the beginning. He is the first to be raised from the dead. That happened so that he would be far above everything. ¹⁹God was pleased to have his whole nature living in Christ. ²⁰God was pleased to bring all things back to himself because of what Christ has done. That includes all things on earth and in

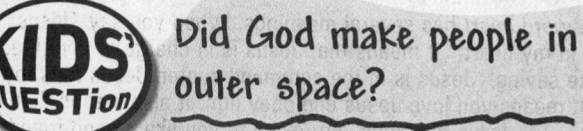

KIDS' QUESTION: Did God make people in outer space?

Some people talk about creatures in outer space. But no one really knows whether there is life on other planets. Most of the talk about other life forms comes from movies and what people think might be true. But if there is life in other parts of the universe, God is in charge of it. God created *everything,* and he is the God of all life everywhere, no matter where it may be.

checkout
Colossians
1:16

Related verses:
Genesis 1:1;
1 Chronicles 29:11

heaven. God made peace through Christ's blood, through his death on the cross.

²¹At one time you were separated from God. You were enemies in your minds because of your evil ways. ²²But because Christ died, God has brought you back to himself. Christ's death has made you holy in God's sight. So now you don't have any flaw. You are free from blame.

²³But you must keep your faith steady and firm. Don't move away from the hope that the good news holds out to you. It is the good news that you heard. It has been preached to every creature under heaven. I, Paul, now serve the good news.

PAUL'S WORK
FOR THE CHURCH

²⁴I am happy because of what was suffered for you. And in my body I fill up my share in Christ's sufferings. I do it for his body, which is the church. ²⁵I serve the church. God appointed me to bring all of his word to you.

²⁶That word contains the mystery that has been hidden for many ages. But now it has been made known to God's people. ²⁷God has chosen to make known to them the glorious riches of that mystery. He has made it known among those who aren't Jews. And here is what it is. Christ is in you. He is your hope of glory.

²⁸We preach about him. With all the wisdom we have, we warn and teach everyone. When we bring them to God, we want them to be perfect as people who belong to Christ.

²⁹That's what I'm working for. I work hard with all of Christ's strength. His strength works powerfully in me.

2 I want you to know how hard I am working for you. I'm concerned for those who are in Laodicea. I'm also concerned for everyone who has not met me in person. ²I want their hearts to be made cheerful and strong. I want them to be joined together in love. Then their understanding will be rich and complete. They will know the mystery of God. That mystery is Christ.

³All the treasures of wisdom and knowledge are hidden in him.

⁴But I don't want anyone to fool you

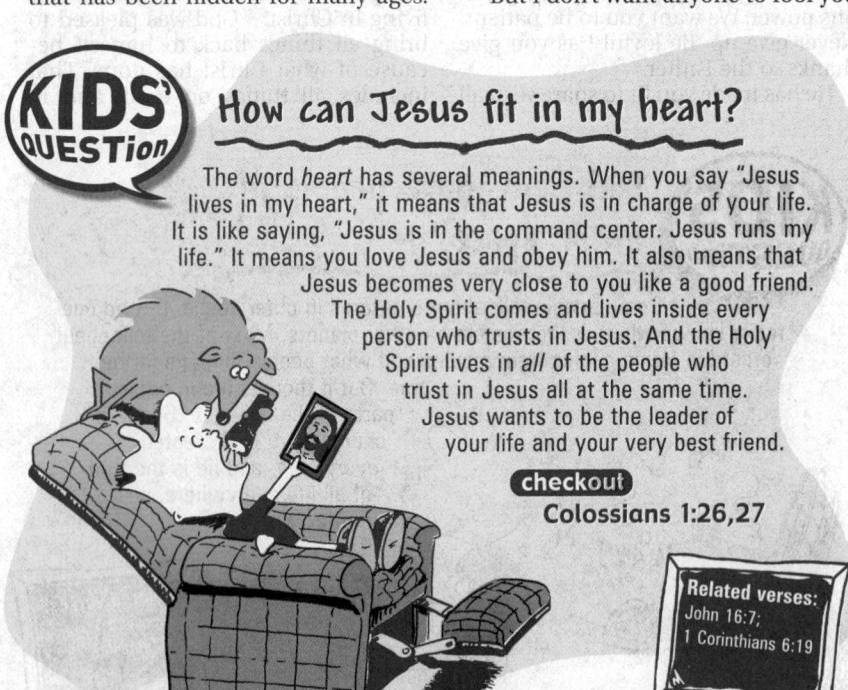

KIDS' QUESTION

How can Jesus fit in my heart?

The word *heart* has several meanings. When you say "Jesus lives in my heart," it means that Jesus is in charge of your life. It is like saying, "Jesus is in the command center. Jesus runs my life." It means you love Jesus and obey him. It also means that Jesus becomes very close to you like a good friend. The Holy Spirit comes and lives inside every person who trusts in Jesus. And the Holy Spirit lives in *all* of the people who trust in Jesus all at the same time. Jesus wants to be the leader of your life and your very best friend.

checkout
Colossians 1:26,27

Related verses:
John 16:7;
1 Corinthians 6:19

with fast talk that only sounds good. [5]So even though I am away from you in body, I am with you in spirit. I am glad to see that you are doing everything in good order. And I am happy that your faith in Christ is so strong.

FREEDOM FROM HUMAN RULES

[6]You received Christ Jesus as Lord. So keep on living in him. [7]Have your roots in him. Build yourselves up in him. Grow strong in what you believe, just as you were taught. Be more thankful than ever before.

[8]Make sure no one captures you. They will try to capture you by using false reasoning that has no meaning. Their ideas depend on human teachings. They also depend on the basic things the people of this world believe. They don't depend on Christ.

[9]God's whole nature is living in Christ in human form. [10]Because you belong to Christ, you have everything you need. He is the ruler over every power and authority.

[11]When you received Christ, you were also circumcised by putting away your sinful nature. Human hands didn't circumcise you. Christ did.

[12]When you were baptized, you were buried together with him. You were raised to life together with him by believing in God's power. God raised Jesus from the dead.

[13]At one time you were dead in your sins. Your sinful nature was not circumcised. But God gave you new life together with Christ. He forgave us all of our sins.

[14]He wiped out the written Law with its rules. The Law was against us. It opposed us. He took it away and nailed it to the cross. [15]He took away the weapons of the powers and authorities. He made a public show of them. He won the battle over them by dying on the cross.

[16]So don't let anyone judge you be-

Why do people say things that aren't true about the stuff they sell on commercials?

Companies want people to buy their products. That is why they make ads. Sometimes the people who make ads do not care whether the ads are true. They just want to get people to buy their stuff. So they make ads that make the product look as though it can do something that it *might* do. And if you do not think about it you may get the idea that the thing will be better than it is. For example, a TV ad may show a group of kids having great fun playing a game. You really do not know from the ad whether the game is fun. You do not know whether *you* would enjoy playing it. But you might get the idea that you would, even if you would not. The kids on TV are actors who were paid to look as though they were having fun. When you see or hear an ad, look and listen carefully.

checkout Colossians 2:8

Related verses:
Jeremiah 9:5,6

cause of what you eat or drink. Don't let anyone judge you about holy days. I'm talking about special feasts and New Moons and Sabbath days. [17]They are only a shadow of the things that were going to come. But what is real is found in Christ.

[18]Some people enjoy pretending they aren't proud. They worship angels. But don't let people like that hold you back from winning the prize. They tell you every little thing about what they have seen. Their minds are not guided by the Holy Spirit. So they are proud of their useless ideas.

[19]They aren't connected to the Head. But the whole body grows from the Head. The muscles and tendons hold the body together. And God causes it to grow.

[20]The people of the world believe certain basic things. You died with Christ as far as things like that are concerned. So why do you act as if you still belong to the world? Here are the rules you follow. [21]"Do not handle! Do not taste! Do not touch!" [22]Rules like that are all going to die out as time goes by. They are only based on human rules and teachings.

[23]It is true that those rules seem wise. Because of them, people give themselves over to their own kind of worship. They pretend they aren't proud. They treat their bodies very badly. But rules like that don't help. They don't stop people from chasing after sinful pleasures.

RULES FOR HOLY LIVING

3 You have been raised up with Christ. So think about things that are in heaven. That is where Christ is. He is sitting at God's right hand. [2]Think about things that are in heaven. Don't think about things that are on earth.

[3]You died. Now your life is hidden with Christ in God. [4]Christ is your life. When he appears again, you also will appear with him in heaven's glory.

[5]So put to death anything that belongs to your earthly nature. Get rid of your sexual sins and unclean acts. Don't let your feelings get out of control. Remove from your life all evil longings. Stop always wanting more

and more. You might as well be worshiping statues of gods. [6]God's anger is going to come because of those things. [7]That's the way you lived at one time in your life.

[8]But now here are the kinds of things you must get rid of. You must put away anger, rage, hate and lies. Let no dirty words come out of your mouths. [9]Don't lie to each other.

You have gotten rid of your old way of life and its habits. [10]You have started living a new life. It is being made new so that what you know has the Creator's likeness.

[11]Here there is no Greek or Jew. There is no difference between those who are circumcised and those who are not. There is no rude outsider, or even a Scythian. There is no slave or free person. But Christ is everything. And he is in everything.

[12]You are God's chosen people. You are holy and dearly loved. So put on tender mercy and kindness as if they were your clothes. Don't be proud. Be gentle and patient. [13]Put up with each other. Forgive the things you are holding against one another. Forgive, just as the Lord forgave you.

[14]And over all of those good things put on love. Love holds them all together perfectly as if they were one.

[15]Let the peace that Christ gives rule in your hearts. As parts of one body, you were appointed to live in peace. And be thankful.

[16]Let Christ's word live in you like a rich treasure. Teach and correct each other wisely. Sing psalms, hymns and spiritual songs. Sing with thanks in your hearts to God. [17]Do everything you say or do in the name of the Lord Jesus. Always give thanks to God the Father through Christ.

RULES FOR CHRISTIAN FAMILIES

[18]Wives, follow the lead of your husbands. That's what the Lord wants you to do.

[19]Husbands, love your wives. Don't be mean to them.

[20]Children, obey your parents in everything. That pleases the Lord.

[21]Fathers, don't make your children bitter. If you do, they will lose hope.

²²Slaves, obey your earthly masters in everything. Don't do it just to please them when they are watching you. Obey them with an honest heart. Do it out of respect for the Lord.

²³Work at everything you do with all your heart. Work as if you were working for the Lord, not for human masters. ²⁴Work because you know that you will finally receive as a reward what the Lord wants you to have. You are serving the Lord Christ.

²⁵Anyone who does wrong will be paid back for what he does. God treats everyone the same.

4 Masters, give your slaves what is right and fair. Do it because you know that you also have a Master in heaven.

MORE DIRECTIONS

²Spend a lot of time in prayer. Always be watchful and thankful.

³Pray for us too. Pray that God will open a door for our message. Then we can preach the mystery of Christ. Because I preached it, I am being held by chains. ⁴Pray that I will preach it clearly, as I should.

⁵Be wise in the way you act toward outsiders. Make the most of every opportunity. ⁶Let the words you speak always be full of grace. Season them with salt. Then you will know how to answer everyone.

FINAL GREETINGS

⁷Tychicus will tell you all the news about me. He is a dear brother. He is a faithful worker. He serves the Lord together with us. ⁸I am sending him to you for one reason. I want you to know what is happening here. I want him to cheer you up and make your hearts strong.

⁹He is coming with Onesimus, our faithful and dear brother. He is one of you. They will tell you everything that is happening here.

¹⁰Aristarchus is in prison with me. He sends you his greetings. So does Mark, the cousin of Barnabas. You have been given directions about him. If he comes to you, welcome him.

If you swear and you're a Christian, do you still go to heaven?

If we have given our lives to Jesus, we will go to heaven even if we do something bad. But our relationship with God will change the way we live. We can do bad things and still go to heaven. But why would we want to? Sin hurts us and it hurts God, and God wants only the very best for us. People who love God love doing good. If we love God, we will want to please him, and we will trust that he knows what is best for us.

checkout
Colossians 3:8

Related verses:
Romans 8:38,39

¹¹Jesus, who is called Justus, also sends greetings. They are the only Jews who work together with me for God's kingdom. They have been a comfort to me.

¹²Epaphras sends greetings. He is one of you. He serves Christ Jesus. He is always praying hard for you. He prays that you will stand firm in holding to all that God has in mind for us. He prays that you will continue to grow in your knowledge of what God wants you to do. He also prays that you will be completely sure about it. ¹³I am happy to tell you that he is working very hard for you. He is also working hard for everyone in Laodicea and Hierapolis.

¹⁴Our dear friend Luke, the doctor, sends greetings. So does Demas.

¹⁵Give my greetings to the brothers and sisters in Laodicea. Also give my greetings to Nympha and the church that meets in her house.

¹⁶After this letter has been read to you, send it on. Be sure that it is also read to the church in Laodicea. And be sure that you read the letter from Laodicea.

¹⁷Tell Archippus, "Be sure that you complete the work the Lord gave you to do."

¹⁸I, Paul, am writing this greeting with my own hand. Remember that I am being held by chains. May grace be with you.

KIDS' QUESTion

If you don't like something a person wears and they ask you if you like it, are you supposed to tell them the truth?

You are not supposed to lie, but that does not mean that you have to be mean. There are many ways to tell the truth. We need to learn *grace*. Grace is when you say the truth in a nice way, even if it is hard for the other person to hear. For example, suppose you do not like the person's new coat. You do not have to say,

"I *hate* that ugly coat!" You can say, "It wouldn't be my choice, but everybody has different tastes." Say things that respect people's feelings. And if the person doesn't ask for your opinion, you don't need to say anything. Sometimes that is the kindest thing to do.

checkout
Colossians 4:6

Related verse:
Luke 6:31

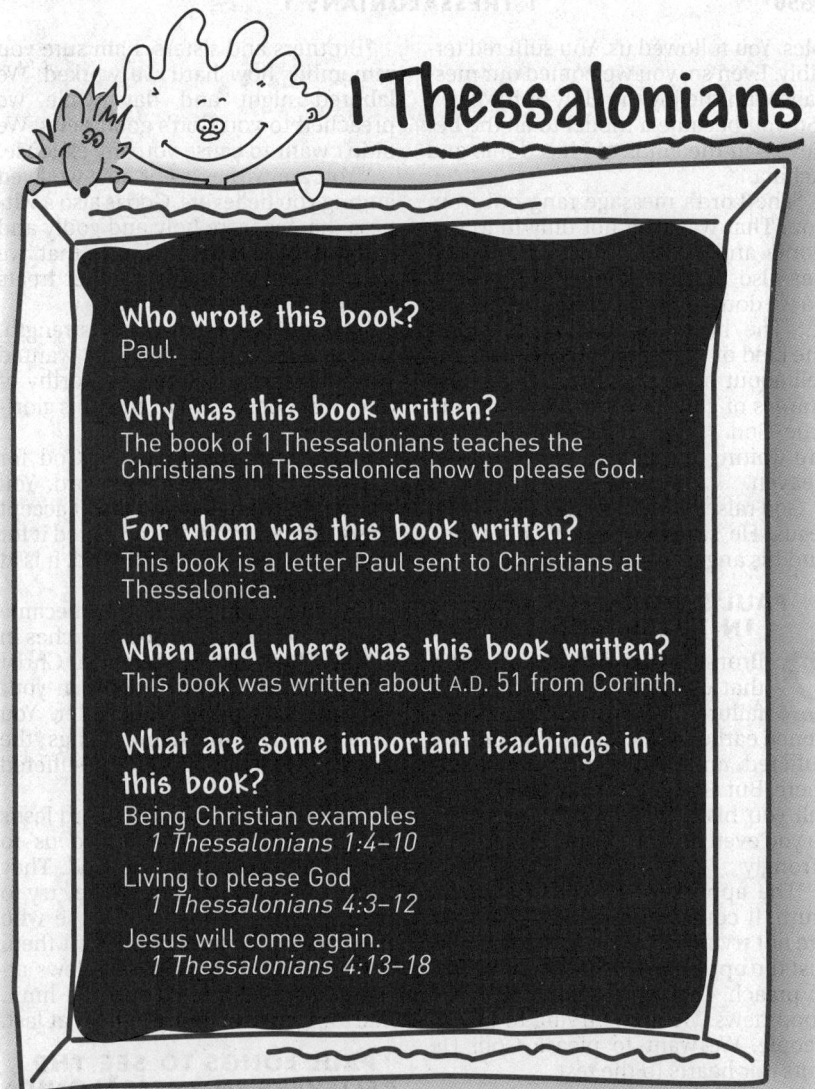

1 Thessalonians

Who wrote this book?
Paul.

Why was this book written?
The book of 1 Thessalonians teaches the Christians in Thessalonica how to please God.

For whom was this book written?
This book is a letter Paul sent to Christians at Thessalonica.

When and where was this book written?
This book was written about A.D. 51 from Corinth.

What are some important teachings in this book?
Being Christian examples
  1 Thessalonians 1:4–10
Living to please God
  1 Thessalonians 4:3–12
Jesus will come again.
  1 Thessalonians 4:13–18

---

1 I, Paul, am writing this letter. Silas and Timothy join me in writing.

We are sending this letter to you, the members of the church in Thessalonica. You belong to God the Father and the Lord Jesus Christ.

May grace and peace be given to you.

PAUL GIVES THANKS

[2]We always thank God for all of you. We pray for you. [3]We never forget you when we pray to our God and Father. Your work is produced by your faith. Your service is the result of your love. Your strength to continue comes from your hope in our Lord Jesus Christ.

[4]Brothers and sisters, you are loved by God. We know that he has chosen you. [5]Our good news didn't come to you only in words. It came with power. It came with the Holy Spirit's help. He gave us complete faith in what we were preaching. You know how we lived among you for your good.

[6]We and the Lord were your exam-

ples. You followed us. You suffered terribly. Even so, you welcomed our message with the joy the Holy Spirit gives. [7]So you became a model to all the believers in the lands of Macedonia and Achaia.

[8]The Lord's message rang out from you. That was true not only in Macedonia and Achaia. Your faith in God has also become known everywhere. So we don't have to say anything about it. [9]The believers themselves report the kind of welcome you gave us. They tell about how you turned away from statues of gods to serve the living and true God. [10]They tell about how you are waiting for his Son to come from heaven.

God raised him from the dead. He is Jesus. He saves us from God's anger, and his anger is sure to come.

PAUL'S WORK FOR GOD IN THESSALONICA

2 Brothers and sisters, you know that our visit to you was not a failure. [2]You know what happened earlier in the city of Philippi. We suffered, and people treated us badly there. But God gave us the boldness to tell you his good news. We preached to you even though people opposed us strongly.

[3]The appeal we make is based on truth. It comes from a pure heart. We are not trying to trick you. [4]In fact, it is just the opposite. God has accepted us to preach. He has trusted us with the good news. We aren't trying to please people. We want to please God. He puts our hearts to the test.

[5]As you know, we never praised you if we didn't mean it. We didn't put on a mask to cover up any sinful longing. God is our witness that this is true. [6]We were not expecting people to praise us. We were not looking for praise from you or anyone else.

As Christ's apostles, we could have caused you some expense. [7]But we were gentle among you. We were like a mother caring for her little children. [8]We loved you so much that we were happy to share with you God's good news. We were also happy to share our lives with you. You had become very special to us.

[9]Brothers and sisters, I am sure you remember how hard we worked. We labored night and day while we preached to you God's good news. We didn't want to cause you any expense.

[10]You are witnesses of how we lived among you believers. God is also a witness that we were holy and godly and without blame. [11]You know that we treated each of you as a father treats his own children.

[12]We gave you hope and strength. We comforted you. We really wanted you to live in a way that is worthy of God. He chooses you to enter his glorious kingdom.

[13]We never stop thanking God for the way you received his word. You heard it from us. But you didn't accept it as a human word. You accepted it for what it really is. It is God's word. It is at work in you who believe.

[14]Brothers and sisters, you became like the members of God's churches in Judea. They are believers in Christ Jesus, just as you are. People in your own country made you suffer. You went through the same things the church members in Judea suffered from the Jews.

[15]The Jews who killed the Lord Jesus and the prophets also forced us to leave. They do not please God. They are enemies of everyone. [16]They try to keep us from speaking to those who aren't Jews. The Jews don't want them to be saved. In that way, the Jews always increase their sins to the limit. God's anger has come on them at last.

PAUL LONGS TO SEE THE BELIEVERS IN THESSALONICA

[17]Brothers and sisters, we were torn away from you for a short time. We were no longer with you in person, but we kept you in our thoughts. We really longed to see you. So we tried very hard to do so. [18]We wanted to come to you. Again and again I, Paul, wanted to come. But Satan stopped us. [19]What is our hope? What is our joy? When our Lord Jesus returns, what is the crown we will delight in? Isn't it you? [20]Yes, you are our glory and our joy.

3 We couldn't wait any longer. So we thought it was best to be left by ourselves in Athens. [2]We

sent our brother Timothy to give you strength and hope in your faith. He works together with God in spreading the good news about Christ. [3]We sent him so that no one would be upset by times of testing.

You know very well that we have to go through them. [4]In fact, when we were with you, we kept telling you that our enemies would make us suffer. As you know very well, it has turned out that way.

[5]That's the reason I sent someone to find out about your faith. I couldn't wait any longer. I was afraid that Satan might have tempted you in some way. Then our efforts would have been useless.

TIMOTHY BRINGS A GOOD REPORT

[6]But Timothy has come to us from you just now. He has brought good news about your faith and love. He has told us that you always have happy memories of us. He has also said that you long to see us, just as we long to see you.

[7]Brothers and sisters, in all our trouble and suffering your faith cheered us up. [8]Now we really live, because you are standing firm in the Lord.

[9]How can we thank God enough for you because of all the joy that comes only from our God? [10]Night and day we pray very hard that we will see you again. We want to give you what is missing in your faith.

[11]Now may our God and Father himself and our Lord Jesus open up a way for us to come to you. [12]May the Lord make your love grow. May it be like a rising flood. May your love for one another increase. May it also increase for everyone else. May it be just like our love for you. [13]May the Lord give you strength in your hearts. Then you will be holy and without blame in the sight of our God and Father. May that be true when our Lord Jesus comes with all his holy ones.

LIVING IN A WAY THAT PLEASES GOD

4 Finally, brothers and sisters, we taught you how to live in a way that pleases God. In fact, that is how you are living. In the name of the

When you're making friends, how do you know what to say?

The best way to start a conversation with someone is to ask questions about that person. You can look for clues to help you know what to ask. For example, if the person is wearing a hat or shirt of a professional sports team, you could ask about the team. If someone is holding a book, you could ask what it's about. It's important to ask people questions about themselves. Talk about them, not just about yourself. Also, look for ways to compliment people. If you hear about a good grade or award that someone received, you could say, "Great job!" If someone did well in a concert, you could say something like, "I really liked your solo." Look for ways to give real compliments. Try to make others feel good about themselves.

Related verses:
Proverbs 16:24;
22:11;
Romans 15:2

checkout
1 Thessalonians 4:9

SO THIS THING-A-MA-BOB MAKES THIS DOO-HICKEY MOVE SO THAT SLIMY GOO STUFF CAN BOIL IN THAT WEIRD LOOKING BOTTLE...

Lord Jesus we ask and beg you to do it more and more.

²You know the directions we gave you. They were given by the authority of the Lord Jesus.

³God wants you to be made holy. He wants you to stay away from sexual sins. ⁴He wants all of you to learn to control your own bodies. You must live in a way that is holy. You must live with honor. ⁵Don't long to commit sexual sins like those who don't know God. ⁶None of you should sin against your brother by doing that. You should not take advantage of him. The Lord will punish everyone who commits those kinds of sins. We have already told you and warned you about that. ⁷God chose us to live pure lives. He wants us to be holy.

⁸So if you refuse to accept my teaching, you turn your back on God, not on people. God gives you his Holy Spirit.

⁹We don't need to write to you about love among believers. God himself has taught you to love each other. ¹⁰In fact, you do love all the brothers and sisters all around Macedonia. But we are asking you to love each other more and more.

¹¹Do everything you can to live a quiet life. Mind your own business. Work with your hands, just as we told you to. ¹²Then unbelievers will have respect for your everyday life. And you won't have to depend on anyone.

THE LORD IS COMING

¹³Brothers and sisters, we want you to know what happens to those who die. We don't want you to be sad, as other people are. They don't have any hope.

¹⁴We believe that Jesus died and rose again. When he returns, many who believe in him will have died already. We believe that God will bring them back with Jesus.

¹⁵That agrees with what the Lord has said. When the Lord comes, many of us will still be alive. We tell you that we will certainly not go up before those who have died.

What will I do in heaven with no friends?

If your friends believe in Jesus, they will be in heaven with you. And you will have a *great* time together. Jesus is preparing a place for you. He will not keep friends and loved ones apart from each other. And we will make new friends in heaven, too. Tell your friends about Jesus if you are not sure whether they will go to heaven. You will all be there together if they put their faith in Jesus too.

Do not worry about heaven being boring. God created butterflies, sunsets, thunderstorms, mountains, laughter and the Grand Canyon. These are all things we can enjoy here on earth. But there will be so much fun, beauty and joy in heaven that you can hardly imagine it now.

checkout 1 Thessalonians 4:13,14

JASON'S IMAGINATION

HEAVEN!

SURPRISE!

HI JASON!

Related verse:
Philippians 3:20

[16]The Lord himself will come down from heaven. We will hear a loud command. We will hear the voice of the leader of the angels. We will hear a blast from God's trumpet. Many who believe in Christ will have died already. They will rise first. [17]After that, we who are still alive and are left will be caught up together with them. We will be taken up in the clouds. We will meet the Lord in the air. And we will be with him forever.

[18]So cheer each other up with these words of comfort.

5 Brothers and sisters, we don't have to write to you about times and dates. [2]You know very well that the day of the Lord will come like a thief in the night. [3]People will be saying that everything is peaceful and safe. Then suddenly they will be destroyed. It will happen like birth pains coming on a pregnant woman. None of the people will escape.

[4]Brothers and sisters, you are not in darkness. So that day should not surprise you as a thief would. [5]All of you are children of the light. You are children of the day. We don't belong to the night. We don't belong to the darkness.

[6]So let us not be like the others. They are asleep. Instead, let us be wide awake and in full control of ourselves. [7]Those who sleep, sleep at night. Those who get drunk, get drunk at night. [8]But we belong to the day. So let us control ourselves. Let us put the armor of faith and love on our chest. Let us put on the hope of salvation like a helmet.

[9]God didn't choose us to receive his anger. He chose us to receive salvation because of what our Lord Jesus Christ has done.

[10]Jesus died for us. Some will be alive when he comes. Others will be dead. Either way, we will live together with him. [11]So cheer each other up with the hope you have. Build each other up. In fact, that's what you are doing.

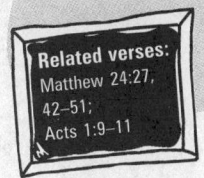

When is Jesus coming back?

No one knows. Right before Jesus left the earth he promised to return some day. He went up into the clouds, and then angels said he would come back. No one knows exactly when that will happen. It could be any day now. Christians look forward to Jesus' return because it will be the end of Satan and the end of all evil in the world. God's people will get to see Jesus in person and live with him forever. We do not know when Jesus will return. But he has told us to be ready at all times. We should live the way he wants us to live, use our time wisely and tell others about God's good news so they can be ready too.

checkout
1 Thessalonians 5:1,2

Related verses:
Matthew 24:27,
42–51;
Acts 1:9–11

FINAL DIRECTIONS

¹²Brothers and sisters, we ask you to have respect for the godly leaders who work hard among you. They have authority over you. They correct you. ¹³Have a lot of respect for them. Love them because of what they do. Live in peace with each other.

¹⁴Brothers and sisters, we are asking you to warn those who don't want to work. Cheer up those who are shy. Help those who are weak. Put up with everyone. ¹⁵Make sure that nobody pays back one wrong act with another. Always try to be kind to each other and to everyone else.

¹⁶Always be joyful. ¹⁷Never stop praying. ¹⁸Give thanks no matter what happens. God wants you to thank him because you believe in Christ Jesus.

¹⁹Don't put out the Holy Spirit's fire. ²⁰Don't treat prophecies as if they amount to nothing. ²¹Put everything to the test. Hold on to what is good. ²²Stay away from every kind of evil.

²³God is the God who gives peace. May he make you holy through and through. May your whole spirit, soul and body be kept free from blame. May you be without blame from now until our Lord Jesus Christ comes. ²⁴The One who has chosen you is faithful. He will do all these things.

²⁵Brothers and sisters, pray for us. ²⁶Greet all the believers with a holy kiss. ²⁷While the Lord is watching, here is what I command you. Have this letter read to all the believers.

²⁸May the grace of our Lord Jesus Christ be with you.

KIDS' QUESTION

Will God be with me all the time in heaven?

Yes! You will get to go right up to God and talk to him. God will be with you all the time, and you will be with him. God will be your friend and you will be his. You will have a great friendship with God forever and ever.

checkout
1 Thessalonians 5:10

Related verses:
1 Corinthians 13:12;
Revelation 21:3,4

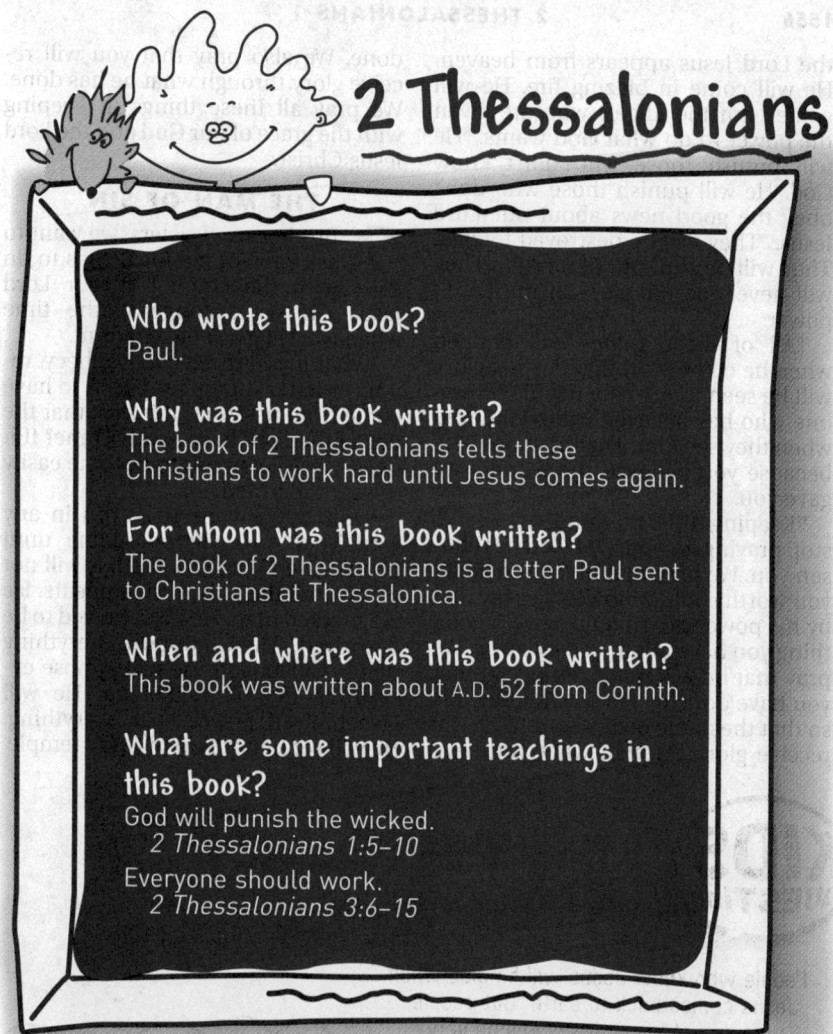

2 Thessalonians

Who wrote this book?
Paul.

Why was this book written?
The book of 2 Thessalonians tells these Christians to work hard until Jesus comes again.

For whom was this book written?
The book of 2 Thessalonians is a letter Paul sent to Christians at Thessalonica.

When and where was this book written?
This book was written about A.D. 52 from Corinth.

What are some important teachings in this book?
God will punish the wicked.
2 Thessalonians 1:5–10
Everyone should work.
2 Thessalonians 3:6–15

1 I, Paul, am writing this letter. Silas and Timothy join me in writing.

We are sending this letter to you, the members of the church in Thessalonica. You belong to God our Father and the Lord Jesus Christ.

²May God the Father and the Lord Jesus Christ give you grace and peace.

PAUL PRAYS AND GIVES THANKS

³Brothers and sisters, we should always thank God for you. That is only right, because your faith is growing more and more. The love you all have for each other is increasing. ⁴So among God's churches we brag about the fact that you don't give up easily. We brag about your faith in all the suffering and testing you are going through.

⁵All of this proves that when God judges, he is fair. So you will be considered worthy to enter God's kingdom. You are suffering for his kingdom.

⁶God is fair. He will pay back trouble to those who give you trouble. ⁷He will help you who are troubled. And he will also help us.

All of those things will happen when

the Lord Jesus appears from heaven. He will come in blazing fire. He will come with the angels who are given the power to do what God wants. [8]He will punish those who don't know God. He will punish those who don't obey the good news about our Lord Jesus. [9]They will be destroyed forever. They will be shut out of heaven. They will never see the glory of the Lord's power.

[10]All of those things will happen when he comes. On that day his glory will be seen in his holy people. Everyone who has believed will be amazed when they see him. That includes you, because you believed the witness we gave you.

[11]Keeping this in mind, we never stop praying for you. Our God has chosen you. We pray that he will consider you worthy of his choice. We pray that by his power he will make every good thing you have planned come true. We pray that he will make perfect all that you have done by faith. [12]We pray this so that the name of our Lord Jesus will receive glory through what you have done. We also pray that you will receive glory through what he has done. We pray all these things in keeping with the grace of our God and the Lord Jesus Christ.

THE MAN OF SIN

2 Brothers and sisters, we want to ask you something. It has to do with the coming of our Lord Jesus Christ. It concerns the time when we will go to be with him.

[2]What if you receive a prophecy, report or letter that is supposed to have come from us? What if it says that the day of the Lord has already come? If it does, we ask you not to become easily upset or alarmed.

[3]Don't let anyone trick you in any way. That day will not come until people rise up against God. It will not come until the man of sin appears. He is a marked man. He is sentenced to be destroyed. [4]He will oppose everything that is called God. He will oppose everything that is worshiped. He will give himself power over everything. He will set himself up in God's temple.

What will happen to bad people when Jesus comes back?

People who know Jesus will be glad when Jesus comes back to earth. But people who do not know Jesus will be very sad and afraid, because they will be judged for their sin. Those who have not believed in Jesus as their Savior will be punished and sent to hell. They will have to go far away from God forever. That is one of the reasons God tells us to tell our friends about Jesus. That way they can join us in heaven.

checkout **2 Thessalonians 1:9**

Related verses:
2 Thessalonians
1:6–10;
Jude 14,15

He will announce that he himself is God.

⁵Don't you remember? When I was with you, I used to tell you those things.

⁶Now you know what is holding the man of sin back. He is held back so that he can make his appearance at the right time. ⁷The secret power of sin is already at work. But the one who now holds that power back will keep doing it until he is taken out of the way. ⁸Then the man of sin will appear. The Lord Jesus will overthrow him with the breath of his mouth. The glorious brightness of Jesus' coming will destroy the man of sin.

⁹The coming of the man of sin will be Satan's work. His work will be seen in all kinds of fake miracles, signs and wonders. ¹⁰It will be seen in every kind of evil that fools people who are dying. They are dying because they refuse to love the truth. The truth would save them.

¹¹So God will fool them completely. Then they will believe the lie. ¹²Many will not believe the truth. They will take pleasure in evil. They will be judged.

STAND FIRM

¹³Brothers and sisters, we should always thank God for you. The Lord loves you. God chose you from the beginning. He wanted you to be saved. Salvation comes through the Holy Spirit's work. He makes people holy. It also comes through believing the truth. ¹⁴He chose you to be saved by accepting the good news that we preach. And you will share in the glory of our Lord Jesus Christ.

¹⁵Brothers and sisters, stand firm. Hold on to what we taught you. We passed our teachings on to you by what we preached and wrote.

¹⁶Our Lord Jesus Christ and God our Father loved us. By his grace God gave us comfort that will last forever. The hope he gave us is good.

May our Lord Jesus Christ and God our Father ¹⁷comfort your hearts. May they make you strong in every good thing you do and say.

PAUL ASKS FOR PRAYER

3 Finally, brothers and sisters, pray for us. Pray that the Lord's message will spread quickly.

When will Jesus come back?

No one knows when Jesus will come back. Not even the angels know. God has chosen not to tell us.

God has also warned us not to listen to people who say they know when Jesus will return. He will come when no one is expecting him. People who say they know when Jesus will return are just trying to trick us.

We do not have to worry about missing him when Jesus returns. It will be plain for everyone to see when Jesus comes back. All people all over the world will know.

checkout

2 Thessalonians 2:2,3

Related verses:
Matthew
24:23–25,36–44

Pray that others will honor it just as you did. ²And pray that we will be saved from sinful and evil people. Not everyone is a believer.

³But the Lord is faithful. He will strengthen you. He will guard you from the evil one.

⁴We trust in the Lord. So we are sure that you are doing the things we tell you to do. And we are sure that you will keep on doing them.

⁵May the Lord fill your hearts with God's love. May Christ give you the strength to go on.

PAUL WARNS THOSE WHO DO NOT WANT TO WORK

⁶Brothers and sisters, here is a command we give you in the name of the Lord Jesus Christ. Keep away from every believer who doesn't want to work. Keep away from anyone who doesn't live up to the teaching you received from us.

⁷You know how you should follow our example. We worked when we were with you. ⁸We didn't eat anyone's food without paying for it. In fact, it was just the opposite. We worked night and day. We worked very hard so that we wouldn't cause any expense to any of you.

⁹We worked, even though we have the right to receive help from you. We did it in order to be a model for you to follow. ¹⁰Even when we were with you, we gave you a rule. We said, "Anyone who will not work will not eat."

¹¹We hear that some people among you don't want to work. They aren't really busy. Instead, they are bothering others. ¹²We belong to the Lord Jesus Christ. So we strongly command people like that to settle down. They have to earn the food they eat.

¹³Brothers and sisters, don't ever get tired of doing the right thing.

¹⁴Keep an eye on anyone who doesn't obey the directions in our letter. Watch that person closely. Have nothing to do with him. Then he will feel ashamed. ¹⁵But don't think of him as an enemy. Instead, warn him as a brother or sister.

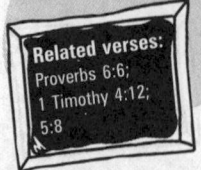

Why do I have to do chores?

Parents do most of the work around the house when children are very young. As children get older, they begin to help out as they can. Many families give special jobs or chores to each person in the family. This way everyone in the family helps make sure the house runs smoothly and the work gets done. Chores can include setting the table, cleaning, dusting, cutting the grass, shoveling the snow, washing clothes, washing windows, cooking meals and caring for animals. Remember that your parents are not just looking for free help. They are getting you ready for life. You need to learn how to work hard and be helpful. You are learning good skills that you will use the rest of your life.

checkout

2 Thessalonians 3:9,10

Related verses:
Proverbs 6:6;
1 Timothy 4:12;
5:8

FINAL GREETINGS

[16]May the Lord who gives peace give you peace at all times and in every way. May the Lord be with all of you. [17]I, Paul, write this greeting in my own handwriting. That's how I prove that I am the author of all my letters. I always do it that way. [18]May the grace of our Lord Jesus Christ be with you all.

Why do I feel afraid if Jesus is with me?

It is natural to feel afraid. In fact being afraid can be good. We should be afraid of danger. Fear can keep us a safe distance from a mean dog or something else that might hurt us.

There is nothing wrong with being afraid.

But being afraid should remind us to trust God and do what he wants us to do. Jesus is always with us, even though we do not see him or always feel that he is there. Jesus wants us to learn to trust him. He wants us to believe that he is there.

Related verses:
Psalm 56:3;
John 14:1

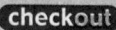

checkout
2 Thessalonians 3:16

Quest Clue

Do you ever get an assignment in school that you just don't want to do? We all have to work no matter what age we are. And God has given your teachers wisdom about what you need to learn so that you can be successful. You'll find Paul's instructions on work in Colossians 3 and 2 Thessalonians 3. How can you apply what he says to your work in school?

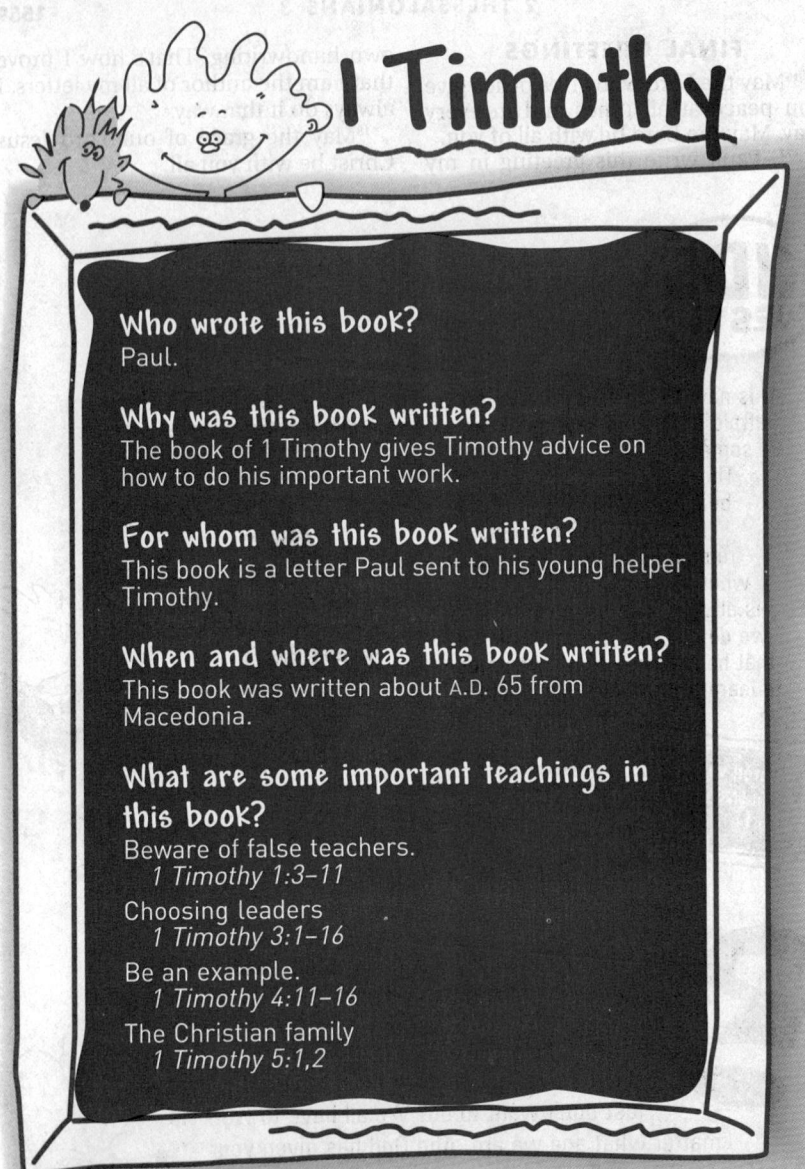

1 Timothy

Who wrote this book?
Paul.

Why was this book written?
The book of 1 Timothy gives Timothy advice on how to do his important work.

For whom was this book written?
This book is a letter Paul sent to his young helper Timothy.

When and where was this book written?
This book was written about A.D. 65 from Macedonia.

What are some important teachings in this book?
Beware of false teachers.
1 Timothy 1:3–11

Choosing leaders
1 Timothy 3:1–16

Be an example.
1 Timothy 4:11–16

The Christian family
1 Timothy 5:1,2

1 I, Paul, am writing this letter. I am an apostle of Christ Jesus, just as God our Savior commanded. Christ Jesus also commanded it. We have put our hope in him.

² Timothy, I am sending you this letter. You are my true son in the faith.

May God the Father and Christ Jesus our Lord give you grace, mercy and peace.

PAUL WARNS AGAINST CERTAIN TEACHERS OF THE LAW

³ Stay there in Ephesus. That is what I told you to do when I went into Macedonia. I want you to command certain people not to teach things that aren't true. ⁴ Command them not to spend their time on stories that aren't completely true. They must not waste time on family histories that never end.

Things like that cause people to argue instead of doing God's work. His work is done by faith.

⁵Love is the purpose of my command. Love comes from a pure heart. It comes from a good sense of what is right and wrong. It comes from faith that is honest and true.

⁶Some have wandered away from those teachings. They would rather talk about things that have no meaning. ⁷They want to be teachers of the law. And they are very sure about that law. But they don't know what they are talking about.

⁸We know that the law is good if it is used properly. ⁹We also know that the law isn't made for godly people. It is made for those who break the law. It is for those who refuse to obey. It is for ungodly and sinful people. It is for those who aren't holy and who don't believe. It is for those who kill their fathers or mothers. It is for murderers.

¹⁰It is for those who commit adultery. It is for those who have a twisted view of sex. It is for people who buy and sell slaves. It is for liars. It is for those who give witness to things that aren't true. And it is for anything else that is the opposite of true teaching.

¹¹True teaching agrees with the glorious good news of the blessed God. He trusted me with that good news.

THE LORD POURS OUT HIS GRACE ON PAUL

¹²I am thankful to Christ Jesus our Lord. He has given me strength. I thank him that he considered me faithful. And I thank him for appointing me to serve him.

¹³I used to speak evil things against Jesus. I tried to hurt his followers. I really pushed them around. But God showed me mercy anyway. I did those things without knowing any better. I wasn't a believer.

¹⁴Our Lord poured out more and more of his grace on me. Along with it came faith and love from Christ Jesus.

¹⁵Here is a saying that you can trust. It should be accepted completely. Christ Jesus came into the world to save sinners.

And I am the worst sinner of all. ¹⁶But for that very reason, God showed me mercy. And I am the worst of sinners. He showed me mercy so that Christ Jesus could show that he is very patient. I was an example for those who would come to believe in him. Then they would receive eternal life.

¹⁷The eternal King will never die. He can't be seen. He is the only God. Give him honor and glory for ever and ever. Amen.

¹⁸My son Timothy, I give you these teachings. They are in keeping with the prophecies that were once made about you. By following them, you can fight the good fight. ¹⁹Then you will hold on to faith. You will hold on to a good sense of what is right and wrong.

Some have not accepted these teachings. By doing that, they have destroyed their faith. They are like a ship that has sunk. ²⁰Hymenaeus and Alexander are among them. I have handed them over to Satan. That will teach them not to speak evil things against God.

DIRECTIONS FOR WORSHIP

2 First, I want all of you to pray for everyone. Ask God to bless them. Give thanks for them. ²Pray for kings. Pray for all who are in authority. Pray that we will live peaceful and quiet lives. And pray that we will be godly and holy.

³That is good. It pleases God our Savior. ⁴He wants everyone to be saved. He wants them to come to know the truth.

⁵There is only one God. And there is only one go-between for God and human beings. He is the man Christ Jesus. ⁶He gave himself to pay for the sins of everyone. That was a witness given by God at just the right time.

⁷I was appointed to be a messenger and an apostle to preach the good news. I am telling the truth. I'm not lying. God appointed me to be a teacher of the true faith to those who aren't Jews.

⁸I want men everywhere to pray. I want them to lift up holy hands. I don't want them to be angry when they pray. I don't want them to argue.

⁹I also want women to dress simply. They should wear clothes that are right and proper. They shouldn't braid

their hair. They shouldn't wear gold or pearls. They shouldn't spend too much on clothes. ¹⁰Instead, they should put on good works as if they were their clothes. That is proper for women who claim to worship God.

¹¹When a woman is learning, she should be quiet. She should follow the leaders in every way. ¹²I do not let women teach. I do not let them have authority over men. They must be quiet.

¹³Adam was made first. Then Eve was made. ¹⁴Adam was not the one who was tricked. The woman was tricked and became a sinner. ¹⁵Will women be saved by having children? Only if they keep on believing, loving, and leading a holy life in a proper way.

LEADERS AND DEACONS

3 Here is a saying you can trust. If anyone wants to be a leader in the church, he wants to do a good work for God and people.

²A leader must be free from blame. He must be faithful to his wife. In anything he does, he must not go too far. He must control himself. He must be worthy of respect. He must welcome people into his home. He must be able to teach. ³He must not get drunk. He must not push people around. He must be gentle. He must not be a person who likes to argue. He must not love money.

⁴He must manage his own family well. He must make sure that his children obey him and show him proper respect. ⁵Suppose someone doesn't know how to manage his own family. Then how can he take care of God's church?

⁶The leader must not be a new believer. If he is, he might become proud. Then he would be judged just like the devil.

⁷The leader must also be respected by those who are outside the church. Then he will not be put to shame. He will not fall into the devil's trap.

⁸Deacons also must be worthy of respect. They must be honest and true. They must not drink too much wine. They must not try to get money by cheating people. ⁹They must hold on to the deep truths of the faith. Even

their own minds tell them to do that. ¹⁰First they must be tested. Then let them serve as deacons if there is nothing against them.

¹¹In the same way, their wives must be worthy of respect. They must not say things that harm others. In anything they do, they must not go too far. They must be worthy of trust in everything.

¹²A deacon must be faithful to his wife. He must manage his children and family well. ¹³Those who have served well earn the full respect of others. They also become more sure of their faith in Christ Jesus.

¹⁴I hope I can come to you soon. But now I am writing these directions to you. ¹⁵Then if I have to put off my visit, you will know how you should act in God's family. The family of God is the church of the living God. It is the pillar and foundation of the truth.

¹⁶There is no doubt that godliness is a great mystery.

Jesus appeared in a body.
　The Holy Spirit proved that he
　　was the Son of God.
He was seen by angels.
　He was preached among the
　　nations.
People in the world believed in
　him.
　He was taken up to heaven in
　　glory.

DIRECTIONS FOR TIMOTHY

4 The Holy Spirit clearly says that in the last days some people will leave the faith. They will follow spirits that will fool them. They will believe things that demons will teach them.

²Teachings like those come from liars who pretend to be what they are not. Their sense of what is right and wrong has been burned as if with a hot iron. ³They do not allow people to get married. They order them not to eat certain foods. But God created those foods. So people who believe and know the truth should receive them and give thanks for them.

⁴Everything God created is good. You shouldn't turn anything down. Instead, you should thank God for it.

⁵The word of God and prayer make it holy.

⁶Point these things out to the brothers and sisters. Then you will serve Christ Jesus well. You were brought up in the truths of the faith. You received good teaching. You followed it.

⁷Don't have anything to do with godless stories and silly tales. Instead, train yourself to be godly. ⁸Training the body has some value. But being godly has value in every way. It promises help for the life you are now living and the life to come.

⁹Here is a saying you can trust. You can accept it completely. ¹⁰We work hard for it. Here is the saying. We have put our hope in the living God. He is the Savior of all people. Most of all he is the Savior of those who believe.

¹¹Command those things. Teach them. ¹²Don't let anyone look down on you because you are young. Set an example for the believers in what you say and in how you live. Also set an example in how you love and in what you

believe. Show the believers how to be pure.

¹³Until I come, spend your time reading Scripture out loud to one another. Spend your time preaching and teaching. ¹⁴Don't fail to use the gift the Holy Spirit gave you. He gave it to you through a message from God. It was given when the elders placed their hands on you.

¹⁵Keep on doing those things. Give them your complete attention. Then everyone will see how you are coming along. ¹⁶Be careful of how you live and what you believe. Never give up. Then you will save yourself and those who hear you.

ADVICE ABOUT WIDOWS, ELDERS AND SLAVES

5 Don't tell an older man off. Make an appeal to him as if he were your father. Treat younger men as if they were your brothers. ²Treat older women as if they were your mothers. Treat younger women

Why isn't there just one Kind of Bible?

There are many kinds of Bibles, because there are many kinds of people. But all Bibles have the same message. They tell us how to live with God on earth, so we can go to heaven when we die. For this reason, Paul encouraged Timothy not to give up reading the Bible.

Some Bibles are very small so we can carry them with us. Others are big so we can see the words better. Some Bibles use everyday words so they are easy to read and the lessons are easy to learn. Some Bibles have notes, maps and charts to help people understand how life in Bible times was different from today. We have all these different Bibles for the same reason. We have them to help us understand and do what God wants.

checkout
1 Timothy 4:13

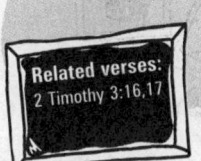
Related verses:
2 Timothy 3:16,17

as if they were your sisters. Be completely pure in the way you treat them.

[3]Take care of the widows who really need help. [4]But suppose a widow has children or grandchildren. They should first learn to put their faith into practice. They should care for their own family. In that way they will pay back their parents and grandparents. That pleases God.

[5]The widow who really needs help and is left all alone puts her hope in God. Night and day she keeps on praying. Night and day she asks God for help. [6]But the widow who lives for pleasure is dead even while she is still living.

[7]Give those directions to the people also. Then no one can be blamed. [8]Everyone should provide for his own relatives. Most of all, everyone should take care of his own family. If he doesn't, he has left the faith. He is worse than someone who doesn't believe.

[9]No widow should be put on the list of widows unless she is more than 60 years old. She must also have been faithful to her husband. [10]She must be well known for the good things she does. That includes bringing up children. It includes inviting guests into her home. It includes washing the feet of God's people. It includes helping those who are in trouble. A widow should spend her time doing all kinds of good things.

[11]Don't put younger widows on that kind of list. They might want pleasure more than they want Christ. Then they would want to get married again. [12]If they do that, they will be judged. They have broken their first promise. [13]Besides, they get into the habit of having nothing to do. They go around from house to house. They waste time. They talk about others. They bother people. They say things they shouldn't say.

[14]So here is the advice I give to younger widows. Get married. Have children. Take care of your own homes. Don't give the enemy the chance to tell lies about you. [15]In fact, some have already turned away to follow Satan.

[16]Suppose a woman is a believer and

KIDS' QUESTION — How are families different now from the way they used to be?

In some ways families are very different. Before cars and planes were invented, families were very close and lots of relatives lived together. Most families were also larger, with more children. New inventions have caused many families to spread far apart. Now people can travel long distances very quickly by car, airplane, bus, boat or train to visit family, and they can stay in touch with each other by phone and through email.

In many ways families are still the same. Families start with a mom and a dad. The parents have parents. Kids have grandparents. And sometimes the grandparents or other relatives live with the family.

(checkout) 1 Timothy 5:3,4

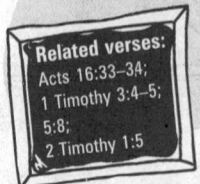

Related verses:
Acts 16:33–34;
1 Timothy 3:4–5;
5:8;
2 Timothy 1:5

has widows in her family. She should help them. She shouldn't let the church pay the expenses. Then the church can help the widows who really need it.

¹⁷The elders who do the church's work well are worth twice as much honor. That is true in a special way of elders who preach and teach. ¹⁸Scripture says, "Do not stop the ox from eating while it helps separate the grain from the straw." *(Deuteronomy 25:4)* Scripture also says, "Workers are worthy of their pay." *(Luke 10:7)*

¹⁹Don't believe a charge against an elder unless two or three witnesses bring it. ²⁰Elders who sin should be corrected in front of the other believers. That will be a warning to the others.

²¹I command you to follow those directions. I command you in the sight of God and Christ Jesus and the chosen angels. Treat everyone the same. Don't favor one person over another.

²²Don't be too quick to place your hands on others to set them apart to serve God. Don't take part in the sins of others. Keep yourself pure.

²³Stop drinking only water. If your stomach is upset, drink a little wine. It can also help the other sicknesses you often have.

²⁴The sins of some people are easy to see. They are already being judged. Others will be judged later. ²⁵In the same way, good works are easy to see. But even good works that are hard to see can't stay hidden.

6 All who are forced to serve as slaves should consider their masters worthy of full respect. Then people will not speak evil things against God's name and against what we teach.

²Some slaves have masters who are believers. They shouldn't show less respect for their masters just because they are believers. Instead, they should serve them even better. That's because those who benefit from their service are believers. They are loved by them.

Teach the slaves those things. Try hard to get them to do them.

LOVE FOR MONEY

³Suppose someone teaches ideas that are false. He doesn't agree with the true teaching of our Lord Jesus Christ. He doesn't agree with godly

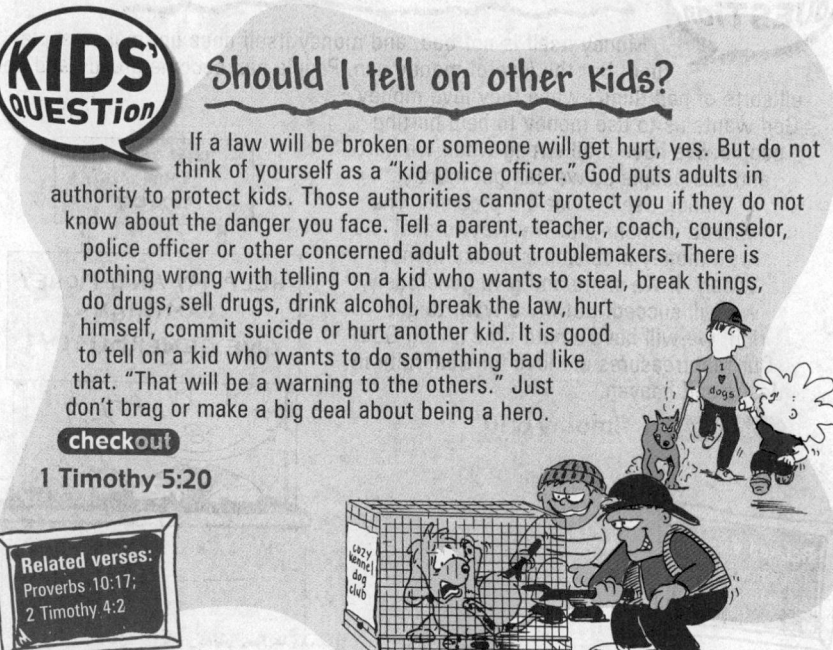

KIDS' QUESTION

Should I tell on other kids?

If a law will be broken or someone will get hurt, yes. But do not think of yourself as a "kid police officer." God puts adults in authority to protect kids. Those authorities cannot protect you if they do not know about the danger you face. Tell a parent, teacher, coach, counselor, police officer or other concerned adult about troublemakers. There is nothing wrong with telling on a kid who wants to steal, break things, do drugs, sell drugs, drink alcohol, break the law, hurt himself, commit suicide or hurt another kid. It is good to tell on a kid who wants to do something bad like that. "That will be a warning to the others." Just don't brag or make a big deal about being a hero.

checkout

1 Timothy 5:20

Related verses:
Proverbs 10:17;
2 Timothy 4:2

teaching. [4]People like that are proud. They don't understand anything. They like to argue more than they should. They can't agree about what words mean.

All of that results in wanting what others have. It causes fighting, harmful talk, and evil distrust. [5]It stirs up trouble all the time among people whose minds are twisted by sin. The truth they once had has been taken away from them. They think they can get rich by being godly.

[6]You gain a lot when you live a godly life. But you must be happy with what you have. [7]We didn't bring anything into the world. We can't take anything out of it. [8]If we have food and clothing, we will be happy with that.

[9]People who want to get rich are tempted. They fall into a trap. They are tripped up by wanting many foolish and harmful things. Those who live like that are dragged down by what they do. They are destroyed and die. [10]Love for money causes all kinds of evil. Some people want to get rich. They have wandered away from the faith. They have wounded themselves with many sorrows.

PAUL GIVES A COMMAND TO TIMOTHY

[11]But you are a man of God. Run away from all of those things. Try hard to do what is right and godly. Have faith, love and gentleness. Hold on to what you believe. [12]Fight the good fight along with all other believers. Take hold of eternal life. You were chosen for it when you openly told others what you believe. Many witnesses heard you.

[13]God gives life to everything. Christ Jesus told the truth when he gave witness to Pontius Pilate. In the sight of God and Christ, I give you a command. [14]Obey it until our Lord Jesus Christ appears. Obey it completely. Then no one can find fault with it or you. [15]God will bring Jesus back at a time that pleases him. God is the blessed

Does money make people bad?

Money itself is not bad, and money itself does not make people bad. But the *love* of money can. People can become greedy and do all sorts of bad things when they love money. God wants us to use money to help hurting people. We have it all wrong when we hurt and use people so *we* can get money.

Money itself is not the problem. The *misuse* of money is. The way to deal with money problems is to use money wisely. If we share and give generously, we will succed. But if we want to get rich, we will have a hard time loving God. Our real treasures are love for God, faith in Jesus and heaven.

checkout 1 Timothy 6:10

Related verses:
1 Timothy
6:17–19

THE EVILS OF MONEY

HELP MY ANTI-MONEY CAMPAIGN! GIVE GENEROUSLY!

and only Ruler. He is the greatest King of all. He is the most powerful Lord of all. [16]God is the only one who can't die. He lives in light that no one can get close to. No one has seen him. No one can see him.

Give honor and power to him forever. Amen.

[17]Command people who are rich in this world not to be proud. Tell them not to put their hope in riches. Wealth is so uncertain. Command those who are rich to put their hope in God. He richly provides us with everything to enjoy.

[18]Command the rich to do what is good. Tell them to be rich in doing good things. They must give freely. They must be willing to share. [19]In that way they will put riches away for themselves. It will provide a firm basis for the next life. Then they will take hold of the life that really is life.

[20]Timothy, guard what God has trusted you with. Turn away from godless chatter. Stay away from opposing ideas that are falsely called knowledge. [21]Some people believe them. By doing that they have wandered away from the faith.

May God's grace be with you.

quest challenge

I Wonder . . .

Why is what I believe about God so important?

Real Life Challenge

You will come across a lot of people who believe different things than you do. A friend may try to convince you that it's okay to lie to keep from getting in trouble. Or you might have a teacher who presents an idea that disagrees with what the Bible teaches. That's why it's important to know what you believe. God wants us to know and believe in his Word because what we believe affects what we do. Ask God to help you know the truth when you hear it.

Quest Clue

Read 1 Timothy 1 to learn what Paul has to say about people who teach ideas that are false. Then find 2 John to hear John's warning about not believing everything you hear.

2 Timothy

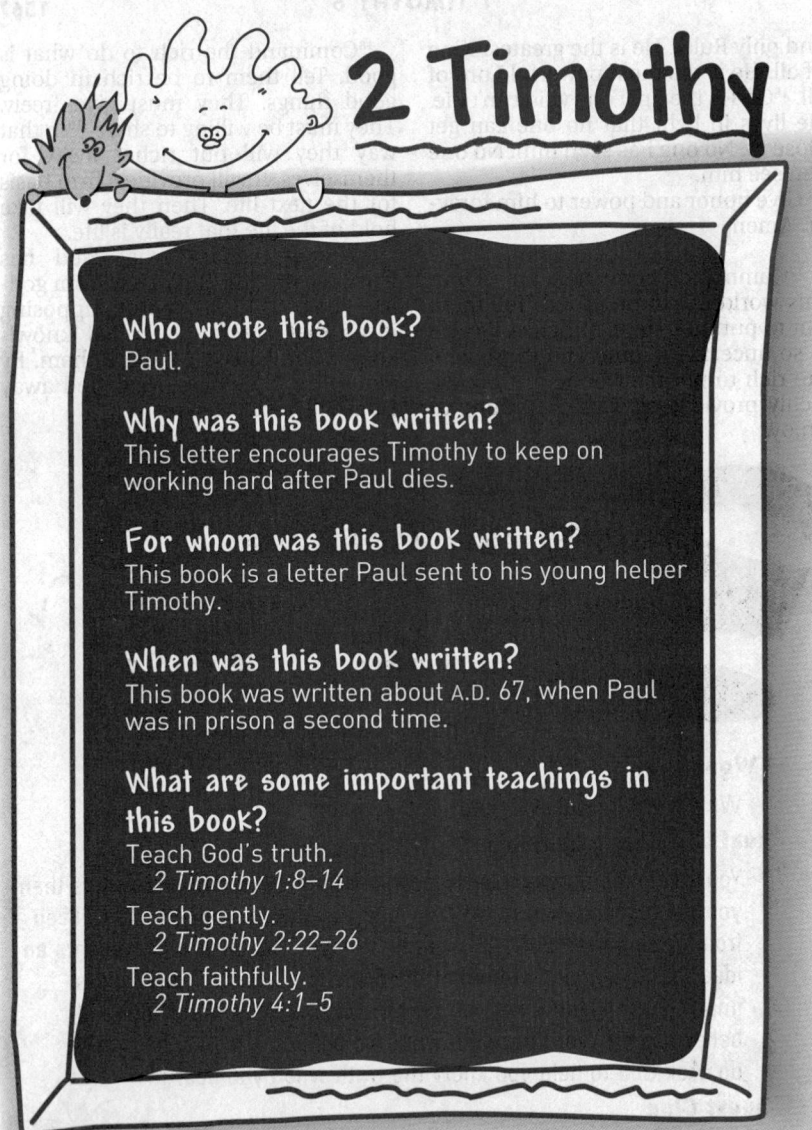

Who wrote this book?
Paul.

Why was this book written?
This letter encourages Timothy to keep on working hard after Paul dies.

For whom was this book written?
This book is a letter Paul sent to his young helper Timothy.

When was this book written?
This book was written about A.D. 67, when Paul was in prison a second time.

What are some important teachings in this book?
Teach God's truth.
  2 Timothy 1:8–14

Teach gently.
  2 Timothy 2:22–26

Teach faithfully.
  2 Timothy 4:1–5

---

1 I, Paul, am writing this letter. I am an apostle of Christ Jesus just as God planned. He sent me to tell about the promise of life that is found in Christ Jesus.

²Timothy, I am sending you this letter. You are my dear son.

May God the Father and Christ Jesus our Lord give you grace, mercy and peace.

PAUL TELLS TIMOTHY TO BE FAITHFUL

³I serve God, knowing that what I have done is right. That is how our people served him long ago. Night and day I thank God for you. Night and day I always remember you in my prayers.

⁴I remember your tears. I long to see you so that I can be filled with joy. ⁵I remember your honest and true faith. It was alive first in your grandmother

Lois and in your mother Eunice. And I am certain that it is now alive in you also.

⁶That is why I remind you to help God's gift grow, just as a small spark grows into a fire. God put his gift in you when I placed my hands on you.

⁷God didn't give us a spirit that makes us weak and fearful. He gave us a spirit that gives us power and love. It helps us control ourselves.

⁸So don't be ashamed to give witness about our Lord. And don't be ashamed of me, his prisoner. Instead, join with me as I suffer for the good news. God's power will help us do that.

⁹God has saved us. He has chosen us to live a holy life. It wasn't because of anything we have done. It was because of his own purpose and grace. Through Christ Jesus, God gave us that grace even before time began. ¹⁰It has now been made known through the coming of our Savior, Christ Jesus. He has destroyed death. Because of the good news, he has brought life out into the light. That life never dies.

¹¹I was appointed to announce the good news. I was appointed to be an apostle and a teacher. ¹²That's why I'm suffering the way I am. But I'm not ashamed. I know the One I have believed in. I am sure he is able to take care of what I have given him. I can trust him with it until the day he returns as judge.

¹³Follow what you heard from me as the pattern of true teaching. Follow it with faith and love because you belong to Christ Jesus. ¹⁴Guard the truth of the good news that you were trusted with. Guard it with the help of the Holy Spirit who lives in us.

¹⁵You know that all the believers in Asia Minor have deserted me. They include Phygelus and Hermogenes.

¹⁶May the Lord show mercy to all who live in the house of Onesiphorus. He often cheered me up. He was not ashamed that I was being held by chains. ¹⁷In fact, it was just the opposite. When he was in Rome, he looked everywhere for me. At last he found me.

¹⁸May Onesiphorus find mercy from the Lord on the day Jesus returns as judge. You know very well how many ways Onesiphorus helped me in Ephesus.

2 My son, be strong in the grace that is found in Christ Jesus. ²You have heard me teach in front of many witnesses. Pass on to men you can trust the things you've heard me say. Then they will be able to teach others also. ³Like a good soldier of Christ Jesus, share in the hard times with us.

⁴A soldier does not take part in things that don't have anything to do with the army. He wants to please his commanding officer. ⁵In the same way, anyone who takes part in a sport doesn't receive the winner's crown unless he plays by the rules. ⁶The farmer who works hard should be the first to receive a share of the crops.

⁷Think about what I'm saying. The Lord will help you understand what all of it means.

⁸Remember Jesus Christ. He came from David's family line. He was raised from the dead. That is my good news. ⁹I am suffering for it. I have even been put in chains like someone who has committed a crime. But God's word is not held back by chains.

¹⁰So I put up with everything for the good of God's chosen people. Then they also can be saved. Christ Jesus saves them. He gives them glory that will last forever.

¹¹Here is a saying you can trust.

If we died with him,
    we will also live with him.
¹²If we don't give up,
    we will also rule with him.
If we say we don't know him,
    he will also say he doesn't know
        us.
¹³Even if we are not faithful,
    he will remain faithful.
    He must be true to himself.

A WORKER WHO PLEASES GOD

¹⁴Keep reminding the believers of those things. While God is watching, warn them not to argue about words. That doesn't have any value. It only destroys those who listen.

¹⁵Do your best to please God. Be a worker who doesn't need to be

ashamed. Teach the message of truth correctly.

¹⁶Stay away from godless chatter. Those who take part in it will become more and more ungodly. ¹⁷Their teaching will spread like a deadly sickness.

Hymenaeus and Philetus are two of those teachers. ¹⁸They have wandered away from the truth. They say that the time when people will rise from the dead has already come. They destroy the faith of some people.

¹⁹But God's solid foundation stands firm. Here is the message written on it. "The Lord knows who his own people are." *(Numbers 16:5)* Also, "All who say they believe in the Lord must turn away from evil."

²⁰In a large house there are things made out of gold and silver. But there are also things made out of wood and clay. Some have honorable purposes. Others do not. ²¹Suppose someone stays away from what is not honorable. Then the Master will be able to use him for honorable purposes. He will be made holy. He will be ready to do any good work.

²²Run away from the evil things that young people long for. Try hard to do what is right. Have faith, love and peace. Do these things together with those who call on the Lord from a pure heart. ²³Don't have anything to do with arguing. It is dumb and foolish. You know it only leads to fights.

²⁴Anyone who serves the Lord must not fight. Instead, he must be kind to everyone. He must be able to teach. He must not hold anything against anyone. ²⁵He must gently teach those who oppose him.

Maybe God will give a change of heart to those who are against you. That will lead them to know the truth. ²⁶Maybe they will come to their senses. Maybe they will escape the devil's trap. He has taken them prisoner to do what he wanted.

TERRIBLE TIMES IN THE LAST DAYS

3 Here is what I want you to know. There will be terrible times in the last days. ²People will love themselves. They will love money. They will brag and be proud. They will tear others down. They will not obey their parents. They won't be thankful or holy. ³They won't love others. They won't forgive others. They will tell lies

---

Why do some Bibles have pictures and some don't?

The people who wrote the Bible did not put pictures in it. But in recent years the people who print Bibles have put pictures in some Bibles. They want to help us better understand the Bible. The pictures help us see what people and places may have been like when the Bible was written. Some of the pictures are drawings or paintings of what an artist thinks something looked like. Usually the artist knows what to draw by learning about that part of the world. Some of the photographs show places and things that still exist. The city of Jerusalem is one of the most famous. All of these things help us learn the Holy Scriptures just like young Timothy did.

Related verses:
2 Timothy 3:16,17

checkout
2 Timothy 3:15

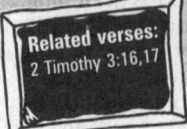

about people. They will be out of control. They will be wild. They will hate what is good.

[4]They will turn against their friends. They will act without thinking. They will think they are better than others. They will love what pleases them instead of loving God. [5]They will act as if they were serving God. But what they do will show that they have turned their backs on God's power. Have nothing to do with those people.

[6]They are the kind who worm their way into the homes of silly women. They get control over them. Women like that are loaded down with sins. They give in to all kinds of evil longings. [7]They are always learning. But they never come to know the truth.

[8]Jannes and Jambres opposed Moses. In the same way, the teachers I'm talking about oppose the truth. Their minds are twisted. As far as the faith is concerned, God doesn't accept them. [9]They won't get very far. Just like Jannes and Jambres, their foolish ways will be clear to everyone.

PAUL GIVES A COMMAND TO TIMOTHY

[10]But you know all about my teaching. You know how I live and what I live for. You know about my faith and love. You know how patient I am. You know I haven't given up. [11]You know that I was treated badly. You know that I suffered greatly. You know what kinds of things happened to me in Antioch, Iconium and Lystra. You know how badly I have been treated. But the Lord saved me from all of my troubles.

[12]In fact, everyone who wants to live a godly life in Christ Jesus will be treated badly. [13]Evil people and pretenders will go from bad to worse. They will fool others, and others will fool them.

[14]But I want you to continue to follow what you have learned. Don't give up what you are sure of. You know the people you learned it from. [15]You have known the Holy Scriptures ever since you were a little child. They are able to teach you how to be saved by believing in Christ Jesus.

What does *inspired* mean?

The word *inspired* is another way of saying that God breathed life into Scripture. It describes the way God used the Bible writers to write the Bible the way he wanted. It does not mean that God always said the words out loud while the writers wrote them down. It means that God gave the writers the ideas. Then God guided them so that they did not make any mistakes. That way the writers wrote what God wanted to say and what we needed to know.

checkout

2 Timothy 3:16

Related verses:
2 Peter 1:20,21

JASON'S IMAGINATION

¹⁶God has breathed life into all of Scripture. It is useful for teaching us what is true. It is useful for correcting our mistakes. It is useful for making our lives whole again. It is useful for training us to do what is right. ¹⁷By using Scripture, a man of God can be completely prepared to do every good thing.

4 I give you a command in the sight of God and Christ Jesus. Christ will judge the living and the dead. Because he and his kingdom are coming, here is the command I give you. ²Preach the word. Be ready to serve God in good times and bad. Correct people's mistakes. Warn them. Cheer them up with words of hope. Be very patient as you do these things. Teach them carefully.

³The time will come when people won't put up with true teaching. Instead, they will try to satisfy their own longings. They will gather a large number of teachers around them. The teachers will say what the people want to hear. ⁴The people will turn their ears away from the truth. They will turn to stories that aren't completely true.

⁵But I want you to keep your head no matter what happens. Don't give up when times are hard. Work to spread the good news. Do everything God has given you to do.

⁶I am already being poured out like a drink offering. The time has come for me to leave. ⁷I have fought the good fight. I have finished the race. I have kept the faith. ⁸Now there is a crown waiting for me. It is given to those who are right with God. The Lord, who judges fairly, will give it to me on the day he returns. He will not give it only to me. He will also give it to all those who are longing for him to return.

PERSONAL WORDS

⁹Do your best to come to me quickly. ¹⁰Demas has deserted me. He has gone to Thessalonica. He left me because he loved this world. Crescens has gone to Galatia. Titus has gone to Dalmatia. ¹¹Only Luke is with me. Get Mark and bring him with you. He helps me in my work for the Lord. ¹²I sent Tychicus to Ephesus.

¹³When you come, bring my coat. I left it with Carpus at Troas. Also bring my scrolls. Most of all, bring the ones made out of animal skins.

¹⁴Remember Alexander, the one who works with metal? He did me a

When I ask a question, why do some people tell me what the Bible says?

The Bible is God's Word. It tells you what God is like and how he wants you to live in this world. Think of the Bible as an instruction book. Your family car has one. The car will run right if you do what the book says. If something goes wrong with the car, you can read the instruction book and find out how to fix it. The Bible is God's instruction book for your life. You need to read and study it so that you will know how to live right and how to fix something when things go wrong with your life.

checkout
2 Timothy 3:17

Related verse:
Psalm 119:105

great deal of harm. The Lord will pay him back for what he has done. ¹⁵You too should watch out for him. He strongly opposed our message.

¹⁶The first time I was put on trial, no one came to help me. Everyone deserted me. I hope they will be forgiven for it.

¹⁷The Lord stood at my side. He gave me the strength to preach the whole message. Then all those who weren't Jews heard it. I was saved from the lion's mouth. ¹⁸The Lord will save me from every evil attack. He will bring me safely to his heavenly kingdom.

Give him glory for ever and ever. Amen.

FINAL GREETINGS

¹⁹Greet Priscilla and Aquila. Greet those who live in the house of Onesiphorus.

²⁰Erastus stayed in Corinth. I left Trophimus sick in Miletus.

²¹Do your best to get here before winter.

Eubulus greets you. So do Pudens, Linus, Claudia and all the brothers .

²²May the Lord be with your spirit. May God's grace be with you.

quest challenge

I Wonder . . .

How can I find the courage to stand up for what's right?

Real Life Challenge

It's hard to stand up for what is right when others choose to do something you know is wrong. What could you do when you see them making fun of another kid at school? Maybe you could ask them to stop. Or you could ask that other kid to come and sit with you at lunch. When you need to stand up for what's right, remember Daniel and his friends, and where they got their courage in a situation like that.

Quest Clue

You can find out how Daniel and his friends were able to handle these tough situations by searching in Daniel chapters 3 and 6. Take a look somewhere in Psalm 118 and 2 Timothy 1 for other clues on where to find courage!

Titus

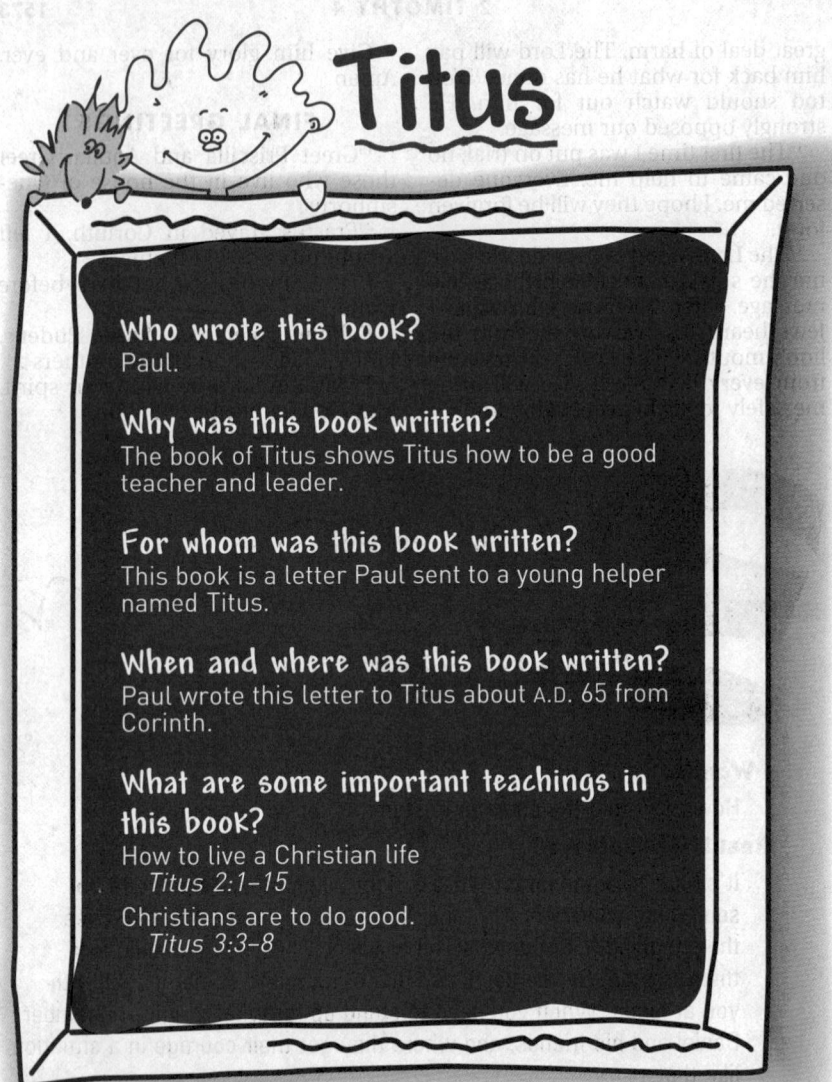

Who wrote this book?
Paul.

Why was this book written?
The book of Titus shows Titus how to be a good teacher and leader.

For whom was this book written?
This book is a letter Paul sent to a young helper named Titus.

When and where was this book written?
Paul wrote this letter to Titus about A.D. 65 from Corinth.

What are some important teachings in this book?
How to live a Christian life
   Titus 2:1–15
Christians are to do good.
   Titus 3:3–8

---

1 I, Paul, am writing this letter. I serve God. I am an apostle of Jesus Christ. God sent me to help his chosen people believe in Christ. I have been sent to help them understand the truth that leads to godly living. ²Faith and understanding rest on the hope of eternal life. Before time began, God promised to give that life. And he does not lie. ³At just the right time he made his word plain. He did it through the preaching that he trusted me with. God our Savior has commanded all those things.

⁴Titus, I am sending you this letter. You are my true son in the faith we share.

May God the Father and Christ Jesus our Savior give you grace and peace.

THE WORK OF TITUS ON CRETE

⁵I left you on the island of Crete. There were some things that hadn't been finished. You needed to sort them out. You also had to appoint elders in every town. I told you how to do it.

⁶An elder must be without blame. He must be faithful to his wife. His children must be believers. They must not give anyone a reason to say that they are wild and don't obey.

⁷A church leader is trusted with God's work. That's why he must be without blame. He must not look after only his own interests. He must not get angry easily. He must not get drunk. He must not push people around. He must not try to get money by cheating people.

⁸Instead, he must welcome people into his home. He must love what is good. He must control his mind and feelings. He must do what is right. He must be holy. He must control what his body longs for. ⁹The message as it has been taught can be trusted. He must hold firmly to it. Then he will be able to use true teaching to comfort others and build them up. He will be able to prove that people who oppose it are wrong.

¹⁰Many people refuse to obey God. All they do is talk a lot. They try to fool others. No one does these things more than the circumcision group. ¹¹They must be stopped. They are destroying entire families. They are teaching things they shouldn't. They do it to get money by cheating people.

¹²Even one of their own prophets has said, "People from Crete are always liars. They are evil beasts. They don't want to work. They live only to eat." ¹³What I have just said is true. So give them a strong warning. Then they will understand the faith correctly. ¹⁴They will pay no attention to Jewish stories that aren't completely true. They won't listen to the commands of those who turn away from the truth.

¹⁵To people who are pure, all things are pure. But to those who have twisted minds and don't believe, nothing is pure. In fact, their minds and their sense of what is right and wrong are twisted. ¹⁶They claim to know God. But their actions show they don't know him. They are hated by God. They re-

KIDS' QUESTION

Why do friends talk behind your back?

Most kids who say bad things about others don't realize that it's wrong and hurtful. They have never learned that they are not only hurting others, they are also hurting themselves by pushing friends away. Some kids give in to pressure from others and go along with what has been said, even if it's about a friend. Many times kids will repeat things they've heard about someone without talking to the person to see if those things are true. This is known as gossiping. Spreading rumors can really hurt people. The Bible says gossiping is wrong—it hurts people and breaks up friendships.

checkout
Titus 1:10-12

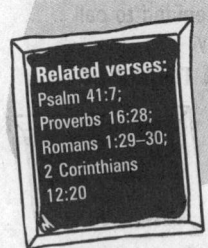

Related verses:
Psalm 41:7;
Proverbs 16:28;
Romans 1:29–30;
2 Corinthians 12:20

fuse to obey him. They aren't fit to do anything good.

TEACHING GOD'S PEOPLE

2 What you teach must agree with true teaching. ²Tell the older men that in anything they do, they must not go too far. They must be worthy of respect. They must control themselves. They must have true faith. They must love others. They must not give up.

³In the same way, teach the older women to lead a holy life. They must not tell lies about others. They must not let wine control them. Instead, they must teach what is good. ⁴Then they can train the younger women to love their husbands and children.

⁵The younger women must control themselves. They must be pure. They must take good care of their homes. They must be kind. They must follow the lead of their husbands. Then no one will be able to speak evil things against God's word.

⁶In the same way, help the young men to control themselves. ⁷Do what is good. Set an example for them in everything. When you teach, be honest and serious. ⁸No one can question the truth. So teach what is true. Then those who oppose you will be ashamed. That's because they will have nothing bad to say about us.

⁹Teach slaves to obey their masters in everything they do. Tell them to try to please their masters. They must not talk back to them. ¹⁰They must not steal from them. Instead, they must show that they can be trusted completely. Then they will make the teaching about God our Savior appealing in every way.

¹¹God's saving grace has appeared to all people. ¹²It teaches us to say no to godless ways and sinful longings. We must control ourselves. We must do what is right. We must lead godly lives in today's world. ¹³That's how we should live as we wait for the blessed hope God has given us.

We are waiting for Jesus Christ to appear in all his glory. He is our great God and Savior. ¹⁴He gave himself for us. By doing that, he set us free from all evil. He wanted to make us pure. He wanted us to be his very own people. He wanted us to long to do what is good.

¹⁵Those are the things you should

Why do they call it Good Friday if that's the day Jesus died?

The day Jesus died is called "Good Friday" because it was a good day for us. Jesus died for us on that day. He died in our place. When he died he paid the price for our sins. Of course, that day was also a sad day. It was sad because Jesus suffered and died. But on Easter morning Jesus came back to life again. Then everyone knew that Jesus had paid the penalty for the sins of the whole world. And because of that, they decided to call it Good Friday.

 Titus 2:14

Related verses: Luke 23:26–56; 24:1–8

teach. Cheer people up and give them hope. Correct them with full authority. Don't let anyone look down on you.

DO WHAT IS GOOD

3 Remind God's people to obey rulers and authorities. Remind them to be ready to do what is good. ²Tell them not to speak evil things against anyone. Remind them to live in peace. They must consider the needs of others. They must be kind and gentle toward all people.

³At one time we too acted like fools. We didn't obey God. We were tricked. We were controlled by all kinds of longings and pleasures. We were full of evil. We wanted what belongs to others. People hated us, and we hated one another.

⁴But the kindness and love of God our Savior appeared. ⁵He saved us. It wasn't because of the good things we had done. It was because of his mercy. He saved us by washing away our sins. We were born again. The Holy Spirit gave us new life.

⁶God poured out the Spirit on us freely because of what Jesus Christ our Savior has done. ⁷His grace made us right with God. So now we have received the hope of eternal life as God's children.

⁸You can trust that saying. Those things are important. Treat them that way. Then those who have trusted in God will be careful to commit them-selves to doing what is good. Those things are excellent. They are for the good of everyone.

⁹But keep away from foolish disagreements. Don't argue about family histories. Don't make trouble. Don't fight about what the law teaches. Don't argue about things like that. It doesn't do any good. It doesn't help anyone.

¹⁰Warn anyone who tries to get believers to take sides and separate into their own little groups. Warn him more than once. After that, have nothing to do with him. ¹¹You can be sure that someone like that is twisted and sinful. His own actions judge him.

FINAL WORDS

¹²I will send Artemas or Tychicus to you. Then do your best to come to me at Nicopolis. I've decided to spend the winter there.

¹³Do everything you can to help Zenas the lawyer and Apollos. Send them on their way. See that they have everything they need.

¹⁴Our people must learn to commit themselves to doing what is good. Then they will be able to provide for the daily needs of others. If they do that, their lives won't turn out to be useless.

¹⁵Everyone who is with me sends you greetings. Greet those who love us in the faith.

May God's grace be with you all.

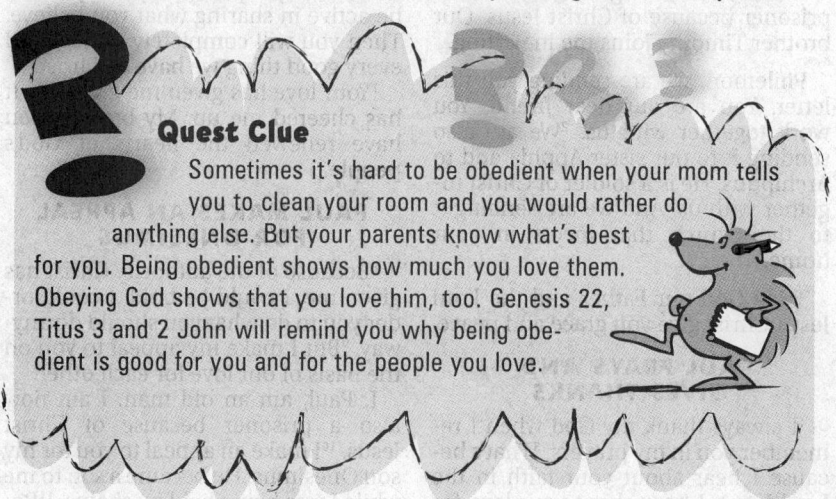

Quest Clue

Sometimes it's hard to be obedient when your mom tells you to clean your room and you would rather do anything else. But your parents know what's best for you. Being obedient shows how much you love them. Obeying God shows that you love him, too. Genesis 22, Titus 3 and 2 John will remind you why being obedient is good for you and for the people you love.

Philemon

Who wrote this book?
Paul.

Why was this book written?
This book asks Philemon to welcome back a runaway slave named Onesimus, who has become a Christian.

To whom was this book written?
This book is a personal letter sent to a Christian named Philemon.

When and where was this book written?
Philemon was written about A.D. 63 while Paul was in prison in Rome.

¹I, Paul, am writing this letter. I am a prisoner because of Christ Jesus. Our brother Timothy joins me in writing.

Philemon, we are sending you this letter. You are our dear friend. You work together with us. ²We are also sending it to our sister Apphia and to Archippus. He is a soldier of Christ together with us. And we are sending it to the church that meets in your home.

³May God our Father and the Lord Jesus Christ give you grace and peace.

PAUL PRAYS AND GIVES THANKS

⁴I always thank my God when I remember you in my prayers. ⁵That's because I hear about your faith in the Lord Jesus. I hear about your love for all of God's people. ⁶I pray that you will be active in sharing what you believe. Then you will completely understand every good thing we have in Christ.

⁷Your love has given me great joy. It has cheered me up. My brother, you have renewed the hearts of God's people.

PAUL MAKES AN APPEAL FOR ONESIMUS

⁸Because of the authority Christ has given me, I could be bold. I could order you to do what you should do anyway. ⁹But I make my appeal to you on the basis of our love for each other.

I, Paul, am an old man. I am now also a prisoner because of Christ Jesus. ¹⁰I make an appeal to you for my son Onesimus. He became a son to me while I was being held by chains. ¹¹Before that, he was useless to you. But now he has become useful to you and to me.

[12]I'm sending Onesimus back to you. My very heart goes with him. [13]I would have liked to keep him with me. Then he could have taken your place in helping me while I'm being held by chains because of the good news. [14]But I didn't want to do anything unless you agreed. Any favor you do must be done because you want to do it, not because you have to.

[15]Onesimus was separated from you for a little while. Maybe that was so you could have him back for good. [16]You could have him back not as a slave. Instead, he would be better than a slave. He would be a dear brother. He is very dear to me. But he is even more dear to you, both as a man and as a brother in the Lord.

[17]Do you think of me as a believer who works together with you? Then welcome Onesimus as you would welcome me. [18]Has he done anything wrong to you? Does he owe you anything? Then charge it to me. [19]I'll pay it back. I, Paul, am writing this with my own hand. I won't even mention that you owe me your very life.

[20]My brother, I wish I could receive some benefit from you because we both belong to the Lord. Renew my heart. We know that Christ is the one who really renews it. [21]I'm sure you will obey. So I'm writing to you. I know you will do even more than I ask.

[22]There is one more thing. Have a guest room ready for me. I hope I can return to all of you in answer to your prayers.

[23]Epaphras sends you greetings. Together with me, he is a prisoner because of Christ Jesus. [24]Mark, Aristarchus, Demas and Luke work together with me. They also send you greetings.

[25]May the grace of the Lord Jesus Christ be with your spirit.

How did Paul send letters to churches if they didn't have mail boxes?

The Roman world of Paul's time did not have a postal service as we have today. Instead people sent letters by messengers or friends. Many of Paul's friends delivered his letters to churches. Paul wrote some letters to only one person. He wrote other letters to whole churches. Paul hoped also that some of his letters to churches would be passed along to other churches to be read over and over again. And that is just what happened. In fact, we are still reading those letters today.

Paul and Timothy wrote the letter to Philemon together, but they asked Philemon right at the beginning to share it.

checkout Philemon 1

JASON'S IMAGINATION

CHURCHING PIGEONS

Related verses: Ephesians 6:21,22

Hebrews

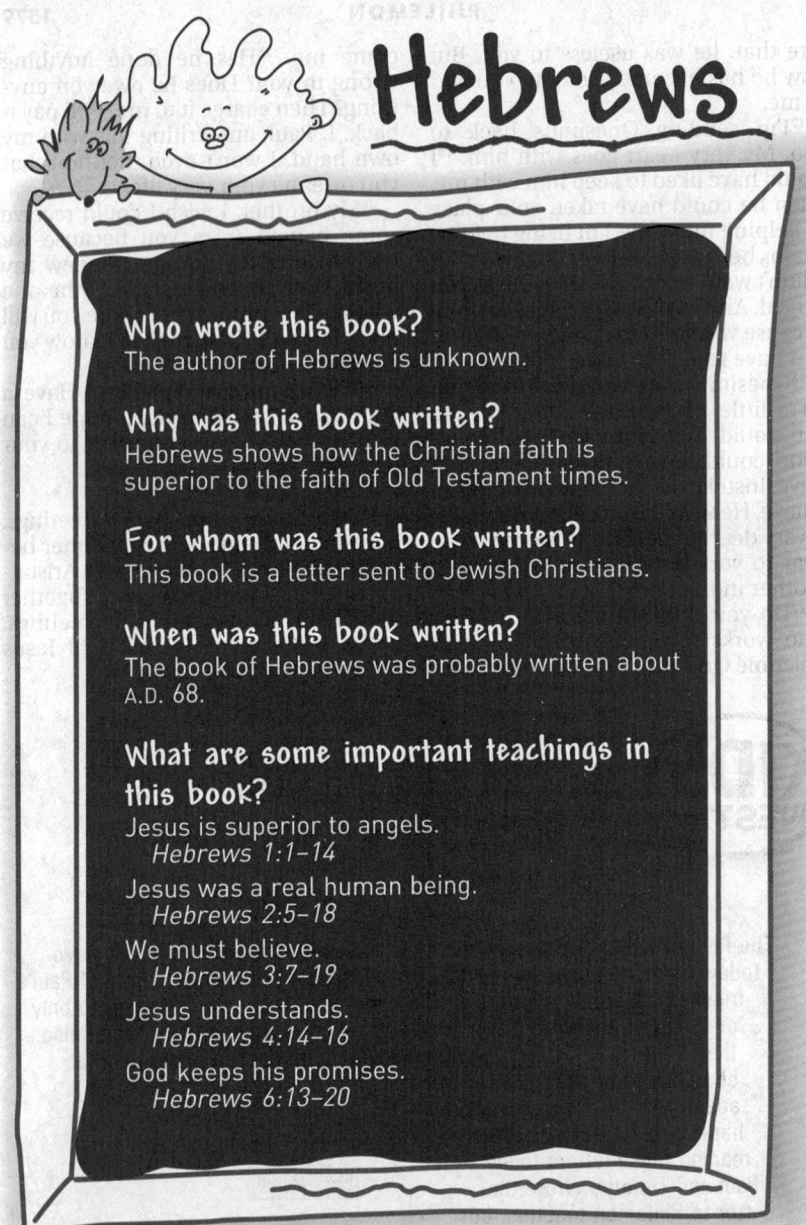

Who wrote this book?
The author of Hebrews is unknown.

Why was this book written?
Hebrews shows how the Christian faith is superior to the faith of Old Testament times.

For whom was this book written?
This book is a letter sent to Jewish Christians.

When was this book written?
The book of Hebrews was probably written about A.D. 68.

What are some important teachings in this book?
Jesus is superior to angels.
Hebrews 1:1–14

Jesus was a real human being.
Hebrews 2:5–18

We must believe.
Hebrews 3:7–19

Jesus understands.
Hebrews 4:14–16

God keeps his promises.
Hebrews 6:13–20

THE SON IS GREATER THAN THE ANGELS

1 In the past, God spoke to our people through the prophets. He spoke at many times. He spoke in different ways. ²But in these last days, he has spoken to us through his Son. He is the one whom God appoint- ed to receive all things. God made everything through him. ³The Son is the gleaming brightness of God's glory. He is the exact likeness of God's being. He uses his powerful word to hold all things together. He provided the way for people to be made pure from sin. Then he sat down at the right hand of

the King, the Majesty in heaven. ⁴So he became higher than the angels. The name he received is more excellent than theirs.

⁵God never said to any of the angels,

> "You are my Son.
>   Today I have become your
>   Father." *(Psalm 2:7)*

Or,

> "I will be his Father.
>   And he will be my Son."
>   *(2 Samuel 7:14; 1 Chronicles 17:13)*

⁶God's first and only Son is over all things. When God brings him into the world, he says,

> "Let all of God's angels worship
>   him." *(Deuteronomy 32:43)*

⁷Here is something else God says about the angels.

> "God makes his angels to be like
>   winds.
> He makes those who serve him
>   to be like flashes of lightning."
>   *(Psalm 104:4)*

⁸But here is what he says about the Son.

> "You are God. Your throne will last
>   for ever and ever.
> Your kingdom will be ruled by
>   what is right.
> ⁹You have loved what is right and
>   hated what is evil.
> So your God has placed you
>   above your companions.
> He has filled you with joy by
>   pouring the sacred oil on your
>   head." *(Psalm 45:6,7)*

¹⁰He also says,

> "Lord, in the beginning you made
>   the earth secure. You placed it
>   on its foundations.
> The heavens are the work of your
>   hands.
> ¹¹They will pass away. But you
>   remain.
> They will all wear out like a piece
>   of clothing.
> ¹²You will roll them up like a robe.
> They will be changed as a person
>   changes clothes.
> But you remain the same.
>   Your years will never end."
>   *(Psalm 102:25–27)*

¹³God never said to an angel,

Can Christians hear God talking to them?

In the Bible we read about people hearing God's voice. But that did not happen very often. Most of the time God gave his messages to people who wrote down what he said. He didn't usually tell them out loud what he wanted them to write, but they knew in their hearts what they should say. God also sent Jesus to teach us about God and to show us what God is like. Then God's people put these messages together in the Bible so everyone could read them. Today God speaks to us mainly through the Bible. That's why it is called "God's Word." The Bible is God's message to us.

Related verses:
1 Samuel 3:1–18;
Psalm 119:1–24

checkout
Hebrews 1:1,2

"Sit at my right hand
until I put your enemies
under your control." *(Psalm 110:1)*

¹⁴All angels are spirits who serve. God sends them to serve those who will receive salvation.

A WARNING TO PAY ATTENTION

2 So we must pay more careful attention to what we have heard. Then we will not drift away from it. ²Even the message God spoke through angels had to be obeyed. Every time people broke the Law, they were punished. Every time they didn't obey, they were punished. ³Then how will we escape if we don't pay attention to God's great salvation?

The Lord first announced that salvation. Those who heard him gave us the message about it. ⁴God gave witness to it through signs and wonders. He gave witness through different kinds of miracles. He also gave witness through the gifts of the Holy Spirit. He gave them out as it pleased him.

JESUS WAS MADE LIKE HIS BROTHERS

⁵God has not put angels in charge of the world that is going to come. We are talking about that world. ⁶There is a place where someone has given witness to it. He said,

"What is a human being that you
think about him?
What is the son of man that you
take care of him?
⁷You made him a little lower than
the angels.
You placed on him a crown of
glory and honor.
⁸ You have put everything under
his control." *(Psalm 8:4–6)*

So God has put everything under him. Everything is under his control.

We do not now see everything under his control. ⁹But we do see Jesus already given a crown of glory and honor. He was made a little lower than the angels. He suffered death. By the grace of God, he tasted death for everyone. That is why he was given his crown.

¹⁰God has made everything. He has acted in exactly the right way. He is bringing his many sons and daughters to share in his glory. To do so, he has made the One who saved them perfect because of his sufferings.

¹¹The One who makes people holy and the people he makes holy belong to the same family. So Jesus is not

Do angels go to work?

The word *angel* means "messenger." Angels do not have jobs where they work for someone for money the way people do. Instead, they serve God. Angels do nothing but serve God all the time without ever getting tired or grumpy.

They are happy to do it.
They do a lot of work.
But they do not go to
work the way your
mom or dad does.

checkout

Hebrews 1:14

Related verses:
Luke 4:10; 16:22

ashamed to call them his brothers and sisters. [12]He says,

"I will announce your name to my brothers and sisters.
I will sing your praises among those who worship you."

(Psalm 22:22)

[13]Again he says,

"I will put my trust in him."

(Isaiah 8:17)

And again he says,

"Here I am. Here are the children God has given me." *(Isaiah 8:18)*

[14]Those children have bodies made out of flesh and blood. So Jesus became human like them in order to die for them. By doing that, he could destroy the one who rules over the kingdom of death. I'm talking about the devil. [15]Jesus could set people free who were afraid of death. All their lives they were held as slaves by that fear. [16]It is certainly Abraham's children that he helps. He doesn't help angels.

[17]So he had to be made like his brothers in every way. Then he could serve God as a kind and faithful high priest. And then he could pay for the sins of the people by dying for them. [18]He himself suffered when he was tempted. Now he is able to help others who are being tempted.

JESUS IS GREATER THAN MOSES

3 Holy brothers and sisters, God chose you to be his people. So keep thinking about Jesus. He is our apostle. He is our high priest. We believe in him. [2]Moses was faithful in everything he did in the house of God. In the same way, Jesus was faithful to the One who appointed him. [3]The person who builds a house has greater honor than the house itself. In the same way, Jesus has been found worthy of greater honor than Moses. [4]Every house is built by someone. But God is the builder of everything. [5]Moses was faithful as one who

KIDS' QUESTION

Are there people inside of angels?

People and angels are different. They live in their own separate spaces. There are not any people inside angels. And people do not become angels when they die. In *cartoons* you may see people die and become angels. But that is not what really happens. People have souls. Our souls live forever as spirit beings, like angels. But we are not bodies inside of angels.

checkout Hebrews 2:5-8

Related verses:
Mark 12:25;
1 Corinthians 6:3

JASON'S IMAGINATION

SHOWER

serves in the house of God. He gave witness to what God would say in days to come. [6]But Christ is faithful as a son over God's house. We are his house if we continue to come boldly to God. We must also hold on to the hope we take pride in.

A WARNING AGAINST UNBELIEF

[7]The Holy Spirit says,

"Listen to his voice today.
[8] If you hear it, don't be stubborn.
You were stubborn when you
    opposed me.
You did that when you were put
    to the test in the desert.
[9]There your people of long ago put
    me to the test.
For 40 years they saw what I did.
[10]That is why I was angry with them.
I said, 'Their hearts are always
    going down the wrong path.
They have not known my ways.'
[11]So in my anger I took an oath.
I said, 'They will never enjoy the
    rest I planned for them.' "

(Psalm 95:7–11)

[12]Brothers and sisters, make sure that none of you has a sinful heart. Do not let an unbelieving heart turn you away from the living God. [13]But build one another up every day. Do it as long as there is still time. Then none of you will become stubborn. You won't be fooled by sin's tricks. [14]We belong to Christ if we hold firmly to the faith we had at first. But we must hold to it until the end. [15]It has just been said,

"Listen to his voice today.
If you hear it, don't be stubborn.
You were stubborn when you
    opposed me."   *(Psalm 95:7,8)*

[16]Who were those who heard and refused to obey? Weren't they all the people Moses led out of Egypt? [17]Who was God angry with for 40 years? Wasn't it with those who sinned? They died in the desert. [18]What people did God promise with an oath that they would never enjoy the rest he planned for them? Wasn't it those who didn't obey? [19]So we see that they weren't able

to enter. That's because they didn't believe.

GOD'S PEOPLE ENTER HIS SABBATH REST

4 God's promise of enjoying his rest still stands. So be careful that none of you fails to receive it.

[2]The good news was preached to our people long ago. It has also been preached to us. The message they heard didn't have any value for them. They didn't combine it with faith. [3]Now we who have believed enjoy that rest. God said,

"When I was angry I took an oath.
I said, 'They will never enjoy the
    rest I planned for them.' "

(Psalm 95:11)

Ever since God created the world, his work has been finished. [4]Somewhere he spoke about the seventh day. He said, "On the seventh day God rested from all his work." *(Genesis 2:2)* [5]In the part of Scripture I talked about earlier God said, "They will never enjoy the rest I planned for them." *(Psalm 95:11)* [6]It is still true that some will enjoy that rest. But those who had the good news preached to them earlier didn't go in. That was because they didn't obey.

[7]So God again chose a certain day. He named it Today. He did that when he spoke through David a long time later. As it was said earlier,

"Listen to his voice today.
If you hear it, don't be stubborn."

(Psalm 95:7,8)

[8]Suppose Joshua had given them rest. If he had, God would not have spoken later about another day. [9]So there is still a Sabbath rest for God's people. [10]God rested from his work. Those who enjoy God's rest also rest from their work. [11]So let us make every effort to enjoy that rest. Then no one will fall into sin by following the example of those who didn't obey God.

[12]The word of God is living and active. It is sharper than any sword that

has two edges. It cuts deep enough to separate soul from spirit. It can separate joints from bones. It judges the thoughts and purposes of the heart. ¹³Nothing God created is hidden from him. His eyes see everything. He will hold us accountable for everything we do.

JESUS IS THE GREAT HIGH PRIEST

¹⁴We have a great high priest. He has gone up into the heavens. He is Jesus the Son of God. So let us hold firmly to what we say we believe.

¹⁵We have a high priest who can feel it when we are weak and hurting. We have a high priest who has been tempted in every way, just as we are. But he did not sin. ¹⁶So let us boldly approach the throne of grace. Then we will receive mercy. We will find grace to help us when we need it.

5 Every high priest is chosen from among men. He is appointed to act for them in everything that has to do with God. He offers gifts and sacrifices for their sins. ²He is able to deal gently with those who have gone down the wrong path without knowing it. He can do that because he himself is weak. ³That's why he has to offer sacrifices for his own sins. He must also do it for the sins of the people.

⁴No one can take that honor for himself. He must be appointed by God, just as Aaron was.

⁵Even Christ did not take the glory of becoming a high priest for himself. God said to him,

"You are my Son.
Today I have become your
  Father."   *(Psalm 2:7)*

⁶In another place he said,

"You are a priest forever,
  just like Melchizedek." *(Psalm 110:4)*

⁷Jesus prayed while he lived on earth. He made his appeal with loud cries and tears. He prayed to the One who could save him from death. God heard him because he truly honored God.

⁸Jesus was God's Son. But by suffering he learned what it means to obey. ⁹In that way he was made perfect. Eternal salvation comes from him. He saves all those who obey him.

¹⁰God appointed him to be the high priest, just like Melchizedek.

Why do we have the Bible?

God gave us the Bible because he wants us to know what he is like and how to live. The Bible is like a lamp or lantern. It shows us the direction to go in life. The Bible is like an instruction manual. It shows us how God wants us to live. And the Bible is like a sword. It cuts the bad out of our lives. The Bible is not just a book. It is God's living word and a powerful help for our lives.

checkout Hebrews 4:12

Related verses:
Psalm 119:105,
130,144;
John 20:30,31

A WARNING AGAINST FALLING AWAY

[11]We have a lot to say about that. But it is hard to explain it to you. You learn too slowly. [12]By this time you should be teachers. But in fact, you need someone to teach you all over again. You need even the simple truths of God's word. You need milk, not solid food.

[13]Anyone who lives on milk is still a baby. That person does not want to learn about living a godly life. [14]Solid food is for those who are grown up. They have trained themselves with a lot of practice. They can tell the difference between good and evil.

6 So let us leave the simple teachings about Christ. Let us grow up as believers. Let us not start all over again with the basic teachings. They taught us that we need to turn away from doing things that lead to death. They taught us that we must have faith in God. [2]They taught us about different kinds of baptism. They taught us about placing hands on people. They taught us that people will rise from the dead. They taught us that God will judge everyone. And they taught us that what he decides will last forever.

[3]If God permits, we will go beyond those teachings and grow up.

[4]What if some people fall away from the faith? It won't be possible to bring them back. It is true that they have seen the light. They have tasted the heavenly gift. They have shared in the Holy Spirit. [5]They have tasted the good things of God's word. They have tasted the powers of the age to come. [6]But they have fallen away from the faith. So it won't be possible to bring them back. They won't be able to turn away from their sins. They are losing everything. That's because they are nailing the Son of God to the cross all over again. They are bringing shame on him in front of everyone.

[7]Some land drinks the rain that falls on it. It produces a crop that is useful to those who farm the land. That land receives God's blessing. [8]But other land produces only thorns and weeds. That land isn't worth anything. It is in danger of coming under God's curse. In the end, it will be burned.

[9]Dear friends, we have to say these things. But we are sure of better things in your case. We are talking about the things that go along with being saved.

[10]God is fair. He will not forget what you have done. He will remember the love you have shown him. You showed it when you helped his people. And you show it when you keep on helping them.

[11]We want each of you to be faithful

Why did Jesus get tempted by the devil?

A "temptation" is a feeling that you might like to do something wrong. Sometimes a person will tempt you by trying to get you to do the wrong thing. The devil tempted Jesus because he hated Jesus. Satan wanted Jesus to sin. But Jesus did not give in. That is why the Bible says that our "high priest," Jesus, was tempted like we are but did not sin. It is not a sin to be tempted. It is a sin only if you give in and do the wrong thing.

Related verses:
Matthew 4:1–11;
1 Corinthians
10:13

checkout
Hebrews 4:15, 16

to the very end. We want you to be sure of what you hope for. [12]We don't want you to slow down. Instead, be like those who have faith and are patient. They will receive what God promised.

GOD KEEPS HIS PROMISE

[13]When God made his promise to Abraham, he took an oath to keep it. But there was no one greater than himself to take an oath. So he took his oath by making an appeal to himself.

[14]He said, "I will certainly bless you. I will give you many children." *(Genesis 22:17)* [15]Abraham was patient while he waited. Then he received what God promised him.

[16]People take oaths by someone greater than themselves. An oath makes a promise certain. It puts an end to all arguing. [17]So God took an oath when he made his promise. He wanted to make it very clear that his purpose does not change. He wanted those who would receive what was promised to know that.

[18]God took an oath so we would have good reason not to give up. We have run away from everything else to take hold of the hope offered to us in God's promise. So God gave his promise and his oath. Those two things can't change. He couldn't lie about them.

[19]Our hope is certain. It is something for the soul to hold on to. It is strong and secure. It goes all the way into the Most Holy Room behind the curtain. [20]That is where Jesus has gone. He went there to open the way ahead of us. He has become a high priest forever, just like Melchizedek.

MELCHIZEDEK THE PRIEST

7 Melchizedek was the king of Salem. He was the priest of God Most High. He met Abraham, who was returning from winning a battle over some kings. Melchizedek blessed him. [2]Abraham gave him a tenth of everything.

First, the name Melchizedek means "king of what is right." Also, "king of Salem" means "king of peace." [3]Melchizedek has no father or mother. He has no family line. His days have no beginning. His life has no end. He remains a priest forever, just like the Son of God.

[4]Think how great Melchizedek was. Even our father Abraham gave him a tenth of what he had captured. [5]Now the law lays down a rule for the sons of Levi who become priests. They must collect a tenth from the people. They must collect it even from those who belong to the family line of Abraham.

[6]Melchizedek did not trace his family line from Levi. But he collected a tenth from Abraham. Melchizedek blessed the one who had received the promises. [7]Without a doubt, the more important person blesses the less important one. [8]In the one case, the tenth is collected by men who die. But in the other case, it is collected by the one who is said to be living.

[9]Levi collects the tenth. But we might say that Levi paid the tenth through Abraham. [10]That's because when Melchizedek met Abraham, Levi was still in Abraham's body.

JESUS IS LIKE MELCHIZEDEK

[11]Suppose the Levites who were priests could have made people perfect. The law was given to the people so they could become perfect through the priests. Then why was there still a need for another priest to come? And why did he need to be like Melchizedek? Why wasn't he from Aaron's family line?

[12]A change of priests requires a change of law. [13]Those things are said about one who is from a different tribe. No one from that tribe has ever served at the altar. [14]It is clear that our Lord came from the family line of Judah. Moses said nothing about priests who were from that tribe.

[15]But suppose another priest like Melchizedek appears. Then what we have said is even more clear. [16]He has not become a priest because of a rule about his family line. He has become a priest because of his powerful life. His life can never be destroyed. [17]Scripture says,

"You are a priest forever,
    just like Melchizedek."
                    (Psalm 110:4)

¹⁸The old rule is done away with. It was weak and useless. ¹⁹The law didn't make anything perfect. Now a better hope has been given to us. That hope brings us near to God.

²⁰The change of priests was made with an oath. Others became priests without any oath. ²¹But Jesus became a priest with an oath. God said to him,

"The Lord has taken an oath and
    made a promise.
He will not change his mind. He
    has said,
'You are a priest forever.' "

(Psalm 110:4)

²²Because of that oath, Jesus makes the promise of a better covenant certain.

²³There were many priests in Levi's family line. Death kept them from continuing in office. ²⁴But Jesus lives forever. So he always holds the office of priest. ²⁵People now come to God through him. And he is able to save them completely and for all time. Jesus lives forever. He prays for them.

²⁶A high priest like that meets our need. He is holy, pure and without blame. He isn't like other people. He does not sin. He is lifted high above the heavens.

²⁷He isn't like the other high priests. They need to offer sacrifices day after day. First they bring offerings for their own sins. Then they do it for the sins of the people. But Jesus gave one sacrifice for the sins of the people. He gave it once and for all time. He did it by offering himself.

²⁸The law appoints men who are weak to be high priests. But God's oath came after the law. The oath appointed the Son. He has been made perfect forever.

THE HIGH PRIEST OF A NEW COVENANT

8 Here is the point of what we are saying. We have a high priest like that. He sat down at the right hand of the throne of the King, the Majesty in heaven. ²He serves in the sacred tent. The Lord set up the true holy tent. A mere man did not set it up.

³Every high priest is appointed to offer gifts and sacrifices. So that priest also had to have something to offer.

⁴What if he were on earth? Then he would not be a priest. There are already priests who offer the gifts required by the law. ⁵They serve at a sacred tent. But it is only a copy and shadow of what is in heaven. That's why God warned Moses when he was about to build the holy tent. God said, "Be sure to make everything just like the pattern I showed you on the mountain." *(Exodus 25:40)*

⁶Jesus has been given a greater work to do for God. He is the go-between for the new covenant. That covenant is better than the old one. It is based on better promises.

⁷Suppose nothing had been wrong with that first covenant. Then no one would have looked for another covenant. ⁸But God found fault with the people. He said,

"A new day is coming, says the
    Lord.
I will make a new covenant
with the people of Israel.
    I will also make it with the
        people of Judah.
⁹It will not be like the covenant
    I made with their people of long
        ago.
That was when I took them by the
    hand.
I led them out of Egypt.
My new covenant will be different
    because they didn't remain
        faithful to my old covenant.
So I turned away from them,
                says the Lord.
¹⁰This is the covenant I will make
    with Israel
after that time, says the Lord.
I will put my laws in their minds.
I will write them on their
    hearts.
I will be their God.
And they will be my people.
¹¹A man will not teach his neighbor
    anymore.
And he will not teach his friend
    anymore.
He will not say, 'Know the Lord.'
Everyone will know me.
From the least important of
    them to the most important,
all of them will know me.
¹²I will forgive their evil ways.

I will not remember their sins anymore." *(Jeremiah 31:31–34)*

[13]God called that covenant "new." So he has made the first one out of date. And what is out of date and getting older will soon disappear.

WORSHIP IN THE HOLY TENT ON EARTH

9 The first covenant had rules for worship. It also had a sacred tent on earth. [2]A holy tent was set up. The lampstand was in the first room. So were the table and the holy bread. That was called the Holy Room. [3]Behind the second curtain was a room called the Most Holy Room. [4]It had the golden altar for incense. It also had the wooden chest called the ark of the covenant. The ark was covered with gold. It held the gold jar of manna. It held Aaron's wooden staff that had budded. It also held the stone tablets. The words of the covenant were written on them.

[5]The cherubim were above the ark. God showed his glory there. The cherubim spread their wings over the place where sin was paid for. But we can't deal with those things more completely now.

[6]That's how everything was arranged in the holy tent. The priests entered it at regular times. They went into the outer room to do their work for God and others. [7]But only the high priest went into the inner room. He went in only once a year. He never entered without taking blood with him. He offered the blood for himself. He also offered it for the sins the people had committed because they didn't know any better.

[8]Here is what the Holy Spirit was showing us. He was telling us that God had not yet clearly shown the way into the Most Holy Room. It would not be clearly shown as long as the first holy tent was still standing.

[9]That's an example for the present time. It shows us that the gifts and sacrifices they offered were not enough. They were not able to remove the worshiper's feelings of guilt. [10]They deal only with food and drink and different kinds of special washings. They are rules that deal with things outside our bodies. People had to obey them only until the new covenant came.

THE BLOOD OF CHRIST

[11]Christ came to be the high priest of the good things that are already here. When he came, he went through the greater and more perfect holy tent. The tent was not made by people. In other words, it is not a part of this creation. [12]He did not enter by spilling the blood of goats and calves. He entered the Most Holy Room by spilling his own blood. He did it once and for all time. He paid the price to set us free from sin forever.

[13]The blood of goats and bulls is sprinkled on people. So are the ashes of a young cow. They are sprinkled on people the Law called unclean. The people are sprinkled to make them holy. That makes them clean on the outside.

[14]But Christ offered himself to God without any flaw. He did this through the power of the eternal Holy Spirit. So how much more will his blood wash from our minds our feelings of guilt for committing sin! Sin always leads to death. But now we can serve the living God.

[15]That's why Christ is the go-between of a new covenant. Now those God calls to himself will receive the eternal gift he promised. They will receive it now that Christ has died to save them. He died to set them free from the sins they committed under the first covenant.

[16]What happens in the case of a will? It is necessary to prove that the person who made the will has died. [17]A will is in effect only when somebody has died. It never takes effect while the one who made it is still living. [18]That's why even the first covenant was not put into effect without the spilling of blood.

[19]Moses first announced every commandment of the law to all the people. Then he took the blood of calves. He also took water, bright red wool and branches of a hyssop plant. He sprinkled the scroll. He also sprinkled all of the people. [20]He said, "This is the

blood of the covenant God has commanded you to keep." *(Exodus 24:8)* ²¹In the same way, he sprinkled the holy tent with blood. He also sprinkled everything that was used in worship there.

²²In fact, the law requires that nearly everything be made clean with blood. Without the spilling of blood, no one can be forgiven.

²³So the copies of the heavenly things had to be made pure with those sacrifices. But the heavenly things themselves had to be made pure with better sacrifices.

²⁴Christ did not enter a sacred tent made by people. That tent was only a copy of the true one. He entered heaven itself. He did it to stand in front of God for us. He is there right now.

²⁵The high priest enters the Most Holy Room every year. He enters with blood that is not his own. But Christ did not enter heaven to offer himself again and again. ²⁶If he had, he would have had to suffer many times since the world was created. But now he has

appeared once and for all time. He has come at the end of the ages to do away with sin. He has done that by offering himself.

²⁷People have to die once. After that, God will judge them. ²⁸In the same way, Christ was offered up once. He took away the sins of many people.

He will also come a second time. At that time he will not suffer for sin. Instead, he will come to bring salvation to those who are waiting for him.

CHRIST'S SACRIFICE IS ONCE AND FOR ALL TIME

10 The law is only a shadow of the good things that are coming. It is not the real things themselves. The same sacrifices have to be offered over and over again. They must be offered year after year. That's why the law can never make perfect those who come near to worship. ²If it could, wouldn't the sacrifices have stopped being offered? The worshipers would have been made clean once and for all time. They

---

KIDS' QUESTION

Why did God make heaven?

God is everywhere. He cannot fit into any one place. When we talk about heaven we are really talking about where God lives. We think of heaven as a place, because that is how we describe going to be with God. That is why we say Jesus went to heaven. He went to be with God. The word *heaven* can refer to several places: (1) the home or place of God, (2) the new Jerusalem, or (3) "the heavens" or sky. Just before Jesus left the earth, he said he would go and prepare a place for us. This is a place where we can live with him. Someday he will come back and take us to that place. He will destroy this world and create a new one. That new world will be for all those who love him. That is the new heaven and new earth that God will make.

 **checkout**

Hebrews 9:24

ROYAL REWARDS SERVICE DESK

ULTIMATE ROYAL REWARDS PROGRAM FREE TRIP TO HEAVEN!

REDEEM YOUR TRAVEL POINTS HERE

REDEEM YOURSELF

SEE HERE FOR DETAILS

Related verses:
Revelation 21:1-3

would not have felt guilty for their sins anymore.

³But those offerings remind people of their sins every year. ⁴It isn't possible for the blood of bulls and goats to take away sins.

⁵So when Christ came into the world, he said,

"You didn't want sacrifices and
    offerings.
Instead, you prepared a body for
    me.
⁶You weren't pleased
    with burnt offerings and sin
    offerings.
⁷Then I said, 'Here I am. It is
    written about me in the scroll.
God, I have come to do what you
    want.' "   *(Psalm 40:6–8)*

⁸First Christ said, "You didn't want sacrifices and offerings. You didn't want burnt offerings and sin offerings. You weren't pleased with them." He said that even though the law required people to bring them. ⁹Then he said, "Here I am. I have come to do what

you want." He did away with the first. He did it to put the second in place.

¹⁰We have been made holy by what God wanted. We have been made holy because Jesus Christ offered his body once and for all time.

¹¹Day after day every priest stands and does his special duties. He offers the same sacrifices again and again. But they can never take away sins. ¹²Jesus our priest offered one sacrifice for sins for all time. Then he sat down at the right hand of God. ¹³Since that time, he waits for his enemies to be put under his control. ¹⁴By that one sacrifice he has made perfect forever those who are being made holy.

¹⁵The Holy Spirit also gives witness to us about this. First he says,

¹⁶ "This is the covenant I will make
        with them
    after that time, says the Lord.
I will put my laws in their hearts.
I will write my laws on their
    minds."   *(Jeremiah 31:33)*

¹⁷Then he adds,

Why do some people believe they will come back to earth as someone else?

Some people do believe they will come back to earth as someone else after they die. We call this belief reincarnation. It says that people never really die once and for all. They keep coming back as something else or as someone else.

Reincarnation is not true. Some people believe in reincarnation because their religion teaches it. Hinduism and Buddhism teach it. Some believe in reincarnation because they want to believe that they will get a second chance to be good. But the Bible does not teach reincarnation. The Bible teaches that we have one life, and then we stand in front of God to be judged.

checkout Hebrews 9:27

Related verses:
Luke 16:19–31

"I will not remember their sins
     anymore.
I will not remember the evil
     things they have done."

(Jeremiah 31:34)

¹⁸Where those have been forgiven,
there is no longer any offering for sin.

A WARNING TO
REMAIN FAITHFUL

¹⁹Brothers and sisters, we are not
afraid to enter the Most Holy Room.
We enter boldly because of the blood
of Jesus. ²⁰His way is new because he
lives. It has been opened for us
through the curtain. I'm talking about
his body.
²¹We also have a great priest over the
house of God. ²²So let us come near to
God with an honest and true heart. Let
us come near with a faith that is sure
and strong. Our hearts have been
sprinkled. Our minds have been
cleansed from a sense of guilt. Our
bodies have been washed with pure
water.
²³Let us hold firmly to the hope we
claim to have. The One who promised
is faithful.
²⁴Let us consider how we can stir up
one another to love. Let us help one
another to do good works. ²⁵Let us not
give up meeting together. Some are in
the habit of doing this. Instead, let us
cheer each other up with words of
hope. Let us do it all the more as you
see the day coming when Christ will
return.
²⁶What if we keep sinning on purpose? What if we do it even after we
know the truth? Then there is no offering for our sins. ²⁷All we can do is to
wait in fear for God to judge. His blazing fire will burn up his enemies.
²⁸Anyone who did not obey the law
of Moses died without mercy if there
were two or three witnesses. ²⁹What
should be done to anyone who has
hated the Son of God or has said no to
him? What should be done to a person
who treated as an unholy thing the
blood of the covenant that makes him
holy? What should be done to someone who has made fun of the Holy
Spirit who brings God's grace? Don't

KIDS' QUESTION

Why do we go to church if God is everywhere?

Something very special happens when God's family gets together.
We pray for each other. We learn from each other. We sing and praise God
together. We serve and help each other. None of this could happen if we
never went to church. Babies, grandparents, children, poor people, rich
people, brown, black, white, American, Asian, African, weak and
strong are all different. But in church we are like brothers and sisters
helping each other.
     It is good to worship God by ourselves. We should
spend time praying and reading the Bible alone. But
it is also very important to pray and read the
Bible with others who follow Jesus. That
way we can cheer each other up
and learn from each other.

checkout Hebrews 10:25

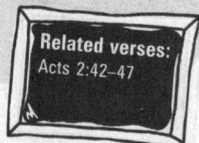

Related verses:
Acts 2:42–47

you think people like that should be punished more than anyone else? [30]We know the One who said, "I am the One who judges people. I will pay them back." *(Deuteronomy 32:35)* Scripture also says, "The Lord will judge his people." *(Deuteronomy 32:36; Psalm 135:14)* [31]It is a terrible thing to fall into the hands of the living God.

[32]Remember those earlier days after you received the light. At that time you stood firm in a great struggle. You did it even in the face of suffering.

[33]Sometimes you were made fun of in front of others. You were treated badly. At other times you stood side by side with people who were being treated like that. [34]You suffered together with people in prison. When your property was taken from you, you accepted it with joy. You knew that God had given you better and more lasting things.

[35]So don't throw away your bold faith. It will bring you rich rewards. [36]You need to be faithful. Then you will do what God wants. You will receive what he has promised. [37]In just a very little while,

"The one who is coming will
    come. He will not wait.
[38] The one who is in the right will
    live by faith.
If he pulls back,
    I will not be pleased with him."
(Habakkuk 2:3,4)

[39]But we aren't people who pull back and are destroyed. We are people who believe and are saved.

LIVING BY FAITH

11 Faith is being sure of what we hope for. It is being certain of what we do not see. [2]That is what the people of long ago were praised for.

[3]We have faith. So we understand that everything was made when God commanded it. That's why we believe that what we see was not made out of what could be seen.

[4]Abel had faith. So he offered to God a better sacrifice than Cain did. Because of his faith Abel was praised as a godly man. God said good things about his offerings. Because of his faith Abel still speaks. He speaks even though he is dead.

[5]Enoch had faith. So he was taken from this life. He didn't die. He just couldn't be found. God had taken him away. Before God took him, Enoch was praised as one who pleased God.

[6]Without faith it isn't possible to please God. Those who come to God must believe that he exists. And they must believe that he rewards those who look to him.

[7]Noah had faith. So he built an ark to save his family. He built it because of his great respect for God. God had warned him about things that could not yet be seen. Because of his faith he showed the world that it was guilty. Because of his faith he was considered right with God.

[8]Abraham had faith. So he obeyed God. God called him to go to a place he would later receive as his own. So he went. He did it even though he didn't know where he was going. [9]Because of his faith he made his home in the land God had promised him. He was like an outsider in a strange country. He lived there in tents. So did Isaac and Jacob. They received the same promise he did. [10]Abraham was looking forward to the city that has foundations. He was waiting for the city that God planned and built.

[11]Abraham had faith. So God made it possible for him to become a father. He became a father even though he was too old. Sarah also was too old to have children. But Abraham believed that the One who made the promise was faithful. [12]Abraham was past the time when he could have children. But many children came from that one man. They were as many as the stars in the sky. They were as many as the sand on the seashore. No one could count them.

[13]All those people were still living by faith when they died. They didn't receive the things God had promised. They only saw them and welcomed them from a long way off. They openly said that they were outsiders and strangers on earth. [14]People who say things like that show that they are looking for a coun-

try of their own. ¹⁵What if they had been thinking of the country they had left? Then they could have returned to it. ¹⁶Instead, they longed for a better country. They wanted one in heaven.

So God is pleased when they call him their God. In fact, he has prepared a city for them.

¹⁷Abraham had faith. So he offered Isaac as a sacrifice. That happened when God put him to the test. Abraham had received the promises. But he was about to offer his one and only son. ¹⁸God had said to him, "Your family line will continue through Isaac." *(Genesis 21:12)* Even so, Abraham was going to offer him up. ¹⁹Abraham believed that God could raise the dead. In a way, he did receive Isaac back from death.

²⁰Isaac had faith. So he blessed Jacob and Esau. He told them what was ahead for them.

²¹Jacob had faith. So he blessed each of Joseph's sons. He blessed them when he was dying. Because of his faith he worshiped God as he leaned on the top of his wooden staff.

²²Joseph had faith. So he spoke to the people of Israel about their leaving Egypt. He gave directions about his bones. He did that toward the end of his life.

²³Moses' parents had faith. So they hid him for three months after he was born. They saw he was a special child. They were not afraid of the king's command.

²⁴Moses had faith. So he refused to be called the son of Pharaoh's daughter. That happened after he had grown up. ²⁵He chose to be treated badly together with the people of God. He chose that instead of enjoying sin's pleasures for a short time. ²⁶He suffered shame because of Christ. He thought it had great value. He considered it better than the riches of Egypt. He was looking ahead to God's reward.

²⁷Because of his faith he left Egypt. It wasn't because he was afraid of the king's anger. He didn't let anything

Will there be a Bible "hall of fame" in heaven?

Some people think that heaven will be just like earth, with shopping malls, schools, stadiums and airports. But heaven will be very different from earth. The spotlight will be on God. We will praise and worship God because no one else's fame can compare with his.

But people *will* be honored in heaven. The Bible says that believers will receive rewards for their good deeds. The greatest reward is just getting to be there. God gives this free gift to all who put their faith in Jesus. He will give other rewards to every believer who does good deeds for God on earth. Everyone who served God will get rewards for the good they did.

Related verses:
Jeremiah 17:10;
Matthew 5:12;
25:31-34

checkout
Hebrews 11:14-16

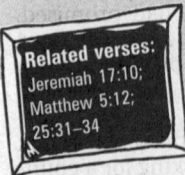

stop him. He saw the One who can't be seen.

²⁸Because of his faith he was the first to keep the Passover Feast. He commanded the people of Israel to sprinkle blood on their doorways. He did it so that the destroying angel would not touch their oldest sons.

²⁹The people had faith. So they passed through the Red Sea. They went through it as if it were dry land. The Egyptians tried to do it also. But they drowned.

³⁰The people had faith. So the walls of Jericho fell down. It happened after they had marched around the city for seven days.

³¹Rahab, the prostitute, had faith. So she welcomed the spies. That's why she wasn't killed with those who didn't obey God.

³²What more can I say? I don't have time to tell about all the others. I don't have time to talk about Gideon, Barak, Samson and Jephthah. I don't have time to tell about David, Samuel and the prophets. ³³Because of their faith they took over kingdoms. They ruled fairly. They received the blessings God had promised. They shut the mouths of lions. ³⁴They put out great fires. They escaped being killed by the sword. Their weakness was turned to strength. They became powerful in battle. They beat back armies from other countries.

³⁵Women received their dead back. The dead were raised to life again. Others were made to suffer greatly. But they refused to be set free. They did that so that after death they would be raised to a better life.

³⁶Some were laughed at. Some were whipped. Still others were held by chains. They were put in prison. ³⁷Some were killed with stones. They were sawed in two. They were put to death by the sword. They went around wearing the skins of sheep and goats. They were poor. They were attacked. They were treated badly. ³⁸The world was not worthy of them. They wan-

Why was Abraham willing to kill his own son?

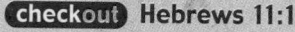

God had promised to make Abraham's family into a great nation. God had said that Isaac would be the first father in this new nation. Abraham believed that God would keep his promise. It is true that God told Abraham to give up Isaac as a burnt offering. But Abraham knew that if God let Isaac die he could also raise Isaac back to life. Abraham did not want Isaac to die. It was *very difficult* for him to take Isaac to the altar. But Abraham knew that God would keep his promise and let Isaac live again. The good news is that something even better happened. God provided a ram to take Isaac's place. God did not want Isaac to die after all! Instead he wanted to teach Abraham how to trust him more.

checkout Hebrews 11:19

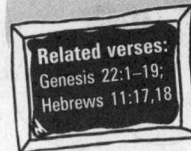

Related verses:
Genesis 22:1–19;
Hebrews 11:17,18

dered in deserts and mountains. They lived in caves. They lived in holes in the ground.

[39]All of those people were praised because they had faith. But none of them received what God had promised. [40]God had planned something better for us. So they would only be made perfect together with us.

12 A huge cloud of witnesses is all around us. So let us throw off everything that stands in our way. Let us throw off any sin that holds on to us so tightly. Let us keep on running the race marked out for us.

[2]Let us keep looking to Jesus. He is the author of faith. He also makes it perfect. He paid no attention to the shame of the cross. He suffered there because of the joy he was looking forward to. Then he sat down at the right hand of the throne of God.

[3]He put up with attacks from sinners. So think about him. Then you won't get tired. You won't lose hope.

GOD TRAINS HIS CHILDREN

[4]You struggle against sin. But you have not yet fought to the point of spilling your blood. [5]You have forgotten that word of hope. It speaks to you as children. It says,

"My son, think of the Lord's
  training as important.
Do not lose hope when he
  corrects you.
[6]The Lord trains those he loves.
He punishes everyone he accepts
  as a son."　　(Proverbs 3:11,12)

[7]Put up with hard times. God uses them to train you. He is treating you as children. What children are not trained by their parents? [8]God trains all of his children. But what if he doesn't train you? Then you are like children of people who weren't married to each other. You are not truly God's children.

[9]Besides, we have all had human parents who trained us. We respected them for it. How much more should we be trained by the Father of our spirits and live!

[10]Our parents trained us for a little while. They did what they thought was best. But God trains us for our good. He wants us to share in his holiness.

[11]No training seems pleasant at the time. In fact, it seems painful. But later on it produces a harvest of godliness and peace. It does that for those who have been trained by it.

[12]So lift your sagging arms. Strengthen your weak knees. [13]"Make level

Can we see people from the Bible in heaven?

Everyone who has ever trusted in Jesus will be in heaven. That includes all the Bible people who ever believed. The Bible calls these people a "huge cloud of witnesses." You will get to know them too. They will be some of your new friends!

checkout Hebrews 12:1

JASON'S IMAGINATION

SAMSON

Related verses:
Matthew 17:1–6

paths for your feet to walk on." *(Proverbs 4:26)* Then those who have trouble walking won't be disabled. Instead, they will be healed.

A WARNING AGAINST SAYING NO TO GOD

¹⁴Try your best to live in peace with everyone. Try to be holy. Without holiness no one will see the Lord.

¹⁵Be sure that no one misses God's grace. See to it that a bitter plant doesn't grow up. If it does, it will cause trouble. And it will pollute many people. ¹⁶See to it that no one commits sexual sins.

See to it that no one is godless like Esau. He sold the rights to what he would receive as the oldest son. He sold them for a single meal. ¹⁷As you know, after that he wanted to receive his father's blessing. But he was turned away. With tears he tried to get the blessing. But he couldn't get his father to change his mind.

¹⁸You haven't come to a mountain that can be touched. You haven't come to a mountain that is burning with fire. You haven't come to darkness, gloom and storm. ¹⁹You haven't come to a blast from God's trumpet. You haven't come to a voice speaking to you. When people heard that voice long ago, they begged it not to say anything more to them. ²⁰What God commanded was too much for them. He said, "If even an animal touches the mountain, it must be killed with stones." *(Exodus 19:12,13)* ²¹The sight was terrifying. Moses said, "I am trembling with fear." *(Deuteronomy 9:19)*

²²But you have come to Mount Zion. You have come to the Jerusalem in heaven. It is the city of the living God. You have come to a joyful gathering of angels. There are thousands and thousands of them. ²³You have come to the church of God's people. God's first and only Son is over all things. God's people share in what belongs to his Son. Their names are written in heaven. You have come to God. He is the judge of all people.

You have come to the spirits of godly people who have been made perfect. ²⁴You have come to Jesus. He is the go-between of a new covenant. You have

come to the sprinkled blood. It promises better things than the blood of Abel.

²⁵Be sure that you don't say no to the One who speaks. People did not escape when they said no to the One who warned them on earth. And what if we turn away from the One who warns us from heaven? How much less will we escape!

²⁶At that time his voice shook the earth. But now he has promised, "Once more I will shake the earth. I will also shake the heavens." *(Haggai 2:6)* ²⁷The words "once more" point out that what can be shaken can be taken away. I'm talking about created things. Then what can't be shaken will remain.

²⁸We are receiving a kingdom that can't be shaken. So let us be thankful. Then we can worship God in a way that pleases him. We will worship him with deep respect and wonder. ²⁹Our "God is like a fire that burns everything up." *(Deuteronomy 4:24)*

FINAL WORDS

13 Keep on loving each other as brothers and sisters. ²Don't forget to welcome strangers. By doing that, some people have welcomed angels without knowing it.

³Remember those in prison as if you were in prison with them. And remember those who are treated badly as if you yourselves were suffering.

⁴All of you should honor marriage. You should keep the marriage bed pure. God will judge the person who commits adultery. He will judge everyone who commits sexual sins.

⁵Don't be controlled by love for money. Be happy with what you have. God has said,

"I will never leave you.
I will never desert you."
(Deuteronomy 31:6)

⁶So we can say boldly,

"The Lord helps me. I will not be afraid.
What can a mere man do to me?"
(Psalm 118:6,7)

⁷Remember your leaders. They spoke God's word to you. Think about

the results of their way of life. Copy their faith.

⁸Jesus Christ is the same yesterday and today and forever.

⁹Don't be carried away by all kinds of strange teachings. It is good that God's grace makes our hearts strong. Don't depend on foods the Law requires. They have no value for the people who eat them. ¹⁰Some worship at the holy tent. But we have an altar that they have no right to eat from.

¹¹The high priest carries the blood of animals into the Most Holy Room. He brings their blood as a sin offering. But the bodies are burned outside the camp. ¹²Jesus also suffered outside the city gate. He suffered to make the people holy by spilling his own blood.

¹³So let us go to him outside the camp. Let us be willing to suffer the shame he suffered. ¹⁴Here we do not have a city that lasts. But we are looking for the city that is going to come.

¹⁵So let us never stop offering to God our praise through Jesus. Let us offer it as the fruit of lips that say they believe in him.

¹⁶Don't forget to do good. Don't forget to share with others. God is pleased with those kinds of offerings.

¹⁷Obey your leaders. Put yourselves under their authority. They keep watch over you. They know they are accountable to God for everything they do. Obey them so that their work will be a joy. If you make their work a heavy load, it won't do you any good.

¹⁸Pray for us. We feel sure we have done what is right. We long to live as we should in every way.

¹⁹I beg you to pray that I may return to you soon.

²⁰Our Lord Jesus is the great Shepherd of the sheep. The God who gives peace brought him back from the dead. He did it because of the blood of the eternal covenant. May God ²¹supply you with everything good. Then you can do what he wants. May he do in us what is pleasing to him. We can do it only with the help of Jesus Christ. Give him glory for ever and ever. Amen.

²²Brothers and sisters, I beg you to accept my word. It tells you to be faithful. I have written you only a short letter.

²³I want you to know that our brother Timothy has been set free. If he arrives soon, I will come with him to see you.

²⁴Greet all of your leaders. Greet all of God's people. The believers from Italy send you their greetings.

²⁵May grace be with you all.

quest challenge

I Wonder . . .
What can I do when I feel lonely?

Real Life Challenge
You discover that none of your friends is in your class next year. Or you want to have a friend over, but everyone already has plans. God knows that we are lonely sometimes, and that's why he reassures us so often in the Bible that he is always with us.

Quest Clue
Read Genesis 28 to see how God encouraged Jacob when he felt alone. Then find Hebrews 13 for more reassurance that God is always with you.

James

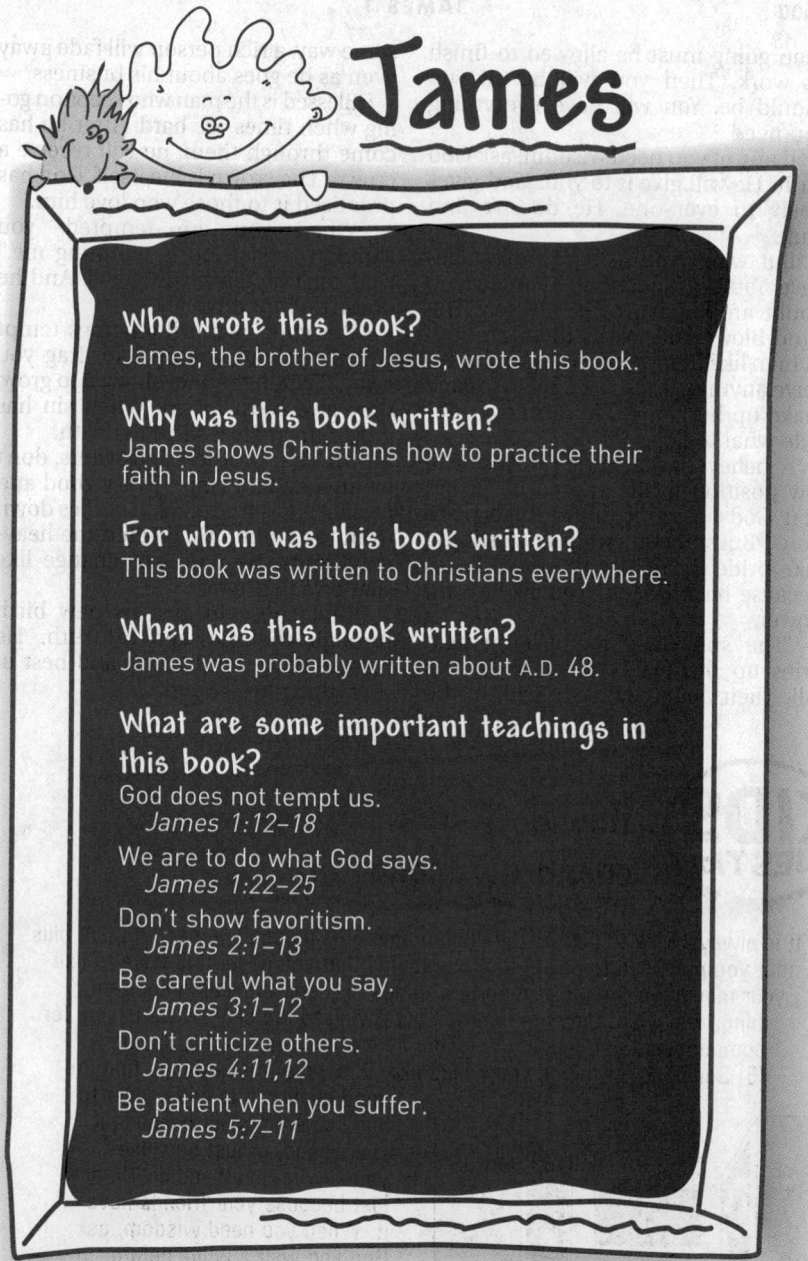

Who wrote this book?
James, the brother of Jesus, wrote this book.

Why was this book written?
James shows Christians how to practice their faith in Jesus.

For whom was this book written?
This book was written to Christians everywhere.

When was this book written?
James was probably written about A.D. 48.

What are some important teachings in this book?
God does not tempt us.
James 1:12–18

We are to do what God says.
James 1:22–25

Don't show favoritism.
James 2:1–13

Be careful what you say.
James 3:1–12

Don't criticize others.
James 4:11,12

Be patient when you suffer.
James 5:7–11

1 I, James, am writing this letter. I serve God and the Lord Jesus Christ.

I am sending this letter to you, the 12 tribes that are scattered among the nations.

Greetings.

FACING ALL KINDS OF TROUBLE

²My brothers and sisters, you will face all kinds of trouble. When you do, think of it as pure joy. ³Your faith will be put to the test. You know that when that happens it will produce in you the strength to continue. ⁴The strength to

keep going must be allowed to finish its work. Then you will be all you should be. You will have everything you need.

⁵If any of you need wisdom, ask God for it. He will give it to you. God gives freely to everyone. He doesn't find fault.

⁶But when you ask, you must believe. You must not doubt. People who doubt are like waves of the sea. The wind blows and tosses them around. ⁷A man like that shouldn't expect to receive anything from the Lord. ⁸He can't make up his mind. He can never decide what to do.

⁹A believer who finds himself in a low position in life should be proud that God has given him a high position. ¹⁰But someone who is rich should take pride in his low position. That's because he will fade away like a wild flower.

¹¹The sun rises. Its burning heat dries up the plants. Their blossoms fall. Their beauty is destroyed. In the same way, a rich person will fade away even as he goes about his business.

¹²Blessed is the man who keeps on going when times are hard. After he has come through them, he will receive a crown. The crown is life itself. God has promised it to those who love him.

¹³When you are tempted, you shouldn't say, "God is tempting me." God can't be tempted by evil. And he doesn't tempt anyone.

¹⁴But your own evil longings tempt you. They lead you on and drag you away. ¹⁵When they are allowed to grow, they give birth to sin. When sin has grown up, it gives birth to death.

¹⁶My dear brothers and sisters, don't let anyone fool you. ¹⁷Every good and perfect gift is from God. It comes down from the Father. He created the heavenly lights. He does not change like shadows that move.

¹⁸God chose to give us new birth through the message of truth. He wanted us to be the first and best of everything he created.

How do I know what is wise to spend my money on?

It is always wise to give to the church and to help people in need, to pay bills that you promised to pay and to buy things that you need. It is wise to use your money for the most important things first and the least important things last. Here they are in order: (1) Giving to the church. (2) Paying for commitments you made. (3) Taking care of your needs. (4) Saving. (5) Spending for things you would like. It is wise to buy things that are good quality. It is wise never to buy something just because it looks good, or just because you saw it advertised on TV, or just because your friends have it. When you need wisdom, ask God and wait a while before deciding. Ask your parents and other wise people too.

checkout

James 1:5

Related verses:
Proverbs 1:8,9;
James 3:17

LISTEN TO THE WORD AND DO WHAT IT SAYS

[19]My dear brothers and sisters, pay attention to what I say. Everyone should be quick to listen. But they should be slow to speak. They should be slow to get angry. [20]A man's anger doesn't produce the kind of life God wants.

[21]So get rid of everything that is dirty and sinful. Get rid of the evil that is all around us. Don't be too proud to accept the word that is planted in you. It can save you.

[22]Don't just listen to the word. You fool yourselves if you do that. You must do what it says.

[23]Suppose you listen to the word but don't do what it says. Then you are like a man who looks at his face in a mirror. [24]After looking at himself, he leaves. Right away he forgets what he looks like.

[25]But suppose you take a good look at the perfect law that gives freedom. You keep looking at it. You don't forget what you've heard, but you do what the law says. Then you will be blessed in what you do.

[26]Suppose you think your beliefs are right because of how you live. But you don't control what you say. Then you are fooling yourselves. Your beliefs are not worth anything at all.

[27]Here are the kinds of beliefs that God our Father accepts as pure and without fault. When widows and children who have no parents are in trouble, take care of them. And keep yourselves from being polluted by the world.

TREAT EVERYONE THE SAME

2 My brothers and sisters, you are believers in our glorious Lord Jesus Christ. So treat everyone the same.

[2]Suppose a man comes into your meeting wearing a gold ring and fine clothes. And suppose a poor man in worn-out clothes also comes in. [3]Would you show special attention to the one who is wearing fine clothes? Would you say, "Here's a good seat for you"? Would you say to the poor person, "You stand there"? Or "Sit on the floor by my feet"? [4]If you would, aren't you treating some people better than others? Aren't you like judges who have evil thoughts?

[5]My dear brothers and sisters, listen to me. Hasn't God chosen those who are poor in the world's eyes to be rich in faith? Hasn't he chosen them to receive the kingdom? Hasn't he promised it to those who love him?

[6]But you have put poor people down. Aren't rich people taking advantage of you? Aren't they dragging you into court? [7]Aren't they speaking evil things against the worthy name of Jesus? Remember, you belong to him.

[8]The royal law is found in Scripture. It says, "Love your neighbor as you love yourself." (Leviticus 19:18) If you really keep that law, you are doing what is right. [9]But you sin if you don't treat everyone the same. The law judges you because you have broken it.

[10]Suppose you keep the whole law but trip over just one part of it. Then you are guilty of breaking all of it. [11]God said, "Do not commit adultery." (Exodus 20:14; Deuteronomy 5:18) He also said, "Do not commit murder." (Exodus 20:13; Deuteronomy 5:17) Suppose you don't commit adultery but do commit murder. Then you have broken the Law.

[12]Speak and act like people who are going to be judged by the law that gives freedom. [13]Those who have not shown mercy will not receive mercy when they are judged. To show mercy is better than to judge.

SHOW YOUR FAITH BY WHAT YOU DO

[14]My brothers and sisters, what good is it if people claim they have faith but don't act like it? Can that kind of faith save them?

[15]Suppose a brother or sister has no clothes or food. [16]Suppose one of you says to them, "Go. I hope everything turns out fine for you. Keep warm. Eat well." And you do nothing about what they really need. Then what good have you done?

[17]It is the same with faith. If it doesn't cause us to do something, it's dead.

¹⁸But someone will say, "You have faith. I do good works."

Show me your faith that doesn't do good works. And I will show you my faith by what I do. ¹⁹You believe there is one God. Good! Even the demons believe that. And they tremble!

²⁰You foolish man! Do you want proof that faith without good works is useless? ²¹Our father Abraham offered his son Isaac on the altar. Wasn't he considered to be right with God because of what he did? ²²So you see that what he believed and what he did were working together. What he did made his faith complete.

²³That is what Scripture means where it says, "Abraham believed God. God accepted Abraham because he believed. So his faith made him right with God." *(Genesis 15:6)* And that's not all. God called Abraham his friend. ²⁴So you see that a person is made right with God by what he does. It doesn't happen only because of what he believes.

²⁵Didn't God make even Rahab the prostitute right with him? That's because of what she did. She gave the spies a place to stay. Then she sent them off in a different direction.

²⁶The body without the spirit is dead. In the same way, faith without good works is dead.

CONTROL WHAT YOU SAY

3 My brothers and sisters, most of you shouldn't want to be teachers. You know that those of us who teach will be held more accountable.

²All of us get tripped up in many ways. Suppose someone is never wrong in what he says. Then he is a perfect man. He is able to keep his whole body under control.

³We put a bit in the mouth of a horse to make it obey us. We can control the whole animal with it. ⁴And how about ships? They are very big. They are driven along by strong winds. But they are steered by a very small rudder. It makes them go where the captain wants to go.

If you say "Jesus" when you're mad, isn't that like praying?

No. It is one thing to talk to God. It is another thing to say God's name because you got hurt or are surprised or angry. Sometimes the same words can have different meanings depending on how you say them. For example, a person might smile and say, "That's great!" But another person might get angry and frown and say, "That's *great*." The same words would have very different meanings. It is the same with God's name. How people say God's name tells us what they mean.

Sometimes people say God's name in anger, in frustration or out of habit. That is called swearing or using God's name *in vain*. You should not do that. You should not even say "My God!" when you're surprised. Treat God with respect and honor his name.

checkout
James 3:10

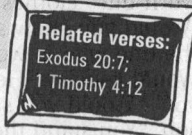
Related verses:
Exodus 20:7;
1 Timothy 4:12

⁵In the same way, the tongue is a small part of the body. But it brags a lot. Think about how a small spark can set a big forest on fire.

⁶The tongue also is a fire. The tongue is the most evil part of the body. It pollutes the whole person. It sets a person's whole way of life on fire. And the tongue is set on fire by hell.

⁷People have controlled all kinds of animals, birds, reptiles and creatures of the sea. They still control them. ⁸But no one can control the tongue. It is an evil thing that never rests. It is full of deadly poison.

⁹With our tongues we praise our Lord and Father. With our tongues we call down curses on people. We do it even though they have been created to be like God. ¹⁰Praise and cursing come out of the same mouth. My brothers and sisters, it shouldn't be that way.

¹¹Can fresh water and salt water flow out of the same spring? ¹²My brothers and sisters, can a fig tree bear olives? Can a grapevine bear figs? Of course not. And a saltwater spring can't produce fresh water either.

TWO KINDS OF WISDOM

¹³Are any of you wise and understanding? You should show it by living a good life. Wise people aren't proud when they do good works.

¹⁴But suppose your hearts are jealous and bitter. Suppose you are concerned only about getting ahead. Don't brag about it. Don't say no to the truth. ¹⁵Wisdom like that doesn't come down from heaven. It belongs to the earth. It doesn't come from the Holy Spirit. It comes from the devil.

¹⁶Are you jealous? Are you concerned only about getting ahead? Then your life will be a mess. You will be doing all kinds of evil things.

¹⁷But the wisdom that comes from heaven is pure. That's the most important thing about it. And that's not all. It also loves peace. It thinks about others. It obeys. It is full of mercy and

KIDS' QUESTion

Why do people cheat just to win a stupid game?

Some people cheat because winning means too much to them. Maybe they like the attention that the winner gets. Maybe they really think they are better people because they win. They may even think that people will like them only if they win. God wants us to work hard at whatever we do and to do it the best we can. We should practice more and try harder if we are not very good at something and want to do better. But we should be a good sport whether we win or lose.

checkout
James 3:14-16

Related verse:
Philippians 2:3

good fruit. It is fair. It doesn't pretend to be what it is not.

¹⁸Those who make peace should plant peace like a seed. If they do, it will produce a crop of right living.

OBEY GOD

4 Why do you fight and argue among yourselves? Isn't it because of your sinful longings? They fight inside you.

²You want something, but you can't get it. You kill and want what others have. But you can't have what you want. You argue and fight. You don't have what you want, because you don't ask God. ³When you do ask for something, you don't receive it. Why? Because you ask for the wrong reason. You want to spend your money on your sinful pleasures.

⁴You are not faithful to God. Don't you know that to be a friend of the world is to hate God? Anyone who chooses to be a friend of the world becomes an enemy of God. ⁵Don't you know what Scripture says? The spirit that God caused to live in us wants us to belong only to God. Don't you think Scripture has a reason for saying that? ⁶God continues to give us more grace. That's why Scripture says,

> "God opposes those who are
>   proud.
> But he gives grace to those who
>   are not." *(Proverbs 3:34)*

⁷So obey God. Stand up to the devil. He will run away from you. ⁸Come near to God, and he will come near to you. Wash your hands, you sinners. Make your hearts pure, you who can't make up your minds.

⁹Be full of sorrow. Cry and sob. Change your laughter to crying. Change your joy to sadness. ¹⁰Bow down to the Lord. He will lift you up.

¹¹My brothers and sisters, don't speak against one another. Anyone who speaks against another believer speaks against the law. And anyone who judges another believer judges the law. When you judge the law, you are not keeping it. Instead, you are acting as if you were its judge.

¹²There is only one Lawgiver and

KIDS' QUESTION: Why do brothers and sisters fight?

Brothers and sisters fight because every person is sinful. No one is perfect. We all do wrong things. We act in ways that displease God and that get us into trouble. We get on each other's nerves and we get angry with one another. We even act selfish toward the people we love, like our parents, brothers and sisters. God has given us rules for living. If we follow his rules, we will get along better.

checkout
James 4:1

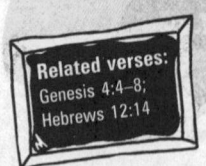

Related verses:
Genesis 4:4–8;
Hebrews 12:14

Judge. He is the One who is able to save life or destroy it. But who are you to judge your neighbor?

BRAGGING ABOUT TOMORROW

13Now listen, you who say, "Today or tomorrow we will go to this or that city. We will spend a year there. We will buy and sell and make money." 14You don't even know what will happen tomorrow. What is your life? It is a mist that appears for a little while. Then it disappears. 15Instead, you should say, "If it pleases the Lord, we will live and do this or that."

16As it is, you are proud. You brag about it. That kind of bragging is evil. 17So when you know the good things you should do and don't do them, you sin.

A WARNING TO RICH PEOPLE

5 You rich people, listen to me. Cry and sob, because you will soon be suffering.

2Your riches have rotted. Moths have eaten your clothes. 3Your gold and silver have lost their brightness. Their dullness will give witness against you. Your wanting more and more will eat your body like fire. You have stored up riches in these last days.

4You have even failed to pay the workers who mowed your fields. Their pay is crying out against you. The cries of those who gathered the harvest have reached the ears of the Lord who rules over all.

5You have lived an easy life on earth. You have given yourselves everything you wanted. You have made your-

Why do countries fight wars with each other?

A war is fought when countries disagree and can't work out their problems by talking together. Sometimes a war will begin when both countries want the same thing, like a certain piece of land. Instead of talking it out, they fight. Other times, a war will begin when one country wants to take over another country.

God wants us to love others and to get along with others. Wars could be avoided if everyone followed God's instructions for loving others. And if each of us chooses to love God and others, we can prevent fights and make the world a little more peaceful.

checkout James 4:2

Related verses:
Psalm 27:3;
Proverbs 30:33;
Matthew 24:6

selves fat like cattle that will soon be butchered. ⁶You have judged and murdered people who aren't guilty. And they weren't even opposing you.

BE PATIENT WHEN YOU SUFFER

⁷Brothers and sisters, be patient until the Lord comes. See how the farmer waits for the land to produce its rich crop. See how patient he is for the fall and spring rains. ⁸You too must be patient. You must stand firm. The Lord will soon come back.

⁹Brothers and sisters, don't find fault with one another. If you do, you will be judged. And the Judge is standing at the door!

¹⁰Brothers and sisters, think about the prophets who spoke in the name of the Lord. They are an example of how to be patient when you suffer. ¹¹As you know, we think that people who don't give up are blessed. You have heard that Job was patient. And you have seen what the Lord finally did for

him. The Lord is full of tender mercy and loving concern.

¹²My brothers and sisters, don't take an oath when you make a promise. Don't call on heaven or earth or anything else to back up what you say. Let your "Yes" be yes. And let your "No" be no. If you don't, you will be judged.

THE PRAYER OF FAITH

¹³Are any of you in trouble? Then you should pray. Are any of you happy? Then sing songs of praise.

¹⁴Are any of you sick? Then send for the elders of the church to pray over you. Ask them to anoint you with oil in the name of the Lord. ¹⁵The prayer offered by those who have faith will make you well. The Lord will heal you. If you have sinned, you will be forgiven.

¹⁶So admit to one another that you have sinned. Pray for one another so that you might be healed. The prayer of a godly person is powerful. It makes things happen.

What if someone is shoplifting and it is your friend—what do you do?

Tell your friend that stealing is wrong and that he or she should not shoplift. If your friend does not want to listen to you, walk away, leave the store and go home right away. You must not stay with a person who is breaking the law. You can get in trouble if you go along with someone who steals even if you do not steal anything yourself. It is a crime not to report a crime. Tell your parents what happened as soon as you get home.

checkout
James 5:19,20

Related verses:
Luke 17:3;
Hebrews 10:24

¹⁷Elijah was just like us. He prayed hard that it wouldn't rain. And it didn't rain on the land for three and a half years. ¹⁸Then he prayed again. That time it rained. And the earth produced its crops.

¹⁹My brothers and sisters, suppose one of you wanders away from the truth and someone brings you back. ²⁰Then here is what I want everyone to remember. Anyone who turns a sinner from going down the wrong path will save him from death. God will erase many sins by forgiving him.

quest challenge

I Wonder . . .

Why should I be careful about what I say?

Real Life Challenge

If you're upset with a friend or a teacher, you might say something mean or negative about them to someone else. How would you feel if the person you were talking about came up behind you and overheard what you said? You'd probably feel pretty bad, and so would that person. What we say can be very powerful and can really help or hurt others. That's why God wants us to be careful about what we say.

Quest Clue

Read Numbers 12 and 2 Kings 2 to see how seriously God takes what we say. Then find a verse in James 5 to learn more about the importance of our words.

I Wonder . . .

How can I become wise?

Real Life Challenge

A friend of yours is really sad, and then shares with you that his parents have been fighting a lot. What do you say? It's hard to know how to help your friend or what kind of advice to give. In situations like these we need to ask for wisdom from God to know what to do. Just because you're young doesn't mean that you can't have wisdom. In the Bible God tells you how to get it.

Quest Clue

Read 1 Kings 3 to learn how King Solomon—who was famous for his wisdom—became wise. Then find the verse in James 1 that will tell you what *you* need to do.

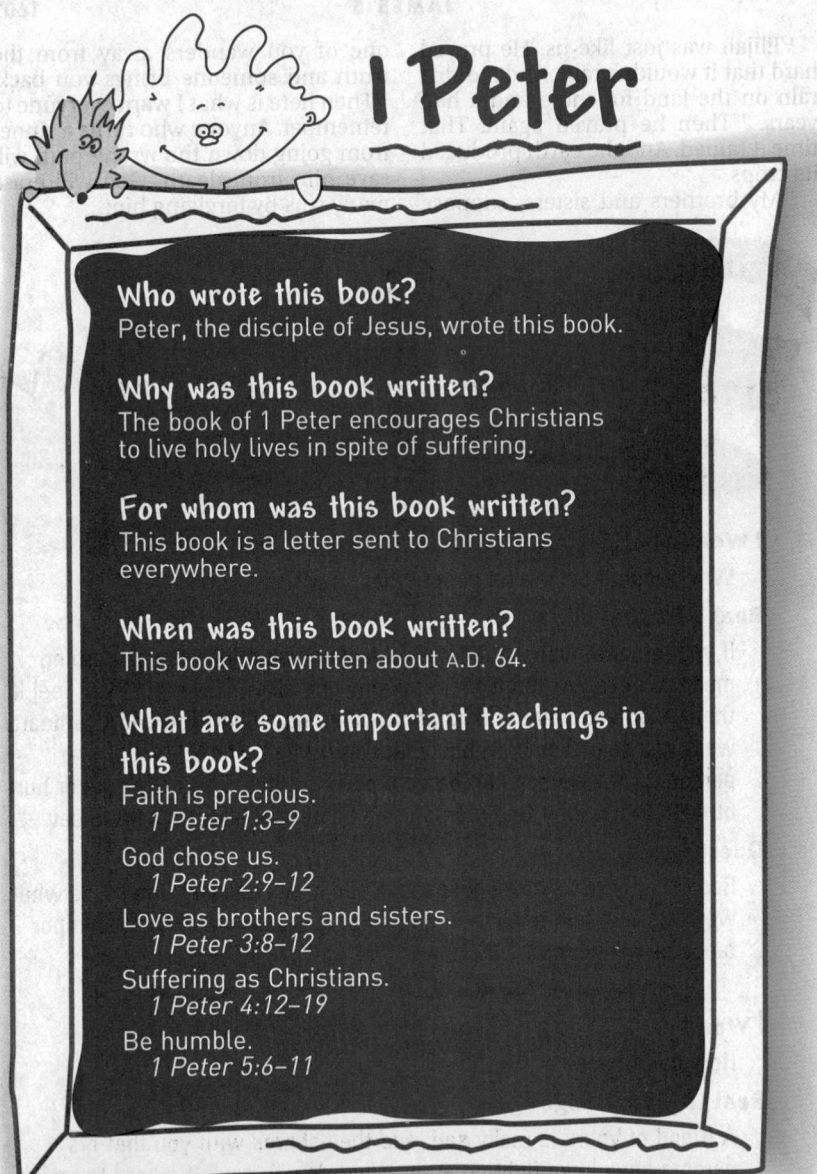

1 Peter

Who wrote this book?
Peter, the disciple of Jesus, wrote this book.

Why was this book written?
The book of 1 Peter encourages Christians to live holy lives in spite of suffering.

For whom was this book written?
This book is a letter sent to Christians everywhere.

When was this book written?
This book was written about A.D. 64.

What are some important teachings in this book?
Faith is precious.
1 Peter 1:3–9

God chose us.
1 Peter 2:9–12

Love as brothers and sisters.
1 Peter 3:8–12

Suffering as Christians.
1 Peter 4:12–19

Be humble.
1 Peter 5:6–11

1 I, Peter, am writing this letter. I am an apostle of Jesus Christ.

I am sending this letter to you, God's chosen people. You are strangers in the world. You are scattered all over Pontus, Galatia, Cappadocia, Asia and Bithynia. ²You have been chosen in keeping with what God the Father had planned. That happened through the Spirit's work to make you pure and holy. God chose you so that you might obey Jesus Christ. He wanted you to be made clean by the blood of Christ.

May more and more grace and peace be given to you.

PETER PRAISES GOD FOR A HOPE THAT IS ALIVE

³Give praise to the God and Father of our Lord Jesus Christ. In his great mer-

cy he has given us a new birth and a hope that is alive. It is alive because Jesus Christ rose from the dead. [4]He has given us new birth so that we might share in what belongs to him. It is a gift that can never be destroyed. It can never spoil or even fade away. It is kept in heaven for you. [5]Through faith you are kept safe by God's power. Your salvation is going to be completed. It is ready to be shown to you in the last days.

[6]Because you know this, you have great joy. You have joy even though you may have had to suffer for a little while. You may have had to suffer sadness in all kinds of trouble.

[7]Your troubles have come in order to prove that your faith is real. It is worth more than gold. Gold can pass away even though fire has made it pure. Your faith is meant to bring praise, honor and glory to God. That will happen when Jesus Christ returns.

[8]Even though you have not seen him, you love him. Though you do not see him now, you believe in him. You are filled with a glorious joy that can't be put into words. [9]You are receiving the salvation of your souls. It is the result of your faith.

[10]The prophets searched very hard and with great care to find out about that salvation. They spoke about the grace that was going to come to you. [11]They wanted to find out when that salvation would come. The Spirit of Christ in them was telling them about the sufferings of Christ that were going to come. He was also telling them about the glory that would follow.

[12]It was made known to the prophets that they were not serving themselves. Instead, they were serving you when they spoke about the things that you have now heard. Those who have preached the good news to you have told you those things. They have done it with the help of the Holy Spirit sent from heaven. Even angels long to look into those things.

Will I see my great-great-grand-parents in heaven?

All people who have ever believed in Jesus will be in heaven. It will not matter how long ago they lived. Your great-great-grandparents will be there if they believed in Jesus. You will be able to meet relatives from long ago. But not every person who ever lived believed in Jesus. So some people will not be there.

checkout 1 Peter 1:4

Related verses:
Revelation 7:9,10

JASON'S IMAGINATION

GREAT GREAT GRANDPARENTS SUNNYSIDE ST.

SUPER GREAT GRANDPARENTS SUNNYSIDE ST.

FABULOUSLY GREAT GRANDPARENTS SUNNYSIDE ST.

BE HOLY

¹³So prepare your minds for action. Control yourselves. Put your hope completely in the grace that will be given to you when Jesus Christ returns.

¹⁴You should obey. You shouldn't give in to evil longings. They controlled your life when you didn't know any better. ¹⁵The one who chose you is holy. So you should be holy in all that you do. ¹⁶It is written, "Be holy, because I am holy." *(Leviticus 11:44,45; 19:2)*

¹⁷You call on a Father who judges each person's work without favoring one over another. So live your lives as strangers here. Have the highest respect for God.

¹⁸The blood of Christ set you free from an empty way of life. That way of life was handed down to you by your own people long ago. You know that you were not bought with things that can pass away, like silver or gold. ¹⁹Instead, you were bought by the price-less blood of Christ. He is a perfect lamb. He doesn't have any flaws at all. ²⁰He was chosen before God created the world. But he came into the world in these last days for you.

²¹Because of what Christ has done, you believe in God. It was God who raised him from the dead. And it was God who gave him glory. So your faith and hope are in God.

²²You have made yourselves pure by obeying the truth. So you have an honest and true love for your brothers and sisters. Love each other deeply, from the heart.

²³You have been born again by means of the living word of God. His word lasts forever. You were not born again from a seed that will die. You were born from a seed that can't die. ²⁴It is written,

"All people are like grass.
All of their glory is like the
    flowers in the field.

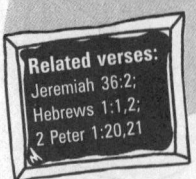

KIDS' QUESTion

How many people wrote the Bible?

God used many people to write the Bible. Moses, King David and the Apostle Paul wrote a lot of it. God also used his spokesmen, the prophets, to write down his words. Isaiah, Jeremiah and Ezekiel were some of them. God used all different kinds of people. He used old people and young people. He used happy people sometimes and very sad people at other times. Some people wrote stories, some wrote poems, some wrote prophecies, and some wrote letters. God used so many people to write the Bible because writing the Bible took thousands of years.

checkout

1 Peter 1:10,11

Related verses:
Jeremiah 36:2;
Hebrews 1:1,2;
2 Peter 1:20,21

JASON'S IMAGINATION

The grass dries up. The flowers fall
    to the ground.
25 But the word of the Lord stands
    forever."   *(Isaiah 40:6–8)*

And that word was preached to you.

2 So get rid of every kind of evil.
Stop telling lies. Don't pretend
to be something you are not.
Stop wanting what others have. Don't
speak against each other.

²Like babies that were just born, you
should long for the pure milk of God's
word. It will help you grow up as believers. ³You can do it now that you
have tasted how good the Lord is.

THE LIVING STONE AND A CHOSEN PEOPLE

⁴Christ is the living Stone. People
did not accept him. But God chose
him. God places the highest value on
him.
⁵You also are like living stones. As
you come to him you are being built
into a house for worship. There you
will be holy priests. You will offer spiritual sacrifices. God will accept them
because of what Jesus Christ has done.
⁶In Scripture it says,

"Look! I am placing a stone in
    Zion.

It is a chosen and very valuable
    stone.
It is the most important stone in
    the building.
The one who trusts in him
    will never be put to shame."
                    (Isaiah 28:16)

⁷The stone is very valuable to you
who believe. But to people who do not
believe,

"The stone the builders did not
    accept
has become the most important
    stone of all."   *(Psalm 118:22)*

⁸And,

"It is a stone that causes people to
    trip.
It is a rock that makes them fall."
                    (Isaiah 8:14)

They trip and fall because they do not
obey the message. That is also what
God planned for them.
⁹But God chose you to be his people.
You are royal priests. You are a holy
nation. You are a people who belong to
God. All of this is so that you can sing
his praises. He brought you out of
darkness into his wonderful light.
¹⁰Once you were not a people. But now

What if the waiter gives me a kid's meal free because he thinks I'm younger than I really am?

It is important to do what is right, even if it costs you money. So if you get a children's price for a meal or a ticket and you are older than a "child," you should tell the truth. Tell the waiter, waitress, ticket seller or whoever is in charge how old you really are. You cannot put a price on honesty.

Remember that God is looking after you. He will meet all your needs and take good care of you if you do things his way. God's way is to be honest. Being honest shows that you trust him.

Related verses:
Psalm 34:11–13;
Colossians 3:9

checkout 1 Peter 2:1

you are the people of God. Once you had not received mercy. But now you have received mercy.

[11]Dear friends, you are outsiders and strangers in this world. So I'm asking you not to give in to your sinful longings. They fight against your soul. [12]People who don't believe might say you are doing wrong. But lead good lives among them. Then they will see your good works. And they will give glory to God on the day he comes to judge.

OBEY YOUR RULERS AND MASTERS

[13]Follow the lead of every human authority. Do it because the Lord wants you to. Obey the king. He is the highest authority. [14]Obey the governors. The king sends them to punish those who do wrong. He also sends them to praise those who do right. [15]By doing good you will put a stop to the talk of foolish people. They don't know what they are saying. God wants you to stop them.

[16]Live like free people. But don't use your freedom to cover up evil. Live like people who serve God. [17]Show proper respect to everyone. Love the community of believers. Have respect for God. Honor the king.

[18]Slaves, obey your masters with all the respect you should give them. Obey not only those who are good and kind. Obey also those who are not kind. [19]Suppose a person suffers pain unfairly because he wants to obey God. That is worthy of praise. [20]But suppose you receive a beating for doing wrong, and you put up with it. Will anyone honor you for that? Of course not. But suppose you suffer for doing good, and you put up with it. God will praise you for that.

[21]Christ suffered for you. He left you an example. He expects you to follow in his steps. You too were chosen to suffer. [22]Scripture says,

Why won't my friend let me play with his stuff?

Your friend may be afraid that his stuff will be broken or misused. Maybe someone recently played with one of his toys and broke it. Remember, the stuff belongs to your friend, so respect his wishes. If you want to play with your friend's things, ask him and promise to take good care of it. If he lets you, show him how careful you can be. If he says no, don't keep asking. Let it go.

checkout
1 Peter 2:17

Related verses:
Romans 12:17;
1 Peter 1:22

I DON'T KNOW HOW IT GOT STUCK IN THERE, BUT IF I CAN GET IT OUT, CAN I PLAY WITH IT?

"He didn't commit any sin.
   No lies ever came out of his
   mouth."   *(Isaiah 53:9)*

²³People shouted at him and made fun of him. But he didn't do the same back to them. He suffered. But he didn't say that bad things would happen to them. Instead, he trusted in the One who judges fairly.

²⁴He himself carried our sins in his body on the cross. He did it so that we would die as far as sins are concerned. Then we would lead godly lives. His wounds have made you whole.

²⁵You were like sheep who were wandering away. But now you have returned to the Shepherd. He is the Leader of your souls.

WIVES AND HUSBANDS

3 Wives, follow the lead of your husbands. Suppose some of them don't believe God's word. Then let them be won to Christ without words by seeing how their wives behave. ²Let them see how pure you are. Let them see that your lives are full of respect for God.

³Braiding your hair doesn't make you beautiful. Wearing gold jewelry or fine clothes doesn't make you beautiful. ⁴Instead, your beauty comes from inside you. It is the beauty of a gentle and quiet spirit. Beauty like that doesn't fade away. God places great value on it.

⁵This is how the holy women of the past used to make themselves beautiful. They put their hope in God. And they followed the lead of their own husbands.

⁶Sarah was like that. She obeyed Abraham. She called him her master. Do you want to be like her? Then do what is right. And don't give in to fear.

⁷Husbands, take good care of your wives. They are weaker than you. So treat them with respect. Honor them as those who will share with you the gracious gift of life. Then nothing will stand in the way of your prayers.

SUFFERING FOR DOING GOOD

⁸Finally, I want all of you to live together in peace. Be understanding. Love one another like members of the same family. Be kind and tender. Don't be proud. ⁹Don't pay back evil with evil. Don't pay back unkind words with

Did Jesus ever do anything bad when he was little?

Nope. Jesus was born as a baby and then grew up, just like you. He was a little boy once and then became a man. When he was a child, Jesus had to learn many things. He had to learn how to hold a cup, how to talk and how to count. He learned things from his parents and went to school to learn. But Jesus never did anything wrong. He never sinned, not even once. He never stole, lied, disobeyed his parents or said bad words. Sometimes Jesus did things that other people did not like. But Jesus always did what was right. He always obeyed God.

checkout
1 Peter 2:22,23

Related verse:
Romans 5:19

unkind words. Instead, pay them back with kind words. That's what you have been chosen to do. You can receive a blessing by doing it.

¹⁰Scripture says,

"Do you want to love life
　and see good days?
Then keep your tongues from
　speaking evil.
Keep your lips from telling lies.
¹¹Turn away from evil, and do good.
　Look for peace, and go after it.
¹²The Lord's eyes look with favor on
　those who are godly.
His ears are open to their
　prayers.
But the Lord doesn't look with
　favor on those who do evil."

(Psalm 34:12–16)

¹³Who is going to hurt you if you really want to do good? ¹⁴But suppose you suffer for doing what is right. Then you will be blessed. Scripture also says, "Don't fear what others fear. Don't be afraid." *(Isaiah 8:12)*

¹⁵But make sure in your hearts that Christ is Lord. Always be ready to give an answer to anyone who asks you about the hope you have. Be ready to give the reason for it. But do it gently and with respect.

¹⁶Live so that you don't have to feel you've done anything wrong. Some people may say evil things about your good conduct as believers in Christ. If they do, they will be put to shame for speaking like that about you. ¹⁷It is better to suffer for doing good than for doing evil if that's what God wants.

¹⁸Christ died for sins once and for all time. The One who did what is right died for those who don't do right. He died to bring you to God. His body was put to death. But the Holy Spirit brought him back to life.

¹⁹By means of the Spirit, Christ went and preached to the spirits in prison. ²⁰Long ago they did not obey. God was patient while Noah was building the ark. He waited, but only a few people went into the ark. A total of eight were saved by means of water.

²¹The water of the flood is a picture of the baptism that now saves you also. The baptism I'm talking about has nothing to do with removing dirt from your body. Instead, it promises God that you will keep a clear sense of what is right and wrong.

Jesus Christ has saved you by rising from the dead. ²²He has gone into heaven. He is at God's right hand. Angels, authorities and powers are under his control.

LIVING FOR GOD

4 Christ suffered in his body. So get ready as a soldier does. Prepare yourselves to think in the same way Christ did. Do it because those who have suffered in their bodies are finished with sin. ²As a result, they don't live the rest of their lives on earth controlled by evil human longings. Instead, they live to do what God wants.

³You have spent enough time in the past doing what ungodly people choose to do. You lived a wild life. You longed for evil things. You got drunk. You went to wild parties. You worshiped statues of gods. The Lord hates that.

⁴Ungodly people think that it's strange when you no longer join them in what they do. They want you to rush into the same flood of wasteful living. So they say bad things about you.

⁵But they will have to explain their actions to God. He is ready to judge the living and the dead. ⁶That's why the good news was preached even to people who are now dead. Human judges said they were guilty as far as their bodies were concerned. But God set their spirits free to live as he wanted them to.

⁷The end of all things is near. So keep a clear mind. Control yourselves. Then you can pray. ⁸Most of all, love one another deeply. Love erases many sins by forgiving them. ⁹Welcome others into your homes without complaining.

¹⁰God's gifts of grace come in many forms. Each of you has received a gift in order to serve others. You should use it faithfully. ¹¹If you speak, you should do it like one speaking God's very words. If you serve, you should do it with the strength God provides. Then in all things God will be praised through Jesus Christ.

Give him the glory and the power for ever and ever. Amen.

SUFFERING FOR BEING A CHRISTIAN

¹²Dear friends, don't be surprised by the painful suffering you are going through. Don't feel as if something strange were happening to you. ¹³Be joyful that you are taking part in Christ's sufferings. Then you will be filled with joy when Christ returns in glory.

¹⁴Suppose people make fun of you because you believe in Christ. Then you are blessed, because God's Spirit rests on you. He is the Spirit of glory. ¹⁵Suppose you suffer. Then it shouldn't be because you are a murderer or a thief. It shouldn't be because you do evil things. It shouldn't be because you poke your nose into other people's business. ¹⁶But suppose you suffer for being a Christian. Then don't be ashamed. Instead, praise God because you are known by that name.

¹⁷It is time for people to be judged. It will begin with the family of God. And since it begins with us, what will happen to people who don't obey God's good news? ¹⁸Scripture says,

"Suppose it is hard for godly
    people to be saved.
Then what will happen to
    ungodly people and
    sinners?"

(Proverbs 11:31)

¹⁹Some people will suffer because God has planned it that way. They

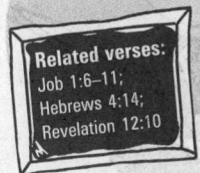

Why can't I see Jesus now?

Jesus went back to heaven to be with his Father. But he has not forgotten about us. He is preparing a place for all who believe in him. He is getting it ready for when they die and go to be with him. The Bible says that Satan brings charges against God's people. He tells God that we are no good. He wants God to reject us. There is an example of this in Job 1:6–11. Whenever the devil accuses a believer, Jesus defends that person. In this way he is acting as our high priest. He can defend us, because he has already paid for our sins.

Jesus has not left us here alone. He sent the Holy Spirit to be with us wherever we go. That is why Jesus said, "It is for your good that I am going away" (John 16:7). One day Jesus will take all believers to live with him forever. Then you *will* be able to see Jesus in person.

checkout 1 Peter 3:22

Related verses:
Job 1:6–11;
Hebrews 4:14;
Revelation 12:10

should commit themselves to their faithful Creator. And they should continue to do good.

TO ELDERS AND YOUNG MEN

5 I'm speaking to the elders among you. I was a witness of Christ's sufferings. And I will also share in the glory that is going to come. I'm making my appeal to you as one who is an elder together with you. ²Be shepherds of God's flock, the believers who are under your care. Serve as their leaders. Don't serve them because you have to. Instead, do it because you want to. That's what God wants you to do. Don't do it because you want to get more and more money. Do it because you really want to serve.

³Don't act as if you were a ruler over those who are under your care. Instead, be examples to the flock. ⁴The Chief Shepherd will come again. Then you will receive the crown of glory. It is a crown that will never fade away.

⁵Young men, follow the lead of those who are older. All of you, put on a spirit that is free of pride toward each other as if it were your clothes. Scripture says,

> "God opposes those who are
>   proud.
> But he gives grace to those who
>   are not."   *(Proverbs 3:34)*

⁶So don't be proud. Put yourselves under God's mighty hand. Then he will honor you at the right time. ⁷Turn all your worries over to him. He cares about you.

⁸Control yourselves. Be on your guard. Your enemy the devil is like a roaring lion. He prowls around looking for someone to chew up and swallow. ⁹Stand up to him. Stand firm in what you believe. All over the world you know that your brothers and sisters are going through the same kind of suffering.

¹⁰God always gives you all the grace you need. So you will only have to suffer for a little while. Then God himself will build you up again. He will make

What mean things does Satan do to people?

Satan does not get to do whatever he wants to do to people. One thing he does is get us to hurt ourselves. Lots of people think that Satan only talks people into doing bad stuff. He does do that. But one of the worst things he does is lie to us. Satan hates God and does not want us to believe what God says. He wants us to believe what is false. He wants us to sin. He wants us to believe that we are no good. Satan lies to us about our worth and about what really matters, so that we will hurt ourselves. One way to see Satan's lies is to know the truth that is in the Bible.

checkout 1 Peter 5:8,9

Related verses: Genesis 3:1–4; John 8:32,44

you strong and steady. And he has chosen you to share in his eternal glory because you belong to Christ.

[11]Give him the power for ever and ever. Amen.

FINAL GREETINGS

[12]I consider Silas to be a faithful brother. With his help I have written you this short letter. I have written it to cheer you up. And I have written to give witness about the true grace of God. Stand firm in it.

[13]The members of the church in Babylon send you their greetings. They were chosen together with you. Mark, my son in the faith, also sends you his greetings. [14]Greet each other with a friendly kiss.

May God give peace to all of you who believe in Christ.

KIDS' QUESTION

Is Kissing wrong?

Kissing is not wrong. Many family members kiss each other. In some countries friends kiss each other on the cheek whenever they say hello. And husbands and wives who love each other often kiss. A kiss can show love and warmth as long as it is OK with the person being kissed.

checkout
1 Peter 5:14

Related verses:
Genesis 27:26;
2 Corinthians
13:12

Quest Clue

When someone hurts you, you may want to get revenge. But God says that he is the one who will protect you and deal with anyone who hurts you. You don't need to do it yourself. Read Romans 12 to hear what Paul says about revenge. Then look at 1 Peter 2 to find out more.

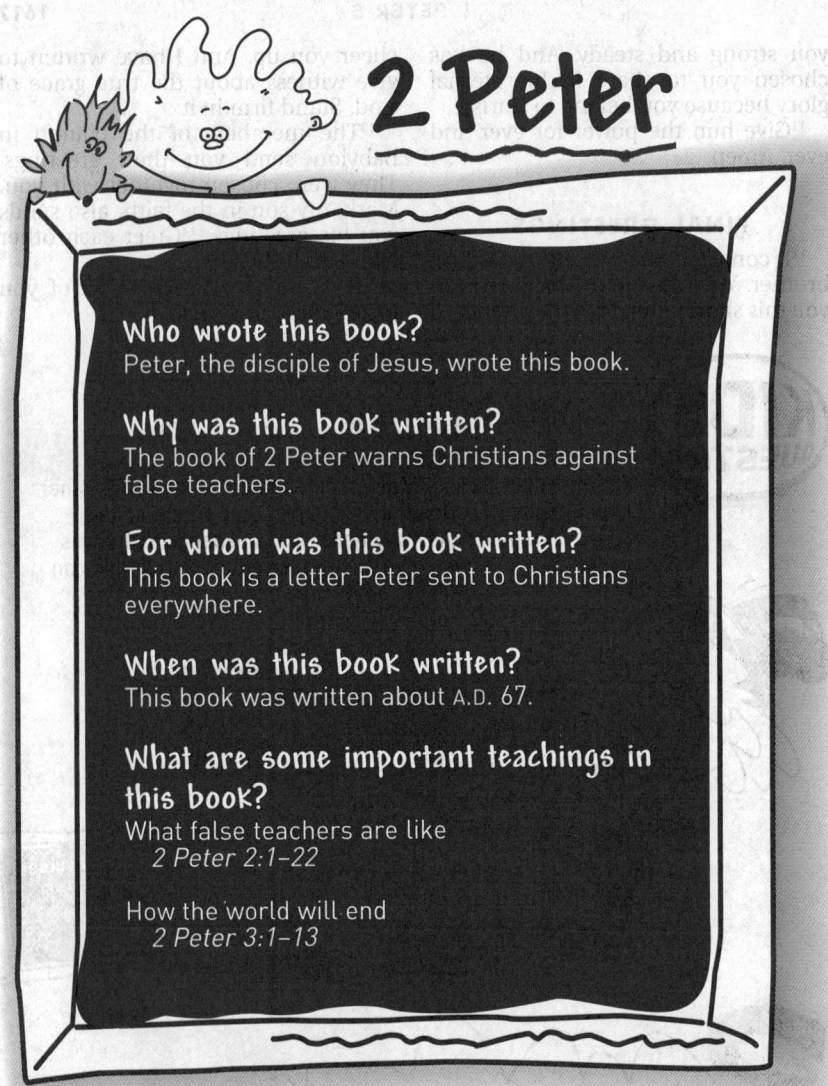

2 Peter

Who wrote this book?
Peter, the disciple of Jesus, wrote this book.

Why was this book written?
The book of 2 Peter warns Christians against false teachers.

For whom was this book written?
This book is a letter Peter sent to Christians everywhere.

When was this book written?
This book was written about A.D. 67.

What are some important teachings in this book?
What false teachers are like
2 Peter 2:1–22

How the world will end
2 Peter 3:1–13

1 I, Simon Peter, am writing this letter. I serve Jesus Christ. I am his apostle.

I am sending this letter to you who have received a faith as valuable as ours. You received it because our God and Savior Jesus Christ does what is right and fair for everyone.

²May more and more grace and peace be given to you. May they come to you as you learn more about God and about Jesus our Lord.

BE SURE THAT GOD HAS CHOSEN YOU

³God's power has given us everything we need to lead a godly life. All of that has come to us because we know the One who chose us. He chose us because of his own glory and goodness.

⁴He has also given us his very great and valuable promises. He did it so you could share in his nature. He also did it so you could escape from the evil in the world. That evil is caused by sinful longings.

⁵So you should try very hard to add goodness to your faith. To goodness, add knowledge. ⁶To knowledge, add the ability to control yourselves. To the ability to control yourselves, add the strength to keep going. To the strength to keep going, add godliness. ⁷To godliness, add kindness to believers. And to kindness to believers, add love.

⁸You should possess more and more of those good points. They will make you useful and fruitful as you get to know our Lord Jesus Christ better.

⁹But what if some of you do not have those good points? Then you can't see very well. You are blind. You have forgotten that your past sins have been washed away.

¹⁰My brothers and sisters, be very sure that God has appointed you to be saved. Be sure that he has chosen you. If you do everything I have just said, you will never trip and fall. ¹¹You will receive a rich welcome into the kingdom that lasts forever. It is the kingdom of our Lord and Savior Jesus Christ.

PROPHECY COMES
FROM GOD

¹²So I will always remind you of these things. I'll do it even though you know them. I'll do it even though you now have deep roots in the truth. ¹³I think it is right for me to remind you. It is right as long as I live in this tent. I'm talking about my body.

¹⁴I know my tent will soon be removed. Our Lord Jesus Christ has made that clear to me. ¹⁵I hope that you will always be able to remember these things after I'm gone. I will try very hard to see that you do.

¹⁶We told you about the time our Lord Jesus Christ came with power. But we didn't make up stories when we told you about it. With our own eyes we saw him in all his majesty. ¹⁷God the Father gave him honor and glory. The voice of the Majestic Glory came to him. It said, "This is my Son, and I love him. I am very pleased with him." *(Matthew 17:5; Mark 9:7; Luke 9:35)* ¹⁸We ourselves heard the voice that came from heaven. We were with him on the sacred mountain.

¹⁹The word of the prophets is made more certain. We have that word. You must pay attention to it. It is like a light shining in a dark place. It will shine until the day Jesus comes. Then the Morning Star will rise in your hearts.

²⁰Above all, here is what you must understand. No prophecy in Scripture ever came from a prophet's own understanding. ²¹It never came simply because a prophet wanted it to. Instead, the Holy Spirit guided the prophets as they spoke. So prophecy comes from God.

FALSE TEACHERS WILL
BE DESTROYED

2 But there were also false prophets among the people. In the same way there will be false teachers among you. In secret they will bring in teachings that will destroy you. They will even turn against the Lord and Master who died to save them. His death paid for their sins. They will quickly destroy themselves. ²Many people will follow their shameful ways. They will give the way of truth a bad name.

³Those teachers are never satisfied. They want to get something out of you. So they make up stories to take advantage of you. They have been under a sentence of death for a long time. The One who will destroy them has not been sleeping.

⁴God did not spare angels when they sinned. Instead, he sent them to hell. He put them in dark prisons. He will keep them there until he judges them. ⁵God did not spare the world's ungodly people long ago. He brought the flood on them. But Noah preached about the right way to live. God kept him safe. He also saved seven others. ⁶God judged the cities of Sodom and Gomorrah. He burned them to ashes. He made them an example of what is going to happen to ungodly people.

⁷God saved Lot. He was a man who did what was right. He was shocked by the dirty, sinful lives of people who didn't obey God's laws. ⁸That good man lived among them day after day. He saw and heard the evil things they were doing. They were breaking God's laws. And his godly spirit was deeply troubled.

⁹So the Lord knows how to keep godly people safe in times of testing. He also knows how to keep ungodly people under guard until the day they will be judged. In the meantime, he continues to punish them. ¹⁰Most of all, this is true of people who follow the evil longings of their sinful natures. They hate to be under authority.

Those false prophets are bold and proud. They aren't afraid to speak evil things against heavenly beings. ¹¹Angels are stronger and more powerful than those people. But even angels don't bring to the Lord evil charges against heavenly beings.

¹²Those people speak evil about things they don't understand. They are like wild animals. They do what comes naturally to them. They are born only to be caught and destroyed. Just like animals, they too will die.

¹³They will be paid back with harm for the harm they have done. Their idea of pleasure is to have wild parties in the middle of the day. They are like spots and stains. They enjoy their sinful pleasures while they eat with you. ¹⁴They stare at women who are not their wives. They want to have sex with them. They never stop sinning. They trap those who are not firm in their faith. They have mastered the art of getting what they want. God has placed them under his curse.

¹⁵They have left God's way. They have wandered off. They follow the way of Balaam, son of Beor. He loved to get paid for doing his evil work. ¹⁶But a donkey corrected him for the wrong he did. Animals don't speak. But the donkey spoke with a human voice. It tried to stop the prophet from doing a very dumb thing.

¹⁷Those false prophets are like springs without water. They are like mists driven by a storm. The blackest darkness is reserved for them.

¹⁸They speak empty, bragging words. They make their appeal to the

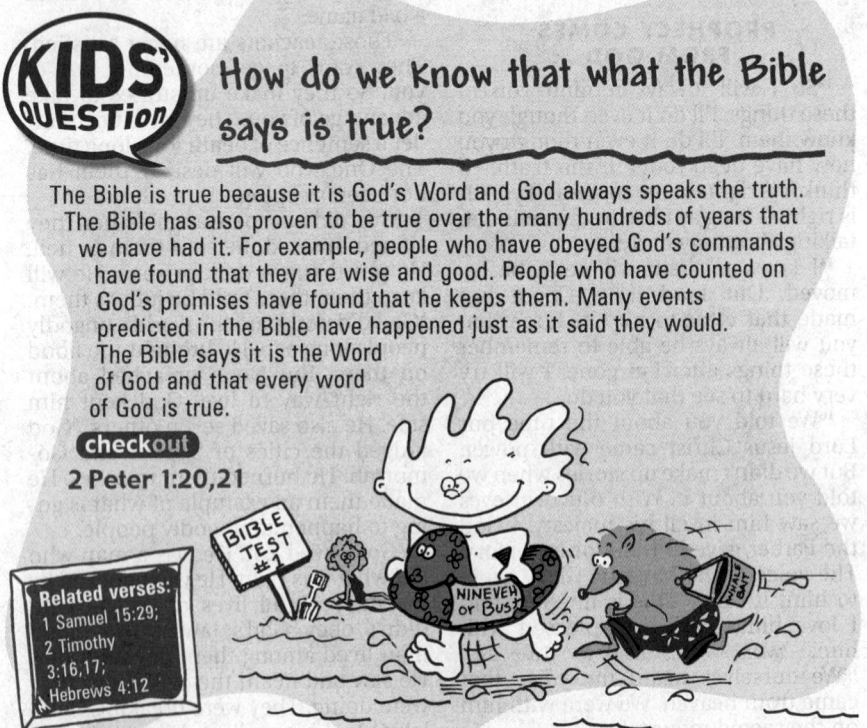

KIDS' QUESTION

How do we know that what the Bible says is true?

The Bible is true because it is God's Word and God always speaks the truth. The Bible has also proven to be true over the many hundreds of years that we have had it. For example, people who have obeyed God's commands have found that they are wise and good. People who have counted on God's promises have found that he keeps them. Many events predicted in the Bible have happened just as it said they would. The Bible says it is the Word of God and that every word of God is true.

checkout
2 Peter 1:20,21

Related verses:
1 Samuel 15:29;
2 Timothy 3:16,17;
Hebrews 4:12

BIBLE TEST #1

NINEVEH or BUST

earthly longings of people's sinful nature. They tempt new believers who are just escaping from the company of sinful people. ¹⁹They promise to give freedom to the new believers. But they themselves are slaves to sinful living. A person is a slave to anything that controls him.

²⁰They may have escaped the sin of the world. They may have come to know our Lord and Savior Jesus Christ. But what if they are once again caught up in sin? And what if it has become their master? Then they are worse off at the end than they were at the beginning.

²¹What if they had not known the way of godliness? That would have been better than to have known it and then to have turned their backs on it. The way of godliness is the sacred command that was passed on to them.

²²What the proverbs say about them is true. "A dog returns to where it has thrown up." *(Proverbs 26:11)* And, "A pig that is washed goes back to rolling in the mud."

THE DAY OF THE LORD

3 Dear friends, this is now my second letter to you. I have written both of them as reminders. I want to stir you up to think in a way that is pure. ²I want you to remember the words the holy prophets spoke in the past. Remember the command our Lord and Savior gave through your apostles.

³First of all, here is what you must understand. In the last days people will make fun of the truth. They will laugh at it. They will follow their own evil longings. ⁴They will say, "Where is this 'return' he promised? Everything goes on in the same way it has since our people of long ago died. In fact, it has continued that way since God first created everything."

⁵Long ago, God's word brought the heavens into being. His word separated the earth from the waters. And the waters surrounded it. But those people forget things like that on purpose. ⁶The waters also flooded the world of that time. It was destroyed.

⁷By God's word the heavens and earth of today are being reserved for fire. They are being kept for the day when God will judge. Then ungodly people will be destroyed.

⁸Dear friends, here is one thing you must not forget. With the Lord a day is like a thousand years. And a thousand years are like a day. ⁹The Lord is not slow to keep his promise. He is not

KIDS' QUESTion

How long is eternity?

We cannot even imagine how long eternity is. Eternity goes on forever. Sometimes we have good times that we wish would never end. A party or a vacation or a visit by a friend from out of town is like that. But even good times come to an end. Eternity, however, never ends. God is eternal and he has given us eternal life. If we know Jesus, we will live forever with him someday in heaven after our lives on earth come to an end.

checkout

2 Peter 3:8

Related verses:
Psalm 90:4;
1 Timothy 1:17

slow in the way some people understand it. He is patient with you. He doesn't want anyone to be destroyed. Instead, he wants all people to turn away from their sins.

10But the day of the Lord will come like a thief. The heavens will disappear with a roar. Fire will destroy everything in them. God will judge the earth and everything in it.

11So everything will be destroyed. And what kind of people should you be? You should lead holy and godly lives. 12Live like that as you look forward to the day of God. It will make the day come more quickly. On that day fire will destroy the heavens. Its heat will melt everything in them.

13But we are looking forward to a new heaven and a new earth. Godliness will make its home there. All of this is in keeping with God's promise.

14Dear friends, I know you are looking forward to that. So try your best to be found pure and without blame. Be at peace with God. 15Remember that while our Lord is waiting patiently to return, people are being saved.

Our dear brother Paul also wrote to you about that. God made him wise to write as he did. 16He writes the same way in all his letters. He speaks about what I have just told you. His letters include some things that are hard to understand. People who don't know better and aren't firm in the faith twist what he says. They twist the other Scriptures too. So they will be destroyed.

17Dear friends, you already know that. So be on your guard. Then you won't be led down the wrong path by the mistakes of people who don't obey the law. You won't fall from your safe position.

18Grow in the grace of our Lord and Savior Jesus Christ. Get to know him better.

Give him glory both now and forever. Amen.

KIDS' QUESTion

How will the world end?

The world will end by God's power. It will not end by accident or by a war that gets out of control. Right now God keeps the world safe from being destroyed. But some day he will decide that the time is right to stop everything and judge everyone. He will burn up the world with fire and intense heat. Then he will create a new heaven and a new earth for all of his people to live forever with him. The Bible tells us that we should not try to figure out exactly when this world will end. But we should always make sure that our hearts are right with God, so that we will be ready at any time.

checkout 2 Peter 3:10–15

Related verses:
Mark 13:7,33, 36,37;
Revelation 21:1

1 John

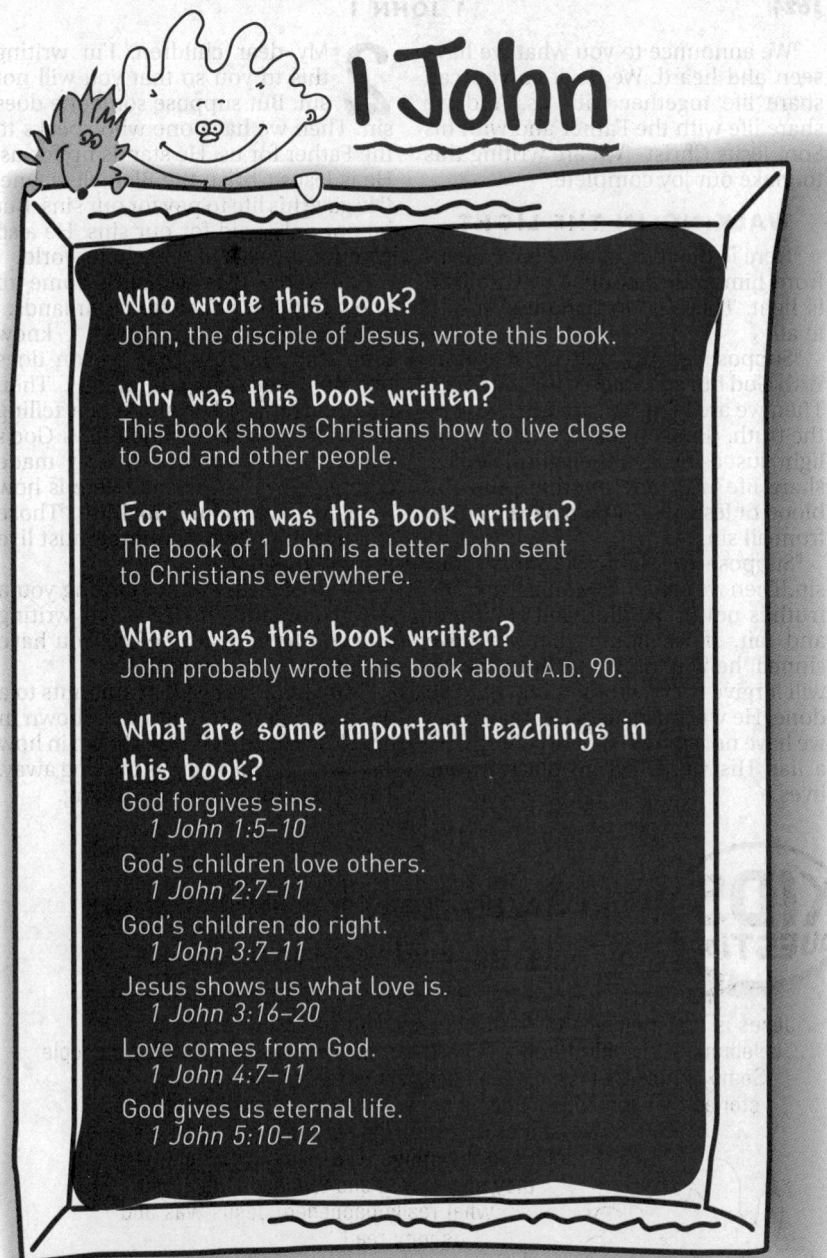

Who wrote this book?
John, the disciple of Jesus, wrote this book.

Why was this book written?
This book shows Christians how to live close
to God and other people.

For whom was this book written?
The book of 1 John is a letter John sent
to Christians everywhere.

When was this book written?
John probably wrote this book about A.D. 90.

**What are some important teachings in
this book?**
God forgives sins.
  1 John 1:5–10
God's children love others.
  1 John 2:7–11
God's children do right.
  1 John 3:7–11
Jesus shows us what love is.
  1 John 3:16–20
Love comes from God.
  1 John 4:7–11
God gives us eternal life.
  1 John 5:10–12

THE WORD OF LIFE

1 Here is what we announce to everyone about the Word of life. He was already here from the beginning. We have heard him. We have seen him with our eyes. We have looked at him. Our hands have touched him. ²That life has appeared. We have seen him. We give witness about him. And we announce to you that same eternal life. He was already with the Father. He has appeared to us.

³We announce to you what we have seen and heard. We do it so you can share life together with us. And we share life with the Father and with his Son, Jesus Christ. ⁴We are writing this to make our joy complete.

WALKING IN THE LIGHT

⁵Here is the message we have heard from him and announce to you. God is light. There is no darkness in him at all.

⁶Suppose we say that we share life with God but still walk in the darkness. Then we are lying. We are not living by the truth. ⁷But suppose we walk in the light, just as he is in the light. Then we share life with one another. And the blood of Jesus, his Son, makes us pure from all sin.

⁸Suppose we claim we are without sin. Then we are fooling ourselves. The truth is not in us. ⁹But God is faithful and fair. If we admit that we have sinned, he will forgive us our sins. He will forgive every wrong thing we have done. He will make us pure. ¹⁰If we say we have not sinned, we are calling God a liar. His word has no place in our lives.

2 My dear children, I'm writing this to you so that you will not sin. But suppose someone does sin. Then we have one who speaks to the Father for us. He stands up for us. He is Jesus Christ, the Blameless One. ²He gave his life to pay for our sins. But he not only paid for our sins. He also paid for the sins of the whole world.

³We know that we have come to know God if we obey his commands. ⁴Suppose someone says, "I know him." But suppose that person does not do what God commands. Then that person is a liar and is not telling the truth. ⁵But if anyone obeys God's word, then God's love is truly made complete in that person. Here is how we know we belong to him. ⁶Those who claim to belong to him must live just as Jesus did.

⁷Dear friends, I'm not writing you a new command. Instead, I'm writing one you have heard before. You have had it since the beginning. ⁸But I am writing what amounts to a new command. Its truth was shown in how Jesus lived. It is also shown in how you live. The darkness is passing away. The true light is already shining.

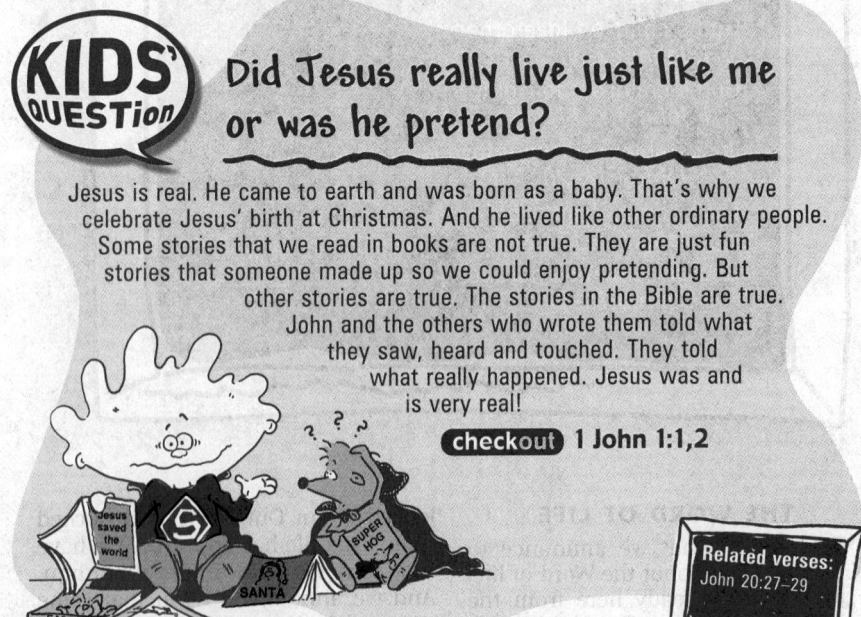

KIDS' QUESTion

Did Jesus really live just like me or was he pretend?

Jesus is real. He came to earth and was born as a baby. That's why we celebrate Jesus' birth at Christmas. And he lived like other ordinary people. Some stories that we read in books are not true. They are just fun stories that someone made up so we could enjoy pretending. But other stories are true. The stories in the Bible are true. John and the others who wrote them told what they saw, heard and touched. They told what really happened. Jesus was and is very real!

checkout 1 John 1:1,2

Related verses:
John 20:27–29

[9]Suppose someone claims to be in the light but hates his brother or sister. Then he is still in the darkness.

[10]Those who love their brothers and sisters are living in the light. There is nothing in them to make them fall into sin. [11]But those who hate a brother or sister are in the darkness. They walk around in the darkness. They don't know where they are going. The darkness has made them blind.

[12]Dear children, I'm writing to you
   because your sins have been
      forgiven.
   They have been forgiven because
      of what Jesus has done.
[13]Fathers, I'm writing to you
   because you have known the
      One who is from the
         beginning.
Young people, I'm writing to you
   because you have won the battle
      over the evil one.

Dear children, I'm writing to you
   because you have known the
      Father.
[14]Fathers, I'm writing to you
   because you have known the
      One who is from the
         beginning.

Young people, I'm writing to you
   because you are strong.
God's word lives in you.
You have won the battle over the
   evil one.

DO NOT LOVE THE WORLD

[15]Do not love the world or anything in it. If you love the world, love for the Father is not in you.

[16]Here is what people who belong to this world do. They try to satisfy what their sinful natures want to do. They long for what their sinful eyes look at. They brag about what they have and what they do. All of this comes from the world. It doesn't come from the Father.

[17]The world and its evil longings are passing away. But those who do what God wants them to do live forever.

A WARNING ABOUT THE ENEMIES OF CHRIST

[18]Dear children, we are living in the last days. You have heard that the great enemy of Christ is coming. But even now many enemies of Christ have already come. That's how we know that these are the last days.

[19]The enemies left our group. They

KIDS' QUESTION

What does God want me to do when I do what's wrong?

The first thing you should do is pray and admit to God what you have done. You should tell him that you are sorry and ask him to help you not to do it again. God will forgive you. You should talk with him about all your problems. Try praying when you first think of doing something wrong. God will help you. If your sin has hurt other people, talk to them and ask for their forgiveness.

checkout 1 John 1:9

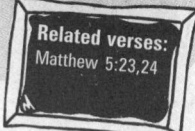

Related verses:
Matthew 5:23,24

didn't really belong to us. If they had belonged to us, they would have remained with us. But by leaving they showed that none of them belonged to us.

²⁰You have received the Spirit from the Holy One. And all of you know the truth. ²¹I'm not writing to you because you don't know the truth but because you do know it. I'm writing to you because no lie comes from the truth.

²²Who is the liar? The person who says that Jesus is not the Christ. People who say that are the enemies of Christ. They say no to the Father and the Son. ²³Those who say no to the Son don't belong to the Father. But anyone who says yes to the Son belongs to the Father also.

²⁴Make sure that you don't forget what you have heard from the beginning. Then you will remain joined to the Son and to the Father. ²⁵That's what God has promised us. We have eternal life.

²⁶I'm writing these things to warn you about those who are trying to lead you down the wrong path.

²⁷But you have received the Holy Spirit from God. He continues to live in you. So you don't need anyone to teach you. God's Spirit teaches you about everything. What he says is true. He doesn't lie. Remain joined to Christ, just as you have been taught by the Spirit.

CHILDREN OF GOD

²⁸Dear children, remain joined to Christ. Then when he comes, we can be bold. We will not be ashamed to meet him when he comes.

²⁹You know that God is right and always does what is right. And you know that everyone who does what is right

What would happen if I accidentally swore in heaven?

You will never accidentally swear in heaven, because no one will be able to sin. Jesus will make all of his people perfect like himself. You will not *want* to sin. Messing up is one thing you will never have to worry about again.

checkout

1 John 3:2,3

JASON'S IMAGINATION

Related verses:
1 Corinthians
13:9,10

has been born again because of what God has done.

3 How great is the love the Father has given us so freely! Now we can be called children of God. And that's what we really are! The world doesn't know us because it didn't know him.

²Dear friends, now we are children of God. He still hasn't let us know what we will be. But we know that when Christ appears, we will be like him. We will see him as he really is. ³He is pure. All who hope to be like him make themselves pure.

⁴Everyone who sins breaks the law. In fact, breaking the law is sin. ⁵But you know that Christ came to take our sins away. And there is no sin in him. ⁶No one who remains joined to him keeps on sinning. No one who keeps on sinning has seen him or known him.

⁷Dear children, don't let anyone lead you down the wrong path. Those who do what is right are holy, just as Christ is holy. ⁸Those who do what is sinful belong to the devil. They are just like him. He has been sinning from the beginning. But the Son of God came to destroy the devil's work.

⁹Those who are born again because of what God has done will not keep on sinning. God's very nature remains in them. They can't go on sinning. They have been born again because of what God has done.

¹⁰Here is how you can tell the difference between the children of God and the children of the devil. Those who don't do what is right do not belong to God. Those who don't love their brothers and sisters do not belong to him either.

LOVE ONE ANOTHER

¹¹From the beginning we have heard that we should love one another. ¹²Don't be like Cain. He belonged to the evil one. He murdered his brother.

How come people put bad movies on TV?

Because lots of people watch them. The moviemakers and the network bosses try to make as much money as possible. If a lot of people watch a certain movie, the television network can make a lot of money through advertising. The networks know that lots of people watch bad shows. Instead of watching bad movies, we should ignore them by changing channels or turning off the TV set. If a lot of people wrote the TV stations and complained about the bad movies, then there would not be things like these on TV anymore.

Remember that bad is bad no matter how many people do it. You don't have to watch bad movies just because they're popular.

checkout
1 John 3:7,8

Related verses:
Psalm 101:3;
Philippians 4:8;
1 John 2:15–16

TELEVISION PRODUCER OF THE YEAR AWARD

BRING THE RATINGS UP BY BRINGING THE STANDARDS UP

And why did he murder him? Because the things Cain had done were wrong. But the things his brother had done were right.

¹³My brothers and sisters, don't be surprised if the world hates you. ¹⁴We know that we have left our old dead condition and entered into new life. We know it because we love one another. Those who do not are still living in their old condition.

¹⁵Those who hate their brothers and sisters are murderers. And you know that murderers do not have eternal life in their hearts.

¹⁶We know what love is because Jesus Christ gave his life for us. So we should give our lives for our brothers and sisters.

¹⁷Suppose someone sees a brother or sister in need and is able to help them. If he doesn't take pity on them, how can the love of God be in him?

¹⁸Dear children, don't just talk about love. Put your love into action. Then it will truly be love. ¹⁹That's how we know that we hold to the truth. And that's how we put our hearts at rest, knowing that God is watching. ²⁰Our hearts may judge us. But God is greater than our hearts. He knows everything.

²¹Dear friends, if our hearts do not judge us, we can be bold with God. ²²And he will give us anything we ask. That's because we obey his commands. We do what pleases him.

²³God has commanded us to believe in the name of his Son, Jesus Christ. He has also commanded us to love one another. ²⁴Those who obey his commands remain joined to him. And he remains joined to them.

How do we know that God lives in us? We know it because of the Holy Spirit he gave us.

PUT THE SPIRITS TO THE TEST

4 Dear friends, do not believe every spirit. Put the spirits to the test to see if they belong to God. Many false prophets have gone out into the world.

²How can you recognize the Spirit of God? Every spirit that agrees that Jesus Christ came in a human body belongs

KIDS' QUESTion

Why did Cain kill his brother?

Because Cain was very, very angry. Both Cain and Abel had offered gifts to God. God was pleased with Abel's gift but not with Cain's gift. The Bible does not tell us why. First Cain became angry at God for not liking his gift. Then he became angry at Abel because God liked Abel's gift. Cain let his anger take control of him. He should have realized that he was wrong and asked God how he could do better. Instead he killed his brother. Anger can make you do terrible things if you let it get to you. Control your anger so you do not hurt the people you love.

checkout 1 John 3:12

Related verses:
Genesis 4:1–16;
Matthew 5:23,24

to God. [3]But every spirit that doesn't agree with this does not belong to God. It is the spirit of the great enemy of Christ. You have heard that the enemy is coming. Even now he is already in the world.

[4]Dear children, you belong to God. You have not accepted the teachings of the false prophets. That's because the One who is in you is more powerful than the one who is in the world.

[5]False prophets belong to the world. So they speak from the world's point of view. The world listens to them. [6]We belong to God. And those who know God listen to us. But those who don't belong to God don't listen to us. That's how we can tell the difference between the Spirit of truth and the spirit of lies.

WE LOVE BECAUSE GOD LOVED US

[7]Dear friends, let us love one another, because love comes from God. Everyone who loves has been born again because of what God has done. That person knows God. [8]Anyone who does not love does not know God, because God is love.

[9]How did God show his love for us? He sent his one and only Son into the world. He sent him so we could receive life through him.

[10]What is love? It is not that we loved God. It is that he loved us and sent his Son to give his life to pay for our sins.

[11]Dear friends, since God loved us that much, we should also love one another. [12]No one has ever seen God. But if we love one another, God lives in us. His love is made complete in us.

[13]We know that we belong to him and he belongs to us. He has given us his Holy Spirit.

[14]The Father has sent his Son to be the Savior of the world. We have seen it. We give witness to it. [15]God lives in anyone who agrees that Jesus is the Son of God. That kind of person remains joined to God. [16]So we know that God loves us. We depend on it.

God is love. Anyone who leads a life of love shows that he is joined to God. And God is joined to him.

[17]So love is made complete among us. We will be bold on the day God judges us. That's because in this world we love as Jesus did.

[18]There is no fear in love. Instead, perfect love drives fear away. Fear has to do with being punished. The one who fears does not have perfect love.

[19]We love because he loved us first. [20]Anyone who says he loves God but in fact hates his brother or sister is a liar. He doesn't love his brother or sister, whom he has seen. So he can't love God, whom he has not seen.

[21]Here is the command God has given us. Anyone who loves God must also love his brothers and sisters.

FAITH IN THE SON OF GOD

5 Everyone who believes that Jesus is the Christ is born again because of what God has done. And everyone who loves the Father loves his children as well.

[2]How do we know that we love God's children? We know it when we love God and obey his commands. [3]Here is what it means to love God. It means that we obey his commands. And his commands are not hard to obey. [4]That's because everyone who is a child of God has won the battle over the world. Our faith has won the battle for us.

[5]Who is it that has won the battle over the world? Only the person who believes that Jesus is the Son of God.

[6]Jesus Christ is the one who was baptized in water and died on the cross. He wasn't just baptized in water. He also died on the cross. The Holy Spirit has given a truthful witness about him. That's because the Spirit is the truth.

[7]There are three that give witness about Jesus. [8]They are the Holy Spirit, the baptism of Jesus and his death. And the three of them agree.

[9]We accept the witness of people. But the witness of God is more important because it is God who gives it. He has given witness about his Son.

[10]Those who believe in the Son of God have accepted that witness in their hearts. Those who do not believe God's witness are calling him a liar. That's because they have not believed his witness about his Son.

[11]Here is God's witness. He has given

us eternal life. That life is found in his Son. [12]Those who belong to the Son have life. Those who do not belong to the Son of God do not have life.

FINAL WORDS

[13]I'm writing these things to you who believe in the name of the Son of God. I'm doing it so you will know that you have eternal life.

[14]There is one thing we can be sure of when we come to God in prayer. If we ask anything in keeping with what he wants, he hears us. [15]If we know that God hears what we ask for, we know that we have it.

[16]Suppose you see your brother or sister commit a sin. But that sin is not the kind that leads to death. Then you should pray for them. And God will give life to them. I'm talking about someone whose sin does not lead to death. But there is a sin that does lead to death. I'm not saying that you should pray about that. [17]Every wrong thing we do is sin. But there are sins that do not lead to death.

[18]We know that those who are children of God do not keep on sinning. The Son of God keeps them safe. The evil one can't harm them. [19]We know that we are children of God. We know that the whole world is under the control of the evil one.

[20]We also know that the Son of God has come. He has given us understanding. Now we can know the One who is true. And we belong to the One who is true. We also belong to his Son, Jesus Christ. He is the true God. He is eternal life.

[21]Dear children, keep away from statues of gods.

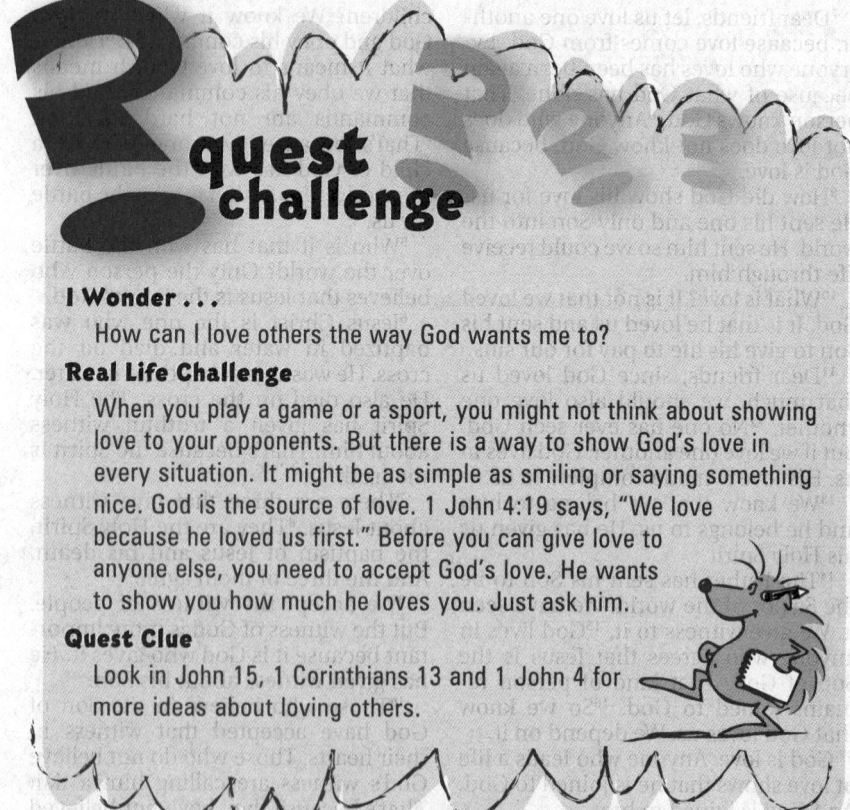

quest challenge

I Wonder . . .

How can I love others the way God wants me to?

Real Life Challenge

When you play a game or a sport, you might not think about showing love to your opponents. But there is a way to show God's love in every situation. It might be as simple as smiling or saying something nice. God is the source of love. 1 John 4:19 says, "We love because he loved us first." Before you can give love to anyone else, you need to accept God's love. He wants to show you how much he loves you. Just ask him.

Quest Clue

Look in John 15, 1 Corinthians 13 and 1 John 4 for more ideas about loving others.

2 John

Who wrote this book?
John, the disciple of Jesus, wrote this book.

Why was this book written?
The book of 2 John shows Christians how to live close to God and other people.

For whom was this book written?
This book is a letter John sent to Christians everywhere.

When was this book written?
John probably wrote this book about A.D. 90.

¹I, the elder, am writing this letter.

I am sending it to the chosen lady and her children. I love all of you because of the truth. I'm not the only one who loves you. So does everyone who knows the truth. ²I love you because of the truth that is alive in us. That truth will be with us forever.

³God the Father and Jesus Christ his Son will give you grace, mercy and peace. Those blessings will be with us, because we love the truth.

⁴It has given me great joy to find some of your children living by the truth. That's just what the Father commanded us to do.

⁵Dear lady, I'm not writing you a new command. I'm writing a command we've had from the beginning. I'm asking that we love one another. ⁶The way we show our love is to obey God's commands. He commands you to lead a life of love. That's what you have heard from the beginning.

⁷Many people who try to fool others have gone out into the world. They don't agree that Jesus Christ came in a human body. People like that try to trick others. They are enemies of Christ. ⁸Watch out that you don't lose what you have worked for. Make sure that you get your complete reward.

⁹Some people run ahead of others. They don't follow the teaching of Christ. People like that don't belong to God. But those who follow the teaching of Christ belong to the Father and the Son.

¹⁰Suppose someone comes to you and doesn't teach these truths. Then don't take him into your house. Don't welcome him. ¹¹Anyone who welcomes him shares in his evil work.

¹²I have a lot to write to you. But I don't want to use paper and ink. Instead, I hope I can visit you. Then I can talk with you face to face. That will make our joy complete.

¹³The children of your chosen sister send their greetings.

quest challenge

I Wonder ...

What does it mean to be part of God's family?

Real Life Challenge

What feelings arise when you think about your family? Perhaps you are happy as you think about family vacations and other times spent together. Maybe you feel sad because your family has had some hard times. No matter how you think about your own family, you are part of an even bigger family with every other Christian around the world. God is your Father, and he cares for you and helps you have good relationships with other Christians.

Quest Clue

Find the verses in Romans 8 and Ephesians 1 that tell you what role God plays in your life. Then read 2 John to see the kind of relationship you can have with other Christians in the family of God.

I Wonder ...

Why is it important for me to stay close to God?

Real Life Challenge

What happens if you don't see or talk to one of your friends for awhile? You probably start feeling like you don't know that person as well as you once did. It works the same way with God. You need to talk to him often in order to feel close to him. God is always close to us, but sometimes we don't realize it if we don't talk to him for awhile.

Quest Clue

Find a verse in John 15 that will encourage you to stay close to God. Then learn why this is so important by reading Jude.

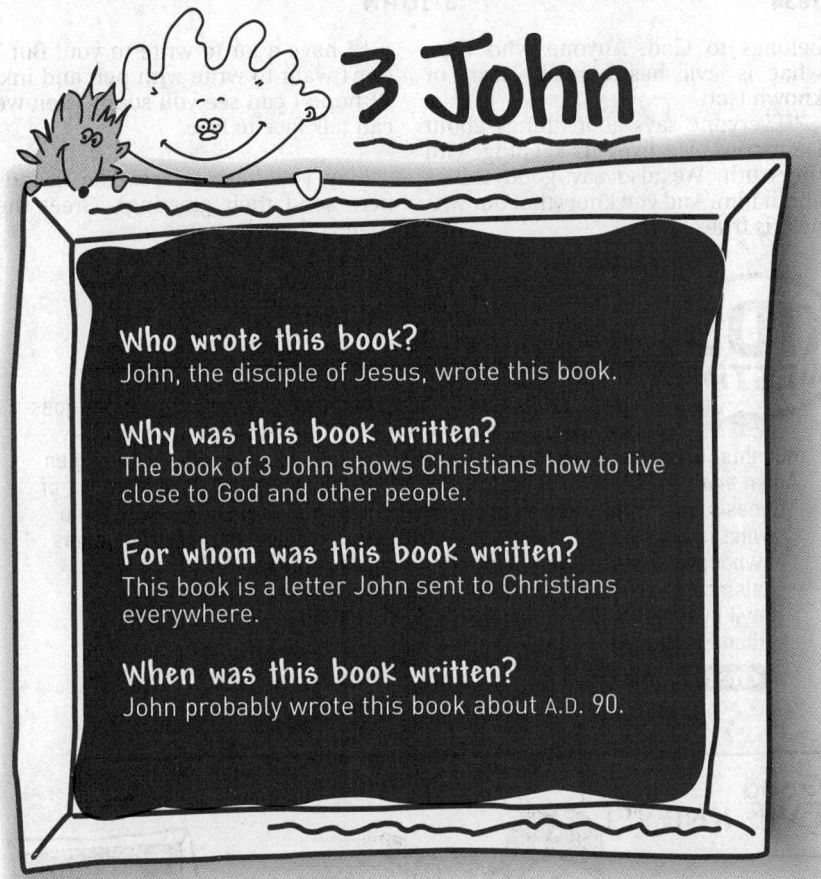

3 John

¹I, the elder, am writing this letter.

I am sending it to you, my dear friend Gaius. I love you because of the truth.

²Dear friend, I know that your spiritual life is going well. I pray that you also may enjoy good health. And I pray that everything else may go well with you.
³Some believers came to me and told me that you are faithful to the truth. They told me that you continue to live by it. That gave me great joy. ⁴I have no greater joy than to hear that my children are living by the truth.
⁵Dear friend, you are faithful in what you are doing for the believers. You are faithful even though they are strangers to you. ⁶They have told the church about your love. Please help them by sending them on their way in a manner that honors God.
⁷They started on their journey to serve Jesus Christ. They didn't receive any help from those who aren't believers. ⁸So we should welcome people like them. We should work together with them for the truth.
⁹I wrote to the church. But Diotrephes won't have anything to do with us. He loves to be the first in everything. ¹⁰So if I come, I will point out what he is doing. He is saying evil things about us to others. Even that doesn't satisfy him. He refuses to welcome other believers. He also keeps others from welcoming them. In fact, he throws them out of the church.
¹¹Dear friend, don't be like those who do evil. Be like those who do good. Anyone who does what is good

belongs to God. Anyone who does what is evil hasn't really seen or known God.

¹²Everyone says good things about Demetrius. He lives in keeping with the truth. We also say good things about him. And you know that our witness is true.

¹³I have a lot to write to you. But I don't want to write with pen and ink. ¹⁴I hope I can see you soon. Then we can talk face to face.

May you have peace. The friends here send their greetings. Greet the friends there by name.

KIDS' QUESTion

What is evil?

Evil is another word for *bad* or *sinful*. Evil is anything that goes against God and goodness. This includes thinking selfish thoughts, doing bad actions and ignoring God. Evil came into the world when Adam and Eve sinned in the Garden of Eden. You can read that in the book of Genesis. Ever since then people have had a part of them that wants to do what is wrong. That is called the "sinful nature." Evil in the world comes whenever sinful human beings do whatever they feel like doing. Evil also comes from Satan. The good news is that we can overcome evil by resisting Satan and obeying Jesus. God is far greater than Satan.

checkout 3 John 11

Related verses:
Genesis 2:9;
Matthew 12:34,
35–37;
1 John 4:4

Jude

Who wrote this book?
Jude, a brother of Jesus, wrote this book.

Why was this book written?
Jude warns Christians about false teachers.

For whom was this book written?
This book is a letter written to Christians everywhere.

When was this book written?
Jude was written about A.D. 66.

¹I, Jude, am writing this letter. I serve Jesus Christ. I am a brother of James.

I am sending this letter to you who have been chosen by God. You are loved by God the Father. You are kept safe by Jesus Christ.

²May more and more mercy, peace, and love be given to you.

A WARNING AGAINST UNGODLY TEACHERS

³Dear friends, I really wanted to write to you about the salvation we share. But now I feel I should write and ask you to stand up for the faith. God's people were trusted with it once and for all time.

⁴Certain people have slipped in among you in secret. Long ago it was written that they would be judged. They are godless people. They use the grace of our God as an excuse for sexual sins. They say no to Jesus Christ. He is our only Lord and King.

⁵I want to remind you about some things you already know. The Lord saved his people. He brought them out of Egypt. But later he destroyed those who did not believe. ⁶Some of the angels didn't stay where they belonged. They didn't keep their positions of authority. The Lord has kept those angels in darkness. They are held by chains that last forever. On judgment day, God will judge them.

⁷The people of Sodom and Gomorrah and the towns around them also did evil things. They gave themselves over to sexual sins. They committed sins of the worst possible kind. They are an example of those who are punished with fire. The fire never goes out.

⁸In the very same way, those dreamers pollute their own bodies. They don't accept authority. They speak evil things against heavenly beings. ⁹But not even Michael did that. He was the leader of the angels. He argued with the devil about the body of Moses. But

he didn't dare to speak evil things against the devil. Instead, he said, "May the Lord stop you!"

¹⁰But those people speak evil things against what they don't understand. They are like wild animals. They can't think for themselves. They do what comes naturally to them. Those are the very things that destroy them.

¹¹How terrible it will be for them! They followed the way of Cain. They rushed ahead and made the same mistake as Balaam did. They did it because they loved money. They are like Korah. He turned against his leaders. Those people will certainly be destroyed, just as Korah was.

¹²They are like stains at the meals you share. They eat too much. They have no shame. They are shepherds who feed only themselves. They are like clouds without rain. They are blown along by the wind. They are like trees in the fall. Since they have no fruit, they are pulled up. So they die twice.

¹³They are like wild waves of the sea. Their shame rises up like foam. They are like falling stars. God has reserved a place of very black darkness for them. He will keep them there forever.

¹⁴Enoch was the seventh man in the family line of Adam. He gave a prophecy about those people. He said,

Are demons red with horns and long tails?

Sometimes cartoons and Halloween costumes show demons in red suits with two horns and a long tail. But that idea came from someone's imagination. It did not come from the Bible. Demons are angels who chose to disobey God. Jude describes some of those evil angels in his letter. Angels are not human beings. They do not have bodies. No one knows what wicked angels look like. Satan, the prince of demons, can take different forms if he wants to. But he does not carry a pitchfork or wear red clothes. He is a real being who lives in the spirit world.

Satan is God's enemy. But Satan is not as powerful as God. Satan was good when God first created him. But later he turned against God and got kicked out of heaven. Jesus called him "the father of lies" (John 8:44). The Bible says he disguises himself as an "angel of light" (2 Corinthians 11:14). Satan can be very tricky. He tries to make bad look good. He lies to us and lies to God about us.

checkout Jude 6

Related verses:
1 Peter 5:8,9

"Look! The Lord is coming with thousands and thousands of his holy ones. [15]He is coming to judge everyone. He is coming to sentence all ungodly people. He will judge them for all the ungodly acts they have done. They have done them in ungodly ways. He will sentence ungodly sinners for all the bad things they have said about him."

[16]Those people complain. They find fault with others. They follow their own evil longings. They brag about themselves. They praise others to help themselves.

REMAIN IN GOD'S LOVE

[17]Dear friends, remember what the apostles of our Lord Jesus Christ said was going to happen. [18]They told you, "In the last days, some people will make fun of the truth. They will follow their own ungodly longings." [19]They are the people who separate you from one another. They do only what comes naturally. They are not led by the Holy Spirit.

[20]Dear friends, build yourselves up in your most holy faith. Let the Holy Spirit guide and help you when you pray. [21]The mercy of our Lord Jesus Christ will bring you eternal life. As you wait for his mercy, remain in God's love.

[22]Show mercy to those who doubt. [23]Pull others out of the fire. Save them. To others, show mercy mixed with fear. Hate even the clothes that are stained by the sins of those who wear them.

PRAISE TO GOD

[24]Give praise to the One who is able to keep you from falling into sin. He will bring you into his heavenly glory without any fault. He will bring you there with great joy. [25]Give praise to the only God. He is our Savior. Glory, majesty, power and authority belong to him. Give praise to him through Jesus Christ our Lord. Give praise to the One who was before all time, who now is, and who will be forever. Amen.

Why doesn't God want us to have fun?

God *does* want us to have fun. Jesus was happy. He told people that they would find joy by following him. Also, God tells us in the Bible that heaven is a place where joy never stops. Some people think the only way to have fun is to sin. Sometimes you can have fun doing what is wrong. But it does not last long. It is like eating something that tastes good but makes you sick later. God wants us to have fun that will last. His fun and joy and happiness are the greatest. And they last forever.

checkout Jude 24

Related verses:
Psalm 5:11;
John 10:10; 15:11

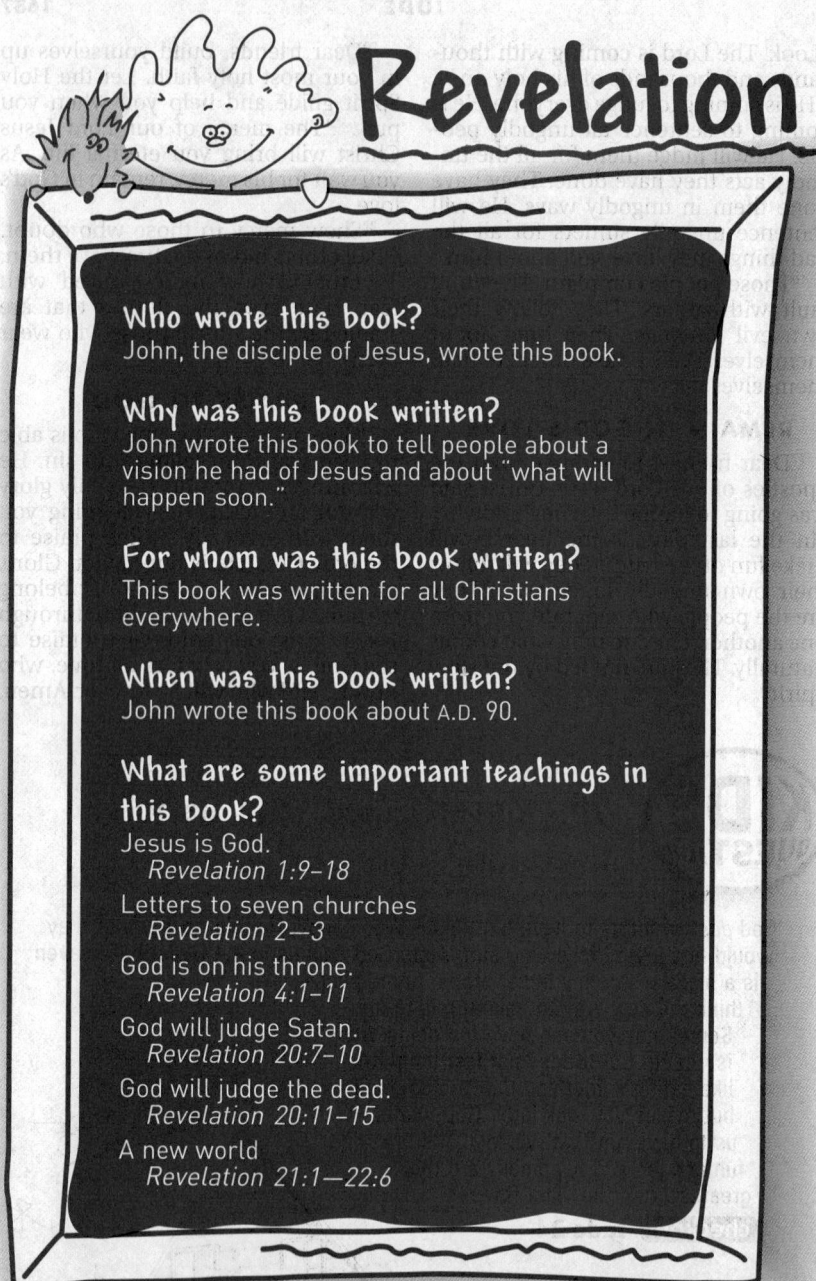

Revelation

Who wrote this book?
John, the disciple of Jesus, wrote this book.

Why was this book written?
John wrote this book to tell people about a vision he had of Jesus and about "what will happen soon."

For whom was this book written?
This book was written for all Christians everywhere.

When was this book written?
John wrote this book about A.D. 90.

What are some important teachings in this book?
Jesus is God.
Revelation 1:9–18

Letters to seven churches
Revelation 2—3

God is on his throne.
Revelation 4:1–11

God will judge Satan.
Revelation 20:7–10

God will judge the dead.
Revelation 20:11–15

A new world
Revelation 21:1—22:6

1 This is the revelation that God gave to Jesus Christ. Jesus shows those who serve God what will happen soon. God made it known by sending his angel to his servant John. ²John gives witness to everything he saw. The things he gives witness to are God's word and what Jesus Christ has said.

³Blessed is the one who reads the words of this prophecy. Blessed are those who hear it and think everything it says is important. The time when these things will come true is near.

GREETINGS

[4]I, John, am writing this letter.

I am sending it to the seven churches in Asia Minor.

May grace and peace come to you from the One who is, and who was, and who will come. May grace and peace come to you from the seven spirits who are in front of God's throne. [5]May grace and peace come to you from Jesus Christ. What Jesus gives witness to can always be trusted. He was the first to rise from the dead. He rules over the kings of the earth.

Give glory and power to the One who loves us! He has set us free from our sins by pouring out his blood for us. [6]He has made us members of his royal family. He has made us priests who serve his God and Father. Give him glory and power for ever and ever! Amen.

[7]Look! He is coming with the clouds!
    Every eye will see him.
Even those who pierced him will
    see him.
All the nations of the earth will
    be sad because of him.
            This will really happen!
                        Amen.

[8]"I am the Alpha and the Omega, the First and the Last," says the Lord God. "I am the One who is, and who was, and who will come. I am the Mighty One."

ONE WHO LOOKS LIKE A SON OF MAN

[9]I, John, am a believer like you. I am a friend who suffers like you. As members of Jesus' royal family, we can put up with anything that happens to us.

I was on the island of Patmos because I taught God's word and what Jesus said. [10]The Holy Spirit took complete control of me on the Lord's Day. I heard a loud voice behind me that sounded like a trumpet. [11]The voice said, "Write on a scroll what you see. Send it to the seven churches in Asia Minor. They are Ephesus, Smyrna, Pergamum, Thyatira, Sardis, Philadelphia and Laodicea."

[12]I turned around to see who was speaking to me. When I turned, I saw seven golden lampstands. [13]In the middle of them was someone who looked "like a son of man." *(Daniel 7:13)*

He was dressed in a long robe with a gold strip of cloth around his chest. [14]The hair on his head was white like wool, as white as snow. His eyes were like a blazing fire. [15]His feet were like bronze metal glowing in a furnace. His voice sounded like rushing waters. [16]He held seven stars in his right hand. Out of his mouth came a sharp sword that had two edges. His face was like the sun shining in all of its brightness.

[17]When I saw him, I fell at his feet as if I were dead.

Then he put his right hand on me and said, "Do not be afraid. I am the First and the Last. [18]I am the Living One. I was dead. But look! I am alive for ever and ever! And I hold the keys to Death and Hell.

[19]"So write down what you have seen. Write about what is happening now and what will happen later. [20]Here is what the mystery of the seven stars you saw in my right hand means. They are the angels of the seven churches. And the seven golden lampstands you saw stand for the seven churches.

THE LETTER TO THE CHURCH IN EPHESUS

2 "Here is what I command you to write to the church in Ephesus.

Here are the words of the One who holds the seven stars in his right hand. He also walks among the seven golden lampstands. He says, [2]'I know what you are doing. You work long and hard. I know you can't put up with those who are evil. You have tested those who claim to be apostles but are not. You have found out that they are liars. [3]You have been faithful and have put up with a lot of trouble because of me. You have not given up.

[4]'But here is something I hold against you. You don't have as much love as you had at first. [5]Remember how far you have fallen! Turn away from your sins. Do the

things you did at first. If you don't, I will come to you and remove your lampstand from its place.

⁶'But you do have this in your favor. You hate the way the Nicolaitans act. I hate it too.

⁷'Those who have ears should listen to what the Holy Spirit says to the churches. I will allow those who overcome to eat from the tree of life in God's paradise.'

THE LETTER TO THE CHURCH IN SMYRNA

⁸"Here is what I command you to write to the church in Smyrna.

Here are the words of the One who is the First and the Last. He is the One who died and came to life again. He says, ⁹'I know that you suffer and are poor. But you are rich! Some people say they are Jews but are not. I know that their words are evil. Their worship is satanic.

¹⁰'Don't be afraid of what you are going to suffer. I tell you, the devil will put some of you in prison to test you. You will be treated badly for ten days. Be faithful, even if it means you must die. Then I will give you a crown. The crown is life itself.

¹¹'Those who have ears should listen to what the Holy Spirit says to the churches. Those who overcome will not be hurt at all by the second death.'

THE LETTER TO THE CHURCH IN PERGAMUM

¹²"Here is what I command you to write to the church in Pergamum.

Here are the words of the One with the sharp sword that has two edges. He says, ¹³'I know that you live where Satan has his throne. But you remain true to me. You did not give up your faith in me, even in the days of Antipas, my faithful witness. He was put to death in your city, where Satan lives.

¹⁴'But I have a few things against you. You have people there who follow the teaching of Balaam. He taught Balak to lead the people of Israel into sin. So they ate food that had been offered to statues of gods. And they committed sexual sins. ¹⁵You also have people who follow the teaching of the Nicolaitans.

¹⁶'So turn away from your sins! If you don't, I will come to you soon. I will fight against those people with the sword that comes out of my mouth.

¹⁷'Those who have ears should listen to what the Holy Spirit says to the churches. I will give hidden manna to those who overcome. I will also give each of them a white stone with a new name written on it. Only the one who receives that name will know what it is.'

THE LETTER TO THE CHURCH IN THYATIRA

¹⁸"Here is what I command you to write to the church in Thyatira.

Here are the words of the Son of God. He is the One whose eyes are like blazing fire. His feet are like polished bronze. He says, ¹⁹'I know what you are doing. I know your love and your faith. I know how well you have served. I know you don't give up easily. In fact, you are doing more now than you did at first.

²⁰'But here is what I have against you. You put up with that woman Jezebel. She calls herself a prophet. With her teaching, she has led my servants into sexual sin. She has tricked them into eating food offered to statues of gods.

²¹'I've given her time to turn away from her sinful ways. But she doesn't want to. ²²She sinned on a bed. So I will make her suffer on a bed. And those who commit adultery with her will suffer greatly. Their only way out is to turn away from what she taught them to do. ²³I will strike her children dead. Then all the churches will know that I am the One who searches hearts and minds. I will

pay each of you back for what you have done.

²⁴'I won't bother the rest of you in Thyatira. You don't follow the teaching of Jezebel. You haven't learned what some people call Satan's deep secrets. ²⁵Just hold on to what you have until I come.

²⁶'I'll give authority over the nations to all who overcome and who carry out my plans to the end. ²⁷It is written,

' "He will rule them with an iron rod.
He will break them to pieces like clay pots." *(Psalm 2:9)*

I have received this authority from my Father. ²⁸I will also give the morning star to all who overcome.

²⁹'Those who have ears should listen to what the Holy Spirit says to the churches.'

THE LETTER TO THE CHURCH IN SARDIS

3 "Here is what I command you to write to the church in Sardis.

Here are the words of the One who holds the seven spirits of God. He has the seven stars in his hand. He says, 'I know what you are doing. People think you are alive, but you are dead. ²Wake up! Strengthen what is left, or it will die. You have not done all that my God wants you to do.

³'So remember what you have been taught and have heard. Obey it. Turn away from your sins. If you don't wake up, I will come like a thief. You won't know when I will come to you.

⁴'But you have a few people in Sardis who have kept their clothes clean. They will walk with me, dressed in white, because they are worthy. ⁵Those who overcome will also be dressed in white. I will never erase their names from the Book of Life. I will speak of them by name to my Father and his angels.

⁶'Those who have ears should listen to what the Holy Spirit says to the churches.'

THE LETTER TO THE CHURCH IN PHILADELPHIA

⁷"Here is what I command you to write to the church in Philadelphia.

Here are the words of the One who is holy and true. He holds the

Will I have my same name in heaven?

We don't know for sure, but we probably will. In the parable in Luke 16:19–23, the beggar Lazarus kept his same name in heaven. When we get to heaven we will see friends and family members who have died and gone there before us. They will recognize us, and we will know them. The Bible says that when we trust Jesus as our Savior our names are written in the "Lamb's Book of Life." That's God's list of who gets into heaven.

Related verses:
Luke 16:19–23

checkout
Revelation 3:5

JASON'S IMAGINATION

key of David. No one can shut what he opens. And no one can open what he shuts. He says, [8]'I know what you are doing. Look! I have put an open door in front of you. No one can shut it. I know that you don't have much strength. But you have obeyed my word. You have not said no to me.

[9]'Some people claim they are Jews but are not. They are liars. Their worship is from Satan. I will make them come and fall down at your feet. I will make them say in public that I love you.

[10]'You have kept my command to put up with anything that happens. So I will keep you from the time of suffering that is going to come to the whole world. It will test those who live on the earth.

[11]'I am coming soon. Hold on to what you have. Then no one will take away your crown.

[12]'I'll see to it that those who overcome will be pillars in the temple of my God. They will never leave it again. I will write the name of my God on them. I will write the name of the city of my God on them. This is the new Je-

rusalem, which is coming down out of heaven from my God. I will also write my new name on them. [13]'Those who have ears should listen to what the Holy Spirit says to the churches.'

THE LETTER TO THE CHURCH IN LAODICEA

[14]"Here is what I command you to write to the church in Laodicea.

Here are the words of the One who is the Amen. What he gives witness to is faithful and true. He rules over what God has created. He says, [15]'I know what you are doing. I know you aren't cold or hot. I wish you were either one or the other! [16]But you are lukewarm. You aren't hot or cold. So I am going to spit you out of my mouth.

[17]'You say, "I am rich. I've become wealthy and don't need anything." But you don't realize how pitiful and miserable you have become. You are poor, blind and naked.

[18]'So here's my advice. Buy from me gold made pure by fire. Then you will become rich. Buy from

If the Bible says we'll live for eternity, why is there an end on earth?

The earth was not made to last forever. Things only last forever if God wants them to. God has determined that the world the way it is now will be destroyed. God will give us a new heaven and a new earth to replace the old one.

But people *will* last forever. When Jesus returns to make the world new, he will judge every person who has ever lived. Those who have received his forgiveness will live with him forever. And those who have refused his forgiveness will be cast into the lake of fire. That is why Jesus came, "so that anyone who believes in him will not die but will have eternal life" (see John 3:16).

Related verses:
Matthew 25:46;
Romans 8:19–22;
2 Peter 3:7;
Jude 1:14–15;
Revelation 21:1

checkout
Revelation 3:10,11

me white clothes to wear. Then you will be able to cover your shameful nakedness. And buy from me healing lotion to put on your eyes. Then you will be able to see.

¹⁹'I correct and train those I love. So be sincere, and turn away from your sins.

²⁰'Here I am! I stand at the door and knock. If any of you hears my voice and opens the door, I will come in and eat with you. And you will eat with me.

²¹'I'll give those who overcome the right to sit with me on my throne. In the same way, I overcame. Then I sat down with my Father on his throne.

²²'Those who have ears should listen to what the Holy Spirit says to the churches.' "

THE THRONE IN HEAVEN

4 After this I looked, and there in front of me was a door standing open in heaven. I heard the voice I had heard before. It sounded like a trumpet. The voice said, "Come up here. I will show you what must happen after this."

²At once the Holy Spirit took complete control of me. There in front of me was a throne in heaven with someone sitting on it. ³The One who sat there shone like jewels. Around the throne was a rainbow that looked like an emerald.

⁴Twenty-four other thrones surrounded that throne. Twenty-four elders were sitting on them. The elders were dressed in white. They had gold crowns on their heads.

⁵From the throne came flashes of lightning, rumblings and thunder. Seven lamps were blazing in front of the throne. These stand for the seven spirits of God. ⁶There was something that looked like a sea of glass in front of the throne. It was as clear as crystal.

In the inner circle, around the throne, were four living creatures. They were covered with eyes, in front and in back. ⁷The first creature looked like a lion. The second looked like an ox. The third had a man's face. The fourth looked like a flying eagle. ⁸Each of the four living creatures had six wings. Each creature was covered all over with eyes, even under the wings. Day and night, they never stop saying,

"Holy, holy, holy
is the Lord God who rules over all.
He was, and he is, and he will come."

How can God move a whole city down to earth?

The apostle John had a vision of God bringing the new Jerusalem down from heaven. We do not know exactly how this will work. But it will happen. God can do anything. He created all the stars and planets. He created all the plants, animals and people. He can certainly create a new city and bring it to earth.

checkout
Revelation 3:12

Related verse:
Revelation 21:2

JASON'S IMAGINATION

DOWN A LITTLE FURTHER PLEASE!

[9]The living creatures give glory, honor and thanks to the One who sits on the throne and who lives for ever and ever. [10]At the same time, the 24 elders fall down and worship the One who sits on the throne and who lives for ever and ever. They lay their crowns in front of the throne. They say,

[11] "You are worthy, our Lord and God!
　　You are worthy to receive glory
　　　　and honor and power.
You are worthy because you
　　created all things.
　They were created and they exist.
　That is the way you planned it."

THE SCROLL AND THE LAMB

5 Then I saw a scroll in the right hand of the One sitting on the throne. The scroll had writing on both sides. It was sealed with seven seals.

[2]I saw a mighty angel calling out in a loud voice, "Who is worthy to break the seals and open the scroll?" [3]But no one in heaven or on earth or under the earth could open the scroll. No one could even look inside it.

[4]I cried and cried because no one was found who was worthy to open the scroll or look inside.

[5]Then one of the elders said to me, "Do not cry! The Lion of the tribe of Judah has won the battle. He is the Root of David. He is able to break the seven seals and open the scroll."

[6]Then I saw a Lamb that looked as if he had been put to death. He stood in the center of the area around the throne. The Lamb was surrounded by the four living creatures and the elders. He had seven horns and seven eyes. The eyes stand for the seven spirits of God, which are sent out into all the earth.

[7]The Lamb came and took the scroll from the right hand of the One sitting on the throne. [8]Then the four living creatures and the 24 elders fell down in front of the Lamb. Each one had a harp. They were holding golden bowls full of incense, which stand for the prayers of God's people.

[9]Here is the new song they sang.

"You are worthy to take the scroll
　and break open its seals.

You are worthy because you were
　put to death.
With your blood you bought
　people for God.
They come from every tribe,
　language, people and nation.
[10]You have made them members of
　a royal family.
You have made them priests to
　serve our God.
They will rule on the earth."

[11]Then I looked and heard the voice of millions and millions of angels. They surrounded the throne. They surrounded the living creatures and the elders. [12]In a loud voice they sang,

"The Lamb, who was put to death,
　is worthy!
He is worthy to receive power and
　wealth and wisdom and
　strength!
He is worthy to receive honor and
　glory and praise!"

[13]All creatures in heaven, on earth, under the earth, and on the sea, and all that is in them, were singing. I heard them say,

"May praise and honor for ever
　and ever
be given to the One who sits on
　the throne and to the Lamb!
Give them glory and power
　for ever and ever!"

[14]The four living creatures said, "Amen." And the elders fell down and worshiped.

THE SEALS

6 I watched as the Lamb broke open the first of the seven seals. Then I heard one of the four living creatures say in a voice that sounded like thunder, "Come!" [2]I looked, and there in front of me was a white horse! Its rider held a bow in his hands. He was given a crown. He rode out like a hero on his way to victory.

[3]The Lamb broke open the second seal. Then I heard the second living creature say, "Come!" [4]Another horse came out. It was flaming red. Its rider was given power to take peace from the earth and to make people kill each other. He was given a large sword.

[5]The Lamb broke open the third seal. Then I heard the third living creature say, "Come!" I looked, and there in front of me was a black horse! Its rider was holding a pair of scales in his hand. [6]Next, I heard what sounded like a voice coming from among the four living creatures. It said, "A quart of wheat for a day's pay. And three quarts of barley for a day's pay. But don't spoil the olive oil and the wine!"

[7]The Lamb broke open the fourth seal. Then I heard the voice of the fourth living creature say, "Come!" [8]I looked, and there in front of me was a pale horse! Its rider's name was Death. Following close behind him was Hell. They were given power over a fourth of the earth. They were given power to kill people with the sword, hunger and sickness. They could also use the earth's wild animals to kill.

[9]He broke open the fifth seal. I saw souls under the altar. They were the souls of people who were killed because of God's word and their faithful witness. [10]They called out in a loud voice. "How long, Lord and King, holy and true?" they asked. "How long will you wait to judge those who live on the earth? How long will it be until you pay them back for killing us?"

[11]Then each of them was given a white robe. "Wait a little longer," they were told. "There are still more of your believing brothers and sisters who must be killed."

[12]I watched as he broke open the sixth seal. There was a powerful earthquake. The sun turned black like black clothes that were made from the hair of a goat. The whole moon turned as red as blood. [13]The stars in the sky fell to earth. They dropped like ripe figs from a tree shaken by a strong wind. [14]The sky rolled back like a scroll. Every mountain and island was moved out of its place.

[15]Everyone hid in caves and among the rocks of the mountains. This included the kings of the earth, the princes and the generals, rich people and powerful people. It also included every slave and everyone who was free. [16]They called out to the mountains and rocks, "Fall on us! Hide us

KIDS' QUESTION

How many angels are in heaven?

There is a huge number. We do not know how many angels are in heaven, because the Bible does not tell us. But there are millions and millions of them. Sometimes the Bible uses the same big numbers to describe the number of angels as it uses to describe the number of stars in the sky and the number of grains of sand on the seashore. That means there are so many that no one has ever counted them!

checkout Revelation 5:11

Related verse: Hebrews 12:22

from the face of the One who sits on the throne! Hide us from the anger of the Lamb! ¹⁷The great day of their anger has come. Who can live through it?"

144,000 ARE SEALED

7 After this I saw four angels. They were standing at the four corners of the earth. They were holding back the four winds of the earth. This kept the winds from blowing on the land or on the sea or on any tree.

²Then I saw another angel coming up from the east. He had the seal of the living God. He called out in a loud voice to the four angels who had been allowed to harm the land and the sea. ³"Do not harm the land or the sea or the trees," he said. "Wait until we mark with a seal the foreheads of those who serve our God."

⁴Then I heard how many people were sealed. There were 144,000 from all the tribes of Israel.

⁵From the tribe of Judah, 12,000 were sealed.

From the tribe of Reuben, 12,000.

From the tribe of Gad, 12,000.

⁶From the tribe of Asher, 12,000.

From the tribe of Naphtali, 12,000.

From the tribe of Manasseh, 12,000.

⁷From the tribe of Simeon, 12,000.

From the tribe of Levi, 12,000.

From the tribe of Issachar, 12,000.

⁸From the tribe of Zebulun, 12,000.

From the tribe of Joseph, 12,000.

From the tribe of Benjamin, 12,000.

THE HUGE CROWD WEARING WHITE ROBES

⁹After this I looked, and there in front of me was a huge crowd of people. They stood in front of the throne and in front of the Lamb. There were so many that no one could count them. They came from every nation,

How will the world end?

We don't know exactly *how* the world will end, but we know that it *will* end—the world will not go on forever. This is not bad news; it is part of God's plan. The world will not be destroyed by people or by things getting out of control. It will be God's doing and in God's timing. It will end in a blaze of fire! God will replace this world with a new one.

But it will not happen until Jesus comes back. He will return, just as he promised, to judge all people who have ever lived and to set up his kingdom. He will replace our damaged world with a new, perfect one, where his people will live with him forever. For those who love him, the end of the world will really be a beginning—a wonderful, awesome beginning!

JASON'S IMAGINATION

OLD   NEW

Related verses:
2 Peter 3:7;
Revelation
21:1–22:6

checkout
Revelation 6:1–17

tribe, people and language. They were wearing white robes. In their hands they were holding palm branches. ¹⁰They cried out in a loud voice,

"Salvation belongs to our God,
who sits on the throne.
Salvation also belongs to the
Lamb."

¹¹All the angels were standing around the throne. They were standing around the elders and the four living creatures. They fell down on their faces in front of the throne and worshiped God. ¹²They said,

"Amen!
May praise and glory
and wisdom be given to our God
for ever and ever.
Give him thanks and honor and
power and strength.
Amen!"

¹³Then one of the elders spoke to me. "Who are these people dressed in white robes?" he asked. "Where did they come from?"

¹⁴I answered, "Sir, you know."

He said, "They are the ones who have come out of the time of terrible suffering. They have washed their robes and made them white in the blood of the Lamb. ¹⁵So

"they are in front of the throne of
God.
They serve him day and night in
his temple.
The One who sits on the throne
will spread his tent over them.
¹⁶Never again will they be hungry.
Never again will they be thirsty.
The sun will not beat down on
them.
The heat of the desert will not
harm them.
¹⁷The Lamb, who is at the center of
the area around the throne,
will be their shepherd.
He will lead them to springs of
living water."

Will we wear clothes in heaven?

The Bible says that people will wear dazzling white robes in heaven. But people will not wear clothes for the same reasons that they wear them here. People on earth wear clothes to protect themselves from bad weather, to cover their nakedness and to impress other people. But in heaven we will not need clothes to protect us from the cold because it will not be cold. We will not need raincoats because it will not be stormy. And we will not need special designer clothes, because we will not need to show off.

checkout **Revelation 7:9**

JASON'S IMAGINATION

HEAVEN

Related verses:
Mark 9:3;
Revelation 4:4

And God will wipe away every tear from their eyes."

THE SEVENTH SEAL AND THE GOLD CUP

8 The Lamb opened the seventh seal. Then there was silence in heaven for about half an hour. ²I saw the seven angels who stand in front of God. Seven trumpets were given to them.

³Another angel came and stood at the altar. He had a shallow gold cup for burning incense. He was given a lot of incense to offer on the golden altar in front of the throne. With the incense he offered the prayers of all God's people. ⁴The smoke of the incense together with the prayers of God's people rose up from the angel's hand. It went up in front of God.

⁵Then the angel took the cup and filled it with fire from the altar. He threw it down on the earth. There were rumblings and thunder, flashes of lightning, and an earthquake.

THE TRUMPETS

⁶Then the seven angels who had the seven trumpets got ready to blow them.

⁷The first angel blew his trumpet. Hail and fire mixed with blood were thrown down on the earth. A third of the earth was burned up. A third of the trees were burned up. All the green grass was burned up.

⁸The second angel blew his trumpet. Something that looked like a huge mountain on fire was thrown into the sea. A third of the sea turned into blood. ⁹A third of the living creatures in the sea died. A third of the ships were destroyed.

¹⁰The third angel blew his trumpet. Then a great star fell from the sky. It looked like a blazing torch. It fell on a third of the rivers and on the springs of water. ¹¹The name of the star is Wormwood. A third of the water turned bitter. Many people died from it.

¹²The fourth angel blew his trumpet. Then a third of the sun was struck. A

Why does God let people die?

People die because sin came into the world when Adam and Eve disobeyed God. Some people die when they're young, some die when they're old and some die when they're in the prime of life.

God can heal people and stop them from dying, and sometimes he does. But even a person who has been healed through a miracle from God will probably die someday.

But God's people know that death is not the end of the story. This life is *not* all there is. People who know God will go to live with him in heaven after they die.

So it is very important for us to be ready to meet him when we die.

checkout

1 Peter 4:5–8

Related verses:
Romans 8:38–39;
1 Corinthians
15:35–58;
2 Corinthians
5:1–8;
Revelation 21:4

third of the moon was struck. A third of the stars were struck. So a third of each of them turned dark. Then a third of the day had no light. The same thing happened to a third of the night.

¹³As I watched, I heard an eagle that was flying high in the air. It called out in a loud voice, "How terrible! How terrible it will be for those living on the earth! How terrible! They will suffer as soon as the next three angels blow their trumpets!"

9 The fifth angel blew his trumpet. Then I saw a star that had fallen from the sky to the earth. The star was given the key to the tunnel leading down into the Abyss. ²When the star opened the Abyss, smoke rose up from it like the smoke from a huge furnace. The sun and sky were darkened by the smoke from the Abyss.

³Out of the smoke came locusts. They settled down on the earth. They were given power like the power of scorpions of the earth. ⁴They were told not to harm the grass of the earth or any plant or tree. They were supposed to harm only the people who didn't have God's seal on their foreheads. ⁵They were not allowed to kill them. But they could hurt them over and over for five months. The pain the people suffered was like the sting of a scorpion when it strikes a man.

⁶In those days, people will look for a way to die but won't find it. They will want to die, but death will escape them.

⁷The locusts looked like horses ready for battle. On their heads they wore something like crowns of gold. Their faces looked like human faces. ⁸Their hair was like women's hair. Their teeth were like lions' teeth. ⁹Their chests were covered with something that looked like armor made out of iron. The sound of their wings was like the thundering of many horses and chariots rushing into battle. ¹⁰They had tails and stings like scorpions. And in their tails they had power to hurt people over and over for five months.

¹¹Their king was the angel of the Abyss. In the Hebrew language his name is Abaddon. In Greek it is Apollyon.

¹²The first terrible judgment is past. Two others are still coming.

¹³The sixth angel blew his trumpet. Then I heard a voice coming from the corners of the golden altar that stands in front of God. ¹⁴The voice spoke to the sixth angel who had the trumpet. It said, "Set the four angels free who are held at the great river Euphrates."

¹⁵The four angels had been ready for this very hour and day and month and year. They were set free to kill a third of all people. ¹⁶The number of troops on horseback was 200,000,000. I heard how many there were.

¹⁷The horses and riders I saw in my vision had armor on their chests. It was flaming red, dark blue, and yellow like sulfur. The heads of the horses looked like lions' heads. Out of their mouths came fire, smoke and sulfur. ¹⁸A third of all people were killed by the three plagues of fire, smoke and sulfur that came out of the horses' mouths. ¹⁹The power of the horses was in their mouths and in their tails. The tails were like snakes whose heads could bite.

²⁰The people who were not killed by these plagues still did not turn away from what they had been doing. They did not stop worshiping demons. They kept worshiping statues of gods made out of gold, silver, bronze, stone and wood, which can't see or hear or walk. ²¹The people also did not turn away from their murders, witchcraft, sexual sins and stealing.

THE ANGEL AND THE LITTLE SCROLL

10 Then I saw another mighty angel coming down from heaven. He was wearing a cloud like a robe. There was a rainbow above his head. His face was like the sun. His legs were like pillars of fire.

²He was holding a little scroll. It was lying open in his hand. The angel put his right foot on the sea and his left foot on the land. ³Then he gave a loud shout like the roar of a lion. When he shouted, the voices of the seven thunders spoke.

⁴When they had spoken, I was getting ready to write. But I heard a voice from heaven say, "Seal up what the

seven thunders have said. Do not write it down."

[5]Then the angel I had seen standing on the sea and on the land raised his right hand to heaven. [6]He made a promise in the name of the One who lives for ever and ever. He took an oath in the name of the One who created the sky, earth and sea and all that is in them. He said, "There will be no more waiting! [7]But in the days when the seventh angel is ready to blow his trumpet, the last part of God's plan will be carried out. God told all this to the prophets who served him long ago."

[8]Then the voice I had heard from heaven spoke to me again. It said, "Go and take the scroll from the angel standing on the sea and on the land. It is lying open in his hand."

[9]So I went to the angel and asked him to give me the little scroll. He said to me, "Take it and eat it. It will become sour in your stomach. But in your mouth it will taste as sweet as honey." [10]I took the little scroll from the angel's hand and ate it. In my mouth it tasted as sweet as honey. But when I had eaten it, it became sour in my stomach. [11]Then I was told, "You must prophesy again about many peoples, nations, languages and kings."

THE TWO WITNESSES

11 I was given a long stick that looked like a measuring rod. I was told, "Go and measure the temple of God and the altar. Count the worshipers who are there. [2]But do not measure the outer courtyard. It has been given to those who aren't Jews. They will overrun the holy city for 42 months.

[3]"I will give power to my two witnesses. They will prophesy for 1,260 days. They will be dressed in black clothes to show how sad they are."

[4]The witnesses are the two olive trees and the two lampstands that stand in front of the Lord of the earth. [5]If anyone tries to harm them, fire comes from their mouths and eats up their enemies. This is how anyone who wants to harm them must die.

[6]These witnesses have power to close up the sky. Then it will not rain while they are prophesying. They also have

power to turn the waters into blood. And they can strike the earth with every kind of plague as often as they want to. [7]When they have finished giving their witness, the beast that comes up from the Abyss will attack them. He will overpower them and kill them. [8]Their bodies will lie in the street of the great city where their Lord was nailed to the cross. The city is sometimes pictured as Sodom, or as Egypt.

[9]For three and a half days, people from every tribe, language and nation will stare at their bodies. They will refuse to bury them. [10]Those who live on the earth will be happy about this and will celebrate. They will send each other gifts, because these two prophets had made them suffer.

[11]But after the three and a half days, a breath of life from God entered the two witnesses. They stood up. Terror struck those who saw them.

[12]Then the two witnesses heard a loud voice from heaven. It said to them, "Come up here." They went up to heaven in a cloud. Their enemies watched it happen.

[13]At that very hour there was a powerful earthquake. A tenth of the city crumbled and fell. In the earthquake, 7,000 people were killed. Those who lived through it were terrified. They gave glory to the God of heaven.

[14]The second terrible judgment has passed. The third is coming soon.

THE SEVENTH TRUMPET

[15]The seventh angel blew his trumpet. There were loud voices in heaven. They said,

"The kingdom of the world has
    become the kingdom of our
    Lord and of his Christ.
He will rule for ever and ever."

[16]The 24 elders were sitting on their thrones in front of God. They fell on their faces and worshiped God. [17]They said,

"Lord God who rules over all, we
    give thanks to you.
You are the One who is and who
    was.
We give you thanks because you
    have taken your great power

and have begun to rule.
¹⁸The nations were angry,
   and the time for your anger has
     come.
The time has come to judge the
     dead.
It is time to reward your servants
     the prophets
and your own people and those
     who honor you.
There is a reward for all your
     people,
     both great and small.
It is time to destroy
     those who destroy the earth."

¹⁹Then God's temple in heaven was opened. Inside it the wooden chest called the ark of his covenant could be seen. There were flashes of lightning, rumblings and thunder, an earthquake and a great hailstorm.

THE WOMAN AND THE DRAGON

12 A great and miraculous sign appeared in heaven. It was a woman wearing the sun like clothes. The moon was under her feet. On her head she wore a crown of 12 stars. ²She was pregnant. She cried out in pain because she was about to have a baby.

³Then another sign appeared in heaven. It was a huge red dragon. He had seven heads and ten horns. On his seven heads he wore seven crowns. ⁴His tail swept a third of the stars out of the sky. It threw them down to earth.

The dragon stood in front of the woman who was about to have a baby. He wanted to eat her child the moment it was born. ⁵She gave birth to a son. He will rule all the nations with an iron rod. Her child was taken up to God and to his throne.

⁶The woman escaped into the desert where God had a place prepared for her. There she would be taken care of for 1,260 days.

⁷There was war in heaven. Michael and his angels fought against the dragon. And the dragon and his angels fought back. ⁸But the dragon wasn't strong enough. He and his angels lost their place in heaven.

⁹The great dragon was thrown down to the earth, and his angels with him. The dragon is that old serpent called the devil, or Satan. He leads the whole world down the wrong path.

¹⁰Then I heard a loud voice in heaven. It said,

"Now the salvation and the power
     and the kingdom of our God
     have come.
The authority of his Christ has
     come.
Satan, who brings charges against
     our brothers and sisters,
     has been thrown down.
He brings charges against them
     before our God day and night.
¹¹They overcame him
     because the Lamb gave his life's
     blood for them.
They overcame him
     by giving witness about Jesus to
     others.
They were willing to risk their lives,
     even if it led to death.
¹²So be joyful, you heavens!
Be glad, all you who live there!
But how terrible it will be for the
     earth and the sea!
The devil has come down to you.
He is very angry.
He knows his time is short."

¹³The dragon saw that he had been thrown down to the earth. So he chased the woman who had given birth to the boy.

¹⁴The woman was given the two wings of a great eagle so that she could fly away. She could fly to the place prepared for her in the desert. There she would be taken care of for three and a half years. She would be out of the serpent's reach.

¹⁵Then the serpent spit water like a river out of his mouth. He wanted to catch her and sweep her away in the flood. ¹⁶But the earth helped the woman. It opened its mouth and swallowed the river that the dragon had spit out.

¹⁷The dragon was very angry with the woman. He went off to make war against the rest of her children. They obey God's commands and hold firm-

13 ly to what Jesus has said. ¹The dragon stood on the seashore.

THE BEAST OUT OF THE SEA

I saw a beast coming out of the sea. He had ten horns and seven heads. There were ten crowns on his horns. On each head was an evil name that was displeasing to God.

[2]The beast I saw looked like a leopard. But he had feet like a bear and a mouth like a lion. The dragon gave the beast his power, his throne, and great authority. [3]One of the beast's heads seemed to have had a deadly wound. But the wound had been healed. The whole world was amazed and followed the beast.

[4]People worshiped the dragon, because he had given authority to the beast. They also worshiped the beast. They asked, "Who is like the beast? Who can make war against him?"

[5]The beast was given a mouth to brag and speak evil things against God. The beast was allowed to use his authority for 42 months. [6]He opened his mouth to speak evil things against God. He told lies about God's character and about the place where God lives and about those who live in heaven with him. [7]He was allowed to make war against God's people and to overcome them. He was given authority over every tribe, people, language and nation.

[8]All who live on earth whose names have not been written in the Book of Life will worship the beast. The Book of Life belongs to the Lamb whose death was planned before the world was created.

[9]Everyone who has ears should listen.

[10]Everyone who is supposed to be
　　captured
　will be captured.
Everyone who is supposed to be
　　killed with a sword
　will be killed with a sword.

So God's people must be patient and faithful.

THE BEAST OUT OF THE EARTH

[11]Then I saw another beast. This one came out of the earth. He had two horns like a lamb. But he spoke like a dragon. [12]He had all the authority of the first beast. He did what that beast wanted. He made the earth and all who live on it worship the first beast. The first beast was the one whose deadly wound had been healed.

[13]The second beast did great and miraculous signs. He even made fire come from heaven. It came down to earth where everyone could see it. [14]He did the signs the first beast wanted him to do. In that way the second beast tricked those who live on the earth. He ordered them to set up a statue to honor the first beast.

The first beast was the one who had been wounded by the sword and still lived. [15]The second beast was allowed to give breath to the statue so it could speak. He was allowed to kill all who refused to worship the statue. [16]He also forced everyone to receive a mark on the right hand or on the forehead. People great or small, rich or poor, free or slave had to receive the mark. [17]They could not buy or sell anything unless they had the mark. The mark is the name of the beast or the number of his name. [18]Here is a problem that you have to be wise to figure out. If you can, figure out what the beast's number means. It is man's number. His number is 666.

THE LAMB AND THE 144,000

14 I looked, and there in front of me was the Lamb. He was standing on Mount Zion. With him were 144,000 people. Written on their foreheads were his name and his Father's name.

[2]I heard a sound from heaven. It was like the roar of rushing waters and loud thunder. The sound I heard was like the music of harps being played. [3]Then everyone sang a new song in front of the throne. They sang it in front of the four living creatures and the elders. No one could learn the song except the 144,000. They had been set free from the evil of the earth. [4]They had not committed sexual sins with women. They had kept themselves pure. They follow the

Lamb wherever he goes. They were purchased from among people as a first offering to God and the Lamb. [5]Their mouths told no lies. They are without blame.

THE THREE ANGELS

[6]I saw another angel. He was flying high in the air. He came to tell everyone on earth the good news that will always be true. He told it to every nation, tribe, language and people. [7]In a loud voice he said, "Have respect for God. Give him glory. The hour has come for God to judge. Worship him who made the heavens and the earth. Worship him who made the sea and the springs of water."

[8]A second angel followed him. He said, "Fallen! Babylon the Great has fallen! The city of Babylon made all the nations drink the strong wine of her terrible sins."

[9]A third angel followed them. He said in a loud voice, "Watch out, all you who worship the beast and his statue! Watch out, all you who have his mark on your forehead or your hand! [10]You, too, will drink the wine of God's great anger. His wine has been poured full strength into the cup of his anger. You will be burned with flaming sulfur.

The holy angels and the Lamb will see it happen. [11]The smoke of your terrible suffering will rise for ever and ever. Day and night, there is no rest for you who worship the beast and his statue. There is no rest for you who receive the mark of his name."

[12]God's people need to be very patient. They are the ones who obey God's commands. They remain faithful to Jesus.

[13]Then I heard a voice from heaven. "Write this," it said. "Blessed are the dead who die as believers in the Lord from now on."

"Yes," says the Holy Spirit. "They will rest from their labor. What they have done will not be forgotten."

THE HARVEST OF THE EARTH

[14]I looked, and there in front of me was a white cloud. Sitting on the cloud was One who looked "like a son of man." *(Daniel 7:13)* He wore a gold crown on his head. In his hand was a sharp, curved blade for cutting grain.

[15]Then another angel came out of the temple. He called in a loud voice to the one sitting on the cloud. "Take your blade," he said. "Cut the grain. The time has come. The earth is ready to be harvested."

Do people walk in heaven, or do they fly to where they need to be?

We do not know for sure how people get around in heaven. The Bible does say that some angels fly. But it never says that people have wings or that they fly around in heaven. Usually when the Bible describes people in heaven they are standing or walking.

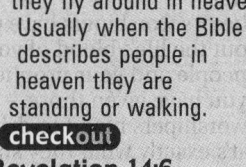

checkout
Revelation 14:6

Related verse:
Revelation 7:9

HEAVENLY
CLOUD WALKERS
$5.00

Fast track to the pearly gates with cloud walkers

[16]So the one sitting on the cloud swung his blade over the earth. And the earth was harvested.

[17]Another angel came out of the temple in heaven. He too had a sharp, curved blade. [18]Still another angel came from the altar. He was in charge of the fire on the altar. He called out in a loud voice to the angel who had the sharp blade. "Take your blade," he said, "and gather the bunches of grapes from the earth's vine. Its grapes are ripe."

[19]So the angel swung his blade over the earth. He gathered its grapes. Then he threw them into a huge winepress. The winepress stands for God's anger.

[20]In the winepress outside the city, the grapes were stomped on. Blood flowed out of the pit. It spread over the land for about 180 miles. It rose as high as the horses' heads.

SEVEN ANGELS WITH SEVEN PLAGUES

15 I saw in heaven another great and miraculous sign. Seven angels were about to bring the seven last plagues. The plagues would complete God's anger.

[2]Then I saw something that looked like a sea of glass mixed with fire. Standing beside the sea were those who had won the battle over the beast. They had also overcome his statue and the number of his name. They held harps given to them by God.

[3]They sang the song of Moses, who served God, and the song of the Lamb. They sang,

"Lord God who rules over all,
  everything you do is great and
    wonderful.
King of the ages,
  your ways are true and fair.
[4]Lord, who will not have respect for
    you?
Who will not bring glory to your
    name?
You alone are holy.
All nations will come
  and worship you.
They see that the things you do are
    right."

[5]After this I looked, and the temple was opened in heaven. The temple is the holy tent where the tablets of the covenant were kept.

[6]Out of the temple came the seven angels who were bringing the seven plagues. They were dressed in clean, shining linen. They wore gold strips of cloth around their chests.

[7]Then one of the four living creatures gave seven golden bowls to the seven angels. The bowls were filled with the anger of God, who lives for ever and ever. [8]The temple was filled with smoke that came from the glory and power of God. No one could enter the temple until the seven plagues of the seven angels were completed.

THE SEVEN BOWLS OF GOD'S ANGER

16 Then I heard a loud voice from the temple speaking to the seven angels. "Go," it said. "Pour out the seven bowls of God's anger on the earth."

[2]The first angel went and poured out his bowl on the land. Ugly and painful sores broke out on the people who had the mark of the beast and worshiped his statue.

[3]The second angel poured out his bowl on the sea. It turned into blood like the blood of a dead person. Every living thing in the sea died.

[4]The third angel poured out his bowl on the rivers and on the springs of water. They became blood.

[5]Then I heard the angel who was in charge of the waters. He said,

"The way you judge is fair.
  You are the Holy One.
  You are the One who is and who
    was.
[6]The beast's worshipers have poured
    out the life's blood of your
    people and your prophets.
So you have given those
    worshipers blood to drink.
That's exactly what they should
    get."

[7]Then I heard the altar reply,

"Lord God who rules over all,
  the way you judge is true and
    fair."

[8]The fourth angel poured out his bowl on the sun. The sun was allowed

to burn people with fire. ⁹They were burned by the blazing heat. So they spoke evil things against the name of God, who controlled these plagues. But they refused to turn away from their sins. They did not give glory to God.

¹⁰The fifth angel poured out his bowl on the throne of the beast. The kingdom of the beast became very dark. People bit their tongues because they were suffering so much. ¹¹They spoke evil things against the God of heaven because of their pains and their sores. But they refused to turn away from the sins they had committed.

¹²The sixth angel poured out his bowl on the great river Euphrates. Its water dried up to prepare the way for the kings from the East.

¹³Then I saw three evil spirits that looked like frogs. They came out of the mouths of the dragon, the beast and the false prophet. ¹⁴They are spirits of demons performing miraculous signs. They go out to gather the kings of the whole world for battle. That battle will take place on the great day of the God who rules over all.

¹⁵"Look! I am coming like a thief! Blessed are those who stay awake and keep their clothes with them. They will not be caught naked. They will not be put to shame."

¹⁶Then the evil spirits gathered the kings together. The place where the kings met is called Armageddon in the Hebrew language.

¹⁷The seventh angel poured out his bowl into the air. Out of the temple came a loud voice from the throne. It said, "It is done!"

¹⁸Then there came flashes of lightning, rumblings, thunder and a powerful earthquake. There has never been an earthquake as terrible as this since man has lived on earth. ¹⁹The great city split into three parts. The cities of the nations crumbled and fell. God remembered Babylon the Great. He gave her the cup filled with the wine of his terrible anger.

²⁰Every island ran away. The mountains could not be found. ²¹Huge hailstones of about 100 pounds each fell from the sky. The hail crushed people. They spoke evil things against God because the plague of hail was so terrible.

THE WOMAN AND THE BEAST

17 One of the seven angels who had the seven bowls came to me. He said, "Come. I will show you how the great prostitute will be punished. She is the one who sits on many waters. ²The kings of the earth took part in her evil ways. The people living on earth were drunk with the wine of her terrible sins."

³Then the angel carried me away in a vision. The Holy Spirit took me into a desert. There I saw a woman sitting on a bright red beast. It was covered with names that say evil things that are displeasing to God. It had seven heads and ten horns.

⁴The woman was dressed in purple and bright red. She was gleaming with gold, jewels and pearls. In her hand she held a golden cup filled with things that God hates. It was filled with her terrible, dirty sins. ⁵Here is the name that was written on her forehead.

MYSTERY
THE GREAT CITY OF BABYLON
THE MOTHER OF PROSTITUTES
THE MOTHER OF EVERYTHING ON EARTH
THAT GOD HATES

⁶I saw that the woman was drunk with the blood of God's people. They are the ones who gave witness to Jesus. When I saw her, I was very amazed.

⁷Then the angel said to me, "Why are you amazed? I will explain to you the mystery of the woman and of the beast she rides on. The beast is the one who has the seven heads and ten horns. ⁸The beast that you saw used to exist. But now he does not. He will come up out of the Abyss. He will be destroyed. Some of the people who live on the earth will be amazed when they see the beast. Their names have not been written in the Book of Life from the time the world was created. They will be amazed because even though the beast used to exist and now does not, he will come again.

⁹"Here is a problem that you have to be wise to understand. The seven

heads are seven hills that the woman sits on. ¹⁰They are also seven kings. Five have fallen, one is ruling, and the other has still not come. When he does come, he must remain for a little while.

¹¹"The beast who used to exist, and now does not, is an eighth king. He belongs to the other seven. He will be destroyed.

¹²"The ten horns you saw are ten kings. They have not yet received a kingdom. But for one hour they will receive authority to rule together with the beast. ¹³They have only one purpose. So they give their power and authority to the beast. ¹⁴They will make war against the Lamb. But the Lamb will overcome them because he is the most powerful Lord of all and the greatest King of all. His appointed, chosen and faithful followers will be with him."

¹⁵Then the angel spoke to me. "You saw the waters the prostitute sits on," he said. "They stand for all the nations of the world, no matter what their race or language is. ¹⁶The beast and the ten horns you saw will hate the prostitute. They will destroy her and leave her naked. They will eat her flesh and burn her with fire. ¹⁷God has put it into their hearts to carry out his purpose. So they agreed to give the beast their power to rule. They will give him that power until God's words come true.

¹⁸"The woman you saw stands for the great city that rules over the kings of the earth."

BABYLON FALLS

18 After these things I saw another angel coming down from heaven. He had great authority. His glory filled the earth with light. ²With a mighty voice he shouted,

"Fallen! Babylon the Great has fallen!
She has become a place where demons live.
She has become a den for every evil spirit.
She has become a nest for every 'unclean' and hated bird.
³All the nations have drunk the strong wine of her terrible sins.
The kings of the earth took part in her evil ways.
The traders of the world grew rich from her great wealth."

⁴Then I heard another voice from heaven. It said,

"Come out of her, my people.
Then you will not take part in her sins.
You will not suffer from any of her plagues.
⁵Her sins are piled up to heaven.
God has remembered her crimes.
⁶Do to her as she has done to others.
Pay her back double for what she has done.
Mix her a double dose of what she has mixed for others.
⁷Give her as much pain and suffering
as the glory and wealth she gave herself.
She brags to herself,
'I rule like a queen. I am not a widow.
I will never be sad.'
⁸But she will be plagued by death, sadness and hunger.
In a single day they will all catch up with her.
She will be burned up by fire.
The Lord God who judges her is mighty.

⁹"The kings of the earth who committed terrible sins with her will sob. They will be sad because they used to share her riches. They will see the smoke rising as she burns. ¹⁰They will be terrified by her suffering. Standing far away, they will exclaim,

" 'How terrible! How terrible it is for you, great city!
How terrible for you, Babylon, city of power!
In just one hour you have been destroyed!'

¹¹"The traders of the world will cry and be sad over her. No one buys what they sell anymore. ¹²Here is what they had for sale.
Gold, silver, jewels, pearls.

Fine linen, purple, silk, bright red
cloth.
Every kind of expensive wood.
All sorts of articles made out of
ivory, valuable wood, bronze, iron
and marble.
¹³Cinnamon, spice, incense, myrrh,
frankincense.
Wine, olive oil, fine flour, wheat.
Cattle, sheep, horses, carriages,
human slaves.

¹⁴"The merchants will say, 'The plea-
sure you longed for has left you. All
your riches and glory have disap-
peared forever.' ¹⁵The traders who sold
these things and became rich because
of her will stand far away. Her suffering will terrify them. They will cry and
be sad. ¹⁶They will cry out,

" 'How terrible! How terrible it is
for you, great city,
dressed in fine linen, purple and
bright red!
How terrible for you, great city,
gleaming with gold, jewels
and pearls!
¹⁷In just one hour your great wealth
has been destroyed!'

"Every sea captain and all who travel
by ship will stand far away. So will the
sailors and all who earn their living
from the sea. ¹⁸They will see the smoke
rising as Babylon burns. They will ask,
'Was there ever a city like this great
city?' ¹⁹They will throw dust on their
heads. They will cry and be sad. They
will cry out,

" 'How terrible! How terrible it is
for you, great city!
All who had ships on the sea
became rich because of her
wealth!
In just one hour she has been
destroyed!
²⁰Heaven, be glad for this!
God's people, be glad! Apostles
and prophets, be glad!
God has judged her for the way
she treated you.' "

²¹Then a mighty angel picked up a
huge rock. It was the size of a large
millstone. He threw it into the sea.
Then he said,

"That is how

the great city of Babylon will be
thrown down.
Never again will it be found.
²²The songs of musicians will never
be heard in you again.
Gone will be the music of harp,
flute and trumpet.
No worker of any kind
will ever be found in you again.
The sound of a millstone
will never be heard in you again.
²³The light of a lamp
will never shine in you again.
The voices of brides and grooms
will never be heard in you
again.
Your traders were among the
world's most important
people.
By your magic spell all the
nations were led down the
wrong path.
²⁴You were guilty of the murder of
prophets and God's people.
You were guilty of the blood of all
who have been killed on the
earth."

HALLELUJAH!

19 After these things I heard
a roar in heaven. It sounded like a huge crowd
shouting,

"Hallelujah!
Salvation and glory and power
belong to our God.
² The way he judges is true and
fair.
He has judged the great prostitute.
She polluted the earth with her
terrible sins.
God has paid her back for killing
those who served him."

³Again they shouted,

"Hallelujah!
The smoke from her fire goes up
for ever and ever."

⁴The 24 elders and the four living
creatures bowed down. They worshiped God, who was sitting on the
throne. They cried out,

"Amen! Hallelujah!"

⁵Then a voice came from the throne.
It said,

"Praise our God,
all you who serve him!
Praise God, all you who have
respect for him,
both great and small!"

[6]Then I heard the noise of a huge crowd. It sounded like the roar of rushing waters and like loud thunder. The people were shouting,

"Hallelujah!
Our Lord God is the King who
rules over all.
[7]Let us be joyful and glad!
Let us give him glory!
It is time for the Lamb's wedding.
His bride has made herself ready.
[8]Fine linen, bright and clean,
was given to her to wear."

Fine linen stands for the right things that God's people do.

[9]Here is what the angel told me to write. "Blessed are those who are invit-ed to the wedding supper of the Lamb!" Then he added, "These are the true words of God."

[10]When I heard this, I fell at his feet to worship him.

But he said to me, "Don't do that! I serve God, just as you do. I am God's servant, just like other believers who hold firmly to what Jesus has taught. Worship God! What Jesus taught is the very heart of prophecy."

THE RIDER ON THE WHITE HORSE

[11]I saw heaven standing open. There in front of me was a white horse. Its rider is called Faithful and True. When he judges or makes war, he is always fair. [12]His eyes are like blazing fire. On his head are many crowns. A name is written on him that only he knows. [13]He is dressed in a robe dipped in blood. His name is The Word of God.

[14]The armies of heaven were follow-ing him, riding on white horses. They

Can we still have birthdays in heaven?

The great thing about birthdays is the parties. We will not grow old in heaven. But we will have lots of parties. The biggest party will be to celebrate "the wedding supper of the Lamb."

That is where we will celebrate our new life in heaven with Jesus. It will be ten times more fun than any birthday party you have ever been to.

The things we enjoy here on earth are like samples. They give us only a taste of what heaven will be like. The things you enjoy here on earth will only be better and greater when you are with God.

checkout Revelation 19:9

Related verses:
Isaiah 25:6–9

JASON'S IMAGINATION

were dressed in fine linen, white and clean.

¹⁵Out of the rider's mouth comes a sharp sword. He will strike down the nations with it. Scripture says, "He will rule them with an iron rod." *(Psalm 2:9)* He stomps on the grapes of God's winepress. The winepress stands for the terrible anger of the God who rules over all.

¹⁶Here is the name that is written on the rider's robe and on his thigh.

THE GREATEST KING OF ALL AND THE
MOST POWERFUL LORD OF ALL

¹⁷I saw an angel standing in the sun. He cried in a loud voice to all the birds flying high in the air, "Come! Gather together for the great supper of God. ¹⁸Come and eat the dead bodies of kings, generals, and other mighty people. Eat the bodies of horses and their riders. Eat the bodies of all people, free and slave, great and small."

¹⁹Then I saw the beast and the kings of the earth with their armies. They had gathered together to make war against the rider on the horse and his army.

²⁰But the beast and the false prophet were captured. The false prophet had done miraculous signs for the beast. In this way the false prophet had tricked those who had received the mark of the beast and had worshiped his statue. The beast and the false prophet were thrown alive into the lake of fire that burns with sulfur. ²¹The rest of them were killed with the sword that came out of the rider's mouth. All the birds stuffed themselves with the dead bodies.

THE THOUSAND YEARS

20 I saw an angel coming down out of heaven. He had the key to the Abyss. In his hand he held a heavy chain.

²He grabbed the dragon, that old serpent. The serpent is also called the devil, or Satan. The angel put him in

KIDS' QUESTION

Will God forgive Satan?

God will never forgive Satan, because Satan hates God and does not want to be forgiven. He does not want a relationship with God or to live in God's presence. He wants to take God's place. But God has already told us what will happen to Satan. Satan will be punished by being thrown in the lake of fire, which is another name for hell. There he will suffer forever for going against God.

checkout
Revelation 20:10

Related verses:
Revelation
20:7–10

chains for 1,000 years. ³Then he threw him into the Abyss. He locked it and sealed him in. This was to keep Satan from fooling the nations anymore until the 1,000 years were ended. After that, he must be set free for a short time.

⁴I saw thrones. Those who had been given authority to judge were sitting on them. I also saw the souls of those whose heads had been cut off because they had given witness for Jesus and because of God's word. They had not worshiped the beast or his statue. They had not received his mark on their foreheads or hands. They came to life and ruled with Christ for 1,000 years.

⁵This is the first resurrection. The rest of the dead did not come to life until the 1,000 years were ended. ⁶Blessed and holy are those who take part in the first resurrection. The second death has no power over them. They will be priests of God and of Christ. They will rule with him for 1,000 years.

SATAN IS JUDGED

⁷When the 1,000 years are over, Satan will be set free from his prison. ⁸He will go out to fool the nations. He will gather them from the four corners of the earth. He will bring Gog and Magog together for battle.

Their troops are as many as the grains of sand on the seashore. ⁹They marched across the whole earth. They surrounded the place where God's people were camped. It was the city he loves. But fire came down from heaven and burned them up. ¹⁰The devil, who fooled them, was thrown into the lake of burning sulfur. That is where the beast and the false prophet had been thrown. They will all suffer day and night for ever and ever.

THE DEAD ARE JUDGED

¹¹I saw a great white throne and the One who was sitting on it. When the earth and sky saw his face, they ran away. There was no place for them. ¹²I saw the dead, great and small, standing in front of the throne. Books

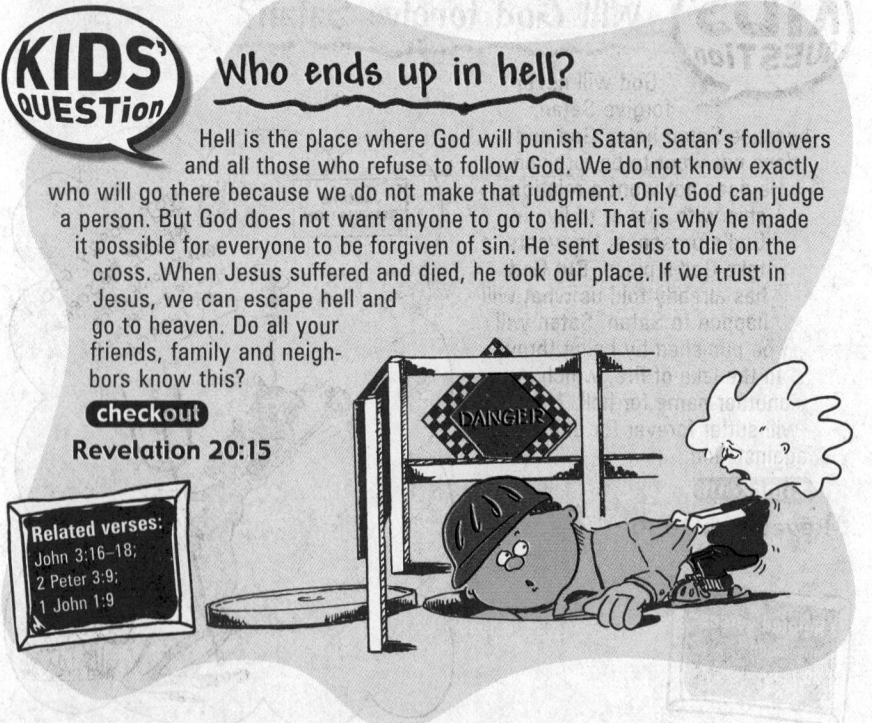

KIDS' QUESTION

Who ends up in hell?

Hell is the place where God will punish Satan, Satan's followers and all those who refuse to follow God. We do not know exactly who will go there because we do not make that judgment. Only God can judge a person. But God does not want anyone to go to hell. That is why he made it possible for everyone to be forgiven of sin. He sent Jesus to die on the cross. When Jesus suffered and died, he took our place. If we trust in Jesus, we can escape hell and go to heaven. Do all your friends, family and neighbors know this?

checkout

Revelation 20:15

Related verses:
John 3:16–18;
2 Peter 3:9;
1 John 1:9

were opened. Then another book was opened. It was the Book of Life. The dead were judged by what they had done. The things they had done were written in the books. ¹³The sea gave up the dead that were in it. And Death and Hell gave up their dead. Each of the dead was judged by what he had done.

¹⁴Then Death and Hell were thrown into the lake of fire. The lake of fire is the second death. ¹⁵Anyone whose name was not written in the Book of Life was thrown into the lake of fire.

THE NEW JERUSALEM

21 I saw a new heaven and a new earth. The first heaven and the first earth were completely gone. There was no longer any sea.

²I saw the Holy City, the new Jerusalem. It was coming down out of heaven from God. It was prepared like a bride beautifully dressed for her husband.

³I heard a loud voice from the throne. It said, "Now God makes his

Will I be able to play games in heaven?

Heaven will be more exciting than you can possibly imagine. Will that mean playing games? Probably not the way you imagine it. You can get bored with games. Life in heaven will *never* be boring. The Bible says that you will always be happy in heaven. If you think games are fun, you should see what is coming next. It will be *much* better than playing games all the time. Isaiah gives us a clue about what we will be doing in heaven. He says we will be shouting and singing praises to God. It will be a great party to celebrate God.

It is OK if you do not understand how singing can be more fun than playing games. God has not told us all there is to know about heaven. How can you really know what to expect if you haven't been there before? You are not *really* able to get excited about it until you get there and see everything up close. But once you are there you will say, "WOW!" That is how it will be when you get to heaven. Just being with God will be more wonderful than you can even imagine.

checkout Revelation 21:3

JASON'S IMAGINATION

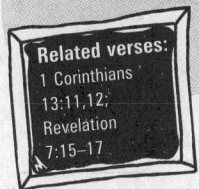

Related verses:
1 Corinthians 13:11,12;
Revelation 7:15–17

home with people. He will live with them. They will be his people. And God himself will be with them and be their God. [4]He will wipe away every tear from their eyes. There will be no more death or sadness. There will be no more crying or pain. Things are no longer the way they used to be."

[5]He who was sitting on the throne said, "I am making everything new!" Then he said, "Write this down. You can trust these words. They are true."

[6]He said to me, "It is done. I am the Alpha and the Omega, the First and the Last. I am the Beginning and the End. Anyone who is thirsty may drink from the spring of the water of life. It doesn't cost anything! [7]Anyone who overcomes will receive all this from me. I will be his God, and he will be my child.

[8]"But others will have their place in the lake of fire that burns with sulfur. Those who are afraid and those who do not believe will be there. Murderers and those who pollute themselves will join them. Those who commit sexual sins and those who practice witchcraft will go there. Those who worship statues of gods and all who tell lies will be there too. It is the second death."

[9]One of the seven angels who had the seven bowls came and spoke to me. The bowls were filled with the seven last plagues. The angel said, "Come. I will show you the bride, the wife of the Lamb."

[10]Then he carried me away in a vision. The Spirit took me to a huge, high mountain. He showed me Jerusalem, the Holy City. It was coming down out of heaven from God. [11]It shone with the glory of God. It gleamed like a very valuable jewel. It was like a jasper, as clear as crystal.

[12]The city had a huge, high wall with 12 gates. Twelve angels were at the gates, one at each of them. On the gates were written the names of the 12 tribes of Israel. [13]There were three gates on the east and three on the north. There were three gates on the

KIDS' QUESTION

What is heaven like?

The best way to imagine heaven is to think about the most exciting place that you have ever visited. Heaven will be like that and much, much better. We know this because the Bible uses wonderful words to tell us what heaven will be like. No one will ever cry or be sad there. The streets will be paved with *gold*. Lions will get along with lambs. We can try to imagine how great it will be, but mostly it will be a really great surprise because it will be so much better than life on this earth.

checkout

Revelation 21:4

Related verses:
Isaiah 65:17–19, 21–25;
Revelation 21:1–21

south and three on the west. [14]The wall of the city had 12 foundations. Written on them were the names of the 12 apostles of the Lamb.

[15]The angel who talked with me had a gold measuring rod. He used it to measure the city, its gates and its walls. [16]The city was laid out like a square. It was as long as it was wide. The angel measured the city with the rod. It was 1,400 miles long. It was as wide and high as it was long.

[17]He measured the wall of the city. It was 200 feet thick. The angel did the measuring as a man would. [18]The wall was made out of jasper. The city was made out of pure gold, as pure as glass.

[19]The foundations of the city walls were decorated with every kind of jewel. The first foundation was made out of jasper. The second was made out of sapphire. The third was made out of chalcedony. The fourth was made out of emerald. [20]The fifth was made out of sardonyx. The sixth was made out of carnelian. The seventh was made out of chrysolite. The eighth was made out of beryl. The ninth was made out of topaz. The tenth was made out of chrysoprase. The eleventh was made out of jacinth. The twelfth was made out of amethyst.

[21]The 12 gates were made from 12 pearls. Each gate was made out of a single pearl. The main street of the city was made out of pure gold, as clear as glass.

[22]I didn't see a temple in the city. This was because the Lamb and the Lord God who rules over all are its temple. [23]The city does not need the sun or moon to shine on it. God's glory is its light, and the Lamb is its lamp.

[24]The nations will walk by the light of the city. The kings of the world will

When Jesus comes to get us, what will happen to earth and everyone else?

Several things will happen when Jesus comes back to rescue all who believe in him: (1) He will bring life on this earth to an end. (2) He will judge everyone. (3) He will create a new heaven and a new earth. (4) We will begin life forever with God. (5) The devil, his demons and all unbelievers will begin their death forever in hell.

checkout

Revelation 21:8

Related verses:
1 Thessalonians
4:16,17;
2 Peter 3:10–14

JASON'S IMAGINATION

bring their glory into it. ²⁵Its gates will never be shut, because there will be no night there. ²⁶The glory and honor of the nations will be brought into it.

²⁷Only what is pure will enter it. No one who fools others or does shameful things will enter it. Only those whose names are written in the Lamb's Book of Life will enter the city.

THE RIVER OF LIFE

22 Then the angel showed me the river of the water of life. It was as clear as crystal. It flowed from the throne of God and of the Lamb. ²It flowed down the middle of the city's main street.

On each side of the river stood the tree of life, bearing 12 crops of fruit. Its fruit was ripe every month. The leaves of the tree bring healing to the nations.

³There will no longer be any curse. The throne of God and of the Lamb will be in the city. God's servants will serve him. ⁴They will see his face. His name will be on their foreheads.

⁵There will be no more night. They will not need the light of a lamp or the light of the sun. The Lord God will give them light. They will rule for ever and ever.

⁶The angel said to me, "You can trust these words. They are true. The Lord is the God of the spirits of the prophets.

Are the streets in heaven real gold or just painted with gold?

All of heaven is real, and none of it is fake. It will be the most beautiful place we have ever seen. The Bible says that the streets will be paved with gold. This may just be a way of saying that it is a great place to be. It may be like saying "It must be a million degrees out here" to describe a really hot day.

But it may refer to real gold streets running through town. It is hard to know *exactly* what heaven will be like, because we really *cannot* understand it now.

Imagine a frog trying to explain frog life to a tadpole. The tadpole would learn that he cannot swim or breathe through his gills on land. It would sound bad. It would sound strange. The frog would not be able to tell the tadpole how good it will be to live on land. Only when the tadpole becomes a frog will the tadpole understand. It is like that with heaven. Only when we get to heaven will we know what the gold will be. But we can be sure that it will not be fake!

JASON'S IMAGINATION

GOLD ST.   GOLD ST.

HEAVEN

DIGGER

checkout

Revelation 21:21

Related verses:
Revelation
21:1—22:21

He sent his angel to show those who serve him the things that must soon take place."

JESUS IS COMING

[7] "Look! I am coming soon! Blessed are those who obey the words of the prophecy in this book."

[8] I, John, am the one who heard and saw these things.

After I had heard and seen them, I fell down to worship at the feet of the angel. He is the one who had been showing me these things.

[9] But he said to me, "Don't do that! I serve God, just as you do. I am God's servant, just like the other prophets and all who obey the words of this book. Worship God!"

[10] Then he told me, "Do not seal up the words of the prophecy in this book. These things are about to happen. [11] Let those who do wrong keep on doing wrong. Let those who are evil continue to be evil. Let those who do what is right keep on doing what is right. And let those who are holy continue to be holy."

[12] "Look! I am coming soon! I bring my rewards with me. I will reward each person for what he has done. [13] I am the Alpha and the Omega. I am the First and the Last. I am the Beginning and the End.

[14] "Blessed are those who wash their robes. They will have the right to come to the tree of life. They will be allowed to go through the gates into the city.

[15] "Outside the city are the dogs and those who practice witchcraft. Outside are also those who commit sexual sins and murder. Those who worship statues of gods, and everyone who loves and does what is false, are outside too.

[16] "I, Jesus, have sent my angel to give

Will God have angels watching over heaven so demons can't get in?

God will let no evil at all into heaven. No sin, no hurting, and no demons will be allowed. The Bible describes one time that Satan was allowed to speak to God. But in the future, God will lock up all demons in a great pit. Then, life in heaven will be completely *safe*. In fact, heaven will be the safest place anywhere. No one in heaven will be afraid of anything. And no one there will ever get hurt.

checkout

Revelation 21:27

Related verses:
Job 1:6;
Revelation 22:3–5

you this witness for the churches. I am the Root and the Son of David. I am the bright Morning Star."

[17]The Holy Spirit and the bride say, "Come!" Let those who hear say, "Come!" Anyone who is thirsty should come. Anyone who wants to take the free gift of the water of life should do so.

[18]I am warning everyone who hears the words of the prophecy of this book. If you add anything to them, God will add to you the plagues told about in this book. [19]If you take any words away from this book of prophecy, God will take away from you your share in the tree of life. He will also take away your place in the Holy City. This book tells about these things.

[20]He who gives witness to these things says, "Yes. I am coming soon." Amen. Come, Lord Jesus!

[21]May the grace of the Lord Jesus be with God's people. Amen.

KIDS' QUESTION

Why can't we put new books into the Bible?

We can't put new books into the Bible, because the Bible is *God's* message, not ours. It contains the words he inspired people to write. Some people have tried to put new books in the Bible, but God is finished writing the Bible. It is the story about how God has saved us. And it is complete. God is not still writing the Bible today, so we do not add to it.

checkout
Revelation 22:18

Related verses:
Hebrews 1:1,2

Quest Clue

In the book of Revelation we read about how the angels praise God in heaven. To learn more about how you can praise God, take the first Quest Challenge at the end of Song of Songs.

Dictionary

Topical Index

Dictionary

A

abyss
A deep pit where evil spirits live. Satan will be held there in chains.

altar
A table or raised place on which a gift, or sacrifice, was offered to God.

amen
A word that means "it is true" or "let it be true."

angel
A spirit who is God's helper. A spirit who tells people God's words. See also cherubim.

anoint
1. To pour olive oil on people or things. This sets them apart for God. 2. To pour oil on people as part of praying for their healing.

anointed
To be set apart as God's special servant.

apostle
One of the twelve men who spent about three years with Jesus. They taught others about Jesus, too. See also disciple.

Aramaic
A language spoken by many people during Bible times. The Jews in Jesus' time most often spoke this language.

ark of the covenant
A large gold box that held the stone tablets of the Ten Commandments. The ark was God's throne on earth.

armor
A special outer covering like clothes made of metal. People wore it to help keep them safe in battle.

Asherah
A false god. People thought she was the Canaanite mother goddess and goddess of the sea.

B

Baal
The name of the most popular false god of Canaan.

Babel
A city where people tried to build a tower up to the sky.

Babylon
1. The capital city of the empire of Babylonia. 2. Any powerful, sinful city.

baptize
To sprinkle, pour on or cover a person with water. It is a sign that the person belongs to Jesus.

Beelzebub
Another name for the devil. Satan.

believe
To accept as true. To trust. See also faith.

blessed
1. Made joyful. 2. Helped by God.

C

cast lots
Something done to find out what God wants. It is like drawing straws to see who will go first.

chariot
A cart with two wheels pulled by horses. People, especially soldiers, rode in them.

cherubim
1. Spirits like angels who have large wings. They were and are a sign that God is sitting on his throne. 2. Spirits who serve God.

chief priest
See high priest.

Christ
A Greek word that means "the Anointed One." It is one of the names given to Jesus. It means the same thing as the Hebrew word Messiah. See also Jesus.

circumcision
Cutting off a male's foreskin (a piece of skin at the end of a penis). It was a sign that the person belonged to God.

clean
1. Something that God accepts. 2. Something that doesn't have sin.

Dictionary

clean animals

Animals that God said were acceptable to eat or to give as offerings.

commandment

A law or rule that God gives. See also law.

concubine

A woman who belonged to a man but was not his legal wife.

Council

See Sanhedrin.

covenant

1. A treaty, or promise, between two persons or groups. In the Bible it is a promise made between God and the people. 2. Promises from God for salvation.

cross

A wooden post with a bar near the top that extends to the right and left. A cross looks like the letter "T." The Romans killed people by nailing them to crosses.

crucify

To kill people by nailing them to crosses.

cud

Food that is chewed again. An animal such as a cow brings its food back from its stomach to its mouth. This food, or cud, can be chewed again. God told the people of Israel they could eat any animal that chews the cud and has hoofs that are separated.

curse

1. A call for God to punish someone. 2. A command of God that punishment will come on someone or something.

D

deacon

A church leader who helps people in Jesus' name.

dedicate

To set apart for a special purpose, often for God's use.

demon

An evil spirit.

devil

The one who tempts people to sin. See also Satan.

disciple

A person who follows a teacher. This person does what their teacher says to do. See also apostle. See also Twelve, the.

divorce

The end of a husband and wife's marriage.

doubt

A lack of faith or trust in something or someone. To not be sure.

E

Eden

The place where God made a garden for Adam and Eve.

elder

The leader of a church, town or nation. This person makes important decisions.

eternal

Forever. Without beginning or end.

evangelist

A person who tells others the Good News of Jesus.

evil

Bad. Wicked. Doing things that do not please God.

evil spirit

A demon. One of the devil's helpers.

F

faith

Trust and belief in God. Knowing that God is real, even though we can't see him. See also believe.

faithful

Able to be trusted or counted on.

famine

A time when there is not enough food to eat.

Dictionary

fast
Going without food and/or drink for a special reason.

Feast of Booths
A celebration or festival when the Israelites thanked God for the harvest of their crops. During the feast they lived in little tents for seven days to help remember when they traveled to Canaan.

Feast of Hanukkah
A celebration praising God that the Israelites and Jews today have to remember the cleaning and rededication of the temple. The temple had been made "unclean" by an enemy.

Feast of Weeks
A festival or celebration day at the beginning of the wheat harvest when the Israelites gave thanks to God. See also Pentecost.

Feast of Passover
See Passover.

Feast of Unleavened Bread
A week for remembering when God set the Israelites free from Egypt. It began the day after the Feast of Passover. During this time the people ate bread made without yeast, like they did when they left Egypt in a hurry.

fig
A sweet fruit that grows on trees in warm countries like Israel.

G

glory
1. God's greatness. 2. Praise and honor.

God
The maker and ruler of the world and all people.

grace
The kindness and forgiveness God gives to people. This is a gift. It cannot be earned.

H

hallelujah
A Hebrew word that means "praise the Lord."

Hanukkah
See Feast of Hanukkah.

harvest
Picking a crop when it is ripe.

heaven
1. God's home. 2. The sky. 3. Where Christians go after they die.

Hebrew
1. Another name for an Israelite. 2. The language spoken by the Israelites. The Old Testament is written in this language.

hell
A place of punishment for people who don't follow Jesus. They go there after they die.

Herod
The first name of five rulers from the same family. They ruled over Israel during the time of the New Testament.

high places
Places where people worshiped false gods. These places were found on top of hills.

high priest
A person from the family line of Aaron. He was in charge of everything in the holy tent or in the temple. He was in charge of everyone who came there to work and worship, too.

holy
Set apart for God. Belonging to God. Pure.

holy bread
Twelve loaves of bread placed in the Holy Room of the holy tent each week. They were a gift to God.

Holy Spirit
God's Spirit who creates life. He helps people do God's work. He helps people to believe in Jesus, to love him and to live like him.

holy tent
Also called the Tent of Meeting. A place where the Israelites worshiped God. They used this tent after they left Egypt and while they were in the desert for 40 years. Years later Solomon built the first temple. Then the people worshiped God there and not in the tent.

Dictionary

honor
To show respect to. To give credit to.

hosanna
A Hebrew word used to praise God.

hymn
A song of praise to God.

hyssop
A plant that smelled like mint. Its branches were used to shake water or blood on something to make it pure.

I

Immanuel
A name for Jesus that means "God with us."

incense
Spices that give a pleasing smell when they are burned. It was placed on the altar in the holy tent.

Israel
1. The new name God gave to Abraham's grandson Jacob. 2. The nation that came from the family line of Jacob. 3. The northern tribes that broke away from Judah to serve their own king.

Israelites
People from the nation of Israel. God's chosen people.

J

jealous
1. How God feels when people worship other things. 2. How we feel when someone else has something we want.

Jesus
The Greek form of the Hebrew name Joshua. It means "the Lord saves." See also Christ. See also Immanuel. See also Savior.

Jews
Another name for the people of Israel. This name was used after 600 B.C.

Jubilee
See Year of Jubilee.

judge
1. To decide if something is right or wrong. 2. A person who decides what is right or wrong in legal matters.

K

kingdom
An area or group of people ruled by a king.

L

law
Rules about what is right and wrong that God gave the people of Israel. See also law, the.

Law, the
The first five books of the Bible.

Levites
Men from the tribe of Levi. They took care of the holy tent and the temple.

locust
A type of insect similar to a grasshopper. A huge number of them sometimes eats and destroys crops.

Lord
A personal name for God or Christ. It shows respect to him as our master and ruler.

lots
See cast lots.

M

manger
A food box for animals.

manna
Special food sent from heaven. It tasted like wafers, or crackers, sweetened with honey. God gave it to the Israelites in the desert, after they left Egypt.

mercy
More kindness and forgiveness than people deserve to get.

Messiah
A Hebrew word that means, "The Anointed One." It means the same thing as the Greek word Christ. See also Jesus.

Dictionary

millstone

A heavy rock used to crush grain to make flour.

miracle

An amazing thing that happens that only God can do. This includes such things as calming a storm or bringing someone back to life.

miraculous signs

Amazing things that God does to point us to him. These things cannot be explained by the laws of nature.

myrrh

A spice with a sweet smell. It came from plants and was made into perfume, incense and medicine.

N

nard

A costly oil made from a plant grown in India. It was used as a perfume to make skin smell good.

Nazarene

A person who came from the town of Nazareth. Jesus was called a Nazarene.

Nazirite

A person who was set apart to God in a special way. Or, a person who promised to do something special for God. They were not allowed to cut their hair, drink any wine or grape juice, eat grapes or raisins, or touch a dead body.

O

oath

A promise made before God.

obey

To do what you are told to do. To carry out God's commands.

offering

Something people give to God. It was and is a part of their worship. See also sacrifice.

oxen

Large cattle that are very strong. They were used to pull carts or plows.

P

papyrus

A tall, grassy plant that grows in shallow water. People made boats with these plants and paper from their stems.

Passover

A feast that happened every year. It reminded the people of the time when God "passed over" their homes in Egypt. Since the people put blood on the doorways, God did not hurt them.

paradise

A perfect place. Another name used for heaven.

pasture

A field of grassy land where cows or sheep may eat.

Pentecost

1. A Jewish celebration held 50 days after Passover. 2. The day the Holy Spirit came in a special way to live in Christians.

Pharaoh

The title of the ruler of Egypt in Bible times.

Pharisees

A group of Jews who carefully followed God's laws and their own rules about God's laws. Some Pharisees were also known as "teachers of the law."

Philistines

Strong enemies of Israel, especially during Saul and David's time.

pierce

To poke through with a sharp instrument.

pillar

1. A tall, upright post that helped to hold up a building. 2. A pillar could also mark a special place.

pillar of cloud

A cloud God used to lead the people of Israel. They could see it all day long when they were in the desert.

Dictionary

pillar of fire

A column of fire God used to lead the people of Israel. They could see it all night long when they were in the desert.

plague

1. A sickness that kills many people. 2. Anything that brings a lot of suffering or loss.

plumb line

A string that has a weight tied to the end of it. It is used to tell whether a wall is straight or not.

pomegranate

A round fruit with a tough skin, many seeds and a juicy red center.

praise

To give glory or honor to someone. To say good things about someone or something.

pregnant

Carrying a baby inside a woman's body until the baby is born.

Preparation Day

The day before the Sabbath day. A day to get all work done so that a person could rest on the Sabbath.

priest

A person who worked in the holy tent or the temple. He was responsible to give his own as well as other people's gifts and prayers to God.

prophecy

Important words or messages that God gives to his people. God gives these words through a special person called a prophet.

prophesy

1. To give a message from God. 2. To tell what the future will be.

prophet

A person who hears messages from God and tells them to others.

proverb

A wise saying.

psalm

A poem of praise, prayer or teaching. The book of Psalms is full of these poems.

Purim

A feast in which the Israelites remembered when God helped Queen Esther save the Jews.

R

Rabbi

The title of a teacher of Jewish law.

resurrection

Coming back to life in a whole new way and never dying again.

right hand

A place of honor and power. Jesus is at the right hand of God.

Rome

1. The empire that controlled a lot of the world when Jesus lived here on the earth. 2. The capital city of that empire. It is in Italy.

S

Sabbath

The seventh day of the week. On that day the Israelites rested from their work and turned their thoughts toward God.

sacred

Set apart for God. Holy.

sacrifice

1. To give something to God as a gift. 2. Something that is given to God as a gift of worship. See also offering.

Sadducees

A group of Jewish leaders. They followed only the first five books of the Bible. They did not believe that people rise from the dead.

salvation

Free from the guilt of sin. Jesus died for our sins and rose up from the dead. With this sacrifice, he paid for our sin. He has saved us if we believe in him.

Sanhedrin

A group of 71 Jewish leaders. They were led by the high priest. They were the most important Jewish court of law in Jesus' time.

Satan
God's most powerful enemy in the spirit world. Also called the devil.

saved
Set free from danger or sin.

Savior
The One who sets us free from our sins. A name belonging to Jesus Christ. See also Jesus.

Scripture
God's written Word to us. We also call this the Bible.

scroll
A long strip of paper or animal skin to write on. It was rolled up on two sticks to make it easy to use and store.

seal
1. A tool or a ring with a drawing or pattern cut into it. 2. A mark made by pressing this tool into clay, wax or paper.

seer
A person who can tell the future with God's help. See also prophet.

shepherd
A person who takes care of sheep or goats.

sin
To disobey or displease God.

Sodom and Gomorrah
Two cities that God destroyed. The people who lived there were very evil.

Son of Man
A name Jesus gave to himself. It shows he is the Messiah. See also Messiah.

soul
A person's true inner self.

spiritual
Having to do with the things of God or the Bible.

staff
A stick a shepherd uses to take care of sheep or goats.

synagogue
A Jewish place of worship and teaching.

T

tambourine
A hand-held drum with metal pieces around the edge. It rattles when it is shaken or tapped.

tassels
Hanging groups of thread that are tied together at one end. God told the Israelites to sew tassels onto their clothing to remind them of God's commands.

temple
1. Any place of worship. 2. The building where the people of Israel worshiped God and brought their sacrifices. God was present there in a special way.

tempt
To try to get someone to do bad things.

Tent of Meeting
See holy tent.

threshing floor
A place where heads, or tops, of grain are beaten or stepped on. This is done to knock the seeds of grain from the stems.

tomb
A place to put dead bodies. It was often a cave with a big, stone door.

treaty
An agreement between two people or groups or nations.

Twelve, the
The men who Jesus chose to be his special followers. See also disciples.

U

unclean
Something that God does not accept. Not pure. Not pleasing to God.

Urim and Thummim
Objects that were worn on the high priest's vest. They were used by the high priest to get a message from God.

Dictionary

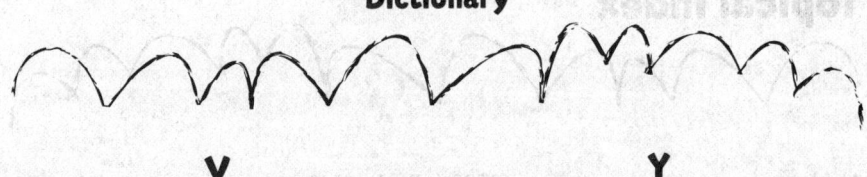

V

vineyard

A place where grapes grow and are picked.

vision

A dream from God. The person who saw it was usually awake. God gave these kinds of dreams to people to show them what he was going to do.

W

wafer

A thin, crisp cracker. Wafers were one kind of offering the Israelites brought to the Lord.

widow

A woman whose husband has died.

winepress

A place where juice is pressed out of grapes to make wine.

wisdom

Understanding that comes from God. Wise thinking.

worship

To give praise, honor and glory to God.

Y

Year of Jubilee

A special year that was to happen every 50 years in Israel. No crops could be planted. Any money that was owed was forgiven. Slaves were set free. Property was given back to its first owner.

yeast

Something added to bread dough to make the bread rise.

yoke

1. A strong piece of wood. It fit on the necks of two oxen so that they could pull carts or plows. 2. A piece of wood put on the neck of a slave or a prisoner.

Z

Zealot

A Jew who was willing to fight to get rid of the Roman rulers. Simon may have been part of this group before becoming one of Jesus' twelve disciples.

Zion

1. The city of Jerusalem. 2. The hill on which King David's house and the temple once stood. 3. Another name sometimes used for heaven.

Topical Index

Guarantee

Zondervan's manufacturer's warranty provides coverage for defective bindings on hardcover, softcover, Leather-Look™ and Italian Duo-Tone™ Bibles for four years, and on bonded and top-grain leather Bibles for six years. This warranty does not apply to normal wear. A lifetime warranty applies to defects within the Bible—for example: missing or misplaced pages, chapters or books. Please return defective Bibles to the original place of purchase for replacement or refund. If this is not possible, please go to www.zondervan.com and click on "Contact Us."

Care

We suggest loosening the binding of your new Bible by gently pressing on a small section of pages at a time from the center. To ensure against breakage of the spine, it is best not to bend the cover backward around the spine or to carry study notes, church bulletins, pens, and the like, inside the cover. Because a felt-tipped marker will "bleed" through the pages, we recommend use of a ball-point pen or pencil to underline favorite passages. Your Bible should not be exposed to excessive heat, cold or humidity. Protecting the gold or silver edges of the paper from moisture will avoid spotting, streaking or fading.